COMPARATIVE COMMERCIAL CONTRACTS

LAW, CULTURE AND ECONOMIC DEVELOPMENT

by

Boris Kozolchyk
Evo DeConcini, Professor of Law,
James E. Rogers College of Law, University of Arizona
Dr.H.c. Universidad Privada Antonio Guillermo Urrelo, Chiclayo, Peru,
Dr. H.c. The Universidad Mayor, Santiago, Chile
Permanent Professor Honoris Causa, Shanghai University of International Business and Economics
Distinguished Visiting Professor of Law and Bailey Lecturer in Residence, Louisiana State University Law Center
Profesor Distinguido, Universidad Carlos III Madrid, Spain
Profesor Distinguido Escuela Libre de Derecho, San Jose, Costa Rica
Former President of the International Academy of Commercial and Consumer Law

HORNBOOK SERIES®

WEST ACADEMIC PUBLISHING

Mat #41508889

444 Cedar Street, Suite 700
St. Paul, MN 55101
1-877-888-1330

Printed in the United States of America

ISBN: 978-0-314-28968-1

This book is dedicated to my loving wife Billie, children Abbie, Raphael , Shaun and grandchildren Sigal, Liana, Alex, Jacob and Ethan. It is also dedicated to my mentors Professors Hessel Yntema, Julius Stone and Adamson Hoebel, and to the United States of America, the country that brought us together and made this book possible.

List of NLCIFT Board of Directors

HONORARY BOARD MEMBERS

Foreword

This magnificent new book draws on Professor Boris Kozolchyk's theoretical and empirical studies over a period of many decades into the development of principles of contract and commercial law in a range of legal families and systems. Founder, President and Director of the National Law Center for Inter-American Free Trade in Tucson, Arizona, since its establishment some 22 years ago, he has brought his wealth of experience to bear on a comprehensive analysis of law as a tool for economic development. The scope of this work is astonishing both in its subject-matter and in the variety of sources on which it draws.

The impact of business practice on the development of commercial law is a topic of endless fascination both to commercial lawyers and jurisprudes. Even such a basic question as "What converts business practice into law?" is fraught with controversy and circular reasoning. This new work focuses on the opposing factors that motivate business practice: altruism and selfishness, co-operation and competition, brotherhood and adversarial behaviour. Interesting too is the contrast in some jurisdictions between commerce between fellow nationals and trading with foreigners. So we are told that in the Japan domestic market co-operation prevails over market freedom, while in the international market Japanese commercial activity is characterised by market competitiveness and low prices.

The span of this book is enormous. In time it ranges from the pre-commercial era, with its emphasis on community and family relationships rather than on contract, through Roman law, mediaeval law and the evolution of powerful guilds to the age of codification and the development of modern commercial law, noting the influence of the economic analysis of law. In space it traverses old and new legal systems in every legal family, covering a vast number of jurisdictions and of legal, economic and anthropological sources.

What has characterised Boris Kozolchyk's writings from long ago is his focus on merchant motivation, on what makes the law work, on the concept of the *bonus vir* and the value added by altruism, and this is the thread that runs throughout this magisterial work of superb scholarship. This is essential reading for anyone seriously interested in the development of commercial law as an instrument of social and economic policy.

ROY GOODE
Oxford

December 2013

Prologue

Officially, this book has been in the making during the 15 years or so that I have taught a course on comparative commercial law at the James E. Rogers College of Law, University of Arizona. My teaching of this course was encouraged by my colleagues David A. Gantz and former Associate Dean Kay Kavanagh; unofficially this book has been in the making during much of my lifetime.

As a young law student in Cuba during the Batista dictatorship, I kept asking myself if all the rule of law could do was to passively watch how bloody and costly violence—albeit periodically clothed in revolutionary garb—was destroying whatever was left of democracy and economic development in my country of birth.

Subsequently, during my LLB studies at the University of Miami and as an LL.M. and S.J.D. student at the University of Michigan, my search for the role of law, and especially commercial law, acquired a direction. It became apparent to me that the U.S.'s legal system was better at resolving pressing socio-economic problems than the one I had left behind. And unlike Cuba, my adopted country did not regard violent revolution as the solution to its injustices and shortcomings, economic and other: elections, statutes, court decisions, law schools, law reviews, law practice, etc. were all legal institutions involved in bringing about non-violent, needed changes.

I remember discussing the topic for my S.J.D. thesis with my University of Michigan mentor Professor Hessel E. Yntema. I told him of my search for a version of the rule of law that could accommodate non-violent, but much needed social change. In response, he asked me about my favorite courses at the University of Miami and I told him about a contracts' course taught by Professor Richard Hausler and a suretyship course taught by Professor Wesley Sturges, a former Dean of the Yale University Law School. He asked why I liked those courses and I told him that they vividly highlighted the judges', law professors' and students' struggle with formulating their versions of commercial justice. Granted, those issues were not as monumental as those of racial integration or curbing abuses of power by the executive branch. Yet they illustrated how judges, lawyers, law professors and students contributed to such a formulation. I also told him how deeply I had been impressed with a Justice Cardozo dissenting opinion in a letter of credit decision in which the paying bank raised the widely accepted principle that when examining letter of credit documents, bankers deal only in documents and not in goods. Thus bankers were not supposed to concern themselves with an alleged fraudulent tender of documents which indicated the shipment of newsprint of a certain tensile strength when in fact it could not be used to print newspapers. While accepting the soundness of the invoked principle, Cardozo explored transactional questions such as: Who was the plaintiff and who was the defendant, and what did they know about the fundamental defects of the goods probably fraudulently described in the tendered documents? Did a confirming bank which had paid the beneficiary of the letter of credit without knowledge of the latter's s fraud have a better right to be paid by the issuing bank than the seller who was a party to the fraudulent presentation? And then he asked the crucial question: Is a fraudulent or forged document a document, let alone a complying document in letter of credit law? I told

Professor Yntema that reading this decision was my first encounter with a jurist who truly knew how to resolve an everyday practical problem of commercial justice.

Yntema must have liked what he heard because he told me that while he could not be my advisor for a thesis that explored the global meaning of the rule of law and its contribution to economic development, he would be glad to be my advisor in my use of the comparative method to help resolve practical problems of justice similar to those tackled by Justice Cardozo. (A month later, while translating one of Professor Yntema's writings into Spanish, I discovered that he had expressed the view that a principal mission of comparative law was precisely to help resolve every day practical problems of justice).

The doctoral work he supervised eventually resulted in a book (Commercial Letters of Credit in the Americas) which together with my subsequent writings on commercial and standby letters of credit enabled my contributions to the resolution of the practical problems of letter of credit justice first as a scholar and commentator and eventually as part of a group of drafters of customary, statutory and treaty letter of credit law. I owe the publication of that book to John (Jack) W. Riehm, who after being my very supportive dean at Southern Methodist University (where I started my teaching career) became the president of the Matthew Bender & Co. His widow Doris remains part of our family and continues to be one of the most faithful supporters of the work of the National Law Center for Inter-American Free Trade (NLCIFT), about which more shortly.

One of my most important intellectual experiences at SMU was the start of my lifelong friendship with Australia's Professor Julius Stone. Julius' wisdom, his vision of the role of law in society and his recognition of the central role of ethical principles have remained a source of inspiration, especially when writing this book. After reading my article, *Fairness in Anglo and Latin American Commercial Adjudication*, he told me how much he enjoyed it and expressed the hope to be around when that article became part of a larger book on what he termed the anatomy and physiology of commercial law making. From the close spiritual distance that always unites us, I toast my mentor and friend Julius Stone and I am glad to report to him that the book he anticipated is here.

My first exposure to commercial law as a tool for economic development took place in Costa Rica where from 1967 to 1969 I directed the United States Agency for International Development (USAID) Law Reform Project. I was lucky to be surrounded by a highly talented and motivated group of law graduates of some of the finest law schools in the United States. Among them were Blake T. Franklin, David A. Gantz and Lorin (Laddy) S. Weisenfeld, who subsequently became highly respected lawyers and life-long friends. Blake is the Vice Chairman of the Board of Directors of the National Law Center and David is one of the nation's top international trade scholars and teachers. He is also the director of a highly successful LL.M. program on international trade and business law at the James E. Rogers College of Law, University of Arizona since its foundation approximately 22 years ago. Laddy has had a brilliant career as a legal advisor to the Overseas Private Investment Corporation (O.P.I.C). and the World Bank.

On the Costa Rican side, we enjoyed the unconditional support of the late and lamented Dean Carlos Jose Gutierrez and Professor Octavio Torrealba, Costa Rica's ablest commercial law scholar and practitioner and my co-author of a commercial law textbook still in use in Costa Rican law schools. The Costa Rican research team consisted of some of that country's most talented young commercial lawyers, including Lic. Rodrigo Oreamuno, who later became Costa Rica's Vice President and Interim President.

Together, Costa Rican and United States lawyers explored the effect of commercial legal institutions upon Costa Rica's economic development. Among these was the failure of the law of business associations to encourage corporate capital formation. In that research project, we learned the importance of familism as a cultural trait. One of our questionnaires, directed to potential middle class investors, inquired why they preferred to invest in second mortgages that yielded an interest rate far inferior to that yielded by the annual dividends of a well-established stock company. The almost unanimous response revealed the distrusting effects of familism: "Why would such a company offer such a good deal to investors who are strangers to them, neither their family nor their friends?" In other words, good deals should only be expected from family and friends and not from contractual strangers.

Mutatis mutandis, the study on access to affordable commercial and consumer credit supported by the law of credit transactions (secured and unsecured) taught us that the predictability of collections could not be based upon penalties even if they were as severe as the imprisonment of defaulting debtors. As stated by a judicial official to our John Finch (one of our insightful researchers and subsequently also a successful lawyer), if he were to enforce such a law, it is likely that a good number of our government officials and judges would have had to spend a considerable time in jail themselves.

Finally, we learned that the mission of commercial law in economic development was to instill trust in its institutions, and that such a trust was not instilled by the severest of the sovereign's commands, but by the fairness of legal institutions that benefitted both regular market participants and third parties. We also learned that commercial fairness was not a utopian or capriciously subjective notion. It was as real as the reasonable expectations of the regular participants and third parties in the Costa Rican marketplace.

Following my return to the United States at the conclusion of my duties at the Law Reform Project, I continued to teach commercial law and jurisprudence at the James E. Rogers College of Law and occasionally as a visiting professor at other United States, European and Latin American law schools. I also represented the United States at UNCITRAL and the United States Council on International Banking (USCIB) at the International Chamber of Commerce. This work was made possible in good measure by my good friend and colleague Professor James E. Byrne of George Mason University School of Law. His first periodical entitled Letter of Credit Update rescued my letter of credit writings from near anonymity. His enthusiastic support of my work continued during his chairmanship of an American Bar Association Task Force for the Revision of Article 5 of the U.C.C. Byrne introduced me to Dan Taylor, the able president of the USCIB, and Dan appointed me the United States Representative to the International Chamber of Commerce for the revision of UCP 400.

Professor Byrne also introduced me to Harold S. Burman, Esq., the Executive Director of the Secretary of State's Advisory Committee on Private International Law.

Burman was responsible for NLCIFT's and my participation in UNCITRAL as part of the team led by Byrne for the drafting of the International Convention on Independent Bank Guarantees and Standby Letters of Credit. My work as one of the drafters of UCP 500 and of the UNCITRAL Convention on Independent Bank Guarantees and Standby Letters of Credit led to my subsequent participation in the revision of Article 5 of the U.C.C., a task in which I worked with Byrne and our common friend James E. Barnes, Esq.

Byrne's introduction to Burman was fateful because subsequently, the Legal Advisor's Office of the United States Department of State appointed me as a United States Delegate to the Organization of American States during the enactment of the OAS Model Law on Secured Transactions. This law that has been adopted by several countries in Latin America and has also influenced the adoption of several other laws in Africa, especially with the world-class expertise of the NLCIFT's Dr. Marek Dubovec.

I often refer to Harold Burman as a soul mate because we share intellectual heroes and one of them is Professor Karl Llewellyn, Harold's teacher at the University of Chicago Law School. At NLCIFT, we owe him much of our success in getting significant commercial treaties, model laws and regulations adopted not only by the OAS, but also by its member countries; we are very happy that his successor, Michael Dennis, Esq., shares his dedication and ideals and is beginning to make his mark in very important UNCITRAL projects.

It was not until Professors Gantz and Kavanagh convinced me to teach a course on comparative commercial law that I was able to reflect pedagogically on the role of commercial law upon economic development. For a good number of years prior to that, I was the beneficiary of the anthropological teachings of E. Adamson Hoebel, the seminal figure of legal anthropology. During Hoebel's visiting professorship at the James E. Rogers College of Law, I learned how useful cultural anthropological analysis was in identifying archetypal legal and commercial behavior. We remained close friends until the end of his life and this book reflects many of his lessons.

The creation of the NLCIFT and the LL.M. and subsequently of the Ph.D. in international trade and business law programs at the James E. Rogers College of Law contributed significantly to the breadth of the comparative commercial law course and of this Hornbook. The NLCIFT was founded in 1992 as a non-profit research institute affiliated with the University of Arizona. This arrangement was made possible by Joel E. Valdez, the then Vice President for Business Affairs of the university, a true community leader and of one of NLCIFT's most loyal and noble supporters and the drafter of the University of Arizona and the NLCIFT Affiliation Agreement. This agreement was signed by former Dean Thomas Sullivan, renewed by former Dean Lawrence Ponoroff, and by his successor Marc Miller, both enthusiastic supporters of joint research and teaching projects with NLCIFT.

NLCIFT's work consists largely in bringing about the uniformity or harmonization of commercial law in developing nations; it began with Latin America and subsequently it was taken to Africa and is now beginning to find its place in Asia. Its initial financial support came from United States congressional appropriations, made possible by the visionary leadership of former Congressman Jim Kolbe, one of the principal architects of the North American Free Trade Agreement (NAFTA) and of the

Central American Free Trade Agreement (CAFTA), some of whose negotiations took place at the NLCIFT headquarters. Following an initial period of federal and state appropriations, the federal congressional funding mandate was assumed by the United States Department of State. NLCIFT is also a contractor with the International Financial Corporation (IFC) of the World Bank, whose secured transactions' program is superbly led by Dr. Alejandro Alvarez de la Campa with the assistance of Elsa Rodriguez Felipe and now of John M. Wilson Esq., a former student and subsequently a staff member and Project Coordinator at NLCIFT and thereafter, Legal Advisor at the Organization of American States.

NLCIFT has also been fortunate in being able to count upon the guidance and assistance of a highly professional, devoted and motivated board of directors presided since shortly after its foundation by Phillip A. Robbins Esq., one of Arizona's most respected lawyers and president of the Arizona-Mexico bar. NLCIFT and I owe much gratitude to the late and lamented Judge John J. Molloy He was NLCIFT's board secretary for more than a decade and in his spare time co-authored and edited with me the four volume NLCIFT treatise on United States Law of Trade and Investment, I am similarly indebted to my friend, former student and board member, Paul Karon and to his wife Patsy for their unfailing support of NLCIFT.

Unlike the traditional uniformity and harmonization work which relies on a transplantation of successful statutes and regulations from other legal systems and cultures, the NLCIFT takes into account those socio-economic and cultural factors that are likely to ensure the success of its joint work with the enacting governments. Thus NLCIFT contextual "roadmaps" on topics such as cross-border truck transportation, check clearing, bank regulations and secured transactions typically take into account variables such as: Archetypal private and public participants, the nations' legal, business and political culture, and the legal institutions that could contribute to or detract from the success of the projected normative work.

This Hornbook incorporates much of the NLCIFT methodology and experience with contextual comparisons. Thus, it is intended for use not only in United States law schools, law offices and legal research and business libraries but also in their counterparts in civil law countries. For this reason, it had to be written in a manner sensitive to what each group of readers is likely to know about the legal institution in question. This explains its large number of footnotes and cross-references designed to provide the quickest possible access to the explanatory comparative data, as it also explains the length of its glossary and topical and conceptual index. The same is true with repeated short explanations of the same legal institution, if that institution is likely to be foreign to one segment of readers or to students who take only one part of the course.

My frequent use of first person style of writing is motivated by a desire to engage the reader in a continuing comparative law dialogue. I do not use cases for purely Socratic or dialectic purposes, as is often done by many case-books, because we have too many contextual gaps to fill. Thus, this book uses court decisions mostly to illustrate and confirm what has been stated in the black letter portion of the principal text.

To conclude, I wish to thank those who have motivated the writing of this book and who have aided and encouraged its completion ever since I became a comparative lawyer under Professors Yntema's, Stone's and Hoebel's tutelage. I have been lucky to count on the support of a loving family starting with my wife Billie, who has doubled as a long time rigorously precise editor, and continuing with my children Abbie, Raphael, Diana, Shaun and David and my grandchildren Sigal, Liana, Alex, Ethan and Jacob, my sister, Marta, the two other Borises (Kozolchyk and Rosen), the extended Kozolchyk and Olchyk families, my lifelong friends Isaac and Sarita Kreps, Nardo Zaias, Jacques and Victoria Ciepielewski and Sam and Lolita Grabb they redefined a close friendship and into a close and caring family. I have also been lucky to enjoy the enduring comradeship of Professors David A. Gantz, James E. Byrne (David and Jim's contributions were noted above) and Roy Spece. Roy has been kind enough to read all the chapters and his comments have always been insightful and helpful. I am similarly indebted to my close friend and colleague Professor Dale Furnish for having used an earlier and shorter version of this book in his teaching of a widely attended undergraduate course at Arizona State University and for his brotherly support since we both started teaching law in this state; Dale is also a devoted NLCIFT board member, researcher and co-author. I also wish to express my gratitude to my former student and present colleague Dr. Marek Dubovec., who has become one of the world's true experts on the law of secured transactions and who was kind enough to comment on several chapters of this book.

I owe to my colleague and former Dean Lawrence Ponoroff the introduction to Louis Higgins of West Academic Press, who has been an understanding and cooperative publisher. Last, but certainly not least, I have been most fortunate in having the support of an extraordinarily capable and giving staff at NLCIFT. It is not an exaggeration to say that without the support and patience of Donna Vulpis, my assistant for many years, this book may not have been written. Keeping track of such a large manuscript and of its many additions and deletions for more than a decade of preparation has often been a super-human task; she discharged it with invariable generosity and good cheer. I am also very grateful to my former students who have doubled as editors and research assistants. The most recent among them is Brad Terry. He, Donna, Cristina Castaneda, Lauren Weiss, Elizabeth Pocock and Billie Kozolchyk comprise the fine team of editors this book has enjoyed during its fifteen year preparation.

As is customary, I assume responsibility for the errors and omissions of this book.

Summary of Contents

Table of Contents

COMPARATIVE COMMERCIAL CONTRACTS

LAW, CULTURE AND ECONOMIC DEVELOPMENT

Part I

OVERVIEW, METHODOLOGY, FORMATION AND EVOLUTION OF COMMERCIAL PROMISES

Chapter 1

GUIDING THEMES AND CONTENT OF THIS BOOK

§ 1.1 INTRODUCTION

This chapter provides a glimpse of what lies ahead in this book and, hopefully, in the growing field of comparative commercial law and economic development studies. I would be the first to acknowledge that this book is not the usual Anglo-American casebook, hornbook or treatise, nor is it the traditional civil law treatise, manual or code commentary. It does study traditional legal texts such as codes, treaties, statutes, court decisions and commentaries as well as compilations of proposed internationally uniform laws and of widely-observed commercial and banking customs. In addition, however, it weaves historical, economic and anthropological materials into the above positive law and normative fabric. The purpose of this weaving is to relate the law of commercial contracts to the values, policies, attitudes and practices from which it sprung.

The breadth of this inquiry is designed to facilitate a deeper understanding of the law of commercial contracts as it fulfills its purpose as an agent of economic development or fails to do so, especially in developing nations.

And while the official or positive law of commercial contracts of developing nations was modeled after that of developed nations, their living law, or the law as actually practiced, is quite different. The following chapters are designed to highlight commonalities and differences as well as the economic consequences that flow from them.

§ 1.2 GUIDING THEMES

A. Whether as a Science or as an Art, the Law Is About People

This section emphasizes the "peopled" nature of law, The law of commercial contracts is about merchants, how they compete and cooperate with each other, strangers or third parties. This is why commercial values, attitudes, courses of dealing, practices and usages of trade require greater attention than legal pedagogy and jurisprudence presently offer them. An important contribution of the peopled nature of commercial contract law is the understanding that those legal institutions that most accurately reflect commercial man's best practices are the most supportive of society's economic development.

One of the first lessons I learned from my mentor Hessel E. Yntema at the University of Michigan was that the study and practice of law could qualify as a science and as an art.[1] As a science, the study of law objectively and accurately

---

[1] See Hessel E. Yntema, Legal Science and Natural Law—Apropos of Viehweg, Topik und Jurisprudenz, 2 INTER-AM L. REV. 207 (1960).

describes its institutions, *i.e.*, its concepts, principles and rules and the manner in which they are created and applied. In this respect, historical and cross-boundary comparisons help to sharpen the key features of legal institutions. But so does the comparison of legal cultures, values, attitudes, customs and practices.

The practice of law relies upon the findings of legal science to determine the applicability of concepts, principles or rules to the issues raised by the particular transaction or litigation. It also relies upon the art of interpretation as a tool with which to persuade judges, arbitrators and juries that the facts and law before them favor their client's position.

Yet, either as a science or as an art, law is about people. As stated by Justice Oliver Wendell Holmes Jr. in a letter to Sir Frederick Pollock, referring to Harvard Professor Christopher Langdell's casebook on the law of contracts, "decisions are reconciled . . . and drawn together by subtle lines which never were dreamed before Mr. Langdell wrote them." He had added that "no one will ever have a truly philosophic mastery over the law who does not habitually consider the forces outside of it which have made it what it is . . . [because] the law finds its philosophy not in self consistency, but . . . in history and the nature of human needs. . . ."[2] In the case of the law of commercial contracts, it is about merchants and how they compete and cooperate with each other and with third parties. The law of commercial contracts, in particular, is shaped by what merchants do, and especially by their standard and best practices. The former are the most widely practiced and thus reflect the reasonable expectations of regular market participants. The latter reflect the behavior of exemplary merchants, respected and often admired for their knowledge, integrity and willingness to be brotherly or altruistic when necessary. Hence, the law of commercial contracts is not a law that can be guided by abstract mathematical concepts, principles and rules, even if supposedly derived from the Roman *Corpus Iuris Civilis*.[3] Neither is it, as claimed by some civil law commentators, a law that can be frozen in time and space because it supposedly embodies eternal, universal and permanent truths.[4]

B. The Shaping Role of Standard and Best Practices

Often in combined fashion, standard and best practices shape the law of commercial contracts. The longevity of these practices and their contribution to economic development reflect the success of their combination.

Commercial law is found in standard and best commercial practices (often referred as living law) and in statutes, court decisions and administrative regulations (often referred to as written or positive law). These laws perform diverse but complementary functions; with greater or lesser success, the living law provides what is often the determinant normative material for the positive law. The positive law is the law that is most frequently invoked in commercial law disputes and almost exclusively taught in most law schools and business schools. Hence it is important to keep in mind what makes these sets of commercial law successful.

---

[2] *See* G. EDWARD WHITE, JUSTICE OLIVER WENDELL HOLMES: LAW AND THE INNER SELF 170 (1993).

[3] *See infra* § 13:1(C) (for a discussion on the teachings of Professor Heinrich Thol and Alfredo Rocco on commercial legal science and the opposite viewpoints of Levin Goldschmidt and Cesare Vivante).

[4] *Id.*

Although standard practices are shaped by everyday commercial behavior, they must all be cost effective and protect the reasonable expectations of regular participants in the chosen transaction. Hence, the standard practices reflect what I have referred to in earlier writings as the "market standard of fairness": Treat the other party to the transaction as a regular {{representative or}} archetypal participant would reasonably expect to be treated when viewing his own advantage.[5] Best practices, in turn, protect not only the reasonable expectations of regular participants, but also those of third parties (or parties who are not regular participants in the transaction) and especially of those whose contractual weakness, ignorance or immaturity makes them entrust regular participants with their assets. Thus, in best commercial practices, the protection given by these practices to such third parties exceeds that given to regular participants and those entrusted regular participants are expected to act in a fiduciary capacity, even if on occasion the fiduciary must behave in an altruistic manner.

Because best practices are designed to induce the trust and creditworthiness of regular participants, traditionally they have shaped the seminal "rules of traffic" of everyday transactions. These are the rules that direct parties on what they have to do to form, amend, assign, cancel or terminate their agreements. Thus, a Roman gratuitous loan agreement (*commodatum*) was not perfected by an exchange of promises between the lender and the borrower, but by the practice that required the delivery of the thing lent to the borrower.[6] Up until that moment, so the practice implied, it was not clear that the lender was serious enough about his promise to allow the recipient to use his thing gratuitously.[7] Similarly, an Anglo American sale agreement still requires, after several centuries as a standard practice, that one party start the contract by giving to the other something of value as consideration for the other's simultaneous or subsequent giving of a thing, a promise, an act or a partial or full performance. When a standard practice (that reflects the right measure of reasonable expectations of profit) is combined with a best practice (that reflects the right measure of concern for the rights of third parties, especially in cases of entrustment), it will succeed in achieving its market building function. This was the case with the English lenders' advance of their loan amounts to their borrowers as the first step in creating a credit market that by the end of the seventeenth century had standardized its transactions and had become the most rapidly developing commercial credit market in Europe.[8]

As will be discussed in Chapter 20, this combination of standard and best practices became a rule of traffic for most other commercial contracts in England and very soon was referred to by merchants, drafters and adjudicators of their contracts as the "consideration" or *quid pro quo* of these contracts. Thus, the simple act of giving something of value clothed the contractual promise with a presumption of validity, even if the promise was executory or one to be performed in the future.[9] In contrast,

---

[5] *See* Kozolchyk, *Fairness,* at 220.

[6] *See* BERGER, ENCYCLOPEDIC DICTIONARY, at 399.

[7] An extension of the principle that validates a gratuitous promise of a loan by delivery is found in Section 518 of the BGB which provides that the failure to execute a donation in formal fashion is cured by the performnce of the donation.

[8] *See infra* ch. 20.

[9] *See infra* chs. 20 & 22 (for the discussion of Slade's case).

the notion of *causa*, which was supposed to be the civil law counterpart to consideration, never became a predictable rule of commercial-contractual traffic. At best, it was a philosophical explanation of the purpose of contracts and why a valid *causa* made them binding. Yet, it could hardly become an initial rule of commercial-contractual traffic when the determination of whether a contract had a valid *causa* usually took place *a posteriori* or when the validity of a contract was challenged in court. Thus, while consideration became a rule of traffic that assured those merchants who had given it that the contract whose sequence they had just started was presumptively binding, *causa* was too removed from what merchants actually did to become a rule of traffic.

C. Successful Standard and Best Practices and Commercial Statutory and Case Law

Commerical statutory and case law areo a product of successful standard and best practices, at times formulated as maxims and principles that best summarize these practices.

At times, these maxims are part of the nation's or region's legal folklore and their authors are unknown, and at other times, the authors are judges or academics.[10] Influential commercial law statutes have benefited from the wise use of these summarizing maxims and principles. One such a statute was the German Law of Bills of Exchange (*Wechselordnung*) of 1848.[11] It relied on maxims that summarized commercial practices of entrustment that dated back to medieval Germany, such as "Where you have put your faith, there you must seek it" (*wo du deinen Glauben gelassen hast, musst du ihn suchen*), and "The (trusting) hand must warrant [the sale or transfer by the] (trusted) hand" (*Hand muss Hand wahren*).[12]

These maxims required the protection of *bona fide* purchasers of movable goods who had acquired them from a person who—thanks to the transferor of the goods—appeared to enjoy their lawful possession and thereby seemed empowered to transfer the goods to innocent third parties. These principles combined the standard practice of allowing a trusting party to recover from an unfaithful bailee or custodian with the best practice that protected the acquisition by an innocent third party purchaser.

When drafting the German law of Bills of Exchange, Judge Dr. Karl Einert treated bills of exchange and other negotiable instruments as transferable goods or movable property. And he relied on the same medieval principles and on German banking practices that protected *bona fide* purchasers or negotiators of bills of exchange and of bearer bonds from claims, or defenses derived from transactions that preceded their purchases or negotiations.[13] As discussed in a later chapter, this law and its guiding principles influenced the English Bills of Exchange Act and the United States Law of Negotiable Instruments, among many other negotiable instrument statutes and

---

[10] *See, e.g.*, Sir Edward Coke's Legal Maxims, *in* SIR EDWARD COKE, THE FIRST PART OF THE INSTITUTES OF THE LAWS OF ENGLAND (Legal Classics Library 1823) (1628), *AVAILABLE AT* THOMAS P. VINCENT, LEGAL HISTORY AND PHILOSOPHY, http://www.commonlaw.com/Coke.html.

[11] *See generally* Peter Ellinger, *Negotiable Instruments*, *in* IX INTERNATIONAL ENCYLOPEDIA OF COMPARATIVE LAW, ch. 4 (K. Zweigert, U. Drobnig eds., 1981).

[12] RUDOLF HUEBNER, A HISTORY OF GERMANIC PRIVATE LAW 409 (Francis S. Philbrick, trans., 1918).

[13] *See infra* ch. 11.

international conventions.[14] Furthermore, at times it is the judicial alertness to changes in standard practices that enables not only the qualification of these practices but the formulation of replacement maxims. This was the case with the eighteenth century English judges who qualified the application of the maxim "buyer be aware" (*caveat emptor*) and initiated its gradual (albeit partial) replacement by "[i]n merchants' sales of wares a sound price warrants a sound article. . . ."[15]

The application of commercial practices, legal maxims and principles is often easier by the use of representative or archetypal commercial behavior. They could illustrate the behavior of either average or exemplary merchants. This law making tradition goes back to classical Roman law. In Chapter IV,[16] the reader will find an opinion by the jurist Ulpian where he suggested that a contractual controversy that involved the use or abuse of a discretionary clause on the sale of a slave be determined in accordance with the behavior of an exemplary man of affairs—the "*Bonus Vir.*"[17] As will be apparent in Chapter IV, Ulpian was not the only one with an in-depth understanding of commercial law and the wisdom to anticipate the consequences that specific practices, laws and judicial decisions could l have on transactions. Such ability and reasoning was shared by jurists such as Lord Mansfield,[18] the drafters of the German Commercial Code (HGB)[19] and Justice Cardozo, among not too many others.[20]

D. Selfishness, Cooperation and Altruism as Integral Parts of Human Nature and Commerce

Recent scientific findings prove that despite man's selfishness, cooperation and altruism are also part of his nature, especially when engaged in commerce.

Commerce, as contrasted with war-making, plundering and exploiting the work of others, is a cooperative endeavor between or among the parties to a contract and also with third parties. This cooperative feature of market life is supported by two corollary principles: The first principle requires that merchants deal with others in the same manner in which regular archetypal market participants would expect to be treated (As will be discussed in Chapter 2, this archetypal standard of market fairness is the most comprehensive; other standards reflect the expectations of one or the other party to the transaction).

The second principle posits that, as was just discussed, those merchants who are the most trusted are likely to treat those who entrust them with their assets with a

---

[14] *See infra* ch. 11. *See also* HUEBNER, *supra* note 12, at 407–10; Kozolchyk, *Transfer*, at 1480, on the effect of this principle upon commercial law and specifically on negotiation.

[15] *See* Karl Llewellyn, *Across Sales on Horseback, 52* HARV. L. REV. 725, 743 (1939); *but c.f.,* James Oldham, *Reinterpretations of 18th-Century English Contract Theory: The View from Lord Mansfield's Trial Notes*, 76 GEO. L.J. 1949, 1972 (1988). For a discussion of the commercial meaning of good faith in connection with express and implied warranties, *see* ch. 23.

[16] *See* § 4:6(C).

[17] *Id.*

[18] *See* Pillans v. Van Mierop, 3 BURR. 1663 [K.B. 1765], it was rejected by the House of Lords in its decision in Rann v. Hughes, 7 T.R. 350 [H.L. 1778]. *See also infra* ch. 22 (for a discussion of this decision).

[19] *See* HGB § 347 (GOREN, 1998).

[20] *See* Meinhard v. Salmon, 249 N.Y. 458, 464 (1928); In re James Estate, 86 N.Y.S.2d 78, 89–90 (1948). *See also* Boris Kozolchyk, *Strict Compliance and the Reasonable Document Checker*, 56 BROOK. L. REV. 45 (1990); U.C.C. § 5–108(a)–(e); United Nations Convention on Independent Guarantees and Stand-by Letters of Credit, arts. 5, 13, 14, http://www.uncitral.org/pdf/english/texts/payments/guarantees/guarantees.pdf.

measure of altruism. In Justice Cardozo's words: "Many forms of conduct permissible in a workaday world for those acting at arm's length, are forbidden to those bound by fiduciary ties. A trustee is held to something stricter than the morals of the market place. Not honesty alone, but the punctilio of an honor the most sensitive, is then the standard of behavior."[21]

While I have been convinced for years that the impulses of altruism (especially as cooperation) and selfishness inter-act and are firmly and deeply imbedded in human nature (as was intuited in the 5th century A.D. by social thinkers starting with a 5th century Talmudic scholar and thereafter social thinkers of the stature of Bernard de Mandeville, Adam Smith and Emile Durkheim),[22] I was not aware of the existence of the scientific verification of this inter-action until rather recently. During the last three decades, Professor Michael Tomasello, co-director of the Max Planck Institute for Evolutionary Anthropology in Leipzig, Germany, and his co-researchers have verified the extent of human cooperation in various comparative experiments.[23]

> [H]umans . . . plan something and divide spoils, or maintain their cooperation over time, this is something that chimpanzees have great difficulty doing. They fight over the food and cannot maintain collaboration over time. Even if they cooperate on something it is not maintained . . . [H]umans put their heads together to do something together that they cannot do alone.[24]

Man's high degree of cooperation starts at an early age. When children see other children doing something in the wrong manner, whether it is playing a game or using a tool, they come to their fellow child's assistance. Thus, a primary and crucial difference between the human and other animal species, including the chimpanzees (our closest genetic relatives), is man's ability to collaborate with each other to achieve shared goals. Reflecting upon these experiments, E.O. Wilson, one of the world's most respected biologists, and the founder of socio-biology, noted that from infancy, man is predisposed to read the intentions of others and is quick to cooperate whenever there is a trace of a shared interest.

---

[21] *See* Meinhard, 249 N.Y. at 464.

[22] *See, e.g.,* Kozolchyk, *Grand and Small Scheme* at 144: where I quoted a passage from the Fable of the Evil Impulse based upon Talmudic writings, at least thirteen centuries old, in which the scholar concluded:

> In scheme divine—a principle sound:
> Vicious forces as passion, avarice and greed
> Are vehicles of progress the world doth need.

Id. (citation omitted).

For references to Bernard Mandeville and Adam Smith, *see infra* ch. 23; and to Emile Durkheim's "duality of human existence," including the co-existence of altruisic and selfish actions in human behavior, *see* STEPHEN INNES, 2 CREATING THE COMMONWEALTH: THE ECONOMIC CULTURE OF PURITAN NEW ENGLAND 7 n.12 & accompanying text (1995).

[23] *See* Michael Tomasello, *Biographical Info*, http://email.eva.mpg.de/~tomas/cv.html [hereinafter Tomasello website]. *See also* The Royal Netherlands Academy of Arts and Sciences, Heineken Prizes—Professor Michael Tomasello, YOUTUBE (Nov. 18, 2010), http://www.youtube.com/watch?v=Dtf2btmfPgw (last accessed Aug. 14, 2013) (transcript on file with author). *See generally* Michael Tomasello et al., *Understanding and Sharing Intentions; The Origins of Cultural Cognition,* 28 BEHAV. & BRAIN SCI. 675 (2005) (on file with author); *see also* Esther Herrmann et al., *Human's Have Evolved Specialized Skills of Social Cognition: The Cultural Intelligence Hypothesis,* SCIENCE 317: 1360–1366 (2007), *in* EDWARD O. WILSON, THE SOCIAL CONQUEST OF EARTH 226–27, 321 (2012), on Tomasello's work.

[24] Tomasello website, *supra* note 23.

In one revealing experiment, children were shown how to open the door to a container. When adults tried to open the (same) door but pretended not to know how, the children stopped what they were doing and crossed the room to help. Chimpanzees who were put in the same circumstance, but are far less advanced in cooperative awareness, made no such effort.[25]

Wilson attributes cooperation, among other features, to the "intentionality" of the human mind, a feature made possible by man's very large working memory, which enables both perception and communication of intentions.[26] This is the very same capability that contracting parties have relied on to enter into agreements since the birth of contracts. Further, as a quintessentially social and cooperative animal, man not only interacts with others as do animals with advanced social organizations, but to a unique degree collaborates and enmeshes himself in social networks including business ventures and transactions.[27] This tendency to socialize and engage in commerce is the product of a drive deeply ingrained in *homo sapiens*. Evolutionary biologists attribute this socialization to a complicated evolutionary process that led man and other animals to "eusociality," *i.e.*, the ability to form groups that include multiple generations who cooperate with each other and *are also prone to perform altruistic acts as part of their division of labor*.[28]

Wasps are among the animals that have attained eusociality—they build nests to raise their young and defend their nests from predators, parasites or competitors often at the the cost of their lives. In addition, while many of the young wasps leave their nests, others stay, thereby enhancing the group's chances of survival. In defending their nests and staying on for the sake of group survival, the species reaches the threshold of eusociality.[29] Bees of solitary species can reach the same threshold when two of them find themselves confined to a space small enough that only one nest or private cell can be built. And, when this happens, "[t]he pair automatically form a pecking order of the kind observed in natural populations of primitively eusocial bees. The dominant female, the 'queen,' stays at the nest and reproduces and guards the nest, while the subordinate female, the 'worker,' forages for food."[30]

The eusociality and altruism among wasps, bees and other animals are traceable to allelles or gene forms that start being selected when parents reach the stage of building nests and feeding their young progressively: "The only thing needed is group selection, acting on group traits that also favors families that stay at home. . . . A new level of biological organization is attained. *One small step for a queen with her newly created worker cast, one giant leap for the insects.*"[31] The cooperation and altruism attributable to insects such as ants, bees, wasps and termites accounts for their large numbers and their ability to thrive as part of a select group. Wilson refers to this select

---

[25] WILSON, *supra* note 23, at 227.

[26] *Id.* at 226.

[27] *Id.* at 226–27.

[28] *Id.* at 16. *See also* Glossary, "Eusociality."

[29] WILSON, *supra* note 23, at 141–42.

[30] *Id.* at 142.

[31] *Id.* at 152.

group as the "social conquerors of the Earth" and its most protean inhabitant is the human species.[32]

According to Professor Wilson, the finding that *instincts* evolve by natural selection belongs to Charles Darwin, who showed how the behavioral traits that define each species are hereditary. In Wilson's words: "They arose and exist today, Darwin said, because in the past they aided survival and reproduction. Darwin's fundamental insight has been verified over and over again."[33] Yet, what does genetics and biology have to say about the moral condition of humans? Are they innately good, but corruptible by the forces of evil? Or are they wicked and redeemable only by the forces of good? Wilson's response is that people are both, and will remain in this condition until a genetic change takes place:[34] "Thus was born the human condition, selfish at one time, selfless at another, the two impulses often conflicted."[35]

This dualism is attributable to individual and group selection. Individual selection results from the competition for survival and reproduction among members of the same group. It shapes instincts in each member that are fundamentally selfish with reference to other members. Group selection stems from the competition between societies or organized groups of individuals: "[It] shapes instincts that tend to make individuals altruistic toward one another (but not toward members of other groups). . . . Together they have created the conflict between the poorer and the better angels of our nature"[36] and are responsible for the "iron rule" of genetic social evolution:

> [S]elfish individuals beat altruistic individuals, while groups of altruists beat groups of selfish individuals. The victory can never be complete; the balance of selection pressures cannot move to either extreme. If individual selection were to dominate, societies would dissolve. If group selection were to dominate, human groups would come to resemble ant colonies.[37]

Some distinguished economists and legal thinkers have taken notice of research of biologists and agree that the biological data shows that altruism may increase the likelihood of the altruist's genes surviving in the competition among populations and they have suggested the term "reciprocal altruism" as a more precise term, especially in social inter-action than just plain altruis. In the words of William Landes and Judge Richard Posner:

> If insect A saves B from some peril, this means B will be alive to save A should he find himself in danger. This "reciprocal altruism" may enhance the survivorship of the group to which A and B belong relative to that of some nonaltruistic insect group).[38]

For the sake of conceptual precision, whenever I use the term "altruism" in this book it will mean, unless otherwise indicated a reciprocal altruism.

---

[32] *Id.* at 10.

[33] *Id.* at 158.

[34] *Id.* at 241.

[35] *Id.* at 17.

[36] *Id.* at 241.

[37] *Id.* at 243.

[38] WILLIAM M. LANDES & RICHARD A. POSNER, ALTRUISM IN LAW AND ECONOMICS 68 AM. ECON. REV. 417–21 (No. 2, 1978), http://www.jstor.org/stable/1816731.

Wilson's iron rule reminded me of two sayings by Jewish sages both alluding to the same dilemma and both frequently mentioned in this book: One was by Hillel, the Elder of biblical times: "If I am not for myself, who will be for me, and if I am only for myself, what am I?"[39] The other belongs to the just mentioned Talmudic "Fable of the Evil Impulse" written during the first centuries of the Common Era, which has been summarized proverbially as: "There is good in evil as there is evil in good."[40]

Professor Wilson suggests another moral command (also authored by Hillel the Elder) that if obeyed wisely may save mankind from the strictures of the moral dilemma created by the pressure of natural selection: *The feeling of empathy for the condition of others.*

> A great deal of recent research has made it possible to see how the impulses might work inside the brain. A promising start has been found in explaining the Golden Rule, which is perhaps the only precept found in all organized religions. The rule is fundamental to all moral reasoning. When the great theologian and philosopher Rabbi Hillel was challenged to explain the Torah in the time he could stand on one foot, he replied, "Do not do unto others that which is repugnant to you. All else is commentary."[41]

In the following chapter, the reader will find a detailed discussion of the "logic of the reasonable," a form of reasoning much relied on for the interpretation of commercial contracts in Anglo-American law. In my opinion, to discern what is reasonable conduct by a contracting party, one party must be able to place himself in the position of an archetypal other and ask himself: "Given what I have said and done in this contractual negotiation and what is generally done or given *by parties similarly situated,* what would the other party expect me to do or give?" This form of reasoning is peculiar to the standard of fairness that I have referred to in my writings, including in this book, as the "market" standard, *i.e.*, treat the other party to the contract as a regular market participant would reasonably expect to be treated. Hence, reasonableness reflects a feeling of empathy for the expectations of others. As reported by Wilson, researchers of the human brain have observed clear manifestations of such an empathy once human subjects are made aware of an imminent harm likely to be experienced by themselves as well as by others.[42]

In sum, the *homo sapiens* either had the proper genetic components or learned early in his development that survival depended upon cooperation with others and that it entailed not only an eye for self-interest but also an instinct for altruistic giving. In fact, the more he gave to others, the more others trusted him and trusted his legal institutions. This was an unforgettable lesson I learned during the 1960s while directing a legal modernization project in Central America.[43] It is also an empirical

---

[39] *See infra* § 5:12(D).

[40] *See also* Morris Silver, Book Review, 20 AJS REV. 197 (1995) (reviewing ROMAN A. OHRENSTEIN & BARRY GORDON, ECONOMIC ANALYSIS IN TALMUDIC LITERATURE: RABBINIC THOUGHT IN THE LIGHT OF MODERN ECONOMICS (1992)) (review on file with author). Silver points out how the Talmud's view on economic self interest as a positive force for economic development preceded Bernard de Mandeville's views in his *Fable of the Bees,* as well as Adam Smith's "invisible hand." *Id.* at 197.

[41] WILSON, *supra* note 23, at 245.

[42] *Id.* at 245 (referring to the work of neurobiologist Donald W. Pfaff).

[43] *See* Kozolchyk, *Toward a Theory of Law,* at 740 ("the indispensable function of the legal system in economic development is that of instilling trust in its institutions.").

verification of Levin Goldschmidt's insight, which was highly admired by Karl Llewellyn, that there is an immanent law of commerce. For those who have trouble with the notion of immanence I would suggest that what Goldschmidt and Llewellyn had in mind was a law that reflects the nature of commercial activity and of commercial man, *i.e.*, a selfish but peculiarly cooperative and on occasion altruistic being.[44] The serious economic consequences of harboring a contrary view of commerce and of the nature of man will be apparent in the chapters that discuss the attitudes and values of France's original commercial court and the effect of Marxism-Leninism upon Soviet commercial contract law.[45]

E. Sub-Standard Contract—Often Simulated—Practices Are Found in All Legal Systems

Simulated contracts are contracts that disguise the intent of the parties by making it appear that they agreed to be bound to perform contract "A" when in fact they agreed to be bound by contract "B." Simulations are pervasive in developing nations as reflected in the saying: "He who invented the law also invented the way around it." Yet, they can also be found in developed nations, and in the last two decades they are quite apparent in major financial transactions. As a "way around the law," simulation is fueled by and fuels corruption and thereby undermines the certainty of the law of contracts.

Not all commercial practices are either standard or best. As Professor E. O. Wilson reminded us, our nature is not always angelical or law abiding and this leads to substandard contractual practices, including many that are caused by bad faith behavior. Bad faith practices are discussed in later chapters.[46] The present section is devoted to simulated contracts, or contracts that disguise their true intent by adopting a label that gives them the appearance of validity even though in fact what the parties intended to accomplish with their disguise is illegal according to the official law. Usually both parties agree to simulate a contractual intent and in that narrow sense it may not be a bad faith practice except *vis a vis* third parties such as a tax collector.

Some of the causes of simulation are traceable to official law rules that are unnecessarily costly and cumbersome. For example, in civil law countries, especially those whose private law has been modeled after the *Code Civil* of France of 1804, certain contracts can be quite expensive or rigidly formalistic and thus unsuitable for the transaction they intend to enter into.[47] As you will soon learn, Roman law relied on the "typification" of its contracts to determine not only the rights and duties, but also the remedies peculiar to each type of contract.[48] Accordingly, it became a standard simulation that when a husband could not use a contract of donation to bequeath valuable property to his wife, he would customarily label the conveyance a purchase and sale (*emptio venditio*), which was allowed, but required the payment of a price that was in fact never paid by the wife.[49] Thus, husband and wife simulated a purchase and sale that actually did not take place.

---

[44] *See infra* § 13:1(C).

[45] *See infra* chs. 9 & 15.

[46] For a detailed discussion of bad faith practices, *see infra* chs. 23 & 24.

[47] *See infra* §§ 7:4–7:5.

[48] *See infra* § 4:4(D)(3)(e).

[49] John P. Dawson, GIFTS AND PROMISES: CONTINENTAL AND AMERICAN LAW COMPARED (1980).

Similarly, medieval European borrowers and lenders of money who wished to enter into loan agreements at the prevailing (but forbidden) market rate of interest, would label their loan a "sale of foreign exchange" (*cambium*) in which the buyer paid a commission equivalent to the interest rate that was secretly being paid by a borrower.[50] Or, consider the transactions used by Mexican sellers of land or buildings located in Mexican coastal and border areas (forbidden zones during the 1950s and 1960s). These sellers would label their sales to foreign purchasers "long term leases" (*arrendamientos a largo plazo*) or "contracts of membership" in a beach resort (*membrecías en clubes turísticos*).[51] By using such labels, Mexican sellers of land in the "forbidden" zones effectuated forbidden sales of land, seemingly without violating the law. Simulations were and are also common in non capitalist countries such as Soviet Russia and the present day socialist People's Republic of China.

During the last decade or so, simulated financial transactions have become popular in developed nations. As with their sisters in developing nations, the purpose of these simulations is to find a way around a law, although the law being circumvented may be as far removed from an ordinary merchant's experience as that which qualifies a country to become a member of the European Union. Take for example Greece's attempt to qualify for admission to the European Union in 2001. To be admitted, the Maastricht Treaty required that Greece's budget deficit not be higher than three percent of its gross domestic product (GDP).[52] The way around this requirement, Goldman Sachs suggested, was for Greece to enter into a cross currency swap with Goldman Sachs where Greek government debt, issued in dollars and yen, was swapped for Euro debt for a certain period of time. The purpose of this swap was to make it appear that by having acquired assets of a higher value than it had conveyed, a significant portion of Greece's government debt disappeared, albeit only for a while. Aside from this swap, Goldman Sachs agreed to lend the Greek government a large amount of money with which to pay some of its imminent obligations. By pushing the swap's termination into the future, the Greek debt statistics meanwhile both hid and obscured the extent of the Greek budget deficit. As observed by a financial analyst, the "reality was that Goldman Sachs had essentially helped Greece cheat on its financial reporting to the European Union as its deficit was much higher than the 3 per cent by the required by the Maastricht Treaty."[53] As noted by Nick Dunbar, the financial reporter and analyst for Bloomberg News who made public the Greek-Goldman Sachs simulation: "When I published my story on Goldman Sachs and Greece in July 2003, the almost-universal reaction was: EU member states were flouting the Maastricht Treaty with the help of investment banks—so what?"[54]

---

[50] *See* Raymond de Roover, *infra* § 5:7(B)(1) n.57 and accompanying text.

[51] *See infra* § 14:4(A)(3)(c).

[52] For a short description of Greece's and Goldman Sachs' simulation, *see* Randy Lacen, *Bailouts And Interest Expense For Greece's Debt Crisis*, SEEKING ALPHA, http://seekingalpha.com/article/701061–bailouts-and-interest-expense-for-greece-s-debt-crisis. For a reference to the story that revealed the use of a swap of foreign currency to mask the loan by Goldman Sachs (one of the world's leading investment bankers), *see* Nick Dunbar, *How Goldman Sachs Helped Mask Greece's Debt*, BBC (Feb. 20, 2012), http://www.bbc.co.uk/news/world-europe-17108367 [hereinafter Dunbar Report].

[53] *See* Lacen, *supra* note 52.

[54] *See* Dunbar Report, *supra* note 52.

Yet, Mr. Dunbar also uncovered analogous simulations by London investment bankers in their dealings with Italian cities and with small and medium-sized business in England.[55]

In the following chapters, the reader will find many other simulations, regardless of the legal system or markets in which they take place, whether in colonial or contemporary Latin America,[56] the Soviet Union,[57] Imperial China or the People's Republic of China.[58] And lest you think that simulation is unknown in United States' commercial marketplace, think of how many of our tax law colleagues earn a respectable living by helping taxpayers to "avoid" or significantly reduce their tax liability by entering into ingenious contracts, seemingly intended mostly, if not solely, for tax avoidance or evasion purposes.

When simulations are as widespread as they are now, they signal a misalignment between the "written" or "positive" law and the law they actually practice, referred to in this book as the "living law."[59] The sharper this misalignment is, the greater the uncertainty in that nation or region's commercial law. And an uncertain commercial law is a sure recipe for higher and often unaffordable costs of doing business. Further, as will be discussed in Guiding Theme 8, contracts, when freely and transparently entered into, are indispensable macro and microeconomic tools for determining realistically the prices and costs involved in the exchanges of goods and services. This makes contract prices and their standard terms and conditions essential tools of economic development. To the extent that many contracts are simulated and non transparent they fail to function as optimal tools for economic development. For only with accurate prices can goods and services be assigned to their most productive use.

F. The Sharp Line Between Civil and Commercial Contracts in Many Civil Law Countries

Countries and regions whose private law stems from the French and Spanish Civil and Commercial Codes draw a sharp line between their "civil" and commercial contracts. These dichotomies and the underlying values and attitudes with respect to commerce as an occupation explain the differences among the respective rules on formation, interpretation and remedies for breach of contract. They might also explain the major differences between the commercial law of England and the United States and that of a French-law-inspired civil law jurisdiction.

1. The Different Meanings of Contract and Promise in Present Day Commercial and Financial Markets

The terms contract and property are the most widely used in private law. Indeed, it is not possible to conceive of a private law or of the law that Immanuel Kant referred to as that of the "mine and the thine"[60] without property and contract. Of these seminal

---

[55] *Id.*

[56] *See infra* § 14:4(A)(3)(c) (on simulations).

[57] *See infra* § 16:4(F)(C) (on the 1967 case of Shorin, involving a contract for conducting a workshop).

[58] *See infra* § 17:5(B) (on simulation in Imperial Law and present day law).

[59] *See* Glossary (on the meaning of the "living" vs. the "positive," "written" or "official" law).

[60] *See generally* Immanuel Kant, *From the Mine and Thine in the State of Nature to the Mine and Thine in the Juridical State*, *in* THE PHILOSOPHY OF LAW: AN EXPOSITION OF THE FUNDAMENTAL PRINCIPLES OF

legal institutions, contract is the most protean and malleable. Depending upon the legal system and jurisdiction in which it was formed, a contract can signify any or all the obligations that are voluntarily assumed by two or more parties simultaneously or on a deferred basis. It can be synonymous with a formal ceremony in front of a notary public or witnesses that results in a solemn document whose terms and conditions are often unchanging or static. A contract can also be synonymous with informal and rapidly-changing terms and conditions without need for novations or new contracts, such a contract often becomes indistinguishable from the parties' or their peers' commercial conduct.

Thus, a contract can mean a firm or enforceable promise by one party in the expectation that the other will accept that promise either expressly or tacitly by acting upon it. It can also mean an enforceable promise issued by one party binding upon it from the moment it was issued and not dependent upon its acceptance by a specified promisee or beneficiary or by an unspecified person or legal entity. A contract can emerge from the parties' contract-like conduct, even though that conduct was not preceded by the issuance of an enforceable promise. Or it can be inferred from a person or legal entity's "adhering" to a pre-established, usually customary form of doing business as set forth in a "master agreement" or in "general conditions of trade."[61] In contrast with the formal and static contract, the preceding contracts are typical of the commercial marketplace and thus are dynamic, of quick birth, change and termination.

By the start of the twentieth century, it became clear that "firm promises,"[62] "options" or "promises to enter into future contracts"[63] were being enforced and at the same time, formalities were being minimized and binding promises could be issued by means of telephone and computer-to-computer communications. And during our time, traders rely more and more on unilaterally-binding promises or instructions encapsulated in single-word computer messages such as: "buy," "sell," "swap" and so on, whose economic importance cannot be overemphasized. Trillions of U.S. dollars exchange hands each day across the trading world with no greater formality than that mentioned above.[64]

Yet, these apparently unilateral promises, acceptances of liability or instructions to intermediaries are neither discrete nor severable units of a one-sided form of liability. They are phases or parts of a complex set of pre-existing bilateral or multilateral contractual relationships. Many are the result of and are supported by a customary form of doing business that presupposes existence of a commercial or financial contract that dictates how each of the binding units will be created, amended or terminated. They may be governed by governmentally-sanctioned compilations of customs, such as with Germany's "General Conditions of Trade,"[65] or by private associations of traders' "master agreements," as those of the International Swaps and

---

JURISPRUDENCE AS THE SCIENCE OF RIGHT (1796), *available at* http://oll.libertyfund.org/?option=com_staticxt &staticfile=show.php%3Ftitle=359&chapter=55818&layout=html&Itemid=27.

[61] *See infra* § 13:2 (for a discussion of the general conditions of trade in German law).

[62] *See infra* § 12:3(D) n.65 and accompanying text.

[63] *Id.*

[64] *See* MAREK DUBOVEC, THE LAW OF SECURITIES, COMMODITIES AND BANK ACCOUNTS: THE RIGHTS OF ACCOUNT HOLDERS (*forthcoming, Edward Elgar 2014*).

[65] *See infra* § 13:2 (on the "General Conditions of Trade").

Derivatives Association (ISDA). In such a socio-economic context, the difference between a unilaterally-binding promise and an executed or completed contract is that between a snap-shot of an event and an entire sequence.

Curiously, this vision of a promise that can become a contract and vice versa is apparent in the juxtaposition of Roman consensual and "real" contracts. Roman law drew a distinction between contracts which sprung to life when an exchange of promises or performances by both parties (however informal) took place. It labeled these contracts "consensual" because, as with sale agreements, they were binding on both sides once they consented on the thing to be purchased and sold and on its price.[66] In contrast, it labeled other contracts as "real" because they required the delivery of a thing (*res*) by one of the parties before the other party became obligated to give it back or to return its equivalent. This was the case with contracts for loans of money (*mutuum*) or with loans of a thing that the borrower could use (*commodatum*).

For the same reason that it would be incorrect to assume that a contemporary unilaterally-binding promise is a discrete legal entity, totally severable from its contractual womb, it would be a mistake to assume that in "real" contracts only one of the parties is obligated to perform by giving or doing something. For he who was obligated to repay a sum of money became obligated after he received the loan from his lender as part of the contract of *mutuum*. What the term "real" contract was intended to address, then, was not the absence of the lender's or borrower's liability, but the time when the borrower's obligation to repay arose, *i.e.*, after receiving the *res* from the lender.

2. The Dichotomy of Civil and Commercial Contracts

Unfortunately, the different meanings of contract are not only the result of what is deemed to be a contract by market participants, but also by legalistic definitions, classifications and dichotomies born under very different socio-economic conditions. One such classification and dichotomy is that of civil and commercial contracts, which was a by-product of the enactment of separate civil and commercial codes in Napoleonic France at the beginning of the nineteenth century and from there spread to the majority of civil law countries. Moreover, with the exception of Germany's civil and commercial codes (among the "model" or influential codes),[67] the French influenced civil and commercial codes draw sharp distinctions between their "civil" and commercial contracts.

The former are usually not-for-profit, formal, static (mostly unchanging during their lifetime) and they are interpreted literally and "causally" (i.e. by paying attention to their transactional causes). The latter are for profit, largely informal, dynamic or changing during their life time, and many are formed by unilateral and abstract promises (or independent from their transactional causes). This dichotomy also explains the sharp differences among the respective rules on formation, interpretation and remedies for breach of contract. Such a dichotomy does not exist in Anglo American law. For example, the remedies associated with a civil (static) and commercial (dynamic) contract differ significantly not only based on their preference for damages (and methods of measuring them) or for specific performance, but also on

---

[66] *See infra* § 4:4(D)(3)(a).

[67] *See infra* chs. 8–12.

the reliance on extrajudicial remedies. While civil or static contracts seldom resort to extrajudicial remedies, commercial or dynamic contracts rely heavily on extrajudicial and equitable remedies. Among these is the unilateral rescission or termination of contracts, especially in cases of anticipatory repudiation, demands for assurance of performance, preclusion, set-off, private repossession of collateral in secured loans, or private sales of that collateral, among others.

As will be apparent in Chapters 8–12, the contract law that has resulted from the civil/commercial contract dichotomy is a major reason why the formation, interpretation and remediation of breaches of commercial contracts are inconsistent with market standard and best practices and are obstacles to economic development. The socio-economic context of the civil/commercial dichotomy assumed the existence of a still largely guild-like society in which merchants, tradesmen and professionals belonged to their own guilds or associations within an essentially agricultural society. Obviously this context is long gone. In our day, farmers and tradesmen are also merchants, and so are the owners and developers of commercial and residential real estate, and members of the liberal professions. And even though in many civil law countries lawyers and physicians are expected to charge "honoraria" instead of fees and to belong to not-for-profit "civil associations," the reality is that those professionals who do not run their offices in a business-like manner are not likely to be in practice for themselves for very long. The same is true for an increasingly large segment of the population who, thanks to computers, conducts businesses and performs services in a commercial fashion from home.

G. Familistic Societies Are Typical of Developing Nations, Regardless of Religion or Political Ideology

Familistic societies are also synonymous with unequal treatment of strangers to the family, clan or tribe. This treatment bears a high and often unaffordable developmental cost. It significantly reduces the size and viability of the marketplace by preventing competition against family and state monopolies. It also increases the cost of doing business for unprotected strangers, also referred to as third parties.

As discussed in connection with our second theme, two types of commercial practices and their respective standards of fairness are indispensable for the creation of a viable commercial society and the economic development that usually accompanies such a society. As noted earlier, one of these standards requires that market participants be treated by their contractual counterparts in a manner consistent with their reasonable expectations when viewing their own advantage. The other requires that highly trusted merchants behave in accordance with a "punctilio the most honorable."

The values and attitudes of a familistic society are often at odds with these standards, which accounts for the differing and often conflicting views on what a binding contract is, how it should be interpreted and how breaches of contract should be remedied. In addition, the familistic values and attitudes have much to do with what can or should be sold, lent or exchanged. For example, a sale of land in a familistic, agricultural-survival society such as China has been governed for most of its history by very different legal institutions than those that govern a commercial society. In the latter, immovable property is a tradable commodity, while in the former it is the sole or major source of family sustenance and thus its sale or mortgage becomes subject to numerous and serious restrictions to its marketability.[68]

What is the principal lesson to be learned from observing the progression that starts with the transactions of pre-commercial societies of families, clans and tribes[69] and concludes with those of our present commercial and financial markets of strangers?[70] In my opinion, the lesson is that for the law of commercial contracts to develop an economy, it must treat these strangers or third parties as a regular participant in the marketplace would reasonably expect to be treated, and, in instances of significant entrustment by that third party, he should be treated as if he were the contracting party's family member or friend.[71]

H. Contracts as *Indispensable* Macro and Micro Economic Tools Especially When Helping to Determine Realistic Prices

When freely and transparently entered into, contracts are indispensable macro and microeconomic tools for determining realistically the prices and costs involved in the exchanges of goods and services. By realistically I mean a determination that is based upon what actual contracting parties are willing to pay for goods and services. As such, contract prices are essential tools of economic development, as dramatically illustrated by what occurred when Soviet, Chinese and Cuban central planners failed to take them into account. To the extent that many contracts are simulated and non-transparent, especially in developing nations, they fail to function as optimal tools for economic development.

Among other functions, commercial archetypes help the legislator or judge to establish the reasonableness of the terms and conditions of a commercial contract, including its prices. As noted by Judge Friendly in his frequently cited decision on the meaning of "chicken" and the reasonableness of its price per pound, it would be unreasonable to accept a meaning that would impose upon the seller a loss for each pound of chicken he sold.[72] As will be discussed especially in connection with the central economic planning of socialist countries,[73] the ability of merchants, legislators, administrators and judges to ascertain realistic prices for what is bought and sold in the marketplace plays an unparalleled role in securing that market's viability.

Where realistic assumptions of the prices of raw materials and final products are unavailable—as was the case with central economic planning in Soviet Russia and its "satellites"—the effects could be disastrous. As concluded by one of the most respected economists in the People's Republic of China, a famine that killed dozens of millions of Chinese farmers during Mao Tse-tung's regime was caused by the inability of these farmers to terminate their membership in unproductive collectives. Unlike what happened during an earlier regulation of collective farms which allowed individual

---

[68] *See infra* chs. 18:1(B).

[69] *See generally infra* § 3:2.

[70] *See infra* ch. 12 (on German codification). *See also infra* chs. 20 (on English) & 21 (on United States law).

[71] *See infra* §§ 3:2, 3:3 & 3:6(A) n.54 and accompanying text (on the treatment of strangers or third parties as family or friends and the implementation of the principle of "peace of the market").

[72] *See infra* § 23:9(G)(4)(a) (transcribing the U.S. case Frigaliment v. BNS International).

[73] *See infra* § 15:4(F)(G)(H) (on the Soviet Union). *See also* Justin Yifu Lin, *Collectivization and China's Agricultural Crisis in 1959–1961*, 98 J. POL. ECON. 1228 (1990) (on Mao's China).

farmers to decide when to join and when to leave collectives based upon what they were able to earn, under Mao they were not allowed to leave or to enter into contracts with other more efficient and fair producers.[74] *The ensuing continuous decline in production was directly attributable to the loss of the contractual option and the inability to estimate profits and losses.*

In the final analysis, the indeterminacy of prices matters as much from a macroeconomic (*i.e.*, entire marketplace) as it does from a microeconomic (*i.e.*, individual contract) vantage point. If individual parties are not allowed to make their contractual decisions based on their perceptions of the reasonableness of the prices they have to pay or are paid for their "factors" of production, their society will continue to be at best one of mere subsistence pre-commercial farming or shepherding as shown by Professor George Dalton's research on production in pre-commercial societies.[75]

§ 1.3 CONTENT OF THE BOOK

This book is divided into six parts and thirty chapters. As the initial chapter of Part I, chapter 1 provides a glimpse of what lies ahead by discussing this book's guiding themes and providing short descriptions of its content, chapter by chapter. Following this overview, Chapter 2 examines the methodology involved in a comparison that in this book is both normative and contextual. It explains why it is important to understand not only the text of representative sources and provisions but also their historical and socio-economic contexts. A description of the legal and business cultures and their representative values, attitudes and practices is at the core of this context. Also at the core of the context are the two methods of legal reasoning in the countries or jurisdictions that have been selected as representative of the civil and common law systems: 1) The Aristotelian inspired scholastic legal logic that to this day governs the civil law lawyers' search for the "legal nature" (read essences)[76] of institutions such as contracts and their substantive and procedural or remedial components; and 2) the "logic of the reasonable" and the "reasoning by example," which provides the persuasiveness of the common law's judicial, statutory and doctrinal law making.

Chapter 3 studies the main features of pre-commercial and "dense" exchange relationships that were devoid of contractual promises and rights; for pre-commercial law was fundamentally a world of duties as set forth in the customs that articulated what was owed as a result of the primary duty of reciprocity. Of particular developmental interest are: 1) the impediment to economic development that resulted from the inability of pre-commercial society to price the factors of production; and 2) the presence of a set of legal principles that had a similar effect, although some of them can still be found in contemporary societies.

Chapter 4 summarizes some of the key features of the Roman legal system, including its contribution of the "legal alphabet" of legal systems around the world. It discusses how the Roman jurists measured rights and duties by using their own "geometric" legal logic as well as by relying on archetypal representatives of desirable contractual behavior such as that of the *Bonus Vir*. Of particular conceptual interest is

---

[74] *See* Lin, *supra* note 74.

[75] *See infra* § 3:3.

[76] *See infra* § 2:2.

their typification and classifications of contracts, including those devoid of enforcement such as the *nuda pacta* in executory promises and agreements.

Part II is devoted to medieval commercial law. Chapter 5 discusses informal, reciprocal brotherly promises of Mediterranean Jewish merchants and the formal notarial deeds of Italian commercial cities. The Jewish brotherly contractual promises and their method of enforcement were instrumental in developing a trusting, long-distance (non-caravan) Mediterranean trade. The formal notarial deeds of Italian cities had the related purpose of enabling the distrusting parties to a contract to enforce otherwise unenforceable executory promises.

Chapter 6 analyzes the guild system of doing business and how it differed from the capitalist system. Because of the importance of notarial law for civil law countries and its frequent misunderstanding by common law lawyers I found it necessary to include a chapter on the Latin notaries (Chapter 7).

Part III comprises Chapters 8–12 and deals with the codification movement, first in its European cradle and thereafter, in representative countries or jurisdictions that adopted the European models for their own codes. Unlike what happened with the Roman law of contracts, the French Civil Code (hereinafter *Code Civil*) made it possible to develop a general theory of contracts that set forth the meaning of contract, its types, parties, formalities, methods of interpretation and remedies for centuries to come, although not necessarily for the benefit of local and international commerce. In fact, despite the presence of commercial codes both in France and Germany, you will soon discover major differences in the effects upon commerce between the *Code Civil* and Germany's *Bürgerliches Gesetzbuch* of 1900 (hereinafter BGB), the two most influential private law codes throughout the civil law world. You should not be surprised that the latter proved much more supportive of commercial transactions than the former.

Among the sequels to the European codification of the law of contracts in general and of commercial contracts specifically, we will cover in Part IV Soviet Russian, Latin American and Chinese statutory and codified law as familistic and socialist variants of the civil law. Since Russia's living law is still governed by attitudes developed during its socialist past and there remain occasional attempts to revive socialist legal theory in Russia and in developing nations, I thought it was important to explore its theoretical bases and their operation in practice, especially because it seems to inevitably lead to what can best be described as an "invertebrate" private law system. This is a system whose private law is governed at the very top by vague pronouncements periodically issued by anointed and presumably infallible leaders who define technical legal concepts as fundamental as "personal" or "private" property or "exploitive" contracts with phrases and exhortations typical of political slogans. Given the vagueness and sloganeering nature of these pronouncements, bureaucratic and judicial decision-makers often fashion their own more specific interpretations of "what is mine and thine" persuaded by bribes or shared profits with the claimants of personal property.

The comparison of Chinese and Latin American laws of commercial contracts was quite educational for someone familiar with Latin American law, but at best a neophyte on Chinese law. Among the lessons I learned in this comparison was that despite the many geographical and cultural differences between these countries, China's Imperial law and colonial Mexico's law of commercial contracts had much in common, including the familistic and monopolistic nature that often accompanies invertebrate private law systems. In addition, China afforded the unique opportunity to observe the uneasy coexistence of traditional familial values and attitudes with a contemporary version of autocratic socialism in the midst of extraordinary prosperity and propelled by a law of commercial contracts designed for free market, non-familistic cultures.

Part V is an introduction to the socio-economic and legal context of English and U.S. commercial law. Chapter 20 describes the commercialized and industrial English society and the gradual transformation of legal institutions originally designed for a feudal, agricultural-based economy, such as the "doctrine of the estates" or "time in the land," into the fragmented rights of ownership and possession of real as well as personal property transformed into business assets. It then focuses on the law of commercial contracts from the sixteenth to the nineteenth century and on the contributions of distinguished commercial law judges and especially of f Lord Mansfield.

Chapter 21 discusses first the socio-economic forces that helped the United States develop not only the largest economy on earth but also the world's most vital commercial and financial marketplace. It starts by focusing on values and attitudes toward commerce in colonial America that helped to shape the archetypal commercial behavior in local and international trade in an America that up until the nineteenth century was an essentially agricultural nation. It then discusses the transformation of that largely agricultural society to the commercial and industrial society it is today. It also examines the interaction between the American version of freedom of contract, which as a principle—together with the principles of reasonableness and good faith—shaped a remarkably flexible substantive and remedial law of commercial contracts.

Part VI discusses in Chapters 22, 23, and 24 respectively, the formation, and interpretation of contemporary commercial contracts and the drafting of the standard and commercial best practices. In doing this, it examines the differences between the major legal systems and cultures, and contrasts two different notions of contract, the *Code Civil* inspired "static"and largely ceremonial version of contract and the U.C.C. inspired "dynamic" constantly changing version of commercial contracts as a reflection of the parties' and their peers' commercial conduct. It contends that depending upon one or another version of contract, they will be formed, interpreted and adjudicated differently and that these differences are easily apparent in the statutory, decisional and doctrinal law discussed in the following chapters. As just noted in the above comparison, the United States law of commercial contracts is analyzed in considerable detail because, following the end of the Second World War and following also the internationalization of its law of commercial contracts, United States commercial law became one of the world's most influential.

Part VI also discusses the judicial and extrajudicial remedial law for the breach of commercial contracts by providing a brief comparative overview of commercial trial procedure in representative jurisdictions. It then studies, in chronological fashion, the various remedies, starting with *culpa in contrahendo* at the pre-contractual stage. It proceeds to study extrajudicial remedies and their growing importance and compares representative methods of pleadings and proof. It examines the remedies for breach of commercial contracts starting with the most commonly-invoked excuses for non-performance, and continues with the remedies for anticipatory repudiation (the phase prior to the maturity of contract obligations) and to the phase where the performance is either defective or non-existent. It concludes with a comparison of the recovery of damages for lost profits in Spanish and United States law, especially when the seller alleges that he lost one or more sales and their profits as a result of the buyer's breach of contract. This comparison provides an opportunity to assess the value of the contemporary jurisprudential theory known as Economic Analysis of the Law in the resolution of important issues of the law of commercial contracts and its possible contribution to economic development.

§ 1.4 APPENDIX: UNDERSTANDING JAPAN'S CORPORATE AND LEGAL CULTURE

"There are truths on this side of the Pyrenees, which are falsehoods on the other." (*Verité en-deçà des Pyrénées, erreur au-delà*)[77]

—Blaise Pascal

A. Introduction

The purpose of this Appendix is to illustrate the importance of culture as a force that shapes a country or region's legal, business and corporate behavior. As we will discuss in Chapter 2, legal culture is a crucial component of the methodology of this book and of a contextual comparison. I hasten to add that legal culture is not the only factor making economic development possible because unless legal culture is combined with sound commercial practices and legal and economic policy making, it will be a necessary but not sufficient condition. The elements of legal culture will be discussed in Chapter 2 and the definitions of some of its component institutions are found in the Glossary.

I will illustrate the importance of culture as a force that shapes a country or region's legal behavior by discussing some aspects of the United States Supreme Court decision *Matsushita Electric Industry Company vs. Zenith Radio Corporation*[78] (hereinafter *Matsushita*), handed down in 1986 and still a subject of academic debate. After discussing its facts, reasoning and failure to take into account what many believe were the necessary legal-cultural perspectives, I will turn to other illustrations of the preeminent role of cultural considerations mostly drawn from my own experience dealing with governmental and transactional policymakers.

B. The Matsushita Decision

Facts[79]

In *Matsushita*, Zenith and National Union Electric Corporation (NUE), two American corporations that manufactured and sold consumer electronic products (CEPs), the majority of which were television sets, sued the defendants, twenty-one Japanese corporations which also primarily manufactured and sold the same products

---

[77] I owe the quote from Blaise Pascal and insightful comments on this decision to my former student Eleni Vaita. Eleni Vaita, The Other Truth: Matsushita Electric Industry Company v. Zenith Radio Corporation 1 (2009) (unpublished research paper, on file with author).

[78] Matsushita Elec. Indus. Co. v. Zenith Radio Corp., 475 U.S. 574 (1986).

[79] *See* David Talenfeld, The Timely Extinction of Homo Economicus (2009) (unpublished research paper, University of Arizona) (on file with author). *See also* Vaita, *supra* note 78. The following summary of facts is based upon excerpts from both of hese research papers.

to consumers in the United States. Zenith and NUE claimed that the defendants conspired to maintain artificially high prices for the sets sold in Japan and artificially low prices for those sold in the United States, thereby intending to drive plaintiffs and other United States producers out of the market.[80] They argued that that this scheme violated various United States anti-trust laws.

The defendants moved for summary judgment. The district court found the bulk of the evidence on which the respondents relied inadmissible and that which was admissible as failing to raise a genuine issue of fact on the existence of the alleged conspiracy; thus, any inference of conspiracy was unreasonable. For these reasons, the district court granted summary judgment for the defendants.

The court of appeals reversed. It determined that much of the evidence excluded by the district court was admissible and held that the district court erred in granting summary judgment and that there was both direct and circumstantial evidence of a conspiracy. It found that the Japanese market for television sets was characterized by oligopolistic behavior in which a small number of firms controlled the market and met regularly to exchange information on prices and other market conditions. Meanwhile, U.S. firms were being prevented from entering the Japanese market by strong tariff and non-tariff barriers.

According to the court of appeals, the defendants needed to operate at full capacity in order to make a profit as their fixed costs were notably higher than those of the plaintiffs. Yet their full capacity production exceeded the demand for their products in the Japanese market, and consequently this required some form of international dumping. For this reason, an agreement was entered into by the defendants in cooperation with Japan's Ministry of International Trade and Industry (MITI) by which the defendants fixed minimum prices for sets exported to the U.S. market. Each Japanese producer agreed to sell only to five U.S. distributors and further undercut their agreed-upon minimum prices with a series of rebate schemes.[81] The court of appeals concluded that a reasonable fact-finder could find a conspiracy to depress prices in the U.S. market in order to drive out U.S. competitors and that this conspiracy was funded by the excess profits obtained in the Japanese market.

The United States Supreme Court granted *certiorari* to determine whether the court of appeals applied the proper standard in evaluating the district court's summary judgment decision. It concluded that the court of appeals erred because the evidence it relied on had little, if any, relevance to the alleged predatory pricing conspiracy and also because it failed to consider the absence of a plausible motive to engage in predatory pricing. It reversed the decision of the court of appeals and remanded it with instructions to consider evidence that petitioners conspired to price predatorily despite the lack of any apparent motive to do so. In the absence of such evidence, the Supreme Court instructed the court of appeals that the petitioners were entitled to have summary judgment reinstated.

C. The Supreme Court's Reasoning

The Supreme Court's main findings of error were that the court of appeals failed to take into account the following: 1) a conspiracy to raise profits in one market

---

[80] Matsushita, 475 U.S. at 577–78.

[81] *Id.* at 581.

[Japan], even if proven, did not tend to show a conspiracy to sustain losses in another [U.S.]; 2) the "absence of plausible motive" for the Japanese companies to engage in such a conspiracy, which "involved substantial profit losses and showed little likelihood of success"[82]; and 3) the factual context of the plaintiff's claim was "implausible" as a claim that "simply makes no economic sense."[83] Yet, as pointed out by one of my former students,[84] the Supreme Court did not clarify *from whose perspective* that claim may or may not make economic sense.

According to the Supreme Court, the predatory pricing conspiracy was speculative because agreements to price products below their competitive level required the conspirators to forgo the profits of free competition.[85] Furthermore, to do this over a long period of time was highly unrealistic. In support of this assertion, the Court quoted (then) Yale Law School Professor Robert Bork on the implausibility of predatory pricing:

> *Any realistic* theory of predation recognizes that the predator as well as his victims will incur losses during the fighting, but such a theory supposes it may be a rational calculation for the predator to view the losses as an investment in future monopoly profits (where rivals are to be killed) or in future undisturbed profits (where rivals are to be disciplined). The future flow of profits, appropriately discounted, must then exceed the present size of the losses.[86]

Based on what to Professor Bork and the Supreme Court seemed to be a universally realistic standard when making business or economic management decisions, the Supreme Court concluded that:

> Absent some assurance that the hoped-for monopoly will materialize, *and* that it can be sustained for a significant period of time, "[the] predator must make a substantial investment with no assurance that it will pay off." For this reason, there is a consensus among commentators that predatory pricing schemes are rarely tried, and even more rarely successful.
>
> . . .
>
> These observations apply even to predatory pricing by a *single firm* seeking monopoly power. In this case, respondents allege that a large number of firms have conspired over a period of many years to charge below-market prices in order to stifle competition. Such a conspiracy is incalculably more difficult to execute than an analogous plan undertaken by a single predator.[87]

Moreover, because success was speculative and depended on the conspirators' willingness to endure losses for an indefinite period, the Supreme Court assumed that "each conspirator has a strong incentive to cheat. . . . [And] if conspirators cheat to any

---

[82] *Id.*

[83] *Id.* at 587.

[84] *See* Vaita, *supra* note 78, at 17.

[85] Matsushita, 475 U.S. at 588, 589.

[86] *See* ROBERT H. BORK, THE ANTITRUST PARADOX: A POLICY AT WAR WITH ITSELF 145 (1978). *See also* John S. McGee, *Predatory Pricing Revisited*, 23 J. LAW & ECON. 289, 295–97 (1980); *cited in* Matsushita, 475 U.S. at 589.

[87] Matsushita, 475 U.S. at 589–590 (citations omitted).

substantial extent, the conspiracy must fail. . . ."[88] Further, by looking at the market for television sets at the time of the trial, the Supreme Court did not find cause for concern of monopolization by the defendants:

> Two decades after their conspiracy is alleged to have commenced, petitioners appear to be far from achieving this goal: the two largest shares of the retail market in television sets are held by RCA and respondent Zenith, not by any of petitioners. Moreover, those shares, which together approximate 40% of sales, did not decline appreciably during the 1970's.[89]

The Supreme Court acknowledged that the defendants' share of the market had risen rapidly during this period, from one-fifth or less of the relevant markets to almost fifty percent.[90] Yet, it noted that neither of the lower courts found that this share allowed them to charge monopoly prices. On the contrary: "The data in the record strongly suggest that that goal is yet far distant."[91] In sum, the majority of the justices were convinced that the defendants "had no motive to enter into the alleged conspiracy," and "[t]o the contrary, *as presumably rational businesses*, [the defendants] had every incentive *not* to engage in the conduct with which they were charged. . . ."[92]

In characterizing the alleged predatory behavior as implausible, nonsensical and economically irrational, the Supreme Court made some unproven assumptions. As summarized by Professor Wesley A. Cann Jr. of the University of Connecticut, the Court assumed that all foreign as well as domestic businesses: "(1) [A]re rational profit-maximizers; (2) have the same level of intensity regarding the incentive to cheat; and (3) would refrain from predatory behavior unless they could recoup their losses in the same market in which those losses were incurred."[93]

Yet, contrary to the Supreme Court's projections, Matsushita Electric Industrial Co. is presently the manufacturer of Panasonic electronics and boasts the top market-share position in the United States plasma display panel television market.[94] "NUE, however, met its demise long before the conclusion of the case"[95] and Zenith managed to avoid corporate fatality in the late 1970's by using "its broad engineering and marketing expertise to diversify,"[96] but ceased to be a major producer and distributor of CEPs in the United States.

---

[88] *Id.* at 590.

[89] *Id.* at 591.

[90] *Id.*

[91] *Id.*

[92] *Id.* at 595 (emphasis added).

[93] Wessley A. Cann Jr., *Internationalizing Our Views Toward Recoupment and Market Power: Attacking The Anti/Dumping/Antitrust Dichotomy Through WTO-Consistent Global Welfare Theory*, 17 U. PA. J. INT'L ECON. L. 69, 75 (1996) (citation omitted).

[94] Jiji Press, *Samsung Expands Lead over Sony in N. American LCD TV Market*, JAPAN'S CORPORATE NEWS NETWORK (Aug. 16, 2008), http://japancorp.net/press_release/19455/samsung_expands_lead_over_sony_in_n_american_lcd_tv_market.

[95] *See* Vaita, *supra* note 78, at 25 & n.142.

[96] Zenith Elec. LLC, *About Us: History* (2010) at http://www.zenith.com/about, *cited in* Vaita, *supra* note 78, at 25 n.140.

D. Whose Legal Cultural Perspective? Whose Rationality?

Did the Supreme Court take into account Japanese corporate culture when making decisions concerning its commercial and consumer contracts? From the above-quoted statements, it is clear that the Court relied on a home-grown perception of economic rationality and efficiency as advocated by the Chicago School of Economics rather than on Japanese corporate culture as reflected in the business practices of Japanese producers and in their relationship with the Japanese government.[97]

In contrast to the Supreme Court's assumptions, Geert Hofstede, a world-renowned Dutch psychologist who studied the impact of national and regional cultures upon management policies, concluded that "there are no such things as universal management theories."[98] Based upon several research projects on the national cultural differences across subsidiaries of the IBM Corporation in more than seventy countries, as well as on subsequent studies, Hofstede identified differing business values attributable to the underlying national cultures.[99] Among these, the presence of the following four values questions the existence of a uniform international version of economic rationality in corporate decision making:[100]

1. Power distance, or the extent to which the less powerful members of organizations and institutions (like the family) accept and expect power within the respective organizations to be distributed unequally.

2. Individualism versus collectivism. In individualist societies, ties between individuals are loose: Everyone is expected to look after him/herself and his/her immediate family. In collectivist societies (which included Japan, among others), people from birth onwards are integrated into strong, cohesive in-groups, often as extended families, which continue to protect their members in exchange for unquestioning loyalty, regardless of the outcome of the business.

3. Uncertainty avoidance deals with a society's tolerance for uncertainty and ambiguity. This dichotomy indicates the extent to which underlying culture programs its members to feel either uncomfortable or comfortable in unstructured situations. *What motivates corporate decisions in uncertainty avoidance cultures, such as Japan's, then, is not so much what other cultures would label rational profit-making as it is the avoidance of uncertainty.*

4. Long—term versus short-term orientation. Values associated with long-term orientation are thrift and perseverance; values associated with short-term orientation are respect for tradition, fulfilling social obligations, and protecting one's "face," above and beyond economic consequences. Again, Japan's business culture scored high in this category while the United States business culture did not.

---

[97] Cann, *supra* note 94, at 73–74 (referring to the dichotomy between anti-dumping and anti-trust policies that was increasingly aggravated by "development of an antitrust regime that relies extensively on Chicago School economic theory.").

[98] Geert Hofstede, *Cultural Constraints in Management Theory*, 7 ACAD. MGMT. EXEC. 81, 81 (1993), *cited in* Cann, *supra* note 94, at 156.

[99] *See* Geert Hofstede, *National Culture, GEERT-HOFSTEDE.COM*, http://geert-hofstede.com/national-culture.html. The study was supplemented by subsequent studies on the behavior of "commercial airline pilots and students in 23 countries, civil service managers in 14 counties, 'up-market' consumers in 15 countries and 'elites' in 19 countries." *Id.*

[100] Hofstede, *supra* note 99, at 89–90.

As pointed out by Professor Cann, Hofstede's studies showed key differences between Japanese and United States business cultures. For example, the United States scored extremely high in the dimension of individualism, which includes "a strong belief in the merits of markets as well as competition between individuals."[101] In contrast, Asian cultures such as China's and Indonesia's scored extremely low in this dimension, and Japan's score fell in the middle between the United States and the Chinese and Indonesian scores.[102] Hofstede also found a significant difference between the United States' low certainty avoidance score and Japan's cultural preference for a more structured, homogeneous and risk avoidance society.[103] As pointed out by Professor Cann, the above and other cultural differences may incline Japanese corporate culture to place national or group interests, "such as employment stability and economic development, above those of either the individual or the single corporate enterprise."[104] In addition, the divergent cultural perspectives between Japan and the United States may affect:

> (1) [T]he willingness and the ability to engage in group activity, such as conspiracies; (2) the desire for consensus and harmony; (3) the degree to which social and business obligations are respected; (4) the likelihood of cheating or undertaking maverick activity; (5) the time horizons for traditional recoupment; and (6) the desirability of pursuing short-term profit maximization as opposed to long-term market growth.[105]

Contrary to the United States business culture, the Japanese corporate culture induces conformity, values harmony and loyalty, encourages nationalism and promotes coordination within the large network of companies horizontally and vertically linked (*keiretsu*) and between these networks and the Japanese government. It also rewards the loyalty of workers and their contribution to the harmonious relations between labor and management. This reward most often results in lifetime employment that requires a policy of "long-term economic growth rather than short-term profit maximization."[106] Hence, the Japanese do not fear cartelization and, "in fact, see cartels as an element of competitive strength."[107] This approach to production and distribution has resulted in a close cooperative relationship between the private sector and the professional government bureaucracy in which the *keiretsu* and MITI forge Japan's industrial policy in a manner that amounts to a living law that preempts its formal or positive law.

As suggested by Professor Cann, this industrial policy must be taken into account to understand the rationality of Japanese business practices.[108] Japanese corporate workers are for all practical purposes tenured, and even when difficult economic conditions no longer permit companies to guarantee lifetime employment, the aspiration to provide it and receive it remains alive.[109] This aspiration has a profound

---

[101] Cann, *supra* note 94, at 157, with references to an earlier Hofstede study including statistical tables.

[102] *See* Hofstede, *supra* note 99, at 91 tbl.1.

[103] Cann, *supra* note 94, at 157.

[104] *Id.* at 157–58.

[105] *Id.* at 158.

[106] *Id.* at 158–59.

[107] *Id.* at 159 (citation omitted).

[108] *Id.* at 160–61.

[109] *Id.* at 161.

effect on the goals and allegiances of Japanese management. Japanese managers' loyalty to their workers influences their decisions concerning:

> [C]apacity level, productivity level, the relative importance of expanded market share and increased return-on-investment, and even the desirability of incurring losses will assume a significantly different dimension.... [T]herefore, the pressures to demonstrate short-term profits or to engage in short-term strategies have been reduced considerably.
>
> A second policy ... concerns the fervent pursuit of economic growth. Two characteristics of Japanese corporations "[are] their unrelenting focus on competitive position" and their preoccupation with market share rather than the Westernized objective of return-on-investment.[110]

E. Professor Dan F. Henderson's Views on Japanese Corporate Culture

Dan Fenno Henderson was the dean of comparative Japanese-United States legal studies and one of the world's leading scholars on Japanese corporate law as well as judicial and extrajudicial adjudication.[111] After practicing law in Japan and the United States, he became a professor of law at Washington University and directed its Asian law program from 1962–91. During his tenure, this program became the most respected around the world. His teachings and writings were always clear, precise and reliable. As a colleague at the International Academy of Commercial and Consumer Law, I looked forward to his presentations at our meetings. During an Academy meeting at the Saint Louis University School of Law in 1995, he spoke on the topic of Foreign Acquisitions and Takeovers in Japan.[112] The majority of the Supreme Court in *Matsushita* would have been well advised to pay attention to his following observations:

> Japan has many special features of finance and business organization, both corporate and supra-corporate, as well as very different business politics and culture: different relationships between law and society, and between business and government. Also, in all political economies there are varying balances between the polity and the market. In Japan, the center of gravity has definitely been with the polity (managed by a politically powerful bureaucracy). With respect, I suggest we err by overemphasizing the freedom of the market in assessing the workings of Japanese business, and thus the potential for acquisitions, as if the political constraints on the "invisible hand" were the same in all countries. Many skew their analysis by too heavily relying on a deterministic ideal of individual wealth maximizing as the unum necessarium of human behavior and public policy. In Japan, without our pronounced individualism, the market lacks requisite freedom and so the polity predominates. Pervasive social organization often prevails over law and free business activity in favor of national, not individual, goals; arguably of

---

110 *Id.* (citation omitted).

111 *See* John O. Haley, *Nachruf, Tribute to Dan Fenno Henderson, 1921–2000,* 11 ZEITSCHRIFT FÜR JAPANISCHES RECHT 5 (2001), *available at* http://www.djjv.org/japrecht/heft11.old/nachruf.html (providing a short list of Professor Henderson's accomplishments). Henderson died in 2000.

112 *See* Dan F. Henderson, *Foreign Acquisitions and Takeovers in Japan*, 39 ST. LOUIS L.J. 897 (1995).

course the individual in the end may reap a fair share of benefits from national achievements. This different nationalistic context clouds our understanding of Japanese corporatism, which is highly focused on international competitiveness and selling cheaply abroad, at the expense of consumerism and buying power at home. This is "contrived" advantage, not Ricardo's "comparative" advantage in resources. This is the reason that I suggested in the late 1960's and early 1970's that rather than thinking of Japanese trading policies as "free enterprise," we should treat her as a "quasi-state trader."

The second barrier to our understanding derives not so much from the obscurity of Japanese differences as from the penchant of our generalists to see Japan in our own image. . . . To an extent, it is true. But, on an individualistic scale, Japan's variance from us is polar, and nowhere is this variance better seen than in the corporatism of Japan business and governance. We do not understand Japanese business organization, which consistently thwarts acquisitions, simply because first, its practices at several levels are anything but transparent, and secondly, too much of our media coverage and too much of our scholarly comment by generalists persists in seeing the Japanese "stock market," "corporate law," "free enterprise" and "democracy" as if these things are or should be fungible worldwide: Just like us. . . . None of this kind of coverage of Japan is helpful in understanding Japanese policy and the sociology of Japanese business the way it really works.[113]

F. Personal Observations on German, Japanese and United States Business and Corporate Cultures

The drafting of the United Nations Convention on Independent Guarantees and Stand-by Letters of Credit,[114] in which I participated as a delegate for the United States, gave me the opportunity to observe the diversity of culturally-influenced policies and how their respective cultures helped shape a new international financial promise. The following observations were made at the time of drafting and represent the beliefs and attitudes held at that point in time. Since then, I have spoken with observers who have noticed changes in the countries throughout the years, but they will not be discussed here.

G. The Transaction, Its Parties and Required Assurances

Independent guarantees and stand-by letters of credit are issued by banks and insurance and bonding companies (hereinafter "issuers") to provide two parallel, but not always consistent, assurances. One assures payment of a stipulated sum of money or its acceptable equivalent to the "beneficiary" of the promise. Such a beneficiary could be a governmental agency in charge of awarding an industrial construction contract to a foreign industrial or construction enterprise. This beneficiary wishes an assurance

---

113 *Id.* at 898–99 (citations omitted).

114 *See* U.N. Convention on Independent Guarantees and Stand-by Letters of Credit, *opened for signature* Dec. 11, 1995, U.N. DOC. A/RES/50/48 (entered into force Jan. 1, 2000), *available at* http://www.uncitral.org/pdf/english/texts/payments/guarantees/guarantees.pdf; *see also* JAMES E. BYRNE, LC RULES AND LAWS: CRITICAL TEXTS 179 (3d ed. 2004).

that if the foreign builder fails to perform in accordance with the terms and conditions specified in the financial promise, the issuer will pay irrevocably the stipulated amount upon presentation by the beneficiary of specified documents supporting the claim.

Another possible beneficiary of such a guarantee or letter of credit may be a fiduciary entity or trustee who represents the numerous holders of financial obligations such as bonds or other negotiable instruments. In such a case, the assurance consists of an irrevocable promise to pay the amount owed to all the holders of these bonds or instruments of indebtedness if a principal paymaster does not pay. Alternatively, the obligation in a "direct pay" standby letter of credit is on the issuing bank, not its account party or customer, and the presentation of documents will be made solely to the issuing bank. As with the promise described in the previous paragraph, this promise of payment is payable upon the presentation of documents in compliance with the terms and condition of the promise. Unlike what is common with the promise of the previous paragraph, the present promise is payable to a trustee or fiduciary entity representing the numerous holders of the bonds or instruments of indebtedness.

The assurance needed by the foreign contractor (who is known as the customer or applicant for the issuance of the letter of credit or as the purchaser of the insurance policy or indemnity bond) is that the order or demand for payment made by the government agency is legitimate in the sense that it was prompted by the contractors' failure to perform as agreed upon in the underlying building or construction contract. This assurance is usually found in the documents tendered by the government agency-beneficiary of the letter of credit, by the beneficiary of the policy or bond or the trustee of the bond indenture. The documents they tender are often accompanied by certificates of third parties or experts stating or certifying that the amounts claimed under the guarantee or letter of credit are due and payable for the reasons stipulated in the guarantees or letters of credit.

H. The Independence or Abstraction of the Promises and Their Assurances

These guarantees and letters of credit are known in the financial world as "independent" or "abstract" promises because their promise of payment is not dependent upon compliance with the terms and conditions stated in or implied from underlying contracts or relationships. In real life, however, the precise boundaries that separate the rights and duties related to the promise of payment and to the underlying transactions or relationships are not as precise as one would wish. One of the most important tasks of this Convention was to provide as much clarity and precision as possible on this abstraction or separation.

Most of the delegations agreed that the issuer of the letter of credit or the bank guarantor should not be able to use the fact that it had not yet been paid by its customer or that it had not obtained a sufficiently reliable assurance of reimbursement from that customer or a trusted third party as an excuse not to pay. They also agreed that the relationship between the issuer or the guarantor and their customers should not interfere with the issuer's or guarantor's obligation to pay the beneficiary. I will refer to this relationship as belonging to a level of abstraction number 1.

However, many delegations disagreed on whether a similar level of abstraction should exist between the issuer's promise and defenses or claims that stemmed from the underlying transactions or relationships between the customer of the bank or of the guarantor and the beneficiaries of their respective promises. This relationship typically involves disputes where, say, a government agency claims that the contractor failed to perform or performed the contract badly and in turn the contractor claims that he or she performed well and that it was the government agency who refused to pay in bad faith. I will refer to this relationship as possibly giving rise to the level of abstraction number 2.

I say "possibly" because often the disputes in this level of abstraction involve not a total failure to perform, but a partial and at times only a minimal failure. Or, as a common law lawyer would characterize these disputes, they involve an inadequacy as opposed to an insufficiency (or failure) of consideration. In addition to these disputes, a number of European delegations were concerned with numerous issuances in which beneficiaries of the Persian Gulf Region took advantage of such an abstraction or independence by submitting documents that on their face seemed to comply, but in fact fraudulently or abusively misrepresented the right to claim payment. Hence, there was no initial agreement on whether the excuses and defenses that belonged in a level 2 abstraction should be excluded from the proposed Convention.

I. The United States Position

The United States advocated the adoption of a fully abstract or independent promise that would remain largely immune from excuses for non-payment or defenses derived from underlying transactions. Accordingly, issuers had to pay except in those instances in which it was manifest and clear to them or to a court of law that the documents presented by the beneficiary had been forged or that the beneficiary's demand for payment had no conceivable basis in fact.[115]

This level of abstraction required that the issuers' promise to pay be conditioned solely upon the presentation of specified documents and not upon the issuers' ascertaining that the act or events that the customer or beneficiary alleged had in fact occurred or not. Neither the banks nor the guarantors were equipped or authorized by law to make their payments dependent upon their examination of, say, engineering calculations on the soundness of a structure any more than they should have been expected to ascertain the tensile strength of paper or the aroma of a Honduran cigar. Bankers are trained and equipped to examine documents and not to act as "detectives of facts."

There was one exception to this principle and it could be invoked when the documents presented by the beneficiary could be easily proven to be forged or fraudulent or to have no conceivable basis in fact. Thus, an issuer could reject payment or a court of law could enjoin it if, say, one government official tendered a document transcribing a governmental award just given to the contractor for having "built a milk plant that had supplied country X with the purest and safest milk available anywhere" while another government agency tendered a certificate stating that payment was due to the beneficiary because the contractor had failed "to supply milk of any acceptable quality. . ."

The United States adopted this position after consulting with the economic sector most affected by the proposed Convention—its banking and financial industry. The

---

[115] *See* U.N. Convention on Independent Guarantees and Stand-by Letters of Credit, *supra* note 114, arts. 19 & 20.

position of this industry was that if issuers were allowed or encouraged to label dependent, weak and uncertain promises as irrevocable letters of credit or independent bank guarantees, the integrity of these promises, even when issued as firm and reliable promises, would be undermined. And even though other participants in the transactions were sought out for their opinions, the policy that shaped the levels of abstraction for the stand-by letter of credit or independent bank guarantee was that of the banking and financial sector. This was unquestionably the sector most directly involved with and affected by the issuance of these promises, regardless of how its contribution to the national GDP or to the nation's exports was ranked.

J. Germany's and Japan's Positions

The German and Japanese delegations, among others, were reluctant to support the United States position. They preferred a promise that could be payable on the basis of stipulated documents and also of the issuers' ascertainment of the occurrence of specified acts or events. In other words, they preferred promises that were neither fully documentary nor abstract.

After intense and prolonged discussions, I asked one of the members of the German delegation how such an uncertain promise could be consistent with the best interests of the German banking industry which, like any other banking industry, profited from the reliability of its promises and suffered from their unreliability. I also asked him why German banks were not present at the discussions while major German industrial exporting companies were present as advisors to his delegation, especially taking into account that the banks seemed to be the commercial entities with most at stake.[116] I reminded him of the statement made to the floor by the representative of the European Bank Federation: If this Convention weakens the promise of the bank or guarantor to the point that it becomes unreliable, the beneficiaries will soon accept nothing else from their foreign contractors-bidders but bars of gold as assurances of seriousness or of good performance.

In response, my German colleague reminded me of an advertisement he had seen on U.S. television in which two investors were seen discussing their respective brokers' recommendations on which stock to purchase when one of them said: "My broker is E.F. Hutton and E.F. Hutton said . . ." Before that investor could finish his statement other investors in the same room rushed to hear what E.F. Hutton was supposed to have recommended. The advertisement concluded with the admonition: "When E.F. Hutton speaks, everybody listens." *Mutatis mutandis* in Germany, he said, "When companies such as Siemens or Mercedes speak, Deutsche Bank or Dresdner Bank must listen." He added that these major exporting companies had a very bad experience with the type of ironclad promises the United States was proposing. Even though these companies had done an excellent job, the government agencies of the beneficiary countries, especially in the Persian Gujlf, instead of encouraging their banks or guarantors to pay, sent documents that in bad faith denied the performance or quality of the work performed by the Siemenses of this world. The result was that the foreign banks paid the local government agency beneficiaries, the German banks had to reimburse their local correspondents, and the German industrial exporters had to reimburse their issuing banks. This is why the policy advocated by Germany was to

---

116 Subsequent to this meeting, German bankers were also present as advisors to the German delegation.

dilute the firmness of the promises by enabling excuses or defenses not to pay bad faith beneficiaries, regardless of whether the dispute involved the inadequacy or the insufficiency of the underlying consideration.

In explaining the culture behind this policy, he pointed out that major industrial exporting companies were Germany's most important producers of wealth and employment. If these companies were seriously damaged by an abusive, albeit foreign government sponsored, policy that xposed them to serious losses, the entire polity would suffer. Hence, Germany had to focus on the national rather than the banking industry's interests.

Upon hearing this explanation, I asked my colleague if he had any objection to my discussing this rationale with our Japanese colleague. He did not and told me that he anticipated a similar explanation by our Japanese colleague. After I told our Japanese colleague about my conversation with our German colleague, I asked him, "Would you agree then that when a major industrial-exporting member of, say, the Mitsui Keiretsu speaks, Sakura Bank [a banking member of the same Keiretsu] must also listen?" Our Japanese colleague smiled and replied, "That is what our German colleague thinks. The reason we prefer a more dependent type of promise is because it is the right thing to do."

In sum, as shown by this comparative experience on normative policy making, the underlying business cultures at the time had much to do with the resulting policies. On the United States side, the policy sprung from consulting with the economic sector most affected by the proposed Convention—the banking and financial industry. As the most directly affected regular participants in the marketplace in question, their voice was first among equals (*primum inter pares*). On the German and Japanese side, what determined who was to be heard first and predominantly was the task assigned to the various participants in a hierarchical and disciplined national campaign of foreign market penetration. If that campaign could best succeed by protecting the interests of the largest and most productive industrial exporters, they had to be heard first and the financial sector had to play second fiddle.

K. Micro-Contractual Policies

I would describe the preceding issues as involving "macro" contractual policies. By a micro-contractual policy, I mean one that shapes the drafting of individual contracts, promises or transactions. Yet, during the transition from a macro to a micro policy, two or more macro policies could compete for application to a given transaction and often they collide to the detriment of the losing policy. This is the case, for example, with the macro-policy of avoiding uncertainty by engaging only in highly structured transactions and the macro-policy of market penetration at all costs. If market penetration is effected by predatory pricing, as in *Matsushita*, it could soon become an assumption of costly and eventually destructive risks. The following incident illustrates just such a situation.

I received a fax containing a detailed schematic rendering of a proposed stand-by letter of credit transaction from someone who identified himself as a loan officer for a foreign bank doing business in the United States. Shortly thereafter, he phoned me and asked if I would be interested in providing a letter opinion on the commercial and regulatory law soundness of the proposed text. He explained that his bank decided to issue such a letter of credit to a state agency so that it could use it as the master promise to finance a large construction project whose streams of revenue would come at first from the public sale of bonds known as "industrial revenue bonds."

The outlined letters of credit promised to pay significant sums to various creditors including builders, architects, and trustees for the holders of bonds and certificates (beneficiaries of the letter of credit). Payments by the issuers of the stand-by letters of credit would be made either upon the beneficiaries' tender of documents certifying to their performance of specified tasks or of a trustee certifying that the terms and conditions of the identified payments had been met.

I told him that I had not seen any reference in the entire set of issuances and underlying transactions to a person or entity that would be the bank's customer or applicant for the credit. As such, this person or entity would be the party responsible for reimbursing the bank or banks involved for all or part of their disbursements. He told me not to worry about that entity because eventually such an entity would be created. He emphasized that his bank had decided to bid for the role of issuer of the standby letters of credit and was prepared to offer the most competitive terms and conditions. He also indicated that he was told that, in my writings and recommendations for customary and statutory law, I had advocated the validity of letters of credit in which the issuer could also be the customer or applicant for the issuance.

I told him that this was true, but if he wanted a letter opinion involving the commercial and regulatory law soundness of the letter of credit, he should first consult with his bank counsel on whether an issuance such as the one contemplated could be silent on its source of repayment or on the collateral that would secure such a repayment. Since I hadn't looked at the state and federal law on point, I was not sure if such an issuance was not in violation of state or federal provisions that may have required such a disclosure. He expressed surprise at my recommendation and asked, "If my bank is willing to accept a risk and has the resources to do so, if its purpose is legitimate, *i.e.*, to gain a foothold in a potentially highly lucrative market for stand-by letters of credit in the United States, why should a state government or any other government be opposed to this issuance?" I reiterated my suggestion that he should consult his own bank counsel. I never heard from him again, except that a few years later I read in a national newspaper how his bank, after having issued many stand-by letters of credit for project finance, failed as a result of having issued large numbers of standby letters of credit secured only by real estate whose value had declined sharply. Clearly, this was an instance where the policy to penetrate markets at all costs had defeated the policy of uncertainty avoidance.

Chapter 2

METHODOLOGY

§ 2.1 THE COMPARATIVE METHOD OF THIS BOOK

A. Scientific Origins

The comparison of data for scientific purposes was practiced in antiquity. Greek geometry, for example, compared figures and dimensions and synthesized observations by means of theorems. Nevertheless, comparative observation and verification as a method of searching for the truth in pure and applied science was not widely adopted in the Western world until the Renaissance. Astronomical observations and oceanographic chart-making by the Spanish and Portuguese ocean voyagers had much to do with this intellectual awakening.[1]

Regrettably, the comparison of legal institutions remained well behind the comparative empirical advances in the physical sciences. Suffice it to say that it was only during the second half of the nineteenth century that the first attempts to engage in systematic comparisons of legal institutions were undertaken and comparative law research societies were created.[2]

B. Different Methods of Comparison

1. The Static Comparison

In its nineteenth century beginnings, the comparison of legal institutions was largely static or non-contextual. Only rarely was it pursued beyond establishing the textual meaning of concepts or rules as found in the laws of other countries or jurisdictions. Law was not examined contextually or "in action" or by measuring its accomplishments or failures and the reasons for both. Thus, much scholarly ink was invested in pinpointing the textual (but not contextual) differences between, say, the French civil law concept of "*causa*" and the common law "consideration" or between the equitable powers of the Roman *Praetor* and the English Chancellor.

Similarly, not an insignificant number of professors in renowned centers of legal scholarship taught comparative law as an annotated lexicography as late as the post-World War II period. For instance, in a graduate course on comparative law that I

---

[1] *See generally* ALLEN G. DEBUS, MAN AND NATURE IN THE RENAISSANCE (Cambridge Univ. Press, 1978).

[2] *See, e.g., Association Internationale de Droit Comparé, Annuaire de Législation Etrangère* (1872–1936), *at* http://www.periodicals.com. *See also* Hessel E. Yntema, *Comparative Research and Unification of Law* 41 MICH. L. REV. 261–268 (1942) [hereinafter Yntema, *Comparative Research*], for a brief but insightful review of some of the leading European and North American ideas on the components of comparative legal research. *See also* Neville Brown, *A Century of Comparative Law in England: 1869–1969*, 19 AM. J. COMP. L. 232 (1971). Professor Brown similarly traces the beginning of comparative law studies in Europe to the foundation of the French Society of Comparative Legislation in 1869, which was also the year when Sir Henry Sumner Maine accepted the Chair of Comparative Jurisprudence at Oxford. According to Professor Brown, from 1869 until 1918 comparative legal studies in England followed the direction provided by Sir Henry Sumner Maine.

attended at the University of Paris in 1958, the professor, after exhorting his students to be comparatists ("*soyez comparatistes*"), proceeded to discuss the meaning of a long list of terms in various languages, followed by short commentaries on each term and by citations to their respective codes or court decisions that used the terms. Obviously, the law that this professor failed to discuss was much more complex and vital (I like to call it "peopled" in the sense discussed in Chapter I) than that reflected in his lists of equivalent terms and summaries of statutory and judicial applications.

Take, for example, some of the commercial aspects of the *causa* and consideration mentioned in Chapters 1 and 22. As will be apparent when comparing the different attitudes toward commerce and especially commercial credit in French, German and Anglo-American law, serious socio-economic consequences followed from French jurists requiring a morality-laden *causa* when determining the negotiability of promissory notes, drafts and government bonds.[3] Our University of Paris comparative law professor failed to tell us that the broad definition of usury in effect in France during the eighteenth and much of the nineteenth century was a major reason why these negotiable instruments were deemed not only non-negotiable but also unenforceable, having been "vitiated" by an illegal cause. Consequently, secondary markets for the discount or purchase of negotiable instruments failed to materialize in nineteenth-century France and French-influenced Spain.

He also failed to tell us that countries whose legal systems did not require a *causa* had developed healthy secondary markets for the same instruments during the same period. I would suggest that the relationship between *causa*, usury and other morality-laden concepts was an infinitely more important legal-contextual datum than our professor's explanation of what Aristotle meant by his "first," "material" and "final" causes.[4] In addition, as the reader will discover when reading Chapter 22 on the formation of contracts, our Parisian class should have also discussed how the giving of something of value as consideration as an initial step in the formation of contracts had much to do with instilling trust between lenders and borrowers; a trust that helped build a commercial credit society in late sixteenth and early seventeenth-century England, the importance of which exceeded that of any development in any other European nation.[5]

2. *The Contextual Comparison and the Purpose of Legal Institutions: Rudolph von Ihering's Views*

Fortunately for comparative law studies, the great Romanist and legal philosopher, Rudolf von Ihering, called attention during the middle of the nineteenth century to the need to connect the study of legal institutions to their purposes. In his words:

> [T]he stone does not fall in order to fall, but because it must fall . . . whilst the man who acts does so, not [necessarily] *because* of anything, but *in order* to attain to something. . . . As there can be no motion of the stone without a

---

[3] *See infra* § 11:4 (on German law including a discussion on the House of Rothschild).

[4] *See infra* § 22:2.

[5] *See infra* § 22:4(C).

> [gravitationally related] cause, so can there be no movement of the will without a purpose.[6]

The importance that von Ihering attributed to the purpose of legal institutions was reflected in his comparison of the Roman law contracts of immediate and simultaneous performance with those whose performance was to take place in the future, a recurrent theme throughout this book:

> Not every contract requires compulsive coercion [such as in action for specific performance] for its [enforcement]; a contract of sale or exchange which is at once carried out . . . leaves nothing to be gotten by coercion. . . . For [its purpose is to facilitate the] simplest form of exchange, *viz.*, a cash business. . . . But this immediate fulfillment on both sides, which makes compulsive coercion unnecessary, is not practicable in all contracts. It is not practicable in a loan—[where] the lender must precede with his performance; the consideration, *viz.*, the payment of the loan, can only follow later. It is not practicable in a contract of lease—whether the rent is paid before or after permission is given to use the object; one of the two parties must come first with his performance and wait for the consideration. Thus certain contracts necessarily presuppose the postponement of the performance on the one side. . . .[7]

The above comparison highlights the diverse functions of two types of contracts, one designed for simultaneous exchanges and the other for extensions of credit. It also makes clear the function of executory promises: to bind their promisors to give or to do something at a future time despite the fact that nothing was given or promised to them prior to the utterance of the promise to perform at a future time. This purposive vision of contracts was behind the suggestion of a functional comparative law analysis by Konrad Zweigert and Heinrich Kötz, two of von Ihering's modern-day followers.[8] In their opinion:

> From this basic principle stem . . . the choice of laws to compare, the scope of the undertaking. . . . The proposition rests on what every comparatist learns . . . the legal system of every society faces essentially the same problems, and solves these problems by quite different means though very often with similar results. . . . [T]he problem must be stated without any reference to the concepts of one's own legal system [but, rather, to the objectives of the mechanisms under analysis]. Thus instead of asking, "What formal requirements are there for sales contracts in foreign law?" it is better to ask, "How does foreign law protect parties from surprise, or from being held to an agreement not seriously intended?"[9]

This is as clear a formulation of a purposive comparison as I have read anywhere, and yet there is more to a purposive comparison if it is truly contextual.

---

[6] VON IHERING, A MEANS TO AN END, at 2 (emphasis added).

[7] *Id.* at 198.

[8] *See* ZWEIGERT & HEINRICH KÖTZ, COMPARATIVE LAW, at 34.

[9] *See* ZWEIGERT & KÖTZ, COMPARATIVE LAW, *supra* note 8, at 34.

3. The Contextual Comparison: Actual Purposes and Practices

The truism that "generalizations are a fertile soil for misperceptions" is worth repeating because static or non-contextual comparative legal analyses are often guilty of misperceptions. Zweigert and Kötz thus assumed that contractual formalities such as the requirement of a writing have a similar purpose, no matter where or when. That purpose, according to these authors, is the prevention of surprise so that the contracting parties do not wind up with a contractual outcome contrary to what they expected. Yet, legal cultures are relentless transformers of the original purposes of legal institutions. For example, the purpose of the requirement of a formal writing for the validity of contracts in Andres Bello's Chilean Civil Code, a code after which many Latin American civil codes were modeled,[10] was not merely to discern the true contractual intent from the literal meaning formally stated in the contract. Bello's purpose was to stamp out the courts' reliance on fraudulent testimonies purchased by the parties or their attorneys from "witnesses" who offered their "testimony" to the highest bidder literally feet away from the courtroom where judges and their clerks adjudicated contractual intent.[11]

The ruptured link between the original and the transplanted purpose of legislation and their respective socio-economic contexts is quite common. I encountered it while discussing a newly drafted chapter on negotiable instruments law with its Nicaraguan drafter during the 1960s.[12] His definition of a negotiable instrument expressly excluded those payable in metal or commodities and quoted as the source for this definition that which appeared in an Italian commercial law treatise.

Yet, my field research in rural Nicaragua revealed that "chips" (*fichas*) issued by the stores of large agricultural producers were among the most popular means of payment in that nation's countryside in the 1950s and 1960s. These chips were issued to company employees or third parties in exchange for the services they rendered to the agricultural company. They entitled their holders to purchase products in the company stores and in some instances they also entitled them to obtain the cash value of products sold by the company store. The chips were commonly transferred by their holders as if they were bearer negotiable instruments. As stated by many of their users, they trusted the intrinsic value of these chips more than they trusted other instruments. Not seeing any reference to these chips in the draft, I asked the drafter why he excluded them. His reply was:

---

[10] *See infra* § 14:5(A)(1).

[11] In his executive message to congress proposing the adoption of Chile's Civil Code of 1855, Chile's then president Manuel Montt made the following testimonial statement on the unreliability of evidence on contractual intent (known to have been written by Andrés Bello): "Well known among inferior classes of the population is the existence of an infamous class of men who earn their living by prostituting their testimonial oath" (*"Conocida es en las poblaciones inferiores la existencia de una clase infame de hombres, que se labran un medio de subsistencia en la prostitución del juramento."*). (*"Mensaje del Ejecutivo al Congreso Proponiendo la Aprobación del Código Civil de 1855"*) [hereinafter President Montt's Executive Message] *See* http://www.chilein.com/c_civil1.htm (for the full text of this executive message). The relevant rules are CÓD. CIV. (Chile) arts. 1708, 1709, 1710 & 1711. For a compendium of essays on Bello's Civil Code, *see* UNIVERSIDAD DE CHILE FACULTAD DE DERECHO, IV ANALES DE LA FACULTAD DE CIENCIAS JURÍDICAS Y SOCIALES (Cuarta Época 1964–1965—No. 4), *available at* http://www.analesderecho.uchile.cl/CDA/an_der_indice/index.html.

[12] Conversation with one of the drafters of a 1968 proposed revision of the Nicaraguan Commercial Code, Managua, Sept. 12, 1968 who preferred to remain anonymous (on file with author) [hereinafter Nicaraguan Conversation].

> Your datum on the use of chips is merely an empirical one. What is important to me as a drafter of a "scientific law" is to find the best scientific definition or concept of a payment instrument. The definition of a payment instrument I chose is by Professor X, my great Italian mentor.[13]

Notice this drafter's dismissal of the circulation of chips in rural Nicaragua as a mere empirical datum and his reliance on an Italian definition of a negotiable instrument as the appropriate datum of commercial legal science regardless of its socio-economic purpose and context. Yet, when shorn of its pseudo-scientific definitional purpose, the common purpose of an Italian and a Nicaraguan negotiable instrument is the same—to provide a widely acceptable means for the payment and extinction of obligations. And if a company store chip was trusted to extinguish obligations more than any other instrument in rural Nicaragua, why deny them the negotiability of bearer instruments that their everyday users were willing to accept in a business and economic environment so different from that of a highly-commercialized Italian marketplace? While ignoring market practices, my Nicaraguan interlocutor revealed an important aspect of his country's legal culture: Legal academics like him disdained empirical facts as a source of law making and preferred to rely on the logical symmetries of foreign legal concepts even though they had been shaped by very different socio-economic conditions and experiences.

In summary, a contextual comparison searches for the purposes of the compared legal institutions, and inquires into the socio-economic and legal needs that these institutions are expected to fulfill. And it does so by examining the relevant commercial practices as well as the official or positive law and the society's legal culture, *i.e.*, the values and attitudes of market participants. This comparison also includes an assessment of the socio-economic consequences of the enactment in question. When a chosen legal institution fails its purpose(s), the comparative analyst must find out the reasons for the failure, and, based upon his findings of successful alternatives, suggest a suitable local or foreign replacement.

4. *Archetypal Behavior and Contextual Analysis*

As noted in Chapter I, the contextual analysis is greatly facilitated by identifying the archetypal behavior that helps to shape both standard and best practices and their resulting legal institutions. Lord Mansfield was one of the first to identify accurately the behavior of the average merchant as he did in a landmark decision in which he stated that the average merchant is someone who does not need to rely on formalities because his word is "his bond."[14] The same was true with Justice Cardozo, whose fiduciary had to evince the punctilio "the most honorable."[15] Please recall that by archetypal behavior, I mean the representative behavior of average merchants, bankers or professionals as reflected in their standard practices as well as in the practices of highly respected and trusted merchants, bankers or professionals, to which I refer as their best practices. It is worth emphasizing that what matters to the

---

[13] *Id.*

[14] Miller v. Race, 97 Eng. Rep. 398 [K.B. 1758]; *infra* notes 80–82 and accompanying text.

[15] *See infra* § 23:9(C).

contextual analyst is whether the conduct of the merchants selected as archetypes is truly representative of the behavior of a class or group of merchants.[16]

Max Weber, one of the founders of modern legal sociology, was among the first to call attention to the importance of representative (he referred to it as "ideal") social behavior in social science research.[17] Think of how hard it would be for social scientists to attribute features to the behavior of social groups or classes without being able to rely on the representative behavior of some of their members. Without it, social scientists and comparative lawyers would have to engage in endless and costly observation and analysis of the behavior of each member of the class or group in question.

a. The Costs of Relying on Inaccurate or Unrepresentative Archetypes of Commercial Behavior When Making Commercial Contract Law

Unfortunately, not all the archetypes relied on by law makers, lawyers and adjudicators are representative of the commercial behavior of the classes or groups they are supposed to represent. Assume, for example, that the comparative analyst was trying to determine how best to resolve the problem of excessive litigation on the alleged intent of contracting parties. Assume further that the analyst was Andres Bello, the principal drafter of Chile's Civil Code of 1857[18] and that the legislative model he used to resolve this problem was the *Code Civil.* This code requires that contracts over a certain sum be executed in a highly formal public or notarial deed (the *titre* or *acte authentique*), and when such a deed is executed it excludes most other evidence on the parties' intent.[19] Finally, assume that Bello blamed the practices of Chilean archetypal court witnesses for the excess and unpredictability of litigation on contractual intent. He referred to these witnesses as "an infamous class of men," and in his introduction to Chile's Civil Code, he accused them of earning their living by offering their testimony on contractual intent to the highest bidder.[20]

Certain that this was the behavior of representative archetypal witnesses in contract litigation, and certain also that contracting parties would use them as witnesses and thereby would not hesitate to testify falsely themselves, Bello's solution was to require a high level of contractual formality that would automatically dispense with the reliance on witnesses to determine a disputed contractual intent.

---

[16] It is important not to confuse the archetypes used in this book with the heroes of Greek or subsequent mythologies. Our commercial archetypes are creatures of commercial cultures. Unlike the Greek mythical heroes, they did not earn emulation and, in some instances admiration, because of their strength or other extraordinary God-like powers but because of their reproducible human features. *See e.g.,* MERRIAM-WEBSTER ONLINE (2011), www.Merriam-Webster.com ("Archetype: the original pattern or model of which all things of the same type are representations or copies; prototype; also a perfect example.").

[17] *See* MAX WEBER ON THE METHODOLOGY OF THE SOCIAL SCIENCES 90 (Edward A Shils & Henry A. Finch trans., 1st ed. 1949). Max Weber describes the research value of archetypal or ideal behavior as follows: "[W]here market-conditioned relationships . . . are discovered or suspected to exist in reality to some extent, we can make the *characteristic* features of this relationship pragmatically *clear* and *understandable* by reference to an *ideal-type.* This procedure can be indispensable for heuristic as well as expository purposes." *Id.*

[18] CÓD. CIV. (Chile) (1857). The code was promulgated on November 22, 1855, but it went into effect (or entered into force) on January 1, 1857.

[19] *See* C. Civ. (FR.) 358–359 (Barrister 1804).

[20] *See* President Montt's Executive Message, *supra* note 11 (on the adoption of Chile's Civil Code of 1855).

Yet, how representative was the behavior of these "infamous men" when compared with the behavior of the much larger class of merchants who entered into their commercial contracts in good faith, and with the intention to cooperate with each other's ability to earn a profit? In addition, because the intent of regular participants in market transactions has to be manifested usually in informal, quick and standardized contracts or parts of them, their intent could best be established by determining what was customary for that trade or business as expressed in informal documents and not in time consuming and costly written and notarial documents. Finally, why assume that the decision to use purchased witnesses was invariably made by the merchants and not by the lawyers to whom they entrusted their litigation?

Justice Oliver Wendell Holmes Jr.'s "bad man" of contracts was another unrepresentative archetyhpe. He was the contracting party ready to breach any contract if paying damages, turned out to be cheaper than performing it. This archetype was as unrepresentative of the contractual behavior of merchants as was Andres Bello's "infamous witness."[21] Yet, the reliance on Bello's "infamous witness" and on Holmes' "bad man" of contracts as archetypes of commercial contractual conduct led Bello to require costly, dilatory and anti-commercial contractual formalities for all contracting parties, and in Holmes' case, led to a presumption of commercial bad faith in the performance (or non-performance) of contracts that is just as costly, if not more, than Bello's. Imagine, for example, the cost incurred by the holders of checks about to be deposited with their banks if the banks' presumption was that their check depositors were (a la Holmes) the "bad men of checks." Such a presumption assumes that check depositors had acquired them in bad faith and that it was their burden to prove that they did not steal, embezzle or fraudulently procure and endorse them. Aside from the high cost of such a negative proof, check depositors could no longer count on receiving provisional credits for their deposited checks as is normally received by check depositors under existing law and practice.[22]

Perhaps one of the most serious misperceptions of the nature of an archetypal banker was that of Alan Greenspan, the former chairman of the Federal Reserve. His archetypal banker was capable and willing to restrain and regulate himself against highly risky forms of lending and hedging. Yet, the Wall Street Journal version of Greenspan's testimony before the House Oversight Committee on October 23, 2008 quotes Rep. Henry Waxman making the following statement to Greenspan: "You had the authority to prevent irresponsible lending practices that led to the subprime-mortgage crisis. You were advised to do so by many others. And now our whole economy is paying its price. . . ." In response, Mr. Greenspan said he made "a mistake" in his hands-off regulatory philosophy, which many now blame in part for sparking the global economic crisis whose consequences we are still suffering. He quoted something he had written in March: "Those of us who have looked to the self-interest of lending

---

[21] *See infra* § 29:2 (on the remedial implications of Justice Holmes' "bad man" archetype).

[22] *See* U.C.C. § 4–214(a) and Comment 1 ("Under current bank practice, in a major portion of cases banks make provisional settlements for items (checks) when they are first received. . . .") (Parenthesis added).

institutions to protect shareholder's equity (myself especially) are in a state of shocked disbelief."[23]

Serious mischaracterizations of archetypal commercial behavior also abound in Marxist-Leninist dogma and legal literature. As will be discussed in later chapters,[24] Karl Marx and Vladimir Illyich Lenin (among others) characterized ordinary merchants in many different ways, such as criminals bent on "exploiting someone else's labor," "speculators" with the goods or money of others, embezzlers of the excess value created by the work of their employees, or avaricious and selfish farmers ("*Kulaks*"). As will also be discussed in these chapters, these inaccurate archetypal characterizations of merchants and farmers became part of the Soviet living law of commercial contracts. Thus, sayings by Lenin on the avariciousness of merchants or farmers and how they profited by hiring and exploiting laborers were soon repeated by self-appointed accusers against the recipients of administrative bonuses who as "model" state employees were awarded: 1) automobiles (but used them as taxis with the help of hired drivers); 2) plots of land (when they were used to grow vegetables with hired help); or 3) *dachas* (country houses or villas) (when rented out and maintained also with hired help).[25]

b. Archetypal Behavior in Simple and Complex Transactions: Standard and Best Practices and Their Economic Significance

Obviously, it is easier to identify archetypal behavior in simpler transactions than in complex ones. The archetypal behavior in a simple transaction such as in a sale of goods in a retail store or market is more easily standardized than that in a complex financial transaction with multiple parties, some supplying goods, others services, and under highly negotiated terms and conditions. Further, the behavior associated with familial (and "civil" or not-for-profit) archetypes such as the French "good father of family" of the *Code Civil*[26] tends to change less over time than that of commercial archetypes. Can you visualize why?

Consider, for example, the changes experienced by an archetypal United States commercial banker in the twentieth century alone. Prior to the enactment of the 1933 Glass-Steagall Act, he could be a deposit banker, a commercial banker and an investment banker or underwriter. After this enactment, he could no longer function as an investment banker.[27] In November of 1999, however, the Gramm-Leach-Bliley Act authorized commercial bankers to engage in some of the same previously-forbidden activities.[28] Quickly thereafter, highly complex new archetypal standard banking practices were engaged in by United States banks with greater powers and rights than ever experienced.

---

[23] See the summary of Greenspan's testimony in Kara Scannel & Sudeep Reddy, *Greenspan Admits Errors to Hostile House Panel*, WALL STREET JOURNAL (Oct. 24, 2008), online.wsj.com/article/SB122476545437862295.html.

[24] *See infra* § 15:3(C)(1).

[25] *See infra* § 16:4.

[26] *See, e.g.*, C. CIV. (FR.) art. 1374 (Barrister 1804). *See also* Kozolchyk, *Commercialization*, at 16–20; *infra* § 23:1(C).

[27] *See* Glass-Steagall Act, 12 U.S.C. § 378 (1933).

[28] Also known as the Financial Services Modernization Act of 1999, Pub. L. 106–102, 113 Stat. 1338 (1999).

As if on cue, shortly after the repeal of Glass-Steagall, an international financial "bubble" grew uncontrollably while new standard practices for complex and often risky transactions continued to be fashioned to meet the demands of a growing national and international clientele. Yet while new standard practices were being created, no attention was paid to their effects upon the welfare of regular participants in those transactions as well as of third parties—among them millions of homeowners who lost their homes and approximately 8 million jobless workers in the United States alone.[29]

Please recall Chapter I's distinction between standard and best practices. There, I described the standard practices as governed by the market standard of fairness which mandates that each party to a contract treat the other as a *regular market participant* would *reasonably expect to be treated* when viewing his own advantage. And I described best practices as those that take into account the effect of their transactions upon third parties and in fiduciary transactions treat the counter party in an altruistic or brotherly fashion.

The fact that recent standard practices in the United States on sub-prime mortgages, including their sales to third parties, were the result of agreements between or among a small group of "primary" market participants should not be missed. For the regular market participants who designed and negotiated the various agreements involved in the creation and distribution of sub-prime mortgage-backed bonds or certificates were the "originating" mortgagee banks, the underwriting banks or securities intermediaries or both, and, of course, their "special purpose" vehicles.

The third party purchasers of the bonds or certificates or of security interests in them were not regular participants in that primary or originating market and were not parties to the negotiation and drafting of the agreements that resulted in the standard practices of that primary market. They belonged to the secondary markets and their reasonable expectations of profitability and safety were taken into account only hypothetically by the drafters of the agreements and creators of the primary market practices. I say "hypothetically" because what the drafters of standard practices on the distribution of mortgage-backed sub-prime bonds or certificates calculated was a likely interest rate that would be attractive to these third parties. They did not truly attempt to assess the risk assumed by their third parties.

5. *Von Ihering's and Justice Cardozo's Contextual Analysis and Cultural Anthropology*

Justice Benjamin Nathan Cardozo was one of the most insightful and influential users of the contextual and purposive legal analysis in Anglo-American law. He attributed its authorship to the "legal sociology" of Rudolf von Ihering. After describing the lawmakers' and especially the judge's function as "thinking of the end which the law serves, and fitting its rules to the task of service,"[30] he added:

> This conception of the end of the law as determining the direction of its growth, which was I]Ihering's great contribution to the theory of

---

[29] These figures were provided by Gary Gensler, chairman of the U.S. Commodity Futures Trading Commission during an interview with Charlie Rose. *Gary Gensler*, CHARLIE ROSE (June 14, 2012), www.charlierose.com/view/interview/12409.

[30] BENJAMIN NATHAN CARDOZO, THE NATURE OF THE JUDICIAL PROCESS 102 (1922) [hereinafter CARDOZO, JUDICIAL PROCESS] (citation omitted).

> jurisprudence, finds its organon, its instrument, in the method of sociology. Not the origin, but the goal, is the main thing. There can be no wisdom in the choice of a path unless we know where it will lead. The teleological [or purposive] conception of his function must be ever in the judge's mind.[31]

By "the method of sociology," Cardozo did not mean today's widely practiced quantitative and statistical analysis of social institutions. His (and von Ihering's) sociological methods relied on their observation of societal developments likely to impact statutory or judge-made law, and especially on those developments likely to prompt serious social or interpersonal conflicts. In Cardozo's time, one such development was the increasing number of accidents related to the industrial manufacture and use of automobiles. Its likelihood of causing injuries to immediate and remote purchasers-users brought into question the manufacturers' duty to foresee the injuries caused by their defective manufacture of vehicles.

Another conflict that attracted Cardozo's attention was the relationship between trusted merchants and financial intermediaries at a time when the latter began to manage the investments of a growing number of savers who were not as professionally capable or economically powerful as managing merchants were. Cardozo's observation of the interests and forces at stake in these conflicts was accompanied by his ability to identify the behavior that was customary among average and model or highly-respected participants in the legal and business relationships, especially when some or all were merchants. Yet, despite Justice Cardozo's references to legal sociology, I would suggest that his method is closer to the one used by legal-cultural anthropologists such as E. Adamson Hoebel and Marcel Mauss, and that Cardozo also relied considerably on archetypal behavior to formulate his concepts, principles and rules of adjudication. The reason why this is such a useful method is because it not only peers into human nature but *focuses specifically on those activities* that eventually become legal institutions.[32]

In pre-industrial societies, the behavior of average merchants when selling their goods was largely governed by the principle "buyer beware" (*caveat emptor*).[33] In contrast, in societies with a developed or developing commercial and financial marketplace, such as the mid-twentieth century United States, similar sales were increasingly accompanied by implied warranties.[34] Further, some commercial relationships required even a higher standard of diligence and concern for the interests of others. This was the case, as noted in the previous section, with trustees when dealing with their settlors and their beneficiaries. Cardozo's observations on the seminal role of trust in certain individuals and legal institutions made him conclude that the behavior that ought to be required from those who were most trusted was that of "a man of the most delicate conscience and the nicest sense of honor."[35]

---

[31] *Id.*

[32] *See infra* § 3:3(C).

[33] *See* GOODE ON COMMERCIAL LAW 201–02, 306 (Ewan McKendrick ed., 4th ed. 2009), on warranties. *See also* LAWRENCE FRIEDMAN, A HISTORY OF AMERICAN LAW 194 (2005). Professor Friedman points out that in McFarland v. Newman, 9 Watts 55 (Pa. 1839), Judge John Gibson restated a United States version of *caveat emptor* when deciding on appeal that "he who is so simple as to contract without a specification of terms, is not a fit subject of judicial guardianship."

[34] *See, e.g.*, D'Onofrio v. First Nat'l Stores, Inc., 68 R.I. 144 (1942) and the discussion of the emergence of implied warranies in English law, *infra* § 30:2(C) (on U.S. law).

[35] CARDOZO, JUDICIAL PROCESS, *supra* note 30, at 109.

Because this behavior was archetypal and took place repeatedly, it could be ascertained objectively and was neither subjective nor capricious. As stated by Cardozo, the standards of behavior required from the highly entrusted were not the product of what some German jurists called "a jurisprudence of mere sentiment or feeling" (*Die Gefühlsjurisprudenz*).[36]

Similarly, although relying on historical observation, von Ihering identified the archetype that inspired the Roman law of contractual fortitude and duress for a considerable period of time. It was the stolid Roman legionnaire, whose standard of contractual behavior was of such fortitude that his contractual will could only be broken by the most severe of physical pressures and for this reason very few contracting parties in classical Roman law were granted the remedy of rescission of contract on the grounds of duress.[37]

The reliance on archetypal behavior to fashion long-lasting commercial law rules is a trait of great jurists from the Ulpians to the Cardozos, also apparent in commercial law adjudication in the Middle Ages, and in the method used by Maimonides, the Jewish medieval sage and rabbinical authority.[38] When instructing lower court judges on whom, between or among the disputing merchants, should take the oath that would decide the controversy, he often resorted to archetypal behavior. For example, where *force majeure* was alleged to have prevented one joint venturer or partner from rendering a proper accounting to the other,[39] he required that in the absence of written, oath-supported promises (such as in a formal promise known as a "*shetar*"), the partner or joint venturer whose behavior varied most from the customary norm had to take the oath reserved for archetypal partners or joint venturers (*Shavuot shutaphim*).[40] As a decissory oath, taking it meant that the disputed fact would be resolved in favor of the oath-taker and a failure to take it would concede the other party's factual allegation.

Similarly, the codifiers of the model European civil and commercial codes resorted to archetypal behavior such as that of the "good father of family" (*bon père de famille*) of the *Code Civil* or the "proper merchant" (*eines ordentlichen Kaufman*) of the German HGB. You will find in Chapter X that I contrast the behavior of this standard but respectable merchant with that of another but more highly trusted archetype, that of Mayer Amschel Rothschild, the international banker in late eighteenth century Germany who protected the assets of his joint venturers in preference to his own.

Archetypal behavior generates what Harvard's Dean Roscoe Pound, the Australian legal philosopher Julius Stone, and the United States founder of legal anthropology E. Adamson Hoebel, among others, referred to as "jural postulates." These postulates express the principles that shape the living law of a given legal

---

[36] *Id.* at 106.

[37] RUDOLF VON IHERING, EL ESPÍRITU DEL DERECHO ROMANO 59, 60 (1962). This translation and abridgement of GEIST DES ROMISCHEN RECHTS concludes that the early Roman law of property was enormously influenced by the model of behavior of the Roman warrior, a man whose favorite means of acquiring property was by the strength of his hands, his sword, and his lance. *See also* Dawson, *Economic Duress—An Essay in Perspective,* 45 MICH. L. REV. 253, 255, 264 (1947), *cited in* Kozolchyk, *Toward a Theory of Law,* at 739 n.199, for an enlightening study of the development of standards and fortitude in the law of duress.

[38] *See infra* § 5:10.

[39] *Id.*

[40] *Id.* at (2) Question 63b (FG).

culture. As such, they epitomize the moral criteria that govern archetypal legal behavior, whether officially or unofficially approved, and are therefore omnipresent throughout the history and geography of commercial contract rights and duties. They range from the pre-industrial postulates such as "buyer beware" to Justice Cardozo's turn of the twentieth century financial centers' "*punctilio*—the most honorable."

6. Micro-loans and Archetypal Women Entrepreneurs: Cultural Anthropology and the Reduction of Poverty.

One of the reasons why the anthropological method is helpful when using commercial legal institutions as tools for economic development is because it not only looks deeply into human nature, but *focuses specifically on those activities* that eventually can become legal institutions and tells us why they have succeeded or failed. Professor James Greenberg of the University of Arizona Anthropology Department is a leading cultural anthropologist much of whose research involves poor indigenous populations among whom he has lived. Recently, he analyzed the use of microfinance as a tool for economic development,[41] and found that many of its advocates made seriously erroneous assumptions about the archetypal entrepreneurial poor women recipients of micro-loans. One assumption was that these women's access to financial services was sure to increase their income and productivity creating self-employment and reducing poverty. Another assumption was that these women not only lacked access to credit but that they wanted such an access regardless of its source. They imagined them as longing to be self-employed and envisioned microcredit as creating successful enterprises that produced cash to pay off their loans and the income to lift them out of poverty. They also assumed that the poor need no special training to do this as they know what is best for them.[42]

Yet, these advocates were unaware that their targeted archetypal poor women entrepreneurs were:

> [U]sually leery of credit, and with good reason as the darker side of credit is debt. Borrowing means being in debt. Borrowing from any kind of institution is fundamentally different from borrowing from friends. Taking loans, even from microcredit associations, is perilous for the poor, as they risk sinking into even deeper economic and social poverty if they cannot repay them. For poor households whose livelihoods are very vulnerable taking on debt increases the risks of falling into a downward debt spiral.[43]

To which Greenberg added:

> The reality is that few microenterprises are very successful for a variety of reasons. One of the major constraints on them is that women already have a full workload: childcare, cooking, cleaning, garden work, fetching water, and tending animals. Rather than having infinite time to devote to a microenterprise, because their time is highly constrained, any microenterprise they undertake must fit into their schedule. Usually this

---

[41] *See* James B. Greenberg, *Microfinance, Law and Development: A Case Study in Mali*, 30 AZ. J. INT. & COMP. L. 135 (2013).

[42] *Id.* at 147.

[43] *Id.* at 148 (citations omitted).

> means that such activities need to be extensions of the kinds of skills and work women do as part of their everyday activities
>
> * * *
>
> If the startup monies come from savings group, or a similar organization, another limiting factor is that most groups require that repayments begin (with some exceptions for agriculture) almost immediately. This means that this activity must produce sufficient revenues from the start in order to make these weekly payments.[44]

One of his findings deserves special attention:

> If microenterprises were really run like business firms, capital invested in the microenterprise would be administered separately from households from household expenses. . . . The reality is that microenterprise and household funds are intermingled. In good times household funds may subsidize microenterprise; in bad times microenterprise may be decapitalized to meet household needs. Given this intermingling of funds, to talk about production or consumption loans is utter nonsense.[45]

Please note how Professor Greenberg's observations are, to paraphrase the interviewing style of a sports television program of a bygone era "up-close and personal." This is how he found out how debt was perceived by many of the poor as "the darker side of credit." The same is true with the women entrepreneurs' practice of commingling business funds with those needed to cure their sick children.

§ 2.2 TWO METHODS OF LEGAL REASONING: LEGAL SCHOLASTICISM AND THE LOGIC OF THE REASONABLE

The methods of legal reasoning are part of a nation's or region's legal culture and as such they influence and are influenced by its attitudes and values, and for this reason they also influence economic development. If as a result of his method of legal reasoning a judge or administrator denies validity to a transaction that is otherwise legal, moral, or consistent with public policy and can contribute to its economic development, there is every reason to question their legal reasoning. For if that transaction's only fault is that it conflicts with a legal definition or classification whose purpose was to better describe and classify transactions used during the life and times of the definer and classifier, but not those who were their necessary replacements, why block their use? After all, commercial legal definitions and classifications should reflect transactional life and not the other way around. The following sections explore the interaction between the two most utilized methods of legal reasoning and economic development.

A. Legal Scholasticism

During the Middle Ages, what eventually became the civil and common law jurisdictions started diverging in varying degrees from their common Roman law ancestry. This divergence was caused largely by the different methods of legal reasoning employed by the jurists, lawyers and law professors within each system.

---

[44] *Id.* at 159.

[45] *Id.* at 160.

Together with the attitudes and values of legislators, judges, lawyers and law professors, these methods shaped the drafting, interpreting, practicing and teaching of law on each side of the systemic divide.

Scholasticism became the prevailing method of legal and theological reasoning in southern and central European universities during the late Middle Ages (mostly from the twelfth to the fifteenth centuries) as well as in some other countries and regions, especially in France, Spain, Portugal and Spanish and Portuguese America. One reason for its popularity was that it aimed at reconciling the teachings of Greek philosophers, especially those of Aristotle, with the prevailing Christian theology.

Christian theology was interested in establishing the permanence and universality of its teachings. Aristotle's writings, particularly on logic and metaphysics, proved very helpful, especially to a mind as keen as that of Saint Thomas Aquinas. For Aristotle, the search for the essence of things was intended to reveal what was unique, universal and permanent about them. Unlike Plato, who believed in a world of forms and ideas that existed separately from the things perceived through our senses, Aristotle believed in universal features that exist within each of the objects discernible to our senses.[46] When successful, this search for the permanent and universal essences leads to definitions such as those admired by my earlier-referred-to Nicaraguan colleague. As stated by Wilhelm Windelband, the distinguished German historian of ancient philosophy:

> [According to Aristotle] . . . human knowledge can obtain a conception of the essential and the permanent only through exact and careful scrutiny of the facts [*i.e.*, what actually exists]. In these teachings Aristotle theoretically adjusted Platonism to empirical science.
>
> The logical form of . . . [his empirical findings is through the process of a] [d]efinition . . . *in which the permanent essence . . . is established as the ground of the changing conditions and manifestations . . . for every single phenomenon* . . . [Hence,] [t]hese determinations of concepts are based *partly upon deduction and partly upon induction* . . .[47]

For example, Aristotle's definitions that apply to animals start with an observation of their peculiarities followed by their classification.[48] Thus a hierarchy was organized in accordance with the complexity and function of animal organs.[49] Similarly, the heirs of the scholastics in pre-codification civil law France[50] (and in many other countries that followed the French example) classified legal institutions such as contracts according to their formalities, mutuality, gratuity, etc., and having done so, placed them within the family of voluntarily-assumed obligations which, in turn, belonged to the genus of obligations (both voluntary as contracts and involuntary as, say, the tort of negligence). The classification was followed by definitions that

---

[46] *See* WILHELM WINDELBAND, HISTORY OF ANCIENT PHILOSOPHY 255 (Herbert Ernest Cushman trans., C. Scribner's Sons 2d ed. 1910) (1901), *available at* www.books.google.com [hereinafter WINDELBAND, HISTORY].

[47] *Id.* at 255–56 (emphasis added) (citations omitted).

[48] UNIV. OF EVANSVILLE, THE ROAD TO MODERN EVOLUTIONARY BIOLOGY, http://faculty.evansville.edu/de3/evolutionweb2/history.html (on file with author).

[49] *Id.*

[50] *See infra* § 8:4(D).

gathered the peculiarities of each species as part of a genus. Thus, a sale agreement could be defined as a "bilateral," "consensual," "synallagmatic" and "onerous" agreement.[51]

Because of their supposedly logical rigor, these scholastic classifications and definitions were particularly well-suited for the synthetic formulation of legal concepts, principles and rules that eventually populated many codes in civil law countries. Thus, the observed practices that had been "incorporated" into the Roman rules on the contract of sale (*emptio-venditio*) receded into the background, and the mere mention of a sale agreement was deemed by courts, lawyers and legal commentators to be the result of the synthesis of concepts such as bilaterality, consensuality, etc. Similarly, it was enough to refer to "property" to suggest the existence of the attendant rights to use, enjoy (and for some, even to abuse), mortgage, pledge or convey the subject property.

The importance ascribed by contemporary civil lawyers to the classification of contracts and to the precise features of the various types classified is in some measure attributable to the "typification" of contracts in Roman law.[52] This is particularly true of those trained to apply codes of the *Code Civil* (definition- and classification-governed variety). Yet, please bear in mind that the Romans typified contracts because of the practical need to enable a high administrative and judicial official (*praetor*) to fashion causes of action and defenses geared to different, albeit standardized, sets of contractual practices. For example, contracts of bailments or deposits of things required that a thing be delivered to their custodian or depositary to be enforceable. In contrast, other agreements such as the *emptio venditio* did not require the delivery of the thing before the parties were bound; their mere agreement sufficed (*nudo consensu*). Thus, the buyer acquired an action to obtain the thing bought or its worth (*actio emptio*) and the seller to receive its price (*actio venditi*) from the time of the agreement.[53]

The reason for the Roman classification of contracts, then, was not the search for universal and permanent essences, but rather for practical, mostly procedural or remedial purposes.

1. Facts and Scholastic Legal Institutions

The scholastic search for essences started (as with Aristotle) with observation and was followed by definitions and classifications. Unlike Aristotle, however, the scholastics[54] were not interested in an empirically-based legal science. Most of their classifications and definitions were intended for theological purposes and for theologically-influenced argumentation and persuasion in law, ethics and politics. In attaining these purposes, they relied not only on Aristotelian logic, but also employed Plato and other Greek philosophers' inspired dialectics. Traces of these methods can still be found in today's civil-law reasoning, and the better one identifies them, the better one can separate what is factual from what is rhetorically persuasive but not necessarily factual.

---

[51] *Id.*

[52] *See* § 4:4(D)(3)(e).

[53] *See infra* § 4:4(D)(3)(a) & § 8:1 (on the scientific method of the Greeks and Babylonians).

[54] *See* Glossary, "scholastic logic."

2. *Dialectics, Axioms and Maxims*

Dialectics in Ancient Greece was a form of dialogue among thinkers who held different ideas and wished to persuade each other by structured, although not necessarily syllogistic, arguments. Plato's dialectics additionally embodied a search for the truth, but this search was not supported by a previous Aristotelian-like collection of facts. In Professor Windelband's words:

> In a strict sense, [Plato's] dialectics consists of . . . suppositions that serve as bridges to enable the discussants to ascend to the principles that embody the truth of the subject under discussion; an axiom was such a principle pure or free of facts. It, in turn, supported the formulation of the sought after definition.[55]

In the Roman law chapter,[56] we will discuss the frequent use of axiomatic reasoning, especially in its rules of law (*regulae iuris*). These were maxims endowed with the persuasive power of self-evident propositions such as: "No one can convey what he does not have." (*Nemo plus iuris in alium transferre potest quam ipse habuit.*) One should not be deceived by the self-evident nature of these maxims, for often they are invoked to reach a conclusion whose factual assumptions have not been proven or have only been proven in part. For example, assume that the above maxim is applied to a conveyance by an owner's agent who lacked an express power of attorney but was clothed by the owner with every appearance of having such a power. Should this maxim apply? As I will discuss in later chapters,[57] at least German and Anglo-American commercial lawyers reject the unqualified application of this maxim for good commercial reasons.[58]

Another method of reasoning used by the Greek dialecticians is the one known in United States law schools as "Socratic." Imitating that which was attributed by Plato to Socrates, this method shows how a given hypothesis (or in our case a legal argument, rule of law or statement about it) can be tested for its reasonableness and can lead to a contradiction or to an absurdity (*reductio ad absurdum*).[59]

3. *The Syllogism*

The main focus of Aristotelian thinking—the essence of things as species which are identified by placing them within their corresponding genus—is the relationship between the universal and the particular. It was based upon this relationship that Aristotle created what Windelband refers to as "the science of logic."[60] In this science, the essence of things is, as noted, what is peculiar to them, and the ultimate mission of Aristotle's science of logic, then, is to make possible the deduction of the particular and peculiar from the general or universal.

---

[55] WILHELM WINDELBAND, HISTORIA DE LA FILOSOFIA ANTIGUA 216 (Editorial Nova 1955) (this author's translation).

[56] *See infra* § 4:2(A)(4).

[57] *See infra* § 11:2(G) (on *Prokura*).

[58] *Id.*

[59] *See, e.g.*, ROBERT C. PINTO, ARGUMENT, INFERENCE AND DIALECTIC: COLLECTED PAPERS ON INFORMAL LOGIC 1 (2001).

[60] WINDELBAND, HISTORY, *supra* note 41, at 249–50.

And since knowledge requires the validation of unknown concepts by known concepts, the "scientific" explanation consists of the deduction of minor (unknown) premises from general (known) premises. Following such a deduction, it is possible to define the thing, whether tangible or intangible. This is why the central point and most-resorted-to feature of Aristotelian logic is its syllogism.[61] I used the word "validation" to remind the reader of my earlier discussion with the Nicaraguan commercial law professor who dismissed his need to include "chips" (*fichas*) in his definition of payment instruments as merely an "empirical" endeavor. His scholastic-legal training required that his proposed rules be validated by "scientific" definitions. Unlike Aristotle, however, he did not think it necessary to take into account the full range of observations or sensorial perceptions of payment instruments used in the Nicaraguan marketplace.[62]

Yet, the validity of what a syllogism concludes depends upon the quality of the data assumed by its major premise. And unlike Aristotle's attempt to verify the accuracy of his observations, however imperfectly at times, the scholastics seldom went beyond what they perceived with their senses. Thus, after having observed an elephant that had been painted white (for whatever reason) they could easily fashion a major premise, such as "Elephants are white"—and this premise would inexorably lead to the conclusion that because X is an elephant, he must be white. Or, as was quipped by Jeremy Bentham (the influential eighteenth and nineteenth century English utilitarian philosopher and jurist) with respect to Aristotle's conclusion that money was a barren commodity therefore not entitled to earn interest when lent, Aristotle missed the fact that, in a credit economy, money does indeed have reproductive organs.[63]

Similarly, and as will be discussed in connection with the "juristic act" of the German *Bürgerliches Gesetzbuch* of the 1900s (hereinafter BGB), an equally faulty observation of the universe of binding promises could lead to a premise such as "contracts are the only binding voluntary obligations."[64] Such a logical major premise would preclude the reliance on promises that in the world of business are binding upon the promisors from the moment they are issued and therefore not the product of a pre-existing contract between the promisor and the promisee.[65]

4. *Economic Development Consequences of Scholastic Classifications and Definitions*

The explicit or implicit aim at permanence and universality of scholastic definitions and classifications was and continues to be at the expense of changing socio-economic reality. In one of my first lectures at a Spanish law school during the nineteen sixties, a professor of "civil law contracts" (non-commercial contracts) objected to the title of my lecture "Conditional Sales or Sales with Retention or Reservation of Title" as follows:

---

[61] *Id.* at 251.

[62] *See supra* § 2:2(A).

[63] JEREMY BENTHAM, DEFENCE OF USURY 100–01 (London 1816).

[64] *See infra* § 12:3(C) (for a discussion in Phillip Heck's views, a follower of von Ihering, on this subject).

[65] *Id.*

> How could such sales *exist*? Has it not been clear for centuries now that sales *are* consensual contracts which transfer title to what is bought from the moment that the buyer and seller agree on the subject matter and price of the sale?[66]

My reply was that if he was referring to the physical existence of conditional sales, the physically verifiable fact was that while he was formulating his objection, millions of these agreements (labeled as contracts) were being concluded throughout the trading world. And if he was referring to their legal existence, all that was required in those jurisdictions that deemed them unenforceable was to replace the invalidating definition or classification with validating ones. This replacement would take into consideration that the former were conceived at a time in which there was little if any commercial and installment credit and that sales were mostly on a "cash on the barrelhead" basis, while the latter would reflect the omnipresence of a credit economy.

Not only did the scholastically-inspired code definitions of "consensual" sales continue to challenge the enforcement of conditional sales in some jurisdictions at least as late as in 1968,[67] but, as I will discuss shortly, other nineteenth century definitions and classifications do the same to other contracts. In their Roman law days, some of these contracts were classified as gratuitous, such as those of deposit or bailment and agency, and continue to be classified as such in the *Code Civil* and its progeny despite the fact that in the transactional life of those countries most depositories, custodians and agents do charge for their services.

Please note that the scholastic definitions of legal institutions use the verb "is" (as in "a deposit is, or an agency is or in the above assertion by my Spanish colleague that sales are consensual) to signify that such is the legal nature (meaning the Aristotelian essence) of deposits, agencies and sales, now and forever, here and elsewhere." Not surprisingly, a contemporary decision by the Spanish Supreme Court distinguished between a loan and a financial lease by comparing their "essences," even though the essence of the loan it was comparing relied upon thirteenth century observations by Saint Thomas Aquinas regarding loans of things "consumed by their use."[68]

From an economic development standpoint, this method of reasoning causes not only the above unjustified and unnecessary obstacles traceable to anachronistic definitions and classifications, it also precludes the validation of new legal institutions by imposing closed-number (*numerus clausus*) criteria to acts of commerce.[69] After all, if the list of contracts, *rights in rem* or "acts of commerce" is supposed to be of all the contracts, *rights in rem* and acts of commerce endowed with uniqueness and universality, how could there be any other? It also undermines trust in legal

---

[66] He was referring to Article 1450 of the Spanish Civil Code of 1887, which states: "The sale agreement is perfected between buyer and seller and is binding on both if the parties had agreed on the subject matter of the sale and on its price, even though neither was delivered or paid." (author's translation)

[67] While teaching at the University of Costa Rica School of Law in 1968, I repeatedly heard the following reasoning from trial court judges on their inability to enforce conditional sales: Article 442 of the Commercial Code of June 1, 1964 provides that even the most informal of oral sale agreements (*a viva voz*) are perfected when the parties agree on subject matter and price, which means that title is transferred to the purchaser *ipso facto* and *ipso iure*. Article 457 of the same Code, in turn, provides the only instance in which title is transferred back to the seller is the event of buyer default, and in such an instance the seller must pay back the price received from the buyer.

[68] *See infra* ch. 30 (on Spanish case law).

[69] *See, e.g.*, § 10:2(B)(1).

institutions in general and commercial legal institutions in particular, especially as interpreted in scholastically-inspired judicial or arbitral disputes. The repeated clashes between judicial or arbitral decisions (or "individual" norms) and marketplace customs and practices creates commercially counterintuitive and thus unpredictable or "irrational" legal institutions.[70] As in some of the decisions discussed in later chapters, many of the courts that apply the scholastic method ignore the inequity or unreasonableness of their decisions and support their reasoning by invoking the scientific truth, comprehensiveness and precision of their scholastic definitions and classifications. That being the truth, there is nothing they could do as judges or arbiters about them.[71]

Hence, the pseudo scientific definitions of a methodology which does not require much by way of factual findings become helpful tools in the hands of corrupt judges who hide their disregard of facts behind such definitions. The bribed judge does not have to explain the irrationality and unfairness of his decisions. All he has to do is to point to a classification such as "obligations to do and to give" with its inherently factual and semantic uncertainties and claim that his hands are tied because the contract before him required say the issuance of a public deed which is an obligation to do, and not one to give and failing such an issuance whatever the parties actually agreed to is irrelevant.[72]

The following are examples of scholastically inspired definitions and classifications of contracts in the *Code Civil*:

Articles 1102—1105 of the *Code Civil*:

> 1102—A contract *is synallagmatical* or *bilateral* when the contractors bind themselves mutually some of them towards the remainder.
>
> 1103—It *is unilateral* when it binds one person or several towards one other or several others, without any engagement being made on the part of such latter.
>
> 1104—It is *commutative* when each of the parties binds himself to give or to do a thing which is regarded as the equivalent for that which is given him, or for that which is done for him.
>
> When the equivalent consists in the chance of gain or loss for each of the parties, in consequence of an uncertain event, the contract is *aleatory*.

---

[70] *See* Philip von Mehren & Tim Sawers, *Revitalizing the Law and Development Movement: A Case Study of Title in Thailand* 33 HARV. INT'L L.J. 67, 68–73 (Winter 1992). These authors aptly summarize Max Weber's typology of legal logic, where economic development was concerned, as including among his four categories of logic a first type which was "formally irrational". It was characteristic of systems that depend on primitive procedures for deciding disputes, such as the Delphic oracle in ancient Greece. Stringent observance of procedural rules is of utmost importance, but the rules have no relationship to the rational determination of the rights and liabilities of the parties in the particular case. One imagines a priest examining the viscera of a goat and proclaiming the guilt or innocence of the accused. A second type of legal logic was the "substantively irrational." Kronman cites as an example "khadi-justice" of the Mideast. Weber characterizes these systems as using an *ad-hoc* process to determine the outcome of a particular case. The system is "irrational" because it espouses no general rules; it is "substantive" because of its willingness to consider the widest range of considerations in determining the outcome of a case. The picture of a Bedouin chief handing out rough-and-tumble justice sprung to the minds of von Mehren and Sawers.

[71] *See infra* ch. 22:10(B)(2).

[72] *See infra* § 22:10(K) (on the Maria Trinidad Gomez decision).

> 1105—The contract of *beneficence* is that in which one of the parties procures for the other an advantage purely gratuitous.[73]

B. The Logic of the Reasonable

In his "Revolt of the Masses," a classic analysis of European philosophical culture and ideas at the turn of the twentieth century, the Spanish philosopher José Ortega y Gasset[74] decried the French and German intellectuals' veneration of the revolutionary spirit; for these intellectuals, if what took place was revolutionary, it had to be good. The French were the elegant masters of rhetoric and the Germans plumbed the depths of metaphysics deeper than others, but both found it very difficult to bring about social change in their own countries in an evolutionary, non-violent manner.

In contrast, the British were neither as elegant in their rhetoric nor as deep in their metaphysics, but through centuries of war, revolution and turmoil had learned how to find practical solutions to the conflicts engendered by social change and did so in an evolutionary manner that was respectful of man's right to "the continuity of his life."[75] After all, Ortega argued that man, unlike other animals, has a memory built up each second of every day by the accumulation of daily experiences. Thus, it is most unnatural for man to go to bed at night believing, on the basis of all those accumulated experiences, that he had a family and a status in life which he acquired by honestly following certain rules only to wake up one morning to be told that he had neither family nor status and that the rules under which he acquired them were no longer in effect—and that all of this radical and unexpected change occurred because of someone else's revolutionary inspiration or whim. This is why Britain, according to Ortega, had to become the "nurse" of a relentlessly revolutionary and violent Europe, a continent that continued to be embroiled in violent and costly social change during most of its history.

He ascribed to the English a "necessary intelligence." As best as I can describe it from a legal standpoint, it is an intelligence that searches for the practical ways to resolve the problems of the here-and-now by relying on past experience as well as by reflecting on the likely consequences of one's actions. Not surprisingly, that intelligence produced a utilitarian school of thought that spent much time calculating the costs and benefits of projected actions and also produced reliance on legal precedents as the products of past experiences. The method of legal reasoning that I am about to describe as the "logic of the reasonable" is a product of Ortega's "necessary" intelligence and although it often relies on utilitarian thinking it is not exclusively utilitarian, for as I will discuss shortly it ascribes absolute value to concern for the "other." Because the nature and importance of this logic, especially for economic development purposes, is not widely appreciated, I will devote the remainder of this chapter to it.

The logic of the reasonable is one of the most common methods of legal reasoning in Anglo-American countries. It is not the only method of reasoning used in these countries, as Anglo-American lawyers, jurists and scholars frequently resort to syllogistic logic or to the absolute value of certain freedoms, such as freedom of expression. Neither is it exclusive to the common law, as more and more commercial

---

[73] C. CIV. (FR.) arts. 302–303 (Barrister, 1804).

[74] JOSÉ ORTEGA Y GASSET, LA REBELIÓN DE LAS MASAS 41 (1956).

[75] *Id.*

lawyers in civil law countries resort to it when drafting statutes, treaties, contracts or arguing cases. Nonetheless, the logic of the reasonable prevails in common law countries when addressing issues as basic as: Is there a contract? What was the intent of the contracting parties? Was there a breach and what remedy or remedies should be granted?

Dr. Luis Recasens Siches was a Spanish legal philosopher who admired Ortega's teachings and became a government official and law professor during the Spanish Republic. He fled Franco's Spain and spent a major part of his academic career as an exiled law professor and researcher at the National University of Mexico School of Law. Despite this background, and as a reflection of the universality of legal phenomena, Recasens Siches' writings (written mostly in Spanish) provide one of the best introductions to the logic of the reasonable.[76]

As did von Ihering when he distinguished between causation in the legal and physical sciences,[77] Recasens Siches singled out purposive action as characteristic of man's legally relevant conduct.[78] The logic of the reasonable guides the choice of legal courses of action, although they are limited in number.[79] In making these choices, man relies on value judgments such as: 1) the appropriateness of the means and purpose[s] to satisfy his perceived need[s]; 2) the utility of the considered action; 3) the morality of the action (for those who regard morals as independent of utility); 4) its justice and fairness; and so on.[80] A law student once asked me for an illustration of the reasonableness between means and ends, as discussed by Recasens Siches. As an answer, I asked him about his reaction to a court decision which required that a sale of a loaf of bread at a local market had to be documented by a notary public's deed (*escritura publica*) or it would be unenforceable. He answered by saying that under the circumstances, such a requirement would be unreasonable. I told him that my illustration was the same given by Professor Lon Fuller in one of his writings in which he stated: "We must preserve a proportion between means and ends; it will scarcely do to require a sealed and witnessed document for the effective sale of a loaf of bread."[81]

I added that the choice of reasonable conduct is guided not so much by the opinions of experts, but by what similarly situated contracting parties would do, as the student said, "under the circumstances." As discussed in earlier sections, these

---

[76] *See generally* Luis Recasens Siches, *The Logic of the Reasonable as Differentiated from the Logic of the Rational (Human Reason in the Making and Interpretation of Law), cited in* AMERICAN SOCIETY FOR LEGAL HISTORY & RALPH A. NEWMAN, *ESSAYS IN JURISPRUDENCE IN HONOR OF ROSCOE POUND 192–221* (Ralph A. Newman ed. Bobbs-Merrill, 1962); *See also* Luis Recasens Siches, *Situación presente y proyección de futuro de la filosofía jurídica*, III ANALES DE LA FACULTAD DE DERECHO (Tercera Época, Jan./Dec. 1956, No. 5) *available at* http://www.analesderecho.uchile.cl/CDA/an_der_articulo/0,1361,SCID%253D2609%2526ISID%253D212,00.html. Because of conflicting pagination, I will cite to this lecture's numbered paragraphs [hereinafter Recasens, ANALES, at ¶ #].

[77] *See* VON IHERING, A MEANS TO AN END, *supra* note 6, at 1–18.

[78] Recasens, ANALES, *supra* note 71, at ¶ 22.

[79] *Id.* at ¶ 24. Although through a different route, *i.e.*, the inherently cooperative nature of viable commercial conduct, I came to the same conclusion and expressed it as one of the principles that guide commercial lawmaking. *See, e.g.*, Kozolchyk, *Modernization,* at 712. I state that the need for commercial cooperation among merchants, no matter where and when, "imposes serious limits upon both the operational and moral components of . . . (its) ingredients." *See also supra* § 1:2 (for the guiding themes ofthis book, including guiding pronciples). *See infra* ch. 21 (for some of the principles that have inspired the drafting and shaping of United Syaes commercial legal institutions).

[80] Recasens, ANALES, *supra* note 71, at ¶ 25.

[81] Lon L. Fuller, *Consideration and Form,* 41 COLUMBIA L. REV. 799, 805 (1941).

similarly situated contracting parties are the archetypes of average (or standard) and best commercial behavior which often become standard and best practices. In addition, and as I will discuss shortly, the logic of the reasonable often resorts to analogies or close similarities between precedents and the facts at hand and the law applicable to them. In addition, when the disputes or competing claims are likely to adversely affect the interests of third parties, the logic of the reasonable is a very helpful tool in shaping best commercial practices by providing the reasons involved in the selection of protected parties and the manner in which they should be protected.

In sum, the logic of the reasonable uses many sources of wisdom, but unlike the exact sciences, it does not intend to uncover the ultimately truthful course of action. Rather, it only aims to suggest the wisest conduct *under the circumstances.* It also operates under the assumption that no general rule, no matter how wisely conceived, is self-executing or automatically implementable. Implementation requires fashioning what Recasens Siches refers to as the appropriate individual norms most often found in court administrative or arbitral decisions and the product of the informed application of general rules to concrete sets of facts.[82] He suggests that the time is ripe for this logic to replace its scholastic counterpart and, as you could have predicted by now, I heartily agree.[83]

Anglo-American commercial legal reasoning makes particular use of two additional features of the logic of the reasonable. I alluded to the first of these sources in previous sections and I would like to identify it now in more precise fashion as a commercially "peopled" logic. This logic compares the behavior of the parties to the contract with the behavior of representative merchants, as in the question "What would 'X,' an average merchant, or 'Y,' an exemplary merchant, have done under the circumstances, *i.e.*, while negotiating or performing the contract?" Thus, much of the behavioral comparison in this book tries to find out the extent to which the contracting parties' behavior approximates that of commercial archetypes.

The use of a commercially peopled logic is not peculiar to Anglo-American law. The reader will find a singularly effective use of it in an opinion by the Roman jurist Ulpian where he measured the conduct expected from a contracting party faced with a discretionary clause against the conduct of a respected man of affairs (*Bonus Vir*).[84] In future chapters, the reader will also find references to exemplary, average and bad faith behavior in French, German, Italian and Anglo-American court decisions. In the following summaries of important Anglo American commercial decisions, please try to identify standard, bad faith or sub-standard and exemplary commercial behavior.

a. Summary of Lord Mansfield's Landmark Decision on the Law of Negotiable Instruments: How Standard and Best Commercial Practices Are Established

In *Miller v. Race*, a decision by Lord Mansfield, one of England's and the Western world's great commercial judges,[85] the main issue was: As between an innocent maker of a stolen promissory note and an equally innocent purchaser of it, who had a better

---

[82] Recasens, ANALES, *supra* note 71, at ¶¶ 30–33.

[83] *Id.* at ¶ 27.

[84] *See infra* § 4:6(C).

[85] Miller v. Race, 97 Eng. Rep. 398 [K.B. 1758].

title to the note. The note was issued by the Bank of England (the defendant) to a "William Finney or bearer on demand." Finney mailed the note to Odenharty who mailed it to a third party. During this mailing, the note was stolen by someone who used it to pay his debt to Miller (the plaintiff). Miller was an innocent innkeeper who took the note in the ordinary course of his business from someone whom Mansfield described as having the "appearance of a gentleman."[86]

Once he learned of the robbery, Finney applied to the Bank of England to stop payment on the note. The Bank did so and Lord Mansfield held that Miller enjoyed the protected status of a good faith purchaser of the note and that his title was superior to that of Finney. He stated: "A bank-note is *constantly and universally*, both at home and abroad, treated as money, as cash; and paid and received, as cash; and it is necessary, for the purposes of commerce, that their currency should be established and secured."[87]

COMMENTS AND QUESTIONS

Please note that Lord Mansfield's analogy between promissory notes and money or cash was predicated upon the behavior of numerous unidentified people. Yet, he gave us an important clue on who these people were: these were people who constantly, both at home and abroad, used banknotes and treated them as cash. Incidentally, what in this reference would lead you to conclude that these people are in fact merchants? Please note also that treating promissory notes as cash has a special connotation in the law of negotiable instruments. It means that notes could be payable on sight or upon their presentation to their maker-payor, although they could also be paid in time. It also means that, as cash, they are easily transferable to another by their delivery (to a "bearer," a term used in the note) or by their endorsement. And it also means that the person obligated to pay must do so when promised and with no excuses, except for a very few and limited legal defenses.

How much would the willingness of merchants to abide by such practices in Lord Mansfield's England as well as in many other European countries have to do with a "law merchant's willingness to treat these practices as binding among merchants"? And what elements lie in these practices that make them binding to merchants and widely enforceable? What if the practice of creating a negotiable promissory note allowed such a note to be stamped on the back of a cow? (as suggested for a negotiable cow by the British humorist A.P. Herbert) Could you see the depositor and the bank's clerk, or more likely clerks, struggling with the effectuation of the deposit of such a negotiable cow? Although Herbert wanted to make fun of the truism that anything can be made to be a promissory note, clearly the medium on which a promissory instrument is drafted must easily accommodate all the functions ascribed to the promissory note, and must do this as easily and inexpensively as possible. This brings us to the first element of a viable standard commercial practice—*its cost effectiveness, and by this I mean nothing more portentous than its ability to fulfill its assigned business and legal purpose as quickly and inexpensively as possible.*

The second element of a standard practice springs from the above described market standard of fairness: The promissory note must treat all the parties who regularly use it as they reasonably expect to be treated when viewing their own advantage. Can you see why? Could bank notes or private notes be used to this day if they would allow makers to take unfair advantage of holders or endorsers or vice-versa. Finally, what about third parties? Please note that Mansfield held that the Bank

---

[86] *Id.* at 402.

[87] *Id.* at 403 (emphasis added).

of England should not have stopped payment on the note to Miller, the innkeeper who gave value to the holder of note whose appearance was that of a "gentleman." In acquiring the note for value from its "bearer" (as authorized by the note), Miller was acting innocently and in good faith as a third party without knowledge of what transpired after the Bank of England issued it to Finney and he mailed it to Odenharty.

When Lord Mansfield concluded that Miller enjoyed the protected status of a good faith purchaser of the note and that his title was superior to that of Finney, he justified his conclusion by saying that for banknotes to continue to be paid and received as cash, "their currency should be established and secured." Was he not saying that for that currency to be established and secured, third parties such as Miller had to be protected in their purchases, discounts or negotiations of banknotes? And if so, was he not laying the basis not only for a standard practice, but also for a best practice, applicable not only to the original parties of the underlying transaction, but also to those who dealt with them or their successors in interest?

b. Judge Friendly's Explanation of What Is "Contractually Reasonable"

In *Frigaliment Importing Co., Ltd.* v. *B.N.S. International Sales*,[88] the issue before the court was seemingly straightforward: What did the parties mean when they agreed on the purchase and sale of animals which their contract described as "chicken?" As it turned out, there were many types of chickens available for purchase in that market and depending upon their variety, prices and profits varied considerably. If the court agreed with the buyer, the type of chicken he claimed to have purchased would have resulted in a significant loss to the seller. After examining numerous sources to establish the meaning of "chicken" and comparing their market prices to the seller's costs, Judge Friendly remarked that: "Plaintiff must have expected defendant to make some profit—certainly it could not have expected defendant deliberately to incur a loss."[89]

COMMENTS AND QUESTIONS ON FAIRNESS AND REASONABLENESS

Why, in the words of Judge Friendly, could the plaintiff not reasonably have expected the defendant to incur a loss? What standard of fairness was Judge Friendly applying: The "brotherly," "market" or "stranger" standard?[90] Could you identify Judge Friendly's resort to the logic of the reasonable in the quoted statement? Could Judge Friendly's response to the Plaintiff's interpretation of the meaning of chicken not be paraphrased as saying: Each contracting party must treat the other in a manner that a regular-archetypal participant in that transaction would expect to be treated when viewing his own advantage?

This standard expectation of reasonableness and fair dealing was codified by the U.C.C. As stated by a California appellate court, the U.C.C. contains "an implied covenant of good faith and fair dealing that neither party will do anything which injures the right of the other to receive the benefits of the agreement."[91] In a later chapter,[92] I will explore the connections between the Anglo-American version of

---

[88] Frigaliment Importing Co., Ltd. v. B.N.S. Int'l Sales Corp., 190 F. Supp. 116 (S.D.N.Y. 1960). This case is fully discussed, *see infra* § 23:9(G)(4)(a).

[89] *Id.* at 120.

[90] *See infra* § 9:2(A) (peace of the market); § 14:4(B) (on brotherly and stranger standards).

[91] Steinmeyer v. Warner Consol. Corp., 42 Cal. App. 3d 515, 519 (1974) (citations omitted).

[92] *See infra* ch. 21.

commercial good faith and reasonableness, but I do not mind anticipating my conclusion that these two concepts have become coupled and seem inseparable throughout the U.C.C., including in Article 5 on letter of credit law that ironically purported to excise their connection.

The concern with treating others fairly, especially in commercial contracts, often relies on the determination of what is reasonable. Reasonableness is, in fact, the favorite logical and empirical tool with which to respond to the issues posed by transactional fairness. As noted in the preceding chapter, reasonableness often requires identifying the behavior of representative or archetypal merchants by asking what Judge Friendly asked himself: Is it reasonable to expect someone who earns his living selling chickens to sell—whatever qualifies as a chicken—for a price that would result in a loss for each pound of chicken sold? This inquiry into the archetypal behavior of a merchant identifies profit-making as the most basic and common feature of commercial reasonableness among regular market participants. But reasonableness can also rely on a more subjective, fact-specific and thus less archetypal inquiry. For example, to be reasonable could mean to place oneself in the shoes of one's counterparty and attempt to act as if one were such a party by asking oneself: What would I have done or expected if I were in his shoes? Or, it could mean a contracting party's willingness to satisfy the contractual expectations of his counterparty when these are known to him, in which case to do what is reasonable would mean to do what is good for the other, as the other sees it.

c. *On Fiduciaries and Their Brotherly Behavior: Justice Cardozo's Decision in Meinhard v. Salmon*[93]

Occasionally, Anglo-American courts and legislators require a commercial behavior that exceeds the standard of good faith practiced by an average merchant. In *Meinhard v. Salmon,* a 1928 decision by the New York Court of Appeals, Justice Cardozo characterized some of practices of a commercial trade or profession as those of the "workaday world" or the ones "trodden by the crowd."[94] He also referred to other practices in more admiring terms. In this case, defendant Salmon entered into a lease with the owner of a building who agreed to convert the building into stores and offices. Plaintiff Meinhard was a third party who invested half of the cost for the reconstruction and in exchange was to receive 40% of the profits for the first five years of the lease and half of the profits for the remaining fifteen years of the lease. Salmon was to be the sole managing partner of the lease. Near the end of the lease, the owner of the building, who also owned the adjoining land, proposed that Salmon tear down the building and build a larger building on the adjoining properties. Without informing Meinhard of the proposed deal, Salmon created a company to manage the new construction and lease. The annual receipts of the new rentals would be almost ten times greater than the amount of the original annual receipts.

Meinhard did not find out about this new lease until the old lease had expired. He sued Salmon, alleging that he had been left out of the new venture wrongfully and that were it not for his original investment, the new venture would not have been possible. As a remedy, he claimed a participation in the new venture. On appeal, the court of appeals held that Meinhard was entitled to almost one half of the interest in the new lease as long as he also assumed half of the liabilities. Cardozo's opinion stressed the

[93] Meinhard v. Salmon, 249 N.Y. 458, 464 (1928).

[94] For a full discussion of this case, *see infra* § 23:9(C).

fiduciary nature of Salmon's position and the forthright conduct required by his status as the sole trustee in charge of managing the original venture. As a trustee, he was required to disclose to Meinhard that a new project had been proposed to him by the owner of the building and adjoining land.

In Cardozo's words, such joint venturers were "subject to fiduciary duties akin to those of partners and owing each other, while the enterprise continued, the duty of the finest loyalty."[95] His following statement became a seminal principle of the United States law of investment trusts, especially in financial ventures, and has been cited on numerous occasions by U.S. and foreign courts:

> Many forms of conduct permissible in a workaday world for those acting at arm's length, are forbidden to those bound by fiduciary ties. A trustee is held to something stricter than the morals of the market place. Not honesty alone, but the punctilio of an honor the most sensitive, is then the standard of behavior. . . . Only thus has the level of conduct for fiduciaries been kept at a level higher than that trodden by the crowd.[96]

C. A Preponderantly Factual and Analogical Logic

1. A Preponderantly Factual Logic

The second feature of the logic of the reasonable as applied in Anglo-American law is that it is preponderantly factual or dependent upon a careful determination of the relevant transactional and disputed facts. Some of its best judges also use sets of facts upon which decisions have been rendered in a legal analogical manner, *i.e.*, they search for a common legal principle behind a similar holding even though the things or objects involved are physically different. And by finding the common legal principle behind the previous judicial decisions involving the use of different things, they develop a justification for extending this principle to a different, but not relevantly distinct, category of acts and things. But before I discuss reasoning "by example," I need to clarify what I mean by the preponderance of facts in Anglo-American judicial decision-making.

Unlike what happens in many a civil law court proceeding, the factual universe of an Anglo American judge is not confined to what was alleged by the parties in their pleadings, as required by the principle of the "Prayed for Justice" (*justicia rogada*) observed in some European and most Latin American jurisdictions.[97] It is also not confined to what the parties managed to prove in court. The adjudicator who relies on the preponderance of facts in arriving at his final decision is not precluded from initiating his own fact finding or allowing facts that were discovered after the filing of the pleadings or after the period of proof to be introduced in evidence. Neither are the parties precluded from delving into the socio-economic context of the dispute and from ascertaining a more realistic meaning of the relevant facts, as the Supreme Court of the United States did when reassessing its own previous conclusion that "separate"

---

[95] Meinhard, 249 N.Y. at 459.

[96] *Id.* at 464.

[97] *See infra* § 25:1(B).

was the functional equivalent of "equal" when it came to the education of African-American children in the United States.[98]

The logic of the reasonable also encourages the lawmaker or adjudicator to examine the socio-economic consequences of the rule he is about to fashion. At times, he is discouraged by what appears to be a reasonable outcome of a rule under consideration, such as its "opening the floodgates of costly and unnecessary litigation;" and for this, among other reasons, he will discard the considered rule. At other times, he will reject a projected outcome as either unlikely or not worth the risk in light of the benefits it would confer upon society at large.

Historically, fact finding was intimately connected to the role of juries since the birth of the common law. At first, jurors as residents in the vicinity were expected to know the facts that allegedly occurred. Yet, as England and the population of its judicial circuits grew, juries heard the facts from the parties and their lawyers and eventually were tasked with determining which version was the most credible and, inferentially, reasonable. This function continues to this day. However, when the facts are highly technical or complicated, the parties may agree to have the judge find the facts, in so-called "bench" trials, or have the fact finding done by a specially designated judicial official. A favorite aphorism of Justice Louis D. Brandeis still sums up the assumption that lies at the root of the preponderance of fact in applying the logic of the reasonable: From the facts the law is born (*Ex Facto Ius Oritur*).

As a short time practitioner in United States courts, I learned the importance of proven facts in jury and bench trials. Often the hardest battles of advocacy were spent in trying to get persuasive evidence before the jury or judge who was the trier of facts. Victory or defeat could be reliably prognosticated once certain facts had "gotten into the record." But it must be remembered that this is a battle that starts during the pre-trial phase of "discovery." During this phase, witnesses, documents and other credible forms of evidence are examined and cross-examined seemingly endlessly in search for a kernel of persuasive evidence. As Alex de Tocqueville is supposed to have commented to an American commercial trial lawyer who asked him about de Tocqueville's trial work in France compared to what he observed in the United States: "In the United States, lawyers spend much of their time finding facts on their own as if they were detective of facts, in France I hear the facts from my client and it is my job to dress them up with the appropriate legal arguments and citations and with that version of facts we march to court."[99]

In a later chapter, I recount how, during a commercial arbitration procedure that I chaired the determinative factor was a motion by the victorious party requesting the surrender by the losing party of non-privileged, informal, communications between the comptroller and the president of the company comptrol;[100] The losing party fiercely fought this request as part of the pre-trial discovery, using every possible argument under the sun, and for good reason. Once the document was surrendered, it contradicted the facts that this party alleged to have occurred in connection with the

---

[98] Brown v. Bd. of Educ., 347 U.S. 483, 488 (1954).

[99] I owe this description of Alexis de Tocqueville's comparison to the late and lamented Professor Saul Litvinoff of the Louisiana State University Law Center. Even though I could not find a reference to it in De Tocqueville's Democracy in America, knowing Saul I am certain he had another good source for it.

[100] *See infra* ch. 27.

losing party's interpretation of the agreement in dispute and conceded the validity of the opponent's version of facts.

Facts also act as an acid test for the validity of what at first sight looks like a highly persuasive logical argument. One such an instance involved Justice Cardozo when he was an appellate judge at the New York Court of Appeals. For a good number of years, courts even in the most sophisticated commercial centers of the world, such as was the New York Court of Appeals, applied letter of credit principles in a syllogistic-formal logical manner. One such a principle was that of the independence of the letter of credit promise from the defenses and equities that the buyers and sellers or other parties of the underlying transactions could raise in connection with the payment of the letter of credit. As in a manner that became customary of the keenness of his factual and purposive analysis, Cardozo taught us all the importance of a factually based distinction.

In *Maurice O'Meara Co. v. National Park Bank*,[101] the underlying contract was for the sale of newsprint paper of a specified tensile strength. The plaintiff presented documents that on their face complied strictly with the terms and conditions of the letter of credit, but the defendant issuing bank refused to pay the drafts. It alleged that upon investigating whether that the plaintiff-beneficiary had acted fraudulently, a reasonable doubt arose in its mind regarding the quality of the newsprint paper.[102] The plaintiff-beneficiary sued the issuing bank for the damages he sustained by the bank's dishonor and the issuer countered by offering to prove that the paper shipped by the beneficiary was considerably inferior to that described in the tendered documents. The majority of the Court of Appeals of New York decided, in a syllogistic manner, that it was established letter of credit law that the issuing bank was concerned only with the strict compliance of draft and documents and if the documents tendered by the beneficiary complied on their face with the terms and conditions of the letter of credit. If that was the case, the bank was absolutely bound to pay, regardless of whether it knew or had reasons to believe that the paper was not of the tensile strength contracted for.[103]

Justice Cardozo agreed that the general rule was indeed that the issuing bank had no duty to investigate the performance of the underlying contract, but he disagreed that if the bank chooses to investigate and discovers that the merchandise tendered is not the merchandise which the documents describe, "it may be forced by the delinquent seller to make payment of the price irrespective of its knowledge."

Then, he focused on the critical facts and the distinction ignored by the majority:

> We are to bear in mind that this controversy is not one between the bank on the one side and on the other a holder of the drafts who has taken them without notice and for value. The controversy arises between the bank and a seller who has misrepresented the security upon which advances are demanded. Between parties so situated payment may be resisted if the documents are false . . . I think we lose sight of the true nature of the transaction when we view the bank as acting upon the credit of its customer

---

101 146 N.E. 636, 637–38 (N.Y. 1925).

102 *Id.* at 639.

103 *Id.*

> to the exclusion of all else. It acts not merely upon the credit of its customer, but upon the credit also of the merchandise which is to be tendered as security . . . I cannot accept the statement of the majority opinion that the bank was not concerned with any question as to the character of the paper. If that is so, the bales tendered might have been rags instead of paper, and still the bank would have been helpless, though it had knowledge of the truth, if the documents tendered by the seller were sufficient on their face.[104]

The first critical yet basic fact was, simply put: Who is the plaintiff? Is it an innocent holder of a draft or negotiable instrument as was Mr. Miller in Mansfield's *Miller v. Race* (the innkeeper who innocently gave value for a stolen and forged draft without knowing anything about its past)? Or, was it the very same person who as a beneficiary tendered the documents that misrepresented the tensile strength of the paper that both the buyer and the issuing bank had every reason to expect? If it was the latter, and "between parties so situated" as the misrepresenting beneficiary and the innocent payor-issuing bank, payment may be resisted. The second critical fact was the meaning of possibly valueless cargo to an issuing bank which in the nineteen twenties and almost through the end of the twentieth century regarded the negotiable bill of lading and the goods it covered as an important component of its security.[105] His analysis showed that the bank's position was supported by both the most relevant facts and the soundest banking practice.

As I said in the preface to my book Commercial Letters of Credit in the Americas, having read this decision as a law student who came from a civil law country in which facts such as those identified by Cardozo were seldom considered by judges, my interest in a letter of credit law such as articulated by Cardozo and my outlook on judges and on the role of facts was a crucial discovery.[106] Add to this discovery Cardozo's analysis of the purpose of documents of title as collateral and as a critical component in the issuance of letters of credit at that time, and an entire new panorama of purposive commercial adjudication opened before my eyes.

2. *Analogy and Reasoning by Example*

My change of outlook was confirmed when I read Justice Cardozo's decision in *MacPherson v. Buick Motor Company*.[107] MacPherson bought a Buick from an automobile dealer and was injured when one of the automobile's tires collapsed as a result of defective spokes. These spokes were manufactured not by the defendant, but by a sub-contractor. Anglo-American law did not have a codified or statutory provision that enabled bringing an action against anyone guilty of negligent conduct in terms such as found in Article 1382 of the *Code Civil*: "Any act whatever of man, which causes damage to another, obliges the one by whose fault it occurred, to compensate it."[108]

---

104 *Id.* at 641.

105 During the nineteen nineties letter of credit banks gradually relied less and less on the bill of lading as collateral and more on prepayments of the amount of the issuance or on perfected security interests on the applicant debtor's inventory, accounts receivable and proceeds.

106 *See* BORIS KOZOLCHYK, COMMERCIAL LETTERS OF CREDIT IN THE AMERICAS ix (1966).

107 MacPherson v. Buick Motor Co., 217 N.Y. 382 (1916).

108 C. CIV. (FR.) art. 1382 (2008).

Under the common law, the MacPhersons of this world could not sue a remote manufacturer seller such as Buick. It was neither in a direct contractual relationship with them ("privity of contract") nor had Buick *directly* harmed them, at least not in a manner that could be easily established. An action on negligence required the existence of a duty recognized by the courts flowing from the defendant to the plaintiff or class of plaintiffs. As framed by Justice Cardozo, then, the main issue before the New York Court of Appeals was "whether the defendant owed a duty of care and vigilance to anyone but the immediate purchaser, that is, to anyone but the dealer."[109]

Cardozo reviewed court decisions he regarded as the foundations of this area of the law. The first involved poison falsely labeled by the druggist-seller as a harmless substance. In this case, the injured customer was awarded damages from the careless seller.[110] The court held that defendant's negligence had put "human life in imminent danger" as any poison falsely labeled was likely to do. To this, Cardozo added that because *the danger is to be foreseen*, there is a duty to avoid the injury. He then turned to a decision in which the defendant, a contractor, built a scaffold for a painter whose employees were seriously injured when the scaffold collapsed.[111] The court held the contractor-builder liable because he knew that an improper construction of the scaffold was also highly likely to injure its user(s). In Cardozo's words, "Building it for their use, he owed them a duty, irrespective of his contract with their master, to build it with care."[112]

He then analyzed a decision which imposed liability upon the manufacturer of a coffee urn which, when heated in preparation for the dispensing of coffee in a restaurant, exploded and injured the plaintiff, a customer of the restaurant.[113] Cardozo reasoned that the manufacturer was liable because the urn "was of such a character inherently that, when applied to the purposes for which it was designed, it was liable to become a source of great danger to many people if not carefully and properly constructed."[114] Cardozo then concluded that although the facts differed in some respects from those in the preceding cases, their governing principle was not limited to poisons, explosives, and things which in their normal operation are implements of destruction. If the nature of a thing is such that it is "reasonably certain to place life and limb in peril when negligently made, it is then a thing of danger. Its nature gives warning of the consequences to be expected."[115]

Please notice how the reasoning employed by Cardozo made use of a legal principle that could be applied analogically to different things only because the principle was the same: liability for the effects caused by negligently manufactured, built, erected, or packaged items. Thus poison was analogized to scaffoldings and the latter to coffee urns and automobile wheels. This was indeed reasoning from example

---

[109] MacPherson, 217 N.Y. at 385.

[110] Thomas v. Winchester, 6 N.Y. 397 (1852). *See also* Kozolchyk, *Roadmap*, at 25–34, for other select decisions by Cardozo.

[111] Devlin v. Smith, 89 N.Y. 470 (1882).

[112] MacPherson, 217 N.Y. at 386.

[113] Statler v. Ray Mfg. Co., 195 N.Y. 478, 480 (1909), *cited in* MacPherson, 217 N.Y. at 387.

[114] MacPherson, 217 N.Y. at 387.

[115] *Id.* at 389.

to example, but the example was a composite of factual and legal considerations.[116] Factually and legally, what they had in common is that they were all negligently manufactured and all injured either buyers or third parties. Thus he chose that legal analogy they had in common—the likelihood of causing injury when negligently manufactured. As a legal analogy, it was "open-ended" and supported by the logic of the reasonable and the principle of foreseeability of likely harm to innocent victims. If the defendant knew of the danger posed by a defective product or should have known of such a danger, he was under a duty to foresee the consequences of his actions and prevent them.[117]

With this statement, Cardozo bridged the gap between a universal duty of diligence toward third parties (as set forth in Article 1382 of the *Code Civil*) and the duty only to those parties who had a cause of action under the traditional conceptual categories of the common law, such as those who were in privity of contract. Reasonableness made this bridging possible by asking the key question: Is it not reasonable to impose the duty to foresee the consequences of a negligently manufactured product upon a defendant with knowledge of the harmful consequences of his acts?

One could hardly miss the central role played by fact finding in *MacPherson v. Buick*, even when expertly and subtly blended with the legal principle of foreseeability in order to make new law. Reasoning by example, then, is used by those appellate judges who are convinced that the state of the law is unsatisfactory and that new judicial and "interstitial" law is more likely to be put in motion by courts than by a legislature. In *MacPherson v. Buick*, the changed socio-economic circumstance was the increased number of victims of automobile accidents caused directly or indirectly by defendants who were not in contractual privity or in direct contractual relationships with the plaintiffs.

§ 2.3 SUMMARY AND CONCLUSIONS: A PROPOSED RESEARCH AND DRAFTING METHODOLOGY

By finding out the purpose of legal institutions, one discovers whether they worked or not and hopefully why they have or have not worked. In the case of the Nicaraguan drafter of a negotiable instruments law, his purpose was "to render an homage to Professor X's theory of negotiable instruments,"[118] not to improve the reliability of all the instruments that circulated in Nicaragua as negotiable instruments. Thus from the very moment the purpose was formulated, one could predict that it was not going to fulfill its economic purpose. His method lacked the right goal, the proper analytical tool and the required data.

Aristotelian-scholastic logic is a useful tool for the purpose of attaining precision and symmetry in the drafting of rules, but because of its aims at permanence and universality (which leads inevitably to a closed number of legal institutions whether they are types of contracts, rights *in rem* or causes of action), it impedes progress and

---

[116] *See* EDWARD H. LEVI, AN INTRODUCTION TO LEGAL REASONING 1–2 (12th prtg. 1968). Mr. Levi was Dean of the University of Chicago Law School and Attorney General of the United States. As far as I know, this term was coined in the United States by Mr. Levi.

[117] *See* JOHN LEWIS, 2 COOLEY ON TORTS 1486 (3d ed., 1906), *cited in* Kozolchyk, *Roadmap,* at nn.71 & 73 and accompanying text.

[118] *See* Nicaraguan Conversation, *supra* note 12.

economic development. This logic could be helpful in adding precision to the formulation of rules, such as by avoiding redundant or contradictory definitions, but it is not helpful in fashioning market sensitive commercial norms.

The logic most suitable for using commercial law as a tool for development is the "logic of the reasonable" because it takes into account past experience with legal institutions as well as the likely future experience with the new institutions, *i.e.*, what the legislator, judge or administrator should reasonably expect to happen once the new institution is operative. In addition, by encouraging law makers and governed alike to consider the reasonable expectations of "the other," including counterparties and third parties, it is the most likely to produce standard and best practices and with them economic development.

Because it is a fact-driven logic, it depends upon the comparative law researchers' ability to collect not only the above described experiences with official legal institutions, but also thorough and accurate versions of commercial and consumer customs and practices and their socio-economic context. This task is greatly facilitated by identifying representative or archetypal behavior of merchants and their counterparties and third parties including consumers. It is also facilitated by the fact that only those commercial legal institutions that are guided by certain immanent principles or standards can aspire to long term viability. Some of them will be discussed in the following chapter, such as the fair competition and cooperation among merchants and the protection of third parties acting in good faith. Others became apparent in Chapter I when discussing the selfish but also altruistic nature of social man, reflected in customs and practices that required the giving of something of value as a means to gain the trust of contracting and third parties.

The logic of the reasonable also serves as a valuable drafting tool. Precise rules are no doubt helpful in bringing about a high degree of predictability, but the more precise the rules are, the narrower is their scope of application. Yet, constantly changing commercial practices need broader guidelines than those offered by the highly precise rules. It is for this reason that the law of commercial contracts of the United States is governed increasingly by standards rather than by rules.[119] And it is precisely in the drafting of such a law that the principles derived from standard and best practices are effective tools, as will be illustrated in the following Appendix..

§ 2.4 APPENDIX: ACCESS TO COMMERCIAL CREDIT AT REASONABLE RATES OF INTEREST[120]

This Appendix illustrates the use of the methodology discussed in this chapter when applied to an economic development project. Assume that the cost of commercial credit in country X, particularly for micro, small and medium-sized businesses—if and when available—is approximately fifty per cent per annum, thereby undermining the creation and growth of micro, small and medium-sized enterprises. Assume also that

[119] On the use of standards and rules in the law of commercial contracts of the United States, see the late Professor Richard E. Speidel, *Restatement Second: Omitted Terms and Contract Method*, 67 CORNELL L. REV. 785 (1982).

[120] X is an abbreviation for a hypothetical Central American country because this Appendix reflects the application of the comparative contextual methodology in research and drafting secured lending law projects done in Costa Rica, Guatemala, Honduras and El Salvador first by the the author and then by NLCIFT over more than thirty years.

many of these enterprises wind up paying rates in excess of 400 per cent per year to usurious lenders. X has requested multi-national organizations to help it fund studies and draft laws that could help it obtain commercial credit at reasonable rates of interest. One of these multi-national financial organizations has heard good things about your law firm and about the fact that you have a group of lawyers trained in the law of comparative commercial contracts. It requests that you send them a proposal outlining what your firm could do for X and what you would charge for it.

The following sections will illustrate what could be an important part of your description of the "technical" work involved in that request. It will also illustrate how to use the comparative contextual method.

A. X's Socio-Economic Context

Up to date socio-economic data on X can be obtained, in part, from widely available printed and electronic sources. The subjects usually covered are wide ranging: 1) X's population including average age, life span and access to medical services; 2) its annual gross domestic product and per capita income; 3) its education and literacy, graduation rates and presence of viable commercial and industrial professionals in various sectors; 4) X's principal sources of income, including exports and the sectors on which its economy depends on most; 5) X's proximity to profitable markets for its goods and services and the adequacy of its infrastructure and means of communication; and 6) governmental institutions, including type of government, role and importance of its branches, taxation, tax evasion and corruption.

These data help identify those goods and services that are the most likely to serve as collateral for commercial loans. For example, if the statistics on health services indicate that a sufficient number of X's residents have regular access to physicians and hospitals, this may bode well for the utilization of medical bills or invoices as accounts receivable collateral for loans made to physicians and hospitals. The same would be true with members of other professions such as artisans and craftsmen. Clearly, this initial statistical data would require further inquiry on, say, the patients' or clients' ability and willingness to repay their credit obligations. Incidentally, a similarly promising initial datum on the importance of tourism for country X led to the suggestion that widely circulating "travel vouchers" be used as collateral for loans granted to travel agencies, and their lodging and transportation contractors or sub contractors who are also holders of travel vouchers. Up until that time, X's travel agencies were under the impression that the only reliable and liquid collateral they could offer were their bank deposits of the amounts paid to them under these vouchers. They were unaware that credit card receipts, and travel vouchers given to them in exchange for their services—while not as liquid as bank deposits—were desirable collateral as contractually promised payments owed by reputable payors. Once X enacted its law on secured transactions, the reliance on credit card receipts and travel vouchers as collateral markedly increased.

Another frequently underestimated datum when visualizing the viability of collateral is the adequacy of a country or region's transportation infrastructure and means of communication. Depending upon its adequacy, it may be possible to increase the utilization of air, rail or truck waybills, ocean bills of lading and warehouse receipts (paper based or electronic) and their transported or stored goods as collateral. In addition, it may be possible to create a national collateral (or personal property security interest) registry either as part of a network of local registries or as a directly accessible central registry or both.

Recall that in the first sentence of this section, I qualified the use of sources of socio-economic data by using the words "in part" in relation to up-to-date standard printed or electronic sources. The other and perhaps most important source of the socio-economic data is that provided by local experts. There is no substitute for the qualitative information provided by national or local researchers and consultants. What may look clear and convincing to foreign eyes, even when armed with the most current statistical reports, may be quite different through discerning local eyes.

For example, certain goods or services may appear at first sight to be highly valuable collateral because of their scarcity and exclusive distribution. Yet, the local expert may be aware of the fact that a monopoly or exclusive franchise for the distribution of product "Y" is scheduled to disappear in the immediate future. The same may be true with a cleverly hidden and corrupt governmental subsidy available only to certain farmers, or with unreliable means of communication. Or, based upon experiences elsewhere, the comparative analyst may be convinced that a secured transactions law could not be enacted in X without the support of the local bankers' association. Yet, the local expert will warn him that bankers would be opposed to the proposed law because it entails taking risks they have never taken. But, thanks to the same local expert,the analyst will find out that that a large demonstration of farmers are willing to show up in front of congress and support a law that will give them access to credit at low interest rates that they had never enjoyed.

B. X's Legal Context

Another guiding theme of this book is the sharp separation between the official or positive law and the unwritten or living law in developing nations. After more than forty years of doing comparative legal studies in developed and developing nations, the only plausible explanation I have for the sharpness and significance of that separation is another guiding theme of this book: the familistic component of the legal culture of developing nations. As will be apparent in later chapters, familism is omnipresent in the legal cultures of Latin America, Russia, and China and is the force that shapes many of their living law institutions as developing nations (another guiding theme of this book). It accounts for the privileged or monopolistic rights of the select few, which, in turn, allow them to write their own rules (or have their governmental connections write them on their behalf). And this continues to occur despite written laws that customarily proclaim the equality of opportunity and the freedom of competition of all.

The vast majority of those who live on the other side of the tracks of economic success in developing nations are unaware of how the other side succeeded. Thus, they have no hesitation in creating their own rules and practices, whose common denominator is that they will obey the official law or the law of the powerful only when it is convenient for them to do so. When it is not, they spend much of their lives avoiding or evading the laws of the "others". As a Spanish serf answered his feudal lord's question: "Don't you obey the King's Command?" "I obey it but I don't fulfill it" (in modern Spanish, "*Lo obedezco, pero no lo cumplo*") whose true meaning is that he only pretends to obey, or simulates his obedience, a contractual attitude which, y as you learned in the preceding chapter, is another guiding theme of this book.

A legal system plagued with such unequal, unfair and deceptive attitudes can best be deciphered by those who live it, understand it and are capable of translating its legal institutions in a coherent manner for the comparative law analyst. Whenever possible, you local experts must become leaders of the drafting effort. Hence, one of the most important staffing decisions for X's project is to find the local legal talent that best understands both the principles that guide the drafting of an effective secured transactions law as well as X's written and living law. Usually the local expeerts are only superficially familiar with the foreign laws that best apply these principles. It then becomes the task of the comparative analysis to serve as a bridge between the foreign experience with the model laws and the local socio-economic and legal data.

Armed with the above described sources of information, the comparative analyst of X's secured transactions law will learn that X's written law provides only two security interests or rights *in rem*; one for real property (the "*hipoteca*" or mortgage) and one for personal or movable property (the "*prenda*" or pledge). And since according to X's civil code, the number of rights *in rem* is closed or is a *numerus clausus* (such definitions being attributable to Aristotle's essences as discussed in this chapter),[121] no more security interests in personal property can exist. These truisms are firmly believed by X's lawyers and judges, who also believe that they came to them directly from Roman law. They must be made aware that this was simply not the case. For Roman jurists, as you will learn in Chapter IV, were non Aristotelian, eminently practical and non-dogmatic and invariably found ways to adapt their legal institutions to the needs of their admittedly rudimentary marketplace by contemporary standards. Thus, in due course, the Roman pledgor of personal property was allowed to remain in possession of the pledge by relabeling this non-possessory pledge a mortgage (*hypotheca*).[122] A similar flexibility will be needed by X's lawyers, law professors and judges with the notions they inherited from the Spanish Civil Code that intangible things such as contract rights, accounts and trade names cannot be pledged because they are not movable or corporeal things.[123]

The comparative law researcher will also quickly learn that under X's law, inventory could be used as collateral only when "immobilized" or locked up in a terminal warehouse, and thus could not be transformed, resold or re-pledged thereby facilitating the repayment of the commercial loan. Yet, was it at least possible under X's law for the seller or a third party custodian to foreclose on the collateral by reselling it publicly or privately without having to ask a court for its judicial remedy? The answer he would hear from the local lawyer was that private parties constantly

---

[121] *See supra* § 2:2(A).

[122] *See* BERGER, ENCYCLOPEDIC DICTIONARY, at 490.

[123] C.C. (Spain) arts. 335, 336 (1889), *available at* http://html.rincondelvago.com/codigo-civil-espanol-de-1889.html. It is true that Article 335 characterizes goods as movable if they are "susceptible of being appropriated . . . and generally all that can be transported from one place to another without harming the immovable property to which they were united" (Se reputan bienes muebles los susceptibles de apropiacion . . . y en general todos los que se pueden transportar de un punto a otro sin menoscabo a la cosa inmueble a que estuvieren unidos). *Id.* art. 335. Yet, Article 336, also includes in the category of movable goods: "the rents or pensions, whether for the life of the recipient or as part of his inheritance. . . ." (las rentas o pensiones, sean vitalicias o hereditarias. . . .). *Id.* art. 336. This inclusion should have suggested to H's legislator that it would have been enough add commercial movable goods such as contract rights, invoices or accounts, and others as part of a growing list new types of movables. Nonetheless, this provision was one of the most contentious and kept on being invoked against the use of such rights as collateral, because "movables are corporeal things."

tried to effectuate such extra judicial remedies and at times got away with them. However, courts continued to insist on the need for judicially ordered repossession or foreclosure and rejected extra judicial remedies as in violation of the civil codes' prohibition against the *Pactum Commissorium* or agreement that enabled the creditor to repossess or foreclose on collateral.

The prohibition of this *Pactum*, incidentally, was enacted more than a thousand years ago by the Roman Emperor Constantine and is still found in most of the civil codes of Latin American nations.[124] Nonetheless, it has remained in force even though its purpose disappeared long ago. Its purpose was to enforce a canonic definition of usury that forbad the charging of any interest, no matter how small, by using the *Pactum* as a subterfuge for the creditor to pocket the value of a thing pledged that was worth much more than the principal and interest due on the loan. It did not matter that the definition of usury in force in most, if not all, of the nations that proscribed the *Pactum* had changed and that a usurious rate was only one that exceeded the maximum allowable rate. And as if this were not enough, any clause that allowed a creditor or third party to repossess or foreclose on collateral, even if it was carried out pursuant to the parties' agreement and without breach of peace, was deemed to have violated constitutional due process by depriving the debtor of a court hearing.

C. The NLCIFT 12 Principles of Secured Transactions Law in the Americas

A comparison of lending scenarios in developed and developing nations by the NLCIFT and by a group of Anglo-American and Latin American experts was concluded in 2001.[125] It showed that X's law shared most of its features with those of the laws of other developing nations. In contrast, while the secured lending laws of Canada and the United States were quite similar, they differed sharply from the laws of developing nations.

In a 2001 meeting of Western Hemisphere experts on secured lending laws, the participants encouraged the NLCIFT to circulate its draft of the principles that inspired the secured transactions laws of Canada and the United States to all the nations in the hemisphere. They also proposed that these principles be used as a guide to draft what a year later became the OAS Model Inter-American Model Law on Secured Transactions of 2002 (hereinafter OAS Model Law).[126] These principles, in turn, became known as the NLCIFT 12 Principles of Secured Transactions Law in the Americas (hereinafter NLCIFT Principles).[127]

What is the importance of these principles as elements of a successful law reform process? Their importance is multi-faceted. First, they provide the justification for the selection of the standard and best practices that will eventually become part of the new law. Second, as justifiers of the proposed law, their legitimacy is earned by the successful legislative experiences that inspired them. In the case of the NLCIFT

---

[124] *See De Commissoria Rescindenda,* Constantine Augustus (Jan. 31, 326); cited and translated by Pharr, The Theodosian Code 3.5.2. at 64 (1952).

[125] *See Meeting of OAS-CIDIP VI Drafting Committee on Secured Transactions Conference Transcript*, 18 ARIZ. J. INT'L & COMP. L. 334, 334–339 (2001).

[126] For the English text of the OAS Inter American Model Law of Secured Transactions of 2002, *see* http://www.oas.org/dil/cidip-vi-securedtransactions_eng.htm.

[127] NLCIFT, *12 Principles.*

Principles, they were inspired by the standard and best secured transactions practices and laws in nations with developed market economies such as Canada and the United States. In the case of Canada the selected statute was its Personal Property Security Act[128] (hereinafter PPSA) and in the United States' it was Article 9 of the U.C.C.

As recommended by the 2001 meeting of hemispheric experts, the NLCIFT Principles, as inspired by the experience with these statutes were to be used as a guide when drafting the OAS Model Law. Thereafter they also continued to be used as a guide for the drafting of the statutes enacted with varying degrees of success by Latin American nations, such as Mexico, Peru, Guatemala, Chile, Honduras, Colombia, El Salvador, and awaiting enactment in Costa Rica.[129] The third reason for the importance of these principles is that they summarize the new law's purposes and as such they act as reminders to those applying the new laws that they may missed or disregarded an important goal.. For the benefit of the reader, the NLCIFT Principles are included below.[130]

1. Secured commercial and consumer credit is an effective tool for economic development because it allows the debtor's use, transformation, sale or barter of collateral (mobilization). The mobilization of these assets leading to their sale or disposition makes possible the payment or self-liquidation of the loan. A single security interest can support a series of loans whose amount and collateral can vary during the life of the loan or loans. By executing a single security agreement and by giving public notice of the loan or line of credit, the secured creditor establishes his priority in the collateral over third parties without having to enter into new credit extension agreements or having to make successive filings. Self liquidation can take place only when the following corollary principles are implemented by legislators, the parties, registries and courts.

2. A security interest is a preferential right to possession or control of personal property. As such, it does not require that the debtor who grants the interest have title to the personal property collateral; his right to its possession, even though co-existent with other possessory rights in the same property by other creditors and debtors, will allow the creation of the security interest.

3. The security interest may be created in any personal property susceptible to monetary valuation whether present or future, tangible or intangible including rights to the same, as well as in the proceeds of this collateral, whether in their first or future generations. Thus, personal property collateral as well as security interests in them are open in number (*numerus apertus*), and these security interests are not limited to pre-existing devices such as the pledge, with or without dispossession of the collateral, chattel mortgages, retention of title or conditional sales, etc.

4. Security interests may be created by contract or by law. The effectiveness of a security interest between the secured creditor and debtor arises from their contract or

---

128 *See, e.g.*, Personal Property Security Act, R.S.O. 1990, c. P. 10 (Can.), *available at* http://www.e-laws.gov.on.ca/html/statutes/english/elaws_statutes_90p10_e.htm.

129 *See* Boris Kozolchyk, *The Implementation of the OAS Model Law: Current Status*, 28 ARIZ. J. INT'L & COMP. L. 1 (2011); Ley de Garantias Mobiliarias [Law on Secured Transactions], Decreto No. 182–2009, tit. VII, ch. 1, 28 de enero del 2010, DIARIO OFICIAL (Honduras); Ley de Garantia Mobiliaria, Decree 51–2007, 16 de noviembrede 2007, DIARIO OFICIAL (Guatemala).

130 *See Boris Kozolchyk, Implementation of the OAS Model Law in Latin America: Current Status* 28 AZ J. INT'L COMP. L. 1 (No. 1, 2011).

from a statutory or judicial imposition without any additional formality. Nevertheless, third party rights, including the rights of judgment creditors and trustees in bankruptcy, will not be affected by the security interest unless proper notice of it is provided to third parties.

5. A principal goal of a secured transactions public notice system is to eliminate secret liens. Public notice can either be attained by the creditor's or designated third party's possession or control of the collateral, or by registration. A perfected security interest in personal property can merge with a negotiable instrument, in which case it will become a negotiable security interest and, thus, an "abstract" undertaking, independent of rights and equities associated with the underlying transaction, thereby allowing its "true sale" or unrestricted negotiation to a *bona fide* purchaser.

6. Effective public notice by a specialized registry occurs when all known or future legal mechanisms with the effect of guaranteeing the payment of a debt against personal property are treated as a unitary security interest. The effect of such a recorded security interest, including its priority, upon third parties (such as other secured creditors and purchasers) commences from the time of its filing, irrespective of the time of its creation.

7. Registration should be inexpensive and should take place in a public registry easily accessible to third parties regardless of nationality or economic sector, if at all possible by electronic means. The filing, in standardized fashion, should contain only the essential data to identify the parties, the amount of the loan or line of credit and collateral, consistent with the needs of actual and potential third parties to discover all recorded liens against the debtor's assets. Generic descriptions of collateral such as "inventory" or "accounts receivable" should suffice. The registry should be indexed generally by the debtor's name and, only exceptionally, by the serial number of the goods.

8. A "purchase money", or "acquisition" security interest should take priority, to the extent that the credit provided is used directly to acquire the collateral, over prior existing perfected security interests in the same kind of collateral, as an incentive to those wishing to provide timely, valuable and needed loans and as a safeguard against the monopolization and immobilization of the collateral available by one or more secured creditors. Perfection of a purchase money security interest should require, in addition to the appropriate filing, a special notice to pre-existing security interests.

9. A buyer in the ordinary course of business takes free of a perfected security interest created by his seller, even when the buyer may know of that security interest. If the sale occurs outside the ordinary course of business, then the buyer takes subject to the security interest even if he pays a fair purchase price.

10. Self liquidation of the security interests requires that repossession of the collateral and foreclosure take place by means of a contractual, rescissory and extrajudicial enforcement that confers upon the creditor or agreed-upon fiduciary the power to repossess or retain and foreclose on the collateral privately or by means of a highly expeditious judicial foreclosure.

11. Whenever possible—and until such time as a perfected and modern bankruptcy system that duly protects debtor and creditor rights has been adopted—the perfected security interest should not become part of bankruptcy proceedings and the law of bankruptcy or any other branch of the law should not become a tool to delay,

avoid and evade secured obligations. Exceptionally, where the bankruptcy takes the form of a business reorganization, collateral may become part of the bankruptcy estate, subject to the exclusive jurisdiction of the bankruptcy court to confirm the perfection of the security interest and establish its priority against the claims of other creditors, to determine the extent and value of the security interest and ultimately to decide whether the collateral is essential to a feasible reorganization that shall protect valid security interests.

12. The harmonization of secured transaction laws—including conflict of law rules—is essential in order to promote cross-border extension of credit.

D. The Drafting of X's Secured Transactions Law: The U.C.C. and the Canadian PPSA as Legislative Models

Experience with the drafting or assisting in the drafting of approximately half a dozen secured transactions laws in Latin America and Africa it became apparent that a three-step process was the most effective. They were: (1) The determination of the compatibility or incompatibility of local law and practice with the NLCIFT Principles by means of a Roadmap study of local secured lending practices. (2) The gathering of as pluralistic a local drafting committee as possible. The committee's need to include all the sectors of the local economy and the legal profession affected by the law familiarize its members with the results of the Roadmap study. (3) The testing of the effectiveness of proposed provisions with lenders and borrowers and to obtain opinions on their constitutionality as well as on other possible difficulties of enforcement with Supreme Court justices, trial judges, practicing lawyers and law professors.

At this time, I would like to return for a moment to the Canadian PPSA and U.C.C. Article 9 as models for the drafting of the OAS Model Law. The reason for this detour is to answer those critics prone to regard the use of foreign legislative models by developing nations as "cultural imperialism." I believe that a conversation I had with a member of the Mexican delegation to the NAFTA agreement in 1991 places the allegation of "cultural imperialism" in its proper perspective.

I had stated to members of the Mexican delegation to the drafting of Nafta's banking provisions that unless Mexico facilitated credit for its small businesses, tens of thousands of them would not be able to compete with their Canadian and United States counterparts who had access to commercial credit at rates of interest below ten percent per year, while their Mexican counterparts had to pay between forty and fifty percent annual rates of interest-when they had access to it. I then suggested that Mexico consider enacting an Article 9 or a PPSA-like law (properly adjusted to Mexico's legal system and civil law tradition). In response to what one member of that delegation perceived as yet another instance of cultural imperialism he asked: "Why is it that Mexico must import its trade and commercial laws from Canada and the United States and the same is not true the other way around?" I responded that the question that he and his Mexican colleagues had to ask themselves was a different one: Does Mexico wish to have commercial credit at affordable interest rates so that its merchants can compete on a level playing field with their Canadian and United States colleagues? If so, a form of commercial credit that started out in England two centuries earlier and from there spread to the United States and Canada was the only one that would make such competition possible. It was a form of credit that allowed commercial, industrial or professional borrowers to remain in possession of the raw materials, equipment, fixtures, inventory and other business assets to enable them to produce, transform, exchange or sell their products and, with the proceeds of the sale or exchange, pay off their "self liquidating" loans. And such a purpose requires certain transactional and legal pre-requisites, without which self liquidating loans could not occur.

In fact, commercial experience has shown that, especially in credit transactions, usually only certain practices could accomplish the necessary cost-effectiveness and fairness that would make them competitive. Starting out with how a credit transaction is structured, how it is documented and who has to give what first to whom, standardization is a pre-requisite of cost-effectiveness.[131] I repeated the example of A.P. Herbert's "negotiable cow" (used earlier in this chapter)[132] and suggested that because of the need for cost-effective practices, a negotiation clause stamped on the back of a cow could not compete with one written or stamped on paper.

Mutatis mutandi, rules that required the debtor's surrender of his assets as security for the loan, could not compete with those that allowed him to make a productive use of those assets. This was a case where using the most appropriate means to attain one's ends was crucial. At this point, our conversation became friendlier and warmer. My interlocutor remembered similar words being uttered by his professor in a course on "Introduction to Law" at the National University of Mexico Law School (UNAM). And this professor was none other than Luis Recasens Siches (whose support for the "logic of the reasonable" was discussed in this chapter).[133] "Yes", he said smilingly, "that is what Don Luis referred to as one of the principal features of reasonableness." (Hopefully, you will now be tempted to re-visit the discussion on the logic of the reasonable in this chapter.)

My newly acquired friend asked me for examples of Mexican legal institutions that were incompatible with such a loan. I repeated to him some of the examples enumerated in the preceding section. I added that the most incompatible was the familistic nature of Mexico's marketplace and legal culture, for secured lending is a form of credit extended to borrowers who are neither members of the lenders' family nor are they his friends. In fact, they are often unknown to the lender. Consequently, the lender must treat family and stranger equally (and so must the borrower) and remember the principle that for a business asset to be relied upon as collateral, it has to have a discernible marketplace value. And one of the legal means to assure equality of treatment is a transparent system of perfection and priority of security interests. Additionally, one of the corollaries of equal treatment and transparency is to protect those who filed or acquired their possession of the collateral first.

However, such a system was certain to be opposed by those who, despite being lenders, labeled themselves in their contracts as conditional sellers, financial lessors or trustors of goods entrusted to their debtors. At root, those transactions simulate or provide the appearance of a legally disguised status. In the case of the above listed lenders, they simulated the status of owners of the collateral, for as owners they would acquire a legal status superior to that of secured creditors even though the latter filed their security interests. And the reason for not wanting to file their security interests was not so much to avoid paying filing fees but to avoid appearing in a public record of

---

131 *See infra* ch. 22 (on formation of contracts).

132 *See supra* § 2:2(1)(a).

133 *See supra* note 71 and accompanying text.

transactions whose transfer taxes alone would be quite significant and worthy of a simulation. Keep in mind that sales or transfer taxes and not income taxes are usually the main source of tax revenue in developing countries. Keep also in mind that in the contemporary marketplace and personal property law most purported owners of this type of property are at best lawful possessors.[134]

My newly acquired friend tried to make a case for those who wish to file to be able to do so and those who did not want to file to be able to do so as well even though the latter's rights or liens would remain secret. (Incidentally, this was the formula first used by Mexico's Decree law, which was the first version of its secured transactions law when enacted in 2003 and was also one of the reasons for its demise a few years later.)[135] In response to his proposal, I quoted a fancy term that legal anthropologists use in connection with such a suggestion, "inherent incompatibility." As translated to lay language by my friend and mentor E. Adamson Hoebel, this term means that "a people cannot cook the same piece of meat and eat it raw."[136] In other words, a commercial self liquidating loan could not be at the same time transparent and secret or unrecorded.

The same would be true with or among many other incompatible legal institutions, including: 1) a principle that requires that the debtor remain in possession of his productive assets in order to be able to repay the loan with their yield, and a definition of a pledge that requires the possession to be transferred to the creditor or to a third party custodian; 2) a definition of movable goods which excludes intangibles such as contract rights, accounts receivable or trade names or trademarks; or 3) a procedure whose purpose is to preserve the value of perishable collateral in the event of debtor default and at the same time require that the remedy of repossession or foreclosure be adjudicated in a lengthy judicial procedure.

E. The Roadmap Study

A Roadmap study describes and analyzes lending practices in representative sectors of the nation's economy. It does this by identifying the archetypal behavior of borrowers, lenders, appraisers of the value of collateral, warehousemen or custodians, and other likely participants in the secured transaction, including lawyers and judges.

The Roadmap refines the socio-economic data at hand by identifying the standard borrowers and lenders and the typical terms and conditions of existing functionally equivalent loans such as conditional sales, chattel mortgages, financial leases or guarantee trusts. It also focuses on the collateral and on how it is used, repossessed or foreclosed on. And it describes and analyzes legal and judicial practices in connection with the loans and their collection and obtains reactions on the effectiveness of proposed new concepts, rules, principles and practices from their likely users.

As a rule, the NLCFIT's Roadmap studies are sectoral in nature. Thus the lending practices are examined having in mind the participation by micro, small and medium-

---

[134] For a historical and comparative background, *see* Boris Kozolchyk, *The Transfer of Personal Property by a Non-Owner: Its Future in Light of its Past*, 61 TULANE L. REV. 1490–99 (1987).

[135] *See* Boris Kozolchyk & Dale Beck Furnish, *The OAS Model Law on Secured Transactions: A Comparative Analysis*, 12 SW. J. L. & TRADE AM. 235, 278–94 (2006).

[136] *Id.*

sized businesses in the agricultural, commercial, industrial and professional sectors.[137] Based upon the statistical socio-economic information for typical, micro, small and medium-sized businesses in X, it became apparent to the Roadmap researchers that the vast majority of these potential borrowers did not have the required business or professional licenses with which to do business and apply for loans from banks or cooperatives or other "non-usurious" sources of credit.

1. *National Identity Card as a Qualifier for the Legal Status of a Securing Debtor (*Deudor Garante*)*

This datum was made known to the designers of the software of the collateral registry. But at the same time, the Roadmap showed that almost all the applicants for bank or cooperative credit had a national identity card with significant data and security features in them to make them acceptable as the functional equivalents of the debtor's personal or business name and address, especially those required for filing or registration purposes. This fact made it possible for the designers of the registry software to use the identity card number instead of the debtor's name as the key reference to the securing debtor in filed financing statements. It also made it easier for the banks and cooperatives to file their security interests and thereby make their lending decisions revolve not on formalities, but on the actual merits of the loan, *i.e.*, whether the debtor had the willingness and ability to repay and whether the source of his repayment was reliable.

2. *Archetypal* Coyotes *and Usurers in Agricultural Loans*

As noted earlier, the sectoral data of the Roadmap concerned the archetypal behavior of typical lenders and borrowers. Thus, in the agricultural sector, it became apparent that many of X's poor farmers (either as micro or small businesses) relied on the credit of the so called "*coyotes*." These were the lenders who advanced moneys to facilitate the growing of the crops and at harvest time, paid the remainder of what became the purchase price for the crops. In other words, the archetypal coyote was a hybrid lender-buyer of the crops. Interestingly, the interviewed farmers did not resent the *coyotes*' financing as much as the interviewers expected, especially when taking into account the cruel connotations of the *coyote* designation.

The reason why they were not resented as expected was because their financing was less oppressive than that of another archetypal lender—the omnipresent usurer and his oppressive rates of interest. What many of these poor farmers did not realize was that if they only had a vehicle or vehicles with which to transport their crops to a market often two or three hours away, they could have sold the same crops for as much as two to three times the price they received from the *coyotes*.

3. *The Negative Effects of the Scholastic Classification of "Principal and Accessory"*

The previous finding underscored the need for financing growing crops, tractors and vehicles for the micro and small farmers. Yet, once the feasibility of such a loan

---

137 For an analysis of the main features outlined in the principal text of micro and small businesses in representative Latin American nations, *see* Boris Kozolchyk & Cristina Castañeda, *Invigorating Micro and Small Businesses Through Secured Commercial Credit in Latin America: The Need for Legal and Institutional Reform*, 28 ARIZ. J. INT'L & COMP. L. 43 (2011).

was explored with banks and cooperatives, their response was that they could not finance the crops unless the borrowers either owned the land where they grew the crops or obtained a subordination agreement from the recorded owner, usufructary or lessor of the land. As you will recall from your reading of this chapter, this reasoning by the bankers, cooperatives and their lawyers was based upon the scholastic classification of "principal" and "accessory" things, and of the resulting principle that the principal things, *i.e.*, the real property or land and the rights in it, invariably absorb the rights to the accessory things (*i.e.*, the growing crops). This finding led the Roadmap to recommend that growing crops and other accessories be given independent status as collateral in the proposed new law.

4. *The Problems with Cattle Loans*

The growing of cattle is also of considerable economic significance in Central America. Yet, surprisingly to the Roadmap researchers, X's lenders only provide loans to the ranchers-cattlemen after their cattle has been slaughtered. Bad experiences and losses suffered with the methods of identifying cattle subject to their security interests, especially when the cattle could be easily moved and commingled with other cattle, discouraged this type of secured lending. It was the view of these potential lenders that unless a reliable system for identifying and tracking the movement of cattle is designed and implemented, they will remain reluctant to provide financing. Some of them suggested that the best solution would be to create a registry of cattle and ranchers and devise a more reliable system of cattle identification.

5. *Loans to Market and Street Stall Operators: Taxes, Legal Culture and Its Effects upon Transparency*

How does an archetypal micro or small business person who operates a stall in a public market or in a street obtain credit with which to purchase and sell his wares in X? The Roadmap study found out that this type of business is still largely dependent upon the credit of an archetypal usurer. The Roadmap also identified the pawn shop-like features of the municipal licenses obtained by usurious lenders to allow their secured borrowers to operate market stalls in X as the lenders' sub-licensees. The usurers as a rule lend paltry sums each week to their sub-licensees, who are then enabled to buy only a minimal amount of wares. Yet these borrowers-sub-licensees pay interest rates that exceed thirty percent a month. If the stall operators fail to repay principal and interest, they will cease to be sub-licensees and will be evicted by their lender licensees.

Contrast such an immobilizing loan with the line of credit financing referred to in the NLCIFT Principles. With such a line of credit, the same stall operator can receive loans from banks or cooperatives at an affordable rate of interest now secured by his inventory, accounts, and proceeds. And, as a line of credit loan, the amount lent by the bank increases in proportion to the operators' sales, proceeds, and profits, and is not limited to a percentage of the original value of the initial collateral. However, the legal culture of tax evasion is a major obstacle to this type of lending in X. When stall operators were asked why they had no books or records with which to document their cash flow and their profits and losses, many were at first reluctant to answer. Finally, some responded by asserting that "*no one pays taxes in X.*"

Even after dramatic illustrations of how much more money the stall operators would make by providing that information to a bank, cooperative or other non-usurious lender and contrasting the costs of a twenty percent per month loan (with a very limited and fixed amount of principal) with a nine or ten percent loan per year with an open-ended line of credit proportional to the volume of sales and profits, many were still reluctant to supply that information. The effect that this aspect of the legal and business culture of X had upon the lenders' willingness to lend was palpable. On the other hand, the transparency of the filings of security interests in the collateral registry evoked fear in the borrowers that the availability of information on their borrowings would prompt the instances of tax collection raids or blackmail by tax collectors.

6. *The Need for Reliable Accounting Data: The Importance of Accounts Receivable Collateral*

Consistent with the findings on the lack of accounting or bookkeeping records among stall operators, the Roadmap showed that micro and small businesses in X kept very few records of their business transactions. Only those who sold on credit, such as the owners of small grocery shops, kept a "booklet" (*libreta*) to document their sales of groceries. This prompted the recommendation of professional accountants that as part of the Roadmap the NLCIFT provide some simple but reliable forms of financial statements. This was done and much to the NLCIFT's surprise and satisfaction, some of X's banks started using these forms and this was soon reflected in the rise in the number of secured loans to small businesses.

A NLCIFT study on lending to micro and small businesses on a secured basis had shown the importance of accounts receivable as collateral. As summarized by a former Superintendant of Banks for Colombia: the invoices signed by the buyers of a delicious ice cream made and sold in his and surrounding buildings by a family of four (two parents and two children), even though payable thirty days later, were more liquid (or collectable) than many of the loans in the Colombian banks' portfolios.

Nonetheless, the Roadmap emphasized that to facilitate reliance on accounts receivable financing by micro-borrowers, their lenders will need to be satisfied that the statement of income flowing from the performance of services or sales of their wares is accurate and reflects a steady and reliable enough clientele (*i.e.*, account debtors) to merit loans or lines of credit. This will require not only the micro-entrepreneur's use of simple but reliable accounting records, but also a higher degree of specialization of the lenders to micro-businesses.

7. *Some Remedial Lessons Learned from Experienced Trial Lawyers*

On the remedial side of the law, asking experienced litigators how they would prevent an extra judicial procedure of repossession or foreclosure from going forward yielded important lessons and a recommendation for new filing provisions. Many of the consulted trial lawyers responded to the Roadmap question by asserting that their mere filing of a request for an interlocutory commercial attachment of all the assets of the defendant-borrower invariably led X's courts to issue such an interlocutory attachment order that froze any other proceeding related to the debtor's property.

This finding led to the inclusion in the draft of X's law of the requirement that whoever wanted to obtain judicially or extrajudicially an attachment of the defendant's assets had to file a notice of the extra judicial or judicial attachment, repossession and foreclosure. Accordingly, for a judicial order of interlocutory attachment to have priority over such a notice, it had to have been filed prior to all the other filers, including those by secured creditors seeking an extra judicial remedy. Similarly, trial lawyers suggested that the naming of an agent for repossession and foreclosure by means of an "irrevocable mandate" (*mandato irrevocable*) had proven more effective in practice and less vulnerable to judicial interference than the naming of a third party depositary or custodian.

F. Conclusions

The Roadmap of X's socio-economic, legal, business and cultural data contained many more findings and recommendations for legislative, contractual, administrative (mostly registry) and judicial practices. However, the main purpose for this Appendix is to illustrate the real life application of the methodology of the contextual comparison discussed in this chapter and advocated by this book. If this illustration is successful, you should be able to start developing your own set of Roadmap-like notes concerning your own future economic development projects as you come across the contextual comparisons that attract your attention in the following chapters.

Chapter 3

THE LAW OF CONTRACTS IN A PRE-COMMERCIAL OR AGRICULTURAL SURVIVAL SOCIETY

§ 3.1 INTRODUCTION: WHY BOTHER WITH PRE-COMMERCIAL SOCIETY?

The legal institutions that gave life to the present law of commercial contracts can be best discerned by contrasting them to their predecessors in ancient times: The sharper their silhouettes, the easier will be our understanding of what has changed and why. Pre-commercial transactions provide such sharply contrasting silhouettes when compared with their contemporary counterparts, although not always. Some of the features of pre-commercial transactions are still with us, although mostly in our poorest or least economically developed societies. Yet, do not be surprised if they are also found in the laws of emerging economic giants such as China or India. Thus, the same comparison that produces contrasts also finds institutional remnants of a distant past. A good starting question, then, would be: Did the kind of contracts were are concerned with exist in a society devoid of merchants or persons who earned their livelihood by selling, exchanging or lending goods or services produced by themselves or by others? The quick answer is that they did not, at least not as the contracts we know.

In a pre-commercial society, the duty to perform a service or provide goods to others was not created by actual promises exchanged between or among suppliers, users or consumers at a time prior to the delivery of the goods or the performance of services. The duties to produce and give one's goods or services to others in such a pre-commercial society were derived from the social "condition" or status of the members of a family, clan or tribe. Their preexisting social status and relationships created the customs and practices that determined what, how and when to produce and exchange. Only when these groups started to earn their living from trade did they start to rely upon contracts which were largely shaped by the customs of those who were the actual traders (and who tended to form their own associations of traders) and not directly from the customs of the community at large.[1]

Moreover, once contracts began to be used in everyday commerce, their practices proved malleable and disposable over time. Consider, for example, the supposedly archetypal practice of exchanging simultaneous promises binding on both parties prior to the performance of the contract. This was a practice that Hugo Grotius (one of the most influential jurists of the seventeenth century as well as the drafters of the *Code Civil*) thought reflected the universal and permanent components and essence of

[1] *See infra* § 3:3 (for a discussion of the work of Professor George Dalton).

binding contracts.[2] As a product of the will of the parties, each party had to express his acceptance to the other's promise. Otherwise, the promise would have been an unenforceable "pollicitation,"[3] an expression often used a century later by Robert Pothier, whose Treatise on Obligations strongly influenced the sections on obligations and contracts of the *Code Civil*.[4] In fact, this assertion did not reflect the full spectrum of Roman contractual practices. Many Roman contracts were enforced even though one party had expressly promised to do or give something and the other did not do so. Instead, the counterparty gave a thing or rendered a service in exchange for the other's promise. Alternatively, one party gave or did something once the other did the same. These transactions were known as "innominate contracts."[5]

Or, consider what happened to Hugo Grotius' "essential" requirement of an acceptance by the promisee prior to enforcing the promisor's promise when the mass merchandising of industrially produced goods, among other nineteenth century economic factors, required the enforcement of "firm" promises, *i.e.*, promises enforceable against the promisor during the period he promised they would be binding even if he had retracted them prior to their acceptance by the promisee.[6] Contrary to Grotius, Pothier, and the *Code Civil* paradigmatic contract formation, commercial offers to sell goods at a certain price and during a specified time period could be enforced as if they had been accepted by their offerees. Similarly, "irrevocable" promises by banks to pay or accept drafts or bills of exchange drawn against them by the "beneficiaries" of their commercial letters of credit were enforceable against them even though the promisees-beneficiaries had not accepted or acted upon such promises when their issuers attempted to revoke them.[7] The life of contracts, then, has been inextricably intertwined with the requirements of trade. For, as will be apparent throughout this book, if there is something essential, universal and permanent about commercial contracts, it is that they are means towards the end of facilitating trade and that as such they must be consistent with the cooperative instinct of the trading man.

§ 3.2 ON STATUS AND CONTRACT

Trade has always depended upon what religion, secular law or observed custom has deemed tradable. Prior to becoming a trader, man and his closely-knit group of nomads hunted and gathered for a living. In this type of society there was very little trade, and what was traded was mostly edible and moveable. Hence, land was not a part of the hunter and gatherer's trade. Yet, neither was it an object of trade once man settled and made his living as a member of a pastoral-agricultural community. The reason for the restrictions on the trading or mortgaging of agricultural or pastoral land was that it had become the principal source of the sustenance of the family, clan or tribe, and thus it was to be sold or mortgaged only when economic necessity required

---

[2] *See generally* Jon Miller, THE STANFORD ENCYCLOPEDIA OF PHILOSOPHY (Edward N. Zalta ed., Fall 2011), http://plato.stanford.edu/entries/grotius/. *See also infra* § 8:2(B)(1), on Grotius' influence on the contract provisions of the *Code Civil*.

[3] *See infra* § 8:2(B)(1)(b).

[4] POTHIER, I OBLIGATIONS, at 5.

[5] *See infra* § 4:4(D)(3)(b).

[6] *See e.g.,* U.C.C. § 2–205.

[7] *See* Boris Kozolchyk, *Commercial and Standby Letters of Credit, in* III UNITED STATES LAW 24–12 to 24–13.

it.[8] Further, once man earned his livelihood as a regular trader, few restrictions applied to his trade of moveables, which soon included incorporeal or intangible objects such as rights to things, or rights to rights in things such as the rights to copyrights, trademarks or patents. Even the ancestral restrictions on the sale of family or communal land started to give way to the process of commodification of anything that had marketable value.[9]

In brief, in those societies that anthropologists describe as dependent upon "dense" social relations,[10] the obligation to give something to one or more members of a family, clan or tribe did not arise from what we refer to as contracts. Such dense exchanges were not preceded by explicit agreements between promisor and promisee. They were and are part of an often undifferentiated set of duties of reciprocity owed to each other by members of the same family, clan or tribe. Eventually, these primitive social groups were able to establish a hierarchy of duties and contributions based on what they perceived as most valuable for their survival. Also, rights and duties within the group eventually became synonymous with hierarchy and social status. Those whose ancestors or who had themselves contributed the most to the group's survival enjoyed the most valuable rights and had to perform the least burdensome duties.

Some legal historians regard this tribal and status-based phase of social life as the beginning of an evolutionary process that culminates in our contemporary contracts' society. Sir Henry Maine, the pioneer historian of "ancient" law, asserts, for example, that the evolutionary process started with social status as the main basis for the entitlement to rights or imposition of duties.[11] As the process evolved, contracts became the basis of entitlement and so it is in our time for most societies. In Maine's opinion, then, the contract as a vehicle for an individualized exchange of goods and services is the main form of entitlement to goods and services in contemporary societies. This entitlement is not based upon the status of the contracting parties, but upon what they contribute to each other's welfare, a contribution whose value is measured by what each contracting party is willing to do for or give to the other.[12]

Following the publication of my Tucker Lecture at Louisiana State University Law Center in 1979,[13] which implicitly endorsed Maine's views as an explanation for the increasing commercialization of civil law, I received a thoughtful letter from Professor Grant Gilmore. Professor Gilmore was one of the most respected and influential commercial law scholars of our time. In his letter, he challenged Maine's "status to contract" and stated that in contrast to Maine's linear view, he discerned recurrent cycles of status and contract in societies such as Czarist, Soviet, and post-Soviet

---

[8] *See infra* note 56 and accompanying text for an explanation of the Indian restriction against "frivolous" or non-necessitous conveyance of family land. *See also infra* § 18:1(F)(6) on the Chinese economic-necessity clause in the conveyance of family land.

[9] *See* NLCIFT, *12 Principles.*

[10] *See generally* CARLOS VELEZ-IBANEZ, BONDS OF MUTUAL TRUST: THE CULTURAL SYSTEMS OF ROTATING CREDIT ASSOCIATIONS AMONG URBAN MEXICANS AND CHICANOS (1983) (describing "dense" relationships in contemporary society).

[11] SIR HENRY SUMNER MAINE, ANCIENT LAW 151 (1905). As noted by Harvard's Dean Roscoe Pound, this meant that status was a condition "that could not be divested voluntarily, and that rights duties and liabilities flow from or are annexed to this condition of a person rather than his volition." Roscoe Pound, *The End of Law as Developed in Juristic Thought*, 30 HARV. L. REV. 200, 211 (1917).

[12] MAINE, *supra* note 11, at 149–51.

[13] *See* Kozolchyk, *Commercialization.*

regimes.[14] While contract may have gained ground over status during the period that immediately preceded the demise of Czarist Russia, or even during the Soviet Leninist period,[15] status reemerged as the dominant form of entitlement to goods and services during most of Soviet Russia only to give way to contract, perhaps only temporarily, in post-Soviet Russia.

Regardless of whether status and contract are benchmarks of an evolutionary process or whether there will always be a combination of both, there can be little question that commercialization can only thrive where, as I will discuss shortly, contracts reflect the parties' intent, especially on the prices they are willing to pay for goods and services. On the other hand, it is also true that many of the legal institutions discussed in this and in following chapters reflect the extent to which familistic and tribal considerations still influence the law of commercial contracts, especially as it applies to the sale of what was family or tribal land and is now land owned by the state.[16] In addition, I describe an incident in a later chapter in which a frustrated United States buyer recounted his Chinese seller's justification for ignoring a contractual promise. The Chinese seller warned that if the U.S. buyer planned to have a profitable business relationship in China, the buyer better understand that it would require that the buyer and seller act as close friends. Such a relationship will only come about from a continuous exchange of reciprocal favors (*Guanxi*), including the disregard of a contractual promise.[17] Yet, please note that one of the most important legal and economic consequences of such a relationship is that it usually is an exclusive relationship. Thus, each of the participants is supposed to enjoy a monopoly with respect to the goods, services and special favors that the other participant provides or can provide. Clearly, then, such a relationship is at the expense of competition and its movement of resources to their most cost effective and productive use.

§ 3.3 DUTIES DERIVED FROM "DENSE" AND RECIPROCAL RELATIONSHIPS

One of the first features of a pre-commercial society that one discerns from contrasting it to our own commercial society is that the former does not depend upon markets for its regular and mercantile exchange of goods and services. Even though markets exist in these societies, they do not decide or significantly influence what members of those societies produce, sell, exchange, lend or donate.

The late Professor George Dalton of the economics department of Northwestern University provided helpful insights on the forces responsible for non-market exchanges of pre-commercial societies. He combined an anthropologist's grasp of the cultural principles that guided pre-commercial transactions with an economist's perception of the economic effects of these principles, especially on the manufacture and distribution of goods. His seminal study, "Traditional Production in Primitive African Economies" published in 1962, profited from a robust anthropological literature on the economies of African tribal societies.[18] Because these societies and economies

---

[14] *See* personal letter to Boris Kozolchyk from Professor Grant Gilmore (on file with author).

[15] *See infra* § 15:4(D)(4).

[16] *See e.g., infra* § 18:3.

[17] *See infra* § 17:5(H).

[18] *See* George Dalton, *Traditional Production in Primitive African Economies*, 76 Q. J. ECON. 360 (Aug. 1962).

remained largely unchanged for thousands of years and often resembled the practices, attitudes and values found in other parts of the pre-commercial world, they enabled him to contrast key transactions and cultural traits of pre-commercial society with their counterparts in the western market economies of the sixteenth and seventeenth centuries.[19] In the following sections, I will summarize some of his findings and conclusions.

A. Absence of Market Dependence: Communal Living vs. A Commercial Association

Professor Dalton found market exchanges of goods and services in many places in indigenous Africa, but typically these exchanges only provided their traders with very minor portions of their income.[20] Thus, these exchanges were not what could be characterized as the dominant economic organization of pre-commercial Africa. Professor Dalton characterized the dominant organization as the "community" of inhabitants, a grouping that he contrasted with an "association" of traders. He quoted the English anthropologist Raymond Wirth for the distinction between these two entities:

> [An] [a]ssociation is a group specifically organized for the purpose of an interest or group of interests which its members have in common. . . . [A] [c]ommunity is a circle of people who live together, who belong together, so that they share not this or that particular interest, but a whole set of interests wide enough and comprehensive enough. . . .[21]

As insightfully pointed out by Karl Polanyi, the distinguished Hungarian economic historian and theorist of social change, this notion of community, a crucial component of primitive economies, was " 'embedded' in society, in the sense that the economic system functions as a by-product of noneconomic institutions. . . ."[22]

To this, Professor Dalton added:

> [In the West] [w]e are used to thinking in terms of "production units" because the Western firm is an association, not importantly affected by kinship, religious, or political affiliation of participants. In Africa, however, production is often undertaken by intimate communities of persons sharing a multitude of social ties and functions, one of which happens to be the production of material goods.[23]

He later concluded:

> [Thus] an African's role in each production process is usually defined by some aspect of his social status—tribal member, husband, cousin, friend, elder. The question, what forces, institutions, or rules direct labor, land and other resources to specific lines of production, can be answered only with reference to community social organization.[24]

---

[19] *Id.*

[20] *Id.* at 361 n.4.

[21] *Id.* at 362 (citing RAYMOND W. FIRTH, THE ELEMENTS OF SOCIAL ORGANIZATION 137 (London 1951)).

[22] *Id.* at 365 (citing KARL POLANYI, THE GREAT TRANSFORMATION 45–58 (1944)).

[23] *Id.* at 362.

[24] *Id.* at 367.

B. The Costs of a Community Method of Production and Distribution

What are the costs that producers and distributors of goods and services pay when they do not depend upon market exchanges for their livelihood? One of these costs, according to Professor Dalton, is that producers are unable to acquire the machinery or technology that enables them to produce more, cheaper and better products and to employ others. Machines, effective technologies, as well as hired labor are considered "factors" of production. He equated a machine or an effective technology with hired labor in the sense that these are productive "factors" that paid for themselves. They were costs of doing business that should be "[i]ncurred . . . to enlarge [the producer or distributor's] sales revenue from which he recovers its cost."[25] He concluded that "without purchased ingredients of production, and without reliance upon market disposition of output, the input and output decisions of producers cannot be based on factor and output prices as guiding parameters."[26] Hence, the cost paid by the pre-commercial community as a producer of goods is not only its inability to produce and sell more and better products, but also the absence of "guiding parameters" of profitability through more realistic pricing. In Professor Dalton's words: "That neither factor nor product prices exist to constrain the indigenous African agriculturalist (as they do the Western) is crucial to understanding why it is that Africans can organize production in such seemingly bizarre 'social' ways."[27]

COMMENTS, QUESTIONS AND CROSS REFERENCES

Professor Dalton pointed out that the variables associated with a dependence on technological and market constraints are fewer and less complicated, and therefore less apt to make the pre-commercial producers and distributors materially insecure.[28] Community producers do not have to fear unemployment due to an ever-advancing technology or too many goods chasing too few consumers. What these producers have to fear most is bad weather or plant disease. Yet I would ask, how about the opposite? Would they have to fear too many consumers chasing too few goods? Probably not in pre-commercial society, but how about in ours?

Later in this book, you will encounter a prescient warning by Austrian economist Ludwig von Mises in 1920 to the central planners of the Soviet economy: Your planning is bound to fail because it did not rely on market prices.[29] Without market prices, argued von Mises, "[T]here is no possibility of allocating resources on the basis of consumer preferences. . . . [or] of calculating costs or revenues and no way of knowing if products most highly valued by consumers have been produced."[30] After reading that portion of the book, you may wish to ask: What do pre-commercial community exchanges and Soviet central planning have in common other than an absence of market prices? What about the absence of a commercial class or of what Professors

---

[25] *Id.* at 363.

[26] *Id.*

[27] Dalton, *supra* note 18, at 363.

[28] *Id.*

[29] *See infra* § 15:4(F).

[30] E. C. Pasour, Jr., *Land-Use Planning: Implications of the Economic Calculation Debate*, 7 J. LIBERTARIAN STUD. 127, 127–28 (1983), *available at* http://mises.org/journals/jls/7_1/7_1_7.pdf. *See* LUDWIG VON MISES, SOCIALISM: AN ECONOMIC AND SOCIOLOGICAL ANALYSIS 113–22 (Liberty Classics (1981) (1951). For related criticisms, as discussed in *infra* § 15:4(F), *see* F. A. HAYEK, INDIVIDUALISM AND ECONOMIC ORDER 149 (Chicago Univ. Press, 1948).

Dalton and Wirth referred to as an "association" as contrasted with a "community of producers"? You may also wish to inquire into what Max Weber, one of the founders of modern legal and religious sociology, regarded as the rationality of his economic man (*homo economicus*)—especially his ability to ascertain costs, profits and losses—which received a notable impulse with double-entry bookkeeping during the thirteenth century AD.[31]

Finally, professor Dalton's analysis of the distinctions between a community association and an association of growers, producers or distributors shows that the latter (unlike the former) are able to gather the factors of production and distribution, thereby being able to estimate prices and costs and likely profits or losses. They do this by engaging in market transactions with their suppliers and buyers by means of contracts. This sequence and its reliance on contracts as the most accurate reflection of the prices that market participants are willing to pay is at the heart of commercial and economic development. Hence, it will not be surprising that where this sequence is missing, such as in Mao's collectivization of agriculture in China,[32] or "Che" Guevara's rejection of Marcelo Fernandez' attempt to introduce cost accounting in the lending policies and procedures of Cuba's National Bank,[33] the economic and social consequences are disastrous. What is ironic and sad is that this is one of the main lessons we should have learned from studying the failures of some pre-commercial societies as they tried to become commercial.

C. Reciprocity and Gift Giving

Dalton defines reciprocity as the giving of gifts and counter-gifts between persons who stand in some socially defined relationship.[34] The gifts of produced items or of other factors of production such as labor are regarded in pre-commercial society as an expression of interest in the social relationship between the gift givers and recipients. He notes that in our own society, significantly, a birthday gift from father to son is just one among many ways of expressing their kinship relation. Yet, reciprocity plays a much more important part in pre-commercial African economies than in our own: The frequency and amount of such gifts are greater; the number of different people with whom one person may engage in gift exchange is larger; the social obligations and sanctions to do so are stronger. Above all, such gift reciprocity in pre-commercial Africa may play an important part in production (especially in labor allocation) which is rarely the case in our own economy.[35]

Professor Barbara Sebek teaches English literature at Colorado State University and has contributed to a better understanding of the role of the gift in both a pre-commercial and commercial society.[36] Despite the generalized assumption that there is little in common between literary analysis, anthropology, economics and law, Professor Sebek, among others of a similar persuasion, disproves that assumption. She points to anthropologist Marcel Mauss's classic 1923 work "The Gift" as a source of unusual insight into the social meaning of gifts in both primitive and contemporary societies.

---

[31] *See* RICHARD SWEDBERG & OLA AGEVALL, THE MAX WEBER DICTIONARY: KEY WORDS AND CENTRAL CONCEPTS 22–23 (Stanford Univ. Press 2005) (on Max Weber's main ideas, including the rational economic man).

[32] *See infra* § 18:3.

[33] *See infra* § 15:4(H).

[34] *See* Dalton, *supra* note 18, at 370.

[35] *Id.* at 371.

[36] *See infra* ch.20, on the origins of English commercialization.

For Mauss, gifts are never "free." His famous question was: "What power resides in the object given that causes its recipient to pay it back?"[37] His answer was that the gift is imbued with "spiritual mechanisms" that engage the honor of both giver and receiver in a way that is almost "magical." Mauss, who studied gift exchange in diverse societies, stated that:

> [I]t is clear in Maori law, the legal tie, a tie occurring through things, is one between souls, because the thing itself possess a soul, is of the soul. Hence it follows that to make a gift of something to someone is to make a present of some part of oneself. . . . In this system of ideas one clearly and logically realizes that one must give back to another person what is really part and parcel of his nature and substance, because to accept something from somebody is to accept some part of his spiritual essence, of his soul.[38]

In a predominantly gift economy, such as the pre-commercial Africa described by Professor Dalton, Mauss contends that the objects that are given remain attached to the givers; they are "loaned rather than sold and ceded." As restated by Professor Sebek, because the identity of the giver is invariably bound up with the given object, the gift has a power which compels the recipient to reciprocate and thereby return them. She further states that:

> [I]n gift exchange, transactors are in a state of "reciprocal dependence" . . . the exchange of gifts creates "personal relations between people". . . . Those who engage in a gift transaction . . . are bound perpetually in a network of giving, receiving, and requiting gifts. These bonds and obligations are the basis of social organization in a culture based on gift exchange.
>
> Mauss proposed that. . . . [g]ift giving confers upon its participants a special relationship of trust, solidarity, and mutual aid. . . . [and] that gifts were the threads of social discourse, the means by which such societies were held together in the absence of specialized governmental institutions.[39]

Given the importance of gifts in a pre-commercial society, and as noted by the distinguished comparative law scholar Professor James Gordley, anthropologists who have studied the relationships of reciprocity in these societies describe two types of reciprocity, one generalized and the other balanced. When reciprocity is generalized, the original benefactor should receive something equivalent to that which he gave, not necessarily at that moment, but eventually. When reciprocity is balanced, each transaction requires that a benefit given be repaid with an equivalent benefit.[40]

Intermediate forms of reciprocity, as part of balanced reciprocity, also exist. For example, the United States anthropologist Professor Marshall Sahlins of the University of Chicago describes an equivalent form of reciprocity among the members of the Kapauku tribe of Papua, a region where fresh meat spoils quickly. When one tribe member gives freshly killed pork meat to another, the recipient ends up supplying

---

[37] MARCEL MAUSS, THE GIFT: THE FORM AND REASON FOR EXCHANGE IN ARCHAIC SOCIETIES 3 (W.D. Halls trans., Routledge 2000) (1950).

[38] *Id.* at 12.

[39] Barbara Sebek, *Good Turns and the Art of Merchandizing: Conceptualizing Exchange in Early Modern England*, ¶ 5 (2001), http://emc.eserver.org/1–2/sebek.html (citations omitted) (on file with author).

[40] Gordley, *Contract in Pre-Commercial Societies,* at 2–8 to 2–9, on generalized and balanced reciprocity.

a type of refrigeration service, without the need for a real refrigerator. A tribe member who gives excess pork to the other member lacking pork does so with the expectation that when he needs pork in the future, the donee will return to him an amount equivalent to what he originally received.[41] This large variety of gifts explains why so much of the production in these societies is "invisible": A gift of labor to help a kinsman clear his land, a gift of cattle to help him acquire a bride, or a gift of a song or a name wind up contributing to the process of production of goods and services.

COMMENT: ON GIFT GIVING AND CONSIDERATION

An online manual on the writing of commercial contracts in the United States makes the following comparison:

> A familiar funny phrase illustrative for the difference between contracts governed by a common law system and European continental contracts are the so-called 'words of agreement': [A common wording in the United States is:]
>
> "NOW, THEREFORE, in consideration of the premises and the mutual covenants set forth herein and for other good and valuable consideration, the receipt and sufficiency of which are hereby acknowledged, the parties hereto covenant and agree as follows."
>
> [The online commentary adds that] [t]he phrase is loaded with common law elements: consideration, as a requirement for the validity and enforceability of any unilateral promise or obligation (*i.e.*, in most cases this is the (purchase) price); this consideration is suggested to be present in all parts of the agreement and whatever may be related but outside the contractual words; this consideration is anyhow sufficient for the obligations to which it pertains; whatever the nature of the *consideration is, it is received*; and, together with some redundant and archaic other wording, the phrase ends with a step-up to the contract provisions themselves.[42]

Please notice the emphasized phrase: ". . . whatever the nature of the *consideration is, it is received*" in the U.S. consideration clause. This wording assumes a transactional sequence in which something of value is given as consideration to someone else in exchange for that person's promise or performance. Do you believe that the giving of something of value prior to the expected promise or counter-performance has anything to do with a culture of gift giving? Could the giving of consideration, then, be regarded as a distant remnant of gift giving and as a form of establishing a bond of solidarity between the contracting parties? If not, would such a gift giving contribute to a greater legal certainty of the enforceability of commercial contracts? These questions will be explored in comparative detail in a later chapter.[43]

D. Redistribution

According to Professor Dalton, redistribution entails obligatory payments of material items, whether as money or labor, to an authority—usually a chief of a tribe or clan or to a king or priest—who reallocates portions of what he receives to provide

---

[41] *Id.* at 2–8.

[42] *See Drafting Principles, Weblog,* WEAGREE.COM, (Mar. 13, 2009), http://www.weagree.com/weblog-detail/14–now-therefore-the-parties-agree.html (emphasis added) (on file with author).

[43] *See infra* ch. 22 (on the formation of contracts).

community services and to reward specific persons.[44] Frequently, the authority also has the power to distribute unused land or hunting sites in exchange for the recipient's tribute as payment or contribution.[45]

Variations of this reciprocity are still discernible in Latin America's subsistence agricultural regions, as part of the reign of the "*caciques*," "*gamonales*," or chieftains. They involve family members and friends as part of close or dense relationships such as among "*compadres*" in Mexico or exchangers of favors in Brazil's *Jeito*.[46] The universality of this contractual or extra-contractual reciprocity can be found in present-day China's *Guanxi*, a widespread method of doing business that relies on close personal connections with other business people or government officials.[47] As in feudal Europe, the overlords or government officials in familistic societies often exchange their political, military and educational "protective" services for part of the commercial or economic output of their subjects.

§ 3.4 IMPERSONAL RELATIONSHIPS IN FREE MARKET SOCIETIES

In contrast with the "densely" personal elements of each transaction in pre-commercial society and in parts of present-day developing nations, many contractual obligations in market societies are "impersonal." They take place frequently among "unknowns" or "strangers." In addition, the legal obligations derived from each contract consummated in the commercial marketplace are limited to each transaction or group of transactions, and as such, they are extinguished with each contract's performance or waiver thereof.

Typical of this commercial context are contracts between parties dealing with each other from a distance (*inter absentes*), such as the purchase of commercial or consumer goods and services from unknown parties, including the performance of such economically significant services as banking, insurance, investment and transportation. Many of these contracts take place every day among millions of strangers in different places of the global commercial and financial market with an aggregate value in excess of trillions of dollars and without greater formality than an electronic bookkeeping entry.[48]

§ 3.5 "DENSE" TRANSACTIONS: A PERENNIAL OBSTACLE TO COMPETITION

Professor Gordley enumerates the legal advantages and disadvantages of a normative system based on dense relationships. One advantage is that the adjudication of disputes is mostly extrajudicial and thus less cumbersome and costly than judicial adjudication. Generally, obligations stemming from dense relationships presuppose a self-regulating, extrajudicial system of adjudication, which punishes serious or repeated breach by expelling the guilty person from the family, clan or tribe. This

---

[44] Dalton, *supra* note 18, at 372.

[45] *Id.*

[46] *See infra* § 14:4(A)(4).

[47] *See infra* § 17:5(H).

[48] *See generally* MAREK DUBOVEC, THE LAW OF SECURITIES, COMMODITIES AND BANK ACCOUNTS: THE RIGHTS OF ACCOUNT HOLDERS (*forthcoming*, Edward Elgar 2014).

extrajudicial remedy of expulsion likely leads to begging as the only means of survival.[49]

From the vantage point of a contemporary market economy, a disadvantage of this system is likely an unfair adjudication of default in individual transactions. Generally, the adjudication of dense obligations does not pay attention to the inequity of the individual breach, especially in relationships of a generalized balance. In these transactions, if the balance over the long term is positive, the inequity of the specific transaction is ignored or deferred. Given the lack of predictability of the outcome of a dispute involving an individual transaction, whoever seriously relies on the likely profit from a single transaction will find it difficult to cope with the uncertainty of disputes emerging from dense relationships.[50] In addition, as pointed out by Professor Gordley,[51] a significant result of this normative system is its stifling effect upon upward mobility. A person who wants to improve his standard of living cannot distinguish himself from the competition and offer better goods or services. Duties and performances are standard and undistinguishable.

I would add that another disadvantage is the damage that dense relationships and their dependence on status do to market economies. Today's marketplace is made up not of family members, close friends of "strangers" or third parties who are unknown to their counterparties. As exemplified by the history of Chinese commercial legal institutions, the status conferred in Imperial China to the members of the same family, clan or tribe frequently prevented competition and fostered exclusive or monopolistic dealings. Thus, third parties were unable to profit from businesses that ranged from distributing salt or lumber, building governmental buildings or operating pawn shops. Interestingly, similar dense relationships of the *Guanxi* variety are responsible for many an investment or business enterprise in contemporary China despite the "socialist" component of its market economy. To understand the "familistic" pre-commercial roots of China's bargains and exchanges is at least—if not more—important in understanding the principles that guide its commercial marketplace as it would be to understand China's interpretation of Karl Marx's "The Capital." For as noted in an earlier section, dense relationships[52] and the familistic marketplace they engender are perennial obstacles to competition.

It is for this reason that a comparative analysis of the contemporary law of contracts must take into account the legal-cultural reasons that justify the entitlement to contractual promises, even if these reasons bear a remarkable similarity to those peculiar to pre-commercial society. For if pre-commercial society attitudes and values, often reflected in concepts, principles and rules, still govern from their graves, the legislator, judge, practitioner and scholar can only ignore them at his peril. As will be apparent in future chapters, the resort to institutions rooted in pre-commercial society's attitudes and values have serious developmental consequences.[53]

---

[49] *See* Gordley, *supra* note 40, at 2–13.

[50] *Id.* at 2–14 to 2–17.

[51] *Id.* at 2–3.

[52] *See supra* § 3:3.

[53] *See, for example,* on Mexico's economy *infra* § 14:4(A)(6), and for the effect on the Chinese economy see *infra* § 17:3(F)(2).

§ 3.6 PRINCIPLES ORIGINATED IN PRE-COMMERCIAL SOCIETIES

The following principles associated with the exchanges of goods and services in pre-commercial society are not the only ones, but are among the most common and characteristic of that society. Nonetheless, and as will be discussed in this and in other chapters, attitudes, values, customs and practices guided by these principles are also found in contemporary societies whose legal and business cultures are either in part or as a whole familistic or tribal.

A. Unequal Treatment of Strangers

In pre-commercial society, strangers to the family, lineage, clan or tribe were often regarded as enemies and thus were not given the benefit of contractual rights similar to those enjoyed by members of the same family, lineage, clan or tribe. Nor did the members in these local or regional associations feel that they owed duties of fair dealing or good faith toward strangers. As we will discuss with respect to the principle of "peace of the marketplace" found in some of the most successful medieval fairs,[54] it was not until this principle was implemented that fairs were able to attract a high enough level of participation by foreign traders. Prior to its implementation, if a foreign trader "A" came from a city "X" and an unknown colleague "B" from the same city defaulted on his obligation to a local merchant "C," C could have A arrested and made subject to severe punishment until he paid the debt owed by B, his unknown colleague. Thus, the "peace of the marketplace" that required all merchants doing business at the fair be treated alike and as if they were local merchants and subject to the same local law was a forerunner to the contemporary free trade principle of "national treatment" that has made possible a volume of international trade undreamt of prior to the Second World War.[55]

B. Valuable Property Is Not to Be Sold, but to Be Kept in the Family Fold

In a pre-commercial society, especially one that depended upon survival agriculture, valuable property was that which provided sustenance for the family or closely-knit social group. Such property was not to be sold, or at least not easily. For example, according to the Hindu law doctrine of "necessity," family or ancestral property could only be sold for an urgent necessity and never for "frivolous" purposes.[56] Even in contemporary Hindu law, if an administrator of a family estate sells valuable property, such as the family land, to support a mistress or to throw lavish parties, the heirs of that estate can recover the land from third parties, regardless of the time of sale.[57] Alternatively, the law can surround the sale of valuable family property with cumbersome formalities, as was the case with the Roman law *mancipatio* which was designed for a real or fictitious conveyance of *res mancipi*.[58]

---

[54] *See infra* § 9:2(A) & (B) (on the fairs and the principle of peace of the marketplace).

[55] *Id.*

[56] Kozolchyk, *Transfer*, at 1469.

[57] *Id.*

[58] According to the Institutes (the rough equivalent of a manual type of legal textbook) by the Roman jurist Gaius, *res mancipi* were properties valuable enough to include buildings and land in Italian soil, servitudes connected with this land, slaves and farm animals. *See* ZULUETA 1 at 1.120. Gaius describes the

Pre-commercial and contemporary property, therefore, seem to have different social and economic functions. During agricultural survival times, ownership was a tool to implement and preserve the power of the tribal or clan leader or subsequently of the Roman head of household ("*paterfamilias*") over valuable family assets. It was not a device to encourage their sale, but to keep them within the tribe, clan or family fold and to fend off strangers' claims. What we presently understand as property, however, is directly related to its marketability. The more certain or unconditional an owner's rights are, the more saleable, marketable or property-like in nature they are.[59]

What is truly remarkable is how this principle continued to govern the sales of family land until as late as the end of the eighteenth century in a society as seemingly commercial as France's. As described by the late Professor John P. Dawson of the Harvard School of law, one of the great comparative law scholars of the twentieth century:

> [The *retrait lignager*] was the power of the owner's kindred to cancel any sale of inherited land and any conveyance, if one had already been made to the purchaser, and then to recover the land, reimbursing the purchaser for any payments he had made. . . . This power, which came to be called the *retrait lignager*, could be exercised by any relative, even distant collaterals, provided that they shared with the seller a common ancestor. . . . The time limit was short, a year and a day from the purchaser's entry into possession. . . . Despite all the disruption it produced and its severe effects in obstructing commerce in land, this power to prevent diversion to strangers through the sale of family land had a long career before it.[60]

The power of a seller's (landowner's) kindred to retract the sale of family land in China has lasted at least as long as that of India. Under Imperial Chinese law, it was sometimes possible for the kindred of the sellers of family land to retrieve the land sold subject to an "economic necessity" clause in the sale agreement for generations.[61] All they had to do was repay the price paid by the original purchaser.[62] Under present law, and as part of the Chinese government's status as absolute owner of the land, its conveyance of land rights (directly or through provincial or municipal entities) does not require the special clauses of revocation of rights of the Imperial law. The official grantor has the power to revoke or expropriate what it gave subject only to a duty of "relevant compensation" that rarely specifies the amount, time, source and procedure for it.[63]

---

ceremony as follows: "in the presence of not less than 5 Roman citizens of full age and also of a sixth person, having the same qualifications, known as the *libripens* (scale-holder). . . ." ZULUETA 1 at 1.119. According to Adolf Berger, "All these things and rights . . . [conveyed as *res manicipi* in the sale procedure known as *mancipatio*] represented the highest value in a primitive rural economy." BERGER, ENCYCLOPEDIC DICTIONARY, at 678.

[59] Kozolchyk, *Transfer,* at 1456. It is no accident that the unconditionality is a central feature of the most saleable of commercial paper. Hence, a negotiable instrument is defined by U.C.C. § 3–104 as an "unconditional promise or order to pay a fixed amount of money. . . ." *See* U.C.C. § 3–104 (2011).

[60] *See* JOHN P. DAWSON, GIFTS AND PROMISES: CONTINENTAL AND AMERICAN LAW COMPARED 31–32 (1980).

[61] *See infra* § 18:1(F)(3).

[62] *Id.*

[63] *See infra* § 19:3(B)(2)(c) on the Property Rights Law of the People's Republic of China, Arts. 42 & 44.

C. Continuous and Unlimited Familial Liability for What Was Conveyed or Sold

Another important feature of the exchange of goods in pre-commercial societies is that the seller or, more accurately, the one who supplies valuable property to others and his family, often remains liable for the defects of the property conveyed for a much longer period of time than is typical in societies with organized markets. Finality of liability seems to be an essential feature of these organized markets but not of pre-commercial society. For example, Jewish sellers of land in fourth century B.C.E. Egypt and their descendants remained liable to defend the title of the land virtually indefinitely.[64] And, as you read the early Imperial Chinese contracts,[65] please notice the standardized reliance on the family's indefinite and unlimited "defension" clauses with respect to attacked or impeached title to the land sold. Similarly, in certain parts of Africa today, a seller of pigs remains liable to his buyer if, following the sale, one of the pigs sold becomes ill or does not eat well during an unspecified period of time, regardless of whether the seller is at fault.[66]

The long-lasting liability of the seller or grantor in pre-commercial societies has forced the creation of commercial law institutions whose effect is to mitigate such liability. For example, in certain regions in India that until very recently depended on a subsistence agricultural economy, unpaid interest on loans was accumulated without limitation from one generation to another on members of the same family of the original debtor. To prevent such accumulation, Hindu law created the doctrine of "*damdupat*" that limits the aggregate amount of interest that can be accumulated: Interest cannot exceed the principal amount of the obligation.[67] Clearly, this rule put an end to the indefinite and overwhelming accumulation of family debts. Similarly, medieval Arab and Jewish traders found it necessary to create business association forms that limited the liability of the silent or investment partners to the amount invested, as did seventeenth century English insurers with respect to maritime risks.[68]

D. A "Harmful" Agency Is Not Binding on the Principal

Another feature of pre-commercial societies that remains the law of some developing nations today, in a slightly modified fashion, is the non-binding effect of promises made or obligations assumed by an agent on behalf of his principal, especially when the latter finds such an agency harmful to his best interests. Typically the principal would not be bound if he can prove that the agent's contract harmed him or was entered into without sufficient authority. This is true even when the latter's identity is disclosed to the third party contracting with his agent or when the agent acted with the apparent authority of his principal.[69]

The reason for the non-binding promise or obligation of the agent *vis-à-vis* his principal in pre-commercial society was the Biblical injunction that an agent can only

---

[64] *See* YARON, INTRODUCTION, at 79–92.

[65] *See infra* § 18:1.

[66] *See* Gordley, *supra* note 40, at 7.

[67] Kozolchyk, *Fairness,* at 257–58.

[68] *See infra* § 5:9(C) (on business association contracts among Medieval Jewish traders).

[69] *See infra* § 5:9(A).

benefit and not harm his principal.[70] This injunction belonged in a setting where agents were fully dependent on their mostly rural principals for their survival and where whatever trade they conducted on behalf of their principals was mostly with parties who knew them. This injunction could hardly support a commercial society of strangers who often deal with each other through intermediaries whose promises must be relied upon, especially when they have been ostensibly empowered to enter into contracts or other obligations by their principals.

Nevertheless, the drafters of the nineteenth century French and Spanish Civil Codes were not fully convinced of the benefits of commercialization and thus retained the Roman characterization of the contract of agency (*mandatum*) as gratuitous service to another, regardless of how necessary such intermediary services were in business transactions.[71] In addition, these civil codes imposed upon the third parties who dealt with the *mandatarius* (or party instructed by his *mandans* to perform a certain act or service on his behalf) the risk of the former exceeding his authority. In other words, the third party could not sue the principal for the obligation assumed by his *mandatarius*; he could only sue the *mandatarius*.[72] In fact, it was not until 1992 that Spain enacted a statute which specified the liability of a principal for the acts of his commercial agent.[73] Following France's and Spain's nineteenth century legislative model, a number of Latin American countries continued to insulate principals from liability entered into by agents on their behalf, in some cases without distinguishing between civil and commercial agents.[74]

E. Unenforceability of Executory Promises

Finally, as reported by Professor Gordley, anthropologists have observed that pre-commercial societies do not enforce executory promises or promises where performance is deferred.[75] I had the occasion to verify this observation in a contemporary and arguably commercial setting, when one of my commercial law students conducted a field study that compared U.C.C. sales law with the tribal law of sales of the Zuni Indians of New Mexico. He reported as follows:

> I asked the silversmith in charge of jewelry production in the tribe how he documented a promise to sell jewelry, *i.e.*, in a contract signed by both parties or by an annotation in a book or record. He seemed perplexed and asked me: "What promise are you talking about?" I responded that it was the promise he made to those buyers who ordered a quantity of jewelry that he couldn't supply at that moment. "I don't make such promises," he stated firmly. "I only sell what I have at hand. I don't know what's going to happen in the future." Similar responses were given to me by virtually all the traders I interviewed.[76]

---

[70] Kozolchyk, *Transfer,* at 1468.

[71] *See* C.C. (SPAIN) ART. 1711.

[72] *Id.* art. 1714.

[73] *See Ley 12/1992, de 27 de Marzo, sobre Contrato de Agencia* (1992).

[74] *See infra* § 5:13(D).

[75] Gordley, *supra* 40, at 7.

[76] Report by former student Chester Jones following his visit tothe Zuni reservation in New Mexico on or about May 12, 1982 (on file with author).

Transactions, such as the delivery of something beyond the normal cycle of its production, consumption, sale or exchange, were too uncertain to be part of ordinary trade. Salomon Nahmad, a Mexican anthropologist and friend who I consulted about this response, told me that he had observed similar behavior among Mexican tribal craftsmen. He linked the unwillingness of Zuni and Mexican tribal traders to issue a promise of future performance to a culture shaped by the inexorability of agricultural or more generally productive cycles, including the cycle to dispose profitably of what one has managed to accumulate.[77]

§ 3.7 ANTHROPOLOGY AND THE FORMULATION OF COMMERCIAL LAW

A. The Work of E. Adamson Hoebel

Even though the law of contracts is, at best, incipient among primitive societies, I found the anthropological analysis of how these societies decide who is entitled to that which has been jointly hunted or fished helpful in the formulation of customary commercial law. The work of the late E. Adamson Hoebel, a great scholar, teacher and dear friend, was especially significant. Together with Karl N. Llewellyn, Hoebel wrote "The Cheyenne Way,"[78] the pioneering work of joint legal and anthropological research which adapted the legal analysis of cases to discern cultural-legal patterns ("law-ways") among the Cheyenne Indians of the United States.

Subsequently, in his equally classic "The Law of Primitive Man," Hoebel described property and possessory bases of entitlement among Eskimos to what they hunted or fished:

> Game and most articles of personal use . . . are objects of property notions. Deep-rooted Eskimo individualism, expressed in the postulate that the self finds its realization through [possessory] action, breeds law-ways in support of private property by way of the corollary idea that the creation of an object makes it the private property of the creator, as it also does, up to a point, in hunting. Game that can be taken by individual effort belongs to the person who makes possible the kill. Consequently, among the Ammassalik of East Greenland the hunter who chops a seal hole "has a potential right to seal caught in it." More definitely, a seal which escapes with a harpoon head in it belongs to the hunter who actually succeeds in capturing and killing the creature, although the harpoon, identifiable with ownership marks, should be returned to its owner. But—any seal harpooned with a bladder float attached to its line goes to the owner of the float no matter who captures it, since it is reasoned that the capture is made possible by the drag and visibility of the float.[79]

---

[77] Conversation between the author and Chester Jones of May 30, 1982 (on file with author).

[78] KARL NICKERSON LLEWELLYN & EDWARD ADAMSON HOEBEL, THE CHEYENNE WAY; CONFLICT AND CASE LAW IN PRIMITIVE JURISPRUDENCE (William S. Hein & Co. 2002) (1941). For an evaluation of Hoebel's contribution to the anthropology of law, *see* Leopold Pospisil, *E. Adamson Hoebel and the Anthropology of Law*, 7 LAW & SOC'Y REV. 537 (1973). *See also* Max Gluckman, *Limitations of the Case-Method in the Study of Tribal Law,* 7 LAW & SOC'Y REV. 611 (1973); *and* A.L. Epstein, *The Reasonable Man Revisited: Some Problems in the Anthropology of Law*, 7 LAW & SOC'Y REV. 643 (1973).

[79] HOEBEL, PRIMITIVE MAN, at 79–80.

Hoebel comments that when the hunting is such that by its very nature more than one man is usually needed, then each man establishes demand-rights for specific portions of the kill. The Baffin islanders furnish a typical example:

> Who first strikes a walrus receives the tusk and one of the forequarters. The person who first comes to his assistance receives the other forequarter; the next man the neck and head; and each of the next two, one of the hindquarters.[80]

> The above entitlement is explained by Hoebel as follows:

> By joining the fray, a hunter exercises his power to open a new legal relation with respect to the other hunters of the moment. They accept a no-power to stop him and so they become bearers of a duty correlative to his claim.

> Against this postulated extension of individualism, however, the postulate that no man can have more than he can effectively use comes into play. It is the giving away of food and goods, not the possession of them, that wins honor and leadership among the simple Eskimos.[81]

B. Anthropology and a Better Understanding of Commercial Law

In Hebbel's opinion, anthropology contributes to a better understanding of law for two reasons. The first is that anthropologists have learned to deal "with cultures as integrated, working wholes. . . . [which] has made possible the development of comprehensive theories of cultural dynamics embracing legal phenomena as but one aspect of culture?"[82] The second is that anthropology is a comparative science. It draws its data from all orders of society—primitive and civilized, prehistoric and contemporary, and even from all portions of the globe. Consequently, it provides the means to check hypotheses as to the nature of man and human behavior (including its normative behavior) by "finding ready-to-order variables somewhere in the anthropological inventory of observed societies."[83]

I believe it would also be useful to re-read carefully the above two paragraphs and see how Professor Hoebel identified a general and influential moral principle, value or postulate when discussing the entitlement to what is hunted or fished by the Eskimos, especially when they join a fray. The principle is: "[N]o man can have more than he can effectively use. . . ."[84] Notice the connection between this norm and the opinions and behavior of the most respected leaders he interviewed. These leaders are characterized by a form of behavior that the rest of the members of that community find worthy of emulation. You will find such a leader in Rome's community of "respected men of affairs" or the *boni viri*. Thus, when Hoebel describes the everyday rules of entitlement to what was hunted or fished, he identifies not only standard behavior represented by what was done or said should be done by archetypal fishermen or huntsmen, but also the behavior of those community leaders that engenders the most respect and desire of emulation in their community. One such honorable behavior is expressed in the rule

---

[80] *Id.* at 80 (citations omitted).

[81] *Id.*

[82] *Id.* at vii (Preface).

[83] *Id.*

[84] *Id.* at 80.

that "the giving away of food and goods, not the possession of them . . . [is what] wins honor and leadership among the simple Eskimos."[85] It becomes obvious, then, that this behavior was inspired by the above principle-postulate ("no man can have more than he can effectively use") and it was exemplified by the behavior of respected, admired and emulated members of the community of fishermen and hunters. But before you dismiss this excursus into the ancestral behavior of pre-commercial society, I would ask you to reserve judgment until you read the following chapter on Roman law[86] and notice why Ulpian, one of the most respected classical Roman jurists, deferred the determination of whether a contractual condition is "illusory" and totally subjective or whether it is objectively ascertainable. Similarly, review the chapter on Anglo law,[87] discussing the influence that the equally pre-commercial giving of gifts had upon the inducement of trust among early commercial contracting parties in England and eventually upon the development of "consideration" as a central element in the development of the Anglo-American law of contracts.

Suffice it to say, that ability to differentiate between ordinary or standard behavior and honorable and highly-respected behavior often distinguishes the good commercial legislator, judge, law professor and litigator from a mediocre one. Depending upon the accuracy of the behavioral features ascribed to such archetypal merchants, key concepts such as "reasonableness," "good faith" or "*uberrima fides*" (the most exacting form of good faith) could be used successfully or fruitlessly when drafting statutory provisions, interpreting a commercial contract or convincing a judge or jury on the diligence, reasonableness or good faith that should be observed by a plaintiff or defendant. And even though "lawmen" (as Professor Karl Llewellyn referred to the above key legal players) should not be expected to engage in the field research that anthropologists engage in, they should become aware of the important legal data that such research can yield.

One of the principal benefits of an anthropological (and social science) vision of law is its facilitation of an analysis of law in its socio-economic context. Hoebel quotes Eugen Ehrlich, as one of the founders of legal sociology, for the proposition that "[a] juristic act is never an individual, an isolated thing, it is part of the prevailing social order."[88]

This vision of the law is divorced from the legal positivistic vision found, among others, in English author John Austin's "Lectures in Jurisprudence." Austin conceived the law to be nothing more than a "command of the sovereign."[89] Hoebel also rejected Austria's Hans Kelsen's "Pure Theory of Law."[90] For Kelsen, as long as a norm is accompanied by a sanction, made effective by an authority which is part of an orderly hierarchy, it can be considered as law. Thus, each norm must be sanctioned by a superior norm, and the ultimate norm from which every legal norm must be derived is what he refers to as the basic norm or the "*Grundnorm*." This basic norm is a purely

---

[85] *Id.*

[86] *See infra* ch. 4.

[87] *See infra* ch. 20 (on English Law).

[88] EUGEN EHRLICH, FUNDAMENTAL PRINCIPLES OF THE SOCIOLOGY OF LAW 397 (1936),*cited in* HOEBEL, *supra* note 79, at 5.

[89] *See* JOHN AUSTIN, I LECTURES ON JURISPRUDENCE, OR, THE PHILOSOPHY OF POSITIVE LAW 89 (Robert Campbell ed., 5th rev. ed. 1885).

[90] *See generally* HANS KELSEN, PURE THEORY OF LAW (Max Knight trans., 1967).

logical construct and is assumed as an initial hypothesis for the existence of a legal system.

The late Julius Stone, another great teacher, friend and highly persuasive advocate of the linkage of law and the social sciences, provides a thoughtful assessment of Austin's and Kelsen's theories. Neither theory is related to an actual society or to an actual law. Theirs is an analysis of legal propositions by reference to their logical consistency and no more.[91] An earthier assessment by other law and society observers is that this positivistic version of the law is "without social content or significance . . . law without flesh, blood or bowels. It is not even zombie-law. . . ."[92]

Is the research methodology of legal positivists such as Austin and Kelsen suitable to describe or explain the validity of commercial law rules? Is it possible that commercial institutions such as contracts or commercial usages or practices could be enforced without an *a priori* validating command by a sovereign or without the threat of a sanction by a hierarchical legal authority? Consider, for example, New York's original non-conforming amendment to 5–102(4) of the U.C.C. (1964 version) which provided:

> Unless otherwise agreed, this Article 5 does not apply to a letter of credit if by its terms or by agreement, course of dealing or usage of trade such letter of credit or credit is subject in whole or in part to the Uniform Customs and Practice for Commercial Documentary Credits fixed by the Thirteenth or any other Congress of the International Chamber of Congress.[93]

While a follower of Austin or Kelsen might say that the above statute should be regarded as the command of the sovereign or the formulation of a hierarchical threat, where does that command or threat appear in the quoted language? If anything, it would be a command reminiscent of that in the notorious Code of the Anarchist: "Article 1. Everyone is free to do whatever one wishes; Article 2. Everyone is free to disregard Article 1." What would be the effects of adopting a positivistic methodology for the identification of commercial law norms, such as proclaimed by Professor Alfredo Rocco, whose treatise "Principles of Commercial Law" was quite popular during the nineteen forties and fifties in Italian, Spanish and Latin American law schools?[94] In its initial chapter he minced no words: "Civil law is not a source of commercial law. . . . 'Commercial law' [positive or enacted statutory law] is the only source. . . . Neither are case law, equity, the nature of things and the general principles of the law, or foreign law."[95] How much would the regular participants in the market feel about an enumeration of sources that excludes their own customs and practices as a source? I witnessed one such a reaction as a member of the legislative committee that drafted the revision of Article 5 of the U.C.C. (on letters of credit) during the early nineteen nineties. As an initial task, the reporter presented the drafting committee with a number of definitions of letter of credit transactions that he faithfully distilled from court decisions, one of them pertaining to the all-important banking term

---

[91] JULIUS STONE, THE PROVINCE AND FUNCTION OF LAW: LAW AS LOGIC, JUSTICE, AND SOCIAL CONTROL, A STUDY IN JURISPRUDENCE 61 (2d prtg. 1950), *cited in* HOEBEL, *supra* note 79, at 6.

[92] Sidney Post Simpson & Ruth Field, *Law and the Social Sciences*, 32 VA. L. REV. 855, 862 (1946).

[93] *See* N.Y. U.C.C. Law § 5–102(4) (McKinney) (1964).

[94] *See infra* § 13:1(C)(2)(b).

[95] ALFREDO ROCCO, PRINCIPIOS DE DERECHO MERCANTIL: PARTE GENERAL (1952).

"confirmation." When these were first shown to the bankers who participated as observers, one of them said to me: "I do not know where Judge X or Professor Y got this definition of a letter of credit confirmation, but that is not what I and my colleagues do when we confirm letters of credit."[96] By now, the reader may have an opinion as to whether any sound reason exists for not taking into account custom and usage and especially best practices in the drafting of commercial contract law.

C. Law and Behavioral Imperatives

Among Hoebel's most important legal-behavioral imperatives were the following:

> [Human behavior is mostly learned, and] [t]his learned behavior in its aggregate isculture, and we say that culture is the integrated sum total of learned behavior patterns which are manifested and shared by the members of a society. . . .
>
> [These] cultural *patterns for behavior* exist prior to the entry of the individual into his society. . . .
>
> Law, which exists in human beings acting, also exists above and beyond the individual as one aspect of culture.[97]

It can no longer be doubted that legal norms, such as in the landmark United States Supreme Court decision *Brown v. Board of Education*[98] forbidding segregation in public schools in the United States, can contribute to the change of cultural patterns. However, there are certain inherent cultural "imperatives" that ultimately limit the choice of legal behavior by a lawmaker or adjudicator. Hoebel refers to one of these imperatives as the "imperative of selection."[99] "[It] is imposed by a number of factors. . . . [including the] *inherent incompatibility* among certain forms of behavior so that contradictory forms may not be performed simultaneously by the same person or persons. [Put simply, a] people cannot cook the same piece of meat and eat it raw."[100]

COMMENTS AND QUESTIONS

What is the likely economic effect of a failure to take into account the imperative of behavioral selection upon the availability of commercial credit at reasonable rates of interest to small- and medium-sized businesses? What about William Graham Summer's reminder that folkways are often the "right ways"?[101] Could this reminder be useful in the above discussion and, if so, what is the merit of consistency between a prescribed legal behavior and a society's folkways or mores? If prescribed behavior need not be consistent with social mores, such as a preference to keep liens as well as other commercial transactions hidden from the public, how can such prevalent commercial mores be changed by law?

---

[96] *See infra* ch. 21 & 24, for a description of the process of drafting U.C.C. Article 5.

[97] HOEBEL, *supra* note 79, at 7–9.

[98] Brown v. Board of Ed. of Topeka, Shawnee County, Kan., 347 U.S. 483 (1954).

[99] HOEBEL, *supra* note 79, at 10.

[100] *Id.*

[101] *Id.* at 15 (citing WILLIAM GRAHAM SUMMER, FOLKWAYS 28 (1906), and pointing out that Graham Summer was addressing the problem that frequently, in society, existing conduct (what "is") takes on the compulsive element of "ought," and hence the folkways are the "right ways.").

§ 3.8 TOPICS OF DISCUSSION

A. Agriculture and the Origin of Contracts

Most of the exchanges described by the anthropologists in this chapter belong to social groups whose survival was based on hunting and fishing and who relied very little, if any, on agricultural exploitation. What effect did agricultural exploitation have in the development of a law of contracts? Does the fact that agricultural societies are more sedentary and stable in character and can often enjoy regularity of crops contribute to their inclination to sell or trade their surpluses to others, especially strangers? Does such a sedentary character contribute to less dense relationships?

B. Cultural Values, Jural Postulates and Legislative Principles

Hoebel points out that viable cultures invariably rely on some criteria of choice to govern or influence the selection of prescribed legal behavior:

> These criteria are the broadly generalized propositions held by the members of a society as to the nature of things and as to what is qualitatively desirable and undesirable. We prefer to call these basic propositions "postulates." Philosophers and sociologists commonly call them "values."[102]

As was apparent in the discussion of "Peopled Logic," cultural values and logic that compares the behavior of actual people is an important aid in the formulation of these jural postulates.[103]

Jural postulates, however, are not only useful in the more accurate formulation of legislative principles, but also in reflecting a society's existing values—values that facilitate considerably not only the legislative process but, more generally, the process of adjudication. This was the mission assigned to jural postulates by Dean Roscoe Pound, one of the most influential legal thinkers of the United States during the twentieth century. Hoebel became intimately familiar with Pound's views not only through his close friend and collaborator Karl N. Llewellyn, but also through Julius Stone, Pound's most insightful exponent and critic.

In Julius Stone's restatement of Pound's thought:

> In order to understand what law in that society should do, the first step . . . must be to observe and record the social phenomena with which the law is concerned, namely, the interests which human beings are actually pressing for recognition by law. From this comprehensive picture the jurist can also draw out, by as impersonal a synthesis as possible, the fundamental principles concerning human conduct (or "the jural postulates") which substantially all of the phenomena presuppose. . . . The jural postulates then are distinct from the actual claims in two respects. First, they are *rationalisations* of these claims, not necessarily coinciding with the actual psychological origins of the claimants' behaviour. Second, they are rationalisations not of all the actual claims but only of *substantially* all. . . . What is their utility when found?

---

102 HOEBEL, *supra* note 79, at 13.

103 *See supra* § 1:2.

> On the one hand, they are working hypotheses which have been found by observation to rationalise, within the limits above stressed, the claims, demands or interests pressing in a given society. They are, therefore, not *mere* speculation. On the other hand, the process of drawing the jural postulates from the mass of claims can scarcely be a very exact one. . . . It must be noticed, further, that they are working hypotheses, not of what the law *is*, but what the *men* in the given society *want the law to do.*[104]

C. Illustration of the Use of Jural Postulates in Drafting Principles for Future Legislation.

As was discussed in the preceding chapter [105] the National Law Center foInter-American Free Trade (NLCIFT) adopted Twelve Principles to facilitate its adoption and implementation by the member states of the OAS.[106] The first two of these principles read as follows:

> Principle 1. Secured commercial and consumer credit is an important tool for economic development because it relies on the self-liquidating nature of the transaction and collateral involved, *i.e.,* the collateral and its proceeds will repay the loan. Self-liquidation can take place only when the following corollary principles are implemented by legislators, the parties, registries and courts.

> Principle 2. A security interest is a preferential right to possession or control of personal property. As such, it does not require that the debtor who grants the interest have title to the personal property collateral; his right to its possession, even though co-existent with other possessory rights in the same property, will allow the creation of the security interest.[107]

Why was it necessary to draft these principles? As once stated to me by the late Raul Cervantes Ahumada, one of Mexico and Latin America's most renowned commercial law writers and draftsman of commercial laws, "A law is not the place to explain or justify its provisions. It would be like Cervantes' depiction of the bad painter, *i.e.*, one who paints a chicken and states in the painting 'This is a chicken and these are the reasons why you should like my chicken.' " What about these principles, should they be used as part of the text of the law? What should be their role in good statutory or code drafting?

---

104 JULIUS STONE, HUMAN LAW AND HUMAN JUSTICE 267–68 (1965).

105 *See Model Law.*

106 *See* NLCIFT, *12 Principles*, at 1 & 2.

107 *Id.*

Chapter 4

ROMAN LAW

§ 4.1 INTRODUCTION: ROMAN LAW AND THE SEMINAL PURPOSES OF PRIVATE LEGAL INSTITUTIONS

Although the importance of historical and interdisciplinary study when attempting to understand contemporary commercial law should be clear by now, one might still ask, why study Roman law? After all, it is a law that treated as gratuitous an everyday agency agreement (*mandatum*) or a loan of things (*commodatum*), regardless of how valuable the services rendered by the agent were or the things lent to their short- or long-term user. Would not these oddities by present day standards reflect an unbridgeable cultural and legal gap between a two-thousand-year-old law and contemporary commercial transactions?[1] As we are about to learn, Roman law provided much of the "legal alphabet" of western civilization for its every day legal institutions. Since viable legal institutions require a formative or seminal purpose, the ability to identify such a pupose –even if it has undergone mutations over time- is a helpful analytical tool. As is shown in Chapter 24, the purpose of securing a "self-liquidating" loan by various forms of creditor and debtor possessions- as articulated by the Romans- is still part of the present day "asset based" commercial loan even though fair and public notice practices had to be added to its purposive nucleus for such a loan to remain viable. Thus, where the law of commercial contracts is concerned history is the conduit to their formative purposes. The analytical and normative accomplishments of the Roman jurists were not accidental. As the reader will soon discover, Roman jurists were highly skilled when resolving what my mentor, Professor Hessel E. Yntema, described as the "practical problems of justice."[2]

§ 4.2 THE PROVIDERS OF A LEGAL ALPHABET

Their first discernible contribution to resolving the practical problems of private law justice or the justice of the "mine and the thine" was the building of a working legal vocabulary. To do this, they relied on the verbs and nouns most commonly used by the parties to the transaction in question and transformed them into terms that could also serve as labels. Two such terms were "purchase" and "sale" (*emptio venditio*). When used sequentially, as in the purchase and sale of goods, these terms reflected the order in which the acts or performances were assumed to have been carried out—first, the buying (*emere*) by a buyer (*emptor*), and then the sale by a seller (*venditor*).[3] Armed with such a rudimentary vocabulary, Romans built their "legal alphabet" or shorthand versions of the key elements of the various transactions. In the purchase and sale, these elements were 1) An informal (consensual) agreement on the quantity and

---

[1] On the basic features of *mandatum* and *commodatum*, *see* BERGER, ENCYCLOPEDIC DICTIONARY, at 399, 574.

[2] *See* Hessel E. Yntema, *Legal Science and Natural Law, Apropos of Viehweg, Topik und Jurisprudenz*, 2 INTER-AM. L. REV. 207, 216 (1960).

[3] BERGER, ENCYCLOPEDIC DICTIONARY, at 452.

quality of the goods purchased and their price (*pretium*); 2) A good faith (*bonae fidei*) performance by the contracting parties, which presupposed that the parties were bound to do what they promised as well as to the obligations derived from what was promised; and 3) The binding effect of a sale from the moment that the parties consented to be bound.[4] Being familiar with these elements made it possible for Paulus ((Paul), a jurist whose opinion is transcribed later in this chapter)[5] to distinguish between a purchase and sale, which required a price, and a barter, which did not.

Professor James Gordley of Tulane University, among other distinguished scholars, points to the "recognition" of the contract of sale by the Roman jurists as one of their signal achievements.[6] What did this "recognition" mean? After all, as pointed out by the famous Romanist and legal historian Friedrich von Savigny,[7] informal sale agreements were among the most widely used (and thus well known) contracts during Roman times. Consequently, to be meaningful, the recognition that Gordley attributes to the Roman jurists had to have not only descriptive but also analytical and prescriptive functions. In other words, in addition to identifying the actual standard market practices involved, the recognition had to prescribe the legal consequences associated with the transaction, *including the parties' rights and duties and their remedies in case of breach.*

In the case of a purchase and sale, the remedies included actions such as the *actio empti* (by an aggrieved buyer),[8] the *actio venditi* (by an aggrieved seller)[9] or defenses such as the *exceptio doli* against the malice or bad faith of either party.[10] However, in the case of barters, as noted earlier, they were only binding and their rights and duties supported by remedies only "long after sale was recognized [as a binding agreement]. . . ."[11]

Professor Gordley also calls attention to the fact that "generic sales," or sales of fungible goods or of goods purchased by sample, were unenforceable under Roman law. In his words:

> In Roman law, the owner of a barn that contained wheat could sell so many bushels of it although they had not yet been measured out. The owner of a field could sell wheat that had yet to be grown on it. A goldsmith could sell a ring he was yet to make. A fisherman could sell whatever his net would catch on the next cast. . . . According to Kaser, the reason is that, originally, sale-like transactions were executed on the spot. Consequently, every sale was of a specific object to be delivered immediately.[12]

---

[4] James Gordley, *The Origins of Sale: Some Lessons from the Romans*, 84 TUL. L. REV. 1437 (2010).

[5] *See infra* § 4:6(A).

[6] Gordley, *supra* note 4, at 1438.

[7] GORLA I, at 30–31.

[8] *See, e.g.*, REINHARD ZIMMERMAN, THE LAW OF OBLIGATIONS: ROMAN FOUNDATIONS OF THE CIVILIAN TRADITION 241–44 (1990) (discussing the use of the *actio empti* when a "thing" had been sold, such as a slave, who was a freeman).

[9] *Id.* at 277.

[10] BERGER, ENCYCLOPEDIC DICTIONARY, at 459.

[11] Gordley, *supra* note 4, at 1439.

[12] *Id.* at 1439–40.

The practice of concluding sale agreements only on the spot was not peculiar to the Roman marketplace. Please recall the Arizona Suni Indian Jeweler's reaction to my student's order for the future delivery of jewelry yet to be crafted.[13] Recall also Professor Salomon Najmad's explanation for a similar attitude among Mexican native tribes who would only sell what they had on hand. His explanation was that their approach to the enforceability of promises of future performances echoed the perennial cycles in the production and distribution of their crops. On the other hand, Polybius, a Greek historian (circa 200–118 B.C.E.) of republican Rome, may have provided a different cultural explanation for the Roman on-the-spot sales. His explanation combined selfishness by all the contracting parties and distrust among them: "In Rome, no one gives anything to another if he is not obligated to do so, and no one pays off an obligation prior to its maturity, even among family."[14] In the case of sales of fungible goods by samples, the lack of juristic recognition may well have reflected the absence of a class of commercial intermediaries among producers, merchants and consumers and of an appropriate institutional setting such as that of the Amsterdam Bourse.[15]

A. Stages in the Development of Roman Law

1. The Archaic Period

The earliest period of Roman law (from 754 to 201 B.C.E.) is known as the "archaic period" because it relied on an adjudication of civil justice directed by pontiffs (*pontifices*). In the words of Adolf Berger, they were the "creators, guardians of, and experts in, divine and pontifical law. . . ."[16] Having coined it, these priests alone knew the procedural law and the legal forms to set it into motion, and they kept this knowledge to themselves. The solemn and ritualistic elements of this archaic law were described by Charles Summer Lobienger as follows:

> "[T]he pleading (*actio*) of the litigant in a civil suit is a religious chant every word and cadence of which must be learnt from the priest; the wager (*sacramentum*) by which the process is stated, is a gift to a temple, and is probably conceived as an atonement for the involuntary perjury of the man who loses his case. . . .[17]

These pleadings were sacramental to the point that if they did not follow exactly the wording known only to the pontiffs, the lawsuit could be lost.[18] In addition to the ritualistic and rigorous nature of this law, it was also highly provincial; it applied only to the city that housed the Roman citizens whose first inhabitants were referred to as *Quirites;* hence the label *ius civile quiritium*.

Side by side with pontifical law, a set of written laws known as the "Twelve Tables" (*Lex Duodecim Tabularum*) was promulgated circa 450 B.C.E. by ten consuls

---

[13] *See supra* § 3:6(E).

[14] THEODOR MOMMSEN, I HISTORIA DE ROMA 1106 (A. Garcia Moreno trans., 1960) (author's translation).

[15] *See infra* § 6:2(F)(5).

[16] BERGER, ENCYCLOPEDIC DICTIONARY, at 635.

[17] CHARLES SUMNER LOBINGIER, THE EVOLUTION OF ROMAN LAW: FROM BEFORE THE TWELVE TABLES TO THE CORPUS JURIS 13 n.5 (1923) (citations omitted).

[18] BERGER, ENCYCLOPEDIC DICTIONARY, at 541 (on *legis actio*).

(supreme magistrates or government officials) who had been empowered to draft the basic laws of the young republic.[19] These laws facilitated the public's prosecution of crimes and enabled injured parties to seek compensation in civil disputes.

Unlike the pontifical chants, there was a clear and rational purpose behind the drafting of the Law of the Twelve Tables: to protect the class of plebeians from legal abuses by the ruling class of patricians, especially in the latter's enforcement of debts. "The important basic principle of [having] a written legal code for Roman law was established, and justice was no longer based solely on the interpretation of judges."[20]

Table III of the Twelve Tables illustrates Warmington's depiction:

> When [a] debt has been acknowledged, or judgment about the matter has been pronounced in court, 30 days must be the legitimate time of grace. After that, then [the] arrest of [the] debtor may be made by laying on hands [and bringing him into court]. . . . If he does not satisfy the judgment, or no one in court offers himself as surety on his behalf, [the] creditor may take [the] defaulter with him. He may bind him either in stocks or in fetters; he may bind him with weight not less than 15 pounds, or with more if he shall so desire. [The] [d]ebtor if he shall wish may live on his own. If he does not live on his own, [the] person [who shall hold him in bonds] shall give him one pound of wheat for each day. He may give more if he shall so desire. . . . On the third market-day, creditors shall cut pieces [divide the debt?]. Should they have cut more or less than their due, it shall be with impunity.[21]

2. *The Pre-Classical Period and the Emergence of Praetors*

During this period (201 to 27 B.C.E.), a new, more flexible law, the *ius honorarium*, emerged. It was designed to soften the rigors of the *ius civile* described above. This new law became the responsibility of administrative officials known as *praetors*. Their role as shapers of the remedial law of contracts cannot be overemphasized. As will be discussed in later sections, *praetors* were responsible for legitimizing causes of action, defenses and remedies related to contractual, among other, private law litigation.[22] Their services were at first free or honorary (hence the name of the new law). As will be discussed in a later section,[23] some of the *praetors* were responsible for the creation of a law applicable to foreign merchants or "peregrines" (the *ius peregrinum*), as well as for the development of the *ius gentium*, a law applicable to non-Roman citizens when dealing with Roman citizens.

3. *The Classical Period and the Crystallization of a Method of Reasoning*

The classical period is the best known and most influential period of Roman law. It lasted roughly the first two-and-a-half centuries A.D. During this period, Roman law reached its highest level of comprehensiveness and analytical refinement. As with their

---

[19] Decemviri Consulari Imperio Legibus Scribundis, *The Twelve Tables*, *available at* http://www.fordham.edu/halsall/ancient/12tables.html.

[20] Kenneth Pennington, *The Twelve Tables*, http://faculty.cua.edu/pennington/law508/12tables.htm.

[21] III REMAINS OF OLD LATIN 437, 439, 441 (G. P. Goold ed., E. H. Warmington trans., Loeb Classical Library 1998) (1938).

[22] *See infra* § 4:4(B).

[23] *See infra* § 4:4(D)(3)(d).

pontifical ancestors, the Roman jurists of the classical period issued legal opinions at the request of public officials, judges or magistrates, and private parties. One of their most important functions was to help *praetors* draft their edicts. Edicts were public announcements of how *praetors* would handle their duties, including what causes of action and legal defenses they would entertain and what procedural formulas had to be followed by magistrates or judges.[24] Not surprisingly, then, much juristic writing was devoted to discussing the application of the *praetor's* edict.[25]

4. *The Greek-Roman Geometric Logic: Analogy and Classification*

By the time Emperor Augustus[26] granted to Roman jurists the power to respond publicly to legal questions (*ius publice respondendi*) on the personal authority of the prince, the legal logic of Roman jurists had been so refined that it compared favorably with that used by their present-day counterparts. This refinement was the product of what I described elsewhere[27] as an ability to objectively measure the legal dimensions of the parties' rights and duties. The Roman jurists' measurements helped ascertain the hierarchy of rights and duties: Which right or duty was superior, inferior, or subordinated to another? What duty corresponded to what right? And equally as important, if not more, which right was actionable and which unfulfilled duties provided a valid defense?

The logic involved in these measurements relied on the ability to analogize or distinguish among legal categories made possible by the continuous development of their legal alphabet with terms such as, for example, persons (*personae*), slaves (*servi*), and things (*res*). As the rights and duties and legal remedies of the persons or entities associated with these terms were identified they became a part of the meaning of the terms. Then, by applying the analogy between, say, slaves and things, slaves were denied full legal personality or the capacity to enter into contracts. Conversely, by applying the analogy between physical persons and certain collective entities that were not human (*personae vice fungi*), such as a decedent's estate (*hereditas*) or a municipality (*decuria*), it was possible to assume the latter's capacity to enter into contracts, [28]

The above described logical tools refined the Roman legal alphabet. By the time the Roman jurist Gaius wrote his *Institutes* in second century A.D.,[29] the term "person" had acquired both a generic and uniform legal meaning throughout the Roman Empire. It included species such as free persons and slaves. When accompanied by certain adjectives, the term *persona* could empower or limit the capacity to enter into contracts. For example, those empowered to conclude contracts or appear in court were *personae legitimae*, whereas those denied such a power because of serious character flaws were *personae turpis*.[30] Thus, the Roman legal system's recognition of new rights and duties associated with the term *persona* led to the coinage and legal recognition of new *personae*.

---

[24] *See infra* § 4:4.

[25] *See infra* § 4:4(B), on Juristic Opinions.

[26] Caesar Augustus lived from 63 B.C.E. to 14 A.D.

[27] Kozolchyk, *Transfer*, at 1469–72.

[28] BERGER, ENCYCLOPEDIC DICTIONARY, at 628 (on *persona, personae vice fungi, hereditas and decuria*).

[29] *See infra* § 4:4(A), (discussing the Institutes).

[30] BERGER, ENCYCLOPEDIC DICTIONARY, at 629 (for *personae legitimae* and *personae turpis*).

Roman jurists often combined analogy with an axiomatic form of reasoning they learned from the Greeks. Consider, for example, the application of juristic maxims such as "No one can transfer greater rights to someone else than he possesses himself." (*nemo plus iuris in alium transferre potest quam ipse habet*),[31] or "No one can [accept a promise by] . . . stipulation on behalf of another. . . ." (*nemo alteri stipulare potest*).[32] In addition to expressing a substantive rule of law, the preceding maxims, or "*regulae iuris*,"[33] contained an axiomatic (albeit redundant) formulation that justified the rule. This formulation rings so self-evident that it creates an impression of inevitability. After all, who besides the person who has or owns something can validly transfer it? Clearly, by using terms such as "owning" or "having," the conclusion is pre-determined. Similarly, by limiting the transferor's power to transfer only a part of the thing sought to be transferred, the conclusion is inevitable that he cannot validly transfer the whole.

The logic used by the Roman jurists who formulated these maxims is not only syllogistic, but also geometrical. It helps distinguish between rights of greater or lesser legal and physical dimensions, such as between a fee simple absolute or absolute right of ownership of property over Blackacre (*dominium*) and lesser rights in someone else's property (*ius in re aliena*), such as a life estate (*usufructus*) or an easement (*servitus*).

Another illustrative use of the Roman geometric logic is its measurement of a custodian or depositary's duties of diligence and care with respect to the thing left in his custody or deposit. The measurement of the degree of diligence and care was provided by a utilitarian consideration—the profitability of his possession (*utilitas contrahentium*): The more he profited from possessing the thing he was caring for, the higher was his duty of care and diligence.[34]

It should be clear, however, that the Roman law method of measuring rights was intended first and foremost as a tool to *determine* which remedy was available to the aggrieved party. It was not intended as the "search engine" that would reveal the permanent and universal essences of rights and duties as was done many centuries later by French scholastics and German Pandectists. Thus, the Roman geometric legal logic was not intended to answer questions such as: Are rights in *personam* or *in rem* closed in number as a result of their permanent and universal legal natures? Or are their permanent and universal natures closed (*numerus clausus*) or open (*numerus apertus*) in number?

In fact, throughout Roman legal history new rights *in personam* or *in rem* appeared without creating much of a juristic reaction to their presence. Consider, for example, the *ius distrahendi*, which presupposed the existence of rights such as of those of the pledgee of personal property in a pledge (*pignus*). The *ius distrahendi* enabled the pledgee to sell the pledge if the debtor and original owner of the pledged thing had failed to pay what he owed on his pledge when it was due. As pointed out by Adolf Berger, even though the *ius distrahendi* originally required an agreement between the debtor and the creditor, eventually it was deemed self understood that the

---

[31] WATSON, DIGEST, 50.17.54. *See also infra* § 4:6.

[32] WATSON, DIGEST, 45.1.38.17.

[33] *See generally* PETER STEIN, REGULAE IURIS: FROM JURISTIC RULES TO LEGAL MAXIMS (1966).

[34] *See infra* ch. 23:4(B)(1) (discussing the French law that attempts to provide a threefold classification of fault as 1) gross negligence, 2) light negligence, and 3) lightest negligence). This classification is geometric in that the degree of fault is directly related to the degree of profitability of the transaction in question.

enforcement of this right *in rem* would proceed unimpeded unless expressly excluded by the pledge agreement.[35] As will be discussed in a later chapter,[36] the Roman method of measurement of rights and duties inspired the drafting of legal definitions and classifications that were treated as self-evident by the first and most influential of all European codes—the *Code Civil* or *Code Napoléon* of 1804—as by its progeny.[37] Yet, as noted in Chapter 2 with respect to scholastic reasoning, despite this reasoning's claim to geometrical universality and truth, it was only as good as the facts of their underlying transactions. To the extent that the scholastic reasoning reflected what was going on in the marketplace, it was helpful. To the extent it did not, and because of its assumed universality and permanence, it precluded new types of rights, whether *in personam* or *in rem*, and became an obstacle to economic development. To illustrate this point, please recall my lecture on contemporary conditional sales delivered at a Spanish law school and a professor's objection to the physical and legal existence of conditional sales simply because they violated a definition of sales in Spain's nineteenth century civil code.[38]

5. *The Logic of the* Bonus Vir

Less noticed than the Roman geometric logic and its *regulae iuris* was a logic used by Roman jurists when attempting to resolve problems caused by contractual clauses that granted broad discretionary powers to one of the parties. This logic analogized the duties of the grantee of such powers to that of a respected man of affairs (*bonus vir*). Some Roman jurists suggested that the judge of facts ask himself: How would such a respected man of affairs behave as the grantee of his discretionary powers?

One of the opinions transcribed below provides a good illustration of how the jurists applied such a standard in the sale of a slave that contained discretionary terms which conditioned the obligor's performance.[39] The reader should pay close attention to this method of measurement of rights and duties because in the ensuing centuries, and to this day, it has made possible greater predictability of contracts containing discretionary clauses. These clauses, incidentally, are quite necessary in contemporary transactions. Can you see why?

6. *The Post-Classical Period*

The post-classical period is characterized by its sterility. As the imperial power was concentrated in fewer hands and an absolute monarchy emerged, the political and economic forces that encouraged the creativity and independence of the mind of the classical period disappeared. After the third century A.D., few new jurists were cited by others and the production of juristic opinions diminished drastically. What emerged in the Eastern empire during the sixth century A.D. was not a new law, but a massive compilation of the pre-existing statutory, juristic, and didactic writings. This was the task of a team of compilers appointed by the Emperor Justinian. They produced the

---

[35] BERGER, ENCYCLOPEDIC DICTIONARY, at 527 (on *ius distrahendi*).

[36] *See infra* § 8:4(C) & (D).

[37] *See infra* § 8:4(D)–(F) (discussing the methodology for the drafting of the *Code Civil*).

[38] *See supra* § 2:2(C)(4).

[39] *See infra* § 4:4(F)(3), (discussing discretionary conditions).

Corpus Juris Civilis,[40] an everlasting scholarly monument to the juristic creativity of earlier periods.[41]

§ 4.3 THE SOCIO-ECONOMIC CONTEXT OF ROMAN COMMERCIAL LEGAL INSTITUTIONS

A. Soldiering as a Gainful Occupation

In another writing of mine, I described an important feature of Rome's economy during the archaic period as follows:

> During the [archaic period and its] [L]aw of the Twelve Tables (*circa* 450 B.C.), Rome was a community of soldiering farmers. These Romans practiced "dry farming," an arduous and skilled form of tilling designed to obtain from a minimum of dry land "the largest amount of vegetable calories." Much of their terrain was rocky and mountainous, requiring them to spend considerable time building terraces and canals and plowing repeatedly to spread moisture deep below the surface. . . .
>
> Horses were also highly valued for their use in soldiering. In fact, ownership of land was lodged, at first, with a small number of families of reputed noble birth (*patricii*) who, as horse-riding knights (*equites*), were the core of the incipient Roman army. These families worked the land in units which included not only the *paterfamilias* [the father-head of the household] but also some slaves. Land not owned by the patricians could be cultivated by plebeians who, in exchange for the right to till the soil, were required to support their patrician benefactors in the latters' wars and politics.
>
> The mutual dependency between patricians and plebeians is apparent in the Twelve Table rules. For example, the patrician who failed to provide for his plebeian ward's necessity could be punished. The allegiance required by this patronage system, coupled with the allegiance owed by members of the family to their *paterfamilias*, provided the organic basis for Rome's famed military hierarchy and discipline.
>
> In due course, military tactics changed and infantry was recruited [almost exclusively] from plebeian farmers. In Professor Kunkel's words, "[t]his class, which had formerly been nothing but a disorganized horde of baggage-carriers in the field of battle, now became the principal bearer of the burdens and spoils of war." In contrast with the clients of the patrician *equites*, the new class of plebeian, the farmer-soldier, was not satisfied with nominal rewards for its war efforts. Soon, Roman generals found it necessary to share their booty with their soldiers.[42]

In his Nobel Prize winning *History of Rome*, Theodor Mommsen drew attention to the fact that ownership of the spoils of war was clearly encouraged as a gainful occupation.[43] The Roman legionnaire's sword legitimized ownership, and the war booty

---

[40] *See infra* § 4:4(A).

[41] *See infra* § 4:4.

[42] Kozolchyk, *Transfer*, at 1457–58 (citations omitted).

[43] MOMMSEN, *supra* note 14, at 1059.

was immediately theirs by the *jus gentium*, including free men who they captured and made their slaves.

However, it was not until the publication of Rudolph von Ihering's *The Spirit of Roman Law* that the profound legal implications of the Roman conqueror's possession became clear. If the God of the Pentateuch granted the Promised Land to the Jews, explained Ihering, the Roman gods gave the Romans the sword and the lance to take the property they wanted.[44] Indeed, ownership and possession in ancient Roman law reflected both a warring and a farming society. In this society, property was valuable if it was useful either in war, in farming, or in both. As Sir Henry Sumner Maine could have observed, contract, albeit an indispensable tool of trade, was not as significant to a warring economy as was the booty and the collection of taxes from those conquered, a consequence of the status of conquerors. As such, status governed society. Valuable things were not acquired by bargain and exchange, but by military acquisition and receipt of taxes.

B. Commerce vs. Roman Archetypal Dignity

Theodore Mommsen's description of trade in pre-republican Rome indicates that despite significant commercial activity since the earliest of times, it was at best a "passive trade."[45] Instead of selling manufactured goods, the Latins sold beasts and slaves to the Etruscans who, in turn, sold their copper to the Romans. When "high commerce," *i.e.*, wholesale and export commerce, finally did arrive, such commerce was in the hands of large aristocratic landholders almost from its inception. Very few other merchants could act as intermediaries between producers and consumers. While most Roman towns had workmen, draftsmen, and petty merchants, theirs was a subsistence trade. Capital was concentrated in very few hands as slavery and poverty grew. Some profit-sharing arrangements existed between the wealthy few and workers, craftsmen, and petty merchants. Generally, however, the supply of capital to non-aristocrats was in the form of loans at exorbitant interest rates.[46]

The picture did not change significantly during the Republic. The city of Rome became a trading center for slaves, agricultural tools, clothing, and especially luxury household items. Most of the goods traded, however, were manufactured elsewhere. The ability to import these goods was given to a privileged few, usually the same landholders who owned merchant ships and large numbers of slaves. During imperial times, there were very few individual farmers who had any surplus to sell. The agricultural surplus that supported Roman towns was produced by millions of slaves. While the city of Rome could rightfully be regarded as the financial center of the civilized world—a marketplace for numerous artisans, shopkeepers, contractors of public works, manufacturers of military wares, moneylenders and tax farmers—commercial prosperity was tied to the monopolies headed by the large landowners.[47]

Rome's brand of capitalistic morality was exemplified by Cato's "Practical Catechism." Cato advised his son that the accumulation of profits was the sign of a life well lived. While a widow need not feel ashamed if her assets declined during her

---

[44] RUDOLPH VON IHERING, I L'ESPRIT DU DROIT ROMAIN 111–19 (3d ed. 1969).

[45] MOMMSEN, *supra* note 14, at 258.

[46] *Id.*

[47] *Id.* at 1100–1115.

lifetime, a Roman gentleman's assets were expected to grow during his life. "[T]he book of accounts which attests that a man left behind more assets than those he inherited is worthy of praise."[48] According to Mommsen, the accretion of a gentleman's assets was possible because of the enforceability of promises in profitable transactions and because of the unenforceability of gratuitous promises. A similar observation led the earlier mentioned Greek historian Polybius' warning about the selfish attitude of Romans who were not prone to give altruistically to others unless obligated to do so and who did not pay off their obligations until the moment they were due, and this was true even among family members.[49]

Yet, while the accumulation of profits was praised, many of today's most respected forms of profit-making were rejected as undignified by well-bred Romans. Romans were taught that it was undignified to charge money for their services, even if these services had significant market value. Thus, someone agreeing to keep another's valuable personal property as a custodian or bailee (*depositum* or *commodatum*) was expected to do so gratuitously. Similarly, someone assisting in the conclusion of another's business (*mandatum* or *procuratio*), however arduous and beneficial his efforts, was supposed to perform them gratuitously. The law not only reflected such expectations, but forbade some persons in the highest levels of Roman society from performing or charging fees for certain commercial services. The *Lex Claudia*, for example, forbade Roman senators and their sons from owning trading vessels except when the commodities carried were gathered from their own lands. Such an attitude was responsible for silent partnerships in which members of the lower social ranks, prominently slaves, engaged in profit-making activities that allowed their silent aristocratic partners to carry on with appropriate dignity. Many of these silent partnerships were engaged in the most undignified of all profit-making activities in Rome: money lending at interest.[50]

This archetypal pattern of transactional selfishness meant that the entrustment of monies, wares or commodities by their ultimate owners for trade purposes frequently had to be made in circumvention of the law, or at least of social respectability. Thus, when entrustment took place, it was generally not to independent merchants with status and power matching those of the trustors, but to members of lower social ranks such as present or former slaves, still dependent upon their trustors for sustenance, protection or both. In this sense, the power that the ancient *paterfamilias* had over the entire household deeply influenced trade and trade-inspired rights and duties, even during the empire. The archetypal pattern also meant that the accumulation of commercial wares or paper was not a sign of fine breeding. In Cato's time (second century B.C.E.), the ideal behavior of a Roman gentleman was still the ancestral farmer-soldier:

---

[48] *Id.* at 1105 (author's translation).

[49] *Id.* at 1106.

[50] Similar situations exist in modern times as well. As a young lawyer in Cuba, I had my first shocking run-in with simulatory culture when I inquired into the fees that should be charged after I had completed hours working on a divorce action for clients. My supervisor simply stated that as dignified legal professionals, we didn't have to charge a fee, but worked paid on "honorarium." In order to file the divorce paperwork, however, the client would have to purchase and pay for filing stamps. The money for these stamps went to the local bar association. I later learned that a large percentage of the money made from purchasing these required filing stamps was collected by the lawyer from the bar association when he filed the documents. In this way, the lawyer in Cuba would maintain his dignified role by charging supposedly a minimal honorarium, yet all the while collecting fees through back channels.

> When our ancestors had to praise a good man, they spoke well of . . . a good farmer. Such was the finest praise. I am aware of the merchant's diligence and pursuit of profit . . . [but], is not agriculture [the activity] that provides the strongest and most vigorous of soldiers? What profit could be more honest than that of the farmer? Those who devote themselves to tilling the soil do not think evil thoughts.[51]

§ 4.4 THE LEGAL CONTEXT

As noted by Professor Yntema, the influence of Roman law has no equal in Western civilization. In Professor Yntema's words:

> There have been, in the Western world, two dominant legal systems, the Roman and the English. Both are functions of empire, the products of people gifted to rule. . . . In the legal systems of these two peoples, accordingly appear significant analogies. In each case, a sharp division was soon made between sacred and secular justice; in each the power of the state was developed at a relatively early stage, the administration of justice was professionalized, and a system of private law, articulated in specific forms of action, superseded the blood-feud and other institutions of the prior communal custom. In each system, the scheme of rights thus elaborated became rigidly formalized and had to be supplemented, corrected, and eventually superseded by a parallel system of equitable remedies, introduced by the authority of a magistrate—the *praetor* in Rome, the chancellor in London. . . . Most noteworthy is the fact that both are essentially systems of case-law, evolved by specialists, generally indifferent to history and with little theory and less philosophy. . . . The theoretical refinement of the modern civil law, however deeply indebted for its inspiration to the Roman sources, is largely post-Roman, and its symmetrical organization in the Code Napoléon and succeeding modern codifications is the product of scholastic attainments or at least interest in synthetic analysis, that neither the Roman jurists nor the English judges customarily displayed.[52]

With some hesitation, I would qualify an assessment as insightful as that of my mentor. While it is true that the Roman jurists were detached specialists with enormous influence when shaping the day-to-day problems of Roman justice, recent studies by economic historians of Rome confirm that these jurists were not as indifferent to their surroundings and status of contract participants as had been generally assumed. In fact, they were very concerned with the impact of their opinions upon the interests of Rome's upper classes, as will be discussed in Chapter 24.[53]

Professor Yntema also points out that of the two legal systems, the Roman had the greater historic and normative significance. As discussed in connection with the archaic period, the ability to reduce law to an authoritative formulation took place as early as with the Law of the Twelve Tables. The fact that following the archaic period Roman jurists were the first to study the practical problems of justice in a non-religious

---

[51] MOMMSEN, *supra* note 14, at 1113–14. M. Porcius Cato was Consul in 195 B.C.E. and Censor in 184 B.C.E. Cicero referred to him as "an expert in *ius civile*, the best of all."

[52] Yntema, *Roman Law*, at 77–78.

[53] *See infra* § 24:3(B)(3).

context, relying on a rich transactional and adjudicative experience, gave its legal institutions an originality and creative freedom denied to then-contemporary as well as subsequent legal cultures. Finally, the decisive influence of Roman law in the Western culture is also owed, according to Professor Yntema, to the fact that a good deal of it was compiled (although far from exhaustively) by the Emperor Justinian in the *Corpus Juris Civilis*. This authoritative document—like the Bible in the religious context and the writings of Aristotle in philosophy—was received as the synthesis of what was not only lawful, but also fair and equitable in later ages.[54]

A. Sources for the Study of Roman Law

Traditionally, the two most important sources for the study of Roman law have been Gaius's *Institutes* and the *Corpus Juris Civilis* of Emperor Justinian. The *Institutes* were authored by the above-mentioned jurist Gaius as a textbook. However, after being taught to numerous generations of students throughout the civil law world as the most authoritative manual of Roman law, it acquired a normative life of its own. Its division of private law into discrete subjects such as persons (*personae*), things (*res*), and legal actions (*actiones*) inspired many sections, parts or chapters of nineteenth and twentieth century civil codes.

Emperor Justinian's *Corpus Juris Civilis*, also mentioned earlier, is a compilation of statutory provisions, lectures and opinions of jurists, drafted by a commission of governmental officials and jurists recruited by Justinian in or around 530 A.D. It included the *Institutes* of Justinian (a slightly revised version of the *Institutes* of Gaius) and the *Digest* (*Digesta Iustiniani*), a collection of the opinions of renowned jurists on issues or disputes brought to their attention by litigants, judges and other officials during the classical period of Roman law. Finally, the *Corpus Juris Civilis* included the *Codex Iustinianus* and the *Novellae Iustiniani* (mostly statutory provisions in their original and updated versions).

The *Corpus Juris Civilis* comprises more than 9,000 texts, divided into fifty books, which in turn were subdivided, with rare exceptions, into titles that contained the texts belonging to the subjects indicated in the heading or rubric of the title. As will become evident in the opinions reproduced below, each text is prefaced by a reference to the jurist whose opinion is transcribed, followed by the book and title from which it is extracted.[55]

The Digest, which is the second component of the *Corpus Juris Civilis* after the *Institutes*, contains passages that are divided into four major sections. The first is the *Sabinus*, which comprises the *ius civile*. This was the basic law of the city of Rome, applicable to the citizens of Rome (*ius civile proprium romanorum*). Sabinus was the author of one of the most famous commentaries on the *ius civile*.[56] As noted earlier, this *ius civile* was regarded by adjudicators as one of strict application. The contrasting counterpart to the *ius civile* was the *ius honorarium* or *pretorium*, whose equitable and more flexible nature prompted Professor Yntema's analogy between the functions of the Roman *praetor* and the English chancellor.[57]

---

[54] Yntema, *Roman Law*, at 79.

[55] *See infra* § 4:6.

[56] BERGER, ENCYCLOPEDIC DICTIONARY, at 527.

[57] *See* Yntema, *Roman Law, supra* note 52 and accompanying text.

The second section contains passages devoted to the *praetor's* edict. It also contains comments on the *praetor's* administrative orders or directives to judges, a good number of which were based upon on equitable principles. The third section is named after the jurist Papinian. It includes the *Questiones* and the *Responsa* of Papiniano, one of the most renowned Roman jurists. Finally, the fourth is the Appendix, which includes sources discovered during the compilation process.

The third component of the *Corpus Juris* is the *Codex Iustinianus*. The *Codex* contains provisions known as "*leges*" voted by popular assemblies during the republican period. These provisions were' complemented by senatorial opinions (*senatus consulta*) completed during the imperial period by a type of decree known as *constitutum principum*.[58] According to another distinguished Romanist, in the classic era, "the Romans apparently were averse to formal legislation as a means of elaborating the law."[59] Like the Digest, the *Codex* is divided into books and titles, and the Justinian compilers made changes to the constitutions of former emperors to adapt these rules to the conditions prevailing during Justinian times.[60] The fourth and final component of the *Corpus Juris* was the *Novellae Iustiani*, a collection of statutes or decrees promulgated after the second edition of the *Codex*.[61]

B. The Contribution of *Praetors*

While the Digest contains numerous opinions on what we consider today as commercial contracts including sales and loans, commercial customs were, according to Professor Yntema, "of distinctly minor importance" among the Romans compared with our time.[62] Nevertheless, the edicts of magistrates—especially those of the urban and peregrine *praetors*—were of great importance to the development of a Roman commercial law:

> [T]he first [urban *Praetor*] inaugurated in 367 B.C. to administer civil justice within the City and the second [*peregrine Praetor* inaugurated] about 242 B.C. to superintend the jurisdiction in cases involving foreigners, proved of the greatest importance in the development of the law. As is commonly known, it was by this means that the *ius honorarium*, the system of remedies supplementing the earlier *ius civile* was created. The fact that this could be accomplished by magistrates, elected for a year . . . can be explained only by the early development in Rome of specialists in private law by whom the magistrates were advised and instructed.[63]

The supplementation alluded to by Professor Yntema should not be underestimated. This was the mechanism that created much of the Roman "living law" of commerce, *i.e.*, the law actually practiced in contrast with the increasingly less practiced formal and strict *ius civile* of Roman commerce. As will be apparent in some

---

[58] BERGER, ENCYCLOPEDIC DICTIONARY, at 410 (*constitutiones principum*).

[59] Yntema, *Roman Law*, at 84 (citing FRITZ SCHULZ, PRINCIPLES OF ROMAN LAW 6–18 (1936)).

[60] BERGER, ENCYCLOPEDIC DICTIONARY, at 392 (*Codex Iustinianus*).

[61] *Id.* at 600 (*Novellae Iustiniani*).

[62] Yntema, *Roman Law*, at 84.

[63] *Id.* at 84–85.

of the juristic opinions that follow, it was the *praetorian* edict that made it possible to circumvent the rigors of the *ius civile*.[64]

Finally, the *Aediles Curules* were also helpful in the creation of the living law of the Roman market. They were members of a group of magistrates created in the year 367 B.C.E.[65] Notwithstanding their broad jurisdiction (from the preservation of public order and the internal security in Rome to the supervision of market transactions), their regulation of the sales of slaves and animals, including the norms over weights and measures, contributed significantly to the certainty of commercial contracts.

C. Civil Procedure

Professor Yntema indicates another similarity between the civil procedure of the Roman law and the common law:

> In the Roman system of civil procedure, which like that of the Common Law was in classical times a contest of the parties, supervised by the magistrate, rather than an officially directed inquisition, a distinction was from the beginning drawn between the proceedings *in iure*, viz., the pleadings leading to the formulations of the issue, and those *apud iudicem*, the actual trial of the case. In the formalistic period of the early *legis actiones*, or actions based upon the Twelve Tables, it was necessary for the parties to recite their claims or defenses in literally exact terms. . . . In the formulary procedure, by which the ancient actions were superseded and which was employed throughout the classical period, the proceedings *in iure* involved the issuance of a formula by the *praetor*, instructing the *iudex* to adjudge as the facts should appear in favor of the plaintiff or the defendant on the conditions stated in the formula and approved by the magistrate as representing the law.
>
> On the other hand, the actual trial took place before a *iudex*, usually agreed to by the parties, who was selected from a panel of leading citizens-laymen. . . . Both the magistrate and the *iudex*, as well as the parties themselves, required the advice of experts who by their studies had acquired authority in law. The consequence was not merely that in its detailed application the law was chiefly developed by jurisconsults who had no recognized part in the procedure itself but acted in an advisory capacity, but even more important, that their attention was necessarily focused upon the very practical problems of law presented in specific cases. . . . This, it would seem, is the underlying explanation of the logical precision that characterized the method and the product of the great Roman jurists.[66]

The formula that guided the judge's ruling normally resulted from the text proposed first to the *praetor* by the plaintiff. The defendant replied with proposed changes, exceptions or defenses. The written document that contained the *praetorian* formulae oriented the judge to rule in favor of the plaintiff or the defendant, depending

---

[64] *See supra* § 4:4(A).

[65] BERGER, ENCYCLOPEDIC DICTIONARY, at 353.

[66] Yntema, *Roman Law*, at 85–86; *but cf. infra* 24:3(B)(3). (Explaining that contemporary economic historians of the Roman Empire have "demonstrated in several areas of the law that jurists were concerned with contemporary social problems, especially ones that impinged directly upon the interests of the upper classes.") DENNIS P. KEHOE, LAW AND THE RURAL ECONOMY IN THE ROMAN EMPIRE 11 (2007).

upon which party was favored by the facts. If the facts supported his claim then condemn accordingly, if not, absolve the defendant (*si paret . . . condemnato, si non paret absolvito*). The written document also set forth possible defenses or exceptions to the complaint. For example, while the formula recognized that certain facts would support the plaintiff's claim that a sum of money was owed to him, it also conditioned the finding in favor of the plaintiff upon a finding that the latter had not waived his claim or that an agreement between the plaintiff and defendant did not exist in which the plaintiff agreed not to pursue his claim (*pactum de non pretendo*).[67]

D. Contracts and Their Enforcement: Why Were Only Certain Types of Contracts Enforced?

1. *The Absence of a General Theory of Contract*

The contemporary law of contracts—whether codified or found in case law—is supported by a general theory of contracts. This theory allows lawyers and judges to answer questions such as: Which contracts are enforceable? Who has the capacity to enter into a contract? What are the elements of a valid contract? What is an offer, what is an acceptance and what are their requirements? What constitutes a breach of contract, and what are the actions and responsibilities related to it? These questions can be answered reliably because a general theory of contract law was formulated that took into account the broadest number of contractual transactions possible and identified their peculiar features. Based on this examination, the theorist can suggest distinctions among them and of the rights and duties of the parties who participate in them. These distinctions were finally incorporated into definitions and classifications of contracts that, depending upon the legal system involved, relied more or less on the Aristotelian "essences."[68]

As noted by the influential English Romanist William Buckland, because Roman law did not have a general theory of contract, its rules applied only to specific contracts or types of contracts.[69] This was manifest in the Roman procedural and remedial law of contracts. As in the Common Law "forms of action" period, Roman law causes of action and remedies were granted only to select transactions and facts related to them.[70]

2. *Binding Promises Because of Their Formality: The* Stipulatio

In early Roman contractual practice, the formal or ritualistic promise expressed in a *stipulatio* played the same role as hydrogen in Mendeleev's periodic table: it was the first "element" of a Roman contractual relationship in which only one of the parties—the promisor—issued a unilaterally binding promise. Recall that in a *stipulatio*, a debtor could bind himself to his creditor by ritualistically answering in an oath taking like fashion a formulated question such as: "Do you promise to pay a hundred?" (*Spondesne centum dare?*) To which, in order to be bound, he would have to answer: "I promise." (*Spondeo*).[71]

---

[67] BERGER, ENCYCLOPEDIC DICTIONARY, at 474–75.

[68] *See supra* § 2:2.

[69] BUCKLAND, MANUAL, at 265.

[70] *See supra* § 4:6.

[71] *See* BERGER, ENCYCLOPEDIC DICTIONARY, at 716.

It is worth noting that the formality of the *stipulatio* was simplified in time and eventually embodied any type of promise and not necessarily those formally agreed to at the end of an interrogation. References to the *stipulatio* were found in juristic opinions on issues as far ranging as the law of property and civil procedure.[72] In addition, the *stipulatio* was for a considerable time available only to Roman citizens.[73] Over time, however, the *stipulatio* could be executed in languages other than Latin and its use in written form increased, especially for economically significant promises. Thus, a *stipulatio* transcribed by a Spanish Romanist attests to a loan agreement in a "Receipt Letter" as follows: "Lucio Ticio greets Sempronio . . . By means of this letter handwritten by my own hand I notify you that I will return to you immediately the 100 coins that you entrusted to me today"[74] This acknowledgment, incidentally, could be regarded as an early precedent of the modern promissory note, which is but one of the many forms of unilateral promises in use in our day. Not surprisingly, as the notaries public gained in importance during medieval times, they became the principal drafters of stipulations involving large sums of money.

3. Contracts Enforced Because of Their Content

As Roman commerce increased, the use of formalities decreased. Thus, while some not-for-profit transactions such as gifts or donations (*donatio*) required the formality of registration with public officials (*insinuatio*), Gaius's *Institutes* called attention to more widely used types of contracts whose enforceability did not depend upon their formality but on their content. He cited the loan of money (*mutuum*) as an example of a binding agreement based not upon a formal agreement, but on the transfer of the money to the borrower.[75] Since it required the transfer or delivery of a thing (*res*) to the borrower, it was referred to as a "real" contract. The reason for its enforceability was not too different from that expressed by those who shaped the English common law form of actions known as "debt" and "detinue." The debtor who failed to repay the amount lent was responsible for tortious conduct for failing to return someone else's property.[76]

a. Nominate Contracts: Consensual and Real

Eight forms of enforceable contracts were referred to by Roman jurists as "nominate" or bearing a specific name or label. Four were "consensual" and included purchases and sale, hires, mandates and partnerships. In E. Allan Farnsworth's words:

> It is as if the Roman jurists of about 100 B.C. had said "Go where you will, you will find that almost everything [that men do in business] can be reduced to four processes: (1) shifting goods permanently from one man's estate to another for a money price; (2) placing one person's property or services temporarily at the disposal of another for a consideration usually in money; (3) the pooling of property, skill, or experience by several persons for a common purpose; and (4) the gratuitous performance of a task by one person on the instructions of another. Moreover the secure and rapid flow of business

---

[72] ZULUETA II, at 151.

[73] ALAN WATSON, THE LAW OF OBLIGATIONS IN THE LATER ROMAN REPUBLIC 1 (1965).

[74] MANUEL JESUS GARCÍA GARRIDO, CASUISMO Y JURISPRUDENCIA ROMANA 95 (2008).

[75] ZULUETA II, at 148.

[76] *See* E. Allan Farnsworth, *The Past of Promise: An Historical Introduction to Contract*, 69 COLUM. L. REV. 576, 586 (1969).

requires that we should think of the relations implied in these processes as commencing not from acts but from promises to act."[77]

These binding agreements did not require the formalities of a stipulation nor that the delivery characteristic of real contracts be "consensual." In these agreements, the parties' "simple consent" binds them.[78] As early as the second century B.C.E., "the revolutionary step was taken of providing actions for the enforcement of the most commercially important consensual agreements, even if concluded informally and without the delivery of a *res*."[79] These were the agreements of sale (*emptio venditio*), hire (*locatio conductio*), partnership (*societas*) and mandate (*mandatum*). Not surprisingly, the great nineteenth century German Romanist Friedrich Carl von Savigny arrived at the same conclusion as did twentieth century Italian Professor Gino Gorla, author of one of the most lucid comparisons of the law of contracts: The Roman consensual transactions (*negocia*) were not only informal in everyday practice, but also the most popular in the Roman marketplace.[80]

Unlike the consensual contracts and their binding bilateral promises, the other four nominate contracts were "real" or requiring, as also noted earlier, the delivery of a thing (*res*) for the agreement to be binding. They included the contracts of deposit; *commodatum*, or loan for temporary use; *mutuum*, or loan for consumption; and pledge, usually a loan secured by the delivery of a thing by the debtor to the creditor. Apart from the loan of money or of other things destined to be consumed by their use (*mutuum*), real contracts encompassed the same transactions that a common law lawyer would classify as bailments. They included: 1) gratuitous loans of things for their borrowers' use and which had to be the same thing that was returned to the lender (*commodatum*); 2) an equally gratuitous deposit of things for safekeeping (*depositum*); and 3) the pledge of personal property (*pignus*).[81] Lawson also points out that these transactions were at first treated in the same way as the common law treated bailments for centuries: not as "real" contracts. Thus, the original Roman law of what eventually became "real" contracts was a law of possession and delict. If a borrower or depositee did not return the thing on demand or at the expiration of the term, or if the pledgee did not return the thing on the repayment of the loan, an expeditious remedy known as "interdict" could be brought against him to recover the pledgor-debtor's possession.[82]

It should be recalled that consensual agreements also differed from real agreements in the manner in which they were interpreted by judges. In an action based upon a consensual agreement such as a sale, the plaintiff, either acting as seller or buyer, typically alleged, first to the *praetor* and subsequently to the *iudex*, that the defendant had failed to perform either by not delivering the promised thing or (if the defendant was the buyer) by not having paid the agreed upon price. Where the plaintiff was successful, the *iudex* was directed to order the defendant to pay the plaintiff whatever he found to be due to him "*ex bona fidei*," or in accordance with the

---

[77] *Id.* at 589–90 (citing F. H. LAWSON, A COMMON LAWYER LOOKS AT THE CIVIL LAW 127 (1955)).

[78] ZULUETA II, at 146.

[79] *Id.* at 147.

[80] GORLA I at 30–31, for studies of Savigny on Roman consensual transactions (*negocia*).

[81] *See* THE ROMAN LAW READER 111 (F. H. Lawson ed., 1969) (describing this classification of contracts and their comparison with the common law counterparts).

[82] *Id.* at 112.

requirements of good faith. This required that the *iudex* (or the jurists that advised him) decide what a defendant acting in good faith would have done under the circumstances. As Professor Lawson reminds us, such an interpretation meant that in contrast with an adjudication based upon a formal *stipulatio*, where all the terms of the agreement had to be expressed or recited lest it not be enforceable, in a consensual sale the parties were bound not only by the terms they had actually agreed to, but by all the terms and conditions that were naturally implied from their agreement.[83]

b. Innominate Contracts

In contrast with the nominate contracts (each of which bore the name of its species as just noted), innominate agreements had no name attached to them. And even though in principle their number could be open, Roman jurists as a rule only referred to four such contracts: "I give so that you give" (*do ut des*); "I give so that you do" (*do ut facias*); "I do so that you give" (*facio ut des*); and "I do so that you do" (*facio ut facias*).[84] Unlike consensual agreements, they were binding only when one of the parties had completed his performance, thereafter requiring a counter-performance known as a *quid pro quo.*

Thus, the enforceability of both nominate and innominate contracts presupposed a simultaneity of performances—once a party performed, the other had the obligation to perform his or her part of the bargain. In contrast, a party's promise to perform in the future, by itself and without the formality of a *stipulatio* or the presence of a simultaneous performance or counter-performance, was deemed a "naked" promise and was not binding. As stated earlier, as a *nudum pactum*, it did not beget an obligation.

c. Typification of Roman Contracts and Contemporary Contracts

While the Roman law of contracts did not provide the interpreter with a general theory of contracts, it did provide him the distinctive features of enforceable contracts, such as the formality of the *stipulatio,* the informality of consensual-nominate contracts, and the *quid pro quo* of innominate contracts. Yet, while typifying these contracts, the Roman jurists were not engaged in the Aristotelian and scholastic task of identifying the universal and permanent essences of contracts. Theirs was the more mundane but profoundly juristic task of determining the actionability of transactions by ascribing actions and defenses or exceptions as well as specific remedies to those contracts selected for enforcement, having been "typified." Thus, when the reader encounters Paulus' (Paul's) opinion later in this chapter,[85] she will notice how the *praetor* fashioned an *actio vendicti* to protect an aggrieved seller from his buyer's breach, and conversely an *actio empti* to protect an aggrieved buyer from his seller's breach. The reader will also note that the *bona fidei* manner in which the contract is interpreted has everything to do with the typification of the sale in question as a consensual contract.

That only a small number of contracts were typified for enforcement in Roman law should not be surprising. Not many types of contracts can be expected in societies where wholesale or intermediaries' markets were unofficially controlled by few large landholder-traders. As long as a relatively small number of traders controlled the

---

[83] *Id.* at 104.

[84] *See* BERGER, ENCYCLOPEDIC DICTIONARY, at 414.

[85] *See infra* note 116 and accompanying text; WATSON, DIGEST, 18.1.1.

markets of intermediaries, it was only those contracts which they were comfortable with that would be enforceable. It is for this reason that both Friedrich Von Savigny and Gino Gorla, among other Romanists, attributed the restricted enforceability of contracts in imperial Rome to their typification.[86]

*d. The Praetor of Peregrines (*Praetor Peregrinus*) and the Remedial Law of Contracts:* Condictio *and* Causa

For those of us interested in the development of commercial contracts, the creation in 241 B.C.E. of a special *praetor* to deal with cases involving *peregrini* may well have marked the beginning of the application of the *ius gentium* in Rome's commercial disputes. This law, loosely translated as the law of nations, could be applied to anyone, as opposed to the *ius civile* or the law of Rome, which was available only to Roman citizens. Highly respected Romanists have suggested that the widespread application of the *ius gentium* was attributable to the promulgation of the *praetor's* edict for suits in which the *peregrini* were parties.[87] This suggestion is warranted because the *ius civile* was not applicable to contracts entered into with or among *peregrini* or between Romans and foreigners. This meant that many contracts among *peregrines*, such as *stipulatios*, were unenforceable, despite their popularity. Moreover, if consensuality was not extended to *peregrini*, how could the informal promises they made to Roman citizens be enforceable?

Upon the taking of office by Consul Quinto Mucio Scaevola in 95 B.C.E., civil causes of action to enforce consensual contracts became recognized. In contrast to the interpretation of the *stipulatio*, which was generally literal and strict (*strictum ius*), the interpretation of the consensual agreements guided by the *praetor peregrinus* sought to establish the real intention of the parties stressing the importance of the good faith element (*bonae fidei*). This intention was established not merely by what had been expressly provided for in the contract, but by all the circumstances and the practices of the previously mentioned archetypal contract party: the respected man of affairs (*bonus vir*).

Finally, during the first and second centuries A.D., a generalized action began to be used in addition to the civil actions available for the enforcement of formal and consensual contracts. This action was designed for contracts in which the performing party had delivered goods on a certain condition or for a certain purpose and that party either had not been paid or the condition presupposed by the delivery had not been fulfilled. This action on the *condictio* enabled the recovery or repossession of goods delivered for a special purpose (*ob causa datorum*).[88]

e. The Roman Typification of Contracts: Its Impact upon Its Own and upon Contemporary Legal Systems

With precision, Professor Gorla summarized the set of enforceable and unenforceable contracts at the end of the Justinian reign as follows:

---

[86] *See* GORLA I, at 30–31 (citing the studies of Savigny).

[87] BERGER, ENCYCLOPEDIC DICTIONARY, at 648 (citing other authorities).

[88] *See* JOHN PHILIP DAWSON, UNJUST ENRICHMENT: A COMPARATIVE ANALYSIS 45 (1969). Some of the cases involving unfulfilled conditions were related to dowries where the expected marriage did not take place, or to donations *mortis causa* where the grantor regained his health, or to the payment made to obtain the emancipation of a slave that did not occur.

> If we set aside the four consensual contracts [purchase and sale, lease, agency, and partnership, which were binding because of their widespread use] we may conclude that the Justinian phase of Roman law ended with two generic groups of binding contracts: one was the formal stipulation and the other was a contract performed by one of the parties while the counterparty promised to do so but did not. However to enforce such a promise, its monetary value had to be susceptible to be measured [*aestimatio*] so as to be able to determine the damages suffered by the victim of the breach. Side by side with these contracts, were the "real" contracts *strictu sensu* which had some features in common with the so called "innominate" [or unnamed] contracts. In contrast with these two groups of binding contracts were the informal contracts and the "naked pacts" which were not binding because there was no action to enforce them. [Among] these were: (1) the promises to lend money [even when interest was to be paid for such loans], or to lend things, to act as a depositary or bailee or to perform services [all of which were deemed gratuitous promises]; (2) the unilateral promise to sell . . . and; (3) the promise to pay for gratuitous past services.[89]

The need for contracts to be typified so that they could be enforceable discouraged reliance not only on contracts that were known to be *nuda pacta*, but also on questionable contracts as well. Conversely, the lack of a remedy to enable the enforcement of untypified contracts encouraged bad faith practices by those aware of the fact the *bona fidei* enforcement of contracts applied only to the contracts typified as consensual.

But perhaps the most damaging consequences of Roman typification were not experienced in the rather incipient Roman marketplace, but in the much more active marketplaces of some contemporary legal systems. To be sure, there were some positive aspects in contractual typification. For example, by ascribing permanent features to the typified contracts, this typification enabled an easier or more objective determination of the parties' standard or stereotypical intent, thus increasing the certainty of commercial contracts.[90] And, as just noted, in the case of consensual contracts such as sale agreements, it ushered in a *bona fidei* method of flexible and contextual interpretation that, when properly applied, made the law of contracts not only fair, but also much more predictable. Further, predictability is best attained when the applicable rules, principles, and concepts reflect the best and most respected among commercial practices. As will be apparent in another juristic opinion transcribed shortly,[91] there is an organic connection between the archetypal behavior of an exemplary merchant such as the "*bonus vir*" and a good faith interpretation of commercial contracts.

On the negative side, however, typification contributed to a legislative and judicial tendency to limit the number of commercial contracts or transactions, thereby reducing them to a closed number of transactions in a manner that conflicted with the continuous transformation of existing contracts and with the creation of new ones, a

[89] GORLA, I, at 35–36 (authors translation).

[90] GORLA I, at 30–31, citing the studies of Savigny, for a summary of the effect of typification in classical Roman law.

[91] *See infra* § 4:6 (excerpts from the *Corpus Juris Civilis* illustrating the reasoning of Roman jurists on issues of contractual formation, interpretation, and remedies).

process typical of vital market economies. Suffice it to say that to this day in many a Romanistically-influenced civil law jurisdiction, only two forms of secured lending are possible: the pledge of moveable property requiring the debtors' dispossession (echoing the Roman *pignus*) and the mortgage of real property in which the debtor can remain in possession of the land or building (*hypotheca*).[92]

Additionally, by focusing on the relations between or among the contracting parties as the holders of rights and duties, actions, and exceptions, the Roman law of contracts, with few exceptions, failed to protect the rights of third party creditors and *bona fide* purchasers of the property involved in those contracts. By failing to regulate the legal effects that contracts such as mandates had upon third parties, many of these third parties were subordinated to the rights of the agents' principal (*mandans*). His instructions to the agent (*mandatary*) were most often undisclosed and thus unknown by third parties who relied to their detriment on the agents' apparent authority to act on behalf of their principals. And as will be discussed in a later chapter,[93] the protection of the third parties' reliance on apparent representation is an indispensable feature of viable marketplaces and market economies.

f. Causa *as an Element of a Valid Contract and a Source of Its Uncertainty*

The Roman *causa* is an element of the validity of typified contracts and has also proven to be a source of uncertainty.[94] According to Gorla, the Roman law notion of *causa* was intimately connected to the type of contract involved. If the contract was "real," then the *causa* consisted of the delivery of the thing to the borrower, lessee, or bailee. This delivery prompted the express or implied promise to return the delivered *res* or its equivalent. If the contract was consensual, *causa* consisted of the performance of the typical undertakings in the most common transactions such as sales, leases, or partnerships. With respect to formal and literal obligations (*obligaciones verbis y litteris*), *causa* alluded not so much to the rationale for legal enforcement, but to the formality itself. So if a given form were used, the contract, whatever its content, was enforceable without more.

However, as also pointed out by Gorla, *causa* as a rationale for enforcing contracts in Roman law was circular. In answer to the question of why contracts with only a certain *causa* were enforceable, the reply was because the law recognizes only certain *causa* as binding.[95] It is true, Gorla notes, that in post-classical and Justinian law, the *actio prescripti verbis*[96] was recognized as a more general contractual action for any promise or bilateral agreement, particularly for atypical or innominate contracts. Nonetheless, this action was recognized only when one of the parties had performed her obligation, *i.e.*, "when she has given or made something in exchange for the promise intended to be recognized in a lawsuit."[97] This obligation to give or to make something, once performed, was the *causa data*. Accordingly, uncertainty prevailed:

---

[92] *See generally* Kozolchyk & Furnish, *A Comparative Analysis*.

[93] *See infra* 5:13(B).

[94] GORLA I, at 31. *See also infra* 22:2(B)–(C) (discussing the contemporary role of *causa* in contract formation in civil law countries).

[95] GORLA I, at 31 (summarizing the effect of typification in classical Roman law).

[96] Berger defines this phrase as: "when the foundation of an action is a bilateral transaction for reciprocal performances which do not conform to the typical and recognized species of contracts." BERGER, ENCYCLOPEDIC DICTIONARY, at 344.

[97] *Id.* at 32 (author's translation).

Until the moment of performance by one of the parties, both promises were revocable as the performance or *causa data* was a required element of formation of the contract. Despite its circularity and uncertainty, Gorla concludes that the *causa data* as a source of enforceability of innominate contracts is one of the most influential in the development of both the civil and common law of contracts.[98] While his conclusion is warranted during the early development of *causa* and consideration, a time when both doctrines seemed largely interchangeable, by the fifteenth and sixteenth centuries, consideration had become a much more commercial doctrine than *causa*.[99] The reasons for such an evolution will be discernible in the following section and more fully illustrated in later chapters. If a third party potential purchaser of a promise of payment in the form of a promissory note, bill of exchange, or government bond needs to ascertain whether the instrument was issued by mostly unknown parties as a result of a morally valid cause, he or she may well decline such a purchase.[100] The following extracts of provisions on *causa* found in the *Code Civil* and transcribed in many a civil code beyond French borders is intended as a preliminary illustration of the importance of this concept in the law of contracts of many civil law jurisdictions. A more in-depth comparison of *causa* and consideration will be undertaken later in this book.[101]

4. *Causa in French and French-Inspired Law*

Articles 1131–1133 of the *Code Civil*:

> Article 1131: An obligation without a cause, or upon a false cause, or upon an unlawful cause, can have no effect.
>
> Article 1132: The agreement is not less valid, although the cause be not expressed therein.
>
> Article 1133: The cause is unlawful when it is prohibited by the law, when it is contrary to good morals or to public order.[102]

In another writing, I commented on the moral features of *causa* in French legal decisions and doctrinal law:

> The Code [*Code Civil*] is concerned with the morality of cause in both gratuitous and onerous contracts. It defines an illicit cause which renders the obligation void as one not only prohibited by law but also contrary to "good morals" and "public order" (*ordre public*). A 1957 decision by the *Cour de cassation* illustrates the meaning of the term "good morals." A French middle-aged, middle-income father of a family, possessed of a modest estate and a lusty sexual appetite, conveyed the beneficial interest in his group life insurance policy to a recently-acquired mistress. His widow and heirs sued the mistress alleging the nullity of her designation as beneficiary. The trial and appellate courts held that there was an immoral cause in the conveyance. This finding, Professor Esmein tells us, is related to the "well-established case law in accordance with which a donation in favor of a concubine is not *per se*

---

[98] *Id.* at 32–33.

[99] *See infra* 22:4.

[100] *See infra* 11:4(F) (discussing the Rothschilds and the development of a bond market in Germany and the opinion of the English barrister).

[101] *See infra* ch. 22.

[102] C. CIV. (FR.) arts. 1131–1133.

invalid . . . as it can be valid in the case of adulterous relationships. It is null, however, for the immorality of the cause, when, appearing to be a donation, it is in reality the payment of a price to bring about or to secure the continuation of the concubinacy."

This rationale could be seen as reflecting a judicial respect only for the purest or the most virile variety of seduction, a distaste for disguised forms of prostitution (*pretium stupri*), or both. Be that as it may, the net effect of the ruling is to discourage conveyances detrimental to one's widow and heirs; for, unless the designated beneficiary could prove that she was conquered only by the grantor's unadulterated erotic powers, the illicitude of the cause would invalidate the conveyance. . . .

What is the moral or religious basis of this indignation? Demogue argued that "good customs," as the basis of the morality of the cause, should be based upon public opinion. Dean Ripert argued in favor of moral or theological foundations which one cannot fail to associate with Judeo-Christian principles of ethical behavior. And Professor Esmein posited that the morality of cause, at least when predicated on the notion of public order, is a malleable concept adaptable to the changing times and needs—a concept shaped by the judge, not by relying upon his own theology, philosophy or personal bias, but inspired by the morality of the entire corpus of law as it relates to the controversy.[103]

Other codes in civil law countries have been more explicit on the meaning of *causa*. For example, Article 1274 of the Spanish Civil Code states:

> In onerous contracts the delivery or promise to deliver a thing or services by the other party is understood as a *causa* for each contracting party; in remuneratory contracts, the services or benefits remunerated, and in those of pure beneficence, the mere liberality of the benefactor.[104]

Article 1467 of the Chilean Civil Code, after stating that pure liberality is a sufficient *causa*, gives the following definition: "By *causa* is meant the motive which induces the act or contract."[105]

Which of the above provisions is truest to its Roman origins?

§ 4.5 TOPICS FOR COMPARATIVE DISCUSSION

A. The German and German-Inspired Rejection of *Causa*

As was just discussed, following the enactment of the *Code Civil,* including articles 1131–1133 above, numerous Roman law-inspired provisions in civil law countries began to require *causa* as an essential element of enforceable contracts.

---

[103] Kozolchyk, *Commercialization*, at 7–8 (citations omitted).

[104] C.C. (SPAIN) art. 1274.

[105] C. CIV. (CHILE) art. 1467. *See also* Alejandro Guzman Brito, *Causa del Contrato y Causa de la Obligación en la Dogmática de los Juristas Romanos Medievales y Modernos y en la Codificación Europea y Americana,* 23 REVISTA DE ESTUDIOS HISTÓRICO-JURIDICOS 209 (2001) (featuring a learned analysis on the reliance on *causa* in the statutory and doctrinal law of civil law jurisdictions since Roman times).

The German Civil Code and the civil codes it inspired are notable exceptions. Why was *causa* as an element of an enforceable contract rejected by the drafters of this code? In his still-influential comparison of *causa* and consideration, Professor Lorenzen attributes the demise of *causa* in the German and German-inspired codes to the policy of freeing the contractual will from formalistic shackles:

> But the dogma of the omnipotence of the human will, the development of which was powerfully assisted by the natural law jurists, survived on the continent of Europe until the present time. . . . It is not strange, then, that the most recent civil codes—those of Brazil, Germany, Japan and Switzerland—omit all reference to the requirement of a *causa* or a consideration for the validity of contracts.[106]

B. The End of the Journey of *Nudum Pactum*?

Consider at this point the fate of the following Roman law-governed transaction: Numerio promises orally or in an informal writing to Salvio that he will sell ten silver jars on a specified date and Salvio agrees to pay him for the silver jars on that date. Numerio offers to deliver the jars to Salvio, Salvio refuses to pay for them. How binding was Salvio's promise under Roman law? How binding was it under the Common Law until Slade's case?[107] When did this type of promise become binding in civil law countries? The above-quoted article by Professor Lorenzen confirms Professor Gorla's findings:

> The abandonment of the Roman theory concerning nude pacts came only through a slow process of development. Seuffert has traced the story of this development. From his account it appears that the new doctrine did not become the prevailing view until the seventeenth century, although it was recognized before that time by eminent writers. It was finally established in the eighteenth century. The change came about in part through the influence of the canon law, which regarded the breach of a promise as a lie and therefore as a sin, the penalty for which was excommunication. The natural law jurists also contributed largely to the establishment of the new doctrine. They taught that the enforceable quality of all agreements was demanded by natural law and that the non-enforceability of pacts was a specific Roman doctrine which was opposed to natural law.[108]

Could there be factors other than canon law and natural law that contributed to the abolition of the *nudum pactum* doctrine? What about the need for commercial credit of a developing marketplace? Was Professor Gorla unnecessarily worried when he referred to the difficulties to sanction the mere promise or *nudum pactum* as the fundamental problem of the enforceable contract?[109] Was this fundamental problem strictly a legal concern, or was the problem also fundamental from a socio-economic standpoint? If it was so fundamental, how could actively trading societies subsist without resolving it? You may wish to keep this question in mind when you read about the early medieval development of a "brotherly" trade among Mediterranean Jewish

---

[106] Lorenzen, *Causa and Consideration*, at 642 (citations omitted).

[107] *See* Slade v. Morley, 76 Eng. Rep. 1074 [K.B. 1602].

[108] Lorenzen, *Causa and Consideration*, at 630–31.

[109] *See generally* GORLA I.

traders and about the late medieval development of the wool trade among Italian bankers and distributors and English producers.[110]

Consideration, Nudum Pactum *and Typification in United States Contract Law*

One of the definitions used in many United States law schools during my days as a student was the following: "Consideration is anything that amounts to an economic benefit to the promisor and a detriment to the promissee."[111] Contrast this definition with that in Section 75 of the *Restatement (Second) of Contracts*: "[*With a few exceptions*], a promise which is bargained for is consideration if, but only if, the promised performance would be consideration."[112] What does this puzzling assertion attempt to say? The comment to this section explains it as follows:

> *The executory exchange*. In modern times the enforcement of bargains is not limited to those partly completed, but is extended to the wholly executory exchange in which a promise is exchanged for promise. In such a case the element of unjust enrichment is not present; the element of reliance, if present at all, is less tangible and direct than in the case of the half-completed exchange. The promise is enforced by virtue of the fact of bargain, without more.[113]

The principle of this section is that, in determining whether there is consideration, one's word is as good as one's deed, but no better. In other words, the promisee must have a reasonable expectation that the promissor's word or deed are what he (the promisee) would deem consideration in exchange for his promise or counter-performance. More detailed rules are stated in sections 76–78 of the Restatement for cases in which the application of this principle has produced problems.[114] Certain cases which have sometimes been thought to be exceptions to this principle are commented upon below.

The following scenarios illustrate the exception to this rule, as well as the principle that the word is as good as the deed but no better:

> "A" promises to pay a debt to "B," or to perform an existing contractual duty to B, or to perform his duty as a public official. The legal duty is neither doubtful nor the subject of an honest dispute, but A would not have fulfilled the duty but for B's return promise. A's promise is not consideration for B's return promise.
>
> A promises B to surrender or to forbear suit upon a claim either against B or against "C." A knows the claim is invalid. A's promise is not consideration for a return promise by B.

The reader should notice that what the Restatement does in these illustrations is not very different from what the Roman jurists will do in their opinions transcribed shortly. It does not identify the "essence" of consideration; rather, it answers a

---

110 *See infra* § 5:9.

111 Currie v. Misa, (1875) LR 10 Exch. 163, *cited in* Lorenzen, *Causa and Consideration,* at 636.

112 RESTATEMENT (SECOND) OF CONTRACTS § 75 (1981).

113 *Id.* cmt. a.

114 *Id.* §§ 76–78.

remedial question: Is someone who promises to pay a pre-existing debt to the other contracting party providing consideration for a new contract so as to be able to sue the other party on it? The answer is in the negative. Thus, the rule referred to by the Restatement as one of the exceptions to the principle that a "promise for a promise" is sufficient consideration is indeed that—an exception. The inclusion of possible exceptions to the reach of a general rule in the formulation of such a rule is a trait found both in Roman law juristic opinions and in the drafting of general rules by Anglo-American jurists. I refer to this trait in this book as the "casuistic" method of legislative and contract drafting.[115] Would the above rules apply to a contract that has an otherwise valid *causa* as defined in Articles 1131–1133 of the *Code Civil*? If not, why not? What influence would the typification of contracts have upon the issues dealt with by the examples in the Restatement?

§ 4.6 ROMAN LEGAL OPINIONS ON TYPES AND INTERPRETATION OF CONTRACTS: THE *BONUS VIR*

The following excerpts from the *Corpus Juris Civilis* illustrate the reasoning of Roman jurists on issues of contractual formation, interpretation and remedies.

A. Barter and Sale: And a Firm Grasp of Transactional Facts

> ***Text:*** PAUL, *Edict, book 33*: All buying and selling had its origins in permutations or exchanges because in ancient times there was no currency as we now have, nor was there a thing named merchandise and another named price; instead, each man exchanged based on the needs of the times [*necessitatem temporum*], because as it frequently happens what one has in excess the other lacks. . . . But since it did not always happen that when you had something which I wanted, I had something that you were willing to receive, a material was selected [*electa materia est*] whose public and perpetual estimation, based on the equal value of the same amount [for both sides] overcame the difficulties with permutations. And this material coined by the mint gives use and ownership [of it] not so much because of the value of its substance or material but because of its amount. And thereafter the things exchanged are not called merchandise but one of them is called the price. But it is doubtful that one can say today that a sale has taken place without the giving of money [for the merchandise] exists. . . .
>
> Thus in the permutation one cannot discern who is the seller and who is the buyer [*Quod in permuatione discerni non potest uter emptor uter venditor sit (est)*].
>
> § 2.—Further, the sale belongs to the law of nations [*iuris gentium*] and thus it is perfected by the mere consent of the parties, it may be entered into *inter absentes*, by messenger and letters.[116]

Notice Paul's grasp of the transactional facts, including the origin and purpose of sale agreements as the main successors to pure barter transactions and of money as a

[115] *See infra* § 5:8.

[116] CUERPO DEL DERECHO CIVIL ROMANO PRIMERA PARTE INSTITUTA.—DIGESTO 18.1.1 (D. Ildefonso L. García del Corral trans., Jaime Molinas ed., 1889), *available at* http://www.bibliojuridica.org/libros/libro.htm?l=600 [hereinafter CUERPO DEL DERECHO CIVIL ROMANO] (translated by author) (emphasis added).

measure of the value and price of what was being sold. Revisiting the "dense relationships" discussed in Chapter 3, could the reciprocal performances described by Paul be part of the "dense relationships" of pre-commercial societies that he characterized as barters? What is the role of negotiation in barter and in dense relationships? Does the concept of transactional balance in the dense relations of the pre-commercial societies fit with the barter in Paul's model? Why is Paul so interested in distinguishing between barter and sale? Does that distinction have any bearing on the determination of the available cause of action to the victim of a defendant's breach?

In contrast with the barter (*permutatio*), which did not attract much Roman juristic attention, sale agreements did. A sale agreement (known as *emptio venditio* for procedural matters) was divided into the phases of buying (*emere*) by the buyer (*emptor*) and the sale (*vendere*) by the seller (*venditor*). Once both parties reached an agreement on the price (*pretium*), their simple consent made it binding to them. But, as pointed out by Adolf Berger, the sale by itself did not transfer the ownership of the object being sold; this transfer occurred through additional juridical acts or transactions such as the *mancipatio*, the *in iure cession*, or the *traditio*.[117] The obligation of the seller consisted of transferring the possession of the sold goods for its peaceful use by the buyer (*ut rem emptori habere* liceat). Some codes such as the Argentinean Civil Code have retained the requirement of a delivery of the thing for the sale (*traditio*) to be fully executed. Thus, Article 577 of the Argentine Civil Code provides that: "Before delivery (*traditio*) of the thing, the creditor does not acquire over it any right *in rem*."[118]

How is this requirement consistent with Paul's characterization of the sale as a contract of the law of nations and so is concluded by mere agreement, by distant parties through messengers, or by correspondence, and consistent is it with the *Code Civil* provision on contracts by distant parties? Are there such provisions in the *Code Civ*il, and it not why not?[119]

The actions corresponding to the breach of a sale agreement were the *actio venditi* by the seller against the buyer for the payment of the agreed price and the *actio empti* by the buyer against the seller if the latter did not comply with certain obligations such as the delivery of the sold object or its custody from the conclusion of the contract until its delivery.[120] The seller was responsible for the loss of possession by the buyer at the hands of third parties (*evictio*) as well as for the hidden defects. Because it is an action of good faith (*bona fidei actio*), the *actio empti* allowed the *iudex* to take into account defects fraudulently hidden by the seller.[121]

The Roman rule that required other acts such as a *mancipatio*, *in iure cessio* or *traditio* for the sale to be concluded and ownership to be transferred to the buyer could be criticized from a point of view of procedural and transactional economy. Why add expensive and meaningless formalities or why provide the prerequisites for various legal actions, when only one could satisfy the remedial need? On the other hand, how common was the sale agreement involved in the *mancipatio*? Or even more to the

---

117 BERGER, ENCYCLOPEDIC DICTIONARY, at 452.

118 C. CIV. (ARG.) art. 577.

119 *See infra* § 8:7(G).

120 BERGER, ENCYCLOPEDIC DICTIONARY, at 452.

121 *Id.* at 453.

point, how common did the Roman adjudicator want the sale of the *res mancipi* to be? As discussed earlier,[122] the formalities in the sale of the *res mancipi* (such as involved in a *mancipatio*) were the product of an ancient policy that restricted as much as possible the sale of goods of high value to the survival of the family. It was not designed for everyday commercial transactions.

On the other hand, the Roman rule which established that a sale, until concluded by a specified formality, transfers the peaceful possession of what was bought has proven useful in the context of contemporary secured transactions law. All that this law requires from a debtor who is about to create a security interest is that he has possessory rights in the collateral and not necessarily ownership of it.[123]

B. Price as an Essential Element

Text: ULPIAN, *Sabinus, book 1:*

. . .

Without a price, there is no sale; however, it is not the payment of the price, but the agreement to pay it that perfects a sale made without a writing [*sine pretio nulla venditio est, non nutem pretii numeratio, sed conventio perfeti sine seriptis habitam emtionem*].[124]

What is the significance of Ulpian's distinction between the necessity of a price and the informality of the sale? Is the price a merely evidentiary requisite (*ad probationem*) or is it a requisite without which there is no contract because of its essential solemnity (*ad solemnitatem*)? Further, is the written form a requisite *ad probationem* or is it *ad solemnitatem*? Would the jurists' characterization of the sale agreement as consensual and *bona fides* support the conclusion that mere agreement on the price and thing sold suffice to enforce a sale agreement in classical Roman law?

C. Discretionary Conditions and the *Bonus Vir* Standard

Text: ULPIAN, *Sabinus, book 28:* The sale of a slave conditioned to his having settled his accounts to his master's [*domini*] discretion [*compatasset arbitrio*] . . . become perfect only when the condition is implemented [*quum impleta fuerit condition*]. [Yet] is this condition implemented by the master's personal discretion [*arbitrio*] or by the discretion of an honorable man [*bonus vir*]? For, if we interpret it as the master's discretion, the sale with such a condition is null because it would be the same case in which someone promised to sell "if he wanted" [*si voluerit*]. . . . [For] it cannot be left to the decision of the obligor [*arbitrium rei*] whether he is obligated or not. Accordingly, it was thought proper by earlier jurists that the obligor's discretion be understood to be that of honorable men [*viri boni*] and not that of the obligor himself.[125]

Would a *bonus vir* be required to disclose to his potential buyer that another seller might be able to give that buyer a better deal than he is prepared to give?[126] Levin

---

122 *See supra* § 3:6(B).

123 *See generally* Kozolchyk & Wilson, *The New Model Inter-American Law*.

124 CUERPO DEL DERECHO CIVIL ROMANO, *supra note* 116, 18.1.2 (translated by author).

125 CUERPO DEL DERECHO CIVIL ROMANO, *supra note* 116, 18.1.7 (translated by author).

126 *See* Kozolchyk, *Commercialization,* at 11.

Goldschmidt, one of the most influential historians of commercial law, referred to the *bonus vir* as a signal contribution of Greco-Roman culture to Western civilization. It was a figure, he said, equidistant from unmitigated greed and from Franciscan selflessness. Would the above disclosure be a case of Franciscan selflessness?[127]

D. The Present and Future *Res* as an Element of the Contract of Sale

> ***Text:*** POMPONIUS, *Sabinus, book 9:* One cannot refer to a sale or purchase without referring to the thing sold. Nevertheless, future produce and offspring are validly purchased and sold so that when the offspring is born, the sale is regarded as complete from the time of the agreement. But if the vendor prevents the birth [of the offspring] or the growing of the produce, he will be liable to the action on purchase [*ex emto aggi posse*].
>
> § 1.—At times even without a thing being in existence a sale is valid as where what is bought is left, as it were, to chance [*quasi ale emitur*]. This is what happens in the purchase of a [future] catch of birds or of fish. . . .[128]

What is the legal source relied on by Pomponius to argue that the vendor is liable to the action on purchase if he takes steps to prevent the birth of animals or the growing of produce? Is it the law of contracts or the law of torts, or is it a possible combination thereof? How about the doctrine of good faith discussed in Chapter 23? How economically and commercially significant is the "aleatory" *quasi ale emitur* (risk assuming contract) referred to by Pomponius? The next time you visit Chicago, you may wish to tour its Mercantile Exchange and acquaint yourself with the significance of its futures transactions.[129]

E. Interpretation: Types of Mistakes

> ***Texts:*** ULPIAN, *Sabinus, book 28:*
>
> § 2.—The next question is whether the mistake was not over the identity of the thing but over its substance [*substantia error sit*], as when vinegar is sold as wine, copper as gold or lead. . . . Marcellus, in the sixth book of the *Digest*, wrote that there is a sale because there is agreement on the thing despite the mistake over its substance. I certainly would agree in the case of the wine, because it is almost the same substance, that is, the wine has soured; however, if it was vinegar from the beginning such as brewed vinegar, then it is deemed that one thing was sold for another, at one thing has been sold as another. . . .[130]
>
> ULPIAN, *Sabinus, book 28*: On the other hand, what if the purchaser were blind or he made a mistake over the subject matter [*materia erratar*] or the

---

[127] *See* WATSON, DIGEST, 18.1.21 (describing why a certain type of obscurity in the terms of an agreement favors the buyer).

[128] CUERPO DEL DERECHO CIVIL ROMANO, *supra note* 116, 18.1.8 (translated by author).

[129] Meanwhile, it may be worthwhile to visit its website: CME GROUP, http://www.cmegroup.com/ (last visited Jan. 3, 2014).

[130] CUERPO DEL DERECHO CIVIL ROMANO, *supra note* 116, 18.1.9 (translated by author) (emphasis added).

mistake was made by an unskilled buyer? Do we say that the parties are agreed on the thing? How can a man agree who cannot see it?

§ 1.—However, if I think that I am buying a virgin when she is, in fact, a [mature] woman [*illam muller*], the sale is valid [*emptio valebit*], there being no mistake over her sex.[131]

What is the difference between an object's substance and its identity? To what extent has the distinction between the substance and the identity of the contract's object been retained in our day? What type of judicial reasoning was used by the above opinions? Is it an *a priori* reasoning that relies on the Aristotelian doctrine of the essence of things, *i.e.*, what universally and permanently characterizes the being of a thing such as wine, gold or sex of the slaves? Or, is it an *a posteriori* reasoning, derived from the observations of the reasonable expectations of buyers of wine, gold or slaves in the Roman market? An illustration of the bad faith exploitation of the a *priori* reasoning in Mexican contractual case law is found in the decision of *Amparo de Teofila Astorga Vda. De Aceves*.[132]

F. Sales by a Non Owner

Texts:

PAUL, *Sabinus*, *book 8*: He who purchases a thing from anyone and believes that it was owned by his seller purchases in good faith [*bona fide emit*]; however a purchase from a pupil [*a pupillo emit*] without the authorization of the pupil's tutor, or with an authorization by a tutor known to the buyer to be not the true tutor is not considered a good faith purchase.[133]

ULPIAN, *Commentaries to Sabinus book 41*: There is no doubt that anyone can sell something that does not belong to him, because there is a purchase and a sale, but the thing sold may be taken [meaning recovered] from the buyer [*sed res emteri auferri potest*].[134]

These two opinions are of considerable significance in the development of the modern commercial law of sales and secured transactions. Can you see why? Implicit in Paul's opinion is the purchaser's right to retain what he purchased in good faith. Also implicit is the connection between ostensible appearances of authorization to sell or pledge and good faith. The purchase from a pupil lacks the ostensible appearance of an authorization or capacity to sell and thus is not in good faith.[135] Ulpian's opinion is as usual wise and influential. He perceived that sales by a non-owner as inevitable, even in a commercial marketplace as incipient as Rome's. In addition, he added that "the thing purchased can be taken from him" (*sed res emteri auferri potest),* which I have re-translated as "recovered from him" to better convey the spirit of his opinion. This was a reminder of the purchaser's relative title to things such as moveable property. It was a wiser opinion than that held by jurists who did not distinguish between something that was stolen and *embezzled* (by someone with authority to resell or pledge), and thus also

---

[131] *Id.* 18.1.11 (translated by author).

[132] Teofila Astorga Vda. De Aceves, Amparo Civil Directo, 125 SJF5a 193 (1955); *see also infra* § 23:9(D).

[133] CUERPO DEL DERECHO CIVIL ROMANO, *supra note* 116, 19.1.8 (translated by author).

[134] *Id.* 18.1.28 (translated by author).

[135] *See infra* § 5:13(B).

believed that the owner could always replevy what his agent sold or pledged against his will.[136] For as also opined by Paul, the ostensible authority or appearance of authority vested by the owner upon the embezzler-seller mattered when disallowing the owner's recovery from a third party purchaser in good faith.

G. Remedies for the Breach of a Sale Agreement

Texts:

Ulpian. *Commentaries to the Edict book 32*: The one who purchases uses the *Ex emto actione.*

§ 1.—[W]hat is adjudicated in this trial [*in hoc judicio*] is whether what was agreed was delivered. Because this is a good faith type adjudication, [and] there is nothing more consistent with good faith than the contracting parties performing what they promised they would [*quam id praestari, quod inter contrahentes actum est*]. But if nothing was agreed about the expected performances, they will be those that are naturally part of this contract.

§ 2.—In the first place, the seller must deliver the same thing [he promised], which, if he was the owner of it will make his buyer a similar owner, and if he was not the owner he will be obligated for the [consequences] of the eviction [or loss of possession of the object sold] [*tantum evictionis nomine venditorem obligat*] if a price was paid or if a bond was provided by the buyer in lieu of the payment of the price.

§ 3.—Labeo and Sabinus opine that *redhibition* [restitution for the damages caused by the hidden defects] is also covered by the action on purchase, and I agree.

§ 4.—The seller of animals must also provide a warranty that they were delivered in a healthy condition [*sana praestari*]. And the seller of beasts of burden usually promises that they feed and drink properly [*esse bibere ut oportet*].

§ 5.—If someone thought he was buying a virgin when in fact a mature woman was sold, and the seller knowing of his buyer's mistake let him persist in it, an action for breach of warranty for latent defects [*redhibitio*] is not justified but an action on the purchase is proper and the purchase will be resolved [terminated] [*ex emto competere actionem ad resolvendam acionem*] and once the price paid was returned to the buyer, he will return he woman [*ut pretio restituto muller reddatur*].

§ 6.—A purchaser of wine gave the seller an earnest money payment [*arrhae*]; subsequently the parties agreed to render the purchase and sale null and void. Julian says that there can be an action on the purchase [*ex emto agi*] to force the return of the earnest money, he also opines that this action is available for dissolving the sale. My question is: If a ring was given as earnest money and the ring was not returned after the sale was executed, including

---

[136] *See* Boris Kozolchyk, *Transfer of Personal Property by a Non Owner*, 61 TUL. L. REV. 1453, 1467 (1987). On the importance of the principle that a secured debtor need not be the owner or have title to the collateral in secured transactions law, see U.C.C. § 9–202 (2013) and *supra* § 3:8(C) (Principle 2 of NLCIFT's Twelve Principles of Secured Transactions Law).

the payment of the price, what should be the action to recover the ring? Should a *condictio* action be brought based on the fact that the cause for the delivery of the ring to the seller no longer existed id [*quasi ob causum data sit*]. Julian would likewise say there can be an action on the purchase and a *condictio* action could also be tried because there was no cause for the ring to remain with the seller.[137]

Ulpian, *Commentaries to Sabinus book 28*: If the thing sold is not delivered, an action lies for what the interest that the buyer has in receiving the thing [*quod rem habere interest emtoris*], but this interest at times exceeds the price of the thing, for it may mean more to the buyer than its price. . . .

§ 1.—If, the seller knowing that the sold land had an easement, hid such a fact from the buyer, he will not be able to evade the buyer's action [*non evadet ex emto actionem*] because all acts against good faith are part of that action. . . . And even if he worded his promise as follows: "Certainly nothing is owed as an easement, but I am not liable even if such an unimagined obligation appears" my opinion is that the seller is still liable on the buyer's action because the easement obligation did exist. . . .[138]

COMMENTS AND QUESTIONS

Did you detect in Ulpian's *Commentaries to Sabinus book 28* and in his Commentaries *to the Edict book 32* a doctrine of reasonable expectations to measure the recovery by an aggrieved party whose "interest" in the thing its price? Notice also that much like Professor Karl Llewellyn in U.C.C. Article 2 provisions on courses of dealing and usages of trade, Ulpian, in the absence of contractual express terms, relied on performances that were "naturally part of the contract" in question to discern the parties' intent.[139] What is the difference between an action based on the sale agreement "*ex emto*" and an action based on the failure of a *condictio*? What did the plaintiffs in these to actions have to prove to the *iudex*? What would be difference between an action on an "express warranty" under U.C.C. § 2–313, or an "implied warranty" under U.C.C. § 2–314 and 2–315 and one based on a *redhibitio?* Adolf Berger's Encyclopedic Dictionary of Roman Law defines *redhibition* as: "The restitution of a purchased thing . . . to the seller because of its essential defects, while the seller returned the price to the buyer. Such rescission of a sale was obtained by the buyer under the *actio redhibitoria*. . . ."[140] Yet, Berger's list of the elements of this *actio* may have missed an important element of this action where the alleged defect was concerned especially as the redhibition action is interpreted in *Code Civil* jurisdictions such as France and Spain. I suggest that you take a look at *infra* § 30:2(E) and try to identify the nature of the actionable defect in the *actio redhibitoria,* and in the U.C.C. actions for breach of warranty of merchantability and fitness for agreed purpose.

Once again the concept of good faith (*bona fide*) appears in Ulpian's *Commentaries to the Edict book 32* in relation to the *Ex emto actio*. Is Ulpian's version of contractual good faith a subjective (honesty in fact) or an objective (usage of trade) standard? These two standards of good faith are commonly used in U.S. commercial contract law. As just noted, one requires that the party not be dishonest and thus is known as the

---

137 CUERPO DEL DERECHO CIVIL ROMANO, *supra note* 116, 19.1.11 (translated by author) (emphasis added).

138 *Id.* 19.1.1 (translated by author).

139 *See infra* § 23:5(A).

140 BERGER, ENCYCLOPEDIC DICTIONARY, at 670; *see also infra* § 30:2(E).

standard of "honesty in fact."[141] The other standard requires that the party not be dishonest, but in addition it requires the party to act in a way consistent with that of a reasonable trader who knows his occupation.[142] Some U.S. jurists make reference to the first category as a person of good heart but without having to behave in a manner that reflects reasonable trade or professional practices. The second is referred to as a person of good heart but evidencing a behavior consistent with reasonable trade or professional practices. Which of these two standards is the prevalent one in the reader's jurisdiction or country? You may wish to peruse through Chapter 23 to obtain an idea of how significant is the concept or doctrine of good faith in today's commercial world.

§ 4.7 CONCLUSIONS: ONCE MORE—WHY STUDY ROMAN LAW?

It should be clear by now that a contemporary commercial lawyer is likely to improve his understanding of his own law as well as that of the countries his clients trade with or invest in if he understands the roots of the respective legal institutions. These roots and their legal alphabet are not mere artifacts of interest to antiquarians; they embody the socio-economic purpose of legal institutions, however enriched or transformed by the passing of time. Even if the practices of the parties governed by such an institution today are significantly different from those engaged in by the Romans and their peregrine trading partners, a kernel of normative purpose always remains. This kernel may be a right or duty that is forever identified with the institution, or a remedy that is still being invoked.

Beyond the benefit of a better understanding of our own law lies the benefit of understanding why Roman law has been so influential and how it facilitates better lawmaking. The Roman jurists were the first keen measurers of rights, duties and their incorporation into remedies. They relied on the logic of analogy, of geometrically-inspired maxims and on the flexible standards of archetypal behavior, such as that of the *bonus vir*. But above all, they relied on a firm grasp of the operative or transactional facts. Their decision-making process shows them to have been firm believers in one of Justice Brandeis' favorite maxims: "*Ex Factum, Ius Oritur.*" Armed with a firm grasp of the facts of the transaction and the dispute it prompted, they ascertained who had which right, what wasits correlative duty and what were the most appropriate remedies. Indeed, one must look very hard into the classical Roman law panoply of contractual rights to find one without a corresponding remedy. Consider, for example, the spectrum of remedies available to an aggrieved buyer in the seller's breach of an everyday sale agreement in Ulpian's *Commentaries to the Edict book 32.* Each of the remedies it summarizes sprung from a sharply delineated set of facts. This is why the *Corpus Juris Civilis* was the main inspiration for what the nineteenth century German Pandectists and their numerous disciples throughout the civil law world proudly referred to as *the* legal science. Hence, only by understanding the Roman legal accomplishments and their limitations will we be able to improve upon the legal science they inspired.

---

141 *See, e.g.,* U.C.C. § 5–102(a)(7) (documentary credit standard).

142 U.C.C. § 2–103(1)(j) (applicable to a sale).

Part II

MEDIEVAL LAW: GUILDS, AGENTS AND NOTARIES.

Chapter 5

MEDIEVAL LAW

§ 5.1 INTRODUCTION: MEDIEVAL LAW AND THE INSTITUTIONALIZATION OF COMMERCIAL TRUST

The timeframe most commonly associated with the Middle Ages starts with the fifth and ends with the fifteenth centuries C.E. From the standpoint of the development of commercial legal institutions, the Middle Ages are a particularly important period. Many of these institutions were imported from Roman law through its mostly Italian "glossators" and (later "commentators"), but these had to be adjusted to the conditions of a resurgent trade after the eleventh century. The trial and error process that these institutions underwent, especially in the Late Middle Ages, prepared them for future use, particularly in continental Europe, and in that respect were their "incubators." The medieval fairs discussed in later chapters[1] also acted as incubators not only of their own legal institutions, but to institutions we use to this day such as bills of exchange and "futures" contracts and their "clearing" mechanisms. In addition, some of the fairs also implemented the principle of the "peace of the marketplace" or equality of treatment of foreign and national merchants, a principle responsible for the resurgence of international trade not only in the Middle Ages, but also after the Second World War when the General Agreement on Tariffs and Trade (GATT) was enacted following centuries of unrestricted mercantilism.[2] An additional incubator of viable business practices was developed during this period, especially from the ninth to the thirteenth centuries, in Mediterranean trade. It helped shape the law and practice of partnerships, joint ventures, secured and unsecured loan agreements, and payment instruments of our day.

Similarly, "double-entry" bookkeeping was developed during the middle of this period.[3] It allowed owners, partners, joint venturers, and third party creditors to ascertain the financial condition of a business by checking how the summary results of transactions had been entered as debits and credits in at least two sets of corresponding accounts: The total of debits had to equal that of credits. This practice made it easier to track the flow of money and the value of goods bought, borrowed, exchanged, sold, manufactured or stored, thereby increasing confidence and cooperation among partners and joint venturers as well as debtors and creditors. Together with the formalization of contracts by the use of notary publics as scriveners (also developed during this period),[4] double-entry bookkeeping provided documentary evidence theretofore unavailable on contractual intent and performance. In sum, all of

---

[1] *See infra* §§ 9:1 & 9:2.

[2] *See* Kozolchyk, *Grand and Small Scheme*, at 137.

[3] *See generally* ALFRED W. CROSBY, THE MEASURE OF REALITY: QUANTIFICATION AND WESTERN SOCIETY, 1250–1600 (1997) (discussing the influence of double-entry bookkeeping upon the commerce of Western societies).

[4] Because of the importance of the notary public in commercial contracts in civil law countries, I have devoted Chapter 7 to the Latin notariat.

these practices contributed to the institutionalization of trust among certain groups of medieval merchants, especially those involved in international trade.

On the other hand, it must be remembered that the medieval period was largely dominated by feudalism. This was a social scheme whose basic tenets discouraged commerce by making the entitlement to land, goods and services depend not on contracts, but on the hierarchical "status" of the claimant. One need only contrast the *unenforceability* of an executory promise made by an "*infanzon*" (a hierarchically superior person in the feudal scheme of the Spanish province of Navarra) with the *enforceability* of an executory promise made by a "*villano*" (his feudal inferior)[5] to realize how seriously feudalism impeded the enforcement of commercial contracts. Similarly, the prevailing medieval definition of usury, which deemed sinful and illegal any rate of interest, however small or comparable to that of the marketplace, prevented the proliferation of agreements to invest, joint venture, sell, or lend. Accordingly, during much of this period, these contracts were confined to certain regions where trade and investment were overtly allowed or where the ruling powers for utilitarian reasons looked the other way.

The reader should not be surprised if, as recently as the twentieth century, norms and attitudes on usury and formalities of commercial contracts closely resembling those of the Middle Ages reappeared in different locations and under different political auspices and social schemes.[6] It may well be, then, that a contracting party's status as a measure of his entitlement to goods and services is a more permanent fixture in man's societal arrangements than Sir Henry Maine was inclined to believe.[7]

A better appreciation of the impact of economic and political forces contrary to the modern law of commercial contracts would be a good reason to learn more about medieval law. In addition, the method of reasoning employed by medieval theologians and jurists deeply influenced the drafting of the first and most influential codes of the nineteenth and twentieth centuries in the civil law world. Our understanding of how Aristotle- and Thomas Aquinas- inspired definitions and classifications of contracts, as discussed in Chapter 2,[8] were used by the drafters of the *Code Civil*, the Spanish Civil Code of 1889, will improve our interpretation of these seminal sources.

Finally, we will focus on one of the less-known contributions of medieval law and commercial practice to the enforcement of executory promises, including those involved in sales, investments, and extensions of credit agreements. This contribution is found in the customs and practices of medieval Mediterranean Arab and Jewish traders and in the Rabbinic *responsa* to disputes prompted by these practices. These customs and practices and the *responsa* helped define the rights and obligations of one set of "religious brethren" when performing contractual and quasi-contractual duties for principals who could be employers or, more frequently, investors, partners or joint venturers. As will be discussed in a later section,[9] this definition brought about a

---

[5] *See infra* § 5:3.

[6] *See infra* § 18:1(B)(1)(a) (on Chinese conditional sales); *infra* § 14:4(A)(3)(c)(i) (on Latin American simulation); and § 15:4(D)(5) (on Soviet era simulations).

[7] *See supra* § 3:3.

[8] *See supra* § 2:2(A)(4).

[9] *See infra* § 5:9(A).

standard of commercial fairness that continues to govern commercial contracts of present-day commercial brethren throughout the trading world.

§ 5.2 CONTRACT AS DELICT, UNJUST ENRICHMENT AND RITUAL IN SOME SOUTHERN EUROPEAN COUNTRIES

Professor Gino Gorla examined the law of southern European countries after the fall of Rome until approximately the eleventh century and found that during this period, the responsibility of a defaulting promisor was based more on tort or delict than on breach of contract.[10] As will be discussed in connection with the formation of contracts in the common law and especially with the development of the concept of consideration, similar rationales supported the contractually-based actions on debt and *detinue* before common law courts.[11] Causes of action based upon a promisor's unjust enrichment at the expense of the promisee were also known in those jurisdictions, particularly when the enrichment resulted from a failure to reciprocate what had been received. The same was true with actions for fraud or deceit because of non-performance. Similarly, formal promises were enforceable not because of what the parties stated as their obligations, but because of their ritual or solemnity or magical or mystical value.[12]

By the eleventh century, the law of some of the Italian provinces started recognizing the notion that an obligation can indeed be derived from a contractual promise, but such a promise could only be enforced when it was preceded by the giving of something, as had been the case with the Roman "real" contracts of loans and bailments.[13] Thus, contractual liability depended upon an unfulfilled exchange where one party had supplied goods or services and the other had not paid for them or failed to reciprocate in kind, a requirement known in medieval Italian law as *"res vel factum."*[14] The need for a *res vel factum, i.e.*, a contractual performance in the broadest meaning of the term, was thus recognized as an element of the formation of the contract. If this element was not present, the promise was revocable. This restriction meant that executory promises or simple promises to perform in the future, even if associated with the four typical-consensual contracts of Roman law (a promise to sell, to hire, to enter into partnership or agency, or not) were not enforced during this period in the Southern European jurisdictions examined by Professor Gorla, and it would take a considerable amount of time before these Roman consensual contracts were enforced in these medieval jurisdictions.[15]

The requirement of an exchange of performances was so deeply rooted in medieval law that a promise to make a donation was only recognized when there was a counter-performance (*Launegild o widerdonum*). The counter-performance could be of symbolic value, like a glove, hat, cap, etc. Meanwhile, the payment of money or something of value as earnest money (*arrhas*) became a method of contracting, although each payment presupposed that performance or part performance was still pending. Finally, penalty clauses played an increasingly important role as remedies for non-performance

---

[10] GORLA I, at 44–45.

[11] *See infra* § 22:4(D).

[12] GORLA I, at 45.

[13] *Id. See also supra* § 4:4(D)(3)(a).

[14] GORLA I, at 45.

[15] *Id.*

in lieu of court-declared damages. This system of contractual sanctions was important also in view of the difficulties—then insurmountable—of a poorly operating judicial system and confusion between the powers and remedies of public and private entities.[16]

§ 5.3 SPAIN'S FORAL LAW

Generally, medieval Spanish law did not enforce promises based upon the mere consent of the parties. As pointed out by Gorla, early medieval Spanish law predominantly enforced obligations derived from tort (*civil delict*) or from contracts whose enforcement required the delivery of the thing (*res*) after having received something of value from the plaintiff-promisee. It will be recalled that these contracts were known as "real" in their Roman law days. Thus, the reader should not be surprised to find that a similar basis for the enforcement of contractual and contractual-tortious liability was relied upon by the English judges until the action of *assumpsit* was developed during the Later Middle Ages.[17]

In addition, contracts lacking an accepted form were enforced in the Southern European countries if *arrhas* had been given by a promisee or if they were concluded after carrying out the ritual of a public handshake (*palmate*). Still, no civil actions existed for non-performance of an executory promise. Criminal actions could be found where the state prosecuted the defaulting debtor and collected and kept the fines imposed upon the debtor. The aggrieved creditor did not benefit from these state proceedings. A creditor's claim could be collected only by means of a cumbersome attachment procedure known as *wadiatio.*[18]

Much of the substantive law of contracts in Spanish medieval law is found in the provincial or "foral" law.[19] As summarized by Professor Ferrandis Villela's comments to Gorla's description of Southern European law, the foral rules varied from province to province but some, such as those in the *Fuero de Navarra,* clearly illustrated the role of feudalism and class distinction in the enforcement of contractual promises.

> *Fuero de Navarra* (undated, assumed to be 12th century): As a general principle, informal promises are unenforceable for unilateral and bilateral contracts . . . but this principle can only be invoked, as a defense and privilege, by noblemen of German ancestry (*infanzones).* In contrast, the lower class residents of Navarra (referred to as *villanos)* were bound by the mere utterance of their promises: *"mas si villano es et promete, deve dar"* (but if he is a resident of the village and he promises, then he must give).[20]
>
> *Fuero de Soria* (undated, assumed to be 12th century): No formal requisites or penalty clauses are required for the enforceability of contracts. Nonetheless, the validity of certain contracts like a sale requires the delivery of *arrhas* or of a token thing or amount.[21]

---

[16] *Id.*

[17] *See infra* § 20:4(B).

[18] GORLA I, at 53–55.

[19] *See* Glossary, "Foral Law."

[20] GORLA I, at 54; Fuero de Navarra, III, 19, 6.

[21] GORLA I, at 54.

> *Fuero Real* (1254 A.D.): Agreements are enforceable whether in writing or not, even when there was no penalty agreed. . . . Nonetheless, the *Fuero* itself allows the parties to unmake the sale before partial or complete payment of the price.[22]

Why was the defense of failure of a necessary formality a "privilege" of the aristocracy and not one available to all contracting parties, including the *villanos*? Does this privilege imply that there were two sets of laws, one applicable to *infanzones* and another to *villanos*? How broad was this class of citizens or residents? Were these *villanos* all the inhabitants of a city (*villa*) much like the central European "burghers," or were they only those inhabitants engaged in trade?[23]

§ 5.4 MEDIEVAL EUROPEAN CITIES AND THEIR "PICARESQUE" MERCHANTS

From the tenth to the fourteenth centuries, many central and northern European cities began an evolution from rural ecclesiastical enclaves or "episcopal cities" to urban centers of professional or commercial trade. Henri Pirenne, the renowned Belgian historian of medieval Europe, described the ninth-century ecclesiastical enclave as having, at most, a small local market that provided for the daily needs of the numerous clergy and their employee serfs.[24] These episcopal cities lived off the surrounding country's rents and dues, as did the fortified castles built by feudal princes to protect their manors from periodic enemy invasions. The castles, referred to as "bourgs" or "burgs," were usually composed of a rampart of earth or stones, surrounded by a moat and pierced with gates.[25] Inside lived the defenders, including the feudal lord and the assigned clergy.

Commerce revived during the second half of the tenth century, and Pirenne attributed this revival to the emergence of a class of free merchants and artisans "from among the landless men, who lived . . . on the margin of a society where land alone was the basis of existence."[26] Many of these men were forced to leave their families simply to lighten the burden of feudal repayment of dues or charges. These men swelled the crowd of vagabonds who roamed through the country, going from abbey to abbey taking their share of alms reserved for the poor, hiring themselves out to the peasants at harvest time or at the vintage, and enlisting as mercenaries in the feudal troops in times of war. According to Pirenne, they were quick to profit from the arrival of ships and merchants along the coasts and in the river estuaries by reselling what they had bought or selling what they had stolen.[27] Many of the more adventurous hired themselves to the Venetian and Scandinavian boats as sailors; others joined the merchant caravans which made their way to the incipient trading ports.

The story of St. Godric of Finchale, an early English merchant, is illustrative of the last resort and archetypally picaresque nature of commerce described by Pirenne

---

[22] *Id.*

[23] For a particularly enlightening view of feudal society and the role trade or the lack of it played in it, see MARK BLOCH, I FEUDAL SOCIETY: THE GROWTH OF TIES OF DEPENDENCE (1989); Mark II FEUDAL SOCIETY: SOCIAL CLASSES AND POLITICAL ORGANIZATION (1989).

[24] HENRI PIRENNE, ECONOMIC AND SOCIAL HISTORY OF MEDIEVAL EUROPE 40 (I. E. Clegg trans., 1956).

[25] *Id.* at 41.

[26] *Id.* at 45.

[27] *Id.*

as prevalent during this period. He was born at the end of the eleventh century in Lincolnshire of a poor peasant family:

> [H]e was a beachcomber, on the lookout for wreckage cast up by the waves. Next, perhaps following some lucky find, he played the role of peddler and went about the country with a pack on his back. Eventually he accumulated a little capital and, one fine day, he joined a band of merchants met in the course of his peregrinations. With them he went from market to market, from fair to fair, from town to town. Thus become a merchant by profession, he rapidly realized profits big enough to enable him to form an association with his fellows, to load a ship in common with them and to engage in coastal trade along the shores of England, Scotland, Denmark and Flanders.[28]

A. A Spanish *Picaro* and Archetypal Tricky Merchant

In Spain, feudalism continued to force the local Godrics of Finchale to struggle for survival aided only by their determination and their quick wit, at least through the sixteenth century. It was not until approximately 1600 that feudalism entered its final crisis in Spain.[29] Thus, in 1554, an anonymous author published the novel *The Life of Lazarillo de Tormes, His Fortunes and Adversities* (*La vida de Lazarillo de Tormes, y de sus fortunas y adversidades*), regarded as a pioneer example of the picaresque genre: a genre devoted to telling the tales of characters who were at times rogues, at times adventurers, and almost always tricky or quick-witted. In the words of Professor John Beverley:

> The [Lazarillo de Tormes novel] tells of a small boy, born poor, whose father dies in war after being exiled for theft and whose mother . . . sends him off as the servant of a blind beggar (colloquially, a *lazarillo*). He works first for this beggar, then for an avaricious village priest, then for an impoverished *hidalgo* or gentleman, all the while experiencing enormous hunger and privation but learning how to "valerse por sí mismo" ("how to fend for himself" or literally, "to e obtain value for himself""). In a series of subsequent jobs his fortunes begin to improve. By the end, he has a wife and a home, which are given to him by a priest, and a position as *pregonero*, or towncrier. He feels himself to be "at the height of my good fortune," but his own telling allows the reader—Your Grace—to see that the wife is the priest's mistress, that Lazarillo is what in Spanish is called a *cabrón, a* man who permits the infidelity of his wife for profit or advantage.[30] (Parenthesis added)

In his many jobs, Lazarillo often had to lie or aid and abet his employer's lies or become a party to pretensions about a social status that neither his employer nor he held. Despite these "adversities," he managed by cunning and determination to develop his own business and eventually his savings:

---

[28] HENRI PIRENNE, MEDIEVAL CITIES: THEIR ORIGINS AND THE REVIVAL OF TRADE 116 (Frank D. Halsey trans., 1969).

[29] John Beverley, *"Lazarillo" and Primitive Accumulation: Spain, Capitalism and the Modern Novel*, 15 THE BULLETIN OF THE MIDWEST MODERN LANGUAGE ASSOC. 29, 38 (1982) (citing PIERRE VILAR, CRECIMIENTO Y DESARROLLO: REFLEXIONES SOBRE EL CASO ESPAÑOL 441 (1964)).

[30] Beverley, *supra* note 29, at 32.

> [O]ne day, when I was in the cathedral, one of the priests gave me a job. He provided me with a donkey, four jugs and a whip and I began to carry water around the city. That was my first step towards becoming a respectable citizen because now my hunger was satisfied. Every day I gave my employer thirty *maravedís* [a small coin] and on Saturdays I worked for myself. [Without telling the priest] I kept whatever I earned every day if it was more than thirty *maravedís*.[31]

B. The Legitimate But Religiously Suspect Archetypal Merchant

In contrast with Lazarillo's non-existent social status as a budding merchant, other merchants with a significant social status and close connections with the Spanish crown and church had emerged in sixteenth-century Spain. However, these were very few in number. In his much-praised account of the rise of one such merchant house, the Ruiz family,[32] Henri Lapeyre notes that the history of commerce during the late Middle Ages, especially during the sixteenth century, is synonymous with the history of the great European commercial dynasties such as the Medicis in Italy, the Fuggers in Germany and in lesser, but nonetheless significant measure, the Ruizes in Spain and France. They were involved in "high commerce": wholesale import and export of commodities, including the increasingly profitable wool trade, and in international banking and insurance.

In contrast with Lazarillo's trade, the Ruiz's was legitimized by its official and church connections. However, this only took place after the Ruiz family established that despite the Jewish sounding name of Simon, one of the founders of the dynasty, the family's blood was "clean," *i.e.*, devoid of Jewish ancestry.[33] Just to be on the safe side, it was not unusual for the Ruiz family to consult priests or theologians whenever a commercial contract could possibly be tainted with usury or the sin of avarice associated with Jewish business practices. The consultation was often accompanied by a request that the correspondent attest to the religious acceptability of the transaction in question.[34]

Despite the religious and social acceptability accorded to merchants devoted to "high commerce" such as the Ruiz family, Cato's (the Roman censor's) view of the merchant[35] as inferior in morality to the farmer-soldier was quite popular in Spain during medieval times and in the centuries that followed, almost to the present day. Henry Lapeyre transcribes part of a report from 1512–1513 by an Italian Ambassador on the lack of a favorable attitude toward business as follows: "The Spaniards are not devoted to commerce because they consider it a dishonorable or shameful endeavor."[36]

He also quotes Ramon Carande, an economic historian of Spain during the reign of Charles V (1516–1556), who described it as a society that definitely regarded commerce as a vile profession while admiring the dignity of the starving nobleman-employer of

---

[31] FRANCISCO DE QUEVEDO, TWO SPANISH PICARESQUE NOVELS 76 (Michael Alpert trans., Penguin Classics 1995)).

[32] HENRI LAPEYRE, UNE FAMILLE DE MARCHANDS: LES RUIZ (1955).

[33] *Id.* at 47.

[34] *Id.* at 134–35.

[35] *See supra* § 4:3(A) & (B).

[36] LAPEYRE, *supra* note 32, at 118.

the Lazarillo de Tormes, who attempted to maintain the appearance of nobility despite lacking the means with which to pay for the services of his valet.[37]

Two centuries later, Wyndham Beawes, an English Consul to the ports of Seville and Sanlucar and author of a popular 1773 English commercial law manual, described the Spanish attitude toward trade as follows:

> They have very considerable ports, equally well situated for commerce, both on the Biscayan and Mediterranean seas, and where large concerns are transacted, though principally by foreigners, as the Spaniards in general consider traffick to be a mean employ, and consequently a derogation from that gentility they almost all affect being born to. . . .[38]

A few years ago, while lecturing at the Law School at the Technological Institute of Monterrey, Guadalajara campus, I was approached by a foreign diplomat who told me about a book on commerce and merchants she was writing for Mexican children. She added that the more she lived in that city, the more she realized how a culture that seemed so accepting of merchants during its pre-colonial period had such a negative view of them following the Spanish colonization.

In conclusion, it is important to keep in mind the contrast between the picaresque version of commerce present in Lazarillo's "fortunes and adversities" and the theologically correct version of commerce exhibited by the Ruiz family in their dealings. Which of these two versions is closest to the reality of the modern commercial marketplace and why? Or is there no single marketplace reality and some marketplaces are more picaresque than others, and if so, where and why? On the other hand, is there any sense in thinking that our vast commercial marketplace could not have come about but for the transformation of the Godrics of Finchale and Lazarillos de Tormes from "bad" to "good" *picaros*? Some of the following sections of this chapter will attempt to shed light on this question.

§ 5.5 CONTEMPORARY VERSIONS OF THE PICARESQUE AND THEIR ECONOMIC DEVELOPMENT COSTS

Lest the reader assume that the picaresque was only a medieval way of doing business and that it was confined to the Lazarillos of that era, I will summarize a section of a fairly recent study of mine on the impact of secured commercial lending on the reduction of poverty.[39]

A 1999 study of the Central Bank of Brazil estimated that one-third of the approximately 40% per annum interest rate paid by Brazilian commercial borrowers was attributable to the difficulties and risks of loan collection and non-repayment.[40] This is neither an unusual finding nor a recent phenomenon, either in Brazil or other Latin American countries. For example, my study, *Law and the Credit Structure in*

---

[37] *Id.*

[38] WYNDHAM BEAWES & JOSEPH CHITTY, I LEX MERCATORIA: OR, A COMPLETE CODE OF COMMERCIAL LAW 24 (6th ed. 1813).

[39] Kozolchyk, *Reduction of Poverty*, at 739–40.

[40] DEPARTAMENTO DE ESTUDIOS E PESQUISA, BANCO CENTRAL DO BRASIL, JUROS E SPREAD BANCÁRIO NO BRASIL (1999).

Latin America[41] showed that the percentages of discounted bills of exchange or drafts protested for lack of payment in Chile from 1958 to 1962 were, respectively, 31.5%, 26%, 34.4%, 37%, and 39.1%.[42] This meant that out of, say, one hundred negotiable and credit instruments in circulation in Chile in 1962, almost 40 had not been paid at maturity. While during the same period the protests of negotiable instruments by Argentine banks fluctuated between one third and one half of the Chilean figures, the percentages of the aggregate uncollected secured and unsecured loans and discounted negotiable instruments in Argentina (gathered under the rubric of "quasi-money") were, respectively: 2.5%, 2.7%, 6%, 9.5%, and 22.9%.[43] In other words, of the total number of bank loans, direct or indirect extensions of credit, and negotiable instruments, as many as 22% during a peak year were in default.

Clearly, neither creditors nor debtors are well served by a legal system that makes collection so difficult and risky for creditors and so expensive for debtors. Inevitably, the cost of credit had to go up to subsidize the many bad loans. In fairness, however, the fault does not lie entirely with the legal system. A business culture of "winner take all, loser take none" and commerce practiced as a "tricky" or "picaresque" occupation have much to do with the cost of credit. The tricky or picaresque aspects of dealing with checks, drafts and promissory notes as credit instruments were reflected in responses given to me by Argentine bankers and merchants as part of the same study.

My first question was: "Why, if protests are so common and collection of negotiable instruments so difficult, are you still willing to take checks, drafts or notes in payment of what is owed to you?" In response, several of my respondents referred to what they described as the "false money psychology." This "psychology" encouraged taking these instruments in payment with the understanding that as with other "false" money, they would be passed on to someone else in payment of what the taker owed to them. The next question was: "Yet, what if that someone else is equally aware of the falseness of the money, why would he take it?" The answer was: "Because the falsity is factored into the prices everyone charges for their goods or services." In other words, a merchant would be willing to take a "false" check after he had charged his customer a much higher price than he would for a cash sale. He would demand a "cash down payment" which would cover a substantial part of his cost, and he would then gamble on the likelihood of collecting the remainder of the check by negotiating it to someone else, who would in all likelihood engage in the same picaresque calculation. I recall the interest that these answers evoked among my RAND Corporation[44] economist-colleagues: Picaresque or tricky commercial behavior acquired an unforeseen economic importance as an explanation for the ever-increasing levels of prices in Argentina's hyperinflation.

As I have stated elsewhere, the business culture of "winner take all, loser take none" is not peculiar to Latin America. It is present in those developing nations that continue to be guided by standards of fairness peculiar to agricultural survival-tribal

---

[41] Boris Kozolchyk, *Law and the Credit Structure in Latin America* (RAND Corporation RM—4918 RC, March 1966). *See* Boris Kozolchyk, *Law and the Credit Structure in Latin America*, 7 VA. J. INT'L L. 1, 24 tbl. 6 (1967), for a somewhat shortened version of the RAND study.

[42] *Id.*

[43] *Id.* at 20–21 (tbl. 4).

[44] RAND CORPORATION, http://www.rand.org/.

societies.[45] In these societies, only the members of one's tribe, clan, family or circle of friends are considered insiders and factually or legally entitled to duties of fair dealing by their fellow insiders. In contrast, those who belong to other tribes, clans, families, or circles of friends are outsiders or "strangers" and, as such, are not entitled to the duties of fair dealing owed to insiders.[46]

This is not to say that strangers are totally without protection in developing nations. They are usually allowed to "purchase" a temporary protected status by paying the notorious bribe. Yet, this status is only temporary because it applies exclusively to a specific transaction or event. It is also temporary because it lasts only until the same or a better protection is made available to another (often competing) stranger willing to pay a similar or higher bribe. At this point, the stranger's protection disappears or becomes subject to a bidding war.

The effects of a culture in which only the most minimal business duties are owed to strangers and the widespread feeling of distrust it inspires in market participants was apparent in the responses provided by middle class Costa Ricans to a 1968 questionnaire on their investment practices. When asked why the respondent, as a potential investor, preferred to invest in real estate mortgages that offered a much smaller return on invested capital than that yielded by the dividends of stock issued year after year by an industrial company, many respondents provided variants of the same answer: If the industrial company's dividend return is such a good deal, why would it be offered to me, neither a member of the family nor a friend of those who run this company?

§ 5.6 LAY LAW, CANON LAW AND *PACTA SUNT SERVANDA*

Side by side with the picaresque ways and the unenforceability of informal promises in lay law stood canon law. In the tenth and eleventh centuries, Roman law was rediscovered, taught and annotated first in Bologna, Italy, and subsequently in other learning centers in Italy and France. Initially, the teaching consisted of annotations (*glosses*) that purported to do nothing more than to clarify the meaning of original texts. These glossators were succeeded by a more intellectually ambitious group of teachers and scholars known as commentators. Unlike the glossators, some of the leading commentators attempted to assess the degree to which Justinian's *Corpus Juris Civilis* could be used as living law for medieval Europe. Thus, Bartolo de Saxoferrato, an Italian fourteenth-century (1313–1357) law professor and the most influential of commentators, concluded that the Roman law refusal to enforce innominate, *i.e.*, non-typified, contracts had little practical consequence in his time because contracts were commonly drafted by public notaries and this added formality

---

[45] *See* Kozolchyk, *Roadmap*, at 4; Kozolchyk, *Fairness*, at 257.

[46] The first time I discussed the findings in my study, Kozolchyk, *Toward a Theory of Law*, with the late and lamented father of legal anthropology, E. Adamson Hoebel, he recalled an incident he witnessed that illustrates the predicament of the stranger in a tribal environment. Hoebel was watching a ritual snake dance that involved an actual snake in the hands of a Native American ritual dancer. This took place at a Native American reservation located near a U.S. national park in the western United States. At one point, the park ranger asked the tribal dancer to stop his dance so that he could have the visitors move back from one of the nearby cliffs lest the snake dart out and scare a visitor who could then easily fall off the cliff. Somewhat annoyed at the interruption, the dancer asked the ranger: "Why are you so concerned, are these your family, or are they your friends, do you even know these people?"

made these innominate contracts enforceable throughout Italy and other European countries.[47]

The jurists charged with interpreting and applying Roman law to contractual disputes in medieval times were familiar with the moral and religious principles found in canon law. These principles not only condemned lies or misrepresentations as sinful behavior, but also decreed the fulfillment of unfulfilled promises (*pacta sunt servanda*). In fact, canon law granted an action of enforcement of promises before its own courts. Nevertheless, positive law (the law officially in force), in contrast to canon law, did not recognize an action for unkept promises, especially as related to atypical or innominate and preparatory contracts.[48]

§ 5.7 METHOD OF REASONING

A. Aristotle's Essences, Commutative Justice and Usury

The Middle Ages marked the resurgence of Aristotle's legal philosophy as taught by the scholastics, particularly St. Thomas Aquinas in his *Summa Theologica*. As discussed in Chapter 2, scholastic legal thinking was characterized by the search for Aristotelian essences, *i.e.*, the properties of objects that made them unique. Once these essences were identified, the scholastics went on to define each object in Aristotelian fashion by placing the species under their genuses. When Aristotle searched for the essence of justice, he found that justice could belong to the genus of virtue or was virtue itself.[49]

Aristotle also identified some species of justice. Prominent among these were the "distributive" justice and the "rectificatory" or "commutative" justice.[50] While distributive justice was concerned with the allocation of political power and resources, commutative justice allocated rights and duties among private parties. In other words, it discerned the meaning of "the mine and the thine" (*meum et tuum*) in transactions such as sales, loans, leases, and other "acts of voluntary commutative justice."[51] A transaction was commutatively just when the parties' performances were equivalent in value; if the transaction were unjust, commutative justice had to bring these performances back to the *status quo ante* point of equivalence.

Thus, Aristotle's was a "static" model of adjudication. It attempted to bring the parties back to where they were before they started to or failed to exchange values. It did not compensate them for foreseeable damages such as the interest lost when unable to use or invest the undelivered monies. However, to grant even such a limited amount of damages, Aristotle would have had to reject his own faulty, but nonetheless influential, view that money was a sterile commodity incapable of earning interest or profits.[52] As will be discussed in connection with the law of damages in civil law

---

[47] *See* Gordley, *Contract in Pre-Commercial Societies,* at 2–8 to 2–17 for an insightful discussion of the dense relationship.

[48] *Id.* at 2–9.

[49] ARISTOTLE, at 701 ¶¶ 15–20. *Id.* at 116.

[50] *Id.* at 1008–14.

[51] *Id.*

[52] *Id.* at 1141:

> For money was intended to be used in exchange but not to increase at interest. And this term interest [*tokos*], which means the birth of money from money, is applied to the breeding of

countries, the Aristotelian static view of contractual adjudication continues to influence the law of compensation for breach of commercial contracts in Spanish and Spanish-influenced Latin American law.

B. Scholasticism,[53] Usury and the Typification of Contracts

1. Repression and Evasion of Usury: Aristotelic Essences and Roman Law

No other scholastic doctrine has exerted more influence on the law of commercial contracts of the Western world—especially those contracts that involved deferred performances—than the doctrine on usury. From the year 1050, usury was considered to be sinful, if not criminal, in most Western European countries.[54] The contract for a loan was the one most generally involved with usury, but usury could be committed by any credit agreement whereby the amount received by the creditor was higher than the one given to the borrower.

Pope Urban III Decree *Consuluit* of 1187 established the bases for the regulation of usury:

> (1) Usury is whatever is demanded in return in a loan beyond the loaned good itself; (2) the taking of usury is a sin prohibited by the Old and New Testaments; (3) the very hope of a return beyond the good itself is sinful; (4) usuries must be restored in full to their true owner; (5) higher prices for credit sales are implicit usury.[55]

The most influential argument in favor of the repression of usury was proposed by St. Thomas Aquinas in his *Summa Theologica*:

> In those things whose use is their consumption, the use is not other than the thing itself; whence to whomever is conceded the use of such things, is conceded the ownership of those things, and conversely. When therefore, someone lends money under this agreement that the money be integrally restored to him . . . it is manifest that he sells separately the use of the money and the very substance [essence] of money [as money is a thing consumed by its use]. The use of money, however as it is said, is not other than its substance [essence]. . . .[56]

More simply, the money lent is such an object that disappears with its use. The influence of Aristotle's essences is clearly present in the previous argument: Money, by essence, is a consumable good. Yet, if it can be empirically proven that money is neither consumable by its use nor that it is a sterile commodity, the Thomistic reasoning, no matter how formally logical, must fall apart. And this proof is readily

---

money because the offspring resembles the parent. Wherefore of all modes of getting wealth, this is the most unnatural.

[53] *See* Glossary, "Scholastic Logic."

[54] *See* JOHN THOMAS NOONAN, THE SCHOLASTIC ANALYSIS OF USURY 11(1957). Noonan cites to the Hadriana collection of ecclesiastical canons and especially to the letter by Pope Leon the Great *Nec Hoc Quoque* as the one with the greatest influence on the doctrine of usury from the years 750–1050 which started the process of uniformity of application of this doctrine. *Id.* at 15.

[55] *Id.* at 20.

[56] *Id.* at 53–54 (citing THOMAS AQUINAS, II SUMMA THEOLOGICA 78(E) (c. 1265)).

available by merely observing what normally happens with commercial loans. Because of these loans, the borrower acquires the ability to obtain and sell goods and with the proceeds of these sales, he can repay the money lent to him; conversely, with each repayment the lender is able to re-lend to the same or to other borrowers.

The Roman typification of the loan agreement as a "real" contract where title to the thing lent (money) is conveyed to the borrower in exchange for a promise of repayment is also clearly apparent in Aquinas' reasoning. Raymond de Roover's description of the most common method used by medieval merchants to avoid being characterized as usurious illustrates the central role of the Roman typification of the loan agreement as a "real" contract when attempting to avoid the imputation of usury:

> Since the [direct] taking of interest was ruled out, the bankers had to find other ways of lending at a profit. The favorite method was by means of exchange bills (*cambium per litteras*). It did not consist in discounting as practiced today, but in the negotiation of bills payable in another place and usually in another currency. Interest, of course, was included in the price of the bill which was fittingly called a "bill of exchange." Although the presence of concealed interest is undeniable, the merchants argued—and most of the theologians accepted these views—that an exchange transaction was not a loan (*cambium non est mutuum*) but either a commutation of moneys (*permutation*) or a buying and selling of foreign currency (*emptio venditio*). In other words, the exchange transaction was used to justify the credit transaction, and speculative profits on exchange served as a cloak to cover interest charges. Nevertheless, it was argued that a *cambium* was not usurious, since there could be no usury where there was no loan.[57]

2. *The Economic Consequences of the Prohibition of Usury*

Despite the weakness of the Thomistic argument and the endless attempts at evasion by merchants and consumers as well as by credit-starved government officials, the scholastic definition of usury and the justification of its prohibition prevented easy access to much-needed commercial, industrial, and consumer credit in medieval Western Europe. The serious economic consequences of this prohibition were apparent during part of the twentieth century in Western European economies such as Spain's, which lacked an effective system of commercial banking until at least the second half of the twentieth century. This distaste for commercial lending was shared by other European government officials. For example, Amintore Fanfani, a high official and defender of the Italian fascist state during his tenure in a fascist office (but *significantly not* thereafter), listed the following merits of the scholastic doctrine of usury:

> In the Middle Ages . . . [it was necessary to support] the intervention of public bodies in economic life as a check to individual activity and to defend the interests of society as a whole; in our own time, by calling for State intervention for the same reasons, the Church has remained faithful to her anti-capitalistic ethics.[58]

---

[57] DE ROOVER, BUSINESS, BANKING AND ECONOMIC THOUGHT, at 32.

[58] *Id.* at 16 (citing AMINTORE FANFANI, CATHOLICISM, PROTESTANTISM, AND CAPITALISM 158–59 (1935)).

Notwithstanding Fanfani, the vast majority of medieval economy historians[59] reach a negative conclusion on the impact of the scholastic doctrine of usury on commerce and economic development. As stated by an English historian: "Under the labyrinthine edifice of Scholastic casuistry . . . competition withered, the flow of credit congealed, and interest rates soared."[60]

Raymond de Roover, the Belgian-American historian of the medieval economy and one of the few historians who found some positive features in the scholastic doctrine of usury, conceded that on balance, its application was quite negative:

> The usury prohibition was designed to protect the borrower but it had the opposite effect. It may have retarded economic growth to the extent that it increased the cost of borrowing. The need for concealment and the use of subterfuges complicated matters. By being forced to operate on the [basis of bills of] exchange payable abroad, bankers had to rely on foreign correspondents paying them fees and commissions which they recovered from borrowers. Loss on the exchange was often so high that it swallowed the profits of the merchant who traded on credit. In this sense, and despite the doctrinal escape-hatches provided by the Schoolmen, the result of the usury prohibition was to increase both the cost and the risk of doing business.[61]

§ 5.8 PRELIMINARY CONCLUSIONS AND A CONTEMPORARY ILLUSTRATION

The combination of a highly formal contract law dependent upon a recovery in tort instead of contract, a feudal law which granted contractual privileges and immunities only to those with the appropriate political or military status, and the scholastic repression of commercial loans as usurious was responsible for a regression to a significant unenforceability of commercial promises during the Middle Ages, except those executed before notary publics. The positive contributions of medieval law to the development of the law of commercial contracts were found elsewhere, as will be discussed shortly. Meanwhile, the reader will profit from the following illustration of how a scholastic definition was relied upon by the Supreme Court of Spain a little over a decade ago. The following decision of May 16, 2000, attempts to distinguish the contract of "leasing," known among United States lawyers as a "financial lease," from a traditional loan agreement in a casuistic manner:

> What is peculiar to the contract of leasing is its facilitation of the acquisition of a certain thing. The ontological reason of this agreement, which explains its socio-economic function, is the [lessee's] need of a given object which according to a . . . 1988 statute, is going to be used for an agricultural, fishing, industrial, commercial, or handicraft or for a professional purpose by the person financed through this device. . . . [This person] accepts this legal formula, because of his need of the thing and his lack of economic resources with which to acquire its ownership . . . although he is given the possibility of such an acquisition by means of an option to purchase the thing at a later

[59] *See* NELSON, THE IDEA OF USURY, at 73–108.

[60] DE ROOVER, BUSINESS, BANKING AND ECONOMIC THOUGHT, at 16 (citing Henry Charles Lea, *The Ecclesiastical Treatment of Usury*, 2 YALE REV. 384–85 (1894)).

[61] *Id.* at 33.

> time. . . . On the other hand, what characterizes the loan of money is the borrower's need for money itself, an object that in addition to being fungible *is consumable by its use* . . . requiring a transmission of ownership with the obligation to return the equivalent, with or without a premium or interest. Therefore, in the case of the loan, its relevance, the reason of being of this contract is to receive money . . . while in the contract of leasing what is financed is the acquisition of an object.[62]

Note that while the prohibition of usury has been eliminated or drastically attenuated in most Western countries, the Aristotelian-Thomistic reasoning seems to retain its influence in the above decision.

Does the reader agree with: 1) the characterization of the legal natures (read: Aristotelian essences) of the loan and the contract of leasing by the Spanish Supreme Court; and 2) the distinction made by the Spanish Supreme Court between the loan and financial lease agreements? Is this not a casuistic distinction without a difference? Isn't an enterprise being financed by the loan of the amount that will make possible its use or the acquisition of an asset needed for its operations and growth? Why would the Supreme Court of Spain in the year 2000 wish to refer to the "consumption by use" feature of a loan as contrasted with the features of a financial lease?

§ 5.9 MEDIEVAL JEWISH COMMERCIAL BROTHERHOOD

More than one thousand letters, books of accounts, and other commercial documents that belonged to medieval Mediterranean and North African Jewish traders were discovered at the end of the nineteenth century in the "Geniza" of the Jewish cemetery in Cairo.[63] This discovery provided a unique opportunity to observe everyday medieval trade as conducted by Jewish merchants in the Mediterranean, North African, and Near Asia regions.

The discovered documents illustrate how a trade formerly conducted by caravans, where merchants closely followed their wares on the backs of camels or mules and did not dare separate themselves from their cargo lest it be lost or stolen, was replaced by a trade of trusted intermediaries. These intermediaries were usually members of the same religion (Jewish or Muslim) and were entrusted with money and wares largely because of the religious-fraternal duties owed to those who had trusted them.[64] Consider, for example, an extract of an eleventh-century letter from an Egyptian Jewish merchant to his Jewish correspondent in Sicily and Tunisia:

---

[62] S.T.S., May 16, 2000 (R.J. No. 2530) (Spain) (translation by this author).

[63] *See* LETTERS OF TRADERS, at 3. Professor S. D. Goitein states that:

> Anyone looking at the title of this book will be tempted to ask: Why Jewish? Why should we single out one of the several communities active in the trade of the Islamic countries during the High Middle Ages? The answer is simple: From that world and that period, only the letters and other papers of Jewish overseas traders have thus far been found. The preservation was due to very special circumstances. All the letters translated in this volume were originally found in the so-called Cairo Geniza. Geniza (pronounced gueneeza) is a place where the discarded writings on which the name of God was or might have been written were deposited in order to save them from desecration.

Id. These documents were collected by several scholars and at the present time can be consulted in their original version at the British Museum.

[64] *See generally* GOITEIN, MEDITERRANEAN SOCIETY (describing trade conditions, customary terms and practices). *See also* AGUS I at 1–21 (describing northwestern European Jewish trade).

> My lord, I have instructed Abu 'l-Bishr . . . to buy saffron for 80 dinars from the sums he owes me and to send everything to you. In case he is unable to buy the goods, he should send you the cash. If God ordains a safe arrival, take 25 dinars from it, add another 25 dinars on your side, and buy whatever God puts into your mind for the entire sum. This should be in partnership between my son Abu Ibrahim and your son Abu Sahl, as we have agreed, so that they should if God, the exalted, wills, follow in the footsteps of their grandfathers. . . . For the balance buy whatever God puts into your mind and send it by boat together with the sal ammoniac and whatever you still owe me.[65]

Please note the expanding "triangle" of entrustment in this letter: "A", the original entrustor, instructed and entrusted "B" (who had previously been entrusted with sums he owed to A) to buy goods for the account of A and send them or their monetary value, again on trust, to C (A's business partner or joint venturer). C, in turn, was entrusted by A to buy goods on behalf of A at his discretion, and to let these goods or their proceeds become the basis of a partnership between A's and C's sons.

A. Customary and Rabbinical Brotherly Duties: The Archetypal Agent

The degree of entrustment apparent in the above-expanding triangle was supported by a set of customary duties among religious and commercial brethren eventually sanctioned by religious ordinances and "*responsas*." The latter were opinions issued by experts on religious law in answer to questions submitted by rabbinical courts or, on occasion, by lay courts. A sampling of the sanctioned duties included the following:

> (a) [W]henever a Jew lost any (money) [property], either by accident or through thievery . . . and another Jew found this property in the hands of a non-Jew and bought it from him—[even if] he did not know that this property originally belonged to a Jew—then if the original owner appeared and recognized his goods, the purchaser must return the goods to the original owner and was entitled to recoup only his expenses.[66]

> (b) Similarly, and in order to prevent unscrupulous gentile creditors-pledgees from taking advantage of necessitous Jewish pledgors, a *responsum* recalled a restrictive customary ordinance that no one shall redeem (from a non-Jew) the pledge of a fellow Jew.[67]

> (c) A Jewish merchant's business relationship with a non-Jew was protected by bans and interdictions restraining other Jewish merchants from interfering with such a relationship (*maarufia).*[68]

> (d) Jewish co-adventurers or passengers in the same commercial voyage were expected to protect a colleague's weak and necessitous dependents in the

---

[65] LETTERS OF TRADERS, at 116.

[66] AGUS I, at 135.

[67] *Id.* at 244.

[68] *Id.* at 206–07.

event of his death or incapacity by picking up his "bundle," i.e., transacting business on his behalf and turning the profits over to his surviving family.[69]

As is apparent in the above customary duties and *responsa*, those Jewish merchants were bound by a standard of fairness that required that each treat his colleague as a brother, meaning altruistically and not necessarily with a view to profit or loss. The measure of the duties owed to the commercial brother, then, was the latter's welfare. This standard of fairness encouraged trust, and by encouraging trust it also encouraged an efficient and highly predictable method of doing business where formalities were rarely of the essence and where reliance was on a brother's word. This is why telling the truth was a central feature not only of business practice, but also of dispute settlement. The truth was often established by the decision of which party (plaintiff or defendant) was supposed to take the "decisory oath."[70] The taking of this oath in vain carried with it tremendous religious and legal consequences because it required invoking the name of God.[71]

B. Evolution of the Biblical Prohibition of Usury and Its Effects upon Brotherhood

Reflecting the agricultural economy of the Jewish people during Biblical times, the Jewish Bible provides:

> If thou lend money to any of my people, even to the poor with thee, thou shalt not be to him as a creditor; neither shall ye lay upon him interest (Exodus 22, 24).
>
> And if thy brother be waxen poor and his means fail with thee, then thou shalt uphold him . . . Take thou no interest of him or increase; but fear thy God . . . Thou shalt not give him thy money upon interest, nor give him the victuals for increase. I am the Lord your God. (Leviticus 25, 36–38).
>
> Thou shalt not lend upon interest to thy brother, interest of money, interest of victuals, interest of anything that is lent upon interest. Unto a foreigner thou mayest lend upon interest; that the Lord thy God may bless thee. . . . (Deuteronomy 23, 20–21).[72]

The application of the above rules obviously turns on the determination of who is a brother, a foreigner, or a stranger. Few times in the history of civilization have so many religious, legal, and economic doctrines depended on the meaning of words as seemingly transparent as "brother." Depending on who was considered a brother, "foreigner," or "stranger," interest would or would not be charged. Depending on the above characterizations, lenders, vendors, partners, and joint venturers could face punishment as usurers.

---

[69] *Id.* at 80–82.

[70] *See infra* § 5:10 (discussing instances of reliance on the decisory oath in the Responsa); *see also* AGUS I, at 158–59; AGUS II, at 440 (comparative evaluation of the oath in the Jewish and Islamic traditions); PEDERSEN, DES EID BEI DEN SEMITEN IN SEINEM VERHAITNIS ZU VERWANDIEN ERSCHEINUNGEN SOWIE DIE STELLUNG DES EIDER IM ISLAM 95–96 (1914).

[71] *See* AGUS I, at 158–59.

[72] HOROWITZ, JEWISH LAW, at 486–87. *But see* NELSON, THE IDEA OF USURY, at 3–29 (stating that on some occasions the Bible commands that strangers (*Gerim*) be treated as brothers).

Benjamin Nelson, a highly respected historian of religious ideas and particularly of the Biblical and post-Biblical notion of "brother," maintains that the evolution of Deuteronomic command started out as a rule of tribal morality and by mid-nineteenth century, after the Reformation and Calvinism, became a rule of "universal brotherhood" which allowed market rates of interest to be charged by and to Jewish and non-Jewish lenders, investors, partners, and joint venturers.[73]

The very notion of usury began to be redefined in the Late Middle Ages.[74] Finally, as a result of Henry VIII's 1545 Statute of Usury, which set forth a permissible or legal rate and punished as usurious the rates charged above that rate, not only England but other trading nations began to adjust their usury rates.[75] This re-definition is the one adopted in most free market economies where the law generally reflects the interest rate that prevails in the marketplace. Accordingly, the vast majority of commercial contracts are presently born free of the opprobrium of usury.

C. Contracts and Medieval Executory Promises

During much of the evolution described by Benjamin Nelson, Jewish merchants were subjected to "ghettoizing" prohibitions that prevented their participation in agriculture, industry and the professions. The result of this policy was to force Jews into the highly unpopular jobs of moneylenders and collectors of taxes.[76] Since major segments of the Jewish community could only survive as moneylenders, rabbinical authorities had to relax the application of the Biblical prohibition of usury. This is how contracts that concealed various types of loans with interest were developed.

As part of this phenomenon, the contracts of partnership or joint venture known as "*heter iska*" were declared valid in various French Jewish communities from the eleventh to the thirteenth centuries.[77] The agreement was embodied in a written instrument called the *shetar iska*. It commonly provided that a passive partner (in fact, the lender) would furnish a specific sum of money to the working partner (in fact, the borrower) for a joint venture. The working partner guaranteed that the passive partner would not lose his investment and also guaranteed a minimum return which was in fact the interest charged for the loan. In return, the passive partner gave complete freedom to the working partner to manage the former's "investment."[78]

George Horowitz, a United States Judaic scholar and lawyer, points out that while at the beginning of this practice it was necessary for the lender to present proof of the loss of his "investment" prior to demanding payment of the guarantee, eventually rabbinical interpretation deemed this evidence redundant; thereafter, the refund promise was payable without the need to present evidence of the loss.[79] Therefore, as we look at the evolution of enforceable executory promises, it becomes apparent that the guarantee of repayment issued by the Jewish borrower in the *shetar* emerged as a

---

[73] NELSON, THE IDEA OF USURY, at xx–xxv.

[74] *See infra* § 5:12.

[75] In England, the Statute of Usury of 1545 under Henry VIII (37 Stat. Henry VIII, c. 9, 1545) established the limit of 10% *per annum,* above which the loan was deemed usurious.

[76] HOROWITZ, JEWISH LAW, at 492.

[77] *Id.* at 493.

[78] *Id.*

[79] *Id.*

medieval antecedent of the late twentieth-century "independent" or "abstract" undertakings discussed in a later chapter.[80]

Classic Roman-law-sanctioned guarantees such as the *adpromissio* (including variants such as *sponsio, fideiussio, fideipromissio*) were executed through the *stipulatio*.[81] However, these guarantees were "accessory" promises or promises dependant on the existence and validity of their underlying principal obligation. If the principal obligation or duty was void, so was the accessory *sponsio, fideiusssio* or *fideipromissio*. In contrast, the *iska* guarantee in the *shetar*, once freed from the condition of having to prove the underlying loss, functioned as an abstract executory promise, independent of the loan *qua* underlying investment. Not surprisingly, the use of the *shetar* became very popular, especially after the incorporation of executory promises similar to those in the contemporaneous promissory note (either in favor of someone named in it or in bearer form).[82] This kind of *shetar* functioned as quasi-currency of considerable circulation among medieval Jewish communities, particularly in Spain.[83]

Meanwhile, approximately two centuries after the transactions described in the Geniza letters and documents of the "brotherly" Mediterranean Jewish merchants took place, evidence of executory contracts for the "advance" or "forward" purchase of wool produced by English, especially Cistercian, monasteries and sold to international traders, many of whom were Italian, began to appear in records of the Exchequer court. We will discuss the significance of these contracts and related documents in a later section. Presently, I will examine important features of the resolution of contractual disputes between Jewish traders by Jewish religious authorities.

§ 5.10 RABBINIC *RESPONSA* BY MAIMONIDES

In his biographic essay about Maimonides,[84] the Uruguayan historian-physician, Dr. Antonio Turnes, relates that Moshe Ben Maimon was born on March 30, 1135 in Cordoba, Spain. Later in life, he became known as Maimonides among non-Jews and as the Rambam among Jews. He lived in Cordoba during the first thirteen years of his life and then had to leave as a result of the conquest of the south of Spain by the religiously fanatic Almohades Islamic tribe. Maimonides' family's long pilgrimage took them to Egypt, where he died in 1204. While in Cordoba, Maimonides was educated in an atmosphere of tranquility and well-being. Despite his young age, he acquired a good knowledge of mathematics, astronomy, philosophy, and physics.[85]

In Egypt, Maimonides became the most famous physician in the Royal Court.[86] He also achieved the status of a most respected theologian and philosopher, being responsible, among other things, for the adaptation of Aristotelian rationalism to Judaism. As a well-known rabbinical authority and community leader, Maimonides

---

[80] *See infra* § 12:3(D).

[81] BERGER, ENCYCLOPEDIC DICTIONARY, at 350.

[82] HOROWITZ, JEWISH LAW, at 517. According to Horowitz, the *Shetar Hamokaz*, or bearer note, was coined as such during the early medieval times by the Jewish communities in Spain. *Id.* at 515.

[83] *Id.*

[84] *See* TURNES, MAIMONIDES. *See also* JOEL L. KRAEMER, MAIMONIDES: THE LIFE AND WORLD OF ONE OF CIVILIZATION'S GREATEST MINDS 293–315 (2008).

[85] TURNES, MAIMONIDES, at 20.

[86] *Id.* at 23.

received numerous consultations from rabbis, rabbinical courts and religious scholars, some of whom officiated as first instance judges in disputes among Jewish merchants in Middle Eastern countries. The following are three of his responses:[87]

1) *Question 20:*[88] The Burden of Proof in the Investment Contract: Executory Promise and Abstraction.

Jewish investor "A" gave money to another Jewish businessman "B" to invest in India. According to the sons of B, the ship in which he was traveling was wrecked and B died.[89] A "sued the dead man's sons. The sons said: Our father died. His ship was wrecked."[90] A replied by saying: "Bring proof that his ship wrecked and that he died."[91] "The sons said: 'We are the heirs [of B, and that declaration, by itself should suffice], we do not have to bring proof. [Instead, if you doubt us,] [y]ou bring proof that . . . [B is] well and alive, and that he is [merely] delayed [in his return from India].' "[92] If you can prove in addition that our father has properties or goods belonging to you, A, we will consider your claim as valid.[93] The rabbi who heard the dispute asked Maimonides how he should decide. "Do the sons have to bring proof that the ship was wrecked and that he died? Or does the investor [A] have to bring proof that . . . [B was] alive and delayed?"[94]

Answer:

The sons of B did not have to bring the proof that B's ship was wrecked and that he died in it demanded by A. Neither did A have to prove that B was well and alive as demanded by the sons of A. "But if the investor [A] will bring proof of the man's death and will produce the bond *shetar*"[95] executed in the presence of other Jewish witnesses and that B died in possession of the money or goods described in the *shetar* to be invested on behalf of A, then A has the right to claim what was stipulated in the *shetar*.[96]

The business transaction in dispute *appears to be* one where A entrusted B with a sum of money for investment in a joint venture. Apparently, it was not a simulated joint venture or one just to hide a true loan because if that were the case, A would have required a repayment guarantee of the capital and the interest in the *shetar*, a common stipulation with interest bearing loans, as noted earlier. The proof of B's death was not as important in Maimonides' eyes as was the presentation of a *shetar* and evidence of A's goods or money in B's possession. He had already found it unnecessary for B's sons to prove his death after they had been validly declared his heirs. However, without presenting a *shetar*, A, not the heirs of B, had the burden to prove the presence of goods that belonged to him and the absence of a profit distribution. Could this burden of

---

[87] Teshuvot ha-Rambam, Responses in Arabic (Joshua Blau & Imre Desser trans., 1961) (compiled and translated into Hebrew by Joshua Blau; translated into English by Imre Desser, who taught Hebrew at the University of Arizona in 1975) (on file with author).

[88] *Id.* at 30–31.

[89] *Id.*

[90] *Id.*

[91] *Id.*

[92] *Id.*

[93] *Id.*

[94] *Id.*

[95] *Id.*

[96] *Id.*

proof result from the commercial custom to rely on a *shetar* to document the entrustment of money and other valuables to an actual or potential joint venturer? Apparently so.

Under your own law, who would have the burden of proof of B's death and presence of goods or money belonging to A and why? In all likelihood, you would have to take into account not only what was stipulated in the operative document, if any, but also the law that deals with the presumption of B's absence or death, the law of successions applicable to his estate, the law of civil procedure on the action(s) brought by A, and of statutes of limitations applicable to the document in question, and so on. Why did all of these different sources of law not come into play in Maimonides' *Responsum*? What presumptions did Maimonides rely on, *i.e.*, rebuttable or irrebuttable, and why? Did he rely on a presumption of good faith as well? In some contemporary legal systems, the holder of an instrument equivalent to a *shetar* (say a promissory note or bill of exchange) is presumed to hold it in good faith unless proven otherwise by the defendant-promisor. Do you think that this presumption was implicit in Maimonides' *Responsum*? How much flexibility does the presence of a solemn oath add to the reliance on presumptions?

2) *Question 63b (G)*[97]: The Implied Promise of an Accounting by the Working Partner and the Decisory Oath.

> R and S were partners (*shutaphim*). [According to their original contract, R was entitled to] . . . three-fourths of the profit and S [to] one-fourth. R kept the accounts (*cheshbon*) [of the partnership]. When the work was completed, S asked R for his share [of the profits]. R gave [S] . . . a small sum [that S felt was too small] and S claim[ed] that his share is larger and [thus] demand[ed] R to go over the accounts with him. R declined saying: "I gave you your share." How shall we decide?[98]
>
> *Answer*:
>
> *R* must go over the accounts with *S*. And if *R* claims that he had forgotten the details, he must take the partners' oath (*shvuat shutaphin*) [and swear] that he gave . . . [*S*] all that he . . . [was entitled to and that he was] . . . unaware of [any other facts or details with respect to the requested accounting]. . . .[99]

Apparently, in the commercial contract disputes adjudicated by Maimonides, the duty to provide a transparent accounting to one's partner was customarily implied in partnership agreements and as such did not have to be specified in the contract, especially because of the fiduciary nature of these transactions. There are some indications (especially from the response discussed below) that the duty of restitution derived from a trusting relationship was not subject to a statute of limitation. *A fortiori*, if restitution is not subject to a statute of limitation, the duty to render transparent accounts when requested by the partner should not have been either.

The implicit promise of rendering transparent accounts relied on the decisory oath for its implementation. In the absence of a detailed accounting, the working partner had to take a special oath tailored to reflect the duties of partners to each other. Thus,

---

[97] *Id.* at 128.

[98] *Id.*

[99] *Id.*

the choice of which of the disputing partners should take the oath, given the fear surrounding such an oath, was in effect decisive and reflected Maimonides' perception of which version of facts was the least credible. His own distrust of the oath taker's version or non-version of events undoubtedly added fear to taking an oath. Notice that Maimonides gave no choice to *R*: either he rendered accounts in a satisfactory manner to *S* or had to take the oath. For *R* to claim that his memory was hazy was unacceptable. If that were the case, he would be ordered to take the feared partner's oath. However, as will be evident in the subsequent *Responsum,* there are some exceptions:

> 3) *Question 71a (TZA)*:[100] An Implicit Executory Promise and the Decisory Oath.
>
> [On his way to Sicily, "R" received objects of value from "S". S said to R]: Take this with you.[101] [There was no further agreement between S and R. R claims that his] intention was to accommodate S's needs, [altruistically, without seeking any profit or commission. Yet,] . . . R did not say so.[102]
>
> Thereafter, R worked on [one of the objects, presumably trying to improve its appearance] . . . and paid . . . with his own money. . . . [for his passage in the boat that was to take him to Sicily].[103]
>
> [R's boat] . . . was captured [by pirates], and they took from him, that which was his, [as well as] . . . that which belong[ed] to others, [as part of] the transaction (*iska*) [goods as well as other] . . . merchandise that he took as an agent (*mishlo-ach).* He, R, paid the ransom—50 dinars—and returned to his family and met S, and other people who gave him merchandise. Nobody [made any claim] because they [all] knew what had happened. Sixteen years went by during which he lived [in peace with all of those who entrusted goods or wares to him]. . . . Then, S . . . [became angry with] R, brought him to court and claimed . . . 42 dinars. . . . [In court, R said]: 'Yes, I took . . . ["X" from S] but we did not have [any specific arrangement]. . . . Rather, I took it from him on my way, [to Sicily] and he left it with me without declaring if this was a profit sharing transaction (*iska*) or if I would be acting as . . . [his] agent (*mishlo-ach*). Most of the profit sharing transactions (*hitasku-yot*) (especially those involve[ing] sailing the ocean) stipulate that the businessman (*mit-a-sek*) gets one-third of the profit [and two-thirds go to the investor], in accordance with Gentile custom. Tell us how to decide: What is R's responsibility? . . . [W]hat about the sixteen years that went by [without a claim]. Can it be considered that S . . . [forfeited his] rights [against R] as the two of them [have lived in the same place all this time]. . . . And what about S's claim that he gave to R a loan, can we treat . . . [their arrangement as a loan or] as a profit sharing transaction (*iska*)? If R is found responsible, [then] for how much?

---

100 *Id.* at 147–49.

101 *Id.*

102 *Id.*

103 *Id.*

> *Answer*:
>
> Where terms are not spelled out and we have only hints [about the parties' intent] from surrounding circumstances, *and the* [*law*] *(halacha)* [*does not have the actual facts or*] . . . *true circumstances* [*before it*], the resolution is left to what lies between man and his Creator. [In order to discern R's] intention. . . . [a] solemn oath is required from R. R must take a solemn oath (upon a sacred object) that . . . [he] was robbed and lost [the items given to him by S], and that he did not take it in any other way than as an agent *(mislo-ach)* and that the circumstances led him to believe so. R must [also] take an oath that he did not take the . . . [objects from S] as a profit sharing transaction *(iska),* and that the circumstances led him to believe that *S* did not give it to him as a sharing transaction (*iska*). S does not have to take an oath unless R [authorizes that] . . . oath and [lets him] take the money [that would result from such an oath]. In this case, S must take . . . [an oath], declaring: "I sold [the objects] . . . to R*,* while the circumstances showed clearly that it was a sale (*mecher*) and not a profit sharing transaction (*iska*). [Finally,] . . . no statute of limitation (*mechila*) [applies] and the law of (*shmita*) (*din shmita*) does not apply either.[104]

In many, if not most cases, Maimonides used the oath to force the party whose version is the most dubious to risk his relation with "his Creator" by taking the decisory oath. On other occasions, however, as in the present case, Maimonides required the oath from the party with the most credible version of what had transpired so that by taking the suggested oath, that party would be immediately exculpated. Evidently, the latter was Maimonides' intention in this case because he was aware of the findings by the original adjudicator that there was no indication that R took the things given to him by S in any capacity other than altruistically. No credible indication of a contrary intent appeared anywhere. Further, sixteen years had gone by since R returned and S did not claim anything during this time. Moreover, the terms of the oath required of R were entirely consistent with what he had already stated to the original adjudicator. Maimonides also empowered R to authorize S's highly incriminating oaths, including the oath that S sold the items of value to R. It seemed a clearly established fact both with the local rabbi and with Maimonides that all that S said to R was, "Take this with you." These words do not, by themselves, reflect a sale agreement. Maimonides's own perception of the facts as found in his initial statement, "When terms are not spelled out and when what all we have is hints [about the parties' intent]" is clearly contrary to what S would have to say in his oath as a seller: "I sold (the objects) to R and the circumstances showed clearly that it was a sale (*mecher*)." In other words, in a contemporary trial lawyer's parlance, Maimonides was "setting up" S to perjure himself if R decided to request the seller's oath, and both parties should have seen this coming.

Would an expression such as "take this with you" be an acceptable basis among contemporary merchants or traders to commence a business arrangement? Seemingly, this was a common method of doing business among the medieval Jewish traders. It was also common not to stipulate the exact percentage to be taken by the active and passive partners of sea voyages, relying instead on the application of "the Gentile

---

104 *Id.*

custom" (a 2/3–1/3 arrangement). Under these circumstances, it is not surprising to find a proliferation of rabbinical law of oaths—one for a seller, another for an agent, another for a partner, and so on. However, these oaths required the support of a substantive law that enumerated the duties of the participants in this religious-brotherly trade. Would they be similar to those listed in § 5:9 above? How seriously enforced were these duties? Why would Maimonides reject the application of a statute of limitation to the duties of a possible partner, joint venturer, or agent? Apart from religious duties, is the reader's opinion that commercial custom played a larger role as a source of commercial contract law among medieval Jewish traders than it does today in his local commercial or civil law, and if so, why? Please recall E. O. Wilson's "iron rule" of genetic social evolution:

> [S]elfish individuals beat altruistic individuals, while groups of altruists beat groups of selfish individuals.[105]

What does that iron law have to say about the above described practices of Medieval Jewish traders?

Finally, and anticipating the discussion in the Appendix, it may be useful to reflect at this early juncture on the limitations of the decisory oath relied upon by Maimonides. "Where terms are not spelled out and we have only hints [about the parties' intent] from surrounding circumstances . . . the resolution is left to what lies between man and his Creator."[106] While Maimonides' may well been the best justification for relying on the decisory oath in his time (including the "confessional" evidence that is still used in many civil law jurisdictions), would not evidence on the parties' course of performance, course of dealing, and usage of trade as proven by witnesses (including the parties) in open court and subject to examination and cross-examination answer much of what was not spelled out by the parties?

§ 5.11 AGENTS' DUTY OF LOYALTY AND THEIR CAUSAL REPRESENTATION IN JEWISH LAW

In ancient Jewish law, the term *Shaliah* was applied to one's agent and meant literally "one who is sent,"[107] regardless of whether he was paid for his services or he acted gratuitously.[108] These agents were subject to two not-necessarily-consistent principles of liability. The first stated "a man's agent is as himself"[109] (*Shelucho shel adam kemoto*) or "one who acts through an agent is in law regarded as if he does the act himself. . . ."[110] Among others, the consequences of this principle of legal identity between principal and agent were:

> If Reuben says to Simeon: "Buy something for me," and Simeon buys without stating whether he purchases it for himself or for someone else, then, in that

---

[105] EDWARD O. WILSON, THE SOCIAL CONQUEST OF EARTH 243 (2012).

[106] Teshuvot ha-Rambam, *supra* note 87, at 149.

[107] *See generally* Israel Herbert Levinthal, *The Jewish Law of Agency*, 13 JEWISH Q. REV. 117, 125 (1922).

[108] *Id.* at 129 (Levinthal distinguishes between the gratuitous agent (*Shaliah*) and the paid agent or commission agent (*Sarsor*)).

[109] *Agency*, ENCYCLOPAEDIA JUDAICA (2008), *available at* http://www.jewishvirtuallibrary.org/jsource/judaica/ejud_0002_0001_0_00524.html.

[110] *See* Levinthal, *supra* note 107, at 133.

> case, Reuben acquires possession [of what was bought by Simeon] from the very moment of delivery. And even if Simeon purchases the article with his own money, he cannot, once the article has been delivered to him, claim that he meant to purchase it for himself.[111]

Such a relationship required loyalty and good faith from the principal as well as the agent. In order to prevent the principal from withdrawing his agent's mandate, it was customary to submit the former to an oath to this effect. This procedure "served as an effective deterrent, but if, despite the oath, the principal revoked it, the revocation is effective. Agency is also terminated upon death of the principal."[112] The second principle as restated by Professor I.H. Levinthal is: "[A]nything done by the agent that tends to work harm to the principal, invalidates the act and cannot affect the principal."[113] One of the consequences of this principle was that acts or contracts entered into by an agent with the apparent authority of his principal that turned out harmful to the latter could be invalidated by him.

Obviously, it is not easy to reconcile this principle with the earlier principle of legal identity between principal and agent, for if they were legally identical, the acts performed by the agent should have been allowed to harm the principal. This conflict between the agent's duty of utmost loyalty to the principal's welfare and a third party's reliance on the apparent authority to negotiate granted to an agent may not have been as significant in medieval "familiar" markets where most of the transactions were among parties known to each other. However, in the globalized marketplace, where most of the contracting parties are strangers to each other, this medieval principle has proven quite harmful.

Yet in due course, Talmudic law forbade the agent to act on the principal's behalf when his act involved the violation of third party rights.[114] Further, as pointed out by the Encyclopaedia Judaica, there are cases in which even if the agent digressed from his authorization or harmed the principal's interests, it was impossible to invalidate his actions with respect to a third party or to return to the original situation.

> In these cases the agent must indemnify the principal for the damage he caused. For example: Where the agent did not present himself as an agent in his dealings with a third party, in other words, where the agency was hidden; where the principal does not succeed in proving that the agency was only for the purpose of repairing and not to damage; and according to some authorities, where the agent intentionally mislead the third party into thinking that he was acting under authorization.[115]

---

111 *Id.* at 134.

112 ENCYCLOPAEDIA JUDAICA, *supra* note 109.

113 *See* Levinthal, *supra* note 107, at 175.

114 ENCYCLOPAEDIA JUDAICA, *supra* note 109.

115 *Id.* (citations omitted).

§ 5.12 ENGLISH WOOL CONTRACTS AND RECOGNIZANCES IN MEDIEVAL LAW

A. Advance Sales and Secured Loans

Studies on the medieval use of "advance" contracts—executory contracts for the sale of wool in England—began appearing shortly around the middle of the twentieth century.[116] That it took this long to unearth the details of these thirteenth-and fourteenth-century executory contracts is surprising when one considers that the wool trade was "the backbone and driving force in the English medieval economy."[117]

As a result of these studies, it now appears that relatively informal English "*recognizances*" of promises to deliver wool at a future time were clearly enforceable in England during those two centuries. As discussed earlier in this chapter, such enforcement was not possible in continental Europe, except when the contracts containing the executory promises were clothed as notarial deeds. Yet, as late as in the nineteen sixties, E. Allan Farnsworth, among the most respected and influential scholars of the common law of contracts, reiterated the conventional wisdom that it was not until Slade's case in 1602 that executory promises were finally enforceable in English law:[118]

> The final triumph of this view came at the beginning of the seventeenth century in Slade's case in which, on a jury finding that "there was no other promise or assumption, but only the said bargain," all the judges of England resolved "that every contract executory imports in itself an assumpsit."[119]

We have also learned since then that when breached, these agreements were regularly and quickly enforced, especially by the Exchequer court, and that English wool producers and their buyers or distributors used binding options and other agreements akin to forward contracts. As summarized by the English historian T.H. Lloyd: "Italian firms were . . . prepared to pay very high prices and to make long term contracts to get [the best English wool]. . . . [Thus] [t]he Italians, for instance, took the lion's share of Cistercian [Monasteries'] wool and in 1294 were buying from 49 out of 74 monasteries."[120] Professors Bell, Brooks, and Dryburgh also refer to an unpublished manuscript by Professor Meir Cohn, a Dartmouth College professor of Development Economics, which shows that Italian merchant societies regularly engaged in other

---

[116] *See generally* ADRIAN R. BELL ET AL., THE ENGLISH WOOL MARKET, C. 1230–1327 (2007). The authors refer to several seminal studies on the English wool trade. *See* EILEEN POWER, THE WOOL TRADE IN ENGLISH MEDIEVAL HISTORY (1941); T. H. LLOYD, THE ENGLISH WOOL TRADE IN THE MIDDLE AGES (1977). I owe to my good friend Professor James E. Byrne of the George Mason University School of Law awareness of and access to these studies. Theodore Plucknett also made a passing reference to these contracts. THEODORE F. T. PLUCKNETT, A CONCISE HISTORY OF THE COMMON LAW 66 (5th ed. 1956) (citing M. M. Postan, *Credit in Medieval Trade* 1 ECON. HIST. REV. 234–61 (1928) ("[f]or an interesting indenture of 12 September 1478, for the sale of wool to be delivered by 2 Feb. 1479 [with some advance payments].").

[117] BELL ET AL., *supra* note 116, at 1, 8. *See also* M. M. POSTAN, MEDIEVAL TRADE AND FINANCE 342 (1973). Postan is frequently quoted for the statement, "The barons of England, sitting in Parliament, asserted in 1297 that wool represented half of England's wealth or, as they put it, 'half the value of the whole land.' " *Id.*

[118] Slade v. Morley, (1602) 76 Eng. Rep. 1074 [K.B. 1602]; *see* E. Allan Farnsworth's, *The Past of Promise: An Historical Introduction to Contract*, 69 COL. LAW. REV. 576, 597–98 (1969) (insightful look at the importance of this case).

[119] Farnsworth, *supra* note 118, at 597–98 (citations omitted).

[120] BELL ET AL., *supra* note 116, at 7; LLOYD, *supra* note 116, at 10.

forward transactions (for a year in advance) that involved English papal tax receipts (with specified precise rates and dates of exchange) as well as future sales of glass and grain and risk transfer contracts such as "sea loans" and other forms of marine insurance.[121]

Such evidence led Bell, Brooks, and Dryburgh to conclude that:

> The needs for derivative instruments and insurance were arguably much greater then than they are now . . . trade and sale[s] were far more risky; transportation was fraught with dangers including piracy or shipwrecks at sea and theft or confiscation by corrupt officials on land. Born of this need for some certainty in a highly uncertain world, wool-growers were willing to forgo some of their revenue for the future sale of their product in order to receive an up-front payment. The merchants with whom the wool producers did business, by contrast, had the financial resources to be able to bear these risks and to diversify them substantially away by transacting with a large number of different producers.[122]

Some historians questioned whether wool was actually sold in these advance or forward sales. They suggested that what may have appeared to have been advance payments for sales were in fact secured loans thereby "thinly disguising the levy of interest and the crime of usury."[123] As discussed earlier in this chapter, the determination of whether a given transaction was a sale of foreign exchange or a loan was not an easy one.[124] Nonetheless, the transactional volume (national and international) of wool transactions was large enough to require that a major portion of the wool involved in these advance or executory contracts had to change hands. Further, official records show that many sales of wool did not even require advance payments, thereby attesting to their nature as sales to be executed in the future.[125]

On the other hand, it is very likely that large numbers of loans secured by wool were negotiated in thirteenth-and fourteenth-century England. As stated by a financial historian, in England it was acceptable that " 'a merchant who forgoes a chance to make a profit [by lending to his borrower] can reasonably take interest provided that his intention was honest and that he was not accustomed to make such loans.' Reasonable rates of interest were argued to be of the order of 5 per cent-12 per cent. . . ."[126]

---

[121] BELL ET AL., *supra* note 116, at 7 (citing Meir Kohn, *Risk Instruments in the Medieval and Early Modern Economy* (Dept. Econ., Dartmouth College, Working Paper No. 99–07, 1999)).

[122] *Id.* at 7–8.

[123] *Id.* at 14.

[124] *See supra* § 5:7(B)(1), on bills of exchange.

[125] BELL ET AL., *supra* note 116, at 21. The following record of a transaction exemplified such sales:

> James of Lissington, a royal clerk . . . and his wife, Agnes, contracted with the Augustinian priory of Newburgh . . . for some 123 sacks of wool to be delivered to him in parcels of 10 ¼ sacks at Trinity each year from 1283 to 1294. . . . James committed himself to payment of £49 a year only upon delivery of the prior's bargain.

Id.

[126] *Id.* at 5 (citing J. GILCHRIST, THE CHURCH AND ECONOMIC ACTIVITY IN THE MIDDLE AGES 107 (1969)). *See infra* chs. 20 & 22 (for a discussion of England as the most advanced commercial credit market in Europe from the seventeenth-to the twentieth-centuries).

B. "Recognizances"

Whether issued in connection with an advance of monies to procure the future sale of wool, with the payment for a future or present sale, or as a loan secured by wool, the *recognizance* (known originally as a *recognicion*) was an acknowledgment by the producer and seller of the wool that he had received an advance of money from the purchaser of the wool against its future delivery. This simple acknowledgment of a debt became so successful a means of collection that William Blackstone's *Commentaries on the Laws of England*, written in 1765–1766, describes a much wider use of *recognizances*:

> A *recognizance* is an obligation of record, which a man enters into before some court of record or magistrate duly authorized, with condition to do some particular act. . . . It is in most respects like another bond: the difference being chiefly this: that the bond is the creation of a fresh debt or obligation *de novo*, the recognizance is an acknowledgment of a former debt upon record; the form whereof is, "that A. B. doth acknowledge to owe to our lord the king, to the plantiff, to C. D., . . . is called the recognizee, "*is cui cognoscitur;*" as he that enters into the recognizance is called the cognizor, "*is qui cognoscit.*" This, being either certified to or taken by the officer of some court, is witnessed only by the record of that court, and not by the party's seal: so that it is not in strict propriety a deed, though the effects of it are greater than a *common obligation; being allowed a priority in point of payment, and binding the lands of the cognizor, from the time of enrollment on record.*[127]

So effective were these *recognizances* as collection devices that a 1929 Publication of the Selden Society, which I will discuss shortly, referred to the recorded *recognizance* as documents "whereby the debtor practically signed judgment against himself."[128]

C. The Registration of Recognizances

Most of the references to contracts in which money was advanced for the sale and future delivery of wool appeared in the section of the Memoranda Rolls of the Exchequer devoted to *recognizances* of debt.[129] The Exchequer was largely an administrative department whose functions were akin to those of present day ministries of the treasury in European and Latin American countries. It collected taxes, managed or supervised the allocation of revenues to expenditures, and was also a court of law and equity whose jurisdiction was originally limited to tax disputes and other matters of interest to the Crown.[130]

Eventually, administrative, fiscal and judicial data were filed in the Exchequer Court. In 1178, its judicial functions were largely transferred to a Court of Common Pleas also referred to as the Exchequer Pleas. This court "entertained every sort of business (including occasional pleas of the crown)" although crown suits were not as high-handed as had been the case in the immediate past.[131]

---

[127] SIR WILLIAM BLACKSTONE, II COMMENTARIES ON THE LAWS OF ENGLAND 802–03 (1922) (emphasis added).

[128] *See* SELDEN SOCIETY *infra* note 134 and accompanying text.

[129] BELL ET AL., *supra* note 116, at 11–12.

[130] *See* PLUCKNETT, *supra* note 116, at 147.

[131] *Id.* at 148 (citation omitted).

> [At that time it became] common practice that the enrolment of debts entered into between private individuals in the Exchequer would be made primarily in the memoranda rolls, the principal records of the business of the Exchequer and its court. . . . [and] as the weight of business grew heavier, a separate section to record acknowledgments of indebtedness—*Recogniciones* (Recognisances)—was created in 1262.[132]

The Selden Society compiled and commented on the sources for the Law Merchant cases, procedures and provenance of these cases, among other subjects.[133] It shows the reliance by merchants, especially those from foreign countries, on the recording of *recognizances* as a means to collect their debts from English wool producers quickly and inexpensively. According to the Selden Society, the right to record *recognizances* was attributable to Edward I:

> Edward I . . . obtained the approval of Parliament for an ordinance, establishing an auxiliary and independent system of inrolling [recording] recognizances of debts whereby the debtor practically signed judgment against himself. This useful measure, strengthened by a supplementary ordinance two years later . . . was reinforced by a parallel provision for the special benefit of merchants visiting the staple towns.[134]

D. Conclusions: Limitations of Brotherly Duties

As reported by Bell, Brooks, and Dryburgh, despite the hundreds of collection writs filed, "it is remarkable how few pleas ended in punishment for one or the other party. Compromise and settlement appear to have been the order of the day."[135]

The components of England's successful medieval collection formula were: first, the parties' use of relatively simple and standard agreements—without such a simplicity and standardization Bell et al. could not have concluded that the agreements "demystified important aspects of the sale, marketing and purchase of wool";[136] second, the recording of this agreement in an office of public records, which meant that the agreement became a "charge" or an enforceable security interest against the debtor or third parties; third, a streamlined enforcement procedure that enabled the creditor (with the initial help of the sheriff) to gain possession of the land and its "issues."

The executory promises to deliver goods, services, or money among religious brethren depended upon a higher morality than that of the then-existing marketplace. Eventually, these religious commercial brotherhoods became lay associations of merchants. Some of the most successful ones relied on various types of limitation of liability.

---

132 BELL ET AL., *supra* note 116, at 12.

133 *See* XLVI THE PUBLICATIONS OF THE SELDEN SOCIETY: SELECT CASES CONCERNING THE LAW MERCHANT A.D. 1239–1633, VOL. II CENTRAL COURTS (Hubert Hall ed., London 1930) [hereinafter SELDEN SOCIETY].

134 *Id.* at xi (citations omitted).

135 BELL ET AL., *supra* note 116, at 15.

136 *Id.* at 25.

Max Weber's *History of Commercial Partnerships in the Middle Ages*[137] describes how the general and limited partnerships of fourteenth-century Italy became engines of capitalist growth despite the severe restrictions on such investments at that time. The ability to limit the investor's liability to what was invested in a partnership fund led to more predictable and confident investments and to the modern corporate form of doing business.

The working and silent partnerships (*commendas*) in which Florentine and other Italian businessmen invested, bore a striking resemblance to the earlier *heter iskas* of the Cairo Geniza letters and Maimonides's *Responsa*. Whether or not these business ventures were the first stage of Weber's "systematic rational pursuit of accumulating profits," a stage which he identified with the beginning of capitalism, or were merely part of an earlier "pre-capitalist" stage,[138] is of less importance than the mechanism that induced trust by the silent partners in their working partners.

In this respect, the lessons learned from the Cairo Geniza letters and Maimonides's *Responsa* are instructive on the interplay between the predictability of outcomes as a result of the limitation of liability *vis-à-vis* third parties and trust among partners or associates. This trust was built on the basis of the standard of conduct of an altruistic brother. The brotherly or altruistic standard of commercial fairness may have existed among other groups of traders, but nowhere was it more apparent than in the above sources. Entrustment of a merchant's money and wares to another was possible even where the commercial journeys were long and the perils serious. As such, the brotherly standard of commercial behavior stood in sharp contrast not only with the downright dishonest behavior of many merchants, but also with the picaresque methods of doing business that had begun to spread throughout the trading world.

These lessons are apparent today in the involvement of Jewish intermediaries in the world's diamond trade and especially in the New York marketplace. As thoughtfully concluded by Duke University Law School Professor Barak Richman:

> Given the importance of credit sales, the diamond industry depends overwhelmingly on the reliable enforcement of executory contracts. However, while most industries can employ state-sponsored courts to enforce payment after the delivery of goods, public courts are toothless to enforce credit sales for diamonds. Diamonds are easily portable and command extreme value throughout the world. A diamond thief encounters little difficulty in hiding unpaid-for or stolen diamonds from law enforcement officials, fleeing American jurisdiction, and selling the valuable diamonds to black market buyers. The courts' failure to prevent flight amounts to a failure to enforce the executory contract. The failure of public courts requires diamond merchants to rely on trust-based exchange. Mutual trust among merchants—which the New York Times has called "the real treasure of 47th street"—assures dealers that by maintaining a trustworthy reputation, they will remain in good community standing and preserve the opportunity to engage in future

---

[137] WEBER, HISTORY, at 196. This writing was also his doctoral dissertation under the tutelage of Levin Goldschmidt. *See also* WEBER, LAW IN ECONOMY AND SOCIETY.

[138] *See* WEBER, HISTORY, at 30–31 (Lutz Kaelber's Introduction).

lucrative transactions. Through this mutual trust, dealers comfortably engage in executory contracts despite the unreliability of state courts.[139]

Yet, what about the protected status of the "strangers" or "third parties" with respect to the brotherly relationship? How protected were they by the standard of fairness when applied only among the brotherly merchants? Not much, as illustrated by the effects of the ancient Hebrew principle of brotherhood between principal and agent (and its modern law variants): "[A]nything done by the agent that tends to work harm to the principal, invalidates the act and cannot affect the principal."[140] It took considerable rabbinic case law to instill a modicum of third party protection in the Hebrew law of agency.

Clearly, the standard of brotherly altruism worked well among a small group of merchants, but failed when it harmed strangers or third parties and ultimately the certainty of the marketplace, a place inhabited largely by strangers and third parties. Consider the impact of brotherly duties such as that of a commercial brother purchasing goods in an "open market." As a commercial brother, he would have to give up to his brother, the victim of an embezzlement or thievery, those goods that were stolen or embezzled from the latter even though he had no knowledge that the goods were embezzled or stolen.[141] Could this duty be imposed upon non-brothers or strangers? If it were so imposed, the vast majority of purchasers would have no certainty of acquisition. *Mutatis mutandis*, consider the duty to tell the truth about the goods or services one provides to the marketplace: If telling the truth were limited to one's brethren, what third party or stranger would be willing to buy in that marketplace?

The inherent limitation of the fairness of brotherhood was pointed out, as a dilemma, by Hillel, a Jewish sage of Biblical times: "If I am not for myself, who will be for me, and if I am [only] for myself, what am I?"[142] Far from being an exceptional dilemma, it is one routinely encountered by marketplace participants and the more powerful the participant, the more routine the dilemma. Consider, for example, the case of J.P. Morgan, without a doubt the most powerful banker and financial intermediary of the United States during the beginning of the twentieth century.[143] On

---

[139] *See* Barak D. Richman, *How Community Institutions Create Economic Advantage: Jewish Diamond Merchants in New York*, 31 LAW & SOC. INQUIRY 383, 392–93 (2006). *See also* Ersoy Zirhlioglu, *The Diamond Industry and the Industry's Dispute Resolution Mechanisms* 30 ARIZ. J. INT'L & COMP. L. 477 (2013).

[140] Levinthal, *supra* note 107, at 175.

[141] *See supra* § 5:9(A).

[142] JOSEPH TELUSHKIN, HILLEL: IF NOT NOW, WHEN? 203 (2010); *see also Hillel*, ENCYCLOPÆDIA BRITANNICA, *available at* http://concise.britannica.com/ebc/article-9367103/Hillel. Hillel is described as a:

> Jewish sage, foremost master of biblical commentary and interpreter of Jewish tradition in his time [first century B.C.—first century A.D.]. [B]orn in Babylonia . . . he went to Palestine in order to continue advanced studies under the . . . Pharisees. . . . As head of a school known as the House of Hillel, he succeeded in winning wide acceptance for his approach, which liberated texts and law from slavishly literal and strict interpretation [and sought to make obedience to the Law feasible for all Jews].

Id.

[143] PBS, American Experience: America 1900, J.P. Morgan, *available at* http://www.pbs.org/wgbh/amex/1900/peopleevents/pande10.html. Provided is the following short biographical note of J. P. Morgan:

> John Pierpont Morgan (1837–1913) began his career in 1857 as an accountant, and worked for several New York banking firms until he became a partner in Drexel, Morgan and Company in 1871, which was reorganized as J.P. Morgan and Company in 1895. Described as a coldly rational

the one hand, he engineered the rescue of many important financial institutions from insolvency with his own monies as well as with monies he collected among fellow bankers. By doing this, he rescued the savings and investments of thousands of depositors and investors in these institutions. He is also credited with protecting the investments of those who bought stocks from his brokerage business by buying those companies who were poorly managed and bringing them to prosperity. In doing this, he was acting much as a Jewish medieval trader would have acted when obeying the duty to pick up his colleague's "bundle."[144] Yet on the other hand, the same J.P. Morgan strongly opposed child labor legislation intended to protect millions of children from suffering the rigors of labor at a premature age and helped create railroad monopolies that fixed shipping prices to the detriment of thousands of farmers and consumers.

In a global marketplace, Hillel's dilemma can be reformulated by asking how widespread the standard of commercial brotherhood should be. The answer started becoming apparent even in J.P. Morgan's time by the movement to enact anti-trust legislation, followed in our own days by the movement to protect the growing number of consumers and investors against commercial abuses. At times, then, duties of a commercial brotherhood have been extended by legislation. But at other times, they have also been extended by wise and compassionate judges. As stated by Justice Benjamin Cardozo, one of the wisest and most compassionate of United States commercial law judges, in my repeated quote from *Meinhard v. Salmon*:

> Many forms of conduct permissible in a workaday world for those acting at arm's length, are forbidden to those bound by fiduciary ties. A trustee is held to something stricter than the morals of the market place. Not honesty alone, but the punctilio of an honor the most sensitive, is then the standard of behavior. . . . Only thus has the level of conduct for fiduciaries been kept at a level higher than that trodden by the crowd.[145]

This decision created a new standard, not only for the protection of the contracting parties, but also for third parties and strangers acting as investors, depositors or even consumers who entrusted their savings to merchants acting in a fiduciary capacity. As stated by Justice Cardozo in this decision (followed in more than 700 other decisions in the Anglo-American legal system), the standard he employed required "an undivided and unselfish loyalty," or in other words, a brotherly standard of fairness.

Yet what about those transactions where such an entrustment did not occur or if it had occurred, could not be predicated upon an altruistic morality, but on the morality of marketplace reciprocity, *i.e.*, on doing what participants in that marketplace would

---

> man, Morgan began reorganizing railroads in 1885, becoming a board member and gaining control of large amounts of stock of many of the rail companies he helped restructure. In 1896, Morgan embarked on consolidations in the electric, steel (creating U.S. Steel, the world's first billion-dollar corporation, in 1901), and agricultural equipment manufacturing industries. By the early 1900s, Morgan was the main force behind the Trusts, controlling virtually all the basic American industries. He then looked to the financial and insurance industries, in which his banking firm also achieved a concentration of control. Morgan was also among the foremost collectors of art and books of his day; his book collection and the building that housed it in New York City are now The Pierpont Morgan Library.

Id.

[144] *See* AGUS I, at 80–82.

[145] Meinhard v. Salmon, 249 N.Y. 458, 464 (1928).

reasonably expect from each other and no more? After all, is this not the most common assumption among marketplace participants? This is precisely the type of expectation envisaged in the English wool trade: on one side was the provider of funds with which to help produce the wool and on the other were the producer and the seller of the wool. If the former was expected to supply funds, he had every reasonable expectation that he would receive the wool in the specified future. Incidentally, this was not, as should be recalled, the common stereotypical or typified transaction common in classical Roman law. What was most common was the simultaneous exchange of goods or services for money or for equivalent goods or services.

The participants in the wool trade came up with a transactional formula that has proven successful to this day. Consider the success of Article 9 of the U.C.C., Canada's Personal Property Security Act, the Model Law of Secured Transactions of the OAS, and a growing number of enactments throughout the commercial world. All require that the secured lender and borrower enter into a security agreement, provide notice of his or her essentials either by recording a summary of it in a public office or by the creditor's possession. They also allow a quick, fair, and inexpensive method of collection. Of these elements, the public notice component seems to be one of the least appreciated.

§ 5.13 APPENDIX: MEDIEVAL AND CODIFIED LAW ON OATHS, MANDATE AND AGENCY

A. The Oath in Civil and Common Law Jurisdictions

Much of the codified law on oath taking in France was modeled after the *jusjurandum* procedure of classical Roman law.[146] The reader will recall from the description of the Roman classical procedure that it was divided into two phases—one before the *praetor* also referred to as *in jure* and the other before the judge (*iudex*) referred to as *apud iudicem* or *in judicio*.[147] Oath taking (*jusjurandum*) could take place during either of these phases. An oath before the *praetor* had the same effect as a confession (*confessio in jure*): it would settle the issue before the *praetor*.[148] When one party proposed to the other that it take the oath, the taking or refusal of the oath decided the dispute and was equivalent to a judgment (*judicium*).[149] A defendant who had taken the oath, won before the *praetor*, and was subsequently sued in an action that involved the same issue was entitled to a *praetorian* defense (*exceptio*) equivalent to the one known in our time as *res judicata*. The Roman Digest's reason for such a decisive outcome was its characterization of the proposal as a deferral to the other party of the adjudicative function of a judge (*iudex*).[150] Such an oath was also referred to by the Digest as non-declinable (*necessarium*); the recipient either had to take it or

---

146 *See* George Long, *Jusjurandum*, *in* A DICTIONARY OF GREEK AND ROMAN ANTIQUITIES 659–63 (William Smith, ed., 1859) (a brief but nonetheless authoritative account on the *jusjurandum* procedure before the *praetor* and *iudex*), *available at* http://penelope.uchicago.edu/Thayer/E/Roman/Texts/secondary/SMIGRA*/Jusjurandum.html.

147 However, for an informal type of oath in this stipulation see § 4:4(D).

148 Long, *supra* note 146, at 663.

149 *Id.*

150 *Id.* (citing Justinian Digest 44.5.1, on "*deferendo ei jusjurandum*").

had to propose that the proponent take it. A refusal to take the proposed oath was equivalent to an acceptance of the other party's claim or defense (*confessio*).[151]

The second type of judicial oath was proposed by the *iudex*, although the parties could suggest it to him. It was not as decisive as the one before the *praetor*. It was a piece of evidence which the *iudex* weighed and could give it as much value as he thought was just and was often used where the *iudex* had to determine the value of the matter in dispute.[152] The *iudex* could disregard it as just another piece of evidence and either acquit the defendant or order him to pay a lower sum than that sworn to by the taker of the oath.[153]

As noted by Professor Pedro A. Malavet of the University of Florida, decisory oaths are still alive, among other civil law countries, in France, Spain and Italy.[154] The oath is generally a subdivision of the testimony of a party to a civil proceeding, known as a "confession" (*confesión* in Spanish), a reference to the fact that a party admission relieves the other party of the duty to prove a fact.[155] Among the provisions referred to by Professor Malavet, the following are particularly relevant to our discussion:

*1. France: The Judicial Oath (*Serment Décisoire*) in the* Code Civil

Article 1357:

The judicial oath is of two types:

1) That which one party defers to the other to make the decision of the case depend on it: it is referred to as the decisory oath;

2) That which is deferred *ex officio* by the judge to one of the parties.

Article 1358:

The judicial oath may be deferred in any kind of dispute.[156]

2. Spanish Civil Code

Article 1235:

The judicial confession must be made before a competent judge and after the party who will benefit from it is on record as having filed an appearance.

Article 1236:

When a judicial confession is requested by means of an oath, the party who is requested to swear under oath will be able to defer the oath to the opposing

---

[151] *Id.* ("*confessionis est nolle nec jurare nec jusjurandum referre*"). "In the Edict ([Justinian] Dig[est] 12.2.34 § 6), the *praetor* says that he will compel the person from whom the oath is demanded to pay or to take the oath." *Id.*

[152] *Id.*

[153] *Id.* (citing Justinian Digest 22.3, on "*de probationibus et praesumptionibus*").

[154] *See* Professor Pedro A. Malavet, *Comparative Law: Class Notes Part 11* (April 2005) (on file with author).

[155] *Id.*

[156] C. CIV. (FR.) arts. 1357–1358 (2008) (translation by author). Unless otherwise indicated, all the English translations of the *Code Civil* provisions belong to Legifrance (*see* Frequently Cited).

party and if that party refuses to do so, it shall be deemed to have confessed [to the facts in question].[157]

3. *Italian Civil Code*

Article 2736:

The oath is of two types:

1) the decisory oath, with which one party charges the other for the purpose of causing the case to be adjudged wholly or in part on the basis of the oath;

2) the supplemental oath, with which the judge on his own initiative charges one of the parties for the purpose of deciding the case when the claim or the defenses have not been fully proved, but are not totally without proof, or for the purpose of ascertaining the value of the subject matter of the claim, if such value cannot be otherwise ascertained.[158]

Stanford Law School's Emeritus Professor John Henry Merryman, co-author of a highly informative and one of the most readable introductions to the civil law tradition, traces the origin of this rule to the concept of "legal proof" in the Middle Ages.[159] The rules regarding the value of particular forms of evidence were used to replace trial by ordeal and other such proceedings. Professor Peter Herzog, another distinguished comparative law scholar cited by Professor Malavet, describes the decisory oath as follows:

> The procedure requires (1) that a party tender the oath and (2) that the court approve the oath. It is as if the court decided that the case would be ready for summary judgment but for the existence of a particular factual finding. Rather than holding a full hearing, the court orders this one fact to be determined. The party may either refuse the oath, in which case they admit the cause of action against them, or may take the oath and win. The facts must be within the knowledge of the oath taker. "Thus, the plaintiff may tender an oath to the defendant on whether he has received money from the plaintiff, but not on whether somebody else (for whom defendant may be a surety) has received money."[160]

Is there such a decisory oath present in your particular jurisdiction? How does the oath described by Professors Malavet, Merryman and Herzog differ from the oath used by Maimonides, and especially from the "partner's oath"? Would such an oath be useful in contemporary commercial contract litigation? How does the "partners' oath" and the above-described civil law confessional-decisory oath differ from an affidavit commonly used in various procedures of common law jurisdictions? Could decisory oaths and affidavits exist without credible deterrents against perjury? What is the relationship between the above-described oaths and the compulsory requirement of a writing for all or most contracts? Remember Andres Bello's description of the sellers of oaths and the

---

157 C.C. (SPAIN) arts. 1235–1236 (1889) (translation by author).

158 C.C. (ITALY) art. 2736 (1942).

159 JOHN HENRY MERRYMAN, THE CIVIL LAW TRADITION: AN INTRODUCTION TO THE LEGAL SYSTEMS OF WESTERN EUROPE AND LATIN AMERICA 117 (2d ed. 1985).

160 Malavet, *supra* note 155, at 4 (citing PETER HERZOG, CIVIL PROCEDURE IN FRANCE 359 (1967)).

importance of the requirement of a writing in the enforcement of contracts?[161] Finally, are decisory oaths and confessional evidence a functional equivalent for pre-trial discovery as well as examination and cross-examination of witnesses, including the parties to the commercial contract? Judging from the increasing number of "oral trial" statutes adopted by Latin American countries, the tide against confessional evidence is turning, and the NLCIFT has been fortunate to be part of a trend that is definitely improving the adjudication of commercial contract disputes.[162]

B. Mandate and Agency and Third Parties

One of my surprises as a first-year law student at the University of Miami Law School law was its offering of a full semester course on the law of agency. Given what I had been taught in Cuba about the twentieth-century version of the Roman contract of mandate (which I assumed was the counterpart to the American law of agency and which was largely confined to the law of powers of attorney), I could not imagine what could possibly be covered in a full semester on the law of agency. Two of my most esteemed University of Miami School of Law teachers, Professors Stojan Bayitch and Richard Hausler, suggested that I read Dean Roscoe Pound's comparison of the Common Law of agency and the civil law mandate in his Treatise on Jurisprudence.[163] It was a very helpful suggestion.

Dean Pound pointed to a major difference in "the form of thinking" between the common law and contemporary versions of the classical Roman law on mandates. The thinking of the common law of agency was apparent in its "relational double titles" such as "Landlord and Tenant," "Master and Servant," "Principal and Agent" and others. These dichotomies reflected a pervasive trait.[164] While the civil law lawyer thinks in terms of contractual rights and duties largely derived from a pre-characterized contractual intent or "will" as reflected in typified and non-typified contracts, the common law lawyer attributes the rights and duties of the parties to these dichotomies to the "incidents" associated with each dichotomous relation.[165]

I would add that when deciding on how to regulate these incidents, common law lawyers took into account what is customary in each relation.[166] In the evolution of the common law of agency, then, custom played a major shaping role. On the other hand, as commerce gradually replaced agricultural subsistence as a form of earning a living among the former feudal tenants and servants, each former feudal relation had to be adjusted to contemporary market circumstances. In common law countries, this was largely the task of judges and lawyers and of the logic described in an earlier chapter as that which was reasonable under the transactional circumstances. That logic provided the openness needed to protect the third parties who dealt with the increasingly distant and unknown principals. It fell to courts and juries to establish what these third parties were customarily promised, what they had reasonably assumed had been promised, or what they relied on as third parties.

---

[161] *See supra* § 2:1(B)(4).

[162] *See* National Law Center for Inter-American Free Trade (NLCIFT), http://natlaw.com/category/training/ (last accessed Aug. 20, 2013), for information on the international trainings provided in this area.

[163] ROSCOE POUND, I JURISPRUDENCE 211–13 (The Lawbook Exchange, Ltd. 2000) (1959).

[164] *Id.* at 211–12.

[165] *Id.* at 212.

[166] *Id.*

Upon reading Pound and thereafter the writings of Wolfram Müller-Freienfels, a professor at the University of Freiburg, a visiting scholar at the University of Michigan School of Law and one of the world's experts on the comparative law of agency, it was clear that the Roman law-inspired contractual mandate of civil law countries was at odds with contemporary commercial realities. As incorporated into the contemporary law of powers of attorney, the Roman law of mandate was hampered by slowness, excessive formalities and costs inconsistent with the needs of the marketplace. In addition, it undermined the certainty of countless market transactions when claims by third parties became subject to excuses or defenses based upon the mandate or principal-agency relationships whose terms and conditions were unknown or should have been unknown to third parties.

Many of the features of the present day law of agency and mandate, "crystallized" in the Middle Ages, remain unchanged in some countries even after their commercialization. In other countries, commercialization began the significant evolution of these features. In order to provide a perspective on these divergent courses, the writings of Professor Müller-Frienfels,[167] a revered master, and of Professor Omar Morales of the University of Guatemala, a graduate of the University of Arizona James E. Rogers College of Law LL.M. program and a promising young scholar, will be surveyed in this Appendix.

1. The Roman Law Mandate

As described by the English Romanists, W. W. Buckland and Arnold D. McNair,[168] in a Roman contract of mandatum:

> If A asks B to render him some service and B undertakes to do it, then, subject to certain rights of revocation and renunciation in both parties, A has an action against B if he fails to carry out the service properly and, on the other hand, B has against A an action for reimbursement of expenses and indemnification.[169]

Thus, the *mandatum* was a gratuitous "typified" or "nominate" contract with little or no application in the profit making world of commercial transactions as it was "nothing more than a friendly service."[170]

The *mandatarius* had the authority to act, but only within the limits of the powers expressly granted by his *mandator*; if the *mandatarius* acted outside those powers, his promises, albeit on behalf of the *mandator,* could not be enforced against the latter. The third party only had recourse against the *mandatarius*. In this respect, the classical Roman law of mandate did not differ much from the biblically-derived legal principle that an agent can only benefit from, but not harm his principal (as was

---

167 Wolfram Müller-Freienfels, *Legal Relations in the Law of Agency: Power of Agency and Commercial Certainty*, 13 AM. J. COMP. L. 193 (1964) (I; *Historical Development*) [hereinafter Müller-Freienfels, *Historical Development*]; Wolfram Müller-Freienfels, *Legal Relations in the Law of Agency: Power of Agency and Commercial Certainty*, 13 AM. J. COMP. L. 341 (1964) (IV, *The Law Today*) [hereinafter Müller-Freienfels, *The Law Today*].

168 Omar Abel Morales Lurssen, *Comparative Study on Agency* (2008) (unpublished LL.M. thesis, University of Arizona) (on file with author), *available at* http://natlaw.com/interam/gu/bk/sp/spgubk00003.pdf (last accessed Aug. 20, 2013)http://www.natlaw.com/interam/gu/bk/sp/spgubk00003.pdf.

169 *See* W. W. BUCKLAND & ARNOLD D. MCNAIR, ROMAN LAW & COMMON LAW: A COMPARISON IN OUTLINE 307–08 (rev. 2d ed. 2008).

170 *Id.* at 308.

discussed in the principal chapter).[171] Thus, biblical and Roman law denied protection to third parties against a *mandator* despite having provided these third parties with every appearance that their *shaliach* or *mandatarius* was authorized to promise or incur the liability they did on behalf of their *mandator* or principal.[172] Clearly this Roman and biblical mandate was very different from the law of agency, which binds principals for the promises or acts of agents whom they clothe with sufficient apparent authority and who consequently promises or acts in what reasonably appears to be a binding or truly "representative" fashion.

2. The Transactional Costs of the Roman and Biblical Mandates

What is at stake when a modern marketplace is governed by the principles underlying the Roman and biblical mandates? Clearly much more is at stake than having to deal with a different nomenclature or even with a requirement of gratuitousness. When a *mandator* and his *mandatarius* become participants in a commercial transaction, it is not only to buy, sell, lend, borrow or exchange goods, services or money with each other but also with third parties, a category which involves most participants in the marketplace, except those who participated in the underlying or pre-existing agreements (in this case of mandate or of agency). Bearing this in mind, ponder the significance of the following example, to which I will refer occasionally in this Appendix.

Retail merchant "TP" heard about the highly discounted price of Pima cotton shirts being offered by "P's" wholesale shirt business. He came to P's business and told "A," P's sales manager that he wished to purchase 80 dozen Pima cotton shirts at the 50% discount he heard about. Unknown to A, P had already sent him an e-mail rescinding the 50% discount two hours prior to TP's arrival at the wholesale business. In the e-mail, P noted a resurgent market demand for those shirts. However, when A dealt with TP, he had not checked his computer. TP paid cash for the shirts to A at the discounted price and immediately rented a truck at a premium freight charge because of his desire to place the shirts for quick sale in his retail business. Subsequently, when TP and the truck he rented arrived at P's warehouse, TP was told by P that he had just fired A for not being a trustworthy sales manager and that the price instruction in effect when the sale took place was the one he had sent to A two hours prior to TP's purchase. P was willing to sell the shirts to TP at the instruction, but not at the discounted price.

Can TP claim from P the delivery of the same shirts he bought from A at the price quoted by him? Can P validly rescind that sale by showing that he had rescinded the discounted price in a timely fashion? How much weight should a contemporary adjudicator of that dispute give to: 1) the instructions that P expressly sent to A; 2) the price quoted by a sales manager who was still employed by P when TP dealt with him? What weight should be given to TP's reliance upon customarily accepted or apparent signs of authority conferred upon the sales manager to bind a principal as his agent? Should there be a requirement that such reliance be followed by acts that reflect the third party's detrimental reliance such as by incurring the costs of hiring a carrier to pick up and deliver the goods?

---

171 *See supra* § 5:11.

172 Morales Lurssen, *supra* note 168, at 8–9.

Such are the issues and determinations peculiar to agency in today's commerce. Depending upon the substantive and procedural approaches adopted in these determinations, commerce could move either in a very slow and costly manner or at a cost-effective and fair pace.[173] There exists a record of a Mexican banking practice inspired by its law of mandate and powers of attorney as interpreted and applied in an unpublished Mexican Supreme Court decision.[174] This decision held that the president of a beer company who contracted to purchase a needed ingredient for the making of beer was not expressly authorized to enter into such a contract by the company's by-laws or powers of attorney; neither his signature in the contract or in the company's check bound the company. It only bound the president in his personal (and insolvent) capacity. Aside from its encouragement, because of the uncertainty that results from bad faith practices, this, among other decisions, caused banks to require that their business clients provide them with their updated by-laws and powers of attorney so that before paying on checks or accepting drafts, the bankers could ascertain the authority of the signers. Can the reader visualize the additional operational costs of such examinations and verifications of signature? If you were a legal adviser to Mexico's Congress or to its Supervisory Banking Commission, what measures would you suggest they adopt to eliminate the artificial costs of the mandate-power of attorney approach to commercial transactions?

3. *Forerunners of the Civil Law of Authority and Representation*

As a result of the emergence of national and international markets for the sales and financing of commodities such as wool (discussed in the principal chapter), Europe's medieval agricultural society became progressively commercialized. Commercialization bred intermediation and intermediation required manifold agencies. Unlike in Cato's Rome, in some European countries, some of the new mandates were paid for. While the "civil" *mandat* was still gratuitous, its commercial counterpart relied on "auxiliaries" of merchants such as sales clerks, commission and "*del credere*" agents (at times also referred to as "factors"). Some earned regular wages, while others were compensated for what they sold, lent, exchanged, insured or shipped. Additionally, some had more discretion to bind their principal than others. Thus, the division of labor and complexity of intermediation practiced by these commercial agents or brokers caused the emergence of more flexible versions of the Roman mandate and of the English agency. As their flexibility increased, so did their similarities.

Interestingly, Canonic and English Church law helped in this rapprochement. For example, a 1298 Canonic Code known as *Bonifatiana* allowed a *mandatarius-procurator* to be designated by a party to a marriage contract to sign it on his behalf even though this contract was deemed highly personal by the secular law and thus not susceptible to being signed by a third party.[175] In turn, the English law of agency was enriched by equity (*aequitas*) as a source of private law.[176] Equity insisted on effectuating the parties' true contractual intent (*fides facta*) especially in connection

---

173 *See supra* § 1:2(B).

174 Unpublished Mexican Supreme Court decision (on file with author).

175 Müller-Freienfels, *Historical Development, supra* note 167, at 194 (citing the *Decretal* titled "*de procuratoribus*" (c. 9, VI, 1, 19), of the Bonifatiana Canonic Code).

176 *Id.* at 195 n.7 and accompanying text ("This idea is stressed very strongly by Hans Würdinger. . . .").

with the church doctrine of *pacta sunt servanda.* In addition, it applied the doctrine of "civil death" to transactions entered into by persons who, as monks, were not supposed to be participating in them. This doctrine required that those who benefitted from transactions entered into by persons considered civilly dead pay for the goods or services acquired by the latter as if they were their agents.[177] Thus, during the reign of Edward I, an abbot was ordered to pay for goods purchased by a civilly dead monk whose monastery (as a tacit principal) benefited from that purchase.[178]

Finally, Hugo Grotius' *De Jure Belli ac Pacis*,[179] a writing that will be discussed in a later chapter and that strongly influenced late eighteenth- and early nineteenth-century civil law codes, especially in Prussia and France,[180] justified the binding effects of a mandate upon the *mandator* because it reflected his true contractual will. Additionally, the *Allgemeine Landrecht fiir die Preussischen* of June 1, 1792 (hereinafter *Landrecht*), the first European enactment that could qualify as a civil code,[181] opened the door to direct ties between the principal and third parties in response to the needs of commerce.[182] Nonetheless, the *Landrecht* lacked a coherent regulation of the independent rights and duties that emerged from the transactions involving the *mandatarius* or procurator and third parties. Issues that remained unanswered were: When was the *mandator* liable for their promises or acts, especially when they had exceeded or disregarded his instructions or powers of attorney? Hence, even though the *Landrecht* influenced both the *Code Civil* and the Austrian General Civil Code,[183] it did not separate or distinguish between the binding effects of a representation of the will of the *mandator* from the rights and duties that flowed between the parties to the original mandate. Such a development took place in nineteenth-century Germany and was essentially due to a doctrinal writing which Müller-Freienfels describes as "one of the major achievements of nineteenth century European legal science."[184]

---

177 *Id.* at 195.

178 *Id.*

179 *Id.*

180 *See infra* § 8:2.

181 *See infra* § 12:3(A).

182 Müller-Freienfels, *Historical Development, supra* note 167, at 196 (discussing *Von Vollmachtsaufträgen* (Powers of Mandate)).

183 *Id.* "As an illustration, the *Code Civil* (arts. 1984 *et seq.*) and the Austrian General Civil Code (Arts. 1002 *et seq.*) still combine power of agency (*pouvoir, Vollmacht*) and mandate (*mandat, Mandat*) and do not acknowledge the existence of "representation," as an autonomous institution." *Id.* (emphasis added).

184 *Id.* Müller-Freienfels notes that Paul Laband had borrowed the concept of abstraction from Karl Einert. *Id.* at 197 n.21. (He wrote: '*Ein Handelspapier zu dem Gebrauche bestimmt, den man beim Wechsel beabsichtigt, ist um so vollkommner. . . . je abstracter es dasteht.*' ") (Attributed the rights of a holder in due course commercial paper an abstraction or independence from the rights, defenses or equities between the original drafter or maker and the payee of the paper) (translation by author). Müller-Freienfel notes that until the seventeenth and eighteenth centuries the common law did not use the term "agent," but used instead designations such as: " 'attornatus,' 'servus,' 'servant,' 'ballivius,' 'camerarius,' 'homo,' 'senscallus,' 'receptor,' 'apprenticius,' 'abroccarius,' " and "procurator." *Id.* at 197. Further, "[a]gency did not emerge as a separate concept distinct from master and servant until after Blackstone's time and not before Livermore and Paley wrote the first American and English books on agency in 1811 and 1812 respectively." *Id.*

4. *The German* Prokura*: Independence or "Abstraction" of an Agent's Authority and Representation*

Müller-Freienfels attributes the modern doctrine of the law of agency in civil law countries to the writings of Professor Paul Laband and to a lesser extent to those of Rudolf von Ihering. Laband's 1866 article "Representation in the Execution of Legal Transactions under the German Commercial Code" (*"Die Stellvertretung bet dem Abschluss von Rechtsgeschaften nach dem Allgemetnen Deutschen Handelsgesetzbuch"*) focused on the *Prokura* as a commonly used form of representation. The *Prokura* is a general power of attorney given to a merchant like "A" (the fired sales manager for the wholesaler of shirts we discussed earlier). It is so drafted as to enable the *Prokurist* or agent to engage in a broad range of commercial transactions on behalf of the principal-owner of the business. *Prokuras* were recorded in the Commercial Register and thereby gave third parties notice of their basic terms and conditions.[185] From the German *Prokura* practice, Laband deduced the "abstract" or independent nature of the *Prokurist's* representation. This means that if his powers as described in their public notice differed from those actually conferred upon him by his principal, third parties had the right to rely on what was public notice regardless of what went on in the pre-existing relationship between the principal and the *Prokurist.*[186]

Laband characterized this principle of separation between the contract of mandate (*Auftrag*) and authority (*Vollmacht*) as one between two independent autonomous relations. He suggested that the law of mandates had to cut the umbilical cord that tied the mandate and the authority and representations it conferred. Otherwise, these legal institutions could not keep up with modern commercial practices and needs.[187] Further, third persons, an always-growing category of participants in a market economy, would be subject to defenses derived from the pre-existing contract of mandate between distant or unknown principals and their agents. Professor Hans Dolle, one of Germany's most respected post-World War private law scholars, called Laband's separation principle one of the most impressive examples of a "legal discovery." Müller-Freienfels agreed with this appraisal and listed a large number of countries that adopted it. Among them, in chronological order, were the civil, commercial or codes of obligations of Germany, Switzerland, Turkey, Greece, Sweden, Denmark, Norway, Finland, Italy, Japan, Thailand, Ethiopia, the Soviet Union, Poland, Czechoslovakia and Hungary.[188]

C. The Common Law of Agency

1. *Status and Contract*

The medieval law of master and servant is in all likelihood the earliest ancestor of the common law of agency, dating back "hundreds of years . . . and dealt with servants who performed physical labor over whom the master had broad control."[189] The term

---

185 *Id.* at 197.

186 *Id.* at 197–98.

187 *Id.* at 198.

188 Wolfram Müller-Freienfels, *Law of Agency,* 6 AM. J. COMP. L. 165, 172–73 (1957).

189 *See* James A. Cohen, *Lawyer Role, Agency Law, and the Characterization "Officer of the Court,"* 48 BUFF. L. REV. 349, 391–92 (2000).

" 'servant' referred to 'wage labor,' commonly manual labor."[190] As noted earlier, because of the commercialization that took place in the fourteenth and fifteenth centuries, a division of commercial labor sprung up that placed numerous intermediaries between producers and distributors or between distributors and consumers. Prominent among them were brokers, agents and factors of various types.[191] The banking business's reliance on branch banking contributed much to the proliferation of financial agents. These agents made it possible for banking headquarters to do business with an increasingly distant clientele, as was the case for the Florentine banks which, as was discussed in the principal chapter, lent to and purchased wool from English wool producers.[192] Yet, common law masters and servants were not thought of as bound by contracts, but by a customary relation in which the status of each party was the determining factor.[193] The master and servant relation led to the development of the concept of *respondeat superior*, which means "[l]et the master answer."[194] By virtue of this doctrine, the master answered for the servant's acts because of his status as master as long as the acts were within the scope of his employment.[195] In other words, because the master controlled the servant's actions, the servant's acts were *ipso iure* the master's and there was no need for contracts to spell out the rights and duties of that relationship; customs sufficed. These customary relations also led to the development of key concepts of the modern law of agency such as "apparent authority" and "disclosed and undisclosed principals," which could bind principals even though they had not expressly authorized, or may have even forbidden, certain acts or promises of their agents.

2. *What Is an Agency*

The Restatement (Third) of Agency, published by the American Law Institute in 2006 (hereinafter Restatement of Agency),[196] defines agency as: "the fiduciary *relationship* that arises when one person (a "principal") manifests assent to another person (an "agent") that the agent shall act on the principal's behalf and subject to the principal's control, and the agent manifests assent or otherwise consents so to act."[197]

As a fiduciary relationship, agency is based on trusting the agent to act on the principal's behalf. Yet the agent is also an intermediary between the principal and a third party. Through its acts, the agent creates rights or obligations for the principal, thus affecting the principal's legal relations with third parties.[198] Finally, in principle, and especially where the principal-agent relationship is concerned, the agent is subject to the principal's control.[199] This is the most critical element of that relationship.[200]

---

190 *Id.* at 392.

191 *See* RENAISSANCE FLORENCE: A SOCIAL HISTORY 183–84 (Roger J. Crum & John T. Paoletti eds., 2006) (discussing the role of intermediaries, especially brokers and factors).

192 *See* Ramon Casadesus-Masanell & Daniel F. Spulber, *Trust and Incentives in Agency*, 15 S. CAL. INTERDISC. L. J. 45, 72 (2005).

193 POUND, *supra* note 163, at 211–13.

194 *See* John Edward Davidson, *Reconciling the Tension between Employer Liability and Employee Privacy*, 8 GEO. MASON U. C.R. L.J. 145, 175 (1998).

195 *See* Daniel S. Kleinberger, *Respondeat Superior Run Amok*, 59 BENCH & BAR MINN. 16, 16–18 (Nov. 2002).

196 RESTATEMENT (THIRD) OF AGENCY (2006).

197 RESTATEMENT (THIRD) OF AGENCY § 1.01 (emphasis added).

198 *See* Deborah A. DeMott, *Disloyal Agents* 58 ALA. L. REV. 1049, 1051 (2007).

199 RESTATEMENT (THIRD) OF AGENCY § 1.01.

However, while this element determines whether an agency relationship exists between the principal and the agent,[201] it does not determine the principal's liability to the third party or parties with whom the agent deals on his behalf, as we will now discuss.

3. *Apparent, Actual, Express and Implied Authority: Disclosed, Undisclosed and Partially Disclosed Principals*

The following are concepts and principles that have shaped many of the rules of United States agency law and as such have found their place in the Restatement of Agency. As illustrated by the sale of shirts by a sales manager at a price below that authorized by his principal, agents, not infrequently, knowingly or not, exceed their actual authority.[202] Yet, such an agent can still bind the principal to the consequences of his acts if he acted with what the Restatement of Agency defines as apparent authority:[203] "[T]he power held by an agent or other actor to affect a principal's legal relations with third parties when a third party reasonably believes the actor has authority to act on behalf of the principal and that belief is traceable to the principal's manifestations."[204]

The two elements for a binding apparent authority, then, are first, the circumstances created by the principal that could reasonably result in a third party believing that the agent is authorized, and second, an "actual and reasonable reliance by the third party upon these circumstances."[205] In the example of the sale of shirts at a price lower than that authorized by the principal, one of the circumstances created by the principal that could induce the third party to believe in such an authorization was the naming of the agent to the position of "sales manager." Furthermore, the third party's reliance on such apparent authority was exemplified by that party's rental of a truck to pick up the shirts.[206]

Apparent authority is distinguished from actual authority based upon the agent's reasonable belief of the principal's intent. As stated by the Restatement of Agency § 2.01: "[a]n agent acts with actual authority when, at the time of taking action that has legal consequences for the principal, the agent reasonably believes, in accordance with the principal's manifestations to the agent, that the principal wishes the agent so to act."[207]

---

200 *See* Kenneth M. Lodge et al., *A Lender's Liability for Agent Misdeeds*, 33 SANTA CLARA L. REV. 811, 820 (1993).

201 *Id.* at 820–21.

202 *See* Thomas A. Simpson, *A Comment on an Inherently Flawed Concept: Why the Restatement (Third) of Agency Should Not Include the Doctrine of Inherent Agency Power*, 57 ALA. L. REV. 1163, 1171 (2006).

203 *See* Luke Meier, *Using Agency Law to Determine the Boundaries of the Free Speech and Establishment Clauses*, 40 IND. L. REV. 519, 522–23 (2007).

204 RESTATEMENT (THIRD) OF AGENCY § 2.03.

205 *See* Lodge et. al, *supra* note 200, at 825.

206 *See* Deborah A. DeMott, *Breach of Fiduciary Duty: On Justifiable Expectations of Loyalty and their Consequences* 48 ARIZ. L. REV. 925, 952 (2006) ("An agent acts with apparent authority when the third party with whom the agent interacts reasonably believes that the agent acts with actual authority on the basis of the manifestation of the principal, which may include placing the agent in a particular position or giving the agent a particular title.").

207 RESTATEMENT (THIRD) OF AGENCY § 2.01.

As noted by Professor Morales, "[t]he third party's belief of the extent of the agent's authority is irrelevant . . . [because] the agent's actual authority is established and determined when the principal [tells] the agent what he is to accomplish."[208] Another commentator stated: "[a]n agent has express actual authority when the principal specifically authorizes the conduct by the agent."[209] "Actual implied authority" comes about when it is reasonably regarded as necessary for the agent to fulfill the task appointed by the principal.[210] Because the agent must act in such a way as to seek to complete the task instructed by the principal through actual implied authority, he can take actions that are incidental to fulfilling his express actual authority.[211] Thus, even though the agent was not specifically authorized to take a certain action, he can reasonably infer that he has authority to do so in order to fulfill his task.[212] Issues of actual authority and actual implied authority usually arise where the agent either seeks payment of his fees or reimbursement for his costs from his principal.

Finally, the Restatement of Agency establishes that "[a] principal is disclosed if, when an agent and a third party interact, the third party has notice that the agent is acting for a principal and has notice of the principal's identity."[213] Further, "[a] disclosed principal is a principal whose identity is known to the third party when the third party transacts with the principal's agent."[214] In contrast, the Restatement of Agency defines an undisclosed principal as follows: "[a] principal is undisclosed if, when an agent and a third party interact, the third party has no notice that the agent is acting for a principal."[215] In a transaction with an undisclosed principal, the third party is unaware of the principal's existence and believes that the agent is acting on his own behalf.[216] I suggest that before inferring an undisclosed principal's exemption of liability, the reader should take a look at the *Cargill* decision summarized in a subsequent section.[217]

D. A Comparison of Civil and Common Law Statutory, Quasi-Statutory and Judicial Rules

1. *The Restatement of Agency in Representative Codes and Uniform Laws*

a. *Drafting Methods*

Even a superficial reading of the Restatement of Agency (which many United States judges and litigators treat as a "quasi-statutory" enactment) shows its

---

208 Morales Lurssen, *supra* note 168, at 59.

209 *See* Meier, *supra* note 203, at 522.

210 *See* Lodge et al., *supra* note 200, at 824.

211 *See* Meier, *supra* note 203, at 522.

212 *See* Eric Rasmussen, *Agency Law and Contract Formation*, 6 AM. L. & ECON. REV. 369, 372 (2004).

213 RESTATEMENT (THIRD) OF AGENCY § 1.04(2)(a).

214 Simpson, *supra* note 202, at 1165.

215 RESTATEMENT (THIRD) OF AGENCY § 1.04(2)(b).

216 *See* Simpson, *supra* note 202, at 1165; Rasmussen, *supra* note 212, at 399.

217 *See infra* § 5:13(D)(1)(d).

judicially-casuistic[218] origins. This form of drafting stands in sharp contrast with the synthesized, algebraic-like concepts of European codes such as the *Code Civil* or the BGB.[219] Notice this contrast in the highly factual distinctions that the Restatement of Agency draws among apparent, actual, express and implied authority and their respective agencies. For example, consider the category of a "Partially Disclosed or Unidentified Principals" which the Restatement of Agency defines as: "[a] principal is unidentified if, when an agent and a third party interact, the third party has notice that the agent is acting for a principal but does not have notice of the principal's identity."[220]

Similarly, the Restatement of Agency selects the judicial rule it deems most consistent with its analysis of case law and recommends to the future adjudicator that: "A principal is partially disclosed if the third party knows that the agent is acting for a principal but is unaware of the principal's identity."[221] In other words, treat the third party in accordance with the rules and exceptions (and perhaps exceptions to the exceptions) that govern the relations with an undisclosed principal.

Compare these provisions of the Restatement of Agency with the following code provisions in Civil Law countries:

> § 164 of the BGB of 1900:
>
> A declaration of intent which a person makes in the name of a principal within the scope of his own power of agency in the name of a principal takes effect directly in favour of and against the principal. . . ."[222]
>
> Or compare with §§ 49 (1) and 50 of the German Commercial Code (*Handelsgesetzbuch,* 1861, hereinafter HGB):[223]
>
> § 49. Scope of the *Prokura*[224]
>
> (1) The *Prokura* constitutes authority to enter into every kind of judicial and non-judicial business and legal transaction related to the operation of a commercial business.
>
> § 50. Limiting the Scope of the *Prokura*
>
> (1) A limitation of the scope of the *Prokura* is ineffective as to third parties.
>
> (2) This applies especially to a limitation whereby the *Prokura* may only be exercised for certain transactions or kinds of transactions, only under certain circumstances, for a limited period of time or at certain specific locations.

---

[218] By legal casuistry is generally meant a formulation of rules that relies heavily on the factual details of litigated cases. For a discussion on causitry in U.S. commercial legislation, *see infra* ch. 21.

[219] For a discussion of the drafting methods of these European codes, *see infra* chs. 8–12.

[220] RESTATEMENT (THIRD) OF AGENCY 1.04(2)(c).

[221] *See* Simpson, *supra* note 202, at 1165.

[222] BGB § 164.

[223] GERMAN COMMERCIAL CODE 66 (Martin Peltzer & Elizabeth A. Voight trans., 2003).

[224] These translators spell this term as *Prokura* while Müller-Freienfels spells it as "*Procura*." Müller-Freienfels, *Historical Development*, *supra* note 167, at 197.

b. Elements of European and Guatemalan Commercial Agency

The European Council Directive 86/653 of 1986 on Commercial Agents states in relevant part:

> 'commercial agent' shall mean a self-employed intermediary who has continuing authority to negotiate the sale or the purchase of goods on behalf of another person, hereinafter called the 'principal', or to negotiate and conclude such transactions on behalf of and in the name of that principal.[225]

At noted by Professor Morales, the European Directive seems to give the same delegated authority to commercial agents that the Restatement of Agency gives to its agents.[226] It states that the commercial agent may negotiate and conclude transactions "on behalf of and in the name of that principal."[227] He notes that the element of actual representation in commercial agency is relied upon by some European courts such as the French *Cour de Cassation* when determining whether commercial agency exists. For example, in *Blanc Canet v. Europcar France SA*,[228] the court held that the status of a commercial agent is not necessarily derived from the intentions expressed by the parties in the contract or from the name that they give to their agreements. It must be found in the manner in which the agency is actually carried out. Thus, Canet could not claim that she was a commercial agent because she did not carry on her activities independently and did not have the power to negotiate or even contract for and on behalf of Europcar.

However, the same European Directive makes it clear that the commercial agent's scope of delegated authority is limited to some transactions such as the sale or purchase of goods:[229] "It does not include other commercial transactions, as even its name, 'commercial agent' suggests."[230] In addition, the European Directive refers to "continuing authority." Do you agree with Professor Morales that an agent's scope of delegated authority is much broader in the common law? If so, why? Does the Restatement of Agency limit the nature of the transactions in which an agent acts on behalf of the principal?

Having examined a decision by the European Court of Justice, Morales concludes that a European commercial agent must complete more than one transaction in order to be considered a commercial agent and thus be entitled to a commercial agency commission. Indeed, in *Poseidon Chartering BV v. Marianne Zeeschip Vof*,[231] Poseidon claimed damages for failure to pay a commercial agent's commission despite the fact that it negotiated a long-term charter party agreement for the defendant. According to the European Court of Justice, the fact that the intermediary maintained relations with the principal throughout the contractual period was insufficient to demonstrate

---

[225] *See* Council Directive 86/653, art. 1, 1986 O.J. (L382) 17 (EC) [hereinafter "European Directive"], *available* at http://eur-lex.europa.eu/LexUriServ/LexUriServ.do?uri=OJ:L:1986:382:0017:0021:EN:PDF.

[226] Morales Lurssen, *supra* note 168, at 20; *see also* RESTATEMENT (THIRD) OF AGENCY § 1.01.

[227] European Directive, *supra* note 225, art. 1(2).

[228] *See* Cour de Cassation [Cass.] [supreme court for judicial matters] Dec. 10, 2003, [2005] ECC 34 (Fr.).

[229] European Directive, *supra* note 225, art. 1(2).

[230] Morales Lurssen, *supra* note 168, at 23.

[231] *See* Case C-3/04, Poseidon Chartering BV v. Marianne Zeeschip VOF and Others, 2006 E.C.R. 2505.

continuing authority. Because Poseidon did not prove continuing authority, it was not a commercial agent for purposes of claiming such an agent's commission; what it characterized as a single contract did not suffice.

Morales points out that this ruling contradicts one of the purposes of the European Directive, which is to protect "commercial agents *vis-à-vis* their principals," including the former's remunerations and commissions.[232] "How ironic," he argues, "that the very protection that is intended by the European Directive is denied to Poseidon by the European Court of Justice."[233]

Guatemala's Commercial Code is in some respects similar to the European Directive. It states that commercial agents act in the name and on behalf of one or many principals.[234] It also states that the commercial agent acts "permanently,"[235] which can be interpreted similarly to the European Directive's "continuing."[236] Thus, a commercial agent in Guatemala may be required to complete more than one transaction in order to be able to collect his commission as a commercial agent, as required by the European Court's interpretation of the European Directive. However, unlike the European Directive, the Guatemalan Commercial Code gives commercial agents a larger scope of action as commercial agents promote and conclude commercial contracts[237] and not just the sale or the purchase of goods.[238]

As a legislator or judge trying to encourage wider participation of commercial intermediaries, especially in a common market setting where massive amounts of goods and services are being traded each day, do you agree with Professor Morales's criticism of the European Court's decision in Poseidon? What is so important about the proof that the commercial agent has been involved in more than one transaction when considering his or her entitlement to a proper remuneration? What if the commercial agent in question wishes to specialize in obtaining multi-year charter parties for a select number of principals? Does it mean that each of these principles can claim he should not be considered their commercial agent, until 1) he procures a charter party agreement with a different carrier than the one originally named in the multi-party agreement?; and 2) the first multi-year agreement is concluded and a new one is negotiated?

---

232 European Directive, *supra* note 225, at 382/17. The recital reads:

Whereas the differences in national laws concerning commercial representation substantially affect the conditions of competition and the carrying-on of that activity within the Community and are detrimental both to the protection available to commercial agents *vis-à-vis* their principals and to the security of commercial transactions; whereas moreover those differences are such as to inhibit substantially the conclusion and operation of commerical representation contracts where principal and commercial agent are established in different Member States. . . . *Id.*

233 Morales Lurssen, *supra* note 168, at 25.

234 *See* CÓDIGO DE COMERCIO DE GUATEMALA art. 280 (1970), *available* at http://guatemala.eregulations.org/media/codigo%20de%20comercio%20decreto%202–70.pdf [hereinafter C. COM. (GUAT.)].

235 *Id.*

236 European Directive, *supra* note 225, art. 1(2).

237 *See* C. COM. (GUAT.) art. 280.

238 *Id.* art. 281.

2. *Civil Law Court Opinions on the Independence of the Agent's Authority*

a. *Germany's* Reichsoberhandelsgericht *(1872)*[239]

A stock company cannot defend itself against a creditor on the ground that the director, who borrowed money for the company, was not authorized to apply for such a loan, and that the creditor knew about this. The court stated:

> The statutory rule, in denying any legal effect to any limitation on the authority of the directors, the *procurists*, or the partners in its various definite, unrestricted, and unconditional provisions, did not intend to draw distinctions either as to whether the third person negotiating with the board of directors had any knowledge of the latter's limitation of authorization nonetheless existing. The third person knew only that a limitation was desired, which, however, the statutory rule declares invalid. Bad faith can not [sic] be held against a party to a contract if he disregards something that the statutory rule expressly declares to be not worthy of consideration.[240]

Insurance Company Germania, another *Reichsoberhandelsgericht* decision, held that a restriction on the authority of the board of directors (*Vorstand*) was registered in the Registry of Companies. Yet, the Court affirmed the principle (of the principal's independent liability toward the third party) in broad terms, and added:

> A third person never needs to permit a limitation of authority to apply against himself, even if that limitation was disclosed by an unlawful entry in the Commercial Register. Such a registered limitation is to be deemed as nonexistent, since the acts of the registrar cannot alter the statutory rule.[241]

Further in *Sander v. Schwarzroc*, *Reichsoberhandelsgericht* held that:

> The mere knowledge of an infringement of the authority to dispose [of things] does not establish the *dolus* [malicious intent] of the third party. Therefore, the third party is not prevented from considering the partner's legal act as one of the partnership itself. However, the third person is not protected with regard to those legal acts which the partner performed under the name of the partnership with the purpose of causing prejudice to the partnership and of which the third party had knowledge and to which he was an accomplice.[242]

On the other hand, the Guatemalan Commercial Code requires that the agent can only agree to contracts and other transactions on behalf of the principal if he is expressly authorized to do so.[243] It also states that contractual offers received from the agent do not bind the principal until he replies that he accepts them.[244] These provisions virtually eliminate the possibility that a commercial agent will bind his principal through apparent authority. However, quasi-contractually and through the transaction known as a *negotiorum gestio,* an agent can bind his principal. As provided

---

239 Müller-Freienfels, *Historical Development, supra* note 167, at 211.

240 *Id.* at 211.

241 *Id.* at 211–12.

242 *Id.* at 212.

243 *See* C. COM. (GUAT.) art. 284.

244 *Id.* art. 286.

for in Guatemala's Civil Code, *negotiorum gestio* occurs when a person conducts negotiations on behalf of another person without an agreement between them and the beneficiary of the other person's actions ratifies the negotiations.[245] By virtue of ratification, those acts are binding to the beneficiary of the negotiations. Though *negotiorum gestio* would appear to be similar to apparent authority in agency, it differs from it in that ratification is still necessary for the transactions to be binding on the principal.

b. A United States Decision on Disclosed and Undisclosed Principals as Secured Creditors: A. Gay Jenson Farms Co. v. Cargill Inc.

In *A. Gay Jenson Farms Co. et al, v. Cargill, Inc.*,[246] 86 individuals, partnerships or corporate farmers sued Cargill, Inc. (Cargill) and defendant Warren Grain & Seed Co. (Warren) to recover losses sustained when Warren defaulted on the contracts made with plaintiffs for the sale of grain. After a trial by jury, judgment was entered in favor of plaintiffs and Cargill appealed. The appellate court affirmed the judgment in an opinion written by Justice Peterson. The following is a summary of his opinion with only isolated citations:

This case arose out of the financial collapse of defendant Warren Seed & Grain Co., and its failure to satisfy its indebtedness to the plaintiffs. . . . Warren operated a grain elevator and . . . was involved in the purchase of . . . grain from local farmers. . . . In addition, it operated a seed business which involved buying seed grain from farmers, processing it and reselling it for seed to farmers and local elevators. Lloyd Hill [owner of Warren] decided in 1964 to apply for financing from Cargill. . . . Warren and Cargill thereafter entered into a security agreement which provided that Cargill would loan money for working capital to Warren on "open account" financing up to a stated limit, which was originally set as $175,000. . . . Proceeds from Warren's sales would be deposited with Cargill and credited to its account. [Loans were secured by a second mortgage on Warren's real estate and a first chattel mortgage on its inventories of grain and merchandise in the sum of $175,000 with 7% interest.] A new contract was negotiated in 1967, extending Warren's credit line to $300,000. . . . Cargill was given the right of access to Warren's books for inspection. . . . Consent by Cargill was required before Warren would be allowed to declare a dividend or sell and purchase stock. . . . Cargill's regional office. . . . examined the annual statement and the accounts receivable, expenses, inventory, seed, machinery and other financial matters. . . . At approximately this time, a memo was given to the Cargill official in charge of the Warren account, Erhart Becker, which stated in part: "This organization (Warren) needs very strong paternal guidance."

. . .

As Warren's indebtedness continued to be in excess of its credit line, Cargill began to contact Warren daily regarding its financial affairs. Cargill headquarters informed its regional office in 1973 that, since Cargill money was being used, Warren should realize that Cargill had the right to make some critical decisions regarding the use of the funds. . . . In 1975, Cargill's regional office began to keep a daily debit position on

---

245 *See* CÓDIGO CIVIL DE GUATEMALA arts. 1605–1615 (2010), *available* at http://biblio3.url.edu.gt/Libros/2011/codigo.pdf.

246 A. Gay Jenson Farms Co. v. Cargill, Inc., 309 N.W. 2d 285 (Minn. 1981).

Warren. . . . In April 1977, an audit of Warren revealed that Warren was $4 million in debt. . . . After Warren ceased operations, it was found to be indebted to Cargill in the amount of $3.6 million. Warren was also determined to be indebted to plaintiffs in the amount of $2 million, and plaintiffs brought this action in 1977 to seek recovery of that sum. Plaintiffs alleged that Cargill was jointly liable for Warren's indebtedness as it had acted as principal for the grain elevator.

. . .

The jury found that Cargill's conduct between 1973 and 1977 had made it Warren's principal. Warren was found to be the agent of Cargill with regard to contracts for:

1. The purchase and sale of grain for market.
2. The purchase and sale of seed grain.
3. The storage of grain.

The court determined that Cargill was the disclosed principal of Warren. It was concluded that Cargill was jointly liable with Warren for plaintiffs' losses, and judgment was entered for plaintiffs. [At trial, plaintiffs sought to establish actual agency by Cargill's course of dealing between 1973 and 1977 rather than "apparent" agency or agency by estoppel, so that the only issue in this case is one of actual agency.] Cargill seeks a reversal of the jury's findings. . . .

1. The major issue in this case is whether Cargill, by its course of dealing with Warren, became liable as a principal on contracts made by Warren with plaintiffs. Cargill contends that no agency relationship was established with Warren, notwithstanding its financing of Warren's operation and its purchase of the majority of Warren's grain. However, we conclude that Cargill, by its control and influence over Warren, became a principal with liability for the transactions entered into by its agent Warren.

Agency is the fiduciary relationship that results from the manifestation of consent by one person to another that the other shall act on his behalf and subject to his control, and consent by the other so to act. In order to create an agency there must be an agreement, but not necessarily a contract between the parties. An agreement may result in the creation of an agency relationship although the parties did not call it an agency and did not intend the legal consequences of the relation to follow. The existence of the agency may be proved by circumstantial evidence which shows a course of dealing between the two parties. When an agency relationship is to be proven by circumstantial evidence, the principal must be shown to have consented to the agency since one cannot be the agent of another except by consent of the latter.

A creditor who assumes control of his debtor's business may become liable as principal for the acts of the debtor in connection with the business. It is noted in comment (a) to section 140 that:

> A security holder who merely exercises a veto power over the business acts of his debtor by preventing purchases or sales above specified amounts does not thereby become a principal. However, if he takes over the management of the debtor's business either in person or through an agent, and directs what contracts may or may not be made, he becomes a principal, liable as a

> principal for the obligations incurred thereafter in the normal course of business by the debtor who has now become his general agent. . . .

A number of factors indicate Cargill's control over Warren, including the following: (1) Cargill's constant recommendations to Warren by telephone; (2) Cargill's right of first refusal on grain; (3) Warren's inability to enter into mortgages, to purchase stock or to pay dividends without Cargill's approval; (4) Cargill's right of entry onto Warren's premises to carry on periodic checks and audits; (5) Cargill's correspondence and criticism regarding Warren's finances, officers salaries and inventory; (6) Cargill's determination that Warren needed "strong paternal guidance". . . .

. . .

We conclude that, on the facts of this case, there was sufficient evidence from which the jury could find that Cargill was the principal of Warren within the definitions of agency set forth in Restatement (Second) of Agency §§ 1 and 140.

. . .

The question of whether payment in good faith to an agent relieves a principal of liability to a third party has not previously been decided in Minnesota. . . . The modern view, which has been adopted by a minority of states, is expressed in Restatement (Second) of Agency § 208 (1958), which provides:

> An undisclosed principal is not discharged from liability to the other party to a transaction conducted by an agent by payment to, or settlement of accounts with, the agent, unless he does so in reasonable reliance upon conduct of the other party which is not induced by the agent's misrepresentations and which indicates that the agent has settled the account.

We now adopt the modern position set forth in the Restatement rule. We believe that this rule is the better principle to be followed since the undisclosed principal is aware that he will become liable under the original transaction, and he should not be able to escape his liability by payment to the agent.

Affirmed.

COMMENTS AND QUESTIONS

Following the Restatement (Second) of Agency, the court refers to agency as a "fiduciary relationship which results from the manifestation of consent by one person to another that the other shall act on his behalf and subject to his control, and consent by the other so to act. . . ."[247] What does the court mean when it says: "In order to create an agency there must be an agreement, but not necessarily a contract between the parties." (Quoting Restatement (Second) of Agency § 1, comment b (1958)? Is this a distinction without a true difference? Would the court have been more accurate if it had said "but not necessarily a *formal contract of agency*"? After all, was it not trying to establish that the plaintiff and defendant acted as if they were a principal and an agent?

---

[247] RESTATEMENT (SECOND) OF AGENCY § 1(1) (1958).

Chapter 6

GUILDS AND THE CAPITALIST SYSTEM AND MARXIST LEGAL SYSTEMS

§ 6.1 THEIR SIGNIFICANCE

It is not always easy to understand what distinguishes our present commercial contracts from their medieval ancestors unless we understand what distinguished the guild system from capitalism. Stated more precisely: What made possible the transition from monopolistic, fixed prices and wages o to free markets for capital and labor?

Equally significant questions could be asked about the connections between the guilds' notion of just price basic tenets of the Marxist-Leninist legal and economic systems. For, as will be discussed in Chapters 15 and 16, Marx perceived the wages a capitalist paid his workers as a principal injustice of the capitalist system. According to him, the capitalists pocketed the difference between what they paid their workers and the added value produced by the combined work of their laborers, thereby enriching themselves at the expense of their "exploited" workers.[1] Were the medieval guilds, perhaps, the model of just compensation that Marxism Leninism had in mind when arriving at their formulas of compensation for workers such as that found in Article 12 of the 1936 Soviet Constitution: "From each according to his ability, to each according to his work."?[2]

The Latin Notariat, as will be discussed in the following chapter, is also a legal institution that owes much to the guild system, including its "tariff" method of compensation. Since the Middle Ages, the Notariat has been a guild-like institution that provided the requisite trust and formality for the execution and enforcement of contractual rights and duties. The following chapter should help the reader understand why a key legal institution like the Latin Notariat became part of important seventeenth- and eighteenth-century commercial statutes and of nineteenth-century codes.

§ 6.2 GUILDS, THE *VERLAGSSYSTEM* AND CAPITALISM

A. The Medieval Guilds and the *Verlagssystem*

The emergence of capitalism has been attributed to factors as diverse as the active presence of Jewish businessmen in central and northern European trade,[3] the

---

[1] *See infra* § 15:3(C)(1)(b).

[2] USSR CONST. art. 12 (1936), *available at* http://www.departments.bucknell.edu/russian/const/1936toc.html.

[3] *See generally* WERNER SOMBART, THE JEWS AND MODERN CAPITALISM (1911). He traced the success of capitalist institutions to the spirit of "acquisitiveness" of Jews and to the Jewish commercial presence in Central and Northern Europe. A controversial historian, Sombart embraced Nazism, which made possible his appointment to the University of Berlin and encouraged his work to be used as proof of Arian superiority over Jewish "acquisitiveness."

perception in the Protestant-Calvinistic ethic that the accumulation of wealth is a sign of divine salvation or election[4] and the "dialectic materialism"[5] of economic forces that placed capitalism as a way-station between feudalism and communism. These and other efforts to trace the roots of capitalism are characterized by a search for ultimate causes, often at the expense of factual evidence.

Factual evidence is not in short supply in the writings of the French economic historian Fernand Braudel. In his monumental trilogy, *Civilisation Matérielle, Economie et Capitalisme, XVe-XVIIIe* (1967) (Capitalism and Material Life, 1400–1800), which first appeared in English in 1973,[6] Braudel pays little attention to the ultimate or metaphysical causes of capitalism, or to what will happen after it is gone, if it is. Braudel's interest lies in describing when, where and how capitalism first showed its face. He seems to rely on a rather basic definition of capitalism: the use of money and of other capital resources by merchants willing to buy or finance labor in a manner that makes profitable production and distribution possible. Accordingly, he searches for the time, place and method when such an organized purchase and financing began.

In this search, he gathers information on all of the possible forces that brought about such a use of capital, regardless of whether the data was related to geographical, cultural, legal, economic or religious factors. This eclectic (or "total history") methodology brought about his conclusion that capitalism started its lengthy process of development in twelfth-century Europe and progressed through cities and states such as Venice, Antwerp, Amsterdam and London to become what it is today. It did so, in Braudel's opinion, by relying on social structures or organized behavior that in due course became transformative legal institutions. On the one hand, capitalism had to struggle against the regulations of guilds that prevented competition and the formation of capital. On the other hand, it was propelled forward by the competition for hired or purchased labor that resulted from the failure of the monopolistic regulations to provide steady and reasonably compensated employment.

The two conflicting social structures that acted as propelling forces of capitalism were: 1) the European associations of artisans or craftsmen known as guilds in

---

[4] *See* MAX WEBER, THE PROTESTANT ETHIC AND THE SPIRIT OF CAPITALISM (Routledge Classics 2005) (1930), *available at* http://xroads.virginia.edu/~HYPER/WEBER/header.html. (This electronic version is available from American Studies at the University of Virginia. Scanned, tagged, copy-edited and published by the University of Virginia American Studies Program 2001.) Charlottesville, Va. (last accessed Aug. 21, 2013). According to Weber, Roman Catholicism allowed the followers of church teachings to be assured of salvation but this was not the case with the Reformation. Protestants looked for signs of their salvation. This search found support in Calvin's doctrine of predestination, according to which God chooses some people for salvation and others for damnation. Success in one's accumulation of capital became an indication of having been chosen for salvation. Weber acknowledged that the religious component was but one of many factors in bringing about capitalism, especially in Western nations, including rational (as opposed to what he described as "magical") thinking, especially as used in science, law and public administration. *Id.* at ch. 4.

[5] Rob Sewell, *What is Dialectical Materialism?—A Study Guide with Questions, Extracts and Suggested Reading*, IN DEFENCE OF MARXISM (Nov. 2, 2002), http://www.marxist.com/what-is-dialectical-materialism.htm. As seen by Rob Sewell, a contemporary Marxist theoretician, the Marxist view of the world is not only materialist, or pre-determined by economic types of considerations, but also dialectical and "[t]he dialectical method is simply an attempt to understand more clearly our real interdependent world." *Id.* He quotes Frederic Engels, Marx's co-author in the Communist Manifesto, as stating that materialist dialectics "is nothing more than the science of the general laws of motion and development of nature, human society and thought." *Id.* As Sewell states, "Put simply, it is the logic of motion." *Id.* According to Marxists, therefore, this motion, as propelled by economic forces, inevitably will lead capitalist society toward communism, and with it, to the withering away of the state.

[6] *See* BRAUDEL I, Translator's Note (preceding the table of contents).

England, *corps de métiers* in France, *Zünfte* in Germany, *arti* in Italy and *gremios* in Spain; and 2) the independent (non-guild) merchants who commissioned manufactured or handcrafted goods from cottage industries. These merchants supplied the money and, in some cases, the raw material necessary for the manufacture of the goods. They were known in Germany as "*Verlegers*" and their work as "*Verlag.*" In France, the commissioned work was known as "*travail à domicile*," and as "domestic" or "putting out" work in England. The following sections summarize, with the help of Braudel's writings as well as the writings of other economic historians, key features of legal institutions whose imprint is still apparent in European civil and commercial codification and, to a much larger degree, surprising though it may sound at first, in socialist economies.[7] Thus, the reader will soon find that relatively recent amendments to the French commercial code still involve guild-like associations of merchants whose function is to make sure that their younger, less expert or well-endowed colleagues succeed, or at least are not wiped out by their competition, or merge their assets with others as best as possible.[8] The will also find that many socialist state sponsored monopolies and cooperatives are still being managed as if they were medieval guilds, except that their hidden profits are distributed not among guild masters, but highly placed party or government officials.[9]

B. Basic Features of European Medieval Guilds

Guilds were associations formed by artisans and craftsmen and later joined by merchants, although in much smaller numbers. While they may have existed from the beginning of commerce,[10] the guilds that immediately preceded the emergence of capitalism started in Europe during the twelfth century and reached their high point three centuries later.[11] The appearance of the European guilds was tied to the incipient money-economy and to the growth of European cities. Before this time, commodity-money and barter were a normal way of doing business.

The main purpose of the guild as a legal institution was to protect its members against competitors and harsh market conditions by assuring them a survival wage, at times paid in money and at times in kind. The fact that Guild members were, among others, manual workers such as bakers, tailors, winemakers, glass and shoemakers, cobblers, blacksmiths and metal workers, played an important role in the development of capitalism. As noted by Braudel, Karl Marx's summary of the typical sequence of a capitalistic transaction had three steps. In the first, the capitalist, the holder of money, paid workers for the goods they produced for him. In the second, he sold those goods

---

[7] In light of this statement, the reader should pay attention to the pricing and cost-cutting consequences of implementing the Soviet and Chinese multi-year plans. *See infra* chs. 15–19 (for a discussion of central planning in Russia and China). As a visiting lecturer at Karl Marx University in Sophia, Bulgaria in the early nineteen nineties, I remember purchasing a blue gabardine tailored suit with a vest and an extra pair of pants for the equivalent in Bulgarian *levas* of $12.00. One of my students during the course was an economist at the Bulgarian Central Bank, and I asked him to give me an estimate of the cost of the raw materials and labor involved in producing such a suit. His reply was "considerably more than the *levas* you paid for it."

[8] *See infra* § 10:5.

[9] *See e.g., infra* § 16:1.

[10] *See* 9 ENCYCLOPEDIA BRITANNICA 356 (1973) (describing Indian guilds in existence much earlier than the Common Era).

[11] BRAUDEL II, at 314–15.

and thereby acquired new money. In the third, he continued to purchase goods with the new money and to accumulate money and goods produced by others.[12]

The fact that manual labor or its product was bought with money, and was not bartered for other goods, was an important step in the road to capitalism because it empowered the holders of money to create their own as well as a residual social wealth. This empowerment of intermediate merchants was destined to collide with the monopolistic franchises granted to the guilds. And the fact that some guilds practiced their trades or professions collectively in the same shop or hall while others practiced them individually in their own shops made this proto-capitalist transaction easier.[13] For merchant guilds were at times as small as that of the providers of drinking water in the Seine River valley of France or as large as that of the international merchants and carriers of the "Hanseatic League," who did their business in and out of northern European sea and river ports.[14] Eventually, the incipient ventures between guild artisans and craftsmen on the one side and merchants on the other broke down when merchants began contracting directly with workers whether or not they were guild members. Once this happened, the conditions were ripe for the emergence of capitalism. What follows, then, is a discussion of the peculiar features of guilds and, as they lost their market dominance, of the key characteristics of the different types of emerging European merchants-capitalists.

1. Monopolies

Guilds enjoyed monopolistic rights given to them, usually as part of a detailed set of regulations, by the king of the realm or by town authorities, and especially by the latter as towns and guilds became highly interdependent entities. As with any monopoly, the purpose of the guild was to protect its market dominance, thereby assuring the basic subsistence of its members and their towns. Thus, medieval guilds were responsible for the reputation of products and regions such as the wine from Champagne and Bordeaux of France, the tin-glazed earthenware from Dutch cities, the lace from Chantilli, and so on. Many centuries later, this reputation gained the protection of commercial and regional trademarks. In exchange for their monopolistic rights, guilds were expected to strictly follow the terms and conditions of their grant, including the payment of taxes, which could often be oppressive.[15]

This monopolistic scheme meant that guilds regulated and policed their craft or profession, exercising control over admission to their ranks and also over the prices and quality of their products.[16] Eventually, the trades represented in the guilds proliferated and subdivided. Braudel notes that in 1260, Paris had more than one

---

[12] *See* KARL MARX, I CAPITAL 247–57 (Ben Fowkes trans., Penguin Classics 1990) (1867); *see also infra* § 15:3(C)(2).

[13] *See generally* ISAÍAS COVARRUBIAS, LA ECONOMÍA MEDIEVAL Y LA EMERGENCIA DEL CAPITALISMO (2004).

[14] *Id.* at 106. The Hanseatic League (from the term "*Hansa*" or group of merchants in German) was an alliance of guilds that included not only traders but also carriers to monopolize the maritime trade in the Baltic and Nordic Seas during the Late Middle Ages roughly between the thirteenth and seventeenth centuries. *Id.* at 81. It was centered in trading towns such as Bruges in the Low Countries and Lubeck and Hamburg in Germany. On the Hanseatic League and its influence in European trade, see BRAUDEL III, at 99–103.

[15] *See* BRAUDEL II, at 315.

[16] *See generally* De Moor, *The silent revolution*.

hundred guilds. At the same time, Nuremberg "was ruled by a strict and vigilant aristocracy, the metal-working guilds . . . divided . . . into several *dozen* independent professions and trades."[17] At the other end of the social spectrum, Basle and Frankfurt sported guilds of beggars who got together for no other purpose than to prevent the competition by colleagues likely to wander in or settle in their towns.[18] Some towns had no guilds and were known as "free" towns. Yet, the number of "free" towns was small, and until the end of the fourteenth century, a significant number of the handicrafts concentrated in urban areas were controlled by guilds.

2. *Hierarchy*

Generally, guilds were formed by masters, journeymen and apprentices. The masters were experts in their field of handicraft. Before a new employee could become a master, he had to undergo a schooling period that lasted several years during which he was first an apprentice and then, after completing his training, a journeyman. Masters earned the highest compensation, and journeymen the lowest. Moreover, journeymen could spend an entire lifetime earning the same wages. For example, a historical survey of customary wages in southern England found that the wage paid to "building [journeymen] craftsmen remained at sixpence a day for 120 years after 1412. . . ."[19] This bare "living wage" feature of the guilds was supplemented by religiously-inspired duties of mutual aid and assistance, especially for handicapped or disabled guild members.[20]

It is apparent from this organizational scheme that guilds favored the interests of masters (who ran them) at the expense of the interests of other members. The Spanish scholar Isaias Covarrubias notes that from the fourteenth century onward, admission to the guilds became even more restricted as the sons of masters were preferred as apprentices over other applicants.[21] Eventually, these sons also became the preferred replacements for their fathers, thereby making the status of guild-master *de facto* hereditary.[22]

3. *Fixed Standards of Workmanship, Fixed Prices and Set Wages in Preference to Profits and Competition*

The overriding purpose of the guilds was not to accumulate profits.[23] In Spain, for example, priests who frequently sat on the guild boards or who appointed board members insisted on the observance of religious and charitable duties, which displaced profit-making when necessary.[24] What really mattered to the guilds was preventing

---

[17] BRAUDEL II, at 315 (citations omitted).

[18] COVARRUBIAS, *supra* note 13, at 108. They were known as *corps de métiers* in France, *Zünfte* in Germany and *gremios* in Spain. The remnants of these guilds were still apparent in cities such as Ghent (in Belgium) and Florence (in Italy) in 1958 where specialized stores sold woolen textiles produced by the descendants of specialized textile guilds. A few decades later, I taught at the University of Aix-en-Provence and some of the best baguettes in that city were advertised as produced "by the centuries-old guild of the bakers."

[19] 10 ENCYCLOPEDIA BRITANNICA 564 (1973), *available at Labour Economics*, ENCYCLOPEDIA BRITTANICA, http://www.britannica.com/EBchecked/topic/326887/labour-economics/66906/Fixing-rates-of-pay.

[20] 4 ENCYCLOPEDIA BRITANNICA 786 (1973).

[21] COVARRUBIAS, *supra* note 13, at 109.

[22] *Id.*

[23] *Id.* at 154.

[24] *Id.*

competition among members and non-members because competition was regarded as a menace to the members' ability to earn a living wage. Thus, guilds forbade their members from diminishing the quality of products by changing their components so as to justify selling the products cheaper than competitors, substituting components in order to change prices, or doing business before or after the designated hours of business and subject to different terms and conditions.[25] Even the addition of rye to wheat when making bread (because it could lead to product differentiation and competition) required approval by the bakers' guild.[26]

The reason behind this apparently unbridled regulation was to enforce fixed prices by standardizing product ingredients and appearance. Products of the same quality were to be sold for the same price. In theory, fixed prices would assure a modicum average income to guild members. This outcome was preferable to that offered by the laws of supply and demand. Additionally, the uniform quality and prices prevented competition among guild members (and non-members) who might otherwise try outselling their competitors by lowering prices. Simply put, anything that could endanger reliance on fixed prices undermined the guild system.

The same fear of competition was apparent in segments of the agricultural sector. Fixed prices supported by uniform quality standards were relied upon in the sale of farm products during the guild period by farmers who grazed their cattle in common lands, also known as "commons" in central and northern Europe.[27] In basic terms, contractual bargaining was not a guild feature.

*4. The Guild Principle of Assurance of Sustenance Over Profits (***Nahrungsprinzip***) vs. Contractual Bargaining*

It is clear from the preceding section that an important legal and economic feature of the guild system was that contracts—the tools that implement supply and demand in capitalist societies—played only a minimal role (or no role at all) in setting the members' wages or the prices of the products. Wages were not the result of individual or collective bargains as is true in many contemporary capitalist societies. They were the product of a principle referred to by Max Weber as *Nahrungsprinzip* (the provision of sustenance, or mere survival, to its members).[28] According to Raymond de Roover, the noted historian of medieval economic thought, there were two influential views on the meaning of a just price among medieval thinkers. One view, which he attributed to Henry of Langenstein, held that a just price was the reasonable charge which would allow the producer "to live and to support his family on a scale suitable to his station in life."[29] If the producer charged more for his labor and expenses to retain his status (*per quanta res suas vendendo statutum suum continuare posit*), he committed the sin of avarice. Max Weber believed this to be the moral foundation of the guild system.

---

[25] *Id.*

[26] *Id.* at 108.

[27] *See generally* ELINOR OSTROM, GOVERNING THE COMMONS: THE EVOLUTION OF INSTITUTIONS FOR COLLECTIVE ACTION (1990). *See generally* De Moor, *The silent revolution* (on the pricing mechanism for products of the common).

[28] *See* Kozolchyk, *Commercialization*, at 11.

[29] Raymond de Roover, *The Concept of the Just Price: Theory and Economic Policy*, 18 J. ECON. HISTORY 418, 418 (1958) (citation omitted).

The other view belonged to Albert Magnus and Saint Thomas Aquinas. It first appeared in a thirteenth-century directive to parish priests: Flocks should be admonished not to charge wayfarers more than the price obtainable in the local market (*quam in mercato vendere possint*); otherwise, the wayfarers can complain to the priest, who is then required to set the price with "humanity."[30] The same reference to the market appears in Albert Magnus' definition of the just price as a price "according to the estimation of the market" (*secundum aestimationem fori*).[31] I should note, however, that the market that Magnus and Aquinas were talking about was one of farmers and producers selling products in a village marketplace, whereas the market discussed in the next section in connection with the *Verlagssystem* was a market of intermediaries where capitalists purchased products from laborers to sell to third parties.

C. The Transition to the Putting Out or the *Verlagssystem* of Contracting and Sub-Contracting of Work

The transition from the guild system to the *Verlagssystem* was summarized by Braudel as follows:

> The purpose of the guilds was to bring together the members of a single trade which they defended against all others. . . . But money, the money economy and external trade—in other words the merchant—were now beginning to intervene. . . . At the end of the twelfth century, woollen [sic] cloth from Provins . . . was being exported to distant Naples, Sicily, Cyprus, Majorca, Spain and even Constantinople. Spires (Speyer), a very modest town . . . which did not even possess a bridge over the nearby Rhine, was in the same period producing a rather ordinary woollen [sic] cloth. . . . And yet this somewhat inferior product was being marketed as far away as Saint-Gall, Zurich, Vienna. . . . And at the same time the towns were being invaded by money. . . . Above the mass rose the profile of a whole community of money-lenders and merchants, Milanese, Venetian, Genoese and Florentine. . . .
>
> [This shows] that [the money] could be accumulated, and that once accumulated it could play . . . [a] role. The unequal struggle had begun: some guilds were to become rich; others, the majority, remained modest. . . . The organization it concealed was the system known to historians as the *Verlaggsystem* or putting-out system. A new age had dawned.[32]

The new age which Braudel refers to consisted of a *Verleger*, or merchant who commissioned or "put out" work that resulted in re-saleable goods. He provided the artisan with the raw materials and a part wage or payment for final products. Upon delivery of the finished product, the *verleger* paid the remainder. In this "putting out" system, guild masters were being transformed into wage earners. Gradually, contracts, occasionally in the form of notarial or public deeds, replaced the system of fixed wages and prices, and, with them, the purportedly assured "station in life" (or status) of the guild system. Braudel notes that "[c]ontracts signed with the weavers were often witnessed by a notary and their conditions could vary."[33] Associations whose specific

---

[30] *Id.* at 421.

[31] *Id.* at 422.

[32] BRAUDEL II, at 315–16 (citations omitted).

[33] *Id.* at 317.

purpose was to profit from the labor of manufacturers of desirable goods began to be formed. For example, a 1400 partnership agreement between two Italian silk merchants stated that its "principal activity . . . [was] to have silk sheets made." (*il trafficho loro serà per la maggiore parte in fare lavorare draperie di seta*).[34] But as a new class of merchant-venturers started to emerge, so did an ancestral prejudice against the merchant, who was suspected to be of non-Christian, (Jewish, or Moorish) blood and regarded as an exploiter or trickster contrasted with the blue-blooded benefactor of his fellow man. A quote by Diego de Colmenares, the historian of the Spanish city of Segovia, reflected this prejudice. While referring to the manufacturers of cloth of his city, he stated:

> [These manufacturers] who are *improperly described as merchants* . . . are *really* the heads of great families, for in their own houses and outside they provide a livelihood for a great many persons (some 200, others 300) employing other men's hands to manufacture all kinds of magnificent cloth.[35]

Prejudice aside, it became clear that the merchants who shaped the *Verlagssystem* were indispensable intermediaries in the production and distribution process. They bought raw materials from the producers, hired of and lent to the artisans, and they also sold to consumers or to retailers, who would in turn sell to consumers. In these activities, the *Verlager* significantly participated in and contributed to the vitality of international fairs which became hubs for networking with other merchants, thereby expanding significantly the volumes of production and the sizes of the consumption markets.[36]

COMMENTS AND QUESTIONS ABOUT THE TRANSITION TO CAPITALISM

1. Causes of the Demise of the Guilds

In *The Wealth of Nations*, Adam Smith attributes the demise of the guilds (which he refers to as corporations) to the following causes:

> It is to prevent his reduction of price, and consequently of wages and profit, by restraining that free competition which would most certainly occasion it, that all corporations, and the greater part of corporation laws have been established. . . . [A]nd when any particular class of artificers or traders thought proper to act as a corporation, without a charter, such adulterine guilds, as they were called, were not always disfranchised upon that account, but obliged to (pay a) fine annually to the king, for permission to exercise their usurped privileges.[37] (Parenthesis added)

2. Mercantilism and Monopoly

The Merriam-Webster dictionary defines mercantilism as:

---

[34] *Id.* (citation omitted).

[35] BRAUDEL II, at 317 (citation omitted) (emphasis added).

[36] Fairs became indispensable for merchants in different trades to establish international networks for selling, exchanging and payment purposes. Thus, in the weavers' trade, Braudel describes how by "the sixteenth century, at the end of winter, the weavers would come to the Spanish fairs, to sell [exchange, etc.] their woollen [sic] cloth. . . ." BRAUDEL II, at 319–20.

[37] ADAM SMITH, AN INQUIRY INTO THE NATURE AND CAUSES OF THE WEALTH OF NATIONS 107 (Penn. State Univ. 2005) (1776) (citation omitted).

> an economic system developing during the decay of feudalism to unify and increase the power and especially the monetary wealth of a nation by a strict governmental regulation of the entire national economy usually through policies designed to secure an accumulation of bullion, a favorable balance of trade, the development of agriculture and manufactures, and the establishment of foreign trading monopolies.[38]

The protection given to some producers, often at the expense of others, first at the town level and eventually at the national or regional level, eventually became a defining feature of European mercantilism.[39] Yet, mercantilism was (and in many countries and regions of the world still is) a product of the selfish (and uncooperative) elements of nuclear commercial transactions. Thus, as a reflection of human nature, these elements are not easily confined to isolated transactions or policies. Sooner or later, they permeate the nuclei of transactions between family and friends in a manner that prevents non-family members or non-friends from engaging in the transactions in question and monopoly or oligopoly becomes not only a macro, but also a micro form of doing business, especially in nations whose markets are week and susceptible of being corrupted.

Thus, when Mexico adopted the North American Free Trade Agreement, it found it necessary to strengthen its antitrust legislation and break down some professional, guild-like monopolies such as those enjoyed by notaries public when drafting formal documents. It then created the profession of "public brokers" (*corredores públicos*) and encouraged their competition with notaries public. Yet, as will be discussed in the following chapter, similarities remained with the monopolistic features of guilds, such as the fact that certain transactions can only be executed in front of notaries. Meanwhile, public brokers are carving out their own exclusive niches. As also discussed, some Central American nations allow any licensed lawyer to easily become a notary public. Could this "open entry" approach to the practice of the notarial profession avoid the objection of it being an officially sanctioned professional monopoly? If so, is there a "slippery slope" here? How about the allegation by many non-lawyers that the legal profession itself is another manifestation of the medieval guild and that its status as a professional monopoly is unjustified?

3. *From Status to Contract and Vice Versa*

The transition from a highly regulated system of production and distribution that attempts to assure subsistence to its participants to one where subsistence is left to the outcome of contractual relations was, as will be recalled,[40] a central theme of Sir Henry Sumner Maine's evolutionary view of the law. Yet, far from being the end of an evolutionary period, many of the features of the guild system reappear in the garb of the Marxist-Leninist socialist "planned economy" in the twentieth century. As will be discussed in connection with Soviet and Chinese commercial transactions law, state monopolies as well as fixed prices and wages, which were designed to assure basic

---

[38] *Mercantilism*, MERRIAM-WEBSTER, http://www.merriam-webster.com/dictionary/mercantilism.

[39] *See infra* § 6:2(D)(1).

[40] *See supra* § 3:2.

sustenance, became part of everyday life under Soviet and Chinese (pre-1978) law, while truly bargained-for contracts faded into the background.[41]

4. The Liberating Power of Credit: What if the Paris Silk Spinsters Had Access to Credit?

In June of 1275, the Provost of Merchants of Paris enacted an ordinance "forbidding the spinsters of silk to pawn the silk the mercers [gave] them to work, or to sell or exchange it, under pain of banishment."[42] At first sight, this would appear to be a reasonable restriction; after all, the silk about to be pledged, sold or exchanged was delivered by the commissioning merchant to the spinsters on the assumption that it was to be the exclusive property of the merchant. Yet, what if the spinsters had asked the merchants to lend them the silk or the money with which to buy it? Assume further that the amount lent on the silk by the merchant to the spinster was considerably lower than the value of the silk, and even lower than the value of the products the spinsters would produce with the lent silk. In that case, would not this prohibition clearly immobilize the silk and the proceeds of its sale, at least while it was in the possession of the spinsters, depriving them of the opportunity to obtain additional credit beyond that which had been extended by the silk merchant?

With the lack of such a "mobilization" of assets, the result of not having access to production and commercial credit at reasonable rates of interest,[43] by laborers such as the Paris spinsters were condemned to the perennial status of barely surviving laborers. What if, instead of deeming the silk merchant an exclusive owner of the silk and the laborer its mere custodian, both parties were deemed holders of rights of possession in the silk? The merchant could still hold a superior right to the possession of the silk or to the proceeds of its sale until his investment and expected profit were paid; the spinsters could produce more, earn more and eventually become merchants themselves.

D. The Emergence of Different Types of Capitalist Merchants in European Commerce

1. The Regulation of Local vs. International Commerce

As will be discussed in connection with the European codification of commercial law,[44] with the exception of those code chapters devoted to ocean navigation,[45] the nineteenth-century French commercial code was designed to apply mostly to local commerce and to merchants who, with few exceptions, were deemed equal before the law.[46] In France, the commercial code was preceded by enactments known as "*Ordonances*" that dealt with both local and international trade, of which the most important was a 1673 *Ordonance* attributed to Minister Colbert, about whom more

---

[41] *See infra* § 16:4(A) (Soviet) and § 17:4(A) (China).

[42] BRAUDEL II, at 317 (citation omitted).

[43] *See* Kozolchyk, *Reduction of Poverty*, at 732.

[44] *See infra* chs. 8–12.

[45] *See, e.g.*, HGB, 1897, Book IV, Maritime Commerce.

[46] *See infra* § 9:2(B) (on the books that had to be kept by certain merchants and not by others). Similarly, *see* HGB (GOREN 1998), at art. 3 (on the exclusion of commercial transactions performed by those who cultivate or exploit farm and forest land).

shortly.[47] The purpose of the *Ordonances* that dealt with international trade was to provide France with the best international trading status and advantages possible. One could find in these policies numerous echoes of the guild system. Not surprisingly, a "mercantilistic" or highly preferential treatment of local merchants and products became the law of France's international commerce.

As just noted, mercantilism had strong ties with the remains of the medieval guild system. However, as noted by Professor Carlton Hayes:

> Industry in the eighteenth century meant far more than baking bread, making clothes, cobbling shoes, and fashioning furniture for use in the town; it meant the production on a large scale of goods to sell in distant places,—cloth, clocks, shoes, beads, dishes, hats, buttons, and what not. Many of these articles were still manufactured under the regulations of the old craft gilds [sic]. For although the gild [sic] system was pretty well broken up in England, it still maintained its hold on the Continent.[48]

2. *Mercantilism and One-Sided Terms of Trade*

The above-mentioned Jean Baptiste Colbert, born in 1619 in Reims, France, was the son and grandson of French merchants.[49] In 1665, he became King Louis XIV's comptroller general of finances and later France's secretary of state of naval affairs. One of his goals was to transform France into an industrially and commercially self-sufficient nation; his policies were largely responsible for France's economic resurgence during the end of the seventeenth century.[50] He encouraged the growth of French industry through subsidies and tariff protection, but also regulated qualities and prices of manufactured and agricultural products often by guilds in order to make them highly competitive, especially against the Dutch and British merchants.

To enhance the reputation of French goods, Colbert painstakingly listed the quality and measure of each article. Thus, he issued numerous regulations on best practices for the dyeing and weaving business so that French dyers and weavers could

---

[47] *See* Note titled "The Codification of Commercial Laws with Special Reference to the French *Ordonnance* of 1673 and to Accounting," *available at* http://sol.cs.trinity.edu/rjensen/readings/history/forrester/a03codes.htm (last visited Oct. 27, 2011), which describes the process of legislative compilation of *Ordonnances* by the Council of Chambers of Commerce on instruction by Louis XIV. From 1664 on, Minister Colbert had met fortnightly with this Council and particularly with a group of distinguished bankers, lawyers and other government officials. One of them was Jacques Savary, the author of *Le Parfait Negociant* (1665), a landmark compilation of commercial and admiralty law opinions and commentaries. The final product of this Commission, also known as the Savary Commission, was the 1673 *Ordonnance* which contained 13 Titles and 122 Articles. They contained rules on remnants of the guild system such as on apprenticeships but also included rules on post-guild subjects such as partnerships and other forms of business associations, bills of exchange and bankruptcy. As pointed out by the anonymous author of this Note, there were some notable omissions that are particularly surprising in light of their importance in present-day commerce: No attention was given to the subject of interest on loans and to long-term contracts. As to the drafting of this *Ordonnance*, the nameless author of the Note also points out that: "The enquiries made by the Savary commission were not of the Parlement [a judicial tribunal that often heard commercial matters] or other lawyers throughout France nor indeed of prior collections of the law. . . . Instead questions [or consultations "*Pareres*"] on acceptable and actual practice were sent out to the main commercial centres of Europe."

[48] CARLTON J. H. HAYES, I A POLITICAL AND SOCIAL HISTORY OF MODERN EUROPE 399 (1916), *available at* http://www.fullbooks.com/A-Political-and-Social-History-of-Modern9.html.

[49] On the life and influence of Colbert, *see generally* CHARLES WOOLSEY COLE, I COLBERT AND A CENTURY OF FRENCH MERCANTILISM (Columbia Univ. Press 6th ed. 2007) (1939).

[50] *Id.*

acquire a reputation for excellence.[51] Breach of his regulations was punished by public exposure, destruction of the goods, and, on the third offense, by the pillory. Similar policies protected inventors and attracted foreign skilled workmen to France, while they forbade French skilled workers from emigrating. Many of his policies were far from subtle. Typical of his "carrot and stick" approach were measures such as: Ships built in France earned a premium, while those bought abroad had to pay a punitive duty, and French workmen forbidden to emigrate and serve foreigners could face the death penalty if they ignored the prohibition. "Privileges, titles of nobility, exemption from taxation, generous grants of money, and other favors were accorded to enterprising business men who undertook to introduce new branches of manufacture."[52]

"The[se] regulations caused much inconvenience and loss to many [competing] manufacturers, and the privileges granted to new enterprises often favored [uncompetitive] industries at the expense of more natural and valuable trades."[53] Yet, France's inability to develop large-scale national and international trade was not all the fault of mercantilism. Trade was hindered by poor roads and the diversity of laws from one province or region to another was as common as the need to change horses in a long and continuous journey.[54] In addition, tolls had to be paid before passing a knight's castle, a bridge, or a town gate, and customs duties were levied on commerce between the provinces of a single kingdom. As noted by Hayes, the cost of transportation was "thus made so high that the price of a cask of wine passing from the Orléanais to Normandy—two provinces in northwestern France—increased twenty-fold."[55]

E. The "Fresh Start" of European Commerce: A Commercial Typology

Despite the mercantilistic European trading policies, as exemplified by Colbert's *Ordonances*, Europe, as a whole, had already experienced what Fernand Braudel referred to as a "fresh start in America"[56] following its discovery in 1492. Europe's international and internal commerce, although still shackled by excessive, diverse and often conflicting regulation, continued to grow and with this growth, capitalism and codified law emerged.

This "fresh start" precipitated unparalleled business opportunities for the European retail and wholesale trades, as well as for industry and banking. Braudel describes many of the transactions associated with this fresh start, many of which found their way into the nineteenth-century commercial codes of France and Germany: First was the commerce practiced in street markets, on the backs of peddlers, in permanent shops, and in periodic fairs. Subsequently, he described how this mostly-

---

[51] HAYES, *supra note* 51, at 400 ("French weavers were given careful orders about the quality of the thread, the breadth of the cloth, and the fineness of the weave. It is said that in 1787 the regulations for French manufacturers filled eight volumes in quarto; and other governments, while less thorough, were equally convinced of the wisdom of such a policy.").

[52] *Id.* at 400.

[53] *Id.* at 400–01.

[54] *Id.* at 401.

[55] *Id.*

[56] BRAUDEL II, at 272.

retail trade was nourished by "higher commerce." This was a commerce carried out by specialized intermediaries in commodity and stock exchanges, warehousing, banking, long-distance carriage and insurance. The following sections summarize Braudel's exhaustive description.[57] As the reader visualizes each form of doing business, he should keep in mind that the types of merchants and commerce described by Braudel are the same ones whose transactions were codified, with greater or lesser precision, by the nineteenth-century codes and which continue to be significant players in the market of our day. I should also note that the following is a broadly-gauged description of European markets. A more detailed description of the French and German markets that are more closely connected with legal institutions regulated by the respective codes will be provided in future chapters when discussing each code.

1. *Street Markets and Transactions* "Inter Praesentes"

The *modus operandi* of these seventeenth and eighteenth-century European street markets can be traced to the manner in which business was conducted by the thirteenth-century merchants who were not members of guilds. The medieval as well as pre-codification (eighteenth century) European street markets were held once or twice per week.[58] In these markets, independent bakers sold their coarse bread, butchers their meats, wholesalers (*grossiers*) their fish, butter and cheese in large quantities together with "piles of produce, slabs of butter, heaps of vegetables, pyramids of cheeses, fruit, wet fish, game. . . ."[59] Occasionally, the butcher would cut up the meat on the spot and he would use the pages of unsold books (just a few years ago I saw French and Spanish butchers using discarded newspapers) to wrap up many of the above purchases.[60] In addition, the countryside also provided these markets with straw, hay, wood, wool, hemp, flax and even fabrics woven on village looms.[61]

Braudel attributes the continued presence of this market to its low and often flexible prices, especially as compared with the prices paid to guild members. In addition, he identified two other features: one was the close inspection of the goods or wares by their purchasers. The German expression that depicted this form of buying was "*Hand-in-Hand, Auge-in-Auge Handel*—selling hand to hand, eyeball to eyeball. . . ."[62] This was a method of immediate exchange of goods for money and it pointed to the presence of another peculiarity: "[*T*]*he goods are sold on the spot, the purchases are taken and paid for there and then. Credit is hardly used between one market and another*."[63] The importance of this description can hardly be overemphasized.

---

[57] *Id.* at 63–100. The following paragraphs summarize extracts from Braudel II.

[58] During my last visit to Paris approximately ten years ago, some of the street markets described by Braudel were still being held twice per week.

[59] BRAUDEL II, at 29 (citation omitted).

[60] *Id.*

[61] *Id.*

[62] *Id.* at 29 (citation omitted). As a child growing up in nineteen forties Cuba, I was often instructed by my parents to accompany my grandmother on her bi-weekly purchases in the old Havana street markets. Her method of inspecting the freshness of the chicken did not endear her or me to the sellers of chickens; nonetheless as with the European street markets, the Cuban street market sellers of chicken did, albeit, grudgingly tolerate her close inspections.

[63] *Id.* (citation omitted) (emphasis added). Braudel adds:

> In the early days, and often until the nineteenth century, shopkeepers would sell, indiscriminately, goods obtained at first, second or even third hand. The name they were

For when Article 1582 of the *Code Civil* defined a sale as an "agreement whereby one party obligates herself to deliver a thing and the other to pay for it," its transactional model was not that of a sale between parties dealing at a distance from each other (*Inter Absentes*). Can you see why such sales require special legal tools, in addition to special means of communication? How about those promises we refer to as offers and acceptances? Can you visualize a butcher patiently awaiting his customer's written acceptance of the price of the meat he has just cut and wrapped in the nearest available newspaper? The butcher's and his customer's transaction was a "cash on the barrelhead" sale agreement, one that was completed once the parties agreed on the meat to be purchased and its price. In this sense, it was—in the terminology of the *Code Civil* and its interpreters—a "consensual" and "synallagmatic" agreement, i.e., one that that transferred title of the meat to its purchaser from the moment of the agreement on its price. This meant that for many code interpreters, sales with retention or reservation of title simply "could not exist."[64]

2. *Shops*

From these street markets eventually emerged the permanent shops. The first people to have shops were the artisans. As described by Braudel:

> 'Real' shopkeepers arrived later: they were the middlemen of exchange, inserting themselves between producer and consumer, and confining their activities to buying and selling: the goods they sold were not (or not entirely at any rate) the work of their own hands. From the start, they were like the capitalist merchant as defined by Marx: he begins with money (M), acquires goods (G) and returns regularly to money, in an MGM pattern.[65]
>
> The middleman, a separate and before long a very frequent figure, was the man of the future. . . .
>
> [Yet] the representatives of commerce were still bewailing the fact in 1788 that even at this date, *négociants* were considered as 'occupying one of the lower classes of society.' One would not have heard this kind of talk in Amsterdam, London or even Italy.[66]
>
> Gradually a distinction appeared between those who sold by weight: [mostly] grocers . . . [and] those who sold by measure: drapers and tailors; [between] those who sold objects: [such as] ironmongers; [and] those who sold used utensils, clothes or furniture: second-hand dealers. . . .
>
> [The] special kinds of shop, encouraged by the development of 'services', were those of the apothecary, the pawnbroker, the money-changer or banker, the

---

> originally given, *mercer* in English (*mercier* in French) is revealing: it comes from the Latin *merx*, *mercies*, merchandise in general. A French proverb says "A shopkeeper (*mercier*) sells everything, makes nothing." And whenever we have records of the stock in such shops, we find the strangest assortment of goods. . . .

Id. at 64.

[64] *See supra* § 2:2(A)(4).

[65] *See* Braudel II, at 62 & 64; *see also supra* note 12 and accompanying text (discussing Marx's archetypal capitalistic transaction).

[66] BRAUDEL II, at 64 (citations omitted).

innkeeper who was [also] often an intermediary for carriers, and the tavern-keepers or 'wine-merchants who keep tables and linen and serve meals. . . .'[67]

Among shopkeepers, most sales were still consensual and credit was extended only in small quantities and mostly just to their well-known customers.[68]

3. Peddlers

Pre-codification Europe evidenced a commercial hierarchy:

> '[S]hopkeeper': at the top, a few very rich merchants, specializing in longdistance trade; at the bottom, the poor pedlars of needles and oilcloth [among many other items], of whom the proverb cruelly says 'small trade, small basket' (*petit merrier, petit panier*) and whom even a servant-girl, especially if she had some savings, would not stoop to marry. . . .[69]
>
> Pedlars were merchants, usually poor ones, who carried on their backs their very meager stock. Nevertheless, taken in the mass, they add up to an appreciable volume of trade. They filled in the gaps in the regular channels of distribution, even in towns, though mostly in villages and hamlets.[70]

As with some shopkeepers, peddlers also extended credit to some of their most trusted customers and, as such, became the beneficiaries of informal, usually oral, executory promises of repayment.[71] And as will be discussed in Chapter 20, English peddlers were much more willing to extend credit to their customers and thus they became a significant source of consumer credit during England's remarkable eighteenth century embrace of consumerism.[72]

4. Fairs as Markets and as Settlement and Clearing Houses

As will be discussed in this section, some of the European fairs, active between the thirteenth and seventeenth centuries, were responsible for institutions such as commercial credit, payment and settlement systems as curators or incubators of commercial legal institutions.

As pointed out by Braudel, there were fairs and then there were *fairs*. Some town or country fairs acting as local or regional markets limited their trade to one or two commodities or products, and if the sole product was, say, wool, and a winter was long enough to prevent the peasants from timely shearing of their sheep, that year's fair had to be cancelled.[73] Other fairs combined the wholesale and retail trade of all sorts of commodities and products, although mostly from an agricultural origin. Larger fairs were not daily or weekly affairs (as were street markets), but were associated with religious holidays. In his inimitably vivid style, Braudel describes fair time near Florence, Italy and in Carpentras, France:

---

[67] *Id.* at 67 (citations omitted).

[68] *Id.* at 73–74.

[69] *Id.* at 68.

[70] *Id.* at 75.

[71] *Id.* at 73–80.

[72] *See infra* § 20:4(B)(1).

[73] BRAUDEL II, at 83.

> Fairs meant noise, tumult, music, popular rejoicing, the world turned upside down, disorder and sometimes disturbances. At Prato near Florence, where the fairs dated back to the fourteenth century, every September the *trombetti* (trumpets) of all the towns of Tuscany would come to *suonare* (make music) in competition in the streets and on the town squares. At Carpentras, the day before the fairs of St Matthew or Saint-Siffrein, the piercing sound of the trumpets would be heard at the four gates of the town, then on the squares, and finally in front of the lawcourts.[74]

The methods of retail sales and pricing at the fairs did not differ much from those practiced in street shops or stalls. This was not true, however, with respect to credit transactions; fairs meant a place to extend or obtain commercial credit and to effectuate payment and settlement of accounts in a quick, efficient and inexpensive manner. The principal instrument of both credit and payment was what we refer in our day as a draft or bill of exchange.[75] This draft or bill of exchange was, and is, a written order of payment drawn by a merchant who could have been the seller of goods or the exchanger of currency or a buyer who bought goods or foreign currency on credit (the drawer). This order of payment was drawn on or directed to another merchant who either had funds that belonged to the drawer or who owed money to the drawer as a result of an unpaid purchase, loan or exchange of currency transaction. Depending upon who owed money to whom, the creditor or person entitled to claim the payment under the bill of exchange was named its payee. The drawer signed his order of payment, and the drawee expressed his willingness to pay the bill by signing it in the drawee-acceptor's column. Often the order was for payment at a future time and at a designated fair where the payee and the acceptor were likely to be present. The mutual presence of debtors and creditors or of their agents facilitated the setting off of debits and credits among numerous traders. It is worth noting that the acceptor's promise to make a future payment was executory, and thus it was the same type of promise denied enforcement because it was deemed a *nudum pactum* both under Roman law and most medieval feudal law, except among Jewish and Arab merchants.[76]

Fairs usually ended with a payment or settlement session where acceptors and payees of bills of exchange settled their accounts, frequently adding up what each owed to the other and paying the unpaid balances either in cash or by issuing another bill of exchange to be collected at a subsequent fair. This method of settlement of accounts was the predecessor of today's bank clearing mechanism used by both local and international banks. As a result of these payment and settlement or clearing sessions, numerous bills of exchange converged upon the most populous fairs. In Braudel's words:

> [D]ebts met and cancelled each other out, melting like snow in the sun: such were the miracles of *scontro* [the discounting of negotiable bills of exchange] [and of] compensation [set off]. A hundred thousand or so *'ecus d'or en or'*—that is *real* coins—might at the clearing-house of Lyons settle business worth millions; all the more so as a good part of the remaining debts would be settled either by a promise of payment on another exchange (a bill of

---

[74] *Id.* at 85 (citation omitted).

[75] *See* Kozolchyk, *Negotiable Instruments*, at 22–2 (discussing the contemporary law of bills of exchange in a comparative fashion).

[76] *See supra* § 5:9(C).

> exchange) or by carrying over payment until the next fair: this was the *deposito* which was usually paid for at 10% a year. . . . So the fair itself created credit.[77]

Eventually, an informal international network of credit, payments and settlements for international traders emerged, and it was centered in fairs such as the one in Piacenza, Italy, which started meeting periodically (usually four times a year) since 1579 and was run by a small group of highly trusted merchant-bankers. Again in Braudel's words:

> No merchandise came to the [Piacenza] fair, and very little cash, but literally masses of bills of exchange, which in fact represented the entire wealth of Europe, with payments by the Spanish Empire as the mainstream. About sixty businessmen attended, Genoese *banchieri di conto* for the most part, a few from Milan or Florence. They were members of a club to which one could not be admitted without paying a very heavy caution [indemnity bond]. These privileged men fixed the *conto*, that is the exchange rate for liquidation at the end of each fair. . . . There was a total of perhaps 200 initiates, behaving with great discretion and handling vast amounts of business, perhaps 30 to 40 million *ecus'* worth at each fair. . . .[78]

The importance of these initiates should not be underestimated. As the reader will recall, it was this very exchange rate mechanism that bankers (*banchieri*) fixed for each fair and that Raymond de Roover, among other scholars of the medieval economy, identified as the most commonly used disguise for the payment of interest for loans that the Roman Catholic Church would have otherwise characterized as usurious.[79] Accordingly, these merchant-bankers acted as "elder commercial brothers" and *boni viri* of fair merchants. They were entrusted not only with overseeing the settlement of vast sums of debt money that belonged to thousands of traders, but also with ensuring that the bills of exchange that these traders used for payment and settlement of their debts, as well as to document their new lines of credit, provided the appearance of legality. Thus, fairs and bills of exchange and the *banchieri di conto* helped institutionalize commercial credit for the first time throughout the trading world.

5. *High Commerce, Wholesalers, Warehousemen and Exchange Houses: The Amsterdam Exchange*

> [I]f the Piacenza fairs were the centre of commercial life in the late sixteenth and early seventeenth century, the new centre of this [commercial] world was soon to be Amsterdam. . . . And while the Amsterdam Exchange took over the vast capital market unchallenged, it also controlled . . . the movement of commodities (pepper and spices from Asia, grain and other products from the Baltic). . . . [W]ith the increase in population, the headlong expansion of the towns, and improvements in consumption, the wholesale trade could not fail to develop too, spilling out beyond the channels offered by the fairs and becoming organized independently. This autonomous organization, through

---

[77] BRAUDEL II, at 90–91.

[78] *Id.* at 91 (citation omitted).

[79] *See* DE ROOVER, BUSINESS, BANKING AND ECONOMIC THOUGHT, at 32.

> the use of depots, warehouses, granaries and stores was tending, with its regularity of supply . . . to replace the periodic bustle of the fairs.[80]

Adopting the terminology of a 1681 commentator, Braudel refers to the merchant who did his business at this Exchange as "The New Businessman" (*Le Nouveau Negociant*).[81] He could be a banker, exchange currency dealer, agent or broker. Regardless of his specialization, "every self-respecting businessman had to look in at the *Bourse* at the end of [every] morning. . . . [Thus], [s]omething like 4500 people were said to crush inside every day between noon and two o'clock, in [1722]. On Saturdays it was less crowded, as the Jews were absent."[82]

The method of purchase in these exchanges, which was much the same throughout Europe, did not rely on the close inspection of each item as in the street markets. It relied on samples of the commodities bought and sold, as it also relied, increasingly, on various types of intermediaries. For example, in the Corn Exchange of Amsterdam:

> [E]very merchant had his *factor* 'who is responsible for bringing there samples of the grains he wants to sell . . . in bags holding about one or two pounds. As the price of grain is fixed as much by [specific] weight as by good or bad quality, there [were] at the back of the Exchange various little scales on which, by weighing three or four handfuls of grain . . . one can estimate the weight of the sack.'[83]

Braudel concludes that one peculiar feature of the Amsterdam Exchange was the speculative freedom of many transactions. As reported by a Spanish visitor merchant, "there was forward buying of herring before it had been caught and wheat and other goods before they had been grown or received."[84] Yet, betting on commodities contracts or on shares, in expert hands, could bring a comfortable income. In his words:

> [S]peculation on the Amsterdam Stock Exchange had reached a degree of sophistication and abstraction which made it for many years a very special trading-centre of Europe, a place where people were not content simply to buy and sell shares, speculating on their possible rise or fall, but where one could by means of *various ingenious combinations speculate without having any money or shares at all*."[85]

6. Questions on the Emergence of a Commercial Typology: From "Eye to Eye and Hand to Hand" to Buying Samples Through Intermediaries

Having read the previous chapter, the reader of this chapter should ask himself: What did *Lazarillo de Tormes'* trade have in common with speculation in the Amsterdam stock exchange? The term "adventure" appears increasingly in the lexicon of business associations and insurance contracts beginning with the eighteenth century: Is there any connection with the behavior of picaresque or even Quixotic

---

[80] BRAUDEL II, at 94–95.

[81] *Id.* at 97.

[82] *Id.* at 100 (citation omitted).

[83] *Id.* (citation omitted) (emphasis added).

[84] *Id.* at 101 (citation omitted).

[85] *Id.* (emphasis added).

characters? Why was such adventurous behavior seldom found in the literature of chivalry during the Middle Ages?

Can the merchants who engaged in what Braudel described as the "ingenious combinations" associated with the Amsterdam Stock or Commodity Exchange be likened to the *Lazarillo's* methods of survival and occasional prosperity in late medieval Spain? What differences existed with respect to their respective "ingeniousness" and honesty? After all, if one is willing to advance a serious commitment to buy or trade based upon a mere sample of the goods or products offered for sale by an intermediary, does not one have to trust the intermediary and the sample's aptness to represent, more or less accurately, the actual goods or products?

During Lazarillo's day, there were numerous merchants or aspiring merchants who were described as "*picaros malos*" (swindlers or evil tricksters). How did their commercial behavior differ from Colbert's mercantilistic policies and from the practices of the "*picaros*" of the Amsterdam Stock or Commodity exchanges who did not hesitate to sell herring yet to be fished or crops yet to be harvested? Could it be that there were some trustworthy and good *picaros* (*picaros buenos*) among the emerging commercial class? If so, what made these intermediaries trustworthy? Recall that trustworthiness in the medieval Mediterranean trade of Arab and Jewish merchants depended upon the religiously inspired duties among commercial-religious brethren.[86] Was there an institutional equivalent in the emerging law of commercial transactions, especially in what Braudel described as "High Commerce"? If so, how did the law reflect and reward desirable and trustworthy conduct? Recall Braudel's reference to the creation of "consular tribunals" in France (to which questions and disputes relating to bankruptcies were referred) and which constituted a privileged and expeditious justice for merchants, "in accordance with commercial law" (*per legem mercatoriam*), designed to safeguard class interests. Could this special legal treatment be justified if it applied preponderantly to *picaros malos*?

7. *Cash, Credit Sales, Brokers and Other Intermediaries*

Can Braudel's following description be generalized to all types of trade: "[G]oods are sold on the spot . . . purchases are . . . paid for there and then. Credit is hardly used between one market and another"?[87] Would it also be true for street markets, shops and peddlers? In interviews with shopkeepers and former peddlers in Central America during the 1960s,[88] many of the interviewees described a form of credit sales that in the case of the shopkeepers was only documented by entries in the shopkeepers' store booklets (*libretas*), and in the case of the peddlers, totally on trust (nothing written) to their occasional customers. Similar practices prevailed in other Latin American countries as far back as the late nineteenth century. From the standpoint of the contemporary law of sales, what difference does it make if the sale is made on a "cash on the barrelhead" basis or on a credit basis? How about the so-called documentary sales such as C.I.F., F.O.B., C.F.A. and others in which payment is supposed to be made not against the tender of samples or of inspected goods, but merely against the presentation of documents? Do these transactions require greater or lesser trust by buyers? Or is it by sellers, or by both buyers and sellers?

---

[86] *See supra* § 5:9.

[87] BRAUDEL II, at 29 (citation omitted).

[88] Kozolchyk, *Toward a Theory on Law*, at 724–25.

What made the replacement of goods and eyeball-to-eyeball, hand-to-hand inspection by mere pieces of paper possible in these sales? If it was the presence of trusted intermediaries such as brokers and commission agents, who were these trusted intermediaries? Were they religious, professional brethren? How important was it for these intermediaries to be properly empowered by their principals? How important was it for third parties dealing with these intermediaries to be able to rely on the appearance of empowerment rather than on the actual terms and conditions of the empowerment? What if third parties were confronted with the allegation that the agents' powers had been exceeded by the agents and that, as a result of restrictions known only to the principal and his agent or intermediary, the principal was not liable for the acts of the intermediary? On this point, it would be worthwhile to revisit the appendix to Chapter 5.[89]

8. Table: Types of Businesses[90] and Their Types of Contracts

	Street Markets	**Shops**	**Peddlers**	**Wholesalers**	**Exchange Houses**
Contract Methods	Oral and face to face	Oral and face to face	Oral and face to face	Oral, face to face, and by correspondence	Oral and face to face
	Hand and eye inspection of actual goods.	Hand and eye inspection of actual goods less frequent.	Hand and eye inspection of actual goods.	Examination of samples.	Examination of samples in commodity exchanges. No examination of samples in stock and monetary or futures contracts.
	Depending upon market conditions—fixed prices or haggling over prices.	Depending upon market conditions—fixed prices or haggling over prices.	No fixed prices, much bargaining	Fixed prices and little bargaining, except for high volume sales.	A combination of fixed prices and open bidding.
	Perfection of contract upon delivery of thing and price ("synallagmatic" performance).	Perfection of contract upon delivery of thing and price ("synallagmatic" performance).	Perfection of contract upon delivery of thing and price (usually in cash).	Perfection of contract upon completion of oral or written agreement; invoices frequently used.	Perfection of contract upon communication of standard symbols of assent, especially among brokers and dealers.

[89] *See supra* § 5:13.

[90] The information for this table came from Braudel's preceding description of seventeenth and eighteenth-century commercial practices, as well as from related descriptions of practices for the same period. WYNDHAM BEAWES, LEX MERCATORIA REDIVIVA 352–521 (1772); *see also* JACQUES SAVARY, 2 LE PARFAIT NEGOCIANT 60–65 (*Parere* IX) (1742) (describing the setting of prices among merchants in French cities). On the utilization of bills of exchange and other commercial instruments in commercial contracts by non-merchants and merchants, see *id.* at 12–27.

No credit given, cash payments only.	Only "book" credit to well-known clients.	Credit commonly given after a trusting, family-like relationship.	Credit given after the establishment of a trusting business relationship; reliance on invoices, promissory notes, and bills of exchange.	Depending upon market conditions—partial or "margin" credit extended. Payment commonly made with promissory notes and bills of exchange, as well as through clearance of account mechanisms.

What contemporary commercial contracts are missing from the above typology? Chapter 21 on the legal institutions that helped shape the United States' capitalist economy provides an additional typology of businesses and contracts which may well help answer this question.

§ 6.3 DUAL CODES FOR FRANCE'S AND GERMANY'S PRIVATE LAW: A REMNANT OF THE GUILD SYSTEM?

To an Anglo-American lawyer, one of the most striking features of the private law (or the law of the "mine and the thine") of many civil law countries is the partitioning of this law into "civil" and "commercial" codes. While this feature will be discussed extensively in the following chapters,[91] now is a good time to call attention to the effect that the guilds had upon this dualism. Regardless of the doctrinal reasons adduced to justify the dualism, and there are many, the gradual departure of merchants from the guild system and their *modus operandi* as individual profit-seeking producers, distributors and intermediaries is reflected in the adoption of commercial codes, whether of the French or German type.[92] Hence, while the commercial codes were designed to apply to the transactions of all the merchants described by Braudel—from the modest peddler to the high powered wholesaler, insurer, carrier or broker—the civil codes were not. They were designed to apply to self proclaimed non-profit transactions whether by individual or associations (the latter being frequently referred to as "civil" as opposed to "business" associations) as well as services rendered by non-merchant artisans, craftsmen and professionals such as lawyers, physicians, engineers or architects. In fact, one of the distinguishing features of professionals is that their members are supposed to charge often regulated "honoraria" or "tariffs," as in the case of notaries public and not "synallagmatic" or negotiated prices for their goods as done by merchants. Hence, the guilds seemed to continue to live in many of the transactions governed by the Civil Code.

Thus, the dualism of codes promotes opposing attitudes with respect to the policies that should govern private law transactions in many countries. This is particularly true in countries or jurisdictions governed or influenced by the French and Spanish

---

[91] *See infra* chs. 8–12.

[92] *Id.*

civil and commercial codes. All too often, "civilists" will oppose—either overtly or covertly—the inevitable commercialization of civil code institutions, such as sales or loan agreements and methods to secure repayment of obligations by secured transactions statutes. As will become apparent in later chapters, this opposition has consequences beyond the endless debates in academic or professional associations. Sadly, to this day, many civilists have failed to realize that by opposing the commercialization of some (though certainly not all) traditional civil law institutions, they are in effect attempting to retain guild like institutions that are inconsistent with economic growth and development. .[93]

While the primary focus of this book is commercial contracts and commercial enactments, such as the various commercial codes, one cannot ignore the influence that civil codes have upon the interpretation of their commercial counterparts. This influence is all the more notable if one considers that civil codes should, in theory, have no involvement with commerce. As will be discussed in connection with the Latin notaries in Chapter 7,[94] civil codes are supposed to deal with a person's (non-commercial) legal status from birth until death, including familial rights and obligations, non-profit contractual obligations, civil associations, liability for torts and not-for-profit acquisition, and the use and disposition (*inter vivos* and *mortis causa*) of personal and real property. On the other hand, many civil codes provide default rules, including general principles that are applicable to commercial disputes.

§ 6.4 CONCLUSIONS

The still present civil-commercial code dualism reflects, albeit opaquely, a momentous but in many cases incomplete evolution in the economic, political and legal history of mankind. This evolution started in societies whose trade was highly restricted and monopolized and where contractual bargaining was lacking in some of its most important legal relationships. Eventually, this evolution led to societies where contractual bargaining was at the center of legal relationships and thus where markets and competition were opened to an increasing number of profit-seeking participants. Thus, when nineteenth-century commercial codes listed the acts of commerce or type of merchants to whom they applied, they took for granted what had been far from evident in medieval societies: Profit-seeking and speculation were inherent in commerce.[95]

---

[93] This point is also made with an increasing degree of urgency in my following publications: Kozolchyk, *Roadmap;* Kozolchyk, *Commercialization*; Kozolchyk, *Reduction of Poverty*.

[94] *See infra* ch. 7.

[95] *See, e.g.,* COD. COM.(MEX) art. 75(1) (2008), which defined acts of commerce as:

> The law considers to be commercial transactions: (I) All purchases, sales and rentals entered into for the purpose of commercial profit, involving maintenance, personality, or merchandise, regardless of their natural state, whether they have been improved or manufactured; (II) The purchase and sale of realty when carried on for commercial speculation. . . .

MEXICAN COMMERCIAL CODE (Abraham Eckstein & Enrique Zepeda trans., West Publ'g 1995).

The model for this definition was Article L110–1 of the 1807 French Commercial Code:

> The law provides that commercial instruments are:
>
> 1° All purchases of chattels in order to resell this, either in kind or after having worked and developed this; 2° All purchases of real property in order to resell this, unless the purchaser has acted in order to construct one or more buildings and to sell these en bloc or site-by-site. . . .

FRENCH COMMERCIAL CODE (English trans.), *available at* http://195.83.177.9/code/liste.phtml?lang=uk&c=32.

By the time France and Germany faced the task of codifying their private law and especially their law of civil and commercial contracts, the socio-economic transition from a guild to a capitalistic system had seemingly been completed. Commerce was in the hands of capitalists or holders of money or its functional equivalent such as highly liquid or trustworthy commercial paper. Not only were parties free to enter all sorts of contracts and free to establish their own prices or fees, but commerce had been institutionalized—starting with peddlers and small retail shops through markets and fairs and all the way up to large importers and exporters, wholesalers, and their banks. The fact that it was institutionalized should not lead the reader to assume that that the codes written in the nineteenth century necessarily reflected how each of these institutional methods of doing business worked in actual practice. Similarly they should lead him to conclude that the Guild mentality was dead and that in some transactgions it was not governing from its grave.

Chapter 7

THE LATIN NOTARIAT AND CONTEMPORARY CONTRACTS

§ 7.1 INTRODUCTION

An estimated seventy percent of the world's population today lives in countries or jurisdictions where the Latin notariat is practiced, as contrasted with the United States and other common law countries' notary. A United States notary public has been defined as:

> [A]n official of integrity appointed by state government—typically by the secretary of state—to serve the public as an impartial witness in performing a variety of official fraud-deterrent acts related to the signing of important documents. These official acts are called notarizations or notarial acts. Notaries are publicly commissioned as "ministerial" officials, meaning that they are expected to follow written rules without the exercise of significant personal discretion, as would be the case with a "judicial" official.[1]

As apparent from this definition, the functions of a notary in the United States are ministerial and mechanical in nature. In contrast, Professor Pedro Malavet of the University of Florida College of Law, a leading comparativist of notarial law and practice, described the Latin notary as the:

> [L]*egal professional* [exclusively] charged with the *public function* of receiving, interpreting, and giving legal form to the intent of the parties, preparing the documents pertinent to the desired end, giving them authenticity; and conserving the originals and issuing copies that attest to their content. This function includes the authentication of facts.[2]

To this definition, the Superior Council of the French Notariat (*Conseil Supérieur du Notariat*) adds:

> The notary [is] a professional who can confer the character of authenticity to deeds. He has to the power to confer the character of authenticity to deeds by signing and adding his seal to instruments. By doing so, he officially recognises the wishes of the persons signing *and personally guarantees the content and the date which appear on the act.* This act is recognised as having the same authority as a court decision.[3]

---

[1] NATIONAL NOTARY ASSOCIATION, *What is a Notary?*, http://www.nationalnotary.org/resources_for_notaries/what_is_a_notary/ (last accessed Nov. 1, 2013).

[2] *See* Pedro A. Malavet, *Counsel for the Situation: The Latin Notary, A Historical and Comparative Model*, 19 HASTINGS INT'L & COMP. L. REV. 389 (1996) (a historical overview of the Latin notariat and a comparative study of its profession and practice from a U.S. legal perspective) [hereinafter Malavet, *Latin Notary*]; *see also* Pedro A. Malavet, *The Foreign Notarial Legal Services Monopoly: Why Should We Care?*, 31 J. MARSHALL L. REV. 945, 952 (1998).

[3] CONSEIL SUPÉRIEUR DU NOTARIAT, PRESS KIT, http://webcache.googleusercontent.com/search?q=ache:v3_YIS-0VqIJ: www.uinl.net/DOCUMENTOS/ARCHIVOSWEB/Dossier%2520presse%2520de%2520la%2520

As legal advisors, drafters, authenticators, record keepers, collectors of transactional taxes, and (in some jurisdictions) escrow agents,[4] Latin notaries often draft and/or officiate the execution of many economically significant contracts in civil law jurisdictions.

This chapter will inquire into the role of Latin notaries in commercial transactions in increasingly commercialized societies, or societies in which real estate mortgages (once upon a time the queen of all security interests and the object of much individual attention by Latin notaries and land registrars) are now massively and quickly traded or collateralized, much as if they were commercial goods or paper. Hence, if up until the middle of the twentieth century, the real estate transactions that were the principal source of revenue of the Latin notary reflected a society where movable property (as contrasted with real property) was, as in the medieval saying, "vile" property (*res mobilis, res vilis*), presently much of the wealth and assets of commercial societies is movable or personal property, including the rights to real property. This was not the society or marketplace for which the Latin notary was designed.

Classical Roman law, with its reliance on "typified" contracts,[5] needed its notaries (some of whom were known as *Tabelliones*)[6] to enforce untypified contracts and especially contracts in which the exchanges of performances were not contemporaneous. Notarial documents and their ritual formalities, many of which echoed those of the *stipulatio*, enabled the enforcement of otherwise unenforceable promises such as the *nuda pacta*.[7]

During the middle ages, the role of notaries gained momentum, especially after the creation of notarial schools and the enactment of notarial laws that standardized entrance and performance requirements much as with guilds.[8] The compensation of

---

profession%2520220608_UK-UINL%2520(EN).doc+%22Because+the+notary+provides+a+public+service,+payments+made+to+notaries+are+strictly+regulated+notaries+charge+clients+a+fixed+rate%22&cd=1&hl=en&ct=clnk&gl=us (emphasis added) [hereinafter CONSEIL SUPÉRIEUR].

[4] *See* Boris Kozolchyk, *Enhancement of Mexican Commercial Adjudication by Improved Transactional Fact-Finding, Application of Equitable Principles, and Drafting of Standard Contracts and Best Contractual Practices*, 27 ARIZ. J. INT'L & COMP. L. 339, 463–64 (2010) (discussing notaries acting as escrow agents). *See also* Ley del Impuesto sobre la Renta [LIR] [Income Tax Law], Diario Oficial de la Federación [DO], 1 de Enero de 2002 (Mex.). Article 154, in its relevant part, states: "In transactions documented in Public Deeds (*escrituras públicas*), the provisional payment [of taxes] shall be done through a statement that must be filed within fifteen days following the date in which the deed or minute was signed. Notaries, brokers, judges and other holders, to whom the law grants notarial powers, shall be responsible for calculating the relevant taxes due and shall pay it to the relevant authorities." *Id.* art. 154. *See also Codigo Fiscal de la Federación* [CFF] [Federal Tax Code], *Diario Oficial de la Federación* [DO], 31 de Diciembre de 1981 (Mex.). Article 26 provides that individuals or entities to which the law grants the power to withhold or collect taxes are joint and severally liable to taxpayers, for the payment of the relevant taxes. *Id.* art. 26. And for a description of the French notaries' role as tax collectors, see Gisela Shaw, *Notaries in France-An Unassailable Profession. Or are they?*, 13 INT'L J. LEGAL PROFESSION 243, 249 (2006) ("The state benefits in a number of very tangible ways from the activity of *notaires*. Firstly, *notaires* calculate and collect state taxes and legal charges (now also including VAT) for each and every transaction performed.").

[5] *See supra* § 4:4(D)(3)(e) (discussing typified contracts and the link of their requirements to the availability of specifically designed actions and defenses).

[6] *See Tabelliones*, ENCYCLOPEDIA BRITTANICA, http://www.britannica.com/EBchecked/topic/579695/abelliones (describing tabelliones as "a humbler class of paid legal documentary experts . . . who were useful in nonlitigious transactions.").

[7] *See supra* § 4:4(D)(2).

[8] Malavet, *Latin Notary*, *supra* note 2, at 416–20.

these was also guild-like: Notarial charges were fixed by tariffs and not by negotiations.

§ 7.2 THE FORMALITIES OR SOLEMNITIES OF LAND AND COMMERCIAL TRANSACTIONS

While Latin notaries have been traditionally associated with real estate transactions,[9] during the sixteenth century, when Holland became Europe's premier commercial power, Dutch notaries were heavily involved in drafting commercial contracts and their offices were where much of the commercial negotiation and deal making took place.[10] Among the commercial contracts drafted by Dutch notaries were sales involving the future delivery of Baltic grain and North Sea herring.[11] Because many of these contracts had to be concluded within a short period of time, they quickly acquired a standardized format. As noted by Dutch economic historians, trade "influenced commercial law and practice, as the thousands of notarial contracts and innumerable agreements to buy and sell at the *Beurs* encouraged uniformity, purchase by sample, and transparency in the distribution of information."[12]

This open-ended approach to the drafting of notarial documents contrasted with the "strictly structured" notarial document pioneered by Bolognese notaries in the thirteenth century.[13] Their document included a reference to the request by the contracting parties for the notarial drafting and referred to an audience with the notary in which the parties described their proposed contract or legal transaction. This audience was intended to elicit some of the factual background of the transaction and its terms and conditions. Once they were established, the notary asserted that he had read his proposed draft to the parties who signed it in his presence and gave them a copy of the notary's document.[14]

With some adjustments, this medieval method of drafting was adopted by France's notaries and was followed by other European and Latin American nations. In due course, provisions of France's Notarial Law of 1803[15] and its *Code Civil* of 1804[16] were also adopted elsewhere, although using a terminology that was not always uniform. For example, Article 1317 of the *Code Civil* defined generically the document issued by notaries as an "authentic act" while the Spanish Civil Code referred to the same notarial document as "*documentos*" or "*escrituras*." Nonetheless, the definition of the *acte authentique* in Article 1317 was the model used in Spanish and Latin American laws and practices:

---

[9] Approximately fifty percent of French notarial work involves real estate sales and mortgages, leasing, and construction.

[10] JAN DE VRIES & AD VAN DER WOUDE, THE FIRST MODERN ECONOMY: SUCCESS, FAILURE, AND PERSEVERANCE OF THE DUTCH ECONOMY, 1500–1815 139, 150, 414, 491, 523 (1997).

[11] *Id.* at 150.

[12] *Id.* at 141.

[13] Malavet, *Latin Notary*, *supra* note 2, at 419.

[14] *Id.*

[15] *Loi Contentant Organisation du Notariat, Loi 25 Ventôse an XI* [French Law on the Notarial System], Mar. 16, 1803.

[16] C. CIV. (FR.) (Barrister 1804).

> The *acte authentique* is one drawn up by public officials having the right to draw up documents in the place where the document was executed, and with the solemnities required.[17]

Please note that implicit in these components are pre-existing and "required solemnities." For example, when drafting a notarial deed of sale of land, some of the solemnities peculiar to this type of contract in representative Latin American jurisdictions include: (1) the notary's identification of the parties based upon their acceptable identity documents; (2) his statement that he has ascertained the parties' capacity to enter into contracts (which, as will be discussed in the appendix, at times requires the notary to go beyond what may appear in the party's identification document); (3) a detailed legal description of the land (including cadastral surveys when these are available); (4) the terms and conditions of the sale; (5) the parties' acknowledgment that they paid taxes and other charges required by law; (6) the notary's reading and explanation of all the stipulations; and (7) the attestations of the parties and witness, acknowledging having read the document and having understood the explanations, followed by their signatures and by the notary and his signature.[18]

As will be discussed shortly, documents so issued enjoyed a presumption of truthfulness and proper formalities or solemnities (*presumptio veritatis et solemnitatis*). Or, as stated by a Canadian commentator: "whatever is written thereon is taken for the truth, and the act is considered to have been drawn in proper form until the contrary be clearly proved."[19]

In contrast with real estate transactions, the French *Code de Commerce* did not require formalities, not even as much as a writing, to prove and enforce its "acts of commerce." As stated by its present Article L110–3: "With regard to merchants, their transactions *may be proven by any means* unless the law specifies otherwise."[20] As will be discussed in a later chapter on the Napoleonic codification,[21] this liberal policy acknowledged both a transactional reality and the minor legal importance attributed by the French codifier to many if not most of its commercial contracts. Further, these transactions were associated with a profession regarded by the bourgeois and the landed gentry as undignified, if not dishonest or usurious.

In contrast, French notaries were tasked with documenting or attesting to non-commercial life's most significant acts or events, such as births and deaths; marriages or their dissolution; gifts; gratuitous loans and wills; agencies as well as the creation, modification or termination of professional or "civil" associations; and the acquisition,

---

[17] C. CIV. (FR.) art. 1317 (Dalloz 1992–93). Compare this definition with that of the "*documento público*" of Article 1216 of the Spanish Civil Code of 1889: "*Son documentos públicos los autorizados por un Notario o empleado public competente, con las solemnidades requeridas por la ley.*" (Public documents are those authorized by a Notary or public employee with the solemnities required by the law) C.C. (SPAIN) art. 1216 (1889). For a similar use of the term Escritura Publica see, for example, Article 1230 of the Spanish Civil Code of 1889. A direct translation of the French *Acte Authentique* (*Actos Autenticos*) was used in the regulations for the recording of documents in the Spanish civil and real property registries. *See, e.g.*, Reglamento del Registro Civil [Rules of Civil Registration] arts. 38, 42, 43 (B.O.E. 1958, 206) (Spain).

[18] The incomplete summary of recitals and terms and conditions in the principal text is based upon the notarial practices that I have observed in Latin American countries.

[19] *Notaries, Their Origin and Office*, 45 CANADA L. J. 279 (Henry O'Brien ed., 1909).

[20] C. COM. (FR.) art. L110–3 (2012) (emphasis added) (author's translation). The original version of this provision was Article 3 of the *Code de Commerce* of 1807. C. COM. (FR.) art. 3 (1807).

[21] *See infra* chs. 8–10.

sale and mortgage of real property. In performing these drafting and attestation services, notaries charged officially fixed honoraria.[22]

Still, life has its own inexorable ways and by the middle of the nineteenth century, France as well as the rest of Europe embraced an economy whose sales and credit transactions had to be executed quickly, informally, and preferably in a standardized and inexpensive form. At the same time, urban real property, despite its *Code Civil* label of "*immeubles*" (meaning immovable), was beginning to be sold, leased and mortgaged in large numbers and for commercial purposes.

Latin notaries became the drafters of those commercial contracts whose transactional value required they be executed in an *acte authentique* or *escritura publica*. To many would-be creditors, the payment of a significant honorarium was justified because these notarial documents empowered them to file actions for summary judgments concomitantly with attachments of the defendants' real or personal property. This feature of the notarial documents labeled them as "self-executory," ("Titulos Ejecutivos") for the defenses allowed against them were very few and exceptional in nature. Among them were the defendant's full payment of his obligation, the falsity or forgery of the document relied upon by the plaintiff and the obligor's contractual incapacity or duress when entering into the formal obligation.[23]

§ 7.3 AUTHENTICATION BY LATIN NOTARIES IN CONTEMPORARY COMMERCIAL TRANSACTIONS

A. The Meaning of Authentication

1. The Wide Geographical Reach of the Latin Notarial Functions

As noted earlier, the French-Latin notariat spread far beyond France and Southern and Central Europe (the ancestral place of birth of this notariat) to the Americas, among other continents. Thus, similar or closely related versions of the Latin notariat are presently found in locations as distant from Napoleonic France as the state of Sonora, Mexico,[24] and the city of San Jose, Costa Rica (about which more later). Accordingly, the notarial law of Sonora defines a notary and his functions as follows:

> Article 5. A notary is a law school graduate who has been granted the public faith [of the government] (*fe pública*) to authenticate those acts and facts which interested parties wish or ought to authenticate in accordance with the law; he is also the person in charge of receiving, interpreting and providing the necessary legal or voluntary formality to juristic acts, thus being in charge of drafting the legal instruments appropriate for such a purpose and conferring authenticity upon these instruments.[25]

---

[22] For a description of present day honoraria, *see* CONSEIL SUPÉRIEUR, *supra* note 3, at 4 ("Because the notary provides a public service, payments made to notaries are strictly regulated; notaries charge clients a fixed rate.").

[23] *See* COD. COM.(MEX.) art. 1397 (1889).

[24] Ley del Notariado para el Estado de Sonora [Notarial Law of the State of Sonora], Boletín Oficial del Estado de Sonora, 4 de Enero de 1996 (Mex.) [hereinafter Sonoran Notarial Law].

[25] *Id.* art. 5 (author's translation). In contrast, the 1803 French Law on the Notarial System defines notaries as: "*public functionaries* designated to receive all acts and contracts to which the parties must or

> Article 6. The notary, while performing his functions, shall act as a legal advisor of the parties who appear before him, guiding their choice of the most appropriate legal means to attain their lawful purposes, shall prepare the necessary documents, shall draft the instrument and shall explain the value and legal consequences of the acts and facts that are granted or take place before him and his public faith; the parties' signatures shall be executed before him, he shall make copies of the instrument and shall preserve the original.[26]

These provisions track the broader definition of the Latin notary provided by the principles of the International Union of Notaries (UINL),[27] a private but influential organization of Latin notaries worldwide: "Notaries are professional lawyers and public officials appointed by the State to confer authenticity on legal deeds and contracts contained in documents drafted by them and to advise persons who call upon their services."[28]

2. *Authentication and Attestation*

Authentication is at the heart of the Latin notary's functions, especially as a recipient of the "public faith" (*publica fides*) of the state. As such a recipient, the notary attests or bears witness to the veracity of those facts he is capable of ascertaining in accordance with criteria set forth by notarial laws, the civil codes and, less frequently, the commercial codes. In addition, he attests to the legality of the transaction.

What are the facts that the Latin notary is allowed to authenticate? As stated by Article 5 of the Sonoran Notarial Code, the notary can authenticate "those acts and facts which interested parties wish or ought to authenticate."[29] To deal with this broad grant of authority, Article 7 of the Notarial Law of Sonora points to the tools that the notary can rely on when attesting to the veracity of facts:

> Article 7. As the person in charge of authentication, the notary, at the request of the interested party, affirms, subject to his [notarial public] faith, the

---

wish to impart the authentic character of a public act and to guarantee the date, keep it deposited and issue copies and testimonies." Malavet, *Latin Notary*, *supra* note 2, at 422. Note that other than the reference to the requirement of a graduation from a law school, the remainder of the Mexican definition comports with the function of providing public faith (implicitly associated with a public functionary) and other essential functions set forth in the French Law on the Notarial System.

[26] Sonoran Notarial Law art. 6 (author's translation).

[27] UNIÓN INTERNACIONAL DEL NOTARIADO (U.I.N.L.), http://uinl.net/presentacion.asp?idioma=ing&submenu=UINL. In addition to the UINL, some European nations belong to the Council of the Notariats of the European Union [hereinafter CNUE]. *See About Us,* NOTARIES OF EUROPE, http://www.notaries-of-europe.eu/about-us/overview. This is a regional organization of European notaries. It covers most of Europe, with a few exceptions such as the United Kingdom, Ireland, and all of Scandinavia. Yet, all the European members of the CNUE are members of the UINL. In addition, Switzerland, Macedonia, Moldava, Monaco, Russia, San Marino, Turkey and the Vatican are members of the UINL. Those European nations that are not members of the CNUE are not members of the UINL either, with the exception of the London Association of Scrivener Notaries, which is also a member of the UINL.

[28] U.I.N.L., http://uinl.net/notariado_mundo.asp?idioma=esp&submenu=NOTAIRE; *see also* CONSEIL SUPÉRIEUR, *supra* note 3 and accompanying text; Malavet, *Latin Notary*, *supra* note 2, at 431 (defining a notary as "a legal professional specially designated to attest the acts and contracts that persons celebrate or perform, to draft the documents that formalize the latter and to give legal advice to those who require the services of his office.").

[29] Sonoran Notarial Law art. 5 (author's translation).

> veracity *of what he sees, hears or perceives by his senses and the certainty and evidentiary weight of the declared intent of the parties* in the [notarial] instrument drafted by him.[30]

Hence, as an officially empowered witness, the notary is instructed to rely on his sensorial perceptions and to assess the certainty and evidentiary weight of the parties' declared contractual intent.

3. **Publica Fides** *and the Evidentiary Weight of a Latin Notary's Authentication*

According to the UINL, the authentication that notaries set forth in their attestations and certifications does not amount to full proof; courts should grant them instead the status of rebuttable presumptions.[31] According to this view, then, a judicial declaration of invalidity, certification or attestation of a notarial document reverses these presumptions and renders the authentication meaningless for all practical purposes.[32]

Professor Malavet offers a more nuanced view when he points out that "[i]n France, a notarial document and the facts included therein, are automatically admissible into evidence and only upon judicial declaration of invalidity does the document lose its [self-enforcing] nature."[33] Indeed, the sweeping language of the first paragraph of Article 1319 of the *Code Civil* supports Malavet's assertion:

> An authentic act gives full faith to the agreement it encompasses both as between the contracting parties and their heirs. . . . (*L'acte authentique fait pleine foi de la convention qu'il renferme entre les parties contractantes et leur heritiers*)[34]

The words "full faith" (*pleine foi*) would support Professor Malavet's reference to an automatic admissibility as evidence which, while not the equivalent to an irrefutable presumption, places a heavier burden upon he who tries to undo its effects. It would seem that where a buyer "B" of property "X" sells or mortgages to a third party "C" what he thought he acquired based upon the automatic admission of the notarial authentication of validity of his purchase, his resale or mortgage to C will not be as easy to undo as it was when the same transaction was subject *ab initio* to a rebuttable presumption. In contrast, the first sentence of Article 1218 of the Spanish Civil Code is more circumspect on the scope of the notarial full faith and authentication:

> Public documents provide evidence, even against third parties, *of the fact that motivates their execution and of their date of execution.*[35] (*Los documentos públicos hacen prueba, aun contra tercero, del hecho que motiva su otorgamiento y de la fecha de éste.*)

---

[30] *Id.* art. 7 (emphasis added).

[31] Malavet, *Latin Notary*, *supra* note 2, at 444.

[32] *Id.*

[33] *Id.*

[34] C. CIV. (FR.) art. 1319 (Dalloz 1992–93) (author's translation).

[35] C.C. (SPAIN) art. 1218 (emphasis added).

The circumspection of the Spanish approach is apparent in the italicized words of Article 1218 above. Only "the fact that motivates their execution"[36] and *not the contents of the document, including the parties contractual intent, are deemed prima facie evidence.*

The difference between the French and Spanish rules on the admissibility of their notarial evidence, and especially on the enforceability of the contract whose conclusion they witnessed, can be illustrated by the following example. A notarial document contains both a loan and a mortgage agreement between "A" and "B." The facts that motivate the execution of such a deed are A's desire to borrow a certain amount of money from B and to provide him with the security of a mortgage. Conversely, from B's standpoint, the admissible facts are his desire to extend such a loan and to become a mortgagee-secured creditor.

According to Article 1319 of the *Code Civil*, the notarial document they signed gives full faith to their security agreement. What does this full faith mean? At a minimum, it must mean that the parties entered into an enforceable agreement between themselves and presumably with effects upon third parties. However, in Spain, the notary's authentication does not extend to the validation of the mortgage, even between the contracting parties, let alone third parties. For under Spanish law, the enforceability of their agreement requires the land registrar's determination that the seller has the right to mortgage based upon the chain of title recorded in the land registry. Indeed, the Spanish Law of Mortgages (*Ley Hipotecaria*)[37] makes it clear that whatever the parties agreed to in their purported mortgage agreement, it would have no legal effect either between A and B or with respect to C (*e.g.*, a *bona fide* purchaser of the mortgaged property) until it was recorded in the land registry.[38]

In other words, unlike the self-enforcing nature attributed by French notarial law to the French notarial document (as in the phrase "and only upon judicial declaration of invalidity does the document lose its [self-enforcing] nature"[39]), the Spanish land registrar, by rejecting what he considers an improperly executed mortgage, can deprive the notarial document of both a recordable and enforceable status and thus of its self-enforcing nature. One must conclude, then, that under Spanish law, where the parties to the loan agreement and mortgage are concerned, the public faith of the notarial document is subordinate to the superior public faith vested upon the land registrar, unless a court reverses the latter's determination.

B. The Limits of the Latin Notary's Factual Authentication

As was discussed in the previous section, whatever is the legal or metaphysical source of the Latin notary's full or public faith, its impact upon authentication is objectively measurable by what is admissible as evidence under the applicable

---

[36] *Id.*

[37] Ley Hipotecaria [Law of Mortgages] (B.O.E. 1946, 58) (Spain).

[38] *See* Kozolchyk, *Mexican Land Registry*, at 316. The current Spanish Mortgage Law, under Articles 20 and 145, requires the drawing of a notarial document and its recording in the land registry for the mortgage to be enforceable among the borrower and lender, as well with respect to the *bona fide* purchaser. Ley Hipotecaria arts. 20, 145. As pointed out above, the language of this statute is quite similar to that of Article 873 of the German Civil Code. Kozolchyk, *Mexican Land Registry*, at 316 n.40 ("For voluntary mortgages to be perfected, it is necessary (1) that there is an agreement expressed in a public deed, (2) that the deed be recorded in the Land Registry set forth in this law.").

[39] Malavet, *Latin Notary*, *supra* note 2, at 444 (citation omitted).

presumption. This is true either with respect to the veracity of transactional facts or with the meaning of the parties' contractual intent.

According to the Superior Council of the French Notariat (*Conseil Supérieur du Notariat*), the French notary "personally guarantees the contents and the date which appear on the act [and] [*t*]*his act is recognized as having the same authority as a court decision*."[40] This assessment would bring the notarial attestation close to the status of an irrefutable presumption. On the other hand, if one reflects on the reasons for the circumspection of Article1218 of the Spanish Civil Code, one may well conclude that its drafters had good reasons to remain circumspect on the scope and effects of the notarial authentication. The negative experience of the *Cour de Cassation* with a doctrine that equated the intent attested to by notaries in *actes authentiques* to the effectuation of justice between the parties is further evidence of the wisdom of circumspection.

*1. Authentication of Contractual Intent and the Doctrine of Contractual Justice (*Justice Contractuelle*)*

Given the higher likelihood of enforcement of statements or promises made before notaries than those made informally, would it be correct to equate the notarial *publica fide* with the judicial adjudication of the rights and duties of the parties to a notarial document? Did the legislature grant adjudicative powers to the notaries by making the literal meaning of what was stated in their contracts the untouchable version of the parties' intent? After all, Article 1134 of the *Code Civil* had declared lawfully executed agreements as *the law between the parties*.[41] Why not elevate the status of that contractual law to the status of a just adjudication of disputes concerning the parties' intent? Despite what may have been wished by notaries and doctrinal writers, the answer, over time, has been in the negative.

A respected early twentieth-century French commentator coined the phrase "contractual justice" ("*justice contractuelle*") to highlight the strong judicial reticence to interpret or re-interpret what the notary attested to as having been agreed to by the parties in their *acte authentique*.[42] This policy of reticence to tinker with the literal meaning of notarial contracts was also applied by the *Cour de Cassation* to other, less formal written contracts, including the so-called contracts of adhesion.[43] Yet, while the

---

[40] *CONSEIL SUPÉRIEUR*, *supra* note 3, at 1 (emphasis added).

[41] *See infra* ch. 8 (on the codification of the *Code Civil*).

[42] *See* Kozolchyk, *Commercialization*, at 13–15 (discussing the meaning and effect of the doctrine of "*justice contractuelle*").

[43] *See* Vera Bolgar, *The Contract of Adhesion—A Comparison of Theory and Practice*, 20 AM. J. COMP. L. 53, 67–68 (1972):

> But in the field of contracts, the *Court of Cassation* steadfastly clings to the letter of article 1134, according to which contracts legally executed are the law as between the parties, and disregards the requirement expressed further in this article—namely, that they should also be performed in good faith. . . . Consequently, the Court almost invariably reverses the more liberal decisions of the lower courts rendered under their famous *pouvoir souverain d'appreciation*—a sovereign power of interpretation which, however, extends only to the interpretation of facts—on the ground that considerations of equity would "denaturalize" the clear and precise terms of the original contract.

(citations omitted). Since that time, and mostly as a result of the consumer protection movement that spread through the nations of the European Union, the *Cour de Cassation* has liberalized its "*justice contractuelle*" approach to adhesion contracts, among others.

Cour de Cassation was partial to literal interpretation as a tool of legal certainty and predictability, it was not about to give up its power to interpret contracts, even if this power was reduced to determining what was the "true" literal meaning.

Lest one loses sight of what is at stake in the literal interpretation of commercial notarial language, it is worth noting that a literal reading of commercial contractual language is often at the expense of the intent reflected in the parties' contractual conduct. Such conduct is apparent in the parties' course of performance of the contract in question or in their course of previous dealings. It is also present in the usages of the trades involved, which are usually the most trustworthy sources of the meaning of commercial terms and transactional practices.[44]

2. *Authentication of Facts Other Than the Contractual Intent*

In principle, the Latin notary is well situated to attest to the existence of some of the facts that he or she witnessed relying on the sensorial perceptions of Article 7 of Sonora's Notarial Law. With the aid of "*what he sees, hears or perceives by his senses*," he can safely attest, say, to the physical presence of the persons who identified themselves as the parties to the contract, or to what they said they had agreed to after he read them the draft contract, and so on. But can he safely attest to the legal implications of facts when such an attestation requires either knowledge of other facts he is unaware of or knowledge that only an expert in those implications would have?

I just asked a leading question, but given the persistence of notarial attestations that disregard the limits of the notarial factual and transactional knowledge, it is a question worth asking. Consider, for example, an actual case related to me by the late Justice of the Supreme Court of Sonora, Lic. Carlos Cabrera.[45] A notary public in Sonora was asked by a victim of an automobile accident to attest to the damages that appeared to have been suffered by the body (*carroceria*) of his vehicle, and also to the location of tire markings at the sight of the collision. After describing the damages that appeared to have been suffered by the body of the plaintiff's vehicle, the notary added that "by observing the strong tire markings left by the vehicle that hit the other on the latter's driver's side, it was apparent that the strong marks made on the pavement by the tires of defendant's [hitting] vehicle were caused by a sudden, almost desperate attempt to stop the vehicle before it hit the plaintiff's vehicle."[46] Lic. Cabrera rightly characterized such an attestation as improper by going beyond what the notary's senses enabled him to see, hear or smell. Further, he attested to causation, to which only an expert on tire markings and vehicle accidents could attest.[47] He then asked me if the attestations he criticized qualified as what U.S. litigants and judges referred to as hearsay evidence in a U.S. television program many watched in Mexico.

In response, I sent him a comment found in McCormick on Evidence which addressed the distinction between hearsay evidence and evidence proffered by a

---

[44] *See infra* ch. 23 (discussing the role of course of dealing and usage of trade in the interpretation of commercial contracts); *see also infra* ch. 24 (discussing the role of standard and best practices in shaping a commercial transactions law that can contribute to economic development).

[45] Letter from Lic. Carlos Cabrera Sr., Justice of the Supreme Court of Sonora, to author (Oct. 12, 1976) (on file with author).

[46] *Id.*

[47] *Id.*

witness who lacked firsthand knowledge of the facts.[48] According to Dean McCormick, a witness is qualified to testify to facts susceptible of observation only if it appears that he had a reasonable opportunity to observe the facts.[49] Accordingly, if a witness testified that an airplane arrived at a certain time and date at a certain airport, but the witness was in a distant city when the arrival took place "and could therefore only have spoken from conjecture or report of other persons," the proper objection is not hearsay, but want of personal knowledge.[50] In contrast, if the witness testifies that his brother told him that he was on the previously mentioned flight and that it arrived at the time stated by that witness, the proper objection is that such a testimony would be that it is based on hearsay. In Dean McCormick's words:

> The distinction is one of the form of the testimony, whether the witness purports to give the facts directly upon his or her own credit . . . or whether the witness purports to give an account of what another has said and this is offered to establish the truth of the other's report.[51]

In response to Dean McCormick's comment, Justice Cabrera noted that in his opinion, notarial attestations were being given too much credit by courts as factual or documentary evidence even though many of them lacked personal knowledge or transcribed hearsay version of facts.[52]

Professor Malavet draws attention to the procedural preference in civil law countries for documentary evidence and for the role of the Latin notaries as trustworthy suppliers of such evidence. Thus, properly empowered public officials are allowed to certify or guarantee the facts stated in the document to which it is attached. Conversely, he notes, common law lawyers are suspicious of authenticated documentary evidence because of its "hearsay concerns and the general common-law preference for in-court testimony [which] justify the inadmissibility of notarized documents as proof of the matter therein asserted."[53] I should add, parenthetically, that many Latin American countries are gradually abandoning the traditional, mostly documentary evidence trial in favor of adversarial trials in which evidence is provided by different sources whose credibility is challenged by the oral and public examination as well as the cross-examination of witnesses.[54]

3. The Problems with the Attestation of the Intent in Commercial Contracts

As with a notary's (non-expert) attestation of the causation of an automobile accident in Justice Cabrera's inquiry, the most that a Latin notary could say about the intent of many a contemporary commercial contract is that he read its terms and conditions to the parties and stated that they understood them and considered themselves bound by them. He cannot attest that they did, in fact, understand the meaning of all the terms and conditions any more than he can say that about himself.

---

[48] II McCORMICK ON EVIDENCE 131 (Kenneth S. Broun ed., 6th ed. 2006).

[49] *Id.*

[50] *Id.*

[51] *Id.*

[52] *Id.*

[53] Malavet, *Latin Notary*, *supra* note 2, at 442–43 (citations omitted).

[54] The NLCIFT is presently training judges and lawyers in Mexico and Colombia to enable their participation in the new "oral" or adversary civil, commercial and criminal trials.

Truth be told, only some of the parties or intermediaries who regularly participate in these complex transactions possess the requisite knowledge to understand all the stipulations associated with, say, the purchase of "derivative" rights or "credit default swaps" or swaps of interest rates or foreign exchange streams of income, including standard provisions on "credit events," "net-net netting," etc.[55]

Conversely, assume that the contract in question is a garden variety real estate transaction with which a Latin notary is familiar, but that following a not uncommon contractual practice in countries like France, Spain and their former colonies in Africa and Latin America, the contract in question hides or "simulates" the true intent of the parties. Please recall that the practice of simulating the execution of ostensibly intended but truly unintended contracts was conceived precisely to hide the true intent of the parties. In such a transaction, is the Latin notary in a position to attest to the true intent of the parties?[56]

Or, assume that one of the parties consented to the terms of a contract that, in his honestly mistaken opinion, reflected faithfully the usage of the trade in question. As will be apparent when we discuss the meaning of good faith and reasonableness in the interpretation of commercial contracts in United States law, the interpretation of a given term or clause by a usage of trade often supersedes, in the eyes of the courts, the parties' understanding of their individual intent.[57]

Finally, assume—as is most commonly the case with commercial contracts—that such a contract starts out as a promise or an act of performance by one of the parties only to be followed shortly thereafter by the other parties' promises or acts of acceptance and that during the relatively short life of their contract (as contrasted, say, with the decades of life of a real estate mortgage or easement), their terms and conditions change with each reciprocal act of performance. Assume also that during the entire life of this commercial contract, no formal document was drafted until the parties appeared before the notary and that the clearest indication of what they agreed to do is found in their course of performance and previous course of dealing—not in an *a priori* ceremonial formulation of a contract.[58] Could a Latin notary realistically and cost effectively decipher the intent of such quickly malleable transactions?

These, among other difficulties with the Latin notary's attestation of the parties' intent in contemporary commercial transactions, render their authentication of these transactions uncertain at best. As will be discussed shortly and in the Appendix, the costliness and ineffectiveness of the Latin notary's participation in commercial transactions is being questioned by nations with legal cultures as diverse as those of, for example, Mexico and Sweden.

C. The German Notarial Experience with Commercial Transactions

In Germany, as in other Latin notariat countries, the notary (*Notar*): (a) satisfies himself as to the identity of the parties that appear before him; (b) verifies that these

---

[55] See, for example, the schedule of events in a typical conference of the Inernational Swaps and Derivatives Association (ISDA). ISDA, http://www2.isda.But in the field of contracts,org/.

[56] *See* § 1:2(E) on contractual simulation.

[57] *See infra* ch. 23:9(G)(4).

[58] *See infra* ch. 22 (for the various scenarios of formation of commercial contracts).

parties are competent to enter into the agreements they seek to notarize; (c) explains to the parties to a contract the contents and legal implications of the instrument; and (d) has the parties and witnesses (where required) sign the contract or other notarial document before him.[59]

Based upon my own experiences with Latin notaries, the German notaries seem to be the ones most attuned to the nature of contemporary commercial contracts. As in France, Spain and Latin America, German notaries play a central role in real estate and corporate transactions of monetary significance, as well as in family and succession matters. Unlike their French colleagues, however, the German notaries seem to have a closer connection with the transactional realities of the marketplace.

For example, the German notary's involvement with the customs and practices of the real estate market makes him aware of transactional facts that are likely to be ignored or disregarded by his French and Spanish counterparts. Since he "handles all aspects of the documentation and effectuation of the transaction",[60] he is charged not only with drafting the real estate contract, but also with checking land registries, working with mortgaging banks, and even holding deposits on behalf of buyers. Thus, the German notary "acts as an independent neutral 'lawyer for the situation' and takes into account the mutual security interests of *all parties* (seller, seller's creditors, purchaser, purchaser's financing bank)."[61] Most importantly, he acts as a facilitator of transactions. For example, where a French, Spanish or Mexican notary would not find it possible to help enforce the seller's supposedly firm promise of selling Blackacre until the actual sale agreement was executed, the German notary would make the enforcement of the seller's firm promise possible by acting as the functional equivalent of an escrow agent.[62] As described by real estate transactions manual:

> Recommended Procedures to Hand-Over of Title Through a Notarial Intervention
>
> In some cases, hand-over (*Grundstücksübergabe*) before payment is agreed. Under German law, this frequently creates the problem that the transfer of ownership represents an advance performance by the seller for which he still has no security. In this case, provisional payment of part of the purchase price is a solution. This money can be deposited with the notary or paid into a special account (*Sperrkonto*) to which the buyer only has access in the event of the complete reversal of the transaction.
>
> Furthermore, to protect the buyer, it is frequently recommended that he should not pay the purchase price direct to the seller but deposit it with the notary. *Notary custody* (*notarielle Verwahrung*) gives the credit institutes and banks the necessary security. Another possibility is to initially *pay the*

---

[59] For basic descriptions of the functions of the German Notar, see *Signature Certification and Full Notarization of a Document*, GERMANY.INFO, http://www.germany.info/Vertretung/usa/en/05__Legal/02__Directory__Services/05__Certificates__Documents/Notarization__Signature__Certification.html; *see also Der Notar*, THE GERMAN WAY & MORE, http://www.german-way.com/germany-notar.html.

[60] PETER L. MURRAY & ROLF STÜRNER, THE CIVIL LAW NOTARY-NEUTRAL LAWYER FOR THE SITUATION 52 (2010).

[61] *Id.* (emphasis added).

[62] *See* Boris Kozolchyk, *Comparative Law on a Standard Option Contract for the Purchase of Real Property and a Guide of Best Contractual Practices*, 27 ARIZ. J. INT'L & COMP. L. 441, 442 (2010); Boris Kozolchyk, *German Notarial Practice*, 27 ARIZ. J. INT'L COMP. L. 463 (2010).

> *purchase price into a special account* to which the seller only has access under conditions previously defined in detail (*Sperrkonto*).
>
> . . .
>
> [A]nother approach to securing the seller's rights is frequently chosen: the conditional transfer of property (*Eigentumsumschreibung unter Vorbehalt*). The conveyance of ownership is already agreed in the purchase contract. However, the notary is instructed by both contracting parties jointly not to file the application for the transfer of property with the land registry office . . . until payment of the purchase price has been verified to the notary. In such cases, a firm promise of payment or confirmation of financing by the bank involved often are considered to be sufficient.[63]

The German notary's role in this transaction reflects both his active participation as a facilitator of an option to purchase or promise of sale that has remained unenforceable to this day in many a Latin notariat jurisdiction and his thorough familiarity with transactional practices, their purposes and functions.

§ 7.4 NOTARIAL ATTESTATIONS IN COMMERCIAL TRANSACTIONS: A NEW BREED OF COMMERCIAL NOTARIES

The preceding discussion of the Latin notary's attestations of transactional facts and contractual intent showed that they are unsuited for the needs of certainty and predictability of the contemporary commercial and financial marketplace. Some countries whose notaries are still members of the Latin notariat have introduced some important variations to it. For example, in 1992, Mexico created the profession of the "public broker" (*corredor público*), which was intended to be a less formal and less costly and dilatory version of the "public notary" (*notario público*).[64] Sweden, in turn, liberalized the practice of the notarial profession to the point that most of its real estate transactions in Sweden are handled by real estate brokers and not by notaries.[65]

In principle, the Latin notary, as a provider of legal certainty, should be a major contributor to national and regional economic development. Yet, is he such a contributor? Or is his intervention so formal, dilatory and costly that it outweighs his possible contribution? These questions are constantly raised when a new commercial law institution such as commercial loans secured with the assets of the debtor-merchant are required to be documented or authenticated by notaries.

Bear in mind that many of the contracts of the contemporary commercial and financial marketplace require specialized knowledge to understand what the parties are doing, let alone intending to do. In addition, it is a marketplace formed in significant measure by strangers or parties who do not know one another and for that reason distrust each other. Thus, this marketplace places a premium on reliable transactional data and is in dire need of trusted and knowledgeable intermediaries

---

[63] *Id.* at 463–64 (citing REAL ESTATE INVESTMENTS IN GERMANY, TRANSACTIONS AND DEVELOPMENT 104 (Michael Multze et al. eds., 2007)).

[64] *See* Ley Federal de Correduría Pública [Federal Law on Public Brokers], Diario Oficial de la Federación [DO] 29 de Diciembre de 1992 (Mex.).

[65] *See infra* § 7:5(A)(4).

who bridge the gaps of insufficient or uncertain information and distrust accurately and inexpensively.

Notaries public could play such a role in some commercial transactions, but they must expand their factual and legal knowledge of the transactions in which they participate and reduce the cost of their participation. They can no longer confine themselves to ascertaining the formalities of traditional sales of real property, including the recitals of ritualistic clauses. They must think of themselves as professional intermediaries with considerable awareness of the transactions and sectors in which they participate. This requires them to be fully familiar with the intent of archetypal parties for the sectors in which they may wish to specialize, an intent that is derived primarily from the parties' prior dealings and the usages of their respective trades.

With such knowledge at hand, notaries could serve not only as drafters or counsel for the drafters of agreements, but also as trusted escrow agents and paymasters. This function would be especially helpful with executory contracts or with contracts whose conditions require that performance be established by independent experts, but whose payment would be effectuated or directed by notarial paymasters familiar with the required experts' certifications. Please note that in that capacity, notaries will not act as inspectors of the quality or quantity of the contractual performance any more than a letter of credit banker would when examining the documents tendered by a beneficiary. Their function, then, would be to ascertain that the documents required by the escrow agreement are the same that were tendered to them, and they would do so based upon their knowledge of these certifications and of the usages of the trades or professions involved. Clearly, this role would require a greater degree of notarial specialization than is presently in existence.

§ 7.5 APPENDIX: THE LIVING LAW OF THE NOTARIAL PROFESSION IN DEVELOPING AND DEVELOPED NATIONS

A. Notarial Practice in Sonora, Mexico, and San José, Costa Rica:

The legal institutions associated with the Latin notariat, as any other legal institutions, cannot help but to be influenced by the attitudes and values that are reflected in a nation or region's legal culture. To date, the formalism and solemnity of the Latin notariat's documents and attestations have proven highly compatible with the legal culture of Latin American nations, as illustrated by notarial practices in Mexico and Costa Rica, among other Latin American nations.

1. Interview Lic. Eduardo Estrella Acedo, from Ciudad Obregón, México[66]

Notarial practice in Mexico is state governed, as is true of all other Mexican states. The State of Sonora has two main sets of laws that govern this profession: (1) the previously mentioned Notarial Law of the State of Sonora,[67] which governs all formal and substantive aspects of the notarial profession, including the process for

[66] Interview with Eduardo Estrella Acedo, Notary Public, Ciudad Obregón, Mexico, in Tucson, Ariz. (June 24, 2008).

[67] *See supra* n.29.

obtaining authorization to practice as a notary, their rights and duties, their use of the special notarial paper for their documents and archives, their seals, and the list of minimum requirements that need to be observed in every public deed they draft; and (2) the Law that fixes the notarial fees for the State of Sonora.[68]

During the month of June of 2008, I interviewed Lic. Eduardo Estrella Acedo. Lic. Estrella is a close friend whom I have known and respected since I first met him in 1969. At that time, he was president of the Sonora Bar Association and a practicing notary public. Since then, he became president of Instituto Tecnológico de Sonora (ITSON), one of Sonora's most respected universities, and deputy governor and mayor of Ciudad Obregon. He is now in private practice as a notary public in Ciudad Obregon and continues to be one of the most respected lawyers and notaries in Sonora. What he says candidly and forthrightly in this interview should explain why he is so respected.

Boris Kozolchyk (hereinafter BK): How did you become a notary?

Lic. Eduardo Estrella Acedo (hereinafter EE): I was appointed by Governor Luis Encinas.

BK: Was there a public examination or competition at that time or was the appointment a decision of the governor?

EE: There was no examination process; the governor appointed whoever he thought was competent.

BK: Is that process of appointment still in effect?

EE: Yes, but only after the examination process has determined who are the successful candidates. In 2008, we had in excess of 100 practicing notaries in Sonora and the governor felt that there were too many of us for a population of roughly two million. If you compare it to the State of Baja California, where the population is ten million and the number of notaries is ten or so, you will see what an enormous disproportion this is.

BK: What are other important qualifications?

EE: Candidates must undergo an eight-year period of study, during which time they apprentice for five years (*aspirantes*) with a notary. After the initial period of five years, they have the right to take the final examination as notarial candidates (*titulares*). However, the governor has also suspended these examinations until further notice.

BK: Does this very cumbersome process (first law school, then the clerkships, then two sets of examinations) weed out the incompetent ones?

EE: Some, but not all.

BK: Is there a continuing legal education requirement?

EE: Yes. The National Association of Notaries (*Asociacion del Notariado Mexicano*) provides interactive computerized courses to the notaries. This is, in principle, a very nice effort. At the end of this course, you get a certificate of

[68] *Ley que Establece el Arancel para los Notarios del Estado de Sonora* [Law that Determines Notarial Fees for Notaries in the State of Sonora] Boletín Oficial del Gobierno del Estado de Sonora, 29 de Diciembre de 1989 (Mex.) [hereinafter Sonoran Notarial Fee Law].

qualification, but very frequently people pay attendance fees and do not attend. In Sonora, I have proposed a similar plan, but with stricter attendance requirements, to the College of Notaries of the State of Sonora, but it has not been accepted by them yet.

BK: Can the College of Notaries expel incompetent or bad faith notaries?

EE: It can. It does have a procedure to investigate accusations of malpractice or incompetence, but once it is completed, it must ask the state government to proceed with its own findings and decisions.

BK: Has the government taken one of these cases to its conclusion?

EE: Yes and no. It did take one such a case to its conclusion, but it was decided not on the merits, but on political grounds.

BK: Let me ask you some questions on *publica fides*, and please respond in whatever order you please: (1) What is your definition of a notary's *publica fides*, *fe pública*? (2) The *Unión Internacional del Notariado* states, with regards to *fe pública*, that *publica fides* gives the notarial attestation or certification a presumption of truth and of legality.[69] Thus, "[t]he facts included in the notarial document are presumed to be true. The legality and proper form of the juridical act it reflects are likewise presumed."[70] However, a judicial declaration of invalidity reverses these presumptions.[71] Do you agree with such a description of *fe pública,* or do you have your own? Finally, (3) As a notary, are you willing to assume responsibility for the truth of facts other than those you can physically ascertain, such as the presence of the parties, their apparent identities and their apparent state of mind, or are you willing to assume more? Please notice the use of the term "apparent" and tell me if you agree with it. When I was drafting some international customs for bankers who had the duty of checking the compliance of documents with requirements in letters of credit, I suggested the use of the term "apparent" as it applied to the compliance of the documents for reasons similar to those that I believe permeate a notary's attestation of facts.

EE: Article 7 of the *Ley del Notariado* of Sonora states that a notary can only attest to the veracity of the acts that he can perceive by the use of his senses. This is the general principle that I follow whenever I have to attest to the occurrence of acts or events with the understanding that the senses may deceive you. I am also guided by the fact that public faith amounts to a rebuttable presumption of veracity or legality. This gives me comfort. Finally, public faith also extends to my determinations of the legality of the document, clause, or statement, based upon my knowledge of the law of contracts, powers of attorney, business associations, mortgages or whatever. I agree with your use of the term "apparent" and like it. One can only go by appearances, such as of mental sanity or lucidity of the party appearing before you. After all, you are not a psychiatrist or a handwriting expert. All you can say is that the contracting party appeared to be sane or that the signature she was affixing to a document appeared to be her signature. Because of the rebuttable presumption attached to my certification, I can say that the party acted in a manner that denoted mental competence or that she

---

[69] Malavet, *Latin Notary*, *supra* note 2, at 444, 448.

[70] *Id.* at 444.

[71] *Id.*

affixed her signature. Perhaps someone, an expert in signatures, can later prove that the signature of the party in question was forged by an impostor.

BK: Are you aware of cases of bad faith behavior by notaries?

EE: Yes. Unfortunately there are a good number of them.

BK: Can you give me some examples.

EE: One of those cases involved a forgery of parts of a contract of sale before a notary that was optically scanned and reproduced in a manner to appear as a power of attorney in favor of an unintended beneficiary. The fraudulent notary actually scanned parts of the public deed of sale and made it appear as a power of attorney.

BK: How could such a forgery be prevented?

EE: By the constant alertness and vigilance of the notary. I will give you a recent example that involved one of my powers of attorney. A colleague in another city in Sonora who knows me professionally called me and asked me to verify whether I had been the notary before whom a certain power of attorney had been issued. I immediately checked the number of the deed against the numbers in my record (protocol) and verified that it was a forged power. The numbers did not match. My colleague was definitely quite alert and vigilant and it paid off.

BK: Is this a frequent occurrence?

EE: Unfortunately, yes. A good number of fraudulent notarial deeds are created by impersonators, people who pretend to be "A" and provide an identity document that belongs to someone else, "B," on the basis of forgery of the identification number. Recently, I heard of a notarial clerk who prevented such a practice by looking carefully at the date of issuance of a driver's license being used by the party appearing before the notary claiming to be someone else. The clerk noticed that the driver's license had been issued a day or two before the appearance and that raised his suspicion because as a rule, such licenses are used as identification devices by people who have held them for much longer periods of time.

BK: Do you rely on some specific indicators to prevent such frauds?

EE: Yes, I have adopted the practice of incorporating the photographs of the contracting parties as part of their notarial deeds. For example, the Mexican voting ID card requires a photograph of the voter. I require it and I append it to all my deeds or powers, and I ask all the witnesses to produce it as well.

BK: Is this a requirement of the notarial code?

EE: Not in so many words, but this code requires that the parties be identified by the notary and leaves it to the notary to employ his own indicators or due diligence in ascertaining the identity of the parties.

BK: How about the mental capacity of the parties? How do you establish it?

EE: By talking with them extensively before the drafting or signing of the notarial act. I ask them questions until it is clear to me that they are lucid and in full command of their faculties. At times, when I have had doubts, I have requested a medical or psychological examination and incorporated the medical certificate as part of the contract.

BK: With what other attestations or certifications do you employ the greatest care?

EE: With ascertaining the legality of the contract and that all the formalities that pertain to the various documents or acts have been complied with.

BK: Do you yourself attest to being a witness to the occurrence or performance of certain acts or the occurrence of certain events?

EE: Yes. Occasionally, we are asked to attest to the service of process upon a defendant in an important lawsuit or that a certain amount of money has been delivered to a contract party or to a third party, or that a certain document has been delivered or produced.

BK: In other words, you attest that a payment has been made or that a payment that was due was not made as in the case of the protest of bills of exchange or promissory notes or checks?

EE: Correct.

BK: Is there a national identity number in Mexico as in some Central American countries?

EE: No. Some Sonora identification numbers exist, but unfortunately, they are being forged much too frequently. This is why it has become common for notaries to require the presentation of two identification documents and why I add photographs.

BK: You told me a few days ago that there is malpractice insurance for Mexican notaries issued by some Mexican insurance companies whose premiums are payable in U.S. dollars. Do you have one? If not, why not?

EE: Yes I do. It is becoming more and more common to do so. Unfortunately, or maybe fortunately, notaries are becoming targets of malpractice lawsuits.

BK: Can you practice throughout the entire state?

EE: No, only in my assigned region of the state. I believe that we should be allowed to practice throughout the entire state and have made such a proposal to the state authorities, but this proposal, together with the others on continuing education, was rejected.

BK: Can you see notaries becoming experts in identifying the elements of important commercial documents and certifying them? For example, Party A produces a document that appears to be a valid proxy that enables Holder X to vote in corporate elections. Or, having examined Deed X, Document D appears to be a valid certificate from a fiduciary requesting payment of a certain amount of principal and interest due with respect to Mortgage Y or Government Bond Z, much as you do presently with powers of attorney.

EE: You know that in Mexico since the 1990s, we have a professional division between notaries and public brokers (*corredores públicos*) and it is reflected in the type of contracts or documents with which we deal. Ours are "civil" transactions governed by state law (mostly state civil codes) and theirs are commercial transactions governed by federal commercial law (the federal commercial code). The documents or attestations that you describe seem to fall within the purview of commercial documents handled by these public brokers. The dividing line, as you point out in your writings, is not as clear as many people think. For example, what about mortgage bonds or notes stemming from mortgage deeds executed before public brokers? Mortgages, as you know, are governed by the state civil codes. On that basis, some Mexican courts have rejected the intervention of public brokers with respect to mortgage deeds, bonds, etc. The same thing is true with the contract of agency or "mandate," which is governed by the state civil codes.

BK: Do you think that the notarial profession is vulnerable in Mexico, and if so, what are the vulnerable areas?

EE: I believe that the Mexican notariat is vulnerable first where it functions as a "hereditary aristocratic" institution. In some states, it is handed down by father to son, and by son to grandson. It should be based upon merit and only merit. Secondly, I believe that the notariat is vulnerable where the services rendered by the notary do not correspond with what he charges for them. Some time ago, there was a national meeting of notaries in Mazatlan. A rather unpleasant, but very telling incident took place following the presentation by a well-known and rather wealthy notary from Mexico City whose office bills out many millions of *pesos* per month in notarial fees. His topic was the notary's certification. After he finished his talk, a notary from the State of Veracruz asked him how many public deeds he certified as having been executed before him during a day. After the Mexico City notary hesitated, the notary from Veracruz said the following: "Sir, you hesitate to tell us because your volume of daily transactions is such that you often certify that as many as fifty such deeds have been concluded in your presence. You and I know that it is not humanly possible to do so. It takes me and other true notaries an average of thirty to forty minutes just to read a deed. In fact, the work you say you do is done for you by secretaries or clerks. Thus, I conclude that you are not acting as a notary, but as an assembly plant (*maquila*). So I am a notary and you are a *maquila*."

2. *Interview with Lic. Joaquín Picado from San José, Costa Rica*[72]

As opposed to Mexico's divided regulation of the notarial profession by state, Costa Rica has a single set of laws that govern notaries throughout the entire country. The substantive law that regulates all formal aspects of the notarial profession—process of authorization, requirements for drafting public deeds, etc.—is the Notarial Code.[73] On the other hand, notarial fees are regulated by a decree issued by the executive branch. This decree not only determines the way in which notarial fees must be calculated, but also includes a section on stamp fees (*timbres*) for the bar association that must be charged and collected by the notary public for each transaction.[74]

The following interview with Lic. Joaquín Picado will provide an illustration of current notarial practices in Costa Rica. Lic. Picado is a professor of commercial law at two Costa Rican law schools and a distinguished Costa Rican lawyer who specializes in commercial and real estate law. Lic. Picado holds an LL.M. from the University of Arizona James E. Rogers College of Law International Trade and Business Law Program and thereafter served as a research attorney and coordinator of the

---

[72] Interview with Joaquín Picado, Notary Public, San José, Costa Rica in Tucson, Ariz. (June 24, 2008).

[73] *Codigo Notarial* [Notarial Code], *La Gaceta*, 22 de Mayo de 1998 (Costa Rica) [hereinafter Notarial Code of Costa Rica].

[74] *Arancel de Honorarios por Servicios Profesionales de Abogacia y Notariado* [Honorarium Fees for Advocacy and Notarial Professional Services], La Gaceta, 18 de Mayo de 2011 (Costa Rica) [hereinafter Decree on Notarial Fees in Costa Rica].

Securitization Law Project at NLCIFT (The National Law Center for Inter-American Free Trade).

Boris Kozolchyk (hereinafter BK): Back in the 1960s, when we were doing research on land titles in rural Costa Rica, we found a peculiar notarial deed in the form of an affidavit that was labeled "Of Affection and Care" (*Afecto y Manutencion*). In it, the affiant promised to take care of the needs of the beneficiary, a designated lady and her immediate family, for an unlimited period of time. Upon further inquiry, it turned out that the affiant was a married man and the beneficiary, his mistress and children from the affiant. When I inquired about its enforceability, I was told by the notary who issued it that he had explained to the parties that the document may not have the full force of a contract, but they insisted on it being in notarial form. To me, this was an indication of the weight attributed to notarial deeds among ordinary Costa Ricans. Are notarial deeds still held in such esteem today?

Lic. Joaquin Picado (hereinafter JP): I'm not so sure about the reputation of notaries in our days. There is no question that there are a good number of reliable notaries in Costa Rica. Yet, I know of notaries who are in jail for repeated fraud and embezzlement. In fact, I know of one who is still in jail. It has gotten to the point that land registries keep a "black book" of suspect notaries. When these registries receive a notarial deed from these notaries that conveys land, creates a mortgage, or subdivides a plot, they examine it very carefully and look for indications of fraud or misrepresentation.

BK: What do you think is responsible for this deterioration? When I lived in Costa Rica in the 1960s, all lawyers were automatically notaries and you seldom heard of notarial misdeeds. In fact, the only misdeed I heard about occurred in some Costa Rican consulates where consuls were bribed to ante-date or post-date deeds of transfer of land.

JP: Well, now there are perhaps ten times as many attorneys and notaries in Costa Rica as when you lived there. The legal profession is not as concerned about ethics and professionalism as it is about making money, sometimes at any cost. On the other hand, the criteria to qualify as a notary today seems more demanding than when you lived there: the Notarial Code of Costa Rica defines a notary public as a "legal professional, specializing in notarial and registry law, and who is legally authorized to practice the notarial function."[75] Thus, to qualify for the status of a notary public, the Notarial Code requires, in addition to proof of "good conduct," that he or she be a graduate of an accredited law school with post graduate work on notarial and registry law, be a membership in the Costa Rican Bar Association for at least two years, and to have applied for the position of notary public. He or she must also be a permanent resident in Costa Rica, except for Costa Rican consuls in foreign countries, and have a "correct" command of the Spanish language.[76] Interestingly, a foreigner who fulfills the above requirements can be a Costa Rican notary as long as in his country of origin, Costa Rican notaries would be entitled to the same treatment.[77]

---

[75] Notarial Code of Costa Rica art. 2.

[76] *Id.* at art. 3.

[77] *Id. See also* Codigo del Notariado [Honduran Notarial Code], La Gaceta, 17 de Enero de 2005 (Hon.). Article 60 states:

BK: So, it is your opinion that the ethics of the notarial profession in Costa Rica could definitely stand improvement?

JP: Yes. The directorate in charge of disciplinary action needs to be much more active in preserving notarial discipline. The open system of access to the notariat had a positive aspect which was to reduce notarial fees through stiff competition among notaries and, as I said, it was in effect at a time of much higher professional ethics. Do not forget that a positive aspect of a more closed system of access, in which notarial practices can be inherited by the notary's heirs, is that the closed system has greater self-discipline. Those who inherit notarial practices tend to be more careful in their handling of their client's affairs because they have a family reputation to protect.

BK: What do you see as positive developments in the practice of the notarial profession?

JP: I see technology, and especially electronic technology and the notarial access to databases, as a very positive development, one that enhances the practice of the profession and the legal certainty of transactions.

BK: Can you provide some examples?

JP: Yes. Now we have immediate access to databases in the registry of persons, business associations, intellectual property law, pledges, real property, and cadastral surveys which enable us to check, say, a person's name or identification number when that person appears before us. The same is true with companies, with the description of land in a deed, and so on. This availability of information imposes a higher duty of diligence on the notary, but it is a welcome one.

BK: Do you carry malpractice insurance as carried by some notaries in Mexico?

JP: Yes. Notarial due diligence is now supported by malpractice insurance policies issued by a quasi-official banking and insurance agency in Costa Rica. This insurance covers the damages suffered by defrauded parties. Unfortunately, because the insurance system is a state system, and a highly bureaucratic one at that, it does not exercise much discipline. Notaries who have committed malpractice are not automatically denied renewal of their existing policies. Yet, the notarial association can expel the notary or subject him or her to criminal sanctions.

BK: Which documents or statements do you most frequently verify?

JP: The identification numbers and filed information on the identity of the parties, their powers of attorney, the previous deeds on the same property, and other data available in databases of the various registries for cross-reference purposes.

BK: How seriously do you take your certification of a contracting party's state of mind?

JP: Very seriously. I have had cases where a person appearing before me appears to be of sound mind, but upon further inquiry, turns out to be legally incapable. For

---

> The parties may agree in their contracts to submit, before a notary public, the procedure for the execution of security interests, whether in moveable or immoveable property, in which case they shall also agree on the minimum price of the immoveable property granted as collateral and of the method for notification, following the procedure set forth in the present Law.

(Author's translation).

example, if I have a contracting party or a testator beyond the age of seventy years or so, I try to engage them in conversation for a while. In one instance, a party who appeared to be of sound mind answered comfortably the first set of questions concerning her name, residence, etc. However, when I asked her about her husband, even though the identification information I obtained from one of the databases indicated that she was a widow, she referred to her husband in one of her answers to me as "still working in our farm." I immediately decided not to be the notary for the transaction.

As the reader compares these interviews, it will be useful to attempt to inquire into the validity of the interviewees' perceptions of the notarial and socio-economic reality around them. For example, do their perceptions on the consequences of open or restricted access to the notarial professions coincide? If not, whose version of consequences sounds most plausible? What do you think about the requirement of appointment to the notarial profession? What do you think about the former Sonoran governor's policy of only appointing notaries in cases of death or incompetence? Is the reader convinced that it is really necessary to pay a significant fee to a notary public to be able to obtain their services as agent or attorney? Or to convey land? Or to sell one's home or place of business? What is wrong with using the various tried and true standard forms for "trust deeds" or "warranty deeds" or "quit claim deeds" that can be so readily found in stationary shops or real estate brokers' offices? Could the need for a Latin notary be the result of a highly distrusting society and marketplace? As noticed throughout this chapter, St. Augustine had a valid point when he noted that in a world of sinners, there was a need for a trusted third party. However, given the content of the preceding interviews, could it be that many trusted third party notaries can no longer be trusted?

B. Sweden and the Liberalized Notariat

Swedish notaries are far less numerous and far less involved in civil and commercial transactions than their Latin counterparts. While drafting the Apostille Convention of 1961,[78] the Hague Conference on Private International Law surveyed

---

[78] Hague Convention Abolishing the Requirement of Legalisation for Foreign Public Documents, Oct. 5, 1961, 33 U.S.T. 883, 527 U.N.T.S. 189, *available at* http://www.hcch.net/index_en.php?act=conventions.text&cid=41. The Hague Conference on Private International Law, on its website, previously provided the following description with regards to said Convention:

> The Hague Convention of 5 October 1961 Abolishing the Requirement of Legalisation for Foreign Public Documents (Hague Apostille Convention) facilitates the circulation of public documents executed in one State party to the Convention and to be produced in another State party to the Convention. It does so by replacing the cumbersome and often costly formalities of a full legalization process with the mere issuance of an Apostille (also called Apostille Certificate or Certificate). The Hague Apostille Convention only applies as between States parties. . . .

This quotation continues to be found on notarial websites around the world. *Steps to Proper Notarization*, AMERICAN ASSOCIATION OF NOTARIES, http://members.usnotaries.net/news.asp?AssetID=576. Simply put, this Convention makes it possible to authenticate public documents issued in a signatory country "A" thereby readying them for execution in signatory country "B." It requires that each country designate the certifying or attesting officials empowered to carry out such a function by affixing a special stamp and seal. Both the United States and Sweden are signatory parties to the Hague Convention. As just noted, under this Convention, each signatory nation selects what authority within its borders is empowered to fix a special stamp or "*apostille*" that attests to the authenticity and validity of the document in question. In the case of Swedish public documents, the Government of Sweden chose Swedish notaries public as their officials, who are designated to certify the authenticity of Swedish public documents, seals and signatures by affixing an *apostille*. In the case of documents originated in the United States, their certification for use in countries signatories to the Hague Convention is done by one of the officials in the jurisdiction in which the document

the role of notaries as certifiers of public documents worldwide. In 2013, there were approximately 250 notaries in practice in Sweden[79] (there are presently 14 notaries in Stockholm).[80]

Various reasons account for the sharp differences in the number of notaries and scope of their work between Sweden and other Latin notarial countries. One is implicit in the Swedish notarial law itself. Swedish law requires that each municipality have at least one notary (referred to as *notarius publicus*) and that the notary be appointed by each county's Administrative Board (*Länsstyrelsen*).[81]

The fact that the Swedish legislator did not seem disturbed by having such a low minimum number of notaries for each county, regardless of its size or number of inhabitants, shows that notaries are no longer significant. The second reason for having fewer notaries is that Sweden, as well as other Scandinavian nations, looks upon restrictive policies on professional practice with disfavor and highly respects notaries.[82]

Accordingly, no centralized register exists in Sweden for its notaries. Also, traditional sources of notarial revenues in Latin notarial countries, such as real estate transactions and protests of unaccepted or unpaid negotiable instruments, are now being handled in Sweden (but not exclusively) by real estate brokers and governmental agencies, respectively.[83] Predictably, as government agencies became involved in formalizing the protests for default on commercial paper, the number of notarial interventions sharply declined in the 1980s.[84] Similarly, and as a result of the policy of

---

has been executed. As pointed out by the United States Department of State through the United States Embassy in Sweden:

> There are three levels of U.S. authorities competent to issue an Apostille certificate depending on what jurisdiction executed the documents: 1. State, territories, and Other jurisdiction: Each state and other jurisdiction in the U.S. have an office that can issue an Apostille certificate. . . . 2. Federal Executive and Administrative Agencies: You must obtain the seal of the federal agency that issued the document before the U.S. Department of State Authentications Office can affix an Apostille to the document. . . . 3. U.S. Courts: Clerks and Deputy Clerks of the Federal Court System can issue Apostilles.

Notary Public Services, EMBASSY OF THE UNITED STATES STOCKHOLM, SWEDEN, http://sweden.usembassy.gov/consulate/acs5.html.

[79] *Designated Competent Authorities*, HAGUE CONFERENCE ON PRIVATE INTERNATIONAL LAW, http://www.hcch.net/index_en.php?act=authorities.details&aid=348#46547.

[80] I am grateful to Elin Hofverberg, an LL.M. student from Sweden, whose paper submitted for my course on Comparative Commercial Law contains valuable information on the Swedish and Scandinavian notaries, including the role of the European notaries and their organization. Elin Hofverberg, A Comparison between Latin and Non-Latin Notariats—The Role of the European Notaries and their Organisations (Apr. 9, 2008) (unpublished substantial paper, University of Arizona, James E. Rogers College of Law) (on file with author and NLCIFT). *But see* CENTRE OF EUROPEAN LAW AND POLITICS (ZERP) ET AL., CONVEYANCING SERVICES MARKET (Dec. 2007), *available at* http://ec.europa.eu/comm/competition/sectors/professional_services/studies/csm_study_complete.pdf (categorically stating that there are zero civil law notaries in Sweden) [hereinafter ZERP, CONVEYANCING SERVICES] (last accessed Nov. 1, 2013).

[81] Hofverberg, *supra* note 81, at 3.

[82] *Id.*

[83] *Id.*

[84] *Id.*

liberalization of access to professional work, Swedish real estate brokers and not notaries are now acting as conveyancers of most of their nation's real estate.[85]

The declining role of Swedish notaries in real estate transactions is described by Peter L. Murray, an English comparative real estate lawyer and consultant to the Conference of European Civil Law Notaries, as follows:

> In studying the Swedish situation, one fact jumped out. In most of the other countries under consideration, only 50–70% of transactions involve the use of real estate brokers. Many sales are negotiated directly by the parties, who then go to conveyancing professionals for the actual transfers. In Sweden, on the other hand, virtually all sales of residential real estate involve the services of brokers. . . .[86]

By adding to this fact the finding by ZERP's Study that civil law notaries are no longer in practice in Sweden, the conclusion can be drawn that an alternative to the notarial profession already exists in a civil law country.

1. The European Union: Notaries and Competition

In August 2006, the Competition Directorate of the European Commission requested a comparative legal and economic study of the various services involved in conveying land in the European Union from a consortium of research institutions coordinated by the Centre of European Law and Politics at the University of Bremen (ZERP) (hereinafter ZERP-Study).[87] Its purpose was to help assess the impact of regulations on the efficiency and performance of the conveyancing services. ZERP prepared a detailed questionnaire to gather reliable information on present regulations of these services in the twenty-one EU countries.[88] Prior to this study, the European Commission had shown an interest in liberalizing and harmonizing the professions within the European Union. There were those "intent on lobbying in Strasbourg and Brussels in favor of the abolition of monopolies enjoyed by notaries in EU civil law jurisdictions, and most specifically resulting from the nationality requirement imposed [upon notaries] by many Member States."[89]

ZERP's task was indeed daunting because of the diversity of functions assigned to the same professionals and the similarity of tasks assigned to different professionals within the European Union. In addition, different standards of diligence were required from the same professionals and similar standards were expected from different professionals. As if this were not enough, the practice of the various professionals often differed from what was stated in their governing law. A brief comparison of the findings in Austria, Belgium and Sweden will illustrate the difficulty of the task.

---

85 Peter L. Murray, Professor, Harvard Law School, Address at the 20th Conference of European Civil-Law Notaries 3–5 (Apr. 25, 2008), *available at* www.notar.at/uploads/murraypaper.pdf (on file with author).

86 *Id.* at 7.

87 ZERP, CONVEYANCING SERVICES, *supra* note 81.

88 The questionnaire was sent to national reporters in Austria, Belgium, the Czech Republic, Denmark, England and Wales, Finland, France, Germany, Greece, Hungary, Ireland, Italy, Luxembourg, the Netherlands, Poland, Portugal, Scotland, Slovakia, Slovenia, Spain, and Sweden. *Id.* at 21–22.

89 Gisela Shaw, *Notaries in England and Wales: Modernizing a Profession Frozen in Time*, 7 *INT'L J. LEGAL PROFESSION 141* (2000); *see also* Gisela Shaw, *The German Notariat and the European Challenge*, 10 INT'L J. LEGAL PROFESSION 37–54 (2003) ("Only Italy, Spain and Portugal promised to withdraw the nationality requirement to avoid being caught up in the formal warning issued by the EU Commission in November 2000.").

In Austria, the finding on "civil law notaries" was that:

> [T]here is no legally mandatory professional to intervene in conveyancing. All steps of conveyancing can be done by the parties themselves, including the mandatory certification of signatures (which can be done at court) and the application for recording a title (with the land register). In practice, however, in more than 90% of all real estate transactions, it is a civil law notary or an advocate who drafts the sales contract, carries out preliminary checks, gives legal advice, certifies the signatures and coordinates the execution of the contract.[90]

This requirement was insisted upon by the banks that financed the purchase price. When this was the case, the notary or advocate also acted as a professional escrow agent. In addition, civil law notaries in Austria were expected to play a central role in the taxation phase of the transaction. As in Mexico, the land transfer tax is normally calculated by the civil law notary as the draft person.[91] As with other Latin notaries, "the Austrian notary is under a duty to comply with professional standards . . . to maintain confidentiality, to act impartially, and to advise the parties objectively."[92]

In contrast, the presence of the notary is mandatory in Belgium.[93] Since only authentic deeds or documents could be registered with the Mortgage Registry Office, a notary, as a public officer, or a judge had to be involved. Without such an authority involved, the transaction had no effect against third parties.[94] Moreover, in certain sales such as foreclosure auctions, the notary was the only person authorized to write the "articles and conditions of sale" (*cahier des charges*) and carry out the sale.[95]

2. *U.S. Notaries*

As compared with the long list of functions of English notaries in Brooke's Notary,[96] the National Notary Association's listing of the functions of a United States notary is quite modest:

> A Notary Public is an official of integrity appointed by state government—typically by the secretary of state—to serve the public as an impartial witness

---

[90] CENTRE OF EUROPEAN LAW AND POLITICS (ZERP), CONVEYANCING SERVICES MARKET STUDY, COUNTRY FICHES 6 (Dec. 2007), *available at* http://ec.europa.eu/competition/sectors/professional_services/studies/csm_study_fiches.pdf (last accessed Nov. 1, 2013).

[91] *Id.*

[92] *Id.* at 10.

[93] *Id.* at 21.

[94] *Id.*

[95] *Id.*

[96] N.P. READY, BROOKE'S NOTARY 65 (11th ed., 1992) (*cited in* Malavet, *Latin Notaries*, *supra* note 2, at 441). Brooke's Notary describes the English notary as an officer of the law authorized to draw legal documents, attest or certify under his official seal the conveyance of real and personal property and power of attorney, and to authenticate such documents as proof of the matters. The notary is also authorized:

> [T]o keep a protocol containing originals of all instruments which he makes in the public form and to issue authentic copies of such instruments; to administer oaths and declarations for use in proceedings in England and elsewhere; to note or certify transactions relating to negotiable instruments, and to draw up protests or other formal papers relating to occurrences on the voyages of ships and their navigation as well as the carriage of cargo in ships.

Id. at 20–21.

> in performing a variety of official fraud-deterrent acts related to the signing of important documents. These official acts are called notarizations or notarial acts. Notaries are publicly commissioned as "ministerial" officials, meaning that they are expected to follow written rules without the exercise of significant personal discretion, as would be the case with a "judicial" official.[97]

Professor Malavet's historical account of the functions of United States notaries supports the National Notary Association's description:

> [I]n the North American colonies, where today each state has its own notary legislation, the occupants of the colonies that would become the United States of America: . . . had little use for the services of a Notary Public. . . . Most agreements for the purchase and sale of land were made public in open court. The buyer and seller met before an official, such as a judge, to advise him of their intention to make an agreement. The judge would make the agreement official and in full force and effect simply by recording the terms in his court record.[98]

The increase in trade between the North American colonies and Europe attracted notaries public. They drew up and witnessed agreements for the purchase and sale of merchandise or certified protests of unaccepted or unpaid bills of exchange drawn on United States importers of British goods. Unlike their English Scrivener-notary counterparts, they did not organize themselves into exclusive or non-exclusive regional or national associations.

The United States notary has remained a clerk with purely ministerial duties. He or she attests to oaths and signatures in his or her individual capacity and not as an employee of the state. As defined, in prototypical fashion, by Arizona law: "An Arizona Notary Public is a public officer commissioned by the Secretary of State to perform notarial acts. A notary is an impartial witness."[99]

As mentioned earlier, the qualifications of such a public officer are modest: he or she is required to be a resident of the particular state for income tax purposes who is at least 18 years old, is a citizen or permanent resident of the United States of America, and has not been convicted of a felony.[100] Once an applicant meets these qualifications, he is required to purchase a five-thousand dollar bond in duplicate form from an insurance agent (which costs approximately thirty dollars). He obtains a check or money order for forty-three dollars (which comprises twenty-five dollars for the filing fee and eighteen dollars for the filing of the notary bond) and within two or three weeks of mailing the application and the money order or check to the secretary of state's office, he will receive the commission to act as a notary for a period of four years. A notary may wish to buy additional insurance against negligent "errors or omissions," but this is not a mandatory requirement. The final expenses include the purchase of

---

[97] NATIONAL NOTARY ASSOCIATION, *supra* note 1.

[98] Malavet, *Latin Notary*, *supra* note 2, at 426–27 (citation omitted).

[99] *Notary Common Questions and Answers*, ARIZONA DEPARTMENT OF STATE, OFFICE OF THE SECRETARY OF STATE, http://www.azsos.gov/business_services/notary/notaryqanda.htm.

[100] *See, e.g.*, ARIZ. REV. STAT. ANN. § 41–312(E) (2013).

the notarial seal (approximately thirty dollars) and a journal (twenty dollars) to record summarily the notarial acts.[101]

Clearly these are not prohibitive requirements, and equally clearly, no special notarial, legal, or any other kind of training is required. Where *publica fides* is concerned, nothing in the Arizona statutory law seems to indicate that notarial acts, attestations or certifications would carry an evidentiary weight different from that of any other "impartial witness."[102] The clerical-ministerial status is equally true in former French and Spanish colonies in the United States. "Louisiana, originally a pure civil law jurisdiction, still retains much of its civilian tradition, but the function of the notary has diminished in importance over the years. Indeed, the truly civilian notary has substantially disappeared. . . ."[103]

As was the case with the English Scrivener notaries' attempt to approximate the functions of Latin notaries, some states in the United States have enacted statutes allowing the appointment of attorneys as civil law notaries with the power to authenticate documents and transactions.[104] Yet, because these attorneys lack *publica fides*, they are far from being able to discharge the functions of Latin notaries.

COMMENTS AND QUESTIONS

Upon evaluating the present day functions of Latin notaries, does the reader conclude that the price paid for their services represents sufficient value to their clients and to society at large? Conversely, does the limited role of notaries in the United States (to administer oaths and take affidavits, to take acknowledgments of deeds and other instruments, and to perform other acts specified by the law of the notary's jurisdiction) make sense given that other agents have to be contracted to fulfill the other functions that a Latin notary alone would handle? Overall, is it more expensive to use a single Latin notary or several transactional agents? Jonathan Taylor, a student reader of this chapter and book concluded that:

> The bottom line comparison is that while the Latin notariat is the product of a guild system which assigns exclusivity to those who qualify for admission to that profession or guild, regardless of market considerations, the U.S. notarial system is more market oriented and assigns Latin notarial functions to other professions or intermediaries such as attorneys, real estate agents or brokers, title insurance companies, escrow agencies, and so on, based on the marketplace participants' determination of who provides them with the needed service at the lowest cost.

Do you agree with this comparison?

---

[101] *See, e.g., id.* §§ 41–126(2), 41–312(B), 41–315, 41–319, 41–321; ARIZ. ADMIN. CODE § 2–12–1103 (2013).

[102] ARIZ. REV. STAT. ANN. § 41–328(B).

[103] D. Barlow Burke, Jr. & Jefferson K. Fox, *The Notaire in North America: A Short Study of the Adaptation of a Civil Law Institution,* 50 TUL. L. REV. 318, 329 (1976).

[104] *See, e.g.,* FLA. STAT. ANN. § 118.10(3) (2013), FLA. ADMIN. CODE ANN. 1N–6.001 (2013); ALA. CODE § 36–20–50(3) (2013).

Part III

EUROPEAN CODIFICATION

Chapter 8

THE FRENCH *CODE CIVIL*; KEY POLICIES AND DRAFTING METHOD

§ 8.1 INTRODUCTION: LAWMAKING THROUGH CODES; A BABYLONIAN AND GREEK ANALOGY

Part III of this book and its constituent chapters, Chapters 8 through 12, are devoted to the civil and commercial codes that have most significantly shaped the contemporary law of commercial contracts in the civil and common law systems. The present chapter is devoted to the *Code Civil* of 1804. The *Code Civil* was selected for special coverage because it has been the most influential of all of the private law codes of the civil law world. Even those codes that have adopted different policies and drafting methods (which by now are many) had to establish their normative "personality" by taking into account what the *Code Civil* did or did not do and either emulate or reject it. This chapter will be followed by others devoted to the French Commercial Code (*Code de Commerce*), the German Civil and Commercial Codes (BGB and HGB, respectively) and their sequels or functional equivalents in Latin America, Russia and China. Once we have discussed these codes, we will turn to key aspects of the English law of commercial contracts to the socio-economic and legal forces that shaped commercial contract law in the United States.

The contrast between lawmaking through codes and case law (and its compilations, including "Restatements" of the law in the United States) is not without interest from the standpoint of the development of scientific ideas and methods of thinking. Recently, I read some of the conversations between Leonard Mlodinow, a talented physicist and fiction writer who spent some time at the California Institute of Technology, and the famous physicist Richard Feynman.[1] Feynman was the theoretical physicist who, in the opinion of many, was the legitimate successor of Albert Einstein. According to Mlodinow, the following is what Feynman told him about two seminal contributions to physics:

> The Babylonians made western civilization's first great strides in understanding numbers and equations, and in geometry. Yet, it was the later Greeks—in particular, Thales, Pythagoras and Euclid—whom we credit with inventing mathematics. This is because Babylonians cared only whether or not a method of calculation worked—that is, adequately described a real physical situation—and not whether it was exact, or fit into any greater logical system. Thales and his Greek followers, on the other hand, invented the idea of theorem and proof—and required that for a statement to be considered true, it had to be an exact logical consequence of a system of

---

[1] *See* LEONARD MLODINOW, FEYNMAN'S RAINBOW: A SEARCH FOR BEAUTY IN PHYSICS AND LIFE 24–25 (2003).

explicitly stated axioms or assumptions. To put it simply, the Babylonians focused on the phenomena, the Greeks on the underlying order.[2]

Despite the enormous disciplinary distances between law and physics, much of what Feynman attributed to the Babylonian approach to physics is equally attributable to the common law method of lawmaking. What he attributes to Greek mathematics and its search for the underlying order of physical reality is present in the European method of private law codification.

While there were a number of earlier private law codes in Europe, the *Code Civil* was the model for much subsequent codification. On the one hand, it incorporated some of the political and economic ideas designed to replace the remnants of French feudalism. On the other hand, the legal institutions (definitions, classifications, principles, and rules) it introduced were regarded by its drafters as components of a legal order that would be not merely of the here and now, but also permanent and universal. As will be apparent in a later chapter, the drafters of the German Civil Code of 1900 (BGB) took this approach to an even higher level of universality and "system building."[3]

Hence, the use of the verb "is"[4] by the French codifiers in the definition of key institutions of the law of contracts was more than a grammatical tool. When Article 1101 of the *Code Civil* stated: "A contract *is* an agreement that binds one or more persons, towards another or several others, to give or to do or not to do something,"[5] it attempted to synthesize the essential features of a legal institution it deemed part of an immutable and universal legal order; simply put, a contract, anywhere and at any time, could not be anything else but what it defined.

These definitions were supported by normative principles of equal permanence and universality. As set forth in the constitutional-sounding proclamation of Article 1134 of the *Code Civil*: "Contracts, lawfully formed, have the force of law among those who made them."[6] The drafting style of this principle, and of many of the *Code Civil* definitions, was inspired by the axiomatic Roman *regulae iuris* previoiusly encountered.[7] However, unlike the original Roman *regulae*, the substance of the French principles, definitions, and classifications bore the imprint of rationalism—an intellectual movement associated with the age of enlightenment and of natural law—and a body of philosophical and theological thought whose meaning often varied with its formulator.

The following sections will first identify the theories that most influenced the written or codified law of contracts of the nineteenth century. Thereafter, it will describe salient socio-economic features of pre-codification France and identify those features that are most closely associated with the archetypal contractual behavior reflected in the *Code Civil*.

---

[2] *Id.* at 24.

[3] *See infra* § 12:2.

[4] *See supra* § 2:2(A).

[5] C. CIV. (FR.) art. 1101 (emphasis added). Unless otherwise indicated, all the English translations of the *Code Civil* provisions belong to Legifrance (*see* Frequently Cited).

[6] *Id.* art. 1134.

[7] *See supra* § 4:2(A)(4).

§ 8.2 THE INFLUENCE OF THE ENLIGHTENMENT AND NATURAL LAW UPON CODIFICATION

For many European intellectuals, the seventeenth and eighteenth centuries comprised the era of "Enlightenment":

> [A] movement of thought and belief concerned with the interrelated concepts of God, reason, nature, [freedom] and man. . . . Although diverse in emphases and interests, the Enlightenment attacked the established ways of European life and, in its conviction that right reason could discover useful knowledge, aspired to the conquest of man's happiness through freedom.[8]

A self-evident axiom by the philosopher Baruch Spinoza (transcribed in the following section) provides a good illustration of an "enlightened" point of view. In it, he praises The Netherlands, a country in which he, as a philosopher, was free to think and express his thoughts, and suggests that for such a freedom to thrive, it must be governed by the rule of law. Similar concerns about the role of freedom and its relation to law in post-feudal states can be found in the writings of John Locke, Voltaire, Jean-Jacques Rousseau and David Hume among many others, including Thomas Jefferson's Declaration of Independence of the United States. Unlike the writings of the scholastics, their writings opposed the view that religious dogma or revelation was the primary source of knowledge and wisdom on how to govern. In varying degrees, these members of the Enlightenment era were influenced by Spinoza's thought that ultimately God and Nature were one, as was the law that emanated from the Supreme Being.

The Enlightenment writers were also inspired by Newton's scientific method.[9] This method was perceived as a combination of a philosophy intended to reveal the orderliness of nature, the universe, and the mathematics of axiomatic proof. Many of the thinkers of the Enlightenment thus asked themselves: Why not apply Newton's method to political and legal philosophy? For God did not seem to rule arbitrarily, but through natural laws observable in His nature.[10] For these thinkers, then, God, reason and nature had to be the ultimate inspirers of codes.

A. Rationalism, Mathematics, Geometric Logic and Humanism

As a by-product of the Enlightenment, rationalism entails a "Reliance on reason . . . as the only reliable source of human knowledge."[11] Rationalism offered an alternative method of thinking to the religious accounts of human nature, conduct and

---

[8] *Enlightenment*, IV ENCYCLOPAEDIA BRITANNICA 887–88 (15th 1974); *see also* § 21:10(B) (on the impact of enlightenment on U.S. law).

[9] *See* WILLIAM DOYLE, THE OXFORD HISTORY OF THE FRENCH REVOLUTION 49 (2d ed. 2002). Doyle states:

> Nevertheless the new principles continued to be taught, and by the 1760s Newtonian physics in one form or another were standard fare in most colleges. Nature was to be evaluated in terms of what could be shown to work and achieve useful results. It could scarcely be expected that some at least of those who learned this lesson should not have thought about judging human affairs by the same standards. . . .

Id.

[10] *Id.* at 53.

[11] Garth Kemerling, *Rationalism*, PHILOSOPHY PAGES, http://www.philosophypages.com/dy/r.htm#ratm (last updated Dec. 30, 2011).

events.[12] More specifically, it asserted that significant knowledge of the world can best be achieved by *a priori* use of a mathematically-inspired logic. Thus, it could be distinguished from the also nascent empiricism (especially in Great Britain) that relied on observation, experimentation, and *a posteriori* verification of suggested explanations.

One of the first codes written during the Enlightenment in 1672 was by Gottfried Whilhelm Leibniz, a German mathematician and philosopher: the *Corpus Juris Reconcinnatum*.[13] Leibniz was convinced that all human knowledge could be summarized through logical calculus. During the same period, Benedict de Spinoza also applied geometric logic and Cartesian mathematics to draft rules of moral behavior capable of creating a perfect social order; an order mindful of the preeminent role of human freedom. In referring to his debt to Holland, where his family escaped after the expulsion of the Jews from Spain in 1492, Spinoza said the following in his *Theological-Political Treatise*:

> Considering the great joy that has been granted to us of living in a republic where there is freedom of opinion for everybody and everybody can observe his religion in the way his conscience dictates . . . it is a task of gratitude and benefit to show that said freedom can be granted without pain to the public good. . . .[14]

Referring to the contribution of reason to attain the best society within the rule of law, Spinoza drafted the following proposition, capable of proof through the logic of geometry:

> Any man guided by reason has more freedom in a State where he lives under the rule of law than if living in solitude and only obeying himself. . . .[15]

Thus, this method contrasted (and measured) the freedom of a solitary life against life under the rule of law, and showed that the radius of freedom is enlarged where human conduct is governed and inspired by law. As will be recalled from our previous discussion of geometric logic,[16] this type of logic was first used by the Greek mathematicians and philosophers and was subsequently applied by Roman jurists, especially in their formulation of legal axioms known as *regulae iuris*. And, as will also be remembered,[17] the Roman jurists were the first to employ the geometric logic in order to measure the dimensions of rights and obligations in actual or potential lawsuits.[18]

Roman juristic measurements were made possible by reliance, beginning with the *regulae iuris* as well as on substantive law rules consistent with the *regulae* and

---

[12] *Id.*

[13] WIEACKER, HISTORY OF PRIVATE LAW, at 257–58.

[14] BENEDICT DE SPINOZA, TRACTATUS THEOLOGICO-POLITICUS 133 (1908).

[15] *Id.* at 134.

[16] *See supra* § 4:2(A)(4).

[17] *Id.*

[18] Geometric logic as applied to legal theory made it so that rights and duties were for the first time measurable and quantifiable. For example, whereas property held in fee simple absolute could be measured as an entire geometrically-measurable circle, a life estate interest in that same property would be a smaller portion of that circle. Geometric logic, therefore, allowed legal rights and duties to be mathematically comparable to one another.

remedial provisions set forth in the *praetor's* edict. Analogy also played a significant role in this analysis. It was supported by Euclidean principles such as "figures equal to a third are equal among themselves." *A fortiori* reasoning, which was frequently relied upon by jurists to remind their readers that *he who can do the greater, must also be allowed to do the lesser,* also depended upon analogy. Such reasoning was supported by Euclid's principle that a total dimension is larger than that of its component parts.[19]

As pointed out by the Chilean legal historian, Professor Alejandro Guzmán,[20] the idea of a revision and consolidation of pre-existing law in a summary or synthetic fashion was already apparent in the sixteenth-century writings of the so-called "Humanistic" movement. One of its aims was to revise Justinian's *Corpus Juris Civilis* as well as the writings of the medieval glossators and commentators in order to adapt them to Renaissance Europe. The Humanists' awareness of the difficulties of adapting Roman legal institutions to the conditions of their time was reflected in the natural law writings of seventeenth-century jurists such as Hugo Grotius and Samuel Pufendorf.

The solution was codification "under the inspiration of the mathematical manner (*mos mathematicus*). . . . to reduce the rules to their most brief and concise formulation."[21] At the root of codification, then, was a mathematically-inspired synthesis of rules. Each codified rule had to be synthesized to encompass the largest possible number of factual situations. And the substantive content of the codified rules, as contrasted with the mathematical or formal logic of their drafting method, was in significant measure provided by the law of nature, as espoused by thinkers who did not always agree on what that law was or how to apply it.

For some, natural law justified an absolute form of monarchy, while for others it tolerated only a form of government with limited rights both for the governing class and for the governed. For some, it dictated that commerce had to be completely free from governmental restrictions, including freedom of contract, property rights, and navigation of the world's oceans. For others, these freedoms were only granted by divine law to those who followed the precepts of the Old or New Testaments as interpreted by a "legitimized" or church-anointed crown. Of the numerous seventeenth- and eighteenth-century versions of natural law, two were particularly influential on the drafting of the first European codes and especially upon the *Code Civil* and the BGB, codes which, as noted in the previous section, filled many gaps and provided many principles of interpretation for their less-intellectually-ambitious commercial counterparts.

B. Right Reason = Logic + Morality: The Writings of Hugo Grotius and Samuel Pufendorf

The codification of the European law of contracts in the nineteenth and twentieth centuries was influenced by political and economic doctrines responsible for the above mentioned replacement of a feudal state by a liberal bourgeois state. As will be discussed shortly,[22] freedom of contract and ownership of property were about to gain a

---

[19] *See* DAVID A. SINGER, GEOMETRY: PLANE AND FANCY (UNDERGRADUATE TEXTS IN MATHEMATICS) 1–2 (1998).

[20] Alejandro Guzmán, *Codificacion y Consolidacion: Una Comparacion entre el Pensamiento de A. Bello y el de A. Teixeira de Freitas*, 10 REVISTA DE ESTUDIOS HISTORICOS-JURIDICOS 269, 280 (1985).

[21] *Id.* at 280–81.

[22] *See infra* § 8:2(B)(1).

firm foothold in the French and German legal systems. This was in large measure due to the marriage between rationalistic and natural law philosophies.

The rationalistic component required the application of the "right reason," i.e., a reason that was not only logical, but also moral. The natural law component provided legitimacy to the applied reason. In a still largely authoritarian world, the legitimacy of a new legal order depended upon showing that its rules and principles were inherently universal and permanent in nature. Two seventeenth-century philosophers, Hugo Grotius and Samuel Pufendorf, provided suggestions, with varying degrees of success, on the best application of the right reason to the codified law of contracts.

1. Hugo Grotius

a. Natural Man and His Sociability

Hugo Grotius was born in Delft, Holland in 1583 and died in Germany in 1645.[23] As a lawyer and legal philosopher, he was one of the most influential natural law thinkers of his time, as apparent not only in the *Code Civil*, but in public international law. His famous treatise, *De Jure Belli ac Pacis* (1625), advocated a *ius gentium*, or law of nations, based on a natural law that relied on the Holy Scriptures, immanent Roman law (in contrast to temporal and, thus, changing law), and on his observation of the "best" natural impulses of man, i.e., man's association with his peers by means of families and social, peaceful and productive groups.[24]

Grotius' natural man was characterized by his "sociability" or cooperation with his peers, especially through commerce. In his polemic monograph, *De Mari Libero*, Grotius advocated freedom of the seas, particularly for maritime commerce and against the monopolistic and absolutistic pretensions of the Portuguese crown.[25] Grotius characterized the notion of contract inherited from Roman law as a voluntary method to acquire goods and services made binding because of the *ius gentium voluntarium*. In this voluntary method of acquisition, the formalistic delivery of the purchased goods (*traditio*) was not required even for "real" contracts such as deposits or bailments, a development which, as Grotius pointed out, was part of the Justinian Digest with respect to a conveyance and secured transaction known as *constitutum possessorium*.[26] As will be discussed shortly, the "consensual" approach to the perfection of contract rights advocated by Grotius entailed the transfer of title to the goods sold from the moment that the parties to a sale agreement agreed on subject matter and price. This

---

[23] *See* WIEACKER, HISTORY OF PRIVATE LAW, at 227–28.

[24] *Id.* at 227–29.

[25] *Id.* at 228. Ironically, the controversy that prompted this writing involved the seizure of a vessel by Grotius' client. Yet, Holland, once it became a maritime and colonial power, adopted similar monopolistic policies as those criticized by Grotius.

[26] *Id.* at 231. *See also* BERGER, ENCYCLOPEDIC DICTIONARY, at 411. Berger refers to the *constitutum possessorium* as a term not used in classical Roman law but in subsequent legal literature as denoting a situation "of a person who transferred possession (*possessio*) of a thing to another but continued to hold it (*detinere*) under another title. Possessory protection is consequently given to the new possessor." *Id.* As will be discussed in Chapter 23, this Roman law institution served as a conceptual basis for the Organization of American States Model Law on Secured Transactions. *See* Kozolchyk & Furnish, *A Comparative Analysis*, at 245–57.

elimination of *traditio* was adopted by the *Code Civil*, but not by others partly influenced by it.[27]

b. The Influence of Grotius' Principles: Consent and Good Faith

Grotius distinguished between what was changeable and temporal and what was "natural" and immanent in Roman law. On this basis, he identified as an immanent feature of contracts their voluntary nature or intent to transfer what was bought and sold regardless of the actual formality of transfer. Consequently, and as just mentioned, contracts of sale, according to Grotius and to the French codifiers, did not require the delivery of the contractual *res* for them to have full legal effect; the mere consent of the parties was sufficient to effect the transfer of the title to the contractual *res*.[28] Moreover, Grotius' consent principle meant that until promises were accepted by promisees, they did not bind promisors and thus were mere "pollicitations." This corollary of the consent principle was also adopted by Robert Pothier,[29] a highly influential doctrinal writer during the pre-codification period whose influence on the *Code Civil* will be discussed later in this chapter.[30]

The consequences of Pothier's adoption of Grotius' view that unaccepted promises are non-binding on the promisor are painfully visible in the *Code Civil*, as will be discussed in a later section.[31] For Grotius, the binding force of the unilateral promise must be found in the duty to behave truthfully as prescribed by moral theology. To those who invoked the lack of binding effects of the *nuda pacta* in Roman law, Grotius answered with the same arguments used against the alleged immanence, or for the continued observance of the requirement of *traditio*. The *nuda pacta* and the requirement of *traditio* were the result of temporal conditions and not of the eternal and immanent features of contracts.[32]

Among other permanent features of contracts was the requirement that they be performed in good faith:

> [The Romans] [l]ike the Germans, since ancient times, valued good faith above any other virtue . . . and they put into practice the idea that all contracts that are based on a *reasonable causa* (*redelicke oorzaek*) deserve a right of action . . . whatever the form and words used, even if the parties were not present in the same place. . . .[33]

---

[27] C. CIV. (FR.) art. 1583 ("It is complete between the parties, and ownership is acquired as of right by the buyer with respect to the seller, as soon as the thing and the price have been agreed upon, although the thing has not yet been delivered or the price paid."). *But cf.* CÓD. CIV. (ARG.) art. 577 ("Before transmission [*traditio*] of the thing, the creditor does not acquire any real property right over it."). *See* Alejandro Garro, *Recordation of Interests in Land*, *in* VI INT'L ENCYCLOPEDIA OF COMP. L., 22–34 (2004) (a thorough and lucid discussion of the evolution of the requirement of *traditio* in civil law systems compared with common law systems).

[28] *Id.*

[29] *See* POTHIER, I OBLIGATIONS, at 5 ("Hence, as I cannot, by my own will alone, transfer to another the property of my goods, if his will does not concur in the acquisition of it. . . .").

[30] *See infra* § 8:4.

[31] *See infra* § 8:2(B)(1).

[32] WIEACKER, HISTORY OF PRIVATE LAW, at 233.

[33] GORLA I, at 67 (citing Grotius).

Professor Gorla construes this quote, and especially its reference to good faith, as applicable to any promise to give an amount or a thing that lacks a traditional *causa*.[34] It does not seem applicable to unexecuted bilateral contracts, as these could be revoked up until the moment of the counter-party's performance. Gorla adds that Dutch law during Grotius's lifetime, unlike the *Code Civil*, did not adopt the natural-law-derived "consensual" principle that "the mere consent binds" (*solus consensus obligat*).[35] On the other hand, Dutch law required a reasonable *causa* and a specific form for formal contracts until well into the twentieth century.[36] The drafters of the *Code Civil* took to heart Grotius' reminder of the value of good faith and made it a requisite in the performance of contractual obligations.[37]

It is worth noting that while Grotius believed that contractual promises were not binding until accepted by the promisee, he also suggested that pre-contractual liability for the damages suffered should be imposed as a result of the negligence of the counterparty while the contract was being negotiated. This suggestion anticipated von Ihering's nineteenth-century doctrine of *culpa in contrahendo*.[38]

2. *Samuel Pufendorf: Axioms Inspired by Natural Law*

Samuel Pufendorf was born in Germany in 1632 and died in 1694. He was the author of *De iure naturae et gentium libri* (1672) and *De Officis hominis ac civis iusta legem naturales libri II* (1673), among others.[39] These writings applied the ideas of rationalist philosophers such as Descartes and Spinoza to legal and ethical behavior. In Franz Wieacker's words:

> In company with Grotius, but in stark contrast with Hobbes, Pufendorf [relies] once again on the natural *socialitas* of man and his need for help from his fellow man (*imbecillitas*); for him, however, these are not features due to the revealed will of the redemptive creator, as they were in the Christian natural law tradition, but qualities inherent in man . . . regardless of his creation.
>
> . . .
>
> [T]his was the critical step, the enormous leap of thought from the idea of a world created by a creator external to it to the idea of a world whose laws immanently evidence the will of the creator. Because of its inherent orderliness this method enabled Pufendorf to construct . . . an architecture of the polity, in which every component could be traced back to mathematically formulated axioms.

---

[34] *Id.*

[35] *Id.* at 71.

[36] *Id.*

[37] LEGIFRANCE C. CIV. (FR.) art. 1134 ("Agreements lawfully entered into take the place of the law for those who have made them. They may be revoked only by mutual consent, or for causes authorized by law. They must be performed in good faith.")

[38] *See infra* ch. 26.

[39] WIEACKER, HISTORY OF PRIVATE LAW, at 243–48 (a thorough and incisive appraisal of Pufendorf's contribution to the codification process). The following paragraphs in the principal text summarize Wieacker's main points.

. . .

> Descartes helped Pufendorf to attain that combination of deduction and induction, axiom and observation, analysis and synthesis, which had characterized thinking in the natural sciences since Galileo's *Discorsi*. This enabled him to stay in close touch with social reality. Whereas Grotius treated as authoritative . . . canonical and literary sources he developed in support of his principles, Pufendorf treated them as merely illustrative and had no hesitation . . . in adducing the evidence of contemporary events and even foreign practices.[40]

Through his rationalism and cultural observation, Pufendorf reached axioms both more general and specific than those of the Roman *regulae iuris.* By incorporating those axioms into a system of natural law, Pufendorf achieved a system of jurisprudence whose traces can be found in both the French and German civil codes. In the BGB, an example can be found in all-encompassing concepts such as that of a "legal transaction" or "juristic act" (*Rechtsgeschäft*) that include contracts, which Pufendorf placed at the center of the universe of private law.

Taking into account man's sociability and the function of contracts as tools for the exchange of wealth, Pufendorf classified them in accordance with the observable nature of the exchanges, i.e., onerous (or profitable), gratuitous or beneficent, or a mixture thereof. After listing the empirically ascertainable transactions by paying attention to their economic content, he searched for those principles and concepts applicable to the entire set. In doing this, Pufendorf became, in Wieacker's words, "the originator of a General Part of the law of obligations [of the BGB]."[41] Hence, his influence could be noted in general provisions such as:

> § 241. [Content of obligation] The effect of an obligation is that the creditor is entitled to claim performance from the debtor. The performance may consist of refraining from acting.[42]
>
> Or:
>
> § 242. [Performance according to good faith] The debtor is bound to effect performance according to the requirements of good faith, giving consideration to common usage.[43]

His influence could also be found in concepts designed to gather a set of rules subsumable under a common heading such as "methods for discharging obligations," which included "performance and substitutes for performance, set-off, release, novation and delegation, change of civil status. . . ."[44] This grouping of closely related rules became a favorite tool of the future private law codes.

§ 8.3 THE DRAFTING OF THE *CODE CIVIL*

The private law of France was so diverse in the eighteenth century that, as observed by Voltaire, anyone traveling through France would change laws as

---

[40] *Id.* at 244–45 (citations omitted).

[41] *Id.* at 246.

[42] THE GERMAN CIVIL CODE 41 (Ian S. Forrester et al. trans., 1975).

[43] *Id.*

[44] WIEACKER, HISTORY OF PRIVATE LAW, at 246.

frequently as horses.[45] This variety of laws was accentuated by the presence of customary law (*Pays de Droit Coutumier*) in the Northern provinces and written law (*Pays de Droit Ecrit*), largely influenced by Roman law, in the Southern provinces.[46] Not surprisingly, a French government account of the codification process found that "[u]nder the [old regime] more than 400 codes of laws were in place in various parts of France. . . . In addition, [by the time of the drafting of the *Code Civil*] the revolutionary governments had enacted 14,000 pieces of legislation."[47]

Military skills aside, Napoleon Bonaparte was a gifted administrator, keenly aware of the need for a uniform law throughout France. Yet, his intervention in the codification process came about a decade or so after it had started. Following the revolution of 1789 and the resultant overturn of much of the existing law, the newly created Constitutional Assembly voted on July 5, 1790 to review and reform "the civil laws" to reach a simple and clear general code of the laws "appropriate to the constitution."[48] Five attempts to codify the new laws were made during the period of the National Convention and the Directorate.

Thereafter, Napoleon appointed experienced administrative officials and government commissioners to prepare the final drafts of what became the *Code Civil*.[49] The most influential of these officials was Jean-Etienne-Marie Portalis, born in Provence to a bourgeois family. After becoming a lawyer at the highest provincial supreme court of Aix (*Parlement*), he practiced law in Paris, where he was elected to an important administrative office. He then became a leader of a moderate party opposed to the Revolutionary Directorate, which led him to flee France when faced with the Directorate's attempts to jail him. When Napoleon established himself as the leader of the highest administrative office (*Consulate*), he named Portalis as a Counselor of State (*Conseiller d'Etat)* and charged him and three other distinguished functionaries (of a similar background) to draw up the final version of the *Code Civil*.[50]

Napoleon participated in thirty-six of the eighty-seven drafting sessions of the *Code Civil* and, according to a French official historian, he contributed "a typically Napoleonic mix of liberalism and conservatism, although basic revolutionary gains—equality before the law, freedom of religion and the abolition of feudalism—were

---

[45] VON MEHREN & GORDLEY, THE CIVIL LAW SYSTEM, at 48.

[46] FREDERICK HENRY LAWSON, A COMMON LAWYER LOOKS AT THE CIVIL LAW 35 (1953); *see also* Francis Deak & Max Rheinstein, *The Development of French and German Law*, 24 GEO. L.J. 551 (1936).

[47] THE NAPOLEON SERIES, THE CIVIL CODE (1995–2008), *available at* http://www.napoleon-series.org/research/government/c_code.html.

[48] VON MEHREN & GORDLEY, THE CIVIL LAW SYSTEM, at 48.

[49] *Id.* at 49. The actual work of codification began under the auspices of the Legislative Convention in 1792 and produced three drafts (a first draft with 715 articles, a second with only 297 articles and a third draft with 1104 articles). *Id.* at 48. Nonetheless, the political crisis was such that this third version was not successful. *Id.* at 49. Ultimately, there was a final version under the auspices of the Napoleonic Consulate from 1799 to 1804. *Id.* On August 13, 1800, Napoleon appointed a drafting commission with the mandate to finish its duties in November of that year. *Id.* The members of the drafting commission were appellate judges, experienced administrative officials and government commissioners. *Id.* The previous versions were examined by the drafting commission, which divided the work according to issues and distributed portions of them to each member. *Id.* After four months of work, the commission submitted its own version to the *Cour de Cassation* and the courts of appeal for comment. *Id.*

[50] The three other officials were Francois Denis Tronchet, Felix-Julien-Jean Bigot de Preameneu and Jacques de Maleville. *Id.*; *see generally* RENE LAVOLLEE, PORTALIS, SA VIE ET SES OEUVRES (1869).

consolidated. . . . Property rights, including the rights of the purchasers of *biens nationaux* [national property] were made absolute."[51]

The final draft of this working group was finished in four months and was forwarded to the General Assembly of the Council of State on July 17, 1801. As pointed out by Professor Gordley,[52] about two-thirds of the texts have close parallels in the works of two legal commentators strongly influenced by natural law writings, the seventeenth century's Jean Domat and the eighteenth century's Robert Pothier. After finishing its review, the Council of State answered favorably and forwarded it to the First Consul, who in turn submitted it to the so-called Tribunate. The Tribunate was comprised of a large number of National Assembly members who were opposed to Napoleon's legislative initiatives. Fearing a contrary vote in the Assembly, Napoleon withdrew the submitted text before its vote. He then reduced the membership of the Tribunate, excluding his enemies, and created a complex procedure that would enable the adoption of the *Code Civil* in March 1804.[53]

In contrast with the BGB of 1900, the *Code Civil* was written in a clear and accessible form to the layman. Its style is epigrammatic, and of such self-evident persuasiveness that even a great prose writer like Balzac recognized his literary debt to the *Code Civil*. Much of the persuasiveness of its epigrams was owed to definitions and classifications of an Aristotelian and Thomastic making and to axiomatic or *regulae iuris* types of rules.[54] Consider, for example, the following provisions:

> Article 1119: As a rule, one may, bind oneself and stipulate in his own name, only for oneself.
>
> Article 1134: Agreements lawfully entered into take the place of the law for those who have made them.
>
> Article 1168: An obligation *is* conditional where it is made to depend upon a future and uncertain event, either by suspending it until the event happens, or by cancelling it, according to whether the event happens or not.
>
> Article 1185: A term differs from a condition, in that it does not suspend the undertaking, of which it only delays the fulfilment.
>
> Article 1226: A penalty *is* a clause by which a person, in order to ensure performance of an agreement, binds himself to something in case of non-performance.
>
> Article 1227: Nullity of the principal obligation involves that of the penalty clause. Nullity of the latter does not involve that of the principal obligation.
>
> Article 2279: In matters of movables, possession *is* equivalent to a title.[55]

While the substantive content of many of the rules on contracts was contributed by the writings of Jean Domat and Robert Joseph Pothier, these articles reflected the

---

[51] THE NAPOLEON SERIES, *supra* note 47.

[52] James Gordley, *Myths of the French Civil Code*, 42 AM. J. COMP. L. 459, 459–61 (1994).

[53] VON MEHREN & GORDLEY, THE CIVIL LAW SYSTEM, at 51.

[54] *See supra* § 4:2(A)(4).

[55] LEGIFRANCE C. CIV. (FR.) arts. 1119, 1134, 1185, 1226, 1227, & 2279 (emphasis added); *see also supra* note 5 and accompanying text.

natural law views of Hugo Grotius and Samuel Pufendorf.[56] At the same time, and as will be discussed in a later section,[57] the newly-enacted rules also reflected the interests of the French bourgeoisie, particularly keen on having, among other contractual legal institutions, unrestricted and certain conveyances of real property.

§ 8.4 POTHIER'S DEFINITIONS AND CLASSIFICATION OF CONTRACTS AND THEIR CONSEQUENCES

A. Definitions

Robert Joseph Pothier was a prolific eighteenth-century legal commentator. His style was clear even when his analysis was not always persuasive. Pothier's command of sources has been dismissed by some highly respected legal historians as superficial.[58] Nevertheless, his *Traité des Obligations*, influenced as it was by Grotius and Pufendorf, was highly instrumental in the drafting of the *Code Civil*. Medieval scholasticism and its Aristotelian inspiration are apparent in Pothier's method of reasoning. Consider the following definitions and classifications:

> A contract *is* a *kind* of agreement. To know what a contract is, it is then previously requisite to know what an agreement is. An agreement or a pact (for these are synonymous expressions) *is the assent of two or more persons, to form an engagement between them, or dissolve or modify one already formed.*[59]

Following the Aristotelian method of definition, Pothier identified what he believed was essential in the defined object, i.e., that feature which is peculiar or unique to the species of agreements known as contracts, the voluntary creation of obligations or engagements. The purpose of this feature was to distinguish contracts—permanently and universally—from other agreements that extinguish or modify previous obligations, but do not form engagements. Once this essence was identified, Pothier proceeded to place contracts within the genus of agreement.[60]

Conceivably, the "species" of contract or agreement could also be placed under the "family" of methods for acquiring property, such as the "voluntary" or "conventional obligations" (as was done by Book III of the *Code Civil*). It could also be placed under the family of voluntary obligations as distinguished from involuntary obligations, such as those derived from the tort of negligence. This interest in classification and taxonomy, surely an Aristotelian legacy, is responsible for distinctions between a contract and an agreement. Despite Pothier's attempt to distinguish between contract and agreement, few lawyers in our day, and possibly in Pothier's as well, would have difficulties with the notion that parties who agreed to modify or extinguish an obligation did not actually contract to do so. One could easily dismiss this distinction as one without a difference, except that when each definition is taken seriously (as it has

---

[56] *See infra* § 8:2(A) & (B).

[57] *See infra* § 8:7.

[58] *See, e.g.*, LAWSON, *supra* note 46, at 54. The assessment by two of the most distinguished comparative law writers of the twentieth century states: "Pothier, an unoriginal compiler who tried from time to time to introduce the sort of order and principle into the law which is necessary for exposition to students." *Id.* For a similar view, *see* John P. Dawson, *Specific Performance in France and Germany*, 57 MICH. L. REV. 495 (1959). *See also infra* § 28:7(B)(3).

[59] POTHIER, I OBLIGATIONS, at 4 (emphasis added).

[60] *Id.* ("The kind of agreement, which has as its object to form [an] engagement, is what is called a contract.")

been to this day by many readers of Pothier), significant legal consequences could follow, such as denying enforceability to otherwise valid promises.

Pothier continued:

> There are other promises, which we make with good faith and with the actual intention to perform them, but without an intention of engaging or binding ourselves and conferring on the party, to whom they are made, the right of requiring their performance. This happens when he, who promises, expressly declares that he does not mean to bind himself, or when this is fairly to be implied and results from the circumstances, or from the relation in which the parties stand to each other.[61]

To illustrate this supposed exception to the family of binding promises, Pothier gave the example of a father who promises a pleasure trip to his law student son to encourage him to be more diligent in his studies. Such a promise, although made in good faith, was, according to Pothier, unenforceable.[62] Nevertheless, Pothier's adherence to this "voluntaristic" principle (only the will of the promisor binds him and only that of the two parties binds both) makes him an advocate of the principle *solus consensus obligat* (the mere consent binds).

Pothier repeatedly refers to Grotius and Pufendorf and their versions of natural law in support of voluntarism and consensual contracts. The reverse side of this bilateral voluntaristic coin is that a promisor cannot make his avowedly "firm" promise binding on himself, except when such a promise is accepted by the promisee. Pothier referred to such an unaccepted promise as a "pollicitation." It cannot become a contract (meaning a contractual type of obligation) for "a contract includes a concurrence of the will of two persons at least, one of whom makes and the other accepts the promise."[63]

Pothier added:

> The pollicitation, according to the principles of mere natural law, produces no obligation, properly speaking. He who makes this promise, may revoke it, as long as it is unaccepted by him to whom it is made. For there can be no obligation without a right acquired, by the person in whose favor the obligation is contracted, against the person who contracts it. Hence as I cannot, by my own will alone, transfer to another the property of my goods, if his will does not concur in the acquisition of it: for I cannot, by my promise, transfer to another a right on my performance, until his will concur in the acquisition of it by his acceptance of the promise.
>
> . . .
>
> It is useless to enquire now, whether pollicitations are obligatory in our law. For as the ordinance of 1731, art. 3, has declared that there shall be but two ways of disposing gratuitously of one's goods, by donation *inter vivos* and by testament, it follows that it rejects the pollicitation.[64]

---

[61] *Id.* at 4–5.

[62] *Id.* at 5.

[63] *Id.*

[64] *Id.* at 5–6.

Predictably, the supporting source was Grotius's natural law.[65]

Please read *Code Civil* Articles 1589–1 and –2 as recently enacted in the case law in the appendix to this chapter,[66] and ask yourself how compatible is the unenforceability of pollicitation with the need to rely on options to purchase and sell real property.[67]

B. Classifications

According to Pothier, the Roman law classification of contracts *bona fidei* and *stricti juris* did not prevail in eighteenth-century France. Instead, contracts were divided into the following categories:[68]

1. Synallagmatic or Bilateral Contracts

According to Pothier:

> [Such contracts] are those in which each of the contracting parties binds himself to the other, as in the contracts of sale, hire, etc. Unilateral [contracts] are those in which one of the parties only binds himself to the other, as in the loan of money. Among the synallagmatic [or bilateral] contracts, we distinguish those that are absolutely so, and those which are so, qualifiedly. The contracts, which are perfectly synallagmatic or bilateral, are those in which the obligation, which each party contracts, is equally a principal obligation of the contract, as contracts of sale, hire, partnership, etc. For example. In the contract for sale, the obligation, which the seller contracts to deliver the thing, and that which the buyer contracts to pay the price, are equally principal obligations of the contract. The contracts which are qualifiedly synallagmatic, are those in which the obligation of one party alone is a principal obligation of the contract. Such are the contracts of mandate, deposit, loan for use, loan for use, and pledge. In these contracts, the obligation which the mandatory contracts to account, those contracted by the depositary, borrower or creditor, to restore the thing deposited, lent or pledged, are the only principal obligations of the contract. Those which are contracted by the mandator . . . are but incidental obligations. . . .[69]

Could it be that Pothier's imperfect synallagmatic contracts reflected not what took place in the France of his day, but in a Rome where mandates and loans for use (*commodatus*) were gratuitous?[70] Can you conceive of a car or equipment leasing company doing business under the assumption that its loans of use (or rentals) are presumptively gratuitous?

---

[65] HUGO GROTIUS, II DE JURE BELLI AC PACIS (THE LAW OF WAR AND PEACE) (1625).

[66] *See infra* § 8:9(C).

[67] *See infra* § 8:9(C)(4) (note however that a number of recent decisions by French courts have significantly qualified the non-binding or revocable effects of a promise or an offer).

[68] POTHIER, I OBLIGATIONS, at 10.

[69] *Id.* at 10.

[70] On the gratuitous nature of the *commodatum* (gratuitous loan of a thing) and *mandatum* (agency) in Roman law, see BERGER, ENCYCLOPEDIC DICTIONARY, at 399, 575.

2. *Consensual and Real Contracts*

Consensual and real contracts are:

> [T]hose which are formed, by the mere assent of the parties, and are therefore called consensual contracts, as sale, hire, mandate, etc. and those in which something else is requisite, as contracts for the loan of money or of things to be used, deposit and pledge, which, from the nature of the contract, require the delivery of the thing that is the object of the contract: These are called *real* contracts.[71]

3. *Problems with Loans as "Real" Contracts*

Why should a loan agreement or a promise to lend be unenforceable prior to the lender's delivery of the amount of the loan? Possibly Pothier was thinking about the Roman loan (*mutuum*) and of the borrower's express or implied obligation to return the amount borrowed plus interest. Yet why not allow enforcement of a promise to lend by a borrower who is the recipient of that promise? After all, borrowers would be better off being able to rely on such a promise and might even be willing to pay a higher rate of interest for it if it were enforceable. Further, in accordance with this classification, could a contemporary line of credit agreement in which a bank gives its client an authorization to draw up to a specified amount be enforceable? The same would be true with promises to make the authorized amounts of credit cards available to the holder of the card. Does the fact that a loan agreement and its corollary promise to lend was classified as a "real" contract mean that unless the amount is delivered by the lender to the borrower at the moment of execution of the contract, there is no contract and thus no liability for the promise?

4. *Problems with Consensual Sales and Notarial or Public Deeds*

Pothier provided a revealing comment on the use of the formal or notarial deed (*acte authentique*) in eighteenth-century France and its effect upon the all-important consensual sale of land, especially as executed by the influential bourgeois segment of the population:

> Although the mere assent of the parties suffices for the perfection of consensual contracts, yet if the parties in a sale, or hire, or any other kind of bargain, agree to have a [notarial] instrument . . . with a view that their bargain be not concluded and perfect[ed], till the instrument shall have received its legal form by the signature of the parties and the notary, the bargain will not be complete until the notarial instrument shall become so; and the parties, although they perfectly agree to the terms of the bargain, will be at liberty to recant at any time before the notarial instrument is subscribed.
>
> [Where] the instrument is required for the perfection of the contract, it is not from the nature of the contract, which of itself requires nothing but the assent of the parties; it is because the contracting parties have required it, and because it is lawful for the parties to a contract to render their obligations dependent on what condition[s] they please.

---

[71] POTHIER, I OBLIGATIONS, at 11.

> It must be observed that an agreement, that a notarial instrument evidencing the bargain shall be drawn, does not of itself render the perfection of the bargain dependent on the instrument. It ought to appear that the intention of the parties was that it should depend on this. Therefore, it has been adjudged, in a case reported by *Mornac, ad. d. l. 17*, that a party could not recede from a contract . . . that there should be a [valid] notarial instrument, although no such instrument had been executed: for it could not be concluded from this clause that the parties had intended to render the completion of their bargain dependent on the execution of a notarial instrument, which might have been thought of in order to provide a lien on the party's lands, which such an instrument procures, or to obviate the danger of losing a private paper.[72]

These comments highlight the difficulties with Pothier's voluntaristic definition of a sales agreement that requires the assent of two or more persons to form an engagement between them or dissolve or modify one already formed. As with the proverbial dog, this definition winds up chasing its own tail and thus contradicting itself.

Assume that a buyer and a seller agree to all of the terms of a sale, including its subject and price, and also agree that they will execute the sale as a notarial deed. The engagement to reduce the agreed-upon terms and conditions to a notarial writing differs from the agreement on subject matter and price in that if either party decides not to sign, there is no agreement at all. Thus, there are two different agreements: one is informal, and the other one depends upon the formality of a public deed. As Pothier admits, if the requirement of a notarial deed were not present and if there were no statute requiring such a formality, the remainder of the consensual agreement would have been enforceable.

This raises the question of what or which was *the* consensual agreement, that on the subject and price or on the need for an execution of a notarial deed. If the notarial clause is fully enforceable as an integral part of *the* agreement, it would appear to be contrary to Pothier's own definition of a consensual sale, which asserts that the consensual sale is enforceable once the parties have agreed on subject matter and price. In other words, contrary to Pothier's definition, the notarial clause would be an agreement subject to a unilateral termination by either party, and thus the voluntaristic explanation of why contracts are binding would start chasing its own tail.

Could this be the reason why the court decision alluded to by Mornac required that the notarial clause be made an express condition precedent and that short of it, the sale agreement be enforceable? Moreover, what happens when the law itself requires a notarial deed as an essential condition if the agreement involves the sale of land whose value exceeds a certain amount? According to Pothier, contracts whose amount exceeded one hundred *livres* could not be proved by witnesses.[73] As will be discussed in a later section, this requirement was adopted in a number of other civil law jurisdictions and especially in Spain and Latin America with serious legal and economic consequences.[74]

---

[72] *Id.* at 11–12. *See also infra* § 22:1(A) (discussing the civil "static-ceremonial" contract).

[73] POTHIER, I OBLIGATIONS, at 12.

[74] *See infra* § 8:7(B) (discussing the formality of contracts).

5. *Onerous, Charitable and Mixed Contracts*

Another category of contracts includes contracts of interest on both sides, charitable contracts and mixed contracts:

> Contracts of interest on both sides are those which are made for the reciprocal interest and advantage of both parties. Such are contracts of sale, exchange, hire, annuity, partnership, and an infinity of others.
>
> Contracts of beneficence [charity] are those which are made only for the advantage of one of the contracting parties. Such are the loan[s] to use, the loan to consume, deposit and mandate.
>
> . . .
>
> Contracts of interest on both sides are subdivided into commutative contracts and aleatory contracts.
>
> Commutative contracts are those in which each of the contracting parties gives and receives ordinarily the equivalent of what he gives. Such is the contract of sale. . . . They are [sub-divided] into four classes, *Do ut des, facio ut facias, facio ut des, do ut facias* [I give so that you give, I do so that you do, I do so that you give, and I give so that you do].
>
> Aleatory contracts are those in which one of the parties, without giving anything on his part, receives something from the other not as a liberality, but as a price of a risk which he runs. All games are contracts of this nature, as are wagers and contracts of insurance.[75]

How realistic are the above types of contracts in the reader's transactional world? For example, would the reader consider a loan that would enable the borrower to use or to consume the lender's object, the contract of deposit or mandate contracts of beneficence? As just noted, is there not an entire financial industry that derives its income from just such types of loans? On the other hand, would donations be deemed contracts in the reader's jurisdiction and thus enforceable as such? Or, would aleatory contracts in our day not require that the speculator give something in exchange for the expectation of a higher gain?

6. *Principal and Accessory Contracts*

> "Principal contracts are those which intervene principally and for themselves. Accessory contracts are those which intervene to insure the execution of another contract. Such are contracts of suretyship and pledge."[76]

This classification has been quite troublesome in banking and financial practice. Consider the following not-so-hypothetical situation. "A," a lawyer for a mortgage bank "MB," asks his legal consultant, "C," whether it would be possible for MB to sell mortgage bonds to the public in the following manner: All the workers of factory "F" interested in buying their F subsidized homes would sign as mortgagors naming MB as the mortgagee and using their homes as the mortgaged collateral. MB would obtain a promise from F, the employer, to guarantee the workers' payments and to deduct the

---

[75] POTHIER, I OBLIGATIONS, at 12–13.

[76] *Id.* at 13.

mortgage payments owed to MB from the salaries it pays its workers-mortgagors. All such executed mortgages would be packaged and sold to the public as mortgage bonds or certificates of participation in the pool of mortgages.

Upon the sale of these bonds or certificates to the public, the proceeds of the sale would be distributed among the builders of the future houses for the workers. As was done by counsel to a Central American government bank, *C* correctly characterized the "sale" of the mortgage bonds to the public as an attempt to borrow construction funds from the buyers of the mortgage bonds. Yet, to sell a mortgage bond (which *C* would characterize as a security device and therefore as an accessory contract in Pothier's and many civil codes' classification), a principal contract (the loan by the buyer of the bond) would have had to pre-exist the sold mortgage. But how could such a loan exist prior to creation of the security interest which by itself embodies the loan? After all, does not the loan come about the moment the security is bought? Thus, a chicken and egg situation results from the fact that an accessory contract such as a mortgage cannot exist prior to the existence of the principal contract. To sell the mortgage bonds to the public, it would be necessary to require that the buyer of each bond first become the lender of each mortgagor-buyer of the future house. However, even this solution would not work because what is sold to the public is not an individual mortgage, but a certificate of participation in a pool of mortgages.

7. *Formal and Informal Contracts*

Finally, a last and very important division of contracts is "those which are subjected by the municipal law to certain rules or forms and those which are regulated *by natural law alone*."[77]

Please note that natural law becomes an actual source of contract law for informal contracts. From a legislative standpoint, and to avoid uncertainty, it does make some sense to suggest a source of law for contracts that have not been classified or "typified." Without a source, they may become unenforceable or their enforcement could be left to the vagaries of analogical interpretation by attempting to apply the law of the closest transactional or legal analogy. Yet, is there not a more certain and predictable source of law to govern informal contracts than an indistinct natural law? If so, what would it be? Would custom, usage of trade, course of dealing, or, for certain contracts, best business practices not be a better source?

In his comment to this classification, Pothier states that the formal contracts in France are the contracts of marriage, donation, bill of exchange and annuity. He adds:

> Other agreements are not subjected . . . to any particular form or arbitrary rule prescribed by the municipal law, provided that they contain nothing contrary to law or good morals, and they be entered into by persons capable of contracting, they are obligatory and give rise to an action. If our laws require that those, the object of which exceeds in value the sum of 100 *livres*, be reduced to writing, it is only with the view to regulate the manner in which they are to be proved, when their existence is denied.[78]

---

[77] *Id.* (emphasis added).

[78] *Id.* at 13–14.

The reader should keep this statement in mind when reading about the Formality of Contracts in a later chapter.[79] Pothier's reference to French law could have helped some appellate courts in Spain and Latin America struggling with another classification: formalities *ad solemnitatem* and *ad probationem*.

C. The *Code Civil*'s Classification of Contracts and Executory Promises

A remarkable similarity exists between Pothier's and the *Code Civil's* classifications of contracts as demonstrated by the following provisions:[80]

> Article 1102: *Synallagmatic or bilateral*
>
> [When] the contracting parties bind themselves mutually towards each other.
>
> Article 1103: *Unilateral*
>
> [When] one or more persons are bound towards one or several others, without there being any obligation on the part of the latter.
>
> Article 1104: *Commutative*
>
> [When] each party binds himself to transfer or do a thing which is considered as the equivalent of what is transferred to him or of what is done for him.
>
> Where the equivalent consists in a chance of gain or of loss for each party, depending upon an uncertain event, a contract is aleatory.
>
> Article 1105: *Benevolence*
>
> [I]s one by which one of the parties procures a purely gratuitous advantage to the other.
>
> Article 1106: *Onerous*
>
> A contract for value is one which obliges each party to transfer or do something.

And while there does not seem to be a counterpart to Pothier's classification of consensual and real contracts, Article 1138 should not be overlooked:

> An obligation of delivering a thing is complete by the sole consent of the contracting parties.
>
> It makes the creditor the owner and places the thing at his risks from the time when it should have been delivered, although the handing over has not been made. . . .[81]

This provision enables the enforcement of a bilateral consensual agreement in which one of the parties undertakes a future delivery. Yet, the requirement of bilateral consent would continue to be essential. Thus, if one of the parties offered the other an option to purchase real estate during a certain period of time, there would have had to be an agreement to the terms and conditions of that option when the option was

---

[79] *See infra* ch. 22.

[80] LEGIFRANCE C. CIV. (FR.) arts. 1102–1106.

[81] *Id.* art. 1138.

granted to the promisee for it to be enforceable. This could be the reason for an amendment to Article 1589 of the same code, which stated:

> A promise of sale is the same as a sale, where there is reciprocal consent of both parties as to the thing and the price.
>
> Where that promise relates to plots already in lots or to be in lots, its acceptance and the agreement that will result therefrom shall be established by the payment of an instalment on the price, whatever the name given to that instalment may be, and by the vesting with possession of the plot.
>
> The date of the agreement, even put into legal form afterwards, is that of the payment of the first instalment.[82]

What about other executory promises such as that of performing a certain service or paying a certain amount of money in exchange for the performance of services or the giving of money—promises that are not agreed upon when issued, but still intended to be firm promises by their issuer? Does Article 1370 of the *Code Civil* take care of the enforceability of these promises or just some of them? Article 1370 states that:

> Certain undertakings are formed without the intervention of any agreement, either on the part of him who binds himself, or on the part of him towards whom he is bound.
>
> Some of them result from the sole authority of legislation; others arise from an act personal to the one who is obligated.
>
> The former are the undertakings formed involuntarily, such as those between neighbouring owners, or those of guardians and other administrators who may not refuse the duties which are imposed upon them.
>
> Undertakings arising from an act personal to him who is bound result either from quasi-contracts, or from intentional or unintentional wrongs; they constitute the subject-matter of this Title.[83]

In answering the above question, the reader should review Articles 1371–1381 of the *Code Civil* (whose official translation is available on the Internet on *Legífrance's* website).[84] Do any of these provisions support generically the enforceability of executory promises to give or to do that have not been accepted by their promisees when issued? What if some of these promises appear in documents such as promissory notes, bills of exchange, corporate or government bonds or certificates of deposit? Where should one look for answers to the latter question, the *Code Civil* or the Commercial Code of France? What is the importance of a provision such as Article 1589–2 of the *Code Civil*, in force since January 1, 2006? Please look up this provision on *Legifrance* and provide your evaluation in light of the preceding discussion.[85]

---

[82] *Id.* art. 1589.

[83] *Id.* art. 1370.

[84] *Id.* arts. 1371–1381, *available at* http://www.legifrance.gouv.fr/.

[85] LEGIFRANCE, http://www.legifrance.gouv.fr/.

D. The Negative Effect of Scholastically Inspired Definitions and Classifications

Pothier and *Code Civil* definitions and classifications offer an appearance of universality, permanence and certainty that are at first sight quite comforting, especially to law students. This comfort comes from the belief that these definitions and classifications are the essence of the law of contracts; the remainder of such a law, as once put to me by a Spanish law student, is mere "*relleno*" (or the filling of the dish). Yet, once he becomes a practitioner, judge or law professor, that student will realize that Pothier's classifications and definitions hinder an easy and effective adaptation of contract law to the ever-changing and often untypified or unclassified marketplace transactions.[86]

As discussed earlier,[87] in their search for abstract concepts to explain or justify conclusions, the scholastics relied on purely deductive techniques and not on empirical research to support their syllogistic major premises. If the facts assumed by their major premises were based on defective or unverified observations, or on observations that were valid only for a given place or time (as with Aristotle's observation that money was a sterile commodity), the effect of making their conclusions permanent and universal rules of law were disastrous indeed.

Recall the medieval regulation of usury:[88] Its major premise was based upon an unempirical supposition that assumed that *any interest rate* was usurious, regardless of whether it was lower than the rate that prevailed in the marketplace. With such a major premise, the conclusion was inevitable that a loan that charged any rate of interest had to be usurious. Similarly, when Pothier drafted the above-transcribed definition of contract ("A contract *is* a kind of agreement. . . . An agreement . . . is the assent of two or more persons, to form an engagement between them, or to dissolve or modify one already formed."[89]), its major premise assumed that a contractual type of obligation—for the promisor of an executory promise—arose from a two-party agreement, even for promises issued as binding on the promisor from the moment of their issuance. Accordingly, it became inevitable that a unilateral promise was not a contractually binding promise and was an unenforceable pollicitation until accepted by the promisee.[90] Such a definition would have denied enforcement to promises that the nineteenth-century marketplace already deemed necessary, such as those enforced under the German HGB (and many others) as "firm promises,"[91] or to promises

---

[86] *See infra* §§ 22:2, 22:4 (discussing the impact of *causa* and consideration on the formation of contract).

[87] *See supra* § 2:2(A).

[88] *See supra* § 5:7(B).

[89] POTHIER, I OBLIGATIONS, at 4.

[90] *See supra* § 8:9(C)(4) (discussing pollicitation).

[91] *See* HGB (GOREN, 1998), art. 376, which in relevant part states:

> (1) Where it is stipulated that performance by one of the parties should be effected at an exact time or within a specific period, the other party may rescind the contract if performance is not made at the exact time or within the period specified, or in the event that the debtor has defaulted, demand payment of damages for non-performance in lieu of performance of the contract. He may only demand performance if he indicates to the other party, immediately following expiration of the time or the period, that he insists on performance.

sanctioned by the twentieth-century international customary banking and commercial law such as commercial or standby letters of credit, among many others.[92]

Perhaps the most important question with respect to Pothier's and the *Code Civil's* classifications pertains to what civil law lawyers refer to as their "constitutive" effect upon rights and obligations, i.e., the power of the classification to validate, invalidate or exclude transactions depending upon whether they fit under the classified categories. If it is a constitutive classification, it is often assumed that, as with the Roman typified contracts, only those contracts that are listed or typified will be enforceable. The burden, then, shifts to the party seeking enforcement who would need to argue that the contract in question is part of the list or is sufficiently analogous to deserve inclusion.

As was discussed in connection with one such classification, *i.e.*, principal and accessory contracts,[93] mortgage bonds or certificates could not be issued in some Central American countries because until there was a loan agreement (as the principal contract) there could not be a mortgage (as the accessory contract).

Yet the price paid for such minimal certainty in terms of foregone individual and socio-economic opportunities could be enormous. For example, in contrast to the opinion by counsel for a central bank in a Central American nation during the 1960s that forbade the creation of mortgage bonds until actual loans had been made (thereby depriving the Central American nation of secondary market financing for its low-income housing), European banking lawyers found it possible to approve the issuance of mortgage bonds to finance public and private housing since the eighteenth century. Similarly, the BGB in 1900 provided for bearer mortgage bonds or certificates as part of the so-called territorial debt (*Grundschuld*).[94]

§ 8.5 NATURAL LAW PRINCIPLES AND CODE INTERPRETATION

In a carefully researched 1994 study quoted earlier,[95] Professor James Gordley offered a dissenting view on the influence of seventeenth-century natural law

---

(2) Where damages are demanded for non-performance and the goods have an exchange or market price, the difference between the purchase price and the exchange or market price at the time and place of the performance due can be demanded.

(3) The result of another sale or purchase can, in the case where the goods have an exchange or market price, only be taken as the basis for the damage claim if the sale or purchase is effected immediately after the performance time or performance deadline has elapsed. If it does not occur at a public auction, the sale or purchase must be carried out at the current price by a broker officially authorized to conduct sales or by a public auctioneer.

(4) The provisions of § 373 Subsection 4 applies to the sale at public auction. The creditor must promptly notify the debtor of the sale or purchase; in case of failure to do this, he is liable for damages.

[92] *See* Kozolchyk, *Commercial and Standby Letters of Credit, in* III U.S. LAW OF TRADE & INVESTMENT, at 24–17.

[93] *See supra* § 8:4(B)(6).

[94] *See* BGB arts. 1191–1198. In 1900, the articles allowed the creation of mortgage bonds or certificates in bearer fashion. For a brief survey on mortgage banking in Europe since the eighteenth century, see BRE BANK HIPOTECZNY, SA, THE HISTORY OF MORTGAGE BANKS AND MORTGAGE BOND (on file with author).

[95] Gordley, *supra* note 52.

philosophies on the drafting of the *Code Civil.* He quoted a number of influential scholars who asserted that the Code's reorganization of contract law turned on "modern individualistic principles"[96] of freedom of ownership, of contract, and liability for one's own fault. In the words of Rene Savatier, these were the "[t]hree pillars [that] support the entire construction of the Napoleonic Code."[97] Gordley disagreed, stating that "these principles were not of the drafters. They were the principles of French 19th century treatise writers who read them into the Code. The drafters subscribed to traditional conceptions of private law that were almost old-fashioned when the Code was enacted."[98]

Two reasons prompted Gordley's dissent. First, the drafters acknowledged that they were not breaking with the past. Second, even if the drafters had wished to rebuild private law on new principles, they did not have the time to do so, as they had to finish their draft in four months. And "[a]lthough no one knows how they spent their time, it is striking that about two-thirds of the texts of the Code have close parallels in the works of Domat and the 18th century jurist Pothier."[99]

Yet, as was apparent in earlier sections, Pothier frequently relied on Grotius and Pufendorf as sources for his natural law voluntaristic principle that enshrined the will and thus the freedom of the parties to a contract. This is how he justified the enforceability of a notarial clause that could impede the execution of an otherwise executed consensual and informal agreement.[100] Moreover, as will be discussed shortly, J.M. Portalis, the principal drafter of the *Code Civil,* is quoted by Professor Gordley as justifying the rule on "objective lesion" by relying on "rules of justice that are anterior to contracts themselves, and from which contracts draw their chief force."[101] Such justification is directly traceable to the type of natural law advocated by Hugo Grotius.[102] Hence, it is not clear why nineteenth-century commentators of the *Code Civil* would have had to read the above-referred-to natural law principles into the *Code* when many of them had already found their way into the *Code* via Pothier's and Domat's major contributions. Professor Gordley's concern, then, must be not so much with the presence of the natural law principles in the *Code*, but with their original authorship, which he traces in many instances to medieval theologians and canonists.

Undoubtedly, legal history benefits from knowing who the original authors of the key contract law principles adopted by the drafting commission of the *Code Civil* were. However, because the principles involved here are as general and all-encompassing as freedom of contract and property ownership, their proper application would require

---

[96] *Id.* at 459. Gordley cited many highly-respected French doctrinal writers. *Id.* at 459 nn. 1, 2; J.–L. HALPERIN, L'IMPOSSIBLE CODE CIVIL 56–57, 276–78 (1992); A.–J. ARNAUD, LES ORIGINES DOCTRINALES DU CODE CIVIL FRANCAIS (1969); J. CARBONNIER, I DROIT CIVIL 66 (11th ed. 1977); A. COLIN, H. CAPITANT & L. JUILLOT DE LA MORANDIERE, I TRAITE DE DROIT CIVIL 129 (1957); G. CORNU, I DROIT CIVIL 107 (4th ed. 1990); GHESTIN & GOUBEAUX, I TRAITE DE DROIT CIVIL 96 (2d ed. 1983); L. JOSSERAND, I COURS DE DROIT CIVIL POSITIF FRANÇAIS 32–33 (1938); H. MAZEAUD, L. MAZEAUD & J. MAZEAUD, I LEÇONS DE DROIT CIVIL 63 (4th ed. 1967); A. WEILL & F. TERRE, DROIT CIVIL INTRODUCTION GENERALE 98 (4th ed. 1979).

[97] Gordley, *supra* note 52, at 459 (citing R. SAVATIER, LES METAMORPHOSES ECONOMIQUES ET SOCIALES DU DROIT PRIVE D'AUJOURD'HUI 5–6 (2d ed. 1959)).

[98] Gordley, *supra* note 52, at 459.

[99] *Id.* at 460.

[100] *See supra* § 8:4(D)(7).

[101] Gordley, *supra* note 52, at 475.

[102] *See supra* § 8:2(B)(1).

concrete illustrations of legislative intent. Two helpful admonitions come to mind: Justice Holmes' "General propositions do not decide concrete cases,"[103] and a more recent one by Professor F. H. Lawson:

> What I want to emphasize in the natural law of the seventeenth and eighteenth centuries is not its importance as affording a basis for political obligation or individual freedom, but the new vision it gave to legal thinkers. For they came to recognize and grasp the chance of deriving the detailed solutions of the law according to the method of Euclidian geometry from the smallest number of axioms and postulates. We are not to think of the theology or even morals: we are in the most secular of centuries, the age of Reason, of deism, and Tom Paine.[104]

Therefore, because of the intellectual atmosphere in which the *Code Civil* was drafted, it was inevitable that the drafters resorted to natural-law-inspired axiomatic formulations. At the same time, it is also worth remembering that Napoleon opposed many of the Revolution's liberal ideas:

> While [Napoleon's] regime did not restore the guilds outright . . . it reimposed restrictive or even monopolistic state regulation on such occupational groups as publishers and booksellers, the Parisian building trades, attorneys, barristers, notaries, and doctors. Napoleon wished to strengthen the ties that bound individuals together, which derived from religion, the family, and state authority.[105]

In light of the tensions between revolutionary and more moderate or conservative Napoleonic policies, the code interpreter becomes all the more dependent upon contextual precision. For this reason, subsequent sections will discuss the socio-economic context of civil code contracts and will identify the distinguishing features of an archetypal "civil" contracting party. This is a party whose contractual predilections were deemed most worthy of attention by *Code Civil* drafters. The contextual and archetypal analyses should enable future contrasts with commercial archetypes as found in the French, German and United States commercial codes.

§ 8.6 SOCIO-ECONOMIC CONTEXT: THE BOURGEOISIE AND ITS INFLUENCE

Perhaps as a result of Napoleon's own policies or perhaps because of the views of other "restorers" of the disrupted order in French society, the *Code Civil* did not reflect the deplorable economic conditions of most of the French population at the time of its drafting. Even after repeated readings of this elegantly and tersely written legislation, I fail to find indications of the economically troubled society for which it supposedly was written. On the contrary, one gets the impression that it was written for a content, stable, and prosperous population largely populated by a strong upper middle class, the Bourgeoisie. Yet, according to a thorough account of French society during the Revolution:[106]

---

[103] Lochner v. New York, 198 U.S. 45, 76 (1905) (Holmes, J., dissenting).

[104] LAWSON, *supra* note 46, at 31.

[105] *See France*, EVERYHISTORY.ORG, http://everyhistory.org/2011countries9.html.

[106] *See* DOYLE, *supra* note 9, at 14–25. The following paragraphs in the principal text will summarize key features of pre-revolutionary France found in this fine scholarly account.

> Poverty was France's most visible social problem. Nobody could overlook it. All travelers noticed the misery of rural housing, and the poor appearance of the peasantry. . . . Bands of roving vagabonds struck terror into the hearts of isolated farmers; and the streets of most towns swarmed with beggars. The poor, meaning those without adequate employment or other assured means of support, numbered at the best of times almost a third of the population; eight million people. In bad times two or three millions more might join them, as crops failed and jobs disappeared. . . .
>
> Peasants accounted for 80 per cent of the French population. . . .
>
> [Despite the large rural migration to the French cities] most town-dwellers were poor, and completely unskilled.[107]

The trades of the artisans and craftsmen, remnants of the guild system, remained exclusive and, with the exception of a few guild-masters, journeymen barely earned a living wage.

> In 1776 an attempt was made to abolish the whole structure of guilds, and Parisian artisans celebrated in the streets at the news. A few months later, however, the old structure was largely restored; and in 1781 new controls were introduced. . . .[108]
>
> By the spring, bread prices in Paris had risen by more than 50 per cent, and riots which began on 27 April . . . spread within a week throughout [France] to the gates of the royal palace at Versailles, and to the bread markets of the capital itself. It took troops, hundreds of arrests, and two public executions to restore order. . . . Only after a bumper harvest in 1787 was the grip relaxed.[109]

In contrast with the penury suffered by most of the inhabitants, the bourgeois, whether of rural or urban origin, did not have to worry "about the price of a four-pound loaf [of bread]."[110] In the countryside, they were the largest employers and owners of agricultural equipment and animals. They were also the principal lenders to needy farmers. And when their debtors defaulted, which was quite common, they would foreclose on their mortgages and thereby accumulate more land. In time, the measure of bourgeois success came to mean being able to retire and live on the yield of their accumulated real property. In the French cities, their number seldom exceeded one fifth of the population, and they made their original fortunes in trade and commerce. Their accumulated wealth enabled them to wield economic and political power.

Perhaps the most important reason for their economic and political power was the taxes they paid as members of the "Third Estate." This was a social class that included peasants, artisans, merchants, and professionals, and did not include the nobility or the clergy. Together this class contributed the largest share of taxes collected in

---

[107] *Id.* at 14, 16, 18.

[108] *Id.* at 20.

[109] *Id.* at 21–22.

[110] *Id.*

France. Quite often, these taxes took the form of periodic payments made by the bourgeois for their massive acquisition of public offices.[111]

The *Oxford History* describes the original source of bourgeois wealth and their attitudes towards this source as follows:

> Among them were always a handful of successful master craftsmen; but [most bourgeois] . . . did not have to work with their hands. . . . There were scarcely more than two million of them. . . . Their share of the national wealth was enormous. Most industrial and almost all commercial capital, amounting to almost a fifth of all French private wealth, was bourgeois owned. Perhaps a quarter of the land belonged to them. . . . [s]o probably did the greater part of the capital invested in a field that had proved peculiarly successful in France since the sixteenth century—venal public offices. Bourgeois competition for such offices was pushing the price of many of them to unprecedented heights in the 1780's. . . .[112] The ultimate source of this enrichment was the extraordinary commercial and industrial expansion of the eighteenth century. All bourgeois fortunes began in business. . . . [Yet] [t]rade and manufacture, however profitable, were not secure; and so as soon as there was money to spare the first instinct was to buy land. . . . Land was safe. . . . Above all, land had prestige. . . . Nobody, therefore, with any aspirations to social consequence could afford to be landless; and those whose ambitions were really serious knew that sooner or later they would have to get out of trade altogether. Very few bourgeois families remained in the business that had enriched them for more than a single generation—unless they were Protestants or Jews debarred by law from everything except making money. Profits not spent on buying property went into buying the next generation a superior education. With that, the way was open to the professions, where mercantile origins could be forgotten.[113]

As an illustration of the embarrassment suffered by the bourgeois with their commercial origins, The *Oxford History* quotes from a 1780 letter by a Lyons litigant (who was also a judge), in which he criticizes his adversary's (another bourgeois') attitude toward merchants:

> I ought not to pass over in silence. . . . I who am the offspring of a generally loved and respected merchant, the outrage done by Mr. Gesse to commerce in describing those who exercise the profession as "persons from the dregs of the

---

[111] *Id.* at 24. As indicated in the following note, many taxes paid by the bourgeois were in the form of payments for the acquisition of public offices.

[112] *Id.* at 22–23. According to the *Oxford History*:

> Originating in the sixteenth century as a way of enabling the king to borrow money . . . the sale of public offices became a basic institution of French social life . . . office-holders were permitted, on payment of an annual tax, to pass them on to their children or re-sell them to third parties. This made offices as sound a social investment as land, and in response to continued demand the Crown made most public functions venal. The whole judicial hierarchy, from the highest presidents in the parlements to the humble tipstaff in the obscurest rural jurisdiction, bought their positions. . . . Under Louis XVI there were over 70,000 venal offices, representing capital value of perhaps 900 million *livres*, increasing rapidly as the market value of most of them went up.

Id. at 25.

[113] *Id.* at 22–24.

people"; it is thus that he speaks of a profession as honorable as it is honoured in this country; yet remember that Mr. Gesse is, as I am, a merchant's son; he disowns his stock, whereas I honour mine.[114]

And as also pointed out by the Oxford History:

> Evidently the paternal calling was chiefly to be honoured for producing enough money to buy the son an office [as a judge]. And nothing testifies more eloquently to the continuing desire of the bourgeoisie to escape from the stigma of commerce than the becoming market for offices [widespread throughout the entire governmental edifice].[115]

The effect of populating judicial offices, among others, with bourgeois venal judges was recently noted by Paul G. Mahoney's description of the judicial system in pre-Revolutionary France:

> The highest courts in pre-Revolutionary France, the *parlements*, were very different from the common-law courts in England. They were part court, part legislature, and part administrative agency. . . . As a practical matter, judicial offices were salable and inheritable. The purchase of a judgeship or other royal office automatically conveyed noble status and qualified the purchaser and his descendants for entry into the *parlements*. The return on the investment was straightforward; in addition to obtaining prestige and serious exemption from taxation that accompanied noble status, *judges enforced the rigidly controlled system of guilds and monopolies that characterized Bourbon France.*[116]

By the start of the French revolution in 1789, however popular the enlightened and rationalistic and natural law proclamations of *liberté, égalité, fraternité* were among the non-bourgeois revolutionaries, the fact was that France's dominant class was the bourgeoisie. As will be discussed now, the *Code Civil* was quite sensitive to its interests in critical areas of the law of contracts.

§ 8.7 THE ARCHETYPAL BOURGEOIS CIVIL CONTRACTING PARTY

The reader will recall the previous discussion of the archetypal *picaro* in connection with Spanish medieval commerce, and then the discussion of the archetypal brotherly merchant and how these forms of model behavior affected the law of commercial contracts. The law of contracts in the *Code Civil* revolves around another archetype: the bourgeois contracting party. The enablement of this archetype was made possible by the *Code Civil* provisions or rules on party autonomy.

A. Party Autonomy

> Article 1101. A contract is an agreement that binds one or more persons, towards another or several others, to give or to do or not to do something.

---

[114] *Id.* at 24.

[115] *Id.*

[116] Paul G. Mahoney, *The Common Law and Economic Growth: Hayek May be Right*, 30 J. LEGAL STUD. 503, 509–10 (2001).

> Article 1134. Contracts, legally formed, have the force of law for those who made them. They cannot be revoked except with their mutual consent or for causes which the law authorizes. They must be executed in good faith.[117]

Had these two provisions been in force from the thirteenth to the eighteenth century in France, there would have been no French guild system. On the contrary, and as was just mentioned, the *parlements* severely restricted the parties' ability to enter into the everyday contracts that threatened the monopolistic powers of guilds.[118] Under such circumstances, the assertion of Article 1134 of the *Code Civil* was more than a simple statement of the binding effects of a contract; it was, in the words of the late Dean Georges Ripert, the equivalent of granting a contractual "franchise to man, [as] it is necessary to unbind the human will from its constraints" (*Il faut donc affranchir l'homme. Il faut dégager de ses entraves la volonte humaine*).[119]

Thus, even though bourgeois *parlement* judges restricted the participation of non-guild members in everyday contracts, the *Code Civil* provided the bourgeois with Dean Ripert's franchise to engage more intensely and securely than ever in the buying and selling of valuable real estate. However, the constraints of typification could still be found with respect to untypified executory promises. As was discussed in an earlier section,[120] those executory promises that were not accompanied by an acceptance shortly after their issuance were, at best, of questionable enforcement. They required qualification under the categories specified by the *Code Civil*[121] or had to become part of the text of an enforceable negotiable instrument such as a promissory note, a bill of exchange, or governmental or corporate bonds. Under these circumstances, is it not significant that the above mentioned Article 1589–1 of the *Code Civil* did not become law until 2006?

B. Formality

In their search for contractual certainty, the bourgeois embraced contractual formalities. Thus, it was not surprising that the *Code Civil* prescribed that if the value of the land purchased, sold or conveyed to an heir exceeded 500 *livres*, either "a notarial deed or a writing under private signature" was required.[122] It will be recalled that in his discussion of consensual contracts, Pothier had indicated an additional reason for the attractiveness of notarial deeds to the bourgeois: They were regularly used as self-sufficient evidentiary instruments with which to obtain judicial liens on their subject property. Could this have been one of the most tangible benefits of what was discussed previously as "*publica fides*"?[123]

As if to underscore the importance of the certainty or predictability of outcome of what had been stipulated in a formal document or notarial deed, the *Code Civil* added:

---

117 C. CIV. (FR.) arts. 1101, 1134.

118 Mahoney, *supra* note 116, at 510.

119 GEORGES RIPERT, LA REGLE MORALE DANS LES OBLIGATIONS CIVILES no. 2 (3d ed. 1935).

120 *See supra* § 8:4(C).

121 *See supra* § 8:4(D).

122 C. CIV. (FR.) art. 1341.

123 *See supra* § 7:3(A)(3).

> [N]o proof by witnesses against or beyond the content of the document, nor as to what is alleged to have been the content previously, at the time or since it was drawn up, shall be allowed, even if the sum or value in dispute is less.[124]

This provision confirmed a principle expressed elsewhere in the *Code*:

> An authentic instrument is conclusive evidence of the agreement it contains between the contracting parties and their heirs or assigns. Nevertheless in case of a criminal complaint for forgery, the execution of the instrument allegedly forged is suspended by the indictment; and in case of allegation of forgery made incidentally, the courts may, according to the circumstances, suspend temporarily the execution of the instrument.[125]

Not surprisingly, resort to parol evidence to establish the parties' course of dealing, usage of trade or custom, a procedural tool quite common in United States commercial contract litigation,[126] was precluded by the *Code Civil*. In addition, the bourgeois-inspired version of contractual justice supported a notion of cause in bilateral or synallagmatic contracts which, but for one notable exception discussed in the following section, required no determination of mutuality of exchange, but merely a correspondence between what the contract stated and what was given and exchanged.[127]

C. Contractual Justice

Bourgeois contractual justice also required good faith in the performance of obligations. However, good faith was measured not by what other promisors, including an ideal or model promisor, would have done or given, but by the meticulous observance of contractual stipulations. Accordingly, the conceptual equality of rights to enter into contracts was confused with the factual equality of bargaining power; it was assumed that the former necessarily entailed the latter. Not surprisingly, Dean Georges Ripert quoted a cryptic but revealing description of what "justice" meant for the drafters and interpreters of the law of contracts in the *Code Civil*: "Simply stated, all justice is contractual or . . . he who says contract says justice."[128]

Hence, in the eyes of its judicial interpreters, the *Code Civil* stood for the view that contracts were not mere repositories of the parties' intent, but also of the parties' binding conception of what was fair or just in their bargain. These contracts were indeed perceived as having been written on stone tablets.[129] This attitude prevailed in France's highest court well into the twentieth century. Surveying its decisions up until 1968, the late and lamented Vera Bolgár, a collaborator and friend of mine and of

---

124 C. CIV. (FR.) art. 1341.

125 *Id.* art. 1319.

126 *See infra* ch. 23.

127 As will be apparent in the discussion of the doctrine of "excessive onerousness" in Italian and Latin American law, this version of contractual fairness is still much alive in the court and doctrinal interpretation of contracts in the above jurisdictions. *See infra* ch. 27.

128 RIPERT, *supra* note 119, at no. 22 ("*Toute justice est contractuelle. Ecrit simplement; qui dit contractuelle dit juste.*").

129 There is support in medieval religious law for the proposition that a fair price is reached by the mere fact that a bargain has been struck. *See* RICHARD HENRY TAWNEY, RELIGION AND THE RISE OF CAPITALISM 40 (5th prtg. 2008). With regard to the notion of cause, legal doctrine since the sixteenth century generally eschewed the use of concepts which by giving greater power to the judges would compromise the stability of contracts. A. WEILL & F. TERRE, LES OBLIGATIONS no. 253 (2d ed. 1975).

Professor Hessel Yntema, assessed the attitude of France's *Cour de Cassation* on contracts of adhesion as follows:

> But in the field of contracts, the Court de Cassation steadfastly clings to the letter of article 1134 . . . and disregards the requirement expressed further in this article—namely, that they should also be performed in good faith. Doctrinally this trend is justified by considerations of legal security that would, in addition, upset standing economic relations through arbitrary judicial power. Consequently, the Court almost invariably reverses the more liberal decisions of the lower courts. . . .[130]

D. Rescission Because of Lesion (*Laesio Enormis*) or Enormous Loss

An exchange of a rough equivalent of value between promisor and promisee (as contrasted with what the contract stated was to be exchanged and what was actually exchanged) was a requirement only when the seller had sold real property and received a price of less than seven-twelfths of the market value of the property. The *Code Civil* provides that if the vendor suffered a loss of more than seven-twelfths of the price of a piece of property, he may demand rescission although he expressly donated the excess.[131]

Please note that the *Code Civil* remedy of lesion is only given to the vendor. This provision reflects the high esteem in which land was held by the bourgeois and the drafters' sympathy for someone who unknowingly or unwillingly conveyed one of his most valuable assets for an amount considerably lower than its market value. The economic harm he or she suffered (*laesio enormis*) could be objectively measured and for this reason was described by doctrinal writers as an "objective" lesion, as distinguished from a "subjective" lesion, or the harm that resulted to a contracting party as a result of his or her inferior bargaining power or physical or mental handicap.[132]

In his enlightening summary of the drafting committee's discussions on *laesio enormis*, Professor Gordley provides ample evidence that its intent was to protect the integrity of the estate of a seller who sold one of his family's valuable and value-stable assets at a price significantly below that of the market:

---

130 Vera Bolgár, *The Contract of Adhesion: A Comparison of Theory and Practice*, 20 AM. J. COMP. L. 53, 67–68 (1972) (citations omitted).

131 C. CIV. (FR.) arts. 1674, 1686.

132 The "subjective" doctrine of lesion, which considered the exploitation of the promisee's contractual weakness and particularly his lack of bargaining power, was not adopted by the *Code Civil*. As noted by Georges Ripert, the *Code Civil* had not provided a remedy for the case of contractual weakness other than the "somewhat brutal theory of incapacity or the hazardous theory of vice of consent." RIPERT, *supra* note 119, at no. 102. *See* BGB, art. 138(2), which provided a remedy of "subjective" lesion when stating in relevant part:

> A legal transaction is also void whereby a person exploiting the need, carelessness or inexperience of another, causes to be promised or granted to himself or to a third party in exchange for a performance, pecuniary advantages which exceed the value of the performance to such an extent that, under the circumstances, the pecuniary advantages are in obvious disproportion to the performance.

THE GERMAN CIVIL CODE, *supra* note 42, at 21.

> According to Portalis, relief would be confined to sales of land because its price was more stable. According to Bonaparte, who took an active part in the discussion, such property was more important. The buyer was denied a remedy, according to Portalis, Tronchet, and Faure, because he was less likely to accept the wrong price through necessity, according to Ségur, because he was less likely to have done so by mistake, and according to Bonaparte, because he was more likely to try to avoid the transaction because his plans had changed. . . . Portalis responded that while faith in contracts must be respected, "there are rules of justice that are anterior to contracts themselves, and from which contracts draw their chief force. . . ."
>
> . . .
>
> Now it is admitted that a contract of sale is a commutative contract, that is to say, one in which each party gives only in order to receive an equivalent, or, if one will, a price proportionate to the value of the thing which he transfers. Therefore, [it] is of the essence itself of the contract that it be rescinded when the equivalent of the thing is not provided. Another maxim that is no less certain in law is that there is no obligation without a *cause*. What are the causes of contracts? In contracts of liberality (*bienfaisance*) the *cause* is liberality itself. But in self-interested contracts, the cause is the interest, that is to say, the advantage that the parties find in making them. In [a] sale, this interest is, for the seller, to have the price that represents the thing sold rather than the thing itself; for the buyer, to have the thing rather than the sum of money that represents its value. These principles granted, one can see that there is no cause in a sale unless the price is in proportion to the value of the thing sold.
>
> . . .
>
> Bonaparte said that "[t]here is not a contract of sale when one does not receive the equivalent of what one gives." Berlier, who wished to abolish the remedy entirely, was outvoted.[133]

Despite the drafters' references to a need for mutuality of exchange in commutative contracts, they afforded protection only to an "objectively-measured" lesion and solely when suffered by the seller when conveying his own or his family's land. This policy was consistent with that of Articles 1118 and 1313 of the *Code Civil* which limit lesion to designated relationships.[134] Yet, what is the "force" alluded to by Portalis in the above quote? Could this "force" be Grotius' Natural Law?

---

[133] Gordley, *supra* note 52, at 475–76 (citations omitted).

[134] LEGIFRANCE C. CIV. (FR.) art. 1118 ("Loss vitiates agreements only in certain contracts and with regard to certain persons, as will be explained in the same Section."); *Id.* art. 1313 ("Adults are entitled to rescission for loss only in the cases and subject to the conditions specially laid down in this Code."); *see also* Kozolchyk, *Commercialization*, at 9 (with the exception of the discussed seller of real property who receives less than one-half of the market price, the others involved familial legal relationships such as between a decedent and his heirs, or between legatees and devisees as a result of an improper division or due to events supervening the acceptance of the inheritance share).

E. *Causa*

Article 1108 of the *Code Civil* lists the elements of a valid contract:

> Four requisites are essential for the validity of an agreement: The consent of the party who binds himself; His capacity to contract; A definite object which forms the subject-matter of the undertaking; A lawful cause in the obligation.[135]

Implementing Portalis' above-quoted principle that there is no obligation without a cause, Article 1131 of the *Code Civil* stated that "[a]n obligation without cause or with a false cause, or with an unlawful cause, may not have any effect."[136] To which Article 1133 added: "A cause is unlawful where it is prohibited by legislation, where it is contrary to public morals or to public policy."[137] This is as far as the clarification of the meaning of *causa* goes in the *Code Civil*.

It is worth recalling that *causa* in Roman law was the basis for typifying contracts. And once contracts were typified, only those contracts whose types were recognized were entitled to enforcement by means of their own actions and defenses. Thus, the *causa* or the reason for enforcing, say, "formal" contracts was their formality, including the delivery of the thing in "real" contracts; the *causa* of consensual contracts was their informality and widespread use, and so on. Eventually, the reason for enforcing innominate contracts, or contracts which were not previously typified, was that their common denominator was a *quid pro quo*. This *quid pro quo* resurfaced in medieval law as the requirement of a *res vel factum* and in the common law as "consideration."[138]

It is also worth remembering that during the codification debate summarized above by Professor Gordley, Portalis tied *causa* to Pothier's classification of contracts. Because of the presence of so many types of performances and counter-performances in Pothier's classification, *causa* could mean any of them. It could mean the promised counter-performance or no counter-performance at all, as with the gratuitous contract of donation (unless the promisee's acceptance of the gift was deemed his counter-performance). It could also mean an objectively determinable expectation of what the counterparty had to perform based upon custom and practice, or it could mean the parties' motivations, as in the case of the so-called "final or psychological" cause.

In the final analysis, as pointed out by Professor Gorla, the common denominator to all of the versions of *causa* was *causa* as *the reason* for the parties to enter into their agreements.[139] Yet, as also pointed out by Gorla, without that common denominator there would be nothing distinctive about the concept of *causa*. It would be a redundant concept, especially when used to establish whether the parties agreed on the essence of their bargain; for if there was an agreement, there had to be a reason for it. In other words, whenever a court found that the parties had a reason for entering into a contract (except for illegal and immoral reasons), the contract had a valid *causa*. If so, what did the concept of *causa* add to that finding? If the parties contended that they had conflicting reasons for entering into the contract, either one of them could claim

---

135 LEGIFRANCE C. CIV. (FR.) art. 1108.

136 *Id.* art. 1131.

137 *Id.* art. 1133.

138 GORLA I at 45.

139 *Id.* at 77–84.

that he or she had been the victim of an essential and contractually disabling mistake. If so, what was the role of *causa*?[140]

The redundancy of *causa* in contemporary Spanish contractual litigation became apparent during class discussions at the doctoral program of Charles III University of Spain during the 2005 and 2006 academic years. Among the doctoral students attending the classes were judges, law professors and practitioners familiar with civil and commercial contract litigation in Spain. Their experience with the judicial application of Article 1275 of the Spanish Civil Code (which transcribes the *Code Civil's* Article 1131),[141] revealed that *causa* was regularly used as a procedural sword or shield whose purpose was to prevent the enforcement of the contract in question. In this procedural context, the moving party usually alleges that the contract not only lacks a *causa* or that it is illegal or immoral, but that he or she was unaware of its non-existence, illegality or immorality when entering into the contract. Further, had the moving party been aware that the counterparty intended an illegal or immoral *causa,* he or she would not have entered into the contract. In other words, in everyday contract litigation in Spain, *causa* quite frequently winds up being indistinguishable from mistake of fact because both equally and fatally vitiate the contract's requisite intent.

F. The Morality of *Causa*

The *Code Civil* was concerned with the morality of *causa* in both gratuitous and onerous contracts and defined an illicit *causa* (which rendered the obligation void) as one not only prohibited by law, but also contrary to "public morals" and "public order." It will be recalled that a gratuitous contract under the *Code Civil* finds its *causa* in the donor's liberality. However, what if the gratuitous conveyance is not to a member of one's family but to a "stranger" such as the grantor's mistress? In such a case, code interpreters drew a distinction between the cause that appears stated in the contract and the so-called "final," "psychological" or "impulsive" cause.[142]

A 1957 decision by the *Cour de Cassation* discussed earlier illustrates the meaning of "public morals" and its connection with the final, psychological or impulsive cause.[143] A French middle-aged father of a family conveyed the beneficial interest in his life insurance policy to a recently-acquired mistress. His widow and heirs sued the mistress alleging the nullity of her designation as beneficiary. The trial and appellate courts decided that the discernible final *causa* of the conveyance was contrary to public morals. They based their decision on the factual findings, on the relationship between the father of family and his mistress, and on established case law. In accordance with the case law, a donation in favor of a concubine was not *per se* invalid. It could be valid when it was made as part of a long-standing adulterous relationship. Yet, the conveyance was null because of the immorality of its *causa* when, appearing to be a

---

140 *Id.*

141 C.C. (SPAIN) art. 1275 ("Contracts without cause or with an illegal cause have no effects whatever. A cause is illegal when it conflicts with law or morals." (*Los contratos sin causa, o con causa ilícita, no producen efecto alguno. Es ilícita la causa cuando se opone a las leyes o a la moral.*)).

142 WEILL & TERRE, *supra* note 129, at nos. 280–81 (a brief review of the morality of cause in gratuitous contracts).

143 Cour de cassation [Cass.] [supreme court for judicial matters] 1e civ., Oct. 8, 1957, JCP 1957 II 10234 (Fr.); for the text of this decision, *see infra* § 8:10, for an earlier discussion *see supra* § 4:4(D)(3)(a), and for a later reference to it *see infra* § 22:2(C).

donation, it was in reality the payment of a price to procure an extramarital relationship.[144]

The net effect of the ruling was to discourage conveyances detrimental to the traditional notion of a bourgeois estate, i.e., one accumulated for the benefit of one's widow and heirs, or perhaps of an extramarital relationship of long duration.

Professor Capitant discusses similar decisions concerning real property rented for purposes of prostitution or for the operation of gambling houses and agreements involving the bribing or corruption of public officials.[145] The courts' distaste for such agreements can be gauged by their unwillingness to order restitution of what was exchanged by the parties during the life of the rescinded contract, despite the fact that normally such restitution is available in rescission cases. As expressed by an indignant court in Bourges in 1889: "Such parties are not worthy of appearing before a court of law."[146] This indignation is reminiscent of that expressed in an earlier section by a litigant son of a merchant who wished to dissociate himself from merchants by referring to them as "persons from the dregs of the people."[147]

G. Contracts *Inter Praesentes* and Disregard of Third Party Rights

Contracting among the bourgeoisie was mostly done on a face-to-face or "*inter praesentes*" basis. If a contract resulted from correspondence, the Code provided very few rules with which to elucidate issues such as whether the mailing of the acceptance by the offeree, its reception by the offeror, or knowledge of its reception by the offeror was when the acceptance became binding. As concluded by Professor Von Mehren, little attention was paid by the French codifier to contracts by correspondence or *inter absentes*.[148] Moreover, while seeming to accept the concept of a third party beneficiary promise, it seriously limited such promises.[149]

The *Code Civil's* concern for the integrity of the family estate of the seller or transferor of land was matched by its lack of concern for third party rights. Thus, the purchaser or mortgagee of real property was subject to secret or unrecorded liens and transfers up until 1855.[150] This situation prevailed because of the legal effect attributed by the *Code Civil* to the will of the contracting parties. By providing that the parties' agreement, without more, was sufficient to effect the transfer of title to property, Article 1138 of the *Code Civil* not only "enfranchised" the will of the parties,[151] it also did away with the formal requirement of physical or symbolic delivery of the thing sold (*traditio*), a Roman law formality which provided a modicum of notice to third parties.

---

[144] See *infra* §8:10.

[145] HENRI CAPITANT, DE LA CAUSE DES OBLIGATIONS 226–27 (3d ed. 1927).

[146] Judgment of 13 June 1889, Bourges, D.P.1889.5.329 (cited in CAPITANT, *supra* note 145 at 243).

[147] DOYLE, OXFORD HISTORY, *supra* note 9, at 24.

[148] Arthur Von Mehren, *The Code and Contract—A Comparative Analysis of Formation and Form, in* THE CODE NAPOLEON AND THE COMMON LAW WORLD 110–11 (B. Schwartz ed., 1956), (a comparative discussion of some of the *Code Civil*'s shortcomings in the regulation of contract law).

[149] *Id.*

[150] Kozolchyk, *Mexican Land Registry,* at 312–13; Kozolchyk, *Commercialization,* at 12.

[151] LEGIFRANCE C. CIV. (FR.), art. 1138 ("An obligation of delivering a thing is complete by the sole consent of the contracting parties.").

Speaking in favor of the principle of immediate transfer of ownership upon execution of an agreement of sale and reflecting the face-to-face nature of bourgeois real estate transactions, Tronchet, one of the drafters, stated: "He who buys does not require that the law adopt special measures for his safety. He has the title before his eyes. He can verify the vendor's possession."[152] To this, Bigot de Preameneu, another drafter, added the need to protect "family secrets": "The system of notice (to third parties) precludes families from preserving the secrecy of their affairs. . . . This secret is always regarded as one of the principal rights of individual liberty."[153]

In 2005, Arizona's neighboring state of Sonora, Mexico announced in a bi-national meeting and press conference that a land registry located in a popular beach resort where many foreigners acquired beach property would be online and available for consultation anywhere in the world. Yet, a Mexican guest onlooker at this press conference was overheard to strongly object to such a development. His objections were very similar to that voiced by Bigot de Preaumeneu: Why should people other than those involved in a recorded transaction be allowed to delve into the private businesses of those who recorded their rights? When a Mexican government official explained that the publicity of the registry was an important inducement to investors and lenders, the onlooker quickly snapped back: "Yes, as it will also immediately attract the kidnappers looking for likely candidates among those who appear to be selling or buying valuable properties lately." How would you respond to such an argument?

Because the contract of sale created, modified or extinguished rights *in rem*, regardless of recordation, a mortgagee who had advanced monies on land on the basis of his mortgagor's recorded ownership could still be subject to an earlier unrecorded transfer of ownership.[154] *Mutatis mutandis*, the contractually-protected owner could "enjoy and dispose of things in the most absolute manner, provided that they are not used in a way prohibited by statutes or regulations."[155]

One of the problems with this "absolutistic" provision was that it encouraged such selfish behavior that it became necessary for the courts, in partnership with doctrine, to develop restraints on "abuses" of rights.[156] Neighbors had to be told that they could not erect fake chimneys simply for their nuisance value, nor could they erect spires with which to prevent the landing of zeppelins on adjoining property in order to extort a higher price for their own property, etc.[157]

---

152 M. PLANIOL, I CIVIL LAW TREATISE 543 (La. St. L. Inst. trans., 1959), *cited in* Kozolchyk, *Commercialization*, at 12 n.42.

153 PIERRE-ANTOINE FENET, 15 RECUEIL COMPLET DES TRAVAUX PREPARATOIRES DU CODE CIVIL 237 (1827). (This author's translation.) This quote is characteristic of the codal attitude toward third party rights, "individual liberties" and "family secrets":

Le système de publicite est une interdiction aux families de garder le secret de leurs affaires. . . . Ce secret a toujours été regarde comme un des principaux droits de la liberte individuelle.

Id. See also Kozolchyk, *Commercialization*, at 12 n.42.

154 Kozolchyk, *Mexican Land Registry,* at 312–13.

155 LEGIFRANCE C. CIV. (FR.) art. 544 ("Ownership is the right to enjoy and dispose of things in the most absolute manner, provided they are not used in a way prohibited by statutes or regulations.").

156 *See generally* Vera Bolgár, *Abuse of Rights in France, Germany, and Switzerland: A Survey of a Recent Chapter in Legal Doctrine*, 35 LA. L. REV. 1015 (1975); Julio Cueto-Rua, *Abuse of Rights*, 35 LA. L. REV. 965 (1975); Shael Herman, *Classical Social Theories and the Doctrine of "Abuse of Right"*, 37 LA. L. REV. 747 (1977).

157 Bolgár, *supra* note 156, at 1021.

§ 8.8 CONCLUSIONS: THE BOURGEOIS ARCHETYPE OF *CODE CIVIL* CONTRACTS

The preceding discussion makes it possible to sketch the main features of a *Code Civil* bourgeois contracting party, especially when selling or buying land: 1) He is fully empowered to acquire and sell it; however, his executory promises in bilateral contracts or promises of deferred performance require an immediate acceptance by the promisee. The enforcement of "firm" promises, or promises that are binding from the time they are issued or reach the promisee, is at best uncertain and at worst unattainable under the *Code Civil*. The same is true with promises extending credit, unless embodied in negotiable instruments. 2) He is as comfortable with formalism and face-to-face transactions as he is uncomfortable with, and distrusting of, informality and *inter absentes* communications. 3) He favors contractual secrecy even where it is at the expense of third party rights. 4) He is a stickler for his rights, occasionally to the point of abuse. 5) He is unscrupulous enough to charge whatever he can get for what he sells and then trusts the doctrine of "contractual justice" to adjudicate his contractual rights and duties. 6) He expects the law to protect him if he sells his land by mistake or duress for less than seven-twelfths of its market value. 7) The *causa* of his contracts (understood as the reason for his contractual undertakings) can have serious anti-commercial effects even when the obligation is attempted to be enforced by third party assignees. Even his "commutative" agreements, i.e., those involving reciprocity of exchange, do not truly assure that the other contracting party will receive an equivalent value to that which that party conferred. If the value conferred upon the other party is the one stated in the agreement, however unequal the bargain, contractual justice will assure that it suffices as the *causa* for the commutative agreement.

The archetypal analysis contextualizes the meaning of public morals in the unlawful cause and adds concrete meaning (contractual justice) to the principle that contracts are the law between or among the parties. At the same time, it warns the interpreter to take the *Code Civil* Article 1135 reference to equity, custom or usage with a grain of salt. This is especially true when interpreting formal contracts such as notarial deeds for the sale or conveyance of land.

Because, as will be apparent in the following chapter, civil code provisions and principles very frequently act as fillers of normative gaps in the Commercial Code, how influential are these bourgeois features in shaping the law of commercial contracts? Or do French commercial contracts reflect the behavior of a different archetype? These questions will be dealt with in the following chapter.

§ 8.9 APPENDIX: CODIFIED, STATUTORY AND CASE LAW

A. Introduction

The purpose of this Appendix is to acquaint the reader with the manner in which French judges and commentators have applied or recommended the application of the *Code Civil* to issues of considerable commercial importance and to explore the contemporary fate of an important executory promise. The selected topics are: 1) the *in rem* enforceability of a promise of sale of immovable property; 2) the meaning of an illegal cause in insurance contracts; and 3) the objective standard for adjudication of the remedy of *lesion*, including the measurement of the value to be compensated.

Citation of French cases is not always standardized. While some cases have names, often they do not and instead use the name of the court, the chamber and the date. Most of the cases refer to decisions by the *Cour de Cassation*, the highest appellate court in France, usually abbreviated "Cass." This court is divided into chambers among which the civil and commercial are the most important for this book. "Civ." denotes civil, "Com." denotes commercial, and "REQ" indicates an appeal. For a listing of some of the most frequently cited statutory, decisional, and doctrinal sources of the law of representative countries or jurisdictions, see the frequently cited section.

B. Promises of Sale of Real Property

The first case to be discussed in this section of the Appendix[158] involves the enforceability of a promise of sale of real property. The decision illustrates a form of analysis popular among mid-nineteenth-century commentators of the *Code Civil* and, subsequently, of other civil codes influenced by it. This form of analysis was taken to new heights of abstraction and dogmatism by nineteenth-century German "*Pandectists*."[159] Theirs was, in the words of Rudolf von Ihering, a world of "heavenly concepts" often at odds with the distant world of the marketplace. Much of the juristic thinking that preceded the enactment of the BGB was of this type, as will be discussed in Chapter 12.

This decision also provides a springboard from which to complete the discussion of the evolution of the promises of deferred performance in French private law, starting with the *Code Civil* and continuing with statutory and judicial additions. The reader will recall that these promises were treated as *nuda pacta* in Roman law and remained as such throughout much of the history of contracts in civil and common law countries. The reader will also recall Hugo Grotius' attempt to trace the binding effect of contracts to the will of the parties.[160] He or she should also recall that by insisting that, a unilateral promise would only be enforceable if the promisee agreed to it. Grotius and Robert Pothier were responsible for the presence of an unenforceable "pollicitation" (or unaccepted executory promise) in the *Code Civil*, as dramatically illustrated by the following provisions prompted by purposes other than those Grotius and Pothier had in mind.

C. Relevant *Code Civil* Provisions

The Promise of Sale:

Article 1589:[161]

The promise of sale shall be deemed a sale when the parties agree on the thing sold and its price.

Article 1589–1:[162]

---

158 All of the decisions discussed in this Appendix have been extracted from HENRY CAPITANT, ALEX WEILL & FRANCOIS TERRE, LES GRANDS ARRÊTS DE LA JURISPRUDENCE CIVILE (7th ed. Dalloz, 1976) [hereinafter ARRÊTS CIVILE].

159 *See* Glossary, "Pandectists."

160 *See supra* § 8:2(B)(1)(a)–(b).

161 C. CIV. (FR.) art. 1589.

162 *Id.* art. 1589–1.

The unilateral promise issued with the purpose of acquiring an immovable thing or right by which the promissor promised to pay or paid an amount for this obligation shall be null and void, regardless of its cause or form of execution.

Article 1589–2:[163]

A unilateral promise of sale of immovable property, a commercial establishment or a right to a lease that involves the whole or part of such immovable property or the shares of stock of business associations referred to in Articles 728 and 1655 of the Tax Code must be confirmed by the execution of a public or private deed and must be recorded within ten days of the date of the acceptance of the beneficiary of the promise.

Earnest Money and the Promise of Sale:

Article 1590:[164]

If the promise of sale was made against the delivery of an earnest money deposit (*arrhes*), each of the contracting parties shall be free to abandon the agreement by forfeiting it if it was the party providing the deposit and by returning double the amount deposited if the abandoning party is the recipient of the deposit.

COMMENTS AND QUESTIONS

As pointed out by Professor Stephane Prigent of the Faculté de Droit de Brest (UBO),[165] the "unilateral promise with the purpose of acquiring an immoveable thing or right" (*engagement unilateral souscrit en vu de l'acquistion d'un bien ou un droit immobilier*) is the one issued by a consumer or non-professional purchaser of immovable property or of a right in that property.[166] The practice that most concerned the drafters of this provision was that of a promise to purchase accompanied by a down-payment. Such a purchaser submitted their promise without receiving from the seller "any guarantee of repayment of that sum in the event of a failure of the execution of the sale" (*un engagement d'achat d'un immueble du versement d'un somme d'argent, sans aucune garantie de restitution des fonds en cas de non-realisation de la vente*).[167] As also pointed out by Professor Prigent, an Article 1589–1 promise or undertaking is an offer to purchase land that would be binding as a contract but only after the offeree's acceptance (still referred to as pollicitation in present-day French law). In theory, this offer can be revoked by the offeror at any time prior to the offeree's acceptance, unless the offeror stipulated a certain time for its acceptance or such a period was customarily observed by offerors.[168] In addition, a number of down-payment practices made these offers and their accompanying down payments unfair practices against purchasers often likely to lose their down payments.[169] The best remedy the legislator could come up with was that of a judicially-enforced nullity or voidness.

---

163 *Id.* art. 1589–2.

164 *Id.* art. 1590.

165 *See* Stéphane Prigent, *Les difficultés d'interprétation de l'article 1589–1 du Code Civil*, AJDI 166 et. seq. (2003) (on file with author).

166 *Id.* at 167.

167 *Id.*

168 *Id.* at 168.

169 *Id.*

Mutatis mutandis, Article 1590 allows the abandonment of a promise of a sale to a buyer willing to forfeit his down payment or to a seller who repays twice the amount of the down payment. My question is whether both parties would not be better and more cheaply protected by their use of a French equivalent of the United States escrow agreement previously illustrated and discussed.[170]

That agreement would assure in the case of an Article 1589–1 situation that the fiduciary-depositary of the buyer's down payment would be responsible for returning the down payment in the event of the seller failing to convey title, or for delivering the full purchase price (on behalf of the buyer) to the seller and conveying title to the buyer. In the case of Article 1590, the trusted third party would be responsible for delivering to the aggrieved party (buyer or seller) the proceeds of their respective forfeitures. Can you see the practical advantages of such a contract, in contrast with the above described procedures?[171]

German notarial practice has developed an extrajudicial and less cumbersome procedure for the options to purchase and promises of sale than that apparent in the above French provisions and in the Mexican Supreme Court decisions. Consider the following advice given by the author of a German manual for real estate transactions:

> Practical Advice: In cases where the purchase price is to be initially deposited with the notary, it is also recommended to agree on the hand-over date.
>
> Hand-over before Payment:
>
> In some cases, hand-over (*Grundstücksübergabe*) before payment is agreed. Under German law, this frequently creates the problem that the transfer of ownership represents an advance performance by the seller for which he still has no security. In this case, provisional payment of part of the purchase price is a solution. This money can be deposited with the notary or paid into a special account (*Sperrkonto*) to which the buyer only has access in the event of the complete reversal of the transaction.[172]
>
> Furthermore, to protect the buyer, it is frequently recommended that he should not pay the purchase price direct to the seller but deposit it with the notary. *Notary custody* (*notarielle Verwahrung*) gives the credit institutes and banks the necessary security. Another possibility is to initially *pay the purchase price into a special account* to which the seller only has access under conditions previously defined in detail (*Sperrkonto*).[173]
>
> . . .
>
> Seller's Strategies:
>
> In Germany, another approach to securing the seller's rights is frequently chosen: the conditional transfer of property (*Eigentumsumschreibung unter Vorbehalt*). The conveyance of ownership is already agreed in the purchase contract. However, the notary is instructed by both contracting parties jointly not to file the application for the transfer of property with the land registry office . . . until payment of the purchase price has been verified to the notary. In such cases, a firm promise of payment or confirmation of financing by the bank involved often are considered to be sufficient.

---

170 *See infra* § 10:9(E).

171 *Id.*

172 REAL ESTATE INVESTMENTS IN GERMANY: TRANSACTIONS AND DEVELOPMENT 104 (Michael Mütze et al. eds., 2007).

173 *Id.* at 105 (emphasis added).

> Practical Advice: The conditional transfer of property has advantages in many cases as a notarised conveyance of ownership already exists. This permits amendments to the contract to be made after the notarisation of the conveyance of ownership in a simple way without renewed notarisation being required (BGH, Urteil vom 6, Mai 1988, BGHZ 104, 277).[174]

Do you see how this German notarial conditional transfer of property has transformed the discrete promises to sell and buy into a binding contract for both sides? Stated differently, with this notarial form of escrow, discrete promises to sell and to buy are no longer executory, but become executed, albeit conditionally. With the increasing commercialization of real property, pressures to enforce executory and conditional promises will only grow in intensity. Consider, for example, the everyday case of a real estate developer who needs to ascertain that the large tract of land that he intends to develop for residential or commercial purposes has proper access to, say, sufficient water and electricity, or that the soil is strong enough to support his projected multi-story buildings or that it does not contain toxic materials. He is willing to pay a certain amount of money to the owner of the land to investigate these potential problems and is willing to pay a certain price for the land. In exchange, he needs the owner's promise that he will not attempt to sell the land to any other person during the period of research. Thus, the buyer is willing to issue his promise of purchase conditioned upon finding that his specified conditions have been met. In exchange, the seller is willing to promise that he will sell the land for the price mentioned in the offer of purchase and will not sell during the research period in exchange for payment of a certain amount of money at the time of issuance of his promise to sell at a certain price. Both are conditional promises, yet they need to be made enforceable so that such a transaction could proceed.[175]

1. Court Decision: Garrone C. Dame Guinde[176]

REPORTER'S TOPICS: Unilateral Promise-Obligation to Do v. Obligation to Give—Rights *in Personam* (Movable Property) v. Rights *in rem* (Immovable Property).

THE COURT: Considering that the unilateral promise of sale transfers to its beneficiary neither the ownership nor any other immovable right [*droit immobilier*] in the property that is the subject of the promise, and that as long as the promisee does not accept the promise in question, the promisor's obligation is not one to give [*donner*] but to do [*faire*] something and it, by itself, creates a *claim that is only movable* in nature, thus the appealed decision has not violated the law or the facts; on the contrary, it applied the law exactly as it should have. . .

OBSERVATIONS BY M. PILON: . . . In this case, the court decided for the first time, from the standpoint of civil law, if a unilateral promise to sell immovable property embodies a movable or an immovable right. This question does not apply to a synallagmatic promise because as stated by Article 1589 of the *Code Civil*: "The promise of sale is deemed a sale from the moment there is agreement by the parties on

---

[174] *Id.* at 106.

[175] *See generally* Boris Kozolchyk et al., *Enhancement of Mexican Commercial Adjudication by Improved Transactional Fact-Finding, Application of Equitable Principles, and Drafting of Standard Contracts and Best Contractual Practices*, 27 ARIZ. J. INT'L & COMP. L. 325, 325–691 (2010). Consult this recent symposium issue if you are interested in how Mexico may be poised to resolve this problem caused by its respect for the *Code Civil* approach.

[176] ARRETS CIVILE, *supra* note 158, at 609–12 (Cour de cassation [Cass.] [supreme court for judicial matters] Nov. 26, 1935, D.P. 1936.1.37 (Fr.) (citations omitted)).

the thing sold and its price. . ." Thus, the transfer of the property [once there is an agreement] occurs from the time of the exchange of promises, and the nature of [the right conveyed by] this promise is immovable. . . and the beneficiary of the promise enjoys a right *in rem* in immovable property.

The nature of the unilateral promise is quite delicate and controversial when. . . the promisee performs acts with respect to this offer that fall short of becoming an acceptance. Some commentators believe that. . . the promisee is entitled to a right that incorporates the nature of the thing involved and thus because it involves a claim to an immovable. . . they label these actions "personal immovable" [*actions personnelles immobilières*]. This is the case with actions for the rescission, termination and nullity of the sale of an immovable. . . The essential point in dispute, however, is whether the promisee-claimant has a right to claim an obligation to do [the payment of damages for the breach of a sale agreement] rather than to claim an obligation to give. . . [the delivery of the immovable]. . . If it is the latter, it can result in a forced sale of the property by the court, in which the court conveys title to the property to the promisee-buyer in the promisor's name. In such a case, the claim by the promisee-buyer would be in the nature of an immovable right [the court in the present case sided with the movable nature of the claim]. The consequences of the court's decision are important. In the present case, the property involved was promised to be conveyed prior to the enactment of a matrimonial property law now in force which transforms property promised to be conveyed into community property.

COMMENTS AND QUESTIONS

Prior to exploring the consequences of this court's analysis, the reader is strongly encouraged to review the facts of Mexico's Supreme Court decision in the 1954 Appeal of María Trinidad Gómez summarized in a later chapter.[177] Please note how the obligation to sign a deed conveying property promised (in a promise of a sale) by the defendant is characterized as an obligation "to do" and thus requiring of a court decision and order to issue the deed of sale. Please also notice the difficulties that commentators have found with this dichotomy, to which I would add that often it is not easy to tell when an obligation to give is not also an obligation to do. For example, if I promise to act as your surety, surely you are expecting me to "give" my promise as surety to your creditor. But how can I give such a promise without "expressing" or "doing" it? See the later discussion in connection with the remedy of specific performance in French law and Professor Dawson's illuminating debunking of the myth of an eternal and universal classification of the obligations into "to do" and "to give."[178]

The reader may have noticed this translator's linguistic difficulties with the Court's conclusion that the promised sale involved neither the ownership nor any *immovable right in the property* (*ni la proprieté, ni aucun droit immobilier sur le bien*). The difficulty with *droit immobilier* is that "immovable" (*immobilier*) modifies "right" (*droit*) and thus renders it an inert object. Literally translated then, *droit immobilier* would mean a right that does not move, a rather odd state for an incorporeal thing such as a right. Yet, this is not the meaning that the *Code Civil*, the courts, and commentators wished to impart.

---

177 *See infra* § 22:10(K).

178 *See infra* § 28:7. *See also* Dawson, *supra* note 58.

2. *The Meaning and Method of the* Code Civil *Provisions*

The meaning the drafters wished to impart on the concept of right can be gleaned first from Article 516 of the *Code Civil.* It proclaimed unhesitatingly, in Aristotelian and scholastic fashion, that things were either movable or immovable. Accordingly, if a right was to be characterized as a thing, it had to be either movable or immovable. Article 517, in a similar fashion, classified things in accordance with their "nature," "destiny" and "the object to which they are applied."[179] Land, buildings, trees and fruits on them, and windmills, among other things, were said to be immovables by their nature.[180] Yet, from the moment grains and fruits were collected, severed or cut, they became movables. So far, then, the *Code Civil* classification was consistent with observable features of things immovable.

Article 524 defines as immovable property by their destiny those "[a]nimals and objects that the owner of an estate placed in it for the service and exploitation of the estate. . . ."[181] Among these it lists, farm animals, plows, seeds provided to tenant farmers for joint venture purposes, and other fixtures related to the various types of industries or businesses carried out in the land.

Much of this category of things was not as easily observable as the preceding one, but it had a plausible transactional reference, i.e., things that the parties wished to incorporate in or associate with an immovable to enhance its value.

The third category is found in Article 526. It applied to the least observable group of things: immovable property based on the object to which the things applied or were related.[182] These were said to be life estates in immovable property, easements in the same immovable, mortgage charges and judicial actions whose purpose was to recover immovables.

The first three of these "things" were what the Romans referred to as rights in the things of others (*iura in re aliena),* and the fourth was a court action to enforce these and other rights to things. Not surprisingly, the followers of the German *Pandectists* who were among the drafters of the BGB, about whom more will be discussed in later chapters,[183] had no hesitation in stating in Article 96 of the BGB that: "*Rights* which are connected with the ownership of a piece of land are deemed to be component parts of the land."[184] Even more confident of the axiomatic existence of this category of things, the drafters of the Mexican Civil Code of 1932 (among others) listed in Section XII of Article 750 as immovable things "the rights *in rem* in immovables" ("*Los derechos reales sobre immuebles*").[185]

The above method of drafting code rules is algebraic in the sense that it ascribes legal consequences to concepts and after having done so, constructs a formula that incorporates those consequences and leads to judicial or administrative actions or

---

179 C. CIV. (FR.) art. 517.

180 *Id.* arts. 518–520.

181 *Id.* art. 524.

182 *Id.* art. 526.

183 *See infra* ch. 12.

184 BGB art. 96 (GOREN, 1994) (emphasis added).

185 Código Civil Federal [CC] [Federal Civil Code], *as amended*, Diario Oficial de la Federación [DO], art. 750 (XII) (Mex.).

remedies. For example, a promise to sell real property is legally characterized as an obligation to do rather than an obligation to give. Obligations to do are characterized as giving right to actions for specific performance, but not for damages. Accordingly, the remedial formula before a court of law asked to enforce a promise to sell real property would be:

"A" (a promise to sell an immovable) + "B" (an obligation to do, i.e., the execution of a deed of sale) = "C" (*in personam* remedy or remedies).

However, the right to demand specific performance of a promised sale or of any other contract, because it is not a right to a thing, but a contractual right against the person, is in turn characterized as movable or personal property. The consequences of this characterization are not only that it must be claimed in a "declaratory" action, which could take several years before it is adjudicated, but also that it cannot be recorded in a land or real property registry as a *lis pendens* because being movable or personal property, it can only be recorded in the registry of personal property (if such a registry exists). Consequently, if the person who obtained and paid for a promise to sell him the property cannot record his right to demand specific performance of that promise in the land registry, he cannot protect his investment and his right to purchase the property against third parties.

Now assume that instead of the promise being one to sell property, the parties actually agreed to such a sale. The legal characterization of such a contract under French law and its progeny is that it is a "consensual" contract, which transfers title to the property to the buyer from the moment that there is agreement on the property and its price. The legal characterization of that right is a right *in rem*, or to the property, "D." D gives right to an action to replevy or obtain the property (*vindicatio rei*) and to a recording in the name of the purchaser in the land registry. Thus:

C (the product of A + B) =D (an *in rem* or *ad rem* remedy).

This method of drafting the codified legal institutions departed from market practices that require that promises to sell convey more than contractual obligations to issue a deed of sale, hard to enforce as these are, but instead the obligation to deliver the land once certain agreed-upon conditions are met.

3. Code Civil *Rules on Promises of Sales and the Commercial Marketplace*

In theory, the above described method of reasoning should render the law more mathematically predictable because it was, after all, an algebraically self-evident law. Yet, as noted in earlier chapters, the self-evidence of this type of rule is only superficial because what made it self-evident was not its empirical verifiability, but the codifier's often redundant classification of obligations "to do" and "to give." In addition, this classification is followed, thanks to the poetic license of scholasticism, by an equally suspect definition of rights (inherently intangible objects) as either moveable or immoveable objects depending upon the object with which they are associated. This definition ignores the legal fact that the right to a moveable object, whether to its possession or ownership, is as much of a right *in rem* or in the thing as the right to the possession of ownership of an immovable. Clearly, legal certainty has not resulted from this type of rulemaking. As once stated to me by a Colombian law professor and commercial litigator: This dichotomy and the fees it has generated in contractual disputes have made it possible for many a litigator to afford his childrens' pretty decent secondary education.

With rules such as these, the judge or code interpreter, especially at the appellate or *Cour de cassation* level, does not have to focus much on the facts of the transaction or the socio-economic problem involved. All he has to ask himself is: "What kind of a (legal) thing is this promise? Is it movable or immovable?" Such a "slot machine" approach to lawmaking and adjudication obscures the true issues, legal and socio-economic.

There may be reasons why a legislator may not wish to facilitate the creation of a more robust real estate market on promises to enter into future contracts or on options. He may wish to retain a *status quo* that restricts the holding of real property to a class such as the bourgeois, as was the case with pre-revolutionary and "commercial-speculation-adverse" Napoleonic France. Or, he may wish to encourage only acquisitions or leases by low-income farmers or urban dwellers.

If the latter was the legislator's intent, it may or may not make sense to state, as was stated by Article 1589–1 of the *Code Civil* (transcribed above), that "[t]he unilateral promise issued with the purpose of acquiring an immovable thing or right by which the promisor promised to pay or paid an amount for this obligation shall be null and void. . . ."[186] This super-"paternalistic" type of consumer protection rule protects some buyers, but will preclude many others, especially low-income potential purchasers or lessees, from acquiring the desired parcel or urban dwelling on terms that they find affordable.

Finally, neither the court decision in question nor code provisions such as Article 1590 would make sense if the desirable socio-economic goal is to encourage the widest possible participation by builders, developers, buyers, lessees and their financiers in an active real estate market. Such a market obviously benefits from increased participation, and one of the most effective means to increase such participation is by allowing the trade-in and enforcement of future rights in real estate, whether by promises of sales or options to buy.

Using a reasoning similar to that in this decision, some civil law jurisdictions treat these promises or options to purchase as unenforceable *in rem,* despite having been paid for by the potential buyers. Hence, it is not unusual for land registrars in these jurisdictions to reject the filing of these promises or options by concluding that options are movable rights and the land registry is only supposed to record immovable rights. This means that he who relied not only on the promisor's express promise to sell, but also on his willingness to accept an earnest money payment,[187] cannot count on the deterrent effect of a recorded right to purchase *vis-à-vis* subsequent but competing buyers. Similarly, the ability to ignore an earnest money payment by taking it back or by paying back double its amount seriously diminishes the certainty and attractiveness of a purchase or sale promise not only for the parties of the original transaction, but also for possibly numerous *bona fide* purchasers in the open marketplace.

In conclusion, the present comment amounts to a plea for legislative and judicial candor. For in the final analysis, the issue is not whether the legal nature of a promise

---

186 C. CIV. (FR.) art. 1589–1 ; *see also supra* § 8:9(C).

187 *Id.* art. 1590.

or option on real estate is such that it can only be a movable or immovable thing (or perhaps, a hybrid?) but, as von Ihering would remind us, "What are the true interests in conflict and what is it that the legal decision-maker truly wishes to accomplish with his legal institutions?"[188]

4. *Commercial Promises and Pollicitations*

The realities of the commercial and consumer-credit marketplace—especially in the era of the Internet—have finally convinced French legislators and judges that at least some promises of deferred payment and performance should be enforceable even prior to the time of their acceptance by the relevant beneficiaries. Even a quick reading of relatively recent statutory and judicial additions to the *Code Civil* should persuade the reader that Robert Pothier's dismissal of unaccepted unilateral promises as *nuda pacta* pollicitations no longer holds axiomatic sway in French law. Von Mehren and Gordley cite a number of decisions where the French courts significantly qualified the non-binding or revocable effects of a promise or an offer. Significantly, these cases involved a commercial context.[189] For example, in *Berthault et Compagnie v. Duchesne et Audiart et Rabier, Thirouin et Compagnie*,[190] the court held that:

> Whereas . . . the court of first instance interpreted properly the intention of the parties and made a proper application of the customs of the Paris Bourse, justified by the needs of commerce and taking into account the circumstances of the negotiations and the difficulty of communication at the time that the offer was made . . . Rabier, Thirouin and Compnay, as appears clearly from previous correspondence between the parties, knew that Duchesne and Audiart, who were negotiating as direct buyers, were buying [the sugar] for immediate resale; as consequently, the offer made on 16 October 1914 could not be withdrawn before the offeree, having had time to contact potential buyers, could accept or refuse; as the period of not more than four hours . . . was not long enough. . . .[191]

In their customary exhaustive manner, these authors also cite to French doctrinal writings supporting a similar approach. For example, A. Colin & H. Capitant, of *the Cours Elémentaire de Droit Civil Français*,[192] under the heading "Case Where the Offer Fixes a Period for the Reply," state:

> The classical theory starts with an exact analysis of the will of the offeror, but this theory generalizes too much. In practice the offeror usually gives the offeree a period within which to accept. . . . Often, although no period is indicated, one results from the nature of the transaction. It can be said that in commerce all offers are accompanied, expressly or implicitly, by such a period. Is it not clear that the offeror cannot be considered free to withdraw

---

[188] *See* VON IHERING, A MEANS TO AN END, at 445–48.

[189] *See infra* § 22:8(C) (for instances of revocable offers in commercial transactions).

[190] Berthault et Compagnie v. Duchesne et Audiart et Rabier, Thirouin et Compagnie, Cour d'appel [CA] [regional court of appeals] Paris 6th ch., Mar. 13, 1917, Gaz. Pal. 1917–1918, 978 (Fr.).

[191] VON MEHREN & GORDLEY, THE CIVIL LAW SYSTEM, at 874–75.

[192] A. COLIN & H. CAPITANT, COURS ELEMENTAIRE DE DROIT CIVIL FRANCAIS 35–36 (10th ed. 1948).

the offer before the expiration of the periods fixed by him? Various systems have, therefore, been proposed to temper the classical doctrine.[193]

a. Statutorily-Enforceable Electronic Pollicitations

The reader is encouraged to review the following legislative additions to the *Code Civil* and to identify formerly-unenforceable pollicitations and ask himself: Why does such a change have to take place? Does it spell the end of unenforceable pollicitations?

Electronic Offers:

Article 1369–4:[194]

Whoever in a professional [and commercial] capacity offers to supply goods or services by electronic means shall make available [to the offeree] the general conditions of trade applicable to the transaction in a manner that allows the preservation of a record thereof as well as their reproduction. Aside from the conditions of validity mentioned in the offer, the offeror shall be bound by his offer as long as it can be accessed electronically as a consequence of its issuance.

In addition, the offer shall mention:

1) The different steps that need to be followed in order to sign the contract by electronic means;

2) The technical means that allow the offeree-user to identify the mistakes committed in the entry of data and correct them prior to concluding the contract;

3) The languages proposed as effective in the conclusion of the contract;

4) Where the contract must be archived, the types of archives made available by the offeror and the conditions of access to the archived contract; and

5) The electronic means of consultation of the professional and commercial rules to which the offeror is willing to submit himself should the need arise.

Validity of an Electronic Purchase Agreement:

Article 1369–5:[195]

For the purchase agreement to be concluded in valid fashion, the offeree must have had the opportunity to verify the total amount of his order and price, as well as to correct possible mistakes prior to the confirmation of his acceptance.

The offeror must acknowledge receipt of what he purchased without unjustified delay and by electronic means.

The purchase order, the confirmation, the acceptance of the offer and the acknowledgment of its receipt will be deemed to have been received when the parties to whom these communications were directed could have access to them.

---

[193] VON MEHREN & GORDLEY, THE CIVIL LAW SYSTEM, at 875.

[194] C. CIV. (FR.) art. 1396–4. Legifrance.

[195] *Id.* art. 1369–5.

Validity of an E-Mail Agreement:

Article 1369–7:[196]

Any simple letter related to the conclusion of a contract can be sent by electronic mail.

The indication of the date of issuance will be the result of an electronic procedure that, unless otherwise proven, is deemed trustworthy in accordance with the requirements set forth by the decree issued by the *Conseil d'Etat*.

Acceptance and Acknowledgment of Receipt:

Article 1369–9:[197]

With the exception of the provisions of Articles 1369–1 and 1369–2, the sending of a writing in electronic format shall be effective when the recipient, after becoming aware of it, acknowledges receipt thereof.

If a legal provision requires that the writing be read by its recipient, the sending of an electronic writing to the interested party in the terms specified in the previous paragraph shall have the same effect of a reading by the recipient of the original writing.

b. Judicially-Enforceable Pollicitations

On a similarly positive note, it is encouraging to find that some judicial decisions have significantly enabled the enforcement of Pothier's unenforceable pollicitations in our time. According to the partial compilation of decisions by Dalloz's annotated versions of the *Code Civil,* it appears that these decisions were first handed down during the early 1960's, although it may have happened earlier.[198] The following is a translation of some of Dalloz's selected holdings:[199]

Civ. 3e, 28 no. 1968 Gaz. Pal. 1. 95:

An offer made to the public and advertised binds the offeror [*policitant*] to the first acceptor of the offer in the same terms and conditions as an offer made to a specified person.

Com. 6 Mar. 1990, JCP 1990, note Gross, Rev. trim. Dr.civ. 1990:

Among merchants, a proposal to enter into a contract is not an offer unless it indicates the intent of the offeror to be bound by it if the recipient accepts.

TGI, Paris, 12 Feb. 1990:

The expiration of the term of validity of an offer without it being accepted renders it automatically unenforceable.

In addition, French courts have expressed conflicting opinions on issues related to enforceable pollicitations, *e.g.*, "Does the death of the offeror of a firm offer render it unenforceable?"[200]

---

196 *Id.* art. 1369–7.

197 *Id.* art. 1369–9.

198 C. CIV. (FR.) 714 (Dalloz 1992–93).

199 *Id.*

200 *Id.* (a list of these decisions).

§ 8.10 ILLEGAL *CAUSA* IN AN INSURANCE CONTRACT

Cie d'assurance Le Secours-Vie et Dame. Avenia C. Veuve Guenebaud et Caisse Nationale d'assurances

REPORTER'S TOPICS: Life insurance . . . immoral or illegal cause, nullity of the designation of the beneficiary.[201]

(Insurance Company *Le Secours-Vie* and Mrs. Avenia C. Widow of Guenebaud. . . .)

SUMMARY:

In a life insurance policy where the mistress of the deceased subscriber of the policy—or, in her absence, any of her successors—was designated as the beneficiary to such policy, the trial court held that all designations were affected by nullity because of its immoral cause. Therefore, in the absence of a (valid) designated beneficiary of the policy, the proceeds of the insurance should benefit the estate of the contracting party, in accordance with Article 66 of the Law of July 13, 1930. Further, having determined that the designation of beneficiary was to convince his mistress (a married woman) to commit adultery, and having dismissed the argument of a possible natural obligation of the insured *vis-à-vis* one of the woman's children born during the cohabitation but who had not been repudiated by the husband, the appeal is rejected.

The contractual relationships in a life insurance policy must be considered separately; on the one hand is the relationship between the insured and the beneficiary, and on the other is the relationship between the insured and the insurance company; these two relationships have different legal grounds, thus the nullity of the former will not affect the latter.

Therefore, if a clause designating a mistress as the beneficiary of an insurance policy is considered immoral, it is of no interest if said clause was the cause that motivated and determined the subscription of the insurance policy, which was freely entered into. The validity of the insurance remains undisputed with respect to the relationship between the insured and the insurance company. . . .

FACTS:

A married man, father of two children, had a mistress (twenty years younger than him) who was, herself, separated from her husband. While he was pursuing separation proceedings from his then wife, the mistress met him in Madagascar where he was sent as the engineer for a company. The trial court noted that, for purposes of convincing her to move there and to live with him, he had designated her as the beneficiary of two group insurance policies with the company where he was employed.

After his death, the mistress claimed the proceeds of the relevant insurance policies. The wife-widow of the deceased informed the two insurance companies that she would object to and challenge all payments made to the designated beneficiary. With respect to one insurance company that—notwithstanding the challenge—had made payments to the mistress, the widow maintained that such payments did not discharge the insurer from its obligation, and that the company should pay such proceeds to his lawful heirs, even though this entailed paying these proceeds for a

---

[201] ARRÊTS CIVILE, *supra* note 158, at 707–12. (Cour de cassation [Cass.] 1e civ., Oct. 8, 1957, JCP 1958 II 10234 (Fr.)).

second time. The court of Paris rendered judgment for the complainant.[202] Appeal to the Supreme Court was filed by the designated beneficiary of the policies and the insurance companies.

DECISION:

THE COURT—On the only issue on appeal No. 2394 Civ. 55 and on the first issue on appeal No. 2072 Civ, 55:

Whereas . . . Guenebaud was the holder of two life insurance policies subscribed through his employer, with the National Insurance Company and Secours-Vie, where he designated as beneficiary, in the first policy, his mistress Mrs. Avenia, and in the second policy the same woman "or her successors"; that after Guenebaud's death, his widow informed the insurance companies that she was going to object to and challenge the payment of the proceeds of the insurance policies from the hands of whoever had them; that the payment from Secours-Vie to Mrs. Avenia is still pending and that the payment from the National Insurance Company had already been made in full.

Whereas, the widow of Guenebaud has, acting on her own behalf and in her capacity as natural and legal guardian of her two children, claimed the nullity of the stipulation in favor of Mrs. Avenia because of its immoral and illegal cause, having complained against the decision in favor of the widow (Paris, June 14, 1955) and holding that the proceeds from the insurance policies should benefit the estate of Guenebaud, since at the time of death of the insured. . . their cause was based on an illegal relationship; that the widow has not answered the arguments. . . that the rights in dispute are legal because their purpose is to repair a damage, and that at least one of the contracts must benefit the "successors" in relation to Mrs. Avenia—*i.e.*, her daughter—and in that regard there cannot be an immoral cause;—Further, the Court of Appeals determined from the documents filed that "the designation as beneficiary under both insurance policies was so that Guenebaud could convince Mrs. Avenia—20 years younger than him—to remain with him and to pursue adulterous relations with him"; hence, this was not a reparation of damages with respect to Mrs. Avenia. . . ." that in light of the findings, the court was able to conclude that the entire designation was affected by nullity for having an immoral cause and that, consequently, in the absence of a designated beneficiary, the proceeds of the insurance policies must go to the estate of the insured in accordance with Article 66 of the Law of July 13, 1930. . . .

ANNOTATION BY MR. ESMEIN: This decision discussed the consequences of an immoral cause underlying a life insurance contract. In the contract, the mistress of the insured is designated as the beneficiary. Following well-established case law, a stipulation benefiting a mistress is not null and void for the sole reason that it benefits a mistress. However, if the contracting parties' purpose or goal is either to initiate or to continue an immoral relationship, then the provision will be null based on the fact that its cause is contrary to good moral standards.[203] Additionally, such a clause or provision will not be considered null if it results from the desire of repairing a damage—i.e., to insure the future or the well-being of a person who dedicated part of

---

[202] Cour d'appel [CA] [regional court of appeal] Paris, June 11, 1955, JCP 1955, II, 9303, note Rabut (Fr.).

[203] Cour de cassation [Cass.] Civ., Mar. 26, 1860, D.P. I 253 (Fr.); Cour de cassation [Cass.] Civ., Oct. 14, 1940, D.H. 1940 174 (Fr.).

his/her life to the person who is granting that benefit,[204] in every case of adulterous relations.[205] In the case at bar, the court determined that the contracts were concluded in order to continue with the adulterous relations, and such provision is null. However, the insurance contract subsists (i.e., remains valid) even without a "formal" designation of a beneficiary.

COMMENTS AND QUESTIONS

Increasingly, insurance policies of all types—including life insurance policies—are used for commercial purposes. For example, before a bank makes a loan or extends a line of credit to a for-profit or not-for-profit corporation interested in building its own headquarters, it may require that the corporate borrower take out an insurance policy on the chief executive officer of the corporation and either name the bank or indorse it to it as the beneficiary. Similarly, merchants requesting a line of credit to acquire inventory or equipment for their business are asked to take out a life insurance policy and follow the same procedure just outlined, thereby securing the bank's collection. Alternatively or additionally, they are asked to take out a fire or accidental destruction of the collateral policy, also naming the secured creditor as beneficiary or endorsing the policy to it.

Why do you think that insurance policies have become such popular collateral? Does the present decision help or hinder the secured creditor's ability to collect on the above described policies?

§ 8.11 LESION

A. Related Statutory Law

Appraisal of the Economic Harm (*Lesion*) in a Sale of Real Property:

Article 1675:[206]

In order to determine if there has been a lesion of more than 7/12ths [of the value of real property], it will be necessary to appraise this value in accordance with its condition and value at the time of its sale.

In the case of a unilateral promise of sale, the lesion will be evaluated on the date it was made.

B. Court Decision: *Soc. Économique de Rennes C. Pailleret et al.*[207]

REPORTER'S TOPICS: Sale, Rescission, Lesion, Objective Nature. December 28, 1932.

SUMMARY OF OPINION:

A *lesion* (economic harm) that has been legally verified is, by itself, sufficient reason to rescind a sale, regardless of the circumstances that were related to or that gave rise to such *lesion*.[208]

---

204 Cour de cassation [Cass.] Civ., Mar. 11, 1918, S. Jur. I 1918, 110 (Fr.).

205 Cour de cassation [Cass.] Civ., Oct. 16, 1956, Gaz. Pal. 1956, 2, 306 (Fr.); *see also* Julliot de La Morandière, Vol. II, No. 742.

206 C. CIV. (FR.) 1675.

207 ARRÊTS CIVILE, *supra* note 158, at 617–19.

Consequently, the right of the harmed seller to request the rescission of the contract cannot be conditioned upon the demonstration of a moral constraint and, furthermore, it cannot be invalidated by the buyer's statements to the effect that the sale had been freely consented to.[209]

FACTS:

Mr. Picard had consented to a promise to sell various real estate properties to *Société Économique de Rennes,* and the latter accepted this promise prior to the death of the promissor. The promissor's heirs initiated an action for rescission based on a *lesion* in excess of seven-twelfths [of the value of the property], and such action was granted by a decision of the court of Rennes dated March 6, 1929. The *Société* appealed.

ALLEGED LEGAL BASIS FOR APPEAL:

Violation of Arts. 1674 and 1677 of the *Code Civil,* because the appealed decision granted the action for rescission brought by the seller's heirs disregarding the buyer's proof that the seller had freely consented to the promise to sell without being the subject of any moral or other constraints—and that only the presence of such constraints, given the spirit of the law, would grant the rescission because of *lesion*. . .

DECISION:

THE COURT: [C]onsidering that pursuant to Article 1674 of the *Code Civil,* if the seller has suffered a loss greater than seven-twelfths of the price of an immovable property, he is entitled to apply for the rescission of the sale; that a *lesion* or loss that has been legally verified is in and of itself sufficient reason to rescind a sale regardless of the circumstances that gave rise to such *lesion*; and consequently, given that the decision under appeal verified existing documentation and, pursuant to Article 1677 of the *Code Civil*, the probability and seriousness of the facts stated by the plaintiffs, such reasoned decision does not violate the articles listed as legal basis; on the contrary, it has made correct application of such articles. For these reasons, appeal is denied.

ANNOTATION BY MR. DUMAS: *Lesion* is defined as the harm suffered by a person due to the inequality between the benefits that such person obtains and the sacrifices she/he must make to obtain them. This is an objective definition which disregards the origin of the *lesion* or its results. Should this, however, be the only consideration? Or would it be necessary, in order to accept the validity of a *lesion*, that the court finds that there was an undue influence—e.g., a moral constraint because the seller was in dire need of the money—or there was an intentional act by the potential buyer to mislead the seller into accepting less-than-favorable conditions?

The drafting process that led to the adoption of the *Code Civil* leaves no doubt as to the fact that the drafters related *lesion* with undue influences or other factors that affected a party's consent. Nonetheless, and however pertinent these considerations might be, the Court of Appeals did not take them into account given that, as a matter

---

[208] C. CIV. (FR.) art. 1674: "Where a seller has suffered a loss greater than seven-twelfths of the price of an immovable, he is entitled to apply for the rescission of the sale, even though he may have expressly renounced in the contract the ability to apply for that rescission and had declared his intention to donate the surplus."

[209] C. CIV. (FR.) art. 1677: "Proof of loss may be allowed only through judgment, and in the case only where the facts alleged are probable and serious enough to induce a presumption of loss."

of fact, none of the actual provisions of the *Code Civil* that deal with *lesion* require that the party who suffered the harm prove that she/he had been under an undue influence. It is not for the court to require more than was required by the legislators. This issue became increasingly important following World War I and the dramatic currency devaluation as reflected in this case: the promise to sell took place before the devaluation, but the promise would have materialized following the devaluation. The seller was not subject to any fraud or to any undue influence. The *lesion* stemmed from circumstances beyond the control of the parties. However, it is likely that such circumstances weighed in on the court's decision.

Article 1676 of the *Code Civil* states that the action for rescission due to *lesion* "shall only be admissible within a period of two years starting from the time of the sale."[210] Still, two years is a long time for a buyer-builder or developer not to know whether his acquisition is final, especially in an active real estate market such as France's. The main chapter explained why the drafters of the *Code Civil* deemed it necessary to grant the protection of this remedy. Having read this chapter and these decisions, how would you summarize those reasons, and how much weight would you still ascribe to the protection of the archetypal bourgeois contracting party among these reasons? Are these reasons as valid in a contemporary urban and commercial society as they were in Napoleon's France? How have commercial buyers, sellers, mortgage lenders, builders and developers of real property adjusted to the *lesion* uncertainty? How would you have adjusted to it as counsel in your jurisdiction? When we discuss Imperial China's "conditional sale contracts,"[211] you will find that given the "familistic" nature of that society, the family or, better still, the household was the owner of most of China's rural land. Often, as a result of economic necessity, the family or household had to sell its ancestral land. And unless the contract contained a qualifier such as "irrevocable sale," the sale was deemed revocable by any member of the family who in the future decided that he could pay back the price originally paid by the buyer. This unlimited right of revocation introduced much uncertainty and endless litigation in Chinese courts. Would that be the case in France, despite its relatively short (two-year) statute of limitations?

---

[210] C. CIV. (FR.) art. 1676.

[211] *See infra* § 18:1(B)(1)(a).

Chapter 9

THE BIRTH OF A CONTINENTAL EUROPEAN COMMERCIAL LAW; FAIR AND COMMERCIAL COURTS

§ 9.1 BIRTHMARKS OF A EUROPEAN COMMERCIAL LAW: THE ROLE OF COMMERCIAL COURTS

Hessel Yntema was not only one of the world's leading conflicts of law scholars and an insightful Romanist, but he was also a learned comparative legal historian. On a bright, snowy night in Ann Arbor, Michigan, during one of his unforgettable visits to the office where I was writing my doctoral dissertation, he reflected on when and where European commercial law acquired its distinct features. These features were acquired, according to Yntema, in the Late Middle Ages in cities such as Florence, Genoa, Siena and Venice in Italy, Barcelona in Spain, and Hamburg in Germany. Seminal inland and seafaring ventures took place not only in the above cities and nearby oceans, but also in fairs like those of Champagne in France, Piacenza in Italy, and Medina del Campo in Spain. He added that while German and Northern European Hanseatic league cities and fairs also contributed important features to the emerging commercial law, the Italian cities and the French fairs were the most fertile incubators of Europe's pre-codified commercial law.

Pre-codified law, however, was dispersed, disorganized and contrasted sharply with the nineteenth-century French and German civil and commercial codes. At this stage, I can best describe these French and German codes of the nineteenth century as sets of rules organized by subject matter, following a sequence that reflected the codifiers' perceived socio-economic importance of the various subjects. Their drafting style was guided by formally logical defined legal concepts and by principles associated either with not-for-profit (civil) or for profit (commercial) activities. When I asked Professor Yntema to please suggest readings on the transition from pre-codified to codified commercial law, he said that the list was long, but that I would do well to start with Levin Goldschmidt's *Universalgeschichte des Handelsrechts* for an insightful panorama of medieval commercial law,[1] and with Paul Huvelin's *Essai Historique sur le Droit des Marchés et des Foires*[2] for the same type of description of the European fairs. The following sections summarize the observations of Goldschmidt, Huvelin, and of contemporary legal historians on the emergence of pre-codified commercial law in Europe and on the role of medieval courts.

The courts of the medieval fairs and consular cities were responsible, *inter alia*, for summary legal procedures of claims supported by "self-enforcing" legal instruments

---

[1] LEVIN GOLDSCHMIDT, UNIVERSALGESCHICHTE DES HANDELSRECHTS 117–28 (1891) [hereinafter GOLDSCHMIDT, HANDELSRECHTS]. *See also* LEVIN GOLDSCHMIDT, STORIA UNIVERSALE DEL DIRITTI COMMERCIALE 23 (V. Pourchain & A. Torino trans., 1913) (an Italian translation).

[2] PAUL HUVELIN, ESSAI HISTORIQUE SUR LE DROIT DES MARCHES ET DES FOIRES (1897).

such as bills of exchange and other writings that acknowledged the obligations of merchants in summary fashion (*scripta obligatoria*). Fairs s and consular courts also helped identify the nature of the commercial transactions heard by them by often referring disputes that involved criminal conduct or non-commercial transactions to other city or provincial courts.

The commercial exclusivity of the jurisdiction of fair courts was echoed, centuries later, in the listing of the "acts of commerce" (*actes de commerce)* by France's *Code de Commerce* of 1807 side-by-side in this code with its rules on the competence and jurisdiction of commercial courts.[3]

The French approach to the codification of commercial law influenced other European and non-European civil law nations such as, among others, Belgium and Argentina. These countries defer the adjudication of commercial disputes to commercial courts which apply their commercial codes only to the acts of commerce listed in them. The adoption of this "objective" approach was another instance in which the life of the law was, Justice Oliver Wendell Holmes Jr. notwithstanding, neither logic nor the product of experience.[4] Whoever thinks of commercial law (and commercial codes) as the products of a strictly logical discipline that applies to transactions easily discernible as acts of commerce has a surprise coming. He or she will find out soon in this chapter that beneath the purported logical rigor lies a human story with shades of greed and passion as in the eighteenth-century French commercial court's "Red Ink" case.[5] He or she will also find out in Chapter 10 how unrealistic and arbitrary can be the application of the acts of commerce criterion by commercial and non-commercial courts alike.[6]

Unfortunately, many interpreters continue to treat the acts of commerce listed in these codes as if they were magical formulas capable of discerning immediately which transactions are "commercial" and governed by the commercial code and which are "civil" and thus governed by the *Code Civil.* This type of interpretation occurred, and continues to occur, without paying attention to why the French codifiers and Napoleon himself were so keen on preventing non-merchants from becoming subject to the same rules as merchants, especially when the non-merchants were not involved in "acts of commerce."

Simply put, Napoleon's favorite citizen was not the merchant but, the bourgeois. Consequently, the reason for listing acts of commerce *was not as much to exclude unlisted commercial transactions from a commercial or commercial-like treatment, as assumed by many to this day, but to prevent the application of code rules to non-merchants.*

This datum explains provisions such as Mexico's Article 385 of its Commercial Code of 1889, which prevents parties to commercial sales from resorting to remedies

---

[3] C. COM. (FR.) art. 1 (1807) (*"Sont commerçants ceux qui exercent des actes de commerce, et en font leur profession habituelle."*) ("Merchants are those who practice acts of commerce as part of their habitual profession.") (author's translation).

The detailed description of the acts of commerce is found in Articles 18 and 19 of the section devoted to the competence and jurisdiction of commercial courts.

[4] *See* OLIVER WENDALL HOLMES, JR., THE COMMON LAW 1 (1881).

[5] *See infra* § 9:2(E)(3)(c).

[6] *See infra* § 10:2.

available to non-merchant sellers of land under the *Code Civil*.[7] According to Article 385, a buyer who is a party to a commercial sale cannot rescind the contract because he paid a price for the goods that exceeds the market value of the goods and thus suffers an economic loss (*lesion*). In contrast, in accordance with Article 1674 of the *Code Civil* (which introduced to the codified world the doctrine of *lesion* as a ground for rescission in the sale of real property), a French landowner who sells his real property for a price that "harms" him economically can petition the court for a rescission of his sale agreement. Please note the significance of the status of the parties and the object of their sale in both provisions. Article 385 of the Mexican Commercial Code is directed at merchants or regular participants in commercial sales, and the principal object of their contract was personal property. Article 1674 of the *Code Civil* is directed at a landowner as seller of real property and its purpose is to protect him from a bad bargain that involved the *Code Civil*'s most valuable asset.

A. Merchant Associations and Consular Courts

As will be recalled, by the twelfth century, associations of merchants had begun to form guilds to control prices and competition.[8] These guilds became powerful as trade in the Mediterranean and across Europe increased. Some, such as those in Genoa, Florence, and Siena, also became dominant in their associations with local governments.[9] In due course, a number of these guild and city-state inspired principles found their way into the European commercial codes of the nineteenth century. As noted by the legal historian Frederic Rockwell Sanborn: "On the one side, in Germany, in northern France, and in England we behold a development of the law through the medium of the fair, while on the other side, in Italy and in southern France, the law is developed in the medieval city state."[10]

B. The Statutes of Mostly Italian Commercial Cities and Consulates

Italy's medieval city-states were heavily engaged in maritime trade with the Middle East, Africa and the Orient. Goldschmidt traces to this maritime trade distinctly commercial legal principles such as: the division of risks among investors and active partners; the methods for allocating profits and management functions especially in partnerships of the *commenda* type; the reliance on double-entry bookkeeping; the allocation of risks in maritime transportation contracts; the binding language of negotiable instruments such as bills of exchange often in a manner

---

[7] *See, e.g.*, Código de Comercio [CCo.] [Commercial Code] art. 385, as amended, Diario Oficial de la Federación [DO] 13 de Diciembre de 1889 (Mex.) ("Commercial sales shall not be rescinded because of lesion. . . .") (author's translation). On the action or defense of lesion, *see infra* ch. 27. *But see* C. Civ. (FR.) art. 1674 ("If a seller was harmed by selling real property for less than seven twelves of its price, he has the right to rescind the contract even though he waived scuch a claim in the sale agreement. . . .").

[8] *See supra* § 6:1.

[9] When I first visited a still largely medieval Siena, aside from being struck by the beauty of its city square, I was impressed by the imposing city hall building whose constituents and officials were mostly merchants. Its size and solidity clearly attempted to match, in importance and lay power, the nearby cathedral.

[10] *See* FREDERIC ROCKWELL SANBORN, ORIGINS OF THE EARLY ENGLISH MARITIME AND COMMERCIAL LAW 127 (1930).

independent from the underlying transaction; and so on.[11] All of this was part of an emerging "corporate commercial law" in the broadest sense of this term.[12]

This corporate commercial law was patterned after a democratic city government in which merchants had a preponderant voice. In fact, as pointed out by Huvelin and Sanborn, since many of these cities were established by the merchants as outgrowths of their markets, their corporations and the municipal bodies in which they participated as citizens resembled each other.[13] In Sanborn's words, "[t]he market was the first franchise granted to the old [merchant] groups, and the right of doing business was the first liberty. From this there developed a privileged situation for these groups, and the organization of the market was the embryo of the organization of the city."[14]

Some of the most commercially-minded cities distinguished between the status of major corporations (often organized as guilds) and minor official corporations.[15] In addition to craftsmen, guilds included merchants and bankers (*cambiatores, campsores nummularii, banchieri, tabulari*) as well as their notaries and physicians. These commercial associations were presided over by an elected *consul* who occasionally also acted as the city's mayor (*podestá*). For his decision-making, the *consul* relied on elected administrative and judicial magistrates whose number varied with the size of the association.[16]

As with the cities, the commercial associations were governed by statutes (*statuta mercatorum*), many of which were enacted between the thirteenth and sixteenth centuries by the municipality (*statuti letti nell' adunanza generale*).[17] The standard of commercial behavior expressed in these statutes was clear. It expected that association members be sworn to "obey their magistrates and behave in a scrupulous and orderly manner" (*condotta scrupolosa e ordinata*).[18]

There were different types of commercial statutes. Some were of general application to all merchants (*dei commerciante in generale*) and were often labeled as "consular" statutes.[19] Other statutes were directed at specialized merchants or guilds (*corporazione* or *gilde*), colonial ventures (*statuti coloniali*), or maritime ventures (*diritti marittimi*).[20]

C. Consular Tribunals

The administration of justice for disputes involving members of a commercial association was carried out by the president or consul and chosen association representatives usually in the premises of the association (*domus-curia mercatorum,*

[11] GOLDSCHMIDT, *supra* note 1, at 117–28.

[12] *Id.* at 117–28.

[13] SANBORN, *supra* note 10, at 172; HUVELIN, *supra* note 2, at 211–13.

[14] SANBORN, *supra* note 10, at 173.

[15] GOLDSCHMIDT, *supra* note 1, at 128–29.

[16] *Id.* at 132–33.

[17] *Id.* at 135.

[18] *Id.* at 133.

[19] Examples include the *Breve Consulum Mercatorum* (Pisa), the *Capitolare dei Consoli di Mercanti* (Venezia), or the *Capitolare dei Sopraconsoli* (Verona). *Id.* at 135.

[20] *Id.* at 136.

casa de la mercanzia dei mercanti). In some cases, these tribunals had an exclusive jurisdiction; in others, they shared it with regular courts.[21]

Generally, the *statuta mercatorum* did not require that the judge or judges (whose number varied with the importance of the case) be legally trained. Certain technical legal issues requiring specialized knowledge could be referred to legally-trained judges or experts (*consilium sapientis*).[22] Nonetheless, the procedures were generally conducted by lay judges. Formalities, including the keeping of records of the proceedings, were entrusted to notaries who, during the trial, ostensibly acted as *consiglieri* to the judge or judges.[23]

Goldschmidt emphasizes that these consular courts were not intended to serve as commercial courts, or as courts for any and all disputes among merchants or among merchants and their lay customers. They were designed as disciplinary tribunals or as our present professional misconduct boards in charge of policing the conduct of the members of the respective associations. And, even in that limited capacity, many acts or transactions were subject to the jurisdiction of ordinary tribunals, especially those that entailed the commission of crimes or required the imposition of fines or imprisonment.[24] Therefore, their jurisdiction was not always clear, as it could only be defined as pertaining generally to proper corporate conduct (*materia di corporazione* or *causa quae ad artem pertinet*).[25]

The procedure before consular courts was summary, including the possibility of compulsory arbitration in cities such as Genoa, where the consular-judicial procedure was not fully developed.[26] Summary procedures, whether before consular or regular courts, were common in Italy starting in the thirteenth century. Their main features were set forth in *Dispendiosam de iudicii*, a 1306 *Decretal* by Pope Clement the Fifth: Judges had to hand out justice plainly, and without artifice or devoid of long and clamorous adjudication (*de plano ac sine figura et longo strepitu iudicii*).[27] Unlike their ecclesiastical counterparts, whose pleading and proof were mostly in writing and filed with and read secretly by the judges, some of the proceedings in these commercial courts were oral and in open court. Evidence, on the other hand, continued to be largely dependent upon private writings and entries made by association members in their books and records. Defenses, especially against claims supported by acceptable writings, were also limited to those specified by statute.

Beginning in the fourteenth century, attachment and foreclosure procedures became widespread and could be supported by private, non-notarial documents provided they were executed and signed by the debtor. Occasionally, commercial books and records could lead to attachment and execution of the assets of the defendant.[28] Appeals were, in many instances, unavailable or highly restricted. They could be made to the higher corporate authorities such as the "super consuls" (*sopraconsoli*) or to the

---

[21] *Id.* at 137.

[22] *Id.*

[23] *Id.* at 138.

[24] *Id.* at 138–39.

[25] *Id.* at 139.

[26] *Id.* at 142.

[27] *Id.* at 139–40. *See also* HUVELIN, *supra* note 2, at 417–18.

[28] GOLDSCHMIDT, *supra* note 1, at 141.

association. Finally, where insolvency was concerned, the consular tribunals had developed what Goldschmidt described as a middle approach, or *via de mezzo*, "between the humane and perhaps excessively relaxed treatment of insolvent debtors in Justinian Roman law and the rough and often cruel provisions of Germany's law of obligations."[29]

D. The Consulates of the Sea (*Consulatus Maris*)

The Consulates of the Sea, mostly located in European port cities, had diverse functions. In some ports, they acted as administrative agencies issuing sailing permits, certifying merchandise as exportable, and issuing other port and customs regulations. In others, they enjoyed judicial powers, thus sitting in disputes among seagoing or homecoming merchants. A third group of consulates, such as the Consulate of Pisa, combined these functions.[30]

Catalonians take pride in a 1494 compilation of commercial maritime and port regulations associated with their Barcelona Sea Consulate. It is referred to by some writers as the *Consolato del Mare*, and it supposedly was the most important compilation of pre-codification European maritime commercial law.[31] Yet, its title, authorship and scope are all uncertain. Some authors characterized this compilation as being confined to the law of the sea and only in times of war while others, based upon better historical sources, attributed to it a much broader scope.[32]

If its scope were as large as the latter writers thought, it encompassed, among other subjects, the following: marine loans, the construction and the buying and selling of vessels, bills of lading, and responsibility for shipped cargo, including proportional sharing of liability among the shippers for the captain's decision to throw cargo

---

[29] *Id.* at 142.

[30] *Id.* at 143.

[31] *See generally* Stanley S. Jados, *Consulate of the Sea and Related Documents* (Aug. 1974), *available at* http://libro.uca.edu/consulate/preface.htm (discussing the *Consolato del Mare*).

[32] *See generally* CONSOLATO DEL MARE (Guiseppe Lorenzo Maria Casaregis ed., 1720). For example, Hannis Taylor, a United States lawyer, diplomat and writer of controversial legal treatises who was appointed Minister or Ambassador to Spain in 1893 during President Grover Cleveland's administration, stated, in his review of important Spanish legal compilations, that one of the most important of these publications was the *Consolato del Mare*, which he said was "probably compiled not later than the fourteenth century by order of the magistrates of Barcelona, the chief seat of the maritime tribunals of Catalonia. In it is contained the earliest collections of the laws and customs of the sea *in time of war*." HANNIS TAYLOR, THE SCIENCE OF JURISPRUDENCE 162–63 (1908) (emphasis added). In contrast, according to Stanley S. Jados, the *Consolato*, to which he refers as the "Consulate of the Sea," was published in a Latin Romance dialect. Jados, *supra* note 31. Its text was inspired by maritime laws traceable to the Phoenicians and the Greeks; its scope far exceeded the laws and customs of navigation in times of war. *Id.* Phoenician maritime law statutes adopted by the Isle of Rhodes and known (unjustifiably according to Mr. Jados) as the Rhodian laws contributed to the contents of the *Consolato* as did some Northern European laws. *Id.* Among the other antecedents quoted by Mr. Jados were Customs of the City of Amalfitina, "written and proclaimed in the year of Our Lord 1010. A second codification was published in 1063 in the city of Trani. In 1509, an edited copy of the Ordinances of Trani of 1063 was incorporated into the statutes of the city of Fermo." *Id.* Baltic and North Seas cities such as Riga, Wisby, Hamburg, Lübeck and other cities of the Hanseatic League adopted some of these laws as early as the ninth century and published them:

> [I]n the thirteenth and fourteenth centuries under the auspices of the Hanseatic League, under the title *Waterrecht*, following a conference of League members in 1407. These compilations were usually referred to as the Laws of Wisby. In the thirteenth century, the Laws of Oléron were promulgated by Louis IX, (1226–1270) king of France. The British *Black Book of the Admiralty* also dates its beginning to the middle thirteenth century. All these compilations contributed significantly to the later formation of internationally acceptable maritime law.

Id.

overboard in order to save the ship and the remainder of the cargo (later referred to in maritime law as "general average").[33] It also prescribed methods of electing the Consuls of the Sea and Judges of Appeal, their jurisdiction, and procedural regulations regarding the adjudication of cases brought before them.[34]

§ 9.2 FAIR COURTS AND THE UNIFICATION OF EUROPEAN COMMERCIAL LAW

In addition to the law that emerged from commercial associations and from the consular tribunals, including the consulates of the sea, the third and most important contributor to European pre-codified commercial law was the large fairs—especially those in the Champagne region of France and in Piacenza, Italy. At this point, the reader would be well advised to re-read Braudel's short description of the various types of fairs and transactions conducted in them.[35]

The uniformity of pre-codified commercial law ("merchant law") owes a great debt to these fairs. In Huvelin's words:

> We owe to the fairs of Champagne in addition to the *rapprochement* between the commercial worlds of France and Germany . . . the encounter of the commercial interests from the entire European continent. Thanks to the fairs, groups of merchants could deal with each other governed by the same enforceable law and under the same tribunals. A central authority existed to which the merchants of all nations could demand, successfully in many cases, protection against overreaching attempts by other merchants intent on applying their local law. This is a fact whose historical importance is unsurpassed by any other in the development of the commercial law of the middle ages. . . .[36]

A. The Early Courts and the Peace of the Market

Policing the fairs so that peace could prevail among participants and visitors was a dual function: One was to keep what Huvelin referred to as the "material" peace,[37] *i.e.*, the prevention or repression of altercations, thievery, assaults, and so on. It also entailed inspecting stores, booths, and the lodgings of merchants to ascertain compliance with fair rules and to assure the safety of the merchants' journeys. The other policing function had to do with adjudicating the many disputes among merchants, money exchangers, lenders and their assistants. This function led to the creation of the "Peace of the Market," a legal institution which has since been associated with European markets and fairs:

> The city was thought to be a permanent market, and the truce of the market became a true peace, justice being available at all times, instead of at certain times. The original peace of the market extended beyond the market's boundaries. . . . to the homes of the merchants, just as it went still further away to the doors of those coming from or going to the markets. . . . The

[33] Jados, *supra* note 31, at 7.

[34] *Id.*

[35] *See supra* § 6:2(F)(4).

[36] HUVELIN, *supra* note 2, at 258.

[37] *Id.* at 392.

> market cross was the traditional symbol of this peace, both in the market and, later, in the city. From this special peace of both market and city it resulted that even the legitimate authorities could not interfere to make arrests for offences committed or debts contracted elsewhere. There was created a true right of asylum, just as in the early fairs. . . . There was a special law of the markets . . . [that] made no distinction between persons, in the interests of commerce, free or servile, villain or noble.[38]

Fairs succeeded in attracting merchants from near and far because, as put by the French legal historian Jean Brissaud:

> Feudalism did not recognize freedom of trade and industry. . . . [In fact, it did everything within its power to erect barriers against trade by imposing all sorts of taxes, duties, tolls, tallies, etc.] Markets and fairs could not be held without a special peace which the public authority (king, seignior, church, or commune, depending on the place) assured by means of heavy penalties. . . . The merchants who attended obtained a safe-conduct or safeguard while they were going and returning. . . . They were drawn to the fairs by exemptions from transit dues (such as tolls, etc.) and from taxes collected on the occasion of sales of merchandise. . . . They were subject neither to escheat dues . . . nor to the right of *marque and reprisal by virtue of which merchants were stopped and their goods seized for the offenses or debts of their fellow citizens or of their seigniors—debts or offenses of whose existence they often had no suspicion; they even enjoyed freedom from arrest, that is, their creditors could neither imprison them nor attach their goods for previous debts or offenses*.[39]

Maintaining the peace of the fair was the function of the Guard or Guards of the Fair (*Custodes Nundinarum*), a term used in official documents for the first time in 1174 in connection with the great fairs of Champagne.[40] Their custodial function resulted from a gradual delegation of jurisdictional powers, first by the feudal count, and later on (as when Champagne was united to France) by the king. This official power was eventually delegated to a special commercially-based jurisdiction (*jurisdiction de marchands et des marches*).[41]

B. Contributions of Early Fair Courts: Permanent Effects of "Peace of the Market," Summary Trials and Equal Treatment

Levin Goldschmidt pointed to the connection between the "Peace of the Market" and the personal nature of medieval law.[42] Itinerant or traveling merchants "carried their law on their backs" and could not claim the protection of the laws of the towns and fairs they visited to do business. This created the possibility of imprisonment or death resulting from the imposition of confiscatory penalties under local law or practice

---

[38] SANBORN, *supra* note 10, at 173 (citations omitted). *See also* GOLDSCHMIDT, *supra* note 1, at 129–30.

[39] JEAN BRISSAUD, A HISTORY OF FRENCH PUBLIC LAW 236, 245–46 (James W. Garner ed., Little, Brown, and Co. 1915) (emphasis added) (citations omitted).

[40] HUVELIN, *supra* note 2, at 390–91.

[41] *Id.* Fair guards were appointed for a period of one year, but later they held office for longer periods, though they could be removed from office for misconduct. *Id.* The number of guards per fair fluctuated yearly from one to three per fair, although generally they were two in number. *Id.* Usually, they were feudal knights (*chevaliers*) or merchants (bourgeois). *Id.*

[42] GOLDSCHMIDT, *supra* note 1, at 31–32.

against defaulting foreign debtors and their compatriots, regardless of the relationship between those compatriots and the defaulting debtors. Often, a debt owed by someone in the foreign trader's home country—unrelated as that other debtor was to the foreign trader present in the host country fair—could be collected from the foreigner present at the fair by any means.

The "Peace of the Market" entitled the foreign trader to a legal treatment equal to that given to national or local merchants. This is the same equal or "national" treatment granted to merchants and their products by the post-Second World War General Agreement on Tariffs and Trade (GATT) and its progeny, such as the World Trade Organization (WTO) and regional agreements such as the North American or the Central American Free Trade Agreements (NAFTA and CAFTA, respectively).[43] Thus, the principle of equal or national treatment, as derived from the medieval "Peace of the Market," has become a cornerstone of contemporary free trade treaties, bi-national as well as multinational.

The early Fair Courts also contributed expeditious judicial or quasi-judicial remedies, especially with respect to foreclosure and execution of acknowledged commercial debts. Some of these remedies were delegated to fair guards. The judicial powers of the guards were enhanced by their designation as keepers of the fairs' seals, an important attribution because most contracts had to be sealed by the guard of the fair. This meant that the guards had jurisdiction over contracts executed at the fair. It also meant that letters, signed by fair guards and with the fairs' seals that requested attachment or sale and foreclosure of assets, could be executed throughout France.[44] Similarly, the letters by the "captains" of Italian commercial associations doing business abroad were entitled to execution against the assets of the member of the association when located in Italy.[45] A fair court decision certified under the seal of the fair was enforceable for thirty years on the goods of the debtor, though the debtor could not be imprisoned after the lapse of one year of the issuance of the decision.[46]

Fairs such as that of Champagne also popularized the use of commercial statutory liens, *i.e.*, liens imposed by statute upon the goods or estate of a commercial debtor in default of his obligations. According to Huvelin, the goods of a debtor were subject to overreaching or "exorbitant" liens under the laws applicable to transactions outside the fairs.[47] Yet, creditors who claimed similar remedies under fair rules had to share their liens on a *pro rata* basis with other creditors of the same fair.[48] This rule fashioned by fair courts also embodied the principle of equality of treatment, a crucial principle in our contemporary treatment of secured creditors and creditors of an insolvent or bankrupt debtor.[49] Similarly, fairs influenced an important institution of the contemporary law of insolvency and creditor-debtor arrangements of "compositions": If a majority of an insolvent debtor's creditors agreed on a monetary or in-kind arrangement with the debtor that released him from liability (*compositio*), this arrangement bound minority creditors.

---

[43] Kozolchyk, *Grand and Small Scheme*, at 137.

[44] HUVELIN, *supra* note 2, at 479.

[45] *See infra* § 9:2(C).

[46] HUVELIN, *supra* note 2, at 475.

[47] *Id.* at 481.

[48] *Id.* at 483.

[49] *Id.* at 489.

The extent of the participation of merchants as judges in the early fair courts has not been fully established. Huvelin finds references to "guards of the fairs and other notables" as members of the fair courts. This would indicate the presence of at least some merchants as judges. At the same time, however, he finds many references in records of proceedings to the absenteeism of guards, and to the imposition of the requirement that guards and adjudicators be subject to a minimum time of compulsory residence in the fairs.[50] As will be discussed shortly, with the decay of feudalism, fair courts became increasingly commercial tribunals.

C. The Post-Fifteenth-Century Fair Courts: Consulates and Commercial Courts

Please recall[51] that the Italian consular tribunals owed their existence to commercial associations. These associations developed a close commercial relationship in France with French merchants of the *Provence* region. The *Societas et Communitas Mercatorum de Francia* was one of the most active French associations in France's commerce with Italy during the thirteenth century and was comprised mostly of merchants from the Montpellier, Provence region.[52] The Montpellier consulate was in charge of naming the head of this association and gave him the title of "captain" (*Capitaneus in Francia et in nundinis Companie*).

As with the Italian commercial associations described by Professor Goldschmidt,[53] the captains and consuls of the French association wielded essentially disciplinary, albeit very broad, powers over members of their association. At the same time, however, a 1278 treaty between France and a number of Italian city-states conferred the right upon Italian merchants to be judged in France in accordance with their own law by their *capitanei, rectores e consules.*[54]

While the number of captains was limited to only one for the entire (Italian or French) association, there could be multiple consuls, each possessing jurisdictional power over the community under his direction. Thus, for example, the powerful Florentine association of drapery merchants had two consuls at the fairs of Champagne.[55] However, it should be emphasized that their jurisdiction depended on the nationality of the persons involved (*ratione personae*). If the judgment were against an Italian member of the association, the captain of the association could enforce the judgment in Italy. If it were against a local merchant, then only the fair's guard could determine its execution under local law.[56]

This power vested upon the guard of the French fair completed the evolutionary process toward a commercial type of adjudication, a process lead by merchants or their representatives. For, as with the procedure in the Italian consular or commercial association courts, the procedure in the fair courts in France was "plain and without delay, without drama or long judicial carryings on" ("*de plano, ac sine figura et longo*

---

[50] *Id.* at 394.

[51] *See supra* § 9:1(A) & (B).

[52] HUVELIN, *supra* note 2, at 398–99.

[53] *See supra* § 9:1(A) & (B).

[54] HUVELIN, *supra* note 2, at 399.

[55] *Id.* at 400.

[56] *Id.* at 401.

strepitu iudici").[57] Huvelin cites the example of a request by the *Consulat* of Lyons that its "short robed" judges replace the "long robed" judges of the ordinary courts in fair commercial disputes. The justification offered for this request was that the procedure followed by regular judges was notoriously lengthy because these non-merchant judges "associate[d] the length of their procedure with their prestige as judges."[58]

The Europeanization of this procedure was prompted by the presence in French, Italian and Spanish fairs of merchants from the entire continent and beyond. When disputes arose among them, treaties that provided for adjudication based upon the respective national laws did not apply either because such laws did not exist or, if they existed, most of the disputants were not members of national commercial associations such as those of the Italians, who had signed treaties of "national treatment." The only available forum was that of the fairs and their courts for "dusty feet" litigants.

D. The Contribution of Consular and Fair Courts

The following summary was insightfully penned by the late Professor Rudolf Schlesinger and his co-authors Hans W. Baade, Peter E. Herzog, and Edward M. Wise:

> The procedure of these merchants' courts was fair, rational and expeditious, in sharp contrast both to the primitive forms of trial (battle, ordeal, or wager of law . . . and to the delays and subtleties of canonistic procedure which in non-commercial matters dominated procedural thinking on the continent from the middle ages until the 19th century. The main characteristics of the substantive law which was created by the commercial courts, were emphasis on freedom of contract and on freedom of alienability of movable property, both tangible and intangible; abrogation of legal technicalities; and most importantly, a tendency to decide cases *ex aequo et bono* rather than by abstract scholastic deductions from Roman texts. No wonder, then, that commercial law was a highly successful institution.[59]

I would only add that a standard *of desirable commercial conduct* (or best commercial practices) was already required by the consular tribunals that heard disputes involving Italian commercial associations. It will be recalled that members of these associations were sworn to obey their consuls and magistrates and *to behave in a scrupulous and orderly manner*.

E. The Successors of the Fair Courts: The French Commercial Courts and Their Failed Promise

1. Consular and Commercial Courts

Towards the end of the sixteenth century, fair courts gradually merged with consular courts, broadening their jurisdiction and increasing their reliance on lay (merchant) judges. In doing this, the expanded fair courts became the ancestors of France's modern commercial courts. As succinctly put by Sanborn: "Finally, the merchants succeeded in getting the jurisdiction of the fair into their own hands."[60]

---

[57] *Id.* at 418.

[58] *Id.* at 419.

[59] RUDOLF B. SCHLESINGER, ET AL., COMPARATIVE LAW 278 (6th ed. 1998) (citations omitted).

[60] SANBORN, *supra* note 10, at 171.

France's commercial-consular courts received their official approval with the enactment of a Royal Decree of December of 1563 by Charles IX. At the instigation of Chancellor Michel de l'Hospital, this decree created the Consular or Merchant courts of Paris and Bordeaux, among other cities.[61] The justification for these courts was that they were to serve "for the public good and the shortening of all suits and differences between merchants."[62] Some merchant courts had jurisdiction over only inland commercial disputes; others, like Nice's Consulate, had jurisdiction over both inland and admiralty disputes.[63] Among other powers, these courts could decree fines or imprisonment, especially with respect to the non-payment of negotiable instruments.[64]

In 2004, Professor Amalia D. Kessler of Stanford University Law School published a thoroughly researched and revealing description of the decisions and *modus operandi* of the Parisian commercial court during the eighteenth century.[65] This court (which she refers to as the Merchant Court and which I will refer to as the commercial court) consisted of one judge and four consuls, all of whom had decision-making powers as members of the *jurisdiction consulaire de Paris*.[66] "The judge and consuls were lay merchants elected on an annual basis through a procedure that, although varying slightly over time, accorded the leading Parisian guilds a prominent role."[67]

The procedure of the commercial court was summary, *i.e.*, it lasted days instead of months or years as was the case in civil and ecclesiastical courts. The commercial court resolved disputes between merchants and occasionally between merchants and non-merchants. It decided, *inter alia*, actions based on bills of exchange, even though one or more parties to these bills were non-merchants.[68] These summary actions inspired the *acciones ejecutivas* (actions based on self-enforcing documents) of the Spanish and Latin American nineteenth-century commercial codes.[69] Typically, these actions enabled the attachment of the defendant's property at the time of the filing of the complaint and certain trustworthy documents as "a conservatory measure."[70] This

---

[61] *See* Michel Bochaca, *The Courts of Bordeaux Competent on Matters of Merchandise before the Creation of the Consular Court (from the mid-15th to mid-16th Century)*, 17 REVUE HISTOIRE DE LA JUSTICE (2007), abstract *available at* http://www.afhj.fr/publications/RHJ17_abstracts.pdf. *See also* Jean Hilaire, *Introduction: The Commercial Jurisdiction from a Historical Viewpoint*, 17 REVUE HISTOIRE DE LA JUSTICE (2007), abstract *available at* http://www.afhj.fr/publications/RHJ17_abstracts.pdf.

[62] IX THE CAMBRIDGE MODERN HISTORY 176 (A. W. Ward, G. W. Prothero & Stanley Leathes eds., 1907) [hereinafter CAMBRIDGE HISTORY].

[63] *Id.* at 176–77.

[64] *See infra* ch. 10 on the drafting of the *Code de Commerce*.

[65] Amalia D. Kessler, *Enforcing Virtue: Social Norms and Self-Interest in an Eighteenth-Century Merchant Court*, 22 LAW & HIST. REV. 71 (2004) [hereinafter Kessler, *Enforcing Virtue*]; *see generally* AMALIA D. KESSLER, A REVOLUTION IN COMMERCE: THE PARISIAN MERCHANT COURT AND THE RISE OF COMMERCIAL SOCIETY IN EIGHTEENTH-CENTURY FRANCE (2007). *See also* G. DENIÈRE, LA JURISIDICTION CONSULAIRE DE PARIS, 1563–1792 (1872), *cited in* Kessler, *Enforcing Virtue,* at 80 n.36.

[66] Kessler, *Enforcing Virtue*, *supra* note 65, at 80. As noted by Kessler, the roles of the "judge and consul differed only in that the former served as the court's chief judge or as its administrative head." *Id.*

[67] *Id.*

[68] SANBORN, ORIGINS, *supra* note 10, at 171. It should be recalled from *supra* chs. 9 & 11 that bills of exchange were not merely instruments of payment, but also of credit and were a commonly-used device to circumvent the prohibition against usury.

[69] *See infra* ch. 25.

[70] *Id.*

characterization of the bill of exchange carried over to the list of acts of commerce in the *Code de Commerce* of 1807 and its progeny.[71]

Bankruptcy disputes were also adjudicated by these courts. However, the ample protection the eighteenth-century courts afforded to bourgeois landowners and creditors contrasted sharply with the minimal protection afforded to secured commercial creditors. It took a major social upheaval in the following century for the secured claims of these merchants to be protected by the newly-enacted bankruptcy law.

Adjudication by the commercial courts was based on the following procedural principles: (1) Judges must be competent in commercial matters; (2) Proceedings must be simple and summary; and (3) Court decisions must be enforced quickly.[72] Despite the consistency of these features with the manner in which business must be conducted in active marketplaces, the French commercial court, a direct descendant of the fair courts, contributed considerably less than its ancestors to a commercial law consistent with the needs of the marketplace.

Take, for example, a subject as vital to commercial intercourse as secured credit: The eighteenth-century commercial court failed to do anything to help modernize the two devices which French law inherited from Roman law, namely, the pledge (*gage*) for personal property security, and the mortgage (*hypothèque*) for real estate lending.[73] In contrast, German judges, whose law was equally (if not more) influenced by the Roman pledge (*pignus*), adapted instead a variant of the *constitutum possessorium* which enables a fiduciary transfer of the pledged assets to the creditor but allows the debtors to remain in possession of them.[74]

Hence, for reasons that will be discussed in detail in the following sections, French commercial law judges, unlike their counterparts in other European jurisdictions such as Germany and England, contributed little to the modernization of commercial law.

---

[71] *See infra* § 10:1(A).

[72] Fabien Valente, *The Consular Courts in the Napoleonic Commercial Code*, 17 REVUE HISTOIRE DE LA JUSTICE, (2007), abstract *available at* http://www.afhj.fr/publications/RHJ17_abstracts.pdf (abstract on file with author).

[73] *See L'ordonnance 2005–171 du 24 février 2005 simplifiant les procédures de constitution et de réalisation des contrats de garantie financière* [Ordinance No. 2005–171 of February 24, 2005 Simplifying Procedures of Formation and Realization of Financial Collateral], JOURNAL OFFICIEL DE LA REPUBLIQUE FRANÇAISE [J.O.] [OFFICIAL GAZETTE OF FRANCE], Feb. 25, 2005, p. 3252:

> *Traditionnellement, le droit français permet le recours à des garanties sous la forme de sûretés réelles sans transfert de propriété (nantissement) principalement sous la forme d'un gage. Le mécanisme du gage présente toutefois un formalisme assez lourd pour sa constitution, nécessitant un acte écrit et une dépossession réelle du débiteur, ainsi qu'une certaine lourdeur dans la mise en œuvre (enchère, intervention du juge). Dans le secteur financier, ces exigences sont rédhibitoires notamment lorsqu'il s'agit de garantir des transactions opérées sur les marchés financiers.*
>
> Traditionally, French law allows the use of *in rem* guarantees without conveying ownership (to the creditor) principally in the form of a pledge. The mechanism of the pledge requires a burdensome formalism requiring a written document and the *in rem* dispossession of the debtor, similarly it overburdens the transaction by (requiring a judicial intervention) in the creation of this guarantee. These requirements inhibit the operations of the financial sector.

(author's translation).

[74] Based upon pre-existing case law, BGB § 223(2) provided that a right may be transferred to secure a claim. This was, in effect, a modern-day adaptation of the Roman *constitutum possessorium*. In German lending practice, this device was used for more than a century under the name of *Sicherungsubertragung*. *See* BGB § 223(2).

This failure remained well into the twentieth century. Take a subject as important to France's local and international trade as commercial letters of credit. Writing in 1957, Dean Jean Stoufflet, France's leading authority on this subject, stated: "We shall see during the course of our study that a large number of issues that have never been decided by French judges have been the subject of decisions by United States and English judges."[75]

2. *Obstacles to a Market-Based Case Law*

If the guiding procedural principles of the commercial court were consistent with commercial needs, what was the obstacle in the way of a more commercially creative role? Could the court's adjudicative policies be responsible for its shortcomings? French legal historians have recently focused on the contrasting values of the commercial court and the marketplace. Professor Silvie Humbert, for example, suggests that the values of the merchant courts conflicted with those of the marketplace and this conflict did not evolve over time, but was apparent from the creation of these courts in the sixteenth century and was present during Honore de Balzac's time (1799–1850).[76] Balzac's novel *Cesar Birotteau*, about a merchant who was also a consular judge, illustrates the central character's awareness "from the beginning [his appointment that] the notions of trade and justice [and] of merchant and judge [in him] seemed to conflict. . . ."[77]

Similarly, Professor Hubert Bonin points to the conflict of an "unrestrained" version of building capitalism vs. a socially aware version of commerce.[78] He refers to the guilt in France associated with doing business as a common characteristic of our country, a feeling he traces to the time of the French Revolution.[79] These views find considerable support in the work of Professor Kessler.

3. *Virtue and French Commercial Court Adjudication*

In Professor Kessler's article, she focuses on the religious roots of the virtuous behavior expected by commercial judges from themselves and merchants.[80] Prior to commenting on the illustrative decisions she compiled, it will be useful to sketch, with the help of Kessler's materials, key features of a typical eighteenth-century Parisian merchant.

a. *A Typical Eighteenth-Century Parisian Merchant*

An important segment of the eighteenth-century Parisian merchant community (and a descendant of the *verlagssystem*[81]) consisted of traders and artisans who produced and sold the goods they made. They received commissions to do work from,

---

[75] JEAN STOUFFLET, LE CREDIT DOCUMENTAIRE 99 (1957) ("Nous verrons au cours de notre etude qu'un assez grand nombre de points qui n'on jamais êtê tranches par les juges français ont été l'objet de decisions aux Etats-Unis et en Grande Bretagne.").

[76] Sylvie Humbert, *Were there Honest Judges and Faithful Merchants in Lille in the 18th and 19th Centuries like César Birotteau?*, 17 REVUE HISTOIRE DE LA JUSTICE (2007), abstract *available at* http://www.afhj.fr/publications/RHJ17_abstracts.pdf (abstract on file with author).

[77] *Id.*

[78] Hubert Bonin, *Justice and Business: a History Revealing Economic and Political Changes (19th-20th Centuries),* 17 REVUE HISTOIRE DE LA JUSTICE (2007), abstract *available at* http://www.afhj.fr/publications/RHJ17_abstracts.pdf (abstract on file with author).

[79] *Id.*

[80] Kessler, *Enforcing Virtue, supra* note 65.

[81] *See supra* § 6:2.

among others, merchants or intermediaries, and this work was usually to be done on a short-term basis.[82] Because these merchants worked out of their own shops, they belonged to a more advanced stage in the evolution of capitalism than the "domicile" workers financed by the *verlegers* described in a previous chapter by Fernand Braudel.

These Parisian merchants had a small volume of business because they lacked the information necessary to predict the demand for their goods or services.[83] I would also add that even if they could predict a future increased demand, they still lacked the credit necessary to fulfill that future demand. As noted earlier, the only secured credit available to attempt to satisfy such a demand was by means of the above-mentioned pledge (*gage*) of tangible assets or the mortgage (hypothèque) of the merchant's place of abode, if he happened to own it. Also, the pledge required that the merchant, as debtor, transfer possession of his productive assets to his creditor, thereby losing their use.

Because the Parisian merchant lacked access to institutional commercial credit, he could only increase his sales by extending (and receiving) credit on a personal "book debt" basis.[84] Book debt was an informal, usually oral, but *ex post facte* form of extending credit. It was not an extension of credit based upon future assets which would have resulted from future, albeit highly likely, transactions. But, was part of an ongoing and often longstanding contractual relationship wherein the debtor would pay in installments, while purchasing additional goods or services from his creditor and, often, vice versa. Only at the end of their credit relationship was there a final settlement where the creditor was paid in full.[85]

As one reflects on this description of book debt, it is difficult not to conclude that whoever extended this credit had to charge interest for it. Had he not recovered his transactional and financial costs, he would not last as an artisan-trader. And here, in my opinion, is where the most damaging conflict between commercial practice and prevailing Christian and commercial court morality existed.

French eighteenth-century church doctrine adhered to the scholastic definition of usury as any amount of interest charged for the use of the principal lent.[86] This doctrine considered any interest charged by the Parisian merchant usurious and, as Professor Kessler acknowledges, usury was "vociferously decried throughout the eighteenth-century."[87] Accordingly, (and this is my assertion, not Professor Kessler's) a double standard of commercial behavior had to exist: One standard for official or public consumption (including that of the court and the church), and the other for the actual business transaction. And again, in my opinion, this double standard undermined attempts to modernize the law of commercial transactions; it prevented the facilitation of the extension of commercial credit.

---

[82] Kessler, *Enforcing Virtue, supra* note 65, at 106.

[83] It will be recalled that in contrast with the French artisan-merchants, the "domicile workers" worked out of their homes and did their work upon receipt of commissions brought to them by the early capitalist intermediaries known as *verlegers*. *See supra* § 6:2.

[84] Kessler, *Enforcing Virtue, supra* note 65, at 107.

[85] *Id.* at 107–08.

[86] It will be recalled from the discussion in an earlier chapter that Pope Urban III issued in 1187 the Decretal Consuluit which, *inter alia*, stated that usury is any amount received by the lender in excess of the amount lent, regardless of how small the interest charged; the mere expectation of usury was sinful and the charge of a higher price for a sale on credit was implicit usury. *See supra* § 5:7(A) & (B) (discussing Saint Thomas's justification of this view).

[87] Kessler, *Enforcing Virtue, supra* note 65, at 74.

b. Commercial Court Decisions

The eighteenth-century Parisian commercial court regarded itself as "a bastion of Christian virtue, actively seeking to promote charitable love and to restrain unbridled self-interest."[88] In contrast to other royal, seigniorial and city courts, the sixty-some merchant courts situated throughout Old Regime France provided justice at no cost. The litigants who came before these courts were not required to pay any fees and, since they were (at least in theory) to represent themselves, they did not have to hire lawyers. Likewise, the lay merchants who served as the courts' judges worked for free:

> [T]he fact that litigants argued without the assistance of lawyers and merchant-court judges received no emolument was crucial to contemporary merchants because it ensured that justice would not be for sale—that it would be . . . shielded from the base commercialization to which the "normal" courts were deemed so susceptible. . . . In the early-modern world, and especially in Catholic France, the age-old Christian belief that the pursuit of profit is sinful continued to exert significant force, and commerce was therefore viewed by many with suspicion and distaste.[89]

Lest the reader dismiss the above description of the court's Christian morality as toothless, Professor Kessler notes the presence of an important enforcer:

> Priests served two critical functions in the merchant court—one clerical, and the other judicial. In their strictly clerical role, priests were responsible for overseeing the religious life of the merchant court and of the community it served. The court itself was housed in a church and contained an internal chapel, built in 1630. In this chapel, Mass was said every Monday, Wednesday and Friday morning, which were the days that the court sat to hear new cases. Generally, the judge and consuls attended this Mass. . . .[90]

c. The "Red Ink Case"

According to the facts provided by a merchant named Bedos,[91] who also sat as presiding judge of the commercial court of Paris when this case was heard, the plaintiff was a destitute young woman who demanded payment of the 10,000 *livres* promised in a bill of exchange of which she was the payee. It was drawn by her lover against a third party (drawee) who presumably owed him the amount of the bill. The drawee refused to pay and the plaintiff sued her lover as the drawer of the bill. She alleged that she had provided him cash in exchange for the bill, that the place of the purchase of the bill of exchange and its payment were different, and that the bill had been properly protested in strict compliance with the requirements of the Commercial Ordinance of 1673.[92]

---

[88] *Id.* at 72.

[89] *Id.* at 73–74.

[90] *Id.* at 81–82 (citations omitted).

[91] According to Kessler, the facts of this case "appear[] in *Le négociant patriote,* an account of Old Regime commercial life and merchant-court practice penned by a successful eighteenth-century merchant named Bedos, who claimed to have served as a merchant-court judge and president of a chamber of commerce." *Id.* at 72 (citation omitted).

[92] *Id.* at 76.

The judge acknowledged compliance with the Ordinance, but expressed his surprise at the color of the bill's ink.[93] Then the plaintiff explained that it was not cash but her virtue that she had surrendered after the defendant promised her that she would receive the payment of the ten thousand *livres*.[94] The red ink was her boyfriend's blood which he obtained by sticking a pin into his vein.[95] Either before or after giving this explanation, the plaintiff fainted.[96] The court did not enforce payment, nor did it deny enforcement as an ordinary court might have done because the "cause" underlying the transaction (prostitution) was immoral.[97] In Professor Kessler's narrative:

> Precisely because the transaction was immoral, the merchant court did not wash its hands of it, but instead tried to save the parties by actively promoting virtue, or Christian love. The court's motto, as Bedos explained, was that "humanity is the primary law." Thus . . . the judge turned to the defendant and said, "Here, sir, is where you have led her, she sinned out of weakness . . . tell her that you will marry her, her restored honor will call her back to life." Properly chastened, the defendant agreed that he ought to marry the plaintiff and promised God that he would make her happy. At this point, the plaintiff immediately revived and recovered sufficiently to ask the court to keep the bill until the day following the marriage, upon which it could be returned to her then husband. Thus assisted by the merchant court in their efforts to remain virtuous, the litigants departed to live happily ever after: "These poor children withdrew satisfied."[98]

COMMENTS AND QUESTIONS

The commercial court's desire to decree a remedy consistent with Christian virtue was quite apparent. Yet, which version of Christian virtue was the one applied? Clearly, the court assumed that its remedy of an imposed marriage was more virtuous than a compensation for the damages inflicted by the defendant's breach of promise of payment of the amount specified in the bill of exchange. What facts, if any, warranted this assumption? Why did the court not discuss the possibility of imposing a jail sentence on the defendant for his breach of a promise contained in a negotiable instrument as was assumed by Napoleon himself during the drafting of the *Code de Commerce*?[99]

As someone who is unfamiliar with the Christian theology on punishment for a breach of promise in a negotiable instrument, I wonder whether Christian theology (if it could speak with one voice) would have imposed the remedy of a marriage that could have easily resulted in a lifetime of unhappiness for the plaintiff. How happy would the plaintiff have been if, having been the victim of a breached promise, she married someone unwilling or unable to keep his future promises? Further, is it consistent with Christian morality not to consult the victim of reprehensible acts about her willingness to marry the person who committed those acts? On the other hand, what if the true

---

[93] *Id.*

[94] *Id.* at 76–77.

[95] *Id.* at 77.

[96] *Id.*

[97] *Id.*

[98] *Id.* at 77–78 (citations omitted).

[99] *See infra* § 10:2(A) & (B).

story were not one of rape or malicious seduction, but of blackmail? This blackmail would take the form of plaintiff's threat of an accusation that the defendant criminally breached his promise to pay a negotiable instrument. The threat was serious because defaulting on such an instrument could, under some circumstances, bring about imprisonment. As the reader will soon discover, a highly influential French legislator, aware of this decision, apparently read the plaintiff's complaint to the commercial court precisely as an attempt to extort money from the defendant.

Judge Bedos may have rejected the remedy of damages because the underlying obligation could have been nullified by its immoral cause of payment for the services of prostitution, as regularly done by civil courts.[100] This possibility was alluded to by Professor Kessler when, in the above quote, she praised Judge Bedos's decision and said: "Precisely because the transaction was immoral, the merchant court did not wash its hands of it, but instead tried to save the parties by actively promoting virtue, or Christian love."[101]

Yet, was a rule applicable to, say, the leasing of residential premises for prostitution purposes equally applicable to a promise of payment in a bill of exchange that did not mention the cause for which it was issued? After all, this was a promise which was supposed to be independent of underlying transaction causes, at least as to certain third parties. Thus, the applicability of the "independence of the cause" rule could depend upon, among other considerations, the identity of the party holding the instrument (a third party in good faith, a holder in due course, or a party to the original transaction) or the party alleging the defense of an immoral or illegal cause.[102]

Professor Kessler herself acknowledges that a bill of exchange is subject to different rules with respect to underlying causes, particularly when the bill is in the hands of someone whom the law deems a third party in good faith or (in Anglo-American legal parlance) a holder in due course.[103] Granted, during Judge Bedos's time there was little if any law on whether or when a payee of a bill of exchange, such as the plaintiff in our case, could become a third party holder in good faith. Moreover, a civil law court may have found it counterintuitive to treat the payee of the bill as a third party or holder in due course when she was in fact the first and only holder of the bill. Yet, by the same token, could a defendant-drawer of the bill object to plaintiff's status as a third party or holder in due course when he himself raised the defense of an immoral cause? Wasn't he, as the drawer of the bill and instigator of the immoral cause, *in pare delictu* with the payee?

Be that as it may, a commercial law judge, especially one who, like his ancestors in the fairs, was supposed to do what was "right and equitable," could have fashioned a remedy to protect an exploited payee against an exploiting and overreaching drawer (if that is what the parties were). Judge Bedos would argue that, having in mind the need to act in accordance with Christian virtue, his remedy was the most consistent with the France of his time. In it, destitute young women such as the plaintiff had few good mating choices, especially after having been seduced by a promise of a monetary reward. Thus, her marriage to a person of means assured her and her future children of continued support. Yet, are commercial courts the best equipped entities to decide on the allocation of rights and duties regarding matrimonial companionship, and family support choices for destitute women, or for prostitutes?

---

100 *See supra* § 9:2(E)(3)(c).

101 Kessler, *Enforcing Virtue, supra* note 65, at 77–78.

102 *See* Kozolchyk, *Commercialization*, at 7.

103 Kessler, *Enforcing Virtue, supra* note 65, at 77.

Finally, Judge Bedos leaves the impression that the plaintiff, a destitute young woman and prostitute, was in full command of the pleading requirements under Colbert's Ordinance of 1673. This would have included inserting two different addresses or locations, one for the place of issuance and acceptance or payment of the bill of exchange and the other for the delivery of the foreign currency, a requirement known among experienced merchants and bills of exchange lawyers as the *distantia loci.*[104] Was this assumption by Judge Bedos realistic? Or was it a "literary license" to dramatize the lay and humanistic nature of his court's justice and the Christian virtue of a court that dealt sympathetically with such destitute members of society?

d. *Other Decisions*

Judge Bedos' "typical day" in the commercial court is intended to illustrate how charitable love for fellow human beings, rather than commercial rules or practices, was the basis of the commercial court's decisions. According to him, he awakened in the middle of the night so that he could conduct a business that was designed not so much for his own profit as it was to help others. Hence, he instructed his cashier to sell "at ten percent below the legal rate."[105]

i. *A Suspension of Payments and Its Charitable Aftermath*

In an equally typical day, a merchant petitioned the court to allow him to suspend his payments because much of his inventory, while headed for France, was seized by pirates. The chief judge granted the suspension and told his colleagues that charity required that all of them pool their resources so that they could help their colleague make up his loss of 240,000 *livres.*[106]

After the suspension hearing, the judge urged a procedure for such charitable undertakings to ensure that all needy and virtuous merchants would receive equal assistance. Pledges were made by the judges to help set up a fund for such unlucky merchants. Next, the judges went to the cathedral to pray for the successful childbirth of the queen and to renew their pledges of contributions to the poor in the hospitals, to the marriage of twenty-four girls with respectable dowries, and to the enablement of

---

[104] The *distantia loci* formalities were designed centuries earlier by Italian merchants and their legal advisers to simulate a sale of foreign exchange instead of acknowledging an interest-bearing loan, thereby helping to prevent an accusation of usury. Such an accusation would have resulted from having a bill of exchange pay a sum of money that included any amount of interest charged for an underlying loan. *See* RAYMOND DE ROOVER, BUSINESS, BANKING, AND ECONOMIC THOUGHT 32 (1974) [hereinafter DE ROOVER, BUSINESS]. In this classic, de Roover describes this method of evading the possible charge of usury as follows:

> Since the taking of interest was ruled out, the bankers had to find other ways of lending at a profit. The favorite method was by means of exchange by bills (*cambium per litteras*). It did not consist in discounting as practiced today, but in the negotiation of bills payable in another place and usually in another currency. Interest, of course, was included in the price of the bill. . . . Although the presence of concealed interest is undeniable, the merchants argued—and most theologians accepted these views—that an exchange transaction was not a loan (*cambium non est mutuum*) but either a[n] [exchange] of moneys (*permutatio*) or a buying and selling of foreign currency (*emptio venditio*).

Id. In other words, the exchange transaction was used to justify the credit transaction and speculative profits on exchange served as a cloak to cover interest charges. Nevertheless, it was argued that a *cambium* was not usurious since there could be no usury where there was no loan. *Id.*; *see also* RAYMOND DE ROOVER, THE RISE AND DECLINE OF THE MEDICI BANK 11 (1963).

[105] Kessler, *Enforcing Virtue, supra* note 65, at 75.

[106] According to Kessler, this was "an extraordinarily large sum in age when the annual income of a tradesman ranged from 300 to 1,000 *livres* and that of a nobleman from 40,000 to 100,000 *livres.*" *Id.* at 75.

poor children as workers in agriculture, shepherding, and the trades (*Arts et Métiers*).[107]

ii. Parrish Priests as Arbiters and Judges: Charity and Just Price

The commercial court often deputized parish priests as mediators and arbiters.[108] In the latter capacity, priests relied for their fact-finding on their knowledge of the moral character of the parties and not as much upon a neutral collection of the actual facts.[109] It was not unusual for a priest to certify that a particular parishioner was "a person who leads a good life and has good morals and is known by everyone as such and that, according to my own knowledge and that of the inhabitants of my parish where she was born and has always lived, she has never failed to pay a debt. . . ."[110]

Such a finding would often be decisive, as was apparent in a number of disputes. In one, a business agent claimed underpayment of his services. After listing the virtues and moral flaws of the parties, the arbiter recommended that the virtuous defendants be awarded damages and that the plaintiff—whom he described as "crafty . . . and whom it is impossible to approach without . . . producing a strong shock"—be made to pay those damages.[111] Similarly, an arbiter-priest recommended that as between two disputant cousins, one's misery "obliterates his debt and it is not to be supposed that [another party], who is more comfortable, would be capable of wanting to be paid . . . by his cousin who is less comfortable than he. . . ."[112]

The just price of goods or services was routinely appraised by the arbiter-priest. For example, a seller of wine claimed that he was underpaid by the owner of a restaurant. After taking into account that the seller had maintained good records of his sales and that the price claimed "seemed reasonable" in the eyes of the arbiter-priest, the commercial court ordered its payment.[113] The same type of subjective appraisal applied to the reasonableness of the amount charged for the discount of a bill of exchange.[114] As noted by Professor Kessler, the basis of such a determination of reasonableness or of absence of lesion was not clear.[115] I should add that I did not find in her survey of cases arbitral findings supported by commercial customs and practices, plentiful though they were throughout France.[116]

4. Summary and Conclusions

a. Professor Kessler's Conclusions

Professor Kessler concludes that the commercial court's Christian values contributed to the "long-term relationships of trust . . . made possible by the

---

107 *Id.* at 79.

108 *Id.* at 82–84.

109 *Id.* at 87.

110 *Id.*

111 *Id.* at 100.

112 *Id.* at 89.

113 *Id.* at 90.

114 *Id.* at 91–92. No references appear in the justification of the finding as to the amounts charged or paid by others in that location or vicinity.

115 *Id.* at 92.

116 *See, e.g.*, CAMBRIDGE HISTORY, *supra* note 62, at 176–79 (referring to these customs and practices and describing the codification process).

institutional context in which most merchant-artisans lived and worked. . . ."[117] In other words, by behaving as virtuous and charitable Christian merchants and by belonging to the same Christian organizations as well as being subject to the same system of commercial justice, the Parisian artisan merchants gained each other's trust, vital business information, and credit. This Christian and virtuous way of doing business and of deciding commercial cases:

> lowered transaction costs sufficiently to make commerce in the relatively undeveloped economy of the Old Regime profitable. Furthermore, because the merchant court could tap into the preexisting network of communal institutions to which it was integrally linked, it was able cheaply and effectively to monitor and regulate behavior by enforcing the community's norms.[118]

b. *My Conclusions*

i. *Selfishness, Charity for Its Own Sake and Normative Charity*

While I find Professor Kessler's scholarship and descriptive skills admirable, I disagree with her conclusions. I agree that belonging to the same religious organizations should lead to greater trust among artisan-merchants. I also agree that the system of book debt may not have been feasible without the same religious bonds ensuring a higher likelihood of repayment. Yet, charity as a form of doing business and of judicial decision-making suffers from inherently crippling limitations.

When charity displaces profit-making, it soon ceases to be a viable business, as outlays and expenses eventually do away with the business's assets. A commonly heard and highly lauded justification for charity as a form of business nowadays is that profit-making is nothing more than selfishness *necessarily* at the expense of the common good.[119] This is a fallacy that often contributes to lively after-dinner conversations and even to dramatic theater such as in Berthold Brecht's "The Good Soul of Szechwan." In it, the good soul poses the "dilemma": If I am good to myself, am I not necessarily bad to others and *vice versa*?

The fallacy of this dilemma was exposed during the first centuries of the Common Era in the Talmudic saying: "There is good in evil, as there is evil in good."[120] This

---

[117] Kessler, *Enforcing Virtue, supra* note 65, at 108.

[118] *Id.* at 72–73.

[119] The reader may be interested in the discussion of the charitable form of doing business as part of micro-lending by the Nobel Prize laureate Mohammed Yunnus, the economist Hernando de Soto, and other lesser known economists and jurists in a televised symposium conducted by the journalist Andres Oppenheimer. *See Oppenheimer Presenta: El Capitalismo Social* (Mar. 21, 2007) (on file with author).

[120] In the Fable of the Evil Impulse based upon Talmudic writings, at least thirteen centuries old, the writer described what would happen to mankind if man's "evil desire" were subdued:

"If you kill him the world will expire!"
For three days the "Evil Yetzer" was imprisoned;
Temptations vanished, greed and pride ceased.
Hurrah! the battle over, the sex-impulse is won—
Alas . . . a fresh egg is needed, there is none.
. . .
At last it dawned—a truth profound
In scheme divine—a principle sound:
Vicious forces as passion, avarice and greed

Rabbinical view was echoed in Bernard Mandeville's "Fable of the Bees" and in Adam Smith's "Invisible Hand" as well as in each of the countless commercial contracts that populate the world's marketplaces and fuel its prosperity. As proven by the evolution of capitalism, selfish profit-making when properly channeled can lead to the common good. As also proven by E. O. Wilson and other socio-biologists, the human species belongs to a select group that has managed to combine selfishness with altruism in a manner that results in cooperation and economic development.[121]

In contrast, charity, for its own sake or without expecting something in return, assists an individual debtor or business person at a given moment, but seldom leads to a community's economic development. If this form of charity were required of merchants and charity is all they provided, it would make the welfare of the needy depend upon the generosity of the benefactors. The more charity is given and the more the needy depend upon the benefactors for their survival, the higher the likelihood that the needy remain will remain needy perennially.

The eighteenth-century French commercial court's version of charity, when practiced virtuously (and not merely to prevent the appearance of usury or of sinful profit-making), was a charity for its own sake. To contribute to personal as well as to a community's economic development, charity would have had to empower the needy to help themselves. For this empowerment to spread, it would have to become institutionalized or incorporated into positive or customary law norms.

Accordingly, the court or legal decision-maker would have to determine, *inter alia*: Which empowering conduct could become the norm for a given transaction or group of transactions? Who would have to contribute to it, how much and for how long? Would there be security or verification mechanisms attached to the giving and to the return? Would there be an educational component attached to it, for example, on how to keep good accounting books or how best to market one's goods or services?

Thus, the normative charity focuses not only on the beneficence of an act, but on its empowering effects, meaning the willingness of some to give up something for the sake of others and the effects of the giving upon a class of merchants and eventually upon society. To illustrate, consider the commercial court decision that suspended the debts of the merchant who lost his inventory to pirates and followed it up with a collection of the amount lost among the judges. What if the decision would have been to

---

Are vehicles of progress the world doth need.

Roman A. Ohrenstein, *Economic Self-Interest and Social Progress in Talmudic Literature: A Further Study of Ancient Economic Thought and Its Modern Significance*, 29 AM. J. ECON. & SOCIOLOGY 59, 62–63 (1970). Professor Ohrenstein, an insightful historian of economic thought, pointed out the obvious parallel between eighteenth-century economic liberal and moral philosophical thought and how Bernard de Mandeville's famous satire, "The Fable of the Bees" was of considerable influence on Adam Smith's, "Wealth of Nations." *Id.* at 61. He also notes the paradox that "[p]arties directly opposite [a]ssist each other as 'twere for spite." *Id.* at 64. Thus, the apparently discordant passions strangely harmonize to the same end such that private vices are turned into public benefits. Further, Adam Smith's *Wealth of Nations* points out that the individual's exertion brings the greatest benefit not only to himself, but also to society. For Adam Smith's individual "neither intends to promote the public interest, nor knows how much he is promoting it. . . . [He is] led by an invisible hand to promote an end which was no part of his intention. . . . By pursuing his own interest he frequently promotes that of society. . . ." ADAM SMITH, AN INQUIRY INTO THE NATURE AND CAUSES OF THE WEALTH OF NATIONS 476 (Edwin Cannan ed., Univ. Chi. Press 1977) (1776).

121 *See* § 1:2(D).

suspend those debts in a manner that enabled the insolvent merchant as well as others in his same position to rehabilitate themselves?

This rehabilitation may have required a temporary forgiveness of a debt, but also, and perhaps more importantly, it would provide access to new credit either from pre-existing creditors or new lenders. Yet, such new credit would not be available unless a realistic and protected source of repayment was assured. Quite possibly a special priority may have to be granted to the new creditors. Clearly, the process of enabling debtor rehabilitation would have to be a much more reflective and well-planned process of decision-making than the instinctive "here and now" charity of Judge Bedos and his colleagues.

It is worth noting that normative charity is not the exclusive domain of enlightened legislatures and commercial courts; it is usually found in viable marketplaces, especially when the transaction or business sector in question has been interrupted by a catastrophe. In such cases, for the transaction or business sector to remain viable, it must regain the trust of regular participants in the marketplace.[122] This was the case of the Mediterranean Jewish traveling merchants whose duty it was to "pick up their deceased colleagues' bundle" and upon doing so, sell their colleague's goods and deliver the proceeds at no charge to the deceased's family. It was also the case of the London goldsmiths who repaid their depositors for the loss of their jewels and other deposits suffered as a result of the London fires—despite the availability of the excuse of *force majeur*.[123] It was also the case of a few solvent New York bankers paying off the debts of their failing colleagues and enabling some of them to continue in business, all of this without charging for their rescue.[124]

These or similar acts became the norms for certain trades, professions or sectors, in some instances as positive law and in others as customary law or as "gentlemen's agreements." Clearly, this normative charity, in contrast with the charity for its own sake, assumes that the benefactors will get something in return (whether greater market stability or a larger volume of future business, etc.) and thus, in some measure, is a selfish act. Yet, it usually benefits not just a handful, but an entire class of merchants, thus contributing to the health of the marketplace and the community's economic development.

ii. Just Prices, Usury, and the Role of Custom and Usage

When the commercial court required what it regarded as commercially virtuous behavior, it discouraged and delegitimized "unchristian" profit-seeking. Such an attitude influenced the commercial court's determinations of a just price, whether of commodities, services or money (as in the case involving the discount rate for a bill of exchange).

The commercial courts and their arbiters' determinations of a just price were not based upon Saint Thomas Aquinas' "*secundum aestimationem fori*" (in accordance with

---

[122] *See generally* Kozolchyk, *Fairness* (discussing the standards of fairness that govern commercial adjudication in different legal systems); Kozolchyk, *Commercialization*.

[123] *See* THOMAS PENNANT, OF LONDON 361–62 (1790) (discussing the trustworthiness, respectability, and integrity of the London goldsmiths).

[124] *See People and Events: J.P. Morgan*, PBS, http://www.pbs.org/wgbh/amex/1900/peopleevents/pande10.html (an interesting description of J. P. Morgan's efforts to rescue failing banks in early twentieth-century America).

the estimation of the market) as discussed in Chapter 5, but upon subjective, if not capricious, criteria. In doing this, they added uncertainty to doing business, particularly for those who may have been interested in extending institutional credit at reasonable rates of interest to merchants or consumers.

When coupled with the prohibition of usury (defined as the charge of any interest for the principal lent), the eighteenth-century commercial court's decision-making discouraged the creation of both credit and capital markets. As concluded earlier in this book by an English scholar: "Under the labyrinthine edifice of Scholastic casuistry . . . competition withered, the flow of credit congealed, and interest rates soared."[125] As similarly concluded by Raymond de Roover, despite its intention to protect borrower-debtors, the prohibition of usury had the opposite effect.[126] The cost of the many subterfuges to evade the usury prohibition was ultimately borne by the same borrowers it was meant to protect.

The cost of evading the usury prohibition, inseparably linked as it was with the commercial court's determinations of just prices, undermined the benefits Professor Kessler attributes to the long-term relationships and to the book debt system. Transactional costs and risks had to increase and competition had to decline as the scarcity of working capital and credit retarded economic growth.

In the final analysis, then, the failure of the charitable rationale as a law-making force by the commercial court described by Professor Kessler was its subjectivity, unpredictability, and resultant inability to become institutionalized. In contrast, predictability was and is a key feature of the type of decision-making based upon observed customs and practices. The certainty of observed custom and practice is earned objectively and only after a laborious process of trial and error. It is, therefore, the certainty that only a "well-trodden practice path" can provide.[127]

From the standpoint of the development of commercial law, the commercial court's failure to rely on observed and sound commercial customs and practices as persuasive, if not binding, sources of law was, in my opinion, its most serious shortcoming. And, while Professor Kessler warns that Christian norms were not the only basis for commercial court jurisprudence, she adds that "though not every case was resolved by applying norms of Christian virtue, such norms were . . . the driving force behind many of the court's decisions and procedures."[128]

§ 9.3 TODAY'S COMMERCIAL COURT

As described by Arnaud de la Cotardiére, Patricia Peterson & Delphine Pujos, three lawyers at Linklaters LLP, a major international law firm with a substantial French litigation practice:

> The [French] Commercial Courts [*Tribunaux de commerce*] are courts of first instance with jurisdiction over:

---

125 DE ROOVER, BUSINESS, *supra* note 104, at 16.

126 *Id.* at 33.

127 Kozolchyk, *Commercialization*, at 38.

128 Kessler, *Enforcing Virtue, supra* note 65, at 81.

• Disputes in connection with undertakings between business persons (*commerçants) such as traders, between credit insitutions or between business persons and credit institutions.*

• Disputes involving commercial corporate entitites.

• Disputes in connection with commercial matters, including a wide variety of instruments such as bills of exchange, promissory notes, security or transactions relating to businesses as a going concern (*fonds de commerce*).[129]

Many of the judges who sit in commercial courts are volunteer businessmen who are elected by their peers and many hold their judicial position on a part time basis. Thus a good number of these judges, especially in smaller cities, are not legally trained.[130] The commercial court is led by a presiding judge.[131] Although judges generally sit in panels of three, usually a reporting judge (*juge rapporteur*) is designated and parties often appear in front of this judge instead of the entire three judge panel.[132]

Jonathon Polier, an international lawyer who practices in Paris and appears before the commercial court, describes the procedural steps in a common type of claim that involves the collection of a contractual debt.[133] It starts out with the plaintiff sending a registered letter addressed to the defendant in which he demands thc payment of his debt or the defendant's carrying out the corrective measures to pay such a debt. This procedure is known as placing the defendant in default or "*mise en demeure*."[134] One of the functions of this date is to start the interest payment clock running.[135]

If payment does not occur within the time stipulated in the letter, a summons and complaint form ("*assignation*") will be prepared by an advocate and will be served by a bailiff ("*huissier*") to the defendant.[136] It states briefly the relevant facts and the applicable law by reference to a code provision.[137]

If the defendant fails to pay:

> [L]egal counsel to the parties will commence a monthly cycle of Tribunal mandated exchanges of pleadings and supporting document wherein they alternately refine the alleged facts and issues of law. These are called

---

[129] *See* Arnaud de la Cotardiére, Patricia Peterson & Delphine Pujos, *Litigation and enforcement in France: overview*, PRACTICAL LAW (July 1, 2012), http://us.practicallaw.com/9–502–0121.

[130] *Id.* They also point out that at least one commercial court exists in most of French administrative departments, totaling approximately 180 courts. *Id.* My own visits to French commercial courts during my stay as a visiting professor to the University of Aix en Provence confirmed the lack of legal training of some commercial judges. I have had difficulties finding contemporary scholarly discussions of practice before commercial courts in France. Most of the published writings on commercial code trial practice that I have had access to date back to the nineteen seventies and eighties. *See generally* Denis Tallon, *Civil and Commercial Law*, VIII–2 INT'L ENCYCLOPEDIA OF COMP. L. (1983).

[131] Cotardiere et al., *supra* note 129.

[132] *Id.*

[133] Jonathon Wise Polier, *French-American Commercial Litigation*, PARIS-LAW.COM, http://www.paris-law.com/articles/Fench_comercial_litigation-en.htm.

[134] *Id.*

[135] *Id.*

[136] *Id.*

[137] *Id.*

> "*conclusions*" and "*conclusions en réponse*". . . . If either Advocate wishes for an expert to be designated by the tribunal, the Advocate files a motion ("*demande d'expertise*") with the TDC. A hearing is scheduled and the tribunal decides to grant or deny the motion. If an expert is appointed, the expertising process becomes a mini proceding where the expert formally notifies the parties of the steps he intends to take (e.g., an inspection of goods or records) and the parties and the Advocates may generally accompany the expert when he effects his inspection, if it is appropriate, as in the case of issues of non-conforming goods.[138]

Polier notes that in rare cases, it may be possible to obtain an interlocutory order to compel the opposing side to produce a precise document or object. But he warns that ordinarily, the French commercial court is "very reluctant to authorize such production and American-type pre-trial 'fishing expedition' discovery procedures are absolutely out of the question."[139]

Cotardiére et al. provide a similar description but emphasize that the complaint not only sets out the factual and legal arguments in support of the claimant's claim, but it must also submit the list of documents on which plaintiff relies as supporting evidence.[140] They also emphasize that:

> Documentary evidence is given greater weight in the French system than the evidence of witnesses, either in written or oral form. In practice, litigants argue their cases on the basis of documentary evidence and tend to resort to witness statements or oral evidence where there is no other choice. Oral testimony is very rare in civil and commercial cases in France.[141]

As will be discussed in a later chapter on comparative trial procedures,[142] one of the problems with this type of complaint is that it confines the facts as well as the legal issues to those that were plead in it and were supported by the documentary evidence it lists in final fashion; facts and issues that may lead to a larger recovery than originally plead will suffer from the fatal procedural sin of *plus peititio* (a larger award than requested or supported). In addition, the inability to rely on the examination and cross-examination of witnesses (including the parties as well as experts) prevents finding what is often the most reliable version of the parties' contractual intent—the parties' course of contractual performance, prior courses of dealings and the usages of their trades.[143]

It is precisely this realization that has led important, emerging commercial nations in Latin America, such as Mexico, Chile and Colombia, to adopt statutory law on "oral trials." These trials open up commercial adjudication to the examination and cross-examination of witnesses and to the reception of the most relevant facts even if obtained at a stage later than the filing of a commercial complaint.[144]

---

138 *Id.*

139 *Id.*

140 Cotardiére et al., *supra* note 129.

141 *Id.*

142 *See infra* ch. 25 (on the comparative commercial trial procedures).

143 *See infra* ch. 23.

144 *See* National Law Center for Inter-American Free Trade, http://natlaw.com/category/training/ (on "oral trials").

It is my opinion that unless France's commercial court and its progeny adopt the key features of the oral trials, it will continue to be an anachronistic institution with little or no chance to contribute to a nation's or region's economic development. Although concluded in 1976, the assessment of the future of French commercial courts by Professor Denis Tallon of the University of Law, Economics and Social Sciences in Paris is still valid in many respects:

> The maintenance of the commercial courts is a matter of considerable dispute in France. They may have advantages by virtue of the better knowledge that the judges have of commercial practices. But because of their very wide jurisdiction, more and more matters are heard by them which call for a thorough legal training, *e.g.* in insolvency and company law. For this reason there is a call at least to restrict their jurisdiction.[145]

To this assessment, I would add that as presently constituted, the French commercial court not only lacks requisite legal knowledge, but also, and at least as importantly, the factual knowledge of the many transactions in which the businessmen judges are not regular participants. The following interview illustrates how a high official of the commercial court views its present and future functions:

Interview with President Perrette Rey on October 1, 2007 on the Reform of Commercial Courts[146]

The interview took place on the bicentennial of the *Code de Commerce*. The interviewers prefaced their questions with a reference to the fact that France is preparing to modernize its approach to commercial law, including the reform of the judicial system, a partial decriminalization of business law, and more effective measures to prevent bankruptcies. According to the interviewers, these were the three pillars of the platform presented by Nicolas Sarkozy on September 6, 2007. Speaking in the name of the French Conference of Lay Judges, Perrette Rey, President of the Paris Commercial Court, gave her views on these developments.[147]

Mme. Perrette Rey was born on August 27, 1942 and has been President of the Paris Commercial Court since 2004. As President of the French Conference of Lay Judges, she represents the country's 185 commercial courts. A former company director, she has been actively involved in commercial law issues for over fifteen years.

Selected Questions and Answers:

Commerce International (hereinafter C.I.): Legal proceedings involving lay lawyers are generally considered as less expensive, quicker, and closer to the sensibility of businesses than their alternatives. Have France's commercial courts been "rehabilitated" after the crisis they recently went through?

Perrette Rey (hereinafter P.R.): France's 3,100 commercial court judges have learned the lessons of those difficult years. Entrepreneurs and company directors, both elected and voluntary, understood that they needed to make continual progress in order to meet the expectations of the businesses that use their services. It seems to me

---

145 Tallon, *supra* note 130, at 140.

146 Interview by Annabelle Pando & Frédérique Perrotin with Perrette Rey, President of the Paris Commercial Court (Oct. 1, 2007), *available at* http://www.actu-cci.com/reflexions-debats/10061–entretien-avec-perrette-rey-sur-les-reformes-en-vue-pour-la-justice-economique-francaise (emphasis added).

147 *Id.*

that it was appropriate that the President, Nicolas Sarkozy, should highlight the efforts made by the Commercial Courts to modernize.

C.I.: Economic and legal competencies, professional ethics, and efficiency are the qualities that you demand from a good lay judge. How can these qualities be developed?

P.R.: Since 2003, the French National Magistrates' College has provided initial training for 300 to 350 lay judges every year. And it dispenses continued training courses to all of France's lay judges. Since 2005, the National Council of Commercial Courts, presided over by the Minister of Justice, half of whose members are lay judges and the other half senior magistrates, directors of the Chancery, and qualified personalities, has been diligent in its efforts to improve professional competencies and the working methods of lay judges by, for example, *concretely defining their duties and obligations in terms of the way they behave and carry out their duties as judges in order to avoid conflicts of interest.*

C.I.: How has the upcoming reform to the judicial system been greeted by the professionals of the lay justice sector?

P.R.: They regard it as the pre-condition for greater efficiency. Commercial law is becoming increasingly complex and voluminous. A good judge of commercial disputes is not necessarily a good bankruptcy judge. Specialization and, consequently, an improvement in the decision-making process, are only possible in jurisdictions over a certain size. Moreover, in 2004, the General Conference of Commercial Courts started to work on a blueprint for reform, which it finalized in 2004 before the subject came under the spotlight. The blueprint is based on a precise and quantified analysis of the activities of all Commercial Courts in regard to the needs of businesses in the area they cover. It recommends not only grouping courts together but also transferring the commercial divisions of the *Tribunaux de Grande Instance* (or 'Courts of First Instance') to Commercial Courts.

C.I.: What about the other announcements: reinforcing the role of the Procurator in the Commercial Courts, developing preventive measures in the field of collective procedures, and partially decriminalizing business law?

P.R.: These reforms should be welcomed. . . . In regard to the criminalization of business life, it is not, by any means, the most appropriate response in most cases. It is often more effective to levy a fine. . . .

C.I.: Is the harmonization of European commercial law a priority?

P.R.: Before harmonizing commercial law, we should get to know one another, familiarize ourselves with each other's legal systems, our specificities in terms of structure, procedure, and execution. The elaboration of a European *jus oeconomicus* is dependent, first and foremost, on working judges participating in dialogue with a view to fostering mutual understanding. As an adjunct to the celebrations of the bicentenary of the French Code of Commerce, we have set up a group including judges and representatives from the French, Belgian and, in the near future, British public prosecutor's offices, as well as business people from our respective countries, to exchange ideas and discuss ways of harmonizing European commercial law. The approach is modest and pragmatic. That is probably what makes it so effective.

C.I.: Will the fact that certain business *milieux* favor arbitration encourage harmonization?

P.R.: Due to the costs involved in the arbitration process, it is mostly favored by large companies. *Compared to the one million judgments handed down annually by the French Commercial Courts, the number of arbitrations is infinitesimal.* It seems to me that those who use the approach are more concerned with choosing the right judge-arbitrator than with serving the cause of European harmonization.

COMMENTS AND QUESTIONS

Please note the absence of references to usages of trade or to the standard and best practices of the various commercial professions. Still, what could have happened to the eighteenth-century "Bastion of Virtue" that made it necessary for the present-day court to get closer to the "sensibility of businesses"? Surely, contemporary French businesses, large, medium and small, are not known for their disdain for profit-making. Nor are the French banks and investment companies known for their reticence to charge interest or hefty commissions. What role, if any, did the enactment of the *Code de Commerce* of 1807 play in this radical change of attitude and value system? Are there remnants of the "Bastion of Virtue" value system in today's commercial adjudication? If not, why would the interviewers ask Mme. Rey about the need to "concretely define their duties and obligations in terms of the way they behave and carry out their duties as judges in order to avoid conflicts of interest?"

Does the volume of commercial decisions handed down annually by the present-day commercial courts in France (approximately one million decisions according to Mme. Rey) sound reasonable for a country whose population is approximately sixty million? If so, how would the volume of France's commercial litigation compare to that of the United States?

In response to a question on the harmonization of European commercial law, Mme. Rey says: "Before harmonizing commercial law, we should get to know one another, familiarize ourselves with each other's legal systems, our specificities in terms of structure, procedure and execution." In light of the experience with the eighteenth-century commercial court and its archetypal merchant and judge, what would you say is missing from the above list of items requiring "familiarization"?

How about the usages of the various trades and sectors whose international compilations of standard and form contracts has been undertaken for many years by entities such as the International Chamber of Commerce (ICC), the International Swaps and Derivatives Association (ISDA), or the Grain and Feed Trade Association (GAFTA)? Are they being relied upon by the parties and the judges of the commercial court?

If not, what are the reasons and consequences of their disregard? While I have read some decisions by the commercial court that apply the Uniform Customs and Practices for Documentary Credits (UCP 500 and 600) and others that attempt to interpret the GAFTA Master Agreement, decisions involving the standard practices of French associations of merchants and their "auxiliaries" do not seem common. If that is actually the case—and it is not caused by the limitations of my own research—why not? Clearly, a body of case law based upon a healthy body of local customary law is only likely to heighten the influence of the commercial court. A disregard of local customary law can only make that court's adjudication less influential.

Chapter 10

THE *CODE DE COMMERCE* OF 1807

§ 10.1 BRIEF BACKGROUND: ENTERPRISES AND WHO IS THE PUBLIC?

The socio-economic picture of pre-revolutionary France drawn by the Oxford History in an earlier chapter[1] remained the same by the time that Napoleon Bonaparte had become France's head of state in 1799. Despite the bleakness of the economic conditions of the post-revolutionary France that Bonaparte governed, Napoleon's view of these conditions was much rosier than that of the Oxford History. On December 31, 1804, only five years after he became the head of the French government, he addressed France's legislature and summed up France's state of affairs as follows:

> Everywhere useful enterprises are in progress. . . .
>
> The civil code has fulfilled the expectations of the public; all citizens are acquainted with it; it serves as their guide in their various transactions, and is everywhere lauded as a benefaction. . . . *The code of procedure and the commercial code are still where they were a year ago, for pressing cares have diverted the emperor's attention elsewhere.*
>
> . . .
>
> The emperor's decrees have reestablished commerce on the left bank of the Rhine. Our manufacturers are improving, although the mercenaries subsidized by the British government vaunt, in their empty declamations, her foreign trade and her precarious resources scattered about the seas and in the Indies, while they describe our shops as deserted and our artisans as dying of hunger. In spite of this, our industries are striking root in our own soil and are driving English commerce far from our shores. Our products now equal theirs and will soon compete with them in all the markets of the world.[2]

Paradoxically, and despite his assessment and prognostication, the loss of net welfare experienced by France during his reign was between three and four percent *per annum*.[3] Given the economic decline experienced by France's population as a whole, it is very unlikely that the commercial class did any better. In fact, as will be discussed shortly, there is every indication that the dominant class continued to be the bourgeoisie and its system of landholding and privileges remained undisturbed. One such privilege was the reliance on expensive notarial deeds, not so much to provide public notice of the transaction, but to insure an easier and quicker attachment and

---

[1] *See supra* § 8:6.

[2] Napoleon Bonaparte's Statement to the Legislative Body on December 31, 1804, *cited in* JAMES HARVEY ROBINSON, II READINGS IN EUROPEAN HISTORY: FROM THE OPENING OF THE PROTESTANT REVOLT TO THE PRESENT DAY 491, 493–94 (1906) (emphasis added).

[3] Kevin H. O'Rourke, *The Worldwide Economic Impact of the Revolutionary and Napoleonic Wars* 28 (Nat'l Bureau of Econ. Research, Working Paper No. 11344, 2005), *available at* http://www.nber.org/papers/w11344.pdf.

foreclosure on the property involved.[4] According to Napoleon, the *Code Civil* had fulfilled the expectations of the public (and particularly that of the bourgeois class) and served as its guide in their various transactions. It is not surprising that the drafting of a commercial code, intended for the class of merchants, was *not* one of Napoleon's pressing cares. In fact, it was quite the contrary.

As noted by a Cambridge University account of the Napoleonic rule (hereinafter Cambridge History), the examination of commercial legislation for codification purposes began in France in 1789.[5] Colbert's 1673 Ordinance on inland commerce and 1681 Ordinance on maritime commerce were still in force,[6] but were "variously interpreted and overspread with a luxuriance of local custom, needed pruning and adaptation."[7] On April 3, 1801, Bonaparte appointed a committee of six to draft a commercial code. That committee produced a draft, but apparently it was submitted to the wrong administrative agency, "where it slumbered peacefully in its pigeonhole for several years."[8]

A. The Final Draft of the *Code de Commerce*

The mistakenly-submitted draft was brought back to life in 1806. The precipitating event was the fraudulent bankruptcy of M. Récamier's bank, a leading financial institution. Napoleon heard about it while campaigning in Germany and sent a rescript to the Council of State (*Conseil d'Etat*) demanding the enactment of a severe bankruptcy law. The *Conseil* replied that such a law would be part of the newly drafted *Code de Commerce*.[9] Thus, the discussions on the redrafted code began on November 4, 1806 and ended on August 29, 1807. Napoleon was mostly interested in two subjects and participated in the drafting of the rules that addressed them.[10]

The first subject was the application of the commercial law to non-merchants who had expressly or tacitly intended to be bound by it, especially when using negotiable instruments such as promissory notes and bills of exchange. Unlike the commercial court's decision in the Red Ink case[11] (which, as will be remembered, acted out of humanitarian and Christian concern for the welfare of a destitute prostitute and her future children), Napoleon worried that non-merchants would sign commercial instruments that could land them in jail because of their lack of familiarity with these instruments. Cambridge History summarizes Napoleon's "rich and effervescent eloquence"[12] on this issue (expressed to the Drafting Commission) as follows:

> [F]or the . . . [non-merchants], credit was a misfortune and a lure to dissipation. For . . . [Napoleon's] part, he was unwilling to see bills of exchange or other negotiable instruments used by those who were not in

---

[4] *See infra* § 10:1(B) (discussing the amendments to the Bankruptcy provisions of the *Code de Commerce*).

[5] IX THE CAMBRIDGE MODERN HISTORY 177 (A. W. Ward, G. W. Prothero & Stanley Leathes eds., 1907) [hereinafter CAMBRIDGE HISTORY].

[6] *Id.* at 176–77.

[7] CAMBRIDGE HISTORY, *supra* note 5, at 177.

[8] *Id.*

[9] *Id.*

[10] *Id.*

[11] *See supra* § 9:2(E)(3)(c).

[12] CAMBRIDGE HISTORY, *supra* note 5, at 177.

> business. Such a practice would lead to the mobilisation of fortunes, and [would] spread alarm among the fathers of families. [In Napoleon's words,] "A courtesan who had extorted a promissory note from a young man might drag him before the commercial Court and get him sent to prison."[13]

This not-so-vague reference to the Red Ink case reflected not only what Cambridge History describes as Napoleon's "hatred of speculation"[14] and distaste for the "mobilisation of fortunes"[15] (implying the destabilization of the bourgeoisie whom he regarded as the strongest economic class in France), but a very different reading of the facts than the one attributed to Judge Bedos. Rather than assuming that the plaintiff was a destitute young woman taken advantage of by a cunning seducer, Napoleon saw her as a "courtesan who had extorted a promissory note."[16] The effect of Napoleon's reading of this case was apparent as recently as in a 1935 version of Article 636 of the *Code de Commerce*:

> Where *pay to the order* bills of exchange bear the signatures of non-merchants and were not issued in connection with commercial, banking or brokerage transactions, the commercial court shall transfer the case to the civil court if requested by the defendant.[17]

Simply put, Napoleon did not want courtesan-inspired extortions or Judge Bedos' type of remedies in connection with bills of exchange. His was not a concern for providing the legal world with a definitive listing of commercial acts for the benefit of merchants in search of commercial code certainty and informal, quick and fair or equitable adjudication; it was to protect non-merchants, and especially the bourgeois, from tricky consequences associated with commercial instruments.

The second major subject of concern for Napoleon was the law of bankruptcy. As described by Cambridge History, the law of bankruptcy of the *ancien régime* assumed that the insolvent merchant had suffered a misfortune, much like the commercial court's unlucky importer of goods seized by pirates, until his fraud on his creditors was proved, "and in other respects it was characterised by objectionable laxity."[18] As part of the new *Code de Commerce*, the *Conseil d'Etat* proposed, at first, to expropriate the bankrupt person's remaining assets and transfer their administration to provisional *syndics*. Thereafter, the bankrupt person's conduct would be subject to an inquiry that might be conducted by a correctional or a criminal court, depending upon whether negligence or fraud was involved. This process was to be in the hands of a public prosecutor, not the creditors.[19] As described by Cambridge History:

> These proposals were severe, but they were not severe enough for Napoleon. "Bankruptcies," he said, "take away men's fortunes without destroying their honour; and that is what it is important to destroy." He argued in favour of

---

[13] *Id.*

[14] *Id.*

[15] *Id.*

[16] *Id.*

[17] C. COM. (FR.) art. 636 (Dalloz 1992–93) (emphasis added): *"Lorsque les billets à ordre ne porteront que des signatures d'individus non négociants et n'auront pas pour occasion des opérations de commerce, trafic, change, banque ou courtage, le tribunal de commerce sera tenu de renvoyer au tribunal de grande instance, s'il en est requis par le défendeur."*

[18] CAMBRIDGE HISTORY, *supra* note 5 at 178.

[19] *Id.*

> incarceration in order to prevent the bankrupt flaunting his triumph of indifference. The creditors could not be trusted to humiliate the bankrupt, for their sole interest was to recover their debts as soon as possible. But prison would do it, even if it were but for an hour. It was also desirable that in every case the woman should share the misfortune of her husband.[20]

Given Napoleon's interest in them, it was not surprising that the rules on bankruptcy occupied a full one third of the original version of the *Code de Commerce*. Recently, Pierre-Cyrille Hautcoeur and Nadine Levratto, French law and economics scholars, summarized the *Code de Commerce's* treatment of bankruptcy as follows:

> Bankruptcy (*faillite*) was defined as the state of having stopped payments (*cessation de paiements*), but the procedure was started only by a judgment stating that a person or a company (*société*) was in that situation. The procedure could be started either at the initiative of the bankrupt himself (. . . *depôt de bilan*), by his creditors (*requête*) or by the court itself (*d'office*). The bankrupt was supposed to be jailed, and the judge to name a trustee (*syndic*) responsible for the management of the [assets and liabilities and the overall] procedure in the interest of the creditors; this supposed either finding a composition (*concordat*), an agreement with the creditors allowing the perpetuation of the firm (which usually included a reduction and a new schedule for the debts), or organizing the complete liquidation of the debtor's estate (*union*). . . . The trustee then divided creditors in secured and ordinary ones. The normal situation was to repay first all creditors holding mortgages, other security or special priority, and then grouping the ordinary creditors in a compulsory class (the *masse*) who had to decide on the *concordat* on a majority basis.[21]

Cambridge History quotes the renowned jurist Pardessus' criticism that the *Code de Commerce* was the most carelessly drafted of any of the Napoleonic series of codes despite that "it was the Code for which there existed the most abundant materials."[22] As examples of neglectful drafting, Cambridge History lists:

> [T]he whole question of purchase and sale is disposed of in a single unimportant clause. There is not a word concerning price, promise of sale, or earnest money; nothing upon the conditions of weights, measures, and assay; nothing on patents or copyrights, on contracts of apprenticeship, or contracts between workmen and manufacturers or shopkeepers, on bank commissions or on the various kinds of loans which are used in commerce. The Second Book . . . [on Maritime Commerce], being copied from the Ordinance of 1681 with little alteration save what was derived from later experience or later laws. . . . The Third Book, on bankruptcy, is said by Pardessus to contain some excellent dispositions, with others so full of objectionable matter that it is difficult to believe they could have passed uncorrected. . . . The Fourth Book, on the competence and procedure of the commercial Courts, is far from

---

[20] *Id.*

[21] Pierre-Cyrille Hautcoeur & Nadine Levratto, *Legal versus Economic Explanations of the Rise in Bankruptcies in 19th Century France* 4 (Paris School of Economics, Working Paper No. 47, 2007), *available at* http://www.parisschoolofeconomics.eu/docs/hautcoeur-pierre-cyrille/wp200747.pdf.

[22] CAMBRIDGE HISTORY, *supra* note 5, at 178.

> being either clear or precise, and is distinguished by the curious omission of any clause dealing with imprisonment for debt. . . .[23]

In the mid-twentieth century, Georges Ripert, the "Dean of French commercial law commentary," was similarly critical, but more understanding of the reasons for its shortcomings:

> The *Code de Commerce* is not comparable to the *Code Civil*, it is a mediocre work with the exception of the Second Book devoted to maritime commerce. . . . The overall plan is not excellent, the drafting is clumsy and archaic. But one must acknowledge that the drafters faced a difficult situation. The corporate [guild] regime had disappeared and no law existed to govern the commerce. The commercial courts had been preserved, but their jurisdiction was uncertain. . . . as was also the extent to which one could do justice to the major principle of civil equality.[24]

B. Early Bankruptcy and Commercial-Credit-Inspired Amendments: Bourgeois v. Merchants

According to Pierre-Cyrille Hautcoeur and Nadine Levratto, "[c]ommercial credit was already a very old practice at the start of the nineteenth century, but the industrial revolution required its extension."[25] In all likelihood, the commercial credit referred to by these authors was the same unsecured credit described by Professor Kessler in the preceding chapter as "book debts."[26] It will be recalled that this credit was unsecured and likely quite costly, largely because of the risks related to nonpayment and to the widespread condemnation of usury.[27]

Nonetheless, as the French economy started growing after the middle of the nineteenth century,[28] larger markets led to a greater need for larger firms producing standardized goods for customized markets, and this "required"" investment in equipment and in distribution facilities. Commercial credit had to be made available for these increasingly complex commercial transactions.[29] The effects on the bankruptcy provisions of the *Code de Commerce* and the increasingly sharp conflict between bourgeois and merchant interests were soon apparent:

---

[23] *Id.* at 178–79.

[24] RIPERT, at 15 (author's translation). As a visiting professor at the University of Aix-en-Provence Law School, I was assigned to lecture in the lecture room *Salle Ripert.* I was frequently told: "There was only one Georges Ripert in French commercial commentary."

[25] Hautcoeur & Levratto, *supra* note 21, at 6.

[26] *See supra* § 9:2(E)(3)(a).

[27] *See generally* ROBERT SOMERS & L. WOLOWSKI, THE SCOTCH BANKS AND SYSTEM OF ISSUE: INCLUDING TRANSLATION OF "LES BANQUES D'ECOSSE" (1873) (comparing bank credit available in France and Scotland). The author is a French Member of a Prestigious Academy; whose views on available credit in France even in 1873, revealed a continuous condemnation of usury, and a pejorative assessment of France's credit system or lack of it, particularly in the countryside. "[M]ortgage is all that exists in lieu of the cash credit; and rude barter still keeps at a distance monetary and civilized exchange." *Id.* at 83.

[28] *See generally* JEAN-LAURENT ROSENTHAL, THE FRUITS OF THE REVOLUTION: PROPERTY RIGHTS, LITIGATION, AND FRENCH AGRICULTURE 1700–1860 (1992). *See also* WORLD HISTORY AT KMLA, *France 1870–1890: The Economy*, http://www.zum.de/whkmla/region/france/france18701890ec.html (revealing statistics on the French economy from 1870–1890, which shows an increase in the French railway net from 15,544 km in 1870 to 33,280 km in 1890; it also includes a table of French governmental revenues and expenditures during the same period of time).

[29] Hautcoeur & Levratto, *supra* note 21, at 6.

> Property-owners, who were to dominate the political elite up to 1830 at least, and owned much of the nation's financial assets, didn't favour the emergence of new elites who could use bankruptcy as an instrument for reneging on their debts, and they preached that reputation and experience should be more valued than risk-taking and innovation. . . . The special protection of mortgage and secured debt under bankruptcy law was the result of a compromise: property-owners accepted that merchants could defect (*sic*) on their debt as long as that debt was due to other merchants, not to them. The organization of the commercial court was another one: their independence in normal operations was counterbalanced by the ultimate control of civil-law judges through the appeal courts and the Cassation court. . . . The power of the civil judges was reinforced by their right to judge a merchant for *banqueroute* (which supposes an offence or a crime). . . .
>
> The 1830 Revolution, bringing to the power liberals and especially bankers (two of the regime's prime ministers), was then essential in the passing of the more liberal 1838 bankruptcy law.[30]

It should be noted that these reforms, enacted barely three decades after the Code's enactment, affected more than one third of its original text.

§ 10.2 THE SCOPE OF AN "OBJECTIVE" COMMERCIAL CODE: ONE OR TWO MORALITIES?

A. Acts of Commerce and the Protection of Bourgeois (Non-Merchant) Fathers of Families

Among the most influential features of the *Code de Commerce* were the rules on its scope, or on the transactions that it would govern. Numerous commercial codes throughout the civil law world adopted its so-called "objective" approach, *i.e.*, a scope determined by the commercial transactions it listed, rather than by the commercial status of those who participated in these transactions. This latter criterion is known as the "subjective" approach and it is usually associated with the German Commercial Code, which will be discussed in a later chapter.[31]

It is worth remembering that Napoleon Bonaparte's goal was to protect non-merchants, particularly from the misfortunes of credit transactions that so frequently led to the "mobilization" and loss of fortunes and to the dissipation of family assets (as in the Red Ink case).[32] As just noted, he strongly wanted to discourage the use of bills of exchange or other negotiable instruments by those who were not in business, and especially by bourgeois fathers of family. Yet, as will be discussed shortly, despite this specific context, the listing of acts of commerce by the *Code de Commerce* was regarded in societies far removed from Napoleon's bourgeoisie and dangerous courtesans as a legal-scientific breakthrough applicable universally to the nascent discipline of commercial code drafting and interpretation.

From a legislative standpoint, it was necessary to ensure that those whom the emperor wanted to protect from the perils of commerce would be governed by the *Code*

---

[30] *Id.* at 6–7 (citations omitted).

[31] *See infra* chs. 11–12.

[32] *See supra* § 10:1(A).

Civil rather than by the *Code de Commerce*. As was discussed in an earlier chapter,[33] such protection applied to transactions that were mostly face-to-face. In transactions that entailed the transfer or mortgage of real property, the *Code Civil* prescribed formalities such as notarial deeds. It encouraged their strict or literal method of interpretation and relied on special remedies such as the rescission of sales of land when their price was below a certain percentage of its market value.[34] Further, their *causa* was omnipresent and traveled with the contractual promises it was supposed to have inspired.[35] Frequently, its immorality or illegality would render such promises unenforceable. Undoubtedly, all of these features reflected a morality peculiar to the civil transactions (meaning not-for-profit transactions) of the *Code Civil*. Such morality contrasted with the morality of the *Code de Commerce*, whose ultimate purpose was to encourage and protect the activities of merchants.

By constructing the *Code de Commerce* around "acts of commerce," its drafters wanted to avoid the impression that its distinguishing features were privileges granted to merchants. Privileges, it should be remembered, were anathema to the revolutionary principle of equality before the law. Thus, if the *Code de Commerce* required fewer contractual formalities and shorter periods for trials and execution and statutes of limitation than the *Code Civil*, it was because of the requirements of the listed types of commercial transactions. Similarly, it was argued by the defenders of the objective scope that if the *Code de Commerce* allowed foreclosure and statutes of limitations or the discharge of debts following bankruptcy, it was because they were attributable to the habitual performance of certain commercial acts or transactions.

Yet the difficulties of using a criterion that would determine the scope of the *Code de Commerce* by separating "*actes de commerce*" from the status of merchants who performed them became apparent from the moment that code was enacted. On the one hand, Article 1 defined merchants as those "who perform acts of commerce and make it their habitual profession" ("*ceux qui exercent des actes de commerce, et en font leur profession habituelle*").[36] On the other hand, Article 721(3) stated that commercial courts had jurisdiction over cases arising from the performance of acts of commerce, *regardless of who performed them*.[37] At its root, the contradiction arose because the drafters of the list of *actes de commerce* attempted to reconcile irreconcilable goals; one aimed at avoiding the appearance of granting privileges to merchants and the other at carving out a legal regime that would encourage the practice of the commercial profession.

---

[33] *See supra* § 8:8.

[34] *Id.*

[35] *Id.*

[36] C. COM. (FR.) art. 1 (1807).

[37] C. COM. (FR.) art. L721–3 (2008). Unless otherwise indicated, all the English translations of the *Code de Commerce* provisions belong to Legifrance (*see* Frequently Cited). This article stated that commercial courts shall take cognizance "of those disputes related to acts of commerce among all persons" ("*3° de celles relatives aux actes de commerce entre toutes personnes*").

B. The List of Acts of Commerce in Original Articles 632 and 633 of the *Code de Commerce*

The original version of the list of acts of commerce appeared in Articles 632 and 633 of the *Code de Commerce*:[38]

> Article 632: The law recognizes, as commercial acts,
>
> Every purchase of merchandise or produce, in order to be sold again, whether in its natural state, or after undergoing some change by labour and art, or even in order simply to let out the use of it.
>
> Every enterprise of manufactures, of commission, of transportation by land or water.
>
> Every contract to furnish provisions or merchandise, every undertaking of agency, or general business, establishments of auctions and theatrical exhibitions.
>
> Every operation of exchange, banking, and brokerage.
>
> All the operations of public banks.
>
> All contracts between merchants, shopkeepers and bankers.
>
> Remittances of bills of exchange, or of money, from place to place, between persons of any description.[39]
>
> Article 633: The law likewise recognises, as commercial acts,
>
> All contracts for the building, the purchase, sale and resale of vessels for foreign and inland navigation.
>
> All maritime shipments.
>
> All purchases or sales of rigging, apparel, and provisions.
>
> All contracts for freight, bottomry, and respondentia loans, insurance, and other contracts concerning maritime commerce.
>
> All agreements and stipulations for the pay and wages of ships' crews.
>
> All engagements of seamen, in the service of merchant vessels.[40]

The above list of acts of commerce did not result from an empirical study of the peculiar features of each of the numerous businesses that existed in pre-codification France.[41] Instead, it was a list that was quickly and carelessly put together. In addition to the omission of businesses that Pardessus noted,[42] it left out others that Fernand

---

[38] *See* THE COMMERCIAL CODE OF FRANCE, WITH THE MOTIVES, OR DISCOURSES OF THE COUNSELLORS OF STATE, DELIVERED BEFORE THE LEGISLATIVE BODY, ILLUSTRATIVE OF THE PRINCIPLES AND PROVISIONS OF THE CODE (John Rodman trans., 1814). This was the closest text to the original version of Article 632 of the *Code de Commerce* that I was able to find in law libraries in the United States. I am very grateful to Mary Johns, Electronic Services Librarian of the Paul M. Herbert Law Center, Louisiana State University for locating this text and double-checking its contents with me.

[39] C. COM. (FR.) art. 632 (1807).

[40] *Id.* art. 633.

[41] In contrast, see § 6:2(F) for Braudel's description of the various types of merchants doing business in France in the 17th and 18th centuries.

[42] *See supra* § 10:1(A).

Braudel had characterized as part of Europe's "high commerce," which included, among others, warehousing and non-maritime insurance.

1. A Closed List of Acts of Commerce: The Exegetes

The *Code de Commerce* list did not specify if it was open or closed in number (*numerus apertus* or *numerus clausus*). The main argument against treating the list as closed was commerce itself, an activity as changing and self-invigorating as the imagination of its practitioners. An argument in favor of a *numerus clausus* interpretation was the repeated presence in Articles 632 and 633 of all encompassing adjectives such as "every" or "all" agreements and the absence of "analogical" clauses such as "and similar transactions" or "like contracts or enterprises."

However, the most important reason in favor of the *numerus clausus* approach was, in my opinion, the scholastic method of reasoning employed by the first and most influential interpreters of the *Code Civil* and *Code de Commerce* known as "*exegetes*." To establish the meaning of ambiguous or incomplete texts, these interpreters relied solely on the existing texts. Nothing outside of those texts was an appropriate tool or basis of interpretation.[43] Thus, the *exegetes*' interpretation was as closed to extrinsic or empirical evidence of legislative intent as was the text of the definitions and classifications of contracts drafted by Pothier, among others.

It will be recalled that when Pothier drafted his definitions and classifications of French contracts, he fixed the meaning of the term "contract" for all places and time (for those who accepted his definition). He did the same thing with his classification of contracts, *i.e.*, contracts could only be bilateral, unilateral, consensual, real, etc. *Mutatis mutandi*, the *exegetes* assumed that the number and meaning of the acts of commerce were limited by what appeared within the decreed list. Not surprisingly, Georges Ripert concluded that it was the "exegetic school that felt obliged to give the list of Articles 632 and 633 a limited [closed] character."[44]

Yet, if the list of acts of commerce was closed, what law applied to acts that, although unlisted, were indispensable to those listed? In Chapter 11,[45] the reader will find a description of how Nathan Rothschild, one of Europe's preeminent eighteenth-century wool merchants, did his buying and selling. In order to buy wool at the best possible price, he supplied many of his English manufacturer-sellers with raw materials and dye. Yet, as literally and strictly interpreted by *exegetes*, Nathan

---

[43] This method of interpretation was not peculiar to France. As will be discussed in Chapter 13, similar tendencies could be found among leading nineteenth and early twentieth century German and Italian commercial law professors such as Heinrich Thöl and Alfredo Rocco. The latter was quite emphatic about the "positivistic" nature of his exegesis. *See* ALFREDO ROCCO, PRINCIPIOS DE DERECHO MERCANTIL, PARTE GENERAL 101 (Revista de Derecho Privado trans., Editora Nacional undated) (1931). In the summary of each of the chapter's headings Professor Rocco states:

> 26. Civil Law is not a source of Commercial Law (*El Derecho civil no es fuente del Derecho mercantil*).
>
> 27. Commercial Law is the only Source (*La "ley mercantil" es la única fuente*). Neither are [sources of commercial law] case law, equity, the nature of things, general principles of the law nor foreign law (*No lo son la jurisprudencia, la equidad, la naturaleza de los hechos y principios generales del Derecho, ni las leyes extranjeras*).

Id. (author's translation).

[44] RIPERT, at 155 (author's translation).

[45] *See infra* § 11:4.

Rothschild's supplies of raw materials and dyes to his manufacturers were not acts of commerce as listed by Articles 632 and 633.

Similarly, consider the case of a retail merchant's purchase or rental of vehicles not for resale or lease, but as the equipment that would deliver goods sold by his business. How could such unlisted purchases or leases be governed by Article 632? Conversely, would the *Code de Commerce* apply to acts such as the purchase of school supplies for their resale (an act listed as commercial) when it was carried out by a non-merchant "civil" professional such as a manager of student housing (*maître de pension*)? Convinced by the exegetic's approach, France's Supreme Court as late as 1931 decided that such an act was civil, despite the housekeeper's intent to profit from it.[46]

2. *Commerce as Defined by Commercial Scholastics*

As a result of the gaps in the lists of Articles 632 and 633 and their progeny, there developed an academic cottage industry of Aristotelian-influenced definitions of the terms "commerce" or "commercial" and of classifications of interstitial acts of commerce. I will illustrate it with selections from the four volume *Elementary Treatise of Commercial Law* by the late Argentine commercial law professor Carlos Malagarriga.[47]

After quoting French, Italian, and English nineteenth- and twentieth-century authors, Professor Malagarriga found what appeared to be a convincing line of thought. He quoted a German author who found the essence of what was commercial in "the massive traffic"[48] of goods. Thereafter, Malagarriga quoted the writings of the respected Spanish professor, Joaquín Garrigues. Garrigues added that a commercial activity requires "a large number of transactions, and that they be of a similar and typical nature."[49] At this point of his enumeration of definitions (three pages into it), Malagarriga referred to the views of Professor Lorenzo Mossa of the University of Pisa, Italy. Mossa found in the notion of "enterprise" the true essence of what is commercial.[50] This is a concept, incidentally, that, despite its literary connotations, was closely connected with Mussolini's fascist attempts to place capital, industry and labor under his political control.

Interestingly, the concept of enterprise (*impresa*) informed not only the drafting of the Italian Civil Code of 1942, but also of commercial codes in Latin America, supposedly imbued with an ideology contrary to fascism.[51] For example, the Commercial Code of Honduras of 1950, unlike the Italian Civil Code of 1942, was drafted by Professor Joaquín Rodríguez Rodríguez, a Spanish Marxist who found refuge in Mexico during the Second World War and whose writings were highly

---

[46] Cour de cassation [Cass.] [supreme court for judicial matters] civ., Apr. 30, 1931, D. 1931, 314, *cited in* RIPERT, *supra* note 24, at 155.

[47] CARLOS C. MALAGARRIGA, I TRATADO ELEMENTAL DE DERECHO COMERCIAL (1963). The author describes how he wrote this treatise and quotes one of its reviewers who compared it favorably to the most erudite publications in foreign lands. *Id.* at IX.

[48] *Id.* at 3 (citing to an otherwise unidentified German author whom he refers to as Hech).

[49] *Id.* at 3 n.13 (citing to Emilio Langle, another Spanish author).

[50] *Id.* at 3 n.14.

[51] *See infra* § 27:4(B) (on the remedy of excessive onerousness and for a discussion on the influence of the Italian Civil Code upon the Honduran Commercial Code and other Latin American codes).

regarded in Mexico and Central America. As will be discussed shortly, the mere fact that the same essence informed codes written by fascists and Marxists is in itself not without significance.

The Italian Civil Code of 1942 was referred to as "unified" because its chapter on obligations applied equally to civil and commercial transactions. Accordingly, Malagarriga quoted Mossa for the definition of commercial law as "the law of an organized economy"[52] and the enterprise (*empresa*) as "the economic person regulated by commercial law."[53] This would suggest that the idea of *empresa* could be regarded as a subjective approach to codifying commercial law, yet in reality, it is a product of commercial legal scholasticism. After a search for what is "commerce," it came up with the notion of "enterprise" or what it means to be "entrepreneurial." Does it help a code interpreter to define the scope of any commercial code in order to ascertain if it is "devoted to enterprise"? In this author's opinion, there is enough reason to doubt its helpfulness; the code's "devotion" to enterprise is ultimately a metaphysical question.

Approaching the end of his lengthy enumeration of definitions of the term "commercial," Professor Malagarriga acknowledged that he was not convinced by the preceding definitions, especially those of the *impresa* type. He reasoned that they did not take into account isolated commercial acts that should still be entitled to be treated as commercial, nor did they answer the criticism by Professor Tulio Ascarelli, another famous Italian professor. Ascarelli had pointed out that commercial codes and their commentators had traditionally regarded agricultural enterprises as non-commercial and yet they were enterprises by Professor Mossa's definition. He also pointed out that the definition of the essence of commerce, as the *intermediation between producers and consumers for a profit,* did not cover such an important commercial activity as the issuance, discount and negotiation of negotiable instruments.[54] As his *pièce de résistance*, Professor Malagarriga offered his own definition of what was commercial. In words at first reminiscent of Pothier's Aristotelian definition of the term contract, he stated:

> Simply, in our opinion, [that which is commercial law is] a branch of private law that deals with certain activities, however not from all points of view, carried out or not in an accidental manner, [activities] which for various reasons have been deemed necessary or convenient not to be the primary object [of regulation] of civil, ordinary or general law.[55]

When I read this definition, I was struck first by its euphemistic use of "simply" and then by the qualifications of each of its elements after taking into account the previous definitions of "commercial." In true scholastic and Aristotelian fashion, Malagarriga started his definition by placing the species, *i.e.*, commercial law, within the genus of "private law," much as Pothier started his attempt to define contract by placing it within the genus of voluntary obligations. Having done this, the empirical support for his definition was found solely within the scholastic definitions of commerce

---

[52] MALAGARRIGA, *supra* note 47, at 3.

[53] *Id.*

[54] *Id.* at 5 (citing to TULIO ASCARELLI, PANORAMA DEL DERECHO COMERCIAL 4–5 (1949)). I have added to Malagarriga's reference to the "intermediation" definition, because this was the definition that I was taught as a commercial law student as providing the truest of essences.

[55] *Id.* (author's translation)

he had listed in the previous five pages. He does not provide a single reference to what were easily observable commercial activities in the professional activities of Argentine merchants. Simply put, observation or any other empirical means of acquiring or refining knowledge on a proffered seminal legal institution such as acts of commerce were not tools of this definitional effort. Either someone else's observation (wherever and whenever it took place) was trusted to have provided the factual universe for the definition or the factual universe was simply secondary.

Take, for example, the assumed non-commercial nature of agri-business referred to in the section devoted to Professor Ascarelli's views above. It just so happens that one of Argentina's most flourishing and vital businesses was agribusiness. To this day, Argentina has remained one of the largest suppliers of grain to the world. Moreover, as a result of man's industrial use and misuse of arable land, presently, more than ever before in its history, agribusiness is an essential component of local and international trade. Are present day commercial codes or statutes supposed to ignore this physical and economic reality because of a definition or classification of commerce inspired by a medieval-feudal view of the nature of land exploitation?

The same question should be asked about the commercialization of real property transactions, especially those involving the public sale of commercial paper backed by mortgages or other real property liens. Despite the fact that low- and middle-income housing is now being financed in many countries and continents by these transactions, should they still be governed by civil codes? This is especially problematic because these codes assume that these transactions seldom take place, are highly individualized, and are at a given point of their existence "causal" (as opposed to abstract or negotiable in nature) and thus subject to costly and lengthy formalities as well as to causal defenses?

Finally, is it not telling that a concept like *empresa* can inspire a code drafted by law professors supported by a fascist state to do its bidding and by a Marxist scholar intent on providing a developing nation with the best of his legal science? Such a use of *empresa* shows its divorce from its socio-economic context and from marketplace realities, so much so that it renders such a reality legally meaningless. Despite its alleged conceptual precision, *empresa* can equally justify unrestricted profit-making and monopoly as it can consumer protection against excessive prices and anti-monopoly legislation.

3. Acts of Commerce Scholastically Classified: Principal and Accessory Acts

While *exegetes* and some later commentators treated all unlisted acts as non-commercial, regardless of whether they were carried out by merchants and contributed to the viability of the listed acts, Georges Ripert pointed out that many of these acts were not merely "accessory," but essentially commercial.[56] As examples of accessory acts, he referred to the earlier mentioned acquisitions of raw materials by merchants intending to finance their craftsmen (*l'achat du matériel*), the rental of vehicles (*la location des véhicules*), and the opening of banking credit (*l'ouverture de crédit chez le banquier*).[57]

---

[56] RIPERT, at 155.

[57] *Id.*

Nathan Rothschild would have heartily agreed with Georges Ripert's analysis. For as it turned out, his success was not as much due to the lower-than-market prices at which he sold his wool, but to his lower costs in the acquisition of the wool. Operating at a much smaller, but also successful scale, my father would have heartily agreed with Nathan Rothschild and Georges Ripert. I once asked him to what he attributed his success in retail and wholesale. He replied: "Once you establish a good reputation for your products and prices, your success will depend upon how much you can lower all your costs, not only of acquisition, but also of production and distribution."[58]

Yet, if they were characterized as "accessory acts of commerce," the transactions that enabled such savings could only come into the list of acts of commerce as interstitial categories under the shadow, so to speak, of listed acts. The application of a commercial law to them thus became questionable. The commercial nature of these accessory acts would require the not so easy proof of how much they contributed to the viability of the listed acts.

4. *Unilaterally Commercial or Mixed Civil and Commercial Acts*

All too frequently, a contract or transaction would take place in which one of the participants performed one of the listed commercial acts and the other an "essentially civil" act. For example, say the seller was an automobile dealer who sold one of his cars and the buyer was a bourgeois father of a family who purchased the automobile strictly for family use. The solution most consistent with the "*cordon sanitaire*," or quarantine line, which Napoleon advocated in an effort to separate the acts of commerce, would apply the *Code de Commerce* to the seller's rights and duties and the *Code Civil* to the buyer's.[59] Yet, aside from the procedural and evidentiary conundrum such a solution would create, what could the judge do about the frequent conflicts between these codes? For example, if according to the *Code Civil* a certain formality was essential for that type of civil contract, would the judge dismiss the case in which a defendant buyer had unjustly enriched himself or would he require restitution and if so, of what or how much?

In the case of another commonly mixed act, the issuance of negotiable instruments such as promissory notes or bills of exchange by a non-merchant and their negotiation by a merchant or banker, Article 636 of the *Code de Commerce* opted, as noted earlier, for an inconclusive solution: the non-merchant signer, endorser or endorsee could have the dispute removed from the commercial to the ordinary civil courts, yet it said nothing about the choice of substantive law for that or any other act of commerce.[60] A decision handed down by the *Cour de Cassation* on May 8, 1907 appeared to supply the rule that governed the choice of substantive law:

> In the case of litigation between two parties in which only one is a merchant or with respect of a non-commercial act for one of them, the party who is not a merchant or who has not engaged in a commercial act has the right to have the case decided by the competent civil jurisdiction, or to bring an action, at

---

[58] Abram Kozolchyk, this author's father (*circa* 1956).

[59] ROBERTO GOLDSCHMIDT, CURSO DE DERECHO MERCANTIL, PARTE GENERAL 32 n.1 (1964).

[60] *See supra* § 10:1(A).

his choice, against the commercial defendant before a civil or commercial tribunal.[61]

Implicit in this choice of law rule was the assumption that the *Code Civil* would be the one applied by the "competent civil jurisdiction."[62] Dalloz's annotated version of the *Code de Commerce* cites similar decisions handed down during 1908, 1930, 1944, and 1965.[63] This choice clearly preferred the interests of the buyer and his likely choice of the *Code Civil*. Accordingly, a seller or lender who acted in good faith (as he is generally presumed to have acted by the *Code Civil*) could not rely on the law with which he was most familiar (including customs, usages, and practices), a law that allowed informal contracts and that he had every reason to believe would apply to the transaction in question. His contract could well lose its binding force under the *Code Civil* because of lack of an essential or solemn formality.

Surprisingly, Georges Ripert's research led him to a contrary conclusion:

> Case law [which Ripert does not cite] do[es] not content itself with deciding that the acts carried out by merchants in the exercise of their profession are commercial, but *presumes* that the acts engaged in by merchants are needed for the exploitation of his business.[64]

Elsewhere, Ripert noted that the choice of law would have been simplified had the courts simply said that acts of commerce are those carried out by professional merchants.[65] While I agree with the wisdom of a presumption in favor of commercial acts, particularly in a world in which many non-traditional merchants continuously perform acts that are either listed as commercial or are interstitial to them, this presumption conflicts with his own suggestion that everything would be easier if acts of commerce were defined as carried out only by professional merchants. Please notice that most of the small and micro-businesses in developing nations are not carried out by professional merchants. What effect would the requirement of professionalism have upon the viability of such businesses?

5. *The Commercial Lawyer's Predicament*

a. Introduction

By now, the reader should be able to envisage the predicament of a commercial lawyer in an acts-of-commerce jurisdiction who is asked to advise his clients on the law applicable to unlisted or interstitial acts of commerce or on unilateral or mixed acts. If his client, say an automobile dealer, asks him to draft a sale agreement for vehicles that will be sold to another merchant who will use them primarily in his business, this seemingly simple task could require considerable research only to conclude that the law is uncertain.

The drafter will have to consider the buyer's intent at the time of purchase, the time devoted to the business use of the vehicles as contrasted with the time for the buyer's personal use, the possibility that the automobiles would be resold or leased

---

[61] Cour de Cassation [Cass.] civ., May 8, 1907, D.P. I 1911, 222 (Fr.).

[62] C. COM. (FR.) art. 631 (Dalloz 1992–93).

[63] *Id.*

[64] RIPERT, at 155 (author's translation).

[65] *Id.* at 155–56.

after a certain period of time, etc. He would then have to weigh the consequences of applying the rules of each possibly applicable code or statute (such as a consumer protection law). These codes may require diverse formalities, methods of interpretation and adjudication, and possibly result in different outcomes depending upon the case being heard by a commercial, civil, or consumer court, or by an administrative body.

While lecturing at the Aix-en-Provence Law School in the early 1980s, I asked French graduate students and practicing lawyers how they coped with the uncertainties caused by the many gaps in their law on acts of commerce. Some agreed with Georges Ripert's conclusion that courts would ordinarily presume the commercial nature of mixed acts. Thus, they would assume that generally the disputes involving merchants and non-merchants would be heard by commercial courts except on issues that were clearly of consumer protection law. Others insisted on the need to consult the latest case law digests. I then asked, "What if you did not have such digests or if the judicial opinions were divided or unclear?" Silence prevailed.

Imagine, then, the predicament of lawyers in jurisdictions that lack a corpus of commercial, civil and consumer law decisions such as France's. The only source of law these lawyers could rely on would be commercial, civil and consumer law doctrinal writings, many of which would be in sharp conflict with each other. It should also be remembered that one of the most serious problems posed by the scholastically-inspired commercial law writings is their inconsistency with market practices and with prevailing custom and usage.

b. *Foreign Doctrine v. Local Customs:* Picado Guerrero v. Rojas Dias

One case illustrates the consequences of disregarding local custom and usage when deciding upon the effects of acts of commerce, even where the custom and usage pertains to something as basic as commercial nomenclature. One of the most famous commercial law disputes in Costa Rica during the 1960's was *Picado Guerrero v. Rojas Dias.*[66] A fraudster forged bonds of the Central Bank of Nicaragua and offered them for sale to one of the few Costa Rican sellers of securities, Sr. Rojas Dias (hereinafter RD). RD was approached by one of Costa Rica's most prominent lawyers, Lic. Picado Guerrero (hereinafter PG), who inquired if he had heard about any good high-yielding government bonds he could purchase. RD told him that he had been told about the availability of high-yielding Nicaraguan bonds. PG asked that the bonds be sent to the Costa Rican Central Bank for verification of their authenticity. RD did this and was informed that the bonds appeared to be genuine. PG paid RD for the bonds; RD retained a commission and paid the remainder of the purchase price to the seller, supposedly a Nicaraguan government official. In fact, the bonds were forged and the fraudster was captured, but not the stolen money. PG decided to sue RD.

PG alleged that he had engaged in a civil purchase of securities from RD whom he characterized as a professional commission agent (*comisionista*). PG also alleged that RD had performed a commercial act which consisted in the resale of forged bonds with the intent to profit therefrom. This commercial act, as listed in the Commercial Code of Costa Rica, differed from the commercial act of brokerage (*corretaje*) in that a

---

[66] BORIS KOZOLCHYK & OCTAVIO TORREALBA, II CURSO DE DERECHO MERCANTIL: TEXTO Y MATERIAL DE ESTUDIO 139 (1971).

commercial agent (as the defendant allegedly was) acts in his own name and warrants to his purchasers the genuineness of what they bought from him.

In his response, RD argued that while it was true that he advertised his services as a *comisionista*, the meaning of this term in the Costa Rican marketplace was similar to that of broker (*corredor*) and that all of his clients, including PG, knew that RD's acts of commerce were only as an intermediary who did not assume liability for what the original seller sold. He and many of his clients testified before the trial court that he always made it clear to his customers that he was a mere intermediary without the staff or resources, including insurance, to warrant anything to his buyers. The marketplace in San Jose was small for his acts of commerce. He estimated that out of a population of approximately 250,000 inhabitants, he sold securities and land to no more than fifty buyers in a good year. He further testified that he and his customers knew each other well and that the plaintiff was one of the most knowledgeable investors and as such, was aware of the conditions under which the defendant acted.

Consistent with the strictly legal appeal ("*casacion*") procedures before the Supreme Court, the only issue before the court was the legal import of the acts of commerce by a "*comisionista*" as opposed to that of a "*corredor*" and whether RD acted as one or the other. Lacking national case law and doctrinal commentary on the legal implications of RD's act, the Supreme Court of Costa Rica turned to Mexican commercial law writings, which were taught in Costa Rican law schools and influenced the drafters of the Costa Rican Commercial Code. These writings convinced the court that RD advertised himself as a *comisionista*, acted as one, and sold on his own behalf. Since he introduced no documentary evidence before the trial court of his customary disclaimer of liability, the court had to assume that RD was responsible for the damages suffered by PG as a buyer of the forged bonds.

During my two-year stay in Costa Rica, I asked a number of RD's clients whether they were all aware that he only acted as a broker, despite his title of *comisionista*. They answered that they were aware he served as a broker. They also said that they would not have expected him to assume liability for the genuineness of the securities that they had bought from a third-party seller through him.

This case illustrates the perils of relying on scholastic definitions and classifications at odds with market practices, course of dealing, usages and customs. It also illustrates how scholastic definitions and classifications disregard the purpose of a list of acts of commerce. Surely acts of commerce were not drafted to provide a battle ground for academics eager to prove the brilliance of their deductive and definitional powers. Their purpose was to provide quick and reliable answers to the most basic of legal questions concerning a participant in a marketplace transaction: What law governs this transaction?

§ 10.3 MEXICO'S EXPERIENCE WITH ITS ACTS OF COMMERCE

The Mexican Federal Commercial Code of 1889 also listed its acts of commerce and broadened the *Code de Commerce's* definition of merchants to include, among others, certain farmers:

> Article 4: Those persons who accidentally, with or without a principal place of business, perform any commercial act, even though they are not legally considered merchants, shall be subject to commercial laws. Therefore,

farmers and manufacturers, and generally those who have set up a warehouse or store in a town in order to sell fruits grown in their land or products manufactured by their industry or work, just as produced in their unaltered state, shall be deemed merchants in everything that is related to [trade in] their stores or warehouses.[67]

Article 75: The law deems acts of commerce:

I. All purchases, sales and leases entered into for the purpose of commercial speculation, of maintenance, [of] moveable property or merchandise, whether in their natural state or after having been worked upon or manufactured;

II. The purchase and sale of realty when carried on with said purpose of commercial speculation;

III. The purchase and sale of participations, shares and bonds of commercial business associations;

IV. Contracts related to governmental obligations and other negotiable instruments currently traded in the marketplace;

V. Enterprises devoted to make provisions and supplies available;

VI. Enterprises devoted to public and private construction work;

VII. Enterprises devoted to manufacturing;

VIII. Enterprises devoted to the transportation of persons or carriage goods, either over land or by water;

IX. Enterprises devoted to the selling of books as well as editorial and printing enterprises;

X. Enterprises devoted to commissions, agency, offices carrying out commercial negotiations and public auctions or sales;

XI. Enterprises devoted to public entertainment;

XII. Transactions of commercial agency;

XIII. Contracts of intermediation [brokerage] in commercial transactions;

XIV. Banking transactions;

XV. All contracts related to maritime commerce and navigation, either by sea or by inland waterways;

XVI. Insurance contracts of all types, as long as they are issued by enterprises;

XVII. Contracts of deposit as a result of commercial transactions;

XVIII. Deposits in warehouses, and all transactions with certificates of deposit and pledge receipts or bonds issued by them;

XIX. Checks, bills of exchange or other transfers of money made from one commercial place [*plaza*] to another among all types of persons;

---

[67] COD. COM.(MEX.) art. 4 (1889).

XX. Commercial receipts or other commercial instruments payable to order or bearer, and other obligations undertaken by merchants; unless it is shown that they stem from non-commercial acts or transactions;

XXI. Obligations among merchants and bankers, unless they are of an essentially civil nature;

XXII. Contracts and obligations of the employees of merchants as long as they are connected with the commercial activities of the merchant who employs them;

XXIII. The sale of agricultural products from the estate or parcel of and by the owner or grower;

XXIV. Operations contained in the General Law of Titles and Credit Operations;

XXV. Any other acts of an analogous nature to those set forth by this Code.

In case of doubt, the commercial nature of an act shall be determined by judicial decision.[68]

. . .

Article 1049: Commercial trials are those whose object is to hear and decide controversies that, pursuant to Articles 4, 75 and 76, derive from acts of commerce.[69]

Article 1050: When, pursuant to the previous Articles 4, 75 and 76, one of the parties to a contract is performing an act of commerce and the other an essentially civil act, and litigation arises from such contract, the dispute will be governed by the provisions of this Book if the party performing the act of commerce is the defendant to the dispute. On the other hand, when the defendant is the party that performed an essentially civil act, the dispute will be governed by the rules of ordinary Law.[70]

A. The Broadened Scope of Mexico's Acts of Commerce

While broadening the scope of Mexico's acts of commerce to include agribusiness, Article 4 characterizes as commercial only that business conducted by the producer of the fruits of the land in his own store or warehouse "in town" (presumably close to where they were produced) as long as the products are in an "unaltered state." On the other hand, Sections I and II of Article 75 are willing to include agriculture and real estate as part of commerce. Why did the Mexican legislator hesitate to include agricultural activities as acts of commerce? Contrast these provisions with Section 3(1) of the German Commercial Code, which includes as merchants agriculture and forestry farmers who voluntarily register as such:

---

[68] *Id.* art. 75.

[69] *Id.* art. 1049.

[70] *Id.* art. 1050.

> § 3(1) [on voluntary registration] § 2 applies to an agricultural or forestry undertaking with the provision that the proprietor is entitled, but not obliged, to effect the registration in the Commercial Register. . . .[71]

B. The Mixed or Unilaterally Civil or Commercial Act in Mexico

Assume that "A" buys a widget from "B" in B's store in a transaction where B intends to make a profit and A intends to use the widget as any other consumer would. In accordance with Article 1050 of the Mexican Federal Commercial Code (1889), this transaction would be governed by a commercial law which is not particularly protective of consumers, especially in their ability to rescind a sale because of "subjective lesion." This is a remedy that the Federal Civil Code of Mexico (not Mexico's Federal Commercial Code) awards when one party takes advantage of the other's "severe ignorance, notorious inexperience or extreme misery."[72]

In contrast with this Civil Code remedy, Article 385 of the Mexican Federal Commercial Code provides, in its relevant part: "Commercial sales shall not be rescinded because of lesion. . . ."[73] On the other hand, Mexico enacted a Federal Consumer Protection Law in 1992 and substantially amended it in 2004.[74] Article 10 of the Federal Consumer Protection Law states:

> Suppliers may not use coercive and unfair commercial practices or methods, or unconscionable clauses or conditions. . . .[75]

Thus, if a commercial seller or supplier uses practices or methods that are coercive or unfair, his consumer buyer does have a remedy which may, and frequently does, differ from the rescission remedy provided by Article 17 of the Mexican Federal Civil Code.

Meanwhile, the history of the amendment of Article 1050 of Mexico's Federal Commercial Code reflects the difficulties experienced with the listing of acts of commerce and the choice of applicable Mexican law. As previously provided, the original (1889) version of Article 1050 stated:

> When, pursuant to the previous Articles 4, 75 and 76, one of the parties to a contract is performing an act of commerce and the other an essentially civil act, and litigation arises from such contract, the dispute will be governed by

---

[71] HGB (GOREN, 1998), at § 3 (1).

[72] Mexican C.C.F. art. 17 (1932). The current version reads as follows:

> When someone, exploiting the extreme ignorance, notorious inexperience or extreme misery of the other, obtains an excessive profit which is evidently disproportionate to what he is obligated to perform, the aggrieved party has the right to elect between requesting the annulment of the contract or the equitable reduction of his obligation, in addition to compensation for the damages suffered.

Mexican C.C.F. art. 17 (2008).

[73] COD. COM.(MEX.) art. 385 (1889). This provision remains unchanged in the Federal Commercial Code currently in effect in Mexico. For a survey of the remedies available for breach of contracts, see chs. 25–30.

[74] Up until the enactment of the Federal Consumer Protection Law in Mexico (L.F.P.C.), Article 385 of the Mexican Federal Commercial Code precluded the application of lesion found under Article 17 of the Mexican Civil Code on "subjective lesion," where the sale was commercial for one of the parties. Consequently, the protection of Article 17 of the Mexican Civil Code was unavailable to consumer purchasers, or to "the weaker party when it is most needed, *i.e.*, when he deals with an expert." Kozolchyk, *Fairness,* at 228 n.40 (citation omitted).

[75] L.F.P.C. (MEX.) art. 10.

> the provisions of this Book if the party performing the act of commerce is the defendant to the dispute. On the other hand, when the defendant is the party that performed an essentially civil act, the dispute will be governed by the rules of ordinary Law [*las reglas del derecho común*].[76]

This rule was similar to that in the landmark decision by the French *Cour de Cassation* discussed earlier.[77] However, the Mexican provision did not make clear what it meant by the term "*derecho común*." Most interpreters assumed that it meant the law found in the civil codes of each of the Mexican states. Was it that of each state or that of the Federal Civil Code, which served as a model for most states? "[T]hose . . . in favor [of] the application of the state civil code [of the defendant's residence] argued that any statute which deprived them of their right to be governed by their own state law [either by applying the Mexican Federal Commercial Code or the Mexican Federal Civil Code] would be unconstitutional."[78] They invoked Article 73 of the Mexican Constitution,[79] which expressly reserves to each state the power to enact its own civil code.[80] "Yet, as if the above constitutional complexities were not enough, some states [such as the State of Sonora] . . . [have] granted state courts concurrent civil and commercial state . . . [trial courts], albeit governed respectively by the state civil code and the Mexican Federal Commercial Code."[81]

In response to the many uncertainties created by its original text, a 1989 amendment was made to Article 1050 of the Mexican Federal Commercial Code. It now reads as follows:

> When, in accordance with commercial law, an act is of a commercial nature to one of the parties, and of a civil nature to the other party, any controversy derived from it will be governed by commercial laws.[82]

However, Mexico's commercial law does not preclude the application of its Federal Consumer Protection Law when the facts and circumstances warrant it. Does this the end the torturous saga of the application of Article 1050 to mixed sales or commercial transactions in Mexico? What do you think?

C. Some Hope in the Americas: The OAS Convention on Choice of Law

If confusion prevails with respect to the law applicable within each jurisdiction as a result of attempting to apply the list of acts of commerce, imagine the confusion that results when the contract involved is international, especially in Latin America, where many such lists are still in force. The amelioration of this confusion was a major reason

---

[76] COD. COM.(MEX.) art. 1050 (1889).

[77] *See supra* § 10:2(B)(4).

[78] E-mail from Lic. Eduardo Estrella Acedo, practicing trial lawyer and notary public, Obregon, Sonora, Mexico to Dr. Boris Kozolchyk, Executive Director of NLCIFT (July 18, 2008) (author's translation) (on file with author).

[79] MEX. CONST. art. 73 (1917).

[80] *See* ROBERTO L. MANTILLA MOLINA, DERECHO MERCANTIL 74–77 (9th ed. 1966).

[81] E-mail from Lic. Eduardo Estrella Acedo, *supra* note 78.

[82] COD. COM.(MEX.) art. 1050 (2008).

behind the enactment of the Organization of American States' (OAS) 1994 Convention on the Law Applicable to International Contracts.[83]

One of this convention's most useful features is the parties' autonomy to choose the applicable law regardless of the connections of such a law with the place where the contracts were entered into or where the acts of commerce took place.[84] Another useful feature is its encouragement to courts to apply widely followed international commercial usages and customs.[85] Hopefully, this convention will convince courts in the Western Hemisphere to turn to more predictable, fair and equitable sources of commercial law than those that now result from the application of the continuously uncertain lists of acts of commerce.

D. Conclusions

What would be the response if one were to ask the Von Ihering-inspired question, "Judging by the experiences with the *Code de Commerce* and the Mexican Federal Commercial Code, did their lists of acts of commerce accomplish their purpose?" The answer would have to be in the negative. Both France and Mexico have had to struggle with serious uncertainty of applicable law, including, in the case of Mexico, constitutional issues, and both have had to add new acts of commerce to their original lists.

If not as a guide to commercial contract dispute resolution, how useful have the lists of acts of commerce been? Aside from helping to justify the enactment of a commercial law that would replace feudal and guild law, were there other problems resolved by the listing of these acts?

The preceding comparative analysis of the socio-economic context of the enactment of the *Code de Commerce* shows that however valid the French commercial-civil code dichotomy was when protecting the bourgeois from a commercialized economy, including dangerous courtesans, present-day French and Mexican societies are quite different and so are their civil codes. Therefore, neither the fear of the commercial, as entertained by Napoleon and the bourgeois, nor the desire to be subject to a civil versus a commercial justice, as supposedly entertained by a large segment of the civil

---

[83] Organization of American States, Inter-American Convention on the Law Applicable to International Contracts, Mar. 17, 1994, O.A.S.T.S. No. 78, 33 I.L.M. 732, *available at* http://www.oas.org/juridico/English/treaties/b-56.html [hereinafter Inter-American Convention]. *See also* Boris Kozolchyk, *The UNIDROIT Principles as a Model for the Unification of the Best Contractual Practices in the Americas* 46 AM. J. COMP. L. 151, 175 (1998) (citing to the transcript of the OAS CIDIP-V Meeting of Experts from November 11–14, 1993).

[84] On the determination of applicable law, Article 7 states:

> The contract shall be governed by the law chosen by the parties. The parties' agreement on this selection must be express or, in the event that there is no express agreement, must be evident from the parties' behavior and from the clauses of the contract, considered as a whole. Said selection may relate to the entire contract or to a part of same.

Selection of a certain forum by the parties does not necessarily entail selection of the applicable law.

Inter-American Convention art. 7.

[85] *Id.* art. 10. The article provides as follows:

> In addition to the provisions in the foregoing articles, the guidelines, customs, and principles of international commercial law as well as commercial usage and practices generally accepted shall apply in order to discharge the requirements of justice and equity in the particular case.

Id.

population, has the same meaning in our society as it did at the beginning of the nineteenth century.

It is true that the Mexican Federal Civil Code echoes some of the general principles of the *Code Civil*. One such principle, subject to some exceptions, is the parties' freedom to bind themselves with the form and substance they choose.[86] Yet its drafters made it very clear that what they understood by civil law, as found in their code, was not a law for the bourgeois, but a "private social code" (*Código Privado Social*), one that reflects that:

> The social revolutions of the present century have prompted a complete revision of the basic principles of social organization, and have brought down the traditional dogmas. . . .
>
> . . .
>
> [And so it replaced a] civil Code, which was the product of the economic and legal needs of other eras. . . . When . . . the legal order was governed by an exaggerated individualism . . .[87]

Moreover, this Code governs large segments of a Mexico that is becoming one of the world's leading exporters of industrial and commercial products and services. It is, in brief, a highly commercialized society with volumes of credit large enough, especially in the construction field,[88] to give Napoleon Bonaparte a fatal dose of concern about the fate of his "fathers of bourgeois families." Is this the civil code, "civil law" or the Mexican *derecho común* that the drafters of the *Code de Commerce* or the Mexican Federal Commercial Code intended to rescue from the clutches of commercialization and such tricky instruments as bills of exchange, checks, credit and debit cards, and investment securities both material and dematerialized, including mortgages and trust deeds?

Further, to the extent that the Mexican Federal Civil Code was concerned with the protection of the weaker, more ignorant or inexperienced contracting parties, as expressed in Article 17,[89] it was not the same concern expressed by the *Code Civil* when protecting the bourgeois seller of land.[90] In fact, the closest parallel was Germany's Civil Code Section 138.[91]

In other words, if Mexico's listing of its acts of commerce is an attempt to protect someone when contracting with merchants, it behooves the legislator or adjudicator to establish who that someone is. If that someone was a consumer, presumptively deemed

---

[86] *See, e.g.*, Mexican C.C.F. arts. 1832 & 1839 (1932). As will be discussed in Chapter 14, despite the broad formulation of these principles, certain formalities and causal elements are still required.

[87] LEYES Y CÓDIGOS DE MEXICO, CODIGO CIVIL: PARA EL DISTRITO FEDERAL 7–8 (Editorial Porrúa, S.A., Mexico 1977) (on the "*Motivos del Código Civil*") (this author's translation).

[88] *See* Kozolchyk, *Closing Remarks*, at 437.

[89] *See supra* note 74 and accompanying text.

[90] *See* C. CIV. (FR.) art. 1674 (Barrister 1804).

[91] Section 138 of the BGB states:

> (1) A legal transaction which is contrary to public policy is void. (2) A legal transaction by which a person exploiting the need, inexperience, lack of sound judgment or substantial lack of will power of another, causes to be promised or granted to himself or to a third party in exchange for a performance, pecuniary advantages which are in obvious disproportion to the performance is also void.

See BGB § 138 (GOREN, 1994).

the weaker party in the transaction with a merchant, then the applicable law should not have been an undefined and unpredictable "civil law," but a narrowly defined and predictable consumer protection law. The inevitable conclusion, then, is that the uncertainty of the Mexican law of acts of commerce is not because its interpreters were concerned with protecting a segment of the population from the perils of commercialization, but rather because they attempted to elucidate the abstract (devoid of socio-economic context) meanings of concepts such as "essentially" civil or commercial acts. The badly-needed legal reform, then, should focus on the elimination of the uncertainty of commercial law, especially as it now affects commercial litigation in Mexico.[92]

As a result of the uncertainty of the applicable commercial law to contractual disputes in Mexico, merchants have been reluctant to bring their disputes before the courts, whether civil or commercial. This complaint about Mexican commercial justice is not only heard from Mexican and foreign merchants doing business in Mexico, it is also heard from appellate judges.[93] A recent study by Mexico's prestigious Autonomous Technological Institute (*Instituto Tecnológico Autónomo de México*) (ITAM) on the execution of contracts in Mexico concluded that judicial procedures were less than good.[94] It blamed many, if not most, of the problems of failed execution of contracts on the lack of judicial resources. Inexplicably, it did not take into account the effects of an uncertain commercial law upon the court's poor performance.

I believe that had the effects of the uncertain commercial law been taken into account, including the scholastic rather than factual or empirical examination of the issues and the application of trade usage and custom, the need for a different legislative and judicial approach to the application of this law would have been starkly apparent and would have encouraged the necessary efforts at legal modernization and reform.

§ 10.4 THE ACCORDION-LIKE PRESENT *CODE DE COMMERCE*

A. Introduction

Another consequence of the uncertain nature of the list provided by Article 632 of the *Code de Commerce* has been the need to enact frequent amendments and expansions of its coverage. This continuous expansion accompanied by some occasional contractions led an exasperated Aix-en-Provence law student, who was having

---

[92] NLCIFT, USAID Project: Mexico Trade Capacity Building Project—Enhancement of the Business and Legal Environment and Trade Capacity through Legal Reform and Improvements in the Administration of Justice by Commercial Courts in Mexico (2006–2012).

[93] *See Enhancement of Mexican Commercial Adjudication by Improved Transactional Fact-Finding, Application of Equitable Principles, and Drafting of Standard Contracts and Best Contractual Practices*, 27 ARIZ. J. INT'L & COMP. L. 325, 434 (2010). "Despite the admonition of Articles 278–279 of the Code of Civil Procedure of the D.F., judges have failed to participate in the development of a case's evidence" ("*desarollo de pruebas*"). *Id.* (citation omitted)

[94] *See e.g.*, CONSEJO COORDINADOR FINANCIERO, *Ejecución de Contratos Mercantiles e Hipotecas en las entidades Federativas, Indicadores de Confiabilidad y Desarrollo Institucional Local* 50 (Mar. 2007), *available at* http://www.abm.org.mx/temas_actualidad/LIBRO%20EJECUCION%20DE%20C131B51.pdf (Baja California, Evaluación de los Poderes Judicial, Ejecutivo y Legislativo, Poder Judicial: "*Estructura y funcionamiento de los tribunales y servicios auxiliares, posición: 15 de 32, puntuación: 1.88.*") *Id.* The average for Baja California is 1.88, which is less than good, according to the indicator scale. *Id.* at 15.

difficulties locating the law in force for one of my research assignments, to refer to the *Code de Commerce* as an "accordion-like" code. The following is the 2008 version of the list of acts of commerce in this code:

TITLE I—The Commercial Act

Article L110–1 [former Article 632 of the *Code de Commerce* (1808)]

The law deems as acts of commerce:

1) All purchases of chattels in order to resell . . . [them], either in kind [as acquired] or after having [been transformed or] worked . . . [upon];

2) All purchases of real property in order to resell . . . [it], unless the purchaser has acted in order to construct one or more buildings and to sell these en bloc or site-by-site;

3) All transactions by intermediaries for the purchase, subscription or sale of real property, sales of commercial establishments [bulk sales], shares or participations in real property companies;

4) All chattels rental undertakings;

5) All manufacturing, commission and land or water transport undertakings;

6) All supply, agency, business office, auction house and public entertainment undertakings;

7) All exchange, banking or brokerage transactions;

8) All public banking transactions;

9) All obligations between dealers, merchants and bankers;

10) Bills of exchange between all persons.[95]

Article L110–2 [former Article 633 of the *Code de Commerce (1808)*]

The law also deems commercial instruments to be:

1) All transactions leading to the construction, and all purchases, sales and resales of ships for inland and foreign-going navigation;

2) All sea shipments;

3) All purchases and sales of ship's tackle, apparatus and foodstuffs;

4) All chartering . . . and bottomry loans;

5) All insurances and other contracts relating to maritime trade;

6) All agreements and conventions on crew wages and rents;

7) All engagements of seamen for the service of commercial ships.[96]

---

[95] C. COM. (FR.) art. L110–1 (2008).

[96] *Id.* art. L110–2.

B. A Summary of the Contents of the 2008 Version of the *Code de Commerce*

What follows is a summary discussion of the "accordion-like" text of the 2008 *Code de Commerce* as illustrated in some of its representative provisions. Therefore, the purpose of this section is to provide the reader with a flavor of what the *Code de Commerce* is in our day. By representative provisions, I mean those that best reflect the policies and values of the French drafters as well as their legislative method. The appendix contains extracts of court decisions that are particularly revealing on the scope of the code.[97]

1. The Status and Capacity of a Merchant

Title II of Book I of the *Code de Commerce* lists the requirements to acquire the status and contractual capacity of a merchant, including the status of foreign merchants doing business in France. One of the features of dispute resolution before fair and consular courts, reflected in Article L110–3 (Title I, Book I), states: "With regard to traders, commercial instruments [acts or transactions] may be proven by any means unless the law specifies otherwise."[98] Similarly, Article L110–4 (Title I, Book I) sets forth a number of short statutes of limitation on commercial obligations or claims.

As was done by the original Article 1 of the 1808 version of the *Code de Commerce*, merchants (traders) are defined as "those who carry out commercial instruments [acts or transactions] and who make this their usual profession."[99] The concern with protecting non-merchants and consumers from the risks and evils of commerce is still apparent in this 2008 version of the Code. Thus, "[m]inors, even when declared of full age and capacity, may not be traders."[100] The "[s]pouses of traders shall be deemed to be traders only if they carry out a separate commercial activity from that of their spouse."[101] And, in a departure from the openness to foreign traders typical of the Champagne and other fairs, the *Code de Commerce* forbids foreign merchants to carry out on French soil a commercial or industrial enterprise or craft that requires registration of the company or trade without the consent of the prefect of the department where the foreigner will initially carry out the activity. However, this provision does not apply to nationals of the European Union member states.[102]

2. Statutory and Administrative Obligations of All Merchants

Chapter III of Title II sets forth the statutory and administrative obligations of a merchant, including the duty to register as a legal person in the Companies' Register. A failure to comply with this duty is punishable with the hefty fine of 3,750 Euros. In addition, the non-compliant merchant may be deprived of the right "to vote in, and to

---

[97] *See infra* § 10:8.

[98] C. COM. (FR.) art. L110–3 (2008).

[99] *Id.* art. L121–1.

[100] *Id.* art. L121–2.

[101] *Id.* art. L121–3.

[102] *Id.* arts. L122–1, L122–2. For an explanation of the status of European Union nationals, especially the free movement of workers, see EUROPEAN COMMISSION, *Free Movement—EU Nationals*, http://ec.europa.eu/social/main.jsp?catId=457&langId=en.

stand in, elections to the commercial courts, the chambers of commerce and industry and the industrial tribunals for a period of up to five years."[103]

Another important obligation is that of keeping accurate books and accounts. Merchants are directed to record their transactions "chronologically" and to take stock at least once every twelve months of the "existence and value of the assets and liabilities of the undertaking."[104] In addition, they are required to prepare annual accounts at the end of the financial year in view of the entries made in the accounts and the stock taking. "These annual accounts shall consist of the balance sheet, profit and loss account [statement] and an annex which shall form an inseparable whole."[105] These provisions still reflect the absence in France of a developed commercial credit system where lenders specialize in different types of loans (on inventory, accounts receivable, equipment, intellectual property, etc.) and thereby require account methods consistent with the need of accurate and timely "snapshots" of the state of their collateral.

3. Special Business Associations and Mutual Support Associations

Title II also governs the life of business associations of the traditional and not-so-traditional types. The not-so-traditional types stem from late nineteenth- and early twentieth-century attempts to support the activities of small businessmen and business associations, particularly by their "bigger brothers." Among these supporting associations are: Cooperative Associations of Retailers (Articles L124–1 to L124–16); Collective Shops of Independent Traders (Articles L125–1 to L125–19); and Mutual Guarantee Schemes (Article L126–1). The last of these associations was designed to facilitate credit, especially for small- and medium-sized "traders, industrialists, manufacturers, craftspeople, commercial companies, members of the professions and owners of property or property rights"[106] by means of suretyships and other assumptions of secondary liability. Another business association in the category of "support of others" is one whose purpose is to help others draft business plans involved in the creation or takeover of a business activity.[107]

As will become apparent during a later discussion of pricing and competition rules and policies, there is a distinct and almost organic link between the duties of larger or more successful business associations and their smaller, weaker brothers.[108]

4. Brokers, Commission Agents, Commercial Agents and Carriers

Title III is devoted to brokers, commission agents, other commercial agents, and carriers. Article L131–1 lists the authorized brokers as "commodities brokers, shipbrokers, and land and water transport brokers."[109] The long shadow of guild exclusivity is apparent in Article L131–3 as it restricts the brokering of land and water transportation exclusively to land and water transport brokers. In addition, these brokers are forbidden from combining "their functions with those of the commodity

---

103 C. COM. (FR.) art. L123–4 (2008).

104 *Id.* art. L123–12.

105 *Id.*

106 *Id.* art. L126–1.

107 *Id.* arts. L127–1—L127–7.

108 *See infra* § 10:4(B)(8).

109 C. COM. (FR.) art. L131–1 (2008).

brokers or shipping brokers designated in Article L. 131–1."[110] An even more pronounced influence of the guild system is found in Article L131–5: It specifies what kind of broker can be involved in the sale or purchase of metals (investment and commodities brokers) and then states that "[t]hey alone shall be entitled to fix the prices of these [metals]."[111]

Unfortunately, traditional methods of doing business, while quaint, are often at odds with contemporary international practices, especially in the financial marketplace. For example, the requirements imposed by Article L132–9 on French issued ocean bills of lading (a provision nestled among the rules on maritime brokers) are at odds with the requirements of banks worldwide that issue, confirm or negotiate commercial letters of credit.[112]

5. *Bulk Sales and Commercial Leases*

Title IV is the French law equivalent of the Anglo-American "Bulk Sale" or "Sale of a Business." It is one of the most detailed sections of the Code. Not only does it set forth all of the requirements of bulk sales, but it also includes ancillary transactions such as the leases of real estate that belonged to the sold business and provides:

> Notwithstanding any clause to the contrary, any contract or agreement under the terms of which the owner or operator of a business or a craft establishment grants the lease thereof totally or partially to a manager who operates it at their own risk shall be regulated by the provisions of this chapter.[113]

Chapter V of Title IV similarly regulates commercial leases.[114] Taking into account the scarcity of commercial space that has prevailed in France's largest cities since the end of the Second World War and the considerable amount of litigation caused by this type of contract, the extended coverage of commercial leases is understandable.

6. *Traditional and Not-So-Traditional Business Associations and Economic Interest Groups*

Book II is devoted to the traditional types of business associations and "economic interest groups." Article L210–1 makes it clear that the mere utilization of a business association format or its object (presumably the acts of commerce it engages in) determines the commercial status of the entity. General partnerships, limited partnerships, limited liability companies and joint-stock companies are commercial "by virtue of their form, irrespective of their objects."[115] Because of its popularity among French businesses, the joint-stock company or the corporation, whether closely or publicly held, is given the most extensive treatment, including a good number of public and criminal law provisions.

---

[110] *Id.* art. L131–3.

[111] *Id.* art. L131–5.

[112] *Contrast id.* art. L132–9.

[113] C. COM. (FR.) art. L144–1 (2008).

[114] *Id.* arts. L145–1—L145–60.

[115] *Id.* art. L210–1.

The *Code de Commerce* allows the creation of limited partnerships with shares of stock[116] and simplified joint-stock companies. The latter statute was used as one of two models in Colombia's simplified business corporation law.[117]

7. *Special Commercial Sales*

Book III governs, in part, transactions seldom regulated in such detail by other codes. They include "closing-down," "warehouse," "clearance" and "factory" (retail) sales.[118] The detail reflects a degree of paternalistic protection that can only be implemented by a huge bureaucracy. In reading the following excerpt of the definition of a "closing down" or "bulk sale," one wonders how many government officials would have to be involved in supervising the compliance therewith. According to Article L310–1, a closing-down sale is one:

> [A]ccompanied or preceded by advertising and presented as being intended, through price reductions, to achieve rapid disposal of some or all of the goods held by a commercial establishment following a decision, regardless of the reason therefore, to cease, seasonally suspend, or change its business activity, or to substantially alter its mode of exploitation, are deemed to be clearance sales.
>
> Clearance sales must be declared in advance to the relevant administrative authority having jurisdiction over the location of the clearance sale. The declaration thus made shall state the reason for and duration of the clearance sale, which shall not exceed two months. It shall be accompanied by an inventory of the goods to be disposed of. If the event giving rise to the clearance sale has not taken place within six months, at the latest, of the declaration being made, the declarant is required to inform the relevant administrative authority thereof.
>
> The offering for sale of goods other than those indicated in the inventory in respect of which the prior declaration was made is prohibited for the duration of the clearance sale.[119]

The policy behind this extensive regulation is not altogether clear. The reader is left wondering if the purpose of these rules is to protect the buying public against misrepresentation, the protection of creditors of the closing business, the protection of the stability of prices in the marketplace or all of the above in similar or varying degrees of interest.

8. *Pricing and Competition: The French Equivalent of the Sherman and Clayton Acts?*

Book IV regulates pricing freedom and competition as well as anti-competitive practices.[120] However, before concluding that these provisions, especially those related

---

[116] *Id.* arts. L226–1—L226–14.

[117] *Id.* arts. L227–1—L227–20. For an enlightening discussion on the legal transplantation of French as well as U.S. law to Latin American legislation, *see* FRANCISCO REYES, II LATIN AMERICAN COMPANY LAW 75–83, *especially* 79 n.284 and accompanying text (National Law Center for Inter-American Free Trade ed., 2013).

[118] C. COM. (FR.) arts. L310–1—L322–16 (2008).

[119] *Id.* art. L310–1.

[120] *Id.* arts. L410–1—L470–8.

to pricing, are the French equivalent of United States antitrust and fair pricing legislation, it would be helpful to review Article L410–2:

> Except in cases where the law specifies otherwise, the prices of goods, products and services . . . shall be determined by the free play of competition.
>
> However, in sectors or areas where price competition is limited by either monopoly situations or long-lasting supply problems, or by acts or regulations, a *Conseil d'Etat* decree may regulate the prices after the Council on Competition has been consulted.
>
> The provisions of the first two paragraphs shall not prevent the government from ordering against excessive price increases or reductions, through a *Conseil d'Etat* decree, temporary measures motivated by a crisis situation, exceptional circumstances, a public disaster or a clearly abnormal situation in the market in a given sector. The decree shall be adopted following consultation of the National Consumer Council. It shall specify its period of validity which may not exceed six months.[121]

Five or so years ago, I had conversation with Horacio Gutierrez, Esq., Deputy General Counsel of Microsoft and a former Member of the Board of Directors of NLCIFT. He, shared some of his impressions on the reasons for the December 28, 2004 *European* Union court dismissal of *Microsoft's* appeal of the 2004 ruling which found the company had abused its dominant position in the European market.[122] According to Mr. Gutierrez, the European Union Court visualized the preservation of competition as a duty of the larger competitors by doing whatever was in their hands to prevent the smaller companies from going under as a result of the technological innovations or other competitive advantages enjoyed by the larger and more successful competitors. I told him that I had the same impression based upon duties of assistance in access to credit and business know-how, including how to best merge with other companies and how best to avoid insolvency imposed upon the larger and better competitors by the *Code de Commerce*.[123] Does this remind you of the guild system or of Judge Bedos' description of the virtuous behavior of the eighteenth-century Commercial Court of Paris?

9. Negotiable Instruments

Book V deals with promissory notes, bills of exchange and secured transactions.[124] France adopted the Geneva Convention on Bills of Exchange and Promissory Notes Providing a Uniform Law for Bills of Exchange and Promissory Notes of 1930,[125] as did a majority of civil law countries. With the exception of Article 10 of the Geneva Convention, the remainder was fully transcribed by the French *Code de Commerce*. As pointed out elsewhere, there are some significant differences between U.C.C. Article 3

---

121 *Id.* art. L410–2.

122 *See* Westlaw, [2004] ECRII-4463 (EU: Case T-201/04).

123 *See infra* § 10:4(B)(13).

124 *See* C. COM. (FR.) arts. L511–1—L526–4 (2008).

125 Convention Providing a Uniform Law for Bills of Exchange and Promissory Notes, June 7, 1930, 143 L.N.T.S. 257, *available at* http://www.jus.uio.no/lm/bills.of.exchange.and.promissory.notes.convention.1930/doc.html.

and the Geneva Convention on the qualifications of a holder in due course, liabilities for fraud and forgery of a drawer and endorser's signature, and others.[126]

10. Secured Transactions Provisions in Book V of the Code de Commerce

The law of secured transactions has become a critical component of the contemporary law of commercial contracts. Increasingly, economic development is tied to the success of secured lending laws. After lagging behind other developed nations for almost a century, France adopted secured lending provisions in its commercial and civil codes in 2003 and 2006. Unfortunately, the results have been disappointing. Because of the leading role of French legislative efforts throughout the civil law world, these statutes will be discussed in some detail hereafter.

Prior to the 2003 compilation of commercial code provisions, the large number of security interests were dispersed among a large number of statutes covering different types of pledges.[127] The 2003 compilation and subsequent revisions did not gather them all under the same legislative roof. The same is true with the 2006 amendments to the *Code Civil*. This dualism of legislative sources creates, by itself, considerable uncertainty in an area of commercial contracts law where certainty is essential for everyday lending. After the 2006 amendments to the *Code Civil*, the interpreter has to ask himself, among many other questions: Is my security interest a commercial security interest governed by the commercial code and perhaps subsidiarily by the civil code, or is it a civil pledge without dispossession, governed principally and finally by the civil code? These problems illustrate the many uncertainties encountered in both sources.

For example, Chapter I of Title II of Book V of the *Code de Commerce* seems to be governed by the principle of "constitutive" notice. According to Article L521–1, a security interest created in connection with a commercial act either by a merchant or a non-merchant must be recorded in compliance with Article L110–3. Such a recording is necessary both to create rights and duties between the contracting parties (lender and borrower) and to give notice to third parties (actual or potential lenders and *bona fide* purchasers of the collateral, and trustees of *syndics* in bankruptcy).

This principle stands in sharp contrast with the "adjective" or pure notice filing system that governs most contemporary secured transaction statutes,[128] and which does not require filing for the purpose of creating rights between the lender and the

---

126 *See* Kozolchyk, III UNITED STATES LAW, at 22–19—22–21, § 16 (some of the main differences between the Geneva Convention and Article 3 of the U.C.C.).

127 *See* Ulrich Drobnig, *Secured Credit in International Insolvency Proceedings*, 33 TEX. INT'L L. J. 53, 58 (1998):

> France is atypical because of the great number and diversity of relevant statutes on pledges. Specific French legislation exists for pledges in no fewer than ten types of assets: enterprises; automobiles; farm equipment and crops; industrial equipment; goods in warehouses; certain raw materials and industrial products; equipment and commercial furniture of hotels; petroleum stocks; films; and, the most recent addition to this catalog, the right to exploit software.

128 *See* U.C.C. §§ 9–201 & 9–203. *See also* MODEL INTER-AMERICAN LAW ON SECURED TRANSACTIONS arts. 5, 10, 34 (2002), *available at* http://www.oas.org/dil/cidip-vi-securedtransactions_eng.htm; Ley de Garantias Mobiliarias [LAW ON SECURED TRANSACTIONS], Decreto No. 51–2007, Vol. CCLXXXIII OFFICIAL GAZETTE, arts. 10, 15 (Nov. 16, 2007), *available at* http://natlaw.com/interam/gu/pp/st/stgubk00031.pdf.

borrower, but does require filing to affect the rights of third parties by placing them on notice of what has been recorded.[129]

The commercial code security interests may be possessory or non-possessory, although some collateral, such as negotiable instruments, require endorsement and possession to perfect the security interest in them. Other instruments such as corporate shares and partnership interests can also be used as collateral, but notice of the creation of the security interest requires a recording in the appropriate corporate or partnership records or in the Registry of Public Debts.

For a commercial type of jurisdiction, the foreclosure procedure set forth in Article L521–3 seems leisurely, if not detrimental to collateral that is highly perishable:

> If payment is not made in the due date, the creditor may, eight days after simple notice served on the debtor and any third party holding a landlord's lien for rent, sell the articles held as security at public auction.[130]

11. Secured Transactions in the 2006 Amendments of the Code Civil

The *Code Civil* provisions on pledges without dispossession compound the confusion created by the 2008 compilation of commercial statutes. The *Code Civil* pledges (whose nature is supposed to be non-commercial) often wander into a gray zone where civil transactions become indistinguishable from commercial ones. For ease of identification, the gray zones will be italicized in the following provisions.

Article 2329 of the *Code Civil* sets forth four types of security interests in movables:

1) Privileged charges over movables;

2) Pledge of corporeal movables;

3) Securities of incorporeal movables;

4) Retention of title as a security.[131]

The *Code Civil* defines a priority charge as a right whose type of debt provides the creditor with priority over other creditors, including real estate mortgagees.[132] Article 2331 lists eight categories of priority charges, which include court costs, funeral expenses, and expenses relating to the latest illness. In addition, this provision lists a large number of owed, or likely-to-be owed, debts to laborers of all types, including wages of domestic staff for the year elapsed and the current year, deferred salary payments, debts of the surviving spouse "*relating to the development of commercial and artisanal undertakings* and to the improvement of their *economic, legal and social environment*,"[133] severance pay, special compensation for lack of job security, allowances for failure to provide proper notice, allowance for paid holidays, and many more. This provision does not make clear whether these priority charges apply to

---

129 *See generally* Kozolchyk & Wilson, *The New Model Inter-American Law*; Kozolchyk & Furnish, *A Comparative Analysis*.

130 *See* C. COM. (FR.) art. L521–3 (2008).

131 C. CIV. (FR.) art. 2329 (2008). Unless otherwise indicated, all the English translations of the *Code Civil* provisions belong to Legifrance (*see* Frequently Cited).

132 *Id.* art. 2324.

133 *Id.* art. 2331 (emphasis added).

collection proceedings against a solvent, insolvent or deceased debtor. Caution would suggest that it could apply to one or two of these three situations.

In addition to the above "general" priority, Article 2332 sets forth special priorities for a number of debts that take precedence in proceedings involving the foreclosure of designated movable property. These specific priority charges resemble the "statutory liens" of United States law, although their scope of application is more specifically laid out. Among them are:

> 1) Rents and farm-rents of immovables on the fruit of the year's crop, and on the price of everything which garnishes the house rented or the farm, *and of everything which is used for the working of the farm: namely, for everything which is due, and for everything which shall become due, where the leases are authentic*, or, where being under private signature, they have an undisputable date; and, in both cases, the other creditors have the right to relet the house *or the farm* for the remainder of the lease, *and to profit by the leases or rents*, on condition, however, that they pay the owner everything which may still be owed to him.
>
> . . .
>
> The same prior charge exists for the repairs incumbent upon the tenant and for everything relating to the execution of the lease. It also exists for all debts resulting, for the benefit of the owner or tenant, from the occupation of the premises, regardless of the basis thereof.
>
> Nevertheless, the *sums owed for seeds, for manure and ameliorators, for anti-cryptogamic and insect products, for products designed for destroying animal or plant parasites harmful to farming, or for the expenses of the year's crop, shall be paid out of the proceeds of the crop*, and those owed for implements out of the proceeds of those implements, in priority to the owner in either case.[134]

The *Code Civil* also introduced amendments to the traditional (dispossessory) pledge. It distinguished between the pledge of corporeal and incorporeal movables, and allowed these pledges to be created for present and future debts.[135] This represents a major advance over nineteenth-century pledges. Yet, immediately in Article 2335, the amendments repeated an ownership requirement which the contemporary law of secured transactions rejects as incompatible with the fragmented and limited nature of ownership in personal property. For it is not only conceivable but also necessary for secured lending that holders of rights to the possession of the same collateral be able to sell or pledge their rights in the collateral, even if they fall short of absolute or historical ownership of that collateral.[136] This development was, ironically, foreshadowed by Article 2279 of the same *Code Civil* (1804 version): "In the case of movables, possession is equivalent to a title."[137]

---

[134] *Id.* art. 2332 (emphasis added).

[135] *Id.* art. 2333.

[136] *See generally* Kozolchyk & Wilson, *The New Model Inter-American Law*; Kozolchyk & Furnish, *A Comparative Analysis*; *see also* NLCIFT, *12 Principles*.

[137] C. CIV. (FR.) art. 2279 (Barrister 1804); *see* C. CIV. (FR.) art. 2276 (2008) (the current language). *See also* Kozolchyk, *Commercialization*; Kozolchyk & Wilson, *The New Model Inter-American Law*; Kozolchyk & Furnish, *A Comparative Analysis*.

Thus, anachronistically and contrary to the spirit of Article 2279 *Code Civil* (1804 version), the current Article 2335 of the *Code Civil* now states:

> The pledge of the thing of another is void. It may give rise to damages where the creditor did not know that the thing belonged to another.[138]

In addition, in a manner contrary to the constitutive notice principle of Article L521–1 of the *Code de Commerce*, which predicates the enforceability of the security agreement between the parties and its notice to third parties upon its recording, Article 2336 of the *Code Civil* rejects such a constitutive effect:

> A pledge is complete by the establishing of a writing which contains the description of the debt secured, the quantity of the pledged units of property, as well as of their species or nature.[139]

Article 2337 emphasizes this differentiation when it states that a pledge is enforceable against third parties by its publicity[140] and does not mention the same requirement for the agreement between the creditor and debtor.

Many other problems occur with the remainder of the *Code Civil* and *Code de Commerce* amendments. Hence, rather than clarifying the import of contemporary secured lending in French law, the amendments to the *Code de Commerce* and *Code Civil* have rendered this law more uncertain. The lack of delineation between a commercial security interest and a civil pledge without dispossession subjects both to numerous and contradictory rules and qualifications, such as rules on formalities, perfection and priorities (both general and special). In addition, the anachronistic requirement that the debtor be the owner of the collateral hangs like a Damocles sword over the enforcement of the security interest or pledge. It would be enough for the debtor, or a third party, to offer evidence that other debtors or creditors hold an ownership interest (of the many co-existing ones in the same collateral) for the transaction to be voided.

In sum, it is clear that both sets of amendments depart significantly from the best national and international secured lending law and practice.[141]

12. Security Interests in Warehouse Receipts, Warrants and Bonds

Chapter II of Title II of Book V of the *Code de Commerce* deals extensively with deposits in bonded warehouses, apparently one of France's most popular security devices.[142] Chapter III deals with the pledges on hotel equipment and furniture,[143] Chapter IV with security interests in oil warrants[144] and Chapter V with security interests in professional tools and equipment.[145]

---

138 C. Civ. (Fr.) art. 2335 (2008).

139 *Id.* art. 2336.

140 *Id.* art. 2337.

141 *See* UNCITRAL, Legislative Guide on Secured Transactions (2010), *available at* http://www.uncitral.org/pdf/english/texts/security-lg/e/09–82670_Ebook-Guide_09–04–10English.pdf; Model Inter-American Law on Secured Transactions arts. 5, 10, 34 (2002), *available at* http://www.oas.org/dil/cidip-vi-securedtransactions_eng.htm; NLCIFT, *12 Principles.*

142 C. Com. (Fr.) arts. L522–1—L522–40 (2008).

143 *Id.* arts. L523–1—L523–15.

144 *Id.* arts. L524–1—L524–21.

145 *Id.* arts. L525–1—L525–20.

Chapter VI of the same title and book provides the French law equivalent of a United States "homestead" protection from attachment of property of the individual businessman and his spouse: "[A] natural person whose name appears in an occupational . . . register or who is engaged in an agricultural or independent business may declare his rights over the real property which constitutes his principal place of residence to be exempt from seizure."[146]

13. Commercial Provisions Other Than in the Code de Commerce

Despite the attempt to include all of the commercial legislation of France in the *Code de Commerce*, some important commercial contracts were left out and are regulated by their own law. One such law is the Insurance Code.[147] It applies to "non-marine" (fire, hail and livestock mortality, personal, bodily injury and material damages, third party liability, natural disasters, terrorism, legal expenses, and technological disasters and life insurance) as well as to marine transportation losses. Marine insurance covers not only the traditional maritime insurance, but also inland waterway and lake transportation insurance. In addition, it sets forth the law applicable to insurance contracts for risks located in the territory of one or more state parties to the European Space Agreement and agreements named therein.

Other examples include the provisions on Maritime Law found in several statutes, such as Law No. 66–420 on Freight Contracts and Maritime Transportation, and the *Code du Domaine Public Fluvial et de la Navigation Intérieure* (Code of Public Waterways and Inland Navigation). Perhaps the most important recent statutory addition on the formalities of commercial contracts is found. Notice that many of those rules are amendments to the civil and not commercial code, why? Notice that they encompass informal electronic contracts, offers and acceptances and promises especially those in an electronic format.[148]

§ 10.5 CONCLUSIONS

Surprisingly, the latest revision of the *Code de Commerce* has adopted a casuistic style of drafting reminiscent of the U.C.C. In addition, it evidences a paternalistic-guild approach which merges with the goals of a socialist or mixed (capitalist-socialist) economy. On the one hand, it interjects governmental bodies into the process of doing business by deciding the better methods for drafting a business plan, preparing for a takeover or merger, avoiding insolvency, etc. And, as if that were not enough, critical institutions for the development of a sound financial marketplace, such as the law of secured transactions, were drafted with little regard for best legal and market practices, both national and international.

Where does this insufficient, confusing and inept coverage leave the merchant and the code interpreter? First of all, it is important to acknowledge the continuous growth in the number of non-merchants who become parties to commercial contracts with merchants and other non-merchants alike. Commercialization has been on the ascent for more than two centuries.[149] Presently, commercialization is especially apparent in

---

[146] *Id.* art. L526–1.

[147] *See generally* CODE DES ASSURANCES [C. assur.] (Fr.).

[148] *See* § 8:9(C)(4).

[149] *See generally* Kozolchyk, *Commercialization.*

the meteoric growth worldwide of countless virtual places such as websites for doing business. In brief, any attempt to limit the acts of commerce to those listed in 1808 and subsequent revisions, or whenever the next addition or amendment is drafted, risks obsolescence as soon as promulgated.

In light of this growth, it is necessary for commercial law to open its doors as widely as possible. Whether the opening mechanism is provided by open lists of acts of commerce or by other approaches discussed in a following chapter is not as important as making sure that the new law reflects sound market practices and protects consumers.

Hardly a legislative term goes by without the enactment of a consumer protection law or the creation of an administrative or judicial office entrusted with such a protection. Whether such a regulation is part of the commercial or a consumer code is often a matter of legislative convenience. However, where it is an essential part of the commercial transaction, such as the protection of "buyers in the ordinary course of business" in secured lending law, its best place is in the commercial statute.[150]

It should also be kept in mind that, as mentioned earlier, in societies where consumers are often merchants and vice versa, the boundaries between consumer protection law and the commercial code are not easily drawn, as the student of the French *Code de Commerce* and the United States' U.C.C. will soon discover. What is fairly safe to predict is that the civil-commercial code dichotomy of Napoleonic France and many of the legal institutions it engendered will soon become a subject mostly for legal historians and antiquarians.

§ 10.6 EXERCISES

The following exercises will familiarize the reader with *Code Civil* and *Code de Commerce* research. Answers are provided at the end of this elementary exercise.[151]

1) *A* and *B* are partners under partnership *C*. *B* was designated as manager of the partnership. *B* decides to purchase a vehicle, both for the use of the company and for his own personal use. Does *B* have sufficient powers to execute the purchase of the vehicle? What provisions of the *Code de Commerce* apply?

2) In a limited partnership, the limited partner is granted a power of attorney in order for him to purchase real estate property for the partnership. After purchasing the real property, the limited partnership accepts no liability for the purchase contract executed by the limited partner. Did the limited partner have the power to execute a purchase-sale agreement for real estate property on behalf of the limited partnership? What provisions of the *Code de Commerce* apply?

---

[150] Kozolchyk & Furnish, *A Comparative Analysis*, at 244 (describing the commercial and consumer credit pyramid that characterizes the credit systems of market economy nations since the late eighteenth century). Retailers, moneylenders and their consumer borrowers were at the base; wholesalers and their bankers and factors were found at the next ascending levels. *Id.* At the top of the pyramid was the Bank of England as lender or discounter of paper produced at the lower levels of the pyramid. *Id.* Unless the consumers at the base of the pyramid were protected in their purchases (as "*bona fide* purchasers" or "buyers in the ordinary course of business"), they would no longer purchase with confidence, and the streams of income flowing from the base of the pyramid to the top would suffer consequently. *Id.*

[151] C. COM. (FR.); C. CIV. (FR.) (in French, English and Spanish).

3) In the same scenario as in Exercise 2 above, what provisions of the *Code Civil* would govern the purchase-sale agreement of real estate property?

§ 10.7 ANSWERS

1) *B* does not have sufficient powers. *See* Article L221–5.

2) The limited partner has no powers to act on behalf of the limited partnership. *See* Article L222–6.

3) Of Contracts and of Conventional Obligations in General, Book III, Title III (Articles 1101 through 1369–11); Articles 1582 *et seq.*

§ 10.8 APPENDIX—CASE LAW RELATED TO THE *CODE DE COMMERCE*[152]

A. Craftsmen and Merchants: Are French Guilds Still Alive?

1. Decision in Cour de Cassation, *Commercial Chamber, May 12, 1969*[153]

U.R.S.S.A.F. de Lyon c. Astruc

Facts:

A hat-maker, who was registered at the occupational registry but not at the registry of commerce, worked as an independent contractor, was assisted only by some employees, and used equipment appropriate for a craftsman but not for a merchant, failed to pay her debts to [a financial entity-lender known as] U.R.S.S.A.F. This entity brought a claim to the commercial court seeking the defendant's involuntary declaration of bankruptcy and also claiming a certain amount as the owed principal and interest. The claim was rejected as inadmissible.

Decision:

THE COURT: On the only issue on appeal: Considering that the lower court (Lyon, May 26, 1967) declared inadmissible the claim for the declaration of bankruptcy filed by U.R.S.S.A.F. of Lyon, against Mrs. Astruc, who owes the principal amount of 17,440.08 Francs, plus interest and fees for the period from January 1, 1963 to June 30, 1965. [Considering that it was] rejected on the ground that Mrs. Astruc is not a merchant . . . the claimant relies on factual evidence that shows that the defendant's business largely exceeds the amount ordinarily associated with a craftsman's business, and that Mrs. Astruc was engaged in commercial speculation by paying for the work of her waged employees and for raw materials and merchandise and reselling the final product, all of which would qualify as a commercial act in accordance with Articles 1 and 632 of the Commercial Code. Yet, on the other hand . . . the court of appeals did not (properly interpret) Article L. 645 C. Secur. Soc., pertaining to the main activity of waged employment and by decree of March 1, 1962 . . . on the conditions under which someone is employed as a craftsman. . . .

---

[152] The cases in this appendix have been translated and abridged by the author, Mariana Silveira, and Cristina Castaneda.

[153] *U.R.S.S.A.F. de Lyon c. Astruc*, Cour de Cassation [Cass.] [supreme court for judicial matters] com., May 12, 1969, Bull. civ. IV, no. 159 (Fr.).

Considering . . . that the court of appeals held that Mrs. Astruc was registered at the registry of her occupation at the time she became indebted of the now disputed debts, that she is not registered at the registry of commerce; that her business is that of a craftsman who makes hats and that she works independently . . . with the help of five waged employees hired as apprentices . . . that she does not use any other equipment apart from three sewing machines, that the value of the labor used is higher than the value of the merchandise used . . . that in fact, the purchase of merchandise is limited to that needed for crafting hats, that she has never had any surplus available stock or that she has not drawn any negotiable instruments; that she has never performed, but exceptionally, two purchases for reselling hats that were crafted in a two-year period on which there was a report; that it has not been established that Mrs. Astruc speculated on the merchandise crafted by others; that from the findings and the holding, the court of appeals was able to find that Mrs. Astruc's main activity is craftsmanship, thus not a commercial activity, and that she does not perform any secondary acts susceptible of being qualified as commercial, therefore not having a commercial nature.

On the other hand, considering that the U.R.S.S.A.F. of Lyon, according to the findings of the appeal, is bound to justify the commercial nature of Mrs. Astruc, without objecting to her craftsman nature. . . . For these reasons it is dismissed. . . .

2. Commentary by R. Houin

Regardless of the silence of the *Code de Commerce*, case law normally has held that a craftsman—meaning an independent manual worker—is not subject to the rules of commercial law. Therefore, it is important to distinguish between a craftsman and a merchant and determine the elements that legally define a craftsman. Case law has provided for the definition of a non-merchant craftsman, and, as happens with most case law, this definition is not devoid of uncertainties. On the one hand, all craftsmen may purchase movable property to resell it, provided that they manually work on it and create a work of their own with it (Article 632, *Code de Commerce*). But on the other hand, case law has recognized that there may be a commercial manufacturing business even in the absence of purchases made for their resale. Nevertheless, case law has recognized that a non-merchant craftsman is the person who performs manual labor, whether independently or with the assistance of the members of his family; in addition, for purposes of his work he may purchase raw materials, use equipment, hire waged employees and apprentices, and have an establishment and a trademark. However, he may not speculate on the products or on the work of others. In summary, the preponderance of manual labor in crafting the products and the absence of speculation are features that identify a non-merchant craftsman.

COMMENTS AND QUESTIONS

Why should France's private and public law insist, in this day and age, on distinguishing between merchants and craftsmen who sell what they produce? As is apparent from this decision, this is not an academic distinction. It requires different registers (for craftsmen or artisans and merchants) and legal regimes (for example, bankruptcy rules that are applicable only to merchants, and which assume that craftsmen make only an exceptional use of negotiable instruments, as indicated by a rather questionable finding of fact). Incidentally, why was it questionable—even in 1969—that a person who employs five employees, who continually buys raw material and sells hats has not, as part of her everyday business, ever drawn commercial paper such as promissory notes, drafts, or the ever-popular French postal or bank *giros*? Is the reason for this distinction an official desire to protect craftsmen from the "sins, perils, and ravages" of "commercial speculation?" Simply put, is the guild system truly dead in French law or is it still ruling from its grave?

What are the economic consequences of enforcing the questionable distinction between craftsmen and merchants? If a craftsman is not a merchant, could commercial credit, *i.e.*, one dependent upon repayment of commercial assets such as accounts receivable, negotiable instruments, and other commercial paper, be made available to them officially, or would it have to be made available only on a clandestine, under-the-table basis? What are the economic implications of barring artisans and craftsmen from the bankruptcy regime?

B. Merchants and Farmers

1. *First Case—Decision in REQ., February 4, 1925*[154]

THE COURT: (Appellant's alleged mistaken interpretations by the lower court): On the first issue on appeal, the infringement of Articles 1, 437, and 638 of the Commercial Code, and 7 of the Law of April 20, 1810, Articles on which the appealed decision was [allegedly] erroneously based to support Mr. Robert's bankruptcy filing in connection with his alleged business operations, [these allegations related to] his work on the forests located on land of his property, however, the agricultural nature of such work does not warrant the holding that he was engaged in commercial transactions.

Considering that the findings of law and facts in the appealed decision indicate that Robert, a merchant of wood in Bourriot-Bergonce, in 1916 made a deal with the Army Intelligence for the supply of 10,000 cubic meters of pine wood; along with several financial stipulations, he, first of all, acquired all of the pines sold by the Viallotte forest; . . . that to succeed in this endeavor he hired Mr. Escudero to cut down the pines and to craft the wood, and that the final amount owed to his creditor was 5,593,75 Francs; that he also agreed to repay some important loans with the successors of A. Pelletier, who were wood merchants in Bordeaux, and that in payment for his debts he signed as acceptor a number of negotiable instruments which are overdue and their payment was claimed on their due date, and that he did the same thing with respect to other unpaid creditors.

Considering that the main findings of fact show that Robert, as a businessperson, in fact processed and crafted the products for their sale, hired labor and conducted . . . a commercial business that involved, among others, making continuous and ordinary commercial transactions. Consequently, considering that, in the appealed decision the court was able to infer from the facts that Robert was a merchant because he performs commercial transactions and such is his ordinary business, and that he filed bankruptcy because he was unable to fulfill payment of his debts; therefore, far from infringing the Articles alleged in this appeal, the court made a proper interpretation of these provisions; for these reasons, the appeal is dismissed. . . .

---

[154] REQ. Feb. 4, 1925, *Robert C. Duffau et autres (et al.),* (D.H. 1925.138).

2. *Second Case—Decision in REQ., December 11, 1944*[155]

THE COURT: The issue at bar pertains to the erroneous application of Articles 631, 632, and 638 of the Commercial Code, the rules of jurisdiction, and Article 7 of the Law of April 10, 1810. . . . The appealed decision found that the commercial jurisdiction was the appropriate one to decide on the claim for damages against M. Brunet (defendant below and appellant). Appellant was an agricultural merchant and the action against him involved an accident that occurred while he was performing his obligations, not as a commercial manufacturing business, but as a business incorporated mainly for farming, given its purpose and the nature of his business operations. Considering the authority and the reasoning discussed in the appealed decision, we find that Brunet, in his ordinary course of business, performed acts consisting of "processing through mechanic means the products he received from producers." Hence, considering that, the decision made by the court of appeals, far from infringing the Articles at issue, applied them properly and the court provided sound legal grounds for its decision; for these reasons, the appeal is dismissed.

3. *Commentaries by Professor Jean Schmidt*

An agricultural business implies the carrying out of commercial transactions—The *Cour de Cassation* held that Mr. Brunet performed commercial transactions by "processing through mechanic means the products he received from producers." Is such an activity regulated by Articles 632 and 633 of the *Code de Commerce* that provide a list of commercial transactions? Article 632 establishes that a processing company is a commercial transaction. On this matter, we first need to take into consideration that the purpose of such companies is to process purchased goods and later proceed to their sale. However, this provision has been slightly modified by doctrine and case law, broadening its scope of application. Therefore, the Court found Mr. Brunet "in his ordinary course of business . . . process[ed] through mechanic means the products he received from producers."

Compatibility of the agricultural and commercial nature of a business—The Supreme Court has implicitly admitted that an agricultural business may have a commercial nature. Therefore, is it important for [a farmer] claiming the performance of acts of commerce to allege that his agricultural business has a commercial nature? Is it required to differentiate between a farmer engaged in the *production* of goods and one in the *trade of goods*?

COMMENTS AND QUESTIONS

The reader may wonder whether the translator of these cases is unaware of redundancies. After all, if a *business* is referred to as agricultural by the courts, why distinguish it from a *commercial* business? Is not a business a business, whether engaged in by shopkeepers or by farmers? Furthermore, is not a business by definition a commercial endeavor? Apparently this is not the case in French judicial decisions, at least for quite a while following the enactment of the *Code de Commerce*. This goes back to one of the issues dealt with throughout this chapter: Why did the legislators, courts and commentators strain so hard to draw these distinctions?

---

[155] REQ. Dec. 11, 1944, *Brunet C. Goutssard* (D. 1945.213, opinion by Gabolde).

In light of the origin of the distinction between farming or owning farmland and commerce involving land or its products, and taking into account the extraordinary importance of agribusiness in our time, what are the legal and economic benefits derived from attempting to preserve this distinction?

C. Agricultural Civil Cooperatives and Acts of Commerce: A Clash Between Commercial and Civil Codes

1. *Applicable Code Provisions*

Code Civil Article 1844–10: Annulment of a company may only result from the infringement of the provisions of Articles 1832, 1832–1, paragraph 1, and 1833 or from one of the general causes for the annulment of contracts.

Any clause of the memorandum or of the articles of incorporation contrary to a mandatory provision of this Title shall be deemed as not written, provided that the infringement of such provision is not penalized with the annulment of the company. Annulment of transactions or resolutions of the branches of a company may only result from the infringement of a mandatory provision of this Title or from one of the general causes for the annulment of contracts.

Code Civil Article 1845: The provisions of this Chapter shall apply to all non-commercial companies, unless they are repealed by the special laws that govern some of these types of companies. Companies to which the law does not grant another form because of their structure, nature or purpose are deemed to be non-commercial.

Code de Commerce Article L210–1: The commercial nature of a company shall be determined by its form or by its objects.

General partnerships, limited partnerships, limited liability companies and joint-stock companies are trading companies by virtue of their form, irrespective of their objects.

2. *Decision in the* Cour de Cassation, *Commercial Chamber, November 20, 2007*[156]

Whereas, according to the appealed decision (Paris, April 1, 2005), the National Union of Agriculture and Farming—Green France—and the Departmental Union for the Defense of the Rights of Farmers and several other entities and individuals have requested the nullity of the regional accounts held by (civil cooperatives/unions) at and by the *Crédit Agricoles Mutuel* (CRCAM), arguing that the commercial nature of the acts pertaining to those accounts results in an illegal object and, therefore, they must be annulled;

Whereas, an appeal was brought against the appealed decision that dismissed the claim for the nullity of the accounts of the CRCAM, claiming:

1) That the main business of a civil cooperative/union may not be a commercial activity; that the accounts held at the CRCAM are of a civil cooperative; that in holding in the appealed decision that they may perform

[156] Case on Appeal No. 05–16219; Appeals No. G05–16.219 and J 05–16.220 before the *Cour de Cassation,* Commercial Chamber, Public Hearing held on November 20, 2007.

acts of commerce provided that they do so in a civil form, the Court of Appeals infringed Articles 1844–10, 1845, second paragraph of the *Code Civil*, and L210–1 of the *Code de Commerce*;

2) That the appealed conclusions are immaterial to the case, that in support of the claim for the nullity of the accounts of the CRCAM, the means used for financing the offer made by CRCAM for an acquisition with Crédit Lyonnais did not take into consideration the mandatory provisions applicable to cooperatives/unions and that its members had therefore been illegally deprived of their property; that in rejecting this argument, the only—yet inoperative—reason was that they conducted an investment operation pursued by CRCAM without there being an investigation on whether the provisions applicable to cooperatives/unions had been taken into consideration and whether the interests of its members had been protected, the Court of Appeals infringed Article 455 of the new *Code Civil* Procedures;

3) That the Judge should have verified that a certain legal provision has been implicitly repealed because it contradicts provisions found in subsequent laws, and that the principles that justified the former legal provision have ceased to be applicable; that in this particular case, a law enacted on April 18, 1922—which is now codified in Article L512–30 of the *Code Monétaire et Financier*—eliminated the obligation of recording the accounts of the CRCAM at the Registry of Commerce and Companies; that this provision is incompatible with Article 44 of the Law of May 15, 2001 which mandates that all companies must be registered at the Registry of Commerce and Companies, and is justified by the fact that the accounts of civil cooperatives/unions have the purpose of providing and guaranteeing activities related to agricultural and farming production and equipment required by its members; that the purpose and scope of several provisions found in laws and regulations have been broadened so as to allow funds and accounts of CRCAM to be used, in general, as they would be used in banking operations, therefore, performing acts of commerce. . . .

However, considering in the first place that the Court of Appeals is not bound to follow the line of argument presented by the parties, the Court of Appeals has rightly held that the exercise of a commercial activity through a credit establishment with the status of a cooperative or union does not necessarily result in the nullity of its activities;

In second place, considering that the specific provisions of Article L512–30 of the French Monetary and Financial Code (*Code Monétaire et Financier*), that exempt CRCAM from registering its accounts at the Registry of Commerce and Companies, are in no way implicitly repealed by Article 44 of the Law of May 15, 2001, unless there is an express provision stating otherwise;

Hence, it follows that none of the claims on appeal have legal grounds to support them. For these reasons, it is dismissed.

COMMENTS AND QUESTIONS

Does the act of investing savings or surplus funds of a civil (*i.e.*, non-commercial or not-for-profit) agricultural cooperative for the presumably-lawful purpose of preserving, if not growing, the cooperative's savings violate French public and private law, including the prohibition of a civil, not-for-profit entity from engaging in commercial acts? In arguing that it does, the National Union of Agriculture and Farming—Green France—pushed the civil versus commercial act dichotomy to its logical limits: Not-for-profit means not-for-profit, and investment with the intent to obtain a profit is a commercial and thus a "speculative" profit-seeking act. Yet, can any entity, for-profit or not-for-profit, survive in an investment-driven marketplace such as ours without earning interest for its deposits? As the Spanish proverb has it: "Stationary vessels earn no freight," and without said freight, it will not be a vessel for much longer. From religious entities at one end of the spectrum, to communist governments at the other end, no one in today's global marketplace can afford to allow surpluses or reserves to remain idle. Yet, if the "civil" not-for-profit category is pushed to its limit, business-minded entities such as civil associations of lawyers or other professionals would also be prevented from investing their savings. Not surprisingly, the *Cour de Cassation* held in this important decision that the exercise of a commercial activity through a credit establishment with the status of a cooperative or union does not necessarily result in the nullity of its activities. One is left to wonder how much a chemically-pure, civil not-for-profit category of transactions will be left in French law in another generation or two.

D. Commercial and Civil Acts: The Performance of Work vs. Agency; Material Acts vs. Juristic Acts

1. Applicable Code Provisions[157]

a. Code Civil

Article 1384: One is responsible not only for the damages caused by one's acts, but also for those caused by persons that one is responsible for or of the things under one's own custody.

. . .

[Paragraph 5] Masters and those who entrust others with the commission of acts [are responsible] for the acts of their employees within the scope of their employment.

Article 1787 [Performance of Work]: When someone is entrusted with performing work the parties may agree that the party doing the work will supply only his work or industry or will also supply the material.

Article 1792–1:[158] The following will be deemed builders (*constructeurs de l'ouvrage*):

1) Any architect, entrepreneur, technician or any other associated with the owner by a contract for the performance of construction work;

2) Any person who sells, once the work of building is finished, a building that he or she has built or has commissioned;

---

[157] The provisions hereafter translated by the author appeared in their original form in C. CIV. (FR.) (Dalloz 1969–70 & 1982–3) which, as best as I was able to ascertain, were still those applied by the court decisions transcribed and referred to in the principal text.

[158] *See* Loi n 78–12 du 4 janvier 1978 [Law 78–12 of January 4, 1978] JOURNAL OFFICIEL DE LA REPUBLIQUE FRANÇAISE [J.O.] [Official Gazette of France], Jan. 5, 1978 (amending *Code Civil* art. 1792 and creating art. 1792–1).

3) Any person who, acting as an agent of the owner, carries out a mission equal to that of the building contractor.

Article 1793: When an architect or builder agrees with the landowner to build the building as detailed in a building plan and for an all-inclusive price, he cannot raise this price even though the price of wages or materials has risen, or changes or augmentations have been made in the plan unless these changes and augmentations appear in a writing agreed by the landowner.

Article 1794: By paying the builder for all the expenses incurred and the profits he would have obtained from the completion of the building, the landowner can rescind an all-inclusive contract unilaterally, even though construction started.

Article 1795: The contract for the performance of work shall be terminated by the death of the worker, the architect or the builder.

Article 1796: However, the landowner shall pay to their [the builder's] heirs the value of his works in proportion to the agreed-upon price.

Article 1984: The mandate or procuration [agency] is an act by which one person gives to another the power to do something for and in the name of the principal (*mandant*). . . .

Article 1986: The mandate is gratuitous, unless otherwise agreed.

Article 1987: It is special or just for one transaction or for certain affairs only, or general or for all the transactions of the principal (*mandant*).

Article 1988: Conceived in general terms, it only covers acts of administration. . . .

b. Code de Commerce

Article L110–1 (Former Article 632):

The law deems as acts of commerce:

3) All transactions by intermediaries for the purchase, subscription or sale of real property, sales of commercial establishments [bulk sales], shares or participations in real property companies. . . .

2. *Decision in* Cour de Cassation, *First Chamber, February 18, 1968,* Dame Montigaud c. Epoux Etchebarne[159]

THE COURT: Whereas, the contract of performing work [*contrat d'entreprise*] is an agreement by which a person [client] directs another, a fully independent contractor [*entrepreneur*] to perform work that entails simple material acts and does not confer upon the contractor any power of representation. Whereas . . . *E* instructed *M* [a specialist in selecting builders for residential homes] to find a builder who could build their home subject to certain specifications such as the type of home and an all-inclusive price, and that this was no more than a simple, vague and gratuitous

[159] *Dame Montigaud C. Epoux Etchebarne*, Cour de Cassation [Cass.] [supreme court for judicial matters] 1e civ., Feb. 19, 1968, D. 1968, 393 (Fr.), *in* HENRI CAPITANT, ALEX WEILL & FRANCOIS TERRE, LES GRANDS ARRETS DE LA JURISPRUDENCE CIVILE 664 (7th ed. 1976). The summary of the facts was done by the author.

mandate. Whereas the proven facts show that Dame O was instructed to perform a juristic act [*act juridique*] in accordance with Article 1984 of the *Code Civil* and not the performance of material acts [as involved in a contract for the performing of work] as was mistakenly concluded by the *Cour d'Appel* Bordeaux 28 Sept. 1964, for this reason this decision is reversed.

Apparently, the *Cour de Cassation* decided to fashion its own category of juristic acts. The following doctrinal comments illustrate the perils of such a venture, particularly when "the facts on the ground" of the respective contracts or transactions do not appear to have been carefully taken into account by the *Cour's* mostly scholastic "juristic versus material acts" dichotomy.

As is customary with decisions that deal only with questions of law, the facts provided by this appellate decision are minimal. Nonetheless, it leads to the conclusion that if *E* entrusts *M*, a residential housing specialist, with the selection of a builder for a family dwelling and gives her the parameters of her choice, such as the type and size of the dwelling and an all-inclusive price, *E's* contractual relationship with *M* amounts to a "vague and gratuitous mandate." Please notice the court's effort to fit *E*'s instructions within a type of contract that, for reasons peculiar to the Rome of two thousand years ago, was characterized by jurists as gratuitous. In the *Cour de Cassation's* words, *E* entrusted *M*, "to find a builder who could build their home subject to certain specifications such as the type of home and an all-inclusive price, *and that this was no more than a simple, vague and gratuitous mandate*."[160]

Notice that the contents of a "simple mandate" have remained fixed as a gratuitous contract since Roman times, regardless of the market practices ever since. And because *E* only asked *M* to perform a "juristic act" in accordance with the provisions of Article 1984 of the *Code Civil* and not a "material act," the lower court's disregard of this distinction misinterpreted Article 1787, among other provisions of the *Code Civil*. I should add that the term "material act" was not defined by this court. Nonetheless, for purposes of our discussion, let us assume that it means an act that produces something material such as movable or immovable property.[161]

In his commentary, an annotator (identified only as Doucet) points out that:

> The distinction between the contract of performance of work [in this case, a building contract] and that of agency carries with it numerous implications, among them: 1) the acts of the builder with respect to third parties do not bind his client [referred to in the law as the landowner]; in contrast, the principal (*mandant*) in an agency relationship is bound by the law of agency and representation; 2) the builder is not a subordinate (*preposé*) of his client in the sense of paragraph 5 of Article 1384 and the client cannot be sued for the crimes or torts committed by the builder during the course of the building work; in contrast, the principal (*mandant*) can be made responsible for the acts of his agent while acting as his subordinate . . .; 3) the client is not responsible for the damages suffered by the builder during the course of the building; on the contrary, Article 2000 of the Civil Code imposes upon the principal the obligation to indemnify his agent for all of the losses suffered

---

[160] *Id.* (emphasis added).

[161] I hasten to add that some codes consider rights in movable property as movable things, and rights to immovable property as immovable.

> during his agency; finally, 4) when an agent is paid a salary, case law has established that his compensation may be revised in a manner to reflect the importance of the mandate, whereas the price convened with a builder is deemed of strict compliance by Article 1793 of the *Code Civil*; however, case law has not been uniform on this point and some courts have not hesitated to apply the rules of agency to building contracts. . . .[162]

Thus, as with the other classifications of contracts in the *Code Civil*, serious consequences follow from the placement of either contract in an assigned legal pigeonhole. Still, it is far from easy to distinguish between "juristic acts" and "material acts" because, contrary to the *Cour de Cassation's* assumption, these are not "chemically pure" categories: Some juristic acts entail the performance of material acts and some material acts are indistinguishable from juristic acts. As pointed out by Doucet:

> The distinction between the contract of agency and that of construction is a subtle one . . . in both cases an individual undertakes a mission on behalf and for the profit of another. . . . [However] this distinction is not one found systematically [in practice] . . . [a] principal can confer wide discretion upon his agent to accomplish his mission [including the performance of material acts] and content himself with receiving a report at the end of the agency . . . conversely a building contract may be so fashioned as to restrict considerably the discretion of the builder . . . as is the case of a builder who is supposed to do his work under the strict control of an architect.[163]

The adoption of a "chemically pure" dichotomy by the *Cour de Cassation* (echoing that of the essentially civil and commercial acts in Article 632 of the *Code de Commerce*) prompted the following commentary by another annotator, (identified only as Cornu):

> It is remarkable that [this decision] adopts as the basis for its legal analysis a contract that the law has not even defined, especially when it is not related to this or that species of contract . . . but to the generic notion of performance of work [*enterprise*].[164]

Doucet adds that the combination of a contract of mandate or agency and performance of work or enterprise is common in commercial practice.[165] For example, in a typical contract of transportation, the carrier agrees to carry out the specific mission of transporting persons or things but also agrees, in an accessory manner, to perform a number of juristic acts for his client such as collecting the cost of the merchandise, insuring the cargo, etc. Conversely, an agent may perform some "material acts."[166] In the final analysis, Cornu concludes that it is up to the trier of facts to determine if the party in question contracted as "a simple intermediary or a subordinate worker."[167]

---

162 CAPITANT ET AL., *supra* note 159, at 665–66.

163 *Id.* at 666.

164 *Id.* at 667 (citing to Cornu, *obs. Rev. trim. dr. civ.* 1968, at 558).

165 *Id.*

166 *Id.* at 668.

167 *Id.*

COMMENTS AND QUESTIONS

Article 1792–1 of the *Code Civil* (transcribed above,[168] please re-read it now) was promulgated in 1978 (approximately ten years after the *Montigaud* decision discussed above). Do you believe it clarified the ambiguities created by the impure dichotomy of mandates (to perform juristic acts) and contracts for the performance of work (to perform material acts)?

Article 1986, also transcribed in relevant part earlier in this Appendix,[169] refers to the mandate as a gratuitous contract, unless otherwise agreed to. Do you believe that this is a realistic definition in our day, or even in its day? Is this true for most present-day recipients of powers of attorney such as lawyers, brokers and commission agents? What is the effect upon the commercial world of each of these recipients of mandates having to prove that their mandate was not a gratuitous transaction? Can you imagine stock brokers having to do this on the floor of the stock exchange in order for a transaction to be deemed concluded?

Article 1787 of the *Code Civil* (also transcribed above)[170] distinguishes between a contract to perform work in which the worker only supplies his work and another in which he will also supply the material involved in doing the work. Implicit in this distinction is the contractual relationship in which the party who commissions the work also supplies the material. Is this the first time the reader has encountered this relationship? How significant does the reader believe this relationship has been in the development of present-day capitalism?

The *Code de Commerce*, whose origin and drafting was discussed in the principal chapter, lists in Article L110–1 (former Article 632 of the *Code de Commerce*) as acts of commerce: "All transactions by intermediaries for the purchase, subscription or sale of real property, sales of commercial establishments [bulk sales], shares or participations in real property companies. . . ." How does this provision differ from Article 1792–1 which, as part of the *Code Civil* (and thus a civil transaction), is applicable to:

> 2) Any person who sells, once the work of building is finished, a building that he or she has built or has commissioned;
>
> 3) Any person who, acting as an agent of the owner, carries out a mission equal to that of the building contractor.

The legal consequences of applying *Code Civil* provisions on the contract of mandate and on the performance of work were illustrated by annotator Doucet. Consider now the consequences of applying *Code Civil* provisions to the following transaction, and after that, consider the consequences of not knowing which provisions of which code to apply:

> The city of *T*, located in a civil law jurisdiction, decides to build a toll road whose construction costs will be paid by the issuance of municipal negotiable bonds sold to the public. The repayment of these bonds, including their principal and interest, will be guaranteed by the receipts of toll fees paid by motorists. In order to put together this arrangement, the city of *T* contacts *ML*, a specialist in this kind of transaction, and provides him with a general description of the project including a maximum amount of construction expenditures, type of road, number of lanes and length of the road. *ML* is

---

168 *See supra* § 10:8(E)(1)(a).

169 *Id.*

170 *See supra* § 10:8(E)(2).

supposed to select a builder, set up an entity that will sell the bonds, collect the toll revenues, pay the builder and repay the bond holders.

How easy would it be to characterize the relationship between *T* and *ML* on the basis of the above-discussed decision and the transcribed provisions of the *Code Civil*? What are the likely consequences of having to apply these provisions to this transaction?

§ 10.9 AN ILLUSTRATION OF THE EFFECTS OF SCHOLASTIC LOGIC UPON NEW CONTRACTS

A. Overview

The illustration below was inspired by discussions on the law of commercial contracts of Mexico during a Judicial Workshop conducted at the Judicial Training School of Mexico's Federal Superior Tribunal during the last week of June 2009 by the NLCIFT.[171] It should highlight the difficulties of applying code provisions (whose drafting was inspired by scholastic methods of legal reasoning) to a present-day transaction unknown to the drafters of the codes, yet much needed in the contemporary real estate marketplace. Since the transaction takes place in Mexico, the applicable provisions would be those of the Mexican Civil and Commercial Codes. Nonetheless, I would like you to examine first the relevant provisions of the French *Code Civil* and *Code de Commerce* as enacted in 1804 and 1808, respectively. The reason for this peculiar sequence is to allow you to assess the lasting effect of some of these provisions on the feasibility of contemporary transactions. The French and Mexican codes are accessible in their original languages as well as in non-official English language translations.[172]

B. The Problem

"B" is a United States real property developer interested in buying real property "X" located on the outskirts of Mexico City from "S," the Mexican owner of the property. B needs to ascertain that the property can be used for certain business purposes and estimates that it will take him 60 days to determine whether these purposes can be met. Accordingly, he needs an option that would bind S not to sell the property during the "due diligence" period. B is willing to pay S's asking price provided S grants him a 60-day option for which he will pay one percent of the asking price upon the signing of the option and the remainder upon obtaining the final deed of sale from S. If the property does not meet his requirements, he will forfeit the one percent; if it does, he will pay the remainder against tender of a signed deed of sale from S. Yet, after studying this book, B becomes aware that options to purchase X are not easily

---

[171] *See* NLCIFT, 16 NOVEDADES (No. 3, Sept. 2009).

[172] The French *Code Civil* and *Code de Commerce* are available in their French language versions in the Dalloz collection of codes available in most United States comparative and foreign law library sections. In this chapter I use C. CIV. (FR.) (Barrister 1804) as an English translation of the original *Code Civil* of 1804, as well as the English translation in C. CIV. (FR.) (2008). The English translation of the *Code de Commerce* is from C. COM. (FR.) (2008). The reader should be aware that the translations are not always accurate and are only available for informational purposes. In the case of the Mexican Federal Civil and Commercial Codes, the original versions, as well as their updated versions in Spanish, are available at http://www.diputados.gob.mx/LeyesBiblio/index.htm; they are also available in annotated versions through Ediciones Fiscales ISEF S.A., as Agenda Civil and Agenda Mercantil, respectively. There is an English translation of the Mexican Federal Civil Code (1932) and of the Federal Commercial Code by Abraham Eckstein and Enrique Zepeda: MEXICAN & COMMERCIAL CODES (Abraham Eckstein and Enrique Zepeda trans., 1995).

enforceable by Mexican courts. As with some Romanistic and medieval laws and as with the *Code Civil,* contractual obligations are classified in Mexico's Civil Code (among other types) as obligations "to do" and "to give" something, and courts derive some unsettling consequences from this classification.[173] S's final obligation under the proposed option to execute a deed of sale conveying the real property to B is generally characterized by Mexican courts as an obligation to do something. As such, S can refuse to sign the final deed of sale until forced to do so by a court of law or the court does it in his name.[174] After becoming aware that his action could entail a long and costly judicial delay,[175] B suggests to S that they execute instead an "escrow account" or "an escrow agency agreement" as used in United States real property transactions.[176] B and S agree to do so and appoint "T", a third party real estate broker located in Mexico whom they both trust. Since the terms "escrow account" and "escrow agent" are unknown to Mexican lawyers, B and S decide to appoint T to act as their "custodian-fiduciary agent" (*depositario-fiduciario*) subject to a set of instructions agreed upon by B and S. Accordingly, T will act as a depositary of the payments (down payment and final payment) that are supposed to be provided by B. Upon receipt of the full purchase price from B and upon receipt from S of his executed deed of sale, T will transfer the payment to S and his deed to B. If S refuses to do so, and based upon the instructions agreed upon by S, T as an empowered fiduciary agent of S will execute the deed of sale to B.

C. The Research

As a scholastically-trained lawyer, you are asked to ascertain if such an escrow agreement is feasible under the *Code Civil* and *Code de Commerce* and subsequently under their Mexican counterparts.

In all likelihood you would commence your search for the applicable law by attempting to ascertain whether the engagement of T amounts to a contract as defined by the *Code Civil.* This was a code that Sir Harry Lawson, one of my most insightful comparative law teachers, referred to as "the constitution of France's private law." Can you surmise the logical reasons why the scholastic searcher would look first at the *Code Civil* for a definition of what is an enforceable "contract"? Does this approach have anything to do with the Aristotelian and scholastic concern with things general and particular? You may wish to consult Chapters 8–9 on the interaction between the civil and commercial codes. You might also wish to review the excerpt from Aquinas' *Summa Theologica* in § 5:7(B)(1) for possible clues on the scholastic reasoning from the "general to the specific."

---

173 C. CIV. (FR.) art. 1101 (2008) states: "A contract is an agreement by which one or several persons bind themselves, towards one or several others, to transfer, to do, or not to do something." In turn, Article 1792 of the Mexican Federal Civil Code defines it as: "an agreement of two or more persons to create, transfer, modify or extinguish obligations." This definition reflects the influence of the German concept of the "juristic act" (*Rechtsgeschäft*), *see infra* § 12:3(C). However, art. 1824 of the same Mexican Federal Civil Code reverts to the *Code Civil's* definition and classification by stating: "The objects of contracts are: (I) the thing that the obligor must give, (II) the thing he must or must not do."

174 *See e.g., infra* § 22:10(K), for a discussion on the Supreme Court decision on the appeal by María Trinidad Gómez, No. 1205/1954.

175 *Id.*

176 *See infra* § 28:2(B) for a shortened version of a typical escrow agreement in use in New York's real estate transactions.

Once immersed in the *Code Civil*, the searcher will find the definition of a contract in Article 1101:

> A contract *is* an agreement by which one or several persons bind themselves, towards one or several others, to transfer, to do or not to do something.[177]

Assuming that this definition answers the question whether the relationship among B, S and T is a contractual one, can you surmise which would be the next scholastic question? What about: "What type of a contract is it"? And indeed, the *Code Civil* definition of contract is followed by classifications of contracts based upon the essential features of each type, such as their mutuality, bilateral or unilateral nature, risk assumption, gratuitousness or onerousness, and so on.[178] Please notice the neutral, almost vague, manner in which the *Code Civil* defines "onerous" contracts as agreements in which each of the parties gives or does something presumably without profiting from their performances.[179] Can you suggest a reason why it does so? Could it be that since the *Code Civil* was not intended for commercial, profit-making transactions it prefers to avoid language that may give the impression that the onerous contract it refers to is or could be a commercial one? And if so, what effect would this fact have upon the application of the *Code Civil* to our factual hypothetical? Would it disqualify the application of the *Code Civil* to our projected escrow agreement as a likely profit-making transaction? These and other features provided by the classification of contracts are intended to facilitate the placement of the contract in question in the normative "box" reserved for each species.

In our case, the contracts involved in the "escrow agency" proposal would have to be identified by their definition and classification. The *Code Civil* has definitions for contracts whose facts seem close enough to those discussed by B and S—in contracts labeled "deposit" and "agency" or "*procuration*."

D. *Code Civil* and *Code de Commerce* Provisions

In the absence of provisions governing the escrow agreement in the Code Civil or Code de Commerce please search for provisions that most closely resemble the escrow transaction: perhaps the contract of deposit?[180] How close is the escrow agreement to any of the transactions covered by these articles? If you do not find them close enough, search for the provisions on the contract of agency or "procuration" (Articles 1984–2010).[181]

Consider also the provisions of the *Code de Commerce* on commercial acts[182] and commercial agents.[183]

---

177 C. CIV. (FR.) art. 1101 (2008) (emphasis added).

178 *See* C. CIV. (FR.) arts. 1102–1106 (2008).

179 *Id.* art. 1106.

180 *Id.* arts. 1915–1963.

181 *Id.* arts. 1984–2010.

182 C. COM. (FR.) art. L110–1 (2008).

183 *Id.* arts. L134–1—L134–4.

E. The Compatibility of the *Code Civil* and the *Code de Commerce* Provisions with Escrow Agreements

How compatible are the provisions on deposit agreements with the intent of the parties as set forth in the factual hypothetical: Article 1915 and its obligation to restore the deposited object in kind; Article 1917 and its "essentially gratuitous" contract; Article 1919 and its "actual" delivery (meaning delivery of the contractual *res*) prior to the existence of obligations on either side? Do these provisions reflect the type of agency desired by B and S? Could an agent act for two counter-parties to a contract or for potentially adversarial principals?

Under which of the above acts of commerce would the escrow agreement be subsumed? What would be the consequence of its failure to qualify for inclusion in this list? Does the commercial agency contract under the *Code de Commerce* fit the mold required by an escrow agreement? What is missing, if anything? What does it contain that is incompatible with the activities of an escrow agent, if anything?

F. Compatibility of the Mexican Civil and Commercial Codes with Escrow Agreements

Please repeat the same search of provisions on contracts and their types in Mexico's Federal Civil and Commercial Codes.

Chapter 11

SOCIO-ECONOMIC CONTEXT OF GERMANY'S CIVIL AND COMMERCIAL CODES

§ 11.1 THE CONTEXT: FROM A DISMEMBERED TO A UNIFIED COMMERCIAL AND INDUSTRIAL GERMANY

I first visited Germany in 1958 while a graduate student at the *Faculté International de Droit Comparé* in Luxembourg. Nazi atrocities, particularly the extermination of my mother's entire family, including my grandparents, aunts, and their infant children, were very much with me. I expected to find the ashes of a monolithic empire, one whose maniacal leader had promised it would last a thousand years. Instead, I found scattered among surprisingly resurging industrial, commercial and financial centers, many remnants of what had been the dismembered Germany of centuries past, a land described by the Encyclopedia Britannica as "dozens upon dozens of small political units. . . . gingerbread [-like] principalities. . . ."[1] Among what was being reborn, I also found a commercial-legal culture whose seeds had been planted by the ancestors of many of those whom the Nazis exterminated.

Scarcely a century earlier, the petty rulers of these principalities had "legislated at will, levied taxes, concluded alliances, and waged wars against each other. . . ."[2] despite being members of the "Holy Roman Empire."[3] Germany had indeed undergone a remarkable economic, political and military transformation between the early years of the Napoleonic empire, during which time it was still "drifting in the backwaters of European politics,"[4] and its emergence as a major world power at the end of the nineteenth century.

The focus of this section is the socio-economic and political transformation that preceded the enactment of Germany's Commercial Code or *Handelsgesetzbuch* (hereinafter HGB) in 1897 and its Civil Code or *Bürgerliches Gesetzbuch* (hereinafter BGB) in 1900. As with France's *Code Civil* and *Code de Commerce*, the German civil

---

[1] *History of Germany*, VIII ENCYCLOPEDIA BRITANNICA MACROPEDIA 98 (15th ed. 1974) [hereinafter BRITANNICA]. The reader will find an excellent historical summary of the political development of Germany on pages 98–121. The principal text summarizes, for purposes of this chapter, the significant points of interest in this development as outlined by Britannica.

[2] *Id.*

[3] Dating back from Charlemagne in the ninth century to King Francis II, who abdicated in 1806 a number of Central European states and principalities, were members of a loose union known as the Holy Roman Empire. It included territories of present-day Austria, Belgium, Germany, Switzerland, Liechtenstein, Luxembourg, Netherlands, the Czech Republic, Slovenia, and parts of Poland, France, and Italy. From the fifteenth century onwards, this union, smaller in size, became known as the Holy Roman Empire of the German Nation. As had been done by its predecessor, it invoked as a source of legitimacy its descent from the Western Roman Empire which had ended with the abdication of Romulus Augustulus in 476. The same source of legitimacy was responsible for the wholesale reception of Roman law in a number of German states in 1495. *See generally* JONATHAN W. ZOPHY, THE HOLY ROMAN EMPIRE: A DICTIONARY HANDBOOK (JONATHAN W. ZOPHY ed., 1980) (discussing the Holy Roman Empire). *See also* VON MEHREN & GORDLEY, THE CIVIL LAW SYSTEM, at 12 (discussing the reception of Roman law in Germany).

[4] BRITANNICA, *supra* note 1, at 98.

and commercial codes, and especially the former, have enjoyed considerable influence among other civil law jurisdictions in Europe, Africa, Asia and Latin America. It is because of their universal appeal that the student-interpreter should be prepared to go beyond mere textual exegesis. As was hopefully made clear by the preceding chapters on the *Code Civil* and *Code de Commerce*,[5] the importance of key code provisions can best be understood if one grasps their purpose and the circumstances that surrounded their enactment. Once familiar with their purposes and circumstances, it will be possible, as was also done with the French materials in the preceding chapters, to identify the archetypal and stereotypical contractual behavior encouraged and protected by German contract law.

A. The French Ideological and Intellectual Influence

While militarily and politically the German principalities, including their Holy Roman Emperor, had enjoyed military and administrative support for a considerable time from the Austrian Hapsburg monarchy, especially in keeping their French neighbors at bay, the French influence on Central European institutions was felt, especially following the French Revolution. The revolutionary promises of liberty, equality and fraternity, followed by Napoleon's initial apparent support for a constitutional state, caused much excitement among German intellectuals, including one Ludwig van Beethoven and his Eroica Symphony.[6]

The ideological enthusiasm, however, was not shared by the princes of the Holy Roman Empire who regarded the French revolution as a dangerous insubordination of the lower classes. Numerous military encounters ensued between member states of the Holy Roman Empire and the French. They were won mostly by the latter and following one of the French victories in 1800, the Holy Roman Emperor Francis II signed the Treaty of Luneville, which ceded the Rhineland to France. Thereafter, the Holy Roman Empire was effectively dismantled and in 1806, Napoleon put in its place a set of French satellite states known as the "Confederation of the Rhine."[7]

By encouraging the creation of satellite confederate states, Napoleon "unwittingly prepared the way for a program of centralization in Germany that helped to frustrate his own plans for the future aggrandizement of France. . . . [as] Germany for the first time felt the stirrings of liberalism and nationalism."[8] In addition, under Napoleonic rule, Germany had experienced efficient centralized government, greater equality before the law, and freedom of opportunity as local governments gradually removed religious disabilities, relaxed economic restrictions and eliminated feudal obligations. Prussia led the way. Between 1806 and 1813, "the statesmen in Berlin initiated a revolution from above in order to transform a rigid despotism into a popular monarchy

---

[5] *See supra* chs. 8–12.

[6] Although some of his biographers are not fully convinced of the veracity of the story, Beethoven, an initial admirer of the French Revolution and Napoleon, is supposed to have erased the dedication of the Eroica Symphony to Napoleon upon hearing of his proclamation as Emperor. *See* JOHN ROBERT SEELEY, II LIFE AND TIMES OF STEIN OR GERMANY AND PRUSSIA IN THE NAPOLEONIC AGE (1878) (an interesting description of the French and Napoleonic influence on the political and legal institutions of Germany in its dismembered days).

[7] BRITANNICA, *supra* note 1, at 102.

[8] *Id.* at 101–02.

supported by the loyalty of a free citizenry. . . . Among their most important achievements was the abolition of serfdom. . . ."[9]

Czarist Russia's defeat of Napoleon in 1812 encouraged Central European governments to line up against France; some of them became allies of the advancing Czarist armies, while others, such as Austria, remained on the sidelines hoping to join in once Napoleon seemed closer to defeat. Following Napoleon's defeat in the battle of Leipzig in 1813, the former members of the Holy Roman Empire gathered in Vienna during the fall of 1814 ("Vienna Congress") to restore peace to Central Europe and devise Germany's new form of government.

B. The Congress of Vienna, the *Zollverein* and Free Internal Trade: A New Commercial Bourgeoisie

The resulting form of government for Germany was a middle course between fragmentation and centralization. Accordingly, the Germany that emerged from the Vienna Congress included a confederation of thirty-nine states "ranging in size from the two great powers, Austria and Prussia, through the minor kingdoms Bavaria, Württemberg, Saxony, and Hanover; through smaller duchies such as Baden, Nassau, Oldenburg [and many others]. . . ."[10] It was a loose political association in which sovereignty, including executive branch decisions, remained with each member government.

Southern German states, imbued with liberal ideas, set up legislative assemblies comprised of propertied voters whose consent was necessary in order to enact legislation. Prussia and Austria, on the other hand, tried to preserve the legitimacy of their landed aristocracy as the ruling class. Yet, as the economy grew, so did the influence of liberals and moderates who advocated a larger measure of both unification and pluralism. They derived their support from a new bourgeoisie that, unlike its French counterpart, included not only owners of valuable real estate, but also industrialists, merchants, promoters, bankers, mine owners, civil servants and even university professors,[11] an increasingly respected class of professionals.

Liberals and moderates favored a monarchical system of government whose power had to be shared, as in the southern states, with a parliament elected by the propertied classes. Unlike the French socialists, however, they "feared the [wild passions of] the proletariat. . . . [and admired] the *juste-milieu* between royal absolutism and mob rule, which had been established in England by the Reform Bill of 1832. . . ."[12] As a result of the growing economic power of this Central European bourgeoisie, the German confederation enacted a Customs Union (*Zollverein*) in 1834 that created a common external tariff and eliminated or substantially reduced the tariffs that encumbered the internal commerce of the member states. Most members of the German Confederation were included, except for Austria and the Northwest states. Its impact was significant:

> [F]or some 25,000,000 Germans the *Zollverein* meant ... commercial unification without the aid of political unification. The Prussian government,

---

[9] *Id.* at 103.

[10] *Id.* at 104.

[11] *Id.* at 106.

[12] *Germany, History: The age of Metternich and the era of Unification: 1815–71*, ANCESTRY.COM, http://freepages.genealogy.rootsweb.ancestry.com/~holmer/links/german-history.html.

moreover, acquired a powerful new weapon in the struggle against Austria for the dominant position in central Germany.[13]

From an ideological standpoint, the creation of the *Zollverein* was one of the first affirmations in the European continent of the importance of free trade as a means to foster economic development, in sharp contrast with the reliance on the war booty that stretched back to at least the days of the original (not Holy) Roman Empire.[14]

C. Political Unification: Prussia and Bismarck's Germany

It took major social upheavals, a substantial economic recovery, plus the political skills of Chancellor Otto Von Bismarck to accomplish Germany's political unification. During the late 1840s, Central Europe underwent an economic depression and famine which considerably slowed industrial growth and prompted large unemployment. This led to hunger riots and eventually to uprisings in early 1848 in some of the Confederation states. At the same time, attempts were made at the legislative level to liberalize and unify the government.

The significant economic upturn came during the 1850s. In the course of a decade, the value of industrial production and foreign trade doubled in the *Zollverein* region. In addition, investment banks started providing risk capital for factories and railroads.[15] The nature of Germany's economy was being transformed from rural and pre-industrial to an industrial one. As wealth shifted from the countryside to the cities, from the landed aristocracy to a commercial and industrial bourgeoisie, "the pressure for a redistribution of political power also gained strength. . . . By the end of the decade a new struggle between the forces of liberalism and conservatism was in the making."[16]

It was at that time that Austrian Emperor Franz Joseph began an experiment with a parliamentary form of government. He promulgated a constitution with a bicameral legislature and an electoral system that recognized the interests of the new bourgeoisie. Similar developments were taking place in Prussia, where King William I was contemplating abdication in favor of his son, who also held liberal views on the role of parliament. Instead of abdicating, he named Otto von Bismarck, the Prussian ambassador to Paris, to a new and all-powerful prime ministry.

Bismarck's plan to attain German unity while preserving the influence of the crown and its nobility gained the support of the bourgeoisie by enabling it to obtain the economic benefits of political consolidation. Following Prussia's victory over Austria in the "Seven Weeks War" (from June to August of 1866), Bismarck created a "North German Confederation" whose executive authority was vested in a presidency held in accordance with hereditary rights by the rulers of Prussia. However, this presidency was assisted by a chancellor responsible only to them. As chancellor, Bismarck encouraged a Franco-Prussian war. The southern states of Germany joined the north in this war and days prior to the French defeat on January 18, 1871, King William I was proclaimed emperor of a finally-united Germany.

---

[13] BRITANNICA, *supra* note 1, at 107.

[14] *See generally* Kozolchyk, *Grand and Small Scale* (more variations on the same theme).

[15] BRITANNICA, *supra* note 1, at 109.

[16] *Id.*

From 1871 to 1879, the economic freedoms sought by the middle class were consolidated and enlarged as the National Liberal Party controlled the legislature. Freedom of enterprise was implemented by various types of business associations, some with and others without limited liability, and work was started on a commercial code intended for those who qualified as merchants and on a civil code designed to enshrine the principles of freedom of contract, ownership and possession of property. The emancipation of rural property from its feudal shackles was encouraged by the support for municipal autonomy. Thus, in 1873, towns were freed from control of the cantonal parliament (*Landrat*) and the way was clear for the development of local government in which Germany led the world. On the same liberal side of the ledger, Bismarck lent his support to advanced social security legislation such as a Sickness Pension Law (enacted in 1883), an Accident Pension Law (enacted in 1884) and an old age pension (enacted in 1889) scheme that accompanied these statutes.[17]

§ 11.2 THE EMERGING GERMAN INDUSTRY, AGRICULTURE, COMMERCE AND FINANCE

A. Industries Big and Small: From Craftsmen to Merchants

In his insightful history of Germany during the period from 1780 to 1918, Harvard's history Professor David Blackbourn points to the period of 1849–1880 as an era of true social and economic transformation.[18] As noted earlier, the value of industrial production and foreign trade doubled from 1850 to 1860 in the *Zollverein* area, and this was accompanied by major infusions of risk capital for factories and railroads.[19] Very soon, commercial, industrial and financial activities began stimulating each other's growth. As Germany's rail system connected more cities, and as the demand for steel and coal increased, the coal fields of the Ruhr Valley raised their production and so did the nascent steel mills. As capital lending and investment for industrial development became more widely available, the chemical industry, followed eventually by the electrical industry, sprang into action.[20]

---

[17] GEORGE LEWIS BOLEN, GETTING A LIVING: THE PROBLEM OF WEALTH AND POVERTY—OF PROFITS, WAGES AND TRADE UNIONISM 583–84, n.2 (Macmillan Co., 1903) (discussing Germany's old age pensions).

[18] DAVID BLACKBOURN, HISTORY OF GERMANY 1780–1918: THE LONG NINETEENTH CENTURY 135–45 (2d ed. 2003) (1997).

[19] *Id.* at 87. For example, according to Professor Blackbourn, railway construction alone accounted for almost a third of all net investments in the 1840's. *Id.* at 88.

[20] *Id.* at 86–87. Professor Blackbourn provides the following statistical indicators of industrial growth in Germany during the period in question:

> [R]aw cotton consumption [for example] in the German Customs Union increased eightfold in the years 1830–50, Austrian output of iron doubled between the 1820s and 1840s, coal production within the borders of the later Germany more than doubled over a slightly shorter period, and so on. Beyond the raw cotton and the raw statistics, we can point to advances in mechanization and the use of new kinds of energy (steam, gas), the development of important industrial branches (engineering, chemicals and sugar, as well as textiles, coal and iron), the appearance on the scene of familiar entrepreneurial names (Krupp, Stumm, Borsig, Maffei, Siemens). Industrialization was more apparent from the 1830s, and in particular regions (the Rhineland and Westphalia, Silesia, Saxony, Bohemia) and subregions [of] (the Neckar valley within largely agricultural Württemberg). Yet the limited extent of industrial change should be recognized. Growth in scale and organization of production generally ran ahead of capital investment and technological innovation, most obviously in the textile sector. The number of weavers grew from 315,000 to 570,000 between 1800 and 1850, but over 90 per cent of looms were hand-operated. Within the overall economy, industry proper continued to be eclipsed by outworking [putting out] and craft production, and even more by agriculture.

While this process of industrialization was going on at the top of the industrial and commercial pyramid, a similarly important one was taking place, although on a smaller scale, at the bottom of the commercial-industrial pyramid. As noted by Fernand Braudel and discussed in earlier chapters, the guild system was replaced by *verlegers* or commercial intermediaries who "put out" or commissioned work to individual or family workers. According to Blackbourn,[21] while the number of *verlegers* and workers involved in the putting out system increased, the number of artisans who worked as guild members decreased:

> The numbers [were] striking. Those engaged in putting-out [increased] from 1 to 1.5 million between 1800 and 1850, when they made up almost 40 per cent of the total manufacturing workforce. Some were rural outworkers, but other[s] included journeyman tailors and struggling small masters forced (like the seamstresses) into a despised piece work, and craftsmen in trades like furniture and bottle making who worked to contract under the direction of merchant capitalists. . . . A good half of all masters worked alone, more in overstocked branches like tailoring, carpentry and shoemaking. They lived on the margins of subsistence. In the 1840s, a meager 400 out of 2800 shoemakers in Berlin earned enough to pay any trade tax; in Elberfeld-Barmen only half of 1100 shoemakers were employed at a given time. The increase of more than a quarter of a million in the number of masters between 1800 and 1850 show[ed] that journeymen could and did set up on their own account, especially in trades that required little initial capital.[22]

B. The Emergence of a Viable Retail Trade: Shopkeepers, Small Merchants, Credit Unions and Non-Usurious Credit

In contrast with the low esteem accorded to merchants generally in Southern Europe, the Cambridge History characterizes merchants in seventeenth and eighteenth-century Italy, Germany and Holland as well-regarded and influential.[23] Professor Blackbourn's description of German cities after 1850 adds interesting features about the status of merchants as members of the emerging lower-middle class:

> Its most important component consisted of those who ran small, independent concerns—master craftsmen, small businessmen . . . [and] shopkeepers. Together they accounted for perhaps 8 per cent of the gainfully employed in the early 1870s. The most important growth came among the shopkeepers, as itinerant traders and hawkers gave way to fixed retail outlets. Of course, there had long been shopkeepers in large mercantile centres, trading imported commodities like tobacco and coffee, but changing popular consumption now established the retailer as a familiar urban figure. Even as

---

Id.

[21] *Id.* at 86.

[22] *Id.* (citations omitted). Professor Blackbourn's conclusions find support in the work of contemporary German historians. *See, e.g.*, Marcel Boldorf, *Institutions and Economic Development: The Cases of Lower Silesia and Northern Ireland (1750–1850)* (*Entwicklung und institutionelle Rahmenbedingungen: Die Beispiele Niederschlesien und Nordirland (1750–1850)*, 90 VSWG 399 (2003).

[23] THE CAMBRIDGE ECONOMIC HISTORY OF EUROPE, V THE ECONOMIC ORGANIZATION OF EARLY MODERN EUROPE 287 (E.E. Rich & C.H. Wilson eds., Cambridge Univ. Press 1977) [hereinafter CAMBRIDGE HISTORY V].

population rose, the ratio of customers to traders fell from 83:1 to 54:1 between 1861 and 1882. By the latter date there were some 450,000 German shopkeepers.[24]

The growth among shopkeepers was largely the result of what Professor David Sorkin refers to as the "multifaceted transformation which German Jews underwent . . . (*circa* 1780–1870)."[25] Sorkin further notes that, "Whereas for centuries the Jews had earned their livelihood primarily from usury, they now gradually shifted to commerce."[26]

> Of the 272 heads of Jewish households in Frankfurt in 1694, for example, 163 were engaged in retailing, especially textiles, while only 109 still lent money and dealt in old clothes. The last complaints about Jews engaged in usury were heard in the Duchy of Kleve in northwest Germany in 1737.[27]

Thus, the Jews, after being forced to earn a living by lending money at interest gradually found themselves engaged in retail and wholesale commerce. As was discussed in Chapter 5, money-lending was an activity prohibited to Christians based on a Biblical prohibition that was interpreted by Christian theologians as preventing Christians from charging interest to their Christian brethren. As Jews were allowed to participate in activities other than money lending, they increased their earnings considerably. If in 1750 nearly fifty percent of the German Jews were only marginally employed or were destitute beggars, in little over a century the tax records revealed that fully eighty percent of the Jewish community was engaged in commerce and sixty percent was in Germany's "upper income brackets."[28]

Meanwhile, commercial credit at approved interest rates was becoming available throughout Germany. An authoritative study on the history of interest rates found that that the so-called "five percent" or "triple" contracts in which the active partner promised his silent partner a five percent return on his investment in the partnership were common in sixteenth-century Germany and were unofficially approved in 1567 by Pope Pius V.[29] The Reformation was more openly accepting of the charge of interest as long as it did not exceed a prescribed or marketplace rate:

> Martin Luther, 1483–1536, declared that a Christian was under no obligation to observe dead Mosaic ordinances [forbidding the charge of interest to religious brethren]. At first, however, he opposed the census [a secured land loan] and the wealthy *rentier* class as even worse than manifest usurers. . . . [Subsequently] Luther's position seemed to change. It was not, he said, complicity in sin to pay usury. The common man must obey the temporal authorities. . . . Reform must come from the princes and not from the people. The Christian man was free to lend his money. Considerations of public

---

[24] BLACKBOURN, *supra* note 18, at 164 (citations omitted).

[25] David Sorkin, *The impact of emancipation on German Jewry: a reconsideration*, *in* JONATHAN FRANKEL & STEVEN J. ZIPPERSTEIN, ASSIMILATION AND COMMUNITY: THE JEWS IN NINETEENTH CENTURY 179 (2004).

[26] *Id.*

[27] *Id.* (citations omitted).

[28] *Id.* (citation omitted).

[29] SIDNEY HOMER & RICHARD SYLLA, A HISTORY OF INTEREST RATES 73 (4th ed. 2005), *available at* http://vnn1.online.fr/Cafeteria/Financial_Accounting_Banking/A.History.of.Interest.Rates.Wiley.Finance.Series.4th.Ed.eBook-YYePG.pdf.

utility should regulate loans at interest. Those who take 5–6% should not be treated as extortioners. Even 8% was permissible as long as it was from redeemable security on land.[30]

Consequently, unlike the concern for usury that prevailed in pre-codification France and Spain, commercial and consumer credit did not evoke fear of prosecution in pre-codification Germany. Not surprisingly, toward the end of the eighteenth century it was neither illegal nor immoral in Germany and Italy to pay interest on periodic payments such as contracts of annuities that fluctuated between four and five percent *per annum*.[31]

Finally, the availability of credit to small merchants received a considerable boost from credit unions (also referred to as cooperatives) as sources of non-usurious commercial loans. While financial cooperatives date back to the beginning of the nineteenth century in England,[32] by the middle of that century "Germany was the first home of credit unions as we know them today. . . ."[33] These unions were volunteer-based, with boards of directors elected by their members. Their founders in 1850 were Hermann Schulze-Delitzsch and Friedrich Raiffeisen. The first credit unions were known as "peoples' banks" (*Vorschussverein*) and their main goal was to build "a credit society to help shopkeepers and urban workers find relief from loan sharks."[34] Accordingly, they would provide production and marketing credit not only to city merchants, but also to farmers who needed credit for their acquisitions of livestock, equipment and seeds, among other goods.[35] Very quickly, cooperative credit became available to tradesmen throughout Germany.[36] By 1859, there were 183 such credit unions with 18,000 members just in Posen and Saxony.[37]

C. Inventory, Accounts Receivable, Financing and a New Law of Executory Contracts

The expansion of commercial and consumer credit in nineteenth-century Germany was supported by different types of loan agreements and collateral. The use of some of these agreements and new types of collateral was described by the Cambridge History as follows:

> Merchants from the town or country regularly bought up agricultural produce from the farmers before it had been harvested against partial or complete cash payment; the rural population was paid cash for linen or cloth that was to be woven later during the winter months. Where the putting-out system

[30] *Id.* at 77.

[31] *Id.* at 176.

[32] *See* Missouri Credit Union Association, *Credit Union Difference*, http://www.branchnearyou.com/cu_difference.html [hereinafter *Credit Union Difference*] (a brief history of financial cooperatives) (on file with author).

[33] *Id.*

[34] *Credit Union History*, INTERNETAUTOGUIDE.COM, http://www.internetautoguide.com/credit-center/credit-union-history.html#ixzz2aTPNskYq (on file with author).

[35] *Credit Union Difference*, *supra* note 32.

[36] ENCYCLOPEDIA BRITANNICA: XXX THE NEW VOLUMES 748–49 (Hugh Chisholm ed., 12th ed. 1922).

[37] Amy Nutt, *More to Know about Credit Unions* (May 27, 2009, 6:56 AM), http://creditusbankinternetbanking.blogspot.com/2009/05/more-to-know-about-credit-unions-by-amy.htmlhttp://creditusbankinternetbanking.blogspot.com/2009/05/more-to-know-about-credit-unions-by-amy.html (on file with author).

> occurred in the towns, similar practices were common. Thus farmers and workers received credit guaranteed by their future harvest[s] or future labour output: sometimes merchants supplied the materials and implements themselves. . . .[38]

A popular form of commercial credit among eighteenth-century shopkeepers and their suppliers relied on the "book entry" method described by Professor Kessler in a previous chapter.[39] In addition, established merchants assigned their accounts receivable to their lenders: "If A was in debt to B and was owed money by a third person C, A could ask C to pay the outstanding balance to creditor B for A's account. . . ."[40]

Please notice that in this assignment of an account or debt, B, A's creditor, could be subject to the same objections or defenses to payment that C had against A, such as the poor quality of A's goods or services. In other words, in the assignment of debts or accounts, if C could raise a valid defense against paying A, he could equally do so against B. This uncertainty had to be eliminated or significantly reduced if the assignment of debts were to be sold "commercially" to third-party financiers or investors, for they would be unwilling to become involved in the disputes between the suppliers of goods or services and their purchasers. In countries whose legal system and commercial culture were not haunted by the fear of prosecution for usury, promissory notes and bills of exchange properly used provided a helpful means of assurance to these third parties.

D. From Cambium to Quasi Money

1. *Sale of Exchange and Usurious Loans; Assignment and Negotiation of Promissory Notes and Bills of Exchange*

Promissory notes, almost since times immemorial, have been two party instruments.[41] Their *maker* promises to pay to their *payee or holder* a sum of money at a specified time. In contrast, a bill of exchange is a three party instrument in which the drawer orders the drawee to accept his order of payment and either pay a third party payee or accept to pay at a future time to the same payee or to his endorsees. This payment can take place upon presentation of the bill (thus paying it "at sight") or it can take place at a future time after the drawee has accepted to do so in the bill's acceptor's column. Both instruments are either assignable or negotiable.[42]

If they are assignable, only the person designated as assignee can collect on them, and such a person does not enjoy rights superior to those of their payee-assignor. If, for example, the payee-assignor owes money to the maker of the note, the latter can invoke this debt as a defense against claims by either the payee-assignor or his assignee. In contrast, if the promissory note was made out to the payee or to the order of the payee, the latter could endorse it to an "innocent" third party, *i.e.*, a party who in good faith

---

[38] CAMBRIDGE HISTORY V, *supra* note 23, at 300.

[39] *See supra* § 9:2(E)(3)(a).

[40] CAMBRIDGE HISTORY V, *supra* note 23, at 301.

[41] *See* KOZOLCHYK & MOLLOY, III UNITED STATES LAW, 22–3–22–5 (discussing promissory notes); *see generally* Benjamin Geva, *The Autonomy of the Banker's Obligation on Bank Drafts and Certified Cheques* 73 CAN. B. REV. 21 (1994).

[42] *See* KOZOLCHYK & MOLLOY, III UNITED STATES LAW, 22–6 (discussing the bill of exchange).

acquired the note for value and was unaware of the maker's claims against the payee. Such an indorsee-holder will not be subject to the defenses that the maker had against the payee-assignor, including an offset by the maker's claim against the payee-assignor. The same legal consequences of the transfer and negotiation apply to the bill of exchange.[43]

As noted in Chapter 5, a variant of the bill of exchange was used in the Middle East and Europe during the middle ages. The southern European and especially the Italian version known as the *Lettera di Cambio* was used to purchase foreign exchange at a place other than that of the payee-holder's place of business. For example, if a merchant "M" in Genoa, Italy needed foreign exchange to purchase lace while in Bruges, Belgium, M would ask banker "B" located in Genoa to send a written instruction to his correspondent "C" in Bruges directing him to supply the local currency needed by M to pay for his purchases of lace.

Prior to B's issuance of his bill of exchange to C, M would pay an amount of Genoese currency needed to buy the lace in Bruges plus an exchange commission or fee (not interest) to B. This payment would be referenced in the bills of exchange by their drawer as the "value clause" and its most common version was that of the "value received" from the buyer of the exchange. The reason why B would charge a fee or commission and not interest was to avoid the characterization of the ostensible purchase of foreign exchange transaction as a usurious loan.[44]

Accordingly, recall that the bill of exchange was quite commonly used to disguise a loan that the church could deem usurious. The disguise or simulation would have M (the actual borrower from B) appear as the buyer of C's foreign exchange to be delivered to him in Bruges. M would then pretend to provide local funds to B which he would notify C were either deposited with him and credited to C's account or he would ask C to debit B's foreign exchange account with C. In fact, however, M's deposit or delivery of local funds to B would not take place until the time when he repaid B's loan and the added commission or exchange fee would in fact mask the payment of interest for B's loan.

2. *Henry Diedrich Jencken's Comparative Analysis of European Nineteenth Century Negotiable Insrument Laws*

Henry Diedrich Jencken (1828–1881) was a London barrister who authored some of the nineteenth century's clearest and most succinct comparative analyses on the differences between, on the one hand, the German and English laws and practices on bills of exchange and promissory notes, and, on the other, the laws and practices of France and France-inspired jurisdictions on the same instruments. His analysis also included important legal and economic consequences of these differences.[45]

---

[43] *Id.*

[44] *See supra* chs. 5 & 9.

[45] *See* Henry Diedrich Jencken, *The Codification on the Law of Bills of Exchange and Negotiable Securities in Europe and the United States, Jurisprudence*, 80–95, *in* THOMAS PITT TASWELL-LANGMEAD, ET. AL., 2 THE LAW MAGAZINE AND REVIEW: A QUARTERLY REVIEW OF JURISPRUDENCE (1877) [hereinafter Jencken, *Codification*]; *see also* HENRY DIEDRICH JENCKEN, A COMPENDIUM OF THE LAWS ON BILLS OF EXCHANGE, PROMISSORY NOTES, CHECQUES, AND OTHER COMMERCIAL NEGOTIABLE INSTRUMENTS OF ENGLAND, GERMANY AND FRANCE (1880) [hereinafter JENCKEN, COMPENDIUM] (his classic monograph).

a. The French and "Latin" System and the Non-Negotiability of Governmental Bonds

The French system, which Jencken described as "all but universally adopted by the Latin races",[46] based the enforceability of the bill of exchange on the above-described contract of exchange (*Contrat de Change*). This contract was perfected by the delivery of the bill of exchange to its payee-holder in exchange for a certain amount of local currency in payment for the delivery of foreign currency at a designated place and time. Accordingly, Jean Marie Pardessus, a leading commentator of the French *Code de Commerce* of 1807, characterized the bill of exchange (*Lettre de Change*) simply as: "[A] contract, by virtue of which one of the parties . . . agrees to pay to the other at a given place a certain sum of money he has received at the former place."[47]

Please notice the above characterizations of the bill of exchange as a contract, as contrasted with its present day characterization as a promise of payment which, when in the hands of a holder in due course or in good faith, is independent of the underlying transactions that prompted its issuance.[48] In addition, unlike Robert Pothier's "*pollicitation*" and the *Code Civil*'s contractual promise, this promise of payment is enforceable from the moment it is issued and does not require its acceptance by the promisee or payee to be binding on the promisor.[49]

Despite his characterization of the bill of exchange as a special contract of exchange, Pothier was aware of the widely used "pay to the order of" endorsement clauses that enabled the payee (one of the parties of the assumed contract) to endorse the bill to third parties who were not parties to the original contract of exchange. In fact, the "pay to the order of" clause which in principle enabled an unlimited number of endorsements was, according to Pothier, "one of the essential characteristics of the Bill of Exchange."[50] Still, Pothier's view of the special contract of exchange characterized its execution as one in which: "A Bill of Exchange coupled with an endorsement, and perfected by delivery, constitutes the mode of fulfilment [sic] of the original contract between the parties."[51] In other words, once the bill of exchange was delivered to its payee, the contract of exchange was deemed executed and whatever rights were transferred to third parties were the result of an assignment of the rights that had been acquired by the original payee, but subject to the terms and conditions of the original underlying contract of exchange (*Cession de Creance*).

As also noted by Jencken, the above characterization of the bill of exchange did not differ from the medieval practice of purchasing and selling (*Emptio Venditio)* of foreign exchange by means of an instrument known as *Lettera di Cambio* or plain *Cambiale*.[52]

---

[46] Jencken, *Codification, supra* note 45, at 85.

[47] *Id.*

[48] *See* KOZOLCHYK & MOLLOY, III UNITED STATES LAW, 22–1. The switch in the statutory characterization of a bill of exchange as a contract to a promise or as the formal act that incorporates such a promise probably took place first in the Prussian draft law of 1847 (S 6). Jencken, *Codification, supra* note 45, at 88; *see also infra* note 63 and accompanying text.

[49] *See supra* § 8:9(C)(4).

[50] Jencken, *Codification, supra* note 45, at 85.

[51] *Id.*

[52] *See, e.g.,* Michele de Cesare, *La questione delle lettere di cambio nel sec.XVII presso la Regia Dogana di Puglia, available at* http://www.bibliotecaprovinciale.foggia.it/capitanata/1988_1993/1988_1993pdf/1988–1993_01_151–156_DeCesare.pdf (describing the seventeenth-century Italian *Lettera de Cambio*) (on file with author).

The parties to the French contract of exchange were the same as those of the Italian medieval version of the *Cambiale.* Most importantly, the legal basis for the payee-holder or his assignee's claim against the drawee was the assignment (*not the negotiation*) of the drawer's monetary claim against the drawee for the deposited funds and this assignment was the above referred transfer of the debt or of the account (*Cession de Creance*).

Clearly, this characterization impeded the negotiability of the bill of exchange because its assignee (even if named an endorsee of the bill) had the same (and no better) rights to the funds deposited with the drawee as the drawer. If the drawer could not claim these funds because of underlying transaction causes, neither could the payee-endorsee. Indeed, it was precisely to insure the drawee's ability to pay according to the instruction by the drawer that the *Code de Commerce* required the drawer to provide the drawee with payment funds in advance of the claim by the payee, his assignee or endorsee and to so signify it in the bill of exchange by means of the above-mentioned "value clause."[53]

In addition, and as the reader will recall from the discussion of the "Red Ink" case in Chapter 9,[54] the reason why the "courtesan" (as Napoleon referred to her) had inserted the *distantia loci* clause in her bill of exchange was to prevent its nullity as a face-to-face or *inter praesentes* usurious loan. Further, since its *raison d'etre* as a *Contrat de Change* was to make foreign exchange available to the payee-holder that was unavailable where the bill of exchange was issued, the bill had to refer to the presumably distant place where the exchange was available for payment (*distantia loci)* or to indicate that it had been forwarded for payment from one place to another (*remise d'un lieu sur un autre*).[55]

Similarly, because the original version of the *Code de Commerce* was vague on the consequences of endorsements and forbad blank endorsements in which the payee-endorser was only required to stamp his signature without mentioning the name of the endorsee, uncertainty prevailed with respect to the rights of these third parties.[56]

Yet, what if the parties to the bill of exchange did not really desire to purchase and sell foreign currency and even less to do it at a distance from each other? What if what they wanted was for one party to borrow money from the other and to have a third party drawee disburse the money either upon presentation of the bill of exchange or at a time after presentment? This was the situation with the promissory notes issued by several European governments since the eighteenth century *in the form of bonds or debentures* and whose purpose was to finance, among other endeavors, their increasingly costly wars. Yet, while it made sense for these governments and their bankers to strengthen their assurance of repayment by identifying the governmental revenues that would repay the bonds and promising to set them aside at a time prior to repayment, it made no economic sense to, in effect, prepay their bonds at the time of their issuance as was required by the value clauses of the *Contrat de Change.*

---

[53] *See* Jencken, *Codification, supra* note 45, at 89 (referring to Articles 115–117 of the original *Code de Commerce*).

[54] *See supra* § 9:2(E)(3)(c).

[55] *See* Jencken, *Codification, supra* note 45, at 89 (referring to Article 110 of the original *Code de Commerce*).

[56] *Id.* at 89–90 (discussing the efforts by the French courts to enable blank endorsements).

In addition, since the identity of the buyers of these bonds in the primary or secondary markets was frequently unknown at the time the bonds were issued, the bankers selected by the various governments as their intermediaries had to be able to endorse and negotiate the bonds to other entities in the primary market or to the individual holders in the secondary market. This could be accomplished by "nominative," "pay to the order of" endorsement clauses; however, at times it was also necessary to enable the intermediary banks to endorse the bonds in blank to their purchasers or creditors or to make the bonds payable to "bearer."

b. The German Negotiable Instruments Law and Government Bonds

Before we discuss the negotiability of German promissory notes and bills of exchange, it is important to understand what makes their promises of payments certain and liquid or money-like. As I stated elsewhere,[57] the promises of payment issued by private parties can differ sharply from paper money or official currency or they can approximate it. Where they approximate paper money, it is because their holder is able to convert these private promises of payment into paper money or official currency quickly and inexpensively.

The ability to monetize private promises requires that their holder be protected as much as possible against claims, defenses or equities raised by the parties to the transaction or transactions that prompted the issuance of the promise. Bear in mind the analogy with the "legal tender" of paper money or currency: The ability of paper money or currency to serve as final payment for private debts would be compromised if such a payment were conditioned upon underlying considerations such as whether their volume of issuance was excessive, or whether the issuing government had adhered to certain fiscal or credit policies.[58] Further, in commercial practice, the objections to being paid with government money must be very few and confined to instances of clearly illegal conduct by the holder or his predecessors such as their forgery, alteration or their use despite an earlier withdrawal from circulation. These objections are incidentally echoed in the short list of "real" defenses that can be raised against negotiable instruments in the hands of holders in due course or in good faith.[59]

In sum, conditionality, whether imposed by statute or by contractual stipulation, introduces crippling uncertainty of payment. It is precisely for this reason that the promises of negotiable instruments are widely, if not universally, defined as unconditional promises to pay sums certain.[60] As was just discussed, this was not the case with the promises that resulted from the assignment of the claims of the *Code de Commerce* of 1807.

---

[57] KOZOLCHYK & MOLLOY, III UNITED STATES LAW, at 22–14.

[58] *See, e.g., Juilliard v. Greenman*, 110 U.S. 421 (1884) (on legal tender).

[59] *See, e.g.,* U.C.C. § 3–302.

[60] *See, e.g.,* Convention Providing a Uniform Law For Bills of Exchange and Promissory Notes (Geneva, 1930) [hereinafter Geneva Convention], *available at* http://www.jus.uio.no/lm/bills.of.exchange.and.promissory.notes.convention.1930/portrait.pdf. Article 1 defines a bill of exchange as an instrument that must contain: "1. The term 'bill of exchange' inserted in the body of the instrument and expressed in the language employed in drawing up the instrument; 2. An unconditional order to pay a determinate sum of money. . . ." *Id.* This Convention has been widely adopted by civil law countries. Common law countries' definition of a negotiable instrument is almost identical. *See* U.C.C. § 3–104(a) ("'negotiable instrument' means an unconditional promise or order to pay a fixed amount of money. . . .").

The promises of payment that were first incorporated into promissory notes and bills of exchange in Germany during the seventeenth and eighteenth centuries were, as their French counterparts, conditioned upon stipulations in the contract of exchange and thus were only assignable and not truly negotiable: They conveyed no better rights to their holder than those of their assignor. Consequently, Jencken assessed the status of German negotiable instruments law during the first decades of the nineteenth century as:

> Tardily introduced, reluctantly adopted, the important juridical questions involved in the creation of a negotiable instrument were not even thought at that time. It was not until the close of the 18th century that [German] jurists turned their attention to the important question of the true juridical character of negotiable instruments.[61]

In retrospect, the tardy introduction and reluctant adoption of bills of exchange and promissory notes as means of payment could well have been a blessing in disguise. For it was only in 1839 that Dr. Karl Einert, a law professor and commercial court judge, provided the proper direction for Germany's (and many other nations') negotiable instruments law in his monograph, "The Law of Bills of Exchange and the Everyday Needs of the Bill of Exchange Business in the Nineteenth Century."[62] In it, he attacked the theory of the *Code de Commerce* that bills of exchange were part of the contract of exchange. As summarized by Jencken, Einert's main points were:

> [A] Bill of Exchange . . . and a Promissory Note . . . partake of the same characteristics, and are, juridically speaking, identical. . . . [t]he only difference between the two instruments consists in this, that the maker or drawer of a Bill of Exchange guarantees not only the payment, but also the acceptance, whilst the maker of a Promissory Note guarantees only payment. . . . A Bill of Exchange . . . in its nature [is] only an acknowledgment of a debt, a promise to pay, rendered, however, negotiable by adding the word[s] [to the] "order" [of]. . . . [Thus the] Bill of Exchange to order partakes of the character of a Bill to Bearer. . . . The usage of bankers of *in blanco* drawings, that is, the issues of drafts [by the drawers] without funds in the drawee's hands, points to the creation of paper money, analogous to bank-notes, only with . . . [the] difference that the acceptor is the surety who guarantees payment.[63]

The support for Dr. Einert's viewpoint did not come from Roman law or from the German *Pandektenrecht*. It came from the usages of bankers and especially from those of Europe's largest banks. As summarized by Jencken:

> [I]n support of his theory, [Dr. Einert] point[ed] to the wide-spread custom of creating a circulating medium by drawings in blank, that is without having funds in the hands of the drawee; a custom resorted to by the great banking firms of Europe to an enormous extent.[64]

---

[61] Jencken, *Codification, supra* note 45, at 86.

[62] *See* KARL EINERT, DAS WECHSELRECHT NACH DEM BEDURFNIS DES WECHSELGESCHAFTS IM NEUNZEHNTEN JAHRHUNDERT (Leipzig Vogel 1879).

[63] Jencken, *Codification, supra* note 45, at 87–88.

[64] JENCKEN, COMPENDIUM, *supra* note 45, at 18.

Einert's theory was at first vehemently attacked by his Pandektist colleagues, but gradually it prevailed and was adopted by most delegates to the National Assembly of the Confederate States of Germany on May 1, 1849.[65] His theory was thus responsible for the first European rejection of the *Code de Commerce*'s contract-of-exchange approach.[66]

By adopting Dr. Einert's recommendations, Germany's negotiable instruments law acquired the same "essential characteristics" as English law. Their similarities were summarized by Jencken as: Bills of Exchange in both countries functioned as negotiable and not merely assignable instruments.[67] Bills of Exchange could be drafted in any manner consistent with their liquid or quasi-monetary nature, although they had to bear the label "Bill of Exchange" on their face.[68] They could be endorsed in blank as well as in a nominative fashion (by naming the endorsee) or they could be endorsed "to the order of" any future endorsee.[69] Drawers as well as previous endorsers were deemed co-principal debtors, but, I would add, only for the amount and terms stated in the instrument. The value clause required by the *Code de Commerce* did not have to be stated. And, importantly, the only defenses allowed against a holder in due course or in good faith were: fraud, forgery, alteration of the debt or "the sum payable after the drawing of a Bill. . . ."[70] The equities or "personal" defenses between the "immediate" parties such as the plaintiff and the defendant in the summary action on negotiable instruments were allowed. Yet, as just noted, neither these equities nor the personal defenses were allowed against third parties, holding in due course or in good faith.[71]

These common statutory and practice features made it possible for Germany, England and other similarly inclined governments to issue bonds for purposes as far apart as the financing of public works or the fighting of local and foreign wars. It also became possible for these governments to create primary and secondary regional and international financial markets governed by the same type of law. The changes in the law and practice of negotiable instruments inspired by Dr. Einert's writings remains a dramatic illustration of how law making at the transactional or micro level can make possible major national, regional and international macro-economic developments.

E. The Importance of Credit and Payment Instruments in Germany's Economic Development

Commercial credit and access to investment capital became major engines of Germany's commercial and industrial growth during the middle of the nineteenth century. At the same time, following the German-French war, Germany emerged as an important financial center for what Braudel referred to as "high commerce" as well as for large industries and railroads.[72] After a careful evaluation of the development of

---

[65] Jencken, *Codification, supra* note 45, at 81.

[66] JENCKEN, COMPENDIUM, *supra* note 45, at 18–19.

[67] *Id.* at 18.

[68] *Id.*

[69] *Id.*

[70] *Id.*

[71] *Id.* at 18–19.

[72] Julia Bersch & Graciela L. Kaminsky, *Financial globalization in the 19th Century: Germany as a financial center* 2 (George Washington University, Ctr. for Econ. Research, Working Paper Sept. 2008), http://home.gwu.edu/~graciela/HOME-PAGE/RESEARCH-WORK/WORKING-PAPERS/Germany-center.pdf (on file with author).

Germany's financial markets in the second half of the nineteenth century, economic historians Julia Bersch and Graciela Kaminsky concluded that the "[F]loatation of domestic securities clearly dominated aggregate issuances, quantitatively and qualitatively, and was closely linked to German economic activity."[73] The rise of German economic activity following its creation of vibrant financial markets was apparent in these scholars' comparison with that of Great Britain from 1880 to 1910. This is dramatically illustrated by statistics on the growth of the gross domestic product (GDP) of both countries during that period.

Economic Activity in Germany and the UK GDP Growth Rates[74]

These statistics attest to the enabling power of a cross-border uniform negotiable instruments law based upon sound legal and market sensitive business principles. The time had arrived when English, German and other European and North American private parties were issuing significant numbers of what economists nowadays refer to as quasi or near money, *i.e.*, privately created assets including liquid promises of payment capable of being converted to cash quickly and inexpensively. These promises have become part of our daily lives and their significance increases (for good and bad) with each passing day as dramatically illustrated by the present world-wide financial crisis.

F. Commercialization of German Rural Property and Agriculture

Prussia, among other German states, abolished serfdom in 1807.[75] According to Professor Blackbourn:

> [P]easant emancipation . . . provided the legal and institutional underpinning of rural production and social relations [for much of Germany]. . . . [While certain feudal rights remained], nowhere did reform "give" peasants the land they worked: it had to be paid for, or "redeemed." The ways in which this was arranged varied by region. . . .
>
> The amount of land under . . . [the plow] grew at an unprecedented rate in the first half of the nineteenth century: by at least 50 per cent [sic] in Germany as a whole, as much as threefold in parts of eastern Prussia. . . . The big estates of the east were increasingly commercial concerns, run by estate managers.[76]

By the seventeenth century, certain standards of commercial-agricultural behavior were discernible in Germany's agricultural and cattle markets. The Cambridge History describes the prevailing standard in cattle trading as follows:

> The cattle market at Wedel, outside Hamburg, was an example of a rural trading-place which blossomed and flourished twice a year in conjunction

---

[73] Kaminsky & Bersch, *supra* note 72, at 3. The authors establish the linkage between railroad construction and trading in railroad equity as the "cornerstone for Berlin's importance as a financial center." *Id.* at 5.

[74] *Id.* at 36.

[75] *See* SEELEY, *supra* note 6, at 186–88. According to Seeley, the Emancipation Edict had been issued by King Frederick William I of Prussia for Prussia only, and not for his other states until nearly three weeks later. *Id.* at 188. *See Documents-Rural and Urban Economy and Labor*, GERMAN HISTORY IN DOCUMENTS AND IMAGES, http://germanhistorydocs.ghi-dc.org/sub_document.cfm?document_id=3613 (an English translation of the text of The Prussian Reform Edict of October 9, 1807, issued by Prussia's King Frederick William III) (on file with author).

[76] BLACKBOURN, *supra* note 18, at 80–82.

> with the cattle drives from north to south. . . . Over all loomed *Roland*, the emblem of the market court of justice, beneath which the court assembled for adjudication. . . . A bargain was concluded when buyer and seller had noted its outcome on their slates. If it concerned a small number of cattle, settlement was effected in cash. Settlement for large lots, on the other hand, would be made via a German factor, who would be reimbursed by the purchaser in ready cash or drafts. . . . Good faith was the rule in the transactions themselves.[77]

The commercialization of agricultural property was evident throughout Germany, and unlike in pre-revolutionary and Napoleonic France, no stigma was attached to it even though it resulted in winners and losers, and the losers (as sellers of land) were not protected by the Napoleonic remedy of lesion (*laesio enormis*). Consider the following description of the effects of commercial diversification of land production by Professor Blackbourn:

> Commercialization . . . reinforced class stratification . . . and eventually led to severe social crisis. This was true to some degree right across Germany, [as] a result of the fact that land was now more obviously a commodity. It was not only that, of course. Agriculture was the axis on which village work and recreation turned. . . . Rising land prices (except for a downturn in the 1820s) encouraged a lively market in rural property. . . . The notary became a more frequent village visitor and rural taverns did well out of "sales-tippling" as the landowning peasantry now pursued its family marriage strategies with Balzacian relish.[78]

In fact, if the historians at the Polish mortgage bank, Bank Hipoteczny SA, are correct, Germany may well have led Europe, if not the world, in the marketing of mortgage bonds to rebuild agriculture in the Silesian region (*Schlesische Landschaft*) following the seventeenth-century Seven Year War, and then applied the same methods of financing to residential construction.[79]

QUESTIONS AND COMMENTS

Having in mind that for much of Europe's commercial life, going back to its Roman law period, land was the most valuable family asset, what would be the likely consequences of Germany's commercialization of land and agriculture for purposes of codification? Would such land transactions (including their yields) belong with the civil or the commercial code?

From the preceding description of the various transactions involving land and its produce in Germany, was there an archetypal figure in German land-contract law equivalent to the French bourgeois? If a family's welfare during agricultural survival times depended on what the land produced, would it not have made sense for the law to make the transfer or conveyance of land very difficult, so as to preserve it within the family estate for as long as possible? What made the transformation of land for survival to land for commercial growth possible in Germany?

---

[77] CAMBRIDGE HISTORY V, *supra* note 23, at 267.

[78] BLACKBOURN, *supra* note 18, at 82.

[79] BRE Bank Hipoteczny SA, *History of Mortgage Banks and Mortgage Bond* [hereinafter BRE Bank Hipoteczny] (on file with author).

In an earlier chapter, I noted that to facilitate its marketability, the BGB did not deem the German territorial debt (*Grundschuld*) an accessory obligation to the principal loan. In other words, the territorial debt was enforceable regardless of whether the security interest attached before the loan was disbursed.[80] This meant that the *Grundschuld* mortgage bonds could be sold despite the fact that their loans had not been dispersed when the mortgage bond was issued. In the *Grundschuld* transaction, then, the loan would occur when the purchaser of the bond paid for it, thereby becoming the issuer's lender. Accordingly, Section 1195 of the BGB states:

> A land charge [*Grunschuld*] may be constituted in such [a] manner that the certificate of the land charge is made out to the bearer. The provisions concerning payable to bearer [instruments] are applicable to such a certificate *mutatis mutandis*.[81]

A clear difference between the real estate mortgage documentation in the United States and Latin American jurisdictions is the execution by a United States borrower-mortgagor of a promissory note that accompanies, physically and legally, the mortgage deed as it is negotiated to a third party, such as a public or private discount or negotiation bank. In Latin American mortgage practice, there is no "merger" between the mortgage deed and the promissory note or other instrument signed by the mortgagor. In other words, in Latin America, the mortgage deed is not a "negotiable" document as it is in the United States. Yet, according to the Bank Hipoteczny SA study,[82] mortgage bonds could be sold as negotiable documents in Germany going as far back as the seventeenth century. Moreover, the BGB enables the land charge to become a bearer instrument. What do you think engendered this difference? Could Pothier's classification of the mortgage deed or contract as an "accessory" contract to the (principal) loan agreement, as reflected in the above quoted Article 2114 of the *Code Civil*, have anything to do with this inability to negotiate the mortgage?

G. A Parenthetical Aside: The Importance of Professional Agents and Intermediaries; The *Prokurist*

With the widespread availability of credit and the growth of commerce and industry in every sector of Germany's economy, it experienced a need for new professionals. This need resulted in an upward social mobility among what Professor Blackbourn referred to as "the new lower middle class of white-collar employees . . . [or support staff for merchants large and small]: clerks, cashiers, *prokurists*, book-keepers and overseers. . . . In the private sector alone, they numbered 400,000 by the beginning of the 1880's, or 3.4 per cent of the labour force."[83]

While the Anglo-American reader should be familiar with Professor Blackbourn's enumeration of the above employees and staff members, he is not likely to be familiar with the *Prokurist*, whose legal nature and functions were explored in Chapter 5 and are summarized by Sections 48–50[84] of the German HGB of 1897:

> § 48. (Conferring of signing power)

---

[80] *See* C. CIV. (FR.) art. 2114 (subjecting the existence of the mortgage to the discharge of a pre-existent obligation, *i.e.*, a loan) and the analysis of its impact upon housing fianance in *supra* §.8:4(B)(6).

[81] BGB (GOREN, 1994) § 1195.

[82] *See* BRE Bank Hipoteczny, *supra* note 79.

[83] BLACKBOURN, *supra note* 18, at 164.

[84] HGB (GOREN, 1998) §§ 48–50 (emphasis added).

(1) Signing power (*Prokura*) may be granted only by the proprietor of the commercial establishment or by his legal representative and only by means of an express declaration.

§ 49. (Extent of signing power)

(1) The signing power authorizes juridical and extra-juridical acts and legal transactions, of all kinds, which are involved in the conduct of a commercial enterprise.

(2) An authorized signatory (*Prokurist*) is empowered to dispose of and encumber real property only if this authority is specially granted to him.

§ 50. (Limitation of signing power)

(1) *A limitation in the scope of the signing power is ineffective as against third parties.*

The protection that Section 50 so firmly grants to the third parties who deal with the *Prokurist* is one of the features that more sharply distinguishes agency in German and German-inspired codes from *Code-Civil*-influenced jurisdictions. This distinction became evident in the contrast between the laws of agency in the United States and in Latin America as discussed in Chapter 5.[85] Unless a corporate agent—no matter how important his position in the operations of the corporation or other form of enterprise—is properly empowered to act in the name of the enterprise when entering into contracts, his signature will not bind the enterprise. Recall the Moctezuma Brewery case in which the president of the brewery successfully avoided the brewery's liability in a large contract for the purchase of hops by proving that his power of attorney did not include the authority to purchase raw materials for the manufacture of beer—that power was conferred expressly only upon a lowly purchase manager.

Given the lack of trust suffered by agents with apparent authority to act on behalf of their principals in familistic legal cultures (to the point that only family members or close friends can be trusted by third parties as binding agents), the *Prokura* should be seriously considered by these developing nations as a helpful, trust-inducing institution. Consider, for example, the following provisions of the Commercial Code of Estonia (1996):[86]

§ 16. Definition of procuration [*Prokura*]

(1) Procuration is an authorisation which grants the representative of the undertaking (procurator) the right to represent the undertaking in all legal acts related to economic activities.

(2) The procurator may transfer or encumber an immovable of the undertaking only if the undertaking grants this right to him or her in the procuration, and this is noted in the commercial register.

(3) If the undertaking restricts a procuration, the restriction shall not apply with regard to third persons, except the restrictions provided for in this Act.

---

[85] *See supra* § 5:13(A)–(B).

[86] COM. CODE (Est.) § 16 (2006) (on file with author).

(4) The provisions concerning representation in the General Part of the Civil Code Act apply to procuration unless otherwise provided for in this Code.

§ 11.3 THE EMERGENCE OF "HIGH COMMERCE" AND BANKERS FOR GOVERNMENTS

When Fernand Braudel talked about "high commerce" in post-Renaissance Europe, he meant one that involved mostly wholesale transactions and was centered in warehouses or staples and commodity exchanges.[87] This was a form of commerce that required specialized trading skills and international networking, but also risky negotiation such as on "futures" and other standardized contracts.

Braudel's high commerce seemed to rely on standardized contracts whenever possible. Two standardized contracts during the sixteenth and seventeenth centuries involved the sale and financing of spices imported by Europe from Asia, the so called "Europe" and "Asia" contracts.[88] Their supply depended upon a Portuguese import monopoly. Pursuant to a "Europe contract," a firm or group of firms committed to "accept imports from the East for one or two years at an agreed price and to undertake the marketing of the goods on its own account."[89] The "Asia contract" was a "financing agreement binding the contractors to deliver eastern spices to the *Casa da India* in Lisbon at fixed prices and on their own account."[90] Control over the European pepper market was held for a while during the sixteenth century by the German brothers Philipp Edouard and Octavian Fugger, who became widely known as bankers to the Spanish kings:

> The Spanish treasury, whose shortage of cash was chronic to the point of its frequently being on the verge of bankruptcy, insisted upon settling the sums due to the Fuggers under the Asia contract with an advance against a Europe contract, adding for good measure a threat to confiscate the Fuggers' funds in Spain-Portugal.[91]

The above-described contracts illustrate the close connection between "high commerce" and international banking with governments as their principal clients. In their inevitable search for valuable and liquid collateral, international lenders such as the Fugger brothers had to rely on commodities such as pepper, or on metals such as the silver mined by Spain in the Americas. It is no surprise then that following the defeat of Phillip II's "Invincible Navy" (*La Armada Invencible*), disenchanted Spaniards complained that the true beneficiaries of the colonization of the Americas were not the *conquistadores*, but the Fuggers.

In due course, the collateral relied upon by German private lenders of governments went beyond the governmental receipts from import monopolies and included an open variety of reliable governmental or quasi-governmental revenues. This was a significant part of the banking business pioneered during the late eighteenth century and early nineteenth century by the House of Rothschild, an

[87] *See supra* § 6:2(F)(5).

[88] CAMBRIDGE HISTORY V, *supra* note 23, at 284.

[89] *Id.* at 284.

[90] *Id.*

[91] *Id.* at 285.

institution that emerged from highly unlikely circumstances to become one of the most successful international commercial and banking businesses ever.

§ 11.4 MERCHANT AND PUBLIC SECTOR BANKING: THE ROTHSCHILDS

Those who practiced high-volume international commerce and banking in post-Renaissance Europe belonged to what Braudel and the Cambridge History characterize as a "commercial aristocracy."[92] The Cambridge History states that:

> With the family as the principal unit of enterprise, family ties—especially when reinforced by religion—sometimes sufficed to sustain [this] trade over long distances. This was so, as Professor Kellenbenz has demonstrated on the basis of genealogical material, with the seafaring Jews between the Iberian peninsula and Hamburg, and between Spain and the Levant.[93]

The reader will recall an earlier discussion of the long distance trade referred to in the above quote by medieval Mediterranean Jewish and Muslim merchants.[94] Yet, that trade was small in scale and was not accompanied by the financial services provided by international banks. The commercial and banking activities about to be described were not only of a very large scale, but also involved a form of collateral no longer confined to commercial goods or agricultural commodities—governmental revenues. Accordingly, governments acted as borrowers and issuers of promises to pay (as promissory notes or bonds), which promises were incorporated into the gradually standardized text of negotiable instruments.

A. The Rothschilds' Multi-National Banking

In his rightly acclaimed biography, *The House of Rothschild*, Oxford's and now Harvard's Niall Ferguson described its business as follows:

> At its zenith from the 1820s until the 1860s, this group had five distinct establishments. In addition to Nathan's in London, there was the original firm of M.A. Rothschild & Söhne in Frankfurt . . . de Rothschild Freres in Paris . . . C.M. von Rothschild in Naples . . . and S.M. von Rothschild in Vienna. . . . they were, to all intents and purposes, the component parts of a multinational bank. . . . Unlike modern multinationals, however, this was always a family firm. . . .
>
> Perhaps the most important point to grasp about this multinational partnership is that, for most of the century between 1815 and 1914, it was easily the biggest bank in the world.[95]

The House was founded by Mayer Amschel Rotschild during the last two decades of the eighteenth century. Rothschild started out as a modest coin dealer doing business and living in Frankfurt's Jewish streets or ghettos (*Judengasse*) where his ancestors had resided at least since the sixteenth century.

---

[92] BRAUDEL I, at 519; *see also* CAMBRIDGE HISTORY V, *supra* note 23, at 286.

[93] CAMBRIDGE HISTORY V, *supra* note 23, at 286–87.

[94] *See supra* § 5:9.

[95] FERGUSON, at 3. Most of the materials discussed in this section have been summarized from this excellent source.

B. Origins

In an earlier section, I used the term "unlikely" when referring to the place of origin of this banking colossus. One need only glance at the pictures of the house and street where Mayer Amschel and his sons were born and read the documents that framed their status as ghetto residents to be amazed at how such a business could have emerged from such humiliating and oppressive circumstances.[96] First was the "The Jews' Sow" (*Judensau*), an obscene graffito that greeted eighteenth-century pedestrians approaching the Frankfurt ghetto. It depicted:

> [A] group of Jews abasing themselves before—or rather beneath and behind—a fierce sow. While one of them suckled at her teats, another (in rabbinical garb) help up her tail for the third (also a rabbi) to drink her excrement. . . . If the traveller looked up, he could also see a second and still more repellent image: that of a dead baby, its outstretched body punctured by countless small knife wounds and beneath it nine daggers. "On Maundy Thursday in the year 1475," read a caption, "the little child Simeon, aged 2, was killed by the Jews". . . .[97]

Second was the city statute that governed the conduct of ghetto inhabitants, to be read each year as a reminder to members of the main ghetto synagogue. Among the terms that remained in force until the end of the eighteenth century were:

> [T]he Jewish population was restricted to just 500 families; the number of weddings was rationed to just twelve a year. . . . No more than two Jews from the outside were allowed to settle in the ghetto each year. Jews were prohibited from farming, or from dealing in weapons, spices, wine and grain. They were forbidden to live outside the Judengasse and, until 1726, were obliged to wear distinctive insignia . . . at all times. They were confined to the ghetto every night, on Sundays and during Christian festivals; at other times, they were forbidden to walk in the town more than two abreast. . . . [and] barred from entering parks, inns, coffee houses and the promenades. . . . They were permitted to visit the town market, but only during set hours, and were forbidden to touch vegetables and fruit there.[98]

Third, and as a reminder of the need to abide by the above "protective measures," were the recurring pogroms, during one of which (in the thirteenth century), the notorious *Judenschlacht* massacred more than three fourths of the Frankfurt Jews.[99]

C. Development

Even in today's global trade, Frankfurt (and especially its airport) enjoys one of Europe's best locations as a hub for north-south and east-west transportation. The same is true for its financial institutions. During the eighteenth century, it was already an important commercial and banking center where two major annual international

---

[96] *Id.* at 38, for the description of the Ghetto during the last decades of the eighteenth century by one of its residents, as transcribed by the poet Luwig Börne.

[97] *Id.* at 35–36 (the graffito appears on page 36).

[98] *Id.* at 37.

[99] *Id.* at 37–38.

trade fairs were conducted and where large amounts and varieties of national and regional coins were needed by the traders.

Not surprisingly, Frankfurt's was one of Germany's most active markets for money changing and lending, including the buying or discounting of commercial and governmental bills of exchange and promissory notes, often issued or endorsed by the borrowing rulers of the region.

> The revenues from their lands and subjects . . . and the expenditures of their courts . . . made these rulers the biggest customers of the pre-industrial German economy. . . . In particular, the fact that the majority spent more than they earned created lucrative if sometimes risky opportunities for German bankers.[100]

Mayer Amschel was the son, grandson and great grandson of small merchants. His great grandfather's gravestone mentioned his "virtue, righteousness, and honesty." In his teens, Mayer Amschel was allowed by the Frankfurt authorities to do a business apprenticeship outside the ghetto. Following his mandatory return to the ghetto, he started selling rare coins apparently as part of his father's cloth business. In 1765, he acquired an important client in William, the Hereditary Prince of Hesse-Kassel, who was his age and who, as a collector of rare coins and medals, shared a common interest with Mayer Amschel. Four years later, Mayer Amschel obtained the Prince's appointment as a court agent, an appointment that enabled him to do business regularly within the court, including the bidding for contracts of supply and finance.

Within the next decade, Mayer Amschel had become Frankfurt's leading coin, medals and antiques dealer, whose "meticulous catalogues" circulated among a widening circle of aristocratic customers. This business provided him with start-up capital for widespread commercial and governmental lending. Meanwhile, he married a rabbi's daughter and had with her nineteen children, of whom ten survived and five joined his commercial and banking business. As his business turned increasingly to banking, the family fortune grew exponentially. By 1797, he was already one of Frankfurt's wealthiest merchant-bankers: His balance sheet showed loans and credits extended to or received from Jewish and non-Jewish merchant-bankers throughout Germany and Austria, as well as Amsterdam, Paris, and London.[101]

This was a time when the effects of the Napoleonic invasion were felt in the *Judengasse*. Napoleon had granted French Jewry its emancipation in 1791. This decree did not apply to Frankfurt Jews (although it was applied shortly thereafter to the Rhineland Jews). However, Napoleon's bombardment of Frankfurt in 1796 destroyed a considerable portion of the *Judengasse*, and this forced the Frankfurt senate, for the first time in centuries, to allow Jews to live outside the ghetto, albeit only for short periods of time. Mayer Amschel was finally able to rent much larger and nicer premises outside the *Judengasse*.

His rented warehouse proved convenient for storing and distributing cloth that he, among other Jewish merchants, started importing from Britain. Because of the manufacturing advances of the British industrial revolution, English textiles of all types flooded the European markets. The volumes of imports were such that German

---

[100] *Id.* at 40.

[101] *Id.* at 46.

wholesalers started locating purchasing agencies in Great Britain. Mayer Amschel was one of the first to send his son Nathan to England as a resident agent and as a partner of the Rothschild business firm. Nathan proved to be a good "chip off of the old block." His correspondence with his father and other members of his family reveals in vivid detail his *modus operandi*. What follows are a few illustrative segments:

a) On buying from the right source:

> As soon as I got to Manchester, I laid out all my money, things were so cheap. . . . I soon found out that there were three profits—the raw materials, the dyeing, and the manufacturing. I said to the manufacturer, "I will supply you with materials and dye, and you will supply me with manufactured goods." So I got three profits instead of one, and I could sell the goods cheaper than anybody. In a short time I made my 20,000£ into 60,000£.[102]

b) On paying cash with borrowed money (Ferguson's and Nathan Rothschild's account):

> Nathan tried as far as possible to pay up front "on present bill terms," which meant "drawing on" (that is, borrowing from) his London bankers "at three months". . . .
>
> [In Nathan's own words]: On Tuesdays and Thursdays the weavers who live in the country twenty miles round Manchester bring here their goods . . . which they sell to the merchants here at two, three and six months' credit. But as there are generally some of them in want of money and willing to sacrifice some profit to procure it, a person who goes with ready money may sometimes buy 15 or 20 per cent cheaper.[103]

Not surprisingly, Ferguson's research reveals that when the profit margins in the textile industry could be as high as twenty percent, Nathan's charges were modest:

> 5 per cent on the cost price for purchases in cash from his warehouse, as little as 9 per cent for goods which had to be despatched [sic] to the continent. This was a deliberate ploy to attract customers and increase his market share. . . .[104]

And that he did, and on terms that would have made the Wal-Marts of our day quite happy. Undoubtedly, Nathan was able to do what he did in 1802, probably not more than a year or two after he came to England, as a result of the significant amount of purchase money made available to him by Mayer Amschel and his brothers. Yet, in assessing his accomplishment, it should also be taken into account that he spoke no English when he arrived in Britain. On the other hand, Meyer Amschel was not happy with his son's disorganization, failure to pay attention to detail and especially to his poorly-kept accounting books and records. In letter after letter, after addressing him as "my dear son" and pleading with him not to be angry with his fatherly advice, Mayer Amschel admonished him in terms that Enron and other large corporations of our day should have heeded:

---

102 *Id.* at 52.

103 *Id.* at 52–53.

104 *Id.* at 53.

> Take on a clerk to manage the despatching [sic] of the consignments . . . be more organised. . . . keep a proper record when [your client] sends you remittances. . . . [and of what] you send us and all that we send you. . . .
>
> [I]f you have many bad debts, which God forbid, and enter them as if they are good, that is simply to pretend that you are rich. . . .[105]

D. Banking and Government Bond Business

Governmental borrowing was very expensive because lenders feared, with good reason, that they would not be repaid, or at least not in time. These methods proved very costly to the crown and polity alike. Taxation was not a solution in part because of the need to obtain the support for its enactment from taxpayers in increasingly representative forms of governments. The British government seemed to have found a solution for its deficit-financing by developing "since the later seventeenth century . . . a relatively sophisticated system of public borrowing (the national debt) and monetary management (the Bank of England)."[106] Yet, by the time the House of Rothschild came on the scene, the high yielding bonds of the British national debt were not being issued because of English fiscal retrenchment and monetary stabilization policies.

As with their coin, antique, and cloth businesses, the Rothschild's banking business started with Mayer Amschel. His relationship with Prince William of Hesse-Kassel proved quite valuable. This principality had a close connection with British colonial policies, especially in North America. Prince William's primary source of revenue for a while was the payment for the services of the Hessian army sold to King George III in his battle against the rebellious colonists. The terms of this sale were quite lucrative for William:

> William received 76 gulden (around £7) per man, plus an additional charge of 25 gulden for each man wounded, and 76 for each man killed. The money was paid . . . in (non-interest-bearing) bills of exchange which were initially paid to William's account at the London bank of Van Notten & Son. When he wanted to convert these into cash before they fell due, he sold them to brokers in Germany. . . . [Thereafter, he invested] his earnings so that they yielded the highest possible interest. And, as the majority of his fellow princes in Germany were frequently in want of money, he had no difficulty in doing so by lending to them.[107]

Mayer Amschel was aware of the profit potential involved in buying the English bills of exchange from William and reselling them to others who wanted them as safe investments or as holdings in pounds sterling in Great Britain. He tried to outbid other brokers by offering lower discount rates than theirs but was repeatedly unsuccessful. At least on one occasion he had to ask for special permission to leave the *Judengasse* on a Sunday (known as a "Sunday pass") to be able to bid on the bills of exchange early on the following day.[108]

---

105 *Id.* at 51 (emphasis added).

106 FERGUSON, *supra* note 95, at 4.

107 *Id.* at 61.

108 *Id.* at 61.

His success as a major bidder did not come until he joined with Karl Friedrich Buderus, a tutor to Prince William's children, and evidently a better-connected courtier than he was. Eventually, Rothschild was permitted to join five established German firms in their successful bids, one of them amounted to 150,000 pounds. This transaction was followed by a "loss leader" bid on war chest bonds in which he lost money. By 1798, however, he was acting as a co-investor, lender and broker with Prince William, by then one of Europe's wealthiest rulers and capitalists.

After Mayer Amschel's silent partnership had developed with William, William no longer extended personal loans, but demanded bearer bonds from his borrowers. Mayer Amschel's commission when buying bearer bonds for William was considerably low by the standard of the day (between 1.75 percent and 2.0 percent).[109] Between 1801 and 1806, he was not only a major buyer of the English bills available for sale, but also participated with William in real estate investments and in extending loans to other governments, including Denmark, Hesse-Darmstadt, Baden and even the Order of St. John. All of this while "continuing to supply . . . [William] with his beloved medals."[110]

Eventually, Mayer Amschel was appointed court agent to most of the nations or principalities, former members of the Holy Roman Empire, including his title of "Imperial Court Agent" awarded by a grateful Austrian Emperor. As summarized by Ferguson, if up until 1806, the Rothschilds had depended upon William and his ilk for their business and privileges, thereafter, it was William who began to depend upon Mayer Amschel and his sons.

E. Integrity and Trustworthiness: The Elector's Treasure

William, the Elector of Hesse-Kassel, lent large sums of money to the Austrian and Prussian rulers. After Napoleon defeated their armies, he decided "to remove the House of Hesse-Kassel from rulership and strike it out of the list of powers."[111] Upon fleeing his estate and principality, William turned to Mayer Amschel and left him in charge of all his moveable assets. Meanwhile, a French general had issued a proclamation confiscating all these assets and threatening anyone who concealed their whereabouts with a military trial.

Ferguson transcribed the following account of the transfer of the Elector's treasure to Mayer Amschel as it appeared in 1836 in an English newspaper:

> The French army was actually entering Frankfurt at the moment when Rothschild succeeded in burying the prince's treasures in a corner of his little garden. His own property, which in goods and money was worth about 40,000 thalers, he did not hide, well knowing that, if he did so, a strict search would be made and that not only his own but the prince's hoard would be discovered and plundered. The Republicans who, like the Philistines of old, fell upon Rothschild, left him not one thaler's value of his own money or property. In truth, he was, like all the other Jews and citizens, reduced to utter poverty but the prince's treasure was safe . . .[112]

---

109 *Id.* at 63.

110 *Id.* at 62.

111 *Id.* at 64.

112 *Id.* at 64–65.

F. The Emergence of an International Bond Market

In England, Nathan and his partner-brothers in Frankfurt and other European cities refined and popularized the House of Rothschild's own variety of governmental bearer negotiable bond. Consider, for example, the loan sought by Prussia after the so-called "War of the Twenty Five Years" in 1818. The Rothschilds had placed a smaller loan on behalf of Prussia with the Elector of Hesse-Kassel in 1817 and Prussia then requested from them a much larger sum to be raised in the London bond market. Nathan specified the terms and conditions of the issuance, which required, among others, a mortgage of Prussian governmental assets and the ratification of the terms of the loan by "an assembly of the estates (*Stände*) or the creation of an independent judiciary. . . ."[113] The Prussians objected and Nathan replied as follows:

> [T]o induce British Capitalists to invest their money in a loan to a foreign government upon reasonable terms, it will be of the first importance that the plan of such a loan should as much as possible be assimilated to the established system of borrowing for the public service in England, and above all things that some security, beyond the mere good faith of the government . . . should be held out to the lenders. . . . [T]he late investments by British subjects in the French Funds have proceeded upon the general belief that in consequence of the representative system now established in that Country, the sanction of the Chamber to the national debt incurred by the Government affords a guarantee to the Public Creditor. . . .[114]

Nathan's terms and conditions were clearly influenced by innovations introduced by the Bank of England's own method of commercial lending and purchasing or discounting commercial paper. It was the first bank at the top of a national credit pyramid to recognize the difference between traditional mortgage and commercial lending.[115] Unlike the security afforded by the traditional real estate mortgage, the security in a commercial loan was assumed to be perishable in the short run. Thus, it required collateral that made the liquidation of the loan possible in a short period of time, and without the need for much judicial or governmental expense. This was the reason for Nathan's insistence not only upon good mortgage security, but also upon a representative legislature's approval of the loan, alternatively or in conjunction with, an independent judiciary willing and able to decree the necessary foreclosure or repossession. The reader will recall that earlier in this chapter we discussed how this type of commercial loan had become popular in some regions of eighteenth-century Germany among merchants and their customers.

The system of governmental financing developed by the House of Rothschild enabled British and other investors in Western Europe to purchase fixed interest bearer bonds secured by various types of governmental revenues. As described by Ferguson:

> [T]his growing international bond market brought together Europe's true "capitalists": that elite of people wealthy enough to be able to tie up money in

---

113 *Id.* at 123 (citation omitted).

114 *Id.* (citation omitted).

115 *See generally* Kozolchyk & Furnish, *A Comparative Analysis; see also* Kozolchyk & Wilson, *The New Model Inter-American Law.*

such assets, and shrewd enough to appreciate the advantages of such assets as compared with traditional forms of holding wealth (land, venal office, and so on). Bonds were liquid. They could be bought and sold five and a half days out of seven (excluding holidays) on the major bourses of Europe and traded informally at other times and in other places. And they were capable of accruing large capital gains. Their only disadvantage was, of course, that they were also capable of suffering large capital losses.[116]

It should be noted that in this process, the House of Rothschild not only influenced the wording of the bonds, but also acted as their principal "market maker," *i.e.*, it assumed responsibility for maintaining a firm "bid and asked" price in the bonds by standing ready, willing and able to buy or sell them at the publicly (bid and asked) quoted prices.

G. Legal Implications of the House of Rothschilds' Issuance of Negotiable Bonds: Archetypal Behavior

For the reader who has been following the slow evolution of executory or deferred performance promises across the centuries and legal systems, it should not be surprising that many of the promises issued by the House of Rothschild were of doubtful enforceability in many of the legal systems that governed their issuance or collection. Nonetheless, I could not find one instance in Ferguson's or other historians' research in which Mayer Amschel's and his children's offers to buy or sell commodities, bills of exchange, or bearer bonds at a future time, were ever defaulted. On the contrary, their promises were as good as their corporate motto: "*Concordia, integritas, industria*" (Harmony, integrity, industry).[117]

With this precedent, it was not surprising that the first European code (commercial or civil) to provide for the enforcement of executory promises was the German Commercial Code, *Handelsgesetzbuch* (HGB) of 1897. It decreed the enforceability of "firm" executory contractual promises (as distinguished from promises in negotiable instruments) once a firm date of payment or performance had been expressed by them.[118] Similarly, it was the BGB in 1900 that set forth the enforceability of offers of rewards, acknowledgment, or acceptances of orders of payments and debts and bonds, including bearer bonds.[119]

While the issuance of securities to the public was eventually regulated, first by the United States Securities and Exchange Act of 1934, and thereafter in many other countries, (*e.g.*, the 2003 version of the French Commercial Code reviewed in the

---

[116] FERGUSON, *supra* note 95, at 5.

[117] *Id.* at 13 (Harmony, integrity, industry).

[118] HGB § 376 (Goren, 1998). Section 376 states in relevant part:

> (1) Where it is stipulated that performance by one of parties should be effected at an exact time or within a specific period, the other party may rescind the contract if performance is not made at the exact time or within the period specified, or in the event the debtor [promisor] has defaulted, [on his promise] demand payment of damages for non-performance in lieu of performance of the contract. He may only demand performance if he indicates to the other party, immediately following the expiration of the time or the period, that he insists on performance.

Id.

See PELTZER & VOIGHT, at 320.

[119] *See* BGB §§ 657–661, 784, 793 (GOREN, 1994).

previous chapter), much of the private law aspects of the Rothschild's financial transactions remained unregulated by commercial codes or similar private law statutes. In fact, it was not until the enactment of Article 8 of the U.C.C. in 1977 that a major financial marketplace turned its attention to the creation, transfer, pledge, cancellation, clearing and setoffs involved with these investment securities.

The question that arises, then, is: What private law governed these transactions? The short answer is a mixture of trade usage and custom, "master" and standardized agreements among participants in trade association, exchanges, or those trade associations' rules such as those of the International Swaps and Derivatives Association (ISDA) and others.

In the absence of codified, statutory or decisional rules, or even where some of these rules exist but are not clear or exhaustive enough on the rights and duties of the parties, how could an adjudicator profit from holding up these transactions to different standards of conduct, particularly to exemplary or archetypal conduct on the one hand, and to average or stereotypical conduct on the other? Please recall how the Roman jurist Ulpian held up the promise to sell a slave, subject to a condition that conferred a certain degree of discretion to the promisor, to the standard of a *bonus vir*. Contrast this standard with the good faith standard applied to an average exchange of promises to buy and sell cattle wholesale in one of the eighteenth-century German cattle fairs described by Professor Blackbourn. In your opinion, which of these two standards demanded greater knowledge, diligence and altruism from its practitioner?

Please recall that among Nathan Rothschild's requested terms and conditions of the bonds issued by Prussia and to be sold in London were ratification of the terms of the loan by "an assembly of the estates (*Stände*) *or the creation of an independent judiciary*."[120] How could an adjudicator, a member of that independent judiciary, determine the meaning of good faith in an everyday type of dispute such as one prompted by the lack a written contract formality? If the standard is one of stereotypical behavior among regular participants in the transaction, the adjudicator must ask himself: "Who is such a person?" Once this person has been identified, he must inquire: "What would he or she regularly do and what would he or she be willing to accept as regular conduct from other participants regarding contract formalities?" Clearly, it would be helpful to an adjudicator attempting to visualize the behavior of such a person to be told more than: "Search for him in the genus of the '*bonus paterfamilias*'" or "Find him among 'prudent reasonable men' or among those who could qualify for membership in the French 'councils of prudent men' " (*conseils de prud'hommes*). Would it be more helpful to tell the adjudicator to examine what is meant by "good faith practices" among respected traders in, say, cattle fairs, bourses, exchanges, etc.?

Let us suppose that the issue did not involve stereotypical but exceptional behavior, *i.e.*, behavior associated with highly-trusted and perhaps also highly-remunerated fiduciaries. In order to establish what behavior would be expected from someone whose duties were not only those of ordinary good faith, but of the highest good faith (*uberrima fides*), the adjudicator would have to resort to archetypal behavior. He would have to ask himself: "What would an *uberrima fides* merchant, banker, or fiduciary have done under the circumstances?" It would have to be someone

---

[120] *See* FERGUSON, *supra* note 95, at 123; *supra* note 113 and accompanying text.

not only highly respected because of his or her transactional expertise, but someone who, because of his or her extraordinary integrity, and perhaps even piousness, had been entrusted with other's property, work, or money and did not disappoint those who trusted him. As with the stereotypical behavior, it would be very helpful to the adjudicator of such a dispute, as it also is to the legislator, to be able to visualize real life examples of such behavior. And, as with stereotypical behavior, the place to start would be among the trades, vocations, or professions in question, and then ask: "Who is the most respected among them and why?"

It would be my contention that Mayer Amschel Rothschild and perhaps some of his children or descendants qualified for archetypal status among the nineteenth-century participants in high commerce and finance. He and some of his descendants were knowledgeable, skillful, careful and meticulous enough in their business transactions to merit the respect and admiration of their peers, including such well-known international bankers as the Barings. Any question about Mayer Amschel's fiduciary integrity was put to rest by his return of the Elector's treasure, even at the cost of losing his own. Moreover, both Prince William and his children's tutor could have testified about his loyalty and cooperative spirit toward both his silent and active partners. As stated by his children's partnership agreement entered into by his five children twenty years after his death:

> We wish to offer a proof of our reverence for the holiest memory of our father, whose virtuous conduct in all of life's relations is a noble example to us all. Through pious acceptance of the higher wishes of God, through faith in God's help, through conscientious honesty and indefatigable industry, this noble and philanthropic man laid the foundation of our good fortune, and when, almost forty years ago, he took his sons into partnership . . . he told them that acting in unison would be a sure means of achieving success in their work, and always recommended fraternal concord to them as a source of divine blessing.[121]

A corollary of the "*concordia*" component of the House of Rothschild motto was the spirit of reciprocal trust instilled among the family partners. A corollary to the principle of unbreakable unity was that of implicit trust in the partners' acting above all for their joint interest. As expressed by Salomon Rothschild to one of his brothers:

> It is an established rule with us that no disapprobation shall be expressed by either of us at the conduct of the other, since as partners we act always for the joint interest and consequently neither of us has the right to blame the other when he has acted for the best.[122]

Ferguson's thorough archival research reveals numerous instances of Mayer Amschel's philanthropy. As an active member of his congregation, he contributed each year the prescribed ten percent of his income to charity, including Jewish and non-Jewish recipients.[123] It would also be my contention that this archetype of "aristocratic" commerce and banking, who separated his charity from his business, and practiced both with equal earnestness, was more likely to shape a commercial law conducive to

---

121 FERGUSON, *supra* note 95, at 78.

122 *Id.* at 83.

123 *Id.* at 74–75.

economic development for Germany and Europe than the one described by Judge Bedos of the eighteenth-century commercial court of Paris.

In sum, by the time Germany's commercial and civil codes were drafted, they governed continental Europe's widest variety of merchants, from small shopkeepers, *verlegers*, clerks, brokers and *Prokurists*, to high-volume bankers, industrial and transportation entrepreneurs. The codes could also rely for commercial decision-making on a growing number of commercial usages and customs as well as on examples of standard and archetypal behavior in high commerce and finance, unhindered by other-worldly visions of commerce and by the scholastic repression of lending at interest.

Chapter 12

THE CODIFICATION OF THE GERMAN CIVIL AND COMMERCIAL CODES

§ 12.1 OPPOSING VIEWS ON CODIFICATION: ROMANISTS AND GERMANISTS[1]

As discussed in the preceding chapter, the goal of a unified Germany was already being actively pursued during the first half of the nineteenth century. Yet, as was the case with France, there was much law to unify. The Napoleonic domination of German states and principalities during the first decades of the nineteenth century resulted in the adoption of the *Code Civil* by the states and principalities west of the Rhine River and Baden. This only added to the large number of local laws extant, including a Roman law that had been received in its totality by many principalities in 1495.[2]

Once a still-dismembered Germany attained its independence from France, writings advocating legal unification began to circulate. The most influential of these was a pamphlet published in 1814 by Anton Thibaut, a professor at the University of Heidelberg. He argued that the Roman culture that was an integral part of the received Roman law was not Germany's and advocated enactments that would reflect German culture, written not in Latin, but in German. This pamphlet spurred a movement that encouraged the enactment of Germany's private law codes: the Commercial Code, *Handelsgesetzbuch*, (hereinafter HGB) in 1897 and the Civil Code, *Bürgerliches Gesetzbuch*, (hereinafter BGB) in 1900.[3]

Thibaut's proposed Germanic law was opposed by the so-called Historical School. This school of thought viewed law as a set of norms developed in response to society's need for change. For the Historical School, it was unreasonable to freeze the law, so to speak, by codifying it, especially when scholars were unable to agree on what law was needed and on how best to draft it. This point of view was advocated by Friedrich Carl von Savigny in his famous pamphlet of 1814, *On the Vocation of Our Times for Legislation and Legal Science* (*Vom Beruf unsrer Zeit für Gesetzgebung und Rechtswissenschaft*).[4] Savigny argued for an intensive study of German legal history, prominently including the received Roman law, especially what he considered its superior analysis.[5]

Although Savigny rejected the idea of natural law as the basis for the new German law, he accepted the natural law point of view that legal science should pursue

---

[1] *See* WIEACKER, A HISTORY OF PRIVATE LAW, at 300–29, 334–70 (a thorough yet illuminating comparison of the views of Romanists and Germanists).

[2] VON MEHREN & GORDLEY, THE CIVIL LAW SYSTEM, at 10–11 (the various reasons for this *en masse* reception of Roman law).

[3] *Id.* at 61.

[4] *Id.* at 62 (citing to a translation of *Vom Beruf unsrer Zeit für Gesetzgebung und Rechtswissenschaft* by A. Hayward in 1831).

[5] *Id.*

principles that would inspire an orderly and coherent legal system. One of his pupils, Georg G. Puchta, devoted himself to "systematizing" Roman law by applying to it a "pyramidal" analysis that would produce general or organizing concepts from which other, more specific ones would be derived.[6]

Puchta also relied on the "national spirit of the German people" (*Volksgeist*) as a natural-law-based principle that would help select the rules most consistent with that spirit.[7] Yet, as also pointed out by von Mehren and Gordley, "[h]owever, abstract, doctrinal thinking dominated Puchta's own writing to such an extent that the Volksgeist had no practical significance in his work."[8]

Bernhard Windscheid, another pupil of Savigny, was less theoretically inclined than Puchta and wrote an exhaustive Roman law treatise, *Lehrbuch des Pandektenrechts*, whose purpose it was to serve as the ultimate reference work for scholars, judges and practitioners. This writing proved influential in the codification of the BGB, which was undertaken shortly thereafter.[9]

By the middle of the nineteenth century, legal positivism[10] had become an ally of German nationalism. Nationalists and legal positivists advocated that, history aside, a national government had the inherent power to promulgate its own law. Legal positivism claimed support from the scientific positivism widespread among the increasingly prestigious German universities and research centers. Scientific positivism maintained that valid knowledge required: (1) empirical observation; (2) formulation of hypotheses based upon what was observed; and (3) a verification of the hypotheses by equally empirical means.

Legal positivists, relying on scientific positivism, rejected natural law as based upon metaphysics instead of the above steps. However, what German legal positivists understood as empirical research differed sharply from what natural or even the pioneering social scientists of the era understood by it. For the natural and social scientists, scientific legal research required not only an objective description of the law as found in written and unwritten or customary sources, but also an equally objective description of the manner in which it was being applied or observed. In addition, it required an analysis of its interaction with society's economic, religious and ethical beliefs.

§ 12.2 PANDECTIST SYSTEM BUILDING

In sharp contrast with the scientific method of the exact and social sciences, the research of the nineteenth-century German "legal scientists," inspired by Puchta's methodology, was confined to what was observed and verified within a finite set of Roman law texts. Puchta's followers looked for what could be identified as essential components of Roman legal institutions as found, for the most part, in the *Corpus Juris Civilis*, known in Germany as the *Pandekts*, and the law derived from it

---

[6] *Id.* at 62.

[7] *Id.* at 65.

[8] *Id.* at 62.

[9] *Id.* The BGB is sometimes referred to as the "Little Windscheid." *See, e.g.*, Robert A. Riegert, *The West German Civil Code, its Origin and its Contract Provisions*, 45 TUL. L REV. 48, 59 (1970) (noting Windscheid's influence).

[10] *See* Glossary, "Legal Positivism."

(*Pandektenrecht*). Accordingly, Puchta's followers were known by the English designation "Pandectists."[11]

A. Illustrations of System Building

If a Pandectist wanted to find out the essential components of, say, the right of possession, he would look at the Roman law remedies for the protection of possession such as in actions and "interdicts" as well as in the defenses against them. He would study the opinion of jurists, the *praetor's* edict and his formulas, Gaius' and Justinian's Institutes, and the collection of laws. Once all these sources were briefed and classified, he would identify the common elements of these remedies and come up with a formula such as:

Possession = Physical control of the thing + The intent to possess it as an owner (*Animus Rem Sibi Habendi* or *Animus Dominii*)

Yet, what if the Pandectists missed an important source or relied on a questionable medieval addition or "interpolation" to a juristic opinion or edict? For example, what if the above components of possession disregarded remedies granted by a *Praetorian* edict not to owners, but to legitimate possessors such as bailees or carriers who did not intend to possess as owners? Or, what if they had unknowingly relied on an interpolation that granted possessory remedies only to Roman citizens ("quiritary owners")? In that case, an adjustment of the earlier "scientific" finding would have to be made and the rewritten formula would lead to a more inclusive concept of possession:

Possession = Physical control + The intent to possess legitimately (*Animus Possidendi*)

In theory, the Pandectists should have produced a "truthful" and precise set of concepts, rules and principles of law making and interpretation, also referred to as "legal institutions." By connecting these institutions and establishing their hierarchy, an analytical system could have been created to give the law maker, adjudicator and interpreter a feeling of "scientific" certainty.

To illustrate, assume that the same research conducted on possession was conducted on ownership and on other rights related to things immovable and movable. Thus, similar *in rem* remedies were given to the following: users of immovables whose rights to use were granted by owners, lawful possessors thereof, holders of life estates, easements or servitudes, and mortgagees and pledgees. Finally, assume that after a thorough study of the Pandectists, the researcher concluded that the only rights *in rem* granted were those just listed. If this finding could not be disproven or qualified by showing that a right may have existed but lacked a remedy such as *ius distrahendi*,[12] the researcher could proudly announce that he or she had discovered an essential feature of the pyramidal or systematic concept of a right *in rem*: by nature or essence, these rights were limited in number (*numerus clausus*). Such a "scientific" finding would lead to the principle or rule that only the rights *in rem* on the researcher's list were entitled to legal protection, including the ability to register them in the appropriate land or chattel registry.

---

[11] *See* Glossary, "Pandectists."

[12] *See* Glossary, "*Ius Distrahendi*."

If the reader finds a resemblance between this method of "system building" and that of French eighteenth-century neo-scholastics such as Robert Pothier, he is not mistaken. For, in order to conclude that because the Pandectists only protected a certain number of rights *in rem*, all rights *in rem* (whether found within or without the universe of the Pandectists) were limited in number, a huge metaphysical and unempirical leap had to intervene and it was buttressed solely by the Aristotelian essences. Both the Pandectists and the neo-scholastics were believers in the Aristotelian essences and in the metaphysical truth of logical sounding definitions and classifications. The major difference between the Pandectists and, say, Pothier, was that their research, albeit much deeper and more detailed, was confined to the universe of rules, concepts, and principles of interpretation found in the received *Corpus Juris Civilis*. Pothier relied not only on Roman law, but also on the writings of legal scholars, including natural law thinkers, and, although less frequently, on his own observations of French contract practice.

B. The Pandectist Disinterest in Socio-Economic Facts and Needs

When it came to adapting the law to changing socio-economic circumstances, both the French neo-scholastics and the Pandectists were equally inflexible. Encouraged by Savigny's high opinion of the analytical skills of Roman jurists, the Pandectist assumed that his "finding" of the applicable Roman law was also a finding of best possible law, and that if factual and socio-economic circumstances changed, all that had to be done was to adjust that best possible law, *i.e.*, Roman law, to the new circumstances.

Yet, what if the found (and received) Roman law prevented such an adjustment? Consider the following incident.[13] In order to rebuild Germany's railroad system after its destruction in the Second World War, a group of lenders agreed to lend, but only if they could perfect their security interests in the railroad equipment, tracks and land beneath them. They took into account that the repayment of their loan required that the railroad operators be allowed to possess and use the above collateral. They also concluded that the best method to secure their loan was to create the equivalent in German law of an Anglo-American security or guaranty trust. In it, the lender-trustee would acquire a right *in rem* in the railroad equipment, rolling stock, tracks and land beneath them, while the rail operator would be the possessor of the collateral. This security interest would have to be recorded in order to protect the lenders against competing rights by other, subsequent creditors and purchasers of the collateral.

At first, the German land registrar rejected such a recording based on the following reasoning:

> The legal nature (meaning the essence) of such a security interest (the trust) is not a right *in rem*. If it is a right *in personam*, obviously it cannot be registered in the Land Registry because it records only rights *in rem*. If the trust purported to have *in rem* effects, especially on the land beneath the rails, it has to qualify as one of the rights set forth in the BGB Sections 873–

[13] This incident, including the notes concerning the Registrar's first opinion, was relayed by the late Professor Milton Katz of the Harvard Law School, one of the United States legal officials involved in the implementation of the Marshall Plan in Germany, to my friend, the late Professor Raul Cervantes Ahumada of the National University of Mexico Law School. Professor Cervantes Ahumada allowed me to copy them shortly before his death in 1994.

928. If it was not one of them, which it does not appear to be, it could not be recorded in the land registry.[14]

When asked whether the enactment of a statute adding this "new" right *in rem* to the list could resolve the problem, his answer was that the list in the BGB was unchangeable because it embodied legal-scientific truth. Such truth, incidentally, came directly from the writings of Roman jurists on rights *in rem* as collated and interpreted by Pandectists. Ultimately, the land registrar was able to find a way to record the rights in question. Yet, had he not done so, would he have been justified in rejecting such a momentous recording, even following the enactment of enabling legislation, based on his "Pandectistically-inspired" findings and conclusions?

Not surprisingly, Rudolf von Ihering, with whom the reader is well acquainted by now, was one of the principal opponents of the "dogmatism" of the Pandectists.[15] Despite having devoted a good part of his academic life to Roman law scholarship, von Ihering objected to concepts, principles, and even rules devoid of a socio-economic purpose and context. In von Ihering's view, the main contribution of law to society stemmed from its ability to harmonize the social and individual interests at stake in judicial disputes and proposed legislation, and when that was not possible, to choose among them. The function of the law, as he saw it, was not to build abstract, permanent and symmetrical structures of rights and duties, but to find the right solution to these conflicts and thereby do justice.[16]

Pandectism did not deal adequately with issues of justice because it was only tangentially interested in the facts and interests at stake in legal disputes or in law-making processes. Its interest was in "abstract" inquiries such as whether rights *in rem* or *in personam* (as with typified contracts) are limited or unlimited in number. Hence, its ultimate goal was to formulate concepts, rules or principles loyal to Roman law and to logical legal symmetry.

§ 12.3 THE DRAFTING OF THE BGB

A. Background: The HGB & ADHGB

Even though the German Civil Code) (BGB) was enacted in 1900, three years after the enactment of the German Commercial Code (*Handelsgesetzbuch* of 1897 HGB), I will discuss the drafting of the BGB first because decades prior to its enactment there was a legislative attempt to harmonize it with the existing version of the HGB. As will be discussed below, in 1857, the lower house of the German parliament (the *Diet*) designated a commission of lawyers and businessmen to draft a general commercial law.[17] The approved version of this law, the *Allgemeines Deutsches Handelsgesetzbuch*, (hereinafter ADHGB), became the federal commercial law of the entire new German Reich in 1871.[18] However, its absorption by the BGB became one of

---

[14] *Id.*

[15] *See* WIEACKER, A HISTORY OF PRIVATE LAW, at 355–57 (an insightful summary of von Ihering's evolution from leading Romanist to founder of the sociological jurisprudence movement in Europe and elsewhere).

[16] Von Ihering's most coherent views on the purpose of the law can be found in his book Law as a Means to an End. *See generally* VON IHERING, A MEANS TO AN END. Of particular interest is his analysis of the idea of justice in commerce. *Id.* at 101–03.

[17] VON MEHREN & GORDLEY, THE CIVIL LAW SYSTEM, at 73.

[18] *Id.* at 73–74.

the major issues during its drafting. This issue was resolved in favor of harmonizing the ADHGB with the BGB.[19] From the inception of the HGB, then, a close, if not organic, connection with the BGB was taken for granted. The BGB eventually provided many rules and principles to fill in the numerous gaps in the HGB.

This harmonization had to take into account that prior to Germany's unification and the creation of its "Second Empire" in 1871, four main systems of civil law were in force: the received Roman common law (*das gemeine Recht*),[20] the Prussian General Land Law of 1794 (*Preussiches Allgemeines Landrecht*),[21] the *Code Civil* of 1804[22] and the Saxon Code of 1863.[23] Once its federal government was empowered to promulgate a code that would govern most aspects of Germany's private law in 1874, a legislative pre-commission was placed in charge of appointing the drafters of the future BGB.[24] It appointed eleven drafters comprised of six appellate judges, three government officials and two law professors.[25]

This drafting commission decided that the civil code should be divided into five parts, beginning with a "general" part. This method was consistent with Puchta's pyramidal or "from the more general to the more specific" approach on how to best organize and summarize Germany's private law. "[T]he commission assigned each of the five major parts of the proposed code to one of its members."[26] It met during the following thirteen years and completed its first draft in 1887.[27]

Serious objections were voiced against its drafting technique, complaining that it was too abstract, confusing, and crowded with cross references, and thus written only for highly trained lawyers and not for the people.[28] In response to these and other objections, including the lack of attention to the needs of the poor,[29] a second drafting commission was appointed in 1890. This commission consisted of twenty-two members:

---

[19] *Id.* at 74.

[20] Riegert, *supra* note 9, at 49. Riegert points out that by the end of the nineteenth century, the Roman common law still covered about 33 percent of the German population. *Id.*

[21] *Id.* at 51. Riegert attributes to the Prussian Code an application that was "partly primary, partly subsidiary . . . over 43 percent of the German population." *Id.*

[22] *Id.* Riegert attributes to the *Code Civil* an application over "17 percent of the German population."

[23] *Id.* at 52. Riegert attributes to the Saxon Code an application over "7 percent of the German population," although he also ascribes to it a predominant influence as "the organizational model for the BGB. . . ." *Id.*

[24] VON MEHREN & GORDLEY, THE CIVIL LAW SYSTEM, at 75.

[25] Riegert, *supra* note 9, at 52.

[26] *Id.*

[27] *Id.*

[28] *See id.* at 53. Riegert points out that:

> Professor Windscheid, the author of what was the leading text on the Pandects, was a member of the commission and his influence on the final product was pervasive. There were charges that the 1887 draft was "Windscheid's book with additions." Those Germans who favored the reception of the Roman law praised the draft, while those who rejected the reception criticized it. A third group, who called for more consideration for the less privileged in society, also joined the opposition.

Id. (Citations omitted.)

[29] *Id. See also* VON MEHREN & GORDLEY, THE CIVIL LAW SYSTEM, at 76 (referring to Otto von Gierke's and Anton Menger's objections based on social and public policy considerations).

ten were lawyers, judges, or law professors, and the other twelve were laymen; the latter were to be consulted on special questions.[30]

Although this group had the appearance of a pluralistic sub-commission, its members were mostly from the business sector: owners of large farms, a bank director, a director of a brewery, a professor of economics and a professor of law.[31] This second commission produced a new draft, including changes prompted by the previously-mentioned objections. Yet, as concluded by Von Mehren and Gordley, while this draft attempted to adapt to the needs of German society and recognize issues of social justice, the language was "not generally rewritten; the number of cross-references was reduced. However, its basic structure was not changed."[32] I would only add that the presence of the business sector in the drafting committee was responsible for the greater sensitivity to the importance of commercial contracts and their inclusion in the code. It was sent to the legislature in 1895 after adding changes on the law of associations, family, successions, and tort law. Finally, a third draft was approved on July 1, 1896 and signed by the Kaiser on August 18 of that year. Its date of effectiveness was January 1, 1900.[33] Its adoption as a model for other civil law countries, while not as widespread as that of the *Code Civil*, was nonetheless impressive. At last count, the following civil law countries used it as a model for their civil codes: Estonia, Greece, Japan, Latvia, People's Republic of China, Portugal, South Korea, Thailand, and Ukraine.

B. Brief Review of the BGB's Contents

It will be recalled that the *Code Civil* was divided into books on persons, things and methods of acquiring property. Each of these books covered a different and purportedly self-contained subject of private law, much as was done by Justinian's and Gaius' Institutes. The BGB was also divided into books, but its first book was labeled a general part and was followed by books on obligations, property, family law and successions.

Because the BGB devotes a separate book to persons, one might be tempted to assume that when it named its first book "General Part," it was just renaming the materials covered by the *Code Civil's* first book on persons. This was not the case. After providing both principles and detailed rules on the subject of physical and legal persons or associations, the general part of the BGB provides the general principles and the nomenclature for the law of things, legal transactions, time limits and statutes of limitations, exercise of rights (including self-help), and security interests.

It is also noteworthy that unlike the *Code Civil*, the BGB, in the first section of the general part, deals with both civil, not-for-profit (non-economic) associations and for profit (economic) associations.[34] And even though it did not regulate the latter in detail, it provided key principles such as the need for a state grant for economic associations

---

[30] Riegert, *supra* note 9, at 53.

[31] VON MEHREN & GORDLEY, THE CIVIL LAW SYSTEM, at 76.

[32] *Id.* at 77 (citation omitted).

[33] *Id.*

[34] BGB § 22 (GOREN, 1994) states:

An association whose object is the carrying on of an economic enterprise acquires legal personality, in the absence of special provisions of [Federal] law, by state grant. The grant is within the competence of the [State] in whose territory the association has its seat.

to enjoy a separate legal personality in the absence of special provisions.[35] Similarly, it set forth the principles and rules that govern the determination of the location or seat of these associations as well as their creation, representation, and management.[36]

The second section of the general part provides the basic concepts and principles for things whose more detailed regulation is found in the BGB's Book 3 on Property. Hence, "corporeal objects are things in the legal sense"[37] and the basic features of fungibles, consumer goods, component parts, fixtures, accessories, fruits, and so on are set forth in the code.[38]

The BGB originally consisted of 2,385 sections, 800 of which had been modified during its first century of existence.[39] Many of these changes were enacted during the Nazi era and subsequently abrogated during the military occupation following the Second World War. Most of the changes took place in family and obligations law.[40] However, the latter was revisited during the new millennium, and in January of 2002, a very substantial reform of the law of obligations (*Schuldrechtsreformgesetz*) became effective.[41]

C. The Juristic Act and the Drafting of the General Part

One of the concepts that inspired the third section of the general part (on legal transactions) was the "juridical act" (*Rechtsgeschäft*). It was not defined in the BGB, although, as suggested in jest by F. H. Lawson, this definition was probably reserved for post-BGB Pandectists.[42] To this remark, he added, also in jest, that he did not know whether the juristic act was "a true conquest of the human mind or an aberration."[43]

In connection with the meaning and purpose of the juristic act, Professor Riegert asked: "What do offer, notice of rescission, and consent to adoption have in common?"[44] One could have added to this list: executory promises of all types (which are less conditional than offers), notices of terminations of tenancies, a grant of authority to an agent, the making of a will, etc. The drafters of the BGB assumed that these acts had in common the embodiment of a juristic act or an act to which the legal order attached consequences even though a contract was not required for such an act to be binding. As stated by E. J. Cohn, the concept of a *Rechtsgeschäft* is wider than that of a contract or even that of an agreement; it includes acts in which one party promises or states something that the law deems binding or *of legal relevance*.[45] An analogy to a precision watch comes to mind—one central part or mechanism that acts as the prime mover for all of the others to follow. In addition, please notice the peculiar meaning of empiricism

---

[35] *Id.*

[36] *Id.* §§ 24–54.

[37] *Id.* § 90.

[38] *Id.* §§ 90–103.

[39] BGB (GOREN, 1994) xviii.

[40] *Id.*

[41] *German Civil Code—Bürgerliches Gesetzbuch*, IUSCOMP.ORG, http://www.iuscomp.org/gla/statutes/BGB.htm (a German-English translation of the reforms). Some of these reforms will be discussed in the following chapter.

[42] F. H. Lawson, Seminar Discussion at the University of Michigan School of Law (Fall 1959).

[43] FREDERICK HENRY LAWSON, A COMMON LAWYER LOOKS AT THE CIVIL LAW: FIVE LECTURES DELIVERED AT THE UNIVERSITY OF MICHIGAN 167 (1955).

[44] Riegert, *supra* note 9, at 59.

[45] E. J. COHN & W. ZDZIEBLO, I MANUAL OF GERMAN LAW 73 (2d ed. 1968).

in the drafters' attempt to find a common denominator of all acts and promises that could be binding.

The Pandectist origins of this concept are apparent. One only has to reformulate Professor Riegert's question in a Pandectist fashion and the answer will become redundantly self-evident: To what manifestations of the human will (whether expressed by one or more persons) does the private law (especially in the *Corpus Juris Civilis* and *gemeines Recht*) attach binding or coercive consequences? A number of such manifestations will be found, and the next "scientific" question will be: What do these manifestations have in common? The inevitable answer will then be: They all are juristic or legal acts or transactions for which the law provides binding or coercive effects to acts or promises by members of German trading society.

How helpful is this analysis? The Pandectist would claim that having identified the common elements of the manifestations of the will to be bound, it will be possible to build an analytical system of code drafting and interpretation. Fewer rules would be necessary than if each possible manifestation were regulated and uncertainty and normative gaps were eliminated. The general principle that guides such manifestations will justify or reject the application of a specific rule to the facts in question. Thus, the interpreter will find it much easier to determine which manifestation of the human will is binding and which is unenforceable, regardless of its label or its location in the BGB. The judge, the arbiter, and the lawyers for the parties engaged in legal transactions will *always* be able to look for the common element(s) of these manifestations of the will and render an exact and true opinion on the enforcement of the transaction(s) in question.

Still, how helpful is it to be told that any manifestation of the will that the law deems binding or coercive is binding or coercive, and that the reason for such a binding effect is because, in a perfectly positivistic mood, the law says so? Clearly, the BGB Pandectists shared the same attraction to circular definitions as the neo-scholastics who drafted much of the *Code Civil*. In addition, they were also attracted by closed numbers of exclusionary rules. Professor Phillip Heck, a von Ihering disciple, pointed to the damaging consequences of one such exclusionary rule.[46]

As stated by Article 305 of the original BGB, "[f]or the creation of an obligation by a juristic act, and for any alteration of the substance of an obligation, a contract between the parties is necessary, unless otherwise provided by law."[47] As noted by Heck, a contract was necessary even when it was established that the person making the unilateral expression of intent was doing so with the intent of obligating himself, and when the person to whom this intent was expressed had, "in good faith, relied upon the existence of an obligation and could reasonably so rely."[48] Heck continued:

> The contractual requirement (*Vertragszwang*) of the BGB stands in contradiction to two protective ideas that are decisive in modern law, the protection of private autonomy and of reliance. . . . What opposing interests are there which can justify such infringement of private autonomy and of the reliance interest? Actually, such opposing interests do not exist. . . . We have

---

[46] VON MEHREN & GORDLEY, THE CIVIL LAW SYSTEM, at 831 (on Phillip Heck's criticism of § 305 of the BGB).

[47] *Id.* at 829.

[48] *Id.* at 830 (citing PHILIPP HECK, GRUNDRISS DES SCHULDRECHTS 122 (1929)).

in the contractual requirement a remnant of the older law, which limited the parties to the use of typical forms.[49]

The general part of the BGB, which Franz Wieacker suggests also includes Book Two, is characteristic of the Pandectist drafting style. In Wieacker's words:

> Whereas the Prussian ALR portrayed rights and duties with a broad brush in concrete situations . . . the BGB "factors out" the common conceptual elements in different legal relationships and places them in two General Parts (Book One; Book Two, §§ 241–432).[50]

Thus, in its attempt to attain a gapless normative system, the BGB often winds up sending the interpreter through the length, height and breadth of Puchta's conceptual pyramid. Von Mehren and Gordley give the example of the search for a buyer's remedies in connection with a recently purchased cow that becomes sick upon its acquisition. The buyer of the cow would have to consult five distinct parts of the BGB before being able to determine his remedies.[51] Even a less factually-circumscribed inquiry presents similar problems. As pointed out by Wieacker:

> [I]n order to find the rules applicable to sale, which is after all a common enough occurrence, one must look to four different sets of norms: to the General Part (§§ 116 ff.; 145 ff.), the general provisions on obligations (such as § 275), the general provisions on *contractual* obligations (§§ 305 ff.; e.g. 323); and finally the provisions on the contract of sale itself (§ 433 ff.; e.g. § 446).[52]

Wieacker's conclusion is that while the General Part "bespeaks a high degree of conceptual and systematic discipline . . . the fact is that it fails to produce that intellectual economy and harmonious clarity which are the hallmark of successful legislation."[53] A similar assessment is shared by many, though not all, von Ihering-influenced scholars.[54]

On the other hand, as Wieacker also points out, another component of the BGB—its *general clauses*—are "[a] better way of avoiding the twin pitfalls of colourless abstraction and clumsy detail. . . ."[55] These clauses are:

> [G]uidelines in the form of maxims addressed to the judge, [and] designed both to control and to liberate him. They constitute a striking and welcome concession by the textual positivists to the judges' sense of responsibility and to a higher social morality; here the legislator was following the example of the Roman *praetor*, who could instruct the *judex* to make his decision on the basis of what was required by *bona fides* or good faith. By such notions as *Treu und Glauben* [good faith], moral conduct, general practice, serious

---

[49] *Id.* at 831.

[50] WIEACKER, A HISTORY OF PRIVATE LAW, at 376 (citation omitted).

[51] VON MEHREN & GORDLEY, THE CIVIL LAW SYSTEM, at 78.

[52] WIEACKER, A HISTORY OF PRIVATE LAW, at 376.

[53] *Id.* at 377.

[54] Riegert, *supra* note 9, at 62–65 (discussing the advantages and disadvantages of the BGB's abstraction). It is surprising to see that Max Rheinstein, a faithful disciple and translator of Max Weber's seminal legal sociology, lines up with the supporters of abstraction. *Id.* at 63–64.

[55] WIEACKER, A HISTORY OF PRIVATE LAW, at 377.

reason, proportionality, and so on the draftsmen were able to render their work more durable and more adaptable to the coming turmoil than they could have realized.[56]

D. The BGB's Commercialization of Civil Contracts

Much of the ideological inspiration for the BGB came from the National Liberal Party, the dominant party in the 1871 parliament (*Reichstag*).[57] In response to the forces described in the previous chapter,[58] the liberals wanted to legislate, *inter alia*, on land law, family law and on the law of associations (civil and commercial). With this in mind, they obtained a crucial amendment to Article 4, Number 13 of the Law of December 20, 1873 which assigned to the future BGB the power to govern all of Germany's private law. This power included contracts emerging from the commercialized agriculture (also described by Professor Blackbourn) and an increased ability to sell land as well as mortgages and other charges or security interests in it.[59] Consistent with the encouragement of the commercialization of real and personal property, the ownership of personal or moveable property being transformed or worked upon was given to the person who transformed or worked on it rather than to the previous owner of original property.[60]

Wieacker dislikes this rule and calls it "nothing but an irritant in the relationship between manufacturer, financier, and supplier of materials on credit."[61] Yet, if the processor was a worker, artisan or craftsman, a rule that had conferred upon him pledgeable rights in the products he processed was bound to be helpful in a credit system that required that the borrower be the owner of the asset he pledged.

COMMENTS AND QUESTIONS

What are the effects of the priority granted to the crafsman vis a vis third parties? There might be other lenders or other *bona fide* purchasers of the goods manufactured as a result of the contribution of labor to the completed goods. Which rule protects the market better?

The BGB helped to commercialize many of the theretofore "civil" (or not-for-profit) transactions. Had the same transactions been governed by the *Code Civil*, they would have been subject to a more restrictive, if not crippling, regulation. For example, the BGB did not declare illegal the Roman *Pactum Commissorium* (as was done by the *Code Civil* and its progeny) whereby creditors could repossess, retain, or resell property pledged or mortgaged. As discussed earlier, unlike the *Code Civil*, the BGB governed a number of aspects of for profit (economic) associations as well as not-for-profit (civil) associations.[62] It also liberally enforced contracts for the benefit of third parties and

---

[56] *Id.* Some of these general clauses, such as §§ 138, 157, & 242, will be transcribed in the following chapter in conjunction with their use in judicial decisions.

[57] WIEACKER, A HISTORY OF PRIVATE LAW, at 371.

[58] *See supra* § 11:1(B).

[59] *Id. See also* WIEACKER, A HISTORY OF PRIVATE LAW, at 371.

[60] *Id.* at 373. *See* BGB § 950 (GOREN, 1994), which states in its relevant part:

> A person, who by processing or transformation of one or several materials produces a new movable thing, acquires the ownership of the new thing, to the extent that the value of the processing or transformation is not substantially less than the value of the material. . . .

[61] WIEACKER, A HISTORY OF PRIVATE LAW, at 373.

[62] BGB §§ 21–79 (GOREN, 1994).

simplified claims by the third party beneficiaries.[63] In contrast with the *Code Civil*, the BGB regulated offers and acceptances *inter absentes*, typical in commercial transactions, including offers binding during a time specified by the offeror and others made during auctions.[64] It made certain oral offers binding upon the offeree as well as the offeror under specified circumstances.[65] The BGB also included several executory promises that could be enforced without the express acceptance of the promisee. Among such are: abstract promises;[66] the acknowledgment of a debt;[67] obligations in bearer instruments;[68] and the public offer of a reward.[69] Furthermore, it enforced "abstract" promises or obligations regardless of the underlying transaction or its cause, thereby deemphasizing, if not doing away with, the requirement of *causa*.[70] The abstraction or separation of conveyances and assignments from their *causa* enabled the negotiation of charges and security interests on land by means of transferable and bearer paper.[71] I should add that this feature of German mortgages and land charges has yet to be attained by a number of countries whose civil codes have followed the "causal" model of the *Code Civil*. For similar market-protection reasons, the BGB rejected the *Code Civil's* rescission of sales of real property when the seller suffered a *laesio enormis*.[72]

E. Summary

While the BGB contained considerable scholastic conceptualism and its application to everyday life was often questionable, it also provided many wise and practical rules that encouraged the entrepreneurial spirit prevalent in Germany at the end of the nineteenth century. It did this, principally, by granting enhanced negotiating freedom to contracting parties and by protecting the buyers of both real and personal property as well as creditors who relied on the security of such property. While its impact upon scholarship and code drafting in other civil law jurisdictions has been exceeded by the *Code Civil*,[73] its impact upon economic development has been much greater, especially because of its closer and supporting relationship with the HGB.

§ 12.4 THE DRAFTING OF THE HGB OF 1897

The HGB was not a product of *Pandektenrecht*. The "spirit" of the HGB can be found in a seminal and early nineteenth-century commercial statute whose method of drafting and key features differed sharply from those of its French counterparts as well as from the BGB.

---

63 *Id.* §§ 328, 330.

64 *Id.* §§ 130, 147–156, 158–163.

65 *Id.* § 295.

66 *Id.* § 780.

67 *Id.* § 781.

68 *Id.* §§ 793, 794.

69 *Id.* § 657.

70 *Id.* §§ 780, 781. *See also* VON MEHREN & GORDLEY, THE CIVIL LAW SYSTEM, at 805–11 (a good commentary on these provisions and the lack of a French counterpart).

71 WIEACKER, A HISTORY OF PRIVATE LAW, at 382.

72 *See* Glossary, "*Laesio Enormis* or Lesion."

73 WIEACKER, A HISTORY OF PRIVATE LAW, at 383–85 (discussing the impact of the BGB upon legal scholarship and code drafting in Austria, China, Greece, Hungary, Japan, Latin America, Poland, Switzerland and Yugoslavia).

A. The Law of Bills of Exchange (*Wechselgesetz*)

While the content and methodology of the proposed national codification was being debated by legal scholars, Germany started its attempts at commercial legal uniformity. The first attempt dated back to the 1830s and involved bills of exchange. As was discussed in the previous chapter, these were the same instruments whose use by non-merchants had troubled Napoleon. Yet, as noted by Dr. Karl Einert's 1839 influential monograph,[74] by the middle of the eighteenth century, bills of exchange and promissory notes were being used not only as a means of payment of commercial obligations, but also as devices with which to provide credit to merchants and governments in England and Germany. The ultimate providers of this credit were third parties to the underlying transactions who, as purchasers in good faith of these instruments (also known as "holders in due course," "holders in good faith," or "protected holders"), enjoyed a higher degree of legal protection than did their predecessors, the original parties to those very same instruments.

Henry Diedrich Jencken, whose important comparison of early European negotiable instruments law we studied in the preceding chapter, referred to the common conviction of the confederate German states to adopt a uniform or general law of bills of exchange (*Allgemeine Deutsche Wechselordnung*); what was at stake was the health of "the commercial and financial intercourse of Germany."[75] This was a wise conviction because as just pointed out bills of exchange were being used in Germany and neighboring countries as instruments of payment and credit. In the latter capacity, they provided financing to governments, banks and merchants, including agricultural, railroad and construction businesses. It is therefore not surprising that in 1847, when the Cabinet of the Confederate States of Germany sitting in Berlin invited all the member states to participate in a conference to draft a uniform law of bills of exchange, most participated. It started its sessions in Leipzig on December 9, 1847 and finished (after 35 drafting sessions) in May 1849 by promulgating what became known as the Law of Bills of Exchange (*Wechselgesetz*).[76]

The Einert-inspired *Wechselgesetz* remained in force only for a short period of time because of the collapse of the National Assembly of Confederate German States. Nevertheless, within fifteen years of this collapse, the individual states promulgated this same law as part of their own law. In 1871, as a result of Germany's final unification, it became a national statute and as such remained in effect without major changes until 1933 when it was replaced by Germany's adoption of the Geneva Convention on Bills of Exchange and Promissory Notes. Nonetheless, the *Wechselgesetz* was adopted as a national or provincial negotiable instrument law by Austria, Finland, Serbia, Sweden and the Swiss cantons.[77] It also influenced the English Bills of Exchange Act of 1882[78] and the United States Uniform Negotiable Instruments Act of

---

[74] *See supra* § 11:2(D)(2)(b).

[75] Henry Diedrich Jencken, *The Codification on the Law of Bills of Exchange and Negotiable Securities in Europe and the United States, Jurisprudence*, *in* II THE LAW MAGAZINE AND REVIEW: A QUARTERLY REVIEW OF JURISPRUDENCE 80 (1877) [hereinafter Jencken, *Codification*]

[76] *Id.* at 81.

[77] *Id.* at 82.

[78] Bills of Exchange Act, 1882, 45 & 46 Vict. c. 61 (Eng.), *available at* http://www.legislation.gov.uk/ukpga/Vict/45–46/61/contents.

1896.[79] The reader is encouraged to refresh his or her memory by revisiting the preceding chapter's comparison of the French and German laws of bills of exchange and to reflect on the reasons for the common features in German, English and subsequently United States law. Could at least one of these reasons be a growing common commercial culture?

B. The Adoption of the HGB

In 1857, the lower house of the transitional German parliament (the *Diet*) designated a commission of lawyers and businessmen to draft a general commercial law.[80] In 1871, it approved the final version of the General Code of Laws Relative to Commerce (*Allgemeines Deutsches Handelsgesetzbuch* (ADHGB)).[81] The purpose of this rather brief code was to guide those it identified as merchants on their rights and obligations in key commercial transactions and on their duties to the local and future national authorities. These duties included the merchants' registration of their business associations, commercial names and marks, and their proper keeping of accounting books and records. In return, they had the right to use their names exclusively and rely on their records as evidence in disputes with other merchants and non-merchants. Because the *Diet* lacked the power to enact national legislation, it recommended passage of this statute by each individual state. Finally, in 1871, the ADHGB became the federal commercial law of the entire new German Reich.[82]

Once the BGB was on the drawing table, one of the major issues was whether it would absorb the ADHGB and become *the* private law code of Germany. This issue was resolved by harmonizing the ADHGB with the BGB, eliminating contradictions and redundancies between the two codes, but leaving in force those texts that were compatible in both. Accordingly, a partly-commercialized BGB became effective January 1, 1900[83] and a harmonized and amended ADHGB was enacted as the HGB in 1897 and became effective in 1901. Its text, enlarged by numerous and continuously incorporated amendments, remains in effect today.[84]

In marked contrast with the BGB, the HGB was largely drafted for merchants and thus it has an easily understandable and close-to-the-marketplace style. Yet, what it gained in clarity, it often lost in precision. In the words of one of its translators:

> [W]hereas in the BGB the same concept is almost always described in identical words . . . in the HGB this is not always the case. On the other hand, the language of the HGB can be described as rather simpler, less convoluted and less impenetrable than the language of the BGB.[85]

Typical of the HGB drafting style were its provisions on a firm name:

§ 17 [Concept]

---

[79] *See* UNIFORM NEGOTIABLE INSTRUMENTS ACT (1896). The Uniform Negotiable Instruments Act was promulgated by the National Conference of Commissioners of Uniform State Laws in 1896 and subsequently enacted in all states in the United States.

[80] VON MEHREN & GORDLEY, THE CIVIL LAW SYSTEM, at 73.

[81] *Id.* at 73–74.

[82] *Id.* at 84.

[83] VON MEHREN & GORDLEY, THE CIVIL LAW SYSTEM, at 77.

[84] *Id.* at 74.

[85] HGB (GOREN, 1998) xiii.

(1) The firm name of a merchant is the name under which he carries on his business and gives his signature

(2) A merchant can sue and be sued in his firm name.[86]

§ 18 [Firm name of sole merchant]

(1) A merchant who conducts his business without a partner or only with a silent partner must use his family name with at least one of his Christian names fully written out as first name. . . .[87]

C. The HGB's "Subjective" Approach to Scope: A Longstanding Misunderstanding

To determine its scope, the HGB first established the status of merchants and did so based upon the businesses or enterprises they were engaged in.[88] As stated by Section 1(1) of the HGB: "A merchant within the meaning of this Code is a person who carries on a commercial enterprise."[89]

It is worth emphasizing that *the listing of the transactions in the HGB, unlike that of the Code de Commerce, had the purpose of making those who habitually practiced the listed transactions automatically eligible for the status of merchants*. The HGB conferred such a status and its privileges unhesitatingly, unlike the *Code de Commerce*, whose conferral was hesitant and fearful of the accusation that the drafters ignored the equality of treatment of all French citizens. Thus, while the policy of the *Code de Commerce* did have a predominantly choice-of-law purpose by making sure that its law applied as little as possible to non-merchants, the HGB cared much less if it applied to non-merchants. Whoever carried on a business was entitled to its privileges and subject to its duties. Once one realizes the differences between these two legislative policies, one also realizes that the longstanding objective-subjective dichotomy relies on the fallacious assumption that both had the same purpose, *i.e.*, to determine when commercial law is the applicable law.

The objective-subjective dichotomy has, indeed, been regarded as the touchstone for the application of commercial law by generations of law professors, especially in France, Spain and Latin America.[90] It assumes that, depending upon whether the commercial code is of an objective or subjective nature, some disputes will be governed by the commercial code and others by the civil code. Accordingly, if the dispute involves acts which are not part of the list of acts of commerce of the *Code de Commerce*, the applicable law will be the *Code Civil*. Similarly, if the dispute does not involve a merchant as defined by the HGB, it will be governed by the BGB as the counterpart to the *Code Civil*.

---

[86] *Id.* § 17.

[87] *Id.* § 18.

[88] *See generally* COHN & ZDZIEBLO, *supra* note 45.

[89] HGB § 1(1) (GOREN, 1998). *But c.f.* INTRODUCTION TO GERMAN LAW 130–31 (J. Zekoll & M. Reimann eds., 2nd ed. 2005). In this book, editors Zekoll and Reinmann separate merchants into three distinctive categories: 1) Merchants by Option; 2) Business Associations; and 3) Merchants by Appearance. It is not easy, however, to see the difference between these categories. *Id.*

[90] *See, e.g.*, RIPERT, at 3–6 (France); RODRIGO URÍA, DERECHO MERCANTIL 5–6 (6th ed. 1968) (Spain); ROBERTO L. MANTILLA MOLINA, DERECHO MERCANTIL 8–9 (1966) (Mexico).

In addition to assigning to it the same choice-of-law purpose, those who affirm the existence of this dichotomy for choice-of-law purposes assume that commercial and civil law each possess peculiar and *unchanging* qualities. For lack of a better term, I will refer to one of these qualities as "civility" and will attribute this quality mainly to the *Code Civil.* It denotes the presence of, among others: non-profit-making transactions, entered into sporadically *inter praesentes* (as contrasted with the *inter absentes* feature of many commercial transactions); a concern with the protection of bourgeois landowners; a preference for contractual *causa* and for notarial formalities; and only a modicum concern for the rights of third parties.[91]

The polar opposite of the quality of civility is supposed to be the commerciality of the transactions regulated by the *Code de Commerce* and its progeny. Its transactions are all motivated by profit making; they are generally standardized and carried out in large numbers, and they are mostly informal and often *inter absentes*. *Causa* still plays a role in these transactions, especially when it is immoral or illegal, and seeks to protect the rights of third parties, but the degree of protection varies with the type of commercial code involved. For example, in addition to the less-protected status of a holder in due course of a French bill of exchange discussed in the preceding chapter,[92] those who relied on the authority conferred upon holders of powers of attorney issued by French merchants under the original regime of the *Code Civil* and *Code de Commerce* were less protected than those who relied on a *Prokura* governed by the HGB.[93]

Yet, as discussed in the preceding section, the BGB absorbed many commercial provisions originally intended for Germany's first General Code of Commercial Laws (ADHGB). This absorption made the BGB a much more commercial code than was the *Code Civil.* Hence, the consequences of applying the BGB to a transaction involving a non-merchant could be much more "commercial" than they would be if the applicable code were the *Code Civil* and its progeny.

For example, the BGB enforced "abstract" promises, *i.e.*, promises binding merely because as stated by Section 780, the promise itself creates the obligation (regardless of the underlying reason or cause of such a promise).[94] Not surprisingly, and in contrast with the BGB, the *Code Civil* and its progeny enforced only those promises whose issuance was supported by a morally- and legally-valid *causa.*[95] As was apparent in the discussion of the business of the House of Rothschild,[96] abstract promises for the payment of sums of money or for the future delivery of investment securities or commodities had become key legal elements of the global financial marketplace. This abstraction became possible in the HGB and in the BGB because their drafters, unlike the drafters of the *Code Civil* and *Code de Commerce*, did not require a legally- and

---

[91] *See* Kozolchyk, *Commercialization*, at 12, 16–17, 22, 26–27.

[92] *See supra* § 11:2(D)(2).

[93] *See supra* § 11:2(G).

[94] BGB § 780 (GOREN, 1994) ("For the validity of a contract whereby an act of performance is promised in such manner that the promise itself is to create the obligation (promise of debt), a written statement of the promise is necessary, unless some other form is prescribed.").

[95] *See* C. CIV. (FR.) art. 1131 (Barrister 1804) ("An obligation without a cause, or upon a false cause, or upon an unlawful cause, can have no effect."); C.C. (Spain) art. 1275 (1889) ("Contracts without a cause, or with an unlawful cause, do not produce effects whatsoever. A cause is unlawful when it conflicts with the law or with morals." (author's translation)).

[96] *See supra* § 11:4.

morally-valid causal connection between monetary promises and their underlying causes.

D. Is the Commercial/Civil Code Dichotomy Presently Justified and Is Unification Possible?

Clearly, the *Code Civil* and the BGB had different legislative goals and levels of civility and commerciality. The different legislative goals of the *Code de Commerce* and the HGB, as well as their discrepancies, rendered the objective-subjective dichotomy questionable. For if the HGB's goal was to provide an inclusive legal umbrella for German merchants, big and small, to do whatever the marketplace regarded as business, it had little in common when it came to policy with the *Code de Commerce*, whose goal was to make sure that only those who performed its short, but in principle exhaustive list of acts of commerce that came under its umbrella. In that light, whether a given transaction was an essentially civil or commercial act was subordinate to the inclusionary or exclusionary goals of the respective codes. Thus, such questions do not belong at the forefront of commercial legal research. At best, they are scholastic exercises that offer no valid reasons in favor of or against unifying our contemporary private law. For this is a law inhabited preponderantly by commercial transactions and by commercialized versions of *Code Civil*, Roman-law-inspired versions of transactions such as sales (*emptio venditio*), agency (*mandatum*) partnerships (*societas*) and loans of things and money (*commodatum* and *mutuum*), whose adaptability to present day commerce has been and will be shown to be impracticable. On the other hand, whether a unification of the law that governs commercial and formerly civil transactions is possible and functional has been proven by the Swiss Code of Obligations of 1911 and the Italian Civil Code of 1942 and, to a more limited extent, by the U.C.C.

Consider, for example, the following sections extracted from the Table of Contents of the Swiss Code of Obligations of 1911 and notice how contracts regarded traditionally as "essentially civil," such as that of a donation or of sale of real property, became part of the same code and were regulated side by side with "essentially commercial" contracts such as residential and commercial leases. In addition, notice how consumer protection provisions, also housed in the same code, protect residential and commercial lessees from abusive practices:

Division Two: Types of Contractual Relationship

Title Six: Sale and Exchange

Section One: General Provisions

Section Two: The Chattel State

Section Three: Sale of Immovable Property

Section Four: Special Types of Sale

Section Five: Contract of Exchange

Title Seven: Gifts

Title Eight: The Lease (Formerly civil and commercial)

Section One: General Provisions

Section Two: Protection against Unfair Rents or other Unfair Claims by the Landlord in respect of Leases of Residential and Commercial Premises.[97]

Similarly, the Italian Civil Code of 1942 includes in the unified Book Four on Obligations, Title III (Individual Contracts), transactions regarded traditionally as "essentially" civil and commercial such as:

Sales of Immovable Property

Agency (Including a Presumption of Profit making)

(Chapter IX, Section 1) Deposit or Bailment (Formerly civil, but now including a Presumption of Non Profit)

(Chapter XII, Section I) Credit Accounts (Commercial)

(Chapter XVI, Section III) Banking Contracts (Commercial)

(Chapter XVIII, Sections I and Following) Perpetual Annuity (Formerly civil now commercial)

(Chapter XIX, Sections I and Following) Life Annuity (Commercial)

(Chapter XX, Sections I and following) Insurance (Commercial)[98]

To this day, no major disruptions of either Swiss or Italian private law have been reported as a result of having unified their law of obligations. In fact, following the fall of fascism, Italian legislators had the opportunity to abrogate the unified arrangement and chose not to do so. What I believe these legislative experiences teach us is that when the unified codes protect non-merchants from the exploitation of the superior expertise or bargaining power of merchants, or when they delegate this protection to other statutes such as for the protection of consumers, they provide a degree of certainty of applicable law that is missing in the objective-subjective, commercial-civil code dichotomies. I will come back to this question when we discuss the scope of the U.C.C. and the various methods of commercial contract interpretation.[99]

§ 12.5 AN OVERVIEW OF THE ORIGINAL AND AMENDED VERSIONS OF THE HGB

A. The Original (1897) Version of the HGB

The original version of Section 1 of the HGB, defined a merchant as follows:

§ 1 [Merchant by virtue of type of business]

(1) A merchant within the meaning of this Code is a person who carries on a commercial enterprise.

(2) Every business enterprise, which has as its objective one of the kinds of business indicated below, is deemed a commercial enterprise:

---

[97] This list of contracts was extracted from the section headings of the Swiss Code of Obligations. Obligationenrecht [OR], Code des obligations [CO], Codice delle Obligazioni [CO] [Code of Obligations] Mar. 30, 1911 SR 220, RS 220 (Switz.), *available at* http://www.admin.ch/ch/e/rs/2/220.en.pdf.

[98] CODICE CIVILE E LEGGI COMPLEMENTARI 513–23 (F. Carnelutti & W. Bigiavi eds., 1964) (source of this extracted list).

[99] *See infra* ch. 22.

1. The acquisition and resale of movable things (merchandise) or of securities, without distinction as to whether the merchandise is resold unchanged, or after treatment or processing;

2. The acceptance for treatment or processing of merchandise for others, provided that the enterprise is not carried on as an artisan one;

3. The underwriting of insurance in exchange for premiums;

4. Banking and currency exchange transactions;

5. Undertakings for the maritime transportation of goods or passengers, the business of carriers or establishments for the transportation of persons overland or on the inland waterways, as well as the business of towing barges;

6. The business of factor[ing], forwarding agent, or warehouse keeper;

7. The business of commercial agent or broker;

8. Publishing as well as other businesses engaged in the book or art trade;

9. The printing trade, provided the enterprise is not carried on as an artisan one.[100]

It is important to note that someone who did not practice one of the listed businesses, such as an artisan printer not falling under subsection 9, could still enjoy the important protection of, for example, the exclusive use of his firm's name by filing this name with the Commercial Register. Up until that filing, he was unprotected because, having failed to qualify for an *ipso facto* status, he was not deemed a merchant. *After* he filed "according to the provisions in effect for the registration of commercial firms,"[101] he was deemed a merchant and his commercial firm's name was protected.

Having a registered firm name was important not only because of the business's ability to prevent competitors from using its established and valuable name, but also because it increased a merchant's credibility in court and among actual and potential lenders or investors. Those who were typified as Section 1 merchants were "automatically" deemed so by virtue of their type of business.[102] Their registration was merely "declarative," *i.e.*, they had the preexisting right to be protected as merchants and the registration merely recognized the existence of these rights.[103]

In contrast, those not typified as merchants, such as the above-mentioned artisans or those engaged in agriculture and forestry, could qualify as merchants only by virtue

---

100 HGB § 1 (1897).

101 *Id.* at § 2, which states:

An artisan or like business enterprise, the carrying on of which is not deemed a commercial enterprise under § 1(2), but which according to its nature and scope requires a business establishment organized in a commercial manner, is deemed a commercial enterprise within the meaning of this Code, insofar as the firm name of the enterprise has been entered in the Commercial Register. The proprietor is obliged to effect the registration according to the provisions in effect for the registration of commercial firms.

102 *See* PELTZER & VOIGHT, at 4.

103 *Id.*

of their registration in the Commercial Register.[104] In their case, their registration was "constitutive" of rights from the time it was granted to the registrants, at which time these rights could be enforced.[105] An additional constitutive right granted to non-Section 1 merchants by their registration as merchants was their ability to convey powers and commercial authority to *Prokurists*. As stated by the original Section 49(1), when a commercial establishment conferred the power to sign in its name (*Prokura*), it "authorize[d] juridical and extra-juridical acts and legal transactions, of all kinds, which are involved in the conduct of a commercial enterprise."[106] And, as made clear by the original Section 50(1): "A limitation in the scope of the signing power is ineffective as against third parties."[107]

As was discussed in the previous chapter,[108] this "abstract" or non-causal approach of the *Prokura* protected those who relied on the appearance of commercial authority of the *Prokurist* and thus encouraged the contracts between these third parties and the frequently unknown or distant principals (acting through their presumably authorized agents or intermediaries). As will become apparent in our discussion of agencies and powers of attorney in jurisdictions that adopted the French and Spanish "causal" (as opposed to the German "abstract") approach to dealings with agents and holders of powers of attorney, the reliance by third parties on the appearance of commercial authority is rendered much more perilous.[109]

With respect to small merchants, Section 4(1) of the original HGB provided that: "The provisions concerning firms, commercial books and authority to sign shall not apply to persons the nature or scope of whose trade does not require a business enterprise equipped in the manner of a commercial business."[110]

B. The Scope of the Amended (1998 and Present) Version of the HGB

Since its enactment, the HGB has undergone a number of amendments. The most substantial of these took place in 1998, especially with respect to its scope.[111] Section 1 of the 1998 amendment now states in an open number (*numerus apertus*) and thus contrasting fashion with the exhaustive listing of the acts of commerce by the *Code de Commerce*: "A merchant within the meaning of this Code is one who conducts a business."[112] In turn, subsection 2 of the same section defined a merchant's business as: "[E]very commercial operation unless the enterprise by type and volume does not require a commercially organized business operation."[113]

This was indeed an open-ended definition, in contrast with the partially closed-ended definition of the 1897 text. In that text, and as just mentioned, only those types of businesses (not mere individualized acts of commerce) listed and described could

---

104 *See* HGB § 3 (GOREN, 1998).

105 *Id.*

106 *Id.* § 49(1).

107 *Id.* § 50(1).

108 *See supra* § 11:2(G).

109 *See supra* § 5:13(B).

110 HGB § 4(1) (GOREN, 1998).

111 *See* PELTZER & VOIGHT, at 1–3.

112 *Id.* at 35.

113 *Id.*

characterize the person or entity that carried them out as a merchant. However, keep in mind that it was only a partially closed list because, say, an artisan's registration of his trade mark or copyright in the commercial registry entitled him to the protection of his intellectual property and to do his business as a merchant.

That the original Section 1 was drafted in the nineteenth century can hardly be missed. For example, while its subparagraph 2, subsection 5 includes the business of maritime overland and inland waterways transportation of goods or passengers and even that of towing barges, it does not mention air transportation. In addition, it left out what Dr. Martin Peltzer and Elizabeth A. Voight, two code annotators and translators, describe as "many service industries which in the meantime had become increasingly important [such as] . . . cinemas, theatres, schools, hotels, advertising [and] . . . the entire construction business."[114]

The 1998 amendment of Section 1 had to take these new businesses and other marketplace facts into account. Wisely, it decided not to engage in a *numerus clausus* exercise by eliminating the list contained in the subparagraph 2 of Section 1. Now "anyone conducting a business is a merchant regardless of his field of commercial activity, be it production, trade, or services."[115]

As pointed out by Peltzer and Voight, there are two exceptions to the applicability of the HGB to those engaged in profit-making transactions. One is guild-like in that it involves the activities of professionals such as lawyers, notaries, and physicians, among others. The other is a remnant of the 1897 system: Where a business is so small that it need not be organized in a formal manner, the person or persons involved in such a business are not deemed merchants. Nonetheless, these small merchants are allowed to apply for registration in the commercial register and, upon registration, they become registered merchants.[116] Peltzer and Voight summarize the amended scope provisions as follows:

> [Now] [a]nyone conducting a business is a merchant, be he registered or not. The revised Commercial Code applies to him. The merchant has a duty to register and can be compelled to file for registration by a coercive fine (§ 14 Commercial Code). Members of the professions do not carry on a commercial business, and, therefore, the Commercial Code does not apply to them. The very small business is exempted from the application of the Commercial Code, but it can file for registration and thereby become a merchant (§ 2 Commercial Code) . . . Agriculture and forestry are also exempted, but can likewise file for registration in the commercial register where a commercially organized business operation is required . . .[117]

These authors raise the question of why small merchants or members of civil law associations would want to file for registration and be subject to the commercial code regime. After all, this regime frequently imposes harsher obligations and stricter duties of diligence on merchants than those applicable to non-merchants under the BGB or other enactments. For example, oral guarantees made by merchants as well as other informal promises are more likely to be enforced against them than when made

---

114 *Id.* at 3–4.

115 *Id.* at 4.

116 *Id.*

117 *Id.* at 4–5.

by non-merchants.[118] Similarly, buyer-merchants, unlike non-merchants, have the duty to examine goods bought by them for defects immediately upon their delivery.[119] Additionally, some types of merchants are deemed to have accepted offers even though they merely remained silent after receipt of these offers.[120]

The reason for the choice of a commercial status under the HGB lies in the considerable benefits that the application of the commercial code brings to borderline or occasional merchants, for example, a "clearly defined and undisputable limitation of liability for the limited partner of a limited partnership."[121] To these benefits, I would add: easier access to commercial intermediaries and commercial credit, and greater credibility of books and records, whether in judicial or extrajudicial procedures.

C. Illustrative Sections of the Amended HGB[122]

1. *Outline of Book One*

As with the *Code de Commerce*, the HGB sets forth in Book One the qualifications for the status of a merchant, the requirements for conducting a commercial business, and the key features of the relationship between merchants and their assistants or auxiliaries. Accordingly, Sections 1 through 58 delineate the rules that govern the existence of a business, its notice to the public, and its bookkeeping and personnel: Merchants,[123] Commercial Register,[124] Commercial Firm Name,[125] Business Books and Records,[126] Commercial Agency (*Prokura*) and Power of Attorney.[127] Thereafter, it

---

118 *Id.* at 5 (citing to § 350 of the German Commercial Code). Section 350 states:

> The formal requirements of § 766 sentence 1 and 2, § 780 and § 781 sentence 1 and 2, of the Civil Code do not apply to a guaranty, an admission of liability or a debt acknowledgement to the extent that the guaranty, for the guarantor, or the admission of liability or debt acknowledgement, for the debtor, is a commercial transaction.

Id. at 307–308.

119 *Id.* at 5 (citing to § 377(1) of the German Commercial Code). Section 377(1) states:

> Where the sale is a commercial transaction for both parties, the buyer must examine the goods promptly following delivery by the seller insofar as this is practicable in the proper course of business. . .

Id. at 321.

120 *Id.* at 5 (citing to § 362(1) of the German Commercial Code). Section 362(1) states:

> Where an offer is made to a merchant whose business includes solicitation or conclusion of business transactions for others, and such offer is from someone with whom the merchant has a business relationship and concerns solicitation or conclusion of such transactions on behalf of the offeror, the merchant is obligated to reply immediately; his silence will be deemed to be acceptance of the offer . . .

Id. at 312.

121 *Id.* at 5.

122 The following summary of illustrative sections was taken from Peltzer and Voight although some of the headings were changed to render them closer to Anglo American terminology.

123 HGB §§ 1–7 (GOREN, 1998).

124 *Id.* §§ 8–16.

125 *Id.* §§ 17–37.

126 *Id.* §§ 38–47b (repealed in 2003).

127 *Id.* §§ 48–58.

governs the status of Commercial Clerks and Commercial Apprentices,[128] Commercial Agents[129] and Commercial Brokers.[130]

What follows is a short description of illustrative sections in Book One and some of the following books.

2. *Commercial Agency*

Chapter Seven of Book One is devoted to the "commercial agent" (*Handelsvertreter*). Its uncharacteristically casuistic regulation reflects the myriad of activities performed by commercial agents throughout the European Union. Accordingly, Section 84 defines this agent as one:

> (1) who, as an independent person engaged in business, is regularly authorized to solicit business for another entrepreneur (the "principal") [*unternehmer*] or to enter into transaction in his name. A person is independent if he is essentially free to structure his activity and determine his hours of work.[131]
>
> The commercial agent is distinguished from an employee in the following fashion:
>
> Any person who, without being independent within the meaning of Sub-section 1, is regularly authorized to solicit business for a principal or to enter into transactions in his name, is deemed to be an employee.[132]
>
> Among the duties of a commercial agent listed by Section 86 are:
>
> The commercial agent is obligated to make efforts towards the solicitation or conclusion of business transactions. In connection herewith he must act in the interests of the principal . . . He shall give the principal all necessary information, i.e. inform him immediately of every solicitation and conclusion of every transaction . . . He must fulfill his duties with the care of a [honest or proper] prudent merchant [*ordentlichen Kaufmanns*].[133]

In turn, the duties of the principal are set forth in equal detail by Section 86(a), among others. The principal must provide the commercial agent with all materials which are necessary for the performance of his duties, such as samples, drawings, price lists, advertising material, and terms and conditions of business.

The principal must keep the commercial agent generally informed. In particular, he must inform him promptly of the acceptance or rejection of a transaction procured by the agent or a transaction concluded by the agent without authority, and of the non-fulfillment of a transaction procured or concluded by him. He must inform him promptly if he desires, or will likely be able to, conclude transactions only on a

---

128 *Id.* §§ 59–83.

129 *Id.* §§ 84–92c.

130 *Id.* §§ 93–104.

131 *See* PELTZER & VOIGHT, at 80.

132 *Id. See* INTRODUCTION TO GERMAN LAW, *supra* note 89, at 136 (describing the second group of intermediaries that act only for the principal's account: "the form most widely used is agency for a commission (*Kommissionsgeschäfte*—§§ 383 *et seq.* HGB). A commission agent . . . is a dealer . . . who makes it his or her business to buy or sell goods in his or her own name though for the account of another. . . .").

133 *See* PELTZER & VOIGHT, at 81.

significantly reduced scale in comparison to that which the agent could expect under normal circumstances.[134]

The same degree of detail is provided with respect to the agents' entitlement to remuneration, its due time and its amount. The regulation takes into account factors such as the type of commercial agency and the agent's guarantee of the fulfillment of the commissioned transaction, the right to an accounting and to the reimbursement of expenses, and the agent's lien or right of retention for what is lawfully owed to him.[135]

3. *Partnerships*

a. *The General Partnership*

Book Two of the revised HGB governs general, limited and silent partnerships. The distinctive features of the general partnership are: (1) its purpose—which is the operation of a commercial enterprise; (2) its form—a common firm name; and (3) its liability—no partner's liability is limited with regard to what is owed to partnership creditors.[136] As a sign of the degree of commercialization of the BGB, the HGB states that "to the extent that this section does not provide otherwise, the provisions of the Civil Code concerning partnership shall be applicable to commercial partnerships."[137]

The concern with the partners' authority to bind the partnership, especially when dealing with third parties, is apparent. After setting forth the broad scope of the partners' powers of representation, including judicial and extrajudicial proceedings, alienation and encumbrance of real property, and conferral and revocation of a *Prokura*, the code states:

> Any limitation of the extent of power to represent is ineffective as against third parties; this is applicable in particular to the limitation that the representation should extend only to certain transactions or kinds of transactions, or that it should be allowed only under certain circumstances or for a certain period or in particular places.[138]

As with the preceding books, Book Two provides a highly detailed regulation of the general commercial partnership including: the extent of the partners' liability;[139] the defenses available to them when sued for partnership debts, including the repayment of partnership loans;[140] the liability of a partner joining an existing partnership;[141] the dissolution of the partnership and withdrawal of partners;[142] the termination of the partnership by the personal creditor of a partner;[143] and continuation of the business with the heirs of a dead partner,[144] concluding with its liquidation.[145]

---

134 *Id.* at 81–82.

135 *See, e.g., id.* at 82–87.

136 HGB § 105(1) (GOREN, 1998).

137 *Id.* § 105(3).

138 *Id.* § 126(2).

139 *Id.* § 128.

140 *Id.* §§ 129–129a.

141 *Id.* § 130.

142 *Id.* §§ 131–134.

143 *Id.* § 135.

144 *Id.* § 139.

145 *Id.* §§ 145–160.

b. The Limited Partnership

As with the general partnership, the limited partnership is distinguishable by: (1) its purpose—the operation of a commercial enterprise; (2) its form—a common firm name; and (3) its liability—limited with respect to one or more partners up to the amount of their capital contributions, a limitation combined with the absence of limitation in the case of the general partners.

Many of the provisions applicable to the general partnerships also apply to the limited partnership, including the formalities of organization, bookkeeping, etc.[146] One additional distinguishing feature is that limited partners are excluded from the management of the business and cannot object to actions taken by the general partners unless these actions "exceed[] the scope of the partnership's ordinary business."[147]

c. The Silent Partnership

The key feature of the silent partnership is that the silent partner makes his capital contribution in such a manner that it is transferred directly to the assets of the owner of the business. Thus, "[t]he owner alone will have the rights and obligations arising from the transactions made in the courses of conducting business."[148] Evidently, the silent partner is more trusting than the limited partner because, in the limited partnership, the limited partner contributes to the partnership's capital while the silent partner's contribution is to the assets of the owner.

Reflecting this higher degree of entrustment, the method for sharing profits and losses does not have to be specified in the silent partnership agreement. Where not specified, the silent partner's share of the profits is that which is "appropriate in the circumstances."[149] His right to profits may not be excluded even if the partnership agreement stipulates that the silent partner is not to participate in the losses.[150]

4. Record and Bookkeeping

The provisions on record keeping in the revised HGB contain some of the most innovative provisions found in contemporary commercial codes, especially as updated for corporate governance in a June 14, 2007 amendment of the 2003 revision.[151] The following are summary illustrations of what was accomplished in these two revisions. According to Section 238 of the 2003 revision, every merchant is obligated to keep books and:

> Make visible his commercial transactions and the state of his assets according to the principles of orderly accounting. The accounting must be in such a condition that an expert third party can have a general insight concerning the operation of the business and concerning the state of the enterprise. . . ."[152]

---

146 *Id.* § 161.

147 *Id.* § 164.

148 *Id.* § 230(1).

149 *Id.* § 231(1).

150 *Id.* § 231(2).

151 *See* DEUTSCHER CORPORATE GOVERNANCE KODEX [DCGK] [GERMAN CORPORATE GOVERNANCE CODE], Feb. 26, 2002, as amended (Ger.), *available at* http://www.ecgi.org/codes/documents/cg_code_germany_june2007_en.pdf.

152 HGB § 238(1) (GOREN, 1998).

In addition, "[i]n the keeping of business books and other required records, the merchant shall employ a living language. . . ."[153]

These principles depart radically from the nineteenth-century Spanish commercial code that required a mandatory set of books and entries, regardless of whether they reflected generally accepted accounting principles.[154]

5. *Commercial Transactions*

Book Four governs selected commercial transactions, such as sales, commission transactions, warehousing, freight forwarding and transport of goods. The reason for including some of these provisions in the HGB rather than allowing the BGB to govern is the commercial status of the parties. For example: the time when performance can be demanded is related to the merchant obligor's "usual business hours";[155] the stipulation of merchandise by means of generic characteristics is to be fulfilled by tendering goods of "average description and quality";[156] the computation of measure, weight, currency, time, and distance is to be made in accordance with what is customary at the location where the contract is to be fulfilled;[157] the silence of a merchant offeree with respect to an offer made to him by someone with whom he has a business relationship is deemed an acceptance if the offeree does not reply immediately.[158]

The provisions on the contract of transportation govern exhaustively the rights and duties of the parties to inland as well as multi-modal transportation and apply to documents that are mere receipts such as truck or rail waybills, as well as to documents of title such as negotiable bills of lading.[159] Negotiable instruments continue to be governed on the whole by the Geneva Convention adopted by Germany, among many other civil law countries, in 1933.[160] Similarly, Book Five of the HGB, devoted to maritime law, applies the Hague-Visby rule on liability for damage to maritime cargo, both to inbound and outbound shipments.[161]

6. *Conclusion*

In contrast with the paternalistic and anachronistic proevisions of the *Code de Commerce* discussed in an earlier chapter,[162] the HGB is a more market-sensitive code. Both its original version as well as its 1998 revision, and especially the latter, allow the market to determine who is a merchant governed by the HGB. Its so-called "subjective" nature, typical of a code written for professionals rather than for certain specified acts, has made its interaction with the BGB more effective than that between the *Code Civil* and the *Code de Commerce*. One of the key ingredients in this positive interaction is

---

153 *Id.* § 239.

154 *See, e.g.*, C. COM. (Spain) arts. 33–63 (1885).

155 HGB § 358 (GOREN, 1998).

156 *Id.* § 360.

157 *Id.* § 361.

158 *Id.* § 362.

159 *Id.* §§ 407–452.

160 *See* Deutsche Wechselgesetz [German Exchange Act], June 21, 1933, RGBl I at 409 (Ger.).

161 *See* International Convention for the Unification of Certain Rules of Law Relating to Bills of Lading, Aug. 25, 1924, 51 Stat. 233; *see also* HGB (GOREN, 1998) Book V (on Maritime Commerce).

162 *See supra* § 10:4(B)(7).

that of German customary law, especially as found in the standard contractual terms and conditions of the various businesses as incorporated into the so-called "general conditions of trade," which will be addressed in the following chapter.[163]

§ 12.6 COMMERCIALIZATION OF CONTRACTS AND THIRD PARTY PROTECTION: *CODE CIVIL* AND BGB

The following comparison of provisions in the French and German civil codes (including one provision located in the HGB, but whose rule is consistent with BGB principles) provides the opportunity to evaluate the effects of applying their respective rules (and underlying principles) to commercial transactions, including their protection of third parties.

Code Civil—France[164]	B.G.B. and H.G.B.—Germany[165]
Formality: Only authentic acts (notarial deeds) and documents under private signature, *i.e.*, documents formally acknowledged by the signing party are given evidentiary value as literal (full) proof of the obligation. *Arts. 1317–1332.*	Where the law requires a writing, then a signature is required; informal contracts can be signed without formal acknowledgment of signatures. Telegraphic communications can be binding, contracts by exchanges of letters are also binding; however, authentication of signatures may be required. *§§ 126* and *127.*
Enforceability of unaccepted promises: Contractual promises require acceptance by the promisee to be enforceable; Recipients of purportedly firm or irrevocable promises are subject to their revocation (as mere pollicitations) prior to their acceptance. *Arts. 1101, 1108.*	Promises can be enforced without the expressed acceptance of a promise. Executory promises (formally *nuda pacta*) such as those found in *§ 780* (Abstract Promise), *§ 781* (Acknowledgment of a Debt), and *§§ 793, 794* (Bearer Instruments), and *657* (Public Offer of a Reward).
Abstract promises: Promises that lack a recognizable legal and moral cause are unenforceable. *Arts. 1108, 1131.*	Abstract promises are enforceable even if their cause is unknown or not ascertainable. *§§ 780–781.*
Causal mortgages: A mortgage is a causal and accessory contract. *Art. 2125 (Original Code Civil and Amendment in Decree of 31 December 1910).*	. Mortgages can be abstract contracts subject to the provisions of the *Grundschuld* and be made out to "bearer." *§§ 1191–1198.*
Contracts *inter absentes*: No regulation for contracts *inter absentes.*	Express regulation of contracts *inter absentes* (*§ 130*), including offers binding during a time specified by the offeror and others made during auctions. *§§ 147–156.*
Benefit of third parties: Restrictive provisions on the enforcement of contracts for the benefit of third parties. *Arts. 1165, 1121.*	Liberal enforcement of contracts for the benefit of third parties. *§ 328.*
Rescission for economic loss on sale of land (lesion): Contracts for the sale of land can be rescinded if the seller sells for a price	A loss suffered while selling land below its market value is not protected except in cases of subjective lesion (*§ 138*). Third parties who

[163] *See infra* ch. 13.

[164] C. CIV. (FR.) (Barrister 1804).

[165] BGB (GOREN, 1900).

lower 7/12th of market value (objective lesion), third parties' rights notwithstanding. *Art. 1674.*	purchase land based on the land registry records are protected. *§ 892.*
Agent exceeds authority to the detriment of third parties: In an agency contract, the principal is not bound to perform if the agent exceeds the principal's instructions. *Art. 1998.*	Apparent authority of the *Prokurist* binds the principal. HGB § 50.
Scope of coverage: Only regulates civil or non-profit associations. *Arts. 1832–1873.*	Regulate civil or non-profit associations, as well as commercial or for-profit associations. *§§ 21–50.*
Third parties and unilateral declarations of intent: No comparable provisions are found in the *Code Civil.*	The BGB protects the third party who relies upon unilateral declaration of intent. *§ 122.*

Chapter 13

CUSTOMS, USAGES AND OTHER SOURCES OF COMMERCIAL CONTRACT LAW IN GERMAN AND OTHER REPRESENTATIVE CODES

§ 13.1 SOURCES AND THEIR HEIRARCHY

A. Custom and Usage

The summary review of the origin and development of European commercial law provided in previous chapters[1] shows that commercial customs and usages were important sources of the nineteenth-century codification, although in some countries more than in others. It also shows that from the time they were first drafted in Italian medieval city-states, commercial customs were corporate in nature. By corporate, I mean that they were mostly drawn as disciplinary rules for members of the various associations of merchants (*corporazioni*). These were the same associations which helped draft the laws of the Italian city-states in which they did their business.[2] Thus, as noted by Levin Goldschmidt and Pierre Huvelin, the laws of the Italian city-states owed much to the commercial customs of the merchants who inhabited them.[3]

As was also discussed in the above-mentioned chapters, corporate commercial customs were compiled during the late Middle Ages at first informally, and thereafter by consulates in ports and other important trading centers. Similar compilations have been drafted in our day by national or international associations of merchants and bankers such as the International Chamber of Commerce (ICC), among others. Accordingly, the ICC's International Commercial Terms (INCOTERMS) standardize the nomenclature as well as the rights and duties of international sellers and buyers of goods, and the Uniform Customs and Practice for Documentary Credits (UCP 500 and 600) govern the use of letters of credit in the payment and finance of sales and other commercial transactions. These two compilations are among the most observed customs and practices in today's trading world.[4]

The corporate origin of commercial customs also finds echo in the standard contract forms and terms issued by national and international trade associations. Some of these govern the trade of commodities such as wool, cocoa, oil, seed and fats, grain and feed, cotton, produce, jute, metal, rubber, sugar, timber and the provision of services, for example, by civil engineers and other service providers in the construction

---

[1] *See supra* chs. 8–12.

[2] *See supra* § 9:1(A).

[3] *Id.*

[4] *See* INT'L CHAMBER OF COMMERCE, PUB. NO. 500, UNIFORM CUSTOMS AND PRACTICE FOR DOCUMENTARY CREDIT (1993); INT'L CHAMBER OF COMMERCE, PUB. NO. 600, UNIFORM CUSTOMS AND PRACTICE FOR DOCUMENTARY CREDIT (2007). *See generally* Kozolchyk, *Towards New Customs* (discussing the observance of these sources).

industry.[5] Other standard forms of commercial and consumer contracts are used in Germany and other European and Latin American nations to cover a wide range of transactions including the retail supply of goods or services, as will be discussed shortly. The availability of these written versions of customs and practices and standard contract forms has facilitated their application in commercial disputes by courts and by arbitration tribunals, especially those that are "sectoral" in nature.[6]

Germany does this in a direct manner by applying standard commercial contracts (a species of customary law) as a primary source of law. It also applies customary law indirectly when its courts reject those standard contracts or clauses that violate the general principles of good faith (*Gebot von Treu und Glauben*),[7] public policy (*boni mores, gute Sitten*),[8] or the behavior of a business-like (also proper, prudent, honest, and decent) merchant (*ordentlicher Kaufmann*). These principles are reflected in the regulation of activities as diverse as the windup of partnerships, sales of goods by retail or wholesale merchants, and the management of maritime vessels.[9] Their application relies indirectly on customary behavior because it must establish those usages or customs that, in the eyes of the court, best embody the good faith and honest behavior referred to by the BGB and HGB.[10] As stated by Zekoll & Reimann, "Under German law, 'good faith' governs commercial as well as plain civil law transactions. Yet, there is a distinctly commercial application of the principle. . . . Furthermore, the Commercial Code affords greater protection to a good faith purchaser of movables when the seller is a merchant."[11]

The reader may wonder why I have waited until now to discuss the sources of commercial contract law in representative civil law jurisdictions. The answer is that Germany is the civil law jurisdiction that relies most on custom and usage as sources of commercial contract law. Consequently, this chapter will discuss commercial custom and usage in conjunction with other important sources of commercial contract law in German and other representative codes.

---

[5] CLIVE M. SCHMITTHOFF, SCHMITTHOFF'S EXPORT TRADE: THE LAW AND PRACTICE OF INTERNATIONAL TRADE 64 (8th ed. 1990). *See also infra* ch. 24; *see generally* 30 ARIZ. J. INT'L & COMP. L. (2013) (This symposium issue is dedicated to reasonableness in standard practices in international trade and business).

[6] Sectoral arbitration is used by various commercial, financial, industrial, and professional associations to decide cases based upon the associations' best practices and rules of procedure. *See, e.g., DRC Trading Standards,* FRUIT AND VEGETABLE DISPUTE RESOLUTION CORPORATION (DRC) (last amended Aug 19, 2013), http://www.fvdrc.com/media/6991/or_part-4_trading_standards.pdf (providing an example of trading standards in the NAFTA region, and especially for agricultural trade between Mexico and the United States); John F. Munger, Importation of Mexican Produce into the US: Procedures, Documentation, and Dispute Resolution (2008) (unpublished LL.M. thesis, Univ. of Ariz.) (on file with author). *See also* Gary T. DOYLE, NORTH AMERICAN STANDARD TRANSPORTATION PRACTICES: A GUIDE TO TRUCK TRANSPORTATION (1998) (discussing road transportation in the NAFTA countries); *Uniform Inter-American Rules for Electronic Documents and Signature Recitals (IAREDS),* ORG. AM. STATES (Oct. 3, 2001), http://www.oas.org/dil/CIDIP-VII_topics_futures_cidips_electroniccommerce_signatures_3oct2001.htm; U.S. COUNCIL ON INT'L BANKING, INC., STANDARD BANKING PRACTICE FOR THE EXAMINATION OF LETTERS OF CREDIT DOCUMENTS (1996).

[7] *See, e.g.,* BGB § 157 (GOREN, 1994) ("Contracts shall be interpreted according to the requirements of good faith, *giving consideration to common usage.*") (emphasis added).

[8] *Id.* §§ 138, 817.

[9] *See* HGB §§ 347, 130a, 497 (GOREN, 1998). That the term *ordentlicher* (which can be translated as "proper", "businesslike", or "prudent") is intended by the HGB to be a generic concept, and thus the need for elucidation by means of commercial usages and customs, is apparent by its application to situations as diverse as the wind-up of partnerships, or other legal entities.

[10] *See, e.g.,* BGB § 157 (GOREN, 1994).

[11] INTRODUCTION TO GERMAN LAW 130 (J. Zekoll & M. Reimann eds., 2d ed. 2005) (references omitted).

B. Case Law

As previously discussed,[12] German and English courts contributed to the development of commercial law, especially in the field of negotiable instruments, while the courts of other countries, such as France, were reluctant to do so. In contrast with their English and German counterparts, French commercial courts continued to look for *causa* in bills of exchange and promissory notes and thus hindered their negotiability until well into the nineteenth century.[13] These courts and their civil counterparts also insisted on a literal interpretation of those formal contracts drafted as "authentic acts" (*actes authentiques*).[14]

The reluctance to apply commercial customs as binding sources of commercial law has continued to this day. For example, in decisions handed down as recently as 1975 and 1997,[15] Spain's Supreme Court rejected the binding effect of widely-observed international and national banking customs such as the Uniform Customs and Practices for Documentary Credits (UCP). There was an attempt to justify these decisions by relying on the doctrine of *opinio iuris vel necessitatis*, which essentially states that the customs and usages must be regarded as binding for a long or "inveterate" period of time by those who are subject to them.

Whether a custom or usage qualifies as binding should not be based upon whether or not it has been observed for a long period of time, such as at least a century as claimed by one of the Spanish decisions, but upon the degree to which those who participate in the transaction in question regard the custom or usage as binding upon them at the time of their decision to participate. The reality is that the UCP has long been recognized by banks, their customers, and courts elsewhere as the "living law" of contemporary letters of credit transactions.[16] This reluctance by the Spanish Supreme Court was not caused by commercial code provisions unsympathetic to commercial custom. On the contrary, Article 2 of the Spanish Commercial Code of 1885, unlike some of its progeny, expressly stated that in the absence of code provisions applicable to acts of commerce, these acts would be governed by "commercial usages observed generally in each market."[17] In sharp contrast, incidentally, Mexico's Commercial Code of 1889 did not even list custom as a binding source of law.[18]

Thus, in order to identify the reasons for the judicial reluctance to apply commercial custom in civil law jurisdictions, one would, again, have to point to the juristic hostility towards commerce. Where commerce was shunned or regarded as a

---

[12] *See supra* § 11:2(D)(2).

[13] *Id.*

[14] Kozolchyk, *Commercialization* at 20.

[15] *See* S.T.S. Oct. 9, 1997 (R.J., No. 899, p.7066) (Spain). This case cites a 1975 Spanish Supreme Court case that referred to the UCP as "mere banking practices *(meras prácticas bancarias)* . . . and if they were to be invoked as custom, Article 6 of the Preliminary Title of the Commercial Code and Article 1 of that Code would demand proof of its existence. . . ." S.T.S. Apr. 14, 1975 (R.J., No. 1517) (Spain) (author's translation).

[16] *See* Kozolchyk, *Towards New Customs*, at 372–76.

[17] C.COM. art. 2, in its relevant part states: "The acts of commerce, whether or not carried out by merchants, and whether or not they are specified in this code, shall be governed by it [the commercial code]; in the absence of code provisions, [they shall be governed] by the commercial usages observed generally in each market. . . ."

[18] CÓD.COM. (Mex.) art. 1 (1889), in its relevant part states: "The provisions of this Code only govern commercial acts." *Id.* at art. 2: "In the absence of provisions in this code, the provisions of the common law [as found in the Civil Code for federal matters] shall apply to commercial acts."

necessary evil at best, commercial customs and usages were ignored by courts. Yet, as shown by the preceding chapters, where commerce was encouraged and widely observed, customary law was unhesitatingly applied by the courts, the certainty required by investors, lenders and traders increased, and so did economic development.

Judicial decisions did not fare better than commercial customs as sources of commercial contract law in the eyes of code draftsmen. Despite their indisputable impact on the entirety of private law, none of the codes listed judicial decisions as binding sources. The desire to preserve the text of the codes as the exclusive repositories of legislative intent was present in the statement attributed to Napoleon upon learning of the first publication of doctrinal and judicial interpretations of his *Code Civil*: "*Mon code est perdu*" (My code is lost).[19]

Yet, the same Napoleon was known to have taken credit for insuring that the *Cour de Cassation* remained as France's highest appellate court. The purpose of this court was to bring about uniformity among the decisions of the lower appellate courts throughout France, thereby obviously empowering it to make "judicial" law. As was apparent with the French decisions reviewed in an earlier chapter, and as will be apparent with the German, French, Mexican and United States decisions discussed hereafter, source of law provisions in the respective codes notwithstanding, court decisions are among the most significant sources of commercial contract law.

C. Doctrinal Law

1. In General

Often the French and German civil and commercial code provisions were drafted in a manner that was either so general or so technical that major gaps soon appeared between the disputed facts and the code provisions under which they were to be subsumed. Court decisions could have been helpful in bridging those gaps, but they were generally unreported and thus widely unavailable. As a result, many of the legislative gaps were and continue to be filled by doctrinal writings, even when applicable decisions are available.

The best of doctrinal writings, including treatises and monographs, annotations to codes or statutory enactments, and commentaries on important court decisions, discuss cases and factual situations. The effect upon the interpretation of commercial contract law by doctrinal writers in France, Germany, Spain and especially in Latin America cannot be overemphasized. As was discussed earlier in connection the Costa Rican case *Picado Guerrero v. Rojas Dias* (which discussed the commission agency versus brokerage characterization of an act of commerce),[20] the doctrinal definition of both a commission agency and a brokerage contract became the law in Costa Rica concerning an intermediary's liability for third party fraud. The Costa Rican Supreme Court, then, decided this landmark dispute based upon the meaning of the term "commission agent" (*comisionista*) as provided by Mexican doctrinal commentators, which reflected the Mexican market practice but not the Costa Rican, and these two meanings were not necessarily consistent. Thus, a doctrinal description of a commercial practice elsewhere

---

[19] MARTIJN WILLEM HESSELINK, THE POLITICS OF A EUROPEAN CIVIL CODE 116 (2006).

[20] *See supra* § 10:2(B)(5)(b).

wound up trumping the meaning of the practice relied upon by the local contracting parties.

This case dramatized a major shortcoming of doctrine as a source of commercial contract law: It is helpful as long as it takes into account the peculiarities of the marketplace to which it is supposed to apply. When its data comes from another different marketplace (or from no marketplace at all, but from formally-logical deductions or inferences derived from other doctrinal writings), it is of little, if not harmful, significance.

2. *Two Influential but Opposite Approaches to Commercial Law by German Doctrinal Writers: Heinrich Thöl and Levin Goldschmidt*

Unlike what happened with the BGB, the HGB was not the subject of serious academic debates or ideological battles. This is surprising because by the time of its enactment in 1897, two sharply different approaches to the "science of commercial law" lurked in the background. The earlier approach pre-dated the HGB and belonged to Professor Heinrich Thöl. A competing approach surfaced during the last quarter of the nineteenth century. Its proponent was Professor Levin Goldschmidt, about whom Professor Yntema had spoken so glowingly to me while I was a graduate student at the University of Michigan. Professor Alfredo Rocco, an early-twentieth-century Italian commercial law professor,[21] and eventually Italy's Minister of Justice at the advent of fascism, was an unqualified admirer of the Pandectist method of "legal science" and most impressed with what Professor Thöl had been able to extract from Roman law. In Rocco's words:

> [F]rom the fragmentary, incidental, and brief expositions that preceded his own . . . the formation of an organized body of doctrine such as is contained in his celebrated treatise on commercial law ("*Das Handelsrecht*"), the first volume of which dated from 1841. . . . [This treatise] can be explained only in the light of the notable development to which German science had brought the study of the history and system of the Pandects. Thöl, in fact, *created German commercial law almost from nothing*, founding it upon an essentially Roman basis. With profound and rigorous logic he succeeded in extracting from that body of legal doctrine, more than a thousand years old, the principal institutions to govern the latest expressions of commercial activity.[22]

a. *Thöl's and Rocco's vs. Goldschmidt's and Vivante's Conceptions of Commercial Legal Science*

I must confess that I was taken aback by Professor Rocco's description of what Professor Thöl had "created." Really, can anyone, no matter how intelligent, create an entire body of law, especially a law as indebted to the goings-on in the marketplace as commercial law, "almost from nothing"? No need to take into account customs, usages, compilations of practices, or experiences with better or poorer practices? All that was required was apparently a "profound and rigorous logic" and a thorough knowledge of a two thousand-year-old law, a law that, as discussed in earlier chapters, was reluctant

---

[21] *See* Alfredo Rocco, *The Commercial Codes*, *in* XI THE CONTINENTAL LEGAL HISTORY SERIES, THE PROGRESS OF CONTINENTAL LAW IN THE NINETEENTH CENTURY 332–43 (1918).

[22] *Id.* at 335 (emphasis added).

to enforce untypified but characteristically commercial contracts and executory promises?

Not surprisingly, Goldschmidt criticized Thöl for failing to explain the commercial and economic origins and purposes or functions of legal institutions, as opposed to their possible analogies with Roman legal institutions. At the time of this critique, he was a young lecturer at the University of Heidelberg and was already considered one of the chief opponents of the Pandectist (which he often referred to as "dogmatic") research methodology.[23]

Goldschmidt was born in Danzig on May 30, 1829, and died in Wilhelmshöhe on July 16, 1897. During a mostly academic career, he wrote important monographs on various commercial law topics. The one with the most lasting impact was *The Universal History of Commercial Law* (*Universalgeschichte des Handelsrecht*), first published in 1864 and frequently cited in earlier chapters.[24] This book influenced some of the most prominent commercial law scholars of the twentieth century, particularly outside of Germany, including Karl Llewellyn, a leading United States commercial law scholar and a principal drafter and advocate of the Uniform Commercial Code of the United States (U.C.C.) and also a co-author with E. Adamson Hoebel of *The Cheyenne Way: Conflict and Case Law in Primitive Jurisprudence*, a pioneering legal anthropological study.[25]

Goldschmidt's *Universalgeschichte* also helped shape the research methodology of many promising European commercial law scholars, including Italy's Cesare Vivante, about whom more will be discussed shortly. Goldschmidt's influence on social science oriented scholars such as Llewellyn and Vivante should not be surprising considering that Goldschmidt was also a teacher and director of Max Weber's Ph.D. thesis on medieval partnerships.[26]

Goldschmidt's teachings could have had a salutary effect upon the development of a commercial law that would have been consistent with the normative needs of developing countries, especially Latin America. I say "especially Latin America" because several generations of Latin American commercial law scholars were educated in Italy where Cesare Vivante, one of Goldschmidt's best disciples, had started a Goldschmidt-oriented research movement. Unfortunately, Italy's turn towards fascism in the 1920s prevented the development of what could have been an empirical commercial legal science for Italy as well as for Latin America.

Cesare Vivante was Italy's preeminent commercial law scholar during the late-nineteenth and early-twentieth centuries. He was born in Venice in 1855 and died in Siena in 1944. His multi-volume *Treaty of Commercial Law* (*Trattato di Diritto Commerciale*), published in 1893 and subsequently in widely read editions (among numerous other publications in fields as diverse as insurance and bill of lading law),[27] evidenced a keen observation of market practices and of the factual background of the

---

[23] *Id.* at 336–37.

[24] *See supra* § 9:1(A).

[25] KARL N. LLEWELLYN & E. ADAMSON HOEBEL, THE CHEYENNE WAY: CONFLICT AND CASE LAW IN PRIMITIVE JURISPRUDENCE (1967).

[26] MAX WEBER, THE PROTESTANT ETHIC AND THE SPIRIT OF CAPITALISM (Talcott Parsons trans., 2003) (1905).

[27] *See generally* CESARE VIVANTE, TRATTATO DI DIRITTO COMMERCIALE (1893).

cases he discussed. Appropriately, he dedicated his *Trattato* to Levin Goldschmidt who, according to Vivante: "Taught me, in exemplary fashion, to search in the intimacy of history for [the components of] the system of the law in force."[28]

As I pointed out earlier, Goldschmidt's "search in the intimacy of history" was not for Pandectist concepts, but for the purposes and functions of legal institutions; their "spirit," in von Ihering's immortal words. Like Goldschmidt, Vivante had the ability to identify the socio-economic consequences of proposed norms, whether judicial or statutory. In his introduction to the fifth edition of his *Trattato*, he refers to his proposal of a unified private law (commercial and civil) code and while contrasting it with the methodology peculiar to civil code drafting, he comments on what *should be the method* of commercial code drafting: "In drafting commercial codes, the empirical method sometimes prevails in the study of technical data [of everyday commerce]. . . . In compiling [this data for future normative use] the spirit of observation and induction is preponderant. . . ."[29]

With these skills and research interests, he was able to build a conceptual and analytical structure that could have refocused Italy's private law agenda in a manner that was both flexible and responsive to the needs of the marketplace. While referring to the role of custom and usage in his proposed unified code, and in a manner highly reminiscent of Goldschmidt's description of law-making in medieval fairs, he stated:

> This innovation would consist of extending the creative force of custom and usage, now restricted in civil codes to the law of contracts, to the entire law of obligations. . . . As a result of it, and without violating the legislative system, because custom cannot derogate statutory law, new influences could potentially break through, [influences] that are presently rejected by civil law . . . which ascribes to tradition a hostile and restraining force against new social functions [for existing or new legal institutions]. [Thus, custom and] usage could emerge freely as legal norms, not only from stock and commodity exchanges, port cities, and banks but also from agriculture [and its manifold transactions]. . . .[30]

b. *Thöl's and Rocco's Views on the Sources of Commercial Law and Their Influence*

Rocco defended Thöl against Goldschmidt's (and implicitly) Vivante's criticisms by asserting that commerce and economics should be left to their respective practitioners. The task of commercial legal scholars, he said, was to build what he and Thöl referred to as the science of commercial law:

> [S]o solid a body of legal doctrine that it was able, until the promulgation of the general German Commercial Code, almost to take the place of law. And upon that codification, for which Thöl's work was in the nature of a preparation . . . [and in which he] exercised a decisive influence.[31]

---

[28] CESAR VIVANTE, I TRATTADO DE DERECHO MERCANTIL dedication page (Cesar Silió Belena trans. 1932) (author's translation).

[29] *Id.* at 16.

[30] *Id.* at 41.

[31] Rocco, *supra* note 21, at 336.

Rocco did not provide a single instance where Thöl's ideas prevailed in the drafting of the HGB. In contrast with his praise for Thöl, according to Rocco:

> Goldschmidt . . . believed in a law derived from the inherent "nature of things" and their relation, alike in all times and all places; hence, for him, the necessity of constant recourse to the "nature of things", which, like all other followers of the historical school, he believed to be the absolute source of law. Every positive law, he said, is the eternal expression and the recognition of those natural norms of law which are permanent and are proper to the relationships of the life of all time. And thus, while Thöl may be placed among the precursors of legal positivism, Goldschmidt (as, indeed, various others of the historical school) must be considered in substance as a late fruit of the school of natural law.[32]

Rocco's summary of Levin Goldschmidt's views left out a critical word and in doing so distorted Goldschmidt's teachings. When he referred to Goldschmidt's belief in the "inherent nature of things" he left out the word "commercial" as the last word of that clause. This omission made Goldschmidt sound like a metaphysician or dreamer instead of one of the most careful students of the development of commercial law, its transactions and socio-economic context from pre-Roman times through its European codification.[33] Whoever reads Goldschmidt's *Universalgeschichte* cannot help but admire his descriptions of commerce and applicable law during each period, the prevailing value systems, and the manner in which merchants resolved their disputes subject to a dynamically changing legal structure.

Goldschmidt's finding that viable marketplaces usually reflect the merchants' predilection for informality of dealing, and for honesty, good faith and archetypal (*bonus vir*) behavior was not a metaphysical concoction; it was an empirically verifiable reality. Of equal importance was his suggestion that concepts such as commercial honesty, good faith, *bonus vir* behavior, and fair dealing have greater legitimacy and lasting power than a positive law that often contradicts them. If there was any doubt about the validity of this inference, one need only correlate the presence of these quintessentially commercial duties and presumptions (reflected in the Roman Digest as well as in Germany's own BGB and HGB) with the economic development of the countries where they were and are practiced.

---

[32] *Id.* at 337.

[33] William Twining makes a similar point with respect to one of Karl Llewellyn's repeated expressions: "situation-sense," which Llewellyn derived from his reading of Levin Goldschimdt's following passage:

> Every fact-pattern of common life, so far as the legal order can take it in, carries within itself its appropriate, natural rules, its right law. This is a natural law which is real, not imaginary; it is not a creature of mere reason, but rests on the solid foundation of what reason can recognize in the nature of man and of the life conditions of time and place: it is thus not eternal nor changeless nor everywhere the same, but is in-dwelling in the very circumstances of life. The highest task of law-giving consists in uncovering and implementing this immanent law.

WILLIAM TWINING, KARL LLEWELLYN AND THE REALIST MOVEMENT 217 (1973) (citations omitted). As insightfully pointed out by William Twining:

> It is significant that both Goldschmidt and Llewellyn were specialists in commercial law and that the context of the quotation from Goldschmidt is a discussion of commercial law. . . . There are few branches of the law which concern directly such a close-knit community with such a wide range of agreement as to what is 'right', 'fair' or 'reasonable.'

Id. at 224–25 (citations omitted).

Rocco's attempt to transform Goldschmidt into a metaphysician was consistent with his own preference for an "objective" commercial law which, in the final analysis, was authoritarian and the product of what John Austin, the English legal positivist, referred to as nothing more than "the command of the sovereign."[34] Indeed, when it was time for Alfredo Rocco to write his own treatise, *Principles of Commercial Law*,[35] he echoed Thöl's and Austin's positivism. In response to the question "What are the sources of commercial law?", he did not hesitate to answer: "Civil law is not a source of commercial law. . . . 'Commercial law' [positive or enacted statutory law] is the only source. . . . Neither are case law, equity, the nature of things and the general principles of the law, or foreign law."[36]

According to Rocco, the only sources worth taking into account were the law that emanates from the state and its appropriate agencies and the custom of the community as tacitly agreed upon by its effective observance. Yet, a custom and usage unsanctioned by the state as law was not a true and proper source of commercial law and once sanctioned, it became law and ceased to be custom.[37]

On case law as a source, his conclusion was equally positivistic and negative:

> Case law, *i.e.*, the theoretical and practical work of the jurists is not a source of law, even though it is a necessary and an excellent tool to *learn about the law*; because this work does not have as an object the creation of law but to study, interpret and apply existing law. . . .[38]

He rejected equity because it was only the result of applying the general norm to the individual case and thus it was so connected with the facts and circumstances of each case that it was not capable of generalization and becoming a generally-observed law.[39] While none of these objections rose above the level of crass sophistry (such as the distinction between case law as an educational as opposed to a creative tool or the impossibility to infer a general rule from individual equitable rulings, and so on), they were said to be warranted by a legal science grounded in the *Pandektenrecht*.[40]

Thöl's and Rocco's rejection of the empirical sources that Levin Goldschmidt and Cesare Vivante found essential for the development of a commercial law (such as commercial custom, case law and equity) had a direct effect on the commercial law of an Italy about to become a fascist state. The Italian Civil Code of 1942 "unified" civil and commercial law and subsumed them under the concept of a state-encouraged enterprise (*impresa*) which watched over (and when necessary imposed) a harmonious cooperation between capital and labor. As discussed in an earlier chapter,[41] this concept of enterprise was soon adopted by admiring Spanish and Latin American academicians. Its vacuous nature has become apparent in its undisturbed presence

---

[34] John Austin was one of the leading nineteenth-century English legal philosophers, and exponent of the doctrine of legal positivism. His definition of the law as a command of the sovereign can be found in his *The Province of Jurisprudence Determined* (1832), and *Lectures on Jurisprudence* (1863).

[35] ALFREDO ROCCO, PRINCIPIOS DE DERECHO MERCANTIL: PARTE GENERAL (Revista de Derecho Privado trans., 1952).

[36] *Id.* at 101 (author's translation).

[37] *Id.* at 104.

[38] *Id.* at 105 (author's translation).

[39] *Id.*

[40] *Id.* at 105–06.

[41] *See infra* § 14:5.

among legal regimes that adhere to fascist and capitalist ideologies alike. Moreover, sixty years after its adoption by the commercial codes of developing nations such as Honduras, its corporate or commercial reality has not changed. To this day, Honduras still has yet to witness the emergence of even one Mussolini-like *impresa*.

A similar attitude among doctrinal writers in Latin American jurisdictions is responsible for the minimal role of customary law as a living law source of commercial contract law. In the case of the Mexican Commercial Code of 1895, with the exception of its reference to the civil code as a subsidiary source, its list of sources could have been drafted by Heinrich Thöl. The only sources applicable to commercial contract law disputes in that code were the codified or statutory commercial and civil laws.[42]

Approximately fifty years later, the Honduran Commercial Code of 1950 seems to have realized the sterility of a commercial law devoid of customary rules and listed customs and usages as binding sources of commercial law.[43] Yet, the sterility of Thöl's and Rocco's approach to commercial legal scholarship and decision-making continued to rule in Honduras from its Pandectist grave. According to the Honduran congressional committee that set forth the reasons for the adoption of this code, it was modern and scientific as a result of its rejection of "empirical and arbitrary doctrines."[44] Clearly, these legislators and their academic advisers continued to equate empiricism with arbitrariness.

c. *Goldschmidt's Influence upon Karl Llewellyn*

Despite the failure of Cesare Vivante's efforts to revitalize Italian and Latin American commercial legal scholarship and lawmaking, Levin Goldchmidt's teachings had a major influence upon one of the key drafters of the U.C.C. In 1960, as a graduate student at the University of Michigan, I visited Professor Llewellyn in his library office at the University of Chicago School of Law. I told him that Professor Yntema had made me aware of his admiration for Levin Goldschmidt's work and I asked him what he liked about Goldschmidt and why. The following is a paraphrased summary of my notes on Llewellyn's assessment of Goldschmidt's contribution to his vision of commercial law, its sources and its normative limits:

> He [Goldschmidt] was the most learned scholar on the history of commercial law that I have encountered. He compressed large volumes of historical and transactional information into capsules of wisdom. One of these had to do with commercial lawmaking. Certainly, its purpose was not to teach merchants how to conduct their everyday business. Once the lawmaker becomes aware of how such a business is conducted, he should assume the merchants' skill, decency, good faith, and willingness to emulate the behavior of respected peers. Most merchants do that and this is because they are inherently decent and also because they are not dummies and know that it is

---

[42] COD. COM.(MEX.) art. 2 (2008). Art. 2 states: "In the absence of the rules provided by this code and other commercial statutes, the acts of commerce shall be governed by the provisions of ordinary law found in the Civil Code on Federal matters." *Id.*

[43] COD.COM (HOND.) art. 1 (1950). Art. 1 states: "Merchants, acts of commerce, and commercial paper shall be governed by this code and other commercial laws, and in their absence by commercial custom and usage and, in their absence, by the Civil Code." *Id.*

[44] Dictamen Presentado sobre el Proyecto de Código de Comercio por la Comisión Especial de Legislación del Soberano Congreso Nacional (Tegucigalpa, 1949). *See also* CÓDIGO DE COMERCIO 102 (TALLERES ARISTON 1950).

in their own best interest to act honestly and decently. If they are dumb enough not to act that way, some may get away with it, but most will not and will not last long in business. As a commercial legislator or adjudicator, then, you need not spend much time writing detailed rules on how the good guys should conduct their business. You should spend your time as a legislator "roping off" the bad guys. These are the ones who act dishonestly and in bad faith, who take advantage of their clients' innocence or of their colleagues' mistakes or of the gaps or ambiguities in the law[45]

Years later, while reading William Twining's intellectual biography of Karl Llewellyn,[46] my attention was drawn to Llewellyn's writings in which he expressed admiration for the same Goldschmidt view that Rocco had rejected as contrary to a commercial law that in Rocco's world came from and was commanded by the sovereign and no one else.[47] Twining also provided materials that confirmed my above observation that Rocco had left out the critical contextual reference to things commercial when referring to Goldschmidt's "nature of things." The Goldschmidt passage that Llewellyn admired and Rocco criticized stated:

> Every problem situation of ordinary life . . . carries within itself its fitting right rule of natural law, its *jus aequum*. Thus, there is a true natural law immanent in the conditions; it is not imaginary, it is not created out of empty reason, but it rests upon the real foundation of the nature of man . . . so that it is of course not eternal and unchangeable and everywhere the same. The highest task of law-making rests in the discovery and implementation of this immanent right law. In this sense what we know as sources of law are never truly creative but on the contrary . . . only tools for discovery. . . . I have therefore striven to find in commercial relations and in the needs of commerce a source for recognition of the law actually in force.[48]

As insightfully noted by William Twining:

> It is significant that both Goldschmidt and Llewellyn were specialists in commercial law and that the context of the quotation from Goldschmidt is a discussion of commercial law. . . . There are few branches of law which concern directly such a close-knit community with such a wide range of agreement as to what is 'right,' 'fair' or 'reasonable'. It is [thus] possible to infer that in Llewellyn's view, a 'sound' decision uncovering the 'immanent' law would be one in which the judge has sufficient experience and understanding of the usages and ethics of the particular trade. . . .[49]

d. Conclusions: Goldschmidt's Suggestions and My Findings

Although unaware of the existence of the above Goldschmidt passage (until I read Twining's book), my comparative commercial legal research pointed to very similar

---

[45] Interview with Karl Llewellyn & Soia Mentschikoff, Former Professors at Univ. of Chi., in Chi., Ill. (Nov. 12, 1960).

[46] TWINING, *supra* note 33.

[47] *Id.* at 217, 224–26, 447 (providing admiring references by Karl Llewellyn to the views of Levin Goldschmidt).

[48] *Id.* at 449 n.91.

[49] *Id.* at 224–25 (citations omitted).

conclusions. In my comparison of Anglo-American and Latin American commercial adjudication, it had become clear that adjudicators were driven by different standards of fairness and that these standards differed depending upon the commercial or non-commercial nature of a society and in the case of the latter, its degree of commercialization.[50]

A society was commercial in the sense that its marketplace(s) enabled the manufacture, distribution and consumption of goods and services to the widest possible number of participants. It was also commercial to the degree that it made possible the widest access to commercial and consumer credit. Thus, in a highly commercialized society, consumers, retailers, wholesalers, manufacturers, and their respective credit providers would have access to their respective credit facilities in a "pyramidal" fashion, with consumers at the bottom and a central bank or a secondary market at the top.

In such a society, the prevailing standard was one in which each party to a contract or commercial or credit transaction owed to the other what I labeled a "market standard of fairness."[51] According to this standard, the counter party, even if he was a total stranger or third party, deserved to be treated as if he were a regular and known participant in that marketplace and was entitled to the protection of his reasonable contractual or transactional expectations.

Occasionally, where one party lacked the bargaining power, contractual skill or capacity of the other party and fully entrusted that other party with his money, goods or services, such an entrustment generated a reasonable expectation of a "brotherly" standard of fairness.[52] This standard imposed contractual duties upon the entrusted party above those of the marketplace standard. In Justice Benjamin Cardozo's words, it required the "punctilio of an honor the most sensitive,"[53] and if the entrusted party had to reduce or give up his profits in order to fulfill the expectations of the trusting party, regardless of the fact that such a behavior was not that of regular participants in the marketplace, so be it.

Conversely, in agricultural survival societies that lacked such developed marketplaces, the prevailing standard with respect to members of other tribes or clans was that of the stranger.[54] This stranger was not owed the duty of enabling the fulfillment of his reasonable expectations, even where his counterparty received all the benefits flowing from the transaction and he received none. Thus, in this type of society, only members of one's own family, clan or tribe are entitled to a marketplace or a brotherly standard of fairness.[55]

The reason I said that my findings were similar to but not the same as Goldschmidt's is because I found the above-described standards of fairness invariably present in the above-described types of society, regardless of time or location. I also

---

[50] *See generally* Kozolchyk, *Fairness.*

[51] *Id.* at 219–20. *See also* Kozolchyk, *Commercialization,* at 17–20.

[52] Kozolchyk, *Fairness,* at 219–20.

[53] In re James' Estate, 86 N.Y.S.2d 78, 89–90 (1948); Meinhard v. Salmon, 249 N.Y. 458, 464 (1928).

[54] Kozolchyk, *Fairness,* at 220, 257.

[55] *Id.* at 257–58.

believe that Karl Llewellyn's constant reliance on the term "reasonable"[56] in Article 2 of the U.C.C. reflects the need to fit disputed facts in commercial controversies under the practices of respected good faith merchants, thereby applying Goldschmidt's *jus aequum*.

Significantly, this method of doing private law justice is clearly traceable at least to Roman and Jewish law. Berger's *Encyclopedic Dictionary of Roman Law* defines the *iustitia aequum* alluded to by Goldschmidt (when referring to the *jus aequum*) in a manner totally consistent with Goldschmidt's:

> Related to justice . . . but distinguished from the positive law. . . . One of the fundamental principles which direct or should direct the development of law; it is the corrective and creative element in such development. A law which is guided by *aequitas* is *ius aequum*, its antonym is *ius iniquum* [or a law of iniquity].[57]

Finally, I believe that the process of "fitting" the law to the facts of each case is precisely what Llewellyn had in mind when he used the obscure term "situation-sense."[58] The consequences of the Goldschmidt-Vivante-Llewellyn and the Thöl-Rocco approaches to the sources of commercial law and commercial legal scholarship and lawmaking are very much with us and will become apparent in the following chapters and as was discussed in Chapter 1, Goldschmidt's and LLeweellyn's intuition has now been confirmed by socio-biological sciences.

D. Commercial Treaties as Sources: Their Hierarchy

Generally, constitutional democracies, whether of the civil or common law variety, set forth the hierarchy of their sources of law applicable to commercial contract disputes in their constitutions, codes or statutory law. As a rule, the constitution occupies the top layer of the hierarchy, although the application of sources below the constitutional level is not always easily determinable. The ranking of these sources often revolves around the federal or unitary nature of the nation and if it is federal, upon the federal or state nature of the case or legislative subject matter; this is true for countries with legal systems as diverse as those of Germany, France, and Mexico on the civil law side and the United States on the common law side.

In addition to the unitary or federal nature of the country in question, the determination of the hierarchy of the various sources also depends upon their ranking by constitutional, statutory and decisional law.

1. Germany

In Germany, the Federal Constitution or Basic Law (*Grundgesetz fur die Bundesrepublik Deutschland*) (hereinafter G.G.), creates both exclusive and concurrent

---

[56] The term "reasonable" appears more than a dozen times in U.C.C. Article 2; it is also omnipresent in the United Nations Convention for the International Sale of Goods (CISG) (1980), which was largely inspired by U.C.C. Article 2, as well as in the UNIDROIT Principles of International Commercial Contracts (2004).

[57] BERGER, ENCYCLOPEDIC DICTIONARY, at 354. *See* H.H Cohn, *Ancient Jewish Equity*, *in* EQUITY IN THE WORLD'S LEGAL SYSTEMS: A COMPARATIVE LEGAL STUDY 45–73 (Ralph Newman ed., 1973) (discussing the role of equitable adjudication in Jewish law).

[58] *See* TWINING, *supra* note 33, at 219–26 (discussing the meaning of this term).

lawmaking jurisdictions.[59] Both the German federation and the states have concurrent powers to legislate on economic and commercial matters,[60] while the public law aspects of trade belong exclusively to the federation, which also has the power to preempt inconsistent lawmaking by the states.[61]

The listing of the sources of commercial contract law and directives on their hierarchy are found throughout the entire HGB. The present Book Four of the HGB is devoted to commercial transactions and its Section 346 instructs code interpreters as follows: "The cutsoms and usages which obtain in commerce shall be taken into consideration among merchants in respect of the meaning and effect of acts and omissions."[62] In addition, the HGB often refers to the BGB either as a primary or subsidiary source of commercial contractual and extra-contractual liability.[63]

Like other European Union countries, Germany is an active participant in commercial treaty making. The power to enter into treaties in Germany belongs to the federal executive branch and ultimately to the President of the German Federal Republic.[64] Treaties negotiated by the executive branch have to be enacted as a legislative act or statute to be binding.[65] Hence, the hierarchy of treaties, enacted in the form of statutes, is the same as that of any other statute; they can abrogate earlier inconsistent statutes or be derogated by subsequent inconsistent statutes.

Mr. Alexander Mayer, a German attorney and LL.M. graduate of the University of Arizona James E. Rogers College of Law provides an important warning concerning Article 25 of the G.G., which states:

Article 25 [Primacy of international law]

---

[59] GRUNDGESETZ FÜR DIE BUNDESREPUBLIK DEUTSCHLAND [GRUNDGESETZ] [GG] [BASIC LAW], May 23, 1949, BGBL. I (Ger.) (Germany's present Constitution), *available at* https://www.btg-bestellservice.de/pdf/80201000.pdf [hereinafter G.G.]. Article 70 states:

> [Division of powers between the Federation and the *Länder*] (1) The *Länder* shall have the right to legislate insofar as this Basic Law does not confer legislative power on the Federation. (2) The division of authority between the Federation and the *Länder* shall be governed by the provisions of this Basic Law concerning exclusive and concurrent legislative powers.

Id. art. 70. I am indebted to Mr. Alexander Mayer, LL.M. 2009 graduate at the James E. Rogers College of Law, University of Arizona, for helping to update the laws on the sources of normative hierarchy in German law.

[60] *See id.* art. 74(11) (which lists as a concurrent power the legislation on "economic matters (mining, industry, energy, crafts, trades, commerce, banking, stock exchanges and private insurance). . . .").

[61] *See id.* art. 71 ("[Exclusive legislative power of the Federation] On matters within the exclusive legislative power of the Federation, the *Länder* shall have power to legislate only when and to the extent that they are expressly authorised [sic] to do so by a federal law.").

[62] HGB § 346 (GOREN, 1998).

[63] *See, e.g., id.* § 347 (on standards of care applicable to commercial contracts pursuant to the BGB).

[64] G.G. art. 59:

[Representation of the Federation for the purposes of international law]

> (1) The Federal President shall represent the Federation for the purposes of international law. He shall conclude treaties with foreign states on behalf of the Federation. He shall accredit and receive envoys.
>
> (2) Treaties that regulate the political relations of the Federation or relate to subjects of federal legislation shall require the consent or participation, in the form of a federal law, of the bodies responsible in such a case for the enactment of federal law. In the case of executive agreements the provisions concerning the federal administration shall apply mutatis mutandis.

[65] *Id.*

The general rules of international law shall be an integral part of federal law. They shall take precedence over the laws and directly create rights and duties for the inhabitants of the federal territory.[66]

According to Mr. Mayer, what Article 25 refers to as "the general rules of international law" are not treaties entered into by Germany, but what some public international lawyers describe as the *general principles of public international law*.[67]

2. *France*

As became apparent during the discussion of the acts of commerce listed in the *Code de Commerce*, from a strictly legislative standpoint, the *Code Civil* remains as the most important subsidiary source of France's commercial contract law.[68] Nevertheless, mostly by court action and with the support of insightful doctrinal commentators, some commercial customs and usages have emerged as important sources of commercial contract and "mercantile specialty" law.[69] The *Cour de Cassation* rested the legitimacy of these customs and usages upon the principle of party autonomy in Article 1134 of the *Code Civil*: "Agreements legally formed have the force of law between the parties. . . ."[70]

Accordingly, as noted by Dean Jean Stoufflet, French courts apply trade usages (*usages professionels*) to establish the parties' rights and duties to commercial letters of credit, among other commercial transactions.[71] Moreover, the *Cour de Cassation* not only routinely accepts appeals from lower court decisions when these decisions have misinterpreted a customary law source such as the Uniform Customs and Practices for Documentary Credits (UCP),[72] but also rely on the opinions of the Banking Commission of the International Chamber of Commerce (the entity responsible for drafting the UCP) as persuasive sources of law.[73]

---

[66] *Id.* art. 25.

[67] According to Mr. Mayer, it is generally accepted by courts and commentators that the *general* rules of international law are the public international customary laws. *See* Statute of the International Court of Justice art. 38 ¶ 1(b)–(c) (Apr. 18 1946), *available at* http://www.icj-cij.org/documents/index.php?p1=4&p2=2&p3=0; *see also* 23 ENTSCHEIDUNGEN DES BUNDEVERFASSUNGSGERICHTS [BVERFGE] [Federal Constitutional Court] 288 § 317 (Ger.); *Ondalf Rojahn, in* INGO VON MÜNCH & PHILIP KUNIG, 2 GRUNDGESETZ-KOMMENTAR [Commentary on the German Constitution] art. 25 Rn.6 (3d ed. 1995).

[68] *See supra* § 10:9(C).

[69] *See* Glossary, "Mercantile Specialty."

[70] C. CIV. (FR.) art. 1134 (2008). Unless otherwise indicated, all the English translations of the *Code Civil* provisions belong to Legifrance (*see* Frequently Cited).

[71] Cour de cassation com., June 10, 1986, Bull. civ. IV, No. 55, note J. Stoufflet (Fr.); Cour de cassation com., Oct. 7, 1987, Bull. civ. IV, No. 861, note J. Stoufflet (Fr.); Cour de cassation 1e civ., (n.d.), Bull. civ. I, No. 86–13.006, note. J. Stoufflet (Fr.).

[72] As far as I have been able to determine, one of the earliest decisions by the *Cour de Cassation* granting the U.C.P. the status of a binding source of law whose misinterpretation is grounds for an appeal is the decision in Discount Bank C. Teboul., *Cass. Commerciale* (Oct. 14, 1851), according to J. Pierre Mattout, a distinguished French banking lawyer and scholar, "this decision is considered by doctrine as an acceptance without reservations by the *Cour de Cassation* of the application of the UCP in France, and of the necessity of lower courts to conform strictly to the Court's interpretation of the UCP lest they find their decisions reversed." See summary by Mattout, *in* INT'L CHAMBER OF COMMERCE, UCP 400 470/37 Int. 6 (1990).

[73] *See, e.g.*, Cour de cassation [Cass] com., July 15, 1992, unpublished, Pourvoi No. 90–18.530 (relying on "an opinion . . . of the Commission which grants the beneficiary the right to demand the return of the documents as long as he has not received payment and to add the modifications and substitutions in view of a second presentation of documents" ("*un parere . . . de la commission bancaire de la chambre de commerce internationale selon lequelle le bénéficiaire est en droit d'exiger la restitution des documents tant qu'il n'a pas*

Where commercial treaties are concerned, Article 55 of the French Constitution was quite direct in its directive on hierarchy: "Treaties or agreements duly ratified or approved shall, upon publication, prevail over Acts of Parliament, subject, with respect to each agreement or treaty, to its application by the other party."[74]

Despite Article 55, however, the coexistence of treaties and municipal statutory law before French tribunals has proved less harmonious than expected. France's *Conseil d'Etat*, its highest administrative tribunal, has had to develop its own theory of "*loi-écran*," according to which the provisions of a subsequent law will prevail over those of an older treaty.[75] Yet, as pointed out by Mr. Hanna Chalhoub, a Lebanese lawyer and graduate of the LL.M. program at the University of Arizona James E. Rogers College of Law, the same court abandoned this theory in 1989 and accepted the absolute supremacy of the treaties, even over subsequent laws.[76] Mr. Chalhoub also notes that France's *Cour de Cassation* had adopted the doctrine of treaty supremacy over municipal law since 1975,[77] except for the "constitutional laws," which are treated as the constitution itself.[78]

3. Mexico

As a federal state, Mexico, as well as Germany and the United States, vests concurrent lawmaking powers in the federal and state congresses.[79] Article 73(X) of the Mexican Constitution of 1917 empowered the Federal Congress to legislate in commercial matters.[80] Thus, Mexico's Commercial Code of 1889 determines the hierarchy of its sources of commercial contract law and does so in the most restrictive of fashions. According to its Article 2, the applicable sources are only "the rules

---

reçu son paiement et peut y apporter toutes modifications et subsitutions en vue d'une seconde présentation dans les délais. . . .")), *available at* http://legimobile.fr/fr/jp/j/c/civ/com/1992/7/15/90–18530/.

[74] 1958 CONST. art. 55 (FR.), *available at* http://www.assemblee-nationale.fr/english/8ab.asp#TITLE%20VI. I am indebted to Mr. Hanna Chalhoub, LL.M. 2008–09 Graduate at the University of Arizona James E. Rogers College of Law, for updated information on the hierarchy of sources of law in Lebanon and France.

[75] *See* Conseil d'État decision [CE] [highest administrative court] Mar. 1, 1968, No. 62814 (Fr.), *available at* http://www.legifrance.gouv.fr/affichJuriAdmin.do?oldAction=rechJuriAdmin&idTexte=CETATEXT000007633957&fastReqId=656405809&fastPos=1.

[76] *See* Conseil d'État [CE] [highest administrative court] Oct. 30, 1998, No. 200286 200287 (Fr.), *available at* http://www.legifrance.gouv.fr/affichJuriAdmin.do?oldAction=rechJuriAdmin&idTexte=CETATEXT000008008495&fastReqId=739589782&fastPos=1.

[77] *See* Cour de Cassation [Cass.] ch. mixte, May 24, 1975, No. 73–13556 (Fr.), *available at* http://www.legifrance.gouv.fr/affichJuriJudi.do?oldAction=rechJuriJudi&idTexte=JURITEXT000006994625&fastReqId=1089903335&fastPos=1.

[78] *See No. 200286 200287, supra* note 76.

[79] Constitución Política de los Estados Unidos Mexicanos [C.P.], *as amended*, art. 40, Diario Oficial de la Federación [DO], 5 de Febrero de 1917 (Mex.) [hereinafter MEX. CONST. (1917)], *available at* http://www.oas.org/juridico/mla/en/mex/en_mex-int-text-const.pdf ("It is the will of the Mexican people to organize themselves into a federal democratic, representative Republic composed of free and sovereign States in all that concerns their internal government; but united in a Federation established according to the principles of this fundamental law."). Article 71 states in part: "The right to introduce laws or decrees belongs: I. To the President of the Republic; II. To the deputies and senators of the Congress; III. To the legislatures of the States. . . ." MEX. CONST. art. 71 (1917).

[80] In accordance with Article 73(X), the Federal Congress is empowered: "To legislate throughout the Republic on hydrocarbons, mining, the motion picture industry, commerce, games of chance and lotteries, credit institutions, and, electric power, to establish a single bank of issue under the provision of Article 28 of the Constitution and to enact labor laws regulating Article 123 of this Constitution." MEX. CONST. art. 73(X) (1917).

provided by this code and other commercial statutes . . . [and] the provisions in the Civil Code on Federal Matters."[81]

Nonetheless, as has been true for centuries in Mexico and elsewhere, treaties that deal with commercial matters are sources of commercial contract law. And as with Germany and the United States, the President of Mexico is empowered to negotiate treaties with foreign nations subject to ratification by the Mexican Senate.[82] This power has become increasingly important for a nation that has entered into dozens of commercial treaties with other nations. The importance of this source of law for the adjudication of disputes in Mexico has been underscored by the Mexican Supreme Court's express adherence to the French approach of treaty supremacy over statutory law, a doctrine followed by its lower courts.[83]

4. *The United States*

As with other federal nations, the United States' federal and state congresses are empowered to enact laws within their sphere of competence as part of a compromise that continues to be, in the colloquial, a "work in progress." Thus, while the United States Constitution states that "No State shall enter into any Treaty, Alliance, or Confederation,"[84] it also states that "The Powers not delegated to the United States by the Constitution, nor prohibited by it to the States, are reserved to the States respectively, or to the people."[85]

Commercial contract law, when faced with intra-state transactions, is part of the laws of individual states. Despite the considerable degree of uniformity among these laws, the U.C.C. is still an individual state's law and as such, subject to frequent "non-conforming" amendments.[86] In addition, the sources of commercial contract law and

---

[81] COD. COM.(Mex.) art. 2 (2008).

[82] Article 76(1) states that: "The exclusive powers of the Senate are: I. To approve the treaties and diplomatic conventions made by the President of the Republic with Foreign Powers. . . ." MEX. CONST. art. 76(1) (1917).

[83] Tesis, Tratados Internactionales, Se Ubican Jerárquicamente por Encima de las Leyes Federales y en un Segundo Plano Respecto de la Constitución Federal [Mexican Supreme Court Thesis], Semanario Judicial de la Federación y su Gaceta, Novena Época, Tomo X, Noviembre de 1999, Tesis P. LXXVII/99, Página 46 (Mex.) (the Supreme Court of Mexico stating "International Treaties rank hierarchically over and above Federal Statutes and rank only below the Federal Constitution.") (author's translation). *See also* Banks Hardwoods California LP v. Jorge Angel Kyriakidez Garcia, Tribunales Colegiados de Circuito [TCC] [Collegiate Civil Courts], Civil Court of First Instance, City of Tijuana, State of Baja California, Agosto de 2005, *available at* http://cisgw3.law.pace.edu/cases/050830m1.html (the Court deeming international treaties superior to federal law and only second to the Federal Constitution). In that decision, the Court stated:

> There is unanimity with regards to the issue that the Federal Constitution is the fundamental law. . . . The problem with regards to the hierarchy of the rest of the legal system . . . [as] found, both in case law and in doctrine, different solutions, amongst those: supremacy of federal law before local law, and the same hierarchy, with regards to "constitutional laws", and the other that says that supreme law will be deemed as such if deemed constitutional. Notwithstanding, this Supreme Court of Justice considers international treaties to be on a second plane immediately following the Fundamental Law, but above federal and local law.

Id. I am grateful to Lic. Raymundo Arenas and to Pankaj Raval, candidates for the LL.M. degree at the University of Arizona James E. Rogers College of Law for providing the above citations.

[84] U.S. CONST. art. I, § 10, cl. 1.

[85] U.S. CONST. amend. X.

[86] *See, e.g.*, the adoption of non-conforming amendments of the original version of Article 5 of the U.C.C. by not only large states such as New York, but also by smaller states such as Alabama and my own state of Arizona. *See also* Boris Kozolchyk, *Letters of Credit, in* IX INT'L ENCYCLOPEDIA OF COMP. L. 11 (1978); I UNITED STATES LAW, at chs. 24–29 (discussing these adoptions).

their hierarchy often vary under the U.C.C. with the contract, transaction or transactional context. A cursory glance at the definitions of key concepts provided by Article 1 of the U.C.C., such as "good faith," "holder" and "notice,"[87] reveals that the sources for these definitions and their hierarchy depend upon what is stated in the respective U.C.C. articles devoted to the various transactions.

Having said this, I hasten to add that where commercial contracts are concerned, the primacy of the law made by the parties is implemented in a fashion not found in any other commercial code. This implementation includes not only the application of the contractual terms and conditions, but also the parties' course of dealing, the usages of the various trades, and the customs of trade centers.[88]

The status and hierarchy of commercial treaties is not as categorical as that of customary law. Article 2, Section 2 of the United States Constitution vests upon the President of the United States the "Power . . . with the Advice and Consent of the Senate, to make Treaties, provided two thirds of the Senators present concur. . . ."[89] And once the United States Senate has ratified the treaty, the United States Constitution does not hesitate to refer to it, in conjunction with "the Laws of the United States" as the "supreme Law of the Land."[90]

Yet, United States law does not rank treaties as superior to statutes. Subsequent statutes may well prescribe a rule inconsistent with an earlier treaty. For example, in *Whitney v. Robertson*,[91] the plaintiff imported sugars from Santo Domingo similar to the ones produced in Hawaii. The Hawaiian sugars, however, were by a subsequent statute admitted free of duty into the United States. According to the plaintiff, the Dominican sugar should have been admitted duty free under the treaty with the Dominican Republic. This treaty provided that no higher or other duty should be imposed on any Dominican article than on like articles of any other foreign country. The Supreme Court held that:

---

[87] U.C.C. § 1–201(b)(20)–(21).

[88] *See* U.C.C. § 1–303.

[89] U.S. CONST. art. II, § 2, cl. 2.

[90] U.S. CONST. art. VI, cl. 2. This clause could not have been more emphatic:

> This Constitution, and the Laws of the United States which shall be made in Pursuance thereof; and all Treaties made, or which shall be made, under the Authority of the United States, shall be the supreme Law of the Land; and the Judges in every State shall be bound thereby, any Thing in the Constitution or Laws of any State to the Contrary notwithstanding.

Id. On the similar ranking of "adopted" treaties and acts of Congress, see Cheung v. U.S., 213 F.3d 82, 94 (2d Cir. 2000), where the Supreme Court stated that "under the Supremacy Clause a self-executing treaty—one that operates of itself without the aid of legislation—is to be regarded in the courts as equivalent to an act of the legislature." Where a state's law, such as a provision of the U.C.C., is in conflict with a treaty, the treaty controls. *See* Clark v. Allen, 331 U.S. 503, 508 (1947) ("[I]f . . . the provisions of the [1923] [T]reaty [of Friendship, Commerce, and Consular Rights with Germany] have not been superseded or abrogated they prevail over any requirements of California law which conflict them."). While a treaty may supersede state law, it does not necessarily do so. Courts will only construe treaties as overruling state law if there is an irreconcilable difference. "It may be inferred from the decisions of the United States Supreme Court . . . that a treaty will, if possible, be given a restricted construction where a broader construction would infringe upon a special power of the state over the subject-matter." 4 A.L.R. 1382 (1919) (citing to Heim v. McCall, 239 U.S. 175 (1915) and Patsone v. Pennsylvania, 232 U.S. 138 (1914)). Since laws on sales, leases, negotiable instruments, letters of credit, secured lending, and investment securities are providence of the states, with respect to intrastate commerce, treaties will only be read to supersede state law if the two are irreconcilable. Consequently, it is possible for a treaty governing a specific transaction to be read so as not to overrule a state statute.

[91] 124 U.S. 190 (1888).

> [The treaty] is a pledge of the contracting parties that there shall be no discriminating legislation, against the importation of articles which are the growth, produce or manufacture of their respective countries, in favor of articles of like character imported from any other country. . . . It was never designed to prevent special concessions, upon sufficient considerations, touching the importation of specific articles into the country of the other."[92]

Accordingly, the Court held that the plaintiff had to pay duty. The Court also found that the law that gave a special concession to Hawaii "was passed after the treaty with the Dominican Republic, and, if there be any conflict between the stipulations of the treaty and the requirements of the law, the latter must control."[93] Moreover, "the courts will always endeavor to construe them so as to give effect to both, if that can be done without violating the language of either; but, if the two are inconsistent, the one last in date will control the other. . . ."[94]

This language is reminiscent of that of the French *Conseil d'Etat*'s "*loi-écran*" mentioned in an earlier section.[95] However, I must call the reader's attention to the fact that in *Whitney*, the legislation pertaining to Hawaii's sugar did not expressly abrogate prior treaties with anyone. The Supreme Court relied on an implicit abrogation of an earlier treaty by a finding of "inconsistency" between the later statute and the earlier treaty. Such a doctrine vests considerable power upon the court or adjudicator of the hierarchy of a given source of commercial law.

5. Conclusions

As a rule, commercial code rules on hierarchies of sources do not provide an accurate portrait of the importance of unlisted sources, such as customary, decisional, doctrinal and treaty law, in everyday commercial contract law practice. Moreover, the listed, as well as the unlisted, sources of commercial contract law are far from being applied in as rigorously hierarchical fashion as it appears in codified rankings. Thus, the outcome of a dispute will often depend upon a flexible application of the listed as well as the unlisted sources of commercial contract law. The following section is devoted to a source that looms very large in many civil law countries and is likely to continue to do so, especially in Germany and other countries influenced by German commercial contract law.

§ 13.2 THE "GENERAL CONDITIONS OF TRADE" IN GERMAN LAW

My first encounter with Germany's General Conditions of Trade involved banking transactions in the *Allgemeine Geschäftsbedingungen für die Banken* (General Conditions of Trade for Banks) (hereinafter AGB), and it occurred in 1970 during a visit to German banks in Hamburg and Frankfurt.[96] The sheer volume and variety of these standard terms and conditions in the contracts entered into by the banks was

---

[92] *Id.* at 193.

[93] *Id.* at 193–94.

[94] *Id.* at 194.

[95] *See supra* § 13:1(D)(2).

[96] I was conducting research on letter of credit law for a chapter in the International Encyclopedia of Comparative Law under the auspices of the Max Planck Institute of Comparative law in Hamburg. *See* Kozolchyk, *Letters of Credit*, *supra* note 86.

overwhelming. Every important aspect or phase of a banking contract was covered, from filling out a deposit slip for a checking account by a bank customer to the diligence of banks while forwarding documents or monetary remittances to each other. I should note that even though some parts of the AGB that I examined during this visit read like standard contract terms, other parts read like mandatory guild directives to its members as well as to the consuming public.

In a subsequent research visit during the 1990s, it became apparent that if at first the AGBs were issued by powerful individual or groups of enterprises, gradually they were also issued by commercial or trade associations as well as by individual businesses. They governed all sorts of sales of goods or provision of services from souvenir shops to rail and tram services. In the words of commentators to a German court decision that will be discussed in a later section:[97]

> The use of general terms and conditions of business (standard terms) is part of the daily bread of international commerce. For some branches and types of business, standard terms have attained such an importance that a separate normative value is ascribed to them and the principles contained within them [fall] under the heading "*lex mercatoria.*"[98]

Some AGBs had to receive governmental approval before coming into force. This was particularly true after the Second World War as a judicial reaction against an excessively Nazi "corporate" state often at the expense of consumer protection. With judicial-governmental intervention also came larger, albeit occasional, public involvement in the drafting process. Eventually, the German law on standard contractual terms and conditions made a decisive turn in the direction of consumer protection.

In 1976, Germany enacted a regulatory statute on the use of standard contracts, the "Regulatory Law on the AGBs" (*Gesetz zur Regelung des Rechts der Allgemeinen Geschäftsbedingungen*) (hereinafter AGBG).[99] In the late 1980s, German banking lawyers who were part of the drafting committee for the Uniform Customs and Practices for Documentary Credits (UCP 500) warned me and other fellow drafters of these customary banking rules against inserting any language that could be regarded by German courts as imposing terms and conditions that had not been disclosed to or bargained with their customers. Finally, in 2002, many of the consumer protection provisions of the AGBG were made part of the revision of the BGB chapter on obligations[100] and became the new Sections 305–310 of this enactment.[101] This revision

---

[97] *See infra* § 13:3(B)(4).

[98] Dr. Martin Schmidt-Kessel, *On the Treatment of General Terms and Conditions on Contracts for the International Sale of Goods (CISG)* (Todd J. Fox trans., 2001) (citations omitted) (criticizing interpretation of the German Federal Supreme Court of Oct. 13, 2001, VII ZR 60/01), *available at* http://cisgw3.law.pace.edu/cases/011031g1.html.

[99] The first version of this statute is from Dec. 9, 1976, and the latest revision available on-line is from Dec. 31, 2001.

[100] The date of these revisions was Nov. 26, 2001 (BGBl. I 2001, S. 3138).

[101] *See* INTRODUCTION TO GERMAN LAW, *supra* note 11, at 189–90 (providing a well-written summary of the consumer protection law provisions).

also implemented a European Union directive on unfair contract terms and consumer protection.[102]

The following is a summary of these provisions. It is intended solely as an illustration of the type of regulation to which standard business terms are subject in Germany and other member nations of the European Union. And while it is an analysis of its legal peculiarities, it should also assist students in their more detailed study of these regulations in connection with a practical exercise in the subsequent section.

A. BGB Sections 305–307

Section 305(1) defines standard business terms as "all contract terms pre-formulated for more than two contracts which one party to the contract (the user) presents to the other party upon the entering into of the contract."[103]

It also provides a hint of the reasonable and non-literal type of interpretation expected of judges. The location, form and typeface of the terms are irrelevant; what matters is their intent. It also distinguishes between contract terms that are negotiated which are not subject to these provisions and those that are not negotiated and which are subject to them. However, as will become apparent in the following subsection, this revision draws a distinction between actual negotiation of contractual terms and disclosure of their existence. Terms that are fully negotiated are not governed by these provisions, while those that are merely disclosed, but not negotiated, are governed by it.

In furtherance of this "contractual awareness" principle and the distinction found in Section 305(1), Section 305(2) states that standard business terms only become a part of a contract if there is full disclosure. This disclosure requires that "the user, when entering into the contract, 1. refers the other party to . . . [these terms] explicitly or, where explicit reference [is very difficult] . . . by posting a clearly visible notice at the place where the contract is entered into, and 2. . . . takes into reasonable account any physical handicap of the other party. . . ."[104]

As long as the above requirements are satisfied, the parties to the contract may agree in advance that specific standard business terms are to govern a given transaction. Thus, this subsection implements the requirement of full disclosure of the business terms referred to in Section 305(1).

Section 305a applies to the instances of special incorporation of the business terms. This incorporation allows a party to disregard the above requirements if the other party to the contract expressly or tacitly agrees to their application. These special instances involve the standard terms and conditions for the supply of public services such as: "railways . . . trams, trolley buses and motor vehicles. . . . Electricity, Gas, Telecommunications, Post and Railway" companies when their standard terms and conditions are "kept available on the business premises of the [issuer-]user. . . ."[105]

---

102 *English Translation of the BGB by Lagenscheidt Translation Service* (last amended July 27, 2011), http://www.gesetze-im-internet.de/englisch_bgb/englisch_bgb.html [hereinafter BGB (2011)].

103 *Id.* § 305(1).

104 *Id.* § 305(2).

105 *Id.* § 305a(1)–(2).

Section 305b sets forth the principle of contract interpretation that gives priority to the agreed upon terms over those in the standard terms.[106] Its companion, Section 305c, contains a rule referred to by the banking lawyers involved in the drafting of UCP 500 as equitable court decisions based on doctrines such as that of contractual good faith (*Gebot von Treu und Glauben*). One such doctrine states that when the outward appearances of a standard term are so unusual that the other party does not expect to encounter them as part of the agreement, courts will exclude them. This rule is buttressed by the principle of *contra proferentem*, *i.e.*, "[a]ny doubts in the interpretation of standard business terms are resolved against the user [issuer]."[107] Along the same lines, Section 306 sets forth some of the consequences of the violations of the provisions:

> (1) If standard business terms in whole or in part have not become part of the contract or are ineffective, the remainder of the contract remains in effect.
>
> (2) To the extent that the terms have not become part of the contract or are ineffective, the contents of the contract are determined by the statutory provisions.
>
> (3) The contract is ineffective if upholding it . . . would be an unreasonable hardship for one party.[108]

Section 307 provides various tests of the unreasonableness of the contents of business terms. For example, they fail this test if, "contrary to the [above] requirement of good faith, they unreasonably disadvantage the other party to the contract with the user [issuer]. An unreasonable disadvantage may also arise from the [contractual] provision not being clear and comprehensible."[109] In case of doubt, an unreasonable disadvantage is "assumed to exist if a provision (1) is not compatible with . . . the statutory provision from which it deviates, or (2) limits essential [fundamental] rights or duties inherent in the nature of the contract to such an extent that attainment of the purpose of the contract is jeopardised."[110]

I would suggest that if the reader finds Levin Goldschmidt's *jus aequum*, Karl Llewellyn's "situation-sense," or my own "marketplace" and "brotherly" standards of fairness looming large behind the above provision, he or she is not far off the mark.

B. An Illustration and an Exercise: A Standard Contract for the Purchase of Souvenirs from *Oktoberfest*

The website for the Munich Oktoberfest Souvenirs[111] contains terms and conditions on, *inter alia*, how to fill out the order, select a form of shipment and delivery, and pay for the goods and shipment utilizing communications as varied as the telephone, internet, e-mail, paper-based writing and fax. The rules are quite explicit and detailed. For example, if I, as a purchaser, were to submit terms and conditions of the standard contract that differed from those posted, the order would be void unless

---

[106] *Id.* § 305b.

[107] *Id.* § 305c.

[108] *Id.* § 306.

[109] *Id.* § 307(1).

[110] *Id.* § 307(2).

[111] *See, e.g.*, OKTOBERFEST.DE, shop.oktoberfest.de; MUENCHEN.DE, http://www.muenchen.de/Rathaus/tourist%y(1)6doffice/oktobfest/127405/oktoberfest_Fragen_Souvenirs.html.

the disparity was explicitly waived by the seller. Presumably, this term and condition would avoid a dispute over whether the merchant had the duty to reject such a disparity or whether the contract could be enforced without it. They also set forth the language of the contract for purposes of its German interpretation, and disclaimed the exactness of the depiction of the goods in the online shop.

The next stipulation is that the seller must notify the customer when the order is received and the period within which the seller accepts or rejects the order (two weeks). Thus, the contract comes into being when the seller notifies the buyer of his acceptance of the offer by e-mail or by a notification that the goods have been shipped or by the delivery of the goods. The time of payment is stipulated as the moment when the acceptance of the order by the seller takes place. The means of payment are fully specified as is the creation of a security interest by a retention of title by the seller until full payment of the purchase price. In addition, there are clauses on the limitation of liability for defects and claims of damages.

This standard contract stipulates that if the seller is held liable for defective products, the liability of slight negligence only applies where the merchant is guilty of *laches* or where the customer is unable to enforce contractual warranties or the merchant is guilty of a violation of an essential contractual obligation. Recovery for damages is limited to the value of the foreseeable usual or typical damages. Yet this limitation of liability does not apply to loss of life or bodily injury of the purchaser. Obvious or patent defects can only be claimed within two weeks after delivery of the goods; e-mails or fax communications constitute adequate notice.

In case of an effective cancellation or revocation of the contract, the seller and purchaser must return the respective performances or benefits conferred, including interest when due. If the customer cannot return the goods received or their value in full, he must compensate the seller for the deficiency. Reflecting the degree of detail that goes into drafting this AGB, it provides that the amount of the return "does not apply to diminished value that is exclusivly [sic] caused by the examination or testing of the goods as it would have for example been possible in a store."[112]

Warranties are provided in accordance with existing law and information about possible additional warranties by the manufacturer of an article are found in the documentation that accompanies the sold products. The AGBs specify that German law is the applicable law, and excludes the application of the Convention for the International Sales of Goods (hereinafter CISG), including orders or sales from outside Germany. Finally, the origination points of the goods as well as the places of payment are designated for jurisdictional purposes.

This summary of the AGB of the Munich Oktoberfest Souvenirs website stands in sharp contrast with the terseness of standard contract conditions of the retail sales websites of United States businesses. Accordingly, I suggest the following exercise. First, the reader should check comparable websites of United States sellers of souvenirs or of books, musical records, CDs or DVDs. The questions to be answered after this comparison are: Do these websites contain comparable standard terms and conditions? Are the terms and conditions that govern the "checkout" and payment stages of the United States websites comparable to the panoply of terms and conditions

---

112 *Terms and Conditions*, OKTOBERFEST.DE, http://shop.oktoberfest.de/en/Terms-and-Conditions/.

of the Munich Oktoberfest Souvenirs website or of those required by Sections 305–307 of the BGB? If not, why not, and what are the legal consequences of not having such an AGB in United States commercial and consumer contract law practice?

§ 13.3 JUDICIAL DECISIONS ON THE SCOPE OF THE HGB, BGB, AGB AND CISG

A. Introduction

The first decision discussed by the German Federal Supreme Court (*Bundesgerichtshof*), while controversial, lays out in detail the journey of an AGB as an enforceable source of law, including its competition against an enforceable treaty such as the United Nations Convention on International Sales of Goods of 1980 (CISG), ratified by Germany on January 1, 1991.

The following decisions should be read as illustrations of when the AGB can be used to limit the liability of their users-issuers and the courts' reliance on principles of good faith, public policy, and proper or decent standards of commercial behavior to determine the validity of contractual stipulations. The final decision on the doctrine of subjective lesion in the BGB provides a vivid contrast with the reliance on the doctrine of objective lesion in the *Code Civil*.[113]

B. *Bundesgerichtshof*, October 31, 2001 [VIII ZR 60/01][114]

1. Applicable Provisions

a. United Nations Convention on the International Sale of Goods (CISG)

Article 2

This Convention does not apply to sales:

(a) of goods bought for personal, family or household use, unless the seller, at any time before or at the conclusion of the contract, neither knew nor ought to have known that the goods were bought for any such use;. . . .[115]

Article 4

This Convention governs only the formation of the contract of sale and the rights and obligations of the seller and the buyer arising from such a contract. In particular, except as otherwise expressly provided in this Convention, it is not concerned with:

---

[113] *See supra* § 8:11.

[114] Bundesgerichtshof [BGH] [Federal Court of Justice] Oct. 13, 2001, ENTSCHEIDUNGEN DES BUNDESGERICHTSHOFES IN ZIVILSACHEN [BGHZ] 149, 113 (Ger.) [hereinafter BGHZ], *available at* http://cisgw3.law.pace.edu/cases/011031g1.html (William M. Barron et al., trans.). The original version of this translation was made available to me by the German Law Archive of the Pace Law School, Institute of International Commercial Law. The following are partial and edited versions of the translation of this decision and commentary which has been transcribed with permission from the Pace Law School. All citations to court decisions and doctrinal sources have been omitted.

[115] The following provisions have been extracted from the United Nations Convention on Contracts for the International Sale of Goods ("CISG"), Apr. 11, 1980, 1489 U.N.T.S. 3, 19 I.L.M 671, *available at* http://www.cisg.law.pace.edu/cisg/text/treaty.html.

(a) the validity of the contract or of any of its provisions or of any usage;. . . .[116]

Article 7

(1) In the interpretation of this Convention, regard is to be [given] to its international character and to the need to promote uniformity in its application and the observance of good faith in international trade. . . .[117]

Article 8

(1) For the purposes of this Convention statements made by and other conduct of a party are to be interpreted according to his intent where the other party knew or could not have been unaware what that intent was.

(2) If the preceding paragraph is not applicable, statements made by and other conduct of a party are to be interpreted according to the understanding that a reasonable person of the same kind as the other party would have had in the same circumstances.

(3) In determining the intent of a party or the understanding a reasonable person would have had, due consideration is to be given to all relevant circumstances of the case including the negotiations, any practices which the parties have established between themselves, usages, and any subsequent conduct of the parties.[118]

Article 35

(1) The seller must deliver goods which are of the quantity, quality and description required by the contract and which are contained or packaged in the manner required by the contract. . . .[119]

Article 45

(1) If the seller fails to perform any of his obligations under the contract or this Convention, the buyer may: . . . (b) claim damages as provided in articles 74 to 77. . . .[120]

Article 74

Damages for breach of contract by one party consist of a sum equal to the loss, including loss of profit, suffered by the other party as a consequence of the breach. Such damages may not exceed the loss which the party in breach foresaw or ought to have foreseen at the time of the conclusion of the contract, in the light of the facts and matters of which he then knew or ought to have known, as a possible consequence of the breach of contract.[121]

---

116 *Id.* art. 4(a).

117 *Id.* art. 7(1).

118 *Id.* art. 8(1)–(3).

119 *Id.* art. 35(1).

120 *Id.* art. 45(1).

121 *Id.* art. 74.

b. HGB

§ 128. Personal liability of a partner [Partnerships in General]

The partners are personally liable as joint debtors for the obligations of the partnership to its creditors. Any agreement to the contrary is ineffective as against third parties.[122]

§ 161. Concept of limited partnership

(1) An association the object of which is the carrying on of a commercial enterprise under a common firm name is a limited partnership, if, in the case of one or more of the partners, their liability to the creditors of the association is limited to the amount of a fixed share in the capital (limited partners), while the rest of the partners have unlimited liabilities (personally liable partners). . . .[123]

§ 162. Registration requirements

(1) The notice for the registration of the partnership shall, in addition to the particulars presented in § 106(2), contain a designation of the limited partners and the amount each has contributed to the capital.

(2) When the registration is published, only the number of the limited partners is to be given; the name, the occupation and the address of the limited partners, as well as the amount of their contributions are not made public.[124]

2. *Facts*[125]

The main Defendant, a German limited liability partnership (hereinafter L) was the German seller of a used rolling-milling machine which was sold to the Plaintiff, a Spanish buyer, for the amount of 370,000 DM. The second Defendant was L's partner without limited liability. This sale was pursuant to L's written confirmation of Plaintiff's purchase dated June 25, 1998. It stated that the confirmation was "based" on the seller's Standard Sales and Delivery Terms (AGB). However, these standard terms and conditions were not transcribed in the confirmation or in any other communication transmitted by the main Defendant to the Plaintiff. One of these neither transcribed nor inserted terms stated that used machines were sold "without any warranty against defects." However, the confirmation did state that the seller would provide a mechanic at the buyer's plant in Spain for one full day at no cost to the buyer to supervise the installation of the machine.

The buyer had the machine installed and connected by a Spanish company. Meanwhile L sent Mechanic A to help with the installation. A was unable to help put the machine into operation during his two visits to Spain in July of 1998. The machine was finally installed with the assistance of a specialist sent by the Defendant during a

---

122 HGB § 128 (GOREN, 1998).

123 *Id.* § 161(1).

124 *Id.* § 162(1)–(2).

125 BGHZ, *supra* note 114. I have summarized the facts set forth hereafter by combining those found in the case text, with extracts from the case commentary.

third visit that took place at the end of September, beginning of October, 1998. Since that time the machine has been working effectively.

The Plaintiff sued L and its principal partner with unlimited liability for the damages it suffered in connection with his losses as a result of the failed installation. The Regional Court, Court of First Instance (*Landgericht*) granted the Plaintiff's claim in the amount of 46,519.18 DM plus interest and dismissed an additional claim. The Court viewed the confirmation of June 25, 1998 as providing the seller's promise to provide a mechanic as assuming responsibility for the installation of the machine. Implicit in this promise was L's obligation to send a qualified technician. Accordingly, it held the Defendant liable for the damages suffered by Plaintiff as a result of not having had a qualified technician and an operative machine until months later.

The Court of Appeals or Court of Second Instance (*Oberlandesgericht*) vacated the judgment of the Court of First Instance and remanded the case to the lower court for new findings of fact consistent with its remand. According to the commentary by Dr. Martin Schmidt-Kessel, the case would have been dismissed by the Federal Supreme Court if the seller had effectively disclaimed its warranty in the confirmation. However, the Supreme Court held that the standard Sales and Delivery Terms were not part of the contract and remanded the case to the appellate court for further proceedings consistent with its holding. The key sentence of its decision stated that: "Under the CISG . . . 'the user [issuer] of general terms and conditions is required to transmit the text [of the standard terms and conditions] to the other party or [to] make it available in another way.' "

3. Reasons for the Decision[126]

The [buyer] has properly pleaded a claim for damages under Arts. 45(1)(b), 35(1) and 74 [of] CISG against the seller, for which Defendant No. 2 is liable under §§ 162(2),128 HGB. The [seller] has not effectively precluded its liability for breach of [warranty]. Because the [seller's] Sales and Delivery Terms were not made applicable to the contractual relationship pursuant to the CISG, the warranty exclusion . . . does not apply. The decision of the lawsuit, thus, depends on whether the rolling-milling machine was afflicted with a defect that was covered by a warranty at the time of the transfer to a freight carrier and what costs arose from its removal. The Court of First Instance must evaluate the evidence relating to this issue.

According to the general view, the inclusion of general terms and conditions into a contract that is governed by the CISG is subject to the provisions regarding the conclusion of a contract (Articles 14, 18 CISG); recourse to the national law that is applicable based on a conflict of laws analysis is generally not available. The CISG does not, however, contain special rules regarding the inclusion of standard terms and conditions into a contract. This was not deemed necessary because the Convention already contains rules regarding the interpretation of contracts.

Thus, through an interpretation according to Art. 8 CISG, it must be determined whether the general terms and conditions are part of the offer, which can already follow from the negotiations between the parties, the existing practices between the parties, or international customs (Art. 8(3) CISG). As for the rest, it must be analyzed

---

126 *See* BGHZ, *supra* note 114 (citations omitted).

[on the basis of] how a "reasonable person of the same kind as the other party" would have understood the offer (Art. 8(2) CISG).

It is unanimously required [by case law] that the recipient of a contract offer that is supposed to be based on general terms and conditions have the possibility to become aware of them in a reasonable manner. An effective inclusion of general terms and conditions thus first requires that the intention of the offeror [as to what] he wants to include . . . into the contract be apparent to the recipient of the offer. In addition, as the Court of Appeals correctly assumed, the Uniform Sales Law requires the user [issuer] of general terms and conditions to transmit the text or make it available in another way.

Insofar as the general terms and conditions at issue become a part of the contract under German non-CISG law . . . where the customer does not know them but has the possibility of reasonable notice—e.g., by requesting them from the user, this does not lead to a different result. In the national legal system, the clauses within one industry sector are often similar and usually known to the participating merchants. To the extent that this does not apply to a commercially-active contract party, it can be expected of him, in good faith, that he make the clauses available to the other party, if he wants to close the deal—as offered by the user [issuer] based on the general terms and conditions. These requirements do not, however, apply to the same extent to international commercial relations, so that, under the principles of good faith . . . a duty to inquire cannot be expected of him [the other party].

The Court of Appeals correctly notes that, pursuant to Art. 1(3) CISG, it is irrelevant to the application of the Convention whether the parties are "merchants or non-merchants," so that, in a different interpretation, non-merchants would also be subject to the heightened duty of inquiry. To the extent that the appeal argues that a "consumer purchase" under Art. 2(a) CISG is excluded from the application of the Convention, this argument cannot be followed. The purchase referred to in Art. 2(a) CISG requires that the seller know or should have known the purpose before or at the time of the conclusion of the contract, whereas, if the buyer is a consumer within the meaning of § 13 BGB, it does not require such knowledge of the seller. This can, therefore, lead to an overlap, where sales contracts are subject to binding national consumer protection laws and, at the same time, to the CISG. In the interest of a practical application of the law as well as to avoid discrimination against non-commercial contract parties, it is, therefore, necessary to make the inclusion of general terms and conditions for contracts governed by the CISG subject to uniform principles.

. . . therefore, [it is necessary to require] the effective inclusion of the Sales and Delivery Terms of the [seller] into its contract with the [buyer]. . . .

The appealed judgment is thus vacated, and the matter remanded to the Court of Appeals for further clarification concerning the defects in the delivered rolling-milling machine alleged by the [buyer] and, if appropriate, concerning the extent of the necessary expenses for removal.

4. *Commentary by Dr. Martin Schmidt-Kessel*[127]

In his commentary, Dr. Martin Schmidt-Kessel points out that because of the very generalized use of general terms and conditions of business (standard terms) as part of what he refers to as the "daily bread of international commerce," they are "suitable to establish usage of trade and guidelines of contract interpretation for the branch of business concerned."[128] However, beneath this threshold as a possible source of usage of trade, and especially in international sales that become subject to the CISG, the question arises: When do these standard terms and conditions apply, especially when they are not made part of the commercial contracts? This was the question before the Federal Supreme Court.

This question is even more pressing in Germany because, as was apparent with the standard contract of the Munich Oktoberfest Souvenirs, the common practice in Germany is to exclude the application of CISG in the standard terms and conditions. Yet, as pointed out by Dr. Schmidt-Kessel and by the Court, whether such standard terms effectively become part of the contract is predominantly decided by the CISG itself and not by autonomous national law.

The reason for this lies in Article 1(1)(b) CISG, which makes the Convention national substantive law for international sales contracts. In Dr. Schmidt-Kessel's opinion:

> Should the parties wish to exclude the Convention in their standard terms, then their rules on inclusion, as part of the national law of the relevant Contracting State designated through the rules of private international law, decide over the effectiveness of that exclusion. The conflicts of law rule that the validity of a choice of law agreement depends on the intended legal system is not applicable to this purely substantive exclusion of the CISG. This result could only be avoided by choosing the law of a Non-Contracting State, which is usually not an attractive option.[129]

Dr. Schmidt-Kessel also points out that apart from the requirement that the counterparty be aware of the user-issuer's intent to include standard terms, the Supreme Court, as a result of this decision, now requires that the terms be transmitted, a position which differs from that supported in the German doctrinal literature. In addition, he notes that the Supreme Court "consciously" deviates from prevailing case law on the inclusion of standard terms as set forth by German law. This case law merely demands the possibility of an appropriate awareness by the counterparty and therefore allows as sufficient the possibility given to the counterparty to request such terms from the user. Finally, Dr. Schmidt-Kessel argues that the decision is unpersuasive; it does not do justice to commercial practice. A general duty to transmit the standard terms and conditions without recognizable exceptions would have the following deleterious effect:

> [O]ther, better known standard clauses—such as Incoterms 2000, the several ECE-Terms, or branch-specific terms such as GAFTA 100 or the rules of the Sugar Association of London—could not become the basis of contracts without

---

127 *See* Schmidt-Kessel, *supra* note 98 (citations omitted).

128 *Id.*

129 *Id.*

being transmitted. For established market participants, a solution to this problem could easily be found through Art. 9(1) CISG; for new market participants, however, this presents a (surely unwanted) access barrier.[130]

QUESTIONS

Do you agree with the court's reasoning or with the criticisms voiced by Dr. Schmidt-Kessel? What do you think of the duty of good faith that the court implied from the fact that contracting parties in other countries may not be aware of the typical wording of German AGBs, including their repeated exclusion of the CISG and the inclusion of disclaimers of all warranties with respect to used goods? Why is it that the CISG is so commonly excluded in German AGBs? Since the drafters of these AGBs are increasingly sensitive to the German courts' policy to protect unwary consumers, is there something in the CISG, the product of a consumer-conscious body such as the United Nations Commission on International Trade Law (UNCITRAL), that is likely to offend consumer protection judges in Germany? If so, what could it be? What about the CISG scope provisions?

C. *Bundesgerichtshof*, September 26, 1989, WM 1989, 1713:[131] Slight Negligence in the AGB for Banks

1. Applicable Provisions of the BGB

Section 675:

The provisions of §§ 663, 665 to 670, 672 to 674 and, if the person bound has the right to give notice without observance of any term of notice, the provisions of § 671(2) also apply *mutatis mutandis* to a contract of service or a contract for work which has for its object the taking care of a matter.[132]

2. Facts and Holding

Plaintiff bought eight new Mercedes Benz automobiles from S for the amount of 385,774.70 DM. To effectuate payment for these cars, the Plaintiff procured the transfer of the purchase price to the Defendant bank and asked in a telex dated August 20, 1986 that the Defendant transfer the money to S as soon as the title to the cars (*Kraftfahrzeugbriefe*), and their registration (*Kraftfahrzeugscheine*) and additional certificates of readiness (*Torpaesse*) were presented to the transferring bank.

On August 21, 1986, merchant S and two other people appeared in branch 65 of the Defendant bank and presented false documents. The bank employee of this branch did not detect the fraud. After checking the documents, the Defendant bank transferred the requested money to S's account and sent the documents to the Plaintiff. Due to the fraudulent nature of the documents presented to the Defendant, the Plaintiff was unable to obtain the eight Mercedes from the Daimler Benz Corporation. The transferred money was traced to R, a thief who had disappeared with it.

The plaintiff claimed damages from the Defendant bank in the amount of DM 42,755.70. The latter argued that: 1) it was impossible for its employee to notice the

---

130 *Id.*

131 Bundesgerichtshof [BGH] [Federal Court of Justice] Sept. 26, 1989, WERTPAPIER-MITTEILUNGEN [WM] 1989, 1713 (Angela D. Paczosa trans.).

132 BGB § 675 (GOREN, 1994).

falsifications and 2) it was not liable for slight negligence since it effectively excluded its liability for slight negligence in term and condition No. 34 of its AGB. The *Landgericht* ruled in favor of the bank. The intermediate appellate court overruled the decision of the *Landgericht*. However, the *Bundesgerichtshof* affirmed the decision of the *Landgericht* in favor of the bank, holding that: 1) The agreement between the defending bank and the plaintiff does not constitute a letter of credit, and 2) The bank can use its AGB to effectively exclude liability for slight negligence.

3. Reasoning

The Plaintiff did not ask the Defendant bank to open a letter of credit in favor of the merchant S. Rather, the Defendant bank and the Plaintiff entered into a special contract for the performance of work that consisted in taking care of another's business (*Geschaeftsbesorgungsvertrag*) governed by Section 675 BGB. Therefore, the UCP (1983) does not apply to the transaction in question.

4. Comment by Angela Daniel Paczosa

The issue of whether or not the UCP is to be applied by analogy in a case not involving the issuance of a letter of credit but of a payment against presentation of documents was left undecided by the court because according to the court the provisions of the UCP are not in conflict with the Defendant Bank's AGB restricting its liability to gross negligence, thereby disclaiming slight negligence.

The court reasoned that it is fair and just to have the bank's customer bear the risk as to whether or not the documents are false since it is the person with whom its customer dealt (and not the bank client himself) who presented the false documents. Thus, the bank should be allowed to exclude its liability for slight negligence.

D. *Bundesgerichtshof*, February 3, 1986, 1986 WM 769–770[133]

This case provides an illustration of the German Supreme Court's Application of the Principles of Good Faith (*Gebot von Treu und Glauben*) and Expected Behavior of a Proper or Businesslike Merchant (*ordentlicher Kaufmann*).

1. Facts

Plaintiff is an insurer of maritime transportation. It insured the transportation of 3,000 bags of coffee from Colombia, South America to Bremen, Germany. Defendant was the shipper of the coffee in March/April 1981. The bill of lading named H of Bremen as the consignee of the goods. H assigned his rights to the plaintiff/insurance company. The insurance company is now suing the Defendant-shipper for reimbursement of the money it had to pay H due to damage to the coffee.

The Defendant [shipper] argues that the *Landgericht* of Bremen does not have jurisdiction to hear the case because the bill of lading contains a forum selection clause that names Bogota as the forum for such litigation. The plaintiff [insurance company for the beneficiary] argues that the forum selection clause did not become part of the contract because it is practicably unreadable.

---

[133] Bundesgerichtshof [BGH] [Federal Court of Justice] Feb. 3, 1986, WERTPAPIER-MITTEILUNGEN [WM] 1986, 769–70 (Angela D. Paczosa trans.).

The lower court denied its jurisdiction. The intermediate appellate court as well as the Supreme Court (*Bundesgerichtshof*) affirm. In its decision, the Supreme Court relied on commentaries to the statute on AGBs (AGBG).

2. Holding

1) Generally, the provisions of a bill of lading that cannot be read even with the help of a magnifying glass, do not become part of the contract [citing its own decision, BGH, May 30, 1983, WM 1983 at 1083–1085].

2) A businesslike or proper merchant (*ordentlicher Kaufmann*) has to act according to the good faith (*Gebot von Treu und Glauben*) and cannot expect that his client impliedly agrees to unreadable provisions written in small print when accepting the paperwork.

3) However, provisions of a bill of lading which are written in small print can become part of the bill of lading contract as long as they are legible.

4) In the case at hand, the forum selection clause printed on the back of the bill of lading did become part of the contract since it was legible and bore a heading printed in bold letters.

3. Reasoning

Before distinguishing the present from its own BGH (*Bundesgerichtshof*) decision of May 30, 1983, WM 1083 (1983), the Supreme Court discusses the AGB-Gesetz (AGBG) and the commentaries which address the issue as to when small printed AGB become part of a contract. It notes that it is the general opinion among scholars that AGB do not become part of a contract when they are illegible because of their small size in print. The court also cites the legislative materials of the AGBG of similar content.

In its AGB-discussion, the Supreme Court points out that this issue (meaning the issue whether or not small print is legible) only plays a role with regard to Section 2 of the AGBG which defines minimum standards for the AGB. Furthermore, the BGH notes that this section of the AGB applies only to non-merchants, while merchants do not get the benefit of Section 2 of the AGBG.

However, the BGH emphasizes that merely because Section 2 of the AGBG does not apply to merchants, merchants cannot conclude that their contracts with non-merchants can incorporate clauses that can only be read by means of a magnifying glass. Rather, the Supreme Court concludes, that merchants have to abide by the doctrine of good faith (*Gebot von Treu und Glauben*) which has been in effect long before the AGBG was enacted. According to the doctrine of good faith, a merchant cannot rely on the fact that the party to his contract agrees to illegible clauses merely by accepting the contract and not commenting or objecting to its contents.

The court distinguishes the case at hand and the discussion of the AGB from its decision dated May 30, 1983, WM 1083 (1983). There, the BGH had ruled that a forum selection clause had not become part of the bill of lading because one could hardly read them with a magnifying glass; in addition, the print was smeared and the letters were printed on very thin paper. In the case at hand, however, the print was easily readable even though it consisted of small letters. The forum selection clause was printed clearly on the back of the bill of lading. The different provisions were printed in black ink on white paper. Furthermore, the different clauses had a heading which was printed in bold letters.

E. *Bundesgerichtshof* (Ninth Civil Senate) 24 February 1994, NJW 1994, 1341:[134]

Subject: Duties of a Merchant Toward a Non-Merchant: BGB Section 138 on Subjective Lesion.

1. *Applicable Provisions of the BGB*

§ 138. [Legal transaction against public policy; usury]

(1) A legal transaction which is against public policy is void.

(2) A legal transaction by which a person exploiting the need, inexperience, lack of sound judgment or substantial lack of will power of another, causes to be promised or granted to himself or to a third party in exchange for a performance [promise], pecuniary advantages which are in obvious disproportion to the performance is also void.[135]

§ 278. [Inability to perform in case of debt described by class]

A debtor is responsible for the fault of his legal representative and of persons whom he employs in performing his obligation, to the same extent as for his own fault. . . .[136]

§ 1618a. [Mutual duty of assistance and respect]

Parents and children owe assistance and respect to one another.[137]

2. *Facts*[138]

The plaintiff's father worked as an [real] estate agent. . . . When, in 1982, he requested the defendant savings bank to increase his borrowing limit for account no. 172429 from DM 50,000 to DM 100,000, the defendant requested him to provide a guarantee from his daughter, the plaintiff in this action. At this time, the plaintiff was twenty-one years old, earned some DM 1,150 net per month as a blue collar worker and did not dispose of any assets. On 29 November 1982, the plaintiff signed at the defendant's premises an absolute guarantee for the amount of up to DM 100,000 plus collateral debts in order to secure all present and future claims which the defendant had against the principal debtor "arising from its business relationship (in particular from current account, credits and loans of any kind, and bills of exchange) as well as bills of exchange handed in by third parties, guarantees, assignments, or subrogation." The following day, the defendant granted the extension of the credit. . . . When his [the plaintiff's father's] assets deteriorated two years later, the defendant called in all credits. From the day when the plaintiff signed the guarantee, the principal's debts

---

134 Bundesgerichtshof [BGH] [Federal Court of Justice] Feb. 24, 1994, NEUE JURISTISCHE WOCHENSCHRIFT [NJW] 1994, 1341 (Ger.), *available at* http://www.iuscomp.org/gla/judgments/bgh/z940224.htm.

135 BGB § 138 (GOREN, 1994).

136 *Id.* § 278.

137 *Id.* § 1618a.

138 *See* BGH, *supra* note 134.

continued to exceed DM 100,000. The plaintiff initially filed a declaratory action, claiming that the contract of guarantee was void. . . . [T]he defendant brought a counterclaim for the payment of DM 100,000 plus interest. . . .

The *Landgericht* allowed the counterclaim. The Appeal Court dismissed it. On appeal by the defendant, this Senate, by judgment of 16 March 1989, restored the judgment of the first instance. This judgment was quashed by the decision of the *Bundesverfassungsgericht* of 19 October 1993, and the case was referred back to this Senate. The appeal did not succeed.

3. Reasons

The Appeal Court refused the action for payment on the ground that the plaintiff had a claim for compensation in pre-contractual liability, which obliged the defendant to relieve the plaintiff from the guarantee.

In the Appeal Court's view, a bank is not required to inform about the risk involved in a guarantee. However, a bank must not trivialize the type, scope or risk of the guarantor's liability and thereby influence his decision, in particular if the guarantor is obviously inexperienced in business matters. Precisely this had happened in this case. According to the . . . plaintiff's father, the . . . [defendant's agent] before signing . . . [said to the plaintiff]: "Would you just sign this here, please, this won't make you enter into any important obligation, I need this for my files." This created the impression on the plaintiff that not much could happen to her at the end of the day. By this, the defendant's agent had grotesquely trivialized the significance of the liability which the plaintiff had assumed. The plaintiff would not have provided the guarantee if the defendant's employee had not trivialized the risk which was connected with this obligation. . . .

Due to the particular circumstances under which the guarantee contract was concluded with the principal debtor's daughter, this contract offends good morals and is thereby void ([under] § 138(I) BGB). . . .

A legal transaction is void under Section 138(I) BGB only if its entire character, as it results from content, motivation, and purpose taken together, offends good morals, for which only those circumstances are to be taken into account which prevailed at the conclusion of the contract (references omitted). The mere fact that the content of the contract placed a considerable burden on the plaintiff and only the plaintiff, cannot in itself question the validity of the guarantee. . . . By its structure, the guarantee is . . . not characterized by an . . . equal consideration of mutual interest but . . . is aimed at providing benefits to one party only.

Likewise, the obligation which has been assumed does not merit disapproval by the law merely because at the time of her declaration of intention, the guarantor did not dispose of the necessary income or assets for performing the obligations for which she was to be liable. The Constitution guarantees freedom of contract within the legal framework, which includes the freedom to design the rules of a contract. This forms an important foundation for the present private legal order. It follows from the freedom of contract that a person must generally be free to enter into risky transactions at his own responsibility and to undertake an obligation which can only be performed under particularly favourable circumstances, if necessary by permanent use of all the income which exceeds the protected earnings rate. . . . As a rule, any person with the unlimited capacity to contract is in a position to realize that a guarantee implies the assumption of a considerable personal risk, to assess the consequences of such conduct accordingly, and to reach a decision on this basis. In principle, this also applies if the guarantor is a close relative of the principal debtor (citations omitted).

However, if the guarantor assumes an obligation the amount of which exceeds by far his present and potential future income situation and assets, such a contract can be void under § 138(I) BGB, if additional circumstances, which can be attributed to the creditor, levy a considerable additional burden on the guarantor and lead to an intolerable imbalance between the parties to the contract. In particular, such burdens can be caused if the creditor exploits the guarantor's inexperience in business matters or a mental predicament, or exerts undue influence on his freedom of decision in another way.

[While] these circumstances primarily characterize conduct which offends good morals in the relationship between the principal debtor and the guarantor. . . . [they also have some] influence on the legal relationship between the guarantor and the creditor bank. It is true that a bank cannot reasonably be expected to investigate in each individual case whether the guarantor was restricted in his freedom of decision, and in particular whether and in which way parents have exerted pressure on their children. However, the abovementioned danger, to which the guarantor is frequently exposed in such cases, influences the kind of conduct which the bank must show as regards the securities which the bank requires and accepts from the borrower. If a bank deems it necessary to require securities for a requested loan, and for this reason makes payment conditional on the borrower procuring a guarantee by his child for an amount which expectedly exceeds by far the child's financial capacity, the question will necessarily arise whether the creditor was aware of the morally and legally unacceptable influence . . . exerted on the guarantor, [and] whether it deliberately closed its mind to such insight. If this is the case, the borrower's conduct, which violates § 1618a BGB, will be attributed to the bank. This will regularly warrant the conclusion that the guarantee in itself is considered void. Therefore, the bank generally must not [request that the client provide a security guarantee by his inexperienced child who has no interest in the credit and] expectedly will be unable . . . to pay the secured debt if the risk materializes. . . . The defendant requested the account holder to provide a guarantee by his daughter for the sum of DM 100,000. The plaintiff's own interests were not involved. The defendant could not help noticing or even positively knew that the plaintiff would be economically overtaxed, as the defendant could not seriously assume that the plaintiff would be in a position to pay DM 100,000 plus all of the accumulated interest within a foreseeable period of time should the occasion arise. . . .

It is also common practice in banking that the securities which need to be provided in order for the loan to be paid out are examined for their value, as without such examination the economic purpose of this security agreement can, as a rule, not be fulfilled. On the other hand, if a bank decides not to make such enquiries in cases where the children of the principal debtor provide securities for very large amounts, this will, as a rule, leave no other possible interpretation than that they were either aware of the guarantor's financial circumstances, or that they deliberately closed their eyes towards the value which this security would provide.

The bank itself exerts undue influence on the guarantor if its employees trivialize the scope of the guarantee, in particular if they purport the signature to be a mere formality (reference omitted). In particular, as regards inexperienced guarantors who additionally are close relatives of the principal debtor, such conduct can create the impression on the guarantor that there is nothing serious to worry about, thereby preventing the guarantor from having a closer look at the content of the document. The representation which S, an employee of the bank, made as regards the meaning and the scope of the guarantee before the plaintiff signed the document, was apt to obscure the risk of such liability and thereby the dangers which this would impose on what the entire future would hold for the plaintiff. This conduct gravely impaired the plaintiff's freedom to reach a matter-of-fact and balanced decision.

Under § 278 BGB, the bank must account for its employee's undue influence on the determination of the plaintiff's will. As regards the subjective requirements under Section 138 I BGB, the findings made *supra* (5) (c) apply *mutatis mutandis*. The above-stated circumstances justify the assumption that the plaintiff signed the guarantee contract as a consequence of the mental predicament which she had been caused. . . .

COMMENTS AND QUESTIONS

Why should a commercial contract practitioner worry about the hierarchy of the sources of law in transnational practice? Imagine that a commercial contracts lawyer in "country A" assumes that the incorporation of a source of contract law such as GAFTA 100 and UCP 600 would govern all the issues concerning formation and method of payment of an international sale of grain and is told by his counterpart in "country B" that neither GAFTA 100 nor UCP 600 would be binding sources. Could such a problem be overcome? If so, how?

One solution, though a very difficult one, may be to draft GAFTA 100 and UCP 600 into the contract, but some of these contractual provisions could be contrary to the law or public policy of the forum. Another solution might be an amendment of the law to make those sources applicable. A third solution might be to enter into a treaty. A fourth solution might be to modify the source provisions in the statutory law to make the provisions of GAFTA 100 and UCP 600 applicable. How would you recommend that country B should proceed?

Part IV

FAMILISTIC AND SOCIALIST VARIANTS OF THE CIVIL LAW

Chapter 14

LATIN AMERICAN CODIFICATION AND ITS ALL-IMPORTANT COLONIAL BACKGROUND

§ 14.1 FAMILISM AND AUTHORITARIANISM IN LATIN AMERICAN AND SOCIALIST LAW

Familism and legalism are prime legal-cultural forces behind much of the law of commercial contracts of developing nations, although in various mixtures or combinations. The living laws of a number of authoritarian regimes in Latin America (although some of them provide the appearance of acting democratically) are a mixture of familism and purported legalism.

By "familism," I mean a legal culture whose institutions are designed to protect the best interests of the family as an economic unit, including actual and family-like or "fictive" kin members (such as the Mexican *compadre* or the Chinese *Guanxi*) and economic dependents, at the expense of the "strangers" or "third parties." In one of the Analects discussed in a later chapter,[1] Confucius, the Chinese sage, is reported to have been asked by an admiring pupil if a Confucian superior moral man was one who would have acted as a son in the questioner's land who turned in his father to the authorities for having stolen sheep from a third person. Confucius replied that in his land, a superior or "upright" man is one who, as a father, "shelters the son, and as the son shelters the father."[2]

Simply put, in a familistic legal culture, family, kin, and at times non-family dependents come first, especially in commercial dealings with non-family members. This culture grants rights and imposes duties upon family members as part of the family's perennial pursuit of survival in a difficult rural environment and the respected and obeyed patrilineal hierarchy is an essential component of that pursuit. Familism encourages family, lineage and clan monopolization, usually by enlisting the support of political and military rulers who are either members of the extended family or are its close friends.

By authoritarian—legalistic cultures, I mean the method of enacting and enforcing laws by authoritarian rulers accompanied by an appearance of having observed lawful procedures. It is only an *appearance* because these rules do not reflect the consent of the governed any more than they are the product of the wisdom or higher morality of the ruler. At their most basic, these legalistic rules reflect the coercive power and pleasure of the sovereign or ruler. Hence, authoritarian legalism does not require the observance of due process by the legislative, administrative or judicial officials that make the rules, nor is it necessary that the rule be wise, fair or moral. If fairness and wise decisions are attained, they are merely byproducts of legalism. For the main concern of the authoritarian legalistic ruler is to benefit those who he thinks deserve it.

---

[1] *See infra* § 17:3(F).

[2] *Id.*

At times, he supports the enactment or enforcement of his legalistic rule with an invocation of his or her authority. At others, he adds a formalistic justification such as by invoking the name of God or his own or by quoting from the writings of political or economic thinkers or ideologues. What matters is that, as expressed by the Latin saying relied upon by some of the Spanish warlords who re-conquered Spain: Whatever pleases the prince enjoys the vigor of law" ("*Quod principi placuit, legis habet vigorem*").

Surprisingly, especially to someone born and raised in Latin America, the early legal cultures of Latin America and China had important elements in common. In addition to the not-very-dissimilar versions of familism and legalism, including a tendency to monopolize commerce and to treat contracting parties who are members of the extended family better than non-members, pre-colonial and colonial Latin America and Chinese "commoners" shared another important attitude: their respect for and obedience to those who were their social, political and military hierarchical superiors. In the case of the family, the obedience was to the patrilineal hierarchy, and where legalism was concerned, the obedience to the chieftain (*caudillo*) warlord or emperor was strengthened by their being equated by the governed to heads of their family households.

The age and size of the Chinese civilization and the continued existence of some of its key legal institutions are unparalleled anywhere in our planet. These facts alone make China's official law, especially its living law, more diverse and encompassing than any other known to man. For this reason alone, familism and legalism in imperial China and pre-colonial and colonial Latin America were not always comparable nor did they interact in the same manner. In addition, while Latin America and China have shared many autocratic rulers, Latin America's rulers and subjects did not experience the every-day influence of a non-official religious doctrine such as Confucianism. Conversely, in modern times, the earlier and more widespread adoption of the European-inspired codes in Latin America made it possible for its law of civil and commercial contracts (including its decisional and doctrinal literature) to enjoy a higher degree of conceptual legal sophistication than that found in imperial China.

Yet, as will be apparent in the following chapters,[3] where third parties are concerned, the interaction between familism and authoritarian legalism spawned much legal uncertainty in Latin America as well as in China. In both regions, it was (and still is) difficult to predict whether a third party or non-family member counterparty would be treated as a family member and at what cost. Similarly, legalism has remained an equally arbitrary, venal, corrupt and unpredictable method to make and enforce law in both regions. And with few notable exceptions, the coexistence, and often merger, of familism and legalism in Latin America and China have prevented the development of trust in legal institutions among third party traders, lenders and investors.

In sum, the official and living laws we will be discussing in this part have enough in common to provide helpful lessons on their causes and their effect upon economic development in many if not most of today's familistic authoritarian-legalistic developing nations.

---

[3] *See infra* chs. 14–19.

§ 14.2 LATIN AMERICA'S ELUSIVE ECONOMIC DEVELOPMENT

When Christopher Columbus observed on October 28, 1492 that "[w]e are in front of the most beautiful land humans have ever laid eyes on," ([e]*stamos frente a la tierra más hermosa que jamás ojos humanos vieron*),[4] supposedly about Cuba (my country of birth), neither he nor his band of adventurer sailors (including several former jailbirds) had the slightest idea about where they actually were or the fate that would await the lands they had discovered. This was a fate that some historians, political scientists and cultural anthropologists would attribute, at least in part, to the type of conquest that followed his discovery.[5]

Despite the splendid flora and fauna, fertile soil, wide variety of minerals for industrial and aesthetic use, and a hard-working, resourceful, hospitable and intelligent population, serious poverty is still far from elimination in Latin America. Mina Goldberg, a research economist at the NLCIFT, reviewed historical and contemporary statistics on poverty in Latin America.[6] She found that colonial legal and political institutions tasked with facilitating the exploitation of mineral wealth and crops such as sugar, coffee, corn, potatoes and tobacco benefitted only a small number of inhabitants. Sharp inequality of income set in at the beginning of the colonial economy which plagues the region to this day. By the mid-1800s, Latin America's per capita income equaled, at best, sixty percent of that of the United States.

One hundred years later, starting in the 1970s and 1980s, overall income grew in Chile, Mexico and Brazil, but poverty reduction was minimal elsewhere. A World Bank study pointed out that one of the key factors in this continued poverty has been that the poor have had very limited access to financial markets and to the possibility of acquiring physical and knowledge capital essential to participate in the growth process.[7]

There are both international and national measures of poverty. The following table relies on both. One international measure of poverty is about $1/day based on a 1985 standard (updated in 1993)[8] and is adjusted to local currency for parity in

---

[4] Alberto Boix Comas, *Así es Cuba* (c. 1950), *available at* http://www.guije.com/cosas/cuba/octubre.htm (on file with author).

[5] *See* CULTURE MATTERS: HOW VALUES SHAPE HUMAN PROGRESS xvii–xxxiv (Lawrence E. Harrison & Samuel P. Huntington eds., 2000) [hereinafter CULTURE MATTERS]; Mariano Grondona, *A Cultural Typology of Economic Development*, *in* CULTURE MATTERS, *supra* note 5, at 44–55; Carlos Alberto Montaner, *Culture and the Behavior of Elites in Latin America*, *in* CULTURE MATTERS, *supra* note 5, at 56–64 (a review of the cultural factor in the fate of Latin American nations, among others in the developing world). *See also* Octavio Barrientos Sánchez, Culture and Legal Dogmatism in an Era of Immaterial Wealth: the Case of Latin America (unpublished manuscript) (on file with author).

[6] Memorandum from former Research Economist Mina Goldberg for Boris Kozolchyk (Sept. 11, 2008) (on file with author) [hereinafter Goldberg, Poverty Memorandum]. *See also* GUILLERMO E. PERRY ET AL., POVERTY REDUCTION AND GROWTH: VIRTUOUS AND VICIOUS CIRCLES (2006), *available at* http://siteresources.worldbank.org/EXTLACOFFICEOFCE/Resources/870892–1139877599088/virtuous_circles1_complete.pdf.

[7] PERRY ET AL., *supra* note 6, at 106.

[8] *See* WORLD BANK, POVERTY IN MEXICO: AN ASSESSMENT OF CONDITIONS, TRENDS AND GOVERNMENT STRATEGY xxi (June 2004), *available at* http://www-wds.worldbank.org/servlet/WDSContentServer/WDSP/IB/2004/07/13/000012009_20040713141715/Rendered/PDF/286120ME.pdf (on file with this author). As of 2004, "[t]he World Bank's 1993 consumption PPP exchange rate for Mexico [was] 2.102." *Id.*

purchasing power (PPP); another, less extreme measure, and equally adjusted for local currency purchasing power, is $2/day.[9]

TABLE: HUMAN AND INCOME POVERTY, HUMAN DEVELOPMENT REPORT 2009[10]

	Human Poverty Index (HPI-1) (%)	Population below income poverty line (%)		
		$1.25/day 2000–2007	$2/day 2000–2007	National poverty line 2000–2006
Argentina	3.7	4.5 **	11.3 **	- - -
Bolivia	11.6	19.6	30.3	65.2
Brazil	8.6	5.2	12.7	21.5
Chile	3.2	<2	2.4	17.0 *
Colombia	7.6	16.0	27.9	64.0 *
Costa Rica	3.7	2.4	8.6	23.9
Cuba	4.6	- - -	- - -	- - -
Dominican Republic	9.1	5.0	15.1	42.2
Ecuador	7.9	4.7	12.8	46.0 *
El Salvador	14.6	11.0	20.5	37.2
Guatemala	19.7	11.7	24.3	56.2
Haiti	31.5	54.9	72.1	- - -
Honduras	13.7	18.2	29.7	50.7
Mexico	5.9	<2	4.8	17.6
Nicaragua	17.0	15.8	31.8	47.9 *
Panama	6.7	9.5	17.8	37.3 *
Paraguay	10.5	6.5	14.2	- - -
Peru	10.2	7.9	18.5	53.1
Uruguay	3.0	<2 **	4.2 **	- - -
Venezuela	6.6	3.5	10.2	- - -
* Data refer to an earlier period outside range specified. ** Estimates cover urban areas only.				

---

[9] According to Goldberg:

> [T]he national measure [of] Latin American countries tend[s] to calculate extreme poverty, based primarily on the cost of a basic food bundle, and moderate poverty, computed as food plus. Measures differ considerably from country to country so that individuals considered poor in one Latin American country would not be so considered in another. . . . In addition, the United Nations has developed a Human Poverty Index (HPI—1), which is based on longevity (proportion of the population not expected to reach forty years of age); knowledge, using adult literacy; and a composite standard of living measured by proportion without clean water or health services and proportion of underweight children. There is also HPI-2, applied . . . to [selected] OECD countries, which applies a longevity standard of age 60 and includes some other components.

Goldberg, Poverty Memorandum, *supra* note 6, at 1 (citation omitted).

[10] Table prepared by Mina Goldberg using data from the 2009 Human Development Report. HUMAN DEVELOPMENT REPORT 2009, OVERCOMING BARRIERS: HUMAN MOBILITY AND DEVELOPMENT, UNITED NATIONS DEVELOPMENT PROGRAMME (UNDP), 176–179 (2009), *available at* http://hdr.undp.org/en/media/HDR_2009_EN_Complete.pdf. Data refer to the most recent available during the period specified. *See id.* at 203–07 (the Reader's Guide to the report).

According to the U.S. Census Bureau, the pre-tax median household income in 2007 was $50,233.[11] Although there are some methodological differences in collecting the figures, the table below,[12] showing median individual income calculated based upon Purchasing Power Parity (PPP), gives an idea of the variation of income between developed countries and Latin American countries.

TABLE: MEDIAN INDIVIDUAL INCOME IN THE U.S. AND MEXICO FOR 2006 AND IN GERMANY FOR 2005

	In U.S. dollars at PPP
United States[13]	$25,800
Germany[14]	$17,860
Mexico[15]	$10,940

As these tables make clear, poverty and a highly unequal distribution of income[16] are still an integral part of Latin American society despite the fact that following the end of the Spanish and Portuguese reign, many of the colonial legal institutions (statutes, administrative, and judicial rules and procedures) were replaced by post-

[11] *USA Statistics in Brief-Income and Poverty*, U.S. CENSUS BUREAU, http://www.census.gov/compendia/statab/2012/files/income.html (on file with author).

[12] *Foreign Exchange Rates—H.10,* THE FEDERAL RESERVE, http://www.federalreserve.gov/releases/h10/Hist/default.htm (on file with author) (providing the foreign exchange rates in different currencies).

[13] *Historical Income Data,* U.S. CENSUS BUREAU, http://www.census.gov/hhes/www/income/data/historical/index.html (on file with author). According to the U.S. Census Bureau, the pretax median individual income in 2006 was $25,795 (the figure in the table above has been rounded to $25,800). *Id.*

[14] The German figure above is equivalent to €15,617. *See* Community Statistics on Income and Living Conditions, EU-SILC (Leben In Europa) 2006, http://circa.europa.eu/Public/irc/dsis/eusilc/library?l=/&vm=detailed&sb=Title. The German figure is for disposable income and uses an:

> [E]quivalence scale [that] assigns a weight to each person in the household. The first adult always gets a weight of 1. Every additional person is given a weight which is [intended] to reflect how much more is needed because of that person: further adults and children from the age of 14 get a weight of 0.5 and children under 14 years a weight of 0.3.

Income, consumption, living conditions, DESTATIS.DE, https://www.destatis.de/EN/FactsFigures/SocietyState/IncomeConsumptionLivingConditions/ExplanationsTerms/PovertyRisk_SILC.html (on file with author).

[15] The Mexican figure above is monetary income per capita, and is figured as the average of the two middle tenths. *See Encuesta Nacional de Ingresos y Gastos de los Hogares* 2006, INSTITUTO NACIONAL DE ESTADÍSTICA Y GEOGRAFÍA (INEGI), http://www.inegi.org.mx/est/contenidos/Proyectos/Encuestas/Hogares/regulares/Enigh/Enigh2006/default.aspx. *See also* INSTITUTO NACIONAL DE ESTADÍSTICA Y GEOGRAFÍA (INEGI), EL INEGI DA A CONOCER LOS RESULTADOS DE LA ENCUESTA NACIONAL DE INGRESOS Y GASTOS DE LOS HOGARES (ENIGH) 2006, *available at* http://www.inegi.gob.mx/inegi/contenidos/espanol/prensa/Boletines/Boletin/Comunicados/Especiales/2007/Julio/comunica1.doc.

[16] *See* UNITED NATIONS DEVELOPMENT PROGRAMME (UNDP), THE HUMAN DEVELOPMENT REPORT 2007/2008, FIGHTING CLIMATE CHANGE: HUMAN SOLIDARITY IN A DIVIDED WORLD, 238–40, 281–84 (2007), *available at* http://hdr.undp.org/en/media/HDR_20072008_EN_Complete.pdf (on file with author). This report indicates inequality measured by the ratio of richest 10% to poorest 10%, as well as by the ratio of richest 20% to poorest 20%, the higher the ratio, the greater the inequality. At the 10% comparison, some representative ratios are Germany (6.9), France (9.1), Spain (10.3), Portugal (15.0), U.S. (15.9), Mexico (24.6), Honduras (34.2), Argentina (40.9) and El Salvador (57.5). *Id.* at 281–83. At the 20% comparison, the ratios are lower, ranging from 4.3 for Germany to 20.9 for El Salvador, but the rank order remains the same. *Id.* Thus, in Germany, the richest 20% garner 4.3 times the amount of income obtained by the poorest 20%. Note that "the underlying household surveys differ in method and in the type of data collected, [so that the distribution data can give an idea of inequality with respect to order of magnitude and variation among countries, but] the distribution data are not strictly comparable across countries." *Id.* at 284.

colonial official law, including civil and commercial codes *à la* France, Spain and Portugal which, in theory, aimed at encouraging economic growth. This chapter will identify key features of these codes and explore the reasons why neither the Spanish colonial law that preceded these codes nor the codes themselves contributed much to Latin America's economic growth. As will become apparent when studying the ineffectiveness of these laws, the operative legal institutions (the "living law"[17]) were elsewhere. The cultural-legal institutions that guided everyday commercial-legal behavior responded to a totally different set of principles than those reflected in Spain and Latin America's official law. One of these living law principles is the citizenry's culture of egalitarianism as manifested in perceived entitlement to rights and subjection to duties. And while the connection between a population's egalitarianism and its economic wellbeing still awaits definitive empirical confirmation, Costa Rica's statistics suggest a possible connection.

The World Bank's 2012 statistics on the Costa Rican economy[18] provide an encouraging picture of the developmental effects of its egalitarian living law than apparent in the above United Nations' 2009 Human Development Report: Access to primary education in Costa Rica continues to be one of the highest in Latin America and the percentage of poverty also continued to be among the lowest in Latin America (approximately 20%).[19] In addition, its per-capita annual income in United States Dollars was $11,600.00 in 2008.[20] As importantly, Costa Rica's egalitarian living law of the ownership of small parcels (*minufundia*) contributed to *a sui iuris* legal status (or a status of legal independence) rarely observed in other Latin American nations.

I first experienced the *sui iuris* egalitarian effects of Costa Rica's widespread ownership of small parcels (minifundia) during a picnic in suburban San Jose. A colleague at the University of Costa Rica where I taught and directed a law reform project during the late nineteen sixties invited my wife and me to a picnic on grounds that he believed were part of his family's parcel. Shortly after our arrival to this parcel, a fourteen year old shabbily dressed boy ran by us chasing a rather noisy goat. Our host, known for his brilliance as well as for his quick temper, yelled at the boy to get out of his property. The adolescent's reply illustrated the support that property ownership provided for Costa Ricans' egalitarian feelings. Addressing the illustrious law professor interchangeably as "tu" and "vos" (equally egalitarian subject pronouns, as contrasted with the respectful Usted") he said, according to my best recollection:

> You may be a famous lawyer, but you have no right to yell at me or to picnic on my family's property. You are lucky that I do not evict you while you are still eating. What kind of a lawyer are you who does not know that your property ends with the Guanacaste tree over there?

Our host humbly apologized and thanked him for letting us finish our picnic on his family's land. In the process we found out that he was the oldest of many children in a rather destitute farming family. The longer I stayed in Costa Rica, the clearer became

---

[17] *See* Glossary, "Living Law."

[18] *See Data Costa Rica,* THE WORLD BANK, http://data.worldbank.org/country/Costa-Rica (last visited Feb. 27, 2014).

[19] *Id.*

[20] *Per Capita Income,* FREE RESOURCES WEBSITE INDEX, http://siakhenn.tripod.com/capita.html (last visited Feb. 28, 2014).

the connection between the rural Costa Ricans' property rights in their minifundia (regardless of wealth or social status) and their egalitarian feelings toward one another.[21] As we will discuss in Chapter 21, a partly similar attitude was apparent among many of the Puritan settlers of the United States.[22] They preferred private over communal property and from this preference stemmed two convictions: 1) The labor that transformed or added value to property justified or strengthened the entitlement to it, and 2) that freedom of contract was the primary means to make one's private property marketable but on the basis of just and reasonable prices.[23] While the Costa Ricans shared the Puritans' first conviction, their official colonial and post-colonial law was unsympathetic to the second, as I will now discuss.

§ 14.3 SPANISH AND COLONIAL OFFICIAL LAW

A. Legalism and Rule of Law

Legalism is a form of law making and enforcement that has little to do with the respect for legal institutions as formulated in the contemporary expression "Rule of Law." The respect for the Rule of Law is not merely for the language of a constitutional, statutory or administrative provision or for the holding of a court decision; it is also for the reasoning and values that justify them and for the manner in which the norms are observed and protected in everyday life, including the judicial, administrative and customary law procedures aimed at preserving these values.

In contrast, as pointed out in the introduction to this part, authoritarian legalism only professes obedience for the law maker and his exalted position as an emperor, king or powerful official, as also noted in the introduction. It is best exemplified in the definition of a Spanish imperial law that we will encounter in the following section:[24] "*Quod principi placuit, legis habet vigorem*" (Whatever pleases the prince, enjoys the vigor of law). In other words, a legalistic law or rule need not be well reasoned nor well intended, although it could be. It may be the product of the ruler's misconceived notion of public welfare or of his individual greed. What matters most is that he who rules and enforces sets forth a discernible and enforceable rule.

The elements of enforceability of a legalistic rule vary with its legal culture. In some, enforceability depends upon the exalted position of the ruler and the ritualistic or magical trappings that surround promulgation and enforcement. In others, it depends upon faithfulness to an official dogma, whether it is "the greatest good for the greatest number" or "employment for the unemployed" or "from each according to his ability and to each according to his needs." In others, what matters most is that the rule be placed in the type of enactment that best expresses the will of the ruler, regardless of what the rule says.

The present chapter on the Latin American law of commercial contracts as well as the Chinese chapters that follow are largely concerned with the interaction between legalism and familism. Unlike legalism, familism is not official law, but a mostly

---

[21] Hugo Fernández, *Adult Education and Alternative Models of Social Organization of Production in Rurual Areas*, *in* International Technical Meeting on Adult Education and Community Enterprises in Development 2 (1978).

[22] *See infra* § 21:2(E).

[23] *Id.*

[24] *See infra* § 14:3(B).

informal or authoritarian living law. It governs the holding of the family's property, including its distribution and conveyance, the family's common budget, including its assets and liabilities, and its contracts with family and non-family members. And all of this contract activity takes place in the midst of an increasingly business world populated by third parties, "strangers," or non-family members.

B. Terminology and Types of Laws

The term "*ley*" is Spanish for the Latin *lex* ("law" in English). Professor Miguel Artola, a member of the Spanish Royal Academy of History, points out that *lex* and *constitutio* (*ley y constitución*) had the same meaning in Imperial Roman law: "Whatever pleases the prince, enjoys the vigor of law" ("*Quod principi placuit, legis habet vigorem*").[25] This vision of the law was shared by the Spanish colonial crown and its viceroys during much of the colonial period. As it turned out, this colonial attitude remained alive in much of the post-colonial commercial contract law.

Based on the legalistic manner in which official Spanish and colonial laws were enacted, *leyes* could be enacted simply because they "pleased the prince," were advised by the king's trusted advisors (*Curia regia*), or were consented to by *Cortes* or assemblies of representatives of the king's subjects, although with far less power of consent than that of parliaments in constitutional monarchies.[26] Many of these *leyes* were promulgated individually and in chronological fashion, and were read out loud by town criers (*pregoneros*). The enactment of the monumental Law of the Seven Parts (*Ley de las Siete Partidas*) by King Alphonse X (the Wise) in 1265—whose purpose was to unify Spanish law—influenced the promulgation of compilations of laws known as *recopilaciónes*. And even though many of these were not organized by subject matter as were the nineteenth-century codes, they provided indexes with which to identify the applicable laws. The "New Compilation of the Laws of Castilla" (*La Nueva Recopilación de Castilla*) in 1567 was the most important of these compilations until it was replaced by another compilation known as "A Critical Assessment of the *Novísima Recopilación*" (*Juicio crítico de la Novísima Recopilación*) which, as pointed out by Professor Artola, was undertaken as a critique of the *Nueva Recopilación*.[27]

Following the unification of the various kingdoms of Spain and the final expulsion of the Jews and Muslims in 1492 (the same year Columbus reached the Americas) by the Catholic Queen Isabella and King Ferdinand, Spain became a global empire. As Europe's strongest kingdom and leading world power during the sixteenth century and the first half of the seventeenth century, its *leyes* reached far beyond Spain and Europe to the Americas and the Philippines. Some of the former kingdoms, such as Castille,

---

[25] Miguel Artola, *El conocimiento de la ley,* MCU.ES, http://www.mcu.es/archivos/lhe/Informacion/introduccion.jsp (on file with author).

[26] *Id.* Professor Artola cites, as examples of the latter, the "*Breviario* de Alarico II, also known as *Lex romana Wisigothorum* was promulgated by an assembly [during the year of] (506) [C.E.] and the *Liber iudiciorum* (c. 654 [of the C.E.]). . . ." (author's translation). These compilations retained their force in the Christian kingdoms that followed the Muslim invasion of Spain until the Christian kings started to govern and promulgate laws with the advice of "*personas de experiencia* and trusted by the King (*Curia regia*)." *Id.* (author's translation). The participation of the attorneys for the important cities of the realm (*procuradores de las ciudades*) in assemblies called by the Kings gave rise to the term "laws with the consent of the royal courts" (*leyes hechas con el consentimiento de las Cortes*). *Id.* The reader will find these terms used occasionally in the compilation known as the "newest" or *Novísima Recopilación*, which will be discussed in a later section. *Id.*

[27] *Id.*

became responsible for the publication of compilations of some of the *leyes*. This compilation omitted laws issued solely with the advice of the *Curia Regis*. Among these were royal decrees (*pragmáticas*), ordinances (*ordenanzas*), or as "agreed upon royal acts" (*actos acordados*) and "royal letters" (*cartas reales*).[28] Their texts remained unpublished in the crown's archives.[29]

Despite Professor Artola's above-listed careful typology, a reader is hard put to find clear distinctions in the hierarchy of these laws, except for the *ordenanzas*, which usually pertained to one subject and attempted to exhaust it, although not always successfully. The rest of these laws seem to share the same hierarchy, although as will be discussed shortly, their observance both in Spain and Hispanic America was an altogether different story.

C. Compilations of Laws in Force in the Americas During the Colonial Period

1. Leyes de Indias*: Inequality and Customary Law*

Spain's relationship with the Americas (referred to by official Spanish law as "the Indies") was governed, in principle, by the Laws of Indies (*Leyes de Indias*).[30] These laws were first compiled in 1573 by order of King Phillip II. They comprised 148 decrees or ordinances that were the first to govern the manner in which military and civilian towns as well religious missions were to be established, including engineering and architectural details. However, as the Spanish and Portuguese colonies grew in size, their governing law became part of more comprehensive compilations.[31] As a rule,

---

[28] *Id.*

[29] *Id.* Some of these enactments will be referred to in later sections either by their full name or abbreviations which may also indicate the participation of the *Curia* or of the *Cortes*.

[30] *See* JUAN MANZANO MANZANO, IV RECOPILACIÓN DE LEYES DE LOS REYNOS DE LAS INDIAS (Ediciones Cultura Hispánica 1973) (1681).

[31] *See* RENÉ DAVID, TRATADO DE DERECHO CIVIL COMPARADO, EDITORIAL REVISTA DE DERECHO PRIVADO 251–52 (1953) (on the sources of colonial Portuguese law). Philip III (*Felipe III*) (April 14, 1578–March 31, 1621) was the King of Spain and King of Portugal and the Algarves, where he ruled as Philip II (*Filipe II*), from 1598 until his death. According to David and Belgian scholars he quotes:

> The institutions in the Portuguese colonies were mostly copied from those of the metropolis, without being, however, adapted to their new destination. Administrative organization never proceeded according to a uniform plan: it was determined by the march of events. The duties of the many officials, their hierarchy and relations of service, were not stipulated by laws or general rules, but by a mass of special decrees, some appointing functionaries for the places, others dealing with the solution of a transitory difficulty or the suppression of some abuse. Often the adjustment of the different pieces of the administrative machinery worked of itself, as a result of habit or routine, sometimes in accordance with the designs of the central government, other times against them.
>
> If the Portuguese Kings since the reign of John II (1481–95) had their lawyers who gave to the laws of the Kingdom the interpretation most suitable to the interests of the crown, the colonial governors also had their own legal authorities, who furnished the texts with the meaning most favorable to the power of the chiefs who respectively employed them. It certainly is not an easy task to describe this administrative machinery, even when one knows the text of the laws and decrees which have organized it, which is not always the case; but it is still more difficult to explain their real working [or application]. It is frequently impossible to distinguish with certainty the laws that were applied from those which were not applied, or which were not applied as they ought to have been, and it is not without difficulty that we are enabled to define with precision the duties of the several authorities.

Id.

these compilations did not distinguish between the laws applicable to Spain proper and to its colonies in the Americas and the Philippines.[32]

The *Leyes de Indias* attempted to regulate each aspect of the interaction between Spain and its colonies, including religion, education, trade, mining, navigation and migration, as well as the civil rights of races or nationalities (such as they were) and duties of the native American population.[33] In 1680, King Charles II ordered the drafting of a new *Recopilación de las Leyes de los Reynos de Indias*. It was published in 1681 and supposedly gathered all the laws which had a direct effect on the Americas. They addressed matters as portentous as whether the presidents (*rectores*) of the universities of Mexico and Peru had King Phillip III's permission to bring with them (supposedly to their workplace or when traveling) "two black servants with swords."[34] At the same time, they reflected the racial prejudices of Spanish and other conquerors during colonial times. Consider, for example, the following response by King Phillip III in a royal letter of April 24, 1618 to the Royal Council of the Indies and the Viceroy of Peru on the question of whether the following racial groups should be excluded from university courses: "[A]nd with respect to the exclusion of the *Mestizos*, *Zambos*, *Mulatos* y *Cuarterones* [I order] that *Constitución* 238 be observed."[35]

The Velazquez Spanish-English dictionary defines a "*mestizo*" as the offspring of a white man and Indian woman (or vice-versa), a "*zambo*" as the son of an Indian and a Chinese woman or vice-versa, a "*mulato*" as the offspring of a white person and a black person, and a "*cuarteron*" as a child of a Creole and a native of Spain.[36] I could not find the full text of *Constitución* 238 in the *Leyes de Indias* and thus do not know whether it decreed the rejection or admission of these groups of students. However, regardless of what it stated, the mere fact that these racial categories existed for educational, administrative and judicial purposes, and that a royal decree was required to decide on their admission to a university is indicative of a prevailing attitude. At the same time, one must question the efficacy of such distinctions in countries that already had a history of continuous racial and ethnic intermingling for almost two centuries. The category of *cuarteron* alone was typical of the blurred and therefore hard-to-enforce nature of the categories. For example, what was the status of the children of two *cuarterones*? Was it equal to the status of Creole or native Spanish children? Clearly, these and other racial categories had sufficiently similar physical and ethnic characteristics to warrant widespread evasion.

These racial and ethnic categories were not peculiar to the Peruvian administration. As insightfully noted by D. A. Brading, a Yale University historian:

---

[32] *See, e.g., infra* § 14:3(C)(3) (for excerpts from the *Novísima Recopilación).*

[33] *See Laws of the Indies,* Encyclopaedia Britannica, http://www.britannica.com/EBchecked/topic/286140/Laws-of-the-Indies. The first laws dealing with the status of the indigenous population were enacted in the sixteenth century. For example, the Laws of Burgos of 1512 and the New Laws of the Indies (*Leyes Nuevas*) of 1542. *Id.* The former established an indenture regime known as "*encomiendas*" whereby groups of Native Americans were "entrusted" to colonizers for their conversion to Catholicism and exploitation of the parcels of land given by the Spanish crown to the colonizers. The abuses of this regime were such that a new set of laws had to be enacted in 1542 in an attempt to improve the conditions of the natives. *Id.*

[34] *See* RECOPILACIÓN DE LEYES DE LOS REINOS DE LAS INDIAS, Book I, Tit. 22, Ley viii (1681) ("*dos Negros lacayos con espadas*"), *available at* http://www.filosofia.org/mfa/fae681a.htm.

[35] *Id.* Ley lvii ("*[Y] en cuanto a la exclusión de los Mestizos, Zambos, Mulatos y Cuarterones se observe la Constitución 238.*").

[36] *Id.*

> [T]he functional distinctions of Europe were replaced [in New Spain or *Nueva España* as Mexico was known during colonial days] by an ethnic stratification based upon the five Estates of Spaniards, *mestizos*, *mulatoes*, Indians and blacks. These categories indicated only the approximate genetic character of an individual and are best regarded as definitions of civic and fiscal status.[37]

Yet, consider the normative implications of such racial and ethnic classifications. If a legislative or administrative law body were to attempt to compile the customs and usages that prevailed among the merchants of New Spain or Peru, compliance with such official classifications would have required identifying the customs and usages peculiar to each racial and ethnic group. This would have been contrary to a culture that, despite the official distinctions, was not one of apartheid. On the contrary, the very existence of so many ethnic and racial categories reflected the large extent of racial and ethnic intermingling. Moreover, commerce, particularly at the retail level, was overwhelmingly interracial and interethnic. Not surprisingly, then, no compilations or manuals of racial or ethnic commercial customs were ever published in Hispanic America.[38] On the other hand, the Spanish merchants and their descendants, by tightly controlling commerce with and in the Americas (as will be discussed shortly), discouraged a pluralistic commercial law, *i.e.*, one that reflected the usages and customs of *all* the regular participants in the various markets. And, as I have concluded elsewhere, commercial law cannot develop unless it provides for equality of treatment in both its official and living law versions.[39]

2. La Nueva *and* Novísima Recopilación

Spain enacted compilations which applied to the mainland and colonies alike. Among these were the *Nueva* and *Novísima Recopilación*. Work on the *Nueva Recopilación* started in 1534 when the *Cortes* of Madrid acknowledged difficulties in determining the applicable laws in a previous privately-drafted compilation. This compilation was not finished until 1537 when a decree (*pragmática*) by King Phillip II ordered its application by all the courts of the realm.[40] It enjoyed a significant circulation and had numerous editions during the seventeenth and eighteenth centuries.

The *Nueva Recopilación* was succeeded by the *Novísima Recopilación*, which was completed in 1805.[41] According to the *Gran Enciclopedia de España* (hereinafter the Spanish Encyclopedia), it was intended as an update of the *Nueva Recopilación*, which

---

[37] *See* D. A. Brading, *Government and Elite in Late Colonial Mexico,* 53 HISP. AM. HIST. REV. 389, 389 (1973) (emphasis added) (citations omitted). *See also* Kozolchyk, *On the State of Commercial Law,* at 12–13 (discussing the importance of equality of treatment in the development of an observed and effective commercial law).

[38] *See generally* BERNAL DÍAZ DEL CASTILLO, THE DISCOVERY AND CONQUEST OF MEXICO: 1517–1521 (A. P. Maudslay trans., Genaro Garcia, ed., Da Capo Press 2003) (1956). Bernal Díaz del Castillo, a Spanish Conquistador in Hernán Cortés' army, published a diary of the conquest of Mexico. In it, he provides interesting details on the manner in which Aztec merchants conducted their every, and mostly barter, activities in Mexican markets. However, his was a chronicle and not a compilation of usages and customs.

[39] Kozolchyk, *On the State of Commercial Law,* at 30.

[40] *See generally* NUEVA RECOPILACIÓN DE LAS LEYES DEL REINO Y AUTOS ACORDADOS (1982).

[41] *See Novísima Recopilación*, GRAN ENCICLOPEDIA DE ESPAÑA, http://www.granenciclopedia.es/derecho/novisima.htm (on file with author) (author's translation) (a historical and analytical summary on the *Novísima Recopilación*, on which this author relied for a general description of this important source of pre-codification commercial contract law in the Americas).

was widely criticized because it ignored some non-royal legislative enactments and included a large number of obsolete royal enactments.[42] Consecutive compilers were appointed during the latter part of the eighteenth century and it was finally submitted for royal approval by King Charles IV in 1805.[43] Because of its date (shortly before the commencement of the independence process in the Americas), it was the last set of Spanish laws for many of the Latin American colonies and it was in effect during the time when these colonies were attaining increasing commercial and economic importance and a growing (though grudgingly-granted) measure of political autonomy.

The *Novísima Recopilación* was divided into twelve books (*libros*) and subdivided into 340 titles (*títulos*) and statutes or laws (*leyes*).[44] The first five books covered numerous topics starting with the Church, its relations with the king and the *Cortes* (the quasi-legislative body), succession to the crown, justice by the king and his *Curia Regis*, civil status, privileges, obligations, charges and contributions of vassals, military service, treasury and the supreme council, municipal government, and laws on hunting and fishing.[45] Of particular interest to us, as will be discussed in a later section, are Books VIII (on the sciences, arts and professions) and IX (on the Board of Trade, money and mines).

Despite the fact that the *Novísima Recopilación* was introduced to the public as "the most complete and varied work both in conception and method,"[46] it was severely criticized almost immediately after publication. One of the critics, the respected jurist Francisco Martínez Marina, referred to it in 1820 as a "vast structure raised from rubbish and ancient ruins; a monstrous edifice comprised of heterogeneous parts and irreconcilable norms; a heaping of old and new laws. . . ."[47] An even harsher criticism appeared in one of the least expected places, the introduction to its 1850 edition by F. de P. Díaz y Mendoza:

> This code, whose purpose was to amend and correct mistakes in its predecessor's references to ancient laws, laws which had fallen into disuse, and [whose purpose was also] to avoid the wrongs committed by relying on mistaken transcriptions of the original texts and which resulted in the inability to determine their true and valid meaning and thus many contrary interpretations existed, failed to fulfill such a purpose. . . . [Consequently,] we live amid the same chaos as we did before its enactment."[48]

---

[42] *Id.*

[43] *Id.*

[44] *Id.*

[45] *Id.*

[46] *Id.* It states: "*la obra más completa y variada en su plan y método.*" *Id.*

[47] Francisco Martínez Marina, *Juicio Crítico sobre la Novísima Recopilación*, *cited in* MANUEL F. LADREDA, ESTUDIOS HISTÓRICOS SOBRE LOS CÓDIGOS DE CASTILLA 184 (1896).

[48] *See* Néstor de Buen, *Derecho y Justicia en Cervantes: Burla Burlando,* 11 REV. DER. PRIVADO 3, 4 (UNAM, May–Aug., 2005) (author's translation), *available at* http://www.juridicas.unam.mx/publica/librev/rev/derpriv/cont/11/dtr/dtr1.pdf. Buen quotes F. de P. Díaz y Mendoza:

> Este Código, formado para corregir y enmendar muchas de las leyes antiguas que por el transcurso de los tiempos habían caído en desuso, y para evitar los males que resultaban de no haberse copiado aquellas leyes de sus verdaderos originales, de lo cual resultaba que era muchas veces imposible atinar con su genuina y legítima aplicación, por aparecer muchas contrarias entre sí, estuvo, sin embargo, muy lejos de corresponder a las esperanzas que su autor hizo concebir. Si hasta entonces había estado el Reino sin una compilación legal que fuera verdaderamente digna de este nombre, y si hasta entonces había carecido de un cuerpo de leyes completo y bien

While the Spanish Encyclopedia is not as harsh a critic as were Martínez Marina or Díaz y Mendoza, it acknowledges the anachronism of this compilation, especially taking into account that it was published a year after France published its *Code Civil*, which it regarded as a much more coherent and precise enactment, and one whose coverage it overlapped considerably. In addition, it was plagued by insufficiencies, contradictions, omissions, and improper citations.[49] Nonetheless, despite its "chaotic" nature, the *Novísima Recopilación* was the fundamental private law text of Spain and its colonies until the enactment of Latin America's civil and commercial codes.

3. *Excerpts from the* Novísima Recopilación[50]

a. *Law No. 2 of King Ferdinand & Queen Isabella on July 25, 1499*[51]

On how no foreigner can engage in the business of money changing in this Realm, even though he holds a letter of naturalization:

We have been informed that some foreign persons [*i.e.,* not born in our kingdoms] . . . try to do business as money changers [in our kingdoms] and engage in such changes inside and outside of our Courts . . . [we have also been informed that] from the currency they change they select the best shaped because they yield the highest profits and then they take these coins out of our realm and leave us with defective coins . . . in order to prevent such conduct from now on and hereafter . . . we order and enjoin by this royal letter that any foreigner who is not born in our Kingdoms, even though he holds a letter of naturalization, shall not be allowed to carry out the trade of money exchanger, nor acquire currency of any kind, inside or outside of our Courts or in any city or town in our kingdoms and [if he does so, he] will forfeit all of his currency plus one half of his entire estate; [The distribution of the proceeds of this fine will be as follows:] half of what is recovered belongs to our [royal] Chamber, the other half will be divided into two parts, one half belongs to his accuser and the other half to the Judge and executor of our judgment. . . .

COMMENTS AND QUESTIONS

Clearly, money changers were not very popular with Isabella and Ferdinand, particularly after these rulers expelled the Jews from their kingdom in part because of

---

> clasificado, que ocurriera a las exigencias y necesidades de la época, bien podemos asegurar sin temor a equivocarnos que, a pesar de la recopilación, siguió en el mismo caos de que creyó haber salido.

Id. at 4. To this, Néstor de Buen added:

> Si la colección fue desordenada, con entrevero de materias diferentes en los mismos libros, asistemática y de dudosa autenticidad de lo transcrito, no es de extrañar que el mundo de las normas haya sido anárquico y desigual en los tiempos en que Miguel de Cervantes corría la legua, viviendo sus miserias y sus hazañas.

Id. at 5.

[49] *See* GRAN ENCICLOPEDIA DE ESPAÑA, *supra* note 35.

[50] IV NOVÍSIMA RECOPILACIÓN DE LAS LEYES DE ESPAÑA (1805) [hereinafter IV NOVÍSIMA RECOPILACIÓN], *available at* http://fama2.us.es/fde/ocr/2006/novisimaRecopilacionT4.pdf. Volume IV includes Book VIII on sciences, arts and trades (*De Las Ciencias, Artes y Oficios*), including the rules pertaining to manufacture of goods; and Book IX on commerce.

[51] *Id.* at 241 (Book IX, Title III, Law II).

their alleged religious and usurious practices. The reader will also recall the connection that existed in European law since medieval times between usury and the contract of exchange and bills of exchange as devices with which to evade it.[52] Yet, strictly from an enforcement standpoint, how could this Royal Letter be enforced in a region such as the Americas where it was extremely difficult, at least during the time of the enactment of this decree, to determine who was born where? Whatever documentation existed during the enactment of this decree came from the Board of Trade of Seville (*Casa de Contratación*) and the consulate of the same city. As will be discussed shortly, these entities were notorious for their corrupt practices, especially in the issuance of identity and other travel documents. In a later section,[53] I will also discuss the serious lack of coin for commercial transactions in the internal trade of New Spain. Could this Royal Letter, which the 1806 *Novísima Recopilación* lists as in force in the Americas at the time of its enactment, contribute to the lack of currency in the commercial markets of New Spain in the seventeenth and eighteenth centuries?

b. Law No. 3 of Charles I & Philip II on October 6, 1552[54]

> Prohibition against exchanges of currency [by means of bills of exchange] that charge interest from the time they were drawn at one fair or place of business to the time of another fair or place of business.
>
> We order, forbid and enjoin from now and hereafter that a person or persons, whatever their status or condition, be they born in these kingdoms or be they foreigners, exchange *maravedis* for other currency, regardless of the amount exchanged, if they charge interest on the amount exchanged, whether it is for sending such currency from one city or location of these kingdoms to another or from one fair to another, and if such moneys were exchanged by paying interest on them, regardless of whether the interest is collectible in currency or kind, whether done publicly or secretly, [as punishment,] these amounts shall be forfeited and the exchanger will be subject to the recovery procedure assigned to usurious loans, including the penalties that prevail for such loans in the laws of our kingdoms. . . .

COMMENTS AND QUESTIONS

This law effectively forbids the use of bills of exchange as devices with which to obtain commercial loans anywhere in the Spanish kingdoms. Considering that commercial credit was generally unavailable in France[55] and Spain[56] except by means

---

[52] *See supra* § 5:7(A)–(B).

[53] *See infra* § 14:4(B).

[54] IV NOVÍSIMA RECOPILACIÓN, *supra* note 45, at 241 (Book IX, Title III, Law III).

[55] *See supra* § 9:2(E)(3)(A).

[56] IV NOVÍSIMA RECOPILACIÓN, *supra* note 45, at 241 (Book IX, Title III, Law III). This law was transcribed in the principal text and was in all likelihood modified in relevant part by the Spanish Law of July 23, 1908 (*Ley de 23 de julio de 1908*), known as the Law of Repression of Usury. *Ley de 23 de Julio de 1908, de la Usura*, NOTICIAS JURIDICAS, *available at* http://noticias.juridicas.com/base_datos/Privado/1230708.html. It redefined usury in its Article 1 as follows:

> A loan agreement shall be null and void if it stipulates a rate of interest which is notably superior to the normal one charged for the loan of money and which is manifestly disproportionate to the circumstances of the case or in circumstances such that is leonine, there being enough reasons to surmise that it was accepted by the borrower because of his penury, inexperience or limited mental faculties.
>
> *Será nulo todo contrato de préstamo en que se estipule un interés notablemente superior al normal del dinero y manifiestamente desproporcionado con las circunstancias del caso o en condiciones*

of bills of exchange or by "book debts" (*i.e.*, sales payable in installments whose price was inflated to include the amounts of unpaid interest), what was the effect of this law upon commercial and consumer transactions? Aside from encouraging reliance on other ingenious circumventions of the letter and spirit of such a law (dangerous and costly as they were bound to be), what effect did this prohibition have upon the emergence of a *legitimate* commercial banking industry in Spain and its colonies? Why is it important for the economic development purposes of market-oriented societies that the commercial lending industry be a legitimate and well-regulated endeavor?

c. Law No. 4 of King Phillip IV on February 10, 1623[57]

> Prohibition of the manufacture and sale of silk and wool cloth without the account and marks required by law as provided by the laws and ordinances of this kingdom.
>
> Because the factories that produce silk and woolen cloth, whether in pure or mixed fashion, *have engaged and continue to engage in much deceit*, and because lacking a standard ["*ley*"] they manufacture their wares with much malice so that they last very little and [wind up causing] great expense to those who use them, we order and enjoin that from now on and hereafter no manufacture or sale be made in our kingdoms [of the above items] whether for clothing or any other purpose . . . under penalty of loss of the products and a fine of one hundred thousand *maravedis*, to be distributed in three equal parts to the Royal Chamber, Judge and accuser . . . [and similarly] merchants who sell this cloth or manufactured products in their shops are equally subject to the above fines.

COMMENTS AND QUESTIONS

Some policymakers who favor a regime of unrestricted freedom of contract and unregulated market decisions tend to forget that without governmental regulation on some of the most essential market components, there would be no "free markets." One of these components is reliance on the truth expressed to each other by market participants. Human nature being the mixture of altruism and selfishness it is; someone must ensure the disclosure and accuracy of key components of commercial transactions, such as their weights and measures.

As an adolescent and part-time silk cloth salesman in my father's store, I experienced the need for truth in the weights and measures of cloth. As a short-statured person, I was replacing a much taller salesman. One of his longtime customers asked me to sell her three *varas* of cloth (a *vara* was roughly three quarters of a meter). I noticed that the salesman I replaced measured the cloth he sold by using the length of his left arm and half of his chest as the equivalent of a *vara*. As I was

---

> *tales que resulte aquél leonino, habiendo motivos para estimar que ha sido aceptado por el prestatario a causa de su situación angustiosa, de su inexperiencia o de lo limitado de sus facultades mentales.*

Id. (author's translation). This provision bears a close resemblance to BGB § 138(2) (GOREN, 1994) . It states:

> A legal transaction by which a person exploiting the need, inexperience, lack of sound judgment or substantial lack of will power of another, causes to be promised or granted to himself or to a third party in exchange for a performance, pecuniary advantages which are in obvious disproportion to the performance is also void.

Id.

[57] IV NOVÍSIMA RECOPILACIÓN, *supra* note 45, at 188 (Book VIII, Title XXIV, Law IV).

about to measure the three *varas* requested by the customer in the same way as the taller salesman, she quickly stopped me and asked me to use a regularly inspected wooden *vara* to measure the cloth. When I inquired why she did not ask the taller salesman to use the same registered *vara*, she told me that she did not distrust me, but since I was much shorter than he, so was the length of my left arm.

The main difference between this exchange and the law transcribed above is that this customer did not distrust my good faith. She recognized that I was acting out of inexperience. Law IV by King Phillip IV truly distrusted all the manufacturers and merchants to whom it referred. Unlike me, they were not presumed to be acting in good faith or inexperience. They were presumed to regularly act in a deceitful manner, a manner usually associated with those who made their living as merchants in the broad sense of this term. My question is: What are the consequences of regulating commerce with an assumption that if *all* merchants are left to their own devices, they will act in bad faith? Please reread my conversation with Professor Karl Llewellyn in connection with Levin Goldschmidt's influence upon his legal thinking.[58]

d. *Law 17 of King Phillip V, December 2, 1737 and King Charles IV, June 3, 1805*[59]

On Contracts between or among merchants; their quality and fulfillment:

1. All the sales, purchases, adjustments or contracts between two or more merchants payable on a cash or installment basis, or on the basis of barter or any other method, shall be effectuated and fulfilled in accordance with the quality and circumstances of the adjustment, unless otherwise agreed or rescinded.

2. In those sales, purchases and adjustments reduced to a writing, the contracts shall be made using the clearest and most intelligible terms (*voces*), avoiding confusion and ambiguities and expressing in all of them the conditions, quantity, quality, marks, numbers and forms of payment.

3. If these agreements are effectuated in the presence of "sworn brokers" (*corredores jurados*) they shall have the same binding force as if they had been executed in public instruments [before notary publics] and whatever difference that appeared in the recollection of the contracting parties with respect to the terms and their adjustments to the circumstances shall be resolved by what appears in the books of the broker and in the consistent entries [in the records] of the transaction kept by one of the parties.

5. When the contracts are entered into solely by the parties and without the intervention of a broker, the parties shall be obligated to reduce these contracts to similar copies (*papel recíproco*) so that each knows what it agreed to and to avoid lawsuits and disputes that usually arise when they do not agree with respect to what has been contracted.

6. In the case of a contract not being reduced to a writing, it will be the obligation of the seller to give the buyer a copy or memory of the transaction and the buyer shall return it duly signed in handwriting with the expression of his agreement to its terms.

---

[58] *Supra* § 13:1(C)(2)(a).

[59] IV NOVÍSIMA RECOPILACIÓN, *supra* note 45, at 253 (Book IX, Title IV, Law XVII).

7. The transactions entered into by persons who are absent from each other, will be documented by what was recorded in their books and original letters received [by the parties] and their copies. . . .

COMMENTS AND QUESTIONS

The manner in which these ordinances were written differs from the style and content present in the preceding Spanish royal laws or decrees. What are the main differences? What are the differences of substance and style between the Bilbao ordinances and the rules on contract formation found in the *Code Civil*? If you conclude that in terms of substance these ordinances are less rigid than the *Code Civil* with respect to, say, the form of contracts and their method of interpretation, what is the reason for such a difference? From the standpoint of the method or style of drafting, which of the two enactments is more precise? Consider, for example, the list in the Ordinances of Bilbao of separate categories of agreements that include "sales, purchases, adjustments or contracts" and contrast it with the definition of a contract by the *Code Civil*. Does the latter's definition of contract include all the categories of the *Ordenanzas*? How would the merchants of the Consulate of Bilbao who drafted these ordinances define the term "contract" and why did they list it as a separate category from purchases, sales and adjustments? Do you detect an association in the *Ordenanzas* between their use of the terms "contract" and "writing," If so, what was the source of their formulation? How does this source differ from that used by the drafters of the *Code Civil*?

4. The Regulation of Colonial Trade

As aptly noted by Professor Matthew Campbell Mirow: "The extraction of wealth and the concomitant exploitation of native and imported labor were the overall aims of colonial commerce."[60] To achieve these aims, the Spanish crown relied on administrative and judicial entities such as the Council of the Indies (*Real y Supremo Consejo de Indias*), the Board of Trade (*Casa de Contratación*), and the commercial consulates (*consulados de mercaderes*) to supervise a regime of both oligopolistic and mercantilistic trade. While the Council of the Indies was the highest administrative, legislative and judicial body with respect to Spanish-American and intra-American trade,[61] day-to-day administrative (and some judicial) decision-making was delegated to the Board of the Trade and some commercial consulates.

a. Board of Trade and Official and Royal Monopolies

It was not by accident that Isabella and Ferdinand were buried in the Cathedral of Seville. When Hispanic America was discovered by Columbus, Seville was the largest and wealthiest city in Spain. Thus, it made sense for them to locate the Board of Trade and Spain's most important commercial consulate in Seville. The Board of Trade was

---

[60] MATTHEW CAMPBELL MIROW, LATIN AMERICAN LAW: A HISTORY OF PRIVATE LAW AND INSTITUTIONS IN SPANISH AMERICA 70 (2004) (citation omitted).

[61] IBERIA AND THE AMERICAS: CULTURE, POLITICS, AND HISTORY 369–70 (John Michael Francis ed., 2006) [hereinafter IBERIA AND THE AMERICAS]. The Council was created in 1524 by Charles I and was the highest administrative and judicial body where Spanish American relations were concerned. *Id.* at 369. It met regularly with the King to advise him on executive, legislative and judicial matters related to the Americas. *Id. See also* ÓSCAR CRUZ BARNEY, EL RIESGO EN EL COMERCIO HISPANO-INDIANO: PRÉSTAMOS Y SEGUROS MARÍTIMOS DURANTE LOS SIGLOS XVI–XIX (1998) (on the judicial function of the Council). Barney includes the text of the Royal Decree of 1795 that created the Consulate of Veracruz. BARNEY, *supra* note 55, at 18. Under the Royal Decree's rule XIII, all the appeals from disputes among merchants are directed in a final instance and only for gross miscarriages of justice to the "Supreme Council of the Indies." *Id.* at 218.

established by royal decree (*decreto real*) in 1503.[62] Its mission was to encourage and regulate commerce and navigation to and from the Indies. Its official title, House and Audience of the Indies (*Casa y Audiencia de Indias*), highlighted its function as the administrative and judicial entity in charge of trade with the Indies. However, from its inception, it became clear that not only the private traders, but the crown itself, wanted to profit from trade with the Indies. As pointed out by Clarence Henry Haring in his classic 1918 study on trade and navigation between Spain and the Americas, while the Board of Trade was originally conceived as a trading house, one of its special missions was to oversee the king's personal investments in the Americas[63] and to ensure the collection of the numerous crown taxes on cargo shipped to and from the Americas.[64]

In due course, the Board of Trade was in charge of every aspect of maritime trade with the Americas, although some of its functions were relinquished to the Council of the Indies in 1543.[65] It regulated, among other activities: shipping (especially the organization of the annual or bi-annual fleet);[66] migration to and from the Americas; relations among merchants and sailors; disposition of the assets of Spaniards who had died in the Indies; qualification of vessels, seamen, and pilots; updating navigational maps; and police and religious activities (which required a permanent jail and a chapel on the Board of Trade's premises). Located on the banks of the Guadalquivir River, Seville was an inland gateway to the Atlantic Ocean, and thus convenient for both shipping and monopolistic control over shippers and their cargo. Seville retained this monopoly until the consulate and most shipping facilities were transferred to the port of Cadiz in 1717.[67]

---

[62] *See generally* ANA CRESPO SOLANA, LA CASA DE CONTRATACIÓN Y LA INTENDENCIA GENERAL DE LA MARINA EN CÁDIZ (1717–1730) (1996). According to the 1503 statute (issued in the city of Alcalá de Henares), the Board of Trade was supposed to "gather and store as long as necessary as many goods and wares, parts and supplies to provide all the necessary things involved in trade with the Indies. . . ." MANUEL DANVILA Y COLLADO, SIGNIFICACIÓN QUE TUVIERON EN EL GOBIERNO DE AMÉRICA LA CASA DE LA CONTRATACIÓN DE SEVILLA Y EL CONSEJO SUPREMO DE INDIAS 18–19 (Madrid, Jan. 7, 1892) (author's translation) ("Para recoger y tener en ella, todo el tiempo necesario, cuantas mercaderías, mantenimientos y otros aparejos fueren menester para proveer todas las cosas necesarias para la contratación de las Indias . . . .")

[63] *See* CLARENCE HENRY HARING, TRADE AND NAVIGATION BETWEEN SPAIN AND THE INDIES IN THE TIME OF THE HAPSBURGS 22–24 (1918).

[64] IBERIA AND THE AMERICAS, *supra* note 55, at 55–56.

[65] *See* DANVILA Y COLLADO, *supra* note 56, at 21–22 (on the administrative and judicial functions of the Board of Trade).

[66] *See Las Carreras de las Indias—1,* HISTORIA Y ARQUELOGIA MARITIMA (July 2007), http://www.histarmar.com.ar/InfGral/AASidoli/CarreraIndias-1.htm (on file with author). Spain's policy was to establish a monopoly, keeping her colonies dependent on her. By law, Spanish colonials could trade only with the authorized Spanish merchant *flotas*. This monopoly was eventually challenged successfully by English, French and Dutch traders. Supposedly these fleets were to sail once or twice a year (though they hardly ever sailed on schedule). The fleets carried manufactured goods for sale to the colonials and returned with gold, silver, emeralds and other gemstones, hides, exotic woods, copper, tobacco, sugar, cochineal, indigo, and other commodities. The fleet would leave Spain (first from Seville and later Cadiz), sail down the coast of Africa until they reached the Cape Verde Islands. From there, they sailed west with the prevailing tradewinds until they entered the Caribbean. At that point the ships split into two separate fleets, the *Nueva España flota* and the *Tierra Firme flota*. The first fleet sailed to Mexico (*Nueva España*'s) port of Vera Cruz, while the second fleet visited the South American mainland ports of Cartagena, Nombre de Dios, and Porto Bello. After loading the return trip cargo, the fleets would meet in Havana, Cuba and sail back to Spain after heading north through Florida. *Id.*

[67] IBERIA AND THE AMERICAS, *supra* note 55, at xxxii.

b. *The Commercial Consulate (*Consulado de Mercaderes*)*

The Commercial Consulate of Seville was created in 1543.[68] It was an association of merchants whose principal purpose was to protect city merchant trading from non-resident (*no burgueses*) competitors.[69] As time went on, the Commercial Consulate absorbed the Board of Trade's civil jurisdiction over disputes between or among the consulate's members. Its operations were governed by a set of 1556 ordinances[70] which required that any merchant who did business with the Indies, as long as he was not a foreigner or an agent or dependent of that foreigner, had to be a member of the consulate.

The Consulate's revenues were derived from the issuance of "general average" maritime insurance policies (*averias*), which were obligatory for anyone doing business with the Americas who shipped merchandise worth more than 1000 *ducates* on one or more occasions. This fee was intended to defray the costs of the royal navy that was to defend the merchant vessels from privateers. However, by the eighteenth century, Seville's role as an exporter and organizer of fleets had drastically diminished and most of the members of the consulate earned their living as "name-lenders" (*prestanombres*) and commission agents for foreign manufacturers and exporters interested in shipping their products through Seville. Nevertheless, powerful vested interests continued to protect Seville's monopoly.[71] In theory, then, only Spaniards could ship their goods or perform their services in the Indies, but in fact bribery by foreign merchant houses and smuggling by locals and foreigners alike were the norm.

§ 14.4 THE LIVING LAW OF COLONIAL COMMERCIAL CONTRACTS: ARCHETYPAL BEHAVIOR

If "official" legal institutions failed to help Latin American societies escape poverty, even though they helped other civil law countries such as the nineteenth- and twentieth-century Germany to become leading commercial and industrial powers, was the failure not of official commercial contract law in Latin America but of its counterpart "living law" institutions?

Some of the most durable living law institutions of the Latin American law of commercial contracts took hold from the seventeenth to the nineteenth centuries. Among them was the archetypal contractual behavior of Latin America's commercial elite. They included the contractual behavior of New Spain's wholesalers (*almaceneros* or *mercaderes*), a Spanish-American version of Fernand Braudel's "high commerce"[72] leading merchants (*hacendados*) of New Spain's agribusiness. Both of these merchants did their business with the strong support of governmental protectors who were frequently New Spain or Latin American "strongmen" (*caudillos*) or their "name lenders" (*prestanombres* y *testaferros*). As will become apparent in the remainder of this chapter, their archetypal behavior was in sharp contrast with that of the Roman *bonus vir* and the German honest, decent merchant. These *almaceneros* and *hacendados* were monopolists or oligopolists who practiced a version of commerce

---

[68] *Id.* at xxviii.

[69] *Id.* at 119.

[70] HARING, *supra* note 57, at xvii–xviii.

[71] IBERIA AND THE AMERICAS, *supra* note 55, at 120.

[72] *See supra* § 5:4(B).

similar to that of a zero-sum game. Their type of commerce never involved the "Christian morality" advocated by Mexico's "good men" (*hombres de bien*), discussed later in this chapter.[73]

A. High Commerce in New Spain: *Picaresque Mercaderes, Flotistas, Almaceneros*, and *Hacendados*

1. *Introduction: Exporters, Importers and Wholesalers*

As aptly put by Professor Stanley Stein of Princeton University in reference to the economy of New Spain: "[I]f (in 1595) [it was true that] 'without silver, nothing happens in this kingdom,' . . . [in 1651 it was also true] that 'in this realm the chief source of wealth is trade.'"[74] He added that "[i]n both sectors the colonial merchant elite flourished"[75] and wound up shaping that colony's commercial practices and living law during its pre-codification days.

As in Europe, New Spain's high commerce was formed by a relatively small group of merchants known generically as "*mercaderes*" or "*comerciantes*." They comprised two groups of merchants.[76] One included the mostly-Spanish exporters and importers (*flotistas*) who shipped their goods from Seville, Spain to Veracruz, New Spain and to the Gulf of Panama and the northern ports of South America.[77] The other was comprised of wholesalers of imported goods (*almaceneros*) who financed their distribution and resided mostly in the Americas.

At first, the fleet's carrying vessels were mostly owned by Seville merchant houses or were chartered by the shippers who qualified as such by the Seville consulate. Two centuries later, however, most of the vessels in the Spanish fleet were owned by foreign merchants and nations. The following pages should help clarify the reasons for this change.

The Seville-based (and duly authorized) shippers exported needed goods and commodities to the colonizers of New Spain. On their return trips, they brought back silver bullion and coins as well as sugar, cacao, dyestuffs (especially cochineal), textiles and other desirable novelties extracted from or produced in New Spain for use in the Spanish and European markets. Their shipments to and from the Americas were carried by fleets (*flotas*). They sailed only once or twice per year, depending upon the availability of accompanying navy vessels and market conditions in the Americas.

Their eventual competitors, the *almaceneros*, lived and did their business mostly in or out of New Spain. The term "*almaceneros*" meant wholesalers ("*almacenistas*" in our day), though it eventually meant much more than that.[78] *Almaceneros* purchased

---

[73] *See infra* § 14:4 (A)(8).

[74] Stanley J. Stein, *Louisa Schell Hoberman's Mexico's Merchant Elite, 1590–1660: Silver, State, and Society*, 73 HISP. AMER. HIST. REV. 151 (Feb. 1993) (book review) (citation omitted).

[75] *Id.*

[76] *See* Jeremy Baskes, *Risky Ventures: Reconsidering Mexico's Colonial Trade System*, XIV COLONIAL LATIN AM. REV. 27–54 (June 2005). In the following description of the *modus operandi* of exporters, importers and wholesalers, I will follow the description provided by Professor Jeremy Baskes. Although I do not agree with all of his conclusions, I consider his facts carefully gathered and sufficiently documented to provide a persuasive version of archetypal commercial behavior in colonial Mexico.

[77] BARNEY, *supra* note 55, at 5–6.

[78] A number of fine studies are available on the *almaceneros. See, e.g.*, D.A. BRADING, MINERS AND MERCHANTS IN BOURBON MEXICO, 1763–1810 (1971); Baskes, *supra* note 70; Jackie R. Booker, *The Veracruz*

imported goods either directly from the *flotistas* upon the arrival of the fleet in Veracruz or from the latter's agents in that port. Upon purchase, they stored and resold the goods throughout New Spain and in neighboring nations as well. Their distribution system relied on commission agents, joint venturers and a widespread credit network. Depending upon market conditions, they would either attempt to resell the goods quickly or hold them until the time for resale was ripe. It did not take long before the leading *almaceneros* became influential members of consulates created in the most important trading cities of New Spain: Mexico City, Guadalajara and Veracruz.[79] And as the most influential members of these consulates, they competed against the *flotistas* for control of New Spain's wholesale and retail markets.

I should note that unlike in pre-codified France, in New Spain, the chief vehicle for upward economic and social mobility was not a bourgeois type of landholding, but an aggressive involvement with commerce and silver mining, although the latter attracted only those *almaceneros* who did not mind a much riskier business. Success in commerce often led to the purchase of recreational or industrial *haciendas*, but their wealth remained tied to commerce.[80]

2. *The Struggle for Control of the New Spanish Market*

At first, the businesses of the *flotistas* and *almaceneros* were often indistinguishable. The same *mercader* whose "house" was a member of the Consulate of Seville shipped goods in his own vessels or consigned them in other merchants' vessels to their Veracruz agents or partners who would then resell them. Depending upon market conditions, the agent of the Seville merchant could store the goods while awaiting propitious market conditions for resale and thereby become an *almacenero*. More frequently, however, he would resell the goods upon arrival. As the eighteenth century progressed, the differences between the *flotista* and *almacenero* methods of doing business became sharper and a battle for control of the New Spain markets ensued, from which the *almaceneros* emerged as the clear victors.

a. *Control of the Supply of Goods: Taxation, Circumvention and Smuggling*

When the fleets were first organized by the Board of Trade, the *flotistas* of Seville, and subsequently of Cadiz, had reasons to believe that they would easily control the supply of goods and thereby market prices and contractual terms in New Spain.

Merchant Community in Late Bourbon Mexico: A Preliminary Portrait, 1770–1810, 45 THE AMERICAS 187, 187–99 (Oct. 1988); BARNEY, *supra* note 55; JOHN E. KICZA, COLONIAL ENTREPRENEURS, FAMILIES AND BUSINESS IN BOURBON MEXICO CITY (1983); Stanley J. Stein, *Tending the Store: Trade and Silver at the Real de Huautla, 1778–1781*, 77 HISP. AM. HIST. REV., 377–407 (Aug. 1997); LOUISA SCHELL HOBERMAN, MEXICO'S MERCHANT ELITE, 1590–1660: SILVER, STATE, AND SOCIETY (1991). These studies have also been used in the following section of this chapter, in attempting to put together an objective description of this most important period in the shaping of Mexican and Latin American commercial archetypes.

[79] The group of wholesalers studied by Hoberman numbered 177, it being the number of persons who called themselves wholesalers in 1689. HOBERMAN, *supra* note 72, at 20. The group studied by Booker was larger. Booker, *supra* note 72, at 192. According to Professor Booker, at least 232 domestic and international merchants occupied the highest rank of the commercial pyramid in Veracruz during the period she studied. *Id.* As with their Mexico City colleagues, Veracruz wholesalers exported a plethora of colonial products and imported large quantities of European merchandise. And as also apparent with their Mexico City colleagues, they controlled Veracruz's social order. *Id.* at 192–93.

[80] *See* Brading, *supra* note 31, at 393–94 (statistics on wealthy merchants and silver miners in various cities of New Spain).

Through their close relationship with the Board of Trade, they controlled both the time and regularity of voyages. Infrequent sailings were supposed to induce higher prices as a result of scarcities. And, by colluding with the Board of Trade, *flotistas* also controlled the quantity and quality of the cargo. In theory, they would also control the supply of goods by making sure that goods could only come into New Spain through the ports whose customs and warehouses they also controlled. Yet, this supposedly air-tight oligopolistic approach to trade was soon circumvented from within and without.

Circumvention from within the fleet system was encouraged by royal taxation. As noted by Professor Jeremy Baskes of Ohio Wesleyan University, commodities shipped legally were much more costly to importers than those smuggled in because of the heavy taxes imposed by the Spanish Crown.[81] Consequently, smuggling within the fleet system became rampant during the sixteenth century and beyond as reflected in the *flotistas*' practices of under-declaring the value of the shipped goods and hiding valuable cargo in the ships' holds. Still, as pointed out by Professor Baskes:

> While illegal, this practice became virtually sanctioned by the Crown's practice of pardoning violators in exchange for a fee, an *indulto*. . . . [Thus,] [s]muggling within the fleet persisted in the eighteenth century and was in fact one of the problems identified by the King in his 1765 instructions to José de Gálvez, the Visitor General to Mexico.[82]

Referring to this practice, a descendant of Veracruz *almaceneros* quoted a proverb to me that was popular among his eighteenth-century ancestors and their colleagues: "He who invented the law also invented the trick to circumvent it" ("*Quien inventó la ley, inventó la trampa*"). Circumvention from without took place in the form of the contraband organized by *almaceneros* with the active assistance of British, French, and Dutch pirates, privateers and buccaneers.[83] Not surprisingly, members of Seville's and later Cadiz's consulate repeatedly accused *almaceneros* of colluding with the foreigners and engaging in "illicit" trade and making only token purchases of fleet goods. In return, *almaceneros* blamed the *flotistas* for delaying shipments to New Spain until they were certain of severe scarcities and therefore able to charge higher prices.[84]

b. Control of Credit: Flotista *and* Almacenero *Credits*

Control of shipments by the *flotistas* and delays in the dates of departures and returns entailed long periods of time, at times years, before the *flotistas* could obtain their profits. Consequently, they were hard pressed for cash with which to repay their Spanish-based "purchase money" loans. As pointed out by Lic. Oscar Cruz Barney, *flotistas* generally depended upon a type of maritime loan known as "*préstamo a riesgo marítimo*" to finance their Spanish and European purchases; the collateral of this loan was the vessel's keel or "bottom" ("bottomry loan").[85] In these loans, the borrower (who was either the owner of the vessel or its *flotista* charterer) had to repay the principal

---

[81] Baskes, *supra* note 70, at 37.

[82] *Id.*

[83] Baskes, *supra* note 70, at 37. Although this effort was less costly than the royal taxes, it was not inexpensive as it required hiding places for the raiders and merchandise, as well as payment of bribes to Spanish and foreign government officials. *Id.*

[84] BARNEY, *supra* note 55, at 10.

[85] *Id.* at 23–64. These loans were also known as "*préstamos a la gruesa ventura*" or simply as "*préstamos a la gruesa.*" *Id.*

and interest owed as soon as the vessel arrived at the destination port where the "risk at sea" clause expired.[86] This meant that the *flotista* was forced to sell the entire or part of the cargo immediately upon arrival. A 1791 chronicler observed that the shipment of *flotistas* "arrived . . . so heavily indebted by *escripturas de riesgo* [bottomry loans] that they had to sell their wares promptly, and only to those who could pay cash immediately."[87]

For a variety of reasons, many of the *almaceneros* enjoyed a much better cash position than the *flotistas*. Because of their residence in major commercial centers such as Mexico City, Guadalajara and Veracruz, they developed extensive networks of family members, friends, apprentices and travelling salesmen in the principal ports and in the urban and rural markets of New Spain. These "trusted allies"[88] could be counted upon to place the *almacenero*'s goods or products as safely and effectively as possible throughout New Spain and neighboring countries. They could also be counted upon to report on market conditions in a timely manner.[89] *Almaceneros* profited significantly from extending credit to or investing with their large scale borrowers, which included silver miners, growers of sugar, dyes, cacao, and wheat or manufacturers of textiles (*obrajes*) or artisans.[90]

Either as lenders or joint venturers, the *almaceneros*' involvement with silver miners, owners of productive land, and textile manufacturers made possible their participation in the commercialization of metals, agricultural products and textiles. Their success in these endeavors led them to purchase public offices including New Spain's Mint. As noted by Professor Louisa Hoberman, collusion with Mint (*Casa de la Moneda*) officials at first linked silver merchants, and afterwards, *almaceneros*. The *almaceneros* purchased the offices of tax farmers (private persons who purchased the right to collect taxes for the Spanish kingdom) and shortly thereafter the office of the Mint's treasurer-director.[91] This meant that the Mint wound up in private hands and "[t]he government also surrendered autonomy over the production of coin."[92] The *almaceneros*' access to an ample supply of metallic coin enabled them to buy cheaper than those who had to borrow or buy the currency in the open market. It also made it

---

[86] *Id.*

[87] Baskes, *supra* note 70, at 36 (citation omitted).

[88] *Id.* at 32.

[89] HOBERMAN, *supra* note 72, at 64–68. *See also* Baskes, *supra* note 70, at 32–33 (on the correspondence between the merchant Francisco Ignacio de Yraeta and his trusted allies).

[90] *See generally* BRADING, *supra* note 72.

[91] HOBERMAN, *supra* note 72, at 93. *See also* John F. Schwaller, Book Review, 23 THE SIXTEENTH CENTURY JOURNAL 400 (Summer 1992) (reviewing LOUISA SCHELL HOBERMAN, MEXICO'S MERCHANT ELITE, 1590–1660: SILVER, STATE, AND SOCIETY (1991)). In his review, Professor Schwaller points out:

> [O]ne of the most important contributions of Hoberman's work is her analysis of the flow of merchants into the royal bureaucracy, and the intimate relationship between royal government and the merchants. Much of this [relationship] came as a result of the sale of public office and the practice of renting tax collection [to the highest bidder]. While sales of public office had developed in the sixteenth century, fiscal pressures of the seventeenth century stimulated their proliferation. Offices sold ranged from the secretariats [clerks] of the high court, to offices within the royal mint, to notarial offices and seats on municipal councils. By the end of the period under study, local magistracies and judicial seats on the high court were added.

Id. at 401. The reader will remember a similar pattern in pre-codification France, where instead of *almaceneros*, the purchasers of the royal offices were the landed gentry bourgeoisie.

[92] HOBERMAN, *supra* note 72, at 93.

possible for them to extend credit at a lower cost than their competitors.[93] The end result was that of all the merchants doing business in New Spain, *almaceneros* could best finance their imports from *flotistas* and their sales to retailers and consumers alike.[94]

Professor Baskes cites to Juan Fernando Meoqui, a prominent Mexico City *almacenero*, in describing the reach of the credit network:

> [T]he extensive network of credit began at the *feria* of Jalapa, where the *almaceneros* sold smaller (but still substantial) amounts . . . to merchants *de tierra adentro* [from the hinterland] who required credit to afford their purchases. Additional portions [after financing by the *almaceneros*] were distributed by the *Consulado* merchants on credit throughout the colony to private storekeepers, often individuals with whom the *almaceneros* enjoyed long-term commercial relations.[95]

Professor Stein confirms the above description when pointing out that "the provincial storekeepers seldom invested any of their own capital into organizing or supplying their stores. Instead, they received their wares on credit from . . . [the *almaceneros*] who shared in any subsequent profits."[96] He also notes that many other "goods were distributed to even more remote corners of Mexico by *viandantes*, traveling salesmen who obtained considerable merchandise on the strength of their word . . . 'spending two years in traveling and the collection of sales made.' "[97] In sum, "[p]roviding credit to retailers and consumers was simply an unavoidable feature of doing business in the cash-scarce, shallow markets of colonial Mexico."[98] Commercial and consumer credit, then, were at the center of the *almaceneros*' dominance of trade and commerce in late-colonial Mexico. Professor D. A. Brading summarizes the status of the *almaceneros* by the turn of the eighteenth century as follows:

> The class which benefited most from the policies of the Spanish monarchy was the colonial merchants. . . . The ensuing [eighteenth] century . . . formed their heyday. The *consulado*, the merchant guild, now farmed the collection of the *alcabalas* [the royal sales or transfer taxes] for a contracted sum. At much the same time the great silver merchants took over the management of the mint, and from this vantage point dominated the credit structure of the silver-mining industry.[99]

---

[93] Baskes, *supra* note 70, at 38. In the words of Baskes:

> These merchants were unique because they alone enjoyed sufficient liquidity to make such substantial purchases in coin. Mexico suffered from an acute shortage of minted coins and so even fairly affluent individuals relied on credit for a preponderance of their acquisitions. The *almaceneros'* ability to pay in cash and buy in bulk allowed them to secure favorable prices.

Id. (citation omitted).

[94] *Id.* at 39.

[95] *Id.* (citation omitted).

[96] Stein, *supra* note 72, at 384.

[97] *Id.* at 381.

[98] *Id.* at 40.

[99] Brading, *supra* note 31, at 408 (citation omitted).

B. The Living Law of Traveling Salesman and their Brotherly Standard of Fairness

The *viandantes* or traveling salesmen alluded to by Professor Stein (presently referred to in many Latin American countries as *viajantes*) were often apprentices of *almaceneros*. Many of them came to the Americas from Spain in the sixteenth through the nineteenth centuries. Usually, they were single and in their late teens, although some were as old as thirty.[100] The most successful were relatives of *almaceneros*, and in guild-like fashion, worked for them as apprentices for many years.[101] They were expected to learn their trade "from the bottom up" and started their training by selling wares entrusted to them by their *almacenero* relatives as traveling commission and "*del credere*" agents.[102] As a *del credere* agent, the young *mercader* assumed responsibility for the repayment of what he sold to his purchasers. This assumption of liability earned him a separate *del credere* commission. If successful, the young *mercader* would start gathering his own startup capital from savings derived mostly from commissions, loans or gifts from his senior relatives and last, but not least, from the dowries that resulted from marrying the daughters of *almaceneros* or other wealthy Creole families (*criollos*).[103]

I learned more about the *modus operandi* of these travelling salesmen in 1965 while gathering materials for a RAND Corporation study on the relationship between law and the credit structure of Latin America.[104] While in Veracruz, I was able to interview Lic. José María Echeverría. He was a descendant of *almaceneros* who came from Spain's Basque provinces to Mexico City via Seville and who was collecting materials to write a biography of one of his ancestors.[105] After creating their import-

---

[100] Booker, *supra* note 72, at 194. Booker makes reference to "research by Brading [that] documented [the] completion of training by most entrepreneurs [*mercaderes*] before age 30." *Id.* Booker continued:

> [Susan] Socolow found that 74 percent of all merchants under 30 were bachelors. . . . A random sampling of Veracruz merchant passports suggests three salient facts: most emigrating European-born Spaniards between 1770 and 1810 were single; their ages were generally in the 20 to 30 cohort; and most intended careers in commerce after serving several years in training.

Id. (citations omitted).

[101] Even as I was growing up in Cuba in the nineteen forties, the sobriquet "*sobrin*" (for *sobrino* or "nephew") was still regularly applied to the nephews or other young relatives of established Spanish merchants who worked in their elders' businesses as apprentices.

[102] *See* Interview with Lic. José María Echeverría, *supra* note 99 and accompanying text. Lic. Echeverría was certain that this practice was widespread both among Mexico City and Veracruz *mercaderes*. He specifically referred to the commission earned by the commission agent because of sales with the guarantee of payment by the commission agent, "*con garantía de pago del comisionista*." He also referred to many disputes among his own ancestors and in other *mercader* families with respect to the nature of the guarantees given by the *mercaderes* acting as *del credere* agents. I have not found exact references to the *del credere* agency in the writings of the historians consulted in this chapter, but their description of the type of credit extended by the *mercaderes* provides strong indications that Lic. Echeverría was correct when I asked him about the sources of his description.

[103] *See* John E. Kicza, Book Review, 66 THE BUSINESS HISTORY REVIEW 398–399 (1992) (reviewing LOUISA SCHELL HOBERMAN, MEXICO'S MERCHANT ELITE, 1590–1660: SILVER, STATE, AND SOCIETY (1991)). This source discusses how dowries were a vital source of venture capital for beginning merchants in New Spain.

[104] *See* Boris Kozolchyk, *Law and the Credit Structure in Latin America*, RAND MEMORANDUM RM-4918-RC (1966). As it turned out, the length of the materials available for this memorandum was such that I had to omit this conversation as well as other historical materials from the memorandum.

[105] Interview with Lic. José María Echeverría (June 12, 1965). I was introduced to Lic. José María Echeverría as a man of letters, knowledgeable on the history of commerce in Veracruz. Unfortunately, after

export business in Mexico City, his ancestors settled in Veracruz during the 1780s and, as many of the members of the new generations of *almaceneros*, started out as *viandantes*. He learned about them by reading their letters and diaries and hearing stories about them from his grandparents. The following are recollections of this interview based upon my notes:[106]

Boris Kozolchyk (hereinafter BK): You said that your ancestors were all born in the Basque country and knew nothing about commerce; they grew up as shepherds. How did they manage to get a permit to travel to lucrative New Spain from Seville when Seville had the monopoly over that trade and it was supposed to be practiced only by merchants? Wouldn't the Board of Trade reject non-Seville Basque shepherds in favor of Seville merchants?

Lic. José María Echeverría (hereinafter JME): [After smiling slyly] Mexicans are under the impression that they invented the bribe (*mordida*) and I tell them that even before there was a country named Mexico, the Andalusians were the world champion bribers and recipients of bribes. My ancestors got their travelling permits or passports by bribing employees of the consulate in Seville who could "arrange for their proper documentation." These officials got them papers indicating that they were members of the merchant guild of Seville. In turn, the consulate employees bribed the Board of Trade officials who placed the label of "*comerciantes*" (merchants) in their passports.

BK: Were your ancestors traveling salesmen before they became *almaceneros*? How did they do business with so many unknown customers?

JME: Most of my ancestors were traveling salesmen when they started their careers at a young age, mostly in their late teens or early twenties. Their *almacenero* relatives entrusted them with wares. They did this because they were family, often as close as nephews. My ancestors soon learned that Mexicans are very good, hard-working and hospitable people, but that there are also some thieves among them, particularly in remote and poor areas of the country, such that at least my great-great-grandfather carried with him a gun or rifle all the time. Remember that they had been entrusted with valuable goods and if these goods were stolen or if they sold them and could not repay their principals, they were responsible for the loss. Nevertheless, family being family, if they offered to repay those goods, but did not have the money to do so, their uncles or other relatives in charge of the business would not fire them. I do not know how much of a commission they were paid, but I am sure that regardless of the commission, they were also getting a small salary and were able to save some money as they were very frugal.

BK: Who were their customers and how did they decide how much credit they would extend to them?

JME: Some of their customers were storekeepers who had already obtained credit from their *almacenero* relatives. In that case, they merely delivered the goods bought by the storekeepers, collected some of the bills due and obtained orders for future deliveries. They earned commissions from these transactions. Their other customers

---

that interview I was not able to locate Lic. Echeverría again. Thus, I do not know if he ever published his family biography.

[106] *Id.*

were mostly peasants, particularly the women who purchased goods for the entire household. They also sold some farming equipment and other implements to their husbands. They had learned that it pays to be nice and family-like to these farmers. They visited their customers regularly, at times once a week. They would start with small credit extensions payable in weekly installments. They would also bring gifts to their customers' children and spend a lot of time talking to them about goings-on in their families and the surrounding cities. Then, and only then, would they collect the weekly installments due. They only felt safe extending significant credit to customers whom they had gotten to know well, as well as their families and close friends. Those who were given credit were like an extended family, many of them were *compadres*. Seldom was credit given to strangers, *i.e.*, people outside the circle of selected families and friends. When they did, the amounts were very little and further credit was discontinued if they failed to pay one weekly installment.

BK: How did the credit-*compadrazgo* system work? What commercial or legal consequences were attributable to it?

JME: As you know, the *compadres* have a very close, family-like relationship. It lasts for a long time, many times for the entire lives of the *compadres*. Usually, the *compadres* are good friends before being asked to be part of a child's baptism. At that time they are named *compadres* or godparents of the newborn by the parents. It is part of the [Catholic] religion. The godfather and godmother (*padrino* and *madrina*), who are like substitute parents of the baptized child, must ensure that if something happens to the parents, they will take care of the child or at least contribute to the child's sustenance and education and make sure that he or she is brought up as a good Catholic.[107] As I just told you, some of my ancestors became godfathers of their customers' children.

BK: Do you have any idea how frequently they accepted such honors and duties?

JME: I do not really know. They covered a lot of territory. On the other hand, I read some letters where they complained that some of their *compadres* apparently expected them to forgive debts they owed them in hard times.[108] That was not very good for their business or family relationships because they (my ancestors) were supposed to repay the *almaceneros* the credit that they had extended and that they could not collect.

BK: On the other hand, I suspect that a *compadre* would not want to default on the debt owed to his *compadre*, and that he would pay his *compadre* before paying anyone else, would not that be the case?

---

107 *See* John E. Kicza, *Life Patterns and Social differentiation among Common People in Late Colonial Mexico City*, 11 ESTUDIOS DE HISTORIA NOVOHISPANA 183 (1991), *available at* http://www.ejournal.unam.mx/ehn/ehn11/EHN01110.pdf (on file with author). This source provides an example of the instances of *compadres* assuming duties of sustenance for destitute parents. Kicza mentions the case of Dr. Antonio Serrano, a physician, who as a *compadre* assumed the duty of sustenance for six children of his destitute *compadre* and providing them with an annuity that ensured their well-being until adulthood. *Id.* at 188. Traditionally among Latin Americans, this relationship formalizes a pre-existing friendship which results in a strong lifelong bond between *compadres. Id.* In its truest form, the *compadre* relationship becomes as strong a bond as the relationship between natural siblings or between a father or mother and his/her children.

108 *See id.* at 196 (citation omitted) (providing an example of debt forgiveness by *compadres*: in one case, the debt appeared forgiven by a manumitted slave to the *compadre* in a last will and testament).

JME: I suppose so. I would not want to borrow money from a *compadre* and not pay it back. I would really feel very bad about it.

BK: What about collateral? What if strangers offered valuable goods as collateral? Would your ancestors extend credit to them?

JME: I do not understand what you mean by goods as collateral. But if what you mean is something like a guarantee, the only guarantee that I saw or heard mentioned was that provided by relatives or close friends of the debtors and of my ancestors.

BK: What about usury? Was that ever a factor?

JME: I did not hear of it being a factor except in one case in which one of my ancestors was accused of being a "usurer" by his customer to the local priest. The reason usury was not a factor was because *viandantes* were taught that it was important not to be accused as usurers and the best way to prevent such an accusation was not to charge interest as such, but to add to the total price of the goods an amount that would cover their risk of non-payment. So they charged more for installments than for cash sales. A father confessor to one of them explained that as long as what they charged was a commission for taking the risk of an installment sale, and not as interest for a loan, they would not be guilty of the sin of usury.

BK: What happened with the accusation of usury against your ancestor?

JME: The priest recommended that he waive his claim against his customer and contribute a certain amount to the Church in the name of Saint Francis of Assisi and that was the end of it.

COMMENTS AND QUESTIONS

There seems to be an organic connection between the availability of coin, particularly good coin, and the volume of commercial credit available in Spain as well as in its colonies. Please reread the excerpt from the *Novísima Recopilación*,[109] and ask yourself whether the *almaceneros*' virtual monopoly over the minting of coin had the same purpose, *i.e.*, monopoly of credit, implicit in the king and queen's prohibition. Is it true that he who holds the coin and its volume in circulation controls credit?

Upon rereading my notes many years later from the above interview, it became clear why the *flotistas* could not win their battle for the control of New Spain's wholesale and retail markets against the *almaceneros*. Simply put, control over the supply of goods had to lose out to control over the supply of credit. The *almaceneros* succeeded because they had instinctively perceived that credit extension in colonial Mexico was the key to success in wholesale and retail trade, which required dealing with trusted allies and close friends as their business associates or joint-venturers and customers. This extended family network kept them safe. Strangers were not to be trusted, and for all practical purposes, they were not part of the *almacenero* credit network, regardless of whether they could offer valuable assets as collateral for their loans. Usury, on the other hand, was not a factor because, especially at the retail level, the local priests were willing to enable consumption as long as the prices of goods paid by their parishioners were affordable.

Stanley Stein asks an important question: Was this merchant elite class one of innovators in a formative phase of Latin America's commercial capitalism? He concludes that it was not because they had too many ways to control and milk the

---

[109] *See* IV NOVÍSIMA RECOPILACIÓN, *supra* note 45, at 241 (Book IX, Title III, Law II).

colonial economy to want to change it and make it a freely competitive one. It was true that their scale of operations, national and international, was such that "these merchant oligarchs approached the archetype of truly independent merchants, to contrast them with the *prestanombres* of Seville or Cadiz."[110] However, I would add that from a law and economic development standpoint, the *almaceneros* provided a genetic imprint for the anti-competitive practices that plagued Mexican and other Latin American markets to this day. In fact, theirs was a model of capitalism in which control of commercial, and ultimately, consumer credit and overt or covert partnerships with, or bribery of, governmental officials assured them the status of perennial winners against other possible competitors. Obviously then, their success was not caused by their better products or lower prices, but by their oligopolistic practices. Beyond excluding competitors, their control prevented the emergence of a class of legally-protected strangers or third parties, such as buyers, creditors and borrowers in the ordinary course of their business. The only protected parties by the living law under which *almaceneros* operated were their families and friends.

1. ***Agribusiness:*** **Hacendados** ***and*** **Caudillos**

a. Hacendados *and Their Exclusive Dealings with Governmental Entities*

Oxford University Professor Alan Knight noted that "notwithstanding a certain traditional, Thomist, aversion to trade"[111] in Spain and Latin America, the search for profit from a certain type of trade was not demeaning in eighteenth-century rural Mexico.[112] Colonial Mexico seemed certainly less concerned with the social impropriety of profiting from agriculturally-based business (agribusiness) by the owners ("*hacendados*") of large estates (*haciendas*) than were the eighteenth-century French bourgeois.

As will be discussed shortly, the possession of large portions of rural land was one of the principal sources of the power of strongmen known as *caudillos* in colonial Hispanic America and especially in New Spain. This possession "conferred a degree of social power and legitimacy which was unmatched by any other calling."[113] The landowner acted as the master, legislator, judge and magistrate of his *hacienda* residents and dependents. In exchange, he expected them to attend to his family's needs and also to bear arms on his behalf.[114] Because the *hacendados*' dependents expected sustenance and protection in exchange for their work and loyalty, and because only few of the landowners were prepared to act as heads of plundering armies (as had their Roman counterparts), profit seeking (rather than warring) was fundamental to preserving their estates.

Yet, agribusiness in colonial Mexico suffered from the high volatility and "chronic weaknesses" of its urban markets. Some markets are characterized by the elasticity of consumer or purchaser demand, rising with higher and falling with lower incomes. Colonial Mexico suffered from an inelastic demand because, despite its status as a world leader in silver mining and production of large amounts of textiles during the

---

110 Stein, *supra* note 68, at 152.

111 ALAN KNIGHT, MEXICO: THE COLONIAL ERA 151 (2002). The traditional aversion to being known as a merchant or trader was "presented as a demonstrable empirical fact, not a simplistic assumption." *Id.* at 151 n.564. Relevant portions of Professor Knight's important study will be summarized in this section.

112 *Id.* at 151.

113 *Id.* (citation omitted).

114 *Id.* at 151–52.

eighteenth century, per capita income began what seemed like an inexorable downward trend. Professor Jamie Rodríguez of the University of California found that in 1800, while the per capita income per year of England and the United States was 196 and 165 respectively (calculated in Mexican pesos), Mexico's income (despite its wealth of silver) was about 116 pesos per year and continuously falling.[115] As discussed in the preceding sections, New Spain suffered chronically from a lack of currency and this condition remained throughout at least the first few decades after Mexican won its independence. In addition, poor communications and transport, especially to and from Mexico's major cities, weighed heavily on agricultural prices and often lowered demand.[116]

Colonial policy favored an *ad hoc* type of market regulation in order to raise governmental revenue and eliminate fluctuations, shortages and social tensions. Public granaries (*pósitos*) and supervised markets (*alhóndigas*) became central entities in the colonial agribusiness. For example, in a city as large as late eighteenth-century Guadalajara (at that time Mexico's second largest city), approximately "two-thirds of the city's grain supply was channelled [sic] through the *pósito*. . . ."[117]

I used the expression "*ad hoc*" in connection with what Professor Knight referred to as market regulation because it was supported by exclusive dealings and oligopolistic arrangements between the governmental agencies and their suppliers. Hence, a city's food supply was guaranteed by agreements between the municipalities and major suppliers in which the latter promised to deliver the grain or meat at a fixed price and during a stipulated time. Even Mexico City (Mexico's largest city) had an oligopolistic meat supply arrangement that dated back to the earliest days of the colony. However, as also noted by Professor Knight, this market was "self-regulated"[118] because the City Council (*cabildo*), whose responsibility it was to oversee the food supply, was usually formed by the *hacendados* themselves. He concludes that "[t]he result was a . . . market hedged about by restrictions, in which producers sought a guaranteed profit on a limited turnover."[119]

Yet, unlike the credit made available by the *almaceneros* to their suppliers and customers, agricultural credit was not always available and when it was, it could be quite expensive. The Church and some *almaceneros* were the *hacendados*' most relied upon sources of commercial credit.[120] The Church provided long-term credit while *almaceneros* provided shorter-term credit. Yet, whatever interest rate was charged by the Church (overt or hidden) had to be augmented by the payment of the ten percent tithe, which was not calculated on the amount of the loan, but on the annual

---

[115] *See generally* Jamie Rodríguez O., *Down From Colonialism: Mexico's 19th Century Crisis*, HISTORICAL TEXT ARCHIVE (1980), http://historicaltextarchive.com/sections.php?action=read&artid=528 (on file with author).

[116] KNIGHT, *supra* note 105, at 154.

[117] *Id.* at 157.

[118] *Id.*

[119] *Id.*

[120] Rodríguez, *supra* note 109. According to Rodríguez:

> The best study of the Church as a banker is Michael P. Costeloe, *Church Wealth in Mexico* (Cambridge, 1976). Richard Lindley discusses the nature of personal credit and its decline in "Kinship and Credit in the Structure of Guadalajara's Oligarchy, 1800–1830" (Ph.D. Dissertation, Univ. of Texas, Austin, 1975).

Id. at n.29.

agribusiness production. In addition, many landholdings were subject to a Church lien known as "*censo*" owed by all the agricultural producers.[121] This lien guaranteed the Church's receipt of a specified percentage of the *hacienda's* annual income, at times payable in kind.[122]

b. Caudillos

The strong presence of *caudillos* in Latin America's political and commercial life has been felt from Argentina to Mexico and indeed as far as Spain, whose General Franco was honored in 1963 with his engraved image on a Spanish *peseta* coin which read: "Francisco Franco, Spain's Caudillo by the Grace of God" ("*Francisco Franco, Caudillo de España, por la gracia de Dios*"). And like the Spanish kings, Latin American *caudillos* usually received a percentage of the profits of merchants and landed gentry.

The power of the *caudillos* came at times from their ownership of large parcels of land. At other times, it was derived from commanding a local militia whose members were also the tenant-farmers who lived on their or their neighbors' land. In Argentina, for example, following its independence from Spain, the authority of the colonial municipal boards (*cabildos*) was replaced by the authoritarian and highly personal power of *caudillos*.[123] As with their Roman and feudal antecedents, these *caudillos* had a patron-client relationship with their dependents; the latter depended upon them for work and protection against enemies real or imagined. In return for their sustenance and protection, the *caudillo* was entitled to his dependents' service as members of a private army.

Starting in 1821, with the ascent to power of General Antonio López de Santa Anna, Mexico commenced its long relationship with *caudillismo*.[124] Upon attaining its independence from Spain, Mexico was unable to establish a stable and enduring form of self-government. Revolts and calls-to-arms in the form of public announcements (*gritos* or *pronunciamientos*) were quite common.[125] Military action preceded or followed them, often unsuccessfully, and meanwhile, every form of government, from monarchy to federal and central republicanism, was attempted. Much damage was caused to the economy by the widespread destruction of property, commerce, and industry (notably mining) and, most importantly, the flight of capital.[126]

Unable to generate sufficient revenues, the various governments defaulted on their debts and were constantly on the edge of bankruptcy. Attempts to increase the amount of currency in circulation by issuing copper coin led to increased poverty and hunger as the new money rapidly lost much of its face value. Loans were forced on the wealthy, and now and again, private assets were confiscated, including those of the

---

[121] KNIGHT, *supra* note 105, at 161.

[122] *Id.*

[123] *See* UNIV. OF NOTRE DAME, POWER AND POLITICS IN THE 19TH CENTURY RIVER PLATE: RISE OF THE CAUDILLOS (2003), http://rarebooks.library.nd.edu/exhibits/riverplate/04–rise/index.shtml.

[124] MICHAEL P. COSTELOE, THE CENTRAL REPUBLIC IN MEXICO, 1835–1846: "HOMBRES DE BIEN" IN THE AGE OF SANTA ANNA 1 (2002). Professor Costeloe is Professor Emeritus and Senior Research Fellow of Hispanic and Latin American Studies at the University of Bristol, England.

[125] *Id.* at 2.

[126] *Id.* at 2–4.

Church.[127] This vicious cycle of robbing Peter to pay Paul was, if not halted, at least seriously diminished when the Mexican army assumed control in 1821 and continued to rule Mexico for almost the entire next century. Professor Costeloe describes the sequence as follows:

> [T]he institution which emerged in 1821 was essentially new in Mexican society. The officer corps, with its love of parades and colorful uniforms, consisted almost entirely of men who made their reputations and acquired their ranks while fighting on either side during the [independence] war. Led by [Agustin] Iturbide [later emperor], they reached a consensus to separate from Spain, and they became immensely popular as a result. . . . It was from their ranks that every president [came], with a couple of interim exceptions, before Benito Juarez was to be drawn, and despite the subsequent rise of powerful civilian politicians and political parties that opposed the preeminence of a military caste, *they successfully defended their status and their privileges*.[128]

Not surprisingly, a profitable alliance developed between Mexico's producers of wealth, especially from rural areas, and the military *caudillos*:

> Tobacco and cotton farmers in Veracruz, textile manufacturers in Puebla, [and] miners in Zacatecas did not hesitate to seek the support of their local military commander in their efforts to influence national economic policy, and merchants in several regions on at least one occasion combined to encourage and finance a revolt.[129]

In sum, the reason for the existence of the *caudillos* was not their charisma, although many of them surely possessed it. It was their ability to recruit subordinates and make things happen in the political or legal order forcefully and violently when necessary. Stated simply, they were able to impose *their* order *manu militare* and to make this order stick for a period long enough so that the dependent population could earn a living. Their subordinates were not only their soldiers and militiamen, *many of whom enjoyed privileges such as immunity from taxation and in some cases, from criminal and civil actions*, but also politicians who, by the very nature of their subordination to the *caudillo* above anyone or everything else, were corrupt. Eventually, the *caudillismo* engendered its own class of name lenders (*prestanombres* y *testaferros*) and devious or "simulatory" methods of doing business (*negocios*).

c. *Bribes,* Negocios *and Simulations*

The personal and authoritarian form of *caudillo* government inevitably breeds corruption. The subordinate government official (whether a member of the legislative, executive, or judicial branch) knows that he owes his position and privileges not to a popular election or to the consent of the governed, but to the *caudillo*. This means that

---

127 *Id.* at 4–5 (citation omitted).

128 *Id.* at 5 (citations omitted) (emphasis added). Professor Costeloe also points out that:

> Between 1821 and 1851, fifteen generals occupied the presidential office, some on an interim basis and some, notably Santa Anna, on several occasions. During the same period, six civilians were acting or interim president but three of these for only a few days.

Id. at 5 n.9.

129 *Id.* at 9 (citation omitted).

he must ultimately discharge his duties and formulate law or policy not based upon his own determination of what is right or wrong, but upon the wishes of the *caudillo*, expressed or deduced.

i. Bribes

Those governed by corrupt politicians, administrators or judges are usually aware of the fact that the *caudillo* expects his appointees to do well (and often pass on the prescribed surplus to the *caudillo*) by carrying out their own corrupt practices. Such practices (dubbed euphemistically as "*negocios*" by the Mexican populace) can adopt the simple form of a bribe ("*mordida*" in Mexico, but known by many other words in the rest of Latin America) or it can become a complex legal transaction by employing a legalistic tool known as a "simulation."

A bribe is a device to obtain preferential treatment from a government official or judge. In agricultural survival societies, such as those found in Latin America well into the twentieth century, preferential treatment was reserved for one's family members or close friends. The reader will remember the reaction of Costa Rican potential investors to the announced high yield of dividends paid on shares of stock of a publically held company: "If the industrial company's dividend return is such a good deal, why would it be offered to me, neither a member of the family nor a friend of those who run this company?"[130] Accordingly, the payment of a bribe is supposed to ensure the preferential treatment afforded to family members or close friends. However, since bribing is available to business competitors as well as to opposing parties to a lawsuit, the payment of a bribe usually becomes a continuous bidding process, one whose winner is often not known until the long and costly conclusion. Meanwhile, costly and often paralyzing uncertainty clouds the rights of bidders and non-bidders alike, including actual or potential investors, sellers, lenders, borrowers and litigators.

ii. Negocios

When Mexicans use the term *negocio* in the context of practices ascribed to politicians acting as government officials, they mean transactions through which these politicians appropriate state funds for their own use or their business associates' use. For example, a government official authorizes a construction company in which he has a secret agreement to build a road, thus entitling him to a major share of the profits or gross revenues of the contract. Or he expropriates a bank and enables a well-known business or professional person, who is also his business associate, to acquire the bank in exchange for his secret share of the bank's profits. Or he instructs a subordinate to purchase raw materials or equipment at a price significantly higher than that typically charged by the supplier. The supplier then forwards the difference between his normal price and the higher price paid by the government entity to a third party who lends his name to the government official and holds the money for that official. In all of these instances, and in infinitely more, the person who acts as a contractor, bank purchaser or recipient of a supplier's rebate is the *prestanombre* or *testaferro*.

iii. Simulations

Simulation is the legal device that creates the necessary contractual language and transactional appearances to mask many of the corrupt practices between *caudillos*,

---

130 *See supra* § 5:5.

the politicians they control, and the name lending or participating merchants. The practice of masking the true transaction with another one that appears to be lawful is regulated in Mexico not only by the applicable Criminal Code, but, surprisingly to the uninitiated, also by the Mexican Civil Code for the Federal District (hereinafter the Mexican Civil Code) as well as by the state civil codes it inspired. Article 2180 of the Mexican Civil Code defines a simulated act as one in which "the parties declare or confess falsely something that in fact has not transpired or has not been agreed upon by them."[131] True to its scholastic roots, the same code goes on to classify simulations as either "absolute" or "relative."[132] An absolute simulation is one in which the simulated act "has no reality whatever" (*no tiene nada de real*). A simulation is relative when a transaction did take place but was different than the one it appears to be ("*cuando a un acto jurídico se le da una falsa apariencia que oculta su verdadero carácter*").[133]

Accordingly, if A and B execute a contract that states that A conveys Blackacre to B and in fact no conveyance takes place, this act will be an absolute simulation that will be null and void. On the other hand, if A states that he has lent X amount of money to B when in fact he has donated that amount to B, the transaction will be deemed a relative simulation. If the simulation is absolute, the Mexican Civil Code states that it will have no legal effects whatsoever.[134] In contrast, "once the true transaction masked by the relative simulation is discovered, such an act will not be null and void unless a law specifically declares it to be."[135]

I recall that while discussing these provisions in a comparative law class in Luxembourg, a Scandinavian lawyer who struggled to capture the meaning of the Mexican Civil Code provisions deemed them worthy of Honore de Balzac's Byzantine machinations. Indeed, the first time I encountered contractual simulation was in the *Code Civil's* provisions on gratuitous transfers between or among family members.[136] Yet, one could easily understand why a loving French parent may have wished to disguise as a loan what was in fact a donation to the neediest of his or her children, thereby avoiding adverse reactions by the other children. Or one could appreciate why a sexually starved middle aged husband would name his occasional mistress the beneficiary of an insurance policy even though some French judges and commentators labeled the transaction a reward for the illicit services of a prostitute.[137] I can even understand why a United States tax lawyer would express his sympathy for Mexican Civil Code provisions that seem to enable what he would consider part of his everyday tax avoidance practice. He would suggest that when he advises his clients to set up a home-based business to be able to deduct certain otherwise non-deductible business

---

[131] Mexican C.C.F. art. 2180 (2008). It is worth noting that a simulation may wind up being perjury, but not necessarily. The civil code does not deal with the crime of perjury but rather with a transaction which may be a contract or a declaration of intent that contains a false description of the intent of the parties, which may or may not be criminal.

[132] *Id.* arts. 2181–2184.

[133] *Id.* art. 2181.

[134] *See id.* art. 2182.

[135] *Id.*

[136] *See* C. CIV. (Fr.) arts. 911, 1099 (2008). *See also id.* art. 1832–1 (discussing gratuitous transfers between spouses contributing to a civil association). Unless otherwise indicated, all the English translations of the *Code Civil* provisions belong to Legifrance (*see* Frequently Cited).

[137] *See supra* § 9:2(E)(3)(c).

expenses or trusts for their children to avoid or reduce the payment of estate taxes, he is also engaging in relative simulations.

Yet, a significant qualitative difference exists between what the U.S. tax lawyer does in order to *lawfully* avoid tax payments and what most of the absolute and relative simulations of the Mexican Civil Code entail. In the tax lawyer's case, he avails himself of tax avoidance (not evasion) transactions expressly or tacitly allowed by the law. Those that are not allowed are treated by United States law as evasions or "abusive avoidance" schemes and are not only null and void, but also criminally punishable. Yet, the latter are precisely the types of simulation *widely engaged in* and seldom punished by Mexican courts. Simply put, simulation is not an occasional practice, but instead *the* method of doing corrupt business (*negocios*) by politicians, their name lending partners, and other parties with whom they deal on a daily and economically-significant basis. It is also a common method of doing business by some of the most economically-powerful private parties. In fact, as will be apparent in a court decision discussed later, the court acknowledged, without punishing, the practice of simulating a transaction in order to reduce or eliminate the payment of real estate transfer taxes.[138]

2. *The Brazilian* Jeito *and the Mexican Simulation*

The *jeito* is in some respects Brazil's counterpart to the Mexican Civil Code's simulation. One major difference is that the *jeito* has remained a purely living law institution and as such, the Brazilian Civil Code does not define, classify or regulate it.[139] A *jeito* may not necessarily require the expenditure of a significant amount of money such as would have to be spent by a Mexican merchant or politician when paying a notary or attorney for the execution of a simulatory public or private deed. The *jeito* was not designed for the exclusive use of the commercial and political elites. It is used, for example, by millions of Brazilians in large cities to try to avoid waiting in a long line. It can be cost free; however, it can also be as costly as Mexico's most expensive *mordida*.

Some Brazilians justify the *jeito* by pointing to the absurdity or capriciousness of Brazil's law or bureaucracy, as noted by my friend and colleague, Professor Keith S. Rosenn: "Once the principle that officials and private citizens may reinterpret or ignore laws they deem overly restrictive or unwise is condoned, its limitation is extremely difficult. Unjust, discriminatory law enforcement and the breakdown of legitimacy may well be the result."[140]

There is no doubt that a rich person has a greater likelihood of obtaining a *jeito* than a poor person, as it is far easier to get it if the provider is well rewarded.[141] Besides through bribes, *jeitos* are also obtained by family members and friends, but the end result is ultimately equally as corrupt because an otherwise unlawful preferential

---

[138] *See infra* § 14:7(G)(2).

[139] *See generally*, Professor Keith S. Rosenn's by now classic study, *The Jeito, Brazil's Institutional Bypass of the Formal Legal System and its Developmental Implications*, 19 AM. J. COMP. L. 514, 514–49 (1971).

[140] *Id.* at 545.

[141] *See* Augusto Zimmermann, *Jeitinho, Brazil's Creative Way to Break the Law and Feel Virtuous about It*, BRAZZIL.COM (2006), http://www.brazzil.com/info/163–april-2006/9588.html (last accessed Nov. 5, 201) (on file with author).

treatment is given not to the one who deserves it most, but to the friend or family member.

Keith Rosenn's breakdown of legitimacy spreads through the entire legal system because, as noted by an Australian scholar, "it is not possible to destabilize some rules without affecting others in the system."[142] I observed this phenomenon in the earlier-cited 1966 RAND Corporation study.[143] Not much has happened since that time to question the validity of that observation.

3. Compadrazgo, *Bribery, Simulation and Violence in Mexican Rural Land Transactions*

To this day, whenever *compadrazgo* combines with bribery and simulation to provide title to indigenous claimants of disputed rural land, as it has done and continues to do in Mexico, the results could be lethal. In his book *Santiago's Sword*, University of Arizona's Anthropology Professor James Greenberg, a most perceptive observer of Mexican indigenous society, identified some of the most important contributors to the bloody and continued violence among residents in the Juquila and Yaitepec townships of the State of Oaxaca as follows:

> The land dispute with the Hacienda de Constancia has its roots in a lease. In 1899 the priest from Juquila, taking advantage of the trust, ignorance, and illiteracy of the Indian authorities in Yaitepec, managed to obtain a lease of more than . . . 1,000 hectares of communal lands for 1,000 pesos. In theory, the Reform Laws of 1857 stripped the church and clergy of property rights. The lease may have been a way of sidestepping the legal issue. . . . The reverend Catholic father was no simple parish priest, but an entrepreneur and a family man with five children. When the priest died . . . his sons [the Navarez brothers] inherited the property, which is now a productive coffee plantation. . . . Then, in 1940, the family divided the estate's 1,178 hectares into five smaller *fincas*, so that each would be under the legal size limits allowed by the agrarian reform laws.
>
> Despite constant troubles with Yaitepec, which saw bloodshed on both sides, the Navarez brothers continued to pay the annual assessment for their lease until about 1970. In 1970, Yaitepec's communal land titles disappeared. . . .[144]

After the Navarez brothers claimed in a letter to the Yaitepec municipal government that they owned the land as private property, they admonished the government as follows:

> There will never be peace in this pueblo, because they [the Juquila claimants] let their secretaries deceive them. They take their money, making them believe it is easy to take away private property. All they do is take trips to

---

142 *Id.* (citing Professor Suri Ratnapala).

143 *See* Kozolchyk, *Law and the Credit Structure in Latin America, supra* note 98; *see also* Boris Kozolchyk, *Law and the Credit Structure in Latin America,* 7 VA. J. INT'L. L. 1, 34–35 (1967) (an early description of the effect of simulation upon the credit structure and economic development of Latin American nations).

144 JAMES GREENBERG, SANTIAGO'S SWORD 75 (1981).

Oaxaca and Mexico. . . . Our private property will never be taken away because it conforms to agrarian codes.[145]

The above is but one example of the many instances in which an original bribe and a simulation whose purpose was to evade the prohibition of the acquisition of land by the church produced a flawed title which became the basis of its land tenure by the Narvaez family and the trigger for a seemingly endless bloody conflict. It was followed in 1940 by another evasion, very likely a bribe, and a simulation of yet another agrarian statute which forbad the holding of parcels that exceeded a certain size. Finally, it was followed by another likely fraudulent claim of a fee simple absolute to land whose chain of title had mysteriously disappeared from the municipal records. The reader is encouraged to watch out for a not-too-dissimilar interplay between "familistic" legal institutions such as the *compadrazgo*, statutory law disputes and violence in the following chapters devoted to Chinese law.[146]

4. *The Effects of Simulation on Mexico's Commerce and Economy*

I will illustrate how simulation affects commercial legal institutions and causes major uncertainty and economic loss by describing a widespread variety of it in Mexico's commercial lending up to approximately five years ago. Assume that I sold computers to Mexican businesses who use them as office equipment and that I was willing to extend credit to my customers. I consulted my attorney, who informed me that I could secure the repayment of the price of these computers by executing a type of secured transaction known as X. X requires that I give notice to the world that I have extended a secured credit to my computer purchasers by filing my security interest in the appropriate registry. This registration used to cost approximately one percent of the value of the transaction. I found this registration fee too expensive. Then I was also told by my attorney that my filings would provide tax authorities with useful information on the annual volume of my credit sales. I press my attorney for other alternatives.

My attorney then told me that I could enter into alternative transaction Y. It is a contract with my purchasers that he would deceptively label it a "financial lease." It would provide the appearance of a lease with an option to purchase, but the option was for a purely symbolic sum because what the parties truly intended was a sale payable in installments. Y did not require the registration of my (hidden, but still intended) security interest because my financial lease contract provides the appearance of a true lease and therefore, ostensibly, I was not a lender but a lessor-owner of the computers made available to my customers. In addition to not having to pay filing fees, if I needed to repossess the computers or sell them in a foreclosure procedure, I did not have to compete with other creditors such as A and B. These creditors had provided earlier loans to my customers and had secured these loans by a clause that encumbered the borrowers' present and future acquired inventory and equipment. Under ordinary, good faith circumstances, the term "equipment" would have been enough to give A and B priority rights in the computers that I had sold to other customers and that were being used by them in their business as either equipment or inventory. Recall that A and B had properly and timely recorded their security interests on my customers prior to my

---

145 *Id.* at 76 (citation omitted).

146 *See infra* § 17:3(F).

actual installment sale. Thus, according to the secured transactions law in force, A and B had perfected their security interest in their respective customers' present and future inventory and equipment (including those that I now purport to have only leased to them) at a time prior to my simulated lease.

I was told by my lawyer that by using Y, I do not have to worry about either A and B's rights or about future secured creditors. Although these properly-secured creditors (prior and future) relied on the fact that no recorded security interests existed or that those that were recorded were for amounts small enough to provide an acceptable cushion of security, my rights are "in a different and superior league." Upon my lawyer's advice, I opted for alternative Y, which saved me registration fees and gave me a priority over all the secured creditors, regardless of when they recorded. In addition, it gives me the opportunity to hide my volume of credit sales from snooping tax collectors as the registry contains no records of these sales. He assured me that my choice was the most popular with suppliers of equipment throughout the nation. I asked him if we should execute this contract before a notary public. He discouraged me because of its cost and also because a notarial document becomes part of a public archive (*protocolo*) and thus there would be a public record of my transactions.[147]

Consider the effects of transaction Y upon the legal system. Secured creditors A and B, who had filed their earlier security interests in the same collateral, are likely to fail in their attempt to rely on what Mexico's law of secured transactions and registry law had assured them was a priority right over all unrecorded security interests. In the future, they would not rely on that secured transactions law and its registry.

Consider also the predicament of another group of creditors, C, D and E, all of whom held claims subsequent in time to those of A and B, as well as to mine. They lent money to the same debtor and the collateral for their loans consisted of the computers that the debtor possessed as inventory or equipment. They searched the registry and found that the only recorded security interests belonged to A and B. If A and B's loans were largely paid up at the time of their loans, the ratio between the unpaid amounts in A and B's loans seemed sufficiently low in relation to the value of the remaining unimpaired collateral so that C, D and E could count on acquiring priority rights over a sufficiently safe margin of unencumbered collateral. Yet they too would become victims of my simulation, for I could still claim that I was the owner of the computers that I deceptively leased. In the future, they too would refrain from lending.

The unreliability of the registry system's notice also affects other third party lenders or purchasers. Therefore, the registry's function of providing accurate and reliable notice of recorded liens becomes a victim of simulation as do the registry's revenues, excessive though they may have been. Tax evasion grows and tax collections diminish. Thus, contrary to my own expectations as a simulator, my volume of credit transactions is eventually sharply reduced because, as one of oldest of living law principles states: "What goes around, comes around," or "What's good for the goose is good for the gander."

Please recall that upon the advice of my attorney, who wanted to avoid having a public record of my loan, I did not ask a notary public to execute the financial lease as a notarial or public deed. Yet, once C, D, and E discovered that my simulated financial

---

[147] *See supra* ch. 7.

lease did not appear in a notarial deed, but in a private document that lacked "public faith,"[148] they found a notary public willing to participate in yet another simulation.[149] The new notarial deed stated that on a date earlier than that of my financial lease, C, D, and E entered into a conditional sale with the purchasers of my computers (These purchasers were willing to go along with this simulation because C, D, and E promised them a significant discount on the price of their computers). Because conditional sales and financial leases did not have to be recorded to be effective against third parties in Mexico,[150] and because ownership of the computers was ostensibly retained by C, D, and E prior to my financial lease, these creditors will claim a better right than mine, especially because they have a document endowed with "public faith" that establishes a certain date (*fecha cierta*) for their earlier priority. In addition, because C, D, and E were ready to offer bribes to the judges and clerks involved in the adjudication of their claims, they would likely prevail against me, unless of course I was willing to join the battle of renewed simulations and bribes.

In sum, the integrity of the laws of commercial contracts, secured transactions, taxation, notarial deeds and court decisions all suffer from the above sequence of simulations and bribes. Meanwhile, aware of the collapse of the notice system, fewer suppliers to small- and medium-sized businesses (or the suppliers' banks) are willing to extend commercial credit based on the assets of their buyers/borrowers; a failure that World Bank economists have estimated affects as much as nine percent of a nation's GDP.[151] Once all of the above individual and social costs are added up, it is clear that simulation and bribery, among other picaresque methods of doing business, seriously impede lasting economic development.

5. *The Business and Legal Ethics of Kinship and Friendship*

Mexico's failure to develop the standards of commercial good faith and honorability hoped for by its *hombres de bien* has been replicated again and again throughout Latin America. With few exceptions, the institutions that took the place of standards inspired by a universal morality were the familistic treatment of kin and close friends and the lack of concern for the predicament of strangers and third parties.

An incident of everyday life illustrates how widespread the lack of concern for strangers is in those developing nations. While visiting a Central American country, I needed my car to be repaired. I noticed a sizeable hole in the sidewalk leading to the repair shop and called it to the attention of the owner so that he could cover it to prevent future accidents. His response was that his family, employees and customers were all aware of it and avoided it. Obviously, he did not take into account the category of strangers, including, perhaps, future customers. A couple of years later, I had an almost identical conversation in another Latin American nation.

In such an environment, those who are not kin or close friends of family or political insiders do not generally expect to receive a fair treatment. When Costa Rica's potential middle class investors were asked why they did not invest in the stock of a

---

[148] *See* Glossary, "Public Faith."

[149] *See supra* ch. 7.

[150] *See generally* Kozolchyk & Furnish, *A Comparative Analysis.*

[151] Heywood W. Fleisig, *The Power of Collateral: How Problems in Secured Transactions Limit Private Credit for Movable Property*, THE WORLD BANK, *available at* http://siteresources.worldbank.org/EXTFINANCIALSECTOR/Resources/282884–1303327122200/043fleisi.pdf (on file with author).

highly successful industrial company with a ten year record of paying a ten percent annual dividend or higher and instead preferred to invest in second mortgages that yielded no more than six percent, the generalized response was: Why would we, strangers to the families that own those companies, be offered such a good deal? There must be something crooked going on.

6. *Politicians and* Hombres de Bien

During the heyday of *caudillismo*, roughly from the beginning of the nineteenth century to the second half of the twentieth century (although it still lives in some Latin American countries under a supposedly Marxist ideology), politicians were and are secondary figures, mere agents and mouthpieces for the *caudillo*. As a rule, *caudillos* make sure that their subordinate politicians and soldiers do well. As was said about Dr. Ramón Grau San Martín, a Cuban president and mini-*caudillo* during the 1940s: "The shark [his nickname] bathes but [those near him also get] splashe[d]" (*El tiburón se baña pero también salpica*).[152]

Starting with Santa Anna, corrupt Mexican politicians earned large fortunes and many displayed them with an "Asiatic lavishness, living in expensively furnished mansions, riding around the city in imported carriages and gambling away large sums in cock-fights."[153] This behavior persuaded *hombres de bien* (men of good) to warn of a potential explosion of anger by the poor against the rich unless a more equitable distribution of wealth could be achieved: "A leveling of incomes is absolutely indispensable if the ruin of society is to be avoided."[154]

Who were these *hombres de bien*? Professor Magali M. Carrera of the University of Massachusetts Dartmouth finds the first description of Mexico's *hombre de bien* in early-nineteen-century literature:

> [T]he specific notions of the *hombre de bien* and the *petimetre* appear as characters in José Joaquín Fernández de Lizardi's (1776–1827) late-colonial novel *El periquillo sarniento* (The Itching Parrot), first published in 1816 and considered to be New Spain's first novel. The story begins with Pedro Sarmiento, a reformed *picáro* or delinquent, telling his children that he was born between 1771 and 1773 in the rich and opulent city of Mexico. Now ill and infirm, Pedro has sincere remorse for his earlier life of debauchery, and proceeds to tell his children his life story so that they may understand and avoid the moral calamity that marked much of his life. . . . He pretends to be a pharmacist, doctor, and storekeeper and is reduced to the status of a beggar and thief.[155]

Toward the end of the story, the author of this novel draws a sharp contrast between Periquillo and his father, who was a true honest, decent, hardworking and caring family man who was also concerned with the welfare of others: a true *hombre de bien*. I find it revealing that the opposite of Lizardi's *hombre de bien* is not only a

---

152 Ilan Ehrlich, *Ramón Grau San Martín: Cuba's Prophet of Disappointment, 1944–1951*, *in* ASSOCIATION FOR THE STUDY OF THE CUBAN ECONOMY, 21 CUBA IN TRANSITION 339 n.6 (2011).

153 COSTELOE, *supra* note 118, at 25 (citation omitted).

154 *Id.* at 25.

155 Magali M. Carrera, *From Royal Subject to Citizen: The Territory of the Body in Eighteenth- and Nineteenth-Century Mexican Visual Practices, in* JENS ANDERMANN, WILLIAM ROWE, IMAGES OF POWER: ICONOGRAPHY, CULTURE AND THE STATE IN LATIN AMERICA 28 (2005).

picaro, but a delinquent *picaro*, the same *picaro malo* we encountered in the medieval literature as a frequent equal of the tradesman-merchant.[156] By the same token, there seems to be a descending order of morality in Lizardi's description of the professions associated with the *hombre de bien*: the pharmacist and the doctor come first, then the storekeeper. I also noticed that lawyers did not appear in Lizardi's list of *hombres de bien*.

The post-Santa Anna *hombres de bien* railed against the political chaos, poverty, collapse of law and order, and some even yearned for a return to colonial days when criminals were punished and things were generally more efficient. One such *hombre de bien*, a resident of Mexico City in 1843, complained that "[m]eat, bread and pulque had never been better or less expensive than in colonial days."[157] The quality of the *pulque* aside, Professor Costeloe concludes that the principal preoccupation of the *hombres de bien* was the declining morality of society: "Without good customs, laws serve no purpose; morality should be the basis and complement of all legislation."[158] Yet, despite the yearning by the *hombres de bien* for a lasting constitutional basis for self-government imbued with a Christian morality that would ensure individual and institutional rights and liberties, Mexico continued to suffer violence and serious economic difficulties "until the iron hand of Porfirio Díaz was able to impose order in the name of economic progress."[159]

In conclusion, after a promising start as Mexico's nineteenth-century conscience, its *hombres de bien* did not succeed in implementing good faith and honorability as guiding elements of Mexico's living law of commercial contracts. A normative bridge was required between the public and private morality advocated by these *hombres de bien* and the archetypal behavior that the HGB and the BGB, as well as pre- and post-Nazi German courts, attributed to their "honest and decent" or "good faith" merchants. Thus, if the issue was one of unequal, unfair, or exploitive treatment of certain merchants or consumers, or a lack of regard by contracting parties for the rights of third parties, or a contracting party's abuse of the letter as opposed to the spirit of the law, the standards of morality advocated by the *hombres de bien* should have been translated into judicial norms or, even more influentially, into enforceable best commercial usages and practices. Yet, this translation of standards would have required real life, everyday examples of *bonus vir* commercial behavior, examples that judges and administrators could point to as worthy of generalized respect and emulation and thus deserving of application to the controversies before them.

7. *Summary and Conclusions*

In a legal and business environment such as the one just described, the role of codified, statutory, administrative or court-made law is secondary. Legislators may take pride in the logical symmetry and even in the fairness of their enactments, but what governs the bulk of marketplace transactions is a different law, namely the "living law." In the case of Mexico and other Latin American nations, this living law stems from a colonial and post-colonial tradition of *caudillismo* and *compadrazgo*

---

156 *See supra* § 5:4(A).

157 COSTELOE, *supra* note 118, at 25.

158 *Id.* at 26.

159 *Id.* at 2.

designed to further tribal, clan or family values typical of agricultural survival societies, but not of free-market economy societies.

In agricultural survival societies, only the associates and clients of the ruling *caudillos* (many of them immune to legal action) and the family members, close friends, and *compadres* of the contracting parties can reasonably expect a favorable outcome from their contracts. This certainly is not a living law designed to support standard transactions among the strangers or third parties who mostly populate market-economy societies. As I have shown elsewhere,[160] in agricultural survival societies, strangers enter into contracts with other strangers at their own risk. The standard of contractual fairness described in earlier chapters as the "market standard"[161] is incompatible with a living law in which only family or close friends of the chieftain, close friends of the contracting parties, or successful bribers and simulators can reasonably expect a successful outcome.

To satisfy the reasonable expectations of contractual strangers, a legal system, especially one in charge of making, applying, interpreting and teaching its law, must make sure that its official and living laws are consistent with one another, and that they all fulfill the developmental purposes assigned to them. A recent study by the World Bank entitled "Where is the Wealth of Nations?"[162] quantifies the positive effect of a legal system that can promote economic growth. As stated by Lic. Octavio Sanchez, a former NLCIFT staff member and present cabinet member in the Honduran government: "What makes . . . [the World Bank] study groundbreaking is that for the first time we are able to quantify how important a legal system is . . . [in bringing about economic] development."[163] According to this study, only four percent of all of the world's wealth is natural capital, eighteen percent is produced or built capital, and seventy-eight percent is intangible capital. Fifty-seven percent of the intangible capital is a direct result of what I would describe as an effective legal system. By an effective legal system, I mean one that can be trusted by good faith merchants, whether acting as contracting or third parties, and by honest and fair government officials and adjudicators to do its task as an agent of economic development.[164]

Because the "winner-takes-all/loser-takes-none" oligopolistic and extended family model of doing business was the one that prevailed in the wholesale trade of both commercial and agricultural goods, Mexico, as well as other Latin American countries, started their independent life without an effective law of commercial contracts.

§ 14.5 LATIN AMERICAN CODIFICATION

After the independence of the Latin American colonies, the above-described colonial law was replaced by numerous codes originally inspired by French and

---

160 *See generally* Kozolchyk, *Fairness;* Kozolchyk, *Commercialization;* Kozolchyk, *Roadmap*; Kozolchyk, *Reduction of Poverty*.

161 *See, e.g.,* § 1:2(B).

162 *See* THE WORLD BANK, WHERE IS THE WEALTH OF NATIONS, MEASURING CAPITAL FOR THE 21ST CENTURY (2006), *available at* http://siteresources.worldbank.org/INTEEI/214578–1110886258964/20748034/All.pdf.

163 *See* SANCHEZ BARRIENTOS, *supra* note 5, at 3. Octavio Sanchez's work is a must read for anyone interested in understanding, *inter alia*, the effect of legal dogmatism in the economic development of Latin American countries.

164 *See* Kozolchyk, *Toward a Theory on Law*, at 681, 738, 740–41 (discussing the effectiveness of and trust in legal institutions in the context of economic development).

Spanish models. The guiding principles of the *Code Civil* and *Code de Commerce* as well as their methods of drafting were discussed in earlier chapters.[165] The extent of the *Code Civil's* influence as a legislative model is highlighted by the Chilean legal historian, Alejandro Guzmán Brito:

> Codification [of civil law] in America [was first strongly] influenced by the French. In fact, the first codes enacted in this part of the world were a clear imitation of the French [codes]: . . . [for example those of Louisiana] (1808 and 1825), Haiti (1825), State of Oaxaca, Mexico (1827–1829) and Bolivia (1830), later adopted by Costa Rica (1841). . . . By the second half of the XIX Century the French influence had started to wane. . . .[166]

At some point, the German Pandectist concept of the juristic act *Rechtsgeschäft* began to emerge as central in the legislative technique adopted by the drafters of various Latin American civil codes.[167]

Despite the yearning for autochthonous codes and the glowing praise of some of the codes in force as "truly" Latin American codes, the fact is that there is little that is truly autochthonous in the enacted codes. Perhaps the most important reason for the lack of authenticity was the codifiers' concomitant belief that codification was a science and as such, was universal and permanent in its formulations. If so, where was the room for purely autochthonous rules, unless they could be shown to rise to the level of universally valid scientific formulations? Accordingly, Latin American codes tend to follow their "scientific" models rather closely, regardless of local socio-economic realities.

During my lectures at Carlos III University in Spain during the summer of 2005, a graduate student discussed his paper on formal contracts in the Spanish Civil Code and included a section on the rental payable in-kind, or "*censo enfiteutico*." This institution traces its ancestry to the Roman law *Emphyteusis* which was "a long term lease of an imperial domain or of private land for a rental in kind."[168] Four of the twenty graduate students present were from Latin America and I asked them whether their civil codes regulated such an institution. Three of them said that their codes did indeed regulate this census. Then I asked them if in their professional lives they had ever encountered such an institution or heard of colleagues who had done so. None had; however, they said that it was a necessary legal institution because after having been identified as a contract in Roman law and being made part of the contracts regulated by seminal nineteenth-century civil codes, no one could dispute their universal and permanent nature.

In addition, and as will be discussed shortly, some legal institutions were selected by Latin American codifiers because they were European scientific "breakthroughs," such as the "juristic act" (*Rechtsgeschäft*) of Pandectist extraction or the concept of "*impresa*" ("*empresa*" in Latin American codes) of fascist-Italian origin. These two

---

165 *See supra* ch. 10.

166 Alejandro Guzmán Brito, *Para la Historia de la Formación de la Teoría General del Acto o Negocio Jurídicos y del Contrato (II): El Sistema y el Vocabulario de la Negociabilidad Jurídica en las Codificaciones,* 19 REV. ESTUD. HIST.–JURÍD. 50 (1997), *available at* http://www.scielo.cl/scielo.php?script=sci_arttext&pid=S0716–54551997000100003&lng=en&nrm=iso&tlng=es (author's translation) (on file with author).

167 *Id.*

168 BERGER, ENCYCLOPEDIC DICTIONARY, at 452.

concepts were given undeserved codified weight at the expense of the archetypal standards of commercial reasonableness and good faith behavior as found in the HGB and BGB. Since these standards are the indispensable tools of a commercially-equitable adjudication, their disregard by Latin American codes has made it very difficult for these codes to encourage such an adjudication, without which it is virtually impossible to develop a law of commercial contracts responsive to the needs of the marketplace and economic development.

A. Latin American "Families" of Civil Codification

By the middle of the nineteenth century, Latin American civil codes affiliated themselves with model codes drafted by local jurists. Prominent among the model codes were the Chilean Civil Code of 1855, the Argentine Civil Code, and the draft of a civil code by Augusto Teixeira de Freitas (1816–1883). This jurist authored a draft of the Brazilian Civil Code (*Esboço de un Código Civil para Brasil*) that was rejected by the Brazilians, but influenced the drafting of the Argentine Civil Code and eventually parts of Brazil's own Civil Code of 1916. As is apparent in Mexico's Civil Code of 1928, the BGB, which was enacted in 1900, replaced, in significant measure, the influence of the *Code Civil* as the exclusive model of codification.

I will now briefly examine the Argentine and Chilean civil codes as progenitors of Latin America's most numerous families of codes.

1. Andrés Bello and the Chilean Civil Code of 1855

In a highly eclectic fashion, the Venezuelan-born jurist and grammarian, Andrés Bello, gathered European codified and legislative material and tried to simplify and consolidate it into one comprehensive civil code.[169] In an article published on June 28, 1833 in the Chilean newspaper *El Araucano*, he expressed his desire to gather dispersed civil law provisions into one well-organized body of law:

> [W]ithout unnecessary prefaces and redundant phrases, without obsolete terms that make them confusing and obscure . . . discarding subject matters that never had or ceased to have application in the world we live in; also, choosing one interpretation from the array of interpretations of issues where commentators of the law are in dispute; as well as coordinating what is currently in effect and extracting all that contradicts it or that is superficial to it. [All of which will result] in a body of law as well organized and complete as possible and ensuring its compatibility with the current laws and regulations that to this day rule in this forum.[170]

As is apparent in this description, Bello, who was an admirer of the English utilitarian philosopher Jeremy Bentham, did not believe that his task as a codifier required the promulgation of a utilitarian philosophy of the civil law. He saw himself as an organizer of compiled materials and drafter of the clearest, most grammatically elegant, and least redundant set of rules. He succeeded in producing a highly elegant, terse, and clear set of rules. He may have even succeeded in providing a constitution

---

[169] Alejandro Guzmán Brito, *Codificación y Consolidación: Una Comparación entre el Pensamiento de A. Bello y el de A. Teixeira de Freitas,* 10 REV. ESTUD. HIST.–JURÍD. 269, 269–84 (1985), *available at* http://www.restudioshistoricos.equipu.cl/index.php/rehj/article/view/135/ (on file with author).

[170] *Id.* at 273–74 (this author's translation).

for Chile's private law as visualized by the aristocratic *hombres de bien* of that era. These men were true to their contractual word and were deeply disdainful, as was Bello, of the "rabble" of purchased witnesses who congregated in courtrooms eager to sell their testimony on the contractual intent of parties they did not even know existed.[171] As will be discussed shortly, he also protected their real property interests in a manner reminiscent of the French bourgeois. However, whether he succeeded in providing the "civil" general framework for a commercial law of contracts is another question which I will leave to the reader to sort out after reading the following provisions from the Chilean Civil Code's section on contracts:

> Article 1438
>
> A contract or convention is an act by which one party is obligated to another to give, to do or not to do something. A party to a contract may be comprised of one or several persons.
>
> Article 1439
>
> The contract is unilateral when one of the parties is obligated to another who assumes no obligation whatever; it is bilateral when the parties are obligated reciprocally.
>
> Article 1442
>
> The contract is principal when it binds by itself without the need of another agreement and is accessory when its object is to guarantee the fulfillment of a principal obligation, so that it cannot subsist without it.[172]

Have you come across this classification before? If so, can you trace its ancestry? Is this likely to be an open-ended (*numerus apertus*) or a closed-ended (*numerus clausus*) classification? How important is the use of the verb "is" in Bello's definitions and classifications of contracts? With respect to Article 1442, can you identify a rather important commercial transaction that would have a very difficult time qualifying as a "principal" contract?

> Article 1445
>
> For a person to bind herself to another by means of an act or declaration of intention it is necessary that: 1) she be legally capable of binding herself; 2) she consents to be bound in that act or declaration and that this consent not be vitiated; 3) the object of the agreement be lawful; [and] 4) its clause also be lawful.
>
> Article 1467
>
> No obligation can exist without a cause that is real and lawful; but it is not necessary to express it. A pure desire to make a gift or an act of beneficence is a sufficient cause. By cause is meant the motive that induces the act or contract; and by an unlawful cause is meant one that is forbidden by the law or that is contrary to good customs and public order. Thus, the promise to give something in payment of a nonexistent debt lacks a cause; and the promise of

---

[171] *See supra* § 2:1(B)(3) (referring to Bello's preface to his Civil Code in which he explains why Article 1708 rejected parole evidence against what appeared stated in written contracts).

[172] C. CIV. (CL.) arts. 1438, 1439, 1442 (1857) (translated by author).

a reward for the commission of a crime or an immoral act has an unlawful cause.[173]

Clearly, (and as expressed with the clarity typical of a good teacher of Spanish grammar and syntax) the Chilean Civil Code belongs squarely within the family that requires a *causa* for contracts to be enforceable. Yet, can you recall important commercial transactions and components of litigation that would suffer from the absence or presence of a "real and lawful" cause?

Article 1708

Testimonial evidence shall not be admitted with respect to an obligation which must be reduced to a writing.[174]

This provision is consistent with Article 1341 of the *Code Civil*,[175] but is contrary to BGB-inspired provisions such as Article 1856 of the Mexican Civil Code which provides that "[t]he usages and customs of the nation shall be taken into account in interpreting the ambiguities of contracts."[176]

While it is true that Bello had in mind the rabble that sold their perjured testimonies on the parties' contractual intent, the language of Article 1708 is broad enough to exclude the testimony of expert witnesses on the customs and usages of the various commercial trades.

Concerning purchases and sales:

Article 1793

The purchase and sale is a contract in which one of the parties is obligated to give something and the other to pay for it in money. The former is said to sell and the latter to buy. The money paid by the purchaser is known as the price.

Article 1794

When the price to be paid consists in part of money and in part of a thing [other than money, the transaction] will be deemed a barter [*permute*] if the thing is worth more than the monetary component and a purchase and sale in the contrary case.[177]

Do you recall another instance where another famous but much earlier jurist drew a distinction between barter and purchase based on the fact that the former required for its fulfillment that goods be exchanged by the parties instead of money? When I called this distinction to your attention,[178] I suggested that the reason for the

---

173 *Id.* arts. 1445, 1467.

174 *Id.* art. 1708.

175 *See* C. CIV. (FR.) art. 1341 (2008). In relevant part, it states: "An act must be made before notaries or under private signature if the sum or value of one hundred and fifty francs . . . and no proof can be received by witnesses against or beyond what is contained in such acts. . . ." *Id.* (author's translation).

176 Mexican C.C.F. art. 1856 (2008). *See also* BGB § 133 (GOREN, 1994) ("In interpreting a declaration of intention the true intention shall be sought without regard to the declaration's literal meaning."); *id.* § 157 ("Contracts shall be interpreted according to the requirements of good faith, giving consideration to common usage.").

177 C. CIV. (CL.) arts. 1793 & 1794 (1857) (author's translation).

178 *See supra* § 4:6(A).

distinction was remedial in nature. Would the same be true in the Chilean Civil Code? If so, why did Bello not specify which cause of action belonged to each transaction?

> Article 1811
>
> The sale of the seller's present and future property is null and void, be it sold in bulk or in quotas; but such a sale will be enforceable if it specifies species, genus, and quantity [sold] in a public deed, even though it comprises all that the seller possesses or expects to acquire as long as it does not include unlawful objects.[179]

It is interesting that in the middle of the nineteenth century, in a mostly rural Chile, bulk sales were known and thought to be deserving of regulation. Do you consider Bello's requirement that the sale be executed in a public deed to be a meaningless or a useful formality?

> Article 1813
>
> The sale of things that do not exist, but are expected to exist, shall be understood to have been made subject to the condition of their existence, unless otherwise agreed, or that because of the nature of the contract it appears that it was intended as a gamble.[180]

As indicated earlier in this section, the Chilean Civil Code shows a preference for the "proper way" to acquire ownership in real property. Accordingly, it downplays the importance of adverse possession as a means to acquire title to land, especially against recorded titles, regardless of the time the recorded title holder had been absent from his fallow land and regardless of the fact that Chile was a country of recent settlers and of vast extensions of uncultivated land.

In his forthcoming monograph on land tenure and land registry regimes in Latin America, the NLCIFT's Lic. Sanchez Barrientos lists some of the features of the real property system of the Bello type of Civil Code adopted in his home country. He points to the protection of the absent landlords against the true users of the land as adverse possessors in provisions such as:

1. Articles 724 and 728, which state that only those persons who recorded their land titles acquired possession of that land. Thus, no matter how many years someone else occupied that property an ownership right could only be claimed by the holder of recorded title to that property.

2. Article 924, which states that possession can only be established legitimately, *i.e.*, by means of a registered title.

3. Article 2505, which stated that adverse possession cannot be invoked against a recorded title.[181]

In addition, the Chilean Civil code requires the execution of a notarial or public deed as the document to be registered. Normally, the fees charged by the notary for

---

179 C. CIV. (CL.) art. 1811 (1857) (author's translation).

180 *Id.* art. 1813 (author's translation).

181 SANCHEZ BARRIENTOS, *supra* note 5.

such deeds were high enough that a large segment of the Chilean population could not afford them.[182]

Despite what Lic. Sanchez Barrientos refers to as its "elitism," the 1855 Chilean Civil Code was the most influential source of Latin American private law codification during the nineteenth century. In addition to Chile, this code was enacted in El Salvador, Ecuador, Venezuela, Nicaragua, Colombia and Honduras. It also inspired the drafting of parts of other nineteenth-century civil codes in Argentina, Brazil, Uruguay, Mexico, Guatemala, Costa Rica and Paraguay.[183]

2. *Dalmacio Vélez Sársfield and the Argentinean Civil Code of 1871*

Despite the claim by some legal historians that the Argentine Civil Code of 1871 was in significant measure the first Latin American product of Pandectism, it is eclecticism that characterizes its drafting method. When drafting this code, Vélez Sársfield relied on the *Code Civil*, the Roman *Corpus Juris Civilis*, Teixeira de Freitas's draft of a Brazilian Civil Code, and Aubry and Rau's Treatise on Civil Law. As pointed out by Professors Kenneth Karst and Keith Rosenn, out of the 4,051 articles of this code, 1,200 were copied from Teixeira de Freitas's Civil Code draft; 700 came from Aubry and Rau's Treatise on Civil Law,[184] 300 from the draft and commentary of a Spanish Civil Code published in 1852 by García Goyena, and 170 were copied from the Chilean Civil Code of 1855.[185] The following provisions illustrate this eclecticism. Can the reader trace their ancestry? This search should also serve as a review of key points discussed in the chapters on French and German codification.

> Article 1137
>
> A contract exists when both parties agree on a common declaration of intention destined to govern their rights.
>
> Article 1138
>
> In this code, contracts are unilateral or bilateral. The first are those in which only one of the parties is obligated to the other; the second are those in which the parties obligate themselves reciprocally one to the other.[186]

The following provision is of mixed or eclectic ancestry. Is the reader able to pinpoint their parentage?

---

[182] *Id.; see also* C. CIV. (CL.) arts. 724, 728, 924, 2505 (1857) (author's translation).

[183] *See generally* Matthew Campbell Mirow, *Borrowing Private Law in Latin America: Andrés Bello's Use of the Code Napoléon in Drafting the Chilean Civil Code*, 61 LA. L. REV. 291 (2001).

[184] Aubry and Rau were professors of civil law at the Strasbourg Law School and their treatise is still influential among Latin American civil law teachers.

[185] KENNETH L. KARST AND KEITH S. ROSENN, LAW AND DEVELOPMENT IN LATIN AMERICA: A CASE BOOK 46 (1975). These authors provide the following illustration of Vélez Sársfiled's eclecticism:

> An idea of the depths and variety of sources can be gleaned from examination of a specific provision of the Argentine Civil Code. Article 923 provides: "Ignorance of the law, or an error of law, shall in no case prevent the legal effects of lawful acts, nor excuse responsibility for unlawful acts." The Code's principal draftsman, Dr. Vélez Sársfield, published annotations to explain his motives and identify his sources. His note to Article 923 includes quotations from Savigny, the famous 19th century German commentator on Roman law, and from several other commentators, principally French.

Id.

[186] CÓD. CIV. (ARG.) arts. 1137, 1138 (author's translation).

Article 1150

Offers may be revoked as long as they have not been accepted, unless the offeror waived his right of revocation or obligated himself when making the offer to remain bound for a fixed period of time.

Article 1184

The following contracts must be executed in a public deed, with the exception of those that are part of a public auction:

1. Contracts that convey immoveable property, whether in fee simple absolute or usufruct (life estate) or create an obligation or lien in the real property or convey rights *in rem* in the immoveable property of others. . . .

Article 1185

Those contracts that should have been executed in a public deed and were executed in a private deed signed by the parties or in a particular instrument in which the parties agreed to execute it in a public deed will be unenforceable as long as the public deed has not been signed.

Article 955

A simulation takes place when the legal nature of an act is masked by the appearance of another, or when the act contains clauses that are deceptive or dates that are inaccurate or when by means of it rights are created or conveyed to persons who lend their names and who are not in fact the participants in the transaction.

Article 957

A simulation is not punished by law when it damages no-one nor has an illegal purpose.[187]

A remarkable similarity exists between the Argentine and Mexican Civil Code provisions on simulation,[188] with the exception of the definition of a benevolent simulation in Article 957 of the Argentine Civil Code. In light of the preceding discussion on the legal and economic effects of simulation, is it possible to agree with Vélez Sársfield that there are simulations that harm no one? Was this drafter thinking of my illustration of a *Code-Civil*-inspired disguise of a donation to the neediest of one's children as a loan so as not to awaken resentment in his or her siblings? Can you think of other instances of "harmless" simulations, particularly in the world of commerce?

3. *Comparison of the Above-Selected Provisions of the Chilean & Argentine Civil Codes*

A Chilean legal historian distinguished the Bello from the Vélez Sársfield and Teixeira de Freitas families of civil codes by stating that the Bello family adopted the French "contractual" model which relied on contracts as the exclusive source of voluntary obligations, while the Vélez Sársfield family turned to the German juristic

---

187 *Id.* arts. 1150, 1184, 1185, 955, 957.

188 *See* Mexican C.C.F. arts. 2180–2184 (2008) (the Mexican Civil Code provisions on simulation).

acts or *Rechtsgeschäft* as their source of such obligations.[189] Yet, upon closer analysis, these supposedly conflicting models turn out not to be conflicting. The *Code Civil*, which inspired the "contractual" model, allowed enforceable unilateral (not contractual) acts such as wills, assignments and waivers of rights. Conversely, the *Rechtsgeschäft* of the BGB required that all voluntary obligations be the result of contracts, to the consternation of commentators such as Phillip Heck, who pointed out why some voluntary unilateral, non-contractual obligations deserved to be binding in German law.[190]

At root, then, the differences between these supposedly opposing families were not caused by technical concepts, but by the degree of their support for commercial contracts and promises that were unenforceable under the *Code Civil*. Accordingly, I would suggest that the reader revisit the "Commercialization" table from a previous chapter[191] and compare it with the provisions of the Bello and Vélez Sársfield family of codes transcribed earlier, as well as with others not included in this listing. Try to find, for example, whether your selected Latin American code enforces: (1) *abstract promises* "whereby an act of performance is promised in such a manner that the promise itself is to create the obligation";[192] (2) *acknowledgments of debt* whereby a written acknowledgment[193] is enforceable without an acceptance of it by the creditor; (3) *bearer instruments* in which a promise in writing to perform an act in favor of a bearer is enforceable;[194] and (4) an *offer of a reward* or a *public announcement* that promises payment of a sum of money for the performances of certain services or the bringing about of a requested result.[195]

Consider, for example, that the Mexican Civil Code of 1928 (which was influenced by the BGB) enables the enforcement of: (1) "firm" offers;[196] (2) public offers of a reward;[197] and (3) "civil" promises of payment of sums certain to the order or bearer.[198] Yet, a word of caution is in order. One ought not to expect that similar texts in, say, the BGB and the Mexican Civil Code will be interpreted by the courts or relied upon by the contractual parties in a similar manner in the two countries. For, as pointed out in the introductory chapter,[199] underlying attitudes toward law in general and commerce in particular weigh as much in the interpretation and application of the law than does the text of positive or "official" law provisions.

---

[189] Guzmán Brito, *supra* note 160. As Guzmán Brito concluded, "that where juristic acts were concerned, two important American codes, the Brazilian and the Argentinean, fully escaped the French contractual tradition and adopted that of the 'juristic act' advocated by the German Pandectist science." *Id.* (author's translation).

[190] *See supra* § 12:3(C) (discussing Phillip Heck's objections).

[191] *See supra* § 12:6.

[192] BGB § 780 (GOREN, 1994).

[193] *Id.* § 781.

[194] *Id.* § 793.

[195] *Id.* § 657.

[196] Mexican C.C.F. art. 1860 (1932).

[197] *Id.* arts. 1861–1867.

[198] *Id.* arts. 1873–1881.

[199] *See supra* § 1:2.

B. Latin American Commercial Codification

1. *Families of Commercial Codes*

Professor Julio Olavarría of Chile points out that as with the Latin American civil codes, the Latin American commercial codes were mainly inspired, at first, by the French, Spanish and Portuguese codes, and later by the German civil and commercial codes and by the Italian civil or "unified" code. Nevertheless, he also believes that:

> [I]t is clear that by the beginning of this [twentieth] Century code drafting was coming into its own and in the future it would rely on its own [socio-economic] characteristics which are more discernible in the field of commercial law than in other legal fields.[200]

Professor Olavarría's prediction has not come about for reasons that I will explore shortly. Similarly, his classification of the Latin American commercial codes in force until the turn of the twentieth century is helpful, but only from a historical and bibliographical standpoint. Many of the codes listed have been so drastically amended as to be unrecognizable and others have been replaced. Olavarría divides the codes into two groups: The first includes those directly based on European codes, among which he distinguishes Haiti (1826) and the Dominican Republic (1884), both derived from the French *Code de Commerce* of 1807; Bolivia (1834) and Costa Rica (1853), derived from the Spanish Code of 1829; and Cuba (1885), Mexico (1889), and Peru (1902), derived from the second Spanish Commercial Code of 1885. Finally, the Brazilian Code of 1850 combined several European sources, including the Spanish Commercial Code of 1826, the French *Code de Commerce* of 1807, and the Portuguese Code of Commerce of 1833.

The second group includes codes that were directly or primarily based on other Latin American commercial codes. Among these are the Chilean Commercial Code of 1865 and the Argentinean Commercial Code of 1862, both of which served to inspire other codes. The Chilean Code was adopted by countries like Colombia in 1869, Ecuador in 1906, El Salvador in 1904, Guatemala in 1877, Honduras in 1898, Nicaragua and Panama in 1869, and Venezuela in 1904; the Argentinean Code was followed by Paraguay and Uruguay.[201]

I should add that in contrast with the influence that the BGB wielded over Latin American civil codes, the German Commercial Code of 1897 has had little influence over its Latin American counterparts. In contrast, the unified Italian Civil Code of 1942, despite its fascist ideology, has influenced the drafting of some Latin American commercial codes. One such code was the Commercial Code of Honduras of 1950, which followed the Italian Civil Code in matters such as its scope, said to be mostly of entrepreneurial activities (*empresa*), its remedies and excuses for non-performance such as "excessive onerousness," and others. Similar scope provisions and rules on excuses for non-performance were adopted by the commercial codes of El Salvador and others, as will be discussed in a later section of this book.[202]

More recently, Professor M.C. Mirow of Florida International University College of Law has called attention to the fact that:

---

200 Julio Olavarra Avila, Los Códigos de Comercio Latinoamericanos 98 (1961).

201 *Id.* at 99.

202 *See infra* ch. 27.

New forms of investment and commerce, such as electronic and internet services and products, are making substantial inroads in Latin America as well. Advances in these areas provide new challenges for legal instituttions and substantive law. Too much freedom in economic activity has also led to problems at times. For example, when Chile privatized its banks the first time, lack of regulation and careless actions sent many of the instiutions into bankruptcy.[203]

The question then is: what made it so difficult for Chile and other Latin American nations to enact the appropriate autochthonous commercial law that Professor Olavarría was predicting was going to be enacted and Professor Mirow suggested was necessary?

2. *Why Autochthonous Commercial Codes Are Unlikely*

The reason why Professor Olavarría's prediction of a wave of thoroughly autochthonous twentieth-century Latin American commercial codes capable of creating sound, long-lasting commercial law did not come to fruition can be easily explained. Commercial law is a law of merchants that is both universal and special to that class (*Lex Mercatoria* and *Lex Specialis*). More than any other branch of the law, it is derived from custom and usage, especially from those that have proven themselves cost effective and fair in the eyes of market participants, starting out with the most active and spreading to the least active markets. Hence, no matter how hard a drafter of a commercial code may try to create new institutions, he or she will run up against customs and practices born and developed in these highly active marketplaces and widely observed elsewhere only after having been thoroughly tried and tested throughout the trading world. Each section, chapter or book of the nineteenth- and twentieth-century commercial codes bears witness to this observation, starting with peculiarly commercial contracts and promises, including negotiable instruments, and continuing with double entry bookkeeping, business associations, and tried and true procedures to terminate, liquidate, or rehabilitate them. To attempt to anticipate the emergence of new commercial institutions or to shape their features in advance of their special and universal developmental sequence has proven futile in most instances.

On the other hand, some promising signs of a more market-oriented, cost-effective, and fair commercial law, capable of encouraging economic development, can be discerned in the last decade of legislation and judicial adjudication in Latin America. On the legislative front, the enactment of the OAS Model Law on Secured Transactions by Mexico, Guatemala, Honduras, El Salvador, Colombia, and Peru is also bringing about a modernization of the law of commercial contracts in general, as well as the laws of civil and commercial procedure.[204] The law of commercial contracts of these countries can now rely on refurbished and autochthonous legal institutions, such as "possessory preferential rights" (derechos posesorios preferenciales), attributable or derived property rights (bienes atribuibles o derivados), brokers and notary publics private adjudication (ventas notariales o por corredores publicos), and so on.

---

[203] M.C. Mirow, Latin American Law: A History of Private Law and Institutions in Spanish America 231 (2004).

[204] See generally Boris Kozolchyk, Implementation of the OAS Model Law in Latin America: Current Status, 28 AZ. J. INT'L & COMP. L 1 (2011).

On the judicial reform front, NLCIFT has been able to train over 3,200 trial and appellate judges, public defenders, attorneys, notaries, law professors and law students in Mexico and Columbia on the subject of "oral trails" and secured transactions and bankruptcy law. This oral trial strongly resembles the typical adversary procedures in American courts. From the standpoint of the modernization and the creation of autonomous legal institutions, this is also a highly promising development because this trial's reliance on factual evidence of all types and of examination and cross-examination procedures is already bringing about local versions of motions, special actions, and enforcement procedures.[205]

Another promising Latin American commercial statute is Colombian Law No. 1258 of simplified corproations (Sociedad Anonima Simplificada or SAS).[206] Its drafter Professor Francisco Reyes has skilfully combined some of the most cost effective and fair United States, French and Colombian corporate practices when creating the most successful business association law in the history of Latin America; presently 96% of all Colombian business associations are of the SAS variety. It has inspired similar legislation in other Latin American and African nations and is now being used as the basis for a Model on Simplified Corporations both at the OAS and at UNCITRAL.

§ 14.6 CONCLUSIONS

The future of commercial codification in the Americas and elsewhere will not rely as much on the drafting ability of renowned commercial law professors as it will on the incorporation of an ever-increasing number of internationally tried and tested customs, usages and practices. It also appears that the drafting function will be confined to isolating general principles of key commercial legal institutions, whether substantive or procedural, and incorporating them into the future "general" or introductory parts of the more modest but uniformly international commercial codes. The accordion-like commercial codes that we witnessed in contemporary French and German efforts to update codification would seem to me creatures of a past that should not be repeated. Further, As apparent in the socio economic conditions of most of the inhabitants of Latin American countries until the past 20 years, neither their civil and commercial codes nor their judicial interpretation contributed much to their economic development. During the last two decades a noticeable improvement in the living conditions of some Latin American countries such as Brazil, Colombia, Costa Rican and Mexico has taken place; nevertheless, unless the proper legal institutions required for a sustainable economic development are in place, nothing will prevent these countries from becoming victims of the "Argentine" syndrome of having been better off at the turn of the 20th century than at the turn of the 21st.

Further, as shown by the history of *almaceneros* and *hacendados*, good commercial practices will not emerge except through entities such as commercial associations,

---

[205] National Law Center for Inter-American Free Trade, Novedades (2013), *available at* http://us6.campaign-archive1.com/?u=42bcba69e83dac012a44b6b33&id=63d14061da. *See also* Arizona Journal of International and Comparative Law, 27 Enhancement of Mexican Commercial Adjudication by Improved Transactional Fact-Finding, Application of Equitable Principles, and Drafting of Standard Contracts and Best Contratual Practices (2010).

[206] Boris Kozolchyk & Cristina Castañeda, *Invigorating Micro and Small Businesses Through Secured Commercial Credit in Latin America: The Need for Legal and Institutional Reform,* 28 AZ. J. INT'L & COMP. L 43, 97 (2011).

chambers of commerce, or other peer legitimizing institutions, and through the rise of new archetypes of commercial behavior whose vision of commerce is not that of a zero-sum game, but a cooperative endeavor that benefits all participants in the marketplace and society at large.

§ 14.7 APPENDIX: COLONIAL AND POST-COLONIAL ATTITUDES

This appendix intends to acquaint the reader with the thoughts of a Spanish priest and author and of a prominent Latin American legal scholar and practitioner. The former helped to shape attitudes toward commerce and commercial contract law, and the latter had a uniquely qualified perspective on the legal culture of an important Latin American nation during the latter half of the twentieth century.

A. A Brief Review of Fray Tomás de Mercado's "Manual of Bargains and Contracts" ("*Suma de Tratos y Contratos*")

The Purposes of the Suma

During much of Spain's colonial regime, Latin America's living law of contracts could not help but be mindful of the Catholic Church's prohibition of usury. Usurers were hauled before the ominous tribunal of the Inquisition (*Tribunal del Santo Oficio de la Inquisición*) in Mexico City and Lima, Peru as money lenders or exchangers who charged interest for their loans, as secret practitioners of Judaism, or both.[207] This contributed to the widespread use of contractual simulations, some of which were described in the main chapter.[208] This fact explains why the *Suma de Tratos y Contratos* (the first manual on enforceable commercial contracts in Spanish and Hispanic American trade) was not written by a jurist, but by a Dominican priest, Fray Tomás de Mercado in 1569.[209] In his Preamble (Nuncupative Epistle) Fray Tomás states the purpose of his writing:

> I started writing this book because I always judged as negligence not to make available to merchants doing business in places like . . . Burgos, Medina del Campo, Lisbon, and others a discussion of what was legal or illegal in their most common transactions, as determined by a board of theologians, so that they do not commit mistakes when entering into the most ordinary or basic of their transactions.[210]

---

[207] *See generally* GENARO GARCÍA, AUTOS DE FÉ DE LA INQUISICIÓN DE MÉXICO (1910). The tribunals of the Inquisition were created by Phillip II, as the *Tribunales del Santo Oficio de la Inquisición*, one in Mexico and the other in Peru. This source provides a record of the prosecutions by the Inquisition Tribunal against suspected Jews, including accused usurers. *See Preguntas Más Frecuentes Sobre el Tribunal de la Inquisición de Lima*, MUSEO DE LA INQUISICIÓN Y DEL CONGRESO, http://www.congreso.gob.pe/museo/inquisicion/histo-inq-catecismo.pdf (on file with author) (on the *Tribunal de la Inquisición* in Lima, Peru, and on prosecutions for usurious lending).

[208] *See supra* § 14:4(A)(3)(c)(iii).

[209] *See* FRAY TOMÁS DE MERCADO, SUMA DE TRATOS Y CONTRATOS [MANUAL OF BARGAINS AND CONTRACTS] (Sevilla, 1587) (1569) (author's translation). *See* Sergio Lucio Torales, *Moral Económica en Suma de Tratos y Contratos de Fray Tomás de Mercado: Estado Actual de la Cuestión*, 21 EL BASILISCO 14, 14–15 (1996), *available at* http://www.filosofia.org/rev/bas/bas22105.htm (on file with author) (a brief biography of this influential priest, whose ideas on freeing up the availability of metallic currency in the Americas and in Spain as a means with which to lower excessively high prices of commodities in both locations, thereby freeing up trade, influenced later European thinkers such as Hugo Grotius).

[210] MERCADO, *supra* note 199, at Prologue.

To this he added:

> Because commerce and money changing are so intertwined . . . it is not enough for the prosperous merchant to purchase and sell, he must also exchange currencies in order to obtain that which he very badly needs to do business in different locations. . . . And since in all of these transactions, usury of every type is present, whether overt or simulated, I thought it convenient to provide an account of all these transactions, that is to say, sales, purchases, exchanges and usuries for the use of merchants and dealers so that that they would know the right path of their art and avoid and reject the wrong and dangerous paths.[211]

B. A Tentative Presumption of Commercial Good Faith Aided by Confessors

It is noteworthy that unlike the fraudulent and deceitful dealings attributed to the manufacturers and retailers of woolen cloth by the Royal Decree in the *Novísima Recopilación* discussed in the principal chapter,[212] Fray Tomás did not attribute such bad faith to the merchants engaged in imports and exports in Spain and the Americas. He blamed the usurious path on the mixing of commerce with the purchase and sale of the badly needed currency. Once involved with currency exchanges, it was too easy to slip into the path of usury. It is for this reason that Fray Tomás regarded the advice of father confessors of merchants as playing a key role when distinguishing what was lawful from what was unlawful and sinful. In his words:

> As Don Antonio de Mendoza, viceroy of New Spain and Peru said: for a good earthly government there is no more important and beneficial thing than good confessors. . . . [A] confessor is to Christianity what the prince is to the city; the person in charge of assuring that everyone lives in and orderly fashion and that the law is obeyed abided and enforced.[213]

In such a capacity, the confessor's task was to dissuade merchants from avoiding their responsibilities in usurious dealings, as well as abstaining from using stipulations that deprived buyers, debtors or lessees from the merchantability of what was sold, borrowed or leased. Usurious dealings comprised, then, both unlawful charges of interest and sales of goods for a price "above their just price." By "above their just price," Fray Tomás meant a sale for a price above that "set by the government or the market."[214]

C. Reasonable Rates of Interest, Just Prices and the Market

This reference to the market as an arbiter of justness of prices did not originate with Fray Tomás. Three centuries earlier, Albertus Magnus and Saint Thomas Aquinas had stated that a just price was to be determined in accordance with the market's appraisal or "*secundum aestimationem fori.*"[215] However, Fray Tomás' inquiry

---

211 *Id.* at prologue ¶ 4.

212 *See supra* § 14:3(C)(2).

213 MERCADO, *supra* note 199, at 26.

214 *Id.* at 36.

215 *See* Kozolchyk, *On the State of Commercial Law,* at 3. This source discusses the concept of fair price in medieval law and other opposing views, arguing that fair price "was limited to amounts that allowed the producer to live and support his family on a scale suitable to his station in life (*per quanto res suas*

on just prices focused on entire categories of contractual behavior and not just on individual contracts.

For example, was it illegal or sinful to sell for prices well below the market when the merchant was in great need of money? He answered that it was neither illegal nor sinful to do so. It was also not illegal to buy the goods offered at the sharply reduced prices, especially if they were purchased in the public market. Contrary to the opinion of other theologians, Fray Tomás stated that a price that would be unjust in private dealings could well be just once the sale was made public and subject to the bargaining of the marketplace.[216] His concept of a just price, then, relied on the inherent publicity of the marketplace. However, it also relied on other transactional factors such as: (1) the cost of the goods; (2) the cost of transportation; (3) the maritime risks; and (4) the time during which the merchant's money was invested in the goods until their sale, including an allowance for a reasonable rate of interest on that money.[217]

The willingness to allow for a charge of interest for a merchant's investment money was striking when one considers that the majority opinion among churchmen during Fray Tomás' time was of absolute prohibition of any charge of any interest above the principal amount lent. Moreover, according to Fray Tomás, there was also a presumption of good faith with respect to the money invested in partnership agreements and its yield of interest. However, this presumption was not absolute, but open to proof of a contrary (usurious) intent. According to him, partnerships could indeed facilitate legitimate deals and profits, especially in long-distance trade. There is good reason to believe that the trade he was alluding to was of the "brotherly" variety described earlier in this book in connection with the Middle Eastern Jewish traders whose disputes were ultimately resolved by rabbinical *responsa*.[218] Fray Tomás specifically notes that contracts that were made "as long as the intermediary is a trustworthy partner" warranted the charge of interest on requisite occasions.[219] However, the price required to enter into a partnership had to be fair (including agreed percentages and interests) and to that extent, it had to take into account and compensate for investment risks, although Fray Tomás admitted that "this principle was rarely applied."[220]

D. Bad Faith and Money Changers

In contrast with Fray Tomás's presumption of good faith in sales and purchases and special commercial and maritime partnerships, his *Suma*, much as Isabella and Ferdinand's earlier decree[221] presumed bad faith in contracts for the exchange of currency and characterized them as simulations of usurious loans. In reference to money changers, he states that "none of them made an exchange that didn't involve

---

vendendo statutum suum continuare possit)," and that of Albert Magnus and Thomas Aquinas, arguing that it was "the price obtainable in the local market (*quam in mercato vendere possint*)." *Id.*

216 MERCADO, *supra* note 199, at 38.

217 *Id.* at 231.

218 *See supra* § 5:10.

219 MERCADO, *supra* note 199, at 34.

220 MERCADO, *supra* note 199, at 34.

221 *See supra* § 14:3(C)(3)(a).

two thousand robberies and usuries."[222] As "prostitutes, they satisfy a need of the kingdom but their profession is, without doubt, sinful."[223]

E. Cash and Installment Sales, Lawful Profits and Unlawful Profiteering

It was not illegal or sinful for merchants and their colleagues or clients to agree on a deferred payment of the purchase price as long as the total contractual price was the same as a cash sale. Yet, it should be recalled that Fray Tomás had accepted "just price" to include "the time during which the merchant's money was invested in the goods until their sale, including an allowance for a reasonable interest rate."[224] Thus, a charge of interest included as part of the total cash price was implicitly acceptable. This may have been the justification used by the father confessor of José María Echeverría's ancestor when allowing him to include a premium on the cash price of the goods sold in installments to his customers in the Veracruz region.[225]

It wasn't illegal or sinful for a merchant to abstain from selling when the market prices where depressed, as opposed to his abstention when there was a severe scarcity of goods or products. In the latter instance, a merchant was assumed to be taking advantage of the scarcity if he refrained from selling goods for more than thirty or forty days from their acquisition, and this was a mortal sin.[226] Similarly, the *Suma* suggested the imposition of penalties for deals where the seller tried to waive his liability for the quality of the goods sold through the use of disclaimers such as:

> "[L]et him see it or wear it," [or] "these goods are conveyed with all their good or bad blemishes." These disclaimers are so often expressed that it is now taken for granted that the more often they are said the more the defects in the goods are accepted knowingly and the tender of defective goods is deemed to have been cured. . . .[227]

Finally, when goods were sold on installments for a deferred price and the buyer defaulted in his payment obligation, the *Suma* allowed for the collection of default interest, even if it could have been characterized as immoderately high:

> It is common not to pay in time. . . [Yet] it is very necessary to abide by [one's obligations] and encourage on time payment so that there is access to credit among men and that they lend and trust each other. Civil laws that understand this truth stipulate that if one defers payment he will then be ordered by a judge to pay the principal amount with usuries, according to what the creditor could, at that time, earn by way of profits from his money, although not the entire amount. This is a law that *if it were to be observed and enforced in actual practice* would be of great use and would prevent many wrongdoings; this law is not only of imperial [origin], but is also [of] divine and natural [origins]. . .[228]

---

222 MERCADO, *supra* note 199, at 80 a.

223 *Id.* at 80 b.

224 *Id.* at 231; *supra* note 207 and accompanying text.

225 *See supra* § 14:4(B).

226 MERCADO, *supra* note 199, at 63 b.

227 *Id.* at 30.

228 *Id.* at 51 & 52 (emphasis added).

F. Conclusions

Fray Tomás's *Suma* expressly or tacitly tolerates an important group of interest-bearing commercial contracts, including sales on installments and partnership agreements. This made it possible for Mexico's *almaceneros* and *viandantes*[229] to extend credit without much concern about usury. The same was true with interest charged for default on the payment of a purchase price or partnership contribution or obligation, even if otherwise immoderate. All of these transactions were deemed to have been priced justly.

Paradoxically, Fray Tomás' conferral of legitimacy on certain otherwise usurious practices came via the unlikely route of the just price of contracts. I say "unlikely route" because usury and just price shared a similar Biblical origin and were regarded by theologians for many centuries as birds of the same feather.[230] Nonetheless, usury remained a serious concern with respect to straight loans and simulated exchanges of money. In a nutshell, then, and as Fray Tomás himself suggested when referring to the courts' reticence to collect default interest, the principles he outlined were not enforced by colonial Mexico's courts but were the ones that guided the confessors' advice. It was this advice, often incorporated into a written opinion-absolution, which constituted, in many instances, Spain's and colonial Latin America's living law on interest and commercial credit.[231]

G. Conversations with Dr. Raúl Cervantes Ahumada

The following extracts of notes are from conversations with my friend, Dr. Raúl Cervantes Ahumada, which took place over a period of several years, but mostly during the decade preceding his death in Mexico City on April 4, 1997. Born in the State of Sinaloa, Mexico on June 24, 1912 (the seventh of eleven children of a humble rural family), Cervantes Ahumada grew up to be one of Mexico's and Latin America's best-known commercial lawyers and law professors. A giant of body and mind, he and two other Mexican professors (Roberto L. Mantilla Molina and Jorge Barrera Graf) were the principal doctrinal writers on Mexico's official commercial law during the second half of the twentieth century. He, more than any of his colleagues, contributed to the understanding of his country's living law.

Some of the conversations transcribed hereinafter were published by the Arizona Journal of International and Comparative Law;[232] others remained unpublished until now and are transcribed from my notes. First, I will include a slightly edited version of the conversations published by the Arizona Journal of International and Comparative Law, and thereafter I will add extracts from subsequent conversations. I should say that some of what Cervantes Ahumada said about Mexico's legal system is no longer true. His reference to the immutable power of the then ruling party (*the Partido Revolucionario Institucional* or PRI) is one. This seemingly permanent hold on Mexico's government was terminated, at least temporarily, by the last two presidential victories

---

229 *See supra* § 14:4(A)(2)(b).

230 *See generally* BENJAMIN NELSON, THE IDEA OF USURY: FROM TRIBAL BROTHERHOOD TO UNIVERSAL OTHERHOOD (1969).

231 *See generally* HENRI LAPEYRE, UNE FAMILLE DE MARCHANDS: LE RUIZ. CONTRIBUTION A L'ETUDE DU COMMERCE ENTRE FRANCE ET L'ESPAGNE AU TEMPS DE PHILIPPE II (1955).

232 *See* Boris Kozolchyk, *Mexican Living Law: An Insider's View*, 5 ARIZ. J. INT'L & COMP. L. 152 (1988) [hereinafter Kozolchyk, *Mexican Living Law*].

of the *Partido de Acción Nacional* (PAN). Similarly, his view of Mexico's courts, especially at the appellate level, while realistic at the time of the 1987 conversation-interview, has changed. Mexico's Supreme Court, for one, is now a more independent institution, capable and willing to take on the challenges of interpreting and making law.[233]

1. On Mexico's Living Law: An Insider's View[234]

This interview with Professor Cervantes Ahumada took place in November of 1987 during the second annual visit of the National University of Mexico Law School (UNAM) professors to the University of Arizona, James E. Rogers College of Law.

Professor Raúl Cervantes Ahumada is one of the most revered law teachers in Mexico and many other Latin American countries. For more than fifty years, his name has been associated with commercial law topics such as negotiable instruments and maritime law. In addition to voluminous scholarly writings, he has authored model uniform negotiable instrument laws for Central and South American countries. He is an integral part of a group of Mexican commercial law professors who, in the late 1940s, began the task of creating a truly Mexican commercial law doctrine. Others in that group included Roberto Mantilla Molina, who combined meticulous exegesis employing every tool of grammar and etymology with a keen sense of what was going on in practice, and Jorge Barrera Graf, who was the most rigorous of conceptualists, subjecting statutory provisions to a most searching conceptual screening.

Cervantes Ahumada was the master maverick. At times his views were expressed in a colloquial fashion familiar even to the central market waiters where he enjoyed his famous Sinaloa breakfasts that few stomachs could withstand. At other times, he was conceptual at the highest academic level, on some occasions, he was even metaphysical (being the fine poet that he was), and on the whole, he was persuasive. His persuasiveness earned him not only many legal victories in courts and legislatures throughout Mexico, but also the position of advisor to Mexican presidents and cabinet ministers. As will be apparent in this interview, his persuasiveness stemmed from a keen sense of reality. He knew the Mexican geographic, animal, human and thus legal landscape as few others did. He understood the feeling behind the gesture and the principle or standard of fairness behind the invoked rule. Thus, he knew how to roll with the punches. Where a lesser academic or litigant would give up the battle when faced with a highly literal and hyper-technical interpretation of existing statutory and decisional law; he turned the interpretation on the interpreter.

His wisdom was inevitably accompanied by his wit. One need only listen to one of his stories to perceive the deep irony that underscores the tale. Each tale brings out a different wrinkle in Mexico's fascinating human and legal landscape. One who understands Raul Cervantes Ahumada understands much of what still moves and shapes "legal" Mexico. His life and deeds are an exhaustive compendium of Mexican living law.

---

233 *See generally* Kozolchyk, *Closing Remarks.*

234 Kozolchyk, *Mexican Living Law, supra* note 222.

2. Caudillos, Caciques *and Simulations*

Boris Kozolchyk (hereinafter BK): Could you please discuss one of the many significant cases in which you have been involved as a litigator before Mexican courts and that in your opinion contributed to the growth of Mexico's substantive or procedural commercial contract law? Perhaps we can start out with the case which established a new approach to the enforcement of fiduciary promises. I gather this case came about early in your career as a litigant and pitted you against some of the most famous litigants in Mexico. As I remember, it involved valuable property conveyed by a debtor facing insolvency to his father, in an attempt to prevent the creditors' possible foreclosure, all of this against the background of bloody battles among local *caudillos* and their chieftains (*caciques*).

Raúl Cervantes Ahumada (hereinafter RCA): The reader will not understand Mexico's law of fiduciary agreements (*pactos fiduciarios*) unless he or she is aware of certain basic facts about Mexico's revolutions. From a legal standpoint, the most significant revolutions Mexico has undergone are the War of Independence, the 1857 Juarez-inspired Laws of Reform (*Leyes de la Reforma*), and the 1910 revolution leading to the Constitution of 1917. As a result of this last revolution, Mexico acquired an entity known as the PRI (the Revolutionary Institutional Party), which is nothing more than an omnipotent branch of the government in charge of electing government officials. The last, like the preceding revolutions, was authentic in the sense that it sprang from the people. Unlike so many other revolutions in Latin America, Mexico's revolutions, and particularly the 1910 revolution, were not mere coups or military takeovers. In a country of approximately 14,000,000 people, this revolution wound up costing as many as a million and a half lives. The enormity of the cost of this revolution, among other factors, gives the 1910 revolution a continuing legitimacy and protects the PRI's hold on power.

I was digressing to dramatize the circumstances under which property was conveyed during the revolution by those who feared losing life and limb at the hands of the various revolutionary groups. The fear was real and the probable consequences of capture or punishment were such that many did not hesitate to convey large estates to fiduciaries. This was going on during the revolution and continued after the enactment of the first agrarian laws distributing the *latifundios* (large landed estates) among landless peasants.

I hasten to add that Mexico did not invent the fiduciary transfer under fear of confiscation. The world has had a long history of such conveyances and, as you pointed out in some of your own lectures in Mexico, the development of the Anglo-American trust is organically connected with feudal conveyances to the Church in England, to the point that the English found it necessary to enact their Mortmain statutes. Juarez' 1857 laws of the *Reforma*, incidentally, echoed the English Mortmain statutes.

In Mexico, however, the fiduciary transfer took a different turn than in English law. The success of the 1910 revolution meant that the professional army that had ruled Mexico for generations was destroyed. In its place emerged a myriad of small armies headed by *caudillos* or their *caciques* who were frequently at war with each other. Political power ebbed and flowed with the success or failure of a particular army. If you had cast your lot with one *cacique* and he was defeated or had to flee the territory, this often meant that you had to do the same. If you had valuable property, often you would leave it with your children's *compadres* (godparents). It was not unusual that, after an initial period of true fiduciary handling by the *compadre*, he would "warm up" to the property and stop sending you the rent or mortgage payments. Then, if you were lucky enough to return after the defeat of the reigning *cacique*, you often had to sue your *compadre* to recover the property.

The ordinary cause of action in this recovery lawsuit was the "action on simulation," alleging that the conveyance to the faithless *compadre*, or to his heirs, was a nullity because the true intent was not to convey but to save the property from a revolutionary takeover. Most courts, however, rejected the simulation argument stating that the intent was not simulated and held that there was an actual intent to convey ownership to the grantee. The intent may have been inspired by whatever founded or unfounded apprehension the grantor had, but nonetheless, there was a true and valid intent to convey.

BK: It seems, then, that the courts' attitude was to ignore the duress that influenced the grantor's conveyance or to refuse to take judicial notice of it. It appears to me that the courts were, in effect, establishing a highly stoic standard of duress while ignoring the effect that the revolutionary wars were having on the grantor's intent to convey.

RCA: Precisely. I do not believe, however, that duress was alleged by the lawyers who sued on the simulation cause of action. What they alleged was the invalidity of the conveyance as a result of an invalid or simulated intent to convey. And the important datum is that these recovery actions were unsuccessful.

This was the state of the law on fiduciary transfers when the widow of a deceased grantor came to see me. Her late husband had conveyed to his father a valuable building which he wished to save from the reach of his creditors and revolutionary chieftains. The assumption was that the father, who was in his seventies, would will the property to his son, who obviously was expected to live longer than the elderly father. Fate had it, however, that the son died sometime after he had conveyed the property and the father, perhaps fearing that the young and very attractive widow would soon remarry to a greedy stranger, or perhaps because he had "warmed up" to the property, refused to re-convey or to include the property in his will.

BK: What about the possibility of using some "constructive" or even "resulting" trust rationale? If I remember correctly, this case was decided after the enactment of Mexico's 1934 Law of Negotiable Instruments, which contains a whole chapter devoted to trusts. There were also some Supreme Court decisions that I read in Professor Batiza's work, *El Fideicomiso, Teoría y Práctica*,[235] which discussed the nature of the trustee's property under Mexican law.

RCA: I am familiar with those decisions collected by Professor Batiza, but unlike the common law trust he aptly described, the Mexican *fideicomiso* does not accept the division of ownership into legal and equitable titles. There is only one owner, and he is the legal owner. The notion of an equitable ownership continues to be foreign to Mexican law. It would have been a perfectly quixotic venture on my part to try to convince a court of the presence of an institution that was not recognized or understood such as that of an equitable ownership or of a reversionary interest. On the other hand, Mexican courts did accept and understand the meaning of a *pacto fidudario*, or

---

[235] *See* RODOLFO BATIZA, EL FIDEICOMISO, TEORÍA Y PRÁCTICA (4th ed. 1980).

fiduciary transaction, and the fact that this type of transaction is governed by a high standard of good faith where the fiduciary is concerned. Accordingly, my argument was that while it was true that the defendant father had acquired legal ownership over the conveyed property, it was also true that he had acquired it subject to an obligation to act as a fiduciary and in good faith. This meant that he was supposed to forward to the son, or the son's surviving widow, those rent proceeds in excess of the sums he was entitled to retain in order to pay for property-related debts and his own living expenses. In addition, he was under a fiduciary, good faith duty to re-convey the property in his will. This duty, I must emphasize, did not arise from a division of ownership into legal and equitable titles, but from the fiduciary's contractual or quasi-contractual obligation in the fiduciary transaction. I recall quoting to the court Cariota Ferrara's study on fiduciary transactions, *Negozi Fiduciari*,[236] to the effect that a fiduciary pact comprises two sub-transactions: the apparent but unreal, and the hidden but real transaction and that the real transaction, unlike the apparent one, should have legal consequences. Unlike my colleagues who had lost in all their preceding attempts to recover, I was not attacking the validity of the contract or conveyance between son and father. On the contrary, I was affirming its validity and enforceability.

Moreover, because I believed the transaction to be valid and enforceable, I was going to introduce evidence of the parties' true intent. My evidence consisted of, *inter alia*, more than 200 letters between father and son in which the father reported punctiliously on the property's income and expenses and repeatedly praised the son's generosity in allowing the father to use some of the income to defray living expenses. I recall one particular letter in which the father asked the son to please relieve him of the duty to include the property in his will and allow him to re-convey it back immediately because he feared disputes among his heirs concerning the property if it appeared in the will as his own. The same letter suggested conveying the property to a corporation and handing over all the shares to the son to assure reversion of the property to its true owner.

The lower court admitted these letters into evidence and ruled for the existence of a fiduciary transaction which imposed the duties I have described. Nevertheless, the court came back with an unexpected procedural twist, saying that I had proved that someone, but not necessarily my client, was entitled to the reversion. Upon the court's inquiry with the land registry, it appeared that neither the plaintiff nor the deceased grantor appeared as having conveyed to the defendant, but that a certain corporation had made the conveyance.

I should add that it was common in Mexico at that time, for fiscal (tax evasion) and other reasons, to record the ownership of valuable real property in the name of a family-held corporation. Thus, said the court, while the defendant is under a duty to return the property to the corporation at the expiration of the fiduciary relationship, the corporation had not been made a party to the lawsuit and thus the petition to insure a re-conveyance to the plaintiff, or indeed to the corporation or to its successor, if any, had to be denied.

---

[236] *See* L. CARIOTA FERRARA, I NEGOZI FIDUCIARI. TRASFERIMENTO, CESSIONE E GIRATA A SCOPO DI MANDATO E DI GARANZIA. PROCESSO FIDUCIARIO (1933).

Naturally, I appealed this decision all the way to the Supreme Court of Mexico on the purely procedural ground of the incongruence or inconsistency between what was proved before the court and the court's decision. My argument was that the court had no power to introduce a new, not alleged or unproven, element into the litigation, nor to rule my action proven on the merits and then deny my prayer for relief on the basis of the not alleged and unproven new element. The appeal to the Supreme Court, then, was on the basis of a violation of procedural due process. The Supreme Court agreed with me and a breach of a fiduciary promise became the method to recover both a beneficial interest in the property as well as, eventually, its legal title.

COMMENTS AND QUESTIONS

Does this rather dramatic use of a simulation change your view of its damaging consequences to the legal system as a whole? Given the political (and life and limb) uncertainty that prevailed in Mexico at the time of the conveyance to the deceased owner's father, a simulated transfer may have been the only method to save the young *hacendado*'s (agribusinessman's) estate. Could it be then that simulated methods of doing business are best suited for politically- and legally-uncertain conditions? I am still skeptical about the value of simulation as a device to gain certainty. First of all, the simulated conveyance to the defendant may not have been as much the product of revolutionary duress (as my highly persuasive friend claimed it was) as it may have been motivated by the desire to evade creditors' claims in a bankruptcy. In such a case, it would have been nothing less than a fraudulent conveyance deserving of invalidation. Second, did you notice the presence of yet another simulation (one involving a conveyance of the same estate to a family corporation that for all practical purposes was nothing more than a "name-lending corporation") whose purpose was primarily that of evading the payment of taxes by the true property owner?

Please notice that this simulation almost derailed my friend's attempt to recover the land by the plaintiff-widow. Had it not been for his superb legal skills, the second simulation would have prevented his recovery. Third, it is interesting that the lower court, on its own, inquired with the land registry as to who appeared as the original owner of the property conveyed to the defendant fiduciary and was willing to return the property to that corporation if it were to be joined as a party plaintiff. This was a rather unusual fact-finding expedition, not only because Mexican civil and commercial courts seldom engage in such *sua sponte* fact finding, especially without notice to the parties, but also because the search for facts was quite limited. I say this because if the court were inquiring into the true ownership of the estate allegedly conveyed, why not inquire into the factual, as opposed to merely formal, existence of the grantor-corporation?

Having gone as far as the court did, why not take the next logical step and find out who was the true owner of the conveyed real property by piercing the corporate veil? Finally, and still within the realm of things factual and equitable (usually inseparable legal categories), why not inquire whether this was not a case where the plaintiff was estopped from attempting to undo what he had willingly done, by preventing him from "going against his own acts" (*venire contra factum proprium*)? Granted, the case law against which RCA rebelled declared the validity of the fiduciary conveyances; however, this declaration was made on the basis that the conveyance was actually intended by the grantor. The equitable and factual inquiry I am asking about would have been of a different nature: As a matter of public policy, should a grantor who provides a false legal appearance be allowed to undo such an appearance once it becomes inconvenient or contrary to his expectations?

3. *The* Caudillo's *and Everyone's Natural Right to Smuggle*

BK: Now that you have given us a picture of some of the difficulties faced by sound judicial lawmaking in Mexico, could you share with us your views on what you say are the many unrealistic statutes made by Mexico's congress? I remember the famous incident involving your one and only appearance on your own weekly national television program. Could you tell us what happened?

RCA: As you know, I had been a law professor to four consecutive Mexican presidents. One such former student, upon becoming president about twenty years ago, accepted another former student's (and former president's) suggestion that I be allowed to have a television program in which I could explain current developments in Mexico's legal system in very simple terms.

During the late 1960s, the Mexican Congress was considering enactment of a new anti-smuggling statute that would have been yet another addition to the long list of such statutes enacted during Mexico's colonial and republican history. I felt this was significant enough to merit some comments because I wanted our legislators to be more realistic. I opened up my discussion of the proposed law by expressing my opposition to it. I justified this opposition on commonsensical and historical grounds. The common sense argument was best expressed in Don Quixote's advice to Sancho Panza when the latter was about to become the governor and supreme lawgiver for the imaginary island of Barataria. Don Quixote advised Sancho not to enact laws that were not likely to be obeyed. This may sound too simple to deserve elaboration, yet it is an example of the supreme wisdom of common sense. Spanish and Mexican legal compilations are pregnant with ineffective, never-obeyed legislative enactments often reflecting nothing more than what I think you once described in one of your writings as the legislator's "lyrical declarations of intent," intended to make the legislator feel good and accomplished by the "mere act of a solemn legislative statement."

The reason why I am certain about the unenforceability of the anti-smuggling statute in Mexico is rooted in Mexico's history. Almost since time immemorial, but at least since colonial days, Mexican citizens and inhabitants have honestly felt that they have a natural or God-given right to smuggle. This has been true for Mexicans in every station of life and is still apparent during our own day and age.

In fact, I related to my viewers a recent incident that fully illustrated the point. Shortly before having been given the opportunity of having my own program, I watched a television program in which the president of Mexico was congratulating a Mexican prize fighter who had just won a world championship in Japan. Much as Soviet leaders talk to their cosmonauts or American presidents congratulate their astronauts after a successful space mission, our president called Tokyo to congratulate our sports hero. At the same time, however, he was catching glances of himself on a nearby television set, a Sony color portable set which could not be imported into the country legally. It happened to have been one of the first models listed on the so-called forbidden list. So, I said, there you have it; the President himself smuggles. And, had I been asked how I knew about the illegality of the import, I would have had to confess that I came across this list when smuggling my own portable color T.V. set into the country.

BK: I gather that, after your Sherlock Holmes-like deduction, your program did not become a permanent fixture in Mexican television.

RCA: You gather correctly.

4. *The Magic Powers of Mexico's Chief Executive*

BK: You once told me about the incident with former President Manuel Avila Camacho and David Alfaro Siqueiros which reflected the enormous (*caudillo*-like) powers possessed by the Mexican president. How does this incident reflect the division of powers and the political system in Mexico?

RCA: Officially, Mexico has had a constitution since 1917 which establishes the division of powers between the three branches of government that we owe to Montesquieu. Nonetheless, the Mexican president exercises more power than he formally or officially possesses. Political scientists often refer to the Mexican presidency as an all-powerful office. They are basically correct, but very few among them suspect the true magnitude of presidential powers. The Mexican president has, in addition to all his worldly powers, Houdini-like powers. He can conceive and execute the most incredible and far-reaching of magical escapes. Consider, for example, the attention the world press gave to a recent escape by a prisoner who managed to fly away from the prison in a helicopter that had landed in the middle of the prison yard. There was a shortage of adjectives with which to describe what went on. I can assure you that this was a non-event compared to what happened to David Alfaro Siqueiros, one of Mexico's foremost muralists and also a notorious militant communist.

During the revolution, Siqueiros had served in one of Mexico's many revolutionary armies. That army's paymaster was a plump young man, affectionately referred to by officers and soldiers alike as *el gordito* (the little fat man). One dreary evening following a lost battle, the plump young man was separated from the rest of the army and desperately searched for his colleagues in arms. A group of his colleagues had found refuge in an abandoned hut. Apprehensively, the paymaster knocked at the door. The soldier who opened the door unceremoniously asked him to leave and find his own refuge. However, Siqueiros, who was in the hut, was more humane and said "*entra hermano, compartiré contigo mi petate*" ("come in, brother, I will share my mat with you"), saving *el gordito* from sleeping on the floor or seeking another shelter hundreds of meters away.

Some years later, Leon Trotsky, the founder of the Red Army and of his own brand of Marxism, was given refuge in Mexico by President Lázaro Cárdenas. Siqueiros was asked by the Soviet Communist Party to arrange for Trotsky's assassination. Accordingly, he organized an assault on Trotsky's place of abode, which ironically had been provided by none other than Diego Rivera, another of the great figures of Mexico's muralism. In this first attempt against Trotsky's life, in which Siqueiros participated, one of Trotsky's bodyguards was killed. Siquieros was captured and sentenced to a long prison term. Once in jail, he feared the worst from the recently elected president. If a leftist such as Cárdenas had placed him in jail, the newly elected president, known to be devoutly Catholic and not an enemy of capitalism, was likely to have him executed at the first opportunity. One night his worst fears seemed to have been confirmed. The prison warden showed up at Siqueiros's cell and asked him to follow him and a special escort. Fearing execution, Siqueiros started to yell desperately that he was about to be executed, in accordance with the classical procedure known in Mexico as the "law of escape." He had to be tied and gagged. He was then taken to a very impressive mansion, which turned out to be the president's official residence. Suddenly a door opened and President Avila Camacho appeared dressed in his most elegant polo attire (he was known as an avid polo player). The president embraced Siqueiros and said,

"David, brother, ever since I was elected, I could not stand the idea of my being in this magnificent mansion, and you rotting away in jail, especially after you shared your *petate* with me one night; I could have been killed were it not for your generosity." In disbelief, Siqueiros kept on muttering, "*este es el gordito del petate*" ("this is the plump little fellow of the *petate*").

Shortly thereafter, then Secretary of the Interior, Miguel Aleman (later one of Mexico's most effective presidents), showed up with a passport and a thick envelope filled with dollars. Siqueiros was taken to a military airport and was told to get ready to fly to Chile, where he would be met and taken care of by none other than the Mexican ambassador. Thus, through a presidential sleight of hand, a prisoner disappeared from Mexico and appeared as a diplomat in Santiago, Chile, where he was to live in considerable comfort for a long time.

5. The Power of Caudillo-*Like Presidents and the "*Letrismo*" of Judges*

BK: President Avila Camacho's were certainly "magical" powers. What effect did such enormous powers have upon the judiciary?

RCA: First of all, I would not limit this almost magical power to our presidents. I would extend it to cabinet ministers, governors (dubbed by the Mexican populace as "provincial viceroys") and other high officials of the executive branch. The judiciary, equally dependent upon the executive branch for its appointment, official or unofficial, and wherewithal, developed an attitude toward decision-making that I labeled for lack of a better term "*letrismo*," or strictest adherence to the letter of the law at the expense of its spirit or purpose. This *letrismo* was the safest way for judges not to appear too independent from their executive branch masters. Any complaint by attorneys about an interpretation contrary to theirs, or to justice, could always be met by the judge's pointing to the literal text of the statute followed by the inevitable: *This is the law, no matter how absurd or unfair the result.*

BK: This brings me to the question of the courts' unwillingness to decide cases based upon equitable grounds. Do you believe that the *letrismo* that you describe is responsible for many decisions that are plainly unfair or inequitable?

RCA: Absolutely. . . . I remember reading your commentary on a 1932 decision by the Mexican Supreme Court and saying to myself, "Boris has joined the select club."

For the sake of the reader unfamiliar with this decision, I will provide a synopsis of its facts. In the 1932 Mexican Supreme Court decision of Gerhard Karras y Cia v. Friedemberg S.A.,[237] the plaintiff was the holder in due course of three bills of exchange accepted (but unpaid) by defendant. He claimed payment of U.S. $1,357 or its equivalent in Mexican pesos. The lower court judge ordered payment of 3,420 Mexican pesos and when payment was refused, decreed execution of judgment against defendant's property.[238] Both parties appealed the execution decree. Plaintiff asserted that the amount of Mexican pesos set forth in the decree corresponded, not to the rate of exchange at the time of the decreed payment by the court, but to the rate in effect at the time of the filing of the complaint. There was a significant difference between these

---

[237] Eduardo García Máynez y Espinosa, *Tercera Sala de La Suprema Corte de Justica de la Nacion: Suplica: 120/32, Recurrentes: Gerhard Karras y Cia. Friedemberg, S.A., in* 5 REVISTA GENERAL DERECHO Y JURISPRUDENCIA 116 (1934).

[238] *Id.* at 117.

two amounts as a result of a monetary devaluation. He contended that the lower court's decision was contrary both to Mexico's monetary law and to the principles of equity. Article 509 of the Mexican Commercial Code in force at that time provided that if the foreign currency stipulated in the bill of exchange was not legal tender, the payment would be in a sum equivalent to that stipulated on the basis of the rate of exchange in effect on the instrument's "due date" (*día del vencimiento*). However, Article 8 of the subsequently enacted monetary law provided that the rate of exchange for the determination of the amount due was that in effect on the date of payment. The Supreme Court chose to read the term date of payment as if it meant the due date of the bill of exchange and not the date of actual payment. This interpretation avoided any possible conflict between the above mentioned provisions.

In reply to plaintiff's contention that defendant was unjustly enriched by such an interpretation, the court stated that "the rise or fall of rates of exchange and their effects upon payment is an economic phenomenon which is independent of the legal necessity to fix, as of the initiation of lawsuits, the quantum of the claim."[239] In addition, the court addressed itself to the role of equitable principles in its adjudication as follows:

> The appellant invokes equity in order to obtain a higher recovery, without taking into account that a court of law, as this court is, except in those cases where the law authorizes resort to equitable principles to resolve concrete cases, cannot apply such principles because it would violate [the principle of] equality before the law which is the basis of social order. As long as there are legal provisions applicable to the case in question there is no reason to attempt to correct them, thereby substituting the legislative by another, entirely subjective will.[240]

In his insightful commentary on this decision, Professor Eduardo García Maynez pointed out that the statutory law in force at the time of this decision directed the courts to decide controversies involving equal rights or rights of the same legal species by "observing the greatest possible equality between the parties," or on the basis of "the maximum amount of reciprocity." Accordingly, even though equity could not, in Professor García Maynez's opinion, alter statutory law, it definitely had a supplementary role, especially where statutory law was unclear or ambiguous. But there is more to this decision than a mistaken assumption of the supplementary role of equity or an excessively formalistic view of pleading (a view that would rather countenance an unjust enrichment rather than allow an amended complaint reflecting the larger sum claimed). The court perceived the market value of the performances involved as "an economic phenomenon" which was "independent" of legal implications. Thus, law was perceived as being concerned with purely legalistic allegations and issues devoid of marketplace implications. Contrary to conventional wisdom, equity, in turn, was perceived as bringing about inequality before the law, because equitable decision-making was assumed to be perforce, highly subjective or arbitrary.

RCA: When I said, "join the club," I meant not only that of Professor Garcia Maynez, but also your and my friend, the late professor, Oscar Morineau. This was one of his mantras in his *El Estudio del Derecho*. He was particularly fond of a Roman

239 *Id.*

240 *Id.* at 120 (author's translation).

proverb that he found in a case decided by a United States Supreme Court justice that you had him read when he visited you in Dallas, something like "from the facts emerges the law" (*Ex Facto Jus Oritur*).[241]

BK: I would like to come back to the point I mentioned earlier with respect to the organic connection between equity and facts or fact finding. Consider your fiduciary pact case. How can anyone deny the impact that those two hundred letters exchanged between the father as a fiduciary owner and his son as trustor had upon the court's perception of the just outcome of the case? How can a judge ignore such a reality when it comes to establishing the real intent of the parties? Clearly, in order to do equity he must have a relevant and reliable set of facts.

RCA: Yes, but it was not easy to get those letters into evidence. The clerk (and I presume the judge as well) kept on rejecting them because they were not truly "documentary," "confessional" or "witnesses" type of evidence. I kept on insisting they were admissible and gave them a mountain of legal arguments. Meanwhile, I was concerned that they wanted a bribe which was common but which I did not want to give. Finally, the clerk hinted that he would be most appreciative if I gave him two autographed copies of one of my books, one for him and one for his girlfriend (apparently also a law student at UNAM). I told him that those were my last two copies (and they were) and that given my good looks, I would be glad to give him my next to last book and his girlfriend an autographed copy of my portrait. Eventually, I had to give up my last two books, but the letters were admitted as evidence.

BK: I would like to ask you about your experience as an author of major commercial laws such as the Model Law on Negotiable Instruments for the Institute for the Integration of Latin America and the Caribbean (INTAL) and your draft of a maritime code for the Mexican government. How did your method of drafting differ from that of other Latin American codifiers?

RCA: Frankly, I liked Andres Bello's style more than that of those who claim to be influenced by the so-called Pandectist legal science. He was a much more direct and clearer codifier than, say, Dalmacio Vélez Sársfield or Teixeira de Freitas and he was not as in love with abstract concepts and definitions. His prose and thought were both terse and I like that. I was once asked why my model law on negotiable instruments did not have a whole bunch of learned definitions, and my reply was that definitions are for the classroom and not for codes. If you want definitions, you should buy yourself a textbook.

BK: How did you decide on what provisions to insert in both of your model laws?

RCA: The Draft of a Maritime Code was largely based on my own experiences with and love for the ocean. As I used to say to my maritime law students, "Life began in the ocean and in man's hour of greatest need it will have to return to it." Hence, I emphasized the need to assure our (Mexico's) legal rights to a fair-sized territorial ocean, but also to a use consistent with the preservation of precious and irreplaceable resources. The negotiable instruments law was more of the standard fare—some

---

[241] The proverb I quoted to Professor Oscar Morineau was *Ex Facto Jus Oritur*, and the United States justice that Raúl Cervantes Ahumada referred to was Justice Brandeis in his dissenting opinion in Adams v. Tanner, 244 U.S. 590 (1917). In its relevant part states: "The judgment should be based upon a consideration of relevant facts, actual or possible—*Ex facto jus oritur*. That ancient rule must prevail in order that we may have a system of living law." 244 U.S. at 600.

provisions were inspired by the Geneva Convention others by our own (Mexico's LTOC) and a few others by your (United States) Uniform Negotiable Instruments Law. My own rules were mostly procedural, *i.e.*, clarifying the peculiarities of actions against parties primarily and secondarily liable, available defenses against these actions, informal methods of protest, quick attachment of assets procedures and so on. Unfortunately, many of these provisions were not popular with the countries likely to adopt them and I had to drop them.

BK: What about customs and practices? Since you were drafting a uniform law for the Americas, did you try to reflect the practices of the various countries?

RCA: Unfortunately, this is where a great void of information exists. There are no compilations of customs and practices in the area of negotiable instruments law in any Latin American country I know of. Surely, there are variations on how the instruments are used and I took notice of a few of those, especially with respect to the check. One of the most common practices was that of transforming checks into credit instruments (as opposed to using them only as payment instruments). By that I mean practices that take advantage of laws that criminalize default on checks. For example, I borrow money from you and you have me sign, not a promissory note promising to pay at a future date, but a postdated check. A check is supposed to be a payment "at sight" instrument, not a payment in the future instrument. Yet, since many Latin American countries make it a crime to issue a check without funds or with insufficient funds, if I do not pay you the check when the postdated time arrives, then you threaten me with filing a criminal action for embezzlement. The threat of such an action is frequently sufficient to induce your payment at least on part of the amount due. I know that this practice is common in Mexico and I heard from colleagues in other countries like Bolivia that the jails were full of postdated check signers. I know that you will say that this is a "pathological" (as you call it) or simulatory practice and I agree because it denaturalizes the check. Yet, this is one of the very few practices I could take into account. I am sure that many more exist, but there were no compilations or manuals that I could examine and obviously the Institute for the Integration of Latin America and the Caribbean (INTAL) did not have the money to pay me to do a country-by-country study of the commercial and banking practices.

COMMENTS AND QUESTIONS

Each one of RCA's responses is related to issues discussed in the principal chapter. As you read his answers, did you find them to be confirming or contradicting the chapter's findings and conclusions? How could RCA's work as a codifier or drafter of a uniform model law be improved by having had access to a compilation of customs? What if the customs were what he and I referred to as "pathological"? Do you have any suggestions on how to eradicate such practices?

Chapter 15

SOVIET COMMERCIAL CONTRACT LAW

Adam Smith, in the Wealth of Nations:

> This division of labor, from which so many advantages are derived, is not originally the effect of any human wisdom, which foresees and intends that general opulence to which it gives occasion. It is the necessary, though very slow and gradual, consequence of a certain propensity in human nature which has in view no such extensive utility; the propensity to truck, barter, and exchange one thing for another.[1]

Vladimir Ilich Lenin:

> [In the USSR] *we do not allow anything private.*[2]

Alphonse the Wise, in the *Siete Partidas*:

> Freely translated as: [T]o do something is a very heavy undertaking, while to undo it is a very light endeavor. . . . ([*E*]*l facer es muy grave cosa, et el desfacer muy ligera. . . .*").[3]

§ 15.1 INTRODUCTION: COMMERCIAL CONTRACTING DURING THE USSR OR ITS FUNCTIONAL EQUIVALENT

A. Scope

This chapter examines the socio-economic context of commercial contracts in a Marxist-Leninist society. As will soon become apparent, Marxist-Leninist dogma, supposedly interpreting the spirit of the socialist revolution, shaped the USSR's official legal institutions such as those rules that stated who owned what, how and for how long and what could be traded and by whom. It also determined which income was properly earned and which was caused by the "exploitation of man by man," which profits were acceptable, if any, and which were illegal or unworthy of a socialist regime.

At times, the Marxist-Leninist dogma was transcribed in constitutional pronouncements such as that of Article 12 of the Soviet Constitution of 1936: "He who does not work, neither shall he eat."[4] At times, the dogma appeared in statutory or administrative laws or in court decisions; more frequently, however, it was distilled from the writings of Karl Marx, Friedrich Engels or Vladimir Ilich Lenin and less frequently from those of Joseph Stalin or Nikita S. Khruschev. Often also, writings and speeches, especially by Lenin, were quoted in popular sayings among administrators and judges.

---

1 Adam Smith, The Wealth of Nations Part 1 55 (1902).

2 HIROSHI ODA, RUSSIAN COMMERCIAL LAW 65–66 (2d ed. 2007).

3 DON ALFONSO EL SABIO, 1 LAS SIETE PARTIDAS 25 (1807) (author's translation) (emphasis added).

4 USSR CONST. ch. 1, art. 12 (1936).

Why was such dogma so popular with so many people inside and outside the USSR? Part of the reason is that Marx and Engels managed to convince many intelligent and non-intelligent sympathizers that Marxism was no mere political or economic doctrine. According to them, it was a science as empirically verifiable and inexorable as Newtonian gravity or Dickens' evolution of the species. In fact, it was, at best, a philosophical exercise based upon unproven scientific hypotheses which explained the evolution of society as caused by dialectical, material and economically-determined causes. This assertion was combined with a passionate cry for social justice for the many victims of the exploitation by the capitalist few. At a time of much social injustice, this cry reverberated among many countries.

Despite Marx's and Lenin's legal training and youthful aspirations to teach law, law played only a marginal role in the asserted inevitable evolution of society from feudalism to communism via capitalism and socialism. The determinant role was played by the capitalist acquisition of goods only to resell them for more money. The orthodox Marxist-Leninist was a "legal nihilist": Law was an incidental tool of the "super-structure" built by economic and materialistic forces. It was condemned to disappear during the communist and final phase of Marxism when everything belongs to everyone and there is no further need for a state or its law.

From approximately 1917 to 1991, the Marxist dogma bolstered by its alleged status of proven science and its claim to the higher morality of social justice became the source of both official or positive and of living law of the USSR, including that law that governed the officially unenforceable commercial contracts. These contracts may have involved a *de facto* joint venture between a factory "dispatcher" and a group of employees who sold a variety of products and services on the black market. Or the private sales, loans, barters or partnerships could be disguised or "simulated" as agreements between collective entities or state agencies and purported expert consultants or advisors who would conduct "workshops" on how to produce and market products.

In theory, general constitutional provisions such as the above-quoted Article 12 of the 1936 Constitution or the statutory prohibition of income derived from hiring wage earners, were supposed to be interpreted in light of the "spirit of the socialist revolution" as enshrined in writings, speeches and sayings by the mostly highly revered leaders and theoreticians. Yet, the interpretations found in these writings or speeches, many of which became popular sayings, were as general and vague as the constitutional or statutory provisions they were supposed to help interpret.

The generality and vagueness of the USSR's official and living law created the endless gaps in and among these laws. These gaps rendered the private law of the USSR "legally invertebrate," *i.e.*, a law whose factual and normative components were so imprecise that they enlarged the power (and all too often filled the pockets) of government officials starting with the policeman who waived a fine or prohibition in exchange for a bribe and extending to the directors of state enterprises and planners of the USSR's economy.

The understanding of how these dogmas affected law making and economic development is not only of historical interest. The reader interested in knowing what was the law that truly determined the resolution of a given claim, dispute or controversy must understand both the invoked Marxist-Leninist science and the political and economic dogmas that resulted from it. The same is true with centralized economic planning—the favorite economic and contract law-making tool of Marxist-Leninists.

B. A Modern Society Without Commercial Contracts?

What would a modern society and legal system whose inhabitants could not legally engage in commercial transactions look like? Such a society was the Union of Soviet Socialist Republics (USSR). During most of its existence, its official law forbad private ownership of most anything of value, conferred such property upon the state and allowed its many agencies to engage in trade, profitably or not, among themselves, with Soviet consumers and with foreign (public or private) buyers, sellers, lenders or exchangers.[5] Private citizens were limited in what they traded, first of all, by what they were allowed to own or possess. They could only own the income and savings from their work, their dwelling units and household furniture, utensils and articles of personal use and convenience (their so-called personal property).[6] From the start of the revolutionary government, the property that could be officially traded was highly restricted: A 1918 decree forbad merchants to enter into profitable transactions involving the production or distribution of textiles, tobacco, glass, leather, cement, woodwork and countless other goods or services.[7] With the exception of a short period during which private trade was possible (roughly from 1921 to 1928), the USSR stuck

---

[5] *Id.* ch. 1, art. 4:

> The socialist system of economy and the socialist ownership of the means and instruments of production firmly established as a result of the abolition of the capitalist system of economy, the abrogation of private ownership of the means and instruments of production and the abolition of the exploitation of man by man, constitute the economic foundation of the U.S.S.R.

Id. See also infra note 98 (discussing the legislative definition of "personal property").

[6] USSR CONST. ch. 1, art. 10 (1936). This source states:

> The right of citizens to personal ownership of their incomes from work and of their savings, of their dwelling houses and subsidiary household economy, their household furniture and utensils and articles of personal use and convenience, as well as the right of inheritance of personal property of citizens, is protected by law.

Id.

[7] *See* Samuel Kucherov, *Property in the Soviet Union*, 11 AM. J. COMP. L. 376 (1962). Who discusses statutes and decrees that implemented the abolition of private ownership. It also provides a list of everyday goods that were prohibited from private trade. *See* Decree of Nov. 21, 1918, *cited in id.* at 377 n.7. Similarly, banks that were not credit cooperatives were declared property of the state even at an earlier time. *Id.* at 377. Kucherov explains:

> [T]he Decree of the All Russian Central Executive Committee "On the socialization of the land" of January 27, 1918 provided that every kind of ownership in land (including that of the peasants), mineral wealth, waters, forests, and all natural resources within the limits of the Russian Federative Soviet Socialist Republic is abrogated forever.

Id. at 376. Kucherov further explains:

> The Decree of August 18, 1921 returned to the former houseowners small houses with not more than 2 apartments (not more than 5 apartments in Moscow and Petrograd) . . . Since all land was nationalized, the owners of small houses retained possession only of the buildings but could use the plots on which the building rested. The possession was limited to personal use of the former owner and his family.
>
> Banks (with the exception of co-operative banks) were declared property of the state by Decree of December 17, 1917. Church property was nationalized by Decree of June 23, 1918 and the Church was prohibited to have any property in the future. The People's Commissariat of Food Supply replaced private commerce in the supply of food and consumer goods to the population.
>
> The first general nationalization decree directed against private industrial enterprises was published on June 28, 1918.

Id. at 376–77 (citations omitted).

with an official non-commercial path. Not since commodities began to be sold, exchanged, leased or borrowed by man, had a national government attempted to implement such an all-encompassing, anti-commercial blueprint.

In order to implement this blueprint, the USSR and the many Marxist-Leninist governments that followed its policies had to act harshly because the non-commercial behavior they were trying to impose did not come naturally to men and women who had been trading for profit for many centuries following what seemed to be as natural an inclination as warring. As stated by Adam Smith, man's progression with private trade was slow and gradual, and was the consequence of his or her "propensity to truck, barter, and exchange one thing for another."[8] It took mankind thousands of years to evolve from hunting and gathering, farming, bartering and selling goods—that they or others had collected or crafted—to actively participating in local, national, regional and eventually global commercial and financial transactions.

This was an evolution that progressively fed, clothed, educated and extended the lives of billions of human beings, although admittedly in some countries or regions more than in others. Put simply, man had evolved naturally into a commercial being albeit with some significant differences on the role of commerce and the degree of economic development of their legal cultures. On the whole, those who embraced private trade as a lawful and morally acceptable way to earn a living did better economically than those who did not. Moreover, those people who developed active commercial and financial markets learned how to create and subject themselves to their own contractual and customary rules and thereby were able to create democratic and pluralistic legal institutions.[9]

C. Merchants and Entrepreneurs in Imperial Russia

1. *Merchants*

Shortly after the then Prime Minister Margaret Thatcher declared Mikhail Gorbachev as someone with whom President Ronald Reagan could do business, she was asked by a reporter whether she envisaged the USSR becoming a vibrant capitalist economy and a democratic society in the near future. Her response went something like this: It will take quite a while for the USSR to become a vibrant capitalistic and democratic society because, among other things, I do not believe that Russia ever developed a class of shopkeepers who knew how to make a decent living and meet their payroll when due.[10] The reader of this chapter will likely find her assessment to be accurate and insightful. There were many shopkeepers in Imperial Russia but they were not the counterparts of Thatcher's inferred archetypal "honest, responsible shopkeeper," especially one who could be counted on to balance his right to profit by doing business with reliable customers and suppliers with his duties to others, not only his customers and suppliers, but also his employees.[11]

---

[8] SMITH, *supra* note 1, at 55.

[9] *See generally supra* § 9:1(B) (on the interaction between Italian municipal law derived from commercial association rules).

[10] *See e.g.* Margaret Thatcher, TV Interview for TV-AM *Frost on Sunday* (Sept. 9, 1990) (transcript available at http://www.margaretthatcher.org/document/108186).

[11] *See generally* DAVID CHRISTIAN, IMPERIAL AND SOVIET RUSSIA: POWER, PRIVILEGES AND THE CHALLENGES OF MODERNITY (1997); and ALFRED RIEBER, MERCHANTS AND ENTREPRENEURS IN IMPERIAL RUSSIA (1982).

Imperial Russia was not a commercial society in the sense described in previous chapters[12] until almost the time of its disappearance. By the time of the Bolshevik revolution of October 1917, still eighty percent of Russia's population earned their living as peasants.[13] Of these, the serfs who tilled the land of private landowners owed feudal obligations including supplying prescribed amounts of goods and services and other dues to their landlords. Feudalism also affected the status of merchants. For a considerable period of time, merchants in Russia's major urban centers were part of a caste and guild system in which they owed duties as suppliers of goods and services to the successive Tsarist regimes and their designees and did so subject to harsh terms and conditions. Consequently, small merchants in Imperial Russia were not doing much better than the peasantry, and neither was doing well economically.[14]

In his Collection of Laws of 1649,[15] Tsar Alexander I designated three hereditary categories, all of which provided services to the feudal state: merchants (part of the urban category), peasants and noblemen. Again, these categories were hereditary.[16] They enjoyed privileges such as "having civil cases tried in their own courts, of being excused from military service, and of being exempted from a head tax."[17] Eventually merchants and peasants became commercially linked, especially after the emancipation of the serfs by Tsar Alexander II on February 19, 1861.[18]

While this decree technically freed twenty-three million serfs from some of their feudal obligations, they were not truly free until they were able to buy the land in which they toiled from their landlords; this could take years, during which time many of the obligations of serfdom continued.[19] The immediate effect of this decree was to force peasants to depend upon what they could sell in the marketplace in order to survive and redeem their land. This is why many emancipated serfs migrated to the cities and tried to join the commercial and trade guilds.

By 1861, two classes were discernible among Russian merchants—the "old guild" merchants who supplied their goods to their traditional state-directed clientele and the new or "third guild" merchants who were former peasants or were dependent upon peasants to supply them with agricultural goods and handicrafts that they could resell to the population at large. Among these goods were hemp, grain, horned cattle, mead, wax, wheels, barrels, wooden utensils and pottery.[20] These merchants often only "scratched out a living at the level of the peasants."[21] Many wound up cultivating their own gardens and selling produce along with dry goods to peasants "either in the town-

---

[12] *See supra* § 6:2(F).

[13] *Emancipation reform of 1861*, WIKIPEDIA.ORG, http://en.wikipedia.org/wiki/Emancipation_reform_of_1861 (last visited Sept. 25, 2013). *See* PETER GATRELL, THE TSARIST ECONOMY, 1850–1917 29 (1986); *see also* ROBERT SERVICE, LENIN: A BIOGRAPHY 145 (2000) (discussing a higher estimate of the size of the peasant population [85%]).

[14] RIEBER, *supra* note 11, at xxi–xxii.

[15] *Id.* at xx–xxi. *See generally* Richard Hellie, *Law Code of 1649, in* ENCYCLOPEDIA OF RUSSIAN HISTORY 828, 830 (James R. Miller et al. eds., 2003).

[16] RIEBER, *supra* note 11, at xxi.

[17] *Id.* at 82.

[18] CHRISTIAN, *supra* note 11, at 83.

[19] *Id.* at 83–84.

[20] RIEBER, *supra* note 11, at 9.

[21] *Id.* at 10.

market stalls or in nearby country-village fairs."[22] Official statistics provided by Professor David Christian of San Diego State University show that the entire merchant class in 1850 numbered 250,000 throughout Russia; despite a continuous growth of the population, forty years later this number had only roughly doubled.[23]

During the second half of the nineteenth century, while shops proliferated in the big cities such as Moscow and Saint Petersburg, merchants in most small and medium-sized towns continued to earn only a subsistence income. In Professor Rieber's words, the rest of the third guild merchants "gave up all pretense of trading for themselves and either toiled in the fields as manual laborers (*chernaia rabota*) or hired themselves out as shop assistants to merchants in the main commercial centers of St. Petersburg and Riga."[24] Yet, as the First World War approached, most of the urban trade was conducted in small shops as opposed to peddlers' carts, temporary stalls in market squares, and so on.[25]

2. *Entrepreneurs and* Kulaks

In contrast with retail urban trade, the number of industrialists and wholesale and banking entrepreneurs grew following the emancipation of the serfs and the availability of cheap labor. According to Professor David Christian, between 1866 and 1903 the number of factories employing more than sixteen workers increased from 2500 to 9000.[26] He illustrated the openness to industrial activities by describing how even a serf could rise to the top if he was able to combine his family's skilled management with the productivity of his cheap labor. In the early 1800s, Fedor A. Gruchkov, while still a serf, obtained permission from his master to set up a weaving factory in Moscow. In the 1820s, his sons joined him in running the business and by the 1840s the Guchkovs owned one of the largest wool factories in Russia; by 1853, the Gruchkovs employed 1800 workers.

In due course, many more peasants became entrepreneurs.[27] In the countryside, those peasant families who were able to generate enough money to buy additional farming equipment, lease additional land or set up small rural-domestic industries became known as "*Kulaks*" or "fists," a term which despite its derisory connotations showed both envy and respect for their ability to accumulate money and dispense of it tightly.[28] These peasant families attracted the attention of socialist revolutionaries such as Vladimir Ilich Lenin, who argued that the *Kulaks* represented not only a steadily growing number of rural entrepreneurs but also (in Marxist-Leninist terminology) the dreaded "emerging rural bourgeoisie."[29]

On the other hand, as the rural population grew, landholding per person shrank between 1860 and 1900 when the average allotment to male peasants had declined by about forty-six percent from 5.2 to 2.8 hectares.[30] These pressures meant that more

---

[22] *Id.*

[23] CHRISTIAN, *supra* note 11, at 117.

[24] RIEBER, *supra* note 11, at 10.

[25] ALAN M. BALL, RUSSIA'S LAST CAPITALISTS: THE NEPMEN, 1921–1929 (1987).

[26] CHRISTIAN, *supra* note 11, at 117.

[27] *Id.* at 118.

[28] *Id.*

[29] *Id.*

[30] *Id.* at 120.

and more peasants had to join the urban marketplace and become wage earners, or producers and suppliers of the all-important grain. According to Professor Christian, in 1850 peasants produced forty-five percent of all marketed grain and by 1914 they produced seventy-five percent.[31] This control at first gave them bargaining power but, as will be discussed shortly, also spelled a zigzagging policy of confiscation of their lands and crops, partial restoration by a tax in kind, and eventually their elimination as a class during Leninist and Stalinist days.

D. The Economic Picture of Pre-Revolutionary Russia

At the turn of the twentieth century, and after many centuries of economic backwardness, Russia seemed poised for an industrial and commercial takeoff. As concluded by Professor Evengii Prussalkov of Cambridge University:

> The economic historians are unanimous on the fact that between 1891 and 1900 the Russian economy really did grow. This period is also known as the period of industrial 'boom' in Russia and it was during that time that the industrial output of the country raised from 5% per annum (figures of 1861–85) to 8–9% *per annum*. Such industrial output ranked among the highest such levels ever measured prior to 1914.[32]

Further, at the conclusion of the Tsarist empire, Russia was the world's fourth largest producer of iron and fifth largest producer of steel. It had also attained significant increases in railroad mileage and oil extraction. On the other hand, Russia lacked investment capital and became dependent upon foreign credit and investments in mining and industry; by the outbreak of the Crimean War in 1905 it was the world's largest debtor. It also depended for its "knowledge" capital on either foreign investors or entrepreneurial minorities such as Jews, Poles or "Old Believers"[33]—groups it had severely discriminated against for centuries.[34] Professor Prussalkov noted that such a rapid pace of industrial development owed much to the common working people, "often regular peasants who flocked to the cities for the new industrial jobs, ending up in abysmal living and working conditions, underpaid and undernourished."[35]

E. The Soviet Experience with Commercial Contracts; Why Were They Not Eradicated?

As just noted, the USSR and Marxism-Leninism not only attempted to transform the political economy of nations but also tried to eradicate private trade, even though by the middle of the nineteenth century this trade was proving itself an economically useful and non-exclusive form of earning a living.[36] Moreover, in contrast to capitalistic

---

[31] *Id.*

[32] *See* Evgenii Prussakov, *The Tsarist Economy Ran Out of Time, Not Out of Potential*, RUSSIANLEGACY.COM, http://www.russianlegacy.com/russian_culture/history/ep_tsarist_economy.htm (last visited Oct. 18, 2013) (on file with author).

[33] *Id.* The term "Old Believers" is applied to those religious groups who abandoned the official Russian Orthodox Church as a protest against introduced church reforms and continued to practice their own traditional rituals. *See* Maria Domnitskaya, *Old believer tradition lives on,* THE VOICE OF RUSSIA (Apr. 8, 2010, 4:07 PM), http://english.ruvr.ru/2010/04/08/6168375.html (on file with author).

[34] *See* Robert V. Daniels, A Documentary History of Communism in Russia: From Lenin to Gorbachev 307–11 (1993).

[35] Prussakov, *supra* note 32.

[36] RIEBER, *supra* note 14, at 82. As stated by Professor Rieber:

societies, the minimal private law enacted by the USSR, such as with respect to the sale, exchange or rental of dwelling units,[37] did not spring from commercial customs and practices.

Pre-revolutionary law was promptly abrogated by the Bolshevik regime; yet, at first no new law of civil or commercial transactions was adopted in part because many felt that the communist phase of Marx's prediction would arrive soon and then there would be no need for law.[38] Nonetheless, a civil code, among others, was enacted in 1922, although as will be discussed in the following chapter[39] it had little effect on the law of commercial contracts. Whatever law was to govern private trade was a law wrought at the top of the governmental pyramid by officials with only themselves as advisers. In addition, it was a law subject to constant and abrupt changes, reversals, and reversals of those reversals, especially during its Leninist phase. After all, it was Lenin who "epitomized" his views on law and legal systems in 1916, one year before the victory of his socialist revolution, as: "law is a political measure, it is [nothing more than] politics."[40]

You might ask: Why would a comparative commercial lawyer be interested in learning about the fate of a law of commercial contracts in an environment as hostile as that of the USSR and its Eastern European, Asian, African and Latin American kin? The answer is that much can be learned from the Soviets' failed attempts to eradicate commercial transactions. Why did their attempts fail? Was it the fault of the official law they employed? Or was there something unworkable in the principles and policies that guided the official law? Or was it a product of both? The failure may have been partly because the Soviet attempt to eradicate commercial transactions stifled human cooperation. The failure also shows here (and in later chapters discussing China,)[41] that the legal system created by authoritarian rule is essentially "invertebrate." In other words, there is no structure and hierarchy (except at the top) to act as the vertebra of the legal system. Do you find some similarities with the invertebration of Latin American *Caudillo* system of law-making?[42]

> The great reforms of the [eighteen] sixties and seventies gradually lowered the barriers that had divided the Russian population into hereditary *soslovia* . . . As regards the merchantry, the *soslovie* principle was deeply eroded by the introduction of the "all-class principle" into the judicial reforms (1864) and more indirectly by the abolition of the legal restrictions on trade (1863–65) . . . Gone were the days when merchants could enjoy the privileges of having civil cases tried in their own courts, of being excused from military service, and of being exempted from a head tax.

Id. at 82 (emphasis added).

[37] *See* Kucherov, *supra* note 7, at 384–85. Here, Kucherov points to the shift of terminology between the RSFSR CIVIL CODE (1922), which referred to a number of things as subject to private ownership, and the USSR CONST. ch. 1, art. 10 (1936), which uses the term "personal" property. Also see his references to primarily statutes as the sources for the determination of what could be bought and sold privately.

[38] *See* HAROLD J. BERMAN, *Codes and Codification, in* ENCYCLOPEDIA OF SOVIET LAW 134 (2d rev. ed. 1985).

[39] *See infra* § 16:2.

[40] V.I. Lenin, *Concerning a Caricature of Marxism and Concerning Imperialist Economism, cited in* JOHN N. HAZARD ET AL., THE SOVIET LEGAL SYSTEM: FUNDAMENTAL PRINCIPLES AND HISTORICAL COMMENTARY 5 n.1 and accompanying text (3d ed. 1977).

[41] *See infra* § 18:4.

[42] *See supra* ch. 14.

Professors John N. Hazard, William E. Butler and Peter B. Maggs[43] wryly point out that natural lawyers such as Professor John C. Wu characterized Soviet official law as paradigmatically positivistic (undoubted heirs, I would add, to John Austin's definition of the law as merely "a command of the sovereign") while Professor Hans Kelsen, himself a refiner of Austin's positivism, regarded Soviet law as a product of natural law that found its source of legitimacy in the dictates of "life" or "nature."[44] Meanwhile, illustrious comparative law scholars such as Professor Rene David of the University of Paris classified Soviet Law as one of the five "principal legal systems of the world"[45] without explaining what was meant by the "legality" of that system. Yet, did not Lenin himself, the principal architect of the Marxist-Leninist "legal system" that governed the USSR, epitomize his views on the law in the above quote as "a political measure"?

Such political measures could often be as cruel and brutal as in Lenin's directives to Bolshevik officials on how to shoot "speculators" (a vaguely-defined group of citizens) or where to hang *kulak*s (an equally vaguely-defined group of rural entrepreneurs)[46] or when Stalin decreed the elimination of entire classes of citizens, whether urban or rural, whom he perceived as political opponents. Alternatively, rules as political measures could be purposely drafted to keep large segments of the population guessing on whether everyday transactions that involved personal property were lawful.[47] This uncertainty was not surprising in a country that rejected reliance on private law as a source of property and contract rights.[48] As tersely stated by the Encyclopedia Britannica, in Soviet law, "[n]o distinction between public and private law existed; all legal matters involved the state. Law was generally thought of as a force for restructuring society and advancing the nation toward communism."[49]

Clearly, private commerce was seriously undermined by such a version of political and uncertain law. Yet, there seemed to be a law that governed the commercial transactions conducted by state entities, their employees and private citizens. As will be discussed in the following chapter,[50] many of the disputes concerning such transactions were governed by a mixture of criminal and administrative law. Would such a version of public law suffice to regulate the relations between informal or unofficial producers, distributors and their customers? These questions will also be among those discussed in the following chapter.

Equally instructive, then, will be the living law of private transactions in the USSR. Where was it found? Who were its makers or drafters? Who applied it? Did it resemble the official or living law of western capitalist countries? Did it address contracts similar to those used for millennia throughout the trading world? And if different transactions emerged under the Soviet living law, how were they enforced and by whom?

---

[43] HAZARD ET AL., *supra* note 40, at xv.

[44] *Id.*

[45] *Id.* at xvi.

[46] *See infra* note 134 and accompanying text. *See also infra* note 170 and accompanying text.

[47] *See* Kucherov, *supra* note 7, at 382 & 390.

[48] *See infra* §§ 16:1–16:2.

[49] *Britannica Concise Encyclopedia: Soviet law*, ANSWERS.COM, http://www.answers.com/topic/soviet-law (last accessed Oct. 18, 2013).

[50] *See infra* § 16:4(F).

Finally, it should be instructive for those comparing the benefits and detriments of the Soviet Marxist-Leninist experience to ascertain the economic effects of replacing marketplace-inspired policies for the production, distribution, intermediation and pricing of goods and services with policies conceived by the autocrats and central economic planners. Were their policies responsible for the USSR's failure to attain a sustainable measure of economic development?

§ 15.2 MARXISM-LENINISM AS A SOURCE OF THE OFFICIAL LAW OF COMMERCIAL CONTRACTS

The guiding spirit of the USSR official law of commercial contracts, as well as its economic plans and anything else that resembled law in that country, came from the writings of Karl Marx, Friedrich Engels and Vladimir Ilich Lenin. The dominance of Marxism-Leninism as a source of the USSR official law of commercial contracts make it imperative to grasp its basics even though at times their numerous writings were often too abstract or unclear. How did this wide array of writings, speeches, directives and letters often become the USSR's official or living law?

The writings of Karl Marx and Vladimir Ilich Lenin were endowed by the Marxist-Leninist government officials with the authority of scientific truths. With such an authority, the rulers of the USSR attempted to instill an unquestioning observance of norms whose infallibility was comparable only to those of Newton's law of gravity or Darwin's evolutionary biology. Despite their Olympian and often vague formulation, Marxist-Leninist principles or tenets were applied to a plethora of issues that ranged from the choice among governmental policies to the resolution of disputes between or among official and private parties as diverse as: What personal property could be sold or rented? What was "unearned" income? Should socialist planning allow for the managerial autonomy of state agencies or firms? Should bonuses or other monetary incentives be given to workers to encourage their good socialist work? Should those who received such rewards—which ranged from housing units to automobiles, salary or pension bonuses—be allowed to profit from them by selling, assigning or renting them?

This chapter will address the above and other related questions and also the temporary resurgence of capitalism during the 1920s, a resurgence largely carried out by commercial intermediaries known in the USSR and the outside world as Nepmen, or "children" of Lenin's New Economic Policy (NEP). Finally, it will focus on the Soviet economic plans as the reaction to the short-lived resurgence of free trade and on the many other costly attempts to cope with the traits of human nature alluded to by Adam Smith and many others. Hopefully by understanding and remembering what went, and is bound to, go wrong we will avoid repeating it.

§ 15.3 MARXISM

A. Biographical Note

Karl Marx (1818–1883) was born in the Prussian border city of Trier. This was the time when Europe, and particularly Britain, was undergoing the harshest period of the industrial revolution. As described in the Norton Anthology of English Literature:

> By the beginning of the Victorian period, the Industrial Revolution had created profound economic and social changes. Hundreds of thousands of workers had migrated to industrial towns, where they made up a new kind of

working class. Wages were extremely low, hours very long—fourteen a day, or even more. Employers often preferred to hire women and children, who worked for even less than men. Families lived in horribly crowded, unsanitary housing.[51]

Marx's attack on capitalism as the culprit for the predicament of industrial workers provided a seemingly convincing justification for the attempts to overthrow the existing political and economic order in Western Europe. He studied law at the Bonn and Berlin universities[52] and after an abortive attempt to become a university professor, he became a journalist and moved to Cologne in 1843 to work as the editor of the "Rhenish Gazette." His criticism of the existing order prompted the Prussian government's ban of its publication. Fearing arrest, Marx fled to France where he edited the "Franco-German Annals" with Friedrich Engels. From France, Marx fled to London in 1849 where he spent the remainder of his life studying and writing. During most of his life, he did not practice a profession, manage a business or hold a regular paying job. Friedrich Engels, like Marx, was interested in economic history, philosophy and political science. He was the son of a wealthy German industrialist, and in short order he became Marx's life-long admirer, close friend, co-author, editor and chief financial supporter.

B. "The Capital" and the Law of Motion of Modern Society

"The Capital" (*Das Kapital*) was Marx's main and most influential publication.[53] Its first volume was published in 1867, and the following two volumes were published in 1885 and 1894. They were edited by Engels who also oversaw their publication. Marx remained an obscure figure in his lifetime; it was only after his death that his ideas exerted a major influence on revolutionary movements throughout the world, culminating with the victorious Revolution of October 1917 in Russia which installed the first Marxist-Leninist government on earth. Despite the decisive effects that his ideas had on the politics and economy of many nations, in the words of Britannica, "Most of his life was spent in a poverty that was only partially alleviated by the benefactions of friends and relatives."[54]

In "The Capital," Marx argued that what made capitalism economically viable was its exploitation of wage earners. His analysis of the conflicting relationship between capitalists and workers and the equally antagonistic struggles between the classes or social groups that preceded capitalism was aimed at revealing what he labeled, with Newtonian overtones, as "The Law of Motion of Modern Society."[55] This was a theory inextricably linked to man's production, use and sale of commodities, including their exchange for other goods, services and money. His purpose was to show, *inter alia*, why

---

[51] *The Victorian Age: Topics*, THE NORTON ANTHOLOGY OF ENGLISH LITERATURE, http://www.wwnorton.com/college/english/nael/victorian/topic_1/welcome.htm (last accessed Oct. 18, 2013) (on file with author).

[52] *See Marx, Karl (Heinrich), in* 6 ENCYCLOPEDIA BRITANNICA Micropædia 660, 660 (15th ed. 1974). This source provides concise but insightful biographical notes.

[53] *See generally* KARL MARX & FRIEDRICH ENGELS, 1 CAPITAL: A CRITIQUE OF POLITICAL ECONOMY (Samuel Moore and Edward Aveling trans., Progress Publishers 1887) (1867), *available at* http://www.marxists.org/archive/marx/works/1867–c1/index.htm. This book provides a readable English version of Volume One of Das Kapital.

[54] *Marx, Karl (Heinrich)*, *supra* note 52, at 660.

[55] *See Preface to the First German Edition* of MARX & ENGELS, *supra* note 53. Marx states "it is the ultimate aim of this work, to lay bare the economic law of motion of modern society . . ." *Id.* ¶ 9.

capital accumulates and eventually (during the penultimate or capitalist phase of this law of social motion) how it concentrates in the hands of a few capitalists in monopolistic fashion only to give way to socialism and finally to communism.

His law of motion of modern society predicted a final trend of declining profits caused by the improvements of technology and by an unstoppable growth in the supply of goods that vastly outpaced demand. Meanwhile, he predicted that wages would continue to fall and so would the standard of living of workers, leading to the final class warfare and the demise of capitalism. He summarized this process in 1848 when he and Engels wrote the Communist Manifesto:

> The history of all hitherto existing societies is the history of class struggles.
>
> Freeman and slave, patrician and plebeian, lord and serf, guild-master and journeyman, in a word, oppressor and oppressed, stood in constant opposition to one another, carried on an uninterrupted, now hidden, now open fight, a fight that each time ended, either in a revolutionary re-constitution of society at large, or in the common ruin of the contending classes.[56]

Unlike the incendiary language of the Communist Manifesto,[57] ("The proletarians have nothing to lose but their chains. . . . Working Men of All Countries, Unite!") "The Capital" was written in aloof, purportedly scientific terms. Its subtitle was "a critique" of the prevailing assumptions of the world's political economy, and Marx's aim was to bring the science of political economy by criticism to the point where it can "bare the economic law of motion of modern society."[58] His hope was that by showing how capitalist development was the precursor of a new, socialist mode of production he would lay bare the scientific foundation for the governance of what he and Engels referred to as a modern socialist society.[59]

C. Marx's Purported Scientific Method

Marx's scientific foundation for the governance of a modern socialist society rested on the identification of: 1) the transactions which distinguished the capitalist marketplace from previous political and economic stages in the development of mankind; 2) the archetypal participants in these transactions; 3) the method of the alleged exploitation; and 4) the scientific verification of his findings.

Capitalist Transactions: Exchange and Use-Value Capital

The first chapter of the first volume of "The Capital" equates the wealth of nations with their ability to accumulate commodities.[60] Commodities and money are forms of capital as are also the equipment and tools which comprise the means of production of commodities. In a pre-capitalist transactional cycle (Marx called them "circuits"), the producer sells the commodities he produces for money ("use-value money") and then

---

[56] KARL MARX & FRIEDRICH ENGELS, MANIFESTO OF THE COMMUNIST PARTY ch. 1, ¶ 1, (Samuel Moore trans., 1969), *available at* http://www.marxists.org/archive/marx/works/1848/communist-manifesto/ch01.htm (on file with author) (citation omitted).

[57] *Id.* ch. 4, ¶ 11.

[58] *Preface to the First German Edition* of MARX & ENGELS, *supra* note 53, ¶ 9.

[59] *Id. See supra* note 55 for a quote by Marx.

[60] *See e.g.*, MARX & ENGELS, *supra* note 53, pt. 1, ch. 1, § 2, n.16. Marx was an avid reader of *The Wealth of Nations* by Smith and seemed always eager to distinguish his views on the value of labor from those of Adam Smith.

purchases other commodities with the proceeds of his sale (C-M-C). In a capitalist cycle, a merchant-intermediary buys commodities in order to resell them at a profit and thereby obtains more money than he started out with and continues the same cycle for as long as it is profitable (M-C-M). The money that circulates in the latter cycle ("exchange-value money") is the one that according to Marx is transformed into capital.[61] This cycle differs from the one in which the peasant sells his corn and with the money he obtains he buys clothes (or the above-mentioned C-M-C).

Please notice the rigidity of these archetypal transactions. In the first, the "producers" of goods or services (to whom he also refers elsewhere as the exploited workers or wage earners) *invariably* sell what they produce in order to consume other commodities or services necessary for their subsistence. In the other, "capitalists" in an equally-fixed fashion sell what they buy in a profitable manner with the purpose of accumulating money as their business capital. Clearly, these descriptions leave no room for the real-life reliance on "use-value" capital in M-C-M transactions and on "exchange-value" capital in C-M-C transactions, as will be apparent in what follows.

1. Archetypal Capitalists and Their Demonology

a. The Imprecise Class of Archetypal Capitalists

As we discussed earlier,[62] contemporary sociology and contextual comparative law benefit much from Max Weber's teachings on archetypal behavior. Recall that Weber's view was that social, economic and historical behavioral research cannot be inductive and supportive of generalizations on social behavior unless the researcher identifies the behavior of representative or archetypal participants in the legal and commercial marketplace. Knowing how these representatives of their various social groups act enables a more accurate description of the behavior of commercial communities. It also enables the identification of standards of behavior against which the various types of commercial behavior can be compared and measured. Recall also that the model merchants are the ones that often inspire higher standards in the behavior of average merchants and their lawyers.[63] However, for any characterization of social behavior to approach objectivity, the described behavior must not be based on conjecture or caricature.

Marx's archetypal capitalist seeks to possess as much exchange-value capital (M-C-M) as possible. From time to time, he may acquire commodities for their use-value (C-M-C), yet when he does so, such an acquisition "*must . . . never be looked upon as the real aim of the capitalist . . .*;[64] [t]he restless never-ending process of profit-making alone is what he aims at."[65] Marx's characterization of the archetypal capitalist, then,

---

[61] *Id.* pt. 2, ch. 4

[62] *See supra* § 2:1(B)(4).

[63] *Id.*

[64] MARX & ENGELS, *supra* note 53, pt. 2, ch.4, ¶ 20 (emphasis added). It goes on to explain: "Commodities (here used in the sense of use-values) are not the terminating object of the trading capitalist, money is his terminating object." THOMAS CHALMERS, ON POLITICAL ECONOMY 165–66 (2d ed., 1832), *cited in id.* pt. 2, ch.4, n.7.

[65] MARX & ENGELS, pt. 2, ch.4, ¶ 20. It goes on to explain: "The merchant counts the money he has made as almost nothing; he always looks to the future." A. GENOVESI, LEZIONI DI ECONOMIA CIVILE: CUSTODI'S EDIT OF ITALIAN ECONOMISTS. PARTE MODERNA 139 (1765), *cited in* MARX & ENGELS, pt. 2, ch. 4, n.8.

excludes any capitalist whose motive or aim in acquiring exchange-value is to obtain commodities for their "use-value."

An objective observation of the universe of capitalists would have revealed that it is full capitalists whose real aim is not necessarily to accumulate more exchange-value for its own sake but to acquire the ownership, use, and all too often, "bragging rights" on the possession of high-value commodities or their functional equivalents. Marx may reply to these instances of use-value motivation by saying that regardless of the ultimate aim for the use of the accumulated exchange capital, what characterizes the archetypal capitalist is his immediate or "real aim" to possess "exchange-value." Yet, by his own admission, Marx's archetypal capitalist rejects the enjoyment of use-value of commodities as his real aim, whether mediate or immediate.

In light of the co-existence of "real aims," could there be others? What about those of capitalists whose motivations are rooted in their religious, political or cultural beliefs or values, or in their "human nature"? If these motivations could similarly encourage the accumulation of exchange-capital, is it not an oversimplification to attribute the emergence and behavior of capitalist types to factors that are said to be economic in nature? To this criticism, Marx and Engels would have answered (as done by an admiring annotator of their Manifesto): "Communism is not 'against human nature' because there is no such thing—only the social values produced by certain kinds of economic organization [are the ones that count]."[66]

It should be clear, then, that Marx's description of archetypal (standard and model) capitalists lacks precision and often belongs to the genre of caricatures. One could explain his imprecision as caused by the indignation he felt when witnessing widespread social injustice and oppression of the working poor. Yet, if one were to dismiss imprecision as an understandable overreaction to injustice, what about the injustice that such imprecise characterizations inflicted upon millions of undeserving victims labeled "bourgeois," "bloodsuckers," "profiteers," "exploiters" and so on?[67]

b. The Demonology of Capitalist Contracts and Private Property: Trade as Inherently Deceitful

Engels claimed that during his and Marx's time, private property was a key factor in the exploitation of the poor by the rich, and blamed capitalist industry for the mass poverty and misery of the working masses and for the large increase of crime and "feudal vices" as reflected in the manner in which capitalists conducted their trade and even their marriages:

> Trade became to a greater and greater extent than ever cheating. The "fraternity" of the [French] revolutionary motto was realized in the chicanery and rivalries of the battle of competition. Oppression by force was replaced by corruption; the sword, as the first social lever, by gold . . . Prostitution increased to an extent never heard of. Marriage itself remained, as before, the

---

[66] KARL MARX AND FRIEDRICH ENGLES, THE COMMUNIST MANIFESTO (1848), *in* 2 READING ABOUT THE WORLD pt. 2, n.15 (Paul Brians et. al. eds., 1999), *available at* http://public.wsu.edu/~brians/world_civ/world civreader/world_civ_reader_2/marx.html (on file with author). This source provides this excerpt and others from KARL MARX & FRIEDRICH ENGELS: THE COMMUNIST MANIFESTO (1848).

[67] *See* n.173 and accompanying text.

legally recognized form, the official cloak of prostitution, and, moreover, was supplemented by rich crops of adultery.[68]

c. The Deification of the Exploited: Select or "Chosen" Classes

In sharp contrast with the invariably sinful capitalists, Marx portrayed the exploited workers, the urban proletariat, as history's chosen people. As pointed out by the late R. H. Tawney of Oxford University, Marx assured the proletariat that:

> [T]he forces of the universe are on the side of the elect as was to be assuaged . . . by the theory of historical materialism. He set their virtues at their best in sharp antithesis with the vices of the established order at its worst, [and] taught them to feel that they were a chosen people, made them conscious of their great destiny in the Providential plan and resolute to realize it.[69]

Engels attributes to Marx, through his "scientific socialism," the identification of the proletariat as the class entitled to "[seize] political power and [turn] the means of production into State property . . . [and] in doing this, it abolishes itself as proletariat, abolishes all class distinctions and class antagonisms, abolishes also the State as State."[70] Yet, the Marxism adopted in the USSR in 1917 added to the proletariat, as if by magic, other supposedly exploited, oppressed and "elect" classes. Lenin's announcement to the "Citizens of Russia" of the passage of power to "the hands of . . . the Petrograd [presently St. Petersburg] Soviet of Workers and Soldiers Deputies, the Military-Revolutionary Committee" of October 25, 1917 did not single out the proletariat as the elected class.[71] He referred to "the cause for which *the people* have struggled" and ended with the proclamation: "Long live the revolution of the *workers, soldiers and peasants*."[72]

2. The Method of Exploitation: Appropriation of the Surplus Value

Some Marxist statements found the iniquitous appropriation in buying cheap anything from anybody (worker, producer or another merchant) and then selling it dearly to anybody: "The increment or excess over the original value (is what) I call 'surplus-value.' "[73] If this were *the* iniquitous appropriation, it closely resembles the religious "sin of avarice," a sin addressed by the medieval theological doctrines on the just price of commodities.[74] For example, Saint Thomas Aquinas' (1225–1274) *Summa*

---

[68] Friedrich Engels, Socialism: Utopian and Scientific 55–56 (Edward Aveling trans., 1910).

[69] R.H. TAWNEY, RELIGION AND THE RISE OF CAPITALISM 99 (1961).

[70] ENGELS, *supra* note 68, at 127.

[71] SERVICE, *supra* note 13, at 311.

[72] *Id.* (emphasis added).

[73] *See* MARX & ENGELS, *supra* note 53, pt. 2, ch. 4.

[74] *See* TAWNEY, *supra* note 69, at 39–54. This source also discusses the Church's medieval condemnation of the "lust of gain" and the "sin of avarice." *See id.* at 37–42. Tawney, I believe insightfully, refers to Karl Marx as "The Last of the Schoolmen." *Id.* at 39. *See also* Laurence M. Vance, *The Myth of the Just Price,* LUDWIG VON MISES INSTITUTE (March 31, 2008), http://mises.org/daily/2918 (on file with author). Vance cites the Book of Acts in the New Testament for formulas of distribution such as, "every man according to his ability . . ." or for the duty of early Christians in Jerusalem when they sold their houses or their land to distribute the money to, "every man according as he had need." *Id.* (internal citations omitted). The influence of the Biblical and Church pronouncements on Lenin's and the USSR's Constitution of 1918 is apparent from the quote, "he who does not work, neither shall he eat." USSR CONST. ch. 1, art. 12 (1936). In the U.S.S.R. work is a duty and a matter of honor for every able-bodied citizen. *Id. See also* Lewis Loflin, *The Apostle Paul Founder of Christianity,* SULLIVAN-COUNTY.COM, http://www.sullivan-county.com/news/paul/

Theologica discusses cheating in buying and selling,[75] and suggests that the just price be established by the "common estimation" of market buyers and sellers (*secundum aestimationem fori*).[76] A century later, Henry of Langenstein (1325–1397), another influential theologian, asserted that the just price of commodities was that which enabled the seller to maintain his station in life. As was discussed in an earlier chapter,[77] Langenstein's theory was the one most commonly associated with the wages paid to guild members and according to their guild status.[78]

Marx and Engels also prescribed a just price for labor: During socialism, the just price was based on the value of what labor produced, and during communism it was based on the amount needed to satisfy labor's needs.[79] Ironically, and contrary to the Marxist doctrine of dialectical materialism,[80] these Marxist materialist formulas were deeply rooted in religious doctrines.[81]

By the time he wrote "The Capital," Marx meant more by the appropriation of surplus-value than the profit obtained by charging more than the cost of one's goods or services.[82] By surplus value he meant the proceeds that resulted from an appropriation by capitalists of what rightfully belonged to the exploited. Reduced to its most elementary formulation, the formula of exploitation was: "[C]apital [or] C . . . as a surplus, [is] the amount by which the value of the product exceeds the value of its constituent elements."[83] He then listed the components of "C" as only two: "c" the money invested by the capitalist to buy the means of production, and "v" the sum he paid to the laborers involved in the production of goods or services. He also referred to "c" as constant capital and to "v" as variable capital. Thus:

> C = c + v: for example, if £500 is the capital advanced, its components may be such that the £500 = £410 [constant capital] + £90 [variable capital). When the process of production is finished, we get a commodity whose value = (c + v) + *s*, where s is the surplus-value; or . . . (£410 const. + £90 var.) + £90 surpl. The original capital has now changed from C to C', from £500 to £590. The difference is *s* or a surplus value of £90.[84]

He did not ascribe independent value as part of the capitalist's investment to his own work and entrepreneurship, goodwill or reputation. He noted, however, that only a fractional value of the constant capital was transferred by the capitalist to the

---

paul.htm (on file with author). This source provides Saint Paul's words: "He who does not work, neither shall he eat" and other sayings by Saint Paul. *Id.*

[75] Raymond de Roover, *The Concept of the Just Price: Theory and Economic Policy* 18 J. ECON. HIST. 418, 422 (1958).

[76] *Id.*

[77] *See supra* § 6:2(B)(4).

[78] *See id.*

[79] *See* Karl Marx, *Critique of the Gotha Program*, in 3 MARX/ENGELS SELECTED WORKS pt. 1 (Progress Publishers 1970) (1875), *available at* http://www.marxists.org/archive/marx/works/1875/gotha/index.htm.

[80] *See infra* § 15:3(D)(1)–(2).

[81] *See, e.g.*, Loflin, *supra* note 74. This source discusses the origin of Marxist-Leninist commands in the following religious injuctions, "every man according as he had need" and "[h]e that doth not work, neither shall he eat." *Id.*

[82] *See* MARX & ENGELS, *supra* note 53, pt. 3, ch. 9, § 1.

[83] *Id.* ¶ 1.

[84] *Id.* ¶ 2.

production process. A similar failure to contribute real value occurred with what the capitalist paid as wages. According to Marx, labor was paid wages to produce a commodity such as yarn whose amount or value was equal only to the value of the commodities that the workers needed for their subsistence ("necessaries") or the value of the money that bought them. Yet, the market price of yarn usually exceeded both the value of "c" (constant capital) as well as "v" (variable capital) or the necessaries paid to labor; and this excess, he said, was appropriated by the capitalist.

According to Engels, then:

> [Marx showed] that even if the capitalist buys the labor power of his laborer at its full value as a commodity on the market, he yet extracts more value from it than he paid for; and that in the ultimate analysis, this surplus-value forms those sums of value from which are heaped up constantly increasing masses of capital in the hands of the possessing classes . . .
>
> These two great discoveries, the materialistic conception of history and the revelation of the secret of capitalistic production through surplus-value, we owe to Marx. With these discoveries Socialism became a science.[85]

This "science" predicted the demise of capitalists (however ill-defined) as the exploiters of the workers. It also prevented the characterization of many transactions among capitalists and workers as profit sharing, for according to Marx, between these two classes there could be nothing but exploitation by the capitalists of their workers. Yet, this "observation" ignored, among others, transactions by the seventeenth and eighteenth century *verlagers* and their "putting out" system,[86] some of whom (as in the description of Nathan Rothschild's purchasing practices in an earlier chapter)[87] provided fabric or money to workers with which the latter could assemble or finish textiles. This form of doing business and increased reliance on commercial credit facilitated the transition especially in Holland, Great Britain and Germany from guild-journeymen to wage earners and from wage earners who had become independent tradesmen to shop owners or industrialists.

This transition was encouraged by the opening of new and profitable trans-Atlantic American markets. As noted by Professor Stanley D. Chapman of the University of Nottingham in his study on the changing roles of merchants and financiers in the eighteenth and nineteenth century English textile industry: "[T]he emergence of the European and then the trans-Atlantic economies led, by degrees, to the insertion of two strata of entrepreneurs between the local manufacturer [or

---

[85] ENGELS, *supra* note 68, at 93.

[86] *See supra* § 6:2(C). *See also* Gay L. Gullickson, *Textile Industry: Europe, 1450 to 1789: Encyclopedia of the Early Modern World,* ENCYCLOPEDIA.COM (2004), http://www.encyclopedia.com/doc/1G2–3404901119.html. This source explains:

> By the sixteenth century . . . [European] merchants had discovered that they could avoid the high wages, labor shortages, and quality controls imposed by urban guilds and governments by hiring peasants to do manufacturing work in their homes. Urban merchants continued to control production, but much of the work force was spread out through the countryside. Alternately referred to as the putting-out system, cottage manufacturing, and the *Verlag* system, merchants (*Verlagers*) found they could save money (rural workers could work for less because they produced much of their own food) and increase production at the same time. . . .

Id.

[87] *See supra* § 11:4(C) (discussing Rothschild's purchasing practices in Germany).

producer] and his widening circles of customers."[88] Frequently, these entrepreneurs had started as craftsmen or wage earners.

D. The Bases of the "Law of Motion of Modern Society"

Marx's "Law of Motion of Modern Society" was not derived from empirically-verifiable findings. What Engels, among other Marxists, refers to as "science" in Marx's writings is an amalgam of: 1) philosophical theories or variations on theories; 2) inferences from historical events (most of them subject to differing interpretations); and 3) unwarranted extrapolations from nineteenth century scientific findings or hypotheses.

1. Dialectics

Engels traced the philosophical bases of Marx's "law of motion of modern society" to the dialectical thinking of Greek philosophers and sophists as refined in the nineteenth century by the German philosopher George Friedrich Hegel.[89] In Engel's words:

> When we consider and reflect upon *Nature at large, or the history of mankind, or our own intellectual activity*, at first we see the picture of an endless entanglement of relations and reactions, permutations and combinations, in which . . . everything moves, changes, comes into being and passes away.[90]

Since this assertion also underlay Hegel's dialectical vision of man's history, Marx and Engels believed that Hegel's philosophy enabled their analysis of the whole world's history (natural or physical, historical and intellectual) as a process of constant motion, change, transformation and development. They argued that because of this philosophy the history of mankind no longer appeared as a wild whirl of senseless deeds of violence but as the evolution of man himself. This is why Lenin kept a "monkey to man" statue of Charles Darwin nearest his desk.[91] As with Marx and Engels, Lenin believed that Darwin's natural selection provided the evolutionary component of Marxist dialectics, including the selection of the proletariat as the class fittest to rule the world.[92]

2. Historical and Economic Materialism

Despite their acknowledged debt to Hegel's dialectics, Marx and Engels concluded that Hegel's philosophy failed to provide a scientific historical pattern because, among other deficiencies, it was "idealist." To Hegel, things and their evolution were only the

---

[88] *See* Stanley D. Chapman, *British Marketing Enterprise: The Changing Roles of Merchants, Manufacturers, and Financiers, 1700–1860*, 53 BUS. HIST. REV. 205 (1979).

[89] ENGELS, *supra* note 68, at 76.

[90] ENGELS, *supra* note 68, at 77 (emphasis added).

[91] *See* SERVICE, *supra* note 13, at 310–11. This section includes this picture contained within a photo display.

[92] *See* ENGELS, *supra* note 68, at 83. Engels refers to Darwin as:

> Nature works dialectically and not metaphysically; that [is] she does not move in the eternal oneness of a perpetually recurring circle, but goes through a real historical evolution. In this connection Darwin must be named before all others. He dealt the metaphysical conception of Nature the heaviest blow by his proof that all organic beings, plants, animals, and man himself, are the products of a process of evolution going on through millions of years.

Id.

physical manifestations of "ideas" of those very things. Hegelian ideas pre-existed things and were forms of thought lodged in eternity even before the universe existed. Marx and Engels claimed that this theory of reality was counter-factual and artificial.[93]

In contrast, their "modern" (Marxist) historical materialism perceived the evolution of humanity as guided by material things. Once the fate of man depended upon the trade of commodities, the forces that shaped his decisions were unmistakably economic.[94] Marx and Engels found scientific support for this materialistic theory in discoveries which, according to them, showed that nature has its own materialistically-determined evolution, including that of celestial bodies and organic species. Upon reviewing "*all* past history" of man, they found parallels to the evolution of nature and deduced that the history of modern society was that of class struggles. And these struggles:

> [A]re always the products of the modes of production and of exchange—in a word, of the *economic* conditions of their time.[95] [Thus], the economic structure of society *always furnishes the real basis, starting* from which we can alone work out the ultimate explanation of the whole superstructure of juridical and political institutions as well as of the religious, philosophical, and other ideas of a given historical period."[96]

Law was part of this economically-directed superstructure. Hence, Marx and Engels proclaimed that "modern materialism is essentially dialectic . . ."[97]

3. Disregard of the Changing Meaning of Property

At the root of the Marxist class struggle and exploitation of the proletariat by the bourgeoisie was the capitalists' ownership of the means of production. So important was the Marxist "finding" that it became part of constitutional and statutory provisions that provided the "essential" definitions of property and, indirectly, of contract in socialist states. For the less a citizen could own, the less he was allowed to convey by contract.[98] Yet property, especially of the means of production was unaffected by the supposedly dialectic ever-changing nature of everything. Marx and Engels' version of capitalistic ownership of private property of the means of production was absolute and static, not very different from that of the most extreme forms of feudalism.

Despite Marx's long-term residence in England, he did not seem aware of the transformation of feudal ownership in that country and in other European countries such as Germany. As aptly described by an English judge, the feudal lord's rights in

---

[93] *Id.* at 87. As diagnosed by Engels:

> [On] the one hand . . . [it asserted] that human history is a process of evolution, which, by its very nature, cannot find its intellectual final term in the discovery of any so-called absolute truth. But, on the other hand, it laid claim to being the very essence of this absolute truth. A system of natural and historical knowledge, embracing everything, and final for all time, is a contradiction to the fundamental law of dialectic reasoning.

Id.

[94] *See supra* § 15:3(C) (on Marx's C-M-C and M-C-M).

[95] ENGELS, *supra* note 68, at 90.

[96] *Id.* at 90–91 (emphasis added).

[97] *Id.* at 88.

[98] *See generally* USSR CONST. (1936).

"his" land, as set forth in the doctrine of the "estates," were not absolute but limited by their holder's "time in the land," *i.e.*, rights that were time-bound, divisible and marketable.[99] This meant that out of English feudalism came a form of "commercial" property rights that could be sold, exchanged, leased or mortgaged to anyone, including the former vassals of the landowner-feudal lord. A similar phenomenon occurred in Germany, Europe's first country to enable the issuance and sale of negotiable mortgage bonds or certificates and with it the acquisition of real property by untold numbers of descendants of the former vassals.[100]

The same or greater degree of negotiation and marketability was true with means of production that were moveable in nature. Even during Marx's time, negotiable documents of title such as ocean bills of lading or warehouse receipts conveyed rights to their holders which were often superior to the rights of their "historical" owners of the goods shipped or stored.[101] Finally, as shown in a seminal 1932 study by Columbia University Law School's Adolf Berle and his economist co-author Gardiner Means,[102] while the ownership of the means of production in the U.S. was ostensibly concentrated in a few hundred of its largest business corporations, the control and disposition of these corporate assets were not in the hands of corporate owners but of a class of professional managers. Moreover, many of the stockholders (owners) of these corporations were workers. Clearly, then, capitalist nations such as Great Britain, Germany and the United States had bestowed a commercial meaning to many, if not most, of the most prized forms of ownership of the means of production, a very different meaning than ascribed to them by Marx and Engels.

4. *The Rhetoric of Marxist Dialectics and Historical Materialism: At Best a Philosophy, Not a Science*

As should be clear by now, science does not support the Marxist findings that the "history of mankind" reveals the presence of the Marxist "law of motion for modern society," dialectic and materialist as it is supposed to be. The exact or physical sciences respond to questions very different from those posed by the mid-nineteenth century philosophical debates that so captivated Marx, Engels and their disciples. A question such as whether the history of the universe and man is dialectic or cyclical, materialistic or idealistic would require considerable re-formulation before it could be scientifically answerable. Marx would have to provide physical scientists with much narrower and factually inspired questions such as: Is it true that a sequence of objectively verifiable events such as "A," "B" and "C" resulted from equally objectively verifiable causes "X," "Y" or "Z"? Nowhere did Marx ask questions such as that, even though he prided himself in his observational faculties.[103]

---

[99] Walsingham's Case, (1579) 75 Eng. Rep. 805 (Q.B.) 817; 2 Plowd. 547, 555 (Exch.).

[100] *See generally supra* § 11:4.

[101] *See generally* Boris Kozolchyk, Evolution and Present State of the *Ocean Bill of Lading* from a Banking Law Perspective 23 J. MAR. L. & COM. 161 (1992); Kozolchyk & Wilson, The New Model Inter-American Law; Kozolchyk & Furnish, A *Comparative Analysis*.

[102] *See generally* ADOLF AUGUSTUS BERLE & GARDINER COIT MEANS, THE MODERN CORPORATION AND PRIVATE PROPERTY (Harcourt, Brace & World 1968) (1932).

[103] ENGELS, *supra* note 68, at 84–85. Consider, for example, the following excerpt from one of Engels' most influential writings:

> An exact representation of the universe, of its evolution, of the development of mankind, and of the reflection of this evolution in the minds of men, can therefore only be obtained *by the methods*

Social science data are equally unsupportive of many of Marx's tenets. Consider, for example, Marx's descriptions of the behavior of archetypal capitalists and of their workers. As previously shown, the Marxist typology of capitalists and proletarians is imprecise, sloganeering and often caricaturesque—keen on demonology and deification. Nonetheless, Marx's followers accepted such assertions as scientific. In fact, Lenin was so convinced of the validity of Marxist science that when his one-time major financial supporter Alexander Bogdanov described Marx's science to him as "old-fashioned poppycock," Lenin referred to Bogdanov as one who believes in nothing and is a "dangerous relativist."[104]

In sum, Marxism is at best a philosophical theory on the political economy of nations. Bertrand Russell, one of the most qualified and articulate philosopher-scientists of the twentieth century, set forth the distinction between these disciplines quite clearly:

> [I]t cannot be [seriously] maintained that philosophy has had any very great measure of success in its attempts to provide definite answers to its [own and even less to scientific] questions. If you ask a mathematician, a mineralogist . . . what definite body of truths has been ascertained by his science, his answer will last as long as you are willing to listen. But if you put the same question to a philosopher, he will, if he is candid, have to confess that his study has not achieved positive results such as have been achieved by . . . [the empirical] sciences.[105]

The fuzziness and unreliability of Marx's dialectical predictions were manifest in his response to a question by Vera Zasulich, one of Lenin's closest collaborators. She asked: Was the Marxist sequence of feudalism to capitalism to socialism to communism predestined to affect every country? Might there not be a chance for a largely pre-

---

> *of dialectics* with its constant regard to the innumerable actions and reactions of life and death, of *progressive or retrogressive changes*. And in this spirit the new German philosophy has worked. Kant began his career by resolving the [issue of a] stable solar system of Newton and its eternal duration, after the famous initial impulse had once been given, into the result of a historical process, the formation of the sun and all the planets *out of a rotating nebulous mass*. From this he at the same time drew the conclusion that, given this origin of the solar system, its future death followed of necessity. His theory half a century later was established mathematically by Laplace, and half a century after that the spectroscope proved the existence in space of such incandescent masses of gas in various stages of condensation.

Id. (emphasis added). It is very unlikely that Engels was referring to the so-called "Big Bang Theory" of the beginning of the universe because the validity of this theory was only established late in the twentieth century and even now it is subject to constant revisions. *See* Dr. Arno A. Penzias & Dr. Robert Wilson *in Press Release: The 1978 Nobel Prize in Physics,* NOBELPRIZE.ORG (Oct. 17, 1978), http://nobelprize.org/nobel_prizes/physics/laureates/1978/press.html. This article explains their Nobel Prize winning work. More likely, the initial impulse mentioned by Engels came from Aristotelian writings which were often quoted by him. If so, this "famous initial impulse" that created the universe was a reference to the Aristotelian notion of a Prime Cause, Prime Mover or an Unmoved Mover, a notion that later Greek philosophers associated with a God-like entity. *See e.g.*, ENGELS, *supra* note 68, at 76. Engels states: "The old Greek philosophers were all born natural dialecticians, and Aristotle, the most encyclopaedic intellect of them, had already analyzed the most essential forms of dialectic thought." *Id.* How verifiable was it that the "sun and all the planets [were formed] out of a rotating nebulous mass" by an Unmoved Mover? *Id.* at 84. Further, were there any *retrogressive* changes during this evolutionary, dialectic process of formation, or was the formation of the universe a process of irreversible and constant expansion or "inflation" and thus without any signs of "retrogression"?

104 SERVICE, *supra* note 13, at 190 & 193.

105 BERTRAND RUSSELL, THE PROBLEMS OF PHILOSOPHY 100 (2008).

capitalist Russia to avoid capitalism altogether and adopt socialism?[106] In response, Marx "accepted that Russia's agrarian economy and peasant communal traditions might allow it to have a socialist transformation without capitalist industrialization."[107]

§ 15.4 LENINISM

A. The Special Meaning of Lenin's Charismatic Authoritarian Leadership

In his "Theory of Social and Economic Organization"[108] Max Weber lists three types of authority whose claims to legitimacy and obedience are based on: 1) rational grounds, which rest on the belief that the norms that grant legal authority to he who governs are lawful; 2) traditional grounds, which are based on the prevailing belief that immemorial traditions, customs and usages grant legitimacy to those authorized by them;[109] and 3) charismatic grounds, which are based on the feelings of exceptional sanctity, heroism or exemplary character evoked by an individual and by the norms of behavior revealed or ordained by him.[110]

Vladimir Ilich Lenin's authority over the inhabitants of the USSR was in many respects absolute, and to many it was charismatic judging from the degree of obedience to the norms ordained by him. Yet this obedience was not based on Weber's widespread feelings of "exceptional sanctity, heroism or exemplary character." As noted by Professor Robert Service, one of Lenin's premier biographers, Lenin was not particularly courageous and only a reluctant participant in street actions; and while he saw himself as the intellectual light of the revolution, even in that capacity he had to be pressured by colleagues to return to Russia when his presence may have made a difference.[111]

He possessed, however, a shrewd and highly persuasive intelligence, an enormous capacity for work and a self-assurance that enabled him to exude authoritativeness even on subjects on which he had little knowledge, let alone expertise. At first, he gained the loyalty of a small circle of intellectual revolutionaries who helped him persuade wider circles of followers. Eventually and with a minimal number of Bolshevik supporters, he became the autocrat and first Chairman of the Council of People's Commissars of the Russian Soviet Federated Socialist Republic (RSFSR) from 1917–1922 and subsequently the Chairman of the Council of People's Commissars of the USSR from 1922 until his death in 1924.[112]

---

106 SERVICE, *supra* note 13, at 88.

107 *Id.*

108 MAX WEBER, THEORY OF SOCIAL AND ECONOMIC ORGANIZATION (A.M. Henderson & Talcott Parsons trans., 1947). *See also Max Weber*, TRIPOD.COM, http://taodesigns.tripod.com/weber/weber47.html (last visited Oct. 21, 2013). This source provides an online summary of WEBER.

109 WEBER, *supra* note 108, at 328.

110 WEBER, *supra* note 108, at 328.

111 *See* SERVICE, *supra* note 13, at 172.

112 *Id.* at 314–15. Lenin was also Chairman of the Council of People's Commissars of the USSR from 1922–1924; Chairman of the Council of Labour and Defense from 1918–1920; and finally, Chairman of the Councils of workers, peasants and soldiers, in effect the entire governmental apparatus (Sovnarkom). *Id.* at 315 & 378.

Despite the popularity of Marx's ideas among Russian intellectual-revolutionaries at the end of the nineteenth century,[113] Russia's socialist revolution did not follow Marx's predicted evolution from feudalism to capitalism and then to socialism and eventually to communism. Nor were the Russian proletarians the unique or most important players in the October revolution and its aftermath. The efforts of Russian revolutionary intellectuals, including, prominently, his own, were as important as the "muscle" or the indignation of the proletarians, soldiers and peasants.

Lenin's ability to persuade and organize must have been enormous for, as stated by Professor Robert Service, it was due largely to Lenin's efforts that the USSR that emerged from the October 1917 revolution became "a beacon to the world's far-left socialists and . . . [it was] Lenin's interpretation of the doctrines of Marx and Engels [that] became holy writ for communists, [to the point that] [ ]at his death [these doctrines were] [ ]designated as Marxism-Leninism."[114] Some of Lenin's character traits that made this revolution and its official and living law possible will be briefly described in the following sections.

B. The October Revolution of 1917

During 1917, industrial and even military strikes proliferated and, after some hesitation, the Bolsheviks (still a small minority compared to other political parties and revolutionary-agrarian movements) joined in demonstrations against the Tsarist government of Nicholas II. As food shortages grew, neither the police nor the army seemed willing to fight the strikers and demonstrators. Tsar Nicholas abdicated on March 13, 1917 and the legislative assembly (*Duma*) he had appointed remained as a legislative body but with little power. Its membership came from liberal and centrist factions as well as from anti-Bolshevik Socialist-Revolutionary and Menshevik factions. They formed a new provisional government which Lenin, still in exile in Switzerland, labeled as "imperialist" and urged that it be overthrown.

C. The April Theses

After some prodding from Bolshevik colleagues, Lenin returned to Russia during April of 1917. By this time, much of the governmental power in large cities such as Moscow and Petrograd was in the hands of loosely-elected "councils" of workers, peasants and occasionally soldiers referred to as "Soviets."[115] Yet, very few of these soviets were controlled by the Bolsheviks. In fact, the total number of Bolsheviks at that time did not exceed 20,000 in a population of 150 million.[116] Lenin presented his program for a revolutionary government in a pamphlet labeled "April Theses."[117] He acknowledged that the Bolsheviks were, in his words, "a small minority" of the Soviets of Workers Deputies and among the proletariat[118] and that there was a need to

---

113 *Id.* at 55–56.

114 *Id.* at 1.

115 *See* SERVICE, *supra* note 13, at 174.

116 *Vladimir Lenin*, *in* GENOCIDE AND CRIMES AGAINST HUMANITY (Dinah L. Shelton & Gale Cengage eds., 2005), *cited in Lenin, Vladimir Genocide and Crimes Against Humanity*, ENOTES.COM, http://www.enotes.com/topics/lenin-vladimir (last visited Oct. 22, 2013).

117 *See* Vladimir Lenin, *The April Theses,* 26 PRAVADA (1917), *cited in* LENIN ON POLITICS AND REVOLUTION: SELECTED WORKS 158–60 (James E. Connor ed., 1968), *reprinted in Lenin's* The April *Thesis (1917)*, THE HISTORY GUIDE, http://www.historyguide.org/europe/april.html (last updated Apr. 13, 2012) (on file with author).

persuade the masses that the "Soviets of Workers Deputies are the *only possible* form of revolutionary government."[119] He urged the rejection of a parliamentary republic as a form of government and advocated the installation of a republic of Soviets of Workers', Agricultural Labourers' and Peasants' Deputies, together with the abolition of the existing police, army and bureaucracy and the replacement of the standing army by arming of the whole people.[120]

He proposed the confiscation of all landed estates and their disposition by the local Soviets of Agricultural Labourers' and Peasants' Deputies.[121] He also suggested "the immediate amalgamation of all banks in the country into a single national bank, and the institution of control over it by the Soviet of Workers' Deputies."[122] On November 8, 1917, the Second Congress of Soviets established the new government headed by the Council of People's Commissars (*Sovnarkom*) with Lenin as Chairman. Shortly thereafter, the *Sovnarkom* presented the draft of the 1918 Constitution to the Congress of Soviets of the Russian Socialist Federative Soviet Republic (RSFSR) and the predecessor to the 1922 USSR. This constitution was enacted on July 10, 1918.[123]

D. Lenin's Law Making: Authoritarian Legalism

1. The Many and Varied Sources of Lenin's Law

Lenin's law could be found in all conceivable formats—officially promulgated laws, decrees, circulars and even a Constitution of 1918 that repeated or closely reflected text that he had proposed in his "April Theses."[124]

In addition, Lenin also made law through what he said in his many writings, including monographs or pamphlets, such as "What is to be Done?,"[125] "The State and the Revolution,"[126] or the above-mentioned "April Theses."[127] He also made law in his directives, letters to national or provincial administrators, speeches and sayings.[128] The normative power of these sources should not be underestimated—many Russians obeyed his utterances as prophetic, and many others did not dare to disobey them

---

[118] *Id.* § 4.

[119] *Id.*

[120] *Id.* § 5.

[121] *Id.* § 6.

[122] *Id.* § 7.

[123] *See* Constitution (Fundamental Law) of the R.S.F.S.R., POLITICSFORUM.ORG, http://www.politicsforum.org/documents/constitution_rsfsr_1918.php (last visited Oct. 22, 2013) (on file with author). This source provides an English translation of this constitution.

[124] *Compare* Lenin, *supra* note 117, *with Constitution (Fundamental Law) of the R.S.F.S.R., supra* note 123.

[125] *See* Vladimir Ilyich Lenin, *What Is To Be Done? Burning Questions of our Movement, in* 5 LENIN'S SELECTED WORKS 347–530 (Foreign Languages Publishing House 1961) (1902), *available at* http://www.marxists.org/archive/lenin/works/1901/witbd/ (on file with author).

[126] Vladimir Lenin, The State and the Revolution: The Marxist Theory of the State & The Tasks of the Proletariat in the Revolution, in 25 COLLECTED WORKS 381 (Charles Farrell et al. eds., 1999), available at http://www.marxists.org/archive/lenin/works/1917/staterev/.

[127] Lenin, *supra* note 117. The complete set of Lenin's Collected Works amount to 45 volumes. *See Lenin Collected Works*, MARXISTS.ORG, http://www.marxists.org/archive/lenin/works/cw/index.htm (last visited Oct. 22, 2013).

[128] *See, e.g., Vladimir Lenin quotes*, THINKEXIST.COM, http://thinkexist.com/quotes/vladimir_lenin/ (last visited Oct. 22, 2013). This source lists quotes by Lenin.

simply because of his announced ruthlessness. The admiration by some and fear by others resulted in a high degree of attempted observance. I said "attempted" observance because, despite the direct tone of his prescriptions, many of them were angry, menacing and choleric enough to leave out essential facts or details needed for their enforcement. Recall, for example, the menaces in the above quotes in the 1918 Constitution to "ruthlessly suppress all exploiters" (What precisely does one do to become an "exploiter"?) or "he that does not work, shall not eat" (What did he mean by work; did he include mental as well as physical? Did not eating mean forced deprivation of food, or lack of payment?).

2. *Obedience Through Didactics and Terror*

Lenin's intellectual elitism and his doubts of the masses' ability to become understanding socialists found its way into one of his often-quoted sayings: "If Socialism can only be realized when the intellectual development of all the people permits it, then we shall not see Socialism for at least five hundred years."[129] Such an attitude was also translated into legislative language such as that of Chapter 1, Section 3 of the 1918 Constitution and into a didactic style designed to explain governmental actions. Jacques Sherry was a long-time resident of Tucson, Arizona who had lived in Russia during the Lenin years and who attended one of these didactic meetings. He described to me Lenin's style as that of a "teacher of small children, even if his audience was comprised of mature men and women." Curiously, a friend of mine who had attended several of Fidel Castro's speeches provided a very similar description.[130]

Yet, presumably to be on the "safe side," Lenin not only spoke to some audiences as a kindergarten teacher but also decided to carry the proverbial "big stick" of authoritarianism. As Lenin's rule wore on, the obedience to his regulations on what could loosely be considered as commercial contracts (as part of his regulation of property and governmental production and distribution of goods) stemmed from the fearful consequences attendant to their non-observance.

In 1917, he urged the enactment of a decree that created "The Whole-Russian Extraordinary Commission for Combating Counter-Revolution and Sabotage" (Cheka). In a short time, it became one of the most feared secret police organizations in contemporary history, rivaling the Nazi Gestapo in its cruelty and countless executions without trial.[131] Barely a year later, he drafted a Resolution of the Central Committee of the Bolshevik Party that forbad the Bolshevik's own press from publishing "defamatory articles" about the Cheka; as Lenin put it: "A good Communist is also a good Chekist."[132]

---

[129] John Reed, Ten Days that Shook the World 303–04 (1922) (emphasis omitted).

[130] *See infra* note 195. This note provides Luis de la Cuesta's description of Castro's speeches.

[131] *See* Service, *supra* note 13, at 10, 321–22, & 337. *See also* Robert GELLATELY, LENIN, STALIN AND HITLER: THE AGE OF SOCIAL CATASTROPHE 57 (2007). *See* Stéphane Courtois et al., The Black Book of Communism: Crimes Terror Repression 9–10 (Jonathan Murphy & Mark Kramer trans., 1999). This source provides a sobering list of the casualties attributable to twentieth-century tyrants such as Lenin, Stalin, Hitler, and Mao Tse-tung, among others.

[132] *Id.* at 79.

Typical of the Cheka's aims and methods of operation is an Instruction of November 1, 1918 by Martin Latsis, a high Cheka official, in which he directs his operatives to proceed as follows:

> We don't make war against any people in particular. We are exterminating the bourgeoisie as a class. In your investigations don't look for documents and pieces of [any other type of] evidence about what the defendant has done . . . The first question you should ask him is what class he comes from, what are his roots, his education, his training . . ."[133]

Latsis was being faithful to Lenin's instructions, including the need for the harshest possible punishment for various classes of culprits. In Latsis' case, the class was that of the bourgeois. In a speech delivered by Lenin to the Workers' Assembly in 1918, the culprits were referred to as "speculators" and enemies of the proletariat:

> The Soviet regime has acted in the way that all revolutionary proletariats should act; it has made a clean break with bourgeois justice, which is an instrument of the oppressive classes . . . [A]s long as we fail to treat speculators the way they deserve—with a bullet in the head—we will not get anywhere at all.[134]

3. *Private Trade During the "War Communism": Bagmen and Entrepreneurial Factory Workers*

Lenin's New Economic Policy was largely a reaction to the failure of a policy known as "War Communism." Following the revolution and the USSR's exit from the First World War, it became engulfed in its own civil war between the military supporters of the revolution (The Red Army) and the conservative defenders of the old regime or of a new parliamentary democracy (The White Army). This war also proved quite costly. During 1918, Lenin's policy was to confiscate private businesses including factories, mines and mills,[135] fix the prices of consumer goods and create a network of state and cooperative stores under the direction of local soviets as the distribution outlets.[136] Shortly thereafter, private sales of commodities were banned and private trade was totally forbidden, especially on agricultural and manufactured products.[137] Yet, by 1920 it was clear that War Communism was an economic and political failure: The majority of the private enterprises, lacking trained management, remained in private hands; and the scarcity of agricultural products was such that hunger spread throughout the land.[138]

Despite the prohibition of private trade, and because of the difficulties in obtaining merchandise from governmental outlets, trade continued and grew in the hands of small merchants described by Professor Alan M. Ball of Marquette University as:

> [H]ighly mobile, small scale operators. Many, known as bagmen, [who] journeyed to the countryside in order to trade for a sack or two of food, which

---

[133] *Id.* at 8.

[134] *Id.* at 59 (citation omitted).

[135] *See* BALL, *supra* note 25, at 5–6.

[136] *Id.* at 6.

[137] *Id.*

[138] *Id.* at 6–7.

they consumed or resold back in the towns. As permanent shops were closed, private trade swelled outdoor bazaars and markets. Here bagmen, peasants (to whom the term *bagmen* was also applied at times), and others offered their wares while the authorities looked the other way . . .[139]

Professor Ball also quotes a vivid description by the Soviet journalist Victor Serge of another type of private trade during War Communism. After explaining how soaring inflation deterred sellers from accepting cash and how this lead to widespread barter, he described trade in "dead factories," among other venues:

> In the dead factories, the workers spent their time making penknives out of bits of machinery, or shoe-soles out of the conveyor-belts, to barter them on the underground market . . . If you wished to procure a little flour, butter, or meat from the peasants who brought these things illicitly into town, you had to have cloth or articles of some kind to exchange . . .[140]

4. The New Economic Policy

In February 1921, Lenin proposed the enactment of a "New Economic Policy" (NEP) in yet another of his pamphlets entitled "The Tax in Kind."[141] This policy compelled peasants to deliver a certain amount of grain as payment of their tax in kind. Having paid this tax, they were allowed to sell the remainder of their production in local markets. However, on May 24, 1921 a decree from the *Sovnarkom*, also enacted at Lenin's urging, "permitted not only the free sale of surplus food . . . but also trade by other citizens of goods produced by small-scale private manufacturers. These sales were not restricted to marketplaces and bazaars but could be conducted from permanent facilities as well as from stalls, booths . . ."[142] Shortly thereafter, the *Sovnarkom* declared "that anyone over sixteen [years of age] could obtain the license that was now required to sell agricultural and manufactured goods from a permanent shop or in a market square."[143]

Lenin's justification for such a fundamental reversal was pragmatic and a bow to the inevitable:

> A wise Communist will not be afraid of learning from a capitalist . . . Did we not in the Red Army (which was partly created from officers and men of the old tsarist army) learn to . . . single out the honest and conscientious, and on the whole, to utilize . . . tens of thousands of military experts? . . . We shall learn to do the same . . . with the commission agents, with the buyers who are working for the state, with the little-cooperator capitalists, with the entrepreneur concessionaires, etc . . .[144]

---

139 *Id.* at 7.

140 *Id.* (citation omitted).

141 V.I. Lenin, *The Tax in Kind (The Significance of the New Policy and its Condition), in* 32 Collected Works 329 (1st English ed., Progress Publishers 1965) (1921), *available at* http://www.marxists.org/archive/lenin/works/1921/apr/21.htm (on file with author).

142 BALL, *supra* note 25, at 20.

143 *Id.*

144 *See Document 5*, DOCUMENT PACKET—THE RUSSIAN REVOLUTION, http://www.historyteacher.net/APEuroCourse/DocPackets/DocsPacket-RussianRevolution.pdf (last visited Oct. 22, 2013) (on file with author). Document 5 describes Lenin's New Economic Policy (NEP) of 1921. *See also infra* § 17:4(A). The

In fact, he was faced with a revolt of peasants and soldiers formerly supportive of Bolshevism, and he only had two choices: either postpone socialism or face the downfall of his revolution. He chose to legalize much of the same private trade he had forbidden two years earlier. Such was the birth of the NEP, a policy that governed internal private trade between 1921 and 1929.[145]

5. *The Nepmen and a Commercial and Economic Revival*

Foreign visitors with different political views were unanimous in their praise of the revival of marketplaces in the USSR shortly after the enactment of the NEP. Professor Ball quotes Emma Goldman, an anarchist and feminist writer, for the following report:

> The new economic policy turned Moscow into a vast market place. Trade became the new religion. Shops and stores sprang up overnight, mysteriously stacked with delicacies Russia had not seen for years. Large quantities of butter, cheese, and meat were displayed for sale; pastry, rare fruit, and sweets of every variety . . . what was but yesterday considered a heinous offense was now flaunted . . . in an open and legal manner.[146]

A similar impression was obtained by the United States industrialist and investor Armand Hammer:

> I rubbed my eyes in astonishment. Was this Moscow, the city of squalor and sadness, that I had left? Now the streets that had been so deserted were thronged with people. Everyone seemed in a hurry, full of purpose, with eager faces . . . workmen tearing down the boarding from the fronts of stores, repairing broken windows, painting, plastering. From high-piled wagons goods were being unloaded into the stores . . .[147]

As noted by Emma Goldman, most of the private trade concerned consumer goods, with food representing, even during the later years of the NEP, approximately forty percent to fifty percent of the NEP trade.[148] Starting in 1921, the government ranked traders, also referred to as Nepmen, in accordance with the nature and size of their businesses. The higher ranks paid the higher fees or licenses and taxes. The lowest ranks were populated by the smaller merchants including bagmen and peddlers, and, in an ascending scale, retailers and wholesalers, who employed a progressively larger number of workers, moved more goods and stored them in larger premises.[149] One of Professor Ball's statistical tables shows that during 1922, 141,400 traders were predominantly bagmen and peddlers while approximately double that number worked as individual merchants in fixed locations.[150]

---

reader will discover a similar utilization of a tax in kind by Chinese emperors attempting to boost agricultural production more than a thousand years earlier. *Id.*

145 BALL, *supra* note 25, at 10. The following sections summarize Professor Ball in *id.*

146 *Id.* at 85. This cites a letter by the renowned U.S. anarchist and feminist Emma Goldman who had been born in Russia and immigrated to the United States.

147 *Id.* This source cites the letter written by Armand Hammer in August 1921 (and is transcribed, in part, by Ball).

148 *Id.* at 86.

149 *Id.* at 87.

150 *Id.* at 91.

Interestingly, state agencies became the principal suppliers of manufactured goods to Nepmen. For example, the number of ordinarily scarce and expensive vehicles sold by state agencies to Nepmen during 1927 was surprising considering the poverty of the USSR at that time: 1,661 cars and trucks and 4,000 motorcycles. The latter would have been sold to the public at several thousand rubles a piece but were purchased by the Nepmen at 400 to 500 rubles each.[151] The difference in the prices paid by the Nepmen to the state agencies and those at which the cars would have been sold to the public by the latter (had they had willing buyers) reflected the breakdown of the pricing system for state manufactured goods. The Nepmen's version of the prices for those manufactured goods was much more realistic than those projected by the state agencies. This is a point to be remembered as we discuss state economic planning.

The same statistics indicated how official cooperative retail stores were being displaced by Nepmen. For every 10,000 inhabitants of the countryside in 1924–1925, there were six cooperative shops, one state store, and thirty-one licensed private trading (Nepmen) operations. In fact, the actual number of private traders was much higher than originally reported because in the countryside it was quite easy to trade on a small scale without a license. According to the Central Statistical Bureau, by the time of their demise Nepmen handled over eighty percent of urban retail trade.[152]

Nevertheless, the economic revival facilitated by the Nepmen was only modest. Poverty in the USSR was far from eradicated by the NEP. During the NEP, much of the authorized trade was still of the survival type: people from different professions and walks of life who had to barter their valuable personal possessions "in quest of food, clothing and fuel."[153]

6. The Nepmen's Informal Commercial Contracts

As apparent from the above government classification of traders, Nepmen included a broad spectrum of merchants, artisans, manufacturers and financiers including a category that both Lenin and Professor Ball referred to as "speculators."[154] Professor Ball adds that Nepmen sprung up as a commercial class not only in the USSR. He found economic policies and legislation "strikingly similar" to that of the USSR in socialist countries such as Yugoslavia, Hungary and China.[155]

During the late 1970s, a recent Soviet immigrant to the United States described to me the genesis of a set of unofficial, informal or black market contracts he and many of his co-workers entered into in the shadow of the economic plans I will discuss shortly. His official job was as a "dispatcher" or clerk in charge of scheduling and supervising the delivery, pick-ups and shipments of the goods produced by a governmental industrial plant. He was supposed to instruct his pick-up drivers on what segments of their shipments they had to deliver to the distributors or users as mentioned in an official list (inspired by an economic plan). He would also indicate to the drivers which portions of the shipments were to be set aside for "unofficial" distribution. The proceeds of the latter would be shared by participants in this unplanned and unofficial

---

151 *Id.* at 110.

152 *Id.* at 111.

153 *Id.* at 88.

154 *Id.* at xvi.

155 *Id.*

distribution scheme, including drivers, clerks, some production workers, informal merchants (retail or wholesale) and, last but not least, plant managers. Clearly, this set of transactions amounted to a more inclusive barter than the one in the USSR's "dead factories" during the War Communism of 1917 and 1918.

He added that this was indeed a widespread method of "doing business" in the informal sector. Factory workers had no qualms about this trade because their families needed the supplemental income and they were also aware of the embezzlement of state property by Communist Party "bigwigs." Participants in these informal or black market schemes routinely relied on informal, mostly oral "commercial" agreements with their counter-parties. Some agreements involved the distribution of the earnings among those involved in the transportation and warehousing of the goods. Others apportioned responsibility for the bribes to government officials, and others for the losses of goods due to accidents or disasters, thereby echoing the role of self-insurance in official commercial legal systems. Others were entered with the clandestine wholesalers which included consignment sale provisions, and so on. They were mostly entered into orally or through highly informal writings but were supported by a firm understanding of who would resolve the disputes among the contracting parties. Disputes were not too frequent, but many transactions were controlled by "a sort of a mafia and if participants did not behave as they were supposed to, they would be punished."[156]

A few years later, a Cuban émigré gave me a similar description of the informal commercial contracts and dispute resolution mechanisms that prevailed in the state-owned plant in which he worked in Cuba. He added that the job of dispatcher was in fact one of the most sought after by plant workers. In some factories, the plant manager would even conduct an informal bidding for such a job. He added that workers in some of the plants in which he worked had invented ingenious profitable schemes that operated across a group of state enterprises. These schemes operated as "recycling cooperatives" designed to supplement the income generated by the sale of plant "dispatched" products. One of these schemes involved the replacement of "healthy" light bulbs in the various plants or government offices with "spent" or "dead" light bulbs. Workers would bring spent bulbs that they had collected from friends and relatives to their plant or office and surreptitiously install them as replacement for the healthy bulbs. The latter would be secreted out and sold "for good money" in the informal or black market; profits would be shared among the participants in the "recycling cooperatives," including plant managers.

a. Speculators, Their Cash and Pricing System

Why did so many Nepmen succeed in selling what state cooperatives and retail outlets had been unable to? The methods employed by a class of traders to whom Lenin referred to as "speculators" provide a good indication. This was a class whom Lenin despised and yet he acknowledged he could not distinguish from other traders: "*It is impossible* to distinguish speculation from "correct" trade if speculation is to be understood in the politico-economic sense. Freedom of trade is capitalism, capitalism is speculation: it would be ridiculous to close our eyes to this."[157]

---

[156] As told to me by this Soviet immigrant taxi driver.

[157] SERVICE, *supra* note 13, at 430.

Nonetheless, to keep one's eyes open to speculative trade meant that upon discovering such a trader the communist's duty was, as Lenin stated in a speech to an assembly of workers in 1918, "to put a bullet through their heads."[158] Thanks to Professor Ball's description of the various types of traders, it is possible to identify some of the archetypal features of the speculators. Their business usually involved more parties or sources than were customary in the lower ranks of retail trade, such as bagmen, peddlers and owners of very small establishments. Their "cooperative retail network" enabled them to acquire and dispose of merchandise more efficiently and resourcefully, or, as Professor Ball suggests, "deviously."[159]

Another feature attributable mostly to speculators would be their access to cash. This access was facilitated by the speculators' realistic pricing system. Being closer to their customers than were the state agencies and cooperatives, speculators knew how much customers would be willing to pay for the goods offered by those state agencies or cooperatives. Usually the realistic price would be one below that being asked by the official sellers, although on many occasions they could obtain higher amounts for the same products offered by the government if they could deliver them sooner or in larger quantities. Another unmentioned factor but one that usually made a difference in the informal trade was the speculator's willingness to extend credit. Being able to offer realistic prices to their customers, they were able to sell more quickly for ready cash than did the state agencies and cooperatives. Aided by their accumulated cash, they were able to purchase at the lowest prices from the chronically cash-starved state agencies, whose cash was limited strictly to central planning allotments for wages and indispensable equipment. Please recall the earlier reference to the vehicles sold by state agencies to Nepmen during 1927. The same vehicles that the state agencies attempted to sell to the public for several thousand rubles a piece wound up being purchased by the Nepmen at 400 to 500 rubles each.[160]

b. Legal and Questionable Transactions

The speculators' cash flow stemmed from transactions that were occasionally legal or above board, and more frequently legally questionable, downright illegal or the product of devious simulations.[161] All of these transactions had something in common: they supplied goods or occasionally services that consumers otherwise would not have been able to obtain, and for a price they were willing to pay.

Professor Ball describes transactions that on their surface appeared to be lawful but below the surface were of questionable legality. In one of them, a Nepman dealt with a state entity whose official function was to publish military literature.[162] The Nepman purchased cartloads of print paper and expensive stationery at extremely low prices. Yet, as that entity's cash flow worsened, the Nepman was able to buy from it other goods of an unexplained origin and usage in that enterprise—musical instruments, first-aid kits and even bicycles. Such a motley inventory indicated that this state entity had been engaged in significant informal and possibly illegal bartering on its own with other producers, suppliers or purchasers. Similarly, another Nepman

---

158 COURTOIS ET AL, *supra* note 131, at 59 (citation omitted).

159 Ball, *supra* note 25, at 109.

160 *Id.* at 110.

161 *See supra* § 14:4(A)(3)(c)(iii) (discussing simulations of commercial contracts).

162 *See* BALL, *supra* note 25, at 110.

dealing with a state agency whose function was to breed livestock acquired from it large numbers of scythes and large quantities of sugar, salt, oats and hay.[163] In due course, the Nepman also purchased from this agency purebred horses which it subsequently sold or rented to private persons for their use in horse races.

In order to obtain goods from official outlets, including cooperatives, Nepmen enlisted their own relatives and friends or hired invalids and unemployed people to stand in for them in the suppliers' long lines.[164] Some of the buyers, such as the invalids, were known to "rent" their subsidy documents to the Nepmen or their surrogates. Professor Ball also notes other practices designed to eliminate the need for a "middleman," such as by obtaining multiple copies of official cooperative membership books and ration cards.[165]

c. *Simulated and Illegal Transactions*

Side by side with these questionable transactions were others that were downright illegal, simulated, or both. As in the case of the "dispatchers" described earlier by the Soviet and Cuban émigrés, some employees provided the proper "façade" for the forbidden transaction.[166] They would open one or more stores or warehouses usually in the name of a relative or business associate who would act as the distributors and joint venturers with the "dispatcher" and his partners in the state entity.

Other Nepmen engaged in both downright illegal and simulated transactions. For example, a Nepman "C" representing a private firm with no capital contracted to supply a state factory "A" with nine hundred tons of oil in return for that firm's large quantity of steel pipe.[167] After promising the steel pipe to state enterprise "B" in exchange for roofing iron, C, with the active cooperation of naval yard employees, stole the oil he had promised to A. He then sold the steel pipe he had received from A to B and wound up with a large amount of roofing iron delivered by B, which he then sold to "D." C shared the proceeds of the sale with the cooperative naval yard employees. Keep this transaction in mind as we study the methods of some of the oligarchs during the beginnings of the Russian federation in the early 1990s in the following chapter.

d. *The Demise of the Nepmen and* Kulaks

Private trade did not last much after Lenin's death in 1924. Already during his life, it had become a significant point of contention within the Communist Party and among the group of his possible successors. In 1924, a year which the orthodox Marxists had labeled "the year of the second revolution," 300,000 private enterprises were closed together with churches and other bastions of the bourgeoisie.[168]

By the end of the 1920s, very few Nepmen could conduct business openly and were relegated to clandestine transactions. *Kulaks* fared the worst. Please recall Lenin's earlier quote: "Freedom of trade is capitalism, [and] capitalism is speculation: it would

---

163 *Id.*

164 *Id.* at 118.

165 *Id.*

166 *See supra* § 15:4(D)(6).

167 *See* BALL, *supra* note 25, at 115.

168 BALL, *supra* note 25, at 39.

be ridiculous to close our eyes to this."[169] Then, ponder the spirit of a letter he sent to a regional group of Bolsheviks on August 11, 1918:

> Comrades! The insurrection of five *Kulak* districts should be *pitilessly* suppressed. The interests of the *whole* revolution require this because 'the last decisive battle' with the *kulaks* is now under way *everywhere*. An example must be demonstrated.
>
> 1. Hang (and make sure that the hanging takes place *in full view of the people) no fewer than one hundred* known *kulaks*, rich men, bloodsuckers.
> 2. Publish their names.
> 3. Seize *all* their grain from them.
> 4. Designate hostages in accordance with yesterday's telegram.
>
> Do it in such a fashion that for hundreds of kilometres around the people might see, tremble, know, shout: *they are strangling* and will strangle to death the bloodsucking *kulaks*.
>
> Telegraph receipt and *implementation*.
>
> Yours, Lenin.
>
> Find some truly hard people.[170]

In line with Lenin's admonition on *Kulaks* and other "rich men and bloodsuckers" and Stalin's own concern about the *Kulaks* leading an insurrection in the Ukraine, millions of *Kulaks* were killed and "liquidat[ed] . . . as a class" by Joseph Stalin during the early 1930s.[171]

E. Economic Planning as a Source of Administrative-Contract Law

Upon Lenin's death, the fate of the NEP was sealed. A hard line faction of the Communist Party which included Joseph Stalin decided to abandon the NEP in favor of a more rapid development of the economy through industrialization and the construction of major public works. The markets opened by the Nepmen, now in the hands of the state, would become a source of funding for the production of consumer and capital goods and large infrastructure and electric power projects.

The economic initiatives of the state would be guided by national economic plans that would replace the private marketplace of the Nepmen as the engine of economic growth of the USSR. As usual, Lenin was also the source. The NEP would be in effect for a few years, but during this time the Central Committee of the Communist Party should make sure that a "uniform economic plan for the entire state" would be prepared.[172]

---

[169] SERVICE, *supra* note 13, at 430.

[170] *Id.* at 365. This letter was repressed during the Soviet period, having been located by Professor Service, it now appears in his biography of Lenin.

[171] *See Stalin's Forced Famine 1932–1933, 7,000,000 Deaths*, THE HISTORY PLACE GENOCIDE IN THE 20TH CENTURY, http://www.historyplace.com/worldhistory/genocide/stalin.htm (last accessed Oct.22, 2013) (on file with author). This source discusses "liquidating the *Kulak*s as a class" and provides a summary of Stalin's policies.

[172] SERVICE, *supra* note 13, at 430.

Under these national economic plans, there was little room for contractual bargaining between or among state agencies that acted as suppliers, manufacturers and distributors of goods and services. Whatever these parties agreed to had to be consistent with central planning goals and requirements.[173] Economic planning, then, acted as the administrative law that governed the production and distribution of goods and services throughout the Marxist-Leninist world.

Soviet economic theorists asserted that planning was "based on a profound knowledge and application of objective socialist economic laws . . . independent of the personal will and desires of individuals."[174] Accordingly, they defined centralized planning as "the conscious application of economic laws to benefit the people through effective use of all natural resources and productive forces."[175]

Planners had to identify production targets, costs and prices and had to allocate necessary resources to each, all of which depended upon the collection of relevant data under the direction of the Central Committee of the Communist Party once it had formulated the economic goals for each economic sector. It is important to emphasize that the goals formulated by the Central Committee guided not only the drafting of the economic plans but also was mandatory administrative-contract law for those entities and officials tasked with executing or implementing the plans. As noted by the Library of Congress:

> Economic plans had the force of law. Traditionally, they had been worked out down to the level of the individual economic enterprise, where they were reflected in a set of output goals and performance indicators that management was expected to maintain.
>
> Operationally, short-range planning was the most important aspect of the planning process for production and resource allocation . . . They covered one calendar year and encompassed the entire economy . . . [they] were broken down into quarterly and monthly plans, which served as . . . blueprints for the day-to-day operation of industrial and other economic enterprises and organizations.
>
> The five-year plan provided continuity and direction by integrating the yearly plans into a longer time frame. Although the five-year plan was duly enacted into law, it contained a series of guidelines rather than a set of direct orders . . .[176]

Once the goals were identified, the methodology of planning was as follows:

> The method used by Gosplan . . . [the state planning commission of the USSR and is constituent republics] was called the system of *material balances* . . . [It] consisted of preparing balance sheets in which available material, labor, and financial resources were listed as assets and plan requirements as

---

[173] *Soviet Union: Economic Planning and Control*, COUNTRY-DATA.COM, http://www.country-data.com/cgi-bin/query/r-12704.html (last accessed Oct. 22, 2013) (on file with author). The discussion on Soviet planning in this section summarizes this fine study found in the Federal Research Division of the Library of Congress, Country Studies Series.

[174] *Id.*

[175] *Id.*

[176] *Id.*

> liabilities. The . . . planners . . . balance[d] resources and requirements to ensure that the necessary inputs were provided . . . [The] central authorities specified detailed output goals, investment projects, and supply plans for only key branches of the economy.
>
> . . .
>
> The control figures were sent in disaggregated form downward through the planning hierarchy to production and industrial associations (various groupings of related enterprises) . . . Individual enterprises at the base of the planning pyramid were called upon to develop the most detailed plans covering all aspects of their operations . . .
>
> [A]s the individual enterprise formulated its detailed draft production plans, the flow of information was reversed . . .[177]

Although Soviet theorists searched for a balance between severe centralization and local initiative, Stalin himself was a "confirmed centralizer."[178] Very few Marxist leaders rejected such a policy. Marshall Tito of Yugoslavia was one of them, and he referred to it as the "cancer of socialism."[179] He attempted a program of decentralization and reduction of planning along the lines suggested by capitalist and socialist critics of central planning. Some of the points made by these critics deserve special attention because they focus on a function of commercial contracts that capitalist lawyers and economists alike tend to take for granted.

F. Market Socialism and Market Prices: Ludwig von Mises' Criticism

Missing or imprecise data on suppliers, producers and consumers, including the desirable quantity, quality and the prices of the produced goods or services, made the calculation of production costs and prices for finished products difficult if not impossible. In 1920, just a couple of years after the instauration of the USSR, the Austrian economist Ludwig von Mises pointed out that Marxist socialism was incapable of rational economic planning precisely because of the lack of reliable information on prices for consumer goods and services, among other indicators.[180] Von Mises warned that without market prices:

> [T]here is no possibility of allocating resources on the basis of consumer preferences . . . [or] of calculating costs or revenues and no way of knowing if products most highly valued by consumers have been produced . . . [For] rational calculation, in the sense of adjusting production to the satisfaction of human wants, is impossible in a centrally directed economy from which prices are necessarily absent. The market, in contrast, allocates resources on the basis of expected profitability . . .[181]

---

177 *Id.* (emphasis added).

178 HAZARD ET AT., *supra* note 40, at 209.

179 *Id.*

180 *See* LUDWIG VON MISES, SOCIALISM: AN ECONOMIC AND SOCIOLOGICAL ANALYSIS, 113–22 (1951), *available at* http://mises.org/books/socialism/contents.aspx. *See also* F. A. HAYEK, INDIVIDUALISM AND ECONOMIC ORDER 149–52 (1963). This source provides related criticisms.

181 *See* E.C. Pasour, Jr., *Land-Use Planning: Implications of the Economic Calculation Debate,* 7 J. LIBERTARIAN STUD. 127, 127–28 (1983) (on file with author).

By focusing on the need for an accurate mechanism to establish prices, von Mises was pointing to the need for negotiated or bargained-for commercial and consumer contracts. Please recall that, as discussed in the previous section, the access to such contractual information was behind the success of many of the Nepmen—for it was only the contractual-bargain mechanism that truly reflected what merchants and consumers were willing to pay for goods and services.

It was for this reason that von Mises' disciple Frederick Hayek, among other distinguished free market economists, predicted that the real and necessary data would continue to be unavailable.[182] Despite these warnings, the Soviet planners "stated goal was to provide basic goods in 'sufficient' quantities at low prices by directing production resources from luxury goods to the production of ... basic goods"[183] without reliable demand and pricing inputs.

G. Yevsey Liberman's Autonomy of Production, Profitability Rate and Economic Planning

During the November 1962 Plenum of the Communist Party of the USSR, Nikita Khruschev (who became First Secretary General of the Communist Party in 1953 following Stalin's death and a bloody period of a violent struggle for succession) quoted one of Lenin's pragmatisms: "Be able if necessary to learn from the capitalists. Adopt whatever they have that is sensible and advantageous."[184] He then endorsed the views of Professor Yevsey Liberman of the Kharkov Engineering and Economics Institute. As reported by Wellesley College Professor Marshall I. Goldman, Liberman proposed three goals for Soviet economic reform and implied the need to fulfill several others.[185]

The first goal was to stimulate Soviet producers to seek higher output targets. Because the economic plans rewarded producers when they fulfilled the quotas or allotments set forth in the national plans, managers of state enterprises set their targets of production as low as possible; the lower they set their targets, the greater was the likelihood of their fulfillment[186] And with fulfillment of such low goals came bonuses and rewards. Liberman's second goal was to encourage the adoption of new technology that could help produce more desirable products.[187] Even though this was a much-needed goal, it was strongly opposed by managers and their superiors who perceived the safety of their jobs as tied to the bureaucratic *status quo*. The third goal was to improve the quality of production. Yet, because incentives were tied to quantity, producers did not care about high quality standards. Their use of better raw materials and components made it difficult to meet the plan's lowest production cost-figures.[188]

---

[182] *Id.* at 130. Hayek's skepticism on the availability of the required data stems from the fact that "the 'data' from which the economic calculus starts are never for the whole society 'given' to a single mind which could work out the implications and can never be so given . . ." *Id.*

[183] David R. Henderson et al., *The Hidden Inequality in Socialism*, 9 INDEP. REV. 389, 390–91 (2005).

[184] *See* Marshall I. Goldman, *Economic Controversy in the Soviet Union*, 41 FOREIGN AFFAIRS 498, 498 (1963), *available at* http://www.foreignaffairs.com/issues/2010/89/4 (on file with author). The principal text summarizes some of the relevant sections in Goldman's excellent essay.

[185] *Id.* at 499.

[186] *Id.*

[187] *Id.*

[188] *Id.* at 499–500.

One of Liberman's anti-centralist suggestions was to eliminate what he called "petty tutelage"[189] and encourage the autonomy of state enterprises. Customarily, senior planners spelled out everything in detail with no room for discretion by the managers of state enterprises. This led to highly costly and inefficient decisions. For instance, in one factory, scrap metal was mistakenly mixed in with brand new metal parts. The manager of the state enterprise requested a budgetary addition to pay for the extra work of sorting the scrap metal and recovering as many of the recently-produced parts as possible. The request was denied because no funds were available under the national or local plans' budgetary allotments for additional personnel. "As a result, 2,000 rubles in wages was saved but 10,000 rubles in metal parts was lost."[190]

Perhaps the most unconventional of Liberman's suggestions was to link bonuses to the plant's profitability rather than on its meeting quantitative targets. Profitability would not take into account the fulfillment of central planning goals except for quantity of production, product assortment and destination and date of delivery. The "profitability rate" did not rely on the traditional socialist and USSR measure of profit which resulted from subtracting imprecise costs from similarly imprecise revenues. Instead, it resulted from establishing a ratio between gross income and fixed and working capital. This ratio would be the sole determinant of the size of the bonus fund awarded to the plant and its employees. It was a more comprehensive and precise ratio than that relied upon by Marx when trying to identify the surplus value supposedly appropriated by capitalists.[191] Any improvement in either of the two components would earn the plant manager and his workers a higher rate and a bonus or other reward. Producers could decrease the cost of labor, raw materials and other resources or they could reduce the amount of fixed and working capital by reducing their request for capital from the national government.[192]

H. The Debate on Libermanism

1. In the USSR

Liberman's proposals provoked a sharp and long debate inside and outside the Soviet Union. As summarized by Professor Goldman, the detractors were a mixture of Marxist purists, opposed to profit making as a goal of state entities, and supporters of heavy industries as a development tool.[193] I would add to that list a Latin American utopian Marxist who was also a harsh totalitarian. The purists asked questions such as: Was not Liberman's reliance on profit in relation to capital tantamount to capitalism with its cyclical unemployment and price fluctuations? Would not factory managers focus on nothing but the maximization of factory profits, shifting away from heavy industry toward the production of consumer goods with higher profit margins?

It should be remembered that the principle of self-sustainability of state enterprises and its rigorous cost accounting was attributable to Lenin's directives, who ordered state agencies in the early 1920s "to operate on a cost-accounting (*khozraschet*) [or *Khozrachiot*] basis. [This meant] . . . that they could no longer rely on the state to

---

189 *Id.* at 500.

190 *Id.*

191 *See supra* § 15:3(C)(2).

192 GOLDMAN, *supra* note 184, at 502.

193 *Id.* at 504–05.

provide them with raw materials, pay their workers, and absorb their finished products regardless of how inefficiently they operated."[194] Ironically, as I just discussed, it was precisely the absence of steady and reliable streams of revenue with which to cover their costs of operation that drove many of these state enterprises into the hands of the Nepmen.

2. *Cuba: The Commercial vs. The New Socialist Man*

The Cuban debate on *khozraschet* and self-sufficiency of state enterprises involved, among others, Marcelo Fernandez Font (Fernandez) one of the Castro revolution's ablest young leaders,[195] and none other than "Che" Guevara (Guevara) who had been entrusted with guiding the economy as presidents of Cuba's National (or Central) Bank. Fernandez's views were supported by some cabinet officers and visiting Marxist intellectuals. Guevara was pretty much on his own. While the debate covered a broad number of issues on the interpretation of Marx's "The Capital," including his theory of value, the issues of most interest arose in connection with Fernandez's proposed adoption by Cuba's National Bank of Liberman's principle of self-sufficiency and profitability of state enterprises and its cost accounting corollary of *khozraschet.*

In an article published in *Cuba Socialista,* Cuba's most authoritative governmental policy journal,[196] Fernandez, just appointed president of the Central Bank, explained why the bank should adopt the *khozraschet* or *khozrachot* accounting principle.[197] This principle had been adopted by some Cuban state entities. As suggested by Liberman, the principle required that:[198] 1) the management of these entities follow the directives of the national economic plans; 2) the enterprise be autonomous, and be empowered to manage its resources; 3) a direct relationship with other state enterprises exist on an egalitarian basis; 4) it be self-sustaining or cover expenses with its own profits; 5) it be enabled to utilize banking credit to supplement its own resources; and 6) it reward especially productive employees with bonuses and other awards.

---

194 BALL, *supra* note 25, at 109.

195 HUGH THOMAS, CUBA, OR, THE PURSUIT OF FREEDOM 910 (Da Capo Press 1998) (1931). Thomas, one of the most reliable chroniclers of the Castro revolution, describes Marcelo Fernandez Font in this book as among the leaders of the 26th of July (Castro's) movement in Havana and refers to him as part of a group of young intellectual leaders including Javier Pazos, Luis de la Cuesta, Manuel Couzeiro and Raul Roa Garcia who became supporters of that movement in 1956. He properly characterized their joinder of that movement as one of the most important intellectual accretions it ever gained. I had met Marcelo Fernandez at the University of Havana through my friend Luis de la Cuesta and was impressed with his idealism, seriousness and studiousness. He became the National Coordinator of the Castro revolution, and subsequently was an Ambassador to the USSR, Minister of Foreign Trade and President of the National Bank of Cuba. Luis de la Cuesta was a fellow student and an extraordinary human being who through his intelligence and selflessness became the informal but effective coordinator of that highly effective group of young intellectuals. With the exception of Marcelo Fernandez, most of the group that Luis de la Cuesta coordinated fled Castro's Cuba after having been given positions of importance. Luis de la Cuesta, for example, acted for a few months as a *de facto* Minister of Culture mostly in charge of educational publications and art programs. Naively, he thought that he could publish the works of the world's great thinkers, novelists and playwrights of the twentieth century in cheap and highly readable editions. Very quickly he was disabused of that notion—his job was mostly to publish Fidel Castro's interminable speeches.

196 Marcelo Fernández Font, *Desarrollo y Funciones de la Banca Socialista en Cuba,* 8 CUBA SOCIALISTA REVISTA MENSUAL 32 (1964) (on file with author).

197 *Id.* at 43–44.

198 *Id.* at 44.

He stressed that for Cuba's National or Central Bank to act as the issuer and supervisor of the use of Cuba's currency and of loans it made to state entities that it had to ascertain and monitor their creditworthiness. If Cuba continued to allow the numerous and repeated defaults of state enterprises on their loans, the Central Bank could no longer safeguard the island's financial stability. He urged that, even if the autonomy of state agencies was not granted, their financial viability and self-sufficiency be accepted as a *sine qua non.*[199]

In his response, Guevara found serious deficiencies in Fernandez's Marxist analysis and urged him to become a more serious student of Marx's "The Capital."[200] Had he been such a student, said Guevara, he would have learned that banking and credit belonged with the last phase of capitalism in its dialectical march toward communism. In that phase, the state acts as an agent for the exploitive monopoly of the banks. Thus, the credit relationships that Fernandez proposed to adopt made no sense once private ownership of the means of production was abolished. If one wished to build socialism as the conduit to communism, said Guevara:

> Collections and payments among state enterprises are inadmissible, as are all credit relationships. The national economy must operate as a large enterprise owned by the people . . . Thus, during the building of socialism all the concepts that governed [capitalist] central banks had to change . . .[201]

Guevara added that the emphasis should be in building up the morality of socialism and creating a new socialist man.[202]

Charles Bettelheim, a French Marxist economist and historian (and an invitee to the debate), pointed out that the changes required by the progression to socialism and to communism (as predicted by Marxist science) require, first of all, improvements in Cuba's productive capacity. The emphasis on a socialist morality and on the creation of a new socialist man were inconsistent with materialist dialectics, which placed economic factors such as production first, with ethical and legal factors in an ancillary position.[203] He added that Guevara's references to a "property of the people" were, given the low level of socialist development, abstract notions of little normative value. Further, the Cuban government was not yet in the position to determine what were Cuba's most urgent social needs because of the infancy of its planning procedures. Thus, while comprehensive planning was still unavailable, commercial considerations, as measured by state entities in Fernandez's proposal, had to continue.[204]

Guevara rejected Bettelheim's advice and insisted on the need to de-commercialize Cuba's marketplace and develop Cuba's new socialist man. He reiterated the Cuban revolution's aversion to the notion of a commercial and commercialized or "merchandised" man, with the attendant cost effectiveness and profit considerations, especially when all of the productive and distributive entities as well as their products

---

199 *Id.* at 47.

200 *See* Mcs. Teresa Machado Hernández, La polémica en torno a la ley del valor y su manifestación en el pensamiento marxista cubano 4 (2008) (unpublished conference paper), *available at* http://www.nodo50.org/cubasigloXXI/congreso08/conf4_machadoh2.pdf (on file with author).

201 *Id.* at 5–6.

202 *Id.* at 6.

203 *Id.*

204 *Id.* at 7.

belonged to the state. And finally, he asserted that the notions of socialist economic planning and market-determined prices and costs were completely incompatible.

In this debate, Guevara did not provide a detailed view of what he meant by a new Cuban socialist man. Elsewhere, in a long letter he sent to the editor of the Uruguayan socialist journal *Marcha*,[205] he attempted to fill in the details of his new socialist man. First, he equated him to the brave and courageous revolutionaries who created the conditions necessary for the victory against the Batista government:[206] "The (socialist) man of the future could be glimpsed in the attitude of our fighters."[207] He then recalled the heroism of those Cubans who selflessly risked life and limb to save others during the passage through Cuba of a 1963 hurricane.[208] It was their heroism and caring for others that had to be taught as part of the new revolutionary ideology and contrasted to the commercialistic attitude that views life "it is a race of wolves: he who arrives does so only at the expense of the failure of others."[209]

After listing the evils of the commercialist mentality, including the transformation of man and his work into a "merchandised man," he predicted an educational system in which the individual's work would be the fulfillment of the daily quota he owed society and his fellow beings. His performance of this duty would not be the result of a contract of sale but a sacred duty; its proper fulfillment was each worker's true legacy.[210] Please notice that this is not a duty that flows to a specific, identifiable person or group of persons; rather, it flows to his society at large and to his fellow beings. As once put to me by the legal philosopher Julius Stone: "A duty to everyone winds up being a duty to no one, except the dictator in charge."

After apologizing for what may have appeared as a "ridiculous" sentimentality, Guevara acknowledged that love for fellow man was central to the new Cuban socialist man. This was missed by many, and he confessed having to endure each day the "great drama of revolutionary leader; he must combine impassioned spirit with a cold mind and make painful decision without flinching."[211]

§ 15.5 CONCLUSIONS: AN INVERTEBRATE LEGAL SYSTEM AND ITS DISREGARD OF HUMAN NATURE

It is now time, then, to answer the related question posed early in this chapter: Why did Marxist-Leninist anti-commercialism fail to eradicate private trade from the USSR? Was it the fault of the official law they employed to banish it? Or was there something unworkable in the principles and policies that guided the official anti-commercial law? The answer to the latter two questions is in the affirmative. There was much that was unworkable in the principles and policies that guided their anti-commercialism, and it started with their mistaken perception of human nature and

---

205 *Letter from Major Ernesto Che Guevara to Carlos Quijano, editor of the Montevideo weekly magazine Marcha, in* ERNESTRO CHE BUEVARA, MAN AND SOCIALISM IN CUBA (Margarita Zimmermann trans., 1967), *available at* http://www.marxists.org/archive/guevara/1965/03/man-socialism-alt.htm.

206 Letter from Major Ernesto Che Guevara to Carlos Quijano, editor of the Montevideo weekly magazine Marcha, supra note 205, ¶ 5.

207 *Id.* ¶ 6.

208 *Id.* ¶ 7.

209 *Id.* ¶ 21.

210 *Id.* ¶ 43.

211 *Id.* ¶ 74.

commerce. They all shared a demonization of capitalism and commerce and a deification of proletarians. None seemed aware of the wisdom in the "Fable of the Bees."[212]

Roman A. Ohrenstein, an insightful historian of economic thought, called attention to the parallel between eighteenth century economic liberal and moral philosophical thought[213] such as in Bernard de Mandeville's famous satire "The Fable of the Bees." This satire was of considerable influence on Adam Smith's "Wealth of Nations,"[214] Thus, the apparently discordant passions strangely harmonize to the same end such that private vices are turned into public benefits. This is the phenomenon of commercial cooperation that one observes frequently in those societies that have managed to develop successful market economies.[215]

Adam Smith's *Wealth of Nations*, which Karl Marx read and cited assiduously, points out that the individual's exertion brings the greatest benefit not only to himself but also to society. For, Adam Smith's individual "neither intends to promote the public interest, nor knows how much he is promoting it . . . [He is] led by an invisible hand to promote an end which was no part of his intention . . . By pursuing his own interest he frequently promotes that of the society."[216] The same observation led Talmudic scholars many centuries earlier to point out that *there is good in evil as much as evil in good.*[217] In other words, even if commercial man were as evil as Lenin and Guevara perceived him to be, which as shown by socio-biologist E.O. Wilson he most definitely he is not, there is still much good in him and vice versa. Hence, much social good could come from self-centered capitalists and much evil surely came from the framers of the supposedly altruistic "new socialist man" under Lenin, Stalin, Mao Tse-tung, "Che" Guevara and others capable of mass murder "without the twitch of a muscle." In sum, for an effective regulation of legal and especially commercial conduct to be a productive tool for economic development, it must be able to rely on accurate perceptions of archetypal behavior. And these perceptions are not the product of the ivory tower of central planners but of the everyday practices of average and model merchants, including prominently their ability to gauge prices and other indicators of the acceptability of goods and services.

---

212 BERNARD DE MANDEVILLE, FABLE OF THE BEES 10 (1724).

213 *See* Roman A. Ohrenstein, *Economic Self-Interest and Social Progress in Talmudic Literature: A Further Study of Ancient Economic Thought and Its Modern Significance*, 29 AM. J. ECON. & SOC. 59, 60–61 (1970).

214 ADAM SMITH, 1 AN INQUIRY INTO THE NATURE AND CAUSES OF THE WEALTH OF NATIONS 87 (Edwin Cannan ed., 1904), *available at* http://www.econlib.org/library/Smith/smWN0.html#I.87. Edwin Cannan, the editor of this 1904 edition, notes in several places where Smith appears to have been influenced by Mandeville, *see id.* at 3, 10, 12, 14, & 102.

215 *See supra* § 1:2(A) (discussing the principle of commercial cooperation).

216 Adam Smith, the Wealth of Nations part 2, 160–61 (1902).

217 *See* Ohrenstein, *supra* note 213, at 63–64.

Chapter 16

THE PECULIAR MEANING OF SOVIET AND POST-SOVIET COMMERCIAL CONTRACTS: AN INVERTEBRATE LEGAL SYSTEM

§ 16.1 THE HIGHER LAW AS SLOGANS: CORRUPTION AND THE INVERTEBRATION OF THE SOVIET LEGAL SYSTEM

The preceding chapter discussed the Marxist-Leninist dogmas that, although voiced in places as distant from the Russian marketplace as Marx's desk no. 7 at the Reading Room of the British Museum or Lenin's University of Geneva classroom, inspired the Soviet enactment of principles such as state ownership of property, the prohibition of private property except for the few items considered "personal property," and the prohibition of income derived from private citizens paying wages or salaries to others. Despite the untried and untested nature of these dogmas, and the imprecise nature of the slogans they engendered, these dogmas became the higher law of the Soviet Legal system, a law whose effects were neither anticipated nor discussed with those whose interests were at stake. It was an authoritarian law promulgated totally by the top and formulated by very few.

This chapter focuses on the effect of the application of "grab by the neck" slogans such as Lenin's "He who does not work, neither shall he eat," which as will be recalled, was promulgated as a constitutional principle by Article 12 of the 1936 Constitution.[1] These slogans appeared in other higher or guiding laws or their functional equivalents as pronouncements of the supreme rulers, especially when attempting to regulate everyday contractual transactions involving both state property and the "personal property" of Soviet citizens.

The reader might ask: Why bother studying such an ineffective and discarded legal system? The main reason is, as also noted in the previous chapter, that this type of invertebrate legal system is apt to reappear at any time and place where law is applied in a totalitarian or autocratic fashion by a supreme leader and a privileged, above-the-law class of bureaucrats, regardless of their political or economic ideology or label. This type of higher law was as apparent in colonial law as it is in present day Latin America, Soviet and present-day Russia, and Imperial and present-day China.[2]

Those closest to the supreme ruler would try to please him by translating his slogans into legal-sounding principles, rules and doctrines of interpretation. But since the final interpreter of these slogans has always been he who issues them, a significant gap inevitably develops between what Justice Holmes referred to as the 'molar' and

---

[1] USSR CONST. art. 12 (1936); *see also* V. I. LENIN, THE STATE AND REVOLUTION 55, (Kessinger Publ'g 2004) (1918).

[2] *See, e.g., infra* §§ 17:4 & 18:3.

'molecular' versions of rules.[3] Totalitarians such as Lenin would be surprised by this chapter because it shows that, against their beliefs, what was "private" could not be eradicated. Through corruption and invertebretation, institutions designed to protect the "mine and thine" have and will reappear—although surely in a weaker fashion—than where private property and contract are the foundation of a thriving private law. The reason for their reappearance is that once man became a trader or "exchanger of commodities" (in the Marxist vocabulary), he also became, among other things, a cooperative being; and there is no cooperation without contract, any more than there is no contract without cooperation.

Hence, in the above-mentioned totalitarian regimes, the vertebrae or links between slogans or guiding principles and the legal institutions that are supposed to implement them start to wither away from the moment the process of implementation begins. And where commerce is concerned, invertebration continues throughout the production, distribution, acquisition and consumption of goods. Consider, for example, the following transactions as gleaned from court and arbitral decisions, administrative and judicial actions, and from commercial practices in Soviet Russia.

"A," a government official acting on behalf of Soviet Russia's central planning agency, directs a factory manager, "B," to produce a certain amount of a consumer goods, "C," at a certain price. This directive is supposed to implement another of Lenin's slogans which provided that "An equal amount of products [should be produced] for an equal amount of labour."[4] Yet, assume that once B receives his instruction from A he discovers that A did not take into account either the availability of all the raw materials needed to meet the overall production quota. He is also certain that A's fixed price was arrived at without surveying the preferences of the likely purchasers of C. Nonetheless, B decides to produce his first monthly share of the assigned quota with the raw materials made available to him. He also assumes that in the past, there was always a certain surplus of raw materials because of the excess amount of raw materials ordered to make it possible for Central planning officials to obtain their unofficial profits from sharing the commissions for exchanging rubbles for hard foreign currencies with foreign money exchangers.

At the end of B's first production cycle, "E," a truck dispatcher in charge of the delivery of C to their official and unofficial outlets, assigned one third of B's trucks to deliver C to unofficial outlets. The purchasers in these outlets were friends or relatives of B's participants in this unofficial scheme as well as friends of friends and relatives of the latter. This diversion from the official outlets, incidentally, occurred on a regular basis with the approval and profit participation of B and the other participants in this distribution scheme, although the percentages of their profits were allotted according to their administrative hierarchy in B. In addition, the participants included policemen in charge of guarding both the official and unofficial outlets and the judges (trial and appellate) in charge of adjudicating disputes concerning the supply of raw materials among agencies subject to the regulation of A as well as the delivery and quality of B's products.

---

[3] S. Pac. Co. v. Jensen, 244 U.S. 205, 221 (1917) (Holmes, J., dissenting) (noting the difference between "molar" (whole body of matter) and "molecular" (atomic components of matter) motions, illustrating the gap between principles and the concrete facts of a case).

[4] LENIN, *supra* note 1, at 80.

Following the end of B's first production cycle, it had no raw materials available with which to go on to the next production cycles. When aware of this problem, A started an inquiry on the reasons for the shortfall of raw materials. It quickly discovered that the shortage was attributable to the use of raw materials in producing goods diverted to unauthorized outlets. However, before A's planner filed his administrative and civil complaint, he was quickly made aware by the potential defendants that A's planners were known to have made tidy profits from the under-the-table commissions they received from the sellers of foreign exchange in return for the planners accepting to pay above-market rates of exchange.

Clearly, even if the most symmetrically hierarchical organizational chart of decision-makers had been set forth by the supreme rulers' most trusted bureaucrats to know how to do away with private property, the eradication of what were in the final analysis private rights and duties was rendered invertebrate by the corrupt behavior of all or most all participants in the production and distribution processes. Ironically, this corruption ushered a perverse version of private law, one where the contribution to social welfare mattered less than the manner in which each participant's take was made to appear consistent with the slogans and the higher law of state ownership. This is a lesson worth remembering by those who, mostly in their younger days, tend to be attracted by the claims to social justice of the revolutionary slogans of competing ideologies. As will be illustrated in the following sections, the cost of legal invertebration and the corruption that it feeds are simply too high for a society truly interested in its welfare and economic development.

A. Sources of Private ("Personal") Law and the Effect of Legal Nihilism

The distinction between the private law (as just defined) and the public law (or the law that governs the relations between the state, its agencies and "the governed") was not present, at least not officially, in Soviet Law, even though its Civil Code of 1922 acknowledged some private property rights such as a limited right to inherit family property.[5] Article 10 of the 1936 constitution of the USSR defined a type of property it referred to as "personal" which included the person's income from his work and savings, his dwelling houses and household furniture and utensils, and articles of personal use and convenience.[6] Yet, for personal property to be protected by official law, it could not be used in a manner that required hiring labor or paying wages (synonymous with the Marxist version of exploitation of man by man). Furthermore, whatever income was derived from using personal property in a manner that involved paying wages qualified as "unearned income"; the earner could wind up in jail and the payments he received could be forfeited together with the personal property involved. Even as late 1986 during Gorbachev's government, yet another official campaign was initiated against unearned income derived from the use of personal property.[7] Russians

---

[5] Samuel Kucherov, *Property in the Soviet Union*, 11 AM. J. COMP. L. 376, 377, 382 (1962) (quoting from a 1918 decree that abolished the right to inherit; and from the RSFSR Civil Code (1922) for the reinstatement of this right subject to severe limitations).

[6] USSR CONST. art. 10 (1936). *See infra* note 67 and accompanying text (citing full text of art. 10); *see also infra* § 16:4(C) (discussing personal property disputes).

[7] DAVID E. HOFFMAN, THE OLIGARCHS: WEALTH AND POWER IN THE NEW RUSSIA 38 (2002).

were confronted with questions such as: "Did you get unearned income by using your "bonus" car as a taxi? Selling your homegrown cucumbers and tomatoes?"[8]

In addition, the sources that governed trade among state entities or with these entities and private citizens, as well as the trade among private citizens, were part of the USSR's public law. This meant that what lawyers in western legal systems would regard as a contractual relationship governed by civil or commercial contract law would be, in the USSR, adjudicated mostly as part of an administrative action or criminal law complaint. The omnipresence of a contracting party who quite often was not only a contracting party, but also an administrator whose version of facts and law were to weigh much more than that of the contracting party, had *de facto* as well as *de jure* consequences.

Thus, an alleged breach of contract by a private consultant performing services for a state agency could easily become an administrative action or criminal law indictment against the private consultant at the instigation of his official client and co-contracting party.[9] Similarly, a breach of a promise to supply raw materials at a stipulated time made by a state entity to another could be characterized by a Soviet Arbitration Tribunal as a violation of an administrative duty owed by the infringer to all the participating state entities in the central economic plan, and called for an administrative fine with little or no relationship to the damages actually suffered by any of the aggrieved parties.[10] As apparent in many of the actions or disputes discussed in this chapter, the higher the political standing of the plaintiff-agent or agency, the more pre-determined was the outcome of the action or complaint. In fact, the mere characterization of the defendant's conduct by an official plaintiff as "exploitive," "capitalistic," "counter-revolutionary," etc., often foretold the outcome of the complaint.

Surely, the manner in which the sources of Soviet law were listed or referred to in official legal publications (such as constitutions, codes, statutes, decrees, decree laws and regulations) closely resembled that of civil law nations. But that is where the similarities ended. As emphasized in the preceding chapter, the writings of Marx and Lenin, despite their lack of official promulgation as laws or regulations (with few exceptions in the case of Lenin's constitutional principles), were the living and, in many instances, the supreme law of the USSR at least for the first two decades of Soviet rule. Further, Lenin's definition of law as nothing more than a "political measure" reinforced a climate of "legal nihilism" inspired by Marx's prophecy of a withering away of the state during the transition from socialism to communism.[11] This climate led some Soviet judges during this period to decide cases based upon what their consciences told them to do.[12]

However, following the chaos of the civil war of 1919–1920, Lenin decided that statutes and codes were needed to enhance the likelihood that the governmental prescriptions would be followed as dictated. Thus, he instituted a period of "legalism" or strict observance of the law. Yet, he made sure that the laws about to be enacted

---

[8] *Id.*

[9] JOHN N. HAZARD ET AL., THE SOVIET LEGAL SYSTEM 189 (3d ed. 1977). *See also infra* § 16:4(F)(1) n.124 and accompanying text.

[10] HAZARD ET AL., *supra* note 9, at 252–53, (Moscow Wool Case).

[11] *See infra* § 16:2(B)(1).

[12] HAZARD ET AL, *supra* note 9, at 5.

provided "escape clauses" that would make it possible for the autocrats to enforce revised versions of what they had enacted. Accordingly, the tsarist principle that conduct could be prosecuted as criminal if it was analogous to that described in codes or statutes was reenacted. Similarly, the Civil Code of 1922 allowed the judge to reject a code rule whose application was "out of keeping with the aims of the new society."[13]

Lenin's and subsequently Stalin's legislative activism was also consistent with a tsarist tradition of centralized legal authority and distrust for customary and judicially-made law, despite some allowances for the ancient customary law of peasant groups and indigenous people.[14] Leninist law distrusted customary and judge-made law because these sources provided an easy inroad for the remnants of a "bourgeois society" into the socialist system.[15] Stalin, on the other hand, enabled the highest court to become a law-making body that was subject to his tutelage. Once he was satisfied that he had a pliant and faithful judiciary, his Judiciary Act of 1938 granted special authority to the Plenum of the Supreme Court "[t]o give interpretations of the laws of the U.S.S.R.," thereby conferring upon it quasi-legislative powers.[16]

Few western legal scholars had the opportunity and ability to observe at close range the application of the law of the USSR, especially during Stalin's pre-World War II reign, as did Columbia University Law School's and Parker School's John Hazard. As the first United States graduate law student at Moscow's Juridical Institute in 1937, he was a witness to many of the events that shaped Stalinist law. His ability to place Soviet law succinctly in the proper socio-economic context and to shed light on the political and economic reasons behind it (and also above it) made him one of the most respected Soviet law experts in the world. In 1958, as a graduate student I attended his lectures at the *Faculté International de Droit Comparé* in Luxembourg and was privileged to be part of many illuminating conversations following these lectures. The following is my brief summary of what Professor John Hazard and his colleagues William E. Butler and Peter B. Maggs said about the hierarchy of the official sources of Soviet law.[17] In later sections, I will summarize some of the judicial decisions they and other Soviet law scholars translated into English to illustrate the application of some of these sources.[18]

B. Hierarchy

Despite the apparent orderly continental civil law-inspired hierarchy of the official law of the USSR, in practice this hierarchy was subject to the whims of the all-powerful executive branch. Hazard, Butler and Maggs pointed out the requirement set forth in the 1936 Constitution that only one body was responsible for legislation. This was a requirement insisted upon by Stalin, yet he among others was responsible for multi-sourced legislation—including through the issuance of numerous decree laws of pre-eminent status. Such disregard of the constitutionally-mandated hierarchy made the hierarchy of the wide array of enactments uncertain. Often, constitutional amendments initiated by executive branch bodies not authorized to do so were formally

---

[13] *Id.* at 6 (citation omitted).

[14] *Id.* at 47.

[15] *Id.*

[16] *Id.* at 48.

[17] HAZARD ET AL., *supra* note 9, at 47–50.

[18] *See infra* § 16:4.

ratified after having been in force for a considerable period of time.[19] Hence, according to these scholars, the conclusion was "inescapable that although the constitution was declared supreme in the hierarchy of Soviet sources of law, there was no adherence to the hierarchy in Stalin's time."[20]

The disregard for the promulgated hierarchy and the large variety of unranked but nonetheless pre-eminent sources of law, such as Marxist-Leninist and Stalinist writings and pronouncements, contributed to the invertebration of Soviet law. As noted earlier, not only were the various types of official and living law enactments that could be regarded as addressing the same set of facts disconnected from each other, but their hierarchy was often hard to establish because of the disconnected manner in which they were related to the sources of their authority. The result was bribery, adjudicative arbitrariness and major legal uncertainty.

§ 16.2 CIVIL AND COMMERCIAL TRANSACTIONS IN CODES AND OTHER ENACTMENTS

A. The Civil Code of 1922 and the Civil Transaction

In order to understand the Marxist-inspired meaning of a "civil" transaction or the typical transaction governed by Soviet civil codes, we must briefly re-visit Karl Marx's description of a pre-capitalist exchange of commodity for money as discussed in the preceding chapter.[21] Recall that Marx referred to transactions in the pre-capitalistic and capitalistic stage where the producer of goods or services sells the commodities he produces for money ("use-value money") and then with that money he purchases other commodities needed for his own use or consumption (C-M-C). In contrast, in the transaction that fully represents the capitalist cycle (M-C-M), the merchant-intermediary buys commodities in order to resell them at a profit and thereby obtains more money with which to continue his cycle of profitable transactions.

The Soviet Civil Code of 1922 was enacted at the time of the New Economic Policy (NEP).[22] This code's principal draftsman, Alexander Goikhbarg,[23] acknowledged the absence of a theoretical scheme to harmonize Marxist dogma with NEP policies and the capitalist policies of its German and Swiss models (the BGB of 1900 and the Swiss Civil Code of 1907). Goikhbarg's reliance on these models, then, was mostly for structure and not for substance. Hence, it took him only four months to draft this code.[24] Its overarching principle was formulated by Lenin in one of his often-repeated sayings: "[In the USSR] *we do not allow anything private*."[25]

Unlike its German and Swiss models, the Soviet Civil Code of 1922 did not include chapters or sections on family law. Such a law was promulgated by the USSR in 1918 and was not made part of the civil code because of the prevailing feeling among Soviet lawyers that the laws of civil transactions, except for non-property transactions and

---

[19] HAZARD ET AL., *supra* note 9, at 49–50.

[20] *Id.* at 50.

[21] *See infra* § 15:3(C)(2).

[22] HIROSHI ODA, RUSSIAN COMMERCIAL LAW 65 (2d ed. 2007).

[23] *Id.* at 65.

[24] *Id.*

[25] *Id.* at 66 (emphasis added).

pure exchange or barter of commodities, would soon wither away while the laws of marriage and family would remain.[26]

The presence of the NEP during most of its first decade of application did not result in rules that protected rights acquired by parties to agreements that pre-existed the code.[27] Under the strong shadow of Lenin's overarching (albeit living law) principle that "we do not allow anything private," Article 1 only protected those rights exercised in a manner consistent with the USSR's social and economic purposes, and Article 30 stated that transactions against the interests of the state were void.[28] Thus, the authority of the code was always subordinated to that of the policies of the executive branch. In fact, even acts as brutal as the deportations of the *Kulak*s and the confiscations of their property from 1928 to 1931 were carried out under the authority of this code.[29]

B. Central Planning and Its Sources of Law: The Fundamental Principles or Bases of the Civil Law of 1961

With the demise of the market economy in 1929, many Soviet lawyers envisaged the disappearance of the civil law found in the Civil Code of 1922. Yet, as noted by Hazard, Butler and Maggs, the same Lenin who had opened markets to private trade had also cautiously begun the planning of national electrification. And Stalin, an innate centralizer of authority, took up central planning of the economy as soon as he thought that the economy's most pressing needs had been met. He then extended the procedures of a planned rural electrification to the planning of an entire economy: "With this act in 1928 the New Economic Policy was phased out of existence, and the problem of public administration became as large as the economy itself, for all but minimal productive resources had been taken from private hands."[30]

As discussed in the preceding chapter, Soviet central plans were, in effect, laws. The identification of economic goals, the listing and allocation of resources, the determination of costs and prices, and the orders to deliver and transport goods were mandatory laws, intended to supplant whatever remnant existed of private contract law. This cataclysmic turn in the life of the economy and society of the USSR required a legal rationalization and perhaps a new legal theory.

1. *Evgeny Pashukanis and a Transitional Law Toward a Stateless and Lawless Society*[31]

Evgeny B. Pashukanis was one of the USSR's most distinguished legal thinkers during the 1920s and early 1930s. He viewed the directives that implemented central planning not so much as full-fledged laws but as administrative commands that were part of a transitional set of rules, a bridge so to speak, between the tsarist legal system

[26] *Id.* at 65.

[27] *Id.* at 66.

[28] *Id.*

[29] RICHARD PIPES, RUSSIA UNDER THE BOLSHEVIK REGIME 402 (1995).

[30] HAZARD ET AL., *supra* note 9, at 185.

[31] *See* EVGENY B. PASHUKANIS, THE GENERAL THEORY OF THE LAW AND MARXISM, ch. IV (Commodity and the Subject) (Peter Maggs trans., 2004) (1924) (on file with author) [hereinafter PASHUKANIS IV] *available at* http://www.marxists.org/archive/pashukanis/1924/law/ch04.htm (discussing the following excerpts).

and a communist society in which there would be no state and no law.[32] Much like the French scholastics and the German Pandectists, Pashukanis did not rely on empirical facts, but rather on a mixture of legal metaphysics and formal logic to support his generalizations. The following statements made in his monograph *The General Theory of the Law and Marxism* (hereinafter *General Theory*), which was published in 1924, illustrate his methodology and the lack of empirical or factual support for his generalizations: "Only in the conditions of a commodity economy is the abstract form of a right created, i.e. the capacity to have a right in general is separated from specific legal claims."[33]

In other words, abstract rights such as the right to own and dispose of property, supposedly enforceable against the world at large, had two essential components: 1) they came about in a commodity economy, and 2) they were separated, abstract or independent from pre-existing claims to the same property.[34] In his own *General Theory*, Pashukanis repeatedly relies on Roman legal institutions to make his points on the legal consequences of a commodity economy.[35] Yet, as discussed earlier in this book, the rights that Pashukanis describes as "abstract," *i.e.*, separated or independent from the rights acquired in pre-existing transactions as well as those *causally* connected with pre-existing transactions were neither in fact nor in law abstract or independent. As shown by Von Ihering, among many other Romanists, the protection of the right to possess personal or real property could not be separated from the violent (law of the booty, and far from an exchange of commodities) manner in which the Roman legionnaire had acquired such property by means of symbols such as the planting of his legion's flag "*sub hasta*"; nor could the less violent form of acquisition of possession and property (*usucapio*) be called the result of an exchange of commodities, nor could it be separated from the use of the land or property for a designated period of time.[36] And where their contractual cause was concerned, these as well as other possessory or proprietary rights were inseparable from the cause and manner in which they had been acquired. In fact, the rights obtained by the possessor of land by means of the *usucapio* was an enforceable right precisely because its holder had done what was necessary to have a superior right to the land he adversely possessed, despite the preexisting rights by previous holders or owners of the land.[37]

Hence, the economy of the civilized world's first major legal system depended in large measure at first upon occupations and taking created rights to own and dispose of things privately—not as a result of the Marxist notion of a peculiarly capitalistic exchanges of commodities. Inexplicably, in another chapter of his *General Theory*,

---

[32] *See Evgeny B. Pashukanis*, MARKISTS.ORG, http://www.marxists.org/archive/%upashukanis/ (English translations of Pashukanis' most important writings, including *State and Law Under Socialism* (1936)).

[33] PASHUKANIS IV, *supra* note 31.

[34] *See supra* § 11:2(G).

[35] *See, e.g.*, PASHUKANIS IV, *supra* note 31, at n.37 and accompanying text. Pashukanis states: "The title of ownership in ancient Roman law, *mancipatio per aes et libram*, shows that it was born simultaneously with the phenomenon of internal exchange." *Id.* Query: Can one say that the notion of title or ownership is abstract from the legal claim by someone who asserts his ownership? How did he know that? Note that this is an anthropological, rather than legal, datum for which no evidence is offered.

[36] Kozolchyk & Furnish, *A Comparative Analysis*, at 252.

[37] Berger defines *usucapio* as an: "Acquisition of ownership of a thing belonging to another through possession of it . . . for a period fixed by law." BERGER, ENCYCLOPEDIC DICTIONARY, at 752.

Pashukanis acknowledges this fact when he states: "Law historically emerged . . . from a claim, and only thereafter did it overlap with the earlier . . . relationship."[38]

In another passage, Pashukanis attempts to delegitimize custom or legal tradition as a source of law and as a perennial participant in any normative universe by stating:

> Custom or tradition, as a higher basis than the individual [conduct] for legal claims, corresponds to the feudal system with its limitations and stagnation. Tradition or custom is in essence something included in notoriously rather narrow geographic boundaries. Therefore, every right is thought of merely as an attribute of a specific concrete subject or of a group of subjects. In the feudal world, "each right was a privilege," (Marx). Each city, each estate, each guild lived according to its law which followed a man wherever he was.[39]

Yet, cultural anthropology shows that customs and customary law as "a higher basis than the individual [conduct] for legal claims" were relied on by primitive tribes much earlier than in any European feudal period.[40] The same is obviously true with any society that actively engaged in commerce, before or after feudalism.

Finally, in Chapter V, Pashukanis asserts:

> The more unstable the authority of the bourgeoisie became, the more compromising its corrections became, the more the *Rechtsstaat* turned into an incorporeal shadow, until finally the extreme intensification of the class struggle forced the bourgeoisie completely to discard the mask of the *Rechtsstaat* and to reveal the essence of authority as the organized force of one class against another.[41]

This statement is reminiscent of "Che" Guevara's "race of the wolves" argument used in his anti-Liberman and anti-Marcelo Fernandez tirade described in the previous chapter:[42] This was a race that according to Guevara was always won by the most ferocious capitalist.[43] As such, it shares the same demonological view of commercial man (or of the bourgeois) held by Marx, Lenin, Stalin and other Bolsheviks. Yet none of these demonologists paid attention to Adam Smith's empirically verifiable observation that at least since man ceased being a hunter-gatherer (and perhaps even then), he had a propensity to trade and cooperate with fellow man. Cooperation, in fact, was recently proven to be the most distinguishing feature between man and his nearest relative in the animal world.[44]

Stated simply, men were much more complicated and cooperative than Marx, Lenin, Stalin, Pashukanis and "Che" Guevara, among many others, gave them credit

---

[38] *See* EVGENY B. PASHUKANIS, THE GENERAL THEORY OF THE LAW AND MARXISM, ch. III (Relationship and the Norm) (Peter Maggs trans., 2004) (1924) [hereinafter PASHUKANIS III], *available at* http://www.marxists.org/archive/pashukanis/1924/law/ch03.htm.

[39] PASHUKANIS IV, *supra* note 31.

[40] *Id. See also generally* HOEBEL, PRIMITIVE MAN; BRONISLAW MALINOWSKI, CRIME AND CUSTOM IN SAVAGE SOCIETY (1926) (discussing the peculiarities of the observance of custom in primitive societies).

[41] EVGENY B. PASHUKANIS, THE GENERAL THEORY OF THE LAW AND MARXISM, ch. V (Law and the State) (Peter Maggs trans., 2004) (1924) [hereinafter PASHUKANIS V], *available at* http://www.marxists.org/archive/pashukanis/1924/law/ch05.htm.

[42] *See supra* § 15:4(H).

[43] *Id.*

[44] *See supra* § 1:2(D) (discussing human versus animal cooperation).

for. Because Marx viewed the exchange of commodities as determinant of man's social behavior, it was Pashukanis's logical conclusion that once such a Marxist M-C-M exchange disappeared and everyone owned everything, there would be no need to protect the holders of the exchanged commodities and law would also disappear.

Sadly, theoreticians such as Pashukanis are not always aware of the danger they represent to tyrants and especially those who suffer from paranoia, for their propensity is always to find an enemy in someone who sounds too intelligent to be clearly understood by them. This was the case with Stalin, who by 1936 was intent on a complete centralization of his power. Yet how could he accomplish that if there is this respected law professor convincing many that law-making was only temporary and not as fearsome as during tsarist days? Or was not this intellectual aware that Lenin's legal nihilism had to be replaced immediately by a policy of "socialist legality" which required that Stalin's and his subordinates' *ukases* had to be made widely known and obeyed by everyone, *or else*? Despite Pashukanis's prominence in legal circles, in the USSR and abroad, and despite his apologies and repeated recantations of his nihilistic theories, he was made to disappear in 1937 while he continued to be labeled officially as "a dangerous deviationist."[45]

2. *The Spastic Journey of Economic Law*

The increasing centralization of economic activity and its regulation by the Law of State Enterprises confirmed Pashukanis's prognosis of a disappearing private law and of a progressively all-encompassing administrative law taking its place as the Soviet transitional law. As an official-mandatory law, the law generated by economic plans displaced the law of contracts between or among state entities and consumers of their goods and services. Thus, while the Civil Code of 1922 remained officially in force until the 1960s, most of it was dead letter.

Hazard, Butler and Maggs point to 1927 as the year when the central economic plan became the law of the land where heavy industry was concerned:

> For the massive equipment of heavy industry every detail of the relationship between the producing corporation and the consuming corporation was planned. For consumers' goods, there was still some permissiveness, as directors were allowed to seek out their counterparts in other corporations and make arrangements for supply of the materials needed. . . .[46]

Stalin could have allowed the legal relations among suppliers, manufacturers and distributors to be governed by their respective contracts. His first choice was to regulate through mandatory law. Accordingly, "[t]he planning orders were then the

---

[45] I had a strange encounter with Pashukanis' theories while attending the 1958 Comparative Law Congress in Brussels, Belgium. Knowing that I would be attending this Congress, the Cuban Bar Association, of which I was a member, asked me to present a resolution condemning the Batista Government for its repeated violations of the rule of law to a Rule of Law Committee chaired by Professor C.J. Hamson of Cambridge University Law School with Professor John Hazard as Reporting Secretary. Upon my reading a two paragraph motion which requested the condemnation of a dictatorial government that had repeatedly violated the human rights of its citizens and thus the rule of law, a Professor Stefan Feodorovich Ketchiakom stood up and proffered endless insults at me, including that of propagating slanderous lies authored by none other than Professor Pashukanis. Fortunately, Professors Hamson and Hazard quickly intervened and reassured me that Ketchiakom was doing a bit of acting for the benefit of a likely "elder brother" present in the audience.

[46] HAZARD ET AL, *supra* note 9, at 242.

sole documents necessary to [govern] production and delivery, supplemented when necessary by agreement on minor details of specifications."[47] Yet, as the plans grew in complexity, they required greater detail and expert knowledge on production and delivery specifications, among others, and this made contracts necessary. Accordingly, a decree of February 1931 reinstated the use of contract and contract forms. To distinguish the contracts used in the production and distribution plans from all others, they were labeled "contract[s] of supply" and the remainder continued to be referred to simply as "contract[s]."[48]

The disputes that arose from contracts of supply were submitted at first to the ordinary courts. However, after the judicial delays threatened to undermine production and distribution goals and timetables, the Stalin administration introduced a new system of administrative courts that relied on arbitration referred to as "State Arbitration."[49] While this system was at first informal and attempted to involve the officials or directors who were parties to the dispute, eventually it became a more formal procedure that relied on the parties' attorneys and their official sources of law, including the Civil Code and supplementary statutes. As noted by Hazard, Butler and Maggs, despite the presence of civil-law-based arguments, some of the lawyers for the state agencies preferred to distinguish between what they referred to as "economic law," or the law and practices peculiar to the economic planning phases and contracts, and the "civil law," or the law applied to the contractual relations between private parties.[50]

As inveterate classifiers and taxonomists, law professors, even in Stalin's Soviet Union, argued for a new type of distinctly Soviet law, a law of a higher hierarchy than the civil law; they labeled this law as "economic" law. It would apply to the relations among the state entities involved in the central planning process. However, many of the proponents of a new and distinct economic law were also converts to Pashukanis's legal nihilism. For this reason, they were also purged together with Pashukanis as enemies of Stalin's state.

Following Stalin's death in 1953, the proponents of an independent economic law were emboldened to try anew. The Encyclopedia of Soviet Law reports that the proposal of an independent branch of economic law with its own "Economic Law Code" was proposed by Professor V. V. Laptev following the 21st Congress of the Communist Party of the Soviet Union in 1959, and that after a debate, this new law was ordered to be codified by decrees of that party, the Council of Ministers of the USSR, and was mentioned supportively in the Soviet Constitution of 1977.[51]

Despite all of these signs of official recognition, economic law was never officially welcomed as a major source of Soviet law. "The Basic Principles of Civil Law and of Civil Procedure"[52] (hereinafter "Basic Principles") "combined the law of public enterprise with that of private individuals, making some exceptions but including both

---

[47] *Id.*

[48] *Id.*

[49] *Id.* at 243.

[50] *Id.*

[51] ENCYCLOPEDIA OF SOVIET LAW 268 (Ferdinand Joseph Maria edlbrugge et al. eds., 2d rev. ed. 1985). *See also* HAZARD ET AL., *supra* note 9, at 274–76.

[52] R. Schlesinger, *The Basic Principles of Civil Law*, 13 SOVIET STUDIES 447 (1962).

types of relationships in the same document."[53] Nevertheless, the merger continued to be severely criticized by supporters of economic law. Despite the sharply different context and possible meaning of "economic law," a growing number of European and Latin American law professors, some of them commercial lawyers, have argued since the 1990s that a new branch of public-private law they refer to as economic law is essential for the understanding of public-private law intersections in their respective economies.

Unlike its Soviet ancestor, however, this branch of the law does not necessarily seem designed to govern the transactions connected with economic plans or contracts between state agencies and their effects upon third parties. At times these new converts to economic law seem to try to harmonize socialist or centrally-planned legal institutions with capitalist or free market contracts, and to this uneasy mix they add a component of "economic analysis" of law.

3. *The Basic Principles of Civil Law and of Civil Procedure of 1961*

The Basic Principles were part of a set that also included the law of civil procedure. As was just discussed, their drafters were under pressure to follow Marxist orthodoxy on the importance of the exchange of commodities for money as a subject of regulation and of an economic law whose concepts, principles and rules would govern, at least transitionally (until the advent of communism), the transactions among state enterprises. Unlike the M-C-M cycle, which according to Marx led inevitably to profiteering and surplus value, state agencies and economic plans would rightfully replace the exploitive capitalist intermediaries of that cycle.

Accordingly, the Preamble to the Basic Principles explained the importance of commodity and money exchange relationships and economic law in a socialist state headed toward communist ownership of the means of production. Upon the enactment of the Basic Principles, "Soviet civil law [would regulate] the property relationships which are governed by the use of money-commodity exchange forms in the building up of communism. . . ."[54] This formulation could not be accused of deviationism because the state-managed commodity exchange would no longer be associated with private enterprise. Thus, as suggested by Rudolph Schlesinger, one of the great comparative law scholars of our time, a new "law . . . associated with commodity exchange need not be regarded as provisional, at least until a fully communist society has been constructed in the more distant future."[55] In relevant part, Article 1 of the Basic Principles stated: "Soviet civil law regulates property relationships and personal non-property relationships connected with them, with the aim of creating the material and technological basis of communism. . . . In [the circumstances provided by law] civil legislation also regulates other non-property relationships."[56]

As referred to by the Basic Principles, an exchange of property is an exchange of commodities for non-commercial purposes. In this respect, the Soviet use of the term "civil legislation" was akin to that of the *Code Civil*, whose exchanges of property

---

[53] HAZARD ET AL., *supra* note 9, at 244.

[54] Schlesinger, *supra* note 52, at 447.

[55] *Id.*

[56] I INTERNATIONAL ENCYCLOPEDIA OF COMPARATIVE LAW: NATIONAL REPORTS U-28 (Viktor Knapp, ed., 1976).

(including not only barters but also sales, leases and bailments) were not supposed to be for commercial profits and whose transactions also involved non-property relations (such as those involving marriage and family).[57] However, as will become apparent shortly, unlike the *Code Civil*, the Basic Principles and related statutory Soviet law disallowed as "unearned income" the payment of wages or honoraria for services performed in civil transactions involving personal property, whereas the *Code Civil* and its progeny allowed and encouraged them.

Some of the provisions in the Basic Principles foreshadowed future liberalization of trade by: 1) enabling the performance of civil transactions other than those defined by it;[58] 2) empowering more juridical persons to participate in the socialist marketplace, such as mixed state and agricultural cooperatives (*kolkhozes*), and conferring property rights to trade unions and other social organizations;[59] and 3) acknowledging the contractual realities of a planned economy in which the nature of the participants as state entities and their subjection to an economic plan were paramount considerations as contrasted with a policy of "mere enforcement of contracts without consideration of their [public law] origin. . . ."[60]

The Basic Principles section dealing with the law of obligations makes it clear that civil law obligations may arise from, among other sources, any agreements or administrative acts which conformed to the "general spirit of Soviet civil law."[61] One such an agreement was found in Chapter IV of the Basic Principles, which dealt with the procurement of agricultural produce. As noted by Professor Schlesinger, this contract contains the usual stipulations concerning delivery dates and prices, but it also sets forth the obligation of the purchasing entity to provide assistance to state and collective farms in producing and transporting produce to the delivery points.[62]

Nevertheless, the liberalization of the law of contracts was still driven by the classification of property and particularly of the types of property that could be traded. Article 25 was an indicator of how far the legislature was prepared to go in embracing a *numerus apertus* approach. As usual, during the reign of Soviet law, "unearned income" or income derived from the payment of wages to workers or joint venturers in connection with the exploitation of "personal property" was a major concern. Based on the same restrictive approach to personal and other forms of property, the Basic Principles limited the ownership of houses to one per family.[63]

§ 16.3 TRANSACTIONS INVOLVING PERSONAL PROPERTY: THE FEDERAL OWNERSHIP ACT OF 1990

According to Dean Yevgeny Sukhanov of the Faculty of Law at Lomonosov Moscow State University,[64] despite the attempts to liberalize some aspects of the law of contracts by the Basic Principles, it was not until the enactment of the federal

---

[57] *See supra* § 8:4(D)(5).

[58] Schlesinger, *supra* note 52, at 448 (citing art. 1).

[59] *Id.* (citing arts. 20 & 24).

[60] *Id.*

[61] *Id.* at 449.

[62] *Id.* (citing art. 52).

[63] *Id.*

[64] *See* Yevgeny Sukhanov, *The Concept of Ownership in Current Russian Law*, VI JURIDICA INT'L 102 (2001), *available at* http://www.juridicainternational.eu/public/pdf/ji_2001_1_102.pdf.

Ownership Act of 1990 that the USSR "considerably expanded and developed the approaches [to private ownership] of the previous law."[65] Dean Sukhanov explained the federal Ownership Act as follows:

> [T]he legislator for the first time abandoned the economic categories of "forms of ownership" . . . and the right of ownership itself became an integral part of a broader concept of rights *in rem*. Thus, the [*Code Civil* and BGB's] concept of real rights—the right of ownership being the most important right—was established in [Soviet] law. In essence, this concept reflects a clear distinction between the economic and legal understandings of the relations to which ownership gives rise.[66]

Prior to this 1990 law, no classification of property was as important to the commerce engaged in by private parties in the USSR as that of personal property. After many official concessions, retractions and restrictions on what a citizen could treat as his personal property and thus set aside for his and his family's unimpeded use and perhaps development and conveyance, Article 10 of the Soviet Constitution of 1936 defined personal property as follows:

> The right of citizens to personal ownership of their incomes from work and of their savings, of their dwelling houses and subsidiary household economy, their household furniture and utensils and articles of personal use and convenience, as well as the right of inheritance of personal property of citizens, is protected by law.[67]

This enumeration tacitly acknowledged the residual nature of personal property; it was a "left-over" property, or one that did not belong to the Soviet state, agencies or cooperatives. Given its importance for informal and black market transactions, it should not be surprising that the enumeration of personal property in Article 10 was temporary and was followed by conflicting legislative and administrative actions. Among these actions were the socialization and "abrogation forever" of every kind of ownership in land including its minerals, waters, forests and all other natural resources; the abolition of private ownership of houses, banks and church property; or the proscription of inheritance by operation of the law or by wills.[68]

Still, after many years of studying Soviet legal institutions, Samuel Kucherov, a Soviet law expert at the United States Library of Congress,[69] quoted his Soviet colleague Raisa Khalfina for the assertion that no other private legal institution attracted as much attention during the heyday of the USSR as personal property.[70] In her words:

> It is difficult to find another legal question which would attract such vivid attention of the public at the present time, as the question of citizens' personal property. Almost in every issue of the central or local papers, articles, feuilletons, letters to the editor, reviews of these letters, concerning

---

[65] *Id.* at 102.

[66] *Id.*

[67] USSR CONST. art. 10 (1936).

[68] *See* Kucherov, *supra* note 5, at 376–77 (citing legislative and administrative decrees).

[69] *Id.* at 376, for his comment.

[70] Please note that Mr. Kucherov wrote his Comment in the early 1960s.

the question of personal property, inheritance, individual housing, gardening, etc., are printed.[71]

In addition to the economic importance of this information, there was an additional legal-cultural factor. Even a quick glance at Soviet legislation and administrative and court decisions on private and personal ownership reveals that one of the main reasons for the citizenry's concern with the scope of personal property was its legal uncertainty. The recurring questions could not be more basic: What rights did ownership of personal property encompass? What personal property could be sold, lent, leased, exchanged or passed on to one's heirs?

Typical of the "off and on," uncertainty-laden approach to the scope of personal property rights was the following, among many other, governmental actions: The right of inheritance of family property was, as mentioned earlier, abolished in 1918,[72] yet farmers were told in 1921 that as former house owners they could get back their houses—but this right was limited to houses with fewer than two apartments except those located in Moscow or Petrograd, which could contain as many as five apartments.[73] Similarly, while private ownership of land had been nationalized, owners of small houses could still rent the plots on which their buildings rested.[74] In addition, possession of land was restricted to the personal use of the former owner (the owner of record at the time of nationalization) and could not be inherited.[75] As commented earlier, the Civil Code of 1922 re-established inheritance rights, although with severe limitations.[76] During the 1920s, this law seemed to have been at its most uncertain point.[77] It was then that "shifting economic policy led alternately to confiscation and denationalization of property on a large scale."[78] This off and on feature of the Soviet law of property led Professor Peter B. Maggs to characterize this entire field of law as complicated and vague: "One may rent out housing space that is not needed but may not profiteer; there is no clear criterion, however, of what is legitimate renting and what is profiteering."[79]

§ 16.4 ALLOCATION OF HOUSING

A. To Whom Are Tenancy Duties Owed? Sources of Tenancy Law

Professor Maggs' quote prompts the question: Why did such a basic question of everyday housing rentals remain unclarified? I believe that a possible answer to the continuing uncertainty on the meaning of profiteering was the difficulty in identifying the victims of such conduct. The victim could hardly be one of the parties to the transaction because, in principle, the transaction was unlawful and the parties to it

---

[71] Kucherov, *supra* note 6, at 376.

[72] Decree of August 20, 1918, *cited in* Kucherov, *supra* note 5, at 376 n.2. For a list of property that could be privately owned in the USSR until the end of the Second World War, see John N. Hazard, *Soviet Property Law,* 30 CORNELL L.Q. 466 (1945).

[73] Kucherov, *supra* note 5, at 376.

[74] *Id.* at 377.

[75] *Id.*

[76] *Id.* at 382.

[77] Peter B. Maggs, *The Security of Individually-Owned Property Under Soviet Law,* 1961 DUKE L.J. 525, 528 (1961).

[78] *Id.* at 525 (citation omitted).

[79] *Id.* at 528.

were presumably "*in pare delictu*." On the other hand, if the victim was "the state," "the proletariat," "the people," or even "the masses," then, as pointed out in the preceding chapter, a duty supposedly owed to everyone winds up being owed to none.

The following discussion on the effect of tenancy duties in housing law during the 1960s is based upon two studies by distinguished Soviet law experts: one by Bernard Rudden Senior Researcher at the University of Leiden[80] and the other by Samuel Kucherov at the United States Library of Congress.[81]

Article 131 of the Constitution of 1936 provided:

> It is the duty of every citizen of the U.S.S.R. to safeguard and strengthen public, socialist property as the sacred and inviolable foundation of the Soviet system, as the source of the wealth and might of the country, as the source of the prosperous and cultured life of all the working people. Persons committing offense against public, socialist property are enemies of the people.[82]

Article 283 of the Civil Code of 1964, in turn, stated: "The tenant is bound to use the property in accordance with the contract and the purpose of the property."[83]

In principle, the preceding and other duties were owed to state-appointed landlords and other administrative authorities, including the Procurator of Justice and communal bodies and parties directly or indirectly related to the use of the premises in accordance with the contract or the purposes of the property as expressed in an economic plan.[84] As the reader will discover in a future section,[85] the USSR was not the only jurisdiction to distinguish between purpose of the property as expressed in a contract and in other documents.

When central economic plans in the USSR listed the property to be used for "plan purposes" (a frequent specification in economic plans), the purpose could not be altered by the parties to the plan without the permission of the planning agency. The effect of the listing of such property was to create duties to an unidentified number of administrative authorities (national and local) as well as to producers, suppliers, distributors and consumers of the goods and services of the plan.[86] Assume, for example, that property "A" was listed in a national plan to serve as a warehouse for the storage of products "B." Assume that "C," the state entity that produced B, found a better place to store it and decided to use B as housing space to be rented to a group of needy employees "X-Z." C's decision could trigger actions by administrative claimants who would allege the infringement of the plan provisions, and by other state entities that could trace the tardiness of delivery of B to the decision to change their storage. Meanwhile, if the change of warehousing space to housing was set aside by the administrative authorities, X-Z would likely file a claim against B for breach of their rental agreement.

---

[80] Bernard Rudden, *Soviet Housing and the New Civil Code,* 15 INT'L & COMP. L.Q. 231 (1966).

[81] Kucherov, *supra* note **5**, at 376

[82] USSR CONST. art. 131 (1936).

[83] Rudden, *supra* note 80, at 234.

[84] *Id.*

[85] *See infra* § 23:9(D) (Teófila Astorga Viuda de Aceves case).

[86] Rudden, *supra* note 80, at 235.

As if the number of possible claimants of tenancy duties were not large enough, Bernard Rudden notes that in 1957 the Communist Party's Central Committee urged the importance of involving the community and the trade unions in the grant of living space, which would also enable these entities to claim tenancy duties. This directive was subsequently adopted by a number of Soviet republics.[87]

B. Allocating Housing Units Without Regard to Market Forces: Administrative Assessment of Needs and Merits

In a 1957 article for the Soviet newspaper *Pravda*, Nikita Khruschev set forth the merit criteria for the allotment of dwellings:

> In building and allotting dwellings we mustn't simply think—because a man is alive, give him a good apartment. You have to take a look at what he's doing, what he's giving to society. In our socialist society, each must give something to the general welfare of the people, must carry a certain load. Only then does he get the right to use the fruits of his labour which are created by society.[88]

This pronouncement was followed by the Housing Ministry's Ministerial Instructions for assessing need and merit and included, as one factor, the applicant's "socially useful work." Yet, soon thereafter, each economic sector started relying on its own indices of housing merit. For example, in the industrial sector reliance was placed on the workers' "productive indices," and this meant that the leaders of production were to be preferred.[89] Yet, who was to be preferred if all of the leaders of production had received their housing or were not interested in the housing available? The following administrative practices illustrate the lack of precision of the archetypes chosen to include or exclude a certain archetypal behavior in an evaluation that was supposed to replace market forces as the adjudicators of the entitlement to apartments.

1. Zamchenko—The Loafer

Assume that a list of applicants for housing existed and one Zamchenko had gradually reached the highest rank. Would a statement by his plant manager that Zamchenko was "a loafer" be enough to: 1) totally bar him from appearing in the list; 2) lower his rank; or 3) send him to the bottom of the list? Or, would an investigation of his productivity be in order? In Zamchenko's case, the answer was to send him to the bottom of the list.

After this decision, those tenants who could not claim that they were leaders of productivity must have been wondering whether they could also be characterized as loafers or whether they had to prove that to housing adjudicators and unidentified claimants of tenant duties. Please notice that this is not a very different characterization from that of the "profiteers" that concerned Professor Maggs.

Rudden referred to another municipal regulation according to which adjudicators, presumably implementing Khruschev's pronouncement, had to take into account the social usefulness of the work they did. Then a local twist was added that required that

---

[87] *Id.* at 236.

[88] *Id.* at 231 (discussing the *Pravda* publication) (citation omitted).

[89] *Id.* at 236.

in order to register, the applicant had to have lived in the city for more than five years; and finally, the regulation required that "[p]ersons not engaged in socially useful labour are denied registration or removed from the list."[90] Clearly, major uncertainty prevailed in this municipal regulation as well.

2. *The Virtuous Tenant?*

On the other hand, apparently once a tenant had qualified for his or her tenancy, then his or her status was highly protected. Thus, Article 328 of the 1964 code provided that;

> The tenant of living accommodation in the building of a local Soviet of Workers' Deputies, or of a State, co-operative or public organisation . . . [had the right] on the expiry of the term of the contract, a right to renewal [for a similar period]. This right may be challenged in court by the landlord only if the tenant has systematically failed to fulfill his duties under the contract.[91]

Rudden refers to this tenant as "the virtuous tenant."[92] I do not know if he used this term ironically, for the diligence required of such a tenant was minimal—all he had to do was not engage in a systematic breach of his duties under the contract. Moreover, the implicit policy of protecting those who had initially qualified was extended to members of their families as well. Accordingly, Article 301 of the same code provided:

> Equally with the tenant[s] . . . the members of his family who live with him acquire the rights and duties which flow from the lease. . . . The following are regarded as members of the tenant's family: his spouse, children and parents, and also other relations and dependants who are unable to work, if they reside with him and carry on a common household.[93]

3. *Making a Wife's Life Impossible as a Ground for Eviction*

An everyday lawsuit illustrates the standard required of a tenant to preserve his status as a "virtuous tenant" and the role of third parties in helping to apply this standard. Goremkyna, wife of Goremkin, brought an action to evict her husband "for making life impossible."[94] The lower court held for her, but the Supreme Court remanded to the lower court:

> The basis for evicting the defendant was that twice he started a fight with the plaintiff . . . His conduct was not considered by the community, either at his place of work or at his residence. Nor was he warned by the court. At work he was classified as satisfactory. His work character was positive . . . The decision of the People's Court to evict the defendant without applying educative measures to him was taken without sufficient foundation.[95]

---

[90] *Id.* (citation omitted).

[91] *Id.* at 236–37.

[92] *Id.* at 237.

[93] *Id.*

[94] *Id.* at 242 (citing original Russian sources on the Goremkyna v. Goremkin case).

[95] *Id.*

Rudden's correct conclusion was that "[t]he Russian lease . . . *straddles contract and delict* [and that] [t]he tenant's duties and liabilities are owed, not merely to the lessor, but to third persons. . . ."[96]

4. Rent, the Withering Away of Law, Prices and Unpredictability

Rudden calls attention to the "unimportance of the regulations on rent"[97] and also quotes a section of the Civil Code that starts out by saying: "Until the establishment of rent-free accommodations. . . ."[98] Thereafter, he refers to supplementary legislation that provided for low rent whose amount depended upon the amenities of the premises and inequalities of social status. For example, Moscow priests had to pay five times the average rate.[99]

The Civil Code's prefatory statement, "Until the establishment of rent-free accommodations," reflects the effect that Lenin's legal nihilism (inspired by Marx's prophecy on the withering away of the state and its law) had upon the law and economics of tenancy. Why bother with careful, equal and detailed regulation if all of the regulation, including perhaps the five-fold extra charges to priests, were bound to disappear in the foreseeable future? The reader will recall that a variant of this view was expressed by "Che" Guevara in the previous chapter.[100] Recall that he dismissed the need for cost accounting and self-sustaining state enterprises or of demanding payment from delinquent state agencies because all that liability structure was soon to disappear when all of the property in society would be in the hands of the state and when such a state would be populated by the "new socialist man." The effects of this attitude upon the legal and economic well-being of a society are not hard to discern: Deferred obligations are less likely to be performed; defaults will proliferate; and credit contracts and, even from a planning standpoint for those so inclined, estimates of prices for supply and final products, are much more difficult to predict for planning and living purposes.

C. The Building of Private Homes and *Dachas*

Official building statistics indicate that in 1959 the largest percentage of the entire dwelling space available in the USSR was personal property which consisted of houses built with state authorization by private citizens.[101] Although these homes and *dachas* (country houses) were built mostly in the outskirts of the big cities and in the countryside, the shortage of dwelling space in the USSR continued to be its "everlasting plague."[102] As an illustration of the "appalling shortage of dwelling space," Rudden quoted a 1960 letter of the hundreds written each day to the editors of newspapers throughout the Soviet Union: "Our family consisted of four persons: father, mother and we two brothers. We lived all four in one room. My brother and I married and got children but we live still in the same room."[103]

---

[96] *Id.* at 242.

[97] *Id.* at 288.

[98] *Id.* (citation omitted).

[99] *Id.* at 238–39.

[100] *See supra* § 15:4(H)(2).

[101] Kucherov, *supra* note 5, at 385.

[102] *Id.* at 386.

[103] *Id.* (citation omitted).

1. *Selected Provisions of the Civil Code of 1964*

As had its predecessors, the Civil Code of 1964 attempted to clarify the scope of the rights of owners of private homes and *dachas*: 1) the owner had the rights to their possession, use and disposition; 2) he could not use those rights to obtain income derived from the work of others, even if he paid wages or shared profits with these others (unearned income); 3) he could only own one dwelling-house or part of one house; and 4) the maximum size of a dwelling-house or parts thereof could not exceed sixty square meters of living space.[104]

Yet, these rights presupposed that the builder of the house or *dacha* had obtained permission for the proposed plan. If he had not done so or deviated substantially from what was allowed, he automatically lost his right of disposition or to the building or parts thereof.[105] The Executive Committee of the local Soviet of Workers' Deputies could order that the house or *dacha* or part thereof be destroyed at the expense of the builder, or a court could decree its confiscation.

Similarly, "[i]f a house, *dacha* (or part thereof) . . . is systematically used by the owner for the extraction of unearned income, then that house, *dacha* (or part thereof) is liable to confiscation without compensation by court procedure at the suit of the Executive Committee of the local Soviet of Workers' Deputies."[106]

2. *Case Law: Unearned Income and Other Accusations Based on Marxist-Leninist Dogma*

The following sub-sections illustrate the everyday application of an invertebrate law whose drafters could be many and unexpected.

a. Lemdyanov's Garden; Speculative and Unearned Income

Lemdyanov owned a sizeable garden and built on it a greenhouse in which he installed a convection stove and an electric heater which enabled him to produce large quantities of vegetables, plants and flowers. In addition, he modernized a hen-house, and kept an average of 100 hens for sale.[107] He sold the vegetables and hens at "speculative prices" and used the proceeds of their sale to build a house and garage. He was accused before the Peoples' Court of un-socialist behavior.

The People's (trial) Court confiscated the above-described properties.[108] The court held that the house and garage he acquired from the proceeds of the sale of vegetables and hen were the product of un-socialist behavior, and were dealt with under another law.

---

[104] Rudden, *supra* note 80, at 247 (quoting various articles of the Civil Code of 1964). Rudden also notes:

> [A] citizen with a large family or a right to extra living space may be allowed by the Executive Committee of the . . . borough Soviet of Workers' Deputies to build, acquire or keep as his property a house, or part of a house, of a larger size. In that case, the living space of the house, or part of a house must not exceed the size determined for the given family according to the norms for tenants in the houses of local Soviets of Workers' Deputies. . . .

Id.

[105] *Id.* at 248 (quoting art. 111 of the Civil Code of 1964).

[106] *Id.* at 249.

[107] *Id.*

[108] *Id.*

QUESTIONS

What made Lemdyanov's use of the greenhouse and hen-house a source of unearned income? Rudden's translation of this case refers to the defendant's use of a "convection stove and an electric heater" to enable him to produce large quantities of vegetables, plants and flowers. Could these machines be the culprits of the production of "unearned income"? Was the rationale of such an income that only a citizen's physical and mental efforts could be the producers of earned income? Even though Lemdyanov had likely paid wages for work related to his garden and hen-house, Rudden's translation does not refer to such payments, but refers to the defendant's sale "at speculative prices." What would you say is a "speculative" price? Is there any connection here with Marx's appropriation of "surplus" value or with the medieval doctrines of the just price, as discussed in the preceding chapter? Could the defendant be guilty of both charging speculative prices and unearned income?

b. *Dembinksy's Case: The Sale of Fruits and Vegetables by Small Farms,* Kulaks *and Behavior Unbecoming a Party Member*

Lemdyanov's case does not clarify the range of a speculator's prices, or the meaning of "unearned income," "behavior unbecoming a party member" and so on—products all of the Marxist-Leninist conceptual demonology. Hopefully, the following deliberations during a meeting of a local communist party concerning the behavior of one of its members and the following court decisions will clarify the meaning of these accusatory concepts.

Following Stalin's death, small plots of land were allocated by the Soviet government to homeowners. Some were given as rewards for productive work and others were given to encourage the growing of fruits and vegetables to increase the nation's short supply.[109] This next case pertains to a Professor Dembinsky of the Faculty of the Industrial Institute of Kuybishev. He decided to become such a gardener, but in the opinion of his colleague Professor Grigor'yev, he had stretched too far the authorization of home gardening.[110] During a meeting of the Industrial Institute faculty in December of 1960, Grigor'yev accused Dembinsky of hiring workers to help him turn his garden into a profitable venture.[111] The following is an extract of the accusation hurled at Professor Dembinsky during a communist party meeting by some of his faculty colleagues:

> Dembinsky was accused of speculation with the products of his huge garden, cultivated with the help of hired workers; the selling of products of the garden permitted him to make a living without having written a line of scientific work within the last twenty years. . . . "in consideration of the question of cars and *dachas* such as Dembinsky possesses, it must be said that he is a new *kulak* and it is we who raised this *kulak*."[112]

This accusation must have sent shivers up Dembinsky's spine as not too many years earlier, "millions of '*kulaks*' were completely dispossessed, physically annihilated, or sent to concentration camps. . . ."[113] Yet, what made Professor Dembinsky a *kulak*?

---

109 Kucherov, *supra* note 5, at 386.

110 *Id.* at 388 (citing Literaturnaya Gazetta (Dec. 20, 1960)) (reporting on this faculty dispute).

111 *Id.*

112 *Id.*

113 *Id.* at 385.

Was there any basis for this accusation in Lenin's dogma? If so, which dogma was it, that of the New Economic Policy? Or was it the need to repress "profiteers," "speculators," and "bloodsuckers" that Lenin also proffered during his three-year interaction with the NEP? Can you distinguish among these anti-socialist types? What was the behavior typical of these "demons"? Would any of them be protected by the provisions of the Civil Code of 1922, the 1936 Constitution or the Basic Principles discussed in the present and preceding chapters?

D. *Dacha* Rentals and Models of Proper Party Behavior: Zikeyev's Construction Materials

A decision of the USSR Council of Ministers of December 1960 forbade the allocation of plots to ordinary citizens for the construction of personal summer homes (*dachas*) in the outskirts of cities.[114] At the same time, a system of incentives and rewards for high-powered communist party officials was put in place. It granted Comrade Zikeyev, the director of a machine building plant and member in good standing of the Communist party, one such a plot. Zikeyev lacked the necessary construction materials, and with help from his colleagues (other plant directors), he collected his construction materials. His *dacha* was built and, according to witnesses, he and his family enjoyed it much.[115]

During one summer while Zikeyev was on travel, his wife rented a part of Zikeyev's *dacha* for a significant number of rubles. However, the Zikeyevs had not counted on the militant party loyalty of their daughter-in-law, a member of the Communist party. She denounced him to the Oblast Party Committee for betraying the party's ideals. According to her, the betrayal started with the building of the *dacha*. Building materials not available to ordinary citizens were available to him. She testified that he once boasted that electric wire and oil that could not be found by others was obtained for him by a plant director friend.[116]

At the meeting of the Party Oblast Committee, several opinions were voiced that criticized reliance on personal property to undermine the party's ideology.

As stated by an exemplary party member identified as "A":

> [H]e too dreamed of a *dacha* for himself and his family. "But then I would be a house owner" thought A. "The word itself is disagreeable . . . though a small landlord, [I would] still [be] a landlord . . . and I have a Party card, I am building Communism. . . ." [Thus A] abandoned his "dream."[117]

Similarly, "B," another highly respected party member, announced that he too had intended to build a *dacha*. But after looking closer into it, he decided that:

> [A]ccording to the opinion of a majority at the meeting, Zikeyev had become such a *money-grabber*. Although no formal decision was taken, the chairman informed Zikeyev that he would be excluded from the Party. In order to avoid it, Zikeyev presented to the Party his *dacha* which he had built himself at his personal expense.

---

114 *Id.* at 386 (summarizing the Decision of the USSR Council of Ministers of December 30, 1960).

115 *Id.* at 386.

116 *Id.* at 387.

117 *Id.*

> [S]ince the story was published in the organ of the Central Committee of the Soviet Union Communist Party, the solution of Zikeyev's case [was regarded as] a semi-official one.[118]

QUESTIONS

Do the accusations by the "exemplary" party members help you connect or "vertebrate" Marxist-Leninist dogma with behavior that Zikeyev was supposed to follow? If so, which exemplary party behavior was the most compatible with Marxist-Leninist dogma? If he could prove that in order to satisfy his family's needs he had to engage in activities that his colleagues said violated the Marxist-Leninist dogma of not being a "money-grabber," would any of the Soviet constitutional provisions transcribed in the present or previous chapter have protected Zikeyev? Had the NEP been in force at the time of his accusation, would he have been authorized to do business as a Nepman? What Marxist-Leninist dogma made the Nepmen lawful during 1921–1929 in the USSR?

E. Economic Significance of the Soviet Commerce in Personal Property

Despite the insults and penalties directed at the alleged *kulaks*, money grabbers and other "profiteers" and "exploiters" of personal property, the economic significance of their transactions could not be ignored by Soviet officials. A mere glance at the statistics provided by the USSR's own Statistical Handbook on Agriculture for 1959 showed that: "The production of . . . individual plots equals and sometimes exceeds the socialized production of animal food, vegetables (45%) and potatoes (70%), and amounts to 82% of the entire egg supply, about [half] of the meat and milk production of the country. . . ."[119]

Samuel Kucherov's analysis of the Soviet policies during the period of collectivization (roughly from 1928 to 1940) is instructive.[120] On the one hand, some policies allowed the building of personal homes, the ownership of personal cars and the cultivation of productive gardens, thereby alleviating the endemic scarcities of housing, transportation and the meager official diet. On the other hand, they imposed severe limitations upon the proliferation of *dachas*, automobiles and productive personal gardens which in the end were counter-productive. Kucherov concludes that the only parties who benefited from the official restrictions were the existing owners of personal property to the detriment of the rest of the population. As stated by a letter of a Communist party member printed by the journal *Kommunist*:

> "The fewer citizens who have their own cars, the more possibilities for automobile owners of receiving unearned income. The fewer citizens who have their own *dachas* and gardens, the more money the owners of *dachas* and gardens will receive by renting the *dachas* and selling vegetables, fruits, and flowers on the market,". . . . Indeed, restrictions will only increase speculation with personal property and foster bribery, which already now is extensively used in matters of allocation of plots for personal housing and gardening.[121]

---

[118] *Id.*

[119] *Statistical Handbook of Agriculture in 1959* (1960), *cited in* Kucherov, *supra* note 6, at 381.

[120] Kucherov, *supra* note 5, at 390–91.

[121] *Id.* at 390.

F. Cases and Disputes Involving Artisans and Small Merchants

The sale of manufactured articles to the public by artisans could be observed during most of the existence of the USSR. Perhaps to acknowledge the inevitable, a Statute on Artisan Handicraft Businesses, enacted on May 3, 1976, defined this activity as "making manufactured articles for sale to the public. . . ."[122] It forbade, however, the employment of wage labor as well as the sale of valuable items whose sale or distribution required state identification marks or certifications.[123] What follows are my brief summaries of Soviet court decisions on the rights and duties of artisans and merchants as translated by Hazard, Butler and Maggs.

1. The 1970 Criminal Case of Fadeev: A Seller of Wagon Wheels[124]

Fadeev, a seller of wagon wheels, was sentenced by a District People's Court to one year of corrective labor, a monetary fine of ten percent of his wages, plus restitution to the state of the proceeds of his sales to the public. The law that he was said to have violated was Article 153 of the section on Private Enterprise and Commercial Activity Intermediaries of the Criminal Code of the USSR. Specifically, he was found guilty of not registering his status as a seller of wagon wheels. This decision was reversed on appeal. The appellate court held that Article 153 only forbade the sale of handicrafts using certain types of business forms, *e.g.*, state, cooperative or other authorized "social forms," whereas Fadeev did not use these forms and acted in a private capacity.

COMMENTS AND QUESTIONS

To a western capitalist observer such as me, the logic employed by the appellate court seems confusing, if not paradoxical. On the one hand, the state only authorized certain forms of doing business, *i.e.*, as a state, cooperative or other authorized form. On the other hand, the defendant disobeyed that requirement and acted as a private, unregistered entity. Yet, he could not have registered without violating Article 153, for he was neither a state nor a cooperative entity. Could the reader draft a coherent, principled and thus predictable commercial rule that would enable him to lawfully sell his handicrafts without violating Marxist-Leninist dogma? How common was Fadeev's predicament in the post-Stalin years of the USSR?

2. The 1967 Case of Shorin: Worker or Joint Venturer? Was It Really a Glass-Blowing Workshop or a Simulation?[125]

Shorin was convicted by the trial court under Article 153 Paragraph 1 of the Criminal Code of the RSFSR and ordered to pay a large fine. He contracted with two collective farms to conduct glass-blowing workshops. In addition, he agreed to receive five percent of the proceeds of the sales following his workshops. On the other side, the workers would receive thirty to thirty-five percent of the remainder. As the organizer of the workshops, he recruited assistants, collected raw materials, got purchasers for the products and established prices. The trial court found that he deliberately hiked the

---

[122] HAZARD ET AL., *supra* note 9, at 187.

[123] *Id.*

[124] This author's summary of the Fadeev transcript cited by Hazard et al. HAZARD ET AL., *supra* note 9, at 189.

[125] The following is my summary of the transcript of a decision by Kalinin County People's Court of 1967. *Id.* at 189–90.

prices of the glass sold to increase his pay. He was accused of engaging in private entrepreneurial activity using a socialistically accepted form of doing business. The appellate court held that Article 153, Paragraph 1 punishes engaging in private entrepreneurial activity using the form of a state or cooperative entity. From its text, it follows that one of the essential elements of the crime is the use of one of the indicated forms of organization of private entrepreneurial activity and the illegal extraction of profit. However, the fulfillment of a labor contract with a collective farm regarding tasks connected with the output of a given type of product cannot by itself be regarded as a private entrepreneurial activity that entails criminal liability. It was factually established that Shorin conducted glass-blowing workshops under a labor contract concluded with the managers of the collective farms and that Shorin conscientiously fulfilled the obligations placed upon him. All of the funds received from the sale of goods produced in the glassblowing workshops were paid to the collective farms. The administrations of the collective farms later paid Shorin the wages due to him. In managing the glass-blowing workshops, Shorin acted in the best interests of the collective farms and fulfilled his labor contract; and these facts do not support the lower court's conclusion that the activity was criminal.

COMMENTS AND QUESTIONS

One does not have to be a specialist on legal simulation[126] to see through the utilization of "workshops" and "labor" agreements by Shorin and the collective farms as generators of additional income for themselves. In western capitalist terms, theirs was a plain and simple joint venture agreement in which he supplied his glass-blowing expertise and raw materials and the collectives supplied their premises, the workers and their business form or corporate shell that enabled the joint venturers to sell their goods and services profitably to the public in exchange for a division of the profits. The lower court chose to characterize this agreement for what it was—a private entrepreneurial activity. The appellate court decided to look the other way. Why do you think it did so? Could it be that, as in the Fadeev case above, it was aware that too many forms of private entrepreneurship were being practiced by the Soviet citizenry to improve their standard of living? Yet, what were the socio-economic costs of not knowing when a trial or appellate court would be as strict in its Marxist-Leninist or Stalinist approach to private entrepreneurship as was the lower court in this case and when a court would be willing to look the other way?

3. The 1968 Case of Utekeshev: A Factory Dispatcher, Nepman or Both?[127]

The facts found by the trial court showed that during 1961–1965, Utekeshev was engaged in speculative activities by buying automobiles and motorcycles and reselling them for an illegal profit of 1670 rubles. He was sentenced to two years in jail, but this sentence was suspended in favor of a two-year probation. Upon review, the Deputy President of the Supreme Court protested before the Judicial Division for Criminal Cases and sought the reversal of the probation arguing that the punishment was unjustifiably soft. According to the Deputy President, the record showed that while the defendant was a foreman at a state entity he engaged in the illegal buying and selling of motorcycles and automobiles to pocket unearned income, failing to register the motorcycles and automobiles as required by law. Further, he bypassed the state stores

---

[126] *See supra* § 14:4(A)(3)(c)(iii).

[127] HAZARD ET AL., *supra* note 9, at 190–92 (extract of this opinion transcribed by Hazard).

and sold them privately for a profit. Upon remand, the People's Court sentenced Utekeshev to an even lighter sentence. The lower court justified its leniency by referring to the fact that this was his first conviction, the (precarious) position of his family, his positive character references and a petition by the members of a collective division of the state agency in which he worked that he be transferred to a re-education facility. The Supreme Court disagreed and sentenced him instead to a punishment in accordance with Article 154 Paragraph 2 of the Criminal Code of the RSFSR.

COMMENTS AND QUESTIONS

The trial court's description of Utekeshev's behavior sounds more than vaguely familiar. Does it remind you of the Soviet and Cuban factory dispatchers described in the preceding chapter?[128] What do you think made Utekeshev such a sympathetic character to the judge or judges that decided in such "an unjustifiably soft" manner in his favor?

§ 16.5 ADJUDICATING COMPLIANCE WITH ECONOMIC PLAN DUTIES: ORDINARY AND SUPPLY CONTRACTS

The reader is now encouraged to refer back to the preceding chapter, which describes the manner in which economic plans were drafted.[129] Meanwhile, remember the differences on the specifications of the economic plan's details depending upon the nature of the goods produced. If the goods were the massive tools and equipment of heavy industry, every aspect between the producing and consuming corporations had to be planned in the greatest of detail. If the goods were for consumer use, "there was still some permissiveness, as directors were allowed to seek out their counterparts in other corporations and make arrangements for [the supplies] needed. . . ."[130] Two different types of centralized planning contracts eventually emerged. One was an ordinary contract between parties to the plan, simply referred to as a contract; and the other was one that contained numerous details and specifications on delivery dates, spare parts and payments. The latter contract required expert knowledge both as to the elements of the contracts and its legal format. A decree of February 18, 1931 referred to it as a "contract of supply."[131]

Article 44 of the Basic Principles defined these contracts as follows:

> Under a contract of supply the supplying organization obligates itself to transfer to the purchasing organization (the buyer) within a given period of time or on a certain date title to, or, in accordance with the provisions of Arts. 21 and 30 of these [Basic] Principles, the right to dispose of a specific product in accordance with a planning order binding on both organizations and relating to distribution of the product concerned; the purchasing organization obligates itself to accept the product and to pay for it at the established prices. A supply contract is also an agreement concluded between organizations in the exercise of their own judgment by which the supplier obligates itself to deliver to the buyer at a time that does not coincide with the

---

[128] *See supra* § 15:4(D)(6).

[129] *See supra* § 15:4(E).

[130] HAZARD ET AL., *supra* note 9, at 242.

[131] *Id.*

moment of conclusion of the contract a product that is not distributed in accordance with a plan.

The supply of a product without conclusion of a contract shall occur only in those circumstances established by the Council of Ministers of the U.S.S.R. or by the Council of Ministers of a union republic.[132]

Please note that the latter supply contract is one entered into by the parties outside the scope of the plan or delivery plan order.

A. Absence of Raw Materials as a Defense

1. *The 1966 Moscow Wool Outlet Case:*[133] *Lack of Raw Materials*

The Moscow Wool Outlet (MWO), a wholesale outlet, filed a claim with the State Arbitration attached to the Council of Ministers of the USSR to obtain a sanction against the Troitskaia Cloth Factory (TCF) for its breach of the contractual obligation to deliver wool fabrics during the second quarter of 1965. TCF reported that the fabric involved was not supplied to the claimant-buyer because of the lack of raw material for the manufacture of that fabric, and requested a finding of an exemption of the duty to pay sanctions, based on the defense of "absence of fault" on its side. The State Arbitration rejected this defense. It stated that the specifications of the fabric were agreed upon by the parties in a 1965 wholesale fair. TCF was obligated to take all necessary measures to take care to obtain the necessary materials. TCF did not take such measures and was not able to deliver the promised wool; and only after the filing of a claim did it disclose the reasons why it was not able to supply the materials. Moreover, it did not present documentary evidence to the State Arbitration showing that it did take all the necessary measures to be able to perform its obligations. Thus, the State Arbitration found no grounds to relieve TCF from the obligation to pay sanctions.

2. *Kharkov Consumer Goods Distributor: Delayed Delivery and Excuses:*[134] *Standards of Diligence and Planning v. Supplier's Fault*

"K" A Kharkov consumer goods distributor filed a State Arbitration claim for the recovery of a 7,500 ruble penalty from the Chernivets Chemical Consumer Products Factory "F" for failure to supply plastic products worth 280,000 rubles in October 1965. F answered that the claimant had overstated the amount of the penalty since the goods were delivered to K albeit with some delay. The delay was due to the fact that F had only fifty to fifty-five percent of the vinyl film needed for the fulfillment of its own plan of production. For this reason, the respondent, citing its absence of fault, asked to be excused. The State Arbiter decided that the measure of damages should be determined according to Article 57 of the Statute of Supply of Consumer Goods. Taking into account the reduction of the production plan for the factory, the claim was allowed in the amount of 1,827 rubles. On appeal, K argued that although the total amount of production for that factory had been reduced, the supply contract of which it was the promisee had not been changed. The Chief Arbiter affirmed the previous decision and

---

[132] JOHN N. HAZARD & ISAAC SHAPIRO, THE SOVIET LEGAL SYSTEM: POST-STALIN DOCUMENTATION AND HISTORICAL COMMENTARY 107 (1962).

[133] HAZARD ET AL., *supra* note 9, at 252–53.

[134] *Id.* at 253–54.

pointed to Article 209 of the Civil Code of the Ukrainian SSR, which imposed a state contractor's liability only in an instance of fault, which in the present case was absent since the failure to supply was the result of non-issuance of allocation permits for raw materials.

B. Comparative Duties of Diligence: The Absence of "Best Efforts" (Good Faith) v. Implied Clause in the Supply Contract

Notice that in the *Wool Outlet Case* TCF was designated as the sole supplier of the wool needed by the claimant. TCF's defense showed an unwillingness to accept responsibility for employing its best efforts in acting as a sole source supplier. In effect, TCF's attitude was: "I will supply what I have and if I do not happen to have the wool at the time that I am supposed to supply it, it is not my fault." TCF's attitude was not: "I better employ my best efforts in obtaining substitute raw materials in a timely manner or I will risk losing my client and pay substantial damages reflected in my profit and loss statement." What duty of diligence does your law of commercial contracts demand from your sole source suppliers? Do you believe that TCF was responsible for damages that it should have foreseen as a result of its failure to supply in time? Or, does the law of administrative sanctions disregard foreseeability? How would you compare the duties of diligence of an economic plan supplier such as TCF (let me refer to him as an average socialist supplier) and that of a reasonable prudent merchant or *bonus vir*? Would any of these archetypes bear the burden of proving that as sole source suppliers they were presumed to know the present and likely availability of what they promised when they promised it? Which is the more predictable amount, that of an administrative sanction or that of damages awarded pursuant to your law of commercial contracts?

§ 16.6 A PERSONAL EXPERIENCE WITH BULGARIAN CENTRAL PLANNING AND STATE PROPERTY

Shortly after the fall of the last Marxist-Leninist government of Bulgaria in 1989, I was invited to lecture on international commercial and banking law topics at Sofia's (then-labeled) Karl Marx Institute for Economics. My baggage was lost by the air carrier, and I had to buy replacement clothes. It was an eye-opening adventure. The only undershirt I could find (even though I visited each of the stores open for business in central Sofia in the company of high government officials) was a colorful tee-shirt that pictured beach volleyball players under a large sign that read "Malibu Beach," a sign so colorful that it could be seen through my white dress shirt. This locally-made t-shirt was sold in a small government shop for the local currency equivalent of fifteen United States dollars. My hosts then took me to the largest government department store in Bulgaria where I found no underwear or shirts, but was able to buy a serviceable three-piece blue suit identical in shape and color to the hundreds on display. Its price was the local currency equivalent of ten United States dollars.

I asked my hosts, all economists, how they could explain: 1) the absence of everyday items such as underwear and dress shirts in the center of Sofia, and 2) an identical price for resplendent colored tee-shirts and for a tailored three-piece suit. In their response, they blamed these "anomalies" on poorly-implemented economic plans. One of them hinted that the equivalence in prices was caused by a vast supply of suits and a demand for tee shirts that outstripped their supply. He added that this should have been anticipated by the drafters of the economic plan. I asked them how it could have been anticipated if the drafters did not have an idea of what the potential purchasers of tee-shirts and three-piece gabardine suits were willing or able to pay for these products.

One of them smiled and asked me if I was referring to the Lieberman debate during the Khrushtchev days. I answered that perhaps I was, and asked him if he agreed with Lieberman. He smiled again and then he said:

> I do. If I did not, why were you invited to teach us about international commercial law, sales, sales financing, negotiation and financing of letters of credit and so on? None of these transactions can work unless they are as self-supporting as Lieberman's state entities and also subject to transparent and rigorous cost-accounting standards.

He added:

> When buying capital goods in capitalist countries, we had to pay with hard currency which we could only acquire with work or commodities whose value was appraised objectively (what participants in a true marketplace were willing to pay for them); but when we were supplying goods and services at home and getting paid for them, the value of these goods had no objective appraisal, and they were worth whatever value someone with the power to do so assigned to them. Each day that went by we kept on losing true value until poverty was too much to bear, especially after we saw how well our capitalist neighbors were doing.

My eye-opening experience continued. A few days later, at the end of one of my lectures, one of the attendees, a government official, asked me to help him invest funds that were deposited in a state Bulgarian bank in a United States bank or banks. He proposed to transfer these funds (which had recently been converted from *levas* to United States dollars) to an investment (*investitions*) account in banks in which I was a legal advisor. I told him that I was an advisor to an umbrella organization for banks but not to a single bank and politely declined his offer. In parting, I asked him whether these funds belonged to the state or to private parties. He quickly answered: "The funds were deposited by state agencies but now there are no more state depositors; now state and private deposits are practically the same." His answer reminded me of a favorite appellation used by some of my Mexican friends disenchanted with their revolution of 1910. Instead of referring to it as "*la revolucion*" (the revolution) as did many others, they called it "*la robolucion*," an intentional mispronunciation that alluded to the widespread governmental robbery (*robo*) of state and private assets in the name of the revolution.

§ 16.7 THE CIVIL CODE OF THE RUSSIAN FEDERATION OF 1995

A. Style and Scope

At first glance, the Civil Code of the Russian Federation (Parts 1 and 2)[135] (hereinafter Civil Code 1995) appears to be a hybrid civil and commercial code much

---

[135] *See* THE CIVIL CODE OF THE RUSSIAN FEDERATION, PARTS I & II (Peter B. Maggs & A.N. Zhiltsov eds. & trans., 1997) (1995) [hereinafter C.C. (Russia)]. The first part of the Code went into effect on Jan. 1,

like the Swiss Civil Code and Code of Obligations (1907, 1912)[136] and the Italian Civil Code of 1942.[137] It also has provisions derived from the more traditionally civil *Code Civil* of 1804 and the BGB of 1900.[138] Its treatment of the many commercial contracts it includes varies in quantity and quality. Its sale provisions, for example, are as comprehensive as those of any traditional or contemporary civil code and seem influenced by the United Nations Convention on Contracts for the International Sale of Goods (CISG),[139] cited and transcribed frequently in this book. Other subjects are not covered as extensively, as I will discuss shortly. Its organization seems influenced by the BGB and its division into a general section that lays out the basic principles of the code followed by specific sections on each of the selected contracts or transactions. Thus, Article 1, titled the Basic Principles of Civil Legislation, reads:[140]

> 1. Civil legislation is based on the recognition of the equality of the participants in the relations regulated by it, the inviolability of ownership, freedom of contract, the impermissibility of arbitrary interference by anyone in private affairs, the necessity of the unhindered realization of civil law rights, ensuring the restoration of violated rights and judicial protection of them.
>
> 3. Goods, services, and financial assets may be moved freely about on the whole territory of the Russian Federation.

Another basic principle and major scope provision is found in Article 2, which in relevant part reads:[141]

> 1. Civil legislation determines the legal position of the participants in civil commerce, the grounds for the origin and the procedure for realization of the right of ownership and other rights in things . . . regulates contractual and other obligations and also other property relations and related personal non-property relations based upon equality, autonomy of will and the property independence of the participants.
>
> Citizens and legal persons are the participants in relations regulated by civil legislation. The Russian Federation, subjects of the Russian Federation, and municipal formations may also participate in relations regulated by civil legislation (Article 124).

1995. The second part of the Code went into effect on March 1, 1996. I thank my former student Ana Sokolova for her gift of this code.

136 THE SWISS CIVIL CODE: OF DECEMBER 10, 1907 (effective January 1, 1912) (Robert P. Shick trans., The Boston Book Co., 1915); I SWISS CODE OF OBLIGATIONS: ENGLISH TRANSLATION OF THE OFFICIAL TEXT (4th ed., Swiss-American Chamber of Commerce 2003). The Swiss Civil Code of 1907, together with a separate Code of Obligations, went into effect in 1912. *See* Fridolin M.R. Walther, *Introduction to the Swiss Legal System: A Guide for Foreign Researchers*, LLRX (Nov. 15, 2000), http://www.llrx.com/features/swiss.htm (an online introduction to the Swiss legal system, including its codes).

137 CC (Italy) (1942), *available at* http://www.jus.unitn.it/cardozo/Obiter_Dictum/codciv/Codciv.htm.

138 *See supra* chs. 8–12 (discussing the features of these codes).

139 United Nations Convention on Contracts for the International Sale of Goods, Apr. 11, 1980, 19 I.L.M. 668, 1489 U.N.T.S. 3.

140 C.C. (Russia), *supra* note 184, at 1.

141 *Id.* at 2.

Civil legislation regulates the relations between persons engaging in entrepreneurial activity or with their participation, proceeding from the position that entrepreneurial activity is independent activity done at one's own risk directed at the systematic receipt of profit from the use of property, sale of goods, performance of work, or rendering of service by persons registered in this capacity by the procedure established by a statute.

3. Civil legislation shall not be applied to property relations based on administrative or other authoritative subordination of one party to another, including tax and other financial and administrative relations, unless otherwise provided by legislation.

B. Epistemology, Political Ideology and Troubling Terminology

These basic principles reveal the Code's epistemology (or theory of knowledge). To the questions "What is the mission of this code and where do its fundamental concepts come from?", Article 2.1 answers that the mission of the Russian Federation's civil legislation is to determine the legal "position" (perhaps meaning "status") of the participants in civil commerce, the grounds for the origin and the procedure for the realization of the right of ownership and other rights in things. In addition to reflecting the difficulty of translating very abstract concepts, it alludes to the paramount position of the concept of ownership in the edifice of the Russian Federation's private substantive and procedural law. From it spring the rights and duties of private law and procedure. Please recall that according to Evgeny Pashukanis, the concept of ownership, in turn, stemmed from the seminal legal relationship involved in the exchange of commodities.[142]

If Pashukanis's ideas provided in his day and place an interesting hypothesis on the origin and eventual disappearance of private law, this is no longer the case. Many of the contemporary commercial transactions do not originate from the need to protect the right of property in the commodities bought and sold, exchanged, lent or used as security by the parties. As discussed in the preceding chapter,[143] ownership of commodities, business assets and even controlling interests in business associations has a very different meaning today than it had for Marx and Engels. In addition, important areas of the law of commercial contracts, such as secured lending, among others, are more dependent upon possessory than upon ownership or title rights. And possession is frequently centered not on tangible assets, but on incorporeal ones, such as the debtor's "streams of income." As stated by U.C.C. § 9–202, with respect to secured lending collateral, it is immaterial who holds title, the debtor or the creditor.[144] Thus, for a commercial code to ascribe superiority to rights of ownership of commercial assets as a basic principle would be, in my opinion, dysfunctional.

From the standpoint of the widely-accepted civil-commercial dichotomy, the concept of "civil commerce" is confusing because it suggests that there is a commerce that is not civil, in which case it is not clear what the code means by "civil." Could it mean a unilateral commercial act where a merchant sells consumer goods to a consumer? Yet that is not the meaning one obtains from looking at the vast number of

142 *See supra* § 16:2(B).

143 *See supra* § 15:3(D)(3) (discussing Marx's mistaken notion of ownership).

144 Kozolchyk & Furnish, *A Comparative Analysis*, at 249.

purely or bilateral commercial contracts, such as for the carriage of commercial goods, freight-forwarding, commercial credit, assignment of accounts receivable, etc. Would "private" perhaps be a better term?

Similarly, the focus of Article 2 on "the relations between persons engaging in entrepreneurial activity or with their participation" is equally troublesome, particularly because of the imprecise and confusing nature of the root term "*impresa*" or "enterprise" as the determinant of the scope of codes such as the Italian Civil Code of 1942 or the Honduran Commercial Code of 1952.[145] The term "enterprise" opens up the question of the status of micro- and small businesses. Surely, micro- and small businesses would not qualify for the status of one of the three "sticks" in the same fascist bundle (*fascio*) that included the state and labor unions in the Italian Civil Code of 1942. At a minimum, small merchants would have had to comply with the often costly requirements of licensing and registration. Was this the entrepreneurial requirement desired by a surely non-fascist Russian Federation? Did it not wish to encourage as many potential micro- and small merchants or "effective owners of businesses" as possible?

In addition, the definition of entrepreneurial activity in Article 2 requires that the enterprise evince an "independent activity done at one's own risk directed at the systematic receipt of profit from the use of property, sale of goods, performance of work or rendering of service by persons registered in this capacity." Yet it does not clarify the meaning of some of its essential components. Take, for example, "independence." Does it mean that a corporation that is part of a conglomerate or holding company but otherwise has a good deal of autonomy running its business is not an entrepreneur? Or, take the requirement of a systematic receipt of profits. Does it mean that one of the largest virtual bookstores in the world, such as Amazon.com, was not an entrepreneur during its first few years of existence when it was not systematically or otherwise earning profits?

On the other hand, there is nothing ambiguous or uncertain about the political ideology of the Civil Code of 1995. It is anti-Marxist and pro-free market economy, as made abundantly clear by Article 1, among many others. The equality of all of the participants in civil code relations is part of a venerable tradition associated with the promulgation of the *Code Civil* of 1804 and, at a much earlier age, with the international commercial fairs and their principle of "peace of the marketplace."[146] The same is true with Article 1's embrace of the inviolability of ownership, freedom of contract and the impermissibility of arbitrary interference by anyone in private affairs. All of these are highly welcome statements for an aspiring free marketplace of goods, services and ideas.

C. Anachronistic and Harmful Provisions

While neither time nor space allow a detailed analysis of the commercial contracts enabled by this code, its treatment of the various types of sale agreements is, as mentioned earlier, among the most comprehensive found anywhere. The same cannot be said, however, about other contracts whose treatment remains anachronistic and harmful. Take, for example, the contract of sale with retention of title. Consistent with

---

145 *See supra* § 14:5.

146 *See supra* § 9:2(B).

the Civil Code's epistemology of ownership as a seminal concept, Article 491 makes the retention of ownership by the seller of goods sold on credit dispositive of the seller's right to recover the goods sold and unpaid, regardless of possibly superior claims by other creditors.

Assume, for example, that a bank "C" helped finance that acquisition of the goods sold on credit by "A" to "B" and that those goods would be temporarily stored in country or jurisdiction "D," where the bank filed its security interest in those goods in a local public registry. Article 491 completely disregards the effects of an earlier and valid registration of a security interest in the same goods. Thus, by allowing the retention of title of Article 491, the Civil Code of 1995 is creating a "secret" (unregistered or recorded) lien which ultimately impedes the access of Russian Federation merchants to a modern and much less expensive commercial credit system than that of the retention of title. The same is true with Article 501 (on the contract of hire-purchase) and with Article 665 (on the contract of financial leasing). Anytime these two transactions are used to disguise their true purpose, which was to lend money to the lessee-purchaser and secure its repayment by using the thing supposedly leased but in reality bought on credit, uncertainty is injected into the system of secured transactions, for these secret liens can defeat recorded ones. Accordingly, the bank C's of this world rightly feel unprotected and would not want to finance such transactions. It would have made much more sense from the standpoint of facilitating commercial credit to do what was done by the OAS Model Inter-American Law on Secured Transactions in 2002: Unify all of the transactions intended as security interests, such as conditional sales or sales with retention or reservation of title, chattel mortgages or mortgages of movable property, pledges of commercial or agricultural assets, hire purchases, financial leases and others, under the category of security interests (*garantías mobiliarias*) in movables and subject them all to the same requirements of notice via registration in a public registry or, in some instances, creditor or third party possession.[147]

Similarly anachronistic and harmful are the provisions on letters of credit. Several of the present provisions (Articles 867–873) ignore, for example, the all-important presence of standby letters of credit (commercial, financial and other) in today's national and international financial markets. Contrary to the widely-observed Uniform Customs and Practices for Documentary Credits of the International Chamber of Commerce (ICC), the Civil Code of 1995 assumes that revocable letters of credit are still in common use and are governed by a presumption of revocability.[148] Further, the Civil Code of 1995 needs to provide a stronger support for widely-observed commercial and especially international customs and practices than provided by its Article 5.

Article 5 presently states that custom and usage of trade is subordinate to an obligatory contractual stipulation by the parties to that contract. Yet what contract is Article 5 talking about? Is it the contract that underlies the issuance of a letter of credit, for example, a contract of sale that specifies a certain number of goods and documents that must be presented by a seller-beneficiary of a letter of credit to a paying bank? Or is it the letter of credit itself? Once a letter of credit has been issued,

---

147 *See* Kozolchyk & Furnish, *A Comparative Analysis*. *See also* OAS, *Model Inter-American Law on Secured Transactions* (2002), http://www.oas.org/dil/Model_Law_on_Secured_Transactions.pdf.

148 *Compare, e.g.,* C.C. (Russia), *supra* note 184, at 293 (Article 868(3), which adopted the presumption of revocability) *with* UCP 500 art. 6(c) *and* UCP 600 art. 2 (2007) (defining credit, which does away with revocable credits).

it governs the relationship between the parties to the letter of credit, especially when it contains its own terms and conditions and is made subject to the Uniform Customs and Practices for Documentary Credits of the ICC (presently the UCP 600). In such a case, the parties to that letter of credit are subject to the terms and conditions of the letter of credit and of its customs and usages, even though some of them are parties to the underlying sale agreement and this agreement will govern their purchase and sale (as opposed to their letter of credit) relationship.

§ 16.8 CONCLUSIONS

The Civil Code of 1995 contains helpful provisions in its general part and in the various sections on some of the most common contemporary commercial contracts such as sale agreements that can certainly encourage the Russian Federation's creation of a viable national and international marketplace. It also contains terms, concepts, principles and rules that are inconsistent with such a goal. In its attempt to generate such an encouragement, the code should empower commercial associations to promulgate sets of standard and best practices for the various sectors of the economy. The empowering provision should enjoy a high-enough hierarchy to make courts, lawyers and, last but not least, merchants observe them as the living law of commercial contracts. One such provision can be found in the Colombian Commercial Code currently in force. Article 3 of that code states:

> Commercial customs shall have the same authority as commercial statutes, provided that they are not expressly or tacitly contrary to the latter, and provided that the facts that create such commercial customs are public, uniform and recurring in the place where the obligations are to be performed or where the parties' relation arose.

In the absence of local customs, the country's general customs shall apply, provided that such customs meet the requirements established in the previous paragraph.[149]

Yet, how effective would such a provision be under an otherwise authoritarian and corrupt regime? A recent book by Gregory Feifer, a journalist and keen observer of Russia's mores,[150] confirms the connections among Russia's authoritarianism, corruption and legal invertebration highlighted in the present and previous chapter. In a recent interview,[151] he pointed out that many Americans cannot understand why Russians:

> [C]ontinue to support their president, the authoritarian Vladimir Putin, who's destroyed democracy along with his political opponents, overseen an explosion of corruption and threatened to direct nuclear missiles at Western Europe. Does that mean e they learned nothing from their very painful past?[152]

He suggests that part of the answer lies in Russia's all-pervasive corruption which provides a relatively easy way for the leaders to exert power by coopting the Russian people "by giving them a feeling they have a stake in the system—because they're

---

[149] C. COM. (Colom.) art. 3 (2010) (this Code is currently in effect).

[150] *See* GREGORY FEIFER, RUSSIANS; THE PEOPLE BEHIND THE POWER (2014).

[151] Justin McDonnell, *Life Under Putin,* THE DIPLOMAT (Feb. 19, 2014), *available at* http://thediplomat.com/2014/02/life-under-putin/ .

[152] *Id.*

getting something in return—and by coercing them because it enables the authorities to prosecute almost anyone."[153] Thus, he concludes that:

> Where we would see corruption and curbs on individual freedom as a threat to our society's viability, many Russians see Putin's presidency and its shortcomings as necessary for providing at least some measure of stability.[154]

As made clear in the present and previous chapter, as well as in Chapter 14 on Latin America's codification of commercial law and in the following chapters on Chinese commercial contract law,what the bribers get in return for their bribes is a monopoly over a piece of the marketplace whose size varies with the size of the bribe and the political or military power of its recipient. But this monopoly can disappear at any time that another briber gives the corrupt official a larger bribe or the corrupt official decides that the bribed arrangement is no longer profitable or convenient. Such are the hallmarks of the predictability y of legal invertebration. Paradoxically, then, legal invertebration is associated with authoritarian attempts to govern the production and distribution of goods and services, regardless of political ideology and geography. Thus, it has been as apparent under Latin American capitalist or fascist dictatorships as it was under the Marxist-Leninist Soviet Union and- as will now be discussing= under Confucian and Neo Confucian Imperial China and under the "socialist market economy" of the Peoples Republic of China.

---

[153] *Id.*

[154] *Id.*

Chapter 17

CHINESE IMPERIAL, MOSTLY LIVING LAW OF CONTRACTS

§ 17.1 INTRODUCTION: LEGAL INVERTEBRETATION AND FAMILISM, CONFUCIANISM AND LEGALISM

Encouraged by former Chinese graduate students, my wife and I toured China in May 2007. We came into contact with one of the world's great civilizations, a striking geographical and human landscape and a huge, time-compressed experiment in economic and social change. As a result of its industrial production, exports and massive construction projects during the last three decades, the People's Republic of China (hereinafter PRC) has become the fastest growing and one of the most important economies of the world.[1] Starting in 1978, the PRC adopted policies for the creation of what it labeled a "socialist market economy" fourteen years later.[2] Many of these policies were to be carried out by what the Plenum of the Central Committee of the Communist Party (hereinafter CCCP) referred to as a "modern entrepreneurial system."[3]

As with other major representative jurisdictions covered in this book, the present chapter will be devoted to the historical and socio-economic context of the Chinese law of commercial contracts. This is a particularly necessary task because one cannot subsume the Chinese legal system in general and its law of commercial contracts in particular under the civil and common law systems any more than one can subsume it, especially today, under a category such as "socialist" law. Chinese law has by now absorbed institutions from the major legal systems while retaining its deeply ingrained cultural values and attitudes toward law, society and, last but not least, family. In fact, if I were asked to isolate the values that have had the greatest influence on China's law of commercial contracts, I would have to say that they are what I described as

---

[1] *See* US-CHINA BUSINESS COUNCIL, US-CHINA TRADE STATISTICS AND CHINA'S WORLD TRADE STATISTICS (1996–2009) (on file with author). According to the China Statistic Yearbook, the total volume of imports and exports of China grew from US$20.64 billion in 1978 to US$360.63 billion in 1999 to US$850.99 billion in 2003 and up to US$2,173.8 billion, *i.e.*, well over two trillion U.S. dollars, in 2007. Meanwhile, the contract value of foreign investment in the PRC grew from US$28.769 billion during the six-year period from 1978 through 1984 to: US$52.009 billion in 1999, US$116.901 billion in 2003 and US$156.588 billion in 2004. *See also* PHOTIUS COUTSOUKIS AND INFORMATION TECHNOLOGY ASSOCIATES, *Amount of Foreign Investment by Type* (2006) (data table going over the amount of foreign investment, by type, that China received in the years 2003 and 2004), http://www.allcountries.org/china_statistics/18_14_amount_of_foreign_investment_by.html. *See generally* Kenneth Dam, *China as a Test Case: Is the Rule of Law Essential for Economic Growth?* (John M. Olin L. & Econ., Working Paper No. 275, 2006) (discussing China's growth and the relationship of this growth with the rule of law), *available at* http://papers.ssrn.com/sol3/papers.cfm?abstract_id=880125.

[2] Although many of the measures that are presently ascribed by the PRC to a "socialist market economy" had been enacted since 1978, the actual term "socialist market economy" was officially sanctioned in October 1992 at the XIV Congress of the PRC. *See* Michele Fabbri, *China—"Socialist market economy" or just plain capitalism?*, IN DEFENCE OF MARXISM (Jan. 20, 2006), http://www.marxist.com/china-socialist-market-economy200106.htm.

[3] *Id.*

"familism" and "legalism"—the former derived from the struggle for agricultural subsistence by the family as an economic unit and the latter from the Chinese's respect and obedience to hierarchy, whether defined in familistic, religious, intellectual, ethical, political or military terms. The respect for and obedience to hierarchy is a value which inspires both familistic and legalistic rules, but produces undesirable results for legal and economic development.

Since familism and legalism are at the center of gravity of the Chinese legal system, the study of China's living law of commercial contracts acquires paramount importance. To determine what law *actually* governs contract making, interpretation and adjudication in China, one must understand how official or written laws interact with their underlying familistic and legalistic norms. Thus, China's living law of commercial contracts is but a reflection of the interaction of these underlying norms. And the age and size of this society, equal to no other in our planet, has made its living law a much more powerful force than any other known to man.

Where was this living law found, who applied it, to whom and how? Upon reviewing recently discovered compilations of contractual documents, it is apparent that contractual practices, including some forms of business associations, are thousands of years old and mostly related to agricultural endeavors.[4] It is also apparent that despite occasional governmental attempts to ban or modify living law institutions following periodic transformations of China's economy, the strong influence of these institutions manifested in family, lineage and clan transactions and informal or customary rules, was still discernible. This was especially true with respect to the sale and distribution of real estate and other valuable family assets. Yet, who within these associations shaped this living law? Was it shaped by the rich who had the power to "promulgate" it as well as by the poor who could only react to it "with their hands and feet," by the landed gentry as well as by the dispossessed?

As we visited rural China and watched malnourished farmers hunched over their buffalo-driven plows in what seemed like an endless reach for the yield of a barely life-sustaining soil, words such as "ancestral" kept coming to mind. To be sure, a major transformation of social and legal institutions was taking place in Chinese cities. As we looked up at the forests of skyscrapers and were told of the large number of rural window cleaners or drove by the endless rows of assembly plants filled with workers of a similar rural extraction, we realized how today's rural presence in the cities is yet another illustration of an ancient predicament; the fate of China's peasantry continues to be decided by others, at times thoughtfully, and many other times arbitrarily and harshly. It did not seem as if these former peasants—now present city dwellers—had much to do with shaping any official or living law of contracts or with what was happening to them and their families, except by their aversion to it and their perennial attempts to circumvent it.[5]

Whether conscripted to fight wars or raise the horses of fighting armies, to relocate to drier or more productive land, to act as the pulling force for difficult river

---

[4] *See infra* § 18:1.

[5] *See* MAX WEBER, THE RELIGION OF CHINA: CONFUCIANISM AND TAOISM 79 (Hans H. Gerth trans., Free Press ed. 1968). As Weber points out, with respect to the constant attempts at land reform by Chinese governments, "The various attempts at land reform by the [Chinese] state led to two results: the absence of rational and large scale agricultural enterprise, and the intensely suspicious aversion of the entire peasantry toward any governmental interference in landownership and land utilization." *Id.*

navigation, or to build and man unproductive furnaces of "household industries" (a project whose end result was one of mankind's most colossal famines), peasants as a group had little to say in these life and death decisions. Only when conditions were wholly intolerable did they rebel, and then with little improvement of their predicament.[6]

It was as if Chinese subsistence farmers, among the world's hardest working and most resilient, were for some undetermined reason kept out of the living law "loop" and were thus likely to experience, again and again, major disasters at the hands of nature or of autocratic rulers, even when these rulers came from their own ranks.[7] In a 2008 speech, Professor Jerome Cohen, one of the West's foremost experts on Chinese law, commented on the lack of representation for large, perhaps the largest, segments of the Chinese population as follows: "Chinese have learned that collective action may be the only effective way to demonstrate the need for resolving their grievances. . . because the legal system has not developed the kinds of institutions necessary to process grievances."[8]

Finally, it was also apparent that despite their revolutionary slogans of radical institutional change, the founders of the PRC, at least in 1949, welcomed a modicum of institutional continuity. The existence of such a policy was confirmed by a United States Library of Congress study, which rejected the conclusion that every traditional institution was changed or was intended to be changed in 1949.[9] According to this study, those who established the PRC in 1949 were not intent on making the new legal institutions a replica of foreign models; yet they also "had an ambivalent attitude

---

[6] Professor Patricia Ebrey transcribes a description of the plight of China's small farmers written by the scholar Chao Cuo in 178 B.C.E. that, in Professor Ebrey's words, "could well have been repeated in most later dynasties":

> They labour at ploughing in the spring and hoeing in the summer, harvesting in the autumn and storing foodstuff in winter, cutting wood, performing labour service for the local government, all the while exposed to the dust of the spring, the heat of the summer, the storms of autumn, and the chill of the winter. Through all four seasons they never get a day off. . . . No matter how hard they work they can be ruined by floods or droughts, or cruel and arbitrary officials who impose taxes at the wrong times or keep changing their orders. . . . Some as a consequence sell their lands and houses, even their children and grandchildren.

PATRICIA BUCKLEY EBREY, THE CAMBRIDGE ILLUSTRATED HISTORY OF CHINA 74 (9th prtg. 2010). While describing life during the Ming Dynasty, she refers to the "160,000 soldiers of the transport army—who pulled loaded barges with ropes where needed—thus bec[oming] the lifeline of the capital." *Id.* at 194. I used the phrase "as a group had little to say" in the principal text to differentiate group or pluralistic decisions from those taken by individual rulers who may have started as conscripts or peasant soldiers and who after a successful military career rose to the ranks of general and emperor as was the case with the founder of the Ming Dynasty, Zhu Yuanzhang, or by a political and military leader such as Mao Tse Tung "born into a peasant family . . . in the province of Hunan. . . ." JUNG CHANG & JON HALLIDAY, MAO: THE UNKNOWN STORY 3 (Anchor Books 2006) (2005); *see also* EBREY, *supra* note 6, at 190; Henry C. K. Liu, *The Abduction of Modernity, Part 3: Rule of law vs Confucianism*, ASIA TIMES ONLINE (July 24, 2003), www.atimes.com/atimes/China/EG24Ad01.html. Liu places the number of Chinese peasant uprisings at "seven . . . in 4,000 years of history. . . ." Liu, *supra* note 6. Yet, I for one am not convinced of the accuracy of such a statement, especially when the same author describes Mao Zedong as the "towering giant in modern Chinese history, with apt insights on Taoist doctrines. . . ." *Id.*

[7] EBREY, *supra* note 6, at 74.

[8] Sky Canaves, *Thirty Years of Chinese Legal Reform*, WALL ST. J. CHINA, Dec. 9, 2008 (reporting on the lecture given by Jerome Cohen at the Foreign Correspondents Club of Hong Kong in December 2008), http://blogs.wsj.com/chinarealtime/2008/12/04/thirty-years-of-chinese-legal-reform/.

[9] U.S. LIBRARY OF CONGRESS, *Traditional Society and Culture*, *in* CHINA: A COUNTRY STUDY (Robert L. Worden et al. eds., 1987) [hereinafter *Chinese Traditional Society*] (on file with author) *available at* http://countrystudies.us/china/42.htm.

toward their country's past and its traditional society, condemning some aspects and praising others."[10] Thus, they attempted to change rural land tenure and education while leaving other institutions, such as the all-encompassing and influential family structure, much as they were.[11]

It was becoming apparent that China's customary (living) law was nourished by an uneasy mix of Confucian and Neo-Confucian moral law ideology and by contractual practices designed to circumvent burdensome or excessively authoritarian-legalistic rules. And, as just noted, these were the forces responsible for imperial China's multi-layered and often contradictory legal fabric. To discern the strands of this legal fabric, it will be necessary to understand first the role of institutions such as the family, lineage and clan and subsequently the transactional values that governed these institutions, including those inspired by Confucian and Neo-Confucian ideologies.

After providing this context, I will focus on influential thinkers, especially Confucius and his disciples, and on merchants as sources of China's living law and will conclude with a discussion of the causes of what some historians and Sinologists refer to as the "Great Divergence."[12] This divide took place mostly during the seventeenth and eighteenth centuries, a time during which China seemed poised to develop a prosperous capitalist economy such as that of Great Britain, but failed to do so.

In previous chapters, I have explored the contribution of commercial legal institutions to Germany's impressive economic takeoff during the three generations that followed its unification. In subsequent chapters, I will examine the takeoffs of Great Britain and the United States and the commercial legal institutions that contributed to them. One of the concerns of this chapter, then, is: What prevented China's capitalist takeoff during the centuries of the Great Divergence? In the absence of viable legal institutions, will China's recent and present economic growth continue to be sustained? When the reader inquires into what is China's present law of commercial contracts, he or she must understand that this law is much like the proverbial iceberg. More than with any other legal system and culture studied in this book—and because of China's long and eventful history—the rules, principles and concepts discussed in this chapter are merely what appear on the tip of its institutional iceberg. They are inseparably tied to the legal, economic and cultural institutions discussed in this chapter. Thus, the meaning of present-day statutes, court decisions, doctrinal writings and even customary law rules must be understood in their peculiarly Chinese historical context.

§ 17.2 THE FAMILY, LINEAGE AND CLAN AS EARLY PRIVATE LAW MAKERS AND ECONOMIC UNITS

In the 1998 edition of their enlightening "new history" of China, Professors John Fairbank and Merle Goldman point out that, until very recently, the Chinese family was a microcosm of the Chinese state:

---

[10] *Id.*

[11] *Id. See also generally* JOHN KING FAIRBANK & EDWIN O. REISCHAUER, CHINA: TRADITION AND TRANSFORMATION (rev. ed. 1989); WILLIAM THEODORE DE BARY, SOURCES OF CHINESE TRADITION (1960). I found these sources, including the U.S. Library of Congress's study, to be quite helpful.

[12] *See infra* § 17:5 (for a discussion of the writings on the "Great Divergence").

> The family, not the individual, was the social unit and the responsible element in the political life of its locality. The filial piety and obedience inculcated in family life were the training ground for loyalty to the ruler and obedience to the constituted authority in the state.
>
> The father was a supreme autocrat, with control over the use of all family property and income and a decisive voice in arranging the marriages of the children. . . . According to the law, he could sell his children into slavery or even execute them for improper conduct.[13]

These authors note that an advantage of the hierarchical ordering of a family and state was to allow each member of the hierarchy to know automatically:

> [W]here he stands in his family or society. He can have security in the knowledge that if he does his prescribed part, he may expect reciprocal action from others in the system.
>
> Within the extended family, every child from birth was involved in a highly ordered system of kinship relations with elder brothers, sisters, maternal elder brothers' wives, and other kinds of aunts, uncles, cousins, grandparents, and in-laws. . . . Family members expected to be called by the correct term indicating their relationship to the person addressing them.[14]

Also significant in terms of hierarchy was that, while family headship passed intact from father to son, family property did not. Early in its history, China abandoned primogeniture as the principle of inheritance of family property in favor of an equal distribution of family land among all of the sons.[15] This made the family not only an economic but also a private law making unit inasmuch as the distribution of family land entailed the conferral of rights and the imposition of duties for those using the land.

In his study "The Traditional Chinese Family and Lineage," David K. Jordan, a research anthropologist at the University of California, San Diego, explained each element of the definition of the Chinese traditional family (*jiā*, 家): a patrilineal, patriarchal, prescriptively virilocal kinship group that shares a common household budget. Of these, it is important to differentiate among patrilineal, lineage and clan associations.[16]

A. Patriarchal Hierarchy

The term "patriarchal" applies to a hierarchically organized family whose prime authority is vested in the senior-most male. In what is also referred to as an "agnatic descent," an individual family member must descend from his or her father. Thus, an agnate is one's genetic relative exclusively through males: a kinsman with whom one has a common ancestor by descent in an unbroken male line. This meant that no two members of a Chinese family had equal authority: "[o]fficially at least, (1) senior

---

[13] JOHN KING FAIRBANK & MERLE GOLDMAN, CHINA: A NEW HISTORY 18 (2006).

[14] *Id.* at 20.

[15] *Id.* at 21.

[16] David K. Jordan, *Traditional Chinese Family and Lineage*, UNIVERSITY OF CALIFORNIA, SAN DIEGO, DIVISION OF SOCIAL SCIENCES, http://weber.ucsd.edu/~dkjordan/chin/familism.html. I am most grateful to my former student and now Professor Ling Zhu of Long Island State University for having corrected the spelling and calligraphy of Chinese terms in the three chapters on Chinese law and practice.

generations were superior to junior generations, (2) older people were superior to younger ones, and (3) men were superior to women. . . . Normatively . . . a family would be headed by a man who was older and/or of more senior generation. . . ."[17] Jordan's discussion of family hierarchy helps to explain central components of the Chinese living law of families and their internal and, at times, external transactions:

> Family hierarchy was very emphatically symbolized in the concept of *xiào* [孝] . . . which is usually translated as "filial piety," but is more accurately rendered "filial subordination." When wills clashed, it was expected (and legally enforced) that the will of a family superior should prevail over the will of a family inferior. Traditional law held a child's insubordination to a parent to be a capital offense, and a daughter-in-law's insubordination to her parents-in-law grounds for divorce.[18]

I should add parenthetically that Jordan's references to a "traditional law" and to its "legal enforcement" do not necessarily mean a law governed by officially promulgated codes, but rather by rules of ethical behavior enforced by unofficial community institutions and influenced largely by Confucius's teachings.[19]

B. Place of Residence

The term "prescriptively virilocal" refers to the expectation that a newly-married couple will live with the groom's family; the men were expected to bring their wives to live on the family estate. "Kinship," in turn, means that members of the family have to be related genealogically, *i.e.*, either by common ancestors or by marriage.[20]

C. Common Budget and the Importance of Family Land for Family Survival

When living together, the members of the family shared a common budget and supporting assets. This meant that possessions, income, and expenses of all family members were pooled, and decisions about resource distribution involved all family members, but were ultimately taken by the patriarchal authority.[21] Jordan, among others, suggests that the common budget is one of the most important features of the internal order of Chinese families.[22] By partaking in the pooling of the assets of a family, an adopted child, for example, could become a member of the family, regardless of kinship. Further, the same family budget could be shared by a family across several households. For example, a family could have members living in farming village "A" and others in small town "B" or in different locations, and all would share a common budget.

Columbia University's Professor Madeleine Zelin has recently drawn attention to the importance of lineage and a common budget in the emergence of the Chinese

---

[17] *Id.*

[18] *Id.*

[19] *See generally* Liang Zhiping, *Explicating Law: A Comparative Perspective of Chinese and Western Legal Culture*, 3 J. CHINESE L. 55 (1989); CHARLES DE SECONDAT, BARON DE MONTESQUIEU, THE SPIRIT OF THE LAWS (Anne M. Cohler et al., Cambridge Univ. Press 1989) (1748); DERK BODDE & CLARENCE MORRIS, LAW IN IMPERIAL CHINA: EXEMPLIFIED BY 190 CH'ING DYNASTY CASES (1973).

[20] Jordan, *supra* note 16.

[21] *Id.*

[22] *Id. See also infra* § 17:5(A).

version of investment trusts.[23] Since male descendants had the responsibility to perform ancestral rites honoring their predecessors in the agnatic chain of descent, "as early as the Song dynasty [960–1279] [A.D.] families were encouraged to ensure the appropriate performance of these rites by sequestering a portion of the patrimony of each generation in the form of an endowment that could not be divided."[24]

Because of the importance of the common budget, then, the division of family assets (*fēnjiā*, 分家) was a critical legal transaction.[25] When family members decided that their union was no longer feasible, they would agree to a division of the family's assets and the creation of new, financially-separate families. This situation occurred typically after the death of a father left two brothers and their wives and children as a common economic unit; differences in the productivity of the brothers or in the number of their children led to disputes settled by such a family division.[26] Traditionally, the mediator of such a dispute was the brother of one of the older married-in women, and usually a contract would commit the settlement to writing. As will be illustrated in the following chapter, this agreement was quite common, even in late imperial law.

As pointed out by the University of Washington's Professor Patricia Ebrey, a fundamental reason why farmers often had difficulties surviving during most of China's history was the above-mentioned equal division of family property among all sons:

> With the decline of feudal tenures and the spread of free buying and selling of land, the division of family property became customary. . . . The Chinese family remained patrilineal, patrilocal, and patriarchal, but it no longer favoured oldest sons in the transmission of [all the family] property. Ownership of land changed hands frequently as those with wealth . . . purchased it and those who inherited land had to sell parts of it to meet expenses. To a family head, the survival of his family depended not merely on the survival of a male heir to continue the ancestral sacrifices, but also on preserving or securing enough family property to allow all the sons to marry and support a family.[27]

This observation explains the remarkable similarity between standard clauses in contracts that conveyed family land subject to the Hindu law's doctrine of "necessity"[28] and to the customs of the Chinese patrilineal, patrilocal family and lineage. The Chinese conveyances of ancestral land, invariably and in a standardized fashion, asserted the serious economic need of the grantor as the reason for the conveyance. On the other hand, as will be discussed shortly, agricultural productivity required that family members be independent and do so by exploiting their own land. This need for greater productivity was the reason why a "frustrated" imperial bureaucrat found it necessary to legalistically impose punitive taxes on family land, thereby forcing the

---

[23] Madeleine Zelin, Informal Law and the Firm in Early Modern China 8–9, 13 (Feb. 23–24, 2007) (unpublished manuscript) (on file with author), *available at* www.international.ucla.edu/cms/files/Zelin_Informal_Law.doc.

[24] *Id.* at 8–9.

[25] Jordan, *supra* note 16.

[26] *Id.*

[27] *See* EBREY, *supra* note 6, at 74.

[28] *See supra* § 3:6(B); see also Kozolchyk, *Fairness,* at 258; *see also* Kozolchyk, *Roadmap,* at 5–6.

departure of many a family member from the family household.[29] This was an early instance in which a Confucian-inspired living law of single-line agnatic family ownership clashed with a "legalistic" attempt to encourage economic development by fragmenting family land ownership.

D. Patrilineal Lineage and Legal Invertebration

A patrilineal lineage (or patrilineage) is a group of families and descendants of a single, specific ancestor, organized in various locations by those heads of families who descended from the same male ancestor. This organization was set up usually for religious or economic purposes.[30] Professor Ebrey points out that these lineages were more common in southern China where migrants from the north had settled in areas with uncultivated land for "many descendants to remain in the vicinity, making for a critical mass of nearby kinsmen."[31] Some of these lineages contributed significantly to the growth of one of the most important commercial clans, the Huizhou (徽州), who will be discussed later in this chapter. Huizhou lineages flourished "in the mid Ming [dynasty] . . . benefiting from the willingness of the many wealthy local merchant families to make donations."[32] Since the basis for the organization of lineages was kinship, lineages included different social classes, from the rich to the poor. Not infrequently, richer members were required to provide money or valuable property to help the poorer members.[33]

Patrilineage relies on binding family rules and requires the ability to identify the ancestor who legitimizes the organization and its rules. Given the number of families that can and usually do claim membership in the lineage, the task of identifying the common ancestor has proven difficult even when carried out by expert genealogists. Anthropologists refer to this ancestor as "apical" because he is at the "apex" of the genealogy by which the lineage membership is determined, and the descent links to this person are known.[34] Where they existed, these lineages owned property that could range from a modest religious hall to venerate ancestors to highly productive rented-out fields.[35] These holdings supported transactions such as loans to members of the lineage, insurance to cover catastrophic events, schools for the benefit of lineage members, and the lineage trusts created at first to ensure the performance of rites to honor ancestors and eventually for commercial investments.[36] On many occasions, the same apical hierarchy was responsible for settling disputes prompted by familial, lineage or intra-clan transactions.[37] In fact, heads of lineage associations were so strong that they were at times charged by the local governments with administrative functions such as tax collection and settlement of disputes.

---

[29] *See infra* § 17:4(A).

[30] Jordan, *supra* note 16.

[31] EBREY, *supra* note 6, at 207.

[32] *Id.*

[33] Jordan, *supra* note 16.

[34] *Id.* Jordan also points out that "[i]n China, as in other lineage systems, it was (and is) regarded as incestuous to marry (or mate with) a member of the same lineage." *Id.*

[35] *Id.*

[36] *Id.*

[37] *Id.*

Lineages, thus, had their own living law. Traditionally, they supplemented their genealogical documents with "family instructions" (jiāxùn, 家训).[38] These were moral directives by elderly members passed down to their descendants, sometimes with rules for the conduct of the lineage business. And since lineages lost face if their members engaged in illegal or immoral acts, they had provisions to punish or eject errant members and expunge their names from genealogies.[39] Indeed, as reported by Professor Ebrey: "By the mid Ming, lineages in some areas of the country were introducing elaborate systems to control and discipline members. In one area of Jiangxi province, for instance, lineages wrote up sets of rules, giving lineage leaders considerable authority to settle disputes and enforce compliance."[40]

Because lineages sought to promote the welfare of their members, and since this could well be at the expense of non-members, conflict between lineages was not unusual. Further, in areas where competing lineages were strong, local warfare was an occasional result. Even in those instances that did not result in open violence, strong underlying tensions existed and this encouraged rules that insisted on residence with those lineage-mates who were close to their kin. The results were the emergence of single-lineage villages, or villages where most residents were members of a single dominant lineage, and this increased the number of conflicts with neighboring villages whose members were not of the same dominant lineage. Predictably, the disciplinary and private law making functions of lineages became unenforceable and invertebrate.

Still, lineages carried with them the prestige of membership. Although one might get the impression that the system of lineages was universal in China, according to Jordan, it was not. The causes, as just noted, were the confusing methods of grouping families and, even more so, the loose rules for membership in clans. Indeed, the "lineage system" was so frail by the advent of the PRC that no official steps were needed to be taken to end the organized lineages that remained. As concluded by Jordan, "[o]nce ownership of private property was restricted, lineages . . . collapsed on their own."[41]

COMMENTS AND QUESTIONS

How do the disciplinary rules and adjudication methods adopted by Chinese lineages differ from those of the Italian medieval "*corporazione*" described earlier in this book[42] by Professor Levin Goldschmidt as forerunners of the consulates and eventually of commercial courts?[43] What are the consequences of membership in the same family in the case of the Chinese lineages? While discussing the transactions of pre-commercial society in Chapter 3, I noted the findings of the late Professor Dalton of Northwestern University with respect to the sharp differences between the productivity of tribes or clans who depended for their survival on associations or groups of members specifically organized for trading purposes and those who relied on communal circles to insure their survival by producing reciprocally or for each other. Could the same be said about Chinese villages whose families were devoted exclusively to agricultural production and lineages such as those of the Huizhou?

---

[38] *Id.*

[39] *Id.*

[40] EBREY, *supra* note 6, at 207.

[41] Jordan, *supra* note 16.

[42] *See supra* § 13:7(A).

[43] *Id.*

E. The Clan

Anthropologists refer to the Chinese clan as "a wannabe lineage,"[44] *i.e.*, a property-holding group made up of descendants of an apical ancestor, but for whom the details of the descent lines from that ancestor are unknown to those who claim to be his descendants. In China, then, clans were created on the basis of a common surname, usually asserting common descent from a real or fictitious ancient person of that name.

A Chinese village may have housed one or more clans, as well as families not organized in clans who were usually the "village poor."[45] In some regions, clans owned large amounts of the land held by their members, which land became part of the clan patrimony. This above-discussed common budget supported by family and lineage rules led to the creation of joint business enterprises. For example, where the clan held jointly-owned land, the business derived from such holdings could be the rental of the land to members and non-members of the clan.[46] As will be discussed shortly, the clan's business could be as varied as weaving, processing rice, distribution of salt or tea, money lending by pawnshops or bank deposits and remittances of funds. Similarly, the proceeds of the clan's business were used for a variety of purposes that ranged from building and maintaining strongholds against bandits, funding schools and providing scholarships for selected clan members, maintaining ancestral family temples, and paying the funeral expenses of poor members.[47]

Some clans, such as that of the Huizhou merchants, were instrumental in the rise of commerce in an entire region by establishing networks of correspondents who serviced different sectors of the economy. Others performed various mutual aid functions. Thus, Chinese who traveled to foreign regions could locate presumed kinsmen and procure assistance from them. Clans also settled disputes that arose between members, forced their observance of community standards by threatening to expel them from the community, and interceded for them with the local or national governments. Clan heads often held government offices.[48] However, the likelihood of conflicts increases with the presence of clans and their selection of certain lineages as their favorites. As pointed out by David Jordan, clan-selected lineages only promoted the welfare of these lineages at the expense of others, and this exacerbated the number and intensity of conflicts between lineages, above and beyond the conflicts between lineages previously discussed.[49] In sum, from the earliest of times, commerce in China was conducted differently between or among members and non-members of familial associations.

---

[44] Jordan, *supra* note 16.

[45] HARRY M. JOHNSON, SOCIOLOGY: A SYSTEMATIC INTRODUCTION 183 (21st reprt. 2006).

[46] *Id.* at 184.

[47] *Id.*

[48] JOHNSON, *supra* note 45, at 184. *See also* Debin Ma, *Law and Commerce in Traditional China: An Institutional Perspective on the "Great Divergence"* 73 KEIZAI-SHIRIN 1 (March 2006) (on file with author), *available at* http://personal.lse.ac.uk/madl/ma_pdf_files/keizai%20shirin%20%20MA1.pdf. According to this study, clan loyalties tend to be strong in southern China, reinforced by ties to an ancestral village, common property, and often a common spoken Chinese dialect unintelligible to people outside the village. Clan structures tend to be weaker in northern China, with clan members that do not usually reside in the same village and typically do not share property.

[49] Jordan, *supra* note 16.

§ 17.3 TRADITIONAL VALUES AND LIVING LAW: CONFUCIUS, DAOISM AND LEGALISM

While in China, I discussed western contemporary commercial contract law sources (including some that I had drafted or participated in drafting) with Chinese judges, scholars and practitioners. Some of their interpretations were based upon principles and value systems unfamiliar to me. Despite being clothed in western analytical terminology, Chinese views on the protection of commercial third parties (such as beneficiaries of letters of credit or holders in due course of their drafts, secured creditors and other financial market participants) who were not members of the obligors' nuclear or extended family were unconcerned with their implications for a market economy. While neither time nor space allows a thorough discussion of their legal reasoning, a brief discussion of the values that influenced present-day official and living law will hopefully be of assistance in understanding these laws.

A. Hierarchy

I had always thought of Confucius as a "humanistic" moral philosopher and not as a religious figure. Surprisingly, we found many religious temples dedicated to him and witnessed how many students brought gifts to him in anticipation or appreciation of a good result in their civil service or university entrance examinations. Yet, as I eventually learned about China, seeming opposites are seldom far apart; humanism and religious rituals were in fact not too distinct. As stated by the eminent Confucian scholar Wing-tsit Chan:

> The movement of humanism began with Confucius (551–479 B.C.). It gained momentum in Mencius [385–303 B.C.E.] and Hsün Tzu [312–230 B.C.E.] and finally reached its climax in Neo-Confucianism. It is a story of more than two thousand years. It is the story of Chinese life and thought. From the time of Confucius to the present day, the chief spiritual and moral inspiration of the Chinese has been the Confucian saying: "It is man that can make the Way great, and not the Way that can make man great."
>
> To say that Confucius was humanistic is not to deny that the Sage showed a reasonable interest in religion. Confucius was, on the one hand, a reformer, a pioneer in universal education for all those who cared to come and for people of all classes, a man who traveled for fourteen years over many states in search of an opportunity to serve the rulers in order that the Moral Law (*Tao*, [or] the Way) might prevail.[50]

Not much is known about Confucius' origins, other than that he was born in Lu, a small feudal state in eastern China.[51] What is known is found in his writings or in writings that his disciples attributed to him such as the *Analects* (a collection of aphorisms, sayings and maxims)[52]—part of a series of the "classics" (*Wujing*, 五经) of

---

[50] Wing-tsit Chan, *The Story of Chinese Philosophy*, in THE CHINESE MIND: ESSENTIALS OF CHINESE PHILOSOPHY AND CULTURE 32 (Charles Alexander Moore ed., 1967) (citations omitted).

[51] EBREY, *supra* note 6, at 42; *see also* Irene Bloom, *Confucius and the Analects*, *in* I SOURCES OF CHINESE TRADITION 41 (Wm. Theodore de Bary & Irene Bloom eds., 2d ed. 1999) (suggesting that "Confucius was born in the feudal state of Lu in eastern China into a family of the lower ranks of the nobility, one that was probably in straitened circumstances.").

[52] Bloom, *supra* note 51, at 42. Professor Bloom explains that "[t]he English word *analects* (from the Greek *analekta)* means 'a selection,' while the Chinese title *Lunyu* may be translated as 'conversations.' "

Confucian literature that included the Book or Code of Rites, which will be discussed in further detail shortly.[53]

Confucius spent time as an advisor in the court of Lu (魯) and also as a teacher (an occupation that earned him many disciples and admirers). He traveled throughout China in search of an opportunity to serve the rulers. China was undergoing yet another period of turmoil, and Confucius was dismayed by the "greed, insincerity, irresponsibility, [and] callous disregard for others' needs and interests. . . ."[54] His teachings on the evils he found and their proposed cures were collected (and very likely supplemented) by disciples and published during the second century B.C.E. as the above-mentioned *Analects* (hereinafter *Analects*, *Lun Yü* or *Lun yu*). Yet, as will be apparent when we discuss the *Analects*, what Confucius meant by "the rights of others" is not necessarily what western legal systems would mean by such rights.

Unlike Plato's utopian "philosopher kings,"[55] Confucius linked moral behavior to actual albeit also archetypal societal occupations and hierarchies with clearly assigned roles, including the preeminent one for the "learned" scholar or "noble" man, "gentleman" or "superior person" (*junzi, 君子*)—someone who, like himself, was not reluctant to do what was good for others, including acting as an advisor to the reigning dynasty.[56] Thus, the preeminent position in the social hierarchy that Confucius assigned to learned men was not in a utopian world. His "learned men" were court advisors to rulers in the actual performance of rituals and ceremonies or setting the official calendar. They also acted as performers of divinations and decipherers of their results, keepers of official records and advisors on how to justify administrative or judicial decisions.[57] In Confucius' ideal society, everyone knew his or her proper place and duties, and the need for a ruler and ruling class were taken for granted. However, Confucian learning and ritual behavior could facilitate upward social mobility.

Confucian rulers had to demonstrate their fitness to govern by their "merits." Heredity alone did not suffice to legitimize the ruler's rule. When asked by an actual ruler about the principles of good government, Confucius replied: " 'Good government consists in the ruler being a ruler, the minister being a minister, the father being a father, and the son being a son'. . . ."[58] Jeffrey Reigel explained the preceding aphorism as follows: "I should claim for myself only a title that is legitimately mine and when I possess such a title and participate in the various hierarchical relationships signified by that title, then I should live up to the meaning of the title that I claim for myself."[59]

Professor Bloom further states that while "[t]he *Analects* is the single most important source for understanding the thought of Confucius. . . . [i]t is clearly . . . not a work that he himself wrote." *Id.*

[53] Burton Watson, David S. Nivison & Irene Bloom, *Classical Sources of Chines Tradition*, *in* I SOURCES OF CHINESE TRADITION 25–26 (Wm. Theodore de Bary & Irene Bloom eds., 2d ed. 1999) (discussing these classics).

[54] EBREY, *supra* note 6, at 42.

[55] *See e.g.*, PLATO, THE REPUBLIC 8 (B. Jowett trans., 1st World Library 2008) (360 B.C.E.) ("We are thus led on to the conception of a higher State [Kallipolis, his utopian or ideal city-state]. . . . 'kings are philosophers' and 'philosophers are kings'. . . .")

[56] EBREY, *supra* note 6, at 42.

[57] *Id.*

[58] Jeffrey Riegel, *Confucius*, THE STANFORD ENCYCLOPEDIA OF PHILOSOPHY (Edward N. Zalta ed., Summer 2013) (citing Confucius's *Analect* (*Lunyu* 12.11)), http://plato.stanford.edu/entries/confucius/.

[59] *Id.*

B. Titles, the Moral Way and Obedience to the Ruler

Lurking behind this nominalistic advice was a belief in the rulers' perennial duty to stay faithful to the moral rule or the above-mentioned Moral Way, or simply "Way," which indicated how the ruler and the ruled ought to behave. In addition, because filial piety or obedience (*xiao*, 孝) was so strongly encouraged by the living law of family and lineage, obedience to the ruler benefited from its similarity to membership in a family or lineage. This was apparent in Confucius' above-quoted saying in which he listed the sons' duties to their fathers as part of the same hierarchy that included rulers and his ministers. Hence, while hierarchy was a fact of life in the governance of families, lineages and public offices in Confucius' time, his teachings contributed to it becoming a permanent fixture of China's public and private law.[60]

C. The Hierarchy of Occupations or Classes: Scholars, Craftsmen, Farmers and Merchants

The Confucian hierarchy of occupations (*sìmín*, 四民) was kind to scholars but not to merchants. Scholars and gentry (*shi*, 士) were at the top and were followed by the artisans and craftsmen or, more generally, workers (*gong*, 工), and the peasant farmers (*nong*, 农); the merchants and traders (*shang*, 商) were at the bottom.[61] According to Fairbank and Goldman, this hierarchical class structure was developed during the early Zhou dynasty by either Confucian or legalist scholars, about whom more will be discussed later.[62] As noted earlier, hierarchy was a central value of Chinese living law and thus was respected and deferred to in everyday life. For example, one of the advantages of the upper classes was the exemption from punishment for some of their violations of official law. The Book of Rites (*Liji*, 礼记), attributed to Confucius, decreed that "Punishments do not extend up to the Great Officials (*xing pu shang tafu*, 刑不上大夫)."[63]

D. Superior Persons

The class of scholars, "Superior Persons" (also referred to as learned men, upright, noble, genteel or gentle men, etc.), to which Confucius attributed the highest social

---

[60] WEBER, *supra* note 5, at 157. Max Weber, for one, finds an organic connection between filial piety and Chinese feudalism: "Residues of feudalism still inhere rather strongly in Chinese status ethics. Piety (*hsiao*) toward the feudal lord was enumerated along with piety toward parents, superiors in the hierarchy of office, and officeholders generally. . . ." *Id.*

[61] FAIRBANK & GOLDMAN, *supra* note 13, at 108. Farmers were in the second place because they produced the food that provided society's physical sustenance. The craftsmen (workers) were third because they produced all the tools and implements needed to survive. Merchants were fourth and last because they did not create goods; rather, they bought them in one place and sold them in another and skimmed profits off the top. As will be illustrated shortly when discussing the *Analects*, Confucius disliked merchants because, according to him, all they cared about was their "gain" or profit-making.

[62] *Id.*

[63] Wallace Johnson, *On Limitations on Legal Privilege in* The Tang Code, 7 J. ASIAN LEGAL HIST. 23, 23 (2007), *available at* http://kuscholarworks.ku.edu/dspace/bitstream/1808/3850/1/johnson2007.pdf. In this study, Professor Johnson calls attention to the influential monograph by the Chinese scholar T'ung-tsu Ch'ü, which describes the legal privileges that separated the upper classes from the commoners and to a great extent protected the former from punishment. *See generally* CH'Ü T'UNG-TSU, LAW AND SOCIETY IN TRADITIONAL CHINA (1961). Professor Johnson adds that these privileges were particularly true in the centuries following the collapse of the Latter Han 後漢 dynasty at the end of the second century B.C.E. "During [that] time, there was a resurgence of feudalism, the great families dominated China, and the central authority was weak." Johnson, *supra* note 65, at 23.

ranking, may not have existed prior to Confucius.[64] In theory, they were supposed to be paid stipends or scholarships (prebends) rather than percentages of collected taxes; and this method of compensation apparently suited Confucius' rejection of acquisitiveness as contrary to the required "poise and harmony of the soul."[65] Confucian scholars gained influence in Chinese society by teaching respect and proper performance of ancestral rituals and by clarifying the meaning of the virtues that Confucius and other respected scholars considered the prerequisites of a superior person's behavior.

These virtues were the following: benevolence, charity and humanity (*ren*, 仁); honesty and uprightness (*yì*, 义, which may be broken down into doing one's best, conscientiousness and loyalty, and reciprocity, altruism, consideration for others, and a Confucian version of the Golden Rule, "[w]hat you do not wish for yourself, do not do to others");[66] knowledge (*zhi*, 智); faithfulness and integrity (*xin*, 信); and correct behavior, or propriety, good manners, politeness, ceremony and worship (*li*, 礼).[67]

The above-stated Confucian version of the "Golden Rule" merits comparison with the western commercial version described earlier in this book as the "marketplace standard of fairness." The latter requires, at a minimum, that one contracting party treat the other, as well as third parties, as regular participants in the marketplace would reasonably expect to be treated.[68] Thus, this version must take into account the others' reasonable expectations. Confucius's version is altruistic enough to direct a first party to treat his counterparty as the first party herself would want to be treated, but it is also paternalistic enough to presume to know better than the counterparty or third parties what they should reasonably expect from the contracting party or parties. Thus, the Confucian version of the Golden Rule is at odds with the western commercial marketplace version of the Golden Rule or marketplace fairness. As just noted, this marketplace thrives when the counterparties' and third parties' reasonable expectations of fair treatment are met, regardless of whether these expectations are consistent with those of the paternalistic and altruistic first party. After all, the first party's expectations may be based upon his own unrealistic or unreasonable assessment of the value that he promised or conveyed to the other party. As the old Spanish saying goes, "*el ojo del amo engorda a la vaca*" (the eye of the owner fattens the cow).

E. Ritual, the (Moral) Way and Confucian Law

Confucius regarded devotion to parents and older siblings as a duty of altruism intended to promote the interests of others before one's own. I hasten to add that the universe of the "others" is not as comprehensive as this term may suggest. As an

---

[64] YU-LAN FUNG, I A HISTORY OF CHINESE PHILOSOPHY 52 (Derk Bodde trans., Princeton Univ. Press 1983) (1931). This author describes this category of scholars under the Confucian school of thought as follows: "[they] were neither farmers, artisans nor merchants, and who did not engage in any kind of productive activity, but depended entirely upon others for their support. This class seems to have been non-existent prior to Confucius. . . ." *Id.* Fung also provides an analogy between the class of Greek Sophists (including Socrates), the Chinese scholars, and Confucius. *Id.* at 46–54.

[65] *See infra* note 94.

[66] Riegel, *supra* note 58 (citing *Lunyu* 12.2, 6.30).

[67] *The Five Virtues of Confucius*, DAVID B. SCHLOSSER, http://www.dbschlosser.com/five-virtues-of-confucius/.

[68] *See* Glossary, "Market Standard of Fairness."

Analect that will be discussed shortly reveals, the term "others" applies to those who are members of the same nuclear and extended family. Beyond this group, the deference may well be more academic than real.

The practice of this deference can be accomplished only by those who have learned self-restraint and discipline. Herein lies the connection between virtue and ritual because learning this virtue involves "mastering *li*, the ritual forms and rules of propriety through which one expresses respect for superiors . . . in such a way that he himself is worthy of respect and admiration."[69] By insisting on the performance of the rituals of deference to the interests of the Confucian others, the teacher instills a behavior consistent with that of a superior person, gentleman or possessor of the ideal or archetypal personality (*junzi*, 君子).[70] Even though the Analects are not explicit on Confucius's view of human nature as good and predisposed to do good, Confucius said that he never came across anyone whose strength was insufficient for practicing the reciprocity and benevolence of *jen* (仁).[71]

In contributing to man's improvement by teaching him to defer to the interests of others (however perceived by the followers of Confucius's Golden Rule), Confucian scholars also hoped to instill faith in the Chinese state and its officials. The legitimacy of a government in Confucius's view depended not upon its military power or even upon the strict enforcement of its laws, but upon that government's higher (Confucian) morality or moral law—a law he referred to, as noted earlier, as the "Way" (*Dao*, 道). This is the most important dividing line between Confucianism and legalism. A scholarly inculcation of such a morality could only lead to greater faith in governmental institutions. Thus, as stated in another analect that will be discussed shortly, even if a state had to give up its military might and its stores of food to preserve faith in governmental institutions, such renunciation was worth it.[72]

Only those who fell beyond the bounds of ritual and moral behavior, *i.e.*, social outcasts, were subject to the ruler's criminal law. As just pointed out, this moralistic and highly restrictive application of official law distinguished Confucian governance from "legalism," *i.e.*, a view that empowered the much wider if not preeminent application of "human law," at least in theory, equally to all the subjects. Hence, in the Confucian legal universe, living law as the Moral Way was supreme, and those who behaved in accordance with the Way were not treated equally with those who did not. In other words, unequal treatment of Confucians and non-Confucians was an essential feature of Confucianism; and official law was implicitly, if not explicitly, inferior to moral (Confucian) law.

---

[69] Riegel, *supra* note 58.

[70] *Id.* (citing *Lunyu* 3.3).

[71] Pei-Jung Fu, *Human Nature and Human Education—On Human Nature as Tending Toward Goodness in Classical Confucianism*, *in* CHINESE FOUNDATIONS FOR MORAL EDUCATION AND CHARACTER DEVELOPMENT 26 (Tran Van Doan, Vincent Shen & George F. McLean eds., 1991), *available at* http://www.crvp.org/book/Series03/III-2/chapter_ii_human_nature_and_huma.htm.

[72] CONFUCIUS, THE ANALECTS (c. 500 B.C.E.) An electronic version of the Confucius's Analects is available online in which the work is divided into four sections, three of which will be used in this chapter. *See* CONFUCIUS, THE ANALECTS (c. 500) [hereinafter CONFUCIUS I], *available at* http://classics.mit.edu//Confucius/analects.1.1.html; CONFUCIUS, THE ANALECTS (c. 500 B.C.E.) [hereinafter CONFUCIUS II]; *available at* http://classics.mit.edu//Confucius/analects.2.2.html; CONFUCIUS, THE ANALECTS (c. 500 B.C.E.) [hereinafter CONFUCIUS III], *available at* http://classics.mit.edu//Confucius/analects.3.3.html.

COMMENTS AND QUESTIONS

Max Weber, the German sociologist who in the eyes of many is the father of modern religious and legal sociology, ascribed much importance to the religious and aesthetic components of Confucius's "gentleman[ly] ideal."[73] Together, the religiously-inspired good spirits, art (expressed in poetry, literature and calligraphy, among other artistic manifestations) and benevolence made up the "work of art" that was supposed to be the Confucian ideal "genteel" man. "Puns, euphemisms, allusions to classical quotations, and refined and purely literary intellectuality were considered the conversational ideal of the genteel man."[74] Not surprisingly, Chinese officials, including emperors, proved their gentility by drafting official communications in the manner of "didactic poems."[75]

On the other hand, Max Weber also points out that since the percentage of aspiring learned or superior men who failed the civil service entrance examinations was extraordinarily high because of small, fixed quotas, many candidates obtained these positions by bribery or outright purchase, much as the "venal" judgeships were purchased by the French bourgeois.[76]

How does Confucius's archetypal superior, genteel, learned man compare with the Greek-Roman *bonus vir,* or with the medieval Jewish brotherly and trusted intermediary, or, more recently, with the German HGB's honest and decent merchant? Clearly, these archetypes were designed for different roles and performed different socio-economic functions. Yet, does Confucius's superior man possess a standard of behavior that could measure the fairness of an average commercial transaction, including the exorbitance of its price, the overreaching effects of its disclaimer of liability, and the control of a market? As you study the *Analects*, please keep these questions in mind.

F. The Analects, Commerce and the Protection of the Third Party

As pointed out earlier, the *Analects* are a collection of widely-read and quoted aphorisms, sayings, maxims and anecdotes embodying teachings attributed to Confucius.[77] Yet, as warned by Jeffrey Riegel, the *Analects* are a problematic and controversial work especially because they were compiled "in variant versions long after Confucius' death by disciples or the disciples of disciples."[78] Despite the controversies and their internal contradictions, Benjamin Schwartz, the late Professor of Harvard University and highly-respected sinologist, counsels against rejecting them as a central source of Confucian and Chinese philosophy.[79] I will heed his advice because for our purposes, the purity of the Confucian texts does not matter as much as does their continued application as a living law of proper behavior.[80]

---

[73] WEBER, *supra* note 5, at 131.

[74] *Id.* at 132.

[75] *Id.*

[76] *Id.* at 134.

[77] *See supra* § 17:3(F). Despite the elapsed millennia, they are alive in the PRC and elsewhere in Asia. Millions read them or cite them, as proven by the recent sale of four million copies of a simplified version. Alberto Serna, *China embraces Confucius again*, MERCATORNET (Nov. 12, 2007), http://www.mercatornet.com/articles/view/china_embraces_confucius_again (discussing the readership of the *Analects*).

[78] Riegel, *supra* note 58.

[79] *Id.*

[80] Based upon the advice of Chinese and U.S. Confucian experts, I have chosen several translations as reliable enough to warrant cross-checking. The first is available online through MIT. CONFUCIUS, *supra* note

While Confucius relied on maxims as his favorite tool of persuasion, they are not normative in the sense that they do not refer to the facts of a given dispute or to a class of disputes as do the Roman *regulae iuris*.[81] Some Confucian maxims were written as narratives capped by a short conclusion, others as aphoristic definitions, and still others as questions which Confucius answered by means of an allegory.

The distinction between maxims in the *Analects* and in the *regulae iuris* points to the limitations of the *Analects* as sources of living or official law, especially when used as principles for decision-making by Confucian-inspired mediators, judges or commentators. Their distance from the actual facts or issues in a given dispute is such that the Analect in question cannot persuasively serve as a rule or principle of adjudication. As a rule, it would not distinguish the relevant from the irrelevant facts; as a principle, it would automatically, without factual evidence, ascribe to the entire class of merchants what has not even been proven with respect to an individual.

1. *On Law, Virtue (the Moral Way) and Essential Faith or Trust in Government*

> 2.3 The Master said, "If the people be led by laws, and uniformity sought to be given them by punishments, they will try to avoid the punishment, but have no sense of shame. If they be led by virtue, and uniformity sought to be given them by the rules of propriety, they will have the sense of shame, and moreover will become good."[82]
>
> 12.11 Tsze-kung asked about government. The Master said, "The requisites of government are that there be sufficiency of food, sufficiency of military equipment, and the confidence of the people in their ruler."
>
> Tsze-kung said, "If it cannot be helped, and one of these must be dispensed with, which of the three should be foregone first?" "The military equipment," said the Master.
>
> Tsze-kung again asked, "If it cannot be helped, and one of the remaining two must be dispensed with, which of them should be foregone?" The Master answered, "Part with the food. From of old, death has been the lot of an [sic] men; but if the people have no faith in their rulers, there is no standing for the state."[83]

Please note that in Analect 2.3, Confucius warned against people being led by law instead of moral principles as provided by the *Analects* and the Code of Rites.

As will be discussed shortly, what Anglo-American lawyers refer to as "law" has at least four counterparts in the Chinese language: order (*li*, 理); rites or the rules of propriety (*li*, 礼), discussed earlier in conjunction with Confucius's Code or Book of

---

72. Additionally, I have relied on two sources with Confucius quotes. A COLLECTION OF CONFUCIUS' SAYINGS, AN ENGLISH-CHINESE BILINGUAL TEXTBOOK (Lao Chenglie et al. eds., 1988); *Confucius Art Quotes*, THE PAINTER'S KEYS, http://quote.robertgenn.com/auth_search.php?name= Confucius. I have cross-checked the translations found in the Riegel and Ebrey sources with the above sources. Riegel, *supra* note 58; EBREY, *supra* note 6.

[81] *See supra* § 4:2(A)(4).

[82] CONFUCIUS I, *supra* note 72.

[83] CONFUCIUS III, *supra* note 74.

Rites; human-made laws (*fa*, 法); and control (*zhi*, 制).[84] And while "human-made laws," especially of a penal nature, were common since the Qin and Han dynasties, the latter dynasty introduced a Confucian component—the adjudication of local disputes by Confucian scholars acting either as arbiters or mediators—and, in so doing, added Confucian morality to the mix of human law.[85] This was a sufficiently important component to warrant the assertion by a respected Chinese scholar that it was the most significant development in China's legal system prior to its twentieth century modernization.[86]

COMMENTS AND QUESTIONS

From a commercial lawyer's standpoint, what is the effect of the numerous meanings of the term "law," and the places where it can be found? Does it add or detract from the certainty of the marketplace? At this point, it would also be helpful to compare Hugo Grotius's and Samuel Puffendorf's versions of natural law (as influences on the French and German Civil Codes) with Confucius's Moral Way. Are they "birds of the same feather," or are they very different animals? What are their normative differences? Which of these differences can be used to fashion more precise rules of contract law?

2. On the Protection of Family and Third Parties

> The governor of She said to Confucius, "In my land there is an upright man. His father stole a sheep, and the son turned him in to the authorities."
>
> The Master responded, "The upright men of my land are different. The father will shelter the son and the son will shelter the father. Righteousness lies precisely in this."[87]

COMMENTS AND QUESTIONS

Why is this version of righteousness commercially important? Why should the innocent victim of a theft of sheep by one's father not be worthy of greater protection than one's thieving father? What effect does the protection of the thieving father and the disregard of the rights of the owner or lawful possessor of the sheep have upon the willingness of sheep owners or possessors to do business in Confucius's family-above-all market place? Assume that "A," the owner of a jewelry store in a busy marketplace, bought a valuable jewel from his son "B" that B had stolen from the rightful owner "C." Should A's sale of this jewel to his other son "D" be allowed to prevail over C's attempt to recover the jewel? Should it prevail over the claim by "E," a stranger who bought the same jewel from A, either before or after it was sold by A to D? How would the previous Analect answer these questions? How would the same questions be answered by the open market (*marché ouvert*) purchase rules in the *Code Civil*, especially Article 2279

---

[84] *See* Zhiping, *Explicating Law*, *supra* note 19, at 56–58 (a thorough and insightful discussion on the various meanings of the Western term "law" (including Anglo-American, Greek and Roman law)).

[85] *See* T'UNG-TSU, *supra* note 63, at 280.

[86] *Id.* at 3.

[87] EBREY, CAMBRIDGE HISTORY OF CHINA, *supra* note 6, at 47. *But cf.* CONFUCIUS III, *supra* note 72:

> The Duke of Sheh informed Confucius, saying, "Among us here there are those who may be styled upright in their conduct. If their father have [sic] stolen a sheep, they will bear witness to the fact." Confucius said, "Among us, in our part of the country, those who are upright are different from this. The father conceals the misconduct of the son, and the son conceals the misconduct of the father. Uprightness is to be found in this."

of the current *Code Civil* and in the English common law?[88] Is it possible to reconcile this Analect with what Professor Ebrey described earlier in this chapter as Confucius's concern with the "greed, insincerity, irresponsibility, [and] callous disregard for others' needs and interests"[89] that he had found in his travels through China?

3. *On Profits and Selfishness*

4.16. The Master said, "The mind of the superior man is conversant with righteousness; the mind of the mean man is conversant with gain."[90]

The Master said, "The gentleman understands moral duty; the petty person knows about profit."[91]

4.14. The Master said, "The superior man thinks of virtue; the small man thinks of comfort. The superior man thinks of the sanctions of law; the small man thinks of favors which he may receive."[92]

The Master said: "He who acts with a constant view to his own advantage will be much murmured against."[93]

Comments and Questions

Please note that while profit-seeking is to be shunned, wealth or being wealthy *per se* was not criticized by Confucius.[94] Does this vision have anything to do with the agricultural-subsistence nature of Confucius's China? Or does it have to do with Confucius's perception of acquisitiveness as contrary to the "poise and harmony of the soul?"[95] Recall Aristotle's rejection of the charge of interest on money lent as unwarranted by the "barren" nature of money.[96] Does this view have anything in common with Confucius's rejection of profit-seeking as an occupation?[97] After

---

[88] C. Civ. (Fr.) art. 2279. Unless otherwise indicated, all the English translations of the *Code Civil* provisions belong to Legifrance (*see* Frequently Cited); *see also* ch. 20 (on British law).

[89] Ebrey, *supra* note 6, at 42; *see supra* note 56 and accompanying text.

[90] Confucius I, *supra* note 72.

[91] Ebrey, *supra* note 6, at 46.

[92] Confucius I, *supra* note 72.

[93] *Id.*

[94] Max Weber proffers a more qualified or perhaps nuanced assessment of Confucius' aversion to profit-making:

> The Master considered acquisitiveness a source of social unrest. Obviously, he meant the rise of the typical, pre-capitalist class conflict between the interests of the buyers or the monopolists and the consumers' interests. . . . Still hostility to economic profit was quite remote, as it was also in the popular mind. . . . Confucius, too, might strive for wealth, "even as servant, with whip in hand," if only the success of the endeavor were fairly guaranteed. But the guarantee does not hold and this fact leads to the one really essential reservation concerning economic acquisitiveness: namely, the poise and harmony of the soul are shaken by the risks of acquisitiveness. Thus, the position of the office prebendary [*i.e.*, the recipient of a government stipend] appears in ethically hollowed form. It is the one position becoming to a superior man because the office alone allows for the perfection of personality.

Weber, *supra* note 5, at 159–60. I am not sure if Max Weber is truly taking exception to the view that Confucius rejected profit-making or if he is more nuanced in his analysis. Be that as it may, is his a proverbial distinction without a difference?

[95] *Id.* at 160.

[96] *See supra* § 2:2(A)(3).

[97] Weber, *supra* note 5, at 159–61.

reviewing the chapters on European codification,[98] do you recall a judge or court that agreed (at least in theory) with Confucius's view on acquisitiveness and virtue? Compare Confucius's view with that of Adam Smith in "The Wealth of Nations":

> Merchants are commonly ambitious of becoming country gentlemen, and when they do, they are generally the best of all improvers. A merchant is accustomed to employ his money chiefly in profitable projects; whereas a mere country gentleman is accustomed to employ it chiefly in expence. The one often sees his money go from him and return to him again with a profit: the other, when once he parts with it, very seldom expects to see any more of it. . . . Whoever has had the fortune to live in a mercantile town situated in an unimproved country, must have frequently observed how much more spirited the operations of merchants were in this way, than those of mere country gentlemen.
>
> . . .
>
> Thirdly, and lastly, commerce and manufactures gradually introduced order and good government, and with them, the liberty and security of individuals, among the inhabitants of the country, who had before lived almost in a continual state of war with their neighbours, and of servile dependency upon their superiors. This, though it has been the least observed, is by far the most important of all their effects.[99]

Whose view, Confucius's or Adam Smith's, is more realistic in today's society? Berthold Brecht, a Marxist playwright who fled Nazi Germany in the 1930s, wrote "The Good Person of Szechuan" (*Der gute Mensch von Sezuan*), a play in which a young prostitute struggles to lead a life that is "good" according to the terms of a morality—inspired by what I perceive as the same morality that inspired Confucius's genteel man. As she tried to be benevolent to others, she observed that she was invariably abused and taken advantage of. At one point, she says (paraphrasing): "If I am good to others, it turns out that I am bad to myself, but if I am good to myself, it turns out that I am bad to others." Would you consider this a real or false dilemma? As between Confucius and Adam Smith, would either of them or both consider it a false dilemma?

4. *Daoism*

Professor Ebrey characterizes Confucius and his followers as "activists."[100] Yet, if Confucius was an activist when drafting the ideology of professional administrators, he was, at best, passive when it came to profit-making in trade as illustrated by the previous Analect. Even his directive to the finder of the beautiful gem—"sell it"—in the preceding Analect was tempered by the passive—"wait for someone to offer a price." The followers of the religion known as "Daoism" (or Taoism), who also enjoyed a wide popularity during Confucius's time, were even more reluctant to get involved in profit-making occupations.[101]

In everyday life, Daoists preferred to yield rather than to assert and to be silent rather than wordy. Their highest good resembled the nature of water: "Water benefits all creatures but does not compete. It occupies places people disdain and thus comes

---

[98] *See supra* chs. 8–12.

[99] ADAM SMITH, AN INQUIRY INTO THE NATURE AND CAUSES OF THE WEALTH OF NATIONS 432–33 (Edwin Cannan ed., Univ. Chi. Press 1976) (1776) (citation omitted).

[100] EBREY, *supra* note 6, at 46.

[101] *Id.* at 47.

near to the Way."[102] An implication of these ideas was that the rulers should leave the ruled alone and enable their "return to a natural state in which the people are ignorant and content. . . ."[103] Professor Ebrey provides an illustrative quote from the Laozi, one of the classic Daoist texts:

> Do not honour the worthy,
>
> And the people will not compete.
>
> Do not value rare treasures,
>
> And the people will not steal.
>
> Do not display what others want,
>
> And the people will not have their hearts confused.[104]

Despite their strong divergence on the role of government, then, the Confucians and the Daoists shared a common distaste for commerce.

5. *Neo-Confucianism*

Once the examination system for ingress to Chinese bureaucracy took hold, efforts began to modernize Confucianism under the authority of the emperor.[105] These reforms assumed respect of the imperial autocracy and perceived:

> [T]he great mass of the common people as passive recipients of the benevolent despotism they sought to guide. They assumed merchants were perniciously addicted to greed and military men to violence. The reformer's job was to keep them in their place and secure a wise application of the unified central power. . . .[106]

Accordingly, during the Song dynasty, the bureaucracy was exhorted to eschew favoritism in the entrance examinations, encourage the sharing of income between the emperor and the peasantry rather than continuing their "squeeze," rely on local militias rather than on national armies for the defense of the provinces, and so on.[107] Professors Fairbank and Goldman refer to these efforts as attempts to keep "the imperial Confucian system going by always trying to remedy its defects and avoid its evils. . . ."[108]

As an aid to this reform effort, the tenets of Neo-Confucianism were summarized in the writings of the scholar Zhu Xi (朱熹, 1130–1200 A.D.). He advocated disciplined self-cultivation as a means to understand the true Way of the moral improvement of the individual and the world, as originally advocated by Confucius and which many centuries later had to be repossessed. Thus, he urged the imperial court and its literati to be less selfish, more rational and humane.[109]

---

102 *Id.* at 48.

103 *Id.*

104 *Id.*

105 FAIRBANK & GOLDMAN, *supra* note 13, at 96.

106 *Id.*

107 *Id.*

108 *Id.* at 97.

109 *Id.* at 98.

The influence of Neo-Confucianism upon China's elite was significant—to the point that it "became the living faith of China's elite down to the twentieth century. . . ."[110] Yet, as will become apparent when we discuss the effect of these ethics upon business practices, its continued emphasis on hierarchy (with merchants at or near the bottom of the heap) and ceremonial and manneristic behavior did not encourage the emergence of truly better (or more ethical) business practices. As also noted by Fairbank and Goldman: "One way in which Neo-Confucianism may have retarded China's modern growth was by its disesteem of trade. The attitude was that merchants did not produce things but only moved them around in search for profit, which was an ignoble motive."[111]

In addition to an anti-commercial attitude, Confucianism and Neo-Confucianism were not equipped to focus on actual practices and their improvement because their classical Chinese method of reasoning and writing made little or no use of "theoretical hypotheses or conditions contrary to fact, nor of inductive and deductive logical reasoning."[112]

§ 17.4 GOVERNMENTAL POLICIES, ECONOMY, MARKETS AND CONTRACTS IN TRADITIONAL CHINA

This section focuses on the interaction between Confucianism and the traditional familial values it reflected or inspired and legalism and the official law it created during China's most influential dynasties. In China, legalism (*fajia*, 法家) was a body of "ideas and practices" associated with the rise of the Chinese imperial bureaucracy and central government control from the fourth to the second centuries B.C.E.[113] These bureaucrats were primarily concerned with the economic problems faced by rural families and how to prevent unrest in the rural population.[114]

Meanwhile, the importance of contracts, mostly in China's predominantly rural marketplace, underwent an evolution similar to that described by Sir Henry Sumner Maine (from "status to contract").[115] Professor Valerie Hansen's illuminating book, *Negotiating Daily Life in Traditional China*,[116] examines a wide spectrum of contracts entered into during the eight centuries that spanned from 600 to 1400 A.D. and involved the purchase, sale or rental of houses or plots of land, draft animals, slaves, concubines and children, and concludes that:

> In 600 [A.D.], officials did not recognize contracts and used government registers to record land ownership. By 1400 [A.D.], the registers had fallen into disuse, and contracts had become the only proof of ownership.
>
> At [first] . . . the central government enjoyed an unprecedented level of control over both the countryside and the cities. Most peasants grew their

---

[110] *Id.*

[111] *Id.* at 100.

[112] *Id.* at 101.

[113] I SOURCES OF CHINESE TRADITION 190 (Wm. Theodore de Bary & Irene Bloom eds., 2d ed. 1999) [hereinafter CHINESE TRADITION].

[114] *Id.*

[115] *See supra* § 2:1(B)(2).

[116] VALERIE HANSEN, NEGOTIATING DAILY LIFE IN TRADITIONAL CHINA: HOW ORDINARY PEOPLE USED CONTRACTS 600–1400 (1995).

> foodstuffs and bought little, except perhaps salt, at local markets. Officials set prices every ten days and supervised weights and measures at the strictly regulated markets. . . . Under the equal-field system . . . *all land belonged to the emperor. Local officials conducted periodic surveys of land and households, reported their findings to their superiors, and redistributed land every three years. Official land registries were the only basis of legal title. Contracts between individuals had no legal status*. . . . As the system of land registration and taxation broke down after 755 [A.D.], the emperor's claim to ownership weakened. . . . Increasingly, people started to buy and sell land . . . and contracts began to be the only reliable record of changes of ownership.[117]

Some of these contracts, as well as those found in additional sources, will be discussed in the following chapter.[118] The next section focuses on the economic and legal policies of contracts of the successive dynasties and especially on those policies that illustrated the interaction between familism-Confucianism and legalism.

A. Feudalism, Taxation and Confucian Adjudication During the Zhou and Qin Dynasties

As with other long-lasting cultures, the Chinese civilization emerged from city-states located along navigable waters, especially those adjacent to the Yellow River.[119] The origins of Chinese culture, including its distinct script, literature, philosophy and methods of farming, became evident in the Zhou dynasty, which reigned from 1122 B.C.E. to 221 B.C.E.[120] It was during this dynasty and especially during what is known as the Eastern Zhou period (770–250 B.C.E.) that "[t]hose engaged in advising rulers about state affairs began analysing basic principles of human society and the natural order. . . . Their ideas began to be written down, and . . . stimulated intellectual debate."[121] As was just discussed, Confucius was the best known and influential of these advisor-scholars.

The large territory occupied by the Zhou led them eventually to share their government with local overlords in a feudal manner not unlike that of Europe.[122] Overlords were appointed first from within the Zhou family and military ranks and subsequently from a growing bureaucracy.[123] The Zhou imposed the obligation to pay tributes, which were collected from the agricultural exploitation of the land, to the dynastic rulers in a pyramidal fashion through nobles, vassals and commoners (in that order). Eventually, the Zhou Dynasty broke apart into individual feudal-like warring states. Finally, in 221 B.C.E., *Qin Shi Huang* (秦始皇, of Terracotta Soldiers mausoleum fame)[124] united the warring kingdoms and created the first Qin and Chinese empire.

---

117 *Id.* at 1–2 (emphasis added).

118 *See infra* § 18:1.

119 THE HISTORY OF CHINA 43 (Kenneth Pletcher ed., 2011).

120 *Id.* at 43, 47.

121 EBREY, *supra* note 6, at 38.

122 *See* ENCYCLOPAEDIA BRITANNICA, *supra* note 119, at 304 (estimating the number of feudal states established by the Chou anywhere from 20 to 70).

123 *Id.* at 303–04.

124 *See Qin tomb,* BRITANNICA.COM, http://www.britannica.com/EBchecked/topic/11785/Qin-tomb.

During this dynasty, government by feudal nobles was replaced by a centralized imperial rule aided by an expanding bureaucratic system. During the fourth century B.C.E., the Qin adopted far-reaching, legalistic-egalitarian and thus anti-Confucian penal and administrative codes on the advice of Lord Shang Yang (商鞅), a powerful bureaucrat.[125] In a collection of his writings known as the Book of Lord Shang (*Shangjun shu*, 商君书),[126] he advocated reliance on strict laws including harsh punishments for violators rather than reliance on what Theodore De Bary and Irene Bloom characterize as "traditional fiduciary relations and family ethics."[127] He also advocated the pursuit of agriculture and the suppression of political parties, particularly those influenced by Confucian scholars.[128]

Lord Shang Yang's enactments were credited with having made possible "the best organized state" during the subsequent Qin dynasty (221–206 B.C.E.).[129] In order to improve agricultural productivity, one of Shang Yang's enactments was aimed at thwarting the effects of China's family law of descent upon landholding. In order to encourage a greater willingness to cultivate arable lands by male members of households, he levied a double tax on any male citizen who was *not* master of an independent (and hopefully) productive household.[130] This was an obvious attempt to break down the strict patrilineal requirement of family lineages.[131] His double tax forced the younger males to move out of their father's household and establish their own productive household wherever a gainful occupation could be found. As a result of this tax, many more economically productive nuclear families could be found in China's countryside. Not surprisingly, Confucian scholars who taught the value of the traditional patrilineage continued to attack Lord Shan Yang's tax levy as violative of the principle of filial piety as late as the second century B.C.E.[132]

B. Monopolies and Corruption in an Agrarian Economy: The Han Dynasty

The Han dynasty, which reigned from 206 B.C.E. to 220 A.D.,[133] came from one of the largest single ethnic groups in the world. It relied upon advances in agriculture to improve its revenues from tributes and taxes. When these collections proved insufficient, Han officials invoked widespread suspicion of commerce as an unsavory speculation and assessed taxes upon commercial transactions and commercial properties such as boats, carts and shops.[134] Further, the Han became responsible for a policy often repeated by their successor dynasties—they competed with merchants by

---

[125] CHINESE TRADITION, *supra* note 113, at 193; *see also* ENCYCLOPAEDIA BRITANNICA, *supra* note 119, at 307 (regarding Shang Yang's reforms).

[126] CHINESE TRADITION, *supra* note 113, at 193. Professors De Bary and Bloom assume that this book is of a date following his being in office and of an "uncertain provenance." *Id.*

[127] *Id.*

[128] *Id.*

[129] THE HISTORY OF CHINA, *supra* note 119, at 55.

[130] *Id.*

[131] *Id.*

[132] *Id.*

[133] *Han Chinese,* NEW WORLD ENCYCLOPEDIA, http://www.newworldencyclopedia.org/entry/Han_Chinese. Han Chinese citizens amount to 92 percent of the population of the PRC and about 19 percent of the world's population. *Id.*

[134] EBREY, *supra* note 6, at 75.

selling back to them and to consumers some of the very commodities they had collected from them as taxes. In 119 B.C.E., still pressed for revenues, the Han established state monopolies for the production and distribution of iron, salt and liquor.[135] This policy deprived merchants, albeit temporarily, of major sources of profit-making.[136] Eventually, it was replaced with a policy of overt or covert shared monopolies with selected merchants or commercial clans.

As was to be the case not only in China but also in colonial Mexico many centuries later, the Han government started as a wholesaler of grain, purchasing it from producers in areas where it was cheap and selling it to the public at a significant premium.[137] The justification for such monopolistic governmental practices was "to eliminate speculation in grain, provide more constant prices, and bring profit to the government."[138] Eventually, the Han abandoned this policy and alternatively associated with private monopolies or embraced *laissez faire* policies. However, the beneficiaries of these policies were the large landowners more so than merchants. In Professor Ebrey's words: "The Chinese economy thus became firmly agrarian, a pattern that was to continue through Chinese history."[139]

Yet, while adopting legalistic policies, the attitudes of the Han bureaucracy were ostensibly shaped by Confucian teachings of "self restraint, concern for others, love of ritual, devotion to principle, and loyalty to superiors. . . ."[140]

On the one hand, the Confucian bureaucracy was guided by a morality proclaimed to be higher and contrary to that of the legalism of the Qin dynasty.[141] On the other hand, Han government officials were the beneficiaries of a generous official and extra-official compensation system. For example, "China already had a civil service divided into twelve grades, each of which received a set annual stipend, from the 100 measures of grain of the lowliest clerk to the 2,000 measures of grain of the highest minister of state."[142]

In due course, some of the taxpayers and suppliers of the monopolized commodities and trades such as the inhabitants of the Huizhou region engaged in wide scale bribery of government officials.[143] This bribery led to the transfer by government officials of a monopolized distribution to selected suppliers. The consequences of such a system of procurement and distribution were to eliminate competition among manufacturers and wholesalers, and the market became dependent on the selected suppliers for its means of payment (mostly metallic coin).

---

135 *Id.*

136 *See infra* § 17:5(A) (for a discussion of the Huizhou family and the replacement of the governmental monopolies by clans of merchants' monopolies).

137 EBREY, *supra* note 6, at 75.

138 *Id.*

139 *Id.*

140 *Id.* at 77.

141 *Id.* at 79–80.

142 *See* STEVEN W. MOSHER, BROKEN EARTH 58 (2008).

143 *See infra* § 17:5(A).

C. An Expansive Empire: Land Contracts and Legalistic Prohibitions—The Tang Dynasty (618–907 A.D.)

During the end of the sixth century A.D. and after the short-lived Sui Dynasty, China's northern and southern provinces were reunited.[144] The succeeding Tang Dynasty (700–800 A.D.) transformed China into an "expansive, dynamic, cosmopolitan empire. . . ."[145] The Grand Canal linked China's northern and southern provinces, and regional and international trade so stimulated economic growth that the Tang capital city of Chang'an became the largest and one of the most prosperous cities in the world.[146]

Money in the form of silver coins began to be used as a means of payment and, as happened in colonial Mexico, the assay and circulation of silver wound up in the hands of private merchants. It was not long before credit and banking institutions emerged: "[S]ilversmiths took money on deposit and arranged for transfers of funds; a complex system of credit transfers arose by which tea merchants would pay the tax quota . . . out of their profits from the sale of the crop . . . and receive reimbursement in their home province."[147]

Meanwhile, government officials started investing personal and government money in commercial transactions, such as oil presses, flour mills, and real estate ventures to the point that "[t]he wall between the ruling class and the merchants . . . was rapidly breaking down in the 9th century. . . ."[148] Yet, despite this revitalized and widespread commerce, no commercial law of any significance was enacted. Instead, the Tang enacted a criminal code in 653 A.D.[149] which decreed penalties from imprisonment to banishment and execution for numerous crimes and ascribed a major role to filial piety and familial hierarchy in their adjudication: "[I]t was [a] more serious [crime] for a servant or a nephew to strike or kill a master or an uncle than vice versa."[150] The absence of a commercial law and the enactment of a criminal code in its place reflected the imperial government's willingness to allow Confucian and traditional family rules to continue to act as the living law of contracts.

This observation is confirmed by Professor Valerie Hansen's research on imperial contracts. She questions whether the Tang dynasty controlled the transfer of imperial land: "The government may have forbidden the sale of land except under exceptional circumstances, but contracts from Turfan show that people did buy and sell land. They also violated the government's strict regulations about the sale of livestock and slaves."[151]

---

144 EBREY, *supra* note 6, at 108.

145 *Id.*

146 *Id.*

147 THE HISTORY OF CHINA, *supra* note 119, at 128–29.

148 *Id.* at 129.

149 EBREY, *supra* note 6, at 111.

150 *Id.* at 112.

151 HANSEN, *supra* note 123, at 10–11.

This fact is particularly significant because the economy during the Tang dynasty was mostly a barter economy. The use of money expanded only slowly during this dynasty and in the centuries following its demise.[152]

D. Monetization, Credit, Wholesale and Retail Contracts, and Manuals: The Song, Ming and Qing Dynasties

1. *The Song Dynasty (960–1127 A.D.)*

Major economic advances in agriculture and industry during the Song dynasty[153] were accompanied by large southward migrations that made the Yangzi river valley "as central to the Chinese economy . . . as the Yellow River regions in the north."[154] In what was described as China's first economic revolution, whole regions of China became market-oriented (rather than just family-oriented) in their production of tea, timber and timber products.[155]

For fear of alienating families who had by then become the most powerful landowning families, the Song funded their wars against nomadic invaders through revenue taxes leveled at every level of exchange rather than through land taxes. Expeditious tax collection and the growth of trade spurred the demand for money in the form of coins (and eventually paper money), thereby consolidating the monetization of China's economy.[156] Song officials granted a monopoly to a small set of shops on the issuance of certificates of deposit for money or goods left with them as bailees or custodians. This private issuance lasted until 1120 A.D. when the government took it over and began issuing paper money. Nonetheless, the process of commercial and financial specialization of China's local and regional trade was set in motion as were a variety of investment, lending and trade contractual arrangements, albeit with the inevitable governmental component:

> Partnerships were common, and commercial ventures were sometimes organized as stock companies, with a separation of owners (shareholders) and managers. Credit was widely available, not only through money-lenders, but also through brokers, wholesalers, and warehousemen. In the large cities merchants were organized into guilds, such as the rice guild which *arranged sales from wholesalers to shop owners and periodically set prices.*[157]

In addition, printed handbooks containing sample contracts became available during this dynasty. The first compilation of vignettes of court cases were published (*Minggong shupan qingming ji*, 名公书判清明集).[158] Together with litigation manuals,

---

152 *Id.* at 11.

153 EBREY, *supra* note 6, at 136.

154 *Id.*

155 Harriet T. Zurndorfer, *Contracts, Property, and Litigation: Intermediation and Adudication in the Huizhou Region (Anhui) in Sixteenth-Century China, in* LAW AND LONG-TERM ECONOMIC CHANGE: A EURASIAN PERSPECTIVE 96 (Debra Ma & Jan Luiten van Zanden eds., 2011).

156 EBREY, *supra* note 6, at 142. Professor Ebrey notes that the T'ang dynasty had stopped using bolts of silk as currency and, by 997 A.D., the Song government was minting 800 million coins per year, which was more than twice the largest amount minted during the T'ang period. *Id.* Yet, less than a century later, in 1085 A.D., the Song supply of coins had increased to over six billion coins a year and, correspondingly, the means of payment of taxes had shifted from commodities such as grain or silk to silver—eighteen million ounces of which had been collected as government revenue in 1120 A.D. alone. *Id.*

157 *Id.* at 142 (emphasis added).

158 Zurndorfer, *supra* note 155, at 92.

they contributed to a considerable increase of contractual litigation.[159] As will be discussed in the following chapter,[160] recently found records of extensive contractual litigation since the days of the Song dynasty force at least a qualification of the scholarly perception that formal law "was not viewed by ordinary Chinese as a tool to resolve private disputes."[161]

Yet, the moralistic hold of Confucius and especially his Neo-Confucian disciples upon Chinese living law (albeit removed from actual business practices) had become apparent during the Song dynasty: The "Song era saw the gradual change of China into an ideological society with a strong sense of orthodoxy."[162] Undoubtedly, this development was aided by the establishment of a meritocratic examination system by the first two Song emperors for aspiring bureaucrats whose schooling including heavy doses of Confucian and Neo-Confucian classics. However, "big families . . . continued to get their candidates [accepted] . . . in disproportionate numbers. . . ."[163]

2. *National Trade, International Trade and Industrialization: The Ming and Qing Dynasties (1368–1644 A.D. and 1644–1912 A.D.)*

Under the Ming Dynasty, the growth of China's industrial sector spawned a technological boom in every area, from silk looms to paper manufacture to the development of new machines for planting, growing and harvesting crops.[164] Consequently, imperial China attained its largest economic expansion: Agriculture, commerce and maritime trade grew dramatically as closer connections with European and other trading partners were established.[165] According to Professor Richard Hooker of Washington State University, Chinese naval-trade expeditions during this period "made China the world's greatest commercial naval power at the time, far superior to any European power."[166]

As a result of all of these advances, China's population and urbanization grew to the point that town and village markets could be found everywhere, including small

---

159 *Id.* at 92–93.

160 *See infra* ch. 18.

161 DANIEL CHOW, THE LEGAL SYSTEM OF THE PEOPLE'S REPUBLIC OF CHINA IN A NUTSHELL 52–53 (2d ed. 2003). After acknowledging that some scholars had recently taken issue with the view that China did not develop a formal civil or commercial law, he summarizes the traditional view of Imperial law in China as follows:

> Citizens viewed law as being administered vertically, from the state upon the individual, as opposed to being used horizontally to resolve disputes between actors with one another. . . . Ordinary subjects who had disputes resolved them through informal means and mediation by various customary and unofficial channels such as through the use of craft or merchant guilds or through the intervention of village elders. The aversion to using the legal system among the general populace meant that China did not develop a civil law system useful in resolving civil disputes. Formal law only served the public interests of the state and was not viewed by ordinary Chinese as a tool to resolve private disputes.

Id.

162 FAIRBANK & GOLDMAN, *supra* note 13, at 100 (Fairbank and Goldman attribute this quote to Professor Denis Twitchett).

163 *Id.* at 94.

164 Richard Hooker, *Ming China: The Commercial Revolution* (1997), http://richard-hooker.com/sites/worldcultures/MING/COMM.HTM.

165 *Id.*

166 *Id.*

businesses that specialized in paper, silk, cotton and porcelain goods.[167] The Ming also built their own merchant marine which carried silks, cotton and porcelain to Manila, where they were traded to the Spanish for silver, firearms and goods from the Americas. Ming porcelain and Chinese tea had become very popular by the mid-seventeenth century in Europe.[168]

This remarkable commercialization was accompanied by despotism under the guise of legalism.[169] On the one hand, the Ming seemed concerned with the fairness of market prices, enacted rules against monopolization of the market in order to force higher prices, and set the lawful rate of interest at approximately three percent per month.[170] On the other hand, government officials continued to exact costly bribes from merchants and the population at large.

Meanwhile, the commercial clans continued to observe as their internal law the strict hierarchy of patrilineal family rules, including resort to a common budget which provided the "seed" or the purchase money for investments, many of which continued to include land as their principal asset. As with other family investments, the decision to invest, purchase or sell family assets of any significance had to be made by the head of the household, lineage or clan.[171] Yet, establishing the hierarchy within these entities (especially families and lineages) required updated genealogies. In southern China, these genealogies were continuously compiled by "educated men." Their services were in demand because the north-south migration often settled in places with sufficient uncultivated land for the many descendants of the same lineage to remain in the same vicinity, "making for a critical mass of nearby kinsmen."[172] This is how one of China's most important commercial clans settled and was able to flourish in the Huizhou region of the Anhui province, as will be discussed shortly.

The Qing dynasty, the last of the imperial dynasties, followed the Manchu chieftains which, in turn, had briefly followed the Ming dynasty. Qing's policies reacted to what Professor Ebrey described as a collapse of the social order in the late Ming and Manchu periods by adopting strongly conservative and inward-looking policies in many aspects of social life.[173] Legalism severely repressed socially and culturally deviant behavior while Confucians attempted to combat the prevailing laxness and the "contamination of Buddhist and Daoist ideas."[174]

The Qing had inherited a highly advanced civilization. Until the beginning of the eighteenth century, China's "material culture" was unrivaled and its standard of living was among the best. Thereafter, however, it started losing ground to the British,

---

167 *Id.*

168 *Id.*

169 EBREY, *supra* note 6, at 190. "The early Ming emperors, struggling to gain personal control over a huge, complex empire, used terror to keep officials in line." *Id.*

170 CONTRACT AND PROPERTY IN EARLY MODERN CHINA 21–22 (Madeleine Zelin, et al. eds., 2004) [hereinafter CHINA CONTRACT AND PROPERTY].

171 Even during the late Imperial period and early "modern" period of Chinese property and contract law, "Chinese property rights . . . operated within a complex of institutions that included partible patrilineal inheritance, weak inheritance rights for women, *ownership vested in the household and not the individual*. . . ." *Id.* at 31. (emphasis added).

172 EBREY, *supra* note 6, at 207.

173 *Id.* at 228–30.

174 *Id.* at 229.

"without anyone in China taking much notice."[175] Ebrey quotes a Qing ruler who, responding to a British envoy's request for an authorization to send a permanent British envoy to Beijing, remarked that "there were too many nations in Europe to allow each an envoy" and added in a letter to the King of England that he saw no use to trade, since "[w]e possess all things."[176]

On the other hand, the private sector and some of their public sector patrons were not as dismissive of foreign capital. Professor Zelin's studies on Chinese partnership contracts during the same period revealed that partnerships that supplied goods or services to the coal mining and related industries were funded by family and outsider capital contributors (*Chengshouren*). Further, these associations were governed by individualized investment contracts that were tolerated, if not encouraged, by the *laissez faire* policies of at least some of the Qing bureaucrats.[177] Clearly, the attempts to reconcile seemingly irreconcilable policies and values had continued until the very end of China's imperial period.

§ 17.5 IMPERIAL CHINA'S FAILURE TO BECOME A CAPITALIST NATION

Could China's failure to become a major capitalist nation during the Ming and Qing dynasties be related to the low regard for commerce and merchants or to other aspects of Confucianism? Max Weber, who asked himself a closely-related question, equated Confucianism with a religion and contrasted it with Puritanism, especially as it related to the resort to family rites.[178] He pointed to a possible link between the continued presence of a "magical-sacramental grace and tradition-strengthening ceremony"[179] and Chinese social, including economic and commercial, behavior: "the unlimited patience and controlled politeness; the strong attachment to the habitual; the absolute insensitivity to monotony; [and] the capacity for uninterrupted work and slowness in reacting to unusual stimuli. . . ."[180] Chinese social behavior also included dishonesty "even toward their own defense attorneys. . . ."[181] To which he added:

> Retail trade, to be sure, seems to know little of such honesty; the "fixed" prices appear to be fictitious even among native Chinese. The typical distrust of the Chinese for one another is confirmed by all observers. It stands in sharp contrast to the trust and honesty of the faithful brethren in the Puritan sects, a trust shared by outsiders as well.[182]

Weber's suggestions on the reasons for a widespread distrust of and among Chinese imperial merchants would lead to the conclusion that Confucianism was indeed the major cause for the late-seventeenth-century "Great Divergence" between imperial China and western capitalism. Yet, why did this cause not prevent the emergence of China's massive commercialization during the Song and Ming dynasties,

---

175 *Id.* at 234.

176 *Id.* at 236.

177 CHINA CONTRACT AND PROPERTY, *supra* note 170, at 5–6.

178 WEBER, *supra* note 5, at 226–27.

179 *Id.* at 230.

180 *Id.* at 231.

181 *Id.* at 232 (although this dishonesty was in contrast with the honesty of Chinese's big businesses).

182 *Id.*

surely an important component of any future form of capitalism? As discussed in earlier chapters,[183] distrust among contracting parties often as not results from "tribalism" or "familism," *i.e.*, the manner in which families, clans and tribes in agricultural survival societies treat strangers or outsiders. Surely some religious doctrines reflect the different treatment given to "brethren" and to the "strangers," such as the prohibition in Deutoronomy to charge interest on loans of money to "thy brethren" but not to strangers.[184]

Nonetheless, the preceding questions are much too big and the available data too sparse to reach verifiable conclusions at least at this stage of the seemingly worldwide inter-disciplinary research efforts. The most a comparative legal researcher can do as part of this effort is to search for those legal principles that enabled the universal transition from a pre-commercial to a commercial society in other countries and legal cultures. The presence of these principles in late-seventeenth-century China could be regarded as a pre-condition of a capitalist economy. And if these are not found or are found only in a weakened state, the chances are that a productive form of capitalism would be unlikely to emerge.

As discussed earlier in this book,[185] among the legal principles that made the transition from a pre-commercial to a commercial society possible in other societies and legal cultures were: (1) the parties' freedom to enter into contracts, including their contractual power to limit their liabilities; (2) equal and fair treatment of merchants and consumers; (3) a view of contracts as the products of the parties' commercial cooperation (including their truthful disclosures of relevant transactional information) and as the receptacles of the parties' reasonable expectations rather than as the result of "zero sum" negotiations; (4) the legal protection of third parties, including good faith purchasers and creditors, from equities and defenses derived from pre-existing or underlying transactions; and (5) a fair and predictable adjudication of disputes among merchants and their customers. The following sections will seek to establish the presence and state of these principles in Chinese imperial commercial practices.

A. The Commercial Practices of an Archetypal Commercial Clan: The Huizhou

Recent records on the Huizhou clan of merchants (*huīzhōu*, 徽州) confirm their importance as a major merchant clan and as trendsetters for other major merchants.[186] After having settled as farmers in the Huizhou region (located in the province of Anhui near the port city of Shanghai), this clan started to trade during the late Song or early Ming dynasties and remained active until the early twentieth century.[187] According to

---

183 *See supra* chs. 1 & 3.

184 *See supra* § 5:9(C).

185 *See supra* § 3:6.

186 *See* Zhang Xuehui, *The Huizhou Documents: A Newly Found, Rich and Precious Source for the Study of Chinese History* (May 23, 2003) (on file with author) (discussing the recent finds of Huizhou documents and the types of contracts found), http://bic.cass.cn/English/InfoShow/Arcitle_Show_Forum2_Show.asp?ID=270&Title=The%20Humanities%20Study&strNavigation=Home-%3EForum-%3EHistory&BigClassID=4&SmallClassID=8; *see also* Qi Zhu, *Shi* in Architecture: The Efficacy of Traditional Chinese Doors 64–95 (Mar. 25, 2008) (unpublished Ph.D. dissertation, Virginia Polytechnic Institute and State University) (on file with author), *available at* http://scholar.lib.vt.edu/theses/available/etd-05152008-193629/unrestricted/Chapter_2.pdf; Zurndorfer, *supra* note 155.

187 *Huizhou Merchants*, CHINA DAILY (May 20, 2009) (on file with author) [hereinafter *Huizhou Merchants*], http://www.chinadaily.com.cn/china/2009–05/20/content_7824807.htm.

the PRC Ministry of Culture, at the beginning of the Song dynasty (907–1276 A.D.), Huizhou merchants were engaged in selling tea, ink, paper and wood throughout China; after Emperor Jiajing's reign in the Ming dynasty, seventy percent of the Huizhou were traders.[188]

B. Sharp Dealing, Bribery and Simulation

In 1132 A.D., the Southern Song dynasty moved its imperial court to the southeastern city of Hangzhou in the Huizhou region. The Huizhou were quick to exploit their proximity to the imperial court. As with Mexico's "*almaceneros*" six centuries later, close contacts between Huizhou merchants and court officials led to a privileged, often monopolistic, supply of goods and services. By the time of the Song dynasty, the Huizhou became the sole suppliers to the court of bamboo, wood and lacquer, among other commodities; in addition, they were heavily represented among the builders of palaces, pavilions, villas, and temples and profited greatly from the salt trade.[189]

The governmental monopoly of salt became lucrative for private merchants once the Ming Dynasty issued a regulation that provided that in exchange for the merchants' bringing needed army supplies to the army's northern outposts, the government would allow suppliers to purchase quotas of salt that they could resell at a profit.[190] Subsequently, another regulation allowed merchants to sell salt without having to journey to the northern frontiers.[191] The Huizhou merchants took advantage of this new regulation and purchased most of the salt available from a government plant ten miles away from Huizhou city at a price of two to three *wen* and resold it to other regions at an average price of sixty to seventy *wen*.[192] As discussed in connection with commercial practices during the Imperial period, this method of trade by major merchants was typical. Over the centuries, they continued to take advantage of such exclusive dealerships and profited from the salt business. By the turn of the nineteenth century, four of the eight largest salt merchants of China were from the Huizhou region.[193]

A similarly lucrative and exclusive dealership trade involved timber needed by the Ming Dynasty for building palaces in Beijing's Forbidden City. Wang Tianjun, a Huizhou merchant, bribed the officials in charge of this project and sold them 16,000 pieces of timber labeled (in a simulated transaction) as "Royal Requisitioned Timber."[194] By obtaining such a classification, he avoided the payment of costly taxes. As noted by Qi Zhu, although bribery was forbidden, many Huizhou merchants used similar "underhanded tricks to reap their profits."[195]

---

188 *Id.*

189 *Ancient China's Merchant Groups and Merchant Culture*, CHINACULTURE.ORG (2003) [hereinafter *Ancient China's Merchant*] (on file with author), http://www.chinaculture.org/gb/en_madeinchina/2006–02/20/content_79481_3.htm.

190 Zhu, *supra* note 186, at 74.

191 *Id.*

192 *Id.*

193 *Id.*

194 *Id.* at 75.

195 *Id.*

As the Huizhou merchants accumulated cash from their salt, timber and other profitable businesses, they placed this cash as loans through a national and international chain of pawnshops. Wang Qi, a Huizhou merchant of the late Ming Dynasty, was known to own more than a dozen shops in Beijing alone;[196] by the time of Emperor Guangxu (光绪, 1875–1909 A.D.), the word Huizhou was synonymous with pawnbroker throughout China.[197]

The implications of this equivalence were not flattering. According to the PRC Ministry of Culture: "The pawn-broking in those days was actually usury. Wei Chaofeng, a [H]uizhou pawnbroker depicted in *Fantastic Stories* [a literary saga], deprived a scholar of [all of] his real estate in three years' time by changing [sic] exorbitant rates of interest."[198] According to this view, Huizhou pawnbrokers were widely regarded as more interested in exorbitant profits than in lending to an appreciative and steady clientele. Professor Chow traces this method of doing business to its agrarian roots. "Instead of channeling capital investment into the support of industrial production, China's agrarian society channeled capital into the practice of usurious money lending for farmers."[199]

The PRC Ministry of Culture describes other features that the Huizhou merchants shared apprenticeship with the eighteenth- and nineteenth-century Mexican *almaceneros* and *hacendados*:[200] "As the saying goes, 'It is a Huizhou practice that thirteen year-olds start their career in town and at seventeen they do business all over the country.' Usually at the age of 12 or 13, Huizhou children began to work as apprentices in town."[201]

I found very few positive images of the business practices of the Huizhou. One such positive practice was that:

> [They] did everything to ensure the quality of the tea they purchased, refusing fake and bad tea. They summarized the experience of selecting raw tea and wrote it in books to warn purchasers. After the tea was brought in, it would be processed under strict rules. The delicately produced tea found a big market overseas.[202]

The PRC Ministry of Culture adds that the Huizhou's success in commerce was a result of what it termed social factors and painstaking efforts and described them, as a group, as " 'properly dressed, well-spoken', 'fully aware of prices, knowing when to buy and sell, and gaining extra profits from selling local goods at other places.' "[203] In all likelihood, the above reference to "social factors" was a euphemism for the Huizhou's reliance on family, lineage, clan and political connections.

---

196 *Id.*

197 *Ancient China's Merchant, supra* note 189.

198 *Huizhou Merchants, supra* note 187 (emphasis added).

199 *See* CHOW, *supra* note 161, at 52.

200 *See supra* § 14:3(A).

201 *Huizhou Merchants*, *supra* note 187.

202 *Ups and Downs of Huizhou Merchants*, CRIENGLISH.COM (July 23, 2009), http://english.cri.cn/6566/2009/07/23/1781s503493.htm.

203 *Huizhou Merchants*, *supra* note 187.

C. Clans and Political Patronage

The common budget of Huizhou families and lineages provided the initial capital to start many of their businesses; even dowries were contributed to this common investment budget.[204] The lineage organization was central to the Huizhou merchants' form of doing business, for it provided:

> [C]redit, capital and commercial intelligence to their members (*Fujii*). . . . Many Huizhou lineages claimed long pedigrees, tracing their ancestry from the time of their southward migration. They maintained their solidarity by keeping their settlements in . . . a few villages, and by regularly meeting to engage in prescribed Confucian rituals. They also periodically issued genealogies. Genealogies would generate consciousness of common identity and prestige. . . .[205]

Once a Huizhou business was organized, it was operated in patriarchal, guild-like fashion by the family clan:

> [Y]ounger members in the same family became apprentices for the more experienced family member. Bonded by the family relationship, the skillful masters generally had complete trust in the younger ones and accepted the mentoring responsibility to teach the apprentice the related skills of running a business. . . . It was eventually through the closely knit family structure that the Huizhou merchants steadily grew their wealth and stepped into the emerging gentry groups.[206]

D. Neo-Confucian Merchants, Bureaucrats and Limited Commercial Risk-Taking

By the sixteenth century, it was clear to the Huizhou that their fortune depended not only upon the support of family, lineage or clan, but also upon that of politicians. Regardless of how these merchants comported themselves, their wealth could be undone almost instantaneously by the whims of high government officials. In response to official arbitrariness and venality, the Huizhou joined the ranks of Neo-Confucian-influenced and trained bureaucrats. They embraced, at least in ritual and appearance, a vague Confucian-like morality of doing business. They adopted the teachings of the Neo-Confucian philosopher Zhu Xi (1130–1200 A.D.) and donated important sums to educational institutions, provided fellowships to their young who wanted to join the Confucian academies, and tutored candidates on how to excel in imperial civil service examinations.[207] Once these Huizhou-supported candidates joined the swelling ranks of government officials, the Huizhou had powerful bureaucratic allies to protect them against bureaucratic avarice and arbitrariness.[208]

The PRC Ministry of Culture describes their strategy as follows:

---

[204] Zhu, *supra* note 186, at 76; *see also supra* §§ 17:5(A) & 17:2(D).

[205] LAW AND LONG-TERM ECONOMIC CHANGE: A EURASIAN PERSPECTIVE 96 (Debin Ma & Jan Luiten van Zanden eds., 2011).

[206] Zhu, *supra* note 186, at 76.

[207] *Id.* at 77.

[208] Ma, *supra* note 48, at 16–17; *see alsoAncient China's Merchant*, *supra* note 189. These sources claim that the Huizhou people were a "disproportionate share in Chinese bureaucracy." Ma, *supra* note 51, at 17; *Ancient China's Merchant*, *supra* note 189.

> The resourceful Huizhou merchants were well versed in the expertise of obtaining a position so as to attach themselves to the court. Their strategy was to "provide funds for academic pursuits with business profits, and get political positions through academic pursuits and ensure business profits from the political positions". . . . [they] went on with large-scale construction, building mansions, ancestral temples, guild-halls, roads and bridges to honor their ancestors and to extend the influence of the clan. . . . [During] the Ming and Qing Dynasties . . . 2,108 people from five counties . . . were granted the title of *jinshi* [equivalent to a doctorate]. . . .
>
> [Thus, it was common for a] "father and son [to] both [be] ministers", [or] "brothers [to] both [be] prime ministers". . . .[209]

Professor Richard Lufrano's studies highlight the manner in which the appearance of Confucian behavior was affected by the Huizhous:

> Through rigorous Confucian-influenced education, apprentices or aspiring merchants learned not only the commercial skills necessary for business but also how to deal with people and how to cultivate appropriate personality traits. In essence, merchants were taught to achieve an "inner mental attentiveness," subdue selfish desires, distinguish good from evil, and practice reciprocity.[210]

This education relied on commercial manuals which advised hard work, obedience, caution, frugality, deference and discretion, as well as other virtues such as generosity, eradication of selfish desires, sincerity, trustworthiness, reciprocity and an enlightened self-interest.[211]

Yet, to teach a Confucian-like commerce, the manuals used mostly general formulations of proper ritualistic behavior rather than descriptions of best business practices such as how to conduct a profitable but fair sale or exchange or how to draft a non-exploitive or excessively selfish loan or security agreement. Thus, on the whole, they did not venture beyond warnings such as not to do business with unsavory characters or not to pursue goals beyond the merchants' means. They also counseled long-term steady profits as opposed to short-term gains. As pointed out by Professor Lufrano, "[t]hose who did turn to mid-level commerce behaved cautiously, rejecting the great risk taking and large-scale deal making of the ideal capitalist merchant."[212] To this, Professor Lufrano added that it "would be surprising for capitalists to emerge from a group of [such] mid-level merchants."[213]

E. Uncompetitive Small Business vs. Monopolistic Clans and Guilds

While monopolies were omnipresent in Europe at the advent of capitalism, they were not as strongly protected by successive governments, nor as long-lasting, as those

---

209 *Huizhou Merchants, supra* note 187. According to Britannica, the title of *jinshi* was equivalent to that of "doctor." *See jinshi article*, BRITANNICA.COM, www.britannica.com/EBchecked/topic/11780/jinshi.

210 RICHARD JOHN LUFRANO, HONORABLE MERCHANTS: COMMERCE AND SELF-CULTIVATION IN LATE IMPERIAL CHINA 2 (1997).

211 *Id.* at 52–67.

212 *Id.* at 178.

213 *Id.* at 216 n.3.

of imperial China. During the Ming and Qing dynasties, commerce was heavily polarized. At one end of the spectrum were major commercial clans and guilds. The latter controlled the prices of numerous items while also providing lodging, warehousing and entertainment services to their members.[214] As was also done by the European guilds, they enforced regulations for their respective trades and discharged important public and civic duties such as maintaining fire-watching towers, soup kitchens in times of famine and other charitable endeavors. In doing this, they exhibited what Fairbank and Goldman describe as a "Confucian 'public-mindedness' " that enabled them to organize militia or boycotts and mediate in trade disputes.[215]

At the other end of the spectrum were the small businesses. Typical was the farm household from which most of the agricultural-based commerce was generated:

> [It] had so little land that sideline and handicraft production especially in silk and cotton became an integral part of its subsistence. The farm household was thus commercialized, to be sure, but through a maximum of labor input, far beyond the point of diminishing returns, and a minimum of input of capital. Both their agricultural income and their handicraft income were necessary for the farm family's mere subsistence.[216]

A major gap existed, then, between the income, market and political power of merchant clans and trading guilds and those of subsistence-farmers and town merchants. The latter, together with the artisans, professionals and laborers, were among the poor. Fairbank and Goldman blamed the agricultural-subsistence origin of their commerce for its lack of progress. Their farm-based production was the victim of an "involution" in which the number of products they produced and sold was not matched by an increase in productivity per hour of labor.[217] Moreover, rural and town merchants alike continued to be the subject of official arbitrariness, corruption and monopoly. The result was that "[m]erchants, bankers, brokers and traders of all sorts were therefore a class attached as subordinates to the bureaucracy."[218] As was just discussed, successful merchants, such as the Huizhou, invested their profits in usurious loans and in real estate rather than in industrial ventures in an attempt to join the "dominant class of landed degree-holders (gentry)."[219] Viewed from a developmental perspective, then, the successful merchant class "produced landlords more readily than independent commercial capitalists."[220]

Meanwhile, merchants continued to be regarded with distrust, especially by those who advocated a return to agrarian values. Professor Richard Lufrano quotes the following set of admonitions to merchants by an advocate of an agrarian economy which reflects the low esteem in which merchants were held during the seventeenth century:

---

[214] FAIRBANK & GOLDMAN, *supra* note 13, at 176–79.

[215] *Id.* at 178.

[216] *Id.* at 179.

[217] *Id.* at 179.

[218] *Id.* at 180.

[219] *Id.* at 179 (as succinctly put by authors Fairbank and Goldman).

[220] *Id.* at 180.

Do not deceive ignorant villagers when fixing the price of goods.

Do not raise the price of fuel and rice too high.

When the poor buy rice, do not give them short measure.

Sell only genuine articles.[221]

F. Absence of Capitalist Intermediaries and the Cotton Cloth Business

In contrast with Fairbank and Goldman's analysis, Dr. Harriet T. Zurndorfer of Leyden University[222] found no commercial or credit intermediaries (*verlegers*)[223] during Ming-Qing China. As customary with Chinese agricultural production, much of the production of rural cotton was done by individual families, lineages and other forms of extended families.[224] By the fifteenth and sixteenth centuries, cotton textile production was commercialized and a division of labor was discernible.[225] Ginned cotton was shipped from cotton growing regions in the north to southern loom houses that spun the cotton and wove the cloth. In 1466, cotton cloth merchants from the principal trading centers established a cotton merchants' guild that sold cotton cloth.[226] By the late Ming dynasty, loom houses increased the production of cotton cloth by families in rural areas where the bulk of the production continued to take place. Unlike in the countryside, however, the urban loom houses were not run by family units but rather they employed "wage workers [who] performed cotton ginning, bowing, carding, spinning, weaving, dyeing and calendaring on a year-round or seasonal basis."[227]

Dr. Zurndorfer identified the following participants in the cotton cloth business: (1) the peasant-producers of raw cotton; (2) those who finished cloth pieces and disposed of them in market towns through licensed cloth brokers (*yaren*); (3) the local merchants-purchasers of these pieces who resold them; (4) long-distance merchants who purchased them from the local merchants (*keshang*); (5) spinners-wage workers who purchased ginned cotton from some of the *keshang*; and (6) local retail merchants who bought yarn and cloth for their mostly local sales from these looms.[228] The *yaren* were residents of the market towns "in possession of the necessary personal connections to both officials and local gentry. . . ."[229] The *keshang*, in turn, "were typically sojourners . . . [who] shipped the finished cotton cloth to other regions. . . . [some of these merchant groups] had access to large amounts of capital and could advance as much as 100,000 taels of silver . . . for large orders of cloth. . . ."[230] With the exception of those who received advances from the long-distance merchants,

---

[221] Tadao Sakai, *Confucianism and Popular Educational Works*, 354–56 (1970), *cited in* LUFRANO, HONORABLE MERCHANTS, *supra* note 210, at 41 n.67.

[222] Harriet T. Zurndorfer, *Cotton Textiles and Ming/Qing China in the Global Economy (1500–1840)*, The London School of Economics & Political Science (Jan. 31, 2006) (on file with author), http://www.lse.ac.uk/economicHistory/Research/GEHN/GEHNPDF/PUNEZurndorfer.pdf.

[223] *See supra* § 6:2(A).

[224] Zurndorfer, *supra* note 222, at 11–12.

[225] *Id.* at 9–11.

[226] *Id.* at 10.

[227] *Id.* at 11.

[228] *Id.* at 13.

[229] *Id.*

[230] *Id.*

participants in this production and supply chain were not financed in the manner made possible by the European *verlegers*.[231]

Accordingly, Dr. Zurndorfer's response to the question why capitalism failed to emerge during the Song and Ming Dynasties in China centers on the absence of Chinese *verlegers*:

> Despite the centrality of merchants to the advancement of cotton textiles in China, this industry, nevertheless, was not evolving toward capitalism. As a number of modern scholars have argued, the system of Ming cotton production cannot be compared to one of the critical phases in Europe's transition to capitalism, i.e. the putting out system whereby merchants advanced capital to rural workers in the form of raw materials, and controlled their product. In contrast to the European putting out merchant . . . the Chinese textile merchant monopolized the market by "buying cheap and selling dear." Consequently, cotton production did not present an opportunity to usher in change to the local social structure or to alter the relations of production.[232]

The absence of European *verlegers* is closely if not causally related to monopolization and exclusive dealing as a form of doing business in China. The European *verleger* was someone who, like Nathan Rothschild,[233] advanced moneys or raw materials to dyers of cotton cloth or to the makers of textiles to be able to compete better with other *verlegers* by selling the same textiles at a cheaper price.[234] The major Chinese merchants who bought large quantities of materials or merchandise cheaply from waged or piece-work producers did it to monopolize the market and be the only ones who could "sell dear" to anyone wanting or needing to buy. The object of the Chinese method of producing and distributing cotton cloth was then, *a priori*, to prevent others than guild or major clan members from competing.

And when during the Ming dynasty China built its own merchant marine and started selling its tea, silk, paper, cotton and porcelain products far and wide it created a large but increasingly unsatisfied demand for its products. Chinese producers needed credit with which to acquire more raw materials and pay more workers and the only institutionally available credit was the Houizhou's monopolistic "pawn shop" and usurious credit which led to higher and eventually uncompetitive prices.

These monopolistic and usurious practices must have continued well into the Qing dynasty. As noted by Professor Zelin, the main focus of the late imperial statutes and codes was the maintenance of fair prices. They equated benefitting from unfair prices to theft and set forth rules against monopolizing the market in order to obtain higher prices for inferior goods or against the buying of goods for prices lower than those of the market.

These practices must have continued well into the Qing dynasty. As noted by Professor Zelin, the main focus of the late imperial statutes and codes was the

---

231 *See supra* § 6:2(A).

232 Zurndorfer, *supra* note 222, at 13–14 (citations omitted).

233 *See supra* § 11:4(C).

234 *See* ROBERT S. DUPLESSIS, TRANSITIONS TO CAPITALISM IN EARLY MODERN EUROPE 127 (1997).

maintenance of fair prices.[235] They equated benefitting from unfair prices to theft and set forth rules against monopolizing the market in order to obtain higher prices for inferior goods or against the buying of goods for prices lower than those of the market.[236]

G. Familism, Unlimited Liability and Business Associations

In her research paper "Informal Law and the Firm in Early Modern China," Columbia University Professor Madeleine Zelin finds that the Chinese family firms (much as their western counterparts) were generally organized as simple partnerships, "relying on household capital and the resources of kin and friends, demonstrating little separation of ownership and control."[237] These features reduced transaction costs and facilitated acquisition of capital; yet, "[they are] also often blamed for limiting firm growth. More importantly, personalization is seen as injecting into the culture of business irrational and corrupt practices grounded in 'familism.' "[238] Professor Zelin also notes an important distinction that took place during late Qing dynasty between commercial and industrial partnerships:

> In the older guild controlled trades, the vast majority of firms appear to be single proprietors or simple partnerships with native place guild affiliations. However, in the burgeoning coal and iron industry [during the late Qing period] . . . the majority of firms are [also] small partnerships [that combined] . . . *investment from unrelated parties, and sometimes incorporating labor shares.*[239]

As long as the investment portfolios of individual households were relatively simple, as was the case in many parts of rural China, the fact that the unit of ownership of property was entrusted solely to the head of the family did not create legal uncertainty as to the liability of members of the family household for family debts. However, in active commercial markets, the property rights and duties of members of the family or lineage could result in serious uncertainties, especially when non-family members invested in businesses that involved family or lineage property.[240] Similar uncertainties and liabilities could also arise for family members, especially when individuals within households began to engage in business activities of their own and such activities involved undivided family property. In Professor Zelin's words: "Common property implied common liability. Because property belonged to the household and not the individual, the debts of the father became the debts of the sons, who themselves could be held accountable for the others' bad business dealings."[241] As with Mexico's "difficult-to-live-with rules," attempts were made to avoid the Chinese unlimited liability of family members by "simulatory" practices, including one which made it appear as if the individual member's business interest was part of his wife's dowry.[242]

---

235 CHINA CONTRACT AND PROPERTY, *supra* note 170, at 21.

236 *Id.* at 21–22.

237 Zelin, *supra* note 23, at 2.

238 *Id.*

239 *Id.* at 5 (emphasis added).

240 CHINA CONTRACT AND PROPERTY, *supra* note 170, at 32.

241 *Id.*

242 *Id.* at 32–33.

H. Exclusive Dealings and the *Guanxi*

By now, it should be clear that Chinese familistic property restrictions on the rights to enter into contracts, especially those that conveyed family property by any person other than the head of the household (and not by an individual owner or co-owner), amounted to a significant obstacle to trade and investment.[243] The protection of the interests of family, lineage or clan members was also at the expense of the rights of outsiders who could not compete in the monopolized or exclusive dealing markets as sought and frequently attained by the Huizhou, among other commercial clans and guilds. Third parties were simply unable to buy the necessary raw materials or components for their products or, if they had managed to do so, they could not sell their products in exclusive or reserved markets. Thus, as the family economic unit grew to become a clan, guild, and, in some instances regional or national monopolies, the number of disenfranchised potential competitors also grew.

The only recourse left to these excluded third parties was to counter the family-centered exclusive dealerships and monopolies with their own exclusivities. To be sure, public officials and powerful personages were bribable, but their help was uncertain because they were likely to be the same public officials who had helped procure (or shared in the procuring of) the original monopoly or exclusive deal. In addition, a reliable patronage would only result after a long-standing relationship of reciprocal services and duties had been established between the parties to this relationship. This relationship and living law institution was, and is still is, known as the *Guanxi* (关系).

> *Guanxi* is constructed and "pulled" . . . when something needs to be done and yet no prior relationship exists, often between individuals not on the same social plane. Once *guanxi* is established, the cultivating of *renqing* (human feelings or human obligations) makes it meaningful. The longer the relationship, the better the *renqing*, and the more effective the interaction. . . . "Once one is inside the *renqingwang* or *guanxiwang*, he is locked into an intricate relationship of interdependence with others. He is, in this case, socially obliged to respond to any request for help from others."[244]

The reader should be able to identify in the long-running *Guanxi* relationship what I described earlier in this book as a "dense" and living commercial law relationship of reciprocity.[245] As with the Mexican dense *compadrazgo*, the parties to this relationship assume brotherly-like duties such as one party's willingness to shoulder the other's losses in the expectation that the long-term balance would be profitable for both. Indeed, as with the Mexican *compadres* or with the beneficiaries of a Brazilian *Jeito,* the *Guanxi* relationship protects its participants, but more often than not this protection is at the expense of the rights of others or those who are, in turn, third parties or strangers to that relationship.

---

[243] Even during the late Imperial period and early "modern" period of Chinese property and contract law, "Chinese property rights . . . operated within a complex of institutions that included partible patrilineal inheritance, weak inheritance rights for women, *ownership vested in the household and not the individual. . . .*" *Id.* at 31 (emphasis added).

[244] LUFRANO, *supra* note 210, at 93.

[245] *See supra* § 3:3.

§ 17.6 CONCLUSIONS: WHY CAPITALISM FAILED TO EMERGE DURING THE MING & QING PERIOD

The preceding analysis of China's imperial commercial practices reveals that most, if not all, were sharply at odds with the above-listed principles[246] of a commercially viable society: from the monopolistic and exclusive dealings, to sharp, zero-sum dealings, especially with non-family members including usurious loans to producers, and eventually leading to uncompetitive prices. It was not only the third parties who were unprotected; the original parties were also frequent victims of legal invertebration. Only some of the transactions entered into by members of the households and the head of the household could provide a modicum of protection. The statistics on homicides that resulted from disputes concerning such rights and duties among holders of divided and undivided family property confirm the degree of prevailing uncertainty.[247] The same uncertainty prevailed with the unlimited liability of family members and outside investors in family businesses when dealing with undivided family property. And, as will be discussed in the following chapters, it is the same uncertainty that stands in the way of the liquidity necessary for the creation of a national and eventually a secondary market for PRC-originated land and real property mortgages.

The ignorance or disregard of the preceding viability principles by China's official and living law contributed to *a non-measurable type of risk*, precisely the kind of risk that capitalists are generally unwilling to assume. Can you visualize, for example, a Nathan Rothschild willing to underwrite the issuance of an imperial Chinese private or public sector housing mortgage bond when faced with any of the above legal uncertainties?[248] The only factor that could still encourage participation in an otherwise questionable transaction would be that of total trust in the counter-party's integrity and skill. Yet, according to some scholars, this is not a trust easily found among non-family counterparties in countries such as China and the Philippines.

A recent collection of essays on business ethics in Asian countries draws a comparison between ethics and trust in the Philippines and China on the one hand and Germany and Japan on the other:

> [E]ver since Max Weber . . . the idea that "familism" is detrimental to economic development has come into circulation. According to the German sociologist, overly restrictive family bonds constrain the development of universal values and impersonal social ties necessary for modern business organizations. . . . For this reason, "familistic" societies such as those of China and the Philippines are considered to be low-trust: They have difficulties in

---

[246] *See supra* § 17:5.

[247] Thomas Buoye, *Litigation, Legitimacy and Lethal Violence: Why County Courts Failed to Prevent Violent Disputes over Property in Eighteenth-Century China, in* CHINA CONTRACT AND PROPERTY, *supra* note 170, at 96 (noting that the author had looked at "literally thousands of homicide reports" and, of these, had analyzed 630 homicides related to disputes over property rights involving, among others, disputes on rent default, eviction, or land boundaries). The magnitude of violence and uncertainty is highlighted by the fact that the 630 homicides he examined took place during the years of 1750–1753 and 1789–80. *Id.* at 7.

[248] Recall Nathan Rothschild's measurement of the transactional risks in a German principality requested for the underwriting and sale of their bonds in the English bond market. After measuring the various determined and determinable risks, he identified the risk of a possible unwillingness to support the judicial and extra-judicial enforcement of defaulted bonds by the principality's parliament. *See supra* § 11:4(C).

> creating large organizations beyond the family; and consequently, the state has had to intervene to promote durable, globally competitive firms. In this regard, a sharp contrast may be drawn with high-trust societies, such as Japan and Germany, capable of spawning large-scale firms not based on kinship ties (i.e., professionally managed).[249]

What remains to be explored is whether two key legal elements for a successful transition from a pre-commercial to a commercial society were present in late imperial China and, if not, why not. One was alluded to as part of the above list of "transitional" legal principles: a fair and predictable adjudication of disputes involving merchants and their customers. The other underlies the drafting and dispute adjudication of contracts in thriving market economies. As described by the late Professor Lon Fuller of Harvard Law School: "the rule must be that you give, so far as possible, what is less valuable to you but more valuable to the receiver; and you receive what is more valuable to you and less valuable to the giver."[250] In other words, contracts must become a tool of commercial cooperation and a product of trust among contracting parties.

If the above-quoted scholars of business ethics are correct in their assessment of the impact of familism in imperial China, how was this impact manifested in the drafting of contracts and especially of their standard clauses? How was it reflected in the manner in which contracts were litigated? And, finally, how could the comparative commercial law of contracts increase reliance on the above-mentioned "universal values" and "impersonal social ties"?

---

[249] Alejo José G. Sison, *Business and culture in the Philippines: a story of gradual progress*, *in* BUSINESS ETHICS IN THEORY AND PRACTICE: CONTRIBUTIONS FROM ASIA AND NEW ZEALAND 151 (Patricia H. Werhane & Alan E. Singer eds., 1999).

[250] LON L. FULLER & MELVIN EISENBERG, BASIC CONTRACT LAW 100 (3d ed. 1972).

Chapter 18

CONTRACTS AND LITIGATION IN IMPERIAL AND MAO'S CHINA

§ 18.1 THE COMMERCIAL AND ECONOMIC IMPORTANCE OF CHINESE IMPERIAL CONTRACTS

Despite the shifting political, economic and legal winds discussed in the previous chapter, the use of contracts during Imperial China grew steadily from the seventh century C.E. to the advent of the Peoples Republic of China (PRC) in 1949.[1] Their variety also increased as they became evidence of title (or of lesser rights) to land conveyed or mortgaged and as they were relied upon as evidence of the parties' intent in a continuously growing number of lawsuits.[2]

As early as the Tang dynasty (618–906 C.E.), contracts were being used for sales, rentals and exchanges of land, livestock, commodities, slaves, concubines, money and even children.[3] Their users varied from the educated gentry who knew how to draft their own contracts with exquisite calligraphy to the uneducated poor who hired the ubiquitous scribes as draftsmen. As a measure of the enormous amount of contractual activity in late imperial China and early modern period, Colorado University Professor Carol H. Shiue quotes an estimate of "upwards of ten million land deeds and contracts. . . ."[4]

A. Free Tenancy and Commercialized Rights in the Land: Commercial and Legal Components of Commercialization

By the sixteenth century C.E., it was clear that China's rural land was being exploited not merely for agricultural subsistence, but commercially by landlords as well as by their tenants. Consider, for example, the following extract of a contract from circa 1500 during the reign of Emperor Hongzhi:

> Hu Sheng, a resident of the fifth *du*, now rents two clumps of land, paddy field and dry land, of the Hong (family). . . . Their location is at the place called 'Atop the Pond and Below the Raised Plot.' Each year (Hu) agrees to pay back four *cheng* and ten *jin* of grain, and each year on the day of the autumn harvest he will allow his master to check the harvest. If there is

---

[1] *See generally* CONTRACT AND PROPERTY IN EARLY MODERN CHINA: RATIONAL CHOICE IN POLITICAL SCIENCE 1–36 (Madeleine Zelin et al. eds., 2004).

[2] *Id.* at 2.

[3] Harriet T. Zurndorfer, *Contracts, Litigation, and Economic Regulation in Imperial China: The Case of Tenant Disputation in Huizhou (Anhui) During the Sixteenth Century* 1–2 (Paper for the Conference, "Law and Economic Development: A Historical Perspective") (Utrecht Univ., Sept. 20–22, 2007) [hereinafter Zurndorfer, *Contracts, Litigation and Economic Regulation*].

[4] ZELIN ET AL., CONTRACT & PROPERTY, *supra* note 1, at 1, *reviewed by* Carol H. Shuie (Economic History Services, 2004) at http://eh.net/book_reviews/contract-and-property-early-modern-china (last accessed October 17, 2013).

additional land to be opened up, [the family will] allow Hu Sheng to open it and work at it. . . .

Signed (in the year) of Hongzhi 13.11.13 (1500.11.13)

The person who sets up the contract Hu Sheng,

scribed by Rao Yongshan[5]

In his lucid description of customary and legal practices on sales, rentals and borrowing of rural land in Imperial and Republican China, Professor Philip C. Huang of UCLA refers to a conveyance practice during the early days of the Ming Dynasty (1368–1644) to illustrate how a certain oceanfront land could be sold subject to two different prices:

> [T]he original "purchase value," or *maijia,* and the "cultivation value," or (*chengjia*) [i.e., the value of the tenant's improvements]. The two [sets of rights] could be bought and sold separately. Generally, the landlord could claim only the *maijia*; the *chengjia* belonged to the tenant. It was an early instance of what amounted to the two-tiered ownership of land.[6]

This contractual practice shows that Chinese agriculture was vital enough to create rights in the land and its products, rights that could be sold or mortgaged to third parties interested in them because of the land's potential to yield reliable streams of income. Having land or crops that others would consider valuable, then, is the first component of what I understand by the commercialization of land rights. The other component is legal in nature and I will address it shortly.

The first of the two transactions discussed above was entered into in the same Huizhou country which, as described in the preceding chapter, was the hub of the commercial transactions of the Huizhou clan.[7] Huizhou landowners relied on "free" and "servile" tenants for the exploitation of their land.[8] And while the legal status of servile tenants was "intermediate between commoners and household slaves,"[9] the status of free tenants was quite close to that of landowners.[10]

Having read Marc Bloch's "*La Société Féodale,*"[11] it appeared that Ming Chinese landlords and free tenants had more rights to convey than did their European

---

[5] Zurndorfer, *Contracts, Litigation and Economic Regulation, supra* note 3, at 25. Zurndorfer cites her source for these contracts as Liu Hehui, "Mingdai Huizhou Hushi dianpu wenyue," *Anhui shixue* 64 (1985).

[6] PHILIP C. HUANG, CODE, CUSTOM AND LEGAL PRACTICE IN CHINA: THE QING AND THE REPUBLIC COMPARED 100 (2001).

[7] *See supra* § 17:5(A).

[8] Zhang Xuehui, *The Huizhou Documents: A Newly Found, Rich and Precious Source for the Study of Chinese History,* CHINESE ACAD. SOC. SCI. 12 (Bureau of Int'l Cooperation, 2003) (discussing the recent finds of Huizhou documents and the types of contracts found), http://bic.cass.cn/English/InfoShow/Arcitle_Show_Forum2_Show.asp?ID=270&Title=The%20Humanities%20Study&strNavigation=Home-%3EForum-%3EHistory&BigClassID=4&SmallClassID=8 (on file with this author). The summaries of contractual clauses in the principal text are based upon summaries provided by this Chinese scholar.

[9] Zurndorfer, *Contracts, Litigation and Economic Regulation, supra* note 3, at 17.

[10] *Id.* The distinctions between language of acknowledgment and of bilateral obligations belong to this author and are based on the excerpts provided by Professor Zurndorfer and discussed in the principal text.

[11] *See* MARC BLOCH, LA SOCIETE FEODALE (2005) (1939), *available at* http://classiques.uqac.ca/classiques/bloch_marc/societe_feodale/societe_feodale.html, *especially*, part 2 (*Deuxieme Partie*: *Les Liens D'Homme a Homme*), section 3 (*Livre troisième: Les liens de dépendance dans les classes inférieures*), ch. 1 (*Chapitre Premier: La seigneurie*).

counterparts. As I will discuss shortly, Chinese free tenants had the right to exploit the "surface of [the] land (*Tian Pi*, 田皮)"[12] and this right could be sold or assigned to others.[13] In fact, the sale of free tenancy rights was standard and was referred to in the Huizhou documents as a "sale of land surface."[14] Further, if the landowner wanted to change free tenants, he had to pay the former free tenant an agreed upon sum to redeem his reversionary right. In addition, as a right *in rem*, the right to exploit the surface of land could also be mortgaged. And if the free tenant of forest land planted trees during his lease, once the trees had grown he had a right to the so-called "Portion of [his] Labour" which allowed him to sell the trees as his property.[15]

The appearance of more rights was confirmed by the provisions on usufruct of the *Code Civil*. Indeed, as defined by Article 578 of the *Code Civil* the usufruct "is the right to enjoy things of which another has ownership in the same manner as the owner himself, but on condition that their substance be preserved."[16] Noticeably absent among the rights of the holder of a usufruct is that of its sale or transfer, for since Roman times the usufruct was deemed a right personal to the usufructuary who could not transfer or sell it.[17]

With such ostensibly valuable rights to the fruits of the land, one could easily have envisaged the emergence of an agile and safe market for the acquisition and financing of free tenancy rights by third parties in imperial China. Yet, this was not the case. Many if not most of the purchasers, renters, assignees or mortgagees did not acquire rights better or at least safer than those held by their sellers, lessors, assignors or mortgagors. Their rights as well as those of their predecessors in interest were subject to pre-existing claims by members of the family unit or household that conveyed the land and at times even by neighbors or members of the same community. Why? This brings us to the legal components of the commercialization of land and its products.

B. The Legal Component: Causal vs. Independent or Abstract Promises and Rights

The most important legal component in the commercialization of land and its products is the nature of the rights obtained by those who buy, exchange, rent or mortgage land or its products. How enforceable are they? By whom? Against whom? Are "third party" rights protected? Do the rights of third parties differ from those of the parties to the original contracts?

In an earlier chapter, while discussing the emergence of a market for negotiable government bonds in Great Britain and Germany,[18] I called attention to the ability to sell and negotiate negotiable bonds in these countries *and the inability to do so* under the *Code Civil* and its progeny. At the root of this inability was the *Code Civil*'s

---

[12] Xuehui, *supra* note 8, at 2. According to Zhang Xuehui, these contracts were also known as the "land of labour (Lifen Tian, 力分田)" or the "land of manure (Fen Cao Tian, 糞草田)."

[13] *Id.*

[14] *Id.*

[15] *Id.*

[16] LEGIFRANCE [C. CIV.] (FR.) art. 578 (translation by author).

[17] BERGER, ENCYCLOPEDIC DICTIONARY, at 755 (*usus fructus*).

[18] *See supra* §§ 11:2(D)(2) & 11:4 (discussing the "Emergence of an International Bond Market").

requirement that only those promises that had a valid *causa* could be enforced.[19] A valid cause was nothing more portentous than the reasons for entering into the original contract.[20] Yet, under the *Code Civil* regime, the party claiming the enforcement of the contract had to allege and prove (if challenged) that the contract or promise had a valid cause. Thus, if "A" leased premises to "B" and the latter used them to run a brothel (a contractual activity considered to be immoral) the rental payments made by B to A by means of drafts or bills of exchange were voidable even if that draft or bill of exchange was in the hands of "C," a banker unaware of the cause of the underlying lease.[21] Needless to say, one could hardly be a protected third party if one became subject to defenses, equities or claims that one was totally unaware of when purchasing real property or lending on its security.

In contrast to the *Code Civil*-inspired law, neither English nor German contractual and negotiable instruments' promises required a valid cause to be enforceable. This meant that if A sold B his rights to the surface of land "X" and B sold the same right or pledged it as security with C, as long as the right was incorporated into an independent or abstract promise, C was immune to most claims or equities invoked by A against B or by A's kin or neighbors, regardless of the causes upon which these claims or equities were based. It should not be too difficult to see why the absence of *causa* in independent or abstract promises of payment was responsible for the emergence of important commercial credit markets, national and international in England and Germany, for these were typically markets of "third parties" or contractual strangers.[22]

As an additional point of terminology—generally only "unconditional" promises can become abstract or independent. Take for example, the promise made by the landlord in the contract transcribed above:[23] "If there is additional land to be opened up, [the family will] allow Hu Sheng to open it and work at it . . ."

Hu Sheng will not be able to claim any additional land for tilling purposes unless the land the landlord referred to as "additional" becomes available. This made the conditional promise become even more uncertain because it was up to the landlord to decide what he meant by "additional" land. Now, if Hu Sheng were to decide to sell that promise to a third party, it would still be a causal, and thus a not very valuable, promise. In contrast, if the landlord had stated: "Today, I irrevocably promise that one day . . . I will rent the following described land to Hu Sheng or whoever he designates in writing. The rental owed will be . . . and this rent will remain the same until the date of the expiration of this lease."

A condition could still be implied in this promise such as the payment of the stipulated rent; nonetheless, the fulfillment of this condition could be easily and objectively verified by the third party. Hence the above-described promise of payment closely approximates the wording of an abstract or independent promise. Abstraction, then, is legal shorthand for lack of conditions or of other stipulations that could render

---

[19] *See* C. CIV. (FR.) art. 1131 (2008). Unless otherwise indicated, all the English translations of the *Code Civil* provisions belong to Legifrance (*see* Frequently Cited).

[20] *See* C. CIV. (FR.) art. 1108 (2008).

[21] *See supra* § 11:4.

[22] *Id.*

[23] *See supra* § 18:1(A).

uncertain the enforcement of the promise. Please keep this point in mind as we examine shortly the causality of Chinese conditional sales of land.

Abstract or independent promises made it possible for third party intermediaries to provide credit to producers, distributors and consumers of agricultural products, among many others. Take the case, for example, of the seventeenth century financial intermediaries who made agricultural and commercial credit available at reasonable rates of interest to farmers, first in Germany and thereafter in Eastern Europe and Scandinavia. Eventually, this credit helped finance large scale cultivation and land, the building of industrial and commercial facilities, and eventually of public housing.[24] In many instances, much of the cash needed to extend this credit was obtained by the sale to the public at large of abstract or independent promises of payment in the form of mortgage bonds or certificates secured by the land, crops and other valuable assets of the borrowers. Following is a discussion of the nature of the rights being conveyed by typical land contracts in imperial China.

1. Land Contracts, Property and Third Party Rights in Imperial China

a. Conditional Sales

One of the most popular sales of rural land in China involved the so-called "redeemable-by-the seller" or "conditional sales." A 1730 "sub-statute" added to the Qing Code defined these redeemable or conditional sales as: " 'contracts (of the property sale) do not contain words like *irrevocable sale*, or [which] specify the period of redemption [of the seller's rights in the land], then (the properties) may all be redeemed.' "[25]

This sale was inspired by an ancient custom known as "*dian*" (典) which allowed the redemption of family land that had to be sold because of the family's economic necessity and which could be redeemed by paying what the family unit owed to the buyer of the land as his purchase price. The above sub-statute limited the right of redemption to sales that the parties had not labeled "irrevocable" or which specified their conditionality by inserting a date for redemption. The two immediate parties to the *dian* agreement were its "maker" or seller of the land and its "holder" or renter or buyer of the land. As insightfully pointed out by Professor Huang:

> The Custom of *dian*, or conditional sales of land, encompassed both a precommercial logic inherited from an earlier day and a market logic of the increasingly commercialized peasant economy of the late imperial period. . . . On the one hand, it gave special consideration to those who could no longer eke out a living from their land, allowing them indefinite time periods in which to try to redeem it, in accordance with a precommercial ideal of permanence. . . . On the other hand, it allowed the buying and selling of the acquired *dian* titles themselves, and even of just the increments of gains from price appreciation, in accordance with a market logic.[26]

---

[24] *See supra* § 11:2(F).

[25] HUANG, *supra* note 6, at 72 (emphasis added) (citation omitted).

[26] *Id.* at 71 (emphasis added).

The reader first encountered references to this pre-commercial logic in an earlier chapter.[27] I then referred to the doctrine of "economic necessity" of Hindu law. Please compare this Hindu law doctrine to the Chinese right of redemption to the *Code Civil's causa*. Recall that the Hindu law doctrine enables the heirs or "co-parceners" of an estate whose executor sells land to third parties to satisfy his own "frivolous purposes" (throwing licentious parties or supporting a mistress) to rescind that sale and retrieve the land or buildings sold. In this respect, it would seem to have the similar effect of a rescission of a contract governed by the *Code Civil's causa* even if a third party purchaser could prove that he was unaware of the reasons or causes of such a sale. What about the Chinese right of redemption? In another writing, I referred to the logic of the Hindu law doctrine of necessity as characteristic of agricultural subsistence or survival societies, in which the family was always the "historical" owner and "once an owner, always an owner."[28] Would the same logic apply to the *Code Civil's causa* and to the Chinese "conditional" sales?

b. Sale of Surface Rights or Topsoil Ownership

As with the conditional sales, the sale of surface rights or the "topsoil" had its origin in the contracting customs of the Chinese imperial agricultural subsistence economy. As described by Professor Huang:

> [A] tenant who contributed markedly to the value of a piece of land through his labor or other investments gained special claims over it. The most common example is the reclaiming of wetlands. The owners of these open lands would rent them out at low cost to tenants, who would make the necessary improvements (in dredging, embanking, irrigating, fertilizing, and so on) to bring them to "ripeness". . . . In return for their contributions, tenants would gain the prerogative of permanent tenure or even topsoil ownership of the plots. Those rights could be threatened only if the tenants failed to pay their rents. In that event, the landlord could take back the land, but only if he compensated the tenant for his contributions.[29]

Please recall the above-transcribed extract of a contract, from circa 1500, in which a Hu Sheng rented two "clumps" of land. This rental agreement illustrates the grant of a right to exploit the surface of land or the topsoil. Similar contracts enabled the tenant to sell or mortgage his right to the surface of the land. Please recall also the commentary to this agreement: If the free tenant of forest land planted trees during his lease, once the trees had grown he had a right to the so-called "Portion of [his] Labour" which allowed him to sell the trees as his property. All of these features indicate that the first component of the commercialization of land, *i.e.*, having something of value to convey, was present in the conveyances of both conditional and topsoil ownership. Yet, what about the *bona fide* purchaser or secured lender on the strength of the rights acquired under a conditional sale topsoil rental or ownership?

---

[27] *See supra* § 3:6(B).

[28] Kozolchyk, *Transfer,* at 1467.

[29] HUANG, *supra* note 6, at 99.

C. Third Party Rights Under a Conditional Sale

The judicial decisions on conditional sales examined by Professor Huang showed that many sales contracts did not specify whether they were irrevocable or redeemable. In accordance with the above transcribed sub-statute of 1730, a descendant of the necessitous seller (*dian*-maker) could invoke his right of redemption many generations after the *dian*-holder's family had come into possession of the land.[30] This invocation trumped the rights of third parties as well as that of the original *dian*-holders. To cure this uncertainty, the Qing Code responded in 1753 by specifying that if the sale was made less than thirty years earlier and did not contain the term "irrevocable," it could be redeemed. The Code added a warning: "Those who muddle things up and argue in court will be punished for violating the code."[31]

The same judicial records indicated that many conditional sale contracts did not make clear the amount that had to be paid by the *dian*-maker to redeem the land from the *dian*-holder: Was it enough to repay the amount originally paid by the buyer-renter (*dian*-holder) regardless of the time that transpired between the sale and its redemption and the amount in which the property had increased in value? What if the market value had significantly increased since the time of the purchase? Professor Huang notes that the above-transcribed Qing sub-statute of 1730 required the *dian* holder to pay the difference between the original sale price and what the land was worth at the time of the redemption claim by the *dian* maker, and this payment could be interpreted as a contemporary quit claim deed (*zhaotie*) by the latter that "he was now selling outright the land. . . . [And the *dian* holder] meaning that he was purchasing the residual title."[32]

Yet, the customs that shaped conditional sale transactions proved too protean for code or statutory law to catch up with. Since a *dian* title conveyed not only possessory, but also conditional, ownership rights in the land and its products, they were valuable and were actively traded either as outright or as conditional sales and these transactions were known as sub-*dians*[33] Professor Huang conjectures that the reason why these transactions lacked regulation was either because they did not cause enough disputes or because the "lawmakers held persistently to a precommercial logic in preference to the market logic. . . ."[34] With infinitely less authority to back up my choice of an explanation, I am inclined to believe that it was the latter. The reason is that the market Huang was referring to was still essentially a familistic market comprised of members of the same families, lineages and clans as discussed in the preceding chapter with respect to Huizhou transactions. In sum, the rights and duties of the parties to a conditional sale were highly uncertain especially where the rights of third parties were concerned. If the sale was revocable or redeemable, the sword of Damocles of the *dian*-maker could come down at any time within the first thirty years of the original conveyance regardless of whether the *dian*-holder was an original or a third party. Similarly, the exact amount that the redeemer was supposed to pay was

---

[30] *Id.* at 73.

[31] *Id.* at 74 (citation omitted).

[32] *Id.* at 75.

[33] *Id.* at 76.

[34] *Id.*

not entirely clear, nor were the rights acquired by the third parties who purchased the land from the *dian*-holders or who lent to them on the security of the land.

D. Third Party Rights Under a Tenancy or Ownership of Surface Land or Topsoil

As noted when describing the rights of tenants of surface land (topsoil), it was their improvement of the land they rented plus their payment of the rents that gained them the right to a permanent tenure of the land they used. The main condition that weighed upon these rights was the continuous payment of the stipulated rent.[35] As with the rights that arose from conditional sales, the rights of the tenants or owners of the surface land or topsoil also had much market appeal. Their rights could be sold conditionally or outright, pledged as security for loans or left to their heirs.[36] One fact that added to the popularity of these conveyances was that payment of transfer taxes could be avoided. Professor Huang quotes another scholar's description of a standard transaction:

> [O]ne peasant who had owned and cultivated land abandoned during the Taiping wars. . . . decided to sell off the subsoil rights and pay regular rent to an absentee owner living in town, who then became responsible for the taxes. The topsoil ownership remained all the while in the original owner's family, passed down from generation to generation, as the subsoil ownership changed hands three times.[37]

Clearly in this and many other cases of abandoned or reclaimed land, the rights to the topsoil that resulted from the improvements were more valuable than the rights to the sub-soil, yet the only officially recorded rights on the land in question (in the land-tax registry) were those of the owner of the subsoil. Further, as best as I could determine from the case records discussed by Professor Huang, the priority between recorded subsoil rights and unrecorded topsoil rights does not appear to have been elucidated by legislators or judges. In fact, as concluded by Professor Huang, in the case of top soil ownership, code and custom rights were "pitted against the other."[38] That being the case, what would prevent the priority of a recorded ownership right in the subsoil over unrecorded rights in the topsoil? It is for this reason that third parties buying from or lending to the family or families who possessed or owned unrecorded rights would be hard put to enforce their rights, except by resorting to the forgery or chicanery of earlier recorded titles.

E. Chinese Families and Communities as Contracting and Litigating Units

As was discussed in the preceding chapter, Chinese families acted as legal and economic units; this meant that under imperial law, ownership of land and its products belonged to the household and not to the individual members of the family unit, until and unless the land and the accompanying budgets were formally divided or partitioned among them, in which case a new family legal and economic unit was

---

[35] *Id.* at 99.

[36] *Id.* at 100.

[37] *Id.* at 102 (citation omitted).

[38] *Id.* at 99.

created.[39] Columbia University's Professor Myron Cohen calls attention to the interaction between contracting families and community ties: "[C]ommunity ties help protect contractual understandings. . . . The witnesses present at the signing committed themselves to becoming involved if the contract was violated. Sensitive contracts at times involved 20 or 25 witnesses . . . and if the contract was breached the guilty party faced ostracization and social uproar. . . ."[40]

The large number of witnesses reflected the interest of the community in real property contracts in which they themselves could participate as likely future owners or creditors of family-owned lands. The familistic and community roots of contractual and property rights explains much of the legal uncertainty including the role of family rituals that at first glance appear to be mystifying. Consider, for example, the references to contracts customarily placed in the purchaser's tomb.[41] Yale University Professor Valerie Hansen explains that the reason for this practice was "to give the dead title to their grave plots as well as to prevent them from being sued in the courts of the underworld."[42] This fear of lawsuits over burial sites, even in the courts of the underworld, indicated how much these sites meant to families and their rituals for an honorable passage of life.

F. The Causality of Chinese Familistic Contracts

1. Causal Statements in an 1894 Sale Agreement

Having discussed the meaning of causality and abstraction or independence of contract and property rights, it is time to discuss how the various causal clauses interact in a typical sale of land agreement. The first agreement selected for discussion was executed in 1894. It was translated by Professor Cohen.[43] After describing how the seller obtained the sold land, from whom, as well as its location in detail reminiscent of the "metes and bounds" descriptions found in contemporary Anglo-American and civil law countries, the scribe provides a number of causal statements. (I have added brackets and numbers to facilitate the following discussion):

> The executor of this contract for the [(1)] *irrevocable* sale of dry field land . . . in the past obtained from his father through succession. . . . [(2)] Now, because my mother needs money [(3)] and after having thoroughly inquired among those closest agnates who are my paternal uncles, each and every one of whom is unable to make the purchase, [(4)] I have relied on a middleman for an introduction to my senior maternal cousin, Zhong Youhe, who is from this village and has come forward to contract [this] purchase. On the same day, through the middleman, the three parties [(5)] [buyer, seller and middleman] have agreed on the basis of market value to a land sale price of twenty silver dollars . . . and on that day money and contract have been

---

[39] *See supra* § 17:2.

[40] Kerstin Ahlgren, *Interview with WEAI Director Myron Cohen*, THE MORNINGSIDE POST (Feb. 26, 2008), http://www.themorningsidepost.com/2008/02/26/interview-with-weai-director-myron-cohen/.

[41] VALERIE HANSEN, NEGOTIATING DAILY LIFE IN TRADITIONAL CHINA: HOW ORDINARY PEOPLE USED CONTRACTS 600–1400, 12–13 & 149–88 (1995) (for her chapter on tomb contracts).

[42] Valerie Hansen—*Professional Webpage*, YALE UNIVERSITY, http://history.yale.edu/people/valerie-hansen (last visited Oct. 1, 2013). *See also* HANSEN, *supra* note 41, at 13 & 189–221 (on the courts of the underworld).

[43] Myron L. Cohen, *Writs of Passage in Late Imperial China*, *in* ZELIN ET AL., *supra* note 1, at 37, 41–42.

straightforwardly exchanged, with no shortchanging and without such thing as use of this property to set off debts. . . . [(6)] Also, should original ownership rights be unclear, this is not something the buyer need be concerned with; it is the seller who is fully responsible. [(7)] Hereafter, *the seller is not to dare speak of redeeming the land* or of gift-money. Upon sale, the seller will immediately settle any possible claims so as to end forever whatever complications there may have been.[44]

COMMENTS AND QUESTIONS

The date of this contract (1894) should help the reader appreciate the longevity of rural customary practices in imperial China. Please contrast its clause (2) with the preamble-clause in a 1234 C.E. defension clause contract discussed later:[45] you will find the wording to be much the same. An additional reason for its selection is its helpful mix of standard causal stipulations.

Clause (1) refers to an "irrevocable" sale. By now, you should know why it was essential to specify that the sale was not conditional and thus not subject to redemption. Because of the unsettling effects of this practice, especially where third parties are concerned, notice how two clauses of this contract (Clause (1) and the first part of clause (7)) attempt to reassure the buyer that it will not be used against him. How does this redemption differ from contemporary United States "conditional sale" practices? A conditional sale is a "secured transaction" (now part of U.C.C. Article 9) in which the seller who sold his goods on a credit basis is assumed to have retained title to the goods sold. In the event of non-payment, he is entitled to repossess the goods without, in most cases, having to claim them in a judicial procedure. Notice that what triggers the right to repossess the goods sold is the buyer-debtor's default in making the payments he owes to the seller. How does this contrast with the conditional sale discussed earlier in this chapter? If you find a difference, what is it, and which of the two transactions, the contemporary conditional sale and the Chinese imperial conditional sale is of a commercial nature and why? Also contrast the latter transaction to the United States real estate practice in which "A," a former owner of a building, signs a "sale and lease back agreement" which entitles him to lease "X," the same building he sold to "B" for a certain amount and within a certain time. Why is a "sale and lease back" not regarded as a dangerous and uncertain agreement by builders, developers, lenders and users in the United States real estate marketplace?

Variants of Clause (2) are found in deeds of conveyance of land in agricultural survival societies not only in thirteenth century China, but also in India, where they are referred to as the "necessity clauses" that gave rise to the "necessity doctrine" of Hindu law, discussed in an earlier section.[46] Recall that this doctrine enables the heirs or "co-parceners" of an estate whose executor sells land to third parties to satisfy his own "frivolous purposes" (throwing licentious parties or supporting a mistress) to retrieve the land or buildings sold. Recall also that this would be true even if the third party purchaser can prove that he was unaware of the cause of such a sale.[47]

Clause (3) refers to the pre-emptive right of relatives (in some other instances also by the neighboring community) to acquire the land offered for sale to third parties. Yet, even after an extensive consultation, it would still be possible for one such a relative to

---

[44] *Id.* at 41 (emphasis added).

[45] *See infra* § 18:1(F)(3).

[46] *See supra* § 3:6(B).

[47] *Id.*

show up after the sale to the third party and claim he was not consulted and exercise his pre-emptive right. Can you visualize the consequences of these pre-emptive causal rights upon the acquisition of rural property by third parties unaware of such a claim or right?

Clause (4) refers to the buyer's status and familial capacity to purchase in this contract as that of a "senior maternal cousin." What if he is not such a cousin and someone validly challenges that status together with his authority to purchase the land? Clause (5) refers to the fact that there was "no shortchanging and without such thing as use of this property to set off debts. . . ." What if a family member of the selling unit can prove that in fact there was shortchanging or that the property was used to set off debts? Clause (6) contains a so-called "defension" clause which dates back to biblical days and whose replica in this section dates back to 1234.[48] In this contract, the statement used by the scribe was: "this is something the buyer need not be concerned with; it is the seller who is responsible." What would happen to this responsibility when the seller dies? As you will recall from an earlier chapter,[49] this "pre-commercial" clause was pre-commercial precisely because it imposed an unlimited and unending liability upon the heirs of the conveying member of the family or of the family unit.

2. *Professor Zelin's Comments on Familistic Clauses in Conditional Sales*

Under the heading of "Limitations Imposed by Custom on Private Agreements," Professor Madeleine Zelin of Columbia University makes the following observations:

> In addition to vesting property in the household, the Chinese family system imposed certain limitations on the alienability of property. Unlike inheritance and succession practices, which were incorporated in the imperial code, customs designed to prevent the dissipation of the household or lineage estate existed strictly in the private realm. . . .[50]

In light of the longevity of these customs, some of which were millenary, how powerful do you believe the Chinese "private realm" referred to by Professor Zelin to have been, and if very powerful, why so? Recall Professor Huang's reference to the "pre-commercial" logic of these customs which he contrasted to the market logic. Why would the prevention of the dissipation of the household or lineage estate not be part of the imperial code, as were the succession practices?

3. *Economic Necessity and a "Defension" Clause (Circa 1234 BCE)*

The following 1234 C.E. extract translated by Professor Hansen[51] is among the oldest relevant texts I was able to find. Despite its age, it contains two clauses that were found in documents that were executed late in the nineteenth century.

> Wu Junfu . . . *needs money to use and otherwise has no means of raising it*, so he puts up [for sale] one plot registered under his name in the southwest part of the Song Family-Estate Village. The plot has a footpath running north to south and totals twenty-five sixth-acres . . .

---

[48] *See supra* § 3:6(C).

[49] *Id.*

[50] ZELIN ET AL., *supra* note 1, at 26.

[51] HANSEN, *supra* note 41, at 115–16.

> He draws up a contract to sell the above plot with its four borders to the Great Teacher Feng of the Longxiang Daoist monastery . . . who will be the owner of the plot permanently. The two sides have discussed and agreed on a price of twenty-five ounces . . . *If afterward there is any obstacle to the sale or anyone encroaches on the land, the seller of the land Wu Junfu must resolve the problem alone without going to court.* Once this is agreed, no one can change his mind about the transaction. Whoever does so first must pay a fine of 10 ounces of silver. For fear that people will not believe this, we accordingly draw [this contract] . . .[52]

COMMENTS AND QUESTIONS

Please note the same reference to an economic need or necessity to sell as in the preceding 1894 agreement. Why do you think this clause appears both in a 1234 and in a 1894 agreement? In fact, it did appear in many of the agreements translated by the various Chinese scholars used in this chapter. For example, one of the contracts collected and translated by Professor Hansen (entered into in 1315 C.E.) reads in relevant part:

> Today, because I am short of money, I willingly have applied to the authorities for a receipt, to draw up a contract for the fields and hills within the above four boundaries and for the cedars, big and small, on the hills, to be sold in full to my fellow sector resident . . . As evaluated and discussed by three sides, the price is paper money from the Zhongtong reign (1260–1264) with a face value of thirteen ingots . . .[53]

Professor Hansen points out that "lack of money" (the reason given by the seller for his having to sell) occurs in most Huizhou contracts.[54] In addition, note the insertion of another familistic clause in which the seller or his family assume the obligation to defend the conveyed title (or "defension" clause). In this agreement, the defension clause is formulated as a seller's agreement to "resolve the problem" of an obstacle to the sale or an encroachment on the land.[55] Is there a counterpart to this clause in the 1894 agreement and if so what is the reason for this clause being used seven centuries apart?

G. Familistic Clauses, Disputes and Violence

Professor Thomas Buoye of the University of Tulsa's research on the violence engendered by sales of land that contain (what I have described in this chapter as "familistic clauses") focused on the eighteenth century, a period of considerable population growth in China (it more than doubled during this century surpassing 300 million inhabitants by its end).[56] The value of land increased and so did the incentives for a more rigorous enforcement of property rights. And while the economic activity was growing, familistic notions of property of land were being eroded: ". . . the evolving

---

[52] *Id.* at 115 (emphasis added)

[53] *Id.* at 120.

[54] *Id.* at 121.

[55] *See* Kozolchyk, *Roadmap*, at 6, (discussing "defension" clauses in which the heirs of the seller remained liable, *sine die*, for any future disturbance of title).

[56] *See* Thomas Buoye, *Litigation, Legitimacy, and Lethal Violence, in* ZELIN ET AL., *supra* note 1, at 94.

concept of land as an alienable commodity increasingly challenged the long-standing notion of land as inviolable [family] patrimony."[57]

The effects referred to by Professor Bouye were apparent in the widespread instances of violence and homicides. A report by one eighteenth century Chinese governor general complained of "endless lawsuits" and violence that sometimes resulted in homicide; another identified conditional sales and " 'evil tenants' who sold land conditionally and continued to till the land. . . ."[58] as the main culprits of this violence. The latter report also states that "the centuries-old practice of conditional land sales had become a source of social unrest . . . [including] demands for supplemental payments, grandsons making claims on land sold by their grandfathers, threats to commit suicide to implicate individuals who refused to accept redemptions. . . ." and so on.[59]

Professor Buoye researched thousands of homicide reports and selected 630 for detailed analysis. Of these, the causes that lead to the fatal disputes were: 1) rent default (135); 2) eviction (74); 3) exercise of the right of redemption (134); 4) boundary disputes (140); and 5) water rights (147).[60] Since the disputes over rights of redemption as well as over boundary and water rights were typically causal clauses more than fifty percent of the homicides were attributable to familistic-causal disputes. Considering what was as stake for China's rural families, such a statistical finding is not surprising. As stated by a peasant who faced eviction: "If you demand that I return this land now is it not the same as killing my family?"[61]

H. Effects of the Typical Land Contracts upon the Economic Growth of Imperial China

What effect, then, did the wide use of enforceable commercial contracts have upon imperial China's economic growth? Professor Carol Shiue among other comparative economists underscores the importance of this question:

> While many economists are now convinced that "good institutions"—common law [type] property rights . . . are deep determinants of economic growth, it has been difficult to identify how exactly specific institutions generate long-run growth. Relating existing notions of good institutions to the different forms that these institutions might take in other societies allows us to get a better view of what is inside the institutional black box.[62]

As also noted by Professor Shuie, in the 1960s, some of the most respected experts on Chinese imperial law assumed that property rights in imperial China were weak and that the frequent expropriation of land by the state was an obstacle to China's economic development.[63] A dissenting view was expressed in a group of essays

---

[57] *Id.*

[58] *Id.* at 96.

[59] *Id.* at 95–96.

[60] *Id.* at 98.

[61] *Id.* at 114.

[62] Shuie, *supra* note 4, at 1.

[63] ZELIN ET AL., *supra* note 1, at 17 (quoting Derk Bodde & Clarence Morris); DERK BODDE & CLARENCE MORRIS, LAW IN IMPERIAL CHINA: EXEMPLIFIED BY 190 CH'ING DYNASTY CASES 4 (1967) (stressing the public law nature of Chinese law and especially its penal component: "The penal emphasis of this [Chinese] law, for

authored and edited by Professors Madeleine Zelin, Johnathan Ocko and Robert Gardella in a helpful collection titled "Contract and Property in Early Modern China," which covers real estate transactions during the Qing Dynasty (1664–1912) and the early years of the Republican Era (1912–1949).[64]

Professor Zelin points to the widely held assumption that the disappearance of state owned land in the late Imperial period also prompted "a *laissez-faire* attitude toward private transactions"[65] which in turn resulted in the emergence of customary practices in the countryside. The state was regarded as having deferred to these practices, thereby:

> [E]ncouraging disputants to seek justice elsewhere, particularly through guild, lineage or village mediation. . . . [Thus] it would be difficult to speak of rights of property except as a highly localized phenomenon. Such a fragmented and fickle property regime could hardly form the basis of a large-scale commercial economy, much less encourage industrial investment.[66]

Yet, she added, once it became possible "to examine property rights in action . . . [mostly] though the [records of] lawsuits . . . in the late Qing [dynasty] and early Republic,"[67] one could not conclude that the state was of marginal importance when establishing property rights:

> Whether the state assumed the role of adjudicator by choice or had that role thrust upon it, county magistrates everywhere were inundated with litigation of an economic nature. That this large body of case law was not collected as precedent for judicial decision making does not mean that the state did not play a role in the establishment of the economic rules of the game and in their enforcement.[68]

Later she adds: "The most powerful evidence for the existence of strong rights of property lies in the imperial statutes relating to theft."[69]

I. Certainty of Family Rights vs. Rights of Third Parties

Professor Zelin's view on the developmental importance of state enforced "strong rights of property" was quite popular among development economists until empirical evidence supposedly linking the presence of these strong rights of property to economic growth was disproven. Peruvian economist Hernando de Soto obtained the support of various governments and international aid institutions for wide distributions of titles and other rights to real property in developing nations thereby hoping to bring about sustainable economic growth.[70] These efforts failed for two good reasons.[71]

---

example, meant that matters of a civil nature were either ignored by it entirely (for example, contract), or were given only limited treatment . . ." *Id.*).

[64] ZELIN ET AL., *supra* note 1.

[65] *Id.* at 18.

[66] *Id.*

[67] *Id.*

[68] *Id.* at 18–19 (citation omitted).

[69] *Id.* at 20.

[70] *See* HERNANDO DE SOTO, THE OTHER PATH: THE ECONOMIC ANSWER TO TERRORISM (2002); & HERNANDO DE SOTO, THE MYSTERY OF CAPITAL: WHY CAPITALISM TRIUMPHS IN THE WEST AND FAILS

The first reason for failure was that the distribution of title to land assumed that credit to micro and small businesses is invariably made possible by the lender's reliance on the borrower's title to land or to personal property as the collateral for his loan. This is not the case in the commercial lending world. What is of greatest interest to commercial lenders is not having a title to the borrower's place of business or even to his inventory or equipment, but to be able to repay themselves from the borrower's sale or productive use of his business assets ("asset-based lending"). As long as the borrower's "streams" of business income can be reliably accessed by the commercial lender, "title to [the] collateral is [immaterial]" in the words of the U.C.C., the most effective enactment in support of commercial credit in the financial world.[72] This rationale applies equally to the lending to agri-business.

The second reason concerns the "undifferentiated" approach to the certainty of contract and property rights. Assume that "A," a member of family "B" sells land "X" to "C" who intends to develop it for agri-business purposes. A also mortgages lot "Y" to banker "D" who will extend a loan that will facilitate A's agri-business plans. A believes that lots X and Y are part of his allotment in a division of the land made by his father "E." E disagrees and believes that lots X and Y were retained by family B under his control. Assume that the division of B's land was not recorded in a registry nor in any other public record, or if registered, the recording cannot be found by anyone interested in buying or obtaining a mortgage in B's land. Assume finally that relying on customary family law or a statutory law, a municipal magistrate decides that the family rights invoked by A and E trump the third party rights of invoked by C and D.

From an economic development standpoint, it makes a difference if the rights of E and family B are deemed superior to those of the third party purchaser-investor and lenders. Following such a decision, third parties such as bankers, mortgagees or *bona fide* purchasers of A's land would not want to buy X or Y or rely on them as collateral. E and family B would be forced to seek development capital among family, lineage or clan members who only proved a good source of capital when they monopolized the business or sector, as was the case with the Huizhou.[73] The frustrated buyers or lenders, in turn, may wish to resort to costly, and in the end, uncertain procedures such as bribery or forgery of deeds and so on. These procedures are invariably costly and uncertain because usually they are subject to reversal by a higher or more powerful bidder. Thus, distributing millions of land titles in developing nations without paying attention to commercial credit requirements and without matching the priority of rights granted by these titles with developmental goals cannot help but fail to produce any discernible measure of economic growth.[74]

Finally, I disagree with Professor Zelin's assumption that the "customary practices of the Chinese countryside" had to result in a "fragmented and fickle" property regime.

EVERYWHERE ELSE (2000). *See also* Kozolchyk, *Reduction of Poverty*, at 737–38 (this author criticizing Hernando de Soto's views).

[71] Kozolchyk, *Reduction of Poverty,* at 737–38 n.37 & accompanying text (referencing studies on Hernando de Soto's title distributions).

[72] U.C.C. § 9–202 (2000).

[73] *See supra* § 17:5(A).

[74] Kozolchyk, *Reduction of Poverty,* at 737–38 n.37 & accompanying text (referencing studies on Hernando de Soto's title distributions).

If a customary practice is cost effective and fair in the eyes of those who regularly participate in such transactions, it has as the potential of becoming a widely, indeed universally, observed rule of law, more effective and growth-promoting than any state enacted commercial statute, particularly in our time.[75] The following sections will examine some of the most common causal clauses in land conveying practices in late Imperial Chinese customary law and their effect upon financial certainty. But first the reader must appreciate the all encompassing role of family and community in the sale of rural land.

J. Preliminary Conclusions

Professor Hansen's research indicates that the history of legal troubles with customary familistic sales clauses and attempts to cure them was in some cases millenary. She points to a 969 C.E. Song dynasty stamp tax that had to be paid within two months of the signing of a land transfer or mortgage contract.[76] This period of time was intended to provide ample time for the exercise of the right of first refusal by the seller's kin and neighbors; thus a customary contract rule emerged by which: "Those who are going to mortgage or sell things should first ask their neighbors if any of them wishes to mortgage or buy the land by writing the inquiry on a placard and waiting for the reply. After two months the contract can be approved and stamped."[77]

Yet realizing that this right of first refusal enlarged the potential number of bidders and of possible transactions involving land or real property, the imperial government enacted a tax and a waiting period for the completion of the conveyance(s). Thus, the initial two months were extended to six or more months to encourage more bids and transactions. Meanwhile, the title to the family land and to related family law duties remained uncertain and subject to endless lawsuits. Still, by the end of the eleventh century, the "process for selling land had become too cumbersome, and the right of [first] refusal was limited to kin unless the neighbors had graves on the plot[s]."[78]

What does this seemingly endless attempt by legalistic rules to cope with familistic causal clauses in China's customary law reveal or at least suggest? One conclusion is apparent—up until the advent of the PRC in 1949, China, despite official policy oscillations, continued to be a deeply familistic and rural society. Yet, it was also a society that had been evolving for centuries in a highly commercial and industrial direction. The research of Professor Zelin provides a vivid illustration of the clash between familistic causal contracting and the need for abstract financial relationships of a growing commercial and industrial society.

She found property rights that "facilitated agreements that extended far beyond face-to-face relationships."[79] She illustrates this finding with the development of industrial and commercial credit facilities, such as that of industrial Zigong (自贡) in 1896, whose financial needs were well "beyond the capacity of traditional pawnshops . . . and remittance banks."[80] The credit facilities that were put together by native

[75] *See infra* §§ 24:6–24:8.

[76] HANSEN, *supra* note 42, at 79.

[77] *Id.* (citation omitted).

[78] *Id.* at 80.

[79] ZELIN ET AL., *supra* note 1, at 31.

[80] *Id.*

businessmen were made possible by "a series of interlocking contracts governing repayment procedures, management structures, and reallocation of assets."[81]

In contrast, she also found that "the Chinese property rights regime . . . operated within a complex of institutions that included patrilineal inheritance, weak inheritance rights for women, ownership vested in the household and not the individual. . . ."[82]

She then concluded that:

> In the long run, however, China's property rights regime could also interfere with the economic efficiency of firms . . . in an environment like that of Zigong, such a property rights regime could result in serious difficulties for investors who were developing large vertically and horizontally integrated industrial and commercial firms. Most of these problems emerged as poorly defined rights and, along with conditional sale and debt, accounted for a large proportion of the property-related suits filed in nineteenth- and twentieth-century Chinese courts.[83]

Apparently, the same problem has continued even in a "socialist market" economy, as confirmed by Pei Chunliang, a Chinese legislator who addressed a national congressional session in 2009 and provided dramatic figures on the contemporary volume of Chinese land disputes: "China's land contract management system faces problems that constrain rural development and affect stability. More than 50,000 land dispute cases arose in 224 cities and counties across the country from 2003 to March 2008."[84]

§ 18.2 FORGERY AND CHICANERY IN IMPERIAL COURT LITIGATION

A. The Assistants in Drafting and Pleading

Litigation over agreements for the sale of land was widespread in China from the time of the Song dynasty (1127–1279 C.E.).[85] As popular sayings had it: "Officials have government law and commoners have private contracts"; or "Officials have government law (zhengfa) and do not accept private agreements as conclusive."[86] I believe that the above translation captured only part of their meaning. An Anglo-American lawyer is likely to deduce from it that in Imperial China there were two sources of the law of contracts, with one (the private law) being subordinated to the other (the governmental or public law).

Yet, after reading the cases and background materials provided by Professors Valerie Hansen and Harriet Zurndorfer, there was more to these sayings than a ranking of sources.

---

[81] *Id.*

[82] *Id.* at 31–32.

[83] *Id.* at 32.

[84] National People's Congress (NPC) of the People's Republic of China, *China's legislature eyes stability with law on rural land disputes meditation*, NPC.GOV (June 29, 2009), http://www.npc.gov.cn/englishnpc/news/Legislation/2009–06/29/content_1508642.htm.

[85] Zurndorfer, *Contracts, Litigation and Economic Regulation, supra* note 3, at 8.

[86] HANSEN, *supra* note 42, at 81.

As just discussed, the familistic way of doing business was having serious difficulties in adjusting to a marketplace increasingly populated by strangers. However, please recall from the preceding chapter that legalistic rulers often shared in the profits of the familistic businesses as official or silent partners or as recipients of bribes. Against this background, it was not surprising that both familistic drafters of contracts and pleadings and their counterparties employed every possible trick to evade, twist or turn legalistic rules and prohibitions to their respective advantage.

Professor Hansen quotes from the initial paragraph in a judicial decision where the judge listed some of the most common contractual forgeries or tricks: "Some use ink that is too heavy or too light. Some use handwriting that is different or the same. Some disguise the amount of land. Some change the name of the plot. Some omit or alter the area or borders. All of these types are difficult to list fully . . ."[87]

To which unidentified judges quoted in the compilation of litigation chronicles, *Qingming ji* (清明集), added:

> Some forgers used old paper with new ink. Or they pasted on emendations in a different handwriting. Or they wrote their personal mark, usually an abbreviated character (*huaya*), on top of a stamp, when the mark should have been underneath the seal. Or they paid the stamp tax on a forgery after the alleged sale had taken place and the case was already in court . . . [despite the fact that] it was illegal to forge official documents, and the punishment was one hundred strokes.[88]

This resort to forgery and chicanery in the judicial process should not be surprising in light of the endless uncertainties that resulted from the clashes between or among familistic clauses or methods of doing business, legalistic statutes or directives, and what Professor Huang refers to as "market logic" as well as official and private corruption. The authors of many of the above-described forgeries and chicanery were known as litigation "assistants" or "masters," a class of people who earned a living by helping others draw up contracts, complaints and evidence for lawsuits. According to Professor Hansen, they were called "those who encourage [law]suits (*jiansong*)' or, more picturesquely, 'those with brushes inserted in their hats' (*erbi*), terms which vividly capture their readiness to draft documents."[89]

B. The Adjudicators

The adjudicators were mostly local magistrates acting as judges, described in the *Qingming ji* as "enlightened, rational, compassionate bureaucrats . . . [in contrast] with an endless stream of quarrels arising among ignorant and recalcitrant locals."[90] Yet at least during the Song dynasty, only a few of these bureaucrats had professional legal training.[91] Some of their decisions reflected a distinct Confucian-moralistic rationale, at times strong enough to deny enforcement of otherwise valid contracts,[92] while others, rendered as tax collectors, reflected a legalistic bent.

---

[87] *Id.* at 98.

[88] *Id.* at 97 (citations omitted).

[89] *Id.*

[90] Zurndorfer, *Contracts, Litigation and Economic Regulation*, *supra* note 3, at 9.

[91] HANSEN, *supra* note 42, at 93.

[92] *Id.*

Dr. Zurndorfer rejects polar views of the system of adjudication as the product of either an authoritarian and "confiscatory state" or of a "weak indifferent dynastic regime."[93] She agrees with Professor Huang that the adjudication of contract disputes was neither the exclusive product of an autocratic official law nor "of community or kin mediation."[94] It was a system in which magistrates functioned more as mediators than as adjudicators.[95] This meant that very frequently they failed to decide cases either because of lack of evidence or the invocation of legalistic grounds by defendant-debtors, such as statutes of limitations.

I would add to the list of missing elements in the adjudication of land disputes the practices of the province or region. Why are there no references to these practices in the vast number of decisions collected by Professors Huang, Cohen, Chihue, Hansen, Zelin, Zurndorfer and others? One possible answer, which is discussed in detail in Ch. 24 infra, is the quality of the practices. In other words practices, certainly must have existed, but were they of the type whose "nuclei" were formed by the right measures of selfishness and altruism, good faith and reasonableness including concern for the rights of innocent third parties? If they were not of this type, if the practice involved was mostly a result of chicanery or of exploitation of a party's political or legalistic power, chances are that they would not be viable. Mutatis mutandis, if the official records of land transactions were chaotic and unreliable how could a claim even by a lineal, male heir of family property succeed in court?

C. An Illustration: A Statute of Limitations and a Clearly Drafted or "Doctored" Contract

The following extract of a magistrate's decision issued in 1194 C.E.[96] illustrates the need for clearly drafted and reliable official documents or their functional (albeit not always truthful) equivalents.

A plot of land had changed hands five times since 1194. The plaintiff who claimed title to this land brought his claim fifty years after that chain of transfers and alleged that the plot was rightfully his because his grandfather had originally mortgaged and not sold it. T he judge cited the statute of limitations and rejected the plaintiff's argument because he had offered as proof of his claim a contract for a different plot.

The magistrate concluded that: "If he says the land was inherited, he [the plaintiff] should have had a land register or a will that can be consulted. If he says it actually was mortgaged by his ancestors, he must have a contract or a mortgage agreement . . . But he has nothing."[97]

---

[93] Zurndorfer, *Contracts, Litigation and Economic Regulation, supra* note 3, at 10. Emblematic of this system of adjudication were the "village elders" of the Song dynasty. In connection with this dynasty, Emperor Taizu (1368–1398) enacted laws intended to cause the moral renovation of the Chinese, including the village elder system for the adjudication of disputes avoiding the magistrates' courts and taming the rampant litigiousness. This experiment with the "Daoist model of little elite of virtuous elders" did not last beyond Taizu's death. Zurndorfer, *Contracts, Litigation and Economic Regulation, supra* note 3, at 13.

[94] *Id.* at 10. (Citation omitted.)

[95] *Id.* at 11.

[96] HANSEN, *supra* note 42, at 98. The following is my reconstruction of some of the relevant facts and reasoning from the text provided by Professor Hansen's summaries, *see Qingmingji* 4: 111–112, 132–133 summary, *cited in id.*

[97] *Qingmingji* 9:313–314, *cited in id.*

A chronicle of disputes during the Qing dynasty, the *Qingming ji*, added that the plaintiff did not know the selling price, the broker's name or the original buyer's name, presumably facts that would have given at least an appearance of the existence of a mortgage. The importance attributed to a sale document as proof of title is emphasized by another judicial statement in another land dispute reported in the *Qingming ji*:[98]

> Today when people take their clothes to the pawnshop to borrow 10 or 100 coins, they use a ticket to redeem their clothes. According to this principle that one cannot redeem clothes if the ticket is lost, how can one redeem land or a house with no proof of ownership?[99]

It is worth noting that the requirement of a written contract by analogy to a pawnshop ticket was a legalistic formality that persuaded this judge and perhaps others as well. However, the problem with the registry of rural land is that it was largely dysfunctional during China's Imperial period and beyond, as will be discussed in a the following chapter.[100]

D. Conclusions: Familistic Clauses, Legal Invertebration, Uncertainty and Third Parties

In a market that attempts to be commercial and encouraging to third parties acting as purchasers, investors and secured lenders, the root cause of the widespread legal uncertainty is a custom that partakes of the worst among familistic customs and legalistic (including judicial) procedures, especially once they became prey to forgery, chicanery and bribery. Familistic clauses were dysfunctional as uncooperative commercial customs, *i.e.*, they were neither cost effective nor fair, especially when failing to protect the crucial third party buyers, investors and lenders. Conditional or redeemable sales, dual tiers of subsoil and topsoil rights, preemptive rights of kin or neighbors, defension and other familistic clauses were unsuited for a growing commercial and industrial society in which third parties had to play a crucial role. *Accordingly, familistic clauses and corrupt legalistic procedures were the principal source of legal invertebration in Imperial contract law.*

This is why attempts to adjust or accommodate these customs with the "logic of the market" failed. As we know, this logic requires that market participants treat each other in a manner that would satisfy reasonable expectations of, among others, profitability and certainty of outcome.[101] In contrast, the familistic logic cares about the welfare and sustainability of the family unit, regardless of its effects upon third parties. Thus, they are irreconcilable forms of doing business and of regulation. This is also why effective commercial customs could not be found in Imperial China as they were found among late medieval and Renaissance European merchants. Because of familism and Confucianism, Chinese merchants did not draft fair and cost effective commercial customs; by and large they were content with drafting exquisite rules of etiquette and courtesy.[102]

---

[98] *Qingmingji* 5: 149, *cited in id.* at 99.

[99] *Id.*

[100] *See infra* ch. 19.

[101] *See* Glossary, "Market Standard of Fairness."

[102] RICHARD JOHN LUFRANO, HONORABLE MERCHANTS: COMMERCE AND SELF-CULTIVATION IN LATE IMPERIAL CHINA 54–55 (1997).

§ 18.3 MAO TSE-TUNG AND HIS SHIFTING MARXIST-LENINIST DOGMA

According to the Encyclopedia Britannica, "looking at the whole period from the foundation of the Communist Party in 1921 to Mao's death in 1976, on can fairly regard Mao Zedong as the principal architect of the new China."[103] This statement was made in 1974 and remained true until Mao's death in September 1976; presently, under "socialist market" conditions it may well have to be qualified.

Unlike Lenin, Mao was from peasant extraction, and also unlike Lenin, he spent at least six months in 1911 soldiering as part of a revolutionary army in Hunan; however, as with Lenin in the USSR, he rose to be both the leading theoretician and practitioner of the dogma of the Chinese communist revolution. When imperial China gave way to the Chinese Republic in 1912, Mao continued searching for his intellectual moorings in institutions as varied as schools of police, business and law while continuing his readings of the "classical works of the Western liberal tradition."[104] In 1918, he became an assistant to the librarian of China's most renowned university, Peking University.[105] That was the time when Peking University Marxist-Leninist intellectuals populated the "May Fourth Movement of 1919, which was to a considerable extent the fountainhead of all of the changes that were to take place in China in the ensuing half century."[106]

In 1920, Mao returned to his native province a primary school principal and started his career as an organizer of small units of the Communist party; a year later he helped to found the national Chinese Communist Party [CCP].[107] At the same time, and as was the case with other of his communist colleagues, he joined the nationalist Kuomintang Party (KMT) coalition led by Sun Yat-sen, widely regarded as the founding father of Republican China, later replaced by Chiang Kai-shek. During his membership in the KMT, Mao edited its principal periodical and served at the Peasant Movement Training Institute.[108] The KMT ruled much of China from 1928 until 1949 when a Mao-led army forced it to leave mainland China and settle in Taiwan.

Mao's reliance on the Chinese peasantry as the principal engine of the communist revolution was a major departure from Marx's Law of Motion of Modern Society. While the *Comintern* advisers continued to insist on a proletarian-led revolution, the Chinese proletarians failed to conquer even one single major city.[109] And when the Central Committee of the CCP was forced to settle in the rural province of Jiangxi (江西), Mao emerged as a political and eventually, military leader. As stated by Fairbank and Goldman:

---

103 23 THE NEW ENCYCLOPAEDIA BRITANNICA: MACROPAEDIA: KNOWLEDGE IN DEPTH 511 (15th ed. 1989); *see also* JOHN KING FAIRBANK & MERLE GOLDMAN, CHINA: A NEW HISTORY, SECOND ENLARGED EDITION 301–11 (2006) (summarizing Mao Zedong's rise and actions while in power).

104 ENCYCLOPAEDIA BRITANNICA, *supra* note 102, at 511.

105 *Id.*

106 *Id.*

107 *Id.* at 512.

108 *Id.*

109 *See* Benjamin Schwartz, *The Essence of Marxism Revisited: A Response,* 2 MODERN CHINA 461, 469–72 (1976).

> From this time on the personality and mind of Mao became a central factor in the CCP revolution. [He exceeded] his colleagues in achieving a unity of theory and practice, a major motif of Confucian philosophy. . . . [As director of the Peasant Movement Training Institute, his] program seems to have stressed an analysis of peasant problems plus an analysis of class structure in the countryside.[110]

It was during 1934–1935 that Mao led the famous "Long March" whose purpose it was to find a place for the CCP in "the periphery of Nationalist [KMT] power."[111] This march started with approximately 100,000 peasants and wound up with almost eight times that many. The CCP had thus found an area it could control and use as its base of operations for future actions against its nationalist and international (mostly Japanese) enemies. It took continuous intra-party struggle for Mao to emerge in 1945 as the "chairman" of the CCP—a position he retained until his death in 1976. After the CCP's victory in 1949 in its civil war with the KMT, the CCP founded the People's Republic of China (PRC) with Mao as its chairman.

As had been done by Lenin, Mao authored a number of writings especially during the period of 1936–1940. Some were inspired by Soviet writers and some by his own experiences including his account of dialectical materialism such as "On Practice" and "On Contradiction" and on subjects more mundane such as on the organization of peasant action groups or on the overall strategy of the revolutionary war.[112] On the whole, Mao's writings were closer to the realities of the Chinese countryside than anything Lenin had ever written about the Russian peasantry. As described by Fairbank and Goldman:

> [U]sing an intensely practical tactic of identifying those classes with whom to work and those classes to work against. . . . [suggesting that] the role of the party worker in the village must be one of a guide and catalyst *rather than a know-it-all.* He must closely examine the villagers' needs and complaints, hopes and fears; [and] only then could he articulate the peasantry's demands and follow the tactic of uniting with the largest possible number to attack the smallest possible target. . . .[113]

Despite Mao's early inclination to formulate "bottom up" policies, he and his triumphant CCP colleagues fully practiced Lenin's "know it all wisdom" once in power. This attitude led Mao (as it had done to Lenin) to continuous shifts and turns of policy and actions which affected the lives of millions. For example, when the PRC was founded in 1949, he stressed total obedience to the CCP only to turn against the CCP's ruling establishment during the so called "Cultural Revolution" in 1966–1969. Similarly, the same Mao who stressed the need for large strides in agricultural production in 1949 switched to a sweeping industrial policy in the largely failed "Leap Forward" of 1957–1958.[114] In the exercise of this autocratic know-it-all attitude, he also shared with Lenin and Stalin a callous disregard for the human costs of his policies. As will be discussed shortly, his collectivization and commune policies were responsible for

---

110 FAIRBANK & GOLDMAN, *supra* note 103, at 302–03.

111 *Id.* at 305.

112 *Id.* at 467.

113 FAIRBANK & GOLDMAN, *supra* note 103, at 303 (emphasis added).

114 *See* ENCYCLOPAEDIA BRITANNICA, *supra* note 103, at 514.

thirty million deaths in the Chinese countryside. And as recalled by a human rights academic website: "Starting in the mid-1950s, Mao repeatedly affirmed his willingness to sacrifice up to a third of the Chinese population in a nuclear war so long as this would help bring about the downfall of world capitalism."[115] Prior to examining Mao's rural land policies and laws, a short detour is necessary on the PRC's initial land reform and its eventual replacement by the values of Mao's "New Socialist Man."[116]

A. The PRC Initial Land Reform

In 1950, Mao enacted an Agrarian Reform Law which distributed land, animals and machinery large masses of hungry and dispossessed peasants; concomitantly, "evil landowners" were found guilty of exploitation and as many as one million were executed between 1949 and 1953.[117] Accordingly the PRC distributed more than half of its arable land to:

> [M]ore than sixty percent of its rural population—on an equitable, per capita basis. Land titles or certificates were issued to farmers as well. This "land to the tiller" campaign lifted hundreds of millions of poor Chinese out of destitution and hunger. Annual crop production increased seventy percent from 113.2 million tons to 192.7 million tons between 1949 and 1956. Similarly, total farm income rose eighty-five percent during the same period.[118]

B. The Abrogation of Pre-Existent Law and the Spirit of the New Socialist Man

After Mao took control of mainland China, all the laws and regulations in force during the tenure of the Nationalist government were repealed.[119] As was the case in the USSR, private farming, industrial manufacturing and distribution and marketing became state assets and as such governed by the central planning system including the five yearly economic plans. In 1950, the Financial and Economic Committee of the State Council promulgated Provisional Measures for Contracts between or among administrative agencies, state enterprises and cooperatives and in the same year, other

---

115 Lorenz M. Lüthi, *Biography, in* 2 GENOCIDE AND CRIMES AGAINST HUMANITY (Dinah L. Shelton & Gale Cengage eds., 2005), *available at* http://www.enotes.com/genocide-encyclopedia/mao-zedong (on file with author).

116 *See infra* § 18:3(B).

117 Zhu Keliang & Roy Prosterman, *Securing Land Rights for Chinese Farmers: A Leap Forward for Stability and Growth*, CATO DEVELOPMENT POLICY ANALYSIS 3–4 (Oct. 15, 2007). *See China 1949 to 1953,* HISTORY LEARNING SITE, http://www.historylearningsite.co.uk/china_1949_to_1953.htm (last accessed Oct. 2, 2013) (summarizing Mao's land reform which started during 1950).

118 Keliang & Prosterman, *supra* note 116, at 3 (citation omitted).

119 *See* Li Zhu, Introduction to Chinese Contract Law (2005) (unpublished substantial paper, University of Arizona) (on file with author) (providing, many of the materials in this research memorandum). This source explains:

> Article 17 of the Common Program of the Chinese People's Political Consultative Conference, also known as the Provisional Constitution of the newly founded People's Republic of China in mainland China provided that it "shall do away with all the laws, decrees and judicial system of the Kuomintang (KMT) reactionary government, because they were oppressing the people, and shall enact laws and regulations which will protect the people, and establish a people's legal system."

CHUNYING XIN, CHINESE COURTS: HISTORY AND TRANSITION 3 (2003), *cited in id.* at 1 n.3 & accompanying text.

state ministries issued decrees regulating the contracts that came under their jurisdiction such as international and local trade and commerce, railways and others.[120]

Also, as in the USSR, disputes among the agencies and third parties were resolved through administrative institutions, including arbitral tribunals. Meanwhile, a wide range of "civil," *i.e.*, non-commercial disputes between individual parties, were adjudicated by local committees of the CCP; they included claims on subjects as varied as housing, funerals, petty quarrels and divorces and often involved the sale, exchange or rental of property that was described earlier as "personal."[121] There was no written or official source of law to govern such controversies except Mao's writings in which he tried to capture the spirit of the revolution as exemplified in what he often referred to as the New Socialist Man (社会主义新人; hereinafter NSM).

I first heard about Mao's NSM from the then dean of a Shanghai law school during his visit to the University of Arizona College of Law in 1980. He spoke of the "hundreds of thousands Chinese law students" who needed a full exposure to commercial law and especially international commercial law. He invited me to teach in Shanghai and asked for permission to translate some of my writings on the law of documentary letters of credit. Thinking about an authoritative and widely observed set of letters of credit customs known as The Uniform Customs and Practices for Documentary Credits of the International Chamber of Commerce (UCP), I asked him whether he considered this source as the "living law" of China's documentary letters of credit or whether international customary law would not qualify as living law in China. He suggested that during Mao's "cultural revolution," China's supreme living law was the NSM; there were multiple references to his virtues in Mao's "Little Red Book" (the Book of Quotations from Chairman Mao).[122] No judge or administrator could ignore Mao's views on the behavior of a NSM. I then asked the dean whether exposing those hundreds of thousands of students to a private (commercial) law whose function was to maximize profit-making was not inconsistent with Mao's NSM or the Little Red Book's "selfless communist man."[123] He tersely assured me that neither I nor my Chinese students would have to worry about any discouragement in Mao's Little Red Book; although it was quite influential in the past, it was not any more.

In his essay on the NSM, Professor Theodore H.E. Chen of the University of Southern California points out that the new society sought by Mao's revolution entailed bringing about a new form of life with "new minds, new ideas, new emotions, and new attitudes."[124] If the old society bred individualists and selfish persons who

---

[120] *See id.* at 3. *See also* YANLONG HAN ET AL, A LEGAL HISTORY OF THE PEOPLE'S REPUBLIC OF CHINA 296 (1998) & DEWU ZHOU, MANUAL OF PRACTICAL KNOWLEDGE OF ECONOMIC CONTRACTS 18, 19 (1988), *both cited in id.* at 2 nn.6–7 & accompanying text.

[121] *See supra* § 18:1(I).

[122] QUOTATIONS FROM MAO TSE TUNG (David Quentin & Brian Baggins trans., 1996), *available at* http://www.marxists.org/reference/archive/mao/works/red-book/. *See also Quotations From Mao Tse Tung: Chapter 28: Communists*, MARXISTS.ORG (2000), http://www.marxists.org/reference/archive/mao/works/red-book/ch28.htm (referencing the virtue of the communist man's selflessness: "At no time and in no circumstances should a Communist place his personal interests first; he should subordinate them to the interests of the nation and of the masses. Hence, selfishness, slacking, corruption, seeking the limelight, and so on, are most contemptible, while selflessness, working with all one's energy, whole-hearted devotion to public duty, and quiet hard work will command respect." *Id.*).

[123] *Id.*

[124] Theodore H.E. Chen, *The New Socialist Man*, 13 COMP. EDUC. REV. 88 (Feb. 1969).

thought only of their personal benefits and ambitions, the NSM had to be a collectivist, completely selfless and ever mindful of his duties to the revolution and party.[125] If the masses did not show enthusiasm for work unless it gave them material benefits and rewards, Mao's directive was to educate the NSM so "that he will not expect personal benefits but will find reward in the increase of production, the fulfillment of state plans, and the success of the proletarian revolution."[126] Accordingly, the CCP started selecting models from different economic sectors and professions, including laborers, peasants, women, and so on.[127] Model laborers, peasants, women and youth were constantly being selected and paraded as examples for the entire population to emulate. Significantly, no model merchants were selected.

"From the virtues extolled in indoctrination and propaganda and from the various 'models' selected to publicize desired behavior,"[128] the key features of the model man envisioned by the Communist planners were: 1) Absolute selflessness, the NSM must also always be ready to sacrifice his own interests for the good of the revolutionary cause;[129] 2) Obedience to the CCP, no matter what the Party or state wants, the NSM must be ready to comply;[130] 3) Class Consciousness, or a willingness to engage in class struggle against landlords and the "bureaucratic bourgeoisie";[131] 4) Labor and Production, the NSM loves labor for its ideological value and contribution to the nation's production. There is no distinction between manual and mental labor and no place for "white collar" persons who disdain to soil their hands in "rough" labor;[132] and 5) Versatility, The NSM must be able to serve in varied capacities, from one productive activity to another in response to the changing needs of the Party-state. Obviously, Mao's selfless man could never engage in hiring another or others for private endeavors for he would be guilty of the same Marxist sin committed in Soviet Russia by those whose income was "unearned."

C. Mao's Collectives, the NSM, the Absence of Contracts, and Its Human and Economic Costs

During most of the 1950s, Mao's policies for "building socialism" followed those of the Stalinist USSR: centralized planning with special emphasis on building capital intensive "heavy" industries. In the countryside too, the stages of land reform, followed in the course of collectivization which were similar to those of the Soviet Union, though the details were somewhat different.[133]

1. Analysis of the Failure of Mao's Collectivization Policies

The details of the implementation of the Soviet-inspired economic growth policies in Mao's China deserve close attention because they reveal a similar pattern of what happened in the USSR. Mao's collectivization policies and China's agricultural crisis of

---

125 *Id.*

126 *Id.*

127 *Id.*

128 *Id.* at 89.

129 *Id.*

130 *Id.* at 89–90.

131 *Id.* at 91.

132 *Id.* at 91–92.

133 ENCYCLOPAEDIA BRITANNICA, *supra* note 103, at 468.

1959–1961 were insightfully examined by Professor Justin Yifu Lin of Peking University (presently on leave of absence as the World Bank's Chief Economist and Senior Vice President for Development Economics).[134]

Professor Yifu Lin traced China's severe agricultural crisis during 1959–1961 to Mao's collectivization policies—thirty million deaths and enormous material losses were largely attributable to these policies.[135] Prior to this crisis, many economists thought that the collectivization movement in China "had avoided the devastating consequences associated with the Soviet Union's collectivization in 1929 and that China provided a model of agricultural development for underdeveloped, densely populated economies."[136] This appraisal had to be discarded as China's agricultural production plunged drastically for the three consecutive years with the above-mentioned catastrophic deaths and material losses.

Professor Yifu Lin describes the economy inherited by Mao's socialist government in 1949 as a war-torn economy "in which 89.4 percent of the population lived in rural areas and industry accounted for only 12.6 percent of national income."[137] Mao's policy of investing in a heavy industrial economy required a massive employment and redeployment of workers that resulted in a sharply increased demand for food and agricultural products. Yet the source of agricultural production continued to be the same independent family farm described in the preceding chapter,[138] a production unit that was too small and fragmented to be able to respond to the large increase in demand. Further, the standard form of contract for land use was that of the free tenancy of the surface land or topsoil described in an earlier section of this chapter.[139] Its rental payments, in kind or in currency, were as high as fifty percent of the output of the main crops which also discouraged productivity.[140]

The CCP had started a land reform program beginning in the 1940s in areas under its control by confiscating lands from the landlords and giving it to their tenants. This program was continued during the revolution until concluded in 1952.[141] Thereafter, three new major forms of cooperatives were set in motion: 1) the "mutual-aid team" in which a handful of neighboring households pooled their labor, farm tools and draft animals for peak seasons or on a permanent basis, but production and income decisions remained with each household;[142] 2) the "elementary cooperative" that involved twenty to thirty neighboring households who combined their productive assets and shared their income either through dividend payments for the use of their respective parcels, animals and farm tools or by remunerating the work performed by each household; and 3) the "advanced cooperative," which as in Stalin's USSR, collectivized all the means of production and in exchange paid the participants solely based on their contribution of labor or "work points." This type of cooperative started

---

[134] Justin Yifu Lin, *Collectivization and China's Agricultural Crisis in 1959–1961,* 98 J. POL. ECON. 1228 (1990).

[135] *Id.* at 1228–29.

[136] *Id.* at 1229 (citations omitted).

[137] Yifu Lin, *supra* note 134, at 1230.

[138] *See supra* § 17:2.

[139] *See supra* § 18:1(B)(1)(b).

[140] Yifu Lin, *supra* note 134, at 1230.

[141] *Id.* at 1231.

[142] *Id.*

with thirty households and eventually encompassed all the households of a village or approximately 150 to 200 households.[143] Please note that the values of the third type of cooperative closely resembled those that Mao expected from the NSM—selflessness and giving up comfort and rewards, compensation solely to make family subsistence possible, retention of class consciousness, especially when dealing with former landlords and maximum productivity and versatility.

At first, peasants were allowed to join the various forms of cooperatives on a voluntary basis; the "advanced cooperatives" were not among the most popular; by 1955, there were only 500 of them. By 1957, however, Mao's encouragement brought up their number to 753,000 and the number of households to 119 million.[144] As the scale of the industrial projects increased, so did the size and scale of agricultural projects; vast irrigation canals and dams that required the participation of dozens of collective farms were customary. Eventually, this approach led to the amalgamation of the 733,000 collective farms into 24,000 "communes" that comprised 120 million households "or over ninety-nine percent of the total rural households in China in 1958."[145] Consistent with the NSM values, "[r]emuneration in a commune was based mainly on the subsistence needs and only partly on the work performed by a peasant."[146]

2. *The Negative Effects of Mao's Collectives and Communes*

The negative effects of Mao's policy were dramatically illustrated in the statistics on the output of grain in collectivized China. From 1958 to 1959, grain output fell by thirty million tons (from 200 to 170 million) and between 1959 and 1960 it fell by 26.5 million tons (from 170 to 143.5 million); meanwhile, a population that had grown from 1958 to 1959 by thirteen million thereafter dropped its number by approximately four million each year until about 1962.[147] Professor Yifu Lin's conclusion was that "the estimated thirty million excess deaths in this crisis were the direct result of the crop failures."[148]

What were the causes of these crop failures? After examining various possible causes from bad weather to mismanagement, Yifu Lin came to the conclusion that the main cause was "the change of the nature of collectivization from a repeated to a one-time game in the fall of 1958."[149] At first, peasants had the right to decide whether or not to join a cooperative but in 1958, Mao promoted the people's commune as "the institutional innovation for quickly realizing communism in rural China."[150] Yifu Lin's analysis showed that when the freedom to quit the collective existed and members could decide what to do at the end of each productive period, productivity was higher. At the same time, since land holdings were highly fragmented and small and often insufficient to raise draft animals, it was possible to increase one's income by pooling the land and farm tools of several households. Yet these gains could be offset by the

---

143 *Id.*

144 *Id.*

145 *Id.* at 1234.

146 *Id.*

147 *Id.* at 1233, (see Table 2: Population, Agricultural Output and Grain Output).

148 *Id.* at 1234 (citation omitted).

149 *Id.* at 1240.

150 *Id.* at 1241.

difficulties and higher costs of supervising the production of the numerous units. Hence:

> To make a collective an efficient institution, some effective substitute for supervision [of its units] is required. A *self-enforcing agreement* among collective members in which each one promises to provide as much effort as on the household farm is an effective alternative when supervision is too costly.[151]

He clarified the meaning of this agreement as follows:

> A self-enforcing agreement does not require a third party to enforce the agreement, to determine whether there have been violations. . . . When the costs of third-party intervention are too high, a self-enforcing agreement is an effective substitute. . . . However, a self-enforcing agreement is sustainable only if the game is repeated. . . .[152]

I would note that the gist of the individual household's implied promise to the collective in a self enforcement collectivization agreement was to produce at least as much as it would have produced prior to joining the collective.

3. *The Economic Value of "Self Enforcing" and Commercial Contracts*

In what Professor Yifu Lin calls a "repeated game"[153] of collectivization, if at the end of a productive period the member feels that he can do better by himself he can withdraw from the collective. If he withdrew, the other members would have had to decide whether they stayed in the collective or withdrew themselves. Self enforcement came into play when the other members of the collective calculated that the losses that would result from the dissatisfied member(s)' withdrawal were larger than the gains derived from staying and reaping the benefits of the collective's economies of scale. If that was the result of their calculus, the collective would disband.

In Professor Yifu Lin's words:

> If the discounted present value of future losses is larger than the one-time gains . . . the member will honor the agreement. Therefore, it is the threat of a collective's collapse that greatly reduces the incidence of shirking [one one's duties or withdrawing from the cooperative]. This implicit threat also guarantees that the production in a voluntarily formed collective will be at least as good as the sum of production of a group of households working separately. . . . [Yet], when a collective [method of production] is imposed . . . [i]t becomes impossible to use withdrawal either as a way to protect oneself or as a means to check the possibility of shirking by the other members. Consequently, the self-enforcing agreement cannot be sustained in a one-time-game collective. . . . If supervision is ineffective and rewards are not closely related to each individual's . . . contribution in production, the incentives [to stay] will be low. . . . A peasant will not work as hard as on the household farm. Therefore, the productivity level of a collective will be lower

---

151 *Id.* (citation omitted) (emphasis added).

152 *Id.* at 1241 n.13.

153 *Id.* at 1241.

than the level reached on the individual household farm. The collective is [then] besieged by the "prisoner's dilemma."[154]

While Professor Yifu Lin used the concept of a self enforcing contract as a construct for his economic analysis, the calculus he describes is similar to that in everyday bilateral or multi-lateral commercial contracts. Elsewhere in this book,[155] I discuss the reason why most commercial contracts are performed and comparatively very few are breached—it is not as much the fear of legal sanctions such as damages, fines or even imprisonment (as Justice Holmes' Jr. would argue),[156] as it is the calculus that contracting parties are better off *in the long run* by performing than by breaching their contracts. Unlike Professor Yifu Lin's prisoner of Mao's commune,[157] commercial contracting parties are free to contract but the logic of their market contracts is usually guided by Jeremy Bentham's "felicific calculus," *i.e.*, the balance that results from subtracting units of pain from units of pleasure.

It is important to recall the lesson learned in a previous chapter with respect to the crucial missing data in the USSR's central planning:[158] the market (and contract)-derived prices and costs. As with central planning, in self enforcing and commercial contracts, their periodic cost-benefit assessment requires the ability to rely on reasonable estimates of what would be the contracting party's gain or loss as based upon actual market prices and costs of production, distribution, etc. Guesses by central economic planners as incorporated into administrative production quotas and non-market inspired prices are of no value to the household decision-maker. In fact, Professor Yifu Lin's assumption that the repeated game scenario would have allowed enough time for the individual household to make a rational decision is, given the chronic absence of relevant data, unduly optimistic. In the final analysis then, the failure of Mao's collectives and communes was caused by the failure to rely on freely-agreed-upon contracts between the households and the collectives.

D. Mediation and Non-Existent Land Contract Litigation During the Collectivization Period

In his studies on dispute resolution and mediation in contemporary China,[159] Stanley B. Lubman draws attention to Maoism as "not simply a way of viewing the world, but a program for changing it."[160] Under Mao, CCP cadres were responsible, among other activities, for the mediation of disputes that arose at the most basic levels of interaction, such as in the streets, business offices, factories and so on. Depending upon the level and type of disputes, the mediators could be "residents committees" (staffed by activities rather than cadres), "security defense committees" and in an ascending ladder of political power "Young Communist Leagues," "Women's Associations" and so on.[161] Some cities had "mediation sections" as part of the municipal governments and their task was to mediate the disputes of the urban

---

154 *Id.* at 1242 (citations omitted).

155 *See supra* § 14:1.

156 *Id.*

157 Yifu Lin, *supra* note 134, at 1242.

158 *See supra* § 15:4(E).

159 STANLEY B. LUBMAN, BIRD IN A CAGE: LEGAL REFORM IN CHINA AFTER MAO 40–70 (1999).

160 *Id.* at 41.

161 *Id.* at 46.

population.[162] I should emphasize that Maoist mediation efforts had a distinctive instructional purpose—to teach the correct behavior in accordance with Mao's socialist dogma, even though, as pointed out by Lubman, this educational function often led to an inconclusive handling of disputes.[163]

Nonetheless, Professor Philip Huang found very few disputes concerning land conveyances during the revolutionary and Mao's land reform period, including transactions between peasants, cooperatives, collectives and communes. During the confiscations of the Land Reform period, the disputes had to do with the resistance by "relatively well-to-do peasants" against the takeover of their land and on the rights and duties of "outsider[s] who had moved into the village."[164] As private land transactions were eliminated during the collective and commune system, so were the disputes "private property no longer figured much in people's [sic] lives, and disputes over inheritance also became very rare."[165]

§ 18.4 CONCLUSION

The system of state-imposed mediation and imposition of decisions on rights in land was supposedly done away by the next phase of Chinese property rights law that was made part of the Socialist Market Economy. Yet was it? Or is there a greater continuity between the authoritarian state-owned property of the past and the contemporary private property ownership system? The reader should be able to arrive at his conclusions after reading the following chapter. From the standpoint of the Imperial substantive law of contracts, there can be little doubt that much of the invertebration of the law of land contracts during the span of many centuries was attributable to familistic clauses and their inter-action with legalistic rules and remedies. The reader should continue to watch for the fate of these clauses under present day Chinese law: Are they still operative, albeit clothed with a different garb and with a different beneficiary although perhaps with the same victims?

---

162 *Id.* at 47.

163 *Id.* at 53.

164 PHILIP C. C. HUANG, CHINESE CIVIL JUSTICE, PAST AND PRESENT 35 (2010).

165 *Id.*

Chapter 19

CONTEMPORARY LAND CONTRACTS, THIRD PARTIES AND JUDICIAL LAW MAKING

§ 19.1 INTRODUCTION

This chapter discusses contemporary land transactions in the People's Republic of China (PRC) such as sales, leases, exchanges and mortgages of land in general and agricultural land in particular.

To a civil-law reader of the *Code Civil* persuasion, the study of land transactions may seem surprising in a textbook devoted to commercial contracts. Yet, PRC land transactions are an integral part of agricultural, industrial and commercial enterprises whose volume and economic importance far exceed those of the PRC's and many other countries' strictly urban commercial trade. Further, the profits from the sale, lease and exchange of land use rights as well as the taxes and fees they generate are among the most important sources of revenue of the PRC.[1] And, of equal importance for our contextual analysis, land transactions may show how the familistic components of yore have fared under a regulatory system in which PRC agencies and collectives are entrusted with the nation's real property.

Because Deng Xiaoping's "socialized market economy" policy started the commercialization of the nation's real property a generation or so ago, the time is ripe to pose the question, "How did the massive selling and mortgaging of land rights fare under the PRC's 'socialized market economy'?" More specifically, how did the Chinese legislators' attempt to combine local and foreign legal institutions succeed when commercializing China's land and real property? Rules aside, was this commercialization governed by the same principles of protection of third party rights apparent in the German law of real property in the nineteenth and early twentieth century[2] and especially in its land registry law? Or was it governed by the often contradictory and unpredictable principles, statutory, administrative and judicial rules encountered in China's imperial history or by the Soviet-like regulation of "personal" and supposedly forbidden private property transactions that failed so miserably in their country of origin?

Finally, the ability to convey, mortgage or pledge land use rights with reasonable certainty to parties who are not members of the sellers' or mortgagees' circle of family, friends and *Guanxi* relationships will serve as the acid test of the success of the PRC's legal institutions used in the process of commercialization.

---

[1] *See infra* § 19:3(B)(2)(c) (on studies by Professor Gregory Stein of the Univ. of Tennessee School of Law).

[2] *See supra* § 12:2(B) (discussing the principles of a commercial society and especially in 19th and early twentieth century German Law); *see also* Kozolchyk, *Roadmap*, at 9–23.

§ 19.2 DENG XIAOPING'S POLICIES

A. Introduction

Prior to our trip to China, I re-read an obituary of Deng Xiaoping, leader of the Communist Party of China (CCP) published by the New York Times.[3] It described Deng as the "political wizard who put China on the capitalist road" and narrated how after having fought as a guerrilla with Mao [Tse-tung] and Zhou Enlai, he became part of the top leadership of the PRC. It also spoke of how after having been installed by Mao as general secretary of the CCP in 1954, he was "dragged down from those heights" twice and purged as a "capitalist roader."[4] Finally, it referred to his remarkable comeback following Mao's death in 1976, and how he became China's paramount leader (in fact, but not in an official position) in 1978 at the age of seventy-four, and thereafter "reigned for a generation."[5]

Deng, as the paramount leader of the PRC, was responsible for an economic boom that significantly improved the lives of China's 1.2 billion citizens. Patrick Tyler summarized the economic improvements experienced by average Chinese during Deng's highly pragmatic rule and the meaning of that rule:

> [I]n cities and in villages, real incomes more than doubled. . . . Most Chinese who have watched a television or used a washing machine or dialed a telephone have done so only since Mr. Deng came to power. . . .
>
> . . .
>
> . . . Deng was best known as a pragmatist who focused on the problems of the day, unencumbered by history or ideology.[6]

Sadly, he will also be remembered for his ordering the June 1989 military crackdown on pro-democracy demonstrators in what history books around the world refer to as the Tiananmen Square massacre.

B. A Socialist Market Economy

Deng was a man of few words and simple maxims. Some of his maxims, much as Mao's and Lenin's, reached the status of constitutional like principles, although expressed in a milder and folksier tone than by his predecessor and revolutionary ancestor. One of these maxims emphasized that there was no road map for economic reform and equated such reform to crossing the river "by feeling out the stones with our feet."[7] His most remembered aphorism was: "It doesn't matter whether a cat is black or white, as long as it catches mice."[8] Clearly, this aphorism justified whatever means or labels were used to attain his goal of a "socialist market economy."

One of Deng's major premises for his socialist market economy was that:

---

[3] Patrick E. Tyler, *Deng Xiaoping: A Political Wizard Who Put China on the Capitalist Road*, N.Y. TIMES (Feb. 20, 1997), http://www.nytimes.com/learning/general/onthisday/bday/0822.html.

[4] *Id.*

[5] *Id.*

[6] *Id.*

[7] *Id.*

[8] *Id.*

> [P]lanning . . . [and] market forces . . . [are] not the essential difference between socialism and capitalism. A planned economy is not equivalent to socialism, because there is planning under capitalism too; a market economy is not capitalism, because there are markets under socialism too. Planning and market forces are both means of controlling economic activity.[9]

This premise fallaciously assumed that both forms of planning were the same regardless of who did the planning, *i.e.*, individual capitalists when deciding what contract to enter into or governmental economists acting for an entire polity. It also assumed that the planning was done in a similar fashion even though central planning does not take into account market prices while private planning does.

1. Decentralization: The Dual and Triple Tracks of Land Use Rights

Stanley Lubman, a scholar and practicing lawyer specializing in Chinese law, has authored helpful analyses of post-Mao economic and legal reforms, and of the decentralization started in the late 1970s.[10] As Mao's rural communes were dismantled, much of China's agricultural production was reassigned to the same familial households drafted into the collective system under Mao. Under Deng Xiaoping, some of the traditional land tenure and leasing practices were revived thereby "expand[ing] the discretion of 185 million peasant families to decide the crops they would grow."[11] Similarly, small scale enterprises could be formed by farmers or merchants.[12] Further, Deng relied on material incentives rather than on political campaigns to motivate the peasantry, allowing them to sell the products of their private plots in the free market.

As a key component of his industrial policy, *Deng shifted from Mao's heavy to light industries—especially those with high export potential—and relied on local municipalities and provinces as the agents for this change.* This shift took place in what Mr. Lubman refers to as a "dual-track" (central and provincial or municipal) approach. First, with respect to central planning, Deng reduced the scope of the state economic plans by loosening price controls and decentralizing budget and project administration functions. Goods produced by state-owned enterprises (SOEs) according to their applicable quota could be sold at the planned prices, while above-quota production could be sold at market prices or at higher specified prices.[13] In approximately two decades, "*by 1997, more than ninety-five percent of China's industrial output was being sold at market price.*"[14] Hence, the planned sector of the economy was being replaced gradually by an "increasingly differentiated nonpublic sector composed of enterprises under widely varying degrees of control by local governments and private owners."[15]

The manner in which Deng and his associates accomplished this shift and dual-track approach was largely through fiscal reform. At first, the central government granted to the local governments the right to retain tax and non-tax revenues that

---

[9] JOHN GITTINGS, THE CHANGING FACE OF CHINA: FROM MAO TO MARKET 253 (2006).

[10] STANLEY B. LUBMAN, BIRD IN A CAGE: LEGAL REFORM IN CHINA AFTER MAO 102–37 (1999).

[11] *Id.* at 103.

[12] *Id.*

[13] *Id.*

[14] *Id.* (emphasis added) (citation omitted).

[15] *Id.* (citation omitted).

would have normally flowed to Beijing.[16] As I will discuss shortly, this policy was replaced by a less generous revenue sharing system; nonetheless, the initial infusion of capital allowed local governments to set up light industries based upon the low cost of labor that generated significant foreign exchange earnings. Eventually, many of these industries, especially in the countryside, were sold by township and village enterprises to businessmen (local and foreign) for cash payments. Meanwhile, in the rural sector, industries were encouraged to take over agricultural processing and then to produce and sell in consumer markets.[17] In due course, this dual (central and local) track ushered in a triple-track regime of rights to use the land and improvements thereon in which private parties and entities played a much larger role.

2. *Hunger for Revenue and Land Use Rights*

Professor Susan Whiting of the University of Washington has shed important light on how the PRC's tax system encouraged the triple track of issuance of land use rights and attendant disputes and litigation.[18] Since 1994, the central government determines tax bases and rates and assigns revenues from the various taxes to central, local and shared categories.[19] As part of central government determination, local agricultural taxes were abolished leading to what she refers to as a "skewed alignment of revenue and expenditure assignments."[20] Local expenditures continued to climb creating a "revenue hunger" at the local levels of government.[21] Hence, the sale of rural and suburban land became one of the most important sources of local government revenue.

The governmental requisition of land in "the public interest" continues to be a favorite means to satisfy this hunger.[22] Accordingly, revenues are earned from: 1) the sale of low-priced land to industrial developers or investors; 2) the promotion of rapid real estate development (presumably by offering the land to commercial and residential developers or by jointly or separately promoting such developments); 3) the legal transfer fees earned by the above transactions; and 4) the use of land as collateral for loans.[23]

Eventually, local governments also started forcing transfers of agricultural land to non-agricultural uses with mostly inadequate compensation. A Chinese survey cited by Professor Whiting showed that of the total amount of the land transfer fee, the local government received on average twenty to thirty percent, the village twenty-five to

---

[16] *Id.*

[17] *Id.*

[18] Susan H. Whiting, Presentation at the Fairbank Center, Harvard University Chinese Justice Workshop: Public Finance and Land Disputes in Rural *China* (Oct. 12–13, 2007) [hereinafter Whiting, Public Finance]; Susan H. Whiting, Presentation at the Yale University Rule of Law Workshop: How Fiscal Pressures Drive Land Disputes and Shape Dispute Resolution Mechanisms in Rural and Peri-Rural China (Apr. 24–25, 2009) (transcript available at http://www.yale.edu/macmillan/ruleoflaw/papers/Whiting_Yale_workshop_041609.pdf) [hereinafter Whiting, Fiscal Pressures]; Susan H. Whiting, *World Bank, Growth, Governance, and Institutions: The Internal Institutions of the Party-State in China* 12, 13, Produced for the World Bank Research Project on the Rise of China and India (Governance) (rev. draft July 28, 2006) [hereinafter Whiting, *Growth, Governance*].

[19] *Id.* at 12–13.

[20] *Id.* at 13.

[21] *Id.* at 12.

[22] Whiting, Fiscal Pressures, *supra* note 18, at 5.

[23] Whiting, Public Finance, *supra* note 18, at 5.

thirty percent, and the farmers only five to ten percent.[24] Not surprisingly, these transfers and readjustments became a major source of often violent protests to the point that during 2005 alone, 87,000 such incidents involving land disputes took place.[25]

§ 19.3 LEGAL REFORMS, PROPERTY RIGHTS AND THEIR RELIABILITY

Introduction: The "Stress" Test of the PRC's Property Rights. Writing in 1999, Stanley Lubman called attention to the weakness of the land titles and especially of the industrial and commercial enterprises by the former townships and village enterprises (TVEs) and their associates or transferees, which as "nonstate enterprises" had "only ambiguous property rights that are poorly protected."[26] Among other reasons, the weakness was traceable to the transfer of ownership from the state to the townships and villages and from them to private owners. This transfer did not come about through a uniform and well-defined process but "through a disorderly variety of devices including the contracting or leasing of public assets, sale to private parties, illicit transfer of ownership to elites, and investment of public funds."[27]

The fact that these legal uncertainties had not visibly diminished the fast pace of investments led some observers to conclude that "individuals may not need to have property rights over enterprise profits for economic growth to occur."[28] I do not share this conclusion. Thirty odd years of "market socialism," a policy that is as internally contradictory as it is untested for society as a whole (including the rural sector), is too short a period to arrive at any conclusion concerning its long term economic, legal and political viability, let alone its supposed path-breaking success. To predict the viability of key legal institutions of market-socialism such as property rights, they must be "stress tested," a term popularized by the recent financial crisis of the United States, but equally applicable to what may well be in store for the PRC for reasons discussed later.

The most basic questions of this test are how certainly, quickly, fairly and inexpensively property rights can be enforced, by whom, against whom, and under what circumstances. This enforceability must be tested not only between the parties to the original conveyance of state-owned land rights by, say, a village committee to a local *Guanxi*-inspired enterprise, but also among the parties who acquire their land use rights thereafter as purchasers, lessees, holders of usufructs or mortgagees from the enterprises who acquired their rights from the village committee.

First I will describe in general terms the nature of the legal system of land use rights and will show why I use the term "invertebrate" when referring to one of its most distinctive features, whether as apparent in the manner in which laws are drafted and implemented, and interpreted by courts and their political superiors. This will be followed by a discussion of the most important constitutional and statutory sources and provisions of the law of land and real property transactions. Having done

---

[24] Whiting, *Growth, Governance*, *supra* note 18, at 14.

[25] *Id.*

[26] LUBMAN, *supra* note 10, at 117 (citation omitted).

[27] *Id.* at 117 (citation omitted).

[28] *Id.* (citation omitted).

this, I will then examine the meaning of key concepts under this law such as ownership, and land use rights, third party rights. The uncertainty of these rights will be tested in representative types of transactions such as the acquisition of residential urban property especially in large cities, or of rural or peri-rural land and in the manner in which typical disputes such as those involving land use certificates, and the right of usufruct are resolved.

A. An Invertebrate Law

The PRC's law on real property transactions is as legally invertebrate as that of the USSR, if not more so. Not infrequently, a governmental entity is one of the parties to a land dispute, and the presumption since times immemorial is that state rights are superior to those of private parties. And then, there is the division of state and collectively owned land, each with its own legal regime, about which more later, Not surprising, land ownership and use law consists of a bewildering array of often hierarchically-disconnected enactments by central and local legislative, executive and judicial branches of government, including directives or instructions by the national or local congresses to the respective courts on how to interpret constitutional statutory and administrative provisions and vice-versa.

1. The Many and Confusing Sources of Legislation

As pointed out by Mitzi Huang, "[t]he manner in which laws are made in China continues to be extremely confusing and vague."[29] Article 2 of the 1982 Constitution [hereinafter Constitution] places the National People's Congress (NPC, but also referred to as the National Congress of the Communist Party of China or NCCPC) at the top of its legislative hierarchy.[30] It has the power to "supervise the enforcement of the Constitution [and] to enact and amend basic laws governing criminal offenses, civil affairs, the State organs and other matters."[31] In addition, the NPC's Standing Committee (NPCSC) is also constitutionally authorized "to supervise the enforcement of the Constitution" and to enact statutes when the NPC is not in session as well as to interpret the constitution and statutes.[32]

Meanwhile, the Local Peoples' Congresses (LPCs), which are the local counterparts of the NPC as established in "provinces . . . municipalities . . . counties . . .

[29] Mitzi Huang, *Seeds of Legal Discontent, The Luoyang Seed Law Case: A Case Study of the Rule of Law in China,* 3 DARTMOUTH C. UNDERGRADUATE J.L. 32 (2005).

[30] PRC, CONST. § 1, art. 2 (1982). This is meant to support the concept that all power in the People's Republic of China belongs to the people. The constitution states:

> The National People's Congress and the local people's congresses at various levels are the organs through which the people exercise state power.
>
> The people administer State affairs and manage economic and cultural undertakings and social affairs through various channels and in various ways in accordance with the provisions of law.

Id. The Chinese government reiterated this point by promoting: "[A]ll power in the People's Republic of China belongs to the people, and the organs through which the people exercise state power are the National People's Congress and the local people's congresses at different levels . . ." *National People's Congress: Organizational System*, CHINA.ORG.CN, http://www.china.org.cn/english/27743.htm (last visited Sept. 16, 2013) [hereinafter *NPC, Organizational System*].

[31] PRC, CONST. § 1, ch. 3, art. 62 (1982), *available at* http://www.npc.gov.cn/englishnpc/Constitution/node_2830.htm.

[32] *NPC, Organizational System*, *supra* note 30, at 3 (NPC Standing Committee (1–3)).

municipal districts, townships . . . and towns"[33] are also authorized by the same Constitution to "ensure the observance and implementation of the Constitution and the law and the administrative rules and regulations in their respective administrative areas."[34] As with the NPC, the LPCs also have the power to adopt local regulations that "must not contravene the Constitution, the statutes and the administrative rules and regulations . . . [and can annul] inappropriate decisions and orders of the [P]eople's government at the corresponding level."[35] If these were meant to be parallel or non-converging lines of authority, in reality they overlap, as will now be illustrated.[36]

2. *Courts and the Weight of Their Decisions: The Luoyang Seed Case*

As prescribed by Article 127 of the Constitution,[37] the Supreme People's Court (SPC) sits at the top of the judicial hierarchy and responds to the NPC and NPCSC as administrative superiors whose powers include the appointment and removal of SPC justices.[38] Below the SPC and in a descending order of hierarchy, seat: 1) the Higher People's Court (HPC) at the provincial level; 2) the Intermediate People's Court (IPC) at the prefecture level; and 3) the Basic People's Court (BPC) at the county level.[39] As with the SPC (which responds to the NPC), the local courts at every level respond to the LPCs. However, Mitzi Huang reminds us that the entire judiciary is subject to the ideology and policies of the Communist Party[40] and Columbia University School of Law Professor Benjamin Liebman, among many others, agrees. While commenting on the designation of a recent president of the Chinese Supreme Court, Professor Liebman noted that:

> Unlike his predecessor, who spent a decade prodding judges to raise professional standards, Wang [Shengjun] isn't trained in the law. He ascended to the position after a career as a Communist Party official. In one of his first big speeches, Wang laid out guidelines for courts to follow: *First they should consider the needs of the Party*, then the needs of society, and finally the requirements of the law.[41]

A similar deference to the CCP officials was reported by Professor Susan Whiting:

---

[33] *China's Political System: II The System of People China*, CHINA.ORG.CN, http://www.china.org.cn/english/Political/26144.htm (last visited Sept. 16, 2013).

[34] *Id.*

[35] Huang, *supra* note 29, at 32 (citing art. 100 of the 1982 Constitution). Huang notes that the adoption of local regulation is by LPC's that are "at and above the county level." *Id.* at 33.

[36] *Id.* at 32. To the conflicting sources in the principal text she adds:

> [O]ther organs of the state also have the authority to legislate. [For example] The State Council, [a rough equivalent of a presidential cabinet of ministers, is considered] the highest executive body, has the power 'to adopt administrative measures' and to 'enact administrative rules and regulations.' [Similarly] [c]entral-level ministries, commissions, agencies and entities (such as . . . the People's Bank of China) directly under the State Council also retain the authority to create legislation. . . . [At the local level, the] local people's governments can issue administrative rules.

Id. (citations omitted).

[37] PRC CONST. ch. 3 § 7, art. 127 (1982).

[38] *See* Huang, *supra* note 29, at 33.

[39] *Id.*

[40] *Id.*

[41] *See* David Hechler, *Lost in Translation*, COLUM. L. SCH. MAG. (2009), http://www.law.columbia.edu/magazine/162122/lost-in-translation (emphasis added).

> [W]hen local cadres, motivated by financial and career interests, become party to land disputes, the role of local courts in resolving such disputes appears to be weakened. Indeed . . . "local policy," which makes reference to State Council directives, now prohibits local courts from accepting land dispute cases.[42]

The Luoyang Seed Case was decided in 2004 by a panel of judges of the Luoyang Municipal IPC only to be reversed by Henan People's Provincial Congress; it illustrates both the supremacy of party policy and the invertebrate state of much of the PRC's commercial contract law.[43] This dispute was between two agricultural companies—one Chinese and the other foreign—and involved a contract for the delivery of corn seed.

Two different statutes appeared applicable, one was national (the National Seed Law of 2000) and the other a local regulation by the Henan's People's Congress. The former required that the damages for breach of contract be calculated according to the difference between the contract and market price for corn seed, the latter decreed that the damages be measured on the basis of government-set prices.[44] The panel of judges held that the National Seed Law applied and gave judgment in favor of the foreign firm. Judge Li, one of the panel members, justified her decision by pointing to the higher normative weight of the national statute.[45]

Unlike cases decided under the supremacy clauses of the constitutions of western nations,[46] the Standing Committee of Henan's People's Congress decided that Judge Li's decision "violated the law by engaging in illegal judicial review and by encroaching on [their] legislative authority."[47] Even though the precise nature of the illegality was not clear, the Standing Committee demanded that the IPC fire Judge Li and another panel judge who agreed with her ruling.[48] At first, the IPC removed the two judges, but as the authorized media objected to the harshness of their disciplinary action, the IPC "softened its stance and reinstated the judges."[49]

This case illustrates the friction among converging sources and institutions of official and living law whose mission was to provide a certain and predictable law of commercial contracts: 1) a national statute; 2) a local administrative regulation; 3) an IPC court decision; 4) a local legislative standing committee order or decree; and 5) an "equitable" adjustment of an administrative order or decree as a result of pressure by the local cadres of the CCP as reflected in media opinion.

---

[42] Whiting, Public Finance, *supra* note 18, at 2.

[43] *See* Huang, *supra* note 29, at 33–34 (for the facts and reasoning of this case).

[44] *Id.* at 33.

[45] *Id.*

[46] *See, e.g.,* U.S. CONST. art. VI, *available at* http://www.archives.gov/exhibits/charters/constitution_transcript.html. In relevant part it states:

> This Constitution, and the Laws of the United States which shall be made in Pursuance thereof; and all Treaties made, or which shall be made, under the Authority of the United States, shall be the supreme Law of the Land; and the Judges in every State shall be bound thereby, any Thing in the Constitution or Laws of any State to the Contrary notwithstanding.

Id. See also MEX. CONST. art. 133 (1917).

[47] Huang, *supra* note 29, at 33.

[48] *Id.*

[49] *Id.*

3. *The Main Constitutional and Statutory Sources of the Reform of Property Law*

Prominent among the national constitutional and statutory sources responsible for the most recent reform of property law as will be discussed in this section are: 1) the Constitution of 1982 as amended, especially in 1988 (Constitution);[50] 2) the Property Rights Law of 2007 (PRL) which is the most important and encompassing statute and as such will receive most of our attention;[51] 3) the Land Administration Law and Registry Measures (LAL, 1986);[52] 4) the Law for the Administration of Urban Real Estate of 1994 (LAURE);[53] 5) the Land Management Law of 1998 (LML); and 6) the Rural Land Contracting Law of 2002 (RLCL).[54] In addition, I will occasionally refer to contract law sources such as The Unified Contract Law of the PRC of March 15, 1999, and to the General Principles of Civil Law of 1985–6.[55]

The original version of Article 10 of the PRC Constitution of 1982 stated:

> Article 10. Land in the cities is owned by the state. Land in the rural and suburban areas is owned by collectives except for those portions which belong to the state in accordance with the law; house sites and private plots of cropland and hilly land are also owned by collectives. The state may in the public interest take over land for its use in accordance with the law. No

---

[50] PRC CONST. (1982).

[51] Lehman et al., *Property Rights Law of the People's Republic of China*, NATIONAL PEOPLE'S CONGRESS (2007), http://www.lehmanlaw.com/fileadmin/lehmanlaw_com/laws___regulations/Propoerty_Rights_Law_of_the_PRC__LLX__03162007.pdf. This is the translation of the PRL that I will primarily use unless otherwise indicated. I will often contrast this translation with: JOHN JIANG, THE REAL RIGHTS LAW OF THE PEOPLE'S REPUBLIC OF CHINA (PART I) (2007), (on file with author). I have also compared the preceding translations against doctrinal summaries of the PRL and practice commentaries, *in* Walter Lee, *China Real Estate Law: Part 1: Land use right,* KNOL.GOOGLE.COM, http://knol.google.com/k/china-real-estate-law-part-1-land-use-right (on file with author) [hereinafter Lee, *Part 1*]; *and* Walter Lee, *China Real Estate Law: Part 2: Property development*, KNOL.GOOGLE.COM, http://knol.google.com/k/china-real-estate-law-part-2-property-development (on file with author). *See also* Feng Wenli, China Land Surveying and Planning Institute, Presentation in Valencia, Spain: Systems of Land Survey and Registration in China (May 21, 2008) (slides on file with author). Mr. Wenli is employed by China Land Surveying and Planning Institute, Ministry of Land and Resources, which brings his version of the selected provisions to an official version of their meaning. Other doctrinal sources that I have used in an attempt to establish the most reliable meaning of the provisions selected for discussion are: Gregory Stein, *Mortgage Law in China: Comparing Theory & Practice*, 72 MO. L. REV. 1315 (2007); *and* Zhu Keliang & Roy Prosterman, *Securing Land Rights for Chinese Farmers: A Leap Forward for Stability and Growth*, CATO Development Policy Analysis (Series No. 3, Oct. 15, 2007), *available at* http://object.cato.org/sites/cato.org/files/pubs/pdf/DPA3.pdf. Among the many other shorter comments, I have found the comments posted by the law firm of Morrison and Foerster, useful. Morrison & Foerster, China Update, *China's New Property Rights Law* (May 31, 2007), http://www.mofo.com/china-update-chinese-real-estate-05-31-2007/. *See also* Valerie Marechal et al., *China's new Property Rights Law—an important step towards improving access to credit for small and medium enterprises*, http://www.doingbusiness.org/~/media/fpdkm/doing%20business/documents/reforms/case-studies/2009/db09-cs-china.pdf.

[52] Stein, *supra* note 53, at 1315 n.2 (on the Land Administration Law [*Tudi guanli fa*]).

[53] *Id.* at 1316 n.6.

[54] Law of the People's Republic of China on Land Contract in Rural Areas No. 73 (promulgated by order of the President, Aug. 29, 2002, effective Mar. 1, 2003), *available at* http://www.gov.cn/english/laws/2005-10/09/content_75300.htm.

[55] *See General Principles of the Civil Law of the People's Republic of China*, THE SUPREME PEOPLE'S COURT OF THE PEOPLE'S REPUBLIC OF CHINA (June 3, 2003), http://en.chinacourt.org/public/detail.php?id=2696. *See also* Lee, *Part 1*, *supra* note 51, art. 2 (emphasis added). *See also* Contract Law of the People's Republic of China (promulgated by the National People's Congress, Mar. 15, 1999) (trans. by John Jiang & Henry Liu) (on file with author). *See Land Administration Law of the People's Republic of China* CHINADAILY.COM.CN (May 8, 2006), http://www.chinadaily.com.cn/bizchina/2006-05/08/content_584128.htm.

> organization or individual may appropriate, buy, sell or lease land, or unlawfully transfer land in other ways. . . .[56]

Consistent with the invertebrate nature of land ownership and use rights, Guoqiang Tian a Chinese economist refers to a collective enterprise as "characterized by two main features, property rights are vaguely defined and there is significant involvement of government officials."[57] My former student Catherine Jiang provides a slightly more precise description:

> A collective economic organization consists of a single or several villages. It is the owner of land in the area of [the] villages and distributes it to the villagers for cultivation of residence. . . . The collective land is not permitted to be used for . . . commercial purposes unless it is converted to the state land.[58]

Despite the bucolic overtones of the property rights of a PRC collective enterprise, Guoqiang Tian, points out that following the introduction of market socialism and especially at the turn of the twenty first century, the PRC's non-state sector was the main engine in China's economy; "with an average annual growth rate of over 20% . . . [and] about 74% of the GNP. Interestingly, collectively owned enterprises comprise about 70% of this sector."[59]

Article 12 of the same Constitution declared that "Socialist public property is sacred and inviolable," and that any "[a]ppropriation or damaging of State or collective property by any organization or individual by whatever means is prohibited."[60] In addition, its Article 13 included a variant of the category of "personal property" found in the USSR Constitution of 1936 that created much uncertainty among hopeful owners of this type of property:[61] "The State protects the right of citizens to own lawfully earned income, savings, houses and other lawful property. The State protects according to law the right of citizens to inherit private property."[62]

During the First Session of the Seventh NPC of April 12, 1988, Article 10 of the 1982 Constitution was amended. Recall that its fourth paragraph provided that: "No organization or individual may appropriate, buy, sell or lease land or otherwise unlawfully transfer land. . . ." It was amended to read: "*The right to the use of the land may be transferred according to law.*"[63]

Thus, what this provision characterized as "the right to the use of land" became transferable and marketable under socialist market conditions. Another supporting amendment to Article 13 was enacted in 2004. At first sight it read as a clear rejection

---

[56] PRC CONST. ch. 1, art. 10 (1982).

[57] Guoqiang Tian, *Property Rights and the Nature of Chinese Collective Enterprises,* 28 J. COMP. ECON. 247, 248 (2000).

[58] Catherine Jiang, Supreme People's Court Directives for Disputes over Land-use in Rural China 1–2 n.3 (2013) (unpublished substantial paper) (on file with author).

[59] Tian, *supra* note 59, at 248.

[60] PRC CONST. ch. 1, art. 12 (1982).

[61] *See supra* § 15:1(B).

[62] PRC CONST. ch. 1, art. 13 (1982).

[63] PRC CONST. ch. 1, art. 10 (amended 1988), *available at* http://www.npc.gov.cn/englishnpc/Constitution/node_2829.htm (emphasis added).

of Lenin's slogan "nothing is private here . . ." and of Articles 5 and 6 of the Soviet Constitution of 1936:[64]

> The lawful private property of citizens is inviolable.
>
> The state protects . . . the right of citizens to own and inherit private property.
>
> The state may, in the public interest, appropriate or requisition private property of citizens for its use in accordance with the law, while making compensations.[65]

Thus, a reporter for the official Chinese newspaper China Today praised its language and quoted Beijing University Professor of Sociology Gao Bingzhong's optimistic assessment that it "signals the end of the system whereby all means of production is publically owned."[66] Professor Gao added that prior to this amendment, a planned economy prevailed and so did a system of public ownership which required no protection of private property. The reporter noted that new forms of ownership encouraged a "non-public economy [which] accounts for one-third of China's aggregate [economic income]"[67] and noted that "[a] 2002 investigation showed that 93 percent of urban citizens wanted an article in the Constitution on private property protection."[68] Professor Gao's and the public's expectations of the new legal regime proved too optimistic.

Only three years later Zhu Keliang and Roy Prosterman (two well-known experts on China's rural development problems) warned in their 2007 study of the insecurity of rural land rights, that:[69]

> Farmers in China face multiple threats to their land rights from local government and village officials. The most prominent threat is land expropriation or acquisition through eminent domain to satisfy demands of industrial growth or urban expansion. Despite a series of central laws and policies, in practice, farmers who lose their land typically receive little or no compensation. Closely related as another source of insecurity of land rights is the persistent "readjustment" or "reallocation" of farmers' landholdings that is administratively conducted by village officials. Today, such land-related problems are the number one cause for rural grievances and unrest in China,

---

[64] USSR CONST. ch. 1, art. 5 (1936). It states: "Socialist property in the U.S.S.R. exists either in the form of state property (the possession of the whole people), or in the form of cooperative and collective-farm property (property of a collective farm or property of a cooperative association)." *Id. See also id.* ch. 1 art. 6. It states:

> The land, its natural deposits, waters, forests, mills, factories, mines, rail, water and air transport, banks, post, telegraph and telephones, large state-organized agricultural enterprises (state farms, machine and tractor stations and the like) as well as municipal enterprises and the bulk of the dwelling houses in the cities and industrial localities, are state property, that is, belong to the whole people.

Id.

[65] PRC CONST. ch. 1 art. 13 (amended 2004), *available at* http://www.gov.cn/english/2005–08/05/content_20813.htm.

[66] Li Wuzhou, *People-Oriented Constitutional Amendments*, 5 CHINA TODAY 10, 12 (2004).

[67] *Id.*

[68] *Id.*

[69] Keliang & Prosterman, *supra* note 51, at 1.

which reported 17,900 cases of "massive rural incidents" of farmers' protests in the first nine months of 2006.[70]

4. A "Sketched" and Loose Style of Legislation

As apparent from the preceding discussion, part of the invertebration that causes the uncertainty referred to by Professors Zhu, Prosterman and Whiting stems from the executive branch's role as supreme decision-maker. As noted by Professor Minxin Pei of Claremont-McKenna College, most legislation in the PRC since 1978 stems from decisions made not by the legislature but by the executive branch, as the legislature mostly endorses bills drafted or sketched out by the executive.[71] Its drafting method is, for lack of a better term, loose. Repeated instances of loosely-drafted legislation will appear throughout this chapter; the following are samples of what can be expected.

Consider, for example, Article 4's enumeration of the rights *in rem* protected by the PRL: "Sanctity of Real Rights: The real rights of the state, the collectives and private persons, *as well as the real rights of other rights holders*, are protected by law, and no entity or individual may infringe on such rights."[72] Who are these "other rights holders"? As we will discuss in connection with the PRC land registry, this imprecision leads to much uncertainty and costly disputes.

The same imprecision is found in Article 12 with respect to the duties of the Registrar of Immovable Property: "The registrar shall perform the following duties: (1) . . . (2) . . . (3) . . . ; and (4) *Other duties prescribed by the relevant Laws and Administrative Regulations*."[73] What laws and what regulations is this provision referring to? Since there are at least more than a dozen laws and regulations that deal with land rights and their registration and some are inconsistent with the others, how can one determine which, among the inconsistent ones, contain duties of the land registrar?

Similarly, assume that the researcher is trying to find out what property falls under the rubric of collective ownership. The PRL directs you to Article 58 which states:

> Scope of Things under Collective Ownership
>
> Immovables or movables owned by a collective *may* include:
>
> (1) Lands, forests, mountains and hills, grasslands, barren lands, and shoals, to the extent their ownership is attributed to said collective under the relevant Laws;
>
> (2) Buildings, production facilities, agricultural field irrigation facilities owned by said collective;

---

[70] *Id.* They add:

> Both Chinese and foreign observers have noted an increase in incidents of rural unrest, including violent confrontations between local governments and farmers. In the first nine months of 2006, China reported a total of 17,900 cases of "massive rural incidents". . . . Approximately 80 percent of these incidents were related to illegal land-takings.

Id. at 3 (citation omitted).

[71] MINXIN PEI, CHINA'S TRAPPED TRANSITION: THE LIMITS OF DEVELOPMENTAL AUTOCRACY 60 (2006).

[72] JIANG, *supra* note 51, at 5 (emphasis added).

[73] *Id.* at 8 (emphasis added).

(3) Educational, scientific, cultural, healthcare, sports facilities owned by said collective; and

(4) *Other immovables or movables owned by said collective.*[74]

What if a collective offers to sell you the right to transform an ordinary rural lake into a profit-making recreational facility, does Article 58 answer whether the collective has the power to sell you the right to convert the lake from agricultural to recreational, profit-making land? Does it define what the collective's "immovable or movable" property was so as to include or exclude lakes? Does it provide a hint of what the relevant laws are that it refers to? Consult, for example, Articles 46 and 153 of the PRL, do they answer the preceding questions?[75]

Typically, the missing rules in the above enumeration enable and encourage official arbitrariness and corruption. Depending upon the magnitude of the problem or conflict, the decisions' missing legislative language are likely to be made by officials and judges influenced by *Guanxi* relationships which are, by definition, contrary to the protection of the rights of third parties.

B. The Results of Invertebration

It is now time to examine the results of legal invertebration, first at the conceptual and subsequently at the transactional and disputation levels.

1. Who Are Owners Under the Property Rights Law (PRL)?

As amended in 2004, Article 10 of the PRC Constitution listed two types of owners:

Land in the cities is owned by the State.

Land in the rural and suburban areas is owned by collectives except for those portions which belong to the State as prescribed by law; house sites and privately farmed plots of cropland and hilly land are also owned by collectives.[76]

Please recall that Article 2 of the Constitution as amended in 1988 had accepted an organization or individual's *right to the use of the land* as well as to its transfer "in accordance with the law."[77] Thus, this provision confirmed the existence of a right *in rem* similar in some respects to the Roman law of usufructs, *i.e.*, the right to use the land and appropriate its fruits without destroying or deteriorating the land.[78] And this

---

[74] *Id.* art. 58 (emphasis added).

[75] Typically, there are other statutes, regulations, ordinances, decrees and judicial interpretations that help decide what the words of high-level laws like those from the PRL mean. While they are sometimes also vague or too general, some are very detailed. *See* Memorandum from Chinese Attorney (Apr. 10, 2011) (on file with author).

[76] PRC, CONST. ch. 1, art. 10 (1982). *See* Lee, *Part 1, supra* note 51, arts. 45–65 (explaining the statutory implementation of this constitutional provision).

[77] *See China's Constitutional Framework* art. 2, CONGRESSIONAL-EXECUTIVE COMMISSION ON CHINA, http://www.cecc.gov/resources/legal-provisions/chinas-constitutional-framework (last visited Nov. 11, 2013) (on file with author).

[78] BERGER, ENCYCLOPEDIC DICTIONARY, at 755. It states:

Ususfructus. [hereinafter usufruct] [entails] The right to use . . . another's property and to take produce (*fructus*) there-from . . . without impairing (*i.e.*, destroying, diminishing, or deteriorating) its substance . . . As a strictly personal right the *ususfructus* is neither transferable nor alienable.

is one of the differences between the Chinese assignment or transfer of the rights to use land and the Roman usufruct—the latter imposed the duty upon its beneficiary not to alter the substance of the land (*salva rerum substantia*) including the inability to build on it.[79] In addition, with some exceptions that allowed the beneficiary to lease part of the property or its fruits, the Roman usufruct was a personal right of the beneficiary and could not be transferred or sold.[80]

As pointed out by Walter Lee, a Chinese practicing lawyer, translator and commentator of the PRL, "before this amendment, the General Principles of Civil Law (enacted in 1985) set out the basic principle . . . that the [persons or] entities who occupy and *use State-owned land can enjoy the land use rights but not the ownership right over the land*."[81] If so, it is necessary to ask what is it that owners own?

2. *What Do Owners Own? The Uncertain Dimensions of Ownership and of Lesser Rights in Rem*

a. *Land Use Rights in General: Grants and Allocations*

The Land Administration Law of the PRC of 1986, as amended in 1988, 1998 and 2004 provides that land in the urban areas of cities is owned by the State and in the rural and suburban areas is owned by peasant collectives, except for those portions of land which belong to the State as provided for by law; house sites and private plots of cropland and hilly land are owned by peasant collectives.[82]

Article 9, makes it possible for state-owned land and land owned by peasant collectives to be used by private units or individuals as long as they protect and manage the land rationally.[83] "People's governments at the county level shall enter into registration in a register, issue certificates in confirmation of the ownership for the land collectively owned by peasants."[84] Similarly, for land owned by peasant collectives to be lawfully used for non-agricultural purposes, the "People's government at the county level shall enter registration into a register, issue certificates in confirmation of the land use right for construction. . . ."[85]

State-owned land used by units or individuals shall also be registered with and recorded by people's governments at or above the county level, which shall, upon verification, also issue certificates to confirm their right to the use of such land.[86] Registration is also required for changes in the ownership of land, in the right to use the land or in the purpose of the registered land.[87]

Id.

[79] *Id.*

[80] *Id.*

[81] Lee, *Part 1*, *supra* note 51, art. 2 (emphasis added).

[82] Land Administration Law in ENGLISH art. 8 (adopted on June 15, 1986, amended Dec. 29, 1988 & Aug. 29, 1998), *available at* sohu.com/2004/07/04/80/article220848071.shtml.

[83] *Id.* art. 9.

[84] *Id.* art. 11.

[85] *Id.*

[86] *Id.*

[87] *Id.* art. 12

Crop cultivation, forestry, animal husbandry or fishery of land owned by peasant cooperatives is governed by a contract between the individual or group of peasants with members of the economic organizations of the peasant collectives. The duration of this contract is 30 years.[88]

The land use rights on urban, state owned land are not found in the PRL of 2007, but in the Provisional Regulations on Grant and Assignment of Urban State-Owned Land Use Rights. Article 12 of these Regulations sets forth the duration of land use rights as follows:

(1) land for residential purposes: seventy years;

(2) land for industrial purposes: fifty years;

(3) land for purposes of educational, scientific and technological, cultural, health care or sports: fifty years;

(4) land for commercial, tourism or recreational purposes: forty years;

(5) land for combined usage or other purposes: fifty years.[89]

The manner in which the state grants rights to the land or buildings matters under its jurisdiction seems more complex than that for lands owned by collectives. The state may grant land use rights for a price, in which case the land use right may be privately sold, mortgaged or inherited. Or, it may "allocate" rights for a public purpose and without any payment. In that case, the allocation is not subject to a disposition other than for the purposes of the grant and to the appropriate entity to discharge such a purpose.[90] The public purposes for which land is allocated could be military, public welfare undertakings, infrastructure projects connected with the production of energy, transportation and many others.[91] Generally, land so allocated is not subject to specified duration or term of use, but cannot be used for any other purpose and by users other than those who can carry out the allocated purpose.[92]

b. *The Legal Nature of Granted Land Use Rights, the Roman* Iura in Re Aliena

Chapter 10 of the "general part" of the PRL grants rights in the things of "others" (meaning the Chinese State or its Agricultural Collectives) much as the Roman law allowed for its *iura in re aliena* among private parties (also known as *iura praediorum*),[93] and as Anglo-American law did with its reversionary interests such as in life estates and easements.[94] As was discussed in the preceding chapter, the Chinese law on free tenancy dates back at least to the seventh century CE.[95] It enabled the coexistence of rights *in rem* in the same land granted by an owner who at one time was

---

[88] *Id.* art. 14.

[89] Provisional Regulations of the People's Republic of China Concerning the Grant and Assignment of the Right to Use State Land in Urban Areas, art. 12 (promulgated on May 24, 1990 by the State Council).

[90] *See* Stein, *supra* note 51, at 1320 n.19 (discussing art. 2 of the Land Administration Law); Lee, *Part 1*, *supra* note 51, art. 73; *and* Wenli, *supra* note 51, at slide 37.

[91] *See* Lee, *Part 1*, *supra* note 51, art. 54 & Walter Lee, *China Real Estate Law: Part 4: Urban Real Property Administration Law* art. 24 (Dec. 31, 2009), http://prclandlaw.wordpress.com/article/china-real-estate-law-part-4-urban-real-zheu88eb3a11-9/ [hereinafter Lee, *Part 4*].

[92] *Id.* art. 76.

[93] *See* BERGER, ENCYCLOPEDIC DICTIONARY, at 522.

[94] *See* JIANG, *supra* note 51, art. 117.

[95] *See supra* § 18:1(A).

the emperor and at another, the feudal lord or the head of a family or household. Occasionally, free tenants were given rights to the topsoil, and others were given rights to the subsoil.[96] At this point, Chinese land law was conferring rights that appeared to be similar to those conferred by the English Doctrine of Estates in the Land.[97] Yet, why did the English Doctrine of Estates in Land make possible a transition to a commercial system whose land and its yield became "commodified," whereas in China, a very different result occurred?

Unlike the Roman usufructs which, as just noted, were deemed personal rights of the original grantee and could not generally be sold or transferred by him, Chinese imperial law allowed the sale and mortgage of land use rights and in some instances, also allowed the tenant to build on the owner's land.[98] Further, unlike Roman law, the PRL allows the holder of a right to build on another's land and in addition grants the rights to inhabit, sell, transfer or mortgage this and other land use rights. However, as also just noted, the PRL also places the state exclusively at the top of the land tenure pyramid with the power to grant rights to "occupy, utilize and obtain profits from . . . resources as owned by the State, or . . . collectively-owned. . . ."[99] And, not to be overlooked, the State has the power to expropriate land or land use rights whenever it deems it in the "public interest" and "in line with the procedure and within the authority provided by the laws."[100] Also not to be overlooked is the fact that the meaning of "public interest" is uncertain especially in land takings under eminent domain and whose "rational" use is subject to questioning.[101] What is even more unsettling is that when deciding what is in the public interest and who is the beneficiary of the taking, the State or the local government often replace the familistic treatment of the Imperial times with the *Guanxi* "favors" accorded to members of non-familial networks of political friendship and bribery.[102]

c. *Hierarchy of Ownership, Land Use Rights and Benefits Under the PRL*

The hierarchical order of land tenure and ownership of rights under the PRL's pyramidal scheme is, then, as follows: 1) the state or collectives are the absolute owners of the rural real property in the manner described by Article 10 of the

---

[96] *See supra* § 18:1(D).

[97] *See* Glossary, "Doctrine of the Estates."

[98] BERGER, ENCYCLOPEDIC DICTIONARY, at 755 (on usufruct).

[99] Lehman et al., *supra* note 51, ch. 1 art. 118.

[100] *Id.* ch. 1 art. 42. It states in relevant part:

> For the purpose of public interest, the collectively-owned land, houses and other real property owned by institutes or individuals may be expropriated in line with the procedure and within the authority provided by laws.
>
> For expropriation of collectively-owned land, such fees shall be paid as compensations for the land expropriated, subsidies for resettlement, compensations for the fixtures and the young crops on land, and the premiums for social security of the farmers whose land is expropriated shall be allocated in full, in order to guarantee their normal lives and safeguard their lawful rights and interests.
>
> Where houses and other real properties of institutes and individuals are expropriated, compensations for demolition and resettlement shall be paid according to law in order to maintain the legal rights and interests of the expropriated; where individual residential house is expropriated, the residential conditions of the expropriated shall be guaranteed.

Id.

[101] *See* Whiting, Fiscal Pressures, *supra* note 18, at 5.

[102] *See supra* § 17:5(H).

Constitution; 2) the holders of land use rights are grantees of the state or collective governments for the purposes and during the time set forth in the Provisional Regulations and often these grantees are provincial or municipal governments who act as conduits for the transfer of land use rights to private parties; and 3) the owners of usufructs or of the rights to use and exploit the land or buildings on it are entitled to the "natural benefits" of that property in the manner and with the priorities specified by Article 116 of the PRL:

> The natural benefits shall be obtained by the *title holder of such properties; where there are both a title holder and an owner of the right to the usufruct of the natural benefits, the property [of the natural benefits or "fruits" of the land or buildings] shall be owned by the owner of the right to the usufruct*; where there are agreements separately made by parties concerned, such agreements shall be observed. . . .
>
> [I]f there is no such or express agreement, the transactional practice shall apply.[103]

Among the most important "natural benefits" in a Chinese usufruct of land are the rights to manage land and build on it (Chapters XI and XII of the PRL) and to use the land for residential and easement purposes (Chapters XIII and XIV of the PRL). Professor Gregory Stein of the University of Tennessee College of law compares the Chinese land use right to the United States ground lease and concludes that the holder of a PRL land use right has greater freedom of action including the ability to build or tear down improvements on the raw land and exploit the surface without being subject to landlord-tenant law restrictions. On the other hand, the purchaser of a PRL right to use the land must pay the purchase price at the execution of the sale and unless he does so, he may not register his right.[104] He points out that this is rarely the case with a United States ground lease, which is usually paid periodically or as the land is being used or developed.[105]

Professor Stein found other differences, such as the prohibition of "flipping" (or reselling) residential land by the initial purchaser of the land use right until he completes twenty-five percent of the proposed construction and the requirement that the holder of the land use right must also own the building constructed on that land.[106] Stein's interviewees qualified their opinions on these practices by referring to the possibility of different or contrary "practices." The fact that these practices carry some normative weight at least with his interviewees is on the one hand a healthy development because it for crop cultivation, forestry, animal husbandry or fishery. to land contracts to fashion a law closer to the needs of the marketplace. On the other hand, to the extent that these practices are guided by traditional familistically-

---

[103] Lehman et al., *supra* note 51, ch. IX art. 116 (emphasis added). This author has made some syntactical corrections to the Lehman translation to facilitate its reading but has tried to preserve the meaning of the translation.

[104] Gregory M. Stein, *Acquiring Land Use Rights in Today's China: A Snapshot from on the Ground,* 24 UCLA PAC. BASIN L.J. 1, 42–43 (2006). Although some of the real estate experts interviewed by Stein referred to practices that circumvent this full payment requirement.

[105] *Id.* at n.114. Although, Professor Stein qualifies this statement by saying that he learned of a recent practice that allows periodic payments.

[106] *Id.* at 43.

inspired, anti-third party rights' clauses they are part of the widespread legal uncertainty.

In sum, an analogy exists between the free tenancies of Imperial law that we previously studied and the land rights of the PRL, albeit with important distinctions. The most important of these is that the PRL replaces the family or household with the PRC as the landlord and grantor of rights and often accords a familistic treatment to the participants in *Guanxi* networks. As part of the government's status of absolute owner, its conveyance of land rights (directly or through provincial or municipal entities) does not require the insertion or disclosure of special clauses of revocation of rights of the Imperial law of land contracts. Under the PRL, the official grantor has the power to revoke or expropriate what it gave subject only to a duty of "relevant compensation" that rarely specifies the amount, time, source and procedure for it.[107] It is also subject to "public interest" and "due procedure" provisions under Article 42 of the PRL.[108]

3. *Who Are the Third Parties of the PRL?*

Third parties[109] are generally defined as parties who despite their not being participants in the transaction in question are likely to be affected by it either as buyers of the same property rights or as creditors who relied on that property as security for their loans. Thus, under the PRL, a large number of third parties are likely to have their ownership or possessory rights negated by competing conveyances or security interests. For example, "B," the buyer of land use rights will certainly suffer from a successful claim by "C," another buyer of the same rights who bought his rights at a later time than B but was given priority over B as a result of a registry or court decision. Or consider the predicament of "D," a mortgagee of the land use rights from C who could not enforce his rights against "E" a purchaser of the same rights because D had relied on a certificate of land use rights that was held unenforceable by the same administrative or judicial decisions or by their political superiors.

Prior to the enactment of the PRL, three possible original grantors were responsible for the creation of third party ownership rights: the central and local governments with respect to urban land and the agricultural collectives for rural-agricultural land. The parties seeking the protection of the PRL, thus, would be the contracting parties (purchasers, lenders, lessees, mortgagees and assignees of rights) in their transactions with: 1) the PRC's central or local governments or governmental enterprises; 2) the collective entities who are the grantors of the rights to use their agricultural land and buildings or who seek the transformation of their land into commercial or industrial property; 3) the public, private, or public and private enterprises who convey their land rights to other private or public and private enterprises; and 4) the owners of the right to inhabit urban and rural dwellings as well as of the rights to the commercial, industrial or agricultural exploitation of lands and buildings. What characterizes the above enumeration of third parties is that all are holders of temporary rights that revert to the government upon the termination of their specified terms. These rights are acquired directly or indirectly from or through

---

107 *See* Lehman et al., *supra* note 51, ch. IV arts. 42 & 44, & ch. X art. 121.

108 *Id.* ch. IV art. 42.

109 *See* Glossary, "Third Parties."

governmental entities and are traceable to government grants, assignments or transfers.

In free market societies, third parties derive their rights occasionally from government grants or assignments but mostly from pre-existing contracts between or among private parties and few of these rights revert back to the government. In contrast, reversion to the government determines the legal nature of land use rights in the PRL. Where the government is the holder of the ultimate reversionary interest, most other rights become expressly or tacitly subordinate to those of the government. This happens often and *en masse* as has been the case with the "readjustments" and reallocations mentioned earlier by Professors Zhu Keliang and Roy Prosterman.[110]

The contrast between the protection of third party rights associated with governmental reversionary rights and those of a free market society is sharp. For example, assume that "A," the owner of Blackacre in a free market society conveys it to buyer "B" who pays part of the purchase price and secures the payment of the remainder by mortgaging Blackacre to A. Assume that shortly after acquiring Blackacre, B sold it to "C," another *bona fide* purchaser who also became the mortgagor of Blackacre for the unpaid portion of his sale price. Finally, assume that B recorded his mortgage prior to the time that A recorded his. In most land registry systems of free market societies, B's recorded right will have priority over A's.[111] In addition, in many such societies B will enjoy a priority over a judicial lien that was not recorded until after his own mortgage was recorded and would enjoy the same priority over an unrecorded administrative expropriation decision.

In contrast, Article 28 of the PRL states:

> Vesting of Real Rights Appropriated by Way of Judicial Instrument or Expropriation Decision.
>
> For [the] creation, alteration, transfer, or extinguishment of a real right resulting from a judicial instrument issued by a People's Court or an arbitration commission, or an expropriation decision issued by the relevant People's Government, etc., the real right is vested at the time of effectiveness of said judicial instrument or expropriation decision of the relevant People's Government, etc . . .[112]

Please note that the priority of the right *in rem* associated with a judicial and an administrative expropriation decision is vested at the time of their extra-registry "effectiveness" and not when recorded in the land registry. This deprives third parties who recorded their rights in the appropriate registry of fair notice of the existence of the judicial or administrative actions.

---

110 *See supra* § 19:3(A)(4).

111 Alejandro Garro, *Recordation of Interests in Land, in* 6 INT'L ENCYCLOPEDIA OF COMP. L. § 8–165 (Athanassios N. Yiannopoulos, ed., 2004).

112 JIANG, *supra* note 51, at 13.

4. *Legal Uncertainties in the Acquisition of Residential Property*[113]

Article 137 of the PRL provides that where the land is developed for industrial, commercial, tourism, entertainment or commercial housing, the procedure for acquiring a land use right by developers and builders is by participating in an auction or in an invitation to bid, rather than by agreements between the state and developers.[114] The purpose of this provision is to prevent the "rampant corruption in the course of assigning land use right[s] [by] . . . agreements between developers and competent government agencies."[115]

The right so acquired by the developer is transferred by him to the individual purchasers of houses with a maximum duration of seventy years. At the end of that term, Article 149 of the Property Law states that land use rights for residential purposes will be extended automatically upon expiration of its term but does not specify what fees, if any, will need to be paid for that extension. It defers such a determination to the by-now customary laws and regulations in effect upon expiration.[116]

Among the key documents that need to be presented by the developer to obtain his building license is his Land Use Right Certificate, issued by the Ministry of State Land Resources.[117] Another is the Developer's License for the presale of a commercial or residential house, which requires the developer to show evidence of prepayment of at least twenty-five percent of the proposed investment in the project. Without this presale license, the presale agreement is null and void. The nature of this nullity is also unclear: Is it one that occurs *ipso iure* or does it need to be invoked by a party to the presale agreement or by an administrative official? What if the party who invokes it is a developer trying to get out of a deal that is less profitable than another one waiting in the wings? In the absence of applicable statutory or case law, a legal scholar suggested to me that the Latin maxim "*Nullus commodum capere potest de injuria sua propria*" (No one should benefit from his own injustice) should apply and would support the enforcement of such contracts.

What are the legal consequences of the lack of recordation of a presale contract? Article 10 of the Rule on Presale of Urban Commercial Houses requires the developer "to record the presale contract with the government agencies in charge within thirty days of signing the contract."[118] This provision does not clarify the effects of the lack of recordation. A Chinese attorney mentioned a Supreme Court Interpretation that

---

113 I am indebted to a practicing and experienced Chinese attorney who preferred to be nameless for many of the real estate practice materials discussed in this section. Memorandum, Chinese Attorney 2 (Mar. 11, 2011) (on file with author) [hereinafter Chinese Attorney 2].

114 Lehman et al., *supra* note 51, ch. XI art. 137. This section is part of the longer description of residential housing, taken from Chinese Attorney 2, *supra* note 113.

115 *Id.* at 2.

116 Lehman et al., *supra* note 51, ch. XI art. 149.

117 *See* Chinese Attorney 2, *supra* note 113, at 3. The list of required documents to be submitted is lengthy. Along with the Land Use Rights Certificate and Developer's License, discussed above, developers must also submit an application form, a business license, a construction project planning license, a project construction license, evidence that the fund invested in the development of the project has exceeded twenty-five percent of the total estimated investment, copies of the project construction contact and specficiation of the construction timetable, and a presale plan, which should include information on location, size, delivery date and plan drawings of the houses involved in the presale.

118 *Id.* at 6.

provides that "the Court shall not consider the contract void for failure of recordation unless otherwise stated in the contract itself."[119] In this scholar's opinion, this interpretation undermines the function of presale contract recordation. Without this recordation, a subsequent third party who purchased the subject house from the developer and recorded the presale agreement is likely to prevail over earlier purchasers with unrecorded presale agreements. Such earlier purchasers would be left with only *in personam* actions against an all-too-probable fraudulent developer.

Once the developer has complied with the administrative requirements, he can either prepare his own contract of sale or rely on the model contract supplied by the Ministry of Construction or other provincial or local governmental entities. The transfer of title to the rights in the sold house, however, will have to await its recording in the Land Registry and shall become effective from the date of its recording.[120]

a. Recent Shanghai Condominium Transactions

As a Chinese attorney stated to me in 2008, "Few people in China will dispute nowadays that to invest in real estate is the quickest way to get rich." This attorney then went on to give the example of her friend "S," a professional person who had made real property purchases and sales her main investment since 2001. In 2001, S bought a condominium in Shanghai. She paid twenty percent of the purchase price as a down payment on the total price of 800,000 RMB (approximately US$100,600). S then immediately leased the property to someone else at approximately US$350 a month. This rent helped her repay her mortgage in a shorter time than anticipated. She then sold the condominium for one million RMB in 2005, and bought her second, third and fourth housing units from the profits she made. The rate of return in these transactions was high by any standard.

In 2007, S decided to buy a condominium worth two million RMB in a prime location in town. It was still under construction but was available for presale. Delivery was scheduled in August 2007; S tried to bargain, but in 2007, housing units were in short supply and so she wound up accepting the asking price. She then executed the sale agreement. Since the purchase of a home with an investment purpose is likely to involve significant sums of money, the Ministry of Construction, developers and local government agencies have published model contracts for the presale of housing units. In S's case, the model contract that she chose to use was prepared by the Shanghai Housing and Land Administration Bureau. Before signing the contract, S checked the License of Presale and confirmed that her unit was within the scope of the license. It is important for a buyer to use a presale agreement as each of these agreements is registered with the real estate administration authority. In many local practices in China, only a template presale agreement such as the one S used will be accepted for registration with authorities; without a presale license, the presale contract would be deemed null and void. On the other hand, where a developer obtains the license before a judicial or administrative action is filed against him, it has been held that the presale contract is valid.[121]

---

119 *Id. See also infra* § 19:4(F).

120 *See* Lehman et al., *supra* note 51, ch. II art. 14.

121 *See Supreme People's Court, Several Issues Concerning the Application of Law to Trial of Disputes over Commodity Premises Sales and Purchase Contracts Interpretation,* CHINA LAW AND PRACTICE art. 2

But what would happen if the developer sold his right to the collection of the payments due to him on the presold units to third parties? How could these third parties—say lenders secured by the developers' right to collect future payments as account receivables—find out if these accounts stem from presale agreements, and further, how could they find out if the developer obtained his license to pre-sell units? Would these third parties be protected against the developer's or other creditors' defense that the presale license was not obtained or was not filed in time? Theoretically, a developer is not permitted to sell his right to the collection of installments on the presale units. All the funds collected by the developer for selling the units during the presale process must be directly paid into an escrow account with the bank which serves as an escrow agent. This escrow account is created under the name of the developer for the purpose of administration of the payments collected in the presale process. The escrowed funds should only be used for the purpose of construction of incomplete units, and the fund will not be released until the units are delivered to home buyers. Therefore, it would not be feasible for the developer to sell or pledge the accounts receivable until the escrow is removed, *i.e.*, until the units have been delivered. In addition to this escrow requirement, it is worth noting that each presale license, including the particulars of the presale units, is published on a website that is easily accessible to the public.

The presale contract registration serves a similar notice function as the registration of the transfer of a complete unit upon which the buyer obtains title.[122] Through the presale agreement registration, the buyer is able to legally secure its prospective title to the target unit. After the registration of the presale agreement, the seller (the developer) will not be able to sell it to other buyers. In other words, if the seller enters into two presale agreements with two buyers in respect to one specific unit; the buyer who has the registered presale agreement will obtain title to that unit, while the other buyer will not, and may only resort to filing a complaint against the seller for breach of contract. Although some suggest that the PRL should have made it clear that neither the filing nor the failure to file should affect the rights of a *bona fide* third party, it has been widely accepted and confirmed by judicial practice that the recordation of the presale agreement confers a quasi-proprietary right upon the filer. As stated by Article 14 of the PRL, the effectiveness of the creation, change, transfer or elimination of a right in real property is at the time of its registration in the Land Registry. In other words, delivery of the house does *not* mean an automatic transfer of title. Article 12 of the Rules on Presale Contacts further states that, "within ninety days of delivery of presale of a commercial house, the buyer shall complete recordation of transfer in order to obtain the Certificate of Housing Ownership and Land Use Right."[123]

b. *Financing Real Estate Transactions in 2008*

Acquisitions such as the one described by the Chinese attorney in the previous section are financed in one of three ways: 1) a lump-sum payment where the buyer will

---

(June 2003), http://www.chinalawandpractice.com/Article/1693138/Channel/9930/Supreme-Peoples-Court-Several-Issues-Concerning-the-Application-of-Law-to-Trial-of-Disputes-over.html.

[122] *See infra* § 19:3(C).

[123] As with other administrative procedures, the completion of the recording of the transfer of title to the use of the house requires the submission of a number of documents.

pay ninety-five percent of the price when signing the contract and remainder at the time of delivery; 2) installments, where the buyer will complete payment of the contract price in a defined number of installments before delivery of the house; and 3) a down payment plus mortgage loans. Presently, this third option is the most common way of financing the purchase of a home; mortgage loans are available through what are known as "Provident Fund Loans" or through commercial housing loans. Chinese employees are required to contribute a certain percentage of their salary to their "personal provident fund account," and the employer is required to provide a matching amount to that fund. Provident Fund Loans thus come from this set-aside money; they have a maximum term of thirty years and a ceiling credit line of 500,000 RMB (as of 2007) to eligible home buyers who make their Provident Fund contributions on time.

Taking Shanghai financing transactions as an example, the use of Provident Fund financing involves four parties: 1) the Shanghai Provident Fund Center (SPFC); 2) the Shanghai Housing Guarantee Company (SHGC); 3) a bank; and 4) a home buyer or loan applicant. The SPFC manages the lending and ordinarily signs a trust agreement with the SHGC by which the SPFC authorizes the SHGC to review and approve Provident Fund Loan applications. It also signs a trust agreement with the banks by which SPFC authorizes the bank to handle and disburse these loans. The next steps taken are: 1) The home buyer applies to a bank or to the SHGC for a provident fund loan and fills out an application form for a Provident Fund Guaranty Loan to purchase a house; 2) The SHGC reviews the form to determine if the applicant is eligible for the loan; 3) If approved, the applicant signs a loan contract with the bank and also signs a home purchase guaranty contract with the SHGC to guarantee the repayment of the loan; 4) The application opens an account with the bank for the purpose of repayment of the loan; 5) The applicant records the mortgage and provides this recordation to the SHGC as a counter-guarantee; 6) Upon receipt of the mortgage certificate, SHGC notifies the bank to disburse the loan to the developer, and the home buyer begins to repay the loan through deposits into the account opened with the bank; and 7) If the loan applicant defaults on his repayment of the loan, the SHGC as guarantor repays the balance of defaulted loans to the SPFC.[124]

c. *2011 Restrictions and Limitations on Second Home Purchases*

Despite the legal uncertainties discussed above, property prices of homes in major Chinese cities continue to rise at an average of 6.4 percent per year.[125] This happened even though the central government raised the minimum down-payment for second home purchases from fifty percent to sixty percent of the property's value on January of 2011 and approved new property taxes for Shanghai and Chongqing.[126] Beijing's new rules allow banks to further raise the down-payment requirements for apartment buyers and raise interest rates on mortgages. In addition, China's central bank has increased interest rates three times since October, and hiked the banks' reserve requirement ratio seven times since the start of last year.

---

[124] *But c.f.*, Mattias Burell, *China's Housing Provident Fund: Its Success and Limitations*, HOUSING FIN. INT'L (Mar. 2006) (arguing that the main tool to enhance the affordability of housing in China continues to be the Housing Provident Fund. However, the author concluded that a serious gap exists between borrowers' earnings and the money needed to buy a housing unit).

[125] Xinhua, *Beijing tightens restrictions on home purchase*, CHINA.ORG.CN (Feb. 17, 2011), http://www.china.org.cn/business/2011–02/17/content_21937249.htm.

[126] *Id.*

And as if these restrictions were little, on February 17, 2011, Beijing's municipal government issued new rules limiting the number of homes each family can purchase in order to "cool the property market."[127] Beijing families who own two or more apartments, such as the Shanghai families described in the preceding section, can no longer make new home purchases and Beijing families who own just one apartment can only buy one additional apartment. These restrictions were issued on the heels of an April 2010 regulation that limited each Beijing family to buying only one extra apartment.[128]

Clearly the Chinese central and local governments are concerned with the rise in the prices of residential investment real estate in China's largest cities which are making homes increasingly unaffordable for most Chinese urban dwellers:

> Prices in . . . Beijing, have more than doubled over the past two years due to easy credit and low lending rates. One square meter in a new apartment in Beijing on average cost 20,000 yuan last year. But the square meter price for apartments within the Third Ring Road, the central urban area, exceeded 30,000 yuan, more than 10 times the monthly income of an average Beijing resident.[129]

To make matters worse, Wang Xiaoguang, chief director of the Macroeconomic Division of the Institute of Economic Research, under the National Development and Reform Commission has forecasted that the prices of residential units in China's largest cities will remain the same for the foreseeable future.[130] Does this rise in prices foretell increasing frictions between those who can afford buying several residential units and those who cannot?

d. Legal Invertebration at the Base of Many of China's Land Rights: The Missing Hukou *for Migrants to Large Chinese Cities*

The Beijing 2011 regulations also forbid non-Beijing registered families who have no residence permit (*hukou*, 户口) or other documents that certify that members of the family have been paying social security or income tax for five straight years are also banned from buying apartments. By the time of my visit to China, I was familiar with the legitimating function of national identity cards in some Latin American countries. They provided their holders not only with the status to claim basic state services such as social security payments, healthcare and so on, but also with legal capacity to enter into binding contracts, file claims or give notice of their rights in public registries.[131] The *hukou* is a small red passbook with information on every family "including marriages, divorces, births, and deaths, as well as the city or village to which each person belongs."[132] One of the differences between this identity card and its Latin American counterpart that I am familiar with is that the *hukou* still treats its holder's family as an economic unit, while the Latin American identity card is given to citizens

---

127 *Id.*

128 *Id.*

129 *Id.*

130 *Id.*

131 *See generally* Kozolchyk & Furnish, *A Comparative Analysis.*

132 Dexter Roberts, *China May Finally Let Its People Move More Freely*, BLOOMBERG BUSINESSWEEK (Mar. 15, 2012). I am indebted to my colleague Dr. Marek Dubovec for bringing this important report to my attention.

or residents in their individual *sui iuris* capacity. An additional difference is that the Latin American identity card is usually national in nature and as such can be used anywhere within the national territory. As described by Bloomberg's Businessweek, that is not the case with the *hukou*:

> What comes attached to the *hukou* are benefits including health care, a pension, and free education for one's children. These benefits are only available if a Chinese citizen lives where he or she is registered. Not having a *hukou* for where one lives makes it more difficult to get a driver's license, buy a house, or purchase a car.[133]

As made clear by the Beijing regulation of February 2011, the legal status of these non-residents and non-holders of valid *hukous* as buyers-mortgagors of homes is precarious at best. Consequently, Bloomberg's Newsweek recently reported that hundreds of millions of Chinese live in China's biggest cities with no access to social benefits and limited ties to the locales in which they work.[134] This non-existent legal status causes the lower consumption and lower productivity of migrant workers and explains why despite China's boom as an industrial nation and as one of the world's largest exporters, the contribution of its private consumption's to its gross domestic product dropped from forty-six percent in 2000 to thirty-three percent in 2010.

For while China's urban population in 2011 approached 700 million, approximately 200 million of them lacked a *hukou*.[135] Add to this legal uncertainty that of the third parties who deal with such a major segment of the urban population by employing them, selling them products or extending credit to them. Add also the fact that quite often these migrant workers obtain fake *hukous* and use them to assure their suppliers of goods and services as well as their lenders as assurances of sources of income and reimbursement that can easily be challenged as non-existent.

In the past, the serious disparity between the rights and access to better salaries and benefits of lawful and unlawful city residents was justified economically because the need for *hukous* forced farmers to remain in their provinces and "produce cheap food to sustain industrialization."[136] Yet, as China's competitiveness in foreign markets declines caused by its higher costs of labor, its top leaders have begun to pay attention to the role of *hukous*. In March of 2012, China's cabinet of ministers announced that it would make it easier for rural migrants to obtain a city *hukou* and Premier Wen Jiabao confirmed this policy to the NPC by promising that migrant workers will become "permanent urban residents in an orderly manner."[137]

Meanwhile, Professor Kam Wing Chan of the University of Washington has shown not only why the *hukou* system is holding up China's desirable urbanization one of the most obvious ways in which China's local consumption could rise to replace China's almost exclusive reliance on exports as the source of its growth. In his words: "The

---

133 *Id.*

134 *Id.*

135 *Id.*

136 *Id.*

137 *Id.*

assumption that China's urbanization will create a very large middle class is proving not accurate."[138]

5. *Legal Uncertainties in Agricultural Land Transactions: Collectives, Who They Are and "Who Is the People?"*

During my visit to Shanghai, our guide continuously pointed to impressive buildings and attributed their ownership to "the people" as with the "people's gymnasium, art museum," etc. After one such a designation, a Chinese passenger startled our guide by asking "Who is the People?" Much as our good guide tried to answer this seemingly naïve question, he could not. The best he could do was to say that "The people is the people."

The PRL equates the state's ownership of land to the ownership of "the whole people" as represented and managed by the State Council.[139] In contrast, the owners of the land of collective-agricultural organizations are not the "whole people," but the members of these collectives,[140] and collectives, as encountered throughout this chapter can own real or personal property.[141] Collectives can also transfer rights *in rem* to real property to third parties.[142] Yet, as now highlighted by Professor Whiting, the term "the collective" is much more centered on the village and its local or Communist part governance than apparent to a first time reader of PRC land rights law:

> In general, "the collective" refers to the village, a rural community organization below the township, which is the lowest level of formal government defined in the constitution. Villages are, in principle, self-governing entities with elected leadership. . . . It is the village that enters into land-use contracts with individual households. According to the Land Management Law, changes to contracted land holdings are permitted with the agreement of two-thirds of the villagers' representatives, as well as the approval of the local government. . . . [V]illages are also led by Communist Party Committees appointed from above.[143]

Moreover, the PRL indicates that "the collective" refers to "members of the collective community," but as also noted by Whiting, this indication does not answer who is empowered to act in the name of the collective, even though it allows its members to sue the collective when the members' rights are violated.[144] She also provides other instances where the land use rights of the collectives are "attenuated" by present law. For example, even when local farmers may have an interest in having the land they occupy being used for industrial or commercial purposes (so as to be able to enjoy a better income), they are precluded from transferring their land use rights to third parties: "In order for land to be transferred from agricultural to non-agricultural

---

138 *Id.*

139 Lehman et al., *supra* note 51, ch. V art. 45.

140 *Id.* art. 59. *See also* Wenli, *supra* note 51, at slide 32.

141 Lehman et al., *supra* note 51, ch. V. art. 58(i)–(iii).

142 *Id.* art. 59 (i)–(v).

143 Whiting, Fiscal Pressures, *supra* note 18, at 6.

144 *Id.* at 7. Professor Whiting also notes that, "Article 60 indicates that the collective exercises ownership rights on behalf of the members and that the members may sue the collective if their rights are violated." *Id.*

use, it must be converted from collective to state land through government requisition or takings."[145]

And as she also points out, compensation for the taking of that collectively-owned land is divorced from the real market value of the land, thereby allowing the opportunity for the local governments to appropriate the difference between the expropriated and market value; furthermore, under Article 26 of the Land Management law, compensation for the taking of the transformed land is made to the collective which then allocates a certain portion of it to the affected individual households.[146] Once the land is converted to state land, the local government can decide on land transfer fees that reflect the true market value of the land whose status as a new "peri-urban" area adjacent to large cities is much more valuable than what would be paid to the farm households' original owners of the agricultural land use rights.[147]

The widespread conversions of agricultural land to state land (or "the people's land") and the subsequent transfers to local and foreign investors or enterprises, was, as we later found, one of the reasons behind his question "Who is the People?" For as he explained to us the official attribution of ownership to an amorphous "people" masked an ownership pillaged by those well situated in the CCP hierarchy. As if the above ambiguity were not enough, a Chinese real property expert interviewed by Professor Gregory Stein of the University of Tennessee Law School added a new layer of rights and ambiguities. He described a practice in which agricultural collectives convert their land to commercial uses and request a permit to build a commercial structure. With that permit comes the authorization to "retain the profits resulting from the change in land use and pass them along to . . . [certain] members of the collective in the form of dividends."[148] Such transactions, while supposedly illegal, are very common.[149] And with this practice comes a new set of ambiguous rights to the dividends yielded by converted commercial structures: Were these rights of the collective as a collective or was it only a right owned only by certain households or individuals and was it saleable by them or inheritable by their heirs?

6. A Land Rights Dispute and the Relative Value of a Land Use Certificate

Based on the facts relayed to Professor Whiting by a local government official,[150] it appeared that the land use rights certificate granted to family household "A" on Blackacre was reassigned to family "B" after A had abandoned it to live with a younger son elsewhere. A was away for two years during which time he did not pay fees and taxes on Blackacre. Following what the official described as local policy and after A's two-year absence, the land was reassigned to B. Yet, A had retained his unchanged certificate of land use rights and B did not receive a new or amended land certificate indicating the transfer in the ownership from A to B.

---

145 *Id.*

146 *Id.*

147 *Id.*

148 PATRICK A. RANDOLPH JR. & LOU JIANBO, CHINESE REAL ESTATE LAW (2000), *cited in* Gregory M. Stein, *Mortgage Law in China: Comparing Theory and Practice* 72 MO. L. REV. 1315, 1326 n.37 (2007).

149 Chinese Attorney 1, *supra* note 75.

150 Whiting, Fiscal Pressures, *supra* note 18, at 10 n.41.

The head of A's household returned to the village and disputed the reassignment action in a local court. Basing its decision on the unmodified text of A's land certificate, the court agreed with A that he had the right to reoccupy his land. Nonetheless, when A tried to execute the judgment, the villagers organized a rally in support of B who in their view was the morally deserving party—he and his family had farmed the land, paid the taxes and fees and had to support a young family. Violence between A and B and their supporters ensued and, in yet another instance of invertebration, the court decision could not be enforced.

As pointed out by Whiting, having reassigned the land, the local officials were "implicitly a party to the dispute";[151] still, the same officials mediated the dispute. Their decision was that A was allowed to continue to hold his land use rights but he was made to agree to rent the land to B for nothing. This nonpayment would last as long as B's children remained in school. Thereafter, A agreed to B's one-time payment for the sale price of the land. Professor Whiting was informed by a county justice bureau official that cases like this were common and reflected the local policy and that courts had decided that they would not hear new land dispute cases and would defer to the mediation of relevant government agencies.[152] She also found that many of the administrative takings were arbitrary and corrupt: Many about-to-be-converted parcels were not sold in auctions but certain buyers were privately indentified by local officials who also arranged for the transfers. Aside from the arbitrariness of the officials' takings, villagers complained about the unfairness of compensations they received for the loss of agricultural land that, once converted into commercial, residential or industrial, became very valuable. They also complained that with their loss of land came the loss of a minimal economic safety net as only a few of the families were allowed to become part of social security schemes.[153]

One cannot help but to ask about the value given by the official mediators-arbitrators to the certificate of land use rights. What is the value of such a document if it can be so easily disregarded by decision makers? I was also surprised by the unabashed judicial deference to the same local officials whose policies and actions had caused the dispute.

7. *Usufructs and Their Priorities: A Typical Dispute*

As transcribed earlier, Article 116 of the PRL sets forth the priorities of claims to the "natural benefits" yielded by the usufructs on land or buildings and their surface and sub-soil.[154] These benefits belong to "the title holder of such properties" (the assignees or holders of usufructs) and where there are both title holders and owners, the natural benefits belong to the latter, unless otherwise agreed and in the absence of an agreement, subject to the practice common with that transaction.[155]

---

151 *Id.* at 10.

152 *Id.* at 13.

153 This has been undergoing a change recently. The social security program theoretically covers all Chinese people. *See* Chinese Attorney 1, *supra* note 75.

154 *See supra* § 19:3(B)(2)(c).

155 Lehman et al., *supra* note 51, ch. IX art. 116. I have made some syntactical corrections to the Lehman translation to facilitate its reading but have tried to preserve the meaning of the translation.

The following dispute illustrates the difficulties of applying Article 116 to competing claims on co-existing usufructs.[156] "A" was the owner of a usufruct granted by "C," an agricultural collective. His usufruct was to enable him to grow milk-producing cattle on Blackacre. "B" was the owner of a usufruct on a segment of Blackacre which C had assigned to the bottling and distribution of the milk produced by the cows grazing in the remaining portion of Blackacre. A was paid a certain amount for the milk produced by his cows but because this amount was minimal, he claimed priority over a certain percentage of the proceeds of the sale of the milk produced by the cows under his care. B claimed that his right to bottle and distribute the milk was independent of A's usufruct and that he should only share the proceeds of the sale of milk with the collective. The main issues in this dispute were whether in the absence of a clear specification in the respective grants, the proceeds from the sale of the milk were a "natural benefit" of A's or B's usufruct or a benefit of whoever registered them, even though no land registry was in operation in the Blackacre area. According to my interlocutor, the result was ultimately found in favor of the collective.

One of the unresolved issues in this dispute was the effect that the lack of recording of both usufructs had upon the rights to the proceeds from the sale of milk. Please recall that Article 10 of the PRL requires that A's and B's land use or usufruct rights be recorded in order to be established and therefore enforceable.[157] Nonetheless, as stated by Jinchang Lai, a Chinese expert on PRC secured lending registries, during an October 19, 2010 meeting of the World Bank, "rural registries are very few in the PRC."[158]

C. The Effectiveness of Land Registry Recordings

An effective system of recording land rights is indispensable for the marketability of these rights. It tells the buyers of the rights as well as to those who lend on the security of these rights that what they are intending to buy or lend on is legally enforceable, for how long, against whom and with what priority. Thus, it enables the setting of prices for what is attempted to be sold and the ratios between amounts lent and value of the land collateral. If taxes are to be imposed upon the value of the land or of the transaction, it enables that imposition. If it is also a "cadastral" registry,[159] it provides a clear and reliable physical description and accurate measurements of the land and or buildings involved.[160] If the parties contemplate obtaining insurance of the title to the land or rights, the registered data enables the assessment of the insurable risk. In short, it is very difficult to conceive of a secondary (third party) market for land use rights, *i.e.*, a market other than that comprised by original sellers and buyers, and lenders and borrowers, in the absence of an affective and reliable land registry.

---

[156] This was an ongoing dispute in a parcel of land in the outskirts of Guilin a city in the authonomous region of Guangxi when we visited it in 2007. The facts were provided to me by one of the participants and they were translated by our tourist guide.

[157] PRC, CONST. ch. 1, art. 10 (1982), *see also supra* § 19:3(B)(3) (on rights to the use of the land).

[158] Jinchang Lai, Sr. Operations Officer, Int'l Finance Corp., Presentation at the FinNet 2010 Practice Group Meeting: Secured Transactions Reform in China: Lessons and Experience (Oct. 19, 2010) (slides on file with author).

[159] *See* Glossary, "Cadastral Survey."

[160] *See* Garro, *supra* note 114, at 24 § 8–32 (describing the German "cadastral" system of land registry, one of the most influential models of such registries. This is by far the clearest, concise and yet complete comparative treatment of the recordation of interests in land).

1. *Multiple Registries and Restricted Access to Recorded Data*

When I visited Shanghai in 2007, I was told by Chinese real estate lawyers that there were "at least six or seven" land registries in the Shanghai province alone and that the most "important ones" were the registries for buildings and for developable land. One of my interlocutors said that interested parties could apply to register their land use rights, building permits and ownership rights in either one of these two registries. The other two were not sure about the availability of interchangeable filings, but indicated that these two registries were required to share their information.

Third party access to the registry was an additional problem. An international law firm with offices in the PRC reported to its clients that the customary practice of the land registries (prior to the enactment of the PRL) was not to make available registry information to interested third parties "except with the registrant's written consent."[161] This firm added that it was unclear under the PRL if "any person will be entitled to search the registry or whether applicants must establish some relationship to the property at issue."[162] These were only a few of the troubling features of a registry system whose data was intended to reassure an increasingly large number of third parties (local and foreign purchasers of land use rights) that their acquisitions, investments or secured loans were legally enforceable.

2. *Is the PRL's a Constitutive or a Notice Registry System?*

Two competing systems of recordation of rights *in rem* in real property existed in Europe during the codification period: the German "constitutive" system whereby the acquisition of the *in rem* right to immovable property depended upon it being recorded, and the French "notice" system in which recordation was only to provide public notice of the existence of the recorded transaction but without "constitutive" effects.[163]

As described by Feng Wenli, an official of the PRC's Ministry of Land (the administrative agency responsible for overseeing this registry), the PRC registration system was inspired by two models: the German registry of land titles (*Grundbuch*) that grants title to the land or buildings after careful scrutiny of the previous recordings and the submitted documents, and Australia's certificate of title issuing Torrens system.[164] Regardless of the models that inspired it, the crucial question is who is protected by it.

---

[161] Morrison & Foerster LLP, *China Update, May 2007: Chinese Real Estate 2* (May 31, 2007), http://www.mofo.com/china-update-chinese-real-estate-05–31–2007/.

[162] *Id.* One Chinese attorney noted that, at least recently in Shanghai, a natural person could check the basic file of a real estate by simply showing his or her identification card. For more detailed information, one need to show his or her lawyer license or court order. *See* Chinese Attorney 1, *supra* note 75.

[163] *See generally* Garro, *supra* note 114, §§ 8–29–34 at 21–26.

[164] Wenli, *supra* note 51, at slide 45. The references to the Torrens system will be, except as otherwise noted to the one adopted in South Australia in 1858 and to the version of the BGB as adopted in Germany in 1900. *See also* Garro, *supra* note 111. I suggest this reading to those interested in an in depth comparison of contemporary land registration systems. Professor Garro's scholarship is characterized, by unusual thoroughness, clarity and precision.

3. *The Torrens System*

The Torrens system[165] (named after his proponent Sir Robert Torrens an Irish-Australian economist and customs collector) was adopted first in South Australia in 1858 and from there it spread to other common and civil law countries.[166] It was modeled after the recordings of transfers of ships under the English Merchant Shipping Act of 1854 which required that every transfer be listed on a separate page of a general register of ships so that title to each ship could be determined "at a glance."[167] Upon registry, a duplicate-certificate of the register page was given to the new owner. When this new owner assigned or transferred his certificate, the transferee would present it to the Registry office where the former entry was canceled, a new page was opened and a duplicate page was issued to the new owner.

As applicable to the registration and transfer of land, the examination of the chains of titles and of recordable documents in the Torrens system was done by officially appointed title examiners. They were and are responsible for the decision to record the creation of an interest in the land or building or of its transfer. Following this recording, a registry certificate was issued. The Torrens certificate was and is enforceable as the title to the land or building except when it is procured by fraud. If a mistake was made by the examiner of titles, an insurance fund pays for the damages suffered by the person who holds the valid claim against the land or relied on the Torrens recording to his detriment.

The key features of the Torrens system, then, are: 1) it "constitutes" or creates rights *in rem*; 2) it grants to the examiner of title a broad scope of examination; and 3) it protects those who rely on what was stated on the face of the certificate by means of an insurance fund which pays for the registry's mistakes.[168] An important drawback of the Torrens system was the inaccuracy of some of the descriptions of the land or buildings. Often these descriptions were inconsistent with those in "cadastral" or surveyed and graphic renderings of the parcels. Some survey plans showed the location of contiguous parcels, but others did not.[169] This led to the scattering of survey records of contiguous parcels and to the inability to rely on a "continuous cadastre" and to disparities between the actual or physical location and dimensions of the parcels and their legal description in the registry and certificates.[170]

Drawbacks aside, Professor Alejandro Garro quotes an English commentator who attributes the success of the Torrens system in England to its requirement that all titles related to land be recorded.[171] This success would not be possible where the law directs the registration of "all other rights" in the land, but does not specify which rights these are, as is the case with the PRL and as will be discussed shortly.

---

165 *See Torrens Title System,* ENCYCLOPEDIA.COM, http://www.encyclopedia.com/doc/1G2–3437704404.html (2005) (providing a summary description of this system). *See* Garro, *supra* note 114, at 42–48 (discussing this system thoroughly).

166 *Torrens Title System, supra* note 165.

167 Garro, *supra* note 160, §§ 8–48–53.

168 *Torrens Title System, supra* note 165. *See supra* § 19:3(B)(4) (on the uncertain recording of the rights of "other holders" in the PRL). *See also* Garro, *supra* note 114, § 8–49.

169 *Torrens Title System, supra* note 165.

170 *Id.*

171 Garro, *supra* note 114, § 8–49 n.213 (citation omitted).

4. *Germany's* Grundbuch

In the *Grundbuch* system,[172] enforceable rights *in rem* do not exist outside the registry. The sale or mortgage of lands or building is executed before a notary public whose deeds contractually bind the original parties to what they promised but this is only an *in personam* liability. As stated by Section 873 of the BGB[173] (in language copied by Article 9 of the PRL),[174] the transfer, acquisition, alteration or loss of a right *in rem* does not take effect until recorded in the *Grundbuch*. This provision made it a constitutive registry, *i.e.*, one without which rights *in rem* cannot be enforced even between the original parties to the transaction, let alone against third parties.

Although the BGB did not expressly list the rights *in rem* susceptible to registration in the *Grundbuch* (as was done by other codes associated with the BGB family such as the Austrian Civil Code),[175] the BGB implicitly restricted the number of rights *in rem* to those governed by Book III. These were: possession, ownership, rights to the use or exploitation of the surface of the land, easements, usufructs or life estates, mortgages and territorial debt.[176]

In addition, the contemporary *Grundbuch* combines the legal description of the land or buildings with data on the actual location and dimensions of the land and individual parcels as found in the surveys of the cadastral office.[177] As the cadastral data accumulated, so did the ability to provide a more precise description of parcels, especially their dimensions and boundaries, as a result of the "parcel identifiers" in cadastral maps. Eventually, these parcel identifiers became part of the recordings in the *Grundbuch* and multi-purpose cadastral survey data such as on soil composition, usage and zoning became easily searchable using the same parcel identifiers of the *Grundbuch*.[178]

---

172 *See* Garro, *supra* note 114, §§ 8–59–8–60; *see also* Kozolchyk, *Mexican Land Registry*, at 314–15.

173 *See* JIANG, *supra* note 51, at 5. Art. 6 states:

Publication of Real Rights

> Creation, alteration, transfer or extinguishment of a real right in an immovable is subject to registration in accordance with the provisions of the relevant Law. Creation or transfer of a real right in a movable is subject to delivery in accordance with the provisions of the relevant Law.

Id.

174 *Id.* at 7. Art. 9 states:

Vesting of Real Rights in Immovables

> Creation, alteration, transfer or extinguishment of a real right in an immovable takes effect upon registration in accordance with the law; and the above shall not take effect unless registration is undertaken, except as otherwise provided by the relevant Law.

Id.

175 *See* Garro, *supra* note 114, § 8–68 n.294 & accompanying text (referencing the Austrian Civil Code § 308 as having "an exhaustive catalog of rights *in rem*").

176 *See* BGB §§ 873–1203.

177 *See* Winfried Hawerk, *Grundbuch and Cadastral Systems in Germany, Austria and Switzerland* (Sept. 1996), http://www.fig.net/commission7/reports/events/delft_seminar_95/paper3.html. Cadastral offices were set up in German and Prussian kingdoms at the beginning of the nineteenth century to facilitate the taxation of the owners of lands and buildings by carefully identifying their real property on the same bases set forth by Napoleon in the occupied areas left of the river Rhine. The first major cadastre in Prussia was completed in 1876. Although the main purpose for the establishing of a cadastre was taxation of land, the idea of using maps and records or graphic and textual data to further tax collection was implemented in the cadastral systems from the beginning. *Id.*

178 *Id.* at 2 (section titled "Historical Review").

a. *The Title Examination of the* Grundbuch

The *Grundbuch* is part of the German court system and is open to public examination of its data and not merely to the parties whose names appear in the registry or their heirs or representatives.[179] Each registry is headed by a municipal or district court judge who acts as the Registrar of Titles and who reviews the legality of recordings and of the certificates issued by land registry officials.

Unlike the Torrens System, the *Grundbuch* system does not have a public compensation scheme or insurance fund to indemnify the parties to the transactions or third parties who relied on what was recorded for errors or omissions in the recording process. The person who makes the mistake bears the loss, including a party to the 111 transaction, a lawyer or notary, or an official of the registry.[180] The quality of the examination of title has been such that the number of complaints has been relatively small.[181]

b. *The Third Parties' Negative and Positive Reliance on the Public Faith of the* Grundbuch

The reader will recall that the concept of public faith attaches to documents executed before the notary publics of countries that belong to the system known as that of the Latin Notariat.[182] This system endows these notarial documents with a *prima facie* presumption of validity. A similar and perhaps even stronger presumption attaches to the recordings in the *Grundbuch.* In a rather circumlocutory fashion, Paragraph 1 of Section 892 of the BGB expresses the *Grundbuch's* guiding principles of "public faith" and of the protection of reliance by third parties:

> For the benefit of a person who by a legal transaction acquires a right *in rem* with respect to a parcel of land, or a right *in rem* with respect to such right, the entries in the land records [of the *Grundbuch*] are deemed to be correct, unless an objection against the correctness has been recorded, or unless the incorrectness is known to the acquirer [of these rights]. . . .[183]

Professor Garro's analysis of this provision provides the needed clarity and precision. He points to the clearer text of Article 973 of the Swiss Civil Code: "Whoever in good faith has relied upon an entry in the land records, and thereby acquired property or other rights *in rem,* is to be protected in such acquisition."[184] Garro clarifies that the principle of public faith (*Öffentlicher Glaube*) and its presumption of correctness of the recordings only benefits he who acquires the right *in rem* in an *inter*

---

179 *See Willkommen zur online Grundbuchabfrage (Osterreich)!*, JUSLINE, http://www.jusline.at/grundbuch.html (last visited Nov. 13, 2013) (for an example of the application for a search in the Austrian *Grundbuch* by a member of the public).

180 MURRAY J. RAFF, PRIVATE PROPERTY AND ENVIRONMENTAL RESPONSIBILITY: A COMPARATIVE STUDY OF GERMAN REAL PROPERTY LAW 210–11 (2003). Professor Raff points out that German notaries have a private indemnity insurance against damages for half a million euros and the judicial officers of the *Grundbuch* also have private professional insurance whose annual premiums in 2003 fluctuated between 110 and 250 Euros per annum for risks between 100,000 to 250,0000, with higher risk coverages being subject to negotiation. *Id.*

181 *Id.* at 211. For example, the North Bremen registry administers 60,000 titles per year, and a city the size of Hamburg has five different registries.

182 *See supra* ch. 7.

183 Garro, *supra* note 114, § 8–162.

184 *Id.*

vivos transfer, as opposed to a *mortis causa* conveyance such as by a will or legacy. Then, he draws attention to the protection of a third party's negative and positive reliance on recorded data.

A negative reliance takes place when the third party is misled by what was required to be recorded and was not recorded. This protection "is the hallmark of the recording systems claiming to protect negative reliance only."[185] In contrast, other systems protect not only against what was not recorded, but also "against . . . claims arising from . . . [what appears] recorded . . . [as an] apparently valid transaction or interest. . . ."[186]

One land registry system where positive reliance was not possible was that of Mexico, at least during the 1970s.[187] In a group of decisions on the protection of third parties, Mexico's Supreme Court questioned the diligence that these parties had to evince in order to be protected as good faith purchasers or creditors. The Court asked: How far back must a diligent searcher go into the chain of title of a parcel to qualify as a *bona fide* purchaser of the recorded property?[188] At first, it held that a diligent and *bona fide* searcher did not have to go back further than to those recordings that immediately preceded the transaction in question. Yet, in subsequent decisions, it extended the time of the search first to earlier recordings and finally to the time of the first recording of the parcel in question, regardless of how far back one had to search and of the sorry state of the Land Registry's records. Simply put, a purchaser could not qualify as *bona fide* unless he exhibited the skill of the most expert and well-endowed of searchers. Clearly such a degree of diligence and good faith would be completely unrealistic and unreasonable under the circumstances of Mexico's land registry and denied third parties the benefits of a positive reliance on the registry's records.

Professor Garro concludes that the Torrens and the *Grundbuch* systems offer the benefits of both a negative and positive reliance protection to third parties. He provides the following supporting quote from E.J. Cohen's Manual of German Law:[189]

> [Section 892 of the BGB] . . . does not require any reliance on the part of the transferee upon the contents of the *Grundbuch*. The transferee is protected in any case in which he did not positively know that the contents of the *Grundbuch* were incorrect. It does not matter whether his ignorance was due to lack of care. It does not even matter whether he ever consulted the *Grundbuch*. Even if he did not know the actual contents of the *Grundbuch* the latter are treated as if they were correct.

D. Third Party Protection and the Land Registry of the PRC

1. *Registry Data: Legal Descriptions and Cadastral Data*

According to Article 10 of the PRL, land rights that are sought to be conveyed, amended or canceled must be registered in a land registry whose location corresponds

---

185 *Id.*

186 *Id.*

187 Kozolchyk, *Mexican Land Registry*, at 353–55 (discussing Eufrasia Rodriguez de Ibarra and Probatio Diabolica).

188 *Id.*

189 Garro, *supra* note 114, § 8–162 n.677.

to that where the land is located.[190] The PRL does not specify if the PRC registry will emulate the *Grundbuch's* joinder of cadastral and legal descriptions of the subject parcels.[191] Only in a vague manner does Article 11 of the PRL allude to the need for such a joinder when it requires that the filer "provide evidentiary materials showing the ownership as well as other necessary materials specifying the site and size of the real property."[192]

This requirement disregards the fact that most filers are often unaware of the information available in governmental cadastral surveys or are unable to integrate such information with the descriptions that appear in the registry's "cards" or "folios" for each parcel. And if the cadastral information is already part of the land registry records, in all likelihood there will be a reference to it in the registry's certificate of ownership or a cross reference in one of the previous entries in the land registry's card of file for the parcel in question. And these records are not usually available to private filers. Clearly, then, the duty to supply cadastral information beyond a cadastral number or other designation should not be the filer's but the Land Registry's, as is the case in Germany.[193]

On the other hand, the history of land and cadastral surveys in the PRC has been as topsy-turvy as that of its land tenure regimes. During the 1949–1952 period of land reform, all rural land was surveyed and registered in village registries, yet in 1956–1978 during Mao's collectivization process, land tenure was consolidated and land registration was abolished; finally, land surveying and registration were reinstated from 1978–1984 during Deng's regime.[194] Meanwhile, the magnitude of the task of creating and cross referencing cadastral and legal description data has only increased by geometric proportions. Feng Wenli reports that after starting a cadastral inventory of the PRC on September of 1989, thirteen years later (on October 31, 2002) a total of 24,200 square kilometers of urban land and 45,160 square kilometers of rural land had been surveyed.[195] If one takes into account that it took three years to survey approximately 70,000 square kilometers of land and that the land surface of the PRC is of 9.6 million square kilometers, one can see why this registry official referred to the number of districts in which a cadastral administration has been established in 2008 with a non-specific, non-committal "many."[196]

2. *The Transactional Sequence Data*

Land registration in the PRC is governed by the Measures for Land Registration, adopted by the Ministry of Land and Resources on November 28, 2007, effective from

---

190 Lehman et al., *supra* note 51, ch. II art. 10.

191 *See* Garro, *supra* note 111, § 8–98. Professor Garro describes the modern cadastre as follows:

> A modern cadastre consists of a series of large-scale maps plotting to scale all parcels of land and building constructions, providing each plot with a parcel identifier number. This identification number allocates a distinct designation or cadastral nomenclature to each parcel, to which all the information provided by the documents filed at the land records regarding that specific parcel may be conveniently linked to facilitate its storage, indexing and retrieval.

Id.

192 Lehman et al., *supra* note 51, ch. II art. 11.

193 *See supra* § 19:3(C)(4) (discussing the German *Grundbuch*).

194 Wenli, *supra* note 51, at slide 8.

195 *Id.* at slide 20.

196 *Id.* at slide 21.

February 1, 2008.[197] Accordingly, the PRL expects the registrars to: 1) examine and weigh the "evidentiary materials" on ownership of rights in the land *as submitted by the filer*; 2) ask the filer to answer questions with respect to any aspect of the registration materials that arise from them; 3) conduct the registration in accordance *with the facts as submitted by the filer* and do so in a timely manner; and 4) perform whatever other duties are required by laws and administrative regulations, including the request for additional materials from the filer and for field surveys if necessary.[198] The result of the above enumerated functions is the entry of the data so gathered in registration "cards" or files for each individual parcel. The data contained in these cards or individual files is the one that proves, in the registrars' opinion, the ownership of land use rights and other rights and interests in land.[199]

For some unexplained reason, however, the registrar's own search for the proper order of succession of conveyances and other transactions, based upon what he independently of the presentation establishes in the pre existent chain of title is absent from his list of functions. Otherwise, how could the examiner satisfy himself that a legally-warranted sequence of rights exists that justifies the validity and effectiveness of the present filing? Should he just rely on the sequence set forth by the filer? This is why the principle of "proper sequence" is central to the *Grundbuch* registries.[200] It can only be relied upon where the registrar is charged to employ his "power of review" or "evaluation of land titles" which include the all the pre-existent recorded documents with respect to Blackacre as well as those submitted by the filer and claimant as the last "link" of a given chain of title.[201]

3. *Certificates of Registration*

Upon registration in the land registry of the PRC, a certificate is issued to governmental units or to individuals holding the rights or interests in the land conveyed by these units. Yet, as noted earlier, PRC governmental units at or above the county level are the "double track" entities referred to by Professor Stanley Lubman as responsible for issuing State-owned Land Use Certificates, Collective Land Ownership Certificates and Collectively Owned Land Use Certificates. And also noted during the discussion of residential land use rights, these certificates are standardized by the Ministry of Land and Resources and are printed by it or its authorized units or entities.[202] Walter Lee, Esq., describes their issuance as follows:

> The owners of the land use rights apply [for the appropriate certificate] to the land administration department . . . at or above county level where the land is situated, and the people's government at the country level will compile a register, verify and issue certificates of State-owned land use right, and confirm the [existence of] land use rights . . .[203]

---

197 Lee, *Part 1*, *supra* note 51, art. 19.

198 Lehman et al., *supra* note 51, ch. II art. 12.

199 *See* Lee, *Part 1*, *supra* note 51, art. 22.

200 *See* Garro, *supra* note 114, §§ 8–140–8–143 (titled "Scope of Review").

201 *Id.*

202 *See* Lee, *Part 1*, *supra* note 51, art.11.

203 *Id.*

> [Typically, a] land use right certificate contains the name of the registered land user, location of the land, permitted usage, term of grant, and will usually attach a site boundary map or floor plan. Some Land Use Right Certificates also contain information on whether the land use right is "granted" or "allocated." If such information is not found in the certificate, it is important for those who carry out due diligence to check the Land Grant Contract.[204]

Please note Mr. Lee's warning about the need for information on whether the land use right was "granted" or "allocated":[205] Granted land use rights require payment of consideration, while allocated rights generally do not require such payments because of their public purpose such as for military, scientific, artistic or other governmental endeavors.[206] Yet, please recall that such allocated rights can only be used for their designated purpose. In contrast, land use rights that were granted in exchange for compensation may be used for their designated use as well as for other purposes. They may also be transferred, leased, mortgaged or inherited.[207] This is one of the reasons for Walter Lee's warning not to rely solely on what appears recorded in the Land Registry, but also to check the land grant contract or allocation.[208] This warning reflects the fact that the data recorded in the land registry are far from being all the relevant data required for determining the existence and scope of land use rights or the grounds for disqualifying a given holder for holding such rights.[209] *Something as basic as the fact that the land attempted to be conveyed for private use may not be so used because of the land's "allocated" status may be missing from the land registry records.*

An equally significant datum is that PRC land use certificates, unlike those of the Torrens system, are not conclusive proof of the creation and transfer of a land use right or security interest or lease of the land use right. While the registration records of the land registry are "conclusive proof" of the above transactions or conveyances, the "land certificate is merely a duplicate *of part of the contents* of the land registration card."[210] In fact as noted earlier in connection with the principle of positive reliance, Article 17 of the PRL makes it clear that in the case of disparity between what is stated in the ownership of rights certificate and what is found or could be found in the registry certificate (most likely the registry ownership card or file), the latter prevails.[211] John

---

204 *Id.* art. 20.

205 *Id.*

206 *See supra* § 19:3(B)(2). *See also* Lee, *Part 1, supra* note 51, art.73 (referencing the Provisional Measures for Allocation of Land Use Rights of March 8, 1992).

207 Wenli, *supra* note 51, at slide 37.

208 *See* Lee, *Part 1, supra* note 51, art. 20. *See also id.* art. 74 (on the "Criteria for allocation"). *See* Walter Lee, *Chinese Real Estate Law: Part 3B: Land Administration Law* art. 54, KNOL.GOOGLE.COM, http://knol.google.com/k/walter-lee/china-real-estate-law-part-3b-land/zheu88eb3a1l/14 (last accessed Sept. 17, 2010) (on file with author) [hereinafter Lee, *Part 3B*]. *See also* Lee, *Part 4, supra* note 91, art. 24. This article lists:

> 1) land to be used by State organs and land for military use; 2) land to be used for urban infrastructure facilities and land to be used for public welfare undertakings; 3) land to be used for infrastructure projects of energy, transportation, water, etc. that have key support from the State; 4) land to be used for other purposes as prescribed by laws or administrative regulations.

Id.

209 Lee, *Part 1, supra* note 51, art. 20.

210 *Id.* art. 22 (emphasis added).

211 Lehman et al., *supra* note 51, ch. II art. 17. This article states:

Jiang's translation of the primacy of land registry records over statements in the certificate of ownership of land use rights is even more categorical:

> The certificate of rights in immovable [property] is the proof establishing that the purported rights [the] holder enjoys . . . in the subject immovable. Items recorded on the certificate of rights in immovable[s] shall be consistent with those recorded in the register of immovables. In case of discrepancy, unless [the] evidence proves that the items recorded in the register . . . are indeed erroneous, [the] items recorded in the register of immovables prevail.[212]

4. *Recordable Rights in* Rem *and Their Uncertain "Holders" or "Obligees"*

For administrative purposes, including zoning, the Land Administration Law[213] grouped the types of land use rights in the preceding sections into three categories: 1) agricultural land or land "directly" used for agricultural production; 2) land used for construction or lands on which buildings and structures could be built, including for residential, industrial, mining, transportation and water conservancy facilities; and 3) land not in use or unused land and thus not part of categories 1 and 2.[214]

Despite the intent to clarify the meaning and scope of land use rights[215] and of the need to record these rights to consider them "established," it is still unclear what rights can or need to be recorded. John Jiang's translation of the list of holders of property rights in Article 4 of the Property Law refers to it as including the state, collective, private persons and "*other rights holders*."[216] The Lehman *et al.* translation, in turn, refers to these unspecified persons or entities as "other obligees." Who are these holders of "other rights" or "obligees" and what *right or rights in rem* do they hold? This is a significant question because depending upon the answer, the PRC registry would be either a "*numerus clausus*" or "*numerus apertus*" registry. If it were the former, it would only allow the recording of a listed number of rights *in rem*. If it were the latter, listed as well as unlisted rights *in rem* could be recorded.

The PRL does not clarify the meaning of "other rights." The above-mentioned Measures for Land Registration[217] refer to "Other interests in land' . . . [as] interests in land other than the land use right and land ownership right, which include interests created by charge . . . lease *and other interests relating to land which are required to be*

> The ownership certificate of real property is the evidentiary material showing the rightful ownership of the obligee in such real property. Items recorded in the ownership certificate of real property shall be in conformity with that registered in the registration certificate, otherwise, the real property registration certificate shall apply.

Id.

212 JIANG, *supra* note 51, at 9–10.

213 *See* Lee, *Part 3B*, *supra* note 208.

214 *Id.* art. 4.

215 Lehman et al., *supra* note 51, ch. I art. 1.

216 *Compare* JIANG, *supra* note 51, at 5(emphasis added), *with* Lehman et al., *supra* note 51, ch. I art. 4. I prefer John Jiang's translation of this Article because it uses the term "right holders" for those who can claim *in rem* right instead of the Lehman, Lee and Xu translation which uses the contractual law and more imprecise term "obligee". Yet, both translations refer to "other" holders, whether right holders or obliges.

217 *See* Lee, *Part 1,* at *supra* note 197 & accompanying text.

registered by laws and regulations."[218] Obviously, this provision also fails to clarify the meaning of "other rights" because the presumably similar term it uses ("other interests") is defined in an illustrative fashion by stating what they include, leaving the door open to other unlisted "interests." Further, it refers the reader to other "laws and regulations" without specifying which ones or where they can be found.

Feng Wenli, the above-mentioned land registry official, defined "other rights on land" as also including: mortgage rights, leasing rights and neighborhood rights.[219] Note his addition of a category not mentioned above by the same Ministry of Land and Resources, *i.e.*, "neighborhood rights" (with overtones of traditional familistic China). Note also that Feng Wenli utilizes the same gerundial "including," thereby acknowledging that his listing of rights is also open-ended and that conceivably there are or may be other recordable rights entitled to registration. Simply put then, under the PRL, the list of recordable rights *in rem* is an open number of rights whose acceptability will be determined in the future perhaps by the legislature, the courts, or by each registrar when properly motivated to record such a right by a *Guanxi* filer.[220]

Since the effectiveness of these "other" rights depends mostly upon registration, unless the potential purchaser or mortgagee of a land use right knows which are "the other" rights or interests, a system of registration that was dysfunctional in 2007 will continue to generate significant uncertainties. Consider the case of "A," a lessee or maybe even a sub-lessee of a land use right in Blackacre who is aware of the fact that a friendly official in the land registry will accept his filing of his land use rights whenever A deemed it appropriate. A finds out that "B" has just acquired from government agency "C" an industrial land use right in Blackacre. At this point, A files his land use right in one of the possibly appropriate registries. B is confronted with the need to have to pay a significant additional sum to have A waive or subordinate his land use right to B's. I was told by some of the lawyers and developers who I met with in Shanghai in 2007 that the above situation is far from unusual.

Professor Garro's comparison of the benefits and burdens of a *numerus clausus* approach supports this analysis. He refers to the *numerus clausus* approach as:

> [A] feature that contributes in turn to the speed, simplicity and security of land transactions. . . . [T]he task of searching the title which a purchaser or mortgagee receives is greatly lightened under a legal system with a limited number of permissible rights in things. . . .[221]

This assertion is especially valid for real property transactions which are less malleable and less apt to produce new types of contracts than transactions involving personal property. And if the economic need for a new or hybrid type of transaction arises such as with a lien that secures rights in both the rolling stock of a railway (personalty) as well as the land surface for its tracks (realty) as was the case with the

---

218 *See* Lee, *Part 1*, *supra* note 51, art. 19 (emphasis added).

219 *See* Wenli, *supra* note 51, at slide 39.

220 *See* Lee, *Part 1*, *supra* note 51, art. 19. As described by Walter Lee, "People's governments at or above the county level are responsible for issuing State-owned Land Use Certificates, Collective Land Ownership Certificates, and Collectively-owned Land Use Certificates." *Id.*

221 *See* Garro, *supra* note 114, § 8–69.

post-World War II reconstruction of the German railroad system,[222] the statutory list should be open to include new legislatively sanctioned rights *in rem*.

E. Conclusions

1. *The Weakness of Third Party Right Under the PRL and Related Statutory and Administrative Law*

On April 22, 2010, China Daily reported that Bank of Communications Ltd., China's fourth-largest publicly traded mortgage lender, disclosed that it made fewer mortgage loans in February and March of that year while trying to rein in lending and property speculation.[223] It also reported that China's bank regulator directed the larger banks to conduct quarterly stress tests on property loans and to ensure that risks are strictly controlled.[224] This regulator also disclosed that Chinese banks extended a less-than-estimated 510.7 billion RMB (US$74.8 billion) of new loans in March after the central bank told lenders to set aside larger reserves and pace credit growth. Further, the housing ministry ordered developers not to take deposits for sales of uncompleted apartments without proper approval.[225]

In light of such a large number of mortgages in the portfolios of their bank-mortgagees, one wonders why the PRC has not developed a private sector-based secondary market for mortgages, especially after the government officials interviewed by Professor Stein recognized the importance and need for such a market.[226] Professor Stein attributes this failure to the "murkiness and unreliability of lending standards, particularly for residential loans. . . ."[227] Much of this murkiness and unreliability results in the creditors' inability to recover a reasonable amount of what they lent by realizing prompt and inexpensive returns on their real estate collateral. As found by Professor Stein and other foreign legal experts, "those who have been buying, selling and lending against Chinese real estate have been operating in a world of significant legal uncertainty."[228] In fact, Professor Stein was also told that the inability to rely on collateral "exists to an even greater degree in the growing automobile loan industry, with lenders having great difficulty tracking down this mobile collateral after a borrower defaults."[229]

Uncertainty, then, lurks behind each stage in the life of a land use right as well as of a personal property security interest. As the preceding discussion shows, the uncertainty exists during the creation, renewal and termination of land use rights. Issues such as who is the private owner or usufructuary of a land use right and what is the scope of his rights cannot be answered by researching the land registry. First, because the land registrars unlike those of the Torrens or *Grandbuch* registries, do not have the duty to establish the enforceable chain of titles to those rights. Second,

---

[222] *See* Glossary, "Scholastic Logic."

[223] *Mortgage Loan Volume Declines: BoCom*, CHINADAILY.COM (Apr. 22, 2010), http://www.chinadaily.com.cn/bizchina/2010–04/22/content_9762770.htm.

[224] *Id.*

[225] *Id.*

[226] Stein, *supra* note 51, at 1329.

[227] *Id.* at 1328.

[228] *Id.* at 1317 (citation omitted). *See* also Keliang & Prosterman *supra* note 51, at 14; *and* Whiting, Public Finance, *supra* note 18, at 11–20 (discussing similar conclusions on the overall legal uncertainty).

[229] Stein, *supra* note 51, at 1328 n.40.

because the exact number as well as the jurisdiction of these registries is far from clear, as contrasted with the government agencies that grant or allot the ownership or possession of land use rights. Third, because the land registries' data is incomplete and often dependent upon what appears in the certificates of land use grants or allocations as issued by other administrative agencies. Fourth, because a recorded right or security interest may well be subject to a superior but unrecorded right that the PRL vaguely refers to as "other rights."[230] Fifth, because the disparities between the "legal" description of the land or real property in the registry and in the cadastral survey are only growing in number. A third party may thus assume—based upon what appears stated in the land registry—that his rights are in a parcel of a certain number of square meters only to find out that the parcel is much smaller or nonexistent once its physical description is found in the cadastral survey or registry.[231]

And where residential urban property is concerned, hundreds of millions of actual or potential buyers and mortgagors presently lack the legal capacity to enter into the required contracts, thereby rendering the contracts they entered into null or subject to nullification. And at the end of the life cycle of many if not most land rights, it is uncertain whether they will be renewed, for how long and at what cost.[232] Conversely, if a land right is terminated abruptly by official expropriation, the amount of compensation is similarly uncertain.[233] There is little question then, that unlike the protection afforded by its supposed Torrens and *Grundbuch* models, the PRL land registry protects neither the positive nor the negative reliance of third parties.[234] In terms of third party protection, their predicament seems not much different from that described in a popular saying during Imperial law rule: The private parties write their contracts but ultimately it is the state who writes the applicable rules.[235]

2. *Regulatory Policies and the Weakness of Third Party Rights*

It is well known by now that "safe and sound" standards of lending were ignored by United States banks and other financial intermediaries that engaged in the issuance and negotiation or resale of "sub-prime" mortgages, as well as by many of their regulators. Professor Stein's study shows that PRC regulators have similarly ignored these standards when lending on the basis of the land use rights of the PRL.[236] Chinese real estate experts interviewed by Stein described the lending policies of PRC bankers as follows:

> [T]he only preconditions of any significance . . . are imposed to ensure that the project is legally permissible and socially desirable. Banks appear to make the decision to lend based solely on the legality of the project and the

---

230 *See supra* § 19:3(C)(3).

231 *See* Glossary, "Cadastral Survey."

232 *See supra* § 19:3(B)(4).

233 *See* Whiting, Public Finance, *supra* note 18, at 12–14.

234 *See supra* § 19:3(E)(4).

235 *See generally* VALERIE HANSEN, NEGOTIATING DAILY LIFE IN TRADITIONAL CHINA: HOW ORDINARY PEOPLE USED CONTRACTS, 600–1400 (1995). This source explains: "Officials have government law, and common people follow private contracts." *Id.* at 46. It also states: "Instead of the phrase which occurs so often . . . 'Officials have government law and commoners have private contracts,' this contract reads, 'Officials have government law (*zhengfa*) and do not accept private agreements as conclusive." *Id.* at 81.

236 *See generally* Stein, *supra* note 51, at 1336–41 (discussing lending standards).

> government's wish to see the project proceed and are far less concerned with the financial viability of the completed development. . . .
>
> . . . The government uses the banking system as an instrument of social policy, subsidizing construction of politically desirable projects even if those projects are not otherwise financially viable.[237]

This lending rationale is reminiscent of the debate on the adoption of the cost accounting principle of *Khozrachet* or of *Khozrachiot* as advocated by the Soviet economist Evsey Liberman and by Marcelo Fernandez, the president of the Cuban central bank during the early 1960s, a principle vehemently opposed by "Che" Guevara, among other radical or utopian socialist leaders.[238] At the root of this debate was whether government agencies, including central banks, should function as self sufficient, profit-seeking entities or whether they should disregard self sufficiency or profit considerations as contrary to socialist dogma.

Professor Stein mentions some possible reasons for the "looseness" of Chinese lending and regulatory policies. These ranged from the expectation that the market price of the collateral would inexorably continue to rise with the governmental encouragement of relaxed attitudes toward the economic feasibility of projects to the *Guanxi* relationships between favorite developers and their silent partner-bankers.[239] He also called attention to increasing governmental concerns with the overheating of the real estate market and the catastrophic consequences for Chinese families if the real estate bubble bursts.[240] It is difficult to ascertain if the PRC had rejected or disregarded *Khozrachet* as a cost accounting regulatory policy. If it had, this would explain the reports of numerous insolvencies among state-owned banks and their being allowed to continue to do business despite their *de facto* insolvency.[241]

Professor Stein explains the bizarre manner in which a seemingly capitalistically-driven PRC real estate market was financed by first posing the central question: "Where do the banks in a rapidly developing but still poor nation come up with the funds their borrower clients are demanding?"[242] His answer was that a major source seemed to be the high rate of savings of China's 1.4 billion citizens and their limited investment choices. The absence of attractive and safe investments led many to invest in residential real estate and bank accounts, despite the low yield of the latter.[243] Some of his interviewees also alluded to the fact that government prints money as needed to keep the construction boom going.[244] One of his interviewees, a surprisingly candid government official, provided what sounds to me as the most accurate description of the government's role in real estate lending:

> [T]he primary source of financial support for China's government, and thus for its lending institutions, is "our ancestors". . . . The Chinese government currently owns all the land . . . aside from land owned by agricultural

---

237 *Id.* at 1336–37.

238 *See supra* § 15:4(H)(2).

239 Stein, *supra* note 51, at 1338–39.

240 *Id.* at 1339–41.

241 *Id.* at 1343.

242 *Id.* at 1341.

243 *Id.* at 1341–42.

244 *Id.* at 1343.

> collectives, and the government retains the power to requisition agricultural land whenever it chooses. . . .
>
> . . . [It] supports its operations in large part by selling off land use rights in this same land, often to the same types of real estate professionals who were the primary targets of uncompensated nationalization during Mao's time. There are currently no *ad valorem* property taxes in China, so . . . China cannot depend on a steady stream of revenues flowing from a stable real property tax base. China relies instead on income taxes, real property transfer taxes, and, most significantly, proceeds from the sale of long term rights to use the same land that the government requisitioned between 1949 and 1982.[245]

As concluded by Professor Stein, the Chinese government funds its operations in significant part by selling land to private parties that it previously seized from other private parties.[246] This datum explains the negative results of the test of third party rights. For in the final analysis, the uncertain or random enforcement of land use rights was not as important to a highly centralized and non-market-determined policy of land marketability as was the government's continuous receipts of revenues derived from land transactions. It is true that the relatively free market system that one now observes in China could well bring down the entire "house of land use rights cards." If individual buyers and lenders are no longer willing or able to buy or lend, or the government is forced to print an exorbitant amount of increasingly valueless money to keep transactions alive, its land rights policy may well fail. Nonetheless, it is worth reiterating that those few who approved the enactment of the PRL were not as keenly interested in having a highly certain and effective law of property rights (despite pronouncement to the contrary) as they were in having a regulatory system that would not interfere with the government's receipt of massive revenues from a hyper-active real estate marketplace. A similar governmental attitude was observed with regard to a brand new form of secured lending that involved moveable property as collateral and particularly accounts receivable. Much attention was given to attaining a high volume of lending as a means of aiding the development of small and medium-sized industries in the free economic zones.

§ 19.4 SECURITY INTERESTS IN MOVABLE PROPERTY

A. The PRL's Generic Mortgage

Chapters 16 and 17 (on mortgages and pledges) of the PRL deal with a form of lending that could help at least in theory to develop internal markets for goods and services; they comprise the law of secured transactions in movable property. Properly drafted and implemented, this law can make it possible to provide credit for micro, small and medium-sized businesses at reasonable rates of interest. Thus, "asset based lending" or secured transactions law has contributed to the reduction of poverty in developing as well as in developed countries.[247] And according to the People's Bank of China (CRC): "One of the constraints to SME [small and medium enterprise] financing in China was the underdeveloped secured transactions system . . . There used to be a

---

245 *Id.* at 1344–45.

246 *Id.* at 1345.

247 *See* Kozolchyk, *Reduction of Poverty*, at 744–49.

law (China Security Law) but it focuses mainly on . . . immovable collaterals (sic) and does not provide effective secured transactions options for SMEs."[248]

The preceding assertion by the CRC does not mention the "Chinese generic mortgage" (*Di Ya*, 抵押) which as its Roman law ancestor[249] encompasses both immovable as well movable property and which does not require a transfer of title or possession to the secured creditor.[250] One can only speculate that this mortgage does not have the business importance that the PRL has assigned to its pledge even though in principle, the generic mortgage is, as will be discussed shortly, more adaptable to contemporary asset based lending than is the pledge.

As just noted, Chinese commentators distinguish the *Di-Ya* regulated by Chapter XVI of the PRL from the common law mortgage in that it does not involve a transfer of title from the mortgagor to the mortgagee and suggest that it is "in substance similar to a common law legal fixed charge, whereby a mortgagor grants a security that attaches to the secured property but does not require [a] transference of title or possession of the asset."[251] They add that "[s]hould the mortgagor default in repayment of the secured sum, the mortgagee is entitled to convert the secured property into money to satisfy the debt. Further, *a properly registered* mortgage will have priority over any other creditor in the event of the mortgagor's insolvency."[252] The reason I added this emphasis is because the words in italics are, in my opinion, crucial when understanding the little use of this device in contemporary Chinese asset-based lending. Without a proper registration of these mortgage rights, *i.e.*, one that would provide public, accurate and timely notice of the creation of the security interest in collateral such as a merchant's equipment, inventory, accounts receivable, proceeds and good will or other forms of intellectual property, this type of generic mortgage is ineffective. For neither its perfection nor its priority vis-à-vis third parties such as other secured and unsecured creditors could be established.

Consider, for example, the economic importance and physical characteristics of the collateral that secures the security interests subject to the generic mortgage in the PRL:

> Article 180:
>
> The following property which the creditor or third person is entitled to dispose of may be mortgaged:
>
> . . . .
>
> (iv) Production equipment, raw materials, semi-finished products and finished products;
>
> (vi) Means of transportation;

---

[248] *See* Xinyan Xu, Manager, Assistant General Manager of Security Registration Dept., People's Bank of China, Presentation at the FinNet 2010 Practice Group Meeting: China Secured Transactions Reform and Security Interest Registry slide 4 (October 19, 2010) (slides on file with author).

[249] *See infra* § 24:3(B).

[250] *See* MARK WILLIAMS, HAITIAN LU & CHIN AUN ONG, SECURED FINANCE LAW IN CHINA AND HONG KONG 69–71 (2010) (discussing the DiYa or generic Chinese mortgage).

[251] *Id.* at 69.

[252] *Id.* (emphasis added).

(vii) Other property that may be mortgaged according to law and administrative rules.

Article 181:

Enterprises, small business of industry and commerce and rural contractors may mortgage their existing and future production equipment, raw materials, semi-finished products and finished products according to the agreement between the parties, if the debtor defaults, the creditor shall have priority in satisfying his claim from such property.[253]

With some exceptions such as selected production equipment and means of transportation under Article 180 (iv) and (vi), the other assets listed in Articles 180 and 181 are not susceptible to easy identification either by serial number or plaques or by their individual dimensions (as is the case with the identification of real property). Thus, the registry that best responds to the need to identify collateral such as generic goods (including equipment, inventory accounts receivable, proceeds as well as raw materials) *is not a registry of ever changing or interchangeable things but of debtors*. Further, it must be a registry quick and responsive enough to provide notice of the existence of the security interest or lien to a vast number of actual or likely third parties. It cannot wait for a registrar to inspect the collateral to ascertain that it is as described in a highly detailed loan or security agreement. It is mostly and essentially a provider of notice of the perfection and priority of the filed security interest in goods generically described, not a grantor of title to the collateral. For much of the asset-based lending collateral can be subject to competing ownership and possessory rights, and as with raw materials, inventory, accounts and proceeds, that collateral is continuously changing. As I will discuss shortly, during my 2007 visit to the PRC I did not encounter one such a functional registry either in Beijing or Shanghai.

B. The PRL's Security Right

Article 2 of the PRL defines "property rights" as "the exclusive right enjoyed by the obligee to directly control specific properties including ownership, usufructuary and security right in property rights."[254] Conceptually, then, it locates a creditor's "security right" within the family of "property rights." Such a characterization would be workable provided that one need not be the owner of the property to be able to create a "security right,"

Article 40 however, makes it clear that: *The owner* shall have the right to establish usufructuary and security right in property rights with regard to its real or movable property. The obligee of the usufructuary and security right shall not do harm to the rights and interests of the owner while exercising their own rights.[255]

This provision is incompatible with contemporary security interests because, as just noted, they do not require that the obligor-debtor be the owner or even to hold title to the collateral to be able to create an enforceable security interest in it.[256] For at the

---

[253] Lehman et al., *supra* note 51, ch. XVI arts. 180–81.

[254] *Id.* ch. 1 art. 2.

[255] *Id.* ch. VI art. 40 (emphasis added).

[256] *See, e.g.*, U.C.C. § 9–202 (2013) (whose heading reads: "Title to Collateral Immaterial"); *See also* NLCIFT *12 Principles*, Principle 2. It states:

root, the security rights that the PRL wanted to define are not propriety but possessory in nature, as we discussed earlier with respect to "rights in the property of others" (the *iura in re aliena* of Roman law). The last sentence of Article 40 is similarly troubling. Assume, for example, that the obligor in a security right transaction is farmer "F" who relies on the crops he has grown in land he has rented but whose ownership belongs to the PRC or to a collective farm "CF". If farmer F cannot repay the loan to Bank "A" this provision subordinates A's repossession or foreclosure on F's crops, unless the PRC or CF authorize it.

Professor Ronald C.C. Cuming of the University of Saskatchewan and one of the world's experts on secured transactions law noted additional concerns in a recent communication to this writer.[257] Of these concerns, I have selected a few to illustrate the magnitude of the law and practice reform task that awaits Chinese and foreign secured transactions experts: (1) The failure of the PRL security right to follow the principle of its "conceptual unity." Under pre-existing as well as under the PRL, security rights can only be acquired on the basis of two statutory categories: The generic (real property and chattel) mortgage and the pledge. Other security agreements such as found in financial leases and title retention or conditional sale agreements are not included and are left to be governed by the Contract Law.[258] (2) The secured rights of the PRL do not extend to proceeds or to those assets received by the debtor as a consequence of the sale or exchange of collateral.[259] As should be readily apparent, the right to proceeds is crucial in both inventory and accounts receivable financing. (3) The PRL does not properly distinguish between the creation or "attachment" of the security interest (which takes place between the secured lender and his debtor and without the need of a filing) and the perfection and priority of the secured right, which requires filing or possession of the collateral by the secured creditor. As noted by Professor Cuming, the term "effectiveness" as applied to the generic mortgage was used in a manner interchangeable with the validity of the transaction between the lender and borrower.[260] (4) The PRL had no rules that validate the very important Purchase Money Security Interest, a security interest which "gives a special first priority to a secured creditor who provides the money to buy tangible collateral"[261]

Article 208 of the PRL states in relevant part that:

> The debtor or a third party transfers the possession of his movables to the creditor as a security for debt. If the debtor defaults, the creditor shall be

---

> A security interest is a preferential right to possession or control of personal property. As such it does not require that the debtor who grants the interest have title to the personal collateral, his right to possession, even though co-existent with other possessory rights in the same property by other creditors and debtors, will allow the creation of the security interest.

Id.

257 E-mail from Ronald C.C. Cuming, Professor, University of Saskatchewan, to author (Oct. 8, 2013 12:30 pm MST) (on file with author).

258 Ronald C.C. Cuming, Professor, University of Saskatchewan, Presentation Notes: People's Supreme Court Meeting Security Transactions Law 3 (Sept. 2013) (on file with author).

259 *Id.* at 6.

260 *Id.* at 8.

261 *Id.*at 10.

entitled to enjoy priority of having his claim satisfied with the proceeds of auction or sale of the pledged property . . ."[262]

This traditional version of the pledge or "pledge with the debtor's dispossession of the collateral" (also known as the "pawn shop pledge") deprives the debtor of the ability to repay his loan by using the pledged property as a "self liquidating" tool or asset that will generate the proceeds with which to repay the loan. Self liquidation, then, makes it necessary for the borrower to remain in possession of the assets acquired through the secured loan until he or she can produce, transform, sell or exchange them and convert them into the accounts and proceeds with which to repay the lender.

In addition, Article 211 of the PRL prohibits clauses that are reminiscent of the *Pactum Commissorium* of Pre-Constantine Roman Law. This *Pactum* was a widely-used clause in Roman secured loans which enabled the secured creditor to repossess and appropriate or resell the goods in the possession of their debtor in an extrajudicial manner if the latter failed to repay the loan or otherwise breached is obligations under the pledge agreement. Article 211 prevents the use of this clause when it states: "A pledgor and a pledgee may not stipulate in the contract that ownership of the pledged property shall be transferred to the pledgee if the obligation is not discharged at its maturity."[263]

As I have discussed elsewhere, this prohibition has done much harm to the modernization of the law of secured transactions in many a civil law jurisdiction.[264] It renders the creditor powerless to bring about a quick, inexpensive and effective liquidation of the secured debt by forcing him to go to court and attempt to recover goods many of which may have lost their value by the time he finally recovers them.

It is true that Article 230 of the PRL provides that when a debtor defaults, the creditor shall be entitled "*to retain the property under legal possession* and to the priority of having the debt paid with the money converted from the property or proceeds from sale or auction of the property. . . ."[265] Yet, the remedy of creditor retention presupposes that the secured creditor is already in possession of the collateral as required by Articles 208 and 212. It is thus inconsistent with self liquidation. It is also true that Article 232 allows the parties to agree that the collateral "shall not be retained" by the creditor,[266] but such a statement falls considerably short of allowing the secured debtor to transform, manufacture, sell or exchange the raw materials, inventory or other assets acquired with the secured creditors loan and then with the proceeds of the sale or exchange repay him.

As a result of the failure to enable the creditor's quick liquidation of the assets whose acquisition, manufacture or transformation he enabled, the PRL renders a loan secured by personal property collateral, especially in corporeal or tangible goods, highly uncertain. Further, 0 one gets the impression that the legislator wanted to link the secured creditor's priorities and remedies not to what was recorded in a secured transactions registry (including his recording of an earlier priority right) but upon the

---

262 Lehman et al., *supra* note 51, ch. XVII art. 208 ¶ 1.

263 *Id.* ch. XVII art. 211.

264 Kozolchyk & Furnish, *A Comparative Analysis,* at 256.

265 Lehman et al., *supra* note 53, ch. XIX art. 230.

266 *Id.* art. 232.

date of an unrecorded right of retention, even if that date was later than the date of the filing of a perfected security interest. Consider, for example, the following priority rule:

> Article 239: Where the movable property that [had] . . . already been mortgaged or pledged are retained at a later time, the lien holder shall enjoy the priority of having the debt paid with the money converted from the property or proceeds from sale or auction of the property.[267]

In other words, secured creditor "One" obtained a generic mortgage without the debtor "D's" dispossession of equipment "X" and filed his security interest in X in the appropriate secured transactions registry on April 1, 2013. On May 1, 20132, D, while in possession of X conveyed it to secured creditor "Two" who took possession of X and retained it as its pledgee until he sold it and paid himself the unpaid amount of his loan to D, even though his loan and security interest were created and perfected at a later time than that of secured creditor One. Creditor One's registered rights were subordinated to the possession subsequently acquired by Two, thus rendering registration meaningless. Predictably, not much secured lending based upon the priority rules of generic mortgages and pledges in tangible goods can beexpected unless the system of priorities is worked out in a fair and cost effective manner.

C. The Pledge of Accounts Receivable

Accounts receivable are intangible goods even if embodied in bills or invoices. What is being used as collateral is the right to collect on records or documents that indicate that amounts they refer to have been earned by the contractual performances of those who assign or sell the accounts to third parties acting as lenders or purchasers and generically designated as assignees. In October of 2010, Chinese secured transactions registry officials reported that over 250,000 security interests involving accounts receivable as collateral had been filed since 2007 in the single national registry and 15,000 of these securities were filed during the preceding fifteen months.[268] As appraised by a World Bank-IFC observer, while the number of filings was not very high in comparison to those of developed markets, their cumulative value was quite large. In Jinchang Lai's words, this enactment "[f]undamentally changed the structure of China's credit market: a new industry developed; and the share of moveables-based loans is now believed to be around 30%" of the total commercial loans.[269]

These are impressive accomplishments. The question remains, however, whether the PRL and the registry of secured transactions will be a sufficiently supportive legal platform for future financing by lenders other than official banks or whether uncertainties similar to those observed with the land use rights and generic mortgages will plague this promising normative and transactional turn in the commercial and consumer credit life of the PRC.

Article 228 of the PRL, one of its key provisions on account receivable lending, states in relevant part:

---

[267] *Id.* art. 239.

[268] *See* Lai, *supra* note 158, at slide 2.

[269] *Id.*

> Where the right of collecting receivables is pledged, the pledgor and the pledgee shall conclude a contract in writing and the right of pledge shall become effective upon registration with the competent authority.
>
> The right of receivables collection, once it is pledged, shall not be transferred unless otherwise agreed by the pledgee and the pledgor. The proceeds from the transfer of the right shall be used to pay in advance the pledgee's claims secured or be deposited with a third party.[270]

The first paragraph of Article 228 contains a rule that is at odds with that of model secured transaction laws and their statutory progeny such as, for example, that of the Organization of American States Article 5: "A security interest is created by contract between the secured debtor and secured creditor." In addition, Professor Cuming points out that there are no priority rules applicable to the pledge of accounts receivable that would replicate those in Article 189 for generic mortgages. He suggests that "the principles of applicable to mortgages of tangible property, with appropriate modifications" should also apply to pledges.[271] This would require that: a) a pledge of accounts be valid between the creditor and debtor without registration; b) pledges of existing and future accounts of the debtor be also valid; c) the pledges could secure all the amounts of debt agreed to by the parties while the pledge agreement is valid; d) the priority of the security rights be based on the date of their registration; e) and, a security agreement providing for a mortgage on tangible property could also include a pledge of the debtor's accounts.[272] I would add that consistent with the absence of a right to proceeds in the PRL's security rights, it would be necessary to clarify that the rights in the accounts also carry-over to the traceable proceeds; thus, a filing as to "accounts" automatically would extend to proceeds.

D. Overlapping Movable Securities Registries

During my 2007 visits to movable security registries in Beijing and Shanghai, I did not find a unified or networked registry system. A considerable overlap of what was to be filed the three different registries I visited. When I inquired about the law that governed the registration of mortgages and pledges I was referred to the PRC Security Law of 1995.[273] A not very reliable English translation of this law by a local firm indicated that, as also required by the PRL, that mortgages and pledges in real and tangible personal property required a filing for the security interests to be valid both *inter partes* and *erga omnes*. When I inquired whether this was the result of importing the *German Grunbuch* model of registry to China, one of the registrars who had been a graduate student in Germany said that this was the case.

Be that as it may. It also appeared from the private English translation that three different and overlapping registries existed: Supposedly, the main registry was housed with the "Administration of Industry and Commerce," but the directive in the Security

270 Lehman et al, *supra* note 53, ch. XVII art. 228.

271 Cuming, *supra* note 258, at 11.

272 *Id.* at 12.

273 PRC Security Law (1995). *See* LU & ONG, *supra* note 250, at 36–37. *See generally* Valerie Marechal et al., *China's new Property Rights Law*, *supra* note 51. (One of the employees of the visited registries had done his own English translation of the law (which he offered for sale) but the English was frequently not understandable. For this reason, its use in this section must be guarded and "impressionistic.")

Law was vague enough to allow "other laws" to dictate registration with other registries.[274] Another registry I visited was the office of a Notary Public, who explained that his registry was for security rights granted by private persons "and owners of the real or movable property mortgaged or pledged." The third category was of registries of collateral based registries, such as for automobiles. Nonetheless during my visit it appeared that registry included all types of "vehicles" such as tractors and mining trucks (generally considered as equipment by registries in the United States and in Latin America). I was also told that security rights in the same "vehicles" were being registered in the Administration of Industry and Commerce as well as in notarial offices.

Needless to say, that such an unpredictable administrative jurisdiction only leads to conflicting claims to the perfection and priority of security rights. As if this overlapping were little, Professor Cuming also informed me of the creation of a Registry for Financial Leases with the "Credit Reference Centre of the People's Bank of China"[275]

E. Supreme Court Land Right Directives and Letter of Credit Judicial Interpretations: Cures of Legal Invertebration?

Article 3 of the PRC Constitution makes it clear that "All administrative, judicial, and procuratorial organs of the state are created by the people's congresses to which they are responsible and under whose supervision they operate."[276] Consequently, the SPC is not an independent entity. It is supervised by the NPC and the NPC is, in turn, controlled by the Chinese Communist Party.[277] Nonetheless the SPC has for some time been empowered to fill statutory gaps and harmonize the often competing statutory, administrative and judicial rules.

This gap filling role has been enhanced during the last decade by its issuance of quasi-statutory directives on land rights such as the "Interpretation of the Supreme People's Court about the Issue Concerning the Laws Applicable to the Trial of Cases of Disputes Over Rural Land Contracting" in 2005 [hereinafter 2005 Directive] and the "Issues Regarding the Adjudication of Administrative Cases Involving Rural Collectively Owned Land" in 2011 [hereinafter 2011 Directive].[278] These directives are published as "official judicial opinions" (Yi Jian), "explanations" (Jie Da), or commentaries (Jie Shi).[279] When necessary, they widen the scope of existing provisions or clarify their reach and occasionally create a new rule. [280]Article 12 of the 2011 Directive provides such a clarification. The Property Rights Law of 2007 (PRL) recognized the need for compensation for the taking of personal as well as real property by the state. However, since constitutionally land is owned by the state, the compensation for fixtures taken in conjunction with expropriated land was uncertain

---

[274] PRC Security Law, art. 42, *cited in* LU & CHIN AUNG ONG, SECURED FINANCING LAW, supra note 273, at 21–22. Per the above private translation, this registry operated under the aegis of article 42 of the Security Law.

[275] Cuming, *supra* note 258, at 2.

[276] PRC CONST. ch. 1, art. 3 (1982).

[277] *Id.* at 2.

[278] JIANG, *supra* note 58, at 15–16.

[279] *Id.* at 14.

[280] Susan Finder, *The Supreme People's Court of the People's Republic of China*, 7 J. CHINESE L. 145, 168 (1993).

and in practice became discretionary. Article Twelve eliminated the administrative discretion and instructed governmental officials to compensate those who had lost personal property attached to the taken land.[281]

Other clarifications were needed by the multiplicity of possible jurisdictions and venues, and their different rules on, among other issues, standing to appear in court or before an administrative entity. Accordingly Article 1 of the 2005 Directive defines who has standing to sue the village or other governmental decision-makers on issues related to the terms and conditions of the contracts of land-use or management, or on the transfer and inheritance of rights under these contracts.[282]

Susan Finder, one of the most respected observers of the SPC during the last two decades, points out that these SPC directives can be considered as "one of the distinctive ways in which the Court *makes* law [in China]."[283] To a distant observer, the above-mentioned directives appear to be distinctive, but are they a preferred way to make law in an invertebrate legal system?

Please note that the drafting style of the above directives is similar to that of statutory rules in their generality and factual opaqueness.[284] Also note that the legitimacy of the Directive's rules is not based on their reasonableness and fairness but on the SPC's exercise of a power vested upon it by the NPC and the Communist Party. Finally, note that the directives' rules are not supported normatively or conceptually by earlier decisions of the SPC or of other influential courts which carefully weighed relevant facts and law and could qualify as precedents.

Mind you, the use of courts as political mouthpieces for political superiors is not a problem unique to the PRC, the same problem is found in many developing nations whose courts lack a tradition of independent judiciousness. This problem is exacerbated when courts are tasked with making a law, and especially a commercial law, that is responsive to the needs of their marketplace and in a manner that only good courts can, *i.e.*, by filling the gaps between the generality of statutory rules and the specificity of the facts in the case or controversy before them.

As apparent in the proceedings of a 2010 Mexican "Commercial-Judicial Workshop,"[285] the gap between the general and the specific, between a sound commercial law and policy and the facts of commercial case can only be filled by judges capable and willing to make "individual norms." These are rules that stem from the facts and issues of the case before them and whose reasoning finds support in broader, universal principles of commercial reasonableness and fairness that make them

---

281 Jiang, *supra* note 58, at 23.

282 *Id.* at 17.

283 Finder, *supra* note 280, at 171.

284 Consider, for example, the following typical language an SPC land right directive in Article 8 of the 2005 Directive:

> [I]f the contractor violates Article 17 of the Rural Land Contracting Law due to using the contracted land for a non-rural construction purpose or causing unrecoverable losses to the contracted land, and if the contract-issuing party requires the contractor to stop the infringement, resume the original status or compensate for the losses, the contract-issuing party shall be supported.

Jiang, *supra* note 58, at 20.

285 *See* Boris Kozolchyk, *Enhancement of Mexican Commercial Law Adjudication by Improved Transactional Fact-Finding, Application of Equitable Principles, and Drafting of Standard Contracts and Best Contractual Practices*, 27 ARIZ. J. INT'L & COMP. L. 441 (2010).

applicable to analogous factual situations. As will be discussed in *infra* Chapters 23 and 243 infra, these principles are often found in standard and best commercial practices which interpret the parties' intent in accordance with the parties' courses of dealing and the usages of their respective trades.

Interestingly, at the same time the some of the SPC justices were drafting the land rights directives, in 1999 others started drafting a set of Letter of Credit "Judicial Interpretations." The mission of these interpretations was to make the PRC law on suspensions of letter of credit payments (prompted by allegations of fraud made by Chinese importers of foreign goods) a reasonable, fair and predictable set of rules.

In his recent monograph, "The Law of Letters of Credit in China"[286] Jin Saibo, the PRC's most knowledgeable and respected letter of credit practitioner-scholar, chronicled the decade of research and drafting of these interpretations and described the main problem they faced as follows:

> In the years between 1994 and 1997, Chinese courts ordered in many cases to suspend LC payments based on unjustified requests by the parties on the grounds unrelated to the LC transactions, which in turn materially affected the international reputation of Chinese issuing banks.[287]

He summarized the work of the PRC's Judicial Interpretations, whose immediate audience is comprised by the PRC's lower court judges as:

> [T]he *LC Judicial Interpretations* include a number of provisions containing tests for LC fraud and fraud exceptions, as well as some procedural issues such as [the standing of] third parties . . . procedures of rulings and review, and the standard of proof and *onus probandi*. The *LC Judicial Interpretations* have made detailed rules on these matters, some of which can be regarded as breakthroughs. . . . [T]he requirements for suspension of payments under an LC are clearly defined, and the threshold for suspension of payment is also clearly defined, which will have the effect of curbing the abuses of discretion by Chinese courts as they did during 1994 and 1995.[288]

I believe that what was accomplished by the LC Judicial Interpretations, modest as it may appear at first sight (especially when compared with the *erga omnes* legislative powers given to the drafters of the Land Use directives) is precisely what is needed to provide a healthy start to the process of judicial vertebration. It does this by letting the SPC and the lower courts do what they are supposed to do best-establish the facts of the judicial problem facing them as lower court judges about to decide the individual case or the SPC in fashioning a decisional policy for the entire set of courts. And once the facts are established, it encourages them to engage in a comparative and sectoral analysis directed to choose the best law and the most widely observed standard and best practices. And once the drafters made their choice publish it and make the reasons for the new rules transparent and accessible to future litigants near and far, as Jin Saibo just did with his fine monograph.

---

[286] JIN SAIBO, THE LAW OF LETTERS OF CREDIT IN CHINA: COMMENTARY AND MATERIALS ON THE CHINESE SUPREME PEOPLE'S COURT'S JUDICIAL INTERPRETATIONS OF LETTERS OF CREDIT (2013).

[287] *Id.* at 39.

[288] *Id.* at 37.

Part V

ANGLO-AMERICAN LAW

Chapter 20

SOCIO-ECONOMIC AND LEGAL CONTEXTS AND ENGLISH COMMERCIAL CONTRACTS

§ 20.1 INTRODUCTION

Chapters 8–12 discussed distinctive civil law institutions mostly associated with codified civil and commercial law. This chapter introduces distinctive legal institutions instrumental in the development of the law of commercial contracts in England. Some of the institutions introduced by this chapter are discussed in comparative detail in Chapters 22–24, devoted to the formation and interpretation of commercial contracts and to the drafting of commercial and financial practices. Accordingly, Chapter 22 will answer questions such as: Why are the rules on commercial contract formation different in the *Code Civil*, BGB and the U.C.C? Or, why are "firm" promises, offers or options to sell or purchase within a specified or reasonable period of time unenforceable under the *Code Civil* and its progeny?

At the root of the above comparison lies the question: What is a commercial contract? Additionally, can a promise to give or do something in the future remain binding on the promisor for a specified or reasonable time even though the promisee did not accept the promise during that time? This is a critical question for commercial promises everywhere because their performance is often deferred to a future time during which the promisor remains bound. Think, for example, of the manner in which present day buyers of stocks and bonds typically issue their terse buy orders in developed financial marketplaces: "Buy X stock at Y price, order valid until 4 pm of Z date." If this purchase order could be revoked at any time prior to the broker's or seller's acceptance, could such an expeditious method of buying securities be viable?

The determination of what is a contract is also critical for the interpretation of commercial promises because if there is no valid contract, there is nothing to interpret and even less to transform into a standard practice. Finally, the question and determination of the validity of executory promises is critical because a code as influential as the *Code Civil* regards them as revocable "*pollicitations*."[1] It is for these reasons that this introductory chapter examines the development of enforceable executory promises in English law (including unconditional promises to pay a sum certain) during the seventeenth and eighteenth centuries, the seminal years of England's world-leading commercialization.

Similarly, Chapter 21 will examine the development of United States legal institutions derived at times directly, at other times indirectly and at times not at all from their English predecessor.

---

[1] *See supra* § 8:9(C)(4).

§ 20.2 ENGLISH LAW

A. Britain's Seventeenth and Eighteenth Century Trade and Tradesmen

As described by an English legal historian, England's beginnings as a commercial and trading nation were humble:

> During the period of history known as the Middle Ages, the industrial attainments of the English were far below the level of their continental rivals, France, Germany, Italy, Spain and the Low Countries. . . . As late as the sixteenth century the type of English society was mainly that of a pastoral and mining community, exchanging its undressed cloth, wool, hides, tin and lead for the manufactures of the continent and the produce of the East.[2]

Nonetheless, by the middle of the eighteenth century, Britain, in large measure thanks to its tradesmen, became a major commercial power, and shortly thereafter thanks to its inventors, entrepreneurs and financiers, it became the world's leading industrial nation.[3] Because our concern in this chapter is with England's commercial pre-eminence our focus will be on its trade and tradesmen.

1. Who Were Britain's Tradesmen?

Daniel Defoe, a popular eighteenth-century English journalist and novelist, (best known for his 1719 novel *The Life and Adventures of Robinson Crusoe*)[4] had only praise for his fellow English tradesmen:

> It is said of England . . . [that] we all value ourselves . . . [as] a trading country; and King Charles II., who was perhaps that prince of all the kings that ever reigned in England, that best understood the country . . . used to say, 'That the tradesmen were the only gentry in England.'[5]

To which he added his own assessment:

> We are the greatest trading country in the world, because we have the greatest exportation of the growth and product of our land, and of the manufacture and labour of our people; and the greatest importation and consumption of the growth, product, and manufactures of other countries from abroad, of any nation in the world. [Why?]
>
> . . .
>
> First, our tradesmen are not, as in other countries, the meanest of our people.

---

[2] E. Wyndham Hulme, *The History of the Patent System under the Prerogative and at Common Law*, 12 L.Q. REV. 141–42 (1896).

[3] *See* C. Knick Harley, *Trade: discovery, mercantilism and technology*, *in* I THE CAMBRIDGE HISTORY OF MODERN BRITAIN 175–203 (Roderick Floud et al. eds., 2004).

[4] DANIEL DEFOE, THE LIFE AND ADVENTURES OF ROBINSON CRUSOE (2010) (1919), http://www.gutenberg.org/files/521/521–h/521–h.htm.

[5] DANIEL DEFOE, THE COMPLETE ENGLISH TRADESMAN 240 (Dodo Press 2013) (1726) [hereinafter DEFOE, ENGLISH TRADESMAN].

> Secondly, some of the greatest and best, and most flourishing families, among not the gentry only, but even the nobility, have been raised from trade, owe their beginning, their wealth, and their estates, to trade; and, I may add,
>
> Thirdly, those families are not at all ashamed of their original, and, indeed, have no occasion to be ashamed of it.[6]

Yet, by tradesmen Defoe did not necessarily mean Braudel's street merchants, shopkeepers or peddlers,[7] or Shakespeare's Shylock (a commonly held view of the moneylender-usurer throughout post Renaissance Europe). The tradesman praised by Defoe was primarily the English international trader:

> By trade we must . . . include navigation, and foreign discoveries, because they are, generally speaking, all promoted and carried on by trade, and even by tradesmen. . . .
>
> . . .
>
> Have not the trade and tradesmen born the burden of the war?—and do they not still pay four millions a-year interest for the public debts? . . . Is not trade the inexhausted fund of all funds, and upon which all the rest depend?[8]

However, the term tradesman had different meanings throughout Great Britain. For example, in the north of Britain and in Ireland:

> [W]hen you say a tradesman, you are understood to mean a mechanic, such as a smith, a carpenter, a shoemaker, and the like, such as here we call a handicraftsman. . . .
>
> But in England, and especially in London, and the south parts of Britain, we take in another sense . . . all sorts of warehouse-keepers, shopkeepers, whether wholesale dealers or retailers of goods, are called tradesmen, or . . . trading men . . . our grocers, mercers, linen and woollen drapers, Blackwell-hall factors, tobacconists, haberdashers . . . glovers, hosiers, milliners, booksellers . . . and all other shopkeepers, who do not actually work upon, make, or manufacture, the goods they sell.
>
> On the other hand, those who make the goods they sell, though they do keep shops to sell them, are not called tradesmen, but handicrafts [men]. . . .[9]

2. Social Classes, Ease of Trade and England's Commercial Revolution

Please recall that the division of labor between the makers of goods and their financiers and merchandisers resulted from the breakdown of the guild system and its eventual replacement by capitalism.[10] Thus, the amalgamation of craftsmen and shopkeepers under the category of tradesmen did much to commercialize the former English guild system. As obligatory apprenticeships, fixed prices and compensation schemes, and uniform standards of quality withered away, it became very difficult to distinguish a tradesman from a businessman. This was true even though England has

---

[6] *Id.* at 240–41 (citation omitted).

[7] *See supra* § 6:3(F)(3).

[8] DEFOE, ENGLISH TRADESMAN, *supra* note 5, at 242.

[9] DEFOE, ENGLISH TRADESMAN, at 1 of the Introduction.

[10] *See generally supra* ch. 6 (on the guilds).

had a deeply ingrained class system in which gentlemen in Daniel Defoe's days felt entitled to converse with their peers undisturbed by the participation of inferior class tradesmen. Thus, Defoe recalls a "smart, but just repartee, [between] a London tradesman [and] a gentleman"[11] in which:

> [A] gentleman, who had a good estate too, rudely reproached him [the London tradesman] in company, and bade him hold his tongue, for he was no gentleman. 'No, Sir,' says he, 'but I can buy a gentleman, and therefore I claim a liberty to speak among gentlemen.[12]

I remind the reader that this classist attitude still esteems international tradesmen. Further it did not translate into a widespread rejection of merchants by other classes and especially those of lesser wealth, as was the case in France and Spain during the same period.[13] As was discussed in earlier chapters,[14] the disdain for merchants as a class was present in Napoleon Bonaparte's reference to England as a "nation of shopkeepers" ("*L'Angleterre est une nation de boutiquiers*").

The English commercial revolution was vitally nourished by the intercontinental trade that followed Spain's, Portugal's and England's voyages of exploration to the Americas and the East Indies. Hundreds of explorers were followed by thousands of traders and colonizers and in short order, their trade was institutionalized with chartered, monopolistic and mercantilistic trading companies such as England's company of Merchant Adventurers[15] and the East India Company.[16]

Trade was also supported by the Bank of England, which was chartered in 1694 and capitalized by a loan of £1,200,000 to the English Government, in return for which the subscribers would be incorporated as the "Governor and Company of the Bank of England."[17] During the Bank's early years, the Government continued to rely on it as a financier and issuer of new coinage,[18] but it also became engaged in "conventional banking business, [by] accepting deposits and discounting bills [of exchange]."[19] The latter became a particularly important source of commercial credit as were the Bank's notes whose unconditional "promises to pay" were widely relied upon.

The ease with which tradesmen could engage in commercial transactions was both a cause and a reflection of how widespread commercialization had become in England. Accordingly, Wyndham Beawes's 1773 commercial manual *Lex Mercatoria Rediviva*[20] did not list the bureaucratic hurdles that merchants had to be prepared to overcome,

---

[11] DEFOE, ENGLISH TRADESMAN, *supra* note 5, at 244.

[12] *Id.* (citation omitted)

[13] *See supra* ch. 8 (for the discussion of the bourgeois and land gentry on French Codification).

[14] *See, e.g.*, § 8:3.

[15] *See generally* Merchant Adventurers, Encyclopaedia Britannica Online, (on a company of English merchants known as the Merchant Adventurers), http://www.britannica.com/EBchecked/topic/375700/Merchant-Adventurers.

[16] *See generally* Encyclopaedia Britannica Online, East India Company, http://www.britannica.com/EBchecked/topic/176643/East-India-Company.

[17] Bank of England, History Timeline, at 1 (The beginnings), http://www.bankofengland.co.uk/about/Pages/history/timeline.aspx.

[18] *Id.* at 2 (Early business—the Bank moves).

[19] *Id.*

[20] WYNDHAM BEAWES, LEX MERCATORIA REDIVIVA (1773) (which is also described as a complete guide to all men in business), *available at* http://babel.hathitrust.org/cgi/pt?id=njp.32101076400819;view=1up;seq=38.

but instead the skills that were expected of him and what he was supposed to know about his trade: (1) To write properly and correctly; (2) All the rules of arithmetic with any affinity or relation to commerce; (3) To keep books of double and single entry; (4) To be expert in the order and forms of invoices, accounts of sales, policies of insurance, charter parties, bills of lading and bills of exchange; and (5) To know the agreement between the monies, weights and measures of all parts.[21]

Noticeably absent in that list were the elements of contracts typified as commercial or as "acts of commerce" in the *Code de Commerce* and its progeny.[22] In fact, when Beawes discusses the formality of commercial contracts, he tersely informs his readers (as heterogeneous a group of tradesmen as those in Defoe's lists) that in England "A Contract for [the Sale of] Goods may be made . . . by Word of Mouth."[23] This informal and undifferentiated approach to contracts sharply contrasted, as you will recall, with the French civil and commercial codes' distinction between civil and commercial transactions. Although the latter listed "acts of commerce," the French codes often required a judicial determination of whether a given transaction was "civil" or not-for-profit and thus governed by the *Code Civil*, or commercial and governed by the *Code de Commerce*.[24]

B. The Honesty of Tradesmen and Their "Poetic" Licenses

Despite the reservations that positivistic-minded legislators, judges and legal commentators have with the ethical components of commercial practices,[25] the undeniable fact is that the viability of these practices, especially when they involve strangers, depends upon trust. And trust can only come about when one party's conduct is morally acceptable to the other. Ethical commercial standards, then, are essential to the trustworthiness of a counterparty or proffered contract. But ethical standards must reflect their commercial context and thus must be realistic enough to assume the for-profit motivation of the parties.

The application of a commercially unrealistic ethical standard was present in the Red Ink case decision discussed in Chapter 9.[26] It involved, as I am sure many of you will recall, a young French lover's promise of payment for a prostitute's sexual favors as signified in a bill of exchange. Perhaps due to the high passion of the moment, the young lover signed the bill with his own blood. As the passion subsided, however, he

---

[21] *Id.* at 26.

[22] *See supra* § 10:2.

[23] BEAWES, *supra* note 20, at 352.

[24] The need for a judicial determination of the civil or commercial nature of transactions is illustrated by the French court decisions, *see* § 10:8 (for excerpts). In England, anyone referred to as a tradesman, shopkeeper or handicraftsman could perform acts of commerce without having to prove that his transaction was part of a legislatively or administratively sanctioned exhaustive list of such acts, or that he kept approved accounting books and records or used special contractual formats when so required by the *Code Civil*.

[25] By positivistic I mean a version of law that views it as nothing more than "the command of the sovereign" in the famous expression by the 19th century "Analytical" legal philosopher John Austin. *See* Bix, Brian, "John Austin", *The Stanford Encyclopedia of Philosophy* 3 (Edward N. Zalta ed., spring 2013) (on "Austin's views" of the law), http://plato.stanford.edu/archives/spr2013/entries/austin-john/. In this book you will find references to other positivistic legal philosophers such as Hans Kelsen (*see* 3:7(B)) and to the United States appellate judge Richard Posner, who as you will find in chapter 23 does not seem comfortable with the "moral overtones" of the doctrine of good faith.

[26] *See supra* § 9:2(E)(3)(C).

reneged on his promise, and when sued by his payee, he alleged the illegality of the act that caused his promise.

Speaking for a commercial court, Judge Bedos decided that regardless of the legality of the underlying transaction, a court such as his, which was concerned with encouraging virtuous conduct, was required to apply a higher standard of morality such as found in the Christian duty of love and compassion for a needy prostitute; accordingly, he ordered the signer to marry the payee of the bill.[27] It is not difficult to see why, realistically, such an ethical standard could not be applied to the payment of everyday bills of exchange in satisfaction of their underlying commercial transactions.

In Chapter 27 of *The Complete English Tradesman*, Defoe attempted to provide a more realistic and commercially-based analysis of a tradesman's honest promises.[28] In his own business dealings, Defoe had encountered outright dishonesty and chicanery as well as borderline unethical conduct. The governing principle of an honest commercial promise was:

> Trade cannot make a knave of an honest man, for there is a specific difference between honesty and knavery which can never be altered by trade. . . .
>
> [Yet] . . . there are some latitudes, like poetical licenses . . . which by the custom and usage of trade he may . . . take some liberties, but within bounds. . . .[29]

One of these poetic (commercial) licenses was a tradesman's "liberty to ask more than he will take." Defoe opined that despite a seller's representations to his potential buyer that his asking price was the final one, he should be forgiven for such a sales tactic. Not only was it a standard practice among sellers, but this practice was usually matched by the buyers' similar misrepresentations of the funds they had available for their purchases.

Another such a license applied to the debtors' assurances of immediate payment when in fact payments could not be made until a later time or not at all. Defoe attributed the predicament of these otherwise honest debtors to a credit market in which payments owed by buyers to sellers or by borrowers to lenders were part of a supply chain. Hence, once a buyer or borrower in the initial links of the chain defaulted, it was likely that subsequent creditors, despite the honesty of their own promises of payment, could not pay their own debts in time.

Defoe's concern with the honesty and morality of a tradesman's promise was also an important trait of his "Complete Tradesman" because it reflected an awareness of what makes a commercial practice trustworthy and thus viable. Chapters 22 and 23 of this book share the same concern and explore the commercial meaning of good faith and its components of honesty, reasonableness and fairness.

---

[27] *Id.*

[28] *See* DEFOE, ENGLISH TRADESMAN, *supra* note 5, at 177–88 (Of Honesty in Dealing, and Lying).

[29] *Id.* at 177.

C. Monopoly and Mercantilism in England's Modern International Trade

Starting in the early fifteenth century, England's international trade was increasingly monopolistic and mercantilistic. The first group of merchants to engage in royally chartered and protected trade was the Company of the Merchant Adventurers, who, starting in the fifteenth century, exported English finished cloth to the Netherlands and Germany.[30] By the middle of the sixteenth century, three-fourths of English foreign trade was controlled by London officers of this company who also served as financiers and advisers to the Tudor monarchs.[31] By 1564, however, they lost an important market in the Spanish Netherlands, and a century later they also lost their monopolistic trading privileges.[32] Still, the Merchant Adventurers started England's own pattern of monopolistic, royally-protected international trade.

This pattern continued during the seventeenth century with the founding of the British East Indies Company. Its 1602 Royal Charter empowered it to trade as Britain's surrogate in the East Indies.[33] Roughly a century and a half later, England was a full competitor with Spain's and Portugal's monopolies and had become a major importer and exporter (in an original or transformed state) of cotton, silk, indigo and salpetre from South India and tea from China. In the case of imported Chinese tea, England soon found itself paying for it with opium, and embroiled in the opium wars with China that lasted until late into the nineteenth century.[34]

This *modus operandi* closely resembled those of Britain's European competitors—monopolistic, mercantilistic and often militaristic. Unlike its European competitors, however, English tradesmen evidenced a greater ability to take advantage of changing economic and political circumstances, especially through their colonial correspondents.

D. Multilateralism and Cooperation with Colonial Tradesmen

Professor C. Knick Harley of Western University of Canada wrote an insightful chapter on England's eighteenth-century trade and mercantilistic practices for Cambridge University's "Economic History of Modern Britain."[35] It shows that European traders imported large quantities of eastern goods, but did not develop a corresponding eastward flow of European goods.[36] Their trade was largely paid with the gold and silver mined in the Americas. As bullion or as coin, these metals repaid Spain's loans from Western European bankers and subsequently these bankers and many English tradesmen used it to pay for their imports from Asia.

In addition, two American crops—sugar and tobacco—played in Harley's words:

> [A] greater role in British (and European) trade than did all trade to the east. . . . Before Columbus' voyages, sugar was expensive—a spice or medicine

---

[30] *See* Britannica, Merchant Adventurers, *supra* note 15.

[31] *Id.*

[32] *Id.*

[33] *See* Britannica, East India Company, *supra* note 16.

[34] *Id.*

[35] *See* C. Knick Harley, *supra* note 3.

[36] *Id.* at 179.

> of the well-to-do as.... Tobacco ... [meanwhile], was [unique and] the Americas' other great export staple.[37]

It was apparent that the English and the merchants doing business in the American colonies had much in common and much at stake in their cooperation. The principal areas of cooperation were: (1) The American colonies acting as key importers of Britain's goods and services;[38] (2) The British merchants and their colonial counterparts acting as commission and *del credere* agents for each other,[39] largely supported by cheap commercial and consumer credit available with English bankers and factors; and (3) Their mutual reliance on slavery to radically lower the costs of producing cotton, sugar and tobacco and to generate unprecedented profits that provided much of the investment and credit capital to both British and colonial entrepreneurs.[40]

In sum, as a result of Britain's central role in this European, Asian and American multilateral trade system, its trade policies were dualistic: Outside its colonial boundaries, England's policies were mercantilistic and at times militaristic. Inside these boundaries, through the medium of colonial tradesmen, mercantilistic laws such as the British Navigation Acts[41] did not prevent the re-export or the import of goods to and from its competitors. Hence, Britain relied on a freer trade system with and through its colonies than did Spain.[42]

E. Samuel Storke: An Archetypal English and Colonial International Trader

A 1965 study by Professor William Roberts, III of Pennsylvania State University examined the Trans-Atlantic business practices of the London House of Samuel Storke, one of the largest English mercantile houses in eighteenth century colonial trade.[43] Storke was born in Hampshire, England late in the seventeenth century to a family of clothiers with close relatives in North America.[44] His father, John Storke, Sr. was a cousin to Judge Samuel Sewall of Boston, Massachusetts. The judge inherited property in England and Storke Sr. helped him collect its rental income for many years. In exchange, Samuel Storke spent two years in Boston with his relatives and upon his return to England set up his own trading company.[45]

---

[37] *Id.* at 181–182.

[38] *Id.* at 184.

[39] *See infra* § 14:3(A)(2)(c).

[40] C. Knick Harley, *supra* note, at 186.

[41] *See* Brankica Radonjic, The Navigation Acts 1650–1969 (David W. Koeller, 1996–1999), http://thenagain.info/webchron/usa/navigation.html. This publication describes the Navigation Acts enacted by the English Parliament from 1650 to 1696 as:

> The Navigation Acts were passed by the English Parliament in the seventeenth century. The Acts were originally aimed at excluding the Dutch from the profits made by English trade. The mercantilist theory behind the Navigation Acts assumed that [the boundaries of] world trade ... [were] fixed and the colonies existed for the parent country.

[42] *See supra* § 14:3.

[43] *See* William I. Roberts, IIII, *Samuel Storke: An Eighteenth-Century London Merchant Trading to the American Colonies*, 39 BUS. HIST. REV. 147–70 (No. 2, 1965).

[44] *Id.* at 148–49.

[45] *Id.* at 149 (citations omitted).

Prior to Samuel Storke's return, Storke, Sr. had sent occasional "ventures" or consignments of cloth to Judge Sewall or to his son-in-law in New England for them to help sell and share in the commissions.[46] The Sewalls reciprocated by channeling colonial purchase orders of English consumer and commercial goods to Storke.[47] From this familial transactional nucleus grew one of the most important trade relationships during England's colonial days in America.

1. Storke's Commission Business

At first, Samuel Storke procured goods in England for his colonial clients and charged a purchase agent's commission. The goods were as varied as hardware, glass, china, tea, spices and textiles including English woolens, silks, linens and cottons.[48] When buying goods on commission for his colonial clients, Storke "seldom had to advance credit to his correspondents. . . . [and did not buy the goods] until he had cash in hand or bills of exchange from them."[49] Conversely, when Storke sold goods on commission to his colonial clients, he made only "the smallest outlay of capital" to pay for transportation and storage costs as well as for customs duties.[50]

The commission business, then, required only small outlays of capital, mostly to pay for the cost of transport and storage of the goods on the English side. As his commission business grew, he also procured maritime insurance policies for his colonial clients which earned him a brokerage fee.[51] Because commercial credit was plentiful in eighteenth-century England,[52] Storke could obtain three to six months credit when purchasing goods for his colonial customers.[53] And even though bad debts were a chronic problem in colonial trade, he did not experience it to a significant degree; apparently his network of traders was sufficiently solvent and trustworthy to render defaults rare. [54]

2. Colonial Executory Promises in Consignments and Joint Ventures

Storke's profits from his sales and consignments to New England and New York were considerable. According to Professor Roberts, European goods destined for the North American retail trade yielded "as much as 500–600 per cent over prime cost, depending on exchange differentials . . . [they earned] proportionately less in the wholesale business."[55] Unlike his commission business, however, many of Storke's consignments required entrustment, especially because some consignments were unsolicited.[56] The consignee, in turn, either expressly or tacitly promised to use his

---

[46] *Id.*

[47] *Id.* at 149–50.

[48] *Id.* at 154.

[49] *Id.* at 155.

[50] *Id.* at 154.

[51] *Id.*

[52] *See infra* § 22:4(C) (for a discussion of the availability of commercial and consumer credit in eighteenth century England).

[53] Roberts, *supra* note 43, at 155.

[54] *Id.* at 155 n.31 and accompanying text.

[55] *Id.* at 155 n.32 and accompanying text.

[56] *Id.* at 148: "Most of the credit Storke extended in the colonial trade resulted . . . from Storke's own initiative in sending consignments to his colonial correspondents."

best efforts in selling the consigned goods. Nevertheless, in some instances, Storke instructed his consignee to sell only for a fixed price.[57]

The central role of executory promises was apparent in Storke's colonial correspondence and records of transactions. They contain numerous references to consignments in which he had made goods available "on account" often by advancing part of the purchase price to his consignees.[58] In fact, in many instances, Storke seemed willing to entrust his consignees or joint venturers with the proceeds of the sale of consigned goods to be used as investments in joint ventures or partnerships with his colonial counterparts. According to Professor Roberts, "Storke seldom ordered the proceeds of his consignments to be returned to him in London. He generally used them for long range investments or speculation [in his colonial businesses]."[59]

Significant entrustment also took place in his many joint ventures to build, outfit and ship trans-Atlantic cargo.[60] These joint ventures often resulted in intricate webs of cooperation between the English and the colonial tradesmen. By relying on the latter's international trade connections, English traders gained access to certain markets dominated by their European competitors. Conversely, some highly popular items in colonial markets that were shipped out of Hamburg or Amsterdam could be obtained in those ports more quickly and cheaply through Storke's contacts.[61] And as joint ventures proliferated, a closer cooperation developed between the English and the colonials by a cross participation in their respective decision making processes. As described by Professor Roberts:

> Storke's relationships with his colonial correspondents exhibit a high order of cooperation and interaction in matters of entrepreneurial initiative, credit, and investment. . . . [62]
>
> Most of the credit Storke extended in the colonial trade resulted not from an inescapable tendency of American merchants to fall behind in paying for English manufactured goods, but from Storke's own initiative in sending consignments to his colonial correspondents.[63]

3. *Some Byproducts of the English Colonial Trade: Fixed Prices and Uniform Weights and Measures*

The highly cooperative and entrusting method of doing business between Samuel Storke and many of his North American consignees, commission agents and joint venturers was certainly facilitated by the quasi-familiar nature of their relationships. Two byproducts of this quasi-familiar trade were: First, the fixed prices of some of the most desirable goods or products as often requested by English consignors.[64] English tradesmen could trust their colonial counterparts to keep the prices of their consigned

---

[57] *Id.* at 157 n.38 and accompanying text: "Storke apparently had ordered that the cloth not be sold for less, and two years later consignment was still unsold."

[58] *See, e.g., id.* at 155 n.32 (on the half a dozen or so price advances on European goods in the colonial market).

[59] *Id.* at 157.

[60] *Id.*

[61] *Id.* at 153.

[62] *Id.* at 170.

[63] *Id.* at 148.

[64] *Id.* at 157 (for an instance of a fixed price directive).

goods—especially those that were in high demand in the colonies—at the level the consignors requested and this made their profitability more predictable. It should also be kept in mind that a market in which consignors and consignees or buyers and sellers are located at long distances from each other (and one in which mail delivery is often tardy) does not lend itself to haggling, which, as many of us have experienced, is usually a face-to-face endeavor.

Markets whose prices were fixed did away with the need for "poetic licenses" and with the haggling described by Daniel Defoe as typical of the early-eighteenth-century English trade.[65] Indeed, the anonymous annotator of the 1726 edition of *The Complete English Tradesman* added in a footnote to Defoe's description of the haggling practices of his time: "The practice of haggling about prices is now very properly abandoned by all respectable dealers in goods, greatly to the comfort of both sellers and buyers."[66] Last, but not least, fixed prices added honesty, fairness and reliability to seller or consignors' price quotations, for they enabled wholesalers to defend themselves against the accusation of price-discrimination or of unequal and uncompetitive pricing.

The second beneficial byproduct of the colonial trade was the standardization of weights and measures throughout the British Empire. In an 1821 Report to the United States Congress, President John Quincy Adams referred to the importance of weights and measures as follows:

> Weights and measures may be ranked among the necessaries of life to every individual of human society. They enter into the economical arrangements and daily concerns of every family. They are necessary to every occupation of human industry; to the distribution and security of every species of property; to every transaction of trade and commerce. . . .[67]

By the eighteenth century, England had achieved a greater degree of standardization of its weights and measures than all its European competitors. The National Aeronautics and Space Administration (NASA), whose calculations depend upon the accuracy of units of weights and measures, eulogized the English units as:

> [W]ell suited to commerce and trade because they had been developed and refined to meet commercial needs. Through English colonization and its dominance of world commerce during the 17th, 18th, and 19th centuries, the English system of measurement units became established in many parts of the world, including the American colonies.[68]

4. *England's Consumer and Comparatively High Wage Society*

Some economic historians attribute England's eighteenth century emergence as a leading trading and manufacturing nation to its powerful consumer society. As the first editor of England's *Annals of Commerce* wrote at the beginning of the nineteenth century: "The home trade is with good reason believed to be a vast deal greater in value

---

[65] *See supra* §§ 20:2 (A)(1 & 2).

[66] DEFOE, ENGLISH TRADESMAN, *supra* note 5, at 187 n.26.

[67] *See* NASA, A Brief History of Measurement Systems, https://standards.nasa.gov/history_metric.pdf.

[68] *Id.*

[and importance] than the whole of the foreign trade, the people of Great Britain being the best customers to the manufacturers and traders of Great Britain."[69]

Consumerism, however, was not thought a complete blessing. As described in 1750 by novelist Henry Fielding in his *Enquiry into the Causes of the Late Increase of Robbers*:

> Nothing has wrought such an alteration in this order of people, as the introduction of trade. This hath indeed given a new face to the whole nation, hath in great measure subverted the former state of affairs, and hath almost totally changed the manners, customs, and habits of the people, more especially of the lower sort. The narrowness of their future is changed into wealth; their frugality into luxury, their humility into pride, and their subjection into equality.[70]

It would not be very long before England enjoyed the highest wage income and standard of living in Europe.[71] As will be discussed in Chapter 21, at the same time English employers were paying the highest wages, English lenders increased their supply of commercial and consumer credit.[72] Thus, as of the middle of the eighteenth century, commercial credit was a significant factor in the sharp rise of England's home trade and the connection between a consumer society's willingness to spend and a commercial (and subsequently industrial) society's higher wages was apparent. Less apparent, but equally significant, was the role of slavery in the rise of a consumer society and in the commercialization of that society.

F. Slavery and England's Welfare

1. Introduction

Britain's experience with slavery during the seminal years of its commercialization and attainment of a world-leading standard of living deserves attention, especially by readers interested in learning about the effects of depriving a sizeable number of highly productive market participants from equal treatment both as producers of goods and services and as human beings.

I will rely on excerpts from studies by Professors Robin Blackburn of Essex University and Simon Schama of Columbia University to evaluate statistical information on the contribution of slavery to Britain's welfare and to obtain a vivid picture of the attitudes of slave owners and of the inhumane condition of plantation slaves. I will also discuss the background and text of a landmark decision by Lord Mansfield on the ownership rights of foreign owners of slaves who resided in England when the decision as rendered. I am indebted to Edmund Heward's biography of Lord Mansfield for the background of this discussion.

[69] *See* NEAL MCKENDRICK ET AL., THE BIRTH OF A CONSUMER SOCIETY 24 (1983) (citation omitted).

[70] *Id.* at 58 (citation omitted).

[71] *See* Robert C. Allen, *The Great Divergence in European Wages and Prices from the Middle Ages to the First World War*, 38 EXPLORATIONS ECON. HIST. 411–14, 433 (2001). *See also* Robert C. Allen, The High Wage Economy in Pre-industrial Britain 8–10 (2006), http://www.helsinki.fi/iehc2006/papers2/Allen77.pdf.

[72] *See infra* § 20:2(F)(2).

2. *Professor Blackburn's Assessment of the Contribution of Slavery to Britain's Welfare*

In a recent BBC presentation, Professor Blackburn summarized his findings on the contribution of slave-based trade with the Americas to the fast-industrializing economy of eighteenth-century Britain.[73] One of his findings was that:

> Slave-owning planters, and merchants who dealt in slaves and slave produce, were among the richest people in 18th-century Britain. . . .
>
> Liverpool merchant bankers, heavily involved in the slave-based trades, extended vital credit to the early cotton manufacturers of its Lancashire hinterland.[74]

Some of these planters contributed to Britain's economy by building highly expensive homes, investing in canals and "of course, many spent their ill-gotten gains on gambling, prize fights and riotous living."[75] According to Professor Blackburn, plantation slavery thrived thanks to the consumer revolution discussed in the preceding section. When Britain and the Netherlands widened their consumer markets in the seventeenth century, "farmers and manufacturers hired wage workers as the best way to expand output and sales. The fact that farmers had to pay rent, and that labourers needed a job if they were to feed their families, was the germ of a new economic system—what we now call capitalism."[76]

As also described in earlier sections, the slave plantation colonies of the Americas supplied highly desirable commodities to England and also to the nations with whom the likes of Samuel Storke traded regularly. In addition, and as also just discussed, the vitality of the trans-Atlantic trade, "including slaving, allowed merchants and bankers to supply credit."[77] This was particularly helpful to some manufacturers such as the early cotton millers, whose mill might have cost them, say, £1,000, but whose payment of wages may have required ten times that amount and whose sales revenues from the colonies might not have been available for a year or more. "[T]his is where the merchants' credit came in."[78]

Consequently, Blackburn estimates that profits created by the low cost of slave labor could have generated enough profits to cover a third of Britain's overall investment needs.[79] He refers to a study on the investments of 23 London merchants heavily involved in the slave trade which shows these merchants alone " 'played their part in building roads and bridges . . . [and] in (other) maritime undertakings, especially whaling. . . .' "[80] His conclusion, then, was that: "Enslaved people on the plantations of the Americas made a large contribution to British prosperity."[81]

---

[73] *See* Robin Blackburn, *Enslavement and Industrialisation*, BBC.CO.UK, http://www.bbc.co.uk/history/british/abolition/industrialisation_article_01.shtml.

[74] *Id.*

[75] *Id.*

[76] *Id.*

[77] *Id.*

[78] *Id.*

[79] *Id.* (on "Profit margins").

[80] *Id.* (citation omitted).

[81] *Id.*

3. Professor Schama on the Inhuman Condition of Sugar Plantation Slaves

In Volume II of his monumental *A History of Britain*, Professor Schama notes that despite the expectation of eighteen-century English statesmen and policy makers to have their rising colonial empire populated by tradesmen and farmers, it was overwhelmingly populated by soldiers and slaves.[82] He then asked the question: How did Britain end up with the wrong empire? His response was vintage Schama:

> From the beginning the British Empire was habit-forming. The general encouragement of addiction was its specialty: a quiet smoke, a nice cup of tea, a sweet tooth (and, a bit later, a pipe of opium)—exotic rarities converted into consumer cravings, exceptional wants turned into daily needs. Where profit beckoned, distaste could be overcome. King James I may have published tracts against the filthy weed *Nicotiana tabacum* . . . but the first settlement the Virginia Company established to grow it still bore his name. . . .[83]

Sugar was another story. In medieval Europe, "its high price and exotic origin meant that it was considered as either a spice or a drug."[84] But before it could be merchandized in large volumes it needed "highly concentrated, task-specific applications of manpower."[85] And here, he gave us a painfully vivid account of what it meant to work as a slave in a Caribbean sugar plantation:

> For the cane was an unforgiving and volatile crop. It could not be farmed and harvested in a single growing year. . . . But once it had reached maturity, the cumbersome grass needed to be harvested quickly to prevent the sugar going starchy. Once stripped and cut, the cane in its turn had to be speedily taken to the ox-powered vertical crushing rollers before the sucrose concentration of the juice self-degraded. Every subsequent stage of production—the boiling of the juice, the arrest of the boiling process at the precise moment for optimum crystallization, the partial refining in clay-stopped inverted cone moulds, the lengthy drying process—demanded the kind of strength, speed and stamina in tropical conditions that indentured white Europeans or captive Native Americans were ill equipped to provide. . . .
>
> So, where to turn for a labor supply that was strong, disease-resistant but obedient, like the cattle that turned the crushers? Where else, of course, but where the Portuguese were already making money from the commerce in ivory, gold and humans—West and Central Africa.[86]

---

[82] SIMON SCHAMA, II A HISTORY OF BRITAIN 405 (2001).

[83] *Id.*

[84] *Id.* at 410.

[85] *Id.*

[86] *Id.* at 410–11. While Professor Schama intends to highlight the horrible plight of African slaves, some readers may think that he is suggesting that only Africans and not Caucasians or Native Americans were suitable as slaves. I do not believe that this was his intent, but if it was I could not endorse these statements.

4. *The James Sommersett Case: A Landmark Lord Mansfield Decision on Slavery*

Chapter 13 of Edmund Heward's short biography of Lord Mansfield[87] supplies helpful background information for one of Lord Mansfield's most important decisions on slavery. Heward notes that "[t]he 18th century was the great age of the English slave merchant . . . [as centered in] London, Bristol and Liverpool. [Of these], Liverpool had only one slave ship in 1709 [but it had] . . . 100 [such ships in constant use] in 1770."[88] Further, [i]n 1768, the English [ships] carried more than half the 100,000 slaves shipped . . . [worldwide].[89] In the eyes of many well-bred Englishmen (quite likely including Lord Mansfield during most of his adult life) it was a respectable trade.[90] The following paragraphs summarize Heward's account of some of the cases that preceded and followed Lord Mansfield's landmark decision in *James Sommersett's Case.*

The "Quakers were the first to . . . [publicly ask] for the abolition of the slave trade but . . . [their] movement did not gain any strength until the end of the 18th century"[91] when other religious groups and incensed members of the population joined them in a movement for the abolition of slavery. One such a person was Granville Sharp, a young worker at the Tower of London who one day in 1765 after visiting his brother William's medical office, "stumbled over Jonathan Strong, a poor negro . . . [slave] waiting for treatment. . . . [who] (seemed ready to drop)."[92] Sharp took Strong to his brother's office and found out that he had been the property of a David Lisle, a lawyer from Barbados who in a fit of temper beat him with a pistol so badly that he could barely move and was nearly blind. After this beating, Lisle concluded that his slave was no longer valuable and left him to die in the streets.[93]

However, after intense medical care, Strong was able to do menial work as an errand boy for an apothecary. He remained in that job for two years when David Lisle accidentally found him and noticing that he could still do some useful work had him kidnapped and sold him to a James Kerr, a Jamaican planter who arranged for his shipment to the West Indies as his slave.[94] Granville Sharp procured a writ from the Lord Mayor of London that freed Strong only to be sued shortly thereafter by Kerr for depriving him of his property. Kerr's claim was accompanied by letter opinions from respected lawyers who cited King's Bench decisions that held that slaves from the West Indies who came or found themselves in England or Ireland either with or without their master were still his property.[95]

Granville Sharp took up the study of law and learned of an opinion by Blackstone in his *Commentaries on the Laws of England* which stated that: "The spirit of liberty is so deeply implanted in our constitution . . . that a slave or negro the very moment he

---

[87] *See* EDMUND HEWARD, LORD MANSFIELD 139–49 (1998) (Freeing the slaves 1772).

[88] *Id.* at 139.

[89] *Id.*

[90] *Id.*

[91] *Id.* at 140.

[92] *Id.* (citation omitted).

[93] *Id.*

[94] *Id.*

[95] *Id.* at 141.

lands in England falls under the protection of the laws and with regard to all natural rights become *eo instante a freeman*."[96] Relying on this opinion, Sharp hired Blackstone as Strong's attorney only to find out shortly thereafter that Blackstone had changed his mind and now believed that the prevailing rule was contrary to his earlier opinion.[97]

Sharp continued to collect opinions by judges and practitioners in favor of Strong's freedom. One of these opinions was by the highly respected Lord Chief Justice Holt (whom we will encounter shortly as an early architect of the English law of negotiable instruments), who stated "that as soon as a negro comes into England he becomes free."[98] Sharp circulated his research memorandum among "well known lawyers in London" and as more lawyers became acquainted with this memorandum, "[t]he lawyers for the plaintiffs Lisle and Kerr took fright and discontinued the action."[99]

By now, Sharp was a well-known and respected advocate for slaves' rights and as such was contacted by a Mrs. Bankes who reported that Thomas Lewis, a freed slave who lived in her house, was also kidnapped by his former owner a Mr. Stapylton who placed him on a vessel bound for Jamaica. Sharp brought criminal proceedings for assault against Stapylton and his accomplices. Stapylton's defense was that he was still Lewis's owner.[100]

At the request of Stapylton, the case was transferred to the King's Bench where, according to Edmond Heward, "Lord Mansfield was clearly anxious not to give a decision . . . which would have such far-reaching social consequences"[101] given the large number of former plantation slaves living in England and Ireland. Nonetheless, Mansfield was able to avoid the substantive law issue of Stapylton's ownership and ordered Thomas Lewis' freedom because Stapylton had failed to prove that he was Lewis's owner.[102]

The preceding judicial proceedings were a prelude to Lord Mansfield's determination of ownership rights over errant slaves in the *James Sommersett's case*.[103] Sommersett was a slave who had been brought to England by his American owner, Charles Stewart. While in England, Sommersett escaped and wasn't captured until two years later by Stewart, who placed him on a slave ship to be sold in Jamaica.

Stewart claimed that American law had granted him the ownership of Sommersett. In a separate court document and prior to rendering judgment, Mansfield urged the parties to agree on a settlement. He identified the case as not involving the validity of a sale of a slave, but the contents of a purported slave owner's property rights in England and under English law regardless of the law in America. He acknowledged the consequences of not recognizing Stewart's right of ownership under American law in his court: No less than 14,000 slaves resided in England with a legal status as uncertain as Sommersett's. Nonetheless, since the parties had not settled, his

---

[96] *Id.* at 142.

[97] *Id.*

[98] *See* Smith v. Brown and Cooper, 91 E.R. 566 [K.B. 1705] (2 Salkeld 666). *See also* HEWARD, *supra* note 87, at 145 (as cited by Francis Hargrave a lawyer for the abolitionists in the James Sommersett's case).

[99] HEWARD, *supra* note 87, at 142.

[100] *Id.* at 143.

[101] *Id.*

[102] *Id.*

[103] James Sommersett v. Stewart 20 State Trials 1 [K.B. 1772], *cited in id.* at 143 n.9.

obligation was to do justice regardless of the consequences of his decision. In his words: "*fiat justitia, ruat coelum*"[104] (justice be done, though the heavens fall). He then held that:

> [T]he return [defendant's answer] states, that the slave departed and refused to serve; whereupon he was kept, to be sold abroad. [Nevertheless] [s]o high an act of *dominium* must be recognised by the law of the country where it is used. The power of a master over his slaves has been extremely different in different countries. The state of slavery is of such a nature, that it is incapable of being introduced on any reasons, moral or political, but only by positive law. . . . It is so odious, that nothing can be suffered to support it, but positive law. Whatever inconvenience, therefore, may [be said to] follow from this decision I cannot say that this case is allowed or approved by the law of England; and, therefore, the black must be discharged.[105]

As concluded by Heward, this decision did not spell the end of slavery, but was "a very important landmark in the road to its abolition."[106] Because of it, 14,000 to 15,000 slaves were in fact freed.[107] Heward also pointed out that despite Mansfield's 1772 decision, blacks were still hunted and kidnapped on the streets of London, Liverpool and Bristol more than a decade later.[108] In fact, in another case that reached the King's Bench in 1783, it appeared that 133 slaves were thrown overboard by the master of the vessel and some of his crew following the calculation that if the slaves died a natural death during what was apparently a rough voyage, the loss would be sustained by their owners. But if they were thrown overboard, supposedly to save the ship from the perils of the sea, the loss would fall on the insurers (underwriters) of the slaves.[109]

5. Conclusions

There is no question that slavery was a crucial part of Britain's commercial emergence. Yet, both Britain and the United States attained their highest levels of economic development following the abolition of slavery and as their societies and marketplaces increasingly treated their citizens, residents and visitors as equal before the law. This is why Mansfield's final rejection of slavery as odious and wanting justification in religion, morality and decency and finding its justification only in positive law was very significant. Because, as you will find in Chapters 22 and 23, he often did not hesitate to treat unjust or inequitable laws inferior to "natural justice." Yet, the fact that even such a natural justice jurist found the slave trade tolerable during a significant part of his judicial career reflected a moral blindness that prevented him from applying to the master-slave relationship the same standards of natural justice he applied to disputes between ordinary merchants.[110]

This moral blindness posed fundamental issues concerning the sustainability of a commercial marketplace whose welfare depended in significant measure on the

---

104 *Id.* at 146 (emphasis added).

105 *Id.*

106 *Id.* at 147.

107 *Id.*

108 *Id.* at 147 (citing F.O. SHYLLON, BLACK SLAVES IN BRITAIN 174 (1974)).

109 *Id.* at 147–48 (citing F.O. SHYLLON, at 184).

110 For one of these standards, *see infra* § 22:7(B).

productivity of slavery. How long could such an inhumane, life-destroying policy last? Unfortunately, as apparent in the present and following chapters, it could last for an inhumanely long time. As stated to me by a Cuban descendant of Caribbean slaves, "No evil can last a hundred years, nor is there a being that can withstand it" (*"No hay mal que dure cien anos, ni cuerpo que lo resista"*). On the other hand, as just stated, evidence abounds on the benefits of inclusiveness and equal treatment in commercial marketplaces and beyond. We witnessed the effects of an equal treatment policy in those medieval fairs that adopted the principle of "Peace of the Marketplace."[111] We witnessed the even more dramatic effects of the General Agreement on Tariffs and Trade (GATT) policy of equal treatment of goods and services in helping war-ravaged segments of humanity gain unprecedented standards of living.[112] On the other hand, Chapter 24 will demonstrate how highly skilled Roman jurists were not able to come up with a viable "nuclear" secured transaction for centuries because of the unequal treatment of slaves and small farmers especially in foreclosure and repossession proceedings. I will re-visit these issues at the conclusion of Part II of this chapter.

G. Judicial Institutions

1. *Common Law Courts*

According to the English legal historian Theodore Plucknett, by the reign of Edward I (1239–1307), the institutional elements of England's judiciary were in place, except for a court of equity.[113] The main common law courts were: (1) the Court of Common Pleas, where the bulk of significant litigation was decided and where many of the most used forms of action (about which more later) were developed;[114] (2) "[T]he King's Bench which had a jurisdiction in error [appeal] from the Common Pleas, and [with] an original jurisdiction over the pleas of the Crown";[115] (3) "Above the King's Bench . . . was the King's Council, ready to supply from the reserves of royal discretion at its command any defects of jurisdiction which might occur in the lower courts. . . ."[116]; (4) The Court of Exchequer Pleas, or Court of the Exchequer, which was part of the King's Council. It dealt with equitable disputes that involved an unjust or wrongful application of the common law as was alleged, for example, had been done by the King's Bench in *Slade's Case* (about which more later).[117]

As will be apparent in our forthcoming discussion of *Slade's Case*,[118] the above courts had their own rules of pleading, procedure and occasionally, their own substantive law. Still, the core of the administration of justice in England was in the hands of a small and tightly knit group of judges and lawyers. Thus, in 1783, when Lord Mansfield decided the *James Sommersett Case*, "there were twelve Common Law Judges—on the King's Bench, Common Pleas and [Court of] Exchequer. . . . [and the number of practitioners before these courts was equally small, and included] 12

---

111 *See supra* ch. 6.

112 *See* § 5:1 (on the principle of the peace of the marketplace); *see also* Kozolchyk, *Grand and Small Scheme*.

113 PLUCKNETT, *infra* note 122 at 155.

114 *Id.*

115 *Id.*

116 *Id.*

117 *See infra* § 20:3.

118 *Id.*

Serjeants and 17 King's Counsels; [all in all] there were less than 350 men at the Bar."[119]

As noted by Professor Lawrence Friedman of the Stanford University Law School in his by now classic *History of American Law*,[120] the royal central courts handled the legal problems of a tiny group of people:

> Leaf through the pages of Lord Coke's reports compiled in the late 16th and early 17th century; here one will find a colorful set of litigants, all drawn from the very top of British society—lords and ladies, landed gentry, high ranking clergymen, wealthy merchants. Common law was an aristocratic law, for and of the gentry and nobility. The masses were hardly touched by this system and only indirectly under its rule.[121]

The guild-like atmosphere of these courts resulted in more uniform pleadings and methods of proof, but also in an excessive reliance on technicalities especially when interpreting contracts. These technicalities also made it easier to reach unfair and occasional corrupt results by blaming the unjust holdings on the rigidities of trial and appellate practice.

On the other hand, the English judiciary was one of the first in the modern world to attain a full measure of independence. The Act of Settlement of 1701[122] consolidated the independence and law making power of England's judiciary. Judges were entitled to "hold [their] office[s] during good behaviour at fixed salaries, and . . . should only be removable by His Majesty upon an address to both Houses of Parliament."[123] You will find indications of this independence when we discuss in a later section how the King's Bench Court created a new form of action on *assumpsit* to avoid the anachronistic features of the actions of debt and covenant in *Slade's Case*. You will also find strong indicators of independence and of competing jurisdictional powers in the forthcoming discussion of the *Earl of Oxford Case*.

The English courts' independence and their struggle for increased jurisdictional powers explains the fact that until the consolidation of the Constitutional Monarchy in the nineteenth century,[124] high courts found themselves frequently acting as umpires

---

119 *See* Bernard L. Shientag, *Lord Mansfield Revisited-A Modern Assessment*, 10 FORDHAM L. REV. 345, 346 (1941) (citation omitted).

120 *See* LAWRENCE M. FRIEDMAN, HISTORY OF AMERICAN LAW (2d ed., rev. 1985).

121 *Id.* at 25.

122 *See* The Official Website of the British Monarchy, The Act of Settlement (for a description of the purpose of this Act, enacted in 1701): "to secure the Protestant succession to the throne, and to strengthen the guarantees for ensuring parliamentary system of government [including an independent judiciary]," http://www.royal.gov.uk/historyofthemonarchy/kingsandqueensoftheunitedkingdom/thestuarts/maryi iwilliamiiiandtheactofsettlement/theactofsettlement.aspx%. Thus, in Plucknett's words: "the complete independence of the [judiciary] bench was therefore permanently established." *See* THEODORE F.T. PLUCKNETT, A CONCISE HISTORY OF THE COMMON LAW 61 (1956).

123 PLUCKNETT at 61.

124 In England's constitutional monarchy, day-to-day power is exercised by Ministers of the Cabinet, and by Parliament. The Official Website of the British Monarchy defers to a description by Walter Bagehot (1826–77):

> One of the most important writers on the subject of constitutional monarchy. . . .
>
> 'The nation is divided into parties, but the crown is of no party. Its apparent separation from business is that which removes it both from enmities and from desecration, which preserves its mystery, which enables it to combine the affection of conflicting parties. . . .'
>
> [T]he Sovereign had three rights: 'the right to be consulted, the right to encourage, the right to warn'.

in disputes between the Crown and the Parliament. In one of these occasions, Lord Chief Justice Coke (one of the advocates in the 1602 *Slade's Case*) famously reminded King James I (1566–1625) of Bracton's (England's most renowned medieval lawyer) admonition: "The King is subject not to men but to God and the Law."[125] But what was that law and where was it found? According to Theodore Plucknett, this was a "fundamental" law which limited both the Crown and Parliament and:

> The nearest we find to an explicit definition of this fundamental law is the assertion of the paramount law of 'reason'. For the rest, the common lawyer's 'reason' is left in as much uncertainty as he [Coke] himself ascribed to the Chancellor's equity. . . . [Still] [h]is doctrine is certainly based largely upon mediaeval precedents. . . .[126]

Whatever Coke meant by the law of reason, it was clear that his doctrine favored the supremacy of the common law over other sources of law.

2. *Equity and Common Law Courts: The Earl of Oxford Case*

The English judicial version of equity served largely to prevent or suspend the application of common law rules that led to unjust results. For a considerable time, the King was the first provider of equity because, in the words of William Blackstone, he was the "fountain of justice."[127] In this respect, he resembled the Roman emperors and their "rescripts" or replies to requests by their subjects for corrective actions to injustices attributable to the trial judges (*iudices*), especially in land disputes (as will be discussed in Chapter 23).[128] Unlike the Roman emperors, the English king relied on his Chancellor (a member of the King's Council) to correct the injustices perpetrated by the common law courts. As of the fifteenth century, this function was lodged with the Court of Chancery.[129]

The enforcement of land use rights was one of the Court of Chancery's most important subjects. *The Earl of Oxford's Case in Chancery*,[130] a landmark decision by this court illustrates its power to undo what it perceived as an injustice by the King's Bench. The dispute before these two courts involved the sale of valuable London real property by the master of the Magdalen College of Cambridge to Queen Elizabeth in 1574. This sale was followed by Queen Elizabeth's transfer of the same property to a Benedit Spinola in payment of a debt that Magdalen College owed him. Thus, the reason behind Magdalen College's sale to the queen was to circumvent a statutory

---

See THE OFFICIAL WEBSITE OF THE MONARCHY, HISTORY AND BACKGROUND, http://www.royal.gov.uk/MonarchUK/HowtheMonarchyworks/History%20and%20background.aspx.

[125] PLUCKNETT, *supra* note 122, at 49 (citation omitted).

[126] *Id.* at 51.

[127] *See* William Blackstone, *Commentaries on the Laws of England: A Facsimile of the First Edition of 1765—1769*, 3 The Founders' Constitution 60 (1979), http://press-pubs.uchicago.edu/founders/documents/a1_8_9s1.html.

[128] *See infra* § 24:3(B)(2).

[129] As pointed out by the Encyclopedia Britannica, as a court of equity under the lord high chancellor it began to develop in the 15th century. In our day, it "comprises the Chancery Division of the High Court of Justice. [Although courts of equity have by now been absorbed by common law courts], [c]ourts of chancery or equity are still maintained as separate jurisdictions in certain areas of the commonwealth and in some states of the United States." *See* Encyclopaedia Britannica Online, *Court of Chancery* (2013), http://www.britannica.com/EBchecked/topic/105336/Court-of-Chancery.

[130] The Earl of Oxford's Case in Chancery 21 E.R. 485 (1615).

prohibition of sales and long-term leases of college properties by masters and fellows of the colleges.[131]

In 1580, following Queen Elizabeth's transfer to Spinola, he sold the subject property to the Earl of Oxford, who spent considerable sums in developing and increasing the market value of this property. However, once the master of Magdalene College became aware of the significant increase in the value of the property conveyed to the Queen and reconveyed to Spinola and the Earl of Oxford, he attempted to regain it from the latter by alleging that the Earl of Oxford's acquisition violated the statutory prohibition against transfers of college property.

As noted by Professor Gary Watt of the University of Warwick School of Law,[132] who refers to this case as "the foundation stone of Equity in modern English law," the Master's attempt to regain the property triggered a battle between the common law courts, led by Lord Chief Justice Coke, and the Chancery Court, led by Lord Chancellor Ellesmere. "Coke was committed to upholding the wording of the statute [that forbad the sale of college property] and to denying exceptions based upon a Royal prerogative. [And] Ellesmere was committed to ensuring that the College did not take unconscionable advantage of the strict letter of the law by denying [the Earl of] Oxford's right to proper compensation for the loss of [his title] . . . [as] he was [also] committed to upholding Royal prerogatives, not least because the Court of Chancery had itself developed from the ancient Royal prerogative of mercy."[133]

Among the precedents relied on by the Lord Chancellor was *Peterson v, Hickman*. This was a case where a husband leased his wife's property and the lessee, unaware of his voidable title, built up the property at great cost. When the husband died, his wife voided the lease, but was compelled by Equity to "yield a Recompence for the Building and Bettering of the Land."[134] Lord Ellesmere also relied on the Hebrew Bible:

> The Law of God speaks for the Plaintiff.
>
> By the Law of God, He that builds a House ought to dwell in it; and he that plants a Vineyard ought to gather the Grapes thereof; and it was a Curse upon the Wicked, that they should build Houses and not dwell in them, and plant Vineyards and not gather the Grapes thereof.[135]
>
> To which he added:
>
> And yet here in this Case, such is the Conscience of the Doctor, the Defendant, That he would have the Houses, Gardens and Orchards, which he neither built nor planted: But the Chancellors have always corrected such corrupt Consciences, and caused them to render *quid pro quo*; for the Common Law itself will admit no Contract to be good without *quid pro quo*, or Land to pass without a valuable Consideration, and therefore Equity must see that a proportionable Satisfaction be made in this Case.[136]

---

131 The Ecclesiastical Leases Act 1571, 13 Eliz. 1, c. 10.

132 Gary Watt, *Earl of Oxford's Case (1615), in* THE NEW OXFORD COMPANION TO LAW 351 (2008), *available at* http://www.griffith.edu.au/%y(2)6ddata/assets/pdf_file/0012/188688/early-intervention.pdf.

133 *Id.*

134 The Earl of Oxford's Case in Chancery 21 E.R. 485, 486.

135 *Id.* at 486.

136 *Id.*

In addition, Ellesmere invoked Cicero's maxim that *summum ius* (strict law) can easily turn into a *summa iniuria*, (the greatest injustice).[137] Thus, "The Cause why there is a Chancery is. . . . [t]hat it is impossible to make any general Law which may aptly meet with every particular Act, and not fail in some Circumstances"[138] And yet, law and equity "both aim at one and the same End, which is, to do Right; as Justice and Mercy. . . ."[139]

Professor Watt summarized the result of the dispute as follows:

> [T]he jurisdictional dispute . . . was referred to King James I. Keen to preserve his Royal prerogatives in the face of Coke's campaign against them, the King determined the matter in favour of the Court of Chancery and thereby established the rule which maintains equity's preeminent status to the present day: *where equity and law conflict, equity shall prevail*.[140]

The absorption of the equity jurisdictions by most common law courts in England, the United States and Commonwealth countries vindicated Ellesmere's view that law and equity could function best when each partook of the other's best features.

3. Equity and Commercial Contract Law

Lord Ellesmere's holding supports commercial legal institutions such as the protection of the good faith purchaser of real property. It also supports the recovery of quasi-contractual rights such as those born from the Earl of Oxford's contribution to the value of the property. In due course, equitable transactional and remedial practices came about that resulted in considerable assistance to commercial transactions and to the viability of their markets. Consider for example the contribution of equitable remedies such as "equitable estoppel" and "preclusion."[141] These remedies have made an invaluable contribution to the entire field of commercial contracts and especially to the smoother operation of instruments of payment and credit such as commercial and standby letters of credit and checks.

In Chapter 23, we will discuss how the equitable remedy of preclusion is being used countless times every day around the world to discourage the tardiness and sloppiness of banks when examining and returning letter of credit documents.[142] The

---

[137] *Id.*

[138] *Id.*

[139] *Id.*

[140] Watt, *supra* note 132, at 352.

[141] Professor Max Radin's defines equitable estoppel (also known as estoppel *"in pais"* in his dictionary) as:

> [W]hen any one by words, acts or abstentions, has induced someone to act as though a . . . relationship existed or had a certain character, this existence or character may not thereafter be legally denied. . . .

See MAX RADIN, RADIN LAW DICTIONARY 115 (Lawrence G. Greene ed., 1955). Civil law lawyers will recognize in this version of estoppel a Roman version of bad faith known as *"Venire contra Factum Proprium," discussed in infra* § 22:10(D).

The equitable remedy of preclusion is but a variety of estoppel *in pais* as just defined.

[142] *See, e.g.*, UCP 500 Sub Article 14(e):

> If the issuing bank . . . fails to act in accordance with the provisions of this Article and/or fails to hold the documents at the disposal of, or fails to return them to the presenter the . . . Bank . . . shall be precluded from claiming that the documents are not in compliance with the terms and conditions of the Credit.

same is true with the payor banks that hold checks without paying for them or returning them beyond their so called "midnight deadline."[143]

§ 20.3 FORMS OF ACTION AND WRITS

The English forms of action were lineal descendants of the Roman formulary procedure.[144] No less a common lawyer than Bracton was amenable to an indefinite expansion of the common law using the Roman law as a model. He counseled that there should be "as many forms of action as there are causes of action. [And that] [t]here ought to be a remedy for every wrong."[145]

Recall that during the Roman formulary procedure Praetors drafted formulas instructing the *iudex* on the elements of a valid action and on the admissible defenses or exceptions to that action.[146] Often the names of these actions reflected the transactions in dispute, such as a pledgee or mortagee's (action on the pledge) *actio pignoraticia* or a seller's (action on the sale) *actio venditi*. In some instances, the actions were named after the Praetor willing to grant the remedy (*e.g.*, the *Actio Publiciana in rem* was named after the Praetor Publicius).[147]

The English forms of action were anonymous, less transparent and more rigid. They relied on labels as opaque as: "Debt," "Covenant," "*Assumpsit*," "Trespass on the Case," "Trover" and so on. As noted by the late Professor Max Radin of the University of California at the Berkeley and Hastings law schools: "For each action a separate writ had to be obtained, and the use of the wrong form of action meant the loss of the plaintiff's case, regardless of the justness of the claim. . . ."[148]

Assume, for example, that H, the lawful holder of a Bank of England promissory note, sent it by mail to C in satisfaction of his debt, but the envelope was stolen by T. H instructed the Bank of England to stop payment on the note. However, T had endorsed the note for value to BFP (plaintiff), a *bona fide* purchaser of it. The Bank of England's clerk (the defendant) refused to pay BFP. In this form of action, the defendant argued that the plaintiff's action was for "trover"—a derivation from the French "*trouver*" ("to find and keep") something that belonged to the plaintiff—which did not entitle him to the relief he sought. In an action on trover, plaintiff was suing "not for the money due upon the note; but for the note itself, the paper, the evidence of the debt."[149]

It was this type of pleading that prompted Lord Mansfield's scolding that neither the negotiations nor the property rights of merchants should depend on subtleties and niceties such as just described, but upon "rules easily learned and easily retained because they are the dictates of common sense drawn from the truth of the case."[150] Recall that this formalistic rigor was in sharp contrast with the Praetor's flexibility and equitable powers. Indeed, as pointed out by Frederic William Maitland (1850–

---

143 *See* U.C.C. § 4–302 (a)(1).

144 *See* Glossary, "*praetor*."

145 PLUCKNETT, *supra* note 122, at 354 (citation omitted).

146 *See supra* § 4:2(A)(2).

147 *See* BERGER, DICTIONARY, at 344.

148 *See* RADIN, *supra* note 141, at 135 (Forms of Action).

149 *See* Miller v. Race 97 E.R. 398, 400 [1758].

150 *See* Hamilton v. Mendes 2 BURR. 1198, 1214 [1761].

1906), widely regarded as the modern father of English legal history, despite their Roman inspiration, the forms of action are distinctively English:

> [B]ut . . . [they are] also, in a certain sense, very Roman. While other nations of Western Europe were beginning to adopt as their own the ultimate results of Roman legal history, England was unconsciously reproducing that history; it was developing a formulary system which in the ages that were coming would be the strongest bulwark against Romanism and sever our English law from all her sisters.[151]

I interpret Maitland's reference to Romanism as the version of Roman law found in a medieval continental civil law heavily influenced by scholastic and abstract definitions, classifications and canonic law maxims such as "*pacta sunt servanda.*" As noted earlier in this book, this was not the practical, factual and problem-oriented Roman law that was often found in the Praetorian formulas.

On the other hand, the early English Writs were *sui generis*. They were not documents "directly instituting litigation."[152] They resembled administrative commands "to an alleged wrongdoer or to some inferior jurisdiction to do justice in a particular manner in such wise that the King shall no more hear complaints concerning it."[153] The justice requested was mostly in the form of restitution. However, by the end of the twelfth century, a new form of writ resembling Praetorian formulas began to be used and it was the one apparent in the seventeenth-and eighteenth-century pleadings that we discuss in the present and subsequent chapters:

> [It] begins with the summons, and the defendant is called on to explain his action. . . . If the old model emphasises the failure to do what is due, the new one rests on a positive misdeed. The misdeed, moreover, is frequently described in the writ as being a breach of peace.[154]

Still, the forms of action used during the seventeenth and eighteenth centuries were capable of producing rules that could govern future cases only when in the hands of great judges. Among these were: Popham, J. in *Slade's Case*,[155] Chief Justice Holt's in *Hussey v. Jacob*,[156] and Lord Mansfield's decisions in *Pillans and Van Mierop v. Rose*,[157] *Miller v. Race*,[158] *and Price v. Neal*.[159]

The extraordinary quality of these decisions stands in sharp contrast with many other decisions by common law courts that were so technical and fact-specific that they could only occasionally be used as precedents or as guides to the enforceability of transactions. The casuistry was such that Jeremy Bentham (1748–1832) criticized this after-the-fact method of law making as "dog law": "When your dog does anything you

---

[151] PLUCKNETT, *supra* note 122 (citing FREDERICK POLLOCK & FREDERIC MAITLAND, 2 THE HISTORY OF ENGLISH LAW BEFORE THE TIME OF EDWARD I, 558 (1898)).

[152] *Id.* at 355.

[153] *Id.*

[154] *Id.* at 366.

[155] Slade v. Morley, 76 Eng. Rep. 1074 [K.B. 1602].

[156] Hussey v. Jacob, 91 E.R. 301 [1696].

[157] Pillans and Rose v Van Mierop and Hopkins, 97 E.R. 1035 [1765].

[158] Miller v. Race, 97 E.R. 398 [1758].

[159] Price v. Neal, 97 E.R. 871 [K.B. 1762].

want to break him of you wait till he does it, and them [sic] beat him for it . . . this is the way judges make law for you and me."[160]

Plucknett reminds us how Jeremy Bentham, whom he refers to as "the prophet" of the new era of liberalism, legal reform and the passionate advocate of legislation and codification, was disappointed as a student at Oxford with William Blackstone's lectures on the common law while "he . . . listened with admiration to the judgments of Lord Mansfield."[161]

§ 20.4 LORD MANSFIELD, JURIES AND MERCHANTS

A. Lord Mansfield

Sir Francis Buller's (a colleague of Lord Mansfield at the King's Bench Court) assessment of Mansfield's accomplishments has withstood the test of time:

> Within the last thirty years the commercial law of this country has taken a very different turn from what it did before. . . . And I should be very sorry to find myself under a necessity of differing from any case on this subject which has been decided by Lord Mansfield, who may be truly said to be the founder of commercial law of this country.[162]

As you will discover when reading Chapter 21, Mansfield's views also influenced the development of United States commercial law. Professor Karl LLewellyn's and U.C.C Article 2's reliance on usage of trade when interpreting commercial contracts, as well as on good faith when judging the manner in which commercial contracts are performed, reflect Mansfield's views. The same can be said about Mansfield's preference for a liberal interpretation of commercial contracts and for the need for the courts' collaboration with merchants when shaping a market-sensitive commercial law. For Mansfield knew that "[B]usiness men have a passion for adding clauses and have no time or inclination to consider the effect of their additions on the contract."[163] Hence, as concluded by C.H.S. Fifoot (another of Mansfield's twentieth-century biographers):

> He realised that the merchant was more competent than the lawyer to prescribe the form of a charter party or to direct the incidence of paper credit. [Hence] [t]he function of the judge was not to dictate, but to interpret and sanction.[164]

This approach to commercial law decision-making separated Mansfield from many other common law judges. It is easy to see why Bentham admired him: With his knowledge of commercial facts, Mansfield could draft rules and principles capable of guiding the parties *ex ante, i.e.*, prior to entering into troublesome transactions. He was also in a position to discern who were third parties acting in good faith and thus

---

[160] *See* Jeremy Bentham, *Truth vs. Ashurst*, *cited in* JEREMY BENTHAM 3 CRITICAL ASSESSMENTS 248 n.11 (Bhikhu C. Parekh ed.,1993), *available at* http://books.google.com/books?id=iOOm8F5_sBcC&pg=PA248&lpg=PA248&dq=jeremy+bentham+dog+law.

[161] PLUCKNETT, *supra* note 122, at 73.

[162] HEWARD, *supra* note 87, at 104–05 (citing Justice Buller, *in* Lickbarrow and Another v. Mason and Others, 2 TERM REP. 63, 74 [1787]; 100 E.R. 35, 40).

[163] *Id.* at 103.

[164] *Id.* at 101 (citing C.H.S. FIFOOT, LORD MANSFIELD 118 (1936)).

deserving of protection. Therefore, the commercial law Mansfield made reflected standard as well as best practices.

Theodore Plucknett makes an important clarification for the civil law lawyer unfamiliar with the Anglo-American jury system. In its origin, the jury was a politically as well as a legally representative institution.[165] It represented the interests of the local community in the administration of justice and was often consulted as a "fact knowing" body.[166] Representativeness, however, is not necessarily consistent with objective fact knowing. Because as members of the community they were likely to be close to the transaction in dispute, the jury was prone to being biased in favor of one of the parties when extrapolating from the facts they thought they knew. Plucknett suggests that by 1468, a jury trial was for all intents and purposes in modern form, a fact-finding body:

> [A] body of impartial men who come into court with an open mind; [and] instead of finding the verdict out of their own knowledge of the events, the parties or their counsel in open court present their evidence to the jury, and witnesses were examined upon oath.[167]

A century later, trial records show not only an examination, but also the "cross-examination of witnesses in the presence of the judge, the parties, their counsel and the jury."[168]

Georgetown University Law School Professor James Oldham has published very helpful materials on Mansfield's juries obtained from Mansfield's trial notes.[169] First, he called attention to the distinction between "special" and "merchant" juries. He corrected the impression that the terms "merchant jury" and "special jury" were synonymous.[170] While many of the special juries impaneled in trials before Lord Mansfield were comprised of merchants, such a status was not a requirement.

The special jury was selected by attorneys for both sides after each side struck twelve names "from a list of forty-eight freeholders. Those remaining twenty-four"[171] persons would be the jurors who tried the case.[172] Accordingly, Mansfield's merchant juries were a species of the genus of special juries, *i.e.*, they became merchant juries after the pool of special jurors (including merchants) had been selected.

In any of these capacities he could ask them a question about a standard practice in a given sector In any of these capacities, he could ask them a question about a standard practice in a given sector or sectors such as, say, the acceptability of promissory notes issued by banks as a means of payment. Based on their responses, he

165 *See* PLUCKNETT, *supra* note 122, at 127–29. The representativeness of the jury, especially as a sign of race, ethnic and gender inclusiveness persists especially in the United States. *See, e.g.*, JEFFREY B. ABRAMSSON, WE, THE JURY: THE JURY SYSTEM AND THE IDEAL OF DEMOCRACY: WITH A NEW PREFACE 99–102 (1994) (Jury Selection and the Cross-Sectional Ideal): "In the United Sates Today, it is common to describe the ideal jury as a 'body truly representative of the community.' " *Id.* at 99.

166 PLUCKNETT, at 126.

167 *Id.* at 129–30.

168 *Id.* at 130.

169 *See generally* JAMES OLDHAM, ENGLISH COMMON LAW IN THE AGE OF MANSFIELD (2004) (introductory chapter).

170 OLDHAM, at 22.

171 *Id.*

172 *Id.* at 22–23.

could confidently state in *Miller v. Race* that bank notes are "constantly and universally, both at home and abroad, treated as money, as cash; and paid and received, as cash; and it is necessary, for the purposes of commerce, that their currency should be established and secured."[173] Or, the standard practice in question could be considerably narrower, such as, what is a reasonable time in the horse trade for returning horses with defects that were only latent at the time of purchase?[174]

The understanding of commercial practices that Mansfield gained from his merchant jurors and consultants transcended the findings of facts in a given case. As he learned more about the relevant practices, he was able to formulate principles that governed a broader spectrum of disputes in the sector in question. For example, from learning about the practices on horse sales, he derived the principle that: "A warranty extends to all faults known and unknown to the seller. Selling for a sound price without warranty may be a ground for an *assumpsit*, but, in such a case, it ought to be laid that the defendant knew of the unsoundness."[175] And it was from his knowledge of the practices on fact disclosures by insureds in insurance contracts that he formulated the governing principle of good faith disclosures in insurance contracts in general:

> The governing principle is applicable to all contracts and dealings.
>
> Good faith forbids either party by concealing what he privately knows, to draw the other into a bargain, from his ignorance of that fact, and his believing the contrary.[176]

He was also able to identify when a higher standard of good faith (*uberrima fides*) required certain disclosures prior to entering into insurance contracts. These disclosures often depended upon a party's actual or imputed knowledge of the relevance of his disclosure to the other party's decision to insure or to become an insured party.

B. Some Key English Contributions to the Substantive Law of Commercial Contracts and Promises

1. *Executory Promises and Commercial and Consumer Credit*

Chapter 22 discusses in detail the famous English *Slade's Case* (1602). Thus the present discussion is only introductory. In *Slade's Case*, the defendant made an unfulfilled executory promise to buy a crop of wheat and rye at a future time. This promise was enforced by the King's Bench even though the seller had not delivered the commodities to the promisor-buyer when he sued the buyer. As described by Professor David Harris Sacks of Reed College, this promise was executory because it promised the performance of "Acts or dispositions intended or capable of taking full effect only at

---

173 Miller v. Race, 97 E.R. 398, 459 [1758].

174 *See* § 23:4(D)(2)(a) (on Mansfield's horse warranty decisions).

175 *See* Stuart v. Wilkins, 99 E.R. 15 [1778] where Lord Mansfield agreed with plaintiff David Stuart that James Wilkins had offered to sell him a mare for a certain "large" price (£31, 10 s) that Stuart had paid him such a sum assuming that the mare was sound only to discover upon delivery that the mare "was unsound, and was afflicted with a certain malady . . . called the windgalls. . . ." *Id.*

176 *See* Carter v. Boehm, 97 E.R. 1162, 1164 [1766].

a future time; its opposite is 'executed,' or where the act or disposition has already occurred and the right or property has already been transferred."[177]

Under the medieval common law, claims seeking the payment of a debt required a writ of debt and proceedings before the Court of Common Pleas, where it could be decided on the basis of an archaic, one-sided and thus uncertain "wager of law." If the defendant decided to take a decissory oath in open court that he did not owe the alleged debt and this oath was supported by a group of his witnesses, he won the lawsuit. By comparison, the procedure before the King's Bench Court for claiming a breach of promise differed sharply. It was based on an action of *assumpsit* (at times referred to also as *indebitatus assumpsit*), which alleged that the defendant had been guilty of a tortious deceit by his failure to pay after promising to do so.

The final judgment in *Slade's Case* was delivered in 1602 by the Lord Chief Justice of the King's Bench, John Popham. It held that:

> [E]very contract executory imports in itself an *assumpsit*, for when one agrees to pay so much money, or to deliver any thing, thereby he assumes or promises to pay, or deliver it, and therefore when one sells any goods to another, and [the other] agrees to pay so much money on such a day, in that case both parties may have an action of debt, or an action on the case on *assumpsit*, for the mutual executory agreement of both parties import in itself reciprocal actions on the case, as well as actions of debt.[178]

By juxtaposing the buyer's and seller's executory promises on equal terms, *Slade's Case* held, then, that the seller's promise to deliver the wheat and rye by a certain date in exchange for the buyer's promise to pay for it was deceitfully breached when the buyer refused to pay the amount he promised to pay when he promised to pay it.

As illustrated by the executory promises of Samuel Storke's consignments and joint ventures, England's ability to grow and develop economically during the seventeenth and eighteenth centuries depended upon the countless numbers of future promises of commercial loans and of investments made by its tradesmen and bankers. You will find many other examples in Chapter 21 of the omnipresent executory promises in the plentiful commercial and consumer credit of the seventeenth and eighteenth centuries.

2. *Negotiability of Promissory Notes and Bills of Exchange*

Chapters 22 and 23 discuss English and United States substantive contract law extensively. However, little space is left in those chapters for a discussion on English negotiable instruments law. Given the importance of this law for English economic development, the remainder of this chapter will be devoted to it.

a. Assignability, Negotiability and Conditionality of Promises of Credit and Payment

Unconditional promises of credit and payment were among the most commonly used executory commercial promises used in seventeenth-and eighteenth-century

---

[177] David Harris Sacks, The Promise and the Contract in Early Modern England: Slade's Case in Perspective, in Rhetoric and Law in Early Modern Europe 47 n.25 and accompanying text (Victoria Ann Kahn & Lorna Lutson eds., 2001).

[178] *Id.* at 33 n.27 and accompanying text.

England. The enforcement of these promises did not depend on future acts or events such as the timely arrival of a vessel or the availability of crops. They were typically expressed in instruments that the English merchants had imported from the continent, especially from Italy, and which some judges and doctrinal writers referred to as commercial "specialties."[179] The two principal specialties were the "promissory note" (or just plain "note") and the "bill of exchange" (also known as "draft").[180] In the note, the maker promised to pay a sum of money at a designated time and place to the payee of the note or to his endorsee or bearer. In the bill of exchange, the drawer ordered the drawee to accept and pay at a future time or pay when the order was presented a specified amount to the designated payee or to his "order."[181]

In contrast with the promissory note, which was at its inception a two-party instrument (*i.e.*, a maker and a payee), the bill of exchange was from its inception a three-party instrument (drawer, drawee (acceptor-payor) and payee).[182] Usually, it presupposed the existence of an account that the drawer had with the drawee and, for centuries, this account was referred to in the "value clause" of bills of exchange. In this account relationship, the drawer had provided money, valuable property or reciprocal credit to the drawee with which he would pay for the draft or reimburse or credit himself after paying. But the draft could also be a two-party instrument at its inception: The drawer could designate himself as the drawee, in which case he would be the party accepting liability for future payment or for payment at sight to the payee, and this liability could be claimed also by his endorsees. Or he could designate himself as the payee, in which case he would still be the party ordering the drawee-acceptor to accept and pay him.

If the law of promissory notes and bills of exchange could eliminate or sharply reduce the maker's or drawer's defenses based on the absence of the above-mentioned conditions, these instruments would be much easier to collect than ordinary contractual (conditional) obligations. As unconditional promises, they could be treated by courts as "independent" or "abstract" promises of payment whose enforcement was insulated from defenses and equities rooted in the underlying transactions. Their easier collection enabled the payee and subsequent endorsees or holders to convert them into cash or valuable property quickly and inexpensively. This ability, which we refer to in our day as "liquidity," makes these instruments desirable to their payees and transferees, especially those who acquire their rights by endorsement (in the case of "pay to the order" instruments) or delivery (as in the case of "bearer" instruments).

A transfer of a promissory note or draft that complies with the requirements of the law of negotiable instruments upgrades the status of transferees from that of assignees to that of holders of independent rights of enforcement. Their legal status is superior to that of assignees because as assignees, they would be subject to the same defenses and equities as their transferor-assignors. In contrast, when transferees acquire their

---

[179] *See* BORIS KOZOLCHYK, COMMERCIAL LETTERS OF CREDIT IN THE AMERICAS 590–91 (1966) (for a discussion of the meaning of commercial specialties—as distinguished from contracts under seal, among other formal contracts).

[180] *See supra* § 11:2(D)(2) (on French commercial codification); *see* Kozolchyk, *Negotiable Instruments* 22–2, 22–11 (for a comparative analysis of the rights and duties of the parties to these instruments).

[181] Kozolchyk, *Negotiable Instruments.*

[182] *Id.*

rights by "negotiation," they become holders in due course or "holders for value" and thereby acquire remedial rights superior to those of their transferors.

b. *Independence of the Negotiable Promise: Hussey v. Jacob and the* Code Civil's Causa

The concept of negotiation in negotiable instruments law contradicts the Roman maxim "no one can transfer what he does not have" (*nemo dat quod non habet)* because, as just noted, the endorser or transferor of an "order" or "bearer" instrument conveys independent and thus more liquid rights than those of the original payees or their previous endorsers.

Hussey v. Jacob,[183] a 1696 decision by Chief Justice Holt of the King's Bench, illustrates the effects of negotiation as contrasted with a mere assignment of a right to payment of a bill of exchange (the names of the parties and some of the less relevant facts will be changed to facilitate an understanding of the impact of this decision). Winner, a gambler, won a certain amount of money when gambling with Loser. In payment of this debt, Loser drew a bill of exchange on himself (ordering himself to accept and eventually pay) the bill of exchange to Winner or to his order. Winner endorsed the bill to Stranger (a stranger to the gambling transaction). Stranger presented the bill for acceptance and payment to Loser. Loser accepted to pay at a future time. According to an anti-gambling statute in force at that time,[184] a gambling obligation was null and void. Nonetheless Stranger sued on *assumpsit* and won. C.J. Holt held:

> If such a note was given to the winner or order, and the winner indorsed it to a stranger for a just debt, and the person upon whom the bill was drawn accepts . . . [the bill] in the hands of the stranger, the acceptor would be liable.[185]

The law in France up until the twentieth century was different. Recall the description of this law in Chapter 11 by Henry Diedrich Jencken (1828–1881), the London barrister who authored a succinct, highly accurate comparison of English, French and German negotiable instruments law available during the early nineteenth century.[186] French law based the enforceability of the bill of exchange on the above-described highly conditional contract of purchase and sale of foreign exchange (*contrat de change*), which was always suspected of hiding a usurious loan.

As a *Code de Commerce* contract of exchange, once the bill of exchange was delivered to its payee, this contract was deemed executed and whatever rights were transferred to third parties were the result of an assignment (not a negotiation) of the rights that had been acquired by the original payee. Consequently, as an assignment (*Cession de la Creance*), the assignee's rights were subject to the terms and conditions

---

183 Hussey v. Jacob, 91 E.R. 301 [1696], *cited in* W.S. HOLDSWORTH 3 A HISTORY OF ENGLISH LAW 166 n.3 and accompanying text (1926).

184 *Id.* at 166 n.4 and accompanying text (on the statute of 16 Charles II, c.7).

185 *Id.* at 166 n.4.

186 *See* HENRY DIEDRICH JENCKEN, A COMPENDIUM OF THE LAWS ON BILLS OF EXCHANGE, PROMISSORY NOTES, CHECQUES, AND OTHER COMMERCIAL NEGOTIABLE INSTRUMENTS OF ENGLAND, GERMANY AND FRANCE (1880) [hereinafter JENCKEN, COMPENDIUM] (his classic monograph). *See also* § 11:2 (D)(2), (Henry Diedrich Jencken's Comparative Analysis of European Nineteenth Century Negotiable Instrument Laws).

of the underlying contract of exchange as well as to related defenses to such an illegal cause because of usury or other violation of the law or public morality.[187] Clearly, this characterization impeded the negotiability of the bill of exchange.

c. *The Questioned and Affirmed Negotiability of Promissory Notes*

Despite Chief Justice Holt's visionary support for the independence of the promise of payment of the bill of exchange in *Hussey v. Jacob*, in *Clerke v. Martin* (a 1702 decision by the King's Bench), he opposed the negotiability of the promissory note.[188] In this case, the plaintiff brought an action on various counts. One was upon *indebitatus assumpsit* (of *Slade's Case* fame) for money lent to the defendant; another was "upon the custom of merchants, as upon a bill of exchange. . . ."[189] It alleged that the defendant gave a promissory note signed by him to the plaintiff in which he promised to pay a certain amount of money to the plaintiff or his order. A verdict including damages was given for the plaintiff. The defendant moved to arrest judgment, alleging that this promissory note was not a bill of exchange within the customs of merchants, and therefore "the plaintiff, having declared upon it as such, was wrong; but that the proper way in such cases is to declare upon a general indebitatus *assumpsit* for money lent, and the note would be good evidence of it."[190] Chief Justice Holt agreed and cited *Horton v. Coggs*, which held that "such a note was not a bill of exchange within the customs of merchants."[191] A subsequent (1704) opinion by Chief Justice Holt described the promissory notes involved as:

> [O]nly an invention of the goldsmiths in Lombard Street, who had a mind to make a law to bind all those that did deal with them; and sure to allow such a note to carry any lien with it were to turn a piece of paper, which is in law but evidence of a parole contract, into a specialty: and besides, it would empower one to assign that to another which he could not have himself. . . ."[192]

Professor James Byrne of George Mason University School of Law, a world-renowned expert on the law of negotiable instruments and letters of credit, quotes Chief Justice Holt's subsequent recollection of a conversation he had with two prominent merchants concerning his *Clerke v. Martin* decision:

> [H]e [Holt] had desired to speak with two of the most famous merchants in London, to be informed of the mighty ill consequences that it was pretended would ensue by obstructing this course [of the negotiability of promissory notes]; and that they had told him, it was very frequent with them to make such *notes*, and that they had looked upon them as *bills of exchange*, and that they had been used for a matter of thirty years, and that not only *notes*, but

---

187 *Id.*

188 Clerke v. Martin, 92 E.R. 6 [1703]; 2 LD. Raym. 757, 758, *in* JAMES E. BYRNE, NEGOTIABILITY: THE DOCTRINE & ITS APPLICATION IN U.S. COMMERCIAL LAW 16–17 (14th ed. 2005). I will be restating segments of the transcript of this decision from this remarkably didactic textbook which I used in my commercial law classes for a half a decade.

189 BYRNE, NEGOTIABILITY at 16 (citing Clerke v. Martin, 92 E.R. 6).

190 *Id.*

191 *Id.* at 17.

192 *Id.* at 18 (citing Buller v. Crips 87 E.R. 793 [Q.B. 1704]; 6 MOD. REP. 29).

> *bonds* for money, were transferred frequently, and indorsed as *bills of exchange*.[193]

Holt asked his interlocutors why they would not want to achieve the same results they sought with their promissory notes by using lawful negotiable instruments such as bills of exchange drawn on themselves and naming their suppliers or lenders the payees of such bills. While he does not refer to their reply to his suggestion, the die was cast in favor of the negotiability of promissory notes. If you are interested in knowing why, please identify the users of promissory notes in the preamble and first "Whereas" of the 1704 Statute of Anne:[194]

> An Act for giving like Remedy upon Promissory Notes, as is now used upon Bills of Exchange, and for the better Payment of Inland Bills of Exchange.
>
> Whereas it hath been held, That Notes in Writing, signed by the Party who makes the same, whereby such Party promises to pay unto any other Person, or his Order, any Sum of Money therein mentioned, are not assignable or indorsible over, within the Custom of Merchants, to any other Person; and that such Person . . . cannot maintain an Action, by the Custom of Merchants, against the Person who first made and signed the same. . . .
>
> Therefore to the Intent to encourage Trade and Commerce, which will be much advanced, if such Notes shall have the same Effect as Inland Bills of Exchange, and shall be negotiated in like manner; be it enacted. . . .
>
> That all Notes in Writing . . . shall be made and signed by any Person or Persons, *Body Politick* or Corporate, or by the Servant or Agent of any Corporation, Banker, Goldsmith, Merchant, or Trader, who is usually entrusted by him, her, or them, to sign such Promissory Notes. . . .[195]

The reference to the Body Politick or Corporate in the above list reflects the significance that promissory notes and their liability format had attained by the turn of the eighteenth century in England: Clothed as government bonds, promissory notes had become important instruments with which to finance public expenditures. The date of the Statute of Anne is also significant. Notice in Chapter 11 the date when Judge Karl Einert persuaded German legislators to abandon the *Code de Commerce's* contract of exchange rationale for their bill of exchange legislation and adopt one that would truly make it and the promissory notes negotiable instruments. It was not until May of 1849 that Judge Einert's draft of a negotiable instruments law was adopted by most delegates to the National Assembly of the Confederate States of Germany.[196]

In contrast, a century and a half earlier, the 1704 Statute of Anne made it possible for England to become a leading financial center for private and governmental borrowers. I should add that England's facilitation of negotiability was not confined to payment and credit instruments; it did the same, although more gradually, for

---

[193] *Id.*

[194] *See id.* at 20 (citing The Statute of Anne 3 & 4 Anne, c. 9 [1704]). This statute was absorbed and thus repealed by the Bills of Exchange Act of 1882 (C.61), S. 96.

[195] *Id.* (emphasis added)

[196] *See supra* § 11:2(B).

documents of title such as ocean bills of lading.[197] In its 1794 decision of *Lickbarrow v. Mason*, the House of Lords established that the consignor-shipper's right to stop the goods before they reached the consignee was subordinate to the rights of the consignee's endorsee holding such a bill. In addition, the special verdict of the jury found that by the "custom of merchants a bill of lading was transferable by endorsement, and capable of transferring title to the goods."[198]

d. *The Economic Effects of Negotiability*

With English law's facilitation of the negotiability of bills of exchange and promissory notes, the Crown becoming a major borrower, and bankers such as the House of Rothschild underwriting the bonds issued by English and other governments, England, as well as the Netherlands and Germany, developed active marketplaces for fixed interest bearer bonds.[199] This was not the case with France as well as other countries whose private law had been inspired by the *Code Civil* and *Code de Commerce*. Please recall that Article 1131 of the Code Civil stated: "An obligation without a cause, or upon a false cause, or upon an unlawful cause, can have no effect" (*L'obligation sans cause, or sur un fausse cause, or sur une cause illicite, ne peut avoir aucune effet*). And as was discussed in Chapters 8–10, usury or other possibly "illegal" or "immoral purposes" continued to hover menacingly over commercial promises of payment well into the twentieth century.[200] Accordingly, if *Hussey v. Jacob* were to have come up before the French *Tribunal de Commerce* at the same time that it came up before the King's Bench, the stranger or endorsee who purchased the bill of exchange would not have been able to enforce it because of the illegality of its underlying gambling obligation.

Toronto University Professor John Munro's recent study entitled *Usury, Calvinism, and Credit in Protestant England* highlights the dramatic economic consequences of not having to worry about a defense of usury (and about the illegality of *causa*) in the development of England's financial markets:

---

[197] I say more gradually because the underlying transaction defenses of lack of privity of contract and lack of agents' powers to issue bills of lading continue to plague English bills of lading well into the twentieth century as will be discussed later in this chapter. *See infra* Section. . . . .

[198] Kozolchyk, *Evolution and Present State,* at 169.

[199] *See supra* ch. 11.

[200] Consider, for example, the effect of a ruling as general as that by an appellate court in Rouen in 1973:

> The agreement that gives birth to an obligation whose cause is illicit is tainted with nullity that *any interested parry may invoke. . .*" (*La convention qui donne naissance a une obligation dont la cause est illicite est attainte d'une nullité que tout interessé peut invoquer. . .*)

Rouen 2, Oct. 1973, D.1974, 378

> Accordingly, if the agreement in question is paid by means of a promissory note or bill of exchange France Ratified the Geneva Convention on Bills of Exchange and Promissory Notes in 1936. *See* United Nations Treaty Collection, http://treaties.un.org/Pages/LONViewDetails.aspx?src=LON&id=547&lang=en. Article 17 of the Geneva Convention states: "Persons sued on a bill of exchange cannot set up against the holder defences founded on their personal relations with the drawer or with previous holders, unless the holder, in acquiring the bill, has knowingly acted to the detriment of the debtor." *See* The League of Nations, Geneva Conventions on the Unification of the Law relating to Bills of Exchange, art. 17 (1930), *available at* http://www.jus.uio.no/lm/en/html/treaties.and.organisations.html#274. Query, is illegality or illicitness a "personal" or a "real" defense, as it is in most laws I am familiar with?

> The consequences of legalizing interest payments, but with ever lower maximum rates, had a far-reaching impact on the English economy, from the 16th century to the Industrial Revolution. The first lay in finally permitting the discounting of commercial bills. Even if medieval bills of exchange had permitted merchants to disguise interest payments in exchange rates, the usury doctrine nevertheless required that they be non-negotiable, [and be] held until maturity, since discounting would have revealed the implicit interest. Evidence for the Low Countries and England demonstrates that discounting, with legal transfers either by bearer bills or by endorsement, with full negotiability, began and became widespread only after the legalization of interest payments in both countries. The importance for Great Britain can be seen in the primary role of its banks during the Industrial Revolution: in discounting commercial bills, foreign and domestic, in order to finance most of the working capital needs for both industry and commerce.

Fully immune to the usury laws, this Financial Revolution permitted the English/British governments to reduce borrowing costs from 14% in 1693 to just 3% in 1757, so that the British economy could finance both 'guns and butter', without crowding out private investments.[201]

---

[201] JOHN MUNRO, USURY, CALVINISM, AND CREDIT IN PROTESTANT ENGLAND: FROM THE SIXTEENTH CENTURY TO THE INDUSTRIAL REVOLUTION (Abstract) (Univ. of Toronto, Dept. of Econ., Working Paper No. 439, 2011), *available at* http://www.economics.utoronto.ca/index.php/index/research/workingPaperDetails/439.

Chapter 21

THE SOCIO-ECONOMIC AND LEGAL CONTEXTS OF U.S. COMMERCIAL CONTRACTS

§ 21.1 INTRODUCTION: PRACTICES, VALUES AND ATTITUDES THAT SHAPED U.S. LAW

"After all, the chief business of the American people is business. They are profoundly concerned with buying, selling, investing and prospering in the world.'

President Calvin Coolidge's address to the American Society of Newspaper Editors, Washington D.C., January 25, 1925.

After reading this chapter, the reader should have little doubt that the law of commercial contracts of a nation whose chief business was aptly described by its 30th president as "business" has been shaped not by statutes, court decisions or even learned treatises, but mostly by commercial practices among other socio-economic forces. This chapter should help answer the questions: What were these practices? Who were their principal shapers? And what were the socio-economic forces, values and attitudes behind such shaping? The answers will not be easy because the number of practices and shapers is large and the socio-economic forces behind them protean. But we will try.

Another purpose of this chapter's identification of practices, participants, attitudes and values is to illustrate how some of the practices inspired the underlying principles of viable commercial institutions under United States law. Consider, for example, the eighteenth-century practice behind some of the chattel mortgage statutes that allowed a debtor to remain in possession of the collateral, thereby enabling him to repay his agricultural and commercial loans, and the principle that such loans should be self-liquidating.[1] As will be discussed in Chapter 24, centuries later, this continued to be the seminal practice for the principle of self-liquidation or payment of secured loans not only in Article 9 of the U.C.C., but also for the regulation of the Federal Reserve Act's "elastic" commercial loans.

Thus, a principal goal of this chapter is to establish the link between key legal principles involved in the development of United States commercial contract law and the practices, values, and attitudes that inspired them. Prominent among these principles are United States' versions of: Freedom of contract and their good faith performance, legal and equitable protection of private ownership and of wealth creating labor, equal protection of equals and a growing inclusiveness of those considered equals, protection of third parties acting in good faith, and a second chance for those who failed in the marketplace, but may succeed under proper circumstances.

---

[1] *See, e.g., infra* § 21:8(A) (discussing eighteenth century chattel mortgage statutes). *See also* NLCIFT, *12 Principles,* at Principle 1.

The shapers of these practices were not always traditional merchants. Consider, for example, the participation of farmers in the development of America's local and international markets. As will become apparent in the next sections, farmers played a crucial role in such development. Not surprisingly, then, the definition of a merchant in U.C.C. § 2–104(1) is among the broadest found in any commercial code:

> (1) "Merchant" means a person who deals in goods of the kind or otherwise by his occupation holds himself out as having knowledge or skill peculiar to the practices or goods involved in the transaction or to whom such knowledge or skill may be attributed by his employment of an agent or broker or other intermediary who by his occupation holds himself out as having such knowledge or skill.[2]

Unlike his French nineteenth-century counterpart, this is not the merchant/suspected usurer whose altruism and virtue had to be proclaimed by Judge Bedos of the Red Ink Case fame lest he be accused of usury.[3] The roots of the U.C.C. § 2–104(1) merchant are found in a professional status "based upon specialized knowledge as to the goods (or as to specialized knowledge as to business practices or both. . .")[4] Indeed, when I first read this definition and comment, I was reminded of a radio interview with Jaume Sabater, Pablo Picasso's friend and agent. In it, Sabater referred to Picasso as one of the most effective salesmen of his art, one who knew exactly how to sell his paintings to New York dealers during the Nazi occupation of France. Picasso, a merchant? Well, Official Comment 3 of the same U.C.C. provision found it necessary to clarify that universities can come within the definition of merchant "if they have regular purchasing departments or business personnel who are familiar with business practices and who are equipped to take any action required."[5]

As we will find in Chapter 23, despite U.C.C. § 2–104, some United States courts characterized farmers as merchants, while others did not. Moreover, while some court decisions denied to farmers the status of merchants (with respect to the requirements of the Statute of Frauds in U.C.C. § 2–201), the Federal Reserve Act characterized negotiable instruments executed by farmers as commercial paper and thereby approved these instruments for discount-advances, especially when secured by "readily marketable staples."[6]

As this introductory chapter will make clear, unlike farmers elsewhere, American eighteenth- and early-nineteenth-century farmers acted as merchants by selling what they had farmed or produced directly to consumers or to wholesalers. Accordingly, as we did with respect to the terms "tradesman" and "merchant" in the preceding chapter on English legal institutions from the seventeenth to nineteenth century, this chapter will identify archetypal merchants in the sale of goods and commercial loans, starting out with those doing business in colonial and independent America.

We will also discuss influential practices, values and attitudes among Puritan settlers and other colonial institutions such as: (1) "General" stores which supplied mostly household goods to the rural population and who initiated America's "consumer

---

[2] *See* U.C.C. 2–204(1). *See also* cmts. (1) & (3) (2013).

[3] *See supra* § 9:2(E)(3)(c).

[4] U.C.C. § 2–104 cmt. 2 (2013).

[5] *Id.* cmt. 3.

[6] *See also infra* § 21:6(C).

revolution," and (2) small family farms that produced and sold their farm products first in their communities and subsequently beyond. Thereafter, we will discuss the practices, values and attitudes of: (1) Wholesalers (including jobbers and factors) who supplied goods and credit to small farmers and producers as well as retail merchants; and (2) post-colonial institutions such as (a) department stores which implemented the consumer revolution by selling the broadest varieties of goods, including in one case, "his and her" actual submarines to loving couples during the Christmas season; (b) bankers who financed manufacturers, wholesalers and retailers; (c) the Federal Reserve Bank as the principal regulator of an unprecedented expansion of commercial and consumer credit following the end of the First World War; and (d) credit rating agencies that supplied data on actual and potential borrowers to their United States lenders. This discussion should help "demystify" certain practices such as the 30, 60, 90 and 180 maturity dates of negotiable instruments (in use in the American marketplace since the second half of the nineteenth century). For all these terms did was to reflect realistic assumptions by representative merchants of how long it would take them to sell the commodities used as collateral and repay their loans.

§ 21.2 PURITAN MERCHANTS-SETTLERS (EARLY SEVENTEENTH TO LATE EIGHTEENTH CENTURY)

A. The Productive Ethic and the Moral Capitalism of the Elect Industrious and Striving

Among the Protestant sects that first settled the United States, the Puritans had the most lasting impact. They were dissatisfied with the reforms of the Anglican Church when it broke with Catholicism in 1535 and insisted in their belief in a spiritual authority based solely on Scripture. They also believed that by substituting king for pope as the head of the church, "England was only recapitulating an unnecessary, corrupt, and even idolatrous order."[7] Nonetheless, many Puritans chose to remain within the Church of England working for reform, and it was from this group that a much larger group of emigrants left from England for New England in the late 1620s and established their colony at Massachusetts Bay.

Even as the Puritans immigrated to New England, "they affirmed their 'Englishness' and saw the main purpose of their new colony as being that of a biblical witness, a 'city on a hill' which would set an example of biblical righteousness in church and state for Old England and the entire world to see."[8] Pilgrims, on the other hand, while sharing some of the Puritan beliefs, wanted to achieve "reformation without tarrying," even if they had to part from their church and their nation. Thus when leaving England they did so in search of a new political and spiritual identity.[9]

In the preceding chapter, we examined an archetypal commercial relationship between the London House of Samuel Storke and its many agents, consignees and joint venturers in colonial North America.[10] This examination revealed key features of

---

[7] *See* CONTEXT AND DEVELOPMENTS: THE PILGRIMS, http://xroads.virginia.edu/~cap/puritan/purhist.html (last visited Dec. 2, 2013) (citation omitted).

[8] *See* Samuel T. Logan Jr. *The Pilgrims and Puritans: Total Reformation for the Glory of God*, PURITANSERMONS.COM, http://www.puritansermons.com/banner/logan1.htm (last visited Dec. 2, 2013).

[9] *Id.*

[10] *See supra* § 20:2(E).

Samuel Storke's Londonbased trans-Atlantic business, but did not dwell on the distinctive features of the local (New England) trade of his correspondents, especially those that followed the 1630 Puritans' settlements. Now we will examine the values, attitudes and commercial practices of New England Puritans when dealing with other local merchants and consumers.

Professor Stephen Innes of the University of Virginia referred to the New England Puritans as possessing a "productive ethic" which was "a fortuitous combination in a New World setting of the Protestant concept of "the calling" with the emergent doctrines of mercantile capitalism, as expressed in the civil culture of the New England Town."[11]

He suggested that the Puritans of the Massachusetts Bay settlement succeeded in establishing their "City upon a Hill" because, among other factors, they linked land ownership to productive labor[12] and premised their productive labor on an "ethically autonomous (grace bearing) individual as the fundamental constituent of society, rather than the order, guild or corporation."[13] This Puritan individual, then, was not only intensely commercial, but was also an assiduous contributor to his family, church and community as well as to schools, especially those "voluntarily organized, or privately controlled."[14] As Calvinist "elect" (or "saints"), these Puritans attempted to bridge what Emile Durkheim (and in our time, the biologist E. O. Wilson) referred to as the "duality of human existence," *i.e.*, the co-existence in the same person of self-interest and altruism, or what Professor Innes labeled a "moral capitalism."[15]

Hence, in Professor Innes's opinion, the Puritan Massachusetts Bay Colony was the New World's "first capitalist commonwealth"[16] whose practices were imbued by an ethic of strong families and town organizations and a religiously inspired "culture of discipline" which fostered:

> *(I)ndustrious and "striving"* behavior, communal responsibility, and a high ratio of savings and investment relative to income by its limitations on leisure . . . both to maximize production and reinvestment and to attend to the needs of the economically vulnerable. It required that human beings "improve every bright and shining moment" while also ensuring that the "rich and mighty" not "eate upp [sic] the poore."[17]

In addition, the pronouncements made by Puritan pastors and theologians:

> (R)eveal the degree to which the labor theory of property developed in William Petty's *Verbum Sapienti* (1665) and John Locke's *Second Treatise* (1690) had its roots in ascetic Puritanism. Work for the saints was the

---

[11] *See* STEPHEN INNES, CREATING THE COMMONWEALTH, THE ECONOMIC CULTURE OF PURITAN NEW ENGLAND 5 (1995).

[12] *Id. See also id.* at 315 note 1 (in which Professor Innes points to research that shows that communal ownership of land in other states had failed precisely because it severed the link between labor and land ownership). The reader will recall that I draw a similar conclusion from the severance of the same link in the USSR and the PRC, *supra* chs. 15–17.

[13] INNES, *supra* note 11, at 6.

[14] *Id.*

[15] *Id.* at 7.

[16] *Id.* at 9.

[17] *Id.* at 9 (citing Reverend John Winthrop, *Model of Christian Charity, in* Winthrop Papers 2:283 (1630)) (emphasis added).

warrant and source of all wealth: God gave the use of the world to the industrious and rational; title to the property came principally from work; the fruits of labor belonged to the worker; men and women only had a right to what they actually could use.[18]

B. Extended Families: Trustworthiness and Credit Networks

As pointed out by Yale University's Professor Edmund Morgan:

> The first duty of a Puritan parent was . . . to give food, shelter and protection to his children. . . . The laws obliged all parents to perform this duty: No New England father could loaf away his time while the cupboard was bare. When a complaint was made in Watertown against Hugh Parsons, "he was Sent For, and advised to imploy his time to the better providing For his Family, and for his incouragement" he was supplied "with some present Corne."[19]

Other Puritans guilty of the same idleness usually received a harsher punishment. For example, one Samuel Mattock was sentenced to incarceration in the house of correction and was made to pay a fine by a court in Suffolk "for Idleness and neglecting his family."[20]

Puritans also took seriously their duty to educate their children in religious matters.[21] Thus, Massachusetts law required parents to teach their children and apprentices to read and understand the doctrines of Christianity.[22] Although the Puritans' educational goal was to promote the observance of their religion, their support for quality, humanistic education resulted in their founding of some of the United States' and the world's leading universities, including Dartmouth, Harvard and Yale.[23]

Another key factor in the commercial success of the Puritan merchant was his familial connections and network of business correspondents. Professor Morgan's collection of letters of prominent Puritan merchants reveals their preference for doing business with relatives, close and distant, who often became their commission agents, consignees and joint venturers. Please recall the pervasiveness of credit extensions in the colonial businesses conducted by Storke in the preceding chapter.[24] Not surprisingly, we re-encountered in Professor Morgan's collection of letters some between the Storke and Seawall families of the preceding chapter.[25] As you may recall, trustworthiness was apparent in the lack of written contracts or of even simple executory promises to pay or perform: Most of these familial transactions were evidenced only as credit and debit entries in Samuel Storke's books of accounts.[26]

---

[18] *Id.* at 90.

[19] *See* EDMUND S. MORGAN, THE PURITAN FAMILY 65 (1965) (citation omitted).

[20] *Id.*

[21] *Id.* at 87.

[22] *Id.*

[23] Ellis Washington, *Harvard, the Ivy League and the Forgotten Puritans,* WND COMMENTARY (June 30, 2007, 1:00 am), http://www.wnd.com/2007/06/42348/.

[24] *See supra* § 20:2(E).

[25] MORGAN, *supra* note 19, at 158–59.

[26] *See supra* § 20:2(E).

C. Maximization of Efforts and of Rights and the Decline of a Puritan Moral Capitalism

Eventually, the industriousness for the sake of one's family welfare acquired a different meaning in non-Puritan America among many a business owner: Every effort that would help the merchant's business grow and expand geographically was owed to that business. While conducting seminars for business lawyers and businessmen on the recently adopted U.C.C. Article 9 on secured transactions law in various states during the early 1970s, I noticed that one of the most popular issues with business lawyers was whether to file their financing statements centrally with the secretary of state's office or locally at the county recorder's office.

One of the variables involved in this determination was that many a secured debt had been assumed by branches or subsidiaries of the same business, and this brought into play the issue of the secured debtor's independence from the head office. It was apparent that many of these businesses were of recent formation and that shortly after signs of success appeared, their owners sought to form as many branches or subsidiaries as they could. My "coffee break" question to business owners was: "Why did you branch out as quickly as you did?" The answer was quick and unanimous: "We owe it to our business."

The more I came in contact with the industriousness and striving of businessmen during the ensuing years, the more it became apparent that one of the signs of a business entity's success was its geographic multiplication. However, with the maximization of its growth often came a maximization of contractual rights, albeit at the expense of rights present in the original Puritan notion of a "moral capitalism."

You will find an illustration of the decline of the Puritan notion of a moral capitalism in my discussion of Justice Cardozo's *Meinhard v. Salmon* decision.[27] In what various New York lawyers have told me was and is not an unusual contractual behavior, a successful joint venturer did not disclose to his investor that as a result of the success of the original joint venture, a larger and potentially more lucrative venture was offered to him, thereby excluding the original joint venturer from participating in the new venture, allegedly because it was about to expire. After characterizing Salmon as a trustee for his joint venturer-investor, Justice Cardozo based his decision on a moral capitalistic principle:

> A trustee is held to something stricter than the morals of the market place. Not honesty alone, but the punctilio of an honor the most sensitive, is then the standard of behavior. . . . [T]he level of conduct for fiduciaries [has] been kept at a level higher than that trodden by the crowd.

Please note that with the maximization of Defendant's Salmon's rights as a managing partner or joint venturer (including his asserted privilege not to disclose an offer made to a joint venture whose life based on a twenty year lease was about to expire) came Cardozo's remedy of a constructive trust on 50% of Salomon's future profits of the defendant in the new joint venture.

---

[27] Meinhard v. Salmon, 249 N.Y. 458, 464 (1928). *See also infra* § 21:9(F) n.55 and accompanying text.

D. Other Religious and Commercial Principles: Just Price and Reasonableness

Harvard University Professor Bernard Bailyn describes the main challenge of Puritan dogma in a commercial environment:

> [C]onstantly exposed to sin by virtue of his control of goods necessary to other people. [And] [s]ince proof of the diligence he applied in his calling was in the profits he made from precisely such exchanges, could a line be drawn between industry and avarice? Puritans answered, as had Catholics for half a millennium, that it could, and they designated this line the "just price."[28]

The meaning of the Puritan just price was provided by the Reverend John Cotton:

> 'A man may not sell above the current price, i.e., such a price as is usual in the time and place, and as another (who knows the worth of the commodity) would give for it, if he had occasion to use it. . . .' A merchant's personal losses or misfortunes ought never to be reflected in an increased valuation, 'but where there is scarcity of the commodity . . . there men may raise their price, for now it is a hand of God upon the commodity, and not the person.'[29]

The reverend's definition of a just price reflects Catholic dogma but adds to it an important element. Please recall that, as formulated by Saint Thomas Aquinas, the just price was determinable in accordance with the "appraisal of the marketplace" (*secundum aestimationem fori*).[30] In the preceding quote, Reverend Cotton added precision to the appraisal by listening to the opinion of an archetypal merchant who "knows the value of the commodity." This addition contributes reasonableness to the determination of the Puritan just price because it relies on the appraisal of a presumptively disinterested, but knowledgeable third party.

As apparent in Puritan sermons, trustworthiness which resulted in the granting of credit to the participants in their networks was central to their social and trade relationships. Puritan preachers were keenly aware that trade required close attention to detail and complete honesty in the performance of its promises or contracts, including avoiding the slightest trace of dishonesty, corruption or nepotism. In fact, it was not unusual for them to quote a Biblical text such as: " 'The LORD abhors dishonest scales, but accurate weights are his delight' (Prov 11:1)."[31]

The emphasis on honest weights and measures also made it easier to instill in the American marketplace the British and European merchants' preference for fixed, posted prices instead of haggled over and thus often "unjust" and not trustworthy prices, especially in the trade of everyday goods.[32]

---

[28] *See* BERNARD BAILYN, THE NEW ENGLAND MERCHANTS IN THE SEVENTEENTH CENTURY 20–21 (1979) (citation omitted).

[29] *Id.* (citations omitted).

[30] *See supra* § 6:2(B)(4).

[31] *See* Erroll Hulse, *The Examples of the English Puritans*, PURITANSERMONS.COM, http://www.puritansermons.com/banner/hulse1.htm (last visited Dec. 2, 2013).

[32] In Europe as well as in the United States, haggling over the prices of everyday items has been shunned by respectable merchants since Daniel Defoe's days, *see supra* § 20:2(E)(3). In contrast, bargaining over high priced items has been more widely acceptable.

E. The Preference for Private Property

As noted earlier by Professor Innes, the Puritan settlers chose private over communal property rights. This choice became apparent during the first half of the seventeenth century, and was a choice later echoed and justified in 1689 by John Locke in his Two Treatises of Government:

> Though the Earth . . . be common to all Men, yet every Man has a Property in his own Person. . . . The Labour of his Body, and the Work of his Hands, we may say, are properly his. Whatsoever then he removes out of the State that Nature hath provided, and left it in, he hath mixed his Labour with, and joyned to it something that is his own, and thereby makes it his Property. . . . that excludes the common right of other Men.[33]

Dr. Gary North of Chalcedon[34] describes how from 1621 to 1623, a Pilgrim colony required that those working in the commonly held fields contribute their work-product to a common storehouse that divided their unequal work product equally among all the participating families.[35] This contribution resulted in an inequality between the work product and the rewards received by all the contributors. When those who worked the fields refused to continue doing so, the colonial Governor abolished the practice of common storage and equal distributions per family. Once this happened, "(i)mmediately, men and women returned to the harvest fields."[36]

In their settlement of New England, Puritan colonies applied the lessons learned from the bad experience of the Pilgrims with common ownership. In addition to an unequal distribution of work product, the common ownership of land caused serious nuisances associated with the settlers' rights to the use of common property day and night. Problems and disputes resulted from such things as: "pigs without rings in their noses running through the town, and midnight tree cutters on the commons."[37] Eventually, the Puritans who had a share in the common pasture and common lands decided to limit the use and distribution of property:

---

[33] JOHN LOCKE, TWO TREATISES OF GOVERNMENT § 2, ¶ 27 (Peter Laslett ed., Cambridge University Press 1988) (1689), *cited in Property and Ownership*, STANFORD ENCYCLOPEDIA OF PHILOSOPHY (Sep. 6, 2004), http://plato.stanford.edu/entries/property.

[34] *See* Gary North, *The Puritan Experiment in Common Ownership*, THE FREEMAN (Apr. 1, 1974), http://www.fee.org/the_freeman/detail/the-puritan-experiment-in-common-ownership#axzz2f5rrIXC6.

[35] *Id. See also Massachusetts Bay Colony,* QUAQUA.ORG, http://www.quaqua.org/pilgrim.htm (last visited Dec. 2, 2013). As this source explains, the Pilgrims who landed at Plymouth, Massachusetts, in 1620 were:

> [A] small religious group that was part of a larger Puritan movement. . . The Puritan movement denoted a loose collection of religious beliefs, not a particular denominational sect. Puritans believed that all institutions, including government, schools, families, communities, and the Church of England, should be "purified" by cleansing away all cultural characteristics regarded by the Puritans as ungodly.
>
> *Id.* The Pilgrim Puritans were persecuted in England and after fleeing first to Holland, they sailed to what is now Plymouth, Massachusetts. From about 1630 onward, other Puritans organized the much larger Massachusetts Bay Colony under the auspices of the Massachusetts Bay Company, located in present day Boston.

Id.

[36] North, *supra* note 34.

[37] *Id.*

In town after town . . . private ownership and private control of property [replaced common ownership] even among men who had grown up in English communities that had used the open field system of farming.[38]

The experience of the Puritan settlements with private property highlighted two convictions: One was the link between the labor that transformed or added value to property and the legitimacy of its original acquisition by Puritan settlers. The other conviction was that freedom of contract was the primary means to make one's private property marketable but only on the basis of just and reasonable prices. And as just noted, the addition of reasonableness in the person of a respected and knowledgeable merchant who knew the market value of the property added precision to what could otherwise be an arbitrary price.

As shown by our earlier discussions of central planning in socialist regimes,[39] the arbitrary and unrealistic pricing of goods and services not only made central planning ineffective but also very costly in economic and human terms. Recall the tragic experience with Mao Tse Tung's decree that forced membership in the PRC agricultural cooperatives. The fact that each family was forced to contribute its animals or produce, year after year, and receive only whatever the collective enterprise distributed was in the end responsible for one of the largest famines in history.[40]

The same consequences will ensue when the price of property ignores the daily inconveniences and costs of nuisances associated with the ownership of shares in a common property. Simply put, the inability of contract prices to reflect what the parties are knowledgeably and freely willing to pay for property deprives purchasers from getting a fair bargain and prevents the property from ever having a realistic market value.

F. Summary and Conclusions

Among the values and attitudes that one can ascribe to the New England Puritans were: (1) A religiously inspired "moral capitalism" which resulted in the energetic pursuit of profit while also caring about the welfare of family and community; (2) A religiously inspired and sanctioned strict work ethic, including frugality, self-discipline and self-denial; (3) A familistic trade that lead to trustworthy contractual networks unburdened by costly legal formalities where commercial credit was routinely made available; (4) An honesty reflected in just prices whose justness could be verified by the opinions of reasonable third parties and by the strict observance of promulgated weight and measures; (5) A preference for private (over communal) ownership whose original title belonged to the contributors of labor that transformed the value of the property. To facilitate the identification of the effects on United States commercial contracts law wrought by some of these values and attitudes as well as of other socio-economic factors, these effects will be summarized at the end of most of the following sections.

---

[38] *Id.*

[39] *See, e.g.,* § 15:4(F).

[40] *See supra* § 18:3(C)(2).

§ 21.3 THE EIGHTEENTH-CENTURY "GENERAL STORE" AND ITS REVOLUTIONARY EFFECTS ON CONSUMERISM

A. The Start of a Consumer Revolution

The Encyclopedia Britannica defines a general store as a "retail store in a small town or rural community that carries a wide variety of goods, including groceries. . . ."[41] In the United States, the general store (at times also referred to as "country" store) succeeded the trading post. A significant portion of its trade consisted of barters among Native Americans, pioneers and early settlers. The general stores served neighboring communities and especially farmers,[42] regardless of their ethnic origin or religious affiliation.

They were usually located at a crossroads or in a village and sold or bartered a wide variety of products made by others. Although they were supposed to be paid in cash because of the scarcity of money in rural areas, much of the rural trade was accomplished through barter. Rowena Olegario, a historian of the culture of credit in the United States estimates that during the general store period the amount of debts paid in cash generally did not exceed one-third of the amounts outstanding.[43] Accordingly, credit played a central role in a consumer revolution that spread from rural to urban America and from there to market economies throughout the trading world.

B. The Fielding Lewis Store of Fredericksburg, Virginia

One of the first urban general stores of colonial America was the Fielding Lewis store of Fredericksburg, Virginia.[44] Its most famous customer was a young George Washington who had grown up on a plantation on the edge of that city and who continued to patronize this store after he moved to Mount Vernon. A letter he wrote to his mother in 1757 asked her to buy cloth, hose and thread from the Fielding Lewis Store. Over a 25-year period, his purchases regularly included items such as shoe buckles, salt, mirrors, and a wide variety of other goods.[45]

The State of Virginia's official history of the Fielding Lewis Store emphasizes the transformation of consumption patterns that general stores helped bring about:

> [T]he consumer revolution of the second half of the eighteenth century . . . changed the American economy and the lives of ordinary people forever. By

---

[41] *General Store,* ENCYCLOPAEDIA BRITANNICA, http://www.britannica.com/EBchecked/topic/228624/general-store (last visited Dec. 2, 2013).

[42] *Id.*

[43] *See* ROWENA OLEGARIO, A CULTURE OF CREDIT: EMBEDDING TRUST AND TRANSPARENCY IN AMERICAN BUSINESS 217 n.52 (2006). She states:

> Local trade also took the form of barter, sometime of a quite complicated sort. . . . In America, transactions represented in journal and ledgers in money terms often involved no currency at all. Instead, the figure merely served as a convenient way to keep track of barter arrangements, which could involve several parties at once. William T. Baxter estimates that only one-third of debts were paid in cash; the remainder was settled by barter.

Id. (citations omitted).

[44] *See The Oldest Retail Building in America?* Historic Fredericksburg Foundation, http://hffi.org/fieldinglewisstore.html (last visited Dec. 2, 2013).

[45] *Id.*

> the middle of the eighteenth century . . . the American colonies . . . [were] making . . . everything from lace tablecloths to brass shoe buckles—cheap enough for ordinary people to buy. Consumer demand skyrocketed, and merchants set up stores . . . to meet the growing demand. This consumer revolution was as fundamental to the lives of ordinary people as the more familiar American Revolution. Indeed, it gave tangible meaning to the ideas of the Revolutionary movement, which appealed to the ambitions of ordinary people for economic and social improvement. The Revolution asserted the right of all Americans to the "pursuit of happiness," which, for ordinary people, included the opportunity to acquire things that had once been reserved to their social superiors. The consumer revolution turned the United States into a nation of shopkeepers and consumers, and redefined the idea of equality.[46]

C. The Commercial and Consumer Credit Practices Associated with General Stores and their Foreign and Local Suppliers

The fact that George Washington, as well as many other inhabitants of rural America, could buy or barter at Fielding Lewis Store items as varied as cloth, hose, thread, shoe buckles, salt and mirrors (among many other products) stood in sharp contrast with the smaller and specialized inventory of eighteenth century European shopkeepers.[47] Moreover, the general store goods were sold or bartered at prices accessible to a large segment of the population that could pay with seasonal cash, credit or through barter. These features, and especially the access to credit made possible acquisitive habits similar to those observed in seventeenth and eighteenth century England. As it turned out, the credit practices associated with these transactions were among the most powerful engines for the consumer revolution alluded to by the State of Virginia.

As was discussed in the preceding chapter,[48] numerous networks of colonial credit originated in Britain and reached both colonial port cities and the interior of the country. As was pointed out by Professor David T. Flynn of North Dakota University,[49] this credit was made possible in part because the colonists had a unit of account, the colonial pound (£), which served as a common denominator for what was lent and repaid. In addition to the colonial pound, other forms of money circulated in the colonies during seventeenth and eighteenth centuries. Among these were gold or silver coins, commodity money, paper currency, and later tobacco and even tobacco warehouse receipts.[50]

Most of these commercial and consumer loans took the form of book credit and promissory notes. Book credits were recorded as debit and credit entries in the merchants' accounting books. Promissory notes, in turn, documented the existence of debts in standardized language that included their makers' unconditional promises of payment, a specified amount of money or of commodities and a date of issue and

---

[46] *Id.*

[47] *See supra* § 6:2(E) (for Braudel's description).

[48] *See supra* § 20:2(E).

[49] *See* David T. Flynn, *Credit in the Colonial American Economy*, EH.NET, http://eh.net/?s=David+T.+Flynn%2C+Credit+in+the+Colonial+American+Economy (last visited Mar. 21, 2014).

[50] *Id.*

payment. Promissory notes had the advantage that they could be assigned or sold prior to their maturity, which gave their holders an early exit to a questionable transaction, although usually at a loss reflected in the amount of the discount or negotiation earned by their endorsees.[51]

The duration of book credit ranged from several months to several years. For example, what were supposed to be cash sales of earthenware concluded on October 1, 1748 were still being paid in installments in April of 1749; thus, Professor Flynn's average duration of these debts to retailers ranged, depending upon the goods sold and the creditworthiness of their buyers between 182 and 211 days.[52] In contrast to book credits, the duration of the credits documented with promissory notes could only be estimated by determining their time of signature and the time of default, or more precisely, when their holders-payees filed their collection lawsuits. On average, this time ranged between 6 and 9 months.[53] Annual interest rates in these loans fluctuated between 3.75% and 7% which, even low by contemporary standards, was surprising in a marketplace still haunted by the possible sin of usury.[54]

It is true that the precise volume of credit transactions, as distinguished from barter and cash, has not been established with precision. Nonetheless, Professor Flynn's analysis of the eighteenth century book entries of Connecticut and Massachusetts merchants showed that most of their purchases were on credit. In fact, "In some regions...credit was so accepted that many employers, including merchants, paid their employees by providing them credit at a store on the [employers'] business's [sic] account."[55] Moreover, probate court records of the inventories of the decedent merchants' estates showed "the frequency of credit through the large amount of accounts receivable recorded for traders and merchants in Connecticut, sometimes over £1,000....[Indeed] [a]lmost 30 percent of the estates of Connecticut 'traders' contained £100 or more of receivables as part of their estate."[56] Accordingly, Flynn points out that credit was a significant form of payment in colonial America and that its duration and cost allowed consumers to consume beyond their current means. In addition, book credit allowed colonists to economize on cash by assigning their "reckonings" and store indebtedness as payment to their workers. He concludes that the variety of credit

---

[51] *Id.*

[52] *Id.*

[53] *Id.*

[54] *See* Mark Valeri, *The Rise of Usury in Early New England: Commerce, bills of exchange, and the morality of money*, 6 COMMON PLACE (2006), *available at* http://www.common-place.org/vol-06/no-03/valeri/. As noted by Professor Mark Valery, the E.T. Thompson Professor of Church History at Union Theological Seminary in Virginia, few topics aroused as extensive a debate in mid sixteenth through the seventeenth century colonial America as the charge of interest on loans. Yet:

> In 1699, the third-generation Boston pastor Cotton Mather informed New Englanders that the Puritan ministers of the Boston area no longer regarded usury as sinful. Meeting as the Cambridge Synod, they had determined that usury, or "an *Advance* on anything lent by contract" (the import of the reference to contract is explained below) was legitimated by the "Divine Law" of the Old Testament, given "countenance" in the New Testament, "Justified" by economic "Necessity and Utility," mandated by the ethical principle of equity, required by the philosophical meaning of money itself, and congruent with the moral "Law of Charity."

Id. Even though the Cambridge Synod's view of usury was not universally accepted in New England, it still introduced a more realistic, market based approach to usury as reflected in the rates reported by Professor Flynn.

[55] Flynn, *supra* note 49 (citation omitted).

[56] *Id.* (citation omitted).

instruments, their duration and the methods of incorporating interest shows credit "as an important method of exchange and the economy of colonial America to be very complex and sophisticated."[57] In this respect, the commercial and consumer credit associated with the general store served as a template for future even more complex and sophisticated methods of trade finance.

As will be described in greater detail in a subsequent section,[58] the assignment of accounts receivable alluded to in passing by Professor Flynn was part of the commercial-financial practice of factoring. It consisted of the assignee merchant either acting as an agent for the collection of the accounts receivable owed to his assignor by his credit customers, or in the factor's outright or "without recourse" purchase of these accounts. Other important features of colonial factoring were described by a contemporary major factoring company:

> By the 1550's AD, Colonial America was accustomed to using merchant agents in Europe to finance shipments of raw materials such as fur, timber, tobacco and cotton overseas. The European merchant bankers would also factor any shipments made to the colonists. Sellers on either shore were paid a discounted amount of the invoice due from the purchaser before goods were shipped and the factor would take a percentage for collecting for collecting the money owed to the seller. Until the early 1700, both English and American law forbade the selling of invoices unless the purchaser [of the goods] or debtor, was notified in advance. Eventually, US state governments adopted a rule that the debtor did not have to be notified, giving rise to non-notification factoring.[59]

Factoring made possible a commercial and consumer credit "pyramid." At its bottom were the consumers and their retailers who generated the upward flow of book debts and other forms of accounts receivable including commercial paper such as promissory notes and bills of exchange. At the top of this private financing system were the factors. By helping to collect or by buying these accounts, the factors helped finance not only the trade of the general stores, but also that of their suppliers and indirectly that of their customers as well. Eventually, with the creation of the Federal Reserve Bank's discount window in the twentieth century, the uppermost layer of the commercial and consumer credit pyramid of the United States was installed. With it came the most robust upward flow (to the Federal Reserve) and downward flow (to the retail merchant and consumer) of financing known to the commercial world.

§ 21.4 THE MULTI-ETHNIC FAMILY FARMER: PRODUCER AND MERCHANT

A. The Economic Importance of Small Farm Family Businesses

By the time of the war of independence, the Puritans' as well as the other settlers' predilection for private property was apparent in rural America: More than 90% of

---

[57] *Id.*

[58] *See infra* § 21:5(A)(5).

[59] *History of Factoring and Credit Cards*, AMERISOURCE, http://www.amerisourcefunding.com/Services/Services-for-Businesses/Accounts-Receivable-Factoring/History-of-Factoring (last visited Mar. 21, 2014).

Americans lived on farms they owned and worked on.[60] And worked they did. As observed by Gordon S. Wood, a distinguished historian of the early American republic,[61] the British embargos of manufactured items during its 1812 war with the United States caused Americans (and especially those in the Northern states) to manufacture and market a wide range of products, of which cotton was one of the key crops. Prior to 1808, only fifteen cotton mills existed in the United States, but only a year later, eighty-seven new mills were added. In New England, small factories were constantly springing up, supporting the common belief that "Spinning yarn and making cloth is. . .our greatest business."[62] Manufacturing was not confined to New England. By 1814, 234 cotton mills operated within fifteen states,[63] and family business was not confined to cotton:

> Even farmers who were not growing crops for export abroad were nonetheless scrambling to create goods to exchange in local markets—working with their wives and children spinning cloth or weaving hats, dressing deer skins and beaver pelts, making hoops and barrels, distilling whiskey or cider, and fabricating whatever they might sell to local stores. . . . [As was the case of] an English-born leather dresser [who] . . . hired country girls to come to his tannery in upstate New York to cut out gloves, which [he] then sent to farmers' wives for sewing and finishing. By 1910 he discovered he had a market for his gloves among households in the Albany area. From these modest beginning grew the flourishing glove and mitten industry of the United States.[64]

Professor Wood provided another telling statistic on the economic and social importance of the above family enterprises: In 1810, 90% of the total $42 million textile production came from family households. Thus, as early as in 1790, a British visitor to Massachusetts and New Jersey noted that "housewives in every farming household kept their families busy carding and spinning woolen and linen cloth in the evenings and when they are not in the fields."[65] A French visitor stated that almost all households of Worcester, Massachusetts "were inhabited by men who were both cultivators and artisans; one is a tanner, another a shoemaker, another sells goods but all are farmers."[66] And as we will discuss shortly, the production and distribution of dairy products such as cheese and butter was another fast growing family business in some states, but especially in New York. It should be kept in mind that these farming, manufacturing and merchandising families came from numerous countries and practiced different religions or none at all.[67]

---

[60] *See* JOHN HARMON MCELROY, FINDING FREEDOM, AMERICA'S DISTINCTIVE CULTURAL FORMATION 57 (1989).

[61] *See generally* GORDON S. WOOD, EMPIRE OF LIBERTY: A HISTORY OF THE EARLY REPUBLIC, 1789–1815 (2009). In this section I will be summarizing Woods' many insightful observations in pages 702–708.

[62] *Id.* at 702.

[63] *Id.* at 703.

[64] *Id.*

[65] *Id* at 704.

[66] *Id.*

[67] MCELROY, *supra* note 48, at 31. In this section the author lists the following countries as contributors to the rural population of seventeen and eighteen century United States:

> During the seventeenth and eighteenth centuries, America received, in addition to Englishmen and communicants of the established state church of England, Scots, Welsh, Swiss, Dutch, Irish,

B. Personal Unsecured Commercial Credit

Unlike the extended and networking Puritan families, most of the farmer-merchant-manufacturing families of late-eighteenth- and mid-nineteenth-century America operated as individual family (not networked) enterprises. And surprisingly to many foreign visitors, these businessmen received credit from distant merchants. A Scottish shopkeeper, known to extend six months to a year of credit to his customers in Chesapeake Bay in the United States, explained his credit policy as follows:

> Scottish storekeepers . . . 'often trust to the labor and industry of many, who are in the Possession of little or no real property.' . . . 'In a young country where land may be got at a low rent, and where a valuable staple is raised, young men soon leave their Parents, and marrying, settle plantations for themselves.' To do this, they need 'household furniture and working tools,' furnished 'upon Credit, by some Factor or Storekeeper.'[68]

C. Effects

The British embargos of manufactured items during its 1812 war with the United States caused Americans to energetically seek economic self-sufficiency in their internal and international trade. Small, privately-owned family farms became the main engine of self-sufficiency and personal, unsecured credit (received and given) was the main lubricant of this engine. As commented by Oxford's Senior Research Fellow Rowena Olegario, instead of relying on real property collateral, the distant suppliers of these American producers relied on the labor and honesty of the settlers[69] and the latter relied on similar character traits when extending credit to their customers. Accordingly, a self-sufficient commercial credit system that did not depend upon the security of real and personal property was set in motion.

§ 21.5 WHOLESALERS AND OTHER NON-BANK SUPPLIERS OF COMMERCIAL AND CONSUMER CREDIT

A. The Migration of the British Model of Commercial Credit to Colonial and Independent America

As became apparent in the preceding chapter, the close familial and religious connections between British and North American colonial merchants and their willingness to extend credit to their contractual counterparties was a major reason for England's commercial success during the seventeenth and eighteenth centuries.[70] The same was true in the nineteenth century despite the hard fought revolutionary and 1812 wars between the United States and England. These connections resulted in what Olegario referred to as a "transmission of mercantile practices from Britain to

---

> French, Germans, Finns, Swedes, Portuguese, Danes, Flemings, Bohemians, Italians, Spanish, Poles, and other European nationalities who were in their religious practices Jews, Shakers, Methodists, Pietists, Presbyterians, Quakers, Congregationalists, and Roman Catholics, among others, and persons of no faith at all.

Id. at 31–32.

[68] OLEGARIO, *supra* note 43, at 23 (citation omitted).

[69] *Id.*

[70] *See infra* § 22:4(C).

America"[71] even though these practices encountered in America: "[A] chronic lack of money, combined with growing markets and ever-increasing competition."[72] The migration of practices occurred in at least two areas:

> First, the British model of strong merchants (rather than banks) as the most important source of trade financing was replicated in the American trade. Wholesalers based in the country's commercial centers-men like the Tappan brothers of New York . . . supplied the bulk of the capital that sustained the mercantile credit system. Second, American merchants, like their British counterparts, extended long credits over great distances to compensate for the shortage of money.[73]

Part of the large amount of commercial credit available in independent America from English sources was often used as start-up capital by ambitious Americans as well as by British immigrants; the same was true with the ample credit made available to United States retail merchants by large United States importers.[74] And while British merchants were aware since the trading days of Samuel Storke that credits to American merchants often remained uncollected beyond the agreed upon repayment period, they also felt that they had to extend it as "a matter of necessity" because of the "competition of other capitalists."[75]

Olegario quotes the French statesman Charles Maurice de Talleyrand for the assertion that it was British credit that truly enabled the commercial-consumer trade in America. (*C'est donc réellement l'Angleterre. . . qui fait le commerce de consommation de l'Amérique*).[76] However, as will become apparent in subsequent sections, even though commercial and consumer credit practices were imported from England, they grew and diversified extraordinarily in the United States, to the point that if Calvin Coolidge was right in saying that the business of America was business, it was also true that the lubricant of that business was credit to fellow merchants and consumers.

B. Commercial Intermediaries: Wholesalers, Factors and Jobbers

Talleyrand notwithstanding, United States wholesalers, at times referred to as such, and at times as "importers," "dealers," "factors" and "jobbers" would soon take over the supply of inventory and commercial credit to smaller merchants in the United States. The terms "importers" and dealers were used as functional equivalents of the wholesaler who buys directly from the manufacturer. By buying directly from United States or foreign manufacturers, the wholesaler made these goods available on a discounted cash basis or on a credit basis to smaller merchants, usually acting as retailers or direct sellers to consumers. Their prices had to be low enough so as to enable their retail clients to sell them at a profit to consumers.

---

[71] OLEGARIO, *supra* note 43, at 21–22.

[72] *Id.* at 22.

[73] *Id.* Professor Olegario adds that:

> Interest was not explicitly charged unless the debtor failed to pay by the agreed-upon time. The cost of carrying the buyer during the period of the loan was folded into the price of the merchandise; thus, cash sales received a "discount."

Id.

[74] *Id.* at 23.

[75] *Id.* at 25.

[76] *Id.*

The term "jobber" applied to a wholesaler who purchased goods in lots (only occasionally including all the marketable types and sizes of a given item of inventory), thus generally stocking only select types and sizes (referred to in the trade as "odd lots"). Their sellers could be manufacturers trying to get rid of items that were not as popular as they expected or they could be insolvent retailers or wholesalers. By buying these lots very cheaply, the jobber was able to buy many of them and sell them to several retailers at one time.[77]

Olegario provides a telling statistic on the importance of wholesaler and jobber credit in mid-nineteenth century America. In an 1858 circular of the Mercantile Agency (a credit reporting agency discussed later) estimated that:

> 157,394 village and country [general] stores owed an average of $14,500 each to city jobbers, an aggregate value of nearly $2.3 billion. . . . Some jobbers advanced to country stores goods worth 'three or four or even five times the amount of his (the jobber's) capital'. . . .[78]

The term "factor" had two meanings in United States nineteenth-century commercial practice. The first applied to merchants who acted as commercial agents for wholesalers or retailers who entrusted them with goods for sale or exchange to third party merchants or non-merchants. For their sales or exchanges, they received a commission. I will refer to this factor as the "factor-agent." Although this meaning of factor is seldom used in present-day commercial practice in the United States, as I will discuss shortly, it had a significant impact on the law of good faith commercial purchases.

The other meaning of factor applies to a financial intermediary who provides funds to manufacturers and wholesalers (and less frequently to retail merchants) in need of working capital and inventory financing. These factors could provide funds as outright purchasers of the accounts receivable of the manufacturer, wholesaler or large retailer, in which case they purchased the accounts "without recourse" on their seller. Or they could act as secured creditors for manufacturers, wholesalers or retailers and lend on the security of their borrower's inventory and accounts payable.[79] They would then attempt to collect the accounts from the account debtors, *i.e.*, the purchasers of the goods or services from the factors' debtors. If he failed to collect or collected only part of the debt, he could demand payment from his borrower of the principal and

---

[77] The definition in the principal text is mine and it reflects my own experience with contracts involving United States twentieth century jobbers but also nineteenth century contracts of some of their ancestors. One of the best dictionary definitions I have found is in the American College dictionary. An incomplete definition of jobber can be found online. *See Jobber,* THE FREE DICTIONARY, http://legal-dictionary.thefreedictionary.com/jobber (last visited Dec. 3, 2013). It defines jobber as:

> A merchant, middle person, or wholesaler who purchases goods from a manufacturer in lots or bulk and resells the goods to a consumer, or to a retailer, who then sells them to a consumer. One who buys and sells on the stock exchange or who deals in stocks, shares, and Securities.

Id.

[78] OLEGARIO, *supra* note 43, at 26 (citation omitted).

[79] *See* GRANT GILMORE, 1 SECURITY INTERESTS IN PERSONAL PROPERTY 128–29 (1965) (for the distinction between the factor who was a commission agent of the selling merchant and the factor as a purchaser of accounts and secured lender).

interest that had become due.[80] The economic and legal significance of both types of factors should not be underestimated.

Professor Grant Gilmore, one of the great commercial law scholars of the twentieth century, pointed out the significance of the so-called Factors' Acts, which were applicable to factor-agents selling their principal's goods in a regional or national market:

> [A] recurrent situation came to be the misappropriation of goods by a faithless agent in fraud of his principal. Classical theory required that the principal be protected and that the risks of agency distribution be cast on the purchaser. The market demanded otherwise.
>
> The reform was carried out through so-called Factor's Acts, which were widely enacted in the early part of the 19th century. Under these Acts any person who entrusted goods to a factor—or agent—for sale took the risk of the factor's selling them beyond his authority; anyone buying from a factor in good faith, relying on his possession of the goods, and without notice of limitations on his authority, took good title against the true owner. In time these Acts were expanded to protect . . . banks, who took goods from a factor as security for loans made to the factor to be used in operating the factor's own business.[81]

And even though these Factor's Acts were absorbed by the twentieth century law of commercial sales and secured transactions (as we will discuss shortly), they were the first to grant protection to the third parties of the secondary markets for the sale and pledge of goods, such as those just mentioned by Professor Gilmore.

Meanwhile, the factors who were purchasers of accounts and secured creditors were the first commercial intermediaries to provide credit based on the security of intangible goods such as accounts receivable. In doing this, they broke with a secured lending tradition in influential continental European countries such as France which restricted chattel mortgages to immovable or real property.[82]

C. Wholesalers as Lenders and Joint Venturers in the Dairy Industry

1. Introduction

By the middle of the nineteenth century, wholesalers, jobbers and factors not only acted as lenders but on occasion, they provided venture capital for the production and distribution of products made or manufactured by family businesses.[83] As discussed

---

[80] The latter practice had its inception in the consignments typical of the colonial trade described in the preceding chapter on British colonial history when factors acted as commission merchants handling goods on consignment. *See Understanding Commercial Factoring and Credit Insurance*, CRFONLINE.ORG, http://www.crfonline.org/orc/cro/cro-3.html (last visited Dec. 3, 2013) (for a basic and more detailed explanation of factoring, especially as practiced presently).

[81] Grant Gilmore, *The Commercial Doctrine of Good Faith Purchase*, 63 YALE L.J. 1057, 1057–58 (1954) (citations omitted).

[82] *See* C. CIV. (FR.) arts. 2118 & 2119. Unless otherwise indicated, all the English translations of the *Code Civil* provisions belong to Legifrance (*see* Frequently Cited).

[83] For a discussion of the role of wholesalers and warehousemen in Europe's seventeenth century "High Commerce" *see supra* § 6:2(F)(5) (for Fernand Braudel's description of "high commerce").

earlier, in some sectors, such as in the sale of dry goods, they remained as principal suppliers of inventory on a credit basis to retail businesses and not as partners or joint venturers.[84] However, in other sectors such as in the production and distribution of dairy products, their role was pervasive and often in conflict with the interests of the small businesses they financed. By participating in the financing, production and sale of milk and dairy products, they often fixed wholesale prices and, with this power, they displaced many a family business.

The following summary of a narrative by the *Encyclopedia of New York State*[85] starts with what was at first an attempt by a railroad carrier to ship fluid milk produced in upstate New York to New York City. This attempt came only after the opening of railroad from upstate New York to New York City by the Erie Railroad line in the mid-nineteenth century.

2. *The Production and Distribution of Fluid Milk in New York State*

Prior to the opening of this service, the dairy farming business was populated by a large number of small and independent family producers of fluid milk and dairy products such as cheese and butter. Their main customers were consumers with whom they did business on an informal, (mostly oral) face-to-face basis. Even so, by 1850, New York State was the nation's leading dairy producer responsible for "almost half of the total cheese production in the United States."[86] But by that time, very few New York State farmers continued to produce "fluid" milk as a cash crop; the lack of sufficient buyers made them turn almost exclusively to the production of cheese and butter.

In 1842, however, a small dairy farmer agreed to participate in a merchandizing experiment proposed to him by an Erie Railroad station master: Fresh country milk would be shipped to the large consumer market of New York City via the Erie Railroad line. In the words of the Encyclopedia of New York State: "The few cans of milk that [this farmer] shipped in an unrefrigerated baggage car became the first upstate milk ever sold in New York City."[87] The number of cans increased from 45 cans per day in 1842 to 273 cans per day in 1843. By 1844, the number increased to 420 cans per day.[88]

One of the reasons for the success of the fresh country milk delivery to the big city was that for a number of years the New York's growing population had consumed only "swill" milk, which is a milk produced by city cows after having been fed brewers' waste.[89] Predictably, this milk turned out to be as bad in appearance as it was dangerous to the health of consumers, especially New York children.[90]

---

[84] *See e.g., Our House,* LEVISTRAUSSSIGNATURE.COM, http://www.levistrausssignature.com/us/about/history.asp (last visited Dec. 3, 2013) (for a description of the history of the dry goods wholesaling business of of Levi Strauss and Co., which started in San Francisco in 1853).

[85] *See* THE ENCYCLOPEDIA OF NEW YORK STATE 433–36 (Peter R. Eisenstadt and Laura-Eve Moss eds., 2005). This account summarizes a perceptive and well told account of what transformed the dairy industry from a family to large corporate conglomerates.

[86] *Id.* at 433.

[87] *Id.*

[88] *Id.*

[89] *Id.*

[90] *Id.*

As the number of fresh cans of milk shipped approached thousands per day, the shippers were no longer the subsistence farmers whose business was seasonal and dependent on the needs of their face-to-face customers. The new dairy farmer had to deliver milk regularly and in large quantities according to the railroad schedule and based on the number of orders placed by milk wholesalers (also known as dealers). Unlike their subsistence trade in upstate New York, the shipping farmers seldom knew their New York City consumers. Meanwhile, the production of butter and cheese started shifting (because of their volume) from the producers' farms to factories which delivered them to wholesalers or to consumers. Thus, the making and selling of cheese and butter was no longer "the the domain of . . . [the farmers' wives] and daughters. . . ."[91] They were part of big business which charged wholesale prices to New York City retail food shops and restaurants that in turn resold the milk or the dairy products to the public, who paid higher retail prices. After 1850, more than 1,500 cheese factories were active across New York State alone.

3. Fixed Prices and Opposing Coalitions

This change in the merchandizing of fluid milk and dairy products meant that farmers surrendered control of the marketing and sale of their milk, butter and cheese to wholesalers and factories. The contractual relationships between dairy farmers as suppliers and their purchasers-dealers as wholesalers (in conjunction with or separately from the factories) consolidated the legal status of dairy farmers as merchants and their contractual relationships with their counterparties as one "between merchants." Consequently, as noted in the introductory section of this chapter, the term merchant was defined a century and a half later by U.C.C. § 2–104(1) and included farmers, among many others, who dealt "in goods of the kind" and who by their occupation held themselves out "as having knowledge or skill peculiar to the practices or goods involved in the transaction. . . ."[92]

In due course, however, United States dairy farmers learned that during the time they were awaiting payment for the fluid milk they had sold on credit, they could sell or pledge their accounts receivable to factors or bankers, especially if the buyers of their milk or daily products and they themselves were credit worthy. It is true that the dairy wholesalers and factors had better financial resources and legal advice than they did.[93] However, the allure of larger sales and profits induced both sides (dairy farmers and wholesalers and manufacturers of dairy products) to attempt to monopolize and restrain the dairy trade. This was a case of industriousness and striving gone awry.

Dairy farmers formed coalitions or cooperatives whose purpose was to restrict the supply of milk and raise its market price. At times, they were joined by the Erie Railroad as a member of their coalition fighting wholesalers and factory owners. Conversely, the factory owners and wholesalers unhappy with what they considered excessively high wholesale prices countered with their own monopolistic or quasi-monopolistic schemes, including the creation of a "Milk Exchange" whose prices they manipulated.[94] The dairy farmers fought back in 1883 and, assisted again by Erie Railroad executives, implemented a strategy of strikes, lawsuits and milk spillings that

---

[91] *Id.*

[92] *See* U.C.C. § 2–104(1) (2013). *See also id.* (cmts. 1–3).

[93] *Id.*

[94] *Id.*

caused serious dairy shortages in New York City and other cities they serviced. These battles continued until non-market forces, including repeated restraint of trade lawsuits, intervened and led to a regulation of the quality, safety and reliable distribution of dairy products and with it, price fixing battles subsided.

4. *Effects of Unregulated Freedom of Contract: Price Fixing and a No Holds Barred Competition*

The migration of British sales and credit practices to colonial America continued after the birth of the United States, including the central role of wholesalers, jobbers and factors as commercial credit providers. Their credit was largely unsecured and relied on established relationships based upon mutual trust. In the case of the New York dairy industry, these intermediaries frequently battled with milk producers in an attempt to lower and fix the prices they were willing to pay.

Worthy of note is how quickly and serendipitously commercial practices came about. Please recall that the new distribution practice of shipping fresh milk from upstate New York to New York City did not come about from contractual negotiations between dairy farmers, wholesalers and factory owners. The negotiations were started by an imaginative, industrious and striving station master of the Erie Railroad line intent on finding cargo for his unused space in baggage cars and an intrigued, but not overly enthusiastic dairy farmer.

Note that these new practices could not have come about if America's dairy farmers and railroad station masters, milk wholesalers and factory owners lacked the Puritan industrious and striving behavior that Reverend John Winthrop exulted in the ship Arabela while sailing to America in 1630.[95] They would not have come about either if the general principle of commercial contracting was: Unless expressly allowed, the contract in question is forbidden. The guiding principle behind the emergence of the new practices had to be: That which the law does not expressly forbid, it allows. This is the reason why a lowly railroad station master felt sufficiently empowered to enter into a transportation contract that was not executed by Erie or another railroad's cargo officials. Such a contractual relationship and its derived practices could not have come about in Stalin's Soviet Union. For as we discussed in Chapter 15, in Stalin's Soviet Union, a rail station master who wanted to use up empty baggage space to carry fresh milk to a big city would have had to join the ranks of the numerous black-marketeers willing to bribe government officials.

On the other hand, the same perceived freedom to enter into any and all contractual relationships led milk farmers to form coalitions with other milk farmers and with the Erie Railroad to fix and defend their fixed prices. On the other side of the fixed pricing battle were the wholesalers and milk factories. It was apparent that both sides' version of freedom of contract included the legitimacy of their respective price fixing. It was also apparent that their common version of competition included conduct that could drive the losing competitor out of business. Thus, theirs was neither a cooperative, let alone a fair type of competition in which both sides could stay in business even though one side emerged with a diminished share of the market as a result of the other's superior products, best prices and services. It was a winner-take-all, loser-take-none type of competition. And as became apparent with the growing

---

[95] *See* INNES, *supra* note 18.

number of restraint of trade lawsuits and "street battles," courts and, subsequently, administrative agencies had to collaborate in setting forth the reasonable boundaries of permissible competition. It became apparent that as family and religious ties subsided, so did the boundaries of permissible competition and the influence of the Puritan principles of a moral type of capitalism. In addition, as pointed out by Steve Pearlstein, a George Mason University Professor and the Washington Post's distinguished economics journalist, prior to the nineteen eighties the ethos of American corporations was concerned with the welfare of society at large:

> The earliest American corporations were generally chartered for public purposes, such as building canals or transit systems, and well into the 1960s were widely viewed as owing something in return to a society that provided them with legal protections and an economic ecosystem in which to grow and thrive. In 1953, carmaker Charlie Wilson famously spoke for a generation of chief executives about the link between business and the larger society when he told a Senate committee that "what is good for the country is good for the country is good for General Motors, and vice versa.[96]

D. Department Stores and Their Progeny

1. *A Seemingly Endless Variety of Goods and Methods of Purchase*

The *American College Dictionary* defines a department store as "A large retail store handling several lines of goods, including dry goods, women's wear, etc. and organized in separate departments."[97] This type of store largely replaced "general" or "country" stores starting in the mid-nineteenth century, especially in well-populated cities.[98] They also introduced commercial practices that resulted from the massive purchases and sales associated with their seemingly ever-growing chains of retail stores.

Department stores also institutionalized and aggrandized, sometimes outlandishly, the consumer revolution referred to by the State of Virginia in its salutation to the Fielding Lewis Store. Having been born and raised in a developing nation, imagine my surprise when I read in a 1963 Nieman Marcus Christmas gifts catalogue that one of its special items was an actual "his and her" submarine in different shapes and colors.[99]

---

[96] Steve Pearlstein, *How the Cult of Shareholder Value Wrecked American Business*, THE WASHINGTON POST (Sept. 9, 2013), http://www.washingtonpost.com/blogs/wonkblog/wp/2013/09/09/how-the-cult-of-shareholder-value-wrecked-american-business/. On the corporate turn towards short term profits and high share value, *see infra* § 21.12(A)(1) and *see also infra* ch. 24 (for the implications of Professor Pearlstein's findings for the procession of creating viable commercial and corporate customs).

[97] AMERICAN COLLEGE DICTIONARY 324 (1963, 64).

[98] *See generally* Jan Whitaker, The History of Department Stores, http://www.departmentstorehistory.net/. *See* The David Sullivan, Department Stores, *in* Encyclopedia of Greater Philadelphia, http://philadelphiaencyclopedia.org/archive/department-stores/ (on some of the Nineteenth century department stores discussed in the principal text).

[99] *God's Christmas Gift,* CROSSWALK.COM (Dec. 2006), http://www.crosswalk.com/print/1450413/ (last visited Dec. 3, 2013). If you happen to be interested on such "his and her" gifts you may finding a description of them in this source. This year's his and her gift is a three hundred thousand dollars Aston Martin, echoing the taste of James Bond. For a readable and insightful description of the history of the retail business in the United States as reflective of consumer real and manipulated tastes, *see* WILLIAM LEACH, LAND OF DESIRE (1993).

While some of the nineteenth century department stores were palatial such as the Turney Stewart "Marble Palace" (New York, 1848)[100] or the John Wanamaker's "Grand Depot" (Philadelphia 1876),[101] others catered to lower-middle-class clientele such as Macy's original store (Haverhill, Massachusetts, 1851)[102] and others to thrifty buyers, such as F.W. Woolworth's Five and Dime stores (Utica, N.Y., 1878).[103] Customers who enjoyed shopping from their homes could also do so by ordering from Montgomery Ward's and Sears and Roebuck's mail order catalogues, which were distributed largely in rural America during the second half of the nineteenth century.[104]

After the Second World War, chains of national and regional "super-markets" changed the method of shopping for a large variety of food and household products. Their customers could select products from stacks located in separate aisles, place them in rolling metal baskets and pay for them to usually smiling cashiers as they exited the stores. Only a generation later, these super-markets had to compete with "hypermarkets" or "big-box" markets exemplified by Wal-Mart (presently the largest chain of stores in the United States and possibly in the world.)[105] Finally, in our day, a new form of shopping originating from our home or place of business computers allows us to shop electronically for an increasingly wide range of products at low prices and with prompt delivery to our homes or places of business.

2. Caveat Emptor *v. "The Customer Is Always Right": An Archetypal Retail Sales Intent and a Presumption of Good Faith*

Having witnessed the displeasure of many retail merchants in my country of birth with customers who returned goods that they had recently purchased, imagine my surprise when a classmate at the University of Michigan told me that Chicago's Marshall Field's (where I had purchased tennis shoes with the naïve expectation that I could use them as skiing boots) would make no fuss about accepting my return of those shoes. He said that it was the practice of many department stores in the United States to accept the return of goods that the customer was unhappy with because their motto was, "The Customer is Always Right." He had heard that a Mr. Selfridge, one of Marshall Field's owners, was the author of that motto and that he had famously instructed his sales staff to "always give the lady what she wants."[106]

---

[100] *About Lower Manhattan: Did You Know at Stewart Department Store,* LOWER MANHATTAN CONSTRUCTION COMMAND CENTER, http://www.lowermanhattan.info/about/history/did_you_know/did_you_know_that_62478.aspx (last visited Dec. 3, 2013).

[101] THE DEPARTMENT STORE MUSEUM, http://departmentstoremuseum.blogspot.com/2010/06/john-wanamaker-philadelphia.html (last visited Dec. 3, 2013).

[102] *Macy's Inc. History,* MACYSINC.COM, http://www.macysinc.com/press-room/macysinc-history/overview/default.aspx (last visited Dec. 3, 2013).

[103] *A Potted History of F.W. Woolworth,* WOOLWORTHSMUSEUM.CO.UK, http://www.woolworths museum.co.uk/aboutwoolies.html (last visited Dec. 3, 2013).

[104] *See* Ann Kim, *Montgomery Ward: The World's First Mail-Order* Business, 53 ILLINOIS HISTORY A MAGAZINE FOR YOUNG PEOPLE 41 (2000), *available at* http://www.lib.niu.edu/2000/ihy000441.html, and Beth Martens, *Sears, Roebuck and Co. and its Effect on Retailing in America,* 53 ILLINOIS HISTORY A MAGAZINE FOR YOUNG PEOPLE 52 (2000), *available at* http://www.lib.niu.edu/2000/ihy000452.html.

[105] *See* ZACHARY COURSE, WAL-MART AND THE POLITICS OF AMERICAN RETAIL (2005), *available at* http://cei.org/pdf/4992.pdf (for an evaluation of the retail business as a result of the emergence of Wal-Mart, as the largest retail store in the world).

[106] *See The Customer is Always Right,* The Phrase Finder, http://www.phrases.org.uk/meanings/106700.html (last visited Dec. 16, 2013).

Years later, I reflected on the sharp difference between a commercial practice that expected mature buyers to "be aware" of what they were buying and to assume responsibility for it, defects and all (*caveat emptor*) and another practice that encouraged merchants to always try to satisfy the reasonable expectations of their customers, even if a sale price of recently purchased goods had to be returned. While writing this book it dawned on me that Mr. Selfridge's attitude provided the retail sales agreement with an archetypal version of its parties' intent and with an equally archetypal presumption of good faith.

3. Title to Consumer Goods: Department Stores as "Open Markets"

One of the least noticed effects of the sales of goods by department stores was the phenomenal expansion of the physical and legal boundaries of the Law Merchant's custom of "*Market Overt.*" According to this custom, purchases in an open market granted good title to the goods bought in it notwithstanding that the seller may have had no title to them.[107]

In nineteenth-century English law the expansion of the *Market Overt* protection was halting: At times it included and at times it excluded the sale of goods that were not sold in a physically "open" market or were sold at the wrong time of the day Even though in principle every shop in the City of London was a *Market Overt*, as Dean Peter M. Smith of the Exeter Faculty of Law noted, the term shops also had a technical meaning. What constituted a *Market Overt* shop varied with the facts of each case. For example, a sale in a tavern was not a sale in a *Market Overt*, nor was a sale of lead from a wharf, while a sale in a building "[that] appears to have been little more than a warehouse was found to be a shop. . . ."[108]

In contrast, § 1–201 of the U.C.C. relies on the notion of a "buyer in the ordinary course of business" and locates such an ordinary course as broadly as with a "person other than a pawnbroker, in the business of selling goods of that kind." It then adds that:

> A person buys goods in the ordinary course if the sale to the person comports with the usual or customary practices in the kind of business in which the seller is engaged or with the seller's own usual or customary practices.[109]

Rather than restricting the *Market Overt* business of the shop and who is protected when purchasing in it, this provision opens the meaning of a shop to the place where seemingly endless types of goods can be purchased by as many methods of purchase as available in department stores. Indeed, as clarified by Official Comment 9 to U.C.C. § 1–201:

> 'Buyer in ordinary course of business.' Except for minor stylistic changes, identical to former Section 1–201 (as amended in conjunction with the 1999 revisions to Article 9). The major significance of the phrase lies in Section 2–403 and in the Article on Secured Transactions (Article 9). . . .[110]

---

107 Peter M. Smith, *Valediction to Market Overt*, 41 THE AM. J. LEGAL HIST. 225 (1997) (citation omitted).

108 *Id.* at 243.

109 U.C.C. § 1–201(9) (2013).

110 See *id.* cmt. 9.

U.C.C. 2–403 is one of the U.C.C. rules that absorbed some of the protections given to *bona fide* purchasers by the Factors Acts including the concepts of "entrustment" to the faithless factor and its validation of good faith purchase. Thus, U.C.C. § 9–320(a) provides: "a buyer in ordinary course of business, other than a person buying farm products from a person engaged in farming operations, takes free of a security interest created by the buyer's seller, even if the security interest is perfected and the buyer knows of its existence."[111]

The connection of this section with purchases made by buyers in the ordinary course of business from the inventory of a retailer, including prominently department store sellers, is direct and immediate. As noted by Official Comment 3 to § 9–320: "Thus subsection (a) applies primarily to inventory collateral."[112]

In sum, the U.C.C. version of the *Market Overt* rule protects a huge segment of the population of the United States as third party purchasers of goods in the ordinary course of business from retailers and especially from department stores. The title to the consumer goods purchased, while subject to the good faith requirements of U.C.C. § 9–320(b), conveys possessory title supported by a document as informal as a retail or wholesale merchant's cash registry or credit card receipt. Such an informal document is found daily in the hands of millions of buyers whose sellers often lack the traditional detailed documentation of ownership of the goods sold. This legal revolution against what Professor Gilmore alluded to earlier as the classical (Roman and English law) world of "No one can transfer what he does not own" (*Nemo Dat Quod Non Habet*) must rank as one of the most significant in the history of commercial law. It is suely one of the factors in the diminution of the status of title to personal property used as collateral as became apparent in the heading of U.C.C. § 9–202, "Title to Collateral Immaterial."[113]

4. *Purchasing Practices, Master Agreements, Standardization of Quality and of Warranties*

Department stores, especially those that were part of chains, had to buy products in large quantities and had to assure their buyers that their products were of a uniform and standardized quality, so that at least their most successful lines of products reflected well on the store's trade name. This uniformity of quality made it easier for manufacturers and sellers to accompany their products with express and implied warranties of merchantability and fitness for the intended use or purpose of their products.

Presently, large department stores do much of their purchasing of inventory through "master" electronic supply agreements.[114] Once such a store's computer's inventory control software detects the need to order or re-order certain items, it issues a purchase order which triggers an electronic request (or application) to its bank for the issuance of a letter of credit to its supplier(s). The notification or confirmation of the issuance of the letter of credit to the supplier's bank or to the supplier triggers the

---

111 *See* U.C.C. § 9–320.

112 *See* U.C.C. § 9–320(a) official comment.

113 *See generally* Boris Kozolchyk, *Transfer of Personal Property by a Nonowner: Its Future in Light of its Past*, 61 TUL. L. REV. 1453 (1987).

114 *See infra* § 22:7(A) (for an analysis of the legal implications of this and related forms of electronic contracting).

supplier's notice to its freight forwarder to request shipping space and procure the issuance of an insurance policy or certificate to cover the shipment(s). Eventually, once the supplier receives the necessary document or electronic message from his carrier, insurer and quality and weight inspector, it will also trigger the supplier's issuance of a draft or demand for payment of the letter of credit from the paying bank.

This form of multi-party contracting (which will be re-visited in Chapter 22) is also used by other large enterprises intent on maximizing their efficiency by receiving and using their raw materials and products "just in time" to save the most costs. In doing this, as will also be discussed in that chapter, it does away with traditional components of purchase and sale agreements and creates another "dynamic" contract.[115]

5. *Consumer Credit Practices: Informality and Contracts of Adhesion*

As just noted, department stores popularized the use of cash registries that issued receipts of cash or check payments to their customers. Generally, this was the only written or printed record of the sale agreement and as such, bolstered informal practices that were consistent with their often massive and rapid sale transactions. They also shaped consumer-credit practices that allowed their customers to charge their purchases directly to their credit account with the store, to their charge card or to both. Charge accounts were among the most popular sources of consumer credit until the end of the Second World War. With proper identification, customers could make purchases on credit subject to a printed set of terms and conditions that were part of contracts of "adhesion" in which customers had no say on their terms and conditions.[116]

Finally, department stores contributed to the widespread use of credit cards, whose world-wide use continues to grow in our time. Although these cards were issued by independent financial intermediaries (many of them by well-known banks), they could be used not only for store purchases, but also for travel and entertainment. The department stores, as a rule, entered into an agreement with the issuers of the cards which enabled the issuer to earn a fee or discount for each use of their cards. Payments with credit cards provided their users with an easier enforcement of contractual warranties of merchantability and fitness of purpose, including by reversing charges for defective or returned products.

6. *Effects*

By increasing the variety of goods, standardizing their quality and easing their acquisition by means of informal transactions, charge accounts and eventually credit cards, department stores contributed significantly to an economy driven by consumption. From a commercial contract standpoint, department stores contributed to new forms of contracting with their customers and suppliers. With their customers, they replaced a "buyer beware" attitude with "the customer is always right" attitude, thereby creating an archetypal good faith intent. For their purchases, they, together with other large public and private entities, introduced multi-party contracts as part of paper-based and later electronic master agreements. These electronic master

---

[115] *Id.*

[116] *See* Friedrich Kessler, *Contracts of Adhesion—Some Thoughts About Freedom of Contract*, 43 COLUM. L. REV. 629 (1943). Incidentally, by that time, other contracts of adhesion were also used by providers of services as diverse as electricity, gas, transportation, insurance, and storage. The classic treatment of contracts of adhesion is still, in my opinion the late Yale University Professor Kessler.

agreements governed contractual relationships with, in principle, a limitless number of suppliers, carriers, insurers and issuers of letters of credit.

In their sales to consumers, they also relied on informal receipts of purchase and master agreements usually associated with charge accounts or cards and eventually credit cards. Today, when most consumer purchases are paid with credit cards, department stores also join the growing number of public and private entities that rely on contracts of adhesion to document their extensions of credit. Payments with credit cards have made it easier to stop payments, return products or claim refunds as extrajudicial remedies for breaches of the warranties of quality. And as payees of credit cards, department stores generate enough discountable or saleable commercial paper to help finance their credit needs.

§ 21.6 COMMERCIAL BANKS AND COMMERCIAL CREDIT

A. Experiments with National and State Banking Systems

When it gained its independence, the United States had neither a central bank nor an official currency.[117] The absence of these two components threatened the liquidity and solvency of the country. Alexander Hamilton, Secretary of the Treasury in President Washington's cabinet, realized that unless the new nation could re-finance its war debts and those of its constituting states, it would lose whatever credit-worthiness it had. With this in mind, he proposed in 1790 the creation of a United States bank modeled, as described in the preceding chapter, after the Bank of England. When the First Bank of the United States opened in Philadelphia in 1791, it had not only "bundled" the state and federal debt and offered repayment bonds at an attractive rate, but also acted as a commercial bank by offering commercial loans to new and established businesses.[118] And as with the Bank of England, its capital and ownership were both public and private—the federal government owned 20 percent of the bank, while private investors owned the rest. The First Bank of the United States achieved some of its creditworthiness goals, but "many politicians objected to the role that the private sector played in its operations; they believed that the government should have controlled it completely."[119]

It was not long before states began authorizing their own banks and issuing their own currency. When the War of 1812 against England broke out, it not only disrupted the trade of the United States but it also sent the federal government back into debt. The federal government then established the Second Bank of the United States in 1816; it was larger than its predecessor (29 branches), had a regulatory role and acted as a depositary bank for private banks. It also "cracked down on financial institutions that appeared to be signing over too many notes."[120] However, its activism disturbed an equally strong-willed President Andrew Jackson who was responsible for the failure to renew its charter in 1836.

---

[117] *See The Complete History of Banks in the United States,* MINT.COM, https://www.mint.com/the-complete-history-of-banks-in-the-united-states/ (last visited Dec. 3, 2013) (for an excellent summary of the United States banking system).

[118] *Id.*

[119] *Id.*

[120] *Id.*

Following this came a "free banking" era that was followed by a "national banking" era. During the free banking era (1837–1864), each state had the power to issue charters for new banks to operate within the state boundaries and many did with little or no regulation. A large number of unregulated banks were opened and, predictably, many had to close because of poor management of difficult market conditions. Shortly after instituting this free banking regime, a financial panic ensued and lingered for several years.

As a result of mounting debts, including those attributable to the Civil War, the federal government created yet another national bank in 1863 which retained some of the principles of free banking. Thus, individual banks could receive charters at either the national or the state levels. Those that chose national charters were required to use government-issued bills and back them with U.S.-issued bonds (which they had to purchase and use as reserves). After the state charter option was phased out, the United States had its first uniform currency in almost a century of existence. Since that time, every bank in the country has used the same federally minted coins and printed bills.

B. The Present Commercial Banking System

At the present time, approximately 8,000 banks are doing business as commercial banks in the United States[121] and some of them were founded at least two hundred years ago.[122] In the United States, commercial banks are the principal players in its payments and credit system. It is through these banks that Americans make most of their payments by "writing checks, swiping credit cards issued by banks or tied to them, and by paying bills via online banking."[123] A financial dictionary defines "near money" or "quasi-money" as "Assets that are easily convertible into cash, such as money market accounts and bank deposits."[124] Much of the money in circulation in the American economy is this private "quasi-money" increasingly in "virtual" form and the remainder is the "legal tender" issued by the Federal Reserve as notes and coins. As pointed out by New York University's Professor Richard Sylla:

> We have confidence in bank money because we can exchange it at the bank or an ATM for legal tender. Banks are obligated to hold reserves of legal tender to make these exchanges when we request them.[125]

As also noted by Professor Sylla:

> The second key function of banks is financial intermediation, lending or investing the money we deposit with them or credit they themselves create to business enterprises, households, and governments. This is the business side of banking. Most banks are profit-seeking corporations with stockholders who provide the equity capital needed to start and maintain a banking business.

---

121 *The Structure of the Federal Reserve System*, FEDERALRESERVEEDUCATION.ORG, www.federalreserveeducation.org/about-the-fed/structure-and-functions (last visited Dec. 3, 2013).

122 *See* Richard Sylla, *The US Banking System: Origin, Development, and Regulation*, THE GILDER LEHRAN INSTITUTE OF AMERICAN HISTORY, http://www.gilderlehrman.org/history-by-era/economics/essays/us-banking-system-origin-development-and-regulation (last accessed Dec. 3, 2013).

123 *Id.*

124 *Near Money,* THE FREE DICTIONARY, http://financial-dictionary.thefreedictionary.com/Quasi-money (last visited Dec. 3, 2013).

125 *See* Sylla, *supra* note 109.

Banks make their profits and cover their expenses by charging borrowers more for loans than they pay depositors for keeping money in the bank. The intermediation function of banks is extremely important because it helped to finance the many generations of entrepreneurs who built the American economy as well as the ordinary businesses that keep it going from year to year.[126]

Banks in the commercial banking system of the United States are either nationally- or state-chartered and regulated. A national bank is "any commercial bank chartered and supervised by the federal government and operated by private individuals."[127] In contrast, a state bank or a state chartered bank is "a commercial bank incorporated under a State charter and not required to be a member of the Federal Reserve System."[128]

Yet, as pointed out by banking law experts Geoffrey P. Miller and Avery I. Belka, even though the dual system of state and national chartering authorities has historically resulted in significant differences on permissible banking activities and in an increased complexity of the regulatory regimes, "federal legislation in the last decade has significantly nationalized banking law by expanding the jurisdiction of the federal regulators and increasingly subjecting state banks to federal banking standards."[129]

The Office of the Comptroller of the Currency (OCC) is the federal entity with the authority to charter these banks. In the case of state banks the regulatory authority is allocated with each state's chartering authority.[130] In addition, because:

> [N]early all banks are required to have deposit insurance, regardless of charter, the Federal Deposit Insurance Corporation (FDIC) also plays a significant regulatory role. Finally, the Board of Governors of the Federal Reserve (Board of Governors) also is a primary regulator of Bank Holding Companies and state chartered banks that are members of the Federal Reserve System.[131]

C. The Federal Reserve and Commercial Lending

1. Goals and Means

The Federal Reserve System of the United States was created on December 23, 1913 by the Federal Reserve Act.[132] Its Board of Governors lists as the main purpose of

---

126 *Id.*

127 *National Bank,* ENCYCLOPAEDIA BRITANNICA, http://www.britannica.com/EBchecked/topic/404493/national-bank (last accessed Dec. 3, 2013).

128 *State Bank,* THE FREE DICTIONARY, http://www.thefreedictionary.com/State+Chartered+Bank (last accessed Dec. 3, 2013).

129 *See* Geoffrey P. Miller and Avery I. Belka, *U.S. Banking System, in* Kozolchyk, IV UNITED STATES LAW 32–i, 32–1.

130 *Id.*

131 *Id.* at 32–4.

132 Federal Reserve Banks Act of 1913, Pub. L. No. 63–43, 38 Stat. 251 (1913).

this system to provide the nation with "a safer, more flexible, and more stable monetary and financial system."[133] Hence, it is charged with the following:

> Conducting the nation's monetary policy by influencing money and credit conditions in the economy in pursuit of full employment and stable prices. [To supervise and regulate] banks and other important financial institutions to ensure the safety and soundness of the nation's banking and financial system and to protect the credit rights of consumers. [To maintain] the stability of the financial system and containing systemic risk that may arise in financial markets. [And, to provide] certain financial services to the U.S. government, U.S. financial institutions, and foreign official institutions, and playing a major role in operating and overseeing the nation's payments systems.[134]

One of the salient characteristics of the Federal Reserve is its considerable independence. The President of the United States selects its chairman, but in the words of its Board of Governors:

> [It is] an independent entity within government. It is not "owned" by anyone and is not a private, profit-making institution.
>
> [It] derives its authority from the Congress of the United States. . . . [but] its monetary policy decisions do not have to be approved by the President or anyone else in the executive or legislative branches of government, it does not receive funding appropriated by the Congress, and the terms of the members of the Board of Governors span multiple presidential and congressional terms. However, the Federal Reserve is subject to oversight by the Congress, which often reviews the Federal Reserve's activities and can alter its responsibilities by statute. Therefore, the Federal Reserve can be more accurately described as 'independent within the government' rather than 'independent of government.'[135]

Congress established 12 regional Federal Reserve Banks and organized them as private corporations, *i.e.*, they issue shares of stock to their member banks as a condition of their membership. Nonetheless, since the Federal Reserve banks are not-for-profit entities, their stock may not be sold, traded, or pledged and their dividends are, by law, six percent per year.[136]

The Federal Reserve Bank of San Francisco describes the supervisory function of the Federal Reserve over banking institutions as follows:

> [T]he Fed promotes the safety and soundness of the banking system, fosters stability in financial markets, and ensures compliance with laws and regulations under its jurisdiction. The Fed encourages banking institutions to meet the financial needs of their communities by making prudent loans, among other actions. Supervision involves examining the financial condition of individual banks and evaluating their compliance with laws and

---

[133] *What is the Purpose of the Federal Reserve System?* BOARD OF GOVERNORS OF THE FEDERAL RESERVE SYSTEM (Aug. 2, 2012), http://www.federalreserve.gov/faqs/about_12594.htm.

[134] *Id.*

[135] *Who Owns the Federal Reserve?*, BOARD OF GOVERNORS OF THE FEDERAL RESERVE SYSTEM (Aug. 2, 2013), http://www.federalreserve.gov/faqs/about_14986.htm.

[136] *Id.*

regulations. Bank regulation involves setting rules and guidelines for the banking system.[137]

As also described by the Federal Reserve Bank of San Francisco, it is the nation's monetary policy authority which empowers it to influence the availability and cost of money and credit in pursuance of a healthy economy. In discharging this mission it pursues the above-mentioned goals of insuring a maximum sustainable output and employment and maintaining stable prices, meaning low, stable inflation. These dual policy goals require moderate long-term interest rates:

> The Fed works to fulfill its dual mandate primarily by setting a target for a key interest rate, the federal funds rate, which is what financial institutions charge each other for loans in the overnight borrowing market. The federal funds rate serves as a benchmark for many other short-term interest rates and consequently broadly influences credit conditions. The Fed uses a number of tools to keep the federal funds rate near its target.[138]

One of these tools makes funds available to the banking system by purchasing government bonds on the market as part of its "open market" operations; "banks take those funds and lend them out in the form of [their depositors'] checking account balances, which amount to a significant multiple over the amount of funds introduced into the system by the government's action."[139] Another tool is by discounting and re-discounting the member banks' commercial paper. The latter is of considerable importance to commercial lawyers.

2. *Paul Warburg and the Federal Reserve Act*

Paul Warburg devoted much of his life to the creation of a functional central banking system in the United States especially through the enactment of the Federal Reserve Act of 1913.[140] He was born in Hamburg Germany in 1868, the offspring of the prominent German banking family M. Warburg & Co. He married an American citizen and became a permanent resident of the United States as well as a partner at his father-in-law's firm, Kuhn, Loeb and Co., one of Wall Street's most important and respected banking houses. As an experienced European banker, he was shocked at the undeveloped status of banking and finances in the United States during the early 1900s.

At that time, the United States was suffering from a rigid system of fixed reserves that prevented the printing of public money when needed, thus discouraging the creation of liquid private or "quasi-money."[141] It was one of the causes of periodic liquidity crises and panics such as the one of 1907.[142] For this reason, manufacturers,

---

137 *See What is the Fed: Supervision and Regulation,* FEDERAL RESERVE BANK OF SAN FRANCISCO, http://www.frbsf.org/education/teacher-resources/what-is-the-fed/supervision-regulation (last visited Dec. 3, 2013).

138 *What is the Fed: Monetary Policy,* FEDERAL RESERVE BANK OF SAN FRANCISCO, http://www.frbsf.org/education/teacher-resources/what-is-the-fed/monetary-policy (last visited Dec. 2, 2013).

139 Miller and Belka, *supra* note 116, at 32–2.

140 *See generally* Michael A. Whitehouse, *Paul Warburg's Crusade to Establish a Central Bank in the United States* (May 1, 1989) http://www.minneapolisfed.org/publications_papers/pub_display.cfm?id=3815.

141 *Id.*

142 *The 1907 Crisis in Historical Perspective,* FAS.HARVARD.EDU, http://www.fas.harvard.edu/~histecon/crisis-next/1907/ (last visited Dec. 2, 2013). According to this source and a study by Paul Warburg, this crisis and subsequent panic resulted from a failed attempt to corner the market on the United Copper

wholesalers, retailers of hard and dry goods and their counterparts in the farming business were unable to obtain credit to finance the acquisition of their respective raw materials, equipment and inventories. As these crises spread, the stock market continued to plunge and bank failures proliferated.

Among the remedies proposed by Warburg was the creation of an American discount market for commercial paper similar to that available to European bankers and their customers-borrowers. He maintained that the United States' central bank supply of money should vary with the short-term legitimate needs of commerce. When these needs increased, the discount by the Federal Reserve Bank of the customer-originated commercial paper held by member banks would provide these customers with ample credit at market rates. When the needs decreased, the supply of quasi-money would also decrease, thereby making it an elastic system of money supply.

The Federal Reserve Bank would accomplish its discount function by advancing to member banks significant portions of the face value of the commercial paper they had indorsed to the regional Federal Reserve Banks. The period for the repayment of the Federal Reserve advances reflected the time during which their member banks' customers would normally repay their indebtedness to those banks. And this time fluctuated with the time it took the member banks' borrowers-clients to sell or to manufacture and sell the respective goods or commodities to their users or consumers. Often the commercial paper (mostly bills of exchange or drafts) that signified the loans made to the merchants who borrowed from the member banks was secured (and accompanied) by documents of title such as ocean bills of lading or warehouse receipts similarly endorsed to the Federal Reserve Bank.

The following are excerpts from Paul Warburg's "The Discount System in Europe"[143] which summarize his speeches and writings in anticipation of the enactment of the Federal Reserve Act of 1913.

3. *Fixed Ratios of Bank Reserves for Demand Obligations v. The Flexible European Discount System*

According to Paul Warburg:

> No mathematical rule can state the correct proportion between reserves and demand obligations. . . . This general principle, however, may be safely laid down: with the present system of immense deposits payable on demand . . . only that structure is safe and efficient which provides for effective concentration of cash reserves [with the central banking authority] and their freest use in case of need, and enables the banks, when necessary, to turn into cash a maximum of their assets with a minimum of disturbance to general conditions. . . . It is now generally acknowledged . . . [European] central bank system. . . . [I]t was a victory of the 'discount system' over the system of cash advances. . . .[144]

Company's stock which led to a string of bank runs and a national panic. The failure of numerous banks and trusts, led to a crisis of faith in the banking system throughout the United States.

[143] Paul M. Warburg, *The Discount System in Europe*, 4 ESSAYS ON BANKING REFORM IN THE UNITED STATES 129 (No. 4, July 1914).

[144] *Id.*

4. *Discounts, Acceptances of Drafts and Documentary Letters of Credit*

Warburg defined the discount of a draft as a temporary indebtedness paid off by the transaction *the carrying out of which the loan was supposed to make possible.* His example was that of a bill of exchange drawn for the sale of cotton while it was being harvested, was in transit for Europe, being manufactured into yarn, or during the time that a merchant had not yet paid for finished articles to the manufacturer, the holder of the bill. Thus, the maturity of the bill depended on the time for the payment of the underlying transaction, which usually was three months.

Bills of exchange or drafts could be drawn by a seller against his buyer and were known as trade acceptances. Or they could be drawn against the European bankers by the seller or exporter of the goods who was frequently also the beneficiary of their letters of credit.[145] Warburg gave the example of an American merchant who bought coffee in San Paolo, Brazil. He generally paid for it by procuring the issuance of a letter of credit by a European bank with a three month maturity. Accordingly, the European banker agreed to accept a three months' bill drawn on him, accompanied by the usual shipping documents such as an invoice, an ocean bill of lading and an insurance policy. The seller-beneficiary would have no difficulty in selling to a bank in San Paolo his bill drawn on a first-class European banking house and thus would promptly obtain the money due him for the goods sold. "The local bank in San Paolo will buy the bill without hesitation (if the shipper is not of the very best standing, the bank will demand that the letter of credit against which the bill is drawn be produced) because it knows that it need only send this foreign bill to England, Germany or France . . . where, owing to the extensive discount market in these countries, it can immediately rediscount the bill, thus securing repayment in cash for the amount invested."[146] Yet:

> [N]o matter how good may be the credit of the American purchaser or of any American bank, whose acceptance the purchaser may offer to the shipper in China, South America, or Europe, no shipper in such countries will, as a general rule, take the acceptance of an American bank or banker, because the American bill has no ready market, while the European bill is of very easy sale.[147]

---

[145] *See Definition of Acceptance,* Financial Times Lexicon, http://lexicon.ft.com/Term?term= acceptance (last visited Dec. 2, 2013). The Financial Times accurately describes a bill of exchange as:

> [An instrument] that binds one party (the acceptor) to pay a specific amount to another at a stated time in the future. A type of time draft used particularly in international trade. If it is drawn directly by the seller of goods on the buyer, it is called a trade acceptance or trade bill. Acceptances can also be issued by finance companies or banks and used as a means of financing trade. A banker's acceptance (BA), also called bank bill, is an acceptance drawn on and accepted by a bank. Such bills are sold by banks at a discount (the banker's acceptance (BA) rate), and redeemed with the same or other accepting banks at face value within a relatively short timeframe (typically one to nine months). As such, the paper is effectively a bank-backed, short-term, non-interest bearing note and qualifies as a money market instrument.

Id.

[146] Warburg, *supra* note 130, at 132.

[147] *Id.* at 133.

5. *The Supply and Demand Elements of a Creditworthy Commercial Contract*

As will be readily apparent in the transcribed portions from the Federal Reserve Act, Warburg's influence on its discount rules of commercial paper was decisive.[148] He persuasively identified the key features of the supply and demand side of the creation of private money. On the supply side, the Federal Reserve Act had to grant its member banks the power to create a market for the commercial paper executed by the customers of these banks and accepted or endorsed (or both) by the member banks. Additionally, it had to concentrate ample enough cash reserves in the central bank to assure the necessary supply of loan funds throughout the system. Finally, to preserve and grow this market, the Federal Reserve had to carefully supervise the quality of the loans, *i.e.*, their liquidity or the member banks' ability to convert them into cash quickly and inexpensively. In identifying these features, Warburg also identified the characteristics of the commercial loans (including the underlying transactions they financed) so as to make them safe and sound to the lending banks and their regulators.

The chief characteristics of these loans were: (1) Faithfulness to their stated purpose so that their performance could be measured against the fulfillment of that purpose; (2) The ability of the loan to be repaid out of the proceeds of the contemplated manufacture, wholesale or retail activity of the borrower, and thus the exclusion of purely financial transactions; (3) The lender's ability to rely on collateral whose market value could be easily and reliably ascertained and realized; (4) A loan maturity that did not exceed the customary period for the repayment of that transaction by the ultimate buyers or users, usually a short period measured in terms of no more than three months; (5) Accessibility to such a loan by anyone who dealt in the goods involved in the loan, regardless of whether such a borrower was an officially licensed merchant, a farmer or a professional producer, supplier or servicer of the goods.

6. *Statutory Rules on Loans That Involve or Are Secured by Readily Marketable Staples*

Section 13 of the Federal Reserve Act (12 U.S.C. § 343) sets forth the powers of Federal Reserve Banks. Among these is the power to discount commercial, agricultural and industrial paper:

> Upon the indorsement of any of its member banks, which shall be deemed a waiver of demand, notice and protest by such bank as to its own indorsement exclusively, any Federal reserve bank may discount notes, drafts, and bills of exchange *arising out of actual commercial transactions; that is, notes, drafts, and bills of exchange issued or drawn for agricultural, industrial, or commercial purposes, or the proceeds of which have been used, or are to be used, for such purposes,* the Board of Governors of the Federal Reserve System to have the right to determine or define the character of the paper thus eligible for discount, within the meaning of this Act. Nothing in this Act

---

[148] *See* Whitehouse, *supra* note 127. Whitehouse shows that at first Warburg had a difficult time convincing Senator Nelson Aldrich, the most influential member of an elite congressional finance committee, on the need to create an elastic method of creating private money modeled after European practices. However after a trip to Europe, Aldrich became an ardent supporter of the European model while Warburg argued for a more balanced approach which was eventually adopted by a Democrat Congress. *Id.*

> contained shall be construed to prohibit such notes, drafts, and bills of exchange, *secured by staple agricultural products, or other goods, wares, or merchandise from being eligible for such discount, and the notes, drafts, and bills of exchange of factors issued as such making advances exclusively to producers of staple agricultural products in their raw state shall be eligible for such discount*; but such definition shall not include notes, drafts, or bills covering merely investments or issued or drawn for the purpose of carrying or trading in stocks, bonds, or other investment securities, except bonds and notes of the government of the United States. Notes, drafts, and bills admitted to discount under the terms of this paragraph must have a maturity at the time of discount of not more than 90 days, exclusive of grace.[149]

Please note the emphasis on the commercial liquidity of the transaction envisaged by the Board of Governors. To improve this liquidity, it precluded the endorser of the commercial paper's reliance on purely formalistic defenses such as lack of notice of non-payment or dishonor. And on the substance of the transaction, it requires that the commercial paper arise solely from *actual commercial transactions* (including factors-lenders as participants in these transactions). Hence, it forbids the discounts of notes, drafts, or bills that were "issued or drawn for the purpose of carrying or trading in stocks, bonds, or other investment securities. . ."[150] In other words, the commercial liquidity it relies on is inconsistent with speculative transactions involving investment securities with few exceptions. Finally, it limited the duration of the discounted notes, drafts and bills to those with a maturity of not more than 90 days, exclusive of grace. Thus, the duration of the discounted commercial paper cannot exceed beyond what the market considers the prudent duration of short term commercial credits.

The Comptroller of the Currency of the United States acting under the aegis of the Department of the Treasury defines a readily marketable staple as:

> [A]n article of commerce, agriculture, or industry, such as wheat and other grains, cotton, wool, and basic metals such as tin, copper and lead, in the form of standardized interchangeable units, that is easy to sell in a market with sufficiently frequent price quotations.[151]

In turn, state statutes that regulate the lending limits of state banks echo the powers granted and limitations imposed by 12 U.S.C. § 343. For example, Oregon's Statutes § 708A.335[152] state in relevant part that "[o]bligations secured by documents covering readily marketable staples" are discountable:

---

149 *Federal Reserve Act Section 13. Powers of Federal Reserve Banks,* BOARD OF GOVERNORS OF THE FEDERAL RESERVE (May 23, 2013), http://www.federalreserve.gov/aboutthefed/section13.htm (emphasis added). This source restates the text found in 12 U.S.C. 343, as amended by act of Sept. 7, 1916 (39 Stat. 752), which completely revised this section; and by act of March 4, 1923 (42 Stat. 1478). As used in this paragraph the phrase "bonds and notes of Government of the United States" includes Treasury bills or certificates of indebtedness. (*See* act of June 17, 1929, amending section 5 of Second Liberty Bond Act of Sept. 24, 1917). As to eligibility for discount under this paragraph of notes representing loans to finance building construction, *see Federal Reserve Act Section 24. Real Estate Loans,* BOARD OF GOVERNORS OF THE FEDERAL RESERVE (May 23, 2013), http://www.federalreserve.gov/aboutthefed/section24.htm.

150 *See supra* note 136 and accompanying text.

151 12 CFR § 32.2 (2013); *see also Readily Marketable Staple Law & Legal Definition,* USLEGAL.COM, http://definitions.uslegal.com/r/readily-marketable-staple/ (last visited Dec. 3, 2013).

152 *§ 708A.335: Obligation Secured by Documents Covering Readily Marketable Staples,* OREGONLAWS.ORG, http://www.oregonlaws.org/ors/708A.335 (last visited Dec. 3, 2013).

> (1) In addition to obligations permitted under ORS 708A.295 (Limitations on amount of obligations to Oregon commercial bank), an Oregon commercial bank may make loans and acquire other obligations of a person secured by documents of title covering readily marketable staples, provided the obligation does not exceed: (a) 15 percent of the Oregon commercial banks capital, where the principle amount of the obligation does not exceed 85 percent of the market value of the staples. . . . [This percentage increases with the higher collateral to loan ratio.] (e) 40 percent of the Oregon commercial banks capital, where the principle amount of the obligation does not exceed 65 percent of the market value of the staples.[153]

7. *Effects: An Archetypal Secured Commercial Loan*

It is true that Warburg's elastic, commercial-loan-inspired supply of quasi-money did not play the pervasive, money supply role he expected. Open market operations consisting of buying and selling government bonds became the primary tool for implementing monetary policy, including establishing interest rates for short-term loans and the total amount of printed money in circulation.[154] Nonetheless, as was just discussed, it was Warburg who identified the elements of discountable commercial paper: Its beneficiaries could be traditional merchants as well as farmers; and whatever were the goods or services involved in the underlying transaction, they had to be true to its purpose and enable the discounted loan paper to be self-liquidating during a short period of time. Thus, paper derived from speculative financial transactions would not qualify for Federal Reserve Bank discount even if its duration was shorter than three months.

By identifying these and related regulatory elements, Warburg did more than institute the discount of commercial paper as a permanent function of the Federal Reserve and state banking systems. He identified the crucial elements of America's archetypal secured commercial loan, including its self-liquidating nature and the consistency between its avowed and real purpose.

---

[153] *Id. See also WAC 208–512A–040: Special rule—Readily Marketable Staples,* LEG.WA.GOV, http://apps.leg.wa.gov/WAC/default.aspx?cite=208–512A–040 (last visited Dec. 3, 2013) (for an analogous provision by the State of Washington but with different loan to collateral ratios, and a rule on aggregate limits). It states:

> Special rule—Readily marketable staples.
>
> (1) Loans and extensions of credit secured by bills of lading, warehouse receipts, or similar documents transferring or securing title to readily marketable staples shall be subject to a limitation of thirty-five percent of capital and surplus, in addition to the general limit set forth in WAC 208–512A–010, if the market value of the staples securing each additional loan or extension of credit at all times equals or exceeds one hundred fifteen percent of the outstanding amount of such loan or extension of credit.

Id.

[154] *See Open Market Operations,* BOARD OF GOVERNORS OF THE FEDERAL RESERVE SYSTEM, http://www.federalreserve.gov/monetarypolicy/openmarket.htm (last visited Dec. 3, 2013).

§ 21.7 CREDIT RATING AGENCIES: THEIR IMPACT ON COMMERCIAL CREDIT

A. Brief History

Because commercial credit was as widespread in the eighteenth century in the United States as it was in England, if not more, the collection and distribution of reliable information on the creditworthiness of actual or potential debtors was a business waiting to happen, and it did during the early decades of the nineteenth century. As will be illustrated in the following sections (and will be discussed in detail in Chapter 22), the omnipresence of commercial credit, fueled by data on the debtors' willingness and ability to repay, stamped American commercial contracts with dynamic and flexible features unlike those of the "civil" or not-for-profit contracts governed by the *Code Civil* and its progeny. It is worth repeating that if the business of America is business, the chief lubricant of that business in the United States, more than in any other nation, is credit, both to merchants and consumers. This role was propitiated by Warburg's vision of an elastic central banking policy on self-liquidating commercial loans and paper as well as by the private sector's collection and distribution of reliable information on creditworthiness.

Indiana University Professor Emeritus of History James Madison's 1974 study on the evolution of credit rating agencies in the United States[155] called attention to the reliance on personal ties for much of their credit information by early nineteenth-century American merchants. Their trade was often conducted with merchants they knew well:

> Country merchants from the West and South traveled to seacoast cities where year after year they purchased their goods from the same wholesalers. Even if the seller did not know a prospective buyer personally, he had available sources of information in the form of the experience and opinions of other merchants.[156]

In his 2008 lecture at the German Historical Institute in Washington, "Civilizing Capitalism? The Beginnings of Credit Ratings in the United States and Germany,"[157] Professor Hartmut Berghoff's of Germany's Gottingen University confirmed the same high level of entrustment found by Professor Madison. Despite the fact that newly arrived businessmen did not know each other and were of different ethnic and cultural backgrounds, their trust in each other was impressive; around 1850, U.S. retailers sold up to three-quarters of their stock on credit and, thus, were dependent on credit from their suppliers.[158] However, as inter-regional markets expanded and business transactions took place increasingly among strangers, defaults "became rampant."[159]

---

155 James H. Madison, *The Evolution of Commercial Credit Reporting Agencies in Nineteenth-Century America*, 48 BUS. HIST. REV. 164 (1974), *available at* http://www.jstor.Org/stable/3112840.

156 *Id.* at 165.

157 Hartmut Berghoff, *Civilizing Capotalism? The Beginnings of Credit Rating in the United States and Germany* (Inaugural Lecture at the German Historical Institute) (Washington, Nov. 14, 2008), http://www.ghi-dc.org/files/publications/bulletin/bu045/bu45_009.pdf.

158 *Id.* at 16.

159 *Id.* at 16.

Olegario refers to a general perception among commercial credit suppliers during the first half of the nineteenth century in England and America "from about the 1840s onward . . . only between 3 and 10 percent of all businesses managed to avoid liquidity problems."[160] One response was for suppliers to "band together into trade protection societies, where members agreed to alert one another regularly about bad debtors."[161] Another response was to obtain information on potential debtors by hiring agents or spies, a method that proved costly and unreliable.[162]

Eventually, Lewis Tappan, a New York merchant, (also known for his anti-slavery and abolitionist views) founded the "Mercantile Agency" in New York in 1841. According to Professor Berghoff, Tappan began to sell credit information at the very moment "[when] the railroads [were creating] interregional anonymous markets" much, I would add, as the one mentioned earlier between milk and dairy producers and consumers in New York State.[163] Paradoxically, as a strict Congregationalist, Tappan regarded credit as evil and so expressed in 1843: "How much wisdom there is in the advice of the apostle Paul—'Owe no man anything.' "[164] Nonetheless, since he had learned that to be in business in America one must have access to credit, he wanted to "purify" the business of credit. With such a celestial and earthly ambition, he created one of America's first credit reporting agencies, one that eventually became the largest in the world.

In 1849, Tappan turned the agency over to Benjamin Douglass, one of his former clerks; Douglass expanded the network of offices and increasingly staffed them with full-time employees.[165] A decade or so later, many of these employees became skilled credit reporters and interpreters of credit information. These skills made them cognizant of sound business and especially credit practices and thus they were respected professionals. Among such former reporters were four U.S. presidents: Abraham Lincoln, Ulysses S. Grant, Grover Cleveland and William McKinley. In 1859, Douglass turned over the agency to his brothe-in-law Robert Graham Dun, who renamed it R.G. Dun & Co. and continued Douglass's expansion; by 1880 it had 69 branch offices and 10,000 correspondents.[166]

Also in 1849, John M. Bradstreet Company set up a competing agency in Cincinnati, Ohio. Its distinguished characteristic was its use of credit ratings. With the publication of the first book of commercial credit ratings, Bradstreet's agency was a genuine competitor of Tappan's and Douglass's Mercantile Agency.[167] It was not until 1933 that these two rivals merged and became what is still today Dun & Bradstreet (D & B).

The information provided by these credit rating agencies was not always reliable during the first decades of operation: Lack of objective (especially accounting) data on the potential borrowers' creditworthiness and frequently shoddy and biased research

---

160 OLEGARIO, *supra* note 43, at 36.

161 *Id.* at 37.

162 *Id.*

163 *See* Berghoff, *supra* note 144, at 16.

164 *Id.* at 16.

165 *See Dun and Bradstreet Company History,* D & B, http://www.dnb.com/company/history.html (last visited Dec. 4, 2013) (for Dun and Bradstreet's own account of its history and accomplishments).

166 *Id.*

167 *Id.*

on the business performance of subject merchants did not portend well. In due course, however, the analysis of creditworthiness improved and enabled commercial credit to grow to unprecedented levels.

During the 1960's, D & B acquired new technologies including a Data Universal Numbering System, The D & B D-U-N-S® Number, which in our day "has become a standard business identifier for the United Nations, the European Commission and the U.S. Government."[168] At present, after having spun off major business information companies such as A.C. Nielsen, Cognizant, Reuben H. Donnelley and Moody's Corporation, D & B provides business and credit information services, including credit ratings, by relying on a global database that "now covers more than 225 million businesses worldwide."[169] For the students of United States' commercial contract practices, the data collected by credit reporting agencies provided as an additional bonus a closer view of the practices, attitudes and values of the contracting parties as well as of those who reported their practices and rated them as practitioners.

B. Character Traits of an Archetypal Mid-Nineteenth Century Credit Worthy Borrower: The Meaning of Honesty

By the late 1840s, credit reporting agencies used a shared set of criteria to "calculate creditworthiness in a systematic way."[170] In addition to the borrower's business ability or capacity to do business and repay their loans, the criteria included some of the same character traits encountered in eighteenth-century Puritan New England: Honesty, punctuality, thrift, sobriety, energy (or a strong work ethic) and focus.[171] These character traits earned for their possessors a presumption of good faith dealing. However, before I discuss the contractual effects of this presumption I would like to briefly explore the meaning of honesty among credit givers with the help of Olegario's helpful source materials.

Olegario found that merchants who had a reputation for honesty and ability, but encountered financial difficulties were frequently allowed by their creditors to continue to operate their businesses in the hope that they would recover.[172] She quotes business writers on the practical value of being honest with one's creditors:

> These houses which have become insolvent or embarrassed, and have made a clean showing of their affairs, have found much sympathy and no difficulty in arranging a settlement.[173]

She also quotes Daniel Defoe's similar advice to British merchants in trouble:

> [H]onesty obliges every man, when he sees his stock is gone . . . and eating into the estates of other men, to put a stop to it; and to do it in time, while something is left. . . . 'call his creditors together, lay his circumstances

[168] *Id.*

[169] *Id.*

[170] OLEGARIO, *supra* note 43, at 82.

[171] *Id.*

[172] *Id.* at 93.

[173] *Id.* (citation omitted).

> honestly before them, and pay as far as it will go . . . By breaking in time you will first obtain the character of an honest, tho' unfortunate man.'[174]

In short, the honesty that credit givers expected to find in the reports or ratings was one that reflected not only a willingness to pay whenever possible, but also a willingness to disclose the debtors' true business condition.

C. Effects of the Presumption of a Debtor's Good Faith

Honesty defined as a willingness to pay and to disclose all the facts relevant to his ability to do so helped the debtor in trouble establish his presumptive good faith and with it acquire a better chance for continuing credit support and perhaps commercial and social rehabilitation.

This presumption played an important role in a society whose state laws were known to be protective of debtors, often at the expense of creditors. As noted by Samuel H. Terry's 1869 The Retailer's Manual:

> Wherever the laws shield a debtor, as they do so generally throughout the United States, the best guarantee for payment, that a creditor can have, is the moral and equitable obligation to pay, in the heart of the debtor.[175]

When such "moral and equitable virtues" (amounting to good faith) were detected in a particular borrower, entrustment followed even if it entailed shipping goods on credit to a distant merchant. As you will recall from our discussion on why the *Code Civil* lacked rules on offers and acceptances *inter absentes*,[176] the main reason behind the uncertainty of communications was the generalized distrust of distant merchants. It would not have helped such merchants to prove their willingness to pay in past transactions or to disclose their present difficulties. Hence, while "rules of traffic" for offers and acceptances, *i.e.*, when and where they bound the offerors and offerees, appeared in English law in the 1818 *Adams v. Lindsell* decision[177] and thereafter in United States law;[178] it took decades before similar rules appeared in jurisdictions governed or influenced by the *Code Civil*.

D. The Problems with Biased Credit Reports

The ability to establish the neo-Puritan-inspired good faith character traits was especially important at a time when income statements and balance sheets (the present reliable indicators of the health of a business) were largely unavailable, and even when they were available, their credibility was questionable in the absence of

---

[174] *Id.* at 93–94 (citation omitted).

[175] *See* SAMUEL H. TERRY, THE RETAILER'S MANUAL: EMBODYING THE CONCLUSION OF THIRTY YEARS' EXPERIENCE IN MERCHANDIZING 196 (1869).

[176] *See supra* § 8:7(M).

[177] *See, e.g.*, Adams v. Lindsell 106 Eng. Rep. 250 [K.B. 1818], *infra* § 22:8(B).

[178] *See* Clarence D. Ashley, *Formation of Contracts* Inter Absentes, 2 COL. L. REV. 1 (1902) (for an early analysis of the impact of this decision on U.S. law); *see also Acceptance By Mail: Adams v. Lindsell*, 25 IND. L.J. 202 (1950), *available at* http://www.repository.law.indiana.edu/ilj/vol25/iss2/6/. It concludes that:

> With the exception of one early Massachusetts case (McCulloch v. Eagle Ins. Co., 1 Pick 278 [1822] the courts of the United States have been unanimous in ruling that a bilateral contract entered into through the medium of the mails is complete at the moment the offeree deposits his acceptance in the mail.

Id. at 202 n.3.

uniform accounting standards.[179] Thus, a simple report would refer to the debtors, whether as individuals or group businesses, in general terms such as:

> John Doe and Richard Roe Buffalo City, Hardware. Both educated to merchandise, and been in business for about 10 years; men of correct business habits; honest, intelligent, and prudent. Doe aged 36, married, *worth $15,000.* Roe aged 30, single, *worth $10,000—about half of their property in real estate,* able friends and engaged in no other business. They are very safe men.[180]

Early credit reporting agencies such as Lewis Tappan's Mercantile Agency relied, then, mostly on unprofessional and unpaid persons (usually bankers, lawyers, aldermen and merchants and other "putative dignitaries") as their sources of information.[181] What mattered to these largely volunteer-reporters were "certain personal traits such as religious faith, moderation in consumption and sexuality, and the 'right' ethnicity":[182] "The message was [neo-Puritanically] clear: a 'good family man'—as the expression usually went—with modest financial security was a better risk than a rich but immoral rake.[183]

Berghoff attributes many of the initial ratings to America's emerging WASP middle class, to which, "not surprisingly, the correspondents belonged" and he added that Tappan:

> [H]oped to improve overall morals by disciplining people by means of credit reports. . . .
>
> On average, Jewish businessmen received lower ratings than Christians. One report said, 'We should deem him safe but he is not a white man. He is a Jew,' subsequently recommending he be kept on a short repayment leash, for 'delay is always dangerous with Jews.' In one case, the correspondent was obviously well versed in the bible and took a very long-term approach to credit history. He held an otherwise very solid [Jewish] merchant house responsible for what had happened during the Jewish exile in ancient Egypt. His report read: 'Are doing an excellent business . . . character and habits good. . . . Considered good by all dealers, but they are Jews, and their ancestors took Jewels of the Egyptians when they left Egypt and never returned them.'[184]

Olegario reports a similar racist attitude with respect to Black businessmen:

> Credit reports almost always indicated when a business was black owned. These individuals were designated as "free men of color," "darky," "negro," "colored," "quadroon," "mulatto," and—infrequently—"nigger." As with Jewish business owners, the agency reports sometimes noted that an individual was a good risk despite belonging to a suspect group.[185]

Women-owned businesses were a minority within a minority (about 145,000 in 1870); they confined their businesses to women's clothing, especially millinery and

---

179 OLEGARIO, *supra* note 43, at 83.

180 *Id.* at 87.

181 Berghoff, *supra* note 144, at 17.

182 *Id.*

183 *Id.* at 18.

184 *Id.*

185 OLEGARIO, *supra* note 43, at 113.

dressmaking and "[e]ven after the Civil War, a reported total worth of only a few hundred dollars was not unusual."[186]

As noted by Professor Berghoff, negative credit reports could be devastating and prevent businessmen from ever obtaining credit:

> If a report read "never trust him, will always be worthless" or took whole families into collective liabilities ("The whole lot of the Weatherbys are Bad Eggs"), relentless social execution took place. Judgments like "he has no energy & will never make a dollar" or "has never succeeded at anything & probably never will" make it clear that people were denied a second or even a first chance forever.[187]

Despite the serious consequences of such reports, the defense-friendly judicial standards of liability for sending erroneous and at times slanderous information on potential debtors discouraged many of the lawsuits brought against them, especially after the financial panic of 1873.[188] Thus, *Ormsby v. Douglass*,[189] an 1868 decision by the Court of Appeals of New York, protected the Douglass agency from a charge of slander by holding that:

> [Defendant] whose business it was to obtain information respecting the credit and responsibility of persons in business, and to furnish the same to those who had just occasion to use it, his communications, made in good faith to a subscriber in respect to the character and standing of the plaintiff, are to be deemed confidential. Where communications are regarded as privileged, they are protected from the presumption of malice which is usually to be inferred from the charge itself.[190]

In addition, the 1867 decision in *Gibson v. R.G. Dun*[191] by the Court of Common Pleas of Hamilton County, Ohio had already set forth a standard of "reasonable diligence" in searching for and supplying such information.[192] This judicial attitude was in contrast to that of various state legislatures that would have imposed liability on the agencies responsible for disseminating the inaccurate reports for the losses they caused.[193] Because of decisions such as the above, by the end of the Civil War, credit reporting and rating agencies had become regular participants in the commercial credit system of the United States with credit evaluation powers that exceeded those that many state legislators would have granted them.

---

[186] *Id.* at 109.

[187] Berghoff, *supra* note 144, at 18.

[188] *See* OLEGARIO, *supra* note 43, at 170.

[189] 37 N.Y. 477 (1868).

[190] *Id.* at 477.

[191] R.G. DUN & COMPANY, OHIO COURT OF COMMON PLEASE (HAMILTON COUNTY), ONTARIO COURT OF QUEEN'S BENCH, AND ONTARIO COURT OF APPEAL, REPORT OF IMPORTANT CASES AGAINST THE MERCANTILE AGENCY AS TO THEIR LIABILITY FOR REPRESENTATIONS, HONESTLY MADE IN THE COUSE OF THEIR BUSINESS: GIBSON VS. DUN, COURT OF COMMON PLEAS, HAMILTON COUNTY, OHIO: MCLEAN VS. DUN, COURT OF QUEEN'S BENCH AND COURT OF APPEAL, ONTARIO, CANADA (1877), *available at* http://www.worldcat.org/title/report-of-important-cases-against-the-mercantile-agency-as-to-their-liability-for-representations-honestly-made-in-the-course-of-their-business-gibson-vs-dun-court-of-common-pleas-hamilton-county-ohio-mclean-vs-dun-court-of-queens-bench-and-court-of-appeal-ontario-canada/oclc/495278915.

[192] OLEGARIO, *supra* note 43, at 152.

[193] *Id.* at 153.

E. Shorter Term Credits, Competition, "Dynamic" Practices and Fairer Prices

Prior to the Civil War the normal terms for the repayment of commercial credits fluctuated between twelve to fifteen months, following the war they fluctuated between one and six months.[194] Olegario attributes the shorter maturities to better transportation and communications facilities and to the specialization of lending: "slower-moving items such as jewelry were sold on longer time than canned goods, which in turn commanded more time than perishable items such as fruits and vegetables."[195] Thus, shorter maturities reflected realistic periods of sales and loan repayment. Not long thereafter, uniform accounting practices made it possible to appraise the market values of self-liquidating loans and their collateral which were also based on their shorter and more realistic maturities.

On the other hand, during the last decades of the nineteenth century, the United States experienced a high jump in productivity accompanied by a slow growth of its population. These were deflationary conditions and were accompanied by a keen competition among wholesalers and retailers.[196] Meanwhile, business manuals counseled merchants to shop for the lowest prices during such pronounced buyers' market conditions: " 'Be tied to no house or man. . . .' 'Buy of the man who offers you the cheapest goods, and guarantees the quality to be equal to that of others.' "[197] Clearly, this advice produced highly competitive conditions in which large buyers were able to extract cheaper prices and better credit terms from "suppliers anxious to obtain their business."[198]

Deflationary and highly competitive conditions encouraged the creation of new dynamic types of contracts which required the parties to remain as contractually flexible as possible so as to adjust to rapidly changing market prices (These and other peculiarities of these contracts will be explored in Chapter 22). Olegario also refers to a popular business manual that recommended to merchants that they should try to turn their inventory every four weeks or so, "for the nimble sixpence is the coin that fills the pocket quickest."[199] One can still discern reflections of these "nimble" practices in U.C.C. Article 2 regulation of when a buyer may reject an allegedly defective tender of goods, on the manner and effect of a rightful rejection and on the buyer's duties as to rightfully rejected goods.[200] They are also discernible in rules that address one party's reasonable concern with another party's inability or unwillingness to perform as

---

194 *Id.* at 27 & 140.

195 *Id.* at 139–40.

196 *Id.* at 141. The statistics are quite telling:

> The 6 billion dollars' worth of goods and services the United States produced in the late 1860s expanded fivefold by the end of the century, to 30 billion in constant dollars. The population, meanwhile, grew much more slowly, about doubling between 1870 and 1900. [Hence] [m]ore goods were chasing fewer customers, and the wholesale price index for all commodities . . . fell—by nearly half in real terms, from one hundred in 1870 to only fifty-four by 1896.

Id. (citation omitted)

197 *Id.* at 142 (citation omitted).

198 *Id.* (citation omitted)

199 OLEGARIO, *supra* note 43, at 144.

200 *See* U.C.C. §§ 2–601, 2–602 & 2–603 (2013).

promised and is given the right to adequate assurance of performance or a cause of action for "anticipatory repudiation."[201]

As noted with respect to the purchasing practices of department stores, standardized production and quality control practices made possible the massive issuance of warranties of quality. And uniform accounting practices made it possible to establish the realistic costs of these warranties and factor those costs as components of wholesale and retail prices. Thus, as standardization led to better quality control, uniform accounting standards led to more competitive and fairer prices.

F. The Continuing Search for Objective Reporting and Rating Criteria

The search for objective criteria of reporting and rating continued during the latter part of the nineteenth century. By 1869, the Bradstreet agency required, in addition to character information, objective data from potential borrowers such as: Time in business; amount of capital, net worth, (after deducting all possible liabilities), estimated wealth including real estate, personal property including investment securities, character, habits, business qualifications, and prospects of success.[202]

Two decades later, the need for reliable accounting practices and standards was voiced by an industrial commission created by the United States Congress in 1898.[203] The purpose of this commission was to examine monopolization as a result of industrial concentration and its effect on railroad fares, the immigration of cheap labor and labor markets.[204] Among its recommendations was the creation of an independent public accounting profession to prevent corporate abuses such as stock watering and that "trusts be required to publish annual audited reports detailing their profits and losses as well as assets and liabilities."[205]

Meanwhile, a National Association of Credit Men (NACM) was created in New York State in 1897. Its goal was to represent the views of the corporate officials in charge of extending credit ("credit men" or "specialists") to other businesses. These specialists were concerned with improving the timeliness, accuracy and transparency of credit reports, and the quality of the financial statements submitted to them. They were also concerned with costly and unreliable commercial practices such as the payment with local checks for purchases or borrowings in other states, stopping "bulk sales" of goods whose purpose was to defraud creditors.

As the NACM grew in importance so did the realization among these specialists that sharing credit information about debtors' payments with other specialists would

---

201 *See* U.C.C. §§ 2–609 & 2–610 (2013), *discussed infra* § 29:2.

202 OLEGARIO, *supra* note 43, at 146.

203 *See* S.N.D. North, *The Industrial Commission*, 168 N. AMER. REV. 708 (June 1899): "The bill creating the United States non-partizan [sic] Industrial Commission was . . . signed by President McKinley, June 18, 1898." ("Conditions which may have led to such legislation were the subject of very full investigation by the industrial commission authorized by Congress by the act of June 18, 1898. 30 Stat. at L. 476, chap. 466"), *cited in* John McLean v. State of Arkansas 211 U.S. 539 ¶ 29 (1909).

204 *See U.S. Industrial Commission Reports (1899–1902)*, BOWLING GREEN STATE UNIVERSITY, http://www.bgsu.edu/colleges/library/assistance/microforms/page41301.html (last visited Dec. 4, 2013) (on the work of this Commission which was created to investigate "issues pertaining to immigration, labor, agriculture, manufacturing, and business").

205 OLEGARIO, *supra* note 43, at 179.

help the entire credit industry.[206] Payment records, then, came to be regarded by many of its members as the most objective indicators of creditworthiness. In due course, NACM circulated a standard trade inquiry among its members on their respective debtors' payments records (also referred to as "ledger information").[207] This information, albeit in more refined fashion, continues to be provided today. The NACM's role as the representative entity of credit professionals in the United States was highlighted in the somewhat grandiose announcement of its 2014 annual meeting:

> For NACM, this marks 118 years of excellence, vision and unity at the nation's largest meeting of business credit practitioners. Share our excitement as the business credit community grows and excels, proving itself as a cornerstone of the world of business.[208]

G. Conclusions

At the turn of the twentieth century, the NACM estimated that "*70% of all the orders* [in the United States] were shipped based on [credit] agency reports."[209] Its *Bulletin* regularly published letters from NACM members praising the credit agencies' services. When Dun and Bradstreet merged in 1933, they became the largest providers of credit information to members of the NCM, banks and other credit providers in the United States and abroad. As noted earlier, D & B was also responsible for the Data Universal Numbering System that is being used throughout the world to identify businesses numerically for data-processing purposes and especially by the European Commission and the U.S. Government. In 2011, its website noted with pride that it had credit relevant information on more than 225 million businesses worldwide.[210] At the end of the twentieth century, this credit was the single largest source of business financing, exceeding the volume of bank loans.[211] As found by Olegario in a Federal Reserve Flow of Funds Report:

> As of the last quarter of 2005, receivables outstanding for nonfarm, nonfinancial corporate businesses was a torrential $2.0 trillion, only slightly smaller than the $2.2 trillion of household consumer debt outstanding for the period.[212]

She concludes that the founders of the credit reporting business in the United States would have marveled at how "the institution became so tightly woven into the fabric of the country's business culture."[213] Thus, while credit reporting practices were

---

206 *Id.* 182.

207 *Id.* at 184. One of the NACM competitors was the Credit Clearing House (CCH) which during its heyday had payment records of "a reported five hundred thousand retail merchants in some thirty lines of trade." *Id.* at 187 (citation omitted). Their members were required to register the names of all their customers and to alert the company when any of them came under investigation, requested unusually high credit lines or slowed down their payments noticeably. It would then distribute this information to all its interested members; however, over time its service proved to be too expensive and slow and went out of business. *Id.*

208 *See* NACM'S 118TH CREDIT CONGRESS & EXPO, http://creditcongress.nacm.org/ (last visited Dec. 4, 2013).

209 OLEGARIO, *supra* note 43, at 191 (emphasis added).

210 *Dun and Bradstreet Company History, supra* note 152.

211 OLEGARIO, *supra* note 43, at 201 (citation omitted).

212 *Id.*

213 *Id.*

practices deeply rooted in the neo-Puritan American business culture, they also contributed to this culture. Recall that one such a contribution rewarded not only those debtors who were willing to pay their obligations when they matured, but also those who disclosed all the facts that could make repayment difficult. And as has been the case with a United States culture of progressive inclusion, credit reporting also contributed to that culture.

I witnessed the impact of the culture of commercial credit inclusion on my family's welfare. Shortly after I started my law teaching career, I befriended a D & B credit examiner. He came to know my father who had just arrived from Cuba with meager resources, after having left behind a highly successful retail and wholesale dry goods business in Cuba (about which more in later chapters). Fortunately, he was able to obtain the records that supported my father's high credit ratings and based on those records, he prepared a favorable credit report. Shortly thereafter, my father, with the help of this credit report, was given a line of credit by a Dallas commercial bank. The small business that obtained financing in significant measure because of this report proved successful enough to support three family partners and several employees for over two decades.

§ 21.8 EARLY TWENTIETH CENTURY SECURED TRANSACTIONS AND BANKRUPTCY LAW

A. Early Secured Transactions Laws

Commercial credit in present day America is not only a product of good credit reports, but also of secured or asset-based lending. According to a 2000 report by the Federal Reserve Bank of San Francisco:

> Banking industry statistics show that commercial loans represent a very large share of the assets of the banking industry. . . . Assets and Liabilities of Commercial Banks in the United States, commercial banks held $1066.5 billion dollars in commercial and industrial loans as of June 2000; these loans accounted for 18.1 percent of all bank assets. Over the ten-year period from 1989 to 1999, commercial and industrial loans outstanding at U.S. commercial banks increased by more than 50 percent.[214]

And as reported by a 1990 study authored by staff members A. N. Berger and G.F. Udell of the Board of Governors of the Federal Reserve, nearly 70% of all commercial and industrial loans of the United States are made on a secured basis.[215] Even if one assumes that one-half of all commercial loans are secured by real estate mortgages and personal guarantees (a highly unrealistic assumption in light of commercial banking loan practices), 35% of all the commercial loans would still be secured by assets such as the borrower's inventory, equipment, contract rights, accounts receivable, proceeds and intangibles such as intellectual property.

---

[214] *How do you define 'Commercial Loans' and what is the economic importance of these types of loans?* FEDERAL RESERVE BANK OF SAN FRANCISCO (Sept. 2000), http://www.frbsf.org/education/publications/doctor-econ/2000/september/commercial-loans.

[215] ALLEN N. BERGER & GREGORY F. UDELL, COLLATERAL, LOAN QUALITY, AND BANK RISK, ISSUE 51 (1988). *See also, generally*, Alberto Franco Pozzolo, *Secured Lending and Borrowers' Riskiness*, BIS.ORG, http://www.bis.org/publ/cgfs19bdi1.pdf (last visited Dec. 4, 2013).

This was not the case at the turn of the twentieth century. As noted by George Lee Flint, Jr. and Marie Juliet Alfaro, early American court opinions revealed that various types of chattel mortgage and pledge statutes allowing debtors to remain in possession of the mortgaged property were on the books since the eighteenth century (first in five Southern states and early in the next century in Northeastern states).[216] And these statutes often had conflicting rules. For example, the first chattel mortgage act passed in New England during the 1830s only covered filing for chattel mortgages. In contrast, chattel mortgage acts of the Southern English-American colonies covered both real estate and personalty, sales as well as mortgages.[217] Because of these conflicting rules, many secured creditors were uncertain whether their security interests perfected in one state were considered perfected in another, and, if not, how and when could they be enforced, especially when debtors were close to insolvency.

A 1917 Manual on Credit and Collections by Richard Prentice Ettinger and David Edwin Golieb vividly described the uncertainty:

> If one creditor had suspicion that a debtor was about to fail, immediately such creditor would rush to court and levy an attachment or execution. Then would begin a mad race for precedence between executions, attachments etc.—between the sheriff, receiver, assignee and mortgagee—to see which one would get possession of the debtor's property first, the receiver frequently finding upon arrival that he was forestalled by the sheriff under a levy or by some preferred mortgagee or assignee placed in possession by the debtor.[218]

Such was the uncertainty by the late nineteenth century that "adjustment bureaus" were being formed "in nearly all major cities to apportion assets more equitably among creditors"[219] Similar institutions were created by a large number of trade groups as "boards of trade" and many creditors preferred trying to collect through them rather than through bankruptcy proceedings.[220]

B. Bankruptcy Law and the "Second Chance" Theology

The notion that Bankruptcy should afford repentant and honest debtors a second chance or a fresh start in business has deep roots in Judeo-Christian theology. Isaiah 43:16–31 is frequently quoted by Christians as one of the bases of a "second chance" theology: "Consider not the things of the past, the things of long ago consider not; see I am doing something new, says the Lord."[221] Similarly, the Gospel of St. John for the Fifth Sunday of Lent reflects on the case of an adulterous woman and Jesus's reaction to those who insisted on stoning her: "Let the one among you who is without sin be the

---

[216] G.L. Flint Jr. and Marie Juliet Alfaro, *Secured Transactions History, The First Chattel Mortgage Acts in the Anglo American World*, 30 WM. MITCHELL L. REV. 1403, 1406–07 (2003–2004).

[217] *Id.*

[218] RICHARD PRENTICE ETTINGER AND DAVID EDWIN GOLIEB, CREDIT AND COLLECTIONS 331 (2nd ed. 1917). This passage is also cited by Olegario in OLEGARIO, *supra* note 43, at 196. This book was translated into Spanish as *Creditos y Cobranzas* (1978) and have seen it in Latin American bookstores as recently as in 2006, even though the Spanish readers had a difficult time with Anglo American legal terminology and its reference to various non-existing legal institutions in Latin America.

[219] OLEGARIO, *supra* note 43, at 196 (citation omitted).

[220] *Id.* at 197.

[221] *See, e.g.*, Fr. Leroy Clementich, CSC, The Theology of Second Chances http://www.catholicanchor.org/wordpress/archives/589.

first to throw a stone at her."[222] The second chance doctrine resonated with Judeo-Christian theologians, preachers and merchants. Olegario quotes from a lecture-exhortation to Boston's Young Men's Christian Union by a preacher named J. H. Allen in the mid-1850s:

> [With] 'the utmost degree of circumspection, losses will occur.' The Creditor 'spurns the idea of an advantage over his neighbor . . . Neither will he, if the bankrupt appears to be honest, oppress the spirit bowed down with sadness.'[223]

The Bankruptcy Act of 1841[224] was the first to adopt debtor protection provisions. It allowed voluntary bankruptcy filings by insolvent debtors, and allowing non-merchants to be debtors who could avail themselves of bankruptcy proceedings, including a discharge of their liability after they turned over their assets to their creditors.[225] The Bankruptcy Act of July 1, 1898, which remained in effect for approximately eighty years[226] enlarged the debtor protection provisions of its 1841 predecessor and provided that anyone owing debts, except a corporation, was entitled to the benefits of the law by filing a voluntary bankruptcy. It also provided that anyone owing debts of $1,000 or more could be adjudged an involuntary bankrupt and be fully discharged of liability, except when he had committed "an offense punishable by imprisonment as provided by the law or, with fraudulent intent to conceal his true financial condition and in contemplation of bankruptcy, had concealed or destroyed or failed to keep records of accounts."[227] The trend to allow bankrupts a second chance by allowing them to file a voluntary petition and discharging them after voluntary or involuntary proceedings led to the institution of corporate and individual debtor reorganization procedures in the 1933–1934 Amendments to the 1898 Bankruptcy Act,[228] later amplified in the Chandler Act of 1938 and by the Bankruptcy Code of 1979.[229]

Meanwhile, Justice Sutherland's opinion in the 1934 the United States Supreme Court decision in *Local Loan Co. v. Hunt*[230] was able to formulate the spirit of the second chance doctrine:

---

[222] *Id.*

[223] OLEGARIO, *supra* note 43, at 96 (citation omitted).

[224] *See Bankruptcy Act of 1841 Dockets, 1842–1843,* NATIONAL ARCHIVES OPA—ONLINE PUBLIC ASSESS, http://research.archives.gov/description/2645683 (last visited Dec. 6, 2013).

[225] *Id.*

[226] The Bankruptcy Act of 1898, ch. 541, 30 Stat. 544. *See Bankruptcy Act of 1898 Case Files, 1898–1963,* THE NATIONAL ARCHIVES OPA—ONLINE PUBLIC ACCESS, http://research.archives.gov/description/566660 (last visited Dec. 4, 2013).

[227] *Id.*

[228] *See e.g.,* 48 Stat. 911 (1934).

[229] *See* Chandler Act, 52 Stat. 840 (1938); Bankruptcy Act of Nov. 6, 1978, Pub. L. No. 95–598, 92 Stat 2549 (as codified and amended); and The Bankruptcy Abuse Prevention and Consumer Protection Act of 2005 (BAPCPA) 11 U.S.C. § 101 (Pub. L. No. 109–8, 119 Stat. 23 (enacted April 20, 2005)). The first bankruptcy law of the United States as was the act of 1800 (which was repealed in 1803). *See Bankruptcy Act of 1800 Case Files, 1800–1830,* THE NATIONAL ARCHIVES OPA—ONLINE PUBLIC ACCESS, http://research.archives.gov/description/1691943 (last visited Dec. 6, 2013). A series of bankruptcy statutes followed only to be amended or abrogated shortly after their promulgation. Where debt protection was concerned, the principal enactments were the 1841 Bankruptcy Law, *supra* note 211, the 1898 Bankruptcy Law, *supra* note 213, and The Chandler Act of June 22, 1938.

[230] 292 U.S. 234 (1934).

> One of the primary purposes of the bankruptcy act is to 'relieve the honest debtor from the weight of oppressive indebtedness, and permit him to start afresh free from the obligations and responsibilities consequent upon business misfortunes. This purpose of the act has been again and again emphasized by the courts as being of public as well as private interest, in that it gives to the honest but unfortunate debtor who surrenders for distribution the property which he owns *at the time of bankruptcy*, a new opportunity in life and a clear field for future effort, unhampered by the pressure and discouragement of preexisting debt.[231]

This was indeed a ringing endorsement of the second chance theology. Nonetheless, the latest, 2005 Bankruptcy law reforms attempted to curb abuses in debtor protection law and practices, thereby attesting to yet another swing of the pendulum of creditor and debtor protection. This shows that bankruptcy law has proven to be as sensitive to Biblically-inspired theology as it is to the advocacy and political pressures of creditor and debtors' rights groups.

§ 21.9 PRINCIPLES DERIVED FROM THE PRECEDING PRACTICES, VALUES AND ATTITUDES

A. Freedom of Contract: That Which the Law Does Not Expressly Forbid, It Allows

As will be discussed in Chapter 22, the principle of freedom of contract in U.S. law and practice is not just the freedom of mentally and physically able citizens and residents to enter into agreements that are binding on them as "their law" (as was proclaimed for the French by Article 1134 of the *Code Civil*).[232] It is also the freedom to select the type and form of contract best suited for the transaction. Such a format could well be that of a pro forma invoice or receipt of payment, a notation on a check that relates the payment to the performance of work under a contract, email message, recorded telephone conference or a "Master" electronically accessed agreement. The reason for the informality of contractual formation is that, as will become apparent in Chapter 22, under the law inspired by U.C.C. Article 2, the parties' contractual conduct (as manifest in their course of dealing, course of performance and usage of trade) is as influential in a court's determination of the existence of a contract and its intent as any other source, and often even more so. Thus, United States law and practice on contract formation attest to the influence of one of its guiding principles: That which the law does not expressly forbid, it allows. It also attests to an often abusive maximization of this principle to the detriment of contracting and third parties. On the other hand, with the proliferation of abusive contractual rights comes a proliferation of remedies such as the earlier discussed constructive trusts, adequate assurances of performance, damages for anticipatory repudiation, and anti-trust and unfair competition remedies. In the final analysis, then, the longevity of this U.S. version of the principle of freedom of contract suggests that despite abuses and the need for continuous new remedies, the U.S. marketplace has been considerably better off with it than with restrictive, *a priori* limitations as apparent in totalitarian legal systems.

---

231 *Id.* at 244 (citation omitted) (emphasis added).

232 *See supra* § 8:7(G).

B. Contracts Must Be Performed in Good Faith, *i.e.*, in an Honest, Reasonable and Fair Manner

One of the remnants of the Puritan's Moral Capitalism is the U.C.C. principle that contracts must be performed in good faith: "Every contract or duty within this Act imposes and obligation of good faith in its performance and enforcement."[233] Please recall the New England Puritans' embrace of honest dealing as manifest in their reliance on honest weights and measures: : "The Lord abhors dishonest scales, but accurate weights are his delight." Honesty, then, was an essential component of what they considered a good faith performance of a contract. But so was a just or fair price and its reasonableness could be ascertained, among other means, by relying on the judgment of a respected and knowledgeable third party. As we will learn in Chapter 23, these are essential elements of U.C.C. Article 2's good faith performance.

In addition, please recall that, while discussing the disclosure practices expected by credit investigators from applicants to commercial loans, we learned that the disclosure of the facts that bore on the applicants' willingness and ability to repay was a component of honesty. You may also recall Lord Mansfield's requirement from applicants for insurance policies in the preceding chapter: If they knew about risks unknown to the insurer and these risks were material to his decision to insure, applicants had the duty to disclose them.

C. Private Ownership of Property Is Preferable to Communal Property

Since the days of the New England Puritan settlements, private ownership was the preferred form of ownership in the United States. Not surprisingly, then, private ownership was protected by the Fifth Amendment of the United States Constitution:

> [N]or [shall any person] be deprived of life, liberty, or property, without due process of law; nor shall private property be taken for public use, without just compensation.[234]

In fact, the thirteen independent states considered private property a significant enough consideration to make the right to vote depend on it.[235]

On the other hand, the increasing commercial reliance (mostly since the nineteenth century) on "documents of title" such as negotiable ocean bills of lading and warehouse receipts contributed to the fragmentation of the ownership of movable or personal property. These documents of title were issued by ocean carriers and warehousemen and their holder acquired rights to the possession of the goods shipped or stored that were superior to those of the "historical" or "legal" owners of the goods (such as an unpaid "conditional" seller or a buyer who had paid a part or even the entirety of their purchase price). Unless they acquired possession of documents of title

---

233 See U.C.C. § 1–203 (1962).

234 *Bill of Rights,* the Charters of Freedom, http://www.archives.gov/exhibits/charters/bill_of_rights_transcript.html (last visited Dec. 4, 2013). This source provides the full text of this amendment.

235 *See Property and the Right to Vote,* Answers.com, http://www.answers.com/topic/property-and-the-right-to-vote (last visited Dec. 4, 2013).

by paying what was owed to their holder, neither the carrier nor the warehouseman would release the goods to them.[236]

In fact, the rights of lawful holders of documents of title could co-exist with the rights of other holders of rights in the same collateral, such as secured creditors with rights in the debtors' business inventory or equipment. The twentieth century proliferation of commercial credit and security interests in commercial assets (as will be discussed in Chapter 24) has continued the fragmentation of ownership rights in commercial assets to the point that much of the contemporary commercial property rights are possessory in nature.[237]

D. Those Whose Labor Creates Wealth Are Entitled to a Share of It

Ascetic Puritanism had much in common with John Locke's theory of value.[238] Industriousness for the Puritan saints was the source of all wealth. And since God gave the use of the world to the industrious and rational, entitlement to property came principally from work and the fruits of labor belonged to the worker. Examples of such values and attitudes abound in United States law and practice. Consider the rights of Homesteaders under the Homestead Act of 1862.[239] It provided that claimants were required to "improve" the plot by building a dwelling and cultivating the land. It then provided that "[a]fter 5 years on the land, the original filer was entitled to the property, free and clear, except for a small registration fee."[240]

Despite the Puritans' seeming failure to take into account the role of capital in providing the wherewithal for the workers' productivity, the Puritanical belief in the productive laborers' entitlement also had a marked effect on commercial practices. In some of these practices, the laborers' entitlement was exclusive, while in others it was shared with other contributors. Consider, for example, a dispute between a merchant whose work has made a trademark widely known to the public but who failed to record it in the trademark registry, and another whose work only consisted in recording such a trademark. The United States' trademark law's adoption of the Puritans' view is apparent in a U.S Patent Office's reply to the following query: Must I register my trademark? "No. You can establish rights in a mark based on use of the mark in commerce, without a registration. . . ."[241]

An example of a practice which shares profits based upon what a worker has contributed to the wealth of the enterprise is that of rewarding "sweat equity." A business dictionary's definition of this term attests to its widespread use:

---

236 *See* Kozolchyk, *supra* note 100, at 1504–1509.

237 *Id.*

238 *See* INNES, *supra* note 11, at 90 (where he also calls attention to Locke's Puritan origins and to his justification for property ownership as based on "acts of improvement").

239 See Chapter LXXV of Act of May 20, 1862 (Homestead Act), Public Law 37–64, 05/20/1862;—An Act to secure Homesteads to actual Settlers on the Public Domain. Record Group 11; *see also Homestead Act (1862),* GENERAL RECORDS OF THE UNITED STATES GOVERNMENT; NATIONAL ARCHIVES, http://www.our documents.gov/doc.php?flash=true&doc=31 (last visited Dec. 4, 2013).

240 *Id.*

241 *See Frequently Asked Questions about Trademarks*, THE UNITED STATES PATENT AND TRADEMARK OFFICE, http://www.uspto.gov/faq/trademarks.jsp#_Toc275426672 (last visited Dec. 4, 2013).

1. Increased worth of a business (over and above the money invested) created by the unpaid mental and/or physical hard work of the founder/owner.

2. Increased value of a property (over and above its purchase price) created by the hard work of the owner/occupant in enhancing its amenities and/or looks.

3. Extra percentage of a firm's common stock (ordinary shares) allocated to the senior executives (over and above their current shareholdings) as an additional motivation for continuing hard work for the firm's success.[242]

Similarly, consider the practice of giving a finder's fee to the intermediary in a business transaction who found the capital or valuable labor needed by the principal of the enterprise. The movie industry is one among many in which finders' fees are commonly agreed upon by movie producers and business agents as a reward to those agents who found the capital or labor used by the principal.[243] In contrast, real estate brokers acting as agents for sellers of real estate in many states customarily, without a pre-existing agreement, reward fellow brokers who produce the eventual purchaser of the real estate.[244]

E. Equal Protection of Equals, and the Growing Inclusiveness of Equals

As discussed in Chapter 9, the principle of an equal protection of merchants regardless of national origin was practiced in the European fairs that granted foreign merchants their "Peace of the Marketplace."[245] This was, in effect, the foreign merchants' safe-conduct against discrimination, including protection against being pursued for debts owed to local merchants by other merchants who were located in their same foreign countries or cities and were not present in the fair.

As pointed out by my colleague, James E. Rogers College of Law Constitutional Law Professor Roy Spece, continuous "trade wars" were common between or among the original thirteen states.[246] In fact, these wars were one of the reasons for the adoption of the United States Constitution—ironically an enactment that would have been deemed unconstitutional under the then-governing Articles of Confederation. The new Constitution greatly enhanced the prospects of trade by giving the central or federal government the right to govern interstate commerce, and, to a lesser extent, by providing in Article IV, Section 2 that "[t]he Citizens of each State shall be entitled to all the Privileges and Immunities of Citizens in the several states."

---

[242] BUSINESSDICTIONARY.COM, *Sweat Equity,* http://www.businessdictionary.com/definition/sweat-equity.html#ixzz2hcZl8JPL (last visited Dec. 4, 2013).

[243] *Generic Finders Fee Agreement,* ENTREPRENEUR.COM, http://www.entrepreneur.com/formnet/form/702 (last visited Dec. 4, 2013).

[244] This practice has been relayed to me in conversations with commercial lawyers in Arizona, California, Florida and Texas.

[245] *See supra* § 9:2(B).

[246] *See* Memorandum from Roy Spece for Boris Kozolchyk (Nov. 22, 2013) (on file with author). I owe the following summary of the law of equal protection and of the constitutional provisions on privileges and immunities under the United States Constitution to my colleague and friend Professor Roy Spece who authored a Memorandum of November 22, 2013 in which he provided very helpful commentary, some of which was too extensive for use in this chapter, but is on file with the NLCIFT for interested readers.

The latter provision at least required that if a state granted its own citizens a right falling within the group of privileges and immunities, it could not discriminate against citizens of other states with respect to that right.[247] Privileges and immunities are limited to rights that are fundamental and thus available to all citizens and residents under all free forms of government. As such, they include the right to travel in and out of other states and to engage in economic activites "such as are necessary to ply one's trade."[248] Accordingly, the United States Supreme Court held in 1870, for example, that a Maryland law that required nonresidents to pay a fee of $300 per year to trade in goods not manufactured in Maryland but exacted a lower fee, ranging from $12 to $150, to resident traders violated Article IV's Privileges and Immunities Clause.[249]

The Articles of Confederation had provided for the free movement of persons and, "to some extent free movement of trade."[250] However, as noted by Louisiana State University's Constitutional Law Professor Emeritus John Baker, the persons who were granted this freedom were only males and who were not slaves.[251] Hence, the equality or non-discrimination aspect of Article IV's protection of privileges and immunities of citizens and residents must be read in the historical context not only of the *de jure*, but also of the *de facto* discrimination against African Americans and other minorities. This was a discrimination that existed despite the adoption of the U.S. Constitution and even after the adoption of the Fourteenth Amendment in 1868. This Amendment guaranteed all persons equal protection: "All persons born or naturalized in the United States, and subject to the jurisdiction thereof, are citizens of the United States and of the state wherein they reside."[252] Yet, de facto discrimination against the newly freed slaves continued and was in some respects, worse after their emancipation. Similarly, women were not even granted the right to vote until adoption of the Nineteenth Amendment in 1920.

This is not the place to review the history of racial and gender discrimination in the United States. Nonetheless, what this history shows is that the plight of racial minorities and women has improved markedly over the years, a process that continues to date. A transformative moment was the adoption of the 1964 Civil Rights Act, which prohibited discrimination based on race or gender. This Act gave these discriminated groups a strong tool to continue their struggles for equality and inclusion in trade and all other aspects of life in the United States.

It is gratifying that a century and a half after the Emancipation Proclamation in 1863 government statistics revealed the willingness of most American people to observe the equality of minorities and women. According to the U.S. Census Bureau's Survey of Business Owners, from 2002 to 2007, the number of black-owned businesses increased by 60.5 percent to 1.9 million, more than triple the national growth rate of

---

247 ERWIN CHEMERINSKY, CONSTITUTIONAL LAW: PRINCIPLES AND POLICIES 485 (4th ed. 2011). According to Dean Erwin Chemerinksky, "a state does not violate this provision if there is a substantial purpose in drawing a distinction and the law in question is closely tailored to that purpose." *Id.*

248 *See* Doe v. Bolton 410 U.S. 179 (1973) (for reference to the privileges and immunities that apply to "plying one's trade in").

249 Ward v. Maryland, 79 U.S. 418 (1870).

250 *See* John S. Baker, *The Constitutional Foundation for the United States Economy, in* Kozolchyk, I UNITED STATES LAW 9–i, 9–22.

251 *Id.*

252 U.S. Const. amend. XIV

18.0 percent. In the words of the Census Bureau's Deputy Director, Thomas Mesenburg:

> Black-owned businesses continued to be one of the fastest growing segments of our economy, showing rapid growth in both the number of businesses and total sales during this time period.[253]

Further, recent data from the Bureau of Labor Statistics confirms that black self-employment has been on the rise, especially in small businesses. The number of self-employed blacks grew by 5.7 percent from 2007 through 2009, in contrast to the 3.4 percent decrease experienced by self-employed whites.[254]

Meanwhile, as of 2004, statistics on entrepreneurship and its ownership showed that women owned 10.6 million businesses in the United States, employed 19.1 million workers—that's one in every seven employees, and their businesses accounted for $2.5 trillion in sales.[255] In addition to leading in the ownership of small businesses,[256] between 1997 and 2013, when the number of businesses in the United States increased by 41percent:

> The number of women-owned firms increased by 59%—a rate 1½ times the national average. Indeed, the growth in the number (up 59%), employment (up 10%) and revenues (up 63%) of women-owned firms over the past 16 years exceeds the growth rates of all but the largest, publicly traded firms—topping the growth rates in number, employment and revenue of all privately held businesses over this period.[257]

F. The Protection of Third Parties as Actual or Potential Market Participants

In commercial contracting, third parties are persons or legal entities likely to be effected, positively or adversely, by the terms and conditions of pre-existent contracts, negotiable instruments, documents of title or investment securities. Examples of such parties abound: A merchant who purchases another merchant's inventory or equipment unaware that the seller had previously pledged those assets to a secured creditor; A lessee of a fleet of automobiles from a lessor who waived the manufacturer's warranties of merchantability and fitness on those vehicles; An indorsee purchaser for value of a negotiable instrument that turns out to be unenforceable because his indorser acquired it for a "past consideration" or as payment of a pre-existing duty or a gambling debt where its enforcement is forbidden; A purchaser of a mortgage bond

---

[253] *Census Bureau Reports the Number of Black-Owned Businesses Increased at Triple the National Rate,* United States Census Bureau Newsroom (Feb. 8, 2011), http://www.census.gov/newsroom/releases/archives/business_ownership/cb11–24.html.

[254] Patrice Peck, *Black Entrepreneurship On The Rise As Self-Employment Becomes An Option For Jobless Black Graduates,* THE HUFFINGTON POST (Oct. 5, 2012), http://www.huffingtonpost.com/2012/08/28/black-entrepreneurship-self-employment_n_1838080.html.

[255] *Women Entrepreneurs,* ENTREPRENEUR.COM, http://www.entrepreneur.com/sbe/women/ (last visited Dec. 4, 2013).

[256] *See* Boris Kozolchyk & Cristina Castaneda, *Invigorating Micro and Small Businesses through Secured Commercial Credit in Latin America: The Need for Legal and Institutional Reform* 28 ARIZ. J. INT'L & COMP. L. 43, 76–79 (2011).

[257] *See Executive Summary to* THE 2013 STATE OF WOMEN-OWNED BUSINESSES Report 2 (2013), *available at* http://www.womenable.com/userfiles/downloads/2013_State_of_Women-Owned_Businesses_Report_FINAL.pdf.

unable to foreclose and collect on the mortgaged property because it was part of a pool of mortgages so "sliced and diced" that it was impossible to identify the mortgaged property; and so on.

As just noted, these third parties amount to a very large group of the everyday participants in the world's commercial and financial markets. Third party protection has been a guiding principle of the commercial and financial contract law of the United States since its inception, although with some notable exceptions. One such an exception was the issuance of documents of title, receipt of shipments, or stored goods by an agent who lacked the authority to do so. For example, in the 1889 United States Supreme Court decision *Friedlander v. Texas & Pacific Railway Co.*,[258] the plaintiff, a secured creditor and holder of a rail bill which on its face stated that a certain number of bales of cotton had been shipped on a railroad car, was unable to obtain the cotton from the carrier at the arrival of the cargo train. The defendant railroad carrier's agent (without the carrier's knowledge) had issued a rail bill on behalf of the defendant, but without actually receiving any cotton from the purported shipper. The Court decided to protect the carrier and held that his agent had acted *ultra vires* and, as such, could not bind his principal. This rejection of third party protection to the holders of rail bills, including the banks which financed the cotton trade of the United States with the rest of the world, proved a serious blow to that industry as well as to cotton exporters who had lost vital financing.[259] Eventually, a uniform state law and a federal statute reversed the United States Supreme Court decision.[260] As noted by *The Cambridge Economic History of the United States*: "American law also enlarged this medium of credit exchange by extending the principle of negotiability beyond British doctrinal limits to include new forms of commercial paper such as municipal and corporate bonds, the bank certificate of deposit, bills of lading, the check, chattel notes and even negotiable instruments paid in such valuables as 'good merchantable whiskey.' "[261]

As it turned out, the United States state and federal legislation that protected holders for value of bills of lading from the *ultra vires* defense attained what I referred to in another study as "the highest level of abstraction available at that time."[262] The innocent holder of the bill who had given value for it in good faith was immunized against the *ultra vires* defense that stemmed from an underlying relationship. I should add that these statutory rules served as a model for the most widely adopted maritime convention on carrier liability. As stated by Article 3(4) of the Brussels International Convention for the Unification of Certain Rules of Law relating to Bills of Lading ("Hague Rules"):

---

[258] 130 U.S. 416 (1889).

[259] *See* ARNOLD W. KNAUTH, THE AMERICAN LAW OF OCEAN BILLS OF LADING 124 (4th ed. 1953); and Boris Kozolchyk, *Evolution and Present State of the Ocean Bill of Lading from a Banking Law Perspective,* 23 J. MAR. L. & COM. 161, 173 (1992).

[260] *See* UNIF. BILLS OF LADING ACT 4 U.L.A. 3 (1922); and the Pomerene Act, 49 U.S.C. app. §§ 81–124 (1988).

[261] *See* THE CAMBRIDGE ECONOMIC HISTORY OF THE UNITED STATES 455 (Stanley L. Engerman & Robert E. Gallman eds., 2000).

[262] Kozolchyk, *supra* note 246, at 173.

> (4). Such a bill of lading *shall be prima facie evidence* of the receipt by the carrier of the goods as therein described in accordance with paragraph 3(a), (b) and (c).[263]

Similarly, Article 2 of the U.C.C. (on Sales of Goods) influenced the UNCITRAL Convention for the International Sale of Goods, especially when assuring the conformity of goods purchased by a third party with the express or implied representations and warranties made by their manufacturer or distributor on the merchantability and fitness of the goods Additionally, Article 9 of the U.C.C. became a worldwide leader on the protection of third party secured creditors and *bona fide* purchasers of collateral. It provided these third parties, *inter alia*, with a highly functional system of perfection and priority of security interests largely based on a functional notice to third parties of the filed security interests and liens.[264]

Some United States judges have also led in the protection of third party purchasers of mass-produced goods.[265] Perhaps the most influential of all such decisions was Justice Benjamin N. Cardozo's opinion in *McPherson v. Buick Motor Co.*[266] A purchaser of an automobile from a dealer (who was not the manufacturer) suffered an accident due to the defectively manufactured spokes of a wheel built by the defendant's sub-contractor. When the purchaser sued the manufacturer, the defendant claimed that there was no direct contractual relationship (privity) between it and the plaintiff and that in the absence of privity, the common law precluded the plaintiff's action. By an ingenious use of analogical reasoning (described earlier as reasoning by example) as well as of the logic of the reasonable,[267] Cardozo circumvented privity and established the manufacturer's duty based on reasonable foreseeability of the harm caused by a dangerous object or instrumentality when negligently manufactured. The precision with which Cardozo fashioned the rule that protected McPherson as a third party in the chain of production and distribution of his automobile continues to be a source of admiration:

> If the nature of a finished product placed on the market by a manufacturer to be used without inspection by his customers is such that it is reasonably certain to place life and limb in peril if the product is negligently made, it is then a thing of danger. Its nature gives warning of the consequences to be expected. If to the element of danger there is added knowledge that the thing will be used by *persons other than the purchaser* [automobile dealer]. . .then irrespective of the contract, the manufacturer of this thing of danger is under a duty to make it carefully.[268]

---

[263] *International Convention for the Unification of Certain Rules of Law relating to Bills of Lading ("Hague Rules"), and Protocol of Signature,* ADMIRALTY AND MARITIME LAW GUIDE INTERNATIONAL CONVENTIONS (Aug. 25, 1924), http://www.admiraltylawguide.com/conven/haguerules1924.html (emphasis added).

[264] *See,* for example, UNCITRAL, UNCITRAL LEGISLATIVE GUIDE ON SECURED TRANSACTIONS, at 99 & 143, U.N. Sales No. E.09.V.12 (2010), *available at* http://www.uncitral.org/pdf/english/texts/security-lg/e/09–82670_Ebook-Guide_09–04–10English.pdf. *See also* Kozolchyk and Furnish, *A Comparative Analysis,* at 9.

[265] *See* Boris Kozolchyk, *A Roadmap to Economic Development Through Law: Third Parties and Comparative Legal Culture,* 23 ARIZ. J. INT'L. & COMP. L. 1, 24–34 (2005).

[266] 217 N.Y. 382 (1916).

[267] *See supra* § 2:2(B).

[268] 217 N.Y. at 389 (1916) (emphasis added).

Meinhard v. Salmon was another highly influential instance of Cardozo's protection of third party investors.[269] As partially transcribed in the Appendix to Chapter 23, the defendant Salmon had entered into a lease with the owner of a building with the obligation to convert it into stores and offices. Plaintiff Meinhard, a third party to the lease agreement, invested half of the cost of its reconstruction in exchange for a percentage of the profits. Salmon was the sole managing partner of the lease and of Meinhard's investment. Near the end of the lease, the owner of the building proposed to Salmon that he tear down the building and build a larger one. Salmon did not inform Meinhard of the proposed deal and created a new company to manage the new business. Upon finding out, Meinhard sued Salmon claiming that he had been wrongfully excluded and that were it not for his original investment and its considerable success, the new venture would not have been possible.

On appeal, Cardozo held that Meinhard was entitled to almost one half of Salmon's interest in the new lease and business venture and stressed Salmon's fiduciary duties and the forthright conduct required by his status as a sole trustee. At a minimum, he was required to disclose to Meinhard the new project proposed to him, for "[such] [j]oint adventurers, like copartners, owe to one another, while the enterprise continues, the duty of the finest loyalty."[270]

Cardozo's following statement is permanently associated with the law of trusts as it intersects with the duties required when managing investments by third parties such as Meinhard's. It is also permanently associated with the standards of fairness and good faith discussed in Chapter 23:

> Many forms of conduct permissible in a workaday world for those acting at arm's length, are forbidden to those bound by fiduciary ties. A trustee is held to something stricter than the morals of the market place. Not honesty alone, but the punctilio of an honor the most sensitive, is then the standard of behavior. . .Only thus has the level of conduct for fiduciaries been kept at a level higher than that trodden by the crowd.[271]

§ 21.10 COMMERCIAL LEGISLATION

Chapters 22 and 23 and their appendices discuss the formation and judicial interpretation of commercial contracts. In addition to discussing the substantive law of contract formation and adjudication, they highlight key features of judicial adjudication in representative jurisdictions. This should enable the reader to form an opinion on how courts in representative jurisdictions function as adjudicators and lawmakers. Chapter 24 focuses on the formation of standard and best commercial practices and on the role of these practices in shaping the future law of commercial contracts. Finally, Chapters 25–30 and their appendices discuss key procedural and remedial aspects of commercial adjudication. Because the emphasis of these chapters is mostly on adjudication, I will devote the remainder of this chapter to an eagle's eye view of the shaping of commercial legislation and to the administrative regulation on commercial contracts.

---

[269] *See* Meinhard v. Salmon, 249 N.Y. 458 (1928). Part of this case was transcribed and discussed, *infra* ch. 23.

[270] 249 N.Y. at 463–64 (1928).

[271] *Id.* at 464.

A. Early Legislators in Independent America: Cultured Gentlemen, the Enlightenment and the Middling Sorts

During the early years of independent America, there were two groups of legislators. In his Introduction to Professor Gordon S. Wood's brilliant history of early independent America, Professor David Kennedy of Stanford University describes the men who made the Revolution and wrote the United States Constitution as:

> [F]or the most part cultured gentlemen, patrician squires who believed in the foundational republican principle of self-government, to be sure, but who also expected the common folk to defer to their "betters" when it came to running the country. The Federalists like Washington, Adams, and Hamilton who presided over the first decade of nationhood were often appalled by the egalitarian excesses unleashed by the Revolution.[272]

The "middling sorts", the other group of legislators, were members of a large segment of the population whom Professor Kennedy identified as a new social class of republicans. They included:

> [U]npriviliged but energetically striving merchants, artisans, and entrepreneurs, [who] arose to dominate politics and define the very essence of the national character. They ferociously opposed all "monarchical" pretensions and insisted on nothing less than a society completely open to talent and industry. . .Their great champion was Thomas Jefferson, the quirky and brilliant Virginia aristocrat who articulated the dearest aspirations of the common people. . . .[273]

These middling sorts also comprised the majority of the legislators in the thirteen independent states. James Madison (the most influential draftsman of the 1789 Constitution and often a supporter of Jeffersonian Republican and eventually "Democratic Republican" Party)[274] complained that the abuses of the state legislatures were "so frequent and so flagrant as to alarm the most steadfast friends of Republicanism."[275] Madison regarded these abuses as caused by men of limited means and education who became:

> [S]elf-appointed leaders, speaking for newly aroused groups. . . . [n]ew petty entrepreneurs . . . [who] had vaulted into political leadership [and]. . . . [in Hamilton's words] '[men] whose ignorance and perverseness are only surpassed by [their] pertinacity and conceit.'[276]

Thus, in the eyes of many of the nation's founders, especially federalists such as Hamilton and Adams, state legislators only cared for their parochial and personal interests and not for the national interests:

---

[272] David M. Kennedy, *Introduction, in* WOOD, *supra* note 49, at XV.

[273] *Id.*

[274] *See* WOOD, *supra* note 49, at 141–73 (on the creation of the DEMOCRATIC-REPUBLICAN PARTY). The Democratic-Republican Party was organized by Thomas Jefferson and James Madison in 1791–93. It opposed the Federalist Party led by Alexander Hamilton. It controlled the Presidency and Congress, and most states, from 1801 to 1824. It split after the 1824 presidential election into two parties: the Democratic Party and the successive ancestors of the present day Republican Party. Most contemporaries called it the Republican Party. *Id.*

[275] *Id.* at 16 (citation omitted).

[276] *Id.* at 17 (citation omitted).

> [F]armers in debt urged the lowering of taxes [and] . . . advocated [for] the suspension of court actions to recover debts and the continued printing of paper money. . . .
>
> [Conversely] [m]erchants and creditors called for high taxes on land in place of tariffs, less paper money, the protection of private contracts, and the encouragement of foreign trade. [Meanwhile] [a]rtisans lobbied for . . . tariff protection. . . . And in the state legislatures representatives of these interests were passing laws on their behalf, in effect, becoming judges in their own causes.[277]

B. The Enlightenment and Some of the Key Principles of United States Public Law

The Stanford Encyclopedia of Philosophy refers to the Enlightenment as a seventeenth- and eighteenth-century period characterized "by dramatic revolutions in science, philosophy, society and politics [that] . . . swept away the medieval world-view and ushered in our modern western world."[278] The ideas debated during this period contributed much to a French Revolution that did away with the absolute monarchy and the exclusive privileges of the French nobility, advocating for freedom and equality for all.

In the case of American thinkers of the stature of Thomas Jefferson, Alexander Hamilton, James Madison and John Adams, the Enlightenment prompted the equally lofty legal and political principles echoed in the opening sentence of the United States Declaration of Independence:

> We hold these truths to be self-evident, that all men are created equal, that they are endowed by their Creator with certain unalienable Rights, that among these are Life, Liberty and the pursuit of Happiness.[279]

They were also echoed in the First Amendment to the 1789 Constitution among others:

> Congress shall make no law respecting an establishment of religion, or prohibiting the free exercise thereof; or abridging the freedom of speech, or of the press; or the right of the people peaceably to assemble, and to petition the Government for a redress of grievances.[280]

Clearly, the Enlightenment in America was more about principles than about detailed norms in response to everyday political and economic conflicts, of which there were many. Meanwhile, at least Washington, Hamilton and Madison were determined to put an end to the egalitarian excesses unleashed by the Revolution. It is not surprising, therefore, that the Constitution of 1789 and its subsequent (1791–1804)

---

[277] *Id.* at 18. *See also* Baker, *supra* note 237, at 9–3 (where he provides striking illustrations of state abuses of citizens of other states by collecting substantial import duties for products destined for states other than the one imposing the duty).

[278] William Bristow, *Enlightenment*, THE STANFORD ENCYCLOPEDIA OF PHILOSOPHY (2011), http://plato.stanford.edu/entries/enlightenment/.

[279] *Declaration of Independence,* THE CHARTERS OF FREEDOM (July 4, 1776), http://www.archives.gov/exhibits/charters/declaration_transcript.html.

[280] *Bill of Rights, supra* note 221.

amendments (1791–1804)[281] had to incorporate a difficult set of compromises that were to be implemented by a limited government except in extraordinary circumstances.

§ 21.11 THE UNITED STATES CONSTITUTION OF 1789 AND ITS COMPROMISES

A. The Federal-State Dualism

One of the most important compromises of the 1789 Constitution was its choice of a dualistic, federal-state government. As stated by Sergio Garcia-Rodriguez, Esq. in his chapter in the NLCIFT's "United States Law of Trade and Investment:"

> The United State government is one of multiple sovereignties. . . . There were thirteen independent states before there was a national government. In the process of amalgamating these separate sovereigns into one government, it was contemplated that certain sovereign powers would remain with each state. As the United States expanded, and new states were added, each State, when admitted, was given the same powers as those recognized in the thirteen colonies, thus perpetuating a dual sovereignty system in all fifty states.[282]

As noted by Garcia-Rodriguez, while these two provisions are in apparent conflict, they are consistent with the original conception of the federal government:[283] As a government "of limited powers," . . . it may act only where authorized by the Constitution and . . . in the areas . . . [where] it is authorized . . . [its power is supreme].[284] According to the doctrine of federal "preemption" "any *valid* federal law or treaty invalidates any inconsistent state constitutional provision, law or practice."[285] And while the dual form of government often results in dual regulation of the same activity, preemption may supersede state law regulation under certain circumstances.[286]

B. A Government with Limited Powers and a Society That Profited from Slavery

Professor Emeritus John Baker sets forth the chief characteristic of a government with limited powers, one we encountered when defining the United States version of freedom of contract as derived from the principle of that which the law does not expressly forbid, it allows:

---

281 *Amendments to the Constitution 1791—1804,* THE FOUNDERS' CONSTITUTION BILL OF RIGHTS, http://press-pubs.uchicago.edu/founders/documents/bill_of_rightss13.html (last visited Dec. 4, 2013).

282 *See* Sergio Garcia-Rodriguez, *Constitutional Law for the Foreign Investor, in* Kozolchyk, I UNITED STATES LAW, 2–i, 2–2.

283 *Id.*

284 *Id.* at 2–2—2–3.

285 *Id.* at 2–3 (citation omitted).

286 *Id.* at 2–5. This author points out that the doctrine of preemption is usually a combination of applying the Commerce of the Constitution (one of the enumerated powers listed in Article I, Section 8, Clause 3 of the Constitution) which states that the United States Congress shall have power to regulate "commerce [with foreign Nations and] among the states" with the above discussed Supremacy clause. *Id.* at 2–4. Hence, preemption occurs (a) "when Congress specifically so provides in its legislation . . . (b) when Congress adopts . . . that it has 'occupied the field' . . . and (c) when state legislation, if permitted, would frustrate the federal purpose in adopting its legislation." Garcia-Rodriguez cites Pacific Gas & Electric Co. v. State Energy Resources Conservation and Development Commission, 461 U.S. 190 (1983). *Id.* at 2–5.

> The Constitution rests on the concept of "liberty under law." This concept postulates that individuals are generally free to act without permission from government unless their action is barred by law. The concept of liberty assumes that individuals will act responsibly; that is to say, successful self-government requires citizens to govern, i.e., to control, themselves.[287]

As a government shared with the governed, the central government was given limited but significant powers, including the powers to tax and to regulate commerce among the states, and these powers were "separated and divided . . . among three co-equal branches."[288] The Constitution divided Congress into two houses, "added a separate . . . co-equal judiciary—not for the sake of convenience or efficiency but to protect liberty both by creating and, at the same time, restraining power."[289] Professor Baker also draws attention to an observation by the French political philosopher the Baron de Montesquieu, one of the greatest political thinkers of the Enlightenment, whose general principles were equally influential with friends and foes of the Constitution:

> 'There can be no liberty where the legislative and executive powers are united in the same person, or body of magistrates,' or, 'if the power of judging be not separated from the legislative and executive powers.'[290]

Yet, what about slavery? Was not their lack of liberty not only morally repugnant but also inconsistent with the building of a nation based on a system of equality enshrined in its Declaration of Independence? Professor Wood summarized the state of the nation after the conclusion of the War of 1812 against England as follows:

> [T]he country became seriously divided over the admission of Missouri as a slave state. . . . Northerners came to realize that slavery was not going to disappear naturally, and Southerners came to realize that the North really cared about ending slavery [in America].
>
> Jefferson. . . . sensed that his 'empire of liberty' had a cancer at its core that was eating away at the message of liberty and equality and threatening the very existence of the nation and its democratic self-government; but he had mistakenly come to believe that the cancer was Northern bigotry and money-making promoted by Federalist priests and merchants. . . .
>
> The Civil War was the climax of a tragedy that was preordained from the time of the Revolution. Only with the elimination of slavery could this nation that Jefferson had called 'the world's best hope' for democracy even begin to fulfill its great promise.[291]

---

[287] Baker, *supra* note 237, at 9–4.

[288] *Id* at 9–5.

[289] *Id.*

[290] *Id.* (citing a Montesquieu quote in The Federalist No. 47 at 314).

[291] WOOD, *supra* note 49, at 737–38 (citation omitted).

C. A Uniform Federal Commercial Law?

1. *Swift v. Tyson and the Long Shadow of Lord Mansfield*

In *Swift v. Tyson*, an 1842 decision by the United States Supreme Court[292] the plaintiff was an endorsee of a bill of exchange and the defendant was the acceptor of the bill. The drawers of the bill were one Norton and another Keith. The bill was accepted by Tyson in favor of Norton as its payee. Norton endorsed the bill to the plaintiff and the defendant dishonored it at maturity.

Trial discovery showed that Swift met the requirements of a holder for value or in due course:[293] He endorsed the bill before it was due in payment of a promissory note due to him by Norton and Keith; he had no notice of a defect in his title to the bill because he understood that the bill was accepted in part payment of some lands sold by Norton to a company in New York. Thus, in the eyes of the lower court he was a *bonâ fide* holder of the bill. The defendant offered to prove, that the bill was accepted by the defendant as a result of fraudulent representations by Norton and Keith. The plaintiff objected to the admission of testimony showing a failure of consideration for the defendant's acceptance of the bill.

The judges of the Circuit Court were divided on whether the defendant, as an acceptor of a bill drawn against him, was entitled to raise the same defense against the third party indorsee he had against the drawers of the bill. This was the issue certified to the Supreme Court. According to Justice Story of the United States Supreme Court, there was no doubt that:

> [A] bona fide holder of a negotiable instrument for a valuable consideration, without any notice of facts which impeach its validity as between the antecedent parties, if he takes it under an endorsement made before the same becomes due, holds the title unaffected by those facts, and may recover thereon, although as between the antecedent parties, the transaction may be without any legal validity. . . . As little doubt is there, that the holder of any negotiable paper, before it is due, is not bound to prove that he is a bona fide holder for a valuable consideration and without notice. . . .[294]

The acceptance of the bill had been made in New York and the defendant argued that as a New York contract, it was governed by the laws of New York and especially by provisions of the thirty-fourth section of Chapter 20 of the Judiciary Act of 1789. Tyson further contended that by the law of New York, as expounded by its courts, a pre-existing debt does not constitute valuable consideration as required by the law of negotiable instruments.

After examining the New York decisions, Justice Story accepted Tyson's version of New York law as correct, but asked whether admitting that the doctrine was fully settled in New York obligated the United States Supreme Court if the New York rule differed from "*the principles established in the general commercial law*."[295] He pointed out that the Courts of New York did not base their decisions on this issue on "any local

---

[292] 41 US 1 (1842).

[293] 41 U.S. at 14–15.

[294] *Id.* at syllabus & 16.

[295] *Id.* at 18 (emphasis added).

statute, or positive, fixed, or ancient local usage: but they deduce the doctrine from the general principles of commercial law."[296] As to the defendant's contention that Chapter 20 of the Judiciary Act of 1789 bound the Supreme Court to follow the decisions of the state tribunals, he replied that in "the ordinary use of language, it will hardly be contended, that the decisions of courts constitute laws. They are, at most, only evidence of what the laws are, and are not, of themselves, laws."[297] Story concluded that in all the cases which had come before the court, it had uniformly assumed "that the true interpretation of the 34th section limited its application to state laws, strictly local, that is to say, to the positive statutes of the state. . . ."[298] Further,

> [T]he law respecting negotiable instruments may be truly declared in the language of Cicero, adopted by Lord Mansfield in Luke v. Lyde, 2 Burr. R. 883, 887, to be in a great measure, not the law of a single country only, but of the commercial world.[299]

Hence, Story decided that a pre-existing debt does constitute valuable consideration where the law of negotiable instruments was concerned. He derived this conclusion from national as well as supra-national general principles of commercial law.[300]

Swift v. Tyson was overturned by *Erie Railroad Co. v. Tompkins*[301] in 1938 because, according to the Supreme Court, federal courts did not have the power to create general federal common law when hearing state law based claims between citizens of diverse states ("diversity jurisdiction"). Despite its reversal on such jurisdictional and public (not commercial) law grounds, *Swift v. Tyson* strongly indicated that America's mid-nineteenth-century commercial and financial marketplace could not be governed by the archaic doctrines of past consideration and pre-existing debt as confirmed by the many negotiable instruments cases applying *Swift v. Tyson* from 1842 until its reversal in 1938.[302] But there is more to *Swift v. Tyson*. Its reliance on Lord Mansfield is significant because of Mansfield's insistence that common law courts should act as courts of equity when needed by the circumstances.[303] This symbiosis between commercial law and equity had a profound influence on Justice John Marshall of the United States Supreme Court and on many of his successors, especially those on the federal bench.

As described by Professor Wood:

> Jefferson [advocated a strict or literal interpretation of the law]. . . . 'Relieve the judges from the rigor of text law, and permit them to wander into its equity,' . . . 'and the whole legal system becomes uncertain.' . . . The goal of judges was . . . 'to render the law more & more certain.' The goal of Mansfield and Blackstone, according to Jefferson, had been the exact opposite. They

---

296 *Id.*

297 *Id.* at 18.

298 *Id.*

299 Id at 19.

300 Id at 20.

301 304 U.S. 64 (1938).

302 *See infra* §§ 22:6 & 22:7.

303 *See* WOOD, *supra* note 49, at 449.

intended 'to render it more uncertain under [the] pretense of rendering it more reasonable.'[304]

Further, Jefferson "believed there was 'so much sly poison' in Mansfield's 'seducing eloquence' that he wanted to forbid American courts from citing . . . decisions . . . by the Court of the King' Bench since Mansfield acceded to the court."[305] In contrast, John Marshall believed Mansfield to be one of the greatest judges who ever sat on any bench and someone responsible for disabling many of the archaic formalisms that prevented English judges from dispensing substantial justice.[306]

2. Casuistry and Prolixity in Statutory and Codified Law

It would be incorrect to assume that Marshall's admiration of Mansfield's contribution was shared by the majority of his fellow judges. In fact, rather than adjudicating in what Karl Llewellyn referred to as the "Grand Style"[307] (much of which he found in Mansfield's decisions), their adjudicative style was casuistic: Their holdings were so narrow that they could only be applicable to almost exact replicas of the facts and arguments they had decided on. Whatever appeared to be beyond the replica was *obiter dicta.* Casuistry provided comfort to lower court judges worried about being overruled because to overrule their narrow decisions appellate judges had to show what facts and applicable rules or doctrines were not taken into account by the lower court, something that appellate judges are supposed to avoid doing as judges of law and not of facts.

By the turn of the twentieth century, it was becoming clear in the writings of highly respected legal thinkers such as Roscoe Pound the long time Dean of the Harvard Law School and later in those of Karl Llewellyn and many other scholars of note (including my mentor Professor Hessel Yntema),[308] that the time had come for a law that reflected what was really going on in American society and especially in its marketplace.

Meanwhile, as discussed in an earlier section, commercial statutes such as on chattel mortgages had begun to appear during the late eighteenth century, although the bulk of the United States' commercial statutory law was enacted during the twentieth century. In fact, one of the most common misconceptions about United States law is that it is "unwritten" in the sense that it is not codified or incorporated into statutes or compilations thereof. The truth is the opposite; there are few countries in the world with a larger amount of statutory law than the United States. This does not mean, as we shall discuss shortly, that statutory and code law are drafted and interpreted in the same manner as they are in civil law countries.

As will be described in the following sections, the majority of federal and state laws are drafted in a casuistic and prolix manner, where one or more illustrations of what is meant by the formulated rules as well as the numerous exceptions and qualifications of it (as well as their illustrations) frequently follow such a rule. Thus, to

---

[304] WOOD, *supra* note 49, at 449 (citations omitted).

[305] *Id.* at 449.

[306] *Id.*

[307] *See infra* § 23:5(D)(1).

[308] *See, e.g.,* Hessel E. Yntema, *American Legal Realism in Retrospect,* 14 VAND. L. REV. 317 (1960–1961).

a civil law lawyer, the United States statutes are often populated by multitudes of narrow rules derived from actual or hypothetical fact situations.

3. *Late Nineteenth- and Early Twentieth-Century Statutory Law*

The Harter Act of 1893 was among the most significant of the late-nineteenth-century statutes of the United States.[309] Its enactment was prompted by a growing practice among United States carriers to insert clauses in their bills of lading that sharply limited their obligations to shippers. In using very broad disclaimer of liability clauses, United States carriers were following the model of the English carriers. The United States Congress stepped in because shippers had no true bargaining power as contrasted with that of the carriers.[310] The Harter Act achieved a compromise between carrier and shipper rights and claims by apportioning their liability depending on where the shipped cargo was at the time the damage took place. The Harter Act was followed a set of important commercial statutes. In 1953, while still lobbying for the enactment of the U.C.C. by some reluctant states, Karl Llewellyn listed the principal early-twentieth-century statutes that it would replace, absorb and modernize:[311]

> I refer especially to the Uniform Negotiable Instruments Law of. . .[312], which is the foundation of banking practice. I refer to the Uniform Sales Act (1906), which has served well . . . I refer to the short-term secured financing covered by the Uniform Trust Receipts Act[313] and the Uniform Conditional Sales Act,[314] one dealing with certain phases of inventory financing, and the other with the financing of individual consumer purchases.

As you will notice in Chapter 23, Professor Llewellyn's opinion of the Uniform Sales Act, largely drafted by Professor Samuel Williston of the Harvard Law School, was quite different from that expressed in the above-quoted article in the Tennessee Law Review. Llewellyn's harsher view of the Uniform Sales Act was, as history has proven, was the most accurate. The Uniform Sales Act was heavily influenced by the English Sale of Goods Act of 1893. And Professor Williston's version was scholarly, but in the casuistic way, not the Grand Style way Llewellyn admired. One of the many examples pertained to standard sales practices among merchants, such as their tolerance for *de minimus* or insignificant deviations from literal terms and conditions

---

[309] 46 U.S.C. § 30702(a). On this Act on its effects on others worldwide, *see also* Kozolchyk, *supra* note 246, at 182. On the commercial law nature of maritime statutes such as Barcelona's Consulato de Mare and Bilbao's Ordenanzas de Bilbao, *see supra* § 9:1(C)–(D).

[310] Kozolchyk, *supra* note 246, at 182.

[311] *Id.* at 186.

[312] *See* LAW OF NEGOTIABLE INSTRUMENTS: STATUTES, CASES, AND AUTHORITIES (Ernest W. Huff ed., 2d ed. 1910), *available at* http://archive.org/stream/cu31924052854415/cu31924052854415_djvu.txt (for the history, text and commentary on the 1891 Negotiable Instruments Act of the United States).

[313] *See* George G. Bogert, *The Effect of the Trust Receipt Act*, 3 U. CHI. L. REV. 26 (1935–1936) (on the history and text of the Uniform Trust Receipts Act as adopted by the State of New York in 1934 and other states in the following years.) Professor Bogert was not a fan of the draftsmanship of the Uniform Trust Receipts Act and criticized it as unnecessarily complex and confusing. *Id.*

[314] *See* William G. Hale, *The Uniform Conditional Sales Act*, 2 OR. L. REV. 1 (1922–1923) (for an introduction to the Uniform Sales Act as concluded by the National Conference of Commissioners of Uniform State laws in 1922).

of the contract (unless expressly otherwise required in the contract). These practices collided with the Sale of Goods Act of 1893's insistence on a "perfect tender" rule.[315]

One of the early-twentieth-century statutes that Llewellyn did not mention was the above-discussed Uniform Bills of Lading Act[316] and its progeny in United States and multinational treaty law. It is an important act not only because of its intrinsic merits, but because of the process of its enactment—it was part of a uniform commercial law movement promoted by two genuinely American law reform and modernization institutions.

By the mid-twentieth century, and largely as a result of the United States' federal system of government, a multiplicity of federal and state legislative and judicial sources of law bore heavily on legal practice and on the predictability of the law, especially inter-state commercial law. The volume of sources of law that were at times unmanageable, multiple and not always consistent was responsible for the creation of two remarkable American legal institutions: The American Law Institute (hereinafter ALI) and the National Conference of Commissioners of Uniform State Law (NCCUSL), now renamed as the Uniform Law Commission (ULC), undertook the task of reviewing existing case law and statutory law for purposes of making them uniform.

The Uniform Law Commission (formally NCCUSL) was established in 1892 to provide non-partisan, carefully drafted legislation intended to provide uniformity to areas of the law governed by diverse and at times contradictory rules, concepts, and principles of interpretation. Members of the ULC must be lawyers qualified to practice law, judges, legislative staff and law professors who are appointed by state governments, the District of Columbia, the U.S. Virgin Islands, to act as researchers, drafters, and facilitators of the enactment of uniform state laws. Without any doubt, the Uniform Commercial Code has been one of its signal accomplishments.[317]

4. *The ALI and Its Restatements of the Law*

The ALI was created on February 23 of 1923 following the recommendation of a group of prominent American judges, lawyers and teachers concerned with the uncertainties of the United States common law.[318] Its purpose was "to promote the clarification and simplification of the law and its better adaptation to social needs, to secure the better administration of justice, and to encourage and carry on scholarly and scientific legal work."[319]

In short order, the ALI became known for its restatements of various areas of the law that were of interest to judges, lawyers and scholars of the law. Thus, the ALI produced restatements for the laws of agency, conflict of laws, contracts, judgments,

---

[315] For such customary tolerances in letter of credit practices (in connection with the payment of the purchase in "documentary" sales, *see*, e.g., UCP 500 sub. art. 3(a) (1993)).

[316] *See* Uniform Bills of Lading Act § 23, 4 U.L.A. 39 (1922); *see also* WILLIAM PORTER BENNETT, HISTORY AND PRESENT POSITION OF THE BILL OF LADING AS A DOCUMENT 82 (1913). According to this author the Commissioners of Uniform State Laws presented this Act to state legislatures for their adoption in 1906. *Id.*

[317] *About the UCL,* UNIFORM LAW COMMISSION, http://www.uniformlaws.org/Narrative.aspx?title=About the ULC (last visited Mar. 18, 2014).

[318] *See* Bennet Boskey, *The American Law Institute: a Glimpse at its Future*, 12 Green Bag 2d 255, 255–56 (2009), *available at* http://www.greenbag.org/v12n3/v12n3_boskey.pdf.

[319] *Id.* at 256.

property, restitution, security, torts, and trusts. Although the ALI's restatements are often referred to as codifications of case law, they are better described as compilations of important cases or cases with precedential value whose holdings are distilled by the restatements as "black letter law," *i.e.*, the rules that courts would apply to similar cases in the future. In doing this, the restatements affirm not only their precedential value, but also the existence of a certain judicial trend which connects holdings to decision-making trends. Thus, this black letter law generally is not framed as a set of codified rules that result from *a priori* formulations of careful definitions and classifications of legal institutions as done by codes such as the *Code Civil* or the BGB. Neither are they deemed binding authority, although in many instances they are followed by courts as persuasive formulations of judicial trends.

Restatements also include comments and illustrations, often as "Reporters' Notes," which include a discussion of all the cases that went into the formulation of a principle summarized in a section. These comments and illustrations help contextualize the rules and thus enable lawyers and judges to rely more confidently on the black letter law set forth in the restatements. In doing this analytical work, albeit confined mostly to case law, the participants in the drafting of the restatements (including black letter law and commentary) craft the United States version of common-law-based legal science. For if by legal science one understands the most accurate and objective description of the state of a given branch of the law, as shaped mostly by court decisions and statutes, the restatements are the best products of American legal science.

My favorite is the Restatement (Second) of the Law of Contracts, whose reporters were two great figures of American contract and private law: Robert Braucher, the father of one of my distinguished colleagues, Jeanne Braucher, and E. Allan Farnsworth, a truly exceptional scholar and drafter. This Restatement is a model of insightful analysis, and of drafting precision and clarity. Its influence is now apparent in a less rigid and still predictable federal and state adjudication of commercial contract disputes (as will become apparent in Chapter 23 on contract interpretation) as it is also in important treaties such as the UNCITRAL Convention on International Sales of Goods law (Vienna Convention) and on the UNIDROIT European Principles of the Law of Contracts.

5. NCCUSL and the Drafting of the U.C.C. Article 5

The ALI and the ULC have been allies in the drafting of a number of important statutes, including the U.C.C. Work on it began during the 1940s. It was first published in 1952, and in periodically revised form it is now the law in all 50 states. The ALI participants in the drafting of the U.C.C. were elected members of the ALI, including prominent judges, practitioners and scholars. The ULC participants, in turn, were state commissioners, officers, staff and representatives of the varioussectors involved in the various articles and underlying trades or professions. On the whole, these entities have done and continue to do a very creditable job of transforming mostly judicially formulated rules into statutory rules. The drafting of Article 5 on letters of credit, however, presented a problem to the drafters because many of the judicially formulated rules they intended to rely on, even for definitional purposes, did not reflect the standard and best letter of credit practices in the United States and worldwide.

As a participant in the drafting process, I witnessed drafters struggling for more than a year with judicial definitions of concepts as basic as "confirmation" or "assignment of the proceeds" which misunderstood and distorted the meaning of those everyday letter of credit transactions. The reason was simple—the courts that authored those definitions did not understand their meaning in letter of credit practice. However, many members of the drafting committee were reluctant to rely on the banking definitions of those terms because banking practices were suspected of being contrary to the best interests of other parties to the letter of credit transactions, such as the customers who applied for the issuance of the letters of credit or the beneficiaries who were paid by the letters of credit.

This perception prompted a vigorous form of drafting pluralism, but such a pluralism misunderstood, as I will discuss shortly, the nature of standard and best practices in the letter of credit business and how these practices are wrought in a manner that they become universally viable (as will be discussed in detail in Chapter 24). With the reader's indulgence, I will discuss the Article 5 drafting process in greater detail than I have discussed legislative drafting in earlier chapters. This is necessary not to illustrate how the U.C.C. was drafted, because in many ways the drafting of Article 5 was atypical, but to illustrate the task that will be faced by other legislators whose main normative sources are standard and best practices that are widely respected in the sector in question as the usages of its trades.

Such was the importance attributed to pluralism during the revision of Article 5 that at first it stood in the way of adopting standard and best practices of the banking industry, even though this industry observed its binding usages in each phase of the letter of credit transaction. For banks were the issuers, notifiers, confirmers, negotiators, transferors and transferees, payors and reimbursers of the letter of letter of credit transaction. And these were the critical and exclusive "operations" of letter of credit banks. Furthermore, in doing so, banks had to act in the above capacities interchangeably, but always watching out for the best interest of their customers-clients as well as their own. And quite frequently, those interests coincided and were not in conflict. The pluralistic method of drafting, set in motion at first by the ALI and the ULC alike, expected that the drafters forcefully advocate what were assumed to be conflicting interests among, say, buyers-applicants for the issuance of letters of credit and seller-beneficiaries of the letters of credit or between issuing, confirming and negotiating bankers. Yet, as will be illustrated in Chapter 24, in the case of letters of credit, this form of drafting misperceived the nature of the letter of credit transaction. For in this transaction, as just noted, all of its regular participants have interchangeable roles or transactional functions instead of roles or functions that are fixed.

This means that today's issuer Bank A, which depended on Bank B as its confirrmer in another issuance, becomes a confirming bank for Bank B as the issuer of the letter of credit. Similarly, today's buyer-applicant for the issuance of the credit could shortly—after acting as a buyer-applicant for the issuance of Letter of Credit 1—act as a seller-beneficiary of the same goods to another buyer-applicant. After all, who could make a commercial living by only buying and not selling or by just issuing and not confirming and negotiating letters of credit? This meant that to designate a drafter "A" to represent the interests of buyers-applicants against the interests of "B," the representative of sellers-beneficiaries was to ignore that this supposed "chemically pure" buyer was an artificial designation because if A succeeded in fashioning a rule that was more favorable to himself as A, he was likely to suffer the consequence of that rule when he acted as B. And the same was true with issuing and confirming banks or with negotiating and transferring banks, etc.

Perhaps the most important legislative lesson to be learned from the Article 5 experience was that statutory rules are best suited as markers of the bright lines of the letter of credit transactional traffic: Some of these are mechanical in nature and others are implementers of legality and public policy. The mechanical rules of traffic are mandatory rules and must be observed by all the participants in the letter of credit transactions. For example, these rules specify what must be done by each regular participant to get the transaction started and make it binding on each of them: When and where is a letter of credit "established" or binding on the issuer, confirmer, etc.? Or what are the time periods, if any, for the execution of subsequent phases?

The provisions that implement public policy and legality are also mandatory but, as a rule, specify what remedies are available to the affected parties. For example, what standards of diligence govern the execution of the various operations or transactions? What are the remedies, contractual, tortious or criminal, available to the aggrieved parties? The transactional or operational rules are those that set forth the meaning of basic practices such as that of issuing an irrevocable and confirmed letter of credit and its negotiation or payment, or of an acceptable commercial invoice, ocean bill of lading or insurance policy and so on. Since these rules are derived from the standard and best practices of letter of credit banking, they usually become widely observed usages of the letter of credit trade. The drafter of statutory law is best advised to rely on these usages rather than on his own legal instincts when setting forth the manner in which rights can be exercised or duties performed.

For example, during the discussion of the duties of a beneficiary or of a bank that presented documents for negotiation or payment to another bank, some drafters at first insisted on requiring the beneficiary and presenting bank to grant the same warranties required of a seller of goods under Article 2 or by the holders of negotiable instruments, documents of title and investment securities under Articles 3, 4, 7 and 8 of the U.C.C.

Yet, such a requirement ran contrary to a fundamental usage of the letter of credit trade which assumed that once a letter of credit was paid by the issuing or confirming banks, the payment was final.[320] As such, its finality could not be re-argued by the issuing or confirming bank, and especially by contending that the beneficiary or presenting banks had presented documents that contained untruthful statements regarding the quantity or quality of the goods paid for by the letter of credit.[321] Nor could the payment by the issuing or confirming bank be reversed by allegation and proof that the paid for documents did not strictly comply with the terms and conditions of the letter of credit.

Regardless of the possible legal analogies between a letter of credit draft or bill of exchange and the warranties ascribed in Articles 3, 4, 7 and 8 of the U.C.C. to the holders of "instruments", "items" and "investment securities , the addition of these warranties to the presentation of letter of credit documents would have ended the

---

[320] *See, e.g.,* UCP 500 sub art. 9(a)–(b) (for the reference to the definiteness of the issuing and confirming banks' undertaking). *See also id.* art. 4. Its principle of abstraction or independence of the issuing and confirming banks' promises: "In credit operations all parties concerned deal with documents and not with goods, services and/or other performances to which the documents may relate." *Id.*

[321] *Id.*

treasured certainty and predictability of the payments of irrevocable-confirmed letters of credit. To their credit, once the advocates of the addition of warranties became aware of the importance of the letter of credit usage, they reversed their position on warranties and agreed to rules consistent with this key letter of credit usage.[322] On the other hand, some of the drafters remained reluctant to adopt widely observed standard and best letter of credit practices when they were inconsistent with established case law. Hoping to persuade them, I sent them an extract of an article written by Francis B. James Esq., one of the first chairmen of the Committee on Commercial law of the Conference of Ccommissioners of Uniform State Laws in 1905:

> A mercantile code should be a clear expression of well recognized commercial customs whether they have or have not yet found their place in judicial decisions. The merchants gave to the law their customs and the law should give their customs back to them clearly expressed and freed from mere technical expressions.
>
> . . .
>
> Where judicial decisions conflict with well recognized, economically and ethically sound customs, the mercantile customs should be embodied in the code in preference to the formal technical rules. . .[323]

6. The United States Legislative Drafting Style

From a civil law codification perspective, the U.C.C. is a compendium of individual norms, with the exception of the overarching application of a principle such as good faith performance and interpretation of obligations as discussed in Chapter 22. As with the ALI restatements, the raw materials for drafting the U.C.C. were an amalgam of case law, commentary thereon and customs and usage of trade. Thus, its rules were not derived from carefully crafted definitions, classifications and general principles as found in European codes such as the *Code Civil* or the B.G.B.

Its casuistry, aided by reasoning by example, is responsible for the narrowness and complexity of many of its rules. As an heir to the Anglo-American (and Roman law) tradition of elucidating the role and place of judicial remedies, the U.C.C. interpreter must learn about the cases that influenced its drafting and must also be able to appraise the effects of the U.C.C. rule upon future litigation. In this respect, the U.C.C.'s main preoccupation is with remedies rather than with transactions. Fortunately for the U.C.C. interpreter, the Official Comments to each rule provide required transactional as well as remedial background by discussing the implications of the various rules and providing the cases whose holdings were adopted and occasionally those that were rejected. The narrowness of the norms also affects the U.C.C's method of definition. Because the definitions in the U.C.C. do not pretend to identify the Aristotelian eternal and universal elements of each institution, they are mere points of reference, declarations of context or at times, mere transcriptions of rules.

---

322 *See* U.C.C. § 5–110 and cmts. (1) & (2) (2013).

323 *See* Francis B. James, *Practical Suggestions on Codifying the Law of Warehouse Receipts*, 3 MICH. L. REV. 282, -284–285. For the effect of James' view on the United States law on warehouse receipts, *see also* Vassil D. Zhivkov, The Warehouse Receipts: A Method To Secure Agricultural Financing 41 (2014) (Doctoral Dissertation, Univesity of Arizona) (on file with author).

Although the U.C.C. is closer to commercial practice than any contemporary commercial code and is also the most faithful to judicial developments, it is not as logically consistent nor as clear and concise as are the commercial codes of major civil law countries. Thus, many U.C.C. definitions are tautological, *i.e.*, they include the defined term as part of the definition. Consider, for example, the definition of a security interest in § 1–201(35) of the U.C.C.: " 'Security interest' means *an interest* in personal property or fixtures which secures payment or performance of an obligation. . . ."[324] Yet, the concept of "interest" remains undefined—is it a right? And if so, is it *in personam* or *in rem*? Nevertheless, if you ask United States judges and commercial practitioners, they would still prefer consistency with actual practices over a sterile clarity, conciseness, and formal logic.

As discussed in Chapter 2, these different methods of defining legal concepts reflect the different roles ascribed by each system to formal logic. The European and Latin-American codes ascribe normative value to definitions and classifications. As discussed earlier, an undefined and unclassified contract or right in rem might not be enforceable in many civil law countries. The same is not true with U.C.C. definitions. Surely, some U.C.C. definitions, such as that of good faith, carry significant normative weight. On the whole, however, the U.C.C. relies on many definitions, mostly to clarify obscure or ambiguous terms, and its classifications carry little, if any, normative weight.

§ 21.12 STATUTORY AND ADMINISTRATIVE REGULATION OF ABUSIVE PRACTICES

A. Overreaching

Because of the living law principle "that which the law does not expressly forbids it allows," and its frequent abuses, the balance between strict regulation and permissibility of contractual practices is a delicate one. Permissibility requires a presumption that the contracting parties act in good faith (and by good faith I mean the same combination of honesty, reasonableness and fairness you will encounter in Chapter 23). Otherwise, the impulse to relentlessly pursue the business opportunities alluded to by Calvin Coolidge would be stifled. Yet, abusive and overreaching practices come in many garbs. Some are even inspired by ideologies espoused by economists as illustrious as Milton Friedman, the Nobel Prize winner who famously pronounced that "The Social Responsibility of Business is To Increase its Profits."[325]

1. Maximizing Share Prices and Shareholders' Value and Social Welfare

As described in a recent Washington Post article by Professor Steven Pearlstein of George Mason University and also a Washington Post economics journalist:

> In the recent history of management ideas, few have had a more profound—or pernicious—effect that the one that says corporations should be run in a manner that "maximizes shareholder value."

---

[324] U.C.C. § 1–201(35) (emphasis added).

[325] Milton Friedman, *The Social Responsibility of Business is to Increase Profits*, NEW YORK TIMES MAGAZINE (Sept. 13, 1970), *available at* http://www.colorado.edu/studentgroups/libertarians/issues/friedman-soc-resp-business.html.

> Indeed, you could argue that much of what Americans perceive to be wrong with the economy these days – the slow growth and rising inequality; the recurring scandals, the wild swings from boom to bust, the inadequate investment in R&D, worker training and public goods – has its roots in this ideology.[326]

Pearlstein shows how the ideology that urges corporate managers to maximize share prices has no foundation in history and law. On the contrary, there is ample evidence that a corporate practice that began during the nineteen seventies and eighties as a "useful corrective to self-satisfied managerial mediocrity has become a corrupting, self-interested dogma peddled by finance professors, money managers and overcompensated corporate executives."[327]

Professor Pearlstein traces the origins of the maximization of share prices to the nineteen seventies and eighties when increased competition spurred by globalization significantly reduced American corporate revenues and share prices. This trend led to hostile takeovers by corporate raiders, many of whom financed their purchases of corporations with "junk" bonds. Disgruntled shareholders were eager to sell their shares and thus the threats of takeovers made corporate executives and directors "[F]ocus on profits and share prices, tossing aside old inhibitions against laying off workers, cutting wages, closing plants, spinning off divisions and outsourcing production overseas."[328]

The corporate infrastructure of maximization of share prices was buttressed by corporate lawyers who invariably advised against any corporate action that might lower the share prices and invite shareholders' lawsuits. It also relied on Wall Street investment advisors, brokers and underwriters who insisted on attractive corporate quarterly earnings and short term trading, and particularly on large pay packages for top executives "tied to the short-term performance of the company stock."[329] He concludes that while maximizing shareholder value has done much for top executives, it has done little for shareholders.[330] The same could be said for the income of average company employees. Moreover, as pointed out by Pearlstein, chief corporate executives are the first to acknowledge that no enterprise can maximize long-term value for its shareholders without attracting excellent employees, producing great products and services, and doing their part to support effective government and healthy communities.[331]

Ironically, this dependence was also acknowledged (albeit tacitly) by the same Milton Friedman who placed the responsibility of corporate duty to pursue profits and high share values above the corporate duty to society's welfare. For, as stated by Cornell University Professor Robert H. Frank, when Friedman proposed his equally

---

[326] Pearlstein, *supra* note 96.

[327] *Id.*

[328] *Id.*

[329] *Id.*

[330] *Id.*

[331] *Id.*

famous "negative" income tax, he became the "architect of the most successful social welfare program of all time."[332]

In light of Friedman's safety net and of his evident compassion for the poor and infirm, the question one needs to address to his doctrine of corporate social responsibility to increase profits and share value is: at what social cost? Surely a Friedman disciple might reply that the duty to provide a safety net for the poor and infirm is the state's responsibility, not the corporate business'. Yet, Friedman's negative income tax could not function unless corporate businesses paid the taxes that made the negative income tax idea possible. In the final analysis, then, the corporate keenness in the pursuit of profits is the selfish side of a coin whose altruistic side consists of a fair treatment of employees and customers, and a brotherly treatment of the community's poor and infirm.

2. *The Maximization of Contractual and Property Rights and Judicial and Administrative Remedies*

As discussed earlier, the United States' legal system has been able to counter (although not always effectively) the maximization and abuse of rights with judicial and administrative remedies. Recall that in the law of sales of goods alone, judicially or statutorily fashioned remedies such as adequate assurances of performance, damages for anticipatory repudiation and constructive trusts followed widespread bad faith attempts to maximize contractual rights. Also recall that the same marketplace that witnessed a large number of predatory and unfair practices also witnessed the proliferation of anti-trust and unfair competition remedies.

---

[332] Robert H. Frank, The Other Milton Friedman: A Conservative With a Social Welfare Program, THE NEW YORK TIMES (Nov. 23, 2006), http://www.nytimes.com/2006/11/23/business/23scene.html?_r=0. As described by Professor Frank, Friedman's negative income tax would replace the multiplicity of existing welfare programs with:

> [A] single cash transfer—say, $6,000—to every citizen. A family of four with no market income would thus receive an annual payment from the I.R.S. of $24,000. For each dollar the family then earned, this payment would be reduced by some fraction—perhaps 50 percent. A family of four earning $12,000 a year, for example, would receive a net supplement of $18,000 (the initial $24,000 less the $6,000 tax on its earnings).
>
> Mr. Friedman's proposal was undoubtedly motivated in part by his concern for the welfare of the least fortunate. But he. . . emphasized the superiority of the negative income tax over conventional welfare programs on purely practical grounds. If the main problem of the poor is that they have too little money, he reasoned, the simplest and cheapest solution is to give them some more. He saw no advantage in hiring armies of bureaucrats to dispense food stamps, energy stamps, day care stamps and rent subsidies.
>
> As always, Mr. Friedman's policy prescriptions were shaped by his desire to minimize adverse economic incentives, a feature that architects of earlier welfare programs had largely ignored. Those programs, each administered by a separate bureaucracy, typically reduced a family's benefits by some fraction of each increment in earned income. Rates of 50 percent were common, so a family participating in four separate programs might see its total benefits fall by $2 for each extra dollar it earned. Under the circumstances, no formal training in economics was necessary to see that working didn't pay. In contrast, someone who worked additional hours under Mr. Friedman's plan would always take home additional after-tax income.

Id. Instead of adopting Friedman's negative tax program, Congress adopted the earned-income tax credit, a program that Professor Frank describes as essentially the same as Friedman's, except that only people who were employed received benefits. Referring to it as one of the few American welfare programs that has been widely adopted in other countries, the earned-income tax credit has proved far more efficient than conventional programs.

In the final analysis, then, the longevity of this U.S. version of the principle of freedom of contract suggests that despite abuses and the need for continuous new remedies, the U.S. marketplace has been considerably better off with it than with restrictive, *a priori* limitations, as apparent in totalitarian legal systems.

On the other hand, there is a contractual or extra-contractual conduct whose mere presence creates a rebuttable presumption of illegality or a violation of public policy. This was the case with the above-discussed nineteenth-century sectorial and inter-sectorial attempts to fix the prices of fresh milk and dairy products. It was also the case with the monopolization of commodities such as sugar, or services such as rail cargo, and "retail price maintenance agreements," among other instances of "*per se*" violations.

B. The Tools to Combat Overreaching

The above unilateral actions or transactions by overreaching merchants prompted the enactment of statutory and administrative prohibitions and their implementation in court adjudication. As with court decisions, statutory and administrative regulations were inspired by the same principles discussed earlier—from freedom of contract (in the broadest sense) and equality of treatment of equals to third party protection.

Accordingly, statutory law enacted at the end of the nineteenth century intended to protect a fair type of competition as well as to curb consumer abuses such as those by the American Sugar Refining Company, which controlled 98% of the sugar production of the United States or by Northern Securities, which controlled the northeastern rail transportation. The principal legislative tool used by President Theodore Roosevelt when he launched his "trust busting era" was the 1890 Sherman Act, which remained largely unused by the Executive until 1902. Its purpose, as defined by the United States Supreme Court, was not:

> [T]o protect businesses from the working of the market; [but] . . . to protect the public from the failure of the market. The law directs itself not against conduct which is competitive, even severely so, but against conduct which unfairly tends to destroy competition itself.[333]

The Sherman Act was supplemented by the Clayton Antitrust Act of 1914, which prohibited, among other transactions, exclusive sales contracts or relationships, local price cutting to freeze out competitors, rebates, interlocking directorates in corporations capitalized at million or more in the same field of business, and inter-corporate stock holdings.

In addition, the enactment of the first and permanent income tax law of the United States on July 2, 1909 as part of the Sixteenth Amendment to the Constitution transformed business and accounting practices, including heightened requirements of transparency of business data. From then on, transparency in the recording and accounting of commercial transactions was no longer discretionary and accounting practices became not only essential when reporting personal and corporate taxes, but also when disclosing likely anti-competitive practices.

---

[333] Spectrum Sports v. McQuillan, 506 U.S. 447, 458 (1992).

C. Disclosure as a Regulatory Tool

The Securities Act of 1933 (also referred to as the Truth in Securities Law) had, two basic objectives: (1) To require the investors to receive financial and other significant information concerning securities being offered for public sale; and (2) Prohibit deceit, misrepresentation and other fraud in the sale of securities.[334]

The disclosure required from the potential seller of securities was the same expected from Puritan merchants and complied with the definition of good faith in U.C.C. § 1–201: "[H]onesty in fact in the conduct or transaction concerned." However, practices such as those of credit examiners required "a clean showing" of all the business affairs of the credit applicants. Query: what did the Truth in Securities Law mean when it required that the potential seller of securities provide the investor with financial and other "significant information"?

If that information appeared in audited reports, the standard of disclosure was likely to be that of the recently created Public Company Accounting Oversight Board (PCAOB), "a nonprofit corporation established by Congress to oversee the audits of public companies in order to protect the interests of investors and further the public interest in the preparation of informative, accurate and independent audit reports."[335]

Yet what about the sellers' of securities own disclosures? My son, Raphael A. Kozolchyk, Esq., a lawyer for the SEC, answered this question (in a personal and non-institutional capacity) from the vantage point of a regulator:

> I believe that smart regulations provide a system wherein any potential investor has access to certain basic facts about an investment before buying it instead of trying to impart an articulated standard of fairness that proves time and again to be highly subjective from court to court and transaction to transaction.

Yet, whether the facts that must be disclosed are "basic" as he suggests or "significant" (as suggested by the Truth in Securities law), both standards are at their best when they take into account the reasonable expectations of archetypal third parties such as representative investors (who, depending upon the type of investment, can range from highly experienced to inexperienced). By relying on the opinions of honest, knowledgeable and identifiable archetypal market participants, the determination of what is reasonable is neither subjective nor arbitrary.

§ 21.13 SUMMARY AND CONCLUSIONS

In the introductory section of this chapter, I expressed the hope that its reader would find answers to questions such as: What were the practices that helped shape the United States law of commercial contracts? Who were the principal shapers of those practices and laws? There can be little doubt that Puritanical character traits such as honesty, industriousness, frugality and willingness to trust counter-parties had much to do with a legal culture of trade (long distance and local) in which private ownership and a labor or transformative work theory of value remained influential to this day. There can also be little doubt that a version of a rural merchant who was a

---

[334] Securities Act of 1933 (as amended through P.L. 112–106, *apprv'd* April 5, 2012), http://www.sec.gov/about/laws/sa33.pdf.

[335] PUBLIC COMPANY ACCOUNTING OVERSIGHT BOARD, http://pcaobus.org/Pages/default.aspx.

manufacturer-producer as well as a distributor of his own goods or products was responsible for the attitude that anyone can be a merchant in America (including farmers) and of the underlying value that commerce is a respectable and honest, if not an honorable, way for anyone to earn a living and more.

The consumer revolution that Virginians associated with the accessibility to the goods of a general store eventually begat department stores and huge multi-acre "big box" stores. Retailers depended upon wholesalers and jobbers for their commercial credit and consumers depended upon retailers for their consumer credit. Meanwhile, department stores popularized informal acknowledgments of their customers' contractual liability and introduced adhesion contracts in their extensions of credit to their customers. Eventually, they also introduced multiparty electronic transactions for "just in time" inventory re-supply.

The commercial and consumer credit practices spawned by the above market participants undoubtedly have acted as lubricants of the economy of the United States. However, they would have been far less effective had courts and administrative agencies not have curbed violations of the Purtians' principle of moral capitalism by maximizations of contractual rights based upon a definition of freedom of contract which presumed any contractual conduct enforceable unless expressly declared as unenforceable. Similarly, the contribution of commercial and consumer credit would have been much less significant were it not for Paul Warburg's vision of the Federal Reserve as a bank that discounted commercial paper in an "elastic" (supply and demand) manner. In doing this, he provided the profiles of both an archetypal lender (observant of short-term, self-liquidating and truly commercial loans) and of an archetypal commercial borrower, able and willing to repay based on his business's cash flow and the "readily marketable" nature of his commodities. After the creation of the Federal Reserve Bank, which was vitally interested in promoting commercial and self-liquidating credit, the United States was likely to acquire a healthy national and international credit market.

At this time, the trading world looks at the United States for its leadership in the protection of good faith and reasonableness in commercial contracting. It also hopes that the United States will continue its leadership in protecting third party purchasers, investors and creditors within its borders and beyond with a requisite dosage of moral capitalism. As will be explored in subsequent chapters, commercial lawyers can play a major role in satisfying these reasonable expectations.

Part VI

FORMATION, INTERPRETATION AND ADJUDICATION OF CONTRACTUAL AND CUSTOMARY LAW DISPUTES

Chapter 22

FORMATION OF CONTRACTS: CEREMONY OR CONDUCT?

"In the beginning of commercial contracts, there was a giving."[1]

§ 22.1 INTRODUCTION: THE STATIC AND DYNAMIC VERSIONS OF "CIVIL" AND COMMERCIAL CONTRACTS

The development of contract law in Roman law and in the early common law was at first remedial, *i.e.*, it grew with the availability of "forms" or causes of action and defenses for a specified group of contracts that were mostly entered into or performed by at least one of the parties. As was apparent during the Roman and Medieval law periods, with some exceptions such as in the Mideastern trade among Jewish merchants, executory promises remained *nuda pacta* in civil and common law countries until credit and promises to give or repay loans became common in the marketplace. As noted by Professor Patrick Atiyah, the distinguished historian of English private law, until the late eighteenth century, the English law of contracts was "largely a law of executed contracts, and not a law of executory contracts."[2] In contrast, the modern law of contracts under both civil and common law legal systems resulted from a "general theory of contract"[3] that identified the basic elements of a binding contract and its constituent promises such as, among others, mutual assent, capacity, cause or purpose (*causa*) and consideration. The questions addressed by this theory were of little or no interest to the Romans or to early common law lawyers. Typical among them were: What is a contract? Why is a contract binding and among whom? What are the constitutive elements of binding contracts and promises? And, of particular interest to this Chapter, how and when is a contract formed?

This chapter focuses on the formation and main elements of contracts. Prominent among these are the *Code Civil* inspired element of "*causa*" and the Anglo-American "consideration." They will be studied mostly from the vantage point of commercial or for-profit transactions. This context excludes gratuitous, charitable contracts or contracts for the rendition of professional services which, like the services of medieval guilds, continue to earn tariff-based "*honoraria*" (instead of negotiated fees) in many a civil law country. As discussed in an earlier chapter,[4] the latter types of contract will also be referred to as "civil" and are largely governed by the *Code Civil* and its progeny.

Despite the for-profit nature of commercial contracts, the reader will soon be introduced to a connection between altruism in the form of gift giving and the development of the Anglo-American contractual element of consideration. As with the comparison of other legal institutions, the main purpose of this chapter's comparison

---

[1] A saying by an anonymous, yet contextual, lawyer.

[2] P. S. ATIYAH, THE RISE AND FALL OF FREEDOM OF CONTRACT 419 (1979).

[3] *See supra* § 4:4(D)(1).

[4] *See supra* § 6:3.

between *causa* (or the reason for the enforcement of a contract) and consideration (or the giving of something of value to initiate the life of a contract or a binding promise) is to determine which of these concepts best facilitates the formation and enforcement of commercial contracts. Stated otherwise, which of these elements, if either, is the true and effective catalyst of a binding promise or agreement? In order to best compare these two institutions, it will be helpful, as is customary in this book, to place *causa* and consideration in their respective normative and socio-economic contexts. This contextual comparison promises to be especially rewarding because of their contrasting intellectual pedigrees—while *causa* traces its pedigree to none other than Aristotle, consideration's pedigree is more pedestrian: It grew up from custom and usage, ancestral as well as medieval, and was invariably associated with the giving of gifts. Why one of these elements (*causa*) never succeeded in performing its mission and the other (consideration) has had a very successful, multi-century career but by now has lost much of its usefulness, is an inquiry pursued throughout this chapter because of the lesson it teaches about sound commercial law making.

Hopefully, the reader will become familiar with the method of forming contracts that emerges from the trust and gift giving that act as catalysts of cooperative behavior between the parties. Only when formative, customary behavior such as gift giving is present will there be room for the so-called "rules of traffic" that delineate when the subsequent steps should be expected and manifested. The more customary a contract law is, as has been the case in Anglo-American law, the more successful will be its legal institutions, as compared to its intellectualized counterparts found in such places as the *Code Civil*.

A. The *Code Civil* (Static-Ceremonial) Contract

The search for the suitability of *causa* or consideration as an encouragement of commercial contracting is part of a broader inquiry into the formation of two contradictory conceptions of contract. One is the product of a bilateral or joint decision that resulted from a face-to-face meeting and a writing often formalized in a ceremony before public officials, notaries and/or witnesses. Typical of this version of contract is the formal deed of sale of real property in the *Code Civil*. As discussed in an earlier chapter,[5] this contract must be executed *inter praesentes*, *i.e.*, by parties or their representatives acting "face-to-face" before a notary public or subject to the official validation of their signatures.[6] The seriousness with which the notarial deed was regarded by Robert Pothier (among other pre-*Code-Civil* commentators) was illustrated in an earlier chapter.[7] He acknowledged that some contracts required no formalities beyond the mere assent of the parties, as was the case with the consensual contracts in Roman law (such as sales, loans, partnership and leases). Yet, if in addition to agreeing on every term and condition of such a consensual contract the parties also agreed to execute a notarial deed, they were, according to Pothier, at liberty to walk away from the remainder of the agreement until a notarial instrument was subscribed. In other words, despite the agreement, there was no contract. What mattered in Pothier's eyes, then, was not that the parties agreed on the substance of the contract, but that such a

---

[5] *See supra* § 8:7(M).

[6] *See* C. CIV. (FR.) art. 1341. Unless otherwise indicated, all the English translations of the *Code Civil* provisions belong to Legifrance (*see* Frequently Cited).

[7] *See generally supra* ch. 7.

substance had not been properly memorialized, as also agreed by the parties. One wonders why Pothier was not willing to grant the victim of the breach (the party who did not walk away) an action to force the reluctant promisor to execute the public deed including the rejected terms and conditions. By doing this, the judge would preserve both the integrity of the substantive agreement and its formality. This, incidentally, is the remedy granted by Article 1279 of the Spanish Civil Code.[8]

I should add that a contract so formally created was generally used in sales and mortgages of land whose transactional life was to last for generations, during which time their terms and conditions usually remained unchanged. The above-described contracts were not peculiar to Pothier's France. A less but still excessively formal contract that required face-to-face negotiation and agreement was also popular among seventeenth-century common law lawyers. As summarized by Professor Kevin Teeven of Bradley University, in this method of contract formation "the parties either emerged from face-to-face negotiations with an agreement or they didn't."[9] And as noted by a seventeenth-century manual on pleading: "If two speak together about an Agreement, and they in the midst of their discussion break off, and they say they will talk further of it tomorrow; this is imperfect, and no Action will arise upon this conference."[10]

Commercial sales, on the other hand, were treated as birds of an entirely different feather by the commercial codes of the same civil law countries whose civil codes were insistent on costly and time consuming formalities for the purchase and sale of real property. Article 109 of the French Commercial Code of 1807 listed the evidence that could establish the existence of a sale of goods as follows:

> Purchases and sales can be established by: (*Les achats et les ventes se constatent)* 1) Notarial or public documents (*par actes publics*); 2) Documents under private signature (*par actes sous signature privée*); 3) Detailed note or memorandum or decision by a foreign exchange agent or broker duly signed by the parties (*par le bordereau ou arrêté d'un agent de change ou courtier, dûment signé par les parties)*; 4) An accepted invoice (*par une facture acceptée*); 5) By correspondence (*par la correspondance);* 6) By accounting books of the parties (*par les livres des parties*); 7) By the testimony of witnesses, when the court deems it admissible (*par la preuve testimoniale, dans le cas o%21g le tribunal croira devoir l'admettre.)*.[11]

This approach to commercial contracts was also widely followed in the civil law world and is apparent in some of the Spanish and Mexican decisions transcribed in the Appendix to this chapter. Its underlying principle is referred to as "spiritualist": Commercial contracts exist even if entered into orally as long as the spirit of the transaction can be found in extrinsic documents or made clear by testimony before the court. Anglo-American readers will readily point out that this is not the approach of the statute of frauds embodied in § 2–201 of the U.C.C.[12] Under this section, oral agreements over $500 require not only "some writing sufficient to indicate that a contract for sale has been made between the parties," but also a written confirmatory

[8] C.C. (SPAIN) (1889) art. 1279.

[9] KEVIN M. TEEVEN, A HISTORY OF THE ANGLO-AMERICAN COMMON LAW OF CONTRACT 177 (1990).

[10] *See* W. SHEPPARD, ACTIONS UPON THE CASE 33 (1663), *cited in* TEEVEN, *supra* note 9, at 203 n.7.

[11] *See* C. COM. (FR.) 109 (1807).

[12] U.C.C. § 2–201.

statement or memorandum "signed by the party against whom enforcement is sought. . . ."[13] Yet, I must warn the reader that despite the view that attributes the "spiritualist principle" to a conceptual breakthrough by keen commercial codifiers, in my view, one must also take into account that the "spiritualistic" approach may well be due to the low esteem with which French citizens held small or retail merchants at the time of codification. For those who regarded retail merchants as dealing with "vile things" (*res mobilis, res vilis*), there was not much of a need for firm evidence on the existence of their transactions.[14] As will be apparent in this chapter, the civil vs. commercial characterization of contract in civil law countries is neither clearly nor uniformly applied by courts. Thus, insurance (supposedly commercial contracts) are treated as ceremonial and essentially formal (*ad solemnitatem*) contracts, and so, are promises to sell commercial land, among others.

B. The "Classic" (Static) Contract of Nineteenth Century United States Decisional Law and Restatement (First) of Contracts

Although much less formal than the "static" *Code Civil* contract, the "classic" contract of United States nineteenth- and early-twentieth-century decisional law evinces static features which were also apparent in the Restatement (First) of Contracts (hereinafter Restatement (First)).[15] Professor Richard Speidel illustrates them in the following example:[16] A and B agree that A will supply a certain service to B for price to be determined in the future. A starts to perform the service but after his initial performance, B repudiates the bargain. A brings an action against B for breach of contract and claims damages based upon what he reasonably expected to profit as a result of his full but interrupted performance. B argues that no contract was formed and Professor Speidel asks, "Who should prevail"?[17] He then traces the answer to Professor Samuel Williston's first edition of his treatise on contracts, and from there to the Restatement (First):

> Professor Williston, in the first edition of his treatise, stated that there could be "no legal obligation" in cases of this sort until the parties had agreed in fact on the price. Because either party could refuse to agree, it was "impossible for the law to affix such an obligation to such a promise." The *Restatement* of which Williston was Reporter, prescribed that an offer "must be so definite in its terms, or require such definite terms in the acceptance, that the promises and performances to be rendered by each party are reasonably certain. . . . The answer, then, was clear: *A* had no contract claim against *B* and, unless part-performance could be severed or had benefited *B*, *A* had not claim for restitution. This followed even though *A* might have been able to establish a reasonable market price for the agreed services.[18]

---

[13] *Id.* § 2–201(1).

[14] For a detailed discussion on the statute of frauds in civil and common law countries, see *infra* § 22:10(C)(1)(a).

[15] RESTATEMENT (FIRST) OF CONTRACTS (1932) [hereinafter RESTATEMENT (FIRST)]; *see also* Richard Speidel, *Restatement Second: Omitted Terms and Contract Method*, 67 CORNELL L. REV. 785, 786–87 (1981–82) (commenting on the "classic" theory of contract espoused in the Restatement First) [hereinafter Speidel, *Omitted Terms*]; Richard Speidel, *The New Spirit of Contract*, 2 J. L. COMM. 193 (1982).

[16] Speidel, *Omitted Terms*, *supra* note 15, at 787.

[17] *Id.*

[18] *Id.* (citations omitted).

The policy behind such a rule, as Speidel points out, is the conclusion that as of the time of formation, it should be certain if a contract exists. To which he added, in typically understated but insightful fashion, that Professor Williston's conclusion was based upon the empirical assumption that bargains are "discrete transactions."[19] This was the same assumption of discreteness of the bargain-contract present in the seventeenth-century English law referred to by Professor Kevin Teeven in which: "the parties either emerged from face-to-face negotiations with an agreement or they didn't."[20] As the reader will recall, this was the same conception of contract formation of the *Code Civil* that I described as "ceremonial." It was, according to Dean Roscoe Pound's characterization, a "mechanical" type of jurisprudence, or one whose rules demand a complete agreement on all the formative terms before a bargain-contract can be formed.[21] Pound's criticism was shared by Professors Arthur Corbin and W.W. Cook. The latter suggested that the "relevant phenomena" for observation should not have focused as much on the judicial doctrines or holdings, but on the transactions involved in those cases as reflected in their factual patterns.[22] Professor Corbin's transactional universe did not just include attention to factual patterns—it was considerably broader than Cook's, including: "[T]he customs, business practices, feelings, and opinions of man—the prevailing mores of the time and place."[23] Not surprisingly, Karl Llewellyn, one of Professor Corbin's most faithful and esteemed disciples (and the guiding spirit behind Article 2 of the U.C.C.), dispensed with the "rigid rules of offer and acceptance contained in the first *Restatement*."[24]

As stated by U.C.C. § 2–204(1) and (3):

> (1) A contract for the sale of goods may be made in any manner sufficient to show agreement, including conduct by both parties which recognizes the existence of such a contract.
>
> (3) Even though one or more terms are left open a contract for sale does not fail for indefiniteness if the parties have intended to make a contract and there is a reasonably certain basis for giving an appropriate remedy.[25]

U.C.C. § 2–305(1):

> The parties if they so intend can conclude a contract for sale even though the price is not settled. In such a case, the price is a reasonable price at the time for delivery if
>
> (a) nothing is said as to price; or
>
> (b) the price is left to be agreed by the parties and they fail to agree; or
>
> (c) the price is to be fixed in terms of some agreed market or other standard as set or recorded by a third person or agency and is not so set or recorded.[26]

---

[19] *Id.* at 787–88.

[20] TEEVIN, *supra* note 9, at 177; *supra* note 9 and accompanying text.

[21] Speidel, *Omitted Terms, supra* note 15, at 788.

[22] *Id.* at 789.

[23] *Id.*

[24] *Id.* at 790.

[25] U.C.C. § 2–204(1), (3).

[26] *Id.* § 2–305(1).

As concluded by Professor Speidel, "A more complete triumph of standards over rules is hard to imagine."[27]

C. Legal and Economic Consequences of the Ceremonial Conception: Parmenides' Transactional World

According to the ceremonial-static conception, one must assume that even if one of the parties promised irrevocably to do or not to do something, the failure to arrive at an agreement on what the parties were supposed to promise and to do precluded the enforceability of such a promise.[28] This version of contract is reminiscent of the being of things espoused by Parmenides (a fifth- and sixth-century Greek philosopher and logician):[29] For something to acquire its individual being, argued Parmenides, once created it remains unchanged. If it is altered, it becomes a different thing, and whoever maintains an opposite view (*i.e.*, that change is inherent in the nature of being) contradicts himself, for the being of a thing, no matter what it is, cannot be equal to its opposite (the non-being).[30]

The constitutive elements of such a Parmenidean contract reflect the nature of its being. Thus, Article 1108 of the *Code Civil* requires: 1) "The consent of the party who binds himself;" 2) "His capacity to contract;" 3) "A definite object which forms the subject-matter of the undertaking;" and 4) "A lawful cause in the obligation."[31] Another constitutive element was the formality, or better still, the solemnity of a contract whose amount was over a certain specified sum. As required by the original version of Article 1341 of the same code:

> An act must be made before notaries or under private signature, respecting all things exceeding the sum or value of one hundred and fifty francs, even in the case of voluntary deposits; and no proof can be received by witnesses against or beyond what is contained in such acts, nor touching what shall be alleged to have been said before, at the time of or subsequently to such acts. . . .[32]

The absence or failure of these elements renders the contract null and void, and according to some codes, such as Mexico's Article 2224 of its Civil Code of 1928, it can be held "non-existent" and without legal effects.[33]

This view of non-existent contracts, deprived of any legal effects, could only exist in a world of an exclusively formal logic and of robotic and lifeless beings. Consider, for example, a classroom exchange in a course entitled "Introduction to Civil Law" that I

---

[27] Speidel, *Omitted Terms, supra* note 15, at 791.

[28] *But cf. infra* § 22:4(D)(2) (discussing *Slade's Case*, decided in 1602, which allows the enforcement of an executory promise, albeit issued in connection with promisee's agreement to deliver a quantity of grain).

[29] John Palmer, *Parmenides*, STANFORD ENCYCLOPEDIA OF PHILOSOPHY (Edward N. Zalta ed., Summer 2012), http://plato.stanford.edu/entries/parmenides.

[30] *Id.* at § 2.3 (Parmenides' views on the being of things).

[31] LEGIFRANCE C. CIV. (FR.) art. 1108.

[32] C. CIV. (FR.) art. 1341 (Barrister 1804). Although somewhat awkward, I have used this translation because this appears to be the closest English version of the original French version.

[33] Mexican C.C.F. art. 2224 (1932) states:

> A nonexistent juristic act by the lack of consent of its parties or the absence of an object shall not produce any legal effect whatsoever. It is not susceptible of being confirmed by the parties, nor by a statute of limitation, and its non existence may be invoked by any interested party.

witnessed at a Mexican law school in 1988. One student asked the professor to give him an illustration of a non-existent contract for lack of a valid object, and he replied that one such a contract was a marriage between homosexuals. He then added:

> Since the object of such a contract is a marriage between a male and a female, the absence of such an object renders the marriage non-existent and without legal effects. As Article 2224 of the Civil Code states, [such a contract] as a non-existent contract . . . is not susceptible of being confirmed by the parties, nor can any rights therein be acquired by a statute of limitations and its non-existence can be invoked by any interested party. In effect it is as if no contract had ever been executed by the parties.[34]

Another student then asked him about the legal status of a child who had been adopted by such a "non-existent" marriage. The professor quickly pronounced the legal status of such a child as non-existent, but apparently realizing the factual and human absurdity of his statement, he quickly added the term "unadopted" or as if the adoption "had never taken place." I then silently asked: "How about the legal status of all the contracts that had taken place as a result of that adoption and while the child lived as an adopted legal person?" Would or should the law require that those transactions, and the many others based upon them, be erased from the legal universe by returning the services rendered, goods sold or moneys paid in connection with the life of a non-existing legal person? Needless to say, my colleague could not have given any answers to these questions even if I had asked them aloud.

Inherent in the Parmenides-like vision of the being and non-being of contracts is not only a denial of the life that goes on outside the confines of a legislature, court of law or notarial office, but also the manner in which contracts must be interpreted. Accordingly, Article 1319 of the *Code Civil* states that: "[A]n instrument in public form [*i.e.*, an *acte authentique* or a notarial deed] is absolute proof of the agreement which it contains between the contracting parties and their heirs or legal representatives."[35] As previously noted, Article 1341 added: "[A]nd no proof can be received by witnesses against or beyond what is contained in such acts. . . ."[36]

One net effect of such a conception of contract is that it threatens the annulment of contracts that involve the largest and poorest segment of the business community, whose joint ventures, partnerships, limited liability or corporate businesses seldom fulfill all the requirements of a static or ceremonial contract.[37] Another effect is the prevention of enforcement of economically important transactions such as options to purchase or promises of sale. While supposedly binding on the promisor, they are not binding on the promisee until he can satisfy himself that the conditions for his purchase or lease or exchange are propitious. Yet, once he does satisfy himself of those conditions, and even within the time period of validity of the option or promise to sell, he cannot enforce his option or the seller's promise because neither is binding until both parties reciprocally agree to be bound. Lawyers and businessmen in highly

---

[34] The class took place during the fall of 1988 at the National University of Mexico UNAM Law School. The professor and students mentioned preferred to remain anonymous.

[35] C. CIV. (FR.) art. 1319.

[36] C. CIV. (FR.) art. 1341 (Barrister 1804).

[37] *See* Boris Kozolchyk & Cristina Castaneda, *Invigorating Micor and Small Businesses Through Secured Commercial Credit in Latin America: The Need for Legal and Institutional Reform*, 28 ARIZ. J. INT'L & COMP. L. 43, 79–95 (2011).

promising developing nations such as Colombia and Mexico have told me that many an important investment did not take place because of such unenforceability.[38]

D. The Commercial (Dynamic) Contract and the Market Forces Behind It: Heraclites' Transactional World

While commercial contracts can also be formed formally, ceremonially and statically, their largest number is formed "dynamically" and "*inter absentes.*" By "dynamically," I mean a contract formed as a result of a unilaterally binding promise or of the conduct of the contracting parties, even though their express or implied promises are not reduced to writing or do not occur simultaneously or reciprocally. Such a contract is usually formed, changed or terminated more quickly than its static or civil counterparts. This is not to say that commercial contracts, even when organically connected, do not enjoy a discreet existence. They do, but as a rule, they exist for a shorter period of time than that of their civil/static counterparts because merchants cannot make a living from buying and holding on indefinitely to the goods they bought, any more than a deposit banker can earn profits by not lending or investing what was deposited with him.

The fact that contemporary commercial contracts are mostly *inter absentes* should not be overlooked. Otherwise, concepts intended for-face-to-face transactions would have to be applied to transactions among strangers dealing at a distance from each other, and relying on internet or catalogue descriptions of the goods or services involved instead of on the "eying and touching" methods used in European medieval street markets. The nature of the market and methods of marketing have changed significantly. As warned by Professor Karl Llewellyn in his 1930 edition of his casebook on the Law of Sales: "The concepts that took shape on the basis of a face-to-face dealing with present goods have in a short century and a quarter been tortured into application to the nationwide indirect marketing structure of today."[39]

Inter absentes formation can be quite varied. Contracts can be formed by: 1) the issuance of a promise followed by a counter promise that accepts the proposed terms and conditions of the initial promise but not infrequently includes new terms and conditions requiring either re-negotiation or excision; 2) performance of the terms and conditions proposed by the offeror or promisor; 3) the issuance of a "firm" or "binding" promise that remains irrevocable and binding on the promisor-offeror for the period stated in his offer or promise even though the offeree or promisee is not bound until he accepts the offer or promise; 4) the conduct (not the promises) of two or more parties that indicates that they are willing to be bound by the same terms and conditions set

---

[38] *See* Boris Kozolchyk, *Enhancement of Mexican Commercial Adjudication by Improved Transactional Fact-Finding, Application of Equitable Principles, and Drafting of Standard Contracts and Best Contractual Practices*, 27 ARIZ. J. INT'L & COMP. L. 349, 361–63 (2010). The legal conundrum faced by those who are governed by static opinion and promise to sell agreements is that even though the option to buy or promise to sell is supposed to be binding on their issuer, it is characterized by a Robert Pothier inspired classification of obligations as an obligation "to do", i.e., to issue the necessary public deed (as contrasted to one "to give" something). As an obligation to do, it must await the court decision directing the promisor to issue the appropriate deed or issue it on his behalf. Thus, even if at the end of a lengthy proceeding the option or promise is deemed enforceable the cost and delay of doing so are serious disincentives. On the other hand, as wrily remarked by the dean of a Colombian law school: "Many of my former students, now civil litigators, have been able to send their children to good schools by litigating options to purchase and promises to sell lawsuits."

[39] KARL LLEWELLYN, CASES AND MATERIALS ON THE LAW OF SALES xvi (1930).

forth in a pre-existing "Master Agreement" or in a "contract of adhesion"; or 5) the commercial conduct of two contracting parties who in the past have entered into contracts with similar terms and conditions and tacitly accepted their course of dealing or usage of trade as binding. The formation of contracts in these five transactions (as well as unlisted others) is dynamic not only because of the likelihood of subsequent changes in rights and duties of the contracting parties without requiring a novation, but also because of the speed with which many of them are formed.

Consider, for example, a bilateral contract that the parties label a "lease of equipment" and that contains a clause that grants to the lessee the option to purchase the equipment at any time by paying an additional sum, thereby converting what was originally a lease into a sale in installments. Notice that such a purchase will be accomplished without any contractual ceremony; the mere payment of a certain amount by the lessee instantaneously transforms such a contract into a sale agreement. Consider also the so-called "short sale" of securities. In such a sale, the seller "S" of the securities borrows the securities from a broker-lender "B" and sells them immediately at the current market price to "P," assuming that shortly after this sale the price of the securities he borrowed and sold will fall and that when the time comes to replace the securities he sold to P, the price will be sufficiently low that he will be able to purchase them cheaply enough to "cover" his "short position." His profit is the difference between the price at which he sold his stock and his cost of buying it back.[40] Accordingly, in a short period of time, S becomes a buyer, seller and borrower of similarly denominated stock in transactions that involve three parties at a minimum, but could involve others as well.

Similarly, in a "line of credit" agreement, the underlying loan can be made subject to constant changes, adjustments or variations that depend upon the proportion between the market value of the borrowers' collateral and the amount of the loan. Normally, the line of credit lender will be able to enforce his rights based upon the time he filed his security interest. However, his rights can also be made subject to special priority rights given to other later-filing creditors such as one with a "purchase money security interest," thereby changing, often unexpectedly, pre-existing priorities.

Yet another clear illustration of the diverse and often progressive or successive formation of contemporary commercial contracts is the "*pro forma*" invoice. It is used by large numbers of buyers and sellers in local and international trade each day. I looked for a description in a source that was likely to be consulted by a large number of lay users, thus reflecting the popularity of its use world-wide. It was provided by Wikipedia, which is usually not a scholarly source, but in this case, a reliable one after I verified its description with commercial lawyers in Europe, Asia and Latin America:

> [A] document that states a commitment from the seller to provide specified goods to the buyer at specific prices. It is [also] used to declare value for customs. It is not a true invoice, because the seller does not record a *pro forma* invoice as an accounts receivable and the buyer does not record a *pro forma* invoice as an accounts payable. . . . [It] is not issued by the seller until the seller and buyer have agreed to the terms of the order. In few cases, [the] *pro forma* invoice is issued for obtaining advance payments from buyer, either

---

[40] *Short Sale*, INVESTOR WORDS, http://www.investorwords.com/4556/short_sale.html (describing short sales and their use in the financial marketplace).

for start production or for security of the goods produced. [Finally, it is followed by a formal invoice when the invoicing party performs.][41]

Please notice its differing uses, and the malleability of its legal features: Its liability is not firm enough to warrant its recording as an account receivable or payable, yet is not issued until there is agreement "on the terms of the order." Meanwhile, once issued, the *pro forma* invoice can help obtain the buyer's advance payment. Would the fact that the "true" invoice is not issued until the contract is deemed performed by the supplier not indicate that in certain agreements, invoices are used to document different and successive parts of the same contract?

Finally, consider a computerized method of doing business pursuant to a "Master Agreement" among various merchants and suppliers of services whose sequence is triggered by a buyer "B" sending a purchase order to the seller "S" of product "X." Immediately upon receipt of B's purchase order, S's computer issues an application for the issuance of a letter of credit or documentary to issuing bank "IB." Prompted by this application, IB issues its letter of credit to S. B's purchase order also triggers S's computer's issuance of a message to a freight forwarder "FF" requesting that he procure shipping space in vessels owned by carrier "D." Upon D's response to FF, the latter issues a communication assuring S of the shipping space requested. B's purchase of X from S depends upon the performance of all the other transactions, which thereby become constitutive elements of the formation of such a sale. Yet, these transactions do not involve B and S directly nor could they be considered to be contracts between them, even though they are the result of a Master Agreement among all the participants. The speed with which unilateral firm promises, such as the present-day computerized "buy order" of stocks and bonds become binding sale agreements, or with which leases can be transformed into installment sales, or loans of securities become part of "short" sales, requires a model of contract formation other than that of the static, bilateral meeting of the minds and its usually ceremonial formation. It requires a conception unnatural to those who associate contracts invariably with a bilateral, simultaneous meeting of the minds' transaction. The dynamic commercial contract can come about unilaterally at first or by the performance of expressed, unexpressed or implied terms and conditions first by one party and then by another. It can also come about by a course of dealing that supersedes terms and conditions originally agreed upon by the parties, but tacitly waived or renounced by the reiterated conduct of the parties.

In sum, commercial contracts are often borne in the perennially flowing waters of commerce. Such a formation is the opposite of that contained in the static conception reminiscent of the teachings on the nature of being by Heraclitus (also a Greek philosopher, *circa* 500 AD): A being which is constantly either changing or subject to change, and thus equal to a "non-being."[42] And as will be discussed in later sections, the notions of "*causa*" and "consideration" reflect these static and dynamic versions of contract: *Causa* reflecting an unchanging and static element of a *Code Civil* "civil" contract ("once a *causa*, always a *causa*" was one of my contracts teachers favorite sayings) and consideration at times taking the form of an act or performance in

---

[41] *Invoice*, WIKIPEDIA, http://en.wikipedia.org/wiki/Invoice.

[42] *See* Daniel W. Graham, *Heraclitus*, STANFORD ENCYCLOPEDIA OF PHILOSOPHY (Edward N. Zalta ed., Summer 2011), http://Plato.stanford.edu/entries/Heraclitus (describing Heraclitus' teachings, contrary as they were to those of Parmenides).

exchange for a unilateral executory promise, at other times a promise, and at others the contractual conduct of the parties.

And the same is true with formalities: While the requirement of a public deed or *acte authentique* in civil-static contracts is often treated by the courts as an essential solemnity without which the contract is either non-existent or absolutely null, the requirement of a writing or of a registration of a commercial (dynamic) contract or transaction is functional or pragmatic; it is used to evidence the seriousness of the contracting party's intent to bind himself, or to provide public notice to third parties of the creation of rights in goods or services, including the performance of a contract or the proceeds of an account.[43] In the final analysis, the catalyst in the formation of a dynamic contract is invariably a form of giving, whether actual or symbolic.

E. The Official and Living Law That Governs Contemporary Commercial Contracts

In principle, a contract, whether statically or dynamically formed, is governed by a nation's "official" or "positive" law, which, as defined earlier,[44] includes not only its constitution, statutes, administrative and court decisions, but also, depending upon the jurisdiction, its "general principles" and legal commentary. In fact, many a commercial contract is governed by the living law of their marketplace and, as just noted, this law will deem the contract formed when it is in compliance with its customs, usages and practices or course of dealing. Among the many commercial contracts so formed are, for example, purchases and sales of cattle in Spanish fairs (with no more than the parties' handshake, although at times forcefully encouraged by a "contract facilitator");[45] sales, consignments, pledges and deposits of diamonds in New York's Diamond District concluded by the pronouncement of a ritual Hebrew saying-blessing followed by a handshake;[46] purchases and sales of present or future commodities expressed by an open outcry of exchanged offers and acceptances by brokers and trading floor specialists in commodity markets in Europe and United States.[47] As technology evolves, transactions diversify and global markets rely on new technologies, there is every reason to expect increased growth of the living law of automated customary rituals.

Yet, while the living law of contract formation progresses at an ever quickening pace (some of it being increasingly compiled as written usages of the trade or profession), its official or positive law counterpart continues to move at a snail's pace and with occasional regressions. Interestingly, this is not just a contemporary phenomenon. It was the case, for example, with the Roman law of pledges during the

---

[43] *See infra* § 22:10 for Spanish and Mexican, Salvadorean and Uruguayan Supreme and appellate court decisions on *ad solemnitatem* and *ad probationem* requirements of civil and commercial contracts.

[44] *See* Glossary, "Positive Law."

[45] *See, e.g.,* CONSEJO SUPERIOR DE CAMARAS DE COMERCIO, INDUSTRIA Y NAVEGACION, RECOPILACION DE USOS Y COSTUMBRES Y PRACTICAS COMERCIALES COMERCIALES SEGUIDAS EN ESPANA 444–56 (1964) (discussing the usages and practices on pricing, place of *conclusión* of the agreement ("by the side of the cattle"), measurement of weight, and role of intermediaries and ritual phrases).

[46] The traditional saying is "luck and blessing" (*mazel und brocha*). TOM ZOELLNER, THE HEARTLESS STONE: A JOURNEY THROUGH THE WORLD OF DIAMONDS, DECEIT, AND DESIRE 188 (2007).

[47] *See, e.g.,* Hank King, *Take a Tour of the Futures Trading Pit*, INVESTOPEDIA (May 26, 2011), http://www.investopedia.com/articles/optioninvestor/07/thepit.asp#axzz1evgSOPG7 (illustrating such a United States market).

middle ages. While the Roman pledge (*pignus*) had become less formal during the classical period of Roman law and some renowned jurists such as Ulpian started characterizing it as an informal "consensual" contract,[48] consensual contracts themselves ceased to be enforceable during the early middle ages in Southern Europe and in Professor Gorla's words, "it took a long time before they became enforceable again."[49]

Another notable regression in the evolution toward a more dynamic law of contracts took place after Lord Mansfield's decision of *Pillans v. Van Mierop* in which he held consideration was unnecessary in commercial contracts once merchants had chosen to express their promises in writing.[50] This informal and dynamic view of contract was rejected thirteen years later by the House of Lords' decision in *Rann v. Hughes*.[51] At times, the regression is motivated by a decline in commercial activity, as during the early middle ages, and at times by the lack of vision of law makers and adjudicators. Hopefully, the frequently-cited UNCITRAL Convention on Contracts for the International Sale of Goods (CISG),[52] the UNIDROIT Principles of International Commercial Contracts (UNIDROIT Principles),[53] and the European Principles of Contract Law (EPCL),[54] whose provisions on the formation of contracts were inspired by best contemporary commercial contract practices, will accelerate the modernization of national positive law.

What is at stake in understanding the static versus dynamic dichotomy is not an exercise in erudition or in showing off fancy legal nomenclatures. It is the realization that depending upon whether a contract is formed in static or dynamic fashion, so will it be interpreted and so will its breaches be remedied, as will be apparent in the subsequent chapters.[55]

§ 22.2 *CAUSA* AND THE PREDICTABILITY OF COMMERCIAL CONTRACTS

The willingness of merchants to enter into commercial contracts generally depends upon their ability to predict outcomes, not only at the end, but also at different stages of the transaction. During the formation stage of, say, a sale agreement, one of the principal concerns of merchants is whether their recently agreed-upon contracts are binding enough and confer upon them proprietary or possessory rights sufficient to enable them to transform, resell or exchange what they bought or replaced. As just discussed, unlike the land-owning bourgeois of the notarial deeds (*actes authentiques*) of the *Code Civil*, retail or wholesale merchants cannot carry out their day-to-day business if they or their attorneys would have to investigate the "historical" or chain of title of their wares. Surely, they need to know that the twenty-year lease that they negotiated for their business premises is enforceable or that they enjoy an exclusivity

---

[48] *See, e.g.*, WATSON, DIGEST, 13.7.1 ("The contract of *pignus* is made not only by delivery but also by mere agreement even in the absence of any delivery.")

[49] GORLA I, at 45.

[50] Pillans and Rose v. Van Mierop and Hopkins (1765) 3 Burr 1663, 97 Eng. Rep. 1035.

[51] Rann v. Hughes (1778) 101 Eng. Rep. 1014.

[52] *See* CISG.

[53] *See* UNIDROIT Principles.

[54] *See* EPCL.

[55] *See infra* § 22:2.

of their patent rights for an even longer period of time, but in their day-to-day transactions they have to be able to assume that, as stated by Article 2279 of the *Code Civil*, "in matters of moveable goods, their possession is the equivalent of title," or as more succinctly stated by the heading of U.C.C. § 9–202, "Title to Collateral [is] Immaterial."[56] Simply put, commercial transactions carry with them peculiar sets of reasonable expectations and thus peculiar rights and duties.

Furthermore, what is reasonable in these expectations cannot be dictated by metaphysical or "ivory tower" criteria absorbed by questions such as "What is the ultimate reason for a contract to be binding?" As discussed in previous chapters,[57] the reasonableness of commercial expectations is based upon what similarly situated contracting parties would have expected when pursuing their own advantage but refraining from interfering with their counterparties' ability and willingness to profit from the same transaction. If the counterparty finds it necessary to sell at a loss, it would not be unreasonable to purchase at the lower price. What would be unreasonable, however, would be to coerce that party to do so by the use of a superior force or economic power. As long as these reasonable expectations are reflected in the outcomes of their agreements, commercial law will be predictable because, as pointed out in these chapters, commerce is at its root a cooperative and not a zero sum game. Hence, *causa* and consideration must be evaluated in light of how each satisfies such reasonable commercial expectations. Of central importance, then, is the study of the evolution of these concepts, including the consequences of their static or dynamic perspectives.

A. *Causa* in Roman and Medieval Law

Causa was an essential element of contracts in Roman and Medieval law. However, the meaning of *causa* in Roman and Medieval law was far from precise. For a considerable period of time, Roman law made the formation of contracts dependent upon the type of contract involved. As was discussed earlier, some contracts, such as the *stipulatio*, were formed once their formal, ritual questions and answers were voiced and, at a later stage, written out.[58] Others, such as sales, rentals, partnerships and agencies (known as consensual contracts), were formed by the parties' mere consent,[59] while the type of contract known as "real" was formed once the thing (*res*) lent or deposited was delivered to the obligor, who thereafter became bound to return it or its equivalent.[60]

Causa was linked by the Romans to the above and other typified contracts in a manner that made its meaning redundant, for *causa* was what characterized each type of contract.[61] If one were to ask a Roman jurist what made the contracts that contained a *causa* enforceable, his answer would likely be that each type of contract had its own *causa* and performance in accordance with such a *causa* is what made them binding.[62] Hence, if the contract was of the type known as "real," its *causa* was the delivery of the

---

[56] U.C.C. § 9–202.

[57] *See supra* ch. 2 & *infra* §§ 23:4(D) & 23:5(A)(2).

[58] *See supra* § 4:4(D)(1).

[59] *See supra* § 4:4(D)(3)(1).

[60] *Id.*

[61] GORLA I, at 30.

[62] *Id.* at 31 (summarizing the effect of typification in classical Roman law).

thing (*res*) to the borrower, lessee or bailee and this delivery prompted the express or implied promise to return it. Or, if it was a consensual contract, its *causa* was what the parties' to everyday transactions such as sales, leases, agencies or partnerships typically agreed upon in those transactions.

It is true that in post-classical and Justinian law, the *actio prescripti verbis*[63] became a more general (less typified) contractual action and applied to any promise or bilateral agreement, particularly to atypical or *innominate* and "synallagmatic" contracts which consisted in reciprocal doing or giving ("I give so that you give," "I do so that you do," or variations thereof). Yet, because of the need for reciprocity, the *actio prescripti verbis* was granted only when one of the parties had performed her obligation, *i.e.*, "when she has given or made something in exchange for the promise intended to be recognized in a lawsuit."[64] This giving or doing something, once performed, was the *causa data* of the contractual obligation.[65] Uncertainty prevailed, then, not only conceptually, but also transactionally: The need for giving or doing something (*causa data*) meant that *until those acts had taken place, all promises were revocable.* Despite the unenforceability of the promise(s) that preceded the giving or performing a *causa data*, Gorla suggests that this initial performance by one of the parties was influential in the development of both *causa* and consideration.[66] As will be discussed in later sections, Gorla seemed on the right track where consideration was concerned; however, where *causa* is concerned, the reader should be the judge.

The medieval glossators' and commentators' search for a more precise meaning of the Roman *causa* of contracts led them to Aristotle's classification of the *causas* of everything that existed. In his books *Physics* and *Metaphysics*, Aristotle discussed four causes for the existence of acts or human behavior and things: 1) the "material" cause or the physical ingredients out of which a thing is made, *e.g.*, the bronze of a statue; 2) the formal cause or that which gives form to the action or thing, such as the shape of the statue; 3) The efficient (also referred to as "impulsive") cause such "as the art of bronze casting" that enabled the transformation of shapeless bronze into a statue; and 4) the "final" cause or the end or purpose for which the thing is made or the acts undertaken, such as the enjoyment or profit of having or selling the statue.[67]

Such was the awe of Aristotle's observations on nature and man among the medieval glossators of the *Corpus Juris Civilis* (incomplete and redundant as Aristotelian observations were) that the twelfth-century glossator Johannes Bassianus relied on two Aristotelian causes to explain not only why but when a contract was unenforceable. As translated by the Chilean legal historian Alejandro Gomez Brito, Bassianus' gloss stated:

> [W]hen there is a giving of something as a contractual (*datio*) and this giving was caused by an (efficient) or impulsive cause (*ob causam impulsivam*), which turns out to be false, (*causa falsa*), an action to recover what was given because of an unfulfilled *causa data* is inappropriate (*condictio causa data*

[63] *See supra* § 4:4(D)(3)(f).

[64] GORLA I, at 32.

[65] *See* WATSON, DIGEST, 12.4.6 ("For one who gives on account of marriage can, if no marriage happens, use the *condictio* as for nonmaterialization of an expected state of affairs. . . .")

[66] GORLA I, at 42–43.

[67] Andrea Falcon, *Aristotle on Causality*, STANFORD ENCYCLOPEDIA OF PHILOSOPHY (Edward N. Zalta ed., Winter 2012), http://plato.stanford.edu/entries/aristotle-*causa*lity/.

causa non secuta u ob causam datorum); whereas, if a thing was given as a final cause (*ob causam finalem*) and such a cause was not fulfilled or could not be fulfilled (*causa non secuta*), then the above action would be appropriate and the plaintiff would succeed in recovering what he gave.[68]

Guzmán Brito suggests that Bassianus's distinction between an efficient or impulsive and a final cause was based on the scholastic principle that once a final cause ceases to exist, so cease the effects of the agreement (*cessante causa (finalis) cessat effectus*).[69] Even though this distinction was advocated by other glossators and appeared in Accursius' influential *Glossa*,[70] it did not explain how an efficient cause that Aristotle characterized "as the art of bronze casting" applies to the formation of a contract, especially with an outcome so contrary to the contract's final cause. Assume, for example, that the efficient cause of my buying the statue is that it is artfully casted, but my final cause for buying is my expectation that I will be able to profit from its resale. The final cause may well be a more precise description of what caused my intent to purchase the statue, but why assume that the failure to obtain an artfully-casted statue is incompatible with my inability to profit from its resale, especially when the "final" cause may well depend upon the fulfillment of the "efficient" one?

B. *Causa* in the *Code Civil* and in Some of Its Progeny

Article 1108 of the *Code Civil* states:

> Four requisites are essential for the validity of an agreement (*convention*): The consent of the party who binds himself; His capacity to contract; A definite object which forms the subject-matter of the undertaking (*engagement*); A lawful cause in the obligation (*Une cause licite dans l'obligation*).[71]

The stark consequences of a lack or failure of a lawful cause were spelled out by Article 1131 of the *Code Civil* in words that echo Bassianus' gloss and the scholastic principle *cessante causa (finalis) cessat effectus*: "An obligation without cause or with a false cause, or with an unlawful cause, may not have any effect."[72]

Please note the draftsmen's difficulty in finding a common term for contract even within the same code provision. The generic term used by the drafters seems to have been *convention*. Yet, they also used *engagement*, which is a term often used in connection with an individual's undertaking or promise, and *obligation,* a term equally applicable either to an individual, mutual or reciprocal undertaking. This multiplicity of terms reflected an unresolved difficulty: Do all the terms have the same meaning or are *engagements* and *obligations* constituent elements of contracts, and if so, what is their relationship with *causa*? If, say, *obligation* is such an element, then a particular obligation (among others) of a contract may be unenforceable while other *obligations* (and at least part of the contract) may be enforceable. If, however, *obligation* is

---

[68] Alejandro Guzmán Brito, *Causa del Contrato y Causa de la Obligación en la Dogmática de los Juristas Romanos, Medievales y Modernos y en la Codificación Europea y Americana,* 23 REVISTA DE ESTUDIOS HISTORICOS-JURIDICOS 209, 279 (2001).

[69] *Id.*

[70] *Id.*

[71] LEGIFRANCE C. CIV. (FR.) art. 1108.

[72] *Id.* art. 1131.

tantamount to a contract, then its falsity or illegality would render the entire contract without effect. As if these possible redundancies were little, why would a false *causa* not be an unlawful one? Was there a true need for the additional category of unenforceability?

These and other difficulties plagued the interpretation of the *Code Civil's causa* provisions from the time of their enactment. Faced with the lack of uniformity and precision rather than doing away with *causa*, the first interpreters of the *Code Civil* suggested further distinctions and classifications of the still imprecisely defined *causa*. For example, Victor Marcadé's 1848 eleven volume commentary on the *Code Civil* states that the cause of a contract reflects the drafters' use of both a technical language (*le langage du droit*) when it refers to the cause of the contract (*la cause du contrat*) and an everyday or "ordinary language" when referring to the cause of the obligation (*la cause de l'obligation*). Then, to clarify the proper application (and meaning) of *causa*, he added two types:

> When I sell you my farm, the cause of my contract or of my obligation, if you will, is the *motive* that prompts my engagement; sometimes it may be the necessity of paying out considerable sums, or sometimes the need to receive rental payments. But in technical legal language, the first motivations [when entering into a contract] ought not be considered; only the last and immediate motive of the obligation are the ones to be considered as their legal cause: when I obligate myself to deliver my farm, my immediate motivation, the legal cause of my obligation, is the counterparty's willingness to pay me a sum of money without regard to the use that I planned for that money.[73]

As apparent in the above-quoted passage, the archetypal contract and contracting parties envisaged by Victor Marcadé were identified in an earlier chapter as of major interest to the *Code Civil* and to its archetypal bourgeois landowner—the occasional, formal and certain conveyance or acquisition of real property—rather than the contracts regularly entered into by everyday businessmen.[74] However, even though the immediate-final cause was more objective and thus more predictable than the subjective motive of each contracting party, the latter version of *causa* is quite alive and one can find it even in connection with the commercial sale of promises such as in an insurance policy, as will be discussed shortly.

Uncertainty as to the meaning of *causa* remained and, not surprisingly, other nineteenth-century Latin American legislators who were generally inclined to follow the *Code Civil* expressed their displeasure with Article 1108's *causa*. Among them was the drafter of the Argentine Civil Code (1871), Dalmacio Velez Sarsfield, whose notes to Article 499 of Argentina's Civil Code indicate that he thought that the cause of an

---

[73] Guzmán Brito, *supra* note 68, at 230–31:

Quand je vous vends (sic) ma ferme, la cause du contrat, ou de mon obligation, si l'on veut, le motif qui m'a déterminé à m'engager, ce sera tantôt la nécessité oğ je me trouve de payer des sommes considérables, tantôt le projet d'acquérir des rentes ou des maisons en remplacement de mes terres, afin de augmenter mon revenu, tantôt de doter ma fille. Mais en droit, ces motifs premiers ne sont pas à considerer; et c'est seulement le motif dernier et immédiat de l'obligation qui constitue sa cause juridique: quand je me oblige à vous livrer ma ferme, mon motif immediate, la cause juridique de mon obligation, c'est l'obligation que vous-même contractez de me payer une somme d'argent, quel que soit l'emploi auquel je destine cette somme.

[74] *See supra* § 8:7.

obligation and of a contract are different entities whose legal features were confused by Article 1108. Accordingly, Article 499 of the Velez Sarsfield's draft of the Argentine Civil Code stated: "There is no obligation without a cause, that is to say without being derived from one *of the facts, or from one of the lawful or unlawful acts, of family relations, or of civil relations.*"[75]

Yet, note how Velez Sarsfield, who had been dissatisfied with the uncertain meaning and scope of Article 1108, added to the confusion by enlarging its scope and extending it to juristic acts or relations (presumably other than contracts) instead of providing *causa* with a more precise meaning. Thus, according to Article 499 of the Velez Sarsfield code, the absence of a valid *causa* could determine the life or death of an obligation that emerged from a fact such as an accident or from a juristic act such as a unilateral promise to pay an amount certain as done in a promissory note or in a government bond, among many others. The reader will recall the effect that a similar evaluation by French interpreters of Article 1108 had upon the absence of a secondary market for government bonds in nineteenth-century France, as contrasted with the presence of such a secondary market in *causa*-free jurisdictions such as Great Britain and Germany.[76]

In the final analysis, the question that the advocates of *causa* as a necessary element of commercial contracts must answer is: Do they wish to encourage the execution and performance of as many lawful contracts as possible or is it their policy to make it possible for lawyers and judges to continue to find grounds with which to invalidate these contracts on hyper-technical grounds prior to or after the parties' performance? The uncertainties that *causa* gives rise to especially after contracts have been performed explain why a significant number of civil and commercial codes enacted during the late-nineteenth and early-twentieth centuries ignored *causa* as a contractual element. Among these were: The Austrian Civil Code (1811); the Portuguese Civil Code of 1865 (whose Article 643 pointedly only required that the parties have the capacity to enter into contracts and give their consent to enter into an agreement which had a valid object); Germany's BGB (1900); Switzerland's *Loi Fedérale qui Complet le Code Civil* (March 1911); Portugal's Civil Code (1966); Holland's Civil Code (1992) and in the Americas, the civil codes of Mexico (1870), Nicaragua (1904), Brazil, (1916), Peru (1936, 1984), Paraguay (1984, 1987) and Quebec (1991).[77]

As pointed out by Professor John Dawson, even in France, the cradle of contemporary *causa*, only a few authors continue to fight a "losing rear-guard action in its defense, but to most it has long been clear that the Code provision means nothing more than that a contract should have a purpose."[78] Yet, there are purposes and there are *purposes*, and an unpredictable number of them as a necessary condition for

---

[75] ÓDIGO CIVIL [CÓD. CIV.] [CIVIL CODE] art. 499 (Arg.), *available at* http://www.archive.org/stream/argentinecivilc00whelgoog/argentinecivilc00whelgoog_djvu.txt (providing the translation of Article 499 (appears now as Article 533)) (emphasis added). *See also* Guzmán Brito, *supra* note 68, at 228–29. According to Professor Guzmán Brito, Andres Bello, the drafter of the Chilean Civil Code, experienced similar difficulties with Article 1108's amalgamation of *convention, engagement* and *obligation.* However, he opted to stay as close as possible to the use of these terms in the *Code Civil. Id.* at 222–25.

[76] *See, e.g.,* §§ 11:2(D)(2) & 11:4(D).

[77] Guzmán Brito, *supra* note 68, at 228.

[78] JOHN P. DAWSON, GIFTS AND PROMISES 114 (1980).

contracting can have uncertain and thus undesirable effects upon economic development.

C. The Long Moral Reach of *Causa*: A 1957 Decision by the French *Cour de Cassation*

Article 1133 of the *Code Civil* states: "A cause is unlawful when the law forbids it, when it is contrary to good morals or to public order."[79]

An often quoted 1957 decision by the *Cour de Cassation* in this book[80], involved an insurance policy with the buyer's mistress as a beneficiary discussed earlier, illustrates one of the possible meanings of the "good morals" component and held that there was an immoral cause in the conveyance. Professor Paul Esmein of the University of Paris tells us that this holding follows well-established case law in accordance with which a donation in favor of a concubine is not *per se* invalid as it can be valid in the case of adulterous relationships. It is null, however, for the immorality of its cause, when, purporting to be a donation, it is in reality the payment of a price to bring about or to secure a concubinacy.[81] The net effect of the ruling may be to discourage conveyances detrimental to one's widow and heirs, but another could well be the discouragement of the purchase of life insurance policies in favor of otherwise "moral" third parties because of the uncertainties of possibly questionable motivations unknown to the insurer or insured at the time of the issuance and sale of the policy. Imagine the mistress—beneficiary having to prove that her much older lover had fully seduced her and she consented to their relationship on a purely amorous basis.

Professor Henry Capitant's classic study on *causa* in French and comparative law discusses similar decisions concerning real property rented for purposes of prostitution or for the operation of gambling houses.[82] The French courts' distaste for such agreements can best be gauged by their unwillingness to order restitution so as to bring about the *status quo ante*. As expressed by an indignant court in Bourges in 1889, "such parties are not worthy of appearing before a court of law."[83]

What is the moral or religious basis of this indignation? Demogue argued that "good customs," as the basis of the morality of the cause, should be based upon public opinion.[84] Dean Ripert argued in favor of moral or theological foundations which one cannot fail to associate with Judeo-Christian principles of ethical behavior.[85] And Professor Esmein posited that the morality of *causa*, at least when predicated on the notion of public order, is a malleable concept adaptable to the changing times and needs—a concept shaped by the judge, not by relying upon his own theology,

---

[79] C. CIV. (FR.) art. 1133.

[80] Cour de cassation [Cass.] [supreme court for judicial matters] 1e civ., Oct. 8, 1957, JCP 1957 II 10234 (Fr.). *See* ALEX WEILL & FRANÇOIS TERRÉ, LES OBLIGATIONS 280–81 (2d ed. 1975) (a brief review of the French Law of *the* morality of cause in gratuitous promises up until 1975). *See supra* § 8:7(F) (this subsection summarizes my discussion in Kozolchyk, *Commercialization*, at 7–9), *see also* its text in *supra* § 8:10.

[81] Cour de cassation [Cass.] [supreme court for judicial matters] 1e civ., Oct. 8, 1957, JCP 1957 II 10234, note Esmein (Fr.) (author's translation).

[82] HENRI CAPITANT, DE LA CAUSE DES OBLIGATIONS 226–27 (3d ed. 1927).

[83] Judgment of 13 June 1889, Bourges, D.P. 1889. 5.329, *cited in* CAPITANT, *supra* note 81, at 243.

[84] 2 RENE DEMOGUE, TRAITE DES OBLIGATIONS EN GENERAL n.773 (1912), *cited in* GEORGES RIPERT, LA REGLE MORALE DES OBLIGATIONS CIVILES, at n.2 (3d ed. 1935).

[85] RIPERT, *supra* note 84, at ¶ 39, n.40.

philosophy or personal bias, but inspired by the morality of the entire corpus of law as it relates to the controversy.[86]

QUESTIONS AND COMMENTS

Why did the *Cour de Cassation* fail to follow Victor Marcadé's advice to not dwell on the motivations of the parties to a contractual relationship and dwell only on their "objective" final motivations or causes? If it followed Marcadé's advice and took into account only the final, objective or standardized cause of a purchase of an insurance policy, what would such a cause have been? How would it have differed from the motivation to protect dear ones—regardless of who they were—from necessitous circumstances? But is not that motivation also the final *causa* for the acquisition of most life insurance policies? *Mutatis mutandis*, would a rental agreement whose landlord was unaware that his lawful business premises were to be used subsequently by his tenant as a house of prostitution be subject to a nullity which may well entail his having to return the rents received before the agreement was declared null? If so, who would be recipient of the returned rents? Obviously it would not be the tenant who would have thereby significantly profited from his immoral contractual behavior. Would it be the same state that at different times in France's history participated in the profits of such establishments? Is it reasonable, then, to impose such a sanction on the unsuspecting landlord?

The Spanish Civil Code of 1889 contains language that intended to clarify what the French draftsmen left unclear with respect to *causa*:

> Article 1274: In onerous [profit-seeking] contracts *causa* is understood, for each contracting party, as the benefit or the promise of a thing or a service by the counter-party, in the remunerative ones the service or benefit remunerated, and in the gratuitous, the gratuitousness of the charitable party.
>
> Article 1277: Even when the *causa* is not mentioned in the contract, its existence and lawfulness is presumed as long as the debtor does not prove the contrary.[87]

Do you think that the Spanish legislature succeeded in clarifying or rectifying what troubled so many interpreters of the earlier transcribed *Code Civil* provisions?[88] Does the presumption of Article 1277 cure the uncertainty of acts or events by the purchaser or renter of goods and services, such as that of the tenant of lawful or moral business premises who turned them into a brothel? Consider also the discussion in an earlier chapter[89] with respect to the approach taken by the BGB to the contractual element of *causa*: The BGB enforced "abstract" promises or obligations regardless of the underlying transaction or its cause, thereby deemphasizing, if not doing away with, the requirement of *causa*.[90]

The BGB enforced "abstract" promises, *i.e.*, promises binding merely because as stated by its Section 780, the promise itself creates the obligation (regardless of the

---

[86] ALEX WEILL, FRANÇOIS TERRE & HENRI CAPITANT, LES GRANDS ARRÊTS DE LA JURISPRUDENCE CIVILE 10–12 (5th ed. 1970).

[87] C.C. (SPAIN) arts. 1274–1277 (1889).

[88] *See supra* § 22:1(A).

[89] *See supra* § 12:3(D).

[90] BGB §§ 780, 781 (GOREN, 1994). *See also* ARTHER TAYLOR VON MEHREN & JAMES RUSSELL GORDLEY, THE CIVIL LAW SYSTEM 805–11 (1977) (a good commentary on these provisions and the lack of a French counterpart).

underlying reason or cause of such a promise).[91] Not surprisingly, and in contrast with the BGB, the *Code Civil* and its progeny enforced only those promises whose issuance was supported by a morally and legally valid *causa*. As was apparent in a previous chapter's discussion of the business of the House of Rothschild,[92] abstract promises for the payment of sums of money or for the future delivery of investment securities or commodities have become key legal elements of the global financial marketplace. This abstraction became possible in the HGB and in the BGB because their drafters, unlike the drafters of the *Code Civil* and *Code de Commerce*, did not require a legally and morally valid causal connection between monetary promises and their underlying causes, especially when purchased or relied on as collateral by third parties acting in good faith.

What are the economic—especially financial market—consequences of not being able to sell abstract (or *causa*-less) instruments or securities to third parties in secondary markets? A secondary market is defined by a financial and investments publication as a "market where investors purchase securities or assets from other investors, rather than from issuing companies themselves. The national exchanges—such as the New York Stock Exchange and the NASDAQ are secondary markets."[93] Who are the third parties of such markets? If each of the securities or assets sold in such a market had to be a proud bearer of a moral *causa*, what effect would such a requirement have upon the third party's decision to purchase it? Finally, would it be reasonable to expect each party (most likely unaware of the security's *causa*) to inquire into the morality of the issuance of the security or of its sale to its previous purchasers?

§ 22.3 CONTEMPORARY INTERNATIONAL PRINCIPLES OF CONTRACT LAW EXCLUDING *CAUSA*

It appears that some of the most respected European contract law scholars have decided to allow *causa* to die the death of a well-intentioned but harmful idea. The following are extracts from the European Union's EPCL and from the UNIDROIT Principles.

A. EPCL

Article 2:101—Conditions for the Conclusion of a Contract

(1) A contract is concluded if:

(a) the parties intend to be legally bound, and

(b) they reach a sufficient agreement without any further requirement.

(2) A contract need not be concluded or evidenced in writing nor is it subject to any other requirement as to form. The contract may be proved by any means, including witnesses.

Article 2:102—Intention

The intention of a party to be legally bound by contract is to be determined from the party's statements or conduct as they were reasonably understood by the other party.

---

[91] *See supra* § 12:4(C).

[92] *See supra* § 11:4.

[93] *Secondary Market*, INVESTOPEDIA, http://www.investopedia.com/terms/s/secondarymarket.asp#ixzz1gfnTKDkS.

Article 2:103—Sufficient Agreement

(1) There is sufficient agreement if the terms:

(a) have been sufficiently defined by the parties so that the contract can be enforced, or

(b) can be determined under these Principles. . . .[94]

B. UNIDROIT Principles

Article 3.1.2:

A contract is concluded, modified or terminated by the mere agreement of the parties, without any further requirement.

COMMENT

The purpose of this Article is to make it clear that the mere agreement of the parties is sufficient for the valid conclusion, modification or termination by agreement of a contract, without any of the further requirements which are to be found in some domestic laws.[95]

The comment goes on to note that there is no need for consideration because:

"[C]onsideration" is traditionally seen as a prerequisite for the validity or enforceability of a contract, as well as for the modification or termination of a contract by the parties. However, in commercial dealings this requirement is of minimal practical importance since in that context obligations are almost always undertaken by both parties.[96]

And there is no need for *causa* because:

[It] is in certain respects functionally similar to the common law "consideration."[97]

While this author agrees with these exclusions, he disagrees with the equation of the functionality of these two elements, as will be discussed hereafter.

§ 22.4 CONSIDERATION: GIFT GIVING, CREDIT AND TRUSTWORTHINESS

The following are observations by persons in different walks of life of instances where gift giving and the need for reciprocity seem to have played an important part in the establishment and continuation of actual or potential contractual legal relationships among the participants.

---

[94] EUROPEAN UNION, THE PRINCIPLES OF EUROPEAN CONTRACT LAW 2002, *available at* http://www.jus.uio.no/lm//eu.contract.principles.parts.1.to.3.2002/portrait.letter.pdf.

[95] INTERNATIONAL INSTITUTE FOR THE UNIFICATION OF PRIVATE LAW, UNIDROIT PRINCIPLES OF INTERNATIONAL COMMERCIAL CONTRACTS 94 (2010), http://www.unidroit.org/english/principles/contracts/principles2010/integralversionprinciples2010–e.pdf.

[96] *Id.* at 95.

[97] *Id.*

A. Instances of Gift Giving, Fairness, Loyalty and Cooperation

1. *Gifts and Benevolence in Nineteenth-Century London*

Writing in 1896 about the benevolence of Londoners a usually acerbic, Mark Twain said:

> In London poor old ragged men and women go up and down the middle of the empty streets, Sunday afternoons, singing the most heart-breakingly desolate hymns and sorrowful ditties in weak and raspy and wheezy voices . . . and the villagers listen and are grateful, and fling pennies out of the windows, and in the deep stillness of the Sabbath afternoon you can hear the money strike upon the stones a block away. . . . The spirit of benevolence is there, there can be no question about that. There is nothing that is quite so marvelous to the stranger as the free way in which England pours out money upon charities. . . . It is not to be disputed that in matters of charity the English are by a long way the most prodigal nation in the world.[98]

2. *Fairness and* Quid pro Quo*: Something for Something and for Nothing at the Tate Museum in 1968*

The great Costa Rican painter Rafael Fernandez ("Rafa") added his own comparative observations on the benevolence and fairness of contemporary Londoners. Rafa and I became close friends in Costa Rica and often shared views on his art and my legal research interests. He seemed particularly interested in my attempts to understand the meaning of fair dealing in different legal cultures. In 1968, as a young and highly talented but largely unknown artist, he traveled to Spain for the first time to exhibit some of his paintings. On his way there, he spent a few days in London visiting the Tate museum, which included Turner's canvasses of stormy seas which we both admired. Soon he ran out of money and tried to earn some by sketching the faces of the Tate's patrons. After a week or so of sketching at Tate's entrance, he managed to collect enough money to resume his trip to Spain. When he arrived, he sent me a note in which he provided some comparative details on the fair dealing of some of Tate's patrons:

> When I handed over my sketches to the English patrons, most thanked me, looked at them politely but at a respectful distance. Having observed other sketchers who did not ask for money when they handed over their sketches, I followed their example. As soon as they looked at the sketches, the English patrons asked me for the price of my sketch, and as did the other sketchers, I raised three fingers and fortunately many of these patrons paid me the three pounds and took my sketches. In contrast, when I tendered my sketches to Spanish or Latin American patrons, they immediately came very close to me, asked me what was my name where I was from, and upon hearing that I was from Costa Rica they embraced me warmly and enthusiastically congratulated on my talent, thanked me profusely and offered to host me in their home countries if I ever visited them. Yet, even though they all took my sketches, very few paid or offered to pay anything for them. I must say that

---

[98] MARK TWAIN, I AUTOBIOGRAPHY OF MARK TWAIN 115–16 (Harriet Elinor Smith ed., 2010).

this comparative experience (using your words) helped me understand a difference between fair and unfair dealing.[99]

3. *The Giving of Credit and Trust at Wildy's and Sons in 1970 London*

Since my days as a law student, I have collected old commercial law textbooks, manuals and guides. I first visited London in 1970 while doing research for my chapter on letters of credit for the Max Planck International Encyclopedia of Comparative Law. It was then that I met Maurice Megrah Q.C., someone whose humanity and writings I admired. When I told him about my interest in acquiring historical commercial law writings, he recommended that I visit the Wildy's and Sons bookstore where he was a customer. I did and found several books for which I had been looking for years. I could only afford one of them but did not have enough money with me to pay for it. An elderly gentleman who introduced himself as a member of the Wildy family asked me if he could be of assistance. I told him that I wanted to buy a book but did not have enough money with me (no internationally-accepted credit cards were available in those days). I told him that I would like to pay twenty dollars or so to put it aside. I explained to him that this was commonly done in "lay away" transactions in the United States. I also told him that I could mail him a cashier's check from the United States and he could then mail me my book. After a few brief questions on what I did and how I came to know Maurice Megrah, he told me that I did not have to leave the twenty dollars as a deposit and that he would be glad to ship the books to me and that I could pay him after I got them in Arizona. Thus started a relationship that allowed me to this day to read and use many otherwise unavailable historical legal materials. In return, I recommended Wildy's and Sons to many of my collector friends and colleagues. Wildy's and Sons advertises itself today as "The World's Best Stocked Law Specialist."[100]

As you reflect upon these London incidents, I would like to tell you about another one that I witnessed thousands of miles away from London in tropical Cuba, my country of birth. As you read it, please consider what the following example of gift giving and fair dealing has in common with the preceding anecdotes, and, if so inclined, ask the question: Could it be that gift giving and altruistic conduct is inherent in successful commerce?

4. *Gifts of Soap: Customer Loyalty Following a Hurricane in Marianao, Cuba*

Hurricanes were frequent summer and fall visitors to Cuba, where my father Abram Kozolchyk was able to build up a substantial retail and wholesale business after very humble beginnings as a rural peddler. Following the visit of a damaging hurricane during the late 1940s to the city of Marianao, where my father had a store named El Encanto de Marianao (across the street from a recently inaugurated Sears and Roebuck store), commodities, including soap, quickly disappeared from the shelves of most stores. Coincidentally, El Encanto de Marianao had just re-stocked its inventory of Palmolive soap and this news quickly spread through Marianao. Shortly thereafter, dozens of steady and first-time customers showed up shouting their

[99] Letter from Rafael Fernandez to Boris Kozolchyk (date unknown).

[100] WILDY & SONS LTD, http://www.wildy.com/.

willingness to pay whatever the asking price was for it. I vividly remember the following exchange between one of my father's clerks and my father:

> Clerk: Abram our cost is five cents per bar, we can easily sell it for fifty cents a bar. No other store has soap in the entire city, everyone will be more than happy to pay it.
>
> Abram: Can you and the other sales clerks single out steady customers in this crowd?
>
> Sales Manager: Yes.
>
> Abram: Give each of our steady customers four bars and charge them nothing; and sell our first time customers four bars at fifteen cents a bar.
>
> Sales Manager: One of the sales people tells me that among the crowd are employees of Sears and Roebuck from across the street who are also our first time customers. What do we do, should we sell it to them as well?
>
> Abram: Yes, do it. I know that we can make a good profit now by selling the soap at fifty or more cents a bar, but if our steady customers are rewarded for their patronage during a time like this, they will always be our customers. And if those who are not our steady customers see how well we treat our steady customers, as well as how fairly we treat them even if they are our competitors, they will either become our steady customers or send us customers when they do not have merchandise we have.

By the time he left Cuba and El Encanto de Marianao was confiscated by the Castro regime, it had a flourishing retail and wholesale business and its relations with the equally-confiscated Sears and Roebuck of Marianao were quite cordial and cooperative.

B. Reciprocity and Gift Giving in Pre-Commercial and Feudal England

While discussing the features of pre-commercial society in an earlier chapter, I referred to the anthropological and economic history work of the late Professor George Dalton of Northwestern University, who defined reciprocity in pre-commercial society as the giving of gifts between persons in a socially-defined relationship.[101] In that society, the gifts of produced items or of other factors of production such as labor were (and are) regarded as an expression of interest in the social relationship between the gift givers and recipients.[102] What was the role of gifts in the "socially defined" relationships (landlords and their tenants, guild masters and their apprentices, and so on) of medieval-feudal Europe?[103] Colorado State University Professor Barbara Sebek's insightful essay "Good Turns and the Art of Merchandizing in Early Modern England"[104] provides some answers to this question. She described the role of gift giving in seventeenth-and eighteenth-century England in a manner surprisingly similar to Dalton's.

---

[101] *See supra* § 3:3.

[102] *Id.*

[103] *See supra* § 3:3(C).

[104] Barbara Sebek, Good Turns and the Art of Merchandizing: Conceptualizing Exchange in Early Modern England (unpublished draft), *available at* http://emc.eserver.org/1–2/sebek.html.

Professor Sebek relied on the cultural anthropological findings on the behavior in primitive societies by Marcel Mauss' 1923 classic "The Gift": Gift giving is significant because it "confers upon its participants a special relationship of trust, solidarity and mutual aid."[105] Mauss' famous question was: "What power resides in the object given that causes its recipient to pay it back?"[106] His answer was that aside from their utilitarian components, gifts are imbued with religious, mythical and magical mechanisms.[107] The giver does not merely give an object, but also part of himself, for the object is tied to the giver: They are "loaned rather than sold and ceded."[108]

England's economy during the period from 1000 to 1500 also relied heavily on gift giving. In fact, according to Richard H. Britnell's painstaking analysis of England's commercialization during this period, the distinction between commercial exchange and reciprocal gift giving was difficult if not impossible to make. In his words:

> Relations between landlords and craftsmen were often tenurial rather than commercial; the village smith often held land on condition that he should maintain the demesne ploughs. The frequent necessity for barter inhibited dependence on market prices. In these circumstances there could be economic interdependence between families without any need for regular markets. . . . The absence of an institutional [market] structure was particularly evident in northern England, where there was little formal organisation of trade outside York in the early eleventh century.[109]

Not surprisingly, a society in which bartered goods and services were frequently indistinguishable from gifts found it helpful to read writings that praised the superior morality of gift giving and its appreciation by gift receivers. One such writing was Arthur Golding's 1540 English translation of Seneca the Younger's *De Beneficiis*. In Professor Sebek's words, "Golding's translation of *De Beneficiis* is a manual for good giving which insistently distinguishes 'benefiting'—the 'doing, receiving, and requiting of good turns'—from merchandizing, or ordinary bargains and loans."[110] *De Beneficiis* focuses on why, when and how gifts should be given and on the proper methods and motives for giving as well how they should be received and reciprocated.

> Despite the centrality of ingratitude in precipitating vice and disorder, benefiting is based on trust rather than legal coercion. Bestowers of benefits who meet with ungrateful recipients do not have recourse to the law; legally-enforced bonds or contracts "stain" the honor of benefits, stripping them of their true estimation or value. . . . This value, however, cannot be measured. The motive for giving benefits is not profit, but fellowship: a benefit is a thing which "most of all other knitteth men together in fellowship" . . . it is a "foul

105 *Id.* at ¶ 5.

106 MARCEL MAUSS, THE GIFT: THE FORM AND REASON FOR EXCHANGE IN ARCHAIC SOCIETIES 3 (W. D. Halls, trans., W. W. Norton & Company 1990) (1950).

107 *Id.* at 24, 26, 38, 43, 45 (among others).

108 *Id.* at 43.

109 RICHARD H. BRITNELL, THE COMMERCIALISATION OF ENGLISH SOCIETY 1000–1500 7 (2d ed. 1996) (citation omitted).

110 Sebek, *supra* note 104, at ¶¶ 10.

shame" to "reckon" or quantify: "It is a vile Usury to keep a reckoning of benefits, as of expenses."[111]

C. Credit and Commerce in Early Modern England

Early modern England (roughly from the sixteenth through the eighteenth centuries) was when new modes of production and organization of markets became apparent in many English cities, especially in Southern England as money became a popular medium of exchange. The need for gift giving as a means to encourage a greater number of exchanges of goods and services was beginning to wither away and historians have pinpointed the beginning of this transition. As noted by R.H. Britnell, even in an increasingly-commercialized southern England as well as in a less-commercialized northern England, the blurring of market and gift forms was still apparent from 1000 to 1500, a period when the distinction between commercial exchange and reciprocal gift giving was often "impossible to make."[112]

The transition from a feudal to a commercialized England sharpened the cultural divide between an agricultural gift-giving economy and one based on commercial-capitalistic and monetary tenets.[113] This divide affected the relations between "friends, family members, husbands and wives, masters and servants, rulers and subjects [all of which] were being reconfigured."[114] The waning past was that of a "status society" in which patronage was particularly important in non-commercial feudal relations. In such a society, one of the common ways to get ahead was by giving things or favors to your landlord if you were his tenant, to your master if you were his servant and so on. Seneca's gifts were not only a moral but a practical imperative. In the emerging commercial and industrial society, the giving was of what could benefit not only the recipient, but also the gift giver and an increasing number of others—the market participants. The increasing use of money in loans and in payments for sales or for the performance of services was an integral part of that transformation.

1. *The Omnipresence of Credit: Self Interest, Trust and Commercial Altruism*

Since Adam Smith's "Wealth of Nations," self-interest and its "invisible hand" became a favorite economic and moral explanation for the formation and growth of commercial contracts and of the markets in which they were concluded. One of Smith's most oft-cited phrases on the role of self-interest was and is: "It is not from the benevolence of the butcher, the brewer, or the baker, that we can expect our dinner,

---

111 *Id.* at ¶ 11:

Thou art deceived if thou think that any judge can help thee; no Law is able to set thee clear again. Only have thou an eye to the faithfulness of the receiver. So shall benefits keep their estimation, and continue honorable. Thou stainest them, if thou make them a matter of Law. In debts it is a most upright speech and agreeable to the Law of all Realms, to say, Pay that thou owest. But it is the foulest word than can be in benefiting, to say, Pay. . . . The estimation of so noble a thing should perish, if we make a merchandise of benefits. . . . Would God that no surety might be taken of the purchaser by the seller, nor bargains and covenants be made under hand & seal: but rather, that the performance of them were referred to the faithfulness and upright meaning of mens' consciences.

112 BRITNELL, *supra* note 109, at 7.

113 *Id.* at 228–37.

114 Sebek, *supra* note 104, at ¶ 2.

but from their regard to their own interest."[115] Less frequently cited are his views on the economic importance of charity, benevolence or commercial altruism as expressed in his "Theory of Moral Sentiments," which also articulated his moral philosophy: "How selfish soever man may be supposed, there are evidently some principles in his nature, which interest him in the fortune of others, and render their happiness necessary to him, though he derives nothing from it except the pleasure of seeing it."[116]

Moreover, Smith's view of self-interest was more benign than a literal reading of the Wealth of Nations might indicate, because he denied that "[s]elf-love was a principle which could never be virtuous in any degree or in any direction."[117] In this respect, as I have noted elsewhere, Smith was part of a long moral-philosophical tradition already present in the fifth-century Talmudist saying: "There is good in [what appears to be] evil and evil in [what appears to be] good."[118] I added the preceding language to emphasize Adam Smith's point that good or virtuosity as well as evil can be part of the same conduct although in degrees that, on balance, would make the conduct more or less evil or good. The importance of this view became apparent in early England's (sixteenth- and seventeenth-century) credit markets.

In the last few decades, some economic historians and social scientists have challenged the assumption that self-interest was the primary motivation behind this growth, which was inspired by Adam Smith's "Wealth of Nations."[119] They contend that the markets that developed in England during these centuries were largely the result of trust between or among contracting parties, especially to credit transactions, and that the "glue" for such a trust was provided by an altruistic conferral of benefits, albeit commercial motivations could not be discounted. My interest in this discussion is not to ascertain which ethical theory (self-interest or transactional altruism) provides the most accurate version of the cause of England's commercialization and economic development. For as I just stated in the preceding paragraph, I do not believe that human behavior is susceptible to such "chemically pure" categorization and that as clearly stated by Adam Smith, self-interest and transactional altruism are not mutually exclusive and what starts out as an act of beneficence or altruism often leads to consequences very dear to the heart of the self-interested and vice-versa.

My interest in this dispute is narrower: to examine the information provided by those who intend to prove that transactional altruism was the engine of the growth of Modern England's markets and see how this information relates to gift giving and transactional altruism in the formation of commercial contracts in Anglo-American law. Along these lines of inquiry, Professor Craig Muldrew of the University of Toronto, among other contemporary historians, maintains that the culture of the early modern English market was explicitly "moral" because:

> [A]part from wholesaling, most buying and selling was done on trust, or credit, without specific legally binding instruments, in which an individual's

---

115 ADAM SMITH, THE WEALTH OF NATIONS 20 (Prometheus Books 1991) (1776).

116 ADAM SMITH, THE THEORY OF MORAL SENTIMENTS pt. I, § I, ch. I, ¶ 1(David Daiches Raphael & Alec Lawrence Macfie eds., Liberty Fund 1982) (1759), *available at* http://oll.libertyfund.org/192/39008/908774.

117 *Id.* at pt. VII, § II, ch. III, ¶ 12.

118 *See supra* § 9:2(E)(4)(b)(1) (discussing the Fable of the Evil Impulse).

119 *See, e.g.*, Craig Muldrew, *Interpreting the Market: The Ethics of Credit and Community Relations in Early Modern England*, 18 SOC. HISTORY 163 (1993).

> creditworthiness in their community was vital. . . . [And] this network of credit was so extensive and intertwined that it introduced moral factors which provided strong reasons for stressing co-operation within the marketing structures of the period. Individual profit and security were important, but neither could be achieved without the direct co-operation of one's neighbours which trust entailed.[120]

Indeed, early modern South England had many weekly markets and often yearly fairs and its towns had many small shops and workshops where tradesmen sold their wares and laborers provided their services mostly on credit. Local merchants were also involved in national and international trade with some tradesmen such as mercers or grocers acting as middlemen between local producers and national or foreign distributors and many of their transactions were also on a credit basis: "[W]hether it was a husbandman selling corn in the market place, a cordwainer selling a pair of shoes or a wholesaler importing coal from Newcastle. . . . by the late sixteenth and seventeenth centuries [credit] was ubiquitous"[121] Professor Muldrew quotes a telling question by Thomas Tusser, the sixteenth-century English poet-farmer and author of a widely-read instructional pamphlet entitled "Who Living but Lends?" He answered: "[B]e lent to they must; else buying [sic] and selling might lie in the dust. . . ."[122]

As pointed out by Professor Muldrew, merchants trading between different communities did not have the same access to knowledge about one anothers' characters as they would have had about their neighbors' and merchants trading on a national scale were more likely to use sealed credit instruments.[123] Yet, many long distance credit relations were performed informally. He cites the case of a young North England merchant who, after ending his apprenticeship, set up his own shop and traveled from Lancaster to London to purchase his inventory and despite being unknown there, London merchants "were still willing to extend him 50 per cent credit."[124] The same was true for merchants engaged in international transactions.[125]

Among other telling indicators of how widespread credit had become were: 1) a typical merchant was owed debts by over 330 people when he died; 2) ninety percent of all the court cases in Southern England in 1640 involved credit transactions and the total number of these cases in the central courts of King's Bench and Common Pleas exceeded 28,000; 3) "in medium sized towns of about 7–10,000 people, such as King's Lynn, Yarmouth, Newcastle and Shrewsbury, it was not uncommon for over 1000 suits to be initiated in a single year!";[126] 4) "most litigation (83 per cent) [in a local borough court such as] King's Lynn, for example, concerned sales credit, and credit extended for services rendered or for work done."[127] Typically, the actions were to recover the unpaid price for the "sale of beer, meat, livestock, wax, fish, bread and even hats or conny wool."[128] It is worth emphasizing that these actions did not seek the debtors'

---

[120] *Id.* at 169.

[121] *Id.* at 171.

[122] *Id.*

[123] *Id.* at 180.

[124] *Id.*

[125] *Id.*

[126] *Id.* at 172.

[127] *Id.*

[128] *Id.*

specific performance or damages for the breach of executory promises (such as the promise to lend or perform a service in the future), but were brought against debtors who had received goods or services from their plaintiffs-creditors and had failed to return them or pay for them.

It is also worth noting that in contrast with the low esteem in which merchants were held during the same period in France and Spain, English merchants and traders "were valued members of the social order, and growth in trade was increasingly seen as advantageous to the commonwealth by increasing its wealth."[129] And unlike their Neo-Confucian Chinese counterparts, whose obedience was to Confucian-inspired rituals of family (and not necessarily commercially-inspired) etiquette,[130] English merchants were aware that their success depended upon being known as trustworthy borrowers and lenders and that such trust was gained by being known as charitable with needy customers, including giving them gifts or granting them interest-free loans. Commercial altruism was thus found in a widely-read diary of a merchant named Thomas Turner, who was often quoted for the assertion that " 'the greatest part of trade [is] trust'. . . ."[131] Similarly, an educational pamphlet quoted earlier counseled that " 'lending to [a] neighbour, in time of his neede, winnes love of thy neighbour, and credit doth breede. . . .' "[132] Such standards were more than lessons on commercial morality or etiquette; they became the living law of a commercialized England. And since credit was a prerequisite for the formation of many commercial transactions, the giving of something of value to the borrower, which was the first step in the transactional sequence of loans, eventually became the rules of traffic that implemented the *quid pro quo* of many other enforceable transactions.

Against this socio-economic background, one must agree with Patrick Atiyah's conclusion that:

> [C]ontract theory until the late eighteenth century was still largely based on the idea that obligations were created by the acceptance of benefits, or by acts of reasonable reliance; obligations . . . were created by what men did, rather than by their pure intentions. . . . [Hence] up to the late eighteenth century [the law was] largely a law of executed contracts, and not a law of executory contracts.[133]

To which he added in an earlier section: "It was the consideration [or the giving something of value] which was the principal ground for the creation of the obligation; the promise played a subordinate role."[134]

2. *Legal Institutions Spawned by the English Credit Society: Standard Practices, Good Faith, Fair Dealing and Reckonings*

In addition to consideration, credit transactions also contributed to the development of other contractual legal institutions. Among them were standard (largely informal) practices, terms and conditions (including pricing) and occasional

---

129 *Id.* at 174–75.

130 *See supra* § 17:3(E).

131 Muldrew, *supra* note 119, at 178.

132 *Id.*

133 P. S. ATIYAH, THE RISE AND FALL OF FREEDOM OF CONTRACT 419 (1979).

134 *Id.* at 140.

good faith requirements for contractual performance, although the practices differed depending upon the status of contracting parties. Wealthier, literate tradesmen used sealed instruments such as bills obligatory,[135] and regularly recorded their transactions in their accounting books or ledgers. In contrast, other lenders and borrowers relied on witnesses as a formality for the execution of their mostly oral transactions.

By regularly involving other members of the community in witnessing the execution of contracts, the participants familiarized them with what eventually became standard terms and conditions of everyday transactions, especially since a large part of the population was illiterate and incapable of drafting contracts and keeping account books and records.[136] Community involvement nourished a communal sense of reciprocity in exchanges often based on the collective awareness of the prices and other terms and conditions of the credit transactions they witnessed. Thus, today's witnesses to a transaction "A" became tomorrow's parties or counterparties in their own transaction "B," which often resembled A in some respects. Gradually, standards for the extension of credit as well as "honesty, of plain dealing and the keeping of promises, dominated the way in which market relations were conceived."[137]

D. The Legal Development of Consideration

Professor Kevin M. Teeven of Bradley University traced the development of consideration from a *causa*-inspired notion to the more commercially influenced notion of *quid pro quo* to sixteenth-century pleadings and court decisions.[138] If what was exchanged was a promise for a promise, courts hesitated at first to enforce the contract for "lack of reciprocity or *quid pro quo*."[139] In other words, what the exchange in question seemed to lack was substance or the giving of something of value. Then, according to Professor Teeven: "[S]uddenly all seemed resolved in 1589, when it was announced in a laconic note reporting the ruling in *Strangborogh v. Warner* that there was consideration because the promises were reciprocal. . . ."[140] Then he quoted an English treatise[141] for the clarification that a promise against a promise will maintain an action upon the case, "as in consideration that you give me ten pounds on such day I promise to give you ten pounds such a day after." In other words, as a *quid pro quo*, the intangible promise (and its implicit consideration) had become material, even as material as ten pounds given as a loan and expected to be paid back.

That giving a *quid pro quo* had become not only an essential component of consideration, but also the first step in concluding a binding commercial contract, was

---

135 A bill obligatory, also known as a "single bill" or "bill of debt" and occasionally also referred to as a promissory note, is a writing by which a merchant acknowledges that owes a certain sum of money to be paid on a certain day and subscribes it at a day and place certain. Some dictionaries state that it is distinguishable from other bills or promissory notes by the fact that it must be under seal. *See* BLACK'S LAW DICTIONARY 211 (4th ed. 1951). *But see* THE FREE DICTIONARY, http://legal-dictionary.thefreedictionary.com/Bill+obligatory (stating that it could have been under seal or not).

136 Muldrew, *supra* note 119, at 173.

137 *Id.* at 177.

138 *See* TEEVEN, *supra* note 9, at 37–43.

139 *Id.* at 43.

140 *Id.* at 43. *See also* Strangborough v. Warner, 4 Leo. 3, 74 Eng. Rep. 686 (1589).

141 CECIL HERBERT STUART FIFOOT, HISTORY AND SOURCES OF THE COMMON LAW: TORT AND CONTRACT 361–63 (1949).

confirmed three centuries later in Leone Levi's two volume treatise entitled *International Commercial Law*, one of England's first nineteenth-century treatises on that subject.[142] Writing in 1863, Professor Levi stated:

> It is essential to the validity of a contract that it be founded on a sufficient consideration. There must be something given in exchange, something which is mutual, or *something which is the inducement to the contract, and it must be a thing which is lawful and competent in value to sustain the assumption.* A contract without consideration is a *nudum pactum*, and not binding in law. . . .[143]

This mid-nineteenth-century reference to consideration as an "inducement of the contract" is persuasive because Professor Levi was not only a knowledgeable commercial law scholar, but one of England's preeminent commercial statisticians, which suggests that his assertion was based upon more than an occasional observation of how contracts were formed. Please also note that by the mid-nineteenth century, Levi and other English commentators applied the same *nudum pactum* characterization applied by the Romans to promises that were not part of typified contracts to the entire genus of contracts that lacked *quid pro quo* consideration.

Finally, as a result of the pervasiveness of credit transactions, many market participants regularly accumulated numerous reciprocal debts and claims against their usual contracting parties. A certain number of these debts were recorded in account books, and then mutually cancelled at convenient intervals.[144] This method of settling debts was referred to as a "reckoning"; it was ubiquitous and involved comparing and crossing out reciprocal entries of debts and thereafter paying the differences in cash.[145] Its use reflected continued courses of dealing among contracting parties; typically, one party's rent obligation to the other was set off against the unpaid price for goods sold or performances of services owed by the landlord. The continued courses of dealing and the ease with which reciprocal obligations could be settled explain why interest was not commonly charged in commercial loans. In contrast with this continuing reciprocal contractual relationship, interest was generally charged in loans given by professional money lenders to their commercial and consumer borrowers.[146]

1. Medieval and Renaissance Meanings of Consideration

Professor J. H. Baker of Cambridge University, a highly precise chronicler of the law of consideration, asserts that "no other doctrine in English law can compete with 'consideration' for greatest diversity of historical explanation."[147] Professor David Harris Sacks of Reed College puts it more harshly: "There is probably no more important or more arcane and complicated concept in the English common law than

---

[142] LEONE LEVI, I INTERNATIONAL COMMERCIAL LAW (1863).

[143] *Id.* at 281 (emphasis added).

[144] Muldrew, *supra* note 119, at 173.

[145] *Id.*

[146] *Id.*

[147] J. H. Baker, *Origins of the 'Doctrine of Consideration*, 1535–85, *in* ON THE LAWS AND CUSTOMS OF ENGLAND: ESSAYS IN HONOR OF SAMUEL E. THORNE 336–58 (Morris S. Arnold ed., 1981) *cited in* RHETORIC AND LAW IN EARLY MODERN EUROPE 23 n.24 (Victoria Kahn & Lorna Hutson eds., 2001).

'consideration.' "[148] In its medieval legal context, as also noted earlier by Professor Teeven, it "emphasized the connection of a given agreement to the reasons or motives the party or parties had in undertaking it."[149] As such, canon law employed it to mean the lawful causes (*causae*) that bound the parties to perform the acts to which they agreed.[150] He quotes from Christopher St. German's English legal textbook "Doctor and Student" (*circa* 1530), in which a Doctor (or teacher) commented to his student:

> [O]ne who made a vow to God "upon a deliberate mind . . . is bound to perform it [and] is bound in conscience to do it. . . . [A] promise made for charitable purposes or in the "service of God" would be binding "though there be no consideration of worldly profit that the grantor had or intended to have for it. . . ." Only "if his promise be so naked that there is no manner or consideration why it should be made then I think him not bound to perform it."[151]

The reference to a vow to God and to the contracting party's conscience reflects the influence that canon law still had upon the law of contracts at that time. The reference to consideration is subsidiary; first a contracting party binds himself in conscience regardless of consideration, only if the promise was so totally devoid of conscience and *quid pro quo* will the purported contract become a *nudum pactum*. Yet, the correction formulated to his teacher's statement by the student underscored the importance that consideration as a material thing had acquired in the common law of the early-sixteenth-century commercial Renaissance: "[A]ll promises lacking any evidence of a quid pro quo, even those for the honor of God or the welfare of the community, would have no obligatory force under the common law. . . ."[152] As further noted by the student: "[H]e to whom the promise is made has a charge by reason of the promise which he has also performed."[153] In other words, the damages claimed by a victim of a breach of promise who performed his side of the bargain may differ from those redressed by the forms of action in debt and *detinue*. As I will discuss shortly, the latter actions were conceived during feudal times and with little or no connection to the commercial world that England was pioneering. Thus, the advent of commercialization bestowed a protean role upon consideration, a meaning closer to the experience of merchants and their *quid pro quo*.

Professor Sacks cites the 1624 edition of John and William Rastell's legal dictionary *Les Termes de la Ley* (first published a century earlier, and which bore a subtitle to explain its purpose: "Certain difficult and obscure words and terms of the common laws and statutes of this realm now in use expounded and explained") as introducing a new definition of consideration.[154] Reflecting William Rastell's scholastic and Aristotelian training,[155] the dictionary defined consideration as "the material

---

148 David Harris Sacks, *The Promise and the Contract in Early Modern England: Slade's Case in Perspective*, *in* RHETORIC AND LAW IN EARLY MODERN EUROPE 28 (Victoria Kahn & Lorna Hutson eds., 2001).

149 *Id.* at 29.

150 *Id.*

151 *Id.* (I have replaced the old English used by Professor Sacks with modern English words).

152 *Id.*

153 *Id.*

154 *Id.* at 30.

155 For a biographical note of William Rastell, a nephew of Thomas More, see 8 ENCYCLOPEDIA BRITANNICA MICROPEDIA 427 (1973).

cause of a contract without which no contract can bind the party."[156] This reference focused on the things of value exchanged between the contracting parties and distinguished this "consideration" from the human and divine purposes—the first and final causes for which an action is undertaken.[157] Consequently, *Les Termes de la Ley* unhesitatingly describes a contract as "a bargain or covenant between two parties, where one thing is given for another which is called '*Quid Pro Quo.*' "[158] The equation between consideration and a *quid pro quo* also reflects the increasing reliance on the form of action known as *assumpsit* for breaches of promise, thereby displacing the action in debt and *detinue* in breach of contract disputes, about which more will follow shortly.

2. Consideration's Connection with the Actions on Debt, Covenant and **Assumpsit***: Slade's Case*

The origins of the English remedial law for breach of contractual promises were apparent in Christopher St. Germain's student's *quid pro quo* version of consideration and in the distinction between the forms of action for "debt" and "covenant." As summarized by Professor J. H. Baker: "The simplest distinction is that debt is a present obligation, arising from an executed contract or a grant, whereas covenant is 'executory' and to be performed in the future."[159] Thus, while to sue on an action on covenant and prove the existence of an executory promise in a manner that made the promise enforceable the plaintiff had to show the deed to the court, this was not the case with actions on debt.[160] The requirement of a deed was confined to covenant because of the tendency in the common law to treat words as inferior to acts or deeds. Hence, legal rights could not arise from the party's mere word; another kind of act or deed, a *factum,* was required.[161] This requirement was best met when the parties gave each other something that they considered valuable. This material version of consideration, one that presupposed a *quid pro quo*, or a bargain and an exchange, helped to bridge the gap between the actions on debt and covenant on the one hand and *assumpsit* on the other. I would suggest that, transactionally speaking, it also helped to bridge the gap of distrust between contracting parties previously unknown to each other, much as Mauss' and Dalton's gifts had done in a pre-commercial society.

The action on the debt was the one most used in breach of contract cases when plaintiffs alleged that they had given something to the defendants who failed to return or pay for it as agreed upon. Columbia University's late and lamented Professor Allen Farnsworth's illuminating study on "The Past of Promise"[162] cites Sir Frederic Pollock's view that in English law, the creditor sued to recover monies after the Norman Conquest in exactly the same manner he would have used to demand possession in land. In other words, "the foundation of the plaintiff's right was not the existence of a

---

[156] Sacks, *supra* note 148, at 30.

[157] *Id.*

[158] *Id.*

[159] J. H. Baker, Book Review, 21 AM. J. LEGAL HIST. 335, 336 (1977) (reviewing A.W.B. SIMPSON, A HISTORY OF THE COMMON LAW OF CONTRACT. VOLUME 1: THE RISE OF THE ACTION OF ASSUMPSIT (1975) and S. J. STOLJAR, A HISTORY OF CONTRACT AT COMMON LAW (1975)) (citation omitted).

[160] *Id.* at 337.

[161] *Id.*

[162] E. Allan Farnsworth, *The Past of Promise: An Historical Introduction to Contract*, 69 COL. L. REV. 576, 587 (1969).

bargain or a promise, but the unjust detention by the defendant of the plaintiff's property or goods."[163] Since the law of debt was unconcerned with bargains or promises generally, it could not be used to enforce oral bargains, especially those in which the parties promised to do or give something in the future.[164]

From a procedural standpoint, the main problem with the action on debt was that the defendant could request a "wager of law" in which he would "make his law" by taking an oath in open court that he did not owe the alleged debt. At a certain day assigned by the court, he would bring eleven neighbors (referred to as compurgators) who would take an oath that they believed that the defendant told the truth. This oath was decissory: Once taken by the defendant and attested to by the compurgators, the plaintiff would lose his action on the debt.[165]

No less an authority than Sir Edward Coke, one of seventeenth-century England's most respected jurists, referred to the widespread concern among creditors-plaintiffs that, as used in actions on debt, the wager of the law was conducive to perjury: "The law presumeth that no man will forswear himself for any worldly thing; but men's consciences do grow so large . . . [thus creditors] choose rather to bring an action *upon*

---

[163] Frederick Pollock, *Contract, in* 7 ENCYCLOPEDIA BRITANNICA 35, 36 (11th ed. 1910) (cited by Farnsworth, *supra* note 162, at 13). *See also* FREDERIC W. MAITLAND, EQUITY, ALSO THE FORMS OF ACTION AT COMMON LAW (Alfred H. Chaytor & William J. Whittaker eds., 1909), *available at* http://www.fordham.edu/halsall/basis/maitland-formsofaction.asp. Maitland describes the action on debt starting with its initial writ: "A writ of debt was addressed to the sheriff; the sheriff is to command the defendant to pay to the plaintiff the alleged debt, or, if he will not do so, appear in court and answer why he has not done so." *Id.* at 299. The court procedure required that the defendant:

> . . . prove his assertion that he owes nothing by his own oath and the oaths of a certain number of compurgators, or oath-helpers. The defendant must then solemnly swear that he owes nothing, and his oath-helpers must swear that his oath is clean and unperjured. If they safely get through this ceremony, punctually repeating the right formula, there is an end of the case; the plaintiff, if he is hardy enough to go on, can only do so by bringing a new charge, a criminal charge of perjury against them.

Id. at 309. A sub-species of debt eventually acquired its own features:

> Meanwhile the actions which came to be known as personal make their appearance. The oldest seems to be Debt-Detinue,' which appears already in Glanvill. I say 'Debt-Detinue'—originally men see little distinction between the demand for a specific chattel and the demand for a certain sum of money. Gradually this action divides itself into two, Detinue for a specific chattel, Debt for a sum of money—this differentiation takes place early in the thirteenth century. As in Detinue the judgment given for the plaintiff awards him either the chattel itself, or its value; and, as the defendant thus has the option of giving back the chattel or paying its value, Bracton is led to make the important remark that there is no real action for chattels. . . .

Id. at 342.

[164] A dispute exists among commentators on whether wager of the law was allowed against attempts to enforce oral or informal covenants. According to Simpson, "there seems never to have been a time when the royal courts regularly allowed actions to be taken on parole covenants," a viewpoint with which Stoljar apparently agrees. Baker, *supra* note 159, at 337. Yet, Baker refers to "recently published rolls of 1248 in which wager of law seems to be regularly allowed against parol covenants." *Id.* As I read Professor Baker's quoted opinion, the implication would be those parol covenants that either were not subjected to a wager of law or somehow survived it, could be enforced. Since I had troubles visualizing a "parol covenant" to begin with, I did a search for such a term and found it used in a decision (circa 1869) by the Supreme Court of Pennsylvania in the sense that a covenant that is attempted to be altered by parol ceases to be a covenant, and can only be enforced if at all as a promise. *A fortiori*, a covenant attempted to be executed orally would meet the same fate.

[165] MAITLAND, *supra* note 163, at 311 (referring to these "old formal modes of proof" as known to the king's court, the same court which "made use of the ordeal until that ancient process was abolished by the Lateran Council of 1215. Trial by battle . . . was not abolished until 1819 and wager of law was not abolished until 1833.")

the case upon his promise wherein [the defendant] cannot wage his law. . . ."[166] The action "upon the case" that Coke was referring to was an action in "*assumpsit,*" developed in the sixteenth century to deal, among others, with deceitful or tortious promises.[167] Over time, *assumpsit* developed as the main remedy for breach of contract promises. In Professor Baker's words: "The bridge was crossed almost invisibly when awards of damages came to represent prospective loss rather than restitution. The way was then clear for *assumpsit* to lie for services, which had happened by the time of *Jordan's Case* in '1528.' "[168]

The late Michigan and Harvard Law School Professor John Dawson also finds that by the 1530s and 1540s, the failure to perform a promise began to be recognized as sufficient ground for the award of damages.[169] However, he notes that consideration "was at the outset, the most pallid" term used mostly in preliminary recitals to laws or conveyances to explain their purpose.[170] Gradually, English courts started connecting what was bargained and sold with what prompted such a sale by using the preposition "for" as the link between the two clauses. For example, in a King Bench's decision rendered in the 1530s, a buyer of malt alleged that the defendant had bargained and promised forty quarters of malt for "two payments . . . and had failed to deliver, so that the plaintiff had had to buy malt elsewhere at a higher price."[171] The cause of action for damages awarded to the plaintiff for the defendant's failure to perform his promise (non-feasance) was "trespass on the case."[172] And, as time went on, the something "for" which the promise was made was described increasingly in pleadings as "the consideration."[173] It was only a short step in the transition from the debt to trespass on the case that made executory promises enforceable.

The landmark decision that completed the transition from debt to trespass on the case and its contractual remedy also known as *indebitatus assumpsit* was *Slade v. Morley,* usually referred to as *Slade's Case.*[174] Slade entered into an informal contract with Morley in which Slade agreed to sell Morley grain still growing in the field. Humphrey promised to pay him sixteen British Pounds for the growing grain at a future date and failed to do so. Slade sued him in *indebitatus assumpsit*, an action that allowed the recovery of special damages that resulted from the defendant's unwillingness to pay for the bargained-for grain. The courts were initially divided over whether the action could be maintained. Some had agreed with the defendant that if he had agreed to pay for a *quid pro quo* such as the delivery of the grain and failed to do

---

166 Sacks, *supra* note 148, at 34 (emphasis added).

167 The action of trespass upon the case to recover debts, in contrast to the action of debt, was based on the wrong done by a broken oral agreement. For the most recent work on the subject, see SIR JOHN SPELMAN, THE REPORTS OF SIR JOHN SPELMAN 255–98 (J. H. Baker ed., 1977); J. H. BAKER, THE LEGAL PROFESSION AND THE COMMON LAW 213–36 (1986); A. W. BRIAN SIMPSON, A HISTORY OF THE COMMON LAW OF CONTRACT (1987).

168 Baker, *supra* note 159, at 338.

169 DAWSON, *supra* note 78, at 199.

170 *Id.*

171 *Id.* at 200–01.

172 *Id.* at 200–01 (citing Pykeryng v. Thurgoode (no date given)).

173 *Id.* at 201.

174 I THE SELECTED WRITINGS AND SPEECHES OF SIR EDWARD COKE (Steve Shepherd ed., 2003) (including a full version of *Slade's Case*), *available at* http://oll.libertyfund.org/index.php?option=com_staticxt &staticfile=show.phpštitle=911&layout=html#chapter_106321. The summary of the fact in the principal text, which was provided by the Liberty Fund, precedes its transcription of the original text.

so when the grain was made available to him, the proper action was that for debt. An action in *assumpsit*, the defendant argued, would have required Morley to issue a new promise following the accrual of the debt, and this promise would had to have been for the payment of the accrued debt.

The King's Bench, contrary to the opinion of its jurisdictional rival, the Court of Common Pleas, held that a person harmed by another's breach of contract could bring an action in *assumpsit*, even though the plaintiff could have also sued in debt, but his recovery would not be the thing owed or misappropriated; it would be monetary damages. As stated by the King's Bench: " '[E]very contract executory imports in itself an *assumpsit*, for when one agrees to pay money or to deliver anything, thereby he assumes or promises to pay, or deliver it.' Thenceforth, the proof of the new promise becomes unnecessary."[175]

The King Bench's willingness to use as sweeping a statement as: "Every contract executory imports in itself an *assumpsit*" appeared, at least to this reader, as a response to a commercial marketplace's need for assurance with respect to a creditor's ability to collect on a promise to pay in exchange for the sale of a retailer's goods or of a farmer's crops. As summarized by Professor J. B. Ames, Harvard Law School's true pioneer among United States' contract law scholars:

> [A]n express *assumpsit* was for a long time essential in the actions of tort against surgeons or carpenters, and bailees. . . . [Furthermore] a defendant who promised to pay a sum certain in exchange for a *quid pro quo* was, before Slade's case, chargeable only in Debt unless he made a second promise to pay the debt. It was only by degrees that the scope of the action was enlarged. . . . In the first place, *Indebitatus Assumpsit* became concurrent with Debt upon a simple contract in all cases.[176]

In sum, the holding in *Slade's Case* that the failure to pay a promised sum of money in exchange for another's performance warrants an action in *assumpsit* led to the conclusion that every executory contract imports an *assumpsit*. This conclusion, in turn, laid the basis for the enforcement of the breach of promises to give or extend credit. Without such enforcement, it is difficult to see how a robust credit economy could function.

§ 22.5 CONTRACT AS A BILATERAL OR MULTI-LATERAL AGREEMENT AND AS A PROMISE

Professor Ames' above-quoted article was written in 1888, a time during which many United States judges frequently cited English case law as persuasive if not primary sources. It started out, however, with a candid criticism of the common law of contracts as wrought by English courts: "Nothing impresses the student of the Common Law more than its extraordinary conservatism. . . . [and] the persistency of archaic reverence for form and of scholastic methods of interpretation."[177]

The increasingly commercialized English and United States economies needed greater clarity and predictability from their law of contracts than that provided by the

---

175 MAITLAND, *supra* note 163, at 364.

176 J. B. Ames, *The History of Assumpsit*, 2 HARV. L. REV. 53, 53–54 (1888).

177 *Id.* at 53.

English sixteenth- and seventeenth-centuries forms of action. *Slade's Case* was helpful in lifting the casuistic restrictions that weighed upon *assumpsit*. Thereafter, an executory promise to pay money by binding the promisor to do so—regardless of the promisee's acceptance or performance—firmed up the legal basis for a commercial *quid pro quo*, one that allowed promises to be exchanged for acts or performances; it was a form of giving (not donating) by promising, and it reinforced the use of what became the ritual wording of countless Anglo-American contracts to this day: "In consideration of. . . ." As will be discussed in a later section,[178] this was a very useful "rule of traffic" for contracting parties to keep in mind. It assured them that what they would in all likelihood have done themselves in a society accustomed to giving something in exchange for something else was not only morally but also legally binding. *Surely, this initial and binding step in the continuum of commercial contracting, which could be counted at a later time by a similar promise or act of performance, was a less formal and more commercial method of contract formation than that of the largely ceremonial and static method of Article 1108 of the* Code Civil.

As with Professor Ames, the best among the common law judges who have contributed to the growth of a commercial and industrial society, whether Mansfield in England or Cardozo in the United States, carry with them the same distaste for hyper-technical scholastic interpretations. As was discussed in an earlier chapter,[179] the search for rules such as that in *Slade's Case* that could invigorate contract law and inspire similar decision-making in the future led United States scholars and judges to draft the American Law Institute's Restatement (First) of Contracts in 1933 and subsequently the Restatement (Second) of Contracts in 1981 (hereinafter Restatement (Second)).

Accordingly, Section 1 of the Restatement (Second) defines contract as follows: "A contract *is a promise* or set of promises for the breach of which the law gives a remedy, or the performance of which the law in some way recognizes as a duty."[180] Notice how this definition differs from that of Article 1101 of the *Code Civil*: "A contract is an agreement which binds one or more persons, towards another or several others to give, to do, or not to do something."[181] Under the *Code Civil*, then, the only promise that can be characterized as a binding contract is one that has been agreed upon by the parties.

As was done by *Slade's Case*, the Restatement (Second) allows an executory promise to bind the promisor contractually, *i.e.*, as a unilateral contractual obligation prior to the time that an agreement can be proved to exist. The comment to Section 1 distinguished between a contract and a promise in that a " 'contract,' like 'promise,' denotes the act or acts of promising. But unlike the term 'promise,' 'contract' applies only to those acts which have legal effect. . . ."[182] In other words, a promise whose legal effect binds the promisor is subsumed under the meaning of "contract." The Restatement (Second) strengthens this connection by defining "promise" in Section 2

---

178 *See infra* § 22:8(B).

179 *See supra* § 20:2(G)(1).

180 RESTATEMENT (SECOND) OF CONTRACTS § 1 (1981) (emphasis added) [hereinafter RESTATEMENT (SECOND)].

181 C. CIV. (FR.) art. 1101.

182 RESTATEMENT (SECOND) § 1 cmt b.

as: "[A] manifestation of intention to act or refrain from acting in a specified way, so *made as to justify a promisee in understanding that a commitment has been made*."[183]

It illustrates the binding effect of such promises by referring to those made by a house builder or inventor of material used in its construction who states to his buyer: "I warrant that this house will never burn down."[184] As noted earlier, similar effects can be attributed to a "firm" offer to sell "X" (real or personal property) "at price 'Y' and valid for a period of thirty days starting on. . . ." They can also be attributed to more succinct "buy" orders of traded investment securities directed by their buyer to a broker-dealer such as: "Buy 200 stock of IBM at a price no higher than X and at a date or time no later than Y."

As discussed in an earlier section, these are "dynamic" versions of contracts and as such are inconsistent with Hugo Grotius' and Samuel Puffendorf's bilateral and static "Will Theory" as enshrined in Article 1101 of the *Code Civil*, among many others. Yet, as pointed out by Allan Farnsworth (Co-Reporter for the Restatement with Professor Robert Braucher), a Will Theory was also in effect in the United States during the first part of the nineteenth century.[185] Nonetheless, by the end of that century, this theory gave way to one in which the contract was based on the parties' bargain. In Farnsworth's words: "[T]he traditional requirement that consideration be either a benefit to the promisor or a detriment to the promisee had begun to be replaced by a requirement that the consideration be 'bargained for.' "[186] The difference lay in the fact all the promissee-plaintiff had to show was not the existence of corresponding benefits and detriments, but that the value given and received was the product of a bargain.

§ 22.6 CONSIDERATION AS BARGAIN: THE SHORTCOMINGS OF THE BARGAIN TEST

A. A Revolution or a Regression to a Motivational *Causa*

According to Yale University Law School Professor Grant Gilmore, the equation between consideration and bargain was a revolutionary invention by Justice Oliver Wendell Holmes.[187] Harvard University Professor John Dawson, an equally illustrious scholar, regarded Gilmore's suggestion as "surprising" and "astonishing," especially when taking into account that the supposed revolution was accomplished by two sentences whose message was as representative of the *status quo* as "between promise and the consideration there must be 'the relation of reciprocal conventional inducement each for the other.' "[188] Dawson's skeptical and ironic assessment of the "bargain" invention was that: "Whatever else Holmes may have invented, we can be sure, at least, that he invented this phrase."[189] Dawson also compared Holmes' bargain-consideration to Chancellor Kent's description of consideration "as something given in exchange, something that is mutual, or something which is the inducement of the

---

183 *Id.* at § 2 (1) (emphasis added).

184 *Id.* at § 2 cmt. d.

185 *See* E. ALLAN FARNSWORTH, CONTRACTS 47 (4th ed. 2004).

186 *Id.* at 47.

187 *See* GRANT GILMORE, THE DEATH OF CONTRACT 19–21 (1974) (cited in DAWSON, *supra* note 78, at 198 n.5, 203 n.12).

188 DAWSON, *supra* note 78, at 203.

189 *Id.*

contract"[190] and noted what Holmes could have added to Kent's requirements had he been more explicit:

> [Holmes] seemed to say that both parties must *agree* that each was induced to promise or act by the promise or act of the other. Perhaps he derived this from the requirement of mutual assent, so that the parties must agree not only on what was exchanged but also why; this would mean that the why—the inducement—for each must be disclosed and agreed to by the other.[191]

Professor Farnsworth's version of Justice Holmes' suggestion agrees in part with Dawson, but does not demand the express disclosure of an agreement on the reciprocal inducements:

> [I]t is not enough that the promise induces the consideration or that the consideration induces the promise, "if the other half is wanting." The Restatement Second reaffirms this by defining bargain to require that the consideration both be "sought by the promisor in exchange for his promise" and be "given by the promisee in exchange for his promise."[192]

This version of bargain appears in Sections 17 and 71 of the Restatement (Second). Section 17 reminds the reader that: "[T]he formation of a contract requires a bargain in which there is a manifestation of mutual assent to the exchange and a consideration."[193] However, the comment to this section indicates that a number of commercial transactions would "not necessarily [be] subject to the requirements of assent and consideration."[194] As enumerated by Section 6, these are: (a) Contracts under seal; (b) Recognizances; (c) Negotiable instruments and documents; (d) Letters of Credit.[195]

Section 71 enumerates the exchanges that constitute consideration and thereby purports to add a clarification to the meaning of bargain:

> (1) To constitute consideration, a performance or a return promise must be bargained for.
>
> (2) A performance or return promise *is bargained for if it is sought* by the promisor in exchange for his promise and is given by the promisee in exchange for that promise.
>
> (3) The performance may consist of
>
> (a) an act other than a promise, or
>
> (b) a forbearance, or
>
> (c) the creation, modification, or destruction of a legal relation.[196]

---

190 *Id.*

191 *Id.* at 204.

192 FARNSWORTH, *supra* note 185, at 55. Could "his" have meant "this"? After all, the party issuing the promise is normally the promisor, at least per Restatement (Second) § 2 (3).

193 RESTATEMENT (SECOND) § 17(1).

194 *Id.* cmt. a.

195 *Id.* § 6.

196 *Id.* § 71 (emphasis added).

Yet, this section does not answer whether the adjudicator must determine what in the language of subsection (1) the promisor sought to obtain from the return promise and vice versa, neither does it say whether the inducement for each must be disclosed and agreed to by the other. If the judge had to make such a determination, he would have to find what the parties, as Dawson suggested, must have agreed on, what was exchanged, and the reasons for each inducement. Needless to say, such a requirement would add considerably more facts and uncertainties to the determination of whether bargain-consideration existed for the contract. Indeed, such a quest could very easily be equated to that in the motivational version of *causa*. Contrast such a determination with one that seeks to find out if what was promised or given can be reasonably regarded as conferring a benefit to the promisor or creating a detriment to the promisee. Clearly, such a benefit-detriment test is more objectively, easily and promptly determinable than a motivationally-inspired bargain test. *In fact, unlike the bargain test, which must wait until the bargain has been concluded to evaluate it, the objective benefit-detriment test can be applied* a priori *by the parties with a reasonable probability of predictive success.*

It is true that Section 81 on "Consideration as Motive or Inducing Cause" tries to discourage a motivational interpretation of the above sections by warning in the heading of Comment b that the motive or cause of the bargain is immaterial and by adding that: "Even in the typical commercial bargain, the promisor may have more than one motive, and the person furnishing the consideration need not inquire into the promisor's motives."[197] Yet what if he does? Or, better still, what if the promisee knows that the promisor's motive is conduct that Article 1108 of the *Code Civil* would refer to as an "unlawful" cause or purpose, a concept that, as shown in the case involving a mistress as a beneficiary of a life insurance policy, included a violation of prevailing morality. How does such awareness affect the enforceability of the contract? Moreover, comment b adds to the uncertainty by stating: "Unless both parties know that the purported consideration is mere pretense, it is immaterial that the promisor's desire for the consideration is incidental to other objectives and that the other party knows it to be so."[198] Given that the use of "peppercorns" as consideration is a well-known pretense by both parties and that this practice is extraordinarily widespread, even this rather narrowly-conceived exception opens up a multitude of bargains for a motivational inquiry.

Professor Farnsworth describes the bargain test of consideration as shifting the concern of judges "from the substance of the exchange to the bargaining process."[199] At the same time, he acknowledges that the requirement of a bargain has little impact on marketplace transactions "[w]here bargain [is] an almost inevitable ingredient" and adds that "bargain might well be lacking in transactions taking place outside or on the periphery of the marketplace."[200] This is another way of saying that such "outside" or "peripheral" transactions do not deserve to be binding because despite the use of words such as "I promise" or "I will agree to," they are not really meant to be binding bargains.

---

197 *Id.* § 81 cmt b.

198 *Id.*

199 FARNSWORTH, *supra* note 185, at 70.

200 *Id.* at 48.

One such a situation would likely be that of a father who promises an expensive trip to his son (a law student of all people) if he did well in school. According to Robert Pothier, that promise is not binding.[201] While such a transaction would be deemed outside the marketplace by most commentators, there are many others that would be considered outside the commercial marketplace because they are entered into by non-merchants and from the computerized comfort of their home; yet, they are quintessentially commercial. These purchases, sales, exchanges and loans with the intent to profit are carried out on the Internet and in virtual marketplaces such as E-Bay which have greatly expanded the physical boundaries of Farnsworth's "periphery" of the marketplace. Clearly, there would seem to be no reason to exclude them from the zone of bargained-for consideration.

B. Adequacy of Consideration, the Peppercorn and the Bargained for Test

One of the elements of bargained-for consideration is its definiteness. It must be definite for the adjudicator to be able to measure the promisee's expectation interest.[202] Otherwise, adds Professor Farnsworth, it would not be possible to calculate the damages that will put the promisee in the same position he would have been had the promise been performed.[203] Yet how can a bargain be regarded as definite and precise enough by a court without delving into the promisee's expectations—as his motivation—to enter into the bargain? For example, was he using the sale price of item "X" as an incentive to induce purchases of item "Y" or as a "loss leader"? If so, he was not necessarily expecting to make a profit from X and this explains the willingness to assume a loss when selling X. Hence, courts will not be able to avoid an immersion into the quicksand of the adequacy and sufficiency of consideration, even though Farnsworth and Section 81 of the Restatement (Second) would much rather they did not.

On the other hand, and despite this preference, the Restatement (Second) does not reject the immersion outright as it could have done by enacting a rule such as: "even a peppercorn—symbolic of something trifling in value—can be consideration. . . ."[204] Instead, the pretense of the peppercorn's bargained-for-consideration is preserved "as long as it is bargained for. . . ."[205] As he usually did, Professor Farnsworth asked the key question: "Will the bargain test tolerate any imbalance, no matter how extreme in the exchange?" He also hinted at what I believe is the correct answer: It does not. The imbalance in the exchange is usually examined by courts of law or equity, not by testing the adequacy of the bargained-for consideration, but by looking into the equities of the transaction when it appears that there was misrepresentation, duress, mistake, incompetence or unconscionability affecting one of the parties to the contract.[206]

In contrast, when the bargain is between parties with similar knowledge of the transaction and bargaining power, as is frequently the case among merchants or their functional equivalents in present-day society, "the adequacy of consideration is not a

---

201 *See* ROBERT POTHIER, I A TREATISE OBLIGATIONS 5 (1802).

202 FARNSWORTH, *supra* note 185, at 108.

203 *Id.*

204 *Id.* at 70.

205 *Id.* at 70.

206 *Id.* at 71.

proper subject for judicial scrutiny."[207] This statement belongs to the 1993 New York Court of Appeals decision that did not involve merchants, but a dentist trying to buy a deceased colleague's practice and good will. The buyer promised to pay a certain amount that turned out to be disproportionately higher than the profits derived from the acquired practice. The court agreed with the holding in another case, which stated that if a buyer "chooses to pay for the expectancy that customers will return to the seller's former location, believing the right to locate there is a valuable asset, and agrees on a price therefor, so be it."[208] In transactional terms, what this ruling means is that the seller of the dental practice and its good will does not need to obtain an opinion from his lawyer prior to entering into this transaction to determine whether the amount offered by the buyer was adequate (or not excessive) given his expectations of profit. Such a reading, incidentally, would have been required under Professor Dawson's interpretation of Justice Holmes' bargained-for consideration. It required that: "[T]he parties must agree not only on what was to be exchanged but also why; this would mean that the why—the inducement—for each must be disclosed and agreed to by the other."[209] Had this been the test, once the buyer's profit expectations were revealed to the seller, he would have been expected to either agree with them or disclaim knowledge of their reasonableness. If he had agreed, the buyer would have had an action for breach of contract, fraud or worse.

§ 22.7 COMMERCIAL CONTRACTS THAT LACK BARGAINED—FOR CONSIDERATION, BUT DESERVE ENFORCEMENT

As acknowledged by Professor Farnsworth, the bargained-for consideration test has little impact on marketplace transactions because in these transactions, bargain—at least as a process—is an almost inevitable ingredient.[210] As discussed earlier, and as illustrated by the purchase of a dental practice in the previous section, the contracts that are negotiated in the periphery of the marketplace are increasingly commercial and thus bargained-for in nature. Those that remain outside of this "periphery" are mostly gratuitous or charitable promises.[211] These are likely to remain outside the periphery because by definition they do not embody an inherently commercial bargain. When they do, there is no longer a reason for them to remain in the periphery. For example, when an employee receives a bonus in the form of an expensive watch and such a gift can be traced to an express or implied policy of reward for the productivity of employees, there is no reason for characterizing it as a gratuitous or charitable promise. Clearly, there are gray areas where the altruism of a gift is questionable, but these areas require case-by-case determinations where facts and equity play the central role, not the doctrine of bargained-for-consideration. In the following sections, I will examine some commercial contracts, old and new, where the positive law has refused enforcement because of the failure of bargained-for consideration while the marketplace and a visionary commercial law judge deemed the transaction binding and commercially necessary.

---

[207] Apfel v. Prudential-Bache Sec. Inc., 616 N.E.2d 1095, 1097 (N.Y. 1993).

[208] Spaulding v. Benenati, 57 N.Y.2d 418, 423 (1982).

[209] DAWSON, *supra* note 78, at 204.

[210] FARNSWORTH, *supra* note 185, at 48.

[211] On the growth of mini and small business associations and their ability to participate in marketplace transactions once they are given access to secured credit, see Kozolchyk & Castaneda, *supra* note 37, at 98–115.

A. Master Agreements and Bargained—For Consideration

Contemporary multi-party agreements that rely on computer-to-computer communications and Master Agreements for their governance face considerable obstacles with the bargained-for consideration theory and its implicit requirement of privity of contract when several sets of contracting parties are involved. Assume that the Master Agreement transaction discussed in an earlier section[212] started when a buyer "B" sent a purchase order for a given commodity at the CIF (Cost, Insurance and Freight) price quoted by the seller "S" from B's to S's computers. S replied to B, accepting B's terms and conditions, but requesting that B procure the issuance of an irrevocable letter of credit to be confirmed by a bank in S's place of business. This letter of credit was to pay S for the CIF cost of the ordered commodities, and included in the cost the transportation of the goods from S's place of business to B's as well as a port-to-port insurance policy. Accordingly, B sent via his computer an application for the issuance of an irrevocable letter of credit to his issuing bank "IB" asking it to issue its own irrevocable letter of credit and requested that IB select a confirmation bank "CB" of its own choice in S's place of business to issue its confirmation to S. B's application also contained an authorization for IB to debit B's checking account with IB for the cost of the issuance and confirmation of the letter of credit to S. IB sent a SWIFT[213] electronic message to CB in S's place of business requesting its confirmation of IB's letter of credit and providing the authorization for CB to debit IB's account for the costs of CB's confirmation.

Upon receipt by S of CB's confirmation, its computer storing the Master Agreement generated requests by S for services by "FF" (a freight forwarder unknown to B), locating shipping space with "OC" (an ocean carrier also unknown to B), and to "IC" (an insurance company similarly unknown to B), requesting the issuance of its port-to-port ship insurance policy covering the shipment of the goods from S's warehouse to B's warehouse. These requests were followed by FF's own computer-to-computer request to OC for shipping space in his ships. In turn, this request was followed by OC's computer-to-computer response supplying FF's requested space. Similarly, FF requested IC to issue the requested policy and IC responded by agreeing to do so. As with the purchase order, by B's and S's acceptance, all the subsequent communication between FF, OC, and IC was subject to the same Master Agreement. Yet this agreement did not state whose promise or performance was consideration for any other.

The Master Agreement involving B, S, FF, OC and IC governed their communications, while the transactions between IB and CB were governed by the S.W.I.F.T. Manual, reference to which was made in the Master Agreement. At the same time, some of the other transactions were set forth in separate sets of promises, offers, acceptances and performances. In addition, the consideration provided by B and S for their purchase and sale agreement, as incorporated into the letter of credit issued by IB and confirmed by CB, provided the money with which to pay for all of the described services, including the payments to S, FF, OC, CB and IB. Nonetheless, even though the bargain between B and S acted as the inducement for all subsequent bargains, B and S were not parties to the bargains between IB and CB or between FF

---

212 *See supra* § 22:1(D).

213 SWIFT, http://www.swift.com/.

and OC or FF and IC. And as implicit in Sections 71 and 75 of the Restatement (Second), consideration for each of these contracts had to be supplied by those who had bargained for them, *i.e.*, those in privity of contract. As stated by Professor Farnsworth, Section 71 required that "the consideration both be 'sought by the promisor in exchange for his promise' and that it be 'given by the promisee in exchange for his promise.' "[214]

In the absence of privity and bargained-for consideration between B and all the other participants except for IB and S, would the rest of the transactions become unenforceable for lack of bargained-for consideration? An agency rationale might be a tempting explanation for such consideration, but CB, FF, OC nor IC were not selected or known by B, nor did B have the power to act as their principal. Another possible resolution to this lack of privity problem was provided by Professor Farnsworth in the quote below, albeit it applied to a transaction involving fewer parties and did not mention a Master Agreement among the participants. Farnsworth suggested that the consideration to the bank (or in our hypothetical CB) may "move" to someone other than the promisor, and illustrates this movement as follows:

> [S]uppose that a bank [CB] says, "We promise you seller, that we will pay you the price of apples if you deliver them to our customer, the buyer." The seller's performance is consideration for the bank's promise, and the seller (the promisee) can enforce that promise, even though the apples are not delivered to the bank (the promisor) but to the buyer (someone other than the promisor).[215]

Yet, if the seller's performance, *i.e.*, the delivery of the apples, is consideration for the paying bank's promise (CB in our hypothetical), it would mean that the bargain for which CB issued the promise of confirmed payment was between CB and S and thus, in exchange for that payment, CB would be the recipient of the apples. Aside from the fact that no self-respecting confirming bank would want to be known for bargaining for the sale of someone else's apples, Farnsworth's scenario raises the question not only of what the true bargain is, if any, between CB and B, but also how that bargain is connected with the bargain between B and IB.

If the CB receives the apples that S shipped to B as required by Professor Farnsworth's bargained-for-consideration "move," IB would not be able to seek reimbursement from the buyer for the amount CB debited to the account of IB. The reason would be that IB's bargain with B was its issuance of the letter of credit to pay for the apples that B was to receive from S. If the delivery of these apples to CB is bargained-for consideration between CB and S, how could it be consideration between B and IB? On the other hand, since CB would not want to unjustly enrich itself by debiting IB's account and keeping B's apples, it would probably want to move the apples back to IB and have IB deliver the apples to B. Otherwise, no consideration would support IB's claim against B, its customer, who is the payor of the letter of credit but would remain apple-less. Thus, if the proposed move of consideration from B to CB would provide support for the bargain between CB and S, it would do away with the

---

[214] FARNSWORTH, *supra* note 185, at 55. As noted earlier, I am confused by this formulation because I would have assumed that the promisee is not the party issuing the promise but the one either accepting it and or performing acts supposedly in exchange for such a promise. *See supra* note 192.

[215] FARNSWORTH, *supra* note 185, at 49.

support for the bargain between B and IB. In addition, please note that it was neither S nor B who bargained with CB for its confirmation of the letter of credit to S, the party who bargained for such a confirmation with CB was IB. Thus, as already decided by Anglo-American courts, if B were to attempt to stop CB's payment to S or CB's keeping the apples, its claims would be rejected precisely because they lacked the requisite privity of contract.[216] Clearly, bargained-for consideration does not belong in this twenty-first century transaction.

B. Past Consideration and Bargained—For Consideration: Lord Mansfield's Decision in Pillans v. Van Mierop

The enforcement of a number of commercial or commercially-related contracts and promises remains uncertain as a result of court decisions that held that where the bargained-for consideration was "past consideration" it did not bind the promisor. Lord Mansfield's opinion in *Pillans and Rose v. Van Mierop and Hopkins* (hereinafter *Pillans v. Van Mierop*)[217] points both to the roots and the reasons for this uncertainty, as well as to its possible remedy.

The plaintiffs were Dutch merchant bankers who had agreed to accept and pay bills of exchange (drafts) drawn on them by White, an Irish merchant doing business in Holland. As merchant bankers, Pillans customarily accepted bills of exchange (also known as drafts) when requested to do so by other bankers with whom they had correspondent relations or who had a reputation for solvency and honesty. Customarily, they would also agree to pay drafts drawn on them by merchants who were their own valued clients or whose promise of reimbursement was guaranteed by another bank of known solvency. The promise that contained such an assurance of reimbursement to Pillans was known at that time as a "confirmation" or a "confirmed credit."[218] In this case, several letters had been exchanged among the plaintiffs, defendants, and White. The relevant ones were written by White to Pillans requesting that it pay his draft to Clifford, a creditor of White, and a letter written by Pillans agreeing to do so, but on condition that White obtain a "confirmed credit upon a house of Rank in London" committing to accept Pillans' draft for the moneys advanced on behalf of White.[219] Van Mierop sent such a letter undertaking to honor a bill of exchange.[220]

However, after Pillans paid Clifford (and one month before Pillans drew its bill of exchange seeking reimbursement from Van Mierop), White became insolvent.

---

[216] See, for example, the following decisions, which hold that because of a lack of privity between the confirming bank and the customer, the confirming bank has no right of reimbursement against the original customer and owes that customer no duty: Dulien Steel Prods., Inc. v. Bankers Trust Co., 298 F.2d 836, 841–42 (2d Cir. 1962); Petra Int'l Banking Corp. v. First Am. Bank of Virginia, 758 F. Supp. 1120, 1130 (E.D. Va. 1991), aff'd sub nom. Petra Int'l Banking Corp. v. Dameron Int'l Inc., 953 F.2d 1383 (4th Cir. 1992).

[217] (1765) 3 Burr. 1663, 97 Eng. Rep. 1035. The discussion of facts and especially of Lord Mansfield's questions during trial, findings and reasoning owes much to C. H. S. Fifoot. C.H.S. FIFOOT, LORD MANSFIELD 129–35 (1936).

[218] Drafts or bills of exchange are "orders" of payment drawn by a creditor or debtor on a third party acceptor, usually a party of known solvency such as a bank or well-known merchant. These drafts could be "time" drafts (if the draft was payable at a future time) or sight drafts (if the draft was payable upon presentation or "at sight"). For a discussion of the legal meaning and economic significance of bills of exchange or drafts, *see supra* §§ 11:2(D)(2) & 11:4.

[219] FIFOOT, *supra* note 217, at 129–30.

[220] *Id.* at 130.

Realizing that White would not be able to reimburse them for the liability they had assumed with Pillans, Van Mierop refused to honor the bills drawn against them by Pillans. Pillans sued Van Mierop on *assumpsit* and the jury held for the defendants on issues related mostly to an allegation of fraud. Lord Mansfield ordered a new trial and in it defendants argued that the only consideration that could be proved was past consideration, *i.e.*, the money that the plaintiffs had paid to Clifford *prior to receiving the defendants' undertaking to reimburse those advances*. According to the defendant's lawyers, since the credit the plaintiffs had given to White was extended one month before the defendants had agreed to accept the plaintiff's draft, the consideration was past and done, before their promise was made.[221]

During a retrial of the facts, Lord Mansfield pursued a distinction between written and oral contracts where consideration was concerned. He asked defendant's counsel whether he had found " 'any case . . . where the undertaking holden to be a *nudum pactum* was in writing'."[222] As surmised by Oxford Professor C. H. S. Fifoot (author of a legal biography of Lord Mansfield), this question took counsel by surprise and the best answer he could muster was that " 'It was anciently doubted' . . . 'whether a written acceptance of a bill of exchange was binding, for want of consideration.' "[223] This reply "revealed a lacuna in the defendants' arguments, of which Lord Mansfield at once took advantage."[224] He thereafter delivered his judgment without the citation of authority. Fifoot suggested that it was short enough to warrant his full transcription; in our case, space is more limited and for that reason the transcription will be shortened.

> This is a matter of great consequence to trade and commerce in every light. . . . Both the plaintiffs and White wrote to Van Mierop and company. They answered "that they would honour the plaintiffs' draughts". . . . A *nudum pactum* does not exist in the usage and law of merchants. I take it, that the ancient notion about the want of consideration was for the sake of evidence only: for when it is reduced into writing, as in covenants, specialties, bonds, [sic] there was no objection to the want of consideration. . . . In commercial cases amongst merchants, the want of consideration is not an objection. This is just the same thing as if White had drawn on Van Mierop and Hopkins, payable to the plaintiffs . . . whether Van Mierop and Co. had effects of White's in their hands or not, if they had accepted his bill. And this amounts to the same thing: "I will give the bill due honour" is, in effect, accepting it. If a man agrees that he will do the formal part, the law looks upon it (in the case of an acceptance of a bill) as if actually done. This is an engagement "to accept the bill, if there was a necessity to accept it, and to pay it, when due": and they could not afterwards retract. It would be very destructive to trade and to trust in commercial dealing, if they could."[225]

Thus, in *Pillans v. Van Mierop*, Lord Mansfield left us with two principles and a rule that even though severely questioned (if not overruled thirteen years later in *Rann v. Hughes*),[226] were later accepted in commercially-minded jurisdictions in the

221 *Id.*

222 *Id.*

223 *Id.*

224 *Id.*

225 *Id.* at 131–32.

226 Rann v. Hughes, 4 Brown 27, 2 Eng. Rep. 18 (H. L. 1778).

common as well as in civil law world. The first principle was that: A *nudum pactum* does not exist in the usage and law of merchants. This was a powerful warning about the importance of differentiating between a commercial and non-commercial context. What could be a valid tenet in the latter could fail to be in the former and vice-versa. The second principle, as mentioned above, was that:

> [T]he ancient notion about the want of consideration was for the sake of evidence only: for when it is reduced into writing, as in covenants, specialties, bonds, [sic] there was no objection to the want of consideration. . . . In commercial cases amongst merchants, the want of consideration is not an objection.[227]

In other words, because of the commercial context of contracts and promises, it was important to understand the historical ("ancient") purpose of consideration: To evidence the seriousness of the parties' intent. But such evidence was not required among merchants when they relied on written and signed promises. This was particularly true when merchants promised to pay money such as in their covenants, specialties and bonds. Formalities such as a writing warn the parties to the contract of the importance of what they are about to write and sign. The rule derived from the preceding two principles was seminal in the creation of a new promise that Mansfield referred to as an undertaking to honor a bill of exchange that is binding upon the party so undertaking, regardless of present, future or past consideration. While the above two principles apply to the entire field of commercial contracts and promises, the rule derived from them as applied to the facts of this case provided the conceptual and normative basis for the enforcement of irrevocably-binding documentary commercial and standby letters of credit as well as for bankers' acceptances of drafts drawn under these letters of credit.[228]

Mansfield's method of reasoning was vintage "logic of the reasonable": His major premise was that "[t]his is a matter of great consequence to trade and commerce in every light. . . ." This premise was based upon Mansfield's review of the relevant facts involved not only in the case before him, but also in related commercial customs and usages. In this decision, he seemed to be saying to his colleagues something like: "My learned colleagues, there is too much at stake in this dispute for you to continue to think about preexisting debts (as was done prior to *Slade's Case*) as the only cause of action for breaches of contractual promises." Mansfield's analysis evaluated past experience with the action on the debt and the salutary effects of a future with an *assumpsit* unshackled by past debt and past consideration. *In sum, Mansfield's was an analysis into the purpose of legal institutions whose ultimate goal was to instill trust in them and in those who used them.*

Despite such clarity and soundness of reasoning, past consideration continues to cloud the judgment of adjudicators and commentators, regardless of whether it is part of a commercial or non-commercial promise or contract and regardless of its transactional context. In the abstract, one may posit that an exchange must be "synallagmatic" or "this for that," but what if the relationship between those who

---

227 FIFOOT, *supra* note 217, at 131.

228 *See* BORIS KOZOLCHYK, COMMERCIAL LETTERS OF CREDIT IN THE AMERICAS 593 (1966) (quoting Dean Rousseau regarding a similar albeit twentieth century explanation of the legal nature of a documentary letter of credit: An acceptance issued in advance of the presentation of the beneficiary's draft and documents).

exchange promises for acts or performances is one in which trust and creditworthiness have created a course of dealing or belong to a trade where it is customary that the promisor issue the promise after the action has been taken by the promisee? This is why I disagree with my admired late colleague, E. Allan Fransworth, when he summarized the rationale of the Restatement (Second) (and underlying decisional support). Professor Farnsworth asserts:

> Imagine an exchange consisting of a promise on one side and some action, either promise or performance, on the other. Only if that action has not yet been taken when the promise is made can the promisor be bargaining for it when making the promise. If the action has already been taken, the promisor cannot be seeking to induce it. Such "past consideration"—action already taken before a promise is made—cannot be consideration for the promise.[229]

As apparent in *Pillans v. Van Mierop*, this non-contextual rationale would reward the Van Mierops of this world who, paraphrasing Lord Mansfield, retracted dishonorably and thereby engaged in conduct "very destructive to trade and to trust in commercial dealing." It would, on the other hand, punish the Pillanses, who acted honorably and in a trusting manner by accepting or paying White's drafts prior to receiving Van Mierop's promised acceptance of their liability. It would also render thousands of security agreements and security interests unenforceable between suppliers and their customers. Often, suppliers sell their product against a promise of the customer to pay the purchase price in ninety days. But, when the customer experiences financial difficulties, the suppliers transform their sale agreements into security agreements that create a security interest in some assets of the customer, and the consideration the sellers provide is the previously-delivered goods on credit, *i.e.*, past consideration.[230] Significantly, Justice Story expressed many of the above concerns in his decision in *Swift v. Tyson*[231] which is discussed in Chapter 21 and which, despite its being overruled on public law considerations in *Eerie R.R. v. Tompkins*[232] still stands as an excellent example of a sound analysis on the minimal role of consideration and pre-existing debts in negotiable instruments law.[233]

§ 22.8 OFFERS, ACCEPTANCES AND CONSIDERATION

A. The Meaning of Offer: Binding When Issued or When Accepted?

Offers and acceptances are species of the genus of promises. Promises can be formulated as generally as in the "save harmless" clauses of maritime letters of indemnity: "[I promise to] indemnify you, your servants and agents and to hold all of you harmless in respect of any liability, loss, damage or expense of whatsoever nature which you may sustain by reason of the ship proceeding and giving delivery of the cargo in accordance with our request." Or they can be expressed with specificity and

---

229 FARNSWORTH, *supra* note 185, at 56.

230 LYNN M. LOPUCKI & ELIZABETH WARREN, SECURED CREDIT: A SYSTEMS APPROACH 143 (7th ed. 2011). Lopucki & Warren state that "The definition of 'value' used in Article 9 [of the U.C.C.] not only encompasses all forms of consideration that would support an ordinary contract, it even includes one form of consideration that does not pass muster in common law contracts: past consideration." *Id.*

231 John Swift v. George W. Tyson, 41 U.S. 1 (U.S. 1842).

232 Erie Railroad Co. v. Tompkins, 304 U.S. 64 (U.S. 1938).

233 *See supra* § 21:11(C)(1).

terseness sufficient for an acceptance to "mirror" their terms and conditions. This difference was accurately captured by Section 58 of the Restatement (Second): "An acceptance must comply with the requirements of the offer as to the promise to be made or the performance to be rendered."[234]

Etymology dictionaries trace the roots of "to offer" in the English, French, Germanic and Scandinavian languages to the acts of giving or presenting something either as part of a religious ritual or as a lay gift.[235] One of the dictionaries traces the first recorded use of the noun offer ("*offre*") to fifteenth-century France, roughly two centuries before Hugo Grotius, the renowned jurist, Romanist and theologian, was exiled there.[236] Hence, by the time Grotius used this term in the seventeenth century in his "Law of War and Peace," it was widely associated in the European continent with a form of giving. This meaning easily blended with the *quid pro quo* version of consideration, thereby adding functionality in England to the giving of consideration as the first step in the standard sequence of contract formation. Professor Reinhard Zimmermann, a distinguished Romanist, asserts that the concepts of contract, offer and acceptance enunciated by Grotius and Puffendorf and restated by Pothier were superimposed upon consideration and adopted during the nineteenth century by English contract law treatise writers, and, one is led to infer, by the English law of contract formation.[237] The reason I am not persuaded by this assertion is because as a rule, Grotius' executory promises were not enforceable when breached except when they had been accepted by the offeree, whereas *Slade's Case* had made this enforcement possible since 1602. Grotius acknowledged that some promises—very few—were binding on the promisor regardless of the promisee's acceptance, but these were part of fully-fledged conveyances of property. Having in mind such a conveyance, Grotius asked:

> [S]ince the Property of a Thing may be transferred by the bare Will, sufficiently declared . . . why may we not in the same Manner transfer to one the right, either of requiring us to transfer to him the Property of a Thing (which is less than the actual Acquisition of the Right of Property itself) or of requiring us to do something in his Favour, since we have as much Power over our Actions as we have over our Goods?[238]

He buttressed the proposition that the right to claim the property transferred does not require an expressed acceptance by the transferee with a reference to the Hebrew

---

234 RESTATEMENT (SECOND) § 58.

235 *Offer*, ONLINE ETYMOLOGY DICTIONARY, http://www.etymonline.com/index.php?term=offer [hereinafter *Offer* Etymology] ("Old English *ofrian* . . . from Latin *offerre* 'to present, bestow, bring before' (in Late Latin 'to present in worship'), from *ob* 'to' . . . + *ferre* 'to bring, to carry'. . . . Non-religious sense reinforced by Old French *offrir* 'to offer,' from Latin *offerre*.") The noun is first recorded in the early 15th century "from Old French *ofre* . . . (12c.), verbal noun from *offrir*. . . . The native noun formation is *offering*." *Id.* Offering is the verbal noun that comes from *offrian*. *Offering*, ONLINE ETYMOLOGY DICTIONARY, http://www.etymonline.com/index.php?term=offering&allowed_in_frame=0. The word offer comes "[f]rom Middle English *offer*, from Old French *offre* ('offer'), from *offrir* ('to offer'), from Latin offerō ('to present, bring before'). Compare North Frisian *offer* ('sacrifice, donation, fee'), Dutch *offer* ('offering, sacrifice'), German *Opfer* ('victim, sacrifice'), Danish *offer ('victim, sacrifice')*, Icelandic *offr* ('offering')." *Offer*, WIKTIONARY, http://en.wiktionary.org/wiki/offer. Thus, the common roots of "to offer" are: to present, bestow or bring before, to bring or carry as part of a sacrifice or donation.

236 *Offer* Etymology, *supra* note 235.

237 REINHARD ZIMMERMANN, THE LAW OF OBLIGATIONS 571 (1996).

238 HUGO GROTIUS, THE RIGHTS OF WAR AND PEACE 280 (The Lawbook Exchange, LTD. 2004) (1738).

Talmud: "Insomuch that the Hebrews maintain that Silence, in an Affair that will not admit of a Delay, has the force of a direct Engagement."[239] Yet, he distinguished the right acquired by the beneficiary of a grant or conveyance of property from that acquired in what he referred to as an "imperfect promise" or a *Pollicitatio*, a pollicitation.[240]

The reader will recall that "pollicitation" was the term borrowed from Roman law by Grotius and Pothier, among other civil law commentators, and meant a "Promise or free Offer" that the promisor made to a city, state or community conditionally and without conveying the right of property as is common with duties of charity and gratitude.[241] Grotius contrasted this "imperfect" promise with the "*compleat*" promise, or one with the same effect as a man's alienation or conveyance of his property.[242] Thus, the English law of contracts seems more advanced than that influenced by Grotius' and Pothier's ideas on the unenforceability of unaccepted offers.

B. Key Rule of Traffic: Offers Clothed with Consideration

Offers and acceptances are integral elements of the dynamic method of commercial contract formation, especially those entered into by distant (*inter absentes)* parties. It is worth reiterating that in this method of contracting, a bargained-for consideration (for example, the offeror's invitation to the offeree to supply his goods or services in exchange for the promisor's payment of something of value) supplies the legal basis for the enforcement of executory promises. Yet, for *inter absentes* contracting to work in the commercial marketplace, even an offer or an acceptance silent as to the time of its binding effect must be able to be relied upon as binding for a duration of time that is commercially reasonable. Otherwise, why would merchants acting as offerees or offerors want to waste their valuable time with offers and acceptances that could be validly revoked at any time? Clearly, then, any rule inspired by the principle of revocability of offers and acceptances, especially when timely accepted or acted upon, is commercially unreasonable and leads to the costliest of commercial uncertainties—that the written word of a fellow merchant, even when expressed in the manner customary to his trade or profession, cannot be trusted.

The Anglo-American laws of formation of contracts *inter absentes* benefitted greatly from a healthy dosage of commercial reasonableness as set forth in two landmark English decisions handed down within one year of each other: *Kennedy v. Lee* in 1817[243] and *Adams v. Lindsell* in 1818.[244] Professor Teeven aptly summarized the importance of these decisions.[245] In *Kennedy v. Lee*, Chancellor Eldon adopted the civilian (presumably Grotius', Puffendorf's and Pothier's) version of binding-but-simultaneous offers and acceptances in the case of an offer accepted by mail. To resolve the problem created by an earlier decision that required the simultaneity of an

---

239 *Id.* at 280 n.10.

240 *Id.* at 281; *see also* Glossary, "Pollicitation."

241 GROTIUS, *supra* note 238, at 281.

242 *Id.* at 701 n.11; *but cf.* BERGER, ENCYCLOPEDIC DICTIONARY at 634 (discussing that the Pollicitatio was binding when the offeror promised to give a gift to a city or municipality in exchange for a post and failed to fulfill his promise).

243 (1817) 36 Eng. Rep. 170 (K.B.).

244 (1818) 106 Eng. Rep. 250 (K.B.).

245 TEEVEN, *supra* note 9, at 178.

acceptance, Eldon held that: "[I]f, within a reasonable time of the acceptance being communicated, no variation has been made by either party in the terms of the offer so made and accepted, the acceptance must be taken as simultaneous with the offer."[246]

As noted by Teeven, this holding may have sufficed as a "complete solution" or as a rule of traffic (as I would call it) "had there not been a concern that if the offeror normally had the right to a notice of assent before being bound, then the offeree ought to have the reciprocal right to know that the offeror had assented."[247] The concern raised in the *Kennedy* case was one of the issues before the King's Bench in *Adams v. Lindsell.* The court held that unless a specific point in time was set forth for the conclusion of the exchanges involving offers and acceptances, "the communications could go on *ad infinitum*."[248] Accordingly, it selected a time for the conclusion of the exchange and it was when the acceptance was sent by the offeree to the offeror. In doing this, the King's Bench had to resort to a legal fiction as a result of the same requirement that Lord Mansfield had to struggle with in *Pillans v. Van Mierop* as discussed in an earlier section: the consideration for the exchange had to be simultaneous, or else it could be characterized as a "past" consideration. The fiction resorted to by the King's Bench was that the offeror was making his offer "during every instant of time" up to the acceptance.[249] Thus, *Adams v. Lindsell*, completed the task of setting forth *the key rules of traffic for offers and acceptances*: Offers as executory promises supported by consideration bind the offeror for a reasonable time until accepted, and acceptances bind the offeree from the moment they are communicated to the offeror.

C. Some Key Rules of Traffic in the Restatement (Second)

Unfortunately, the above English decisions were not properly implemented by the Restatement (Second) where commercial, *inter absentes* transactions are concerned. Section 24 of the Restatement (Second) defines an offer as: "[T]he manifestation of willingness to enter into a bargain, so made as to justify another person in understanding that his assent to the bargain is invited and will conclude it."[250]

To qualify as a binding offer subject to acceptance, the Restatement (Second) first distinguishes among the degrees to which promises bind parties. For example, it places the offers of options to buy or sell at the highest obligation level because "is a promise which meets the requirements for the formation of a contract" and thus "limits the promisor's power to revoke an offer."[251] It then accepts the possibility of conduct other than a writing as a means of assent,[252] and requires precision and clarity from the offer such as on the determination of "the person or persons in whom is created the power of acceptance,"[253] the form or format of the acceptable acceptance,[254] and the reasonable

[246] *Id.*

[247] *Id.*

[248] *Id.*

[249] *Id.*

[250] RESTATEMENT (SECOND) § 24.

[251] *Id.* § 25. Contrast this rule with the interpretation of what was supposed to be a counterpart provision in the Mexican Federal Civil Code and its interpretation by the Supreme Court of Mexico in the Maria Trinidad Gomez case, *infra* 22:10(K).

[252] RESTATEMENT (SECOND) §§ 18, 19.

[253] *Id.* § 29.

[254] *Id.* § 30.

certainty of an offer's terms and conditions.[255] Here, a transactional and not litigation-inspired or judge-made test of Restatement (Second) § 33(2) would have been preferable. The judge-made text posits that: "The terms of a contract are reasonably certain if they provide a basis for determining the existence of a breach and for giving an appropriate remedy."[256] A transactional test would require the testimony of respected merchants or commercial experts on what they would deem as a reasonably certain offer in the field of commerce involved in the contract in question.

Consistent with the *Kennedy* and *Adams* decisions, Restatement (Second) § 35 grants to the offeree-acceptor "a continuing power to complete the manifestation of mutual assent by acceptance of the offer."[257] Similarly, Section 41 underscores the role of a reasonable time as a rule of traffic for offers and acceptances, especially as analyzed in the *Adams* case:

> (1) An offeree's power of acceptance is terminated at the time specified in the offer, or, if no time is specified, at the end of a reasonable time.
>
> (2) What is a reasonable time is a question of fact, depending on all the circumstances existing when the offer and attempted acceptance are made.
>
> (3) Unless otherwise indicated by the language or the circumstances and subject to the rule stated in Section 49, an offer sent by mail is seasonably accepted if an acceptance is mailed at any time before midnight on the day on which the offer is received.[258]

Yet, despite this language, and despite Comment b to Section 25's acknowledgment of the need for irrevocable offers (unless they state that they are not revocable so that offerees can depend on their binding force), and despite the acknowledgment that the presumption of irrevocability is the rule "in many legal systems,"[259] it also pledges loyalty to "[t]he common law rule, resting on the requirement of consideration, permits the revocation of offers even though stated to be firm."[260]

Somewhat lamely, Comment b to Section 25 of the Restatement suggests that the offeree's need for a dependable basis for a decision to rely on the seemingly binding offer "is met in part by the common-law rule that a mailed acceptance prevents revocation. Where more is needed, the option contract is available."[261] In other words, the useful legal fiction of *Adams v. Lindsell* that the offeror was making his offer "during every instant of time up to the acceptance" was not taken up by the Restatement (Second), thereby reviving the "archaic reverence for form and of scholastic methods of interpretation" that Professor Ames and other students of the common law of contracts found so counter-productive.[262]

---

[255] *Id.* § 33.

[256] *Id.* § 33(2).

[257] *Id.* § 35(1).

[258] *Id.* § 41.

[259] Maria del Pilar Perales Viscasillas, *The Formation of Contracts & the Principles of European Contract Law*, 13 PACE INT'L L. REV. 371, 384 (2001); BGB art. 145; United Nations Convention on Contracts for the International Sale of Goods art. 16(2), Apr. 11, 1980, 19 I.L.M. 668, 1489 U.N.T.S. 3.

[260] RESTATEMENT (SECOND) § 25 cmt. b.

[261] *Id.* (citation omitted).

[262] *See supra* note 176 and accompanying text.

The thrust of this comment is the rule in Section 42, although it is stated in an oblique and almost apologetic fashion: "An offeree's power of acceptance is terminated when the offeree receives from the offeror a manifestation of an intention not to enter into the proposed contract."[263] Comment a to this provision is blunter—under the heading of revocability of offers, it states:

> Most offers are revocable. Revocability may rest on the express or implied terms of the offer, as in the case of bids at an auction. But the ordinary offer is revocable even though it expressly states the contrary, because of the doctrine that an informal agreement is binding as a bargain only if supported by consideration. Inroads have been made on that doctrine by statute and by rules giving effect to nominal consideration and to action in reliance on that promise. Where such rules are applicable, or where the offer is itself a formal contract or an agreement binding as a bargain, the case is governed by Section 37 rather than by this Section.[264]

The major premise that "most offers are revocable" is not supported by the transactional facts of a contemporary marketplace. This is a marketplace whose innumerable offers are in the form of millions if not billions of advertisements of goods or services at specified prices with set time limits for "special deals," "close outs" and "liquidations." In fact, irrevocable offers encompass every sector of merchandising, from retail or wholesale dry goods businesses to automobile dealerships and the airplane or travel industries. These offerors actually depend upon this type of mass merchandizing to attract many if not most of their customers. If asked by legislators or judges, these offerors would be the first ones to tell them that their profitability is deeply tied to their customers' trust in the irrevocability of what is stated in their offers as printed in newspapers, broadcasted in television sets or communicated through the Internet.

Irrevocability is so necessary that it has led to the "commodification" and liquidity (or easy negotiation and redemption) of vast numbers of "bearer" supermarket coupons, redeemable by their bearers' tender to a supermarket cashier. Would such a transaction be possible if each time a supermarket cashier is ready to credit their bearers with a certain amount of the price rings up in his cash register, a warning flashed in her computer indicating that the irrevocable offer as widely announced has been revoked a week, a day or hour earlier? Did the drafters of the above comment take into account the effects that a presumption of revocability would have upon banks or savings and loan institutions whose offers to pay, say, a certain amount of interest for savings or deposit accounts is what attracts a substantial part of their depositor-investors? Or did they consider what this presumption would do to the letter of credit business, especially now that its best customs and practices world-wide have had to adopt the principle of irrevocability?[265]

---

263 RESTATEMENT (SECOND) § 42.

264 *Id.* § 42 cmt. a.

265 UCP 600 art. 3 (2007).

D. Irrevocability and § 2–205 of the U.C.C.

As stated by § 2–205 of the U.C.C.:

> An offer by a merchant to buy or sell goods in a signed writing which by its terms give assurance that it will be held open is not revocable, for lack of consideration, during the time stated or if no time is stated for a reasonable time, but in no event may such period of irrevocability exceed three months, but any such term of assurance on a form supplied by the offeree must be separately signed by the offeror.[266]

As noted by Official Comment 1 to this section, a firm offer no longer requires consideration to be binding on the offeror; now it is binding by "merely be[ing] characterized as such and expressed in signed writings."[267] Further, the meaning of the requirement of a signature reflects the influence of electronic messaging by making "authentication" its functional and reasonable equivalent. Nonetheless, since authentication by a writing (or its functional equivalent) is "the essence of this section," even though "settled" courses of dealing or usages of trade allow for oral communications as firm offers, this provision would still require a writing.[268]

§ 22.9 CONCLUSIONS AND RECOMMENDATIONS

One of the purposes of a general theory of contract is not only to help litigators and judges "prophesy" what the courts will do in fact (*a posteriori*), but also to help the parties and their attorneys identify *a priori* its formative elements and their validity. For it is this identification that will allow the parties to predict when and how their contracts will be formed and from that moment on, when and how to assume further obligations, manufacture, transform, sell, buy, lend or borrow, based upon the existence of the formed contract.

For centuries now, consideration has been one of these elements and one of the purposes of this chapter is to evaluate its usefulness, especially as compared with *causa*, its civil law counterpart. There is no doubt that without the enforcement of executory promises, a credit economy could not have come about. This enforcement was made possible in English law by the King's Bench decision in *Slade's Case* that the defendant-promisor's failure to pay the plaintiff "sixteen British Pounds for the growing grain at a future date" warranted an action on *indebitatus assumpsit. In this respect, requiring the giving of something of value as the factual and legal predicate for the enforcement of executory promises was an extremely useful legal institution in the development of a credit economy.*

Yet, as economies develop, some of the formative legal requirements are either discarded or de-emphasized for the sake of simplicity. As a law student, I remember reading Arthur Corbin's warning that a number of contracts or promises may exist without bargained-for consideration. The latest edition of his *magnum opus* contains the same warning: "There are many agreements that are not bargains; and there are many contracts that involve no bargain. . . ." (Among these he listed contracts under

---

[266] U.C.C. § 2–205.

[267] *Id.* § 2–205, cmt. 1.

[268] For a discussion on the negative effects of this requirement in the contemporary marketplace, *see infra* 22:10(F).

seal as well as the lesser known "informal contracts" without assent or consideration.)[269] As shown in this chapter, the number of commercial transactions exempt from consideration has been growing during the last century, almost from one generation to another.

Meanwhile, as this chapter also shows, *causa* and bargained-for consideration are a hindrance to many an important commercial transaction—from the immoral *causa* that prevented French negotiable bonds, from being marketable for a considerable part of the eighteenth and nineteenth centuries, to the equally unenforceable insurance policies because of their immoral purpose. The same uncertainty could affect United States contract rights and accounts receivable as one of the most popular forms of collateral in secured lending if subjected to the acid test of "bargained-for consideration" and to defenses derived from it such as the presence of past consideration. It is therefore appropriate to reassess the contribution or hindrance of motivational *causa* and bargained-for consideration in the formation of commercial contracts.

To the extent that contractual elements that the parties thought were present at the time of formation could subsequently be found to be non-existent or seriously flawed by a judge or arbiter, the certainty of the supposedly binding promises or agreements is undermined. Meanwhile, as commercialization and financial globalization grow, so does the demand for certain contractual promises that can yield a reliable and profitable stream of income. Contract rights and accounts receivable derived from such promises have by now become an essential component of that marketplace.[270] Consider this datum: In a recent trip to Chile, I found out that approximately thirteen percent of its GDP is comprised of "factoring" activities, *i.e.*, the purchase or negotiation of accounts receivable and factoring. Consider also that factoring began in Chile in 2005,[271] and less than two generations ago Chile was a developing South American nation, not the developed nation it is now.

Moreover, depending upon the certainty of collection of accounts receivable *and their proceeds*, they are not only more desirable by factors, but Chileans are also willing to purchase or negotiate them "without recourse" on their previous holders, sellers or assignors. Thus, reducing the uncertainty of collection by giving lending factors access to the proceeds of the contracts and accounts receivable free from underlying contractual claims and equities (including their "bargained-for consideration" or *causas*) enlarges their pool of liquid assets and induces their willingness to lend. Finally, consider that the ability of an original holder of accounts to sell or negotiate his accounts "without recourse" (*i.e.*, without the factor's ability to sue him for a failure to collect on the account assigned or sold). This would be possible when a negotiable instrument states that it is negotiated without recourse on its endorser or transferor, or when the account debtor waives his actions or defenses against the assignee of the account. In such cases, it may be possible for micro- or small

---

269 I CORBIN ON CONTRACTS 27 (Joseph Perillo ed., Rev. Ed. 1993).

270 *Compare* U.C.C. § 9–102 (1998) *and* U.C.C. § 9–102 (1962). The latest revision of U.C.C. Article 9 does not include a separate definition for "contract rights," as it was absorbed by the definition of "accounts."

271 Kozolchyk & Castaneda, *supra* note 37, at 62–63.

businesses to have more unimpaired assets and thereby gain access to additional commercial credit.[272]

As with the ease of negotiability of eighteenth-century governmental bonds in France and Spain, then, the need for greater ease of assignment and sale of contract rights and accounts is an additional reason why *causa* and bargained-for consideration should not be allowed to undermine their certainty. The need for certain and liquid promises was recognized in some instances by both the Restatement (Second) and the U.C.C. when they exempted contracts under seal, negotiable instruments and documents, recognizances or public or formal acknowledgments of debt of unperformed conditions or duties, firm promises and letters of credit from the need for consideration.[273] In fact, the entire genus of "abstract" or independent promises, *i.e.*, promises whose enforcement is independent from their underlying contract's *causa* or bargained-for consideration, is highly sought after by creditors and investors. As noted by Oxford's Sir Roy Goode, England's leading commercial law scholar: "[T]he rule that a contract must be supported by consideration is not absolute. An important exception is the abstract payment undertaking, a promise which the law will enforce as a matter of mercantile usage despite the absence of consideration or even reliance."[274]

Similarly, Professor Farnsworth reminds us that Mansfield's "heresy" (that putting a promise in writing should operate as an alternative to consideration) has a continuous appeal, especially after consideration started playing a larger role in the formation of contracts once the requirement of a seal was abolished.[275] He also calls attention to notable attempts to excise consideration from the law of contracts, including a 1937 Recommendation by the English Law Revision Committee to enact a statute to make signed written promises enforceable without regard to consideration; and although this recommendation was not followed in Britain, some American states have enacted legislation along similar lines:

> Pennsylvania has the most sweeping statute, under which any promise, even a purely gratuitous one, is not "unenforceable for lack of consideration, if the writing also contains an additional express statement, in any form of language, that the signer intends to be legally bound." A more common variety of legislation, found in over a dozen states including California, makes a writing "presumptive evidence of consideration." New York has enacted statutes making a writing a substitute for consideration in a limited number of situations, including promises supported only by "past consideration."[276]

In sum, once consideration is found in the mere issuance or in the exchange of a promise for a promise, a "bargained for" requirement is unnecessary and redundant.

---

[272] *Id.* at 63.

[273] RESTATEMENT (SECOND) § 6; U.C.C. § 2–205.

[274] GOODE ON COMMERCIAL LAW 77–78 (Ewan McKendrick ed., 4th ed. 2009; *see also* Roy Goode, *Abstract Payment Undertakings*, *in* ESSAYS FOR PATRICK ATIYAH (Peter Cane and Jane Stapleton eds., 1991). In addition to the above mentioned letters of credit and bank guarantees, Profesor Goode lists performance bonds. I would add to the list of abstract undertakings the promise to deliver the goods said to be stored or carried by a warehouseman or a carrier in his negotiable document of title if duly negotiated to a holder in due course. *See, e.g.*, U.C.C. § 7–502; Boris Kozolchyk, *Evolution and Present State of the Ocean Bill of Lading from a Banking Law Perspective*, 23 J. OF MAR. L. & COMMERCE 161, 173 (1992) (commenting on the abstraction of the U.S.-issued negotiability of ocean bills of lading).

[275] FARNSWORTH, *supra* note 185, at 89.

[276] *Id.* (citations omitted).

This is why Pennsylvania's statute best embodies the wisdom of Mansfield's solution. Where the enforcement of the original contract between its parties is concerned, eliminate the need for consideration, but make sure that the expression of the party's intent (in the case of unilateral promises) or the parties' promises faithfully portray their respective intent to be bound. And where what is sought is the protection of third parties interested in purchasing or negotiating contract rights and accounts, helpful international conventions and model laws as well as national statutes are now paving the way for progressively more abstract and liquid commercial promises. They allow for the account-debtors' waiver of defenses related to the account holder's improper performance or failure to supply adequate consideration as well as for the account debtor's agreement to raise such defenses only against the original holder or assignor of the account.[277]

In a world where three-quarters of the securities transactions in the contemporary marketplace are done over the computer and are based on preexisting forms of "dynamic" contracting, neither *causa* nor the bargained-for version of consideration can be regarded as "catalysts" of this type of contracting. Nonetheless, a form of giving, whether an initial promise, an act or a symbol of both, continues to be the catalyst for such transactions. Accordingly, contemporary legislators, judges and commentators cannot ignore such facts and the official law that they are shaping should follow the trends apparent in international conventions such as the CISG and compilations of customs such as the UCP, the International Standard Banking Practice (ISBP) of the ICC, or ISDA and other sources of law, both official and customary.

§ 22.10 APPENDIX: FORMALITIES AND SOLEMNITIES IN COMPARATIVE CASE LAW

A. Ibero-American and United States Case Law

This Appendix is devoted mostly to the study of formalities and solemnities in Ibero-American and United States court decisions and related statutory and customary law. As emphasized in the principal chapter, formality as a key element of the validity of contracts reflects a view of contract as a ceremonial event fixed in time and space (the latter by the terms and conditions set forth in the contractual document). In contrast, where contract is regarded as the parties' commercial conduct, formality is no longer a key element. The main purpose of this Appendix is to illustrate the normative and economic importance of this dichotomy through court decisions, comments, and questions.

The jurisdictions chosen as representative of contrasting views on contractual formality are those of Spain and Latin America on the one hand, and the United States on the other. The reason for this choice is that many jurisdictions in the two camps have opposite views on the formalities required of commercial contracts. It is my hope that the compiled decisions will help us understand the reasons for the sharply different rules. Do they reflect conflicting normative views on the nature of the transactions involved—some more in need of a formal-evidentiary record than others—

---

[277] United Nations Convention on the Assignment of Receivables in International Trade art. 9, Dec. 12, 2001, *available at* http://www.uncitral.org/pdf/english/texts/payments/receivables/ctc-assignment-convention-e.pdf.

or are they caused by contrasting methods of legal reasoning: A scholastic as opposed to a pragmatic or "logic of the reasonable" method of thinking.

In addition, while some of the Spanish decisions apply a principle of informality that resembles that of court decisions of the United States, many Latin American court decisions still cling to formality and solemnity as essential elements of the validity of a contract as commercial in nature as a life insurance policy. Is this divergence caused by the continuing presence of the Latin notaries and their *modus operandi* as discussed in Chapter 7? If so, what are the economic consequences, for example, of a small business not being able to obtain a loan secured by its inventory, equipment, or accounts receivable as collateral unless it is formally documented by a costly notarial deed that describes in detail all the goods that comprise the collateral? Can you visualize the cost of formally drafting and amending such a document each time new collateral is added to the secured loan or, when the goods described in detail as collateral are sold and others, similarly detailed, replace them? Finally, a reminder that I do not include cases on *causa* and consideration in this Appendix, important as these legal institutions are to the formation of commercial contracts, because court decisions on these issues are already an integral part of the discussion in the principal chapter.

B. Parmenides' Logic and the Validity of an Insurance Contract Under Uruguayan Law

1. *Applicable Law*

a. *Civil Code of Uruguay*

Article 1596. Testimony of the parties' witnesses will not be admitted as evidence to prove something different from the content of instruments [documents] or to justify something that was stated at the time of or subsequent to the granting of the instrument [document], even if its amount or value is less than 100 re-adjustable units.

Article 1574. Public instruments are all those official documents drafted or granted by authorized officials, according to the required forms and within their powers. Every public instrument is an authentic title, and as such it provides full proof, provided that it is not otherwise challenged by a claim of forgery. It is considered a public deed when the document is granted before a Notary Public and incorporated in the protocol [official paper used by Notaries] or recorded at a public registry. It is also considered a public deed when it is granted before an official authorized by law and in accordance with the requirements of law.

b. *Commercial Code of Uruguay*

Article 644. An insurance contract requires a written policy which may be public or private (Article 202).

Article 645. All insurance policies or contracts, except for life insurance, require: 1) Date on which the contract is granted; 2) Name of who requests the insurance, whether in his name or on behalf of a third party; 3) A sufficiently clear identification of what is insured and its actual or given fixed value; 4) The amount of the insurance; 5) Risks undertaken by the insurer; 6) The effective term in which the insurer's coverage of risks will begin and terminate; 7) The insurance premium; and 8) In general, all circumstances that might be of real interest to the insurer, as well as any other stipulations made by the parties.

2. *Decision by the Supreme Court of Uruguay, 1991, Volume 102, LJU Case 11695*[278]

. . .

SECOND:

The appellant filed her appeal to the Supreme Court alleging the violation and erroneous application of Articles 350 and 434 of the Code of Civil Procedure . . . and Articles 1596 [and] 1574 . . . of the Civil Code. . . . The appellant argues that the Trial Court erroneously evaluated the evidence presented in trial, especially the documents . . . which are public documents and as such prove that the insurance policy existed and was effective at the time of the incident.

She argues that it is prima facie evidence and thus the existence of the aforesaid contract cannot be disputed. . . . She further adds that because they are public documents, "according to Art. 1575 of the Civil Code, it cannot be disputed that . . . [the documents] are absolute legal proof of having entered into a contract and of its date. . . ."

WHEREAS:

The Court unanimously dismisses the appeal filed by the appellant, affirms the reasoning and holding of the first and second courts . . . and imposes the costs and fees of this appeal on the appellant. . . . The issue of the appeal is whether the Trial Court erroneously applied the legal provisions related to the evaluation of evidence, especially that of public documents. The "findings of facts" [according to the Trial Court] . . . can be summarized as follows: It begins by affirming that it "fundamentally shares the final conclusion on the dismissal of the complaint; that *there was never an insurance contract between the parties that allows recovery of the claimed compensation*."[279]

Forthwith the Court concludes: . . . that the original insurance policy in our records on file . . . shows that the document was never executed [because it lacked required formalities]. . . . In conclusion, there is no legal proof of compliance with the requirements stated under Articles 644 and 645 of the Commercial Code . . . [a] fact that has been acknowledged by the appellant when the appellant alleged the existence of a "material policy," one which does not include [the essential requirement of] a price. . . . [The] main issue is to determine whether the contract really existed, and whether payment of the price enabled it to produce all of its effects upon the occurrence of the incident at issue.

Based on the previous facts, the Civil Court held that an insurance policy was never executed. Because the insurance policy is a solemn contract, it is an unavoidable consequence that the legal relationship was never perfected; and if this is true, the alleged beneficiary of the insurance policy cannot claim payment of the price. . . . An insurance policy must be executed in a public or private deed [Art. 644 of the Commercial Code], and even when executed in a public deed it must comply with the

---

[278] Volume 102—Year 1991, LJU CASE 11695, Supreme Court of Justice. Appeal to the Supreme Court, Montevideo, July 16, 1990.

[279] Emphasis added.

requirements of law; this is the first evidentiary standard that Art. 1574 of the Civil Code regulates.

Summarizing: The Civil Court evaluated the evidence according to the rules of reason and sound judgment [Articles 402 and 349 of the Code of Civil Procedure] . . . in order to know if the contract existed or not. . . . [T]he law provides no other way for the Court to determine it. If the Court would have accepted the existence of an insurance policy [*i.e.*, that the contract was executed according to the requirements of law], then the solemnity of the insurance contract would have given it the value of prima facie evidence. However, in this case, deciding whether the contract was executed requires the use of reason and sound judgment, and the use of all means of evidence that may prove or deny the existence of said contract, including the use of assumptions, indications, circumstances, and even testimony. This proves that in order to determine whether the insurance contract existed, the Court used and correctly applied normal means of evidence.

COMMENTS AND QUESTIONS

Parmenides' axiomatic affirmation that opposite terms (such "being" v. "non-being") cannot each be valid is logically self-evident, but it does little to answer the basic issue of this case: Is a contract only a contract when it has been formally completed with all its t's crossed and i's dotted, or could a contract be valid if the parties behave as if they are governed by it? The Court's reasoning was that if there is no formally completed contract (meaning a document whose price or premium has not been specified), no evidence exists that such a contract was concluded. However, this argument is factually untenable.

The Supreme Court of Uruguay concludes that: "[T]here is no legal proof of compliance with the requirements stated under Articles 644 and 645 of the Commercial Code . . . [a] fact that has been acknowledged by the appellant when the appellant alleged the existence of a 'material policy,' one which does not include [the essential requirement of] a price." Yet, why is it essential that the insurance policy itself be the only possible document or record that sets forth the premium or price paid for it? Would the Court's opinion have been different if insurance experts in Uruguay had testified that a side note between the agent for the insurance company and the insured agreeing to a certain premium is evidence of an agreement on the price of the policy and that such a price can be filled in subsequently and be made part of the issued policy?

Furthermore, what if the insured submitted receipts signed by the insurer acknowledging the insured's payment of premiums? Or, what if the insurer's accounting records showed the policy in question as one "in force"? How would the above case have been decided in the reader's jurisdiction? Would the courts in the reader's jurisdiction look at the parties' conduct as suggested by the German author Christopher-Lehmann Haupt,[280] and as done by a ruling by a German court (that this author discusses) which found that a contract had been formed between a car driver and a security guard of a parking lot as a result of their repeated conduct or course of performance? When a court ignores the contract made evident by the parties' course of performance, course of dealing, or by commercial or economic sectors' usage of trade, is

---

[280] *See* PHILLIP HECK, GRUNDRISS DES SCHULDRECHTS 122 (1929) (*cited in* VON MEHREN & GORDLEY, *supra* note 90, at 830–31).

it not protecting and encouraging contractual bad faith, as was made clear by the Roman Praetor's "*exceptio doli*"?[281]

C. Heraclites' Being: Informality in the Formation of United States Agri-Business Contracts

1. The Informality of the Commercial Sale of an Automobile

a. Roy Buckner Chevrolet, Inc. v. Robert Cagle[282]

OPINION:

ALMON, Justice

Robert Cagle brought an action for breach of contract against Roy Buckner Chevrolet, Inc. A jury fixed his damages at $11,522.17.

In November, 1977, Cagle went to Roy Buckner Chevrolet to discuss the purchase of a 1978 Chevrolet Corvette, known as a "Limited Edition Corvette CP". General Motors Corporation produced only a limited number of these automobiles, which were referred to as "Indy Vettes" because one or more of them were used as pace cars at Indianapolis.

Cagle talked to the assistant used car manager, who referred him to Joel Kelly, the new car sales manager. The assistant used car manager partially filled out a "buyers order" form which was then presented to Kelly. After the initial discussion, Kelly agreed to sell Cagle an "Indy Vette" at list price. Kelly wrote "list price" and signed his name on the "buyers order". His signature did not appear in the space provided for the signature of an officer of Roy Buckner Chevrolet, but rather was signed in the middle of the page. The form was only partially completed at the time of Kelly's signature. Cagle also signed the order form and gave Kelly a $500 deposit. When the form was signed, Roy Buckner Chevrolet did not have an "Indy Vette" in its possession, but later received two such automobiles.

Roy Buckner Chevrolet notified Cagle that it would not sell him one of these cars and attempted to return his deposit. Cagle refused the attempted return of the deposit and brought suit.

There is no disagreement about damages, as the market value of this limited edition "Indy Vette" was substantially higher than the manufacturer's suggested list or sticker price. . . .

The appellant argues several issues for reversal, however. The principal one is whether a valid contract was consummated. Appellant asserts that there was never a meeting of the minds and that the memorandum was insufficient under Code 1975, § 7–2–201(1). That section states:

> (1) Except as otherwise provided in this section a contract for the sale of goods for the price of $500.00 or more is not enforceable by way of action or defense unless there is some writing sufficient to indicate that a contract for sale has been made between the parties and signed by the party against whom enforcement is sought or by his authorized agent or broker. A writing is not

[281] *See* § 23:1(C) (discussing the *exceptio doli's* role in shaping the Roman law doctrine of good faith).

[282] 418 So. 2d 878 (Ala. 1982).

> insufficient because it omits or incorrectly states a term agreed upon, but the contract is not enforceable under this paragraph beyond the quantity of goods shown in such writing.

The appellant claims that the "buyers order" was only partially complete and several important spaces were left blank, and therefore, that it does not comply with § 7–2–201(1). The "buyers order" is characterized by the appellant as nothing more than an agreement to enter into a future agreement. We do not agree [especially if due consideration is given to the testimonies of key participants of this transaction].

Kelly testified as follows:

Q: And you recall the situation and the dealings with Mr. Cagle on that occasion?

A: Yes, sir.

Q: Did you offer to sell that car to Mr. Cagle for list price?

A: Yes, sir.

Q: Did he accept that offer?

A: Yes.

Q: Did he make a down payment of $500 to Roy Buckner Chevrolet?

A: Yes, sir.

Q: Was he given a receipt for that down payment?

A: Yes, sir.

Q: Was he told that when the car came in, the first Indy 'Vette would be his?

A: Yes, sir.

Q: And when the car came in was he told it will not be sold to [sic] you?

A: Yes.

It is undisputed that Kelly was acting in his capacity as sales manager and was an agent for Roy Buckner Chevrolet, with the authority to contract. In light of Kelly's testimony, it is obvious that he intended to bind the parties immediately and not merely to agree at a future date. The question then becomes whether the "buyers order" form is a sufficient memorandum under the statute of frauds contained in § 7–2–201(1).

It is true that the order form is only partially complete and is not signed in the designated place by an officer of Roy Buckner Chevrolet. *However, open terms in a contract are not conclusive on the indefiniteness of the contract.*[283]

[As stated in § 2–204:]

> (1) A contract for sale of goods may be made in any manner sufficient to show agreement, including conduct by both parties which recognizes the existence of such a contract.

---

[283] Emphasis added.

(2) An agreement sufficient to constitute a contract for sale may be found even though the moment of its making is undetermined.

(3) *Even though one or more terms are left open a contract for sale does not fail for indefiniteness if the parties have intended to make a contract and there is a reasonably certain basis for giving an appropriate remedy.*

Code 1975, § 7–2–204.

The Official Comment to § 7–2–204 adds:

If the parties intend to enter into a binding agreement, this subsection recognizes that agreement as valid in law, despite missing terms, if there is any reasonably certain basis for granting a remedy. The test is not certainty as to what the parties were to do nor as to the exact amount of damages due the plaintiff. Nor is the fact that one or more terms are left to be agreed upon enough of itself to defeat an otherwise adequate agreement. Rather, commercial standards on the point of "indefiniteness" are intended to be applied, this Act making provision elsewhere for missing terms needed for performance, open price, remedies and the like.

The more terms the parties leave open, the less likely it is that they have intended to conclude a binding agreement, but their actions may be frequently conclusive on the matter despite the omissions.

The form is signed by both parties, and states the quantity and price of the car. Even though the price is stated to be the list price, we feel this is sufficiently definite. Code 1975, § 7–2–305, provides that parties may conclude a contract even though the price is not settled. In agreeing to let the price be fixed at the amount stated on the list, both parties were bound by the obligation of good faith contained in Code 1975, § 7–1–203.

. . .

Accordingly, the judgment is affirmed.

COMMENTS AND QUESTIONS

Please note that the court's principal goal was to satisfy the parties' reasonable expectations, even when some of the formal elements of the sale agreement were missing. Also note how the parties' disclosure of evidence with respect to the will of the parties prior to trial is influential on the result of the dispute. Each question asked during the oral hearing was matched to that which was previously discovered in the pre-trial discovery stage.[284] This is because one of the cardinal rules of the U.S. oral evidence procedure with regard to witness testimony is that the examining or cross-examining lawyer should not ask questions whose answer he or she cannot anticipate. The best way to achieve this result is through pre-trial discovery. Finally, also remember the flexible type of claim that is required for filing such complaints[285] under federal and most states' procedural law—one which allows the court to arrive at a decision that is consistent with current usage and practices in the marketplace.

The principle that one or more terms can be left open in a sale agreement (including its price) if the parties intended to make a contract and a reasonably certain

---

[284] *Id.* at 879–80. *See also infra* § 25:6 (discussing pre-trial discovery).

[285] *See infra* § 25:6 (discussing pre-trial discovery & complaint).

basis existed for giving an appropriate remedy (as formulated in U.C.C. § 2–204 and its Official Comment) is one of the core principles of the United States law of sales of goods. It was affirmed and expanded by the not yet adopted amendments to Article 2. Amended U.C.C. § 2–201(1) raises the contractual amount that requires a formality to $5,000.00.[286] Additionally, instead of referring only to the formality of a writing (as did the original § 2–201), it refers to a "record sufficient to indicate that a contract for sale has been made between the parties and signed by the party against which enforcement is sought. . . ."[287] Amended U.C.C. § 2–103, in turn, defines "record" as "information that is inscribed on a tangible medium or that is stored in an electronic or other medium and is retrievable in perceivable form."[288]

Reflecting the often quick and fluid nature of the negotiation of commercial contracts, the Official Comment to Amended § 2–201(1) states that:

> The record required by subsection (1) need not contain all of the material terms of the contract, and the material terms that are stated need not be precise or accurate. All that is required is that the record afford a reasonable basis to determine that the offered oral evidence rests on a real transaction. The record may be written on a piece of paper or entered into a computer. . . . The only term which must appear is the quantity term.[289]

b. *Heraclitean Features of Commercial and Financial Contracts*

Mid-South Packers, Inc. v. Shoney's, Inc.[290]

OPINION:

Per Curiam:

I.

The facts, as viewed in the light most favorable to Shoney's, are as follows. In the spring of 1982, Mid-South and Shoney's engaged in negotiations for the sale by Mid-South to Shoney's of various pork products including bacon and ham. . . . The discussion concerned prices and terms at which Mid-South could supply bacon and ham to Shoney's. At this meeting, Mid-South submitted a letter styled "Proposal" that set forth prices and terms at which Mid-South would supply Shoney's with various types of meat. The letter also provided that Shoney's would be informed forty-five days prior to any adjustment in price. The letter contained neither quantity nor durational terms. Shoney's expressed neither assent to nor rejection of the prices outlined in the letter. Shoney's estimated its needs from Mid-South at 80,000 pounds of meat per week. The legal effect of the letter proposal is the center of the controversy.

In July 1982, Shoney's began purchasing goods from Mid-South. The transactions were initiated by Shoney's, either through purchase orders or through telephone calls. On the day following each shipment, Mid-South sent invoices to Shoney's containing additional provisions for payment of both fifteen percent per annum interest on accounts not paid within seven days and reasonable collection costs, including attorney's fees. Shoney's bought vast quantities of bacon from Mid-South until August

---

[286] Amended U.C.C. § 2–201(1) (2003).

[287] *Id.*

[288] *Id.* § 2–103(1)(m).

[289] *Id.* § 2–201, cmt. 1.

[290] 761 F.2d 1117 (5th Cir. 1985).

12, 1982. On that date, Mid-South informed Shoney's at a meeting of their representatives that the price for future orders of bacon would be raised by $0.10 per pound, due to a previous error in computation by Mid-South. Shoney's objected to the price modification, apparently in reliance on the forty-five day notice provision contained in the disputed letter proposal. After negotiations, Mid-South agreed to increase the price by only $0.07 per pound. Shoney's neither agreed nor refused to purchase at the new price. Mid-South's new proposal was never reduced to writing.

On the first Shoney's purchase order sent after the August 12 meeting, Shoney's requested shipment at the old lower price. When Mid-South received the purchase order its representative, Morris Ates, called Shoney's representative, Ray Harmon, and advised Harmon that Mid-South would only deliver at the new higher price. The uncontradicted testimony of Ates is that Harmon told Ates to ship the bacon and to note the higher price on Shoney's purchase order. The bacon was shipped, and an invoice at the new price followed as did Shoney's payment, also at the new price.

From August 18 until October 5, 1982, Shoney's placed numerous orders for goods, including bacon, with Mid-South. Some if not all of these orders involved telephone conversations between representatives of the two companies, at which time Mid-South again quoted its increased selling price. . . . Shoney's paid Mid-South's quoted prices in all instances except the final order. On the final order . . . Shoney's offset the amount due on the invoice by $26,208, the amount allegedly overcharged on prior orders as a result of the $0.07 price increase.

Mid-South then brought this action to recover the amount offset plus interest and reasonable collection costs, including attorney's fees, as provided in the invoices. Shoney's admits that it owes $8,064.00 of the offset to Mid-South, inasmuch as this amount is attributable to orders placed after the expiration of the forty-five day notice period which, Shoney's contends, commenced on August 12 when Mid-South asked for the price increase.

II.

Shoney's contends that it accepted the proposal of Mid-South to supply it meat by placing orders with Mid-South, thereby [because of the parties' conduct] forming a binding contract between the parties. Shoney's characterizes the contract as a "requirements contract" and asserts that the quantity term under the contract was that amount it reasonably and in good faith required. Accordingly, Shoney's argues that the notice provision contained in the letter proposal contractually bound Mid-South to notify Shoney's forty-five days before increasing its prices.

Mid-South asserts that the proposal was at most a "firm offer." Mid-South argues that under Miss. Code Ann. § 75–2–205 (1972), Uniform Commercial Code § 2–205, (hereinafter referred to as U.C.C. or the Code), a firm offer is irrevocable despite a lack of consideration "during the time stated or if no time is stated for a reasonable time; but in no event may such period of irrevocability exceed three (3) months." Thus, Mid-South contends that under any construction of the document, the offer must have expired three months after April 17, 1982, the date of the letter proposal, or on approximately July 17, 1982; therefore, it asserts the right on August 12, 1982, to increase the selling price without notice.

The district court, on consideration of cross summary judgment motions, adopted Mid-South's theory, holding that no long-term requirements contract was created and that each purchase order constituted a separate contract for the amount stated at the price required by Mid-South.

Requirements contracts are recognized in Mississippi and are not void for indefiniteness. Miss. Code Ann. § 75–2–306(1). However, an essential element of a requirements contract is the promise of the buyer to purchase exclusively from the seller either the buyer's entire requirements or up to a specified amount.

Ray Harmon, Shoney's agent in the transaction, maintained that Shoney's at all times had the right to purchase goods from suppliers other than Mid-South. . . . Thus, by Shoney's own admission, no requirements contract could have arisen from the April 17 letter proposal and the meeting at which it was discussed.

Under the Code, the letter proposal and surrounding negotiations constituted, at most, a "firm offer" which was irrevocable, without consideration, only for a period of three months commencing on April 17 and ending on July 17, 1982. Miss. Code Ann. § 75–2–205. Thus, Mid-South had the right, after July 17, to raise its offered price as it did and the district court was correct in so holding.

The district court was also correct in holding that each purchase order stood on its own as a contract between Shoney's and Mid-South. . . . Thus, each time Shoney's manifested its assent, in telephone calls or purchase orders to Mid-South, a new and independent contract between the parties was created. . . . Finally, the parties' "course of performance" is consistent only with Mid-South's expressed offer and Shoney's expressed acceptance of the new price.

Shoney's remedy under the circumstances was either to reserve whatever right it might have had to the old price by sending its purchase orders with an "explicit reservation," Miss. Code Ann. § 75–1–207, or to find a supplier who would sell at an acceptable price. No rational theory of the law of contracts could permit Shoney's to manifest acceptance of Mid-South's new offer, thus inducing performance, and then revoke that acceptance and demand compliance with the terms of the prior, withdrawn offer. *See* Miss. Code Ann. § 75–2–606(1)(b); § 75–2–607(1). Hence, the entire $26,208 offset by Shoney's is due and owing Mid-South and the district court's judgment, to this extent, was proper.

. . .

AFFIRMED.

COMMENTS AND QUESTIONS

Please note that the court finds that at the center of this controversy is a "letter proposal" that Mid-South submitted to Shoney's. What is the precise legal nature of this letter? The court found that this letter set forth prices and terms at which Mid-South would supply Shoney's with various types of meat. It also stated that the buyer of the meat would be informed forty-five days prior to any adjustment in price. Yet, the letter was said by the court to contain "neither quantity nor durational terms." Hence, based upon U.C.C. § 2–201, as discussed in *Buckner* case, could this letter form the basis for a binding sale agreement? Further, Shoney's did not, according to the court, express either assent or rejection of the prices outlined in the letter, although it estimated its needs at 80,000 pounds of meat per week.

In light of the difficulties of determining the U.C.C. elements of formation of contract, what made for a binding contractual relationship between these parties? Shoney's and the United States Court of Appeals for the Seventh Circuit refer to the contract involved as a requirements contract. However, contractual classifications or typification do not seem to play any significant role in the previous or subsequent United States decisions. Why would the court have found it necessary to typify such a contract? It added that these contracts "are recognized in Mississippi and are not void for indefiniteness."[291] What made such a recognition and enforcement possible? I suggest that you read the subsequent *Warder & Lee Elevator* decision before you attempt to answer this question.

Financial Transactions: The Short Sales and "Naked" Short Sales of Investment Securities

In *Whistler Investments, Inc. v. Depository Trust and Clearing Corp.*, Judge Sidney Thomas described short sales and naked short sales as investment securities:

> "A short sale is a term of art used for a security trading practice in which a party 'speculates that a particular stock will go down in price and seeks to profit from that drop.'" The seller sells a security he does not own, borrows the security from a broker to meet the delivery obligation, and then purchases an identical security to return to the broker. If the security has declined in price between the sale and the purchase, the seller profits. In contrast, "a 'naked short sale' occurs when a seller sells a security without owning or borrowing it and does not deliver the security when due."[292]

What formalities, if any, are used in the short sale transactions such as those described? Given the quickness of their sequence, how detailed and solemn could these formalities be? You can assume that the amounts of money involved in each of these transactions vastly exceed the $500 that U.C.C. § 2–201 requires for a writing to be used or the $5,000 that Amended U.C.C. § 2–201 requires for a record to be kept. Then, what would be the likely text of the documents or records that contain the parties' intent? What tools does a judge or arbitrator have to interpret such intent?

D. Heraclites and Contract Formation as a Result of the Parties Conduct in Agri-Business

Warder & Lee Elevator, Inc. v. Britten[293]

OPINION:

McCormick, Justice

The question in this action for breach of an oral contract to sell grain is whether the trial court erred in holding defendant's statute of frauds defense under the Uniform Commercial Code was defeated by promissory estoppel. We affirm the trial court.

. . .

Plaintiff Warder & Lee Elevator, Inc., operates a grain elevator in the town of Webster. . . . [On] July 4, 1974 . . . Defendant John W. Britten, a farmer in the area, came to the office during the morning with a friend. The elevator had purchased Britten's grain for years, and he and Lee were well acquainted. At Britten's request

---

291 *Id.* at 1120.

292 539 F.3d 1159, 1162–63 (9th Cir. 2008) (citations omitted).

293 274 N.W.2d 339 (Iowa 1979).

Lee quoted him the price the elevator would pay for new-crop corn and soybeans for fall delivery based on market prices of the prior day.

Britten offered to sell and Lee agreed for the elevator to purchase from Britten 4000 bushels of corn at $2.60 per bushel and 2000 bushels of beans at $5.70 per bushel for October–November delivery. [A bushel is a measurement equivalent to 35.24 liters.]

The elevator did not at that time require a seller to sign a memorandum or other writing to show the agreement. Instead, the only writing consisted of notes showing the terms of sale made by Lee for internal bookkeeping purposes. All of the elevator's prior purchases from Britten had been upon oral agreement, and Britten had kept his promises on each occasion. In fact, no seller had previously refused to perform an oral agreement with the elevator.

It was the custom of the elevator not to speculate in grain but to act essentially as a broker. Thus on July 5, 1974, the elevator sold the same quantities of corn and beans as were involved in the Britten purchase for fall delivery to terminal elevators at Muscatine for a few cents more per bushel.

Grain prices increased substantially during July. On July 29, 1974, Britten called Francis Lee and said he wished to "call the deal off". Lee told him: "You cannot call it off. We sold this grain, and we expect delivery this fall." Britten said he would not deliver the grain.

In an effort to mitigate its loss and to enable it to meet its commitment to sell the grain, the elevator purchased appropriate quantities of new-crop corn and beans from other farmers on and shortly after July 29.

In August 1974, James Lee met Britten on a street in Webster. Britten initiated a conversation in which he said he would not fulfill his agreement and offered $500 in settlement. Although counsel for Britten objected to the admissibility of the evidence at trial, the objection was untimely and no motion to strike was made. Lee rejected the offer. He told Britten the elevator had sold the grain and expected him to perform under his contract.

Britten sold his 1974 crop elsewhere.

The elevator brought this action against Britten for breach of the oral agreement, seeking as damages the loss it sustained in covering its delivery obligation under the July 5 contracts by which it sold the quantity of grain purchased from Britten. *See* § 554.2712 of the Code. That loss was $6478.34, which was the amount, plus interest, for which the trial court entered judgment.

Britten offered no evidence at trial. He relied solely on the statute of frauds in § 554.2201 of the Code. The elevator urged promissory estoppel in bar of the defense.

The statute of frauds applicable to the sale of crops is § 554.2201. Under this statute an oral contract for the sale of goods for a price of $500 or more is unenforceable, with certain stated exceptions. The elevator does not contend any of those exceptions is applicable. Promissory estoppel is not among them.

Authority for use of promissory estoppel to defeat the statute of frauds, if it exists, must be found under § 554.1103. It provides:

> Unless displaced by the particular provisions of this chapter, the principles of law and equity, including the law merchant and the law relative to capacity

to contract, principal and agent, estoppel, fraud, misrepresentation, duress, coercion, mistake, bankruptcy, or other validating or invalidating cause shall supplement its provisions.

We have not had occasion to decide whether the provisions of § 554.2201 displace the doctrine of estoppel which would otherwise be available in accordance with § 554.1103. However, other courts which have considered the question have held the doctrine is available. Several of those decisions involved grain sales in circumstances analogous to those in the present case.

. . .

We have long recognized promissory estoppel as a means of defeating the general statute of frauds in § 622.32. We see nothing in § 554.2201 which purports to require a different rule under the Uniform Commercial Code.

The listing of exceptions to the statute of frauds in § 554.2201 is plainly definitional. The provision does not purport to eliminate equitable and legal principles traditionally applicable in contract actions. . . .

If § 554.2201 were construed as displacing principles otherwise preserved in § 554.1103, it would mean that an oral contract coming within its terms would be unenforceable despite fraud, deceit, misrepresentation, dishonesty, or any other form of unconscionable conduct by the party relying upon the statute. No court has taken such an extreme position. Nor would we be justified in doing so.

. . .

The issue is whether one has acted to his detriment in reliance upon the promise of another, and it is immaterial whether that promise was unilateral or bilateral.

Specific circumstances which justify use of the doctrine as a means of avoiding a statute of frauds defense are now expressed in Restatement (Second) of Contracts § 217A (Tent. Draft 1–7, 1973) as follows:

> (1) A promise which the promisor should reasonably expect to induce action or forbearance on the part of the promisee or a third person and which does induce the action or forbearance is enforceable notwithstanding the Statute of Frauds if injustice can be avoided only by enforcement of the promise. The remedy granted for breach is to be limited as justice requires.

. . .

In order to obtain the benefit of the doctrine of promissory estoppel to defeat a statute of frauds defense, the promisee must show more than the nonperformance of an oral contract. Under § 217A the defense cannot be overcome, when it is otherwise applicable, unless the promisee proves (1) the promisor should reasonably have expected the agreement to induce action or forbearance, (2) such action or forbearance was induced, and (3) enforcement is necessary to prevent injustice.

. . .

AFFIRMED.

COMMENTS AND QUESTIONS

As apparent from the preceding decisions, U.S. courts do not typically discuss if they are dealing with a consensual, synallagmatic, commutative, or other type of contract. Rather, they focus their analysis on the facts, applying a pragmatic criterion with respect to the role that formality plays in the existence of a contract. A phone conversation, a partially completed and incorrectly signed purchase order, and telex communications can all be considered a contract, as well as a check with an annotation related to the transaction for which it was used. This case in particular reflects the importance that courts attribute to the parties' contractual conduct, whether manifested in the course of performance in the contract in question or the parties' prior course of dealing, and the usages or customs of the trade. Recall Judge McCormick's findings of fact:

> The elevator had purchased Britten's grain for years, and he and Lee were well acquainted. At Britten's request Lee quoted him the price the elevator would pay for new-crop corn and soybeans for fall delivery based on market prices of the prior day.
>
> . . .
>
> The elevator did not at that time require a seller to sign a memorandum or other writing to show the agreement. . . . All of the elevator's prior purchases from Britten had been upon oral agreement, and Britten had kept his promises on each occasion. In fact, no seller had previously refused to perform an oral agreement with the elevator.
>
> It was the custom of the elevator not to speculate in grain but to act essentially as a broker.[294]

These facts, which can be summarized as the contractual conduct of the parties and their usage of trade, are closely connected with the equitable doctrine of estoppel. As is the case with many of our contemporary legal institutions, the Roman Praetor led the way when refusing to enforce conduct that contradicts the parties' previous and relied upon conduct. It is for this reason that he enjoined a party's *venire contra factum proprium*.

E. Spanish Case Law: Formalities *ad Solemnitatem* and *ad Probationem*

Informality of contractual promises under Spanish civil law has a long, but not always aristocratic tradition. It will be recalled that according to the thirteenth century *Fuero de Navarra*, promises to do or give something in the future entered into by German-Spanish aristocracy (or that of the limited nobility or *infanzones*) did not bind them. However, villains (*villanos,* meaning not only peasants or miscreants, but also city dwellers) were bound to comply with promises of deferred performance by mere consent: "if a villain promises, he shall give."[295]

F. The Spiritualistic Principle in the Spanish Civil Code

The Spanish Civil Code of 1889 adopted a "spiritualistic" (or "formality is not required") principle, particularly found in Articles 1254, 1258, 1278, 1279 and 1280 that provide, in their relevant parts:

Article 1254: A contract exists from the moment one or several persons consent in obligating themselves. . . .

---

294 *Id.* at 340–41.

295 FUERO DE NAVARRA, III, 19, 6.

Article 1258: Contracts are perfected by mere consent. . . .

Article 1278: Contracts are binding in whichever form they are granted, provided that they comply with the essential conditions required for their validity.

Article 1279: If the law requires that for a contractual obligation to be effective it needs to be granted in a public deed or by means of other special forms, the parties may compel each other to comply with said formality from the time of their consent and from the moment they comply with other elements required for its validity.

Article 1280: The following shall be granted in a public deed:

1. Acts and contracts, whose purpose is to create, transfer, modify or terminate any *in rem* rights over real estate property.

2. Lease agreements of the aforesaid assets, for a term of six or more years, provided that they are effective against third parties.

3. Marriage agreements and their amendments.

4. Assignments, rejections and disclaimers to hereditary rights or marital agreements.

5. Powers of attorney to enter into marriage, general power to litigate and special powers to be used in trials; powers to manage assets and any others whose purposes are acts that have to be granted in or drafted to be granted in a public deed, or that is effective against third parties.

6. Assignments of claims or rights resulting from an act granted in a public deed.[296]

It is also required to grant in writing, at least in a private document, any other contract where the value of the obligations, of at least one of the parties, exceeds 1,500 pesetas. As will be discussed,[297] the renowned Professor Ernst Rabel, one of the pioneers of the comparative law of sales, characterized this principle in the 1950s as embodying modern legal science and urged Professor Llewellyn not to adopt it for Article 2 of the U.C.C.

G. Supreme Court Decision No. 1743, March 12, 1994, Civil[298]

Mr. Ricardo L.G. filed an ordinary declarative claim for breach of contract against Mrs. Lucia U.U. and the Real Estate Agency J.M.I. The Trial Court of Amurrio issued its opinion on April 10, 1990 in favor of the plaintiff. On appeal, the Court of Appeals partially reversed the Trial Court's decision in favor of the co-defendant, the Real Estate Agency. The Supreme Court hereby dismisses the appeal.

Opinion by Honorable Mr. D. Pedro Gonzalez Poveda

Findings of Law:

First:

In the lawsuit filed before the Trial Court, the now appellee sought judgment for specific performance for the signature of public deeds for the sale of real

---

[296] C.C. (SPAIN) (1889) arts. 1254, 1258, 1278, 1279, 1280.

[297] *See infra* § 23:5(D)(2)(b).

[298] S.T.S., Mar. 12, 1994 (R.J., No. 1743) (Spain).

estateproperty, and for the buyer to grant full title over the acquired property by delivering the keys to it [the property] and by providing notice that upon non-performance within the given peremptory term, the Judicial Authority would perform it, and also to pay the legal fees of the complainant, or to reimburse the down payment to the buyer for the amount of two million pesetas [2.000.000] plus legal interest and legal fees. The basis for such claim is that the plaintiff bought a property from Mrs. Lucia U.U., who had given a power of attorney to the Real Estate Agency J.M.I. to sell the real estate property, and having entered into the sale agreement with Mr. José María C., son-in-law of the owner, on behalf of whom he was acting, and having fixed the price on seven million pesetas, the buyer gave the aforesaid Agency the amount of one million pesetas as down payment.

The Second Division of the Provincial Court of Appeals of Bilbao rendered judgment in appeal partially reversing the Trial Court's judgment, affirming the judgment against Mrs. Lucia U.U. to perform her obligation to grant full title over the property located in Ugarte (Llodio), and to perform her obligation to sign the public deeds of sale within the term of ten days after full payment was effected; or upon non-performance, then judicial performance would follow.

Second:

The first issue on appeal is based on Article 1692 numeral 5 of the Law of Civil Procedure, alleging a violation of Article 1280.1 of the Civil Code because the power of attorney under which Mr. José María C. acted is not evidenced in the files of the proceedings. There is no public deed containing a power of attorney authorizing the sale of real estate property. In a February 3, 1987 decision (RJ 1987, 674), it is stated that case law has established that according to Articles 1278 and 1279 of the Civil Code, the provisions of Article 1280 do not require formalities "*ad solemnitatem*" but only "*ad probationem*," meaning that a trial court judge can decide on the existence of a contract that complies with the requirements of Article 1261 of said Code without necessarily having to rely on a written document; the Court "*a quo*" may grant its existence through the evaluation of evidentiary instruments provided therein; the decisions of February 21, 1987 (RJ 1987, 727), September 30, 1988 (RJ 1988, 6939) and November 23, 1989 (RJ 1989, 7905) follow the same reasoning. A doctrine long applied by this Court with respect to powers of attorney is found in the holding of the October 30, 1906 decision which states that express powers of attorney granted by the principal to his brothers exclude the principal's need to personally deal with the buyer; it presupposes the principal's agreement to sell and may be granted verbally, as provided in Article 1710 of the Code. Thus, what Article 1280 requires in its last paragraph is that all contracts that exceed the amount of 1.500 pesetas have to be executed in writing; but it does not say that this is a requirement for their perfection. Case law without the need of further arguments renders the issues on appeal inadmissible. . . .

COMMENTS AND QUESTIONS

In this case, the Supreme Court distinguished between the formality of written documents as requirements *ad solemnitatem* and requirements *ad probationem*. It is a requirement *ad solemnitatem* when, without the written formality, the contract is not perfected. On the other hand, it is a requirement *ad probationem* when it is required to prove the existence of the contract, or to allow its registration. The Court concluded that a power of attorney is not a solemn contract. It held that Article 1280 of the Civil Code "requires in its last paragraph . . . that all contracts that exceed the amount of

1.500 pesetas have to be executed in writing; but it does not say that this is a requirement for their perfection." What is the source of law used by the Supreme Court to make such a distinction between *granting* and *perfecting* contracts? Is it a legislative, judicial, or doctrinal source of law? What would justify making such a distinction? Finally, if the distinction is not based on a legislative source of law, would the aphorism "where the law makes no distinction, the interpreter must not distinguish" be applicable?

H. Supreme Court Decision No. 6424, July 4, 1994, Civil[299]

Mito, S.A. filed a small claim against Aleaciones de Metal, S.A. to recover damages for breach of a requirements contract. The Trial Court number 12 of Barcelona decided on January 7, 1991 partially in favor of the plaintiff, ordering the defendant to pay for damages to be determined in the execution of the judgment; this decision was affirmed by the First Division of the Provincial Court of Appeals of Barcelona on April 22, 1991. The defendant filed an appeal to the Supreme Court. The Supreme Court dismissed the appeal.

Opinion by the Honorable Mr. D. Jesús Marina Martínez-Pardo

. . .

Third:

The allegation on appeal claims the erroneous application of Article 1280, based on Article 1692 numeral 5, specifically in the paragraph dealing with the violation of laws of the legal system, both Articles of the Civil Code. The appellant argues that the Court infringed said Articles by accepting the existence of a contract based on the freedom of forms and on assumptions, and by concluding that the contract was a requirements contract. The appellant leaves the issue of assumptions for the next allegation, and concludes by citing Articles 1278, 1279 and 1280 of the Civil Code, where the last paragraph of Article 1280 of the Civil Code states that: "It is also required to grant in writing, at least in a private document, any other contract where the value of the obligations, of at least one of the parties, exceeds 1,500 pesetas." In the case at issue, there was no public deed granted.

According to the continuous and consistent interpretation of these Articles, the argument of the appellant is completely at odds with the content of the cited legal provisions—in such a way that it should be enough to remind the appellant that in our Law there is absolute freedom of forms (Articles 1255 and 1278); that where the law establishes a written formality, it can either be *ad probationem* or *ad solemnitatem*; that in the case at issue, a solemnity cannot be required by Law because the Law does not regulate this type of contract; that where the Code refers to a non-solemn public deed or private document, the correct interpretation of Article 1280 in relation to 1279 is that the parties can compel each other to grant the contract in such way.

Fourth:

For all the aforesaid, the appeal to the Supreme Court is hereby dismissed and legal fees and loss of the deposit are on the appellant in accordance with Article 1715 of the Law of Civil Procedure.

---

[299] S.T.S., July 4, 1994 (R.J., No. 6424) (Spain).

COMMENTS AND QUESTIONS

In the previous case, the Spanish Court distinguished the requirements of Article 1280 of the Civil Code from those of Article 1279. Article 1279 states that:

> If the law requires that for a contractual obligation to be effective it needs to be granted in a public deed or by means of other special forms, *the parties may compel each other* to comply with said formality from the time of their consent and from the moment they comply with other elements required for its validity.[300]

What is the connection between the "spiritualistic" principle, the natural law of European pre-codification,[301] and the parties' freedom of contract? How do these principles contribute to the certainty of contracts? Which of the principles used by the courts in the previous decisions are more compatible with the needs of a globalized market?

I. Salvadoran Case Law: Solemnity of a Waybill and Classification of Contracts[302]

Heraclites or Parmenides?

The Bill of Lading[303] as a Formal Requirement for All Transportation Contracts: Decision of the Supreme Court of El Salvador

CIVIL COURTROOM OF THE SUPREME COURT OF JUSTICE: San Salvador, at the Tenth hour of the 22nd of December 2002.

Analysis of the Appeal:

The appellant has two allegations on appeal: the first is for erroneous interpretation of the law in violation of Articles 1330 and 1331 of the Commercial Code; and the second, for erroneous application of the law pertaining to testimonial evidence in violation of Article 321 of the Code of Civil Procedure. On the first allegation, the appellant argues that the Court *ad quem* gave a special legal connotation to transportation contracts because it considered the bill of lading as the only means of evidence to prove the parties' agreements, providing it with a legal nature that it does not have, *i.e.*, a solemnity *per se* and not a solemnity *ad probationem* as is the spirit and sense of the law. Furthermore, even if the reasoning of the Court of Appeals that the bill of lading is a means to prove a transportation contract is true, it is not so given the way that the Court reasoned in its decision because Article 1331 of the Salvadoran Commercial Code does not exclude other means of evidence, and it does not require that for the use of these other means it is necessary to prove that the bill of lading pre-existed and was subsequently misplaced or destroyed.

The Court of Appeals' reasoning was that the cause of the debt that the defendant claims results from a transportation contract entered into by an individual whose course of business is transportation and a corporation and therefore, the contract is governed by the provisions of the Commercial Code. This Code regulates said contract

---

300 C.C. (Spain) (1889) art. 1279 (emphasis added).

301 *See supra* § 8:2.

302 El Salvador: Case law, No. C 1003 (Dec. 21, 2002), *available at* http://natlaw.com/natlaw-world/.

303 The term "bill of lading" in this decision refers to a non-negotiable bill of lading.

under Article 1313 and defines it as the contract where the carrier is bound to transport people or goods from one place to another in exchange for a price. In the instant case, we are dealing with the transportation of goods and not people; thus, Article 1319 of the Commercial Code is applicable, and it establishes that the carrier bears all obligations and liabilities regarding the transportation of goods. Generally, this contract is granted and formalized by the mere consent of the parties, which can be verbal, as it is a consensual contract; it is a bilateral contract because there are two parties involved, with reciprocal stipulations or obligations; it is an onerous contract as all other commercial contracts are, because the person who provides the service is entitled to receive a price.

Notwithstanding the fact that it is a consensual contract, Article 1330 of the Commercial Code requires the bill of lading as a formality of the contract, a document with no constitutive effects but only required for evidentiary purposes. The carrier has the obligation to issue a bill of lading which, as was previously stated, is a way to prove the existence and content of the contract. This view is shared by Professors Joaquin Rodríguez Rodríguez and Emilio Langle Rubio, among others. The content of the bill of lading will decide any issues on the enforcement and performance of the contract, only allowing claims or defenses for forgery of the document or material error in its wording. In accordance with Article 1338 of the Commercial Code, the bill of lading should be returned by the shipper to the carrier upon performance of the contract and at that moment, all rights and obligations are deemed to be extinguished. All of the above reaffirms that the bill of lading is used as a means of evidence; and furthermore, Article 1338 of the Commercial Code states that if the shipper cannot return the bill of lading because he lost it, the shipper will then issue and provide the carrier with a receipt of delivery of the goods, and this receipt will have the same effects as returning the bill of lading.

The legal provisions of the Salvadoran Commercial Code which were supposedly infringed are the following:

Art. 1330. The bill of lading is the document that proves the contract between the shipper and the carrier, upon which issues on the enforcement and performance of the contract will be decided, only allowing claims or defenses for forgery of the document or material error in its wording.

Art. 1331. When the original and copy of the bill of lading are lost, any issues pertaining to it will be decided according to the evidence provided by the parties. Any condition omitted from the document can also be proven.

From the analysis of these provisions it is clear that the contract for the transportation of goods is proven with the bill of lading; that matters regarding its enforcement and performance will be decided in light of what was agreed in said document; that the bill of lading only allows for claims or defenses for forgery of the document or material error in its wording; and that when the bill of lading is lost, the issues arising from it shall be decided according to the evidence that the parties may provide.

After analyzing the Court of Appeals' reasoning, this Court finds that the alleged violation by the Court *ad quem* has no grounds, because, contrary to what the appellant argues, the Court has given the correct legal interpretation to the law. In fact, in applying the law to the case at issue, the Court of Appeals has established that the transportation contract is a consensual contract, that it is generally granted verbally, and that for evidentiary purposes the contract shall be stated in the bill of lading; but in lack thereof, its content may be proven through other means of evidence. . . .

Notwithstanding the consensual nature of the contract, for evidentiary purposes, the agreement between the one who provides the service and the beneficiary of that service is materialized in a bill of lading. This is stated under Article 1330 which is previously cited, but in its absence, the contract may be proven through other means of evidence as provided by law, such as testimony, which is evidence permitted by law for this type of contract. This is why testimony is indeed relevant to the case at issue. However, as previously stated, in this type of contract, the law establishes that only in the absence of a written contract can other means of evidence be used.

In the present case, it can be deduced from the statements in page one of the claim that the transportation contract between the defendant Central American Shippers, S.A. and the appellant Mr. Humberto Hernán Fuentes Valle was verbal; hence there was no bill of lading, and, therefore, he filed a commercial declarative summary complaint to establish the existence of the defendant's obligation to pay the price agreed in the contract and default of payment. . . . In addition to the fact that there was no written contract, there is a letter sent to the appellant by Mr. Lincoln J. Martín Jr. on behalf of the defendant, where he accepts the existence of a contractual relationship and the existence of payment due. . . .

The witnesses . . . established that Mr. Humberto Hernán Fuentes Valle . . . provided transportation services to the company Central American Shippers, S.A. from Santo Tomás de Castilla, Republic of Guatemala, to the Ground Customs Administration in our country, El Salvador . . . [and] that resulting from such services, the aforesaid company originally owed Mr. Fuentes Valle the amount of 374,516.04 Colones. . . . The Court *ad quem* erred as a matter of law in the evaluation of the evidence presented, violating the provisions of Article 321 of the Code of Civil Procedure which establishes the legal value of testimonial evidence. The Court failed to give the testimonial evidence the correct evidentiary value established by law, as they are the correct and pertinent evidence to this case. And for these reasons it is appropriate to reverse the appealed decision, it is so declared.

COMMENTS AND QUESTIONS

Apparently, in the Court's opinion, the transportation contract is consensual and obligatory from the moment it is agreed on. Therefore, the Court considers that the document that embodies the bill of lading is a requirement *ad probationem*—that when it is missing, it can be proven through other means. Where does the consensual nature of the Salvadoran transportation contract come from? All that Article 1313 of the Salvadoran Commercial Code, cited by the Court, states is:

> In the contract of transportation, the carrier is bound to transport people or goods from one place to another in exchange for a price. This contract will be commercial when it is provided by companies that provide this service to the public in the ordinary course of their business.

Notice that there are different types of transportation contracts and different documents related to them. In maritime transportation, the bill of lading, especially the negotiable one, represents title to the transported goods. If the consignee or its beneficiary does not have these bills of lading, then they are simply missing the required documents to claim the goods from the carrier. This does not apply to transportation via train, air, or ground. In such transportation, the document issued by the carrier is a mere receipt and not a required document or a document of title. Based on the law as well as on customs and practices of international and local transportation pertaining to the classification of this contract as consensual, what is the importance of this distinction?

If the legislator does not classify the transportation contract as consensual, is it possible that the parties in their own contract can agree that it is their intention that the contract be consensual? What is the importance of the parties' ability to classify a contract as consensual? Or is a "higher authority" required for this? Would the opinion of a doctrinal commentator be considered this higher authority?

J. Mexican Case Law on Contractual Formality and Solemnity

Definition of Constitutive and Declarative Documents

Séptima Época, Third Chamber, October 15, 1956

Mexican Law also distinguishes between requirements *ad probationem* and *ad solemnitatem*. The following is an excerpt of a court's decision that adheres to the Spanish and Salvadoran perspective:

> Next to constitutive or *ad solemnitatem* documents are those declarative or *ad probationem* documents. The former are those without which the legal act that they incorporate cannot be brought to life, and it is said that they are constitutive of the act itself, as is the case with marriage contracts, promissory notes, checks, etc. The latter are used to prove the act or contract incorporated within them, but do not exclude the possibility of the parties proving the act or contract through other means, as is the case with sale agreements where form is not a constitutive element, although it may be for its effects against third parties; and form is so far from being a constitutive element of sale agreements that even when the law requires that the contract be granted in a public deed, its ineffectiveness may be eliminated, regardless of its lack of form, if the parties willingly perform it.[304]

COMMENTS AND QUESTIONS

According to this decision, lacking the formality of a public deed will render the contract relatively null, but not absolutely null and void or nonexistent. However, other Mexican decisions do require formalities *ad solemnitatem*. For example, according to a court of appeals:

> A contract for the assignment of rights as a gift, granted in the State of Quintana Roo, is found to be absolutely null and void because it was not recorded at the Public Registry of Property. Based upon a harmonious interpretation of Articles 2228, 2397, 2610, 2616, 2617, 3159 and 3160 of the Civil Code of the State, this legal act constitutes a contract of donation, which is a solemn contract that requires registration for its legal existence. Such registration is an essential element for the existence of this type of contract; if

---

[304] La Forma No es Elemento Constitutivo de la Compraventa, Pleno de la Suprema Corte de Justicia [SCJN] [Supreme Court] Semanario Judicial de la Federación y su Gaceta, Séptima Época, tomo XC, Octubre de 1956, Tesis Tercera Sala, Cuarta Parte, Página 59 (Mex.), *available at* http://ius.scjn.gob.mx/paginas/externas/detalle.aspx?id=241259 (also on file with this author) (this author's translation). I am thankful to Lic. Manuel Pliego from the LL.M. program in International Trade Law at the James E. Rogers College of Law, University of Arizona 2004–2005, for providing me with this source.

this requirement is not complied with, the contract cannot produce any legal effects.[305]

What might be the reasoning for requiring a solemnity for the assignment of rights as gifts and not for the sale agreement of personal property or real estate property?

K. Preparatory Contracts and Public Deeds Under Mexican Law

Maria Trinidad Gómez Jiménez—Direct Amparo[306]

(Supreme Court dismisses the amparo.)

PROMISE TO SELL (LAW OF JALISCO): A promise only creates obligations to do, which are included in the corresponding contract and are in accordance with what has been offered. For its effectiveness, it is required that it be granted in writing, that it has the essential elements and characteristics of the final contract, and that it be limited to a specific term.

Articles 2163 to 2167 of the Civil Code clearly state that a promise to sell must include the elements particular to a sale agreement, *i.e.*, its determination and price. A promise does not transfer ownership of the offered good; it only creates an obligation to do—that of the granting of the final contract by the obligated party provided that the other party requests it within the term stipulated in the promise. In this case, the parties consent that their agreement is not regarding an actual transaction but rather a future contract; thus the buyer's payment on consignment does not grant him the right to receive the contractual good.

OPINION:

. . .

Second: The appellant alleged that the lower court reached its decision based on the opinions of foreign authors instead of basing it on the Civil Code of the State of Jalisco. This statement is incorrect; the court based its opinion in the first place on the provisions of the Civil Code of said State in effect at the time of the execution of the document and only secondarily did it refer to the opinions of foreign commentators.

Third: In summary, the appellant then refers to the violation of [various articles of the Civil Code of the State of Jalisco] and others of the Code of Civil Procedures. According to the appellant, the court disregarded the law which, for the existence of a sale agreement and transfer of property rights, only requires that the parties agree on an identifiable thing and its price, even when the former has not been delivered or the latter has not been paid, in the absence of an agreement otherwise.

This allegation has no grounds because Articles 2163 to 2167 of the Civil Code of the State of Jalisco regulate preparatory contracts, specifically that of a promise. In those provisions it is established that one can undertake the obligation to execute a

---

[305] Cesion de Derechos. El Contrato no Inscrito en el Registro Público de la Propiedad está Afectado de Nulidad Absoluta, Segundo Tribunal Colegiado del Décimo Cuarto Circuito [TCC] [Collegiate Circuit Court], Semanario Judicial de la Federación y su Gaceta, Novena Época, tomo IV, Noviembre de 1996, Tesis XIV.2o.15C, Página 411, *available at* http://ius.scjn.gob.mx/paginas/externas/detalle.aspx?id=200886 (on file with this author).

[306] Maria Trinidad Gómez Jiménez, 125 SJF5a 355 (1955), *in* WOODFIN L. BUTTE, SELECTED MEXICAN CASES 305–08 (1967) (any changes made are to aid in clear understanding).

future contract, allowing for this contract to be a preliminary contract or a promise, whether unilateral or bilateral. The promise only creates an obligation to do, consisting of granting the contract in accordance with what was offered. To be valid, the promise must be set out in writing, contain the characteristic elements of the definitive contract and be limited to a certain period of time.

From these provisions it is clear that a promise to sell must have the elements and characteristics of a sale, *i.e.*, determination of the good and the price. Thus Article 2819 of the 1934 Civil Code of Jalisco provided:

> For a simple promise to sell to have legal effects, when dealing with real estate property or non-fungible movable property, it is necessary to determine the type of asset. With fungible movable property, it is only necessary to determine its genre and quantity. In every case price must be determined.

Determination of the good and price are essential requirements, as is also the term for which the promise will remain in force, *i.e.*, which time period the interested party must compel performance for the granting of the final contract.

Therefore, a promise does not transfer ownership of the offered good, but only creates an obligation to do, *i.e.*, granting the final contract, provided that the other party so requests it within the term of the promise. In this case, the parties' agreement and will pertains to a future contract and not to a present transaction. Consequently, the contract granted in a public deed which supports this claim is not a sale agreement under which property rights have been transferred even though the good and price have not yet been delivered or paid, respectively. It is a simple contract promising to sell under which property rights were not transferred and where payment on consignment of the aforementioned amounts in favor of the defendants did not grant the appellant the right to receive the assets at issue. The appellant indicates that the term of one year as agreed in the contract was not for her to accept the contract because she had already accepted it, but rather was agreed on for payment of the price. This argument is incorrect, because the period agreed on in the promise to sell was for the effective term of the promise and within which Mrs. Gómez Jiménez could compel performance of the final sale agreement.

Fourth: The appellant, based on the legal provisions mentioned in the preceding allegation which she believed had been infringed, argues that the corresponding authority found that the sale transaction was not completed because the price was not paid in due time. This statement is incorrect. The court did not hold that the sale agreement ceased to have effects because its price was not paid in due time, but rather the court merely held that in the instant case there was no sale agreement and that the appellant had allowed for the term of the promise to elapse, because the term expired on the last day of August 1935. The appellant also alleges the court's failure to apply several theses published in the Appendix to Volume XCVII of the Semanario Judicial de la Federación. This allegation is dismissed because the theses referred to by the appellant (240 to 243) refer to sale agreements and not to contracts of promises to sell. Thesis 848, published in said Appendix, clearly states that "a promise to sell does not transfer property rights to goods because it only creates an obligation to do consisting on the granting of the final contract."

Fifth: The appellant makes reference to [the course of dealing that preceded] the contract in dispute. For instance, she refers to a mortgage claim filed against her father in which, according to her, it was decided that the defendants had, in one single act, entered into a first contract as buyers and entered into a second contract selling and transferring property rights to the appellant. This allegation has no grounds since, as previously said, the clear wording of the contract is that of a promise to sell.

Additionally, the appellant cites a decision of the Auxiliary Chamber of the Supreme Court of Justice, amparo number 7326–50, arguing that in said decision it was held that the contract at issue was a true sale agreement and not a promise to sell. This is incorrect. The facts argued in the aforementioned amparo resulted from a claim filed by Mrs. María Trinidad Gómez Jiménez and her brothers against the Mestas and requesting a declaration of ineffectiveness, inexistence or nullity of the contracts granted in the public deed of August 31, 1934. That constitutional claim was decided against Mrs. Gómez Jiménez and her brothers in a holding that makes no reference, of any kind, to the contract being a sale agreement rather than a promise to sell. It is worth noting that in the claim on which the previously-mentioned amparo was based, the appellant herself established that there was a promise by the Mestas to sell to her, as well as a sale agreement granted by her parents to the Mestas, and that both transactions were simulations, and that in fact it was a loan agreement secured with a mortgage. Consequently, the present arguments made by the appellant and those argued in the original lawsuit where the facts of this amparo are being discussed are contradictory.

. . .

Seventh: Since the infringements alleged by Mrs. María Trinidad Gómez Jiménez have no grounds, it is appropriate to deny Constitutional protection because there was no violation of her guarantees as stated in Articles 14 and 16 of the Constitution.

Given the aforementioned . . . we hold that:

[This Court] does protect Mrs. María Trinidad Gómez Jiménez against the [decisions] of the First Chamber of the Supreme Court of Justice of the State of Jalisco and the Fourth Civil and Treasury Judge of Guadalajara. . . .

COMMENTS AND QUESTIONS

Although the terms and conditions of the contract are not included in the findings of facts, from the facts summarized by the Court, it is possible to infer that the appellant had an option to purchase real estate property at a given price within a one-year term from the date of the option, and that when she tried to pay the agreed price, *before the term elapsed*, the defendant refused to transfer the real estate property. Apparently, the reason for the refusal was that the appellant omitted to take the middle step of obtaining a public deed from the seller that would convey title to the real estate. The Supreme Court concluded that the buyer could not have exercised his option unless he compelled the seller to grant the final contract. Because the appellant filed her complaint to force the granting of the public deed after the term of the promise had elapsed, her claim was dismissed.

Notice that in concluding this, the Court classified the contract as a preparatory contract as opposed to a final contract. Hence, a contract that created an obligation to do (grant the sale contract) instead of an obligation to give (transfer property rights to the real estate property). If one needed a clear illustration of the importance of classifications of obligations and contracts in Mexican law, this one should suffice. Yet, how far is this precedential decision or "individual norm" from the usages of the real estate trade in Mexico? Is the method described by the Court on the execution of promises to purchase real estate property the way in which they are actually executed in the Mexican real estate market? Is it the common practice of sellers or their brokers or agents to wait until a buyer files a lawsuit compelling the granting of the public deed, and then drafting the document before receiving payment of the price or assurance of payment?

Such a transactional method does not seem reasonable, especially given the possibility of the buyer deciding not to purchase once the seller has sustained the costs of preparing the public deed. If one were to ask Mexican real estate brokers or investors about the common procedure used in acquiring real estate property through promises to sell, what would be the traditional *modus operandi* before the term of the promise elapses? Would it be: 1) File a formal lawsuit requesting that the seller grant the sale document, specifying a date for compliance; 2) After this additional term has elapsed, file a claim before the courts for specific performance; or 3) Go to the courthouse and deposit the sale price and receive a court's decision on the performance of the promise? Or would it be more efficient, reasonable, and thus a better practice to do what the buyer did in this case: Notify the seller that the buyer is willing to purchase the real estate property under the conditions stipulated in the contract of promise to sell, and inquire where to pay or deposit payment of the price, whether directly to the seller, before a notary, or through a bank account deposit especially designated for payment of the promise? Unfortunately, it was not common usage that had a greater influence on the determination of a transactional formula in this decision, but rather the classification of the contract, regardless of the unnecessary costs and uncertainty resulting from the transactional formula applied in this decision.

Two Mexican real estate brokers from the AMPI (the prestigious *Asociación Profesional de Intermediarios o Corredores Inmobiliarios* (Professional Association of Real Estate Intermediaries and Brokers)) who preferred to remain anonymous described their practice with options to purchase or promises to sell in July of 2009 as follows:

> As real estate brokers, we could not engage in transactions to purchase real estate property through the use of these options or promises if we had to judicially (or extrajudicially) claim the granting of the public deed of sale from the seller after he had in fact agreed to sell that property based upon the terms and conditions specified in the agreement. How could we justify the time and expense of entering into such an agreement? More specifically to your question, we do not think that the procedure established by the Supreme Court in the Amparo of Maria Trinidad Gómez is in touch with market reality.

Chapter 23

TWO GUIDING PRINCIPLES FOR THE INTERPRETATION OF COMMERCIAL CONTRACTS: GOOD FAITH AND REASONABLENESS

§ 23.1 INTRODUCTION AND SUMMARY

A. From a Formalistic to a Commercial-Sectoral Interpretation

The enactment of Articles 1 and 2 of the U.C.C. and the Restatement (Second) of Contracts (hereinafter Restatement (Second)) signaled a radical departure from a contract interpretation that searched for intent primarily "within the four corners" of the written contract or in the "plain meaning of its words."[1] These U.C.C. articles, the Restatement (Second) and the case law gradually built around them have led to a commercial-sectoral form of interpretation that discerns the parties' intent not only in light of what their contracts state, but also from what they do when performing them, especially when their conduct is part of their courses of dealing and usages of their trades.

It could not be otherwise. As we discussed in the preceding chapter, little of what the parties intended in their dynamic contracts is captured in the limited space provided by invoices, memoranda, telegraphs, telephone calls, telexes, "master agreements" and e-mail messages. By the time Professor Arthur L. Corbin published the third edition of his magnum opus in 1960 and read every United States decision of consequence to contract interpretation, it was clear to him that extrinsic or "parol" evidence, *i.e.*, proof of the parties' intent found outside of the four corners of their contracts, had to be an integral part of the process of discerning intent.

This contextual view of intent was shared by Karl Llewellyn. Llewellyn was also aware of the importance that the BGB and HGB and German courts attributed to their "super eminent" principles of good faith and loyalty. BGB § 157 directed courts to interpret contracts "as required by good faith, taking customary practice into consideration."[2] Similarly, BGB § 242 obligated the debtor to perform his side of the bargain in accordance "with the requirements of loyalty and good faith while observing the usages of trade."[3] And § 346 of the HGB linked the commercial duties of "doing and

---

[1] For a thorough description of the statutory and case law evolution from nineteenth-century formalistic interpretation of contracts and its "within the four corners" and plain meaning formalism to the contemporary U.C.C. and Restatement (Second) regime, *see* Harold Dubroff, *The Implied Covenant of Good Faith in Contract Interpretation and Gap Filling: Reviling a Revered Relic*, 80 ST. JOHN'S L. REV. 559 (2006).

[2] BÜRGERLICHES GESETZBUCH [BGB] [CIVIL CODE], Aug. 18, 1896, REICHSGESETZBLATT [RGBL] 195, as amended, § 157 [hereinafter BGB], *available at* http://www.gesetze-im-internet.de/englisch_bgb/englisch_bgb.html.

[3] BGB § 242 (1896). The original version as transcribed in the principal text referred to duties of loyalty and good faith. The present version deleted the reference to loyalty and states: "An obligor has a duty

omitting to do certain things" with the "customs and usage in force in business relations."[4] In addition, HGB § 347 as well as sister provisions stated that a commercial transaction "obliges to use care in the interest of a third party [and] is responsible to such third party for the use of the ordinary care of a prudent trader (*Ordentlichen Kaufmanns*)."[5]

These were overarching or "super eminent" principles because they applied to the entire field of contract law, civil and commercial, and to the life cycle of a contract—from formation to extinction—and, if you agreed with Rudolf von Ihering, they also applied to its negotiation even though it may have resulted in no contract.[6]

During my regretfully short and only conversation with Karl Llewellyn,[7] he expressed admiration for the sweeping formulation of the above provisions and expressed the hope that the U.C.C. captured their "spirit." He also drew my attention to Professor Levin Goldschmidt's insight when trying to identify the singularity of commercial legal institutions as part of "the nature of things."[8]

Goldschmidt's detractors thought that his reference to the nature of things was a metaphysical excursion into the vagaries of natural law.[9] I believe that Goldschmidt's observation referred to the nature of things commercial and thus to legal institutions (as one would have expected from the most respected historian of commercial law). If my assumption is correct, Goldschmidt intuited that legal principles such as good faith, reasonableness and fair dealing are products of commercial man's instinctive cooperation with his fellow men.

Even though Llewellyn did not literally copy the above BGB and HGB provisions in his version of U.C.C. Articles 1 and 2, the latter bore their imprint by relying on honesty, reasonableness and fairness as elements of good faith.[10]

This chapter confirms the validity of the U.C.C.'s and Llewellyn's elements of good faith. It also shows that when implementing the duty of commercial cooperation, honesty, reasonableness and fair dealing carry out two missions: 1) They guide contracting parties in their attempts to behave honestly, reasonably and fairly; and 2) They warn parties attempting to overreach at the expense of others of the consequences of their acts or omissions. This chapter also illustrates the usefulness of realistic archetypes of commercial behavior when shaping the sets of rights and duties consistent with honest, reasonable and fair behavior.

The following chapter (devoted to the drafting of commercial practices) will show how and why some sets of rights and duties are universally observed, in some cases for

---

to perform according to the requirements of good faith, taking customary practice into consideration." BGB § 242.

[4] THE COMMERCIAL CODE FOR THE GERMAN EMPIRE 146 (Bernard A. Platt trans., 1900) [hereinafter CODE FOR THE GERMAN EMPIRE]. To establish between traders the extent and importance of the doing and omitting to do certain things, account must be taken of the customs and usage in force in business relations.

[5] CODE FOR THE GERMAN EMPIRE, *supra* note 4, at 146.

[6] *See infra* ch. 26 (*Culpa in Contranendo*).

[7] *See supra* § 13:1(C)(2)(c) (customs as a source of law).

[8] *Id.*

[9] *Id.*

[10] *Id.*

centuries, while others never gain such observance. It will also show how the massive number of standard commercial contracts used in our marketplace requires the identification of the contractual intent characteristic of the sectors involved. I refer to this intent as "sectoral" and note that it is the most frequently used tool for an everyday, non-judicial as well as judicial application of good faith.

B. An Illustration of Embedded Good Faith in Usages of Trade

I have chosen a set of sellers' and buyers' rights and duties in the International Chamber of Commerce's (ICC) INCOTERMS 2010 to illustrate how good faith duties become part of internationally observed usage of trade.[11] The purpose of INCOTERMS, incidentally, is to provide:

> [A] set of international rules for the interpretation of the most commonly used trade terms in foreign trade. Thus, the uncertainties of different interpretations of such terms in different countries can be avoided or at least reduced to a considerable degree.[12]

The chosen set of rights and duties is from INCOTERMS' "Ex-Works," one of eleven such sets. Each INCOTERM reflects what representative exporters and importers accept as their rights and duties when performing a given aspect of the export-import transaction. Ex-Works requires that the buyer pick up the goods at the seller's warehouse, factory or place of business and demands very few duties from the seller-exporter. The seller is expected to deliver the goods to the buyer and the latter is expected to pick them up and arrange for all subsequent transport, insurance and customs clearances. Accordingly, an Ex-Works price quote by the seller typically includes only the invoice value of the goods.

As was done by earlier versions of INCOTERMS, the 2010 version displays the above set of rights and duties in symmetrical fashion, *i.e.*, for most of the sellers' rights there are corresponding buyers' duties and vice versa. Among the duties of the sellers are:

> A4 Delivery
>
> The seller must deliver the goods by placing them at the disposal of the buyer at the agreed point, if any, at the named place of delivery, not loaded on any collecting vehicle. If no specific point has been agreed within the named place of delivery, and if there are several points available, the seller may select the point that best suits its purpose. The seller must deliver the goods on the agreed date or within the agreed period.
>
> A7 Notice to the buyer

---

[11] INT'L CHAMBER OF COMMERCE (ICC), INCOTERMS 2010 15–21(2010) [hereinafter INCOTERMS 2010].

[12] INT'L CHAMBER OF COMMERCE (ICC), INCOTERMS 2000, *available at* http://www.tradegoods.com/helper/03rules/rules_101.html. However, please bear in mind that INCOTERMS has a narrow scope and only applies to the the rights and obligations of the parties' arising from the shipmnent and delivery of the sold goods. Thus it does not concern itself with issues such as who is the owner of the goods or who has better right to their possesson.

The seller must give the buyer any notice needed to enable the buyer to take delivery of the goods.[13]

While the preceding are considered traditional Ex-Works sellers' duties, the following, especially the second paragraph, were enacted in 2010:

A9 Checking—packaging—marking

The seller must pay the costs of those checking operations (such as checking quality, measuring, weighing, counting) that are necessary for the purpose of delivering the goods in accordance with A4.

The seller must, at its own expense, package the goods, unless it is usual for the particular trade to transport the type of goods sold unpackaged. The seller may package the goods in the manner appropriate for their transport, unless the buyer has notified the seller of specific packaging requirements before the contract of sale is concluded. Packaging is to be marked appropriately.[14]

B THE BUYER'S OBLIGATIONS

B1 General obligations of the buyer

The buyer must pay the price of the goods as provided in the contract of sale.

B4 Taking delivery

The buyer must take delivery of the goods when A4 and A7 have been complied with.

B7 Notices to the seller

The buyer must, whenever it is entitled to determine the time within an agreed period and/or the point of taking delivery within the named place, give the seller sufficient notice thereof.[15]

The parties' choice of Ex-Works is not a reflection of a seller's strength of bargaining power or of the buyer's weakness. In fact, presently, Ex-Works is used by many inexperienced and low budget exporters. On the whole, the choice of a given set of rights and duties results from the parties' respective calculus of cost effectiveness as well as supply and demand.

Because Ex-Works 2000 and its predecessors imposed so very few duties on sellers-exporters, some of them took advantage of inexperienced buyers during the decade that this version of INCOTERMS was in force by shifting a higher cost of "late" packing to buyers. Typically, these sellers would refrain from asking their buyers for their packing instructions until the buyers' truckers or freight forwarders arrived at the seller's place of business. They would then let them know that the goods had already been assembled and were ready to be packaged if the buyers paid an additional (and usually a sizeable) amount for it.

Attorneys for one such an unfairly surprised buyer asked my opinion on the good faith of such a practice: My response was that the described practice was dishonest and

---

[13] INCOTERMS 2010, *supra* note 11, at 16, 18.

[14] *Id.* at 20.

[15] *Id.* at 17, 19.

unreasonable and therefore in bad faith.[16] Eventually, the authoritative response to similar other disputes came in the above transcribed Second Paragraph of A9 of INCOTERMS 2010, which in relevant part refers to the seller's duty to package as follows:

> The seller must, at its own expense, package the goods, unless it is usual for the particular trade to transport the type of goods sold unpackaged. The seller may package the goods in the manner appropriate for their transport, unless the buyer has notified the seller of specific packaging requirements before the contract of sale is concluded. . . .[17]

Note this section's addition of the following duties of cooperation: 1) The buyer's disclosure of the need for packaging; and 2) The seller's payment of the cost of packaging, which according to custom was included in his invoice and could payable ahead of time credit or wire transfer, or upon delivery of the goods. However, note also that this duty had an important component of reasonableness: The buyer's request for packing would be unreasonable when the goods involved were customarily shipped without packing or special packing in the trade. Finally, note how these duties are consistent with each party's duty of cooperation. Because the buyer is in the best position to know what goods need packing, he has the duty of timely notice. And because the seller is in the best position to establish the cost of packing, it is his duty to specify its cost and when and how payment is to take place.

In sum, the 2010 addition to Ex-Works shows how merchants wishing to perform their Ex-Works duties in good faith can turn to it for guidance. It also shows how new duties of good faith performance are now imbedded in a new practice. Truth to tell, the "new" practice had existed for many years except that it was not specified in Ex-Works and reflected only what good faith exporters and importers ordinarily agreed to. In 2010, the same practices attained the rank of usages of trade. As such, they also became reliable tools for the discernment of Ex-Work (sectoral) contract intent by parties, lawyers and courts.

C. Good Faith in Representative Civil and Common European Law

Good faith as found in nineteenth- and early twentieth-century European codes (French as well as German) had only a tenuous relationship with the Roman Praetor's *exceptio doli*. This possible defense by a victim of the counterparty's deceit or abusive interpretation of contract language was part of the Praetor's remedial formula designed to encourage a just and equitable interpretation of contracts.

Under a *Code Civil* generalized form of interpretation, the justness and equitable components of the Roman good faith doctrine were often set aside by a sole reliance on a literal reading of the parties' intent, often in the name of "contractual justice."[18] The harshness of this doctrine prompted some code commentators to advocate reliance on

---

[16] These attorneys requested that their names and that of their clients to remain anononymous. For a freight forwarder's description of the reasons for the addition to Ex Works, A.9 and the "tricky" nature of disputes prompted by the previous silence, see Maria, *Incoterms 2010—Ex-Works (EXW)*, POINT TO POINT EXPORT SERVICES (May 1, 2013, 2:26 PM), http://ptp-maria.blogspot.com/2013/05/incoterms-2010-ex-works-exw.html.

[17] INCOTERMS 2010, *supra* note 11, at 20.

[18] *See infra* § 23:4(B).

the doctrine of abuse of rights to prevent injustices similar to those feared by the Roman Praetor.[19]

The majority of French courts and commentators preferred to measure a party's good faith in its performance of contractual obligations against standards of care and diligence, at times related to the utility derived by the debtor, and at times by the abstract archetypal behavior of a "good father of family" or of his professional or commercial counterparts. A basic question to keep in mind when discussing the various standards of diligence or care provided by French law will be: Precisely, what is the relationship between standards of diligence and of good faith; are these standards and underlying concepts their functional legal equivalents?

The German law section will show how good faith was used by the highest German appellate court in the years following the First World War to curb debtors' abuses of the nominalist (strict law) theory of payments. It will also show how the German courts' rewriting of contracts in the name of a good faith replaced not only the parties' intent, but also the will of the legislature. Finally, it will inquire into the reasonable limits of the courts' efforts to rewrite contracts they found to be inequitable.

On the common law side, the reader will be exposed first to Lord Mansfield's good faith as, above all, honesty. Thereafter, we will assess the impact of Articles 1 and 2 of the U.C.C and related sections of the Restatement (Second). It will also assess why Llewellyn failed when drafting "merchant" rules unsupported by courses of dealing and usages of trade. The chapter will conclude with a detailed analysis of one of Judge Richard Posner's much discussed decisions. The purpose of this analysis is to show the difficulties that everyday merchants, their legal advisors and the adjudicators of their disputes have with an *"a posteriori"* (after litigation) based formulation of good faith performance. This analysis should prepare the reader for the *a priori* method of drafting standard practices in which honesty, reasonableness and fairness are imbedded.

§ 23.2 CONTRACT TYPES, STAGES AND SOURCES OF INTERPRETATION

At any given time, a commercial contract can be more (or less) than its wording. As discussed in the preceding chapter, a commercial contract can bind one, two or more parties. If the promisor issued a firm promise, he will be the only party bound during the time stipulated in his promise; yet, once the promisee promises a counter-performance, he will be equally bound. If the contract is bilateral, both parties will be bound from the moment of their exchange of promises or thereafter as a result of their course of performance or dealing. Finally, a "Master" agreement[20] binds multiple parties even though some of them join at different times and their promises are made to all or just some of the participants. My colleague, Professor Simone Maria Sepe, divides this vast array of transactions into idiosyncratic and non-idiosyncratic contracts.[21] The former are characterized by highly specific terms and conditions that

---

[19] *See infra* § 23:4(C)(2).

[20] For a description of a Master agreement, *see supra* § 22:7(A).

[21] Simone Maria Sepe, Good Faith and Contrct Interpretation: A Law and Economics Perspective 48–51 (University of Arizona James E. Rogers College of Law Arizona Legal Studies Discussion Paper No. 10–28, 2010), *available at* http://papers.ssrn.com/sol3/papers.cfm?abstract_id=1086323.

reflect individually bargained transactions.[22] The latter take place between parties who deal regularly with each other and rely on widely accepted customary practices.[23] They tend to include boilerplate provisions supplied by industrial, financial or trade organizations.[24] This dichotomy highlights the manner in which the respective contracts are not only formed, but also interpreted—the non-idiosyncratic ones relying more on standard practices and trade usages and the idiosyncratic ones paying greater attention to the terms and conditions as well as the surrounding circumstances of each contract.

However, there is more to the interpretation of contracts than the manner in which they were formed. Many commercial contracts undergo multiple transformations, starting with their negotiation and continuing with their formation, performance, amendment and termination. During the negotiation stage of, say, a sale agreement, the promisor or offeror may communicate all or just some of his proposed terms and conditions. Often he does so orally, by e-mail or by a preliminary document such as a pro-forma invoice that summarizes the seller's version of the future contract and facilitates the buyer's preliminary interpretation of its terms and conditions. And often these are the only documentary embodiments of contractual intent. Thus, the promisor's conduct may be the only source to warrant the promisee's detrimental reliance, and if so, he may be liable for damages even though the contract was not technically formed.[25] In countries or jurisdictions in which bad faith negotiations (not leading to the conclusion of a contract) are actionable,[26] the adjudicator will focus his interpretation not on the final terms and conditions of the unexecuted contract, but on the manner in which negotiations were carried out and on the reasonableness of the plaintiff's expectations.

Once a contract is successfully formed and during its performance or termination, disputes may spring from the seemingly narrow *ambiguities in a term or condition of its text,* such as: Was the price quoted for "chicken" applicable to "broilers" or "fryers"?[27] Are "Coromandel groundnuts" the same edibles as "machine-shelled groundnut kernels?"[28] And as just discussed in the introductory section, if the parties agreed to be governed, say, by an INCOTERMS Ex-Works contract, the cost effectiveness of shipping may well depend upon who is responsible for the cost of packaging the goods.[29]

The manner in which these performances are interpreted differs depending on the contract's static or dynamic (commercial) nature.[30] The civil or static contracts are mostly idiosyncratic and are usually interpreted by relying on what is stated within the four corners of the relevant document; only exceptionally will evidence be allowed

---

[22] *Id.* at 50.

[23] *Id.* at 48–49.

[24] *Id.*

[25] *See infra* ch. 26.

[26] *Id.*

[27] *See* Frigaliment Importing Co. v. B.N.S. Int'l Corp., 190 F.Supp. 116, 118 (S.D.N.Y. 1960); *see also infra* § 23:9(G)(4)(a).

[28] *See* J.H.Rayner & Co v. Hambro's Bank, Ltd., 1 K.B. 36 (1943).

[29] *See* INCOTERMS 2010, *supra* note 11, at 15 (reflecting a common dispute respecting who has the obligation to load the goods).

[30] *See supra* ch. 22.

on the parties' intent as found outside those corners. In contrast, a dynamic commercial contract is often interpreted using "extrinsic" evidence, including, in our day, a healthy dosage of phone and e-mail communications, despite the warning of the Parol Evidence Rule of U.C.C. § 2–202:

> Terms with respect to which the confirmatory memoranda of the parties agree or which are otherwise set forth in a writing intended by the parties as a final expression of their agreement with respect to such terms as are included therein may not be contradicted by evidence of any prior agreement or of a contemporaneous oral agreement. . . .[31]

However, the same rule allows such a writing to be "explained or supplemented a) by course of performance, course of dealing or usage of trade. . . ."[32] This allowance is inevitable because most commercial contracts are informal and their terms and conditions are summarily expressed often using the parties' or their trade's terms or idioms.

The sources of commercial contractual law and practice frequently determine the outcome of a dispute on contractual interpretation. Indeed, courts, especially in the United States, at times find it necessary to replace the parties' expressed intent with the intent characteristic of the usage of trade to which the transaction in question belongs.[33] This attitude, incidentally, has provided special meanings to the so called "objective" theory of the parties' intent. One version states that the intent is "what a reasonable person in the position of the other party would conclude his manifestation to mean."[34] Another version, which I refer to as archetypal (and which I prefer as the most realistic) is found in Article 8(2) of CISG: "(S)tatements made by and other conduct of a party are to be interpreted according to the understanding that a reasonable person of the same kind as the other party would have had in the same circumstances."[35] Please note that while the former version looks at the position of "the other party," the latter looks at the position of a person "of the same kind as that of the other party." This formulation makes the latter's behavior that of an archetype and thus a more objectively identifiable one. Not surprisingly, this archetype, often acting as an expert witness on usages of trade, becomes a primary source for the interpretation of contractual intent in courts in the United States.

What about statutes or court decisions that deal with neighboring fields of the law of commercial contracts? A contractual dispute may involve damages to the property or person of one of the contracting parties caused by the manner in which the other party discharged his duties as a manufacturer of dangerous goods, or as a depositary, bailee, lessee or business manager of the other party's business or business assets. In such a case, the interpretation of contractual duties will focus not only upon the text of the contract or of the law of contracts, but also on the law of torts and especially on its standards of care or diligence and on its archetypes of diligent behavior. Nonetheless, I

---

[31] U.C.C. § 2–202. If anyone ever doubted Arthur Corbin's powers as the visionary of the contemporary law of contracts, I recommend reading Arthur L. Corbin, *The Interpretation of Words and the Parol Evidence Rule*, 50 CORNELL L. Q. 161, 161–70 (1965).

[32] U.C.C. § 2–202(a).

[33] *See, e.g., infra* note 165 (discussing the holding in *Colombia Nitrogen* in the United States).

[34] *See, e.g.,* Lucy v. Zehmer, 84 S.E.2d 516, 522 (Va. 1954) (holding that a party's intention will be held to be what a reasonable person in the position of the other party would conclude his manifestation to mean).

[35] *See* CISG.

must caution the reader not to assume, as has been done by French commentators and courts, that statutory or decisional standards of care also double as sources of good faith behavior.[36]

Last but not least are the overarching principles of honesty, reasonableness and fair dealing, which are the "nuclear" components of good faith. At times they are found in statutory law, at times in case law and doctrinal writings, but most frequently they are imbedded in standard and best practices. Regardless of the type of contract and its life-stage (from negotiation to termination) or the number, timing and symmetry of their performances, these principles are by now an integral part of the interpretation of commercial contracts, particularly in German and United States law. As noted in the Introduction, they are overarching because they apply during the entire life of a contract or ongoing commercial relationship. Consider, for example, the commercial relationship in *Meinhard v. Salmon*,[37] one of Justice Cardozo's most influential contract and fiduciary law decisions and therefore, repeatedly cited in this book. Once an investor had in good faith entrusted his savings to someone whom Cardozo characterized as a partner acting in a fiduciary capacity, the entrusting-investor had to be offered a subsequent investment regardless of whether the first contract had expired. In other words, because of the fiduciary nature of the defendant's management of the plaintiff's investment, the latter's duty to act in good faith exceeded those of the average marketplace participant: It was a duty expected from a father or elder brother when handling the affairs of an infant (*uberrima fides*). Thus the fiduciary was expected to do what was best for his trusting partner even if the fiduciary could lose significant profits by allowing this partner to participate in a new investment.

§ 23.3 GOOD FAITH INTERPRETATION: JUDICIAL AND MARKET BASED VERSIONS

Rather than search for "essential" or Aristotelian definitions of good faith, an effort in which much print continues to be wasted, I will discuss two approaches to the use of good faith in the law of commercial contracts. One is judicially based and was one of those selected by Professor Franz Wieacker, one of Europe's most respected historians of private law, as an important source of the good faith performance of contracts. In Wieacker's view, good faith is essentially a legal concept and its meaning and method of application should be researched in predominantly legal sources such as in Roman legal maxims, national and international landmark court decisions, influential legal treatises, commentaries and compilations of "general principles of the law," among others.[38] He prefers using these judicial and doctrinal sources over others because they are "objective" and technical-legal versions of good faith rather than the parties' subjective opinions and are thus more apt to be uniformly acceptable.

Wieacker lists one Roman and one Germanic legal maxim as illustrations of what his sources yield. The Roman maxim, similar to estoppel, rejects as in bad faith procedural behavior that goes against the pleader's own previous acts or statements

[36] *See infra* § 22:3(B) (discussing good father of family and obligations of result).

[37] 249 N.Y. 458, 464 (1928); *infra* § 22:9(C)(1).

[38] *See* FRANZ WIEACKER, EL PRINCIPIO GENERAL DE LA BUENA FÉ 59–85 (Jose Luis Carro trans., 1977) (author's translation).

("*venire contra factum proprium*").[39] The German maxim addresses the reverse or passive side of estoppel and provides that a party cannot claim a right that it repeatedly and consistently failed to invoke, thereby creating an expectation of its non-use (*Werwirkung*).[40] It is worth noting that these trial- or dispute-inspired maxims are narrower than the Roman principles which address the behavior expected from a good citizen living a useful life. One such principle appears in Justinian's *Institutes*: "[L]ive honestly, not to injure another, and to give to each one that which belongs to him" (*honeste vivere, alterum non laedere, suum cuique tribuere*).[41]

As with the Justinian's *Institutes* precept, the market- or transaction-based version of good faith is not confined to the conduct of the parties or their lawyers during litigation. It does not exclude conduct during litigation from the overall assessment of good faith conduct. But because only a small percentage of commercial contracts is litigated and much interpretational guidance is needed in the everyday life of a commercial contract, one must not lose sight of what the parties as participants in the marketplace understand and abide by as good faith in their everyday transactions, as was apparent in the above Ex-Works illustration.

However, what is to be done when a usage of trade known to both parties seems to contradict a contractual stipulation? Consider a contract where the seller-appellant claims, relying on a usage of trade known to both parties, that he is entitled to be paid the market price of the chemical product he sold to the defendant-buyer instead of the lower, fixed price stipulated in the contract.[42] But add to this claim that the sale agreement contained a merger clause which stated that "No verbal understanding will be recognized by either party hereto; this contract expresses all the terms and conditions of the agreement, shall be signed in duplicate and shall not become operative until approved in writing by the Seller." Finally, assume that the lawyer for the buyer-defendant confidently relies on the same Roman doctrine of "*venire contra factum proprium*" that Professor Wieacker suggests as paradigmatic of contractual bad faith. In just such a situation,[43] Judge Butzner, writing for the United States Circuit Court for the Fourth Circuit, concluded, appropriately in my opinion, that:

> The contract does not expressly state that course of dealing and usage of trade cannot be used to explain or supplement the written contract. The contract is silent about adjusting prices and quantities to reflect a declining market. It neither permits nor prohibits adjustment, and this neutrality provides a fitting occasion for recourse to usage of trade and prior dealing to supplement the contract and explain its terms.[44]

Official Comment 2 to § 8.2–202 of the Annotated Code of Virginia added:

---

[39] The Anglo-American equitable estoppel is the counterpart to this Roman doctrine. For example, the definition of estoppel is "a bar which precludes a person from denying the truth of a fact which has in contemplation of law become settled by the acts and proceedings of judicial or legislative officers, or by the act of the party himself. . . ." Lewis v. King, 157 La. 718, 726 (1925).

[40] KOZOLCHYK, EL DERECHO COMERCIAL, at 263; *see also* WIEACKER, *supra* note 38, at 60–62.

[41] *See* JUSTINIAN, THE INSTITUTES, Book 1, Title 1, *available at* http://www.constitution.org/sps/sps02_j1-1.htm.

[42] *See infra* § 22:9(E)(1) (discussing the *Columbia Nitrogen* decision).

[43] Columbia Nitrogen Corp. v. Royster Co., 451 F.2d 3 (1971).

[44] *Id.* at 9–10.

> Paragraph (a) makes admissible evidence of course of dealing, usage of trade and course of performance to explain or supplement the terms of any writing stating the agreement of the parties *in order that the true understanding of the parties as to the agreement may be reached. Such writings are to be read on the assumption that the course of prior dealings between the parties and the usages of trade were taken for granted when the document was phrased.* Unless carefully negated they have become an element of the meaning of the words used. Similarly, the course of actual performance by the parties is considered the best indication of what they intended the writing to mean.[45]

Judge Butzner's interpretation, bolstered by Official Comment 2 to § 8.2–202, is distinctly market-oriented because it takes into account understandings arrived at by the parties in their prior dealings and in the usage of their trade when attempting to give meaning to their contracts. This "taken for granted" understanding of the terms of the contract acquired through the prysms of course of dealing and usage of trade is consistent with Llewellyn's "merchant" version of good faith in U.C.C. § 2–103(b)[46] as well as with the above mentioned Article 8(2) of CISG, which also relies on the understanding that a reasonable person of the same kind as the other party would have had in the same circumstances.

§ 23.4 GOOD FAITH IN THE JUDICIAL INTERPRETATION OF COMMERCIAL CONTRACTS

A. Good Faith (*Bona Fides*) in Roman and Medieval Law

As pointed out by Professors Reinhard Zimmerman and Simon Whittaker, the concept of *bona fides* originated in Roman law with a standard clause in the Praetor's formula directed to the trier of facts (*iudex)* in contractual disputes.[47] This clause was known as the *exceptio doli* and its purpose was to prevent plaintiffs from acting deceitfully by taking advantage of the rigors of strict law.[48] The instruction to the *iudex* directed him to ascertain "if in this matter nothing has been done, or is being done, in bad faith by the plaintiff" (*si in ea re nihil dolo malo . . . factum si neque fiat.*).[49] Thus, the meaning of good faith in Roman law was, as suggested by Professor Franz Wieacker, a judicial (and I would add remedial) one: The judge had to determine whether the plaintiff was acting deceitfully, in bad faith, with "*dolus malus,"* or had otherwise done something inequitable. If he found that such conduct had taken place, the plaintiff's action was dismissed. This instruction allowed the judge to decide the case before him in what Zimmerman and Whittaker also refer to as a "fair or reasonable manner."[50]

---

[45] VA. CODE ANN. § 8.2–202 cmt. 2 (2012) (emphasis added).

[46] U.C.C. § 2–103(b) (1962) (" 'Good faith' in the case of a merchant means honesty in fact and the observance of reasonable commercial standards of fair dealing in the trade."). *See, e.g.*, MICH. COMP. LAWS ANN. § 440.2103(b) (2013) (the State of Michigan's version of this provision), *available at* http://www.michigan.gov/documents/entireuccbook_18831_7.pdf.

[47] Cambridge Studies in International and Comparative Law, Good Faith in European Contract Law 16 (Reinhard Zimmerman & Simon Whittaker eds., 2000) [hereinafter Good Faith].

[48] *See supra* § 23:1(C) for a discussion of the Praetorian formulas and equitable clauses.

[49] GOOD FAITH, *supra* note 47, at 16.

[50] *Id.*

Bona fides was not as precise a concept as *dolus* (deceit) because, among other reasons, the purpose of *dolus* was invariably "to defraud, deceive or cheat another," while good faith conduct may have manifold purposes and ways of manifesting itself.[51] In addition, *bona fides* was meant to apply to the widest spectrum of contracts—from the formal and ritual *stipulatio* (which was subject to the strict law (*stricti iuris*) action *par excellence*) to the informal consensual agreements. Further, unlike the strict law *stipulatio*, the Praetor's formula for consensual-informal agreements did not need an *exceptio doli* or other special language to be interpreted *ex bona fide* because these agreements were supposed to be interpreted in this manner automatically.[52]

Among the significant consequences of the flexible *bona fides* interpretation of contracts were remedial implications above and beyond those normally associated with bad faith conduct. For example, a seller was deemed to have acted in good faith when he did not invoke the defense of buyer beware (*caveat emptor*) against unwary buyers.

The wide-ranging effects of the *bona fides* doctrine continued to benefit the flexibility and fairness of the law of commercial contracts during the middle ages and in the modern era. By Justinian's time, the requirements of the formulary procedure were liberalized and contract actions could be brought regardless of whether the contracts in question were part of the actionable or typified sets. Given the growing volume of commerce and especially of international commerce, merchants benefited from the *bona fides* related doctrine of equity (*aequitas*). As pointed out by Zimmerman and Whittaker:

> Throughout the Middle Ages, and in the early modern period, *aequitas* remained in the forefront of discussion as a counterpoise to the *ius strictum* (strict law), but it was commonly identified with *bona fides*.... [which] became a fundamental principle of . . . *lex mercatoria*. "*Bona fides est primum mobile ac spiritus vivificans commercii*" (good faith is the prime mover and lifegiving spirit of commerce) . . . in the same vein Baldus had stated "*bonam fidem valde require in his, qui plurinum negotiantur*" (good faith is much required of those, who trade most).[53]

B. Good Faith (*Bonne Foi*) in the *Code Civil* and in French Judicial and Doctrinal Interpretation

If Article 1134(3) of the *Code Civil* intended to clarify the manner in which contracts had to be executed and interpreted, it fell considerably short of its goal: "Agreements legally formed . . . must be executed in good faith."[54] Among other things, it did not say was what it meant by good faith. It was not until 2007 that a drafting

---

[51] *See, e.g.*, BERGER, ENCYCLOPEDIC DICTIONARY, at 440 (the Jurist Labeo defines Dolus as "any cunning, deceit, or contrivance used to defraud, deceive or cheat another."). Further, Berger translates *dolus bonus* as simple "shrewdness." *Id.*

[52] GOOD FAITH, *supra* note 47, at 16. *See also* BERGER, ENCYCLOPEDIC DICTIONARY, at 440. The reader may also recall that the *bona fides* of consensual agreements was one of the features that Hugo Grotius considered admirable and linked to his natural law ideas. The reader will recall that these were the ideas that influenced Robert Pothier, among other French commentators, whose writings became part of the *Code Civil*. *See supra* § 8:2.

[53] GOOD FAITH, *supra* note 47, at 17–18 (citations omitted). *See also Baldus de Ubaldis*, THE CATHOLIC UNIVERSITY OF AMERICA, http://faculty.cua.edu/pennington/baldbio.html (discussing the medieval commentarist Baldus de Ubaldis, also referred to as Baldus de Perugia).

[54] *See* C CIV. (FR.) art. 1134.

commission for the reform of France's Law of Obligations (the *Projet Catala*) attempted a clarification of good faith as a tool of contractual interpretation. This commission included judges, some of whom were members of France's *Cour de Cassation*. Unfortunately, the commission's attribution of numerous broad missions to good faith did not provide the needed clarification either: "Broadly understood, good faith (*i.e.*, loyalty, solidarity, proportionality and concern for contractual balance) is present during each phase of the life of a contract. . . ."[55]

The same tendency to extol good faith without identifying it in marketplace transactions persists. A lawyer who practices before the *Cour de Cassation* affirms, without explaining why or how, that the above quoted sentence of Article 1134 is "one of the fundamental rules of civil law."[56] Similarly, the author of a 2006 doctoral thesis on judicial practices quotes Jean Domat's and Jean-Étienne-Marie Portalis' exhortation: "*il faut de la bonne foi, de la réciprocité et de l'égalité dans les contrats*" (we need good faith, reciprocity and equality in contracts).[57] Still, after reviewing appellate decisions on Article 1134(3), she concludes that: "Despite [Article 1134(3)] [French] case law has failed to employ [meaningfully] either the notion of good faith or Article 1134(3)."[58] She added that "one had to wait until 1985 to encounter the *Cour de Cassation's* first remedy based on paragraph 3 of Article 1134."[59] Because (as known by now to the common law reader) the *Code Civil* has been the most influential model of private law codification in civil law countries, and because decisions by French courts and commentaries by French scholars are followed in many of these countries, it is necessary to examine them in some detail.

*1. Contractual Diligence, Fault (*Culpa*) and the* Bon Pére de Famille

French courts frequently rely on the archetypal behavior of a good father of family (*bon père de famille*) and on Roman-law-inspired classifications of contractual diligence to bridge the gap between litigated facts and good faith. Nevertheless, it has not been easy to apply this standard in a legal system in which judges traditionally rely on a literal interpretation of the intent of the parties, especially in formally written contracts or *actes authentiques*. The reader will recall that for much of the twentieth century, French judges relied on a method of interpretation that Dean Georges Ripert referred to as "*Justice Contractuelle*," *i.e.*, the expressed intent is not only the law of the parties, but it is also their contractual justice. Hence, a judge should not add his own sense of justice, equity or fairness to a deal that the parties, by their agreement to execute a formal or public deed, adjudicated as just. Not surprisingly, many French judges preferred a literal interpretation of the text of the contract. Given that attitude,

---

[55] *See Bonne Foi*, LEXINTER.NET, http://www.lexinter.net/JF/bonne_foi.htm (author's translation). On the *Projet Catala* on the law of obligations, concluded in 2007, see COUR DE CASSATION, http://www.courdecassation.fr/jurisprudence_publications_documentation_2/autres_publications_discours_2039/discours_2202/2007_2271/groupe_travail_10699.html.

[56] *L'obligation d'exécution de bonne foi ne survit pas au contrat*, PIERRE FERNANDEZ (Jan. 5, 2006), http://aufildudroit.over-blog.com/article-1539846.html.

[57] Amandine Assaillit, La bonne foi et la loyaute contractuelle (Oct. 2006) (unpublished thesis), *available at* http://www.masterdroit.fr/3_Ressourccs_Fichcs_fichiers/FICHES_PDF/FICHES_OBLIG_PDF/1_bonne_foi_et_loyaute.pdf.

[58] *Id.* at 1.

[59] *Id.*

one of the first issues on the application of the *bon père de famille* standard was whether the parties could waive it.[60]

Another peculiarity of the French standard of good faith is its connection with a three-tiered system of contractual fault in which the diligence expected from the parties is dependent upon the degree to which the party allegedly at fault benefitted from the transaction. This connection predated the *Code Civil*[61] and was used when finding contractual fault (*culpa*) in classical Roman law. Accordingly, the *Justinian Digest* quoted a respected jurist for the statement that "There is no *culpa* if everything was done that a very careful man should have done."[62]

French law attempted to provide the precision not found in Roman texts by resorting to a threefold classification of fault that made the degree of care expected from a defendant dependent upon the utility or profit derived from the transaction (*utilitas contrahentis*). Accordingly, contracting parties are liable for: 1) gross negligence (*faute grave* or *lourde*) if they watch over the goods for others without pay or profit; 2) light negligence (*faute legere*) if they charge for their services; and 3) the lightest negligence (and highest diligence) (*faute très légère*) if the party at fault was the only one who benefitted from the transaction.[63] One of the difficulties of using these utility or profit-dependent standards of care in conjunction with the *bon père de famille* is the latter's abstract and malleable nature, often only vaguely associated with a given transaction and equally often associated with no discernible transaction.

Robert Pothier, for example, defined *faute lourde* (gross negligence) as a failure to devote to the affairs of others "the level of care which even the least careful and most stupid of people would not fail to devote to their own business, such a fault being opposed to good faith."[64] This minimalist version of good faith was applied by some French judges, while others applied the utilitarian test when dealing with merchants, but, again, without specifying the behavior that amounted to the expected diligence (and good faith) of, say, a "good" restaurant owner, banker, jeweler, stock broker, travel agent or ship owner, among others.

A survey of French appellate decisions during the mid-1980s found that the standard of the archetypal good father of family was applied to tradesmen and professionals, commercial agents, paid custodians or bailees and suppliers of goods and personal services.[65] The courts described such a multifaceted good father of family as:

> [A] careful, diligent, vigilant man . . . the average man having a sense of his responsibilities; an abstract type [devoid of] exaggeration [one] who does not

---

[60] *See, e.g.*, Margaret Phillips, The Standard of Bon Père de Famille in French Law; Its Application by the French Courts and a Comparison with the Standard of Reasonableness, 2–3 (Fall 1982) (unpublished paper, University of Arizona) (on file with author).

[61] *Id.* at 7.

[62] BERGER, ENCYCLOPEDIC DICTIONARY, at 419.

[63] *See supra* § 4:2(A)(4) (discussing the Roman jurists' method of resoning that I refer to as geometric logic).

[64] WilliamTetley, *Good Faith in Contract: Particularly in the Contracts of Arbitration and Chartering*, 35 J. MAR. L. & COM. 561, 577 n.80 (2004). Professor Tetley refers to Art. 1474 of the Québec Civil Code of 1994's exclusion or limitation of a party's liability for material injury caused to another through "an intentional or gross fault; a gross fault is a fault which shows gross recklessness, gross carelessness or gross negligence" as an illustration of the reach of Pothier's definition of *faute lourde*. *Id.*

[65] Phillips, *supra* note 60, at 9–10.

exceed *"le juste milieu"* (right middle ground) and maintains himself at the pivot point of reason and equity; reasonable and just.[66]

Their standards of diligence also varied with the nature of their businesses:

> [A] ship's captain was held to the standard of a prudent and diligent sailor; for a [restaurant owner] the standard of a prudent . . . and well informed [restaurant owner], for a nurse that of a nurse endowed with the knowledge necessary to competently practice her trade. . . . [And] a professional person is held to a different level of competence; that of an average, prudent professional.[67]

Not surprisingly, judicial decision making could not help but to become capricious and unpredictable in the absence of a careful delineation of the transactional facts to which such standard of diligence applied. Thus, one judge held that where a competent jeweler acting as his client's agent bought gems for his client at a price considerably higher than the market price, he had acted carelessly and in bad faith. It was not clear in this decision if the defendant jeweler had the required expertise to obtain the types of gems he had been requested to buy at the best possible price, nor was there a basis established for determining what was a fair market price for the jewels in question.[68] Similarly, another judge held that a travel agency that advertised itself as a "worldwide travel agency" was liable for its failure to advise a customer (who purchased a ticket to travel to and in Brazil) that Brazil's local transporters did not carry insurance against accidental injuries suffered by their passengers.[69] The court did not state what evidence it relied on to arrive at its decision. Its decision did not mention whether a code of conduct existed for international travel agents to follow with respect to warnings that ought to be given to travelers or whether respected international travel agents had testified on warnings that they would have reasonably given to travelers to foreign countries. In a thorough commentary on the duty of care of French travel agents under French case law, Professor Thérèse Rousseau-Houle of the Faculty of Law of the University of Laval (Canada) concluded that:

> A travel agent's liability normally differs according to whether he merely acts as a middleman between clients and service suppliers or whether he himself organizes travel. Court decisions reveal nevertheless that proper qualification of the relationship is not necessarily a prerequisite as to the rules applicable. The overriding criterion appears rather to be consumer protection. Consequently, the burden of proof on the consumer has been slightly reduced and travel agents are more often than not held liable under an obligation of result.[70]

---

[66] *Id.* at 7–8 (citations omitted).

[67] *Id.* at 9 (citations omitted). Phillips attributes the features she listed to the several doctrinal writers, who extracted them from court decisions. *See* LEOBON LAROMBIERE, I THEORIE ET PRATIQUE DES OBLIGATIONS 491 (1857); JEAN CARBONNIER, 4 DROIT CIVIL, LES OBLIGATIONS 251 (1956); MARCEL PLANIOL & GEORGES RIPERT, 6 TRAITE PRATIQUE DE DROIT CIVIL FRANÇAIS no. 834 (2d ed. 1954).

[68] Phillips, *supra* note 60, at 10.

[69] Wagons—Lits c. Duchiron, Cour d'appel [CA] [regional court of appeal] Paris, Nov. 25 1955, JCP 1956, II, 9240. For a useful comment on the diligence expected by French courts from travel agents, see Thérèse Rousseau-Houle, *La responsabilité des agences de voyages: les tendances de la jurisprudence récente*, 24 LES CAHIERS DE DROIT 643 (1983), *available at* http://www.erudit.org/revue/cd/1983/v24/n3/042562ar.pdf.

[70] Rousseau-Houle, *supra* note 69, at 643.

In the following section, I will explore the meaning of an obligation to produce a certain contractual result as contrasted with the obligation to employ ordinary diligence in the discharge of one's contractual duties. Still, it is not too early to point out that the fundamental question on diligence as a standard determinative of good faith remains unanswered by French judges and commentators: Why should diligence alone determine whether or not a party has performed the contractual stipulations in good faith? Isn't there more to contractual good faith than making sure that the proverbial T's were crossed or the I's dotted? Recall that the Roman Praetor found it necessary to provide an *exceptio doli* precisely to avoid a party's bad faith reliance on strict compliance with a contract's terms and conditions.

2. *The Obligation to Produce a Result or to Employ Ordinary Diligence*

René Demogue, a renowned early-twentieth-century commentator of the *Code Civil,* attempted to bring predictability to the interpretation of contractual duties of diligence and, directly or indirectly, of the required good faith. He did this by proposing to measure these duties against the fulfillment of two alternative obligations. One was to produce a certain contractual result, such as completion of an office building (*obligations de resultat*); the other to perform services employing the archetypal average diligence of a good father of family (*obligations de moyens*). As summarized by a French commentator:

> It all depends on the contractual stipulations and on the type of contract. . . . In a transportation contract the carrier undertakes to transport the passenger or the merchandise to a specified destination. He is [then] held to an *obligation de résultat.* Hence, the debtor [promisor] must obtain for his creditor a precise result. Whereas, if he only engages to employ the means appropriate to attain a result envisaged by the promisee-creditor such as when a physician undertakes to treat a disease but not [necessarily] to cure it; similarly, when the advocate undertakes to make sure that his client is defended but not [necessarily] to win his lawsuit.[71]

In the obligation to produce a promised result, the promisor's expected diligence requires strict liability (*responsabilite objectif*) for its breach unless the promisor could prove that he could not conclude the promised construction or work because of an "act of God" (*force majeure*), a fortuitous event (*cas fortuit*) or an extraneous cause (*cause étranger*). In contrast, where the promise is to use the diligence of a *bon père de famille,* the promisor is liable only for ordinary negligence.[72]

---

[71] Stephanie, *La faute contractuelle: une notion hétérogène et imprécise*, LEGALETIC (Nov. 23, 2008) (on file with author).

[72] *See* RENE DEMOGUE, 5 TRAITE DES OBLIGATIONS EN GENERAL § 1237 (1923). *See also* James Gordley, *Impossibility and Changed and Unforeseen Circumstances*, 52 AM. J. COMP. L. 513, 518–19 (2004). Although not in the same league as Professors Demogue and Gordley, Stephanie concludes, validly in my opinion, that the liability in the case of the *obligation de résultat* is strict or "objective." Stephanie, *supra* note 71. This viewpoint is confirmed by one among many decisions by France's *Cour de Cassation*. As stated by the *Cour*: "The obligation to produce a certain result entails both a presumption of fault and of cause and effect between the promisor's performance and the damages claimed." (*L'obligation de résultat emporte à la fois présomption de faute et présomption de causalité entre la prestation fournie et le dommage invoqué).* Cass. civ 1ère., 16 février 1988, Bull civ. I, nË 42, p. 27, RTD civ. 1988.767, obs. P. Jourdain. Stephanie added that "[t]he promisor-debtor will not be freed from liability unless he can prove an Act of God, acts by a third party or an extraneous cause." (*Le débiteur ne pourra se libérer que par la preuve d'un cas de force majeure, fait du*

In a manner reminiscent of the synthesis of the universal order of things that the ancient Greek mathematicians attempted to leave us with,[73] and of a Roman jurist who referred to a related classification of obligations as the ultimate or most encompassing dichotomy (*Summa Divisio*),[74] Demogue's classification was to cover the entire spectrum of contractual diligence. He found support for this classification in Articles 1147 and 1138 of the *Code Civil.* In relevant part, Article 1147 stated: "[T]he obligor will be liable for damages, either for the absence or delay in the performance of his obligation unless he proves that the failure to perform resulted from an outside cause that cannot be imputed to him, and further that there was no bad faith on his part."[75] Nonetheless, Demogue's supposedly all-encompassing categories are both overlapping and incomplete by failing to cover the entire spectrum of contractual liability. For example, when a contracting party promises that he will finish the construction of a building (as he is supposed to assert in an *obligation de resultat*), is he not also asserting that in completing the building he also used a certain measure of diligence? Otherwise, why call it a "building" and not just a "shack" or a temporary warehouse? In other words, a certain degree of diligence is implicit in the very description of a *résultat.* Conversely, when a contracting party claims to have employed average diligence while constructing the building, does not the nature of the building being built (as promised) figure into the determination of the contractor's diligence? And last but not least, why does even the most punctilious performance of a contractual stipulation amount to good faith? What if I am an experienced builder of warehouses and my client asks me to build him a warehouse in which to store certain fruits and vegetables for a minimal period of time. At the same time, my client inserts an addendum listing highly expensive but unnecessary equipment and parts used for storing perishables over a much longer period of time than required by the described warehouse. Don't I owe my client a good faith duty to inform him of the unnecessary costliness of his list of specifications? Restatement (Second) § 161(b), for one, imposes such a duty.[76]

3. *Conclusion: Diligence and Completion of a Performance Are Not Necessarily Determinative of Good Faith*

The preceding discussion shows that not only is the standard of an archetypal good father of family (or its professional variants) not a reliable indicator of the expected good faith in commercial contracts, but neither are the classification of

---

tiers ou d'une cause étrangère.) Stephanie, *supra* note 71, at n.17 and accompanying text (citing other *Cour de Cassation* decisions).

[73] *See supra* chs. 8 & 10 (on French codification).

[74] *See* Eric Descheemaeker, *The Roman Division of Wrongs: A New Hypothesis*, 5 ROMAN LEGAL TRAD. 1, 12 (2009), *available at* http://www.romanlegaltradition.org/contents/2009/RLT5–DESCHEEMAEKER.PDF (attributing to the Roman jurist Gaius (G.3.88) the expression "*summa divisio*" of obligations).

[75] C. CIV. (FR.) art. 1147. Unless otherwise indicated, all the English translations of the *Code Civil* provisions belong to Legifrance (*see* Frequently Cited).

[76] Section 161(b) states the non-disclosure of a fact known is the equivalent to an assertion that thte fact does not exist:

> [W]here [the contracting party] knows that disclosure of the fact would correct a mistake of the other party as to a basic assumption on which that party is making the contract and if non-disclosure of the fact amounts to a failure to act in good faith and in accordance with reasonable standards of fair dealing.

Restatement (Second) of Contracts § 161(b) (1981).

obligations based on their profitability, the average diligence or the completion of promised results. As will be shown in subsequent sections, good faith has its own moral components. As Baldus, the medieval commentator,[77] reminded us, *bona fides* is expected most from those who trade most. One of the implications of Baldus' reminder is that unlike the sporadic nature of disputes in civil (not for profit) transactions, the volume and speed of commercial transactions require that the parties to the transaction be able to predict *ex ante* (prior to entering into a transaction) what it would mean to perform each party's share of that transaction in good faith.

C. Good Faith, Trade Usage and Archetypal Behavior in the BGB, HGB and Court Decisions

1. BGB and HGB Provisions on Good Faith and an Imperial Court's Monetary Revaluation

According to Professors Zimmerman and Whittaker, ever since the enactment of the BGB, the German doctrine of good faith became inseparable from that of "Fidelity and Faith" (*Treu und Glauben*) and both were equally applicable to civil and commercial transactions.[78] Among the synonyms for *Treu* in an everyday English German dictionary are fidelity, loyalty, commitment, devotion, allegiance, reliability, dependability, steadfastness, staunchness and trustworthiness.[79] Please note that some of the listed terms connote *a priori* duties to the world at large, although BGB § 157 requires that "contracts are to be interpreted as required by good faith, taking customary practice into consideration."[80] Similarly, § 242 obligated the debtor to perform his side of the bargain in accordance "with the requirements of loyalty and good faith while observing the usages of trade."[81] These provisions seem directed at two not necessarily mutually exclusive recipients: § 157 is directed to those who interpret the contract, presumably courts, but also the parties themselves, while § 242 is directed solely to the obligor about to perform his side of the bargain. Arguably, there is some redundancy in this formulation. Nonetheless, from the standpoint of commercial contract interpretation, the redundancy is a healthy one because it reinforces the interpretive role and objective features of usages of trade. In contrast, other sections refer to a more abstract duty as that found in § 138(1), which states that "a [contract] which is contrary to public policy is void."[82]

Perhaps the most dramatic and far reaching application of § 242 of the BGB occurred when the courts had to decide whether it could be invoked against obligors who insisted on paying their monetary obligations in a currency whose value had been reduced to virtual nothingness by Germany's hyperinflation during the decade following its defeat in the First World War. The German Imperial Court protected the creditor against the literalistic (or "nominalist") interpretations of the currency

---

[77] *See supra* note 53 and accompanying text.

[78] GOOD FAITH, *supra* note 47, at 18.

[79] *Treu* is translated into English as loyal, and the synonyms referred to are those of the word loyal. *reu*, REVERSO.NET, http://www.reverso.net/translationresults.aspx?lang=EN&direction=german-english.

[80] BGB § 157.

[81] BGB § 242 (1896); *supra* note 3 and accompanying text.

[82] *Id.* § 138(1).

stipulations by revaluing this currency in light of the principle of good faith in the performance of obligations. In the words of Zimmerman and Whittaker:

> The Court thus tried to steer a middle course: neither was it regarded as sufficient if the plaintiff merely acted inequitably nor was judicial intervention to be confined to the extreme case where the only purpose of exercising a right had been to cause damage to another. The application of § 242 BGB soon became a bone of contention in the great methodological disputes of the first part of this century. . . .[83]

The requirement to observe the usages of trade gave the BGB's version of good faith a distinctly commercial character, a trend that reappeared half a century later in the U.C.C.[84] Please recall that § 346 of the HGB had already linked the commercial duties of "doing and omitting to do certain things" with the "customs and usage in force in business relations."[85] In addition, as was discussed in an earlier section,[86] § 347 of the HGB as well as sister provisions provide that a commercial transaction "obliges to use care in the interest of a third party [and] is responsible to such third party for the use of the ordinary care of a prudent trader (*Ordentlichen Kaufmanns*)."[87] This was an archetypal merchant whose standard of care was expected from agents, business partners or joint venturers, among others.[88] Further, as pointed out by Professors Zekoll and Reimann, "the Commercial Code affords greater protection to a good faith purchaser of movables when the seller is a merchant."[89] By the turn of the twentieth century, then, the legislative seeds had been planted in German law for a version of commercial good faith that took into account the subjective *exceptio doli* (a cousin of the U.C.C.'s "honesty in fact" standard)[90] as well as an objective standard of reasonableness based upon commercial archetypal behavior.

It is also worth emphasizing that the Imperial Court's rejection of contractual claims on the basis that the plaintiff had acted inequitably or abusively went beyond what the drafters of the BGB or HGB anticipated in their provisions on subjective and objective good faith. This court rejected the principle of nominalism in its decision of November 28, 1923.[91] Nominalism required payment of the face amount of the obligation in the stipulated currency even if one gold mark was traded at that time for as many as 522 billion paper marks.[92] In doing this, the Imperial Court also refused to allow a debtor to discharge a monetary obligation secured by a mortgage by paying the nominal value of the debt in paper marks. It further held that the creditor did not have to consent to a deletion of the mortgage from the land registry and was also entitled to a new court-fixed exchange rate.[93]

---

[83] GOOD FAITH, *supra* note 47, at 20 (citations omitted).

[84] *See infra* § 23:5(A)(1).

[85] *See* CODE FOR THE GERMAN EMPIRE, *supra* note 4, at 146.

[86] *See supra* § 23:1(A).

[87] CODE FOR THE GERMAN EMPIRE, *supra* note 4, at 146.

[88] *See* HGB §§ 130(a), 347, 497 (GOREN, 1998).

[89] INTRODUCTION TO GERMAN LAW 130 (Joachim Zekoll & Mathias Reimann eds., 2005).

[90] *See infra* note 152 and accompanying text.

[91] GOOD FAITH, *supra* note 47, at 20–21.

[92] *Id.*

[93] *Id.* at 21.

The justification for these decisions was found in § 242 of the BGB. After all, how could anyone believe that he or she was acting in good faith when she was attempting to pay a monetary obligation in paper money whose purchasing power was only an infinitesimal fraction of the nominal amount printed on it? Hence, by relying on the overarching norms (also known as "general clauses" or *generalklauseln*) of the general part of the BGB, this court revalued all the legal transactions subject to the nominalistic approach and thereby it also rendered ineffective the Parliament's currency laws.[94] In Zimmermann and Whittaker's words: "This decision hit the German legal community like a bombshell. . . . [for] [t]he fixing of exchange rates was certainly not the business of the courts and it was irreconcilable with the *exceptio doli generalis* even in its most extended version."[95]

After studying the German rate adjustment decisions from 1915 to 1924 and comparing them to those in the United States during the Civil War period, Professor John Dawson wisely assessed the limits of reliance on § 242's good faith as a tool to ameliorate the impact of inflation.[96] It was true that German courts had helped ameliorate the impact of hyper-inflation upon contractual obligations whose purely symbolic performance discouraged not only credit, but overall productivity.[97] However, while judicial intervention had played a useful role in a hyper-inflationary period, especially when the legislative or executive branches had done little if anything about it, its role during moderate inflationary periods was negative. Judicial intervention based upon good faith or other equitable doctrines during the latter periods could have interfered with sound legislative and administrative policies to allow inflation in some instances to serve as a device to facilitate much needed debt relief. This was a function that central banking officials or even expert congressional staff members were much better equipped to discharge than judges. In addition, a judicial intervention that would place in doubt the parties' own terms and conditions could also undermine the very legitimacy of contracts as the best tool for the orderly exchange of goods and services.[98]

2. *Good Faith, Reasonableness and Abuse of Rights* **(Unzulassige Rechtsabüsung,** ***or*** **Rechtsmissbrauch)**

Following Germany's hyperinflationary period, German courts continued to apply the good faith doctrine liberally, but without attempting to legislate for an entire category of obligations such as those requiring monetary payments. As noted by Dr. Nathalie Hofmann, a winner of the annual Albert Kritzer award, the good faith doctrine was applied to prevent acts which could harm the purpose of the contract.[99] In

---

[94] *Id.*

[95] *Id.*

[96] *See generally* John P. Dawson, *Effects of Inflation on Private Contracts: Germany, 1914–1924,* 33 MICH. L. REV. 171 (1934); James J. White & David A. Peters, *A Footnote for Jack Dawson*, 100 MICH. L. REV. 1954, 1959 (2002).

[97] White & Peters, *supra* note 96, at 1959.

[98] *See generally* John P. Dawson & Frank E. Cooper, *The Effect of Inflation on Private Contracts: United States 1861–1879* (pts. 1 & 2), 33 MICH. L. REV. 706, 852 (1935); *see also* White & Peters, *supra* note 96, at 1959.

[99] Nathalie Hofmann, *Interpretation Rules and Good Faith as Obstacles to the UK's Ratification of the CISG and to the Harmonization of Contract Law in Europe*, 22 PACE INT'L L. REV. 145, 160 n.88 (2010) (citing German case law discussing the obligation to refrain from acts that could harm the purpose of the contract).

addition, until the reform of the German Law of Obligations in 2002, the good faith doctrine supported: a) the modification of contracts in cases of hardship or frustration of the contractual purpose (as done in common law countries), and b) the cancellation of long-term contracts for just cause.[100] Moreover, it supported an action against the bad faith conduct of a contracting party during the pre-contractual or negotiation phase of the transaction (*culpa in contrahendo*) as now enshrined in § 311(2) of the BGB.[101] Furthermore, it was used against interpretations of contracts (in the broad sense) that entailed an abuse of rights. The late professor, Rudolf B. Schlesinger, the principal author of one of the twentieth century's finest comparative law textbooks, illustrated the application of the good faith doctrine to an abuse of shareholder's rights. One of his illustrations involved a 1935 decision by Germany's Imperial Court, which found that:

> Defendant had alleged and offered to prove that the plaintiff, who had been active in other stock corporations as a professional oppositionist bent on obtaining personal rather than corporate benefits, was here engaged in the same kind of practice . . . [H]e carried on obstruction solely for the purpose of acquiring the shares of the W. family at a cheap price and to compel either his election as a director or the distribution of a higher dividend; and that the present action, again, was to serve plaintiff's own selfish rather than corporate purposes. The legal relevance of these allegations should not have been denied. . . . [T]he statutory scheme shows that the shareholder's special need for legal protection results from the sole fact of his membership in the corporation . . . by virtue of which . . . he is given the right to attack those resolutions of the corporation which are inconsistent with law or charter, even though they may cause no detriment to him personally. But this right has its limits where it conflicts with the duty of faithfulness which the shareholder owes the corporation and which permeates all the rules of corporate law. . . . The idea of the impropriety of an abuse of rights has found statutory recognition in . . . Section 226 of the [BGB]. . . . Beyond the confines of that provision, however, the same principle must apply whenever the exercise of a right constitutes a gross violation of the maxim dominating the entire field of private law, the maxim of *bona fides*. . . . Decisions of this court have repeatedly recognized that the principle of *bona fides* contained in Section 242 of the [BGB] constitutes a general limitation upon the exercise of rights also in the law of stock corporations and of limited liability companies.[102]

---

[100] *Id.* at 160–61.

[101] BGB § 311:

(1) In order to create an obligation by legal transaction and to alter the contents of an obligation, a contract between the parties is necessary, unless otherwise provided by statute.

(2) An obligation with duties under section 241(2) also comes into existence by

1. the commencement of contract negotiations
2. he initiation of a contract where one party, with regard to a potential contractual relationship, gives the other party the possibility of affecting his rights, legal interests and other interests, or entrusts these to him, or
3. similar business contacts.

[102] RUDOLF B. SCHLESINGER ET AL., COMPARATIVE LAW 574–75 (5th ed. 1988).

Section 226 of the BGB states: "The exercise of a right is improper if it cannot have any purpose other than that of harming another."[103] As was customary with Professor Schlesinger's analysis, he clearly and precisely identified the abuse of right doctrine as a consequence of the duty to act in good faith. I would add that consistent with that analysis, abuse of rights appears as a species of bad faith whose frequency and harmfulness has persuaded some legal systems, such as Germany's, to provide an injunctive remedy against it. Reasonableness plays a central role in this remedy because in principle, the holder of a right, whether *in rem* or *in personam*, is entitled to exercise it; otherwise, why refer to it as a right? The remedial issue is then framed as: What is an unreasonable use of the right? The contrary assertion that a right would not be a right if it could not be exercised and that an abuse of right is only a meaningless play on words ("logomachy") (as voiced by Marcel Planiol, an influential early twentieth century French jurist)[104] can thus be discarded as yet another instance of formally logical sophistry attempting to retain a waning *status quo*.

3. Conclusions

BGB §§ 157 and 242 and § 346 of the HGB were the first code rules to rely on good faith not only to resolve judicial disputes, but also to help the parties determine *ex ante* how to perform their contractual duties by referring the interpreter to the customs and usages of the trade in question. The German version of good faith was also independent of the law of torts (particularly negligence) and of promised contractual results; instead, German law chose to associate it with reasonableness and fairness. The use of this conceptualization in the monetary revaluation cases, while revolutionary and on the whole helpful to the stabilization of Germany's economy, was in some instances regarded by lawyers and commentators as an arbitrary judicial substitution for the parties' clearly expressed contractual intent. Accordingly, German codified law can rightfully be regarded as the legislative pioneer of operational good faith norms and, as a result of Karl Llewellyn's admiration for the BGB, it inspired his version of commercial good faith.[105]

D. Good Faith and Reasonableness in English Law

U.C.C. § 1–203 states that "Every contract or duty within this Act imposes an obligation of good faith in its performance or enforcement." This generalized obligation to perform or enforce contracts in good faith was a clear departure from the English law, as observed by courts to this day and by courts in the United States until the turn of the twentieth century. With the exception of decisions by Lord Mansfield that set

---

[103] *Id.*

[104] Shael Herman, *Classical Social Theories and the Doctrine of "Abuse of Right"*, 37 LA. L. REV. 747, 747 (1977). "Planiol, who opposed the doctrine, called the formula 'abusive use of rights' a logomachy, 'for if I use my right, my act is licit; and when it is illicit it is because I exceed my right. . . .' " *Id.* The Merriam Webster online dictionary defines a logomachy as a "dispute over or about words". *Logomachy*, MERRIAM-WEBSTER.COM, http://www.merriam-webster.com/dictionary/logomachy.

[105] WILLIAM TWINING, KARL LLEWELLYN AND THE REALIST MOVEMENT 197 (1973). While discussing Llewellyn's perception of the beauty of legal accomplishments (Legal Aesthetics), Twining states: "The great monument to this esthetic ideal is the German Civil Code, read not as it stands on the page, merely, but read also against the rigorous, almost rigid German theories of construction and dogmatics which were in vogue for a decade after its adoption." *Id.*

forth a general obligation to perform contracts in good faith,[106] English case law did not embrace such a general obligation. Sir Roy Goode of Oxford University explains why:

> The reluctance of English courts to recognize a duty to negotiate in good faith or to interfere with bargains freely made is an aspect of a general mistrust of what are perceived to be over-broad principles not susceptible to clear or consistent application. Thus in contrast to Continental and American legal systems, English law does not possess any general requirement of good faith. A duty of good faith is owed in particular situations or relationships. For example, a person seeking to displace another's title or obtain priority over an earlier security interest must show that he himself took in good faith. . . .[107]

Professor Goode also notes that, under English law, contracting parties are expected to act in good faith when seeking equitable remedies and although English courts do not rely on a general duty to act in good faith, they do impose closely related duties in some contracts. For example, in sale agreements, sellers have a duty to sell goods of a satisfactory quality and not conceal their defects, as they also have a duty to refrain from interfering with the counterparty's performance or from making misrepresentations.[108] Professor Goode concludes:

> At the heart of the judicial caution concerning the introduction of a general concept of good faith is that there is no consensus on its content. The central question is how to resolve the tension between the legitimate pursuit of self interest by a party who has entered or is negotiating to enter into a contract and a proper regard for the legitimate interests of the other party. English law does . . . distinguish between relationships *that are essentially adversarial*, where the guiding principle is that each party has to look after itself, from those which are essentially cooperative because the relationship between the parties or the circumstances in which they come together imposes on one of them an obligation to subordinate its own interests to that of the other, as in the case of an agent or other fiduciary.[109]

I would add that those English decisions that regard contracting parties as adversaries also assume that the contracting parties are presumed to be "of age" or savvy enough to fend for themselves and if they do not, they should. A holding of the King's Bench in a still widely cited 1934 decision can be summarized as: "In the absence of fraud or misrepresentation parties who have put their contract in writing and signed it will not be heard to say that they have not read it or did not know, understand or assent to its contents provided the document is legible however small the print."[110]

This assumption continues to apply to contracts between merchants even after the enactment of the Unfair Contract Terms Act of 1977[111] because this Act is not

---

[106] *See e.g., infra* § 23:4(D)(2) (Lord Mansfield's decisions).

[107] *GOODE ON COMMERCIAL LAW* 105 (Ewan McKendrick ed., 4th ed. 2009) (citations omitted).

[108] *Id.* at 105–106.

[109] *Id.* at 106 (emphasis added).

[110] Friedrich Kessler, *Contracts of Adhesion—Some Thoughts About Freedom of Contract*, 43 COLUM. L. REV. 629, 630 n.3 (1943) (discussing L'Estrange v. F. Graucob Ltd., 2 K.B. 394 (1934)).

[111] Unfair Contract Terms Act, 1977, c. 50 (Eng.):

concerned with contractual good faith or fairness generally, but mostly with the effect of overreaching exemptions of liability clauses by manufacturers or distributors in their notices or warnings to consumers.[112]

1. *Adversarial v. Cooperative/Fiduciary Transactions; Standard and Best Practices*

What about the assumed *adversarial* nature of commercial contracts in English decisional law? Is it accurate to characterize all commercial contracts as adversarial? Certainly, some commercial contracts are adversarial. At one end of the economic scale are Professor Sepe's idiosyncratic sales, leases, mortgages or exchanges of highly valuable commercial assets, whether real or personal property, whose cost or availability may affect the economic viability of the contracting parties.[113] In such cases, the parties are likely to regard themselves as adversaries and when they can afford it, they will hire experienced contract lawyers, top economists, statisticians and other experts to go over every word or clause with the proverbial fine tooth comb to assure their gain, even if at the expense of the other's loss.

At the other end of the commercial spectrum are the parties to flea market transactions who are similarly likely to regard themselves as adversaries and to take every possible precaution against their counterparties misrepresentation and chicanery.[114] Nonetheless, it should also be remembered that in these representative sets of adversary contracts, each contracting party also has a strong interest in satisfying the other's reasonable expectations of profitability. Assume, for example, that the large, highly complex and negotiated transaction involves a long term supply of raw materials that are as essential to the economic viability of the supplier as they are to the purchaser. If the prices negotiated by adversaries wind up preventing the long-run profitability and performance of the supplier, it will hurt both parties. The same would be true in the dickered flea market transaction; sooner or later, the winning adversary's trickery will become known by others and will prevent the trickster's ability to do business in that market.

Despite the number of these sharply negotiated or dickered contracts, the vast majority of contracting parties regard themselves mostly as cooperating with each other. Prominent among these are the standard transactions entered into by merchants as sellers, lenders, borrowers, investors, shippers, carriers, insurers, brokers and so on. Their format is standardized and so are their rights and duties. Thus, the text of these contracts embodies, as illustrated with the Ex-Works

---

> An Act to impose further limits on the extent to which under the law of England and Wales and Northern Ireland civil liability for breach of contract, or for negligence or other breach of duty, can be avoided by means of contract terms and otherwise, and under the law of Scotland civil liability can be avoided by means of contract terms. . . .

Id. See also GOODE, *supra* note 107, at 108–112.

112 *Id.* at 108.

113 Aluminum Co. of America v. Essex Group, Inc., 499 F. Supp. 53, 56–57 (W.D. Penn. 1980).

114 While visiting Mexico City's famous "Lagunilla" flea market I discovered a wordier but ingenious version of *caveat emptor*: Beware, purchaser: You are the one who purchases and I am only who sells you what you want to purchase (*Atencion, Comprador: Usted es quien compra y yo solo quien le vende lo que usted quiere comprar*).

INCOTERM, not only individual intent, but, above all, intent that is representative of the sector, trade or profession involved.[115]

Last but not least, it is important to distinguish between the practices that are standard for the regular participants of a given trade, which in due course become *the* usages of that trade, and those practices that take into account not only the best interests of regular participants, but also those of occasional participants and of third parties whose rights are likely to be affected by the usages.[116] It is worth emphasizing that parties whose conduct during litigation is deceitful are very likely the same parties who at the earlier (transactional and everyday practice) stage of their contracts evaded compliance with standard, let alone best, practices. Thus, to the extent that their bad faith conduct is monitored at the transactional stage by their trade, industry or profession—as it was with some of the medieval guilds[117]—the need for litigation and for judicial versions of good faith, such as those enumerated by Professor Wieacker, diminishes.

2. *Lord Mansfield on Truth Telling, Contractual Warranties and Good Faith*

Contractual warranties, especially those that are implied as contrasted with those that are expressed, have a close connection with the good faith expected from contracting parties during the negotiation and performance of their contracts. As will be apparent shortly, the connection between good faith and telling the truth was organic with Lord Mansfield. His ambition was to "go through life with the character of an honest man. . . . I am not afraid of calumny. I had rather be the object of it than the author of it."[118] Thus, in some contracts of insurance whose expectations of truth telling were highest, he implied a warranty of truthfulness. The following sections benefit from a study of Lord Mansfield's trial notes by Emery V. Anderson (a graduate student of Professor Karl Llewellyn at Columbia University Law School) and by Georgetown University Law School Professor James C. Oldham.[119] Their studies shed considerable light on Mansfield's views on good faith.[120]

a. *Warranties Associated with Horses Sold for a Sound Price: Express and Implied Warranties*

The Anglo-American law on the sale of goods relies on two types of warranties: express and implied.[121] Professor Llewellyn observed that the law of contract warranties in England from 1780–1850 "divides conveniently . . . into horse and non-

---

115 *See* ch. 22 (describing the various types of "dynamic" commercial contracts and the role of usage of trade in the formation of these agreements).

116 For a preliminary dicussion of the importance of these practices in the formation of commercial contract law, *see supra* § 1:2(B). For a full discussion of the compilation and drafting of these practices, *see infra* ch. 24.

117 *See supra* § 6:2(A).

118 C.H.S. FIFOOT, LORD MANSFIELD 143 (1936).

119 James Oldham, *Reinterpretations of 18th-Century English Contract Theory: The View from Lord Mansfield's Trial Notes*, 76 GEO. L.J. 1949 (1988).

120 The study of Mansfield's trial notes was first done by Emery W. Anderson, a student of Karl Llewellyn.Mr. Anderson's study resulted in an LL.M. Thesis. Emery W. Anderson, New Light on Warranty of Quality 1350 to 1800, (undated, circa 1940) (unpublished Master of Laws Thesis, Columbia University).

121 *See* U.C.C. §§ 2–314, 2–315.

horse (cases)."[122] Anderson's and Oldham's studies confirmed the validity of this observation: The sale of horses was the most often litigated sale of goods in Mansfield's court with "at least forty such cases, and thirty-three of these involved proof of an express warranty" and most were won by the buyers of the horses.[123] Despite the large number of express warranty cases, the decisions and notes evidenced Mansfield's willingness to consider implied duties of quality associated with some sales and also to hear evidence on what was a reasonable time for plaintiffs to return defective goods such as horses.[124] As was discussed in Chapter 20,[125] expert commercial juries were known in the city of London as far back as the fourteenth century. Judge Learned Hand provided a summary description of their *modus operandi*:

> The custom was . . . exceedingly common in the city of London throughout the fourteenth century in trade disputes. . . . The mayor . . . summoned a jury of men of that trade, and their verdict decided whether the defendant had offended the trade regulations and upon it the mayor gave a sentence. . . . So we find in 1645 that the court summoned a jury of merchants to try merchants' affairs "because it was conceived they might have better Knowledge of the Matters in Difference that were to be tried, than others could, who were not of that Profession."[126]

Lord Mansfield made the most and best use of merchant juries.[127] His instructions to these jurors were meant to elicit a reliable version of commercial custom or usage of trade. In addition, his adjudication profited from his ability to identify those usages whose ethical components, such as honesty of word and deed and cooperativeness, assured them of recognition as a living commercial law. This was the case of his conclusion in *Pilans v. Van Mierop*, which led to the principle that a "[commercial] man's word is his bond."[128] Using the same method of reasoning, he would instruct the jury in warranty cases to determine whether a sold horse was sound or whether, if unsound, it was returned by the buyer in a timely manner.

As pointed out by Professor Oldham, the sale of horses usually provided a specified time in which the horse could be returned, but if that time were so short that it would be "impossible to make a full discovery of latent faults," the jury was to assess whether the horse was returned "in a reasonable time."[129] Accordingly, Mansfield coupled the reasonable time for the return of the horse with the buyer's ability to inspect the horse (the purpose of the allowed time) and with the buyer's good faith. His version of good faith in these horse cases was also related to what the buyer knew about the horse when he bought it (which in the case of many buyer-traders was significant). Those were the facts that allowed him to assess the reasonableness of the time of return. Hence, after referring to the reasonable time of return of the horse,

---

[122] Oldham, *supra* note 119, at 1970 (citation omitted).

[123] *Id.* at 1971.

[124] *Id.*

[125] *See supra* § 20:4(A).

[126] Learned Hand, *Historical and Practical Considerations Regarding Expert Testimony*, 15 HARV. L. REV. 40, 41–42 (1901–1902).

[127] *See supra* § 20:4(A).

[128] THOMAS CURRY, XV REPORTS OF CASES ARGUED AND DETERMINED IN THE SUPREME COURT OF THE STATE OF LOUISIANA 332 (1841).

[129] Oldham, *supra* note 119, at 1971.

Mansfield usually added, "according to the law."[130] Professor Oldham seems to agree with the preceding observation when he states that Mansfield's trial notes "demonstrate that the knowledge of the buyer remained pertinent, and if he were aware of the alleged defect at the time of the sale, his claim would be defeated."[131] In other words, even if the buyer returned the horse within a reasonable time, his awareness of the defect at the time of sale was bad faith that would disqualify any finding of reasonableness.

Some of Lord Mansfield's decisions on warranties on the sale of horses did not presuppose such knowledge and required evidence that the seller knew of the defective condition. For example, in *Stuart v. Wilkins*,[132] the seller-defendant expressly warranted the quality of the horse. The plaintiff chose to sue on *assumpsit* instead of on the breach of the express warranty and the procedural issue was whether *assumpsit* was the proper action. The court concluded that it was, to which Mansfield added: "A warranty extends to all faults known and unknown to the seller. Selling for a sound price without warranty may be a ground for an *assumpsit,* but, in such a case, it ought to be laid that the defendant knew of the unsoundness."[133] Thus, Mansfield stood ready to impose a duty upon sellers not to sell for a sound price without a corresponding warranty. In doing this, he may have been the first common law judge to have perceived the inherent symmetry and reciprocity of commercial good faith performances. Simply stated, commercial cooperation requires that performances be balanced.

b. Implied Warranties in the Sale of Beer

In *Harding v. Enkell,* a brewer-seller of ale sued a tavern keeper for the price of ale delivered to the latter, which according to the tavern keeper-buyer was "so bad in quality as to be quite undrinkable."[134] Mansfield's decision was a clear opening to an implied warranty of merchantability that did not require proof of the brewer's knowledge of the defect. His decision was summarized as follows:

> "[a]fter . . . [an] examination of a great number of respectable people on the part of the defendant, who proved the gross badness of the ale in question, his Lordship declared, he thought it consistent with reason and justice, that brewers should be accountable to their customers for the quality of the beer they send in; and if it turned out bad, they were bound to receive it back again." The jury agreed, giving a verdict for the defendant, which, according to the *Morning Chronicle,* "may be no unuseful guide for the future conduct of brewers in general."[135]

---

130 *Id.*

131 *Id.*

132 99 Eng. Rep. 15 (1778); *see also* Oldham, *supra* note 119, at 1972.

133 Oldham, *supra* note 119, at 1972.

134 *Id.* at 1974. According to Oldham, this case was recounted in the *Morning Chronicle* on December 8, 1781. *Id.* at 1974 n.159.

135 *Id.* at 1974 (citation omitted).

c. *Good Faith, Implied Warranties in Insurance Contracts and the Importance of Telling the Truth*

That Lord Mansfield's association of a party's good faith with the absolute duty to tell the truth expected of him was applicable to commercial transactions in addition to sales became apparent in *Carter v. Boehm*,[136] another one of his landmark decisions. As governor of an English fort in Sumatra, Indonesia, Carter purchased an insurance policy from Boehm to cover the risk that the fort might be overrun by a foreign enemy. A credible witness testified that Carter knew that the fort could resist the attacks from natives, but not from European military powers such as France. He also testified that Carter was aware of this fact when he applied for Boehm's insurance and was also aware that the French were likely to attack this fort. When the French attacked and the fort was overrun, Boehm refused to pay the insurance policy, alleging Carter's above mentioned knowledge. Lord Mansfield decided in favor of Boehm, saying that Carter had failed his duty of highest good faith. In Mansfield's words:

> Insurance is a contract [based] upon speculation. The special facts upon which the risk is to be computed lie most commonly in the knowledge of the assured only. The under-writer trusts to his representation and proceeds upon the confidence that he does not keep back any circumstance in his knowledge to mislead the underwriter into a belief that the circumstance does not exist and to induce him to estimate the risk as if it did not exist.[137]

He made it clear that the policy would be equally void against the underwriter if he concealed anything exclusively within his knowledge, such as when he had learned that the ship to be insured had arrived safely at its destination, and would be compelled to refund the premium that he had fraudulently obtained.[138] To which he added:

> This governing principle is applicable to all contracts. Good faith forbids either party, by concealment of what he alone knows, to draw the other into a bargain which he would certainly avoid if the information were equal. But either party may innocently be silent as to matters upon which both may equally exercise their judgment. . . . There are many matters as to which the assured may be innocently silent. He need not mention what the underwriter knows or ought to know . . . as the difficulties of the voyage, the variations of the seasons, or the probability of lightning, hurricanes and earthquakes. So the underwriter is bound to know every cause which may occasion political perils. . . .[139]

A similar analysis is apparent in *Schoolbred v. Nutt*.[140] One of Lord Mansfield's jury instructions was: "It is a condition, or implied warranty, in every policy, that the Ship is seaworthy; and therefore there need be no representation of that." However, if a statement or representation was made that was not truly factual, he would not hesitate to find the bad faith that is associated with dishonesty. For example, when the

---

[136] 97 E.R. 1162 [1966].

[137] Edmund Heward, Lord Mansfield 101–02 (1979).

[138] *Id.* at 102.

[139] *Id.*

[140] 495 NB 73 [London, May 27, 1782], *cited in* Oldham, *supra* note 119, at 1973 n.154; *see also* JAMES ALLAN PARK, A SYSTEM OF THE LAW OF MARINE INSURANCE 300–01 (6th ed. 1809).

issue in a sale of goods by auction to the highest bidder was whether the seller-owner could employ a "puffer" or agent to raise the price by his fictitious bidding, Lord Mansfield's response was:

> The matter in dispute is of small pecuniary value, but it involves principles of the highest importance to society. The basis of all dealings ought to be good faith; so more especially in these transactions where the public are brought together upon a confidence that the articles set up to sale will be disposed of to the highest real bidder. That can never be the case if the owner may secretly enhance the price by a person employed for that purpose. Yet tricks and practices of this kind daily increase, and grow so frequent that good men give into the ways of the bad, and become dishonest. . . . I cannot listen to the argument that it is common practice. Gaming, stock-jobbing, and swindling are all very common; but the law forbids them all.[141]

3. *Conclusions: Mansfield's Good Faith and Reasonableness*

Unlike the versions of good faith relied upon by French courts and commentators, Lord Mansfield's decisions helped to predict what constituted good faith conduct in a given trade. He made predictability possible by linking the duties of truthfulness and reasonableness with archetypal behavior and usages of trade. Thus, he coupled the meaning of, say, the reasonable time for a buyer's return of a defective horse with the time that it generally took professional or alert buyers to inspect horses (prior and after their sale). In contrast, ordinary tavern keepers could hold the brewer accountable in a manner "consistent with reason and justice" without having to prove their lack of knowledge of the beer's defects when they bought it.

The same considerations held true with respect to expected disclosures by the insured in various types of insurance contracts. Mansfield's version of good faith and reasonable conduct in the trade in question were also grounded in his command of the transactional facts, and especially what I will refer to as the "nuclear elements of a commercial practice" in Chapter 24.[142] Please note how succinctly and accurately he identified the nuclear elements of the insurance practice: "Insurance is a contract [based] upon speculation. The special facts upon which the risk is to be computed lie most commonly in the knowledge of the assured only. The underwriter trusts to his representation and . . . [assumes] that he does not keep back any circumstance in his knowledge. . . ."[143] Hence, the transactional facts, including the type of insurance and the actual or imputed knowledge of these facts determined the reasonableness of the duty to disclose. But honesty in fact, as detectable by any regular participant in the transaction, was above transactional practice: Recall his rebuke of puffery in public bidding: "I cannot listen to the argument that it is common practice. Gaming, stock-jobbing, and swindling are all very common; but the law forbids them all."[144]

Mansfield's good faith, then, was shaped first of all by the moral duty to be honest and disclose the truth. Disclosure was unnecessary only when it was clear beyond a reasonable doubt that the counterparty would not be aware of the relevant facts. And

---

141 HEWARD, *supra* note 137, at 102–03.

142 *See infra* § 24:2.

143 HEWARD, *supra* note 137, at 102.

144 *Id.* at 103.

when what was reasonable could not be discerned from course of dealing or usage of trade, he relied on what was described early in this book as the logic of the reasonable.[145] Among the questions associated with this logic were: What was the business and legal relationship of the parties—buyers and sellers, insurers and insured, brewers and distributors? What were their transactional goals and how were these goals reflected in the alignment of their respective rights and duties? Were the alignment and the goals reasonable based upon the expectations of archetypal counterparties? What was the effect of the alignment of rights and duties upon the rights of third parties and upon the community of traders or society's welfare?

Doubts about the effectiveness of Mansfield's logic are quickly dispelled by contrasting the principles or rules that resulted from his logic with those that resulted from the formally logical rules of the common law of his time. One example will suffice. The formally "logical" common law rule encountered by Mansfield when deciding *Pillans v. Van Mierop* was (as was discussed in the preceding chapter) that a promise whose consideration was past was unenforceable for lack of present consideration. In contrast, Mansfield's rule (which resulted from his observation of what was honest and reasonable in commercial practice and from his evaluation of its impact upon the community of merchants and their clients) was: "A *nudum pactum* does not exist, in the usage and law of merchants."[146] It is difficult to estimate how many trillions of dollars' worth of "line of credit" agreements would have been unenforceable beyond their first disbursements had they been governed by the formally logical common law rule of past consideration.[147] Further, the commercial letter of credit practice central to the financing of global trade for more than one hundred years would not have come into existence if the issuing bank's promise had to be supported by present consideration supplied by its beneficiary-promisee.[148]

§ 23.5 GOOD FAITH IN THE U.C.C. AND RESTATEMENT (SECOND)

A. Articles 1 and 2 of the U.C.C. and Restatement (Second) § 202

Lord Mansfield's requirements of honesty in fact and reasonableness, as often reflected in usages of trade, amounted to the first effective formula of a commercial duty of good faith in Anglo-American decisional law. Yet, despite such an auspicious beginning, to this day no generalized doctrine of good faith exists in English decisional or statutory law. The task of creating such a doctrine of good faith was undertaken in the United States primarily by Llewellyn's Articles 1 and 2 of the U.C.C.[149]

---

145 *See supra* § 2:2.

146 FIFOOT, *supra* note 118, at 131.

147 In a line of credit agreement, the lender, *ex ante,* agrees to lend a variable amount of money that depends upon the borrower's ability to repay it and whatever was the initial consideration for that agreement remains supporting future loans for the life of the agreement.

148 For a discussion of the problems posed by the formal requirements of present consideration, *see infra* §§ 22:5 & 22:6. For a discussion of the non-role of consideration in the issuance of letters of credit, *see* BORIS KOZOLCHYK, COMMERCIAL LETTERS OF CREDIT IN THE AMERICAS 575–84 (1966).

149 Other U.C.C. articles, such as Article 5, adopted the standard of "honesty in fact" for letter of credit transactions, while Article 9 adopted the "honesty in fact and the observance of reasonable standards of fair dealing" for secured transactions. *Compare* U.C.C. § 5–102(a)(7) *with* U.C.C. § 9–102(a)(43). In principle, there is no reason for adopting different standards. The reasons for the adoption of an honesty in

As will be recalled from Chapter 20, the National Conference of Commissioners of Uniform State Laws and the American Law Institute first adopted the U.C.C. in 1951.[150] It had three sections on good faith. U.C.C. § 1–201(19) defined it as "honesty in fact in the conduct or transaction concerned." Section 1–203, in a manner reminiscent of the *Code Civil*'s Article 1134 ("Agreements legally formed . . . must be executed in good faith.") and the BGB's § 157 ("contracts are to be interpreted as required by good faith. . . ."), declared that "Every contract or duty within this Act imposes an obligation of good faith in its performance or enforcement."[151] In addition, the 1951 version of the U.C.C. contained a special definition for good faith in commercial sales: § 2–103(1)(b) defined good faith for purposes of Article 2 as: " 'Good faith' in the case of a merchant means honesty in fact and the observance of reasonable commercial standards of fair dealing in the trade."[152]

In turn, § 202 of the Restatement (Second) (as revised in 1981) provided its own "Rules in Aid of Interpretation," which closely followed the spirit of U.C.C. Articles 1 and 2, and the views of Professors Corbin and Llewellyn.[153] For example, § 202(1) states:

> Words and other conduct are interpreted in the light of all the circumstances, and if the principle purpose of the parties is ascertainable it is given great weight.[154]

Similarly, § 202(4) and (5) state:

> (4)Where an agreement involves repeated occasions for performance by either party with knowledge of the nature of the performance and opportunity for objection to it by the other, any course of performance accepted or acquiesced in without objection is given great weight in the interpretation of the contract.
>
> (5) Wherever reasonable, the manifestations of intention of the parties to a promise or agreement are interpreted consistent with each other and with any relevant course of performance, course of dealing, or usage of trade.[155]

U.C.C. Article 1 was revised in 2001 and § 1–201 re-defined good faith as "honesty in fact and the observance of reasonable commercial standards of fair dealing."[156] Section 1–304 also restated the obligation to observe good faith as: "Every contract or duty within [the Uniform Commercial Code] imposes an obligation of good faith in its performance and enforcement."[157] Finally, Article 2 of the U.C.C. was amended in 2003

---

fact standard in a code that relies as much as does the U.C.C. on course of performance, course of dealing and usage of trade as a prime interpretive tools.

150 For the sequence of adoptions and amendments of the provision on good faith in Articles 1 and 2, *see* Dubroff, *supra* note 1, at 559 n.2.

151 U.C.C. § 1–203.

152 U.C.C. § 2–103(1)(b) (1951).

153 James Byrne, *Publisher's Note* to RESTATEMENT 2D OF CONTRACTS & UNIDROIT PRINCIPLES: THE TEXTS, THE COMMENTS & THE ILLUSTRATIONS v. (Institute of International Banking Law and Practice ed., 2001).

154 Restatement (Second) of Contracts § 202(1) (1981).

155 *Id.* § 202 (4)–(5).

156 U.C.C. § 1–201(b)(20).

157 *Id.* § 1–304.

to remove the special definition of good faith for purposes of Article 2, presumably because the general provisions of Article 1 had taken care of all the definitions of good faith, except that of Article 5, about which more later.

1. A Sectoral Version of Contractual Intent: Course of Dealing and Usage of Trade as Sources of Commercial Intent (U.C.C. § 1–205)

In the preceding as well as in earlier sections of this chapter, we learned about course of performance, dealing and usage of trade as engines of the formation of commercial contracts. Because of these engines, and despite the purportedly exclusionary circles of intent of U.C.C. § 1–205(4) in real-legal life, the interpretation of commercial contracts under the U.C.C. is as influenced by the parties' conduct as it is by contractual language. U.C.C. § 1–205 identifies the principal manifestations of contractual conduct and their use as sources of interpretive and remedial law. As stated by U.C.C. § 1–205(1): "A course of dealing is a sequence of previous conduct between the parties to a particular transaction which is fairly to be regarded as establishing a common basis of understanding for interpreting their expressions and other conduct."[158] The interpretive value of usage of trade is similarly highlighted by U.C.C. § 1–205(2): "A usage of trade is any practice or method of dealing having such regularity of observance in a place, vocation or trade as to justify an expectation that it will be observed with respect to the transaction in question."[159]

Then U.C.C. § 1–205(3) sets forth the interpretive function of course of dealing and usage of trade as the providers of the "particular" or *sectoral meaning* of contractual terms and conditions: "A course of dealing between parties and any usage of trade in the vocation or trade in which they are engaged or of which they are or should be aware *give particular meaning to and supplement or qualify terms of an agreement*."[160]

Aware of the major departure from traditional or purely textual methods of interpretation espoused by the "literal," "plain meaning" and "within the four corners" approaches,[161] the Official Comment tried to soften the innovative blow of the contextual approach it introduced by assuring lawyers and judges that:

> This Act deals with "usage of trade" as *a factor* in reaching the commercial meaning of the agreement which the parties have made. The language used is to be interpreted as meaning what it may fairly be expected to mean to parties involved in the particular commercial transaction in a given locality or in a given vocation or trade. . . . Part of the agreement . . . to which such rules yield is to be sought for in the usages of trade which furnish the background and give particular meaning to the language used, and are the framework of common understanding controlling any general rules of law which hold only where there is no such understanding.[162]

---

158 *Id.* § 1–205(1). Henceforward, and unless otherwise noted, course of dealing will include course of performance.

159 *Id.* § 1–205(2).

160 *Id.* § 1–205(3) (emphasis added).

161 On the misleading and contextual meaning of the "plain meaning" approach to the interpretation of contract, see the terse but highly insightful Comment b to § 212 of the Restatement (Second): "It is sometimes said that extrinsic evidence cannot change the plain meaning of a writing, but meaning can almost never be plain except in a context." RESTATEMENT (SECOND) OF CONTRACTS § 212 cmt. b (1981).

162 U.C.C. § 1–205 cmt. 4 (emphasis added).

Similarly, U.C.C. § 1–205(4) tried to reassure the traditional, textual interpreters of contracts by providing them with a simple, almost graphic, set of concentric and exclusionary circles of contractual intent in which that closest to the express terms excludes the application of the others:

> The express terms of an agreement and an applicable course of dealing or usage of trade shall be construed wherever reasonable as consistent with each other, but when such construction is unreasonable express terms control both course of dealing and usage of trade and course of dealing controls usage of trade.[163]

Despite this reassurance, the significance attributed to an intent that was not individual, but commercial, contextual and sectoral, was unmistakable. To be persuasively established, such intent required the admissibility of extrinsic evidence on course of dealing and usage of trade. This was not as easily accomplished as one may have thought because of the earlier discussed Parol Evidence Rule of U.C.C. § 2–202.[164]

The admissibility of parol evidence required a creative or "Grand Style" judicial decision making (in Karl Llewellyn's lexicon and about which more in the following section). When this creativity was aptly employed, the results were welcomed by some (such as myself) and rejected by textual interpreters. Consider, for example, Judge Butzner's reliance on comment 2 of U.C.C. § 2–202 in *Columbia Nitrogen*, which is found in the Appendix.[165] Simple as the explanation in this comment may appear to be, it reflected a transformation in the discernment of commercial intent. This was a transformation presaged in other decisions such as in a 1968 opinion by Chief Justice Traynor of the California Supreme Court.[166] Its epistemology assumes that words as well as conduct are tools to express a contractual intent whose ultimate meaning depends upon its transactional context. Comment b to § 212 of the Restatement (Second) also supports this contextual method of interpretation: "It is sometimes said that extrinsic evidence cannot change the plain meaning of a writing, but meaning can almost never be plain except in a context."[167] The contextualization of commercial contract intent is also apparent in the U.C.C.'s relaxed requirements for proof of a binding commercial custom. Its requirements differ markedly from those of traditional English and continental law.[168] In fact, in the U.C.C., customary law became a genus

---

[163] *Id.* § 1–205(4).

[164] *Id.* § 2–202; *supra* note 31 and accompanying text.

[165] *See infra* § 23:9(E). As reported by my research assistant Brad Terry, *Columbia Nitrogen* is good law. The only negative treatment it has received was in Southern Concrete Services, Inc. v. Mableton Contractors, Inc., 407 F.Supp. 581, 583 (N.D. Ga. 1975). However, the Mableton case merely distinguished Royster based upon a factual difference. *Columbia Nitrogen* has been discussed in seventy four subsequent cases and has been favorably cited by courts in nearly all of the U.S. federal circuits.

[166] Chief Justice Traynor's test for the admissibility of extrinsic evidence:

> The test of admissibility of extrinsic evidence to explain the meaning of a written instrument is not whether it appears to the court to be plain and unambiguous on its face, but whether the offered evidence is relevant to prove a meaning to which the language of the instrument is reasonably susceptible.

Pacific Gas & Elec. Co. v. G. W. Thomas Drayage & Rigging Co., 69 Cal. 2d 33, 37 (1968).

[167] RESTATEMENT (SECOND) OF CONTRACTS § 212 cmt. b; *see supra* note 161 (referring to this comment).

[168] As noted by Professor Roy Goode, the legal criteria that validate custom in English law are "certainty and consistency of practice, reasonableness, notoriety, and conformity with mandatory law. Moreover, in order to constitute a usage the practice must be observed from a sense of legally binding obligation, not as a matter of mere courtesy or convenience or a desire to accommodate a customer's wishes."

whose most often relied upon species are course of performance, course of dealing, and usage of trade. Official Comment 5 of § 1–205 tells us why:

> A usage of trade under subsection (2) must have the "regularity of observance" specified. The ancient English tests for "custom" are abandoned in this connection. Therefore, it is not required that a usage of trade be "ancient or immemorial", "universal" or the like. Under the requirement of subsection (2) full recognition is thus available for new usages and for usages currently observed by the great majority of decent dealers, even though dissidents ready to cut corners do not agree. There is room also for *proper recognition of usage agreed upon by merchants in trade codes.*[169]

2. *The Sectoral Meaning of Reasonableness: Placing Oneself in the Position of "An Archetypal Other," A Personal Anecdote*

Reasonableness is frequently used to denote the behavior of many, if not most, similarly situated people, regardless of their occupation or social status. But reasonableness also has a distinctly commercial meaning, especially when the counterparty is another merchant. I beg the reader's indulgence for relying on another personal anecdote that illustrates the importance of commercial reasonableness as a full partner of good faith when interpreting contractual conduct, even at the earliest of stages of a possible negotiation. My father had just come to the United States after having had all his business assets confiscated in Cuba. He was undergoing a very difficult time adjusting to a life without a business or a paying job. At that time, I was teaching at the Southern Methodist University School of Law and thanks to Professor Bayless Manning, the future dean at the Stanford Law School, I was invited to visit that law school to explore the possibility of my teaching there. To lighten his mood, I invited my father to come along. We spent an afternoon touring downtown San Francisco and at his request, we visited shops in Chinatown.

While at a souvenir store and after he spent some time looking at different items and comparing their prices to those he used to charge in his Cuban store, the shop owner approached us and asked a question that I could not understand as it seemed to have been more in Chinese than English. Surprisingly, my father, in his very limited English, answered her almost immediately by repeating the same sounds that were part of her question. After she heard his reply, she nodded politely and in more understandable English wished us a good day. I was surprised by this exchange and after we left the store I asked, "Papá, you must tell me what she asked us and explain to me how you could possibly answer her with so little English and no Chinese." He slowly uttered what he heard her say and I recognized the sounds of the English

---

GOODE, *supra* note 107, at 14. The last criterion is also known as the *opinio juris sive necessitates*, *i.e.*, the conviction that the custom is binding and together with the preceding criteria are also pretty uniform in continental civil law. Some countries continue to insist that for a commercial custom to be valid, it must be "inveterate." By inveterate, the Spanish Supreme Court at one point meant that it had to be a custom observed widely by merchants for generations, if not centuries, regardless that commercial practices had changed significantly during those intervals. Thus, its reluctance to apply commercial customs as binding sources of commercial law has continued until a decade or so ago. For example, in decisions handed down as recently as 1975 and 1997, Spain's Supreme Court rejected the binding effect of widely observed international and national banking customs such as the Uniform Customs and Practices for Documentary Credits (UCP).

[169] U.C.C. § 1–205 cmt. 5 (emphasis added).

expression "looking around." But how did he know the meaning of looking around in English? His answer was remarkable. "At that time, I didn't know their meaning, but I put myself in her position, watching a couple of unlikely customers and wondering if she should waste her time with us or pay attention to other, more likely customers. That was certainly what I would have asked in her shoes, 'Are you interested in buying something or are you just looking around?' That is why I repeated as an answer the sound of what I thought was her question, 'looking around.' "

Being able to place oneself in the position of one's commercial counterparty and perceiving what that merchant wants to know or expects to hear are crucial components of commercially reasonable behavior. It is the attitude that enables a successful merchant to anticipate what goods, services, prices, terms and conditions would satisfy the reasonable expectations of his counterparties. It is an attitude contrary to that of *caveat emptor* or of the picaresque vendor reputed to have said somewhere in medieval Europe, "I don't care if you get what you want or expect, as long as I get my profit." Granted, this stage of a contractual negotiation had not been reached by my father and the shop owner, but it could not have been reached unless my father instinctively knew to ask himself, "What would I have done if I were in her shoes?" Still, if you dig deeper into what made my father act the way he did, you realize that he was not really placing himself in her shoes, as was the scenario assumed by the earlier mentioned *Lucy v. Zehmer* definition of reasonableness.[170] All he knew about her is that she was a fellow merchant interested in making a sale. He was not even placing himself in his own shoes. He was placing himself in the shoes of a representative or archetypal merchant (*i.e.*, someone like him or her having to make a commercial decision). Years later, Professor John Honnold, the exemplary teacher, scholar and human being, then Secretary General of UNCITRAL, to whom I had told my father's Chinatown story, sent me the final draft of the United Nations Convention on the International Sale of Goods for my comments. As I read Article 8(2), I had a feeling that I knew the reasonable person that this provision was referring to quite well: "[S]tatements made by and other conduct of a party are to be interpreted according to the understanding that a reasonable person of the same kind as the other party would have had in the same circumstances."[171]

B. Llewellyn's Archetypal "Decent" Merchant and His German Antecedent

Article 2's archetypal decent merchant had a counterpart in the HGB. As discussed in Chapters 11 and 12, the archetypal merchant in this code was a proper, business-like and prudent merchant (*Ordentlichen Kaufmanns*).[172] The polar opposite of this archetype was a merchant to whom Llewellyn referred to as the "sharpy," "dirty" or "corner-cutting" merchant, someone prepared to rely on legal formalisms or hyper-technical interpretations of contracts or of the law to renege on contracts when changes in market price had made the contract price onerous.[173] As he stated in an article advocating the adoption of the U.C.C.:

---

170 *See supra* note 34 and accompanying text.

171 CISG art. 8(2); *see supra* note 35 and accompanying text.

172 *See* HGB §§ 130(a), 347, 497 (GOREN, 1998).

173 *See, e.g.*, U.C.C. § 1–205 cmt. 5 (referring to the U.C.C.'s full recognition for new usages and "for usages currently observed by the great majority of decent dealers, even though dissidents ready to cut

> It just happens under the law as it now stands . . . when you deliver goods in pursuance of a contract to deliver, you have no right to a receipt. If the fellow at the other end refuses to give you a receipt but insists upon delivery, you come into default in your contract if you insist upon the receipt. Now, no decent business man would refuse to give a receipt. Look, however, at the opportunity this offers to the sharpy. A man has made a contract for the purchase of goods, the time for delivery has come, the price has gone down, the contract has become extremely uncomfortable to the buyer. So what does he do when the goods arrive, having been advised by a lawyer as crooked as he? He refuses to give a receipt.[174]

Llewellyn's archetypal decent merchant combined good faith (meaning honesty) with reasonableness: "I am willing to admit a certain amount of bad faith and stupidity on the part of anybody today, but I am reasonable and I don't think general standards ought to be drawn with the assumption that there is going to be unreasonableness."[175] To which he added:

> The way to write good law is to indicate what you want to do, and you assume within reason that the persons the law deals with will try to be decent; then after that, you lay down the edges to take care of the dirty guys and try to hold them in, which means that every statute ought to have two essential bases, one to show where the law wants you to go, and one to show where we will put you if you don't.[176]

C. The Exclusion of Reasonableness in Article 5 of the U.C.C. on Letters of Credit

The unamended text of U.C.C. § 2–103(1)(b) incorporates reasonableness as an element of good faith: "Good faith in the case of a merchant means honesty in fact and the observance of reasonable commercial standards of fair dealing in the trade."[177] This formulation combined Lord Mansfield's element of honesty with his reliance on course of dealing and trade usage, often through the findings of fact by merchant jurors. With these findings, he was able to determine what was reasonable in addition to whether the parties were being honest. U.C.C. § 2–103(1)(b) also seemed to have borrowed from the references to customary practices and usages of trade as sources for the application of the good faith requirement found in BGB §§ 157 and 242. Thus, § 2–103(1)(b) became U.C.C. Article 2's "objective" standard and the antipode of the subjective version of good faith. Eventually, other U.C.C. articles adopted the same objective standard.[178]

---

corners do not agree."). For another reference to the sharpers, see Zipporah Batshaw Wiseman, *The Limits of Vision: Karl Llewellyn and the Merchant Rules*, 100 HARV. L. REV. 465, 515, 518–19, 529 (1987).

[174] Karl Llewellyn, *Why a Commercial Code?*, 22 TENN. L. REV. 779, 780–81 (1953).

[175] *Id.* at 782.

[176] *Id.*

[177] *Id.* § 2–103(1)(b); *see supra* note 46.

[178] U.C.C. §§ 1–201(b)(20); 2A–103(3) (financial leases); 3–103(a)(4) (negotiable instruments); 4–104(c) (bank deposits and collections); 4A–105(a)(6) (fund transfer by banks); 8–1029(a)(10) (investment securities); 9–102(43) (secured transactions).

Notably absent from the list of adoptions of the objective standard is Article 5 on letters of credit. Since the reasons for the rejection of reasonableness by Revised Article 5 were in my opinion ill-advised, I will summarize now my objections during the drafting of this revision.

Prior to the enactment of Article 5 and UCP 500, the prevailing standard for the bank's examination of letter of credit documents was their strict compliance with the terms and conditions of the letter of credit.[179] Strict compliance was understood by many court decisions as the result of a mechanical "mirror image" examination of the documents against the terms and conditions of the letter of credit. These examinations were used as excuses for banks not to pay on letters of credit when they could not be certain of reimbursements by their customers. And many of these customers were known to rely on the same examination when the prices of the goods they bought had unexpectedly dropped and their profits were imperiled. Thus, prior to the revision of Article 5, I advocated the adoption of a different standard for the examination of the documents based on reasonableness as found in the examination by an archetypal "reasonable document checker."[180] Article 13(a) of UCP 500 adopted this standard as found in "International Standard Banking Practice."[181] Similarly, the drafters of revised Article 5 required in U.C.C. § 5–108(e) that the issuing bank "observe standard practice of financial institutions that regularly issue letters of credit."[182]

In light of these provisions, a document checker could no longer rely on his "strict compliance" (mirror image and often bad faith) examination to reject documents that would have complied had they been examined in accordance with standard (and reasonable) banking practice.[183] In other words, honesty in fact (without reasonableness) could no longer support the increasingly common bad faith practice of mirror-image examination and rejection of documents. Not surprisingly, and despite Article 5's adoption of the honesty in fact standard, because of the parallel adoption of Article 13(a) of UCP 500 and § 5–108(e) of the U.C.C., courts in the United States have since required the bankers to rely on the reasonableness found in standard banking practice as a measure of their good faith examination of documents.[184] This meant that the rejection of the standard of reasonableness by the drafters of Revised Article 5, unlike the rest of its many admirable provisions, was a discordant note in an otherwise highly sound enterprise.

D. The Merchant Rules of U.C.C. Article 2

Readers used to the drafting style of nineteenth-century European formally logical civil and commercial codes, whose definitions and classifications are based upon the Aristotelian essences of the respective concepts, will find the drafting of Articles 1 and

---

179 *See generally* Boris Kozolchyk, *Strict Compliance and the Reasonable Document Checker*, 56 BROOK. L. REV. 45 (1990) [hereinafter Kozolchyk, *Strict Compliance*]. *See also infra* ch. 24 (a detailed examination of the letter of credit practices and the governing stamdards).

180 Kozolchyk, *Strict Compliance*, *supra* note 179, at 72–80.

181 UCP 500 art. 13(a) (1993).

182 U.C.C. § 5–108(e).

183 For the reasons why standard letter of credit banking practices have an inbuilt component of reasonableness, *see infra* ch. 24.

184 *See, e.g.*, Voest-Alpine Trading USA Corp. v. Bank of China, 167 F. Supp. 2d 940, 946–48, (S.D. Tex. 2000); Brenntag Int'l Chemicals, Inc. v. Norddeutsche Landesbank GZ, 9 F. Supp. 2d 331, 342 (S.D.N.Y. 1998).

2 of the U.C.C. too loose, imprecise and their definitions tautological. Nonetheless, their apparent looseness was not caused by carelessness. Professor Karl Llewellyn's drafting style reflects his distaste for what he deemed a mechanical, formalistic and narrow method of drafting commercial law as apparent in the Uniform Sales Act. He referred to that statute as a 'rebuilt machine' of what was contained in the English Sales of Goods Act of 1893.[185] As pointed out by Professor Ziporah Batshaw Wiseman of the University of Texas Law School, this enactment reflected a nineteenth-century commerce in which the prototypical sales transaction was:

> [T]he face-to-face sale in which the buyer paid cash and took her goods home. Llewellyn sought, instead, a model that reflected the reality of a twentieth-century "nationwide indirect marketing structure." In the modern world of sales, Llewellyn's and ours, most commercial sellers and buyers of goods do not deal face-to-face and do not immediately take the goods home. Rather, they contract for a sale in the future; their agreement is usually on the buyer's or seller's printed form; their sale is on credit; and their relationship has just begun. In addition, there may be one or more middlemen between the seller-manufacturer and the buyer, who may be buying for resale or for use. . . . Williston's law of sales, reflecting faithfully the English Act on which it was modeled, took no cognizance of these complexities."[186]

As shown by the good faith provisions of Articles 1 and 2 that he authored, for Llewellyn as well as for Baldus (the medieval commentator), good faith was a fundamental principle of the *lex mercatoria*.[187] And commerce was an activity that was dynamic, cooperative and trusting enough to require a law sensitive to marketplace behavior and flexible enough to allow the judges' application of standards of interpretation that would implement the policies behind the rules. And when unforeseen factual situations emerged, the law had to allow courts to shape new rules and standards consistent with these policies in what he labeled the "Grand Style" of judicial decision making.[188]

1. *The Grand Style of Interpreting Contracts and Llewellyn's Merchant Rules*

As the chief draftsman of Article 2 of the U.C.C., Llewellyn, as much as any other scholar-draftsman in the common or civil law world, tried to institutionalize commercial custom as a key source for the interpretation of commercial contracts. He was responsible for visionary provisions that enabled the application of customary law sources and commercial practices as an official and living law of contracts. Deep down, however, his favorite tool for the interpretation of commercial contracts was the Grand Style, which encouraged the judge's reliance on purposive, equitable and policy-oriented tools. Hand in hand with his encouragement of judicial creativity were Llewellyn's own rules, often clothed as commercial practices.

---

185 Karl Llewellyn, Cases and Material on the Law of Sales xvi (1930).

186 Wiseman, *supra* note 173, at 475–76.

187 *See supra* text accompanying note 53; Wiseman, *supra* note 173, at 510 ("Llewellyn's proposal of a substantial performance rule in merchant sales is a clear example of his concern for fairness and good faith in merchant transactions.").

188 *See infra* note 200 and acompanying text.

As defined by § 2–104(1), the archetypal merchant for whom Karl Llewellyn drafted Article 2's "Merchant Rules" was one with knowledge and skills related to his goods or transactions. This was not just a good father of family or even an ordinary citizen endowed with an unusual amount of common sense. This was someone with a sense of what was reasonable based upon what he and other merchants like him knew and did for a living:

> "Merchant" means a person who deals in goods of the kind or otherwise by his occupation holds himself out as having knowledge or skill peculiar to the practices or goods involved in the transaction or to whom such knowledge or skill may be attributed by his employment of an agent or broker or other intermediary who by his occupation holds himself out as having such knowledge and skill.[189]

The emphasis on the need for a merchant to possess knowledge and skill with goods or services and their transactions suggests a subjective approach to the scope of a commercial code such as that of the HGB, *i.e.*, the code is only for merchants and their transactions.[190] Section I of this Code defined a merchant (or "trader" in B.F. Platt's translation) broadly as "he who carries on a trade."[191] In addition, as noted by A.F. Schuster, another early translator of the HGB, those who qualified as merchants enjoyed certain privileges such as the ability: a) to trade under a firm name; b) to appoint an ostensibly empowered agent who bound his principal even if he exceeded his actual authority *(Prokurist)*; c) to trade in the stock exchange; d) to claim commissions for his services when acting as an intermediary; and others.[192] Conversely, the HGB merchant was subject to mandatory duties such as the retention of copies of all business letters forwarded to him as well as certain accounting books and records.[193] If he was declared bankrupt and failed to fulfill these or other mandatory duties, he was subject to criminal punishment. Moreover, when he dealt with non-merchants, his transactions (with few exceptions) were still governed by the commercial code even though the counterparty was a consumer.[194]

Unlike the HGB, the U.C.C. does not limit the transactions that confer the status of merchants. Nor does it confer special trading privileges or impose special commercial duties such as the preservation of correspondence or the use of a specific method of bookkeeping; it defers these requirements to other state or federal enactments. On the other hand, U.C.C. Article 2's treatment of certain typically commercial promises or transactions differs from that in which the counterparty is a non-merchant. Further, Article 2's permissive approach to the status of merchants and their transactions anticipated the use of the same approach in Germany's 1998 amendment to its commercial code (HGB). Section 1 of the HGB now tersely states: "A merchant within the meaning of this Code is anyone who conducts a business."[195] The mere fact that

---

189 U.C.C. § 2–104(1).

190 *See supra* § 12:3(A)(4) (discussing the *Allgemeines Deutsches Handelsgesetzbuch* (ADHGB) of 1871); *see also* CODE FOR THE GERMAN EMPIRE, *supra* note 4, at 146.

191 CODE FOR THE GERMAN EMPIRE, *supra* note 4, at 1.

192 THE GERMAN COMMERCIAL CODE xi (A. F. Schuster trans., 1911), *available at* http://ia700408.us.archive.org/3 /items/cu31924025030150/cu31924025030150.pdf.

193 *Id.*

194 For the exceptions of the application of the HGB to nonmerchants, *see id.* §§ 346, 352, 369, 377.

195 *See* GERMAN COMMERCIAL CODE (Martin Peltzer & Elizabeth A. Voight trans., 5th rev. ed. 2002).

many businesses that used to be associated with the status of licensed merchants are now being conducted by non-licensed or otherwise qualified merchants from their home computers suggests the need for a reexamination of the scope of rules that presuppose a sharp divide between licensed and non-licensed merchants.

2. *A Contemporary Evaluation of the Merchant Rules in Article 2 of the U.C.C.*

Professor Llewellyn's so-called merchant rules of Article 2 of the U.C.C. have been the subject of two fine studies on his vision and methodology, one of which is critical and the other admiring, but both acknowledge the difficulties encountered by the application of his merchant rules. The first of these studies was published in 1985 by Professor Ingrid Michelsen Hillinger of the Boston College School of Law.[196] After she examined how some of the merchant rules fared in court, she concluded that while in the abstract, the discrimination between merchants and non-merchants had some justification, the relevant basis for discriminating rules was not between merchants and non-merchants, but between consumers and non-consumers.[197] She quoted Llewellyn for the assertion that "[t]hese are rules which lay upon a person professionally involved in the field those obligations which should properly be laid upon such persons."[198] Contrary to this assertion, Professor Hillinger concluded that Llewellyn's "merchant rules did not codify merchant reality, but rather Llewellyn's view of what that reality should be."[199]

The other study, done by Professor Zipporah Batshaw Wiseman, was published in 1987. She identified one of the purposes of the merchant rules was to "take into consideration merchant reality and permit Grand Style judging. . . ."[200] As discussed previously, Grand Style judging pursued fairness without being hindranced by "formal" or "mechanical" jurisprudence.[201] She acknowledged that the original conception of the merchant rules of Article 2 "has essentially disappeared. . . . [a]nd when a conflict arises, courts frequently apply the remaining rules in a manner that Llewellyn would

---

[196] Ingrid M. Hillinger, *The Article 2 Merchant Rules: Karl Llewellyn's Attempt to Achieve The Good, The True, The Beautiful in Commercial Law*, 73 GEO. L.J. 1141 (1985).

[197] *Id.* at 1184.

[198] *Id.* at 1160.

[199] *Id.*

[200] Wiseman, *supra* note 173, at 503. By "Grand Style," Llewellyn alluded to many decisional features. Wiseman summarizes them:

> Llewellyn's Grand Style of the common law described a general period of judicial creativity and flexibility. At its best it was an "ongoing renovation of doctrine," not in a brusque break with tradition, but in a "harmonization of vision with tradition, of continuity with growth, of machinery with purpose, of measure with need." Llewellyn saw the best courts of this period as seeking justice—a "right and fair solution"—by both "look[ing] back upon the heritage of doctrine and also . . . look[ing] forward into prospective consequences and prospective further problems. "Precedent," Llewellyn wrote, "is carefully regarded, but if it does not make sense it is ordinarily re-explored; 'policy' is explicitly inquired into; alleged 'principle' must make for wisdom as well as for order if it is to qualify as such. . . ." Thus, the Grand Style or the Style of Reason was the very opposite of mechanical jurisprudence. It described a period of decisionmaking and decision-writing that took account of both the heritage of the law and of the social context.

Id. at 496 (citations omitted).

[201] *Id.*

describe as the essence of Formal [not Grand] Style judging."[202] Why did Llewellyn's merchant rules fail to accomplish their purpose?

a. Perfect Tender v. Substantial Performance

One of the main goals of the merchant rules was to have the law "reflect to a degree, if not explicitly incorporate, the better standards and practices, as well as the understandings and needs, of merchants."[203] The merchant rules on substantial performance of sale agreements were among those that attempted to incorporate these better standards and practices. The common law as well as the writings of Professor Samuel Williston of Harvard Law School[204] distinguished between the sale of goods, which could be rejected for any deviation from the contract terms under the perfect tender rule, and non-sales contracts, whose substantial performance prevented their rescission, but in some instances allowed damages. The rationale of the perfect tender rule was that the contracting parties expected that each item specified in the contract had to be tendered as specified in the contract.[205]

Llewellyn proposed replacing this rule with one of substantial performance for those sales that took place between merchants.[206] He believed that unlike merchants, consumers were more prone to "find goods unuseable because of an error in color or finish, but he considered merchant contracts to be another matter."[207] Further, he perceived twentieth-century commercial practice as one in which buyers and sellers generally know that exact compliance with the terms of the contract is often not practicable and for this reason, merchants are regularly willing to make adjustments for unsubstantial deviations from contract specifications.[208]

Llewellyn's substantial performance rule authorized courts to make adjustments to contract specifications. These adjustments would also prevent bad faith buyers from using the perfect tender rule as an excuse to rescind contracts whose prices were higher than those that prevailed at the time of payment. Thus, Llewellyn's proposal of a substantial performance rule reflected a policy to align the law of sales with what he perceived as the most effective market practices and also to discourage bad faith practices. Still, how accurate were his perceptions of commercial and consumer behavior? His conclusion that consumers were more likely to reject imperfect or deviant goods than merchants may have reflected the behavior of some consumers and merchants, but certainly not that of many of their counterparts. I have searched diligently, but have found no empirical studies on merchant or consumer expectations of a perfect or substantial compliance that supported his proposed new rules.

If Llewellyn's rules were based on what juries or judges may have found as facts in a given case, it is fair to ask, again, if these findings were consistent with the actual commercial and consumer practices. Consider, for example, the widely known practices

---

202 *Id.* at 538.

203 *Id.* at 504.

204 *See* WILLISTON ON CONTRACTS (Richard E. Lord ed., 4th ed. 2012). For relevant sections of the Uniform Sales Act of 1906, see The Uniform Sales Act of 1906, *available at* http://www.drbilllong.com/HistSales/USAXI.html.

205 Wiseman, *supra* note 173, at 510.

206 *Id.* at 509–10.

207 *Id.* at 510 (citation omitted).

208 *Id.*

of wholesale and retail merchants who establish their reputation as sellers of high quality and specially manufactured goods. Would they be willing to risk their reputation and clientele by not insisting on exactly the color or finish ordered by their clients? Conversely, consider that many consumers we all know, perhaps ourselves, would not mind overlooking a minor imperfection in the color or finish of goods we are interested in purchasing if the price of an otherwise high quality product were to be significantly reduced. In fact, the success of many a "discount" store is attributable precisely to that consumer attitude.

Indeed, as Professor Hillinger showed, Llewellyn never hid the fact that he was creating business duties or practices where none had existed. One such instance was the U.C.C. § 2–201 duty to send out a confirmation letter after the conclusion of an oral deal and a duty to read a confirmation letter received.[209] He supported this creation with a venerable case law tradition: "The fact is, and the cases show, that different responsibilities have been imposed both by explicit law and by the cases upon persons who have professional responsibilities as contrasted with other persons."[210] Thus, at least some of what he referred to as commercial practices had been deduced from case law findings that may have reflected individual or isolated practices.

The substantial performance rule ran into significant opposition when made dependent on the following definition of a substantial performance:

> Performance is substantial whenever, disregarding any supervening change in the market price, the delivery offered in no material manner increases the risks which would rest on the buyer under exact performance, and is of such character as reasonably to meet the buyer's operating requirements, so that an appropriate reduction of price can serve as adequate compensation for failure of exact performance.[211]

As Professor Wiseman pointed out:

> [I]n practice, its application invites a battle of experts, with the jury ultimately required to choose among them in determining the substantiality of the seller's performance, the materiality of any increase in the buyer's risks, and the extent to which the buyer's operating requirements had been met. The only answer . . . was to allow the parties the option by agreement to submit the issue of the substantiality of the breach to conclusive arbitration.[212]

Thus, despite Llewellyn's efforts to modify and weaken it, a qualified version of the Perfect Tender Rule still reigns in U.C.C. § 2–601.

b. The Need for Writings: The Statute of Frauds and Confirmatory Memoranda

Another merchant rule carved out an exception to the Statute of Frauds, which in U.C.C. § 2–201 provides that "a contract for the sale of goods for the price of $500 or more is not enforceable . . . unless there is some writing sufficient to indicate that a

---

209 *See* U.C.C. § 2–201.

210 Hillinger, *supra* note 196, at 1168.

211 Wiseman, *supra* note 173, at 511. Professor Wiseman cites to the 1940 Uniform Act § 21(2)(a) (the full text of the provision in question appears in footnote 199 of her article).

212 *Id.* at 511.

contract for sale has been made between the parties and signed by the party against whom enforcement is sought. . . ."[213] The reference to "some writing sufficient" makes it clear that the writing need not be as formal as a French or Spanish public deed (*acte authentique* or *escritura publica*).[214] However, what if this informal writing is used not as part of the contract ceremony, but as a subsequent confirmation of what was agreed orally? U.C.C. § 2–201(2) addresses such a transaction:

> Between merchants if within a reasonable time a writing in confirmation of the contract and sufficient against the sender is received and the party receiving it has reason to know its contents, it satisfies the requirements of subsection (1) against such party unless written notice of objection to its contents is given within 10 days after it is received.[215]

In other words, an oral agreement may be enforceable if one of the parties sends the other an informal writing in confirmation of that agreement within a reasonable time after the agreement was concluded. And unless the recipient of the confirmatory writing sends a written objection within 10 days after its receipt, the oral agreement will be enforceable against him. Llewellyn's goal in setting forth a ten-day limit for the objection to the written confirmation was to protect one of his archetypal decent merchants (the sender of the confirmation) from a bad faith or abusive practice by a sharpy (the silent receiver of the confirmation).

The sharp practice he was trying to eradicate allowed the recipient of the confirmatory writing to sit on it, thereby neither accepting nor rejecting it until he was satisfied that the market prices were likely to go up in the immediate future. If he assumed that they were going to go down, he would disregard his earlier oral assent and use his silence to subsequently claim that he had rejected the confirmation.[216] To enforce his new rule, Llewellyn was counting on courts deciding statute of fraud disputes in the Grand Style manner he advocated, *i.e.*, justice over formalism by paying attention to the purpose and reason of the rule rather than to its literal meaning. The definition involved in applying Llewellyn's exception to the Statute of Frauds was that of the above discussed professional "merchant."[217]

During the 1970s, much litigation revolved around the meaning of the term "merchant" as related to farmers' futures contracts for the sale of grain. Professor Hillinger describes a typical scenario of an abuse of the U.C.C. definition of a merchant in relation to the application of § 2–201(2):

> Farmer periodically calls Grain Elevator Company to check on current grain prices. During one call Farmer likes what he hears and the parties conclude a contract on the phone, the grain to be delivered some months later. Shortly after the oral deal, Grain Elevator Company . . . sends a written confirmation of the phone deal to farmer. Farmer does not respond. Grain Elevator Company then contracts to sell Farmer's grain to a third party. At the time scheduled for delivery, the price of grain has skyrocketed, and . . . Farmer no longer likes the contract price. He sells his grain to someone else at the

---

213 U.C.C. § 2–201(1).

214 *Id.*

215 *Id.* § 2–201(2).

216 Wiseman, *supra* note 173, at 530.

217 U.C.C. § 2–104(1).

> higher market price. Farmer's breach forces Grain Elevator Company to cover at the current market price to meet its contractual obligations. It ultimately sues Farmer to recover its loss. . . . Farmer inevitably makes two responses to Grain Elevator Company's contract action: (1) "We never made a contract" and, (2) "Even if we did, I am a farmer, not a merchant, and therefore, the contract is unenforceable because I never signed anything." . . . As Article 2 is presently understood, the result of the litigation turns on the issue of the farmer's status.[218]

While some courts applied the confirmatory statement "between merchants" to farmers,[219] others concluded that the terms "farmer" and "merchant" were mutually exclusive. Ironically, the latter view found support in Llewellyn's writings, which did not consider most farmers to be merchants;[220] although some of his articles distinguished the horse and haystack farming America from the contemporary "wares-in-commerce" America.[221]

As it happens, Llewellyn was a firm believer in the value of writings in commercial transactions, apparently regardless of when or where they were used. He argued for retaining the Statute of Frauds among merchants because it embodied the better practice: "the general indirect effect of the statute, in urging men to get their deals into writing, is highly salutary; and . . . the practice of 'confirming' oral or telephone deals is today so ingrained that the statute no longer costs the price in occasional hardship which it cost a century ago."[222]

During the late 1980s, I conducted an informal survey on letter of credit amendment and re-presentation practices among the United States banks. Most of the respondents told me that when discussing amendments to the letter of credit and possible re-presentation of documents, they did not send confirmatory memoranda, but used recordings of their phone conversations authorized by their interlocutors as records of what had been agreed upon. And while this practice may not have met all the requirements of a usage of trade, it certainly was a course of dealing of many banks. Significantly, if I were to ask the same question a decade or so later, the same bankers would have responded that similar communications were now being made increasingly via computers. Thus, a paper-based writing was replaced within twenty years in an important commercial and financial sector: first by recordings of phone conversations and subsequently by computer-to-computer communications, many of them standardized.

---

[218] Hillinger, *supra* note 196, at 1176–77.

[219] *Id.* at 1177.

[220] *Id.* (Referring to a comment to an early draft in which Llewellyn discussed the case of an apple farmer who marketed three to six hundred bushels a year.). Although this farmer would extend the same implied warranty of merchantability associated with merchants or with "goods" merchant, he would not be subject to the rule in U.C.C. § 2–207 that additional minor terms stated in a confirmation became part of the parties' contract. *Id.* The reason for this distinction was because the invocation of § 2–207(2) depends upon the established practice of regular merchants to attend and reply promptly to correspondence. *Id.* And quoting Llewellyn: "No such practice exists among small farmers . . . his occupation does not hold him out as familiar with any practice 'of the kind involved' or as having the general knowledge or skill in that aspect of a person in trade." *Id.*

[221] *Id.* at 1178.

[222] Wiseman, *supra* note 173, at 518.

I should also note that most European and Latin American commercial codes do not require a writing for their commercial contracts and rely instead on what some judges and commentators referred to in the previous chapter as the "spiritualist" principle of evidence of contract formation. This contrast with the proposed U.C.C. Statute of Frauds prompted Professor Ernst Rabel[223] to oppose vigorously its enactment, referring to it as "The most striking example of ultra-conservatism. . . . a thoroughly antiquated legislative trick . . . and 'the refuge of a welcher.' "[224] He added that no civil law country had such a statute, "[n]ot even the small farmers of Poland and Italy have been considered to need this guard" and asked, "Do we rate American businessmen as less intelligent, more naive?"[225]

In sum, as with the draft provisions on substantial performance, the merchant rules that require commercial contracts over $500 to be in writing as well as the confirmatory memoranda for oral contracts have proven largely ineffective because the meaning of both merchant and a writing were too restrictive, the latter in particular. Since the time when Llewellyn visualized the importance of a writing for the certainty of commercial transactions as a paper-based, record keeping practice, both technology and commercial practices have changed. Thus, as shown by the farmers "sitting on their written confirmation" cases, Llewellyn's (not the market's) confirmatory memoranda practice contributed to, rather than prevented, bad faith and sharp practices.

In sum, Llewellyn's merchant rules failed because what he attributed to merchants were judicial and litigation responses, as opposed to market-inspired responses to bad faith practices used in anticipation of litigation or during litigation practices. Thus, as with Franz Wieacker's version of bad faith practices, Llewellyn's merchant rules did not involve the transaction-based good faith practices which preceded and could have prevented the bad faith practices that took place during litigation. Had his merchant rules reflected widely observed good faith practices, they would have had to carefully set forth, among other aspects of the transaction: a) the meaning of the terms commonly associated with the transaction or practice; b) the steps that regular participants in it undertake in order to conclude their sales and purchases, including the time and place related to each step; c) the transaction's standard terms and conditions; and d) the rules and procedures for dispute resolution and so on. Stated simply, Llewellyn's merchant rules did not set forth what good faith buyers and sellers, directly or through brokers or intermediaries, promised, did, or reasonably expected from their counterparties.

---

223 Ernst Rabel was one of Europe's foremost commercial and private international law scholars during the twentieth century. After he fled from Nazi Germany to the United States, he contributed his comparative law skills to conflicts of law and the law of sales. For a discussion of his relationship with Llewellyn and attempts to marry a Rome Institute Project for the Unification of the Law of Sales with the U.C.C., see WILLIAM TWINING, KARL LLEWELLYN AND THE REALIST MOVEMENT 312–13 (1973).

224 Ernst Rabel, *The Sales Law in the Proposed Commercial Code,* 17 U. CHI. L. REV. 427, 433 (1950).

225 *Id.* For a discussion of the informal ("spiritualist") approach to commercial contracts, see ch. XXI(A)(1) and the Spanish and Mexican Supreme Court decisions in the Appendix to that chapter. Please notice the caution I expressed in the preceding chapter with respect to the purpose of the principle of "spiritualism" in the European and Latin American commercial codes. While there is little evidence on why Article 109 of the French Commercial Code of 1807 adopted this principle and allowed oral evidence to prove the existence of a sale agreement, during a 1959 seminar discussion at the University of Paris presided by Professor Andre Tunc that I attended it was obvious that the two most frequently mentioned reasons by French commercial law specialists were 1) the relatively low value of the average goods as compared with real property (*res mobilis, res vilis*) and 2) the quickness of these transactions.

Nevertheless, Llewellyn's contributions to a better interpretation of commercial contracts by combining honesty, reasonableness and fairness as well as by empowering courses of dealing and trade usages as indispensable sources for the interpretation of contracts far outweighed the failure of his merchant rules.

§ 23.6 SCHOLARLY VIEWS ON GOOD FAITH: LAW AND ECONOMICS AND THE BAD FAITH EXCLUDER

As with many other Law and Economics analyses, the pioneering and most influential analysis of good faith as a tool for the interpretation of contracts was by Judge Richard Posner. I will use his opinion in *Market Street Associates Ltd. Partnership v. Frey*[226] as a starting point for the comparison of his judicial- and litigation-inspired views on good faith with those inspired by a course of dealing and usage of trade version.

A. The Facts[227]

In 1968, J. C. Penney (hereinafter Penney) a large chain of retail stores and owner of commercial real property entered into a contract to sell and then lease back the same property it sold to General Electric Pension Trust (hereinafter PT). The sale price was one million dollars and the leaseback was for 25 years. Among other stipulations, paragraph 34 of the sale-leaseback stated that the lessee could request the lessor (PT) to finance the costs and expenses of construction of additional improvements on the premises sold and leased back, provided the amount of the costs and expenses was at least $250,000. PT promised:

> [T]o give reasonable consideration to providing the financing of such additional Improvements and Lessor and Lessee shall negotiate in good faith concerning the construction of such Improvements and the financing by Lessor of such costs and expenses.[228]

The same paragraph also provided that "should the negotiations fail, the lessee shall be entitled to repurchase the property at a price roughly equal to the price at which Penney sold it to the pension trust . . . plus 6 percent a year for each year since the original purchase."[229]

One of the properties leased back from PT was a shopping center in Milwaukee. In 1987, Penney assigned its lessee's interest in this shopping center to Market Street Associates (hereinafter MA), a real estate investment, managing and brokerage firm.[230] A year later, MA received an inquiry from a drugstore chain (hereinafter DSC) interested in opening a store in the Milwaukee shopping center. As was its course of dealing with owners and lessees of commercial property, DSC required that MA either build the store for it or procure financing for it and supervise its building. At first, MA sought financing from third parties to build the future drug store premises but failed because only mortgage financing was available with these parties and this financing

---

226 941 F.2d 588 (7th Cir. 1991).

227 The following is a summary of Judge Posner's version of facts.

228 941 F.2d at 591.

229 *Id.*

230 MARKET STREET, http://www.marketstreetservices.com/market-street-report.

required that MA, the mortgagor, be the owner of the mortgaged property. MA then decided to try to buy back the shopping center from PT.

MA's managing partner, one Orenstein, tried repeatedly to reach one Erb, the chief executive officer at PT by phone. Erb did not return his calls, so Orenstein wrote to him expressing an interest in buying the property. In this communication, Orenstein asked Erb to "review the file" and call him back to discuss the purchase after his review. A few days later, in June of 1988, Orenstein received a call from an associate of Erb indicating an interest in selling the property for $3 million. Orenstein found this price excessive. Approximately a month later, he wrote to PT requesting a $2 million loan to finance improvements of the shopping center presumably to satisfy the needs of DSC. This letter did not mention paragraph 34, nor did it alert Erb to the consequences of failed negotiations over the financing that Orenstein had requested.

In what Judge Posner referred to as Erb's "habit of unresponsiveness,"[231] he also failed to respond to this letter. Orenstein then sent him a certified letter in which he asked again about whether PT was willing to provide financing pursuant to the lease. If Erb was willing, Orenstein suggested they enter into negotiations to "*amend the ground lease appropriately*."[232] The day after Erb's receipt of this letter, he replied by turning down the request for financing because it "did not 'meet [PT's] current investment criteria,' " which was to make improvement loans only for projects worth more than $7 million.[233] Approximately a month later, Orenstein wrote to Erb telling him that MA was exercising its option to purchase the property as set forth in Paragraph 34 of the sale and leaseback.

PT refused to sell and MA filed a suit for specific performance of the purchase option. District Judge Reynolds granted summary judgment in favor of PT on two grounds. The first was that "by failing in its correspondence with the pension trust [PT] to mention paragraph 34 of the lease, Market Street Associates [MA] had prevented the negotiations over financing that are a condition precedent to the lessee's exercise of the purchase option from taking place."[234] The second was that "this same failure violated the duty of good faith, which the common law of Wisconsin, as of other states, reads into every contract."[235] He relied on statements made by Orenstein's in his deposition in which he said that:

> [I]t had occurred to him that Erb mightn't know of paragraph 34, though this was unlikely . . . because Erb or someone else at the pension trust [PT] would probably check the file and discover the paragraph . . . [which would enable MA] to walk off with the property for [what Judge Posner referred to as] (perhaps) a song.[236]

---

[231] 941 F.2d at 591.

[232] *Id.* (emphasis added).

[233] *Id.*

[234] *Id.* at 592.

[235] *Id.*

[236] *Id.*

B. A Subjective "State of Mind" Approach to Discerning Good or Bad Faith

Judge Reynolds inferred from Orenstein's deposition that MA did not want financing from PT, but was looking for an opportunity to buy the property at a bargain price. Had MA not been acting in bad faith, Judge Reynolds assumed, it would have advised PT that it was requesting financing pursuant to paragraph 34 so that PT would understand the penalty for refusing to negotiate. Judge Posner was aware of the limitations of the trial record that made it necessary for him to conjecture on the possible reasons for MA's alternative proposals: "Whether Market Street Associates [MA] was pessimistic about obtaining financing from the pension trust [PT] . . . or *for other reasons,* it initially sought financing for the project from other sources."[237] Posner and Reynolds also assumed that the Orenstein's prime motive was to buy the shopping center for a heavily discounted price or "for a song."

Yet, why did a fact so central to the determination of Orenstein's bad faith remain conjectural? If the likely price of the property was not known as a fact to be considerably higher than that of paragraph 34, or if Orenstein had not conceded that his intent was to walk away with the property for a song, what was the basis for the summary judgment? Further, during a full trial it would have been easy to establish the market price of the property by means of certified value appraisals, as is the usual practice in the commercial real estate leasing trade.[238] Nonetheless, Judge Posner conjectured that the market price had to be higher than the one at which MA tried to purchase the shopping center: "The market value must be higher, or Market Street Associates [MA] wouldn't be trying to coerce conveyance at the paragraph 34 price; whether it is as high as $3 million, however, the record does not reveal."[239]

C. Judge Posner's Ordered Search for Orenstein's State of Mind

For Judge Posner, the dispositive question was whether MA tried to trick ("opportunistically") PT into rejecting the requested financing so that MA "would be entitled to walk off with the property for (perhaps) a song,"[240] thereby acting in bad faith by violating its "duty of good faith performance. . . ."[241] Posner found "much common sense in Judge Reynolds' conclusion" that MA did not act in good faith and conjectured that MA was aware that PT was run by a "sluggish and hidebound bureaucracy unlikely to have retained . . . or to be able at short notice to retrieve, the details of a small lease made twenty years earlier."[242]

However, Posner also pointed out that when deciding PT's motion for summary judgment, Judge Reynolds' recital of facts agreed with PT's version and that by construing the facts favorably to PT, Judge Reynolds had misapplied the standard for summary judgment, which requires that facts be construed as favorably as possible to MA, the nonmoving party. If the latter standard were applied, opined Posner, MA had

---

237 *Id.* at 591 (emphasis added).

238 *See infra* § 23:8 (comments about the case by the author's cousin, Boris Kozolchyk, an experiencd and well respected Florida Commercial Real Estate Broker).

239 941 F.2d at 592.

240 *Id.*

241 *Id.* at 596.

242 *Id.* at 597.

not acted in bad faith: The $3 million price demanded by PT could appear as grossly excessive and the $1 million plus 6 percent for approximately twenty years offered by MA may not have conferred so great a windfall to MA and may have even been a fair market price. Because MA's version of facts did not support a finding of its bad faith, Posner decided then that a new trial was required to determine MA's true "state of mind" when trying to exercise his right to purchase the shopping center per paragraph 34.

Judge Posner also noted the speciousness of one of PT's arguments. PT argued that MA could not exercise the purchase option because it required previous negotiations on MA's request for financing and these negotiations did not take place. However, it was PT that pre-empted the negotiations by its offhanded dismissal of them and its failure to give "reasonable consideration" to MA's request per paragraph 34.[243]

He acknowledged that he usually would not excuse contracting parties from failing to read and understand the contents of their contracts; and that in this case "an immensely sophisticated enterprise simply failed to read the contract."[244] Yet, he added that such enterprises make mistakes deliberately to take advantage of a contracting partner's mistake during the performance stage of a contract is a breach of good faith:

> To be able to correct your contract partner's mistake *at zero cost to yourself*, and decide not to do so, is a species of opportunistic behavior that the parties would have expressly forbidden in the contract had they foreseen it. The immensely long term of the lease amplified the possibility of errors but did not license either party to take advantage of them.[245]

I am not certain what Judge Posner meant by correcting a counterparty's mistake at zero cost. If the correction expected from MA required that it request PT to review paragraph 34 before rejecting the courses of performance proposed by MA, this "correction" was implicit in Orenstein's earlier request to Erb to "review your file on this matter [the proposed purchase of the shopping center] and call me so that we can discuss it further."[246]

Further, once Orenstein asked Erb to be advised immediately if Erb was "willing to provide the financing. . . . [And] [i]f you are willing, we propose to enter into negotiation *to amend the ground lease appropriately*", Erb had good reasons to review the file immediately given the likely change in the status of an important lease.[247] Bear in mind that from the standpoint of any landlord interested in the marketability of his shopping center, the prospect of a lease or sublease to a drugstore chain is an event significant enough to review the terms and conditions of the ground lease. Thus, a likely amendment of the ground lease would certainly have required a very careful examination of the sale-leaseback agreement and of its paragraph 34.

---

243 Please note that this bad faith pleading was the same behavior addressed by one of the oldest Roman equitable maxims in Professor Wieacker's illustrative list discussed in an earlier section and characterized then as a judicial form of bad faith: "No one may set himself in contradiction of his own previous conduct" (*Venire contra factum proprium*). *See supra* § 23:3. Please note also that this Roman maxim inspired the procedural version of estoppel in English and common law countries.

244 941 F.2d at 597.

245 *Id.*

246 *Id.* at 591.

247 *Id.* (emphasis added).

If Oreinstein's request for Erb's review of the file was not a sufficient means to correct Erb's conjectured unawareness of the presence of paragraph 34, what would have been? Was MA expected to explain to PT why its sustained indifference and subsequent rejection of MA's requests could harm its best legal and business interests? Needless to say, such an explanation would not have come at a zero legal and accounting cost to MA. On the other hand, what if Erb or his associates did review the file and for some unexplained reason thought that paragraph 34 was inapplicable or, if applicable, ignorable, because of the unlikelihood that MA would obtain non-personal, mortgage financing? What if PT had decided, for entirely selfish reasons (*i.e.*, the elimination of a costly intermediary in its direct negotiations with DSC), to get rid of MA as a tenant by discouraging it from seeking potentially profitable sublessees or purchasers of the shopping center? If so, did PT not violate its good faith duty of cooperation with its lessee?[248]

Because of the slimness of the factual record, the above assumptions about Erb's state of mind are as plausible as those by Judges Reynolds' and Posner's about Orenstein's state of mind. Yet, apparently the factual gaps concerning Orenstein's state of mind could not be filled upon remand. An editorial note following the text of Judge Posner's opinion in the official report stated that despite the unresponsiveness of the remand court to Judge Posner's instruction to determine Orenstein's "state of mind," the original decision by Judge Reynolds was reaffirmed on a second appeal.

D. The Law and Economics Justification for Judge Posner's Opinion

Judge Posner regards the duty to act in good faith as "a stab at approximating the terms the parties would have negotiated had they foreseen the circumstances that have given rise to their dispute."[249] Yet, as is typical with judicial versions of good faith, they are shaped by the twists and turns of litigation. Thus, the required divination of the good faith conduct would have to be done *a posteriori*, *i.e.*, after the parties' original intent and subsequent conduct had been filtered through their allegations and proof, including in this case the limitations on fact finding imposed by a successful motion for summary judgment. The discernment of good faith in a litigation setting then seldom resembles one obtained from examining the duties expected from contracting parties as set forth from courses of dealing and from usages of trade.

Elsewhere, Judge Posner enunciated a principle on the function of contract law that is broad enough to encompass what he views as the function of good faith: "the fundamental function of contract law (and recognized as such at least since Hobbes's day) is to deter people from behaving opportunistically toward their contracting parties, in order to encourage the optimal timing of economic activity and (the same point) obviate costly self-protective measures."[250]

And indeed, Hobbes's assigns to the law of contracts the function of deterring the very likely breaches that would have resulted from the frailty of human promises.

---

[248] *See* AMPAT/Midwest, Inc. v. Illinois Tool Works Inc., 896 F.2d 1035, 1041 (7th Cir. 1990) ("The parties to a contract are embarked on a cooperative venture, and a minimum of cooperativeness in the event unforeseen problems arise at the performance stage is required even if not an explicit duty of the contract.").

[249] 941 F.2d at 595.

[250] RICHARD POSNER, ECONOMIC ANALYSIS OF LAW 103 (5th ed. 1998).

However, bear in mind that Hobbes' contracting man had only recently emerged from a "state of nature" in which each man was free to take from nature or others whatever he could keep and this led to him to become his fellow man's wolf.[251] The Hobessian social contract entered into between such a creature and the state made it possible to enforce contracts between man and man with the state acting as an enforcer:

> And the same are the 'bonds' by which men are bound and obliged: bonds that have their strength not from their own nature, for nothing is more easily broken than a man's word, but from fear of some evil consequence upon the rupture.[252]

This is a view that Thomas Hobbes and Judge Posner share with Justice Oliver Wendell Holmes Jr., who famously stated: "The duty to keep a contract at common law means a prediction that you must pay damages if you do not keep it,—and nothing else."[253] The key feature of this Hobbesian-inspired scenario, then, is Hobbes' assessment of human nature. In his view, the man of contracts is a man whose promises are enforceable not by man's cooperation with man, or by his religious or moral views, but from his fear of the evil consequence that the state will impose on him.

As the reader may have anticipated by now, my reaction to the view shared by these (and other) illustrious legal thinkers is that it is at odds with man's cooperative biology as well as with the reality of his marketplaces. For no matter where you are, the number of performed contracts is incomparably larger than that of those breached. And factors such as one's reputation for honesty and reasonableness as well as the sustained likelihood of long-run profits that results from trust and probity continue to be valued more highly by most men than are the profits that flow from dishonesty and unreasonableness.

Accordingly, Posner's justification for requiring good faith performance in this decision is not the desirability of good faith behavior, *per se*, but its ability to deter bad faith conduct. Please note that Judge Posner's dispositive question on Orenstein's state of mind was: Did Orenstein try to trick ("opportunistically") PT into rejecting the requested financing so that MA would be entitled to walk off with the property for (perhaps) a song? This is not a dissimilar question from that typically asked of jurors with respect to the criminal defendant's criminal intent (*mens rea*). And as became apparent in this case, this method of analysis transformed the discernment of good faith into a highly subjective, costly, and, in the end, inconclusive determination.

E. Professor Summer's Negative Excluder

Professor Robert Summers' inquiry into the meaning that courts in the United States as well as the U.C.C. draftsmen give to the phrase "good faith" has been highly influential in contractual case law and in the drafting of the Restatement (Second). In a brief description of his view, he stated:

---

[251] *See generally* Sharon A. Lloyd & Susanne Sreedhar, *Hobbes Moral and Political Philosophy*, STANFORD ENCYCLOPEDIA OF PHILOSOPHY (Edward N. Zalta ed., Summer 2013), http://plato.stanford.edu/entries/hobbes-moral/#StaNat.

[252] THOMAS HOBBES, LEVIATHAN 85 (George Routledge & Sons Ltd. 1907) (1651).

[253] O. W. Holmes, *The Path of the Law*, 10 HARV. L. REV. 457, 462 (1897).

> [A]s used in the case law, [good faith] is best understood as an "excluder"—it is a phrase which has no general meaning or meanings of its own, but which serves to exclude many heterogeneous forms of bad faith. It will also be suggested that if the Code draftsmen had perceived this, they would not have given the term the general, invariant meaning: "honesty in fact in the conduct or transaction concerned."[254]

Professor Summers compiled a representative list of excluded bad faith behavior that shows how varied this behavior can be: from subterfuges and evasions to overt or hidden actions, from lack of diligence and slacking off to willful rendering of imperfect performance, and from abuse of the power to specify contractual terms to interference with or failure to cooperate in the other party's performance.[255]

I disagree with Professor Summer's version of good faith and especially with his epistemology. Because he believes that good faith has no *general meaning or meanings of its own*, he relies on what he labels a bad faith excluder. Aside from what I believe is a mistaken empirical assumption that I will address momentarily, Summers' excluder is impractical: If a businessman or lawyer needs to ascertain *ex ante* if a good faith performance is about to occur, he will have to try to find if one or more of his colleagues behaved in a manner that courts considered as in bad faith and then try to convert that finding into its accurate good faith antipode. Clearly, even if this were an accurate conversion, it could not be done quickly or inexpensively enough to guide everyday merchants and their lawyers with their everyday transactional concerns on good faith.

Simply put, Summer's epistemology assumes that while bad faith is knowable, good faith is not. In this assumption, Summers seems to agree with Thomas Hobbes', Judge Posner's and Justice Holmes' view of human nature, whose most common trait is the propensity to breach his promises or to behave in bad faith, hence the discernibility of bad faith in contrast with the difficulties in discerning good faith.

But there is more to the exclusive discernibility of bad faith. Whoever believes in such a view of human nature winds up adopting a presumption of perennial bad faith, unless it is timely deterred. Yet, as we now know from contemporary biology, altruism in competition with selfishness is responsible for the cooperative building of social institutions such as commerce. And as the renowned economist William Landes and Judge Posner acknowledged having learned from biological findings, nothing short of survival may well be at stake for the cooperative human species:

> The biologists have done more work on this question than the economists. They have shown that altruism may increase the likelihood of the altruist's genes surviving in the competition among populations. If insect A saves B from some peril, this means B will be alive to save A should he find himself in danger. . . . this "reciprocal altruism" may enhance the survivorship of the group to which A and B belong relative to that of some nonaltruistic insect group.[256]

---

[254] Robert S. Summers, *"Good Faith" in General Contract Law and the Sales Provisions of the Uniform Commercial Code*, 54 VA. L. REV. 195, 196 (1968); U.C.C. § 1–201(19) (1962).

[255] Restatement (Second) of Contracts § 205(d).

[256] William M. Landes and Richard A Posner, *Altruism in Law and Economics*, 68 AM. ECON. REV. 417, 418–19 (1978).

Empirical findings about human nature aside, consider the effect that Summers' epistemology and Hobbes', Holmes' and Posner's presumption of bad faith conduct would have for a nation's economic development: Its marketplace would be one without trust and every public or private representation of fact would be subject to a costly and uneconomical verification process, as is or has been the case in some developing countries.[257]

On the other hand, there is a purposive aspect of Professor Summer's "open ended" analysis of good faith that I agree with: Good faith as a guarantee that substantive justice will be applied to contractual relations by imposing moral standards capable of overriding explicit terms of the contract when they do not satisfy requirements of decency, fairness, or reasonableness.[258] It is for this reason I find the formulation in the Restatement (Second) of the mission of good faith a wise *reformulation* of Professor Summer's excluder theory: "[I]t [good faith] excludes a variety of types of conduct characterized as involving "bad faith" *because they violate community standards of decency, fairness or reasonableness*."[259] In other words, good faith behavior has its own knowable meaning and the ultimate sources of this meaning are not individual disputes or court decisions that state what constituted bad faith behavior in the case or dispute in question, but the objective or sectoral sources of commercial reasonableness, decency and fairness.

F. An Objective, Sectoral Version of Good Faith Commercial Leasing

U.C.C. § 1–205(3) validated the interpretive function of courses of dealing and usages of trade as providers of the sectoral or vocational meaning of contractual terms and conditions: "A course of dealing between parties and any usage of trade in the vocation or trade in which they are engaged or of which they are or should be aware *give particular meaning to and supplement or qualify terms of an agreement*."[260] And as was brilliantly intuited by E. Allan Farnsworth at the time when he started to leave his indelible mark on the law of contracts of the United States:

> Good Faith performance has always required the cooperation of one party where it was necessary in order that the other might secure the expected benefits of the contract. And the standard for determining what cooperation

---

[257] Boris Kozolchyk, *The UNIDROIT Principles as a Model for the Unification of Best Contractual Practices in the Americas*, 46 AM. J. COMP. L. 151, 157–58 (1998). The article provides a description of a Mexican customs procedure (circa 2000 A.D.) shaped by an unwritten presumption of bad faith:

> If the shipment is large or significantly valuable, it will be inspected by the Mexican customs broker prior to its entry and customs' inspection in Mexico. Mexican customs brokers have their forwarding agents in the U.S. side of the border inspect many shipments prior to their entry into Mexico because as brokers, they are subject to heavy fines and loss of their professional licenses if the import documents incorrectly describe the goods or their customs status. [Often this inspection requires purchasing or renting expensive inspection facilities on the U.S. side of the border.] Thus the Mexican government suspects the brokers and the brokers suspect the exporters-importers' description especially if a poor description can save significant custom duties. This costly and time consuming pre-entry inspection practice is therefore driven by an unwritten presumption of bad faith.

Id.

[258] Summers, *supra* note 254, at 197–200.

[259] Restatement (Second) of Contracts § 205(a) (emphasis added).

[260] *Id.* § 1–205(3) (emphasis added).

was required has always been an objective standard, based on the decency, fairness or reasonableness of the community and not on the individual's own beliefs as to what might be decent, fair or reasonable. Both common sense and tradition dictate an objective standard for good faith performance.[261]

Good faith performance, however, comes in different qualities, especially where those performing are fiduciaries. At the lower end of the spectrum of fiduciary good faith performance are sellers who sell on standard terms to unknown buyers and who are entrusted with payments in advance of their shipments. These are fiduciaries who Judge Posner would expect to treat their "principals" as if those principals were the fiduciaries themselves. Thus, they are not expected to "take advantage of the principal's [buyer's] incapacity, ignorance, inexperience, or even naïveté."[262] In contrast, if one of the contracting parties is a trusting investor and the entrusted managing partner or joint venturer was given full powers of management and negotiation, his fiduciary duties would be more demanding than those of Judge Posner's fiduciary. As Justice Cardozo taught us in *Meinhard v. Salmon,*[263] when an investor entrusts his savings to a managing partner or joint venturer and by such an entrustment makes it possible for his entrusted party to receive other lucrative offers of investments, the fiduciary owes his investor an "utmost" quality of good faith, or the "punctilio the most honorable" (*uberrima fides*). This means that the fiduciary must refrain from accepting such investment opportunities without giving notice to his entruster and providing him the opportunity to participate in the new investment.

This version of good faith has helped develop both trusting relationships and certain locations such as, say, the City of London or Wall Street, as major financial marketplaces. Please note that such a development takes place not despite the "moralistic overtones" of *uberrima fides* that seem to concern Judge Posner,[264] but precisely because of the higher morality of fiduciaries acting as "their brothers' keepers" and the willingness of judges such as Justice Cardozo to help raise the morality of the marketplace.[265]

As discussed in an earlier section, the meaning of reasonableness is inextricably linked with concern for the reasonable expectations of others, including archetypal

---

[261] E. Allan Farnsworth, *Good Faith Performance and Commercial Reasonableness under the Uniform Commercial Code*, 30 U. CHI. L. REV. 666, 672 (1963). United States court decisions that confirm Professor Farnsworth's objective or comunitarian vision abound even at a time when the United States was not the commercial, financial and industrial power it is today. *See, e.g.*, Patterson v. Meyerhofer, 97 N.E. 472 (N.Y. 1912). Judge Posner cites to a more modest version of contractual cooperation: "The parties to a contract are embarked on a cooperative venture, and a minimum of cooperativeness in the event unforeseen problems arise at the performance stage is required even if not an explicit duty of the contract." Market St. Assocs. Ltd. P'ship v. Frey, 941 F.2d 588, 595 (7th Cir. 1991) (citing AMPAT/Midwest, Inc. v. Illinois Tool Works Inc., 896 F.2d 1035, 1041 (7th Cir. 1990)).

[262] 941 F.2d at 593.

[263] 164 N.E. 545 (1928). For an edited and shorter version of this landmark decision, *see infra* § 23:9(C).

[264] Judge Posner states:

> The particular confusion to which the vaguely moralistic overtones of "good faith" give rise is the belief that every contract establishes a fiduciary relationship. A fiduciary is required to treat his principal as if the principal were he, and therefore he may not take advantage of the principal's incapacity, ignorance, inexperience, or even naïveté.

941 F.2d at 593.

[265] *But cf.* 941 F.2d at 595 ("It would be quixotic as well as presumptuous for judges to undertake through contract law to raise the ethical standards of the nation's business people.").

others. Although fairness or fair play was not defined in the U.C.C. or in the Restatement (Second), it has an objectively ascertainable meaning as discussed in connection with the equality of treatment granted to traders in some medieval fairs by the so called "Peace of the Marketplace."[266] It was the commercial nature of the traders and the activities of the fair that made it possible to forbid the discriminatory treatment of foreigners by local merchants. Since then, fairness in commercial law has had the connotation of an equalitarian treatment of equals. Thus, as part of commercial good faith, fairness watches over the discriminatory or exclusionary treatment of merchants by other merchants. As also discussed in earlier chapters, this is a treatment usually associated with familistic and command economy societies as well by the guild system. Consequently, U.C.C. § 2–103(1)(b) was the United States' first statutory provision on commercial good faith to acknowledge the combined participation of honesty, reasonableness and fairness.

The task of discerning good faith in commercial contracting is obviously facilitated by a well drafted set of rights and duties. However, often such a set is unavailable either because of the dynamic and informal nature of the contract or because of the inadequate legal/business training of the drafters.[267] In the absence of such a clear formulation, the adjudicator must rely on the parties' course of dealing and usages of trade. And, in the absence of the latter, he must identify the archetypal market practice in the testimony of knowledgeable, experienced and respected practitioners.

In the instant case, such a determination would have focused first on the functions of paragraph 34, especially the clause related to lessee's request for the financing of a likely mutually profitable improvement. Was this clause commonly used in Milwaukee's or the region's commercial leases? If so, why? How did it reflect the reasonable expectations of commercial lessors and lessees? Could it be regarded as implementing the duty of cooperation between lesssor and lessee, especially when the former's financing of improvements could demonstrably lead to larger revenues for both parties? If the purpose of the request for financing was not to implement a central duty of cooperation to the commercial lease in question, why link the failure of the financing negotiations to a provision designed to undo the commercial lease by enabling a sale at a price presumably attractive to the purchaser?

I am aware of Judge Posner's warnings that Economic Analysis of the Law has long ago abandoned the model of a "hyperrational, emotionless, unsocial, supremely egotistic, nonstrategic man (or woman). . . ."[268] Nonetheless, a justification for good faith that focuses solely on its deterrence of an undefined bad faith and dismisses the "moral overtones" of good faith strikes me as sounding the same skeptical note on human nature (including its good faith) as Hobbes did in his Leviathan's "nothing is more easily broken than a man's word. . . ."[269]

The inaccuracy of the archetypal behavior that Judge Posner associates with the choice of good faith conduct is apparent in his definition of "rational choice." For

---

[266] *See supra* § 9:2(B).

[267] In my experience, these drafting skills are equally lacking in law schools in both civil and common law countries. Consequently, law graduates must pursue their post-graduate instruction on the peculiarities of contracting in the various sectors of the economy while practicing law.

[268] Richard A. Posner, *Rational Choice, Behavioral Economics, and the Law*, 50 STAN. L. REV. 1551, 1552 (1998).

[269] HOBBES, *supra* note 252, at 85.

Posner, a rational choice is nothing more portentous than "choosing the best means to the chooser's ends."[270] When applied to the choice of a good faith performance, this definition suggests that the choice must be that of each party's choosing. But this is an inaccurate archetypal behavior because the good faith of commercial contracts requires that each party's choice satisfy not only the chooser's ends but also the reasonable expectations of the other party or parties. And it is precisely for this reason that the discernment of commercial good faith must so frequently rely on transactional or sectoral intent.[271]

In sum, commercial good faith means much more than the sword with which to punish an opportunist or the shield with which to defend against him. And rather than trying to rely on subjective and often hypothetical versions of contractual intent, the everyday concerns involving the good faith of merchants, lawyers and judges are best answered by examining the parties' well drafted sets of duties and, in their absence, their courses of performance, dealings and usages of the trade. And when written versions of these sources are unavailable, adjudicators should turn to the versions of good faith provided by knowledgeable and respected members of the respective trades.

§ 23.7 CONCLUSIONS: GOOD FAITH AND THE PROPHECY OF WHAT COURTS WILL DO IN FACT

I paraphrase Justice Oliver Wendell Holmes Jr.'s famous definition of law because it reminds us of one of the central themes of this chapter: There is more to good faith than its judicial version, so dear to so many distinguished judges and academics, and it is the good faith of the marketplace. Early in this chapter, we learned from the Roman Praetor that *bona fides* was incompatible with deceitfulness (*dolus*), especially during litigation after one party tried to take advantage of missing inconsequential formalities or excessively strict interpretations to claim an unearned right or to evade an assumed duty. Then we learned from Lord Mansfield the importance of honesty as an element of good faith, inside or outside the courtroom. Karl Llewellyn added reasonableness and fair dealing in the trade in question as additional elements in the 1951 version of the U.C.C. He learned about this connection both from his studies of the BGB and HGB as well as from his Yale Law School professor, Arthur Corbin, who was also the teacher of us all. It was Corbin who opened our eyes to the critical role of reasonable expectations in the interpretation of contracts. It was then E. Allan Farnsworth who linked these expectations to community values.

This chapter stresses the interpretive role of commercial sectoral values and maintains that when determining the meaning of good faith, judges and lawyers should pay more attention to the objective sectoral sources of reasonableness and fairness. Ordinarily, these include codes of ethics or manuals of conduct that compile standard and best practices as courses of dealings or usages of trade. They also include the opinions and testimony of knowledgeable and well respected merchants. The chapter also illustrates the highly significant role of great commercial law judges such

---

[270] Posner, *supra* note 268, at 1551.

[271] It is true, that contracts of "adhesion" usually reflect the performance preferences of the offeror of goods or services. Nevertheless, unless the "adhesion" seller, lender, exchanger or provider of services is a state agency part of a command economy, he will have take into account seriously the preferences of his consumers, lest he be quickly displaced by others who do so.

as Lord Mansfield and Justice Cardozo as architects of the better application of good faith standards to various transactional settings.

Finally, this chapter illustrates how a determination of what is reasonable profits from identifying what an archetypal participant in the same trade or profession of the counterparty would have done under the circumstances. Lawyers and social scientists alike have much to thank Max Weber and E. Adamson Hoebel for drawing attention to the usefulness of representative (archetypal) behavior as a tool with which to measure what is reasonable and fair in judicial and marketplace settings.

Given the importance that good faith, meaning honesty, reasonableness and fair dealing have in the interpretation of contracts, especially in a brave new world of a global marketplace of third parties and contractual strangers, it is high time for legal education to teach how best to use these tools of market-sensitive contractual interpretation and economic development.

§ 23.8 APPENDIX 1: COMMENTS BY A RESPECTED COMMERCIAL REAL ESTATE BROKER

Cooperation Between a Lessor and Lessee of a Commercial Lease

This section summarizes the views of my cousin, also named Boris Kozolchyk, a knowledgable and respected Florida Commercial Real Estate Broker and consultant on the cooperative business practices associated with commercial leasing.

One of the aspects of Market Street Associate's (MA) dispute with Pension Trust (PT) that struck him as particularly significant was PT's uncooperative attitude as a landlord toward MA (its assignee-lessee's) efforts to attract a national drugstore chain (DSC) as a tenant of its Milwaukee shopping center. Lack of cooperation in this case was particularly manifest in failures to reply to requests for finance of necessary improvements that could redound to the benefit of PT and MA.

In my cousin's view, regardless of the size of a commercial lease, a commercial lessor has a vested interest in cooperating with his lessee's attempts to attract such tenants. This is especially true for pension funds that depend upon lease revenues in order to pay out their long-term obligations to their pensioners. Bear in mind that tenancies such as that by DSC determine the market value of shopping centers. Bear in mind also that a DSC lease represents not only a reliable stream of income, but also a marketable asset. When such a lease is sold, which is not an infrequent event, its market value is determined by DSC's credit rating and by the actual terms and conditions of the lease, including its length, options to renew and other economic terms or incentives, mutual obligations and so on. Therefore, in the ordinary course of business, PT should have had a strong interest in fully cooperating with MA in obtaining marketable terms and conditions for the DSC lease. In this respect, paragraph 34 reflects the importance that both parties, as well as the industry, place on financial cooperation between the lessor and the lessee.

What happens in the marketplace when one of the parties willingly or negligently fails to communicate or respond to a communication on an important aspect of its commercial lease? One example involves the Option to Renew Clause (OR), which in essence provides the mechanism to extend the term of the commercial lease. Although there are different OR formats, one that is commonly used in Florida gives the lessee the right to extend the lease term if the lessee gives written notice within a stipulated time frame—for example, 6 months or a year—prior to the expiration of the then running term. In the event that lessee fails to notify the lessor as indicated, the lessor has no responsibility to notify the lessee of the lease expiration, and the lessee loses his right to the option. My cousin has been involved in several leases when a lessee negligently failed to exercise the option to renew at a great cost to him. The landlord may have been aware of lessee's failure to exercise the option, but elected not to make the lessee aware of the requirement. I am not aware of a single instance in which such failure of communications had judicial repercussions. The assumption in the community of commercial lessors, lessees and brokers with whom he is familiar is that as long as the parties involved are professional or experienced in the commercial lease business, they are responsible for their acts as well as their omissions.

From a commercial real estate broker's perspective, a typical real estate transaction requires that the broker act honestly and disclose the facts that affect, or may affect, the value of the property when such facts are not otherwise available to either party to the transaction. If he were a broker in this transaction, he would want to make sure that the parties were aware that at the time of the request of financing to bring in DSC as a tenant, there were less than 5 years left in the original lease and that a lease with DSC would have required a minimum of a new 20-year lease.

In connection with these negotiations, he would question PT's good faith when refusing to enter into a negotiation with MA that could have resulted on a higher final value for their property and could have brought PT closer to their asserted $7 million investment threshold.

Ordinarily, MA's financing request would include information about DSC and the terms of the proposed sublease. If so, PT would have been aware of the potential value of the sublease and MA's inability of obtain financing from another source. One cannot ignore the possibility that PT's perception of its privileged position may be reason for its repeated failures to respond to MA's inquiries, as it could have decided that it was in a better position to put the deal together with DSC than MA and was thereby eliminating a costly intermediary. Keep in mind that at the time of the financing request, there were less than 5 years left in the original term and a new lease with DSC would have required a minimum term of 20 years. Conjectural as this explanation of PTs behavior is, it is at least as realistic as the one assumed by the lower and appellate courts. It would explain both PT's $3 million asking price and its $7 million financial investment threshold.

In conclusion, he found it surprising that the courts did not try to avail themselves of the most widely used method of value determination in real estate, namely, a certified appraisal. Once such a value is established, some of the questions of "good faith" on PT's side (how reasonable was the $3 million asking price and what is a basis for a "reasonable negotiated solution") could have been much more easily established.

§ 23.9 APPENDIX 2: COMPARATIVE CASE LAW

A. Introduction

The cases selected for discussion are divided into three sections (B, C and D). Viteri's Heirs, the first case in Section B, illustrates a method of interpretation in which the court examines the commercial contract as a logical construct isolated from basic transactional facts as well as from considerations of good faith, reasonableness and from what is fair under the circumstances. The predominant interpretive criteria are: 1) Is the contract in question highly personal in nature (*intuitu personae*) or can it be performed by anyone? and 2) Do the pleadings contain the appropriate prayers for relief? The answers to these questions, and nothing more, dictate what each party was entitled to receive under the contract, if anything.

Teofila Astorga Viuda de Aceves, the third case, exemplifies the shortcomings of relying on traditional tools for the interpretation of civil contracts such as the plain meaning of words found within the four corners of the contract. In this case, the contract is for a lease of a residential unit, part of which will be used as an ice cream parlor. Not receiving court consideration are the parties' course of performance and course of dealing as well as the commercial usage of residential units in the unit's neighborhood. Also absent are considerations of plaintiff's bad faith and possible abuse of rights.

Each of the above cases is juxtaposed against their polar opposite in method of reasoning (including fact finding) and result: Justice Cardozo's landmark opinion in *Meinhard v. Salmon* and Judge Butzner's opinion in the *Columbia Nitrogen* case. Cardozo's opinion is credited with having provided vital legal support to financial markets in which fiduciaries are central players. And Judge Butzner's decision may well have cemented the role of usage of trade as the final interpreter of the meaning of commercial and sectoral terms and conditions. From the standpoint of economic development, how significant are these accomplishments? Section F concludes with the *Haakjoeringskoed* decision by the German Imperial Court. It underscores the corrective function of a usage of trade with respect to the meaning of key terms and conditions of commercial contracts, even when the two parties to the sale agreement agreed on a term that turned out to have a mistaken meaning.

B. How a Formal Logical Intent Can Do Away with Good Faith, Reasonableness, Fairness and Justice

The Heirs of Viteri[272]

The appellants, heirs of Engineer Jorge Viteri (hereinafter Viteri), set out a number of arguments of misapplication (referred to in Mexico's appellate terminology as violations-"*violaciónes*") of the law by the lower court requiring reversal by the Supreme Court. The following is the author's summary and translation of their arguments followed by a summary of Mexico's Supreme Court reply to these arguments and final decision.

The following are the appellant's arguments:

I. The appellants argue that the lower court mistakenly applied or failed to apply Articles 78[273] of the Commercial Code and 1796[274] and 1858[275] of the Civil Code.

---

[272] Jorge Viteri, Suc de., 125 SJF5a 315 (1955), Amparo Civil Directo No. 4215 of 1953, Sec 1ª. Summary by the author of a translation kindly made available by the late Professor Woodfin Butte of the University of Texas School of Law. WOODFIN LEE.BUTTE, SELECTED MEXICAN CASES 309–12 (1967). Any errors and omissions due to the summarization of Professor Butte's excellent translation are the sole responsibility of the author. On the procedural aspects of an *amparo* appeal, *see* Glossary, "*Amparo* Appeal."

[273] Article 78 states: "In commercial contracts, each party is bound in the manner and terms in which it appears that it wanted to be bound, without having the validity of the commercial act depend upon the observance of formalities or specified requisites." Código de Comercio [CCo.] [Commercial Code], *as amended*, Diario Oficial de la Federación [DO], 7 de octubre de 1889 (Mex.) (author's translation).

They further argue that the court below disregarded the true intent of the contract on which the action was based. The parties' intent was to bring an unproductive oil well into full production by using both Viteri's technical expertise and his considerable investment of time and money. Viteri completely performed his contractual obligations. The complaint below demanded payment of 50% of the profits accumulated after a surplus amount of production was reached. This royalty was to be paid for Viteri's technical services as an oil engineer and as the manager of the oil well once it became profitable. The latter functions are accessory to the principal agreement of making the oil well productive and could be carried out by any competent manager now that Viteri is deceased; on the other hand, the initial task of making the well productive could not have been done without him. Without his work, the oil well would have been plugged and abandoned. The accessory nature of the management obligations is proven by the fact that after Viteri's death, the management of the well continued to be profitable under someone else's management.

II. Despite Viteri's death, the partnership agreement between Viteri and the owners of the well continued in existence and the court below erroneously applied Article 1854 of the Civil Code.[276] The principal object of the contract at issue was to make the well commercial, and this is why it was agreed that the contract would last as long as the well was profitable. The death of Viteri was an unavoidable accident (*caso fortuito*) for which no one is responsible and from which Viteri's heirs share in the partnership should not suffer. The governing principle should therefore be that what is accessory in a contract is subordinated to what is principal. A finding that the contract is terminated without awarding Viteri's share to his heirs causes unjustified and harmful injury to the appellants' interests. The lower court's reliance on a formal and rigid view of the contract involved and of the need to rescind it without awarding the corresponding share of royalties to the appellants has misapplied Article 78 of the Commercial Code.[277]

III. Article 1858 of the Civil Code was misinterpreted by the lower court's failure to give effect to Clause 6 of the contract, which supports the characterization of this contract as one for the performance of construction work payable by the royalties derived from the surplus oil production. There is no basis for treating Viteri's

---

[274] Article 1796 states in relevant part:

> Contracts are perfected by the mere consent of the parties, except for those that must have the form set forth by law. . . . they bind the parties not only to the fulfillment of what was expressly agreed upon, but also to the consequences that according to their nature are consistent with good faith, the usages and the law.

Código Civil Federal [CC] [Federal Civil Code], *as amended*, Diario Oficial de la Federación [DO], 26 de mayo, 14 de julio, 3 y 31 de agosto de 1928 (Mex.) (author's translation).

[275] Article 1858 states:

> Contracts that are not expressly regulated by this code shall be governed by the general rules of contracts, by the parties' stipulations and with respect to those provisions of the contract that were silent on the rules applicable to them, by the rules that are applicable to the most analogous provisions applicable to other contracts regulated in this code.

Id. art. 1858 (author's translation).

[276] Article 1854 states: "Contract clauses must be interpreted jointly by taking into account what each of them states when interpreting the others and by attributing to the doubtful clauses the meaning that emerges from the entire set of clauses." *Id.* art. 1854 (author's translation).

[277] *See supra* note 273.

performance of his promise to rebuild the oil well and corresponding royalties as income from a regular partnership contract because such a partnership is invariably based on the sharing of losses and profits, and the contract on which this action is based stipulated that the losses were to be born entirely by Viteri if the oil well was not profitable.

IV. The court below acknowledges that it would not be proper to deprive Viteri of his rights, and that it would be necessary to liquidate the partnership, but that on the basis of the cause of action chosen by the plaintiffs, it is not possible to protect these rights. This finding misinterprets Article 1327 of the Commercial Code,[278] which instructs the court to deal exclusively with actions and defenses raised by the parties in their complaint and answer, because the court should have preserved the rights of the appellants to bring about the liquidation of the partnership in accordance with Article 230 of the Law on Commercial Companies, or should have laid the basis for such liquidation by the application of Article 85 of the Code of Civil Procedure.[279]

V. The lower court's decision fails to recognize the appellants' rights as successors to Viteri's interest in the well. . . . The decision also fails to apply Article 1857 of the Civil Code, which should have been applied because it requires that when a doubt exists on how to interpret a contract, the court should interpret it in a manner that insures the highest measure of reciprocity between the parties. . . .[280]

OPINION:

The appellant presents two fundamental arguments. The first is that the contract on which the action is based has two parts: 1) a principal part that consists of Viteri's bringing into production an oil well which was to be plugged as non-productive; and 2) an accessory part that consists of Viteri's managing the production of the well and maintaining its profitability. In exchange for these obligations, Viteri was supposed to receive 50% royalties of the oil produced after a certain level of surplus production had been reached. According to the appellant, the second part of the contract was accessory to and followed the completion of the first one. The appellant alleges that because that which is accessory follows what is principal, if the principal phase of the contract was carried out and completed as of 1941, from that time forward, Viteri and his heirs acquired the right to receive 50% of the profits from the surplus oil.

This argument is unpersuasive. The work of making the well commercial, although more significant during the first part of Viteri's performance, was not his entire expected performance under the contract. His obligations lasted until his death and Viteri performed considerable management work in the years following his initial work of making the well productive. Considering these facts, it is not possible to

[278] Article 1327 states: "The court decision (*sentencia*) shall deal exclusively with the actions and exceptions brought respectively before the court by the complaint and answer." CCo. art. 1327 (Mex.) (author's translation).

[279] These articles address the liquidation of a partnership.

[280] In relevant part, Article 1857 states:

> When it is absolutely impossible to resolve the doubts on how to interpret a contract by following the rules set forth in the preceding articles . . . if the contrast was of a gratuitous type, the doubt shall be resolved in favor of the smallest conveyance of rights and interests; if the contract was for profit (*oneroso*) the doubt shall be resolved in favor of the highest measure of reciprocity (*mayor reciprocidad de intereses*) [between the parties].

CC art. 1857 (Mex.) (author's translation).

establish for royalty purposes what is the accessory and what is the principal object of this contract. The conclusion should be that since Mr. Viteri can no longer render those services he was supposed to perform, the condition subsequent of Article 1949 of the Civil Code and the rescission of the contract between Viteri and owners of the well is triggered.[281] Once triggered, it dispenses with the need to characterize the contract as one of a regular partnership or of the performance of construction work subject to royalty payments. That is to say, the obligations are to be reciprocally terminated in view of the fact that one of the parties can no longer perform his obligations.

The appellant's statement that the well continues to produce and that this shows that Viteri's oil management work can be performed by some other person is unpersuasive as well. The important thing is not that the technical work of Mr. Viteri can be done by someone else, but that since the work is of a strictly personal nature, if Mr. Viteri can no longer perform it, the other party to the contract has the right to rescind it. The court below is correct in deciding that the defendant company is not required to accept the appointment of a third party by the heirs of Viteri since this would be an interference with the freedom of the company to designate its own employees or to reach agreement with anyone it chooses. It follows that, since the profitability of the well does not depend on one single performance of work by Viteri, but on his continuing work of keeping the well in this productive condition, the rights acquired by virtue of the contract by Mr. Viteri, being strictly personal, cannot be inherited and the heirs of Viteri cannot require the performance of the contract which terminated with the death of Mr. Viteri.

The appellants' second argument is that the court below should have preserved the rights of the plaintiffs as Viteri's heirs to move for the liquidation of the partnership and for the distribution of its share. And in the event that they did not receive their share, their action on unjust enrichment should be allowed to proceed. This argument fails because of the form of the complaint submitted by the appellant.

It is possible that the first task carried out by Viteri (to bring the well into commercial production) was of greater economic importance and might justify greater compensation than did the permanent work of maintaining the well in a profitable state. That is to say, it is possible that this first task might represent, for example, 25% of the surplus oil production and that the permanent work would correspond to another 25% so that if the first task was completed, Viteri acquired a right of 25% of the shares that can be transmitted to his heirs.

The lower court agreed with this reasoning. Nevertheless, the complaint was drafted in such a manner that it made it impossible to render a decision against the defendant company. In the complaint, the claim was made solely for the entire 50%, without any deduction and under the assumption that the heirs would assume all of the obligations of Mr. Viteri (it was later indicated that the heirs would pay a third party who would carry out the permanent or ongoing work entrusted to the deceased). Thus, there was no attempt to distinguish between the initial work and the permanent or ongoing work, nor was there any attempt to have any expert evaluation of the two. In this manner, and given the way in which the controversy was brought to the court, if

[281] In relevant part, Article 1949 states: "The power to rescind [contractual] obligations is deemed implicit when they are reciprocal when one of the parties does not fufill what he was supposed to." *Id.* art. 1949 (author's translation).

the court had reached a decision against the defendant company by taking into consideration questions which were not presented by the appellants, the nature of the litigation would have been completely altered and Article 1327 of the Commercial Code would have been violated.

The lower court correctly stated the following:

> The heirs of Viteri may have a right to their portion of the agreed upon 50%; but of course not to all of it, which is what is sought in the complaint. Such an award would be inconsistent with the evidence before us as well as with what was pleaded by the appellants. It would therefore violate Article 1327, which limits the recovery to what was pleaded and proven. Only expert testimony could have given a basis on which to reduce the value of any such decision to a monetary figure, and such testimony is not on the record.

For the foregoing reasons the appellants' *amparo* appeal is rejected.

1. Factual Gaps and Non-Reliance on Course of Dealing and Usage of Trade

Gaps abound in the factual record relied upon by Mexico's Supreme Court. It is clear that Viteri, an oil production engineer, entered into a contractual arrangement with the owners of a well in which he agreed to contribute his engineering skills, time and money (including building materials) to develop the defendant's oil well in Mexico. It is also clear that Viteri assumed the risk of failure of his efforts to develop the well: If he did not succeed in making the oil well profitable, he would not recover what he invested. Finally, it is also a fact that he succeeded in making the oil well profitable and continued to manage the well for a period of time that the Supreme Court describes only as "prolonged." Then Viteri died and his heirs initiated an action against the owners of the well, demanding payment of the 50% royalty on the surplus oil as apparently agreed upon.

Among the many relevant unanswered factual questions were: 1) Was Viteri ever paid the 50% royalty while he was alive? 2) What did this payment include? Did the royalties paid include what was owed to him as a result of his engineering work as well as for his management of the well? 3) What was meant by the term production surplus? Was it the amount arrived at after deducting costs, including overhead such as a salary for Viteri as project manager and after reimbursing him for the costs of production he advanced? 4) The Supreme Court held that it could not grant the 50% royalty agreed upon because there was no evidence regarding how much of the 50% claimed was for the engineering work involved in developing the well and how much for his managerial work. The Court referred to the absence of an accounting report among the evidence that should have been submitted by the plaintiffs-appellants. If so, could the Supreme Court have instructed the lower court to appoint such an expert and award the amount he found due and payable for the engineering work? 5) On the other hand, why did the Supreme Court assume that the 50% royalty was not for the entirety of Viteri's contribution and allow the managerial part of the contribution to be performed by a competent manager paid by Viteri's heirs? 6) The Supreme Court repeatedly referred to Article 1327 of the Commercial Code, which directs courts to keep their decisions within the bounds set by the "actions and exceptions brought respectively before the court by the complaint and answer."[282] Yet this directive does not deny the power of the courts to grant, deny or reduce the amount claimed. If so, and bearing in mind that appellants did claim the 50% royalty (as the upper limit of their claim (*peititio*), why not instruct the lower court to find the amount owed based upon proper evidence, or, if that was not procedurally possible, dismiss the case without prejudice and allow the refilling of an action for the proper amount? 7) Why was there no reference in the lower court decision or in its discussion by the Supreme Court to the usages of the oil production trade on compensation for "sweat equity" partners or joint venturers? After all, Article 1856 of the Civil Code of 1932 expressly directed the courts to take into account customs and usages when interpreting the ambiguities of contracts.[283] 8) Since at the time of this dispute private oil wells were allowed to be developed and exploited in Mexico by private parties, what were the Mexican customs and usages concerning the distribution of profits in oil development contracts? Did they regard contributions such as Viteri's to be part of a regular partnership or a performance of work contract where the party who performs the work is entitled to a fixed royalty for the productive life of the well?

2. *Law, Legal Culture and Limitations to Equitable Decision Making: Prayed for Justice, Literalism and Contract Typification*

Had the Supreme Court decided to resolve this dispute equitably, Article 1857 would have supported such a decision. It imposes a duty on the Mexican judge to decide the case equitably where doubts on the parties' intent were "impossible to resolve" as was concluded by the Supreme Court in this case:

> When it is absolutely impossible to resolve the doubts on how to interpret a contract by following the rules set forth in the preceding articles . . . if the contract was for profit (*oneroso*) the doubt shall be resolved in favor of the highest measure of reciprocity (*mayor reciprocidad de intereses*).[284]

Had the Supreme Court provided the measure of reciprocity mentioned in this provision, it would have encouraged the Viteris of this world to contribute their skills, time and money to productive endeavors. Having denied such reciprocity, the conclusion is inescapable that others such as Viteri will probably choose not to participate as partners, joint venturers or risk assuming builders and managers, except when provided with expensive, ironclad reassurances such as irrevocable letters of credit or payment bonds.

The Mexican Supreme Court invoked as an excuse for not acting equitably a procedural principle invoked by many other courts in civil law countries as part of the their Roman inheritance: "Justice can only be granted for what is prayed for and proven" (*Pluspetitio*).[285] In other words, the court should grant no more (and some countries say no less as well) than what the parties requested in their complaint, answer or counterclaim. As noted earlier, the Supreme Court repeatedly quoted Article

---

[282] CCo. art. 1327 (Mex.) (author's translation).

[283] Article 1856 states: "The custom and usage of the country shall be taken into account when interpreting the ambiguities of contracts." *Id.* art. 1856 (Author's translation).

[284] *Id.* art. 1857 (author's translation).

[285] BERGER, ENCYCLOPEDIC DICTIONARY, at 633.

1327 of the Commercial Code as limiting its equitable and related fact-finding functions. Yet, as is also discussed in that Chapter 23, other countries supposedly governed by the same legal system, such as Germany, have found ways around this limitation. Why not Mexico? The late Professor Eduardo Garcia Maynez, one of the great legal thinkers of the hemisphere, as well as his highly respected colleagues, Lic. Oscar Morineau Rodriguez, Professor Raul Cervantes Ahumada and now presently, Magistrate Juan Luis Gonzalez Alcantara, attributed this aversion to equitable interpretation of contractual and statutory law to a legal culture of literalism ("*letrismo*") which protects the judge from being accused of being capricious, venal or worse.[286]

Closely related to literalism is the judicial tendency in Mexico and other countries that have adopted many of the legislative principles of the *Code Civil* to rely on the "typification" of contracts as an important tool to determine the parties' intent. This is done directly when determining that the contract in question is, say, unilateral or bilateral, consensual or real, gratuitous or onerous, etc., or by applying analogous types of contracts to those without regulation. As stated by Article 1858 of Mexico's Civil Code:

> Contracts that are not expressly regulated by this code shall be governed by the general rules of contracts, by the parties' stipulations, and with respect to those provisions of the contract that are silent on the rules applicable to them, by the rules that are applicable to the most analogous provisions applicable to other contracts regulated in this code.[287]

In Viteri's case, the typification relied on by the Supreme Court was that of an *intuitu personae* contract, *i.e.*, a contract entered into because of the personal features of Viteri's performance in contrast with contracts whose participants contribute solely their capital. Having determined that the contract is of an *intuitu personae* nature, a legal consequence follows: The death or absence of such a party requires the termination or rescission of the contract.

Yet, even if one were to assume that the management of the well could not have gone on without Viteri (contradicted as this assumption was by the facts), why not liquidate the partnership or joint venture in a manner that was fair to all concerned? The Supreme Court's answer placed the blame of this unfairness on an improperly drafted complaint. Wasn't such a result—one that enabled one party's unjust enrichment as a result of its deceitful invocation of a strict remedy—precisely why the Praetor formulated his *exceptio doli*? Or, as M. Tullius Cicero, among many other Roman notables (including Praetors) were known to have suggested to decision-makers to ask themselves: "Who profited from the decision or deed?" (*Cui bono fuerit*).[288]

---

[286] *See supra* § 14:6(G).

[287] CC art. 1858 (Mex.) (author's translation).

[288] MARCUS TULLIUS CICERO, THE PHILIPPIC ORATIONS OF M. TULLIUS CICERO 55 (2nd rev. ed. 1878). This saying was attributed to the jursit Lucius Cassius, the proposer of the Lex Tabellaria. *Id.* at 55 n.6. Cicero argues that after Caesar's death, Antony had derived more advantage than anyone else from it. *Id.*

3. The Fairness of the Marketplace

The Viteri decision is clearly contrary to a standard of fairness that I refer to in this book and other writings as the "fairness of the marketplace."[289] This fairness requires that each contracting party treat the other as a regular market participant in that trade or profession would want to be treated when viewing his own advantage. The decision belongs to a category of fairness typical of familistic and tribal societies discussed previously.[290] Viteri's heirs were treated as members of a rival family, tribe or clan who lacked the support or protection of influential politicians and judges; no duties of equity and fairness were owed to them.

What is the connection between the stranger standard of fairness and a good faith interpretation of contracts? Clearly, the stranger standard of contractual treatment can be traced to pre-commercial societies[291] and thus it precedes the pleadings in the Viteri case. The defendant owners of the oil well had made up their minds to prevent the plaintiffs from getting what was rightfully theirs once Viteri died, or perhaps even before that. They must have learned from the picaresque way of doing business that "he who invented the law also invented the way of getting around it."[292] All they had to do was find the adjudicators able and willing to implement this method of doing business. Therefore, the most effective cure for the bad faith and injustice in the outcome of Viteri's case would have been found first in fair, standard engineering agreements and thereafter in the usages of the oil well development trade.

C. Good Faith Among Co-Adventurers

Meinhard v. Salmon[293] *(249 N.Y. 458)*

Appeal from a judgment of the Appellate Division of the Supreme Court in the first judicial department, entered June 28, 1928, modifying and affirming as modified a judgment in favor of plaintiff entered upon the report of a referee.

OPINION:

CARDOZO, Ch. J.

On April 10, 1902, Louisa M. Gerry leased to the defendant Walter J. Salmon the premises known as the Hotel Bristol at the northwest corner of Forty-second street and Fifth avenue in the city of New York. The lease was for a term of twenty years, commencing May 1, 1902, and ending April 30, 1922. The lessee undertook to change the hotel building for use as shops and offices at a cost of $200,000. Alterations and additions were to be accretions to the land.

Salmon, while in course of [negotiating a contract] with the lessor as to the execution of the lease, was in course of [negotiating a contract] with Meinhard, the plaintiff, for the necessary funds. The result was a joint venture with terms embodied in a writing. Meinhard was to pay to Salmon half of the moneys requisite to

---

289 *See* Glossary, "Market Standard of Fairness." Kozolchyk, *Fairness*, at 220, 233, 234.

290 *See, e.g., supra* § 1:2(G).

291 *Id.*

292 *See supra* § 5:4 (describing the *picaresque* form of doing business).

293 249 N.Y. 458 (1928).

reconstruct, alter, manage and operate the property. Salmon was to pay to Meinhard 40 per cent of the net profits for the first five years of the lease and 50 per cent for the years thereafter. If there were losses, each party was to bear them equally. Salmon, however, was to have sole power to "manage, lease, underlet and operate" the building. There were to be certain pre-emptive rights for each in the contingency of death.

The two were coadventurers, subject to fiduciary duties akin to those of partners. . . . The heavier weight of duty rested, however, upon Salmon. He was a coadventurer with Meinhard, but he was manager as well. During the early years of the enterprise, the building, reconstructed, was operated at a loss. If the relation had then ended, Meinhard as well as Salmon would have carried a heavy burden. Later the profits became large with the result that for each of the investors there came a rich return. For each, the venture had its phases of fair weather and of foul. The two were in it jointly, for better or for worse.

When the lease was near its end, Elbridge T. Gerry had become the owner of the reversion. He owned much other property in the neighborhood, one lot adjoining the Bristol Building on Fifth avenue and four lots on Forty-second street. He had a plan to lease the entire tract for a long term to some one who would destroy the buildings then existing, and put up another in their place. . . . Then, in January, 1922, with less than four months of the lease to run, he approached the defendant Salmon. The result was a new lease to the Midpoint Realty Company, which is owned and controlled by Salmon, a lease covering the whole tract, and involving a huge outlay. The term is to be twenty years, but successive covenants for renewal will extend it to a maximum of eighty years at the will of either party. The existing buildings may remain unchanged for seven years. They are then to be torn down, and a new building to cost $3,000,000 is to be placed upon the site. The rental, which under the Bristol lease was only $55,000, is to be from $350,000 to $475,000 for the properties so combined. Salmon personally guaranteed the performance by the lessee of the covenants of the new lease until such time as the new building had been completed and fully paid for.

The lease between Gerry and the Midpoint Realty Company was signed and delivered on January 25, 1922. Salmon had not told Meinhard anything about it. Whatever his motive may have been, he had kept the negotiations to himself. Meinhard was not informed even of the bare existence of a project. The first that he knew of it was in February when the lease was an accomplished fact. He then made demand on the defendants that the lease be held in trust as an asset of the venture, making offer upon the trial to share the personal obligations incidental to the guaranty. The demand was followed by refusal, and later by this suit. A referee gave judgment for the plaintiff, limiting the plaintiff's interest in the lease, however, to 25 per cent. The limitation was on the theory that the plaintiff's equity was to be restricted to one-half of so much of the value of the lease as was contributed or represented by the occupation of the Bristol site. Upon cross-appeals to the Appellate Division, the judgment was modified so as to enlarge the equitable interest to one-half of the whole lease. With this enlargement of plaintiff's interest, there went, of course, a corresponding enlargement of his attendant obligations. The case is now here on an appeal by the defendants.

Joint adventurers, like copartners, owe to one another, while the enterprise continues, the duty of the finest loyalty. Many forms of conduct permissible in a workaday world for those acting at arm's length, are forbidden to those bound by fiduciary ties. A trustee is held to something stricter than the morals of the market place. Not honesty alone, but the punctilio of an honor the most sensitive, is then the standard of behavior. As to this there has developed a tradition that is unbending and inveterate. Uncompromising rigidity has been the attitude of courts of equity when petitioned to undermine the rule of undivided loyalty by the "disintegrating erosion" of particular exceptions. Only thus has the level of conduct for fiduciaries been kept at a level higher than that trodden by the crowd. It will not consciously be lowered by any judgment of this court.

The owner of the reversion, Mr. Gerry, had vainly striven to find a tenant who would favor his ambitious scheme of demolition and construction. Baffled in the search, he turned to the defendant Salmon in possession of the Bristol, the keystone of the project. He figured to himself beyond a doubt that the man in possession would prove a likely customer. To the eye of an observer, Salmon held the lease as owner in his own right, for himself and no one else. In fact he held it as a fiduciary, for himself and another, sharers in a common venture. If this fact had been proclaimed, if the lease by its terms had run in favor of a partnership, Mr. Gerry, we may fairly assume, would have laid before the partners, and not merely before one of them, his plan of reconstruction. The pre-emptive privilege, or, better, the pre-emptive opportunity, that was thus an incident of the enterprise, Salmon appropriated to himself in secrecy and silence. He might have warned Meinhard that the plan had been submitted, and that either would be free to compete for the award. If he had done this, we do not need to say whether he would have been under a duty, if successful in the competition, to hold the lease so acquired for the benefit of a venture then about to end, and thus prolong by indirection its responsibilities and duties. The trouble about his conduct is that he excluded his coadventurer from any chance to compete, from any chance to enjoy the opportunity for benefit that had come to him alone by virtue of his agency. This chance, if nothing more, he was under a duty to concede. The price of its denial is an extension of the trust at the option and for the benefit of the one whom he excluded.

No answer is it to say that the chance would have been of little value even if seasonably offered. Such a calculus of probabilities is beyond the science of the chancery. Salmon, the real estate operator, might have been preferred to Meinhard, the woolen merchant. On the other hand, Meinhard might have offered better terms, or reinforced his offer by alliance with the wealth of others. Perhaps he might even have persuaded the lessor to renew the Bristol lease alone, postponing for a time, in return for higher rentals, the improvement of adjoining lots. We know that even under the lease as made the time for the enlargement of the building was delayed for seven years. All these opportunities were cut away from him through another's intervention. He knew that Salmon was the manager. As the time drew near for the expiration of the lease, he would naturally assume from silence, if from nothing else, that the lessor was willing to extend it for a term of years, or at least to let it stand as a lease from year to year. Not impossibly the lessor would have done so, whatever his protestations of unwillingness, if Salmon had not given assent to a project more attractive. At all events, notice of termination, even if not necessary, might seem, not unreasonably, to be something to be looked for, if the business was over and another tenant was to enter. In the absence of such notice, the matter of an extension was one that would naturally be attended to by the manager of the enterprise, and not neglected altogether. At least, there was nothing in the situation to give warning to any one that while the lease was still in being, there had come to the manager an offer of extension which he had locked within his breast to be utilized by himself alone. The very fact that Salmon was in control with exclusive powers of direction charged him the more obviously with the duty of disclosure, since only through disclosure could opportunity be equalized. If he might cut off renewal by a purchase for his own benefit when four months were to pass before the lease would have an end, he might do so with equal right while there remained as many years. He might steal a march on his comrade under cover of the darkness, and then hold the captured ground. Loyalty and comradeship are not so easily abjured.

Little profit will come from a dissection of the precedents. None precisely similar is cited in the briefs of counsel. What is similar in many, or so it seems to us, is the animating principle. Authority is, of course, abundant that one partner may not appropriate to his own use a renewal of a lease, though its term is to begin at the expiration of the partnership. The lease at hand with its many changes is not strictly a renewal. Even so, the standard of loyalty for those in trust relations is without the fixed divisions of a graduated scale. . . . To say that a partner is free without restriction to buy in the reversion of the property where the business is conducted is to say in effect that he may strip the good will of its chief element of value, since good will is largely dependent upon continuity of possession. Equity refuses to confine within the bounds of classified transactions its precept of a loyalty that is undivided and unselfish. Certain at least it is that a "man obtaining his *locus standi*, and his opportunity for making such arrangements, by the position he occupies as a partner, is bound by his obligation to his co-partners in such dealings not to separate his interest from theirs, but, if he acquires any benefit, to communicate it to them." Certain it is also that there may be no abuse of special opportunities growing out of a special trust as manager or agent. . . . A constructive trust is then the remedial device through which preference of self is made subordinate to loyalty to others. Many and varied are its phases and occasions.

We have no thought to hold that Salmon was guilty of a conscious purpose to defraud. Very likely he assumed in all good faith that with the approaching end of the venture he might ignore his co-adventurer and take the extension for himself. He had given to the enterprise time and labor as well as money. He had made it a success. Meinhard, who had given money, but neither time nor labor, had already been richly paid. There might seem to be something grasping in his insistence upon more. Such recriminations are not unusual when coadventurers fall out. They are not without their force if conduct is to be judged by the common standards of competitors. That is not to say that they have pertinency here. Salmon had put himself in a position in which thought of self was to be renounced, however hard the abnegation. He was much more than a coadventurer. He was a managing coadventurer. For him and for those like him, the rule of undivided loyalty is relentless and supreme. A different question would be here if there were lacking any nexus of relation between the business conducted by the manager and the opportunity brought to him as an incident of management. For this problem, as for most, there are distinctions of degree. If Salmon had received from Gerry a proposition to lease a building at a location far removed, he might have held for himself the privilege thus acquired, or so we shall assume. Here the subject-matter of the new lease was an extension and enlargement of the subject-matter of the old one. A managing coadventurer appropriating the benefit of such a lease without warning to his partner might fairly expect to be reproached with conduct that was underhand, or lacking, to say the least, in reasonable candor, if the partner were to surprise him in the act of signing the new instrument. Conduct subject to that reproach does not receive from equity a healing benediction.

. . .

The judgment should be modified by providing that at the option of the defendant Salmon there may be substituted for a trust attaching to the lease a trust attaching to the shares of stock, with the result that one-half of such shares together with one additional share will in that event be allotted to the defendant Salmon and the other shares to the plaintiff, and as so modified the judgment should be affirmed with costs.

1. Cardozo's Awareness of Relevant Facts

In contrast with the dearth of relevant facts in Viteri's case, Justice Cardozo was armed with all the relevant facts needed to form his perceptions of archetypal behavior in *Meinhard v. Salmon*. His legal analysis reflected a clear and deep understanding of the transaction, what lead to the dispute and the reasons behind the parties' behavior. He understood what Gerry (the new landlord) would be looking for in an investor to help him develop his grandiose plan. He knew why the right to the possession of the Bristol property initially developed by Salmon and in which Meinhard had been the critical investor was "the keystone of the project."[294] Please note that while Cardozo had no difficulties in quickly and accurately identifying this keystone, the Mexican Supreme Court could not make up its mind on whether Viteri's engineering contribution was the "principal object" of his contract or whether it was a combination of his engineering and well management services.

Similarly, Cardozo quickly discerned why Salmon, the defendant in possession of the Bristol property, would prove a likely customer to the landlord. In addition, he understood why to an average businessman, such as Gerry, Salmon would appear as the owner of the lease of the Bristol property. Cardozo was aware of what signs of apparent ownership of a lease would suffice to create an impression of ownership in the real estate transactions common in the Manhattan of his day. *Pari passu*, from the moment he looked at Meinhard and Salmon's investment agreement, Cardozo perceived that Salmon was in fact holding the property as a fiduciary for himself and for Meinhard in the common venture in which Salmon was the principal contributor of capital.

Cardozo also perceived the crucial fact that if Salmon had disclosed to Gerry that the lease was owned by a partnership, Gerry very likely would have made Meinhard aware of his plan to rebuild the former Bristol Hotel property as part of a larger complex. This disclosure to Meinhard, who apparently had sufficient cash and other valuable assets on hand to have become Gerry's capitalist partner, may have deprived Salmon of his "pre-emptive opportunity" to be the sole bidder because Meinhard could have become Salmon's competitor at least to finance Gerry's project.[295]

These facts led to Cardozo's first major finding of fact. It was that Salmon's conduct excluded his co-adventurer from competing to become Gerry's new partner, investor or lender. The gathered facts also led to his second finding that the opportunity to hide the deal from Meinhard came to Salmon "by virtue of his agency.

[294] 249 N.Y. at 464.

[295] *Id.* at 464–65.

This chance, if nothing more, he was under a duty to concede."[296] This second finding prevented Salmon from defending his conduct by alleging that the opportunity to bid would have been of little value to Meinhard because, in Cardozo's memorable words because of their elegance, terseness and truth, "[s]uch a calculus of probabilities is beyond the science of the chancery."[297]

Despite the fact that a court of equity did not have to determine why and how Salmon could have succeeded in convincing Gerry to accept his offer of financing, and despite the fact that Meinhard was not a real estate operator, but a woolen merchant, Cardozo listed a few conjectures that further revealed his firm grasp of the transactional facts:

> Meinhard might have offered better terms, or reinforced his offer by alliance with the wealth of others. Perhaps he might even have persuaded the lessor to renew the Bristol lease alone, postponing for a time, in return for higher rentals, the improvement of adjoining lots. We know that even under the lease as made the time for the enlargement of the building was delayed for seven years. All these opportunities were cut away from him through another's intervention.[298]

It is also noteworthy that Cardozo's awareness of the usages and practices involved in New York's real estate marketplace at the turn of the twentieth century filled many a gap in the court's awareness of the relevant facts.

2. *Typification v. The Duties of a Commercial Relationship as the Ratio Decidendi: Average Good Faith (Honesty in Fact) v. Uberrima Fides*

Unlike the appellants' and the Mexican Supreme Court's reasoning in Viteri's case, very little was riding on whether the contract between Meinhard and Salmon bore the label of a regular partnership, a joint venture or another type of financing agreement. What mattered were the duties inherent in the commercial relationship entered into by the parties. Cardozo referred to the contract between plaintiff and defendant simply as that between "co-adventurers." Yet, when referring to the duties engendered by such a contract, he described them as "fiduciary duties akin to those of partners. . . ."[299] And once he characterized the commercial relationship between the parties as one between co-adventurers akin to partners, his *ratio decidendi* was inevitable: "joint adventurers and partners . . . owe to one another, while the enterprise continues, the duty of the finest loyalty."[300] This is the same type of good faith, incidentally, that Lord Mansfield, inspired by his spiritual Roman ancestors, had referred to in his day as "*uberrima fides*."

To underscore the higher duties expected from such a fiduciary, Cardozo distinguished their good faith: "[m]any forms of conduct permissible in a workaday world for those acting at arm's length, [are forms of conduct that] are forbidden to

---

296 *Id.* at 465.

297 *Id.*

298 *Id.* at 465.

299 *Id.* at 462.

300 *Id.* at 463–64.

those bound by fiduciary ties."[301] The words of Cardozo that follow still reverberate in many courtrooms in developed financial centers. They have been credited with having instilled a standard that has protected the investments and other fiduciary transactions of millions and millions of market participants:

> A trustee is held to something stricter than the morals of the market place. Not honesty alone, but the punctilio of an honor the most sensitive, is then the standard of behavior. As to this there has developed a tradition that is unbending and inveterate.[302]

D. Plain Meaning of the Words Within the Four Corners of a Deed vs. Market Intent

Teofila Astorga Vda. de Aceves[303]

Brief Synopsis of Facts: A lessee of a residential house located in what became a highly commercial section of the city of Culiacan, Sonora transformed the front part of it into an ice cream parlor. This was part of a trend that involved most of the neighborhood in which this house was located. For a number of months, the landlord-owner of the house did not object to this use but some time thereafter she brought an action to rescind the lease agreement and evict the present tenant alleging that the house was being used for a purpose other than allowed in the lease agreement. Apparently, more lucrative offers had been made to the landlord and her action for rescission was caused by her desire to accept one of these offers. This fact was apparently not known by defendant when filing his answer and additional pleadings.

OPINION:

The lower court found that the lease agreement did not specify the use to be given to the property in question. Hence, there was no prohibition laid upon the tenant against establishing an ice cream parlor in the rented house. The fact that the latter was installed is not sufficient cause for finding that the property has been devoted to a use different from that agreed upon, or even a use contrary to its proper nature or purpose; this quite apart from the fact that it is quite common—the appellate court adds—that in the city of Culiacán, Sinaloa, there are established small industries such as ice cream shops, tinware shops, nixtamal mills, etc., in ordinary urban properties.

Nonetheless, since the contracting parties did not stipulate the use which would be given to the house in question, the tenant had the duty of using it in accordance with its natural use and purpose, under penalty—if this duty is violated—of giving grounds for rescission (Articles 2371, Paragraph II, and 2307, Paragraph III of the Civil Code). The use which, according to the nature of the property, should have been given to the property appears quite clearly from the contents of the first clause of the contract, which provides: "First.—Senora Teófila Astorga viuda de Aceves, gives in leasehold the urban property designated as No. 37 of calle Rafael Buelna West, of this City, composed of two rooms on the front and one interior room, entrance, kitchen, bath, washroom, scullery, toilet, cement floor, plaster walls, tile roofs and wooden beams."

---

301 *Id.* at 464.

302 *Id.*

303 Teofila Astorga Vda. de Aceves, 125 SJF5a 193 (1955), *in* BUTTE, *supra* note 272, at 293–94.

The natural conclusion would be that, according to the structure and nature of the property, it was to be used as living quarters. The defendant, in answering the bill of complaint, maintained that in addition to living quarters the property would be used for the establishment of a small ice cream parlor business and as an office for the business affairs of the defendant, but he did not prove for the record the existence of such an agreement. His adversary, on the other hand, clearly proved that the house was being used, in addition to living quarters, for the business of an ice cream parlor. From the judicial inspection which was carried out, it appears that it was shown that the ice cream parlor is indeed installed in the property and even Torres Mejia himself admitted that he has in the house all of the equipment of the ice cream parlor. The unquestionable result is that in this case, contrary to what the lower court found, the tenant has violated his obligation to use the property according to its nature and purpose, and for this reason the allegations of violation are well founded as brought by the complainant.

The *amparo* for which she petitions should be granted to her in order that the appellate court, in compliance with this decision, should revoke the decision complained of and in place thereof should find that the plaintiff did prove her action of rescission and should decide the other natural consequences of this finding, and should also, on the basis of evidence presented for this purpose, make proper decision as to the damages sought in the complaint.

Fact Finding Under the Civil Procedure Code in Force in Sinaloa

As one can best ascertain, the relevant facts were: 1) The plaintiff rented a residential house and did not specify the permissible uses of the property in the lease or rental agreement; 2) The defendant, like many other renters in that same vicinity, rented a residential property to conduct a business, in this case, opening an ice cream parlor; 3) The plaintiff/lessor attempted to rescind the contract by alleging that the rented house was being used in a manner contrary to the "nature" of the property; 4) The court decided that pursuant to the "nature" of the property (which had bedrooms and other features associated with a residence), such property was to be treated as a residence and could only be used for such purpose.

Could a landlord/lessor's action for rescission of a lease alleging the lessee's use of the property as one contrary to its nature be deemed in good faith if the landlord plaintiff was shown to be aware of the purpose of the rental when he signed the lease? Wouldn't his claim for rescission be subject to what Anglo-American lawyers label estoppel and what a Roman lawyer would characterize as an instance of *venire contra factum proprium*? Clearly, there were a number of reliable indicators of the parties' intent that this court did not take into consideration. Among these were: a) the course of contractual performance, *i.e.*, the several months during which the plaintiff landlord was aware of the use of her premises as an ice cream parlor, including her continued collection of rent without objection to the presence of an ice cream parlor; b) The fact that the amount paid by the renter was higher than that paid for similarly sized houses in purely residential neighborhoods; c) The fact that similar properties in the parties' and surrounding neighborhoods were all used as commercial shops or parlors; d) The fact that the description of the property relied upon by the court is a standard description of residential and commercial property for cadastral or tax purposes and not for the purpose of establishing a contractual intent. Could such findings of facts based upon credible evidence be added to the complaint, or was the defendant impeded from adding these facts given the civil procedural rules in force at the time of the filing of his answer?[304]

E. Usage of Trade as Provider of Sectoral and Contractual Intent

Columbia Nitrogen Corp. v. Royster Co.[305]

Action for breach of contract for purchase of phosphate by plaintiff from defendant, wherein defendant asserted antitrust defense and counterclaim based on plaintiff's alleged reciprocal trade practices. The United States District Court for the Eastern District of Virginia, at Norfolk, John A. MacKenzie, J., entered judgment for plaintiff and defendant appealed.

OPINION:

BUTZNER, Circuit Judge.

Columbia Nitrogen Corp. appeals a judgment in the amount of $750,000 in favor of F. S. Royster Guano Co. for breach of a contract for the sale of phosphate to Columbia by Royster. Columbia defended on the grounds that the contract, construed in light of the usage of the trade and course of dealing, imposed no duty to accept at the quoted prices the minimum quantities stated in the contract. . . . The jury found for Royster on both the contract claim and the antitrust counterclaim. We hold that Columbia's proffered evidence was improperly excluded and Columbia is entitled to a new trial on the contractual issues. . . .

I.

Royster manufactures and markets mixed fertilizers, the principal components of which are nitrogen, phosphate and potash. Columbia is primarily a producer of nitrogen, although it manufactures some mixed fertilizer. . . . In the fall of 1966, Royster constructed a facility which enabled it to produce more phosphate than it needed in its own operations. After extensive negotiations, the companies executed a contract for Royster's sale of a minimum of 31,000 tons of phosphate each year for three years to Columbia, with an option to extend the term. The contract stated the price per ton, subject to an escalation clause dependent on production costs. In pertinent part, the contract provides:

> Contract made as of this 8th day of May between COLUMBIA NITROGEN CORPORATION, a Delaware Corporation, (hereinafter called the Buyer) hereby agrees to purchase and accept from F. S. ROYSTER GUANO COMPANY, a Virginia Corporation, (hereinafter called the Seller) agrees to furnish quantities of Diammonium Phosphate 18–46–0, Granular Triple Superphosphate 0–46–0, and Run-of-Pile Triple Superphosphate 0–46–0 on the following terms and conditions.
>
> . . .
>
> *Price*-In Bulk F.O.B. Cars, Royster, Florida.
>
> Diammonium Phosphate 18–46–0 $61.25 per ton

[304] *See supra* § 5:13(B)(2).

[305] 451 F.2d 3 (4th Cir. 1971).

Granular Triple Superphosphate 0–46–0 $40.90 per ton

Run-of-Pile Triple Superphosphate 0–46–0 $0.86 per unit

. . .

Escalation—The escalation factor up or down shall be based upon the effects of changing raw material cost of sulphur, rock phosphate, and labor as follows. These escalations up or down to become effective against shipments of products covered by this contract 30 days after notification by Seller to Buyer.

No verbal understanding will be recognized by either party hereto; this contract expresses all the terms and conditions of the agreement, shall be signed in duplicate and shall not become operative until approved in writing by the Seller.

Phosphate prices soon plunged precipitously. Unable to resell the phosphate at a competitive price, Columbia ordered only part of the scheduled tonnage. At Columbia's request, Royster lowered its price for diammonium phosphate on shipments for three months in 1967, but specified that subsequent shipments would be at the original contract price. Even with this concession, Royster's price was still substantially above the market. As a result, Columbia ordered less than a tenth of the phosphate Royster was to ship in the first contract year. When pressed by Royster, Columbia offered to take the phosphate at the current market price and resell it without brokerage fee. Royster, however, insisted on the contract price. When Columbia refused delivery, Royster sold the unaccepted phosphate for Columbia's account at a price substantially below the contract price.

II.

Columbia assigns error to the pretrial ruling of the district court excluding all evidence on usage of the trade and course of dealing between the parties. It offered the testimony of witnesses with long experience in the trade that because of uncertain crop and weather conditions, farming practices, and government agricultural programs, express price and quantity terms in contracts for materials in the mixed fertilizer industry are mere projections to be adjusted according to market forces.

. . .

Columbia also offered proof of its business dealings with Royster over the six-year period preceding the phosphate contract. Since Columbia had not been a significant purchaser of Royster's products, these dealings were almost exclusively nitrogen sales to Royster or exchanges of stock carried in inventory. The pattern which emerges, Columbia claimed, is one of repeated and substantial deviation from the stated amount or price, including four instances where Royster took none of the goods for which it had contracted. Columbia offered proof that the total variance amounted to more than $500,000 in reduced sales. This experience, a Columbia officer offered to testify, formed the basis of an understanding on which he depended in conducting negotiations with Royster.

The district court held that the evidence should be excluded. It ruled that "custom and usage or course of dealing are not admissible to contradict the express, plain, unambiguous language of a valid written contract, which by virtue of its detail negates the proposition that the contract is open to variances in its terms."

A number of Virginia cases have held that extrinsic evidence may not be received to explain or supplement a written contract unless the court finds the writing is ambiguous. E.g., *Mathieson Alkali Works v. Virginia Banner Coal Corp.*, 147 Va. 125, 136 S.E. 673 (1927). This rule, however, has been changed by the Uniform Commercial Code which Virginia has adopted. The Code expressly states that it "shall be liberally construed and applied to promote its underlying purposes and policies," which include "the continued expansion of commercial practices through custom, usage and agreement of the parties. . . ." The importance of usage of trade and course of dealing between the parties is shown by § 8.2–202[306] [U.C.C. § 2–202], which authorizes their use to explain or supplement a contract. The official comment states this section rejects the old rule that evidence of course of dealing or usage of trade can be introduced only when the contract is ambiguous. And the Virginia commentators, noting that "[t]his section reflects a more liberal approach to the introduction of parol evidence . . . than has been followed in Virginia," express the opinion that *Mathieson*, *supra*, and similar Virginia cases no longer should be followed. We hold, therefore, that a finding of ambiguity is not necessary for the admission of extrinsic evidence about the usage of the trade and the parties' course of dealing.

We turn next to Royster's claim that Columbia's evidence was properly excluded because it was inconsistent with the express terms of their agreement. There can be no doubt that the Uniform Commercial Code restates the well established rule that evidence of usage of trade and course of dealing should be excluded whenever it cannot be reasonably construed as consistent with the terms of the contract. Royster argues that the evidence should be excluded as inconsistent because the contract contains detailed provisions regarding the base price, escalation, minimum tonnage, and delivery schedules. The argument is based on the premise that because a contract appears on its face to be complete, evidence of course of dealing and usage of trade should be excluded. We believe however, that neither the language nor the policy of the code supports such a broad exclusionary rule. Section 8.2–202 [U.C.C. § 2–202] expressly allows evidence of course of dealing or usage of trade to explain or supplement terms intended by the parties as a final expression of their agreement. When this section is read in light of Va. Code Ann. § 8.1–205(4),[307] it is clear that the test of admissibility is not whether the contract appears on its face to be complete in every detail, but whether the proffered evidence of course of dealing and trade usage reasonably can be construed as consistent with the express terms of the agreement.

---

[306] VA.CODE ANN. § 8.2–202 (U.C.C. § 2–202) provides:

Terms with respect to which the confirmatory memoranda of the parties agree or which are otherwise set forth in a writing intended by the parties as a final expression of their agreement with respect to such terms as are included therein may not be contradicted by evidence of any prior agreement or of a contemporaneous oral agreement but may be explained or supplemented (a) by course of dealing or usage of trade (8.1–205) or by course of performance. (8.2–208); and (b) by evidence of consistent additional terms unless the court finds the writing to have been intended also as a complete and exclusive statement of the terms of the agreement.

[307] VA. CODE ANN. § 8.1–205(4) (U.C.C. § 1–205) states:

The express terms of an agreement and an applicable course of dealing or usage of trade shall be construed wherever reasonable as consistent with each other; but when such construction is unreasonable express terms control both course of dealing and usage of trade and course of dealing controls usage of trade.

The proffered testimony sought to establish that because of changing weather conditions, farming practices, and government agricultural programs, dealers adjusted prices, quantities, and delivery schedules to reflect declining market conditions. For the following reasons it is reasonable to construe this evidence as consistent with the express terms of the contract:

The contract does not expressly state that course of dealing and usage of trade cannot be used to explain or supplement the written contract.

The contract is silent about adjusting prices and quantities to reflect a declining market. It neither permits nor prohibits adjustment, and this neutrality provides a fitting occasion for recourse to usage of trade and prior dealing to supplement the contract and explain its terms.

Minimum tonnages and additional quantities are expressed in terms of "Products Supplied Under Contract." Significantly, they are not expressed as just "Products" or as "Products Purchased Under Contract." The description used by the parties is consistent with the proffered testimony.

Finally, the default clause of the contract refers only to the failure of the buyer to pay for delivered phosphate. During the contract negotiations, Columbia rejected a Royster proposal for liquidated damages of $10 for each ton Columbia declined to accept. On the other hand, Royster rejected a Columbia proposal for a clause that tied the price to the market by obligating Royster to conform its price to offers Columbia received from other phosphate producers. The parties, having rejected both proposals, failed to state any consequences of Columbia's refusal to take delivery—the kind of default Royster alleges in this case. Royster insists that we span this hiatus by applying the general law of contracts permitting recovery of damages upon the buyer's refusal to take delivery according to the written provisions of the contract. This solution is not what the Uniform Commercial Code prescribes. Before allowing damages, a court must first determine whether the buyer has in fact defaulted. It must do this by supplementing and explaining the agreement with evidence of trade usage and course of dealing that is consistent with the contract's express terms. Va. Code Ann. §§ 8.1–205(4), 8.2–202. Faithful adherence to this mandate reflects the reality of the marketplace and avoids the overly legalistic interpretations which the Code seeks to abolish.

. . .

Course of dealing and trade usage are not synonymous with verbal understandings, terms and conditions. Section 8.2–202 [U.C.C. § 2–202] draws a distinction between supplementing a written contract by consistent additional terms and supplementing it by course of dealing or usage of trade. Evidence of additional terms must be excluded when "the court finds the writing to have been intended also as a complete and exclusive statement of the terms of the agreement." Significantly, no similar limitation is placed on the introduction of evidence of course of dealing or usage of trade. Indeed the official comment notes that course of dealing and usage of trade, unless carefully negated, are admissible to supplement the terms of any writing, and that contracts are to be read on the assumption that these elements were taken for granted when the document was phrased. Since the Code assigns course of dealing and trade usage unique and important roles, they should not be conclusively rejected by reading them into stereotyped language that makes no specific reference to them.

Indeed, the Code's official commentators urge that overly simplistic and overly legalistic interpretation of a contract should be shunned.

We conclude, therefore, that Columbia's evidence about course of dealing and usage of trade should have been admitted. Its exclusion requires that the judgment against Columbia must be set aside and the case retried.

COMMENTS AND QUESTIONS

Judge Butzner's interpretation of this contract, bolstered by Official Comment 2 to U.C.C. § 2–202 is, as noted in the principal chapter, distinctly market oriented. It takes into account the understandings arrived at by the parties in their prior dealings and in the usage of their trade when attempting to give meaning to their contracts. As also noted in the principal chapter, in developed commercial and financial markets, course of performance, course of dealing and usage of trade enjoy a degree of legitimacy in the everyday, "living law," extrajudicial interpretation of contracts to which few statutory rules or court decisions can aspire. It stems from the comfort felt by those who regularly exchange their goods and services with words or expressions that are part of their courses of dealing and usages of trade.

The court distinguished between additional or supplemental terms and conditions that one party claims or alleges were agreed upon (even though they were not set forth in writing in the contract) and the course of dealing and usage of trade—in the sense that the latter can be admitted as extrinsic evidence, whereas the former cannot. Because in the eyes of the court these are different concepts, U.C.C. § 2–202 excludes terms and conditions that were subject to a verbal agreement, but remains silent with respect to the course of dealing and usage of trade. Do you agree with this distinction, and if so, which of the two is more likely to create more uncertainty or unpredictability of judicial interpretations?

Hypothetically, assume that the diammonium phosphate trade was significant enough to encourage its three main manufacturers and suppliers to draft standard practices for the sale and distribution of their chemical product. Assume also that these standard practices included terms and conditions that excluded consideration of market prices for the purpose of adjusting prices listed in the agreement with the distributors of mixed fertilizers, the principal purchasers of diammonium phosphate. In addition, these practices included a clause that expressly excluded any terms and conditions other than those in their standard contract practices. You are an attorney for a small company that regularly purchases phosphate and sells mixed fertilizers. Your client asks you if he should sign such a standard agreement. You consulted with a more experienced colleague who suggested you re-read Official Comments 5 and 6 to U.C.C. § 1–205 on reasonable, decent and "indecent" practices. After you re-read it, would you characterize the proffered standard practices as reasonable, decent or indecent?

F. Usage of Trade Versus a Mutually Mistaken Term

1. Haakjöringsköd *Case*[308]

Facts:

On November 18, 1916, defendant sold plaintiff a certain amount of *Haakjoeringskoed* for DM 4.30 per kilo, CIF Hamburg, payable in cash in exchange for

308 Reichsgericht [RG] [Federal Court of Justice] Aug. 6, 1920, RGZ 99, 147 (Ger.).

the bill of lading and an insurance policy. Plaintiff and defendant thought that *Haakjoeringskoed* was the Norwegian word for whale meat, when in reality it was the Norwegian word for shark meat. At the end of November, plaintiff paid defendant the stipulated amount in exchange for the documents. When the goods arrived in Hamburg they were seized by the Zentral-Einkaufsgesellschaft m.b.H. (a group or center in charge of controlling the quality and source of certain imports into Berlin).

Plaintiff argued that the goods sold to him were supposed to be whale meat but they turned out to be shark meat, and that if whale meat had been delivered it would not have been seized. Thus, plaintiff demanded that defendant had to pay him the difference between the price already paid and the lower price he received from the Zentral-Einkaufsgesellschaft m.b.H due to the seizure because defendant delivered goods that were not in compliance with the sales contract.

2. *Holding of the* Reichsgericht *(Supreme Court of Germany in 1920)*

The Court established that both the plaintiff and defendant had erred about the real meaning of the word *Haakjoeringskoed* when they entered into the contract because neither was familiar with this word. Even though the goods that arrived in Hamburg were exactly what the defendant was supposed to deliver according to the plain language of the contract, namely *Haakjoeringskoed* (shark meat), the defendant did not deliver what he really owed, namely whale meat. Both parties intended to enter into a contract about whale meat. They chose a word (*Haakjoeringskoed*) that did not express their real intent. Thus, their relationship has to be construed as if they had chosen the correct word (whale meat). Therefore, defendant had the obligation to deliver whale meat.

The Court found that the delivered goods had a defect as to quality. Accordingly, the plaintiff could claim the difference between the price he had already paid to the defendant and the price he received from the *Zentral-Einkaufsgesellschaft.*

Please re-read the following opinion by the Roman Jurist Ulpian on mistakes that invalidate contracts that was previously discussed in Chapter 4,[309] which may or may not agree with the opinion by the *Reichsgericht*:

> ***Texts:*** D.18.1.9 Ulpian, Sabinus, book 28. It is obvious that an agreement is of the essence in a sale and purchase; the purchase is not valid if there be disagreement over the contract itself, the price, or any other element of the sale. Hence, if I thought that I was buying the Cornelian farm and that you were selling the Sempronian, the sale is void because we were not agreed upon the thing sold. The same is true if I intended to sell Stichus and you thought that I was selling you Pamphilus, the slave himself not being there: Because there is no agreement on the object of sale, there is manifestly no sale. 1. Of course, if we are merely in disagreement over the name but at one on the actual thing, there is no doubt that the sale is good; for if the thing be identified, a mistake over its name is irrelevant.

Did the *Reichsgericht* agree with Ulpian and if so, on what basis?

---

309 *See supra* § 4:6(C).

G. Strict Compliance, Good Faith, Fraud and Abuse of Rights in German Letter of Credit and Bank Guarantee Law

1. Introduction

Please recall from the discussion on the origins of the doctrine of good faith in Roman law that its *exceptio doli* was designed to discourage deceitful pleadings linked with the enforcement of strict compliance (*stricti iuris*) promises. In German judicial and banking practice, the letter of credit law principle of strict compliance is referred to as *Dokumentenstrenge* and is applicable to commercial and standby letters of credit as well as to independent bank guarantees. The first two cases of this section involve the application of the strict compliance principle in typical disputes involving letter of credit and independent bank guarantee litigation. German decisional law is the most explicit when applying the good faith and reasonableness principles as well as the defense of abuse of rights against a payment supported by the strict compliance doctrine. You will be able to observe how the key sections of the BGB on good faith and reasonableness discussed in the principal chapter are applied in remedial letter of credit and bank guarantee settings. Prominent among these provisions is § 157, which, as you will recall, states that "contracts are to be interpreted as required by good faith, taking customary practice into consideration."[310] Prominent also is § 242, which obligates the promisor-debtor to perform in accordance with "the requirements of good faith, taking customary practice into consideration."[311]

Often, these sections are invoked by a beneficiary whose presentation of documents has been rejected by the bank for spurious or hyper-technical reasons. They are also invoked by a bank's customer (the party who procured the issuance of a letter of credit or independent bank guarantee) who tries to prevent payment to the beneficiary by alleging that the documents presented by him are fraudulent or are the product of his abuse of the right to claim a payment for the presentation of documents that on their face comply with the strict requirements of the letter of credit, but in fact he has no right to claim such payment.

The summary action whose goal is to protect victims of fraudulent or abuse of right claims relies on an injunctive remedy known as *Einstweilige Verfuegung*. This action may be brought against the bank that issues the letter of credit or independent bank guarantee or against the so called "counter-guarantor" (*Antragsgegnerin*). This is the bank in the customer's place of business that issues the payment or performance guarantee to the guarantor bank in the beneficiary's place of business. The guarantee issued by the latter bank is known as a direct guarantee. The counter-guarantee issued at the customer's place of business names as its beneficiary the bank that acts as the direct guarantor at the beneficiary's place of business. The counter-guarantee promises the direct guarantor that upon his payment of the direct guarantee to the local contracting party, it will reimburse him for that payment.

Often the party that requests the issuance of a direct guarantee is a local government agency. Because of its superior bargaining power in places where the number of hopeful suppliers far exceeds the demand for their goods or services, this agency often stipulates that the direct guarantee will be paid by its presentation of a

---

310 BGB § 157.

311 BGB § 242.

simple demand of payment, unaccompanied by documents that attest to or certify to the default of the supplier of goods or services. The counter-guarantee, in turn, stipulates that its promise payment will be paid upon the direct guarantor's presentation of a statement asserting that it has paid the local government agency, the beneficiary of its direct guarantee. To illustrate: "A" is the bank that issues its counter-guarantee on behalf of "S," a construction company in Tucson, Arizona. It requests bank "B" in Riyadh, Saudi Arabia to issue its guarantee to the city of Riyadh. In the event that S does not perform as promised in its successful bid to build a business facility, the city of Riyadh will present a document stating that the building built by S did not meet the contract specifications and request, upon simple demand, that B, the direct guarantor, pay the city of Riyadh the amount stipulated in the direct guarantee. Once B pays the city of Riyadh on its direct guarantee, it can present a simple demand for reimbursement from the counter-guarantor in Tucson stating that it paid the amount for which it seeks reimbursement.

As will be discussed by the following court decisions, the remedy of *Einstweilige Verfuegung* requires proof that the beneficiary whose payment is sought to be enjoined has either tendered fraudulent documents or abused his right to demand payment by presenting a document that although facially in compliance with the letter of credit or bank guarantee, in fact it is not. This is particularly the case with bank guarantees that are payable on the basis of the beneficiary or direct guarantor's simple demand of payment. For even though the required document is a simple statement that payment is due, it presupposes that the customer who procured the issuance of the guarantee failed to perform its part of the bargain. The customer would then argue that the beneficiary, usually a foreign government or contracting party, is acting in bad faith, either fraudulently or abusively, *i.e.*, with no valid or conceivable grounds to make the demand for payment of the direct guarantee.

The following judicial decisions[312] illustrate how the overarching principle of good faith and the archetypal behavior of a proper merchant (*Ordentlichen Kaufmanns*) as well as reasonable and customary conduct among the participants in these transactions are used by German courts in conjunction with claims of bad faith or abuse of rights by bank customers against the beneficiaries of standby letters of credit, direct guarantees or counter-guarantees.

2. Landgericht *Stuttgart, June 15, 1978, WM 1056 (1978)*[313]

Facts:

The plaintiff, a Lebanese company, sued an issuing bank and demands payment of the performance guarantee shortly after it expired. The plaintiff argues that it is entitled to payment in accordance with the principle of good faith (*Treu und Glauben*) of BGB Section 242 since it was prevented from requesting payment in a timely fashion because of a force majeur (*hoehere Gewalt*, *i.e.*, the war going on in Beirut and the closing of all banks for several days). The court of first instance (*Landgericht*) of Stuttgart ruled for the defendant and stated that the doctrine of *Treu und Glauben* cannot be used to extend the deadline set forth in a letter of credit. It added that if the

---

312 I am indebted to my former student and research assistant Angela Daniel, who is now a practicing lawyer in Germany, for her English translation of the judicial decisions.

313 Landgericht Stuttgart [OLGZ] [Regional Court], June 15, 1978, WERTPAPIER-MITTEILUNGEN [WM], 1056, 1978 (Ger.).

plaintiff wanted a more flexible deadline he could have negotiated it when entering into the contract.

Decision:

The doctrine of *Dokumentenstrenge* applies to both letters of credit and performance guarantees. In conformity with that doctrine, banks may only accept documents if they clearly comply with the requirements stated in the letter of credit. Thus, all the documents have to be presented within the time periods stated in the letter of credit. The purpose of the doctrine of *Dokumentenstrenge* is to protect the customer (*Auftraggeber*). Only in cases where the bank has reason to believe that the customer approves of the intended deviations from the letter of credit requirements is the bank allowed to not comply strictly with the letter of credit. As stated by a commercial code commentary, the bank is only entitled to deviate from the letter of credit if it is able to determine beyond a reasonable doubt (*voellig einwandfrei*) and without the help of experts that the deviation: 1) is unimportant (*unerheblich*) and 2) does not hurt the interests of the bank's customer. If the bank is acting against the customer's directions, the customer can prevent the bank from seeking reimbursement against him for wrongful payment.

Accordingly, after the date of expiration of the letter of credit, the bank is entitled to refuse to honor the beneficiary's request for payment, especially since the bank would be entitled to such refusal according to the terms of the letter of credit. . . . Articles 11 and 37 of the Uniform Customs and Practices for Documentary Credits (UCP 290) provide that letters of credit cannot be extended beyond their original expiration date even in the event of war, strike, etc. The above mentioned provisions also apply to performance guarantees.

3. OLG Frankfurt, March 3, 1983, WM 1983, 575[314]

Facts:

In October 1981, the *Antragstellerin* (applicant for a temporary injunction), who had its principal place of business in Germany, entered into a contract with Company A in Saudi Arabia and agreed to deliver equipment in the amount of 1,150,000.00 marks. Company A opened a documentary letter of credit with the *Antragsgegnerin* (counter-guarantor bank against whom the temporary injunction is sought). Company A requested a bank guarantee in the amount of ten percent of the contract value. The applicant obtained a performance bond and the counter-guarantor bank at the customer's place of business issued a bank guarantee in which it agreed to pay to Bank B in Saudi Arabia (that was also the direct guarantor for the Saudi contractor) that was payable upon first demand. Bank B sent a telex on behalf of Company A to the counter-guarantor bank on April 25, 1982 and requested payment of its counter-guarantee.

Meanwhile, the customer who procured the issuance of the counter-guarantee successfully obtained a temporary injunction in Germany on April 28, 1982. The *Landgericht* reversed and set aside the temporary injunction. The appellate court

---

[314] Oberlandesgericht Frankfurt [OLGZ] [Regional Court], Mar. 3, 1983, WERTPAPIER-MITTEILUNGEN [WM], 575, 1983 (Ger.).

(OLG Frankfurt) affirmed the decision of the *Landgericht* and refused to reinstate the temporary injunction.

Holding:

1) The doctrine of *Treu und Glauben* applies to bank guarantees. Therefore, the bank customer (*Garantieauftraggeber*) who requested the bank to issue it can generally procure a temporary injunction and prevent the bank from paying the beneficiary the guaranteed amount, if the demand for payment is legally abusive or fraudulent.

2) If the bank's customer provides the cash [or equivalent bond] to the guaranteeing bank after the beneficiary requests payment, a temporary injunction is generally available to prevent such payment rather than to prevent the debiting of the bank accounts of the customer through the guaranteeing bank after payment was made.

Reasoning:

The doctrine of *Treu und Glauben* does apply to bank guarantees. Generally, a temporary injunction is available to prevent payments through the guaranteeing bank if the demand for payment is obviously abusive or fraudulent. However, the customer and applicant for the issuance of the injunction in the case at hand did not successfully prove the requirements of a temporary injunction.[315] According to the dominant opinion in legal literature,[316] those defenses related to the underlying contract(s) cannot be raised by a participant in these contracts who is also a party to the guarantee or letter of credit to prevent the bank from paying on the bank guarantee or letter of credit, unless the request for payment by the beneficiary of the letter of credit or bank guarantee is legally abusive or fraudulent and thus in violation of the doctrine of *Treu und Glauben*. Another prevailing doctrine in letter of credit and bank guarantee law provides that the promise in the letter of credit or bank guarantee is independent of the defenses or equities that the parties could have raised based upon their underlying contract. This doctrine requires, then, that the [issuing or confirming] bank first pay on the letter of credit and then the parties may litigate their underlying rights and duties based upon the contract. Only in cases of abuse of the principles of strict compliance and independence, where it is either obvious or it can be proven with clear and convincing proof that the letter of credit or the bank guarantee [promises of payment] are being abused,[317] can the doctrine of the independence of the underlying transaction from the bank guarantee be set aside.

---

[315] Note by Angela Daniel: The court distinguishes the decision of the OLG Frankfurt, NJW 1981, 1914 and states that the bank in that decision would have been forced to pay the bank guarantee with its own means, while the *Antragsteller* in the present case provided the cash for the payment. Thus, the court concluded that appropriate relief in the case at hand could have been obtained only by issuance of a temporary injunction.

[316] Oberlandesgericht Saarbruecken [OLGZ] [Regional Court], RECHT DER INTERNATIONALEN WIRTSCHAFT [RIW] 338, 1981 (Ger.); Oberlandesgericht Hamburg [OLGZ] [Regional Court], RECHT DER INTERNATIONALEN WIRTSCHAFT [RIW] 615, 1978 (Ger.); Oberlandesgericht Frankfurt [OLGZ] [Regional Court], BB 954, 1974 (Ger.); Horn, Buergschaften und Garantien zur Zahlung auf erstes Anfordern, NEUE JURISTISHE WOCHENSCHRIFT [NJW] 2153, 1980 (Ger.); Liesecke, Rechtsfragen der Bankgarantie, WERTPAPIER-MITTEILUNGEN [WM] 22, 1982 (Ger.); Schuetze, 83, 1981 (Ger.).

[317] Oberlandesgericht Saarbruecken [OLGZ] [Regional Court], RECHT DER INTERNATIONALEN WIRTSCHAFT [RIW] 338, 1981 (Ger.); Oberlandesgericht Frankfurt [OLGZ] [Regional Court], NEUE JURISTISHE WOCHENSCHRIFT [NJW] 1914, 1981 (Ger.).

The request for payment of the bank guarantee in the case at hand is not legally abusive. As required by law, Company A: 1) complained several times by telex that the goods were not fully delivered or were delivered damaged, and 2) set a deadline of one month for corrected redeliveries and repairs. Witness K, who was supervising the installation of the equipment in Saudi Arabia, corroborates these facts. Thus, the demand for payment of the bank guarantee by its Saudi beneficiary was neither legally abusive or fraudulent in light of these facts.

In support of her position, the customer-applicant for the injunction signed an affidavit, alleging compliance with her contractual obligations. Such general allegations are not sufficient to prove that the beneficiary abused his right to demand collection. Instead, the applicant should have confirmed and corroborated her statement with 1) a signed list of those items that had to be delivered to Company A as required by the contract and 2) corresponding bills of lading which would have demonstrated shipment and delivery of these goods.

Rather, the statements of the application were too vague and general, preventing any investigation as to whether or not those statements were truthful and correct. With such statements, the customer cannot obtain an injunction that would prevent bank guarantee payments. Simply put, by merely presenting an affidavit that alleges compliance with contractual obligations and further alleging that the request for payment is not justified, the plaintiff-applicant for the injunction has not met its burden of proof.

Furthermore, the counter-guarantor bank also has a substantial interest in the compliance of her obligations under the bank guarantee. Its reputation is on the line when it refuses to pay with clear and convincing reasons for doing so. . . .

Affirmed.

COMMENTS AND QUESTIONS

The first case makes clear the unwillingness of the Stuttgart District Court (*Landesgericht*) to allow the good faith doctrine to replace a strict rule of expiration of a letter of credit. Apparently, the German fondness for timeliness would not allow good faith to bend an expiry deadline.

The second case acknowledges that the doctrine of good faith in the performance of obligations does apply to letters of credit and bank guarantees. However, it also sets forth the standards of evidence that govern the invocation of a fraudulent or abusive tender. The bank's invocation of lack of good faith or abuse of rights is limited to instances where the beneficiary was very likely to have perpetrated an egregious fraud, *i.e.*, when the goods represented by the documents were not the same as the goods shipped. Another form of preclusion occurs when, as in the first case, an issuing bank unreasonably delays its examination of the non-complying documents and/or failed to notify the beneficiary or presenting bank in time for them to attempt to cure the defect.

In sum, unlike the French decisions discussed in the principal chapter,[318] these decisions view the good faith and reasonableness expected from the archetypal proper merchant as equitable defenses. By identifying the factual patterns that did or did not amount to good faith or reasonable behavior, these decisions provide greater predictability than available in the French decisions. In addition, they show how good

---

[318] *See supra* § 23:4(B).

faith, reasonableness, waiver and estoppel interact with each other in the practices endorsed by the Uniform Customs and Practices for Documentary Credits (UCP), whose format may well qualify for what the Official Comment to U.C.C. § 1–205(5) refers to as a "Trade Code."

4. *Trade Usage, Reasonableness and Unconscionability in United States and German Court Decisions*

a. *Frigaliment Importing Co. v. B.N.S. Int'l Sales Corp.*[319]

OPINION:

FRIENDLY, Circuit Judge.

The issue is what is chicken? Plaintiff says "chicken" means a young chicken, suitable for broiling and frying. Defendant says "chicken" means any bird of that genus that meets contract specifications on weight and quality, including what it calls "stewing chicken" and plaintiff pejoratively terms "fowl." Dictionaries give both meanings, as well as some others not relevant here. To support its [definition], plaintiff sends a number of volleys over the net; defendant essays to return them and adds a few serves of its own. Assuming that both parties were acting in good faith, the case nicely illustrates Holmes' remark "that the making of a contract depends not on the agreement of two minds in one intention, but on the agreement of two sets of external signs—not on the parties' having meant the same thing but on their having said the same thing." I have concluded that plaintiff has not sustained its burden of persuasion that the contract used "chicken" in the narrower sense.

The action is for breach of the warranty that goods sold shall correspond to the description. Two contracts are in suit. In the first, dated May 2, 1957, defendant, a New York sales corporation, confirmed the sale to plaintiff, a Swiss corporation, of

"US Fresh Frozen Chicken, Grade A, Government Inspected, Eviscerated 2½–3 lbs. and 1½–2 lbs. each all chicken individually wrapped in cryovac, packed in secured fiber cartons or wooden boxes, suitable for export

75,000 lbs. of 2 ½–3 lb. [chickens] @ $33.00

25,000 lbs. of 1 ½–2 lb. [chickens] @ $36.50

per 100 lbs. FAS New York

scheduled May 10, 1957 pursuant to instructions from Penson & Co., New York."

The second contract, also dated May 2, 1957, was identical save that only 50,000 lbs. of the heavier "chicken" were called for, the price of the smaller birds was $37 per 100 lbs., and shipment was scheduled for May 30. The initial shipment under the first contract was short but the balance was shipped on May 17. When the initial shipment arrived in Switzerland, plaintiff found, on May 28, that the 2½–3 lbs. birds were not young chicken suitable for broiling and frying but stewing chicken or "fowl"; indeed, many of the cartons and bags plainly so indicated. Protests ensued. Nevertheless, shipment under the second contract was made on May 29, the 2½–3 lbs. birds again being stewing chicken. Defendant stopped the transportation of these at Rotterdam.

---

[319] 190 F. Supp. 116 (S.D.N.Y. 1960).

. . .

Since the word "chicken" standing alone is ambiguous, I turn first to see whether the contract itself offers any aid to its interpretation. Plaintiff says the 1½–2 lbs. birds necessarily had to be young chicken since the older birds do not come in that size, hence the 2½–3 lb. birds must likewise be young. This is unpersuasive—a contract for "apples" of two different sizes could be filled with different kinds of apples even though only one species came in both sizes. Defendant notes that the contract called not simply for chicken but for "US Fresh Frozen Chicken, Grade A, Government Inspected." It says the contract thereby incorporated by reference the Department of Agriculture's regulations, which favor its interpretation; I shall return to this after reviewing plaintiff's other contentions.

The first hinges on an exchange of cablegrams which preceded execution of the formal contracts. The negotiations leading up to the contracts were conducted in New York between defendant's secretary, Ernest R. Bauer, and a Mr. Stovicek, who was in New York for the Czechoslovak government at the World Trade Fair. A few days after meeting Bauer at the fair, Stovicek telephoned and inquired whether defendant would be interested in exporting poultry to Switzerland. Bauer then met with Stovicek, who showed him a cable from plaintiff dated April 26, 1957, announcing that they "are buyer" of 25,000 lbs. of chicken 2½–3 lbs. weight, Cryovac packed, grade A Government inspected, at a price up to 33¢ per pound, for shipment on May 10, to be confirmed by the following morning, and were interested in further offerings. After testing the market for price, Bauer accepted, and Stovicek sent a confirmation that evening. Plaintiff stresses that, although these and subsequent cables between plaintiff and defendant, which laid the basis for the additional quantities under the first and for all of the second contract, were predominantly in German, they used the English word "chicken"; it claims this was done because it understood "chicken" meant young chicken whereas the German word, "Huhn," included both "Brathuhn" (broilers) and "Suppenhuhn" (stewing chicken), and that defendant, whose officers were thoroughly conversant with German, should have realized this. Whatever force this argument might otherwise have is largely drained away by Bauer's testimony that he asked Stovicek what kind of chickens were wanted, received the answer "any kind of chickens," and then, in German, asked whether the cable meant "Huhn" and received an affirmative response. Plaintiff attacks this as contrary to what Bauer testified on his deposition in March, 1959, and also on the ground that Stovicek had no authority to interpret the meaning of the cable. The first contention would be persuasive if sustained by the record, since Bauer was free at the trial from the threat of contradiction by Stovicek as he was not at the time of the deposition; however, review of the deposition does not convince me of the claimed inconsistency. . . .

Plaintiff's next contention is that there was a definite trade usage that "chicken" meant "young chicken." Defendant showed that it was only beginning in the poultry trade in 1957, thereby bringing itself within the principle that "when one of the parties is not a member of the trade or other circle, his acceptance of the standard must be made to appear" by proving either that he had actual knowledge of the usage or that the usage is "so generally known in the community that his actual individual knowledge of it may be inferred." Here there was no proof of actual knowledge of the alleged usage; indeed, it is quite plain that defendant's belief was to the contrary. In order to meet the alternative requirement, the law of New York demands a showing that "the usage is of so long continuance, so well established, so notorious, so universal and so reasonable in itself, as that the presumption is violent that the parties contracted with reference to it, and made it a part of their agreement." *Walls v. Bailey*, 49 N.Y. 464, 472–73 (1872).

Plaintiff endeavored to establish such a usage by the testimony of three witnesses and certain other evidence. Strasser, resident buyer in New York for a large chain of Swiss cooperatives, testified that "on chicken I would definitely understand a broiler." However, the force of this testimony was considerably weakened by the fact that in his own transactions the witness, a careful businessman, protected himself by using "broiler" when that was what he wanted and "fowl" when he wished older birds. Indeed, there are some indications, dating back to a remark of Lord Mansfield [in] Edie v. East India Co. 2 Burr. 1216, 1222 (1761), that no credit should be given "witnesses to usage, who could not adduce instances in verification." 7 Wigmore, Evidence (3d ed. 1940), § 1954. While Wigmore thinks this goes too far, a witness' consistent failure to rely on the alleged usage deprives his opinion testimony of much of its effect.

. . .

Defendant makes a further argument based on the impossibility of its obtaining broilers and fryers at the 33¢ price offered by plaintiff for the 2½–3 lbs. birds. There is no substantial dispute that, in late April, 1957, the price for 2½–3 lbs. broilers was between 35 and 37¢ per pound, and that when defendant entered into the contracts, it was well aware of this and intended to fill them by supplying fowl in these weights. It claims that plaintiff must likewise have known the market since plaintiff had reserved shipping space on April 23, three days before plaintiff's cable to Stovicek, or, at least, that Stovicek was chargeable with such knowledge. It is scarcely an answer to say, as plaintiff does in its brief, that the 33¢ price offered by the 2½–3 lbs. "chickens" was closer to the prevailing 35¢ price for broilers than to the 30¢ at which defendant procured fowl. *Plaintiff must have expected defendant to make some profit—certainly it could not have expected defendant deliberately to incur a loss.*[320]

. . .

When all the evidence is reviewed, it is clear that defendant believed it could comply with the contracts by delivering stewing chicken in the 2½–3 lbs. size. Defendant's subjective intent would not be significant if this did not coincide with an objective meaning of "chicken." Here it did coincide with one of the dictionary meanings, with the definition in the Department of Agriculture Regulations to which the contract made at least oblique reference, with at least some usage in the trade, with the realities of the market, and with what plaintiff's spokesman had said. Plaintiff asserts it to be equally plain that plaintiff's own subjective intent was to obtain broilers and fryers; the only evidence against this is the material as to market prices and this may not have been sufficiently brought home. In any event it is unnecessary to determine that issue. For plaintiff has the burden of showing that "chicken" was used in the narrower rather than in the broader sense, and this it has not sustained.

This opinion constitutes the Court's findings of fact and conclusions of law. Judgment shall be entered dismissing the complaint with costs.

---

320 Emphasis added.

b. *Trade, Sector and Commercial Reasonableness: Profit Seeking as a Common Denominator?*

Please note the number of sources and possible indicators of contractual intent considered by the court to determine the meaning of "chicken": 1) English language dictionaries; 2) German language dictionaries; 3) U.S. Department of Agriculture quality manuals; 4) Manuals of the Association of Poultry Industries; 5) Testimony or witness statements regarding the usage and customs of the marketplace; 6) Wholesale price in the New York market during the negotiations; and 7) Timing of the reservation of shipping space by the buyer. All of these sources were supposed to shed light on how other contracting parties in the same trade would characterize what they meant by the term "chicken."

The comparison with the behavior of others as hopefully found in these sources brings to mind the search for reasonable behavior. Still, this search needs the refinement provided by the trade-sectoral context of the transaction. First of all, who are the relevant others? Clearly, the relevant behavior was not that of the retail purchaser of chicken, who, like my grandmother, eyed and touched each chicken, often to the displeasure of daily or weekly market vendors. Unlike my grandmother, the buyers of chicken in *Frigaliment* were professional merchants who bought and sold poultry based not upon their "eye and hand" inspection, but upon the types of chicken described in catalogues or other printed descriptions of their key features.

The buyers and sellers of these chickens were keenly aware of the differences among their types and of the prices of each type, as well as the price variations caused by their seasonal availability, cost of warehousing, refrigeration, transportation, inspection and so on. As such, these merchants qualified for the status of regular participants in the trade and sector in question and were expected to behave in accordance with a standard of reasonableness and fairness that I have described earlier in this book (and in other writings) as that of the "market" standard: Treat the other party to the contract in the same manner that a regular participant in that trade would want to be treated when viewing his own advantage.[321]

Judge Friendly agrees with the application of this standard, but warns against imputation of the knowledge peculiar to the chicken trade to a party (including the meaning of chicken) unless that party (in this case the defendant) was a regular participant in that trade. In *Frigaliment*, the defendant seemed to have just started doing business in that trade and "when one of the parties is not a member of the trade or other circle, his acceptance of the standard must be made to appear" by proving either that he had actual knowledge of the usage or that the usage is "so generally known in the community that his actual individual knowledge of it may be inferred." How would you prove actual knowledge of the meaning of chicken to Judge Friendly? He would consider the testimony of regular participants in that trade, but would also heed Lord Mansfield's warning that: "[N]o credit should be given to witnesses to usage, who could not adduce instances in verification." Thus, depending upon a party's membership in a trade, not only the meaning of chicken, but also the reasonableness and fairness associated with that meaning, could cause different legal and economic consequences.

---

[321] *See* Glossary, "Market Standard of Fairness." *See also* Kozolchyk, *Fairness*, at 220, 233, 234.

Nonetheless, in the final analysis, and regardless of the trade or of the "circle" of merchants involved, the meaning of chicken *had, in Judge Friendly's view, a common commercial denominator*. No merchant, regardless of his trade, would agree, save under exceptional and temporary circumstances, to sell chicken (or any other product or service) for a price that would inevitably cause him to lose money with each sale.

Chapter 24

DRAFTING COMMERCIAL PRACTICES AND THE GROWTH OF COMMERCIAL CONTRACT LAW

§ 24.1 INTRODUCTION

The importance of commercial practices as a source of commercial contract law in today's global marketplace is beyond dispute. Massive numbers of commercial and financial transactions are governed by rules freshly harvested from commercial practices by global, regional and local associations. Among these practices are the International Commercial Terms (INCOTERMS)[1] and the Uniform Customs and Practices for Documentary Credits (UCP),[2] both of which were compiled and published by the International Chamber of Commerce (ICC); the Credit Derivatives Definitions and Master Agreement, which was compiled and drafted by the International Association for Swaps and Derivatives (ISDA);[3] and the standard trading terms for quality, warranties, shipping documents, payment terms, insurance, default and breach of contract remedies drafted by the Grain and Feed Trade Association (GAFTA).[4] In addition, there are countless standard terms and conditions for the performance of commercial and professional services compiled by their respective national and international as well as public and private associations.[5]

For each subject transaction, the above compilations establish, in varying detail, who does what, when, and how and who is responsible for the failure to comply. This chapter discusses the development of secured lending practices in Republican and Imperial Rome and draws lessons from the difficulties experienced in generating practices acceptable to lenders and borrowers alike. It compares the Roman experience with that of twentieth century bankers from many nations relying upon contemporary standard practices to draft viable commercial letter of credit practices for banking associations worldwide. Why was it that six centuries of contractual and extra-contractual practices, accompanied by countless administrative and judicial decisions, did not produce viable secured transactions practices in Rome, while it took only half of

---

[1] *The new Incoterms 2010 Rules*, INTERNATIONAL CHAMBER OF COMMERCE, http://www.iccwbo.org/products-and-services/trade-facilitation/incoterms-2010/ (last visited Nov. 14, 2013). The Incoterms are internationally recogized and are used throughout the world in contracts for the sales of goods.

[2] *See infra* §§ 24:6(D) & (E). The UCP has been the living law for letters of credit throughout the world for nearly a century.

[3] *ISDA Master Agreement*, INTERNATIONAL ASSOCIATION FOR SWAPS AND DERIVATIVES, http://www.isda.org/publications/isdamasteragrmnt.aspx (last visited Nov. 14, 2013). The ISDA publishes and sells a Master Agreement, which was last published in 2002.

[4] *Contracts*, GAFTA, http://www.gafta.com/contracts (last visited Sept. 12, 2013).

[5] Performing a Google search for "General Terms and Conditions of Trade" illustrates this point. Because of the importance of this topic, the Arizona Journal of International and Comparative Law has developed an issue to contemporary standard and best practices, *see Commercial Practices & the Growth of Commercial Contract Law* 30 ARIZ. J. INT'L & COMP. L. (No. 3, 2013).

a century to draft viable LOC practices for bankers and their customers throughout the world?

Compilations of commercial and financial practices, as well as of the rules of law derived from them, can encourage or discourage the viability of their respective transactions. They encourage it when regular market participants observe and trust them as cost effective, reasonable and fair. They discourage them when they induce or facilitate sharp dealing, abuses of rights, and spurious excuses for non-performance. Consider, for example, a contract in which "A", a manufacturer of restaurant equipment and fixtures, sells some of them to "B", the owner of a small restaurant. This sale is subject to standardized terms and conditions adopted by the "World Wide Association of Manufacturers of Restaurant Equipment and Fixtures."[6] One of these terms provides:

> This agreement contains all the terms and conditions agreed upon by the parties and is effective between or among them as well with respect to their assignees, purchasers or creditors without need for further formality or notice than the execution of this contract. In the event of B's failure to pay any owed installment, A is authorized to repossess all the sold fixtures and equipment sold by A.

Shortly before defaulting on his debt to A, B sold his restaurant to C for its cash market value, which included the unpaid price of the fixtures and equipment bought from A. Based upon his standardized agreement with B, and prior to C taking possession of the restaurant, A repossessed all the equipment and fixtures he sold to B. While this conditional sale practice fulfills the reasonable expectations of A and B, it ignores those of C. Surely C could sue B for breach of contract, conversion or unjust enrichment, but by that time B is likely insolvent or incarcerated. Hence, a practice that fails to provide notice to actual or potential third parties and thus renders the transaction secret where third parties are concerned discourages loans to a going concern and lowers the market price. It discourages future secured lenders because they cannot determine prior to lending which of the going concern's assets are subject to a prior and superior security interest. Additionally, it discourages future buyers because they do not know which assets should be relied on as part of their offered purchase price.

§ 24.2 THE NUCLEAR ELEMENTS OF A VIABLE COMMERCIAL PRACTICE

The nuclear elements of a viable commercial practice are: cost effectiveness, selfishness, altruism, honesty, reasonableness and fairness.

Adam Smith, Emile Durkheim and E. O. Wilson, among other prescient observers of human nature remind us, that selfishness and altruism are indispensable impulses of commercial cooperation. And although their dosage per practice is not subject to precise measure (at least not with the present tools of social science), their presence in what I will refer to metaphorically as the nucleus of a viable commercial practice is always discernible.

---

[6] This is a hypothetical entity and any similarity with an actual one is coincidental.

While I do not know enough legal history (let alone biology) to draw a precise analogy between the elements of a viable commercial practice and those of a cell's nucleus, I have observed enough commercial practices (some from their infancy to their demise) to ascertain that they stem from a transaction whose DNA-like features are replicated in the practices of their offspring. I have also observed that regardless of the economic sector, a viable, cost-effective practice is one that takes into account a business's fixed, variable and marginal costs[7] while tempering the selfish impulses of its practitioners with altruism and with the duties to act honestly, reasonably and fairly.

A. Selfishness

Selfishness is commonly equated with the pursuit of profit exclusively or primarily for oneself. However, unless a merchant can convince his counter-parties that he has taken into account their reasonable expectations of profitability, he will soon have no counter-parties with whom to deal. This is true even when the selfish merchant fully discloses the terms and conditions of his promised (selfish) performance and expressly disclaims any responsibility for it. Consider, for example, a practice in which a "jobber" offered goods at a price advertised as "At least 50% of their prevailing market price."[8] The meaning of this disclosure and disclaimer came into question in a recently mediated dispute.[9] In it, the sale of industrial products was subject to an "as is" clause that expressly disclaimed their merchantability. The buyer asked the seller about the portion of the entire lot that was likely to be worth "very little if anything," to which the seller replied: "Probably less than 10% of the goods purchased." But he then repeated the disclaimer to his buyer and added: "Please remember that in this 'as is' sale we do not warrant the quality of what we sell, regardless of the percentage of merchantable goods." Soon after buying the goods, the buyer discovered that at least 80% of the goods were seriously defective and could not be resold.

After interviewing three respected jobbers who sold the same type of goods on the same "as is" basis, I expressed my opinion as follows:

> Even in an "as is" practice, the seller has a duty to act honestly and reasonably. . . . An "as is" price that is advertised as "At least fifty percent of the market value" of the goods must honestly and reasonably reflect such a value. These duties were not fulfilled in this case and therefore a serious downward adjustment of the price paid by the buyer is in order.

The major premise of this opinion is that even a fully-disclosed, selfish version of a practice is subject to the requirements of honesty, reasonableness and fairness, especially because more than a fair price was paid by the "as is" purchaser. Please recall also the warning of U.C.C. § 1–203, as discussed in the preceding chapter: "Every contract or duty within this Act imposes an obligation of good faith in its performance

---

[7] *See Economics Basics for Civil Engineers: Lesson 1*, CONCRETE BASISCS, http://www.concretebasics.org/articlesinfo/conceptsofcost.php (last visited Sept. 12, 2013) (for simple illustrations on the concepts of these costs).

[8] *Jobber*, THE FREE DICTIONARY, www.thefreedictionary.com/jobber (last visited Sept. 12, 2013). In United States' trade parlance, a jobber is a merchant who buys merchandise or equipment from manufacturers and sells it to retailers.

[9] I was consulted by one of the attorney-mediators who asked me to report on jobbers' practices. While I was authorized to publish the above redacted version of my opinion, I am not at liberty to disclose the name of the parties, the mediators and experts including my interviewees.

or enforcement."[10] Good faith means "honesty in fact in the conduct or transaction concerned"[11] but also, as stated in U.C.C. § 2–103(b), "[I]n the case of a merchant [good faith] means honesty in fact and the observance of reasonable commercial standards of fair dealing in the trade."[12] To this definition, I would add Lord Mansfield's maxim which I have paraphrased as "A fair price demands a fair warranty."[13] A literalist may argue that the "as is" disclaimer in the dispute above renders inoperative the seller's public representation that the price charged warrants at least 50% of the commercial value. But, if so, what is the legal import of a representation that clearly exceeds the boundaries of puffery?

Finally, bear in mind that as a variant of justice, fairness requires equal treatment of equals and thus it potentially involves a larger number of "constituents" than does reasonableness. The term reasonable, at least in my linguistic experience, generally involves the behavior of the parties of a representative transaction or relationship. Thus, as discussed in the preceding chapter, where commercial contracts are concerned, what is reasonable is determined by asking how an "archetypal other" contracting party would act under the circumstances. The question of what is fair can be asked in connection with performance in a contract or relationship, but it is also frequently asked in connection with the impact that a contract, course of dealing or usage of trade will have or is likely to have on an entire class of third parties such as consumers.

B. Altruism

Altruism is at times reflected in one party's willingness to be the first in giving something of value to the other, although in doing so, she usually expects that her giving will be followed by a comparable giving by her counter-party. This everyday contractual practice is mostly utilitarian because the initial giving is part of a business strategy to induce the trust and continuing business of the recipient. The same is true with the "loss leader" pricing practice so common among retailers world-wide. In this practice, the seller foregoes profits in some of his sales with the intent to attract a larger clientele for profitable transactions.

At times, however, altruistic conduct involves a significant giving of time and money by one or more members of a class of merchants or bankers whose intent is to assure the survival of the larger group. This was the case when J. P. Morgan (one the most influential financiers in the United States at the turn of the twentieth century), with a group of financiers he gathered, was able to rescue a growing number of insolvent banks by restoring their liquidity and thereby ending the "Panic of 1907."[14]

J. P. Morgan's "restoration of liquidity" practice was not new and continues to be used in many countries with a comparable mixture of altruistic-utilitarian motives. Finally, there is the plain altruism of merchants, bankers and other professionals who are willing to sacrifice some of their profits or incur some losses to help out a colleague, a client or (more rarely) third parties in dire need.

---

[10] U.C.C. § 1–203 (2013).

[11] *Id.* § 1–201(19).

[12] *Id.* § 2–103(1)(b).

[13] *See supra* § 23:4(D)(2)(A).

[14] *See generally* ROBERT F. BRUNER & SEAN D. CARR, THE PANIC OF 1907: LESSONS LEARNED FROM THE MARKET'S PERFECT STORM (2009).

Of the preceding practices, only those with a utilitarian component become elements of the nucleus of commercial and financial practices. Recall Adam Smith's observation that good or virtuosity as well as selfishness can be part of the same economic conduct, and recall how this observation echoed a similar one in a fifth century observation by a Talmudic scholar who pointed to the instances in which selfish and at times evil motives lead to virtuous results and vice-versa.[15] As was discussed in Chapter 20, the large volume of commercial credit found in sixteenth- and seventeenth-century England—the largest per capita usage of commercial credit known at that time—was attributable to lending practices that combined an altruistic initial giving with the lender's profit-making. Similarly, recall how Meyer Rothschild's willingness to assume the risk of the loss of his own property to safeguard that of his princely client earned him a reputation for probity and integrity that eventually yielded untold riches for him and his family.[16]

C. The Importance of Factual (Non-Formally Logical) Research When Identifying the Nuclear Elements of a Practice

To understand a commercial or financial practice, one must first identify its nuclear or formative elements. As discussed in Chapter 2, this is an empirical, fact-based, search for answers to questions such as: What is the socio-economic context of the practice? And as part of such a context, what are the economic forces that drive the practice? Is it urban- or rural-based? Who are its regular participants and shapers and who are the most likely third parties? Who are its most and least respected practitioners and why? Clearly, the answers will not be found in pre-existent formally logical definitions and classifications, inspired as they may or may not have been by other and very different practices. In fact, almost invariably, attempts to capture the gist of new practices using formally logical methodological lenses leads at best to inertia and at worst to normative blockage.[17] Recall also in that chapter the skeptical question voiced by a scholastically trained professor: How could conditional sales exist if sales are consensual agreements that transfer the title to the purchaser from the moment he and the seller agree on the goods sold and their price?[18]

Or recall a similar skepticism of the practice of issuing mortgage bonds to finance the construction of public housing by selling them to the public as voiced by a lawyer to the housing authority of a developing nation.[19] Her questions were: Is not a mortgage an accessory obligation to the loan agreement, the principal obligation? As an accessory obligation (as her nineteenth century civil code said it was) how could a mortgage bond exist or be created for a loan that does not yet exist? In fact, no money has been advanced in that practice to the borrower mortgagor until someone, an underwriter or secondary market buyer, pays the purchase price of the bond. As with the rejection of the conditional sale practice, this formally logical reasoning ignores the empirical fact that mortgage bonds or certificates were used successfully at least since the seventeenth century in European nations and that the BGB devotes several of its

---

[15] *See supra* § 22:4(C)(1).

[16] *See supra* § 11:4(E).

[17] *See supra* § 2:2(A)(4).

[18] *Id.*

[19] *See supra* §§ 11:2(D)(2) & 11:4(D).

provisions to the so called "territorial debt" which relies on mortgage certificates as financing tools.[20]

D. The Nuclear Elements of a Contemporary Secured Transaction

The nucleus of a practice is best examined once that practice has reached maturity or when its archetypal participants and third parties regard it as cost effective, reasonable and fair.[21] One of the main purposes of a secured commercial loan is to encourage commercial lenders to lend to merchants who are unable to obtain unsecured loans, or even if they were able to obtain them, the interest rates would be prohibitive. The secured loan enables lending at reasonable rates of interest to such merchants by financing their acquisition of business assets such as raw materials and inventory that when transformed (with the use of equally financed equipment) and resold, facilitate significantly the repayment of the secured loan. Thus, a peculiar feature of secured or asset-based lending is what the *NLCIFT 12 Principles of Secured Transactions Law in the Americas* refer to as the loan's self-liquidation.[22]

Further, the practice of "line of credit financing," which enlarges or shrinks the amounts lent depending upon the debtor's streams of revenue and reliability of repayment, has shown that it is possible, and indeed necessary in many cases, to perfect a security interest in collateral prior to the time when the loan is disbursed. Accordingly, collateral can be a future thing that comes into existence after the security has been created or it can be the right to demand the performance of a contract or it can be the account receivable that is a *prima facie* indication that such performance has taken place. Similarly, collateral can be not only the thing pledged or mortgaged, but also the proceeds obtained from the sale of the collateral.

The contemporary security interest or right *in rem* in the collateral can be created by means of a consensual or informal contract as well as by a statutory, administrative or judicial provision. Surprising to many a contemporary civil law lawyer who believes that in Roman law only owners could pledge their assets, Roman law actually allowed some non-owner debtors to pledge or mortgage things they did not own, but lawfully possessed.[23] In United States' secured transactions law, this practice became a legal principle. Thus, the heading of U.C.C. § 9–202 proclaims, "Title to Collateral Immaterial." The practice that required that the debtor only have rights in the collateral (as contrasted with his ownership of it) also became a nuclear element of the security interest of § 9–203(b). It enables a debtor who has "rights in the collateral or the power to transfer rights in the collateral to a secured party" to create a security interest in the collateral.[24]

Additionally, to be effective and quickly convertible into cash, the *in rem* right of a secured transaction, especially in the case of moveable and perishable goods, requires a

---

[20] *See supra* § 11:2(F).

[21] NLCIFT, *12 Principles*. What follows is a summary of the Twelve Principles of Secured Transactions Law of the NLCIFT.

[22] *Id.* Principle 1.

[23] *See, e.g.*, WATSON, DIGEST, 13.7.20. The quoted opinion states: "Property belonging to another can be given as a *pignus* with its owner's consent. Even if the pledge is made without his knowledge and he later ratifies, the *pignus* is valid." *Id.*

[24] U.C.C. § 9–203(b)(2) (2012); *see generally* Boris Kozolchyk, *What to do About Mexico's Antiquated Secured Financing Law*, 12 ARIZ. J. INT'L & COMP. L. 523 (1995).

summary repossession or foreclosure procedure that in most instances should be extrajudicial and by means of the creditor's self-help. Finally, another nuclear element of a security interest against third parties (defined as any party other than the original secured creditor and debtor) is that it be publicized by a functional and accurate form of public notice.

§ 24.3 SECURED LENDING IN IMPERIAL ROME: ARCHETYPAL PARTIES

A. Socio-Economic Context: The Republican and Imperial Commercial Archetypes

In Chapter 4, I quoted Cato's depiction of the small farmer-soldier, lauded by the ancestors as a model man (*virum bonum*) who, unlike merchants, "do[es] not think evil thoughts."[25] Professor Jo-Ann Shelton of the University of California, Santa Barbara also quotes Cato's views on the profitability of property ownership in contrast with the profitability and morality of money lending. After listing raising livestock and crops as the most profitable, the questioner asked Cato: "What about moneylending?" to which Cato replied: "What about murder?"[26] Apparently, Cato's distaste for money lending as an occupation was even stronger than that for commerce. At the same time, he made his fortune through investing and lending in maritime (bottomry) loans.[27]

Cato's hypocrisy reflects the radical change in social attitudes and values that Republican Rome was undergoing. One of Cato's writings was a manual on how to run a farm (*De Agricultura*) "On Agriculture"[28] (a vital component of Rome's internal commerce). This writing, among others, enabled Theodor Mommsen (the great Swiss historian of Rome) to provide a compelling description of the evolution of Cato's archetypal farmer-tenant in *Historia de Roma*. I rely on Mommsen's analysis for the following summary of the socio-economic context of practices associated with secured lending during the late Roman Republic and Empire.[29]

During most of the Republic, the farmer was still viewed as:

> [R]obust and practical . . . "the earliest to rise and latest to go to bed; as severe and demanding of himself as of those who work for him, aware of how to earn the respect of the woman who makes his home; forever vigilant of his workers and his farm animals; ready to lend his hand in farm chores, but without reaching the point of exhaustion as is the case with his slaves,

---

[25] THEODOR MOMMSEN, I HISTORIA DE ROMA 1114 (A. Garcia Moreno trans., 4th ed., Aguilar 1960) (1855–56) (translated by author); *see also supra* § 4:3.

[26] JO-ANN SHELTON, AS THE ROMANS DID: A SOURCEBOOK IN ROMAN SOCIAL HISTORY 126 (2d. ed. 1998).

[27] MOMMSEN, *supra* note 25, at 1114 n.2. Mommsen tried to mitigate the clear appearance of Cato's hypocrisy:

> Cato, as well as others, placed his capital in cattle and analogous commercial enterprises. But he tried not to violate the law . . . he did not belong to commecial companies that profited from usurious loans. . . . The maritime loan [bottomry] in which he repeatedly participated was not, by far, a prohibited usurious loan.

Id. (translated by author)

[28] *Cato: De Agricultura,* PENELOPE.UCHICAGO.EDU, http://penelope.uchicago.edu/Thayer/E/Roman/Texts/Cato/De_Agricultura/home.html (last visited Sept. 16, 2013).

[29] As in Chapter 4, I will be relying in this chapter on the Spanish translation of Theodor Mommsen's *Römische Geschichte*, which was written in 1855–56. *See* MOMMSEN, *supra* note 25.

> unwilling to borrow or lend; host banquets or worship gods other than the domestic ones. Finally, glad to leave commercial dealings in the hands of . . . his landholder. . . .[30]

Yet this version of the Roman farmer did not last much longer. The long-term or life tenancy was disappearing in the late Republic, where the most common tenancy was of short duration and was of the "half and half" variety. In it, profits were split evenly between landowners and tenants, although the latter bore the costs of planting and cultivation.[31] By the end of the Republic, the most typical form of land tenure was by absentee landowners. Many of them owned several plots which they occasionally visited but primarily managed through employees and increasingly, slaves. In Mommsen's words:

> [T]he agrarian economy in Italy was being transformed while at the same time ignoring the best uses of the various forms of capital. [For this economy] everything was the same, cattle or slaves. "A good guard-dog—said a Roman agronomist—should not be sweet with his fellow slaves." As long as the ox and the house servant did their work, they were equally fed . . . when they could no longer perform they were sold as old furniture. . . . "The slave—stated a Cato aphorism—, must work whenever he is not asleep." Compassion had no place [in this economy]. . . .[32]

The sharp decline in the price of cereal grains was a major factor in the transformation of rural land tenure and in the emergence of a new dominant commercial and financial archetype. In an attempt to satisfy the populist clamor for lower prices for grain by the urban population, Rome's official policy was to increase the imports of the cheapest possible cereal grains and to encourage the acquisition of small farms by large landholders and money lenders. By manning these farms with large numbers of slaves, the cost of production of grain was reduced, but this was at the expense of the small farmers.[33] Their loss of a decent livelihood broke down their moral values, to the point that the "sobriety of their customs" was lost.[34] They were replaced by "herds of slaves, unburdened by women and children."[35]

According to Mommsen, the new archetypal merchant was a financier or money lender (*fenerator* or the generator or recipient of interest). He was the principal player in the commercial agriculture and finance of late Republican and Imperial Rome.[36] Where commercial agriculture was concerned, he was much more than the traditional money lender. He helped manage large commercial farms, both in Italy and abroad. In that capacity, he shaped the lending and collection practices that we will be discussing in the following sections. He did this as a monopolist of agricultural and related commercial credit. Mommsen attributes to this money lender the wide use of informal contracts which he could easily enforce by his contacts with administrative and judicial

---

[30] *Id.* at 1089 (quoting Cato) (translation by author).

[31] *Id.* at 1082.

[32] *Id.* at 1088 (translation by author).

[33] *Id.* at 1091–1095.

[34] *Id.* at 1095 (translation by author).

[35] *Id.* at 1096 (translation by author).

[36] *Id.* at 1099–1100.

officials.[37] He did not believe in giving without receiving something in return. And as stated by the historian Polibius: "In Rome . . . no one gives, if he is not obligated to do so, no one pays a penny prior to the date of maturity of the debt, even among relatives!"[38]

Mommsen summarizes the behavior of a thoroughly commercialized imperial Rome as a society and community corrupted to the core in which "the most unbridled selfishness took the place of humanity and of love of country."[39] It is now time to turn to the secured lending practices that came out of the socio-economic transformation Mommsen so painstakingly described.

B. The Creditor's Fiduciary Ownership (*Fiducia*), His Possesory Pledge (*Pignus*) and His Non-Possessory Mortgage (*Hypotheca*)

A review of juristic opinions on pledges and mortgages in the Justinian Digest and of imperial and praetorian responses to queries by officials and disputants in the Justinian Code (*Rescripta principum*)[40] reflects a widespread and imaginative use of these security devices. In the words of the Jurist Marcian:

> Property can be mortgaged for any obligation, such as loan, dowry, sale, hire, or mandate, whether immediate, future, or conditional and whether the contract is present or past. It can also be mortgaged for a future obligation; for part as well as the whole sum; and for a civil, praetorian, or natural obligation. . . . [And] [t]he difference between *pignus* and *hypotheca* is purely verbal.[41]

Having this description in mind, I will briefly examine the characteristics of each of these security devices and subsequently their nuclear elements despite Marcian's observation of functional equivalence.

1. The Fiducia, *the* Pignus *and the* Hypotheca

In his epoch-making *Das Recht des Besitzes*[42] (translated as "Treatise on Possession: Or, the Jus Possessionis of the Civil Law"), Friedrich Karl von Savigny referred to the possession of the pledgee as a "derivative" right based on the pledge agreement (*contractus pignoris*).[43] Savigny acknowledged that the holders of non-contractual pledges such as the so-called praetorian pledges also had rights to the

---

[37] *Id.* at 1105–06.

[38] *Id.* at 1106 (translation by author).

[39] *Id.* at 1112 (translation by author).

[40] BERGER, ENCYCLOPEDIC DICTIONARY, at 680.

[41] WATSON, DIGEST, 20.1.5.

[42] FRIEDRICH KARL VON SAVIGNY, DAS RECHT DES BESITZES (1803). The book was later translated into English and is the version I cite to: FRIEDRICH KARL VON SAVIGNY, VON SAVIGNY'S TREATISE ON POSSESSION; OR THE JUS POSSESSIONIS OF THE CIVIL LAW (Erskine Perry trans., S. Sweet 1848) (1803). Rudolf von Ihering referred to the Recht des Besitzes as the book that helped us regain the juridical method of the Romans and with it the birth of modern jurisprudence. It should be noted that von Ihering made this assessment despite his disagreement with one of Savigny's principal findings with respect to the intent to own the thing possessed (*animus dominii* or *rem sibi habendi*) as an essential element for the protection of possession in Roman law. *See supra* § 12:2(A).

[43] VON SAVIGNY, *supra* note 42, at 215.

things, but these rights were not equivalent to those derived from the contract of pledge.[44]

As a predecessor of the *Pignus,* the *Fiducia* was a transfer in trust of the ownership of the collateral to the creditor. This was a simulated transfer because despite its appearance as a formal conveyance of rights *in rem*, the creditor was not supposed to acquire such rights. In fact, according to typically undisclosed agreements, the debtor retained the right described by Savigny as the re-delivery of the thing at some future time by means of the *actio pigneraticia*. And as he emphasized, the creditor had "no *animus domini*, and, consequently, no original Possession [was transferred]. . . ."[45]

Professor Rudolf Sohm was a distinguished late nineteenth- and early twentieth-century Roman and Canonic law scholar. His version of the *Fiducia* varies somewhat from Savigny's.[46] Sohm characterized the security interest of the pledgee-creditor in the pledge agreement as an *in rem* right which enabled the creditor to secure payment of what was owed to him "through the medium of a thing."[47] As did Savigny, Sohm noted that the *Fiducia* was the pledge's principal ancestor in Roman law and its creation was by means of a formal, simulated formal conveyance (*mancipatio, imaginaria venditio nummo uno*) by the debtor to the creditor with the understanding that once the debtor paid, the creditor would reconvey the entrusted thing to him.[48] But then Sohm added an important fact: As the ostensible fiduciary owner, the secured creditor was in strict law entitled to deal with the conveyed property as he liked, including reselling it to satisfy his claim if the debtor defaulted.[49] Yet, this fiduciary's resales were often at the expense of the debtor's remaining or reversionary rights. Consequently, debtors were reluctant to use this device and gradually the *Fiducia* was replaced by the *Pignus*.

The *Pignus* avoided the debtor's insecurity by not requiring him to part with his ownership. In the pledge, the secured creditor acquired his security interest in the collateral by becoming its possessor; his security interest was perfected by the delivery of the thing (*traditio*) to the creditor. However, the *Digest* quotes an opinion by the invariably subtle Ulpian (who, as you will recall, introduced us to the archetypal *Bonus Vir* in Chapter 4).[50] In this opinion, Ulpian focuses on the elements of creation of a security interest and implicitly on its perfection:

> The contract of *pignus* is concluded not only by the delivery of the thing pledged but by simple agreement even if no delivery [of the pledged thing] is made [*Pignus contrahitur non sola traditione, sed etiam nuda conventione, etsi non traditium est*]. If, therefore, an agreement alone suffices for the formation of *pignus*, what if someone points out gold as the thing about to be

---

[44] *Id.* at 216. Berger's ENCYCLOPEDIC DICTIONARY OF ROMAN LAW defines the praetorian pledge as a pledge taken by the creditor upon an order from a magistrate including the Praetor to secure, among other obligations, those flowing from an execution of a judgment debt. BERGER, ENCYCLOPEDIC DICTIONARY, *supra* note 40, at 631.

[45] VON SAVIGNY, *supra* note 42, at 216.

[46] RUDOLF SOHM, THE INSTITUTES OF ROMAN LAW 272 (James Crawford Ledlie trans., 1892).

[47] *Id.*

[48] *Id.*

[49] *Id.*

[50] *See supra* § 4:6(C) (on *Bonus Vir*).

pledged and hands over bronze instead? In consequence, did he [still] pledge the gold? [*Et consequence est, ut aurum obligatur*] And the consequence of such an agreement is that the gold is pledged and not the bronze because the parties did not agree on it as the pledge.[51]

Thus, this opinion expressly requires only the agreement to create the pledge and allows the inference that the transfer or delivery of the thing, to which he also refers, as the means to perfect the enforcement of a right *in rem* not only against the pledgor but also against third parties in possession of the pledge. For as an owner of the thing pledged, the debtor could recover it from anyone who obtained possession of it wrongfully, and as soon as he repaid the secured loan, the creditor had to return it to him.[52] The debtor-pledgor also had a special action for the recovery of the pledge against its wrongful retention by the secured creditor (the above mentioned *actio pigneraticia*).[53] On the other hand, as pointed out by Professor Reinhard Zimmermann, while the possessory pledge was a standard practice in early Roman law, in classical law the debtor could remain in possession of the pledged thing while a lesser possessory right in favor of the pledgee could still be carved out.[54] At a later time, this right was recognized as a right in the property of others (*ius in re aliena*).[55]

Meanwhile, the praetor fashioned summary remedies known as possessory interdicts in favor of lawful possessors who had been deprived of their possession.[56] These remedies did not require or determine ownership rights, as was the case with the *actio rei vindication*, and for this reason they often failed to recover goods in the hands of *bona fide* purchasers or adverse possessors.[57] To resolve this problem, the secured creditors resorted to yet another practice in which an agreement or clause stipulated that in the event of debtor default, the ownership of the pledged collateral would be forfeited and transferred to the creditor as a penalty. This practice was sanctioned by the *Lex Commissoria.* During early days of Imperial Rome, this agreement or clause was supplemented by another agreement that gave the creditor the right to sell the collateral to satisfy the debtor's obligation ("*Pactum Venditionis*").[58] Thus, in contrast with the *fiducia,* the debtor did not transfer ownership of the pledged thing to the creditor, but instead transferred possession. Finally, the praetor's edict was also instrumental in popularizing the *Hypotheca* practice. This practice seemed to provide greater certainty to both parties than the *Fiducia* and the *Pignus*. It allowed the debtor to retain ownership (and in many instances also possession) of the collateral. In addition, the debtor of a *Hypotheca* could agree with his creditor on the application of the *Lex Commissoria*, which, by rescinding the *convenio pignoris*, allowed the creditor to gain possession of the collateral. In addition, a *Pactum Venditionis* allowed the creditor to sell the collateral and pay himself out of the

---

[51] CUERPO DEL DERECHO CIVIL ROMANO PRIMERA PARTE INSTITUTA.—DIGESTO 13.7.1. (D. Ildefonso L. García del Corral trans., Jaime Molinas ed., 1889) (translated by author), *available at* http://www.biblio juridica.org/libros/libro.htm?l=600 [hereinafter CUERPO DEL DERECHO CIVIL ROMANO] (emphasis added).

[52] SOHM, *supra* note 46, at 273.

[53] REINHARD ZIMMERMANN, THE LAW OF OBLIGATIONS: ROMAN FOUNDATIONS OF THE CIVILIAN TRADITION 221 (1996).

[54] *Id.*

[55] *See supra* § 4:2(A)(4) (on *iura in re aliena).*

[56] SOHM, *supra* note 46, at 273.

[57] *Id.*

[58] *Id.* at 273 n.2.

proceeds of the sale. Armed with these agreements, the mortgagee could defeat third parties holding lesser rights *in rem*.[59]

The *Hypotheca* enabled small and tenant farmers to mortgage their farming stock *(invecta et iliata)* and their mortgagee-lenders could obtain the possession of this collateral when the farmers defaulted by means of the *Interdictum Salvianum* as well as by means of the *Actio Serviana*.[60] Unlike the *Pignus*, then, the *Hypotheca* allowed the debtor to remain in productive possession of the real or personal property collateral, thereby allowing the debtor to generate revenues with which to repay the loan.

In sum, the nuclear element of a *Fiducia* consisted of an "imaginary" or simulated transfer of ownership, but a transfer nonetheless. It exposed the debtor-transferor to the risk of losing his collateral to bad faith practices by creditors. The nuclear elements of the Roman pledge were an agreement to pledge, however informal, whose purpose was to secure loans and a contemporary or subsequent transfer of possession to the creditor, but not as an essential requisite for the creation of the pledge. As with the pledge, a mortgage could be created informally by a consensual contract and the mortgagor could remain in possession of the thing pledged. Thus, many mortgagor-farmers remained in possession of the land, farm animals and crops during the life of the *hypotheca*.[61]

If you find only minor differences between Roman pledges and mortgages, you are in good company. Please recall that after comparing these practices, the above quoted jurist Marcian concluded that: "The difference between *pignus* and *hypotheca* is purely verbal."[62] When I first read this opinion, I found its simplification of the seemingly contrasting features of pledges and mortgages reassuring, but after recalling the phenomenon of legal invertebration in Latin American, Soviet and Chinese law, I wondered if the Roman law and practice on pledges and mortgages did not evidence a similar invertebration in the above laws and practice. Recall that when it came to the enforcement of rights against a member of the same family, close friend or business associate of the judge or administrator, legal precision and the rule of law gave way to simulatory and fraudulent practices that blurred the distinctions between established legal institutions, but I am jumping ahead of the story.

2. *The Sale of Collateral by Creditors in the Justinian Digest and Code*

Please recall Professor Sohm's reference to the practice in which an agreement or clause enabled the creditor's sale of the debtor's pledged thing (*Pactum venditionis.*) Its purpose was to allow the pledgee to repay himself with the proceeds of the sale of the pledged thing. A review of the Justinian Digest and Code reveals that this practice was the subject of numerous disputes reflecting conflicting policies of creditor and debtor protection. On the one hand, the creditor's sale was viewed by Ulpian and some Imperial Rome rescripts as valid and desirable, even in the absence of an enabling agreement or clause. On the other hand, other Imperial Rescripts evince concern with

---

[59] *Id.* at 274.

[60] *Id.*

[61] *See* CHARLES PHINHEAS SHERMAN, II ROMAN LAW IN THE MODERN WORLD 185 (1917). It states: "The essence of hypotheca is the agreement to hypothecate—that is, the retention of possession by the debtor." *Id.*

[62] WATSON, DIGEST, 20.1.5.

depriving debtors of their rights in the collacteral and try to establish, albeit feebly, some due process standards for the creditors' sales.

Ulpian, *Sabinus, book 41*:

If it has been agreed to sell the *pignus* at the time of concluding the pledge agreement or subsequently [*Si convenit de distrahendo pignoris sive ab initio sive postea*], not only is the sale valid but the purchaser becomes the owner of the thing. Nonetheless, even if there is no agreement for the pledge to be sold, we apply the rule that unless such a sale is forbidden in the agreement the sale will be allowed. The rule we apply is that the sale is still allowed, unless it was agreed that the sale was not allowed in which case the the creditor who sold will be guilty of theft [*creditor si distraxerit furti obligatur*] except where the debtor gave three notices of default and the debtor did not respond.[63]

The Emperors Diocletian and Maximian, and the Caesars, to Eudemia.

Where property has been pledged according to law, and the creditor makes a legitimate sale of the same, the debtor by afterwards offering to refund the price to the purchaser, or by tendering the amount of the debt to the creditor, cannot evict the possessor of the property.[64]

The Same Emperor [Justinian] to Julian, Praetorian Prefect.

And, as We have found in agreements made with reference to pledges or hypothecations that relief is not only ordinarily granted to the creditor in possession, but also, when he is deprived of the property pledged, whether by his own fault, or not, or through accident, We have thought it to be more humane to assist the creditor by means of the praetorian pledge, no matter how he may have lost possession of the property. . . . For even though he ought to take such care of his pledge that it may not suffer any damage, still, in order not to deal harshly with creditors, We incline to a liberal interpretation of the law, and grant them the right of recovery.[65]

The Same Emperors [Diocletian and Maximian] and Caesars to Rufinus.

If, however, he [the creditor] should purchase it from the debtor, who sold it to him, it would establish a bad precedent to set aside the sale made with the consent of both parties, if neither the fraud of the adverse party, nor the employment of duress by him is proved. Therefore, if you can show by clear, positive evidence that the creditor always held possession through a fictitious purchaser, and that he afterwards bought in good faith the property which was fraudulently disposed of, you can compel the creditor to make restitution of the same, after having tendered him the payment of the debt with interest.[66]

---

[63] CUERPO DEL DERECHO CIVIL ROMANO, *supra* note 51, 13.7.4 (translated by author) (emphasis added).

[64] THE JUSTINIAN CODE FROM THE CORPUS JURIS CIVILIS 8.10.2 (Samuel Parsons Scott ed. & trans., 1932), *available at* http://www.freewebs.com/vitaphone1/history/justinianc.html [hereinafter THE JUSTINIAN CODE].

[65] *Id.* 8.22.2.

[66] *Id.* 8.28.10.

Notice how the first rescript describes the prevailing attitude of creditor protection. Notice also how the second rescript acknowledges the widespread use of creditor-inspired, simulatory, bad faith practices.

3. Unbridled Selfish Practices and Legal Invertebration

Tulane University Professor Dennis P. Kehoe's recent study "Law and the Rural Economy in the Roman Empire" dates the imperial concern with creditors and large landholders' simulatory and fraudulent practices to the reign of Marcus Aurelius (121–80 A.D.), who in a rescript insisted that the creditors use the courts rather than self-help to proceed against the debtor.[67] He also quotes the jurist Modestinus' (a student of Ulpian's) reference to emperor Julian's law on the use of private force (*lex Iulia de vi privata*) by a creditor who unlawfully and coercively seized the property of a debtor. Such a creditor would be subject to serious sanctions, including the loss of one third of his property and the declaration of infamy with a possible loss of civil rights and a removal from decent society.[68] Still, please keep in mind that the use of the *Lex Commissoria* and the debtor's forfeiture of his rights in the collateral as well as his authorization to resell the collateral (*Pactum Venditionis*) remained valid until emperor Constantine's decree nullifying them in 326 A.D.[69] Could the jurists have harmonized such seemingly contradictory policies by establishing the meaning of concepts such as the U.C.C.'s "breach of the peace"[70] or the French abuse of rights (*abus de droit*) as applicable to the Roman secured creditors' sales of collateral?[71] Or were the Roman jurists too biased in favor of landholders and lenders' secured creditors' rights and remedies? The answer to both of these questions is yes. According to Professor Kehoe, although many of these jurists adhered to a "closed intellectual tradition, one divorced from social concerns and largely subject to its own internal logic," they were in fact sympathetic to the interests of large landholders.[72] And in several areas of the law these jurists were more concerned with those problems that "impinged directly on the interests of the upper classes" than they were with debtor protection.[73]

In addition, Professor Kehoe found a substantial disparity "between the written law and the practice of the courts."[74] This disparity may have been caused by the large volume of litigation, the aristocratic extraction of judges and their lack of legal training. But more likely, it was caused by conflicting policies and contradictory legal directives. These factors, plus the pervasive presence of corruption (as the usual companion of simulations and fraudulent schemes), explain why so many small farmers turned for relief not to the courts, but to the emperor.[75] Further, the injustices inflicted upon the small farmers and tenants paled into insignificance when compared with the inhumanities inflicted upon the slaves who worked the farms. Not

---

[67] DENNIS P. KEHOE, LAW AND THE RURAL ECONOMY IN THE ROMAN EMPIRE 152 (2007).

[68] *Id.*

[69] *See infra* note 88 and accompanying text.

[70] U.C.C. § 9–609(b)(2) (2012).

[71] *See infra* § 8:7(M).

[72] KEHOE, *supra* note 67, at 12.

[73] *Id.*

[74] *Id.* at 14.

[75] *Id.* at 18.

surprisingly, slave revolts and insurrections were not uncommon. In one of these revolts alone, 7,000 slaves were condemned to death.[76] This explains why agricultural lending practices not only failed to mature into clearly and precisely formulated concepts, principles and rules, but also why legal invertebration persisted until secured agricultural and commercial lending lost its vigor as a formula of economic growth and why Rome's rural population suffered a significant decline.[77]

4. *Questions, Comments and Conclusions*

No reasonable and fair commercial and financial practices can be expected from the interaction between sharply unequal participants, regardless of whether the inequality stems from their vastly different economic or political powers or from their different functions in the transactions in question. It is still hard to decipher how such an unequal bargaining environment produced the "half and half" practice apparent in late Republic short-term leases. Yet, regardless of how that practice came about, it is a testimony to its reasonableness and fairness that many centuries later it is still found in nations who pride themselves in the Romanistic roots of their civil law tradition.[78]

The contrast between the viable "half and half practice" and the failed, one-sided sale of collateral practices highlights the importance of honesty, reasonableness and fairness when shaping viable and long-lasting commercial practices. The failure of the Roman practices was not because the jurists did not identify the nuclear elements of the sale of collateral practice as they did with so many other practices. Review the above opinions of Ulpian and Marcian, among others, and you will soon realize how many of these elements they correctly identified. Consider, for example, their identification of the pledge agreement as the principal nuclear element in the formation of the pledge, regardless of the transfer of possession to the creditor. In fact, for much of the twentieth century, the civil codes of several civil law countries failed to appreciate the wisdom of Ulpian's previously discussed opinion on the ancillary role of transfer of possession in the creation of a pledge.[79] Or consider the jurists' observation that an open number of things could be used as collateral. As stated by Gaius: "Future property can be mortgaged, for example, unharvested crops, offspring of a female slave, and the young of animals once born."[80] Such collateral was unavailable in the secured transactions laws of many civil law countries well into the twentieth century.[81]

Unlike many of their intellectual heirs, Roman jurists also discerned the collateral value of groups of similar animals or things as units of assets, as they also discerned the value of continuing the security interest in the things or animals that replenished their original number. Thus, as opined by the Jurist Marcian: "If a flock is mortgaged, later born animals are included. Indeed, if the whole flock dies and is renewed, it remains subject to mortgage."[82] Similarly, Roman jurists and emperors or their legal

---

[76] MOMMSEN, *supra* note 25, at 1118.

[77] *Id.* at 1117–19 (For an analysis of the decline of Rome's rural population and its causes during the late Republic and early Empire).

[78] *Id.* at 1082 n.1 (referring to art. 1818 of the *Code Civil* as an heir to the Roman half and half practice with respect to cattle raising). The same practice can be observed in Central and South American share cropping.

[79] Boris Kozolchyk, *Law and the Credit Structure in Latin America*, 7 VA. J. INT'L L. 1, 3 (1967).

[80] WATSON, DIGEST, 20.1.15.

[81] Kozolchyk, *supra* note 79, at 4–8.

[82] WATSON, DIGEST, 20.1.13.

assistants perceived the value of contract rights as collateral, even though these rights were incorporeal things. In the words of emperors Diocletian and Maximinian: "After it was settled that the contracts of debtors could be given in pledge, it seemed to be the rule that equitable actions could be granted to the creditor himself who made the demand (as has already been decided) after the sale of the claim."[83] In contrast, one of the most influential civil codes in the Western Hemisphere to this day still requires that the thing pledged must be corporeal.[84] Finally, consider a rescript by Emperor Septimius Severus that stated that crops from a property held as security should be credited against the debt owed and that any crops left over should be returned to the debtor.[85] It was not until well into the twentieth century that Latin American statutes allowed the use of crops and their fruits as collateral separate from the land on which they grew.

Despite all these visionary contributions to the future law of secured transactions, the Roman standard secured transactions practice reflected in the Justinian Digest and Code of Justinian still missed two of the most important nuclear elements: (1) a fair and functional notice system to alert third parties interested in lending on the strength of the collateral or in buying it that a pledge or mortgage would be senior to their potential rights, and (2) a fair and reasonable self-help procedure that would (a) enable the secured creditor to repossess the collateral upon the debtor's default, (b) sell it for a fair market price, and (c) at the same time protect the remainder rights of the debtor in the sold collateral. Hence, while the jurists visualized most of the nuclear elements that would have made it possible for parties with relatively similar bargaining power and equal information on the facts of the transaction to maximize their respective rights, they did little to remedy the unreasonableness and unfairness of overreaching and oppressive practices between unequal contracting parties and with respect to third parties.

It was not until the twelfth century that potential secured lenders in the former Roman colonies such as Britain were able to lend to parties other than those with whom they had close relationships. This was because they lacked accurate and timely notice of the pre-existence of pledges and mortgages. According to Sir Roy Goode, during the reign of Richard I (in twelfth-century England), debtors were, as with the Roman law *Hypotheca*, allowed to remain in possession of the collateral.[86] However, unlike the *Hypotheca*, the "Jewish" mortgage practice in Britain required that secured creditors provide public notice of their security interests by a filing in a public registry.[87] This critical mutation of the Roman nuclear secured lending practice made it possible for many more potential secured lenders and purchasers to become interested in lending or purchasing.

---

[83] THE JUSTINIAN CODE, *supra* note 64, 4.39.7 (for a reply by Emperors Diocletian and Maximian to Manassa).

[84] *See, e.g.*, CÓD.CIV. art. 2384 (1857) (Chile). It states: "By means of the pledge agreement a moveable thing is delivered to the creditor for his security. The delivered thing is called a pledge." *Id.* (translation by author). Obviously, a delivered thing must be a corporeal thing. Recall that Chile's Civil Code served as a model for many other civil codes in the Western Hemisphere. *See supra* ch. XIV § 14:4(A) (on Latin American law).

[85] KEHOE, *supra* note 67, at 153. Additionally, Professor Kehoe refers to emperor Caracalla's citations to rescripts that upheld the exclusive authority of a judge to alienate property pledged as security. *Id.*

[86] GOODE ON COMMERCIAL LAW 627 n.50 (Ewan McKendrick ed., 4th ed. 2009).

[87] *Id.* at 585. This source states: "An exception was the Jewish mortgage, a non-possesory security interest perfected by local registration under a system established by King Richard I." *Id.* at 585 n.50.

And as was concluded in the previous section, the reason for the inability to work out the appropriate legal and equitable formula of creditors' sales and foreclosures was not the absence of highly skilled and pragmatic legal professionals and administrators. Instead, the reasons were deeper: A pronounced and unbridgeable inequality between creditors and debtors. Even those practices that seemed ready to incorporate reasonable and fair nuclear elements were quickly undermined by the continuing resort to simulations and other bad faith practices. The final blow to the Roman practices of self-help came when the *Pactum Commissorium* was outlawed by Emperor Constantine in 326 A.D. His justification for outlawing this *Pactum*, which he referred to as *Lex Commissoria*, albeit terse, bears reflection:

> Since among other captious practices the harshness of the provision for forfeiture *(lex commissoria)* is especially increasing, it is our pleasure that this provision shall be invalidated [and that hereafter all memory of it shall be abolished].[88]

In sum, the nuclear elements present in both the pledge and the mortgage (as aided by the *Pactum Commissorium* and the *Pactum Vendendi*) conferred rights of possession, either actual or future, upon a secured creditor once the debtor defaulted in his repayment obligation. Nevertheless, the manner in which these potential elements of the secured transactions nucleus were being used, especially by large landholders and lenders, made them unreasonable and unfair, and thus failed practices.

§ 24.4 DRAFTING COMMERCIAL LETTER OF CREDIT (LOC) PRACTICES

A. Why LOC Practices?

In the following sections, I examine the compilation of practices and drafting of rules associated with the commercial letter of credit (LOC) transaction.[89] LOC practices originated during the first half of the nineteenth century and are still used today throughout the trading and financial worlds. Thus, enough information exists about them to answer questions such as: How did they come about? What are their "nuclear" elements? What made some practices viable and others not? How did they mutate into new practices? Who are the principal drafters of practice-based rules and what characterizes their drafting? What is the role of lawyers as advisors and assistants in the drafting of rules based on LOC practices?

One reason for selecting LOC practices is that they illustrate how relatively equally-situated bankers compiled them and drafted what eventually became binding rules of practice throughout the banking world. By "relatively equal" I mean bankers who, despite the differing size of their assets or of their economic or political powers, still perform interchangeable functions with and for each other and earn standardized commissions, fees or rates of interest when discharging those functions. As will be discussed shortly, bank A, who issued a LOC this morning and asked bank B to

---

[88] THE THEODOSIAN CODE 65 (Clyde Pharr ed. & trans., 1952), *cited in* Kozolchyk & Furnish, *A Comparative Analysis*, at 16 n.57.

[89] *See* Boris Kozolchyk, *The Emerging Law of Standby Letters of Credit and Bank Guarantees*, 24 ARIZ. L. REV. 319 (1982) (for a disctinction between commercial and stand-by letters of credit); *see also* Boris Kozolchyk, *Commerical and Standby Letters of Credit, in* 3 UNITED STATES LAW ON TRADE AND INVESTMENT (Boris Kozolchyk & John F. Molloy eds., 2001).

confirm it and authorized Bank C to negotiate it, can be asked later during the same morning by bank B to confirm its LOC and can be authorized by bank C to negotiate its LOC.

Another reason for the choice of topic is to allow the reader to compare the rules arrived at by banks and by representatives of commercial sectors with the "merchant rules" drafted by Professor Llewellyn discussed in the preceding chapter.[90] A final reason is that I have spent a major part of my professional life studying, testifying, arbitrating and, on occasion, compiling and drafting rules based on these practices. This familiarity allowed me to witness the birth, development, mutation and demise of LOC practices and observe what made some of them work and others not. And even though LOCs are not as widely used now as they were a decade ago (having often been replaced by a secured transaction practice known as "supply chain fainancing"),[91] much can still be learned from what made LOCs the highly popular means of payment and finance for close to two centuries.

B. The Basic Commercial LOC Transaction

An irrevocable LOC promises to pay its beneficiary (usually the supplier or seller of goods or services) a stipulated amount against his presentation of documents specified in the LOC. Typical among these documents are an invoice describing the goods, their quantity and price, a negotiable ocean bill of lading attesting to the shipment of the goods in apparent good order, an insurance policy or certificate covering the risk of loss or destruction of the goods, and possibly other documents such as certificates attesting to the origin, quality or weight of the goods shipped.

As a payment instrument, the LOC promises to pay to the named beneficiary, his transferees, or *bona fide* holders of the draft the amount specified therein. It can be paid upon the presentation of the documents or at a stipulated time thereafter. In the latter case, it is also a credit instrument. As a credit instrument, it enables the bank's applicant for the credit to wait a certain period of time before providing the issuing bank the funds necessary to pay the beneficiary. The draft or bill of exchange accepted by the issuing or confirming bank also becomes an instrument of credit for the beneficiary. He is able to negotiate the LOC draft prior to its maturity with the bank that issued or confirmed it or with another bank the issuing bank authorized to negotiate it. In doing this, the beneficiary or the holder of the draft obtains the amount stated in the draft less the discount or negotiation commission charged by the negotiating bank.

To perform its global payment and credit functions, the LOC relies on a network of correspondent banks acting as issuers, advisers or notifiers, confirmers of the issuing banks' and their own liability to the beneficiaries, presenters of the beneficiaries' documents to the issuers or confirmers, negotiators of the beneficiaries, payors of the LOC and reimbursers of this payment. Of these, the issuing and confirming banks are the central participants because their promises of payment or acceptance of the beneficiary's draft are highly liquid, i.e., easily and inexpensively convertible into cash. As will be discussed in the following section, the fact that the functions of LOC bankers

[90] *See supra* § 23:5(D) (discussing merchant rules in the U.C.C.).

[91] *See generally* Boris Kozolchyk, *Supply Chain Financing, Straight Bills of Lading and Standby Letters of Credit*, 2 GEO. MASON J. INT'L COM. L. 100 (2011).

are interchangeable provides an easier and almost organic path to reasonable and fair practices.

Three legal features make the LOC promises highly liquid:[92] (a) Their irrevocability from the moment they are issued; (b) their primary liability, (i.e., the fact that the beneficiary can claim payment first from the issuing or confirming bank without having to show that he tried to collect first from the bank's applicant-buyer or from any other party); and (c) their independent or abstract liability (i.e., its promise of payment does not depend upon the occurrence of acts, events, or transactions underlying the issuance of the LOC, but only on the compliance of the documents presented to the issuing or confirming banks). Thus, if the goods shipped do not meet all the specifications of the underlying sale agreement, but the tendered documents meet the specifications of the LOC, the issuing or confirming banks must pay. Only when the fraud perpetrated by the beneficiary is egregious enough to leave the banks with worthless paper are extraordinary or equitable remedies granted to the paying bank or its applicant, such as injunctions against payment or attachments of funds related to the LOC.

C. The Interchangeable Functions of Correspondent LOC Banks and Their Organic Marketplace Standard of Fairness

As just noted, the roles and functions of the above listed banks, and especially those of the issuing and confirming banks, are interchangeable. This interchangeability incorporates, organically so to speak, a marketplace standard of fairness as the governing standard of correspondent banks' transactions. The issuing banker who questions whether his confirming banker acted properly when paying or checking documents can obtain his answer by asking himself: What would I have done as an archetypal confirming bank? Such a marketplace standard of fairness is not as easily ascertainable in other trades or when the parties to the contract belong to different trades or professions. The functional need for reasonable and fair practices for LOCs makes it easier to discern their nuclear elements.

D. Standard and Best Practices for the Examination of LOC Documents

1. *The Birth of a Nuclear LOC Practice, Its Shapers and Practitioners*

During the early nineteenth century, English merchant bankers developed a multi-faceted form of banking which included loans to governments and reputable merchants. Their success obviously depended upon their knowledge of the trades they practiced and financed. The House of Brown,[93] one of the oldest and most respected merchant banking houses, started its business in Ireland by trading in linen, a commodity it knew well.[94] It sold its and others' goods on commission and extended

---

[92] Kozolchyk, *supra* note 89, at 331.

[93] EDWIN J. PERKINS, FINANCING ANGLO-AMERICAN TRADE, THE HOUSE OF BROWN, 1800–1880 17 (1975). Among the members of the House of Brown were Alexander Brown and Sons in Baltimore, Brown Brothers & Co. in New York, William and James Brown & Co. in Liverpool, and Brown and Shipley & Co. in London.

[94] *Id.* at 19. The House of Brown was founded by Alexander Brown, a successful Irish linen merchant who immigrated to the United States in the late 1790's. *Id.*

credit to importers and exporters, especially to and from the United States.[95] Most of these credits were documented by an accepted bill of exchange or draft that the beneficiary seller or exporter drew on the House of Brown as the acceptor and payor of the draft. Such drawing was based upon a previous authorization to draw given by the House of Brown to the beneficiary in question.

By the mid-nineteenth century, the House of Brown was a major issuer of promises to accept bills of exchange based on the above mentioned "authorizations" to draw. An 1838 communication by the House of Brown to its correspondent in New Orleans summarized this practice in connection with a possible purchase of cotton from a seller's commission agent:

> You are aware that our usual custom is to advance 2/3rd's or 3/4th's of the cost of the cotton. . . . We would arrange the business as follows. You may give him [the seller's commission agent or factor] an order for one thousand Bales or more on such terms as you may think proper and we will confirm the same *by authorizing him to draw on our New York house or here if to be done on as good terms as 60 days sight. . . .*[96]

The House of Brown would purchase the cotton and issue its "authorization" to the seller of the cotton at the same time so that it could be assured of acceptance and payment by a banker of known solvency. The time of payment was set at sixty days from the time the bill of exchange was presented. This authorization to draw the draft when followed by the presentation of a draft and accompanying documents to be accepted and/or paid by the issuing merchant banker became the first element of the nuclear practice of the commercial letters of credit, especially when issued not only on behalf of the House of Brown, but on behalf of other importers.[97] The above quote illustrates the birth of a nuclear practice: It started as a course of performance in a small number of contracts between the House of Brown and its initial clients. Eventually, it was transformed into a course of dealing involving a larger number of clients and a longer period of time, and eventually, after being tested in the marketplace it became the nuclear practice of a usage of trade.

The practice of authorizing and accepting the beneficiary's draft largely replaced another practice in which a draft and documents were presented to a bank or other trusted third party located at the buyer's place of business. The bank or trusted third party notified the buyer that the seller's draft and shipping documents had arrived and that the latter (mostly as a negotiable ocean bill of lading) would be delivered to the buyer if he paid for them at sight or if he signed as an acceptor of the bill of exchange or draft promising to pay it at a designated future time. Clearly, in this transaction, known as "documents against (the buyer's) payment or acceptance," the seller assumed the risks of the buyer's non-payment and possession of documents "of title" to the goods, such as the negotiable ocean bill of lading. This risk was eliminated by the House of Brown LOC, which embodied an irrevocable promise by an issuing or

---

[95] *Id.* at 19–22.

[96] *Id.* at 283 (emphasis added). Professor Perkins estimated that based on an average price of 8 cents per pound and bale weight of 400 lbs, this order was in the range of $32,000. *Id.*

[97] *Id.* at 25. Professor Perkins found the first reference to a LOC in the House of Brown records for 1820. *Id.*

confirming bank of known solvency at a time prior to the presentation of the draft and documents.

Please note that the nuclear LOC practice of issuing the authorization to draw a draft against the issuing merchant banker was initiated by giving something of value to the beneficiary (the authorization to draw) without receiving an immediate equivalent from him. The beneficiary's giving in return did not happen until the documents required by the LOC were presented to the issuing or confirming bank. And even though some English judges were not satisfied with the absence of an immediate *quid pro quo* as consideration for the issuing bank's promise,[98] the issuing bank gained the trust of the beneficiary and of subsequent participants in the transaction, including its correspondent banks; for the issuing bank, that was sufficient consideration.

Each of the nuclear participants in the LOC had to trust each other, some when issuing their binding promises, others (such as the beneficiary) by procuring shipping documents prior to being paid by the LOC, and still others (such as the issuing or confirming banks) by paying against documents instead of the actual goods. Because of this ever present trust, all of these regular participants were expected to act honestly, reasonably and fairly. Put simply, the elements of Karl Llewellyn's version of good faith that encompassed honesty, reasonableness and fairness were the essential elements of the nucleus in which the other elements of the LOC lived and interacted with each other. Once the above described "authorization to draw" nuclear practice came about and its regular and occasional participants were identified and their functions tested in the marketplace, the living law of LOCs was created first by courses of dealing and eventually by trade usages.

2. Macro and Micro-Economic Forces That Encouraged or Discouraged LOC Practices in the United States

In 1962, almost a century and a half after its initial use by a small number of Anglo-American merchant bankers, 55% of the international sales of the United States were paid or financed by LOCs[99] and much of the world's significant LOC litigation took place in the United States. The United States' markets for goods and services and banks were the engine that moved the LOC transaction worldwide. Yet it was not until 1962 that Article 5 of the U.C.C., the first LOC statute of the United States, was enacted.[100] It seemed apparent that LOCs did not require a code or statute to enable them to attain the commercial, financial and economic prominence they had.

In fact, however, the prominence of the LOC as an international payment and financial device occurred in the United States because of the enactment of the Federal Reserve Act of 1913.[101] It made it possible for United States banks to do what the House of Brown was doing in England since the middle of the nineteenth century: Authorize the presentation of the beneficiaries' drafts and accept and discount U.S. dollar-denominated drafts regardless of their provenance. As described by Wilbert Ward of Citibank, a lawyer's lawyer who was also a banker's banker and chairman of

---

[98] BORIS KOZOLCHYK, COMMERCIAL LETTERS OF CREDIT IN THE AMERICAS: A COMPARATIVE STUDY OF CONTEMPORARY COMMERCIAL TRANSACTIONS 573–90 (1966).

[99] *Id.* at 32.

[100] *Id.* at 351.

[101] Federal Reserve Act, 12 U.S.C. §§ 221–522 (1913); *see also* KOZOLCHYK, *supra* note 98, at 609–10. *See also* Paul Warburg's role in the enactment of this act, *supra* § 21:6(C)(1).

the New York Commercial Credit Conference,[102] as well the principal architect of LOC law and practice in the United States until the end of the Second World War:

> The federal reserve banking system brought the gold reserves of the [United States] . . . into the federal reserve banks, and the reserves of the member banks were carried primarily as credits on the books of the federal reserve banks. The secondary reserve of the member banks consisted of paper eligible for rediscount with the federal reserve banks. . . . In order to mobilize our mercantile credits, however, *it was necessary to change the business habits of the nation by converting these credits from book accounts and promissory notes into trade acceptances. The ability of the national banks to finance foreign trade was assisted by authorizing them to accept bills having not over 6 months to run and growing out of the importation or exportation of goods."*[103]

The italicized text summarizes the principal statutory basis for the issuance of LOC's as part of the business of banking. But it was more than that: It was the mechanism that enabled member banks to create their own highly liquid form of money (also referred to as quasi-money) in the form of widely marketable trade acceptances and not merely as accounts in the books of the issuing bank ("book accounts" in Mr. Ward's terminology). Thus, the Federal Reserve Act was not only the pioneering, but also the visionary statute and the macro-economic force behind the pre-eminent role played by United States banks in LOC transactions world-wide following the First World War.

Mr. Ward was also a shrewd observer of the effect that micro-economic market forces had upon commercial and banking practices, including the abandonment of good faith by many importers when expected profits were likely to dwindle or unexpected losses were about to occur. He noticed that differences in the interpretation of LOC terms did not lead to too many disputes as long as the prices of exports continued to rise. In good times, importers were willing to forego disputes knowing that prompt possession of the goods meant higher profits. As a reaction to those attitudes by their commercial applicants, New York banks adopted a policy of liberal interpretation of credit terms "in the interest of the prompt movement of goods . . ."[104] Yet, as prices stabilized, and in some cases dropped sharply, attitudes changed and the number of disputes grew geometrically.

Typically, when prices dropped sharply, issuers were instructed by applicants to "reject documents if the least irregularity appeared."[105] Ambiguous terms became

---

[102] *See* Dan Taylor, *U.S. Council on Int'l Banking and the UCP, A Brief History*, 6 LETTER OF CREDIT UPDATE 11, 11–12 (1990). This Conference was a study group of LOC practices comprised of thirty-four experienced international bankers from New York. For its history and influence on the drafting of the earliest compilation of LOC practices.

[103] WILBERT WARD, AMERICAN COMMERCIAL CREDITS 15–16 (1922) (emphasis added). *See also* JAMES E. BYRNE ET AL., UCP 600: AN ANALYTICAL COMMENTARY iii (2010) (attributing to Wilbert Ward the chairmanship of the ICC Committee of Bills of Exchange and Cheques, which later became the ICC Commission on Banking Technique and Practice, and oversaw the adoption of UCP 82 (1933) and its 1951 revision (UCP 151)). Byrne also quotes from a communication by Ward to the ICC dated October 1926 in which he stated that: "the International Chamber of Commerce could render a practical service to international trade by seeking to obtain international uniformity . . . by adopting uniform regulations for export commercial credits." *Id.*

[104] WARD, *supra* note 103, at 22.

[105] *Id.* at 23.

excuses to reject payment or reimbursement. One such term during Ward's time was an ocean bill of lading "evidencing shipment" of the merchandise. Because of the scarcity of vessels following World War I, carriers started issuing "received for shipment" or "received for transportation" bills of lading instead of the traditional "on board" bills of lading. A received for shipment bill was issued prior to the actual loading of the merchandise and evidenced receipt of the goods by the carrier, but not on board the carrying vessel. Therefore, unlike the "on board" bill of lading, the arrival of received for shipment goods could not be predicted or estimated. As Ward observed: "Merchants welcomed the new received-for-shipment [bills of lading] when they were exporters, and objected to it when they were importers."[106]

The banks found themselves in the middle of such disputes and their solution was to state as clearly as possible to United States beneficiaries and to foreign correspondent banks what documents and clauses were acceptable. Nonetheless, the importer bank's clients' reactions to unexpected lower profits or higher losses or the unavailability of cargo space in the port of New York created bad faith practices calculated to avoid having to reimburse banks that had used reasonable care in the examination of LOC documents. Most often these selfish practices resorted to specious and hypertechnical objections to the bankers' examination of the LOC documents.

§ 24.5 THE LIMITED ROLE OF JUDICIAL, STATUTORY OR CODIFIED LOC LAW

Prior to the enactment of Article 5 of the U.C.C., Article 3 of the U.C.C., which replaced the Negotiable Instruments Law, did not enforce promises or authorizations to draw unless they were accepted and signed in the draft or bill presented for acceptance and payment.[107] Yet if the nuclear promise of the LOC transaction was to accept the beneficiary's draft *written in advance of the presentation of his draft or bill of exchange and accompanying documents*, as just noted, how could such an acceptance enforce the draft if such a draft did not exist at the time the bank issued its promise of acceptance?

It is true that there was substantial case law on acceptances signified in documents other than the bill of exchange itself, and indeed some of these were called "extrinsic" and others "virtual" acceptances.[108] Yet these practices were not of much assistance to the various LOC banks, especially when the LOC practice required an organic connection between the obligation to pay upon the presentation of a specified set of documents (as signified in the extrinsic document) and the negotiation, endorsement and payment functions lodged with the draft or bill. What if these two documents did not travel together or contained inconsistent stipulations? Consequently, the transactional innovation introduced by the House of Brown authorization and acceptance practice lacked a statutory or judicial basis for its enforcement.

---

106 *Id.* at 25.

107 U.C.C. § 4–110 (1962). This section, as well as its present version in § 3–409(a) (2013), require that the acceptance must be written on the bill of exchange.

108 HERMAN N. FINKELSTEIN, LEGAL ASPECTS OF COMMERCIAL LETTERS OF CREDIT 42–92 (1930). To this day, the best treatment of the subject of virtual and extrinsic acceptances in English and United States law is by Herman Finkelstein.

The enforcement of such a legally unpedigreed promise was at first only handled by Anglo-American court decisions, some of which were responsible for either enunciating or validating some of the basic principles and rules for the judicial or arbitral enforcement of LOC rights and duties. However, starting in the 1950s with promulgation of the 1951 and, much later, 1962 revisions of the UCP, courts in important United States financial centers, such as New York, Massachusetts, Illinois, Pennsylvania and California, relied on the UCP as the principal source for the adjudication of documentary compliance issues in a growing number of judicial, albeit equitable, actions for remedies.

Not surprisingly, and much to the chagrin of the drafters of Article 5 of the U.C.C., the state of New York (among other states) adopted a "non-conforming" amendment to Article 5 in 1964. Accordingly, Original Article 5 was applied only if the credit did not expressly incorporate the UCP. If the LOC stated that it was governed by the UCP, it governed instead of the U.C.C.[109] This New York amendment illustrated the power enjoyed by the UCP as a positive law source of LOC law. Even though the UCP was a usage of trade and thus a customary law source, it displaced statutory law as the pre-eminent source and it did so in the most important LOC jurisdiction in the world.[110]

I have selected the process of drafting of UCP 500, which was published in 1993, as the focal point for discussion and comparison with the Roman secured lending practices because as a participant in that process, I had the opportunity to observe the transformation of standard practices into practice-inspired and formally adopted rules. In addition, UCP 500 was the revision that promulgated the largest amount of significant new rules and profited most from interaction between bankers and lawyers. But before we study the drafting of UCP, it will be helpful to be able to contrast its distinctive features with some of the UCP's customary law predecessors.

---

[109] U.C.C. § 5–102(4) (1964). New York adopted a non-conforming amendment to this section that provided:

> Unless otherwise agreed, this art. 5 does not apply to a LOC if by its terms or by agreement, course of dealing or usage of trade such LOC or credit is subject in whole or in part to the Uniform Customs and Practice for Commercial Documentary Credits fixed by the Thirteenth or any other Congress of the International Chamber of Congress.

N.Y. U.C.C. LAW § 5–102(4) (McKinney 1964). Similar non-conforming amendments were enacted by Alabama, Arizona, and Missouri. *See* ALA. CODE § 7–5–102(4) (1977); ARIZ. REV. STAT. ANN. § 47–5102(D) (1967); MO. REV. STAT. 400.5–102(4) (West 1983).

[110] It is also worth mentioning as an indication of the legitimating and remedial power of banking practice that even France's *Cour de Cassation* (whose preference for positive law over commercial customary law is well known) had been granting appeals based on the misinterpretation of the UCP as positive law. For examples of appeals to the *Cour de Cassation* based upon the lower courts' misinterpretation of law, *see* Cour de cassation [Cass.] [supreme court for judicial matters] com., Apr. 9, 1996, Bull. Civ. IV, No. 94–20.407 (Fr.) (where one of the grounds for the cassation type of appeal was that "*la cour d'appel a viole l'article 1134 du Code civil, ensemble les articles 44 et 45 des regles et usances uniformes*" (the court of appeals misinterpreted article 1134 of the Civil Code and articles 44 and 45 of the UCP)); Cour de cassation [Cass.] [supreme court for judicial matters] com., Nov. 29, 1994, Bull Civ. IV, No. 92–15175 (Fr.) (where the basis for appeal was the misinterpretation of Article 16 of UCP 400). Similar deference to the UCP as a primary source of LOC law was apparent in Japanese and German decisions. For Japanese decisions that defer to the UCP as a primary source of law, *see* Tōkyō Chihō Saibansho [Tōkyō Dist. Ct] Aug. 28, 1989, Kinyu Shoji Hanrei 8–9, 33–38 (court upheld UCP 290 Articles 3 and 4 exemptions for the loss of documents by a correspondent bank "unless the choice or supervision of a correspondent was grossly negligent. . . .") (translation by Professor Kazuaki Sono); Tōkyō Chihō Saibansho [Tōkyō Dist. Ct] May 29, 1987, Kinyu Shoji Hanrei 781, 38–43 (court applied and upheld UCP 290 Article 12 (a)'s allocation of the risk because "reliance upon the UCP has become a commercial custom . . .") (translation by Professor Kazuaki Sono). For German decisions, *see supra* § 23:9(F). Consequently, by the 1970s and 80s, the UCP was regarded as both positive and living law throughout most of the commercial banking world, especially on issues of documentary compliance.

§ 24.6 PREDECESSORS OF UCP 500

A. The New York Bankers Regulations Affecting Export Commercial Credits of 1920 (New York 1920 Regulations)[111]

These New York 1920 Regulations were directed to the correspondent banks of the New York bank members of the New York Commercial Credit Conference and not to any other parties of the LOC transaction such as the issuing bank's applicant or to the beneficiary of the LOC. Other significant features flow from the micro-economic force that prompted the bad faith practices of importers identified earlier by Ward. Such bad faith practices explain the presence of two other features of the New York 1920 Regulations: 1) A stipulated nomenclature, and 2) the role of the New York bank members of the New York Commercial Credit Conference as the exclusive coiners of the meaning of the terms used in the LOC and in the documents presented for payment by their correspondent banks.

Accordingly, the New York 1920 Regulations were addressed: "TO CORRESPONDENTS" and Regulations 2 and 3 stated in relevant part:

> 2. We will interpret the terms "documents," "shipping documents" and words of similar import, as comprehending only ocean bills of lading (sailor bill of lading included) and marine and war risk insurance, in negotiable form, with invoices.
>
> 3. Unless specifically otherwise instructed, we will accept "received for transportation" bills of lading in the form customarily issued in New York. (The steamship lines constituting the Transatlantic Conference state that the customary procedure necessitated by American port conditions, is to issue bills of lading against the receipt of goods into the custody of the steamship owners or agents, for transportation by a named steamer, and failing shipment by said steamer, with liberty to ship in and upon a prior or following steamer.[112]

Please note first the use of the corporate "we" as the coiners or definers of the meaning of LOC and documentary terms. However, there was more than style to the use of the corporate "we": It was a unilateral and binding declaration by the New York bankers of what was acceptable to them as advisers or notifiers, confirmers, negotiators and payors of foreign-issued LOCs.

Note also the prominence of the disparities between the shipping and bill of lading practices that resulted in the issuance of a "received for transportation" bill of lading and a "received on board" or plain "on board" bill of lading. These disparities were significant enough that the bankers who preferred the on board practice found it necessary to ask the Transatlantic Conference why they would issue only "for transportation" rather than "on board the vessel" bills of lading. Was it because of the very crowded conditions of American ports, especially at the conclusion of the First

---

111 *See* Dan Taylor, *Text, First U.S. Rules Affective Export Credits*, 6 LETTER OF CREDIT UPDATE 40 (1990) (for the full text of these 1920 Regulations). The complete title of these regulations is: Regulations Affecting Export Commercial Credits Adopted by the New York Bankers Commercial Credit Conference of 1920. Letter of Credit Update is presently published by the Institute of International Banking Law & Practice as Documentary Credit World.

112 *Id.* at 41.

World War? Finally, note the importance given to a broad disclaimer clause, which is also explained, at least in part, by the bad faith practices alluded to by Ward:

> 1. We assume no liability or responsibility for the form, sufficiency, correctness, genuineness or legal effect of any documents, or for the description, quantity, quality, condition, delivery or value of the merchandise represented thereby, or for the good faith or acts of the shipper or any other person whomsoever; but documents will be examined with care sufficient to ascertain whether on their face they appear to be regular in general form.[113]

Some of the principles that guided merchant banking practices for years to come were implicit in this wording. For example, the disclaimer of responsibility for the sufficiency, correctness and genuineness of the tendered documents was a consequence of the principle of independence between the LOC promise of payment and the underlying transaction's claims, defenses or equities. Further, the reference to "care sufficient to ascertain whether on their face they appear to be regular in general form" implemented the requirement of mere facial compliance, which was a corollary of the principle of independence.

B. The Uniform Customs and Practices for Documentary Credits (UCP)

As the bankers of other continents began to master the LOC business and acquired the necessary solvency and liquidity to act as confirming and negotiating banks of the LOCs issued by their correspondent banks in other nations, the drafting of LOC practices on the examination of documents underwent a fundamental shift. They were no longer the practices of a group of banks in a major financial and trading center. The time had come for truly international practices. The ICC seemed to be at the right place and time to help develop such practices by acting as the host for their compilation and drafting.

The ICC was created during an international congress of chambers of commerce and industrial associations in Atlantic City, New Jersey in 1919. A year later, it opened its doors in Paris as a non-governmental federation of world-wide commercial, industrial and professional associations.[114] Unlike other organizations, it could rely on a vast network of national associations representing economic sectors gathered under umbrella organizations or councils. Proposals for international harmonization or standardization of commercial and financial practices could be initiated by national members through their respective councils or directly by national members participating in the ICC international sectoral committees.[115] Before we turn to these formal, institutionally sponsored or hosted international compilations of checking practices, we need pay a short visit to individual bank sources of LOC practices.

---

[113] *Id.*

[114] ERIC A. CAPRIOLI, 27 LE CREDIT DOCUMENTAIRE: EVOLUTION ET PERSPECTIVES 119–20 (1992). *See generally* GEORGE L. RIDGEWAY, MERCHANTS OF PEACE: THE HISTORY OF THE INTERNATIONAL CHAMBER OF COMMERCE (1959) (for a more detailed history and description of activities of the ICC).

[115] In the case of LOCs, the sectoral committee was at first called Checks, Bills of Exchange and Documentary Credits, and eventually renamed the Commission on Banking Technique and Practice.

C. Bankers' Documentary Examination Manuals and Checklists

As part of their daily business of examining documents, the most experienced and respected LOC bankers started drafting internal manuals full of directives on the acceptability or rejection of documents. Known in the LOC trade as checklists, these manuals were exchanged with correspondent banks and at that stage of the interaction often served as an initial laboratory of the viability of the practice. Generally, the checklists were nothing more than terse, unexplained instructions on how to examine the document in question, what statements or descriptions to look for, and so on. Occasionally, a highly experienced and respected banker would also provide the reasons for a suggested practice in an examination manual. One such a manual was Frank Sauter's *Random Notes on Commercial Credits*, a set of two booklets.[116] Sauter was a vice president of First National City Bank of New York during the 1950s and 60s. He was not only a model document checker, but also a teacher of standard and best practices in the United States and other countries where his bank had offices. He attributed his motivation for writing *Random Notes on Commercial Credits* to a request by a young banker who came to him "not seeking information alone or trying to learn whether the answers were yes or no. . . . [but wanting] to know the 'why' behind the answers . . ."[117]

His discussion of "stale" bills of lading illustrates why this young banker sought him out. Article 43 of the UCP (1933) had attempted to define a stale bill of lading, but had done so in a circular manner:

> Documents must be presented without delay. Banks may refuse documents if presented to them too late, in other words at a date not justified by the usual time to cover the distance between the place of dispatch and the place where payment is made.

Yet, terms such as "too late" or "usual time," when related to the time it took to cover the distance between the place of dispatch and where payment was to be made, did not explain why a bill of lading was truly stale. Sauter rightly pointed out that the above provision "is the rule but not the answer which so many seek to this frequently heard question."[118] He added that this rule seems to give the banks the last word on what constitutes a stale bill of lading when in fact it is not the bank's judgment of what is the usual time, but transactional considerations such as the availability of the bill of lading to the bank's applicant when the vessel arrives at its port of destination:

> [A]t one time it was popular [for bankers] to say offhand and with some authority that a bill of lading was stale if presented so many days late. . . . When this question is put to us in New York, *we answer it by saying that as a rule if we can airmail the documents in time to reach their destination on or before the arrival of the vessel carrying the goods*, we will not regard the documents as stale.[119]

---

116 FRANK SAUTER, I RANDOM NOTES ON COMMERCIAL CREDITS (1960) [hereinafter SAUTER I]; FRANK SAUTER, II RANDOM NOTES ON COMMERCIAL CREDITS (1963) [hereinafter SAUTER II].

117 SAUTER I, *supra* note 116, at *Foreword*.

118 *Id.* at 24.

119 *Id.* (emphasis added).

Note that in contrast with Article 43 of UCP 1933, Sauter's version of staleness was focused on the unavailability of the bill of lading at the time of the arrival of the vessel. The reason for this focus was that the arrival of the goods prior to the arrival of the bill of lading can cause significant costs to the applicant. They include the need to store the goods in expensive refrigerated warehouses as well as the payment of costly demurrage and damages owed by the applicant-consignee of the goods to third parties as result of their failure to receive them at a promised date. This transactional fact meant that a bill of lading could be stale even if it arrived within the usual time to cover the distance between the place of dispatch and the place where payment is made. In my opinion, Sauter's version of staleness is still the best explanation for a practice of presentation of transport documents that the UCP, for sound pragmatic reasons, limits to a twenty-one day period.[120]

The same was true with the proverbial formulation of a nuclear element of the LOC cellular transaction, imbedded in the UCP since its 1951 revision: "In documentary credit operations, all parties concerned deal in documents and not in goods."[121] He illustrated the centrality of this proverbial principle with an anecdote in which an applicant requested that his bank "sell" him an LOC that would assure him that the same olive oil in a bottled sample he handed over to the bank would be the one received from the foreign seller. In response to this request, Sauter stated:

> Of course, we could have accommodated him if we had wanted to, but experience has taught us to "mind our own business," and that is the banking business. . . . No bank that knows the commercial credit business would enter into a transaction of this kind just to accommodate this stranger, or even its very best customer. It would be impractical for a bank to do so anyhow when you stop to think about it, as the stranger did after a while.[122]

Clearly, the practices suggested and explained by Sauter had a discernible purpose that was cost effective, profitable, reasonable and fair to correspondents, whether customers or third parties.

D. The Uniform Customs and Practices for Documentary Credits (UCP 1933 Revision)

Despite the occasional presence of enlightened practice manuals that could contribute to a better understanding of LOC practices everywhere, the time had come for a truly international compilation of standard and best LOC practices. Given its international, world-wide character, the natural host entity for such a compilation was the ICC and the vehicle was a set of internationally uniform customs and practices. The first version of the UCP, known as the "Uniform Customs and Practices for Documentary Credits Fixed by the 7th Congress of the International Chamber of Commerce," was published in 1933 by the ICC as Brochure 82. It was heavily influenced by a set of banking practices labeled *Uniform Regulations for Commercial Documentary Credits*, which were adopted during the ICC's 1929 Amsterdam Congress and whose authorship was attributed by an ICC brochure to United States bankers.

---

[120] *See, e.g.*, UCP 500 art. 43(a); UCP 600 art. 14(c).

[121] INT'L CHAMBERS OF COMMERCE, UNIFORM CUSTOMS AND PRACTICE FOR COMMERCIAL DOCUMENTARY CREDITS [UCP] No. 151, art. 10 (1951) [hereinafter UCP 151].

[122] SAUTER II, *supra* note 116, at 45.

The purpose of these regulations was to harmonize those previously adopted and published by banking associations in various countries. As with the New York 1920 Regulations, the Amsterdam Regulations continue the emphasis on setting forth a uniform nomenclature and thus define "commercial documentary credits"[123] as well as the main types. It also set forth the issuing and confirming bank's standard of care for the examination of the LOC documents and instructed the banker to "ascertain that on their face they appear to be in regular form."[124] And it enunciated the so-called independence principle as follows: "Commercial Documentary Credits are essentially distinct transactions from sales contracts on which they may be based and with which banks are not concerned."[125]

This 1933 revision adopted, albeit in a more succinct form, the same principle of independence found in the 1929 Uniform Regulations. Thus, LOCs were "[D]istinct transactions from sales contracts, on which they may be based, with which Banks are not concerned."[126] Similarly, it adopted a standard for the examination of documents and papers that required "care so as to ascertain that on their face [the documents and papers] appear to be in order."[127] *The absence of a reference to strict compliance as the standard for the LOC documents in this first version of the UCP is noteworthy. It reflected the foreignness of this judicial doctrine of strictness for the sake of strictness to what bankers regarded as their examination practice.*[128] The fact is that the judicially created principle of strict compliance had misperceived the kind of compliance that archetypal document checkers regarded as reasonable and desirable, as I will discuss in a later section.

E. The Uniform Customs and Practices for Documentary Credits (UCP 1951 Revision)

Two features of the 1951 revision of the UCP deserve attention. The first was Article 10's proverbial formulation of the principle of independence or abstraction: "In documentary credit operations, *all parties concerned deal in documents and not in goods.*"[129] I should add that when the principle behind a commercial practice can be expressed in such a proverbial fashion, it is a sign that the underlying practice has gained widespread, if not universal, acceptance.[130] The second feature was its reference to "all parties concerned," suggesting an inclusion of occasional participants in the circle of regular participants and an incipient concern with the status of third parties. This revision was not characterized by the inclusion of new practices, but by

---

[123] *See* INT'L CHAMBERS OF COMMERCE, UNIFORM REGULATIONS FOR COMMERCIAL DOCUMENTARY CREDITS, § A (1)–(9) (1929).

[124] *Id.* § B(1).

[125] *Id.* § A(1).

[126] INT'L CHAMBERS OF COMMERCE, UNIFORM CUSTOMS AND PRACTICE FOR COMMERCIAL DOCUMENTARY CREDITS [UCP] No. 82, art. 1 (1933).

[127] *Id.* art. 10.

[128] *Id.* Article 10 only requires from a bank that negotiates or pays and seeks reimbursement for it that its payment or negotiation be "in conformity with the terms and conditions of the relevant letter of credit." *Id.*

[129] UCP 151, *supra* note 121, art. 10 (emphasis added).

[130] In fact, this proverbial formulation had been used in the beginning sentence of art. 10 of UCP 1933, but perhaps because of the much larger number of LOCs issued in 1951, this version was often credited as being the one that introduced this proverbial principle.

widespread adoptions of the UCP, as it stood in earlier versions, by many banking associations around the world.

F. The 1962, 1974 and 1983 Revisions: Bernard Wheble and Lawyers as Participants in the Drafting Groups

In 1961, the British Bankers' Association (BBA) joined the ICC Working Group in drafting the 1962 revision of the UCP[131] and named Bernard S. Wheble, at first an observer, and subsequently a participant in this group. Wheble was a senior LOC banker for London's Brown and Shipley's (of House of Brown fame). He was Great Britain's and one of the world's most respected LOC bankers. Soon after joining the ICC's Commission on Banking Technique and Practice, he became the leading draftsman and principal author of the two subsequent (1974 and 1983) revisions of the UCP.

Times were changing and fast. By the time Wheble chaired the 1974 and 1983 revisions, the regular participants in the LOC transaction and their third parties were a much more heterogeneous group than those he dealt with at Brown and Shipley's. The group included Charles Bontoux, one of France's most distinguished banking lawyers and one of the draftsmen of the 1951 revision of UCP, as well as of the 1962, 1974 and 1983 revisions.[132] I was fortunate to have corresponded with this fine jurist and banker for a number of years and as a result became aware of the differing points of view between him, Bernard Wheble and myself on the role of lawyers as draftsmen of the UCP.

UCP 290 (1974) was largely drafted by Wheble and was adopted by bank associations in over 150 countries, including most socialist nations.[133] It ushered in a new group of transport documents prompted by the container revolution.[134] It also added certainty to one aspect of the issuer's and confirmer's promise to the beneficiary: It made it clear that the issuer's undertaking to purchase or negotiate the beneficiary's draft was without recourse on the beneficiary, thereby making their payment final.[135]

From Bontoux, I learned of Wheble's reluctance to accept my suggestion of a reasonable document checker standard for the examination of documents despite the repeated references to the document checker's reasonable care in earlier versions of the UCP.[136] The same was true with legal or equitable remedies. Wheble agreed that given

---

[131] This was the first revision designated not only by its date but also by the number of the ICC publication. The 1962 revision of the UCP was also referred to as ICC Publication 222.

[132] *See* INT'L CHAMBERS OF COMMERCE, TRIBUTE TO CHARLES BONTOUX, No. 470/496 (1987).

[133] *See* Boris Kozolchyk, *Towards New Customs and Practices for Documentary Credits; The Methodology of the Proposed Revision*, *in* COMMERCIAL LAW ANNUAL 1993 371, 377 (Louis F. Del Duca & Patrick Del Duca ed., 1992).

[134] *See* INT'L CHAMBERS OF COMMERCE, UNIFORM CUSTOMS AND PRACTICE FOR DOCUMENTARY CREDITS [UCP] No. 290, art. 23 (1974) [hereinafter UCP 290].

[135] *See id.* art. 3(a)(iii) ("to purchase/negotiate, without recourse to drawers and/or bona fide holders. . . ."). *See also* E.P. Ellinger, *The Uniform Customs and Practice for Documentary Credits—The 1993 Revision*, 3 L.M.C.L.Q. 377, n.17 (1994). As noted by Ellinger, "without such a provision, the law of negotiable instruments would lead to the opposite conclusion: Bills of Exchange Act 1882, ss. 43(2)." *Id.*

[136] *See* Boris Kozolchyk, *In Which the Writer Takes a Tongue-In-Cheek Look at American v. British English*, 3 DOCUMENTARY CREDIT INSIGHT (1997) (where I refer to an article written by Wheble in the same publication under the pseudonim Mercator). In this article, he criticized my suggestion of using the standard of reasonableness in connection with the banker's examination of the documents as being contrary to its ordinary usage in England. The article states:

the private status of the ICC as a law giver, the UCP could not be drafted as a supra-national mandatory law. Its usage of trade status should be maintained and strengthened. Additionally, in his view, it was not necessary for the UCP to rely on equitable remedies or sanctions because LOC bankers are as good as their word and if they did not observe the UCP or acted in bad faith, they would not remain in the LOC business for long. That, he concluded, was as much of a sanction as the UCP could or should provide.

When I became one of the drafters of UCP 500 in the early 1990s, Wheble sill retained these views. Wheble and I became friends and in many enjoyable exchanges of opinions he heard my reasoning. For example, on the need for the UCP to consider relying on equitable remedies, I pointed to Article 16 of UCP 400, whose preclusion rule was the UCP's most cost effective non-judicial dispute resolution practice. It addressed the situations in which an issuing or confirming bank did not return the supposedly non-complying documents to the beneficiary in a manner timely enough to enable the cure of the discrepancies and re-presentation of the documents or when an issuing or confirming bank returned the documents in a timely manner, but did not state the reason for their rejection.

According to Article 16 of the UCP 400, if an issuing or confirming bank found discrepancies that merited the refusal of the documents, it was obligated to give timely notice of the defects and of the fact that the documents were being held at the disposal of the beneficiary or presenting bank. If the issuing or confirming bank failed to do so, the bank was "precluded from claiming that the documents are not in accordance with the terms and conditions of the credit."[137] This preclusion was strict in the sense that the beneficiary did not have to show that the bank's dereliction caused him material damage. In addition, it relied on an extrajudicial remedy effected by merely debiting the account of the derelict bank or crediting the account of the diligent bank with a paying bank. Despite its informality, this remedy or sanction had saved and continues to save banks, their applicants and beneficiaries incalculable sums in transactional and judicial costs and fees.

I also reminded Wheble of another living law remedy that saves considerable transactional and judicial costs—the abandonment of goods with the negligent or bad faith banker by the applicant or beneficiary. An aggrieved applicant can abandon the goods improperly paid for by the issuing bank by leaving them with the bank. And an aggrieved beneficiary can abandon the goods with the bank that wrongfully dishonored his presentation of complying documents. While this remedy would still be unacceptable in civil law jurisdictions that require all contractual rescissions to be

---

> According to the said Wheble, 'reasonable' in British English denoted someone who was neither particularly good nor bad at what he or she was doing . . . just middling; certainly he or she could not be one who could persuasively testify in court on what honest and knowledgeable bankers would do under the circumstances. Consequently, argued Wheble, the term "reasonable banker" or "reasonable document checker" would be misleading to British courts, bankers and banking lawyers. He suggested the use of other terms more consistent with British English such as "reasoned" checker.

Id. I pointed out that learned English judges starting with Lord Mansfield to many in our time relied on the term reasonable to depict a merchant or bank that not only knew his trade but had the interest of other traders in mind when selecting a course of dealing and eventually a practice. *Id.*

137 INT'L CHAMBERS OF COMMERCE, UNIFORM CUSTOMS AND PRACTICE FOR DOCUMENTARY CREDITS [UCP] No. 400, art. 16(e) (1983) [hereinafter UCP 400].

judicial,[138] it is widely used in other less formalistic jurisdictions and in private negotiations, mediation and arbitration. Towards the end of our discussions, and sadly shortly before his death, I had the impression that he was beginning to relent in his opposition to what he referred to as "lawyers' intrusions" into the sacred domain of banking practices.

§ 24.7 UCP 400 PROBLEMS AND UCP 500 CURES

With the marked increases in the world-wide use of LOCs and despite Wheble's best efforts when drafting UCP 400, bad faith practices proliferated during its lifetime (1984–1993).[139] Some of these practices involved applicants and issuing banks attempting to mislead beneficiaries and third parties into thinking that the credits issued were irrevocable when in fact they could be revoked. Others took place during the negotiation of the drafts and documents and resulted in the charge by purported negotiating banks of fees or commissions in exchange for insignificant or valueless services. UCP 400 also granted to FIATA, a Belgian-based association of freight forwarders, the exclusive right to issue ocean bills of lading as agents for the carrier, a right that was not enjoyed by other freight forwarders, whether acting as associations or as individuals.[140]

The large majority of bad faith practices were associated with a hypertechnical strict examination of the documents by issuing banks.[141] In this respect, the challenge faced by UCP 500 when trying to encourage good faith practices in the marketplace and in the courtroom was reminiscent of that faced by the Roman praetor when he had to resort to the *exceptio doli*.[142] Please bear in mind as we proceed with the analysis of UCP 500 that the same praetorian rationale that disallowed reliance on strict law as a shield for abusive or malicious practices could have applied to the judicial versions of strict compliance of LOC documents that will be discussed shortly.

A. Revocability-Express or Hidden and Uncertainty of the Credit Promise

One of the main goals of UCP 500 was to support the integrity and reliability of the documentary credit promise.[143] The Working Group was aware of complaints by national delegations concerning the periodic issuance of LOCs that were silent or ambiguous on their revocability. It agreed that the generalized uncertainty about

---

138 *See infra* § 28:3.

139 UCP 400, *supra* note 137; *see also* James E. Byrne, *The 1983 Revision of the Uniform Customs and Practice for Documentary Credits*, 102 BANKING L. J. 151, 171–172 (1985); *see generally* Boris Kozolchyk, *The 1983 Revision, Trade Practices and Court Decisions: A Plea for a Closer Relationship*, 9 CAN. BUS. L. J. 214 (1984).

140 *See* Boris Kozolchyk, *The Unwarranted Comeback of the FIATA Bill of Lading*, *in* ANNUAL SURVEY OF LETTER OF CREDIT LAW & PRACTICE 135 (James E. Byrne & Christopher S. Byrnes eds., 2006) (for a brief account of the decision to remove the FIATA privilege and an attempt to reinstate it) [hereinafter Kozolchyk, *The Unwarranted Comeback*].

141 *See* Kozolchyk, *Towards New Customs*, *supra* note 133, at 407–08 (for a graphic illustration of the problems reported by LOC to the Working Committee that drafted UCP 500).

142 *See supra* § 23:1(C) (discussing the *exceptio doli's* role in shaping the Roman law doctrine of good faith).

143 Kozolchyk, *Towards New Customs*, *supra* note 133, at 376.

revocability among beneficiaries and correspondent banks required UCP 500's reversal of the presumption of revocability.[144]

Another problem with the uncertainty of revocability was the issuance of revocable LOCs disguised as irrevocable. These LOCs were labeled irrevocable, but contained conditions that left the irrevocability of the LOC in the hands of issuing banks and their applicants. A popular disguise of irrevocability was that of LOCs known in LOC practice as "pre-advices." Typically, the issuer of a pre-advice informed the beneficiary that his payment would be made upon receipt of funds from the applicant. Other pre-advices, such as that in the 1999 decision of *Hamilton Bank, N.A. v. Kookmin Bank*, listed as a condition to the issuer's payment the presentation of "a copy of authenticated. . .telex *from issuing bank* to advising bank, indicating quantity to be shipped, destination and nominating transporting company."[145] In other words, despite the irrevocable designation of its LOC, Hamilton Bank would instruct its correspondent not to pay until Hamilton had submitted an authenticated telex authorizing payment.[146]

Having in mind the serious effects that these bad faith practices had against applicants, beneficiaries and correspondent banks, the Working Group warned banks not to issue such pre-advices unless their issuer was prepared to issue "the operative credit instrument or amendment thereto." Where such a pre-advice had been issued, unless the recipient disclosed that it was not binding, Article 11(c) of UCP 500 deemed the deceptive issuer "irrevocably committed to issue or amend the Credit, in terms not inconsistent with the pre-advice, without delay."[147] Thus, this rule applied another equitable, extrajudicial remedy (a species in the genus of specific performance) and thereby strengthened the aggrieved beneficiary's or correspondent bank's extrajudicial remedy in an arbitration proceeding and facilitated the claim for specific performance before a court of law.

B. An Issuer or Confirmer's Primary Liability

Uncertainty also prevailed among regular participants and third parties, including secured creditors interested in using the LOC as collateral. The main uncertainty was created by the manner in which UCP 290 and 400 referred to the LOC as an undertaking. According to Article 10(a)(i) of UCP 400, an irrevocable LOC was "a definite undertaking of the issuing bank . . . if the credit provides for sight payment—to pay, *or that payment will be made. . . .*"[148] The words "or that payment will be made" were being used by banks in some Asian countries to place primary liability not on the issuing or confirming banks, but on the applicant and his surety or sureties. Thus, it was not clear to potential secured creditors, among others, whether the beneficiary or his transferee who presented the required documents to the issuing bank had to claim

---

144 UCP 290, *supra* note 134, art. 1(c). It states: "In the absence of such indication the credit shall be deemed to be revocable." *Id.* This presumption was repeated in UCP 400, *supra* note 137, art. 7(c). It was reversed by UCP 500. UCP 500, *supra* note 120, art. 6(c). Art. 6(c) states: "In the absence of such indication the Credits shall be deemed to be irrevocable." *Id.*

145 Hamilton Bank, N.A. v. Kookmin Bank, 44 F. Supp. 2d 653, 655 (S.D.N.Y 1999) (emphasis added).

146 *Id.* at 656. As apparent in this court decision, this deceitful practice was the object of a complaint to the Office of the Comptroller of the Currency of the United States.

147 UCP 500, *supra* note 120, art. 11(c).

148 UCP 400, *supra* note 137, art. 10(a)–10(a)(i) (emphasis added).

first from the applicant or sureties, and then only if they did not pay could they claim the definite undertaking of the issuing or confirming bank. Considering that such a definition led to uncertainty and to bad faith practices, the words "or that payment will be made" were eliminated.

C. An Uncertain Time of Establishment

An additional uncertainty was caused by not knowing when liability of an irrevocable LOC was established. Assume that a correspondent bank that had been asked to confirm an LOC by telex (still a popular method of inter-bank communication during the 1980s) had issued such a confirmation only to receive a phone communication by the issuing bank instructing it to cancel it a few hours later. During my interviews with both money center and inland bank document checkers in the United States, it became clear that a confirming bank could not be reasonably expected to rely on the Society for Worldwide Interbank Financial Telecommunication (hereafter S.W.I.F.T.) message asking it to confirm an LOC via S.W.I.F.T. if it was going to be instructed to retract that message hours or minutes later by a phone message. Consequently, the unanimous opinion of the Working Group of UCP 500 was that the time of establishment of liability should be fixed when the LOC was issued and sent to the correspondent bank or beneficiary by whatever means.

This practice was unacceptable to some of the banking associations and it was shelved only to be adopted by Article 5 of the U.C.C. and by the United Nations Convention on Independent Guarantees and Stand-By Letters of Credit.[149] Eventually, Article 7(b) of UCP 600 reverted to the original version of the UCP 500 establishment rule: "An issuing bank is irrevocably bound to honour as of the time it issues the credit."[150]

D. Uncertain Finality of Payment by the Confirming Bank

Many banks were uncertain whether the rule of finality of payment of the issuing bank in UCP 290 and 400 was also applicable to issuing banks. In other words, was the payment by the confirming bank to the beneficiary at the maturity of the LOC or at an earlier time as a result of its negotiation of the beneficiary's draft? This was an important clarification because the issuing and the confirming banks performed equal and parallel undertakings. It was also important because a growing number of confirming banks, when acting as negotiators of the LOCs they had confirmed, treated their negotiations of the beneficiaries' drafts as subject to recourse against the beneficiary if they were not reimbursed by the issuing banks that nominated them as confirmers. Article 9(a)(iv) and (b)(iv) of UCP 500 clarified that the negotiations by both the issuing and the confirming bank were without recourse on the beneficiary.

---

[149] U.C.C. § 5–106 (2012). It states: "A letter of credit is issued and becomes enforceable according to its terms against the issuer when the issuer sends or otherwise transmits it to the person requested to advise or to the beneficiary." *Id.* Similarly, art. 7 (1) of the United Nations Convention on Indpendent Guarantees and Stand-By Letters of Credit states that: "Issuance of an undertaking occurs when and where the undertaking leaves the sphere of control of the guarantor/issuer concerned." G.A. Res. 50/48. art. 7, U.N. Doc. A/RES/50/48 (Jan. 26, 1996). Sub-section 3 adds: From the time of issuance of an undertaking, a demand for payment may be made . . ." *Id.* art. 7 subsec. 3.

[150] UCP 600, *supra* note 120, art. 7(b).

E. Negotiation of the LOC Draft and Commissions: Good Faith and Reasonableness

The responses to the surveys conducted by Charles del Busto, then the president of the ICC Banking Commission, as well as to my questionnaires and interviews, showed that the term negotiation was in urgent need of clarification. From an operational standpoint, a major source of disputes regarding negotiation among beneficiaries and negotiating, issuing, or confirming banks was the charge of a negotiation commission that beneficiaries thought was unjustified. In some of these disputes, different banks acting as negotiating, issuing or confirming banks claimed to have been the true negotiators and thus entitled to the negotiation commission.

From a strictly legal and procedural standpoint, the most important disputes on negotiation concerned the holder in due course status claimed by banks who allegedly had negotiated the beneficiary's drafts drawn against the issuing or confirming bank. When such a bank succeeded in attaining the status of holder in due course, it was immunized in most jurisdictions against claims by the applicant and the issuing or confirming bank that it had negotiated fraudulent documents and thus was not entitled to payment or reimbursement of the amount due on the LOC.[151] As often happens with rules based upon commercial or banking practices, symmetry must exist between the operational and legal terminology—in our case between the operational meaning of negotiation and the legal meaning of holding the beneficiary's draft in due course.

Since the claims of fraudulent tender of documents multiplied during the 1980s, especially with the large volume of shipments to and from China, this legal clarification was of considerable commercial and economic significance. The UCP 500's mission was to provide an answer that was satisfactory to correspondent bankers disputing their claims to negotiation commissions and to the courts, lawyers and bankers involved in LOC fraud disputes. The meaning of negotiation was central in four different practices and in the determination of whether a given bank was a holder in due course.

According to Practice One, negotiation meant that the issuing or confirming banks would examine the documents submitted to them at a date prior to the specified date for the acceptance of the draft or for payment of the LOC. This examination was followed by the negotiating bank's acceptance or payment of an amount that reflected the discounted value of the acceptance or advanced payment. This negotiation was without recourse on the beneficiary and thus it amounted to a final payment of the LOC.

In Practice Two, the acceptance or payment was made by a bank that had been authorized to negotiate the LOC as part of a general or individual authorization. The commission or fee for negotiation would also take into account the discounted value of the advanced acceptance or payment as well as whether it was negotiated with or without recourse on the beneficiary.

---

151 Boris Kozolchyk, *Letters of Credit*, *in* IX INTERNATIONAL ENCYCLOPEDIA OF COMPARATIVE LAW 113–34 (Jacob S. Ziegel et. al. ed., 1979) [hereinafter Kozolchyk, *Letters of Credit*]; *see also* Boris Kozolchyk, *The Immunization of Fraudulently Procured Letter of Credit Acceptances: All Services Exportacao, Importacao Comercio, S.A. v. Banco Bamerindus Do Brazil, S.A. and First Commercial v. Gotham Originals*, 58 BROOK. L. REV. 369 (1992).

In Practice Three, the same negotiating bank as in Practice Two would examine the documents, report to the issuing or confirming bank that, in its opinion, the documents were in compliance with the LOC and would ask the issuing or confirming bank if it wished the negotiating bank to accept or pay on the credit. If the LOC required payment at sight, the negotiating bank would request the issuing or confirming bank to wire the payment to it. With this remittance, it would pay the beneficiary, charge a commission for negotiation and assume the risk that if the documents were refused by the issuing or confirming bank, it would reimburse these banks for the amount previously wired and paid to the beneficiary.

In Practice Four, the same bank would inform the issuing or confirming bank that, in its opinion, the documents were in compliance, inform the beneficiary of the same and ask the issuing or confirming bank to wire the funds with which to pay the beneficiary. Upon receipt of the funds wired by the issuing or confirming bank, it would pay the LOC and charge a negotiation commission or fee. However, this negotiating bank would not assume responsibility for recovering from the beneficiary the amount it had paid on behalf of the issuing or confirming bank, nor would it warrant to the issuing or confirming bank or the beneficiary that the documents it had examined complied with the LOC.

During my surveys and interviews on the meaning of negotiation, I prefaced my request for the bankers' definition of negotiation in connection with respect to Practice Four by stating:

> In characterizing this practice as a negotiation, please place yourself in the position of an issuing or confirming bank that wired the funds paid to the beneficiary to the presenting-negotiating bank. Assume that when you deduct your commission for your negotiation, your beneficiary asks you if you are not charging a commission for the same service performed earlier by the negotiating presenting bank.

The gist of the responses to this question, at least of those that can be summarized in polite company, was:

> Imagine the chutzpah of such a presenting-negotiating bank. It charges a negotiation commission for providing the beneficiary with no money or promise of payment of it is own. In contrast, we provide the money and because the presenting-negotiating bank charged a commission for negotiation, our charge, which is legitimate, is jeopardized.

Most respondents agreed that Practices One and Two entitled the negotiating bank to a payment of negotiation commission. A majority agreed that Practice Three also allowed for a negotiation commission. Only one banker, among dozens, agreed with the practice that entitled the purported negotiator in Practice Four to a negotiating commission. Clearly, in the first three practices, the negotiating bank gave tangible value to the beneficiary when acquiring his draft, whereas in Practice Four, the purported negotiator did not give such value. The result of this inquiry, then, led to the negotiation practice sanctioned by Article 10(b)(ii) of UCP 500:

> Negotiation means the giving of value for Draft(s) and/or document(s) by the bank authorised to negotiate. Mere examination of the documents without giving of value does not constitute a negotiation.[152]

Please note that the reasonableness that this provision relies on is objective and archetypal. It takes into account what a negotiating bank would consider reasonable if it acted as an issuing or confirming bank that made a final (non-recourse) payment on the LOC in advance of its date of maturity.

F. Elimination of a Monopolistic Bill of Lading Practice

The increased involvement of other sectors of the economy in the issuance of documents that triggered payment of LOCs, such as the transportation sector, soon resulted in attempts by members of this sector to monopolize the issuance of documents such as "port to port" ocean bills of lading when they were not issued by the ocean carriers or their agents. Article 25(d) of UCP 400 made this monopolistic practice possible by providing that: "Unless otherwise stipulated . . . banks will reject a transport document issued by a freight forwarder unless it is the FIATA Combined Transport Bill of Lading . . . or otherwise indicates that it is issued by a freight forwarder acting as a carrier or agent of a named carrier."[153] If a freight forwarder was not a member of FIATA, he could only issue bills of lading if he was the owner of the vessel or was appointed by the owner of the vessel as his agent, a status not easily earned.

After a review of the legality and fairness of such a practice, the position paper submitted by the United States Council on International Banking (USCIB), which represented the banks doing LOC business in the United States, stated in relevant part:

> The USCIB disagrees with the [UCP's] Sub-Working Group's continuing endorsement of FIATA documents on an exclusive basis. In our view, the UCP should state the banking criteria for accepting or rejecting transport documents. Whatever document meets these criteria should be acceptable, regardless of the business logo or professional association of the issuer. We believe it was a mistake to endorse one particular entity (an endorsement which is invariably at the expense of unendorsed entities). . . ."[154]

The Working Group and UCP 500 adopted this recommendation and eliminated the FIATA monopoly.

G. Bad Faith Excuses Not to Pay or Reimburse: A Judicial Mirror Image Version of Strict Compliance

By the 1980s, the doctrine of strict compliance had become "judicialized" by courts throughout the United States and other countries. There was even a Florida version of Lord Sumner's dictum in *Equitable Trust Co. of New York v. Dawson Partners Ltd*: "there is no room for documents which are almost the same or which will do just as

---

152 UCP 500, *supra* note 120, art. 10(b)(ii).

153 UCP 400, *supra* note 137, art. 25(d).

154 *See* Kozolchyk, *The Unwarranted Comeback, supra* note 140, at 135 (for a more detailed explanation of the reasons for the objection to the FIATA endorsement.)

well."[155] As found in a 1979 Florida state court decision, the standard for the examination of documents was as demanding as Lord Sumner's, but more reminiscent of Florida's sun and fun than of London's wet and dreary Mincing Lane: "[c]ompliance with the terms of a letter of credit is not like pitching horseshoes. No points are awarded for being close."[156] Nonetheless, the courts' understanding of the function of these documents and how they should be examined (and interpreted) according to standard banking practices was equally thin on both sides of the Atlantic Ocean.

Lord Sumner's principle assumes mirror image compliance. On the one side is a detailed, unambiguous formulation of requirements in the operative credit instrument. On the other are the required documents, replicating to the last minute detail the credit terms and conditions. The issuing, confirming, negotiating or paying banks are supposed to hold the mirror image of the credit terms to the tendered documents. Any deviation, no matter how slight, is unacceptable. Yet, in actual banking practice, this assumed mirror image practice of examination more often than not results in a blur.

Countless issuances contain shorthand formulations of trade terms whose full import is explained in extrinsic sources such as INCOTERMS.[157] And LOCs seldom specify what each required document must state in response to the shorthand reference or trade term. Consequently, the document checker must ascertain that, for instance, a seller's FOB invoice tendered in response to a credit's stipulation of FOB terms does not contain a charge for marine insurance. After all, under FOB terms, it is the responsibility of the buyer to procure the marine insurance even though the letter of credit itself does not specify that the FOB invoice should not contain an insurance charge.

Second, the mirror image examination is also unhelpful when a credit requirement does not mean in the beneficiary's and confirming bank's place of business what it means in the applicant's. Take, for example, the amended requirement in the LOC in the *Equitable Trust* case, which asked for the beneficiary's tender of a certificate of quality supplied by experts and signed by the Chamber of Commerce of Batavia.[158] It so happened that there was no Chamber of Commerce in Batavia. There was, however, a Commercial Association of Batavia which was in every respect, including legal status, the functional equivalent of chambers of commerce elsewhere. Invoking as discrepancies an improper and insufficient number of signatures, the applicant refused to reimburse the plaintiff bank. The Lords of Appeal held that the evidence indicated that the Commercial Association of Batavia could be regarded as the equivalent of a chamber of commerce.[159]

Thus, *Equitable Trust,* the paradigmatic version of judicial strict compliance, seemed ready to allow a certification by a "Commercial Association" instead of by a "Chamber of Commerce" once it was apparent that the former was the latter's functional legal equivalent. This functional legal equivalence of documents or terms may be interpreted either as an exception, or as an approval of a version of strict

---

[155] Boris Kozolchyk, *Is Present Letter of Credit Law Up to Its Task?*, 8 GEO. MASON U. L. REV. 285, 319 (1985–1986).

[156] Fid. Nat'l Bank v. Dade County, 371 So. 2d 545, 546 (Fla. Dist. Ct. App. 1979).

[157] *See* INT'L CHAMBER OF COMMERCE, INCOTERMS (2010) (for the most recent version of INCOTERMS), *available at* http://www.iccwbo.org/products-and-services/tradefacilitation/incoterms-2010/.

[158] Kozolchyk, *Is Present Letter of Credit Law, supra* note 155, at 320.

[159] *Id.* at 320–321.

compliance that acknowledges commercial and legal realities of the place of tender. Indeed, several UCP revisions have exempted paying banks from liability for having paid credits because of requirements of foreign law and usage.[160]

Third, the mirror image requirement is unhelpful when verifying that the statements in some documents are consistent with the statements in others. The mirror image examination assumes that these statements must be identical, whereas UCP 400 was based on the more liberal standard that the statements in one document are not inconsistent with those in the other.[161] Thus, a document checker who insisted on inter-documentary mirror image compliance violates the UCP's own standard of examination.

Fourth, mirror image examination is singularly damaging to the trustworthiness of the LOC undertaking when used by bad faith bankers or applicants to avoid the formers' failure of reimbursement and the latters' losses from a bad bargain. Accordingly, bad faith bankers resorted to mirror image examination to reject an otherwise complying tender of documents to prevent the loss caused by the lack of reimbursement by an insolvent applicant. To validate such bad faith practices in the name of strict compliance tips the contractual balance sharply in favor of applicants and against beneficiaries. It also undermines the indispensable trust among the correspondent banks.

As noted earlier, the roles and functions of correspondent banks are inherently interchangeable. Where roles and functions are so easily switched, retaliation is never out of the question and the fear of retaliation adds to the prevailing uncertainty. Moreover, if the issuing bank is deemed to have a right to raise such mirror image hypertechnicalities against the beneficiary or confirming bank, why should such a right be denied to the issuer's applicant in its refusal to reimburse the issuing bank that honored the LOC?

H. The Issuing Bank's Discretion to Approach the Applicant for a Waiver of Discrepancies

A sharp division of opinion existed between large "money center" and smaller inland banks in the United States on the acceptability of the issuing banks' approach to the applicant. The opposing camps agreed that the distrust felt by beneficiaries and many money center bankers on the one hand, and by inland issuing banks and their applicants on the other, had to be overcome. They also agreed that the principle of independent and neutral checking of documents by the banks had to be preserved, but did not agree on what the issuing bank could say about the nature of the discrepancy to the applicant or when it could be said.

One of the lawyers of the Working Group proposed a combination of rights and duties based on the following principles: First, the issuing bank that approached its

---

160 *Id.* at 321.

161 UCP 400, *supra* note 137, art. 15. It states:

> Banks must examine all documents with reasonable care to ascertain that they appear on their face to be in accordance with the terms and conditions of the credit. Documents which appear on their face to be inconsistent with one another will be considered as not appearing on their face to be in accordance with the terms and conditions of the credit.

Id.

applicant for a waiver was expected to act as a fiduciary for both the beneficiary and the applicant. Second, the issuing bank's fiduciary duties stemmed from being allowed to utilize *its sole judgment* on whether to approach the applicant and what to disclose about the discrepancies and when. This fiduciary duty was to be discharged reasonably and reasonableness would determine the timing of the approach based upon considerations such as the curability of the discrepancy and the time it would take to cure it. The result was Articles 14(b) and (c) of UCP 500, which in relevant part stated:

> b. Upon receipt of the documents the Issuing Bank and/or Confirming Bank, if any, or a Nominated Bank acting on their behalf, must determine on the basis of the documents alone whether or not they appear on their face to be in compliance with the terms and conditions of the Credit. . . .
>
> c. If the Issuing Bank determines that the documents appear on their face not to be in compliance with the terms and conditions of the Credit, it may in its sole judgment approach the Applicant for a waiver of the discrepancy(ies).

I. Consequences of the Judicial Mirror Image Compliance: Costly Defensive Practices

The uncertainty of the judicial standard of strict compliance and the likelihood of confirming banks being saddled with the risk of not being reimbursed as a result of bad faith discrepancies caused a large number of banks to adopt highly defensive examination practices. Some confirming banks refused to confirm foreign irrevocable credits without full pre-payment and waiver of discrepancies. Negotiating banks were unwilling to negotiate beneficiaries' drafts without specifying their recourse against the beneficiary. Others were only willing to act as collecting agents and not as negotiating banks for beneficiaries. The same was true with confirming and negotiating banks, which instructed their document checkers to reject any questionable tender and to list as many discrepancies as possible for submission by the issuing bank so that it obtained a waiver of all possible discrepancies from its applicant. A growing number of issuing banks inserted clauses in their application agreements that authorized their payment and reimbursement regardless of discrepancies. Not surprisingly, document checkers also increased their reliance on bank counsel for everyday documentary compliance decisions, frequently replacing sensible banking practices with hypertechnical legal excuses for non-acceptance or payment of the LOCs in anticipation of possible lawsuits.[162]

---

[162] In July 1987, Letter of Credit Update published a survey of documentary compliance practices in the United States. Bankers were asked what percentage of documents presented by the beneficiaries or beneficiaries' banks contained discrepancies. *See Reader Survey Brings Out Reactions to Minor Discrepancies*, 3 LETTER OF CREDIT UPDATE 13, 14 (July, 1987).; *see also* James E. Byrne, *Letters of Credit*, 43 BUS. LAW. 1353, 1355–1356 (1988); *Beginning a Series on Discrepancies: Five Timely Steps*, 1 LETTER OF CREDIT UPDATE 10 (1985); *LC Update Trends, Issues & Alerts*, 3 LETTER OF CREDIT UPDATE 2, 2 (1987); *Chase Looks at Discrepancies*, 3 LETTER OF CREDIT UPDATE 15 (1987). The majority of the respondents indicated that 90% of the documents initially tendered contained discrepancies. A similar survey conducted by this writer in the 1970s among representative bankers of major financial centers produced estimates in the same range. *See* Kozolchyk, *supra* note 151, at 14 & 149. While most perceived discrepancies were eventually cured or waived (estimating that the number of incurable tenders was no more than 1%), the high rate of widespread initial rejection was responsible for high transactional costs. SITPRO, a British international trade facilitation entity, estimated in 1985 that the annual cost to English exporters of correcting LOC discrepancies was approximately 50 million pounds. SITPRO, LETTER OF CREDIT MANAGEMENT AND CONTROL 1 (1985). The high rate of rejection and cure also caused higher operational costs for LOC banks whose review and correction of documents continued to be highly labor intensive. The

§ 24.8 THE UCP 500'S RESPONSE TO BAD FAITH DISCREPANCIES AND THE ISBP

UCP 500's response to the proliferation of bad faith discrepancies encouraged by the mirror image version of strict compliance was provided by Article 13(a), which in relevant part stated:

> Banks must examine all documents stipulated in the Credit with reasonable care, to ascertain whether or not they appear, on their face, to be in compliance with the terms and conditions of the Credit. Compliance of the stipulated documents on their face with the terms and conditions of the Credit, shall be determined by international standard banking practice as reflected in these Articles.[163]

A question raised by lawyers and judges alike throughout the LOC world was: Where do we find such a standard practice? The first such compilation was prepared in 1996 by the above mentioned USCIB, the Mexican Bankers' Association and the National Law Center for Inter-American Free Trade (NLCIFT). It was labeled "Standard Banking Practice for the Examination of Letter of Credit Documents" (SBPED).[164]

The SBPED reflected the requirements of UCP 500, but as a harmonized set only for the United States' and Mexican checking practices. A world-wide harmonization of practices came about in 2002 when most of the other national association members of the ICC summarized the most widely observed documentary examination practices into what was named the International Standard Banking Practice (ICC Publication 645).

§ 24.9 FACTORS THAT DETERMINE DOCUMENTARY CHECKING PRACTICES

A. Extrinsic Factors

The volume of daily examinations of LOC documents could be as high as 20 LOC presentations per day in a money center bank and a handful per day in inland banks. This factor alone was responsible for a more distant or closer relationship between the document checker, the beneficiary or the beneficiary's bank and last but not least, the applicant.

Thus, the directive of Article 16(b) of UCP 400 to the document checker to establish compliance "*on the basis of the documents alone*" resonated more naturally with a document checker of a money center bank than with his inland bank colleague.[165] The last time I visited the document checking shop of the Manufacturers Hanover Bank in lower Manhattan, one the busiest LOC checking departments in the

---

highest operational cost of all, however, was the distrust fueled by the perception that the irrevocable confirmed LOC was no longer the reliable means of payment and finance it was a generation earlier. A bank could no longer take for granted its correspondent's cooperation, good faith and reasonableness.

163 UCP 500, *supra* note 120, art. 13(a).

164 *See* Boris Kozolchyk, *Foreword* to U.S. COUNCIL ON INTERNATIONAL BANKING, INC., STANDARD BANKING PRACTICE FOR THE EXAMINATION OF LETTER OF CREDIT DOCUMENTS (1996).

165 UCP 400, *supra* note 137, art. 16(b) (emphasis added).

U.S at that time, I must have been the only non-document checker present in a hall that housed dozens of checkers, their eyes glued solely to their sets of documents and their respective LOCs. By contrast, the atmosphere in the three inland banks I visited was quite different. Document checkers were usually also in charge of advising, issuing or confirming LOCs. They were much fewer in number than those in the money center banks and their LOC applicants or beneficiaries could easily access them. In two of these three banks, the document checkers also advised their applicants on how to draw the terms and conditions of an LOC in a manner in which they were protected from a fraudulent beneficiary. Clearly, these inland bankers were not the isolated paymasters envisaged by Bernard Wheble's Article 13 of the 1962 revision, which made the applicant responsible for precise instructions on "the documents against which payment, acceptance or negotiation is to be made"[166] and led to a practice of accepting tenders that, albeit in compliance with stated instructions, did not make much sense to an experienced applicant or document checker.

B. Intrinsic Factors: Archetypal Bad and Good Faith Bankers

The most important intrinsic factors in the viability of document checking practices are the checker's knowledge of the LOC business, his skill and integrity.

1. *Bad Faith Bankers*

As we discussed earlier, the mirror image version of document examination provides an easy cover for bad faith practices and for the temptation to use such practices by invoking hypertechnical reasons not to pay. This temptation is not exclusive to applicant-buyers. It also affects the document checker who finds out that his applicant is unable or unwilling to reimburse him.

2. *Honest but Selfish Bankers*

The selfish document checker acts honestly when he detects a discrepancy that on its face is serious enough to warrant rejection. But he is selfish when he decides not to approach the applicant for a waiver of a discrepancy that in his judgment the applicant would be likely to waive because it might expose him to possible risks. He is aware that Article 14 of UCP 500 allows him "in its sole judgment (to) approach the Applicant for a waiver of the discrepancy."[167] But he is also aware that there are some risks inherent in this approach, although these are risks that an archetypal reasonable document checker would be willing to assume as illustrated in the practice commentary by Vincent Maulella, one of the United States' most respected LOC document checkers.[168]

3. *A Reasonable Document Checker*

In making the decision to approach the applicant for a waiver, Maulella's archetypal banker would have acted reasonably because he would take into consideration not only the interests of his client-applicant, but also those of the

---

[166] UNIFORM CUSTOMS AND PRACTICE FOR DOCUMENTARY CREDITS [UCP] No. 222, art. 13 (International Chamber of Commerce [ICC] 1962). This article states: "All instructions to issue, confirm, or advise a credit must state precisely the documents against which payment, acceptance or negotiation is to be made." *Id.*

[167] UCP 500, *supra* note 120, art. 14(c).

[168] Vincent M. Maulella, *UCP Art 16 Proposal on Notifying the Applicant*, 7 LETTER OF CREDIT UPDATE 6 (1991).

beneficiary or "other" party in the LOC transaction. Contrary to the bad faith document checker, the archetypal reasonable document checker's highest duty is to the integrity and reliability of the LOC promise: As a knowledgeable, trusted paymaster and critical participant in the nuclear LOC transaction, he would try to find ways to pay a beneficiary who tendered documents that in the eyes of other reasonable document checkers should have been acceptable to their applicants, and, if not acceptable, could have been rejected by them in a timely manner.

As noted earlier, a reasonable document checking practice belongs to the family of fair practices, but the latter encompasses more market participants than does the former by including not only the actual participants in the transaction, but also third parties likely to be affected by it.

§ 24.10 SUMMARY AND CONCLUSIONS

The first group of questions posed in the introductory section of this chapter pertained to the elements of a viable LOC practice: 1) How did this practice come about and what were its nuclear elements? 2) Why were some practices and their mutations viable and others were not? The second set of questions pertained to the most appropriate drafters of these practices: 3) Who were they and how helpful were lawyers as drafters or co-drafters?

In answer to the first question, we should keep in mind that the reason for the LOC was to replace unreliable promises of payment made by distant buyers who were often unknown to their sellers. When issued as an irrevocable, primary and independent promise by banks of known solvency, the LOC provided the reliability sought by seller-beneficiaries and holders in due course of the drafts. Accordingly, the first nuclear element of the LOC promise was the issuing and confirming banks' promises to accept or pay the seller-beneficiary's draft when accompanied by specified documents. Transactionally speaking, this firm promise was an initial giving of something of value without receiving *immediate* comparable value from the beneficiary. In fact, the beneficiary could have ignored the issuance of the LOC without incurring any liability to the issuing bank. However, this initial giving by the issuing bank cemented the trustworthiness of the LOC transaction for all the subsequent participants.[169]

The second nuclear element of the LOC promise was the beneficiary's tender of the set of documents specified in the LOC. A crucial feature of this tender was that the documents had independent value; independent, that is, from the value of the goods to which they referred. This value was measured by their acceptability to document checkers as in compliance with the LOC requirements and by providing, in the case of the negotiable ocean bill of lading, the symbolic "key" with which to obtain the goods shipped. Since this second nuclear element was predicated upon trust, each of the nuclear participants had to act honestly and reasonably: The beneficiary was trusted to make a good faith tender of documents that would meet the requirements of the LOC and the reasonable expectations of the issuing bank and its applicant, the document checker was trusted to exercise reasonable care and good faith in his examination of the documents, and the applicant was trusted by the issuing bank to act in good faith when reimbursing it and doing so in a reasonably timely manner.

---

[169] *See supra* § 22:4.

The answer to the second question then, is that for the LOC nuclear practice to be viable, its elements must be part of a balance between selfish (profitable) and altruistic promises and performances that is acceptable to the participants in the transaction, including banks as well as merchants, and their intermediaries, such as, among others, carriers and insurers. This balance, initiated by the altruistic giving of a firm commitment by the issuing bank, can produce not only standard practices or the practices acceptable to the regular or everyday participants in the transaction, but also best practices. These practices are the ones that reflect not only the interests of regular participants, but also protect third parties from discriminatory or unfair practices, such as the one that excluded freight forwarders who did not belong to an arbitrarily selected organization.

Examples of nuclear practices that lost or could have lost their viability as a result of the disruption of an agreed upon balance abound. Consider, for example, the mutation introduced by Article 10(a)(i) of UCP 400, which allowed an irrevocable LOC to promise "to pay or that payment will be made. . . ." This mutation upset the acceptable balance of a nuclear LOC promise that must be certain, documentary and independent. One of the questionnaires I circulated prior to the drafting of UCP 500 asked whether banks would be willing to confirm LOCs that contained words to the effect that the issuer "would see to it or procure that payment would be made." Not surprisingly, there were no willing confirmers of such a promise.

The question about the most appropriate drafters of standard and best practices and about the role of lawyers as co-drafters was also answered by the UCP 500 experience. Clearly, the principal drafters of commercial and financial practices are its *boni viri*, the most experienced, knowledgeable and respected practitioners: The Wilbert Wards, Frank Sauters, Bernard Whebles, Charles del Bustos and Vincent Maulellas of the banking world, whose courses of dealing are capable of creating viable usages of trade because of their cost effectiveness, honesty, reasonableness and fairness.

However, the UCP 500 experience also showed that lawyers thoroughly familiar with LOC practices have much to contribute to the drafting of rules based on these practices. Their role is made possible not only by their familiarity with banking practices and the law applicable to them, but also by their mastery of the logic of the reasonable. The understanding of the transactional facts and their legal and socio-economic implications enabled the lawyers who participated in the drafting of UCP 500 to assess the legality as well as the reasonableness and fairness of existing or proposed practices. It also enabled them to draft rules that harmonized the views of the opposing groups of bankers, such as large money-center banks and smaller inland banks, with respect to the practice of approaching the applicant for his waiver of discrepancies. Most importantly, what made the wording of UCP 500 Article 14(c) viable was a lawyer's understanding of the importance of imposing fiduciary duties on banks entrusted with decisions that could seriously affect the interests of their entrusting clients and of third parties This would not have been possible without the lawyers' ability to visualize the larger picture of transactional rights and duties in the LOC transaction.

What can be learned from the comparison of Roman secured lending and contemporary LOC bankers' practices? The first lesson is that practices whose participation is interchangeable are the likeliest to attain reasonableness. When this morning's issuing bank of a letter of credit confirmed by a confirming bank will be this afternoon's confirming bank of a letter of credit issued by the morning's confirming bank, each of these participants will have to ask himself: what should I reasonably expect from my archetypal counter-party when acting as an issuing or confirming bank? Obviously such an interchangeability can only be expected from regular participants in the same trade or profession. When, as in the case of the Roman repossession and foreclosure practices, the powerless borrowers were always the borrowers and the lenders were always the lenders, someone other than these participants had to be willing and ready to prevent the abuses from coming into being; To attempt to stamp them out once the practices are in wide use is always riskier and costlier. For such abuses are invariably countered by attempts to bribe the enforcers, and when corruption fails, by violence. Eventually, the abusive practices lead to legal invertebration and to Emperor Constantine's abrogation of the Lex Commissoria.

It is also true that the larger the number of trades or professions involved in drafting a common practice, the stronger will be the need to cope with bargaining inequalities. At NLCIFT, we learned this lesson while drafting the practices for the carriage of goods by trucks among Canada, the United States and Mexico. Quite often, lawyers had to mediate between the opposing interests of shippers (small and large) and then between shippers and carriers (small and large). And if this were not hard enough, the interests of the insurers for the above groups also had to be satisfied. The lesson learned from such a drafting was the importance of identifying the practice that was the nuclear component of all the others. In the case of truck carriage, the nuclear component was an acceptable measure of the liability of the carriers for damages suffered by the goods they carried. Once such a measure was agreed to it was possible to draft acceptable invoices, manifests, bills of lading, insurance policies, notices of claims and so on. The importance of a nuclear component acceptable to all the participants in the truck carriage of goods also highlighted the importance of drafting under the auspices of a neutral but knowledgeable host such as UNCITRAL, the Organization of American States, UNIDROIT, the ICC, and NLCIFT.

Underlying all the lessons learned in this chapter is the universality and permanence of Lord Mansfield's dictum, which I have paraphrased proverbially as "a fair price calls for a fair warranty." No viable commercial or financial practice can ignore this dictum. But what is fair is not the result of a mathematical calculus; it is the result of honesty and reasonableness. Karl Llewellyn's definition of commercial good faith as discussed in the preceding and the present chapters must be kept in mind. This good faith can have no better guardian than a commercial lawyer who understands the facts of a practice as well as its governing law, its economic reason for being and the socio-economic consequences of proposed practices. And at a time when lawyers' drafted or approved financial practices have led nations into recessions that impoverished much of their population, the attitude of "client ueber alles" must be replaced by one in which commercial lawyers act as the principal guardians of transactional good faith.

However, the UCP 500 experience also showed that lawyers thoroughly familiar with LOC practices have much to contribute to the drafting of rules based on these practices. Their role is made possible not only by their familiarity with banking practices and the law applicable to them, but also by their mastery of the logic of the reasonable.[170] The understanding of the transactional facts and their legal implications as well as the mastery of the logic of the reasonable enabled the lawyers who participated in the drafting of UCP 500 to act as devil's advocates testing the legality, reasonableness and fairness of existing or proposed practices. It also enabled them to draft rules that harmonized the opposing groups of bankers, such as large money-center banks and smaller inland banks, with respect to the practice of approaching the applicant for his waiver of discrepancies. It was a lawyer's understanding of the fiduciary duties the law imposes upon a party entrusted with decisions that could seriously affect the interests of the entrusters and their clients that made the wording of UCP 500 Article 14(c) acceptable.[171] It also made possible the viability of the new practice to this day. Among these practices were self-help remedies, such as preclusion and abandonment of goods when the issuing or confirming banks failed to pay or rejected the documents in a timely and reasonable manner.

What can be learned from the comparison of Roman secured lending and contemporary LOC bankers' practices? The first lesson is the importance of equality among the participants in the practice. The equality I am referring to pertains not necessarily to the parties' economic or political bargaining power; it refers to the equality of their transactional functions. The Roman secured lenders' attempt to create viable extrajudicial practices that would facilitate the quickest repayment of their loans and/or the easiest and cheapest way to acquire the property of their borrowers was doomed by both inequalities. The second of these inequalities was the subordination of the borrowers (small farmers and tenants) to their landowners-creditors' directions on the functions assigned to them by the lenders. This dual inequality was responsible for the onesidedness, harshness and corruption evidenced by the secured lending practices and especially by sale and acquisition of collateral practices. Eventually, these practices led to contradictory rules, legal invertebration and to Constantine's decision to invalidate them as "captious" and "harsh" practices deserving to have their memory abolished.

And while it is true that the largest and busiest participants in a commercial or financial practice are often its most influential drafters, their influence is usually tempered by the interchangeability of their functions. Unlike the subordinated and fixed duties of the Roman small farmers and tenant-borrowers, during a typical business day of a small LOC banker, he would act as an issuer of an LOC that would be confirmed, negotiated or paid by a much larger correspondent bank and vice versa. Such an interchangeability of functions requires a modicum of reasonableness from all of the participants in the LOC transaction because all these participants are potential "others" in the eyes of their correspondents and whatever they reasonably expect for themselves, they must also expect for the others in whose shoes they may find themselves at any time.

The second lesson is a corollary of the first: The larger the number of trades or professions involved in drafting a common practice, the larger are the bargaining and functional inequalities and the harder is the task of drafting and the greater the need for legal participation. At NLCIFT, we learned this lesson while drafting the practices

---

[170] *See supra* § 2:2(B).

[171] *See supra* § 24:9(B)(2).

for the carriage of goods by truck among Canada, the United States and Mexico.[172] Quite often, lawyers had to mediate between the opposing interests of shippers (small and large) and then between shippers and carriers (small and large). And if this were not hard enough, the interests of the insurers for the above groups also had to be satisfied. This lesson suggests that participants in the same trade or profession should be involved in the first attempt at drafting commercial and financial practices. And even when a multi-trade or profession is attempted as it was with NASTRAPS, it is much easier to agree on viable multi-sector or professional practices when their respective practices have been agreed upon. The importance of functional sectoral or professional equality highlights the role of a neutral host such as the ICC or the NLCIFT for the drafting of the practices. Among the most important functions of such an entity is establishing the transactional facts, including the most accurate terminology possible and a catalogue of the most pressing disputes and issues. It also emphasizes the importance of furthering cross sectoral equality of bargaining by educational and training efforts of those with the least knowledge and experience. For example, at NLCIFT we are planning to train micro and small borrowers in the use of real life line-of-credit secured financing with the help of bankers and law and business school graduates. At the same time, accountants will help borrowers develop reliable financial statements acceptable to bankers, and bankers will develop manuals of best practices for secured lending. These educational and training efforts should contribute to the birth of new viable standard and best practices of secured lending.

There are many more lessons to be learned from what has been discussed, but time and space only allow for a third lesson. Underlying all the lessons learned in this chapter is the universality and permanence of Lord Mansfield's dictum, which I have paraphrased proverbially as "a fair price calls for a fair warranty." No viable commercial or financial practice can ignore this dictum. But what is fair is not the result of a mathematical or even algebraic calculus; it is insperable from good faih as a combination of honesty, and reasonableness. And this good faith can have no better guardian than a commercial lawyer who understands the facts of a practice as well as its governing law and its economic reason for being. In this connection, it would be wise to heed the wise warning made in 1905 by Francis B. James, the chairman of the made f the committee on commercial law of the National Conference of Commissioners of Uniform State Laws. I : quoted in an earlier chapter:[173]

> The proposed code governing warehouse receipts is a commercial code and therefore ought to be based on the mercantile rather than the legal view. . .A mercantile code should be a clear expression of well recognized commercial customs whether they have or have not yet found their place in judicial decisions. The merchants gave to the law their customs and the law should give their customs back to them clearly expressed and freed from mere technical expressions.

. . .

---

[172] NATIONAL LAW CENTER FOR INTER-AMERICAN FREE TRADE, NORTH AMERICAN STANDARD TRANSPORTATION PRACTICES: A GUIDE TO TRUCK TRANSPORTATION (Gary T. Doyle ed., 1998).

[173] *See supra* § 21:11(C)(5) n. 323 and accompanying text.

Where judicial decisions conflict with well recognized, economically and ethically sound customs, the mercantile customs should be embodied in the code in preference to the formal technical rules."[174]

I would also suggest that the reader pay special attention to James' reference to "ethically sound customs." For as technology grows and proliferates so do unethical practices, such as those designed to maximize shareholders' values but which truly result in the payment of exhorbitant salaries and bonuses to coporate managers and directors,[175] or those by brokers who profit by trading "in front" of their clients or by engaging in rigged high frequency trading practices.[176]

---

[174] Francis B. James, *Practical Suggestions on Codifying the Law of Warehouse Receipts*, 3 MICH. L. REV. 282, 284–285 (1904–1905), *See supra* § 21:11(C)(5).

[175] *See supra* § 21:12 (A)(1).

[176] For a thoughtful suggestion on some of the latest questionable practices, *see* Editorial Board, *Is High-Frequncy Stock Trading Stepping Over a Legal Line?,* WASHINGTON POST, http://www.washingtonpost.com/opinions/is-high-frequency-stock-trading-stepping-over-a-legal-line/2014/04/10/c18e2b80-bf50-11e3-bcec-b71ee10e9bc3_story.html (last accessed Apr. 15, 2014).

Chapter 25

BRIEF OVERVIEW OF COMMERCIAL TRIAL PROCEDURE

§ 25.1 INTRODUCTION

Most of the judicial decisions discussed in this book are by appellate courts. This may lead the reader to assume that these decisions were the product of similar pleading and proof practices at the trial level. They were not. Some of the pleading and proof differences are attributable to the presence of a jury as a chief finder of facts in common law jurisdictions or to the heavier reliance on written pleadings and proof in civil law countries. Other differences are the product of even deeper disparities among distinct legal cultures. Some of these contrasts are clearly observed among Spanish and Latin American jurisdictions on the one side and Anglo-American jurisdictions on the other. It is for this reason that our comparison will focus largely on these jurisdictions.

In Spain and Latin America, trial court disputes for breach of contract fall into two procedural categories: One is the ordinary or declarative trial (*juicio ordinario* or *declarativo*) where the court starts out in *tabula rasa* fashion to establish all of the relevant facts and at the end of the procedure "declares" the parties' rights and duties. The other procedural category is that of a summary or executive trial (*juicio sumario* or *ejecutivo*) where many of the most important facts are presumed to have been established by the highly credible documents tendered to the court at the start of the procedure. These documents could be notarial or public deeds, negotiable instruments or court decisions that have "declared" the parties' rights and are awaiting execution. The purpose of this proceeding, then, is to decide whether or not a decree of execution against assets of the defendant is in order.

In contrast with Latin-American law, U.S. law does not distinguish between declarative and executive actions. While summary actions and even trials exist, they do not arise from a separate trial procedure but from "motions" or requests for summary hearings or actions, including equitable relief, as part of the same procedure before trial courts. Following is a basic description of an ordinary Latin-American trial court procedure for breach of a commercial contract. Thereafter, we will discuss its U.S. counterpart. It should be noted that while some Latin American jurisdictions have special commercial courts, most assign commercial and civil trials to the same courts of first instance.

A. General Overview of Ordinary or Declarative Judicial Procedures in Latin America and Spain[1]

Because the rights and duties of the parties in a declarative or ordinary trial have to be established and fully proven, the process is much longer than in an executive or summary trial. In some Mexican state jurisdictions, for example, an ordinary civil trial can often last several years, and once one includes appeals, the final decision may take as long as a decade.[2] Even thought commercial disputes are often heard in declarative and ordinary trials (because evidentiary documents are unavailable or insufficient to support an executive trial), a vast number of commercial disputes are disposed of in executive or summary trials.

The most important source of law that governs civil procedure in Spain and Latin America is the code of civil procedure. A typical description of what the codes of civil procedure require for ordinary trials may be found in a description provided by the Mexican Institute for Legal Research:

> [T]he ordinary trial procedure sets forth the requirements of a complaint and notice of it; admissible evidence, and how it can be obtained, proffered and weighed by the court; the manner in which allegations have to be presented; the term during which the court must issue its opinion; and the necessary requirements to execute the judgment and give it *res judicata* effect.[3]

Normally, the codes of civil procedure list the elements of an ordinary commercial or civil complaint. For example, in Mexico a complaint alleging a commercial cause of action must comply with the provisions of Article 1061 of the Federal Commercial Code;[4] similarly, a Colombian complaint must comply with the requirements of Article 75 of the Colombian Code of Civil Procedure.[5]

---

[1] I am thankful to the following former LL.M. students from the University of Arizona, James E. Rogers College of Law, for their helpful contributions and suggestions: Ana María Rivera (Colombia), Flavia Figueredo Omodei (Uruguay), Manuel Pliego (Mexico), Samuel Barbosa (Brazil), Ana Cristina Castaneda, Research & Development Director, NLCIFT (El Salvador).

[2] STEPHEN ZAMORA ET AL., MEXICAN LAW 321–335 (2004).

[3] INSTITUTO DE INVESTIGACIONES JURÍDICAS, MEXICAN LEGAL DICTIONARY 1862 (1988).

[4] CÓD. COM. (MEX.) art. 1061 (1889). It states:

The first pleading must have attached:

I. The power of attorney that authorizes the litigant to act on behalf of another person;

II. The document or documents that establish the authority of the litigant in the dispute, when acting as the legal representative of an individual or corporation or when the right claimed was assigned to him by another person;

III. The documents on which the plaintiff supports his claim and those on which the defendant supports his defenses. If the plaintiff is missing a document, he must state in the complaint that he has requested that such document be issued and prove it with a simple copy of the document bearing the stamp of the registry, protocol, office or place in which the original document is filed, so that the certification of said document is issued at his expense, as provided by law. In the case of the defendant, he must prove that he has requested the issuance of the document that he is missing by attaching a simple copy of the document bearing the stamp of the registry, protocol or office when answering the complaint or within three days following the term to answer the complaint.

The parties are deemed to have access to the documents if they can legally request an authorized copy of the originals and if there is a duty to issue them to the parties. If the parties do not have access to the documents or for any other reason cannot file the documents supporting their claims or defenses, they shall state before the judge and under oath the reason why they cannot present said documents. After such statement, the judge shall order the issuance of the document to

Typically, the complaint in an ordinary trial must be filed before the competent judge, who will determine its admissibility. Once it has been admitted, notice must be given to the defendant, granting him a term to respond or to file a counterclaim. When responding, the defendant may completely or partially deny the facts, dispute the law being invoked and file defenses or counterclaims. Where the defendant files a counterclaim, the court will decide on its admissibility once the period of reply by the plaintiff has elapsed. The same rule applies to any defenses, provided they do not require the production of evidence; if they require it, the judge will grant a period in which evidence must be obtained and will rule on the defense at the preliminary and conciliation hearings.

If the parties settle during this conciliation hearing, the process will end; otherwise, it will proceed to the evidentiary stage and will continue until a judgment is

---

> whoever is responsible for it, at the expense of the interested party, ordering its seizure as provided by law.
>
> Unless otherwise provided by law, or in case of supervening evidence, if the parties fail to comply with any of the previous requirements, no documentary evidence will be admitted if it is not attached to the complaint or answer thereto; the same will apply if the complaint and answer to the complaint do not identify the documents in a way that will allow the court to request and receive them in due time.
>
> IV. In addition to the provisions of numeral III, the parties must attach to the complaint or answer thereto every document that they have in their power and that will be used as evidence; and any document filed thereafter in breach of this provision will not be admitted, unless it is supervening evidence; and,
>
> V. A simple legible copy of the complaint and all the documents referred to herein, including those that are filed for evidentiary purposes in accordance with the preceding paragraphs, in order to give notice to the opposing party.
>
> The immediately preceding provision will also apply to writs claiming the defense of set-offs or counterclaims or other incidents in the process.

Id. (translation by author).

[5] C.P.C. (Colom.) art. 75 (1970). It states:

> The complaint for any process must include:
>
> 1. Designation of the judge to whom the complaint is addressed.
>
> 2. Name, age and domicile of the plaintiff and defendant; if no domicile is available, residency must be expressed, and if the defendant's domicile or residency is not known to the plaintiff, this must be stated under oath, which will be deemed granted upon the filing of the complaint.
>
> 3. Name and domicile or residency in absence thereof of the legal representatives or agents of the parties, if they cannot or do not act on their own behalf. If this information is unknown, such circumstance must be expressed as provided in the previous numeral.
>
> 4. Name of the judicial representative of the defendant, if any.
>
> 5. What is being sought with the claim, which must be precisely and clearly stated. If there are several claims, they must be stated separately, complying with the provisions of Article 82.
>
> 6. The facts supporting the claims, duly determined, classified and listed.
>
> 7. Law that supports the claim.
>
> 8. Amount claimed, when the estimation of the amount is necessary for determining jurisdiction or type of process.
>
> 9. Indication of the type of process applicable to the claim.
>
> 10. Request of the evidence that the plaintiff attempts to make effective.
>
> 11. Address of the office or residence where the plaintiff and his agent will receive personal notices; address where to give notice to the defendant or his agent, unless the defendant or his agent provide a different address, or a statement under oath that such address is unknown, and this oath shall be deemed to be granted upon the filing of the complaint.
>
> 12. All other requirements that the code provides on this matter.

Id. (translation by author).

handed down. The ordinary procedure concludes with the commencement of the appellate stage. During this stage, the hierarchically superior courts may revoke, modify or affirm a decision handed down by the lower courts.

As is apparent from the preceding summary, the Code of Civil Procedure holds a tight reign over the proceedings: the parties are not allowed to conduct, let alone design, ancillary procedures as is done by United States litigators during pre-trial discovery. Just as important, adjudication is strictly based upon what the pleadings (and especially the complaint) asks for, as required by the principle of *"justicia rogada"* (only that which is expressly requested or "prayed for" will be granted).

B. *Justicia Rogada*, *Ultra Petita* and the Remedial Finality of the Pleadings

Despite its seemingly innocuous nature, Section 5 of Article 75 of the Colombian Procedural Code, as transcribed above, must not be overlooked. It requires that the complaint specify: "What is being sought with the claim, which must be precisely and clearly stated. If there are several claims, they must be stated separately, complying with the provisions of Article 82."[6]

This provision is a corollary of the procedural principle of *justicia rogada*. In plain words, it means that the court should grant neither more nor less than what the parties requested (prayed for) in their pleadings and especially in the complaint, answer or counterclaim. If the decision goes beyond or fails to rule on any of the prayers for relief, it is very likely to be appealed and reversed.

Consider, for example, the statute that governs the jurisdictional powers of the Supreme Court of El Salvador (*Ley de Casación*) and a typical decision rendered under it. Judges must decide in direct response to the express petitions of the litigants; if they do not, the parties may request reversal of the decision in the cassation procedure. The law reads as follows:

> The Law on Appeals involving only Violations of the Law (*Ley de Casación*):
>
> Art. 3. An appeal because of violation of the law or judicial doctrine shall be granted on the following bases:
>
> 4°—If the decision was contrary to the petitions formulated by the litigants, by granting more than what was asked for or failing to rule on any of the petitions. . .[7]

As stated in the following summarized excerpt of the decision of the Civil Branch of the Supreme Court of El Salvador in *ASSA v. AIG*:[8]

> III. SPECIFIC ARGUMENTS FOR THE APPEAL
>
> 3. Because the lower appellate court's decision is inconsistent with what was requested by the parties by granting more than what they requested. . . as set forth by Article 3 of the Cassation Law. . .

---

[6] *Id.* art. 75 § 5.

[7] Law No. 1135 Ley de Casación, Apr. 9, 1953, [161] Diario Oficial (El Sal.). Since then the law has undergone several reforms, the latest on Aug. 21, 2002.

[8] Sala do lo Civil de la Corte Suprema de Justicia [the Civil Branch of the Supreme Court of Justice], 31 de marzo de 2003, "ASSA v. AIG" No. 1466 S.S. (El Sal.).

> The appellants allege that the lower appellate court decision is inconsistent with the request made by the litigants because it grants more than they requested... They assert that the above-mentioned provision has a twofold purpose; on the one hand it prevents baseless claims and on the other it forces the judge to examine the parties' petitions solely in the context of their respective pleadings...
>
> In the proceedings below, the plaintiff presented documentary evidence to support its factual allegations without objection by the defendant... In addition, the trial judge ordered an accounting of commingled assets by an expert witness whose testimony he took into account when ruling that: "Having established that the plaintiff is entitled to be compensated for the unilateral and unjustified termination of its distribution contract with the defendant... it is therefore appropriate to grant the plaintiff's petition with the exception of personal unsecured loans extended by the plaintiff... as well as mortgage loans granted with its own and not with AIG assets, and on which ASSA assumed the risk of non-payment and cannot claim their losses from AIG..." This Branch of the Supreme Court finds that the points on appeal are: that the appellant disagrees with the payment decreed below which includes amounts allocated to furniture, equipment and land in the amount of ¢1.451.750.40 and for the above-mentioned loans in the amount of ¢864.248.00 which although they involved insurance policies issued by AIG the risk of loss had been assumed by ASSA. For these reasons we find that the appealed decision included items that were not requested in the pleadings below, neither before the first nor the second instance courts. Therefore, the lower appellate court did not limit itself to those facts and claims submitted to it, thereby ignoring the procedural requirement of consistency between what was requested and what was granted... Simply put, the lower appellate court granted more than what was requested by the parties in their pleadings and its decision is therefore an *ultra petita*...

COMMENTS AND QUESTIONS

Would a United States federal or state court judge be limited in his award of damages or of other remedies to what was stated in the complaint? What is gained or lost by adopting the principle of *justicia rogada* and its corollary of *ultra petita*?

Brazilian civil procedural rules introduce an unexpected and somewhat perplexing twist by granting appeals based not only on *ultra petita* but also on *infra petita* which can be resolved on appeal by the appellate judge without the need of remanding the case to the trial court for further proceedings. In December 2001, a reform to the Code of Civil Procedures added Section 3 to Article 515, allowing the appellate court to resolve issues on appeal within certain limits. This section states: "Where a process is concluded without a decision on the merits (Art. 267), the court may rule forthwith on the matter, provided that the issue at bar is exclusively on a matter of law and the circumstances require an immediate ruling."[9]

---

[9] Decreto No. 5869, 17 de janeiro de 1973, Diario Oficial da Uniao [D.O.U.] de 17.1.1973 (Braz.) art. 515 (translation bu author).

Furthermore, a decision of the Appellate Civil Court of Brazil in 2004[10] decided that Section 3, transcribed above, gives a broader interpretation with regards to its scope of application. It held that:

> Although the instant case is not a process concluded without a ruling on the merits, the court considers that it is possible to give § 3 of Art. 515 of the Code of Civil Procedures a broader interpretation. Therefore, it is appropriate to cite the Honorable Paulo Afonso Brum Vaz: "*. . .I believe that it is possible to give § 3 of Art. 515 of the Code of Civil Procedures . . . a broader interpretation, so that the concept of a process concluded without a ruling on the merits also covers cases where the judge a quo has issued a decision that is not related to the petitions formulated by the claiming party. . . Therefore, a court will be able to rule on the merits of the petitions in cases of* extra petita *or* infra petita *rulings, provided that the requirements of the final part of the cited provision are met ('. . .is exclusively on a matter of law and the circumstances require an immediate ruling.').*"

The following section contains two typical complaints: the first initiates an ordinary or declarative action claim before a trial court in Uruguay; the second is a generic breach of contract complaint before a trial court in the United States. The reader will note that, consistent with the principle of *justicia rogada*, the Uruguayan complaint is more formal, structured and specific in its "petition" section.

The Uruguayan complaint's caption reflects the remaining influence of Roman law typification: it typifies the action by averring that it is an action for the rescission of a contract and for payment of a penalty clause. Its allegations of fact and offer of evidence must bear out this assertion; if not, its effectiveness can be objected to as self-contradictory, and this may be fatal. It is filed by an attorney acting as a representative of the plaintiff and proving her representation by means of a notarial power of attorney attached to the complaint. The reader will note that the filing attorney refers to this power to establish his authority to appear on behalf of her client.

The U.S. complaint is much simpler and is limited to naming the parties, the facts as alleged by the plaintiff, and the cause or causes of action; it does not require that the attorney establish his power to act on behalf of his stated client. Thus, as an "officer of the court" (a concept seldom heard in Spanish and Latin American jurisdictions), the lawyer is trusted (and presumed) to be telling the truth about his power of representation. However, if he lied about it, he could easily face disciplinary action, including disbarment.

Even though both documents make reference to the facts that led to the breach of the contract, the reader will notice certain differences. The U.S. complaint makes a general reference to facts and no express reference to the law applicable to that specific case, with the exception—in this example—to the laws of the State of Arizona where both corporations were incorporated. In contrast with its U.S. counterpart, the Uruguayan complaint, when stating the facts and alleging non-performance of contractual obligations, makes reference to the specific clauses that were breached. It also lists the evidence pertaining to the facts, and includes the names of witnesses and key evidentiary documents. In addition, it has a section dedicated to the law applicable to the case at bar. In this section, the complaint finds its grounds in specific legislation citing provisions from the applicable codes or statutes.

---

[10] S.T.F., Ap. Civ. No. 2003.71.05.000320–8/RS, Relator: Des. Federal VALDEMAR Capeletti, 22.09.2004, Diario Oficial da Uniao [D.O.U.], 27.10.2004 (Braz.), *available at* http://www.natlaw.com/interam/br/bk/cl/clbrbk00071.htm.

Finally, the last section of the Uruguayan complaint known as the "petition" section, states *all* the remedies and relief (including the amount of the compensation) sought by the complaint and authorizes the attorneys to receive notices related to the process. If a remedy does not appear requested in this section, in all likelihood it will be deemed to have been waived. Similarly, because of the *ultra petita* corollary of the principle of "prayed for justice," the amount claimed stands as the limit of the recovery. Thus, from a remedial standpoint, the Uruguayan complaint is intended to be the final, polished document.

The U.S. complaint is a more informal, flexible and inconclusive document intended essentially to request the court's intervention in order to obtain judicial remedies whose scope and extent is yet to be fully determined. As the trial proceeds, new facts and new remedies may be added, including a larger or smaller amount of the claim. Thus, the U.S. complaint operates much as the opening salvo of a remedial request than as the plaintiff's remedial blueprint.

§ 25.2 A TYPICAL URUGUAYAN COMPLAINT[11]

COMPLAINT FOR RESCISSION OF CONTRACT AND ENFORCEMENT OF PENALTY (URUGUAY)

JUDGE OF FIRST INSTANCE IN CIVIL MATTERS ON DUTY IN MONTEVIDEO.

Lucía González, with Identification Document No. 3.455.818–3, acting as a legal representative of XXX, SRL, according to the power of attorney attached as Exhibit A to this complaint, with domicile in Avda. Gral. Rivera No. 3089–302, Montevideo, and for purposes of this process, establishes as her domicile, Plaza Independencia 810, of this city; to the Judge, I state:

That acting in the capacity previously mentioned, I come to pursue an ordinary trial for breach of contract and enforcement of a penalty stipulated under clause 8 of the contract of which rescission is requested, against ZZZ, S.A. domiciled in Avda. 18 de Julio No. 2233, pursuant to the allegations of facts and statements of law that I proceed to exhibit.

I. FACTS

1. XXX, SRL (hereinafter "XXX") is the owner of a renowned flower shop (The Flower Shop) established in this city since 1980, through which she supplies flower arrangements upon the request of its customers, not only within the city of Montevideo, but to anywhere in the country.

Until the year 2004, XXX supplied its own products, but as the business grew it was not able to comply in due time with the requests of its clients.

2. Therefore, in July 12, 2004, XXX entered into a contract (the "Contract") with ZZZ, S.A. (hereinafter "ZZZ") under which ZZZ would provide delivery services for XXX.

3. To render the services, ZZZ had to keep twenty vehicles available for any requests of XXX under the conditions stated in the Contract. ZZZ had the

[11] Example of a complaint prepared by Dr. Flavia Figueredo, graduate of the Master of Laws in International Trade and Business Law (LL.M.) program at the James E. Rogers College of Law of The University of Arizona (2005).

duty to send a vehicle to XXX establishment within fifteen minutes of the latter's request (Clause 2 of Annex I of the Contract). The Contract (Clause 4) also stipulated a timeframe in which deliveries had to be performed, taking into consideration the distance to the place of delivery.

4. Soon after entering into the Contract, ZZZ began facing considerable delays in the expected deliveries, not only because of the time that it took for the vehicles to arrive at XXX establishment to pick up the flower arrangements that had to be delivered, but also in the time of delivery to its customers.

5. Such delays damaged XXX's image and resulted in monetary losses—because in several cases it could not charge its customers since the flower arrangements were not delivered on time; it also lost many old and new customers by turning down several orders because it was not able to deliver them on time. Paradoxically, a contract that was entered into to improve XXX's services ended up almost ruining the business.

6. According to Clause 12 of the Contract, the parties would automatically be in breach of contract upon non-performance of their obligations, without the need of a special notice or claim of default. However, after having several meetings with Mrs. White, General Manager of ZZZ, requesting that services be provided as agreed and not having any positive results, XXX sent, extrajudicially, a claim on January 20, 2005, demanding ZZZ to comply with the services pursuant to the Contract (document C). Nevertheless, ZZZ continued to breach the contract.

7. XXX tried to negotiate the termination of the Contract so that it could begin using the services of another company, in order to improve such services and prevent the loss of existing customers and potential new business; however, ZZZ refused.

8. It must be pointed out that to this day XXX has complied with every payment to ZZZ in accordance with the Contract, as is shown by the receipts attached herein (document D).

9. For all the aforementioned, it is the interest of the party that I represent to request the rescission of the Contract, and the enforcement of the penalty stipulated in Clause 8 of said Contract for the amount of $250,000.00.

II. LAW

I support my claim with the law found in Articles 1341 to 1347 and 1336 of the Civil Code and under Chapter III and Articles 337 et seq. of the Code of Civil Procedure.

III. EVIDENCE

1. Documentary Evidence

i) Document A: Power of Attorney.

ii) Document B: Contract between XXX and ZZZ dated July 12, 2004.

iii) Document C: Extrajudicial claim sent by XXX to ZZZ on January 20, 2005.

iv) Document D: Payment receipts issued by ZZZ upon payments made by XXX from July 2004 to March 2005.

2. Testimonial Evidence

Judicial notice to the following witnesses is requested for them to give testimony as witnesses:

i) María Gómez, Identification Document No. 1.222.333–4, with domicile in Pte. Barrio No. 1212, who will testify as customer of The Flower Shop on the delays suffered when ZZZ began providing its delivery services.

ii) Lucy González, Identification Document No. 1.222.333–5, with domicile in Avda. 18 de Julio 6464, a former customer of The Flower Shop who will testify on the same issue.

iii) Geraldine White, Identification Document No. 1.222.333–6, who will receive notice at ZZZ's domicile in Avda. 18 de Julio No. 2233, and who will testify on the several meetings held with Mr. Luis González, legal representative of XXX, who requested changes in the services provided by ZZZ and explained the damages that resulted from ZZZ's breach of contract.

iv) Luis González, Identification Document No. 1.222.333–7, with domicile in Pereira de la Luz No. 8789, who will testify on the same issue as Mrs. White, and on the complaints of customers resulting from delays on the delivery of The Flower Shop's products.

v) Sylvia Pereira, Identification Document No. 1.222.333–8, with domicile in Charrúa No. 7889 and Gilberto Jiménez, Identification Document No. 1.222.333–9, with domicile in Calle Colonia 1234–405; both will testify on the complaints of customers resulting from delays in the delivery of The Flower Shop's products and on the cancellation and rejection of orders because of the inability to comply with the time of delivery.

IV. PETITIONS

For the aforementioned reasons, I respectfully petition the Judge that he:

1. Receive the complaint and documents attached and acknowledge the sufficiency of the power of attorney granted in my favor, and accept the actual and contractual domiciles as stated.

2. Give notice of this complaint to ZZZ at the domicile previously indicated, in accordance with the corresponding procedures.

3. Following the notice, declare the rescission of the Contract and order ZZZ to pay the penalty established in Clause 8 of the Contract.

And I state: That I hereby authorize Dr. Laura González, Juan Pérez and the Paralegal Cristina Campos to receive notifications of any resolution issued in this process, and to have access to the file and to retrieve the file if necessary.

§ 25.3 THE SUMMARY OR EXECUTIVE PROCESS IN COLOMBIA, MEXICO AND SPAIN[12]

A. Introduction

A commercial substantive law that is secreted from "the interstices of procedure" happens only when courts are willing to facilitate commercial transactions by mitigating excessive procedural rigidity, encouraging good faith and protecting third parties otherwise unprotected by the substantive law extant.

In theory, such a power should be more willingly and easily wielded by courts in countries such as France with a long tradition of commercial courts. Yet, as was discussed in connection with the codification of commercial law in France, as a result of a deeply imbedded disdain for commerce such a remedial power was not exercised by the Commercial Court to the degree desired or welcomed by French merchants.[13] Neither has it been used by other countries such as Mexico that enacted federal commercial procedural rules as part of its federal commercial code.[14] On the other hand, countries such as Colombia seem to have made some significant statutory progress in liberalizing commercial procedure, especially in connection with summary or executive trials.

In this section, we will study how summary trials involving formal commercial contracts as well as negotiable instruments, among other commercial transactions, are conducted and appealed. What is discussed hereafter, and especially its comparison with United States' motions for summary judgment is of importance to practical and theoretical commercial lawyers in civil and common law countries. For these procedures are supposed to serve best those who have little time for protracted trials and can submit the type of evidence best found in uncontroverted standardized documents such as those regularly used by merchants. Hence what follows should help evaluate the ability of the executive process and the motion for summary judgment to resolve commercial disputes quickly and fairly.

B. Essential Elements of an Executive-Summary Procedure

The petitioner of a summary process must accompany his petition with a document worthy of immediate enforcement, also known as an "executive" or "enforcement title" ("*título ejecutivo*"). This document provides credible evidence of the existence of a clear, express, and liquid or immediately enforceable obligation. An express obligation is one that appears clearly and unequivocally from the document. Its immediate enforcement feature has been defined by the Supreme Court of Colombia as one "due forthwith and not subject to any terms or conditions and thus a pure, simple and already declared obligation."[15] This is a broad enough criterion to include a wide

---

[12] I am thankful to Ana María Rivera, graduate of the Master of Laws in International Trade and Business Law (LL.M.) program at the James E. Rogers College of Law of The University of Arizona (2005), for her help in preparing the materials used in this Section.

[13] *See supra* § 9:3.

[14] *See* CÓD. COM. (MEX.) Book V (1889). In that respect, art. 1063 provides: "All commercial disputes will be conducted in accordance with the applicable procedures in this Code, special commercial laws and, in lack thereof, by the Federal Code of Civil Procedure." *Id.* art 2063.

[15] *See* Corte Suprema du Justicia [C.S.J.] [Supreme Court] augusto 31, 1942, Gaceta Judicial [G.J.] (No. LIV, p. 383) (Colom.).

range of documents such as *res judicata* or final decisions in declarative trials, a notarial or public deed recorded in a land registry endowed with the power to issue land titles where the recorded owner wishes to quickly evict a trespasser, a negotiable instrument or document of title in the hands of a holder in due course, a court document in which the defendant confesses judgment in favor of the plaintiff, etc.

Most civil law countries require that these executive titles be in writing; however, as will become apparent in the following section, in Colombia an obligation which is not in writing may also qualify as an enforcement title. For example, according to Article 488 of the Code of Civil Procedure of Colombia:

> Express, clear and enforceable obligations may be enforced by means of a summary procedure; for that purpose, they must be incorporated in a document granted by the debtor or assignor and constitute undisputed evidence against the latter, or [the obligation may be] declared in a court's decision—of any jurisdiction—or other court order enforceable by law, or [in decisions] that result from administrative or police procedures, where legal fees are approved or legal honoraria of justice functionaries are specified. *A confession* [in answer to interrogatories made during a trial] is not an enforcement title, but the confession regulated under Article 294 is an enforcement title.[16]

Yet, some countries, such as Turkey, would also allow the use of additional executive documents such as arbitration awards for appeals and executions of judgments.[17] Aware of the growing need for documents that could reduce litigation time and cost, the Code of Civil Procedure of Colombia does not provide an exclusive list of documents or of "titles" that can trigger the initiation of an executive-summary process. As noted by Professor López Blanco, "it is untrue that only certain obligations may be enforced [in an executive trial] because every obligation that complies with the provisions and general requirements of Article 488 has the right to its summary process."[18] By contrast, Article 407 of the Mexican Federal Code of Civil Procedure provides a clearly exhaustive list of civil enforcement titles,[19] and Article 1391 of the Federal Commercial Code provides a similar list for commercial enforcement titles.[20] In

---

[16] C.P.C. (Colom.), *supra* note 5, art. 294 (emphasis added). It states:

> When a person plans to file a claim or fears to be claimed against, this person may make a single request, so that the other party answers an interrogatory of the facts that will be discussed in the process. The request must include a brief statement of what it is intended to be proven.

Id.

[17] Code of Civil Procedure (CCP) (Turkey) art. 434 (1927).

[18] HERNÁN FABIO LÓPEZ BLANCO, INSTITUCIONES DEL DERECHO PROCESAL CIVIL 378 (3d ed., 1998) (this author's translation).

[19] C.F.P.F. (Mex.) art. 407 (2008). It states:

> The following may be enforced:
>
> I. Final judgments;
>
> II. Public documents that according to this code provide full proof;
>
> III. Private documents recognized before a notary or a judicial authority; and
>
> IV. All other documents that according to the law are deemed enforceable.

Id. (translation by author).

[20] CÓD. COM. (MEX.) art. 1391 (1889). It states:

> The summary process is available for claims based on a document authorized to be enforced. The following are documents that are authorized to be enforced:

this writer's opinion, Colombia's "open number" of enforceable titles embodies the most desirable legislative policy from a commercial law standpoint because it enables the judge—where the evidence before him warrants it—to fashion his remedy with greater flexibility and fairness than allowed by the exhaustive list approach. Even though this flexibility may be regarded by some as injecting uncertainty, the ability of the judges to obtain actual facts in a dispute results in much better commercial adjudication and better "individual judicial norms" that can be followed by precedents.[21]

Another feature of the Colombian summary process is that it is not necessary to have a written enforcement title. Professor López Blanco gives the example of a tape recording of a debtor confessing his default. As provided by Articles 11[22] and 12[23] of Law 446 of 1998, any document provided by the parties is authentic, whether written or incorporated into another media. Nevertheless, written documents continue to be the most commonly used in Colombian and Mexican summary procedures.

C. Cautionary Measures

Before the order of execution is issued by the Colombian trial court, some preliminary procedures, also known as "cautionary measures," are usually available to the petitioner, including provisional attachments and garnishments of assets that the plaintiff has grounds to believe the debtor may attempt to hide. In addition, Article 489 of the Code of Civil Procedure of Colombia provides for cautionary measures intended to facilitate the execution procedure such as notice of default to the defaulting debtor,[24]

> I. Final judgments or *res judicata* and final arbitral awards that do not allow for appeals pursuant to Article 1346 and following the provisions of 1348;
>
> II. Public instruments, official copies of public documents and copies of said documents certified by authorized public officials;
>
> III. The debtor's judicial confession pursuant to Article 1288;
>
> IV. Documents of credit;
>
> V. Insurance policies in accordance with the provisions of the laws on this matter;
>
> VI. The decision of insurance appraisal experts fixing the value of the incident, in accordance with the provisions of the laws on this matter;
>
> VII. Invoices, checking accounts and any other commercial contracts signed and judicially recognized by the debtor; and
>
> VIII. All other documents that according to the law or because of their characteristics are deemed to be enforcement titles.

Id. (translation by author).

[21] *See* Boris Kozolchyk, *The Individual Norm in Mexican Commercial Adjudication*, 27 ARIZ. J. INT'L. & COMP. L. 339 (2010).

[22] L. 466, 8 de julio de 1998, Diario Oficial [D.O.] art. 11 (Colom.).

[23] *Id.* art. 12. It states: "Documents that comply with the requirements of Article 488 of the Code of Civil Procedure are deemed authentic when they can be used as an enforcement title." *Id.* (translation by author).

[24] LÓPEZ BLANCO, *supra* note 18, at 393. It states:

> Notice of default to a debtor is used in cases where enforcement does not coincide with default; on the other hand, notice of the assignment of receivables must be used when the instrument containing the receivable cannot be assigned through endorsement, because if it is possible to transfer or assign a receivable through endorsement notice is not required.

Id.

notice of the assignment of receivables to the attaching creditor[25] and notice of enforceable titles directed to the debtor's heirs.[26]

D. Types of Summary Processes: Large and Small Claims

In Colombia, a summary process may be for a large, small or minimum amount claimed; this amount determines the competency of the court. Until very recently, large and small claims followed the same procedural rules, and minimum claims were subject to a different one. Since the enactment of Law 794 in 2003, all summary processes must follow the same procedure, with the only difference that large and small claims are now subject to appeals and conciliation, while minimum amount claims have a single instance and, therefore, do not allow appeals or others.[27]

According to the Attorney General of Colombia, the reasoning behind having a single-instance process for minimum amount claims and a two-instance process for large and small claims is that "the minimum amount claim process is characterized by its briefness, expedited resolution, and balance between judicial economy and the right to legal representation and access to justice. . ."[28]

Most civil-law countries have a similar procedure for summary trials. Its steps are the following: First the complaint is filed before the competent judge, and it is accompanied by the enforcement title which, as just discussed, must incorporate a clear, express and immediately enforceable obligation. If applicable, it is also accompanied by a petition for cautionary measures to preserve assets for the purpose of execution by means of a preliminary order of attachment, garnishment or sequestration.

If the court is persuaded that the requirements for the summary procedure are met, it will issue an order directing the defendant to pay or else to face the attachment, garnishment or sequestration of assets available for execution.[29] If the complaint was accompanied by a request for cautionary or preliminary attachment and it is accepted

---

[25] *Id.* Notice of the assignment of receivables is done by presenting the instrument, "which will have an annotation with the transfer or assignment of the right, designating the assignee and bearing the signature of the assignor." CÓD. COM. (COLOM.) art.1961 (1971). It is important to clarify that according to the provision of arts. 1960–1963 of the Colombian Commercial Code, the assignment of receivables has no effects against the debtor or third parties unless due notice has been provided.

[26] CÓD. COM. (COLOM.), *supra* note 25, art. 1434. It states: "Negotiable instruments enforceable against a decedent are equally enforceable against his heirs, but creditors may not file a claim or enforce it until after eight days following judicial notice of these instruments." *Id.* (translation by author).

[27] L. 794, 9 de enero de 2003, Diario Oficial [D.O.] art. 70 (Colom.). It states:

> This law repeals all provisions that are contrary to it and especially the following: (. . .) b) Articles 544 to 549 of the Code of Civil Procedure that regulate the minimum amount summary process. These processes will be resolved in a single instance under the rules established for summary processes for large and small claims.

Id. (translation by author).

[28] Term used by the nation's Attorney General in Corte Constitucional [C.C.] [Constitutional Court] 2005, Sentencia C–103/05, *available at* http://www.corteconstitucional.gov.co/relatoria/2005/C–103–05.htm (translation by author).

[29] *See, e.g.,* C.P.C. (Colom.), *supra* note 5, art. 497. It states:

> Upon filing of the complaint in accordance with the law and with the enforcement title attached thereto, the judge will issue an order to the defendant, ordering him to comply with the obligation as requested in the complaint, if possible, or to comply in any way that he considers legal.

Id. (translation by author).

by the court, an order of attachment, garnishment or sequestration will be issued to the sheriff or court official in charge of such actions.

The judge may find that the document attached to the complaint was not an enforcement title because it did not comply with the requirements of law or may determine that the complaint is not sufficiently clear—in such cases the complaint may be dismissed by the judge, with or without prejudice.

If an order to pay is issued, notice must be given to the defendant. Forthwith, the official that is enforcing the order will request payment, and if the defendant pays or had previously paid then the process is suspended. However, if the defendant did not or does not pay, then the official will attach the defendant's assets, and following this stage in the process the defendant will be notified and will have a reasonable amount of time to comply with the obligation or to oppose the enforcement by filing defenses.[30]

If the defendant fails to comply within the time provided, he will be summoned to appear in court to hear the pronouncement of judgment; if he does comply with the obligation within the time, the process will end. However, if the defendant files any or all of the limited defenses allowed by the code of civil procedure there will be a short evidentiary period followed by the pronouncement of judgment within a short period of time.

1. Example of a Colombian Complaint in a Summary Process

TO THE CIVIL JUDGE OF THE CIRCUIT OF CALI

E.S.D.

REF.: INDIVIDUAL ACTION FOR SUMMARY PROCESS FILED BY IGNACIO JARAMILLO CABAL AGAINST JOSE MARIA ACEVEDO CASTRO

Daniel López, authorized lawyer, of age and of this domicile, as identified by my signature, acting as attorney for Mr. Ignacio Jaramillo Cabal, of age and of this domicile, in this writ filed in this court to start an individual summary process for a large claim against Mr. José María Acevedo Castro, of age and of this domicile, so that an order to pay is issued against the defendant and in favor of the plaintiff, for the amount that I will indicate in the petitions of this complaint.

FACTS

FIRST: The defendant issued check No. 023 in favor of the plaintiff on the defendant's checking account number 0003458761 at Bank Santander, with main offices in this city, for the amount of one hundred million pesos ($100,000,000.00). **SECOND:** That when trying to cash the check the bank did not pay it because of insufficient funds. **THIRD:** That all cash stamps have been removed from the check and its lack of payment has been formally protested. **FOURTH:** The debtor has not paid the check, therefore producing a current, clear, express and enforceable obligation. **FIFTH:** The plaintiff as

[30] JORGE A. CLARIA OLMEDO, DERECHO PROCESAL 314 (1982) (this author's translation). It states: "The purpose of filing defenses is to 'avoid being subject to what the plaintiff claims as a definite result of the process filed by the latter.' " *Id.* (this author's translation)

payee and holder of the check granted me the necessary powers of representation to file this claim.

CLAIMS

To the Honorable Judge, I request that you issue an order against the defendant and in favor of the plaintiff for the following amounts:

1. One hundred million pesos ($100,000,000.00) for the amount of the check;

2. Twenty million pesos ($20,000,000.00) equivalent to 20% of the amount of the check, as penalty pursuant to the provisions of Article 731 of the Commercial Code;

3. Banking default interest from the moment it was due until the defendant fulfills payment of these claims; and

4. Legal fees of this process.

LAW

The provisions of law supporting this claim are: Articles 619 to 670 and 712 to 751 of the Commercial Code and 488 et. seq. of the Code of Civil Procedure, and other corresponding or complementary laws.

PROCEDURE

This is a summary process for a large amount, and the process is regulated under Title XXVII, Chapter I through VI of the Code of Civil Procedure.

COMPETENCE AND AMOUNT CLAIMED

Your Honor is competent to hear this claim because of the place where the obligation is supposed to be complied with, because of the parties' domicile and because of the amount of the claim, which I estimate at one hundred and twenty million pesetas ($120,000,000.00).

EVIDENCE

I file as evidence, to support this claim, the negotiable instrument incorporated in check number 023 on the checking account number 0003458761 at Bank Santander, with main offices in this city.

ATTACHMENTS

I attach to this complaint the power of attorney granted in my favor, the previously-cited negotiable instrument, a copy of this complaint for the court files, a certification of bank interest issued by the Bank Supervising Agency, and a copy of the complaint to provide notice of it.

NOTIFICATIONS

I may be notified at the courthouse office, or at my office located at 4563 Street #11–33 of this city.

The plaintiff may be notified at 8965 Street #45–99 of this city.

The defendant may be notified at his place of residency, at 3256 Street #88–11 of this city.

Sincerely,

To you the Honorable Judge,

____

Daniel López

C.C. No. 12345678 of Cali

T.P. No. 87654321 of the Superior Judicial Council

2. *Example of a Mexican Complaint in a Summary Process*

FILE No. _______

COMMERCIAL SUMMARY PROCESS
LA FLOR COMPANY, S.A. DE C.V.
v.
LA 14, S.P.R. DE R.I.

JUDGE OF FIRST INSTANCE

CIVIL COURTROOM ON DUTY

SEBASTIAN QUIJANO, of Mexican nationality, of legal age, acting in my capacity as attorney at law in charge of disputes and collections for the company La Flor Company, S.A. de C.V., capacity that I demonstrate with a certified copy of public deed number 14137, volume 333, of the public notary 31, Pedro Gomez Esq., practicing and domiciled in this city, I hereby establish as place to receive notifications my law firm located at Street Tetabiate, No. 89, of this city; and pursuant to Articles 1069 of the Commercial Code in force and Articles 71, 72 and 174 of the Code of Civil Procedure of the State of Sonora, I hereby authorize as senior lawyer, Camilo Arango Esq. with Professional Identification Number 1493973 issued by the General Department of Professions, and pursuant to the last of the above-mentioned articles, I hereby authorize José Reyes, Daniel Cervantes and Martin Caicedo; I respectfully appear before you to state that:

By means of this writ and based on section IV of Article 1391 of the Commercial Code in force, I come to file a summary commercial claim against the company La 14, S.P.R. de R.I. which may receive service of process at its domicile located at Calle Coahuila, No. 872–8 of this city, claiming payment and compliance of the following obligations:

a) Payment of the principal amount of US$18,080.00 (Eighteen thousand and eighty US dollars).

b) Payment of normal interest of 15% per annum, as stated in the document that supports this claim.

c) Payment of default interest of 18.75% per annum, until the date of full payment of the debt.

d) Payment of the tax on normal and default interest at a rate of 15% or the rate in effect as of the time it is owed.

e) Payment of legal fees and expenses sustained because of this trial.

I base the claim on the following facts and law:

FACTS

1. On June 12, 2001, the company La 14, S.P.R. de R.I. through its legal representatives issued a promissory note in favor of La Flor Company, S.A. de C.V. for the amount of US$18,080.00 (Eighteen thousand and eighty US dollars) payable on November 30, 2001.

2. In said promissory note, the company La 14, S.P.R. de R.I. had the obligation to pay normal interest of 15% per annum and default interest of 18.75% per annum until the date of full payment.

3. Since the date for payment as stated in number 1 above has elapsed and the issuer has not fully paid it, despite several extrajudicial requests of payment made by the company I represent, for this reason it is necessary to judicially claim its payment.

EVIDENCE

I offer the following evidence:

1. Certified copy of public deed number 14137, volume 333, of the public notary 31, Pedro Gomez Esq., practicing and domiciled in this city, with which I prove my capacity as general attorney for disputes and collections for the company La Flor Company, S.A. de C.V.

2. Original promissory note Number D1–000142 issued by the company La 14, S.P.R. de R.I. on June 12, 2001 payable on November 30 of the same year.

LAW

Articles 175 to 196 of the General Law of Negotiable Instruments and Credit Operations are applicable to the substance of this claim.

With respect to the procedure available for this claim, Articles 1391 to 1414 of the Commercial Code apply.

Based on all the aforementioned, to you honorable Judge I hereby petition:

FIRST. To recognize my capacity as attorney for the company La Flor Company, S.A. de C.V. as evidenced by the certified copy of the public deed containing the power of attorney that is attached to this complaint; upon this recognition of my capacity, I ask you to admit this complaint against the company La 14, S.P.R. de R.I. in a commercial summary process, exercising the right for payment of the stipulations of the amounts claimed.

SECOND. To issue a resolution containing an order requesting the defendant to pay and upon non-compliance, to attach the defendant's assets up to the amount owed and to place them in deposit with the person appointed by the creditor, and to provide the defendant with notice of this complaint so that it can present its arguments.

THIRD. Once all legal procedures have been completed, to issue judgment against the defendant as requested in this complaint and order public auction of the attached assets to pay the creditor with the proceeds of the auction.

FOURTH. To accept my authorization of the professionals hereby appointed by me to intervene on my behalf in this process.

I DECLARE ALL THAT IS NECESSARY.

City of Obregon, Sonora, February 12, 2002.

Sebastian Caicedo Quijano, Esq.

§ 25.4 A LANDMARK SPANISH DECISION ON DEFENSES IN AN EXECUTIVE PROCEDURE

The following Spanish appellate decision illustrates the fallacy of the widespread assumption in civil law countries that negotiable instruments such as promissory notes and bills of exchange are *ipso iure* executive documents. This fallacious assumption is heard even when the plaintiffs in the executive actions are the original payee-holders of these instruments and their defendants are the original debtors of the underlying transaction acting as makers-signers of the notes or as acceptors of the bills of exchange. The truth is that the only parties whose status as holders of negotiable instruments is undisputed as plaintiffs in executive actions are those who are holders in due course. Because the legal status of all the holders of negotiable instruments (whether in due course or not) is governed not only by the codes of civil procedure but also by the laws of negotiable instruments, and because the latter list the defenses against holders in greater detail than the former, the laws of negotiable instruments should be given the preeminent status of a "*lex specialis*" or of the more specific law and therefore prevail. Yet as will be apparent in the following decision, Spanish appellate courts seem evenly divided on this point. One of the questions for the reader to keep in mind, then, is whether the same "virus" that seemed capable of infecting the executive status of the promissory note in this case can also infect other documents that involve the original parties to the underlying transaction as plaintiffs and defendants. Another question is whether reasoning by the Spanish appellate court is not surprisingly close to that of a United States court considering whether there are grounds to grant a motion for summary judgment. And if that is the case, could not this decision be regarded as inhabiting the grey area between the facts required to be proven in executive actions and those in motions for summary judgment?

Gamma Due, SL v. SMACC SpA[31]

In the city of Castellon, on the sixteenth day of June of two thousand and one. The First Branch of the Provincial Appellate Court of Castellon comprised by the undersigned judges has considered the present appeal against the lower court decision of. . . the thirteenth day of October of nineteen hundred and ninety nine. This opinion is drafted by D. Fernando Martínez Sanz.

FACTS:

First: The lower court decision literally ordered:. . . to proceed with the execution of judgment against the attached goods of defendant Gamma Due, SL and obtain payment with the proceeds of these goods to plaintiff SMAC, SPA for an amount of

[31] Gamma Due, SL v. SMACC SpA, 1st Branch of the Provincial Appellate Court of Castellon (Spain), June 16 2001 (originally Oct. 13, 1999) (unpublished version on file wit author).

8,068,900 pesetas, as well as payment of all the legal interest owed on this debt. . . by the defendant.

Second: Upon notification of this decision to the parties by the representatives of Gamma Due, SL a timely appeal was lodged against it and this appeal having being admitted. . . service of process was issued and the parties appeared before this court.

Third: By this court's order of November 24, 1999 the present record of proceedings was created. . . A hearing was held with the parties present. During this hearing, the appellant requested the reversal of the lower court decision with the issuance of another decision in its favor and imposing costs upon the plaintiff below. Appellee requested the confirmation of the lower court decision with the imposition of costs upon the appellant. . .

LEGAL BASES FOR THE PRESENT DECISION:

The legal bases of the appealed judgment are accepted and confirmed based on the following reasons:

FIRST. The appellee is the payee-holder of a promissory note validly issued and signed by the appellant. The parties had entered into a purchase and sale agreement, the executing appellee is an Italian company who had sold a tile polishing machine to the appellant. . . The note was presented for payment after its due date and was dishonored. Thereafter a series of collection actions were undertaken by the appellee. . . and when these failed the appellee brought an executive action against the appellant.

Appellant, Gamma Due, SL, raised first the defense of lack of proper formalities alleging that the note was presented for payment in an untimely manner on November 21, 1997. Such a defense is rejected as it was below. It is true that the holder of a note has the burden of presenting it on its due date or during the next two working days. Nevertheless, the consequence of failing to present the note during such a date is the loss of an action against the parties secondarily liable such as endorsers or drawers, etc. (who would otherwise lack notice of the presentment and be deprived of an opportunity to timely pay themselves or force payment by the defendant). Thus, the failure to present the note during those early days does not entail the loss of an action by a party primarily liable such as the appellee who as holder of the note was not affected by the above-mentioned period of presentation.

SECOND. The second ground for appeal which consists of the allegation that funds were not provided to the appellant for the payment of the note by the appellee appears to create greater difficulties for the appealed decision. One of the components of this defense is that appellee breached his contractual duties as seller of the equipment purchased by the appellant. Article 67.1 of the applicable law of negotiable instruments points out, in relation to Article 96 of the LCCH, that the "the debtor of a negotiable instrument may raise against the holder of the bill of exchange all the defenses that emerge from their personal (contractual) relationship." In the case before us, the defense would have been the defects that appellant alleges he found in the tile polishing machine that made it unfit for the purpose it was acquired.

The law links this defense to the bill of exchange. . . It is true that the provision in question may seem to warrant such a defense when it states that "to the promissory note will be applicable, the provisions related to the bill of exchange. . . as long as they are not incompatible with its nature (arts. 49–60, 62 and 68)" (art. 96 LCCH). . . If applicable, these rules would allow defenses such as the extinction, nullity, or breach of the underlying contract. We are mindful of the existence of numerous decisions by provincial appellate courts which reject the application to promissory notes of the defense that funds for its payment were not provided to the maker-appellant. We are also mindful of the existence of an equal number of decisions that allow such a defense. Our survey of case law shows, then, that the law of defenses is far from uniform.

The critical issue, then, is whether the causal or underlying contract defenses, such as a breach of contract by the appellee against the appellant, are incompatible with the nature of the promissory note. It is obvious that the promissory note differs from the bill of exchange in some fundamental respects: While the note embodies a pure and simple promise of payment by its maker-signer, the bill of exchange is an order of payment directed by the drawer to the drawee. On the other hand, it is also true that once a drawee accepts the bill, his position does not differ much from that of a signer or maker of a promissory note, for his acceptance will also be "pure and simple.". . . And no one *dares to assert that a drawee cannot raise the defense of lack of provision of funds to the holder of a bill of exchange that claims it.* From the standpoint of the certainty of the holding of negotiable instruments, is there a reason to treat any differently the maker or signer of a note and an acceptor of a bill of exchange?. . . If one were to prevent the maker or signer of a note to raise causal defenses, the promissory note would be transformed into something it is not: the so-called "first demand guarantee," in which the guarantor promises in an unconditional and absolute fashion to pay once its beneficiary demands payment. . .

At a time when the instrument has not yet left the immediate parties (the debtor and creditor of the original or underlying transaction) and is not yet in circulation there are no valid reasons to. . . "immunize" the original creditor from the causal or underlying contract defenses. . . since he is not a third party in good faith as required by Article 20 of the LCCH. As long as there are not such third party holders, the "personal" or causal defenses between the appellant and appellee may be raised. (art. 67.1 LCCH). The lower court judge is therefore correct when he states that it is possible to raise the defense of the lack of provision of funds against the party seeking to execute on a promissory note.

The fact that such a defense may be raised does not mean that it is appropriate in the present case. What the appellant alleges by way of underlying or causal contract defense was that the machine had a number of defects that made it unfit for its business purpose. This argument is unacceptable. . . Despite the large volume of materials on record, no precise indication appears on the purpose of the machine. By not supplying the actual sale agreement and its exact specification on the object of this contract, its payment schedule, etc., it is very difficult to deduce if there was a breach by the seller. We only find a document related to the terms of its delivery (franco destination)[32] and an addendum whereby the buyer agrees to test the machine for a period of five days allowing its return if it does not perform as it did in the factory and that the period of thirty days to claim hidden or latent defects (*vicios ocultos*) set forth by Article 342 of the Commercial Code lapsed. . .

For purposes of admissibility in an executive procedure, our case law distinguishes between the defense of total breach or lack of performance (*exceptio non adimpleti*

[32] *See* Glossary, "Franco Destination."

contractus) and a defective performance short of a total breach (*exceptio non rite adimpleti contractus*). While the effect of the first is unambiguous and easily provable in an executive trial—even if the debtor's promissory note is the basis for this trial—the same is not true with a merely defective performance. . . The reason for this distinction is that a defective performance often is a matter of degree and therefore it cannot be easily proven by a procedure restricted to objectively and quickly ascertainable evidence. . . for this reason such evidence is best heard in an ordinary or declarative action as held by a vast number of decisions.

In the case before us, while defects of the polishing machine are alleged it is not certain whether they are major or structural or they arise in normal usage. These are issues beyond the evidentiary capability of a summary trial. . . In addition, as stated by our Supreme Court, one ought to distinguish between the case of latent defects and a breach due to the mistaken delivery of one thing for another (*aliud pro alio*). . . As stated by the Supreme Court in its decision of December 1, 1977, where one thing has been delivered for another, a total breach has occurred and the aggrieved buyer may rely on articles 1101, 1106 and 1124 of the Civil Code without having to prove the total inability to use the thing. . . and the latent defects required by articles 1484, 1485 and 1486 of the Civil Code. An executive summary procedure is not suitable also for the determination of whether there is an "*aliud por alio*."

No matter how strenuous the efforts of the plaintiff, this court is in no position to determine if there was such a delivery in this case. . . Here and now what we can only establish is whether or not the machine fulfilled satisfactorily at the time of its delivery and installation as we can also establish that after such a delivery and installation the plaintiff signed the promissory note in question. . . even though he had no obligation to do it if it was not to his satisfaction. . . This court thus shares the conclusions arrived by the court below after examining the expert's findings on the lack of sufficient evidence for a claim of total breach. . . For all these reasons, we decide that:

The appeal is rejected and the lower court decision is confirmed. . .

§ 25.5 A COMMENTARY, A SUGGESTION AND A FEW QUESTIONS

This decision should be highly influential on the issue of admissible defenses in executive actions for commercial contracts and promises of payment. It is factually based and well researched from a jurisprudential, although not always from a transactional, standpoint (as will be discussed shortly). What it says about the enforcement of promissory notes as executive titles could be easily applied to checks, bills of exchange, public deeds and, in some Latin American countries, even to invoices signed by the debtor-purchaser (*facturas cambiarias o conformadas* or the Brazilian *duplicatas*), precisely for the purpose of enabling the filing of executive-like actions.

One need not be a legal oracle to divine the reason behind the use of these instruments in an executive trial, a use that crossed national boundaries and appears in the trade between Spain and Italy, two members of the European Union: to avoid the extraordinary lengths and costs of a declarative-ordinary, breach of contract action. Yet, has this promissory note-based practice achieved its purpose?

First, let me address some of the transactional shortcomings of the decision. When comparing the promissory note to the bill of exchange, the court follows what seems to have become a tradition among Spanish courts and litigants. They equate the historical defense of lack of a provision of funds (peculiar to bills of exchange) to the generic "causal" defense because of breach or failure to perform related to the underlying (*exceptio non adimpleti contractus* and *exceptio non rite adimpleti contractus*).

The lack of a provision of funds is a defense in mostly obsolete bill of exchange law because, it was based on the acceptance that a bill of exchange was supposed to document an underlying contract for the purchase or trade of foreign exchange.[33] It will be recalled that its typical transaction was as follows: The purchaser of the exchange, say in Genoa, Italy, provided Genovese currency to the drawer of the bill of exchange in Genoa so that he would order or instruct (by means of the bill) his correspondent or business partner drawee in Salamanca, Spain to pay a similar or corresponding amount of Spanish pesetas in Spain. The bill of exchange also acted as an authorization to debit the drawer's account with the drawee for the amount paid out to the holder of the bill. A failure to provide funds to the drawer could be used by the drawee as his justification for not accepting the bill of exchange (if the bill required acceptance) or for not paying it, if it was payable "at sight."

Only by a rather distant factual analogy could this justification for non-acceptance or non-payment by the drawee (a third party) be equated to the breach of contract by the payee of the promissory note against the maker of the note. For unlike the drawee and the payee-holder of the bill of exchange, the maker and payee of the note were in a direct contractual relationship. Their relationship was referred to by English judges as in "privity of contract," and the breach of this contract was directly suffered by the maker of the note, unlike what happened with the drawee of the bill. If the same sale had been paid by a bill, it may not have necessarily been suffered by its acceptor-payor because his relationship was with the drawer and its ostensible "cause" was a foreign exchange transaction and not a forbidden loan or even installment sale transaction.

Further, as will be recalled from the discussion about the effect of *causa* upon French, German and English negotiable instruments law,[34] the underlying cause played a disabling role with respect to French negotiable instruments in contrast with its very different (if existent) role with respect to German and English bills of exchange.

In light of the different weight given to the cause of the underlying transaction in France and Spain on the one hand and Germany and Britain on the other, and to the increased willingness by European consumer protection legislation to replace the warranty against hidden defects by a broader warranty of merchantability,[35] the following waiver of defenses by the maker of the note may be a useful tool for summary procedures: "The maker of this note irrevocably waives the defense of breach of contract, whether total or partial, except for the defenses of payee's fraud, malice or grave fault in the performance of the underlying transaction."[36]

---

[33] *See supra* § 11:2(D).

[34] *Id.*

[35] *Id.* Perhaps the most important source for the increasing acceptability by civil law nations of its warranty and merchantability is CISG art. 35(2), which was replaced by U.C.C. § 2–314 & § 2–315.

[36] The text of this quote is this author's proposal.

Yet, would such a waiver be possible under the Geneva Convention on Bills of Exchange and Promissory Notes?[37] Would it be possible under U.C.C. Articles 3 and 9?[38] Would you agree that if such a waiver were upheld, the promissory note and perhaps other instruments such as the check, the bill of exchange or a signed invoice could truly become effective tools of a quick and inexpensive executive procedure? In light of the importance of contemporary consumer protection law, should this waiver be restricted only to merchants in their commercial transactions?

When drafting the preceding waiver, I was fully aware that, as I stated in the introductory paragraph to this case, a fundamental difference exists between the status of an "immediate" party to the transaction such as the seller of the polishing machine and his buyer in this case, and a third party holder in due course or innocent purchaser of the promissory note. The latter should enjoy immunity from the underlying defenses while the immediate party, in principle, does not deserve to be "immunized."[39] Yet, buyers may well agree to such a waiver if in exchange for their signature they get a considerable reduction in the price or other beneficial terms or conditions, including a beneficial interest in a reasonably-priced insurance policy.

§ 25.6 UNITED STATES PROCESS: DISCOVERY, COMPLAINT AND DECISION

A. From Common Law Forms of Action to Code Pleadings[40]

Although the United States inherited a rigid system of pleading and proof known as "forms of action" from English law (whereby unless plaintiffs or defendants repeated ritualistic formulas in their "writs" they risked losing their actions or defenses) such has not been its procedural law for over two centuries. During the nineteenth century, many if not most states adopted a "code" or statutory pleading that dispensed with the old forms of action. It relied instead on a generic complaint or declaration followed by an answer, rejoinder, rebutter and surrebutter, and other unnamed pleadings. Eventually, code pleading was also discarded in favor of a less formalistic and technical system as embodied in the rules of civil procedure adopted by the United States federal district courts in 1938 and eventually by most state courts as well.

United States procedural law, whether in federal or state courts, does not distinguish between civil and commercial trials; the trial of what a civilian would consider a commercial or civil case is subject to the same unified rules of pleading and proof in United States law. This unified trial system is divided into several stages: 1) pleadings; 2) disclosure of the essence of the claims and defenses, and pre-trial discovery; 3) oral presentation of evidence before the judge or jury, as the case may be;

---

[37] The League of Nations, Convention Providing a Uniform Law for Bills of Exchange and Promissory Notes, (Geneva, 1930), *available at* http://www.jus.uio.no/lm/bills.of.exchange.and.promissory.notes.convention.1930/doc.html.

[38] U.C.C. art. 3 (2012) & U.C.C. art. 9 (2012).

[39] This is a distinction that I advocated in earlier writings and which was quoted approvingly in some unpublished Spanish, Chinese and Korean court decisions. *See* Boris Kozolchyk, *The Immunization of Fraudulently Procured Letter of Credit Acceptances: All Services Exportacao, Importacao, Comercio S.A. v. Banco Bamerindus Do Brazil., S.A. and First Commercial v. Gotham Originals*, 58 BROOK. L. REV. 369 (1992–1993).

[40] John F. Molloy, *Civil Procedure*, *in* 1 UNITED STATES LAW OF TRADE AND INVESTMENT 7–iii–7–76 (2001). This section is a summary of chapter 7 on U.S. Civil Procedure.

and 4) final judgment. This judgment can take the form of a summary judgment in which case there is no need for the presentation of evidence or for discovery, because, based on what the parties themselves alleged, there is no issue of fact to be tried. A fifth and final stage consists of the appeal.

During the entire process, facts "drive the vehicle we call law," as stated by Judge F. Molloy, a litigator and friend of the author—or "*Ex Factum Ius Oritur*," as more elegantly stated by Justice Brandeis of the Supreme Court of the United States. This is the reason why under U.S. law the initial pleadings or complaint have to be sufficiently broad and flexible, enabling the parties to discover and then add, remove or modify its content at any of the previously mentioned stages—prior to final judgment.

As described by Judge Molloy, "the complaint is a written declaration of a claim [a term that now includes electronic communications between the court and the parties], which can be founded on either legislative or common law. The claim need not state facts but may be based on legal conclusions."[41] The Rules of Civil Procedure specify that the complaint requires a " 'short and plain statement' of the grounds of jurisdiction of the court and a 'short and plain statement' of the claim."[42] Also, "pleading in the alternative and adoption by reference [are] permitted."[43]

A typical U.S. complaint (as the one provided in this section)[44] is divided into different counts that state different legal grounds for the claim. Unlike what happens with the Colombian and Mexican complaints, in the U.S. complaint, "[i]t is not material that the counts are phrased in the alternative, or even that one count is not consistent with another."[45]

Judge Molloy continues: "Contrary to the practice in many legal systems with Roman ancestry . . . it is *not* necessary to allege: . . . [t]he capacity of a party to sue or to be sued."[46] To which I would add that it is also unnecessary to allege and prove before trial that the parties or of their judicial or extrajudicial representatives have the powers of attorney under which the complaint is filed. Under the U.S. law of procedure there is a presumption of good faith of the parties and of the professionals.

Moreover, under U.S. civil procedure there is no difference between declaratory and summary judgments, because the latter is a generic motion for judgment by which the moving party petitions the court to issue its ruling before trial. This motion is known as motion for summary judgment or motion for judgment on the pleadings, and it requires that there be no "genuine dispute as to the material facts concerning one or more issues";[47] the *quid iuris* is only on the applicable law, a matter that can be decided by the judge without determining the facts of the case, and hence the process is bound to be resolved summarily.

Under U.S. law, this concept of a trial revolved around the distinct nature of the judicial hearing and its components, both evidentiary and decisional, all of them

---

[41] *Id.* at 7–22.

[42] *Id.* at 7–48.

[43] *Id.* at 7–49.

[44] *See infra* 2.

[45] Molloy, *supra* note 40, at 7–49.

[46] *Id.* at 7–38.

[47] *Id.* at 7–58.

contributors to the proverbial "day in court." This concept is in contrast to the civil procedure in many countries with Roman roots, in which the judicial hearing is a stage in a civil or criminal process and which occurs serially.[48] In fact, "[i]n the U.S., the trial is in the nature of a single public event, essentially oral in nature, commencing at a time certain, solely and only for the presentation of evidence and the questioning and the cross-examining of witnesses. This event commences on a date and hour fixed by the court, with its object the determination of the facts of the case [and may last a few hours, weeks or, sometimes, even months or years]. [Similarly], [c]ontests over what the applicable law may be [or certain procedures, especially evidentiary ones], are often determined by the trial judge in rulings upon various pre-trial motions [and special rulings]."[49]

B. Summary Judgment Decisions

In U.S. civil trials, there is an action and procedure for obtaining a summary judgment. Summary judgment procedures are available for actions based on commercial contracts and negotiable instruments, as well as for actions based on other evidentiary documents or titles that prove the certainty of the rights claimed (for example, final judgments or a party's confession). As was mentioned in the previous section, the procedural theory behind the U.S. action and procedure for summary judgment is that there is no dispute on the material facts of the claim as alleged by the moving party and not objected by the other party; the only dispute is on the law applicable to such facts. The moving party—whether the plaintiff or defendant—is the one that must prove that there is no genuine dispute as to the material facts. In addition, it is the non-moving party who has to prove that there is a genuine dispute as to the material facts; hence, the nature of the evidence is open and unlimited and, therefore, different from that of summary processes under civil law systems.[50] It will be recalled that under the latter, defenses are listed in the law and, therefore, they are closed in number.

C. Filing a Civil Action

1. Pre-Trial Discovery

One of the most important distinguishing features of the U.S. civil and commercial trial procedure is the ability of the parties to obtain disclosure of facts from opposing parties. The right to discover the factual and legal bases of the opposing party's case extends not only to material evidence, but also to any fact which may "lead to the discovery of admissible evidence."[51] This revolution in judicial procedure commenced with the adoption by the U.S. Congress of the Federal Rules of Civil Procedure in 1938—rules which, as noted earlier, have served as the model for similar rules in the great majority of the U.S. states and their courts.[52]

---

[48] *Id.* at 7–19.

[49] *Id.* at 7–18. *See also* Boris Kozolchyk, *in Transcript of the Symposium on Judicial Cooperation Between the United States and Mexico* 1985 ARIZ. J. INT'L & COMP. L 11–13 (1985) (for additional information on this comparison, and the dialogue between Mexican and U.S. lawyers).

[50] Molloy, *supra* note 40, at 7–58.

[51] Rule 26(b)(1) of the Rules of Civil Procedure for the United States District Courts, *cited in id.* at 7–4.

[52] *Id.* at 7–4.

The result of this procedural revolution is that the parties are free to investigate the facts from any type of evidence (documental, testimonial, expert testimonies) before it is presented in trial. This leads to the preparation of very elaborate questionnaires and petitions for documents or other evidence and to the close examination of answers to these questionnaires and to testimony presented by the other party. It must be emphasized that although the parties proceed to this disclosure in their individual and private capacities, the procedure for requesting and disclosing pre-trial evidence is of a mandatory nature.

It is also mandatory to hold private hearings or meetings in which the plaintiff has the right to question the truthfulness of the information provided by the other party—whether provided in the pre-trial discovery stage or during the private hearing. The party answering the questionnaire may object directly before the trial court during the stage of production of evidence, or during the private hearing. In general, an objection may be to the irrelevance, broadness, excessiveness or abusive petition of documents or other type of evidence; or on the examination or cross-examination made by the plaintiff during the private hearing. An objection made during the private hearing must be made to the party conducting the hearing, normally a private lawyer. All objections will be evaluated by the court during a special hearing, and its decision will either order the corresponding party to provide the evidence or the requested answer, or will exempt it from doing so.

This procedure shapes the manner in which the complaint is drafted, leaving the facts, applicable law and petition of evidence open to everything that may be discovered during this pre-trial discovery. This pre-trial process also has a profound effect on the way the parties present their allegations and evidence during trial and on the drafting of the final judgment.

At the end of this section, there is an example of an arbitral award governed by the Arbitration Rules of the United Nations Commission on International Trade Law (UNCITRAL),[53] which was influenced by U.S. pre-trial discovery rules and practice. This arbitration award illustrates the significant impact that pre-trial discovery of facts had on the findings of facts and the resolution of that dispute.

2. *Complaint*

Under the U.S. trial system, a complaint is a writ (usually delivered to the court in electronic form) which contains factual and—to a lesser extent—legal grounds on which the action is based. The applicable law may be found in statutes or in common law. As is clearly shown in the complaint provided herein, there are very few formalities required in pleadings. For the complaint, Rule 8 of the Federal Rules of Civil Procedure specifies a "short and plain statement" of the grounds of jurisdiction of the court and a "short and plain statement" of the claim.[54] Therefore, pleadings are usually schematic, which justifies some judges granting petitions requesting that the plaintiff provide a clearer or more comprehensive complaint. Finally, it is worth mentioning that not all actions seek to obtain damages, but that there are some special forms of action to claim specific performance of obligations. Unlike the *justicia rogada*

---

[53] Arbitration Rules of the United Nations Commission on International Trade Law (UNCITRAL). G.A. Res. 31/98, U.N. GAOR, 31st Sess., Supp. No. 17, U.N. Doc. A/31/PV.99, (Dec. 15, 1976).

[54] Molloy, *supra* note 40, at 7–48.

approach, it is not necessary to state the precise relief requested in order to receive damages. These are called actions in "equity," in which the judge, rather than a jury, is the fact-finder and where what is sought by the plaintiff is recovery of title to real estate property or specific performance of contracts as well as remedies to do or not to do something (injunctive relief).

a. Sample of a U.S. Complaint

Law Offices of John P. Green

SBN 111111

2000 E. Main St.

Tucson, Arizona, 00000

(520) 888–8888

IN THE SUPERIOR COURT OF THE STATE OF ARIZONA IN AND FOR THE COUNTY OF PIMA

LISA SMITH, a single woman, and JEREMEY JONES and CHERYL JONES, husband and wife, plaintiffs,

v.

GENERAL PROPERTIES, INC., an Illinois corporation, and ABC LIMITED PARTNERSHIP, a limited partnership, defendants,

COMPLAINT: Rescission of Contract, or, in alternative, Damages for Fraud assigned to: _______.

FACTS: The plaintiffs, Lisa Smith, a single woman, and Jeremey Jones, and Cheryl Jones, husband and wife, for their causes of action against the defendants, and each of them, allege as follows:

COUNT ONE—Rescission

1. The defendant, GENERAL PROPERTIES, INC., is an Illinois corporation, doing business in Pima County, State of Arizona; defendant ABC LIMITED PARTNERSHIP is an Arizona limited partnership; all events giving rise to the causes of action herein stated occurred in Pima County, Arizona.

2. Plaintiff, Lisa Smith is a single woman; plaintiffs, Jeremey Jones and Cheryl Jones are husband and wife.

3. In early September of this year (2000), and prior to September 18, 2000, the defendants, and each of them, by their agent Michael Morgan, made representations and promises to the plaintiffs to induce them to enter into a certain transaction with the defendants, by which the plaintiffs were to purchase through a corporation to be formed and owned by them, a certain space in the "Patron Place," a shopping center owned and controlled by the defendants, located on East Broadway, Tucson, Arizona (hereinafter referred to as "the Mall"). Among such representations made, which induced the plaintiffs to so act, were the following:

a. That the Mall had traffic levels of approximately 50,000 people per day and that the traffic would at least double over the Christmas and New Year holidays;

b. That the other spaces in the Mall similar to the one being sold to the plaintiffs had present sales levels of a minimum of $2000 per day, and some were doing over $12,000 per day;

c. That in the Mall, during November and December of 1999, the space which had the least amount of sales grossed $70,000 monthly and there were similar spaces that grossed as much as $120,000 monthly during this time.

4. That in reliance upon these representations, the plaintiffs: (a) commenced the organization of a corporation, Body Color, Inc., which was to be the buyer of the space promised to them by the defendants; (b) paid the defendants $100,000 as a partial payment of the purchase price estimated at $500,000; (c) purchased merchandise to retail in the space bought by the plaintiffs from the defendants; (d) employed personnel to administer the retail store to be established; and (e) devoted hundreds of hours of their own time in promoting and conducting said business.

5. The plaintiffs have received no benefit from the space so purchased from the defendants, and in addition to the amounts paid to the defendants as part of the purchase price, the plaintiffs have lost substantial sums of money in carrying out the business.

6. Upon discovering that the representations above stated were materially false and that the marketing campaign in newspapers and television that the defendants as owners of the shopping center had promised had not occurred before or at the time of this complaint, the plaintiffs gave written notice to the defendants, to the effect that they elected to rescind the above-described contract, and offered to deliver back the purchased space in exchange for the $100,000 initially paid.

7. The defendants refused to rescind the contract.

8. In connection with the bringing of this action, the plaintiffs have incurred several costs, including legal fees.

WHEREFORE, plaintiffs ask for judgment as follows:

1. That this court declares that the contract between the parties has been rightfully rescinded by the plaintiffs, and that the defendants must return the sum of $100,000, plus interest at legal rate.

2. That the plaintiffs recover their reasonable legal fees, the costs of this action, and any other that this court deems appropriate.

COUNT TWO—Damages

In the event that the relief sought in the prior count cannot be promptly granted, the plaintiffs adopt by reference the allegations of paragraphs 1 through 4, inclusive, of Count One, *supra*, and allege the following:

With regard to the said representations and promises, the plaintiffs allege: (a) that these misrepresentations were deliberately made by the defendants; (b) that the representations made were known by the defendants to be false when made; (c) that the defendants had no intention of performing future acts promised; (d) that the representations were deliberately made to induce the plaintiffs to enter into the aforesaid contract, and to induce the plaintiffs to pay to the defendants $100,000; (e) that the plaintiffs were ignorant of the falsity of said representations and promises and reasonably believed the representations made to be true, and that the promised activities would be performed; and (f) that the plaintiffs relied upon the representations and promises made by the defendants and, as a result thereof, they incurred expenses in an amount in excess of $300,000, and expended considerable amounts of their time and energy calculated at a reasonable value of $150,000.

WHEREFORE, plaintiffs ask for judgment as follows:

For judgment against the defendants and each of them for damages sustained in the sum of $450,000, and for the costs incurred in this action, including attorneys' fees.

For judgment against the defendants for punitive damages in the sum of $300,000, or in such greater amount as the jury and court may deem appropriate, with the purpose of discouraging similar conduct.

For such other relief as the court may deem appropriate.

LAW OFFICES OF JOHN P. GREEN

By: ______________________

John P. Green
Attorney for plaintiffs

STATE OF ARIZONA
PIMA COUNTY ss

Lisa Smith and Cheryl Jones stated under oath that they have read the foregoing complaint and that the statements therein are true, in substance and in fact.

______________________ ______________________

Lisa Smith Cheryl Jones

b. Importance of Pre-Trial Discovery: Arbitration Between Plaintiff "PC" and Defendant "MC," Case Number XXX of the AAA

Given the importance of pre-trial discovery, I will now transcribe sections of an arbitral award in connection with a major commercial contract dispute, where this type of discovery played a central role and where I was Chair of the Arbitral Tribunal that applied the Arbitration Rules of the UNCITRAL[55] signed by Mexico and, therefore, part of the Mexican arbitration procedure that allowed discovery prior to arbitration. Please pay special attention to Section C of this award.

---

[55] Arbitration Rules of the United Nations Commission on International Trade Law (UNCITRAL), *supra* note 53.

The names of the parties and disputed facts have been modified in order to preserve their anonymity.

Arbitral Award issued with majority of votes, in Mexico September 17, 1996.[56]

I. BACKGROUND

A. FACTS

1. JOINT VENTURE

On June 15, 1985 the Mexican companies PC and MC, each a subsidiary of U.S. corporations PC Inc. and MC Corp. respectively, concluded a contract of joint venture (hereinafter JV).[57] The purpose of the contract was to market "fertilizer PC" in Mexico.

Under the contract, MC provided the product and trademark, while PC had to distribute and market the product, including selling, invoicing, collecting, advertising and promoting the product. The parties agreed to equally receive profits or sustain losses, *i.e.*, at a 50/50 rate.

2. CONTRACTUAL REFERENCES TO MEXICAN PESOS AND U.S. DOLLARS

The JV's daily operations were kept in Mexican pesos, as well as the resulting distribution of dividends and tax obligations. However, their contract referred to the initial investment of the parties as: "the amounts in Mexican Pesos then equivalent to US$560,000. . ."

3. CONTRACTUAL STIPULATIONS ON MC'S TERMINATION OF THE CONTRACT WITHOUT RIGHTFUL CAUSE

Article 10 of the JV stipulates the termination of the contract with or without rightful cause. Article 10.2.1 establishes the terms and conditions applicable to MC if MC decides to terminate the contract without rightful cause. This article grants MC two options for terminating the contract:

If MC notifies PC of its termination of the contract without rightful cause, MC must comply with one of the following alternatives:. . . (b) MC will pay PC, or whoever PC appoints, a severance payment equal to 175% of the net aggregated sales of the product received in the last twelve months prior to the notice of termination.

On January 23, 1995, MC notified PC of its intention to terminate the JV effective as of July 31 of the same year, because it considered that, although there were good economic results, the JV was not consistent with its objectives. In the notice, MC indicated that the amount of 112,602,000 new Mexican Pesos was equal to what it calculated was 175% multiplied by the net aggregated sales of fertilizer PC received in the last twelve months prior to this notice, in consideration of the half of the fertilizer business owned by

---

[56] The text of the original arbitral award has been modified because of its length. The original arbitral award was ratified by the Supreme Court of Mexico.

[57] Art. 252 of the Ley General de Sociedades Mercantiles [LGSM] [General Law of Commercial Corporations], *as* amended, Diario Oficial de la Federación [DO], 4 de agosto de 1934 (Mex.). It defines the atypical contract of joint venture as: "A joint venture is a contract by which one person grants another person or persons that provide goods or services to the former a share in the profits and losses of the commercial activity or of one or several commercial transactions." *Id.* (translation by author).

PC. On August 1, 1995, MC delivered payment to PC on the basis of the above calculation and deposited the aforesaid amount. . . in a bank account with Citibank, NY, where it is still deposited awaiting the resolution of this dispute.

The dispute between the parties is on the amount offered by MC to PC. The amount offered in payment by MC is based on the net sales of the product in Mexican Pesos, during the twelve months prior to the notice of termination, multiplied by 175%. The amount of 112,602,000 new Mexican pesos according to MC was equal to US$19,478,262. Only just a month before MC's assessment, the Mexican currency was devaluated by approximately forty percent with respect to the U.S. dollar. If the Mexican peso had not been devaluated and if MC would have based the estimations on the net sales on the JV's profit and loss statement of that year, the amount that MC would have to pay would have reached US$32,783,986.

Therefore, although there are several facts in dispute in the arbitral complaint, in the responsive pleadings to the complaint and in the counterclaim, this dispute is fundamentally on the meaning of the phrase: "*the net aggregate sales of the product received in the last twelve months prior to the notice of termination.*"

The plaintiff, PC, argues that the parties' intention was to include a clause in connection with the severance payment section of the contract on the aggregate amount that resulted from the monthly conversion of the value from Mexican pesos into U.S. dollars. This process is known as the dollarization of the Mexican peso, and its main purpose is to preserve in U.S. dollars the value of income from sales received in Mexican Pesos. PC argues that the conversion of Mexican pesos to U.S. dollars was accustomed by the parties and consistent with the obligation of providing periodical financial reports to both holding companies in the U.S. and to the U.S. supervising authorities.

The defendant, MC, argues that the parties' intention was that of simply paying the amount in Mexican pesos based on the annual volume of sales at the end of the period and not on a monthly and dollarized basis. MC argues that, after all, they are both Mexican companies that conduct their daily operations in Mexican pesos, including tax payments and dividends, as required by Mexican Law.

. . .

1. HEARINGS

During the preliminary hearing held on April 24, 1996, the tribunal decided that it would apply Mexican Law in deciding on the substantive matter and it would use the AAA rules on the process. The tribunal decided that the documents of the arbitration would be in English, with Spanish translations where applicable; and that the hearing would be held in English and in a manner consistent with other hearings governed by the AAA, meaning that the parties could perform pre-trial discovery in accordance with the Arbitration Rules of the UNCITRAL.[58]

Prior to the final hearing, this Tribunal decided on MC's refusal to provide documents requested by an order of this Tribunal; here MC was requested to provide evidentiary documentation requested by PC. MC objected to this order alleging that such order was contrary to Mexican law and its provisions on public order. The answer to the defendant's objection was issued by a majority of votes and drafted by the same arbitrator that drafted this award. It held that the order did not violate said legal provisions and that, to the contrary, an Arbitral Tribunal has to focus on the facts of the dispute and reject the use of procedural hyper-technicalities that may shadow the relevant facts. Therefore, it held as follows:

In the case at bar, the facts—substance of the dispute—revolve around the intention of the parties in the text of the termination clause. The Mexican Constitutional provisions—including those on due process—in no way prevent this Tribunal from ordering the parties to provide evidence, including files and documents, that may shed light on what was the real intention of the parties. . . If there was any type of commercial practice or negotiation path followed by the parties, then it must be proven. If the parties had expressed their understanding of the contractual clauses in documents other than the JV, then these documents are subject to pre-trial discovery. After all, once the study of the contractual provision is exhausted, there is no better method to establish the parties intention than that of looking into documents related to prior negotiations and the parties understanding of the contractual clauses. In the absence of such type of evidence, commercial usage or practices in the marketplace must be taken into consideration with regard to the disputed contract. . .

Pursuant to this decision, both parties provided the required documents, exchanged their list of witnesses and provided a summary of what they anticipated their witnesses' testimony would be. . . The final hearing was held in the city of Mexico, on the 24–28 of June, 1996.

II. FACTS

A. Meaning of Net Aggregate Sales

There is no dispute on the meaning of the term "sales." The meaning of the term "net" was clarified during the hearing as follows: "The term net is used to differentiate between the term gross, the latter being the listed price." Therefore, what is pending to be clarified is how to aggregate the income derived from the net sales of the contract. The contract establishes a twelve-month period for aggregating sales, but is silent as to the way in which this has to be done. More specifically, it is necessary to determine if the net sales made in pesos should be converted into dollars at the end of each month, as is argued by the plaintiff. Or, must the monthly sales made in pesos be added until the end of the fiscal or calendar year, without converting them into dollars, as is argued by the defendant?

---

[58] *See supra* § 25:6(C)(1) (on pre-trial discovery).

After researching and analyzing several meanings of the word "aggregate" contained in technical and common dictionaries, this Tribunal concluded that the meaning corresponds to the commercial context and purpose of its use. In this case, the context and purpose was to establish the value of the JV at the time of termination, in case one of the parties wanted to purchase half of the business held by the other party.

The contract which is the object of this dispute makes constant reference to amounts in dollars or their immediate equivalent amount in pesos. For instance, when it makes reference to the amounts invested by the parties, it is so done in dollars and provides an immediate equivalent amount in pesos; the same is true of the amounts stating the limits for capital expenses and indebtedness. In this context, the Tribunal may only ask itself: *Is it reasonable that the parties wanted to stipulate the amounts for measuring the limits of the JV daily operations in dollars or their immediate equivalent in pesos, and that they did not want to stipulate the same values and amounts with respect to one of the most important transactions in the life of the JV,* i.e., *the purchase price to be paid by one of the partners?*

Although companies like those partnered in the JV, who have issued shares and bonds for public offering, are subject to a strict duty of transparency and authenticity with regards to their accounting and measure of the value of their assets and liabilities, they cannot ignore the need for a coherent measure of assets and liabilities on a daily basis and at the time of sale. Furthermore, in order to guarantee their shareholders and creditors that their assets are constantly protected from devaluation, the only sound commercial and accounting practice is that of converting the assets to the most stable currency as soon as it is possible to convert it. Therefore, it is not reasonable to think that they would use different standards and methods for measuring value, to measure their limits on expenses and debts, and to measure the value of sale of the same assets.

B. REBUTTAL OF MC'S ALLEGATION

Even though the JV contract is silent regarding the way in which the aggregation of net sales must be done, MC argues that the parties' intention was clear, since all purchases and sales made by the JV in Mexico were done in pesos and both companies were incorporated in Mexico. Despite the fact that it is true—as argued by MC—that the contract does not stipulate that the aggregation of net sales of the product had to be done in dollars, it is also true that the contract does not state that it had to be done in pesos. In fact, as is argued by PC, the contract makes reference to seven different amounts of money, six of which are made in dollars and only one of which—found in the appendix to the contract—is done in pesos.

C. PURPOSE OF THIS DISPUTE AND EVIDENCE RESULTING FROM PREVIOUS DISCOVERY

The real purpose of this dispute is not to determine if the payment must be done in dollars, excluding the Mexican pesos as payment currency, or if it must be done directly in pesos.[59] *The real dispute is on the amount of pesos that MC must pay pursuant to the aggregation method agreed to by the parties in the JV, or, if the JV does not provide for such method, pursuant to Mexican law and the applicable commercial uses and practices.*

MC argues that according to the provisions of Mexican laws on the interpretation of contractual intent. . .: "unless otherwise stipulated, the only currency that may be used to determine monetary obligations and to perform commercial transactions is the Mexican peso"—Article 635 of the Commercial Code. The arbitrator agrees with this interpretation; however—as previously stated—the issue is not to determine what currency must be used for paying the obligation, but on the amount of Mexican pesos and the method for aggregating them.

The fact that both companies are Mexican does not mean that its partners had the intention of measuring the severance payment *in pesos, whose devaluation—both because of official policy and market behavior—has been continuous during the existence of the JV.* Both the Mexican Supreme Court and the Appellate Courts ordinarily uphold as effective contractual clauses that stipulate the dollar as currency for measuring payments in pesos.[60]

Furthermore, and more convincingly, the evidence produced in pre-trial discovery by the plaintiff PC shows that the vice-president of the International Division of the defendant MC interpreted the clause at bar in the exact same way as it is claimed by PC. An internal memorandum addressed to the President, in which the author evaluated the various alternatives that MC had, indicated that: "in fact, and in all honesty, the payment that we should make should be 32.4 million dollars or the amount that results from multiplying the factor 1.75 times the total sales of last year." To that he added that, depending on the forensic ability of the lawyers hired by PC for this claim, "the amount owed could result in being less onerous in the arbitration process."

. . .

. . .

V. DECISION

In accordance with the preceding analysis, this Tribunal holds in favor of the plaintiff, dismisses the defendant's petitions and grants the plaintiff the amount in Mexican pesos, equivalent to US$33,493,250 according to the exchange rate effective on the date in which payment had to be performed, plus six percent legal interest pursuant to the provisions of Article 362 of the

[59] Mexican monetary laws clearly, expressly and certainly stipulate that every monetary obligation payable in Mexico must be paid in pesos.

[60] *See* Amparo Directo 8364/81, María Palacio Viuda de Suárez, 10 de octubre de 1983; Amparo Directo 6286/80, Carlos Villareal Alanís y María Elena Medina Ríos de Villareal, 1 de octubre de 1981; and Amparo Directo 1390/80, Arturo Cortés Villada y otros, 31 de octubre 1990, *cited in* Semanario de la Suprema Corte de Justicia [SCJN] [Supreme Court], tercera sala, Séptima Época, tomo 175–180 (undated), Tesis Aislada, Página 115 (Mex.). *See also* Amparo Directo 1149/82, Kenworth Mexicana, S.A. de C.V. 22 de noviembre de 1982, *cited in* Semanario de la Suprema Corte de Justicia [SCJN] [Supreme Court], tercera sala, Séptima Época, tomo 163–168, (undated) Tesis Aislada, Página 46 (Mex.).

Commercial Code, in the concept of total and final payment of PC's fifty percent in the JV.

Chapter 26

PRE-CONTRACTUAL LIABILITY: *CULPA IN CONTRAHENDO*[1]

§ 26.1 INTRODUCTION

This chapter is devoted to the doctrine of "*culpa in contrahendo*" (fault while negotiating a contract). It imposes liability upon parties whose bad faith negotiation injures a party who relied to his detriment upon another's representation of an intent to be bound or more generally upon the false appearance of good faith bargaining. Even though the distant origins of this doctrine can be found in the Roman remedies for a failure to act with the requisite *bona fides* in consensual contracts, its modern use can be traced to a study published by Rudolf von Ihering in 1861.[2] Concerned about the deficient protection that the pre-BGB German civil law afforded commercial endeavors, von Ihering proposed that "damages should be recoverable against the party whose blameworthy conduct during negotiations for a contract brought about its invalidity or prevented its perfection [particularly if the other party had relied on the validity of the contract]."[3] Von Ihering maintained that, when faced with such non-compliance or inadequate compliance, the law should reinstate the *status quo ante* by providing to the injured party restitution for the damages suffered. Von Ihering further noted that the careless promisor had only himself to blame when he created in the mind of his counterparty the false appearance of agreeing to a binding obligation.[4]

As elaborated by von Mehren and Gordley:

> For example, the Pandekten School considered the parties' agreement ineffective to form a contract if it contemplated an impossible performance or was based on a mistake. Ihering argues that in treating the contract as void and excluding creation of an obligation to perform, we need not deny all effect to the agreement. In these circumstances, he would protect the negative contractual interest—the reliance interest—of the party to whom the impossible performance was [mistakenly] promised. For him, this liability is

---

[1] I am thankful to Rodrigo Novoa Urenda, (LL.M. 2005–University of Arizona and currently an NLCIFT Board Member and Director of the NLCIFT Chilean branch at the Universidad Mayor, Law School) for his authorization to use a portion of his article as a part of this chapter. Rodrigo Novoa, *Culpa in Contrahendo: A Comparative Law Study: Chilean Law and the United Nations Convention on Contracts for the International Sale of Goods (CISG)*, 22 ARIZ. J. INT'L & COMP. L. 583 (2005) (prepared for my class on International Commercial Transactions).

[2] *See* Rudolf von Ihering, *Culpa in contrahendo oder Schadenersatz bei nichtigen oder nicht zur Perfection gelangten Vertriigen,* 4 JAHRBUCHER FUR DIE DOGMATIK DES HEUTIGEN ROMISCHEN UND DEUTSCHEN PRIVATRECHTS 1 (1861), *reprinted in* 1 VON IHERING, GESAMMELTE AUFSIITZE 327 (1881), *cited in* VON MEHREN & GORDLEY, at 837.

[3] Friedrich Kessler & Edith Fine, *Culpa in Contrahendo, Bargaining in Good Faith, and Freedom of Contract: A Comparative Study*, 77 HARV. L. REV. 401, 401 (1964).

[4] *Id.* at 402 n.3 and accompanying text.

based on *culpa* although, in many cases, he conceded that fault is being used in a rather special sense.[5]

It is noteworthy that von Ihering limited the application of his theory to contracts that had been agreed to by mistake or to those in which negotiations had reached the point of manifest acceptance, but did not extend it to negotiations that had failed and to contracts that were not concluded because of a faulty behavior by one of the parties. E. Allen Farnsworth added that "[i]t was a French scholar, Raymond Saleilles, who in 1907 advanced the view that after parties have entered into negotiations, both must act in good faith and neither can break off the negotiations 'arbitrarily' without compensating the other for reliance damages."[6] This amplified version of *culpa in contrahendo* was the one that was ultimately adopted by many civil law countries. In contrast, the version of *culpa in contrahendo* that prevails in common law countries is of a different nature, as will be analyzed below.

§ 26.2 A BRIEF SURVEY OF *CULPA IN CONTRAHENDO* IN CIVIL LAW COUNTRIES

A. Germany

The BGB did not adopt von Ihering's version of *culpa in contrahendo*. Instead, German courts were the ones who used von Ihering's article in conjunction with certain broadly-formulated provisions of the BGB to fashion a judicial doctrine of pre-contractual liability. Accordingly, the German Federal Supreme Court (*Bundesgerichtshof*) decided that the fault (*culpa*) that imposes liability for damages can also arise when one party raises in the other an imminent expectation that a contract will be concluded and, ultimately, the contract is not concluded, and such failure is to blame for the expenses incurred by the aggrieved party.[7] In my opinion, Saleilles' view was the most equitable and consistent with best business practices. Further, I see no reason to exempt from liability a bad faith negotiating party who finally enters into a contract but that is highly detrimental to his counter party.

Thus, Sections 122, 179, 307 and 309 of the BGB were relied upon by German courts as supportive of *culpa in contrahendo*. Of these, Section 122 was one of the most frequently invoked by the courts:

> 1) If a declaration of intention [*Willenserklärung*] is void under § 118, or rescinded under §§ 119, 120, the declarant shall, if the declaration was required to be made to another party, compensate that party, or otherwise any third party, for the damage which the other or the third party has sustained by relying upon the validity of the declaration not, however, beyond the value of the interest which the other or the third party has in the validity of the declaration.

---

[5] VON MEHREN & GORDLEY, *supra* note 2, at 838 (emphasis added) (citations omitted).

[6] E. Allan Farnsworth, *Precontractual Liability and Preliminary Agreements: Fair Dealing and Failed Negotiations*, 87 COLUM. L. REV. 217, 240 (1987).

[7] Kessler & Fine, *supra* note 3, at 404.

2) The obligation to compensate does not arise if the injured party knew the ground of the nullity or rescission or did not know it due to negligence (should have known it).[8]

In spite of the numerous amendments that the BGB has undergone since its promulgation, Articles 122 and 179 have remained in force without significant modifications. However, this has not been the case with Articles 307 and 309, which were replaced when the BGB incorporated the provisions of the Law Governing Standard Business Terms and Conditions.[9] Following the amendments introduced to the Code in 2002, the doctrine of *culpa in contrahendo* was specifically set forth as follows in Section 311(2). In relevant part, it states:

(2) An obligation with duties under section 241(2) also comes into existence by

1. the commencement of contract negotiations

2. the initiation of a contract where one party, with regard to a potential contractual relationship, gives the other party the possibility of affecting his rights, legal interests and other interests, or entrusts these to him, or

3. similar business contracts.[10]

B. France

The *Code Civil* does not impose an obligation to act in good faith during the time period prior to the conclusion of the agreement or during the negotiations; consequently, it fell upon the courts to establish and regulate *culpa in contrahendo*. French courts have expressly recognized the application of rules pertaining to good faith during the stage of business negotiations.[11] However, if one of the parties suffers damages because of the other party's fault during the negotiations, the affected party will have to initiate a claim based on non-contractual liability and will have to prove: (1) the existence of damages to be compensated; (2) a culpable act; and (3) a nexus between such act and the damages.

---

[8] BGB art. 122 (GOREN, 1994).

[9] VON MEHREN & GORDLEY, *supra* note 2, at 837–39. Article 179 provides as follows:

(1) Whoever has entered into a contract as agent is, if he has not given proof of his authority, bound to the other party at his choice either to carry out the contract or to compensate him, if the principal refuses to ratify the contract.

(2) If the agent did not know that he had no authority, he is bound to compensate only for the damage which the other party has sustained by relying upon the authority; not, however, beyond the value of the interest which the other party has in the validity of the contract.

(3) The agent is not liable, if the other party knew or should have known of the lack of authority. The agent is also not liable if he was limited in his competency to enter into transactions, unless he had acted with the consent of his legal representative.

BGB art. 179 (GOREN 1994). Prior to the 2002 amendments, Article 307 provided that: "a person, in concluding a contract the performance of which is impossible, knew or should have known that it was impossible, he is obliged to make compensation for any damage which the other party has sustained. . . ." *Id.* art. 307. Finally, prior to the amendments, Article 309 extended the application of Article 307 "[i]f a contract is contrary to a statutory provision. . . ." *Id.* art. 309.

[10] BGB art. 311(2).

[11] Cour d'appel [CA] [regional court of appeal] Paris, Feb. 13, 1883, Gaz. Pal. 1883, 2, 414 (Fr.); Cour d'appel [CA] [regional court of appeal] Lyon, July 10, 1896: D. 1896, 496; Cour de cassation [Cass.] [supreme court for judicial matters] com., Mar. 20, 1972, Bull. civ. IV, No. 93, note J. Schmidt (Fr.); Cour de cassation [Cass.] [supreme court for judicial matters] com., Jan. 11, 1984, Bull. civ. IV,.No. 16. (Fr.).

C. Italy

Articles 1337 and 1338 of the Italian Civil Code of 1942 specifically contemplate the application of the good faith principle to pre-contractual negotiations. In fact, Article 1337 provides that "[t]he parties, during negotiations and the formation of the contract, shall conduct themselves according to good faith."[12] In turn, Article 1338 provides that "[a] party who knows of or should know of the existence of a reason for invalidity of the contract and does not give notice to the other party is bound to compensate for the damage suffered by the latter as a result of relying on the validity of the contract."[13]

In this regard, the Italian Supreme Court (*Corte di Cassazione*), in the 2001 decision *Orsoni v. Santoli*,[14] resorted to Article 1337 to reverse the first and second-instance decisions, which rejected the pre-contractual liability of the defendants who had without justification withdrawn from the negotiations for the sale of their property. In the words of the Italian Supreme Court:

> [T]he pre-contractual liability regulated under Article 1337 may exist both during the formation of the contract and during its negotiations . . . in the latter, the parties only evidence their intention to conclude a contract, without acting to such effect. When negotiations reach a point where the party is convinced that the contract will be concluded, if a party withdraws without good reason, in violation of the good faith obligation, that party will have to compensate the damages. . . .[15]

D. Peru and Argentina

Peruvian and Argentine law are strikingly similar when it comes to *culpa in contrahendo*. The 1984 Peruvian Civil Code provides under Article 1362 that "[c]ontracts must be *negotiated*, concluded, and performed *in accordance with good faith and the common intent* of the parties."[16] Similarly, Article 1198 of the Argentine Civil Code provides that "[c]ontracts must be *concluded*, construed and performed in *good faith* and pursuant to the parties' understanding or what they were likely to understand, acting in a careful and prudent way."[17] Both articles, in addition to having very similar text, share a striking similarity to Article 1337 of the Italian Civil Code, referenced above. In turn, Argentine courts have corroborated the application of *culpa in contrahendo* within the Argentine system. As concluded by an Argentine federal appellate court in a 1989 decision: "We may note the existence of pre-contractual

---

[12] C.C. (Italy) art. 1337 (1942) (author's translation).

[13] *Id.* art. 1338.

[14] Cass., sez. III, 4 marzo 2002, n. 3103, Corr. giur., 2002, p. 909 (It.), *cited in* Adriana Tempesta & Veneranda Aguirre, Culpa in Contrahendo: Precontractual Liability in Italy and in the United States (Spring 2004) (unpublished paper, James E. Rogers College of Law, University of Arizona) (on file with author).

[15] *Id.* (author's translation).

[16] C.C. (Peru) art. 1362 (1984) (author's translation) (emphasis added). *See generally* Olga Alejandra Alcántara Francia, La Obligación de Informar en el Período Precontractual y su Repercusiones en la Formación de los Contratos de Consumo (April 2005) (unpublished paper, Carlos III University, Madrid) (on file with author).

[17] CÓD. CIV. (Arg.) art. 1198 (1869) (author's translation).

liability resulting from an arbitrary and sudden rupture of the negotiations conducted by the parties so as to enter into a contract."[18]

The evolution of legislative trends in Argentina is of particular interest in light of the link that has been established—to varying degrees—between *culpa in contrahendo* and contractual protection of consumers in the context of consumer protection law. Following the Argentina Civil Code's recognition of *culpa in contrahendo*, Argentina's Consumer Protection Law further provided that:

> If the offeror *were to violate the duty of good faith during the stage prior to the conclusion of the contract* or during performance, or failed to comply with the duty of information underlying competition policy or commercial honesty, the consumer will be entitled to demand the invalidation of the contract or that of one or more clauses.[19]

E. Chile

As was the case in Germany and France, Chilean courts were responsible for introducing *culpa in contrahendo* in Chilean contractual and extra-contractual law. In contrast to France and Germany, the source relied upon by the Chilean courts was the Commercial Code, especially Articles 99[20] and 100.[21] Chilean superior courts have established the pre-contractual protection of the parties pursuant to the principle of good faith. In this regard, the Appellate Court of Talca, Chile, decided that:

> [T]he principles of good faith and equity are the basis for the pre-contractual liability doctrine, and their breach creates the right to recover damages. *[I]t is evident that the basis for such liability is the respect of the good faith and loyalty that must underlie the relations between those who undertake negotiations aiming at the conclusion of a contract; the breach of this duty of good faith brings about the defendant's obligation to compensate the damages caused to its counterpart.*[22]

Other Chilean courts have applied the notion of *culpa in contrahendo* to various cases. By way of example, a 1999 decision by the Civil Court of First Instance of

---

[18] Cámara de Apelaciones en lo Civil y Comercial [CApel.CC] [provincial court of appeals in civil and comercial matters], sala 2, 2/5/89, La Ley [L.L.] (1989–D–416) (Arg.) (author's translation).

[19] Law No. 24240, Sept. 22, 1993, [LIII–D] A.D.L.A. 4125 (Arg.) (author's translation) (emphasis added). *See generally* Francia, *supra* note 16 (referring to Peruvian consumer protection legislation and precontractual liability).

[20] CÓD. COM. (Chile) art. 99 (1865):

> The offeror may withdraw the offer during the time between the moment the offer is sent and the moment of the acceptance, except when such offer also includes a commitment to await the acceptance or not to do away with the object of the contract unless the offer had been rejected or a certain time period had elapsed. Withdrawals may not be presumed.

(Author's translation).

[21] *Id.* art. 100:

> A sudden withdrawal imposes on the offeror the obligation to compensate all expenses incurred by the person to whom the offer had been addressed, as well as any damages arising from such withdrawal. However, an offeror may be exempted from the obligation to compensate provided such offeror complies with the proposed contract.

(Author's translation).

[22] Corte de Apelaciones de Talca [C. Apel. de Talca] [Talca Court of Appeals], 8 noviembre 1999, "Espinoza c. Bobadilla," (Chile) (emphasis added).

Concepción ruled in favor of the plaintiff based on the pre-contractual liability of the defendant:

> Modern doctrine—unlike traditional doctrine—believes that even though prior to a contract the parties may unilaterally withdraw from the negotiations, *such ability is restricted by virtue of the parties' duty to act in good faith*, which must be reflected in an honest and loyal behavior, that is to say, a behavior that must, at the very least, avoid damaging the other party's interests, respect other people's property and be harmonious with conflicting interests. Social and ethical values demand a minimum level of loyalty and honesty . . . and the absence of such values is somewhat analogous to negligence by omission—by allowing the other party to be unaware of the reality and, hence, creating an expectation that should be dispelled. This is what brings about the right to recover damages.[23]

§ 26.3 *CULPA IN CONTRAHENDO* IN COMMON LAW JURISDICTIONS

Even though common law jurisdictions acknowledge and sanction a certain negligent behavior during the pre-contractual stage, such sanctions are not based on the lack of compliance with a good faith principle. Indeed, pre-contractual good faith has been characterized by some English courts as "repugnant to the adversarial position of the parties when involved in negotiations," so long as there are no misrepresentations.[24] Likewise, United States courts have also been reluctant to acknowledge the application of the good faith principle to pre-contractual negotiations.[25]

However, as noted by Kessler and Fine, even though "[t]he common law appears to have no counterpart to the German doctrine of culpa in contrahendo," there are other mechanisms that serve a similar function.[26] The late E. Allan Farnsworth points out that unjust enrichment resulting from the negotiations, misrepresentation and

---

[23] Primer Juzgado Civil de Concepción [1° J.Civ. Concepción] [First Civil Tribunal of Concepción], 13 abril 1999, "Empresa de Telecomunicaciones Asintec S.A. c. Club Hípico de Concepción S.A.," ¶ 26 (Chile) [hereinafter *Club Hípico*] (emphasis added).

[24] Walford v. Miles, [1992] 2 A.C. 128 (H.L.) (Eng.). The court's full discussion went as follows: "However, the concept of a duty to carry on negotiations in good faith is inherently repugnant to the adversarial position of the parties when involved in negotiations. Each party to the negotiations is entitled to pursue his (or her) own interest, so long as he avoids making misrepresentations." *Id.*; *see also* Courtney & Fairbairn Ltd. v. Tolaini Brothers (Hotels) Ltd., [1975] 1 All E.R. 716 (Eng.).

[25] Farnsworth, *supra* note 6, at 239. Farnsworth explained:

> Some scholarly writers have generalized from the cases decided on the grounds of misrepresentation and specific promise to argue that a general obligation of fair dealing may arise out of the negotiations themselves, at least if the disappointed party has been led to believe that success is in prospect. Thus Summers wrote that if courts follow *Red Owl*, "it will no longer be possible for one party to scuttle contract negotiations with impunity when the other has been induced to rely to his detriment on the prospect that the negotiations will succeed." American courts, however, have been unreceptive to these arguments and have declined to find a general obligation that would preclude a party from breaking off negotiations, even when success was in prospect. Their reluctance to do so is supported by the formulation of a general duty of good faith and fair dealing in both the Uniform Commercial Code and the Restatement (Second) of Contracts that, at least by negative implication, does not extend to negotiations.

Id. (citations omitted).

[26] Kessler & Fine, *supra* note 3, at 401.

promissory estoppel are the doctrinal equivalents to *culpa in contrahendo* in the common law.[27]

By using terms that go beyond *culpa in contrahendo*, the common law does not restrict liability to the stage prior to the conclusion of the contract. Indeed, in the civil law jurisdictions discussed above, the conclusion of the contract generally precludes the possibility to claim damages based on the *culpa in contrahendo* theory.[28] However, in the common law system, damages resulting from a party's behavior during the pre-contractual negotiations may be claimed even after the contract has been concluded. However, in order for such pre-contractual behavior to be brought forward, such behavior must fall within one of the causes of action recognized by common law, and it may not be characterized merely as being contrary to good faith, as would be the case in a civil law system.[29] In other words, in order to recover damages, the plaintiff must show evidence that the defendant's actions satisfy the requirements of causes of action such as unjust enrichment, misrepresentation or promissory estoppel.[30]

A. Determination of Damages Under *Culpa in Contrahendo*

Both in civil and common law countries, the scope and extent of the damages to be recovered by virtue of *culpa in contrahendo* or pre-contractual liability, respectively, have been extensively debated by the courts. There seems to be some consensus in both systems as to limiting recovery to what has been described as the "negative interest," or losses directly attributed to the fault.

Farnsworth notes the following:

> The law of precontractual liability is relatively undeveloped, even on the grounds that are already recognized. This may be due in part to the considerable uncertainty that surrounds the measure of recovery under any of these grounds. I believe that courts are willing to be more generous in this regard than is commonly supposed and that recognition of this generosity will encourage the development of the law of precontractual liability.[31]

---

[27] *See* Farnsworth, *supra* note 6, at 223. *See also* Steven A. Mirmina, *A Comparative Survey of Culpa in Contrahendo, Focusing on its Origins in Roman, German, and French Law as well as its Application in American Law*, 8 CONN. J. INT'L L. 77, 94–96 (1992).

[28] *Club Hípico*, at ¶ 22. The court explained:

> The first item to clarify with respect to this action is that all facts pertaining to the alleged pre-contractual liability must focus on the time period subsequent to May 2, 1997, that is to say, subsequent to the termination of the promissory contract. Indeed, in light of that contract, entered into on February 27, 1997, all prior negotiations resulted, in fact, in that contract and, hence, become part of the contract since preliminary negotiations end when the next stage begins, in this case, the signing of the referenced preparatory contract, a stage that clearly must be governed by the rules pertaining to contractual liability. *Consequently, both the time period prior to February 27, 1997 as the one subsequent to such date, and up until May 2, 1997—which is the period of validity of the promissory contract agreed by the parties—do not fall under a pre-contractual situation and, consequently, anything that could exist with relation to preliminary negotiations or dealings must be subsumed into the subsequent stage."*

Id. (emphasis added).

[29] *See supra* § 20:3.

[30] Farnsworth, *supra* note 6, at 229–43.

[31] *Id.* at 223.

Cases such as *Satellite Broadcasting Cable, Inc. v. Telefónica de España, S.A.*[32] (United States) and *Empresa de Telecomunicaciones Asintec S.A. v. Club Hípico de Concepción S.A.*[33] (Chile) evidence that the two different jurisdictions, one common law and the other civil law, have resolved this issue in similar fashion. Indeed, the *Satellite Broadcasting* decision followed the interpretation of Justice Davila in *Producciones Tommy Muniz, Inc. v. Copan*[34] and an opinion of the Italian Supreme Court, limiting the measure of recovery by the plaintiff to the negative interest.[35] Meanwhile, the Chilean court decided as follows:

> [I]t should be noted that *during the negotiations the damages to be recovered should be limited to the expenses and losses that are directly dependent upon such negotiations*, that is to say, in this case, to what doctrinal writings have designated as "provoked expenses" [or negative interest], *i.e.*, those that are based upon the will of both parties or those that the plaintiff was led to believe were essential to continue the negotiations, thus excluding "spontaneous expenses," *i.e.*, those that do not fall under the previous categories and which must be deemed to have been incurred in each party's benefit—in this case, that of the plaintiff. Consequently, in this particular case, *we rule against the plaintiff's claim for compensation of loss of earnings (*lucro cesante*) and moral damages (*daño moral*), since such categories do not fall under the notion of provoked expenses [or negative interest]*, particularly because the former consists exclusively of the potential profits to be obtained as a result of the final contract (a contract that was never concluded and which, consequently, had no legal effects), and with respect to the latter [moral damages], there has not been any clear evidence of the alleged damage to the commercial reputation as a direct consequence of the defendant's withdrawal of the offer to enter into a contract.[36]

B. *Culpa in Contrahendo* from an International Perspective

The UNIDROIT Principles of International Commercial Contracts (2010) (hereinafter UNIDROIT Principles) have recognized the application of *culpa in contrahendo*. Article 1.7 states that "[e]ach party must act in accordance with good

---

[32] 807 F. Supp 218 (D.P.R. 1992).

[33] *Club Hípico*, at ¶ 26.

[34] Producciones Tommy Muñiz, Inc. v. Comité Organizador de los VIII Juegos Panamericanos (COPAN), 13 P.R. Offic. Trans. 664 (1982).

[35] *Satellite Broadcasting*, 807 F. Supp. at 221; *Producciones Tommy Muñiz*, 13 P.R. Offic. Trans. at 693–94. Justice Davila explained:

> I believe I should also pronounce myself on the type of damage that should be compensated in these cases. We have a good example in the opinion of the Italian Court of Cassation, as summarized by Mariano Alonso Pérez: "precontractual liability does not suppose the recovery of all the contractual damages sustained by the other party, but only of those comprised within the so-called 'negative interest' "—*id quod interest contractum initium non fuisse*—; that is to say, those expenses incurred by the other party in foresight of the future contract—travels, expertise, advise, etc.—as well as the losses caused by not being able to take advantage of favorable opportunities to execute a contract with other persons.

13 P.R. Offic. Trans. at 693–94. *See also* Novoa, *supra* note 1, at 596.

[36] Club Hípico, at ¶ 18 (emphasis added).

faith and fair dealing in international trade," and "[t]he parties may not exclude or limit this duty."[37] Furthermore, Article 2.1.15 expressly provides that:

> (1) A party is free to negotiate and is not liable for failure to reach an agreement.
>
> (2) However, a party who negotiates or breaks off negotiations in bad faith is liable for the losses caused to the other party.
>
> (3) It is bad faith, in particular, for a party to enter into or continue negotiations when intending not to reach an agreement with the other party.[38]

As for the United Nations Convention on Contracts for the International Sale of Goods (CISG), recognition of *culpa in contrahendo* has been and continues to be significantly debated.[39] Unlike the UNIDROIT Principles, the CISG contains no explicit provision that imposes a duty of good faith on the parties to international contracts. Article 7(1), however, provides that "[i]n the interpretation of this Convention, regard is to be had to its international character and to the need to promote uniformity in its application and the observance of good faith in international trade."[40] Given the general nature of this provision, adoption of the *culpa in contrahendo* concept by the Convention is and will continue to be seriously debated.

C. Case Law

1. *Chile:* Juan Antonio Luna Espinoza v. Sergio Bobadilla Valenzuela et. al., *Appellate Court of Talca, Chile (Nov. 8, 1999)*

a. *Findings of Fact*

In September 1992, Juan Luna Espinoza (buyer-plaintiff) entered into an agreement with Sergio Bobadilla Valenzuela (seller-defendant) for the purchase of real property adjacent to his land—the approximate surface area of the land was 3,182 square meters. The sale could not be perfected at the time because the defendant first had to obtain clean title to the land. The defendant received $8,000,000 Chilean pesos for the property and both parties personally proceeded to delimit the boundaries of the property that was to be sold, which is where the plaintiff was living. Once all issues pertaining to the title were resolved, and even though defendant had, in fact, materially delivered possession of the property, defendant refused to grant the relevant public deed on the basis that there were differences with respect to the measurements and boundaries of the land that had been sold to the plaintiff. The plaintiff, after coming into possession of the land, had made significant investments in the property including filling and leveling the property with Highway Five South, adding a fence

---

[37] International Institute for the Unification of Private Law (UNIDROIT), UNIDROIT Principles of International Commercial Contracts art. 1.7, 2010, http://www.unidroit.org/english/principles/contracts/principles2010/integralversionprinciples2010–e.pdf.

[38] *Id.* art. 2.1.15.

[39] *See, e.g.*, Diane Madeline Goderre, *International Negotiations Gone Sour: Precontractual Liability under the United Nations Sales Convention*, 66 U. CIN. L. REV. 257 (1997).

[40] United Nations Convention on Contracts for the International Sale of Goods art. 7(1), Apr. 11, 1980, *available at* http://www.uncitral.org/pdf/english/texts/sales/cisg/CISG.pdf. For an excellent perspective on this Convention and its main features, see María del Pilar Perales Viscasillas, El Contrato de Compraventa Internacional de Mercancías (2001), http://www.cisg.law.pace.edu/cisg/biblio/perales1.html.

with an extension of over 5,000 square meters, making additions to the existing service-center and inn, including the addition of bungalows, dining rooms and a pool.

b. Procedural History

The plaintiff filed a claim for specific performance and recovery of damages against the defendant. The court of first instance rejected the claim to the effect that the defendant should be ordered to grant and sign the relevant public deed for the sale of the property and, instead, accepted the motion that the defendant should compensate damages assessed at 100 million pesos. Both parties appealed the decision; the defendant also appealed before the Supreme Court (*recurso de casación*).

c. Issue

The main issue was whether there was pre-contractual liability on the part of the defendant.

d. The Court's Opinion

The Court ruled that damages should be paid to the plaintiff, thus disregarding the defendant's claim that there was no contract between the parties and, consequently, that it would have been impossible to accept the plaintiff's reasoning which was based on legal provisions pertaining to contractual liability.

e. The Court's Reasoning

The court stated that the basis of pre-contractual liability lies in good faith and equity; non-observance of these principles gives rise to the right to recover damages. The only relevant provisions are those that pertain to the formation of contractual consent; hence, the Commercial Code applied to the case at hand.

The court held that in order for the contract to be perfected, the only missing element was compliance with the relevant formality (*solemnidad*). Consequently, this was the issue that needed to be addressed. The court asked: What are the effects of contractual consent when such consent exists but does not comply with the formality to originate the contract? Are these mere negotiations or, alternatively, are we facing a situation where an offer and acceptance have been validly exchanged? In other words, at which point of the pre-contractual stage do the parties find themselves? In the court's opinion, there was a meeting of the minds, and even though this is not sufficient to perfect the contract, it may have been enough to bring about the liability of the offeror to the extent that there is a quasi-contractual relationship between the parties which makes the offeror liable in the event of withdrawal and forces such offeror to compensate the damages suffered. Consequently, in this type of contract, where there is consent and agreement, even though such consent is insufficient to perfect the contract, there remains a right of withdrawal that may be exercised by either party up to the time where the formality has been complied with or there is delivery of the property. The court continued, however, that in the event of withdrawal, the party withdrawing may incur pre-contractual liability for the damages caused to the other party by virtue of such withdrawal. Such liability is based on the general principles embodied in the Commercial Code, which are the basis for pre-contractual liability and the true criterion whereby claims for compensation must be assessed.

The court thus held that regardless of the doctrine applied—*i.e.*, whether the opinion is that in these circumstances the rules pertaining to contractual liability should apply, or whether the rules that apply are those that govern torts both intentional and negligent—it was evident that the basis for such liability was the application of the principle of good faith and loyalty that must underlie all relations between parties who are negotiating a contract. The court stated that the disregard of such good faith brings about an obligation to compensate the damages caused to the other party. In this regard, the court held that as long the contract had not been perfected and notwithstanding the right to withdraw, such right cannot be exercised arbitrarily, or, in the words of Professor Pablo Rodríguez, merely based "on the text of the provisions applied pursuant to an outdated literal criterion."

DISCUSSION TOPICS

How would the reader describe the Chilean notion of *culpa in contrahendo* as embodied in the judgment referenced above? Is it a contractual notion? Non-contractual? Quasi-contractual? If it were quasi-contractual, why did the court not quantify the defendant's unjust enrichment and, had it done so, what criteria should it have followed? In the reader's opinion, what damages should be recovered based on the court's wide-ranging reasoning? How would the reader compare the reasoning and judicial policy in this judgment vis-à-vis other judgments, including the United States *Satellite Broadcasting* case and the Chilean *Empresa de Telecomunicaciones* case, referenced before?

Following these discussions, and bearing in mind the need for international business certainty, would the reader recommend the adoption of an international convention on *culpa in contrahendo* based on the UNIDROIT Principles? What would be the arguments, both in favor of and against it? Consider, for example, the following argument by a hypothetical Minister of the Economy:

> As the party responsible for attracting productive investments to my country, I have to seek and safeguard the creation of an attractive investment climate. If potential investors perceive that our legal framework is open to all types of claims deriving from unconcluded negotiations pertaining to investment projects, it is likely that such investors would prefer to invest in a neighboring country that does not impose such pre-contractual liability.

Chapter 27

EXCUSES FOR NON-PERFORMANCE OF CONTRACTS

§ 27.1 INTRODUCTION

The law of excuses for non-performance has become increasingly important, especially with respect to large construction and service contracts which require continuous and deferred performances. Non-performance of these contracts is often related to the economic and monetary adversity that periodically affects many regions of the world. Because the U.S. economy and its dollar-denominated payments have not been historically as volatile as those of European, Asian and Latin American economies (although this stability is being severely tested at the time of this writing), U.S. contracting parties have not had to turn to excuses for non-performance with the same frequency as their non-U.S. counterparts. Hence, U.S. case law and doctrine regarding excuses for non-performance is not as extensive as that of some European and Latin American countries. For this reason, this chapter will focus largely on the latter and less on the U.S.

The excuse for non-performance chosen as the focus for our study is the "excessive onerousness" (hardship) of the promised, but unfulfilled, contractual obligation. Various reasons prompted this particular excuse selection. The first is that the comparison of excessive onerousness with other possible excuses for non-compliance provides a good overview of the remedies available to parties who contemplate discontinuing a highly onerous performance. Some of these performances may have just been initiated while others may have been going on for a significant part of the agreement.

Secondly, since excessive onerousness is intimately associated with promises of deferred performance, this excuse provides a good opportunity to observe the problems endemic to such a promise. This fits well given that the enforceability of these promises has been one of the continuing themes of this book.

Finally, I felt that in light of the remedies for breach of contract that will be discussed in the following chapters, the Anglo-American reader would benefit from an introduction to some of the most common remedies in civil law countries as they apply to an actual transaction. Here, serendipity intervened and I was asked to participate as an expert witness in an international arbitration whose main legal issue was the legal nature of the remedy of excessive onerousness as compared to other remedies existing in civil law jurisdictions. What follows is a summary of my opinion in this arbitration procedure. In order to preserve the anonymity of this arbitration, the names of the parties and disputed facts have been modified.

§ 27.2 FACTUAL BASIS FOR THE ARBITRATION

In the second trimester of 1993, the Gas Company of El Salvador (GCES) announced the opening of public bidding for the construction and operation of a production plant of natural gas in the Republic of El Salvador. The bidders had to comply with certain terms and conditions, among which was abiding by the method of calculation of the price of the gas produced by the plant. This method assured the winning bidder of a "cost plus" formula which would take effect after the winner was given the right to subscribe to a purchase-sale contract of gas (PCG). After a large investment to build and operate one production plant of gas, this contract would make the winner the provider of gas to GCES for a fixed term of twenty years. In turn, the GCES would be obligated to purchase 100% of the gas produced by the plant.

On February 2, 1994, the bid was awarded to a foreign joint venture that eventually assigned its rights to the AGPC S.A., the defendant in the arbitration proceeding before us. The bidder's plant initiated operations on September 1, 1995, and consequently the parties began complying with the obligations stipulated in the contract. Months later, the President of El Salvador announced the gradual privatization of the GCES.

In 1996, the Salvadoran Congress enacted the Law for Distribution of Natural Gas. The enactment of this law forced the GCES to grant subsidies to its customers—the large majority of the Salvadoran consumers—by discounting the price of gas below what GCES paid. The GCES alleged that the cited law was a supervening act, unpredictable and extraordinary and that, by itself, was sufficient basis for the resolution (termination), without compensation, of the contract with the defendant. For this purpose, the plaintiff invoked the remedies in Article 994 of the Salvadoran Commercial Code (hereinafter S.Com.C.) and filed the corresponding arbitral claim before the tribunal. Defendant AGPC S.A. requested an expert opinion (discussed below) on the meaning of this provision in light of its purpose and application in other jurisdictions.

§ 27.3 ELEMENTS OF THE ARBITRAL DECISION

A. The Plan of the Comparative Analysis

The GCES based its claim to the "resolution" of the contract (a term that is the rough Spanish and Latin American equivalent of the United States termination or rescission) on excessive onerousness and quoted Article 994 of the S.Com.C. to support its claim:

> Article 994: Where in a contract of continuous, periodic or deferred performance, the performance of one of the parties becomes excessively onerous because of supervening acts that occur in the marketplace and that are extraordinary and unpredictable, the party who owes such performance has the right to rescind or terminate the onerous performance; however, the other party will also have the right to oppose such resolution, through a proposal of an equitable and proportionate modification of the contract. In case of disagreement of the parties, the judge will refer the matter to an expert's opinion.

The excuse of non-performance of the contract, to which this article refers, is reminiscent to a family of codes, of which the Italian Civil Code of 1942 (hereinafter It.C.C.) is the most influential. Accordingly, this Code will be discussed first. Thereafter, I will discuss those codes that are closest to the Salvadoran code in order of geographic and systemic proximity, *i.e.* the Honduran, Argentinean, German, Swiss and French civil and commercial codes in addition to the United States Uniform Commercial Code.

From an educational standpoint, this comparison should help familiarize the reader not only with excessive onerousness in the S.Com.C. and its Italian model, but also with analogous remedies used in other civil and common law jurisdictions. As customary in this book, the legal analysis will be accompanied by relevant transactional and socio-economic data.

B. The Exceptional Nature of Excuses for Non-Performance

While the contracting world continues to adhere to the principle of the faithful observance of contracts (*pacta sunt servanda*), the excuses for non-performance relied upon by the plaintiff GCES remain exceptional in nature. Prominent among these excuses, in addition to excessive onerousness, are: 1) "*rebus sic stantibus*" or a substantial unforeseen alteration of the circumstances prevailing at the time of contracting; and 2) the need to rely, when changed circumstances occur, not on the letter of the contract but on: a) its "fundamental presuppositions," b) "hypothetical presuppositions of intent," and c) "implied conditions." In addition, some of the most popular excuses across the English Channel and the Atlantic Ocean have been the "frustration of the contractual purpose" and the "impossibility of performance."

The exceptional nature of *rebus sic stantibus*, one of the first and still one of the most relied-upon excuses, was made clear by an arbitral decision issued under the aegis of the International Chamber of Commerce (ICC), one of the principal arbitration bodies of the commercial world. In its arbitral decision, the arbitrators stated: "The principle *rebus sic stantibus* [also known as that of unforeseen changed circumstances . . . or *force majeure*] is universally considered as being of strict and narrow interpretation, [and] as a dangerous exception to the principle of sanctity of contracts."[1]

As will become apparent throughout this comparison, the same exceptional nature is true for the other excuses. Their exceptionality stems from the same reason that impeded Justice Holmes Jr.'s "bad man's" choice between performing or paying damages from becoming the guiding principle of contractual performance. Legitimating such a choice would have contradicted the most elemental need for certainty in any viable commercial marketplace.

C. Summary of the Expert's Opinion

The factual presuppositions of Article 994 S.Com.C. and its remedial purpose, as found in the legal doctrine that inspired it, lead to the conclusion that it is inapplicable to the contract in question. The facts show that the occurrence of the extraordinary and unforeseeable acts to which this Article refers, were foreseeable by the plaintiffs. This is especially true when one takes into account the plaintiffs' prominent position both in the Salvadoran government and business world. The plaintiffs' advanced knowledge of the harmful change of the legal regime was inevitable given their governmental and business prominence. Additionally, such status made them direct or indirect participants in shaping these events.

---

[1] *See* NAGLA NASSAR, SANCTITY OF CONTRACTS REVISITED: A STUDY IN THE THEORY AND PRACTICE OF LONG-TERM INTERNATIONAL COMMERCIAL TRANSACTIONS 201 (Nijhoff, 1998), citing ICC Award in case no. 1512.

Similarly, the economic results of the parties' respective performances place in serious doubt the alleged excessive onerousness, especially if one takes into account the profits obtained by GCES after its privatization and sale of assets.

From a legal standpoint, the roots and remedial purposes of Article 994 S.Com.C. are directly attributable to its Italian ancestry. A careful analysis of the Italian case law and doctrinal commentary shows that this provision was intended for the occurrence of truly catastrophic and unforeseen events with significant effects on the marketplace. Typical among these events were a sudden and unexpected inflation or a drastic devaluation of the national currency.

Finally, the performance of the present contract lacks the elements of onerousness required by leading Italian judicial decisions and doctrinal writings because these, as a minimum, presuppose a "synallagmatic" imbalance (which we will discuss shortly) and an inability to foresee the supervening acts or events that brought about the plaintiffs' onerousness. In addition, there were serious indications that the plaintiffs assumed what Italian and Salvadoran law refer to as the "aleatory" risk of this contract.

D. Basic Concepts Supporting This Opinion

1. The Synallagmatic Balance of Article 994 S.Com.C.

Under Italian law, one of the causes of excessive onerousness is the loss of what courts and doctrinal writers refer to as the synallagmatic balance of promised performances. The concept of synallagmatic balance was described at the end of the eighteenth century by Robert Pothier in his Treatise on Obligations, as part of what he considered the object or purpose of a contract:

> [T]hings which one of the contracting parties stipulates shall be given to him, and which the other promises to give him; or something which one of the parties stipulates to be done or not *to be* done, and which the other party promises to do or not to.[2]

According to this view, in order to determine if a synallagmatic balance exists in a contract, it is necessary to analyze the parties' stipulations. In Pothier's words:

> [Perfect synallagmatic or bilateral contracts are those in which] each party's obligation is also a principle obligation of that contract, the as with sales, leases, partnerships and so on . . . For example, in the contract of sale, the seller's obligation to deliver the thing and the buyer's obligation to pay the price are also the principle obligations of the sale agreement.[3]

Hence, what characterizes Pothier's synallagmatic balance is not only the presence of bilateral promises, but also the supposed negotiating equality of the parties and the reciprocity of the performances stipulated by the parties. For this reason, a synallagmatic imbalance does not merely occur when the values of both performances are arithmetically unequal. For Pothier, as well as for his Italian and Latin American followers or adherents, a synallagmatic balance occurs when the parties negotiate the contract under an assumed negotiating equality and *receive what they stipulated to.*

---

[2] POTHIER, I OBLIGATIONS, at 37.

[3] *Id.* at 14.

Thus only on rare occasions is it necessary to examine the imbalance beyond what was stipulated in order to establish a price or an equitable balance of performances.

Professor Roberto Lara Velado, the principal draftsman of the S.Com.C. and a scholar who shares Pothier's views, deems the performances stipulated in a synallagmatic contract equivalent[4] as the basis for this affirmation is found in Article 1312 of the Salvadoran Civil Code (hereinafter S.C.C.).[5]

Moreover, as Professor Lark Velado points out, the more a synallagmatic contract is negotiated and amended and the more the parties rely on objective measuring devices to determine the value of their performances, such as price indexes and mathematical formulas for costs and profits, the more inevitable is the conclusion that an objectively fair synallagmatic balance exists.[6] The statutory regulation for this conclusion is found under Article 963 of the S.Com.C. in reference to the determination of a fair price.[7]

Professor Lark Velado's observation points to the possible dichotomy between an agreed-upon, *a priori* and binding synallagmatic balance, and an *a posteriori* objectively-measured balance which may or may not come into place in cases of excessive onerousness. As will become apparent in the following sections, it is the former balance (*i.e.*, *a priori* or agreed-upon balance) that most Italian courts look to in order to determine the applicability of excessive onerousness. One reason why the *a posteriori* form of imbalance comes into play only exceptionally is because of the strong presumption in favor of an *a priori* balance. This is especially true when a contract is carefully negotiated and, even more so, when any need for an *a posteriori* balance is expressly or impliedly waived by the parties.

2. *The Synallagmatic Balance of a Group of Contracts*

Both the *a priori* and *a posteriori* synallagmatic balance of a contract can result from the performances stipulated in a single contract or in a group of contracts, as long as they are all part of or related to the same negotiation. This view was espoused in a

---

[4] ROBERTO LARA VELADO, INTRODUCION AL ESTUDIO DEL DERECHO MERCANTIL 205 (1969). It states:

> Consequently, two obligations are derived from the sale agreement: 1) the obligation of the seller to convey to the buyer the ownership of the object sold; and 2) the buyer's obligation to pay to the seller the price for the object bought. Both performances are deemed equivalent.

Id. (translation by author).

[5] CÓD. CIV. (EL. SAL.) art. 1312 (1858). It states:

> The onerous contract is commutative when each of the parties obligates itself to give or do something that is regarded [by the other party] as equivalent to what the other party must give or do; and if the equivalent [performance] consists of an uncertain contingency of profit or loss, then it is known as aleatory.

Id. (translation by author).

[6] LARA VELADO, *supra* note 4, at 200. It states:

> The fair price of objects, as well as the current market price will be determined in accordance with any of the following methods, each displacing the other in the order listed: 1) Official price lists when these are determined by the government; 2) Price lists issued by banks, stock exchanges and chambers of commerce, deeming them as evidentiary appraisal documents; 3) Experts appraisal.

Id. (translation by author).

[7] *See* CÓD. COM. (EL. SAL) art. 963 (1983). It states: "In the absence of official lists to determine the fair price and current market price, these will be determined by the lists issued by banks, stock exchanges or the chamber of commerce. In the absence of these lists, prices will be determined by experts." *Id.* (translation by author).

decision of the Supreme Court of Spain in 1956 which states that: ". . . no onerousness exists in the legal sense if the [stipulated] exchange (of values) takes place in other contracts . . ."[8]

3. *Foreseeability of the Synallagmatic Imbalance*

Article 994 S.Com.C. also requires the claimant's inability to foresee the acts or events that caused the subsequent imbalance or lack of mutuality. Foreseeability under Article 994 S.Com.C. takes into account the personal and professional traits of the claimant. If the claimant was in possession of privileged information because of his official or quasi-official nature or as a result of his conduct, then the claimant clearly cannot assert that the consequences derived from what he knew, or even should have known, would happen were unforeseeable.

4. *Permissive Nature of Article 994 S.Com.C.*

Under Salvadoran private law, mandatory or imperative contractual provisions are exceptional. If the Salvadoran legislator intends to forbid a contractual waiver of a right or claim, then he will generally do so and often explicitly.[9] Thus, Article 12 of the S.C.C. allows the waiver of rights as long as such a waiver does not affect third parties. Relying on this Article and taking into account that its waiver is not forbidden, Article 994 S.Com.C. has to be considered as a permissive provision; hence, the excuse for excessive onerousness can be waived under Salvadoran law. As was confirmed by Italian court decisions, discussed in a later section, Article 1467 of the It.C.C. (the inspiring provision of Article 994 of the S.Com.C.) can be waived and so can its Salvadoran counterpart.

§ 27.4 TRANSACTIONAL AND LEGAL BASES FOR THE OPINION

A. Normative Lineage and Main Features of Article 994 S.Com.C. and Article 1467 of the It.C.C.

The immediate inspiration of Article 994 of the S.Com.C. came from Articles 750, 755 and 757 of the Honduran Commercial Code of 1950 (hereinafter H.Com.C.).[10] However, the Salvadoran and Honduran provisions were both inspired by Article 1467 of the C.C (Italy).

---

[8] *Cf.* Sentencia de 12 junio de 1956, *cited in* AUGUSTO PINO, LA ECCESSIVA ONEROSITA DELLA PRESTAZZIONE 8 (Cedam, Padua 1951), FEDERICO DE MALLOL, LA EXCESIVA ONEROSIDAD DE LA PRESTACION 72 (Federico de Mallol trans., Bosch, Barcelona, 1959) [hereinafter PINO & MALLOL].

[9] *See* CÓD. COM. (EL. SAL), *supra* note 7, art. 998 (as an example of a mandatory provision under Salvadoran commercial law). It states: "Parties cannot modify the legal regime of caducity [lapsed rights]; neither can they waive it if set forth by law." *Id.* (translation by author).

[10] CÓD. COM. (HOND.) art. 757 (1950). It states:

> If a contract of continued, periodic or deferred performance becomes excessively onerous to one of the parties as a consequence of unforeseen or extraordinary acts, the affected party can request its resolution with the consequential effects established under Article 750. The other party may proceed as indicated in Article 755.

Id. (translation by author). Art. 750 of the Honduras Commercial Code states: "The resolution of a contract as a result of non-performance has retroactive effect among the parties, excluding those stipulations already performed under contracts of continued or periodic performance." *Id.* art. 750 (translation by author). And art. 755 of the commercial code explains: "The defendant may oppose to the resolution if it offers an equitable modification of the contract." *Id.* art. 755 (translation by author).

The C.C (Italy) of 1942 is one of a few codes regarded as a "unified" code—*i.e.*, a single code that covers what was covered separately by nineteenth-century civil and commercial codes. The C.C (Italy) is divided into six books, 2969 articles and, like its French and German civil and commercial counterparts, it is accompanied by an ever-growing body of commercial legislation including that on maritime navigation (*Il Codice della Navigazione* of 1940), insurance, bankruptcy and liquidation procedures, and so on.[11]

Considering its fascist origins, one could have hardly predicted that many, if not most, of the provisions of the original C.C (Italy) would have remained in force in our time.

Nonetheless, because many Spanish and Latin American commercial law scholars did their graduate work in Italy, especially after the Second World War (and many still do), the C.C (Italy) became an inspiration for Latin American codes such as the H.Com.C. of 1950.[12]

B. Foreseeability of the Assumption of Risks by the GCES

S.Com.C. drafter Professor Lara Velado shared Professor Joaquin Rodríguez's (main drafter of the H.Com.C.) strong support for freedom of contract. Additionally Professor Velado took into account that this is not an absolute principle and that exceptions must be considered, such as the one in Article 965 of the S.Com.C. In reference to this exception, Professor Velado stated:

> There is an exception [to freedom of contract] under commercial law found in the concessions granted to governmental enterprises ... and the concessionaires of state or municipal services. [These suppliers]. . . . can fix the price of their goods and services, because they are the only ones who offer them or because a group of enterprises have agreed on a common price. [Yet, in exchange for this privilege or monopoly, these concessionaires] may be forced to contract with any other person under the same contractual conditions as they have contracted with others . . .[13]

It is undisputed that the GCES was aware of this S.Com.C. provision, which does not preclude price fixing but forbids the unwillingness to provide an exclusive service. Furthermore, the S.Com.C. compels the rendering of said services by imposing the remedies of damages or specific performance against the unwilling concessionaire. It was also clear to the GCES that since 1970 it had the duty to provide said public services, regardless of whether the prices for the services were fixed or freely negotiated by the parties. This duty undoubtedly carried with it a major risk. However, it was a completely foreseeable risk to its provider, in this case the GCES.

---

[11] *See* MARIO BELTRAMO, I THE ITALIAN CIVIL CODE AND COMPLEMENTARY LEGISLATION (Mario Beltramo et. al. trans., 1996) [hereinafter Beltramo I], and MARIO BELTRAMO, II THE ITALIAN CIVIL CODE AND COMPLEMENTARY LEGISLATION (Mario Beltramo et. al. trans., 1996) [hereinafter BELTRAMO II].

[12] *See* REPUBLICA DE HONDURAS, CODIGO DE COMERCIO 6–7 (Ariston ed., 1950). Despite the rejection of fascist or authoritarian ideas, this works adopts the C.C. (ITALY) concept of "empresa" and its "massive" acts of commerce as central to that code's scope.

[13] LARA VELADO, *supra* note 4, at 203. *See also* CÓD. COM. (EL. SAL), *supra* note 7, art. 965 (translated by author).

C. Determining the Fair Price of Natural Gas Under the PCG

Article 963 of the S.Com.C. provides a method to determine the fair or just price of a commodity when it is not pre-established in official lists or quotations of prices:

> In the absence of official lists to determine the fair price and current market price [of goods, securities or commodities widely traded (also known as escalator clauses)], these will be determined by the lists issued by banks, stock exchanges or the chamber of commerce. In the absence of these lists, prices will be determined by experts.

This provision supports the parties' freedom to refer to lists of prices or price indices in their contractual stipulations. Thus, the S.Com.C., in an *a posteriori* fashion, validates the synallagmatic balance of performances in contracts with escalator clauses as done by the PCG.[14] On this point, the S.Com.C. is entirely consistent with its Italian progenitor and Italian court interpretations.

D. The Remedies for Excessive Onerousness Under Italian Law

The remedy related to excessive onerousness under the It.C.C. is that of the termination (*risoluzione*) of the contract. Article 1467 of the It.C.C. states:

> In contracts of continuous and periodic performance or of deferred performance, if extraordinary and unforeseeable events make the performance of one of the parties excessively onerous, the party who owes such performance can demand the termination of the contract, with the effects set forth in Article 1458.
>
> Termination cannot be demanded if the supervening onerousness is part of the normal risks of the contract.
>
> A party against whom termination is demanded can avoid it by offering to equitably modify the conditions of the contract.

Accordingly, excessive onerousness becomes one more cause of judicial and extrajudicial termination of contracts in Italian law. This is not surprising in light of the fact that contractual termination is the main remedy of contractual law under the It.C.C. The generic cause for judicial termination can be found in It.C.C. Article 1453:

> "In a contract with continuous performance, when one of the parties does not comply with its obligation, the other party may request the specific performance or the termination of the contract, subject to compensation for damages suffered in either case . . ."[15]

It should be noted that unlike what occurs under the French and Spanish civil codes, the remedy of an extrajudicial termination of the fully or anticipatorily-breached contract is available under Italian and German law.[16] As stated by Articles 1454 and 1456 of the It.C.C.:

---

[14] *Id.* art. 963. This article, as does C.C. (ITALY) art. 1474, addresses the issue of fair price, especially when it has not been stipulated in the contract. Both provisions rely on the negotiations between the parties or on the prices customarily fixed by the seller in comparable transactions, or on the prices publicly listed whether in the form of stock exchange or other public market quotations.

[15] C.C. (ITALY) art. 1453 (translation by author).

[16] *See id.* arts. 1454 & 1456.

> Art. 1454. The counterparty of the non-complying party may request from the other party compliance with the contract within a reasonable time; if by the end of the reasonable term for compliance the obligation remains unfulfilled, the contract will be deemed terminated.
>
> The term cannot be less than fifteen days, unless the parties agree otherwise, or unless given the nature or purpose of the contract, a shorter term is considered reasonable.
>
> Upon expiration of the term for compliance, the contract will be considered terminated by law.
>
> Art. 1456. The parties to a contract may expressly stipulate the termination of a contract when a given obligation is not complied with according to their stipulations.
>
> Once one of the parties expresses its intention to apply the termination clause, the contract is deemed terminated by law.

E. Comparison of Remedies Under Italian Law

As will be illustrated in later chapters,[17] both the judicial and private termination of contracts coexist with other remedies and these remedies are often confused, notwithstanding their distinctive characteristics. Among these are remedies based upon codified provisions such as lesion and subjective lesion discussed in earlier chapters.[18] In the case of rescission caused by the "lesion" (economic harm or damages), the plaintiff suffers harm by the rescinding party as a result of a sale price of real property significantly lower than its market value. In the case of "subjective lesion," the plaintiff, a contracting party with weaker bargaining power, suffers by being exploited by the other stronger party. These doctrines are similar to the code-supported remedy known as the annulment of the contract as a result of "vices" of consent; this annulment is caused by the physical or mental handicaps of one of the contracting parties or the duress or coercion imposed upon that party by the other. The following is a discussion of some of these codified and statutory remedies in the It.C.C.

1. Rescission

The It.C.C. limits the remedy of rescission to the following situations: a party may rescind a contract when, according to Article 1447 of the It.C.C., it was entered into under "unfair conditions, known by the other party, and caused by the need of saving himself or his family from a present danger of personal injury."[19]

The factual assumption of this remedy is not that of excessive onerousness since the latter presupposes a contract entered into by equals and a synallagmatic imbalance of performances in contracts of continued or deferred performance. Along the same lines, Article 1448 of the It.C.C. allows a general claim for rescission as a result of the serious patrimonial injury (*lesione*) suffered by the Plaintiff:

> If there is a disproportion between the performance of one party and that of the other, and such disproportion was the result of a state of need of one

---

[17] *See infra* chs. 28–30.

[18] *See, e.g.,* § 8:7(J).

[19] C.C. (ITALY) art. 1447 (translation by author).

> party, of which the other has availed himself for his advantage, the injured party can demand the rescission of the contract.
>
> The action is not admissible if the injury [*lesione*] does not exceed one-half of the value of the performance made or promised by the injured party at the time of the contract.
>
> To be actionable, the injury must continue until the time when the action is filed.
>
> Aleatory contracts cannot be rescinded for injury.
>
> The provisions concerning rescission as a result of partitions are not affected [by this provision].
>
> An action for rescission can entail not only the termination of the contract and the restitution of the amounts unlawfully gained by the defendant and damages, but it can also lead to a criminal action.

This remedy differs from excessive onerousness because it requires that there be a state of need by the contracting party affected by the injury, and also because it limits the remedy to contracts of which the injury is of a certain amount.

2. *Annulment and Mistake*

Under the It.C.C., contracts can be annulled because of a party's incapacity,[20] mistake, duress or fraud.[21] According to Article 1428 of the It.C.C., a mistake is ". . . a cause for the annulment of a contract when it is essential and acknowledged by the other party."[22] A mistake is "essential" when, *inter alia*, "1) it affects the nature of the purpose of the contract; or 2) it affects the identity or quality of the object of the performance which, according to the parties' stipulations, has to be considered determinative of their consent . . ."[23]

In our case, GCES is not alleging incapacity, mistake, duress or fraud as an excuse to its claim for the termination of the contract. The aforementioned causes of termination or rescission of a contract affect the parties' capacity to consent to what was agreed to. This lack of consent is in contrast with the excessive onerousness alleged by GCES which does not question GCES' capacity or free will to enter into the PCG.

Excessive onerousness as a cause of termination of a contract occurs *after* the contract has been validly entered into by the parties. The It.C.C. also distinguishes between the various remedies as forms of action and as exceptions or defenses. For example, even though the parties have the right to claim (or not claim) the nullity of a contract, they cannot waive its annulment or rescission. In contrast, excessive onerousness is not listed among the actions or defenses not allowed to be waived, thus it is impliedly waivable.

---

[20] *Id.* art. 1425.

[21] For these vices of consent, *see id.* arts. 1427–33 (mistake); 1434–38 (force, duress and coercion); 1439–40 (fraud and malice).

[22] *Id.* art. 1428 (translation by author).

[23] *Id.* art. 1429 (translation by author).

3. Rebus Sic Stantibus

Unfortunately, there is only minimal legislative history with respect to excessive onerousness, especially in relation to its differences with other excuses for non-performance, such as *rebus sic stantibus.* Among the few legislative history references available on Article 1467 of the It.C.C., there is one provided by the Italian Minister of Internal Affairs (*Ministro Guardasigilli*) at the time of its enactment: "Thus, i[t] [excessive onerousness] introduced expressly and generally for contracts with reciprocal performances [implementing] the principle of implicit subjection to the *clausula rebus sic stantibus* . . . consistently with a singularly Italian tradition . . ."[24]

This reference to the *rebus sic stantibus* doctrine has been shown to be historically inaccurate and thus unreliable. As pointed out by Professor Augusto Pino, the *rebus sic stantibus* doctrine is applied to contracts of all types, whereas Article 1467 of the It.C.C. applies only to specific contracts, such as commutative contracts and contracts whose performance is deferred.[25]

As concluded by Professor Pino: "In effect, the general principle that was deemed . . . Article 1467 of the It.C.C. can be deducted and established fully only by means of a rigorous interpretation of this provision and not by a reference to a historical principle with which it may not even coincide."[26]

As will be apparent during the discussion of the German excuses for non-performance,[27] the hyperinflation of post-World War I Germany (during a time in which numerous Italian legal scholars did their graduate work in that country) was a dramatic laboratory on the effects of unforeseen circumstances upon the performance of commercial and civil contracts alike and how to deal with such circumstances. The vast amount of German judicial and doctrinal literature on the various remedies analogous to excessive onerousness is continuously referred to by Italian commentators and court decisions to this day. In light of the influence of other German contractual law institutions, such as the *Nachfrist*[28] (or preparatory notice for an extrajudicial resolution of contracts) upon the It.C.C.,[29] it is likely that German literature influenced the Italian drafters of the It.C.C.

4. Aleatory Contracts and the Waiver of Excessive Onerousness

For some of the Italian commentators, the purpose and scope of Article 1467 is easier to understand when it is juxtaposed with Article 1469 of the same code which allows the waiver of excessive onerousness as a defense or grounds for resolution of the

---

[24] *See* CARLO BRACCIANTI, DEGLI EFFETTI DELLA ECCESSIVA ONEROSITA SOPRAVENIENTI NEI CONTRATTI 62 (2nd ed. 1947). On March 16, 1942, the Italian Minister of Internal Affairs (or *Ministro Guardasigilli),* in an explanation to the then proposed art. 1467 (*Relazione al rogetto Ministeriali delle Obbligazioni*), stated: "Thus, i[t] introduced expressly and generally for contracts with reciprocal performances, the principle of implicit subjection to the *clausula rebus sic stantibus* . . ." *Id.*

[25] *See* Pino & MALLOL, *supra* note 8, at 72. These sources discuss where the reliable sources showed that the clause was applied indistinctively to "all legal relations . . . of private and public law." *Id.*

[26] *Id.* at 133.

[27] *See infra* § 27:4(H)(1).

[28] *See* Glossary, "*Nachfrist.*"

[29] C.C. (ITALY), *supra* note 14, art. 1454.

contract when the contract is aleatory, *i.e.*, when its participants are willing to gamble on its positive or negative results.[30]

In contrast to Article 1312 of the S.C.C., which will soon be discussed, Article 1469 of the It.C.C. does not define aleatory contracts. However, as is customary in civil law countries, such gaps are usually filled by doctrinal definitions. One of the most influential doctrinal definitions of an aleatory contract belongs to the late Professor Francisco Messineo:

> Aleatory contracts, by their nature, are those where the element of sacrifice is related to the element of profit-that is to say, while the risk to which one party is exposed cannot be quantified at the time of formation of the contract, it will be subsequently revealed by the course of events . . . [and by the outcome of the contract].[31]

On the other hand, Article 1312 of the S.C.C. acknowledges that commutative contracts can easily become aleatory:

> The onerous contract is commutative when each of the parties obligates itself to give or do something that is regarded [by the other party] as equivalent to what the other party must give or do; and if the equivalent [performance] consists of an uncertain contingency of profit or loss, then it is known as aleatory.[32]

In the same vein, Article 1469 of the It.C.C. refers to a commutative contract that can be transformed into an aleatory contract by the intent of the parties.[33] It should not be surprising, then, that when the parties decide to create an aleatory contract Article 1469 of the It.C.C. allows them to waive the application of Article 1467.

Professor Carlo Braccianti, one of the first commentators of Article 1467 of the It.C.C.,[34] lists aleatory contracts, by nature, as those that involve "sales of futures, pensions and insurance plans, betting games, authorized lottery, and some stock exchange contracts, etc."[35] Agreeing with this doctrinal observation, Italian case law has also contributed to the determination of implied aleatory contracts and has classified supply contracts with price adjustment clauses as one of the most common aleatory categories. As stated by a 1985 decision by the *Corte di Cassazione*:

> If extraordinary events occur during the performance of supply contracts, where the parties have included adjustment mechanisms to mitigate prices, termination may not be obtained even in cases where the adjustment mechanism turns out to be inappropriate in reestablishing equilibrium between the economic value of the performances. The adjustment

---

[30] *Id.* art. 1469. *See* Glossary, "Aleatory Contracts."

[31] F. MESSINEO, II MANUALE DI DIRITTO CIVILE E COMMERCIAL 203 (7th ed., 1946), *cited in* BRACCIANTI, *supra* note 24, at 74.

[32] CÓD. CIV. (EL SAL.), *supra* note 5, art. 1312 (translation by author).

[33] C.C. (ITALY), *supra* note 14, art. 1469. It states: "The provisions of the preceding articles do not apply to contracts which are aleatory by their nature or by the intention of the parties." *Id.* (translation by author).

[34] *See generally* BRACCIANTI, *supra* note 24.

[35] *Id.* at 74.

> mechanisms . . . imply the will of the parties to assume the risks of supervening events . . .[36]

The equation of indexation clauses with assumption of market risks is clear in a 1991 decision of the *Corte di Cassazione*: "A contract of sale is aleatory [with respect to its market price] when it expressly stipulates the automatic revaluation of the purchase price in relation to the rate of exchange between the Italian Lira and the Swiss franc."[37]

These courts also expanded on the validity of the waiver of defenses provided by Article 1467 of the It.C.C. As the reader may recall, Article 1469 of the It.C.C. allows the parties to implicitly transform a commutative contract into an aleatory one, thereby waiving the application of Article 1467 of the It.C.C. Additionally, Article 1341 of the It.C.C. allows the party who drafted a standard contract to stipulate limitations to contractual and extra-contractual responsibilities, as long as the other party agrees to those covenants in writing.[38] Therefore, the previously-cited Italian case law and statutory provisions leave no doubt that the action for excessive onerousness can be waived by the fact of entering into an implied aleatory contract. These sources concur with Professor Pino's reference to Article 1467 of the It.C.C. as a "dispositive provision," or a provision whose application can be excluded by the parties.[39]

On repeated occasions Italian courts have characterized as aleatory those contracts in which the claimant should have foreseen the risks involved. For example, in a 1994 decision by the court of Genoa,[40] a buyer of stock on margin claimed the resolution of his purchase agreement after the administrator of the stock exchange issued an administrative order forbidding future margin contracts. The court held that the issuance of such an order was foreseeable by a person with average negotiating capacity, average shrewdness and knowledge of stock exchange transactions, and added: "in stock exchange-margin agreements, termination because of excessive onerousness is not possible where an administrative authority forbids *sine die* new stock purchases . . ."[41]

The court also held that in order to terminate a contract because of excessive onerousness, three conditions must be met: 1) extraordinary and unforeseeable events that cause contractual imbalance; 2) excessiveness of that imbalance; and 3) the occurrence of a risk above and beyond that which is normal for that type of contract. The court considered that in this case the three conditions were not met; even though an administrative order is not statistically predictable, it is likewise not necessarily unforeseeable. It is well known that regulators of stock exchanges have the power to demand cash payment of margin transactions; thus, payments in cash instead of margin should be considered as part of the "rules of the game."[42]

---

[36] *Corte di Cassazione Civil,* Cass. Civ. I., 1985, n.3730.

[37] *See Corte di Cassazione* Civil, Cass. 7 giungo 1991, n. 6542 Foro It. Rep. 1991, n.401.

[38] C.C. (ITALY), *supra* note 14, art. 1341.

[39] PINO & MALLOL, *supra* note 8, at 139. For a definition of a dispositive provision see LUIS RIBO DURÁN, DICCIONARIO DE DERECHO (not dated). It states: "In contrast to the imperative are the so called dispositive norms, also known as *ius dispositivum,* which are those that the private parties can apply, incorporating them or replacing them as agreed by the parties . . ." *Id.* (emphasis added).

[40] Corte D'Appello di Genova, sentenza 9 maggio 1984, Foro Italiano I, 1985.

[41] *Id.*

[42] *Id.* at 267.

Italian courts refer to contractual risk or "*alea*" as a notion connected to the particular market and type of business.[43] Therefore, any risk that is common to that market and business should be considered as assumed by the parties unless otherwise stipulated. As was previously discussed, the parties have the freedom to include clauses or covenants by which they are bound to assume or waive risks, even to the point of having to perform the contract when this performance could be categorized as impossible.[44] For this reason, courts have held that if a contract were entered into in time of war, the parties necessarily had to assume or waive certain business risks. Courts have also held that share price fluctuation may be considered a normal risk depending on the current market conditions.[45]

5. *Foreseeability and the* "Uomo Medio"

As will be discussed in following sections, in some countries, such as France, that have not adopted the legislative remedy of excessive onerousness, it is possible to claim unforeseeable consequences of a contract as an excuse for non-performance, although this excuse is limited to administrative concessions. If the costs of performing an administrative concession exceed the limits of what could have been foreseen by the parties when entering into the contract, a French court, although reluctantly, can adjust them.

Even a cursory review of Italian case law on excessive onerousness will reveal that courts closely link foreseeability and synallagmatic imbalance, especially when the latter can be measured objectively. In doing this, it is clear that excessive onerousness is a broader doctrine than the French doctrine of foreseeability since it is not restricted to administrative concessions.

For example, in a 1994 decision by the Court of Monza (Italy), the plaintiff was the seller of 1,000 tons of steel. In the case, the plaintiff proved that the cost of the raw materials required to produce the steel had increased thirty percent above the final agreed-upon price. He also proved that at the time of performing the contract, the market price of the product was forty-five percent higher than it was when the agreement was entered into. Nevertheless, he did not prove that the increase in costs was caused by an extraordinary and unforeseeable event rather than by his own delay in acquiring the raw materials. The claim was rejected by the court as follows: "The claimant had to prove that the fluctuations of prices, far from depending upon the normal and inherent transactional risk, found its origin in abnormal economic or financial causes, general or particular (as the case may be) that affected the price in an extraordinary and unforeseeable fashion."[46]

Because of the close relationship between the synallagmatic imbalance and what is foreseeable by the parties, a doctrinal commentator of this decision aptly concludes that excessive onerousness often varies from case to case; simply put, it is as much a

---

[43] Sentenza, Trib. Napoles, 13 marzo 1947, Sorrentino c. Filippone, Foro Italiano, at 656.

[44] As it was discussed, this contractual power is granted by the second paragraph of art. 1341 of the Italian Civil Code. For case law affirming this rule, see Sentenza, App. Milan, 15 Iunnio 1948, L'Ausiliare c. Borrelli, en Riv. dir. comm., 1948, II, p. 360, *cited in* PINO & MALLOL, *supra* note 8, at 88.

[45] *Id.* at 89 (it lists more than a dozen appellate court decisions).

[46] Tribunale di Monza, 29 marzo 1993, Foro It. I, 1994, at 916, 922, citing Cass.14, dicembre 1982 n.6867, *Id.*, nn 292–294; 18 ottobre 1978, .4647 id.; Rep. 1978,

factual as a legal determination.[47] Not surprisingly then Italian courts have had to resort to a flexible, albeit objective and archetypal, standard of behavior to measure foreseeability. The chosen standard is the behavior of an "average person" (*uomo medio*) under the circumstances of the marketplace in question.[48] This standard seldom requires highly-specialized knowledge, unless it involves professional contracting parties; and instead it leads to an evaluation of the foreseeability "in relation to the situation in existence at the moment of the conclusion of the contract . . . in relation to the nature of the transactions and the conditions of the market [as known or as should have been known by an average person]."[49] Therefore, if the transaction involves the purchase of stock in a stock exchange, the standard of an average person will be that of a person with "average capacity, average shrewdness and knowledge of the stock exchange transactions," but not necessarily a specialist.[50]

This standard of foreseeability is also inextricably tied to the determination of "normal risk assumption" (*alea normale*) and has led some courts to establish a group of risks that can be considered as foreseeable within certain markets, such as the fluctuation in the value of currencies, inflation, and variations in production costs or in the price of certain merchandise, such as fungible goods.[51]

*6. Contractual Presuppositions (*Presupposizione*)*

Paolo Cendon, another well-known commentator of the It.C.C., notes that despite the objective (synallagmatic balance) approach generally used by Italian courts, some judicial decisions rely on the doctrine of contractual presupposition. This doctrine assumes that the excessive onerousness of the It.C.C. is merely a restatement of *rebus sic stantibus*.[52] As noted earlier, this equation was also made without much support by the Minister of Internal Affairs of Italy at the time of the It.C.C.'s enactment. According to this judicial viewpoint, events that were not assumed as likely to occur, and thus were not taken into consideration by the parties at the time of contracting, might lead to the termination of the contract if they took place once the contract was to be performed.

Cendon objects to this point of view because he considers that, in order to determine a synallagmatic imbalance, the only thing that a judge needs to do is to compare the performances and counter-performances stipulated by the parties. In his opinion, it is beyond the judicial function to speculate on what was taken, or should have been taken, into consideration by the parties, when and where. Professor Pino adds to this objection that the nineteenth century German writings already distinguished between the *rebus sic stantibus* and the contractual presuppositions doctrines. When applying the *rebus* doctrine, the adjudicator first examines the express language of the contract and then compares it to the supervening events that affected

---

[47] *Id.* at 917. Case Annotation identified as S. di. Paola at 920.

[48] GIUSEPPE MIRABELLI, COMENTARIO DEL CODICE CIVILE, DELLE OBBLIGAZIONI DEI CONTRATTI IN GENERALE 656 (1980) (citing different sources).

[49] *Id.*

[50] Corte D'Appello di Genova, sentenza 9 maggio 1984, Foro Italiano I, 1985, at 266, 267. *See also* PAOLO CENDON, IV COMENTARIO AL CODICE CIVILE 859 & 863 (1991) (with reference to Cass. 2684/55 that took into consideration the "alle qualità dei contraenti"—the capacity and status of the parties).

[51] For examples of "normal risks" that are excluded as causes for the remedy of excessive onerousness, *see also* Cass. 2904 /87, Cass. 1913 /85, and Cass.1/83, *id.* at 863.

[52] *Id.* at 860.

the parties' ability to perform. If the contractual language did not contemplate the supervening events, the *rebus* doctrine applied. In contrast, when applying the doctrine of contractual presuppositions, the adjudicator disregards the explicit language of the contract and looks for the hypothetical agreement between the parties based on what he conjectures was their contractual intention; the adjudicator will then take this intention into account and try to enforce it in light of the supervening acts, regardless of their foreseeability.[53]

Additionally, Professor Pino points out that the doctrine of contractual presuppositions is a serious limitation upon the parties' freedom of contract since it creates a new type of implied condition, or "super-condition," of reasonability justified, paradoxically, by the argument that if the parties had taken those facts into consideration when entering into a contract, they would have included them as part of their stipulations.[54] Thus, the express contractual intent, or what the parties had actually agreed on, would be subordinated to what they *should have agreed on* in the eyes of the judge; accordingly, the parties' contract would become enforceable only if the judicially-presupposed facts had been made part of the contract.

This reasoning leads Professor Pino to conclude that the doctrine of contractual presuppositions and Article 1467 of the It.C.C. are incompatible. For if they were compatible, the parties to "contracts of continuous or periodic performance or for deferred performance"[55] would have to subordinate the enforcement of their obligations to the verification of unforeseeable events, even under circumstances that were not considered by the parties precisely because they were unforeseeable.[56]

Another reason why the doctrine of contractual presuppositions has not succeeded with the majority of Italian courts is that it encourages the debtor's bad faith by allowing him to contradict his own contractual acts with impunity. As was pointed out in Giuseppe Mirabelli's Commentary to the Italian Civil Code: "[T]he events must be strictly accidental or imputable to a party other [than] the party who invokes their relevance."[57] Therefore, an Italian court would not apply Article 1467 of the It.C.C. to the dispute between GCES and AGPC S.A. because GCES's claim of an unforeseeable act (privatization by the Salvadoran government) was not only foreseeable, but could have been directly or indirectly attributable to GCES itself. In this respect, Mirabelli considers that:

> [Any conduct] imputable to the debtor may exclude the application of the remedy not only in the case where the debtor did not foresee, because of his negligence, an event that was clearly foreseeable or in the case where the debtor suffered the effects of excessive onerousness having been placed in default but also because he had participated in the aggravation of his own indebtedness . . .[58]

---

[53] PINO & MALLOL, *supra* note 8, at 150.

[54] *Id.* at 155.

[55] *Id.*

[56] *Id.* at 156.

[57] MIRABELLI, *supra* note 48, at 656.

[58] *Id.* at 25.

7. *Subjective Excessive Onerousness*

Anticipating the occurrence of a result like that of the above-discussed 1994 decision by the Court of Monza, Paolo Cendon reiterated the role of a bilateral or synallagmatic imbalance analysis as:

> [Contemporary interpretation has] overcome the temptation to subsume excessive onerousness within ambit of hardship or the more general doctrine of difficulty of performing the obligation . . . thus reflecting a strictly objective notion onerousness; case law too excludes the subjective component of the debtor's difficulties in performing, maintaining that the impairment of the debtor's ability to perform is not by itself a cause for termination, unless that impairment is also accompanied by a marked increase in the value of his performance.[59]

This same author points out that the crucial moments for measuring the contractual imbalance are i) when performances are due and ii) when performances are finally carried out.[60] As noted earlier, Professor Pino, another proponent of the objective criteria for measuring onerousness,[61] suggests that since the law is not an exact science, it can hardly measure the mathematical equivalence of performances. Hence, the legal equivalence of performances must be understood as the value that each party, *ex ante*, is willing to grant to the performance of the other party in exchange for one's own performance.

Where the present dispute is concerned, Professors Cendon and Pino would point out that the main issue is not the size of the alleged loss suffered by plaintiff GCES when selling the gas it purchased from AGPC S.A. at the agreed-upon contract price. Instead, reflecting the majority opinion in Italy, these authors would conclude that the main issue would be whether the payments made by the GCES to AGPC S.A. gave the latter a completely disproportionate value compared to that which would have been given as required by their contract.

In a similar vein, in one of its decisions, the International Court of Arbitration of the International Chamber of Commerce equated excessive onerousness to its version of hardship and rejected its application as follows:

> Faced with a number of unforeseen difficulties which substantially increased the cost of the construction, the contractor requested the renegotiation of the contract invoking hardship according to Articles 6.2.2 and 6.2.3 of the UNIDROIT Principles . . . the Arbitral Tribunal held that the provisions of the UNIDROIT Principles on hardship do not correspond, at least presently, to current practices in international trade.[62]

---

[59] *See supra* note 46 & accompanying text, on the Monza Appellate decision. *See also* CENDON, *supra* note 50, at 859–860.

[60] *Id.*

[61] PINO & MALLOL, *supra* note 8, at 56–57 (includes citations of authors with an opposite point of view).

[62] *See* Case 8873, 1997 ICC INT'L COURT OF ARBITRATION (English abstract) *available at* http://www.unilex.info/case.cfm?pid=2&do=case&id=641&step=Abstract (on file with this author).

F. Judicial and Doctrinal Circumscription of the Remedial Criteria of Article 1467 of the It.C.C.

There can be little doubt that Italian case law and doctrinal comments have circumscribed the scope of application of Article 1467 of the It.C.C. and that they continue do so. This trend confirms the restrictive nature of this excuse for non-performance in Italian law. Among the categories of contracts that cannot be terminated because of excessive onerousness are: i) unilateral contracts, or contracts in which only one party acquires obligations, *i.e.*, the contract of donation;[63] ii) executed contracts, as opposed to executory promises or promises whose performance is deferred;[64] iii) cases in which the plaintiff fails to prove his contractual diligence as manifested in an absence of reasonable foreseeability;[65] iv) leases that include express or implied conditions that prohibit the lessee to use the leased asset to compete with the lessor or for purposes other than specified if the lease is subject to a statutory minimum term;[66] v) loans of fungible goods;[67] and finally, vi) loans and other contracts in which the beneficiary has received payment of a sum of money intended to cover the risk of loss caused by a supervening inflation.

Moreover, according to Professor Pino, for a considerable period of time, Italian case law rejected the application of Article 1467 of the It.C.C. to loans of all types. This rejection was due to the prevalence of the nominalistic principle that established that the beneficiary only owed the expressly stated or nominal amount of the loan, plus interest.[68] Furthermore, as noted by a 1980 decision of the highest Italian court, the *Corte di Cassazione*, it is a well-established judicial doctrine that "[e]xcessive onerousness will not lay where the damage suffered by the plaintiff is imputable to his own behavior."[69]

To summarize, Italian judicial interpretation is characterized by a continuous search for a circumscribing formula to determine objectively whether or not the performances agreed upon resulted in a reasonably unforeseeable synallagmatic imbalance. The main issue is not the amount of damages caused to the plaintiff or the

---

[63] *See* Relazione al Progetto Ministeriale, No. 246, cited by BRACCIANTI, *supra* note 31, at 99. Doctrine points this out based on the *Relazione Ministeriale* of the Italian Ministry of Justice. It states,

> The law of excessive onerousness does not cover contracts where only one of the parties is obligated (for example, donations of deferred execution). Because such a contract does not involve reciprocal performances, it is not conceivable that one of the parties will offer a performance designed to stabilize an imbalance . . .

Id.

[64] C.C. (ITALY), *supra* note 14, art. 1467. This article only applies to pending-deferred performances, not to those already executed. *See* Cassazione, 13 dicembre, 1980, no. 6470 p. 178, Societa Fina Italiana v. Rescaldini.

[65] Tribunale di Monza, Foro It. 1994, at 916, 922, citing Cass. 14 dicembre 1982, n. 6867, For example, if the plaintiff fails to prove to the court that the increase in costs was not caused by his own delay in acquiring raw materials. Similarly, art. 1467 of the Italian Civil Code does not apply in the case where a supplier fails to prove that it was impossible to comply with his contractual obligation with the raw materials acquired before there was an increase in its price. Arch.ric.giur., 1948, at 170, Dict., 7 gennaio 1947, *cited in* PINO-MALLOL, *supra* note 8 at 27.

[66] Pretura di Roma, Ordinanza 24 novembre 1984, Coc. Sassoufulfin e Soc. inocea c. Soc. Camar, *cited in* BRACCIANTI, *supra* note 31, at 13.

[67] *See* PINO & MALLOL, *supra* note 8, at 49–51. Given that they lack a measuring device, such as money, to establish its onerousness.

[68] Cass.7 iunio 1948, Quattrocchi c. Modo, Giur. Compl. Cass., 1948 III. p. 76, *cited in id.* at 58.

[69] Cass. 6464/80.

profits that he failed to receive, but the excessive disproportion between the value received by the claimant and that, which according to the contract, he should have conferred to the defendant at the time of performance. Therefore, it is in the imbalance of the stipulated performances where excessive onerousness must be found. Finally, a finding of foreseeability of the onerousness depends upon the standard of an average market participant, the *uomo medio*; a flexible standard that is adjusted to the typical assumptions of risks and profit-making in different types of markets.

G. Excessive Onerousness Under Argentinean Law

1. Article 1198 of the Argentinean Civil Code

Article 1198 of the Argentinean Civil Code of 1968 (hereinafter A.C.C.) was inspired by Italian and German law.[70] It states:

> Contracts shall be created, interpreted and executed in good faith and in accordance with what the parties probably intended or could have intended, operating with care and foresight. Where in bilateral commutative contracts and unilateral onerous and commutative contracts of deferred or continued performance the performance owed by one of the parties becomes excessively onerous as a result of extraordinary and unforeseeable events, the affected party may claim the termination of the contract. The same principle will apply to aleatory contracts where excessive onerousness results from causes extraneous to the very risk of the contract.
>
> In contracts of continued performance, its termination will not affect the already-executed performances.
>
> Termination will not apply if the affected party was in fault or in default.
>
> The other party may prevent termination by offering to equitably improve the provisions of the contract.[71]

This article applies the principle of good faith in a more open-ended manner than its German model. Section 157 of the BGB provides that contracts must be ". . . interpreted as required by good faith, taking customary practice into consideration."[72] As will be recalled from the discussion in the preceding chapter of *culpa in contrahendo*,[73] this provision of the A.C.C. goes beyond its German counterpart by requiring good faith, not only in the execution of contracts, but also in their creation.

While Article 1198 of the A.C.C. has elements in common with Article 1467 of the It.C.C., it also departs from this model by allowing excessive onerousness in aleatory contracts, as long as it arises from causes extraneous to the very risk of the contract. The consequences of using such broad language do not appear to have been considered by the Argentine legislators. For example, assume that the contract is a purchase agreement in which the seller, knowing that the market is highly volatile, binds himself to sell gas at a price fixed by the parties. According to Article 1198 of the A.C.C., the provisions on excessive onerousness would not be applied in the case of a

[70] CÓD. CIV. (ARG.) art. 1198 (translated by author).

[71] *Id.*

[72] BGB art. 157.

[73] *See supra* ch. 26.

significant increase in the price of gas because this would be considered as the "very risk of the contract." Nevertheless, according to this same rule, the excuse would apply in a case in which the production plant was destroyed by an earthquake since Article 1198 of the A.C.C. provides that "[t]he same principle will apply to aleatory contracts where excessive onerousness results from causes extraneous to the very risk of the contract." But would it? What did the Argentine legislator mean by an "extraneous cause"? Given the openness of this exception, an earthquake could be an extraneous cause and, as such, would allow for the resolution of the contract *based on the excessive onerousness* doctrine.

However from a strictly conceptual point of view, why should the consequences of a *force majeuer* (a force of nature or an act of God) such as those of an earthquake (extrinsic events to the risk assumed in the contract) also be considered aleatory? Such causes would only be aleatory if the parties had assumed the risk of their occurrence at the time of entering into a contract. Accordingly, Article 1198 of the A.C.C. would not apply to such situations because they would be part of the "very risk of the contract." And from the standpoint of commutative fairness, why should the debtor and victim of a *force majeure* be forced to the standard of proof required by excessive onerousness, when the *force majeure* itself could free him from having to comply with his obligation to continue to supply natural gas? Or does Article 1198 of the A.C.C. exclude the application of these rules when there is a *force majeure*?[74] It is obvious that Article 1198 of the A.C.C. should have been drafted more clearly so as to avoid questions like these.

2. *Argentinean Case Law and Hyperinflation*

Argentinean case law has helped to clarify the open-ended nature of its civil code provisions and application of excessive onerousness, especially in a hyperinflationary marketplace. In Argentina during the 1970s and 1980s, the high increase of litigation for excessive onerousness was described by a judge as the result of the "hurricane" of hyperinflation that hit the country in the early 1970s. When reading the numerous decisions on this matter, it is clear that this hurricane was perceived by Argentineans as man-made and not a force of nature. In most of the decisions there is reference to the "*Rodrigazo*," an administrative decree formulated as an intensive economic shock therapy ordered by a minister whose first name was Rodrigo but whose last name, for unknown reasons, was never mentioned. Many judges and commentators attributed the hyperinflation to this decree that occurred following June 1975.

After 1975, the *Rodrigazo* prevented debtors' claims of excessive onerousness by supporting the argument that the parties should have been aware of the hyperinflation and should have considered it in their contracts. At this time, most of the litigation involved the sale of real estate property, and most of the transactions, ranging from small lots to apartments, houses and condominiums, were paid through installments.

---

[74] *See* Aziz T. Saliba, *Rebus sic stantibus: A Comparative Survey,* 8 MURDOCH UNIV. ELEC. J. L. 1, 2 (2001). As noted:

> Rebus sic stantibus should not be confused with *force majeure*. *Force majeure* excuses the obligor to perform only if there is an irresistible (and unforeseeable) obstacle. In *force majeure*, the performance must be physically or legally impossible and must not be merely more onerous to perform. Thus, in a nutshell, the fundamental difference is that, unlike *rebus sic stantibus*, *force majeure* does not include economic hardship nor even economic impossibility.

Id. (emphasis added).

Landowners, builders and landlords claimed that their sales or lease prices had become "laughable" as a result of hyperinflation. Thus "what started [as a] regular sale or lease, inflation turned into a donation."[75] A 1980 decision from the Appellate Court of Cordoba illustrates how the argument of a "laughable" counter-performance became the basis for the termination of contracts.[76] In this case the plaintiff had purchased real estate property whose value substantially increased as a result of the devaluation of the Argentinean peso with respect to the U.S. dollar. The purchase agreement was documented in a Public Deed and recorded at the Registry of Real Estate Property. However, the defendant refused to deliver the property alleging the application of Article 1198 of the A.C.C. because: "the purchaser's counter-performance has become laughable." The court took judicial notice of the hyperinflationary process and stated: "In 1972, I held, remembering Italian case law, that a claimant cannot claim *sopravenienza* when what is involved is the mere depreciation in value, but once an extraordinary monetary depreciation has taken place, the termination or revision of the contract because of excessive onerousness should be applied."[77]

The court determined that the inflationary rate at the time of the purchase agreement (45% per year) had increased by 100%. It also examined the cost of living and found that this factor had increased from 346.7% in January 1973 to 439% in January 1974. In 1975, this index reached 952.5%, and by December of that same year it had increased to 2,595.2%.[78]

Based on these statistics and on their impact on the defendant's payments of installments, the court decided that Article 1198 of the A.C.C. had to be applied. Yet, the influence of Italian case law and its insistence upon the element of lack of foreseeability as measured by the standard of an *uomo medio* can be found in another Argentine appellate decision that excludes the application of Article 1198 of the A.C.C.[79] As stated in that 1980 decision:

> The theory of unforeseeability (imprevisión) embodied in Article 1198, second paragraph, does not apply when the contract was entered into after the month of June 1975, because [that time] is the determining and significant landmark that unchained a surprising and extraordinary inflation, from which time onwards an adequate diligence impeded the ignorance of subsequent effects.[80] (emphasis omitted).

The same reasoning is present in a 1979 appellate decision:

> The ground (for appeal) based upon the "theory of unforseeability" has no basis because at the time of the Public Deed—October 1975—the party that now claims to have been damaged could more than reasonably have been

---

[75] See the numerous citations of doctrine found in LILY R. FLAH AND MIRIAM SMAYEVSKI, TEORIA DE LA IMPREVISION, APLICACION Y ALCANCES, DOCTRINA Y JURISPRUDENCIA (1989).

[76] 2ª Instancia, Córdoba, Marzo 28 de 1980, Dipietro y Navili Soc. Col. Torres de Horrock, Maria y Otros. La Ley, T. 1980B at 420.

[77] *Id.* at 423.

[78] *Id.* at 424.

[79] CNCI v. Sala C., Noviembre 5, 1978, Busetti, Oscar J.y otros c. Asociación Civil Santísima Cruz. La Ley, 1980 D, at 744.

[80] *Id.*

aware of the profound hyper-inflationary process that had been shaking the Argentine population since the beginning of June 1975.[81]

Considering that Article 1198 of the A.C.C. and Article 994 of the S.Com.C. share the same normative lineage, the Argentine judicial experience with the element of foreseeability is very useful in determining the application of the latter to the Salvadoran dispute central to the arbitration.[82]

H. Excessive Onerousness in German Law

1. *Legal and Economic Background*

The BGB adopted a very restrictive policy on excuses for non-performance as a result of supervening circumstances.[83] While it is true that Section 275 of the BGB freed the debtor from the duty to perform when he was not responsible for the circumstances that created the change,[84] in order to terminate the contract he had to prove that compliance had become impossible.[85] Bernhard Windscheid suggested that courts should, when fairness required, apply the doctrine of "tacit presuppositions."[86] This doctrine, which sought to ascertain the implied intent of the parties, shared much with the Italian doctrine of contractual presuppositions, discussed earlier. Windscheid's suggestion was not accepted by the other drafters of the BGB.

Two decades after its enactment, following Germany's defeat in World War I and the supervening inflation, the BGB rules that were initially formulated for exceptional cases became the norm in Germany's everyday life. Initially, the Supreme Court (then the *Reichsgericht*) refused to admit excuses for non-performance. During the 1920s, the *Reichsgericht* held that "a rise in market value or procurement cost of a commodity or service was no excuse to a seller from his promise to sell it,"[87] notwithstanding the fact that in a five-month period, wholesale prices within the country had tripled. However, two of the "Chambers" (or divisions) of the Supreme Court did order the revision of the

---

[81] Montegriffo Nestor y Otra c. Asociación Civil Santísima Cruz R. D.J.1979–7–13 sum. 49 La Ley, Repertorio XXXIX, A-1, at 402 (1979).

[82] CÓD. CIV. (Para.) art. 672 (1985) and CÓD. CIV. (ARG.) art. 1198. Both of these articles followed the Italian model, which states:

> In contracts of deferred performance, if supervening unforeseen and extraordinary events would make the performances excessively onerous, the debtor may claim the termination of the contract's pending performances. Termination will not apply when the supervening onerousness is considered within the normal risks of the contract, or if the debtor was in fault. The defendant may avoid the resolution of the contract by offering an equitable modification of it. If the contract was unilateral, the debtor may claim the decrease in the value of the performance or an equitable modification as to the way in which to execute it.

C.C. (ITALY) art. 1467 (translation by author).

[83] John Philip Dawson, *Judicial Revision of Frustrated Contracts: Germany*. 63 B.U.L. REV. 1039 (1983). In this section, my opinion summarizes the study in this article. Citations of the BGB are from BGB (GOREN, 1994).

[84] BGB § 275 ¶ 1. It states: "The debtor is relieved from his obligation to perform if the performance becomes impossible because of a circumstance, for which he is not responsible, occurring after the creation of the obligation." *Id.*

[85] *Id.*

[86] It should be recalled that Windscheid, *supra* §§ 12:1 & 12:2, was a central figure of the German pandects during the second half of the XIX Century and a member of the first drafting Commission of the BGB.

[87] Dawson, *supra* note 83, at 1044. It discusses a contract to manufacture a tugboat, to be delivered after the war; by 1919, and that its production cost had tripled.

terms and conditions of those contracts in which the supplier's costs of production had increased in such a way that could lead to his economic ruin.[88]

The systematic expansion of the judicial power to review contracts began in 1921 through the writings of Paul Oertmann, a commentator who merged the *rebus sic stantibus* doctrine and Windscheid's "tacit presupposition" into the concept of "foundation of the transaction" or "basis of the business" (*Geschäftsgrundlage*).[89] According to Oertmann, the *rebus* doctrine did not assume an impossibility to perform because the parties could not prove at the moment of entering into the contract that *both* were anticipating the unforeseeable events that could eventually lead to the contract's resolution.[90] Oertmann suggested that it should be enough for one of the parties to consider a term or condition or the occurrence of an event as a presupposition or basis of the contract, and for the term to be known by the other party, even if it was not mentioned in the contract or in discussions that preceded the contract.[91] This is how Oertmann attempted to narrow and make more objective the scope of application of Windscheid's proposed rule. In contrast to Windscheid, Oertmann focused the attention of the court on the effects of the unforeseen events and not on the contractual intent or expectations of the parties. Oertmann's theory was based on the legislative objective standard established in Section 242 of the BGB, which provides: "the debtor is bound to effect performance according to the requirements of good faith, giving consideration to common usage [in accordance to the commercial usage that prevails in the market]."[92]

By 1922, courts began to apply the Oertmann-inspired remedy in cases in which one party was heavily burdened by unforeseen events. This remedy was known as "Adjustment" (*Anpassung*), or the judicial adjustment of the performance. Based on this remedy, courts held that, for example, a buyer had to pay a higher price than the stipulated one, in order to compensate for the unforeseen increase in the costs of the seller.[93]

2. *The* Anpassung *and Judicial Activism*

Dawson's analysis of five decades of German decisional law, starting in the 1920s and including the post-World War II period, shows the basic requirements of the *Anpassung* and other judicial doctrines that attempted to rise up in its place. His analysis began with a November 28, 1923 decision of the *Reichsgericht* that deprived the German mark of its status as a compulsory legal tender once its value reached almost zero.[94] In this case, a creditor was freed from his obligation to receive payment in marks as stipulated in a mortgage note signed seven years prior to the date of execution. According to the Court, the statute that granted marks the status of legal tender currency was enacted in a prosperous and stable time; therefore, drafters could not foresee the effects of a devastating war and hyperinflation.

---

[88] *Id.* at 1044 n.13 (includes citations of authorities).

[89] *Id.* at 1040 and 1046 (citation omitted).

[90] *Id.* at 1046.

[91] *Id.*

[92] BGB (GOREN, 1994), *supra* note 83, § 242.

[93] Dawson, *supra* note 83, at 1039 & 1052. However, as noted by Dawson, it was never envisioned by this author that the courts would use his theory to fully review the terms and conditions of contracts. *Id.*

[94] *Id.* at 1047.

As Dawson points out, this decision not only abolished a simple contractual provision, but also the binding effect of monetary legislation. That claim was based on Section 242 of the BGB, which according to the court "rules over the whole of our legal order."[95] The court reasoned that no one, acting in good faith, could believe that paying a debt with meaningless currency would ever fulfill a duty of payment.[96]

In contrast with the judicial activism of the 1920s, the 1930s witnessed little judicial revision of agreed-upon contractual performances with only few exceptions. A 1933 decision of the *Reichsgericht* regarding clauses to preserve the value of an agreed-upon currency was one of the few holdings that revised original contractual terms. In this case, the parties agreed on measuring the value of the debt originally in marks, with a rate of exchange in British sterling pounds.[97] The plaintiff argued that, for both parties, the basis of the contract was payment measured by the value of the sterling pound as "the firmest currency in the world." Yet, at that time the British currency had devaluated thirty percent since the granting of the contract. As such the court of appeals considered that the court of first instance "might be justified . . . in awarding the plaintiff the full prize due before the rate of exchange had been unexpectedly altered."[98] However, in another case, the court rejected this type of revaluation because the decrease of the purchasing power had not exceeded fourteen percent.[99] Similarly, another decision rejected a purely arithmetic ratio to determine the loss of the basis of the contract.[100] Thus, a loan granted in sterling pounds that had to be paid in the same currency and that had resulted in a loss of less than a third of the value of that currency was not entitled to revaluation.[101] During this time it became apparent how the theory of judicial adherence to the "foundation of the contract" was open to arbitrary interpretation.

Since the 1950s, German courts applied the *Anpassung* as their preferred remedy and one that allowed them to review "all kinds of contracts that had been unbalanced through the discovery of unknown facts or the occurrence of unexpected events."[102] As Dawson pointed out, this remedy "rested on the premise that since a contingency had occurred for which the contract had not provided, [and that] a court must step in and fill the gap."[103] In the words of Dawson, "the conclusion had no connection whatsoever with the premise."[104]

---

[95] *Id.* at 1048.

[96] *Id.* at 1048–1049.

[97] *Id.* at 1071 (citation omitted).

[98] *Id.*

[99] *Id.* at 1072.

[100] *Id.*

[101] *Id.*

[102] *Id.* at 1075.

[103] *Id.*

[104] *Id.* According to Professor Saliba, in Brazil, the first judicial intervention in the same fashion described by Dawson for German law was in a 1932 decision (without further citation) in which a lessee of a building property of a religious group in Rio de Janeiro decided to exercise a purchase option that had been stipulated in a much lower price than that of the building's market value. The Judge of First Instance held that the imbalance between the performances would have been so clear that the *rebus sic stantibus* doctrine had to be applied to that contract. OLIVEIRA, JOSÉ DE ANISIO, A TEORIA DA IMPREVISÃO NOS CONTRATOS (1991), *cited in* Saliba, *supra* note74, at 7 n.19.

The courts' enthusiasm for the revision of contracts during the 1950s and 1960s began to decrease thereafter. In the following decade, sellers of real estate were denied adjustments to increase the payments owed by buyers, even when the argument before the court was that the cost of living in Germany had increased by fifty-two percent since the time the parties had entered into the contracts.[105] Accordingly, the lessor of a gas station was denied the adjustment of a lease agreement despite his argument that during the course of the twenty-one year lease, the cost of living had increased sixty-six percent.[106]

Dawson finds that the clearest test of the attitude of German courts regarding performance imbalances occurred during the 1972–1973 "oil shock," an event that saw an unprecedented increase in the price of the middle-eastern oil. This increase caused a serious imbalance in the value of performances; in some cases the cost of oil was ten times higher than actually stipulated in the original contract. Notwithstanding such a disproportion, most German courts held that the increase in oil prices was no excuse for the judicial adjustment of those contracts.[107]

I. The *Rebus Sic Stantibus* Clause Under Swiss Law

Article 373 of the Swiss Code of Obligations of 1912,[108] another of the few "unified" civil and commercial codes, contains a *rebus sic stantibus*-like rule with regard to sale agreements. This rule allows the seller to increase the price in the case of extraordinary events. Moreover, if such an event were to prevent or impede the normal performance of the contract, the court, in its discretion, might increase the contract price or order its termination. Regardless of the apparent openness of this provision, Swiss courts have been quite reluctant to apply the *rebus sic stantibus* doctrine, as is apparent in the decision by the Swiss Federal Court in the matter of *Rogenmoser v. Tiefengrund A.G.*[109]

In this case, the plaintiff leased a restaurant from the defendant for a fifteen-year term but, after a short period of doing business, the plaintiff requested that the defendant-lessor consent to a reduction of the installment payments because of the serious effects of the economic downturn in Switzerland at the time. The commercial court of the Canton of Zurich dismissed the complaint and the Federal Court affirmed the dismissal stating:

> Like the other modern codifications, the positive law of Switzerland has not adopted this view (*clausula rebus sic stantibus*). Nevertheless, this Court has recognized that a promisor must be discharged if extraordinary and unforeseeable circumstances render his duty to perform the promise so onerous that insistence upon [such] performance would cause his economic ruin . . . Upon renewed examination, we cannot adhere to this criterion without qualification. If the principle of *bona fides* is the yardstick for the

---

105 *See* Dawson, *supra* note 83, at 1080.

106 *Id.* at 1081.

107 *See, e.g., id.* at 1081.

108 *See* Federal Act on the Amendment of the Swiss Civil Code, (Part Five: The Code of Obligations) (Status as of Jan. 1, 2013) art. 373 ¶ 2 (March 30, 1911), *available at* http://www.admin.ch/ch/e/rs/2/220.en.pdf.

109 1st Civil Division, October 10, 1933, BGE 59 II 372, *translated in* RUDOLF B. SCHLESINGER ET. AL., COMPARATIVE LAW 816 (1987)

> application of the *clausula* [*rebus*], then the decision cannot be made to depend solely upon the effect which the change of circumstances had upon the *obligor's duty* to perform. The effect of the change on the entire legal relationship must be examined. The criterion of threatened ruin of the obligor would in the last analysis depend upon his subjective ability to perform . . . [The court points out that this subjective criterion would be inconsistent with the provision of the Code which prescribes that only objective but not subjective impossibility shall excuse performance.] The contract of lease was entered into for not less than fifteen years. This long duration contained a speculative element, at least on the part of the plaintiff. Also the nature and size of the premises rendered it clear [from the beginning] that the contractual risk was a substantial one.[110]

The final part of the decision indicates that the Swiss courts, as well as their counterparts in Italy, rejected the application of the doctrine of excessive onerousness to both express and implied aleatory contracts. Consequently, this Swiss decision, as well as the Italian ones discussed earlier, is based on a synallagmatic imbalance that can be measured objectively and granted on a case-by-case basis depending on the facts and the specific rules applicable to them.

J. Theory of Unforeseeability Under French Law

Under French law there is no legislative provision similar to that of Article 994 of the S.Com.C., Article 1467 of the It.C.C., Article 1198 of the A.C.C., Article 275 of the BGB nor Article 373 of the Swiss Code of Obligations. Normally, civil and commercial appellate courts in France have insisted on the principle of sanctity of contracts (*pacta sunt servanda*), thus rejecting petitions to adjust or revise contracts due to an unforeseen change in circumstance.[111]

After World War I and the devaluation of the French franc that followed, many French parties to contracts tried to obtain the revision of their contracts, not because their duty became impossible to perform but because it was so onerous and because they had not been able to foresee such an event. Some of their allegations were based on the principle of contractual good faith under Article 1134 of the *Code Civil*. While others argued for the application of Article 1156 of the same code that allowed parties to obtain judicial revision of their contracts to reflect the true intention of the parties.[112] However, the French civil and commercial courts were not persuaded by these arguments and continued to apply the *pacta sunt servanda*.

On the other hand, the *Conseil d'Etat*, the highest administrative court in France, adopted a more liberal criteria on the revision of administrative contracts in the matter of *Compagnie Générale d'Eclairage de Bordeaux v. Ville de Bordeaux*.[113] In this case, the plaintiff had promised to supply gas to the city of Bordeaux on a fixed tariff rate

---

110 *Id.* at 40–41.

111 *See* Boris Kozolchyk, *The Commercialization of Civil Law and the Civilization of Commercial Law,* 40 LA. L. REV. 3, 14–16 (1979–1980) (in relation to the principle of strict interpretation of contracts and the so-called contractual justice).

112 Saliba, *supra* note 74, at 3.

113 *Compagnie Generale d'Eclairage de Bordeaux v. Ville de Bordeaux*, Conseil d'Etat, March 30, 1916, D. 1916. III.25 (concl. Chardenet, note), S. 1916. III.17 (concl. Chardenet, note Hauriou) *cited in* VON MEHREN & GORDLEY, THE CIVIL LAW SYSTEM, at 545.

and for a specific number of years. As a result of World War I and an increase in the price of coal, the price of gas increased dramatically. The plaintiff requested a revision of the contractual tariff rate but her petition was dismissed by the corresponding authorities. However on appeal, the *Conseil d'Etat* overturned the local administration's decision.[114]

According to the *Conseil d'Etat*, providers or concessionaries generally have to take into consideration the variations of costs when they bid for contracts under a fixed tariff rate. However when the increments are such that exceed the limits of what could have been foreseen by the parties at the time of contracting, the dispute must be presented to a first instance judge in order for adjustment.[115]

It is important to emphasize that under French law, the Doctrine of Unforeseeability (*Imprévision*) only applies to administrative contracts. According to Marcel Planiol, a well-respected treatise writer of the early twentieth century, "one should not compare these two rules, for the administrative tribunals are inspired solely by the necessity of assuring public service, and do not modify the contract except under such necessity."[116] More recently, a North American scholar concluded that:

> [I]n France, the *théorie de l'imprévision* did not develop into anything more than a method for relieving governmental contractors of unforeseeable hardships to insure the uninterrupted functioning of public services. In practice, the theory has been applied only to three contracts 1) public works, 2) governmental supplies, and 3) concessions such as gas and electricity. Attempts to expand the doctrine of *imprévision* to private contracts have been regularly frustrated by the *Cour de Cassation*, France's highest court, which has been inclined to excuse performance of contractual obligations only if such performance is literally impossible."[117]

K. Excuses for Non-Performance Under U.S. Law: Injury, Impossibility, Impracticability and Frustration of the Purpose

As was mentioned in the introduction in the United States the law regarding excuses for non-performance of contracts do not have the judicial and doctrinal importance that they do in civil-law countries such as Germany and Italy. Taking into consideration the economic reasons mentioned at the beginning of this chapter, we must also consider that the equity jurisdiction (even when absorbed by common law, as was the case in the United States) provides the decision-maker with considerably more flexibility to evaluate circumstances that "shock the judge's conscience" regarding what is fair and equitable.[118]

---

114 See the commentary to this decision, Saul Litvinoff, *Force Majeure, Failure of Cause and Theorie de l'Imprevision: Louisiana Law and Beyond*. 46 LA. L. REV. 1, 15 (1985–1985).

115 *See* the discussion of this decision in Saliba, *supra* note74, at 3 & 4. *See also* Litvinoff, *supra note* 114, at 15.

116 MARCEL PLANIOL, TREATISE ON CIVIL LAW § 1168A (11th ed. 1939).

117 Saliba, *supra* note 74, at 4 (emphasis added) (citation omitted).

118 *Id.* at 7. According to Professor Saliba, Uruguay is the only country of the MERCOSUR that does not provide for a doctrine equivalent to the *rebus sic stantibus*. He ascribes this absence to the fact that art. 1291 of the Civil Code of Uruguay was inspired by arts. 1134 & 1135 of the C.Civ. (Fr.),in the same way as art. 1796 of the Mexican Federal Civil Code. *Id.*

On the other hand, the U.C.C. provides for various excuses for non-performance, including a *sui generis* version of the subjective injury (lesion) under Section 2–302.[119] The U.C.C. also provides a rule on the impossibility to perform under Section 2–607[120] and on the impracticability to perform under Section 2–615.[121]

In United States judicial practice it is not easy to distinguish between the doctrines of impossibility and impracticability to perform. For example, in a state court decision[122] in which the issue was the contractual responsibility of a railroad company for the suspension of services as a result of the expropriation of land close to the areas where they receive and provide services that ultimately would impede their normal functioning in the overall area, the court defined the excuse for non-performance as follows:

> Where, from the nature of the contract, it is evident that the parties contracted on the basis of the continued existence of the person, thing, condition, or state of things, or of facts, to which it relates, the subsequent perishing of the person or thing, or cessation of existence of the condition or state will excuse the performance, or terminate the contract, a condition to that effect being implied, in spite of the fact that the promise may have been unqualified . . . limited to the situation where neither party is at fault and neither has assumed the risk. It has been referred to as the doctrine of supervening impossibility of performance.

However, the same court also cited the Restatement of the Law of Contracts, V. II, Chapter 14, Section 454, and Section 457 when providing that: "In the Restatement of this Subject, impossibility means not only strict impossibility but impracticability because of extreme and unreasonable difficulty, expense, injury or loss involved."

From this it might be understood that the distinction can be between what is physically and legally impossible and what can lead to economic ruin and therefore be impracticable. Nevertheless, such an inference would not result from the precision of these concepts. The same is true for the doctrine of the "frustration of the purpose of the contract," as its formulation continues to be amorphous and thus, its application to cases of impossibility and impracticability become uncertain. As it was stated in a 1956 decision of the House of Lords in the case of *Davis Contractors Ltd. v. Fareham U.D.C.*:

> [F]rustration occurs whenever the law recognizes that, without default of either party, a contractual obligation has become incapable of being performed because the circumstances in which performance is called for

---

[119] U.C.C. § 2–302 (2012). It states:

> (1) If the court as a matter of law finds the contract or any clause of the contract to have been unconscionable at the time it was made the court may refuse to enforce the contract, or it may enforce the remainder of the contract without the unconscionable clause, or it may so limit the application of any unconscionable clause as to avoid any unconscionable result. (2) When it is claimed or appears to the court that the contract or any clause thereof may be unconscionable the parties shall be afforded a reasonable opportunity to present evidence as to its commercial setting, purpose and effect to aid the court in making the determination.

Id.

[120] U.C.C. § 2–607 (2012).

[121] U.C.C. § 2–615 (2012).

[122] Kansas, Oklahoma & Gulf RY. Co. v. Grand Lake Grain Co., 434 P.2d 153 (1967).

would render it a thing radically different from that which was undertaken by the contract. *Non haec in foedera veni.* It was not this that I promised to do.[123]

§ 27.5 THE RESTATEMENT 2ND OF CONTRACTS: ISSUES FOR CLASS DISCUSSION

Instead of the customary factual and legal conclusions found at the end of expert opinions, I have included some of the sections of the Restatement 2nd of the Law of Contracts. The purpose of this is to allow the reader to recall the information previously discussed. This review will require that the reader compare the scope of the provisions that will follow with the contractual excuses for non-performance discussed throughout this chapter, including: *The Rebus Sic Stantibus Clause, Contractual Presuppositions, the Basis of the Contract or Basis of the Transaction, Unforeseeability and Excessive Onerousness.*

Restatement 2nd, Chapter 11—Impracticability of Performance and Frustration of Purpose[124]

Section 261 Discharge by Supervening Impracticability

Where, after a contract is made, a party's performance is made impracticable without his fault by the occurrence of an event the non-occurrence of which was a basic assumption on which the contract was made, his duty to render that performance is discharged, unless the language or the circumstances indicate the contrary.

Section 262 Death or Incapacity of Person Necessary for Performance

If the existence of a particular person is necessary for the performance of a duty, his death or such incapacity as makes performance impracticable is an event the non-occurrence of which was a basic assumption on which the contract was made.

Section 263 Destruction, Deterioration or Failure to Come into Existence of Thing Necessary for Performance

If the existence of a specific thing is necessary for the performance of a duty, its failure to come into existence, destruction, or such deterioration as makes performance impracticable is an event the non-occurrence of which was a basic assumption on which the contract was made.

Section 264 Prevention by Governmental Regulation or Order

If the performance of a duty is made impracticable by having to comply with a domestic or foreign governmental regulation or order, that regulation or order is an event the non-occurrence of which was a basic assumption on which the contract was made.

Section 265 Discharge by Supervening Frustration

Where, after a contract is made, a party's principal purpose is substantially frustrated without his fault by the occurrence of an event the non-occurrence

---

123 Davis Contractors Ltd. v. Fareham Urban DC, [1956] A.C. 696 (H.L.) [696] (appeal taken from Eng.) (*emphasis added*).

124 Restatement (Second) of Contracts, §§ 261–265 (1981).

of which was a basic assumption on which the contract was made, his remaining duties to render performance are discharged, unless the language or the circumstances indicate the contrary.

QUESTIONS

What arguments would the reader advance in favor of a liberal application of the aforementioned contractual excuses for non-performance, especially with respect to excessive onerousness? What arguments would she use against the proposed liberal application? How much have markets in countries like France, Mexico or Uruguay suffered because of the lack of excuses like those provided in German and Italian law? Apart from these excuses, are there any other means under the reader's legal system to avoid the excessive onerousness of contractual obligations without affecting the predictability of the law of contracts?

Chapter 28

EXTRAJUDICIAL REMEDIES AND THE REMEDY OF SPECIFIC PERFORMANCE

§ 28.1 INTRODUCTION

Having completed the review of pre-contractual remedies and excuses, we now turn to the remedies for breach of a contract whose performance is due and cannot be excused. The claim for a breach of contract can arise from the fact that the due date has elapsed without performance by the obligated party, or as the result of a breach of the promised performance after performance has commenced. In addition, a claim for breach of contract can be sustained in some jurisdictions prior to the due date of performance. Such a remedy usually requires that the behavior of one of the parties strongly indicates to the other his inability or unwillingness to comply when compliance is due. Alternatively such a claim can be sustained if the potentially non-compliant party fails to provide assurances of his willingness and ability to comply. The remedies for these pre-due-date breaches are known in some jurisdictions as "anticipatory." This and the following chapters are devoted to the most common remedies for actual (or due-date) breaches, as well as for anticipatory breaches of contracts.

Two of the remedies that are studied in these chapters are well known to the reader: one is the "specific" or judicially-decreed performance of the party in breach and the other is the action for damages. A third group of lesser-known remedies are "extrajudicial remedies" or remedies carried out by the parties themselves and without the intervention of judicial or arbitral authorities. This chapter examines the most common extrajudicial remedies as well as the judicial remedy of specific performance. The following chapter will examine the judicial remedy of damages.

§ 28.2 EXTRAJUDICIAL REMEDIES

Extrajudicial remedies are especially necessary in international sales where parties are separated by geography and different legal systems. Litigating one's contract in a foreign court is neither easy nor cost effective. On the other hand, when dealing with perishable goods, speedy delivery is required to be successfully completed. Such speed of delivery requires that the goods be represented by "documents of title" which in many instances could be made to arrive at the destination before the goods. Because of the reliance of these documents of title by means of anticipating the goods, a new type of sale—documentary sales[1]—emerged. If the nineteenth century law of domestic sales uniformly allowed the buyer a "reasonable time" to inspect the goods sold prior to requiring payment, international documentary sales law required the buyer's payment or acceptance of a draft or bill of exchange at the time of presentation of the shipping documents (not the goods) to the buyer. Thus, in these sales, payment

[1] *See* Glossary, "Documentary Sales."

against documents would come first, and the inspection of the goods and the claim for non-performance or breach would come later.

This reversal of the "cash on the barrelhead" sequence of transactions (a variety of what Roman jurists referred to as "I give so that you give" (*do ut des*)) was dubbed by some courts and commentators as a "*Solve et Répéte*" (first pay then claim) method of doing business. Not surprisingly, the twentieth-century remedial law of sales reflected the same need for expediency not only for international but also for local sales. Some jurisdictions facilitated extrajudicial remedies in their domestic codification and case law early in the twentieth century. Less than a century later (a short time span in the development of commercial legal institutions, and getting shorter with each passing decade), other jurisdictions introduced the same remedies in international sales law treaties and related sources. To facilitate a better understanding of the law of extrajudicial remedies and because these treaties and related sources set forth the remedies in their clearest and most succinct fashion, we will turn to them first.

Before beginning the examination of these treaties and rules, a clarification of terminology is in order. As was discussed in the preceding chapter and as will become apparent in the following discussion, there are significant differences in the use of the remedial terminology on breaches of contract among common and civil lawyers. For example, common-law lawyers also use the term "rescission" in a generic manner to include the remedy of unilateral or bilateral "termination" that civil lawyers of the French, Italian and Spanish family of codes refer to as "resolution." In addition, Anglo-American lawyers use the term rescission in connection with remedies that apply to cases of duress, coercion and unconscionability. This is the usage that most closely approximates that of civil-law lawyers especially in French, Italian and Spanish legal writings, who (as discussed in the preceding chapter) associate rescission with the suffering of a serious economic, physical or psychological harm or threat of harm (*lesion*) by the plaintiff.

On the other hand, the United Nations Convention on Contracts for the International Sale of Goods (1982) (hereinafter CISG), in an attempt to provide a generic term that would embrace not only the above common and civil law terminology but also that used by the German family of codes, used the term "avoidance" while referring to the unilateral termination of contracts. The use of such a term by the United Nations makes sense when its fundamental purpose is to bring about legislative and judicial uniformity. However, since the purpose of this book is educational and thus must highlight the conceptual differences, I will use the term resolution in a manner consistent with its French, Italian and Spanish code usage. Accordingly, the term resolution will include the Anglo-American remedy of unilateral termination for the counterparty's breach and also the remedy that CISG refers to as "avoidance"; however, it will not include the remedies for duress, coercion or unconscionability unless otherwise indicated by the discussion.

A. CISG

Article 25 (Essential breach): A breach of contract committed by one of the parties is fundamental if it results in such detriment to the other party as substantially to deprive him of what he is entitled to expect under the contract, unless the party in breach did not foresee and a reasonable person of the same kind in the same circumstances would not have foreseen such a result.

Article 26: A declaration of avoidance of the contract is effective only if made by notice to the other party.

Article 39

(1) The buyer loses the right to rely on a lack of conformity of the goods if he does not give notice to the seller specifying the nature of the lack of conformity within a reasonable time after he has discovered it or ought to have discovered it.

(2) In any event, the buyer loses the right to rely on a lack of conformity of the goods if he does not give the seller notice thereof at the latest within a period of two years from the date on which the goods were actually handed over to the buyer, unless this time-limit is inconsistent with a contractual period of guarantee.

Article 47

(1) The buyer may fix an additional period of time of reasonable length for performance by the seller of his obligations.

(2) Unless the buyer has received notice from the seller that he will not perform within the period so fixed, the buyer may not, during that period, resort to any remedy for breach of contract. However, the buyer is not deprived thereby of any right he may have to claim damages for delay in performance.

Article 48

(1) Subject to Article 49, the seller may, even after the date for delivery, remedy at his own expense any failure to perform his obligations, if he can do so without unreasonable delay and without causing the buyer unreasonable inconvenience or uncertainty of reimbursement by the seller of expenses advanced by the buyer. However, the buyer retains any right to claim damages as provided for in this Convention.

(2) If the seller requests the buyer to make known whether he will accept performance and the buyer does not comply with the request within a reasonable time, the seller may perform within the time indicated in his request. The buyer may not, during that period of time, resort to any remedy which is inconsistent with performance by the seller.

(3) A notice by the seller that he will perform within a specified period of time is assumed to include a request, under the preceding paragraph, that the buyer make known his decision.

(4) A request or notice by the seller under paragraph (2) or (3) of this article is not effective unless received by the buyer.

Article 49

(1) The buyer may declare the contract avoided:

(a) if the failure by the seller to perform any of his obligations under the contract or this

Convention amounts to a fundamental breach of contract; or

(b) in case of non-delivery, if the seller does not deliver the goods within the additional period of time fixed by the buyer in accordance with paragraph (1) of article 47 or declares that he will not deliver within the period so fixed.

(2) However, in cases where the seller has delivered the goods, the buyer loses the right to declare the contract avoided unless he does so:

(a) in respect of late delivery, within a reasonable time after he has become aware that delivery has been made;

(b) in respect of any breach other than late delivery, within a reasonable time:

(i) after he knew or ought to have known of the breach;

(ii) after the expiration of any additional period of time fixed by the buyer in accordance with paragraph (1) of article 47, or after the seller has declared that he will not perform his obligations within such an additional period; or

(iii) after the expiration of any additional period of time indicated by the seller in accordance with paragraph (2) of article 48, or after the buyer has declared that he will not accept performances.

B. U.S. Escrow Agreement as an Extrajudicial Remedy

The following escrow agreement was discussed with Mexican judges, litigants, notary publics and real estate brokers as an alternative extrajudicial remedy to be used instead of "Promises of Sale" or options to purchase that were declared unenforceable by Mexican courts when accompanied by a lawsuit for specific performance which could last several years.[2] After you read this agreement and the Astorga decision, do you think that having such an agreement enforced would restore the inadequacy of the judicial enforcement of options to purchase and promises to sell?

A New York Real Estate Escrow Agreement With Consumer Protection Ingredients[3]

DOWN PAYMENT ESCROW AGREEMENT

(For Residential Sales in New York State [for low and mid-income buyers])

Escrow agreement between the buyer and seller of real property and their attorneys as escrow agents. The use of the singular in this agreement shall be deemed to include the plural, and vice versa, whenever the context requires. [FN2] If more than one person is buying or selling the premises covered by this agreement, their obligations shall be joint and several.

The buyer and seller have entered into a contract to purchase and sell residential real estate. The premises to be conveyed to the buyer are located at: _______.

As a term of the contract of sale, the buyer is obligated to provide the seller with a down payment on the purchase price, to be held in escrow. To safeguard the down payment from loss, the buyer and seller, and their attorneys, agree to the escrow arrangement set forth in this agreement. For that purpose, this agreement designates

---

[2] *See* Teófila Astorga Vda. De Aceves, The Supreme Court of the Justice of the State of Sinaloa (*El Supremo Tribunal de Justicia del Estado de Sinaloa*), Semanario Judicial de la Federación [SJF], Quinta Época, tomo CXXV, 1953, tesis 5313, Sec. 1a, Pagina 193 (Mex.).

[3] Boris Kozolchyk, *Symposium: Enhancement of Mexican Commercial Adjudication by Improved Transactional Fact-Finding, Application of Equitable Principles, and Drafting of Standard Contracts and Best Contractual Practices: English Material: Working Group Reference Materials*, 27 ARIZ. J. INT'L COMP. L. 441 (2010). *A New York Real Estate Escrow Agreement with Consumer Protection Ingredients*, 27 ARIZ. J. INT'L & COMP. L. 465 (2010).

the buyer and seller as "escrow beneficiaries"; their attorneys as joint "escrow agents" and the buyer's down payment as the "escrow deposit."

Escrow agents acknowledge the receipt of the escrow deposit in the amount of $ _______.

Escrow agents acknowledge their fiduciary obligations to the escrow beneficiaries to safeguard the escrow deposit in a special bank account, and to provide to them a complete accounting of all financial transactions relating to that escrow deposit. [FN3]

[Optional clause for certain type of sales:] Escrow agents will make no claim for compensation for their services as escrow agents.

Escrow agents will deposit the escrow deposit in a bank account with the following banking institution in the State of New York at its branch located at the following address: _______.

No later than 10 business days after the date of this agreement, escrow agents will provide the escrow beneficiaries with written notice confirming the escrow *466 deposit required by this agreement, the title and number of the bank account and, if such account is interest-bearing, the initial rate of interest.

[Consumer Notice: Section 778 of the New York . . . Law sets forth the fiduciary obligations of escrow agents in possession of down payments in the sale of residential real estate . . .]

Upon closing, the escrow agents will deliver the escrow deposit to the seller, together with interest, if any. [Optional clause specially designed to Facilitate the Process of Transferring Title to the Property in various States and added to this text by the NLCIFT: "Seller authorizes X (employee, officer or representative of the escrow agents) as his agent, pursuant to the power of attorney for the transfer of real property, which provides broad and sufficient powers to carry on the agency, so that when the escrow agent gives notice of payment of the full purchase price as agreed in the option agreement, the seller's agent X will sign the deed of sale in favor of the buyer."] In the event the closing does not occur, the escrow agents will refund the escrow deposit to the buyer, together with interest, if any. Upon payment of the escrow deposit to the seller, or its refund to the buyer, escrow agents will be fully released from all liability and other obligations with respect to the escrow deposit . . .

[Consumer Notice: Section 1006 of the New York Civil Practice Law and Rules provides a judicial procedure for resolving conflicting claims to property that is held by stakeholders, including escrow deposits held by escrow agents.]

This agreement may be canceled by a written notice signed by the escrow beneficiaries and delivered to the escrow agents. [FN4]

Escrow agents will be jointly and severally liable to the escrow beneficiaries for any loss of the escrow deposit which results from gross negligence, bad faith, or wilful [sic] misconduct. Escrow agents will not be liable for any error in judgement [sic], or any act taken or omitted in good faith, any mistake of law, or any mistake of fact . . .

In Witness Whereof, the buyer and seller and their attorneys have signed this agreement on the ___ day of _______, 199_.

C. UNIDROIT Principles on International Commercial Contracts (2004) (Hereinafter UNIDROIT Principles)

Chapter 7—Non compliance

Section 1: Non-Performance in General

Article 7.1.1 *(Non-performance defined)* Non-performance is failure by a party to perform any of its obligations under the contract, including defective performance or late performance.

Article 7.1.3 *(Withholding performance)*

(1) Where the parties are to perform simultaneously, either party may withhold performance until the other party tenders its performance.

(2) Where the parties are to perform consecutively, the party that is to perform later may withhold its performance until the first party has performed.

Article 7.1.4 *(Cure by non-performing party)*

(1) The non-performing party may, at its own expense, cure any nonperformance, provided that

(a) without undue delay, it gives notice indicating the proposed manner and timing of the cure;

(b) cure is appropriate in the circumstances;

(c) the aggrieved party has no legitimate interest in refusing cure; and

(d) cure is effected promptly.

(2) The right to cure is not precluded by notice of termination.

(3) Upon effective notice of cure, rights of the aggrieved party that are inconsistent with the non-performing party's performance are suspended until the time for cure has expired.

(4) The aggrieved party may withhold performance pending cure.

(5) Notwithstanding cure, the aggrieved party retains the right to claim damages for delay as well as for any harm caused or not prevented by the cure.

Article 7.1.5 *(Additional period for performance)*

(1) In a case of non-performance the aggrieved party may by notice to the other party allow an additional period of time for performance.

(2) During the additional period the aggrieved party may withhold performance of its own reciprocal obligations and may claim damages but may not resort to any other remedy. If it receives notice from the other party that the latter will not perform within that period, or if upon expiry of that period due performance has not been made, the aggrieved party may resort to any of the remedies that may be available under this Chapter.

(3) Where in a case of delay in performance which is not fundamental the aggrieved party has given notice allowing an additional period of time of reasonable length, it may terminate the contract at the end of that period. If the additional period allowed is not of reasonable length it shall be extended to a reasonable length. The

aggrieved party may in its notice provide that if the other party fails to perform within the period allowed by the notice the contract shall automatically terminate.

(4) Paragraph (3) does not apply where the obligation which has not been performed is only a minor part of the contractual obligation of the non-performing party.

§ 28.3 JUDICIAL OPPOSITION TO EXTRAJUDICIAL REMEDIES

The extrajudicial remedies of the CISG and UNIDROIT Principles as well as the escrow practices just illustrated have facilitated international and national commerce by discouraging litigation and, slowly but surely, have influenced domestic law.[4] Yet, too many civil-law jurisdictions remain attached to the notion that termination or resolution of a contract are judicial remedies "by nature" and therefore should not be made available extrajudicially. This attitude prevails even where courts could reverse or correct the import of these remedies *a posteriori*, *i.e.*, after the extrajudicial remedies had already been resorted to.[5]

The judicial opposition to extrajudicial remedies is unrealistic and harmful to the smooth flow of trade. The reality is that for every contract or binding legal relationship that is judicially terminated, resolved or rescinded, there are millions that are harmlessly resolved or terminated by the complying party or by both parties. After all, extrajudicial termination saves the time, money and aggravation that usually accompany a protracted and expensive lawsuit. Further, the aggrieved party's inability to resell or repurchase the goods or services at a profit involved in the failed transaction while awaiting a judicial resolution results in the significant loss of business and economic opportunity.

Despite these commercial, legal and economic realities, the reader will soon encounter some code provisions and court decisions that force the aggrieved parties of the actual or likely breach to act in a "Spartan" way.[6] In other words, the aggrieved party who wishes to claim the other party's breach has the duty to perform his side of the bargain even if he has every reason to believe that the counterparty will not perform his. And if the non-culpable party does not act in a Spartan manner and sues,

---

[4] *See* RAFAEL ILLESCAS ORTIZ & PILAR PERALES VISCASILLAS, DERECHO MERCANTIL INTERNACIONAL: EL DERECHO UNIFORME [INTERNATIONAL COMMERCIAL LAW AND UNIFORM LAW] 197–332 (2003) (for a general overview of remedies under Spanish law). *See also* MARIA DEL PILAR PERALES VISCASILLAS, EL CONTRATO DE COMPRAVENTA INTERNACIONAL DE MERCANCÍAS (CONVENCIÓN DE VIENA DE 1980) (2001), *available at* http://www.cisg.law.pace.edu/cisg/biblio/perales1.html (on the Vienna Convention); and Maria del Pilar Perales Viscasillas, *El derecho uniforme del Comercio Internacional: los principios de Unidroit (ámbito de aplicación y Disposiciones Generales) [Uniform International Commerical Law: The UNIDROIT Principles (scope of application and general provisions)]* 223 REVISTA DE DERECHO MERCANTIL 221 (1997) (on the UNIDROIT General Principles); *and* Maria del Pilar Perales Viscasillas, *UNIDROIT Principles of International Commercial Contracts: Sphere of Application and General Provisions*, 13 ARIZ. J. INT'L & COMP. L. 381, 390–441 (1996). *See also* Boris Kozolchyk, *The UNIDROIT Principles as a Model for the Unification of the Best Contractual Practices in the Americas*, 46 AM. J. COMP. L. 151 (1998).

[5] *See infra* §§ 29:5–29:7. *See also* Kozolchyk, *Fairness*, at 229–30 & 257–58.

[6] *See, e.g.*, CÓD. COM. (MEX.) art. 376 (2008) (translation by author). It states, "In commercial sales, once the contract is perfected, the *complying* party will have the right to claim to the *non-complying* party the resolution or compliance of the contract, and reparation, apart from damages." *Id.* (Emphasis added.) The reference to the Spartan behavior belongs to William Hedrick, a former student and distinguished lawyer. See his path-breaking article: William Headrick, *La Rescisión de la Compraventa,* 49 REVISTA DE LA FACULTAD DE DERECHO DE LA U.N.A.M. 83 (1963).

he will be part of a lengthy and costly procedural standoff; all the counterparty has to do is to raise the defense of the plaintiff's own failure to perform (*exceptio non adimpleti contractus*). Under these circumstances, this *exceptio* will freeze judicial adjudication *sine die*, or indefinitely. A review of the above-transcribed UNIDROIT Principles 7.1.3(1) and 7.1.5(2) will quickly reveal that these code provisions stand in sharp contrast.

Furthermore, a court operating under such Spartan assumptions is likely to decide (as was decided by a Mexican court in a case discussed in a later section) that an aggrieved seller who resells property extrajudicially after his buyer *failed to pay the purchase price* criminally misappropriated the defaulting buyer's property. The basis of such a ruling was that in accordance with the "consensual" nature of sale agreements, the resold property belonged to the defaulting buyer from the moment he and the seller agreed on a stipulated (albeit unpaid) price.[7] The only remedy left to the aggrieved seller in this case was to sue the defaulting buyer either for damages or specific performance.

Those who are opposed to extrajudicial resolution fail to take into account that since Roman law days, certain complying parties have been allowed to terminate the breached contract partially or completely and even allowed to appropriate the assets in their possession that prior to the breach belonged to the non-performing party. Consider, for example, the contractual implications of the creditors' right of set-off. The Roman *compensatio* and its progeny in civil codes throughout the civil-law world allowed a depository-creditor in possession of the liquid amount owed by a defaulting debtor to set off what he owed without having to go to court.[8] A variant of this type of termination takes place in unlimited fashion in everyday business, and especially in connection with deposit accounts held by banks and other financial intermediaries. They are known as "clearing," "netting" and "settling" operations. Without the implicit set-offs in these operations, the banking and securities industries would start each business day owing each other truly incalculable amounts.

---

[7] *See infra* § 29:6 (for the decision by the Magistrate Judge Agustín Mercado Alarcón in Pedro J, González 1637/63). It states:

> If the defendant executes a contract agreeing to transfer a piece of land to the state government and then transfers it to a private party, the defendant will be criminally guilty of embezzlement. He is not excused from such a crime by alleging that he acted the way he did because the state government did not perform according to the draft of the contract and that he does not consider himself bound to such a document . . . The fact that the state government as an entity and acting in its private capacity did not perform its contractual obligations does not give the defendant the right to consider the contract as terminated, nor does it allow him to transfer the rights at issue . . .

Id.

[8] *See* BERGER, ENCYCLOPEDIC DICTIONARY, at 401 (for an illustration on how the *compensatio* operated under Roman Law.) The author explains that in classical law, the judge could, when the creditor acted in good faith and as part of a good faith inspired decision (*bona fide iudicum*) take into account what the plaintiff owed the defendant from another transaction and condemn the defendant to pay the balance if the debt was larger. Berger states:

> Later a set off of reciprocal debts was available under certain circumstances [without judicial intervention] through the *exceptio doli*. The practice of the *cognitio extra ordinem* favored the development of the institution [of *compensatio*] and *thus it became a general form of extinction of obligations which operated beyond the judicial courts . .* "

Id. (emphasis added).

The same would be true with laws that grant to certain creditors the right to retain possession of assets that belong to non-performing parties after their breach (thereby sanctioning a unilateral termination or resolution)[9] such as for: 1) the innkeeper in possession of the luggage of guests who have not paid for their lodging thus breaching their lodging contracts;[10] 2) the provider of unpaid repair services who is in possession of the repaired goods;[11] and 3) the carrier of goods who may retain delivered goods when the receiver has not paid for the delivery service.[12] Curiously, while this extrajudicial remedy is allowed as a lien or right of retention without court intervention, the same remedy is rejected by the same jurisdictions in the case of other, more formally-established claims.

Despite the widespread prohibition of the *Pactum Commissorium* in civil-law countries, as was discussed in Chapter 24, none of the above lien creditors and others like them are required to obtain judicial decisions in order to exercise their right to terminate their contracts.

It is obvious that the notion of a judicial monopoly over the termination or resolution of contracts is inconsistent with the needs of contemporary commercial transactions, including their volume, expeditiousness, and the fact that creditors or their agents often are or can easily be in possession of money and assets that belong to their debtors. It is also worth considering, as noted earlier, that the previously-described extrajudicial resolutions of contracts, as well as others not described, can always be subject to an *a posteriori* form of judicial review. Furthermore, if the debtor can prove that the creditor exceeded or abused his rights to extrajudicially terminate the contract or otherwise enriched himself, nothing should prevent that debtor from obtaining adequate judicial relief. Yet, unlike its *a priori* counterpart, such a relief would encourage the smooth flow of commerce.

§ 28.4 THE INCREASING ROLE OF EXTRAJUDICIAL REMEDIES

A. Anticipatory Repudiation, Substitute Transactions and *Nachfrist*

Article 7.3.1 and especially sub-article (d) of the UNIDROIT Principles enable the aggrieved party to exercise his right to terminate the contract unilaterally when the breach is substantial. This right can be exercised even when the breach occurs before the due date of performance as long as the party has sufficient indications that that performance will not be forthcoming.[13] This provision was modeled after the U.C.C.

---

[9] *See* CÓD. COM. (EL. SAL.) arts. 957–959 (1983); CÓD. COM. (HOND.) arts. 703–706 (1950); and CÓD. COM. (GUAT.) arts. 682–687 (1877) (on the right to retain possession of goods).

[10] *See, e.g., id.* art. 870. It states: "The innkeeper has priority over the guest's luggage and personal property to cover unpaid lodging, and for that effect, he can retain possession over these assets until he receives payment of the amount owed by the guest." *Id.* (translation by author). *See also* CÓD. CIV. (EL. SAL.) art. 2221(1) (1858).

[11] *See id.* art. 916 & CÓD. CIV. (GUAT.) arts. 1981–1982 (1877).

[12] *See* CÓD. COM. (EL. SALUPON EFFECTIVE NOTICE OF CURE, RIGHTS OF THE AGGRIEVED PARTY THAT AR.), *supra* note 9, art. 1322; CÓD. CIV. (EL. SAL.), *supra* note 10, art. 2221(2); and CÓD. COM. (HOND.), *supra* note 9, art. 1081.

[13] *UNIDROIT Principles of International Commercial Contracts* art. 7.3.1, UNIDROIT INTERNATIONAL INSTITUTE FOR THE UNIFICATION OF PRIVATE LAW (2010), http://www.unidroit.org/english/principles/contracts/principles2010/integralversionprinciples2010–e.pdf. Article 7.3.1 UNIDROIT Principles provides:

Article 2 provisions that will be discussed in the following chapter[14] and also by the German *Nachfrist* as found in Article 321 of the B.G.B.:

> 1) A person who is obliged to perform in advance under a reciprocal contract may refuse to render his performance if, after the contract is entered into, it becomes apparent that his entitlement to consideration is jeopardised [sic] by the inability to perform of the other party. The right to refuse performance is not applicable if consideration is rendered or security is given for it.
>
> (2) The person required to perform in advance may specify a reasonable period in which the other party must, at his choice, render consideration or provide security reciprocally and simultaneously against performance. If the period ends without result, the person required to perform in advance may revoke the contract. Section 323 applies with the necessary modifications.[15]

This provision will be discussed in more detail in Chapter 29.[16] Similarly, as discussed in the preceding chapter,[17] the UNIDROIT Principle finds support in Article 1456 of the Italian Civil Code:

> Article 1456. The parties to a contract may expressly stipulate the termination of a contract when a given obligation is not complied with according to their stipulations.
>
> Once one of the parties expresses its intention to apply the resolution clause, the contract is deemed terminated by law.

B. The Aggrieved Party's Duty to Mitigate Damages

The policy of facilitating the flow of commerce is also responsible for the remedial rules that attempt to reduce the economic waste that results from a breach of contract. These rules compel the aggrieved party who unilaterally terminates a contract to

---

> ARTICLE 7.3.1 (Right to terminate the contract)
>
> (1) A party may terminate the contract where the failure of the other party to perform an obligation under the contract amounts to a fundamental non-performance.
>
> (2) In determining whether a failure to perform an obligation amounts to a fundamental non-performance regard shall be had, in particular, to whether
>
> (a) the non-performance substantially deprives the aggrieved party of what it was entitled to expect under the contract unless the other party did not foresee and could not reasonably have foreseen such result;
>
> (b) strict compliance with the obligation which has not been performed is of essence under the contract;
>
> (c) the non-performance is intentional or reckless;
>
> (d) the non-performance gives the aggrieved party reason to believe that it cannot rely on the other party's future performance;
>
> (e) the non-performing party will suffer disproportionate loss as a result of the preparation or performance if the contract is terminated.
>
> (3) In the case of delay the aggrieved party may also terminate the contract if the other party fails to perform before the time allowed it under Article 7.1.5 has expired.

Id. See also id. arts. 7.3.3. & 7.3.4.

[14] *See infra* § 29:7.

[15] BGB § 323, art. 321 (2012).

[16] *See infra* § 29:7.

[17] *See infra* § 27:4(D).

minimize the damages claimed from the defaulting party by acting as diligently as possible in reducing the waste. Thus, if he is a seller the law encourages him to seek timely, profitable and cost-effective resales, and if he is the aggrieved buyer he is encouraged to do the same by repurchasing as diligently and cost-effectively as possible.[18] The manner in which courts decree these remedies will be illustrated in the following chapter.

C. Preclusion

As the current technology of the financial marketplace develops the pressure upon its participants to use inexpensive and speedy methods of financing and payment of commercial contracts, the parties are also increasingly forced to rely on equitable remedies designed to encourage a modicum of diligence and finality of payment or settlement. One of these equitable remedies is that of "preclusion," used extensively by correspondent bankers.

A variant of this extrajudicial remedy was first used by Article 8(f) of the 1974 version of the Uniform Customs and Practice for Documentary Credits of the International Chamber of Commerce:

> If the issuing bank fails to hold the [non-complying] documents at the disposal of the remitting bank, or fails to return the documents to such bank, the issuing bank shall be precluded from claiming that the relative payment, acceptance or negotiation was not effected in accordance with the terms and conditions of the credit.[19]

As was discussed in Chapter 24, the purpose of this rule was to encourage the timely examination of documents by a nominated bank placed in charge of paying or negotiating these documents on behalf of the bank that issued the documentary credit. The standard practice is for the nominated bank to examine the documents tendered by the beneficiary of the documentary credit; once they are found to be in compliance with the terms and conditions of the credit the bank will accept the draft drawn by the beneficiary—promising to pay at a future time—or to pay the draft. If the documents are not in order, the bank must reject the presentation within a specified period of time and explain the reasons for the rejection.

If the issuing bank does not object to the payment or negotiation performed by the nominating bank, or if it does not reject and send the examined and rejected documents to the nominated bank within a specified time frame, then the nominated bank will deem the credit as paid and be reimbursed by debiting the issuing bank's account in its own books, or by drawing against the issuing bank's account with a reimbursing bank. This is all done without the nominated bank appearing before a court or independent adjudicator prior to its unilateral debiting or drawing against the account of the negligent issuing bank—*i.e.*, it is an extrajudicial solution.

This rule has remained in force in subsequent revisions of the UCP because of its evident procedural and transactional efficiency: If each and every case of untimely failure to accept or pay or to reject the presentation had to be litigated by

---

[18] *UNIDROIT Principles of International Commercial Contracts*, *supra* note 13, art. 7.4.8.

[19] INT'L CHAMBER OF COMMERCE, UNIFORM CUSTOMS AND PRACTICE FOR DOCUMENTARY CREDITS [UCP] No. 290, art. 8(f) (1974). For a discussion of the origin and the effect of this provision, *see supra* § 24:6(F).

correspondent banks, the fate of billions of dollars would remain unsettled for unaffordable long periods of time. However, as mentioned above with respect to the remedy of set-offs and netting, nothing would prevent an *a posteriori* judicial revision of the extrajudicial settlement.

The same is true with the rule known as the "midnight deadline" used in the collection of checks in markets such as the United States, which can be found under Section 4–302(a)(1) of the U.C.C.:

> (a) If an item [check or bill of exchange] is presented to and received by a payor bank, the bank is accountable for the amount of:
>
> (1) a demand item, other than a documentary draft, whether properly payable or not, if the bank, in any case in which it is not also the depositary bank, retains the item beyond midnight of the banking day of receipt without settling for it or, whether or not it is also the depositary bank, does not pay or return the item or send notice of dishonor until after its midnight deadline; or. . . .

§ 28.5 THE PROHIBITION OF THE *PACTUM COMMISSORIUM*, IN A COSTA RICAN DECISION

A strong link exists between the prohibition to terminate or resolve a contract extrajudicially and a Roman contractual clause that enabled the parties' resolution known as the *Pactum Commissorium*. I described this clause earlier as one that allowed the party who had performed his side of the bargain to appropriate and dispose of the defaulting debtor's property in order to repay himself for the latter's unpaid debts.[20] The *Pactum* was widely used in Roman law to effectuate the extrajudicial resolution of loan agreements until it was forbidden by Emperor Constantine in his 326 A.D. Constitution. Constantine justified his prohibition asserting: "As with other deceptive practices, the constant harsh use of the *lex commissoria* [by creditors] has increased and it is our pleasure that this law be invalidated."[21]

The harshness to which Constantine was referring resulted from the use of the *pactum* to guarantee payment of what he considered usurious loans. Yet, he (and early Christian doctrine) deemed usurious any loan that charged interest, regardless of how insignificant the amount paid or the rate charged. Even though some European jurisdictions redefined usury as involving only those amounts charged over and above the market rate,[22] the prohibition of the *Pactum* continues to be in force in many civil law countries.

The following extract of a Costa Rican decision illustrates the continued application of the prohibition of the *pactum* as a restriction on the parties' ability to

---

[20] *See supra* § 24:3(B)(4).

[21] *See* THE THEODOSIAN CODE AND NOVELS AND THE SIRMONDIAN CONSTITUTION 65 (Clyde Pharr trans., 1952) (citation omitted), *cited in* Kozolchyk & Furnish, *A Comparative Analysis* 235 & 256 n.76.

[22] *See* Boris Kozolchyk, *Law and the Credit Structure in Latin America*, 7 VA. J. INT'L L. 1, 10–11 (1966–1967) (on the interaction of the illegality of the *Pactum Commissorium*, usury and secured transactions loan in Latin America). *See also supra* § 9:2(E)(4) (for a discussion of the impact of the strict definition of usury upon commerce during pre-codification France).

rescind their contracts extrajudicially.[23] There are certain legal provisions that must be considered while reading this decision:

Civil Code of Costa Rica:

Article 627: For the validity of an obligation it is indispensably essential that there be:

(1) [Legal] capacity of the party who is acquiring an obligation;

(2) Certain and possible purpose or object matter of the obligation; and

(3) Legal cause.[24]

Article 421: Any stipulation authorizing the creditor to take possession of mortgaged assets upon the debtor's default is null and void.[25]

Commercial Code of Costa Rica:

Article 536: Any stipulation authorizing the creditor to take possession of the pledged assets or to dispose of them upon de debtor's default is null and void. At the time the contract is executed it is possible to authorize the creditor to foreclose the collateral through an authorized broker and without undertaking any judicial procedures. In which case, it is the obligation of the authorized broker in charge of foreclosure to make one publication of the foreclosure notice in the Official Gazette with eight days in advance of the date of sale—including in those days the date of publication and the date on which the foreclosure sale will take place.[26]

Second Civil Court, First Section Decision No.264: Jose Luis Garcia Abarca v. Guillermo Pana Rodriguez and Elizabeth Pana Fernández (2005):

BY Judge BRENES VARGAS

WHEREAS:

On September 4, 1997, José Luis García Abarca and Guillermo Pana Rodríguez entered into a contract of "assignment of rights in real property," rights which at that time had been granted by the National Housing and Urbanization Institute [NHUI] in favor of defendant Guillermo Pana Rodriguez . . . The contract provided that José Luis García Abarca lent Guillermo Pana Rodríguez one million colones, payable in two months with a one-month extension and stipulated a five percent monthly interest rate. It also established that in case of the debtor's default, the agreement would be deemed a fully-fledged assignment of rights in the said property in favor of the plaintiff lender . . .

[T]he defendant, Guillermo Pana Rodríguez, did not repay the money lent by the plaintiff, and the latter requested to the NHUI that ownership of the property be transferred to him. This request was denied because in December 2001 the defendant had conveyed his right of ownership to his daughter and co-defendant, Elizabeth Pana

---

[23] I am thankful to Joaquin Picado Esq. from San José, Costa Rica, an LL.M. student, for the text of this decision.

[24] CÓD. CIV. (COSTA RICA) art. 627 (1841) (translation by author).

[25] *Id.* art. 421 (translation by author).

[26] CÓD. COM. (COSTA RICA) art. 536 (1964) (translation by author).

Fernández. That donation was accepted by the NHUI, and on the February 18, 2002 it executed a public deed [*Escritura Publica*] in favor of Ms. Pana Fernández, which was recorded in the Public Registry . . .

The plaintiff, José Luis García Abarca, in his appeal against the decision that dismissed his complaint, alleges a wrongful application of Article 330 of the Code of Civil Procedure . . . He also argues the failure to apply Article 457 of the Civil Code, because according to him the donation in favor of Ms. Pana Fernández, by Mr. Guillermo Pana Rodríguez, constitutes a fraud against his creditors by disposing of property that his creditors could foreclose on . . . He concludes that Ms. Pana Fernández cannot be protected by the registration of the conveyance provided by the cited Article 457, and for this reason the lower court judgment should be reversed and his appeal granted.

This Court considers that the defendant's defense of plaintiff's lack of entitlement to sue is appropriate . . . Apart from the reasons stated by the trial court, there are others that can be raised *ex-officio* by this Court. These grounds are related to the legality of the contract discussed before the trial court . . . According to the contract labeled by the parties an "assignment of rights in real property" . . . the plaintiff and defendant . . . stipulated that in case of the debtor's non-performance the creditor would become the owner of the property *ipso jure*, which at the time had been granted by the NHUI in favor of the debtor . . . [This] agreement to rely on the assignment of rights in real property as collateral for a commercial loan amounts to a violation of the prohibition of the *Pactum Commissorium* [and] for this reason it cannot be used as a basis for a lawsuit to recover the property allegedly conveyed to the creditor in accordance with the doctrine that inspires numbers 19, 421 and paragraph 3) of Article 627 of the Civil Code, and [thus the agreement is deemed] absolutely null . . . Given that the cause of the obligation is illegal, it is not possible to accept the allegations of the complaint, because the plaintiff lacks the *in rem* right that he alleges to have . . .

THEREFORE: The appealed decision is affirmed.

COMMENTS AND QUESTIONS

Does Article 627 of the Costa Rican Civil Code forbid the *Pactum Commissorium*, if so where? How much freedom of action does Article 627 of the Costa Rican Civil Code allow a judge trying to determine the legality of a clause that resolves a loan agreement in the event of non-payment? Would the outcome of this case have been different if the transaction was a commercial transaction? What does the reader think was the intention of the legislator in including Article 536 in the Commercial Code? How much weight does the reader ascribe to the amount of interest charged by the plaintiff to the defendant for his "commercial loan" (approximately sixty percent per annum)? Does the reader believe this amount to be usurious and, if so, on what basis? Would the reader be surprised to learn that this rate of interest did not greatly exceed that which was ordinarily charged for "commercial" loans in San Jose, Costa Rica at that time? The prohibition of the *Pactum Commisorium* in civil-law jurisdictions and developing nations has been a major obstacle when trying to enable those jurisdictions to enact secured transactions laws that have proven to be essential tools for economic development.[27] On the other hand, as discussed in Chapter 24, the abuse of the *Pactum Commisorium* by creditors had equally damaging consequences.

§ 28.6 THE *SICHERUNGSÜBEREIGNUNG* UNDER GERMAN LAW[28]

Susan Jacqueline Butler, a German and U.S. attorney and LL.M. graduate, describes the *Sicherungsübereignung* as a secured transaction in which the debtor keeps possession of the collateral and assigns to the creditor a fiduciary ownership right over the security, bound by the terms and conditions of an agreement where the parties stipulate the conditions and way in which to execute the security such as returning the collateral and its ownership to the performing debtor.[29]

Butler also summarizes a 2000 decision of the German Federal Supreme Court (*Bundesgerichtshof*) as follows:

A brewing company granted a loan to two restaurant and bar owners in exchange for their promise to exclusively acquire the beer produced by the plaintiff-creditor. The security interest was granted in a portion of the equipment of the two restaurants-bars. Given the non-performance on the payment of the loan by the defendant, the brewing company unilaterally terminated the loan agreement and filed suit for the amount owed, 65,500 German marks, which was the remaining balance of the loan after the extrajudicial enforcement of the security interest that resulted in a total of 11,500 German marks. Finding that the resolution clause in the contract and the extrajudicial remedy to enforce the creditor's security interest were legal, the Court dismissed the objection made by the defendant to both legal institutions.[30]

A. Interviews with German Bankers in Frankfurt and Hamburg—July 11, 1971

As the drafter of the chapter 5 on Letters of Credit of the Encyclopedia of Comparative Law of the Max Planck Institute of Hamburg, I conducted various interviews with many German bankers in charge of issuing and examining documentary credits at the beginning of 1971. Following are two sample questions from the Supplementary Questionnaire given to the bankers:

> Question 13, Supplementary Questionnaire: What security interest is most commonly used in the issuance of a documentary credit (excluding amounts deposited in special accounts or in any other form of prepayment of the documentary credit)?
>
> Question 14: What percentage of the credits issued are guaranteed by this security interest and approximately what is the amount granted annually in

---

[27] Organization of American States [OAS], *Model Inter-American Law on Secured Transactions*, adopted at the Sixth Inter-American Specialized Conference on Private International Law (CIDIP-VI), (Feb. 8, 2002) art. 17, *see also* Kozolchyk & Furnish, *A Comparative Analysis,* at 16–17.

[28] I am thankful to Susan Jacqueline Butler, German and U.S. Attorney, and a former student of mine, for providing me with this decision and its translation on May 15, 2002.

[29] *Id.*

[30] *Id.*

this type of credits by your banks: a) more than 10 million; b) more than 50 million; or c) 100 million marks?[31]

Seven of the nine interviewed bankers that answered Question 13 indicated that they predominantly use the *Sicherungsübereignung*. On the approximate amount of money loaned annually, only one of the bankers estimated this amount at fifty million marks, while the rest of bankers estimated the amount in excess of 100 million marks for each of their banks.[32]

B. Economic Significance of Resolution Clauses and Extrajudicial Remedies in the Law of Commercial Loans

The previous figures illustrate the importance that secured transactions have acquired in the German credit industry. In the U.S. market, the figures on secured lending—including dematerialized securities such as stock and bonds—exceed trillions of dollars per year.[33] Not surprisingly, World Bank economists have estimated that the gross domestic product of a country and especially that of a developing country can be increased by significant percentages through the use of secured transactions with express agreed resolution that allows the use of extrajudicial remedies for collection and repossession.[34] Some developing countries such as Guatemala, Honduras, Colombia, El Salvador, and Mexico have introduced or enacted laws that in effect create the bases for a national and regional commercial credit market with interest rates much below that in the above-discussed Costa Rican decision. The parties and especially the lender's ability to terminate the loan agreement unilaterally and pursue the extrajudicial remedy of repossession and foreclosure play a critical role in these laws discussed in the following sections.

C. Honduran Law on Secured Transactions—2010[35]

Article 57. General Principles on Enforcement: Enforcement of security interests will be conducted based on the following general principles:

1. Enforcement will always be conducted on an extrajudicial basis by means of a public auction before a notary public, in compliance with the provisions of this Law and, in a subsidiary manner, with those of the Notarial Code . . .

The conditions pursuant to which enforcement shall be conducted will be determined in the agreement that creates the security interest. Such conditions shall be used as a guide by the judge or notary for purposes of the auction of the security interests.[36]

---

[31] Interviews with German Bankers conducted by Boris Kozolchyk, James E. Rogers Colleg of Law, Univ. of Ariz. (1971).

[32] *Id.*

[33] *Id.*

[34] Heywood Fleisig, *Secured Transactions: The Power of Collateral*, 33 FINANCE & DEVELOPMENT 44, 46 (1996), *available at* at http://www.worldbank.org/fandd/english/0696/articles/0150696.htm.

[35] Honduras, Law of Secured Transactions, Decree no. 182–8009, La Gaceta, Diario Oficial de la Republica de Honduras, Num. 32, 125 (Jan. 28, 2010) (Ley de Garantias Mobiliarias, Decreto no. 182–2009), La Gaceta, Diario Oficial de la Republica de Honduras (28, Enero 2010) [hereinafter Honduras, Sec. Trans. L.], http://www.garantiasmobiliarias.hn/ley.pdf.

[36] Id. art. 57 (translation by author).

Article 66. Agreement on the Conditions for Sale or Auction: At any time, before or during the enforcement proceeding, the secured debtor may reach an agreement with the secured creditor on terms other than those previously established, either for the delivery or repossession of the goods, the terms of sale or auction, or any other matter, provided such agreement does not affect other secured creditors or buyers in the ordinary course of business, and is not contrary to the applicable law.[37]

COMMENTS AND QUESTIONS

Is Constantine's justification to preclude the use of the *Pactum Commissorium* valid in our days? And if so, could you think of practices that would be considered "harsh" or "deceptive"? As just noted, World Bank studies show significant increases of the GDP of developing countries by enacting a law like that provided under Article 9 of the U.C.C. or like the OAS Model Law of 2002 or the laws of Guatemala and Honduras previously quoted.[38]

One of the many reasons for such an assertion is the high cost of credit and the large number of loans that cannot rely on enforceable security interests. For instance, the Central Bank of Brazil estimated that the risks of credit collection were the cause of at least thirty percent of the cost of commercial loans in Brazil, loans that only two years ago charged interest rates exceeding forty percent per year.[39]

§ 28.7 SPECIFIC PERFORMANCE AS A REMEDY FOR COMMERCIAL CONTRACTS

A. Introduction

Despite the assertion of Justice Holmes, Jr. that a defaulting party always has the option to breach his contract as long as he is willing to pay damages, specific performance obtained within a reasonable time after the breach is, in principle, the remedy most consistent with the needs of a busy marketplace.[40] For, where parties enter into their contracts in good faith, specific performance is the remedy most consistent with their expectations. Nevertheless, the trial practice of civil and common law countries reveals that an award of damages is the remedy most commonly sought by and granted to the aggrieved parties.

It could be that the preference for damages is at root semantic: What some litigators regard as damages others see as specific performance. Consider, for example, an action for repayment of the principal and interest due on a loan. On the one hand, the action asks for the very same performance stipulated in the loan agreement, but on the other hand it is intended to compensate the lender for the monetary damages suffered as a consequence of the breach.

Similarly, an underlying obligation to pay an amount of money could be characterized as an obligation to "give" (what was promised) and an obligation to "do" (also what was promised), especially when one takes into account that "giving" is a

---

[37] *Id.* art. 66 (translation by author).

[38] Decree 51 art. 3, Law on Secured Transactions, Diario Oficial [D.O.] (2007) (Guat.), *available at* http://db.natlaw.com/subscribe.php?url=/interam/gu/bk/tn/stgubk00034.pdf. *See also* Honduras, Sec. Trans. L., *supra* note 35; [OAS], *Model Inter-American Law*, *supra* note 27; The World Bank Group, *Mexico Country Brief* (2000) (on file with this author).

[39] *See* Kozolchyk & Furnish, *A Comparative Analysis,* at 242 (in relation to these studies).

[40] *See* J. Holmes, *The Path of the Law*, 10 Harv. L. Rev. 457, 462 (1897).

form of "doing" and vice versa. The reason for mentioning the dichotomy of "giving" and "doing" is not to sharpen the reader's sophistic skills but to prepare him or her for the following comparative and historical excursus that explains why in many if not most legal systems a distinction continues to be made between obligations to do and to give as they relate to the remedies of damages and specific performance.

Regardless of why the remedy of damages is preferred by merchants and litigators, the historical path of specific performance and its scope of application are of great interest to comparative commercial law. The following discussion should teach us how remedial law was formed, by whom and for what purpose(s). It will also educate us on the cultural reasons responsible for the contrast between the "official" substantive law and the "unofficial" or living law. Based on what this section teaches, the reader might be able to contribute to the making of a more effective remedial law.

B. John P. Dawson and Specific Performance Under French, German and North American Law

The understanding of the law of specific performance everywhere has been greatly aided by Professor John P. Dawson's study, "Specific Performance in France and Germany."[41] In this study, Dawson outlines, step by laborious step, the development of specific performance since its beginnings in Roman law to the mid-twentieth century. In the following pages I will try to summarize Dawson's findings. I say that I will "try," because synthesizing the writings of such a great scholar is (in keeping with one of the main themes of this section) easier said than done.

1. Roman Law

According to Gaius, the *praetorian* procedure of classical Roman law only knew of monetary awards—meaning that the measure of the breach was in money and not through the delivery of the promised goods. This affirmation was based on his description of an ordinary *praetorian* formula:

> In all formulas containing a condemnation, the condemnations are expressed through valuation in money. And so, even though the action is to recover a specific thing, such as land, a slave, a garment, gold or silver, the *iudex* does not order the defendant to deliver the specific thing, as was the practice in early times, [but] orders him to pay money after estimating its value.[42]

This clear description of judicial practices during the Classical period became clouded during the preparation of Justinian's *Corpus Juris Civilis*. One of the few remedial law texts of Classical Roman Law updated by the compilers of the *Corpus Juris Civilis* was an opinion by Ulpian with reference to the *Rei Vindicatione*, or the action given to an owner to recover his property in hands of a non-owner. Ulpianus restated the rule that the standard remedy for an unlawful possession was measured in terms of money and could be increased if the defendant was guilty of fraud.[43] However, the Justinian compilers added the following clause: "If the defendant has the

---

[41] John Philip Dawson, *Specific Performance in France and Germany* 57 MICH. L. REV. 495 (1958–1959). The numerous citations to specific pages of Dawson's article have the purpose of facilitating the reader with access to rich sources of information that this author uses, and hopefully some of the readers of this book will too.

[42] *Id.* at 496 (citation omitted).

[43] *Id.* at 500–501.

property sued for, it will be taken from him 'by military force on the authority of the *iudex*' (*manu militari officio iudicis*)."[44] Dawson notes that the goal of the compilers was to express the usual practices in the times of Justinian. Nonetheless, this simple addition contradicted Gaius' formulation of the rule. As pointed out by Dawson, the Justinian compilers could hardly have foreseen the consequences of this addition.[45]

The compilers also cited two opinions by Celsus, a contemporary of Gaius (second century A.D.). In one of these, Celsus discussed the guarantor's liability for the contractual losses and concluded that in case there were losses, the guarantor had to be sentenced to pay a sum of money "as happens in all obligations to do."[46] While it is true that the Classical jurists often referred to obligations to "do" or to "give," they did so without ascribing precise legal consequences to these terms.[47] A possible explanation to what Celsus had in mind when referring to obligations to do is found in another text where Ulpianus suggested a monetary judgment as the appropriate solution. It involved cases where several persons were obligated to perform an indivisible obligation such as that of transferring an *in rem* right over indivisible real estate such as a house or in an easement, obligations that because of their indivisibility could not be easily partitioned and allocated among the obligors. In this context, Ulpianus cites Celsus' statement that in case of non-performance of an obligation to do, the non-performing party will have to comply by making a monetary payment.[48] Yet, neither this statement by Celsus nor the related opinion by Ulpianus provides a basis with which to distinguish between obligations to give and to do something. In fact, according to Ulpianus, the obligation to do something not only included acting or abstaining to act, but also the delivery of a thing.

2. *Roman Law-Inspired Medieval Law*

The Bologna-based glossators who reinitiated the study of Roman law circa 1100 by relying exclusively on the Justinian *Corpus Juris Civilis* could not know that the reference to a "military force" (*manu militare*) procedure to implement the replevin action (*vindicatio rei*) was an addition by the Justinian compilers to the Ulpianus text. Nevertheless, the Bolognese scholars did find a conflict between texts related to specific performance especially with respect to sale agreements. If a seller refused to deliver the thing sold, was it lawful to force the delivery of the thing sold, and if so what was the importance of the maxim "*nemo potest praecise*," or "no one can be forced into contract"?[49] With the exception of one of the jurists, the rest concluded that force could not be used and maintained that the remedy was monetary as provided in the Classical texts.

---

[44] *Id.* at 501.

[45] *Id.*

[46] *Id.* (citation omitted).

[47] *Id.* For example, D.45.1.2 states that: "Some stipulations involve giving and some involve doing." The formulas that make reference to *iudices* normally say that they are addressed to what the defendant must "give or do." *Id.* at 501 n.17. But in D. 50.16.218, Paul was cited as follows: "The term 'to do' (*facere*) includes every kind of doing such as giving, paying, judging . . ." *Id.*

[48] *Id.* at 502 (citation omitted).

[49] *Id.* at 503.

The dissenting view belonged to Martinus, who was known for his often radical views.[50] Martinus argued that since the seller's obligation was to deliver a specific thing, he should be compelled into doing so to the extent possible. He supported his view with a distressful, almost *ad misericordiam*, question: "If you have sold bread, have not delivered it, and I have died of hunger, will a money judgment suffice?"[51] Despite the lack of support for Martinus' opinion in Roman sources, his opinion and the *manu militare* addition of the Justinian compilers to Ulpianus' text were the most influential during the following centuries. This meant that specific performance would be available against a breach of contract of a sale agreement when the breach consisted in a failure to obtain the delivery of a specified thing that was in existence, and that it could be enforced in some instances *manu militare.* It would not be available generally in contracts whose obligations could be characterized generally as "to do something."

During the time of the "commentators" (fourteenth to sixteenth centuries), there was strong support among these writers for the use of *manu militare* against a seller of a specific thing who had refused to deliver it.[52] In somewhat less dramatic terms than Martinus, the commentator Baldus de Ubaldis tempered the application of the remedy of specific performance by arguing that he who had promised to build a house (possibly over an extended period of time) could not be compelled to specifically perform such a promise (*non cogitur praecise ad factum*) because "this would be a kind of servitude."[53]

Bartolus de Saxoferrato (1314–1357), one of the most respected commentators (the mostly Italian-based jurists who replaced the glossators as more ambitious interpreters of the *Corpus Juris Civilis* and framers of Roman medieval law), objected to the weak logical and juristic support behind Celsus' and Martinus' remedial dichotomy. He asked: "Why would one result in obligations to give and another in obligations to do? . . . I have searched the gloss and it gives no answer. So far as the writers discuss this question, they can give no answers that are necessarily conclusive, only some that appear to be somewhat persuasive."[54] Bartolus then turned to Baldus' analogy between specific performance and slavery when the act involved required the performance of acts over an extensive period (*quaedam species servitutis*). His reply was that only certain contracts required a long period of performance and that most of the promised acts in contracts were for a short period of time and thus their forced performance would not entail slavery. Nonetheless, given the weight of juristic opinion in favor of the dichotomy of doing and giving, he was willing to accept its application.

3. France: **"Nemo Potest Praecise Cogi ad Factum"** *as a Self-Evident Truth*

High Appellate Courts (*Parlements*) in feudal France did not feel bound by the medieval Roman law dichotomy and applied both remedies to obligations to do as well as to give, with few distinctions.[55] Thus, when the drafters of the 1804 *Code Civil* promulgated this dichotomy it was not because of pre-existing law. According to

---

[50] *Id.* at 503. It states, "The facts known of Martinus are collected by KANTOROWICZ, STUDIES IN THE GLOSSATORS OF THE ROMAN LAW 86–87 (1938)." *Id.* at 503 n.19.

[51] *Id.* at 503.

[52] *Id.* at 504 (citations omitted).

[53] BALDUS, COMMENTARY ON C.4.49, *cited in id.* at 504 n.26.

[54] *Id.* at 504.

[55] *Id.* at 508.

Dawson, the source responsible for this rule was Pothier's "Treatise of Obligations" (a source frequently discussed in this book). Dawson was not an admirer of Pothier's scholarship. He described him as a superficial writer, incapable of original ideas but with an easy-to-follow writing style that provided the impression that what was being described as the law was invariably self-evident.[56]

As did his Roman and medieval predecessors, Pothier distinguished between obligations "to give a thing" and "to do something"; in the latter, the debtor could only be forced to pay damages, because, as in Baldus' analogy to slavery: "no one can be forced into doing something" (*nemo potest praecise cogi ad factum*). Pothier considered that the same was applicable to obligations "not to do something", taking into account that in this negative type of obligation, if the obligor had done something that could be undone, the obligee could have it undone at the obligor's expense.[57]

The drafting commission that approved the first draft of the 1804 *Code Civil* accepted Pothier's views without debate. The only reference to the dichotomy was found in the "Motives" of the Code. It contained a paraphrase of Baldus' opinion as repeated by Pothier: "No one can be constrained to do or not to do a thing, and if it were possible such constraint would constitute violence, which cannot be a means for enforcing contracts."[58] This was the principle that inspired Article 1142 of the *Code Civil*: "Every obligation to do or not to do resolves itself into damages, in case of non-performance on the part of the debtor."[59]

With respect to obligations to give, such as to deliver a specific thing (that included sales, donations and barters), the applicable rule was that because the contracts involved were "consensual" (meaning that title was transferred by the mere consent of the parties) the appropriate remedy was specific performance. With it, the plaintiff could obtain or regain possession of the identifiable promised thing.[60]

Dawson suggests that there were cultural and historical reasons that supported the French choice of *nemo potest praecise cogi ad factum* with respect to obligations to do. The fall of the *ancien régime* and the popularity of liberal ideas were behind the distrust of a powerful judiciary, one that could force *manu militare* on the missing performances. Pothier's dichotomy curtailed such a power by limiting the judge's ability to enforce the performance of an open-ended category of contractual obligations that could be characterized as obligations to do.[61]

In my opinion, there was another reason why the drafting commission did not challenge Pothier's dichotomy, and it had to do with the maxim that supported it. *Nemo potest praecise cogi ad factum* was a Roman legal maxim and a *regulae juris*. As it was noted in the section on European codification,[62] the axiomatic approach to civil code drafting invested numerous of its provisions with the aura of self-evident truths.

---

[56] *Id.* at 509.

[57] POTHIER, I OBLIGATIONS, at 84, 87, 92–93 (in reference to §§ 141, 146, 156–158).

[58] Dawson, *supra* note 42, at 510.

[59] C. CIV. (FR.) 1142 (Barrister 1804).

[60] Dawson, *supra* note 42, at 511 (citing arts. 1136, 1138, 1583, 938, 1703 of the *Code Civil*).

[61] *Id.* at 510.

[62] *See supra* § 8:7(G) (on the persuasiveness of legal maxims).

Pothier contributed to this aura, not only by advocating the adoption of the dichotomy but also by characterizing the *nemo potest praecise cogi ad factum* as a "legal maxim."[63]

A few decades following the enactment of the *Code Civil*, French courts began decreeing fines, sometimes in high amounts, to force parties in default to do or not to do what the court had ordered should be done or not done. This order was known as an "*astreinte*"; and its scope was broad enough to encompass the rendering of accounts, the filing of required documents or the delivery of things.[64]

Yet, what seemed on its face a return to a more powerful judiciary and the adoption of a method of enforcing contracts that disregarded the equation between slavery and specific performance turned out to be just an appearance. The *astreinte* proved ineffective in forcing the performance of contractual obligations to do or not to do something. Its ineffectiveness was and still is a result of its limited and "simulatory" purpose: It was designed to scare the debtor into compliance by raising the amount of a fine (that existed only on paper) until compliance took place. It was conceived strictly as a temporary and revocable remedy which was cancelled the moment the party in default complied. When the debtor did not perform, meaning that he was not scared enough by the *astreinte* (as was and is usual with well-advised debtors), the *astreinte* was not enforceable. It was unenforceable because as a fine for an action in contempt of a judicial order it was an unsanctioned crime—a crime not included in the French Penal Code. Therefore, the enforcement of an *astreinte* was contrary to another equally self-evident maxim "no crime without a law" (*nulla poena sine lege*).[65]

The reluctance to enforce the *astreintes* seemed destined to disappear as a consequence of the housing crisis following World War II. During this time, thousands of residents of apartments and other family dwellings ignored the *astreintes* ordered by the French courts in support of eviction notices in favor of the owners or lessees dispossessed during the war period. For fear that the non-compliance of judicial orders would lead to a generalized anarchy, many French courts began to issue *astreintes* that were automatically transformed into final rulings or judgments (in effect as punitive damages) for the amount of the fine.[66] However, as a result of populist pressures, the French Congress enacted the Law of July 21, 1949 which reinstated the *astreinte* as a mere warning and forbad its transformation into punitive damages, only allowing as damages those that were directly attributable to the non-performance of lessees or squatters.[67]

In concluding his study on specific performance in France, Dawson summarizes the status of the law on specific performance in 1950 as follows:

> As to one class of promises—to transfer land or goods that can be reached by a bailiff—specific relief is available, it seems, to any promisee who wants it if rights of third parties have not intervened. This is a large percentage of the potentially enforceable promises, and its importance should not be minimized.

---

[63] Dawson, *supra* note 42, at 509.

[64] *Id.* at 512–14.

[65] *Id.* at 513 & 524.

[66] *Id.* at 521.

[67] Loi n. 49–972 du 21 juillet 1949 donnant le caractère comminatoire aux astreintes fixées par les tribunaux en matière d'expulsion, et en limitant le montant (1949), *available at* http://www.legifrance.gouv.fr/affichTexte.do?cidTexte=LEGITEXT000006068069&dateTexte=20120531.

> Outside this group, for promises in general, the authors have been saying for more than a century that the 'principle' is always specific performance. The only reservation that is usually admitted is for that very rare case where the performance promised involves a high degree of personal creativity—the usual illustration is the artist who promised to paint a picture . . . [In support of the remedy inspired on this principle we continue citing the *astreintes*] . . . An outside observer will be excused, I hope, for describing such a principle as almost wholly meaningless where the *astreinte* is the only means employed for its realization.[68]

In 1998, Konrad Zweigert and Heinrich Kötz, two renowned German comparative law scholars, evaluated the status of specific performance before French courts in 1998 as follows: "French Law generally admits the issuance of judgments for performance in kind but enforces them in a very grudging manner."[69] A 2004 comparative survey by Henrik Lando and Caspar Rose reached the same conclusion.[70] Thus, the large gap between the French positive law of specific performance and its living law counterpart persists and with it the preeminence of the underlying attitudes toward the real power of the judiciary.

4. Germany

The comparison of the laws of specific performance in France and Germany illustrates some of the key cultural differences between these two pillars of the civil law system. On the one hand, the Germany of the second half of the nineteenth century was a society shaped by Prussian values that stressed respect for authority (often blindly) and for the law it handed down, including the penalties for non-performance of obligations. At the same time, as was discussed in an earlier chapter,[71] Germany had been the most serious recipient and user of Roman legal institutions, especially after it received Roman law officially in the sixteenth century as the "*ius commune*" of many of its provinces. This reception made German lawyers familiar with the medieval Roman law dichotomy between "doing" and "giving" as relied upon by the earlier quoted commentators. French society, on the other hand, as was discussed in the preceding section, was distrustful of authority. Thus, it also discouraged truly enforceable *astreintes* by pretending or simulating an enforcement that did not exist.

Before the enactment of the BGB, German jurists were very familiar with the preference that classical Roman law had for the remedy of damages, and thus the main issue they had to deal with was how to best apply the remedy of specific performance in connection with sale agreements.[72] Most courts and commentators concluded that a buyer could sue for specific performance when the real or personal property sold was one susceptible of being attached.[73] The same was not true for obligations "to do"

---

[68] Dawson, *supra* note 42, at 524–25.

[69] KONRAD ZWEIGERT & HEIN KÖTZ, INTRODUCTION TO COMPARATIVE LAW VOLUME II—THE INSTITUTION OF PRIVATE LAW 165 (Tony Weir trans., 2d rev. ed. 1987).

[70] Henrik Lando & Caspar Rose, *On the Enforcement of Specific Performance in Civil Law Countries*, 24 INT'L REV. L. & ECON. 473, 478 (2004).

[71] *See supra* § 12:1 & 12:3(A).

[72] Dawson, *supra* note 42, at 525.

[73] *Id.* at 525. It states, "REFERENCES TO OPPOSING VIEWS ARE COLLECTED BY Ziebarth, die Realexecution Und die Obligation § 16 (1866)," *cited in id.* at 525 n.83.

because courts and commentators generally assumed that these obligations could not be subject to specific performance.

In 1870, the Drafting Commission of the German Code of Civil Procedure unanimously agreed that, as provided by Articles 1143 and 1144 of the *Code Civil*, only those acts that could be assigned to someone else—that could be performed by a third party—could give rise to an action for specific performance whose cost would be borne by the defendant. The Commission also agreed that the incarceration of the debtor for acts whose performance could be delegated or substituted was a violation of the prohibition of debtors' imprisonment.[74] However, the majority of the same Commission also agreed that it was "intolerable and inconsistent with the basic principles of the modern law of obligations that an obligor without property should be able to defeat the execution of a judgment [of specific performance] merely through his own disobedience."[75]

This Code's "Motives," published in 1872,[76] assured the citizenry that no effort was spared to limit the use of fines and arrests to those cases in which performance could not be obtained through any other means. The Motives added that if the claimed performance was only to obtain an amount of money from an insolvent obligor, then a fine or arrest was not appropriate because the purpose of specific performance was not to punish insolvency.[77]

It was not hard to discern the internal contradictions in the "Motives." Hence, the Code of Civil Procedure, effective as of 1879, included a number of mutually exclusive remedies. One of them applied to court decrees for the delivery of identifiable personal or real property. For such property, the appropriate procedure was the attachment of the property by a court officer.[78] A second remedy applies to court decrees that authorized the substituted or delegated performance at the expense of the defendant.[79] The third remedy applies to a court decree that ordered the performance of an unfulfilled unilateral promise known as a "declaration of will." Typically, such a promise involved the conveyance of title to real estate property, and the remedy consisted in the judicial order compelling the defendant-promisor to execute or to allow for the public deed of transfer to be executed. This decision was self-enforceable because it provided for the execution of the transfer by the judicial authority itself.[80]

In Dawson's opinion, the most interesting type of remedy is that in which the court orders performance of an act that cannot be delegated to or be performed by a third party and whose performance depends exclusively on the will of the defaulting defendant. In this case, the applicable remedy is that of an arrest or a monetary fine initially limited to 1,500 marks (but unlimited since 1924).[81] An obligation "to refrain from doing something" is equated to the types of acts whose performance cannot be

---

[74] *Id.* at 526.

[75] *Id.*

[76] BEGRUENDUNG DES ENTWURFS EINER DEUTSCHEN CIVIL Prozessordnung 573–77 (1872), *cited in id.* at 526 n.86 and accompanying text.

[77] *Id.*

[78] *See* Zivilprozessordung [ZPO] [Code of Civil Procedure], Jan. 30, 1877, Reichsgesetzblatt [RGBI.], 83, as amended, arts. 883 & 886 (Ger.). [hereinafter ZPO]; *see also* art. 884 ZPO, for a similar provision.

[79] *Id.* art. 888.

[80] *Id.* arts. 894–896.

[81] *Id.* art. 888.

delegated, and for this reason the defaulting defendant can be arrested for a maximum of two years or subject to an equivalent fine.

In an apparent departure from what was the most common remedy in classical Roman law, the BGB "Motives" stated that the specific performance of breached promises was the normal and preferred procedure. This principle informed the applicable substantive law in the BGB which was to act in harmony with the remedies set forth in the Code of Civil Procedure. Accordingly, Section 241 of the BGB states: "By virtue of an obligation the obligee is entitled to claim performance from the obligator. The performance may also consist in forbearance."[82]

This rule made damages an exceptional remedy, applicable to cases of "injury to a person or damage to a thing,"[83] or to cases in which specific performance was "not possible or is not sufficient to compensate the obligee,"[84] and when the aggrieved party gave formal notice of his claim for damages in terms of money and allowed for a reasonable time for its performance.[85] The debtor also had the right to a monetary compensation instead of specific performance when the latter required "disproportionate expenses" compared to the amount of the debt.[86]

Apart from the rigorous definition of all of the remedies associated with specific performance, another characteristic of the German remedial system is that German courts, in contrast with the French, have frequently granted the remedy of substitute performance (performance by somebody else) or compliance. Nevertheless, a shared characteristic with the French is that most of the German litigants resort to the remedy of damages for the majority of contractual non-performance suits and especially in relation to sale agreements and other commercial contracts.[87] Both Zweigert and Kötz in 1998[88] and Lando and Rose in 2004[89] agree with Dawson's analysis. In the words of Zweigert and Kötz:

> In Germany . . . where the claim to performance is regarded as the primary legal remedy, it does not in practice have anything like the significance originally attached to it, since whenever the failure to receive the promised performance can be made good by the payment of money commercial men prefer to claim damages rather than risk wasting time and money on a claim for performance whose execution may not produce satisfactory results.[90]

Zweigert and Kötz note that specific performance has been used in Germany, albeit not exclusively, to obtain performance of building contracts, thereby vindicating Bartolus' reply to Baldus' comment,[91] and for the delivery of goods or personal property in existence.[92] A study cited by Lando and Rose makes reference to a court decision on

---

[82] BGB, *supra* note 15, § 241.

[83] *Id.* § 249.

[84] *Id.* § 251.

[85] *Id.* § 250, 283 & 326.

[86] *Id.* § 251 ¶ 2.

[87] Dawson, *supra* note 42, at 530.

[88] KONRAD ZWEIGERT & HEIN KÖTZ, AN INTRODUCTION TO COMPARATIVE LAW VOLUME 484 (Tony Weir trans., 3d rev. ed. 1998).

[89] Lando & Rose, *supra* note 71, at 478.

[90] ZWEIGERT & KÖTZ, *supra* note 89, at 484.

[91] *See supra* § 28:7(B)(2).

[92] Lando & Rose, *supra* note 71, at 479.

specific performance of service contracts such as a contract to supply electricity to a hotel or to repair a computer system; nonetheless, in the words of Lando and Rose, "specific performance is rarely used, especially in commercial transactions."[93]

5. *United States*

Dawson notes that by 1450 the common law had already adopted the remedy of damages as its preferred one for contractual non-performance, with the exception of actions for the attachment of movable and immovable property such as replevin or other extraordinary remedies such as the *mandamus*. Since then, a "mixed system" was developed, which to this day uses both damages and specific performance dependent on the adequacy test of the latter remedy.[94]

The elements for this adequacy test have been determined by the U.S. courts through the use of an exclusion formula: The remedy of specific performance will be granted by a court of equity in its discretion when there is no other adequate remedy under common law (a jurisdiction which was assumed to be stricter than the equity jurisdiction before both merged).[95] Generally the remedy at law has been found inadequate by courts in two situations: 1) where damages would be insufficient given the special nature of the subject matter of the contract; and 2) where damages are impracticable—in other words, when it is impossible to arrive at a legal measure of damages with enough certainty.[96]

An example of the difficulty in arriving at a legal measure of damages is found in a case before the Supreme Court of the State of Arkansas in 1948.[97] The action for specific performance was brought seeking the purchase of a Ford automobile. The Supreme Court held that: "While equity will not ordinarily enforce a contract for the sale of chattels, it will do so where special and peculiar reasons exist which render it impossible for the injured party to obtain adequate relief by way of damages in an action at law."[98] Hence, if the automobile at issue would have "peculiar, unique or sentimental value to the buyer not measurable in damages,"[99] then specific performance should be granted.

Dawson, among others, criticizes this "adequacy test" of the remedy because of its vagueness and suggested as a better rule that specific performance be available for any asset that can be attached by a sheriff as done under German Law. It is true that specific performance would not be used in cases involving markets where the expeditiousness of the transaction is of the essence, and where the markets are reasonably well organized, in such a way that complying sellers and buyers may easily obtain substitute performances. But Dawson sets out the question: Why not leave the choice to the aggrieved and complying party? And to this Dawson concludes by

---

[93] *Id.*

[94] Dawson, *supra* note 42, at 495–96.

[95] See, among other decisions, Portnoy v. Brown, 430 Pa. 401 (1968); Roth v. Hartl, 365 Pa. 428 (1950); and First National State Bank of New Jersey v. Commonwealth Federal Savings and Loan Association, 610 F.2d 164 (3d Cir. 1979).

[96] *See* Girard Bank v. John Hancock Mut. Life Ins. Co., 524 F. Supp. 884, 895 (Pa. 1981).

[97] McCallister v. Patton, 214 Ark. 293 (1948).

[98] *Id.* at 293.

[99] *Id.*

affirming that the adequacy test is so well rooted in the U.S. system that in order to eliminate it, it would be necessary to enact a special law.[100]

The reader is asked to evaluate if the Sections of the U.C.C. that follow are that "special law" to which Dawson makes reference:

Section 2–702. *Seller's Remedies on Discovery of Buyer's Insolvency*

(1) Where the seller discovers the buyer to be insolvent he may refuse delivery except for cash including payment for all goods theretofore delivered under the contract, and stop delivery under this Article [Section 2–705].

(2) Where the seller discovers that the buyer has received goods on credit while insolvent he may reclaim the goods upon demand made within ten days after the receipt, but if misrepresentation of solvency has been made to the particular seller in writing within three months before delivery the ten day limitation does not apply. Except as provided in this subsection the seller may not base a right to reclaim goods on the buyer's fraudulent or innocent misrepresentation of solvency or of intent to pay.

(3) The seller's right to reclaim under subsection (2) is subject to the rights of a buyer in ordinary course or other good faith purchaser under this Article [Section 2–403]. Successful reclamation of goods excludes all other remedies with respect to them.

Section 2–704. *Seller's Right to Identify Goods to the Contract Notwithstanding Breach or to Salvage Unfinished Goods*

(1) An aggrieved seller under the preceding section may

(a) identify to the contract conforming goods not already identified if at the time he learned of the breach they are in his possession or control;

(b) treat as the subject of resale goods which have demonstrably been intended for the particular contract even though those goods are unfinished.

(2) Where the goods are unfinished an aggrieved seller may in the exercise of reasonable commercial judgment for the purposes of avoiding loss and of effective realization either complete the manufacture and wholly identify the goods to the contract or cease manufacture and resell for scrap or salvage value or proceed in any other reasonable manner.

Section 2–709. *Action for the Price*

(1) When the buyer fails to pay the price as it becomes due the seller may recover, together with any incidental damages under the next section, the price

(a) of goods accepted or of conforming goods lost or damaged within a commercially reasonable time after risk of their loss has passed to the buyer; and

(b) of goods identified to the contract if the seller is unable after reasonable effort to resell them at a reasonable price or the circumstances reasonably indicate that such effort will be unavailing.

---

[100] Dawson, *supra* note 42, at 532.

(2) Where the seller sues for the price he must hold for the buyer any goods which have been identified to the contract and are still in his control except that if resale becomes possible he may resell them at any time prior to the collection of the judgment. The net proceeds of any such resale must be credited to the buyer and payment of the judgment entitles him to any goods not resold.

(3) After the buyer has wrongfully rejected or revoked acceptance of the goods or has failed to make a payment due or has repudiated [Section 2–610], a seller who is held not entitled to the price under this section shall nevertheless be awarded damages for non-acceptance under the preceding section.

Section 2–712. *"Cover"; Buyer's Procurement of Substitute Goods*

(1) After a breach within the preceding section the buyer may "cover" by making in good faith and without unreasonable delay any reasonable purchase of or contract to purchase goods in substitution for those due from the seller.

(2) The buyer may recover from the seller as damages the difference between the cost of cover and the contract price together with any incidental or consequential damages as hereinafter defined [Section 2–715], but less expenses saved in consequence of the seller's breach.

(3) Failure of the buyer to effect cover within this section does not bar him from any other remedy.

Section 2–716. *Buyer's Right to Specific Performance or Replevin*

(1) Specific performance may be decreed where the goods are unique or in other proper circumstances.

(2) The decree for specific performance may include such terms and conditions as to payment of the price, damages, or other relief as the court may deem just.

§ 28.8 SPECIFIC PERFORMANCE AND THE JUST-IN-TIME PAYMENT AND DELIVERY: AN ILLUSTRATIVE CASE

Throughout the first part of this book, we have followed the evolution of the enforcement of promises of deferred performance, and we have reached the conclusion that after achieving a high degree of enforceability and abstraction, these promises have become the most popular in our time in matters where the amounts involved exceed billions of dollars per day. Even though according to Roman law the promises of purchase, sale, barter, payment, and lease of are not exclusively personal ones, they clearly should allow for damage awards.

On the other hand, non-performance of many of these promises may result in a similar (and more generalized) situation visualized by the glossator Martinus when he put himself in the place of a starving buyer awaiting the delivery of bread.[101] Think for example of a case where Bank "X" has promised to pay the principal amount and

---

[101] *See supra* § 28:7(B)(2).

interest owed from the emission of bonds in the amount of one billion euros issued by country "Y" to thousands of bearers in the entire financial industry. Payment will be made through a standby letter of credit or through an independent bank guarantee. It is very possible that many of these bearers would rely on the immediate payment of the interest of these bonds to pay other obligations or imminent expenses that cannot be postponed. It is also probable that if there is no immediate payment of the bonds, Y would lose credibility in the international financial market, and with that any future issuance of bonds would have much higher costs.

Assume *X* announces on December 31, 2005 at noon that it will postpone payment of Y's bonds, originally due the following day, for an "additional week" until it receives full payment of a deposit prior to payment required in a contract with "Z" (a broker and endorser of Y who negotiated with X the issuance of the letter of credit or bank guarantee). Should X's non-performance deserve an extremely expedited specific performance based on highly enforceable remedies of fines or imprisonment?

Along the same lines, consider the current transactional practice known as the "just-in-time delivery" that a producer or distributor must rely on to be able to fulfill a number of vital commitments. This practice requires that delivery of goods and services promised by the supplier be just in time to meet all these impending commitments. Management experts and economists alike would testify that success of many contemporary producers of goods, especially industrial goods, depends on having the necessary goods and parts in their inventory to be able to serve their customers. This method of management is but a modern version of the old Spanish saying: "an anchored vessel earns no freights," This principle is responsible for a large number of typical contracts for the different economic sectors and industries, most of which are now in electronic form. What would be the role of a modernized remedy for specific performance in order to encourage reliance on these practices?

Why does the reader think that French and German substantive law on specific performance has been replaced by the living law of damages? Could this be attributable to the artificiality of the dichotomy derived from the corrupted and inconclusive texts of the classical Roman law? Looking back, what would you think was the flaw in the French and German codification processes with respect to specific performance? What would the reader suggest in order to repair these flaws? How could a current legislator obtain a clearer view of the purpose of specific performance? How useful would it be to conduct an analysis of the different types of contracts that are mostly used in a market or markets, including those that are of a personal nature as well as those whose performance can be delegated or substituted? Would it be relevant to research how to increase reliance on "just-in-time delivery" performances? From an economic development perspective, does specific performance deserve to be encouraged or discouraged? Could countries poorer than France and Germany afford an ineffective remedial law in a world market that is highly competitive and dependant on the commercial practice that reduces the existence of "anchored vessels that earn no freight"?

The following is a summary of a 2009 decision by the Supreme Court of New York's Kings County, written by the Judge Jack M. Battaglia. In this case, purchasers-plaintiffs brought an action against a vendor-defendant, seeking specific performance of a contract for sale of a cooperative apartment. The plaintiffs moved for preliminary injunction to prohibit the defendant from conveying or otherwise encumbering the apartment, pending adjudication of action, for summary judgment, and to amend caption. Ultimately, the court held that the purchasers were not entitled to summary judgment on specific performance claim. This case is particularly important because it shows how a thoughtful judge attempts to achieve equity by looking at conditions of the marketplace and not simply legal doctrines in the abstract.

Joseph Lezell and Yachiel Michael Jaffe v. David Forde[102]

Supreme Court, King's County, New York

> Specific performance is an equitable remedy, and so the requirement . . . that there be no adequate remedy at law for it to be ordered. Satisfaction of the requirement is, in effect, presumed when real property is the subject of the contract. "The pleading itself is sufficient to show that the plaintiff has no adequate remedy, or not one, at least, which may be full, adequate, and perfect."
>
> "(A)s to contracts pertaining to personal property," however, "(t)he rule is that . . . a party should be confined to his action for damages, unless it appears that he is entitled to the thing contracted for in specie, which to him has some special value and which he cannot readily obtain in the market, or in cases where it is apparent that compensation in damages would not furnish a complete and adequate remedy.
>
> Specific performance of a contract for the purchase and sale of stock was ordered where the stock "had never been listed on any exchange or had any quoted value or any definite market price or any certain value capable of exact ascertainment" and "the defendant was the owner of at least ninety-two percent of the stock and controlled the balance." ("[T]rading in defendant's stock was so thin that plaintiff would be unable to purchase the number of shares to which it is entitled on the open market, and nearly half of the outstanding shares were held by insiders or members of their families.")
>
> Similarly, "while specific performance is available in appropriate circumstances for the breach of a commercial or residential lease, this equitable remedy is not awarded as a matter of course to enforce real property leases." ("[S]pecific performance of a lease can only be awarded upon a showing of uniqueness.") "The word 'uniqueness' is not . . . a magic door to specific performance." "A distinction must be drawn between physical difference and economic interchangeability." "The point at which breach of a contract will be redressable by specific performance thus must lie not in any inherent physical uniqueness of the property but instead in the uncertainty of valuing it."
>
> Where specific performance of a lease is sought, the distinction between physical difference and economic interchangeability may not always be evident.
>
> The question is whether, for purposes of an action for specific performance, the ownership interest in a cooperative apartment, comprised of shares of the corporate owner of the property and a long-term proprietary lease, should be

---

[102] Joseph Lezell et. al. v. David Forde, 26 Misc. 3d 435, 442–47 (2009) (citations omitted).

treated as real property, requiring no showing as to an adequate remedy at law, or "irreparable harm" for purposes of preliminary injunctive relief, or should be treated as personal property, requiring a showing of "uniqueness," however conceived. In other words, should the whole be found greater than the sum of its parts?

The ownership interest in a co-operative apartment is *sui generis*. . . .

The growth of co-operative ownership of apartment buildings. . . . especially in New York City, has created legal problems not resolved by uncritical resort either to the rubrics governing real property or those governing personal property . . .

"Neither the stock certificate nor the lease, inseparably joined, can appropriately be viewed or valued in isolation from the other. Nor may a dynamic jurisprudence ignore the manner in which economic affairs are conducted or the perception that the members of society have in conducting their affairs."

As a result, "stock in a residential cooperative corporation with its appurtenant proprietary lease are subject to various characterizations as realty or personalty depending upon the purpose of the characterization."

Specific performance and related preliminary injunctive relief are available remedies, in the appropriate case, for the breach or threatened breach of a contract for the purchase and sale of a cooperative apartment. For the most part, however, the decisions do not address the "adequate remedy at law" or "irreparable injury" requirements for specific performance and related injunctive relief.

An exception is *Seitzman v. Hudson River Associates*, in which the First Department upheld a preliminary injunction in an action for specific performance, finding irreparable injury in part by reason of a provision in the contract that "(purchaser) shall have such remedies as he is entitled to at law or on equity, including but not limited to specific performance because the Apartment and possession thereof cannot be duplicated." But the court also found that "[i]f plaintiffs are relegated to monetary damages by denial of injunctive relief, they will be prevented from having an office in the same building in which they live—not a minor consideration, in Manhattan."

Although not addressing the requirements for equitable relief, another First Department opinion states that "a proprietary lease is no different from any other type of lease" and "[c]ooperative apartment stock is . . . like any other stock in a corporation owning real estate." "It does not appear that the pairing of the two together does anything to create a new classification of real estate."

It is clear that a contract for the purchase and sale of the ownership interest in a cooperative apartment is governed, as a contract for the sale of goods, by Article 2 of the U.C.C., including Article 2's remedy provisions. But none of the decisions that address specific performance of a contract for the purchase and sale of a cooperative apartment makes mention of U.C.C. section 2–716, Buyer's Right to Specific Performance or Replevin.

Section 2–716(1) provides that "[s]pecific performance is no longer limited to goods which are already specific or ascertained at the time of contracting. The test of uniqueness under this section must be made in terms of the total situation which characterizes the contract." "[T]he use of the term 'unique goods' is not intended to revive the common-law tests of equity jurisdiction and is not the sole test for relief." "[U]niqueness is not the sole basis of the remedy under this section for the relief may also be granted 'in other proper circumstances' and inability to cover is strong evidence of 'other proper circumstances."

The reference to "cover" is to the remedy provided by section 2–712. "[T]he buyer may 'cover' by making in good faith and without reasonable delay any reasonable purchase of or contract to purchase goods in substitution for those due from the seller." "The buyer may recover from the seller as damages the difference between the cost of cover and the contract price together with any incidental or consequential damages . . ., but less expenses saved in consequence of the seller's breach." Referring to "the section on specific performance of contracts for unique' goods," the Official Comment states that "availability of the goods to the particular buyer for his particular needs is the test for that remedy."

The intended meaning of "unique" and its relationship to "other proper circumstances" as requirements for specific performance under section 2–716 is not entirely clear. But a legislative policy to broaden the circumstances in which the remedy would be appropriate does seem clear, and, particularly with the reference to the cover remedy, the availability of substitute goods in the market-in other words, "uniqueness" in an economic sense-is central to the determination. The policy appears consistent with the "distinction between physical difference and economic inter-changeability" and the availability of substitute goods as a central consideration is hardly a recent innovation.

The upshot of all this seems to be that a claim for specific performance of a contract for the purchase and sale of a cooperative apartment is not treated like real property for purposes of an assessment of the adequacy of a remedy at law or the existence of irreparable injury, but those assessments are tied to the operative market for cooperative apartments at the time and place of actual or threatened breach of the contract. The result is consistent with equity, the attempt to achieve fairness in the individual case.

One might question, therefore, the persistence of the special benefit given to real property, grounded in the culture and economics of more than a century ago, over the cooperative form of ownership, on which the real estate market in modern New York City depends. And what of the condominium unit, declared "for all purposes" to "constitute real property?" A claim for specific performance of a contract for the purchase and sale of a condominium apartment is deemed to involve real property . . . but this Court is unaware of any decision that expressly addresses the requirements for an equitable remedy. These are questions for another day, and, ultimately, a higher court.

Plaintiffs' Verified Complaint, or at least the incomplete copy included with the motion papers, contains no allegation as to the "uniqueness" of apartment

F1 at 446 Kingston Avenue, or as to the inadequacy of a remedy at law or irreparable injury if specific performance is not ordered. . . .

The contract of sale does contain a provision that, in the event of Seller's default, "Purchaser shall have such remedies as Purchaser is entitled to at law or in equity, including specific performance, because the Unit and possession thereof cannot be duplicated." . . . But, although not insignificant, the provision in itself is insufficient to establish entitlement to an equitable remedy.

Plaintiffs have, therefore, failed to demonstrate a likelihood of success on the merits of their cause of action for specific performance or irreparable injury if preliminary injunctive relief is not granted.

Plaintiffs' motion is denied in its entirety.

COMMENTS AND QUESTIONS

As noted by Judge Battaglia, "Specific performance is an equitable remedy . . . and so the requirement is that there be no adequate remedy at law for it to be ordered. Satisfaction of the requirement is, in effect, presumed when real property is the subject of the contract."[103] Why should the requirement that there be no adequate remedy at law be presumed in the case of real property and not, say, in the case of valuable personal property? Is it a reflection of the uniqueness that rural America attributed to real property and especially to land or buildings on it? Was this the "rural" attitude that Professor Karl Llewellyn was referring to in his landmark article "*Across Sales on Horseback*"?[104] Curiously, many of the civil law jurisdictions studied in this book arrive at the same conclusion as that alluded to by Judge Battaglia but through a different reasoning—the obligation to convey land usually entails the obligation to sign a public deed, which is an obligation "to do" as opposed to an obligation to "to give." A person cannot be compelled to do something he does not want to for that would be tantamount to some form of slavery, thus there must be a substituted performance often by a judge signing the deed of conveyance of Blackacre.[105] No one has traced the development of the dichotomy of obligations "to give" and "to do" and their relationship to specific performance as insightfully as did Professor Dawson whose landmark study I summarized in this chapter.[106] Please re-read his comments on the adequacy test and see if you are satisfied with Judge Battaglia's analysis. If the uniqueness of the personal property is no longer a "magic door" to specific performance, what is? Do you agree with Judge Battaglia (and an increasing number of other judges) that the test of uniqueness is no longer "the inherent physical uniqueness of the property but instead in the uncertainty of valuing it." If so, why? In attempting to establish the legal nature of a lease of real property accompanied inseparably with the stock in the cooperative building where the premises are located, Judge Battaglia states: "Stock in a residential cooperative corporation with its appurtenant proprietary lease is subject to various characterizations as realty or personalty depending upon the purpose of the

---

103 26 Misc. 3d 435, at 442.

104 Karl Llewellyn, *Across Sales on Horseback*, 52 HARV. L. REV. 725 (1939).

105 *See supra* § 22:10(K).

106 *See supra* § 28:7(B).

characterization."[107] Does any particular school of comparative and historical legal thought come to mind as agreeing with this analysis? After reading this decision, would you conclude that the law of specific performance has declined in importance in United States law given the prevalence of actions for damages? Or would you conclude, that specific performance, or aspects of it, must now be found in cases involving the law of injunctions (temporary restraining orders and preliminary injunctions), in the law of cover and substitute performance, in actions for the price, and impossibility or impracticability of performance, among others?

---

107 26 Misc. 3d 435, at 444.

Chapter 29

JUDICIAL AND EXTRAJUDICIAL TERMINATION

§ 29.1 REMEDIES FOR BREACH OF COMMERCIAL OR DYNAMIC CONTRACTS

If the contract in question is one that, according to Chapter 22, qualifies as commercial and dynamic (as contrasted with the "civil" or static type), the remedies for its breach should compensate the innocent victim (also known as the "the aggrieved party"[1]) as quickly and closely to the moment of the actual or "anticipatory" breach as possible, thereby stimulating the constant flow of commerce.[2] This is not what would happen if the remedy were that of Article 376 of the Mexican Commercial Code: "In commercial sale agreements, once the contract is perfected, the *complying party* will have the right to claim [*in court*] *from the non-complying party*, the rescission or performance of the contract, and compensation and damages."[3]

According to this provision, the only party entitled to terminate the contract and seek damages is he who complies with the contract by performing his side of the bargain. If that party is the seller, he must deliver what he sold; if he is the buyer, he must pay for what he bought. Having so performed, the aggrieved party may claim, *in court*, the termination of the contract and the damages.[4] Thus, during the entire period of non-compliance, and while an aggrieved party wearily weighs the consequences of complying with a breached contract, valuable goods, services and payments remain in legal and transactional limbo, unused and unproductive.

It should not be surprising if very few if any aggrieved parties would be willing to comply with their contractual obligations once the other party failed to perform his. All that Article 376's requirement of compliance by the aggrieved party does, then, is to freeze the breached or certain-to-be-breached transaction with the attendant and accumulating economic losses.[5]

A commercially-inspired remedy then would require that the aggrieved party be allowed to terminate the contract without having to be involved in a lengthy and costly judicial proceeding. If he is the seller, he would be able sell what the original buyer did not buy to another buyer and claim the difference between the price of the original and

---

[1] *See Party,* LEGAL DEFINITION http://law.yourdictionary.com/party (last visited Oct. 30, 2013) (for the definition of an aggrieved party: "a party whose pecuniary, personal, or property rights have been negatively affected by the actions of another or by a court's [sic] ruling." *Id.*)

[2] See the definition of an anticipatory breach in U.C.C. § 2–610 (2013) later in this section.

[3] CÓD. COM. (MEX.) art. 376 (2008) (translation by author) (emphasis added).

[4] This is one instance in which a code in a civil law country uses the term rescission to mean the same thing as termination.

[5] William Headrick, *La Rescisión de la Compraventa,* 49 REV. DE DERECHO U.N.A.M. 83 (1963). As noted in the preceding chapter, to my knowledge, this point was first made in Mexican legal literature by William Headrick in this landmark article.

breached contract and that of his resale and in doing so he has the duty to mitigate the breaching party's damages.[6] The same would remedy would be applicable *mutatis mutandis* to the aggrieved buyer. In broad terms, this is the approach of the Vienna Convention on the International Sale of Goods (CISG)[7] and the sections of the U.C.C. that follow.

As was also discussed in the preceding chapter, the current international remedial trends, then, are open to extrajudicial remedies, such as mediation, arbitration and express or implied resolution of contracts by the parties. We will now discuss the U.C.C. remedies related to judicial and extrajudicial resolution of contracts. Subsequently we will discuss counterpart remedies in civil law systems. The reader might be well advised to revisit Chapter 2's discussion of Holmes' bad man of contracts with the role of archetypal commercial transations in the formation, interpretation and remedies of the law of commercial contracts.[8]

§ 2–609. *Right to Adequate Assurance of Performance*

(1) A contract for sale imposes an obligation on each party that the other's expectation of receiving due performance will not be impaired. When reasonable grounds for insecurity arise with respect to the performance of either party the other may in writing demand adequate assurance of due performance and until he receives such assurance may if commercially reasonable suspend any performance for which he has not already received the agreed return.

(2) Between merchants the reasonableness of grounds for insecurity and the adequacy of any assurance offered shall be determined according to commercial standards.

(3) Acceptance of any improper delivery or payment does not prejudice the aggrieved party's right to demand adequate assurance of future performance.

(4) After receipt of a justified demand failure to provide within a reasonable time not exceeding thirty days such assurance of due performance as is adequate under the circumstances of the particular case is a repudiation of the contract.

§ 2–610. *Anticipatory Repudiation*

When either party repudiates the contract with respect to a performance not yet due the loss of which will substantially impair the value of the contract to the other, the aggrieved party may

(a) for a commercially reasonable time await performance by the repudiating party; or

(b) resort to any remedy for breach (Section 2–703 or Section 2–711), even though he has notified the repudiating party that he would await the latter's performance and has urged retraction; and

---

[6] *See* Pioneer Bank and Trust Co., v. Seiko Sporting Goods, 184 Ill. App. 3d 783 (1989) (for a judicial qualification of the aggrieved party's duty to mitigate damages).

[7] *See* CISG arts. 74–77.

[8] *See supra* § 2:1(B)(4).

(c) in either case suspend his own performance or proceed in accordance with the provisions of this Article on the seller's right to identify goods to the contract notwithstanding breach or to salvage unfinished goods (Section 2–704).

§ 2–701. *Remedies for Breach of Collateral Contracts Not Impaired*

Remedies for breach of any obligation or promise collateral or ancillary to a contract for sale are not impaired by the provisions of this Article.

§ 29.2 JUSTICE HOLMES' BAD MAN AND SECTION 2–609 ASSURANCES

Contrary to Justice Holmes' assumption that all the common law requires from the party who has chosen to breach a contract is the payment of damages, Section 2–609 imposes an obligation not to impair "the other's expectation of receiving due performance." Hence, "when reasonable grounds for insecurity arise with respect to the performance of either party the other may in writing demand adequate assurance of due performance." Clearly, this duty to provide assurances of performance would not have been required if the contracting party's duty were merely that of paying damages for his chosen breach.

The enforcement of the duty to provide assurances of performance starts out extrajudicially but can be subsequently pursued in court and can include damages beyond those discussed in the common law decisions relied upon by Justice Holmes.[9]

According to Section 2–609 of the U.C.C., this extrajudicial claim coexists with the suspension of performance by the party that has reasonable grounds for insecurity; and, as just noted, it may then be followed by a unilateral and extrajudicial termination of the contract. Consider the following example: Buyer "C" purchases 100 computers [on] credit (with a small down-payment) from an intermediate Seller "S" who purchases them from a third party, the producer "P." C gives S a check for ten percent of the total price as a partial payment of the transaction. The bank dishonors payment of the check due to insufficient funds. This situation gives S grounds for insecurity with respect to C's performance, grounds that are serious and reasonable. Thus, it would be unfair to force S to enter into the obligation with P, unless C is able to give him adequate assurance of his performance. Consequently, S would suspend his performance until he receives this assurance.[10]

Another situation that can lead to a claim for adequate assurance of performance is where an intermediate "X" finds out that producer "P" has been delivering defective products to brokers "C" and "D." Additionally X finds out that his exclusivity agreement is not being honored by P who has sold the same product to other intermediates in the area where he has exclusive distribution. These facts can be

---

[9] *See infra* § 30:3(D)(2) (discussing the damages available against a contracting party who acts with bad faith).

[10] U.C.C. § 2–609 cmt. 1 (2012). In relevant parts it states:

> The section rests on the recognition of the fact that the essential purpose of a contract between commercial men is actual performance and they do not bargain merely for a promise, or for a promise plus the right to win a lawsuit and that a continuing sense of reliance and security that the promised performance will be forthcoming when due, is an important feature of the bargain.

Id.

reasonable grounds for X to claim adequate assurance from P and eventually terminate the contract.

The element of reasonableness has to take into consideration the type of contract, as well as the rights and obligations stipulated in it.[11] For instance, if it is a CIF[12] sale agreement (or any other "documentary agreement" in which payment is due not upon delivery of the goods but the documents), the buyer cannot suspend payment until he inspects the goods based on rumors about their bad quality. Given that payment is due upon delivery of documents, it would be contrary to the CIF terms to hold an inspection of the goods prior to payment.

On the other hand, in an ordinary sale or non-documentary sale, where the seller has a good reputation in the market, his verbal assurance to fix the defective products could be sufficient. Therefore, the standard used for this remedy is not *that of subjective fear* but one which results from an objective or commercially-reasonable evaluation, taking into consideration the type of contract, the course of dealing between the parties, and usages of the trade. As with the market standard of fairness so often referred to in this book, the "insecure" party must place himself in the position of a regular participant in that type of transaction ("the other") and inquire whether such a person would reasonably require assurances. This remedy, as well as its U.C.C. Article 2 companions, reflects the dynamic nature of contemporary commercial contract law. Can you see how and why?

§ 29.3 ANTICIPATORY REPUDIATION

If a contracting party is certain that the other party will not perform, he can claim the second of the above-transcribed remedies. U.C.C. § 2–610 grants an action for extrajudicial termination of the contract against a defendant's anticipatory repudiation. This action is intended to terminate the duty to carry out performances not yet due. However, for the anticipatory repudiation to be effective against the defendant, it has to be easily and clearly proven. Additionally, plaintiff has to prove that he will be substantially impaired as a consequence of the non-performance of the other party.

U.C.C. § 2–610 requires an overt communication of intention or an action by the repudiating party that renders performance impossible or demonstrates a clear intention not to continue to perform or counter-perform.[13] In measuring the seriousness of non-performance, how would a request from the supposedly breaching seller, say, for a higher price or an increase in the volume of the agreed-upon goods or services be characterized? Could this request be considered an objective indication of repudiation?

According to the Official Comment 2 of this Section, this would not in itself be considered repudiation. However, it will be repudiation if such request for a higher price or an increase in the volume of performance includes a statement that the requesting party will not continue to perform unless the difference in the price is paid or the additional volume of the performance is granted. The remedies aforementioned

---

[11] *See id.* cmts. 3 & 4.

[12] *See* Glossary, "Documentary Sales."

[13] U.C.C. § 2–610 cmt. 1 (2012).

and especially their interrelation are illustrated in the following decision, which has
1309

been considerably reduced in length from its original full version but still contains a succinct catalogue of the U.C.C. Article 2 remedies.

§ 29.4 A JUDICIAL EXCURSUS OF BREACH OF CONTRACT REMEDIES UNDER THE U.C.C.

AMERICAN BRONZE CORPORATION, APPELLEE, v. STREAMWAY PRODUCTS, APPELLANT[14]

No. 44828

Court of Appeals of Ohio, Eighth Appellate District, Cuyahoga County

8 Ohio App. 3d 223; 456 N.E.2d 1295; 1982 Ohio App. LEXIS 11256; 8 Ohio B. Rep. 295; 37 U.C.C. Rep. Serv. (Callaghan) 687

December 16, 1982, Decided

DISPOSITION: *Judgment reversed and remanded on counterclaim.*

SUMMARY: Defendant-customer filed a counterclaim against plaintiff-producer alleging that the producer breached its contract to construct for and deliver to the customer a stated number of bronze castings. The producer had filed suit to recover funds due on account. A trial court, Cuyahoga County (Ohio) determined that the producer had not breached the contract and was entitled to the funds due, and the customer appealed to this court.

The defendant-customer contended that the parties entered into three binding contracts and that the producer repudiated the binding agreements; that the producer's refusal to perform was an anticipatory repudiation of the contracts; that the producer terminated the contractual relationship and in so doing failed to give reasonable notice; that the producer was bound to the contracts after receiving adequate assurances of performance from the customer; and that the producer breached the contract.

The court held that (1) the parties entered into the three contracts at issue; (2) the producer anticipatorily repudiated the contracts and became liable to the customer; (3) the action taken by the producer was not "rescission" as defined by the Ohio Uniform Commercial Code (U.C.C.), Ohio Rev. Code Ann. § 1302.12; (4) the producer did not "terminate" the contractual relationship because the contracts were for a definite duration so were not subject to termination pursuant to Ohio Rev. Code. Ann. Section 1302.22(B); (5) the producer was not entitled to unilaterally breach the contract; and (6) when the producer repudiated the contracts, the customer was free to pursue its remedies under the Ohio U.C.C.

OUTCOME: The trial court erred in its conclusions of law, so the judgment was reversed and remanded on the customer's counterclaim.

OPINION BY: PRYATEL

---

[14] American Bronze Corp. v. Streamway Products, 8 Ohio App. 3d 223 (1982).

FINDINGS OF FACTS

Streamway, the defendant-customer, called in orders from American, plaintiff-producer, and then confirmed through written purchase orders. From November 21, 1979 to January 3, 1980, American partially performed—meaning that they only delivered part of the products they had promised to deliver.

On January 17, 1980, American's Vice-President, in a telephone conversation, informed Streamway's Plant Manager and Streamway's President that American would no longer accept new Purchase Orders from Streamway but that American would produce all open orders then in existence. American requested adequate assurances from Streamway in order to continue production of castings. The assurances requested were bringing their account current, paying future invoices within ten days, arriving at an agreed price for scrap returned, and holding American harmless for any failure to produce the castings. Streamway, on January 18, 1980, delivered a check in excess of $66,000.00, which brought its account current with American.

On January 14, 1980, Streamway had placed an order, before American's Vice-President informed them of their decision not to accept new purchase orders. On January 18, of that same year, American returned said order refusing to produce the requested castings. On January 24, 1980, American informed Streamway that they would not produce the castings which were on open order, and in addition, that they had melted down any of the castings which had been previously produced for said open orders. As a result of this information Streamway placed orders with another company to cover for said castings. This lead to the following additional costs: difference in price—$16,301.30; cost to Streamway in converting some castings—$2,374.11; cost of retooling—$2,970.00; and other miscellaneous costs—$3,500.00. The total cost incurred by Streamway as a result of American's alleged anticipatory repudiation was twenty-five thousand one hundred forty-five dollars and forty-one cents ($25,145.41).

The trial court held that American had not breached any of the contracts because it was not a commercially unreasonable period of time, from November 21, 1979 to January 24, 1980, for American to unilaterally rescind its acceptance of part of the purchase orders, and the totality of the final purchase order. There being no breach of contract, Streamway had no right to damages. Judgment was granted on the complaint in favor of American in the sum of $9,489.64, with statutory interest at the rate of 8% per annum from December 3, 1981, and against Streamway with costs to Streamway.

STREAMWAY'S ALLEGATIONS

Streamway appeals citing three assignments of error. First, that American's refusal to perform was an anticipatory repudiation of the contracts. Although "anticipatory repudiation" is not defined in Ohio's Revised Code, the case law and official comments to the Ohio Revised Code Section 1302.68 provide a detailed definition. "Anticipatory repudiation" occurs where one party "repudiates the contract with respect to a performance not yet due the loss of which will substantially impair the value of the contract to the other." On this issue we have to mention the case *Columbia Gas Transmission Corp. v. Larry H. Wright, Inc.* (S.D. Ohio 1977), 443 F. Supp. 14, 21 and the Official Comment 1 to R.C. 1302.68 that states: "anticipatory repudiation centers upon an overt communication of intention or an action which renders performance impossible or demonstrates a clear determination not to continue with performance."

In the case at hand, American's Vice-President, Gerald Goldstein, unequivocally stated on January 24, 1980 that from that moment American would not perform any further on the three contracts and in fact had melted down those units already produced. Consequently, Streamway then rightfully removed the tooling necessary to produce these parts. The value of the contracts to Streamway was substantially impaired in that a new producer of the parts had to be found at substantial cost to Streamway. Therefore, American anticipatorily repudiated these contracts . . . The total cost incurred by Streamway as a result of American's actions was $25,145.41.

Nevertheless, the trial court concluded as a matter of law that American rescinded these contracts within a commercially reasonable time, thus causing no breach of the contracts. These conclusions are erroneous. The action taken by American was not "rescission" as defined by the Ohio Uniform Commercial Code. The Official Comment 3 to R.C. 1302.12 defines "rescission" as including "abandonment or other change (in the contractual relation) by mutual consent" (parenthesis added); it does not include unilateral termination or cancellation in the concept of rescission.

FINDINGS OF LAW

The trial court held that American had not breached any of the contracts because it was not a commercially unreasonable period of time, from November 21, 1979 to January 24, 1980, for American to unilaterally rescind its acceptance of part of the purchase orders, and the totality of the final purchase order.

I. Termination and Repudiation

We cannot agree to this categorization of American's acts. What American did was to unilaterally terminate its contracts with Streamway. This termination is explicitly defined in R.C. 1302.01(A) (13) as occurring "when either party pursuant to a power created by agreement or law puts an end to the contract otherwise than for its breach". This is supplemented by the language of R.C. 1302.22(B) and (C) and with the Official Comments 7 and 8 to those sections stating that "termination" deals with contracts indefinite in duration. The contracts in the instant case were for a definite duration, an inherent characteristic to the production of a specific number of units; therefore these contracts are not subject to termination as provided in R.C. 1302.22(B).

The R.C. Section 1302.22(B) and (C) and with the Official Comments 7 and 8 provide that:

> Section 1302.22
>
> (B) Where the contract provides for successive performances but is indefinite in duration it is valid for a reasonable time but unless otherwise agreed may be terminated at any time by either party.
>
> (C) Termination of a contract by one party except on the happening of an agreed event requires that reasonable notification be received by the other party and an agreement dispensing with notification is invalid if its operation would be unconscionable.
>
> Official Comments
>
> 7. Subsection (2) applies a commercially reasonable view to resolve the conflict which has arisen in the cases as to contracts of indefinite duration. The "reasonable time" of duration appropriate to a given arrangement is

limited by the circumstances. When the arrangement has been carried on by the parties over the years, the "reasonable time" can continue indefinitely and the contract will not terminate until notice.

8. Subsection (3) recognizes that the application of principles of good faith and sound commercial practice normally call for such notification of the termination of a going contract relationship as will give the other party reasonable time to seek a substitute arrangement . . .

American's actions in repudiating the contracts in the case *sub judice* led to Streamway's removal of its tooling on January 24, 1980 . . . Repudiation of a contract by one party leaves the other free to cancel and resort to its remedies for breach. In *Pillsbury Co. v. Ward* (Iowa 1977), 250 N.W. 2d 35, 41, the buyer unreasonably extended the date for delivery (and collection) of the sold goods, thus reducing the value of the contract to the seller. This was found to constitute a repudiation of the contract and to entitle the seller to cancel and resort to his remedies for breach. In the instant case, American refused to perform further under these contracts thus allowing Streamway to cancel and resort to its extrajudicial remedies under R.C. 1302.85, including "cover" (substitute purchases) as defined in R.C. 1302.86. Accordingly, Streamway's first assignment of error is sustained.

On its relevant parts the R.C. 1302.85 reads:

Section 1302.85

(A) Where the seller fails to make delivery . . . or the buyer rightfully rejects or justifiably revokes acceptance then with respect to any goods involved, . . . as provided in section 1302.70 of the Revised Code, the buyer may cancel and whether or not he has done so may in addition to recovering so much of the price as has been paid:

(1) "cover" and have damages under section 1302.86 of the Revised Code as to all the goods affected whether or not they have been identified to the contract; or

(2) recover damages for non-delivery as provided in section 1302.87 of the Revised Code.

The R.C. 1302.86 defines the remedy to "cover" as:

Section 1302.86

A) After a breach within the preceding section, the buyer may "cover" by making in good faith and without unreasonable delay any reasonable purchase of or contract to purchase goods in substitution for those due from the seller.

(B) The buyer may recover from the seller as damages the difference between the cost of cover and the contract price together with any incidental or consequential damages as defined in section 1302.89 of the Revised Code, but less expenses saved in consequence of the seller's breach.

II. Adequate Assurance

The trial court erred in concluding, as a matter of law, that the defendant was justified in unilaterally rescinding the contracts with appellant after receiving adequate assurances of performance from the appellant. Streamway here argues that

American was bound to these contracts after receiving adequate assurances of performance from Streamway.

Under R.C. 1302.67, either party may require adequate assurances of performance from the other when there are reasonable grounds for insecurity. According to Section (B), between merchants, the reasonableness of the grounds for insecurity as well as the adequacy of the assurances offered will be determined according to commercial standards, including the obligation of good faith. Furthermore, the reasonableness of the grounds for insecurity is a question of fact.

In the instant case, American asked for assurances of performance in the form of payment of all outstanding accounts, payment of all new accounts within ten days of delivery, a new policy on return of scrap metal . . . One day after this request, Streamway tendered a check in full payment of its past due accounts and agreed to pay all future invoices within ten days of delivery. American in return agreed to produce all open orders then in existence. The reasonableness of this request is not contested, only the adequacy of the assurances given is in issue.

As a matter of law, the trial court held these assurances to be adequate but that American was still justified in unilaterally rescinding the contract. We agree that the assurances given were commercially reasonable to insure Streamway's performance, but we cannot agree that American was still entitled to unilaterally breach the contract. Having received adequate assurances, American was bound to perform and its failure to do so rendered it liable to Streamway. Accordingly, Streamway's second assignment of error is sustained.

The trial court's judgment is reversed . . .

COMMENTS AND QUESTIONS

Professors Luis Díez Picazo and Antonio Gullón summarize the following remedies with respect to the ineffectiveness of contracts:

> Following the regulations of the Spanish Civil Code, a contract can be declared:
>
> 1) Absolutely null. It is the maximum penalty provided by the legal system, because it disallows the transaction to have any legal consequences. As a distinct legal category, in some case law and doctrine it is contrasted with the non-existence of the contract;
>
> 2) Annullable. It brings about a relative ineffectiveness of the agreement, and is characterized by the fact that the contract produces effects from the moment of its perfection. . . But these effects are relative, because an action for annulment will render the transaction ineffective, or, conversely, if the parties confirm the transaction by their words or conduct it will render it effective; similarly, the expiration of the statute of limitations for bringing an action for nullity will render it effective;
>
> 3) Rescindable. Rescission is a supervening ineffectiveness of a contract which has all of its essential elements and fulfills all the requirements that are particular to that type of contract. But, because of the harm that the contract inflicts on protected parties, the legal system grants an action (action of rescission) to cease its effectiveness. One of its outstanding features is that it is an action *in extremis* because it is given only when no other remedies are available.

> Apart from these categories there are others such as resolution (for non-performance), revocation (for example, a donation that is revoked because of an ungrateful beneficiary) and reduction, which entails a partial loss of the contractual goods (*e.g.*, a donation that affects forced heirship assets). In all of these cases, there is a total or partial termination of the transaction as a result of supervening events . . .[15]

As indicated in earlier chapters, in order to avoid a purely semantic conflict, the term "termination" (instead of "rescission") is used in this book as the English equivalent for the Spanish and Latin American law "resolution." Rescission will be used only when applicable to cases of what the French, Spanish and Latin American civil codes (and exceptionally some commercial codes) refer to as lesion or the U.C.C. refers to as unconscionability.[16]

With regard to the above categorization, how do the remedies described by Justices and Professors Luis Díez Picazo and Antonio Gullón compare to the ones described in the *American Bronze* decision? It should be recalled that in that decision the following remedies were discussed: 1) adequate assurance; 2) extrajudicial resolution as a result of anticipatory repudiation; 3) termination of the contract; 4) rescission; 5) substitute performance or cover; and 6) damages resulting from the substitute purchases. Apart from these remedies, Section 2–106 (4) of the U.C.C. adds the remedy of "cancellation": " 'Cancellation' occurs when either party puts an end to the contract for breach by the other and its effect is the same as that of "termination" except that the canceling party also retains any remedy for breach of the whole contract or any unperformed balance."[17]

Which of the above remedies require judicial intervention and which do not?

When Díez Picazo and Gullón refer to resolution as a remedy, do they include in this remedy the following situations? 1) Seller "X" affected by buyer "B's" non-performance decides to resell the goods previously sold but undelivered to B to a third party "C." After this resale, X claims from B payment of the difference in the price from the original price of sale and that of the sale to C, and assuming that this price is lower than the original price of sale, then he claims the difference in price plus interest for the time of sale until its collection; or 2) Seller "A" affected by buyer "B's" non-performance determines the market price of the sold good at the time of breach and then claims payment to B for the difference between the price of a hypothetical sale at the time of breach and the contractual price plus interest. If these situations are not considered as part of the Spanish concept of resolution, are they likely to be included under the same remedy in the Spanish and Latin American remedial systems?

§ 29.5 ANTICIPATORY REPUDIATION UNDER SPANISH LAW: SPANISH DECISION NO. 7491, OCTOBER 20, 1994[18]

DECISION of OCTOBER 20, 1994, Civil Decision 7491. The Supreme Court orders dismissal of the appeal.

By: Honorable Mr. D. Gumersindo Burgos Pérez de Andrade

---

[15] LUIS DÍEZ PICAZO & ANTONIO GULLÓN, 2 SISTEMA DE DERECHO CIVIL 102–04 (9th ed. 2001) (translation by author).

[16] *See* U.C.C. § 2–302 (2012).

[17] *Id.* § 2–106(4).

[18] S.T.S., Oct. 20, 1994 (R.J., No. 7491) (Spain).

POINTS OF LAW AND AUTHORITIES

FIRST—This appeal was brought before the court on the basis of three arguments; the first two were made . . . under former Section 4, Article 1692 of the Law of Civil Procedure (*Ley de Enjuiciamiento Civil*), and were dismissed in the proceedings below because they did not fall within the scope of said Section; therefore all allegations were reduced to the alleged violation of Article 1124 of the Civil Code . . . According to the appellant, this provision allows him to unilaterally terminate reciprocal obligations when one of the parties believes that the other party has stopped performing as stipulated, even when the latter believes otherwise and opposes the intended resolution—or, in other words, the unilateral will of a party in a reciprocal obligation is sufficient to declare the resolution of an obligation, rendering judicial intervention unnecessary, despite the argument of the other party.

This position, if accepted, would render unnecessary the provision of Article 1256 of the said code, leaving all contractual dealing without substance, because the mere opinion of one of the parties would be enough to breach any agreement, alleging as an excuse that the other party has not performed as agreed. The right to the resolution of obligations is implicit in all reciprocal obligations, but only Courts have the right to order such resolution upon the claim of a party against the opposition of the other; and this order will only be granted based on the following evidence: non-performance of the defendant and the full performance by the plaintiff. Case law is vast and unanimous in this issue, . . . holding that the declaration of resolution enclosed in a telegram dated August 21, 1987 was not accepted by the plaintiff, who opposed it through notarial summons on August 28 of that same year, and through the filing for injunctive relief on the following month of September, which resulted in a favorable decision on November 21, 1987.

The document dated December 19, 1987, in which repossession was agreed, did not include the waiver that the appellant was seeking, but rather the complete opposite. And never has the appellant correctly proven the alleged non-performance of the other party; furthermore, the opposite of that is presumed . . .

For all the previous reasons, the only allegation that was admitted to this process is dismissed, thus dismissing the entire appeal and costs are on the appellant . . . and the deposit granted forfeited . . .

COMMENTS

As with Article 376 of the Mexican Commercial Code, in order to obtain the resolution of a contract for non-performance, the plaintiff in this case must show that he has fully performed. Additionally, Spanish courts hold that such a decision can only be granted by the courts themselves, meaning that the aggrieved party cannot extrajudicially terminate the contract. Can you see how this remedy is an outgrowth of the static ceremonial native of civil contracts? How much influence does Article 1124 of the Spanish Civil Code have on the availability of this remedy not only in Spain but in Latin American nations such as Mexico.[19]

> Article 1124: The right to the resolution of obligations is implicit in all reciprocal obligations where one of the parties does not perform what is stipulated.

[19] *See generally* Headrick, *supra* note 5.

> The aggrieved party may choose to claim specific performance or resolution of the obligation, with damages and interest in both cases. Even after the aggrieved party has chosen specific performance, if performance becomes impossible, he may also claim resolution. . . .[20]

According to the Spanish Supreme Court, the only way to interpret this provision is by denying the possibility of extrajudicial resolution; if not, then it would be: "[[L]eaving all contractual dealing without substance,] because the unilateral opinion of one of the bound parties would suffice to leave unfulfilled any agreement, with the pretextual argument that the counterparty has incurred in breach of contract."[21]

What is the basis used by the Supreme Court in order to affirm that if extrajudicial resolution is allowed, it would "leav[e] all contractual dealing without substance"? Is this argument of an empirical or a dogmatic nature? If it were empirical, then this affirmation obviously disregards the day-to-day contractual life in Germany, Italy, the U.S. and other countries. If it were dogmatic, what is the dogma that supports it? Would it be the judicial monopoly over all contractual non-performance disputes? If so, why aren't the following commercial legal institutions considered illegal? Bankers' set-offs of reciprocal debts in clearing houses or with amounts on deposit by their customers; or the right to retain possession of assets granted to carriers, innkeepers and other suppliers of services when their clients fail to pay for their services—a right that presupposes a prior unilateral resolution of the contract by the obligee. Finally, one has to question the assumption made by the Supreme Court in its analysis of the contracting parties' conduct. Did it assume the contracting parties' good or bad faith? Did it assume the aggrieved party's bad faith?

§ 29.6 EXTRAJUDICIAL RESOLUTION UNDER MEXICAN CASE LAW[22]

Number 1637, February 13, 1964

Plaintiff: Pedro J. González

Opinion by: Minister Agustín Mercado Alarcón

If the defendant executes a contract agreeing to transfer a piece of land to the state government and then transfers it to a private party, the defendant will be criminally guilty of embezzlement. He is not excused from such a crime by alleging that he acted the way he did because the state government did not perform according to the draft of the contract and that he does not consider himself bound to such a document, and for this reason he transferred the land at issue to another party.

The fact that the state government as an entity and acting in its private capacity did not perform its contractual obligations does not give the defendant the right to consider the contract as terminated, nor does it allow him to transfer the rights at issue. The defendant has the right to file the corresponding claim before a judicial authority in order to obtain the termination or the non-performance of the contract; therefore, until the time a court decision is granted, the defendant-seller has no right to transfer the piece of land to another person. Even when in the contract it was established that it was a "draft of the contract," from its wording and the fact that it is

---

[20] C.C. (SPAIN) art. 1124 (1889) (translation by author).

[21] S.T.S., Oct. 20, 1994 (R.J., No. 7491) (Spain) (translated by author).

[22] Pedro J. Gonzales, Tribunales Colegiados de Circuito [TCC] [Collegiate Circuit Court], Semanario Judicial de la Federación, Sexto Época, tomo LXXX, febrero de 1964, tesis 1637/63 (Mex.).

not subject to any subsequent approval by the defendant or any other party, it is hence clear that it is not a draft but the contract itself.

The fact that the contract was not recorded at the Real Property Public Registry only means that it has no effects against third parties; the contract binds the parties to perform in accordance with the provision of Article 3003 of the Civil Code of the State of Baja California. Finally, with regard to the defect of its form in that the contract was not granted in a public deed, this does not mean that the contract is null and void, but rather that it grants the parties the right to claim to the other that the contract be granted in a public deed, without diminishing the rights and obligations stipulated therein.

COMMENTS

Mexican law and other civil-law jurisdictions allow contractual clauses that expressly terminate the agreement upon the happening of certain acts or events. In principle, this clause should bring about a unilateral termination of a contract upon non-performance of a party. However, decisional law is far from unanimous among Mexican state courts; one state supreme court may hold that the clause is self-executing and does not require a judicial order, while another may state that it does not matter if the contract allows the parties to rescind the contract under certain circumstances, because there is always the need for judicial intervention.

The following decision by another Mexican appellate court illustrates how, in some cases, judicial intervention would in the opinion of this court not be required:

> In accordance with the provision of Article 1949 of the Civil Code of the State of Guerrero . . . the right to terminate is implicit in reciprocal obligations, where one of the parties does not perform what is stipulated; that is why the *doctrine refers to this right to resolution as an implied pactum commissorium, because it is implied and understood as part of bilateral contracts. However, there is also an express pactum commissorium, where the parties stipulate this right as part of the contractual covenants and it is considered legal,* because, according to Articles 1832 and 1839 of the cited civil code, in matters of contracts the will of the parties is the supreme law, because they can include the covenants that they deem convenient, apart from the fact that in civil contracts each party binds itself to the terms and conditions that it intended to be bound to. Following this line of thought, contrary to what happens with the implied *pactum commissorium*, in the case of an express clause of resolution the contract can be resolved or automatically terminated by the mere non-performance of one of the parties; *i.e.*, by the fact that in practice some of the stipulated causes for rescission can be updated without requiring court intervention to that effect; in other words, as a result of the express *pactum commissorium*, the contracting parties have the right to rescind the contract by and before themselves where one of the parties has failed to perform their contractual obligations. Second Collegiate Court of the Twenty First Circuit.[23]

Compare the following decision by Mexico's Second Collegiate Court of the Seventeenth Circuit:

---

[23] Tribunales Colegiados de Circuito [TCC] [Collegiate Circuit Court], Semanario Judicial de la Federación, Octava Época, tomo XIII, Marzo de (undated) Pagina 413 (Mex.) (emphasis added).

> Articles 1745 to 1751 and 1684 to 1691 of the Civil Code of the State of Chihuahua do not imply that the *pactum commissorium* has the effect of allowing the contracting parties to unilaterally rescind the contract upon non-performance; instead, they require that a judicial authority determine if the rescission of the contract is adequate or not. Second Collegiate Court of the Seventeenth Circuit.[24]

§ 29.7 THE *NACHFRIST* IN GERMAN CASE LAW

Section 326 of the BGB, in effect until the 2002 amendments of the BGB,[25] influenced the drafting of Articles 48 and 49 et. al. of the CISG and Article 7.3.1 of the UNIDROIT Principles and were applied in the following decisions by German appellate courts. Its 2002 amendment will be transcribed thereafter.

Section 326 of the BGB:

> If, in the case of a mutual contract, one party is in default in performing, the other party may give him a reasonable period within which to perform his part with a declaration that he will refuse to accept the performance after the expiration of the period. After the expiration of the period he is entitled to demand compensation for non-performance, or to withdraw from the contract, if the performance has not been made in due time; the claim for performance is barred. If the performance is only partly made before the expiration of the period, the provision of § 325 (1) sent. 2 applies *mutatis mutandis*. If, in consequence of the default, the performance of the contract is of no use to the other party, such other party has the rights specified in (1) without giving any period.[26]

A. ***Bundesgerichtshof*, October 30, 1991—VIII ZR 9–91**[27]

FACTS

On March 29, 1989, plaintiff bought from defendant (a car and yacht dealer) a yacht and a trailer for DM 42,500. Plaintiff knew that defendant had to import the yacht from the U.S. According to the sales contract, defendant had to deliver the yacht in eight to ten weeks. Ultimately, defendant was able to deliver the yacht on August 5, 1989; defendant had delivered the trailer in July 1989. Also on March 29, 1989 plaintiff authorized defendant to sell his car for at least DM 65,000. Plaintiff paid defendant the

---

[24] Tribunales Colegiados de Circuito [TCC] [Collegiate Circuit Court], Semanario Judicial de la Federación, Octava Época, tomo V (undated) Pagina 435 (Mex.).

[25] GERMAN CIVIL CODE—BÜRGERLICHES GESETZBUCH, http://www.iuscomp.org/gla/statutes/BGB.htm (last visited Oct. 31, 2013). This source explains:

> When the Act to Modernise the Law of Obligations *(Schuldrechtsmodernisierungsgesetz)* entered into force on 1 January 2002, this marked the most sweeping reform of the German Civil Code or *Bürgerliches Gesetzbuch* since it was enacted on 1 January 1900. The following is a bilingual edition of those provisions of the BGB's Book 1 (General Part) and Book 2 (Law of Obligations) which are affected by the reform. Some unaltered provisions were added to this translation for context, whereas some minor alterations to less central provisions are only mentioned as such without having been reproduced. The English translation by Geoffrey Thomas and Gerhard Dannemann was made possible through the generous support of the Zeit-Stiftung Ebelin und Gerd Bucerius.

Id.

[26] *Id.* § 326.

[27] Translation by Susana-Jacqueline Butler, Esq.

difference between the purchase price of the yacht and the price for the car, namely DM 22,500, on March 30, 1989. On July 26, 1989, plaintiff told defendant that he had revoked the sales contract of the yacht because he had not received any notice when the yacht would be delivered.

Plaintiff argued that he was entitled to terminate the contract because defendant had told him several times before that he was not going to be able to determine when he would be able to deliver the yacht. He further argued that defendant knew that he, the plaintiff, intended to use the yacht for a family vacation in July 1989. Accordingly, he had told the defendant on July 13, 1989 that he should provide a yacht at least on July 20, 1989. This deadline and also several calls by plaintiff's brother-in-law until July 26, 1989 did not produce any positive results. Essentially, the plaintiff claimed reimbursement of the purchase price of DM 42,500.

REASONING AND HOLDING OF THE *BUNDESGERICHTSHOF*

The Court of Appeals (*Oberlandesgericht*) found that under Section 326 of the BGB, plaintiff was entitled to terminate the sales contract for the yacht. Thus, the defendant had the obligation to reimburse the purchase price (Sections 346 and 347 of the BGB). According to the sales contract, defendant was obliged to deliver the yacht within the first half of June 1989. At least at the beginning of July, plaintiff could have expected that defendant would inform him of a precise date of delivery. Plaintiff's reaction on July 13, 1989 had to be interpreted as a demand for delivery. Consequently, defendant was in default of delivery. With his appeal, defendant is not questioning that his obligation was due and that he was in default.

The *Bundesgerichtshof* pointed out that a further requirement for a lawful revocation of a sales contract, and consequently for reimbursement or damages to the revoking party under Section 326 Abs. 1 of the BGB, is that the obligee grants the obligor an additional period ("*Nachfrist*")[28] to perform his obligations. In combination with this period, the obligee also has to warn that he will reject the performance after the granted period lapses.

The Court of Appeals ruled that in the case at bar, plaintiff did not have to comply with this requirement because the defendant refused several times to name a precise date of delivery. According to the *Oberlandesgericht*, the grant of an additional period to perform would not have changed the situation because defendant did not know when his supplier in the U.S. could deliver the yacht to him. Thus, plaintiff must have been allowed to clarify the situation by revoking the contract without a *Nachfrist*. It would have been unfair to plaintiff if defendant were still entitled to deliver the yacht even after plaintiff's vacation had started.

The *Bundesgerichtshof* stated that this finding of the *Oberlandesgericht* was erroneous because plaintiff had to comply with all of the requirements of Section 326 Abs. 1 of the BGB. Thus, he should have granted defendant an additional period to perform and stated that after the lapse of this period he would reject the performance. Only if defendant had refused to perform in due time or within a suggested reasonable time would the additional period not have been required. Under those circumstances, the grant of an additional period to perform makes no sense because the obligor does not need a second chance to perform. In such a case, the obligee would have the rights

---

[28] *See* Glossary, "*Nachfrist*" for its latest legislative formulation in § 321 of the BGB.

under Section 326 Abs. 1 of the BGB, without granting an additional time, to revoke the contract (with reimbursement) or to claim damages for non-performance.

In the instant case, defendant did not refuse to perform. He did not even refuse to inform of the date of delivery. He simply said that he was not able to answer this question due to his own lack of information as to when his supplier in the U.S. would deliver. The *Bundesgerichtshof* stated that there could be one other reason why plaintiff might not have been required to grant a *Nachfrist* which the *Oberlandesgericht* failed to examine: where delivery of the yacht was made after plaintiff's vacation, when it would no longer be of interest to him.

The case was remanded.

COMMENTS AND QUESTIONS

In this case, the Court of Appeals interpreted that Section 326 of the BGB would apply only if there were no anticipatory repudiation, as it is known under the U.C.C. In other words, it is not required that a party allow for an additional time period to perform if the other party has unequivocally shown his repudiation of the contract, and the aggrieved party wants to suspend performance of his own obligations and proceed as if the other party had breached. However, according to the German Supreme Court, the BGB requires previous notice and an additional time period to perform, even when there are signs of possible repudiation of the contract. It would be useful to determine how the *Nachfrist* is formulated under the United Nations Convention on Contracts for the CISG. Is its regulation similar to that of the above German decision, or is it more similar to the U.C.C.'s anticipatory repudiation? How is this legal concept regulated under the UNIDROIT Principles and the European Principles for Contracting?

B. *Bundesgerichtshof*, December 12, 1985—VIII ZR 47–85[29]

FACTS

Defendant-seller was a car dealer in Vienna. Defendant entered into a sales contract for a sailing ship with Plaintiff-buyer. The sailing ship was to be delivered from Duesseldorf, Germany to Hamburg, Germany. Part of the conditions of the contract were defendant's "General Terms and Conditions of Trade or Business" (*Allgemeine Geschaeftsbedingungen*), which established that defendant would be entitled to twenty-five percent of the sale price as flat rate damages if the plaintiff terminated the contract without justification.

After entering into the contract, plaintiff and defendant had discussions pertaining to several contractual conditions and the sailing ship. The parties reached an agreement on the date for delivery in Hamburg. Plaintiff-buyer traveled to Hamburg with his legal counsel. First, he noticed that the interior of the ship had a different color than the one they had agreed on. Second, he saw a sign in the same ship he already bought offering it for sale. Plaintiff told defendant that he was terminating the sales contract, and his counsel confirmed this in a letter. Defendant's counsel responded that defendant was not accepting such termination and that he intended to claim damages. Plaintiff's counsel answered that plaintiff was upholding his decision to terminate the contract. Defendant then sold the sailing ship to a third party and reimbursed DM 40,950 for plaintiff's down payment, keeping the remaining amount of

[29] Translation by Susana-Jacqueline Butler, Esq.

DM 43,549.50. He considered that DM 42,250 was equivalent to the twenty-five percent flat rate damages that he was entitled to according to the contract and that he was also entitled to DM 1,299.50 in additional damages for his attorney's fee.

REASONING AND HOLDING OF THE *BUNDESGERICHTSHOF*

The *Bundesgerichtshof* found that plaintiff's termination of the contract was unjustified. Termination of the contract was not justified by the fact that at the time of delivery in Hamburg the color of the ship was different than what was agreed on—and plaintiff had not allowed the defendant to modify the color. However, this did not give defendant the right to the flat-rate damages stipulated in the contract. Because both plaintiff and defendant were merchants, the statute that governs the General Conditions of Trade (*Gesetz ueber die Allgemeinen Geschaeftsbedingungen* (AGBG) and *Allgemeine Geschaeftsbedingungen* (AGB) respectively) is only applicable with the least degree of strict scrutiny for merchants under Section 24 of the AGBG. But even under this less strict standard, a merchant is not allowed to use the AGBG which generally entitles him to damages without a previous grant of an additional time period to perform (*Nachfristsetzung*). For this reason . . . defendant's AGBG is void, and the defendant is not entitled to the flat-rate damages.

The *Bundesgerichtshof* remanded the case to the Court of Appeals to determine if there might be other provisions of the law that enable defendant to recover damages.

COMMENTS AND QUESTIONS

It is understood from this case that the requirement of a prior notice may be waived or voided among merchants or participants in the same sector or market, and that a flat rate for damages can be stipulated in the contract. However, the court does not appear eager to make a broad definition of the concept of merchants of the same sector or market. In this case, a car dealer is not in the same sector or market as a seller of sailing ships; yet they were both merchants and thus it was possible to argue that in accordance with Section 24 of the AGBG a less strict standard could be applied (this section assumes that the parties are informed). The plaintiff should have granted the *Nachfrist* to the defendant.

Could it be understood that the *Nachfrist* is a middle-ground between the extrajudicial resolution for anticipatory repudiation under U.S. law and the Mexican judicial resolution, as it was held in the case of Pedro J. Gonzalez? Is there any similar concept regulated under the reader's legal system? Is it found in case law, customs, or under the general terms and conditions of contracting? During one of our class discussions a German lawyer compared the *Nachfrist* and the U.C.C.'s extrajudicial resolution for anticipatory repudiation as follows:

> The concept of the *Nachfrist* seems to have a fundamentally different orientation than that of the U.C.C. Its purpose is to protect both the obligor and obligee; for this reason it requires an additional period to perform. The U.C.C., on the other hand, seems more oriented to protect the obligee, using a standard [of notice even] less strict than that of the *Nachfrist*, and allowing for a declaration of non-performance at an earlier stage. The *Nachfrist* also protects the obligor in other ways, apart from allowing him additional time to

perform. German law requires that the obligee who wants to terminate a contract must communicate its intentions with time in advance . . .[30]

Does the U.C.C. require the granting of an additional period of performance in addition to the notice of termination? What is the significance of this requirement?

The present-day version of the *Nachfrist* is found in Section 323 of the BGB.

C. BGB Section 323

Withdrawal for nonperformance or for performance not in conformity with the contract:

(1) If, in the case of a reciprocal contract, the obligor does not render an act of performance which is due, or does not render it in conformity with the contract, then the obligee may withdraw from the contract, if he has specified, without result, an additional period for performance or cure.

(2) The specification of a period of time can be dispensed with if

1. the obligor seriously and definitively refuses performance,

2. the obligor does not render performance by a date specified in the contract or within a specific period and the obligee, in the contract, has made the continuation of his interest in performance subject to performance being rendered in good time, or

3. there are special circumstances which, when the interests of both parties are weighed, justify immediate revocation.

(3) If the nature of the breach of duty is such that setting a period of time is out of the question, a warning notice is given instead.

(4) The obligee may revoke the contract before performance is due if it is obvious that the requirements for revocation will be met.

(5) If the obligor has performed in part, the obligee may revokethe whole contract only if he has no interest in part performance. If the obligor has not performed in conformity with the contract, the obligee may not revoke the contract if the breach of duty is trivial.

(6) Revocation is excluded if the obligee is solely or very predominantly responsible for the circumstance that would entitle him to revoke the contract or if the circumstance for which the obligor is not responsible occurs at a time when the obligee is in default of acceptance.[31]

§ 29.8 CONTEMPORARY VARIANTS OF EXTRAJUDICIAL TERMINATION REMEDIES

The following are contemporary variants of extra judicial termination remedies prompted by the breach or default of borrowers in loans secured by commercial assets (also known as secured transactions or asset based loans, or (in Spanish) as *prestamos con garantias mobiliarias*). As shown by a study of the Central Bank of Brazil, as well

[30] Susana-Jacqueline Butler, Materials for the Comparative Commercial Law Course—Spring 2000 (2000) (unpublished manuscript) (on file with author) (translated by author).

[31] GERMAN CIVIL CODE—BÜRGERLICHES GESETZBUCH, *supra* note 25, § 323.

as other economic studies, the cost of the uncertainty of collection subject to the prevailing judicial procedures accounts for at least one third of the amount of interest rates of commercial loans in that country.[32]

A. U.C.C. Section 9–609 Secured Party's Right to Take Possession After Default[33]

(a) [Possession; rendering equipment unusable; disposition on debtor's premises.] After default, a secured party:

(1) may take possession of the collateral; and

(2) without removal, may render equipment unusable and dispose of collateral on a debtor's premises under Section 9–610.

(b) [Judicial and nonjudicial process.]

A secured party may proceed under subsection (a):

(1) pursuant to judicial process; or

(2) without judicial process, if it proceeds without breach of the peace.

(c) [Assembly of collateral.]

If so agreed, and in any event after default, a secured party may require the debtor to assemble the collateral and make it available to the secured party at a place to be designated by the secured party which is reasonably convenient to both parties.

B. OAS Model Law of 2002[34]

Article 61. At any time, before or during the enforcement proceeding, the debtor may reach an agreement with the creditor on terms other than those previously established, either for the delivery or repossession of the goods, the terms of the sale or auction, or any other matter; this agreement will be obligatory, provided that said agreement does not affect other secured creditors or buyers in the ordinary course of business.

Article 62. In any event, the debtor will retain the right to claim damages for the abuse of his rights by the creditor.

C. Guatemalan Decree Number 51–2007[35]

Article 65. Voluntary enforcement. The secured creditor and secured debtor may agree in the security agreement or at any time, before or during the judicial enforcement proceedure established in this law, that the enforcement against the collateral be performed privately under the terms and conditions that they may freely agree on.

---

[32] Kozolchyk & Furnish, *A Comparative Analysis,* at 242.

[33] U.C.C. § 9–609 (2012).

[34] Organization of American States [OAS], *Model Inter-American Law on Secured Transactions,* Final Act, 3(F), *adopted at the Sixth Inter-American Specialized Conference on Private International Law (CIDIP-VI),* (Feb. 8, 2002).

[35] Decreto No. 51–2007 [Decree Number 51–2007] Diario Oficial [DO], 16 de noviembre de 2007 (Guatemala), *available at* http://natlaw.com/natlaw-world/.

They may agree on the delivery and repossession of the collateral, the form and conditions of sale or auction, and any other matter, provided that they do not infringe the parties' and third parties' constitutional rights.

In case of chattel mortgage bonds and guarantee trusts, the parties may agree that enforcement be done in accordance with the Law of Warehouses and the Code of Commerce, as the case may be.

Article 66. Secured debtor's right. In any event, the secured debtor will retain the right to claim damages for the abuse of rights by the secured creditor.

D. Honduran Law of Secured Transactions of February 24, 2008[36]

Article 57. General Principles on Enforcement. Enforcement of security interests will be conducted based on the following general principles:

1. Enforcement will always be conducted on an extrajudicial basis by means of a public auction before a notary public, in compliance with the provisions of this Law and, in a subsidiary manner, with those of the Notarial Code.

2. Notwithstanding the preceding provision, the secured creditor may directly take possession of the collateral when he has a right of retention derived by law or created by contract. The same right will be available when the collateral has an agreed-upon value under twenty minimum wages at the highest end of the scale, or upon an agreement for the resolution of a contractual obligation that expressly allows it.

3. Judicial intervention may only be requested in those cases where it has been agreed that enforcement will take place before a judge or when the obligation attempted to be extrajudicially enforced has already been paid by the secured debtor, that the secured debtor has defense based on forgery of its signature or on the alteration of the documents text, in these cases a summary trial shall be followed.

The conditions pursuant to which enforcement shall be conducted will be determined in the agreement that creates the security interest. Such conditions shall be used as a guide by the judge or notary for purposes of the auction of the security interests.

J. Extra Judicial Remedies Among Correspondent Letter of Credit Banks

E. UCP 500 Sub Article 14d[37]

i. If the Issuing Bank and/or Confirming Bank, if any, or a Nominated Bank acting on their behalf, decides to refuse the documents, it must give notice to that effect by telecommunication or, if that is not possible, by other expeditious means, without delay but no later than the close of the seventh banking day following the day of receipt of the documents. Such notice shall be given to the bank from which it received the documents or to the Beneficiary, if it received the documents directly from him.

---

[36] Decreto No. 182–2009 [Decree No. 182–2009], Diario Oficial [DO], 28 de enero del 2010 (Honduras), *available at* http://www.garantiasmobiliarias.hn/ley.pdf.

[37] *See* INT'L CHAMBER OF COMMERCE, UNIFORM CUSTOMS AND PRACTICE FOR DOCUMENTARY CREDITS [UCP] No. 500 sub-art. 14(d)(i–iii) (1993).

ii. Such notice must state all discrepancies in respect of which the bank refuses the documents and must also state whether it is holding the documents at the disposal of, or is returning them to, the presenter.

iii. The Issuing Bank and/or Confirming Bank, if any, shall then be entitled to claim from the remitting bank refund, with interest, of any reimbursement which has been made to that bank.

F. UCP 500 Sub-Article 14e[38]

If the Issuing Bank and/or Confirming Bank, if any, fails to act in accordance with the provisions of this Article and/or fails to hold the documents at the disposal of, or return them to the presenter, the Issuing Bank and/or Confirming Bank, if any, *shall be precluded from claiming that the documents are not in compliance with the terms and conditions of the Credit.*[39]

§ 29.9 CONCLUSION

An aggrieved party's right to terminate commercial contracts quickly and extrajudicially is a necessity of a marketplace that places a premium on the contracting parties' ability to compete. But please notice that at root the justification of a unilateral termination by an aggrieved commercial party is the opposite of a breach of contract by Justice Holmes' "bad man" or Judge Posner's economic rational man: It is not to allow the breaching party to reduce his losses but to minimize the accumulation of transactional damages and wasted social resources that would occur when the aggrieved innocent party must (in some jurisdictions) quixotically, as it were, perform his side of the bargain (even though the other party has breached) and then sue for damages the party in breach. The justification for this course of action is also to increase the competiveness of regular and *bona fide* participants in the marketplace by allowing them to participate more quickly in another possibly profitable transaction, whether it is by reselling what was not bought or repurchasing what was not sold.

The tendency to grant to aggrieved parties the right to terminate contracts and other commercial relations is also a result of the need to provide finality to transactions and courses of dealings that could not exist without them. Consider, for example, the finality of an extrajudicial set off between a bank and its client depositor. Both the bank and its depositor are better off by knowing what is the net amount owed to each other, so that they can invest it or enter into another banking or commercial transaction as quickly as possible. Add to the amount involved in a two party set off, the amounts accumulated by countless banks involved when clearing their respective debits and credits at the end of each banking day in a city, region, country or group of countries. Can you visualize the economic costs of having courts of law approve or reject the set offs that take place among the participants to a clearing house? The longer it takes to know what each entity can dispose of or pay, the costlier its business cycle. The same is true with the strict "preclusion" rule of the Uniform Customs and Practices for Documentary Credits sub-Article 14d, transcribed above. By being precluded to claim that documents not examined in a timely manner do not comply with the terms and conditions of the credit, the decision of the issuing or confirming

---

[38] *See id.* sub-art. 14(e).

[39] *Id.* (emphasis added.) *See supra* § 24:6(F) for a discussion on the importance of this remedy.

bank becomes final and the equivalent of payment. Even though it could be litigated, having agreed to be governed by such a rule, the bank that breached it will not be likely to succeed and most often than not, do what a colorful New York bank lawyer once referred to me as "eat the documents." It is clear that this extrajudicial remedy has saved an immeasurable amount of trips to court and dollars spent on court proceedings.

An unnamed counsel for an unnamed central bank in a developing nation once told me that such inter-bank or private party "adjudications of rights" (billions of which take place each banking day) deprived objecting banks and parties of their due process of law. My reply was that what he described as a deprivation of due process in the clearing and set off procedures was, at worst, a temporary deficit in claimant's credit column that if proven could be adjusted during the next clearing day. The same argument applies to the breaching party who believes that the resale or repurchase by the aggrieved party resulted in him having to pay more damages. For in our day, it would be rare to find a legal system that did not grant such a party an action for, in ascending scale of gravity, 1) an accounting; 2) damages; 3) unjust enrichment; 4) fraud or abuse of rights if the facts warranted them. So the problem of extrajudicial adjudication is not due process but the competitive consequences of its absence.

Chapter 30

DAMAGES FOR BREACH OF WARRANTY IN U.S. ECONOMIC ANALYSIS INFLUENCED LAW

§ 30.1 BASIC NOTIONS OF U.S. LAW ON THE RECOVERY OF DAMAGES

The *American Bronze* decision, discussed in the previous chapter, illustrates the diversity and flexibility of remedies in Article 2 of the U.C.C. for the recovery of damages caused by the breach of sale agreements. The remedies for sellers and buyers are set forth in parallel and symmetrical fashion, with the exception of the buyer's remedy for the seller's breach of an express or implied warranty which for obvious transactional reasons has no counterpart seller's remedy. Can you see why? Most importantly from a comparative standpoint-it allows for the unilateral termination of the contract by the victim of an anticipatory repudiation by the counter-party, a remedy unavailable to this day under the Spanish and Spanish influenced codes as was also discussed in the preceding chapter.

In connection with this unilateral termination, Article 2 sets forth two sets of remedies: the first relies on an actual purchase or sale (depending upon who is the aggrieved party) and the second on a hypothetical purchase or sale (also depending upon who is the aggrieved party).

The third remedy is judicial and subsidiary in nature: it is available to the party who can prove in court that, having chosen the remedy of resale or re-purchase, the recovery fell short of what he would have recovered had the defendant fully performed his contractual obligations. The fourth remedy is also judicial and also provides damages but is only available to buyers who can prove the seller's breach of the express or implied contractual warranties provided by the U.C.C.

As will become apparent throughout this chapter, the aggrieved party's power to terminate contracts extra judicially is at the root of the variety and flexibility of remedies found in the U.C.C. and United States case law. The following provisions on actual and hypothetical resales and re-purchases or covers as well as on the action for the price and for breach of warranty are transcribed to facilitate the subsequent discussion of their meaning in case law and commentary. The reader is encouraged to return to them during the ensuing discussion

A. Actual Resales

According to § 2–706 (1), the first remedy available to the seller allows him to recover the difference between the contract price and the resale price of the goods in an actual, substitute sale.

§ 2–706. Seller's Resale Including Contract for Resale.

(1) Under the conditions stated in Section 2–703 on seller's remedies, the seller may resell the goods concerned or the undelivered balance thereof. Where the resale is made in good faith and in a commercially reasonable manner the seller may recover the difference between the resale price and the contract price together with any incidental damages allowed under the provisions of this Article (Section 2–710), but less expenses saved in consequence of the buyer's breach.

(2) Except as otherwise provided in subsection (3) or unless otherwise agreed resale may be at public or private sale including sale by way of one or more contracts to sell or of identification to an existing contract of the seller. Sale may be as a unit or in parcels and at any time and place and on any terms but every aspect of the sale including the method, manner, time, place and terms must be commercially reasonable. The resale must be reasonably identified as referring to the broken contract, but it is not necessary that the goods be in existence or that any or all of them have been identified to the contract before the breach.

(3) Where the resale is at private sale the seller must give the buyer reasonable notification of his intention to resell.

(4) Where the resale is at public sale

(a) only identified goods can be sold except where there is a recognized market for a public sale of futures in goods of the kind; and

(b) it must be made at a usual place or market for public sale if one is reasonably available and except in the case of goods which are perishable or threaten to decline in value speedily the seller must give the buyer reasonable notice of the time and place of the resale; and

(c) if the goods are not to be within the view of those attending the sale the notification of sale must state the place where the goods are located and provide for their reasonable inspection by prospective bidders; and

(d) the seller may buy.

(5) A purchaser who buys in good faith at a resale takes the goods free of any rights of the original buyer even though the seller fails to comply with one or more of the requirements of this section.[1]

B. Hypothetical Resales

If § 2–706 requires an effectively executed resale of the goods by the aggrieved seller, § 2–708 gives the seller the option to hypothetically resell and calculate damages as if he would have actually resold the goods.[2] Therefore, under this provision the seller has the right to recover the difference between the contractual price and the market price he would have received if the goods were sold in due contractual time and place. Additionally, this formula allows the seller to suspend production of the contractual goods.

---

[1] U.C.C. § 2–706(1) (2011).

[2] *Id.* § 2–708.

§ 2–708. Seller's Damages for Non-acceptance or Repudiation.

(1) Subject to subsection (2) and to the provisions of this Article with respect to proof of market price (Section 2–723), the measure of damages for non-acceptance or repudiation by the buyer is the difference between the market price at the time and place for tender and the unpaid contract price together with any incidental damages provided in this Article (Section 2–710), but less expenses saved in consequence of the buyer's breach.[3]

As we mentioned earlier, the third formula is subsidiary to the one discussed above; it pertains to the profits that the seller would have received according to § 2–708(2). As a subsidiary remedy it can only be used if the formula of § 2–708(1) fails to put the seller in a similar position to that in which he would have been had the contract been performed as originally agreed.

§ 2–708. Seller's Damages for Non-acceptance or Repudiation.

(2) If the measure of damages provided in subsection (1) is inadequate to put the seller in as good a position as performance would have done then the measure of damages is the profit (including reasonable overhead) which the seller would have made from full performance by the buyer, together with any incidental damages provided in this Article (Section 2–710), due allowance for costs reasonably incurred and due credit for payments or proceeds of resale.[4]

The consequences of this rule for the recovery of damages for lost profits as a loss volume seller will be discussed in a later section. Finally, under certain circumstances § 2–709 grants the seller payment of the full contractual price.

C. Specific Performance and the Seller's Action to Recover the Price

§ 2–709. Action for the Price.

(1) When the buyer fails to pay the price as it becomes due the seller may recover, together with any incidental damages under the next section, the price

(a) of goods accepted or of conforming goods lost or damaged within a commercially reasonable time after risk of their loss has passed to the buyer; and

(b) of goods identified to the contract if the seller is unable after reasonable effort to resell them at a reasonable price or the circumstances reasonably indicate that such effort will be unavailing.[5]

Depending on the remedy chosen by the seller and the circumstances of each case of non-performance, the measurement of damages based on the previous formulas may be substantially different. It should also be pointed out that the remedies provided to the seller in the previous rules are also granted in a parallel, yet not symmetrical, way to aggrieved buyers as follows:

---

[3] *Id.* § 2–708(1).

[4] *Id.* § 2–708(2).

[5] *Id.* § 2–709(1).

D. The Buyer's Action for Cover

§ 2–712. "Cover"; Buyer's Procurement of Substitute Goods.

(1) After a breach within the preceding section the buyer may "cover" by making in good faith and without unreasonable delay any reasonable purchase of or contract to purchase goods in substitution for those due from the seller.

(2) The buyer may recover from the seller as damages the difference between the cost of cover and the contract price together with any incidental or consequential damages as hereinafter defined (Section 2–715), but less expenses saved in consequence of the seller's breach.

(3) Failure of the buyer to effect cover within this section does not bar him from any other remedy.[6]

E. Buyer's Damages from a Hypothetical Re-Purchase

§ 2–713. Buyer's Damages for Non-Delivery or Repudiation.

(1) Subject to the provisions of this Article with respect to proof of market price (Section 2–723), the measure of damages for non-delivery or repudiation by the seller is the difference between the market price at the time when the buyer learned of the breach and the contract price together with any incidental and consequential damages provided in this Article (Section 2–715), but less expenses saved in consequence of the seller's breach.

(2) Market price is to be determined as of the place for tender or, in cases of rejection after arrival or revocation of acceptance, as of the place of arrival.[7]

F. Buyer's Action for Breach of Warranty

§ 2–714. Buyer's Damages for Breach in Regard to Accepted Goods.

(1) Where the buyer has accepted goods and given notification (subsection (3) of Section 2–607) he may recover as damages for any non-conformity of tender the loss resulting in the ordinary course of events from the seller's breach as determined in any manner which is reasonable.

(2) The measure of damages for breach of warranty is the difference at the time and place of acceptance between the value of the goods accepted and the value they would have had if they had been as warranted, unless special circumstances show proximate damages of a different amount.

(3) In a proper case any incidental and consequential damages under the next section may also be recovered.[8]

§ 2–716. Buyer's Right to Specific Performance or Replevin.

(1) Specific performance may be decreed where the goods are unique or in other proper circumstances.

---

[6] *Id.* § 2–712.

[7] *Id.* § 2–713.

[8] *Id.* § 2–714.

(2) The decree for specific performance may include such terms and conditions as to payment of the price, damages, or other relief as the court may deem just.[9]

§ 30.2 DAMAGES FOR NON-PERFORMANCE OF CONTRACTUAL WARRANTIES IN U.S. LAW

A. Express and Implied Warranties Under the U.C.C.

Apart from the remedies previously described, buyers also have the right to recover losses caused by defects in the quality of the purchased goods. Obviously, this remedy is available only after the seller has delivered the goods or provided the services to the buyer and, as will be discussed shortly, features idiosyncratic pleading and proof. Similarly, damages recovered because of it may be higher than those recovered from a failure to deliver the purchased goods.

The remedy for breach of warranty has a discernible component from the Anglo American law of torts, a branch of the law referred to in Spanish and Latin American jurisdictions as of "extra-contractual" or civil "delictual" liability (*responsabilidad extra-contractual* o *por delito civil).* Thus, it is not unusual under United States law that a victim from the breach of an express or implied warranty is granted damages that result both directly from the breach and indirectly from it as incidental or consequential damages.

The Official Comment 1 to § 2–313 provides a description of both types of warranties:

> 1. "Express" warranties rest on "dickered" aspects of the individual bargain, and go so clearly to the essence of that bargain that words of disclaimer in a form are repugnant to the basic dickered terms. "Implied" warranties rest so clearly on a common factual situation or set of conditions that no particular language or action is necessary to evidence them and they will arise in such a situation unless unmistakably negated.[10]

An express warranty does not require special or customary wording or language such as "this description of the product is an express warranty of its characteristics or purpose." According to the Official Comments 5 and 6 of U.C.C. § 2–313, catalogues or publications given to the buyer, containing technical specifications, blueprints, samples or models of the sold good, may be considered express warranties.[11]

There are two types of implied warranties in the U.C.C.: merchantability and fitness for a particular purpose.

§ 2–314. Implied Warranty: Merchantability; Usage of Trade.

> (1) Unless excluded or modified (Section 2–316), a warranty that the goods shall be merchantable is implied in a contract for their sale if the seller is a merchant with respect to goods of that kind. Under this section the serving

---

[9] *Id.* § 2–716(1)–(2).

[10] *Id.* § 2–313 cmt.1.

[11] *Id.* § 2–313 cmts. 5 & 6.

for value of food or drink to be consumed either on the premises or elsewhere is a sale.

(2) Goods to be merchantable must be at least such as

(a) pass without objection in the trade under the contract description; and

(b) in the case of fungible goods, are of fair average quality within the description; and

(c) are fit for the ordinary purposes for which such goods are used; and

(d) run, within the variations permitted by the agreement, of even kind, quality and quantity within each unit and among all units involved; and

(e) are adequately contained, packaged, and labeled as the agreement may require; and

(f) conform to the promise or affirmations of fact made on the container or label if any.

(3) Unless excluded or modified (Section 2–316) other implied warranties may arise from course of dealing or usage of trade.[12]

§ 2–315. Implied Warranty: Fitness for Particular Purpose.

Where the seller at the time of contracting has reason to know any particular purpose for which the goods are required and that the buyer is relying on the seller's skill or judgment to select or furnish suitable goods, there is unless excluded or modified under the next section an implied warranty that the goods shall be fit for such purpose.[13]

To summarize the main features of the aforementioned U.C.C. warranties, let us assume that I purchase a vehicle at a price paid in the market for similar vehicles and the vehicle does not do what similar vehicles do, i.e. transport me from A to B. I do not have to worry about proving to the court that the defendant-seller promised that the vehicle would provide me with transportation from A to B. All I have to allege is the breach of the implied warranty of merchantability. On the other hand, if I told the seller that I was going to participate in a car race and wanted to buy a vehicle that would enable me to compete in it and the vehicle I bought transported me from A to B but lacked the speed with which to compete in that race I could claim damages for the breach of the implied warranty of fitness for the specific purpose made known to the seller.

The recovery of damages resulting from the breach of these warranties has different legal grounds from that of breach of contract before performance is due. According to the Official Comment 13 of § 2–314:

In an action based on breach of warranty, it is of course necessary to show not only the existence of the warranty but the fact that the warranty was broken and that the breach of the warranty was the proximate cause of the loss sustained. In such an action an affirmative showing by the seller that the loss resulted from some action or event following his own delivery of the goods can

---

[12] *Id.* § 2–314 (2011).

[13] *Id.* § 2–315 (2011).

operate as a defense. Equally, evidence indicating that the seller exercised care in the manufacture, processing or selection of the goods is relevant to the issue of whether the warranty was in fact broken. Action by the buyer following an examination of the goods which ought to have indicated the defect complained of can be shown as matter bearing on whether the breach itself was the cause of the injury.[14]

Damages are measured using the criterion of what was objectively or reasonably foreseeable. Therefore, the defendant would be liable for all damages regardless of any amount previously recovered, if those damages were reasonably contemplated or foreseen by the parties as the probable result if the contract were breached. This criterion of what is foreseeable can be traced to the English decision in *Hadley v. Baxendale*, a rule still in force in common law jurisdictions.[15]

B. Historical Background of Contractual Warranties in Common Law

Independent actions for breach of express or implied warranties which are resolved on a case-by-case basis result from the diverse background of causes of action in common law contracts. Sir Roy Goode concisely and clearly restates the evolution of the remedial law of sales in common law.[16]

As will be recalled, in the historical description provided by Professor Farnsworth, common law as well as Roman law were in principle hostile to providing for an action for breach of executed performances without the *quid pro quo*. The Common law required that either the seller deliver the goods and the buyer failed to pay for them or that the buyer pay their price and receive nothing in order to grant an action for "*debt*". The absence of actions for failure to perform executory promises is explained by the fact that Medieval England was primarily agricultural. Thus, its common law did not focus on commercial sales or on sales of movable property to be paid or delivered in the future except to the extent that these things had been given to the indebted defendant.

Most of the claims for breach of commercial sales were pleaded before merchant courts referred to as Court of Piepowders or before criminal courts. The former applied rules based on commercial customs, and the latter relied on rules designed to punish those who tampered with products such as beer or wine or who used false weights and measures. With the exception of the sale of edibles and beverages by suppliers, sellers were not bound by implied warranties of quality and quantity. Generally, also, sellers had no obligation to disclose latent defects known to them, nor to expressly or impliedly warrant that they had transferred good title of property or possession of the sold goods. This absence of implied warranties was part of a legal system governed by the principle of "*caveat emptor*" or "*caveat emptoris*" (let the buyer beware).[17] The following phrase, cited by Goode, illustrates the harshness of the regime: "The buyer had eyes; let him use them, or suffer the consequences."[18]

---

[14] *Id.* § 2–314 cmt. 13.

[15] *E.g.*, Bongam v. Action Toyota, Inc., 14 F. App'x 275, 282 (4th Cir. 2001)

[16] ROY GOODE, COMMERCIAL LAW 187–94 (3d ed. 2004).

[17] *Id.* at 185.

[18] *Id.* at 184.

The remedial result was that, with very few exceptions, only expressed contractual warranties supported causes of action based on the *tort of deception*. This action would only stand if the plaintiff proved that the seller had knowingly made a false affirmation with respect to the nature, quality or title of the goods or services. However, if the affirmation could be tied to an express warranty of truthfulness, the buyer could file a claim of tort of deception without having to prove that the seller acted fraudulently or knowingly.

Even though common law courts in the XVI Century began to allow claims for breach of contractual undertakings not based on claims in tort but in *assumpsit*, it was not until 1778 that a court finally held that a claim for breach of a contractual warranty had to be filed in *assumpsit*.[19] From there, it was only a short step to holding that claims could be brought for "implied" warranties. Nevertheless, as Goode points out, the path taken for implied warranties was unnecessarily long and tortuous, largely because of the influence of real property law, its closeness to the principle of *caveat emptor* and because it was apparently easier to verify if the purchased land was productive or inhabitable.

Almost a century after the 1778 decision, *Jones v. Just* an 1868 decision, held that implied warranties in sales of goods existed where the buyer had not been able to inspect them.[20] If the buyer had inspected them, the seller was not liable for the defects even if these were latent or hidden. It was not until the end of the XIX Century that an action for breach of implied warranties was granted: 1) where the buyer had relied on the description of the goods provided by the seller, and 2) in the purchase of goods said to be fit for a particular purpose known to the seller, and in which the buyer had relied on the seller's skills and judgment to manufacture them. The judicial grant of an implied warranty against replevin or deprivation of the buyer's title did not take place until an 1864 decision.[21]

This brief historical excursus shows that, from its inception, the U.C.C. protected the commercial buyer in a broader fashion than that of the nineteenth and early twentieth century English common law. Interestingly, the broader protection of the U.C.C. started with upgrading the binding effect of the seller's description of goods in his oral or written presentation of his products. As was previously mentioned, under the U.C.C., descriptions of goods even when only included in catalogues or blueprints became *express warranties*, which the buyers could not waive even if the waiver appeared in an express clause.

Secondly, the U.C.C. eliminated the link between the inspection of the goods and the seller's liability for breach of implied warranties of the inspected goods. Regardless of inspection, implied warranties could be claimed by the buyers. Exclusion of these *implied warranties* under the U.C.C. is only effective if the seller expressly and clearly stipulates in the contract that they are excluded.

Under Anglo-American law, buyers of goods of lesser quality or quantity than those agreed upon, including those defectively manufactured, also have the right to claim damages for breach of implied warranties in actions that are largely predicated

---

[19] *Id.* at 186.

[20] *Id.* at 187.

[21] *Id.* at 188 n.37 and accompanying text.

upon the law of negligence. It is worth noting that the same legislative trend can be found in an increasing number of civil law countries.[22] Under Anglo-American law, a claim for breach of an implied warranty is allowed despite the lack of privity of contract (or absence of a direct contractual relationship) between plaintiff and defendant. Therefore, an airplane manufacturer or its main distributor may be sued for breach of warranty of merchantability by a user-buyer of the airplane that has been affected by a mechanical flaw, even though the buyer did not purchase the airplane from the manufacturer or its main distributor, but from a subsequent purchaser-user.[23]

C. Damages for Breach of Warranties; Consequential Damages in Taylor and Gaskin Inc. v. Chris Craft Industries[24]

KRUPANSKY, Circuit Judge. In this appeal the defendant-appellant Chris-Craft Industries (Chris-Craft) has challenged the district court's refusal to award Chris-Craft consequential damages which assertedly resulted from plaintiff-appellee's negligence and breach of express and implied warranties of merchantability. . . .

. . .

Sometime in mid-1970, Chris-Craft decided to produce a pleasure boat called MXA-25. As conceived, the MXA-25 design . . . [had] the fuel tank located at the stern of the craft. . . . Chris-Craft began production of a prototype MXA-25.

Chris-Craft had submitted a blueprint design for the MXA-25 fuel tank to Taylor & Gaskin. . . . Chris-Craft . . . discussed with Taylor & Gaskin the feasibility of utilizing a less expensive "slush compound tank". . . . Although Chris-Craft had used painted tanks on its diesel boats, it had never used them on gasoline engine powered boats such as the MXA-25. Further, Taylor & Gaskin had no previous experience with the then-new slush compound method of construction. Accordingly, the trial court found that Chris-Craft and Taylor & Gaskin had equal degrees of expertise with respect to the design and manufacture of slush compound fuel tanks.

. . .

Subsequently, Taylor & Gaskin offered to produce the slush compound unit at a cost which was approximately ten dollars per unit less than the hot dipped galvanized tank. Taylor & Gaskin had also obtained B.I.A. approval of the slush compound tank, which was predicated upon assurances that the tanks would be covered with 1.5 mils of paint; the B.I.A. did not, however, perform any tests to determine the corrosion resistance of painted tanks. Taylor & Gaskin covered the tanks with one coat of red enamel paint, which did provide at least a 1.5 mil thickness.

Wilkins (Taylor & Gaskin's contractor) knew that these fuel tanks would be exposed to the marine environment and, although he was unaware of Chris-Craft's intentions relative to the unique placement on the MXA-25 of the tanks, he were found to have known—prior to production—that the tanks would be unable to resist corrosion in the marine environment and were therefore not suited for marine use. Wilkins' own

---

[22] *See* Alejandro Hernandez Maestroni, *Part 1: Introduction: Overview of the Study Undertaken by the National Law Center for Inter-American Free Trade*, 20 ARIZ. J. INT'L COMP. L. 1, 14–15 (2003) (discussing briefly Chilean, Argentine, Uruguayan, and Brazilian laws).

[23] *See id.* at 18–19 (referencing different countries' laws in the late 20th century that established liability for all participants in the distribution of defective products).

[24] Taylor & Gaskin, Inc. v. Chris-Craft Indus., 732 F.2d 1273 (6th Cir. 1984).

estimate was that the tanks would last one year, two at the most. Nevertheless, Wilkins did not communicate this knowledge to Chris-Craft. . . .

Chris-Craft remained unaware of the tank's inability to withstand the marine environment when, between September 1972 and June 1973, it purchased 550 tanks from Taylor & Gaskin. Sometime in July 1973, Chris-Craft learned that the B.I.A. intended to delete the Taylor & Gaskin tank from its approved equipment list as of August 1st of that year. Upon learning of the impending change, Chris-Craft began ordering hot dipped galvanized tanks for the MXA-25. Prior notice of this change notwithstanding, Chris-Craft installed another 100 slush compound units before the B.I.A. acted to officially withdraw its approval. . . .

In April 1974, Chris-Craft received the first of numerous customer complaints regarding corrosion of the slush compound fuel tanks on the MXA-25. . . . By May 1974, Chris-Craft began to suspect that the Taylor & Gaskin fuel tanks were "built in failures". Later that month, Chris-Craft notified Taylor & Gaskin of the complaints and suggested that the two companies effect a joint recall of the slush compound tanks. Taylor & Gaskin responded that the responsibility for tank problems was on Chris-Craft and that Taylor & Gaskin would not participate in a recall effort.

. . .

On March 28, 1975, Chris-Craft initiated a voluntary recall campaign to replace the painted tanks with hot dipped galvanized units. Taylor & Gaskin responded to the recall by threatening Chris-Craft with a trade libel suit.

On June 3, 1975, Taylor & Gaskin initiated this diversity action to obtain $10,681.39 due and owing as payment for the slush compound tanks. Chris-Craft admitted the amount was unpaid and counterclaimed alleging negligence and breach of warranties. . . .

Pursuant to trial, the district court found that Taylor & Gaskin had provided Chris-Craft with express and implied warranties of merchantability. However, because Chris-Craft did not rely on Taylor & Gaskin's "expertise", and because the two companies were found to have equal levels of expertise, the district court concluded that no warranty of fitness for a particular purpose had been made by Taylor & Gaskin.

. . .

The credited testimony of Chris-Craft's expert Arthur Claess established that the tank would begin rusting at one to two months and would rust through at two years. Such evidence is sufficient to prove that the tanks were not merchantable at the time they left the control of the manufacturer, that is that they were not fit for the ordinary purpose of holding fuel in a marine environment, U.C.C. 2–314.

. . .

In arriving at its damage award, the trial court found that the value of the tanks at the time they left the manufacturer was zero; accordingly, Chris-Craft was awarded the contract price of the tanks, $25,114.58, offset by the stipulated unpaid amount, $10,683.19, for an ultimate award of $14,431.39 on the breach of warranties claim. Taylor & Gaskin has not appealed this judgment.

Chris-Craft's counterclaim had included a claim for consequential damages which represented the costs of the campaign to recall and replace the defective fuel tanks. The trial court held that this was not the proper case for the award of consequential damages because, (1) "Chris-Craft has failed to present any evidence that the costs of recall were within the reasonable contemplation of the parties, either by applicable industry regulations or trade practices", (2) "Chris-Craft failed to perform corrosion tests", (3) rusting was also attributable to installation and design, (4) "the evidence does not establish that removal and replacement of all 550 tanks was 'proximately caused' by Taylor & Gaskin's breach", and (5) because "it cannot fairly be said that a reasonable person would have contemplated at the time of contracting that the entire result of a recall campaign would ultimately be borne by the manufacturer". Chris-Craft has appealed this resolution of its claim for consequential damages.

. . .

This action was initiated to recover on a contract for the sale of goods, to a buyer for resale and damages thereunder must therefore be resolved within the dictates of the Uniform Commercial Code. . . . The damages which are available to the buyer as compensation for the seller's breach under Michigan's Uniform Commercial Code "are intended to place the injured party in as good a position as he would have been in had the promised performance been rendered".

. . .

The pertinent text of 2–714 reads thus:

> (2) The measure of damages for breach of warranty is the difference at the time and place of acceptance between the value of the goods accepted and the value they would have had if they had been as warranted, unless special circumstances show proximate damages of a different amount.
>
> (3) In a proper case any incidental and consequential damages under the next section may also be recovered.

Section 2–715. Mich.Comp.Laws 440.2715, in its relevant portion, states:

> (2) Consequential damages resulting from the seller's breach include:
>
> (a) any loss resulting from general or particular requirements and needs of which the seller at the time of contracting had reason to know and which could not reasonably be prevented by cover or otherwise;

While the U.C.C. does not define or explicate the section 2–714 phrase "in a proper case", it is well-settled that consequential damages for the breach of warranties are available where such damages occur. That is to say, a proper case for the award of consequential damages is a case in which damages satisfy the requisites of section 2–715(2). The Michigan state courts have consistently applied this principle to cases arising under the Uniform Commercial Code as adopted by the state. . . . The facts of *Ambassador Steel Co. v. Ewald Steel Co.*, 33 Mich. App. 495, 190 N.W.2d 275 (1971), are similar to those of the case at bar. Therein, the appeals court allowed consequential damages which had resulted from the seller's breach of warranties of merchantability with respect to steel sold to the buyer for subsequent resale. The state appellate court explained (citations deleted):

> In the instant case, after the defect in the steel was discovered, the railroad cars [in which the steel had been incorporated by the defendant buyer's customer] had to be recalled, stripped and refabricated. Defendant was charged for these operations by his customer. There is scant authority to support a contention that defendant should not be reimbursed by plaintiff for these charges. Indeed, defendant must recover these charges against him if he is to be put in as good a position as he would have been if the steel had been of commercial quality. If the steel had been of commercial quality in the first place, defendant would not have suffered these charges.

. . .

The rule which has thus emerged from the state court analyses of sections 2–714(3) and 2–715(2) is that consequential damages which result from the seller's breach of warranties are recoverable to the extent that the seller had reason to know such damages would follow a breach. . . .

. . .

Consistent with the foregoing, this court finds that the district court erred as a matter of law when it found that Taylor & Gaskin completely breached its express and implied warranties of merchantability, but denied Chris-Craft its consequential damages.

D. Issues for Class Discussion

How does the amount of damages that could possibly be recovered under U.C.C. section 2–714 compare with those damages that could possibly be recovered from a substitute sale or purchase?

§ 2–714:

> (2) The measure of damages for breach of warranty is the difference at the time and place of acceptance between the value of the goods accepted and the value they would have had if they had been as warranted, unless special circumstances show proximate damages of a different amount.
>
> (3) In a proper case any incidental and consequential damages under the next section may also be recovered.[25]

How do these elements differ from those which the plaintiff would have had to claim and prove if Taylor & Gaskin had not delivered the promised goods in due time? How would this case have been decided if, instead of applying the U.C.C. provisions, the court applied the English case law described by Professor Goode and applied until the late XIX Century? Why did the defendant not try to prove that Chris-Craft had examined the tanks at the time of delivery? If both parties had technical expertise on fuel tanks in a marine environment, why is it that both the trial court and the court of appeals determined that the manufacturer had breached the warranty of merchantability? On the other hand, why is it that both courts dismissed the claim for breach of the warranty of fitness for a particular purpose? It must be noted that in the decision at hand the losses suffered by the plaintiff were considered as foreseeable *by the parties*. Nevertheless, in the previous section we made reference to the rule in

[25] U.C.C. § 2–714(2)–(3) (2011).

Hadley v. Baxandale in which foreseeability is required on behalf of the *defendant, seller or manufacturer*. What are the consequences of this distinction? Which criterion would the reader prefer as attorney to the plaintiff? Finally, would this type of recovery of damages be granted in your country? When answering this question, the reader must ask himself the question that Von Ihering would: What is the purpose that the law ascribes to claims for breach of implied warranties? If there is no legal concept that performs such purpose, would the reader suggest its creation?

E. The U.C.C. Implied Warranty of Merchantability and the Spanish Civil Code Redhibitory Action (*"Accion Redhibitoria"*)

The following comment is based on a presentation made in my comparative commercial law seminar at the Carlos III University Law School of Madrid during the spring of 2004 by Dr. Cristian Larraín (presently Professor Cristian Larrain in his native country of Chile). His topic was the comparison between the Spanish Civil and Commercial Code actions for breach of sale agreements and actions for breach of the implied warranty of merchantability under U.C.C. Article 2. What follows is a summary of Professor Larraín's oral presentation.[26]

Articles 1484 and 1486 of the Spanish Civil Code set forth the remedies for the sale of goods with patent and latent defects but fall short of the U.C.C. remedies for the seller's breach of the implied warranty of merchantability and fitness for purpose. The Spanish remedy that comes closest to the U.C.C. remedies for breach of warranty is the redhibitory action for defects in the goods sold. Normally a redhibitory defect is a latent defect, of such magnitude, that it renders the good inappropriate for its normal use or purpose, or that it so diminishes its value to the purchaser that he would have only purchased it for a much lower price.

Professor Fernando Sanchez Calero, one of Spain's most respected commentators of the Civil Code distinguishes between a flaw and a defect. A flaw refers to the lack of certain promised or guaranteed qualities. (Thus, I would add parenthetically, that such a flaw presupposes an express warranty). In addition, the redhibitory action enabled by the flaw includes an action to reduce the price paid *quanti minoris* (or reduction of the price paid).[27]

The redhibitory action then is mostly for latent flaws and these flaws are not measured against what other merchants would have deemed a merchantable good, in their trade. Hence, the implied warranty of merchantability is a concept and a remedy foreign to the Spanish Civil Code. According to Professor Larraín, perhaps the most important difference between the U.C.C. conceptual and remedial scheme and that of the Spanish Civil Code is that in the latter, *the goods uselessness is a consequence of a physical flaw or defect. If the good cannot be used by its purchaser for reasons other than a patent or latent defect but simply because it does not qualify as merchantable (say because it is obsolete by the standards of similar goods) a redhibitory action is*

---

[26] Cristián Andrés Larrain Páez, Las Garantías Contractuales en el Derecho Español [Contractual Warranties in Spanish Law] (2004) (on file with author).

[27] Fernando Sanchez Calero, *Latent Defects in Commercial Sales and the Exercise of Actions that result from them*, (*"Los Vicios Ocultos y el Ejercicio de las Acciones que de ellos derivan en la Compraventa Mercantil"*) (Comment to a Supreme Court decision of Dec. 2, 1954.); COMMERCIAL LAW REVIEW, Madrid, April–June 1956, No. 60, pg. 449, cited by Cristian Larraín, Contractual Warranties under Spanish Law (2004) (hereinafter Larraín, Warranties).

unavailable. Additionally, the Civil Code requires that the *flaws or defects be latent.* If they are patent or evident, the legislator assumes that the buyer knows of them and acknowledges their existence, which would probably lead only to the remedy of reduction in the price. As provided in Article 1484 of the Civil Code, the seller "*won't be liable for patent defects, or others that are not apparent, if the buyer given his occupation or profession has the necessary skills to easily identify them.*"

Article 336 of the Spanish Commercial Code also provides remedies for the defects in the quality of the goods sold; however, Sánchez Calero and Larraín find its regulation imprecise. On one hand, the buyer who examines the goods upon delivery will have no right to claim against the seller for flaws or defects, and if he does not examine them, he is granted four days from the time of delivery to claim such defects. The imprecision resides in the shortness of the terms; the law could hardly be referring to latent flaws and defects. Also, releasing the seller from liability when the buyer has examined the goods upon delivery seems to be referring to flaws and defects that are evident to the eye. But if they are latent, the buyer will hardly ascertain them in four days, and even worse, upon their receipt.[28]

I would suggest that the reader reflect on what makes the U.C.C. breach for the implied warranty of merchantability such a foreign concept to the Spanish Civil Code.

§ 30.3 RECOVERY OF LOSS PROFITS BY THE "LOST VOLUME" SELLER IN ANGLO-AMERICAN LAW

A. R.E. Davis Chemical Corp. v. Diasonics Inc.[29]

CUDAHY, Circuit Judge

. . .

I.

Diasonics is a Delaware corporation engaged in the business of manufacturing and marketing medical diagnostic equipment. R.E. Davis Chemical Corporation (Davis), an Illinois business, contracted to purchase one such device, a .35 tesla nuclear magnetic resonance instrument (MRI), from Diasonics at the price of $1,500,000 pursuant to a written agreement dated February 23, 1984. By the terms of the agreement, upon payment of the full purchase price Davis was to be furnished a $225,000 research grant "based on [an] approved program of development activities." . . . The agreement also afforded Davis the option to upgrade the MRI to a high field/spectroscopy system by June 1, 1985—approximately 15 months after delivery of the MRI was scheduled—at an additional cost of $700,000. Davis advanced a $300,000 deposit for the MRI but failed to take delivery, thereby breaching the contract. After Davis repudiated the contract, Diasonics resold the MRI to a third party at the contract price.

When Diasonics refused to refund the $300,000 deposit, Davis filed suit demanding return of the down payment pursuant to section 2–718(2) of the U.C.C. (1985). Diasonics counterclaimed, alleging that it was entitled to recover the profit it lost on the sale under U.C.C. 2–708(2) (1985) because it was a lost volume seller. The district court entered summary judgment for Davis, holding that lost volume sellers

[28] This is convincingly argued by Fernando Sánchez Calero, supra note 742, pg. 454.

[29] 924 F.2d 709 (7th Cir. 1991).

are not eligible for recovery of lost profits but rather are limited to damages measured by the difference between the resale price and the contract price together with incidental damages under U.C.C. 2–706(1). Concluding that the Illinois Supreme Court would follow the majority of jurisdictions, which allow lost volume sellers to recoup their lost profits under U.C.C. 2–708(2), we reversed and remanded the case with instructions that

> the district court calculate Diasonics' damages under 2–708(2) if Diasonics can establish, not only that it had the capacity to make the sale to Davis as well as the sale to the resale buyer, but also that it would have been profitable for it to make both sales . . . [and that Diasonics] probably would have made the second sale absent the breach.

On remand, Diasonics filed a motion *in limine* to preclude Davis from introducing evidence of the additional expenses Diasonics would have been forced to incur had Davis performed its part of the bargain and elected to exercise the upgrade option. The district court granted this motion at the start of the three-day bench trial. Concluding that Diasonics had adequately established damages for its lost profit amounting to $453,050, the district court ultimately entered judgment for Diasonics in the sum of $153,050 ($453,050 less the $300,000 deposit which Diasonics retained).

On appeal, Davis . . . contends that the district court erred by refusing to allow it a $225,000 credit for the research grant and by excluding evidence of the loss Diasonics would have sustained had Davis exercised its upgrade option.

II.

Ordinarily, a seller's damages for a buyer's breach of contract are measured by the difference between the contract price and the market price. In some situations, however, this sum is inadequate to place the seller in as good a position as performance would have done. For example, a broken contract costs a lost volume seller—one with a finite quantity of customers and the capacity to make an additional sale—its profit on one sale. To be made whole, a lost volume seller must thus recover damages equal to the profit it lost on the sale.

In accordance with this reasoning, in *Diasonics I*, 826 F.2d at 681, we adopted for the first time in Illinois the rule that a lost volume seller is entitled to recoup its lost profit. We held that in order to qualify as a lost volume seller, a plaintiff must establish the following three factors:

> (1) that it possessed the capacity to make an additional sale,
>
> (2) that it would have been profitable for it to make an additional sale, and
>
> (3) that it probably would have made an additional sale absent the buyer's breach.

A. LOST VOLUME SELLER STATUS

Diasonics has adduced ample evidence to establish its status as a lost volume seller. The evidence is undisputed that Diasonics possessed the capacity to manufacture one more MRI. Diasonics also demonstrated that it was, in the words of Judge Kocoras, "beating the bushes for all possible sales." . . . Based upon this evidence, the district court's finding that Diasonics probably would have made an additional sale but for Davis' breach is not clearly erroneous.

Davis offers no evidence to controvert the proof adduced by Diasonics that it both possessed the capacity to manufacture additional MRIs and was actively soliciting every possible customer for MRI sales in 1984. Instead, Davis clutches at one footnote in our previous opinion to justify its contention that Diasonics must precisely identify the resale buyer. . . . The mere fact that Diasonics was unable to specify the particular unit Davis contracted to buy and trace the exact resale buyer for that unit thus should not foreclose it from recovering lost profits. Without more evidence, we decline to impose upon Diasonics the burden of proving the exact buyer who purchased this particular system in order to qualify as a lost volume seller.[30]

Footnote 13 of Diasonics I sets forth one commentator's three factor test for determining whether a buyer's breach ahs resulted in loss of sales volume:

(1) the person who bought the resold entity would have been solicited by plaintiff had there been no breach and resale (in other words, if the resale buyer would have been an additional buyer itself) (Parenthesis added.)

(2) the solicitation would have been successful, and

(3) the plaintiff could have performed the additional contract.[31]

B. DAMAGE CALCULATIONS

. . . . Diasonics need only prove its damages with reasonable certainty, not with mathematical precision.Moreover, the district court's conclusions regarding Diasonics' computations constitute factual determinations that cannot be overturned unless clearly erroneous. . . .

C. RESEARCH GRANT

The district court refused to deduct $225,000 from Diasonics' damages, ruling that the conditions precedent to provision of the research grant—payment payment of the full contract price and approval of a program of development activities—had not been satisfied. Simple reliance upon Davis' failure to comply with the conditions precedent to payment of the research grant, however, effectively skirts the true question at issue here—whether the research grant was what it purported to be or was really a discount masquerading in other garb. If the research was indeed genuine and would have redounded to Diasonics' benefit, then Diasonics is not obliged to dole out $225,000. But if both parties understood the research grant to be a type of rebate, automatically payable upon receipt of the MRI in return for practically worthless information, then Davis should receive a $225,000 credit on the damages it must pay Diasonics. Davis' breach does not entitle Diasonics to gain more than the benefit of its bargain. Upon remand, the district court must thus determine whether the research grant served merely as a disguised discount from the purchase price, or whether it constituted an independent exchange supported by genuine consideration.

D. UPGRADE OPTION

The last and most complex issue entails a similarly fact-intensive inquiry into whether the upgrade arrangement constitutes a true option or, rather, an integral and enforceable provision of the original contract. Illinois courts generally hesitate to

---

[30] *Id.* at 710–12 (citations omitted).

[31] *Id.* at 712 n.3.

enforce options unless the option holder has clearly availed itself of the right by performing all conditions precedent to its exercise. . . . This particular care probably reflects the potential for unfairness when allowing an option holder to benefit from an agreement by which it could not have been bound. Reasoning that Davis failed to comply strictly with the condition precedent to exercise of the option by repudiating the contract, the district court accordingly excluded evidence of the losses Diasonics would allegedly have sustained had it performed the upgrade.

If the upgrade were a virtual certainty, however, the expenses of conveying a highfield/spectroscopy system that Diasonics avoided as a result of Davis' breach should certainly figure in the lost profits damage calculus. Davis presented some evidence to suggest that the upgrade provision, though couched in option terminology, was actually an integral part of the original bargain. (As footnoted in the decision: Davis introduced evidence that it specially designed the MRI building to house the more powerful highfield/spectroscopy system. Moreover, it appears that Diasonics itself initially characterized the upgrade provision as an enforceable part of the original agreement when it counterclaimed seeking additional damages for the profits it lost by Davis' failure to upgrade.)

Courts are often forced to divine the true meaning of such ambiguous arrangements.

. . .

Attempting to realize the true intentions of the parties does not require us to engage in abstract calculations of theoretical probabilities. Avoiding the thicket of academic economics, we opt for a pragmatic approach. Only when the evidence demonstrates a substantial likelihood that the option would have been exercised and persuasively establishes the value of the option should that value figure in the calculation of damages. . . .

Without more evidence, it is impossible to determine whether Davis' upgrade option should enter into the calculation of Diasonics' lost profits. . . . Upon remand, the district court should determine the probability that the option would have been exercised by examining the following non-exhaustive set of factors:

(1) the importance of the option to the original bargain,

(2) the relationship between the option's value and the additional $700,000 Davis was required to pay, and

(3) the relationship between the value of the MRI Davis contracted to buy and the original contract price.

If the original contract price was inflated and the additional $700,000 essentially nominal in relation to the value added to the MRI by the upgrade, then both parties may have understood that the only economically rational course available to Davis was to purchase the upgrade. Under such circumstances, Davis would probably have exercised its option. But if the additional $700,000 even roughly approximated the value added to the MRI by the upgrade, Davis may well have chosen not to exercise the option.

III.

Diasonics is entitled to the benefit of its bargain, no more, no less. Although we hesitate to burden district courts with impossibly complex damage computations, we remand for further consideration of the evidence with respect to the research grant and the upgrade option. The district court's entry of judgment is thus AFFIRMED IN PART, REVERSED IN PART, and REMANDED for further proceedings not inconsistent with this opinion.[32]

B. The "Economic Analysis of Law"; A Propos of the Lost Volume Seller

The loss of profits to a seller who claims damages because of the loss of volume of sales caused by the buyer's failure to buy the goods he promised when he was supposed to has caught the attention of scholars interested in an "Economic Analysis of Law" (hereafter abbreviated as EAL). This analysis has become quite popular among legal theorists in the United States, Europe and Japan and is beginning to spread to Spanish-America. As noted by Professor David Ramos from the University Carlos III de Madrid:[33]

> One of the most influential lines of thought in contemporary legal writings, especially where private law is concerned, is the EAL. One of its seminal writings was Professor Ronald Coase's article *The Problem of Social Cost.*[34] In his article, Professor Coase applies his theory on the costs of market transactions to the analysis of legal phenomena . . . Whether one agrees or not with this type of argument, the truth is that there are some areas of law where it is impossible to understand the consequences of certain rules or points of view without taking into account the economic considerations set forth by the EAL. Such is the case of the law of contracts and, more precisely, the issue at hand: what should be the recovery of lost profits for a lost volume seller.

The following extended comment expresses my views on EAL not merely as a body of knowledge that can help discern the economic consequences of the statutory and decisional law that governs commercial contracts but also as a method for prescribing better, or in the language of EAL, "more efficient" commercial contract law rules. For this reason the following section is written a *propos* of the issues raised by the damages for lost volume, i.e., using the discussion of these damages as a springboard for the wider consideration of the province and function of EAL. Having this dual purpose in mind, it will be necessary to delve, albeit elementarily and summarily, on the main analytical tools (principles, corollaries and concepts) relied upon by EAL.

---

[32] *Id.* at 712–14 (citations omitted).

[33] David Ramos was part of the Doctorate Course at the Universidad Carlos III de Madrid, taught by the author, May–June 2004, and provided the comments here transcribed as part of his main coursework.

[34] Ronald H. Coase, *The Problem of Social Cost*, 3 J. L. & ECON. 1 (1960). *See generally* RICHARD POSNER, ECONOMIC ANALYSIS OF THE LAW (8th ed. 2011) (providing a history of EAL).

C. Analytical Tools of EAL: Principles, Corollaries, Theorems and Concepts

1. The First Two Principles: On the Law of Demand and on the Relationship Between Prices and the Costs of Opportunity

As described by Judge Richard Posner, the most influential of EAL writers:

> . . . [E]conomics is the science of rational choice in a world—our world—in which resources are limited in relation to human wants. The task of economics, so defined, is to explore the implications of assuming that man is a rational maximizer of his ends in life, his satisfactions—what we shall call his "self interest."[35]

Central to Judge Posner's EAL, then, is the assumption that man is a rational self-interest (or utility) maximizer in all areas of life, not just in his economic affairs. This assumption implies that people respond to incentives—"that if a person's surroundings change in such a way that he could increase his satisfaction by altering his behavior, he will do so."[36] From this utilitarian proposition he derives three fundamental principles of economics. The first is the law of demand, which poses an ". . . inverse relation between price charged and quantity demanded. . . . If the price of . . . [a commodity] rises [significantly]. . . . [b]eing rational and self-interested, the consumer will react by investigating the possibility of substituting goods that he preferred less. . . ."[37] The relative or alternative relationship between lowest prices charged by sellers and their costs of opportunity.

This relationship is relative (my term) or alternative (his) because the "lowest price that a rational self-interested seller would charge. . . . is the price that the resources consumed in making (and selling) the seller's product would command in their next best use—the alternative price."[38] Put more simply, if I am to manufacture *X*, which requires a capital input of *Y* and a labor input of *Z*, the price I pay for these inputs must exceed that which would have been paid by another bidder for the same inputs, otherwise they would have been sold to that bidder and not to me.

As apparent from this illustration, the economic concept of cost is more inclusive and subtle than the mere addition of the prices of all the resources consumed by the seller. Hence, Posner refers to the cost of opportunity as "the second fundamental principle of economics" because of its corollary notion that a cost is incurred whenever someone, in what he refers to as the world of economic affairs, is denied the use of that resource.

> Since I can breathe as much air as I want without depriving anyone of any of the air he wants, no one will pay me to relinquish my air to him; therefore air is costless [although this is not to say that clean air is costless]. . . . [Thus] the principal cost of higher education is not tuition; it is the foregone earnings

---

[35] POSNER, *supra* note 35, at 3 (citations omitted).

[36] *Id.* at 5.

[37] *Id.* at 4.

[38] *Id.* at 7.

that the student would have if he were working rather than attending school.[39]

As part of the economic measurement of costs, Posner adds a "slightly oversimplified" version of Professor Coase's theorem: if, as with the breathing of unclean air, the transactions are costless, the initial use to which property is put by its owner or possessor (Posner refers to this use as its initial assignment) will not affect the ultimate use of the property. He gives the example of the farmer entitled to compensation for the destruction of his crops by sparks from the adjacent railroad.

> Assume that his [the farmer's] crops are worth $100 and are flammable, that the value to the railroad of unimpeded use of its right-of-way is $120, but that at the cost of $110 the railroad can install spark arresters that will eliminate the fire hazard. On these assumptions, the real value of the crops to the farmer is not $100 but somewhere between $100 and $110, since at any price above $110 the railroad would install spark arresters rather than buy the farmer's property right, but that at any proice below $110 the railroad would buy the property. The farmer is better off selling his property to the railroad at a price between $100 and $110; he will do this because the railroad will buy at aprice in that range; and as a result his land will be shifted into some fire-insensitive use, just as if the railroad had owned it in the first place.[40]

The conclusion Posner draws from Coase's theorem is that the forces of competition tend to make opportunity cost the maximum as well as the minimum price of economic resources. And that a "price above the opportunity cost is a magnet drawing resources into the production of the good until, in accordance with the Law of Demand, the increase in output drives price down to cost. . . ."[41]

The concept of marginal cost serves is an additional analytical tool for the measurement of costs. Posner refers to it as "the change in total costs brought about by a one-unit change in output; in other words, it is the cost that would be avoided by producing one unit less."[42] As the reader will recall, this concept was at play in the determination of the damages for lost sales in the Diasonics decision. It is also at play in the definition of price equilibrium: "a point at which, unless the conditions of demand or supply change, there is no incentive for sellers to alter the price or output."[43]

2. *The Third Principle: Economic Efficiency*

Armed with the above two principles, their corollaries, a theorem and related conceptual tools, Posner explains his third principle or that of economic efficiency:

> [R]esources tend to gravitate toward their most valuable uses if voluntary exchange—a market—is permitted. . . . By a process of voluntary exchange, resources are shifted to those uses in which the value to consumers, as measured by their willingness to pay, is highest. When resources are being

---

[39] *Id.* at 8 (citations omitted).

[40] *Id.* at 10.

[41] *Id.* at 10.

[42] *Id.*

[43] *Id.* at 10–11.

> used where their value is highest, or, equivalently, when no reallocation would increase their value, we are saying that are being employed efficiently.[44]

This principle was so dear to Posner's original pan-economic world of policy choices that at one point he advocated reliance on the price paid by the highest bidder as the most efficient (and thus socially preferable) method for allocating the adoption of abandoned children.[45] Presently, Judge Posner acknowledges that the term "efficiency" to denote that allocation of resources in which value is maximized in a utilitarian Jeremy Bentham like fashion ("the greatest good for the greatest number" or the "felicific" calculus of excess of pleasure over pain) is flawed as an ethical criterion.[46]

> . . . First, most people don't believe . . . that maximizing happiness, or contentment, or joy, or preference satisfaction, or the excess of pleasure over pain, or some other version of utility is or should be one's object in life. . . .
>
> Second, by aggregating utility across persons, utilitarianism treats people as cells in the overall social organism rather than as individuals. This is the source of a number of well-known barbarisms seemingly implied by utilitarian ethics, such as the deliberate sacrifice of innocents to maximize the total amount of happiness. . . .[47]

The objections to the link between economic efficiency and utilitarianism have "turned many economists to a definition of efficiency that confines the term to outcomes of voluntary transactions."[48] Judge Posner is among them, and he places himself among the economists that have adopted the Kaldor-Hicks concept of transactional efficiency or wealth maximization. This concept takes into account the wealth maximization effects not only between the parties directly involved in the transaction but also upon third parties.[49]

Thus, a sale of a wood carving that A (the seller) values at $50 and B (the buyer) values at $120, if sold for a price anywhere between these two figures would yield a total benefit to the parties of $70. If the harm (if any) done to third parties (minus any benefit to them) does not exceed the $70, then taking into account the wealth maximization effects upon the contracting parties and third parties, the result would be an efficient transaction.[50] He adds that "when an economist says that free trade or competition or the control of pollution or some other policy or state of the world is efficient, nine times out of ten he means Kaldor-Hicks efficient."[51]

Finally, Judge Posner expresses awareness that his reader may be troubled by what appear to be severely unrealistic assumptions that underlie economic theory such as the rationality of human behavior. Yet, his version of rationality is a minimalist one:

---

[44] *Id.* at 13.

[45] *See* Anthony D'Amato, *Globalizing Adoption: Linking Children and Adoptive Parents*, 116 CHRISTIAN CENTURY 668, 669 (1999) (on file with author), *available at* http://anthonydamato.law.northwestern.edu/Pages-papers/globalizing-adopt-cc.pdf.

[46] POSNER, *supra* note 35, at 16.

[47] *Id.*

[48] *Id.* at 17.

[49] *Id.*

[50] *Id.*

[51] *Id.* at 18.

"rationality is objective rather than subjective; it is the ability and inclination to use instrumental reasoning to get on in life and thus does not assume consciousness (rational decisions are often intuitive)."[52]

Despite the minimalism of its rationality, "the assumptions of economic theory are one-dimensional and pallid when viewed as descriptions of human behavior—especially the behavior of such unconventional economic 'actors' as the judge, the litigant, the parent, the rapist, and others whom one encounters in the economic analysis of law."[53] To these actors, and because our subject is the law of commercial contracts, I would add the behavior of everyday merchants as well as of the *Bonus Vir*. Before we examine the usefulness of EAL in the context of the law of commercial contracts it is necessary to contrast the behavior of Posner's rational-maximization-of-wealth-person, whom we will refer to as Posner's *Homo Economicus* with that of ordinary, everyday merchants and with the *Bonus Vir*.

D. Posner's *Homo Economicus*, Ordinary Merchants and the *Bonus Vir*

Posner himself refers to the compendium of principles, corollaries and other conceptual tools that comprise the economic theory that explains the behavior of his *Homo Economicus* as abstract. He defends its abstraction, however, by stating that "abstraction is of the essence of scientific inquiry, and economics aspires to be scientific. . . . [I]ts lack of realism in the sense of descriptive completeness, far from invalidating a theory, is a precondition of theory. A theory that sought faithfully to reproduce the complexity of the empirical world in its assumptions would not be a theory—an explanation—but a description."[54]

With due respect, Posner's justification of the abstract economic theory that informs the behavior of his economic man and his rejection of the description of complexities is semantics and not science. To be sure, abstraction is a child of mathematics and especially of the mathematical ability to "simplify" or synthesize observable data by reducing it to its most comprehensive yet tersest formula possible. Yet, these mathematical formulas are as scientifically valid as the data they synthesize. As an example of an abstract yet highly useful scientific formulation, he refers to Newton's law of falling bodies, even though this law was, according to Posner, unrealistic in its assumption that bodies fall in a vacuum and for this reason was superseded by Einstein's general theory of relativity.[55]

Yet, even if Newton's theory of what explains the falling of bodies was "unrealistic" it still illustrates the need for a precise and accurate description of the phenomena the scientist intends to explain and predict. Without it, a lay observer such as Posner may reach the conclusion that it was an unrealistic theory. In Newton's case, his description of the phenomena he was trying to explain by mathematical laws took place in the universe of our every day life. He chose a seminal factual assumption in

---

[52] *Id.* at 20.

[53] *Id.* at 21.

[54] *Id.*

[55] *Id.*

the analogy between the falling apple and a "falling" moon and explained it by a verifiable force, the law of gravity.[56]

Newton's factual assumptions work for the observable world, although not for Albert Einstein's universe in which space and time become a continuum. Einstein's general theory or relativity sprung from an equally seminal factual assumption-no matter how fast an object might accelerate; it will never catch up with a beam or wave of light.[57] Einstein's "realistic facts," then, were those of a world of objects attempting to move at the speed of light, where time slows down, space stretches and gravity is the result of a space-time curvature. These facts were not those of Newton's everyday world of falling apples and the moon being attracted by the earth's gravity.[58] Thus, both theories, in their respective contexts, were built upon equally realistic and ultimately verifiable set of seminal facts.

Significantly, the reason Einstein considered Galileo Galilei the father of modern physics was precisely because he was the first to synthesize mathematically his carefully described observations and experiments on the motion of falling bodies, and especially their acceleration.[59] The importance of a valid observation and description in the formulation of a scientific theory was illustrated by Galileo's discarding Aristotle's unrealistic view that heavier bodies fall faster than lighter ones and that the reason why all bodies fall is because "they long to be united with earth".[60]

In contrast with Galileo's, Newton's and Einstein's seminal factual assumptions, Posner's *Homo Economicus* is governed by principles, corollaries and concepts so broad and abstract that they predict only the most basic of commercial behavior.

Yet, will these principles, corollaries and concepts help a merchant decide whether or not to do any of, for example, the following: 1) reduce his prices significantly to a) introduce a product in the market as a "loss leader", b) reduce the same prices to long term clients who suddenly find themselves in serious economic difficulties but who may recover and continue to buy his products at regular prices? 2) fulfill his "brotherly" duty to "pick up the bundle" of a seriously ill or deceased colleague and deliver the profits to the colleague's family? 3) increase the salary of his employees beyond the minimum wage if his profit margins are still healthy; 4) assume a risk of loss, even though it was not brought about by his willful or negligent acts, thereby increasing the credibility of his promises and trust among fellow merchants and customers? Or would they help a legislator allocate a risk such as described in 4) among various non culpable parties?

I doubt that Posner's economic analysis will answer these questions with a modicum of accuracy. The reason is because the behavior he ascribes to the rational

---

[56] The following remarks on Newton and Einstein's assumptions, paraphrase those by theoretical physicist Michio Kaku in Michio Kaku, Brilliant Minds, Galileo Galilei, Isaac Newton, Albert Einstein and Stephen Hawking (Science Channel, DVD, 2008). [hereinafter Brilliant Minds]. The late and lamented Professor William Sears of the University of Arizona Aeronautical Engineering Dept. and one of the premier aeronautical mathematicians and physicist of the Twentieth Century described Professor Kaku's writings and television programs on leading theoretical physicists as among the most lucid and accessible to the general public.

[57] Brilliant Minds, *supra* note 57.

[58] *Id.*

[59] *Id.*

[60] *Id.*

man is often at odds with the behavior of an archetypal merchant. Recall his failure to take into account the appraisal practices of commercial real estate brokers' in the J. C. Penney case. Recall also his agreement with Justice Holmes' (and Thomas Hobbes') archetypal "bad man's" entitlement to breach his contracts as long as he is willing to pay the damages. Note also that his rational man's decisions are snapshots of individual transactions and seldom take into account the merchants' concerns with the streams of related, including future, transactions between the same and third parties. Finally, notice the lesser role he attributes to the presumed contractual good faith (honesty, reasonableness and fairness of the archetypal merchant) while he is willing to rely on a conjectural subjective state of mind of the defendant in the J.C. Penney decision, a conjecture based upon "bad man" inspired assumptions of his contractual behavior.

1. The Gap Between EAL Economic Theory and Desirable Commercial Behavior: Price v. Neal and Section 204 of the New Payment Code

In 1985, the so called Articles 3–4–8 Committee appointed by the Permanent Editorial Board of the U.C.C. completed a third draft of the proposed Uniform New Payment Code. Its purpose was to replace many of the provisions that dealt with the transfer of funds whether by electronic or paper based means, including negotiable instruments and some investment securities. It contained two major changes in the allocation of losses caused by the forgery of the drawer's signature and of subsequent endorsements. Of these, only the former allocation will be discussed, especially because EAL influenced its justification.[61]

Section 204 of the proposed New Payment Code (NPC) dealt with allocation of loss among the payor bank, collecting banks, presenting banks and other prior transferors of checks and drafts deposited with collecting banks and forwarded "downstream" toward the payor-drawee banks or banks where the drawer of the check or draft had a deposit and checking account. Under the pre-existing § 3–418 the U.C.C. rule, inspired by Lord Mansfield's landmark 1762 decision in Price v. Neal,[62] payment of an item[63] is final if the party presenting it to the payor bank is a holder in due course or is someone who in good faith relies on the finality of that payment.[64]

The drawee bank, which pays on an item with a forged signature, also had the duty under U.C.C. Article 4 to re-credit the innocent customer's account because such a payment was deemed as unauthorized by its drawer and thus "improperly" payable.[65] As pointed out by Professors Steven B. Dow and Nan S. Ellis, the payor bank may assert defenses in response to its customer's demand for re-credit, such as preclusion by having acted negligently in facilitating the forgery or by failure to promptly report

---

[61] *See* Steven B. Dow & Nan S. Ellis, *The Proposed Uniform New Payments Code: Allocation of Losses Resulting from Forged Drawers' Signatures*, 22 HARV. J. ON LEGIS. 399 (1985) (evaluating the changes to the pre-existing law allocation of the risk of loss for these signatures).

[62] Price v. Neal, (1762) 97 Eng. Rep. 871 (K.B.); 3 Burr. 1354; U.C.C. § 3–418 (App'x. G 2012) which stated in relevant part: "[P]ayment or acceptance of any instrument is final in favor of a holder in due course, or a person who has in good faith changed his position in reliance on the payment."

[63] The term item is used generally in bank deposits and collection law to denote an instrument such as a draft or check deposited for collection and forwarded or presented to the payor bank for its payment.

[64] U.C.C. § 3–418 (1972) and *id.* cmt. 1.

[65] U.C.C. § 4–401(c) (2012) (stating in relevant part: "A bank may charge against the account of a customer a check that is otherwise properly payable from the account. . . .").

the forgery after reviewing the item.[66] However, even if the payor bank can prove the customer's negligence, the bank's own negligence may disqualify its defense of contributory or comparative negligence.[67] Thus, the combination of Price v. Neal (as adopted by U.C.C. § 3–418) and U.C.C. § 4–401(1) resulted in a powerful protection of both customers whose signatures were forged in checks that they had not issued and of equally innocent third parties who in good faith gave value on these instruments by discounting or negotiating them. It was the protection of the latter which had prompted Lord Mansfield to analogize the discounted or negotiated drafts to money.[68]

The drafters of the NPC justified the removal of the protection of holders in due course of instruments with forged signatures with, among others, factual or transactional and an EAL inspired arguments. They rejected the traditional justification for the rule of *Price v. Neal* that asserted that the payor bank was in a better position to detect the forgery of its own customer's signature because it was inconsistent with modern banking practices in which a large number of items are processed by computers. The second argument against the two hundred year old rule was it was impractical and uneconomic. The impracticality and economically inefficient nature of the rule was reflected by the alleged reality that banks do not check signatures under a certain dollar amount even though they will be liable on them.[69]

This argument seems inspired by the principle of cost opportunity and its corollary notion that a cost is incurred whenever someone, in what Judge Posner referred to as the world of economic affairs, is denied the use of that resource as well. It is also influenced by the concept of marginal cost. In other words, if the bank's resources are more productive and capable of being maximized by not checking for the forgery of signatures for amounts below a certain figure, why continue to insist on a rule that will only be ignored by the banks in favor of a more "efficient" allocation of their resources? Why not exempt them from the liability for an undiscovered forgery and allow them to maximize their wealth more efficiently? How such a reasoning would satisfy the Kaldor-Hicks requirement of taking into account the third party's (i.e. holder in due course's) wealth maximization was left unanswered. Similarly, the consequences of a marginal cost analysis did not seem to be taken into account.

As pointed out by Professors Dow and Ellis,

> Implicit in these statements is the idea that at some dollar amount [for each item], it would be economical for the payor bank to verify its customer's signature given the costs of verification and the certainty and extent of liability.[70]

Thus, as pointed out by Dow and Ellis, even if what the drafters of NPC assumed as a transactional fact was true, then why not allow the rule to remain in effect for those large amount items whose cost of examination was justified by the amount of the

---

[66] Dow & Ellis, *supra* note 62, at 409.

[67] *Id.* at 410.

[68] *See* Lord Mansfield's decisions in Miller v. Race (1758) 97 Eng. Rep. 398 (K.B.); 1 Burr. 452 & Peacock v. Rhodes, (1781) 99 Eng. Rep. 402 (K.B.); 2 Doug. 633.

[69] N.P.C. § 202 cmt. A, *cited in* Dow & Ellis, *supra* note 62, at 426 n.153 and accompanying text (this also references the fact that a factual assumption underlying the impractical and uneconomic nature of the rule that "banks do not check signatures under a certain amount" was unproven).

[70] *Id.* at 246–27.

item, especially when the drafters had used the same economic cost argument to abolish the rule.[71]

The NPC was rejected as a whole and one of the reasons that prompted that rejection was its abolition of *Price v. Neal*. This was very surprising to some of the members of the Permanent Editorial Board who could not understand why a rational banker intent on maximizing his wealth and reducing his exposure to risk would not welcome a rule that eliminated such an exposure. When one of them asked me this very question, my reply was by way of another question: did you establish with the bankers what they deemed as the most rational and efficient rule to maximize their wealth when allocating the risk of forgery of their customers' signatures?

One such a banker and lawyer in charge of his bank's risk management department stated his bank's reasons for rejecting the abolition of *Price v. Neal* as follows:

> It is true that we might derive a short-term benefit from the elimination of liability *vis-à-vis* holders in due course. Yet, we need to weigh this apparent gain against the loss in the volume of circulation of checks and the willingness of third parties to discount or negotiate them and then bring them to us for final payment. We are happy with our volume of check circulation. In addition, we have already internalized the cost of this risk by including it in our insurance coverage for errors and omissions. By now it is a perfectly acceptable cost. Therefore, we could not see stopping a trust and business inducing practice because of an assumption by economic theorists that an exemption from liability is our most efficient way of doing business. Frankly, we believe we know our business and its efficiency better than those who fashioned the new rule.[72]

Clearly, the drafters of the NPC would have greatly profited from taking into account the above "best practice" considerations as expressed by everyday merchants and market participants.

In the final analysis then, the reason why the help of these principles, corollaries, theorems and concepts is in my opinion quite limited is because of what Judge Posner refers to as the "one dimensional and pallid" assumptions of economic theory and their failure to capture "the full complexity, richness, and confusion of the phenomena. . . ."[73]

As became apparent in the bankers' rejection of the NPC, this is a richness that must take into account factors such as the nature of the business and marketplace and their variants on costs and profit margins, longer-term considerations such as caused by relationships with customers, colleagues and third parties and last but not least, the reasonable expectations of bank customers.

---

[71] *Id.* at 427.

[72] The above quoted text is the result of a conversation with the head of the risk management department of a major United States bank, during the month of April 1989 in New York City. This banker and lawyer requested that his name not be revealed.

[73] POSNER, *supra* note 35, at 21.

2. *EAL's Contribution to Commercial Contract Adjudication*

As apparent in the discussion of the NPC's failed abolition of *Price v. Neal*, EAL draftsmen's reliance on the behavior of an archetypal economic man making short run, marginal cost and utility decisions, without more, had serious normative shortcomings. On the other hand, as shown by the research of Professors Charles Goetz and Robert Scott, among others,[74] economic theory can contribute to a better adjudication of commercial contract disputes. Consider, for example, their analysis of the decision in *Neri v. Retail Marine Corp.*[75]

Retail Marine, a boat manufacturer, sold Neri a boat for the price of $12,587.40, against which they made a down payment of $4,250.00. Soon after the sale, Neri repudiated the contract. Four months later, Retail Marine sold the same boat to another buyer for the same price as previously contracted with Neri. As in *Diasonics*, Neri claimed the refund of his down payment of $4,250.00; Retail Marine opposed it and counterclaimed arguing that had it not been for Neri's breach, Retail Marine would have had two separate profits, one resulting from the contract with Neri and the other from the subsequent sale of a similar boat. The Court of Appeals of the State of New York admitted the counterclaim and held that the measure of damages by calculating the difference between the market price of the boat that Neri failed to purchase and the price stipulated in the breached contract was not enough to place the seller in as good a financial position as Neri's performance would have done. Therefore, Retail Marine had reason to claim the lost profits from Neri as a lost volume seller.[76]

As noted by Goetz and Scott, "[t]he court categorized Retail Marine's situation as that of a dealer with an 'inexhaustible' supply of boats; consequently, the second buyer did not replace the first."[77] Because they were considered independent transactions, it follows that recovery as a lost volume seller was granted. However, the undisputed facts did not support such a conclusion: "Mere *ability* to supply additional volume in no way implies that such volume could have been supplied profitably."[78]

From this point on, these authors analyze the restrictive effects that factors such as the market in which Retail Marine operated and the effects that the costs of inventory could have over the seller's expected profits.[79] For example, in a market with perfect competition, meaning one in which supply and demand were in balance as a result of an unlimited number of sellers and buyers with equal access to goods and prices, Retail Marine would have no control over the price of its boats. These would sell for the equilibrium price between supply and demand in the market. Its capacity of selling with profits would be limited by, among other factors, increasing production costs.[80]

If Marine were to operate in a market where it had power and control over its sale prices, and if the prices had to be reduced in order to keep up with competition,

---

[74] Charles J. Goetz & Robert E. Scott, *Measuring Sellers' Damages: The Lost-Profits Puzzle* 31 STAN. L. REV. 323, 331–32 (1979).

[75] *Id.* at 331–38 (discussing Neri v. Retail Marine Corp., 30 N.Y.2d 393 (1972)).

[76] *Id.* at 332.

[77] *Id.*

[78] *Id.*

[79] *Id.* at 333.

[80] *Id.*

Marine's volume of sale would also be influenced by the price levels, because if it was not able to pay its production costs then the volume of sales would also be affected.[81]

Other factors could also lead to the conclusion that if there were a market to resell boats, then the re-sales in that market would not necessarily be considered "new" but rather replacement sales for those breached and therefore would not allow for recovery of damages as a lost volume seller. Thus, profits from sales in a market for new boats have different characteristics from those from sales in a market for used boats. The same would be true of a market of spare parts in contrast with a market of fully assembled goods.

In fact, the remedy for non-performance of sales of spare parts or those in process of production is commonly that of lost profits but only pertaining to the breached sale. This is so because damages for lost profits as a lost volume seller are measured by the difference between the contractual price and the price of a substitute sale and both require that the boat be manufactured and be ready to be resold. Yet, in the case of sales of spare parts or products in process of production, the producer that does not have firm purchase orders can easily decide not to continue with the production of the contracted spare parts or goods.

There are other important analytical differences caused by markets where purchases are made directly from the producer or indirectly through intermediaries, or by markets where the goods are homogenous or standard and subject to normal sale standards, as opposed to the sale of goods that are "custom made" or manufactured upon specific requirements from the buyer. Once the differences have been identified, it is the job of the analyst to determine the microeconomic consequences of breached sales and their effects on possible substitute or new sales.

As just noted, production costs have a great influence in determining a realistic measure of damages. Economic analysis takes into consideration whether the costs alleged by the seller are fixed (e.g., lease of the place where the production plant or sales offices are located) or variable (e.g., raw materials or labor invested in the production of a specific group of boats). If fixed, they would be equally divided among all of the boats produced or sold. If variable, they would be apportioned to each boat upon which these costs were invested.

The same is true with the analysis of average and marginal costs. Average costs are those which result from dividing total costs of production by the total number of produced boats. However, in order to determine possible profits of future lost sales, several analysts use the formula for the earlier described marginal costs, i.e. the cost of producing the next unit. For instance, if 10 boats are produced at a total cost of $10,000, the average cost of each boat is $1,000. However, if production of an eleventh boat results in a total cost of $11,500 (for all the boats including the one about to be produced) then the marginal cost of that one boat is $1,500 and this is the cost used by analysts to determine whether there are profits or not from the sale that immediately follows the breach.

Obviously, if the market sale price of that boat were lower than its marginal cost, then far from receiving profits from the lost sale the producer would most likely not produce that additional boat and instead avoid the losses which he could have

[81] *Id.* at 334.

incurred. In this case, it would not be possible to claim lost profits as a lost volume seller.

Summarizing, EAL can help in perfecting or correcting the application of law of damages by identifying analytical mistakes such as made by the court in *Neri*: first, when it assumed that a seller like Retail Marine could have an inexhaustible supply of boats, and second, when it decided that such a possibility characterized every future sale as a new sale, hence justifying the award of damages for lost volume.

Similarly, this analysis may prevent errors in measuring damages by suggesting when to take into consideration factors that either limit or qualify the lost volume of sales in relation to types of markets, products and their costs. *Diasonics* illustrates how a basic economic analysis was significant to the courts determination of the lost volume of sales. It should be recalled that in this decision a list of factors suggested by Professor Harris are cited as follows:

> 1. the person who bought the resold entity would have been solicited by the seller to buy had there been no breach and resale [in other words, if the resale buyer would have been an additional buyer himself];
>
> 2. the solicitation would have been successful; and
>
> 3. the plaintiff could have performed the additional contract.[82]

Later, Robert Casey, another economic analyst, suggested a fourth factor to be added to Harris' list:

> [A] lost-volume situation exists only when the breached sale would have provided the seller with an increase in total profit [within that fiscal or calendar year].[83]

3. *Closing the Gap Between Economic Theory and Commercial Contract Law Making: The Average Merchant and the* Bonus Vir

As shown by Goetz and Scott's analysis of the Neri decision, the gap between the economic theory assumptions that Judge Posner himself characterizes as "one dimensional and pallid when viewed as descriptions of human behavior" and the behavior of average and exemplary merchants is one that empirical data can and must narrow. Yet, this gap is sharply apparent in Judge Posner's own assumptions especially one related to what he refers to as the contracting parties' opportunistic behavior and how to deal with it. According to Judge Posner:

> . . . [I]t is not always obvious when a party is behaving opportunistically. Suppose A hires B to paint his portrait "to A's satisfaction." B paints a portrait that connoisseurs of portraiture admire. . . . A rejects the portrait and refuses to give any reason for the rejection. If the rejection is not made in good faith, A will be held to have broken the contract. . . . *No one would voluntarily place himself at the mercy of the other party*, so it is reasonable to assume that had the parties thought about the possibility of bad faith they would have forbidden it expressly.

---

[82] *See supra* note 32 and accompanying text.

[83] Robert M. Casey, *An Economic View of the U.C.C. Seller's Damage Measures and the Identification of the Lost-Volume Seller*, 49 ALB. L. REV. 889, 909 n.115 (1984–1985).

> Should the law go further, and read into the contract an implied duty of reasonableness on A's part? It should not (and does not). The parties *probably meant A to be the sole judge of the adequacy of B's performance.* The language of the contract so suggests, though not conclusively; and the suggestion is reinforced by reflecting *on the incompetence of a judge or jury to determine whether A . . . dissatisfied with the portrait, ought to have liked it.*[84]

Contrast this statement with that by the Roman jurist Ulpian in D.18.1.7 (Ulpian, *Sabinus, book 28*) discussed during the First Part of this book.

> The sale of a slave "if he shall have settled his accounts to his master's satisfaction" is conditional; now conditional sales become perfect, only when the condition is satisfied. Does the condition mentioned refer to the master's personal satisfaction or to the satisfaction of an honorable man? If we accept the former interpretation, the sale is null as also would be the case where a man would sell, if he chose to do so, or if he promised in a stipulation, "I will give ten if I want to"; it cannot be left to the decision of a contracting party whether he is under an obligation. Accordingly, it was settled by the earlier jurists that one looks to the judgment of an honorable man and not to that of the master himself. Hence, if the accounts were acceptable, but he refused them or if he, in fact, accepted them, but pretended not to, the condition of purchase would be realized and the vendor could be sued by the action on purchase.[85]

While Ulpian would seem to agree with Judge Posner that it is highly unlikely that someone would contractually place himself at the mercy of the other party, his normative solution was quite different, and in my opinion wiser and perhaps even more economically efficient. Ulpian would adopt the normative solution he attributes to the earlier jurists and rely on the judgment of an honorable man (*bonus vir*) and not to on that of the master himself. Hence, if the accounts were acceptable to that honorable man the condition of purchase would be realized and the vendor could be sued by the action on purchase.

When relying on the judgment of an honorable man, Ulpian gained the assistance of someone of not only a superior morality to that of Posner' *homo economicus* but that of a respectable and wise merchant. This archetype had likely participated in or heard about instances where one contracting party had placed himself at the mercy of another. Thus, he could more easily tell what the parties truly meant when they agreed that A should be sole judge of the adequacy of B's performance. Did they really mean it, or were their words only "code" words for another meaning? For this was a personage familiar with the customary practices of various contracting parties, their honorability as well as their reasonableness.

Consequently, while the *homo economicus* often ends up being a creature of the laboratory capable of producing only highly narrow, and short lasting rules, the *bonus vir*, as a flesh and bones merchant is the beneficiary of commercial contract trial and error and of the well trodden contractual and remedial paths. Empirically and intuitively, the *bonus vir* knows what claims are regarded as fair by the regular

[84] POSNER, *supra* note 35, at 117 (Emphasis added).

[85] *See supra* § 4:6(C).

marketplace participants and that in the final analysis it is that fairness as much as his business acumen which earns him the trust of his peers, perhaps the most valuable asset in commerce. Hence, he is highly respected by his peers and is one of the most reliable sources of good commercial practices, long run rules and consequently of a sustainable substantive and remedial law.

At the same time, there is no question that the gap between economic theory and commercial contract law making should be narrowed also by having access to the compilations of the standard and best contractual practices of average merchants. As discussed in Chapter 24, the practices that attain such a status of viability earn it because of their proven cost effectiveness and fairness to market participants, whether parties to the contract or third parties. With such an assistance, the task of the legislator and judge become much easier and their norms can truly contribute to the economic development of the jurisdiction or region.

Epilogue

I am sure that having had to study more than a thousand pages of text, innumerable footnotes—often alluding to exotic sources and a similarly large number of cross references—you will not mind an epilogue that is short. I will also assume that you would probably want to have an answer, tentative though it may be, to the question of what lies ahead for the law of commercial contracts, including its continuing and hopefully accelerated, contribution to economic development.

Because law—whether positive or living—is invariably contextual (as this entire book illustrates) and if one takes into account the proven failure of centrally planned economies, what lies ahead for the law of commercial contracts will depend on the fate of two versions of market economies. In the first, commercial contracts are used extensively, but they reflect mostly the selfish impulses of merchants and of their governmental, usually corrupt, partners and as counselled by submissive-client-*ueber-alles*-lawyers. Clearly these are free markets in name only: Monopolies and oligopolies, corruption, invertebration and economic stagnation will eventually prevail as they did shortly after China's eighteenth century imperial commerce reached its developmental peak and as they continue to prevail in many of the developing nations discussed in this book.

In the second market economy, where commercial contracts are formed by the right mix of altruism and selfishness and where disputes are adjudicated on the basis of what is reasonable and fair (often as illustrated by the archetypal behavior of knowledgeable and respected merchants), standard and best practices will consolidate their place as the main source of the living, as well as of the positive commercial law. Standard practices will continue to be applied to regular participants in their trade or sector and the number of these practices will continue to grow. What is uncertain is whether best practices will keep pace. Recall that best practices can apply either to transactions between regular participants and third parties or to transactions only between regular participants, but with a marked effect on the interests of third parties, especially of those not capable of bargaining on equal terms with regular participants.

In theory, the number of best practices are also likely to increase because the contemporary marketplace is one in which the largest number of participants are contractual strangers. This book shows that to protect the participation of these third parties or strangers in the marketplace is to protect the vitality of the marketplace and to improve the wellbeing of regular participants and third parties.

Yet, for the third party participation to increase significantly, the ethics of the marketplace will need to undergo a change that reflects the importance of cooperation, not only among regular participants, but also with third parties. They should be protected by the same duties of honesty, reasonableness and fairness that characterize successful standard practices. This will require a change in the role of commercial lawyers so that while they continue to be devoted and capable advocates for their clients, a new version of professional good faith also requires them to be guardians of the honesty, reasonableness and fairness of the transaction they counsel.

Such an attitude will require a redirection in the teaching of commercial contract law and in its everyday application by lawyers and adjudicators. Once familiar with the nuts and bolts of the transactions, they will need to identify sectoral and archetypal contractual behavior and to discern both, the existing mix of selfish and altruistic practices and the mix is most likely to satisfy the reasonable expectations of the archetypal contracting parties. They will also need to ascertain the likely effect of standard and best practices upon third parties bearing in mind that the greater the number of market participants acting in different commercial capacities, the greater will be the likelihood of economic development for all.

And once students learn to identify standard and particularly best practices, they will also have to learn how to formulate them as the legal principles, maxims, concepts and rules that will shape the future law of commercial contracts. Finally, it is worth recalling that the practices that proved most successful in the Anglo-American facilitation of commercial and consumer credit and economic development were those that induced the most trust among participants. And that trust was induced most by practices whose transactional sequence was initiated by an act of giving.

Frequently Cited

ADOLF BERGER, 43 ENCYCLOPEDIC DICTIONARY OF ROMAN LAW, PART 2 (1953), *available at* http://books.google.com/books?id=iklePELtR6QC&printsec=frontcover&source=gbs_v2_summary_r&cad=0 [hereinafter BERGER, ENCYCLOPEDIC DICTIONARY].

ANTONIO L. TURNES, MAIMONIDES: EL SABIO SEFARDÍ (Granada ed. 2004) [hereinafter TURNES, MAIMONIDES].

ARISTOTLE & RICHARD MCKEON, THE BASIC WORKS OF ARISTOTLE (Richard McKeon ed., 1914) [hereinafter ARISTOTLE].

ARTHUR CORBIN, 2 CORBIN ON CONTRACTS (Joseph M. Perillo & Hellen H. Bender ed., rev. ed. 1995) [hereinafter CORBIN, ON CONTRACTS].

ARTHUR TAYLOR VON MEHREN & JAMES RUSSELL GORDLEY, THE CIVIL LAW SYSTEM: AN INTRODUCTION TO THE COMPARATIVE STUDY OF LAW (2d ed. 1977) [hereinafter Von MEHREN & GORDLEY, THE CIVIL LAW SYSTEM].

BAUMBACH ET AL., HANDELSGESETZBUCH (27 ed. 1987).

BENJAMIN NELSON, THE IDEA OF USURY: FROM. TRIBAL BROTHERHOOD TO UNIVERSAL OTHERHOOD (2d ed. 1969) (1949) [hereinafter NELSON, THE IDEA OF USURY].

BETRIEBS-BERATER, http://www.betriebs-berater.de/ (last visited Dec. 16, 2013).

Boris Kozolchyk, *A Roadmap to Economic Development Through Law: Third Parties and Comparative Legal Structure*, 23 ARIZ. J. INT'L & COMP. L. 1 (2005) [hereinafter Kozolchyk, *Roadmap*].

Boris Kozolchyk, *Closing Remarks on the Rule of Law, Democracy, and Economic Development (a hemispherice conference sponsored by LexisNexis and Inter-American Bar Associations) (Mexico City, 2007)* 25 ARIZ. J. INT'L & COMP. L. 437 (2008) [hereinafter Kozolchyk, *Closing Remarks*].

Boris Kozolchyk, *Fairness in Anglo and Latin American Commercial Adjudication*, 2 B.C. INT'L & COMP. L. REV. 219 (1979) [hereinafter Kozolchyk, *Fairness*].

Boris Kozolchyk, *Highways and Byways of NAFTA Commercial Law: The Challenge To Develop a Best Practice in North American Trade*, 4 U.S. MEX. L.J. 1 (1996) [hereinafter Kozolchyk, *Highways and Byways*].

BORIS KOZOLCHYK, LA CONTRATACIÓN COMERCIAL EN EL DERECHO COMPARADO (2006) [hereinafter KOZOLCHYK, EL DERECHO COMERCIAL].

Boris Kozolchyk, *Law of the U.S. in Comparative-Legal Reasoning-Perspective, in* I UNITED STATES LAW OF TRADE AND INVESTMENT 1-12 (Boris Kozolchyk & John F. Molloy eds., 2001) [hereinafter Kozolchyk, I UNITED STATES LAW 1-12].

Boris Kozolchyk, *Modernization of Commercial Law: International Uniformity and Economic Development* 34 BROOK. J. INT'L L. 709 (2009), *available at* http://www.brooklaw.edu/students/journals/bjilcurrent.php [hereinafter Kozolchyk, *Modernization*].

Boris Kozolchyk, *NAFTA in the Grand and Small Scheme of Things*, 13 ARIZ. J. INT'L & COMP. L. 135 (1996) [hereinafter Kozolchyk, *Grand and Small Scheme*].

Boris Kozolchyk, *Negotiable Instruments and Bank Deposits and Collections*, *in* III U.S. LAW OF TRADE & INVESTMENT 22-2 (Boris Kozolchyk & John F. Molloy eds., 2001) [hereinafter Kozolchyk, *Negotiable Instruments*].

Boris Kozolchyk, *On the State of Commercial Law at the End of the 20th Century*, 8 ARIZ. J. INT'L & COMP. L. 23 (1991) [hereinafter Kozolchyk, *On the State of Commercial Law*].

Boris Kozolchyk, *Secured Lending and Its Poverty Reduction Effect*, 42 TEX. INT'L L.J. 727 (2007) [hereinafter Kozolchyk, *Reduction of Poverty*].

Boris Kozolchyk, *Transfer of Personal Property by a Non-Owner: Its Future in Light of its Past*, 61 TUL. L. REV. 1453 (1987) [hereinafter Kozolchyk, *Transfer*].

Boris Kozolchyk, *The Commercialization of Civil Law and the Civilization of Commercial Law*, 40 LA. L. REV. 3 (1979) [hereinafter Kozolchyk, *Commercialization*].

Boris Kozolchyk, *The Mexican Land Registry; a Critical Evaluation*, 12 ARIZ. L. REV. 308 (1970) [hereinafter Kozolchyk, *Mexican Land Registry*].

Boris Kozolchyk, *The UNIDROIT Principles as a Model for the Unification of the Best Contractual Practices in the Americas* 46 AM. J. COMP. L. 151 (1998) [hereinafter Kozolchyk, *UNIDROIT Principles*].

Boris Kozolchyk, *Toward a Theory of Law in Economic Development, the Costa Rican USAID-ROCAP Law Reform Project,* LAW & SOC. ORDER 681 (1971) [hereinafter Kozolchyk, *Toward a Theory of Law*].

Boris Kozolchyk, *Towards New Customs and Practices for Documentary Credits; The Methodology of the Proposed Revision*, in COMMERCIAL LAW ANNUAL (Louis F. Del Duca & Patrick Del Duca eds., 1993) [hereinafter Kozolchyk, *Towards New Customs*].

Boris Kozolchyk & Dale Beck Furnish, *The OAS Model Law on Secured Transactions: A Comparative Analysis*, 12 SW. J. L. & TRADE AM. 235 (2005–2006) [hereinafter Kozolchyk & Furnish, *A Comparative Analysis*].

BORIS KOZOLCHYK, DALE BECK FURNISH & MAREK DUBOVEC, LAW OF SECURED TRANSACTIONS IN A COMPARATIVE AND ECONOMIC DEVELOPMENT PERSPECTIVE (forthcoming) [hereinafter KOZOLCHYK, FURNISH & DUBOVEC, DEVELOPMENT PERSPECTIVE].

Boris Kozolchyk & John M. Wilson, *The Organization of American States: The New Model Inter-American Law on Secured Transactions,* 7 UNIF. L. REV. 69 (2002) [hereinafter Kozolchyk & Wilson, *The New Model Inter-American Law*].

BORIS KOZOLCHYK ET. AL, UNITED STATES LAW OF TRADE AND INVESTMENT (Boris Kozolchyk & John F. Molloy eds., 2001) [hereinafter Kozolchyk, I, II, III or IV UNITED STATES LAW].

CLAUS-WILHELM CANARIS ET AL., HGB: STAUB GROSSKOMMENTAR (1983). DER BETRIEB, http://www.der-betrieb.de/content/ (last visited Dec. 16, 2013).

DON FELIPE II, NOVÍSIMA RECOPILACIÓN DE LAS LEYES DE ESPAÑA (1805), *available at* http://fama2.us.es/fde/ocr/2006/novisimaRecopilacionT1.pdf [hereinafter NOVÍSIMA RECOPILACIÓN].

EDWARD ADAMSON HOEBEL, THE LAW OF PRIMITIVE MAN: A STUDY IN COMPARATIVE LEGAL DYNAMICS (Harvard University Press 2006) (1954) [hereinafter HOEBEL, PRIMITIVE MAN].

Ernest G. Lorenzen, *Causa and Consideration in the Law of Contract*, 28 YALE L.J. 621 (1919) [hereinafter Lorenzen, *Causa and Consideration*].

FERNAND BRAUDEL, I THE STRUCTURES OF EVERYDAY LIFE: CIVILIZATION & CAPITALISM 15TH–18TH CENTURY (Siân Reynolds trans., William Collins Sons & Co., & Harper & Row, Publishers, Inc. 1981) (1979) [hereinafter BRAUDEL I].

FERNAND BRAUDEL, II THE WHEELS OF COMMERCE: CIVILIZATION AND CAPITALISM 15TH – 18TH CENTURY (Siân Reynolds trans., William Collins Sons & Co., & Harper & Row, Publishers, Inc. 1981) (1979) [hereinafter BRAUDEL II].

1161 words from pp. 29, 62, 64, 67, 68, 73–4, 75, 85, 90–1, 94–5, 97, 100, 101, 315–16, 317, 319–20 from CIVILIZATION AND CAPITALISM 15TH–18TH CENTURY, VOL. 2: THE WHEELS OF COMMERCE by FERNAND BRAUDEL. Copyright (c) 1979 by Librairie Armand Colin, Paris. English translation copyright (c) 1982 by William Collins Sons & Co. Ltd and Harper & Row, Publishers, Inc. Reprinted by permission of HarperCollins Publishers.

FERNAND BRAUDEL, III THE PERSPECTIVE OF THE WORLD (Siân Reynolds trans., William Collins Sons & Co., & Harper & Row, Publishers, Inc. 1984) (1979) [hereinafter BRAUDEL III].

FRANCIS DE ZULUETA, 1 INSTITUTES OF GAIUS BOOK I (1946) [hereinafter ZULUETA 1].

FRANCIS DE ZULUETA, II THE INSTITUTES OF GAIUS (1953) [hereinafter ZULUETA II].

FRANZ WIEACKER, A HISTORY OF PRIVATE LAW IN EUROPE: WITH PARTICULAR REFERENCE TO GERMANY (Tony Weir trans., 1995) [hereinafter WIEACKER, HISTORY OF PRIVATE LAW].

FRITZ SCHULZ, HISTORY OF ROMAN LEGAL SCIENCE (1952) [hereinafter SCHULZ, HISTORY].

GEORGE HOROWITZ, THE SPIRIT OF JEWISH LAW (1953) [hereinafter HOROWITZ, JEWISH LAW].

GEORGES RIPERT, I TRAITE ÉLEMENTAIRE DE DROIT COMMERCIAL (5th ed. René Roblot, 1963) [hereinafter RIPERT].

Germany, Encyclopædia Britannica, http://www.britannica.com/EBchecked/topic/231186/Germany/58171/Germany-from-c-1760-to-1815 (last accessed June 26, 2013) [hereinafter Britannica].

GINO GORLA, I EL CONTRATO:EXPOSICION GENERAL (Jose Vilella ed., Bosch 1959) (1955) & GINO GORLA, II EL CONTRATO: CASUISTICA Y PROBLEMAS (Jose Vilella ed. 1959) [hereinafter GORLA I & GORLA II].

H.E. Yntema, *Roman Law and its Influence in Western Civilization*, 35 Cornell L. Q. 77 (1949-1950) [hereinafter Yntema, *Roman Law*].

INSTITUTES OF GAIUS E.G.: G. INST. 1.1 (F. de Zulueta trans., 1946).

IRVING ABRAHAM AGUS, I URBAN CIVILIZATION IN PRE-CRUSADE EUROPE (1965) [hereinafter AGUS I].

IRVING ABRAHAM AGUS, II URBAN CIVILIZATION IN PRE-CRUSADE EUROPE (1965) [hereinafter AGUS II].

ISAIAS COVARRUBIAS, LA ECONOMÍA MEDIEVAL Y LA EMERGENCIA DEL CAPITALISMO (2004), *available at* http://www.eumed.net/cursecon/libreria/2004/icm/icm.htm (on file with autor) [hereinafter COVARRUBIAS].

J. VON STAUDINGER, KOMMENTAR ZUM BÜRGERLICHEN GESETZBUCH MIT EINFÜHRUNGSGESETZ UND NEBENGESETZEN (13th ed. 1996).

James R. Gordley, *Contract in Pre-Commercial Societies and in Western History*, *in* 7 INTERNATIONAL ENCYCLOPEDIA OF COMPARATIVE LAW (Arthur T. von Mehren et. al. eds., 1997) [hereinafter Gordley, *Contract in Pre-Commercial Societies*]. This citation is to Von Mehren and Gordley's *The Civil Law*, and not to the Encyclopedia.

John Beverley, *"Lazarillo" and Primitive Accumulation: Spain, Capitalism and the Modern Novel*, 15 BULL. MIDWEST MODERN LANGUAGE ASSOC. 29 (1982) [hereinafter Beverley, *Lazarillo*].

JOHN PHILIP DAWSON, UNJUST ENRICHMENT: A COMPARATIVE ANALYSIS (1969).

JOHN THOMAS NOONAN, THE SCHOLASTIC ANALYSIS OF USURY (1957).

KONRAD ZWEIGERT & HEINRICH KOTZ, I INTRODUCTION TO COMPARATIVE LAW (Tong Weir trans., 2d rev. ed. 1987) [hereinafter ZWEIGERT & KOTZ, COMPARATIVE LAW].

LETTERS OF MEDIEVAL JEWISH TRADERS (S.D. Goitein trans., 1973) [hereinafter LETTERS OF TRADERS].

MANUEL CUADRADO, CÓDIGO CIVIL: CONCORDADO Y ANOTADO CON JURISPRUDENCIA (S.L. Dykinson ed., 2007).

MANUEL JESÚS GARCÍA GARRIDO, CASUISMO Y JURISPRUDENCIA ROMANA: PLEITOS FAMOSOS DEL DIGESTO (1965) [hereinafter GARCÍA GARRIDO, CASUISMO Y JURISPRUDENCIA].

MARTIN PELTZER & ELIZABETH A. VOIGHT, GERMAN COMMERCIAL CODE (5th rev. ed. 2003) [hereinafter PELTZER & VOIGHT].

MAX WEBER, HISTORY OF COMMERCIAL PARTNERSHIPS IN THE MIDDLE AGES (Lutz Kaelber trans., 2003) [hereinafter WEBER, HISTORY].

MAX WEBER, LAW IN ECONOMY AND SOCIETY (Max Rheinstein ed., 1966) [hereinafter WEBER, LAW IN ECONOMY AND SOCIETY].

National Law Center for Inter-American Free Trade [hereinafter NLCIFT].

NATIONAL LAW CENTER FOR INTER-AMERICAN FREE TRADE, NLCIFT *12 Principles of Secured Transactions Law in the Americas* (2006), http://db.natlaw.com/bci9.pdf [hereinafter NLCIFT, *12 Principles*].

National Law Center for Inter-American Free Trade, *North American Transportation Practices* (1998), http://natlaw.com/pubs/purchase/nast.htm [hereinafter *NASTRAPS*].

NIALL FERGUSON, I THE HOUSE OF ROTHSCHILD: MONEY'S PROPHETS: 1798–1848 (1999) [hereinafter FERGUSON]. Reprinted by permission of Penguin Publishers.

OTTO PALANDT ET AL., BÜRGERLICHES GESETZBUCH (61st ed. 2002).

RAYMOND DE ROOVER, BUSINESS, BANKING AND ECONOMIC THOUGHT IN LATE MEDIEVAL AND EARLY MODERN EUROPE (A COLLECTION OF ESSAYS) (Julius Kirshner ed., 1974) [hereinafter DE ROOVER, BUSINESS, BANKING AND ECONOMIC THOUGHT].

REINHARD ZIMMERMANN, THE LAW OF OBLIGATIONS: ROMAN FOUNDATIONS OF THE CIVILIAN TRADITION (1996).

REUVEN YARON, INTRODUCTION TO THE LAW OF THE ARAMAIC PAPYRI (1961) [hereinafter YARON, INTRODUCTION].

RICARDO OLIVERA GARCIA, CÓDIGO DE COMERCIO ANOTADO (1998).

ROBERT JOSEPH POTHIER, I A TREATISE ON OBLIGATIONS, CONSIDERED IN A MORAL AND LEGAL VIEW (Martin & Ogden trans., 1802) [hereinafter POTHIER, I OBLIGATIONS].

RUDOLPH B. SCHLESINGER, HANS W. BAADE, PETER HERZOG & EDWARD M. WISE, Comparative Law (6th ed. 1998) [hereinafter SCHLESINGER ET AL., COMPARATIVE LAW].

RUDOLF VON IHERING, LAW AS A MEANS TO AN END (Isaac Husik trans., 1913) [hereinafter VON IHERING, A MEANS TO AN END].

S.D. GOITEIN, A MEDITERRANEAN SOCIETY: THE JEWISH COMMUNITIES OF THE ARAB WORLD AS PORTRAYED IN THE DOCUMENTS OF THE ARAB GENIZA VOLUMES I & II (1967) [hereinafter GOITEIN, MEDITERRANEAN SOCIETY].

TESHUVOT HA-RAMBAM, RESPONSES IN ARABIC (Joshua Blau trans 7th ed., 1961) (on file with author) [hereinafter TESHUVOT HA-RAMBAM].

THE AMERICAN LAW INSTITUTE, RESTATEMENT OF THE LAW SECOND: CONTRACTS 2D (1979) [hereinafter RESTATEMENT (SECOND) OF CONTRACTS].

THE AMERICAN LAW INSTITUTE, RESTATEMENT OF THE LAW THIRD: AGENCY (2006) [hereinafter RESTATEMENT (THIRD) OF AGENCY].

THE CAMBRIDGE ECONOMIC HISTORY OF EUROPE, V THE ECONOMIC ORGANIZATION OF EARLY MODERN EUROPE (E.E. Rich & C.H. Wilson eds., 1977) [hereinafter CAMBRIDGE HISTORY VOL. V].

THE CAMBRIDGE MODERN HISTORY, IX NAPOLEON (A.W. Ward et al. eds., 1906), *available at* http://archive.org/stream/cambridgemodern09actouoft/#page/n5/mode/2up.

IX THE CAMBRIDGE MODERN HISTORY, (A.W. Ward, et al. eds., Norwood Press, 1909) (1906) [hereinafter IX CAMBRIDGE HISTORY].

I THE DIGEST OF JUSTINIAN (Alan Watson ed., University of Pennslyvania Press 1998) (1985) [hereinafter WATSON, DIGEST].

II THE DIGEST OF JUSTINIAN (Alan Watson ed., University of Pennslyvania Press 1998) (1985) [hereinafter WATSON, DIGEST II].

Tine De Moor, The Silent Revolution. The Emergence of Commons, Guilds and Other Forms of Corporate Collective Action in Western Europe From a New Perspective. Paper presented at The Return of the Guilds Symposium, Utrecht University (5-7 October 2006), *available at* http://www.iisg.nl/hpw/papers/guilds-demoor.pdf [hereinafter De Moor, *The silent revolution*].

THEODOR MOMMSEN, HISTORY OF ROME VOLUMES 1 & 2 (1868) [hereinafter MOMMSEN, HISTORY].

WILLIAM WARWICK BUCKLAND, A MANUAL OF ROMAN PRIVATE LAW (2d rev ed., Scientia Verlag 1981) (1953) [hereinafter BUCKLAND, MANUAL].

WM GRUPPE, http://www.wmrecht.de/index.php (last visited Dec. 16, 2013).

International Organizations:

European Union, *The Principles of European Contract Law 2002 (Parts I, II, and III)*, LEXMERCATORIA.ORG (2002), http://www.jus.uio.no/lm/eu.contract.principles.parts.1.to.3.2002/landscape.pdf [hereinafter EPCL].

INT'L CHAMBER OF COMMERCE, INCOTERMS 2010 (2010).

INT'L CHAMBER OF COMMERCE, UNIFORM CUSTOMS AND PRACTICE FOR DOCUMENTARY CREDITS [UCP] No. 500 (1993) [hereinafter UCP 500].

INT'L CHAMBER OF COMMERCE, UNIFORM CUSTOMS AND PRACTICE FOR DOCUMENTARY CREDITS [UCP] No. 600 (2007) [hereinafter UCP 600].

ORGANIZATION OF AMERICAN STATES, INTER-AMERICAN RULES ON ELECTRONIC DOCUMENTS AND SIGNATURES (IAREDS) (2001), *available at* http://www.oas.org/dil/CIDIP-VII_topics_futures_cidips_electroniccommerce_signatures_3oct2001.htm [hereinafter IAREDS].

Organization of American States [OAS], *Model Inter-American Law on Secured Transactions* CIDIP-VI/RES. 5/02, *adopted by the Sixth Inter-American Specialized Conference on Private International Law*, (Feb. 27, 2002) [hereinafter *Model Law*].

U.N. INT'L INSTITUE FOR THE UNIFICATION OF PRIVATE LAW [UNIDROIT], UNIDROIT PRINCIPLES OF INTERNATIONAL COMMERCIAL CONTRACTS (2010), http://www.unidroit.org/english/principles/contracts/principles2010/integralversionprinciples2010-e.pdf [hereinafter UNIDROIT Principles].

Uniform Commercial Code [U.C.C.] § xx [hereinafter U.C.C. § xx].

United Nations Convention on Contracts for the International Sale of Goods, Apr. 11, 1980, 19 I.L.M. 668, 1489 U.N.T.S. 3 [hereinafter CISG].

Argentina:

CÓDIGO CIVIL [CÓD. CIV.] [CIVIL CODE] art. xx (Arg.) (translated by author) [hereinafter CÓD. CIV. (ARG.)].

CÓDIGO DE COMERCIO [CÓD. COM.] [COMMERCIAL CODE] art. xx (Arg.) (translated by author) [hereinafter CÓD. COM. (ARG.)].

China:

Constitution:

Constitution, THE NATIONAL PEOPLE'S CONGRESS OF THE PEOPLE'S REPUBLIC OF CHINA, http://www.npc.gov.cn/englishnpc/Constitution/node_2830.htm (last visited Dec. 10, 2013) [hereinafter PRC CONST. ch. xx, § xx (1982)].

Constitution, THE NATIONAL PEOPLE'S CONGRESS OF THE PEOPLE'S REPUBLIC OF CHINA, http://www.npc.gov.cn/englishnpc/Constitution/2007-11/15/content_1372962.htm (last visited Dec. 10, 2013) [hereinafter PRC CONST. ch. xx, § xx (2004)].

Other Laws:

Contract Law of the People's Republic of China (adopted & promulgated by the Second Session of the Ninth National People's Congress March 15, 1999), NOVEXCN.COM, http://www.novexcn.com/contract_law_99.html (last visited Dec. 10, 2013) [hereinafter PRC, Contract Law (1999)].

General Principles of the Civil Law of the People's Republic of China (Adopted on April 12, 1986), THE SUPREME PEOPLE'S COURT OF THE PEOPLE'S REPUBLIC OF CHINA: PRL LAWS (Mar. 6, 2003), http://en.chinacourt.org/public/detail.php?id=2696 [hereinafter PRC, General Principles (1986)].

LEHMAN, LEE & XU LLX TRANSLATION DEPARTMENT, PROPERTY RIGHTS LAW OF THE PEOPLE'S REPUBLIC OF CHINA (2007), *available at* http://www.lehmanlaw.com/fileadmin/lehmanlaw_com/laws___regulations/Propoerty_Rights_Law_of_the_PRC__LLX__03162007.pdf [hereinafter Lehman et al., PRL (2007)].

THE REAL RIGHTS PROPERTY LAW OF THE PEOPLE'S REPUBLIC OF CHINA (John Jiang trans., adopted & promulgated, 2007), *available at* http://www.cclaw.net/library/real_rights_law_part_i.pdf (full text on file with author) [hereinafter John Liang PRL].

France:

Civil Code:

CODE CIVIL [C. CIV.] art. xx (Fr.) (2008), *available at* http://www.legifrance.gouv.fr/home.jsp, (translated by author) [hereinafter C. CIV. (FR.) arts. xx].

CODE CIVIL (Georges Rouhette & Anne Rouhette-Berton trans.) (2006), *available at* http://www.legifrance.gouv.fr/Traductions/en-English/Legifrance-translations (translated by author) [hereinafter LEGIFRANCE [C. CIV.] (FR.) arts. xx].

WHEN CITING TO Barrister of the Inner Temple:

CODE NAPOLEON OR THE FRENCH CIVIL CODE (Barrister of the Inner Temple trans., Claitor 1960) (1824) (translated by author) [hereinafter C. CIV. (FR.) page (Barrister 1804)].

When citing to Dalloz:

CODE CIVIL [C. CIV.] art. xx (Codes Dalloz 1992-1993) (translated by author) [hereinafter C. CIV. (FR.) page (Dalloz 1992-93)].

Commercial Code:

When citing to Dalloz:

CODE DE COMMERCE [C. COM.] art. xx (Petits Codes Dalloz) (translated by author) [hereinafer C. COM. (FR.) page (Dalloz year)].

When citing to Legifrance *Code de Commerce* (2008) version:

CODE DE COMMERCE [C. COM.] art. XX (FR.) (2008) *available at* http://www.legifrance.gouv.fr/initRechCodeArticle.do (translated by author) [hereinafter C. COM. (FR.) arts. xx (2008)].

When citing to original:

CODE DE COMMERCE [C. COM.] art. XX (FR.) (1807) (translated by author) [hereinafter C. COM. (FR.) article (1807)].

Germany:

Civil Code:

German Civil Code BGB, JURIS GMBH, SAARBRUCKEN (2007), *available at* www.juris.de (on file with author) [hereinafter BGB].

THE GERMAN CIVIL CODE, REVISED ED., AS AMENDED TO JAN. 1, 1992 (Simon L. Goren trans.) (1994), [hereinafter BGB (GOREN, 1994)].

Commercial Code:

HANDELSGESETZBUCH [HBG] [COMMERCIAL CODE], May 10, 1897, Reichsgesetzblatt [RGBl] 219 (Ger.) [hereinafter HGB, 1897].

THE GERMAN COMMERCIAL CODE, 2D ED., REVISED AND AMENDED TO OCT. 28, 1994 (Simon L. Goren trans.) (1998), [hereinafter HGB (GOREN, 1998)].

Constitution:

GRUNDGESETZ FUR DIE BUNDESREPUBLIK DEUTSCHLAND [GRUNDGESETZ] [GG] [BASIC LAW], May 23, 1949, BGBI (Ger.) [hereinafter G.G.].

Italy:

Codice civile [C.c.] (It.) (1942) [hereinafter C.C. (ITALY) (1942)].

Mexico:

Civil Code:

Código Civil Federal, NATLAW.COM, http://www.natlaw.com/interam/mx/hl/hlmxcu.htm (last accessed Oct. 3, 2008) (translated by author) [hereinafter Mexican C.C.F. (2008)].

Codigo Civil para el Distrito y Territorio Federales [Civil Code for the Federal District and Territories], Diario Oficial de la Federación [DO], *as amended,* 1 de Septiembre de 1932 (Mex.) (translated by author) [hereinafter C.C.D.T.F. (1932)].

Código Civil para el Distrito y Territorios Federales en Materia Común, y para toda la República en Materia Federal [Civil Code for the Federal District and Territories in Ordinary Matters, and for the entire Republic on Federal Matters], Diario Oficial de la Federación [DO], 26 de Mayo de 1928 (Mex.) (translated by author) [hereinafter Mexican C.C.F. (1932)].

MÉXICO (D.F.), CODIGO CIVIL: PARA EL DISTRITO Y TERRITORIO FEDERALES (1955) [hereinafter C.C.D.T.F. (1955)].

Commercial Code:

Código de Comercio [CCo.] [Commercial Code], Diario Oficial de la Federación [DO], 13 de Diciembre de 1889 (Mex.) (translated by author) [hereinafter COD. COM.(MEX.) art. xx (1889)].

Código de Comercio [CCo.] [Commercial Code], Diario Oficial de la Federación [DO], *as amended,* 30 de Diciembre de 2008 (translated by author) [hereinafter COD. COM.(MEX.) art. xx (2008)].

Constitution:

Constitución Politica de los Estados Unidos Mexicanos [C.P.], *as amended,* Diario Oficial de la Federación [DO], 5 de Febrero de 1917 (Mex.), *available at* http://natlaw.com/interam/mx/any/pr/prmxany00121.htm (translated by author) [hereinafter MEX. CONST. (1917)].

Other laws:

Ley Federal Protección al Consumidor [LFPC] [Federal Consumer Protection Law], Diario Oficial de la Federación [DO], 24 de Diciembre de 1992 (Mex.), *available at* http://natlaw.com/interam/mx/cs/st/stmxcs00007.htm (translated by author) [hereinafter L.F.P.C. (MEX.) art. xx].

Russia:

1936 Constitution of the USSR Adopted December 1936, BUCKNELL.EDU, http://www.departments.bucknell.edu/russian/const/36cons01.html (last visited Dec. 10, 2013) [hereinafter USSR CONST. ch. xx, art. xx(1936)] (on file with author).

Grazhdanskii Kodeks Rossiinskoi Federatsii [GK RF] [Civil Code] art. xx (USSR) (1922) [hereinafter RSFSR CIVIL CODE (1922)].

Spain:

C.C., B.O.E. n. 206, July 25, 1889 (Spain) (translated by author) [hereinafter C.C. (SPAIN) (1889)].

C. Com. (Spain) (translated by author) [hereinafter C.Com.].

United States of America:

Constitution of the United States, THE CHARTERS OF FREEDOM, http://www.archives.gov/exhibits/charters/constitution_transcript.html (last visited Dec. 10, 2013) [hereinafter U.S. CONST. (1787)].

West's National Reporter System [NRS] (1879), *available at* www.lawschool.westlaw.com.

United States Code [U.S.C.] § xx [hereinafter U.S.C. § xx].

United States Code Annotated [U.S.C.A] § xx [hereinafter U.S.C.A. § xx].

Table of Abbreviations

ADHGB	General Code of Commercial Laws (Germany) *Allegemeines Deutsches Handelsgesetzbuch*
ALI	American Law Institute
BGB	Civil Code (Germany) *Bürgerliches Gesetzbuch*
CCCP	Central Committee of the Communist Party (China)
CCP	Chinese Communist Party
CISG	United Nations Convention on International Sale of Goods
Code Civil	French Civil Code
Code de Commerce	French Commercial Code
Cour de Cassation	French Court of Final Civil, Commercial and Criminal Appeals.
D.	Recueil Dalloz
EPCL	Principles of European Contract Law (European Union)
GAFTA	Grain and Feed Trade Association
HGB	Commercial Code (Germany) *Handelsgesetzbuch*
ICC	International Chamber of Commerce
INCOTERMS	International Commercial Terms of the ICC
ISDA	International Swaps and Derivatives Association
JCP	*Juris-Classeur Périodique, Edition Commerce et Industrie*; *Code de Commerce*
LOC	Letter of Credit
NAFTA	North American Free Trade Agreement
NCCUSL	National Conference of Commissioners of Uniform State Law

NLCIFT	National Law Center for Inter-American Free Trade
OAS	Organization of American States
PPSA	Personal Property Security Act (Canada)
PRC	People's Republic of China
PRL	Property Rights Law of 2007 (China)
SBPED	Standard Banking Practice for the Examination of Letter of Credit Documents
SJFG	*Semanario Judicial de la Federación y su Gaceta*
SWIFT	Society for Worldwide Interbank Financial Telecommunication
UCC	Uniform Commercial Code (United States)
UCP	Uniform Customs and Practices for Documentary Credits of the ICC
ULC	Uniform Law Commission
UNCITRAL	United Nations Commission on International Trade Law
UNIDROIT	International Institute for the Unification of Private Law
USCIB	United States Council for International Business
WM	*Wertpapier-Mitteilungen*

Table of Cases

Table of Statutes

Glossary

A Posteriori – A reasoning or assertion based on proven experience.

A Priori – A form of reasoning not based on factual observation or experience, but on formal logic or on theoretical assumptions unsupported by facts.

Abstract or Independent Obligation or Promise – An obligation or promise whose enforcement depends on terms and conditions incorporated into a reliable medium of communication. Thus, its enforcement is not dependent on equities or defenses derived from underlying and unincorporated transactions. A United States treasury bill endowed with legal tender is a promise at the highest level of abstraction. A banker's acceptance of his or her client's or third party's bill of exchange drawn on him is a notch below the treasury bill in its abstraction. This is because it is subject to defenses such as fraud in its inception or *ad factum*. An ordinary contractual promise lacks abstraction because, in principle, it is subject to all the defenses and equities of the present and underlying contractual relationships.

Acceptance of a Negotiable Promise – The act of assuming a primary and abstract liability by an acceptor of a bill of exchange by signing his name in the acceptor's column. When the acceptor is a banker, his acceptance is known as a banker's acceptance and as an abstract promise is negotiable in numerous financial markets.

Acte Authentique – A formal document executed before a French Notary or Government Official empowered to authenticate its enforcement.

***Actes de Commerce* (Acts of Commerce)** – The transactions that are listed as part of the scope provisions in commercial codes of civil law countries that were influenced by the French *Code de Commerce* of 1807. Their purpose is to indicate that the listed transactions will be governed by the commercial code, although commonly civil code provisions will also be applied where there are gaps in the coverage of the commercial code.

Actio Empti, Actio Venditi – Roman law actions associated with sale and purchase agreements (*Emptio-Venditio*). The former action was brought by the buyer to recover the thing he bought and paid for, but had not been delivered or was defective. The latter was brought by the seller to recover the price of what he sold but was still not paid for by the buyer.

***Actio Pignoraticia* (Action on the Pledge)** – The Roman law action brought by the secured creditor (pledgee) to foreclose on the pledged thing.

Ad Probationem* and *Ad Solemnitatem – Expressions used mostly in civil law countries to characterize the type of formality required in different contracts and their effects upon the enforcement of those promises. Those contracts that are enforceable despite the absence of formalities, such as the sale of goods, are deemed to rely on formalities only for evidentiary purposes (*ad probationem*) and to facilitate proving the parties' intent. In contrast, those contracts whose absence of specified formalities renders them null and void, as is the case with the sale (or in some jurisdictions the mortgage) of real property, are deemed to be contracts *ad solemnitatem*; they are null and void without their solemnity.

Aleatory Contracts – Contracts in which one of the parties assumes the risk that a specified act, event or performance will or will not take place. Insurance and credit default swaps are typical aleatory contracts.

***Amparo* Appeal** – *Amparo* appeals are the most common in Mexican law. They are present in most of the Mexican decisions discussed in this book. In a so called Direct *Amparo*, the appellant complains that his constitutional right to a due process of law was violated by the lower court when it ignored or misapplied the law. The Mexican *Amparo* (unlike other Latin American amparos) shares with the French *Cassation* appeal the allegation that the lower court erred when applying the law to the facts of the case, and for this reason it is a strictly a legal (non-factual) appeal. It differs from the French *Cassation* in that French appellants do not claim that their constitutional rights of due process were violated by the alleged judicial mistaken application of the law.

Archetypal Merchant – A merchant whose behavior is representative of the group or sector in which he does his regular business. This behavior could be morally exemplary such as that of Justice Cardozo's entrusted fiduciary who behaved with the punctilio "the most honorable," or it could be reprehensible such as that of the "picaresque" (tricky and deceitful) merchant. He could also be could also be crassly utilitarian, such as Justice Holme's "bad man" of contracts.

"Bad Man" of Contracts – Justice Oliver Wendell Holmes Jr.'s archetypal contracting party who would not hesitate to breach his contractual promise when he calculates that he would be economically better off by breaching it and paying damages than by performing it.

Bonus Paterfamilias – The most commonly used archetypal standard of contractual diligence in the *Code Civil* and in its progeny. Literally it refers to the diligence of a good father of a family, but it has remained an excessively vague standard and has been extended by French courts and commentators with equal vagueness to the diligence of a good ship captain, restaurant owner, travel agent and other merchants.

Bonus Vir – A Roman law designation for an upright, honest and knowledgeable merchant, or a "man of affairs" to whom disputed issues of contract interpretation are submitted for his usually decisive opinion.

Breach of Warranty – A generic action against a seller of goods who has either failed to fulfill an express promise with respect to the quality of the goods sold, or who has failed to fulfill his duties with respect to two major implied warranties or representations of quality: a) merchantability, or fitness of the goods, for the purposes ascribed to them in the usages of the trade in question (U.C.C. § 2–314) or fitness for the particular purpose implied in the contract in question (U.C.C. § 2–315).

"Brotherly" Standard of Fairness – A standard of fairness that requires that a contracting party treat the other in an altruistic enough manner so that his own contractual interests are subordinated to those of the entrusting party. This standard is usually applied to fiduciaries entrusted with the assets of the other contracting party. This standard was common during the early middle ages among Jewish merchants engaged in long distance Mediterranean trade, especially those entrusted with goods or money by their religious "brethren."

Cadastral Survey – A detailed metes and bounds description of property for preponderantly fiscal purposes which usually includes a physical representation of the property either by aerial photography or computerized images of parcels and subdivisions.

Casuistry – A method of drafting and interpreting statutory, administrative or judicial rules which narrowly and exclusively circumscribe their application to the proven facts that prompted the drafting or interpretation. At its most extreme, casuistry rejects an analogical and reasonable application of rules.

Causa – A term common in civil law countries whose codes have been modeled after the *Code Civil.* At its most basic, it is the reason why the parties enter into their contracts and thus it is a requirement for their validity. This validity presupposes that its *causa* does not violate the law, public policy and morality.

Causa Data – The actual performance of a contractual obligation commonly consisting of the giving of something to the other party that entitles the performing party to demand the counter-party/s performance.

Caveat Emptor – A medieval English law doctrine whose literal meaning was "Buyer beware." It assumed that in the absence of express statements or representations with respect to the quality of the goods purchased, the buyer assumed the risk of the seller's lesser quality and patent, as well as latent defects of the goods purchased. Gradually, this doctrine was replaced by the actions for implied warranties of merchantability and fitness for the particular contract purposes. *See* Breach of Warranty.

Commercial Letter of Credit – A banking instrument for the payment and financing of mostly international sales. It is usually payable against the presentation of documents indicating the shipment of specified goods, their price, quantity, quality and origin, as well as their insurance coverage. This letter of credit is most frequently referred to as a "documentary letter of credit."

Commercial Transaction – In addition to its lay meeting which connotes a for-profit contract, it is also used in this book as a technical legal term that encompasses three contractual relationships: One is the traditional two party relationship in which the contracting parties are bound to each other as a result of simultaneous or successive exchanges of promises, acts, goods or things. Another is a contemporary version which involves multiple parties and a series of promises and performances by them, although not in a "synallagmatic" (or direct and sequential exchange of promises or performances) fashion. As parties to a "Master Agreement," promises and performances depend upon the promises and performances by third (non-synallagmatic) parties. For example, even though a freight forwarder was contacted by a seller to obtain shipping space for his goods, what triggers his request for space to the carrier was a notification that the buyer electronically procured the issuance of an irrevocable confirmed letter of credit by a third party bank. Thus a computer-generated program of purchase of inventory may start out by a buyer's request to his bank to issue a letter of credit to a seller beneficiary, and at the same time trigger a request to the seller's freight forwarder to procure shipping space, and will proceed with a request by that freight forwarder to an insurer to issue a maritime policy, etc. The third type of commercial transaction frequently discussed in this book refers to a "firm" or irrevocable promise that cannot be revoked by its issuer during a specified or reasonable time of enforcement. Depending upon the legal system, this promise is binding on the promisor from the moment of its issuance regardless of whether it was or was not accepted by the promisee or offeree during that time.

Compadrazgo – *See Guanxi.*

Consensual Contracts – In Roman law as well as in the *Code Civil,* the term consensual contract refers to a type of contract that is enforceable despite its lack of formality. Thus the parties' agreement on its subject matter and price in a sale of goods sufficed to bind the parties. This practice supported the principle that the parties' mere consent binds them (*solus consensus obligat*). U.S. contract and secured transactions legal literature often uses the terms consensual and contractual interchangeably. Thus, even though the contract in question may have to fulfill formal requirements, such as those set forth in the statute of frauds for sale agreements (U.C.C. § 2–201) or in the "attachment" or requirements for the creation of security agreements (U.C.C. § 9–203), the term consensual is still applied to such agreements.

Constitutum Possessorium – A classical Roman law agreement, under which a debtor owner of property agreed to hold the property as an authorized user or usufructuary for the benefit of his secured creditor. The latter could become its fee simple owner if the debtor defaulted in his repayment obligation.

Contra Proferentem – A principle of contractual interpretation commonly resorted to by courts in the United States. It posits that an ambiguous contractual clause should be interpreted against its draftsman or against the party that provided the wording.

Culpa in Contrahendo – Actionable tortious or bad faith behavior during the period of the negotiation of the contract or prior to its formation.

Customs – The set of practices (standard and best) generally observed in a trading center or by a given sector of the economy.

Derivatives and Swaps – Derivatives and swap transactions are aleatory, or risk, assuming as well as hedging transactions. In one type of derivative transaction, one party guarantees to the other that all or part of the latter's investment securities will retain a fixed value over a certain period of time. Thus, under a price swap derivative, when the value of the guaranteed assets decreases, the counterparty must deliver stock or other collateral to offset any losses.

Doctrine – The writings by commentators who are sufficiently respected by their legal peers to be quoted as reliable versions of the state of the law or as advocates of a given theory of interpretation, or as authors of concepts, principles or rules eventually adopted by legislators and judges.

Doctrine of the Estates – An English feudal legal institution that made it possible for land-users who were not fee simple absolute owners of the land to hold fragmented possessory rights for a specified period of time. However, unlike with the Roman law rights in the property of others (*iura in re aliena*) these estates in the land could be transferred and encumbered as rights of "time in the land" of others.

Documentary Credit – A term often used interchangeably with commercial letters of credit.

Documentary Sales – Sales payable against the presentation of documents and not upon the inspection of goods by the buyer. Among the most common documents associated with documentary sales are: invoices, negotiable ocean bills of lading, sea waybills, air waybills, insurance policies and certificates of insurance, brokers and cover notes, certificates of quality, quantity, weight and origin of the goods. The International Chamber of Commerce's International Commercial Terms (INCOTERMS), which are the most widely observed compilation of international sale terms, classified these sales on the basis of the rights and duties of buyers and sellers. Among the most prominent of these terms are CIF, where the seller's invoice bills include the price of the goods and the cost of insurance and freight, and F.O.B., where the invoice bills the buyer for the price of the goods but the buyer assumes the cost of transportation as well as of the insurance of the goods.

Eusociality – The ability of certain animals and human beings to form groups that include multiple generations who cooperate with each other and who are capable of performing altruistic deeds as well as selfish acts. The right combination of such altruism and selfishness is responsible for the viability of standard and best commercial practices.

Executory Promise – A promise to perform a contractual duty or duties at a future time. Firm executory promises, especially in credit or financial transactions, bind their issuer during their specified or reasonable period of duration.

Extra-Contractual Liability – A term used in many civil law countries, especially in Latin America, to refer to tortious, including negligent conduct.

Foral Law – As used in the principal text, the term "foral law" is mostly applicable to Spanish medieval provincial sources of law. The term "*fuero*" referred to the authority to enact laws granted to a province, region, community or group of communities, including those governed by the Roman Catholic Church.

Guanxi – **A** long-standing Chinese informal relationship in which the participants are expected to perform reciprocal services, many of which are contractual or relate to contracts. The Chinese *Guanxi* has a close counterpart in the Mexican *compadrazgo* in which close friends become "*compadre,*" or part of a "dense" relationship for their own and their families' benefits.

Innominate Contracts –Contracts that are not typified or generically described contracts in which some parties give something or issue promises in exchange for a counterpart giving or issuances of promises by the others.

Inter Absentes – Transactions between parties who deal at a distance from their counter-parties and consequently require reliable means of communications for their promises, especially for those that can be categorized as offers and acceptances.

Inter Praesentes – Face to face transactions in which oral or other informal means of communication can perfect contracts or contractual relationships.

"Invertebrate" legal system – A legal system whose rules are unpredictable because they are arbitrarily fashioned and applied by administrative or judicial officials at each level of decision-making and adjudication without regard for pre-existing rules or principles, except those (mostly in the form of slogans) attributable to officials at very top of the normative pyramid. This type of legal system is, paradoxically, common in authoritarian societies.

Ius Distrahendi – The right to foreclose or repossess on the collateral of a secured transaction either as a result of the parties' security agreement or of statutory or judicial liens.

Laesio Enormis* or Lesion in the *Code Civil – The ability of a seller of immovable property to rescind a sale if the price paid for the property is less than a statutorily specified percentage of its market value at the time of the sale.

Legal Culture: The set of attitudes and values that determine the manner in which a nation or region formulates and applies or interprets its positive and living law legal institutions.

Legal Institution – A concept, principle or rule (substantive, procedural or remedial, whether embedded in a nation's positive or living law), that makes it possible for that nation to allocate public or private rights, duties, powers and privileges among its physical persons or legal entities.

Legal Positivism – A school of legal thought distinguishable from legal realism. Some of the most influential legal positivists view the law as nothing more than "the command of the sovereign" in the famous expression by the 19th century "Analytical" legal philosopher John Austin. Others, such as the Austrian born Hans Kelsen, require that the sovereign's command's coerciveness be supported by a hierarchical set of norms at whose base lies a hypothetical norm (*grundnorm*) which justifies the enforcement of all the other norms.

Legal System (effective) – The sum of a nation's or region's legal institutions, including those that allocate the ranking (or hierarchy), scope and method of the application of its laws. From a developmental standpoint, the effectiveness of a legal system and its institutions is best measured by their success in attaining the developmental goals assigned to them.

Living Law – A non-official law that is nonetheless observed by market participants as the law that shapes and governs their day-to-day transactions.

Market Standard of Fairness – According to this standard of interpretation of contracts and adjudication of contractual dispute, each participant in a market transaction is expected to treat the other as an archetypal market participant would reasonably expect to the treated by the counterparty.

Nachfrist – Notice of termination of performance which is due under a bilateral contract when the obligee reasonably believes that the obligor is not likely to perform. It is presently described in BGB article 321.

Negotiable Instrument – A transferable, signed document that promises to pay the holder or bearer a sum of money at a future date or on demand and that can be endorsed "to the order of" the endorsee or to "bearer."

Nuda Pacta – An unenforceable promise or bargain as a result of the absence of an essential (*ad solemnitatem*) formality or of a substantive element of the contract such as its *causa* or consideration.

Numerus Clausus – A doctrine that prevails mostly in civil law countries which posits that certain transactions or rights are limited in number. Accordingly, some civil codes apply this doctrine to the rights *in rem* and only allow those rights listed to be recorded in the land registry and enforced against the property in question. Similarly, some commercial codes are interpreted as limiting the transactions governed by the code as those listed in the *Actes de Commerce* (Acts of Commerce) *See Actes de Commerce.*

Obiter Dictum or Dicta – A fundamental principle of Anglo-American judicial interpretation that dictates that the only judicial pronouncements entitled to precedential value are those made by courts with respect to the factual and legal issues before them. Other statements made by the court (*obiter dictum or dicta)* are entitled only to persuasive but not precedential or binding value.

Pandectists – German Roman law scholars who regarded the Roman *Corpus Iuris Civilis* (also referred to as the Pandects) as the supreme manifestation of legal science and as the primary inspiration for German private legal institutions. They were especially active and influential during Germany's 19th century pre-codification and codification periods. While their precision and thoroughness was legendary, presently they are regarded as "dogmatic" or unconcerned with the here and now of German law, and especially with its living law.

Picaresque Behavior – A "take advantage of the stranger" method of doing business in medieval Europe, Imperial Spain, colonial Latin America and Imperial China, which results in a view of commerce as a "zero sum game."

Pollicitation – An unaccepted and thus revocable executory promise in the *Code Civil.* This legal institution was heavily influenced by Hugo Grotius's view of contracts, and is also a result of the will of the contracting parties and the meeting of their minds that held sway in *Code Civil* France for two centuries. However, it is beginning to disappear from the French law of commercial transactions.

Positive, Written, or Official Law – Law which is governmentally enacted and enforced or is subject of enforcement. It includes not only a county's constitution, statutes, administrative and court decisions, but also, depending upon the jurisdiction, its "customs and practices," and its "general principles."

Praetor – A high administrative or judicial official in the Roman Empire who fashioned many innovative and equitable procedures and rules of interpretation of contracts.

Principle – A summary of standard and best practices expressed in a normative and at times didactic manner (as is done by legal maxims or proverbs) and whose purpose is to justify and induce the observance of rules derived from or consistent with it.

Promissory Estoppel and Preclusion – An equitable doctrine that provides that when a party to a contractual or pre-contractual relationship changes his position to his significant detriment by acting or failing to act in a beneficial manner to his own interest when relying on the counter-party's promise, he can enforce that promise. And this enforcement is possible even though other elements of the contract may not be present, or in the case of "strict" preclusion where he cannot prove that he experienced serious damages. The Roman law doctrine that approximates this Anglo-American equitable doctrine is the doctrine of *Venire Contra Factum Proprium* (or contradicting one's own conduct). A companion Anglo-American equitable doctrine of preclusion forbids a negligent contracting party from invoking a defect in the counter-party's performance if his diligent conduct would have enabled the counterparty to cure the defect in a timely manner.

Public Faith (*Publica Fide*) – A critical element of the Latin Notariat which vests notarial documents and acts with a rebuttable presumption of truthfulness and legality. Thus, unless the facts and assertions contained in the notarial documents are effectively disproven, they must be taken as truthful and valid.

Reasonable and Fair Contract Behavior – A reasonable contractual behavior takes into account what an "archetypal other" contracting party would have done or expected to be done under the circumstances. A fair contractual behavior takes into account not only what an archetypal other contracting party's behavior, but also the effects of the contract upon the interests of third parties.

Repudiation, Anticipatory and Final – Some civil codes and codes of civil procedure in civil law countries only allow actions for breach of contract to those parties who have performed their side of the agreement. In contrast, Anglo-American law allows a party who has suffered the other party's breach or is certain that the other party will breach the contract in the immediate future to sue for anticipatory or final repudiation. Among the remedies provided for such an actual or suspected repudiation are: the demand for assurance of performance, an action for rescission and damages (without actually reselling to another party or purchasing the same goods from another party (cover), and specific performance. *See Nachfrist* for comparable German law.

Scholastic Logic – A method of reasoning which dominated the thinking and teaching of twelfth and thirteen century Catholic theologians, such as Saint Thomas Aquinas whose writings influenced many definitions and classifications of the *Code Civil*. Scholastic logic is a formal type of logic because it is concerned with the internal consistency of its premises, but not with the consistency of these premises with empirically verified facts. Thus, if the major premise of a formal logic syllogism stated that "All elephants are white," scholastic reasoning could well conclude that any elephant must be white.

Secured Credit and Secured Transactions – An Anglo-American term that refers to loan agreements and functionally similar transactions whose repayment is guaranteed by the debtor's providing the creditor personal or real property collateral capable of facilitating such a repayment. The United States Law on secured credits as governed by article 9 of the U.C.C. ranks as the most advanced, exhaustive and casuistic in the world.

Short Sale – A financial transaction involving investment securities, such as common stock, in which an investor-speculator borrows the stock from a dealer betting that the price of the borrowed stock will decline in value and that by buying them later at the lower value, he will be able to recover an equal number of the shares he borrowed and retain the remainder of the stock to realize a profit in their sale.

Simulation – A legal subterfuge used by contracting parties when attempting to evade the undesirable consequences of mandatory rules. The evasion would provide the appearance of the parties entering into a contract that does not bear such consequences. For example, "A" and "B" are interested in participating in a secured loan; however such a loan would have to be recorded in a public registry to be enforceable against third parties. Still, the registration may be too expensive or it may reveal information of interest to tax authorities which A and B would prefer remained secret. Accordingly, instead of entering into a secured loan, A and B would enter into a lease agreement in which B will also have an option to purchase the goods at a certain period and for a certain symbolic amount. In that jurisdiction, such a lease would not have to be recorded and would still protect A's rights in the goods he was relying on as collateral. Clearly, this evasion would be detrimental to third parties, such as B's secured creditors who had recorded their security interests prior to the execution of the lease but whose rights would be inferior to those of A (the ostensible lessor) and as such owner of the leased goods. It would also prevent tax authorities from tracing the income generated by the hidden loan.

Stipulatio – One of the first binding Roman promises whose validity was made possible by its ritualistic formalities.

Third Parties – Third Parties are generally defined as parties who despite their not being participants in the transaction in question are likely to be affected by it, either as buyers of the same property rights or as creditors who relied on that property as security for their loans. Depending upon the transaction or legal issue involved, they are also referred to as "strangers" to the contracting parties, their families or close friends, clans or tribes.

Usufruct and Life Estate – The right to use land and appropriate its fruits without deteriorating that land. In Roman law, this right was part of a group of rights known as rights in the property of others *(iura in re aliena).* In Common law countries, this right or interest in land was part of the Doctrine of the Estates and when it was granted for the life of the grantee, it was referred to as a "Life Estate."

Usury – The practice of charging interest above the allowable rate for the use of money, such as interest rates on loans. The medieval canonic definition of usury was absolute: any interest charged for the use of money was usurious. Following King Henry VIII's definition of usury, the definition of usury gradually changed, especially in Northern European jurisdictions, to interest charged above the permissible rate.

Venire Contra Factum Proprium – *See Promissory Estoppel and Preclusion.*

Index

References are to Pages